Road trip Germany. Caravanning delight.

Expect unspoilt countryside, delightful historic towns and a range of excellent camping and caravanning facilities when visiting Germany. Whether you're exploring the great outdoors or follow Germany's classic scenic routes, the possibilities are endless. www.germany.travel

Holidays in Germany: www.germany.travel

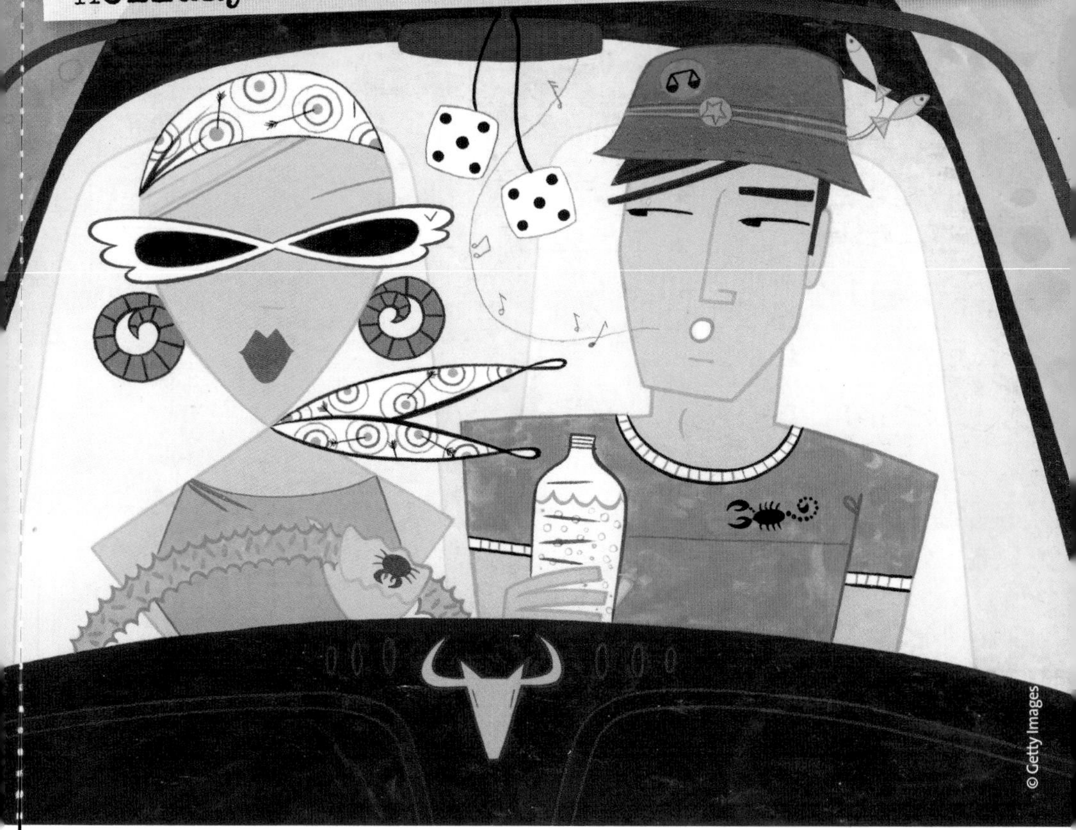

© Getty Images

Travel Destination Germany © German National Tourist Board
Supported by:

on the basis of a decision
by the German Bundestag

Germany
The travel destination

Explanation of a Campsite Entry Caravan Europe 2012/2013

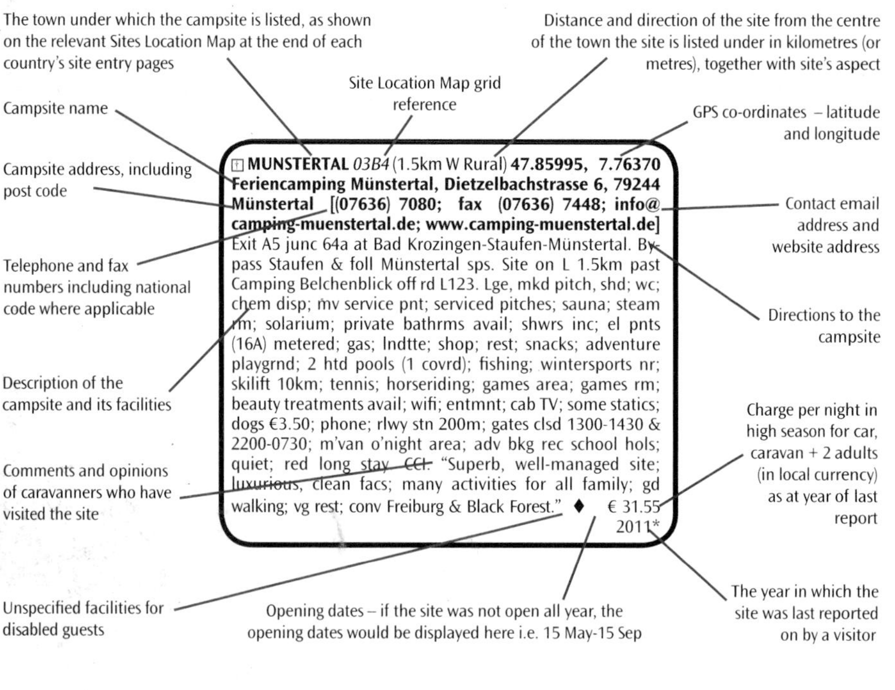
The town under which the campsite is listed, as shown on the relevant Sites Location Map at the end of each country's site entry pages
Site Location Map grid reference
Distance and direction of the site from the centre of the town the site is listed under in kilometres (or metres), together with site's aspect
Campsite name
GPS co-ordinates – latitude and longitude
Campsite address, including post code
MUNSTERTAL 03B4 (1.5km W Rural) 47.85995, 7.76370 Feriencamping Münstertal, Dietzelbachstrasse 6, 79244 Münstertal [(07636) 7080; fax (07636) 7448; info@camping-muenstertal.de; www.camping-muenstertal.de] Exit A5 junc 64a at Bad Krozingen-Staufen-Münstertal. By-pass Staufen & foll Münstertal sps. Site on L 1.5km past Camping Belchenblick off rd L123. Lge, mkd pitch, shd; wc; chem disp; mv service pnt; serviced pitches; sauna; steam rm; solarium; private bathrms avail; shwrs inc; el pnts (16A) metered; gas; Indtte; shop; rest; snacks; adventure playgrnd; 2 htd pools (1 covrd); fishing; wintersports nr; skilift 10km; tennis; horseriding; games area; games rm; beauty treatments avail; wifi; entmnt; cab TV; some statics; dogs €3.50; phone; rlwy stn 200m; gates clsd 1300-1430 & 2200-0730; m'van o'night area; adv bkg rec school hols; quiet; red long stay CCI. "Superb, well-managed site; luxurious, clean facs; many activities for all family; gd walking; vg rest; conv Freiburg & Black Forest." ♦ € 31.55 2011*
Contact email address and website address
Telephone and fax numbers including national code where applicable
Directions to the campsite
Description of the campsite and its facilities
Charge per night in high season for car, caravan + 2 adults (in local currency) as at year of last report
Comments and opinions of caravanners who have visited the site
Unspecified facilities for disabled guests
Opening dates – if the site was not open all year, the opening dates would be displayed here i.e. 15 May-15 Sep
The year in which the site was last reported on by a visitor

Popular Abbreviations

(for a full list of abbreviations please see page 11).

Site Description

sm: max 50 pitches | **med**: 51–150 pitches | **lge**: 151-500 pitches | **v lge**: 501+ pitches | **hdg**: hedged
mkd: marked | **sl**: sloping site | **pt sl**: sloping in parts | **terr**: terraced site | **shd**: plenty of shade
pt shd: part shaded | **unshd**: no shade | **hdstg**: some hard standing or gravel pitches

Popular Abbreviations for Site Facilities

Adv bkg: advanced booking accepted
CCI or CCS: Camping Card International or Camping Card Scandinavia accepted
chem disp: dedicated chemical toilet disposal facilities
chem disp (wc): no dedicated point; disposal via wc only
CL-type: very small, privately-owned, informal and usually basic, farm or country site
El pnts: mains electric hook-ups
Eng spkn: English spoken
entmnt: entertainment (facilities or organised)
Indtte: washing machine(s) with or without tumble dryers
NH: suitable as a night halt;
quiet: peaceful, tranquil site
rest: restaurant
shwrs: hot showers available at a fee
shwrs inc: cost included in the site fee quoted
tradsmn: tradesmen call at the site, e.g. baker
SBS Site Booking Reference - Ref No. for a site included in the Caravan Club's network i.e. bookable through the Club
ssn season

Popular Generic Abbreviations

Adj: adjacent, nearby; **app**: approach, on approaching; **arr**: arrival, arriving **bef**: before **bet**: between **c'van**: caravan; **ccard acc**: Credit and/or debit cards accepted; **CChq acc**: Camping cheques accepted; **clsd**: closed **E**: East; **ent**: entrance/entry to **excel**: excellent; **facs**: facilities; **foll**: follow; **fr**: from; **gd**: good; **inc**: included/inclusive; **L**: left; **M'van:** motorhome/motor caravan; **narr**: narrow **N**: North; **o'fits**: outfits; **R**: right; **rec**: recommend/ed; **red**: reduced/reduction; **rte**: route **S**: South; **sp**: sign post/signposted; **strt**: straight, straight ahead **sw**: swimming **vg**: very good; **W**: West

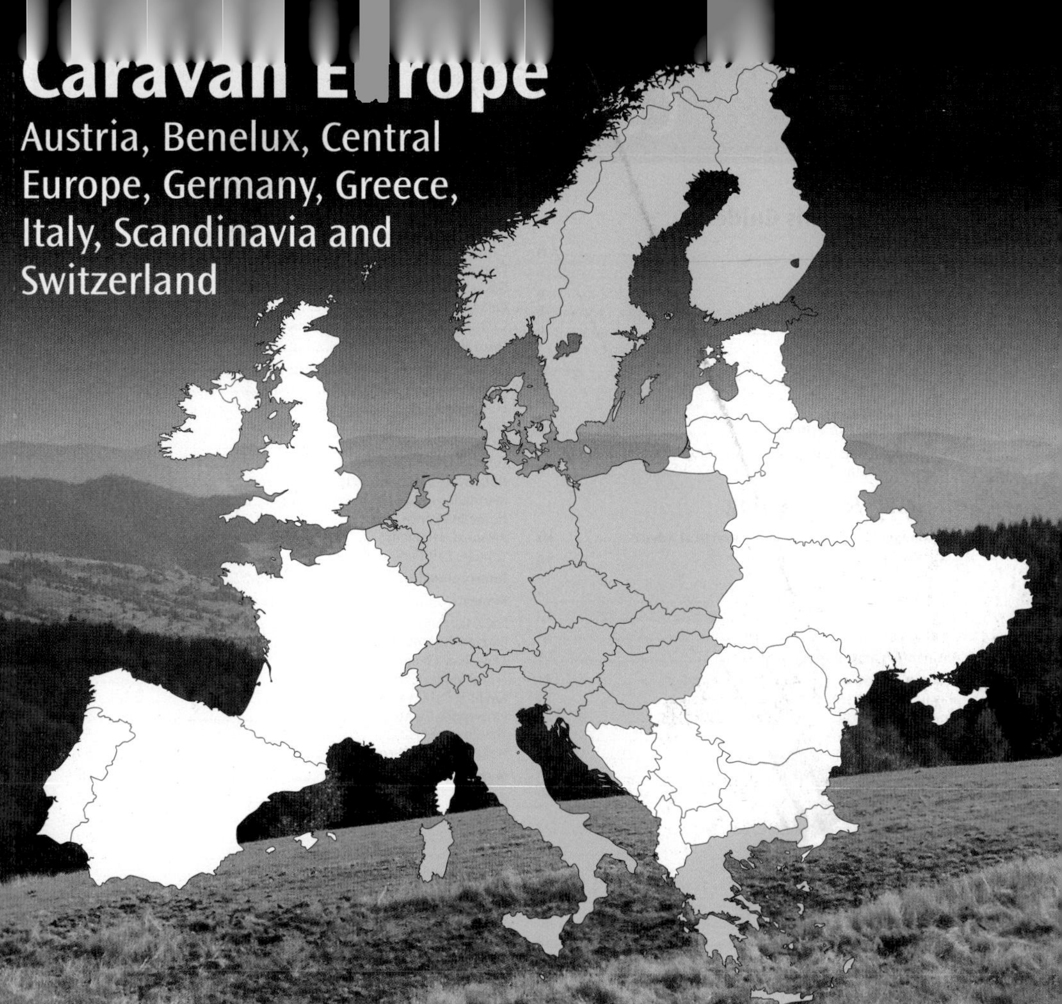

© The Caravan Club Limited 2012

Published by The Caravan Club Limited
East Grinstead House, East Grinstead
West Sussex RH19 1UA

General Enquiries: 01342 326944
Brochure Requests: 01342 327410
Travel Service Reservations: 01342 316101
Red Pennant Overseas
Holiday Insurance: 01342 336633
Website: www.caravanclub.co.uk
Email: enquiries@caravanclub.co.uk

Editor: Rowena Sait
Email: rowena.sait@caravanclub.co.uk

Printed by Elanders Ltd
Newcastle-upon-Tyne

ISBN 978-0-9569510-2-1

Maps and distance charts generated from Collins Bartholomew Digital Database

Maps © Collins Bartholomew Ltd 2011, reproduced by permission of HarperCollins Publishers

Except as otherwise permitted under Copyright, Design and Patents Act, 1998, this publication may only be reproduced, stored or transmitted in any form, or by any means, with the prior permission in writing of the publisher.

The contents of this publication are believed to be correct at the time of printing. Nevertheless, the publisher and copyright owner(s) can accept no responsibility for errors or omissions, changes in the detail given, or for any expense or loss thereby caused.

Front cover photo: Main Image Austria by Pamela Murphy, Temple of Poseidon, Greece © iStockphoto.com/DenGuy, Neuschwanstein Castle, Germany © iStockphoto.com/stockcam, Venice by Milcie Aldersley

Contents

How To Use This Guide

Introduction ... 6
Handbook ... 6
Country Introductions ... 6
Campsite Entries ... 6
Campsite Fees ... 6
Sites Location Maps ... 7
Satellite Navigation ... 7
Site Report Forms ... 8
Win a Sat Nav ... 8
Explanation of a Campsite Entry ... 10
Abbreviations – Site Description & Facilities ... 11
Other Abbreviations & Symbols Used ... 12

Planning & Travelling

Caravaning and Touring Abroad – Practical Advice ... 16
Before You Travel ... 16
On the Journey ... 19
During Your Stay ... 21
Checklist ... 22
Technical Leaflets ... 23
Continental Campsites ... 24
Booking a Campsite ... 24
Caravan Club Overseas Site Booking Service ... 24
Camping Cheques ... 25
Caravan Storage Abroad ... 25
Electricity Supply ... 25
Facilities & Site Description ... 26
Finding a Campsite ... 26
Lunch Breaks ... 27
Motorhomes – Overnight Stops ... 27
Municipal Campsites ... 27
Naturist Campsites ... 27
Opening Dates ... 28
Pets on Campsites ... 28
Prices ... 28
Registering on Arrival ... 29
Sites' Contact Details ... 29
General Advice ... 29
Complaints ... 29
Specimen Site Booking Letters (4 Languages) ... 30-33
Customs Regulations ... 34
Travelling to the UK from the EU ... 34
Travelling to/from Non-EU Countries ... 34
Travelling Within the EU ... 35
Boats ... 35
Currency ... 35
Food & Plants ... 35
Medicines ... 36
Motor Vehicles & Caravans ... 36
Personal Possessions ... 37
Prohibited & Restricted Goods ... 37
Documents ... 38
Camping Card International (CCI) ... 38
Driving Licence & International Driving Permit (IDP) ... 38
European Health Insurance Card (EHIC) ... 39
MOT Certificate ... 39
Passport ... 39
Pet Travel Scheme (PETS) ... 40
Travelling with Children ... 40
Vehicle Excise Licence ... 40
Vehicle Registration Certificate ... 41
CRIS Document ... 41
Visas ... 41
Ferries & the Channel Tunnel ... 42
Planning Your Trip ... 42
Booking Your Ferry ... 42
Table of Ferry Routes ... 43
Channel Tunnel ... 44
Gas – Safety Precautions & Regulations ... 44
Pets on Ferries & Eurotunnel ... 44
Caravan Club Sites Near Ports ... 44
Insurance ... 46
Car, Motorhome and Caravan Insurance ... 46
Green Card ... 46
European Accident Statement ... 47
Caravans Stored Abroad ... 47
Legal Costs Abroad ... 47
Holiday Travel Insurance ... 48
Holiday Insurance for Pets ... 48
Marine Insurance (Car Ferries/Boats) ... 49
Home Insurance ... 49
Personal Belongings ... 49
Vehicles Left Behind Abroad ... 49
International Holidays ... 50
Money ... 51
Local Currency ... 51
Foreign Currency Bank Accounts ... 51
Travellers' Cheques ... 51
Travel Money Cards ... 52
Credit & Debit Cards ... 52
Emergency Cash ... 53
The Euro ... 53
Holiday Money Security ... 53
Motoring – Advice ... 55
Preparing for Your Journey ... 55
Driving on the Continent ... 56
Driving Offences ... 56
Fuel ... 57
Low Emission Zones ... 58
Motorhomes Towing Cars ... 58
Motorway Tolls ... 58
Parking ... 59
Priority & Roundabouts ... 59
Public Transport ... 59
Road Signs & Markings ... 59
Speed Limits ... 60
Traffic Lights ... 61
Winter Driving ... 61
Fuel Price Guide Table ... 62
Speed Limits Table ... 63
European Distance Chart ... 64
Route Planning Maps ... 66-69
Motoring – Equipment ... 70
Bicycle & Motorbike Transportation ... 70
Car Telephones ... 70
First Aid Kit & Fire Extinguisher ... 70
Glasses (Sight) ... 70
Lights ... 70
Nationality Plate (GB/IRL) ... 71
Radar/Speed Camera Detection ... 71
Rear View External Mirrors ... 71
Reflective Jackets ... 71
Route Planning ... 71
Satellite Navigation/GPS ... 72
Seat Belts ... 72
Spares/Spare Wheel ... 72
Towing Bracket ... 72
Tyres, Winter Tyres & Snow Chains ... 73
Warning Triangles ... 73
Essential Equipment Table ... 74
Mountain Passes & Tunnels ... 75

Advice & Information for Drivers ... 75
Major Mountain Passes Table – Alpine ... 77
Major Rail Tunnels Table – Alpine ... 86
Major Road Tunnels Table – Alpine ... 87
Mountain Passes & Tunnels Maps – Alpine ... 90-93

During Your Stay

Conversion Tables ... 94
Electricity & Gas ... 96
Electricity – General Advice ... 96
Electrical Connections – CEE17 ... 96
Hooking up to the Mains ... 97
Reversed Polarity ... 98
Shaver Sockets ... 98
Gas – General Advice ... 98
Keeping in Touch ... 100
Emails & The Internet ... 100
Text Messages (SMS) ... 100
International Direct Dial Calls ... 100
Global Telephone Cards ... 100
Radio & Television ... 101
Using Mobile Phones Abroad ... 102
Medical Matters ... 104
Before You Travel ... 104
European Health Insurance Card (EHIC) ... 104
Holiday Travel Insurance ... 105
First Aid ... 105
Vaccinations ... 105
Claiming Refunds ... 106
Accidents & Emergencies ... 106
Calling The Emergency Services ... 106
Insect Bites ... 106
Rabies ... 106
Swimming ... 107
Sun Protection ... 107
Water & Food ... 107
Returning Home ... 107
Safety & Security ... 108
Overnight Stops ... 108
Around the Campsite ... 108
Children ... 109
Fire ... 109
Swimming Pools & Water Slides ... 109
Beaches, Lakes & Rivers ... 110
On The Road ... 110
Personal Security ... 111
British Consular Services Abroad ... 112

Countries

Austria
Country Introduction ... 113
Site Entries ... 120
Distance Chart / Sites Location Map ... 146/147
Belgium
Country Introduction ... 149
Site Entries ... 155
Distance Chart / Sites Location Map ... 168/169
Croatia
Country Introduction ... 171
Site Entries ... 178
Distance Chart / Sites Location Map ... 190/191
Czech Republic
Country Introduction ... 193
Site Entries ... 200
Distance Chart / Sites Location Map ... 212/213
Denmark
Country Introduction ... 215
Site Entries ... 222
Distance Chart / Sites Location Map ... 243/244
Finland
Country Introduction ... 245
Site Entries ... 252
Sites in Aland Islands ... 257
Distance Chart / Sites Location Map ... 259/260
Germany
Country Introduction ... 261
Site Entries ... 269
Map of Federal States ... 352
Distance Chart / Sites Location Maps ... 347/348
Greece
Country Introduction ... 353
Site Entries ... 359
Sites in Greek Islands ... 368
Distance Chart / Sites Location Map ... 370/371
Hungary
Country Introduction ... 373
Site Entries ... 380
Distance Chart / Sites Location Map ... 388/389
Italy
Country Introduction ... 391
Site Entries ... 399
Sites in Sardinia ... 461
Sites in Sicily ... 464
Map of Regions & Provinces ... 470
Distance Chart / Sites Location Maps ... 471/472
Luxembourg
Country Introduction ... 475
Site Entries ... 479
Sites Location Map ... 484
Netherlands
Country Introduction ... 485
Site Entries ... 492
Distance Chart / Sites Location Map ... 523/524
Norway
Country Introduction ... 525
Site Entries ... 535
Sites in Lofoten & Vesteralen Islands ... 560/561
Distance Chart / Sites Location Maps ... 563/564
Poland
Country Introduction ... 567
Site Entries ... 574
Distance Chart / Sites Location Map ... 582/583
Slovakia
Country Introduction ... 585
Site Entries ... 591
Distance Chart / Sites Location Map ... 595/596
Slovenia
Country Introduction ... 597
Site Entries ... 602
Distance Chart / Sites Location Maps ... 606/607
Sweden
Country Introduction ... 609
Site Entries ... 617
Sites in Öland Islands ... 639
Distance Chart / Sites Location Maps ... 641/642
Switzerland
Country Introduction ... 645
Site Entries ... 653
Distance Chart / Sites Location Map ... 680/681

MOUNTAIN PASSES & TUNNELS REPORT FORM Back of Guide

SITE REPORT FORMS Back of Guide
See also alphabetical index at the back of the guide

This free brochure brings you the best of Europe

Kopie, on the Lakes & Mountains Grand Tour

Summer 2012

The Ultimate Guide to

Continental

Caravanning

Discover over 200 quality campsites throughout Europe

01342 316 101

www.caravanclub.co.uk

THE CARAVAN CLUB

The Caravan Club has handpicked over 200 quality campsites throughout Europe, inspecting each one to make sure they deliver to the highest standards you expect.

This year we've added some terrific new sites for you to discover, from the foot of the Pyrénées to the beautiful Loire Valley.

Our ever-popular tours now include an amazing 33-night Grand Tour of Lakes & Mountains across Europe, a Celtic Grand Tour of Ireland & Brittany and a seven-night Champagne Tour of such famous names as Moët & Chandon and Tattinger.

There are escorted tours for those who've never travelled abroad before, GB Privilege motorhome-only tours, Atlantic Adventures, tours of the Dutch Bulbfields and so much more.

Download your free copy today or phone us to start enjoying the best of Europe.

Find out more in our free 'Continental Caravanning' brochure available online at www.caravanclub.co.uk/brochures or call for your copy on 01342 327 410

Welcome

to Caravan Europe 2012/2013

We are very pleased to be able to bring you the 2012/2013 edition of Caravan Europe, the dedicated guide to touring and campsites. This volume of the comprehensive handbook contains practical information with helpful hints and advice on touring and travelling in Austria, Belgium, Croatia, Czech Republic, Denmark, Finland, Germany, Greece, Hungary, Italy, Luxembourg, Netherlands, Norway, Poland, Slovakia, Slovenia, Sweden and Switzerland, as well as over 3,500 sites for you to choose from in these countries, the majority of which have been recommended by Caravan Club members.

Within Caravan Europe you will find campsites to suit all needs and requirements. Whether you're looking for a peaceful holiday in the countryside or mountains, or a lively resort by the sea or city, there really is something for everyone. What's more, every site entry has comments and reviews from fellow caravanners and tourers, giving you unique eyewitness accounts of each campsite.

In order to be able to include as many recommended campsites as possible we have continued to use our abbreviation list for site entries, which means you are able to choose from a wide variety of campsites across Europe. We have included some of the most popular abbreviations on the bookmark page, so you can now always have these to hand whenever you check a site entry. You can also find the full list of abbreviations on page 11.

Caravan Europe has been put together to help you get the most out of your holiday and we hope that you find it a useful and enjoyable resource when planning your trip. Without you, the reader, Caravan Europe wouldn't be such an invaluable source of information. If you visit a campsite please fill in a site report form and share your experience with us. This will also give you automatic entry into our competition to win a Snooper Ventura Caravan Club Edition Sat Nav, the perfect satellite navigation system for anyone with a caravan.

We wish you a wonderful time on your travels and look forward to receiving your site reports!

Rowena Sait

Rowena Sait, Editor

Read on to discover 1,000s of sites

www.caravanclub.co.uk

How to use this guide

Introduction

The information contained within Caravan Europe is presented in the following categories:

The Handbook

This includes general information about touring in Europe, such as legal requirements, advice and regulations. The Handbook chapters are at the front of the guide under the section headings:

Planning and Travelling

During Your Stay

These two sections are divided into chapters in alphabetical order, not necessarily the order of priority. Cross-references are given where additional information is provided in another chapter.

Country Introductions

Following on from the Handbook chapters you will find the Country Introduction chapters containing information, regulations and advice specific to each country. You should read the Country Introductions carefully in conjunction with the Handbook chapters before you set off on your holiday. Cross-references to other chapters are provided where appropriate.

Campsite Entries

After the Country Introduction you will find the campsite entries listed alphabetically according to the towns and villages in, or near to, where they are located. Where several campsites are shown in and around the same town they will be listed in clockwise order from the north.

To find a campsite all you need to do is look for the town or village of where you would like to stay in or nearby. If a campsite is not shown under the name of the particular town or village that you are searching for, then a cross-reference may indicate an alternative village or town under which it may be found in the guide. For example, for the town Ceriale (Italy) the cross-reference will direct you to campsites listed under Albenga.

To maintain consistency we have used local versions of town or city names. For example, Firenze is used instead of Florence and Praha is used instead of Prague.

In order to facilitate such a large number of campsites within Caravan Europe we have used

abbreviations in the site entries. For a full and detailed list of these abbreviations please refer to the chapter Explanation of a Campsite Entry. We have also included some of the most popular abbreviations used, as well as an explanation of a campsite entry, on the tear-out bookmark page for your convenience. Simply pull out the bookmark page at the front of Caravan Europe and you can then always have it to hand whenever you need to check a site entry in the guide.

Campsite Fees

Campsite entries show high season fees per night in local currency for a car, caravan, plus two adults, as at the year of the last report. In addition a deposit or booking fee may be charged, which might not be refundable. Prices given do not necessarily include electricity or showers, unless indicated, or local taxes. Outside of the main holiday season many sites offer discounts on the prices shown and also some sites may offer a reduction for longer stays.

Campsite fees may vary to the prices stated in the site entries. You are advised to always check fees when booking, or at least before pitching, as those shown in site entries should be used as a guide only.

Sites Location Maps

Each town and village listed alphabetically in the site entry pages has a map grid reference number, e.g. 3B4 or C2. The map grid reference number is shown on each site entry. The maps can be found at the end of each country's site entry pages. The reference number will show you where each town or village is located. Place names are shown on the maps in two colours:

Red where there is a site open all year (or for at least approximately eleven months of the year)

Black where only seasonal sites which close in winter have been reported.

Please note: these maps are for general campsite location purposes only; a detailed road map or atlas is essential for route planning and touring.

Town names in capital letters (**RED**, **BLACK** or in *ITALICS*) correspond with towns listed on the Distance Chart.

The scale used for the Sites Location Maps means that it is not possible to pinpoint every town or village where a campsite exists. Where we cannot show an individual town or village on a Sites Location Map for reasons of space, we list it under another nearby town which then acts as a central point for campsites within that particular local area. With some exceptions, such as Berlin, sites are listed under towns up to approximately 15 kilometres away. The place names used as a central point are usually, but not always, the largest towns in each region; some may be only small villages.

Satellite Navigation

Most campsite entries in this guide now show a GPS (sat nav) reference. It is in the format 41.89051(latitude north) and 12.49424 (longitude east), i.e. decimal degrees. Readings shown as -1.23456 indicate that the longitude position in question is west of the 0 degrees Greenwich meridian. This is important to bear in mind when inputting co-ordinates into your sat nav device for campsites in Western France, most of Spain and all of Portugal. Readings given in other formats such as degrees + minutes + seconds or degrees + decimal minutes can be converted using www.cosports.com then click on GPS Lat/ Long Conversion, or simply use Google maps (http://maps.google.co.uk) and input a GPS reference in any format to locate a town, village or campsite.

Please be aware if you are using a sat nav device some routes may take you on roads that are narrow and/or are not suitable for caravans or large outfits.

The GPS co-ordinates given in this guide are derived from a number of reliable sources but it has not been possible to check them all individually. The Caravan Club cannot accept responsibility for any inaccuracies, errors or omissions or for their effects.

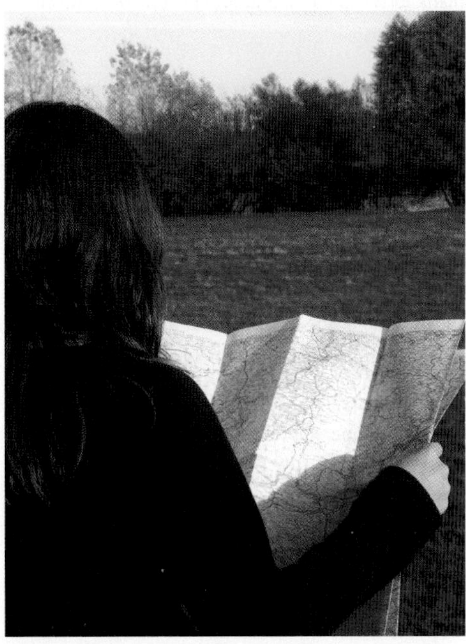

Site Report Forms

With the exception of campsites in the Club's Overseas Site Booking Service (SBS) network, The Caravan Club does not inspect sites listed in this guide. Virtually all of the site reports in Caravan Europe are submitted voluntarily by both members and non-members of The Caravan Club during the course of their own holidays.

We rely on you, the users of this guide, to tell us about campsites you have visited

Sites that are not reported on for five to six years may be deleted from this guide. We therefore rely very much on you, the users of this guide, to tell us about campsites you have visited – old favourites as well as new discoveries.

You will find some site report forms towards the back of this guide which we hope you will complete and return to us by freepost. An abbreviated site report form is provided if you are reporting no changes (or only minor changes) to a site entry. Additional site report forms are available online and on request.

You can complete both the full and abbreviated versions of the site report forms on our website. Simply go to www.caravanclub.co.uk/europereport and either complete the form online or download blank forms to fill in later and post to The Caravan Club.

Complete site report forms online – www.caravanclub.co.uk/europereport

For an explanation of the abbreviations that are used in the site entries, please refer to the chapter ***Explanation of a Campsite Entry*** or use the tear-out bookmark page at the front of the guide which shows some of the most popular abbreviations used.

Please submit reports as soon as possible. Information received by **mid September 2013** will be used wherever possible in the next edition of Caravan Europe. Reports received after that date are still very welcome and will be retained for entry in a subsequent edition. The editor is unable to respond individually to site reports submitted due to the large quantity that we receive.

Win a Sat Nav

If you submit site reports to the editor during 2012 and 2013 – whether by post, email or online – you will have your name entered into a prize draw to win the Snooper Ventura Caravan Club Edition Sat Nav (terms and conditions apply). Four runners up will also receive the latest editions of Caravan Europe.

The Snooper Ventura Caravan Club Edition Sat Nav will already have the GPS co-ordinates programmed in for the majority of campsites within the current edition of Caravan Europe as well as Club sites throughout the UK, allowing you to find sites around your present or future location at the touch of a button. It has been specifically designed for caravanners and will calculate routes that avoid obstacles such as narrow roads and low bridges, based on the size of your vehicle. The perfect equipment for anyone with a caravan or large motorhome!

Tips for Completing Site Reports

- If possible it is best to fill in a site report form while you are at the campsite or shortly after your stay. Once back at home it can be difficult to remember details of individual sites, especially if you visited several during your trip.
- When giving directions to a site, remember to include the direction of travel, e.g. 'from north on D137, turn left onto D794 signposted Combourg' or 'on N83 from Poligny turn right at petrol station in village'. Wherever possible give road numbers, together with junction numbers and/or kilometre post numbers,

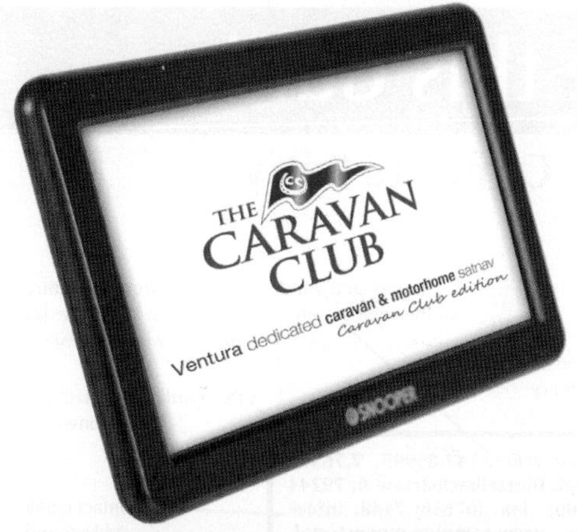

snooperventura
Caravan Club edition

SNOOPER

where you exit from motorways or main roads. It is also helpful to mention useful landmarks such as bridges, roundabouts, traffic lights or prominent buildings, and to advise whether the site is signposted. If there are any roads that are difficult to access or narrow please also mention this in the report.

- When noting the compass direction of a site **this must be in the direction FROM THE TOWN the site is listed under TO THE SITE, and not the direction from the site to the town.** Distances are measured in a straight line and may differ significantly from the distance by road.
- If you are only amending a few details about a site there is no need to use the longer version form. You may prefer to use the abbreviated version but, in any event, do remember to give the campsite name and the town or village under which it is listed in the guide. Alternatively, use the online version of the form – www.caravanclub.co.uk/europereport
- If possible, give precise opening and closing dates, e.g. 1 April to 30 September. This information is particularly important for early and late season travellers.

The editor very much appreciates the time and trouble you take submitting reports on campsites that you have visited; without your valuable contributions it would be impossible to update this guide.

Every effort is made to ensure that information contained in this publication is accurate and that the details given in good faith in the site report forms are accurately reproduced or summarised. The Caravan Club Ltd has not checked these details by inspection or other investigation and cannot accept responsibility for the accuracy of these reports as provided by members and non-members, or for errors, omissions or their effects. In addition The Caravan Club Ltd cannot be held accountable for the quality, safety or operation of the sites concerned, or for the fact that conditions, facilities, management or prices may have changed since the last recorded visit. Any recommendations, additional comments or opinions have been contributed by caravanners and people staying on the site and are not generally those of The Caravan Club.

The inclusion of advertisements or other inserted material does not imply any form of approval or recognition, nor can The Caravan Club Ltd undertake any responsibility for checking the accuracy of advertising material.

Acknowledgements

The Caravan Club's thanks go to the AIT/FIA Information Centre (OTA), the Alliance Internationale de Tourisme (AIT), the Fédération International de Camping et de Caravaning (FICC) and to the national clubs and tourist offices of those countries who have assisted with this publication.

How to use this Guide

Explanation of a Campsite Entry

The town under which the campsite is listed, as shown on the relevant Sites Location Map at the end of each country's site entry pages

Distance and direction of the site from the centre of the town the site is listed under in kilometres (or metres), together with site's aspect

Site Location Map grid reference

Campsite name

GPS co-ordinates – latitude and longitude

Campsite address, including post code

Telephone and fax numbers including national code where applicable

Description of the campsite and its facilities

Comments and opinions of caravanners who have visited the site

Contact email address and website address

Directions to the campsite

Charge per night in high season for car, caravan + 2 adults (in local currency) as at year of last report

MUNSTERTAL *03B4* (1.5km W Rural) **47.85995, 7.76370 Feriencamping Münstertal, Dietzelbachstrasse 6, 79244 Münstertal [(07636) 7080; fax (07636) 7448; info@camping-muenstertal.de; www.camping-muenstertal.de]** Exit A5 junc 64a at Bad Krozingen-Staufen-Münstertal. By-pass Staufen & foll Münstertal sps. Site on L 1.5km past Camping Belchenblick off rd L123. Lge, mkd pitch, shd; wc; chem disp; mv service pnt; serviced pitches; sauna; steam rm; solarium; private bathrms avail; shwrs inc; el pnts (16A) metered; gas; Indtte; shop; rest; snacks; adventure playgrnd; 2 htd pools (1 covrd); fishing; wintersports nr; skilift 10km; tennis; horseriding; games area; games rm; beauty treatments avail; wifi; entmnt; cab TV; some statics; dogs €3.50; phone; rlwy stn 200m; gates clsd 1300-1430 & 2200-0730; m'van o'night area; adv bkg rec school hols; quiet; red long stay. CCI. "Superb, well-managed site; luxurious, clean facs; many activities for all family; gd walking; vg rest; conv Freiburg & Black Forest." ♦ € 31.55 2011*

Unspecified facilities for disabled guests

The year in which the site was last reported on by a visitor

BALATONSZEPEZD *C1* (4km SW Rural) *46.82960, 17.64014* **Balatontourist Camping Napfény, Halász út 5, 8253 Révfülöp [(87) 563031; fax 464309; napfeny@balatontourist.hu; www.balatontourist.hu]** Take m'way E71/M7 & exit junc 90 along N shore of lake, passing Balatonalmádi & Balatonfüred to Révfülöp. Site sp. Lge, mkd pitch, pt shd; wc; chem disp; mv service pnt; baby facs; private san facs avail; shwrs inc; el pnts (6A) inc; Indtte (inc dryer); shop; supmkt 500m; tradsmn; rest; snacks; bar; BBQ; playgrnd; paddling pool; lake sw & beach adj; fishing; watersports; cycle & boat hire; tennis 300m; horseriding 5km; games area; games rm; wifi; entmnt; TV rm; 2% statics; dogs HUF900; twin-axles acc (rec check in adv); phone; adv bkg; quiet; ccard acc; red low ssn. "Warm welcome; excel, well-organised lakeside site; gd pitches; gd for families; fees according to pitch size & location." ♦ 27 Apr-30 Sep. HUF 7150 (CChq acc) SBS - X06 2011*

Opening dates

The site accepts Camping Cheques – see the chapter ***Continental Campsites*** for details

Reference number for a site included in The Caravan Club's Site Booking Service network i.e. bookable through the Club

Site Description Abbreviations

Each site entry assumes the following unless stated otherwise:

Level ground, open grass pitches, drinking water on site, clean wc unless otherwise stated (own sanitation required if wc not listed), site is suitable for any length of stay within the dates shown.

aspect

urban – within a city or town, or on its outskirts
rural – within or on edge of a village or in open countryside
coastal – within one kilometre of the coast

size of site

sm – max 50 pitches
med – 51 to 150 pitches
lge – 151 to 500 pitches
v lge – 501+ pitches

pitches

hdg pitch – hedged pitches
mkd pitch – marked or numbered pitches
hdstg – some hard standing or gravel

levels

sl – sloping site
pt sl – sloping in parts
terr – terraced site

shade

shd – plenty of shade
pt shd – part shaded
unshd – no shade

Site Facilities Abbreviations

adv bkg

Advance booking accepted;
adv bkg rec – advance booking recommended

baby facs

Nursing room/bathroom for babies/children

beach

Beach for swimming nearby;
1km – distance to beach
sand beach – sandy beach
shgl beach – shingle beach

bus/metro/tram

Public transport within an easy walk of the site

CCI or CCS

Camping Card International or Camping Card Scandinavia accepted

chem disp

Dedicated chemical toilet disposal facilities;
chem disp (wc) – no dedicated point; disposal via wc only

CL-type

Very small, privately-owned, informal and usually basic, farm or country site similar to those in the Caravan Club's network of Certificated Locations

dogs

Dogs allowed on site with appropriate certification (a daily fee may be quoted and conditions may apply)

el pnts

Mains electric hook-ups available for a fee;
inc – cost included in site fee quoted
10A – amperage provided
conn fee – one-off charge for connection to metered electricity supply
rev pol – reversed polarity may be present

(see ***Electricity and Gas*** in the section ***DURING YOUR STAY***)

Eng spkn

English spoken by campsite reception staff

entmnt

Entertainment facilities or organised entertainment for adults and/or children

fam bthrm

Bathroom for use by families with small children

gas

Supplies of bottled gas available on site or nearby

internet

Internet point for use by visitors to site;
wifi – wireless local area network available

lndtte

Washing machine(s) with or without tumble dryers, sometimes other equipment available, eg ironing boards;
lndtte (inc dryer) – washing machine(s) and tumble dryer(s)
lndry rm – laundry room with only basic clothes-washing facilities

Mairie

Town hall (France); will usually make municipal campsite reservations

mv service pnt

Special low level waste discharge point for motor caravans; fresh water tap and rinse facilities should also be available

NH
Suitable as a night halt

noisy
Noisy site with reasons given;
quiet – peaceful, tranquil site

open 1 Apr-15 Oct
Where no specific dates are given, opening dates are assumed to be inclusive, ie Apr-Oct – beginning April to end October (**NB: opening dates may vary from those shown; check in advance before making a long journey, particularly when travelling out of the main holiday season**)

phone
Public payphone on or adjacent to site

playgrnd
Children's playground

pool
Swimming pool (may be open high season only);
htd – heated pool
covrd – indoor pool or one with retractable cover

poss cr
During high season site may be crowded or overcrowded and pitches cramped

red CCI/CCS
Reduction in fees on production of a Camping Card International or Camping Card Scandinavia

rest
Restaurant;
bar – bar
BBQ – barbecues allowed (may be restricted to a separate, designated area)
cooking facs – communal kitchen area
snacks – snack bar, cafeteria or takeaway

SBS
Site Booking Service (pitch reservation can be made through the Caravan Club's Travel Service)

serviced pitch
Electric hook-ups and mains water inlet and grey water waste outlet to pitch;
all – to all pitches
50% – percentage of pitches

shop(s)
Shop on site;
adj – shops next to site
500m – nearest shops
supmkt – supermarket
hypmkt – hypermarket
tradsmn – tradesmen call at the site, eg baker

shwrs
Hot showers available for a fee;
inc – cost included in site fee quoted

ssn
Season;
high ssn – peak holiday season
low ssn – out of peak season

50% statics
Percentage of static caravans/mobile homes/ chalets/fixed tents/cabins or long term seasonal pitches on site, including those run by tour operators

sw
Swimming nearby;
1km – nearest swimming
lake – in lake
rv – in river

TV
TV available for viewing by visitors (often in the bar);
TV rm – separate TV room (often also a games room)
cab/sat – cable or satellite connections to pitches

wc
Clean flushing toilets on site;
(cont) – continental type with floor-level hole
htd – sanitary block centrally heated in winter
own san – use of own sanitation facilities recommended

Other Abbreviations

AIT	Alliance Internationale de Tourisme
a'bahn	Autobahn
a'pista	Autopista
a'route	Autoroute
a'strada	Autostrada
adj	Adjacent, nearby
alt	Alternative
app	Approach, on approaching
arr	Arrival, arriving
avail	Available
Ave	Avenue
bdge	Bridge
bef	Before
bet	Between
Blvd	Boulevard
C	Century, eg 16thC
c'van	Caravan
ccard acc	Credit and/or debit cards accepted (check with site for specific details)
CChq acc	Camping Cheques accepted
cent	Centre or central

clsd	Closed
conn	Connection
cont	Continue or continental (wc)
conv	Convenient
covrd	Covered
dep	Departure
diff	Difficult, with difficulty
dir	Direction
dist	Distance
dual c'way	Dual carriageway
E	East
ent	Entrance/entry to
espec	Especially
ess	Essential
excel	Excellent
facs	Facilities
FIA	Fédération Internationale de l'Automobile
FICC	Fédération Internationale de Camping & de Caravaning
FFCC	Fédération Française de Camping et de Caravaning
FKK/FNF	Naturist federation, ie naturist site
foll	Follow
fr	From
g'ge	Garage
gd	Good
grnd(s)	Ground(s)
hr(s)	Hour(s)
immac	Immaculate
immed	Immediate(ly)
inc	Included/inclusive
indus est	Industrial estate
INF	Naturist federation, ie naturist site
int'l	International
irreg	Irregular
junc	Junction
km	Kilometre
L	Left
LH	Left-hand
LS	Low season
ltd	Limited
mkd	Marked
mkt	Market
mob	Mobile (phone)
m'van	Motor caravan
m'way	Motorway
N	North
narr	Narrow
nr, nrby	Near, nearby
opp	Opposite
o'fits	Outfits
o'look(ing)	Overlook(ing)
o'night	Overnight
o'skts	Outskirts
PO	Post office
poss	Possible, possibly
pt	Part
R	Right
rd	Road or street
rec	Recommend/ed
recep	Reception
red	Reduced, reduction (for)
reg	Regular
req	Required
RH	Right-hand
rlwy	Railway line
rm	Room
rndabt	Roundabout
rte	Route
RV	Recreational vehicle, ie large motor caravan
rv/rvside	River/riverside
S	South
san facs	Sanitary facilities ie wc, showers, etc
snr citizens	Senior citizens
sep	Separate
sh	Short
sp	Sign post, signposted
sq	Square
ssn	Season
stn	Station
strt	Straight, straight ahead
sw	Swimming
thro	Through
TO	Tourist Office
tour ops	Tour operators
traff lts	Traffic lights
twd	Toward(s)
unrel	Unreliable
vg	Very good
vill	Village
W	West
w/end	Weekend
x-ing	Crossing
x-rds	Cross roads

Symbols Used

◆ Unspecified facilities for disabled guests check before arrival

⊞ Open all year

* Last year site report received (see Campsite Entries in Introduction)

Discover the overseas travel goes the extra mile for you

You'll enjoy touring in Europe so much more with The Caravan Club

Even if you have toured Europe before, you'll find your holiday so much more enjoyable with The Club. You can rely on our help and expertise to make your time abroad truly carefree.

We can arrange everything: Continental site bookings, ferry crossings at great prices and the finest travel insurance, all handled with care and expertise.

With over 200 hand-picked sites across Europe, from France's famous wine regions or sun-kissed Spanish coastal gems to exploring the Swiss Alps, there's something for everyone.

"We called The Club's Travel Service and were immediately put at ease – they were really helpful and organised everything, including ferries, campsite, insurance – the lot!"

Alan Godfrey

Request a brochure or talk to a dedicated overseas advisor

www.caravanclub.co.uk/continental or call **01342 488 062**

service that

Relax, we can do it all for you:

- The best possible negotiated ferry fares
- Pitch bookings at over 200 Club-inspected sites
- Wide choice of Tours & Excursions from short breaks to Grand Tours
- Camping cheques, ideal for off-peak travel
- Unbeatable overseas holiday insurance
- Advice & information from our team of overseas advisors
- The indispensable Caravan Europe Guides
- Everything for new or experienced travellers abroad

Inset one: Les Saules (LOI), France

Inset two: Château de l'Epervière (LIZ), France

Planning and Travelling

Caravanning and Touring Abroad – Practical Advice

You may be new to caravanning abroad, or perhaps it has been a while since you last toured in Europe. If so then this section of the handbook will offer you practical and useful advice, giving you the knowledge and confidence that you need to make the most of your trip and enjoy your holiday.

Travelling through Europe can be a daunting prospect. That's why the practical advice offered in this chapter has been put together, providing you with a summary of the comprehensive information contained elsewhere within the guide. Please be aware that laws, customs, regulations and advice differ in each country so you are recommended to make sure you are familiar with these for each country that you are planning to visit.

Before You Travel

Choosing Your Campsite

The great thing about touring is the freedom that it offers you. However, if you are new to travelling in Europe we would suggest that it might be wise not to be overly ambitious and to plan your trip carefully.

The great thing about touring is the freedom that it offers you

There is a wide range of campsites available across Europe offering a choice of different facilities and amenities, but we would recommend that you stay in a campsite close to port on your first night of arrival. This will give you a little time to get used to driving on the right hand side of the road and you can then make a fresh start to your journey the next day, or spend a couple of days (or indeed your whole holiday) enjoying the campsite and surrounding area.

When choosing your campsite (or campsites) there are some important factors that you need to keep in mind. Firstly, the location, do you want to be by the sea or near to a city, or perhaps you have a specific interest such as museums or hiking?

You need to consider what facilities and amenities are available as well, both on the campsite and in the nearby area. If you have children then you may want to make sure there is a playground and entertainment on site, or maybe you would like a good restaurant within easy walking distance.

These are all important factors to consider before you decide on where to stay during your holiday in order to avoid disappointment.

You should also take into account the time of year you are planning on travelling. If you are going in low season then many facilities and amenities may be closed. If you are going in high season or during public holidays it is likely there will be a high number of traffic and tourists, therefore advanced booking is often recommended.

For further information to help you choose the right campsite for your holiday, please refer to the chapter ***Continental Campsites***. This chapter includes useful information on campsites in Europe and also has a site booking letter, both in English, German, Italian and French, for you to use when making a reservation.

Overseas Site Booking Service

For peace of mind you may prefer to use The Caravan Club's Overseas Site Booking Service which offers Club members pitch bookings on over 200 campsites throughout Europe. This gives you freedom and flexibility of travel while eliminating

language problems, international deposit payments or waiting for replies by letter or email. Furthermore, you will have the reassurance of a confirmed pitch reservation and pitch fees paid in advance.

The Club's Continental Caravanning brochure (available from November every year) gives full details of the Overseas Site Booking Service and of the sites to which it applies, as well as information on the Club's range of package tours and excursions for caravanners. Campsite only bookings, which do not include a ferry crossing are subject to a £25.00 booking fee. Sites in the service may be booked via the Club's website, www.caravanclub.co.uk/overseas

All the sites in the Club's Overseas Site Booking Service are listed in this guide and are marked 'SBS' in their site entries. The Caravan Club cannot make advance reservations for any other campsites listed in this guide.

Choosing Your Ferry Crossing

There is a wide choice of ferry operators and routes available. The use of ferry crossings, or the Channel Tunnel, is a matter of personal preference and convenience. The Channel Tunnel and crossings from Dover to Calais are quickest, but if you have a long drive from home to your departure port, you may prefer a longer crossing giving you the chance to relax for a few hours and enjoy a meal onboard. The chapter ***Ferries and the Channel Tunnel*** contains a list of ferry routes and additional information.

Make sure you know the overall length, as well as the height, of your vehicle(s), as vehicle decks on some ferries have areas where height is restricted, and this should be checked when making your booking.

The Club's website has a direct link through to a number of the most popular ferry operators' reservations systems and Club members can make their own reservations while still taking advantage of the Club's negotiated offers as well as the ferry companies' own early booking offers – see www.caravanclub.co.uk/overseas

Insurance

UK motor vehicle policies will usually give you the legal minimum of insurance for EU countries, however it is very important to check whether your comprehensive cover becomes third-party-only when you leave the UK. It may be necessary to pay an additional premium for comprehensive cover abroad.

Having insurance for your vehicles does not cover any other risks that may arise when you are on holiday, for example, emergency medical and hospital expenses, or loss or theft of personal belongings. The Caravan Club's Red Pennant Overseas Holiday Insurance gives you maximum protection against a variety of mishaps which might otherwise ruin your holiday and is tailor-made for the caravanner and motorhome tourer. This is backed by the Club's own helpline with multi-lingual staff available 24 hours a day, 365 days a year.

If you are going to leave your home unoccupied for any length of time, check your house and contents insurance policies regarding any limitations or regulations.

You will find further details, information and advice in the ***Insurance*** chapter or see www.caravanclub.co.uk/redpennant and www.caravanclub.co.uk/insurance

Documents

All members of your party must have a valid passport, including babies and children. The chapter ***Documents*** sets out the requirements and explains how to apply for a passport.

In some countries a passport must be carried at all times as a form of photographic identification. You should also keep a separate photocopy of your passport details and leave a copy of the personal details page with a relative or friend.

You are best to carry a full valid photocard driving licence with paper counterpart. If you have an all green license issued before 1991, which does not conform to EU standards or have a pictorial representation of what you are allowed to drive/tow, we would strongly recommend that you change this for a photo-card license or carry an International Driving Permit (IDP). Police overseas may have problems understanding the all green license, and subsequently you may be delayed on your journey if they have to wait for help in translating it. International Driving Permits (IDP's) can be obtained from selected Post Offices, The AA and the RAC.

Carry your vehicle's Vehicle Registration Certificate (V5C), insurance certificate and MOT road worthiness certificate, if applicable, together with a copy of your CRIS document (proof of ownership) in respect of your caravan.

For hired or leased vehicles (including company cars) you will not normally have the V5C and therefore will need to get a VE103 Vehicle on Hire Certificate from the vehicle owner instead.

See the ***Documents chapter*** in the section ***PLANNING AND TRAVELLING*** for full details.

Vehicles and Equipment

Ensure your car and caravan or motorhome are properly serviced and ready for the journey, paying particular attention to tyres and tyre pressures.

Make sure caravan tyres are suited to the maximum weight of the caravan and the maximum permitted speed when travelling abroad - see the chapter ***Motoring - Equipment*** and, if you're a member of The Caravan Club, the Technical Information chapter of the Club's UK Sites Directory & Handbook.

Take a well-equipped spares and tool kit. Spare bulbs, a warning triangle (two are required in some countries), a reflective jacket/vest, fire extinguisher and a first-aid kit as these are legal requirements in many European countries. Nearside and offside extending mirrors are essential to give the best possible vision, together with a spare tyre/wheel for both car and caravan.

In many countries drivers who leave their vehicle when it is stationary on the carriageway must by law wear a reflective jacket or waistcoat, but it is sensible to do so in any country. A second jacket is a commonsense requirement for any passenger who also gets out of your vehicle to assist. Keep the jackets readily to hand inside your vehicle, not in the boot.

If headlights are likely to dazzle other road users, they must be adjusted to deflect to the right instead of the left using suitable beam deflectors or (in some cases) a built-in adjustment system.

Even if you are not planning to drive at night, you will need to switch your headlights on in tunnels or if visibility is poor. Some countries require dipped headlights to be used during daylight hours.

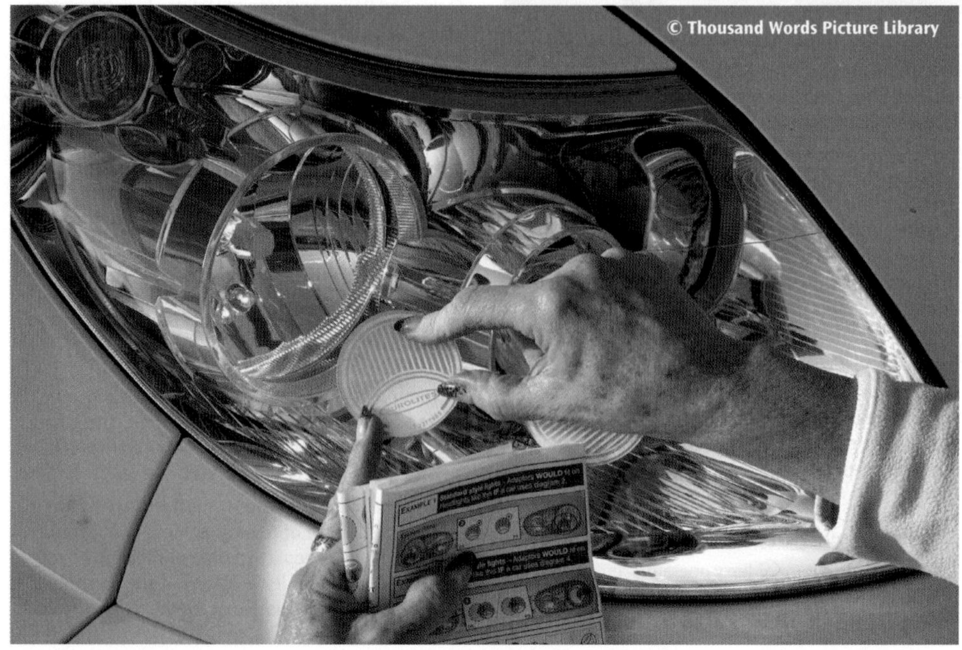
© Thousand Words Picture Library

Bulbs are more likely to fail with constant use and therefore it is always recommended to carry spares, whether it is a legal requirement or not.

For a checklist of equipment please see page 25.

Towing

Before you tow make sure you know your car well and have the correct mirrors suitable for your car and caravan. Plan carefully to avoid roads that are too narrow or may have low bridges, and never stop where it is unsafe to do so, i.e. on bends, narrow roads, etc.

Pull over safely to allow any build up of traffic behind you to pass wherever it is possible to do so and always keep a safe stopping distance between you and the vehicle in front. If you are overtaking or pulling across a main road allow yourself plenty of time to do this safely.

If you are new to towing, or if you would like to gain some valuable experience and knowledge, The Caravan Club runs 'Practical and Caravan Manoeuvring' courses, as well as 'Motorhome Manoeuvring' courses. These courses are open to both members and non-members of The Caravan Club and are designed to help you enjoy caravanning and touring more confidently.

For more information please visit www.caravanclub.co.uk/courses

Money

It is a good idea to carry a small amount of foreign currency, including loose change, for countries you are travelling through in case of emergencies, or when shopping. Many credit/debit cards issued in the UK will allow you to obtain cash from cash dispensers but it is best to check with your bank before you leave. Look for the same symbol on the machine as on your debit or credit card. Cash dispensers are often found in supermarkets as well as outside banks. The rate of exchange is often as good as anywhere else but there may be a charge.

Travellers' cheques are not widely accepted in some countries and credit cards issued by British banks may not be universally accepted, therefore it is wise to check before incurring expenditure. In some countries you may be asked to produce your passport for photographic identification purposes when paying by credit card.

*See the chapter **Money** and the **Country Introduction** for further information.*

On the Journey

Ferries and Eurotunnel

Report to the check-in desk at the ferry port or Eurotunnel terminal allowing plenty of time before the scheduled boarding time. As you approach the boarding area after passport control and Customs, staff will direct you to the waiting area or the boarding lane for your departure. As you are driving a 'high vehicle' you may be required to board first, or last. While waiting to board stay with your vehicle so that you can board immediately when instructed to do so. Virtually all ferries operate a 'drive on – drive off' system and you will not normally be required to perform any complicated manoeuvres, nor to reverse.

While waiting, turn off the 12V electricity supply to your fridge to prevent your battery going flat. Most fridges will stay adequately cool for several hours, as long as they are not opened. If necessary, place an ice pack or two (as used in cool boxes) in the fridge. You may be required to show that your gas supply has been turned off correctly.

Neither the ferry companies nor Eurotunnel permit you to carry spare petrol cans, empty or full, and Eurotunnel will not accept vehicles powered by LPG or dual-fuel vehicles. However Eurotunnel will accept vehicles fitted with LPG tanks for the purposes of heating, lighting, cooking or refrigeration, subject to certain conditions.

If your vehicle has been converted and is powered by LPG, some ferry companies require a certificate showing that the conversion has been carried out to the manufacturer's specification.

You will be instructed when to drive onto the ferry and, once on board, will be directed to the appropriate position. Treat ferry access ramps with caution, as they may be steep and/or uneven. Drive slowly as there may be a risk of grounding of any low point on the tow bar or caravan hitch. If your ground clearance is low, consider whether removing your stabiliser and/or jockey wheel would help.

Once boarded apply your car and caravan brakes. Vehicles are often parked close together and many passengers leaving their vehicles will be carrying bags for the crossing. It may, therefore, be wise to remove extended rear view mirrors as they may get knocked out of adjustment or damaged.

Make sure your car and caravan are secure and that, wherever possible, belongings are out of sight. Ensure that items on roof racks or cycle carriers are difficult to remove – a long cable lock may be useful.

Note the number of the deck you are parked on and the number of the staircase you use. You will not usually be permitted access to your vehicle during the crossing so take everything you require with you, including passports, tickets and boarding cards.

On ferry routes where you are permitted to transport pets, animals are usually required to remain in their owners' vehicles or in kennels on the car deck. On longer ferry crossings you can make arrangements at the onboard information desk for permission to visit your pet at suitable intervals.

*See also **Pet Travel Scheme** under **Documents** in the section **PLANNING AND TRAVELLING**.*

If you have booked cabins or seats go to the information desk immediately after boarding to claim them. Many ferries have a selection of restaurants and cafés, a shop, a children's play area, even a cinema, disco or casino to while away the time during the crossing. If you wish to use the main restaurant it may be advisable to make a reservation.

Listen carefully to onboard announcements, one of which will be important safety information at the time of departure. A further announcement will be made when it is time to return to your vehicle. Allow plenty of time to get down to the car deck. Don't start your engine until vehicles immediately in front of you start to move. Once off the ferry you may want to pull over into a parking area to allow the queue of traffic leaving the ferry to clear.

If you have made an advance booking on the Eurotunnel proceed to the signposted self check-in lanes. You will need to present the credit or debit card used when you made your booking. Having checked in you may, if you wish, visit the terminal to make any last minute purchases, etc, and then follow signs to passport control and customs. Your gas cylinder valves will be closed and sealed as a safety precaution and you will be asked to open the roof vents.

You will then join the waiting area allocated for your departure and will be directed onto the single-deck wagons of the train and told to park in gear with your brake on. You then stay in or around your vehicle for the 35 minute journey but will not be allowed to use your caravan until arrival. Useful information and music are supplied via the on-board radio station. On arrival, close the roof vent and release the caravan brake. When directed by the crew, drive off, remembering to drive on the right hand side of the road!

Motoring on the Continent

For comprehensive advice please see the chapters ***Motoring Advice*** and ***Motoring Equipment*** and the Country Introduction chapters. The following additional points may be helpful if you are feeling nervous about driving abroad.

Many roads are not as busy as those in the UK, but try to avoid rush hours in larger towns. There are fewer lorries on the roads at weekends and generally you will find that roads are quieter between 12pm and 2pm.

Don't attempt long distances in a single stint. Share the driving, if possible, and plan to break your journey overnight at a suitable campsite. There are thousands of sites listed in this guide, many of which are located near to motorways and main roads.

You are most likely to forget to drive on the right when pulling away from a parked position. It may be helpful to make yourself a sign and attach it to the dashboard to remind you to drive on the right. This can be removed before driving and replaced each time you stop. Alternatively, make a member of your party responsible for reminding the driver every time you start the car. Pay particular attention when turning left or when leaving a rest area, service station or campsite, and after passing through a one-way system.

Speed limit signs are in kilometres per hour - not miles per hour

Make sure the road ahead is clear before overtaking. Stay well behind the vehicle in front and, if possible, have someone with good judgement in the left-hand seat to give you the 'all clear'.

You will be charged tolls to use many European motorways. Credit cards are widely accepted as payment but not always. The Country Introduction chapters contain more details. Motorways provide convenient service stations and areas for a rest and a picnic en-route but, for your own safety, find an established campsite for an overnight stop.

Beware of STOP signs. You will encounter more of them than you find in the UK. Coming to a complete halt is compulsory in many European countries and failure to do so may result in a fine.

The maximum legal level of alcohol in the blood in most European countries is lower than that permitted in the UK. It is better not to drink at all when driving as penalties are severe.

If you are unfortunate enough to be involved in a road accident, take some photographs to back up the written description on your claim form.

During Your Stay

Arriving at the Campsite

Go to the campsite reception and fill in any registration forms required. A Camping Card International/Camping Card Scandinavia is recommended and usually accepted in lieu of handing over your passport.

If you have not booked in advance it is perfectly acceptable to ask to have a look around the campsite before deciding whether to stay or accept a particular pitch.

Pitches are usually available when the site re-opens after the lunch break and not normally before this time. Aim to arrive before 7pm or you may find the campsite reception closed; if this is the case you will probably find a member of staff on duty in the bar. It is essential to arrive before 10pm as the gates or barriers on most sites are closed for the night at this time. If you are delayed, remember to let the site know so that they will keep your pitch. When leaving, you will usually need to vacate your pitch by midday at the latest.

Many campsites offer various sporting activities, such as tennis, fishing, watersports, horseriding and bicycle hire, as well as entertainment programmes for children and/or adults in high season. Many also have a snack bar, restaurant and bar. Restrictions may apply to the use of barbecues because of the risk of fire; always check with site staff before lighting up.

Dogs are welcome on many campsites but some sites will not allow them during the high season (or at all), or will require them to be on a lead at all times. Check in advance. In popular tourist areas local regulations may ban dogs from beaches during the summer months.

If you have any complaints, take them up with site staff there and then. It is pointless complaining after the event, when something could have been done to improve matters at the time.

Food and Water

There is a limit to the amount of food which may be imported into other countries. In the light of animal health concerns in the UK in recent years, authorities abroad will understandably take a cautious approach and there is no guarantee that meat and dairy products, if found, will not be confiscated by Customs officers.

Be reasonable with the amount of food that you take with you and stick to basic items and/or children's special favourites. On occasion it may be difficult to obtain supplies of fresh milk, bread and cereals at campsite shops, particularly outside the summer season, so stock up before your arrival on site. It's often helpful to take your own supply of carrier bags and a cool box in hot weather.

Drinking water is normally clean and safe in the countries covered in Caravan Europe, but you may find the taste different from your own local mains supply and prefer to drink bottled water.

Electricity and Gas

Calor Gas is not normally available on the continent. Campingaz is widely available but you will need an adaptor to connect to a standard regulator. Alternatively carry sufficient gas for your stay, subject to the cross-Channel operator's regulations which may restrict you to three, two or even only one gas cylinder. Always check when making your booking.

Voltage on most sites is usually 220V or 230V nominal but may be lower. Most UK mains appliances are rated at 220V to 240V and usually work satisfactorily. Many sites have the European standard EN60309-2 connectors (formerly known as CEE17), into which you can plug your UK 3-pin connector and mains lead. However, on some sites you may need a continental 2-pin adaptor available from UK caravan accessory shops.

Caravanners may encounter the problem known as reverse polarity. This is where the site's 'live' line connects to the caravan's 'neutral' and vice versa and is due to different standards of plug and socket wiring that exist in other countries. The Club recommends checking the polarity immediately on connection, using a polarity tester, obtainable from a caravan accessory shop before you leave home.

The caravan mains electrical installation should not be used while a reversed polarity situation exists. Ask the site manager if you can use an alternative socket or bollard, as the problem may be restricted to that particular socket only. Frequent travellers to Europe who are electrically competent, often modify an adaptor to reverse the live and neutral connections. This can be tried in place of the standard connector, to see if the electricity supply then reverts to 'normal'. It is important that you are electrically competent or use an electrician to carry out the modification.

*See the chapter **Electricity and Gas** and **Country Introduction** for further information.*

Medical Matters

Before leaving home obtain a European Health Insurance Card (EHIC) which entitles you to emergency health care in the EU and some other countries. An EHIC is required for each individual family member, so allow enough time before your departure to obtain them. You can apply online on www.ehic.org.uk or by phoning 0845 6062030, or you can get an application form from a post office.

Specific advice on obtaining emergency medical treatment in the countries covered in this guide is summarised in the relevant country chapters and is also covered on the NHS website, www.nhs.uk/nhsengland/healthcareabroad. Alternatively obtain a copy of the Department of Health's leaflet, T7.1 Health Advice for Travellers which is downloadable from www.dh.gov.uk, email: dh@prolog.uk.com or call 08701 555455.

Check with your GP for the generic name of any prescription medicines you are taking. If you need more, or lose your supply, this will help a doctor or pharmacist to identify them. Keep receipts for any medication or treatment purchased abroad, plus the labels from the medicines, as these will be required if you make a claim on your travel insurance on returning home.

*For further advice and information see the chapter **Medical Matters**.*

Safety and Security

Safety is largely your own responsibility – taking sensible precautions and being aware of possible hazards won't spoil your holiday, but neglecting your safety and ignoring possible risks might.

The chapter entitled ***Safety and Security*** covers aspects of your own and your family's personal safety whilst on holiday. You are strongly advised to read this section carefully and follow the advice contained.

Other Information

Tourist Boards

Many European countries maintain tourist offices in the UK and they will supply you with information on their respective countries on request. In addition, a great deal of information can be obtained from the tourist board websites. Contact details of relevant tourist boards are given in the Country Introduction chapters.

Route Planning

It is wise to plan your route beforehand wherever possible. We have a ***Route Planning Map*** chapter under the ***Planning and Travelling*** section for your reference.

Both the AA and RAC have useful websites offering a European route planning service with access for non-members: www.theaa.com and www.rac.co.uk. Please be aware that some routes may not be suitable for caravans or large vehicles.

Satellite Navigation

GPS co-ordinates are given for most site entries in this guide. Your sat nav is a valuable aid in finding a campsite, but it is important to realise that such systems are not perfect and they may take you on routes that are not suitable for caravans or large vehicles. It is wise, therefore, to use your sat nav in conjunction with an up to date map or atlas or use a sat nav that has been designed specifically for caravanners and motorhome owners such as the Snooper Ventura Caravan Club Edition.

*For further advice see the chapter **Motoring – Equipment**.*

Checklist

It is assumed that users of this guide are well aware of the domestic and personal items necessary for trips away and of the checks to be made to vehicles before setting off. The Caravan Club's Technical Office will supply a copy of a leaflet 'Things to Take' to Club members on request, or you can download it from www.caravanclub.co.uk

The checklist is intended as a reminder only and covers some of the necessary items:

Car

Extending mirrors
Fire extinguisher
First aid kit
Fuses

Headlight converters/deflectors

Jack and wheelbrace

Mobile phone charger

Nationality stickers – GB or IRL (car and caravan) if not included within number plate

Puncture kit (sealant)

Radiator hose

Reflective safety jacket(s)/vest(s)

Satellite navigation device

Snow chains (if possibility of using snow covered roads)

Spare bulbs

Spare key

Spare parts, e.g. fan belt

Spare wheel/tyre

Stabiliser

Tool kit

Tow ball cover

Tow rope

Warning triangle/s

Caravan

Awning and groundsheet

Bucket

Chemical toilet and fluid/sachets

Corner steady tool and pads

Electrical extension lead and adaptor(s)

Extra long motorhome water hose pipe

Fire extinguisher

Gas cylinders

Gas regulator (Campingaz) if planning to use Campingaz, or as a back-up in case other gas is not available

Gas adaptor and hoses (where regulator is fitted to the caravan) to suit 'local' gas cylinders

Hitch and/or wheel lock

Levelling blocks

Mains polarity tester

Nose weight gauge

Peg mallet

Spare bulbs, fuses and lengths of wire

Spare key

Spare 7-pin plug (12S plug is especially vulnerable to damage)

Spare water pump (submersible types are vulnerable to failure)

Spare wheel/tyre

Spirit level

Step and doormat

Water containers - waste/fresh

Water hoses – waste/fresh

Documents and Papers

Address book, contact telephone numbers

Camping Card International/Camping Card Scandinavia

Car/caravan/motorhome insurance certificates

Campsite booking confirmation(s)

Caravan Club membership card

Caravan Europe guide book/s

Copy of your CRIS document

Credit/debit cards, contact numbers in the event of loss

Valid driving licence (not provisional)

European Health Insurance Card (EHIC)

European Accident Statement

Ferry booking confirmation and timetable

Foreign currency

Holiday travel insurance documents (Red Pennant)

International Driving Permit (if applicable)

Letter of authorisation from vehicle owner (if applicable)

Maps and guides

MOT roadworthiness certificate (if applicable)

NHS medical card

Passport (plus photocopy of details page) and visas (if applicable)

Pet's passport and addresses of vets abroad

Phrase books

Telephone card

Travellers' cheques and/or travel money card

Vehicle Registration Certificate V5C or Vehicle on Hire Certificate VE103

Technical Leaflets

The Caravan Club publishes technical leaflets for its members (some available to non-members) on a wide range of topics, many of which are relevant to caravanning abroad.

You are advised to request copies or see:

www.caravanclub.co.uk/expert-advice

Planning and Travelling

Continental Campsites

© *iStockphoto.com/Antony McAulay*

Introduction

There are thousands of excellent campsites throughout Europe belonging to local municipalities, families, companies or camping, touring and automobile clubs. Most sites are open to everyone but a few are reserved for their own members.

Compared with Caravan Club sites in the UK, pitches may be small and 80 square metres is not uncommon. Pitches may also be very close together, particularly in Germany and Italy where it is not uncommon to put your hand out of your caravan window and touch the caravan on the next pitch. This may present problems for large outfits and/or outfits with awnings. In the summer season it may also be difficult to put up awnings because of hard ground conditions in hot climates.

Generally the approaches and entrances to campsites are well signposted, but often only with a tent or caravan symbol or with the word 'Camping', rather than the site's full name.

There are usually sinks for washing up and laundry rooms containing washing machines and dryers. Many sites have a shop in high season, even if only for basic groceries, however some shops stock a wide variety of items. Often there is a restaurant or snack bar, Wi-Fi access, swimming pool and playground. Occasionally there may be a car wash, sauna, solarium, bureau de change, tourist information office and other facilities on site.

In the high season all campsite facilities are usually open and some sites offer organised entertainment for children and adults as well as local excursions. However, bear in mind that in the months of July and August, toilet and shower facilities and pitch areas will be under the greatest pressure.

Booking a Campsite

It is advisable to pre-book pitches during the high season. If you are planning a long stay then contact campsites early in the year. Some sites impose a minimum length of stay in order to guarantee their business. Usually there are one or two unreserved pitches available for overnight tourers.

Often it is possible to book directly via a campsite's website using a credit or debit card to pay a deposit if required. Otherwise you can write (enclosing a reply envelope or letters may be ignored) or email the campsite. A word of warning: **some campsites regard the deposit as a booking or admin fee and will not deduct the amount from your final bill.**

Site booking letters in English, German and Italian are provided at the end of this chapter. Detachable response letters are also provided which should encourage site operators to reply. It is worth remembering that a site will very rarely reserve a special place for you. The acceptance of a reservation merely means you will be guaranteed a pitch; the best being allocated first or for repeat visitors. Not all campsites accept advance bookings.

If you do not book ahead you should plan to arrive no later than 4pm (even earlier at popular resorts) in order to secure a pitch, after that time sites fill up quickly. You also need to allow time to find another campsite if your first choice is fully booked.

Caravan Club Overseas Site Booking Service

The Caravan Club's Travel Service offers Club members an Overseas Site Booking Service (to which terms and conditions apply) to over 200 campsites throughout Europe. This service gives freedom and flexibility of travel but with the reassurance of a confirmed pitch reservation and pitch fees paid in sterling in advance. Full details of this service, plus information on special offers with ferry operators, tours & excursions programmes (some specifically aimed at motorhomes) and details of Red Pennant

Overseas Holiday Insurance appear in the Club's Continental Caravanning brochure – telephone 01342 327410 to request a copy, or visit www.caravanclub.co.uk/overseas

Booking a site through The Caravan Club gives you a price guarantee and no matter what happens to exchange rates, there will be no surcharges. Campsite only bookings, which do not include a ferry crossing, are subject to a £25.00 booking fee.

All Overseas Site Booking Service sites are listed in this guide and are marked 'SBS' in their site entries. Many of them can be booked via the Club's website, www.caravanclub.co.uk. **The Caravan Club cannot make advance reservations for any other campsites listed in this guide.**

Except in the case of those campsites included in the Club's pre-bookable Continental Caravanning network and marked SBS (Site Booking Service) at the end of their site entries, the Caravan Club has no contractual arrangements with any of the sites featured in this guide. Furthermore, even in the case of sites with which the Club is contracted, it has no direct control over day-to-day operations or administration. Only those sites marked SBS have been inspected by Caravan Club staff.

It is assumed by The Caravan Club Ltd, but not checked (except in the case of sites marked SBS), that all campsites fall under some form of local licensing, which may or may not take account of matters of safety and hygiene. Caravanners are responsible for checking such matters to their own satisfaction.

Sites Direct

In addition to the sites in the Site Booking Service network, Club members now have a greater choice of campsites available to book direct through the Club's website. The Club has implemented a link to enable direct reservations within, for example, a particular region, or on sites with specific facilities. These sites (approximately 500) have not been inspected by Caravan Club representatives and all the information about them has been input by site owners themselves. Payment is direct to the site and any booking made through this channel is subject to the individual site's terms and conditions. For more information see www.caravanclub.co.uk/sitesdirect

Camping Cheques

The Caravan Club operates a low season scheme in association with Camping Cheques offering Club members flexible touring holidays. The scheme covers approximately 622 sites in 29 countries.

Camping Cheques are supplied through The Caravan Club as part of a package which includes return ferry fare and a minimum of seven Camping Cheques. Each Camping Cheque is valid for one night's low season stay for two people, including car and caravan/motorhome/trailer tent, electricity and one pet. Full details are contained in the Club's Continental Caravanning brochure.

Those sites which feature in the Camping Cheques scheme and which are listed in this guide are marked 'CChq' in their site entries.

Caravan Storage Abroad

The advantages of storing your caravan on a campsite in Europe are obvious, not least being the avoidance of the long tow to your destination, and a saving in ferry and fuel costs. Some campsites advertise a long-term storage facility or you may negotiate with a site which appeals to you.

However, there are pitfalls and understandably insurers in the UK are reluctant to insure a caravan which will be out of the country most of the time. There is also the question of invalidity of the manufacturer's warranty for caravans less than three years old if the supplying dealer does not carry out annual servicing.

*See also **Insurance** in the section **PLANNING AND TRAVELLING.***

Electricity Supply

For your own safety you are strongly advised to read the chapter ***Electricity and Gas*** in the section ***DURING YOUR STAY.***

Many campsites now include electricity and/or shower facilities in their 'per night' price and where possible this has been included in site entries. Where these are not included, a generous allowance should be made in your budget. It is not unknown for sites to charge up to the equivalent of £4 per night or more for electric hook-ups and £2 per shower. In winter sports areas, charges for electricity are generally higher in winter – the prices given in this guide are usually those charged during the summer months.

Facilities and Site Description

Campsite descriptions, facilities, directions, prices and other information are reported to the editor by users of this guide. Within individual site entries the comments (in inverted commas) are from people who have visited the site and it must be understood that people's tastes, opinions, priorities and expectations can differ greatly. Please also bear in mind that campsites change hands, opening dates and prices change and standards may rise or fall, depending on the season.

Facilities Out of Season

During the low season (this can be any time except July and early August) campsites may operate with limited facilities. Shops, swimming pools, bars and restaurants may be closed. A municipal site warden may visit in the morning and/or evening only to collect fees, which are sometimes reduced during the low season.

Sanitary Facilities

Facilities normally include toilet and shower blocks with shower cubicles, wash basins and razor sockets. Toilets are not always fitted with seats and do not always have toilet paper. The abbreviation 'wc' indicates the normal, pedestal type of toilet found in the UK. Some sites have footplate 'squatter' toilets and, where this is known, it is indicated by the abbreviation 'cont', i.e. continental.

It is recommended that you take your own universal flat plug (to fit all basin sizes) and toilet paper. During the low season it is not uncommon for only a few toilet and shower cubicles to be in use on a 'unisex' basis and they may not be cleaned as frequently as they are during the site's busy season. Hot water, other than for showers, may not be generally available.

In recent years many campsites have upgraded their sanitary facilities in line with visitors' expectations, but you may find that some are still unheated and may not offer items such as pegs on which to hang clothes/towels, or shelves for soap and shampoo. Rarely, there may be no shower curtains or shower cubicle doors and hence little or no privacy.

Waste Disposal

Site entries in this guide indicate (when known) where a campsite has a chemical disposal facility and/or a motorhome service point, which is assumed to include a waste (grey) water dump station and toilet cassette-emptying point.

Continental caravanners in general tend to prefer to use a site's toilet and shower facilities, together with its dishwashing and vegetable preparation areas, more than their British counterparts who prefer to use their own facilities in their caravan. Caravanners used to the level of facilities for the disposal of waste water on Caravan Club sites may well find that facilities on Continental campsites are not always of the same standard.

Chemical disposal points are occasionally difficult to locate and may be fixed at a high level requiring some strenuous lifting of cassettes in order to empty them. Disposal may simply be down a toilet – continental or otherwise. Wastemaster-style emptying points are not very common in Europe.

Formaldehyde chemical cleaning products are banned in many countries. It is recommended to always use formaldehyde free cleaning products that are kinder to the environment and the overwhelming proportion of current products are now formaldehyde free. In Germany the 'Blue Angel' (Blaue Engel) Standard, and in the Netherlands the 'Milieukeur' Standard, indicates that the product has particularly good 'green' credentials.

Rubbish bins are normally provided and at many campsites you will also find recycling bins. At some campsites, notably in Switzerland and Germany, you may have to purchase special plastic bags for the disposal of rubbish or pay a daily rubbish or environmental charge.

Finding a Campsite

Directions are given for all campsites listed in this guide and most also have GPS co-ordinates. Where known full street addresses are also given. The directions have been supplied by users of this guide and The Caravan Club is unable to check each one in detail for accuracy.

*See the chapter **Motoring – Equipment** in the section **PLANNING AND TRAVELLING** for more information on satellite navigation.*

Lunch Breaks

Some campsites close for a long lunch break, sometimes up to three hours, and occasionally there is no access for vehicles during this period. The time during which a site's entrance gate or barrier is closed may be reduced or extended according to the time of year. This may also apply to the overnight closure of gates and barriers. In addition, use of vehicles within the site may be restricted during certain hours to ensure a period of quiet. Check with individual campsites for their regulations.

Motorhomes – Overnight Stops

Towns and villages across Europe may provide dedicated overnight or short stay areas specifically for motorhomes, many of which have good security, electricity, water and waste facilities. These are known as 'Aires de Services', 'Stellplatz' or 'Aree di Sosta' and are usually well signposted with a motorhome pictogram.

Likewise, to cater for this growing market, many campsites in popular tourist areas have separate overnight areas of hardstanding with appropriate facilities often just outside the main campsite area. Fees are generally very reasonable.

A number of organisations publish guides listing thousands of these sites. Alternatively see www.campercontact.nl for details of thousands of sites for motorhomes in many countries in Europe.

For reasons of security The Caravan Club strongly advises against spending the night on petrol station service areas, ferry terminal car parks or isolated 'aires de repos' or 'aires de services' along motorways. *See the chapter **Safety and Security** in the section **DURING YOUR STAY.***

Where known, information on the availability of public transport within easy reach of a campsite, as reported by caravanners, is given in the site entries in this guide.

Municipal Campsites

Municipal sites are found in towns and villages all over Europe, in particular in France, and in recent years many municipalities have improved standards on their sites while continuing to offer good value for money. However, on some municipal sites you may still find that sanitary facilities are basic and old-fashioned, even though they may be clean. Bookings for a municipal site can usually be made during office hours through the local town hall or, increasingly, the local tourist office.

Outside the high season you may find significant numbers of seasonal workers, market traders and itinerants resident on sites – sometimes in a separate, designated area. In most cases their presence does not cause other visitors any problem (other than early morning traffic noise as they leave for work) but where they are not welcome some sites refuse entry to caravans with twin-axles ('deux essieux' in French) or restrict entry by caravan height, weight or length, or charge a hefty additional fee. Check if any restrictions apply if booking in advance.

Recent visitors report that bona fide caravanners with twin-axle or over-height/weight/length caravans may be allowed entry, and/or may not be charged the higher published tariff, but this is negotiable with site staff at the time of arrival.

When approaching a town you may find that municipal sites are not always named and signposts may simply state 'Camping' or show a tent or caravan symbol.

Naturist Campsites

Details of a number of naturist sites are included in this guide and are shown with the word 'naturist' after their site name. Some, shown as 'part naturist' have separate areas for naturists. Visitors to naturist sites aged 16 and over usually (but not always) require an INF card or Naturist Licence and this is covered by membership of British Naturism (tel 01604 620361 or www.british-naturism.org.uk). Alternatively, holiday membership is available on arrival at any recognised naturist site (a passport-size photograph is required). When looking for a site you will find that naturist campsites generally display the initials FNF, INF or FKK on their signs.

Opening Dates

Opening dates (where known) are given for campsites in this guide, many of which are open all year. Sometimes sites may close without notice for refurbishment work, because of a change of ownership or simply because of a lack of visitors or a period of bad weather.

Outside the high season it is always best to contact campsites in advance as some owners have a tendency to shut campsites when business is slack. Otherwise you may arrive to find the gates of an 'all year' campsite very firmly closed. Municipal campsites' published opening dates cannot always be relied on at the start and end of the season. It is advisable to phone ahead or arrive early enough to be able to find an alternative site if your first choice is closed.

Pets on Campsites

See also ***Pet Travel Scheme*** *under* ***Documents*** *and* ***Holiday Insurance for Pets*** *under* ***Insurance*** *in the section* ***PLANNING AND TRAVELLING.***

Dogs are welcome on many campsites provided they conform to legislation and vaccination requirements, and are kept under control. Be prepared to present documentary evidence of vaccinations on arrival at a campsite.

Please be aware however that some countries authorities do not permit entry to certain breeds of dogs and some breeds will need to be muzzled and kept on a lead at all times. You are advised to contact the appropriate authorities of the countries that you plan to visit via their embassies in London before making travel arrangements for your dog.

Campsites usually have a daily charge for dogs. There may be limits on the number of dogs allowed, often one per pitch, or the type or breed accepted. Some campsites will not allow dogs at all or will require them to be on a lead at all times. Some campsites may also not allow dogs during the peak holiday season or will forbid you to leave your dog unattended in your caravan/motorhome, which can make going out for an evening meal or a day trip difficult. Dog owners must conform to site regulations concerning keeping dogs on a lead, dog-walking areas and fouling, and may find restricted areas within a site where dogs are not permitted.

In popular tourist areas local regulations may ban dogs from beaches during the summer.

Think very carefully before taking your pet abroad. Dogs used to the UK's temperate climate may find it difficult to cope with prolonged periods of hot weather. In addition, there are diseases transmitted by ticks, caterpillars, mosquitoes or sandflies, particularly in southern Europe, to which dogs from the UK have no natural resistance. Consult your vet about preventative treatment well in advance of your holiday. You need to be sure that your dog is healthy enough to travel and, if in any doubt, it may be in its best interests to leave it at home.

Visitors to southern Spain and Portugal, parts of central France and northern Italy, from mid-winter to late spring should be aware of the danger to dogs of pine processionary caterpillars. Dogs should be kept away from pine trees if possible or fitted with a muzzle that prevents the nose and mouth from touching the ground. This will also protect against poisoned bait sometimes used by farmers and hunters.

In the event that your pet is taken ill abroad a campsite will usually have information about local vets. Failing that, most countries have a telephone directory similar to the Yellow Pages, together with online versions such as www.pagesjaunes.fr.

Most European countries require dogs to wear a collar at all times identifying their owners. If your dog goes missing, report the matter to the local police and the local branch of that country's animal welfare organisation.

Prices

Campsite prices per night (for a car, caravan and two adults) are shown in local currencies. In EU member states where euros is not the official currency they are usually accepted for payment of campsite fees and other goods and services.

Payment of campsite fees should be made at least two hours before departure. Remember that if you stay on site after midday you may be charged for an extra day. Many campsites shown in this guide as accepting credit card payments may not do so for an overnight or short stay because of high transaction charges. Alternatively, a site will impose a minimum amount or will accept credit cards only in peak season. It is always advisable to check the form of payment required when you check in.

On arrival at a campsite which has an automatic barrier at the entrance you may be asked for a deposit, returnable on departure, for the use of a swipe card to operate the barrier. The amount will vary from site to site; €25 or €30 is usual.

Campsites may impose extra charges for the use of swimming pools and other leisure facilities, showers and laundrette facilities.

Registering on Arrival

On arrival at a campsite it is usual to have to register in accordance with local authority requirements, and to produce an identity document which the campsite office may retain during your stay. Most campsites now accept the Camping Card International (or Camping Card Scandinavia) instead of a passport and, where known, their site entries are marked CCI or CCS. CCIs are available to Caravan Club members at a cost of £6 by calling 01342 336633 or are free to members if you take out the Club's Red Pennant Overseas Holiday Insurance.

Alternatively, a photocopy of your passport may be acceptable and it is a good idea to carry a few copies with you to avoid depositing your passport and to speed up the check-in process.

Sites' Contact Details

Telephone numbers are given for most campsites listed in this guide together with fax numbers, website and email addresses where known.

The telephone numbers assume you are in the country concerned and the initial zero should be dialled, where applicable. If you are telephoning from outside the country concerned you should dial the international country code and the initial zero is omitted. For more details see the chapter ***Keeping in Touch*** and the ***Country Introduction*** chapter.

General Advice

Most campsites close from 10pm until 7am or 8am, however, late night arrival areas are sometimes provided for late travellers. Motorhomes in particular should check the gate/barrier closing time before going out for the evening in their vehicle. Check out time is usually between 10am and 12pm. Advise reception staff if you need to leave very early, for example, to catch a ferry.

If possible inspect the site and facilities before booking in. If your pitch is allocated at check-in ask to see it first to check the condition and access, as marked or hedged pitches can sometimes be difficult for large outfits. Riverside pitches can be delightful but keep an eye on the water level; in periods of heavy rain this may rise rapidly and the ground becomes boggy.

If the weather has been bad early in the season you may find that site staff have not been able, for example, to cut grass or hedges and prepare the site fully for visitors. At the end of the season grass pitches may be well worn and could be muddy or slippery after rain.

Often campsites have a daily discounted charge for children, however it is not unknown for site owners to charge the full adult daily rate for children from as young as three years old.

A tourist tax may be imposed by local authorities in some European countries. VAT may also be payable on top of your campsite fees. These charges are not usually included in the prices listed in this guide.

Speed limits on campsites are usually restricted to 10 km/h (6 mph). You may be asked to park your car in a separate area away from your caravan, particularly in the high season.

Some campsites ban the wearing of boxer shorts-style swimming trunks in pools on the grounds of hygiene. This rule may be strictly enforced.

The use of the term 'statics' in the campsite reports in this guide in many instances refers to long-term seasonal pitches, chalets, cottages, tour operators' fixed tents and cabins, as well as mobile homes.

Complaints

If you have a complaint take it up with site staff or owners at the time so that it can be dealt with promptly. It is pointless complaining after the event, when action to improve matters could have been taken at the time. In France, if your complaint cannot be settled directly with the campsite, and if you are sure you are within your rights, you may take the matter up with the Préfecture of the local authority in question.

The Caravan Club has no control or influence over day to day campsite operations or administration. Except in the case of a small number of sites in the Club's Overseas Site Booking Service with which it is contracted (marked SBS in site entries) and on which it has made a booking for you, it cannot intervene in any dispute you may have with a particular site.

Site Booking Letter – English

Date: Address (block caps)..

....

....

Tel No: (0044) ....

Fax No: (0044) ....

Email ....

Dear Sir/Madam

I wish to make a reservation as follows:

Arriving (date and month)................. **Departing** (date and month)................. (........nights)

Adults	....	**Children (+ ages)**		....			
Car	☐	**Caravan**	☐	**Motor Caravan**	☐	**Trailertent**	☐
Electrical Hook-up			☐	**Awning**	☐	**Extra tent**	☐

I look forward to an early reply and enclose an addressed envelope. When replying please advise all charges and deposit required. I look forward to meeting you and visiting your site.

Yours faithfully,

[Name in block capitals after signature]

Caravan Club Membership No........................

✂--

Reply

Date: Address..

....

....

Dear Mr/Mrs/Ms ....

Thank you for your reservation from .... to .... (........ nights).

- **YES, OK** – I am pleased to confirm your reservation (with/without electrical hook-up) and look forward to welcoming you.
- **NO, SORRY** – I regret that the site is fully booked for the dates you request.

Yours sincerely

....

Site Booking Letter – German

Datum: Anschrift (in Großbuchstaben)...

....

....

Telefonnummer.: (0044)..

Faxnummer: (0044)..

Email ....

Sehr geehrter Herr/sehr geehrte Dame

Ich möchte wie folgt reservieren:

Ankunft (Tag und Monat) .... **Abreise** (Tag und Monat).................... (... Nächte)

Erwachsene .... Kinder (in Alter von) ....

Auto ☐ **Caravan** ☐ **Wohnmobil** ☐ **Klappwohnwagen** ☐

Strom ☐ **Vordach** ☐ **Extra Zelt** ☐

Ich sehe einer baldigen Antwort entgegen und lege einen addressierten Umschlag bei. Bitte führen Sie in Ihrem Antwortschreiben sämtliche erforderlichen Gebühren und Anzahlungen an. Ich freue mich auf den Aufenthalt auf Ihrem Campingplatz und hoffe, Sie dort zu treffen.

Mit freundlichen Grüßen

(Unterschrift und Name in Großbuchstaben)

Caravan Club Mitgliednummer ....

✂---

Antwort

Datum: Anschrift: ....

....

....

....

Herrn/Frau/Fräulein...

Vielen Dank für Ihre Reservierung von .... bis .... (.......Übernachtungen).

- **JA, OK** – Ich kann Ihre Reservierung (mit/ohne elektr. Anschluß) bestätigen und freue mich, Sie hier zu begrüßen.
- **NEIN, LEIDER** – Ich bedaure, daß der Campingplatz für die von Ihnen gewünschte Zeit voll belegt ist.

Mit freundlichen Grüßen

....

Site Booking Letter – Italian

Data:

Indirizzo (stampatello)..

....

....

N° Tel: (0044)...

N° Fax: (0044)...

Email..

Egregio Signore/Signora

Desidero fare una prenotazione come segue:

Arrivo (giorno e mese)...................... **Partenza** (giorno e mese)........................(...notti)

Adulti............... **Bambini** (+ età)...................................

Automobile ☐ **Roulotte/Caravan** ☐ **Camper** ☐ **Tenda a rimorchio** ☐

Allacciamento elettrico ☐ **Tendone** ☐ **Tenda addizionale** ☐

Attendo un sollecito riscontro con busta indirizzata. Quando risponde, la prego di farmi sapere tutte le tariffe ed il deposito richiesti. Attendendo di incontrarla e di visitare il suo campeggio, la prego di gradire i miei distinti saluti.

[Nome in stampatello dopo la firma]

No d'associazione al Caravan Club.............................

✂--

Risposta

Data:

Indirizzo..

....

....

Egregio Signore/Signora...............

La ringrazio per il modulo di prenotazione da............a............. (......notti).

- **SI, OK** – Sono lieto di confermare la sua prenotazione (con/senza allacciamento elettrico) e attendo di incontrarla.
- **NO, MI DISPIACE** – Mi dispiace ma il campeggio è completamente prenotato per le date da lei richieste.

Distinti saluti.

....

Site Booking Letter – French

Date: Adresse (lettres majuscules)..

....

....

Tél : (0044)..

Fax : (0044)..

Email...

Monsieur/Madame

J'aimerais désire effectuer la réservation suivante :

Arrivée (jour et mois) .... **Départ** (jour et mois)...................... (.........nuits)

Adultes .... **Enfants (+ âges)** ....

Voiture ☐ **Caravane** ☐ **Camping car** ☐ **Tente-remorque** ☐

Branchement électrique ☐ **Auvent** ☐ **Tente supplémentaire** ☐

Ci-joint une enveloppe avec mon adresse. En vous remerciant par avance pour votre réponse je vous demanderais de bien vouloir me communiquer vos tarifs complets ainsi que le montant des arrhes à verser.

En attendant le plaisir de faire votre connaissance et de séjourner sur votre terrain, je vous prie de croire, Monsieur/Madame, à l'assurance de mes sentiments les meilleurs.

(Nom en lettres majuscules après la signature)

No. d'adhérent du Caravan Club ....

✂---

Réponse

Date: Adresse ....

....

....

Monsieur/Madame/Mademoiselle

J'accuse réception de votre bulletin de réservation pour la période

du....................... au ....(........nuits).

- **OUI** – Je confirme votre réservation (avec/sans branchement électrique) en attendant le plaisir de faire votre connaissance.
- **NON** – Je suis au regret de vous informer que le terrain est complet pendant la période de votre choix.

Veuillez croire, Monsieur/Madame/Mademoiselle, à l'assurance de mes sentiments les meilleurs.

....

Planning and Travelling

Customs Regulations

Travelling to the UK from the European Union

On entry into the UK no tax or duty is payable on goods bought tax-paid in other EU countries which are for your own use and which have been transported by you. VAT and duty are included in the price of goods purchased and travellers can no longer buy duty-free or tax-free goods on journeys within the EU.

The following are guidance levels for the import of alcohol and tobacco into the UK but Customs do not enforce any absolute limits. However, if you bring in more than the following quantities Customs may suspect that they are for a commercial purpose and may ask questions and make checks. If you break the rules Customs may seize the goods – and the vehicle(s) used to transport them – and may not return them to you.

800 cigarettes
400 cigarillos
200 cigars
1kg tobacco
10 litres of spirits
20 litres of fortified wine (e.g. port or sherry)
90 litres of wine
110 litres of beer

No one under 17 years of age is entitled to the tobacco or alcohol allowances.

When entering the UK from another member state of the EU without having travelled to or through a non-EU country, you should use the blue Customs channel or exit reserved for EU travellers, provided your purchases are within the limits for imports from that country and you are not importing any restricted or prohibited goods, details of which are given later in this chapter.

Travelling to/from Non-EU Countries to/from the UK

Customs allowances for countries outside the EU apply to the following countries: Andorra, Croatia, Gibraltar, Norway and Switzerland.

You may purchase goods free of duty if travelling from the UK direct to a country outside the EU. Duty-free allowances for travellers returning to the UK (or entering any other EU country) from a non-EU country are generally as follows:

200 cigarettes, or 100 cigarillos, or 50 cigars, or 250gms tobacco
1 litre of spirits or strong liqueurs over 22 per cent volume, or 2 litres of fortified wine, sparkling wine or any other alcoholic drink that's less than 22 per cent volume
4 litres of still wine
16 litres of beer
£390 worth of all other goods including perfume, gifts and souvenirs without having to pay tax and/ or duty (or £270 if you arrive by private plane or private boat for pleasure purposes)
No one under 17 years is entitled to the tobacco or alcohol allowances.

When entering the UK from a non-EU country, or having travelled to or through a non-EU country, you should go through the red Customs channel or use the telephone at the Red Point if you have exceeded your Customs allowances, or if you are carrying any prohibited, restricted or commercial goods. Use the green Customs channel if you have 'nothing to declare'.

All dutiable items must be declared to Customs on entering the UK; failure to do so may mean that you forfeit them and your vehicle(s). Customs officers are legally entitled to examine your baggage and your vehicles and you are responsible for packing and unpacking. Whichever Customs channel you use, you may be stopped by a Customs officer and you and your vehicles may be searched.

If you are caught with goods that are prohibited or restricted, or goods in excess of your Customs allowances, you risk a heavy fine and possibly a prison sentence.

For further information contact HM Revenue & Customs National Advice Service on 0845 010 9000 (+44 2920 501 261 from outside the UK).

Travelling Within the European Union

While there are no limits on what travellers can buy and take with them when travelling between EU countries (provided the goods are for personal use and not for re-sale), the guidance levels are below:

800 cigarettes or 400 cigarillos or 200 cigars or 1kg tobacco
10 litres spirits over 22 per cent volume or 20 litres fortified wine not over 22 per cent volume
90 litres wine
110 litres beer

Boats

Virtually all boats of any size taken abroad must carry registration documents when leaving UK waters. Contact the Maritime and Coastguard Agency on 0870 6006505 or www.mcga.gov.uk for details. The Royal Yachting Association recommends that all boats have marine insurance and can provide details of the rules and regulations for taking a boat to countries bordering the Atlantic Ocean and the Baltic, Mediterranean and Black Seas – tel 0845 345 0400 or 023 8060 4100, www.rya.org.uk. Some countries require owners of certain types of vessels to have an International Certificate of Competence and information is contained in RYA publications.

If planning to take a boat abroad check with the appropriate tourist office before departure as rules and regulations for boat use vary from country to country. Third party insurance is compulsory in most European countries and is advisable elsewhere.

Currency

Any person entering or leaving the EU will have to declare the money that they are carrying if this amounts to €10,000 (or equivalent in other currencies) or more. This includes cheques, travellers' cheques, money orders etc. This ruling does not apply to anyone travelling within the EU.

For further information contact HMRC Excise & Customs Helpline on 0845 010 9000.

Food and Plants

Travellers from within the EU may bring into the UK any fruit, vegetable or plant products without restriction as long as they are grown in the EU, are free from pests or disease and are for your own consumption. For food products Andorra, the Channel Islands, the Isle of Man, San Marino and Switzerland are treated as part of the EU.

From most countries outside the EU you are not allowed to bring into the UK any meat or dairy products. Other animal products may be severely restricted or banned and it is important that you declare any such products on entering the UK.

HM Revenue & Customs publish leaflets broadly setting out the rules, entitled 'Bringing Food Products into the UK' and 'Bringing Fruit, Vegetable and Plant Products into the UK'. These can be downloaded from their website or telephone the National Advice Service on 0845 010 9000.

Rules regarding food and plants can change at any time without notice. For up to date information please contact the Food and Environment Research Agency (Fera) on 0844 248 0071. If you are unsure about any item you are bringing in, or are simply unsure of the rules, you must go to the red Customs channel or use the phone provided at the Red Point to speak to a Customs officer.

In the light of animal health concerns in recent years in the UK, authorities abroad will understandably take a cautious approach to the import of foodstuffs. There is no guarantee that such products, if found, will not be confiscated by Customs officers.

Medicines

If you intend to take medicines with you when you go abroad you should obtain a copy of HMRC Notice 4, 'Taking Medicines With You When You Go Abroad', from HM Revenue & Customs National Advice Service on 0845 010 9000 or download it from www.hmrc.gov.uk. Alternatively contact the Drug Enforcement Policy Team, HM Revenue & Customs, New King's Beam House, 22 Upper Ground, London SE1 9PJ, tel 020 7865 5767.

There is no limit to the amount of medicines obtained without prescription, but medicines prescribed by your doctor may contain controlled drugs (i.e. subject to control under the Misuse of Drugs legislation) and you should check the allowances for these – in good time before you travel – in case you need to obtain a licence from the Home Office. In general, the permitted allowance for each drug is calculated on an average 15 days' dose.

Motor Vehicles and Caravans

Travellers between member states of the EU are entitled to import temporarily a motor vehicle, caravan or trailer into other member states without any Customs formalities.

Motor vehicles and caravans may be temporarily imported into non-EU countries generally for a maximum of six months in any twelve month period, provided they are not hired, sold or otherwise disposed of in that country.

Temporarily imported vehicles should not be left behind after the importer has left, should not be used by residents of the country visited and should not be left longer than the permitted period.

If you intend to stay longer than six months, take up employment or residence, or dispose of a vehicle you should seek advice well before your departure from the UK, for example from one of the motoring organisations.

Anyone temporarily importing into another country a vehicle – either hired or borrowed – which does not belong to them should carry a letter of authority from the vehicle owner and/or a VE103 Vehicle on Hire Certificate from the vehicle owner (this includes company cars).

*See the chapter **Documents** in the section **PLANNING AND TRAVELLING** for further details.*

Use of Caravan by Persons other than the Owner

Many caravan owners reduce the cost of a holiday by sharing their caravan with friends or relatives. Either the caravan is left on the Continent on a campsite

or it is handed over at the port. In making these arrangements it is important to consider the following:

- The total time the vehicle spends abroad must not exceed the permitted period for temporary importation.
- The owner of the caravan must provide the other person with a letter of authority. It is not permitted to accept a hire fee or reward.
- The number plate on the caravan must match the number plate on the tow car used.
- Both drivers' motor insurers must be informed if a caravan is being towed and any additional premium must be paid. If travelling to a country where an International Motor Insurance Certificate (Green Card) is required, both drivers' Certificates must be annotated to show that a caravan is being towed.
- If using The Caravan Club's Red Pennant Overseas Holiday Insurance, both drivers must be members of The Caravan Club and both must take out a Red Pennant policy.

*See the chapter **Insurance** in the section **PLANNING AND TRAVELLING.***

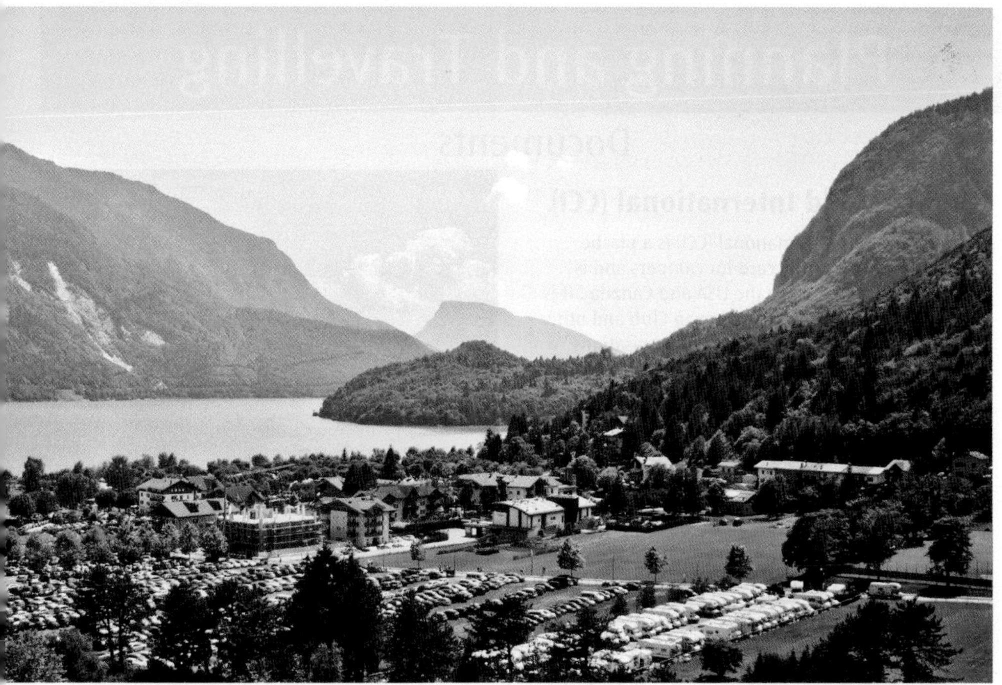

© iStockphoto/Giorgio Magini

Personal Possessions

Generally speaking, visitors to countries within the EU are free to carry reasonable quantities of any personal articles, including valuable items such as jewellery, cameras, laptops, etc, required for the duration of their stay. It is sensible to carry sales receipts for new items, particularly of a foreign manufacture, in case you need to prove that tax has already been paid.

Visitors to non-EU countries may temporarily import personal items on condition that the articles are the personal property of the visitor and that they are not left behind when the importer leaves the country.

Prohibited and Restricted Goods

Just because something is on sale in another country does not mean it can be freely brought back to the UK. Regardless of where you are travelling from, the importation into the UK of some goods is restricted or banned, mainly to protect health and the environment. These include:

- Endangered animals or plants including live animals, birds and plants, ivory, skins, coral, hides, shells and goods made from them such as jewellery, shoes, bags and belts even though these items were openly on sale in the countries where you bought them.
- Controlled, unlicensed or dangerous drugs e.g. heroin, cocaine, cannabis, LSD, morphine, etc.
- Counterfeit or pirated goods such as watches, CDs and sports shirts; goods bearing a false indication of their place of manufacture or in breach of UK copyright.
- Offensive weapons such as firearms, flick knives, knuckledusters, push daggers or knives disguised as everyday objects.
- Pornographic material depicting extreme violence or featuring children such as DVDs, magazines, videos, books and software.

This list is by no means exhaustive; if in doubt contact HM Revenue & Customs National Advice Service for more information or, when returning to the UK, go through the red Customs channel or use the telephone at the Red Point and ask a Customs officer. It is your responsibility to make sure that you are not breaking the law.

Never attempt to mislead or hide anything from Customs officers; penalties are severe.

Documents

Camping Card International (CCI)

The Camping Card International (CCI) is a plastic credit card-sized identity card for campers and is valid worldwide (except in the USA and Canada). It is available to members of The Caravan Club and other clubs affiliated to the international organisations: the AIT, FIA and FICC.

A CCI may be deposited with campsite staff instead of a passport and is therefore essential in those countries where a passport must be carried at all times as a means of identification. A CCI is also recommended for other countries but it is not a legal document and campsite managers are within their rights to demand other means of identification. More than 1,100 campsites throughout Europe give a reduction to holders of a CCI, although this may not apply if you pay by credit card.

The CCI is provided automatically, free of charge, to Caravan Club members taking out the Club's Red Pennant Overseas Holiday Insurance, otherwise it costs £5.50 (2012). It provides extensive third party-liability cover and is valid for any personal injury and material damage you may cause while staying at a campsite, hotel or rented accommodation. Cover extends to the Club member and his/her passengers (maximum eleven people travelling together in the same private vehicle) and is valid for one year. The policy excludes any claims arising from accidents caused by any mechanically-propelled vehicle, i.e. a car. Full details of the terms and conditions and level of indemnity are provided with the card.

When leaving a campsite, make sure it is your card that is returned to you, and not one belonging to someone else.

*See the **Country Introductions** for more information and www.campingcardinternational.com*

Driving Licence & International Driving Permit (IDP)

Driving Licence

A full, valid driving licence should be carried at all times when driving abroad as you must produce it when asked to do so by the police and other authorities. Failure to do so may result in an immediate fine. If your driving licence is due to expire while you are away it can normally be

renewed up to three months before the expiry date. If you need to renew your licence more than three months ahead of the expiry date contact the DVLA and they will advise you.

All European Union countries should recognise the pink EU-format paper driving licence introduced in the UK in 1990, subject to the minimum age requirements of the country concerned (normally 18 years in all the countries covered in this guide for a vehicle with a maximum weight of 3,500 kg and carrying not more than 8 people). However, there are exceptions in some European Countries e.g. Slovenia, and the Country Introduction chapter contains details. It is strongly recommended that you upgrade your license to the current photocard license, which conforms to European Union standards.

Holders of an old-style green UK paper licence or a licence issued in Northern Ireland prior to 1991, which is not to EU format, should update it to a photocard licence before travelling in order to avoid any local difficulties with the authorities. Alternatively, obtain an International Driving Permit to accompany your UK licence. A photocard driving licence is also useful as a means of identification in other situations, e.g. when using a credit card, when the display of photographic identification may be required. Application forms are available from most post offices or apply online at www.direct.gov.uk

If you have a photocard driving licence, remember to carry both the plastic card and its paper counterpart.

Allow enough time for your application to be processed and do not apply if you plan to hire a car in the very near future. Selected post offices and DVLA local offices offer a premium checking service for photocard applications but the service is not available for online applications.

Driving licence – carry both the photocard and its paper counterpart

International Driving Permit (IDP)

If you hold a British photocard driving licence, no other form of photographic identification is required. If you plan to travel further afield then an IDP may still be required and you can obtain one over the counter at selected post offices (search on www.postoffice.co.uk or call 08457 223344) and from motoring organisations, namely the AA or the RAC, whether or not you are a member. An IDP costs £5.50 (2011) and is valid for a period of 12 months from the date of issue but may be post-dated up to three months.

To apply for an IDP you will need to be resident in Great Britain, have passed a driving test and be over 18 years of age. When driving abroad you should always carry your full national driving licence with you as well as your IDP.

European Health Insurance Card – Emergency Medical Benefits

For information on how to apply for a European Health Insurance Card (EHIC) and the medical care to which it entitles you, see the chapter ***Medical Matters*** in the section ***DURING YOUR STAY.***

MOT Certificate

You are advised to carry your vehicle's MOT certificate of road worthiness (if applicable) when driving on the Continent as it may be required by the authorities if your vehicle is involved in an accident, or in the event of random vehicle checks. If your MOT certificate is due to expire while you are away you should have the vehicle tested before you leave home.

Passport

Many countries require you to carry your passport at all times and immigration authorities may, of course, check your passport on return to the UK. While abroad, it will help gain access to assistance from British Consular services and to banking services. Enter next-of-kin details in the back of your passport, keep a separate record of your passport details and leave a copy of it with a relative or friend at home.

The following information applies only to British citizens holding, or entitled to hold, a passport bearing the inscription 'United Kingdom of Great Britain and Northern Ireland'.

Applying for a Passport

Each person (including babies) must hold a valid passport. It is not now possible to add or include children on a parent's British passport. A standard British passport is valid for ten years, but if issued to children under 16 years of age it is valid for five years.

All new UK passports are now biometric passports, also known as ePassports, which feature additional security features including a microchip with the holder's unique biometric facial features. Existing passports will remain valid until their expiry date and holders will not be required to exchange them for biometric passports before then.

Full information and application forms are available from main post offices or from the Identity & Passport Service's website, www.direct.gov.uk where you can complete an online application. Allow at least six weeks for first-time passport applications, for which you will probably need to attend an interview at your nearest Identity and Passport Service (IPS) regional office once you have submitted your application – telephone the IPS helpline on 0300 2220000 to arrange one. Allow three weeks for a renewal application and at least one week for the replacement of a lost, stolen or damaged passport.

Main post offices offer a 'Check & Send' service for passport applications costing £8.17. To find your nearest 'Check & Send' post office call 08457 223344 or see www.postoffice.co.uk

Passport Validity

Most countries covered in this guide merely require you to carry a passport valid for the duration of your stay. However, in the event that your return home is delayed for any reason, and in order to avoid any local difficulties with immigration authorities, it is advisable to ensure that your passport is valid for at least six months after your planned return travel date. You can renew your passport up to nine months before expiry, without losing the validity of the current one.

Schengen Agreement

All the countries covered in this volume of Caravan Europe - except Croatia - are party to the Schengen Agreement, which allows people and vehicles to pass freely without border checks from country to country within the Schengen area. Where there are no longer any border checks you should still not attempt to cross land borders without a full, valid passport. It is likely that random identity checks will continue to be made for the foreseeable future in areas surrounding land borders.

The United Kingdom and Republic of Ireland do not fully participate in the Schengen Agreement.

Last but not least: your passport is a valuable document. It is expensive, time-consuming and inconvenient to replace and its loss or theft can lead to serious complications if your identity is later used fraudulently.

Pet Travel Scheme (PETS)

The Pet Travel Scheme (PETS) allows owners of dogs, cats and a number of other animals from qualifying European countries, to bring their pets into the UK (up to a limit of five per person) without quarantine, providing the animal has an EU pet passport. It also allows pets to travel from the UK to other EU qualifying countries. All of the countries covered in this guide are qualifying countries. However, the procedures to obtain the passport are lengthy and the regulations, out of necessity, are strict.

Be aware that some countries may not allow entry to certain types or breeds of dogs and may have rules relating to matters such as muzzling and transporting dogs in cars. You are advised to contact the appropriate authorities of the countries you plan to visit via their embassies in London before making travel arrangements for your dog. You should also check with your vet for the latest available information or call the PETS Helpline on 0870 2411710, email: quarantine@animalhealth.gsi.gov.uk.

More information is available from the website for the Department for Environment, Food & Rural Affairs (Defra), www.defra.gov.uk and you are advised to visit this website before you travel. Please note as of the 1st January 2012 rules for pets re-entering the UK have changed. Details are available on the Defra website.

The PETS scheme operates on a number of ferry routes between the Continent and the UK as well as on Eurotunnel services and Eurostar passenger trains from Calais to Folkestone. Some routes may only operate at certain times of the year; routes may change and new ones may be added – check with the PETS Helpline for the latest information.

Pets normally resident in the Channel Islands, Isle of Man and the Republic of Ireland can also enter the UK under the PETS scheme if they comply with the rules. Pets resident anywhere in the British Isles (including the Republic of Ireland) will continue to be able to travel freely within the British Isles and will not be subject to PETS rules. Owners of pets entering the Channel Islands or the Republic of Ireland from outside the British Isles should contact the appropriate authorities in those countries for advice on approved routes and other requirements.

It is against the law in the UK to possess certain types of dogs (unless an exemption certificate is held) and the introduction of PETS does not affect this ban.

For a list of vets near Continental ports, look in the local equivalent of the Yellow Pages telephone directory. Campsite owners or tourist offices located near Channel ports will be familiar with the requirements of British visitors and will probably be able to recommend a vet. Alternatively, the local British Consulate may be able to help, or the ferry company transporting your pet.

Adequate travel insurance for your pet is essential

Last but by no means least, adequate travel insurance for your pet is essential in the event of an accident abroad requiring veterinary treatment, emergency repatriation or long-term care if treatment lasts longer than your holiday. Travel insurance should also include liability cover in the event that your pet injures another animal or person or damages property whilst abroad. Contact The Caravan Club on 0800 0151396 or visit www.caravanclub.co.uk/petins for details of its Pet Insurance scheme, specially negotiated to take into account Club members' requirements both at home and abroad.

*See **Holiday Insurance for Pets** under **Insurance** in the section **PLANNING AND TRAVELLING**.*

Travelling with Children

Some countries require documentary evidence of parental responsibility from single parents travelling alone with children before allowing them to enter the country or, in some cases, before permitting children to leave the country. The authorities may want to see a birth certificate, a letter of consent from the other parent and some evidence as to your responsibility for the child.

If you are travelling with a minor under the age of 18 who is not your own, you must carry a letter of authorisation, naming the adult in charge of the child, from the child's parent or legal guardian.

For further information on exactly what will be required at immigration contact the Embassy or Consulate of the countries you intend to visit before your visit.

Vehicle Excise Licence

While driving abroad it is necessary to display a current UK vehicle excise licence (tax disc). If your vehicle's tax disc is due to expire while you are abroad you may apply to re-license the vehicle at a post office, by post, or in person at a DVLA local office, up to two months in advance. If you give a despatch address abroad the licence can be sent to you there.

Vehicle Registration Certificate (V5C)

You must always carry your Vehicle Registration Certificate (V5C) when taking your vehicle abroad. If you do not have one you should apply to a DVLA local office on form V62. If you need to travel abroad during this time you will need to apply for a Temporary Registration Certificate if you are not already recorded as the vehicle keeper.

Telephone DVLA Customer Enquiries on 0300 7906802 for more information.

Caravan – Proof of Ownership (CRIS)

In Britain and Ireland, unlike most other European countries, caravans are not formally registered in the same way as cars. This may not be fully understood by police and other authorities on the Continent. You are strongly advised, therefore, to carry a copy of your Caravan Registration Identification Scheme (CRIS) document.

Hired or Borrowed Vehicles

If using a borrowed vehicle you must obtain a letter of authority to use the vehicle from the registered owner. You should also carry the Vehicle Registration Certificate (V5C).

In the case of hired or leased vehicles, including company cars, when the user does not normally possess the V5C, ask the company which owns the vehicle to supply a Vehicle On Hire Certificate, form VE103, which is the only legal substitute for a V5C. See www.bvrla.co.uk or call them on 01494 434747 for more information.

If you are caught driving a hired vehicle abroad without this certificate you may be fined and/or the vehicle impounded.

Visas

British citizens holding a full UK passport do not require a visa for entry into any countries covered by this guide. EU countries may require a permit for stays of more than three months and you should contact the relevant country's UK embassy before you travel for information.

British subjects, British overseas citizens, British dependent territories citizens and citizens of other countries may need visas that are not required by British citizens. Again check with the authorities of the country you are due to visit at their UK embassy or consulate. Citizens of other countries should apply to their own embassy, consulate or High Commission for information.

Planning and Travelling

Ferries and the Channel Tunnel

Planning Your Trip

If travelling in July or August, or over peak weekends during school holidays, such as Easter and half-term, it is advisable to make a reservation as early as possible. Space for caravans on ferries is usually limited, especially during peak holiday periods. Off-peak crossings, which may offer savings, are usually filled very quickly.

When booking any ferry crossing, account must be taken of boats, bicycles, skylights and roof boxes in the overall height/length of your car and caravan or motorhome. Ferry operators require you to declare total dimensions. It is important, therefore, to report the dimensions of your outfit accurately when making a ferry booking, as vehicles which have been under-declared may be turned away at boarding.

Individual ferry companies may impose vehicle length or height restrictions according to the type of vessel in operation on that particular sailing or route. Always check when making your booking.

Report the dimensions of your outfit accurately when making a ferry booking

Advise your booking agent at the time of making your ferry reservation of any disabled passengers. Ferry companies can then make the appropriate arrangements for anyone requiring assistance at ports or on board ships.

For residents of both Northern Ireland and the Republic of Ireland travelling to the Continent via the British mainland, Brittany Ferries, Irish Ferries and P & O Irish Sea offer special 'Landbridge' or 'Ferrylink' through-fares for combined crossings on the Irish Sea and the English Channel or North Sea.

The table on the following page shows current ferry routes from the UK to the Continent and Ireland. Some ferry routes may not be operational all year, and during peak holiday periods the transportation of caravans or motorhomes may be restricted. Current ferry timetables and tariffs can be obtained from The Caravan Club's Travel Service, from a travel agent or from ferry operators' websites.

Booking Your Ferry

The Caravan Club is an agent for most major ferry companies operating services to the Continent, Scandinavia, Ireland and the Isle of Wight, and each year provides thousands of Club members with a speedy and efficient booking service. Our Continental Caravanning brochure (available from November) and Winter Escapes brochure (available from July) feature a range of special offers with ferry operators – some of them exclusive to The Caravan Club. The brochure also includes full information on the Site Booking Service for campsites on the Continent, the Tours & Excursions programme, and Red Pennant Overseas Holiday Insurance. Telephone 01342 327410 to request a brochure or see www.caravanclub.co.uk/planning-your-trip/overseas-trips

During the course of the year, new special offers and promotions are negotiated and these are featured on the Travel Service News page of The Caravan Club Magazine and on the Club's website.

The Club's website has a direct link to a number of ferry operators' reservations systems allowing Club members to make their own reservations and still take advantage of the Club's negotiated offers and the ferry companies' own early booking offers. A credit card deposit is taken and the balance collected ten weeks before departure date. Some ferry operators are imposing fuel surcharges but these will be included in all fares quoted by The Caravan Club. Reservations may be made by telephoning The Caravan Club's Travel Service on 01342 316101 or on www.caravanclub.co.uk/planning-your-trip/overseas-trips

Route	Operator	Approximate Crossing Time	Maximum Frequency
Belgium			
Hull – Zeebrugge	P & O Ferries	12½ hrs	1 daily
Ramsgate – Ostend†	Transeuropa Ferries	4 hrs	5 daily
Denmark			
Harwich – Esbjerg	DFDS Seaways	18¼ hrs	3 per week
France			
Dover – Calais	P & O Ferries	1½ hrs	22 daily
Dover – Calais	SeaFrance	1½ hrs	17 daily
Dover – Dunkerque	DFDS Seaways	2 hrs	12 daily
Folkestone – Calais	Eurotunnel	35 mins	3 per hour
Newhaven – Dieppe	Transmanche Ferries	4 hrs	2 daily
Plymouth – Roscoff	Brittany Ferries	6 hrs	2 daily
Poole – Cherbourg	Brittany Ferries	2¼ hrs	1 daily
Poole – St Malo (via Channel Islands)	Condor Ferries	5 hrs	1 daily (May to Sep)
Portsmouth – Caen	Brittany Ferries	3¾ / 7½ hrs	4 daily
Portsmouth – Cherbourg	Brittany Ferries	3 / 4½ hrs	3 daily
Portsmouth – Cherbourg	Condor Ferries	5½ hrs	1 weekly (May to Sep)
Portsmouth – Le Havre	LD Lines	3¼ / 8 hrs	2 daily
Portsmouth – St Malo	Brittany Ferries	9 hrs	1 daily
Weymouth – St Malo (via Channel Islands)	Condor Ferries	9½ hrs	1 daily
Ireland – Northern			
Cairnryan/Troon – Larne	P & O Irish Sea	1 / 2 hrs	11 daily
Liverpool (Birkenhead) – Belfast	Stena Line	8 hrs	2 daily
Cairnryan – Belfast	Stena Line	2 / 3 hrs	7 daily
Ireland – Republic			
Cork – Roscoff†	Brittany Ferries	14 hrs	1 per week
Fishguard – Rosslare	Stena Line	2 / 3½ hrs	3 daily
Holyhead – Dublin	Irish Ferries	1¾ / 3¼ hrs	4 daily
Holyhead – Dublin	Stena Line	3¼ hrs	4 daily
Holyhead – Dun Loaghaire	Stena Line	2 hrs	2 daily
Liverpool – Dublin	P & O Irish Sea	8 hrs	2 daily
Liverpool (Birkenhead) – Dublin	Stena Line	7 hrs	2 daily
Pembroke – Rosslare	Irish Ferries	4 hrs	2 daily
Rosslare – Cherbourg†	Irish Ferries	19½ hrs	3 per week
Rosslare – Cherbourg†	Celtic Link Ferries	17 hrs	3 per week
Rosslare – Roscoff†	Irish Ferries	19½ hrs	4 per week
Swansea – Cork†	Fastnet Line	10 hrs	3 per week
Netherlands			
Harwich – Hook of Holland	Stena Line	6½ hrs	2 daily
Hull – Rotterdam	P & O Ferries	10¼ hrs	1 daily
Newcastle – Ijmuiden (Amsterdam)	DFDS Seaways	15½ hrs	1 daily
Spain			
Portsmouth – Bilbao	Brittany Ferries	24 hrs	2 per week
Portsmouth or Plymouth – Santander	Brittany Ferries	24 / 20 hrs	4 per week

† Not bookable through the Club's Travel Service.

Note: Services and routes correct at time of publication but subject to change.

Channel Tunnel

The Channel Tunnel operator, Eurotunnel, accepts cars, caravans and motorhomes (except those running on LPG and dual-fuel vehicles) on their service between Folkestone and Calais. While they accept traffic on a 'turn up and go' basis, they also offer a full reservation service for all departures with exact timings confirmed on booking.

All information was current at the time this guide was compiled in the autumn of 2011 and may be subject to change.

Gas - Safety Precautions and Regulations on Ferries and in the Channel Tunnel

UK based cross Channel ferry companies usually allow up to three gas cylinders per caravan, including the cylinder currently in use. However some, e.g. Brittany Ferries, DFDS Seaways, SeaFrance and Stena Line, restrict this to a maximum of two cylinders, which have to be securely fitted into your caravan. It is always advisable to check with the ferry company before setting out as regulations may change.

Cylinder valves should be fully closed and covered with a cap, if provided, and should remain closed during the crossing. Cylinders should be fixed securely in or on the caravan in the manner intended and in the position designated by your caravan's manufacturer. Ensure gas cookers and fridges are fully turned off. Gas cylinders must be declared at check-in and ships' crew may wish to inspect each cylinder for leakage before shipment. They will reject leaking or inadequately secured cylinders.

Eurotunnel will allow vehicles fitted with LPG tanks for the purposes of heating, lighting, cooking or refrigeration to use their service, but regulations stipulate that a total of no more than 47 kg of gas can be carried through the Channel Tunnel. Tanks must be switched off before boarding and must be less than 80% full; you will be asked to demonstrate this before you travel. **Vehicles powered by LPG or equipped with a dual-fuel system cannot be carried through the Channel Tunnel.**

Most ferry companies, however, are willing to accept LPG-powered vehicles provided they are advised at the time of booking. During the crossing the tank must be no more than 75% full and it must be turned off. In the case of vehicles converted to use LPG, some ferry companies also require a certificate showing that the conversion has been carried out to the manufacturer's specification.

The carriage of spare petrol cans, whether full or empty, is not permitted on ferries or through the Channel Tunnel.

It is your responsibility to check current safety precautions and regulations on ferries and channel tunnels before you travel.

Pets on Ferries and Eurotunnel

It is possible to transport your pet on a number of ferry routes to the Continent and Ireland, as well as on Eurotunnel services from Folkestone to Calais. At the time this guide was compiled the cost of return travel for a pet was between £30 and £50, depending on the route used. Advance booking is essential as restrictions apply to the number of animals allowed on any one departure. Make sure you understand the carrier's terms and conditions for transporting pets.

It's important to ensure that ferry staff know that your vehicle contains an animal

On arrival at the port ensure that ferry staff know that your vehicle contains an animal. Once on board pets are normally required to remain in their owner's vehicle or in kennels on the car deck and, for safety reasons, access by pet owners to the vehicle decks while the ferry is at sea may be restricted. On longer ferry crossings you should make arrangements at the on-board information desk for permission to visit your pet at suitable intervals in order to check its well-being.

Information and advice on the welfare of animals before and during a journey is available on the website of the Department for Environment, Food and Rural Affairs (Defra), www.defra.gov.uk

*See also **Pet Travel Scheme** under **Documents** and **Holiday Insurance for Pets** under **Insurance** in the section **PLANNING AND TRAVELLING**.*

Caravan Club Sites Near Ports

Once you have chosen your ferry crossing and worked out your route to the port of departure you may like to consider an overnight stop at one of The Caravan Club sites listed in the table on the opposite page, especially if your journey to or from home involves a long drive.

Book online using the Club's UK Advance Booking Service at www.caravanclub.co.uk or call 01342 327490. Otherwise when sites are open, contact them direct.

Advance booking is recommended, particularly if you are planning to stay during July and August or over Bank Holidays.

Port	Nearest Club Site and Town	Tel No.
Cairnryan, Stranraer	New England Bay, Drummore	01776 860275
Dover, Folkestone, Channel Tunnel	Bearsted, Maidstone	01622 730018
	Black Horse Farm*, Folkestone	01303 892665
	Daleacres, Hythe	01303 267679
	Fairlight Wood, Hastings	01424 812333
Fishguard, Pembroke	Freshwater East, Pembroke	01646 672341
Harwich	Cambridge Cherry Hinton*, Cambridge	01223 244088
	Commons Wood*, Welwyn Garden City	01707 260786
	Round Plantation, Mildenhall	01638 713089
Holyhead	Penrhos, Benllech, Anglesey	01248 852617
Hull	Beechwood Grange, York	01904 424637
	Rowntree Park, York	01904 658997
Newcastle upon Tyne	Old Hartley, Whitley Bay	0191 237 0256
Newhaven	Sheepcote Valley*, Brighton	01273 626546
Plymouth	Plymouth Sound, Plymouth	01752 862325
Poole	Hunter's Moon*, Wareham	01929 556605
Portsmouth	Rookesbury Park, Fareham	01329 834085
Rosslare	River Valley, Wicklow	00353 (0)404 41647
Weymouth	Crossways, Dorchester	01305 852032

** Site open all year*

When seasonal Club sites near the ports are closed, the sites listed below may be useful overnight stops for early and late season travellers using cross-Channel or Irish Sea ports. Although they may not be 'on the doorstep' of the ports in question they are open all year or most of the year. All 'open all year' sites offer a limited supply of hardstanding pitches.

Port	Nearest Club Site and Town	Tel No.
Dover, Folkestone, Channel Tunnel	Abbey Wood, London	020 8311 7708
	Alderstead Heath, Redhill	01737 644629
	Amberley Fields, Crawley	01293 524834
	Crystal Palace, London	020 8778 7155
Fishguard, Pembroke, Swansea	Pembrey Country Park, Llanelli	01554 834369
Portsmouth	Abbey Wood, London	020 8311 7708
	Alderstead Heath, Redhill	01737 644629
	Amberley Fields, Crawley	01293 524834
	Crystal Palace, London	020 8778 7155

Alternatively, consider an overnight stay at a CL (Certificated Location) site within striking distance of your port of departure. Many CLs are open all year.

Full details of all these sites can be found in the latest edition of The Caravan Club's Sites Directory & Handbook and on the Club's website, www.caravanclub.co.uk

NB Amberley Fields, Commons Wood, Daleacres, Fairlight Wood, Hunter's Moon, Old Hartley, Rookesbury Park and Round Plantation are open to Caravan Club members only. Non-members are welcome at all the other Caravan Club sites listed above.

Planning and Travelling

Insurance

Car, Motorhome and Caravan Insurance

Insurance cover for your car, caravan, motorhome or trailer tent whilst travelling abroad is of the utmost importance. In addition, travel insurance, such as The Caravan Club's Red Pennant Overseas Holiday Insurance (available only to Club members), not only minimises duplication of cover offered by your motor and caravan insurance, but also covers other contingencies such as despatch of spare parts, medical and hospital fees, vehicle hire, vehicle recovery, etc.

*See **Holiday Insurance** later in this section.*

In order to be covered for a period abroad the following action is necessary:

- **Caravan** – Inform your caravan insurer/broker of the dates of your holiday and pay any additional premium required. The Caravan Club's 5Cs Caravan Insurance gives free foreign use cover for up to 182 days.
- **Car or Motorhome** – If your journey is outside the EU or EU Associated Countries (listed on the next page) inform your motor insurer/broker of the dates of your holiday, together with details of all the countries you will be visiting, and pay any additional premium. Also inform them if you are towing a caravan and ask them to include it on your Green Card if you need to carry one.

The Caravan Club's Car Insurance and Motorhome Insurance schemes extend to provide full policy cover for European Union or Associated Countries free of charge, provided the total period of foreign travel in any one annual period of insurance does not exceed 180 days for car insurance and 270 days for motorhome insurance. It may be possible to extend this period, although a charge will apply. The cover provided is the same as what a Club member enjoys in the UK, rather than just the minimum legal liability cover required by law in the countries that you are visiting.

Should you be delayed beyond the limits of your insurance you must, without fail, instruct your insurer/broker to maintain cover.

For full details of The Caravan Club's caravan insurance telephone 01342 336610 or for car and motorhome insurance products, telephone 0800 0284809 or visit our website, www.caravanclub.co.uk/insurance

Taking Your Car or Motorhome Abroad – Evidence of Insurance Cover (Green Card)

All countries require visiting motorists to have motor insurance cover for their legal liability to third parties. An International Motor Insurance Certificate, commonly known as a Green Card, is evidence of compliance with this requirement. However, motorists visiting EU and Associated Countries do not need a Green Card as, under EU legislation, a UK Motor Insurance Certificate is now accepted in all such countries as evidence that the obligatory motor insurance cover is in force.

Travellers outside of the EU and Associated Countries will need to obtain a Green Card document, for which insurers usually make a charge. If a Green Card is issued, your motor insurers should be asked to include reference on it to any caravan or trailer that you may be towing. If you do not have evidence of the obligatory insurance cover, you may have to pay for temporary insurance at a country's border.

Irrespective of whether a Green Card is required, it is advisable to notify your insurer/broker of your intention to travel outside of the UK and obtain confirmation that your policy has been extended to include use of the insured vehicle abroad, as your motor insurer may not automatically provide you

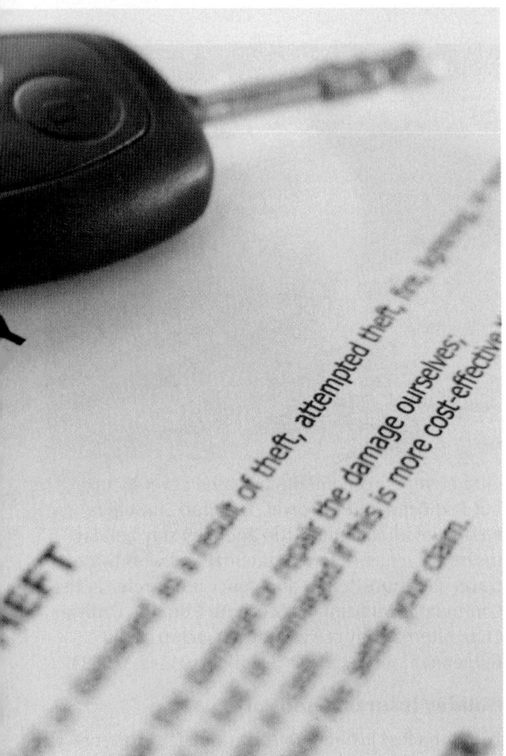

with full policy cover when abroad. You should ensure that your vehicle and motorhome policies provide adequate cover for your purposes, rather than the minimum cover that the country you are visiting obliges you to have.

European Accident Statement

You should also check with your motor insurer/broker to see if they provide a European Accident Statement to record details of any accident you may be involved in with your motor vehicle. Travelling with your Vehicle Registration Certificate, (V5C) or vehicle on hire certificate (VE103), MOT certificate (if applicable), certificate of motor insurance, copy of your CRIS document, European Accident Statement and valid UK pink EU-format paper driving licence or photocard driving licence should be sufficient in the event that you are stopped for a routine police check or following an accident whilst travelling within the EU or an Associated Country. These documents should never be left in your vehicle when it is unattended.

European Union and Associated Countries

European Union: Austria, Belgium, Bulgaria, Cyprus, Czech Republic, Denmark, Estonia, Finland, France, Germany, Greece, Hungary, Ireland, Italy, Latvia, Lithuania, Luxembourg, Malta, Netherlands, Poland, Portugal, Romania, Slovakia, Slovenia, Spain, Sweden and the United Kingdom.

Associated EU Countries (i.e. non-EU signatories to the motor insurance Multilateral Guarantee Agreement): Andorra, Croatia, Iceland, Norway, Switzerland and Liechtenstein.

Although EU Countries, you may still wish to obtain a Green Card if visiting Bulgaria or Romania in order to avoid local difficulties which can sometimes arise in these countries. If you do not take a Green Card you should carry your certificate of motor insurance. If you plan to visit countries outside the EU and Associated Countries, and in particular central and eastern European countries, you should check that your motor insurer will provide the necessary extension of cover.

Croatia

If you are planning to visit Croatia and intend to drive through Bosnia and Herzegovina along the 20 km strip of coastline at Neum on the Dalmatian coastal highway to Dubrovnik you should obtain Green Card cover for Bosnia and Herzegovina. If you have difficulties obtaining such cover before departure contact the Club's Travel Service Information Officer for advice, email: travelserviceinfo@caravanclub.co.uk. Alternatively, temporary third-party insurance can be purchased at the country's main border posts, or in Split and other large cities. It is understood that it is not generally obtainable at the Neum border crossing itself.

For Club members insured under the Caravan Club's Car Insurance and Motor Caravan Insurance schemes full policy cover is available for the 20 km strip of coastline from Neum.

Caravans Stored Abroad

Caravan insurers will not normally insure caravans left on campsites or in storage abroad.

In these circumstances specialist policies are available from Towergate Bakers on 0800 4961516, www.towergatebakers.co.uk, email bakers@towergate.co.uk or K Drewe Insurance, tel 0845 4085929, www.lookinsuranceservices.co.uk, email support@lookcaravans.co.uk

Insurers will not normally insure caravans left on campsite or in storage abroad

Legal Costs Abroad

A driver who is taken to court following a road traffic accident in a European country runs the risk of being held liable for legal costs, even if cleared of any blame.

Motor insurance policies in the UK normally include cover for legal costs and expenses incurred (with insurer's consent) which arise from any incident that is covered under the terms and conditions of the policy. The Caravan Club's Car Insurance and Motorhome Insurance schemes incorporate such cover, together with optional additional legal expenses cover for recovering any other losses that are not included in your motor insurance policy. Similar optional legal expenses insurance is also offered as an addition to the Club's 5Cs Caravan Insurance scheme.

Holiday Travel Insurance

Having insured your vehicles, there are other risks to consider and it is essential to take out adequate travel insurance. The Caravan Club's Red Pennant Overseas Holiday Insurance is designed to provide as full a cover as possible at a reasonable fee. The Club's scheme is tailor-made for people with caravans, motorhomes or trailer tents and includes cover against the following:

Recovery of vehicles and passengers
Chauffeured recovery
Towing charges
Emergency labour costs
Spare parts location and despatch
Storage fees
Continuation of holiday travel, i.e. car hire, etc
Continuation of holiday accommodation, i.e. hotels, etc
Emergency medical and hospital expenses
Personal accident benefits
Legal expenses
Loss of deposits/cancellation cover
Emergency cash transfers
Personal effects and baggage insurance
Loss of cash or documents
Cost of telephone calls

If you are proposing to participate in dangerous sporting activities such as skiing, hang-gliding or mountaineering, check that your personal holiday insurance includes cover for such sports and that it also covers the cost of emergency mountain and helicopter rescue.

Look carefully at the exemptions to your insurance policy, including those relating to pre-existing medical conditions or the use of alcohol. Be sure to declare any pre-existing medical conditions to your insurer.

Club members can obtain increased cover by taking out Red Pennant **Plus** cover. The Club also offers a range of annual multi-trip and long stay holiday insurance schemes for Continental and worldwide travel. For more details and policy limits refer to the Continental Caravanning brochure from the Caravan Club. Alternatively see www.caravanclub.co.uk/redpennant for details or telephone 01342 336633.

Holiday Insurance for Pets

The Club's Red Pennant Overseas Holiday Insurance can be extended to cover extra expenses in respect of your pet that may arise as part of a claim for an incident normally covered under the Red Pennant policy, such as pet repatriation expenses. It does not, however, cover costs arising from an injury to, or the illness of your pet, or provide any legal liability cover to you as a pet owner.

For this you will require separate pet insurance, such as that offered by The Caravan Club, which covers treatment abroad, quarantine costs, emergency expenses, including boarding fees, as well as holiday cancellation costs. It also covers legal liability in the event of injury or damage caused by your pet.

Contact The Caravan Club on 0800 0151396 or see www.caravanclub.co.uk/petins for details of the Club's Pet Insurance scheme, specially negotiated to take into account Club members' requirements both at home and abroad.

See, www.caravanclub.co.uk/petins for details of our Pet Insurance scheme

It is advisable, therefore, to ensure that you have adequate travel insurance for your pet in the event of an incident or illness abroad requiring veterinary treatment, emergency repatriation due to illness or long-term care in excess of the duration of your holiday.

Marine Insurance

Car Ferries

Vehicles driven by their owner are normally conveyed in accordance with the terms of the carrying companies' published by-laws or conditions, and if damage is sustained during loading, unloading or shipment, this must be reported at the time to the carrier's representative. Any claim arising from such damage must be notified in writing to the carrier concerned within three days of the incident. Nonetheless it is unwise to rely upon the carrier accepting liability for your claim so it would be prudent to have separate transit insurance.

The majority of motor policies provide transit insurance cover for vehicles during short sea crossings up to 65 hours normal duration – check this with your insurer/broker.

The Caravan Club's 5Cs Caravan Insurance policy automatically covers you for crossings of any length within the area covered by Red Pennant Overseas Holiday Insurance.

Boats

The Royal Yachting Association recommends that all boats have marine insurance. Third party insurance is compulsory for many countries, together with a translation of the insurance certificate into the appropriate language(s). Check with your insurer/broker before taking your boat abroad.

Medical Insurance

It is important to make sure your travel insurance also covers medical emergency expenses. Regardless of whether you have a European Health Insurance Card (EHIC), medical expenses can still be incurred so make sure your travel insurance policy will cover you.

The Caravan Club's Red Pennant cover is available to members. Please visit www.caravanclub.co.uk/redpennant for further information or telephone 01342 336633.

*See the chapter **Medical Matters** in the section **DURING YOUR STAY** for further information.*

Home Insurance

Most home insurers require advance notification if you are leaving your home unoccupied for 30 days or more. They often require that mains services (except electricity) are turned off, water drained down and that somebody visits the home once a week. Check your policy documents or speak to your insurer/broker.

The Caravan Club's Home Insurance policy provides full cover for up to 90 days when you are away from home (for instance when touring) and requires only common sense precautions for longer periods of unoccupancy.

Contact 0800 0284815 or see www.caravanclub.co.uk/homeins for details of our Home Insurance scheme, specially negotiated to suit the majority of Club members' requirements.

Personal Belongings

The majority of travellers are able to cover their valuables such as jewellery, watches, cameras, laptops, bicycles and, in some instances, small boats, under the All Risks section of their Householders' Comprehensive Policy. This includes The Caravan Club's Home Insurance scheme.

Vehicles Left Behind Abroad

If you are involved in an accident or breakdown whilst abroad which prevents you taking your vehicle home, you must ensure that your normal insurance cover is maintained to cover the period that the vehicle remains abroad, and that you are covered for the cost of recovering it to your home address.

You should remove all items of baggage and personal belongings from your vehicles before leaving them unattended. If this is not possible you should check with your insurer/broker to establish whether extended cover can be provided. In all circumstances, you must remove any valuables and items which might attract Customs duty, including wine, beer, spirits and cigarettes.

Planning and Travelling

International Holidays 2012 and 2013

International Holidays, Important Dates & UK Bank Holidays

2012				2013	
January	1	Sunday	New Year's Day	1	Tuesday
	2	Monday	Bank Holiday	-	-
	6	Friday	Epiphany	6	Sunday
February	22	Wednesday	Ash Wednesday	13	Wednesday
March	1	Thursday	St David's Day	1	Friday
	17	Saturday	St Patrick's Day	17	Sunday
	18	Sunday	Mother's Day	10	Sunday
	25	Sunday	British Summer Time Begins	31	Sunday
April	1	Sunday	Palm Sunday	24 Mar	Sunday
	6	Friday	Good Friday	29 Mar	Friday
	8	Sunday	Easter Day	31 Mar	Sunday
	9	Monday	Easter Monday	1	Monday
	23	Monday	St George's Day	23	Tuesday
May	7	Monday	May Bank Holiday	6	Monday
	17	Thursday	Ascension Day	9	Thursday
	27	May	Whit Sunday	19	Sunday
June	4	Monday	Spring Bank Holiday UK	27 May	Monday
	5	Tuesday	Queen's Diamond Jubilee (Bank Holiday)	-	-
	7	Thursday	Corpus Christi	30 May	Thursday
	17	Sunday	Father's Day	16	Sunday
July	20	Friday	1st Day of Ramadan*	9	Tuesday
August	15	Wednesday	Assumption	15	Thursday
	18	Saturday	Ramadan Ends*	7	Wednesday
	27	Monday	Bank Holiday UK	26	Monday
September	17	Monday	Jewish New Year (Rosh Hashanah)	5	Thursday
	26	Wednesday	Jewish Day of Atonement (Yom Kippur)	14	Saturday
October	28	Sunday	British Summer Time ends	27	Sunday
	31	Wednesday	Halloween	31	Thursday
November	1	Thursday	All Saints' Day	1	Friday
	11	Sunday	Remembrance Sunday	10	Sunday
	15	Thursday	Al Hijra – Islamic New Year	4	Monday
	30	Friday	St Andrew's Day	30	Saturday
December	25	Tuesday	Christmas Day	25	Wednesday
	26	Wednesday	St Stephen's Day; Boxing Day UK	26	Thursday

** Subject to the lunar calendar*

NOTES *1) Outside the UK when a holiday falls on a Sunday it will not necessarily be observed the following day.*

2) Public holidays in individual countries are listed in the relevant Country Introductions.

3) Dates listed here and in the Country Introduction Chapters are believed to be correct at time of publication, however please note some dates may not have officially been confirmed and may be subject to change.

Planning and Travelling

Money

Take your holiday money in a mixture of cash, credit and debit cards and travellers' cheques or pre-paid travel cards and keep them separately. Do not rely exclusively on only one method of payment.

*See **Customs** in the section **DURING YOUR STAY** for information about declaring the amount of cash you carry when entering or leaving the EU.*

Local Currency

It is not necessary to carry a large amount of cash but it is a good idea to take sufficient foreign currency for your immediate needs on arrival, including loose change if possible. Even if you intend to use credit and debit cards for most of your holiday spending, it makes sense to take some cash to tide you over until you are able to find a cash machine (ATM), and you may need change for parking meters or the use of supermarket trolleys.

You can change money at ports and on ferries but the rates offered do not generally represent the best value. The Post Office, many High Street banks, exchange offices and travel agents offer commission free foreign exchange, some will charge a flat fee and some offer a 'buy back' service. Most stock the more common currencies such as Euros, but it is wise to order in advance in case demand is heavy, or if you require an unusual currency.

Shop around and compare commission and exchange rates to make sure you get the best deal

Currency can also be ordered by telephone or online for delivery to your home address on payment of a handling charge. Online providers such as the Post Office or Travelex and most of the High Street banks offer their customers an online ordering service which usually represents the best value. It can pay to shop around and compare commission and exchange rates, together with minimum charges.

If you pay for your currency with a credit or debit card the card issuer may charge a cash advance fee in addition to the commission and/or handling charge.

Banks and money exchanges in central and eastern Europe are not willing to accept Scottish and Northern Irish bank notes and may be reluctant to change any sterling which has been written on, is creased or worn, or is not in virtually mint condition.

Exchange rates (as at September 2011) are given in the Country Introductions in this guide. Up to date currency conversion rates can be obtained from your bank or national newspapers. Alternatively, www.oanda.com updates currency rates around the world daily and allows you to download a currency converter to your mobile phone.

Foreign Currency Bank Accounts

Frequent travellers or those who spend long periods abroad may find a euro bank account useful. Most such accounts impose no currency conversion charges for debit or credit card use and allow fee-free cash withdrawls at ATMs. Some banks may also allow you to spread your account across different currencies, depending on your circumstances. Your bank will advise you.

Travellers' Cheques

Travellers' cheques can be cashed in many countries, and are the safest way to carry large sums of money. They can be replaced quickly – usually within 24 hours – in the event of loss or theft. However, their popularity has declined in recent years and increasing numbers of foreign retailers and merchants are not accepting travellers' cheques, instead preferring debit/credit cards or cash. Recent visitors report difficulties in finding a bank that will cash them for non-account holders, and where they are accepted high commission charges may be incurred. Travellers' cheques may still be useful if you are travelling off the beaten track or in far-flung locations, but bear in mind that small bank branches may not offer foreign exchange services.

Commission is usually payable when you buy the cheques and/or when you cash them in. See the Country Introduction for more information.

Travel Money Cards

Travel money cards are issued by the Post Office, Travelex, Lloyds Bank and American Express amongst many others. For a comparison table see www.which-prepaid-card.co.uk

They are an increasingly popular and practical alternative to travellers' cheques as a pre-paid PIN protected travel money card offers the security of travellers' cheques, with the convenience of plastic. Load the card with the amount you need (in euros, sterling or US dollars) before leaving home, and then simply use cash machines to make withdrawals and/or present the card to pay for goods and services in shops and restaurants as you would a credit or debit card. You can obtain a second card so that another user can access the funds and you can also top the card up over the telephone or online while you are abroad.

These cards can be cheaper to use than credit or debit cards for both cash withdrawals and purchases as there are usually no loading or transaction fees to pay. In addition, because they are separate from your bank account, if the card is lost or stolen there is less risk of identity theft.

The Caravan Club has teamed up with Caxton FX to offer members a euro prepaid MasterCard travel money card. See www.caravanclub.co.uk/eurocard

Credit and Debit Cards

Credit and debit cards offer a convenient way of spending abroad. You can use a card to pay for goods and services wherever your card logo is displayed and also to obtain cash from ATMs using your PIN. ATMs usually offer an English language option once you insert your card.

For the use of cards abroad most banks impose a foreign currency conversion charge (typically 2.75% per transaction) which is usually the same for both credit and debit cards. If you use your credit card to withdraw cash there will be a further commission charge of up to 3% and you will be charged interest (possibly at a higher rate than normal) as soon as you withdraw the money.

In line with market practice, Barclaycard, which issues The Caravan Club's credit card, charges a 2.75% fee for all card transactions outside the UK. Cash withdrawals abroad are subject to a further 2% handling charge as in the UK. A £2 minimum fee applies with a maximum charge of £50 (information correct at time of publication).

Contact your credit card issuer before you leave home to let them know you will be travelling abroad

Check the expiry date of your cards before you leave and memorise the PIN for each one. If you have several cards, take at least two in case you come across gaps in acceptance of certain cards, e.g. shops which accept only MasterCard or only VISA.

If you are planning an extended journey arrange for your credit or charge card account to be cleared each month by variable direct debit, ensuring that bills are paid on time and no interest is charged.

Credit and debit 'chip and PIN' cards issued by UK banks may not be universally accepted abroad and it is wise to check before incurring expenditure.

Contact your credit or debit card issuer before you leave home to let them know that you will be travelling abroad. In the battle against card fraud, card issuers are frequently likely to query transactions which they regard as unusual or suspicious. This may result in a cash withdrawal from an ATM being declined, or a retailer at the point of sale having to telephone for authorisation and/or confirmation of your details. Difficulties can occur if there is a language barrier or if the retailer is unwilling to bother with further checks. Your card may be declined or, worse still, temporarily stopped. In this instance you should insist that the retailer contacts the local authorisation centre but, in any event, it is a good idea to carry your card issuer's helpline number with you. You will also need this number to report the loss or theft of your card.

Dynamic Currency Conversion

When you pay with a credit or debit card, retailers may offer you the choice of currency for payment, e.g. a euro amount will be converted into sterling and then charged to your card account. You may be asked to sign an agreement to accept the conversion rate used and final amount charged and, having done so, there is no opportunity to change your mind or obtain a refund. This is known as a 'dynamic currency conversion' but the exchange rate used is unlikely to be as favourable as that used by your card issuer. You may also find retailers claiming that a sterling bill will automatically be generated when a UK-issued credit card is tendered and processed. If this is the case then you may prefer to pay by cash.

Some ATMs may give you the option to convert your withdrawal into sterling when you withdraw euros. It is often best to decline and opt to pay in the national currency.

Emergency Cash

If an emergency or robbery means that you need cash in a hurry, then friends or relatives at home can use the MoneyGram instant money transfer service available at post offices and branches of Thomas Cook.

This service, which does not necessarily require the sender to use a bank account or credit card, enables the transfer of money to over 233,000 money transfer agents around the world. Transfers take approximately ten minutes and charges are levied on a sliding scale.

As a last resort, contact the nearest British Embassy or Consulate for help

Western Union operates a similar secure, worldwide service and has offices located in banks, post offices, travel agents, stations and shops. You can also transfer funds instantly by telephone on 0800 833833 or online at www.westernunion.co.uk

As a last resort, contact the nearest British Embassy or Consulate for help. The Foreign & Commonwealth Office in London can arrange for a relative or friend to deposit funds which will be authorised for payment by embassy staff. See individual Country Introductions for embassy and consulate addresses abroad.

Most travel insurance policies, including the Club's Red Pennant Overseas Holiday Insurance, will cover you for only a limited amount of lost or stolen cash (usually between £250 and £500) and you will probably have to wait until you return home for reimbursement.

The Euro

The Euro is the currency in use in many countries in Europe. Each country's versions of banknotes and coins are valid in all the countries of the single currency euro zone.

Police have issued warnings that counterfeit euro notes are in circulation on the Continent. You should be aware and take all precautions to ensure that €10, €20 and €50 notes and €2 coins that you receive from sources other than banks and legitimate bureaux de change, are genuine.

Holiday Money Security

Treat your cards as carefully as you would cash. Use a money belt, if possible, to conceal cards and valuables and do not keep all your cash and cards in the same place. Split cash between members of your party. Memorise your PINs and never keep them with your credit/debit cards.

If you keep a wallet in your pocket, place a rubber band around it, as it is then more difficult for a pickpocket to slide the wallet out without your noticing.

To avoid credit or debit card 'cloning' or 'skimming' never let your card out of your sight. In restaurants follow the waiter to the till or insist that the card machine is brought to your table. This is particularly important as you may frequently find that a signature on a transaction slip is not checked against the signature on your card. If you do allow your card to be taken and it is gone for more than a minute, become suspicious.

If you suspect your card has been fraudulently used, or if your card is lost or stolen, or if a cash machine retains it, call the issuing bank immediately. All the major card companies and banks operate a 24-hour emergency helpline.

If you are unlucky enough to become a victim of fraud your bank should refund the money stolen, provided you have not been negligent or careless.

Keep your card's magnetic strip away from other cards and objects, especially if they are also magnetic. If the card is damaged in any way electronic terminals may not accept your transaction.

If you use travellers' cheques keep a separate note of their serial numbers in case of loss, and a record of where and when you cash them. If they are lost or stolen, contact the appropriate refund service immediately.

Carry your credit card issuer/bank's 24 hour UK helpline number with you in the event of loss or theft

Carry your credit card issuer/bank's 24-hour UK helpline number with you. You might also want to consider joining a card protection plan so that in the event of loss or theft, one telephone call will cancel all your cards and arrange replacements.

Take care when using cash machines. If the machine is obstructed or poorly lit, avoid it. If someone near the machine is behaving suspiciously or makes you feel uneasy, find another one. If there is something unusual about the cash machine do not use it and report the matter to the bank or owner of the premises. Do not accept help from strangers and do not allow yourself to be distracted.

Always log off from internet banking upon completion of your session

Be aware of your surroundings and if someone is watching you closely do not proceed with the transaction. Shield the screen and keyboard so that anyone waiting to use the machine cannot see you enter your PIN or transaction amount. Put your cash, card and receipt away immediately. Count your cash later and always keep your receipt to compare with your monthly statement.

If you bank over the internet and are using a computer in a public place such as a library or internet café, do not leave the PC unattended and ensure that no-one is watching what you type. Always log off from internet banking upon completion of your session to prevent the viewing of previous pages of your online session.

The cost of credit and debit card fraud is largely borne by banks and ultimately its customers, but the direct cost to cardholders should not be under-estimated in terms of inconvenience and frustration, not to mention the time taken for incidents to be investigated and fraudently withdrawn funds to be returned to your account. There is the additional danger of identity theft.

Learn more about card fraud and preventative measures to combat it on www.cardwatch.org.uk

*See also **Security and Safety** in the section **DURING YOUR STAY.***

Planning and Travelling

General Motoring Advice - Europe

Preparing For Your Journey

Adequate and careful preparation of your vehicles should be your first priority to ensure a safe and trouble free journey. Make sure your car and caravan, or motorhome, are properly serviced before you depart and take a well equipped spares kit and a spare wheel and tyre for your caravan to avoid any unnecessary disruptions to your holiday.

If you are a member of The Caravan Club re-read the Technical Information section of your UK Sites Directory & Handbook as it contains a wealth of information which is relevant to caravanning anywhere in the world.

Whether you are newcomers to caravanning or old hands, The Caravan Club offers a free advice service to Club members on technical and general caravanning matters, and also publishes information leaflets on a wide range of topics, all of which members can download from the Club's website. Alternatively, write to the Club's Technical Department or telephone for more details. For advice on issues specific to countries other than the UK, Club members should contact the Travel Service Information Officer, email: travelserviceinfo@caravanclub.co.uk

Documentation

Along with your driving licence always carry your Vehicle Registration Certificate (V5C) or the Vehicle on Hire Certificate (VE103), insurance certificate and MOT certificate (if applicable) when taking your vehicle abroad. You are also strongly advised to carry a copy of your Caravan Registration Identification Scheme (CRIS) document. You may be asked to show these documents when entering some countries.

If you are driving a hired or borrowed vehicle you must be in possession of a letter of authorisation from the owner, or a hire agreement.

*See **Documents** in the section **PLANNING AND TRAVELLING***

Weight Limits

From both a legal and a safety point of view, it is essential not to exceed vehicle weight limits. European authorities are alert to the danger of over-weight vehicles and drivers are advised to carry with them documentation confirming their vehicle's maximum permitted laden weight. If your Vehicle Registration Certificate (V5C) does not clearly state this, you will need to produce alternative certification, e.g. from a weighbridge.

If your vehicle(s) are pulled over by the police and you cannot produce this documentation you may have to accompany police to a weighbridge. Subsequently if your vehicle(s) are found to be overweight you will be liable to a fine and may have to jettison items. The Caravan Club, therefore, recommends a trip to a local weighbridge with your vehicle(s) fully laden before embarking on your holiday.

Some Final Checks

Experienced caravanners will be familiar with the checks necessary before setting off and the following list is a reminder:

- All car and caravan lights are working and sets of spare bulbs are packed
- The coupling is correctly seated on the towball and the breakaway cable is attached
- All windows, vents, hatches and doors are shut
- All on-board water systems are drained
- All mirrors are adjusted for maximum visibility
- Corner steadies are fully wound up and the brace is handy for your arrival on site
- Any fires or flames are extinguished and the gas cylinder tap is turned off. Fire extinguishers are fully charged and close at hand
- The over-run brake is working correctly
- The jockey wheel is raised and secured, the handbrake is released.

Driving On The Continent

Probably the main disincentive to driving abroad, particularly for caravanners, is the need to keep to the right-hand side of the road. However, for most people this proves to be no problem at all after the first hour or so. There are a few basic, but important, points to remember:

- Buy a good road map or atlas and plan ahead to use roads suitable for towing. See ***Route Planning and GPS*** in the chapter ***Motoring – Equipment.***
- In your eagerness to reach your destination, don't attempt vast distances in a single stint. Share the driving, if possible, and plan to break your journey overnight at a suitable campsite. There are many sites listed in this guide and a lot of them are well situated near to motorways and main roads.
- Adjust all your mirrors for maximum rear-view observation. The vast majority of towed caravans – whatever the type of towing vehicle – will require extension mirrors to comply with legal requirements for an adequate rearwards view.
- Make sure the road ahead is clear before overtaking. Stay well behind the vehicle in front and, if possible, have someone with good judgement in the left-hand seat to give you the 'all clear'.
- If traffic builds up behind you, pull over safely and let it pass.
- Pay particular attention when turning left, when leaving a rest area/petrol station/campsite, or after passing through a one-way system, to ensure that you continue to drive on the right-hand side of the road.
- If your headlights are likely to dazzle other road users, adjust them to deflect to the right instead of the left, using suitable beam deflectors or (in some cases) a built-in adjustment system. Some lights can have the deflective part of the lens obscured with tape or a pre-cut adhesive mask, but check in your car's handbook if this is permitted or not. Some lights run too hot to be partially obscured in this way.
- When travelling, particularly in the height of the summer, it is wise to stop approximately every two hours (at the most) to stretch your legs and take a break.
- In case of a breakdown or accident, use hazard warning lights and warning triangle(s). Remember to wear a reflective jacket or waistcoat if you leave your vehicle.

Another disincentive for caravanners to travel abroad is the worry about roads and gradients in mountainous countries. Britain has steeper gradients on many of its main roads than many other European countries and traffic density is higher.

The chapter ***Mountain Passes and Tunnels*** under ***PLANNING AND TRAVELLING*** gives detailed advice on using mountain passes.

Another worry involves vehicle breakdown and language difficulties. The Caravan Club's comprehensive and competitively priced Red Pennant Overseas Holiday Insurance is geared to handle all these contingencies with multi-lingual staff available at the Club's headquarters 24 hours a day throughout the year – see www.caravanclub.co.uk/redpennant

Driving Offences

You are obliged to comply with the traffic rules and regulations of the countries you visit. Research shows that non-resident drivers are more likely to take risks and break the law due to their feeling of impunity. Cross-border enforcement of traffic laws is the subject of a European Directive which is being ratified by EU member states. This will bring an end to flagrant disregard of traffic rules and make them equally enforceable throughout the EU. In the meantime, a number of bi-lateral agreements already exist between European countries which means that there is no escaping penalty notices and demands for payment for motoring offences.

Make sure you are familiar with traffic laws in the countries you plan to visit, including speed limits and equipment you are legally required to carry. See the ***Speed Limits*** and ***Essential Equipment*** tables later in this guide and the additional information contained in the Country Introduction chapters.

Some foreign police officers can look rather intimidating to British visitors used to unarmed police. Needless to say, they expect you to be polite

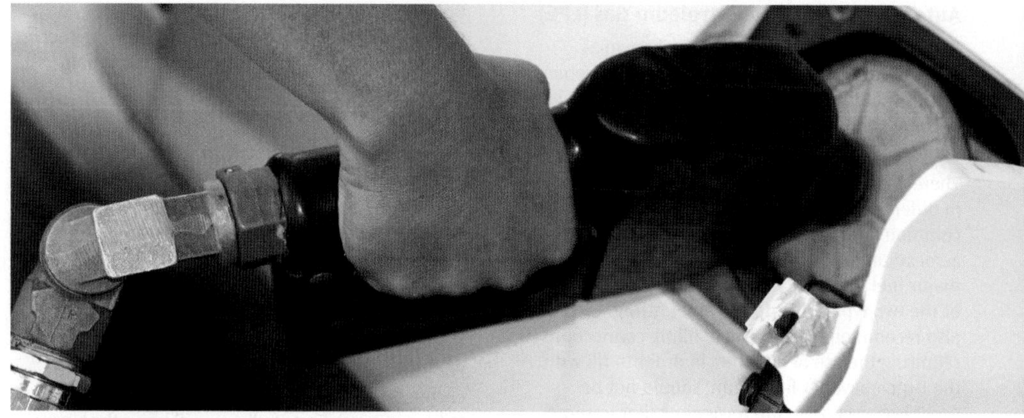

and show respect and, in return, they are generally helpful and may well be lenient to a visiting motorist. Never consider offering a bribe!

The authorities in many countries are hard on parking and speeding offenders. Visiting motorists should not be influenced by the speed at which locals drive; they often know where the speed traps are and can slow down in time to avoid being caught! In general, it is no use protesting if caught, as anyone who refuses to pay may have their vehicle impounded.

Be particularly careful if you have penalty points on your driving licence. If you commit an offence on the Continent which attracts penalty points, local police may well do checks on your licence to establish whether the addition of those points renders you liable to disqualification. If so you would then have to find other means to get yourself and your vehicle(s) home.

Many police forces are authorised to carry out random breath tests

Drink-Driving

The maximum legal level of alcohol in the blood in most Continental countries is lower than that in the UK (in some it is zero), and many police forces are authorised to carry out random breath tests. It is wise to adopt the 'no drink when driving' rule at all times; offenders are heavily fined all over Europe and penalties can include confiscation of driving licence, vehicle(s) and even imprisonment. For more detailed information see the Country Introduction chapter.

On-the-Spot Fines

Many countries allow their police officers to issue fines which must be paid immediately, up to certain limits. The fine may be a deposit for a larger fine which will be issued to your home address. In most countries credit cards are not accepted in payment of on-the-spot fines and you may find yourself accompanied to the nearest cash machine. Always obtain a receipt for money handed over.

Fuel

During ferry crossings make sure your petrol tank is not over-full. Don't be tempted to carry spare petrol in cans; the ferry companies and Eurotunnel forbid this practice and even the carriage of empty cans is prohibited.

Grades of petrol sold on the Continent are comparable to those sold in the UK with the same familiar brands; 95 octane is frequently known as 'Essence' and 98 octane as 'Super'. Diesel is sometimes called 'Gasoil' and is normally available in all the countries covered in the Caravan Europe guides. The fuel prices given in the table at the end of this chapter were correct according to the latest information available in September 2011. Members of The Caravan Club can also check current fuel prices by visiting www.caravanclub.co.uk/overseasadvice

In sparsely populated regions it is a sensible precaution to travel with a full petrol tank and to keep it topped up. Similarly in remote rural areas in any country you may have difficulty finding a manned petrol station at night or on Sundays. Petrol stations offering a 24-hour service may involve an automated process which occasionally work only with locally issued credit cards.

*See the **Fuel Price Guide Table** at the end of this chapter.*

Automotive Liquified Petroleum Gas (LPG)

The increasing popularity of LPG – known as 'autogas' or GPL – and use of dual-fuelled vehicles means that the availability of automotive LPG has become an important issue for some drivers, and the Country Introductions provide more information.

There are different tank-filling openings in use in different countries. Pending the adoption of a common European filling system, UKLPG, the trade association for the LPG industry in the UK, and the major fuel suppliers recommend the use of either of the two types of Dutch bayonet fitting. UKLPG also recommends that vehicle-filling connections requiring the use of adaptors in order to fill with the Dutch bayonet filling gun, should not be used. However, the Club recognises that in some circumstances it may be necessary to use an adaptor and these are available from Autogas 2000 Ltd on 01845 523213, www.autogas.co.uk

Lead Replacement Petrol

Leaded petrol has been withdrawn from sale in many countries in Europe and, in general, is only available from petrol stations in the form of a bottled additive. Where lead replacement petrol is still available at the pump it is generally from the same pumps previously used for leaded petrol, i.e. red or black pumps, and may be labelled 'Super Plus', 'Super 98' or 'Super MLV', but it is advisable to check before filling up if this is not clear from information at the pump.

Low Emission Zones

Many cities in countries around Europe have introduced 'Low Emission Zones' (LEZ) in order to regulate vehicle pollution levels. Some schemes require you to buy a windscreen sticker, pay a fee or register your vehicle before entering the zone and you may need to show proof that your vehicle meets the required standard.

Before you travel visit the website www.lowemissionzones.eu for maps showing the location of the LEZ and for further information.

Motorhomes Towing Cars

A motorhome towing a small car using an A-frame or towing dolly is illegal in most European countries, although such units are sometimes encountered. Motorhome users wishing to tow a small car abroad should transport it on a braked trailer so that all four of the car's wheels are off the road.

Motorway Tolls

For British drivers who may never, or rarely, have encountered a toll booth, there are a couple of points to bear in mind. First of all, you will be on the 'wrong' side of the car for the collection of toll tickets at the start of the motorway section and payment of tolls at the end. If you are travelling without a front seat passenger, this can mean a big stretch or a walk round to the other side of the car. Most toll booths are solidly built and you should be careful of any high concrete kerbs when pulling up to them.

On entering a stretch of motorway you will usually have to stop at a barrier and take a ticket from a machine to allow the barrier to rise. Avoid the lanes dedicated to vehicles displaying electronic season tickets. You may encounter toll booths without automatic barriers where it is still necessary to take a ticket and, if you pass through without doing so, you may be fined. On some stretches of motorway there are no ticket machines as you enter and you simply pay a fixed sum when you exit.

Your toll ticket will indicate the time you entered the motorway. Be warned that in some countries electronic tills at exit booths calculate the distance a vehicle has travelled and the journey time. The police are automatically informed if speeding has taken place and fines are imposed.

Payment can be made by credit cards in most, but not all countries.

*See the **Country Introduction** chapters for specific information.*

Parking

Make sure you check local parking regulations, as fines may be imposed and unattended vehicles clamped or towed away. Look out for road markings and for short-term parking zones. It might be helpful to make a note of the words for the days of the week in the local language and the words for 'height', 'length', 'over' for example.

Ensure you are in possession of parking discs in towns where they are required. As a general rule, park on the right-hand side of the road in the direction of traffic flow, avoiding cycle and bus lanes and tram tracks. Vehicles should not cause an obstruction and should be adequately lit when parked at night.

The following are some signs that you may encounter.

No parking on Monday, Wednesday, Friday or Sunday

No parking on Tuesday, Thursday or Saturday

Fortnightly parking on alternative sides

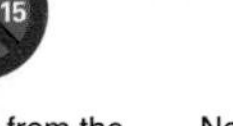

No parking from the 1st-15th of the month

No parking from the 16th-end of the month

In parts of central Europe car theft may be a problem and you are advised to park only in officially designated, guarded car parks whenever possible.

Parking Facilities for the Disabled

The Blue Badge is recognised in most European countries and it allows disabled motorists to use the same parking concessions enjoyed by the citizens of the country you are visiting. Concessions differ from country to country, however, and it is important to know when and where you can and, more importantly, cannot park. If you are in any doubt about your rights, do not park.

Explanatory leaflets describing the concessions in countries inside and outside the EU are available from the Department for Transport's website, www.dft.gov.uk/transportforyou/access/bluebadge, or telephone 0300 1231102 to request copies. See also www.fiadisabledtravellers.com

Priority and Roundabouts

When driving on the Continent it is essential to be aware of other vehicles which may have priority over you, particularly when they join from the right into the road you are using. Road signs indicate priority or loss of priority and motorists must be sure that they understand the signs.

Never rely on being given right of way, even if you have priority

Care should be taken at intersections and you should never rely on being given right of way, even if you have priority, especially in small towns and villages where local, often slow-moving, traffic will take right of way. Always give way to public service and military vehicles and to buses, trams and coaches.

In some countries in Europe priority at roundabouts is given to vehicles entering the roundabout (i.e. on the right) unless signposted on the contrary. This is a reversal of the UK rule and care is needed.

See the ***Country Introduction Chapters*** for more information.

Public Transport

In general in built-up areas be prepared to stop to allow a bus to pull out from a bus stop when the driver is signalling his intention to do so. Take particular care when school buses have stopped and passengers are getting on and off.

Overtaking trams in motion is normally only permitted on the right, unless on a one way street where you can overtake on the left if there is not enough space on the right. Do not overtake a tram near a tram stop. These may be in the centre of the road. When a tram or bus stops to allow passengers on and off, you should stop to allow them to cross to the pavement. Give way to trams which are turning across your carriageway.

Do not park so as to obstruct tram lines or force other drivers to do so; trams cannot steer round obstructions! Take care when crossing tram tracks, especially if the rails are wet, and be particularly careful when crossing them at shallow angles, on bends and at junctions.

Road Signs and Markings

Many road signs have the same general design in most countries in Europe making them fairly easily recognisable. Blue and green direction and marker signs are used to identify motorways and main roads but their use may be the opposite of that in the UK, i.e. motorways marked by green signs and main

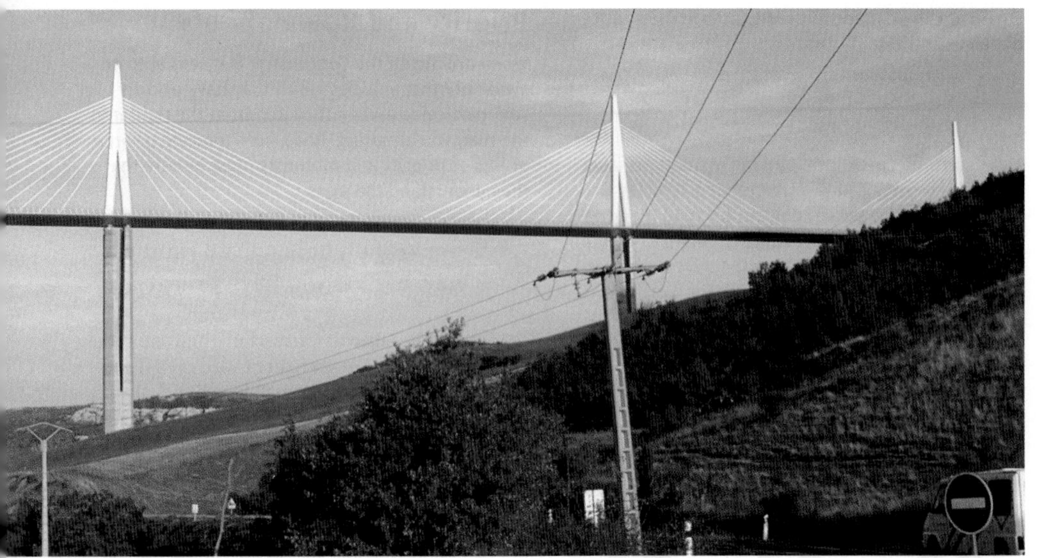

roads by blue. This can be particularly confusing, for example when crossing from France where motorway signs are blue, into Switzerland or Italy where they are green.

Where text descriptions rather than symbols are used on information signs it can be helpful to make a note of a few basic words for flood, diversion, by-pass, etc. The country introductions lists a few such basic words and phrases in the local language for your reference.

You will often encounter STOP signs in situations which, in the UK, would probably be covered by a Give Way sign. Be particularly careful – coming to a complete halt is usually compulsory, even if local drivers seem unconcerned by it, and failure to do so may result in a fine. Be careful too in areas where maintenance of roads may be irregular and where white lines have been worn away.

A solid single or double white line in the middle of the carriageway always means no overtaking.

Direction signs in general may be confusing, giving only the name of a town on the way to a larger city, or simply the road number and no place name. They may be smaller than you expect and not particularly easy to spot.

Across the EU you will find that major routes have not only an individual road number, such as A6, but also a number beginning with an 'E' displayed on green and white signs. Routes running from east to west have even 'E' numbers, whereas routes running from north to south have odd 'E' numbers. This can be helpful when planning long-distance routes across international frontiers.

In some countries, particularly in Scandinavia and Belgium, through routes or motorways may only show the 'E' road numbers, so it would be advisable to make a note of them when planning your route. The E road system is not recognised in the UK and there are no such road signs.

Pedestrian Crossings

Stopping to allow pedestrians to cross at zebra crossings is not nearly as common a practice on the Continent as it is in the UK. Pedestrians often do not expect to cross until the road is clear and may be surprised if you stop to allow them to do so. Check your mirrors carefully when braking as other drivers behind you, not expecting to stop, may be taken by surprise. The result may be a rear-end shunt or, worse still, vehicles overtaking you at the crossing and putting pedestrians at risk.

Speed Limits

Remember speed limit signs are in kilometres per hour, not miles per hour. General speed limits are given in the table at the end of this chapter. Refer to the Country Introduction for detailed information.

Radar-detection devices, whether in use or not, are illegal in many countries on the Continent and should not be carried at all. If you have one in your vehicle remove it before leaving home.

Speed cameras are becoming more widespread throughout Europe but you should not expect them to be highly visible as they are in the UK. In many instances, for example on the German motorway network, they may be hidden or deliberately inconspicuous. The use of unmarked police cars using speed detection equipment is common. See the item ***Radar/Speed Camera Detectors*** in the chapter ***Motoring – Equipment.***

Traffic Lights

Traffic lights may not be placed as conspicuously as they are in the UK, for instance they may be smaller, differently shaped or suspended across the road, with a smaller set on a post at the roadside. You may find that lights change directly from red to green, by-passing amber completely. Flashing amber lights generally indicate that you may proceed with caution if it is safe to do so but must give way to pedestrians and other vehicles.

Be cautious when approaching a green light, especially in fast-moving traffic

A green filter light should be treated with caution as you may still have to give way to pedestrians who have a green light to cross the road.

You may find that drivers are not particularly well-disciplined about stopping as they approach a light as it turns red and if they are behind you in this situation, they will expect you to accelerate through the lights rather than brake hard to stop. Therefore be cautious when approaching a green light, especially if you are in a relatively fast-moving stream of traffic. Similarly, be careful when pulling away from a green light and check left and right just in case a driver on the road crossing yours has jumped a red light.

Winter Driving

If you regularly caravan in wintry conditions a four-wheel drive car or all-terrain vehicle may be a good investment. An ABS braking system offers significant advantages as do other comforts such as heated seats and steering wheels.

Winter driving abroad requires extra preparation and caution, especially if you are heading for mountainous areas or to northern Europe. Major mountain passes are kept open in winter except in particularly extreme conditions - see the chapter ***Mountain Passes and Tunnels*** for details. Otherwise keep to main roads wherever possible as they are more likely to be clear of snow and ice, and adjust your speed and driving technique to the road conditions. Scenic diversions are probably not a good idea in the depths of winter.

The law in some countries requires the fitting of winter tyres and/or the use of snow chains – see ***Winter Tyres and Snow Chains*** in the chapter ***Motoring – Equipment.***

You can also visit www.caravanclub.co.uk/overseasadvice to access and download the Winter Equipment Requirements leaflet.

Fuel Price Guide

Prices per litre as at September 2011

Country	Unleaded		Diesel	
	Unleaded	Translation of Unleaded	Diesel	Translation of Diesel
Andorra (EUR)	1.20 (95) 1.26 (98)	Sans plomb or sin plomo	1.09	Gazole or gasóleo
Austria (EUR)	1.40 (95) 1.53 (98)	Bleifrei	1.34	Diesel
Belgium (EUR)	1.65 (95) 1.68 (98)	Sans plomb or loodvrije	1.46	
Croatia (HRK)	9.88 (95) 10.24 (98)	Eurosuper or bez olova	8.92	Dizel
Czech Republic (CZK)	34.93 (95)	Natural or bez olova	34.27	Nafta
Denmark (DKK)	12.83 (95) 11.86 (98)	Blyfri	10.72	
Finland (EUR)	1.57 (95) 1.62 (98)	Lyijyton polttoaine	1.36	
France (EUR)	1.52 (95) 1.56 (98)	Essence sans plomb	1.34	Gazole
Germany (EUR)	1.58 (95) 1.61 (98)	Bleifrei	1.42	Diesel
Greece (EUR)	1.74 (95) 1.92 (98)	Amoliwdi wensina	1.52	Petreleo
Hungary (HUF)	391 (95)	Olommentes uzemanyag	379	Dizel or gázolaj
Italy (EUR)	1.60 (95) 1.75 (98)	Sensa piombo	1.56	Gasolio
Luxembourg (EUR)	1.32 (95) 1.36 (98)	Sans plomb	1.18	Gazole
Netherlands (EUR)	1.74 (95) 1.80 (98)	Loodvrije	1.40	Diesel or gasolie
Norway (NOK)	14.32 (95) 14.63 (98)	Blyfri bensin	13.43	Diesel
Poland (PLN)	5.18 (95) or 5.40 (98)	Bezolowiu	5.11	
Portugal (EUR)	1.59 (95) 1.65 (98)	Sem chumbo	1.37	Gasóleo or diesel
Slovakia (EUR)	1.38 (95)	Natural or olovnatych prisad	1.28	Nafta
Slovenia (EUR)	1.29 (95) 1.30 (98)	Brez svinca	1.24	
Spain (EUR)	1.35 (95) 1.46 (98)	Sin plomo	1.30	Gasóleo A or Gas-oil
Sweden (SEK)	14.38 (95) 14.78 (98)	Blyfri normal, premium	14.14	Diesel
Switzerland (CHF)	1.69 (95) 1.75 (98)	Bleifrei or sans plomb or sensa piomba	1.78	Diesel or gazole or gasolio
UK (GBP)	1.36 (95) 1.43 (98)		1.40	

Fuel prices courtesy of the AIT/FIA Information Centre (OTA) (September 2011)

Prices shown are in local currency, price per litre. The contents are belived to be correct at the date of publication but should be used for guideline purposes only. Differences in prices actually paid may be due to currency and oil price fluctuations as well as regional variations within countries.

For the most recent fuel prices please visit www.caravanclub.co.uk/overseasadvice

Speed Limits

Kilometres per hour (see Conversion Table below for equivalent miles per hour)

Country	Open Road			Motorways		
	Solo*	Towing	Motorhome (3,500-7,500kg)	Solo*	Towing	Motorhome (3,500-7,500kg)
Andorra	60-90	60-90	60-90	n/a	n/a	n/a
Austria	100	80***	70	100-130	100***	80
Belgium	90	90	90	120	120	90
Croatia	90-110	80	80	110-130	90	90
Czech Republic	80-90	80	80	130	80	80
Denmark	80-90	70	70	110-130	80	70
Finland	80-100	70-80	80	100-120 (100 for motorhome under 3,500kg)	80	80
France**	90-110	80-110**	80-100	110-130	90-130**	90-110
Germany	100	80	80	130	80	100
Greece	90-110 (80 for motorhome under 3,500kg)	80	80	130 (90 for motorhome under 3,500kg)	80	80
Hungary	90-110	70	70	130	80	80
Italy	90-110	70	80	130	80	100
Luxembourg	90	75	90	130	90	130
Netherlands	80-90	80-90***	80	120	90***	80
Norway	80	80	80	90-100	80	80
Poland	90-120	70-80	70-80	140	80	80
Portugal	90-100	70-80	70-90	120	100	100
Slovakia	90	90	80	130	90	80
Slovenia	90-100	80	80	130	80	80
Spain	90-100 (70-80 for motorhome under 3,500kg)	70-80	70-80	120 (90 for motorhome under 3,500kg)	80	90
Sweden ****	70-100	70-80	70-100	90-120	80	90-120
Switzerland	80-100	60-80	80	100-120	80	8+0

Converting Kilometres to Miles

km/h	20	30	40	50	60	70	80	90	100	110	120	130
mph	13	18	25	31	37	44	50	56	62	68	74	81

*** Also including motorhomes under 3,500kg unless otherwise stated.**
**** Speed limits when towing a caravan/trailer in France is based on the gross train mass of your car/vehicle combination. If the gross train mass of the car/vehicle is over 3,500kg the speed limit is 90kph on motorways and 80-90kph on open roads. If the gross train mass of car/ vehicle is under 3,500kg the speed limit is 130kph on motorways and 90-110kph on open roads. To work out the gross train mass of your car/vehicle you need to add the fully laden weight of your car to your cars towing limit. For further information and for an example please visit www.caravanclub.co.uk/overseastravel. Please note in France speed limits are reduced in adverse weather.**
***** If the combined weight of your car and caravan is over 3,500kg then the speed limit is the same as a motorhome over 3,500kg.**
****** Speed limits vary greatly in Sweden and are dependent on the quality and safety of the road.**

NOTES: 1) *See Country Introductions in the relevant guides for further details, including special speed limits, where applicable.*
2) *Speed limits in built-up areas are generally much lower, and in some countries speed limits in residential areas may be as low as 20kph.*
3) *All information on this page is believed to be correct at the time of publication but may be subject to change. Speed limits often vary and some countries may trial new speed limits on certain roads and motorways. Check before you travel and always look for signs advising of speed limits on the journey. Please visit www.caravanclub.co.uk/overseasadvice to check the latest speed limits before you travel and for more detailed information and advice.*

European Distances

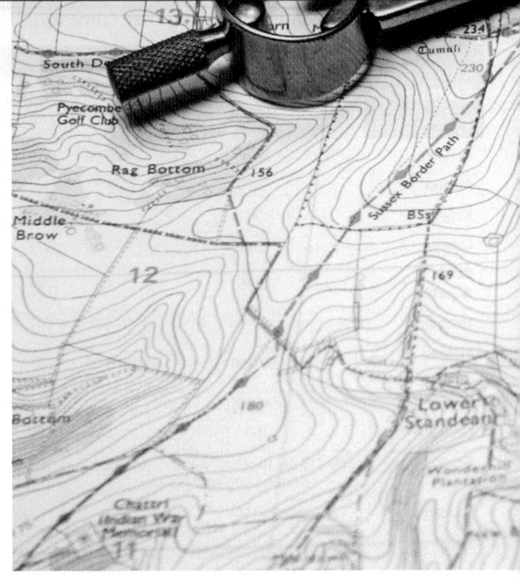

Distances are shown in kilometres and are calculated from town/city centres along the most practical roads, although not necessarily taking the shortest route.

1km = 0.62 miles

Amsterdam	Athini (Athens)	Barcelona	Bergen	Berlin	Bilbao	Bordeaux	Bruxelles (Brussels)	Budapest	Calais	Dubrovnik	Firenze (Florence)	Frankfurt am Main	Genève (Geneva)	Göteborg (Gothenburg)	Hamburg	Helsinki	Kobenhavn (Copenhagen)	Lisboa (Lisbon)	Ljubljana	Luxembourg	Lyon	Madrid	Marseille
2836																							
1552	2090																						
1507	4017	2817																					
668	2584	1856	1320																				
1426	3422	613	2866	1974																			
1085	3240	566	2525	1632	338																		
211	2792	1365	1625	776	1235	893																	
1407	1510	1910	2179	852	2258	2061	1363																
368	2926	1381	1672	917	1196	866	195	1549															
2024	1265	2049	3204	1771	2381	2199	1970	787	2024														
1340	2115	1084	2476	1226	1432	1232	1185	929	1390	1074													
446	2396	1324	1537	538	1491	1149	401	970	595	1583	973												
909	2446	761	2120	1074	1109	678	721	1280	740	1405	604	588											
1043	3205	2354	791	656	2404	2063	1162	1517	1316	2392	1851	1061	1644										
467	2780	1778	1050	284	1828	1486	585	1145	752	1967	1428	488	1071	584									
1204	2540	2388	1186	505	2525	2182	1316	1030	2016	1893	1766	1101	1656	662	776								
780	2938	2091	1029	392	2141	1799	898	1253	1058	2125	1587	798	1381	241	321	795							
2269	4320	1241	3709	2817	883	1188	2077	3133	2061	3279	2307	2333	1983	3246	2669	3423	2982						
1239	1580	1451	2119	993	1778	1587	1191	429	1394	658	474	810	798	1262	1187	2023	1493	2640					
381	2637	1153	1655	766	1271	929	215	1184	409	1758	973	237	510	1192	625	1302	938	2113	974				
920	2559	634	2186	1224	982	531	733	1431	750	1518	695	691	151	1722	1146	1758	1459	1857	938	521			
1779	3760	618	3219	2326	394	697	1586	2510	1578	2719	1683	1842	1360	2755	2179	2913	2492	622	2038	1621	1234		
1231	2621	504	2496	1535	852	652	1044	1446	1057	1580	619	1003	439	2033	1456	2069	1769	1727	993	831	313	1104	
1040	2128	982	2165	1034	1330	995	885	944	1088	1087	296	673	318	1690	1117	1575	1427	2205	500	672	443	1581	509
834	1621	1347	1835	585	1696	1242	729	654	966	567	637	397	593	1209	786	490	946	2570	411	514	744	1947	1002
1807	2443	1551	2943	1693	1899	1699	1652	1396	1868	1675	466	1440	1071	2318	1895	1599	2054	2774	951	1439	1161	2150	1078
1049	993	2359	472	972	2409	2068	1167	1833	1620	1058	2167	1078	1661	320	592	907	557	3252	2055	1206	1727	2761	2039
501	946	1040	1941	1049	923	581	309	1487	287	1097	1133	575	504	1478	902	736	1215	1765	1243	354	459	1274	771
2076	2189	1131	3516	2624	690	994	1883	2907	1851	2671	2081	2139	1758	3052	2476	2311	2789	304	2429	1918	1631	571	1503
855	1753	1700	1659	338	1942	1600	890	514	1069	257	1020	497	918	997	625	431	734	2784	655	723	1067	2299	1380
1608	2244	1352	2744	1494	1700	1500	1453	1197	1668	1476	267	1241	872	2119	1696	1400	1855	2575	751	1240	962	1951	879
2483	4683	3844	2824	2129	3862	3519	2635	3038	2827	3870	3330	2530	3112	1528	2050	837	1745	4760	3269	2660	3214	4250	3625
977	1777	1510	1978	728	1858	1381	885	547	1127	632	629	540	732	1352	929	633	1089	2733	288	670	883	2110	1038
2305	2418	1010	3745	2856	920	1223	2112	2910	2100	2838	2084	2324	1761	3281	2705	2511	3018	400	2431	2152	1634	529	1506
1387	1126	2698	1009	1000	2748	2406	1505	1861	1662	1086	2195	1405	1988	481	928	1234	585	3590	2097	1545	2066	3100	2378
601	1277	1123	1751	752	1406	1065	432	1012	618	734	788	219	402	1276	702	406	1012	2249	773	219	490	1723	803
2350	511	2604	3531	2098	2936	2754	2306	1024	2491	779	1629	1910	1960	2719	2294	2054	2452	3834	1145	2151	2073	3274	2135
1200	1645	323	2640	1758	452	248	1007	1812	1101	1740	985	1225	662	2177	1600	1412	1913	1294	1347	1054	536	701	407
3041	5241	4402	1893	2687	4420	4077	3193	3596	3260	4428	3888	3088	3670	2570	2608	1367	2303	5316	3699	3218	3772	4808	4083
1899	2335	357	3164	2203	602	796	1711	2257	1717	2185	1430	1670	1107	2700	2124	1857	2437	970	1788	1499	981	347	852
1242	1928	1236	2311	1061	1584	1257	1137	692	1351	1043	255	829	580	1685	1262	966	1422	2459	240	925	705	1835	763
1223	2149	2339	1907	591	2531	2190	1332	670	1472	567	1502	1062	1557	1084	874	948	982	3374	1041	1289	1706	2883	2019
1151	1970	1793	1943	622	2147	1805	1107	243	1300	540	812	714	1024	1281	909	807	1017	3016	376	928	1174	2393	1321
1347	2166	1592	2348	999	1940	1614	1303	356	1476	917	611	910	936	1704	1299	1003	1441	2815	133	1087	1062	2192	1120
810	1418	1046	1914	837	1394	935	627	984	847	819	580	397	286	1438	865	569	1175	2269	717	414	436	1645	726

Luxembourg - Warszawa (Warsaw) = 1289 km

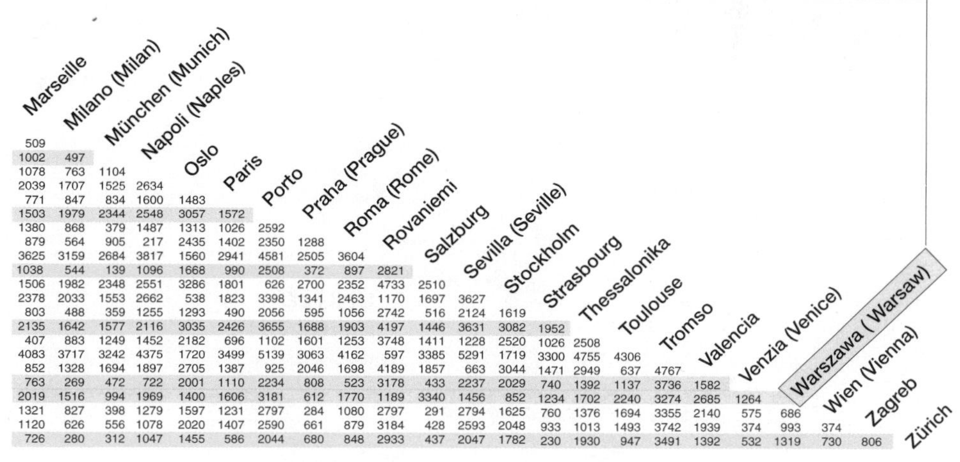

Marseille	Milano (Milan)	München (Munich)	Napoli (Naples)	Oslo	Paris	Porto	Praha (Prague)	Roma (Rome)	Rovaniemi	Salzburg	Sevilla (Seville)	Stockholm	Strasbourg	Thessalonika	Toulouse	Tromso	Valencia	Venzia (Venice)	Warszawa (Warsaw)	Wien (Vienna)	Zagreb	Zürich
509																						
1002	497																					
1078	763	1104																				
2039	1707	1525	2634																			
771	847	834	1600	1483																		
1503	1979	2344	2548	3057	1572																	
1380	868	379	1487	1313	1026	2592																
879	564	905	217	2435	1402	2350	1288															
3625	3159	2684	3817	1560	2941	4581	2505	3604														
1038	544	139	1096	1668	990	2508	372	897	2821													
1506	1982	2348	2551	3286	1801	626	2700	2352	4733	2510												
2378	2033	1553	2662	538	1823	3398	1341	2463	1170	1697	3627											
803	488	359	1255	1293	490	2056	595	1056	2742	516	2124	1619										
2135	1642	1577	2116	3035	2426	3655	1688	1903	4197	1446	3631	3082	1952									
407	883	1249	1452	2182	696	1102	1601	1253	3748	1411	1228	2520	1026	2508								
4083	3717	3242	4375	1720	3499	5139	3063	4162	597	3385	5291	1719	3300	4755	4306							
852	1328	1694	1897	2705	1387	925	2046	1698	4189	1857	663	3044	1471	2949	637	4767						
763	269	472	722	2001	1110	2234	808	523	3178	433	2237	2029	740	1392	1137	3736	1582					
2019	1516	994	1969	1400	1606	3181	612	1770	1189	3340	1456	852	1234	1702	2240	3274	2685	1264				
1321	827	398	1279	1597	1231	2797	284	1080	2797	291	2794	1625	760	1376	1694	3355	2140	575	686			
1120	626	556	1078	2020	1407	2590	661	879	3184	428	2593	2048	933	1013	1493	3742	1939	374	993	374		
726	280	312	1047	1455	586	2044	680	848	2933	437	2047	1782	230	1930	947	3491	1392	532	1319	730	806	

Route Planning – North

Murmansk
Tromsø
Ivalo
Narvik
Kiruna
Kemijärvi
Boda
NORWAY
Luleå
Oulu / Uleåborg
Kajaani
FINLAND
Gulf of Bothnia
SWEDEN
Umeå
Kuopio
Vaasa / Vasa
Petrozavodsk
ondheim
Östersund
Jyväskylä
RUSSIAN FEDERATION
Sundsvall
Ladozhskoye Ozero
Tampere
Pori
Lahti
Sankt Peterburg
Pushkin
Mora
HELSINKI / HELSINGFORS
Gävle
Turku / Åbo
Hamar
Falun
Gulf of Finland
Narva
Vårdö
Novgorod
Uppsala
TALLINN
OSLO
Västerås
ESTONIA
Karlstad
STOCKHOLM
Örebro
Tartu
Pärnu
Pskov
Linköping
Gulf of Riga
Velikiye Luki
Jönköping
Gotland
Visby
LATVIA
Göteborg (Gothenburg)
Oskarshamn
Jūrmala
RĪGA
Frederikshavn
Jelgava
Aalborg
Kalmar
Öland
Liepāja
Daugavpils
Navapolatsk
Vitsyebsk
Halmstad
Šiauliai
Panevėžys
Kattegat
Grenaa
Baltic Sea
Karlskrona
Klaipėda
LITHUANIA
KØBENHAVN
Malmö
VILNIUS
Mahilyow
ENMARK
Kaunas
RUSSIAN FEDERATION
Rønne
Bornholm
Marijampolė
MINSK
Kaliningrad
Gedser
Sassnitz
Gdańsk
BELARUS
Babruysk
Kiel
Hrodna
Rostock
Olsztyn
Baranavichy
Białystok
Hamburg
Schwerin
Szczecin
POLAND

Route Planning – South

BELARUS
Chernihiv
Gorzów Wielkopolski
POLAND
WARSZAWA
Brest
Berlin
Poznań
KYIV
Łódź
Lublin
Rivne
Zhytomyr
Leipzig
Wrocław
Kielce
Dresden
Opole
UKRAINE
Liberec
Katowice
L'viv
Vinnytsya
Hradec Králové
Kraków
Rzeszów
Ternopil'
Khmel'nyts'kyy
Karlovy Vary
PRAHA
Ostrava
Ivano-Frankivs'k
Plzeň
CZECH REPUBLIC
Olomouc
Zlín
Žilina
Prešov
České Budějovice
Brno
Trenčín
Košice
Uzhhorod
Chernivtsi
Bălți
Rîbnița
SLOVAKIA
MOLDOVA
Suceava
CHIȘINĂU
Trnava
Nitra
Miskolc
Nyíregyháza
Baia Mare
Iași
Tighina
Linz
WIEN
BRATISLAVA
Debrecen
Zalău
Bistrița
Piatra Neamț
BUDAPEST
Salzburg
Sopron
Győr
Bacău
Szolnok
Oradea
Târgu Mureș
Szombathely
Kecskemét
AUSTRIA
Veszprém
Békéscsaba
Sfântu Gheorghe
HUNGARY
Graz
Hódmezővásárhely
Alba Iulia
Focșani
Sibiu
Klagenfurt
Nagykanizsa
Szeged
Arad
Deva
Brașov
Maribor
Tulcea
ROMANIA
Pécs
Subotica
Buzău
SLOVENIA
Timișoara
LJUBLJANA
ZAGREB
Slobozia
Ploiești
Târgu Jiu
Constanța
Osijek
Novi Sad
Reșița
Pitești
Trieste
Zrenjanin
Călărași
Slavonski Brod
Drobeta-Turnu Severin
BUCUREȘTI
Karlovac
Silistra
Venezia
Rijeka
BEOGRAD
CROATIA
Banja Luka
Craiova
Ruse
Dobrich
Tuzla
Šabac
Varna
Pula
SERBIA
Razgrad
BOSNIA-HERZEGOVINA
Kragujevac
Pleven
Shumen
Zenica
Kraljevo
Veliko Tŭrnovo
Zadar
Vratsa
SARAJEVO
Kruševac
Gabrovo
Sliven
Burgas
SAN MARINO
Niš
BULGARIA
Ancona
Split
Mostar
Mitrovicë
SOFIYA
Stara Zagora
MONTENEGRO
Pejë
PRISHTINË
Kyustendil
Perugia
Nikšić
KOSOVO
Kirklareli
Dubrovnik
Prizren
Blagoevgrad
Edirne
ITALY
Kumanovo
Kŭrdzhali
PODGORICA
Shkodër
L'Aquila
Pescara
SKOPJE
Veles
Tekirdağ
Adriatic Sea
MACEDONIA
TURKEY
Prilep
ROMA
Campobasso
Durrës
TIRANË
Bitola
Çanakkale
Elbasan
Thessaloniki
Bari
ALBANIA
Napoli
Vlorë
Korçë
Potenza
Limnos
Mytilini
Larisa
Lesvos (Lesbos)
Tyrrhenian Sea
Ioannina
Kerkyra (Corfu)
Chios
Evvoia
Aegean Sea
GREECE
Nicastro
Catanzaro
ATHINA
Andros
Keffalonia (Cephalonia)
Patra
Tinos
Agios Dimitrios
Messina
Palermo
Reggio di Calabria
Naxos
Zakynthos (Zante)
Ionian Sea
Sicilia (Sicily)
Catania
Gytheio
Siracusa
Kriti (Crete)
Mediterranean Sea
Chania
Irakleio (Iraklion)
MALTA
VALLETTA

Motoring - Equipment

Please note equipment requirements and regulations change frequently. To keep up to date with the latest equipment information please visit www.caravanclub.co.uk/overseasadvice

Bicycle and Motorbike Transportation

Regulations vary from country to country but as a general rule separate registration and insurance documents are required for a motorbike or scooter and these vehicles, as well as bicycles, must be carried on an approved carrier in such a way that they do not obscure rear windows, lights, reflectors or number plates. Vehicles should not be overloaded, i.e. exceed the maximum loaded weight recommended by your vehicle manufacturer.

Car Telephones

It is illegal to use a hand-held car phone or mobile phone while driving. Hands-free equipment should be fitted in your vehicle if you feel you must use the phone while travelling.

First Aid Kit

A first aid kit, in a strong dust-proof box, should be carried in case of an emergency. This is a legal requirement in several countries in Europe and is a must have item regardless.

*See **Essential Equipment Table** at the end of this chapter and the chapter **Medical Matters**.*

Fire Extinguisher

As a recommended safety precaution, an approved fire extinguisher should be carried in all vehicles. This is a legal requirement in several countries in Europe.

See ***Essential Equipment Table*** at the end of this chapter.

Glasses

It is a legal requirement in some countries for residents to carry a spare pair of glasses if they are needed for driving and it is recommended that visitors also comply. Elsewhere, if you do not have a spare pair, you may find it helpful to carry a copy of your prescription.

© iStockPhoto.com/36clicks

Lights

When driving on the Continent headlights need to be adjusted to deflect to the right, if they are likely to dazzle other road users, by means of suitable beam deflectors or (in some cases) a built-in adjustment system. Do not leave headlight conversion to the last minute as, in the case of some modern high-density discharge (HID), xenon or halogen-type lights, a dealer may need to make the necessary adjustment. Remember also to adjust headlights according to the load being carried and to compensate for the weight of the caravan on the back of your car.

Even if you do not intend to drive at night, it is important to ensure that your headlights will not dazzle others as you may need to use them in heavy rain or fog and in tunnels. If using tape or a pre-cut adhesive mask remember to remove it on your return home.

Dipped headlights should be used in poor weather conditions such as fog, snowfall or heavy rain and in a tunnel even if it is well lit. You may find police waiting at the end of a tunnel to check vehicles. In some countries the use of dipped headlights is compulsory at all times, day and night, and in others they must be used in built-up areas, on motorways or at certain times of the year.

Take a full set of spare light bulbs. This is a legal requirement in several countries.

See ***Essential Equipment Table*** at the end of this chapter.

Headlight-Flashing

On the Continent headlight-flashing is often used as a warning of approach or as an overtaking signal at night, and not, as is commonly the case in the UK, an indication that you are giving way, so use with great care in case it is misunderstood. When another driver flashes you, make sure of his intention before moving.

Hazard Warning Lights

Generally hazard warning lights should not be used in place of a warning triangle, but they may be used in addition to it.

Nationality Plate (GB/IRL)

A nationality plate of an authorised design must be fixed to the rear of both your car and caravan on a vertical or near-vertical surface. Checks are made and a fine may be imposed for failure to display a nationality plate correctly. These are provided free to members taking out The Caravan Club's Red Pennant Overseas Holiday Insurance – see www.caravanclub.co.uk/redpennant

Regulations allow the optional display on number plates of the Euro-Symbol which is a circle of stars on a blue background with an EU Member State's national identification letter(s) below – e.g. GB or IRL. On UK-registered vehicles whose number plates incorporate the Euro-Symbol, the display of an additional GB sticker on a vehicle is unnecessary when driving within the EU and Switzerland. However, it is still required when driving outside the EU even when number plates incorporate the Euro-Symbol, and it is still required for all vehicles without Euro-Symbol plates.

GB is the only permissible national identification code for cars registered in the UK. Registration plates displaying the GB Euro-Symbol must comply with the appropriate British Standard.

Radar/Speed Camera Detectors

The possession or use of a radar-detection device, whether in use or not, is illegal in many countries on the Continent and you should not carry one in your vehicle. Penalties include fines, vehicle confiscation or a driving ban. Some countries also ban the use of GPS satellite navigation devices which pinpoint the position of fixed speed cameras and you must, therefore, deactivate the relevant Points of Interest (PoI) function.

Rear View External Mirrors

In order to comply with local regulations and avoid the attention of local police forces, ensure that your vehicle's external mirrors are adjusted correctly to allow you to view both sides of your caravan or trailer – over its entire length – from behind the steering wheel. Some countries stipulate that mirrors should extend beyond the width of the caravan but should be removed or folded in when travelling solo, and this is common-sense advice for all countries.

Reflective Jackets/Waistcoats

Legislation has been introduced in many countries in Europe (see individual Country Introductions in relevant guides) requiring drivers to wear a reflective jacket or waistcoat if leaving a vehicle which is immobilised on the carriageway outside a built-up area. This is a commonsense requirement which will probably be extended to other countries and which should be observed wherever you drive. A second jacket is also recommended for a passenger who may need to assist in an emergency repair. Carry the jackets in the passenger compartment of your vehicle, rather than in the boot. The jackets should conform to at least European Standard EN471, Class 2 and are available from motor accessory shops and from the Club's shop – see www.caravanclub.co.uk/shop

Route Planning

An organisation called Keep Moving www.keepmoving.co.uk provides information on UK roads including routes to ferry ports, tel 09003 401100 or 401100 from a mobile phone. The Highway Agency has information for roads in England, including channel port access, visit www.trafficengland.com. Both the AA and RAC have useful websites offering a route planning service: www.theaa.com and www.rac.co.uk. Other websites offering a European routes service and/or traffic information include www.viamichelin.com and www.mappy.com which, amongst other things, provides city centre maps for major towns across Europe.

Detailed, large-scale maps or atlases of the countries you are visiting are essential. Navigating your way around other countries can be confusing, especially for the novice, and the more care you take planning your route, the more enjoyable your journey will be. Before setting out, study maps and distance charts.

If you propose travelling across mountain passes check whether the suggested route supplied by the route-planning website takes account of passes or tunnels where caravans are not permitted or recommended.

See the chapter ***Mountain Passes and Tunnels.***

Satellite Navigation/GPS

Continental postcodes do not, on the whole, pinpoint a particular street or part of a street in the same way as the system in use in the UK. A French five-digit postcode, for example, can cover a very large area of many square kilometres.

GPS co-ordinates are given for most site entries in this guide and wherever possible full street addresses are given, enabling you to programme your sat nav as accurately as possible.

Your sat nav device is a valuable aid in finding a campsite in an area you are not familiar with, but it is important to realise that such equipment is not perfect. For example, sat nav routes are unlikely to allow for the fact that you are towing a caravan or driving a large motorhome. Use your common sense – if a road looks suspect, don't follow it.

It is probably wise therefore to use your sat nav in conjunction with the printed directions to campsites in this guide, which have been supplied by users of the guide based on their own experience of driving to the site, together with an up-to-date map or atlas. You may find it useful to identify a 'waypoint' (a nearby village, say) mentioned in these written directions and add it to your route definition when programming your sat nav to ensure you approach from a suitable direction. Please note the directions given in the site entries have not been provided by The Caravan Club but by users of Caravan Europe. The directions have not been checked in detail for accuracy, therefore always use in conjunction with an up to date map or atlas.

Update your sat nav device regularly and remember that, in spite of detailed directions and the use of a sat nav, local conditions such as road closures and roadworks may on occasion make finding your destination difficult.

*See the chapter **Introduction** in the section **HOW TO USE THIS GUIDE** for more information on satellite navigation.*

Seat Belts

The wearing of seat belts is compulsory in all the countries featured in this guide. On-the-spot fines will be incurred for failure to wear them and, in the event of an accident and insurance claim, compensation for injury may be reduced if seat belts are not worn.

As in the UK, legislation in many countries in Europe, requires all children up to a certain age or height to use a child restraint appropriate for their weight or size and, in addition, some countries' laws prohibit them from sitting in the front of a car.

Rear-facing baby seats must never be used in a seat protected by a frontal airbag unless the airbag has been deactivated.

Spares

Caravan Spares

On the Continent it is generally much more difficult to obtain spares for caravans than for cars and it will usually be necessary to obtain spares from a UK manufacturer or dealer before you travel.

Car Spares Kits

Some motor manufacturers can supply spares kits for a selected range of models; contact your dealer for details. The choice of spares will depend on the vehicle, how long you are likely to be away and your own level of competence in car maintenance, but the following is a list of basic items which should cover the most common causes of breakdown:

Radiator top hose • Fan belt • Fuses and bulbs • Windscreen wiper blade • Length of 12V electrical cable • Tools, torch and WD40 or equivalent water repellent/dispersant spray

Spare Wheel

Your local caravan dealer should be able to supply an appropriate spare wheel. If you have any difficulty in obtaining one, The Caravan Club's Technical Department will provide Club members with a list of suppliers' addresses on request.

Tyre legislation across Europe is more or less fully harmonised and, while the Club has no specific knowledge of laws on the Continent regarding the use of space-saver spare wheels, there should be no problems in using such a wheel provided its use is strictly in accordance with the manufacturer's instructions.

Towing Bracket

The vast majority of cars registered after 1 August 1998 are legally required to have a European Type approved towing bracket (complying with European Directive 94/20) carrying a plate giving its approval number and various technical details, including the maximum noseweight. The approval process includes strength testing to a higher value than provided in the previous British Standard, and confirmation of fitting to all the car manufacturer's approved mounting points. Your car dealer or specialist towing bracket fitter will be able to give further advice. Checks may be made by foreign police. From 29 April 2011 for brand new motorhome designs (launched on or after that date) and 29 April 2012 for existing designs (those already being built before 29 April 2011), all new motorhomes will need some form of type approval before they can be registered in the UK and as such can only be fitted with a type approved towing bracket. Note also that some manufacturers are type approving their vehicles ahead of these required dates, so check carefully with any vehicle built from 2009 onwards. This change will not affect older vehicles, which can continue to be fitted with non-approved towing brackets.

Tyres

Safe driving and handling when towing a caravan or trailer are very important and one major factor, which is frequently overlooked, is tyre condition. Your caravan tyres must be suitable for the highest speed at which you can legally tow, not for any lower speed at which you may choose to travel. Some older British caravans (usually over ten years old) may not meet this requirement and, if you are subject to a police check, this could result in an on-the-spot fine for each tyre, including the spare. Check your tyre specification before you leave and, if necessary, upgrade your tyres. The Caravan Club's technical advice leaflet 'Caravan Tyres and Wheels', available to members on the Club's website or by post, explains how to check if your tyres are suitable.

Most countries require a minimum tread depth of 1.6 mm over the central part of the whole tyre, but motoring organisations recommend at least 3 mm across the whole tyre. If you plan an extended trip and your tyres are likely to be more worn than this before you return home, replace them before you leave.

Tyre Pressure

Tyre pressure should be checked and adjusted when the tyres are cold; checking warm tyres will result in a higher pressure reading. The correct pressures will be found in your car handbook, but unless it states otherwise it is wise to add an extra four to six pounds per square inch to the rear tyres of a car when towing to improve handling and to carry the extra load on the hitch.

Make sure you know what pressure your caravan tyres should be. Some require a pressure much higher than that normally used for cars. Check your caravan handbook for details.

Tyre Sizes

It is worth noting that some sizes of radial tyre to fit the 13" wheels commonly used on older UK caravans are virtually impossible to find in stock at retailers abroad, e.g. 175R13C.

After a Puncture

The Caravan Club does not recommend the general use of liquid sealants for puncture repair. Such products should not be considered to achieve a permanent repair, and may indeed render the tyre irreparable. If sealant is used to allow the vehicle to be removed from a position of danger to one of safety, the damaged tyre should be removed from the vehicle, repaired and replaced as soon as practically possible.

Following a caravan tyre puncture, especially on a single-axle caravan, it is advisable to have the opposite side (non-punctured) tyre removed from its wheel and checked inside and out for signs of damage resulting from overloading during the deflation of the punctured tyre. Failure to take this precaution may result in an increased risk of a second tyre deflation within a very short space of time.

Winter Tyres and Snow Chains

Winter tyres should be used in those countries with a severe winter climate and in some it is a legal requirement. Winter tyres are designed to minimise the hardening effect of low temperatures which in turn leads to less traction on the road, and to provide extra grip on snow and ice and in wet conditions. If you intend to make an extended winter trip or to travel regularly to where there may be snow or ice on the roads, it would be advisable to buy a set of winter tyres. Your local tyre dealer will be able to advise you.

Snow chains may be necessary on some roads in winter. They are compulsory in some countries during the winter where indicated by the appropriate road sign, when they must be fitted on at least two drive-wheels. They are not difficult to fit and it's a good idea to carry sturdy gloves to protect your hands when handling the chains in freezing conditions. For further information see the Country Introductions.

Polar Automotive Ltd sells and hires out snow chains (10% discount for Caravan Club members), tel 01892 519933 www.snowchains.com, email: polar@snowchains.com

Warning Triangles

In almost all European countries it is a legal requirement to use a warning triangle in the event of a breakdown or accident; some countries require two. It is strongly recommended that approved red warning triangles be carried as a matter of course.

A warning triangle should be placed on the road approximately 30 metres (100 metres on motorways) behind the broken down vehicle on the same side of the road. Always assemble the triangle before leaving your vehicle and walk with it so that the red, reflective surface is facing oncoming traffic. If a breakdown occurs round a blind corner, place the triangle in advance of the corner. Hazard warning lights may be used in conjunction with the triangle but they do not replace it.

*See **Essential Equipment Table** at the end of this chapter.*

Technical information compiled with the assistance of the Automobile Association.

Planning and Travelling

Essential Equipment in Europe

See also the information contained in the Handbook chapter and in the Country Introductions within the relevant Caravan Europe Volumes. For up to date information on essential equipment requirements for countries in Europe please visit www.caravanclub.co.uk/overseasadvice

Country	Warning Triangle	Spare Bulbs	First Aid Kit	Reflective Jacket	Additional Equipment to be Carried/Used
Andorra	Yes (2)	Yes	Rec	Yes	Dipped headlights in poor daytime visibility. Winter tyres recommended; snow chains when road conditions or signs dictate.
Austria	Yes	Rec	Yes	Yes	Winter tyres from 1 Nov to 15 April.*
Belgium	Yes	Rec	Rec	Yes	Dipped headlights in poor daytime visibility.
Croatia	Yes (2 for vehicle with trailer)	Yes	Yes	Yes	Dipped headlights at all times from the last Sunday Oct to the last Sunday in Mar. Snow chains in winter months in certain regions is compulsory.*
Czech Rep	Yes	Yes	Yes	Yes	Dipped headlights at all times. Replacement fuses. Winter tyres or snow chains from 1 Nov to 31st March.*
Denmark	Yes	Rec	Rec	Rec	Dipped headlights at all times. On motorways use hazard warning lights when queues or danger ahead.
Finland	Yes	Rec	Rec	Yes	Dipped headlights at all times. Winter tyres Dec to Feb.*
France	Yes (2 rec)	Yes	Rec	Yes	Dipped headlights recommended at all times.
Germany	Yes	Rec	Rec	Rec	Dipped headlights recommended at all times. Winter tyres to be used in winter weather conditions.*
Greece	Yes	Rec	Yes	Rec	Fire extinguisher compulsory. Dipped headlights in towns at night and in poor daytime visibility.
Hungary	Yes	Rec	Yes	Yes	Dipped headlights at all times outside built-up areas and in built-up areas at night. Snow chains may be compulsory on some roads in winter conditions.*
Italy	Yes	Rec	Rec	Yes	Dipped headlights at all times outside built-up areas and in poor visibility. Snow chains from15 Oct to 15 April.*
Luxembourg	Yes	Rec	Rec	Yes	Dipped headlights at night and in daytime in bad weather.
Netherlands	Yes	Rec	Rec	Rec	Dipped headlights at night and in bad weather and recommended during the day.
Norway	Yes	Rec	Rec	Rec	Dipped headlights at all times. Winter tyres compulsory when snow or ice on the roads.*
Poland	Yes	Rec	Rec	Rec	Dipped headlights at all times.
Portugal	Yes	Rec	Rec	Yes	Dipped headlights in poor daytime visibility, in tunnels and in lanes where traffic flow is reversible.
Slovakia	Yes	Yes	Yes	Yes	Dipped headlights at all times. Winter tyres compulsory when compact snow or ice on the road.*
Slovenia	Yes (2 for vehicle with trailer)	Yes	Yes	Yes	Dipped headlights at all times. Hazard warning lights when reversing. Use winter tyres between 15 Nov and 15 March or carry snow chains.
Spain	Yes (2 Rec)	Rec	Rec	Yes	Dipped headlights at night and in tunnels and on 'special' roads (roadworks).
Sweden	Yes	Rec	Rec	Rec	Dipped headlights at all times. Winter tyres from 1 Dec to 31 March.
Switzerland (inc Liechtenstein)	Yes	Rec	Rec	Rec	Dipped headlights recommended at all times, compulsory in tunnels. Snow chains where indicated by signs.

NOTES:
1) *All countries: seat belts (if fitted) must be worn by all passengers.*
2) *Rec: not compulsory for foreign-registered vehicles, but very strongly recommended*
3) *Headlamp converters, spare bulbs, fire extinguisher, first aid kit and reflective waistcoat are strongly recommended for all countries.*
4) *In some countries drivers who wear prescription glasses must carry a spare pair.*
5) *Please check information for any country before you travel as rules and regulations change. This information is to be used as a guide only and it is your responsibility to make sure you have the correct equipment.*

** For information and regulations on winter driving in these countries, please see the Country Introduction chapters in the relevant Caravan Europe guide.*

Planning and Travelling

Mountain Passes and Tunnels

The mountain passes, rail and road tunnels listed in the tables are shown on the following maps. Numbers and letters against each pass or tunnel in the tables, correspond with the numbers and letters on the maps.

Please read the following advice carefully.

Advice for Drivers

Mountain Passes

The conditions and comments in the following tables assume an outfit with good power/weight ratio. Even those mountain passes and tunnels which do not carry a 'not recommended' or 'not permitted' warning may be challenging for any vehicle, more so for car and caravan outfits.

If in any doubt whatsoever, it is probably best to restrict yourself to those mountain passes which can be crossed by motorway. In any event, mountain passes should only be attempted by experienced drivers in cars with ample power and in good driving conditions; they should otherwise be avoided.

In the following table, where the entry states that caravans are not permitted or not recommended to use a pass, this generally – but not always – refers to towed caravans, and is based on advice originally supplied by the AA and/or local motoring organisations, but not checked by The Caravan Club. Motorhomes are seldom prohibited by such restrictions, but those which are relatively low powered or very large should find an alternative route. Always obey road signs at the foot of a pass, especially those referring to heavy vehicles, which may apply to some large motorhomes.

Do not attempt to cross passes at night or in bad weather. Before crossing, seek local advice if touring during periods when the weather is changeable or unreliable. Warning notices are usually posted at the foot of a pass if it is closed, or if chains or winter tyres must be used.

Caravanners are obviously particularly sensitive to gradients and traffic/road conditions on passes. Take great care when negotiating blind hairpins. The maximum gradient is usually on the inside of bends but exercise caution if it is necessary to pull out. Always engage a lower gear before taking a hairpin bend and give priority to vehicles ascending. Give priority to postal service vehicles – signposts usually show their routes. Do not go down hills in neutral gear.

Keep to the extreme right of the road and be prepared to reverse to give way to descending/ascending traffic.

On mountain roads it is not the gradient which taxes your car but the duration of the climb and the loss of power at high altitudes: approximately 10% at 915 metres (3,000 feet) and even more as you get higher. Turbo power restores much of the lost capacity.

To minimise the risk of the engine overheating, take high passes in the cool of the day, don't climb any faster than necessary and keep the engine pulling steadily. To prevent a radiator boiling, pull off the road safely, turn the heater and blower full on and switch off airconditioning. Keep an eye on water and oil levels. Never put cold water into a boiling radiator or it may crack. Check that the radiator is not obstructed by debris sucked up during the journey.

A long descent may result in overheating brakes; select the correct gear for the gradient and avoid excessive use of brakes. Note that even if using engine braking to control the outfit's speed, caravan brakes may activate due to the action of the overrun mechanism, causing them to overheat. Use lay-bys and lookout points to stop and allow brakes to cool.

In alpine areas snow prevents road repairs during the winter, resulting in road works during the summer, which may cause traffic delays. At times one-way traffic only may be permitted on some routes. Information will be posted at each end of the road.

Main roads crossing major passes are rarely totally unguarded; but minor passes may be unguarded or simply have stone pillars placed at close intervals. If you do not have a good head for heights consider a different route.

Leave the blade valve of your portable toilet open a fraction when travelling at altitude. This avoids pressure build-up in the holding tank. Similarly, a slightly open tap will avoid pressure build up in water pipes and fittings.

Tunnels

British drivers do not often encounter road tunnels but they are a common feature in Europe, for example, through mountain ranges. Tolls are usually charged for the use of major tunnels.

Ensure you have enough fuel before entering a tunnel. Emergency situations often involve vehicles stranded because of a lack of fuel.

When approaching a tunnel in bright sunshine, slow down to allow your eyes to adjust and look out for poorly-lit vehicles in front of you and for cyclists. Take sunglasses off before entering a tunnel and take care again when emerging into sunshine at the other end.

Signposts usually indicate a tunnel ahead and its length. Once inside, maintain a safe distance from the vehicle in front in case the driver brakes sharply. Minimum/maximum speed limits usually apply. Dipped headlights are usually required by law even in well-lit tunnels, so switch them on before you enter. Some tunnels may be poorly or totally unlit.

Snow chains, if used, must be removed before entering a tunnel in lay-bys provided for this purpose.

'No overtaking' signs must be strictly observed. Never cross central single or double lines. If overtaking is permitted in twin-tube tunnels, bear in mind that it is very easy to under-estimate distances and speed once inside. Watch out for puddles caused by dripping or infiltrating water.

In order to minimise the effects of exhaust fumes close all car windows and set the ventilator to circulate air, or operate the air conditioning system coupled with the recycled air option. If there is a traffic jam, switch your hazard warning lights on and stop a safe distance from the vehicle in front. Sound the horn only in a real emergency. Never change direction unless instructed to do so by tunnel staff or a police officer.

If you break down, try to reach the next lay-by and call for help from an emergency phone. If you cannot reach a lay-by, place your warning triangle at least 100 metres behind your vehicle. Passengers should leave the vehicle through doors on the right-hand side only. Modern tunnels have video surveillance systems to ensure prompt assistance in an emergency.

Mountain Pass Information

The dates of opening and closing given in the following tables are approximate and inclusive. Before attempting late afternoon or early morning journeys across borders, check their opening times as some borders close at night.

Gradients listed are the maximum which may be encountered on the pass and may be steeper at the inside of curves, particularly on older roads.

Gravel surfaces (such as dirt and stone chips) vary considerably; they can be dusty when dry and slippery when wet. Where known to exist, this type of surface has been noted.

In fine weather winter tyres or snow chains will only be required on very high passes, or for short periods in early or late summer. In winter conditions you will probably need to use them at altitudes exceeding 600 metres (approximately 2,000 feet).

Abbreviations

MHV	Maximum height of vehicle
MLV	Maximum length of vehicle
MWV	Maximum width of vehicle
MWR	Minimum width of road
OC	Occasionally closed between dates stated
UC	Usually closed between dates stated
UO	Usually open between dates stated, although a fall of snow may obstruct the road for 24-48 hours.

Mountain Passes and Tunnels Report Form

The Caravan Club welcomes up-to-date information on mountain passes and tunnels from caravanners who use them during the course of their holidays. Please use the Mountain Passes and Tunnels report forms at the back of the book and complete and return them as soon as possible after your journey.

Converting Gradients

20% = 1 in 5	11% = 1 in 9
16% = 1 in 6	10% = 1 in 10
14% = 1 in 7	8% = 1 in 12
12% = 1 in 8	6% = 1 in 16

Much of the information contained in the following tables was originally supplied by The Automobile Association and other motoring and tourist organisations. Additional updates and amendments have been supplied by caravanners who have themselves used the passes and tunnels. The Caravan Club has not checked the information contained in these tables and cannot accept responsibility for their accuracy, or for errors, omissions or their effects.

Major Alpine Mountain Passes

Before using any of these passes, PLEASE READ CAREFULLY THE ADVICE AT THE BEGINNING OF THIS CHAPTER

	Pass Height In Metres (Feet)	From *To*	Max Gradient	Conditions and Comments
1	**Achenpass** (Austria – Germany) 941 (3087)	Achenwald *Glashütte*	4%	UO. Well-engineered road, B181/307. Gradient not too severe.
2	**Albula** (Switzerland) 2312 (7585)	Tiefencastel *La Punt*	10%	UC Nov-early Jun. MWR 3.5m (11'6") MWV 2.25m (7'6") Inferior alternative to the Julier; fine scenery. **Not recommended for caravans**. Alternative rail tunnel. See ***Rail Tunnels*** in this section.
3	**Allos** (France) 2250 (7382)	Colmars *Barcelonette*	10%	UC early Nov-early Jun. MWR 4m (13'1") Very winding, narrow, mostly unguarded pass on D908 but not difficult otherwise; passing bays on southern slope; poor surface, MWV 1.8m (5'11"). **Not recommended for caravans**.
4	**Aprica** (Italy) 1176 (3858)	Tresenda *Edolo*	9%	UO. MWR 4m (13'1") Fine scenery; good surface; well-graded on road S39. Narrow in places; watch for protruding rock when meeting oncoming traffic. Not recommended for caravanners to attempt this pass E or W. Poor road conditions, repairs reduce width drastically.
5	**Aravis** (France) 1498 (4915)	La Clusaz *Flumet*	9%	OC Dec-Mar. MWR 4m (13'1"). Fine scenery; D909, fairly easy road. Poor surface in parts on Chamonix side. Some single-line traffic.
6	**Arlberg** (Austria) 1802 (5912)	Bludenz *Landeck*	13%	OC Dec-Apr. MWR 6m (19'8"). Good modern road B197/E60 with several pull-in places. Steeper fr W easing towards summit; heavy traffic. **Pass road closed to caravans/trailers.** Parallel road tunnel (tolls) available on E60 (poss long queues). See ***Road Tunnels*** in this section.
7	**Ballon d'Alsace** (France) 1178 (3865)	Giromagny *St Maurice-sur-Moselle*	11%	OC Dec-Mar. MWR 4m (13'1") Fairly straightforward ascent/descent; narrow in places; numerous bends. On road D465.
8	**Bayard** (France) 1248 (4094)	Chauffayer *Gap*	14%	UO. MWR 6m (19'8") Part of the Route Napoléon N85. Fairly easy, steepest on the S side with several hairpin bends. Negotiable by caravans from N-to-S via D1075 (N75) and Col-de-la-Croix Haute, avoiding Gap.
9	**Bernina** (Switzerland) 2330 (7644)	Pontresina *Poschiavo*	12.50%	OC Dec-Mar. MWR 5m (16'5") MWV 2.25m (7'6") Fine scenery. Good with care on open narrow sections towards summit on S-side; on road no. 29.
10	**Bracco** (Italy) 613 (2011)	Riva Trigoso *Borghetto di Vara*	14%	UO. MWR 5m (16'5") A two-lane road (P1) more severe than height suggests due to hairpins and volume of traffic; passing difficult. Rec cross early to avoid traffic. Alternative toll m'way A12 available.

Before using any of these passes, PLEASE READ CAREFULLY THE ADVICE AT THE BEGINNING OF THIS CHAPTER

	Pass Height In Metres (Feet)	From *To*	Max Gradient	Conditions and Comments
11	**Brenner (Europabrücke)** (Austria – Italy) 1374 (4508)	Innsbruck *Vipiteno/Sterzing*	14%	UO. MWR 6m (19'8") On road no. 182/12. Parallel toll m'way A13/A22/E45 (6%) suitable for caravans. Heavy traffic may delay at Customs. **Pass road closed to vehicles towing trailers.**
12	**Brouis** (France) 1279 (4196)	Nice *Col-de-Tende*	12.50%	UO. MWR 6m (19'8") Good surface but many hairpins on D6204 (N204)/S20. Steep gradients on approaches. Height of tunnel at Col-de-Tende at the Italian border is 3.8m (12'4) **Not recommended for caravans.**
13	**Brünig** (Switzerland) 1007 (3340)	Brienzwiler Station *Giswil*	8.50%	UO. MWR 6m (19'8") MWV 2.5m (8'2") An easy but winding road (no. 4); heavy traffic at weekends; frequent lay-bys. On-going road improvement (2009) may cause delays – check before travel.
14	**Bussang** (France) 721 (2365)	Thann *St Maurice-sur-Moselle*	7%	UO. MWR 4m (13'1") A very easy road (N66) over the Vosges; beautiful scenery.
15	**Cabre** (France) 1180 (3871)	Luc-en-Diois *Aspres-sur-Buëch*	9%	UO. MWR 5.5m (18') An easy pleasant road (D93/D993), winding at Col-de-Cabre.
16	**Campolongo** (Italy) 1875 (6152)	Corvara-in-Badia *Arabba*	12.50%	OC Dec-Mar. MWR 5m (16'5") A winding but easy ascent on rd P244; long level stretch on summit followed by easy descent. Good surface, fine scenery.
17	**Cayolle** (France) 2326 (7631)	Barcelonnette *Guillaumes*	10%	UC early Nov-early Jun. MWR 4m (13'1") Narrow, winding road (D902) with hairpin bends; poor surface, broken edges with steep drops. Long stretches of single-track road with passing places. **Caravans prohibited.**
18	**Costalunga (Karer)** (Italy) 1745 (5725)	Bolzano *Pozza-di-Fassa*	16%	OC Dec-Apr. MWR 5m (16'5") A good well-engineered road (S241) but mostly winding with many blind hairpins. **Caravans prohibited.**
19	**Croix** (Switzerland) 1778 (5833)	Villars-sur-Ollon *Les Diablerets*	13%	UC Nov-May. MWR 3.5m (11'6") A narrow, winding route but extremely picturesque. **Not recommended for caravans.**
20	**Croix Haute** (France) 1179 (3868)	Monestier-de-Clermont *Aspres-sur-Buëch*	7%	UO on N75. MWR 5.5m (18') Well-engineered road (D1075/N75); several hairpin bends on N side.
21	**Falzárego** (Italy) 2117 (6945)	Cortina-d'Ampezzo *Andraz*	8.50%	OC Dec-Apr. MWR 5m (16'5") Well-engineered bitumen surface on road R48; many blind hairpin bends on both sides; used by tour coaches.

Before using any of these passes, PLEASE READ CAREFULLY THE ADVICE AT THE BEGINNING OF THIS CHAPTER

	Pass Height In Metres (Feet)	From *To*	Max Gradient	Conditions and Comments
22	**Faucille** (France) 1323 (4341)	Gex *Morez*	10%	UO. MWR 5m (16'5") Fairly wide, winding road (N5) across the Jura mountains; negotiable by caravans but probably better to follow route via La Cure-St Cergue-Nyon.
23	**Fern** (Austria) 1209 (3967)	Nassereith *Lermoos*	8%	UO. MWR 6m (19'8") Obstructed intermittently during winter. An easy pass on road 179 but slippery when wet; heavy traffic at summer weekends. Connects with Holzleiten Sattel Pass at S end for travel to/from Innsbruck – see below.
24	**Flexen** (Austria) 1784 (5853)	Lech *Rauzalpe (nr Arlberg Pass)*	10%	UO. MWR 5.5m (18') The magnificent 'Flexenstrasse', a well-engineered mountain road (no. 198) with tunnels and galleries. The road from Lech to Warth, N of the pass, is usually closed Nov-Apr due to danger of avalanche. **Not recommended for caravans.**
25	**Flüela** (Switzerland) 2383 (7818)	Davos-Dorf *Susch*	12.50%	OC Nov-May. MWR 5m (16'5") MWV 2.3m (7'6") Easy ascent from Davos on road no. 28; some acute hairpin bends on the E side; bitumen surface.
26	**Forclaz** (Switzerland – France) 1527 (5010)	Martigny *Argentière*	8.50%	UO Forclaz; OC Montets Dec-early Apr. MWR 5m (16'5") MWV 2.5m (8'2") Good road over the pass and to the French border; long, hard climb out of Martigny; narrow and rough over Col-des-Montets on D1506 (N506).
27	**Foscagno** (Italy) 2291 (7516)	Bormio *Livigno*	12.50%	OC Nov-May. MWR 3.3m (10'10") Narrow and winding road (S301) through lonely mountains, generally poor surface. Long winding ascent with many blind bends; not always well-guarded. The descent includes winding rise and fall over the Passo-d'Eira 2,200m (7,218'). **Not recommended for caravans.**
28	**Fugazze** (Italy) 1159 (3802)	Rovereto *Valli-del-Pasubio*	14%	UO. MWR 3.5m (11'6") Very winding road (S46) with some narrow sections, particularly on N side. The many blind bends and several hairpin bends call for extra care. **Not recommended for caravans.**
29	**Furka** (Switzerland) 2431 (7976)	Gletsch *Realp*	11%	UC Oct-Jun. MWR 4m (13'1") MWV 2.25m (7'6") Well-graded road (no. 19) with narrow sections (single track in place on E side) and several hairpin bends on both ascent and descent. Fine views of the Rhône Glacier. Beware of coaches and traffic build-up. **Not recommended for caravans.** Alternative rail tunnel available. See ***Rail Tunnels*** in this section.
30	**Galibier** (France) 2645 (8678)	La Grave *St Michel-de-Maurienne*	12.50%	UC Oct-Jun. MWR 3m (9'10") Mainly wide, well-surfaced road (D902) but unprotected and narrow over summit. From Col-du-Lautaret it rises over the Col-du-Telegraphe then 11 more hairpin bends. Ten hairpin bends on descent then 5km (3.1 miles) narrow and rough; easier in N to S direction. Limited parking at summit. **Not recommended for caravans.** (There is a single-track tunnel under the Galibier summit, controlled by traffic lights; caravans are not permitted).
31	**Gardena (Grödner-Joch)** (Italy) 2121 (6959)	Val Gardena *Corvara-in-Badia*	12.50%	OC Dec-Jun. MWR 5m (16'5") A well-engineered road (S243), very winding on descent. Fine views. **Caravans prohibited.**

Before using any of these passes, PLEASE READ CAREFULLY THE ADVICE AT THE BEGINNING OF THIS CHAPTER

	Pass Height In Metres (Feet)	From *To*	Max Gradient	Conditions and Comments
32	**Gavia** (Italy) 2621 (8599)	Bormio *Ponte-di-Legno*	20%	UC Oct-Jul. MWR 3m (9'10") MWV 1.8m (5'11") Steep, narrow, difficult road (P300) with frequent passing bays; many hairpin bends and gravel surface; not for the faint-hearted; extra care necessary. **Not recommended for caravans.** Long winding ascent on Bormio side.
33	**Gerlos** (Austria) 1628 (5341)	Zell-am-Ziller *Wald im Pinzgau*	9%	UO. MWR 4m (13'1") Hairpin ascent out of Zell to modern toll road (B165); the old, steep, narrow and winding route with passing bays and 14% gradient is not rec but is negotiable with care. Views of Krimml waterfalls. **Caravans prohibited.**
34	**Gorges-du-Verdon** (France) 1032 (3386)	Castellane *Moustiers-Ste Marie*	9%	UO. MWR probably 5m (16'5") On road D952 over Col-d'Ayen and Col-d'Olivier. Moderate gradients but slow, narrow and winding. Poss heavy traffic.
35	**Grand St Bernard** (Switzerland – Italy) 2469 (8100)	Martigny *Aosta*	11%	UC Oct-Jun. MWR 4m (13'1") MWV 2.5m (8' 2") Modern road to entrance of road tunnel on road no. 21/E27 (UO), then narrow but bitumen surface over summit to border; also good in Italy. Suitable for caravans using tunnel. Pass road feasible but not recommended. See ***Road Tunnels*** in this section.
36	**Grimsel** (Switzerland) 2164 (7100)	Innertkirchen *Gletsch*	10%	UC mid Oct-late Jun. MWR 5m (16'5") MWV 2.25m (7'6") A fairly easy, modern road (no. 6) with heavy traffic at weekends. A long winding ascent, finally hairpin bends; then a terraced descent with six hairpins (some tight) into the Rhône valley. Good surface; fine scenery.
37	**Grossglockner** (Austria) 2503 (8212)	Bruck-an-der-Grossglocknerstrasse *Heiligenblut*	12.50%	UC late Oct-early May. MWR 5.5m (18') Well-engineered road (no. 107) but many hairpins; heavy traffic; moderate but very long ascent/descent. Negotiable preferably S to N by caravans. Avoid side road to highest point at Edelweissespitze if towing, as road is very steep and narrow. Magnificent scenery. Tolls charged. Road closed from 2200-0500 hrs (summer). Alternative Felbertauern road tunnel between Lienz and Mittersil (toll). See ***Road Tunnels*** in this section.
38	**Hahntennjoch** (Austria) 1894 (6250)	Imst *Elmen*	15%	UC Nov-May. A minor pass; **caravans prohibited.**
39	**Hochtannberg** (Austria) 1679 (5509)	Schröcken *Warth (nr Lech)*	14%	OC Jan-Mar. MWR 4m (13'1") A reconstructed modern road (no. 200). W to E long ascent with many hairpins. Easier E to W. **Not recommended for caravans or trailers.**
40	**Holzleiten Sattel** (Austria) 1126 (3694)	Nassereith *Obsteig*	12.50%	(12.5%), UO. MWR 5m (16'5") Road surface good on W side; poor on E. Light traffic; gradients no problem but **not recommended for caravans or trailers.**
41	**Iseran** (France) 2770 (9088)	Bourg-St Maurice *Lanslebourg*	11%	UC mid Oct-late Jun. MWR 4m (13'1") Second highest pass in the Alps on road D902. Well-graded with reasonable bends, average surface. Several unlit tunnels on N approach. **Not recommended for caravans.**

Before using any of these passes, PLEASE READ CAREFULLY THE ADVICE AT THE BEGINNING OF THIS CHAPTER

	Pass Height In Metres (Feet)	From *To*	Max Gradient	Conditions and Comments
42	**Izoard** (France) 2360 (7743)	Guillestre *Briançon*	12.50%	UC late Oct-mid Jun. MWR 5m (16'5") Fine scenery. Winding, sometimes narrow road (D902) with many hairpin bends; care required at several unlit tunnels near Guillestre. **Not recommended for caravans.**
43	**Jaun** (Switzerland) 1509 (4951)	Bulle *Reidenbach*	14%	UO. MWR 4m (13'1") MWV 2.25m (7'6") A modern but generally narrow road (no. 11); some poor sections on ascent and several hairpin bends on descent.
44	**Julier** (Switzerland) 2284 (7493)	Tiefencastel *Silvaplana*	13%	UO. MWR 4m (13'1") MWV 2.5m (8'2") Well-engineered road (no. 3) approached from Chur via Sils. Fine scenery. Negotiable by caravans, preferably from N to S, but a long haul and many tight hairpins. Alternative rail tunnel from Thusis to Samedan. See ***Rail Tunnels*** in this section.
45	**Katschberg** (Austria) 1641 (5384)	Spittal-an-der-Drau *St Michael*	20%	UO. MWR 6m (19'8") Good wide road (no. 99) with no hairpins but steep gradients particularly from S. Suitable only light caravans. Parallel Tauern/Katschberg toll motorway A10/E55 and road tunnels. See ***Road Tunnels*** in this section.
46	**Klausen** (Switzerland) 1948 (6391)	Altdorf *Linthal*	10%	UC late Oct-early Jun. MWR 5m (16'5") MWV 2.30m (7'6") Narrow and winding in places, but generally easy in spite of a number of sharp bends; **no through route for caravans** as they are prohibited from using the road between Unterschächen and Linthal (no. 17).
47	**Larche (della Maddalena)** (France – Italy) 1994 (6542)	La Condamine-Châtelard *Vinadio*	8.50%	OC Dec-Mar. MWR 3.5m (11'6") An easy, well-graded road (D900); long, steady ascent on French side, many hairpins on Italian side (S21). Fine scenery; ample parking at summit.
48	**Lautaret** (France) 2058 (6752)	Le Bourg-d'Oisans *Briançon*	12.50%	OC Dec-Mar. MWR 4m (13'1") Modern, evenly graded but winding road (D1091), and unguarded in places; very fine scenery; suitable for caravans but with care through narrow tunnels.
49	**Leques** (France) 1146 (3760)	Barrême *Castellane*	8%	UO. MWR 4m (13'1") On Route Napoléon (D4085). Light traffic; excellent surface; narrow in places on N ascent. S ascent has many hairpins.
50	**Loibl (Ljubelj)** (Austria – Slovenia) 1067 (3500)	Unterloibl *Kranj*	20%	UO. MWR 6m (19'8") Steep rise and fall over Little Loibl pass (E652) to 1.6km (1 mile) tunnel under summit. **Caravans prohibited.** The old road over the summit is closed to through-traffic.
51	**Lukmanier (Lucomagno)** (Switzerland) 1916 (6286)	Olivone *Disentis*	9%	UC early Nov-late May. MWR 5m (16'5") MWV 2.25m (7'6") Rebuilt, modern road.
52	**Maloja** (Switzerland) 1815 (5955)	Silvaplana *Chiavenna*	9%	UO. MWR 4m (13'1") MWV 2.5m (8'2") Escarpment facing south; fairly easy, but many hairpin bends on descent; negotiable by caravans but possibly difficult on ascent. On road no. 3/S37.

Before using any of these passes, PLEASE READ CAREFULLY THE ADVICE AT THE BEGINNING OF THIS CHAPTER

	Pass Height In Metres (Feet)	From *To*	Max Gradient	Conditions and Comments
53	**Mauria** (Italy) 1298 (4258)	Lozzo di Cadore *Ampezzo*	7%	UO. MWR 5m (16'5") A well-designed road (S52) with easy, winding ascent and descent.
54	**Mendola** (Italy) 1363 (4472)	Appiano/Eppan *Sarnonico*	12.50%	UO. MWR 5m (16'5") A fairly straightforward but winding road (S42), well-guarded, many hairpins. Take care overhanging cliffs if towing. The E side going down to Bolzano is not wide enough for caravans, especially difficult on busy days, not recommended for caravans.
55	**Mont Cenis** (France – Italy) 2083 (6834)	Lanslebourg *Susa*	12.50%	UC Nov-May. MWR 5m (16'5") Approach by industrial valley. An easy highway (D1006/S25) with mostly good surface; spectacular scenery; long descent into Italy with few stopping places. Alternative Fréjus road tunnel available. See ***Road Tunnels*** in this section.
56	**Monte Croce-di-Comélico (Kreuzberg)** (Italy) 1636 (5368)	San Candido *Santo-Stefano- di-Cadore*	8.50%	UO. MWR 5m (16'5") A winding road (S52) with moderate gradients, beautiful scenery.
57	**Montgenèvre** (France – Italy) 1850 (6070)	Briançon *Cesana-Torinese*	9%	UO. MWR 5m (16'5") An easy, modern road (N94/S24) with some tight hairpin bends and with good road surface on French side; road widened & tunnels improved on Italian side, in need of some repair but still easy. Much used by lorries; may be necessary to travel at their speed and give way to oncoming large vehicles on hairpins.
58	**Monte Giovo (Jaufen)** (Italy) 2094 (6870)	Merano *Vipiteno/Sterzing*	12.50%	UC Nov-May. MWR 4m (13'1") Many well-engineered hairpin bends on S44; good scenery. **Caravans prohibited.**
	Montets (See **Forclaz**)			
59	**Morgins** (France – Switzerland) 1369 (4491)	Abondance *Monthey*	14%	UO. MWR 4m (13'1") A lesser used route (D22) through pleasant, forested countryside crossing French/Swiss border. **Not recommended for caravans.**
60	**Mosses** (Switzerland) 1445 (4740)	Aigle *Château-d'Oex*	8.50%	UO. MWR 4m (13'1") MWV 2.25m (7'6") A modern road (no. 11). Aigle side steeper and narrow in places.
61	**Nassfeld (Pramollo)** (Austria – Italy) 1530 (5020)	Tröpolach *Pontebba*	20%	OC Late Nov-Mar. MWR 4m (13'1") The winding descent on road no. 90 into Italy has been improved but not rec for caravans.
62	**Nufenen (Novena) (Switzerland)** 2478 (8130)	Ulrichen *Airolo*	10%	UC Mid Oct-mid Jun. MWR 4m (13'1") MWV 2.25m (7'6") The approach roads are narrow, with tight bends, but the road over the pass is good; negotiable with care. Long drag from Ulrichen.
63	**Oberalp** (Switzerland) 2044 (6706)	Andermatt *Disentis*	10%	UC Nov-late May. MWR 5m (16'5") MWV 2.3m (7'6") A much improved and widened road (no. 19) with modern surface but still narrow in places on E side; many tight hairpin bends, but long level stretch on summit. Alternative rail tunnel during the winter. See ***Rail Tunnels*** in this section. **Not recommended for caravans.**

Before using any of these passes, PLEASE READ CAREFULLY THE ADVICE AT THE BEGINNING OF THIS CHAPTER

	Pass Height In Metres (Feet)	From *To*	Max Gradient	Conditions and Comments
64	**Ofen (Fuorn)** (Switzerland) 2149 (7051)	Zernez *Santa Maria-im-Münstertal*	12.50%	UO. MWR 4m (13'1") MWV 2.25m (7'6") Good road (no. 28) through Swiss National Park.
65	**Petit St Bernard** (France – Italy) 2188 (7178)	Bourg-St Maurice *Pré-St Didier*	8.50%	UC mid Oct-Jun. MWR 5m (16'5") Outstanding scenery, but poor surface and unguarded broken edges near summit. Easiest from France (D1090); sharp hairpins on climb from Italy (S26). **Closed to vehicles towing another vehicle.**
66	**Pillon** (Switzerland) 1546 (5072)	Le Sépey *Gsteig*	9%	OC Jan-Feb. MWR 4m (13'1") MWV 2.25m (7'6") A comparatively easy modern road.
67	**Plöcken (Monte Croce-Carnico)** (Austria – Italy) 1362 (4468)	Kötschach *Paluzza*	14%	OC Dec-Apr. MWR 5m (16'5") A modern road (no. 110) with long, reconstructed sections; OC to caravans due to heavy traffic on summer weekends; delay likely at the border. Long, slow, twisty pull from S, easier from N.
68	**Pordoi** (Italy) 2239 (7346)	Arabba *Canazei*	10%	OC Dec-Apr. MWR 5m (16'5") An excellent modern road (S48) with numerous blind hairpin bends; fine scenery; used by tour coaches. Long drag when combined with Falzarego pass.
69	**Pötschen** (Austria) 982 (3222)	Bad Ischl *Bad Aussee*	9%	UO. MWR 7m (23') A modern road (no. 145). Good scenery.
70	**Radstädter-Tauern** (Austria) 1738 (5702)	Radstadt *Mauterndorf*	16%	OC Jan-Mar. MWR 5m (16'5") N ascent steep (road no. 99) but not difficult otherwise; but negotiable by light caravans using parallel toll m'way (A10) through tunnel. See ***Road Tunnels*** in this section.
71	**Résia (Reschen)** (Italy – Austria) 1504 (4934)	Spondigna *Pfunds*	10%	UO. MWR 6m (19'8") A good, straightforward alternative to the Brenner Pass. Fine views but no stopping places. On road S40/180.
72	**Restefond (La Bonette)** (France) 2802 (9193)	Barcelonnette *St Etienne-de-Tinée*	16%	UC Oct-Jun. MWR 3m (9'10") The highest pass in the Alps. Rebuilt, resurfaced road (D64) with rest area at summit – top loop narrow and unguarded. Winding with hairpin bends. **Not recommended for caravans.**
73	**Rolle** (Italy) 1970 (6463)	Predazzo *Mezzano*	9%	OC Dec-Mar. MWR 5m (16'5") A well-engineered road (S50) with many hairpin bends on both sides; very beautiful scenery; good surface.
	Rombo (See **Timmelsjoch**)			
74	**St Gotthard (San Gottardo)** (Switzerland) 2108 (6916)	Göschenen *Airolo*	10%	UC mid Oct-early Jun. MWR 6m (19'8") MHV 3.6m (11'9") MWV 2.5m (8'2") Modern, fairly easy two- to three-lane road (A2/E35). Heavy traffic. Alternative road tunnel. See ***Road Tunnels*** in this section.

Before using any of these passes, PLEASE READ CAREFULLY THE ADVICE AT THE BEGINNING OF THIS CHAPTER

	Pass Height In Metres (Feet)	From *To*	Max Gradient	Conditions and Comments
75	**San Bernardino** (Switzerland) 2066 (6778)	Mesocco *Hinterrhein*	10%	UC Oct-late Jun. MWR 4m (13'1") MWV 2.25m (7'6") Easy modern road (A13/E43) on N and S approaches to tunnel, narrow and winding over summit via tunnel suitable for caravans. See ***Road Tunnels*** in this section.
76	**Schlucht** (France) 1139 (3737)	Gérardmer *Munster*	7%	UO. MWR 5m (16'5") An extremely picturesque route (D417) crossing the Vosges mountains, with easy, wide bends on the descent. Good surface.
77	**Seeberg (Jezersko)** (Austria – Slovenia) 1218 (3996)	Eisenkappel *Kranj*	12.50%	UO. MWR 5m (16'5") An alternative to the steeper Loibl and Wurzen passes on B82/210; moderate climb with winding, hairpin ascent and descent. **Not recommended for caravans.**
78	**Sella** (Italy) 2240 (7349)	Selva *Canazei*	11%	OC Dec-Jan. MWR 5m (16'5") A well-engineered, winding road; exceptional views of Dolomites; **caravans prohibited.**
79	**Sestriere** (Italy) 2033 (6670)	Cesana-Torinese *Pinarolo*	10%	UO MWR 6m (19'8") Mostly bitumen surface on road R23. Fairly easy; fine scenery.
80	**Silvretta (Bielerhöhe)** (Austria) 2032 (6666)	Partenen *Galtur*	11%	UC late Oct-early Jun. MWR 5m (16'5") Mostly reconstructed road (188); 32 easy hairpin bends on W ascent; E side more straightforward. Tolls charged. **Caravans prohibited.**
81	**Simplon** (Switzerland – Italy) 2005 (6578)	Brig *Domodóssola*	11%	OC Nov-Apr. MWR 7m (23') MWV 2.5m (8'2") An easy, reconstructed, modern road (E62/S33), 21km (13 miles) long, continuous ascent to summit; good views, many stopping places. Surface better on Swiss side. Alternative rail tunnel fr Kandersteg in operation from Easter to September. See ***Rail Tunnels*** in this section.
82	**Splügen** (Switzerland – Italy) 2113 (6932)	Splügen *Chiavenna*	13%	UC Nov-Jun. MWR 3.5m (11'6") MHV 2.8m (9'2") MWV 2.3m (7'6") Mostly narrow, winding road (S36), with extremely tight hairpin bends, not well guarded; care also required at many tunnels/galleries. **Not recommended for caravans.**
83	**Stelvio** (Italy) 2757 (9045)	Bormio *Spondigna*	12.50%	UC Oct-late Jun. MWR 4m (13'1") MLV 10m (32') Third highest pass in Alps on S38; 40-50 acute hairpin bends either side, all well-engineered; good surface, traffic often heavy. Hairpin bends too acute for long vehicles. **Not recommended for caravans.**
84	**Susten** (Switzerland) 2224 (7297)	Innertkirchen *Wassen*	9%	UC Nov-Jun. MWR 6m (19'8") MWV 2.5m (8'2") Very scenic and well-guarded road (no. 11); easy gradients and turns; heavy traffic at weekends. Eastern side easier than west. Negotiable by caravans (recommended for small/medium sized only) with care, but not for the faint-hearted. Large parking area at summit.

Before using any of these passes, PLEASE READ CAREFULLY THE ADVICE AT THE BEGINNING OF THIS CHAPTER

	Pass Height In Metres (Feet)	From *To*	Max Gradient	Conditions and Comments
85	**Tenda (Tende)** Italy – France 1321 (4334)	Borgo-San Dalmazzo *Tende*	9%	UO. MWR 6m (19'8") Well-guarded, modern road (S20/ND6204) with several hairpin bends; road tunnel (height 3.8m) at summit narrow with poor road surface. Less steep on Italian side. **Caravans prohibited during winter.**
86	**Thurn** (Austria) 1274 (4180)	Kitzbühel *Mittersill*	8.50%	UO. MWR 5m (16'5") MWV 2.5m (8' 2") A good road (no. 161) with narrow stretches; N approach rebuilt. Several good parking areas.
87	**Timmelsjoch (Rombo)** (Austria – Italy) 2509 (8232)	Obergurgl *Moso*	14%	UC mid Oct-Jun. MWR 3.5m (11'6") Border closed at night 8pm to 7am. The pass (road no 186/S44b) is **open to private cars without trailers only** (toll charged), as some tunnels on Italian side too narrow for larger vehicles. Easiest N to S.
88	**Tonale** (Italy) 1883 (6178)	Edolo *Dimaro*	10%	UO. MWR 5m (16'5") A relatively easy road (S42); steepest on W; long drag. Fine views.
89	**Tre Croci** (Italy) 1809 (5935)	Cortina-d'Ampezzo *Auronzo-di-Cadore*	11%	OC Dec-Mar. MWR 6m (19'8") An easy pass on road R48; fine scenery.
90	**Turracher Höhe** (Austria) 1763 (5784)	Predlitz *Ebene-Reichenau*	23%	UO. MWR 4m (13'1") Formerly one of the steepest mountain roads (no. 95) in Austria; now improved. Steep, fairly straightforward ascent followed by a very steep descent; good surface and mainly two-lane; fine scenery. **Not recommended for caravans.**
91	**Umbrail** (Switzerland – Italy) 2501 (8205)	Santa Maria-im-Münstertal *Bormio*	9%	UC Nov-early Jun. MWR 4.3m (14'1") MWV 2.3m (7'6") Highest Swiss pass (road S38); mostly tarmac with some gravel surface. Narrow with 34 hairpin bends. **Not recommended for caravans.**
92	**Vars** (France) 2109 (6919)	St Paul-sur-Ubaye *Guillestre*	9%	OC Dec-Mar. MWR 5m (16'5") Easy winding ascent and descent on D902 with 14 hairpin bends; good surface.
93	**Wurzen (Koren)** (Austria – Slovenia) 1073 (3520)	Riegersdorf *Kranjska Gora*	20%	UO. MWR 4m (13'1") Steep two-lane road (no. 109), otherwise not particularly difficult; better on Austrian side; heavy traffic summer weekends; delays likely at the border. **Caravans prohibited.**
94	**Zirler Berg** (Austria) 1009 (3310)	Seefeld *Zirl*	16.50%	UO. MWR 7m (23') South facing escarpment, part of route from Garmisch to Innsbruck; good, modern road (no. 171). Heavy tourist traffic and long steep descent with one hairpin bend into Inn Valley. Steepest section from hairpin bend down to Zirl. **Caravans not permitted northbound and not recommended southbound.**

Technical information by courtesy of the Automobile Association. Additional update and amendments supplied by caravanners and tourers who have themselves used the passes and tunnels. The Caravan Club has not checked the information contained in these tables and cannot accept responsibility for their accuracy, or for any errors, omissions, or their effects.

Major Alpine Rail Tunnels

Before using any of these tunnels, PLEASE READ CAREFULLY THE ADVICE AT THE BEGINNING OF THIS CHAPTER

	Tunnel	Route	Journey Time	General Information and Comments	Contact
A	**Albula** (Switzerland) 5.9 km (3.5 miles)	**Chur – St Moritz** Thusis to Samedan	80 mins	MHV 2.85m + MWV 1.40m or MHV 2.50m + MWV 2.20 Up to 11 shuttle services per day all year; advance booking required.	Thusis (081) 2884716 Samedan (081) 2885511 www.rhb.ch
B	**Furka** (Switzerland) 15.4 km (9.5 miles)	**Andermatt – Brig** Realp to Oberwald	15 mins	Hourly all year from 6am to 9pm weekdays; half-hourly weekends.	(027) 9277777 www.mgbahn.ch
C	**Oberalp** (Switzerland) 28 km (17.3 miles)	**Andermatt – Disentis** Andermatt to Sedrun	60 mins	MHV 2.50m 2-6 trains daily (Christmas-Easter only). Advance booking compulsory.	(027) 9277777 www.mgbahn.ch
D	**Lötschberg** (Switzerland) 14 km (8.7 miles)	**Bern – Brig** Kandersteg to Goppenstein	15 mins	MHV 2.90m Frequent all year half-hourly service. Journey time 15 minutes. Advance booking unnecessary; extension to Hohtenn operates when Goppenstein-Gampel road is closed.	Kandersteg (0)900 553333 www.bls.ch/autoverlad
E	**Simplon** (Switzerland – Italy)	**Brig – Domodossola** Brig to Iselle	20 mins	10 trains daily, all year.	(0)900 300300 http://mct.sbb.ch/mct/autoverlad
	Lötschberg/Simplon Switzerland – Italy	**Bern – Domodossola** Kandersteg to Iselle	75 mins	Limited service Easter to mid-October up to 3 days a week (up to 10 times a day) and at Christmas for vehicles max height 2.50m, motor caravans up to 5,000 kg. Advance booking compulsory.	(0)900 553333 www.bls.ch
F	**Tauerbahn** (Austria)	**Bad Gastein – Spittal an der Drau** Böckstein to Mallnitz	11 mins	East of and parallel to Grossglockner pass. Half-hourly service all year.	(05) 1717 http://autoschleuse.oebb.at
G	**Vereina** (Switzerland) 19.6 km (11.7 miles)	**Klosters – Susch** Selfranga to Sagliains	18 mins	MLV 12m Half-hourly daytime service all year. Journey time 18 minutes. Restricted capacity for vehicles over 3.30m high during winter w/ends and public holidays. Steep approach to Klosters.	(081) 2883737 www.rhb.ch

NOTES: Information believed to be correct at time of publication. Detailed timetables are available from the appropriate tourist offices. Always check for current information before you travel.

Major Alpine Road Tunnels

Before using any of these tunnels, PLEASE READ CAREFULLY THE ADVICE AT THE BEGINNING OF THIS CHAPTER

	Tunnel	Route and Height above Sea Level	General Information and Comments
H	**Arlberg** (Austria) 14 km (8.75 miles)	**Langen to St Anton** 1220m (4000')	On B197 parallel and to S of Arlberg Pass which is closed to caravans/trailers. **Motorway vignette required; tolls charged.** www.arlberg.com
I	**Bosruck** (Austria) 5.5 km (3.4 miles)	**Spital am Pyhrn to Selzthal** 742m (2434')	To E of Phyrn pass; with Gleinalm Tunnel (see below) forms part of A9 a'bahn between Linz & Graz. Max speed 80 km/h (50 mph). Use dipped headlights, no overtaking. Occasional emergency lay-bys with telephones. **Motorway vignette required; tolls charged.**
J	**Felbertauern** (Austria) 5.3 km (3.25 miles)	**Mittersill to Matrei** 1525m (5000')	MWR 7m (23'), tunnel height 4.5m (14'9"). On B109 W of and parallel to Grossglockner pass; downwards gradient of 9% S to N with sharp bend before N exit. Wheel chains may be needed on approach Nov-Apr. **Tolls charged.**
K	**Frejus** (France – Italy) 12.8 km (8 miles)	**Modane to Bardonecchia** 1220m (4000')	MWR 9m (29'6"), tunnel height 4.3m (14'). Min/max speed 60/70 km/h (37/44 mph). Return tickets valid until midnight on 7th day after day of issue. Season tickets are available. Approach via A43 and D1006; heavy use by freight vehicles. Good surface on approach roads. **Tolls charged.** www.sftrf.fr
L	**Gleinalm** (Austria) 8.3 km (5 miles)	**St Michael to Fiesach (nr Graz)** 817m (2680')	Part of A9 Pyhrn a'bahn. **Motorway vignette required; tolls charged.**
M	**Grand St Bernard** (Switzerland – Italy) 5.8 km (3.6 miles)	**Bourg-St Pierre to St Rhémy (Italy)** 1925m (7570')	MHV 4m (13'1"), MWV 2.55m (8'2.5"), MLV 18m (60'). Min/max speed 40/80 km/h (24/50 mph). On E27. Passport check, Customs & toll offices at entrance; breakdown bays at each end with telephones; return tickets valid one month. Although approaches are covered, wheel chains may be needed in winter. Season tickets are available. **Motorway vignette required; tolls charged.** For 24-hour information tel: (027) 7884400 (Switzerland) or 0165 780902 (Italy), www.letunnel.com
N	**Karawanken** (Austria – Slovenia) 8 km (5 miles)	**Rosenbach to Jesenice** 610m (2000')	On A11. **Motorway vignette required; tolls charged.**
O	**Mont Blanc** (France – Italy) 11.6 km (7.2 miles)	**Chamonix to Courmayeur** 1381m (4530')	MHV 4.7m (15'5"), MWV 6m (19'6") On N205 France, S26 (Italy). Max speed in tunnel 70 km/h (44 mph) – lower limits when exiting; min speed 50 km/h. Leave 150m between vehicles; ensure enough fuel for 30km. Return tickets valid until midnight on 7th day after issue. Season tickets are available. **Tolls charged.** www.tunnelmb.net

Before using any of these tunnels, PLEASE READ CAREFULLY THE ADVICE AT THE BEGINNING OF THIS CHAPTER

	Tunnel	Route and Height above Sea Level	General Information and Comments
P	**Munt La Schera** (Switzerland – Italy) 3.5 km (2 miles)	**Zernez to Livigno** 1706m (5597')	MHV 3.6m (11'9"), MWV 2.5m (8'2"). Open 24 hours; single lane traffic controlled by traffic lights; roads from Livogno S to the Bernina Pass and Bormio closed Dec-Apr. On N28 (Switzerland). **Tolls charged.** Tel: (081) 8561888, www.livigno.eu
Q	**St Gotthard** (Switzerland) 16.3 km (10 miles)	**Göschenen to Airolo** 1159m (3800')	Tunnel height 4.5m (14'9"), single carriageway 7.5m (25') wide. Max speed 80 km/h (50 mph). No tolls, but tunnel is part of Swiss motorway network (A2). **Motorway vignette required.** Tunnel closed 8pm to 5am Monday to Friday for periods during June and September. Heavy traffic and delays high season. www.gotthard-strassentunnel.ch
-	**Ste Marie-aux-Mines** 6.8 km (4.25 miles)	**St Dié to Ste-Marie-aux Mines** 772m (2533')	Re-opened October 2008; the longest road tunnel situated entirely in France. Also known as Maurice Lemaire Tunnel, through the Vosges in north-east France from Lusse on N159 to N59. **Tolls charged.** Alternate route via Col-de-Ste Marie on D459.
R	**San Bernardino** (Switzerland) 6.6 km (4 miles)	**Hinterrhein to San Bernadino** 1644m (5396')	Tunnel height 4.8m (15'9"), width 7m (23'). On A13 motorway. No stopping or overtaking; keep 100m between vehicles; breakdown bays with telephones. Max speed 80 km/h (50 mph). **Motorway vignette required.**
S	**Tauern and Katschberg** (Austria) 6.4 km (4 miles) & 5.4km (3.5 miles)	**Salzburg to Villach** 1340m (4396') & 1110m (3642')	The two major tunnels on the A10, height 4.5m (14'9"), width 7.5m (25'). **Motorway vignette required; tolls charged.**

NOTES:

Dipped headlights should be used (unless stated otherwise) when travelling through road tunnels, even when the road appears well lit. In some countries police make spot checks and impose on-the-spot fines. During the winter wheel chains may be required on the approaches to some tunnels. These must not be used in tunnels and lay-bys are available for the removal and refitting of wheel chains. For information on motorway vignettes, see the relevant Country Introductions.

Much of the information contained in the table was originally supplied by The Automobile Association and other motoring and tourist organisations. Updates and amendments are supplied by caravanners and tourers who have themselves used the passes and tunnels. The Caravan Club has not checked the information contained in these tables and cannot accept responsibility for their accuracy, or for any errors, omissions, or for their effects.

Have you got Europe covered?

2012/2013

Caravan Europe

Guide to Sites and Touring in Spain and Portugal

THE CARAVAN CLUB

Over 700 sites in **Spain** and **Portugal** as recommended and reviewed by Caravan Club members

2012/2013

Caravan Europe

Guide to Sites and Touring in France

Over 3,500 sites in **France** and **Andorra** as recommended and reviewed by Caravan Club members

THE CARAVAN CLUB

Complete your collection of these indispensable guides to sites and touring throughout Europe

Available to members at the below *exclusive* prices via The Caravan Club

Spain and Portugal £5.99 **France** £8.99

Plus 1st class postage and packing £2.50 per order within the UK.

Available to non-members through all good book retailers and via The Caravan Club website.

www.caravanclub.co.uk/caravaneurope

or telephone 01342 327410

Alpine Countries – East

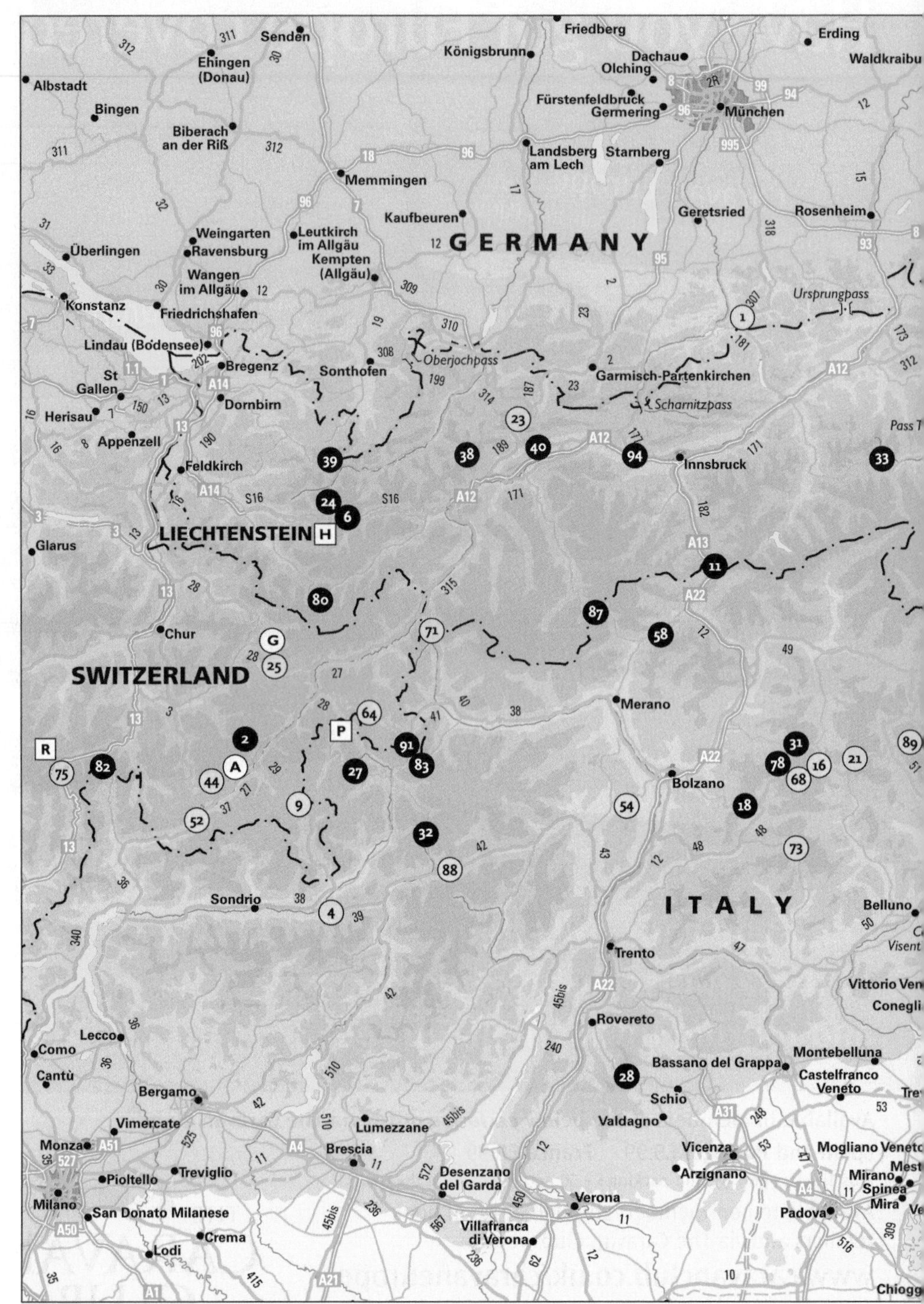

AUSTRIA
SLOVENIA
St Pölten
Traun
Wels
Amstetten
Steyr
Salzburg
Kapfenberg
Leoben
Graz
Wolfsberg
Villach
Klagenfurt
Dravograd
Maribor
Pesnica
Radlje ob Dravi
Ravne na Koroškem
Slovenj Gradec
Jesenice
Tržič
Radovljica
Kranj
Kamnik
Mozirje
Velenje
Slovenske Konjice
Slovenska Bistrica
Šmarje pri Jelšah
Žalec
Celje
Šentjur pri Celju
Laško
Trbovlje
Hrastnik
Zagorje ob Savi
Domžale
LJUBLJANA
Litija
Sevnica
Krško
Brežice
Trebnje
Novo Mesto
Grosuplje
Cerknica
Tolmin
Škofja Loka
Idrija
Vrhnika
Logatec
Ajdovščina
Nova Gorica
Gorizia
Udine
Pordenone
Monfalcone
Portogruaro
San Donà di Piave
Jesolo
Piran
Izola
Zellerrain
Lahnsattel
Hengstpass
Semmering
Pyhrnpass
Pfaffensattel
Pass Gschütt
Schoberpass
Solker Tauern
Perchauer Sattel
Gaberl
Obdacher Sattel
Packsattel
Kartitscher Sattel
Motorway
Motorway (Proposed)
Motorway Road Tunnel
Major/Main Roads
Minor Mountain Passes (suitability for caravans not checked)
Major Mountain Passes Suitable for Caravans
Major Mountain Passes Unsuitable for Caravans
Major Rail Tunnels
Major Road Tunnels
0 10 20 30 40 50 km
These maps should be used in conjunction with the information in the Mountain Passes and Tunnels tables in this chapter.
2000m – +3000m
1000m – 2000m
100m – 1000m
0 – 100m
© Collins Bartholomew Ltd 2011

Alpine Countries – West

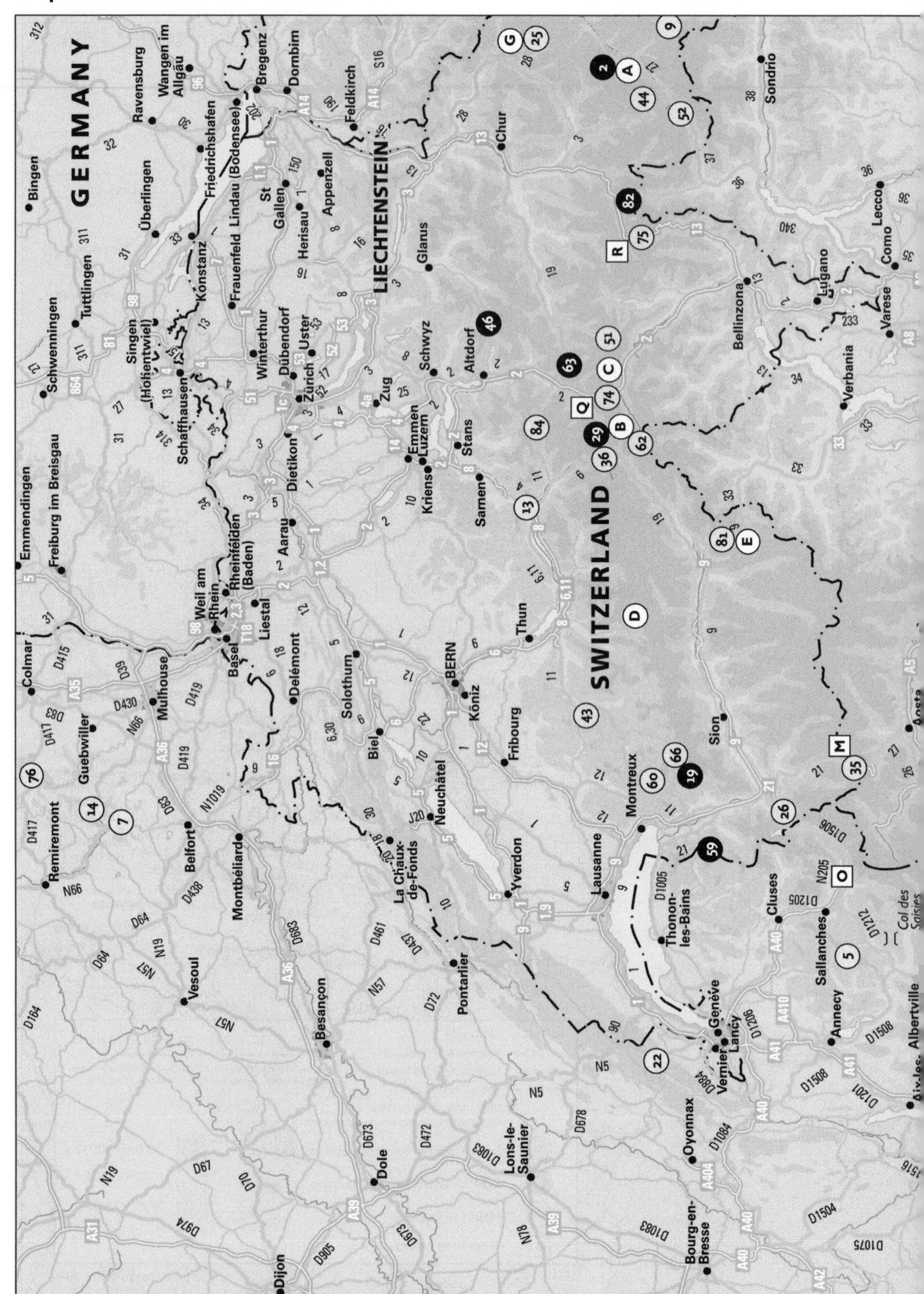

Motorway
Motorway (Proposed)
Motorway Road Tunnel
Major/Main Roads
Minor Mountain Passes (suitability for caravans not checked)
Major Mountain Passes Suitable for Caravans
Major Mountain Passes Unsuitable for Caravans
Major Rail Tunnels
Major Road Tunnels
0 10 20 30 40 50 km
These maps should be used in conjunction with the information in the Mountain Passes and Tunnels tables in this chapter.
2000m – +3000m
1000m – 2000m
100m – 1000m
0 – 100m
© Collins Bartholomew Ltd 2011
FRANCE
ITALY
MONACO
Voiron
Col du Granier
Col de la Croix de Fer
Fontaine
Grenoble
Échirolles
Col de la Bataille
Col de Rousset
Col du Festre
Gap
Col de Maure
Col des Champs
Col de la Croix
Col Agnel
Col de la Traversette
Ivrea
Novara
Magenta
Milano
Pioltello
San Donato Milanese
Crema
Lodi
Vercelli
Vigevano
Pavia
Cremona
Venaria
Chivasso
Casale Monferrato
Rivoli
Torino
Orbassano
Moncalieri
Valenza
Piacenza
Voghera
Pinerolo
Carmagnola
Asti
Alessandria
Tortona
Bra
Alba
Acqui Terme
Novi Ligure
Fossano
Passo della Cisa
Cuneo
Mondovì
Genova
Rapallo
Chiavari
Sestri Levante
Savona
La Spezia
Albenga
Imperia
San Remo
Ventimiglia
Menton
Monte-Carlo
Nice
Manosque
Aix-en-Provence
Grasse
Antibes
Cannes
Draguignan
Fréjus
St-Raphaël
Col de Gratteloup
Marseille
Aubagne
Col de la Bigue
La Ciotat
Toulon
La Valette-du-Var
Hyères
Six-Fours-les-Plages

Conversion Tables

Length & Distance

Centimetres/Metres	Inches/Feet/Yards	Inches/Feet/Yards	Centimetres/Metres
1 cm	0.4 in	1 in	2.5 cm
10 cm	4 in	1 ft	30 cm
25 cm	10 in	3 ft/1 yd	90 cm
1 m	3 ft 3 in	10 yds	9 m
100 m	110 yds	100 yds	91 m
Kilometres	**Miles**	**Miles**	**Kilometres**
1	0.6	1	1.6
10	6.2	10	16.1
25	15.5	25	40.2
50	31.1	50	80.5
100	62.2	100	160.9

Kilometres to Miles

km/h	20	30	40	50	60	70	80	90	100	110	120	130
mph	13	18	25	31	37	44	50	56	62	68	74	81

Weight

Grams/Kilograms	Ounces/Pounds	Ounces/Pounds	GramsKilograms
10 gm	0.3 oz	1 oz	28 gm
100 gm	3.5 oz	8 oz	226 gm
1 kg	2 lb 3 oz	1 lb	453 gm
10 kg	22 lb	10 lb	4.54 kg
25 kg	55 lb	50 lb	22.65 kg

Capacity

Millilitres/Litres	Fluid Ounces/ Pints/Gallon	Fluid Ounces/ Pints/Gallon	Millilitres/Litres
10 ml	0.3 fl oz	1 fl oz	28 ml
100 ml	3.5 fl oz	20 fl oz/1 pint	560 ml
1 litre	1.8 pints	1 gallon	4.5 litres
10 litres	2.2 gallons	5 gallons	22.7 litres
50 litres	11 gallons	10 gallons	45.5 litres

Area

Hectares	Acres	Acres	Hectares
1	2.5	1	0.4
5	12.4	5	2
10	24.7	10	4
50	123.5	50	20.2

Tyre Pressures

Bar	PSI (lb/sq.in)	Bar	PSI (lb/sq.in)
1.00	15	3.05	44
1.50	22	3.50	51
2.00	29	4.15	60
2.50	36	4.75	69

Map Scales

Scale	Equivalent Distance	
1:100 000	1 cm = 1 km	1 in = 1¾ miles
1: 200 000	1 cm = 2 km	1 in = 3¼ miles
1: 400 000	1 cm = 4 km	1 in = 6¼ miles
1: 500 000	1 cm = 5 km	1 in = 8 miles
1: 750 000	1 cm = 7.5 km	1 in = 12 miles
1:1 000 000	1 cm = 10 km	1 in = 16 miles
1:1 250 000	1 cm = 12.5 km	1 in = 20 miles
1: 2 000 000	1 cm = 20 km	1 in = 32 miles

You'd have to go a long way to beat our ferry prices

We can make your trips to Europe much more rewarding in so many ways. We have over 200 hand-picked sites, chosen and checked by Club members. We also have dedicated overseas advisors to help you every step of the way.

But did you realise that The Caravan Club's travel service can save you money? We have negotiated special deals with all the major ferry operators that give you prices you'll find hard to beat even if you booked direct.

Book your ferry crossing and sites together with The Caravan Club and you're on your way to savings and a great holiday too.

Request a brochure or talk
to a dedicated overseas advisor
www.caravanclub.co.uk/continental
or call 01342 488 062

THE
CARAVAN
CLUB

During Your Stay

Electricity and Gas in Europe

Electricity – General Advice

The nominal voltage for mains electricity has been 230 volts across the European Union for more than ten years, but varying degrees of 'acceptable tolerance' have resulted in significant variations in the actual voltage found. Harmonisation of voltage standards remains an on-going project. Most appliances sold in the UK are rated at 220-240 volts and usually work satisfactorily. However, some high-powered equipment, such as microwave ovens, may not function well and you are advised to consult the manufacturer's literature for further information.

Appliances which are 'CE' marked should work acceptably, as this marking indicates that the product has been designed to meet the requirements of relevant European directives.

The site entries in this guide contain information on minimum amperage supplied on campsites and the Country Introduction contains additional information (where known). Frequently you will be offered a choice of amperage and the following table gives an approximate idea of which appliances can be used (erring on the side of caution). You can work it out more accurately by noting the wattage of each appliance in your caravan. The kettle given is the caravan type, not a household kettle which usually has at least a 2000 watt element. Note that each caravan circuit also has a maximum amp rating which should not be exceeded.

Electrical Connections – EN60309-2 (CEE17)

Whilst there is a European Standard for connectors, namely EN60309-2 (formerly known as CEE17), this does not apply retrospectively and you may find some

Continental campsites where your UK 3-pin connector, which is to European Standard, will not fit. Accurate information is not easy to come by, but based on The Caravan Club's overseas sites booking service, approximately 80% of campsites in Europe do have some, or all, UK 3-pin hook-ups, leaving approximately 20% of campsites with only 2-pin hook ups. Therefore it is a good idea to carry a 2-pin adapter. See the relevant Caravan Europe titles and Country Introductions for more information.

Different types of connector may be found within one campsite, as well as within one country. If you find your CEE17 connector does not fit, ask campsite staff to borrow or hire an adaptor.

Even with a European Standard connection, a poor electrical supply is possible. The existence of the EN60309-2 (CEE17) standard should not be taken as an automatic sign of a modern system.

Amps	Wattage (Approx)	Fridge	Battery Charger	Air Conditioning	Colour TV	Water Heater	Kettle (750W)	Heater (1KW)
2	400	✓	✓					
4	800	✓	✓		✓	✓		
6	1200	✓	✓	*	✓	✓	✓	
8	1600	✓	✓	✓**	✓	✓	✓	✓**
10	2000	✓	✓	✓**	✓	✓	✓	✓**
16	3000	✓	✓	✓	✓	✓	✓	✓**

* *Possible, depending on wattage of appliance in question*

** *Not to be used at the same time as other high-wattage equipment*

Other Connections

French – 2-pin, plus earth socket. Adaptors available from UK caravan accessory shops.

German – 2-pin, plus 2 earth strips, found in Norway and Sweden and possibly still Germany.

Switzerland – 3-pin (but not the same shape as UK 3-pin). Adapters available to purchase in Switzerland. Most campsites using the Swiss 3-pin will have adaptors available for hire or to borrow.

If the campsite does not have a modern EN60309-2 (CEE17) supply, ask to see the electrical protection for the socket outlet. If there is a device marked with IDn = 30mA, then the risk is minimised.

Hooking Up to the Mains

Connection

Connection should always be made in the following order:

- Check your caravan isolating switch is at 'off'.
- Uncoil the connecting cable from the drum. **A coiled cable with current flowing through it may overheat.** Take your cable and insert the connector (female end) into the caravan inlet.
- Insert the plug (male end) into the site outlet socket.
- Switch caravan isolating switch to 'on'.
- Preferably insert a polarity tester into one of the 13-amp sockets in the caravan to check all connections are correctly wired. **Never leave it in the socket.** Some caravans have these devices built in as standard.

It is recommended that the supply is not used if the polarity is incorrect *(see **Reversed Polarity** overleaf)*.

WARNING

In case of doubt or, if after carrying out the above procedures the supply does not become available, or if the supply fails, consult the campsite operator or a qualified electrician.

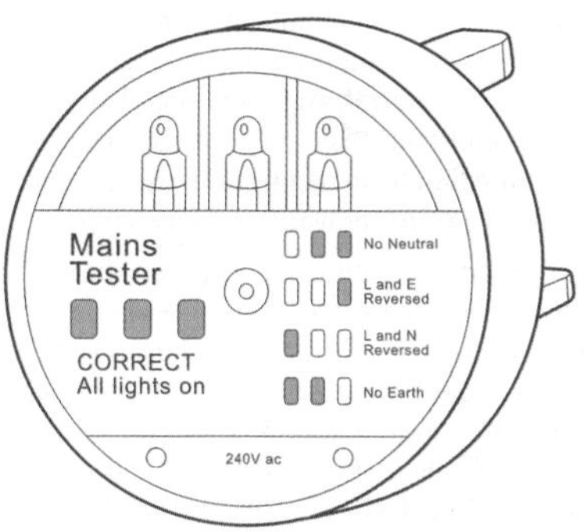

From time to time, you may come across mains supplies which differ in various ways from the common standards on most sites and your test equipment may not be able to confirm that such systems are satisfactory and safe to use. While it is likely that such systems will operate your electrical equipment adequately in most circumstances, it is possible that the protective measures in your equipment may not work effectively in the event of a fault.

Site Hooking Up Adaptor

(MAINS CONTINENTAL)

ADAPTATEUR DE PRISE AU SITE (SECTEUR) CAMPINGPLATZ-ANSCHLUSS (NETZ)

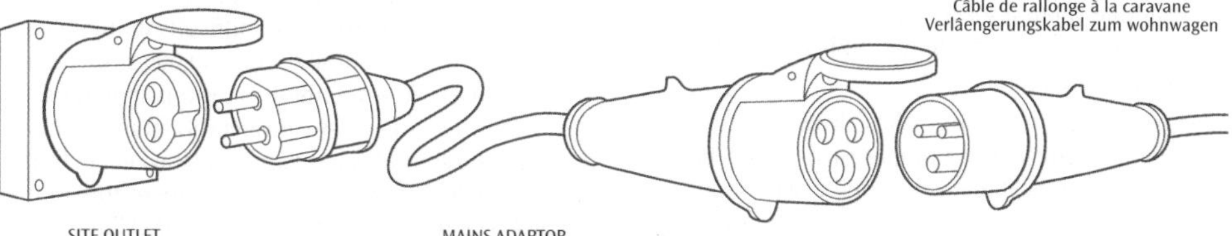

If your test equipment is not built into your caravan it should be readily available for everyday use.

To ensure your safety, the Club recommends that unless the system can be confirmed as safe, it should not be used.

Disconnection

- Switch your caravan isolating switch to 'off'.
- At the site supply socket withdraw the plug.
- Disconnect the cable from the caravan.
- Motorhomes – if leaving your pitch during the day, do not leave your mains cable plugged into the site supply, as this creates a hazard if the exposed live connections in the plug are touched or if the cable is not seen during grass-cutting.

Reversed Polarity

Even when the site connector is to European Standard EN60309-2 (CEE17), British caravanners are still likely to encounter the problem known as reversed polarity. This is where the site supply's 'live' line connects to the caravan's 'neutral' and vice versa. The Club strongly recommends that you always check the polarity immediately on connection, using a polarity tester available from caravan accessory shops.

The caravan mains electrical installation **should not be used** while reversed polarity exists. Try using another nearby socket instead, which may cure the problem. Frequent travellers to the Continent who are electrically competent often make up an adaptor themselves, clearly marked 'reversed polarity', with the live and neutral wires reversed. (The 'German' plug can simply be turned upside down, so no further adaptor is required.) If these steps do not rectify the reversed polarity, the site supply may be quite different from that used in the UK and we recommend, for your own safety, that you disconnect from the mains and **do not use the electrical supply.**

Always check the polarity immediately on connection

Using a reversed polarity socket will probably not affect how an electrical appliance works BUT your protection in the event of a fault is greatly reduced. For example, a lamp socket may still be live as you touch it while replacing a blown bulb, even if the light switch is turned off.

Even when polarity is correct, it is always a wise precaution to check that a proper earth connection exists. A good indication of this can be achieved using a proprietary tester such as that shown on the previous page. However, there are earth faults that these simple devices are unable to identify and if there is any doubt about the integrity of the earth system, **DO NOT USE THE ELECTRICITY SUPPLY.**

Shaver Sockets

Most campsites provide shaver sockets on which the voltage is generally marked as either 220V or 110V. Using an incorrect voltage may cause the shaver to become hot or to fail. The 2-pin adaptor obtainable in the UK is sometimes too wide for Continental sockets. It is advisable to buy 2-pin adaptors on the Continent, where they are readily available. Many shavers will operate on a range of voltages and these are most suitable when travelling abroad.

Gas – General Advice

The rate of gas consumption is difficult to predict as it depends on many factors, including how many appliances you use in your outfit, whether you use a mains electric hook-up when available, how much you eat out and, of course, what the temperature is! As a rough guide plan to allow 0.45 kg of gas a day for normal summer usage.

With the exception of Campingaz, LPG cylinders normally available in the UK, e.g. Calor gas (both butane and propane), cannot be exchanged abroad. If possible, take sufficient gas with you for your holiday and bring back the empty cylinder(s). If additional capacity is required beyond what you would normally carry, check with cylinder suppliers to see if you can swap to a larger one (if there is room in your gas locker to carry it) or check if it is economic to carry a second cylinder. Note that ferry and tunnel operators may restrict the number of cylinders you are permitted to carry.

The wide availability of Campingaz means it is worth considering it as a fall-back if you run out of your 'normal' gas. However, prices vary widely from country to country, and maximum cylinder sizes are quite limited (2.75 kg of gas in a 907 cylinder), making it less practical for routine use in larger vehicles with several gas appliances. A Campingaz adapter is relatively inexpensive, though, and is widely available in the UK. It can be a prudent purchase prior to travelling, especially if taking a long holiday. It is also wise to hold a spare Calor gas cylinder in reserve in case you experience difficulty in finding a Campingaz supplier locally. With 130,000 stockists in 100 countries, however, these occasions should be rare, but prices may vary considerably from country to country. Alternatively, adaptors are available from Campingaz/Calor stockists to enable use of the normal Calor 4.5 kg regulator with a Campingaz cylinder.

If you are touring in winter or wherever cold weather conditions may be encountered, it is advisable to use propane gas instead of butane. BP Gaslight (propane) cylinders, which have been gaining in popularity in the UK, are available in several European countries. However, you cannot exchange cylinders bought in other European countries, nor bring ones back to other European countries for exchange. For news of further developments check the BP Gaslight website, www.bpgaslight.com

Take sufficient gas with you for your holiday

Many other brands of gas are available in different countries and, subject to the availability of suitable regulators, adapters and connecting hoses, as long as the cylinders fit in your gas locker these local brands can also be used with your outfit. If you regularly visit a country, it may well be worth buying a 'local' cylinder, as you can then exchange it in that country when necessary. If you are travelling across several countries this may not be a viable option.

The use of 30 mbar has been standardised for both butane and propane within the EU, replacing several different pressures previously used. On later model UK-specification caravans and motorhomes (2004 models and later) a 30 mbar regulator suited to both propane and butane use is fitted to the bulkhead of the gas locker. This is connected to the cylinder by means of a connecting hose (and sometimes an adaptor) to suit different brands or types of gas. Older outfits and some foreign-built ones may use a cylinder-mounted regulator, which may need to be changed to suit different brands or types of gas.

Hoses and adapters to suit the most common brands and types of gas are available in the UK from suppliers such as Gaslow (0845 4000 600 or www.gaslow.co.uk) or from good dealerships, and it may be easier to buy these before travelling, rather than rely on local availability when you are abroad.

WARNING

Refilling your own UK standard cylinder is prohibited by law in most countries, unless it is carried out at certain designated filling plants. Since these plants are few and far between, are generally highly mechanised and geared for cylinders of a particular size and shape, the process is usually not practical. Nevertheless, it is realised that many local dealers and site operators will fill your cylinders regardless of the prohibition. **The Caravan Club does not recommend the user-refilling of gas cylinders WHICH HAVE NOT BEEN SPECIFICIALLY DESIGNED FOR THIS PURPOSE; there is real danger if cylinders are incorrectly filled.**

- Cylinders must never be over-filled under any circumstances.
- Regular servicing of gas appliances is important. A badly adjusted appliance can emit carbon monoxide, which could prove fatal. Check your vehicle or appliance handbook for service recommendations.
- Never use a hob or oven as a space heater.

*For information about the carriage of gas cylinders on ferries and in the Channel Tunnel, including safety precautions and regulations, see the chapter **Ferries and the Channel Tunnel** in the section **PLANNING AND TRAVELLING.***

The Caravan Club publishes a range of technical leaflets for its members (some available to non-members) including detailed advice on the use of electricity and gas. You are advised to request copies or see www.caravanclub.co.uk/expert-advice

During Your Stay

Keeping in Touch

Emails and the Internet

Wi-Fi hotspots are increasingly available on lots of campsites in Europe and many (but not all) offer Wi-Fi to their guests free of charge.

A Wi-Fi enabled laptop, tablet (such as an iPad) or a mobile 'smartphone' should enable the sending and receiving of emails, photos and video clips, together with website browsing, plus numerous other internet functions.

Alternatively there are internet cafés all over the world where you can log on to the internet and collect and send emails. You will be charged for the time you are logged on, however some public libraries in many countries offer free internet access.

WARNING:

Wi-Fi internet surfing abroad by means of a dongle (which uses a mobile phone network) is still prohibitively expensive, as is data roaming on internet enabled mobile phones. The reduction in international mobile phone roaming charges does not currently apply to data streaming.

Text Messages (SMS)

Using a mobile phone to send text messages is a cost-effective way of keeping in touch. There is a charge for sending texts but receiving them abroad is free.

A number of websites offer a free SMS text message service to mobile phones, e.g. www.cbfsms.com or www.sendsmsnow.com

International Direct Dial Calls

International access codes are given in the relevant Country Introduction chapters. To make an IDD call, first dial the international access code from the country you are in, followed by the local number you wish to reach including its area code (if applicable), e.g. from the UK to Hungary, dial 0036 – the international access code for Hungary – then the local number omitting the initial 0 of the area code.

Most, but not all countries include an initial 0 in the area code. With the exception of Italy, where the 0 must be dialled, this initial 0 should not be dialled when calling from outside the country in question. Some countries' telephone numbers do not have area codes at all (e.g. Denmark, Luxembourg, Norway). If this is the case simply dial the international access code and the number in full. The international access code to dial the UK from anywhere in the world is 0044.

International calls can be made from telephone boxes in most countries using coins or, more commonly, phonecards or credit cards, and often instructions are given in English.

Ring Tones

Ring tones vary from country to country and the UK's double ring is not necessarily used in other countries.

Global Telephone Cards

Rechargeable global telephone cards offer rates for international calls which are normally cheaper than credit card or local phonecard rates. Payment methods vary, but are usually by monthly direct debit from your credit card or bank account. Also widely available are pre-paid international phonecards available on-line or locally from post offices, newsagents, kiosks or shops. There are many websites selling international phonecards for use all over the world such as www.planetphonecards.com and www.thephonecardsite.com

Making Calls from your Laptop

If you download Skype to your laptop you can make free calls to other Skype users anywhere in the world using a Wi-Fi broadband connection. Rates for calls to

non-Skype users (landline or mobile phone) are also very competitively-priced. You will need a computer with a microphone and speakers, and a webcam is handy too. It is also possible to download Skype to an internet-enabled mobile phone to take advantage of the same low-cost calls – see www.skype.com

Radio and Television

Radio and Television Broadcasts

The BBC World Service broadcasts radio programmes 24 hours a day from a worldwide network of FM/AM/SW transmitters and you can listen on a number of platforms: online, via satellite or cable, DRM digital radio, internet radio or mobile phone. In addition, many local radio stations broadcast BBC World Service programmes in English on FM frequencies. You can find detailed information and programme schedules at www.bbc.co.uk/worldservice

Listeners in northern France can currently listen to BBC Radio 5 Live on either 693 or 909 kHz medium wave or BBC Radio 4 on 198 kHz long wave. Whereas analogue television signals will be switched off in the UK during 2012 no date has yet been fixed for the switch off of analogue radio signals.

BBC News Online is available on internet-enabled mobile phones, palmtop computers and other wireless handheld devices – text 81010 from your mobile phone or type www.bbc.co.uk/mobile into your browser for set-up information. Mobile phone network providers also have links to the BBC or Sky News from their own portals for breaking news and headlines.

Digital Terrestrial Television

As in the UK, television transmissions in most of Europe have been (or soon will be) converted to digital. The UK's high definition transmission technology may be more advanced than any currently implemented or planned in Europe. This means that digital televisions intended for use in the UK, whether for standard or high definition, might not be able to receive terrestrial signals in some countries.

Satellite Television

For English-language TV programmes the only realistic option is satellite, and satellite dishes are a common sight on campsites all over Europe. A satellite dish mounted on the caravan roof or clamped to a pole fixed to the drawbar, or one mounted on a foldable free-standing tripod, will provide good reception and minimal interference. Remember however that obstructions to the south east (such as tall trees or even mountains) or heavy rain, can interrupt the signals. A specialist dealer will be able to advise you on the best way of mounting your dish. You will also need a satellite receiver and ideally a satellite-finding meter. Many satellite channels are transmitted clear, or 'free-to-air', which means they can be received by any make of receiver, but others are encrypted and require the use of a Sky viewing card and digibox.

For the free-to-air channels, there is a choice of receivers including Sky, Freesat and generic makes. There is nothing to stop you taking a Sky digibox from home unless your Sky contract says you have to keep your Sky digibox connected to your phone line, in which case charges may apply. Alternatively you can take a Freesat receiver or a generic free-to-air receiver. There is also a camping kit which comprises a receiver, dish and stand, and 10m of cable all enclosed in a convenient plastic carrying case. They are available from caravan accessory shops and a variety of other outlets.

Freesat boxes are widely available on the high street, or you can buy a non-subscription Sky digibox from a number of online suppliers. To watch any encrypted channels, there is no option other than to use a Sky digibox, equipped with a viewing card. However, although it is not illegal to use a Sky viewing card outside the UK, it is against Sky's terms and conditions and it will be within their rights to cancel the card. The digibox itself is your own personal property and can be taken abroad without restriction. It will provide access to most free-to-air channels without having a viewing card in it. However, do note that if you intend to take a Sky+ box with you, it will not perform any of the record or playback functions without its designated Sky card. A Freesat+ recorder on the other hand has no such restrictions and can be used freely across Europe.

There are hundreds of English-language TV channels and national radio stations that can be received anywhere in the UK and, in some cases, large parts of Europe. The main entertainment channels such as BBC1, ITV1 and Channel 4 have for a number of years been more difficult to pick up in mainland Europe than others such as Channel 5. Unfortunately in 2012 these channels will be joined by others, including the Channel 5 family, due to the arrival of a new narrow-beam satellite. A 60cm dish will still suffice for most of France, Belgium and the Netherlands, as well as those parts of Germany, Switzerland and Spain that immediately border them, but as you travel further afield, you'll need a progressively larger dish to pick up the entertainment channels. On the plus side, those affected channels will no longer need a Sky viewing card, and users of Freesat and free-to-air receivers will have a greater choice of viewing. The news channels such as Sky News, BBC News and France 24 will almost certainly remain accessible across most of Europe.

As Caravan Europe went to press, the precise impact of the new satellite was still unknown. See the website www.satelliteforcaravans.co.uk (created and operated by a Caravan Club member) for the latest changes and developments, and for information on how to set up your equipment.

Television via a Laptop

With a modern laptop this is straightforward. In order to process the incoming signal the laptop must, as a minimum, be fitted with a TV tuner and a TV-in connector – basically an aerial socket. Some laptops have them built in, but if not you can obtain a plug-in USB adaptor. An alternative connection is the HDMI socket (High Definition Multimedia Interface) which is fitted to some of the more expensive laptops, for which you will need an HD digital receiver. For more information see www.radioandtelly.co.uk

Currently television programmes via BBC iPlayer are only available to users to download or stream in the UK . This is due to rights agreements, however the BBC are aware that there is a demand for an international version. Most radio programmes are available outside of the UK via BBC iPlayer as well as highlights from many BBC News programmes and BBC Sport video content. Check for updates before you travel www.bbc.co.uk/iplayer

Using Mobile Phones Abroad

Mobile phones have an international calling option called 'roaming,' which will automatically search for a local network when you switch your phone on, wherever you are in Europe. You should contact your service provider to obtain advice on the charges involved as these are partly set by the foreign networks you use and fluctuate with exchange rates. Most network providers offer added extras or 'bolt-ons' to your tariff to make the cost of calling to/from abroad cheaper.

There are no further formalities and the phone will work in exactly the same way as in the UK. When you arrive at your destination, your mobile will automatically select a network with the best service. You should also be able to access most of the features you use in the UK, including voicemail and pay-as-you-go top-up.

When calling UK landline or mobile phone numbers prefix the number with +44 and drop the initial 0 of the area code. Enter telephone numbers in your phone's memory in this way, and you will get through to those numbers when dialling from the memory, whether you are in the UK or abroad.

Because mobile phones will only work within range of a base station, reception in some remote rural areas may be patchy, but coverage is usually

excellent in main towns and near main roads and motorways. Approximate coverage maps can be obtained from many dealers.

If you are making calls to numbers within the country you are visiting, you only need to use the standard dialling code without the international code, rather like using your phone in the UK. To make a call to a country other than the UK from abroad, simply replace the +44 country code with the applicable country code, e.g. +36 for Hungary.

You should note that if you receive an incoming call while abroad, the international leg of the call will be charged to your mobile phone account because the caller has no way of knowing that they are making an international call. It is possible to bar or divert incoming calls when abroad and your service provider will supply a full list of options.

Mobile service providers have responded to pressure from the EU to reduce roaming charges but while mobile phone charges are coming down, sending and receiving video messages is still expensive – check with your network provider.

Global SIM Cards

As an alternative to paying your mobile service provider's roaming charges it is possible to buy a global SIM card which will enable your mobile phone to operate on a foreign mobile network more cheaply.

When you go abroad you simply replace the SIM card in your phone with the new card, remembering to leave a voicemail message on the old card telling callers that you have temporarily changed number. This service is offered by a number of network providers as well as companies such as www.roameo.co.uk, www.truphone.com and www.0044.co.uk

You may, however, find it simpler to buy a SIM card abroad but before doing this, check with your UK service provider to find out whether it has locked your phone against the use of a different SIM card and what, if anything, it will charge to unlock it. The website www.0044.co.uk has instructions on how to unlock mobile phones. If you plan to use a mobile phone a lot while abroad, e.g. to book campsites, restaurants, etc, then give some thought to buying a cheap 'pay-as-you-go' phone in the country you are visiting.

Hands-Free

Legislation in Europe forbids the use of mobile or car phones while driving except when using hands-free equipment. **If you are involved in an accident whilst driving and, at the same time, you were using a hand-held mobile phone, your insurance company may refuse to honour the claim.**

Internet & Wi-Fi-Enabled Phones

As technology advances VoIP (voice-over internet protocol) permits you to be contacted on and make calls from your usual mobile phone number while abroad. Part of your call is routed over the internet – see www.truphone.com for information about the latest mobile apps. You will need a Wi-Fi or 3G internet-enabled phone.

Mobile Internet Costs - Data Roaming

Please be aware that accessing the internet overseas via your mobile can be very expensive. It is recommended that you disable your internet access by switching 'data roaming' to off, in order to avoid a large mobile phone bill on your return. If you need to go online or check your email, find a free Wi-Fi hotspot. These are now often available on some campsites or in some cafes, bars and restaurants.

Finally.....

Make a note of your mobile phone's serial number, your own telephone number and the number of your provider's customer services and keep them in a safe place separate from your mobile phone.

Remember to pack your charger and travel adaptor. Charging packs, available from major mobile phone and other retailers, provide a power source to recharge your phone if you do not have access to a mains supply. Whichever network you use, check that you have the instructions for use abroad.

During Your Stay

Medical Matters

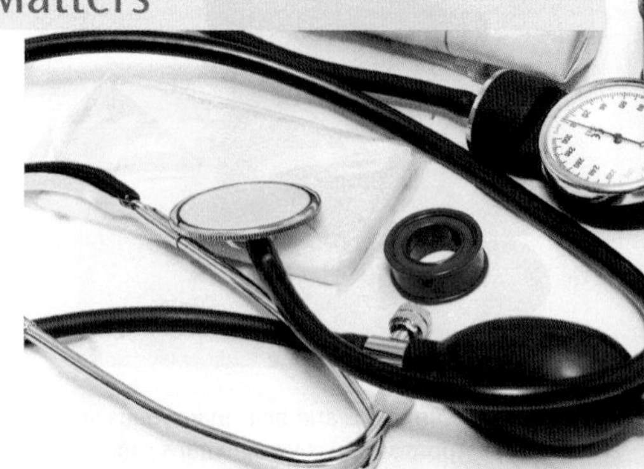

This chapter offers advice and information on what to do before you travel, how to avoid the need for healthcare when you are away from home and what to do when you return.

Specific advice on obtaining emergency medical treatment in European countries is comprehensively covered country-by-country in the Healthcare Abroad section of the NHS Choices website, www.nhs.uk. Alternatively obtain a copy of the Department of Health's leaflet, T7.1 Health Advice for Travellers which is downloadable from www.dh.gov.uk, or call 020 7210 4850.

Very few countries offer such easy access to medical facilities as Britain. Obtaining medical treatment abroad may seem complicated to UK residents who are used to the NHS. Also in most countries around the world you will have to pay, often large amounts, for relatively minor treatment.

Before You Travel

If you have any pre-existing medical conditions it is wise to check with your GP that you are fit to travel. If your medical condition is complex then ask your doctor for a written summary of your medical problems and a list of medications currently used, together with other treatment details, and have it translated into the language of the country, or countries, that you are visiting. This is particularly important for travellers whose medical conditions require them to use controlled drugs or hypodermic syringes, in order to avoid any local difficulties with Customs.

*See **Customs Regulations** in the section **PLANNING AND TRAVELLING**.*

Check the health requirements for your destination; these may depend not only on the countries you are visiting, but which parts, at what time of the year and for how long. If you are travelling to an unusual destination, heading well off the beaten track, or if you simply want to be sure of receiving the most up-to-date advice, your first step should be to get a MASTA Travel Health Brief. This is designed to meet your specific travel health needs, helping you understand the travel health risks you may face together with any relevant vaccination, antimalarial and other protective advice. To obtain a MASTA Travel Health Brief free of charge simply log on to www.masta-travel-health.com

Always check that you have enough of your regular medications to last the duration of your holiday and carry a card giving your blood group and details of any allergies or dietary restrictions (a translation of these may be useful when visiting restaurants). Your doctor can normally prescribe only a limited quantity of medicines under the NHS so if you think you will run out of prescribed medicines whilst abroad, ask your doctor for the generic name of any drugs you use, as brand names may be different abroad. If you don't already know it, find out your blood group. In an emergency this may well ensure prompt treatment.

If you have any doubts about your teeth or plan to be away a long time, have a dental check-up before departure. An emergency dental kit is available from High Street chemists which will allow you temporarily to restore a crown, bridge or filling or to dress a broken tooth until you can get to a dentist.

A good website to check before you travel is www.nathnac.org/travel. This website gives general health and safety advice and reports of disease outbreaks, as well as highlighting potential health risks by country.

European Heath Insurance Card (EHIC)

Before leaving home apply for a European Health Insurance Card (EHIC). British residents who are temporarily visiting another EU member state, as well as Iceland, Liechtenstein, Norway or Switzerland, are entitled to receive state-provided emergency treatment during their stay on the same terms as residents of those countries. As well as treatment in the event of an emergency, this includes on-going medical care for a chronic disease or pre-existing illness, i.e. medication, blood tests and injections. The card shows name and date of birth and a personal identification number. It holds no electronic or clinical data.

Apply online for your EHIC on www.ehic.org.uk or by telephoning 0845 6062030 or by obtaining an application form from a post office. An EHIC is required by each individual family member, so allow enough time before your departure for applications to be processed. A child under 16 must be included in a parent or guardian's application as a dependant, and will receive his/her own card.

The EHIC is free of charge, is valid for up to five years and can be renewed up to six months before its expiry date. Before you travel remember to check that your EHIC is still valid.

Before you travel remember to check that your EHIC is still valid and allow enough time to apply

Private treatment is generally not covered by your EHIC, and state-provided treatment may not cover everything that you would expect to receive free of charge from the NHS. If charges are made, these cannot be refunded by the British authorities but may be refundable under the terms of your holiday travel insurance policy.

An EHIC is not a substitute for travel insurance and **it is strongly recommended that you arrange full travel insurance before leaving home (see below) regardless of the cover provided by your EHIC.** Some insurance companies require you to have an EHIC and some will waive the policy excess if an EHIC has been used.

An EHIC issued in the UK is valid provided the holder remains ordinarily resident in the UK and eligible for NHS services. Restrictions may apply to nationals of other countries resident in the UK. For enquiries about applications see www.ehic.org.uk or call EHIC Enquiries on 0845 6062030. For other enquiries call 0845 6050707. If your EHIC is stolen or lost while you are abroad contact 0044 191 2127500 for help.

Residents of the Republic of Ireland, the Isle of Man and Channel Islands, should check with their own health authorities about reciprocal arrangements with other countries.

Holiday Travel Insurance

Despite the fact that you have an EHIC you may incur thousands of pounds of medical costs if you fall ill or have an accident, even in countries with which Britain has reciprocal health care arrangements. The cost of bringing a person back to the UK, in the event of illness or death, is **never** covered by reciprocal arrangements.

Therefore, separate additional travel insurance adequate for your destination is essential, such as The Caravan Club's Red Pennant Overseas Holiday Insurance, available to Club members – see www.caravanclub.co.uk/redpennant

First Aid

A first aid kit containing at least the basic requirements is an essential item and in some countries it is compulsory to carry one in your vehicle (see the ***Essential Equipment Table*** in the chapter ***Motoring – Equipment***). Kits should contain items such as sterile pads, assorted dressings, bandages and plasters, hypo-allergenic tape, antiseptic wipes or cream, painkillers, gauze, cotton wool, scissors, finger stall, eye bath and tweezers. Add to that travel sickness remedies, a triangular bandage, medicated hand cleaner or wipes, a pair of light rubber gloves and a pocket mask in case you ever find yourself in a situation where you need to give mouth-to-mouth resuscitation. Also make sure you carry something for the treatment of upset stomachs, which often spoil more holidays than anything else.

A first aid kit is an essential item and it is compulsory to carry one in many countries

It is always wise to carry a good first aid manual containing useful advice and instructions. The British Red Cross publishes a comprehensive First Aid Manual in conjunction with St John Ambulance and St Andrew's Ambulance Association, which is widely available. First aid essentials are also covered in a number of readily-available compact guide books.

Emergency Multilingual Phrasebook

The British Red Cross, with the advice of the Department of Health, produces an Emergency Multilingual Phrasebook covering the most common medical questions and terms. It is aimed primarily at health professionals but the document can be downloaded as separate pages in a number of European languages from the Department of Health's website. See www.dh.gov.uk/publications and use the search facility.

Vaccinations

The Department of Health advises long stay visitors to some eastern European countries to consider vaccination against hepatitis A. See the Country Introductions in the relevant edition of Caravan Europe for further information. Polio and tetanus booster injections are no longer routinely administered unless you are at particular risk – see www.nhs.uk

Tick-Borne Encephalitis (TBE) and Lyme Disease

Hikers and outdoor sports enthusiasts planning trips to forested, rural areas in some parts of central and eastern Europe, including many countries popular with tourists, such as (amongst others) Austria and Croatia, should seek medical advice well ahead of their planned departure date about preventative measures and immunisation against tick-borne encephalitis which is transmitted by the bite of an infected tick. TBE is a potentially serious and debilitating viral disease of the central nervous system, with the risk highest between spring and autumn when ticks are active in long grass, bushes and hedgerows in forested areas and in scrubland and areas where animals wander, including in and around campsites and at rural motorway rest areas. It is endemic in many countries in mainland Europe.

There is no vaccine against Lyme disease, an equally serious tick-borne infection, which, if left untreated, can attack the nervous system and joints. Early treatment with antibiotics will normally halt the progress of the disease, but you should be vigilant about checking yourself and your family for ticks and be aware of signs and symptoms of the disease.

If you think you might be at risk use an insect repellent containing DEET, wear long sleeves and long trousers, inspect the body for ticks after outdoor activity and remove with tweezers. Avoid unpasteurised dairy products in risk areas. See www.tickalert.org or telephone 01943 468010.

During Your Stay

Take your NHS medical card with you if visiting a non-EU country as you may be asked for it when seeking medical assistance. Some UK Primary Care Trusts will only issue medical cards on request.

If you require treatment in an EU country but do not have an EHIC, or are experiencing difficulties in getting your EHIC accepted, telephone the Department for Work & Pensions for assistance on the overseas healthcare team line 0044 (0)191 218 1999. The office is open from 8am to 5pm Monday to Friday and they will fax documents if necessary.

Claiming Refunds

If you are entitled to a refund from the authorities of the country in which you received treatment you should make a claim in that country either in person or by post before you return home. You must submit the original bills, prescriptions and receipts (keep photocopies for your records). The booklet T7.1 contains details of how to claim refunds, as does NHS Choices on www.nhs.uk/nhsengland/Healthcareabroad. If you cannot claim until your return home you should contact the Department for Work & Pensions on 0191 218 1999. The DWP will liaise with overseas authorities on your behalf to obtain a refund, which may take some time.

Accidents and Emergencies

If you are unfortunate enough to be involved in, or witness a road accident, or become involved in an emergency situation, firstly summon help early by any means available, giving the exact location of the accident or emergency and the number of casualties. Notify the police; most police officers have first aid training.

If you witnessed an accident the police may question you about it. Before leaving the scene, make a brief note and a rough sketch to indicate details of the time you arrived and left, the position of the vehicles and the injured, the surface of the road, camber, potholes, etc, the weather at the time of the accident, skid marks and their approximate length – in fact anything you feel might be relevant – then date it and sign it. Take photographs if possible. You may never be called on to use these notes, but if you are you have a written record made at the time, which could be of great value.

Calling the Emergency Services

The telephone numbers for police, fire brigade and ambulance services are given in each Country Introduction within each of the relevant Caravan Europe Guides. In all EU member states the number 112 can be used from landlines or mobile phones to call any of the emergency services. In most instances operators speak English.

In all EU member states dial 112 to call any of the emergency services

Insect Bites

Most of the temperate parts of Europe have their fair share of nuisance insects such as mosquitoes and midges, particularly near lakes, and it is wise to use an insect repellant. A number of products are available including impregnated wrist and ankle bands and insect repellant sprays and coils. Covering exposed skin with long trousers and long-sleeved shirts is recommended after dark. Also see information earlier in this chapter about tick-borne encephalitis and Lyme disease.

Rabies

Rabies incidence across Europe has reduced in recent years, in large part due to EU-sponsored vaccination programmes. Apart from isolated incidents, rabies is now confined to a few member states in the east of the EU, principally Romania and Latvia.

Despite this, **DO NOT** bring any animals into the UK without first complying with the legal requirements.

Always seek medical attention immediately if you get bitten by an animal. Rabies is an acute viral infection and can be fatal.

Swimming

Pollution of sea water at some Continental coastal resorts, including the Mediterranean, may still present a health hazard. Where the water quality may present risks, e.g. in rivers and lakes, as well as at the coast, or where it is simply unsafe to bathe, signs are usually erected, often accompanied by warning flags, which forbid bathing:

French: Défense de se baigner or Il est défendu de se baigner

Italian: Vietato bagnarsi or Evietato bagnarsi

Spanish: Prohibido bañarse or Se prohibe bañarse

Warning flags should always be taken very seriously – red is for danger, when you should not enter the water; usually yellow or orange means you may paddle at the water's edge, but may not swim. A green flag normally indicates that it is ok to swim. A chequered flag generally means that the lifeguard is temporarily absent. You should never go swimming alone and you should always make sure you know what each flag means and be aware of any risks before you decide to enter the water.

*See **Safety and Security** in the next chapter for further information.*

Sun Protection

Never under-estimate how ill careless exposure to the sun may make you. If you are not used to the heat it is very easy to fall victim to heat exhaustion or heat stroke. The symptoms include headache,

tiredness, weakness and thirst, leading to confusion, disorientation and, in very extreme cases, coma and death. Anyone showing signs of serious over-exposure to the sun should be placed indoors or in the shade, encouraged to sip water and kept cool by fanning or sponging down with cool water. Call a doctor if the patient becomes unconscious or delirious

Take sensible precautions: avoid sitting in the sun between 11am and 3pm; use a good quality sun-cream with high sun protection factor (SPF) and re-apply frequently; wear a sun hat and cover up with a cotton T-shirt when swimming; wear good quality sunglasses which filter UV rays, and finally take extra care at high altitude, especially in the snow and in windy conditions.

Children need extra protection as they burn easily, tend to stay out in the sun longer and are unaware of the dangers of over-exposure. Keep babies out of the sun at all times.

Water and Food

Water from mains supplies throughout Europe is generally good but the level of chemical treatment may make it unpalatable and you may prefer to use bottled water.

Food poisoning is a potential risk anywhere in the world, but in extremely hot conditions a common-sense approach is called for. Avoid food that has been kept warm for prolonged periods or left unrefrigerated for more than two to four hours. If the source is uncertain, do not eat unpasteurised dairy products, ice-cream, under-cooked meat, fish or shellfish, salads, raw vegetables or dishes containing mayonnaise.

Returning Home

If you become ill on your return home do not forget to tell your doctor that you have been abroad and which countries you have visited. Even if you have received medical treatment in another country, always consult your doctor if you have been bitten or scratched by an animal while on holiday.

If you were given any medicines in another country, it may not be legal to bring them back into the UK. If in doubt, declare them at Customs when you return.

If you develop an upset stomach while away or shortly afterwards and your work involves handling food, tell your employer immediately. If after returning home you develop flu-like symptoms, a fever or rash, contact your GP or NHS Direct.

Claim on your travel insurance as soon as possible for the cost of any medical treatment. Holders of an EHIC who have not been able to claim while abroad should put in a claim for a refund as soon as possible – see ***Claiming Refunds*** earlier in this chapter.

During Your Stay

Safety and Security

Cars and
contents left
at owners risk

The European Union has strong and effective safety legislations. Nevertheless, safety is largely your own responsibility. Taking sensible precautions and being aware of possible hazards won't spoil your holiday, but a careless attitude might. The following advice will help you and your family have a safer and hopefully trouble-free holiday.

Overnight Stops

The Caravan Club strongly recommends that overnight stops should always be at campsites and not at motorway service areas, ferry terminal car parks, petrol station forecourts or isolated 'aires de services' or 'aires de repos' on motorways where robberies, muggings and encounters with illegal immigrants are occasionally reported. If you ignore this advice and decide to use these areas for a rest during the day or overnight, then you are advised to take appropriate precautions, for example, shutting all windows, securing locks and making a thorough external check of your vehicle(s) before departing. Safeguard your property, e.g. handbags, while out of the caravan and beware of approaches by strangers.

Having said that, there is a wide network of 'Stellplätze', 'Aires de Services', 'Aree di Sosta' and 'Áreas de Servicio' in cities, towns and villages across Europe, many specifically for motorhomes, and many with good security and overnight facilities. It is rare that you will be the only vehicle staying on such areas, but avoid any that are isolated, take sensible precautions and trust your instincts. For example, if the area appears run down and there are groups of people hanging around who seem intimidating, then you are probably wise to move on.

Around the Campsite

The Caravan Club gives safety a high priority at its UK sites but visitors to the Continent sometimes find that campsites do not always come up to Club standards on electrical safety, hygiene and fire precautions.

Take a few minutes when you arrive on site to ensure that everyone, from the youngest upwards, understands where safety equipment is, how things work and where care is needed to avoid an accident. Once you've settled in, take a walk around the site to familiarise yourself with its layout and ensure that your children are familiar with it and know where their caravan is. Even if you have visited the site before, layout and facilities may have changed.

Locate the nearest fire-fighting equipment and the nearest telephone box and emergency numbers.

Natural disasters are rare, but always think about what could happen. A combination of heavy rain and a riverside pitch could lead to flash flooding, for instance, so make yourself aware of site evacuation procedures.

Be aware of sources of electricity and cabling on and around your pitch. Advice about electrical hook-ups is given in detail in the chapter ***Electricity and Gas*** in the section ***DURING YOUR STAY*** – read it carefully.

A Club member has advised that, on occasion, site owners and/or farmers on whose land a site is situated, use poison to control rodents. Warning notices are not always posted and you are strongly advised to check if staying on a rural site and accompanied by your dog.

Common sense should tell you that you need to be careful if the site is close to a main road or alongside a river. Remind your children about the Green Cross Code and encourage them to use it. Adults and children alike need to remember that traffic is on the 'wrong' side of the road.

Incidents of theft from visitors to campsites are rare but when leaving your caravan unattended make sure you lock all doors and shut windows. Conceal valuables from sight and lock bicycles to a tree or to your caravan.

Children

If staying at a farm site, remember that the animals are not pets. Do not approach any animal without the farmer's permission and keep children supervised. Make sure they wash their hands after touching any farm animal. Do not approach or touch any animal which is behaving oddly or any wild animal which appears to be tame.

Watch out for children as you drive around the site and observe the speed limit (walking pace).

Children riding bikes should be made aware that there may be patches of sand or gravel around the site and these should be negotiated at a sensible speed. Bikes should not be ridden between or around tents or caravans.

Children's play areas are generally unsupervised. Check which installations are suitable for your children's ages and abilities and agree with them which ones they may use. Read and respect the displayed rules. Remember it is your responsibility to know where your children are at all times.

Be aware of any campsite rules concerning ball games or use of play equipment, such as roller blades and skateboards. Check the condition of bicycles which you intend to hire.

When your children attend organised activities, arrange when and where to meet afterwards.

Make sure that children are aware of any places where they should not go.

Never leave children alone inside a caravan.

Fire

Fires can be a dangerous hazard and it is important to follow a few basic safety rules. Any fire that starts will spread quickly if not properly dealt with. Follow these rules at all times:

- Never use portable paraffin or gas heaters inside your caravan. Gas heaters should only be fitted when air is taken from outside the caravan.
- Never search for a gas leak with a naked flame or change your gas cylinder inside the caravan. If you smell gas (or in the event of a fire starting), turn off the cylinder immediately, extinguish all naked flames and seek professional help.
- Never place clothing, tea towels or any other items over your cooker or heater to dry.
- Never leave a chip pan or saucepan unattended.
- Keep heaters and cookers clean and correctly adjusted.
- Know where the fire points and telephones are on site and know the site fire drill. Establish a family fire drill. Make sure everyone knows how to call the emergency services.
- Where regulations permit the use of barbecues, take the following precautions to prevent fire:

  Never locate a barbecue near trees or hedges.
  Have a bucket of water to hand in case of sparks.
  Only use recommended fire-lighting materials.
  Do not leave a barbecue unattended when lit and dispose of hot ash safely.
  Do not let children play near a lit or recently extinguished barbecue.

Swimming Pools

Make the first visit to the pool area a 'family exploration' - not only to find out what is available, but also to identify features and check information which could be vital to your family's safety. Even if you have visited the site before, the layout may have changed, so check the following:

- Pool layout – identify shallow and deep ends and note the position of safety equipment. Check that poolside depth markings are accurate and whether there are any sudden changes of depth in the pool. The bottom of the pool should be clearly visible.
- Are there restrictions about diving and jumping into the pool? Are some surfaces slippery when wet? Ensure when diving into a pool that it is deep enough to do so safely.
- Check opening and closing times. For pools with a supervisor or lifeguard, note any times or dates when the pool is not supervised, e.g. lunch breaks or in low season. Read safety notices and rules posted around the pool. Check the location of any rescue equipment.
- Establish your own rules about parental supervision. Age and swimming ability are important considerations and at least one responsible adult who can swim should accompany and supervise children at the pool at all times. Remember that even a shallow paddling pool can present a danger to young children. Even if a lifeguard is present, you are responsible for your children and must watch them closely.
- Do not swim just after a meal, nor after drinking alcohol.

Water Slides

Take some time to watch other people using the slides so that you can see their speed and direction when entering the water. Find out the depth of water in the landing area. Ensure that your children understand the need to keep clear of the landing area.

Consider and agree with your children which slides they may use. Age or height restrictions may apply.

Check the supervision arrangements and hours of use; they may be different from the main pool times.

Check and follow any specific instructions on the proper use of each slide. The safest riding position is usually feet first, sitting down. Never allow your children to stand or climb on the slide.

Do not wear jewellery when using slides.

Beaches, Lakes and Rivers

Check for any warning signs or flags before you swim and ensure that you know what they mean. Check the depth of water before diving and avoid diving or jumping into murky water as submerged swimmers or objects may not be visible. Familiarise yourself with the location of safety apparatus and/or lifeguards.

Children can drown in a very short time and in relatively small amounts of water. Supervise them at all times when they are in the water and ensure that they know where to find you on the beach.

Use only the designated areas for swimming, windsurfing, kayaking, jetskiing, etc. Always use life jackets where appropriate. Swim only in supervised areas whenever possible.

Familiarise yourself with tides, undertows, currents and wind strength and direction before you or your children swim in the sea. This applies in particular when using inflatables, windsurfing equipment, body boards, kayaks or sailing boats. Sudden changes of wave and weather conditions combined with fast tides and currents are particularly dangerous.

Establish whether there are submerged rocks or a steeply shelving shore which can take non-swimmers or weak swimmers by surprise. Be alert to the activities of windsurfers or jetskiers who may not be aware of the presence of swimmers.

On the Road

Do not leave valuable items on car seats or on view near windows in caravans, even if they are locked. Ensure that items on roof racks or cycle carriers are locked securely.

Beware of a 'snatch' through open car windows at traffic lights, filling stations, in traffic jams or at 'fake' traffic accidents. When driving through towns and cities keep your doors locked. Keep handbags, valuables and documents out of sight at all times.

In view of recent problems with stowaways in vehicles on cross-Channel ferries and trains, check that your outfit is free from unexpected guests at the last practical opportunity before boarding.

If flagged down by another motorist for whatever reason, take care that your own car is locked and windows closed while you check outside, even if someone is left inside. Be particularly careful on long, empty stretches of motorway and when you stop for fuel. Even if the people flagging you down appear to be officials (e.g. wearing yellow reflective jackets or

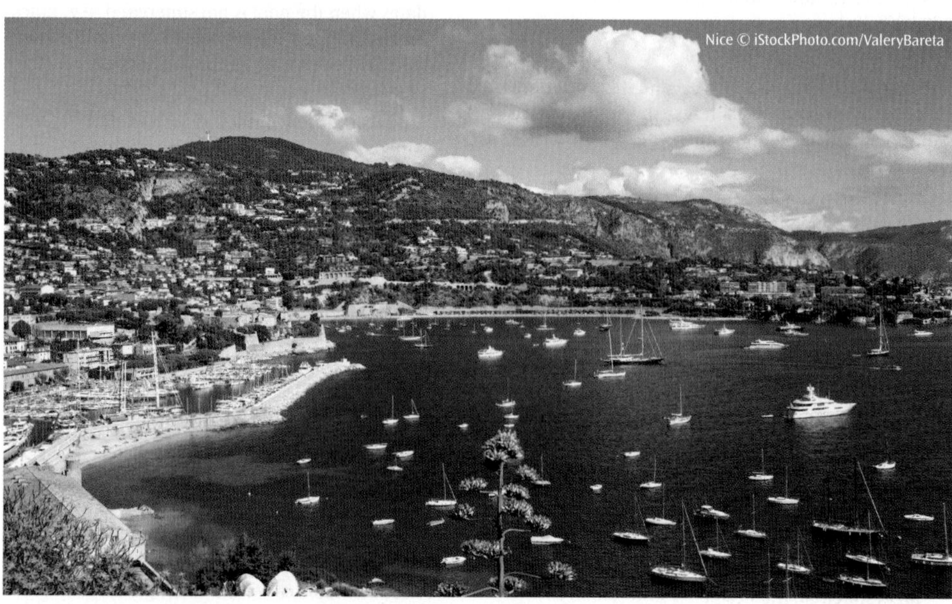

Nice © iStockPhoto.com/ValeryBareta

dark, 'uniform-type' clothing) show presence of mind and lock yourselves in immediately. They may appear to be friendly and helpful, but may be opportunistic thieves prepared to resort to violence. Have a mobile phone to hand and, if necessary, be seen to use it.

Road accidents are a significant risk in some countries where traffic laws may be inadequately enforced, roads may be poorly maintained, road signs and lighting inadequate, and driving standards poor. The traffic mix may be more complex with animal-drawn vehicles, pedestrians, bicycles, cars, lorries, and perhaps loose animals, all sharing the same space. In addition you will be driving on the 'wrong' side of the road and should, therefore, be especially vigilant at all times. Avoid driving at night on unlit roads.

Pursuing an insurance claim abroad can be difficult and it is essential if you are involved in an accident, to take all the other driver's details and complete a European Accident Statement supplied by your motor vehicle insurer.

It's a good idea to keep a fully-charged mobile phone with you in your car with the number of your breakdown organisation saved into it.

Personal Security

There is always the risk of being the victim of petty crime wherever you are in the world. As an obvious tourist you may be more vulnerable, but the number of incidents is very small and the fear of crime should not deter you from holidaying abroad.

The Foreign & Commonwealth Office produces a range of material to advise and inform British citizens travelling abroad about issues affecting their safety, including political unrest, lawlessness, violence, natural disasters, epidemics, anti-British demonstrations and aircraft safety. See the FCO's travel advice for all the countries covered by the Caravan Europe guides on www.fco.gov.uk or see BBC2 Ceefax, page 470.

Specific advice on personal security in countries covered in Caravan Europe are given in the Country Introduction chapters. The following points are a few general precautions to help ensure you have a safe and problem-free holiday:

- Leave valuables and jewellery at home. If you do take them, fit a small safe in your caravan and keep them in the safe or locked in the boot of your car. Do not leave money or documents, such as passports, in a car glovebox, or leave handbags and valuables on view. Do not leave bags in full view when sitting outside at cafés or restaurants. Do not leave valuables unattended on the beach.
- When walking be security-conscious. Avoid unlit streets at night, walk well away from the kerb and carry handbags or shoulder bags on the side away from the kerb. The less of a tourist you appear, the less of a target you are. Never read a map openly in the street or carry a camera over your shoulder.
- Carry only the minimum amount of cash. Distribute cash, travellers' cheques, credit cards and passports amongst your party; do not rely on one person to carry everything. Never carry a wallet in your back pocket. A tuck-away canvas wallet, moneybelt or 'bumbag' can be useful and waterproof versions are available. It is normally advisable not to resist violent theft.
- Do not use street money-changers; in some countries it is illegal.
- Keep a separate note of bank account and credit/debit card numbers and serial numbers of travellers' cheques. Join a card protection plan so that in the event of loss or theft, one telephone call will cancel all your cards and arrange replacements. Carry your credit card issuer/bank's 24-hour UK contact number with you.
- Keep a separate note of your holiday insurance reference number and emergency telephone number.
- Your passport is a valuable document; it is expensive and time-consuming to replace and its loss or theft can lead to serious complications if your identity is later used fraudulently. Keep a separate record of your passport details, preferably in the form of a certified copy of the details pages. Fill in the next-of-kin details in your passport. A photocopy of your birth certificate may also be useful.
- Many large cities have a drug problem with some addicts mugging and pickpocketing to fund their habit. Pickpockets often operate in groups, including children. Stay alert, especially in crowds, on trains, undergrounds and stations, near banks and foreign exchange offices, and when visiting well-known historical and tourist sites.
- Beware of bogus plain-clothes policemen who may ask to see your foreign currency or credit cards and passport. If approached, decline to show your money or to hand over your passport but ask for credentials and offer instead to go to the nearest police station.
- Laws vary from country to country and so does the treatment of offenders; find out something about local laws and customs and respect them. Behave and dress appropriately, particularly when visiting

religious sites, markets and rural communities. Be aware of local attitudes to alcohol consumption. Do not get involved with drugs.

- Do respect Customs regulations. Smuggling is a serious offence and can carry heavy penalties. Do not carry parcels or luggage through Customs for other people and do not cross borders with people you do not know in your vehicle, such as hitchhikers. If you are in someone else's vehicle do not cross the border in it – get out and walk across; you do not know what might be in the vehicle. Do not drive vehicles across borders for other people.
- Hobbies such as birdwatching and train, plane and ship-spotting, combined with the use of cameras or binoculars, may be misunderstood (particularly near military installations) and you may risk arrest. If in doubt, don't.
- In the event of a natural disaster or if trouble flares up, contact family and friends to let them know that you are safe, even if you are nowhere near the problem area. Family and friends may not know exactly where you are and may worry if they think you are in danger.

The Risk of Terrorism

There is a global underlying risk of indiscriminate terrorist attacks, including in places frequented by foreign travellers, but it is important to remember that the overall risk of being involved in a terrorist incident is very low. Injury and death are far more likely through road accidents, swimming, alcohol-related occurrences or health problems.

Most precautions are simple common sense. Make sure you are aware of the political situation in the country you are visiting and keep an eye on the news. Report anything you think is suspicious to the local police. The FCO Travel Advice for each country within the Caravan Europe guides is summarised in the Country Introduction chapters, but situations can change so make a point of reading the FCO's advice before you travel and register for its email alerts, www.fco.gov.uk

British Consular Services Abroad

British Embassy and Consular staff offer practical advice, assistance and support to British travellers abroad. They can, for example, issue replacement passports, help Britons who have been the victims of crime, contact relatives and friends in the event of an accident, illness or death, provide information about transferring funds and provide details of local lawyers, doctors and interpreters. But there are limits to their powers and a British Consul cannot, for example, give legal advice, intervene in court proceedings, put up bail, pay for legal or medical bills, or for funerals or the repatriation of bodies, or undertake work more properly done by banks, motoring organisations and travel insurers.

Most British consulates operate an answerphone service outside office hours giving opening hours and arrangements for handling emergencies. If you require consular help outside office hours you may be charged a fee for calling out a Consular Officer. In countries outside the European Union where there are no British Consulates, you can get help from the embassies and consulates of other EU member states.

If you have anything stolen, e.g. money or passport, report it first to the local police and insist on a statement about the loss. You will need this in order to make a claim on your travel insurance. In the event of a fatal accident or death from whatever cause, get in touch with the nearest consulate at once.

If you commit a criminal offence you must expect to face the consequences. If you are charged with a serious offence, insist on the British Consul being informed. You will be contacted as soon as possible by a Consular Officer who can advise on local procedures, provide access to lawyers and insist that you are treated as well as nationals of the country which is holding you. However, they cannot get you released as a matter of course.

If you need help because something has happened to a friend or relative abroad contact the Consular Assistance Service on 020 7008 1500 (24 hours).

FCO's LOCATE Service

The FCO encourages ALL British nationals travelling abroad to register for this service, even for short trips. If a major catastrophe, crisis or natural disaster occurs the local British embassy or consulate will be able to contact you to check that you are all right and give advice, and if friends and family at home need to get in touch, you can be contacted easily. For more information see www.fco.gov.uk/locate

British and Irish Embassy and Consular Contact Details can be found in the Country Introduction chapters of the relevant Caravan Europe Guides.

Austria

Country Introduction

© iStockphoto.com/wingmar

Austria: mountain view

Population (approx): 8.3 million

Capital: Vienna (population approx 1.7 million)

Area: 83,8758 sq km

Bordered by: Czech Republic, Germany, Hungary, Italy, Liechtenstein, Slovakia, Slovenia, Switzerland

Terrain: Mountainous in south and west; flat or gently sloping in extreme north and east

Climate: Temperate; cold winters with frequent rain in the lowlands and snow in the mountains; moderate summers, sometimes very hot

Highest Point: Grossglockner 3,798m

Language: German

Local Time: GMT or BST + 1, i.e. 1 hour ahead of the UK all year

Currency: Euros divided into 100 cents; £1 = €1.14, €1 = 87 pence (September 2011)

Telephoning: From the UK dial 0043 for Austria and omit the initial zero of the area code of the number you are calling. To call the UK from Austria dial 0044, omitting the initial zero of the area code

Emergency numbers: Police 133; Fire brigade 122; Ambulance 144, or dial 112 for any service (operators speak English).

Public Holidays 2012

Jan 1, 6; Apr 6-9 (Easter); May 1, 17, 28; Jun 7; Aug 15; Oct 26 (National Day); Nov 1; Dec 8, 25, 26.

Public Holidays 2013

Jan 1, 6; Mar 29-Apr 01 (Easter); May 1, 9, 20, 30; Aug 15; Oct 26 (National Day); Nov 1; Dec 8, 25, 26.
School summer holidays last the whole of July, August and early September

Tourist Office

AUSTRIAN NATIONAL TOURIST OFFICE
9-11 RICHMOND BUILDINGS
LONDON W1D 3HF
Tel: 0845 1011 818
www.austria.info/uk
holiday@austria.info

The following introduction to Austria should be read in conjunction with the important information contained in the Handbook chapters at the front of this guide.

Camping and Caravanning

There are approximately 500 campsites in Austria. Most campsites and local tourist boards issue a 'Gaste Karte' entitling the holder to reduced charges at some attractions and facilities, such as cable cars. Discounts vary from region to region. There are around 150 campsites that are open all year, mostly in or near to ski resorts.

A Camping Card International (CCI) is essential and entitles you to a reduction at some sites. A cash deposit is often payable on arrival against a site barrier 'swipe' card. You may find that you are also charged a tourist tax and a daily amount for rubbish disposal.

Casual/wild camping is not encouraged and is prohibited in Vienna, in the Tyrol and in forests and nature reserves. Permission to park a caravan should be obtained in advance from the owners of private land, or from the local town hall or police station in the case of common land or state property.

Country Information

Cycling

There is an extensive network of cycle routes, many of which follow dedicated long-distance cycle and foot paths, such as the 360 km cycle lane that follows the Danube from Passau, on the German border, to Hainburg, near the Hungarian and Slovakian borders.

Many cities encourage cyclists with designated cycle lanes. In one-way streets cyclists may travel in a cycle lane in contraflow if this is allowed by signs. A Citybike hire scheme operates in Vienna from more than 60 rental offices situated close to underground/metro stations. For more information see www.citybikewien.at or telephone 0810 500500 in Austria. There are eight signposted mountain bike routes between 10 and 42 kilometres long in the Vienna woods. You are allowed to transport bicycles on metro trains.

The wearing of cycle helmets is compulsory for children under 12 years.

Transportation of Bicycles

Bicycles may be carried on the roof of a car as well as at the rear. When carried at the rear, the total width must not extend beyond the width of the vehicle (including the external mirrors), and the rear lights and number plate must remain visible. The driver's view should not be obstructed.

Electricity and Gas

Current on campsites varies between 4 and 16 amps. Plugs have two round pins and increasingly campsites have CEE connections. Electricity points tend to be in locked boxes, making it necessary to check polarity quickly on arrival before the box is locked. Arrangements also need to be made for the box to be unlocked if making an early departure.

Some sites in Austria make a one-off charge – usually of €2 or €3 however long your stay – for connection to the electricity supply, which is then metered at a rate per kilowatt hour (kwh) of between 60 and 75 cents. This connection charge can make one-night stays more expensive.

The full range of Campingaz cylinders is widely available.

*See **Electricity and Gas** in the section **DURING YOUR STAY.***

Entry Formalities

There are no identity checks at the borders with EU countries or Switzerland nor are there Customs controls with EU countries but checks on goods may still be carried out at the border with Switzerland.

British and Irish passport holders may stay in Austria for up to three months without a visa. Visitors arriving at a campsite or hotel must complete a registration form.

Regulations for Pets

*See **Pet Travel Scheme** under **Documents** in the section **PLANNING AND TRAVELLING.***

Medical Services

Minor matters can be dealt with by staff at pharmacies (apotheke). Pharmacies operate a rota system for night and Sunday duty; when closed a notice is often displayed giving the addresses of the nearest pharmacies that are open.

Treatment by doctors and hospital outpatient treatment is free of charge provided the doctor or hospital is contracted to the local health insurance office (Gebietskrankenkasse). To be covered for hospital treatment you will need a doctor's referral. In-patient treatment will incur a daily charge for the first 28 days and this is generally non-refundable.

Only a limited amount of dental treatment is covered under the state healthcare system. You will need to present your European Health Insurance Card (EHIC) – check the expiry date before you travel.

It is possible to get a refund of up to 80% from one of the regional health insurance offices in Austria for any private medical treatment (including dentists).

If you enjoy hiking and outdoor sports you should seek medical advice before you travel about preventative measures and immunisation against tick-borne encephalitis, a potentially serious and debilitating viral disease of the central nervous system which is endemic from spring to autumn. Lyme disease is an equally serious tick-borne infection for which there is no preventative vaccine. Ticks are found in rural and forested areas, particularly in long grass, bushes, hedgerows and woods, and in scrubland and areas where animals wander. If you think you might be at risk use an insect repellent containing DEET, wear long sleeves and long trousers, inspect the body for ticks after outdoor activity removing them with tweezers, and avoid unpasteurised dairy products in risk areas. See www.tickalert.org, email info@tickalert.org or telephone 01943 468010.

You are strongly recommended to obtain comprehensive travel and medical insurance before travelling to Austria, such as The Caravan Club's Red Pennant Overseas Holiday Insurance – see www.caravanclub.co.uk/redpennant

*See **Medical Matters** in the section **DURING YOUR STAY.***

Opening Hours

Banks – Mon-Fri 8am-12.30pm & 1.30pm-3pm (5.30pm Thu), main branches do not close for lunch; closed Saturday and Sunday.

Museums – Mon-Fri 10am-6pm (summer), 9am-4pm (winter); Sat, Sun & public holidays 9am-6pm.

Post Offices – Mon-Fri 8am-12pm & 2pm-6pm; city post offices do not close for lunch; in some towns post offices open on Sat 9am-12pm.

Shops – Mon-Fri 8am-6pm; some open until 7.30pm Thu; some close 12pm-2pm for lunch; Sat 8am-5pm.

Safety and Security

Most visits to Austria are trouble-free, but visitors should take sensible precautions to avoid becoming a victim of crime at crowded tourist sites and around major railway stations and city centre parks after dark. Pickpockets and muggers operate in and around the city centre of Vienna, including in restaurants, cafés and on public transport.

Drivers, especially on the autobahns in Lower Austria, should be wary of approaches by bogus plain clothes police officers, possibly wearing baseball caps marked 'Polizei' and travelling in unmarked cars. In all traffic-related matters police officers will be in uniform and unmarked vehicles will have a flashing sign in the rear window which reads 'Stopp –Polizei – Folgen'. Police officers may be in plain clothes but in any case will identify themselves unasked. If in any doubt contact the police on the emergency number 133 or 112 and ask for confirmation that plain clothes police officers are patrolling the area. Drivers have the right to ask to speak to a uniformed police officer.

The winter sports season lasts from December to March, or the end of May in higher regions. If you plan to ski you are recommended to contact the Austrian National Tourist Office in London for advice on weather and avalanche conditions before travelling, and take local advice throughout your stay. Proper protection from the weather is essential, as well as provisions for emergencies. Seek avalanche information locally – there are helpline telephone numbers for the Avalanche Warning Service in all the major ski areas or visit www.avalanches.org. Most avalanches occur in spring. In most areas of the country children under the age of 15 are legally required to wear a helmet when skiing.

Austria shares with the rest of Europe an underlying threat from terrorism. Attacks could be indiscriminate and against civilian targets.

*See **Safety and Security** in the section **DURING YOUR STAY.***

British Embassy

JAURESGASSE 12
1030 VIENNA
Tel: (01) 716130
http://ukinaustria.fco.gov.uk/en/
E: viennaconsularenquiries@fco.gov.uk

There are also Honorary Consulates in Bregenz, Graz, Innsbruck and Salzburg.

Irish Embassy

ROTENTURMSTRASSE 16-18, 5th FLOOR
1010 VIENNA
Tel: (01) 7154246
www.embassyofireland.at E: viennaembassy@dfa.ie

Customs Regulations

Alcohol and Tobacco

For import allowances for alcohol and tobacco products see ***Customs Regulations*** in the section ***PLANNING AND TRAVELLING.***

Documents

Driving Licence

If you hold a UK driving licence which does not bear your photograph you should carry your passport as further proof of identity, or obtain a photocard licence.

Passport

You are advised to carry your passport at all times.

Vehicle(s)

You should carry your vehicle registration certificate (V5C), insurance details and MOT certificate (if applicable). If you are not the owner of your car or motorhome, you should carry a letter of authority from the owner permitting you to drive it.

*See also **Documents** in the section **PLANNING AND TRAVELLING.***

Money

Travellers' cheques can only be changed in banks. They are not generally accepted as a means of payment.

Cash dispensers (Bankomaten) have instructions in English.

The major credit cards are accepted by shops, restaurants, and petrol stations but not as widely as elsewhere in Europe. Small shops and supermarkets, restaurants and hotels may not accept them.

Carry your credit card issuers'/banks' 24-hour UK contact numbers in case of loss or theft of your cards.

Motoring

Alcohol

The maximum permitted level of alcohol in the bloodstream is 0.049%, i.e. lower than that permitted in the UK. Penalties for exceeding this limit are severe. A lower limit of virtually zero applies to drivers who have held a full driving licence for less than two years.

Breakdown Service

The motoring organisation, ÖAMTC, operates a breakdown service 24 hours a day on all roads. The emergency number is 120 throughout the country from a land line or mobile phone. Motorists pay €117 during the day and €156 at night (2011); towing charges also apply. Payment by credit card is accepted.

Members of AIT and FIA affiliated clubs, such as the Caravan Club, qualify for reduced charges on presentation of a valid Club membership card.

Essential Equipment

*See **Motoring – Equipment** in the section **PLANNING AND TRAVELLING.***

Lights

The use of dipped headlights during daytime is no longer compulsory but they must be used in poor visibility or bad weather. Headlight flashing is used as a warning of approach, not as an indication that a driver is giving way.

Reflective Jackets/Waistcoats

If your vehicle breaksdown or you are in an accident you must wear a reflective jacket or waistcoat when getting out of your vehicle (compliant with EU Standard EN471). This includes when setting up a warning triangle. It is also recommended that a passenger who leaves the vehicle, for example, to assist with a repair, should also wear one. Keep the jackets within easy reach inside your vehicle, not in the boot.

Child Restraint System

Children under 14 years of age and less than 1.5 metres in height, must use a suitable child restraint system for their height and weight when travelling in the front and rear of a vehicle.

Vehicles that do not have such protection i.e. two seater sports cars, must not be used to transport children under 14 years of age at all. Children under 14 years of age but over 1.5 metres in height must use the adult seat belt.

Children under 14 years of age but over 1.35 metres are allowed to use a 3-point seat belt without a special child seat, on the condition that the seat belt does not come across the child's throat or neck.

Winter Driving

From 1 November to 15 April vehicles, including those registered abroad, must be fitted with winter tyres marked M&S (mus & snow). The use of snow chains on the driving axle will only be allowed as an alternative where roads are fully covered by snow and/or ice and providing road surfaces will not be damaged by the chains.

From 15 November to 15 March all vehicles over 3,500 kg must have winter tyres fitted on at least one driving axle and carry snow chains, whether there is snow on the road or not. Snow chains are compulsory where there are signs indicating that they are required on a particular road.

Snow chains can be hired or purchased from Polar Automotive Ltd, tel 01892 519933, www.snowchains.com, email: polar@snowchains.com (10% discount for Caravan Club members).

The maximum recommended speed for vehicles with snow chains is generally 50 km/h.

Fuel

*See **Fuel** under **Motoring – Advice** in the section **PLANNING AND TRAVELLING.***

Most petrol stations are open from 8am to 8pm. Motorway service stations and some petrol stations in larger cities stay open 24 hours. Fuel is normally cheaper at self-service filling stations.

LPG (flüssiggas) is available at a limited number of outlets – a list should be available on www.oeamtc.at

Parking

Regulations concerning the parking of motorhomes and caravans vary according to region, but basically severe restrictions apply in areas protected for their natural beauty or landscape and beside lakes.

A zigzag line marked on the road indicates that parking is prohibited. Blue lines indicate a blue zone (Kurzparkzone) where parking is restricted to a period fof upto two hours and you need to purchase a voucher (Parkschein) from a local shop, bank or petrol station.

Most cities have 'Pay and Display' machines, parking meters or parking discs, and in main tourist areas the instructions are in English. Ilegally-parked cars may be impounded or clamped. In some cities signs indicating 'm-parking' or 'mobile-parking' mean that local residents can pay parking fees via a mobile phone.

Large areas of Vienna are pedestrianised and parking places are limited. However, there are several underground car parks in Vienna District 1.

You may be required to leave your sidelights on when parking on the road at night. A red road sign or a red band attached to lamp posts indicates where street lights are switched off at midnight.

*See also **Parking Facilities for the Disabled** under **Motoring – Advice** in the section **PLANNING AND TRAVELLING.***

Priority

Outside built-up areas, road signs on main roads indicate where traffic has priority. On roads where there are no such signs, priority at intersections is given to traffic from the right. On steep mountain roads there is no binding priority rule; the vehicle which can more easily reverse to a parking place is obliged to do so.

Buses have priority when leaving a bus stop. Do not overtake school buses with flashing yellow lights which have stopped to let children on and off. Trams have priority even if coming from the left and priority must always be given to emergency vehicles.

In heavy traffic, drivers must not enter an intersection unless their exit is clear, even if they have priority or if the lights are green.

Roads

Austria has a well developed and engineered network of roads classified as: federal motorways (A roads), expressways (S' roads), provincial (B roads) and local (L roads). There are over 12100 km of motorways and expressways. Many roads have a name as well as a number, the name referring to the area through which the road passes, e.g. the Brenner Autobahn (A13), the Tauern Autobahn (A10), the Süd Autobahn (A2) and the West Autobahn (A1).

Road Signs and Markings

Most signs conform to international usage. The following are exceptions:

Diversions

Street lights not on all night

Tram turns at yellow or red

Recently we have been advised by members that they have been stopped and fined in Austria for using roads that prohibit trailers and caravans. This is indicated by the below sign:

If there is an additional sign which shows a weight limit, then this means the gross vehicle weight of the trailer and you have to stay below this gross vehicle weight if you wish to use the road. You can also find these signs with a length limit.

Some other signs that are also in use which you may find useful Include:

Abblendlicht – *Dipped headlights*

Alle richtungen – *All directions*

Bauarbeiten – *Roadworks*

Durchfahrt verboten – *No through traffic*

Einbahn – *One-way street*

Fussgänger – *Pedestrians*

Beschrankung für halten oder parken – *Stopping or parking restricted*

Lawinen gefahr – *Avalanche danger*

Links einbiegen – *Turn left*

Raststätte – *Service area*

Rechts einbiegen – *Turn right*

Strasse gesperrt – *Road closed*

Überholen verboten – *No passing*

Umleitung – *Detour*

Do not cross a continuous white or yellow line in the centre of the carriageway.

Traffic Lights

At traffic lights a flashing green light indicates the approach of the end of the green phase. An orange light combined with the red light indicates that the green phase is imminent.

Speed Limits

*See **Speed Limits Table** under **Motoring – Advice** in the section **PLANNING AND TRAVELLING.***

Exceptions

If the total combined weight of the car and caravan outfit or a motorhome exceeds 3,500 kg the speed limit on motorways is reduced to 80 km/h (50 mph) and on other roads outside built-up areas to 70 km/h (43 mph). A built-up area starts from the place name sign at the entrance to a town or village.
On motorways where the general speed limit for solo vehicles is 130 km/h (81 mph) overhead electronic message signs may restrict speed to 100 km/h (62 mph). Between 10pm and 5am solo cars are restricted to 110 km/h (68 mph) on the A10 (Tauern), A12 (Inntal), A13 (Brenner) and A14 (Rheintal). There is a general speed limit of 60 km/h (37 mph) on most roads in the Tyrol, unless indicated otherwise.

The minimum speed limit on motorways, as indicated by a rectangular blue sign depicting a white car, is 60 km/h (37 mph).

A number of towns have a general speed limit of 30 km/h (18 mph), except where a higher speed limit is indicated.

Navigation systems equipped with speed camera/speed gun detectors are prohibited, but those with maps indicating the location of speed cameras are tolerated.

Towing

The Austrian authorities are concerned about overloaded caravans and motorhomes and may check at border crossings to ensure the towed vehicle does not exceed the kerbside weight of the towing vehicle, or the weight stipulated on your Vehicle Registration Certificate (V5C).

Traffic Jams

In recent years traffic has increased on the A1 from Vienna to the German border (the West Autobahn) because of the growth in the numbers of visitors to the Czech Republic, Slovakia and Hungary. There are usually queues at the border posts with these countries too. As a result, traffic has also increased on the ring road around Vienna and on the A4 (Ost Autobahn).

Other bottlenecks occur on the A10 (Salzburg to Villach) before the Tauern and Katschberg tunnels, the A12 (Kufstein to Landeck) before the Perjen tunnel and before Landeck, and the A13 (Innsbruck to Brenner) between Steinach and the Italian border. Busy sections on other roads are the S35/S6 between Kirchdorf or Bruck an der Mur and the A9, the B320/E651 in the Schladming and Gröbming areas, and the B179 Fern Pass.

Violation of Traffic Regulations

Police are authorised to impose and collect on-the-spot fines from drivers who violate traffic regulations and you may pay with cash or a credit card. For higher fines you will be required to pay a deposit and the remainder within two weeks. An official receipt should be issued. A points system operates which applies to drivers of Austrian and foreign-registered vehicles.

Motorways

Emergency telephones on motorways are orange in colour and are 2 km to 3 km apart. A flashing orange light at the top of telephone posts indicates danger ahead.

Motorway Tolls – Vehicles under 3,500 kg

Drivers of all motor vehicles under 3,500 kg with two or more axles using motorways and expressways (A and S roads) must purchase a motorway vignette (sticker). One vignette covers your caravan as well.

Vignettes may be purchased at all major border crossings into Austria and from OeAMTC offices, larger petrol stations and post offices in Austria. A two-month vignette is available for a car (with or without a trailer) or a motorhome at a cost of €23. Also available is a 10 day vignette at €7.90 and a one year vignette at €76.50 (2011 tariffs, subject to change).

Failure to display a vignette incurs a fine of at least €120, plus the cost of the vignette. Credit cards or foreign currency may be used in payment. If you have visited Austria before, make sure you remove your old sticker.

There are special toll sections in Austria which are excluded from the vignette and where the toll needs to be paid at respective toll points. These include A10 Tauern tunnel, A13 Brenner motorway and S16 Alberg tunnel.

Motorway Tolls – Vehicles over 3,500 kg

Tolls for vehicles over 3,500 kg are calculated according to the number of axles and EURO emissions category and are collected electronically by means of a small box (called the GO-Box) fixed to your vehicle's windscreen. The GO-Box uses a high frequency signal to communicate with around 400 fixed-installation toll points covering the whole country, making it possible to effect an automatic toll deduction without slowing traffic. They are available for a one-off handling fee of €5 from approximately 220 points of sale – mainly petrol stations – along the primary road network in Austria and neighbouring countries (although the availability of GO-Box facilities may not be well advertised), and at all major border crossing points. Automatic vending machines are also being installed in order to extend the network of points of sale.

Drivers can either pre-pay by means of a stored toll credit system, or post-pay with a credit card. Tolls are calculated according to the number of axles on a vehicle; those with two axles are charged between €0.146 and €0.178 per kilometre + 20% VAT, according to the vehicle's emissions rating.

This system can seem complex and you may like to visit www.go-maut.at/go or www.asfinag.at for more information, including a list of points of sale and general instructions on how to use the GO-Box. Alternatively telephone 0043 19551266 or email info@go-maut.at for help before you travel, or call 0800 40012400 (from Austria, Germany or Switzerland) or 00800 40012400 from the UK. Operators speak English.

Drivers of vehicles close to the 3,500 kg limit are advised to carry with them documentation confirming their vehicle's maximum permitted laden weight. If your Vehicle Registration Certificate (V5C) does not clearly state this, you will need to produce alternative certification, e.g. from a weighbridge.

This distance-related toll system does not apply to a car/caravan combination even if its total laden weight is over 3,500 kg, unless the laden weight of the towing vehicle itself exceeds that weight.

Korridor Vignette

A special vignette, the 'Korridor Vignette' is required on the A14 in the region of Bregenz. Vehicles up to 3,500 kg without a standard motorway vignette need this special vignette to drive along the 23 km stretch (corridor) between Hohenems (junction 23 on the A14) and Hörbranz (junction 1) at the German border. The vignette is available from petrol stations in the area and at the border and costs €2 for a single journey, €4 return. Vehicles over 3,500 kg must use a GO-Box – see above.

In addition, separate tolls are payable on many roads and tunnels in mountainous regions.

*See the sections **Alpine Passes** and **Major Alpine Road Tunnels** in the chapter **Mountain Passes and Tunnels.***

Touring

Austria is divided into nine federal regions, namely Burgenland, Carinthia (Kärnten), Lower Austria (Niederösterreich), Salzburg, Styria (Steiermark), Tyrol (Tirol), Upper Austria (Oberösterreich), Vienna (Wien) and Voralberg.

Culinary specialities include 'backhendl' (fried chicken in batter), 'Wiener schnitzel' (veal escalope), goulash and cakes such as 'apfel strudel' (apple pastry) and 'sacher torte' (chocolate gateau). Wines are good and local beers are pleasant and light.
A 10-15% service charge is included in restaurant bills, but it is customary to add a further 5% tip if satisfied with the service.

The Vienna Card offers unlimited free public transport and discounts at museums, restaurants, theatres and shops. The Card is valid for three days and is available from hotels, tourist information and public transport offices; see www.wienkarte.at

A Salzburg Card and an Innsbruck Card are also available – see www.austria.info/uk or contact the Austrian National Tourist Office for more information.

Local Travel

All major cities have efficient, integrated public transport systems including underground and light rail systems, trams and buses. Two to five people travelling as a group by train can buy an Einfach-Raus-Ticket (ERT), which is good for a day's unlimited travel on all Austrian regional trains – see www.oebb.at (English option) for more information or ask at any station.

In Vienna there are travel concessions on public transport for senior citizens (show your passport as proof of age). Buy a ticket from a tobacconist or from a ticket machine in an underground station. Otherwise single tickets are available from vending machines in the vehicles themselves – have plenty of coins ready. Tickets are also available for periods of 24 and 72 hours. Children under six travel free and children under 15 travel free on Sundays, public holidays and during school holidays.

Car ferry services operate throughout the year on the River Danube, and hydrofoil and hovercraft services transport passengers from Vienna to Bratislava (Slovakia) and to Budapest (Hungary).

All place names used in the Site Entry listings which follow can be found in the Strassen & Städte Superatlas for Austria and Europe published by Freytag & Berndt, scale 1 cm to 1.5 km and 1 cm to 3.5 km, see www.freytagberndt.com

ABERSEE *B3* (Rural) *47.73348, 13.42826* **Campingpark Abersee, Reith 22, 5342 Abersee (Salzburg) [(06227) 3512; fax 35124; campingpark.abersee@aon.at]** Fr St Gilgen on B158 dir Abersee. Turn L under underpass into Seestrasse, in 1km L at site sp, site on R in 250m. Call at farm opp (not guesthouse adj) if recep clsd. Sm, mkd pitch, pt shd; wc; chem disp; shwrs inc; el pnts (16A) metered; shop 1km; rest, snacks 500m; playgrnd; htd, covrd pool 5km; lake sw 200m; 20% statics; dogs €2.20; bus 1km; quiet. "Vg farm site in beautiful setting; excel walking, boating activities."
1 May-31 Oct. € 19.30 2008*

ABERSEE *B3* (2km E Rural) *47.71336, 13.45138* **Camping Schönblick, Gschwendt 33, 5342 Abersee (Salzburg) [(06137) 7042; fax 704214; laimer.schoenblick@aon.at; www.camping-schoenblick.at]** Fr B158 at km 36 dir Schiffstation & site in 1km on L. Med, mkd pitch, pt sl, terr, some hdstg, pt shd; wc; chem disp; shwrs €0.80; el pnts (10A) €1.80; gas; lndtte; shop & 1km; tradsmn; rest, snacks 300m; lake sw adj; 40% statics; dogs €1; quiet; ccard acc; CCI. "Beautiful, friendly, family-run site nr lakeside opp St Wolfgang town; ferry stn; excel san facs but stretched at busy times; walks & cycle path fr site." 1 May-15 Oct. € 17.20 2008*

There aren't many sites open at this time of year. We'd better phone ahead to check the one we're heading for is open.

ABERSEE *B3* (1km NW Rural) *47.73910, 13.40065* **Camping Birkenstrand, Schwand 18, 5342 Abersee (Salzburg) [tel/fax (06227) 3029; camp@birkenstrand.at; www.birkenstrand.at]** Fr B158 fr St Gilgen, on ent Abersee turn L at km 32 twds lake. Site on both sides of rd in 1km. Med, mkd pitch, pt sl, unshd; wc; chem disp; shwrs €0.70; el pnts (10A) metered; lndtte (inc dryer); shop 100m; rest, bar 100m, snacks; BBQ; playgrnd; lake sw adj; boat & cycle hire; golf 15km; entmnt; TV rm; 20% statics; dogs €2.50; Eng spkn; adv bkg; quiet. "Excel area for walking, cycling; lovely situation; immac site." 15 Apr-15 Oct. € 17.80 2009*

ABERSEE *B3* (1km NW Rural) *47.73656, 13.43250* **Camping Wolfgangblick, Seestrasse 115, 5342 Abersee (Salzburg) [(06227) 3475; fax 3218; camping@wolfgangblick.at; www.wolfgangblick.at]** Fr B158 fr St Gilgen, on ent Abersee turn L at km 32 twds lake. Site in 1km adj Camping Birkenstrand. Med, mkd pich; hdstg, pt shd; wc; chem disp; shwrs €0.70; el pnts (12A) metered; lndtte; shop; rest; snacks; bar; playgrnd; lake beach adj; 50% statics; dogs €2.90; poss cr; Eng spkn; quiet; ccard acc. "Pleasant site; gd, friendly family run site by lake; helpful owners; beautiful scenery; excel for walking & cycling; on bus route to Salzburg and local vills; can be crowded, adv bkg helpful." 1 May-30 Sep. € 19.70 2011*

ABERSEE *B3* (3km NW Rural) *47.73945, 13.40245* **Romantik Camping Wolfgangsee Lindenstrand, Schwand 19, 5342 St Gilgen (Salzburg) [(06227) 32050; fax 320524; camping@lindenstrand.at; www.lindenstrand.at]** Fr St Gilgen take B158 dir Bad Ischl. In 4km at km 32 foll sp Schwand, site on L on lakeside. Lge, mkd pitch, hdstg, pt shd; htd wc; chem disp; serviced pitches; shwrs inc; el pnts (10A) metered; shop; tradsmn; rest 1km; playgrnd; lake adj; watersports; 10% statics; dogs €3.20; phone; bus & boat to local towns & Salzburg; Eng spkn; adv bkg; quiet; ccard acc; red low ssn; CCI. "Lovely site; rec adv bkg for lakeside pitches."
Easter-15 Oct. € 19.00 2009*

⊞ **ACHENKIRCH** *C2* (3km S Rural) *47.49955, 11.70641* **Alpen-Caravanpark Achensee, Achenkirch 17, 6215 Achenkirch (Tirol) [(05246) 6239; fax 6626; info@camping-achensee.com; www.camping-achensee.com]** Fr A12/E60 exit Wiesing/Achensee turn L on B181 (Achenseestrasse), sp to camp on L at N end of lake. Lge, pt sl, pt shd; htd wc; chem disp; shwrs €1; el pnts (16A) €2.50; gas; lndtte; shop; rest; snacks; bar; playgrnd; lake beach & sw; skilift; skibus; TV; bus; phone; noisy; 20% statics; dogs €4; adv bkg. "Sm pitches; steamer trips, boating on lake; beautiful scenery; chair lifts; lake deep, not suitable for children." € 21.00 2008*

AFRITZ *D3* (500m N Rural) *46.73701, 13.76874* **Camping Bodner, Seestrasse 27, 9542 Afritz-am-Zee (Kärnten) [(04247) 2579; fax 29990; office@camping-bodner.at; www.camping-bodner.at]** Fr Villach, take B94 twd Feldkirchen, turn L after 4km onto B98 sp Radenthein. N of Afritz, after Gassen, turn L, site sp. Med, some hdstg, pt sl, pt shd; wc; chem disp; mv service pnt; shwrs €1; el pnts (4-6A) inc; gas; lndtte; shop 1.5km; rest; snacks; bar; BBQ; playgrnd; lake sw adj; sailing; dogs €1.50; quiet. "Family-run site; gd walking country - both mountains & flat." 1 May-30 Sep. € 19.80 2010*

ALTAUSSEE *C3* (1.5km S Rural) **Bauernhofcamping Temel, Puchen 39, 8992 Altaussee (Steiermark) [(03622) 71968]** N fr Bad Aussee dir Altausseer See, site sp. Sm, hdstg, pt sl, unshd; wc; chem disp; mv service pnt; shwrs €0.50; el pnts €2; shop 1.5km; rest 800m; lake sw 800m; dogs €1; quiet. "Well-kept, peaceful site amidst beautiful scenery; friendly owner; idyllic." 1 May-30 Sep. € 13.60 2009*

⊞ **ALTENMARKT IM PONGAU** *C3* (800m S Rural) *47.37145, 13.41915* **Camping Passrucker, Zauchenseestrasse 341, 5541 Altenmarkt (Salzburg) [(06452) 7328; fax 7821; camping.passrucker@sbg.at; www.camping-passrucker.at]** Exit A10 junc 63 onto B99 to Altenmarkt. In town cent turn R & foll site sp. Med, pt shd; htd wc; chem disp; mv service pnt; baby facs; sauna; solarium; shwrs inc; el pnts (13A) metered; lndtte; shop high ssn; playgrnd; sm pool; fitness rm; skibus; TV rm; 50% statics (sep area); dogs €1.50; Eng spkn; adv bkg; quiet; red long stay; CCI. "Pretty town in lovely area; gd walking; higher prices in winter; excel san facs; friendly owner." ♦ € 21.00 2010*

ANGER *C4* (Rural) **Camping Anger, 8184 Anger (Steiermark) [(03175) 2211]** Fr N on B72 go strt over town rndabt, ignore 1st green sp on R with icons (inc camping) & foll next green sp at junc. Go strt on, campsite ent after hedge & bef car park. Fr S go to rndabt & double-back, then as above. Sm, shd; wc; shwrs inc; el pnts (10A) metered; shop, rest, snacks, bar in town; playgrnd; pool adj; games area; Eng spkn; rd noise in day, quiet at night. "Excel, simple, friendly site; gd walking, cycling in area; if site locked ask at adj pool." € 11.50 2008*

ASCHACH AN DER DONAU *B3* (6km N Rural) *48.42026, 13.98400* **Camping Kaiserhof, Kaiserau 1, 4082 Aschach-an-der-Donau (Oberösterreich) [(07273) 62210; fax 622113; kaiserhof@aschach.at; www.pension-kaiserhof.at]** Fr town cent foll site sp. Site adj rv & Gasthof Kaiserhof. Sm, pt shd; htd wc; chem disp; mv service pnt; shwrs; el pnts; Indtte; shop 6km; tradsmn; rest; snacks; bar; playgrnd; 80% statics; poss cr; Eng spkn; ccard acc; red long stay/CCI. "Beautiful location on Danube." ♦ 15 Apr-30 Sep. € 19.00 2010*

ATTERSEE *B3* (1km S Rural) *47.9121, 13.5307* **Camping Wimroither Mühle, Mühlbach 5, 4864 Attersee (Oberösterreich) [tel/fax (07666) 7749]** Exit A/E60/E551 junc 243 twd Attersee. In 2km at town sp turn R to site down unclass rd in 200m. Narr lane. Med, pt sl, pt shd; wc; chem disp; shwrs €1; el pnts (16A) €2.20; Indtte; sm shop & 300m; rest 300m; snacks; lake sw 250m; 60% statics; dogs; poss cr; adv bkg; quiet. "Conv Salzkammergut & Dachstein with lovely scenery." 1 Apr-31 Oct. € 13.00 2008*

ATTERSEE *B3* (15km S Rural) *47.80100, 13.48266* **Inselcamping, Unterburgau 37, 4866 Unterach-am-Attersee (Oberösterreich) [(07665) 8311; fax 7255; camping@inselcamp.at; www.inselcamp.at]** Leave A1 at junc 243 St Georgen/Attersee, foll B151 to Unterach fr Attersee vill. Site sp on app to Unterach. Med, pt shd; wc; chem disp; mv service pnt; shwrs €1; el pnts (6A) €2; gas; shop; supmkt nr; tradsmn; snacks; lake sw; shgl beach; 25% statics; dogs €2; clsd 1200-1400; poss v cr; Eng spkn; adv bkg; quiet; CCI. "Excel site; helpful owner; 5 min walk to attractive town; conv Salzburg & Salzkammergut; lots to see locally; gd boat trips; extra for lakeside pitches - some with boat mooring." 1 May-15 Sep. € 15.50 2009*

⊞ **AU** *C1* (500m S Rural) *47.31604, 9.99881* **Camping Köb, Neudorf 356, 6883 Au-im-Bregenzerwald (Voralberg) [(05515) 2331; fax 23314; info@campingaustria.at; www.axtres.net/campingaustria/]** Fr W on B200 fr Dornbirn sp Bregenzerwald, take 2nd turn R after tunnel at end of Au. Site immed on L. NB B200 not open to c'vans Au to Warth. Sm, pt shd; htd wc; chem disp; mv service pnt; shwrs €0.70; el pnts (6A) metered; Indtte; shop 100m; tradsmn; rest, bar 300m; pool 200m; internet; 10% statics; no dogs; phone adj; bus 100m; poss cr; adv bkg; quiet; CCI. "Mountain scenery; excel, secluded, well-run, family site; helpful owner." € 22.00 2009*

⊞ **BAD AUSSEE** *C3* (2.5km NE Rural) *47.61651, 13.81248* **Camping Staud'nwirt, Grundlseerstrasse 21, 8990 Bad Aussee-Reith (Steiermark) [(03622) 54565; fax 52427; gh.staudnwirt@aussee.at; www.aussee.at/staudnwirt]** Fr B145 E or W turn into Bad Aussee & foll sp thro vill cent twd Grundlsee. Gasthof Staudnwirt on L, with site sp opp on R. Sm, pt sl, shd; wc; chem disp; mv service pnt; shwrs inc; el pnts (16A) €2.10; gas; shop; rest; playgrnd; lake sw; 50% statics; dogs; skibus; poss cr; quiet; ccard acc; red CCI. "Pitches both side of rd - site away fr hotel in orchard easier access; friendly site; gd rest." € 16.00 2008*

I'll go online and tell the Club what we think of the campsites we've visited – www.caravanclub.co.uk/europereport

BAD AUSSEE *C3* (10km NE Rural) *47.63884, 13.90212* **Camping Veit-Gössl, Gössl 145, 8993 Grundlsee (Steiermark) [(03622) 8689; fax 86894; office@campingveit.at; www.campingveit.at]** Turn R off B145 (Bad Ischl to Mitterndorf) thro Bad Aussee foll sps Grundlsee, onto Gössl at end of lake. Site on lakeside, ent adj gasthof off mini-rndbt. Sm, sl, terr, pt shd; wc; chem disp; shwrs €1.10; el pnts (10-16A) €2; gas; Indtte; shop, rest, snacks, bar adj; tradsmn; playgrnd adj; sand beach; lake sw; dogs €1; bus; adv bkg; quiet but some rd noise; Eng spkn. "Excel, well-kept site; gd san facs; friendly, helpful owner; lovely setting; boat hire or ideal for own boat; beautiful views fr all pitches; gd walking country." 1 May-30 Sep. € 14.60 2008*

BAD AUSSEE *C3* (10km NE Rural) *47.63783, 13.90365* **Campingplatz Gössl, Gössl 201, 8993 Grundlsee (Steiermark) [(03622) 81810; fax 81814; office@campinggoessl.com; www.campinggoessl.com]** Fr B145 foll sp to Grundlsee, then along lake to Gössl at far end. Ent adj gasthof off mini-rndbt, go thro Camping Veit, then on L. Med, pt shd; wc; shwrs inc; el pnts (10A) metered + conn fee; Indtte; shop adj; tradsmn; shop, rest, snacks, bar 500m; playgrnd adj; sand beach & lake sw adj; fishing; boating (no motor boats); dogs €1; bus; adv bkg; quiet. "Excel walking cent; scenery v beautiful; local gasthofs vg; daily bus & ferry services; v clean facs." 1 May-31 Oct. € 17.00 2008*

⊞ **BAD GASTEIN** *C2* (3km N Rural) *47.13421, 13.13137* **Kur-Camping Erlengrund, Erlengrundstrasse 6, 5640 Bad Gastein (Salzburg) [(06434) 30205; fax 30208; office@kurcamping-gastein.at; www.kurcamping-gastein.at]** Exit A10/E55 at junc 46 onto B311 thro St Johann to Lend, then S on B167 thro Bad Hofgastein. On N o'skts of Bad Gastein turn L 300m after BP g'ge to avoid narr town streets. Lge, mkd pitch, some hdstg, pt shd; htd wc; chem disp; mv service pnt; serviced pitches; baby facs; shwrs; el pnts (16A) metered; mains gas conn to some pitches; Indtte (inc dryer); shop; tradsmn; rest adj; playgrnd; htd pool; tennis; golf; fishing; ski bus; skilift 4km; wifi; cab TV; 30% statics; dogs €2.50; adv bkg; quiet; ccard acc; red CCI. "Excel ski area with over 50 ski lifts & 9 x-country trails." € 25.50 2011*

⊞ **BAD GLEICHENBERG** *C4* (3km SE Rural) *46.87470, 15.93360* **Camping Feriendorf in Thermenland, Haus Nr 240, 8344 Bairisch-Kölldorf(Steiermark) [(03159) 3941; fax 288411; camping.bk@aon.at; www.bairisch-koelldorf.at]** Exit A2 at Gleisdorf Süd onto B68 dir Feldbach. Take B66 dir Bad Gleichenberg & at 2nd rndabt turn L, site sp. Med, unshd; htd wc; chem disp; mv service pnt; baby facs; shwrs; el pnts (16A) metered; gas; lndtte (inc dryer); tradsmn; rest; snacks; bar; BBQ; playgrnd; covrd pool; lake sw; tennis 600m; cycle hire; games area; golf 3km; 10% statics; dogs €0.70; adv bkg; quiet. ♦ € 20.00 (CChq acc) 2009*

⊞ **BAD HOFGASTEIN** *C2* (1km S Rural) *47.14323, 13.12140* **Kur-Camping Bertahof, Vorderschneeberg 15, 5630 Bad Hofgastein (Salzburg) [(06432) 6701; fax 67016; camping@bertahof.at; www.camping-bertahof.at]** Fr B167 site at km 18.8, opp Erlengrundstrasse. Med, pt shd; htd wc; chem disp; shwrs inc; el pnts (16A) metered; gas; lndtte; shop 1.5km; tradsmn; rest; wifi; 50% statics; dogs €3.50; phone; skilift 2km; skibus; quiet. "Gd san facs." € 22.70 2008*

⊞ **BAD MITTERNDORF** *C3* (500m W Rural) *47.55501, 13.92241* **Kur-Camping Grimmingsicht, Haus Nr 338, 8983 Bad Mitterndorf (Kärnten) [(03623) 2985; fax 29854; camping@grimmingsicht.at; www.grimmingsicht.at]** Site on R (S) of B145 fr Bad Aussee to Liezen, sp. Sm, mkd pitch, pt shd; htd wc; shwrs inc; el pnts (10A) metered (long lead req); lndtte; shop 500m; tradsmn; bar; BBQ; rest, snacks 500m; bar; playgrnd; 20% statics; phone; Eng spkn; adv bkg; quiet but occasional rd & rlwy noise; red CCI. "Superb mountain scenery; gd san facs." ♦ € 16.50 2008*

BAD RADKERSBURG *D4* (500m W Rural) *46.68751, 15.97633* **Bad Radkersburg Camping, Thermenstrasse 20, 8490 Bad Radkersburg (Burgenland) [(03476) 2677556; fax 267503; camping@parktherme.at; www.parktherme.at/camping]** Sp in town cent, adj rv. Med, mkd pitch, hdstg, unshd; wc; chem disp; mv service pnt; serviced pitches; shwrs inc; el pnts (16A) metered; lndtte; shop 500m; rest, snacks 100m; BBQ; playgrnd; pool complex adj; 30% statics; dogs €2; phone; adv bkg; quiet; ccard acc; CCI. "Spa adj; cycle path to pretty town; v helpful owner; excel, modern facs; gd NH on way to Croatia, Slovenia." 1 Mar-11 Nov. € 21.40 2008*

⊞ **BLUDENZ** *C1* (6km E Rural) *47.14110, 9.92716* **Walch's Camping & Landhaus, Arlbergstrasse 101, 6751 Innerbraz [(05552) 281020; info@landhauswalch.at; www.landhauswalch.at]** Fr A14/S16 E from Feldkirch dir Arlberg, exit Braz. Site further 2km on L, sp. Med, unshd; wc; chem disp; mv service pnt; baby facs; sauna/solarium; shwrs inc; el pnts (16A) metered + conn fee; lndtte (inc dryer); shop, rest; bar; playgrnd; pool 1km; games rm; wifi; dogs €3.50; bus nr; site clsd Nov; Eng spkn; adv bkg; quiet; CCI. "Mountain activities & golf avail nrby; vg site; excel facs." ♦ € 24.80 2010*

⊞ **BLUDENZ** *C1* (5km SE Rural) *47.14628, 9.90236* **Camping Gasthof Traube, Klostertalerstrasse 12, 6751 Braz (Voralberg) [(05552) 28103; fax 2810340; office@traubebraz.at; www.traubebraz.at]** Site behind Gasthof Traube in middle of Braz vill, which is sp off dual carriageway S16. Med, some hdstg, sl, pt shd; htd wc; chem disp; baby facs; sauna; shwrs inc; el pnts (6A) inc (rev pol); lndtte (inc dryer); shop 1km; tradsmn; rest, snacks in gasthof; playgrnd; 2 htd pools (1 covrd); paddling pool; tennis; solarium; skilift 6km; skibus; golf 1.5km; wifi; entmnt; 40% statics; no dogs; poss v cr; quiet but some rlwy noise; ccard acc; red CCI. "Clean & tidy, family-run site; poss muddy pitches; conv Liechtenstein." € 25.60 2010*

⊞ **BLUDENZ** *C1* (1km S Rural) *47.14651, 9.81630* **Auhof Camping, Aulandweg 5, 6706 Bürs (Vorarlberg) [(05552) 67044; fax 31926; auhof.buers@aon.at; www.buers.at]** Exit A14/E60 junc 59 dir Bludenz/Bürs, then Brand. Site sp in 300m at Zimba Park shopping cent on edge of sm indus est. Med, unshd; htd wc; shwrs inc; el pnts (4A); gas; lndtte; shop & 300m; rest, snacks 300m; some rd noise. "Friendly, tidy, clean site on working farm; conv Arlberg Tunnel, Liechtenstein & mountain resorts; muddy in wet; conv NH for m'way." € 19.50 2011*

⊞ **BLUDENZ** *C1* (5km S Rural) *47.14268, 9.77875* **Heidi's Camping, Boden 7, 6707 Bürserberg (Voralberg) [(05552) 65307; fax 053074; info@burtschahof.at; www.burtschahof.at]** Exit A14/E60 at junc 59 twd Bürs/Brand. Site in 4km on L - 10% climb with bends. Sm, mkd pitch, some hdstg, terr, pt shd; htd wc; chem disp; baby facs; fam bthrm; shwrs inc; el pnts (16A) €1.50; lndtte (inc dryer); shop, rest, bar 200m; BBQ; playgrnd; pool; 25% statics; dogs; bus 200m; phone; poss cr; adv bkg; quiet. "CL-type site in lovely situation - worth the climb; sm/med o'fits only - manhandling poss req." € 23.50 2010*

BLUDENZ *C1* (2km W Rural) *47.16990, 9.80788* **Terrassencamping Sonnenberg, Hinteroferstrasse 12, 6714 Nüziders (Vorarlberg) [(05552) 64035; fax 33900; sonnencamp@aon.at; www.camping-sonnenberg.com]** Exit A14/E60 junc 57 onto B190 N, foll sp Nüziders & foll site sp thro Nüziders vill. Med, mkd pitch, hdstg, terr, pt shd; htd wc; chem disp; mv service pnt; shwrs inc; el pnts inc (5-13A) inc; lndtte (inc dryer); shop 500m; tradsmn; rest, snacks 300m; bar; playgrnd; wifi; entmnt; TV rm; dogs €3.50; phone; sep car park; poss cr; Eng spkn; adv bkg; quiet; ccard not acc; red low ssn/long stay. "Friendly, v helpful owners; superb facs; beautiful scenery - extra for Panorama pitches at top of site; excel mountain views; excel walking; lifts to mountains; ltd opening hrs for recep - use phone at building on L at main entrance; no arrivals after 2200 hrs but sep o'night area; rec bk in adv in high ssn; gd for m'vans; highly rec." 28 Apr-3 Oct. € 26.60 2011*

⊞ **BLUDENZ** *C1* (500m NW Rural) *47.16171, 9.8168* **Camping Seeberger, Obdorfweg 9, 6700 Bludenz (Vorarlberg) [(05552) 62512; fax 69984; camping.seeberger@aon.at; www.camping-seeberger.at]** Exit A14/E60 dir Bludenz-Mitte or Bludenz-West. Foll sps fr cent of town or fr main app rds. Med, hdg pitch, pt sl, pt shd; wc; chem disp; mv service pnt; shwrs inc; el pnts (10A) €2.50; gas; Indtte; shop; tradsmn; rest adj; playgrnd; sw 1km; skilift 5km; 40% statics; dogs €2; site clsd mid-Apr to mid-May & mid-Nov to mid-Dec; some Eng spkn; adv bkg; quiet; red CCI. "Tractor avail for tow to pitch; scenic site adj fruit orchard; vg, modern san facs; gd alpine walking." ♦ € 19.60 2008*

BRAZ see Bludenz *C1*

BREGENZ *C1* (2km W Rural) *47.50455, 9.71345* **Camping Mexico am Bodensee, Hechtweg 4, 6900 Bregenz (Voralberg) [tel/fax (05574) 73260; info@camping-mexico.at; www.camping-mexico.at]** App Bregenz fr Feldkirch. At bottom of hill on ent town, turn L at camping sp. Fork L at next junc & foll sps, or, fr Bregenz take Bahnhofstrasse (sp St Gallen). In approx 1km site on R sp. Fr Bregenz by-pass foll sps to Bregenz (city tunnel). At end of tunnel turn L at T-junc (sp St Gallen). In 500m turn R at camping sp. Site adj Seecamping. Sm, pt shd; wc; chem disp; shwrs inc; el pnts (6A) €2.60; gas, shop 1km; tradsmn; Indtte; rest 1km; BBQ; playgrnd; lake beach 200m; canoe/bike hire; internet; 50% statics; dogs €1.50; phone 100m; Eng spkn; adv bkg; quiet; ccard acc; red long stay. "Well-run, friendly, family-run site; gd san facs; rec arr early." ♦ 1 May-30 Sep. € 23.60 2008*

When we get home
I'm going to post
all these site report
forms to the Club
for next year's guide.
The deadline's mid September 2013

BREGENZ *C1* (2km W Rural) *47.50583, 9.71221* **Seecamping Bregenz, Hechtweg, 6900 Bregenz (Vorarlberg) [(05574) 71896; fax 718961; geisselman.guenter@aon.at; www.seecamping.at]** App Bregenz fr Feldkirch. At bottom of hill on ent town, turn L at camping sp. Fork L at next junc & foll sps, or, fr Bregenz take Bahnhofstrasse (sp St Gallen). In approx 1km site on R sp. Fr Bregenz by-pass foll sps to Bregenz (city tunnel). At end of tunnel turn L at T-junc (sp St Gallen). In 500m turn R at camping sp. Site adj Camping Mexico. Lge, pt shd; htd wc; chem disp; shwrs inc; el pnts (10A) inc; Indtte; shop; tradsmn; snacks; bar; shgl beach for lake sw adj; 10% statics; dogs free; poss cr; Eng spkn; quiet; red CCI. "Footpath to town cent; site in 2 halves; vg san facs." ♦ 15 May-15 Sep. € 24.00 2008*

BREITENWANG see Reutte *C1*

BRIXEN IM THALE see Kitzbühel *C2*

⊞ **BRUCK AN DER GROSSGLOCKNERSTRASSE** *C2* (SW Urban) *47.28386, 12.81736* **Sportcamp Woferlgut, Krössenbach 40, 5671 Bruck-an-der-Grossglocknerstrasse (Salzburg) [(06545) 73030; fax 73033; info@sportcamp.at; www.sportcamp.at]** Exit A10 junc 47 dir Bischofshofen, B311 dir Zell-am-See. Take 2nd exit to Bruck, site sp fr by-pass, & foll sps thro town to site. Lge, pt shd; wc; chem disp; mv service pnt; serviced pitches; baby facs; sauna; shwrs inc; el pnts (16A) metered + conn fee; gas metered + conn fee; Indtte; rest; snacks; bar; farm produce; playgrnd; htd pool; lake sw adj; tennis; indoor play area; games rm; gym & fitness cent; ski cent; wifi; entmnt; TV; many statics; dogs €4.50; phone; bus to Zell-am-Zee & glacier; poss cr; Eng spkn; adv bkg; some rd & rlwy noise; red long stay; ccard acc. "Extended facs area with R numbered pitches preferable; excel site for short or long stay; big pitches; helpful recep; tour ops tents & statics; excel for young/teenage families; noisy tannoy announcements high ssn; vg san facs; warm welcome; small supmkt nrby & plenty of rests & cafes; excel." ♦ € 30.80 2011*

BRUCK AN DER MUR *C4* (3km W Urban) *47.40311, 15.22755* **Camping Raddörf'l, Bruckerstrasse 110, 8600 Oberaich (Steiermark) [(03862) 51418; fax 59940; info@gasthofpichler.at; www.gasthofpichler.at]** Fr S6 take Oberaich exit 4km W of Bruck, Foll site sp (in opp dir to vill of Oberaich), go under rlwy bdge, turn L at T-junc. Site is 300m on L at Gasthof Pichler, ent thro car park. Sm, pt shd; wc; shwrs inc; el pnts (10A) inc; Indtte; shop 3km; rest; snacks; bar; playgrnd; dogs €2; poss cr; some rlwy noise; CCI. "Gd NH; site (10 outfits max) in orchard at rear of Gasthof; gd rest." 1 May-1 Oct. € 22.00 2010*

DELLACH IM DRAUTAL *D2* (500m S Rural) *46.73085, 13.07846* **Camping Waldbad, 9772 Dellach-im-Drautal (Kärnten) [(04714) 288; fax 2343; info@camping-waldbad.at; www.camping-waldbad.at]** Clearly sp on B100 & in vill of Dellach on S side or Rv Drau. Med, hdg/mkd pitch, pt shd; wc; chem disp; mv service pnt; baby facs; shwrs €1; el pnts (6A) inc; gas; Indtte; shop; rest; snacks; bar; playgrnd; htd pool complex adj inc paddling pool, waterslide etc; games area; games rm; entmnt; internet; 5% statics; dogs €2.50; poss cr; adv bkg; quiet; ccard acc. "Peaceful,wooded site; vg leisure facs adj." ♦ 1 May-30 Sep. € 25.00 2010*

⊞ **DOBRIACH** *D3* (1km S Rural) *46.77020, 13.64788* **Komfort Campingpark Burgstaller, Seefeldstrasse 16, 9873 Döbriach (Kärnten) [(04246) 7774; fax 77744; info@burgstaller.co.at; www.burgstaller.co.at]** Fr on A10/E55/E66 take exit Millstätter See. Turn L at traff lts on B98 dir Radenthein. Thro Millstatt & Dellach, turn R into Döbriach, sp Camping See site on L by lake after Döbriach. V lge, hdg/mkd pitch, pt shd; wc; chem disp; mv service pnt; baby facs; sauna; private bthrms avail; shwrs inc; el pnts (6-10A) inc; gas; Indtte; shop; rest, snacks, bar adj; playgrnd; htd pool; lake sw; boating; solarium; games area; horseriding; cycle hire; cinema; golf 8km; entmnt; internet; TV; 10% statics; dogs €4; poss cr; Eng spkn; adv bkg; quiet; red snr citizens/low ssn; CCI. "Organised walks & trips to Italy; excel rest; some pitches tight." ♦ € 29.50 2009*

DOBRIACH *D3* (1km S Rural) *46.77463, 13.65511* **Schwimmbad Camping Mössler, Glanzerstrasse 24, 9873 Döbriach (Kärnten) [(04246) 7735; fax 773513; camping@moessler.at; www.moessler.at]** Exit Spittal for Millstätter See & Döbriach & at end of lake turn to Döbriach See, cont to T-junc & turn L where site sp. Lge, pt shd, mkd pitch; htd wc; chem disp; mv service pnt; sauna; baby facs; shwrs inc; el pnts (4A) inc; gas; Indtte; shop; rest; snacks; bar; playgrnd; htd pool; lake; statics; dogs €2.30; phone; Eng spkn; adv bkg; quiet; red long stay/low ssn; CCI. "Well-equipped site; excel pool; beautiful mountain & lake scenery; walks & drives; vg facs." ♦ 15 Mar-31 Oct. € 30.10 2008*

⊞ **DOBRIACH** *D3* (1km SW) *46.76811, 13.64809* **Camping Brunner am See, Glanzerstrasse 108, 9873 Döbriach (Kärnten) [(04246) 7189 or 7386; fax 7837; camping.brunner@aon.at; www.camping-brunner.at]** Fr Salzburg on A10 a'bahn take Seeboden-Millstatt exit bef Spittal. Foll rd 98 N of Millstattersee to camping sp. Med, pt shd; wc; chem disp; mv service pnt; fam bthrm; baby facs; shwrs inc; el pnts (6A) inc; rest; snacks; bar; shop; pool 300m; playgrnd; tennis; watersports; poss cr; dogs €4.50; adv bkg; ccard acc; CCI. "Great site with excel, spotlessly cln san facs; gd size pitches; lakeside location; supmkt nrby & rests in vicinity; superb scenery." ♦ € 35.00 2011*

DORNBIRN *C1* (1.5km SE Rural) *47.39931, 9.75645* **Camping in der Enz, Gütlestrasse, 6850 Dornbirn (Vorarlberg) [(05572) 29119; camping@camping-enz.at; www.camping-enz.at]** Exit A14/E60 for Dornbirn-Sud, foll dir Ebnit-Rappenlochschlucht gorge for 1.2km, camp sp beyond cable car base. Med, pt shd; wc; chem disp; shwrs inc; el pnts (6A) €2.50; Indtte; shop; rest; snacks; playgrnd; lge pool 200m; cable car stn opp; adv bkg; ccard acc; red CCI. "Nice site in attractive location; conv Lake Constance, Bregenz, Lindau; sep o'night area." 1 Apr-30 Sep. € 17.00 2009*

DROBOLLACH see Villach *D3*

EBERNDORF see Völkermarkt *D3*

⊞ **EHRWALD** *C1* (1.5km NE Rural) *47.41142, 10.92360* **Comfort Camping Dr Lauth, Zugspitzstrasse 34, 6632 Ehrwald-Eben (Tirol) [(05673) 2666; fax 26664; info@campingehrwald.at; www.campingehrwald.at]** On ent Ehrwald, foll sps Tiroler Zugspitz Camping, turn R immed bef rlwy bdge (R turn nearest rlwy; do not go under rlwy bdge). Sp on R 1.5km fr Ehrwald, same rd as for Zugspitzbahn Camping. Fr Lermoos take 1st L after rlwy bdge. Med, pt sl, pt shd; htd wc; chem disp; baby facs; shwrs inc; el pnts (4A) metered; gas; Indtte (inc dryer); shop; tradsmn; rest; snacks; bar; BBQ; playgrnd; pool 4km; wifi; 50% statics; dogs €2.20; poss cr; Eng spkn; adv bkg; quiet; red long stay; CCI. "Excel san facs; mountain walks, skiing & cycling; conv Innsbruck & Fern Pass; v beautiful; vg bistro." € 26.00 2010*

⊞ **EHRWALD** *C1* (4km NE Rural) *47.42689, 10.94093* **Tiroler Zugspitz Camp, Obermoos 1, 6632 Ehrwald (Tirol) [(05673) 2309; fax 230951; camping@zugspitze-resort.at; www.zugspitze-resort.at]** Foll sp fr Ehrwald to Obernoos & Zugspitzbahn. Med, mkd pitch, pt terr, pt shd; wc; chem disp; mv service pnt; baby facs; sauna; shwrs inc; el pnts (16A) metered; gas; Indtte (inc dryer); shop; tradsmn; rest; playgrnd; 2 pools (1 htd, covrd); paddling pool; games rm; 60% statics; dogs €4; phone; Eng spkn; adv bkg; quiet; ccard acc; red CCI. "Excel site in beautiful location; some awkward, sm pitches; vg facs; adj cable car to summit Zugspitz." ♦ € 32.00 2010*

⊞ **EHRWALD** *C1* (2km W Rural) *47.40250, 10.88893* **Happy Camp Hofherr, Garmischerstrasse 21, 6631 Lermoos (Tirol) [(05673) 2980; fax 29805; info@camping-lermoos.com; www.camping-lermoos.com]** On ent Lermoos on B187 fr Ehrwald site located on R. Med, pt sl, pt shd; htd wc; chem disp; mv service pnt; shwrs inc; el pnts (16A) metered; gas (metered); Indtte (inc dryer); shops 200m; rest; playgrnd; htd pool 200m; tennis; skilift 300m; wifi; cab TV; 40% statics; dogs; phone; site clsd 1 Nov-mid Dec; adv bkg; quiet; ccard acc. "Ideal for walks/cycling; v picturesque; adj park; ask for guest card for discount on skilifts etc." € 23.00 2010*

⊞ **EHRWALD** *C1* (4km W Rural) *47.40693, 10.86976* **Camping Lärchenhof, Gries 16, 6631 Lermoos (Tirol) [(05673) 2197; fax 21975; info@camping-lermoos.at; www.camping-lermoos.at]** On B187, adj to BP petrol stn & gasthof. Sm, unshd; wc; chem disp; sauna; shwrs inc; el pnts (6A) €2.50; Indtte; shop adj; rest, snacks adj; tradsmn; pool 200m; ski bus; skil-lift 800m; skibus; drying & ski rm; 40% statics; dogs; poss cr; Eng spkn; some rd & rlwy noise. "Gd walks & cycling fr site; views; vg site & san facs." € 17.00 2008*

EISENSTADT *B4* (10km E Rural) *47.84401, 16.68720* **Campingplatz Oggau, 7063 Oggau-am-Neusiedlersee (Burgenland) [(02685) 7271; fax 72714; office@campingoggau.at; www.campingoggau.at]** Fr N or S exit A2 at Neustadt Süd, S4 sp Eisenstadt. Foll sps Eisenstadt on S4/S31, exit at Eisenstadt Süd & foll sps to Rust & Oggau; site sp thro vill. Lge, hdg pitch, shd; wc; chem disp; mv service pnt; shwrs €0.80; el pnts (16A) €2; gas; shop; rest; snacks; bar; playgrnd; pool adj; wifi; 60% statics; dogs; poss cr; adv bkg; ccard acc. ♦ 1 Apr-31 Oct. € 18.80 2009*

EISENSTADT *B4* (10km E Rural) *47.80132, 16.69185* **Storchencamp Rust, Ruster Bucht, 7071 Rust-am-Neusiedlersee (Burgenland) [(02685) 595; fax 5952; office@gmeiner.co.at; www.gmeiner.co.at]** Fr Eisenstadt take rd to Rust & Mörbisch. In Rust foll sps to site & Zee; lakeside rd to ent. Lge, pt shd; wc; chem disp; shwrs inc; el pnts (16A) €2.30; Indtte; shop; rest; snacks; pool 200m; lake sw 500m; boating; 60% statics; dogs €2.90; poss cr; quiet. "Nr Hungarian border; attractive vill with nesting storks." ♦ 1 Apr-31 Oct. € 20.20 2010*

EMMERSDORF AN DER DONAU see Melk *B4*

ENGELHARTSZELL *B3* (500m NW Rural) *48.51238, 13.72428* **Camp Municipal an der Donau, Nibelungenstrasse 113, 4090 Engelhartszell (Oberösterreich) [(0664) 8708787; tourismus@engelhartszell.ooe.gv.at; www.engelhartszell.at]** Fr Passau (Germany) exit SE on B130 along Rv Danube. Site on L in approx 28km just bef Engelhartszell adj municipal pool complex. Sm, unshd; wc; chem disp; shwrs; el pnts (6A) metered; Indtte; tradsmn; snacks; bar; playgrnd; pool adj; 50% statics; bus nr; poss cr; quiet. "Excel, clean, friendly site on rvside; Danube cycleway passes site." ♦ 15 Apr-15 Oct. € 15.00 2009*

FAAK/FAAK AM SEE see Villach *D3*

FEICHTEN IM KAUNERTAL see Prutz *C1*

FELDKIRCH *C1* (2km NW Urban) *47.25880, 9.58336* **Waldcamping Feldkirch, Stadionstrasse 9, 6803 Feldkirch (Vorarlberg) [(05522) 76001-3190; waldcamping@feldkirch.at; www.waldcamping.at]** Exit A14 at Feldkirch Nord, strt over next 2 rndabts sp Nofels. Cont to foll sp Nofels/Gisingen, then site sp. Site adj open air pool & leisure cent. Med, mkd pitch, pt shd; htd wc; chem disp; shwrs inc; el pnts (6A) €2.20; (poss rev pol); Indry rm; tradsmn; rest 800m; BBQ; playgrnd; htd pool adj, TV rm; 50% statics; dogs €2.75; bus 200m; poss cr; adv bkg; noise fr adj leisure cent; red CCI. "Vg." 1 Apr-31 Oct. € 22.00 2009*

The opening dates and prices on this campsite have changed. I'll send a site report form to the Club for the next edition of the guide.

⊞ **FERLACH** *D3* (500m SW Urban) *46.52166, 14.29222* **Messeparkplatz Schloss Ferlach, 9170 Ferlach (Kärnten) [(04227) 4920; office_schloss@ferlach.net; www.ferlach.at]** Fr B85 foll sp Ferlach, parking sp adj rv (top half of car park). Sm, hdstg, pt shd; own san rec; chem disp €1; mv service pnt (water) €1; shop, rest, snacks, bar 500m; quiet. "Free to stay but €4 parking charge; vg, conv NH for Loibl pass; c'vans & m'vans acc; pleasant town." € 4.00 2011*

FIEBERBRUNN see St Johann in Tirol *C2*

FRAUENKIRCHEN *B4* (6km S Rural) *47.79160, 16.91619* **Camping Zicksee, 7161 St Andrä-am-Zicksee (Burgenland) [tel/fax (02176) 2144; info@st.andrae-tourism.or.at; www.tiscover.com/st.andrae.zicksee]** Fr B51 site sp on lake 1.5km W of vill of St Andrä. Fr St Andrä foll sp Zicksee, fork R at junc after rlwy x-ing, site on L. Lge, mkd pitch, some hdstg, shd; htd wc; chem disp; mv service pnt; baby facs; shwrs €0.50; el pnts (10A) €1.80 (long cable poss req); gas; Indtte (inc dryer); shop; tradsmn; rest adj; snacks; playgrnd; lake sw; fishing; watersports; phone; no dogs; poss cr; quiet; CCI. "Excel facs; gd cycling & birdwatching E of lake; remote part of Austria; height restriction on ent of 3.20m." ♦ 1 Apr-30 Sep. € 17.90 2011*

FRAUENKIRCHEN *B4* (7km W Urban) *47.85424, 16.82665* **Strandcamping Podersdorf-am-See, Strandplatz 19, 7141 Podersdorf-am-See (Burgenland) [(02177) 2279; fax 227916; strandcamping@podersdorfamsee.at; www.podersdorfamsee.at]** Foll sp fr cent of Podersdorf on shore Neusiedlersee. Lge, mkd pitch, hdstg, pt shd; wc; chem disp; mv service pnt; shwrs €0.50; el pnts (12A) inc; shop; Indtte; rest; snacks; playgrnd; lake sw adj; sand beach; windsurfing; boating; internet; poss cr at w/end; 25% statics; dogs €4.90; quiet; red CCI. "Nature reserves & birdwatching lakes to S; many cycle paths in flat region; gd views fr site; bread baked daily." ♦ 1 Apr-1 Nov. € 27.00 2009*

⊞ **FREISTADT** *B3* (500m N Urban) *48.51444, 14.5100* **Freistädter Freizeit Club-Camping, Eglsee 12, 4250 Freistadt (Oberösterreich) [(07942) 72570; fax 725704; ffc@nusurf.at; www.freistadt.at/ffc]** Fr Linz turn R at rndabt N of town cent onto B38 twds Weitra/Gmund, site on R in 500m. Sm, pt shd; wc; chem disp; mv service pnt; shwrs inc; el pnts (16A) €2; Indtte; snacks; rest 400m; bar; pool 1.5km; dogs €0.90; quiet; red CCI. "NH; recep in bar - book in 1st; helpful, friendly owners; conv for old town & Czech Rep." € 15.60 2008*

FROHNLEITEN *C4* (2.5km S Rural) *47.2555, 15.3187* **Camping Lanzmaierhof, Ungersdorf 16, 8130 Frohnleiten (Steiermark) [(03126) 2360; lanzmaierhof@tele2.at; www.frohnleiten.or.at]** Fr S35 exit Frohnleiten S. Foll sp for stn (bahnhof) & cont 2km twd Ungersdorf. Site on L behind Gasthof Lanzmaierhof, narr ent. Sm, pt sl, pt shd; wc; chem disp; shwrs; el pnts (10A) inc; tradsmn; rest; snacks; bar; BBQ; sm plunge pool; tennis; dogs €0.90; Eng spkn; quiet but some rd & rlwy noise; 10% red CCI. "Gd restful spot bet Graz & Vienna; conv Austrian o'door museum; basic, clean facs." 1 Apr-15 Oct. € 17.80 2008*

⊞ **FUGEN** *C2* (1km N Rural) *47.35949, 11.85223* **Campingplatz Hell, Gageringerstrasse 1, 6263 Fügen/Zillertal (Tirol) [(05288) 62203; fax 64615; info@zillertal-camping.at; www.zillertal-camping.at]** On A12/E45/E60 exit junc 39 exit onto B169. Site well sp. Med, mkd pitch, some hdstg, terr, pt shd; wc; chem disp; mv service pnt; sauna; fam bthrm; shwrs inc; el pnts (10A) metered (long lead poss req); gas; Indtte (inc dryer); shop; supmkt 500m; rest; snacks high ssn; bar; playgrnd; htd pool; paddling pool; cycle hire; games rm; golf 10km; wifi; entmnt; dogs €2.50 (not acc Jul/Aug); Eng spkn; adv bkg; some rd noise daytime only; red 8+ days; CCI. "Wonderful site; superb san facs; lge pitches; friendly, helpful staff; excel." € 34.00 2011*

FURSTENFELD *C4* (500m W Rural) *47.05631, 16.06255* **Thermenland Camping, Campingweg 1, 8280 Fürstenfeld (Steiermark) [(03382) 54940; fax 51671; camping.fuerstenfeld@chello.at; www.camping-fuerstenfeld.at]** Exit A2/E59 sp Fürstenfeld onto B65. Site well sp fr town cent. Med, pt sl, pt shd; wc; chem disp; shwrs inc; el pnts (10A) €2.30 (poss long lead req); Indtte (inc dryer); shop 500m; tradsmn; rest 1.5km; snacks; bar; pool; paddling pool; waterslide; rv fishing; golf 5km; entmnt; 25% statics; dogs €2; phone; quiet; rec CCI. "Pleasant rvside site; ltd facs but clean; conv Hungarian border." 15 Apr-15 Oct. € 20.00 2010*

FUSCH AN DER GLOCKNERSTRASSE *C2* (S Rural) *47.22452, 12.82658* **Camping Lampenhäusl, Grossglocknerstrsse 15, 5672 Fusch-an-der-Glocknerstrasse (Salzburg) [(06546) 2150; fax 215302; gasthof@lampenhaeusl.at; www.lampenhaeusl.at]** E of rd, on S o'skts of Fusch. Sm, pt shd; wc; shwrs inc; el pnts (16A) €3.80 or metered; lndtte (inc dryer); shop & 100m; rest; snacks; bar; playgrnd; htd pool 100m; TV rm; 50% statics; phone; bus; Eng spkn; adv bkg; quiet; ccard acc; red long stay; CCI. "Vg, clean facs but stretched if site full; vg site." 10 May-26 Oct. € 17.50 2010*

FUSCHL AM SEE *B3* (800m SW Rural) *47.79230, 13.29682* **Camping Seeholz, Dorfsrtrasse 36, 5330 Fuschl-am-See (Salzburg) [tel/fax (06226) 8310; camping-fuschl@aon.at]** Exit A1 at junc 274 onto B158 dir Hof & St Gilgen. Foll sp to Fuschl & site. Med, shd; wc; chem disp; shwrs inc; el pnts (8A) inc (long lead poss req); gas; lndtte; shop; rest; snacks; lake sw & shgl beach adj; 25% statics; dogs; poss cr; adv bkg; some rd noise. "Helpful staff; basic, gd san facs; beautiful lake." 1 Apr-31 Oct. € 23.20 2009*

GALTUR *C1* (5km W Rural) *46.97786, 10.12516* **Camping Zeinissee, Zeinisjoch 28, 6563 Galtür (Tirol) [tel/fax (05443) 8562; zeinissee@galtuer.at; www.camping-zeinissee.galtuer.at]** On B188 travelling W, site sp 2.5km after cent of Galtür, along gently climbing rd. Sm, hdstg, unshd; htd wc; chem disp; shwrs inc; el pnts metered; lndtte; tradsmn; rest, bar adj; playgrnd; lake sw adj; TV rm; no statics; dogs; bus 100m; Eng spkn; adv bkg; quiet. "Excel site o'looking sm lake at 1800m; wonderful views; walking; conv Silvretta Stausee." 15 Jun-31 Oct. € 19.00 2008*

⊞ **GASCHURN** *C1* (1km N Rural) *46.99765, 10.01431* **Camping Nova, Campingstrasse 13A, 6793 Gaschurn (Voralberg) [(05558) 8954; fax 8962; info@campingnova.at; www.campingnova.at]** Leave A14 at junc 61 onto B188 dir Schruns. After Schruns cont for approx 15km, site on R bef ent Gaschurn. Med, mkd pitch, pt shd; htd wc; chem disp; mv service pnt; sauna; shwrs €1.20; el pnts (13A) inc; gas; lndtte; shop 1km; tradsmn; rest 500; snacks; bar; playgrnd; pool 1km; games area; internet; TV rm; 85% statics; phone; bus; site clsd 1st week Apr to 1st week May; poss cr; Eng spkn; some rd noise; CCI. "Gd." ♦ € 21.50 2008*

GMUND (KARNTEN) *C3* (5km W Rural) *46.93482, 13.52344* **Camping Kurt Zechner, Fischertratten 17, 9853 Gmünd (Kärnten) [tel/fax (04732) 2192; tanja.zechner@aon.at; www.camping-zechner.com]** Fr Gmünd, foll sps Maltatal. In 5km turn 1st L after sp Fischertratten, site in 100m on rvside. Sm, pt sl, pt shd; wc; own san; chem disp; mv service pnt; shwrs inc; el pnts (10A) €2.50; gas; lndtte; shop; tradsmn; snacks; bar; htd pool 2km; dogs free; phone; bus 100m; Eng spkn; adv bkg; quiet; CCI. "Gmünd medieval town; vg walking area; conv NH." ♦ 1 May-30 Oct. € 16.00 2008*

GMUND (KARNTEN) *C3* (8km NW Rural) *46.94950, 13.50940* **Terrassencamping Maltatal, Malta 6, 9854 Malta (Kärnten) [(04733) 234; fax 23416; info@maltacamp.at; www.maltacamp.at]** Exit A10/E14 onto B99 to Gmünd. Foll sp Malta & after 6km site sp, on R next to filling stn. Lge, mkd pitch, terr, pt shd; htd wc; chem disp; mv service pnt; 20% serviced pitches; sauna; shwrs inc; el pnts (10A) inc; lndtte (inc dryer); sm supmkt; tradsmn; rest; snacks; pizzeria; bar; BBQ; playgrnd; htd pool; paddling pool; canoeing; trout-fishing; games area; games rm; tennis; guided walks; children's mini-farm; wifi; 5% statics; dogs €2.90; phone; poss cr; adv bkg; quiet; CCI. "Gmund & Spittal gd shopping towns; Millstättersee 15km, Grossglocknerstrasse 1hr's drive; magnificant area with rivers, waterfalls, forests & mountains; vg rest; excel site." ♦ 1 Apr-31 Oct. € 26.50 (CChq acc) 2010*

I'll fill in a report online and let the Club know – www.caravanclub.co.uk/europereport

This is a wonderful site.

GMUNDEN *B3* (4km SE Rural) *47.90295, 13.7695* **Camping am Traunsee Schweizerhof, Haupstrasse 14, 4813 Altmünster (Oberösterreich) [(07612) 89313 or 87276; fax 872764; office@schweizerhof.cc; www.schweizerhof.cc]** Exit A1 at Regau onto B145 dir Gmunden. Fr Gmunden foll sp Bad Ischl, site well sp on L. Sm, hdstg, terr, pt shd; wc; chem disp; mv service pnt; shwrs €1; el pnts (10A) €2; lndtte; shop 500m; tradsmn; rest; snacks; bar; htd pool 500m; playgrnd; lake sw & boating adj; tennis adj; 5% statics; dogs; poss cr; Eng spkn; adv bkg; rd noise; red CCI. "Beautiful area; gd walking/cycling." 1 May-30 Sep. € 20.80 2008*

GNESAU *D3* (2km W Rural) *46.77966, 13.95062* **Camping Hobitsch, Sonnleiten 24, 9563 Gnesau (Kärnten) [(04278) 368; fax 3684; office@camping-hobitsch.at; www.camping-hobitsch.at]** Site sp on B95. Sm, pt shd; wc; chem disp; shwrs inc; el pnts €2.80; lndtte; shop, rest 2km; snacks; bar; playgrnd; pool; tennis; games area; no statics; dogs €1.50; Eng spkn; quiet. "Beautiful setting in meadow; excel san facs; adj to cycle path." 1 May-30 Sep. € 13.30 2010*

⊞ **GOLLING AN DER SALZACH** *C2* (2km W Rural) *47.60176, 13.14382* **Camping Torrenerhof, Torren 24, 5440 Golling-an-der-Salzach (Salzburg) [(06244) 5522; fax 552222; hotel@torrenerhof.com; www.torrenerhof.com]** Fr S on B159 in Golling (past fire stn on R) turn R over rlwy & foll rd for 2km. Fr E55/A10 take L fork on ent vill. Turn L 300m over level x-ing. Site in 2km behind hotel. Fr N level x-ing is opp hidden castle. Sm, pt sl, pt shd; wc; chem disp; mv service pnt; shwrs inc; el pnts (10A) €2.50; lndtte (inc dryer); shop; rest; snacks 1.5km; playgrnd; golf 15km; dogs €1; Eng spkn; adv bkg; quiet. "Scenic area nr beautiful waterfall; excursions fr vill; inadequate facs poss stretched if full; gd base for Salzburg; gd cycling; sh stay/NH only." ♦ € 18.00 2008*

GRAN *C1* (4km W Rural) *47.50825, 10.49468* **Panoramacamp Alpenwelt, Kienzerle 3, 6675 Tannheim (Tirol) [(05675) 43070; fax 430777; alpenwelt@tirol.com; www.tannheimertal-camping.com]** Fr N leave A7 junc 137 Oy-Mittelberg onto B310 to Oberjoch, then B199 to Tannheim. Fr S on B198 dir Reutte, turn onto B199 at Weissenbach to Tannheim. Med, mkd pitch, hdstg, terr, unshd; htd wc; chem disp; some serviced pitches; baby facs; sauna; shwrs inc; el pnts (16A) metered; Indtte; shop; tradsmn; rest; bar; playgrnd; pool 4km; lake sw 4km; entmnt; internet; cab TV; 30% statics; dogs €3.50; ski bus; skilift 2km; adv bkg; quiet; CCI. "Excel site; gd walking, cycling area." ♦ 20 Dec-19 Apr & 1 May-30 Oct. € 22.00 2010*

GRAZ *C4* (6km SW Urban) *47.02447, 15.39719* **Stadt-Camping Central, Martinhofstrasse 3, 8054 Graz-Strassgang (Steiermark) [(0316) 697824 or 0676 3785102 (mob); guenther_walter@utanet.at; www.tiscover.at/camping central]** Fr A9/E57 exit Graz-Webling, then dir Strassgang onto B70, site sp on R after Billa supmkt & filling stn. Med, mkd pitch, some hdstg, pt shd; wc; chem disp; mv service pnt; shwrs inc; el pnts (6A) inc; gas; Indtte (inc dryer); supmkt 200m; rest, snacks adj; bar; BBQ; playgrnd; pool, paddling pool adj; tennis; 80% statics; dogs free; bus to city; poss v cr; quiet. "Pleasant, conv site; regular bus service fr the nrby main rd (no traff noise); free entry to superb lido (pt naturist); site mngr v helpful." ♦ 1 Apr-31 Oct. € 30.00 2011*

GREIFENBURG *D2* (1km E Rural) *46.74744, 13.19448* **Fliergercamp am See, Seeweg 333, 9761 Greifenburg (Kärnten) [(04712) 8666; info@fliegercamp.at; www.fliegercamp.at]** On rd 100/E66, site clearly visible fr rd on app Greifenburg. Med, mkd pitch, pt shd; htd wc; chem disp; mv service pnt; baby facs; shwrs inc; el pnts (16A) inc; Indtte; shop 1km; tradsmn; rest; snacks; bar; BBQ; playgrnd; lake sw adj; dogs; Eng spkn; adv bkg; quiet; CCI. "Gd cycling; vg site." ♦ 1 Apr-15 Oct. € 17.60 2009*

GREIFENBURG *D2* (1km W Rural) *46.74805, 13.16416* **Familien-Camping Reiter, Hauzendorf 3, 9761 Greifenburg (Kärnten) [tel/fax (04712) 389; campingreiter@gmx.at; www.camping-reiter.at]** Fr Greifenburg on B100, site on L. Sm, pt shd; htd wc; chem disp; baby facs; shwrs €1; el pnts (10A) metered; Indtte (inc dryer); shop; tradsmn; rest; snacks; bar; BBQ; playgrnd; htd pool; dogs €1; quiet. "Beautiful area." 1 Apr-15 Nov. € 21.00 2011*

GREIN *B3* (200m SW Urban) *48.22476, 14.85428* **Camping-platz Grein, Donaulände 1, 4360 Grein (Oberösterreich) [(07268) 21230; fax 2123013; camp@camping-grein.net; www.camping-grein.net]** Sp fr A1 & B3 on banks of Danube. Med, pt shd; wc; chem disp; shwrs inc; el pnts (6-10A) €3; gas; Indtte; shop adj; rest in vill; snacks; bar; playgrnd; htd, covrd pool 200m; open air pool 500m; fishing; canoeing; wifi; 10% statics; dogs €1.50; poss cr; some rd/rlwy noise; red long stay; CCI. "Friendly, helpful owner lives on site; recep in café/bar; vg, modern san facs; lovely scenery; quaint vill; gd walking; excursions; conv Danube cycle rte & Mauthausen Concentration Camp." 1 Mar-31 Oct. € 18.00 2008*

GRUNDLSEE see Bad Aussee *C3*

HALL IN TIROL *C2* (500m NE Urban) *47.28423, 11.49658* **Schwimmbad-Camping, Scheidensteinstrasse 26, 6060 Hall-in-Tirol (Tirol) [(05223) 4546475; fax 4546477; h.niedrist@hall.at; www.hall.ag]** Exit A12/E45/E60 at junc 68 at Hall-in-Tirol. Cross rv strt into town & foll camp sp fr 2nd turn L; site on B171. Difficult ent. Med, pt shd; wc; chem disp; mv service pnt; shwrs inc; el pnts (6A) €2; Indtte; shop high ssn; supmkt 500m; tradsmn; rest; playgrnd; htd pool adj; tennis, minigolf adj; wifi; 15% statics; dogs; bus; poss cr; Eng spkn; adv bkg; some rd noise & church bells; red long stay/CCI. "Well-cared for site; friendly welcome; vg, modern facs, poss stretched high ssn; local excursions, walking; part of sports complex; Hall pretty, interesting medieval town; frequent music festivals; less cr than Innsbruck sites; no twin-axles; walk to town; conv for m'vans; NB m'vans only 1 Oct-30 Apr for €7.50 per night." ♦ 1 May-30 Sep. € 20.30 2011*

⊞ **HALL IN TIROL** *C2* (2km E Urban) *47.2816, 11.5308* **Camping Landhotel Reschenhof, Bunderstrasse 7, 6068 Mils-bei-Hall (Tirol) [(05223) 5860; fax 586052; landhotel@reschenhof.at; www.reschenhof.at]** Fr Innsbruck leave A12 & turn L twd Hall-in-Tirol onto B171 dir Wattens. Go L at traff lts & over bdge, then R at traff lts. Site approx 2km on L behind Landhotel Reschenhof on ent Mils. Sm, pt sl, pt shd; htd wc; chem disp; sauna; shwrs inc; el pnts (6-12A) inc; gas; Indtte (inc dryer); rest; snacks; bar; BBQ; playgrnd; pool; paddling pool; skilift 2km; internet; 15% statics; quiet. "Conv Innsbruck by bus; gd NH." € 21.20 2008*

HALL IN TIROL *C2* (5km E Rural) *47.28711, 11.57223* **Schlosscamping Aschach, Hochschwarzweg 2, 6111 Volders (Tirol) [tel/fax (05224) 52333; info@schlosscamping.com; www.schlosscamping.com]** Fr A12 leave at either Hall Mitte & foll sp to Volders, or leave at Wattens & travel W to Volders (easiest rte). Site well sp on B171. Narr ent bet lge trees. Lge, mkd pitch, pt sl, pt shd; wc; chem disp; mv service pnt; shwrs inc; el pnts (16A) €2.70 (long cable req some pitches; adaptor lead avail); gas; Indtte; shop; tradsmn; 2 supmkts 500m; rest; snacks; bar; BBQ; playgrnd; htd pool; horseriding, tennis; TV rm; dogs €2.50; phone; bus 250m; Eng spkn; adv bkg; quiet but church bells, clock & some rlwy noise at night; red long stay; ccard acc (for 4+ days); CCI. "Well-run, clean site with vg, modern facs & helpful management; few water & waste points; grassy pitches; beautiful setting & views; gd walking/touring; arr early to ensure pitch." 1 May-12 Sep. € 22.00 2010*

HALLEIN *B2* (3km NW Rural) *47.70441, 13.06868* **Camping Auwirt, Salzburgerstrasse 42, 5400 Hallein (Salzburg) [(06245) 80417; fax 84635; info@auwirt.com; www.auwirt.com]** Exit A10/E55 junc 8 onto B150 sp Salzburg Süd, then B159 twd Hallein. Site on L in 4km. Med, pt shd; wc; chem disp; mv service pnt; shwrs €1; el pnts (10A) €2.80; Indtte; rest; snacks; bar; playgrnd; dogs; bus to Salzburg at site ent; poss cr; Eng spkn; adv bkg; CCI. "Mountain views; cycle path to Salzburg nr; helpful staff; v friendly site; gd san facs & rest; gd disabled rm; conv salt mines at Hallein & scenic drive to Eagles' Nest; conv for Berchtesgaden." ♦ Easter-15 Oct & 1 Dec-7 Jan. € 21.40 2011*

AUSTRIA

AUSTRIA

HALLSTATT *C3* (4km SE Rural) *47.54874, 13.67779* **Campingplatz am See, Winkl 77, 4831 Obertraun (Oberösterreich) [(06131) 265; camping-am-see@chello.at; www.camping-am-see.at]** Fr Hallstatt foll sps for Obertraun. Site immed on L on ent vill of Winkl. Med, some hdstg, pt shd; wc; chem disp; mv service pnt; baby facs; shwrs inc; el pnts (10A) €3 (long lead req); lndtte (inc dryer); shop; supmkt 1.5km; tradsmn; snacks; bar; BBQ; lake sw & shgl beach adj; wifi; dogs €1.50; Eng spkn; adv bkg; quiet; ccard acc; red CCI. "Nr Dachstein ice caves, Hallstatt salt mines, Gosau valley." 1 May-30 Sep. € 31.50 2010*

HALLSTATT *C3* (500m S Rural) *47.55296, 13.64786* **Camping Klausner-Höll, Lahnstrasse 201, 4830 Hallstatt (Oberösterreich) [(06134) 83224; fax 83221; camping@hallstatt.net; http://camping.hallstatt.net/home/]** On exit tunnel 500m thro vill, site on R nr lge filling stn. Med, pt shd; wc; chem disp; shwrs inc; el pnts (16A) €3; lndtte; shop; rest adj; snacks; bar; playgrnd; pool adj; lake sw; boat trips; dogs; poss cr; Eng spkn; ccard acc; red long stay/CCI. "Excel, level site; gd, clean san facs; chem disp diff to use; conv Salzkammergut region, Hallstatt salt mines, mountains, ice caves; pretty town 10 mins walk." 15 Apr-15 Oct. € 22.00 2009*

HARTBERG *C4* (200m S Rural) *47.2803, 15.97218* **Camping Hartberg, Augasse 35, 8230 Hartberg (Steiermark) [(03332) 6030 or 06769 414939 (Mob); fax 60351; camping@hartberg.at; www.hartberg.at]** Fr A2/E59 exit junc 115 sp Hartberg, site sp off B54 in vill. Med, pt sl, shd; wc; chem disp (wc); shwrs; el pnts (16A) €2; lndtte; shop 300m; rest, bar in vill; htd, covrd pool 100m; 20% statics; dogs €1; poss cr; red long/stayCCI. "Sh walk to vill." 1 Apr-1 Nov. € 14.50 2008*

⊞ **HASELGEHR** *C1* (1km NE Rural) *47.31527, 10.49722* **Freien-Camping Rudi, Luxnach 122, 6651 Häselgehr [(05634) 6425; info@lechtal-camping-rudi.at; www.lechtal-camping-rudi.at]** On rd B198 fr Reutte (N), in Häselgehr cross rv bdge, turn R bef church. In 100m take R fork, site on R in 500m. Med, hdstg, unshd; htd wc; chem disp; mv service pnt; shwrs inc; el pnts (13A) metered; lndtte (inc dryer); shop 5km; rest 500m; pool 500m; skilift 5km; skibus; few statics; dogs €1.50; bus 400m; Eng spkn; adv bkg; quiet; red long stay; CCI. "Cycling & x-country skiing fr site; rafting cent on site; gd." € 20.40 2010*

HEILIGEN GESTADE see Ossiach *D3*

HEILIGENBLUT *C2* (2.5km S Rural) *47.02164, 12.86244* **Camping Möllfuss, Pockhorn 25, 9844 Heiligenblut (Kärnten) [(04824) 24645; fax 24684; hoopfnstuben@gmx.at]** On B107 at S end of Grossglockner Pass. Med, pt shd; htd wc; chem disp; mv service pnt; shwrs inc; el pnts (16A) metered; gas; lndtte; shop; rest; snacks; bar; playgrnd; pool; dogs; quiet; ccard acc; red CCI. "Conv NH bef x-ing Grossglockner Pass." 1 Jun-15 Oct & 1 Dec-15 Apr. € 16.40 2009*

⊞ **HEILIGENBLUT** *C2* (8km S Rural) *46.97908, 12.88574* **Camping Zirknitzer, Döllach 107, 9843 Grosskirchheim (Kärnten) [tel/fax (04825) 451; camping.zirknitzer@utanet.at; http://web.utanet.at/zirknitp]** B107 fr Grossglockner Pass, S thro Heilingenblut dir Winklern & Lienz, site sp. Sm, pt shd; wc; sauna; shwrs; el pnts (16A) €2.60; lndtte; shop 500m; tradsmn; rest; bar; playgrnd; pool, tennis 500m; fitness rm; site clsd Nov & end Apr; adv bkg; quiet. "Well-run, scenic site; friendly & helpful; gd, modern san facs; gd walking; conv Grossglockner & Italian border." € 15.00 2009*

⊞ **HEILIGENBLUT** *C2* (1km W Rural) *47.03682, 12.83887* **Nationalpark-Camping Grossglockner, Hadergasse 11, 9844 Heiligenblut (Kärnten) [(04824) 2048; fax 24622; nationalpark-camping@heiligenblut.at; www.heiligenblut.at/nationalpark-camping]** At S end Grossglockner. Keep R in Heiligenblut, down hill & foll sp to site. Med, pt sl, unshd; wc; shwrs inc; el pnts (16-20A) €2.50; gas; lndtte; shop 500m; rest; snacks; bar; playgrnd; pool 200m; dogs €2; site clsd mid-Oct to end Nov; Eng spkn; quiet; CCI. "In Hohe Tauern National Park; sh, steep walk to vill; gd NH bef/after Grossglockner Pass; v ltd facs low ssn." € 19.70 2009*

HEITERWANG see Reutte *C1*

⊞ **HERMAGOR** *D3* (2km E Rural) *46.63090, 13.39630* **Sportcamping Flaschberger, Vellach 27, 9620 Hermagor (Kärnten) [(04282) 2020; fax 202088; office@flaschberger.at; www.flaschberger.at]** On B111 on R hand bend, site sp. Med, hdg/mkd pitch, hdstg, pt sl, pt shd; htd wc; chem disp; mv service pnt; shwrs inc; el pnts (16A) inc; lndtte; shops, rest, snacks adj; playgrnd; pool; tennis; sports hall; wifi; cab TV; 10% statics; dogs €1.80; Eng spkn; quiet but some rd & rlwy noise; red snr citizens. "Superb site, hard to fault; excel facs." ♦ € 20.40 2008*

HERMAGOR *D3* (6km E Rural) *46.63048, 13.45416* **Camping Presseggersee Max, Presseggen 5, 9620 Hermagor (Kärnten) [(04282) 2039; fax 20394; info@camping-max.com; www.camping-max.com]** Site on S side of B111 to E of Hermagor twd Villach. Sharp turn at site ent. Med, sl, pt shd; wc; chem disp; mv service pnt; shwrs inc; el pnts (10A) €2.50; gas; lndtte; shop; sm playgrnd; lake sw adj; dogs €3; quiet; adv bkg; CCI. "Excel; well-kept, family site; friendly, helpful owner." 1 May-15 Oct. € 18.50 2008*

⊞ **HERMAGOR** *D3* (6km E Rural) *46.63163, 13.4465* **Naturpark Schluga-Seecamping, Vellach 15, 9620 Hermagor-Presseggersee (Kärnten) [(04282) 2051 or 2760; fax 288120; camping@schluga.com; www.schluga.com]** Exit A2 dir Hermagor, site sp on rd B111. Lge, mkd pitch, pt shd; htd wc; chem disp; mv service pnt; serviced pitches; baby facs; fam bthrm; sauna; private san facs avail; shwrs; el pnts (6A) €2.10; gas; lndtte (with dryer); supmkt, rest, snacks high ssn; bar; playgrnd; htd pool 4km; lake sw, fishing 300m; tennis 500m; games area; cycle hire; fitness rm; wifi; entmnt; TV rm; dogs €2.60; 20% statics; phone; adv bkg; quiet; ccard acc; red snr citizens. "In beautiful situation." ♦ € 25.90 (CChq acc) 2008*

⊞ **HIRSCHEGG** *C3* (200m N Rural) *47.02300, 14.95325* **Campingplatz Hirschegg, Haus No. 53, 8584 Hirschegg [info@camping-hirschegg.at; www.camping-hirschegg.at]** Exit A2 junc 224 Modriach N. At T-junc foll sp to Hirschegg & in cent of vill turn R at petrol stn. Site in 300m on L by fire stn. Med, hdg/mkd pitch, pt shd; wc; chem disp; shwrs inc; el pnts (10A) €2; Indtte; shop, rest, bar in vill; playgrnd; pool; lake sw adj; wifi; 30% statics; dogs €1; adv bkg; quiet. "Excel, family-run site." € 16.00 2009*

HOPFGARTEN see Wörg *C2*

We can fill in site report forms on the Club's website – www.caravanclub.co.uk/europereport

IMST *C1* (1km E Rural) *47.23972, 10.7450* **International Camping am Schwimmbad, Schwimmbadweg 10, 6460 Imst (Tirol) [(05412) 66612; camp1@gmx.at; http://members.aon.at/camp1]** Exit A12/E60 at Imst onto B171 N dir Imst; then exit B171 onto B189; in 500m turn R, then immed L into Schwimmbadweg. Foll camp sps fr by-pass to avoid Imst town & narr streets. Poss easier to foll Schwimbad (sw pool) sps. Med, mkd pitch, pt sl, pt shd; wc; chem disp; shwrs inc; el pnts (6A) €2; gas; Indtte (inc dryer); shop; pool adj; cycle hire; wifi; dogs €1.50; poss cr; Eng spkn; red long stay. "V pleasant in mountain setting; gd walking; helpful owner; ltd san facs low ssn." 1 May-15 Sep. € 18.00 2009*

⊞ **IMST** *C1* (1.5km S Rural) *47.22861, 10.74305* **Caravanpark Imst-West, Langgasse 62, 6460 Imst (Tirol) [(05412) 66293; fax 63364; fink.franz@aon.at; www.imst-west.com]** Fr A12/E60 exit Imst-Pitztal onto B171 N dir Imst. In 1km at rndabt take last exit heading W then immed sharp L opp Citroën dealer into Langgasse. In 750m turn L, site on R. Med, mkd pitch, pt sl, pt shd; wc; chem disp; mv service pnt; shwrs inc; el pnts (6-10A) €3; gas; Indtte; shop 200m; rest 200m; snacks; bar; playgrnd; pool 1.5km; skilift 2km; free skibus; dogs €2; Eng spkn; quiet. "Gd cent for Tirol, trips to Germany & en rte for Innsbruck; lovely views; clean facs; gd." € 19.50 2011*

INNSBRUCK *C1* (11km SE Rural) *47.26002, 11.50509* **Campingplatz Judenstein, Judenstein 42, 6074 Rinn-bei-Innsbruck (Tirol) [(05223) 78098; fax 7887715; camping@kbrinn.at; www.kbrinn.at/camping]** Exit A12/E45/E60 junc 68 & foll Tulfes sp. Thro Tulfes & 2km onto Rinn, site sp, just bef church with clock. App rd narr & steep in places. Med, hdg/mkd pitch, pt sl, pt shd; wc; chem disp; mv service pnt; shwrs inc; el pnts (6A) €2; gas; Indtte; shop adj; tradsmn, rest, bar adj; lake sw 5km; golf 1km; cab TV; 50% statics; dogs; Eng spkn; quiet but church bells adj; CCI. "Gd, clean, well-run site; site yourself; office open evenings; helpful, friendly staff; ample pitches; bus service to area & city cent." 1 May-30 Sep. € 13.00 2011*

⊞ **INNSBRUCK** *C1* (6km SW Rural) *47.23724, 11.33865* **Camping Natterersee, Natterer See 1, 6161 Natters (Tirol) [(0512) 546732; fax 54673216; info@natterersee.com; www.natterersee.com]** App Innsbruck fr E or W on A12 take A13/E45 sp Brenner. Leave at 1st junc sp Innsbruck Süd, Natters. Foll sp Natters - acute R turns & severe gradients (care across unguarded level x-ing), turn sharp R in vill & foll sp to site. Take care on negotiating ent. Narr rds & app. Fr S on A13 Brennerautobahn exit junc 3 & foll dir Mutters & Natters. Med, pt shd, sl, terr; htd wc; chem disp; mv service pnt; baby facs; shwrs inc; el pnts (6-16A) inc; gas; Indtte (inc dryer); shop; rest; snacks; bar; BBQ; playgrnd; lake sw; waterslide; tennis; cycle hire; games area; games rm; wifi; entmnt; games/TV rm; no dogs Jul/Aug, otherwise €4; bus to Innsbruck; train 2.5km; sep car park high ssn; guided hiking; clsd 1 Nov-mid Dec; poss v cr; Eng spkn; adv bkg; ccard acc; red low ssn; CCI. "Well-kept site adj local beauty spot; lakeside pitches gd views (extra charge); gd, scenic cent for walking & driving excursions; gd for children; friendly, helpful staff; excel modern san facs; some sm pitches & narr site rds diff lge outfits." ♦ € 31.50 (CChq acc) SBS - G01 2011*

⊞ **INNSBRUCK** *C1* (5km W Rural) *47.26339, 11.32629* **Camping Kranebittehof, Kranebitter Allee 216, 6020 Innsbruck-Kranebitten (Tirol) [(0512) 279558; info@camping-kranebitterhof.at; www.camping-kranebitterhof.at]** Fr W fork L after Zirl bef main rd rv bdge, sp Innsbruck & foll B171 for 3km. Fr S on A13 fr border foll dir Bregenz on A12 exit Kranebitten & foll sp to site. Sharp ent on R. Med, mkd pitch, hdstg, terr, pt sl, pt shd; wc; chem disp; mv service pnt; shwrs inc; el pnts (6-10A) inc; Indtte; shop; pizzeria; hiking; skilift 5km; wifi; 20% statics; dogs; bus; poss cr; Eng spkn; some m'way & airport noise; ccard acc; red low ssn/long stay/CCI. "Excel, refurbished site in lovely situation; vg, modern san facs; friendly, helpful staff." € 25.00 2010*

⊞ **INNSBRUCK** *C1* (5km W Urban) *47.25307, 11.32661* **Campingplatz Pizzeria Stigger, Bahnhofstraße 10, 6176 Völs (Tirol) [(0512) 303533; campingvoels@aon.at; www.camping-stigger.at]** Exit A12/E60 at Völs exit & foll site sp. Sm, pt shd; wc; chem disp; mv service pnt; shwrs inc; el pnts inc; Indtte; shop 100m; rest (pizzeria); snacks; bar; pool 200m; bus adj; Eng spkn; ccard acc; CCI. "Gd; conv Innsbruck." € 28.00 2010*

⊞ **INNSBRUCK** *C1* (8km W Rural) *47.2605, 11.25575* **Farmcamping Branger Alm, Haus Nr 32, 6175 Unterperfuss (Tirol) [(05232) 2209; fax 22094; brangeralm@aon.at; www.brangeralm.at]** Fr A12/E60 exit at Zirl-West, junc 91 & turn R at T-junc on m'way exit & foll sp Unterperfuss. Turn L at next T-junc. Site on R in 2km at ent to vill, immed after church on R. Med, pt shd; htd wc; chem disp; shwrs inc; el pnts (6A) metered; gas; Indtte; snacks; rest adj; bar 1km; pool 3km; skilift 4km; 90% statics; dogs €1; bus to Innsbruck; Eng spkn; quiet but some rlwy & rd noise. "Excel clean, modern facs; site poss untidy low ssn; if recep not in office, go to rest; vg rest." ♦ € 20.00 2009*

ITTER BEI HOPFGARTEN see Wörgl *C2*

AUSTRIA

KAUMBERG *B4* (4km E Rural) *48.01958, 15.94335* **Campingplatz Paradise Garden, Höfnergraben 2, 2572 Kaumberg (Niederösterreich) [0676 4741966 (mob); fax (02765) 3883; grandl@camping-noe.at; www.camping-noe.at]** B18 Hainfeld-Berndorf rd, site sp. Med, unshd; htd wc; chem disp; mv service pnt; baby facs; shwrs inc; el pnts (12A) €2; gas; lndtte (inc dryer); shop & 4km; rest 1.5km; snacks; bar; playgrnd; cycle hire; games rm; 60% statics; dogs free; phone; Eng spkn; adv bkg; quiet; red long stay; CCI. "Gd walking; helpful owner; superb san facs; easy access Vienna; lovely rural area." ♦ 1 Apr-31 Oct. € 22.00 2011*

⊞ **KERNHOF** *B4* (2km NW Rural) *47.81975, 15.53278* **Camping Gippelblick, Oberkeer 1, 3195 Kernhof (Niederösterreich) [(02768) 2544 or 0664 5035981 (mob); camping@pgv.at; www.campingkernhof.at]** Fr N exit A7 junc 59 St Pölten onto B20 S, then take B214. At junc with B21 turn W dir St Aegyd-am-Neuwalde & on to Kernhof. Site well sp in vill. Med, hdg pitch, pt shd; htd wc; chem disp; mv service pnt; shwrs €0.50; el pnts; lndtte; shop 2km; rest 400m; playgrnd; wintersports; skilift 4km; some statics; adv bkg; dogs; quiet. "Off beaten track; excel for mountain activities." € 12.00 2008*

KEUTSCHACH AM SEE *D3* (3km E Rural) *46.58673, 14.22778* **Camping Reautschnighof, Reauz 4, 9074 Keutschach-am-See (Kärnten) [tel/fax (0463) 281106; camping-reautschnighof@gmx.at; www.camping-reautschnighof.at]** Exit A2 at Klagenfurt West S to Viktring on S side of Wörthersee. Foll sp Keutschach & site. Sm, mkd pitch, pt sl, terr, unshd; wc; chem disp; shwrs €0.50; el pnts (6A) inc; shop 3km; rest 600m; pool 8km; lake sw 200m; dogs €1.50; quiet. "Lovely rural walks from area" 1 May-30 Sep. € 20.50 2011*

KEUTSCHACH AM SEE *D3* (3km E Rural) *46.58348, 14.22878* **Camping Reichmann, Reauz 5, 9074 Keutschach-am-See (Kärnten) [(0699) 1500057; info@camping-reichmann.at; www.camping-reichmann.at]** Exit A2 at Klagenfurt W onto B91 S to Viktring. Foll sp Keutschach-am-See, site sp. Lge, pt sl, pt shd; wc; chem disp; shwrs inc; el pnts (6A) inc; lndtte (inc dryer); shops 2km; rest; snacks; bar; BBQ; playgrnd; lake sw adj; fishing; games rm; internet; dogs €1.50; phone; poss cr; Eng spkn; quiet; ccard acc; red low ssn; CCI. "Excel." ♦ 1 May-20 Sep. € 25.70 2009*

KEUTSCHACH AM SEE *D3* (2.5km S Rural) *46.58472, 14.17225* **Strandcamping Sud, Dobeinitz 30a, 9074 Keutschach-am-See (Kärnten) [(04273) 2773; fax 27734; info@strandcampingsued.at; www.keutschachsued.at]** Fr Klagenfurt (N) take rd 91 (E94) sp Loibl Pass & turn R for Viktring & bypass Keutschach. At Keutschach See turn L off main rd at rndabt & foll sp past Strandcamping North. Lge, mkd pitch, some hdstg, pt sl, pt shd; wc; chem disp; mv service pnt; shwrs inc; el pnts (10A) inc; gas; lndtte (inc dryer); shop; tradsmn; rest; snacks; bar; BBQ; playgrnd; beach; lake sw adj; 80% statics; dogs €2.30; poss cr; Eng spkn. "Gd walking, sw, cycling & views." 1 May-30 Sep. € 27.50 2010*

KEUTSCHACH AM SEE *D3* (5km SW Rural) *46.57781, 14.15173* **FKK Camping Sabotnik (Naturist), Dobein 9, 9074 Keutschach-am-See (Kärnten) [(04273) 2509; fax 2605; info@fkk-sabotnik.at; www.fkk-sabotnik.at]** Fr Klagenfurt take B91 dir Loibl Pass; turn W at sp Viktring & Keutschach. W of lake turn S & foll camp sp past Camping Müllerhof. Lge, pt sl, pt shd; wc; chem disp; shwrs inc; el pnts (16A) inc; gas; lndtte; shop; rest; playgrnd; lake sw & beach; sailing; cycle hire; golf 4km; wifi; entmnt; TV; dogs €2; poss cr; adv bkg; quiet; cc acc. "Gd, friendly cent for families & lake area; gd forest walks; gd san facs." ♦ 1 May-30 Sep. € 20.00 2008*

KEUTSCHACH AM SEE *D3* (6km SW Rural) *46.57796, 14.14821* **FKK Camping Müllerhof (Naturist), Dobein 10, 9074 Keutschach-am-See (Kärnten) [(04273) 2517; fax 25175; muellerhof@fkk-camping.at; www.fkk-camping.at]** Exit fr A2 junc 335 sp Velden West dir Velden. In 1km at rndabt foll sp Keutschach; in 3km turn L at site sp. Or fr Villach, take B83 E twd Velden. Turn R approx 3km bef Velden sp Keutschach & foll site sp. Fr Klagenfurt, take B91 S, turn W to Keutschach. Cont on main rd past vill & foll site sp. Lge, mkd pitch, some hdstg, pt shd; htd wc; chem disp; mv service pnt; sauna; baby facs; shwrs inc; el pnts (6A) inc; lndtte (inc dryer); shops adj; tradsmn; rest; snacks; bar; playgrnd; sw in lake; games area; games rm; wifi; entmnt; TV; 10% statics; no dogs; phone; adv bkg; quiet. "Gd for lakes, walks, sailing." 15 Apr-30 Sep. € 30.00 2011*

KEUTSCHACH AM SEE *D3* (1km W Rural) *46.59080, 14.16490* **Camping Brückler Nord, Keutschachsee 5, 9074 Keutschach-am-See (Kärnten) [tel/fax (04273) 2384; camp.brueckler@aon.at; www.brueckler.co.at]** On N point of Keutschacher See at exit of Reifnitz rd fr Velden-Viktring rd. Med, pt shd; wc; chem disp; mv service pnt; shwrs inc; el pnts (6A) €4; lndtte; shop, rest adj; snacks; BBQ; playgrnd; lake sw; fishing; cycle hire; wifi; 25% statics; dogs €2.50; quiet. "Excel facs for children." 1 May-30 Sep. € 28.00 (CChq acc) 2009*

There aren't many sites open at this time of year. We'd better phone ahead to check the one we're heading for is open.

⊞ **KITZBUHEL** *C2* (1.5km W Rural) *47.45906, 12.3619* **Campingplatz Schwarzsee, Reitherstrasse 24, 6370 Kitzbühel (Tirol) [(05356) 62806 or 64479; fax 6447930; office@bruggerhof-camping.at; www.bruggerhof-camping.at]** Site sp fr Kitzbühel dir Kirchberg-Schwarzsee. Lge, pt sl, pt shd; htd wc; chem disp; mv service pnt; fam bthrm; sauna; shwrs inc; el pnts (16A) metered; mains gas conn some pitches; lndtte; shop; rest adj; snacks; bar; playgrnd; pool 2km; lake sw 300m; cab TV; 80% statics; dogs €5.50; phone; bus; poss cr; Eng spkn; adv bkg; ccard acc; CCI. "Gd walks, cable cars & chair lifts; vg, well-maintained site; poss mosquito prob; some pitches in statics area; friendly owner." ♦ € 34.80 2009*

⊞ **KITZBUHEL** *C2* (11km W Rural) *47.44583, 12.25721* **Campingplatz Brixen-im-Thale, Badhausweg 9, 6364 Brixen-im-Thale (Tirol) [(05334) 8113; fax 8101; info@camping-brixen.at; www.camping-brixen.at]** Fr A12 take B170 twd Kitzbühel. In Brixen 200m after church (opp rdside shrine) turn R into Winterweg, turn L 200m & foll sp to site. Lge, mkd pitch, pt shd; wc; chem disp; mv service pnt; shwrs €0.70; el pnts (16A) €2.50; Indtte; shop; rest; bar; playgrnd; pool 300m; lake 300m; cycle hire; 70% statics; dogs €2.50; Eng spkn; adv bkg; quiet but some rlwy noise; CCI. "Superb mountain scenery; excel walking & skiing; excel facs; organised activities; sm pitches for m'vans; rec cable car ride up Hahnenkamm; higher charges in winter." ♦ € 16.00 2008*

⊞ **KITZBUHEL** *C2* (14km W Rural) *47.43333, 12.20218* **Panorama-Camping, Mühltal 26, 6363 Westendorf (Tirol) [(05334) 6166; fax 6843; info@panoramacamping.at; www.panoramacamping.at]** On B170 fr Kitzbühel, site on L 1.5km after passing Westendorf stn, immed after tractor showrm. Med, mkd pitch, terr, unshd; wc; chem disp; mv service pnt; serviced pitch; sauna; shwrs inc; el pnts (12A) metered; gas metered & conn fee; Indtte; tradsmn; snacks; playgrnd; pool 200m; fitness rm; games rm; ski-lift 1km; cab TV; 80% statics; dogs €3.30; site clsd mid to end Nov; Eng spkn; adv bkg; some rlwy noise; red long stay; CCI. "Visits to silver mine, Swarovski crystal works; caves; excel location, conv Kitzbuhel, Innsbruck, Salzburg; excel facs; gd value rest/ snacks; access poss diff lge o'fits." ♦ € 20.00 2008*

KLAGENFURT *D3* (4km W Rural) *46.61826, 14.25641* **Campingplatz Strandbad, Metnitzstrand 5, 9020 Klagenfurt (Kärnten) [(0463) 5216391; fax 5216395; camping@stw.at]** Fr A2/E66 take spur to Klagenfurt-West, exit at Klagenfurt-Wörthersee. Turn R at traff lts & immed L at rd fork (traff lts), then foll sp to site. Lge, shd; wc; chem disp; sauna; shwrs inc; el pnts (10A) €1.50; Indtte; shop; rest; playgrnd; sand beach adj; cycle hire; entmnt; 10% statics; bus; quiet; ccard acc. "V clean facs." ♦ 1 May-30 Sep. € 25.50 2008*

KLOSTERLE AM ARLBERG see Zürs *C1*

KLOSTERNEUBURG *B4* (250m NE Rural) *48.31097, 16.32810* **Donaupark Camping Klosterneuburg, In der Au, 3402 Klosterneuburg (Niederösterreich) [(02243) 25877; fax 25878; campklosterneuburg@oeamtc.at; www.campingklosterneuburg.at]** Fr A22/E59 exit junc 7 onto B14, site sp in cent of town behind rlwy stn. After passing Klosterneuburg Abbey on L turn 1st R (sharp turn under rlwy). Site immed ahead. Med, mkd pitch, pt shd; htd wc; chem disp; mv service pnt; shwrs inc; el pnts (6-12A) €3; gas; Indtte (inc dryer); shop; rest 200m; snacks; BBQ; cooking facs; playgrnd; leisure cent & htd pools adj; cycle & boat hire; tennis; wifi; TV rm; 5% statics; dogs free; phone; bus; train to Vienna; poss cr; quiet; ccard acc; red CCI. "Well-organised, popular site; vg san facs; helpful staff; sm pitches; conv Danube cycle path & Vienna; church & monastery worth visit." ♦ 15 Mar-31 Oct. € 26.00 (CChq acc) 2011*

⊞ **KOSSEN** *B2* (2.5km W Rural) *47.65388, 12.41544* **Eurocamping Wilder Kaiser, Kranebittau 18, 6345 Kössen (Tirol) [(05375) 6444; fax 2113; info@eurocamp-koessen.com; www.eurocamp-koessen.com]** Leave A12 at Oberaudorf/Niederndorf junc, head E on 172 thro Niederndorf & Walchsee to Kössen. Strt across at rndabt, in 1km turn R sp Hinterburg Lift. At next junc turn R & site located after 400m. Lge, mkd pitch, pt shd; htd wc; chem disp; mv service pnt; serviced pitches; sauna; solarium; baby facs; shwrs inc; el pnts (6A) metered + conn fee; gas; Indtte; shop high ssn; tradsmn; rest, snacks high ssn; bar; playgrnd; htd pool adj; tennis; games area; golf 2km; entmnt; internet; cab TV; 50% statics; dogs €4; poss cr; Eng spkn; adv bkg; ccard acc; CCI. "Lovely site; excel play area & organised activities; rafting, hang-gliding & canoeing 1km; excel." € 23.50 2009*

⊞ **KOTSCHACH** *D2* (800m SW Rural) *46.66946, 12.99153* **Alpencamp, Kötschach 284, 9640 Kötschach-Mauthen (Kärnten) [tel/fax (04715) 429; info@alpencamp.at; www.alpencamp.at]** At junc of rds B110 & B111 in Kötschach turn W onto B111, foll camp sps to site in 800m on L. Med, mkd pitch, pt shd; htd wc; chem disp; mv service pnt; sauna; shwrs inc; el pnts (16A) inc; Indtte (inc dryer); sm shop; supmkt 400m; rest 100m; snacks; playgrnd; 2 pools (1 htd, covrd); waterslide; tennis; games area; games rm; boat & cycle hire; tennis 400m; wifi; TV; dogs €2.50; phone; site clsd 1 Nov-14 Dec; poss cr; Eng spkn; quiet; ccard acc. "Useful for Plöcken Pass; cycle tracks on rv bank nrby; vg san facs; friendly, helpful owner; vg site." ♦ € 26.90 (CChq acc) 2010*

KRAMSACH AM REINTALERSEE see Rattenberg *C2*

KREMS AN DER DONAU *B4* (1km SW Urban) *48.40305, 15.59194* **Donaupark-Camping, Yachthafenstrasse 19, 3504 Krems-Stein (Neiderösterreich) [tel/fax (02732) 84455; donaucampingkrems@aon.at; www.donauparkcamping-krems.at]** Fr B3 along N of Danube in Stein, foll site & 'Schiffstation' & camping sps to site on rvside. Med, unshd; htd wc; chem disp; mv service pnt; shwrs inc; el pnts (16A) €2; gas; Indtte (inc dryer); shop 500m; tradsmn; rest adj; snacks; bar; playgrnd 200m; pool 500m; cycle hire; 5% statics; phone; poss v cr; Eng spkn; adv bkg rec high ssn & pub hols; some rd & rv traffic noise; ccard acc; CCI. "Well-run site; excel, clean facs; office open 0730-1000 & 1630-1900; sm pitches; conv Danube cycle rte." 1 Apr-31 Oct. € 17.60 2009*

KREMS AN DER DONAU *B4* (7km SW Rural) *48.38998, 15.51678* **Campingplatz Rossatzbach, Rossatzbach 21, 3602 Rossatz (Neiderösterreich) [(02714) 6317; fax 6249; gemeinde@rossatz-arnsdorf.at; www.rossatz-arnsdorf.at]** Exit A1 junc 80 sp Melk & Donau Brücke. Cross Rv Danube & turn R along Danube L bank. After Dürnstein re-cross Danube on metal box bdge & turn R sp Melk & Rossatzbach. In 3km turn 1st R in Rossatzbach vill & foll sp to site in 200m. Sm, pt shd; htd wc; chem disp; shwrs inc; el pnts (16A) metered; Indtte; shop 1km; rest; snacks; bar; playgrnd; games area; 20% statics; dogs; poss cr; adv bkg; quiet; CCI. "Pleasant site on opp site of Danube to Dürnstein; most pitches on rvside; interesting area." Easter-31 Oct. € 17.25 2009*

⊞ **LANDECK** *C1* (500m W Urban) *47.14263, 10.56147* **Camping Riffler, Bruggfeldstrasse 2, 6500 Landeck (Tirol) [(05442) 64898; fax 648984; info@camping-riffler.at; www.camping-riffler.at]** Exit E60/A12 at Landeck-West, site in 1.5km, 500m fr cent on L. Sm, pt shd; wc; chem disp; shwrs inc; el pnts (10A) €2.70 (poss rev pol); gas; Indtte; shop adj; snacks, rest adj; playgrnd; pool 500m; cycle hire; dogs free; poss cr; site clsd May; ccard acc; red CCI. "Well-kept, clean, friendly site; sm pitches; narr rds; recep open 1800-2000 low ssn - site yourself & pay later; excel NH." € 23.50 2011*

⊞ **LANGENFELD** *C1* (400m S Rural) *47.07228, 10.96450* **Camping Ötztal, Unterlängenfeld 220, 6444 Längenfeld (Tirol) [(05253) 5348; fax 5909; info@camping-oetztal.com; www.camping-oetztal.com]** Exit A12 junc 123 at Ötztal onto B186 dir Sölden. On ent Längenfeld foll sp sports cent, site on R immed bef bdge over Rv Fischbach. Med, some hdstg, pt shd; wc; chem disp; mv service pnt; baby facs; solarium; sauna; shwrs; el pnts inc (6A) metered; gas; Indtte; shop adj; rest; bar; playgrnd; htd pool adj; rafting; tennis 500m; wifi; sat TV; 15% statics; dogs €3.10; poss cr; Eng spkn; quiet. "Gd rest & bar; mountain views; thermal springs, open air museum & Tirolean folk museum nr; vg site." ♦ € 22.50 2011*

⊞ **LANGENWANG** *C4* (N Rural) *47.56875, 15.62008* **Europa Camping, Siglstrasse 5, 8665 Langenwang (Steiermark) [(03854) 2950; europa.camping.stmk@aon.at; www.campsite.at/europa.camping.langenwang]** Exit S6 sp Langenwang, site sp in town cent. Sm, hdg pitch, pt shd; htd wc; chem disp; shwrs €0.80; el pnts (16A) €1.90; Indtte; shop, rest, snacks, bar 100m; playgrnd adj; htd, covrd pool 7km; lake sw 4km; ski facs; 30% statics; dogs; bus; Eng spkn; adv bkg; quiet; red long stay. "Pleasant, friendly site; family atmosphere; excel facs." € 15.00 2008*

LEIBNITZ *D4* (700m W Urban) *46.77864, 15.52891* **Camping Leibnitz, Rudolf-Hans-Bartsch-Gasse 33, 8430 Leibnitz (Steiermark) [(03452) 82463; fax 71491; leibnitz@camping-steiermark.at; www.camping-steiermark.at]** Fr A9 take exit Leibnitz onto B74, site not well sp, but nr sw pool, on rvside. Med, hdg/mkd pitch, pt shd; wc; chem disp; mv service pnt; fam bthrm; shwrs €1; el pnts (10-16A) €1.80; Indtte (inc dryer); shop 700m; rest; snacks; bar; playgrnd; pool adj; waterslide; rv sw adj; tennis; no statics; dogs; Eng spkn; ccard acc; CCI. "Gd NH; excel san facs; gd sports & leisure facs; interesting town." ♦ 1 May-15 Oct. € 15.50 2009*

LERMOOS see Ehrwald *C1*

LEUTASCH see Seefeld in Tirol *C1*

LIENZ *C2* (5km SE Rural) *46.80730, 12.80350* **Camping Seewiese, Tristachersee 2, 9900 Tristach (Tirol) [tel/fax (04852) 69767; seewiese@hotmail.com; www.campingtirol.com]** On B100 to Lienz dir Tristach, turn sharp L after rlwy underpass & rv bdge to by-pass Trisach. Turn R after 4km opp golf course. Steep (11%) climb to site. Sp. Med, some hdstg, sl, pt shd; wc; chem disp; mv service pnt; shwrs inc; el pnts (6-16A) €2.70; gas; Indtte (inc dryer); sm shop & 5km; rest & 500m; bar; playgrnd; htd pool 5km; lake sw 200m; tennis; cycle hire; wifi; TV rm; dogs €3; bus high ssn to Tristach; phone; poss cr; Eng spkn; quiet; red low ssn; CCI. "Fairly secluded, relaxing site; mountain views; gd walks; gd san facs; helpful owner." 7 May-25 Sep. € 24.50 (CChq acc) 2008*

LIENZ *C2* (500m S Urban) *46.82255, 12.77111* **Comfort-Camping Falken, Falkenweg 7, 9900 Lienz (Tirol) [(04852) 64022; fax 640226; camping.falken@tirol.com; www.camping-falken.com]** On B100 to town cent, foll sp Tristacher See, site sp adj leisure cent. Med, pt shd; htd wc; chem disp; mv service pnt; baby facs; shwrs €0.75; el pnts (6A) inc; gas; Indtte (inc dryer); sm shop; tradsmn; rest, snacks, bar high ssn; playgrnd; htd, covrd pool 500m; skilift 2km; ski bus; golf 4km; wifi; TV; 30% statics; dogs €3.50; poss cr; quiet; ccard acc; red long stay. "Gate closes 1300-1500; easy walk to vill with beautiful scenery - nearest site to Lienz; sm pitches; vg site." ♦ 20 Dec-20 Oct. € 27.50 2010*

⊞ **LIENZ** *C2* (2km SW Rural) *46.81388, 12.76388* **Dolomiten-Camping Amlacherhof, Amlach 4, 9900 Lienz [(04852) 62317; fax 6231712; info@amlacherhof.at; www.amlacherhof.at]** S fr Lienz on B100, foll sp in 1.5km to Amlach. In vill, foll site sp. Med, hdg/mkd pitch, pt shd; htd wc; chem disp; mv service pnt; baby facs; shwrs €0.80; el pnts (16A) metered; Indtte (inc dryer); rest 500m; snacks; bar; BBQ; playgrnd; htd, covrd pool; tennis; cycle hire; games rm; golf 7km; wifi; TV rm; 10% statics; dogs €2.90; bus adj; site clsd 1 Nov-15 Dec; poss cr; Eng spkn; adv bkg; quiet. "Excel touring cent; many mkd walks & cycle rtes; cable cars, ski lifts 3km; attractive, historic town; excel, scenic site; gd facs for children." ♦ € 21.70 2010*

LINZ *B3* (10km E Rural) *48.23527, 14.37888* **Camping-Linz am Pichlingersee, Wienerstrasse 937, 4030 Linz-Pichling (Oberösterreich) [(0732) 305314; fax 3053144; office@camping-linz.at; www.camping-linz.at]** Exit A1/E60 junc 160 onto B1, site sp on lakeside. Med, mkd pitch, pt shd; htd wc; chem disp; mv service pnt; shwrs inc; el pnts (6A) inc; gas; Indtte; sm shop & 2km; tradsmn; rest; snacks; bar; cooking facs; lake sw adj; tennis; internet; 40% statics; dogs €1.90; bus; site clsd 1300-1500; poss cr; adv bkg; some noise fr m'way; red long stay. "Excel, well-run, family-run site; friendly staff; gd walks around lake; monastery at St Florian worth visit; conv NH; gd." ♦ 15 Mar-31 Oct. € 20.60 2011*

⊞ **LOFER** *C2* (1km S Rural) *47.57500, 12.70804* **Camping Park Grubhof, St Martin 39, 5092 St Martin-bei-Lofer (Salzburg) [(06588) 82370; fax 82377; camping@lofer.net; www.grubhof.com]** Clear sps to camp at ent on rd B311 Lofer to Zell-am-See. Lge, pt shd; htd wc; chem disp; mv service pnt; baby facs; serviced pitches; shwrs inc; el pnts (10A) €2; Indtte; supmkt 700m; rest; bar; pool 1km; playgrnd; wifi; dogs €3; phone; adv bkg; bus to Salzburg; quiet; CCI. "Beautiful scenery; roomy, peaceful site; excel san facs; lge rvside pitches; sep sections reserved for visitors without children or with dogs; sh walk to vill; highly rec." ♦ € 21.20 2010*

⊞ **LUNZ AM SEE** *B4* (300m E Urban) *47.86194, 15.03638* **Ötscherland Camping, Zellerhofstrasse 23, 3293 Lunz-am-See (Niederösterreich) [tel/fax (07486) 8413; info@oetscherlandcamping.at; www.oetscherlandcamping.at]** Fr S on B25 turn R into Lunz-am-See. In 300m turn L, cross rv & take 1st L, site on L on edge of vill. Sm, hdstg, pt shd; htd wc; chem disp; mv service pnt; shwrs €1; el pnts (16A) inc; Indtte; shop, rest in vill; lake sw 500m; winter skiing; 80% statics; dogs €1; Eng spkn; quiet. "Excel walking; immac facs; vg site on Rv Ybbs & Eisenstrasse." € 15.00 2009*

MAISHOFEN see Zell am See *C2*

MALTA see Gmünd (Kärnten) *C3*

MARBACH AN DER DONAU *B4* (1km W Rural) *48.21309, 15.13828* **Campingplatz Marbacher, Granz 51, 3671 Marbach-an-der Donau (Niederösterreich) [(07413) 20733; fax 20735; info@marbach-freizeit.at; www.marbach-freizeit.at]** Fr W exit A1 junc 100 at Ybbs onto B25. Cross Rv Danube & turn R onto B3. Site in 7km. Fr E exit A1 junc 90 at Pöchlarn, cross rv & turn L onto B3 to Marbach, site sp. Med, mkd pitch, pt shd; htd wc; chem disp; mv service pnt; shwrs inc; el pnts (16A) €2.50; Indtte (inc dryer); shop 500m; tradsmn; rest 500m; BBQ; rv sw; watersports; tennis 800m; boat & cycle hire; internet; entmnt; 5% statics; Eng spkn; adv bkg; rlwy & rv noise; ccard acc; red CCI. "Beautiful, well-managed site; sm, narr pitches; excel facs & staff; gd cycling & watersports." ♦ 1 Apr-31 Oct. € 17.60 (CChq acc) 2010*

MARIAZELL *B4* (3km NW Rural) *47.79009, 15.28221* **Campingplatz am Erlaufsee, Erlaufseestrasse 3, 8630 St Sebastien-bei-Mariazell (Steiermark) [(03882) 4937; fax 214822; gemeinde@st-sebastian.at; www.st-sebastian.at]** On B20 1km N of Mariazell turn W sp Erlaufsee. Site in 3km on app to lake, turn L thro car park ent to site. Med, pt sl, pt shd; wc; chem disp; shwrs €0.50; el pnts (12A) metered; Indtte; shop 3km; rest, snacks adj; beach nr; bus high ssn; dogs €1.90; quiet. "Cable car in Mariazell; pilgrimage cent; all hot water by token fr owner." 1 May-15 Sep. € 16.30 2011*

MATREI IN OSTTIROL *C2* (500m S Rural) *46.99583, 12.53906* **Camping Edengarten, Edenweg 15a, 9971 Matrei-in-Osttirol (Tirol) [tel/fax (04875) 5111; info@campingedengarten.at; www.campingedengarten.at]** App fr Lienz on B108 turn L bef long ascent (by-passing Matrei) sp Matrei-in-Osttirol & Camping. App fr N thro Felbertauern tunnel, by-pass town, turn R at end of long descent, sps as above. Med, pt shd; wc; chem disp; mv service pnt; shwrs €0.50; el pnts (10A) €2.20; gas; Indtte; supmkt, rest, snacks adj; bar; playgrnd; pool 300m; 10% statics; dogs; bus; poss cr. "Gd mountain scenery; helpful owner." 1 Apr-30 Oct. € 17.40 2008*

MAURACH see Schwaz *C2*

⊞ **MAYRHOFEN** *C2* (1km N Rural) *47.17617, 11.86969* **Camping Mayrhofen, Laubichl 125, 6290 Mayrhofen (Tirol) [(05285) 6258051; fax 6258060; camping@alpenparadies.com; www.alpenparadies.com]** Site at N end of vill off B169. Lge, mkd pitch, hdstg, pt shd; wc; chem disp; mv service pnt; sauna; shwrs inc; el pnts (10A) €2.50 or metered; gas; Indtte; shop 1km; rest; snacks; playgrnd; pool; cycle hire; wifi; 50% statics; dogs €3; site clsd 1 Nov-15 Dec; adv bkg; poss cr; some factory noise; CCI. "Modern san facs." ♦ € 20.30 2009*

MELK *B4* (1km N Rural) *48.23347, 15.32888* **Camping Fährhaus Melk, Kolomaniau 3, 3390 Melk (Niederösterreich) [tel/fax (02752) 53291; jensch@brauhof-wieselburg.at]** Skirt Melk on B1, immed after abbey at traff lts, turn N on bdge over rv (sp). Site in 700m. Sm, pt shd; wc; shwrs; el pnts (6A) inc; shop & 1km; rest at Gasthaus; snacks; bar; BBQ; playgrnd; fishing; quiet. "Lovely, basic site but adequate; abbey adj & boating on Danube; NB all sites on banks of Danube liable to close if rv in flood." 1 Apr-31 Oct. € 17.60 2010*

MELK *B4* (5km N Urban) *48.24298, 15.34040* **Donau Camping Emmersdorf, Bundesstrasse 133, 3644 Emmersdorf-an-der-Donau (Niederösterreich) [(02752) 71707; fax (2752) 7146930; office@emmersdorf.at; www.emmersdorf.at]** Fr A1 take Melk exit. Turn R, foll sp Donaubrücke, cross rv bdge. Turn R, site 200m on L, well sp. Sm, mkd/hdg pitch, pt shd; wc; chem disp; baby facs; shwrs inc; el pnts (6A) inc; Indtte (inc dryer); shops 300m; supmkt 3km; rest 300m; BBQ; pool 13km; fishing; tennis; cycle hire; games rm; dogs; phone; noise fr rd & disco w/end; ccard acc; CCI. "Liable to close if rv in flood; clean facs; attractive vill; vg." ♦ 1 May-30 Sep. € 16.10 2010*

MELK *B4* (5km NE Rural) *48.25395, 15.37115* **Campingplatz Stumpfer, 3392 Schönbühel (Niederösterreich) [(02752) 8510; fax 851017; office@stumpfer.com; www.stumpfer.com]** Exit A1 junc 80. Foll sp for Melk on B1 as far as junc with B33. Turn onto B33 (S bank of Danube) for 2km to Schönbühel. Site on L adj gasthof, sp. Sm, pt shd, wc; chem disp; shwrs €0.50; el pnts (10-16A) €2.40 or metered; gas; Indtte; shops 5km; rest; snacks; rv adj; dogs; poss v cr; Eng spkn; adv bkg; ccard acc; red long stay/CCI. "On beautiful stretch of Danube; arr early for rvside pitch; abbeys in Melk & Krems worth visit; lower end site unrel in wet; helpful staff; vg facs but poss stretched high ssn; cycle path adj." 1 Apr-31 Oct. € 17.40 2010*

MILLSTATT *D3* (2km SE Rural) *46.79581, 13.59768* **Terrassencamping Pesenthein (Part Naturist), Presenthein, 9872 Millstatt (Kärnten) [(04766) 2665; fax 202120; camping-pesenthein@aon.it; www.pesenthein.at]** Exit A10/E55 dir Seeboden & Millstaff. Lake lakeside rd B98 fr Millstatt to Dellach. Site on L just beyond Pesenthein. Lge, mkd pitch, terr, pt shd; htd wc; chem disp; mv service pnt; baby facs; shwrs inc; el pnts (6A) €1.75; Indtte; shop; rest; playgrnd; lake sw & beach adj (via tunnel); TV; 17% statics; dogs free; phone; Eng spkn; adv bkg; quiet; CCI. "Lovely views over lake; excel facs." 1 Apr-30 Sep. € 25.20 2010*

MILLSTATT *D3* (4km SE Rural) *46.78863, 13.61418* **Camping Neubauer, Dellach 3, 9872 Millstatt-am-See (Kärnten) [(04766) 2532; fax 25324; info@camping-neubauer.at; www.camping-neubauer.at]** Exit A10/E55 dir Seeboden & Millstatt. Take lakeside rd B98 fr Millstatt to Dellach, R turn & foll camping sp. Med, mkd pitch, some hdstg, terr, pt shd; htd wc; chem disp; baby facs; shwrs inc; el pnts (6A) inc; gas; Indtte (inc dryer); shop; tradsmn; rest adj; snacks; bar; BBQ; playgrnd; lake sw; watersports; tennis; cycle hire; golf 6km; wifi; entmnt; 10% statics; dogs €2; poss cr; no adv bkg; quiet; ccard acc. "Gd touring base; easy access to Italy; superb scenery with lakes & mountains; gd walks; excel facs; boat trips nr; gd rest." 1 May-15 Oct. € 24.50 2011*

MITTERSILL *C2* (E Rural) *47.27761, 12.49267* **Camping Schmidl, Museumstrasse 6, 5730 Mittersill (Salzburg) [(06562) 6158]** Fr Zell-am-See or Kitzbühel, exit to Mittersill, fr town sq foll camping sp past hospital. Sm, pt shd; wc; chem disp; shwrs €0.60; el pnts (15A) inc; Indtte; shops 1km; rest, snacks 100m; 40% statics; dogs; poss cr; quiet. "Friendly & welcoming; useful stop bef Felbertauern tunnel; conv Krimml waterfall & Grossglockner." 1 May-30 Sep. € 12.00 2009*

MONDSEE *B3* (3km N Rural) *47.86640, 13.30621* **Camping Mond-See-Land, Punz Au 21, 5310 Tiefgraben (Oberösterreich) [(06232) 2600; fax 27218; austria@campmondsee.at; www.campmondsee.at]** Exit A1/E60/E55 junc 265 for Mondsee, turn N on B154 dir Strasswalchen. After 1.5km turn L dir Haider-Mühle on narr country rd to site in 2km. Site sp fr B154. Med, mkd pitch, pt sl, pt shd; htd wc; chem disp; shwrs inc; el pnts (16A) €3.20; gas; Indtte (inc dryer); shop; tradsmn; rest; snacks; bar; BBQ; playgrnd; pool; boating; internet; entmnt; dogs €2.90; phone; adv bkg; quiet; red long stay; "Beautiful mountain scenery; spacious pitches; excel new san facs; lovely countryside; serviced pitches avail for extra charge; somewhat isolated & away fr main rd." ♦ 1 Apr-31 Oct. € 19.80 2011*

MONDSEE *B3* (5km SE Rural) *47.82956, 13.36554* **Austria Camp, Achort 60, 5310 St Lorenz (Oberösterreich) [(06232) 2927; fax 29274; camp.mondsee@inode.at; www.oberoesterreich.at/austria-camp]** Exit A1/E55/E60 junc 265 onto B154. In 4km at St Lorenz at km 21.4 turn L onto unclassified rd to site in 600m at lakeside. Fr SW via Bad Ischl, at St Gilgen take Mondsee rd; 500m after Plomberg turn R at St Lorenz; Austria Camp sps clear. Med, shd; wc; chem disp; mv service pnt; sauna; baby facs; sauna; shwrs inc; el pnts (6A) €2.90; Indtte (inc dryer); rest; snacks; bar; shop; playgrnd; lake sw; fishing; boat-launch; tennis; cycle hire; golf nr; entmnt; 45% statics; dogs €2.90; poss cr (Jul-Aug); adv bkg; quiet; 10% red CCI. "Gd, clean san facs; gd rest; friendly, family-run site." ♦ 1 May-30 Sep. € 22.50 2010*

⊞ **MURAU** *C3* (5km W Rural) *47.10791, 14.13883* **Camping Olachgut, Kaindorf 90, 8861 St Georgen-ob-Murau (Steiermark) [(03532) 2162 or 3233; fax 21624; office@olachgut.at; www.olachgut.at]** Site sp on rd B97 bet Murau & St Georgen. Med, pt shd; wc; chem disp; mv service pnt; baby facs; sauna; shwrs inc; el pnts (16A) metered; gas conn; Indtte (inc dryer); shop 2.5km; rest; snacks; bar; playgrnd; lake sw; games area; cycle hire; skilift 2.5km; horseriding; entmnt; internet; 40% statics; dogs €2.20; adv bkg; quiet. ♦ € 21.00 2010*

MURECK *D4* (500m S Rural) *46.70491, 15.77240* **Campingplatz Mureck, Austrasse 10, 8480 Mureck (Steiermark) [(03472) 210512; fax 21056; m.rauch@mureck.steiermark.at]** Fr Graz on A9, turn E at junc 226 onto B69 sp Mureck. NB: Low archway in Mureck. Med, mkd pitch, some hdstg, shd; wc; chem disp; shwrs €0.50; el pnts (10A) inc; Indtte (inc dryer); shops adj; rest; snacks; bar; BBQ; playgrnd; htd pool complex inc waterslide adj; fishing; tennis; cycle hire; games area; wifi; 30% statics; dogs €3.50; phone; adv bkg; quiet; red long stay; ccard acc; red CCI. "Off beaten track in pleasant country town; part of leisure complex; gd, modern san facs." ♦ 1 May-15 Sep. € 22.90 2010*

⊞ **MURECK** *D4* (10km W Rural) *46.71611, 15.68277* **Gasthof Dorfheuriger, Unterschwarza 1, 8471 Unterschwarza-Murfeld (Steiermark) [(03453) 21001; dorfheuriger@gmx.net; www.dorfheuriger.eu]** On B69 fr Mureck or exit A9 junc 226 at Gersdorf & take B69 E for 2km. Sm, mkd pitch, unshd; wc; chem disp; mv service pnt; el pnts; rest, bar adj; tennis; wifi; quiet. "Vg NH for m'vans only." 2010*

NASSEREITH *C1* (1km N Rural) *47.34043, 10.81585* **Romantik-Camping Schloss Fernsteinsee, Fernsteinsee, 6465 Nassereith (Tirol) [(05265) 5210157; fax 52174; camping@fernsteinsee.at; www.fernsteinsee.at/camping]** 5km S of Fern pass. Immed prior to rd bdge. Ent sp by Hotel - use S ent, not ent by bdge/hotel. Med, pt sl, shd; htd wc; chem disp; sauna; solarium; some serviced pitches; shwrs inc; el pnts (6A) inc; Indtte; shop & 4km; rest 400m; snacks; playgrnd; sw in lake adj; boating; sat TV; dogs €2; quiet; ccard acc. "Immac facs; excel rest; stunning scenery for walking/cycling." ♦ Easter-31 Oct. € 31.00 2011*

⊞ **NASSEREITH** *C1* (1.5km E Rural) *47.30975, 10.85466* **Camping Rossbach, Rossbach 325, 6465 Nassereith (Tirol) [tel/fax (05265) 5154; camping.rossbach@aon.at; www.campingrossbach.com]** On ent vill of Nassereith turn E & foll dir Rossbach/Dormitz, site in 1.5km. Foll sm green sps. Narr app. Med, mkd pitch, pt shd; htd wc; chem disp; mv service pnt; baby facs; shwrs inc; el pnts (6A) inc; Indtte (inc dryer); shop; tradsmn; rest; snacks; bar; BBQ; playgrnd; htd pool; paddling pool; fishing; games rm; skilift 500m; skibus; TV; 5% statics; dogs €1.50; phone; adv bkg; quiet; CCI. ♦ € 18.90 2011*

NATTERS see Innsbruck *C1*

⊞ **NAUDERS** *C1* (2km S Rural) *46.85139, 10.50472* **Alpencamping, Bundestrasse 279, 6543 Nauders (Tirol) [(05473) 87217; fax 8721750; info@camping-nauders.at; www.camping-nauders.at]** On W side of B180 just bef Italian border. Sm, some hdstg, unshd; htd wc; chem disp; baby facs; shwrs €0.50; el pnts €1.90; gas conn; Indtte; shop & 2km; rest; snacks; bar; no statics; dogs €2; phone; site clsd 1 Nov-19 Dec; poss cr; ccard acc; CCI. "Conv NH for Reschen pass; gd touring base; excel cycling, walking; excel san facs." € 18.00 2009*

⊞ **NENZING** *C1* (2km SW Rural) *47.18313, 9.68238* **Alpencamping Nenzing, Garfrenga 1, 6710 Nenzing (Vorarlberg) [(05525) 624910; fax 624916; office@alpencamping.at; www.alpencamping.at]** Exit A14/E60 or B190 at Nenzing, foll camping sps thro Nenzing for 3km up Gurtis rd, narr & winding in parts, camp on L sp. When leaving site, vehicles routed away fr Nenzing on sp country rds for 10km back to B190. Lge, mkd pitch, hdstg; terr, pt sl, pt shd; wc; chem disp; mv service pnt; baby facs; sauna; shwrs inc; el pnts (4-12A) metered; gas; Indtte; shop; tradsmn; rest; snacks; bar; playgrnd; htd pool; paddling pool; ski-lift 1.5km; games rm; wifi; entmnt; TV; many statics; dogs €4.50; clsd 31 Mar-24 Apr; skibus; poss cr; Eng spkn; adv bkg ess; quiet; 10% red low ssn. "Close to ski school & lifts; gd views & beautiful walks; excel san facs; gd rest; recep poss unmanned in winter - phone box adj; excel." ♦ € 31.00 2008*

⊞ **NEUSTIFT IM STUBAITAL** *C1* (E Rural) *47.11076, 11.31021* **Camping Stubai, Dorf 115, 6167 Neustift-im-Stubaital (Tirol) [(05226) 2537; fax 29342; info@campingstubai.at; www.campingstubai.at]** S fr Innsbruck on B182 or A13, take B183 dir Fulpmes & Neustift. Site sp, in vill opp church & adj Billa supmkt. If app via A13 & Europabrucke, toll payable on exit junc 10 into Stubaital Valley. Med, some mkd pitch, pt sl, pt terr, pt shd; htd wc; chem disp; mv service pnt; baby facs; fam bthrm; sauna; shwrs inc; el pnts (6A) €2.90; Indtte; shops adj; rest, bar adj; playgrnd; htd pool 500m; games rm; 50% statics; dogs €2.60; Eng spkn; adv bkg; quiet but church bells (not o'night) & rd noise fr some pitches; debit cards acc; CCI. "Friendly, family-run site; pitches nr rv poss flood; recep open 0900-1100 & 1700-1900 - barrier down but can use farm ent & find space; excel mountain walking & skiing." € 17.10 2009*

⊞ **NEUSTIFT IM STUBAITAL** *C1* (6km SW Rural) *47.06777, 11.25388* **Camping Edelweiss, Volderau 29, 6167 Neustift-im-Stubaital (Tirol) [tel/fax (05226) 3484; info@camping-edelweiss.at; www.camping-edelweiss.com]** Fr B182 or A13 exit junc 10 take B183 to Neustift, site on R at Volderau vill. Med, hdstg, unshd; htd wc; chem disp; mv waste; shwrs inc; el pnts (4A) €2; gas; Indtte; shop 6km; tradsmn; rest; snacks; 30% statics; dogs €1.50; phone; bus; quiet. "Excel peaceful site in scenic valley; vg, modern san facs; haphazard mix of statics & tourers; winter skiing." € 15.00 2010*

NUZIDERS see Bludenz *C1*

⊞ **OBERNBERG AM INN** *B3* (500m SW Rural) *48.31506, 13.32313* **Panorama Camping, Saltzburgerstrasse 28, 4982 Obernberg-am-Inn (Oberösterreich) [tel/fax (07758) 2203; obernberg-panoramacamping@aon.at]** Exit A8/E56 junc 65 to Obernberg. Then take dir Braunau, site well sp. Med, hdg pitch, pt sl, pt shd; wc; chem disp; serviced pitches; shwrs inc; el pnts (10A) metered or €2 (poss rev pol); Indtte; shop 200m; rest 400m; pool, tennis 800m; o'night area for m'vans; Eng spkn; adv bkg; quiet. "Friendly, excel sm site; site yourself if office clsd; nr to border; spectacular views; san facs clean; gd walking, birdwatching; network of cycle paths around vills on other side of rv; interesting walled town." € 19.00 2011*

OBERSAMMELSDORF see Völkermarkt *D3*

OBERTRAUN WINKL see Hallstatt *C3*

OBERWOLZ *C3* (1km E Rural) *47.20076, 14.29296* **Camping Rothenfels (Part Naturist), Bromach 1, 8832 Oberwölz (Steiermark) [tel/fax (03581) 76980 or 0664 1412514 (mob); camping@rothenfels.at; www.rothenfels.at]** Fr E on B96 to Niederwölz, then B75 to Oberwölz. Site sp on edge of town. Med, terr, pt shd; htd wc; chem disp; mv service pnt; shwrs inc; el pnts (6A) inc; Indtte (inc dryer); shop 1km; tradsmn; rest, snacks, bar 1km; tradsmn; playgrnd; rv fishing; games rm; 15% statics; dogs €1; Eng spkn; no adv bkg; quiet; ccard acc; red long stay. "Magnificent setting; Oberwölz worth visit - m'vans use car parks outside gates; clean facs; site not suitable disabled." 1 Apr-31 Oct. € 18.50 2010*

⊞ **OETZ** *C1* (8km S Rural) *47.13533, 10.9316* **Ötztal Arena Camp Krismer, Mühlweg 32, 6444 Umhausen (Tirol) [tel/fax (05255) 5390; info@oetztal-camping.at; www.oetztal-camping.at]** Fr A12 exit junc 123 S onto B186 sp Ötztal. S of Ötztal turn L into Umhausen vill & foll site sp. Med, mkd pitch, pt sl, pt shd; wc; chem disp; shwrs €0.75; el pnts (10A) metered (poss rev pol); gas; Indtte; shop 200m; tradsmn; rest; snacks 200m; bar; BBQ; playgrnd; pool 200m; lake sw; internet; 30% statics; dogs €2.60; phone; Eng spkn; adv bkg (dep); quiet. "Well-run site; immac facs; lots of local info given on arr; friendly owners; poss diff pitching on some sh pitches; excel cent for Stuibenfal waterfall (illuminted Wed night high ssn) & Ötztaler Valley; pool & lake sw 200m; wonderful scenery; gd walking fr site." € 20.00 2011*

OGGAU AM NEUSIEDLERSEE see Eisenstadt *B4*

OSSIACH *D3* (3km E Rural) *46.68558, 14.01233* **Familien-Camping Jodl, Alt-Ossiach 6, 9570 Ossiach (Kärnten) [(04243) 8779; fax 87794; info@camping-jodl.at; www.camping-jodl.at]** Site on S shore of Ossiachersee at E end, fr Feldkirchen take B94 rd in 6km turn S sp Ossiach-Villach, at rd junc turn W, site on R in 1km (approx). Sp at site ent. Fr W on B94 thro Bodensdorf & Steindorf turn S as above. Med, mkd pitch, terr, pt shd; wc; chem disp; mv service pnt; shwrs inc; el pnts inc (16A) inc; Indtte; shop high ssn; tradsmn; supmkt 2km; rest; snacks; playgrnd; shgle beach adj; lake sw; watersports; dogs €3; o'night facs for m'vans; Eng spkn; adv bkg; quiet; red snr citizens; CCI. "Excel site; beautiful scenery; friendly owners; facs for sm boats; oldest established site on Ossiachersee." 11 Apr-30 Sep. € 26.30 2009*

OSSIACH *D3* (2km S Rural) *46.66528, 13.97680* **Wellness-Seecamping Parth, Ostriach 10, 9570 Ossiach (Kärnten) [(04243) 27440; fax 274415; office@parth.at; www.parth.at]** Exit A10/E55/E66 at Villach-Ossiachersee. Foll sp for Ossiachersee Süd. Site on L, 2km bef Ossiach. Med, mkd pitch, some hdstg, pt sl, terr, pt shd; htd wc; chem disp; mv service pnt; serviced pitches; baby facs; sauna; shwrs inc; el pnts (10A) inc; gas; Indtte (inc dryer); shop; rest; snacks; bar; BBQ; playgrnd; shgl beach for lake sw adj; waterslide; solarium; watersports; tennis; fitness rm; cycle hire; golf course; wifi; entmnt; cinema & TV rm; wifi; TV; 25% statics; dogs €3; site clsd 8 Nov-26 Dec; poss v cr; Eng spkn; adv bkg ess; quiet; red CCI. "Excel; lake views; helpful staff; busy site." ♦ 1-6 Jan & 1 Apr-31 Oct. € 26.70 (CChq acc) 2008*

OSSIACH *D3* (1km SW Rural) *46.66193, 13.9728* **Camping Kölbl, Ostriach 106, 9570 Ossiach (Kärnten) [(04243) 8223; fax 8690; camping-koelbl@net4you.at; www.camping-koelbl.at]** Fr Villach to Feldkirchen on S bank of Ossiachersee. Med, pt sl, pt shd; wc; chem disp; mv service pnt; shwrs inc; el pnts (10A) €1.20; gas; Indtte; shop 100m; rest; playgrnd; pool 1.5km; boat-launching; lake sw; skibus; 15% statics; poss cr; quiet. "Gd cent for Carinthian lakes; cycle path; clsd 1300-1500." ♦ 1 Apr-31 Oct & 15 Dec-15 Jan. € 20.50 2008*

AUSTRIA

OSSIACH *D3* (1km SW Rural) *46.66388, 13.97500* **Terrassen Camping Ossiacher See, Ostriach 67, 9570 Ossiach (Kärnten) [(04243) 436; fax 8171; martinz@camping.at; www.terrassen.camping.at]** Leave A10/E55/E66 at exit for Ossiachersee, turn L onto B94 twd Feldkirchen & shortly R to Ossiach Süd. Site on lake shore just S of Ossiach vill. Lge, mkd pitch, terr, pt shd; htd wc; chem disp; mv service pnt; baby facs; fam bthrm; shwrs inc; el pnts (4-10A) €3; gas; Indtte; shop; rest; snacks; bar; BBQ; playgrnd; lake sw & beach; watersports; windsurfing; fishing; horse riding; tennis; games area; cycle hire; games rm; cash machine; wifi; entmnt; TV rm; dogs €3; twin-axles acc (rec check in adv); poss cr; clsd 1200-1500 low ssn, parking adj; quiet; ccard acc; red long stay/low ssn; CCI. "Ideal Carinthian lakes, Hochosterwitz castle & excursions into Italy; beautiful scenery; many activities; excel san facs." ♦ 1 May-30 Sep. € 31.00 SBS - G05 2011*

OSSIACH *D3* (4km SW Rural) *46.65321, 13.93344* **Seecamping Berghof, Ossiachersee Süduferstrasse 241, 9523 Heiligengestade (Kärnten) [(04242) 41133; fax 4113330; office@seecamping-berghof.at; www.seecamping-berghof.at]** Exit Villach on rd sp Ossiachersee; take R turn Ossiachersee Süd, site on L bet rd & lake. Lge, terr, pt sl, pt shd; htd wc; chem disp; mv service pnt; serviced pitches; fam bthrm; baby rm; private bthrms avail; shwrs inc; el pnts (6A) inc; gas; Indtte (inc dryer); shop, rest; snacks high ssn; bar; playgrnd; lake beach & sw; sailing; fishing; tennis; games area; cycle hire; golf 10km; wifi; entmnt; 10% statics; dogs €3 (in sep area); phone; poss cr; adv bkg; quiet; red snr citizens/long stay/low ssn. "Excel site; gd cent for excursions to castles & lakes; many sports & activities; extra for lge/lakeside pitches; muddy when wet." ♦ 1 Apr-17 Oct. € 32.10 2010*

OSSIACH *D3* (4km SW Rural) *46.65376, 13.93735* **See-Camping Mentl, Süderstrasse 265, 9523 Heiligen-Gestade (Kärnten) [(04242) 41886; fax 43850; camping@mentl.at; www.mentl.at]** Fr A10/E55/E65 turn N onto B94 twd Feldkirchen. Almost immed turn R sp Ossiach, site on L adj lake in 4km. Lge, mkd pitch, terr, pt shd; wc; chem disp; some serviced pitches; baby facs; shwrs inc; el pnts (6A) inc (check pol); Indtte (inc dryer); shops adj; snacks; rest adj; playgrnd; lake sw; watersports; cycle hire; entmnt; no dogs high ssn; poss cr; Eng spkn; adv bkg; quiet; red long stay. "Beautiful setting; gd facs & entmnt for children; helpful staff; excel, modern, clean san facs." ♦ 1 Apr-15 Oct. € 28.80 2010*

OSSIACH *D3* (4km W Rural) **Seecamping Plörz, Süduferstrasse 289, 9523 Heiligen-Gestade (Kärnten) [(04242) 41286 or 0676-3221494 (mob); info@camping-ploerz.at; www.camping-ploerz.at]** Fr A10/E55/E65 turn N onto B94 twd Feldkirchen. Almost immed turn R sp Ossiach, site on R just past Camping Mentl. Sm, pt sl, pt shd; htd wc; chem disp; mv service pnt; baby facs; shwrs inc; el pnts (16A) inc; Indtte; shop, rest, snacks, bar nrby; play equipment; lake sw adj; TV rm; dogs €2; phone; Eng spkn; quiet. "Excel sm farm site with gd facs; friendly helpful owners; quiet alternative to other busy lakeside sites; lge pitches; v clean facs; cycle paths & gd walks; bus stop at gate; ltd facs for children." Apr-25 Sep. € 24.00 2011*

⊞ **PETTENBACH** *B3* (4km N Rural) *47.99116, 14.02231* **Camping Almtal, Pettenbach 49, 4643 Pettenbach (Oberösterreich) [(07586) 8627; fax 862733; office@almtalcamp.at; www.almtalcamp.at]** Exit A1/E60/E55 dir Vorchdorf & foll sp to Pettenbach, then foll dir Sattledt, site in 4km on L, well sp. Lge, pt shd; htd wc; chem disp; mv service pnt; shwrs inc; el pnts (6A) inc (long lead poss req); Indtte; shop & 4km; rest; snacks; playgrnd; htd pool; tennis; cycle hire; entmnt; phone; poss noisy. "Conv Salzburg lakes; san facs poss unclean low ssn (2008)." ♦ € 23.00 2008*

PETTNEU AM ARLBERG see St Anton am Arlberg *C1*

PODERSDORF AM SEE see Frauenkirchen *B4*

I'll go online and tell the Club what we think of the campsites we've visited – www.caravanclub.co.uk/europereport

POYSDORF *A4* (1km W Urban) *48.66454, 16.61168* **Veltlinerland Camping, Laaerstrasse 106, 2170 Poysdorf (Niederösterreich) [(02552) 20371; fax 37131; veltlinerlandcamping.poysdorf@gmx.at; www.poysdorf.at]** Fr rd 7/E461 at traff lts in Poysdorf turn W onto rd 219 dir Laa an der Thaya. Site sp on R in approx 1km on edge of park. Sm, mkd pitch, some hdstg, terr, unshd; htd wc & shwrs at park adj (key issued); chem disp; mv service pnt; el pnts (6A) €2.20; Indtte; shop 1km; rest; playgrnd; rv sw adj; tennis; 50% statics in sep area; dogs; Eng spkn; quiet. "Gd, under-used site 1 hr N of Vienna; no other site in area; conv Czech border." 1 May-31 Oct. € 12.10 2010*

⊞ **PRUTZ** *C1* (200m E Rural) *47.07955, 10.6588* **Aktiv-Camping Prutz, Pontlatzstrasse 22, 6522 Prutz (Tirol) [(05472) 2648; fax 26484; info@aktiv-camping.at; www.aktiv-camping.at]** Fr Landeck to Prutz on rd B180 turn R at Shell stn over rv bdge, site sp. Med, hdg/mkd pitch, pt shd; htd wc; chem disp; mv service pnt; baby facs; shwrs inc; el pnts (16A) inc; gas; Indtte; shop high ssn; rest, snacks high ssn; bar; playgrnd adj; pool complex in vill; lake sw 1km; cycle hire; internet; TV rm; 20% statics; dogs €3; o'night area for m'vans; site clsd Nov; poss cr; Eng spkn; adv bkg; some rd noise; ccard acc; red low ssn/long stay/snr citizens; CCI. "Excel, clean facs; gd views; office clsd 1000-1700 - find pitch & pay later; walks & cycle rtes; conv NH en rte Italy & for tax-free shopping in Samnaun, Switzerland." ♦ € 30.00 2010*

PRUTZ *C1* (7km SE Rural) *47.05310, 10.75012* **Camping Kaunertal, Platz 30, 6524 Feichten-im-Kaunertal (Tirol) [(05475) 316; fax 31665; info@weisseespitze.com; www.weisseespitze.com]** Fr Prutz sp Kaunertal. Site R over sm bdge at Platz, sp. Med, unshd; htd wc; chem disp; shwrs; el pnts (4A); Indtte; rest in hotel adj; playgrnd; pool adj; tennis; summer ski; internet; dogs €2; adv bkg; v quiet; ccard acc. "Lovely scenery & walks; friendly staff; vg rest; conv for tax-free shopping in Samnaun, Switzerland." ♦ 1 May-31 Oct. € 17.00 2008*

PURBACH AM NEUSIEDLERSEE *B4* (1km SE Rural) *47.90958, 16.70580* **Storchencamp Purbach, Türkenhain, 7083 Purbach-am-Neusiedlersee (Burgenland) [(02683) 5170; fax 517015; office@gmeiner.co.at; www.gmeiner.co.at]** Exit A4/E6 junc 43 onto B50 at Neuseidl-am-See to Purbach. Site sp in town nr pool complex. Sm, pt shd; htd wc; chem disp; mv service pnt; baby facs; shwrs inc; el pnts (6A) €2.30; lndtte; shop; rest; bar; BBQ; playgrnd; pools, waterslide adj; games area; 80 statics; dogs €2.90; bus/train 1km; Eng spkn; quiet. "Open field for tourers; excel sw complex adj free with local visitor card + free public transport & red ent to museums etc; modern facs; conv NH." 1 Apr-31 Oct. € 17.40 2010*

⊞ **RADSTADT** *C3* (300m N Rural) *47.38751, 13.46108* **Tauerncamping, Schloss-strasse 17, 5550 Radstadt (Salzburg) [(06452) 4215; fax 42154; info@tauerncamping.at; www.tauerncamping.at]** Exit A10 junc 63 onto B99, site sp in Radstadt. Med, some hdstg, terr, pt shd; htd wc; chem disp; mv service pnt; baby facs; shwrs €1; el pnts (10A) metered; gas; lndtte (inc dryer); shop adj; tradsmn; rest; snacks; bar; BBQ; playgrnd; htd pool; tennis 200m; 50% statics; dogs; poss cr; adv bkg; quiet except church bells. "Conv NH." € 24.80 2010*

⊞ **RATTENBERG** *C2* (4km N Rural) *47.45670, 11.88084* **Seen-Camping Stadlerhof, Seebühel 15, 6233 Kramsach-am-Reintalersee (Tirol) [(05337) 63371; fax 65311; camping.stadlerhof@chello.at; www.camping-stadlerhof.at]** Exit A12/E45/E60 junc 32 Rattenberg dir Kramsach. At rndabt turn R, then immed L & foll sp 'Zu den Seen' & site sp. Site on L at Lake Krumsee. Lge, mkd pitch, some hdstg, pt sl, pt shd; htd wc; chem disp; sauna; baby facs; shwrs inc; el pnts (10A) inc; gas; lndtte (inc dryer); shops 2km; rest; snacks; bar; BBQ; playgrnd; htd pool; paddling pool; lake sw 200m; fishing; tennis; cycle hire; games rm; wifi; cab TV; 50% statics; dogs €3.50; phone; adv bkg; quiet. "Beautiful, well laid-out site in lovely setting; gd san facs." ♦ € 24.50 2011*

⊞ **RATTENBERG** *C2* (3km NE Rural) *47.46121, 11.9066* **Camping Seeblick Toni, Moosen 46, 6233 Kramsach-am-Reintalersee (Tirol) [(05337) 63544; fax 63544305; info@camping-seeblick.at; www.camping-seeblick.at]** Exit A12/E45/E60 junc 32 sp Kramsach. Foll sps 'Zu den Seen' for about 5km. Drive past Camping Seehof site to Brantlhof site, 3rd site on Reintalersee. Med, mkd pitch, pt shd; wc; chem disp; mv service pnt; baby facs; sauna; serviced pitches; private bthrms avail; shwrs inc; el pnts (10A) €3.50 + conn fee; mains gas conn; lndtte (inc dryer); shop; rest; snacks; bar; playgrnd; lake sw; fishing; cycle hire; games area; games rm; fitness rm; guided walks; x-country skiing; wifi; entmnt; TV rm; 10% statics; dogs €5.50; adv bkg; quiet; ccard acc. "Excel site; lovely lakeside setting; superb san facs, inc for children; excel meals; gd for ski & walking; conv NH fr a'bahn." ♦ € 27.00 (CChq acc) 2009*

⊞ **RATTENBERG** *C2* (3km NE Rural) *47.46198, 11.90708* **Camping Seehof, Moosen 42, 6233 Kramsach-am-Reintalersee (Tirol) [(05337) 63541; fax 6354120; info@camping-seehof.com; www.camping-seehof.com]** Exit A12/E45/E60 junc 32 sp Kramsach, foll sp 'Zu den Seen' for 5km. Site immed bef Camping Seeblick-Toni Brantlhof. Med, mkd pitch, pt shd; htd wc; chem disp; mv service pnt; baby facs; shwrs inc; el pnts (6-13A) €2.80; lndtte; shop; tradsmn; rest; snacks; bar; BBQ; playgrnd; pool; lake sw; cycle hire; gym; solarium; horseriding nr; internet; cab TV; 30% statics; dogs €3; phone; poss cr; Eng spkn; adv bkg; quiet; ccard acc; red long stay; CCI. "Friendly staff; gd views fr some pitches; gd, modern san facs; gd rest." ♦ € 23.00 2009*

REISACH *D2* (1.5km N Rural) *46.65467, 13.14906* **Alpenferienpark Reisach, Schönboden 1, 9633 Reisach (Kärnten) [(04284) 301; fax 302; info@alpenferienpark.com; www.alpenferienpark.com]** Turn E in Kötschach on B111 to Hermagor. At Reisach turn L immed past bdge. Foll sps up hill & across bdge & cont. Bear R up long 1 in 8 slope into wood. Site on L at sp Schonboden. Med, mkd pitch, pt sl, pt shd; htd wc; chem disp; fam bthrm; shwrs inc; el pnts (10A) €2.50; gas; lndtte; shop & 4km; rest; snacks; bar; playgrnd; pool; tennis; some statics; dogs €2; Eng spkn; adv bkg; v quiet. "Friendly site; only suitable sm outfits." 15 Dec-31 Oct. € 20.00 2009*

⊞ **REUTTE** *C1* (600m N Rural) *47.47763, 10.72258* **Camping Reutte, Ehrenbergstrasse 53, 6600 Reutte (Tirol) [(05672) 62809; fax 628094; camping-reutte@aon.at; www.camping-reutte.com]** Take Reutte by-pass sp Innsbruck. Enter Reutte at end of by-pass, site sp in 1.5km on L. Med, mkd pitch, some hdstg, pt shd; wc; chem disp; mv service pnt; shwrs €1; el pnts (16A) €2.40; lndtte; shop; tradsmn; rest; snacks; pool adj; skilift 500m; cab TV; dogs €2; phone; Eng spkn; adv bkg; quiet; ccard acc; CCI. "Conv for Fern Pass; adj Neuschwanstein Castle; barriers clsd 2100; clean, popular site; excel." € 22.80 2010*

REUTTE *C1* (11km E Rural) *47.48635, 10.83951* **Campingplatz Sennalpe, 6600 Breitenwang (Tirol) [(05672) 78115; fax 63372; agrar.breitenwang@aon.at]** Heading S fr Reutte on by-pass, turn L outside town sp Oberammergau/Plansee. Foll rd to lake for approx 10km up 14% hill, sh steep climb. Foll lake approx 7km to Am Plansee, turn 1st turn R at end of lake after hotel. Site over bdge on L. Lge, unshd; wc; chem disp; mv service pnt; shwrs €1; el pnts (12A) €1.50 + conn fee; lndtte; shop adj; playgrnd; lake sw & shgl beach adj; 10% statics; dogs €2.50; poss cr; Eng spkn; no adv bkg; quiet; 10% red long stay; CCI. "Beautifully situated on lakeside in remote area; gd base Neuschwanstein Castle." ♦ 15 Dec-15 Oct. € 18.50 2008*

REUTTE *C1* (6km SE Rural) *47.47448, 10.78511* **Camping Seespitze, Planseestrasse 68, 6600 Breitenwang (Tirol) [(05672) 78121; fax 63372; agrar.breitenwang@aon.at]** S fr Reutte on by-pass turn L outside town sp Oberammergau/Plansee. Site on L in 5km. Med, pt sl, terr, pt shd; wc; chem disp; shwrs €1; el pnts (12A) metered (long lead poss req) + conn fee; lndtte; shop; tradsmn; rest adj; snacks; bar; playgrnd; lake sw adj; 10% statics; dogs €2.50; Eng spkn; adv bkg; quiet; CCI. "Beautiful position, mountain scenery; gd walks; v clean san facs; well-maintained site." 1 May-15 Oct. € 24.00 2009*

⊞ **REUTTE** *C1* (10km SE Rural) *47.45547, 10.75937* **Camping Heiterwangersee, Fischer-am-See, 6611 Heiterwang (Tirol) [(05674) 5116; fax 5260; hotel@fischeramsee.at; www.fischeramsee.at]** Fr Reutte on B179 dir Ehrwald turn R to Heiterwang, foll sp to Hotel Fischer & to lakeside (1.5km). Med, some hdstg, pt shd; htd wc; chem disp; mv service pnt; sauna; shwrs inc; el pnts (10-16A) metered; Indtte (inc dryer); shop; tradsmn; rest; snacks; bar; lake sw; fishing; boating; ski-lift 2km; 70% statics; dogs €2; skibus; poss cr; adv bkg rec high ssn; quiet; ccard acc. "Lovely location; vg san facs." € 29.00 2010*

RINN BEI INNSBRUCK see Innsbruck *C1*

RUST AM NEUSIEDLERSEE see Eisenstadt *B4*

ST ANDRA AM ZICKSEE see Frauenkirchen *B4*

When we get home I'm going to post all these site report forms to the Club for next year's guide. The deadline's mid September 2013

⊞ **ST ANTON AM ARLBERG** *C1* (8km E Rural) *47.14809, 10.34668* **Arlberg Panoramacamping, Sportranch 45a, 6574 Pettneu-am-Arlberg (Tirol) [(05448) 8352; fax 83524; info@arlberg-panormacamping.at; www.arlberg-panoramacamping.at]** Fr S16 exit at E end Arlberg Tunnel sp St Anton. Turn L (E) onto B197/B316 to Pettneu. After 3km at ent to vill, keep R skirting vill. Sportranch 1km on R, ent downhill to L of fire stn. Access only suitable sm/med o'fits. Sm, mkd pitch, pt shd; wc; chem disp; mv service pnt; all serviced pitches; shwrs €1; el pnts (10-13A) €2.50 or metered; Indtte; shop 1km; snacks; rest 500m; bar; games rm; horseriding; Wellness-Park nrby; TV; dogs free; bus; adv bkg; quiet but some rd/rlwy noise; ccard acc; red low ssn/long stay/CCI. "Clean facs; friendly owner; owner prefers long stay (significant reduction); geared for winter ssn; gd cent walking, skiing." € 26.00 2010*

ST GILGEN see Abersee *B3*

⊞ **ST JOHANN IM PONGAU** *C2* (1km S Urban) *47.34141, 13.19793* **Camping Kastenhof, Kastenhofweg 6, 5600 St Johann-im-Pongau (Salzburg) [tel/fax (06412) 5490; info@kastenhof.at; www.kastenhof.at]** Take A10 S fr Salzburg onto B311 for Alpendorf. Go over rv & turn L into Liechtensteinklamm twd St Johann, site on L, sp. Med, unshd; htd wc; chem disp; mv service pnt; sauna; shwrs €1; el pnts (15A) metered + €2 conn fee; Indtte (inc dryer); shop; rest, snacks 500m; playgrnd; paddling pool; bus; cab TV; some statics; dogs free; adv bkg; quiet; CCI. "Conv Tauern tunnel, Grossglockner Hochalpenstrasse, Zell-am-See; gd clean site." € 20.00 2010*

⊞ **ST JOHANN IM PONGAU** *C2* (5km SW Rural) *47.3249, 13.16658* **Sonnenterrassen Camping, Bichlwirt 12, 5620 St Veit-im-Pongau (Salzburg) [(06415) 57333; fax 57303; office@sonnenterrassen-camping-stveit.at; www.sonnenterrassen-camping-stveit.at]** Exit A10 at Bischofshofen onto B311 S dir Zell-am-See. After St Johann exit St Veit, site on R in 700m. Med, mkd pitch, terr, pt shd; htd wc; chem disp; mv service pnt; baby facs; shwrs inc; el pnts (16A) metered; gas mains conn; Indtte; shop, rest 2km; snacks; bar; playgrnd; htd, covrd pool 2.5km; lake sw 2.5km; horseriding 1km; golf 3km; wifi; TV; 30% statics; dogs free; ski bus; drying rm; site clsd mid-Apr to mid-May & part Nov; adv bkg; quiet; ccard not acc. "Excel, clean, tidy,well-managed site & superb facs." € 20.00 2008*

⊞ **ST JOHANN IM PONGAU** *C2* (1km W Urban) *47.34605, 13.19276* **Camping Wieshof, Wieshofgasse 8, 5600 St Johann-im-Pongau (Salzburg) [(06412) 8519; fax 8292; info@camping-wieshof.at; www.camping-wieshof.at]** On rd B163 dir Zell-am-Zee, past Agip petrol stn, above rd. Med, terr, unshd; htd wc; chem disp; mv service pnt; shwrs €1; el pnts (15A) metered; Indtte; shop 500m; rest adj; playgrnd; golf 6km; 80% statics; dogs; poss cr; Eng spkn; quiet. "Pleasant site; gd views; vg san facs; friendly & helpful owners." € 18.00 2011*

ST JOHANN IN TIROL *C2* (10km SE Rural) *47.46845, 12.55440* **Tirol Camp, Lindau 20, 6391 Fieberbrunn (Tirol) [(05354) 56666; fax 52516; office@tirol-camp.at; www.tirol-camp.at]** Fr St Johann thro vill of Fieberbrunn, site sp at end of vill. Turn R up to Streuböden chair lift, site 200m on L. Lge, terr, pt shd; htd wc; chem disp; mv service pnt; baby facs; fam bthrm; sauna; shwrs inc; el pnts (6A) metered; Indtte (inc dryer); shop; rest, snacks, bar high ssn; playgrnd; 2 htd pools (1 covrd); waterslide; lake sw; games area; tennis; wellness cent; internet; entmnt; TV rm; 30% statics; dogs €3; phone; train; poss cr; adv bkg; quiet; red senior citizens; ccard acc; red low ssn/snr citizens. "Superb site & facs; gd base for skiing, gd walking; trips to Innsbruck & Salzburg." 1 Jan-30 Apr & 20 May-6 Nov. € 25.00 2008*

⊞ **ST JOHANN IN TIROL** *C2* (1.5km SW Rural) *47.51078, 12.40888* **Sonnencamping Michelnhof, Weiberndorf 6, 6380 St Johann-in-Tirol (Tirol) [(05352) 62584; fax 625844; camping@michelnhof.at; www.camping-michelnhof.at]** On L of B161 St Johann-Kitzbühel, heading S. Turn L in 2km at sp, fork L after level x-ing. Site on R in 500m. Med, mkd pitch, hdstg, sl, pt shd; htd wc; chem disp; mv service pnt; baby facs; shwrs inc; el pnts (10A) €2.70; Indtte; supmkt 1.5km; rest; snacks; playgrnd; pool 2km; golf 4km; 50% statics; dogs €4; phone; Eng spkn; quiet; CCI. "Friendly warden; higher prices in winter; vg." ♦ € 18.40 2009*

⊞ **ST MICHAEL IM LUNGAU** *C3* (S Rural) *47.09685, 13.63706* **Camping St Michael, Waaghausgasse 277, 5582 St Michael-im-Lungau (Salzburg) [tel/fax (06477) 8276; camping-st.michael@sgb.at]** Exit junc 104 fr A10/E55, site sp at turn into vill, then on L after 200m bef hill. Sm, pt shd; wc; chem disp; mv service pnt; shwrs inc; el pnts (16A) €3.50 (poss rev pol); gas; Indtte; shop adj; rest, snacks adj; playgrnd; pool adj; skilift 1km; dogs; poss cr; adv bkg; ccard acc; red CCI. "Delightful site adj vill; excel san facs (shared with adj sports club); poss full if arr after 6 pm, but o'flow area avail." € 20.00 2010*

ST PETER AM KAMMERSBERG *C3* (2km SE Rural) *47.17905, 14.21671* **Camping Bella Austria, Peterdorf 100, 8842 St Peter-am-Kammersberg (Steiermark) [(0898) 1892745; booking@camping-bellaitalia.it]** Fr B96 turn N onto L501 into Katschtal Valley dir Oberdorf, Althofen & St Peter-am-Kammersberg. Site sp. Lge, some hdstg, pt shd; wc; chem disp; mv service pnt; sauna; shwrs; el pnts (16A) inc; Indtte; shop; rest; snacks; bar; playgrnd; htd pool; lake sw; games area; cycle hire; wifi; entmnt; TV rm; some statics; Eng spkn; adv bkg; quiet. "New site - opening April 2011; superb walking area." ♦ 1 May-30 Sep. € 16.60 (CChq acc) 2010*

ST PRIMUS *D3* (800m N Rural) *46.58569, 14.56598* **Strandcamping Turnersee Breznik, Unternarrach 21, 9123 St Primus (Kärnten) [(04239) 2350; fax 235032; info@breznik.at; www.breznik.at]** Exit A2 at junc 298 Grafenstein onto B70. After 4km turn R & go thro Tainach, St Kanzian twd St Primus. Site is on W side of Turnersee. Lge, mkd pitch, pt shd; htd wc; chem disp; mv service pnt; serviced pitches; baby facs; shwrs inc; el pnts (6A) inc; Indtte (inc dryer); shop; rest; bar; BBQ; playgrnd; lake sw; fishing; tennis 500m; games rm; games area; cycle hire; golf 2km; wifi; entmnt; cinema rm; TV rm; 30% statics; dogs €3.30; adv bkg; quiet; CCI. "Lovely situation; excel site." ♦ 16 Apr-2 Oct. € 26.60 (CChq acc) 2009*

ST VEIT IM PONGAU see St Johann im Pongau *C2*

ST WOLFGANG IM SALZKAMMERGUT *B3* (1km E Rural) *47.73286, 13.46375* **Seecamping Appesbach, Au 99, 5360 St Wolfgang-im-Salzkammergut (Oberösterreich) [(06138) 2206; fax 220633; camping@appesbach.at; www.appesbach.at]** Turn L off main St Gilgen-Bad Ischl rd, foll rd thro Strobl twd St Wolfgang; camp on L by Appesbach Hotel on lake shore. Med, pt sl, pt shd; htd wc; chem disp; mv service pnt; shwrs inc; el pnts (10A) metered or €2.80 (poss rev pol); gas; Indtte; shop; tradsmn; rest; bar; playgrnd; lake sw; boat-launching; tennis; 50% statics; dogs €2; bus; adv bkg; ccard acc. "Busy, clean, family-run site; gd, reasonable rest; v helpful owners; beautiful scenery; poss diff in wet." ♦ 1 Apr-31 Oct. € 21.20 2008*

⊞ **ST WOLFGANG IM SALZKAMMERGUT** *B3* (2km SE Rural) *47.73063, 13.47795* **Komfortcamping Berau, Schwarzenbach 16, 5360 St Wolfgang-im-Salzkammergut (Oberösterreich) [(06138) 2543; fax 254355; camping@berau.at; www.berau.at]** Turn N off B158 at Strobl at sp for St Wolfgang & foll sps. Easy to miss - look for Gasthaus/Hotel Berau just after soccer field on L. Med, mkd pitch, pt shd; wc; chem disp; mv service pnt; sauna; baby facs; shwrs inc; el pnts (6A) inc; gas; Indtte (inc dryer); shop; tradsmn; rest; snacks; bar; BBQ; playgrnd; lake sw; watersports; cycle hire; wifi; entmnt; dogs €3.10; phone; poss cr; Eng spkn; adv bkg; quiet; ccard acc; red long stay; CCI. "Immac san facs; excel site." ♦ € 29.00 2010*

ST WOLFGANG IM SALZKAMMERGUT *B3* (1km W Rural) *47.74277, 13.43361* **Camping Ried, Ried 18, 5360 St Wolfgang-im-Salzkammergut (Oberösterreich) [tel/fax (06138) 3201; camping-ried@aon.at; http://members.aon.at/camping-ried]** Fr Salzburg take B158 thro St Gilgen dir Bad Ischl. Exit at sp Strobl & foll sp St Wolfgang. Go thro tunnel to avoid town cent, foll rd along lake to site. Sm, pt sl, terr, pt shd; htd wc; chem disp; mv service pnt; baby facs; shwrs €0.80; el pnts (16A) metered; gas; Indtte; shop; tradsmn; rest; snacks; bar; playgrnd; lake sw, fishing, watersports adj; tennis nr; TV rm; 10% statics; dogs €1.80; phone; poss cr; Eng spkn; quiet; ccard not acc; CCI. "Mountain rlwy stn nr; lake views; gd touring base; easy walk into town; friendly site; v clean san facs." Easter-31 Oct & Christmas. € 35.35 2011*

SALZBURG *B2* (2km N Urban) *47.82683, 13.06296* **Camping Nord-Sam, Samstrasse 22a, 5023 Salzburg-Sam [tel/fax (0662) 660494; office@camping-nord-sam.com; www.camping-nord-sam.com]** Heading E on A1/E55/E69 exit junc 288 Salzburg Nord exit & immed take slip rd on R; then over to L-hand lane for L-hand turn at 2nd traff lts, up narr rd to site, sp. If thro Salzburg foll Wien-Linz sps thro city; turn onto B1 on exit o'skts, camp site posted on L. Med, hdg pitch, hdstg, pt sl, pt shd; htd wc; chem disp; mv service pnt; baby facs; shwrs inc; el pnts (10A) €3; Indtte (inc dryer); shop; supmkt 10m; snacks; playgrnd; htd pool; dogs €3; bus adj; poss cr; Eng spkn; adv bkg ess; rlwy noise; ccard not acc; red long stay/CCI. "Sm pitches & high hdges; san facs clean but old & stretched when site full; friendly staff; many attractions nrby; site sells Salzburg Card; cycle track to city cent; recep open 0800-1200 & 1600-2030 high ssn." ♦ 27 Mar-17 Oct. € 29.00 2011*

SALZBURG *B2* (2km N Rural) *47.82843, 13.05221* **Panorama Camping Stadtblick, Rauchenbichlerstrasse 21, 5020 Salzburg-Rauchenbichl [(0662) 450652; fax 458018; info@panorama-camping.at; www.panorama-camping.at]** Fr A1/E55/E60 exit 288 Salzburg Nord/Zentrum & at end of slip rd turn R & sharp R at traff lts, site sp. If coming fr S, foll ring rd to W then N. Med, mkd pitch, hdstg, terr, pt shd; htd wc; chem disp; mv service pnt; shwrs inc; el pnts (4A) inc (long lead req some pitches); gas; Indtte; shop; tradsmn; rest/café high ssn; bar; wifi; dogs €2; phone; bus to town nr (tickets fr recep); poss cr; Eng spkn; adv bkg; rd noise; ccard not acc; red 3+ days; CCI. "Conv a'bahn; views of Salzburg; cycle track by rv to town; trav cheques exchanged (not Amex); Salzburg card avail fr recep; sm pitches - rec phone ahead if lge o'fit; v helpful family owners; vg rest; excel, modern san facs; rec arr early; also open some dates in Dec & Jan; excel." 20 Mar-5 Nov. € 28.00 2011*

SALZBURG *B2* (5km SE Urban) *47.78058, 13.08985* **Camping Schloss Aigen, Weberbartlweg 20, 5026 Salzburg-Aigen [tel/fax (0662) 622079; camping.aigen@elsnet.at; www.campingaigen.com]** Fr S leave A10/E55 at junc 8 Salzburg-Süd & take B150 twds Salzburg on Alpenstrasse. Turn R at rndabt dir Glasenbach, then L into Aignerstrasse. 1km S of Aigen stn turn R into Glasenstrasse & foll sps to site. Lge, pt sl, pt shd; wc; chem disp; shwrs inc; el pnts (6-16A) €2; gas; washing m/c avail; shop; rest; snacks; bar; bus to town 700m; poss cr; adv bkg; quiet except nr bar/rest; red long stay/CCI. "Friendly, family-run site; sl pitches v slippery & boggy when wet; excel rest; conv for city." 1 May-30 Sep. € 16.00 2011*

AUSTRIA

⊞ **SCHLADMING** *C3* (500m NE Rural) *47.39901, 13.69328* **Camping Zirngast, Linke Ennsau 633, 8970 Schladming (Steiermark) [tel/fax (03687) 23195; camping@zirngast.at; www.zirngast.at]** Exit B320 at sp Schladming Ost. Proceed past Planai lift & turn R at rndabt. Cont for 1km, under rd bdge & over rv, site on R behind rest. Med, pt shd; wc; chem disp; shwrs inc; el pnts (10A) €3.50; Indtte; shop & 500m; tradsmn; rest; snacks; bar; pool 200m; cab TV; 60% statics; dogs; phone; adv bkg; rd & rlwy noise; ccard acc. "Gd base walking/skiing; summer pass for mountain lifts inc in tariff; pitches cramped bet statics high ssn; sh walk to attractive town." € 31.00 2008*

SCHONBUHEL see Melk *B4*

⊞ **SCHRUNS** *C1* (1km S Rural) *47.06760, 9.91615* **Camping Zelfen, Zelfenstrasse 79, 6774 Tschagguns (Voralberg) [(0664) 2002326; kunsttischlerei.tschofen@utanet.at; www.camping-zelfen.at]** Fr Bludenz to Schruns. After x-ing rlwy turn R at traff lts, foll rd L in front of Spar. Site on L in 1.6km, sp. Med, pt shd; htd wc; chem disp; shwrs €1; el pnts (6A) inc; Indtte; shop & 1.6km; rest, snacks, bar 1.6km; playgrnd; pool 200m; 50% statics; dogs; phone; poss cr; Eng spkn; adv bkg; quiet; ccard acc; CCI. "Free sw & children's activities at nrby Activpark; site conv Montafon valley; office open 0800-0900 & 1800-1900 - other times use freephone by office door." € 22.00 2009*

⊞ **SCHWAZ** *C2* (7km N Rural) *47.42156, 11.74043* **Camping Karwendel, 6212 Maurach (Tirol) [(05243) 6116; fax 20036; info@karwendel-camping.at; www.karwendel-camping.at]** Exit A12/E45/E50 junc 39 onto B181. Foll sp Pertisau & Maurach. In 8km (climbing fr a'route turn L at Maurach. Foll rd thro vill,turn L at T-junc, then strt across rndabt twd lake. Site sp past recycling cent. Med, unshd; htd wc; chem disp; shwrs €1; el pnts (10A) €2; Indtte; shop 500m; rest; snacks; bar; playgrnd; lake sw 500m; golf 4km; internet; TV; 80% statics; dogs €2; site clsd Nov; poss cr; quiet; ccard acc. "In open country, glorious views of lake & mountains; diff access lge o'fits." € 18.00 2009*

SCHWAZ *C2* (6km W Rural) *47.30613, 11.64926* **Alpencamping Mark, Bundesstrasse 12, 6114 Weer (Tirol) [(05224) 68146; fax 681466; alpcamp.mark@aon.at; www.alpencamping mark.com]** Exit A12/E45/E60 junc 61; cont E on B171. Site on R after Weer vill. Ent mkd by flags. Med, hdg pitch, pt shd; htd wc; chem disp; mv service pnt; baby facs; shwrs inc; el pnts (6-10A) €2.70; Indtte (inc dryer); shop 500m; tradsmn; rest; snacks; bar; BBQ; playgrnd; htd pool; lake sw 2km; tennis; horseriding; cycle hire; dogs €3; Eng spkn; adv bkg; quiet; ccard acc; red long stay/CCI. "Well-maintained site in scenic location; cln pleasant site with nice rest; friendly, welcoming owners & staff; lavish sports facs; gd san facs; nr town of Weer; many local attractions; rec." ♦ 1 Apr-31 Oct. € 21.00 2011*

⊞ **SEEFELD IN TIROL** *C1* (1km N Rural) *47.33661, 11.17756* **Alpin Camp, Leutascherstrasse 810, 6100 Seefeld (Tirol) [(05212) 4848; fax 4868; info@camp-alpin.at; www.camp-alpin.at]** Fr N on B177/E533 turn W into Seefeld. Thro main rd, turn R sp Leutasch, site on L in 2km. Apps fr SE & SW via v steep hills/hairpins, prohibited to trailers. Med, hdstg, pt sl, terr, pt shd; wc; chem disp; mv service pnt; sauna & steambath inc; shwrs inc; el pnts (16A) €2.80 or metered; gas (metered); Indtte; shop & 2km; rest adj; playgrnd; htd, covrd pool, golf 1.5km; cycle hire; wifi; 10% statics; dogs €3; bus to town; site clsd Nov; adv bkg; Eng spkn; quiet; red snr citizens. "Excel site; excel facs; friendly owners; vg walking; delightful setting; ski tows at gate." ♦ € 21.50 2010*

The opening dates and prices on this campsite have changed. I'll send a site report form to the Club for the next edition of the guide.

⊞ **SEEFELD IN TIROL** *C1* (8km NW Rural) *47.39832, 11.17941* **Holiday Camping, Reindlau 230B, 6105 Leutasch (Tirol) [(05214) 65700; fax 657030; info@holiday-camping.at; www.holiday-camping.at]** Fr B2 fr Germany & passing S thro Scharnitz on B177 & take minor rd W in 4km sp Leutasch. Foll sps to site approx 11km. Do not use Mittenwald-Leutasch rd, v narr & steep gradients. Rte fr S fr A12 via Telfs not rec for c'vans. Med, unshd; htd wc; chem disp; mv service pnt; private bthrms avail; serviced pitches; sauna; baby facs; shwrs inc; el pnts (12A) €3.20 or metered; gas; Indtte (inc dryer); drying rm; shop; rest; snacks; bar; htd, covrd pool; paddling pool; fishing; tennis; golf driving range; golf 10km; skilift 3km; skibus; wifi; sat TV each pitch; dogs €3; site clsd 11 Nov-6 Dec; adv bkg; quiet; ccard acc. "Gd walking & skiing cent; immac facs; superb location; gd walking, cycling; excel." ♦ € 28.00 2010*

SEEKIRCHEN AM WALLERSEE *B2* (1km NE Rural) *47.90249, 13.14232* **Strandcamping Seekirchen, Seestrasse 2, 5201 Seekirchen-am-Wallersee (Salzburg) [tel/fax (06212) 4088; strandbad.seekirchen@hotmail.com; www.camping-seekirchen.at]** Exit A1 junc 281 Wallersee & foll sp Seekirchen, then dir Neumarkt (Seekirchen by-pass), exit Wallersee-Zell. In 2km dir Schloss-Seeburg cross rlwy, turn L then R to site. Med, unshd; wc; chem disp; baby facs; shwrs €0.90; el pnts (16A) €1.50; Indtte; shop; lake sw; fishing; boating; dogs €2; poss cr; some noise fr rlwy. "Easy access fr a'bahn; helpful management." 1 May-15 Sep. € 18.00 2008*

⊞ **SILLIAN** *D2* (2.5km E Rural) *46.74583, 12.46315* **Camping Lienzer Dolomiten, Tassenbach 191, 9920 Strassen-bei-Sillian (Tirol) [(04842) 5228; fax 522815; camping-dolomiten@gmx.at; www.camping-tirol.at]** B100 fr Sillian dir Lienz, turn R after filling stn, over level x-ing, then immed R; site sp. Med, mkd pitch, some hdstg, pt sl, unshd; wc; chem disp; mv service pnt; shwrs inc; el pnts (6A) €2; Indtte; shop, rest 3km; tradsmn; bar; lake sw; skilift 3km; 25% statics; dogs €2; red long stay. "Informal site; clean facs; helpful staff; mountain views." € 21.00 2010*

⊞ **SOLDEN** *C1* (1km S Rural) *46.95786, 11.01193* **Camping Sölden, Wohlfahrtstrasse 22, 6450 Sölden (Tirol) [(05254) 26270; fax 26725; info@camping-soelden.com; www.camping-soelden.com]** Turn L off main rd at cable car terminal. Turn R at rv & foll narr track on rv bank for about 200m, turn R into site. Med, mkd pitch, pt sl, terr, pt shd; wc; chem disp; mv service pnt; serviced pitches; sauna; shwrs inc; el pnts (10A) metered; gas; Indtte; shop 200m; snacks 500m; rest 20m; playgrnd; gym; wifi; dogs €3; dog-washing facs; site clsd mid-Apr to mid-Jun approx; adv bkg; quiet; Eng spkn; ccard acc. "Excel for touring or climbing in upper Ötz Valley; pitches tight for lge outfits; superb site; excel san facs." ♦ € 27.90 2009*

⊞ **SPITAL AM PYHRN** *C3* (3km N Rural) *47.6912, 14.3260* **Campingplatz Pyhrn-Priel, Gleinkerau 34, 4582 Spital-am-Pyhrn (Oberösterreich) [(07562) 7066; pyhrn-priel@aon.at; www.pyhrn-priel.at]** Exit A9 junc 52 - Gleinkerau; cross rndabt on m'way access rd & turn L at T junction; foll sp for approx 500m & turn R to site. Med, unshd; wc; chem disp; shwrs; el pnts (10A) €2.50; Indtte; shop 3km; tradsmn; rest; snacks; bar; playgrnd; pool 3km; 60% statics; dogs €2.20; Eng spkn; adv bkg; quiet; ccard acc; CCI. "Gd views; walking; para/hang-gliding school; summer toboggan run; pleasant owners." ♦ € 18.00 2011*

SPITTAL AN DER DRAU *D3* (500m S Rural) *46.78513, 13.48669* **Camping Draufluss, Schwaig 10, 9800 Spittal-an-der-Drau (Kärnten) [(04762) 2466; fax 36299; drauwirt@aon.at; www.drauwirt.com]** Exit A10 Salzburg-Villach junc 146 Spittal-Ost. In Spittal foll site & 'Goldeckbahn' sp. Cross bdge & site on L - book in at hotel recep. Site on rvside. Med, pt shd; htd wc; chem disp; shwrs inc; el pnts (10-16A) €3; Indtte (inc dryer); shop in town; rest, bar at hotel; htd, covrd pool 800m; rv fishing adj; boating; tennis; games/TV rm; dogs €1.30; Eng spkn; quiet; red CCI. "Modern san facs; conv NH." 15 Apr-1 Oct. € 23.30 2011*

STAMS see Telfs *C1*

STEYR *B3* (3km NE Urban) *48.06117, 14.43764* **Camping Forelle, Kematmüllerstrasse 1a, 4400 Steyr-Münichholz (Oberösterreich) [tel/fax (07252) 78008 or 06764 729445 (mob); forellesteyr@gmx.at]** Fr W on B122 foll camping sp to Amstetten on B115/309 & then 122a to Steyr-Münichholz. Site on Rv Enns. Sm, hdstg, unshd; htd wc; chem disp (wc); shwrs inc; el pnts (16A) inc; Indtte; shop 500m; rest, snacks, bar 1km; BBQ; playgrnd; pools 1km; watersports, tennis nr; cycle hire; dogs €2.20; phone; quiet; red long stay; CCI. "Pleasant rvside site; Steyr interesting, historic town." ♦ 1 Apr-31 Oct. € 20.00 2010*

SULZ IM WIENERWALD *B4* (500m N Rural) *48.10510, 16.13348* **Camping Wienerwald, Leopoldigasse 2, 2392 Sulz-im-Wienerwald (Niederösterreich) [(0)664 4609796; fax (02238) 8855; ww-camp@aon.at; www.camping-wienerwald.at]** Leave A21/E60 at junc 26 dir Sittendorf, Foll sp to site at Sulz (7km fr m'way). Sm, mkd pitch, pt sl, pt shd; wc; chem disp; mv service pnt; shwrs inc; el pnts (6A) €1.90 (poss long lead req); Indtte; shop, rest in vill; tradsmn; wifi; few statics; dogs €1.20; poss cr; quiet. "Conv Vienna - 25km; gd walks." 15 Apr-15 Oct. € 14.00 2010*

⊞ **TELFS** *C1* (8km W Rural) *47.27510, 10.98661* **Camping Eichenwald, Schiess-Standweg 10, 6422 Stams (Tirol) [tel/fax (05263) 6159; info@camping-eichenwald.at; www.tirol-camping.at]** Exit A12 at exit Stams-Mötz, foll B171 sp Stams. Turn R into vill, site behind monastery nr dry ski jump; steep app. Med, terr, pt shd; htd wc; chem disp; mv service pnt; baby facs; private bthrms some pitches; shwrs inc; el pnts (6A) €2.70; gas; Indtte (inc dryer); shop 400m; rest; snacks; bar; playgrnd; sm htd pool high ssn; tennis 500m; games area; games rm; cycle hire; wifi; TV rm; statics in sep area; dogs €2.50; Eng spkn; adv bkg; quiet but monastery bells & rlwy noise; CCI. "Beautiful views; friendly owner; vg site." ♦ € 17.90 (CChq acc) 2011*

TRAISEN *B4* (500m W Rural) *48.0423, 15.60335* **Terrassen-Camping Traisen, Kulmhof 1, 3160 Traisen (Niederösterreich) [(02762) 62900; fax 64391; info@camping-traisen.at; www.camping-traisen.at]** Exit A1 junc 59 S onto B20 to Traisen, turn W in vill. Sp to site up hill for 400m. Med, mkd pitch, terr, pt shd; wc; chem disp; mv service pnt; shwrs €0.50; el pnts (6A) metered; shop 1km; bar; sm htd pool; playgrnd; internet; 60% statics; dogs €1; Eng spkn; quiet; red CCI. "Pleasant with beautiful views; clean, well-kept site; helpful, friendly owners; central water point." 15 Feb-15 Nov. € 19.50 2008*

TRISTACH see Lienz *C2*

TULLN *B4* (2km E Urban) *48.33277, 16.07194* **Donaupark-Camping Tulln, Donaulände 76, 3430 Tulln-an-der-Donau (Niederösterreich) [(02272) 65200; fax 65201; camptulln@oemtc.at; www.campingtulln.at]** Fr S on A1 take exit 41 sp St Christopher & foll B19 to o'skts of Tulln, then turn R onto B14 Südring. Foll B14 round past commercial areas, eventually over rlwy bdge to T-junc. Turn L into Langenlebarnerstrasse, site on R (if reach BP g'ge you have overshot). Fr N foll B19 across rv on Rosenbrucke (bdge) & cont on B19 to B14 Südring, then as above. Site sp (Camping des ÖAMTC) often shown on local sp or on green sports complex sp. Med, some hdg/mkd pitch, pt shd; htd wc; chem disp; mv service pnt; baby facs; sauna; shwrs inc; el pnts (6A) €3; gas; Indtte (inc dryer); shop; supmkt 1km; rest; snacks; bar; BBQ; playgrnd; pool 400m; fishing, lake sw, water skiing nrby; horseriding 2km; cycle hire; tennis; games rm; wifi; entmnt; recep 0730-1930 high ssn; 20% statics; dogs; bus/train to Vienna; Eng spkn; adv bkg; quiet; ccard acc; red low ssn/CCI. "Welcome pack; helpful staff; gd base for area; gd walks, cycling, birdwatching; bus/train to Vienna; poss cr & sm pitches; 15 mins walk to town." ♦ 15 Apr-15 Oct. € 26.50 (CChq acc) 2011*

UNTERACH AM ATTERSEE see Attersee *B3*

UNTERPERFUSS see Innsbruck *C1*

UNZMARKT *C3* (W Rural) *47.19847, 14.44121* **Camping im Freizeitpark, Am Sportplatz 27, 8800 Unzmarkt (Steiermark) [(03583) 2956; www.unzmarkt-frauenburg.at]** W fr Judenburg on B317, site sp opp Agip petrol stn. Sm, terr, pt shd; wc; shwrs inc; el pnts €1.10 (long lead poss req); Indtte; shop 200m; rest; bar; playgrnd; sports field adj; quiet, some rlwy noise. "Gd site, part of lge leisure complex; recep in café." 1 May-30 Sep. € 10.00 2009*

AUSTRIA

VELDEN AM WORTHERSEE *D3* (5km E Rural) *46.61890, 14.10565* **Camping Weisses Rössl, Auenstrasse 47, Schiefling-am-See, 9220 Velden-Auen (Kärnten) [(04274) 2898; fax 28984; weisses.roessl@aon.at; http://members.aon.at/weisses.roessl]** Fr A2 exit 335 dir Velden. At rndabt bef town fol sp twd Maria Wörth for 9km on S side of Wörthersee. Site on R up hill. Lge, some hdstg, terr, pt sl, pt shd; htd wc; chem disp; mv service pnt; baby facs; shwrs inc; el pnts (16A) inc; gas; lndtte (inc dryer); shop; rest; bar; BBQ; playgrnd; pool; beach & lake sw nrby; TV; dogs; phone; poss cr; Eng spkn; some rlwy noise; CCI. "Gd." 1 May-30 Sep. € 27.60 2010*

VIENNA see Wien *B4*

VILLACH *D3* (8km NE Rural) *46.65641, 13.89196* **Campingbad Ossiachersee, Seeuferstrasse 109, 9520 Annenheim (Kärnten) [(04248) 2757; fax 3606; office@camping-ossiachersee.at; www.camping-ossiachersee.at]** Fr A10/E55/E66 exit sp Villach/Ossiacher See onto B94. Turn R for St Andrä sp Süd Ossiacher See. Site on L in 300m. Lge, pt shd; htd wc; baby facs; chem disp; mv service pnt; shwrs inc; el pnts (10-16A) inc; lndtte; shop; rest; snacks; bar; playgrnd; lake sw adj; sailing; watersking; tennis; games area; 5% statics; phone; no dogs; barrier clsd 1200-1400; poss cr; adv bkg; quiet; ccard acc. "Well-kept site; handy NH even when wet; Annenheim cable car." ♦ 15 May-15 Sep. € 25.50 2009*

⊞ **VILLACH** *D3* (3km SE Rural) *46.59638, 13.89333* **Camping Mittewald, Fuchsbichlweg 9, 9580 Drobollach (Kärnten) [(04242) 37392; fax 373928; camp.mittewald@gmail.com]** Exit A2/E55 sp Villach/Faakersee. At end slip rd turn R onto B84 to Faakersee, site sp on L. Sm, pt sl, pt shd; htd wc; chem disp; shwrs; el pnts (10A); gas; lndtte; shop 3km; rest; bar; playgrnd; some statics; dogs; some Eng spkn; quiet. "Lovely location; extensive grass pitches; excel san facs." ♦ € 28.90 2011*

VILLACH *D3* (6km SE) *46.58953, 13.91483* **Wisencamping Marhof, Greutherweg 19, A-9580 Drobollach-Faaker See, Kärnten [(4254) 2888; office@marhof.at; www.marhof.at]** Foll sps in Villach marked Faaker Nord. Site on N side of rd at vill of Greuth. Sm, pt sl, pt shd; wc htd; chem disp; mv waste; shwrs; el pnts (metered); lndtte; BBQ; tradsmn; playgrnd; pool; dogs €0.70; quiet. "Delightful site; beautiful views; conv for lakes; excel facs; gd cycling/walking area; v peaceful; Eng not spkn; v helpful & friendly owners; excel." 01 Mar-30 Nov. € 28.10 2011*

VILLACH *D3* (8km SE Rural) *46.56986, 13.90701* **Familiencamping Poglitsch, Kirchenweg 19, 9583 Faak-am-See (Kärnten) [(04254) 2718; fax 4144; poglitsch@net4you.at; www.kindercamping.at]** Exit A11/E61 junc 3 & foll sp for Faakersee. Site in vill, bet church & lake. Med, mkd pitch, pt shd; wc; chem disp; mv service pnt; some serviced pitches; baby facs; shwrs inc; el pnts (10-16A) inc; gas; lndtte (inc dryer); shop; tradsmn; rest; snacks; bar; playgrnd; lake beach & sw; watersports; cycle hire; games area; golf 1km; wifi; entmnt; TV; 15% statics; dogs €3.50; phone; Eng spkn; adv bkg; quiet; CCI. "Excel, well-run site; friendly owner; quiet imposed after 2300." ♦ 1 Apr-15 Oct. € 27.00 2010*

VILLACH *D3* (8km SE Rural) *46.57266, 13.93268* **Strandcamping Gruber, 9583 Faak-am-See (Kärnten) [(04254) 2298; fax 22987; gruber@strandcamping.at; www.strandcamping.at]** When app down Drau Valley fr Lienz foll sp round Villach to Faakersee. This will bring round N of lake to Egg. Site 800m beyond on R. Fr A11/E61 exit junc 3 & foll sps to Faakersee/Egg. Med, shd; wc; chem disp; shwrs inc; el pnts (10A) €2.50; gas; lndtte (inc dryer); shop; rest; playgrnd; lake sw; golf 2km; wifi; 10% statics; dogs €2; poss cr; adv bkg; quiet; ccard acc. "Excel for touring Carinthian Lake District; gd for children; v beautiful situation on lakeside; friendly staff." ♦ 1 May-20 Sep. € 30.90 2010*

VILLACH *D3* (9km SE Rural) *46.57416, 13.93694* **Strandcamping Arneitz, Seeuferlandesstrasse 53, 9583 Faak-am-See (Kärnten) [(04254) 2137; fax 3044; camping@arneitz.at; www.camping-arneitz.at]** On B83 Klagenfurt to Villach at Velden, foll sp to Faakersee. Thro Egg to site on R. Fr Villach foll sp to Faakersee. Clearly sp. Lge, mkd pitch, shd; wc; shwrs inc; el pnts (16A) inc; gas; lndtte (inc dryer); shop; rest; snacks; bar; BBQ; playgrnd; lake sw; tennis; entmnt; internet; TV; dogs free; adv bkg; quiet. "Excel facs, but ltd low ssn." ♦ 1 May-30 Sep. € 32.00 2010*

VILLACH *D3* (10km SE Rural) *46.56828, 13.9293* **Strandcamping Sandbank, Badeweg 3, 9583 Faak-am-See (Kärnten) [(04254) 2261; fax 3943; info@camping-sandbank.at; www.camping-sandbank.at]** Exit A11/E61 junc 3 & foll sp to Faakersee. Site last on R on E side of lake. Med, pt shd; wc; chem disp; serviced pitches; shwrs inc; el pnts (12A) €2.20; lndtte (inc dryer); supmkt 1km; rest adj; snacks; playgrnd; lake sw; tennis adj; games area; golf 15km; entmnt; TV; 10% statics; dogs €1.80; rd/rlwy noise; red snr citizens. "Surcharge for lakeside pitch; boats & surfboards for hire." 1 May-30 Sep. € 25.70 2010*

⊞ **VILLACH** *D3* (3km NW Urban) *46.61503, 13.80684* **Camping Gerli, Badstrasse 23, 9500 Villach (Kärnten) [(04242) 57402; fax 582909; gerli.meidl@utanet.at; www.campgerli.com]** Fr A10/E55/E66 exit junc 172. Fr rndabt at end of slip rd foll campsite sps. Med, pt shd; wc; some serviced pitches; baby facs; shwrs €0.75; el pnts (4-16A) metered or €2; lndtte (inc dryer); sm shop; rest; playgrnd; paddling pool; lake sw nr; solarium; tennis; entmnt; 20% statics; dogs €1.10; phone; poss cr high ssn; adv bkg; poss noisy; 10% red CCI. "Ski lift close by." € 15.70 2009*

VOLDERS see Hall in Tirol *C2*

⊞ **VOLKERMARKT** *D3* (9km S Rural) *46.58376, 14.62621* **Rutar Lido FKK See-Camping (Naturist), Lido 1, 9141 Eberndorf (Kärnten) [(04236) 22620; fax 2220; fkkurlaub@rutarlido.at; www.rutarlido.at]** Take B82 S fr Völkermarkt to Eberndorf. At rndbt on vill by-pass turn R. Site sp on L. Camp ent in 700m down narr rd. Lge, pt shd; wc; chem disp; mv service pnt; sauna; shwrs inc; el pnts (10A) inc; gas; lndtte; shop; rest; snacks; playgrnd; 4 pools (1 htd, covrd); paddling pool; shgl beach & lake sw 2km; tennis adj; games area; 30% statics; dogs; o'night area for m'vans; adv bkg; quiet; ccard acc; red CCI. "Gd family site." ♦ € 28.80 2009*

VOLKERMARKT *D3* (6km SW Rural) *46.58613, 14.58080* **Terrassencamping Turnersee, 9122 Obersammelsdorf (Kärnten) [(04239) 2285; fax 22854; ferienparadies@ilsenhof.at; www.ilsenhof.at]** Turn off B82 dir Klopeinersee & St Kanzian. Just bef Turnersee foll sp L for site. Med, mkd pitch, some hdstg, terr, pt shd; wc; chem disp; mv service pnt; baby facs; shwrs; el pnts (10A) inc; gas; Indtte (inc dryer); shop 1km; tradsmn; rest 300m; snacks; bar; BBQ; playgrnd; pool; covrd pool 8km; shgl beach & lake sw 500m; 20% statics; dogs €2.90; v quiet; red CCI. "Excel views of mountains beyond Turnersee." ♦ 1 May-10 Sep. € 27.70 2011*

VOLS see Innsbruck *C1*

WAIDHOFEN AN DER THAYA *A4* (500m SE Rural) *48.81113, 15.28839* **Campingplatz Thayapark, Badgasse, 3830 Waidhofen-an-der Thaya (Niederösterreich) [(02842) 50356 or 0664 5904433 (mob); stadtamt@waidhofen-thaya.gv.at; www.waidhofen-thaya.at]** Site sp fr town cent. Med, pt shd; wc; chem disp; mv service pnt; baby facs; shwrs €0.50; el pnts (10A) €2.30; Indtte; shop, rest, snacks, bar 500m; tradsmn; playgrnd; pool 300m; cab TV; 5% statics; no adv bkg; quiet; CCI. "Quiet site nr attractive town; recep open 0800-1000 & 1600-1800." ♦ 1 May-30 Sep. € 11.00 2010*

⊞ **WALCHSEE** *B2* (300m W Rural) *47.64881, 12.31433* **Sonnencamping Seespitz, Seespitz 1, 6344 Walchsee (Tirol) [(05374) 5359; fax 5845; info@camping-seespitz.at; www.camping-seespitz.at]** Exit A93/E45/60 junc 59 onto B172 thro Niederndorf to Walchsee (11km). Site on R by lake after rd on R to Südsee at beginning of Walchsee vill. Lge, pt shd; htd wc; chem disp; mv service pnt; serviced pitches; extra for lakeside pitches; baby facs; shwrs inc; el pnts (6A) €3; gas; Indtte (inc dryer); sm shop; supmkt adj; rest; snacks; bar; playgrnd; lake sw; fishing; boating; games area; 60% statics; dogs €3.50; poss cr; adv bkg; quiet; red CCI. "Excel; attractive lakeside setting with mountain views; vg san facs." ♦ € 21.00 2010*

⊞ **WALD IM PINZGAU** *C2* (1km W Rural) *47.24343, 12.21071* **SNP Camping, Lahn 65, 5742 Wald-im-Pinzgau (Salzburg) [(06565) 84460; fax 84464; info@snp-camping.at; www.snp-camping.at]** Sp fr both dir on B165 Gerlos-Mittersill rd. Sm, unshd, mkd pitch; wc; chem disp; mv service pnt; shwrs €1; el pnts (10A) €4; gas; Indtte; shop 1km; snacks; bar; playgrnd; pool 1km; site clsd Nov; Eng spkn; adv bkg ess; quiet; ccard acc; red long stay/CCI. "Gd walks; friendly, helpful owner; gd san facs, bus nearby for Krimul waterfalls." € 30.70 2011*

WEER see Schwaz *C2*

WERFEN *C2* (2km S Rural) *47.44501, 13.21165* **Camping Vierthaler, Reitsam 8, 5452 Pfarrwerfen (Salzburg) [(06468) 57570; fax 56574; vierthaler@camping-vierthaler.at; www.camping-vierthaler.at]** Fr A10 exit 43 or 44 sp Werfen/Pfarrwerfen. Turn S onto B159 twd Bischofshofen. After 2km site on L bet rd & rv. Sm, pt shd; wc; chem disp; mv service pnt; shwrs €1.30; el pnts (10-16A) €1.30; gas; Indtte; shop; rest; snacks; bar; playgrnd; htd pool 2km; walking; fishing; rafting; wifi; few statics; dogs free; quiet but some rd & rlwy noise; ccard acc. "Scenic site; friendly owners; Werfen castle & ice caves worth a visit; cycle path." 15 Apr-30 Sep. € 16.50 2011*

WESENUFER *B3* (500m S Rural) *48.45460, 13.81615* **Camping Nibelungen, 4085 Wesenufer (Oberösterreich) [tel/fax (07718) 7589; nibelungen.camping@utanet.at; www.nibelungen-camping.com]** On B130 bet Passau & Linz, sp in Wesenufer on rvside. Sm, mkd pitch, pt shd; wc; chem disp; mv service pnt; shwrs inc; el pnts (6-12A) €1.80 + metered; Indtte; snacks; rest 500m; playgrnd; 60% statics; dogs €0.70; Eng spkn; quiet. "In beautiful position; cycling & walking; Danube boat trips; helpful owner; clsd 1200-1400." Easter-30 Sep. € 11.60 2009*

WESTENDORF see Kitzbühel *C2*

WIEN *B4* (8km E Urban) *48.20861, 16.44722* **Aktiv-Camping Neue Donau, Am Kaisermühlendamm 119, 1220 Wien-Ost [tel/fax (01) 2024010; neuedonau@campingwien.at; www.wiencamping.at]** Take A21-A23, exit sp Olhafen/Lobau. After x-ing Rv Danube turn R, sp Neue-Donau Sud. In 150m turn L at traff lts after Shell g'ge; site on R. Fr E on A4 turn R onto A23 & take 1st slip rd sp N-Donau after x-ing rv Danube. Lge, unshd; htd wc; chem disp; mv service pnt; 20% serviced pitches (extra charge); shwrs inc; el pnts (16A) €4 (poss rev pol); Indtte; shop; rest; snacks; sm playgrnd; rv 1km; tennis; games area; wifi; dogs €4.50; bus/metro to city 1km; Eng spkn; adv bkg; rd & rlwy noise; ccard acc; red CCI. "Conv Vienna; lovely site; excel facs but poss stretched high ssn; poss v cr due bus tours on site; cycle track to city cent (map fr recep); 3 classes of pitch (extra charge for serviced); recep clsd 1200-1430." ♦ 15 Apr-15 Sep. € 26.40 2010*

WIEN *B4* (8km S Urban) *48.15065, 16.30025* **Camping Wien-Süd, Breitenfurterstrasse 269, 1230 Wien-Atzgersdorf [(01) 8673649; fax 8675843; sued@campingwien.at; www.campingwien.at]** A1 fr Linz/Salzburg take A21 at Steinhausl (35km W of Vienna), merges with A2 dir Wien sp A23 Altmansdorf. At end a'bahn turn L dir Eisenstadt/Vösendorf, in 500m turn R at 1st set traff lts into Anton Baumgartnerstrasse. Then turn R at 6th traff lts into Breitenfurterstrasse. Site on R adj Merkur supmkt. Fr N on A22 foll A23 to m'way A2 dir Graz. At junc 5 (Vösendorf) take A21 to junc 36 (Brunn am Gebirge & foll 'Zentrum' sp for 5km. At Merkur supmkt on R, turn R to site. Med, mkd pitch, pt shd; htd wc; chem disp; shwrs inc; el pnts (16A) €4; Indtte; supmkt adj; snacks; playgrnd; no statics; dogs €4.50; bus; metro; Eng spkn; adv bkg; quiet; ccard acc; CCI. "Gd bus & metro connections to city; sep tent area; v pleasant site; gd san facs; lovely disabled rm; conv for Wien; v friendly; recep open 0800-1600." ♦ 1 Jun-31 Aug. € 24.60 2011*

WIEN *B4* (10km SW Urban) *48.13583, 16.25555* **Camping Rodaun, Breitenfurterstrasse 487, An der Au 2, 1236 Wien-Rodaun [tel/fax (01) 8884154]** Fr W exit A1/E60 at junc 23 sp Pressbaum. At traff lts turn R onto B44. In 5km turn R onto B13 to Rodaun, site sp on R in 15km.. Med, some hdstg, shd; htd wc; chem disp; mv service pnt; shwrs €0.50; el pnts (6A) metered; gas; Indtte (inc dryer); shop 500m; rest 500m; pool 2km; dogs; tram nr (tickets fr recep); adv bkg; quiet. "Conv Vienna, wine-growing vill, Mayerling, Vienna woods, spas; excel, clean san facs; friendly, helpful, efficient owners." 1 Jul-10 Oct. € 23.80 2010*

Terrassencamping Schlossberg Itter

Familie Ager • A-6305 Itter • Brixentalerstr. 11
Tel. 05335/2181 • Fax 05335/2182
www.camping-itter.at • E-mail: info@camping-itter.at

Summer: table tennis, enormous children's playground, heated swimming pool. All pitches with TV connection. Wild water boating.
Winter: only 2 km away from the extended ski area Wilder Kaiser - Brixental with 96 lifts and 250 km of ski fields. Free skibus.

Top quality sanitary block with individual cabines. Sauna hut. Internet corner. WLAN on all pitches. Restaurant.

GPS: N 47°27'58.60" / E 12°08'22.20"

⊞ **WIEN** *B4* (6km W Urban) *48.21396, 16.2505* **Camping Wien-West, Hüttelbergstrasse 80, 1140 Wien [(01) 9142314; fax 9113594; west@campingwien.at; www.campingwien.at/ww]** Fr Linz, after Auhof enter 3 lane 1-way rd. On app to traff lts get into L hand (fast) lane & turn L at traff lts. At next lts (Linzerstrasse) go strt over into Hüttelburgstrasse & site is uphill. Fr Vienna, foll sp A1 Linz on W a'bahn & site sp to R 100m bef double rlwy bdge. After this turn L on rd with tramlines & foll to v narr section, R at traff lts. Lge, mkd pitch, hdstg, pt shd; wc; chem disp; mv service pnt; shwrs inc; el pnts (16A) €4; Indtte; shop & 2km; tradsmn; snacks; playgrnd; wifi; some statics; dogs €4.50; bus; sep car park; site clsd Feb; poss v cr; Eng spkn; adv bkg; noisy in day but quiet at night; ccard acc; red CCI. "Rec arr early; gd bus service to U-Bahn & city cent - tickets fr recep + Vienna Card; clean facs, but poss stretched high ssn & ltd low ssn; poss itinerants; site poss unkempt low ssn; sm pitches." € 23.90 2010*

I'll fill in a report online and let the Club know – www.caravanclub.co.uk/europereport

WILDALPEN *C3* (500m N Rural) *47.66673, 14.98692* **Camping Wildalpen, Hopfgarten 239, 8924 Wildalpen (Steiermark) [(03636) 342; fax 313; camping@wildalpen.at; www.wildalpen.at]** On B24 in Wildalpen turn down hill by church, site 500m on R by rv. Med, pt shd; wc; chem disp; mv service pnt; shwrs €0.85; el pnts (12A) inc; rest, snacks & shop in vill; tradsmn; pool 1.5km; tennis; 40% statics; dogs €1; poss cr; adv bkg. "Remote site, cent for white water canoeing instruction; excel for walking, photography, botany, bird life." ♦ 15 Apr-31 Oct. € 17.00 2009*

⊞ **WORGL** *C2* (7km SE Rural) *47.46627, 12.13950* **Terrassencamping Schlossberg-Itter, Brixentalerstrasse 11, 6305 Itter-bei-Hopfgarten (Tirol) [(05335) 2181; fax 2182; info@camping-itter.at; www.camping-itter.at]** E fr Wörgl on B170 twd Kitzbühel. Site sp on L (N) side of rd in 7km, below castle & by rv opp Peugeot g'ge. Fr A12/E45 exit at Wörgl Ost & turn L at 1st T-junc sp Brixental for 4km. Turn R onto B178 at sp Brixental, then L on B170 for Hopfgarten. Med, mkd pitch, terr, pt sl, pt shd; htd wc; chem disp; mv service pnt; baby facs; fam bthrm; sauna; shwrs inc; el pnts (8-10A) €2.80; gas; Indtte (inc dryer); sm shop; tradsmn; rest; snacks; bar; BBQ; playgrnd; htd pool; paddling pool; solarium; canoeing; golf 15km; wifi; cab/sat TV; 25% statics; dogs €3.50; site clsd 15-30 Nov; poss cr; Eng spkn; adv bkg; quiet, but some rlwy noise; ccard not acc; CCI. "Superb site; highly rec, espec for children; immac pool; easy pitching on flat area but tractor assistance for pitching on steep terrs; luxury san facs; gd winter ski cent with drying rm; practice ski-run on site; gd walks; excursions arranged." ♦ € 26.00 2011*

See advertisement

⊞ **WORGL** *C2* (10km SE Rural) *47.43068, 12.14990* **Camping Reiterhof, Kelchsauerstrasse 48, 6361 Hopfgarten (Tirol) [(05335) 3512; fax 4145; info@campingreiterhof.at; www.campingreiterhof.at]** Fr Wörgl S on B170, thro Hopfgarten, site sp on R dir Kelchsau. Med, mkd pitch, pt shd; htd wc; chem disp; mv service pnt; baby facs; shwrs €1; el pnts (10A) €2.80; Indtte (inc dryer); shop 2km; tradsmn; rest, snacks, bar adj; playgrnd; htd pool 200m; skilift 2km; free ski bus; wifi; 45% statics; dogs €2.20; poss cr; Eng spkn; adv bkg; quiet but some rd noise; CCI. "V friendly, v welcoming, helpful staff; immac san facs; excel for families or couples; lge recreation park adj; excel walking & cycling area; excel." ♦ € 17.80 2011*

⊞ **ZELL AM SEE** *C2* (6km N Rural) *47.37740, 12.79583* **Campingplatz Bad Neunbrunnen, Neunbrunnen 56, 5751 Maishofen (Salzburg) [(06542) 68548; camping@neunbrunnen.at; www.camping-neunbrunnen.at]** Foll B311 N fr Zell-am-See dir Saalfelden; 500m after Maishofen turn L bef tunnel & foll site sp. Med, mkd pitch, some hdstg, unshd; wc; chem disp; mv service pnt; shwrs inc; el pnts (10A) €2.20; Indtte (inc dryer); shop; tradsmn; rest; snacks; bar; playgrnd; lake sw; fishing; games rm; winter sports area; wifi; dogs; quiet; ccard acc;. "Vg, scenic site; cycle & walking tracks fr site." € 17.00 2010*

⊞ **ZELL AM SEE** *C2* (2km NE Rural) *47.33975, 12.80896* **Seecamp, Thumersbacherstrasse 34, 5700 Zell-am-See (Salzburg) [(06542) 72115; fax 7211515; zell@seecamp.at; www.seecamp.at]** Fr S end Zellersee take B311 N thro tunnel sp Zell-am-See Centrum. Cont thro town cent & in 500m turn R over rlwy x-ing sp Thumersbach. Site on R past yacht club. Med, pt shd, mkd pitch, hdstg; wc; chem disp; mv service pnt; shwrs inc; el pnts (16A) metered + conn fee €2.50; metered gas; Indtte; shop (high ssn); tradsmn; rest; snacks; bar; playgrnd; sand beach adj; lake sw; sailing; watersports; fishing (free); cycle hire; wifi; dogs €4.30; bus at site ent; poss cr; Eng spkn; quiet but some rd & rlwy noise; ccard acc; red low ssn; CCI. "Lge sports cent nr; lger 'Komfort' pitch avail for extra; gd, clean san facs; gd walk town cent; site clsd 1100-1600; ltd pitch care low ssn; mountain views." ♦ € 29.40 2010*

⊞ **ZELL AM SEE** *C2* (3km SE Rural) *47.30133, 12.8150* **Camping Südufer / Panorama Camping, Seeuferstrasse 196, 5700 Thumersbach (Salzburg) [(06542) 56228; fax 562284; zell@camping-suedufer.at; www.camping-suedufer.at]** S fr Zell on B311 sp Salzburg (using tunnel). At 3rd rndabt turn L dir Thumersbach, site on L in 1.5km, sp. Med, hdg pitch, pt shd, 50% serviced pitch; mv service pnt; wc; chem disp; baby facs; shwrs inc; el pnts (16A) metered + conn fee; Indtte; shop; tradsmn; playgrnd; lake 300m; TV; 30% statics; dogs €3.50; bus; Eng spkn; adv bkg; quiet; red long stay; CCI. "Conv Salzburg & Krimml falls; clsd 1200-1330; cycle & footpaths round lake adj; helpful owners; excel facs; peaceful site; campsite being renamed in the future to Panorama Camping; nicely laid out site with adequate pitches; owners take you to pitch and make elec conn; shops & rest 500m; pizzas & rolls fr recep." € 25.30 2011*

⊞ **ZELL AM ZILLER** *C2* (3km N Rural) *47.26326, 11.8995* **Erlebnis-Comfort-Camping Aufenfeld, Aufenfeldweg 10, 6274 Aschau-im-Zillertal (Tirol) [(05282) 2916; fax 291611; info@camping-zillertal.at; www.camping-zillertal.at]** Fr A12 turn S at junc 39 Wiesing onto B169. At Kaltenbach take rd to Aschau, site sp. Lge, mkd pitch, terr, pt shd; htd wc; chem disp; mv service pnt; serviced pitches; baby rm; fam bthrm; sauna; shwrs inc; el pnts (6A) €2.30; gas; Indtte (inc dryer); shop; rest; snacks; bar; playgrnd; htd, covrd pool; padding pool; lake sw; boating; tennis; games area; skiing; cycle hire; wifi; entmnt; TV; car wash; 30% statics; dogs €3.50; phone; train 500m; site clsd Nov; adv bkg rec public hols & high ssn; quiet; ccard acc. "Excel site; wonderful facs for children." ♦ € 30.90 2008*

⊞ **ZELL AM ZILLER** *C2* (500m SE Rural) *47.22830, 11.88590* **Camping Hofer, Gerlosstrasse 33, 6280 Zell-am-Ziller (Tirol) [(05282) 2248; fax 22488; info@campingdorf.at; www.campingdorf.at]** Fr A12/E45/E60 exit junc 39 onto B169 dir Zell-am-Ziller. In vill, site on R, sp. Med, mkd pitch, pt shd; htd wc; chem disp; mv service pnt; baby facs; shwrs inc; el pnts (10A) €3.50 or metered; gas; Indtte (inc dryer); shops adj; rest; snacks; bar; BBQ; playgrnd; htd pool; cycle hire; games rm; wifi; entmnt; dogs €2.50; phone; poss cr; quiet but rd noise; Eng spkn; adv bkg; debit cards acc; red long stay; CCI. "1st class site with clean, well-equipped facs; poss fly problem high ssn; friendly, welcoming family; some pitches tight for lge o'fits; gd walking & cycling; owner arranges guided walks; site discount for funicular; excel." € 21.80 (CChq acc) 2010*

ZWETTL *A4* (15km SE Rural) *48.58956, 15.31805* **Campingplatz Lichtenfels, Friedersbach 69, 3533 Friedersbach (Niederösterreich) [(02826) 7492 or 0664 5746866 (mob); forstverwaltung@thurnforst.at; www.thurnforst.at]** Fr E on B38 fr Zwettl on app Rastenfeld look for rv bdge & ruins of castle. Site sp on L. Med, pt shd; wc; chem disp; shwrs; no el pnts; bar; BBQ; lake sw & shgl beach 100m; games area; 40% statics; dogs; quiet. "Pretty lake setting; open air concerts in ruins of castle high ssn; friendly owner; v clean facs." 1 May-10 Oct. € 15.50 2011*

AUSTRIA

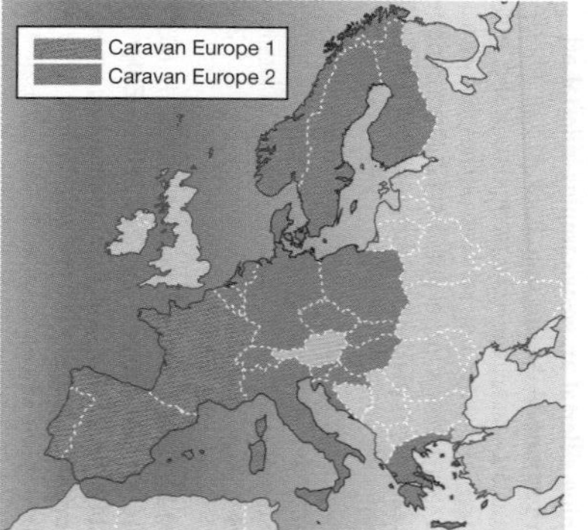

Distances are shown in kilometres and are calculated from town/city centres along the most practical roads, although not necessarily taking the shortest route. 1km = 0.62miles

Landeck to Wien (Vienna) = 550km

	Bludenz	Braunau-am-Inn	Bregenz	Bruck an der Mur	Eisenstadt	Fürstenfeld	Gmünd	Gmunden	Graz	Innsbruck	Judenburg	Kitzbühel	Klagenfurt	Landeck	Leibnitz	Lienz	Liezen	Linz	Mariazell	Radstadt	Reutte	Salzburg	Schärding	Sillian	Spittal an der Drau	St. Pölten	Villach	Wien (Vienna)	Wörgl
Braunau-am-Inn	324																												
Bregenz	59	451																											
Bruck an der Mur	562	263	620																										
Eisenstadt	66	345	722	129																									
Fürstenfeld	658	388	715	123	126																								
Gmünd	552	213	611	246	190	369																							
Gmunden	399	80	455	187	280	311	164																						
Graz	590	322	646	56	174	68	299	243																					
Innsbruck	148	245	204	421	513	510	405	251	444																				
Judenburg	503	239	563	63	195	155	261	164	88	354																			
Kitzbühel	243	138	299	291	403	415	296	143	347	95	260																		
Klagenfurt	487	292	544	161	292	215	340	242	140	340	97	243																	
Landeck	70	323	128	498	596	588	482	330	522	79	432	173	415																
Leibnitz	627	359	686	94	200	357	340	282	39	469	126	386	130	547															
Lienz	337	233	395	301	421	227	391	235	290	190	224	94	149	266	280														
Liezen	464	168	521	97	229	308	187	90	126	315	70	190	150	392	198	229													
Linz	454	113	510	185	231	59	99	68	241	304	189	197	268	383	279	293	115												
Mariazell	585	263	643	63	135	186	184	199	118	438	126	329	223	517	155	363	119	149											
Radstadt	367	134	425	167	331	291	291	142	224	220	136	124	182	297	260	158	67	184	187										
Reutte	110	338	133	511	604	601	494	344	535	90	446	187	432	76	558	280	399	397	529	311									
Salzburg	338	64	395	230	331	353	221	68	285	190	198	82	252	269	322	176	126	123	255	75	281								
Schärding	442	47	501	270	309	379	177	74	309	295	237	186	305	372	355	279	151	79	231	183	384	110							
Sillian	368	264	425	331	452	388	422	269	320	222	254	124	181	297	311	32	260	322	394	189	310	208	311						
Spittal an der Drau	413	216	470	210	342	281	393	237	212	263	150	170	75	344	204	76	163	279	276	95	356	155	266	109					
St. Pölten	559	238	617	141	113	196	117	171	198	410	207	304	302	491	236	398	204	125	80	252	503	229	202	430	355				
Villach	449	255	506	189	320	253	368	269	178	303	124	205	38	381	168	113	201	297	253	131	392	191	302	142	36	331			
Wien (Vienna)	619	299	678	150	50	171	141	234	198	470	215	363	312	550	221	440	265	186	140	361	561	300	264	469	386	65	349		
Wörgl	127	180	273	325	437	449	330	177	381	66	394	34	277	144	420	128	224	131	363	158	158	110	220	158	204	338	239	397	
Zell am See	299	141	352	239	408	365	299	145	296	150	209	56	211	230	310	91	142	198	261	74	240	84	188	122	106	305	143	366	90

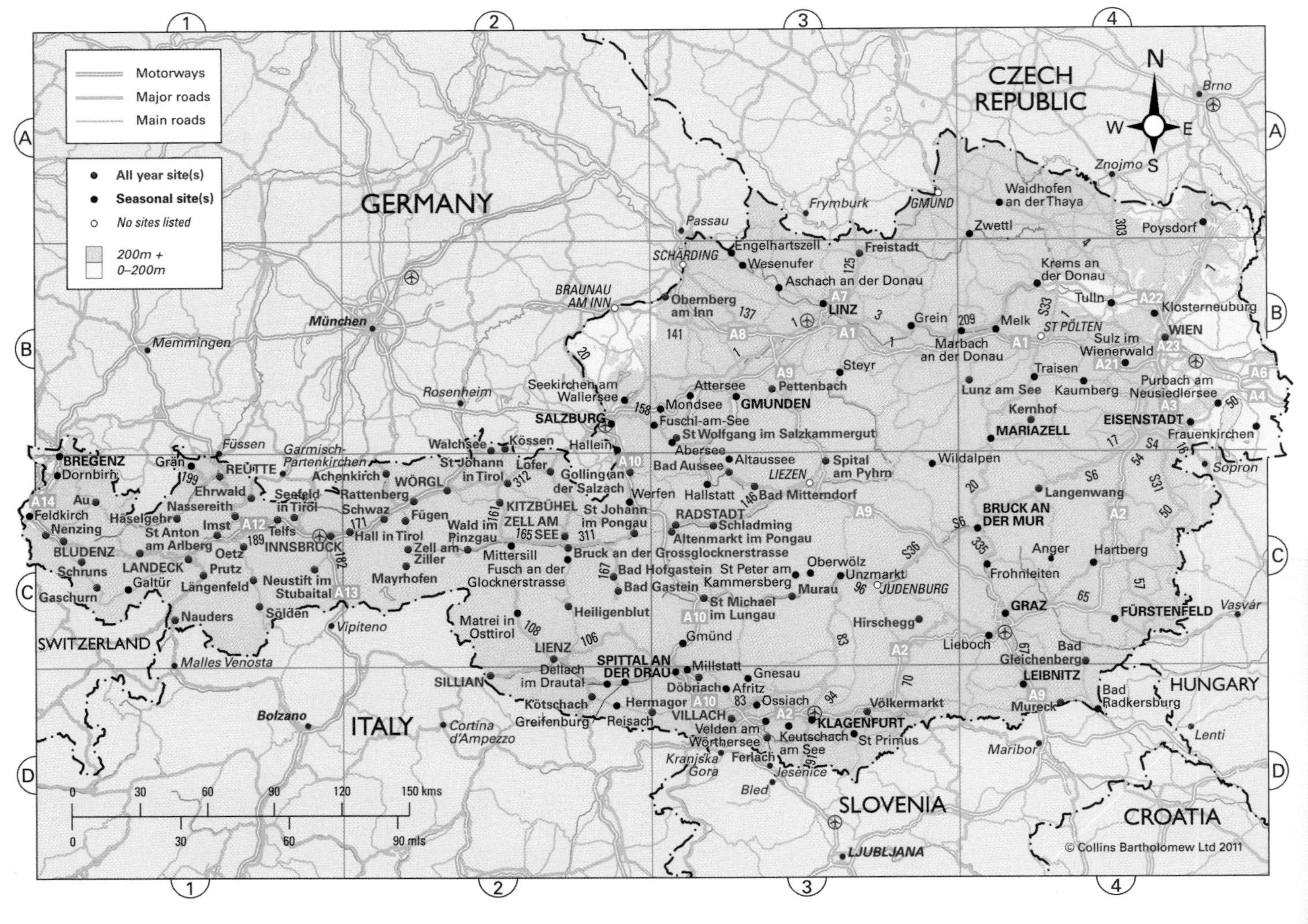
Motorways
Major roads
Main roads
All year site(s)
Seasonal site(s)
No sites listed
200m +
0–200m
GERMANY
CZECH REPUBLIC
N
W
E
S
Brno
Znojmo
Waidhofen an der Thaya
GMÜND
Frymburk
Passau
Zwettl
Poysdorf
SCHÄRDING
Engelhartszell
Freistadt
Wesenufer
Aschach an der Donau
Krems an der Donau
Tulln
Klosterneuburg
BRAUNAU AM INN
Obernberg am Inn
LINZ
Grein
Melk
ST PÖLTEN
WIEN
München
Memmingen
Marbach an der Donau
Sulz im Wienerwald
Steyr
Traisen
Purbach am Neusiedlersee
Rosenheim
Seekirchen am Wallersee
Attersee
Pettenbach
Mondsee
GMUNDEN
Lunz am See
Kaumberg
Kernhof
SALZBURG
Fuschl-am-See
St Wolfgang im Salzkammergut
MARIAZELL
EISENSTADT
Frauenkirchen
Walchsee
Kössen
Hallein
Abersee
Füssen
Garmisch-Partenkirchen
Altaussee
Spital am Pyhrn
Wildalpen
BREGENZ
Grän
REUTTE
Achenkirch
St Johann in Tirol
Lofer
Bad Aussee
LIEZEN
Sopron
Dornbirn
WÖRGL
Golling an der Salzach
Ehrwald
Seefeld in Tirol
Rattenberg
Werfen
Hallstatt
Bad Mitterndorf
Langenwang
Au
Nassereith
Schwaz
KITZBÜHEL
St Johann im Pongau
Feldkirch
Häselgehr
Fügen
RADSTADT
BRUCK AN DER MUR
Nenzing
Imst
Schladming
St Anton am Arlberg
Telfs
Hall in Tirol
Wald im Pinzgau
ZELL AM SEE
Altenmarkt im Pongau
Anger
Hartberg
BLUDENZ
Oetz
INNSBRUCK
Zell am Ziller
Mittersill
Bruck an der Grossglocknerstrasse
Oberwölz
LANDECK
Prutz
Bad Hofgastein
St Peter am Kammersberg
Schruns
Fusch an der Glocknerstrasse
Unzmarkt
Frohnleiten
Galtür
Längenfeld
Neustift im Stubaital
Mayrhofen
Bad Gastein
Murau
JUDENBURG
Gaschurn
St Michael im Lungau
GRAZ
FÜRSTENFELD
Vasvár
Nauders
Sölden
Heiligenblut
Matrei in Osttirol
Hirschegg
Vipiteno
SWITZERLAND
LIENZ
Gmünd
Lieboch
Bad Gleichenberg
Malles Venosta
SPITTAL AN DER DRAU
Millstatt
Dellach im Drautal
Gnesau
SILLIAN
Döbriach
Afritz
LEIBNITZ
HUNGARY
Kötschach
Hermagor
Ossiach
Völkermarkt
Bad Radkersburg
Bolzano
ITALY
Greifenburg
Reisach
VILLACH
KLAGENFURT
Mureck
Cortina d'Ampezzo
Velden am Wörthersee
Keutschach am See
St Primus
Lenti
Maribor
Kranjska Gora
Ferlach
Jesenice
Bled
SLOVENIA
CROATIA
LJUBLJANA
0
30
60
90
120
150 kms
90 mls
© Collins Bartholomew Ltd 2011

Belgium

Country Introduction

© iStockphoto.com/Franky De Meyer

Brussels

Population (approx): 10.4 million

Capital: Brussels (population approx 1 million)

Area: 30,528 sq km

Bordered by: France, Germany, Luxembourg, Netherlands

Terrain: Flat coastal plains in north-west; central rolling hills; rugged Ardennes hills and forest in south-east; south and west criss-crossed by canals

Climate: Mild winters but snow likely in the Ardennes, cool summers, rain any time of the year; coast can be windy

Coastline: 66km

Highest Point: Signal de Botrange 694m

Languages: Flemish, French, German

Local Time: GMT or BST + 1, i.e. 1 hour ahead of the UK all year

Currency: Euros divided into 100 cents; £1 = €1.14, €1 = 87 pence (September 2011)

Telephoning: From the UK dial 0032 for Belgium and omit the initial zero of the area code of the number you are calling. To call the UK from Belgium dial 0044, omitting the initial zero of the area code. When dialling within the Brussels area use the code 02 before the telephone number

Emergency numbers: Police 112, Fire Brigade 112, Ambulance 112.

Public Holidays 2012

Jan 1; Apr 8, 9; May 1, 17, 27, 28; Jul 21 (National Day); Aug 15; Nov 1, 11 (Armistice Day); Dec 25.

Public Holidays 2013

Jan 1; Mar 31; Apr 1; May 1, 17, 19, 20; Jul 21 (National Day); Aug 15; Nov 1, 11 (Armistice Day); Dec 25.

School summer holidays extend over July and August.

Tourist Offices

BELGIAN TOURIST OFFICE
Tel: 0800 9545 245 (brochure requests) or 020 7537 1132
www.opt.be
info@opt.be

TOURISM FLANDERS-BRUSSELS
Tel: 0800 9545 245 (brochure requests) or 020 7307 7738
www.visitflanders.co.uk
info@visitflanders.co.uk

...uction to Belgium should ...ction with the important ...ntained in the Handbook chapters ...f this guide.

...ping and Caravanning

...ere are more than 900 campsites in Belgium, most of which are near the coast or in the Ardennes. They are classified into five categories. Coastal sites tend to consist largely of mobile homes/statics and can be very crowded at the height of the holiday season. A local tourist tax is usually included in the rates charged.

Twin-axle caravans are not permitted on municipal sites in and around Antwerp. Caravans and vehicles longer than 6 metres are prohibited from Liège city centre.

The Camping Card International is not compulsory but in some cases holders of a CCI benefit from a reduction in overnight charges.

Casual/wild camping is prohibited in Flanders. Elsewhere permission must first be sought from the landowner or police. Camping is not permitted alongside public highways for more than a 24-hour period, nor is it permitted in lay-bys, in state forests or along the seashore, or within a 100 metre radius of a main water point, or on a site classified for the conservation of monuments. There are approximately 50 stopovers throughout the country specifically for motorhomes.

Country Information

Cycling

Belgium is well equipped for cyclists, with an extensive network of signposted cycling routes. Cycle lanes are marked on the carriageway by means of a broken double white line or by circular signs depicting a white bicycle on a blue or black background.

Transportation of Bicycles

A bicycle may be carried at the rear of a vehicle providing its width does not extend beyond the width of the vehicle or more than one metre from the rear, and providing the rear lights and number plate remain visible.

Electricity and Gas

The current on most campsites varies between 4 and 16 amps although on some it is as low as 2 amps. Plugs have two round pins. CEE connections are not yet available at all sites.

When using a mains tester to test a connection before hooking-up recent visitors have reported problems that may be more common in Belgium than in other countries. Tester readings appear to indicate reverse polarity, possibly no earth and/or an incorrectly alternating current. In this situation The Caravan Club advises you not to use the connection.

The full range of Campingaz cylinders are available.

*See **Electricity and Gas** in the section **DURING YOUR STAY.***

Entry Formalities

British and Irish passport holders may visit Belgium for up to three months without a visa.

*See also **Documents** in the section **PLANNING AND TRAVELLING.***

Regulations for Pets

*See **Pet Travel Scheme** under **Documents** in the section **PLANNING AND TRAVELLING.***

Medical Services

The standard of health care is high. Emergency medical and hospital treatment is available at a reduced cost on production of a European Health Insurance Card (EHIC). Check whether a doctor you wish to see is registered with the national health service (conventionné/geconventioneerd) or offers private healthcare. In any event you will have to pay for services provided but 75% of the cost of treatment and approved medicines will be refunded if you apply to a local Sickness Fund Office with your EHIC.

At night and at weekends at least one local pharmacy will remain open and its address will be displayed in the window of every pharmacy in the locality.

You are strongly recommended to obtain comprehensive travel and medical insurance before travelling, such as The Caravan Club's Red Pennant Overseas Holiday Insurance – see www.caravanclub.co.uk/redpennant

*See **Medical Matters** in the section **DURING YOUR STAY.***

Opening Hours

Banks. Open hours vary from one bank to another, however usual open hours are – Mon-Fri 9am-12pm & 2pm-4pm; Sat 9am-12pm (some banks).

Museums – Tue-Sun 10am-5pm; most museums close Monday

Shops – Mon-Sat 09am-6pm or 8pm (supermarkets); some close 12pm-2pm; most shops closed Sunday.

Safety and Security

Belgium is relatively safe for visitors but you should take the usual sensible precautions to avoid becoming a victim of muggers, bag-snatchers and pickpockets, especially at major railway stations and on the underground, buses and trams in Antwerp and

Brussels. Take particular care in Brussels, both on foot and on public transport, in the area of the Gare du Midi (Eurostar terminal), the Gare du Nord, and around the EU quarter at Rondpoint Schuman. Avoid walking in areas near the stations at night, particularly if you are on your own

While driving keep car doors and windows locked at all times and do not leave valuables visible in your car. It is not uncommon for thieves, usually on motorbikes, to break a window and snatch valuables from the front or back passenger seat when a vehicle is stationary at traffic lights. Car-jacking, especially of up-market vehicles, remains a risk.

Belgium shares with the rest of Europe an underlying threat from terrorism. Attacks could be indiscriminate and against civilian and tourist targets. The area around Brussels hosts a number of international institutions (EU, NATO) which are sensitive locations where you should be vigilant.

*See **Safety and Security** in the section **DURING YOUR STAY**.*

British Embassy

AVENUE D'AUDERGHEM 10
OUDERGEMLAAN
1040 BRUXELLES
Tel: (02) 2876211
http://ukinbelgium.fco.gov.uk/en/

Irish Embassy

CHAUSEE D'ETTERBEEK 180
1040 BRUXELLES
Tel: (02) 2823400
www.embassyofireland.be
brusselsembassy@dfa.ie

There is also an Honorary Consulate in Antwerp.

Customs Regulations

Alcohol and Tobacco

For import allowances for alcohol and tobacco products see ***Customs Regulations*** in the section ***PLANNING AND TRAVELLING.***

Documents

Passport

You should carry your passport at all times as Belgian law requires everyone to carry some form of identification.

Vehicle(s)

You should carry your vehicle registration certificate (V5C), insurance details and MOT certificate (if applicable). If you are not the owner of your car or motorhome, you should carry a letter of authority from the owner permitting you to drive it.

*See **Documents** in the section **PLANNING AND TRAVELLING.***

Money

Travellers' cheques are unlikely to be accepted as a means of payment in shops, restaurants, etc, and recent visitors report that sterling travellers' cheques and, on occasion, sterling notes, may be difficult to cash in banks. Travellers are advised to take traveller's cheques in Euros.

Supermarkets often do not accept credit cards. Cash machines are widespread but may be few and far between outside town centres.

Carry your credit card issuers'/banks' 24-hour UK contact numbers in case of loss or theft of your cards. If you have difficulty reporting the theft of your card(s) to your UK bank or credit card company, ask the Belgian group 'Card Stop' to send a fax to your UK company to block your card. Card Stop's telephone number is (070) 344344.

Motoring

Accidents

The police must be called after an accident if an unoccupied stationary vehicle is damaged or if people are injured. In the case of other accidents when it is not necessary to call the police to the scene, you must still report the matter at a police station as soon as possible.

Alcohol

The maximum permitted level of alcohol is 49 milligrams in 100 millilitres of blood, i.e. lower than in the UK (80 milligrams). Penalties for exceeding this limit are severe including suspension of driving licence and a possible jail sentence.

Breakdown Service

The Touring Club Royal de Belgique (TCB) operates a breakdown service 24 hours a day throughout the country, tel (070) 344777. On motorways, use the roadside telephones called 'telestrade' which are controlled by the police and are situated approximately every 2 km. Ask for 'Touring Secours' or, when in the north of the country, 'Touring Wegenhulp'. It will be necessary to pay a fee which is variable depending on the time of day.

Essential Equipment

*See **Motoring – Equipment** in the section **PLANNING AND TRAVELLING.***

Reflective Jacket/Waistcoat

If you have brokendown or are in an accident where stopping or parking is prohibited, you must wear a reflective jacket or waistcoat when getting out of your vehicle. Passengers who leave the vehicle, for example to assist with a repair, should also wear one. Keep the jacket(s) to hand in your vehicle, not in the boot.

Child Restraint System

Children under 1.35m must be seated in a child seat or child restraint when travelling in the front or rear seat of a vehicle. If a child seat/restraint is not available, i.e. when two child restraint systems are being used on rear seats and there is not adequate space for a third child restraint system to be placed, a child must travel in the back of the vehicle using an adult seat belt. If the child is three years or under they must not travel in a vehicle without being seated in a child seat/restraint.

The child restraint must correspond to the child's weight and be of an approved type. A rear facing child restraint must not be used on a front seat with a frontal airbag unless it is deactivated.

Fuel

Petrol stations on motorways and main roads are open 24 hours and credit cards are generally accepted. Others may close from 8pm to 8am and often all day Sunday.

LPG, also known as GPL, is widely available at many service stations. For a list of outlets by region see www.primagaz.be/fr/lpg-automobile/autogasstations-in-belgie/

*See also **Fuel** under **Motoring – Advice** in the section **PLANNING AND TRAVELLING**.*

Parking

Blue zones indicating limited parking are used to denote where vehicles must display a parking disc on working days, including Saturdays, from 9am to 6pm. Discs are available from police stations, petrol stations and some shops. Outside blue zones a parking disc must also be used where the parking sign has a panel showing the disc symbol. Parking areas are also regulated by parking meters and if these exist inside a blue zone parking discs must not be used, except if the parking meter or ticket machine is out of action. Illegally parked vehicles may be towed away or clamped.

Do not park in a street where there is a triangular sign 'Axe Rouge/Ax Rode'.

*See also **Parking Facilities for the Disabled** under **Motoring – Advice** in the section **PLANNING AND TRAVELLING**.*

Priority

You should take great care to obey the 'priority to the right' rule which was tightened in 2007 and is designed to slow traffic in built-up areas. Drivers must give priority to vehicles joining from the right, even if those vehicles have stopped at a road junction or stopped for pedestrians or cyclists, and even if you are on what appears to be a main road. Exemptions to this rule apply on motorways, roundabouts and roads signposted with an orange diamond on a white background.

Trams have priority over other traffic. If a tram or bus stops in the middle of the road to allow passengers on or off, you must stop.

Roads

Roads are generally in good condition and are well lit at night, including the entire motorway network. Traffic is fast and the accident rate is high, especially at weekends, mainly due to speeding.

Road Signs and Markings

Roads signs and markings conform to international standards. A sign has been introduced prohibiting the use of cruise control. This sign will normally only be encountered on motorways where there is a risk of multiple crashes due to congestion or road works. Where this particular sign shows a weight limit, the prohibition applies to drivers of vehicles with a higher maximum permitted weight.

Roads with the prefix N are regional roads; those with numbers 1 to 9 radiate from Brussels. Motorways have the prefix A and have blue and white signs. When route planning through Belgium follow the green European road numbers with the prefix E which may be the only road numbers displayed.

Road signs you may see include the following:

You may pass right or left

Cyclists have priority over turning traffic

Cyclists have priority at junction

Use of Cruise Control prohibited

Destination road signs can be confusing to foreigners because a town may be signposted either by its French or its Flemish name, according to the predominant language in that particular area. The most important of these towns are listed below:

Flemish	***French***
Aalst	*Alost*
Aken (Aachen)	*Aix-la-Chapelle (Germany)*
Antwerpen	*Anvers*
Bergen	*Mons*
Brugge	*Bruges*
Brussel	*Bruxelles*

Doornik	*Tournai*
Edingen	*Enghien*
Gent	*Gand*
Geraardsbergen	*Grammont*
Ieper	*Ypres*
Kortrijk	*Courtrai*
Leuven	*Louvain*
Luik	*Liège*
Mechelen	*Maline*
Namen	*Namur*
Rijsel	*Lille (France)*
Roeselare	*Roulers*
Ronse	*Renaix*
Tienen	*Tirlemont*
Veurne	*Furnes*

Generally signposts leading to and on motorways show foreign destination place names in the language of the country concerned. e.g. German. Exceptions do occur, particularly on the E40 and E314 where city names may be given in Flemish or French.

Speed Limits

*See **Speed Limits Table** under **Motoring – Advice** in the section **PLANNING AND TRAVELLING.***

Whilst the general speed limit in built-up areas is 50 km/h (31 mph), lower limits of 30 km/h (18 mph) or 20 km/h (13 mph) may be imposed and indicated by signs in residential areas, town centres and near schools. Brussels city centre is a 30 km/h (18 mph) speed limit zone. The start and finish points of these zones are not always clearly marked.

Vehicles over 3,500 kg in weight are restricted to 90 km/h (56 mph) outside built-up areas and on motorways.

A car navigation system with maps indicating the location of fixed speed cameras is permitted but the use of radar equipment which actively searches for speed cameras or interferes with police equipment is prohibited.

Traffic Jams

During periods of fine weather roads to the coast, the Ardennes and around Brussels and Antwerp are very busy on Friday afternoons and Saturday mornings, and again on Sunday evenings.

Other busy routes are the E40 (Brussels to Ostend), the E25 (Liège to Bastogne and Arlon), the E411 (Brussels to Namur and Luxembourg), and the N4 from Bastogne to Arlon around the border town of Martelange caused by motorists queuing for cheap petrol in Luxembourg. Routes to avoid the worst of the jams have been established and these are indicated by orange and green road signs. In general avoid traffic on the E40 by taking the R4 and N49, and on the E411 by taking the N4 Bastogne to Marche-en-Famenne and Namur. These routes are heavily used and consequently the road surface is subject to excessive wear and tear which can be challenging for caravanners.

Traffic Lights

A green light (arrow) showing at the same time as a red or amber light means that you can turn in the direction of the green arrow providing you give way to other traffic and to pedestrians. An amber light, possibly flashing, in the form of an arrow inclined at an angle of 45 degrees to the left or to the right, shows that the number of traffic lanes will be reduced. Leave the lane as quickly as possible in the direction indicated by the arrow.

Tunnels

Three road tunnels go under the River Scheldt at Antwerp. In the Liefkenhoeks tunnel on road R2 to the north of the city a toll of €16.35-18 (2011) is levied on vehicles over 2.75 m in height. Solo cars are charged €4.60-5.50. The Kennedy Tunnel on road R1 to the south of the city is toll-free but is heavily congested in both directions for much of the day. The smallest tunnel, the Waasland Tunnel is part of the N59a and is also toll-free.

Violation of Traffic Regulations

The police may impose on-the-spot fines on visitors who infringe traffic regulations such as speeding and parking offences. Penalties may be severe and if you are unable to pay on the spot your vehicle(s) may be impounded or your driving licence withdrawn. Fines can be paid in cash or with a debit or credit card. An official receipt must be issued.

In an effort to improve road safety the authorities have increased the number of speed traps throughout the country in the form of cameras and unmarked police vehicles.

Vehicles of 3,500 kg or over are not allowed to use the left lane on roads with more than three lanes except when approaching a fork in a motorway when vehicles have to move to the left or right lane, depending on their destination.

Motorways

Belgium has an extensive network of approximately 1,750 km of motorways (A roads), one of the densest in the world. Although Belgium motorways are toll free, the introduction of a motorway sticker is planned for 2013.

Service areas usually have a petrol station, restaurant,

shop and showers. Rest areas have picnic facilities. For detailed information about the motorway network see www.autosnelwegen.net

Recent visitors report that some motorways are so heavily used by lorries that the inside lane has become heavily rutted and/or potholed. These parallel ruts are potentially dangerous for caravans travelling at high speed and vigilance is necessary. It is understood that parts of the A2/E314 and A3/E40 are particularly prone to this problem.

Touring

Flemish is spoken in the north of Belgium, whilst French is spoken in the south. Brussels is bi-lingual. English is widely spoken. German is spoken in the extreme east of the country.

Belgian pastry-cooks have a worldwide reputation for the variety and richness of their cream and chocolate confections, and no trip is complete without sampling the Belgian national dish 'moules et frites' (mussels and chips served with mayonnaise). Towns in the Ardennes specialise in a variety of sausages and hams. Beer is the national drink and there are several hundred speciality beers on offer, as well as well known brands of lager. Prices in restaurants are quoted 'all inclusive' and no additional tipping is necessary. Smoking is severely restricted in public places including restaurants and cafés.

Plastic carrier bags are generally not provided in supermarkets, so take your own.

When visiting Brussels visitors may buy a Brussels Card, valid for 24, 48 or 72 hours, which offers free access to virtually every major museum in the city and unlimited use of public transport, together with discounts at a number of other attractions. The pass is available from the tourist information office in the Hotel de Ville and from many hotels, museums and public transport stations. Or buy online from www.brusselscard.be

Local Travel

Anyone under the age of 25 years is entitled to free or reduced price travel on public transport in the Brussels region. During periods of severe air pollution public transport in that region is free to all passengers.

Brussels and Antwerp have metro systems together with extensive networks of trams and buses. Tram and bus stops are identified by a red and white sign and all stops are request stops; hold out your arm to signal an approaching bus or tram to stop. Tickets, including 10-journey and one-day travel cards, are available from vending machines at metro stations and some bus stops, newsagents, supermarkets and tourist information centres.

Most of Belgium is well connected by train and most main routes pass through Antwerp, Brussels or Namur. Trains are modern, comfortable and punctual and fares are reasonably priced. Buy tickets before boarding the train or you may be charged a supplement. Eurostar tickets to Brussels allow free, same day transfers to domestic Belgian stations.

Bikes are allowed on some buses in the Flanders area of the country.

Plans are in hand to to introduce a unified smart card ticketing system covering all public transport, irrespective of company or mode of transport. This system will use chip cards, card readers and on-board computers.

All place names used in the Site Entry listings which follow can be found in Michelin's Benelux & North of France Touring & Motoring Atlas, scale 1:150,000 (1 cm = 1.5 km).

AALTER *A2* (1km N Rural) **Camping Isabel-Novel, Manewaarde 13A, 9880 Aalter [(09) 3744589; fax 3747515]** Fr A10/E40 Ostend-Gent, exit Aalter. Take N44 sp Maldegem. L at 2nd set traff lts (lts are v close together), turn immed R thro indus est. Turn L into narr low at site sp (diff to spot), site 650m on R. Ent to site diff for lge o'fits/m'vans. Med, pt shd; wc; shwrs €0.50; el pnts €1.50; shops 4km; playgrnd; fishing; 50% statics; quiet but rd & rlwy noise; CCI. "Friendly site; in field adj old residential site; conv NH." 1 Apr-30 Sep. € 12.00 2010*

ADINKERKE see De Panne *A1*

AISCHE EN REFAIL *B3* (S Rural) *50.59977, 4.84335* **Camping du Manoir de Là-Bas, Route de Gembloux 180, 5310 Aische-en-Refail [(081) 655353; europa-camping.sa@skynet.be; www.camping-manoirdelabas.be]** Fr E411/A4 exit junc 12 & foll sps to Aische-en-Refail. Site on o'skts of vill. Lge, pt sl, pt shd; wc; chem disp; shwrs €1; el pnts (6A) inc; gas; Indtte; shop; snacks; htd pool; paddling pool; fishing; tennis; games rm; entmnt; 80% statics; dogs; poss cr; Eng spkn; adv bkg; quiet; CCI. "Friendly staff; site little run down; ltd hot water; basic san facs; some site rds are narr; recep far side of chateau; gd rest & bar." ♦ 1 Apr-31 Oct. € 18.00 2011*

AMBERLOUP/STE ODE see Tenneville *C3*

ANTWERPEN *A3* (15km NE Urban) *51.30548, 4.58536* **Camping Floreal Club Het Veen, Eekhoornlaan 1, 2960 Sint Job-in't-Goor [(03) 6361327; fax 6362030; het.veen@florealclub.be; www.florealclub.be]** Fr A1/E19 exit junc 4 to Sint Job in't Goor. Strt over traff lts & immed after canal bdge turn L, 1.5km to site alongside canal. Lge, hdg/mkd pitch, pt shd; htd wc; chem disp; mv service pnt; baby facs; shwrs inc; el pnts (10A) inc; Indtte (inc dryer); shop; rest; snacks; bar; playgrnd; tennis; games rm; 80% statics; dogs €3.40; phone; bus 1.5km; Eng spkn; adv bkg; CCI. "V helpful recep; pleasant site & town; gd cycling along canal; gd NH." 1 Mar-31 Oct. € 25.00 2010*

ANTWERPEN *A3* (1km NW Urban) *51.23347, 4.39261* **Camping De Molen, Jachthavenweg 2, St Annastrand, 2020 Antwerpen [tel/fax (03) 2198179; toerisme@stad.antwerpen.be; www.camping-de-molen.be]** Clockwise on ring rd, take 1st exit after Kennedy tunnel, exit 6. R at traff lts, 3rd L where cannot go strt on (rv on R), site on R in 1km on bank of Rv Schelde. Or on ent Antwerp foll sp Linkeroever, go strt on at 3 traff lts, then turn L & foll camping sp. Fr A14/E17 exit junc 7 & foll sp for Linkeroever Park & Ride until site sp appear, then foll sp. Med, pt shd; wc; chem disp; shwrs; el pnts (10A) €2.50 (poss rev pol) - €25 deposit for adaptor/cable; shops 1km; supmkt by metro; rest adj; pool nr; wifi; bus nrby; metro 1km; poss cr; Eng spkn; adv bkg rec; quiet, but some rv traff noise & poss noise fr local bar; ccard not acc; red low ssn. "Popular site; max 14 nt stay; pedestrian/cycle tunnel to city cent 1km; gd for rollerblading, cycling; friendly, helpful staff; mosquitoes poss a problem; san facs satisfactory; 30 min walk to city cent." ♦ 16 Mar-15 Oct. € 23.00 2011*

⊞ **ARLON** *D3* (2km N Urban) *49.70310, 5.80763* **Camping Officiel, 373 Rue de Bastogne, Bonnert, 6700 Arlon [tel/fax (063) 226582; campingofficiel@skynet.be; www.campingofficielarlon.be]** Fr E411 exit junc 31 onto N82 Arlon for 4km, turn twd Bastogne on N4. Site sp on R. Med, pt sl, pt shd; wc; chem disp; fam bthrm; shwrs inc; el pnts (6A) €2.40 (check earth); gas; Indtte (inc dryer); shop 2km; tradsmn; rest; snacks; bar; BBQ; playgrnd; pool; wifi; TV rm; dogs €2; Eng spkn; poss cr; adv bkg; some rd noise; red long stay; CCI. "Charming, clean site; levelling blocks/ramps req - supplied by site; c'vans tight-packed when site busy; 5km approx to Luxembourg for cheap petrol; Arlon interesting town; vg NH & longer stay." € 18.50 2011*

ARLON *D3* (7km N Rural) *49.74833, 5.78697* **Camping Sud, 75 Voie de la Liberté, 6717 Attert [(063) 223715; fax 221554; info@campingsudattert.com; www.campingsudattert.com]** Off N4 Arlon rd on E side of dual c'way. Sp to site fr N4 (500m). U-turn into site ent. Med, hdg/mkd pitch, some hdstg, pt shd; htd wc; chem disp; shwrs €0.50 (high ssn); el pnts (5-10A) €2.50 (check earth); Indtte; shop; tradsmn; rest; snacks; bar; BBQ; playgrnd; pool; no statics; dogs €2; phone; bus; adv bkg; Eng spkn; quiet, some rd noise; red long stay; CCI. "Vg, well-organised site; special NH pitches; fishing & walking." 1 Apr-25 Oct. € 18.00 2010*

ATTERT see Arlon *D3*

AVE ET AUFFE see Han sur Lesse *C3*

⊞ **BASTOGNE** *C3* (500m NE Urban) *50.00340, 5.69525* **Camping de Renval, 148 Route de Marche, 6600 Bastogne [tel/fax (061) 212985; info@campingrenval.be; www.campingrenval.be]** Fr N leave A26 exit 54, foll Bastogne sp. Fr Marche-en-Famenne dir, exit N4 at N84 for Bastogne; site on L in 150m opp petrol stn. Fr E foll Marche, in 1km site on R opp petrol stn. Med, hdstg, pt sl, terr, pt shd; htd wc; chem disp; baby facs; shwrs inc; el pnts (10A) inc (poss rev pol); Indtte (inc); shops 1km; snacks; BBQ; playgrnd; tennis; games area; wifi; entmnt; 95% statics; dogs €3; site clsd Jan; quiet; ccard acc; red low ssn. "Take care speed bumps; helpful staff; clean san facs but long walk fr tourers' pitches; gd security; facs ltd low ssn; gd NH." € 20.00 2010*

⊞ **BERLARE** *A2* (1km N Rural) *51.04350, 3.98960* **Camping Roosendael, Schriekenstraat 27, 9290 Berlare-Overmere [(09) 3678742; fax 3657355; hugoscalafilm@skynet.be; www.ideal-caravans.be]** Fr A14/E17 junc 11 onto N449 dir Laarne. At T-junc turn L onto N445 past Overmere & Donk. Approx 2.5km after Overmere at rndabt with Shell g'ge turn R onto N467 past Donkmeer to Berlare. After 1.5km turn L in front of 'Café de Kalvaar', site at end of rd. Med, hdg/mkd pitch, pt shd; htd wc; chem disp; shwrs; el pnts (6A) inc; Indtte; shop, rest, snacks, bar 500m; BBQ; playgrnd; lake beach & sw 500m; fishing 500m; games rm; tennis 500m; many statics; phone; quiet; Eng spkn. "Nice site; lge pitches, mainly sandy soil; warm welcome; clean, modern san facs, but ltd; poss under-used low ssn; local vet comes to site; gd NH." ♦ € 17.00 (CChq acc) 2011*

DISCOVER THE BELGIAN ARDENNES & CAMPING BERTRIX

Camping Bertrix

- Beautiful nature
- Charming villages
- Tasteful Belgian beers
- Superb walking area
- Impressive memorials
- Traditional Belgian meals

- Spacious pitches
- Panoramic views
- First class facilities
- Heated swimming pools
- Excellent restaurant
- Hospitable atmosphere

Enjoy your holiday in a Four Star Quality setting for affordable prices
Internet: www.campingbertrix.be Tel.: 0032 61 412 281 (English spoken)

BERTRIX *D3* (2km S Rural) *49.83942, 5.25360* **Ardennen Camping Bertrix, Route de Mortehan, 6880 Bertrix [(061) 412281; fax 412588; info@campingbertrix.be; www.campingbertrix.be]** Exit A4/E411 junc 25 onto N89 for Bertrix & foll yellow sps to site. Lge, mkd pitch, terr, pt shd; htd wc; chem disp; mv service pnt; baby facs; fam bthrm; some serviced pitches; sauna; shwrs inc; el pnts (10A) €4; gas; Indtte (inc dryer); shop high ssn; tradsmn; rest; snacks; bar; playgrnd; htd pool high ssn; paddling pool; tennis; cycle hire; internet; TV rm; 35% statics; dogs €5; poss cr; Eng spkn; adv bkg; quiet; ccard acc; red low ssn/snr citizens; red low ssn/CCI. "Excel site; scenic location; friendly, helpful owners; gd for families; excel clean facs; gd rest; lovely site with big pitches; big pool; lovely setting." ♦ 1 Apr-14 Nov. € 28.00 (CChq acc) 2011*

See advertisement

BOUILLON *D3* (800m S Rural) *49.78247, 5.06212* **Camping Moulin de la Falize, Vieille Route de France 62, 6830 Bouillon [(061) 466200; fax 467275; moulindelafalize@swing.be; www.moulindelafalize.be]** Fr A4 exit junc 25 & foll N89. Turn R dir Bouillon. At end of town 1-way system turn R then immed L up hill, site on L in 800m. Med, pt sl, terr, unshd; wc; chem disp; sauna; shwrs inc; el pnts (6A) inc; Indtte; shop 1km; rest; snacks; bar; BBQ; playgrnd; pool; rv 1km; tennis; fitness cent; entmnt; 95% statics; phone; dogs; quiet; Eng spkn; ccard acc; CCI. "V ltd touring pitches; steep inclines; conv Orval Abbey, brewery; NH only." 1 Apr-31 Dec. € 17.50 2009*

BOUILLON *D3* (6km W Rural) *49.79479, 5.01352* **Camp Municipal Halliru, 1 Route de Corbion, 6830 Bouillon [(061) 466009; fax 468048; halliru@bouillon.be; www.bouillon.be]** Fr Bouillon pass under castle, turn L twd Corbion on N810; site on R in 6km. Steep descent into site. Med, pt shd; wc; shwrs €1; shops 1.5km; el pnts (10A) €2.08 (long lead poss req); playgrnd; fishing; 50% statics; dogs; poss cr; phone; quiet. "Peaceful, rvside site; conv historic town; fair." ♦ 1 Apr-30 Sep. € 10.42 2011*

BREDENE see Oostende *A1*

BRUGES see Brugge *A2*

BRUGGE *A2* (12km NE Rural) *51.28937, 3.33332* **Camping Hoeke, Damse Vaart Oost 10, 8340 Damme [(050) 500496; www.campinghoeke.be]** Fr Brugge ring rd, take minor rd to NE, sp Damme on S side of canal. At Damme, cont by canal to Siphon. Cross canal, turn L in front of cafe, R & cont 4km by canal to Hoeke. Site behind pub building on R bef bdge at Hoeke. Or fr N fr junc N49 & N376 take N49 dir Maldagem for 3.5km. Site sp both sides of canal in Hoeke. Keep canal on R twd Damme, site 300m on L, sp on building. Sm, hdg/mkd pitch, pt shd; wc; chem disp; 10% serviced pitches; shwrs €1; el pnts (6A) inc; gas; shops 4km; rest; bar; BBQ; playgrnd; sand beach 8km; 90% statics; phone; quiet; CCI. "Picturesque town, conv Bruges fishing in canal; tight access to pitches; charge for all hot water; NH/sh stay only." ♦ 1 Mar-15 Nov. € 16.25 2010*

⊞ **BRUGGE** *A2* (3km E Urban) *51.20722, 3.26305* **Camping Memling, Veltemweg 109, 8310 Sint Kruis [(050) 355845; fax 357250; info@camping-memling.be; www.camping-memling.be]** Exit A10 junc 8 Brugge. In 2km turn R onto N397 dir St Michiels & cont 2km to rlwy stn on R. Turn R under rlwy tunnel & at 1st rndbt take dir Maldegem onto ring rd & in a few kms take N9 sp Maldegem & St Kruis. After 3km at traff lts adj Macdonalds, turn R & immed L sp Camping to site on R in 400m past sw pool. Fr Gent exit E40 sp Oostkamp & foll Brugge sp for 7km to N9 as above. Med, mkd pitch, some hdstg, pt shd; htd wc; chem disp; mv service pnt; shwrs inc; el pnts (6A) inc (poss rev pol); Indtte; shops 500m; 3 supmkts nrby; rest, snacks, bar 500m; htd pool adj; cycle hire; wifi; 13% statics; dogs €2; bus 200m; poss v cr; Eng spkn; adv bkg ess high ssn; poss noisy at w/ends & rd noise; ccard acc; red low ssn/long stay; CCI. "Busy site; conv Brugge & ports; red low ssn as no shwrs/rest/bar; friendly, helpful owners; recep open 0900-1200 & 1700-1900 (all day to 2200 high ssn); arr early high ssn to ensure pitch; low ssn site yourself & report to recep; conv Zeebrugge ferry (30mins) & allowed to stay to 1500; adv bkgs taken but no pitch reserved; m'van pitches sm, rec pay extra for standard pitch; clean san facs but stretched high ssn (refurb planned in 2012); cycle rte to Bruges; 35 min walk to Brugge cent; conv bus." € 26.00 2011*

BELGIUM

⊞ **BRUGGE** *A2* (500m S Urban) *51.19634, 3.22573* **Motorcaravan Park, Off ring rd R30, Buiten Katelijnevest, Brugge** Exit A10 at junc 7 twd Brugge. After going under rlwy bdge, turn R under ring rd after old bus stn to dedicated mv parking adj coach parking, nr marina. Sm, hdstg, pt shd; chem disp €0.50; el pnts (10A) inc; washrm nr; water €0.50; shop 500m; dogs; noisy; m'vans only; red low ssn. "In great location - gd view of canal, sh walk to town cent thro park; rec arr early high ssn; if full, take ticket & park in coach park opp; NH only." € 22.50 2011*

⊞ **BRUGGE** *A2* (9km SW Urban) *51.18448, 3.10445* **Recreatiepark Klein Strand, Varsenareweg 29, 8490 Jabbeke [(050) 811440; fax 814289; info@kleinstrand.be; www.kleinstrand.be]** If travelling fr W leave A10/E40 at Jabbeke exit, junc 6; turn R at rndabt & in 100m turn R into narr rd. Foll site to statics car pk on L & park - walk to check-in at recep bef proceeding to tourer site in 400m. If app fr E leave A10/E40 at junc 6 (Jabbeke) turn L at 1st rndabt. Drive over m'way twd vill. Turn L at next rndabt & foll site sp into site car pk as above. V lge, hdg/mkd pitch, pt shd; wc; chem disp; mv service pnt; baby facs; shwrs €0.75; el pnts (10A) inc; gas; Indtte (inc dryer); shop & 1km; 2 rests (1 open all yr); snacks; 3 bars; BBQ; playgrnd; paddling pool; direct access to lake sw adj; tennis; fishing; watersports; cycle hire; games rm; wifi; entmnt; TV; 75% statics; dogs €2; no c'vans/m'vans over 12m; bus to Brugge; poss cr with day visitors; Eng spkn; quiet but background m'way noise; ccard acc; red low ssn/CCI. "Busy site; vg touring base; lge pitches; wide range of entmnt & excursions; bus to Bruges every 20 mins." ♦ € 36.00 (up to 4 persons) SBS - H15 2011*

BRUSSELS see Bruxelles *B2*

We can fill in site report forms on the Club's website – www.caravanclub.co.uk/europereport

BRUXELLES *B2* (10km NE Rural) *50.9346, 4.3821* **Camping Grimbergen, Veldkantstraat 64, 1850 Grimbergen [(0479) 760378 or (02) 2709597; fax (02) 2701215; camping.grimbergen@telenet.be]** Fr Ostend on E40/A10 at ringrd turn E & foll sp Leuven/Luik (Liège)/Aachen. Exit junc 7 N sp Antwerpen/Grimbergen N202. At bus stn traff lts turn R twd Vilvourde N211. Turn L at 2nd traff lts (ignore no L turn - lorries only). Site sp 500m on R. Ent via pool car pk. Med, pt sl, pt shd; wc; chem disp; shwrs inc; el pnts (10A) €2.50; Indtte; shops 500m; tradsmn; rest adj; pool adj; cycle hire; dogs €1; phone; hourly bus to city 200m; Eng spkn; adv bkg; quiet but some aircraft noise & cock crowing; CCI. "Well-run, popular site - rec arr early; gd, clean, modern san facs; helpful staff; sh walk to town; train to Brussels fr next vill; red facs low ssn; gates clsd 1130-1400; gd rest by bus stop; conv Brussels; excel."♦ 1 Apr-31 Oct. € 17.00 2011*

BRUXELLES *B2* (10km E Urban) *50.85720, 4.48506* **RCCCB Camping Paul Rosmant, Warandeberg 52, 1970 Wezembeek [(02) 7821009; camping.wezembeek@hotmail.com; www.rcccb.com]** Leave ringrd RO at junc 2 sp Kraainem turning E. In 600m at rndabt at end of dual c'way take 3rd exit, then 1st L into residential rd. At end turn L, then R at end. Foll rd to crest of hill, site on L, sp. Med, mkd pitch, hdstg, terr, pt sl, pt shd; wc; chem disp; shwrs inc; el pnts (6A) inc (poss rev pol & no earth); gas 3km; Indry rm; shop, rest, snacks 1km; bar; playgrnd; 65% statics; dogs €1; metro nr; gates clsd 1200-1400 & 2200-0800; Eng spkn; adv bkg; some rd & aircraft noise; ccard acc; CCI. "Poss diff for lge outfits due narr site ent, v tight corners, raised kerbs; poor san facs (2011); gd for metro into Brussels fr Kraainem; welcoming wardens." 1 Apr-30 Sep. € 20.00 2011*

BURE/TELLIN see Tellin *C3*

CHIMAY *C2* (Urban) *50.04578, 4.30963* **Camping Communal, Allée des Princes 1, 6460 Chimay [(060) 211843; fax 214099]** Fr N (Beaumont) site sp in town cent on R. Med, mkd pitch; wc; shwrs inc; el pnts (6A) inc; Indry rm; shop; snacks; BBQ; playgrnd; htd pool 500m; 75% statics; dogs; quiet. "Site guarded at night." ♦ 1 Apr-31 Oct. € 12.50 2008*

DAMME see Brugge *A2*

DE HAAN *A1* (2km E Coastal) *51.28330, 3.05610* **Camping Ter Duinen, Wenduinesteenweg 143, Vlissegem, 8421 De Haan [(050) 413593; fax 416575; lawrence.sansens@scarlet.be; www.campingterduinen.be]** Exit A10/E40 junc 6 Jabbeke onto N377 dir De Haan. Go thro town dir Wenduine, site on R in 4km. Med, mkd pitch, unshd; htd wc; chem disp; mv service pnt; baby facs; shwrs €1.20; el pnts (16A) inc; Indtte (inc dryer); shop; snacks; bar; BBQ; playgrnd; htd pool 200m; water complex 1km; sand/shgl beach 500m; lake sw adj; fishing, cycle hire 200m; horseriding 1km; golf 4km; wifi; 85% statics; dogs €3; phone; tram nrby; poss cr; Eng spkn; adv bkg ess; fairly quiet; CCI. "Neat, clean, well-managed site; friendly staff; poss long walk to excel san facs inc novelty wcs!; conv ferries, Bruges; excel." ♦ 15 Mar-15 Oct. € 23.00 (CChq acc) 2010*

DE HAAN *A1* (W Urban/Coastal) *51.26123, 2.99836* **Camping 't Rietveld, Driftweg 210, 8420 De Haan [(0475) 669336; camping.rietveld@telenet.be; www.campingrietveld.be]** Fr Ostend on N34; fork R onto Driftweg bef golf club dir Vosseslag & Klemskerke, site sp. Sm, unshd; htd wc; chem disp; baby facs; shwrs €1.10; el pnts (16A) €1.75; Indtte; shop, rest, snacks, bar in town; playgrnd; sand beach 1km; 80% statics; dogs €1.85; poss cr; Eng spkn; quiet; CCI. "Friendly, helpful staff; clean san facs." 1 Apr-15 Oct. € 21.90 2010*

BELGIUM

⊞ **DE PANNE** *A1* (2km W Rural) *51.08288, 2.59094* **Camping Ter Hoeve, Duinhoekstraat 101, 8660 Adinkerke [(058) 412376; camping.terhoeve@skynet.be; www.camping-terhoeve.be]** Leave Calais-Ostend m'way at junc 1 (ignore junc 1a) dir De Panne. Foll rd past theme park (Plopsaland), L at filling stn, site 1km on L. Lge, hdg pitch, pt shd; wc; chem disp; mv service pnt; shwrs inc; el pnts (4A) €1.50 (poss no earth); Indtte (inc dryer); shop; supmkt 500m; snacks; playgrnd; beach 2km; 60% statics; no dogs; tram 500m; poss cr; some daytime noise fr nrby theme park; ccard not acc. "Nice pitches; friendly, helpful owner; gd, modern san facs; lge grassed area for tourers & hdstg area for late arr/early dep; barrier clsd 2200-0800 - go to visitors' car park on R bef booking in; san facs clsd 1100-1600 low ssn; v busy site high ssn, phone to check opening times low ssn; conv Dunkerque ferries & Plopsaland park." € 12.00 2011*

⊞ **DE PANNE** *A1* (2.3km W Rural) *51.07666, 2.58663* **Familie Camping Kingervreugde, Langgeleedstraat 1, 8660 Adinkerke [(058) 411587; fax 421129; admin@kindervreugde.be; www.familiecamping.net]** Leave Calais-Ostend m'way at junc 1 (ignore junc 1a) dir De Panne. Foll rd past theme park (Plopsaland), L at filling stn, site 1.3km on L. Med, hdg pitch, pt shd; htd wc; chem disp; shwrs inc; el pnts (6A) €2.50; Indtte; shop, rest, snacks, bar 1km; BBQ; playgrnd; dogs; 50% statics; phone; bus 800m; Eng spkn; adv bkg; quiet; ccard not acc; red CCI. "Conv Dunkerque/Calais ferries." ♦ € 20.50 (3 persons) 2008*

DEINZE see Gent *A2*

DINANT *C3* (4km S Rural) *50.22178, 4.92230* **Camping Parc de Vacances Villatoile, Ferme de Pont-à-Lesse, Route de Walzin, 5500 Anseremme [(082) 222285; fax 227151; info@villatoile.be; www.villatoile.be]** Leave E11 at junc 20 onto N97 dir Philippeville, then onto N94 dir Dinant. At T-junc facing rv turn L onto N95 to Anseremme. Go thro vill & turn L just bef rv bdge, site 1.5km on L. NB App rd has v lge, brick-built speed ramp. Med, pt shd; wc; chem disp; mv service pnt; shwrs €1.20; el pnts (10A) inc (poss rev pol); gas; Indtte (inc dryer); shop; tradsmn; rest, snacks; high ssn; bar; playgrnd; pool 300m; rv sw adj; canoeing; games area; wifi; entmnt; 40% statics; dogs; phone; Eng spkn; adv bkg (winter); quiet; ccard acc; CCI. "On loop of Rv Lesse; busy, not particularly clean site used by canoeists, rock climbers & hikers; extra for rvside pitch; scenic area; gd san facs; gd walks; hign ssn music Sat nights; gates locked 2200-0800; poss lge, noisy youth groups; gd fun for older children otherwise NH only." 1 Apr-15 Oct. € 17.80 2010*

DINANT *C3* (10km SW Rural) *50.19094, 5.00611* **Camping de la Lesse, Rue du Camping 1, 5560 Houyet [(82) 666100; fax 667214; lafamiliale@coolweb.be; www.campingdelalesse.be]** S on N95 fr Dinant for about 13km; turn L onto D929 sp Houyet. Cross rlwy & immed turn L along Rv Lesse. Lge, pt shd; htd wc; chem disp; shwrs; el pnts (15A) inc; Indtte; shop 500m; rest; snacks; bar; playgrnd; pool adj; tennis; kayaking; fishing; 50% statics; dogs €2; train; poss noisy; CCI. "Pleasant area for walking/cycling; caves at Han-sur-Lesse worth visit; basic san facs." 1 Apr-31 Oct. € 17.00 2008*

⊞ **DINANT** *C3* (1.5km NW Urban) *50.27722, 4.89694* **Camping Communal Devant-Bouvignes, 1 Quai de Camping, 5500 Dinant [(082) 224002 or (477) 619873 (mob); fax 224132; devantbouvignes.dinant@gmail.com; www.dinant.be]** Exit E11 junc 20 onto N936; drive to cent of Dinant (steep descent) to T-junc; turn R onto N92; cont along rv for 1.5km; site on L after bend. Med, pt shd; htd wc; chem disp; mv service pnt; baby facs; shwrs €1; el pnts (16A) €3; Indry rm; supmkt 1km; drinks avail; playgrnd; rv sw; 50% statics; dogs free; bus at ent; adv bkg; quiet, but some rd & rlwy noise; ccard not acc. "Excel situtation on rv bank; site undergoing modernisation (2011), inc pitch layout, when completed it should be excel." € 17.00 2011*

⊞ **DINANT** *C3* (9km NW Rural) *50.33557, 4.99534* **Camping Durnal - Le Pommier Rustique, Route de Spontin, 5530 Durnal [(083) 699963; fax (0475) 407827; info@camping-durnal.net; www.camping-durnal.net]** Leave E411 at junc 19. Turn S dir Spontin onto D946, then N937, foll site sp. Sm, mkd pitch, terr, unshd; wc; chem disp; fam bthrm; sauna; shwrs inc; el pnts (10A) inc (check rev pol); Indtte (inc dryer); shop; tradsmn; rest; snacks; playgrnd; games area; child entmnt high ssn; cab TV; mainly statics; dogs free; 4 nights for price of 3; Eng spkn; quiet; ccard acc. "Friendly, helpful owner; well-run, well-maintained site; ltd touring pitches; sm pitches; modern san facs; conv NH fr m'way." € 20.00 2011*

⊞ **DOCHAMPS** *C3* (S Rural) *50.23080, 5.63180* **Panoramacamping Petite Suisse, Al Bounire 27, 6960 Dochamps [(084) 444030; fax 444455; info@petitesuisse.be; www.petitesuisse.be]** Fr E25, take rd 89 sp Samrée. Turn N in Samrée to Dochamps, turn R bef vill, site sp. Lge, some hdstg, pt sl, terr, unshd; htd wc; chem disp; mv service pnt; htd shwrs; baby facs; el pnts (16A) inc; gas; Indtte (inc dryer); shop; rest; snacks; bar; playgrnd; htd pool; paddling pool; waterslide; tennis; games area; wifi; TV rm; adv bkg; 50% statics; dogs €5; phone; quiet; poss cr; ccard acc; red low ssn/snr citizens; CCI. "Gd facs; beautiful spot; busy, popular site." € 32.50 (CChq acc) 2011*

ECAUSSINNES LALAING *B2* (2km W Rural) *50.58397, 4.19279* **Camping La Dime, Rue Hayette 2, 7191 Ecaussinnes-Lalaing [(067) 442780; info@offim.be]** Exit A7/E17 at junc 20 onto N534 dir Ronquières. Turn L in approx 4km, then R in 2km opp white house. Foll site sp along narr rds - few passing places. Med, pt sl, pt shd; wc; chem disp; shwrs €1; el pnts (10A); bar; playgrnd; pool; TV rm; 75% statics; dogs; Eng spkn; adv bkg; quiet; CCI. "Friendly, family-owned site; facs neglected; take care polarity/earth; conv Ronquières, Thuin; NH only." 1 Apr-31 Oct. € 15.00 2008*

⊞ **EEKLO** *A2* (7km E Rural) *51.18093, 3.64180* **Camping Malpertuus, Tragelstraat 12, 9971 Lembeke [(09) 3776178; fax 3270036; campingmalpertuus@telenet.be; www.vkt.be]** Exit A10/E40 junc 11 onto N44 dir Aalter & Maldegem. Foll sp Eekloo onto N49 & then foll sp Lembeke, site sp. Med, pt shd; htd wc; chem disp; mv service pnt; shwrs €1; el pnts (4A) €3; gas; Indry rm; shop 2km; rest 200m; snacks; bar; 85% statics; dogs; phone; bus 300m; Eng spkn; adv bkg; quiet; 10% red CCI. "Gd site in lovely area; friendly staff; entmnt/events at w/end; gd size pitches; gd site." ♦ € 15.50 2011*

EPINOIS see Binche *C2*

BELGIUM

⊞ **EREZEE** *C3* (1.5km S Rural) *50.27923, 5.54779* **Camping Le Val de l'Aisne, Rue du TTA, 6997 Blier-Erezée [(086) 470067; fax 470043; info@levaldelaisne.be; www.levaldelaisne.be]** Fr Marche-en-Famenne take N86 dir Hotton. In Hotton cross Rv Ourthe & immed turn R dir Soy & Erezée. In 9km at lge rndabt foll sp La Roche-en-Ardenne, site in 900m on L. Med, hdg/mkd pitch, pt shd; htd wc; chem disp; baby facs; shwrs; el pnts (16A) €3; gas; Indtte (inc dryer); shop 1.5km; rest; snacks; bar; BBQ; playgrnd; htd, covrd pool 10km; lake beach & sw adj; fishing; kayaking; tennis; games area; wifi; entmnt; cab/sat TV; 70% statics; dogs €3; train 8km; phone; poss cr; Eng spkn; adv bkg; quiet; ccard acc; red long stay/low ssn/CCI. "Beautiful situation; excel, well-maintained facs; friendly, helpful staff; vg, peaceful site." ♦ € 18.00 2010*

ESNEUX *C3* (500m N Rural) *50.53941, 5.56986* **Camping Les Murets, Chemin d'Enonck 57, 4130 Hony-Esneux [tel/fax (041) 3801987; lesmurets@skynet.be; www.lesmurets.be]** On rd A26/E25 take exit 41 or 42 dir Esneux. In vill of Méry, directly after green bottle bank turn R over bdge & immed L at end of bdge sp Hony/Hôni. Foll sp Les Murets, under rlwy bdge Les Murets on L. Med, pt shd wc; chem disp; shwrs €0.90; el pnts (4A) inc; gas; shops, rest 500m; tradsmn; supmkt in Méry; BBQ; playgrnd; pool 5km; TV rm; dogs; phone; poss cr; Eng spkn; adv bkg rec high ssn; quiet but some rlwy noise. "Friendly; facs basic but clean; conv touring base." 1 Apr-31 Oct. € 16.80 2009*

⊞ **EUPEN** *B4* (2km SW Rural) *50.61457, 6.01686* **Camping Hertogenwald, Oestraat 78, 4700 Eupen [(087) 743222; fax 743409; info@camping-hertogenwald.be; www.camping-hertogenwald.be]** Fr German border customs on E40 a'bahn for Liège, take 2nd exit for Eupen. In Eupen L at 3rd traff lts & 1st R in 100m. Drive thro Eupen cent, foll sp to Spa. Camping sp immed at bottom of hill, sharp hairpin R turn onto N629, site on L in 2km. Med, unshd; htd wc; chem disp; shwrs inc; el pnts (6A) inc (long lead req & poss no earth); Indtte; shop 2km; rest; snacks; bar; playgrnd; htd, covrd pool 3km; games area; 90% statics; dogs €1.60; phone; poss cr; Eng spkn; quiet. "Sm tourer area; clean site adj rv & forest; muddy after rain; gd walking & cycling beside rv; conv Aachen." ♦ € 17.90 2011*

⊞ **EUPEN** *B4* (2.5km SW Rural) *50.61250, 6.01128* **Camping Wesertal, Rue de l'Invasion 66-68, 4837 Membach-Baelen [(087) 555961 or 555076; fax 556555; info@wesertal.com; www.wesertal.com]** Fr E40 junc 38 onto N67, turn R at 1st rndabt & foll sp Baelen & Membach, site sp in 7km. Med, shd; htd wc; chem disp; sauna; baby facs; shwrs €1; el pnts (16A) inc (check pol & poss no earth); Indtte; shops 3km; tradsmn; playgrnd; pool 2km; 90% statics; dogs €2; poss cr; Eng spkn; adv bkg; quiet; CCI. "Site adj rv & forest; friendly welcome; poss run down, scruffy; ltd space for tourers; some pitches well away fr (poss grubby) san facs; gd walks; NH only." € 19.60 2009*

FAUVILLERS *D3* (SE Rural) *49.84716, 5.70297* **Camping Beau Rivage, Wisembach 15a, 6637 Fauvillers/Wisembach [(063) 600357; fax 601004; info@campingbeaurivage.be; www.campingbeaurivage.be]** Fr Martelange foll sp to Wisembach. Site sp nr cent of vill. Sm, mkd pitch, pt shd; htd wc; chem disp; shwrs €0.50; el pnts (16A) €1.50; gas; Indtte; shop; bar; playgrnd; rv sw adj; 80% statics; phone; Eng spkn; quiet. "Friendly owner; pleasant pitches adj rv." 1 Apr-1 Nov. € 14.00 2008*

FLORENVILLE *D3* (8km E Rural) *49.69208, 5.40866* **Camping du Faing, Rue du Faing 16, 6810 Jamoigne [(061) 320272; fax 464867]** Exit A4/E25 junc 30 onto N83 W or junc 29 onto N87/N83 thro Tintigny. Site at W end of Jamoigne - track to site adj lge concrete materials depot. Sp diff to spot. Med, pt shd; wc; chem disp; shwrs inc; el pnts inc; Indtte; supmkt in vill; bar; rest; playgrnd; covrd pool & sports adj nr; 80% statics; dogs; phone; quiet; ccard acc. "NH only; san facs need refurb - more facs avail in recep/rest/bar building at site ent." ♦ Mar-Dec. € 22.00 2009*

FLORENVILLE *D3* (13km E Rural) *49.6849, 5.5206* **Camping Chênefleur, Norulle 16, 6730 Tintigny [(063) 444078; fax 445271; info@chenefleur.be; www.chenefleur.be]** Fr Liège foll E25 dir Luxembourg. Exit junc 29 sp Habay-la-Neuve to Etalle, then N83 to Florenville. Site sp off N83 at E end of Tintigny vill. Med, pt shd; htd wc; chem disp; shwrs inc; baby facs; el pnts (6-8A) inc; gas; Indtte (inc dryer); shop; tradsmn; rest; snacks; bar; playgrnd; htd pool; paddling pool; games area; cycle hire; wifi; entmnt; dogs €4; Eng spkn; adv bkg; quiet; ccard acc. "Orval Abbey, Maginot Line worth visit; friendly staff; gd, clean site & modern san facs." ♦ 1 Apr-30 Sep. € 32.25 (CChq acc) 2011*

GEDINNE *C3* (1km SW Rural) *49.97503, 4.92719* **Camping La Croix Scaille, Rue du Petit Rot 10, 5575 Gedinne [(061) 588517; fax 588736; camping.croix-scaille@skynet.be; www.campingcroixscaille.be]** Fr N95 turn W to Gedinne on N935. Site sp S of vill on R after 1km. Lge, mkd pitch, some hdstg, terr, pt shd; htd wc; chem disp; shwrs inc; el pnts (16A) €1.60; gas; Indtte (inc dryer); snacks; bar; playgrnd; TV; pool; tennis, fishing adj; cycle hire; 75% statics; dogs; poss cr; quiet; ccard acc; CCI. 1 Apr-15 Nov. € 12.65 2010*

⊞ **GEEL** *A3* (9km N Rural) *51.22951, 4.97836* **Camping Houtum, Houtum 51, 2460 Kasterlee [(014) 85 92 16; fax 853803; info@campinghoutum.be; www.campinghoutum.be]** On N19 Geel to Turnhout rd 1km bef Kasterlee site sp on R at windmill opp British WW2 cemetery. Foll sps to site 500m on rd parallel to N19, cross next rd, site in 300m. Lge, mkd pitch, pt shd; htd wc; chem disp; shwrs €1; el pnts (4-6A) €2; Indtte; shops adj; snacks; lge playgrnd; pool 2km; adj to rv with boating, canoeing, fishing; tennis & mini-golf 300m; cycle hire; nature trails adj; 60% statics; phone; poss v cr; adv bkg; v quiet; ccard acc; red long stay/CCI. "Orderly, attractive site; lots for children all ages." € 17.00 2011*

BELGIUM

GENT *A2* (10km SW Rural) *51.00508, 3.57228* **Camping Groeneveld, Groenevelddreef 14, Bachte-Maria-Leerne, 9800 Deinze [(09) 3801014; fax 3801760; info@campinggroeneveld.be; www.campinggroeneveld.be]** E or W E40/E10 on Brussels to Ostend m'way exit junc 13 at sp Gent W/Drongen. Take N466 sp Dienze. Approx 1km beyond junc with N437, turn L just after 2nd 70 km/h sp down narr side road - house on corner has advert hoarding. Site on L opp flour mill. Sm sp at turning. Med, some hdg pitch, pt shd; htd wc; chem disp; mv service pnt; shwrs inc; el pnts (10A) inc (poss no earth); shops 2km; rest (bkg ess), snacks, bar (w/end only low ssn); playgrnd; fishing; entmnt; TV; 40% statics; dogs €2; phone; Eng spkn; adv bkg; quiet; red low ssn/long stay; CCI. "Gd welcome; additional san facs at lower end of site; office open 1800-1900 low ssn but staff in van adj san facs opp, or site yourself; barrier closed until 0800; do not arr bef 1400; 1km fr Ooidonk 16thC castle." 1 Apr-31 Oct. € 22.00 2010*

GENT *A2* (3km W Urban) *51.04638, 3.68083* **Camping Blaarmeersen, Zuiderlaan 12, 9000 Gent [(09) 2668160; fax 2668166; camping.blaarmeersen@gent.be; www.blaarmeersen.be]** Exit A10/E40 Brussels-Ostend m'way at junc 13 sp Gent W & Drongen. At T-junc turn onto N466 twd Gent. In 4km cross canal then turn R to site, sp (3 rings) Sport & Recreatiecentrum Blaarmeersen. Fr Gent cent foll N34 twd Tielt for 1km past city boundary & turn L to site; adj lake & De Ossemeersen nature reserve. NB Due to rd layout, rec foll camping sp on app to site rather than sat nav. Lge, hdg/mkd pitch, pt shd; htd wc; chem disp; mv service pnt; serviced pitch; shwrs inc; el pnts (10A) metered + conn fee €1.25 (poss rev pol); Indtte (inc dryer); shop; tradsmn; rest; snacks; bar; playgrnd; pool & full sports facs adj; lake sw adj; watersports; tennis; frequent bus to Gent; 5% statics; dogs €1.25; phone; bus to town nr; no departure bef 0815 hrs; Eng spkn; rd/rlwy noise; ccard acc; passport req. "Clean, well-organised, busy site; beautiful lake with path around; helpful staff; rest gd value; gd cycle track fr site; cycle into cent avoiding main rd; gd location for walks & activities; poss itinerants low ssn; pitches muddy when wet; some m'van pitches sm & v shd; excel." 1 Mar-31 Oct. € 18.50 2011*

BELGIUM

⊞ **GERAARDSBERGEN** *B2* (4km NE Urban) *50.78990, 3.92351* **Camping Domein De Gavers, Onkerzelestraat 280, 9500 Geraadsbergen [(054) 416324; fax 410388; gavers@oost-vlanderen.be; www.degavers.be]** Fr N on A10 exit junc 17; S for 26km on N42 to Geraardsbergen. After level x-ing turn L at traff lts, L at rndabt & foll sp De Gavers for 4.3km. Fr S on N42 foll sp Geraardsbergen to rndabt, turn L then turn R at 2nd traff lts sp De Gavers. Lge, hdg pitch, pt shd; htd wc; chem disp; mv service pnt; baby facs; shwrs €0.50; el pnts (10A) inc (long lead req); Indtte; shop, rest, bar 400m; playgrnd; lake sw & sand beach adj; TV; 80% statics; dogs; phone; train 4km; poss cr; Eng spkn; adv bkg; quiet but some rd noise; ccard acc; red long stay/CCI. "Sep area for tourers; many leisure facs; excel touring region." € 25.00 2010*

GODARVILLE *B2* (1km S Rural) *50.48794, 4.29318* **Camping Domaine Claire-Fontaine, 11 Ave Clémenceau, 7160 Godarville [(064) 443675; sites.voiesdeau@hainaut.be]** Exit A15/E42 junc 18 onto N59 to Godarville, site sp. Lge, unshd; wc; chem disp; shwrs inc; el pnts (6A) inc; Indry rm; tradsmn; shop 1km; snacks; bar; BBQ; playgrnd; lake sw; games area; 85% statics; dogs; phone; ccard acc; CCI. "Facs better than 1st impression but avoid san facs nr touring area & avoid area outside barrier; helpful warden; NH only." 1 Mar-31 Oct. € 22.00 2010*

GRIMBERGEN see Bruxelles *B2*

⊞ **HAN SUR LESSE** *C3* (Urban) *50.12727, 5.18773* **Camping Aire Gîte d'Etape, Rue du Gîte d'Etape 10, 5580 Han-sur-Lesse [(084) 377441; gite.han@gitesdetape.be]** Exit A4/E411 junc 23 sp Ave-et-Auffe & Rochefort. Go over 2 rv bdges then immed L & 1st R. Site on L. Sm, hdstg, unshd; wc; mv service pnt; shops, rests etc nr; playgrnd nrby; games area; entmnt; motor caravans only. "Gd; attendant calls." € 5.00 2009*

HAN SUR LESSE *C3* (Urban) *50.12621, 5.18610* **Camping Le Pirot, Rue Joseph Lamotte 3, 5580 Han-sur-Lesse [(084) 377280; fax 377576; han.tourisme@skynet.be; www.valdelesse.be]** Exit A4/E411 junc 23 sp Ave-et-Auffe & Rochefort. Go over 1st bdge then L immed bef 2nd bdge in Han cent; sh, steep incline. Sm, unshd; wc; chem disp; shwrs inc; el pnts (10A) inc (poss rev pol); Indtte; shop nr; rest, snacks, bar 200m; no statics; dogs; bus adj; poss cr; adv bkg; quiet; ccard acc; CCI. "Excel position on raised bank of rv; adj attractions & rests; interesting town; helpful staff; basic, dated san facs; conv NH." 1 Apr-15 Nov. € 20.00 2011*

HAN SUR LESSE *C3* (500m S Rural) *50.12330, 5.18587* **Camping La Lesse, Rue du Grand Hy, 5580 Han-sur-Lesse [(084) 377290; fax 377576; han.tourisme@skynet.be; www.valdelesse.be]** Site 500m off Han-sur-Lesse main sq adj Office de Tourisme. If app fr Ave-et-Auffe, turn R at Office du Tourisme, take care over rlwy x-ing to site on R in 150m. Med, mkd pitch, pt shd; htd wc; chem disp; shwrs inc; el pnts (3-6A) inc; gas; Indtte; shops, rests 200m; playgrnd; canoeing adj; rv adj; 80% statics; dogs; phone; poss cr; adv bkg ess high ssn via Tourist Office; phone adj; noisy; ccard not acc; CCI. "Gd touring base; underground grotto trip; take care on narr rds to site - v high kerbs; san facs immac." 1 Apr-15 Nov. € 22.00 2009*

⊞ **HAN SUR LESSE** *C3* (4km SW Rural) *50.11178, 5.13308* **Camping Le Roptai, Rue Roptai 34, 5580 Ave-et-Auffe [(084) 388319; fax 387327; info@leroptai.be; www.leroptai.be]** Fr A4 exit 23 & take N94 dir Dinant. At bottom of hill turn R onto N86. Turn L in vill of Ave, foll sp, 200m to L. Med, mkd pitch, hdstg, pt sl, terr, pt shd; wc; chem disp; mv service pnt; shwrs €0.90; el pnts (6A) €1.80; gas; shop & 5km; tradsmn; snacks; bar; playgrnd; htd pool; TV; 80% statics; dogs €1.50; site clsd Jan; poss cr; Eng spkn; adv bkg; quiet; CCI. "Some pitches awkwardly sl; generally run down & poor facs; ltd facs low ssn; NH only." € 20.00 2008*

HASSELT *B3* (9km N Rural) *50.99775, 5.42537* **Camping Holsteenbron, Hengelhoefseweg 9, 3520 Zonhoven [tel/fax 011 817140; camping.holsteenbron@skynet.be; www.holsteenbron.be]** Leave A2 junc 29 twd Hasselt; turn L at 1st traff lts in 1km, foll sp thro houses & woods for 3km. Site is NE of Zonhoven. Med, hdg/mkd pitch, hdstg, pt shd; htd wc; chem disp; shwrs €1; el pnts (6A) inc; Indry rm; snacks; bar; playgrnd; games area; TV; 30% statics; dogs €1; phone; Eng spkn; quiet; CCI. "Pleasant, happy site in woodland; gd touring base; friendly owners." 1 Apr-13 Nov. € 22.00 2011*

HOGNE see Marche en Famenne *C3*

⊞ **HOUTHALEN** *B3* (500m E Rural) *51.01439, 5.46651* **Recreatiepark Hengelhoef, Tulpenstraat 141, 3530 Houthalen-Helchteren [(089) 382500; fax 844582; info@recreatieparkhengelhoef.be; www.hengelhoef.be]** Fr A2/E314 exit 30, turn N & foll sp to Houthalen, site sp. Obtain pass card bef app barrier. Lge, mkd pitch, shd; htd wc; chem disp; mv service pnt; baby facs; some serviced pitches; sauna; shwrs inc; el pnts (10A) inc; gas; Indtte (inc dryer); shop; rest; snacks; bar; BBQ; playgrnd; 2 pools (1 htd covrd); paddling pool; waterslide; wave machine; jacuzzi; lake beach & fishing adj; wildlife park; tennis; cycle hire; wifi; entmnt; TV; 80% statics; no dogs; phone; bus adj; poss cr; adv bkg; ccard acc; CCI. "Part of lge leisure complex; v busy high ssn but quiet after 2200; excel pool complex; gd facs for disabled; gd local footpaths." ♦ € 39.30 (4 persons) 2008*

HOUTHALEN *B3* (3km E Rural) *51.03222, 5.41613* **Camping Kelchterhoef, Binnenvaartstraat, 3530 Houthalen-Helchteren [(011) 526720; info@kelchterhoef.be; www.kelchterhoef.be]** Exit A2/E314 junc 30 N. In 2km at x-rds turn L, in 2km at rndabt turn R into Binnenvaartstraat, then foll site sp. Lge, mkd pitch, pt shd; htd wc; chem disp; shwrs; el pnts (6A) inc; Indtte; shop; snacks; playgrnd; lake sw adj; entmnt; internet; TV; 40% statics; adv bkg; Eng spkn; quiet. "Use entry phone for access; fair site." 1 Apr-1 Nov. € 22.00 2008*

HOUYET see Dinant *C3*

HUY *B3* (2km E Urban) *50.5337, 5.2596* **Camping Mosan, Rue de la Paix 3, 4500 Tihange [(085) 231051; fax 251853; ces.huy@skynet.be]** Exit A15 junc 8 & proceed to Huy town cent, then along S bank of Rv Meuse dir Liège for 2km (past bdge on L) beyond town cent. Immed bef lge cooling towers on L, turn R (unmkd). In approx 200m sharp L turn into Rue de la Paix. Site recep at house beyond community cent. Sm, pt shd; wc; chem disp; mv service pnt; shwrs; el pnts inc; shop 1km; adv bkg; ccard not acc. "Fair site; easy access to town; recep opens 1630 - site yourself." 1 Apr-30 Sep. € 15.00 2009*

JABBEKE see Brugge *A2*

KASTERLEE see Geel *A3*

KEMMEL/HEUVELLAND see Ypres/Ieper *B1*

KNOKKE HEIST *A2* (500m SE Urban) *51.33530, 3.28959* **Camping Holiday, Natiënlaan 70-72, 8300 Knokke-Heist [(050) 601203; fax 613280; info@camping-holiday.be; www.camping-holiday.be]** On N49/E34 opp Knokke-Heist town boundary sp. Site ent at side of Texaco g'ge. Med, unshd; wc; chem disp; shwrs inc; el pnts (6A) €1.90 (poss rev pol); supmkt opp; rest, snacks 500m; playgrnd; beach 1.5km; cycle hire; phone; 60% statics; poss cr; quiet but rd noise. "V clean, tidy site but ltd san facs; may need to manhandle c'van onto pitch." ♦ Easter-30 Sep. € 20.00 2010*

KOKSIJDE *A1* (500m NE Urban) *51.11105, 2.65215* **Camping De Blekker, Jachtwakersstraat 12, 8670 Koksijde ann Zee [(058) 511633; fax 511307; camping.deblekker@skynet.be; www.deblekker.be]** Fr E40 Brugge-Calais exit dir Veurne & foll sp Koksijde. At rndabt turn R for Koksijde Dorp then Koksijde ann Zee. Site sp on R. Lge, hdg/mkd pitch, pt shd; htd wc; chem disp; mv service pnt; serviced pitches; mv service pnt; baby facs; shwrs €1; el pnts (10A) inc; gas; Indtte (inc dryer); shop 300m; rest; snacks; bar; BBQ; playgrnd; htd, covrd pool 400m; sand beach 1.8km; games rm; TV; 80% statics; no dogs; phone; poss cr; adv bkg; quiet; Eng spkn; ccard acc; CCI. "Warm welcome; relaxing site; modern san facs but insufficient for size of site." ♦ 15 Mar-15 Nov. € 30.00 2010*

KOKSIJDE *A1* (500m SW Rural) *51.11114, 2.67082* **Camping Amazone, Westhinderstraat 2, 8670 Koksijde ann Zee [(058) 513363; fax 522512; info@camping-amazone.com; www.camping-amazone.com]** Fr A18/E40 exit junc 1A dir De Panne, foll sp Koksijde on N8. Pass airfield & turn R to Koksijde, site on L in 500m. Med, mkd pitch, unshd; wc; own san; chem disp; shwrs €1; el pnts (6A) €2; sand beach 1.2km; 80% statics; Eng spkn; quiet. "Ltd touring pitches, but conv NH Dunkerque/Ostend ferries." 1 Apr-30 Sep. € 18.00 2009*

⊞ **KOKSIJDE** *A1* (2km W Rural) *51.10536, 2.62987* **Camping Noordduinen, Noordduinen 12, 8670 Koksijde aan Zee [(058) 512546; fax 512618; roos@campingbenelux.be; www.campingnoordduinen.be]** Exit A18/E40 junc 1a onto N8. Foll sp Koksijde to rndabt, strt over into Leopold III Laan, site on L. Sm, hdg pitch, hdstg, pt shd; wc; shwrs €1; el pnts €2.50; Indtte; supmkt 300m; sand beach 3km; wifi; 80% statics; dogs €2.50; bus 500m; Eng spkn; adv bkg; quiet; CCI. "Gd site; adj cycle rte to Veurne - attractive, historic town." € 25.00 2010*

LEMBEKE see Eeklo *A2*

LIEGE *B3* (10km S Rural) *50.56770, 5.58826* **Camping du Syndicat d'Initiative de Tilff, Rue du Chera 5, 4040 Tilff-sur-Ourthe [(04) 3881883]** Exit m'way at Tilff junc 41 or 42 & foll sp to site. Sm, v sl, pt shd; wc; chem disp; shwrs; el pnts (4A) €2.48; Indtte; shops 500m; playgrnd; pool 2m; poss cr; 95% statics; dogs; quiet; CCI. "Basic site; ltd space for tourers; NH only." ♦ 1 Apr-31 Oct. 2009*

LILLE-GIERLE see Turnhout *A3*

⊞ **LONDERZEEL** *B2* (2km NE Rural) *51.02194, 4.31926* **Camping Diepvennen, Molenhoek 35, 1840 Londerzeel [(052) 309492; fax 305716; info@camping-diepvennen.be; www.camping-diepvennen.be]** On A12 exit at Londerzeel, foll sp Industrie Zone & Diepvennen. Foll Diepvennen sp to site. Site on W side of A12. Lge, pt shd; wc; shwrs €1; el pnts €2.60; Indtte; shop; rest; snacks; playgrnd; pool; fishing pond; tennis; games area; 95% statics; rd noise; red long stay. "Long walk to san facs block; easy access by train to Antwerp & Brussels." ♦ € 17.40 2009*

There aren't many sites open at this time of year. We'd better phone ahead to check the one we're heading for is open.

⊞ **MALMEDY** *C4* (3km E Rural) *50.42008, 6.07059* **Familial Camping, Rue des Bruyères 19, 4960 Arimont-Malmédy [tel/fax (080) 330862; info@campingfamilial.be; www.campingfamilial.be]** Take St Vith rd (N62) out of Malmédy; in 2km over level x-ing turn L in 300m at sp Arimont & 2nd camping sp. Site on L, 1.5km up winding (but easy) hill. Med, pt sl, terr, pt shd; htd wc (some cont); chem disp; mv service pnt; shwrs €1; el pnts inc (4-6A) €2; gas; Indtte (inc dryer); sm shop; tradsmn; rest; snacks; bar; sm pool; playgrnd; games rm; wifi; entmnt; TV; bus 1km; 50% statics; dogs free; phone; site clsd last week Oct to 2nd week Dec; Eng spkn; adv bkg; ccard not acc; CCI. "Pleasant but untidy site with excel views over hills; gd facs; conv Ardennes, Spa motor racing circuit; lorry noise fr rd to quarry behind site." € 17.50 2011*

MALONNE see Namur *C3*

⊞ **MARCHE EN FAMENNE** *C3* (4km NW Rural) *50.24911, 5.27978* **Camping Le Relais, 16 Rue de Serinchamps, 5377 Hogne [(0475) 423049; info@campinglerelais; www.campinglerelais.com]** Sp fr N4 bet Marche-en-Famenne & Namur. Fr Namur ent immed R under new bdge. Med, pt sl, unshd; htd wc; chem disp; baby facs; shwrs inc; el pnts (10A) €2.50; Indtte; rest; snacks; playgrnd; lake adj; TV; 30% statics; dogs free; adv bkg; some rd noise; CCI. "V pleasant; gd facs." € 20.00 2009*

MEMBACH-BAELEN see Eupen *B4*

MOL *A3* (5km E Rural) *51.20945, 5.17181* **Camping Zilverstrand, Kiezelweg 17, 2400 Mol [(014) 810098; fax 816685; info@zilverstrand.be; www.zilverstrand.be]** Exit A13 junc 23 dir Geel onto N19 then N71 to Mol, site sp on N712 twd Lommel. Lge, pt shd; htd wc; chem disp; mv service pnt; baby facs; fam bthrm; el pnts (6A) inc; Indtte (inc dryer); shop; tradsmn; rest; snacks; bar; BBQ; playgrnd; htd covrd pool; paddling pool; waterslides; lake sw & beach; tennis 1km; cycle hire; golf 1km; wifi; 60% statics; dogs; adv bkg; quiet. ♦ 22 Apr-31 Oct. € 30.50 (CChq acc) 2011*

⊞ **MONS** *B2* (E Urban) *50.45155, 3.96312* **Camping Du Waux-Hall, Ave St Pierre 17, 7000 Mons [(065) 337923 or 335580; fax 356336; ot1@ville.mons.be; www.mons.be]** Site nr ring rd to E of town. Join Mons inner ring (anti-clockwise traff only) foll 'Autres Directions' to N90 Charleroi exit (sp bef tunnel Beaumont-Binche) where turn R; take 1st R in 100m, then immed R down sliprd then R at end. Site sp on L in 200m at end of park. Or fr Binche on N90 pass barred ent to park to traff lts, keep L-hand lane strt across lts, in 50m to U turn in sq to return across lts, then as above. Med, some hdg/mkd pitch, pt shd; htd wc; chem disp; serviced pitch; shwrs inc; el pnts (6-10A) metered; Indtte (inc dryer); shops 600m; tradsmn; rests, bars in town; dogs free; bus to town cent; poss cr; Eng spkn; quiet; ccard acc; red low ssn/CCI. "Excel, clean & tidy, but old san facs; friendly welcome; gd supmkt 2 mins drive; adj attractive park with ponds & playgrnd; 15 min walk to town cent; lge pitches; grass pitches poss diff/waterlogged when wet; conv Waterloo battlefield." € 13.50 2011*

⊞ **MUNKZWALM** *B2* (500m E Rural) *50.87573, 3.74058* **Camping Canteclaer, Rekegemstraat 12, 9630 Munkzwalm [(055) 499688; fax 316150; camping.canteclaer@telenet.be; www.campingcanteclaer.be]** Fr A10 exit junc 17 onto N42 S. At junc with N46 turn R & in 7km turn L to Munkzwalm on N415 Noordlaan which becomes Zuidlaan. Turn L again into Zwalmlaan, site by rlwy. Lge, pt shd; wc; chem disp; shwrs €0.75; el pnts (6A) inc; Indtte; shops 1km; rest; snacks; bar; playgrnd; statics; phone; adv bkg; quiet, some rlwy noise; 80% statics. "Sm touring area." € 13.00 2009*

NAMUR *C3* (11km S Rural) *50.37233, 4.86966* **Camping La Douaire, 43 Rue du Herdal, 5170 Profondeville [(081) 412149]** Fr Namur take N92 S twds Dinant. At approx 8km 100m after rndabt take slip rd sp Profondeville. In 100m turn R into Chemin du Herdal, site on L, narr ent. Med, mkd pitch, sl, pt shd; wc; chem disp; shwrs €1.25; el pnts €3; gas; shop, rest 300m; playgrnd; pool 4km; 95% statics; dogs; quiet. "Conv Namur & Dinant; not suitable twin-axles; only 2 (poor) touring pitches, no hdstg." 1 Apr-15 Oct. € 8.80 2009*

NAMUR *C3* (5km SW Rural) *50.44164, 4.80182* **Camping Les Trieux, 99 Rue Les Tris, 5020 Malonne [tel/fax (081) 445583; camping.les.trieux@skynet.be; www.campinglestrieux.be]** Fr Namur take N90 sp Charleroi, after 8km take L fork sp Malonne (camp sp at junc). After 400m turn L at camp sp & site at top of 1 in 7 (13%) hill, approx 200m. To miss steep hill, fr Namur take Dinant (N92) S. In 2km R at camping sp. Take care at hairpin in 200m. Foll site sps. Located up steep, but surfaced rd. Med, mkd pitch, terr, pt shd; htd wc; chem disp; mv service pnt; shwrs €1; el pnts (10A) €2; Indtte; shop; tradsmn; snacks; playgrnd; TV; 50% statics; phone; Eng spkn; quiet; ccard not acc; red low ssn; CCI. "Friendly owners; pretty site, but steep - take care ent pitch; pitches diff for lge o'fits; basic san facs but clean; NH only." 1 Apr-15 Oct. € 17.50 2008*

BELGIUM

NEUFCHATEAU *D3* (3km S Rural) *49.83502, 5.41640* **Camping Val d'Emeraude, Route de Malome 1-3, 6840 Neufchâteau [tel/fax (061) 277076; heleenluisman@hotmail.com; www.valdemeraude.be]** Take Florenville rd out of town. In 2km site at lge cream house on L. Med, pt sl, unshd; wc; chem disp; shwrs; el pnts €3 (poss rev pol); Indry rm; shop 3km; rest, snacks, bar 1km; playgrnd; fishing 500m; 70% statics; dogs €1.50; quiet but some rd noise; CCI. "Friendly owner; well-kept, flat pitches; basic, ltd san facs (unclean 6/09); attractive location; gd NH." ♦ 1 Apr-31 Oct. € 16.00 2009*

⊞ **NEUFCHATEAU** *D3* (2.5km SW Rural) *49.83305, 5.41721* **Camping Spineuse, Rue de Malome 7, 6840 Neufchâteau [(061) 277320; fax 277104; info@camping-spineuse.be; www.camping-spineuse.be]** Fr A4/E411 exit junc 26 or junc 27 fr E25 to Neufchâteau. Take N85 dir Florenville, site is 3rd on L. Ent easy to miss. Med, pt shd; htd wc; chem disp; mv service pnt; shwrs; el pnts (16A) €3; Indtte; shops 1km; tradsmn; rest; snacks; bar; playgrnd; sm pool; wifi; TV; 30% statics; dogs €1.25; phone; Eng spkn; quiet; ccard acc; red low ssn/snr citizens. "Pleasant, pretty site; poss diff lge outfits if site full; vg san facs; some flooding after heavy rain." € 16.00 2011*

NIEUWPOORT *A1* (2km E Rural) *51.12960, 2.77220* **Kompas Camping, Brugsesteenweg 49, 8620 Nieuwpoort [(058) 236037; fax 232682; nieuwpoort@kompascamping.be; www.kompascamping.be]** Exit E40/A18 at junc 3 sp Nieuwpoort; in 500m turn R at full traff lts; after 1km turn R at traff lts; turn R at rndabt & immed turn L over 2 sm canal bdgs. Turn R to Brugsesteenweg, site on L approx 1km. Fr Ostende on N34 (coast rd) turn L at rndabt after canal bdge as above. V lge, hdg/mkd pitch, some hdstg, pt shd; htd wc; chem disp; baby facs; shwrs inc; el pnts (10A) €2.20; gas; Indtte (inc dryer); shop & 2km; rest; snacks; bar; playgrnd; 2 pools (1 htd, covrd); paddling pool; waterslide; tennis; sports/games area adj; cycle hire; golf 10km; wifi; entmnt; 90% statics; dogs €2.30; poss cr; adv bkg; quiet; red long stay/CCI. "Well-equipped site; helpful staff; boat-launching facs; sep area for sh stay tourers; v busy w/ends; excel cycle rtes; conv Dunkerque ferry." 1 Apr-14 Nov. € 34.00 (4 persons) (CChq acc) 2011*

⊞ **NIEUWPOORT** *A1* (2km E Rural) *51.13324, 2.76031* **Parking De Zwerver, Brugsesteenweg 16, 8620 Nieuwpoort [(0474) 669526; de_zwerver@telenet.be]** Nr Kompass Camping - see dirs under Kompass Camping. Site behind De Zwerver nursery. Sm, mkd pitch, all hdstg, unshd; wc; mv service pnt €2.50; shwrs & hot water; Indtte; BBQ; playgrnd; m'vans only. "Coin & note operated facs; modern & efficient; walking/cycling distance to town cent & port." ♦ € 0.50 (per hour) 2010*

⊞ **OLLOY SUR VIROIN** *C3* (1km SW Rural) *50.06876, 4.59643* **Camping Try des Baudets, Rue de la Champagne, 5670 Olloy-sur-Viroin [tel/fax (060) 390108; masson_p@yahoo.Fr]** Fr N99 turn to Olloy-sur-Viroin sp Fumay. At end of main street (where Fumay rd turns L), cont strt then R, site sp up fairly steep, narr rd with passing places. Lge, mkd pitch, sl, unshd; wc; chem disp; shwrs inc; el pnts (6A) inc; Indtte; shop, bar 1km; playgrnd; fishing; 80% statics; dogs; bus; Eng spkn; adv bkg; quiet; CCI. "Gd walking, cycling; steam rlwy in valley; friendly proprietor; vg." ♦ € 18.00 2009*

⊞ **OOSTENDE** *A1* (2km NE Coastal) *51.24882, 2.96710* **Camping 17 Duinzicht, Rozenlaan 23, 8450 Bredene [(059) 323871; fax 330467; info@campingduinzicht.be; www.campingduinzicht.be]** Fr Ostend take dual c'way to Blankenberge on N34. Turn R sp Bredene, L into Driftweg which becomes Kappelstraat & turn R into Rozenlaan. Site sp. Lge, mkd pitch, hdstg, unshd; htd wc; chem disp; mv service pnt; serviced pitches; baby facs; shwrs €1; el pnts (10A) inc (poss no earth); gas; Indtte (inc dryer); shop 500m; rest; snacks, bar adj; BBQ; playgrnd; sand beach 500m; wifi; 60% statics; dogs; phone; security barrier; poss cr; Eng spkn; adv bkg; quiet; ccard acc; red low ssn; CCI. "Excel site; poss long walk to san facs; take care slippery tiles in shwrs; Bredene lovely, sm seaside town." € 23.00 (4 persons) 2011*

⊞ **OOSTENDE** *A1* (4km E Urban/Coastal) *51.24970, 2.96834* **Camping Astrid, Koning Astridlaan 1, 8450 Bredene [(059) 321247; fax 331470; info@camping-astrid.be; www.camping-astrid.be]** Foll tourist sp. Med, unshd; wc; chem disp; serviced pitch; shwrs; el pnts (10A) inc; shops 100m; sand beach adj; cab/sat TV; 80% statics; phone; poss cr; Eng spkn; ccard not acc. "Most sites nrby are statics only; friendly, helpful owners." ♦ € 23.50 2009*

⊞ **OOSTENDE** *A1* (4km E Rural) *51.24366, 2.98002* **Camping T Minnepark, Zandstraat 105, 8450 Bredene-Dorp [(059) 322458; fax 330495; info@minnepark.be; www.minnepark.be]** Fr Ostend take N34 sp Blankenberge. After tunnel under rlwy turn R sp Brugge. Cross canal & in 300m turn L at filter sp Bredene-Dorp. In 2km immed after blue/white water tower on R, turn L at x-rds. At mini-rndabt turn R passing Aldi supmkt. Site on L after Zanpolder site. Fr A18 exit junc 6 & take N37 sp De Haan. In 5km turn L at rndabt onto N9 sp Oostende. In 5km turn R sp Bredene-Dorp, then R in 2.5km at rndabt into Zandstraat, then as above. V lge, unshd; wc; chem disp; shwrs €1; el pnts (16A) €1 (poss rev pol); Indtte (inc dryer); shops 1km; tradsmn; playgrnd; sand beach 2km; wifi; cab TV; 75% statics; dogs €3; Eng spkn; adv bkg; quiet. "Lge pitches; friendly, helpful staff; warm welcome; excel, well-run site; vg san facs; conv ferries, Bruges & coast." € 24.00 2011*

⊞ **OPGLABBEEK** *B3* (1km S Rural) *51.02825, 5.59745* **Camping Wilhelm Tell, Hoeverweg 87, 3660 Opglabbeek [(089) 854444; fax 810010; receptie@wilhelmtell.com; www.wilhelmtell.com]** Leave A2/E314 at junc 32, take rd N75 then N730 N sp As. In As take Opglabbeek turn, site sp in 1km. Med, mkd pitch, pt shd; wc; chem disp; mv service pnt; shwrs €0.90; el pnts (10A) inc; gas; Indtte (inc dryer); shop high ssn; rest; snacks; bar; BBQ; playgrnd; 2 htd pools (1 covrd); paddling pool; waterslide; tennis; cycle hire; golf 10km; wifi; entmnt; TV rm; 55% statics; dogs €4; phone; adv bkg; red long stay/low ssn; quiet; CCI. "Nice site; narr ent; superb pools, wave machine; site in nature reserve; helpful staff." ♦ € 32.00 (CChq acc) 2011*

BELGIUM

OTEPPE *B3* (1km N Rural) *50.58239, 5.12455* **Camping L'Hirondelle Château, Rue de la Burdinale 76A, 4210 Oteppe [(085) 711131; fax 711021; info@lhirondelle.be; www.lhirondelle.be]** App fr E A15/E42 at exit 8; turn W on N643 for 1.5km; turn at sp on R for Oteppe. In vill 3km pass church to x-rds & R by police stn: site 150m on L. Fr W exit A15 at exit 10 onto N80, turn R onto N652 at Burdinne for Oteppe - easier rte. V lge, pt sl, shd; wc; shwrs €1; el pnts (6A) inc; gas; Indtte; shop; rest; snacks; bar; BBQ; playgrnd; 2 pools; waterslide; tennis; games area; internet; 75% statics; dogs €2.50; poss cr; quiet; ccard acc; red CCI. "Site in grounds of chateau; excel facs for children; touring pitches at top of site poss diff (steep); gd area for walking, fishing; conv NH." 1 Apr-31 Oct. € 21.00 2010*

OVERIJSE see Bruxelles *B2*

POLLEUR *C4* (1.5km W Rural) *50.53140, 5.86320* **Camping Polleur, Rue du Congrès, 4910 Polleur [(087) 541033; fax 542530; info@campingpolleur.be; www.campingpolleur.be]** Exit A27/E42 junc 7 or 8, site sp. Steep, narr access unsuitable lge c'vans or twin-axles. Lge, pt sl, unshd; wc; chem disp; shwrs €1; el pnts (16A) inc; Indtte; shop; rest; bar; BBQ; playgrnd; htd pool; waterslide; games area; cycle hire; golf 7km; entmnt; internet; 30% statics; dogs €2; phone; bus 100m; poss cr; Eng spkn; adv bkg; ccard acc; CCI. "NH only." Easter-31 Oct. € 24.75 2008*

PROFONDEVILLE see Namur *C3*

⊞ **ROCHE EN ARDENNE, LA** *C3* (2km E Rural) *50.17697, 5.59847* **Camping Floréal La Roche, 18 Route de Houffalize, 6980 La Roche-en-Ardenne [(084) 219467; camping.laroche@florealclub.be; www.florealclub.be]** Outside town on N860 dir Houffalize on rvside, sp. V lge, mkd pitch, unshd; htd wc; chem disp; mv service pnt; baby facs; shwrs inc; el pnts (10A) inc; gas; Indtte (inc dryer); shop; tradsmn; rest; snacks; bar; playgrnd; htd pool, paddling pool nr; fishing; tennis; cycle hire; games area; wifi; TV rm; 70% statics; dogs; bus; poss cr; Eng spkn; adv bkg; some rd noise; ccard acc; red long stay/CCI. "La Roche interesting town; vg, well-run, friendly site; lge pitches." ♦ € 20.65 2010*

ROCHE EN ARDENNE, LA *C3* (800m S Rural) *50.17465, 5.57774* **Camping Le Vieux Moulin, Rue Petite Strument 62, 6980 La Roche-en-Ardenne [(084) 411507; fax 411080; info@strument.com; www.strument.com]** Off N89 site sp fr La Roche town cent (dir Barrièr-de-Champlon), site in 800m. Med, some hdg pitch, pt sl, shd; htd wc; chem disp; shwrs €2; el pnts (6A) €2.50 (poss no earth); gas 800m; Indtte; shops 800m; fishing; canoeing; 70% statics in sep area; dogs €2; poss cr; Eng spkn; adv bkg; quiet; CCI. "Beautiful site; gd pitches; poss unclean san facs & dishwashing (7/09); poss youth groups; poor security; gd walking (map avail)." Easter-Nov. € 13.90 2011*

ROCHEFORT *C3* (500m E Rural) *50.15801, 5.22606* **Camping Communal Les Roches, 26 Rue du Hableau, 5580 Rochefort [(084) 211900; fax 312403; campingrochefort@lesroches.be; www.lesroches.be]** Fr Rochefort cent on N86 & turn L at rndabt, then 1st R. Site well sp. Lge, hdg/mkd pitch, hdstg, pt sl, unshd; htd wc; chem disp; mv service pnt; baby facs; serviced pitches; shwrs inc; el pnts (6A) metered; Indtte (inc dryer); shop, rest, bar nrby; BBQ; playgrnd; pool high ssn adj; tennis; games area; games rm; internet; entmnt; TV; 50% statics; dogs; phone; bus 250m; train 2km; Eng spkn; quiet; ccard acc. "Vg, well-managed, refurbished site; gd walking." ♦ 1 Apr-31 Oct. € 25.00 2010*

ST VITH *C4* (9km S) *50.24229, 6.09402* **Camping Hohenbusch, Grufflingen 44, B-4791 Burg Reuland [80 22 75 23; info@hohenbusch.be; www.campinghohenbusch.be]** Fr St Vith take the E421 towards Grüfflingen; site on R of the rd sp. Med, hdg pitch, pt shd; htd wc; chem disp; MV service pnt; baby facs; shwrs (metered); el pnts (6A) €2.50; Indtte; rest; playgrnd; pool; games rm; entmnt; wifi; dogs €2.50. "Eng spkn; v helpful owner; v lge pitches; fully serviced immac modern san facs." 01 Apr-06 Nov. € 22.00 2011*

SART LEZ SPA see Spa *C4*

SINT JOB IN'T GOOR see Antwerpen *A3*

SINT KRUIS see Brugge *A2*

SINT MARGRIETE *A2* (2km NW Rural) *51.2860, 3.5164* **Camping De Soetelaer, Sint Margriete Polder 2, 9981 Sint Margriete [(09) 3798151; fax 3799795; camping.desoetelaer@pandora.be; www.desoetelaer.be]** Fr E on N49/E34 to Maldegem or fr W on N9 or N49 turn N onto N251 to Aardenburg (N'lands), then turn R twd St Kruis (N'lands) - site situated 1.5km strt on fr St Margriete (back in Belgium). Med, mkd pitch, pt shd; wc; chem disp; all serviced pitches; shwrs inc; el pnts (6A) inc; Indry rm; shops 3km; no dogs; Eng spkn; adv bkg; quiet; ccard not acc; CCI. "Vg, clean site; excel, modern san facs; peace & quiet, privacy & space; highly rec for relaxation." Easter-15 Oct. € 19.50 2011*

⊞ **SOUMAGNE** *B3* (1km S Rural) *50.61099, 5.73840* **Domaine Provincial de Wégimont, Chaussée de Wégimont 76, 4630 Soumagne [(04) 2372400; fax 2372401; wegimont@prov-liege.be; www.prov-liege.be/wegimont]** Exit A3 at junc 37 onto N3 W twd Fléron & Liège. In 500m at traff lts turn L sp Soumagne. In Soumagne at traff lts form R dir Wégimont, site on top of hill on R directly after bus stop. Med, hdg pitch, pt sl, pt shd; htd wc; chem disp; baby facs; shwrs inc; el pnts (16A) inc poss rev pol; shop; rest; bar; communal BBQ; playgrnd; pool adj high ssn; tennis; games area; some entmnt; 70% statics; dogs; bus; site clsd Jan; poss cr; some rd noise; CCI. "Welcoming site in chateau grnds (public access); clean facs; conv sh stay/NH nr motorway." € 13.50 2011*

Parc La Clusure is perfectly situated in the centre of the Ardennes, near charming villages such as St. Hubert and Rochefort. Both young and old can enjoy the numerous recreational possibilities offered by the campsite and its surroundings.

- Minimum pitch size 100 m² + electricity (16 A)
- Bar, restaurant and heated swimming pool
- Super-market and daily fresh bread
- English speaking personnel
- British television station
- New sanitary units
- Near the Grottoes of Han, Euro Space Center
- 8 km from motorway E411 Namur-Luxembourg

Parc La CLusure - Chemin de La Clusure 30 - 6927 Bure (Tellin) - Belgium
Tel. 0032 (0)84 360 050 - www.parclaclusure.be

SPA *C4* (4km NE Rural) *50.50806, 5.91928* **Camping Spa d'Or (TCB), Stockay 17, 4845 Sart-lez-Spa [(087) 474400; fax 475277; info@campingspador.be; www.campingspador.be]** App fr N or S on m'way A27/E42, leave at junc 9, foll sp to Sart & Spa d'Or. Lge, pt sl, pt shd; htd wc; chem disp; baby facs; shwrs & bath inc; el pnts (10A) €3 (check earth); gas; Indtte; shop high ssn; rest; snacks; BBQ; playgrnd; htd pool; cycle hire; entmnt; 60% statics; dogs €5; poss cr; quiet; ccard acc; red CCI. "Conv F1 Grand Prix circuit Francorchamps & historic town Stavelot; vg." 1 Apr-14 Nov. € 27.65 (CChq acc) 2009*

SPA *C4* (1.5km SE Rural) *50.48559, 5.88385* **Camping Parc des Sources, Rue de la Sauvenière 141, 4900 Spa [(087) 772311; fax 475965; info@parcdessources.be; www.parcdessources.be]** Bet Spa & Francorchamps on N62, sp on R. Med, mkd pitch, pt sl, pt shd; htd wc; chem disp; mv service pnt; baby facs; shwrs €1; el pnts (10A) €2.75; gas; Indtte; shops 1.5km; snacks; bar; playgrnd; pool; 40% statics; dogs €2; 60% statics; phone; poss cr; quiet. "San facs old; poss poor pitch care low ssn; NH only." ♦ 1 Apr-31 Oct. € 17.50 2010*

⊞ **STAVELOT** *C4* (3km N Rural) *50.41087, 5.95351* **Camping L'Eau Rouge, Cheneux 25, 4970 Stavelot [(080) 863075; fb220447@skynet.be; www.eaurouge.nl]** Exit A27/E42 junc 11 onto N68 twd Stavelot. Turn R at T-junc, then 1st R into sm rd over narr bdge. Med, mkd pitch, pt sl, pt shd; htd wc; chem disp; mv service pnt; baby facs; shwrs €0.50; el pnts (6-10A) €3; Indtte (inc dryer); shop 2km; tradsmn; snacks; bar; BBQ; playgrnd; games area; archery; wifi; TV; 50% statics; dogs €1; poss cr; Eng spkn; quiet. "Vg rvside site; friendly, helpful owners; twin-axles not acc; conv Francorchamps circuit." ♦ € 17.00 2011*

⊞ **STEKENE** *A2* (2.5km SW Rural) *51.18366, 4.00730* **Camping Vlasaard, Heirweg 143, 9190 Stekene [(03) 7798164; fax 7899170; info@camping-vlasaard.be; www.camping-vlasaard.be]** Fr N49 Antwerp-Knokke rd, exit sp Stekene. In Stekene, take dir Moerbeke, site on L in 4km. V lge, mkd pitch, unshd; htd wc; chem disp; serviced pitches; shwrs €1.25; el pnts (16A); Indtte; supmkt adj; rest; snacks; bar; playgrnd; pool; games area; 75% statics; poss cr; Eng spkn; poss noisy; ccard acc. ♦ € 16.00 2009*

⊞ **TELLIN** *C3* (5km NE Rural) *50.09665, 5.28579* **Camping Parc La Clusure, 30 Chemin de la Clusure, 6927 Bure-Tellin [(084) 360050; fax 366777; info@parclaclusure.be; www.parclaclusure.be]** Fr N on A4 use exit 23A onto N899, fr S exit junc 24. Foll sp for Tellin & then take N846 thro Bure dir Grupont vill. At rndabt at junc N803 & N846 take 2nd exit to site, sp. Lge, hdg/mkd pitch, pt shd; htd wc; chem disp; mv service pnt; baby facs; shwrs inc; el pnts (16A) inc (check rev pol); Indtte (inc dryer); shop; tradsmn; rest; snacks; bar; playgrnd; htd pool; paddling pool; rv fishing; tennis; games area; games rm; wifi; entmnt; TV rm; 35% statics; dogs €5; phone; poss cr; Eng spkn; adv bkg; some rlwy noise; ccard acc; red low ssn/CCI. "V pleasant, popular rvside site; conv m'way; conv for limestone caves at Han-sur-Lesse & gd touring base Ardennes; friendly owners; clean facs; a lovely site - one of the best; excel." ♦ € 34.90 (CChq acc) 2011*

See advertisement

⊞ **TENNEVILLE** *C3* (1km N Rural) *50.07644, 5.55529* **Camping Pont de Berguème, Berguème 9, 6970 Tenneville [(084) 455443; fax 456231; info@pontbergueme.be; www.pontbergueme.be]** Fr N4 Brussels-Luxembourg fr NW; twd end of Tenneville past g'ge turn R sp Berguème. Almost immed turn L & foll sp to Berguème. Fr SE turn R off N4 50m after x-ing Rv Ourthe & foll sp to Berguème & site in 1.5km. Well sp fr N4. Med, unshd; htd wc; chem disp; baby facs; shwrs; el pnts (4A) inc (poss rev pol &/or earth prob); gas; Indtte; shop; snacks; playgrnd; pool; fishing; canoeing (winter only); wifi; 40% statics; dogs €1.75; phone; Eng spkn; adv bkg; quiet; red CCI. "Excel site; clean, modern facs." € 16.00 2010*

TENNEVILLE *C3* (8km S Rural) *50.02637, 5.51292* **Camping Tonny, Tonny 35, 6680 Amberloup/Ste Ode [(061) 688285; camping.tonny@skynet.be; www.campingtonny.be]** Fr N4 take N826 S; in 4km turn R to Tonny. Site on L. Med, mkd pitch, shd; htd wc; chem disp; mv service pnt; baby facs; shwrs €0.50; el pnts (4-6A) €2.50-3.50; gas; Indtte (inc dryer); ice; tradsmn (high ssn); rest; snacks; bar; BBQ; playgrnd; fishing; games area; games rm; entmnt; TV; 10% statics; dogs €2; bus adj; poss cr; Eng spkn; adv bkg; quiet; CCI. "Friendly, helpful owners; excel walking & cycling." 15 Feb-15 Nov. € 17.50 2010*

TILFF SUR OURTHE see Liège *B3*

⊞ **TOURINNES LA GROSSE** *B3* (500m SW Rural) *50.77952, 4.73657* **Camping au Val Tourinnes, Rue du Grand Brou 16A, 1320 Tourinnes-la-Grosse [(010) 866642; info@campingauvaltourinnes.com; www.campingauvaltourinnes.com]** Fr N on E40/A3 m'way exit junc 23 onto N25 S dir Hamme-Mille. In Hamme-Mille turn L at traff lts, site on R in 2km. Or fr S on E411/A4 exit junc 8 onto N25 to Hamme-Mille & turn R at traff lts, then as above. Sm, hdg/mkd pitch, shd; htd wc; chem disp; mv service pnt; baby facs; shwrs €0.50; el pnts (10A) €5; Indtte (inc dryer); tradsmn; rest; bar; playgrnd; lake fishing; wifi; some statics; dogs €2.50; Eng spkn; quiet. "Pleasant touring pitches on lakeside (take care goose droppings!); friendly owners; vg, modern san facs; access tight for lge o'fits; airshow 1st w/end July." € 18.00 2010*

⊞ **TOURNAI** *B2* (2km E Urban) *50.59988, 3.41377* **Camp Municipal de l'Orient, Jean-Baptiste Moens 8, 7500 Tournai [(069) 222635; fax 890229; campingorient@tournai.be]** Exit E42 junc 32 R onto N7 twd Tournai. L at 1st traff lts, foll sp Aquapark, L at rndabt, site immed on L (no sp). Sm, hdg pitch, some hdstg, pt shd; htd wc; chem disp; some serviced pitches; shwrs inc; el pnts (10A) inc (poss rev pol/no earth) or metered; gas; Indtte (inc dryer); shops 1km; tradsmn; rest, bar & playgrnd at leisure complex; htd indoor pool adj; leisure cent/lake adj (50% disc to campers); poss cr; Eng spkn; adv bkg ess high ssn; some rd noise daytime & fr leisure cent adj; ccard not acc; CCI. "Well-kept site in interesting area & old town; facs stretched high ssn, but excel site; take care raised kerbs to pitches; max length of c'van 6.50m due narr site rds & high hdges; helpful warden; E side of site quietest." € 15.00 2011*

⊞ **TURNHOUT** *A3* (7km SW Rural) *51.2825, 4.8375* **Recreatie de Lilse Bergen, Strandweg 6, 2275 Lille-Gierle [(014) 557901; fax 554454; info@lilsebergen.be; www.lilsebergen.be]** Exit A21/E34 junc 22 N dir Beerse; at rndabt foll sp Lilse Bergen. Site in 1.5km. Lge, mkd pitch, shd; htd wc; chem disp; mv service pnt; baby facs; shwrs €0.20 per min; el pnts (10A) inc; Indtte (inc dryer); shop; tradsmn; rest; snacks; bar; BBQ; playgrnd; pool; lake sw; watersports; tennis; cycle hire; games area; wifi; entmnt; 60% statics; dogs €5; phone; sep car park; poss cr; Eng spkn; adv bkg; poss noisy; ccard acc; red low ssn/CCI. "Site sep pt of lge leisure complex; pitches amongst pine trees; modern san facs, poss streteched high ssn; excel for children/teenagers." € 26.50 (4 persons) 2011*

⊞ **VEURNE** *A1* (500m S Urban) *51.07056, 2.66535* **Aire Naturelle, Kaaiplaats, 8630 Veurne [stadsbestuur@veurne.be; www.veurne.be]** M'van parking area sp on inner ring rd, nr canal quay. No facs & no fee; shops, rest, nrby; busy in day, quiet at night. 2009*

VIELSALM see Manhay *C3*

⊞ **VIELSALM** *C4* (Rural) *50.24013, 5.75396* **Camping aux Massotais, 20 Petites Tailles, Baraque de Fraiture, 6690 Vielsalm [(080) 418560; info@auxmassotais.com; www.auxmassotais.com]** Exit A26/E25 junc 50 onto N89 dir Vielsalm. At 1st rndabt turn R onto N30 dir Houffalize. Site on L in 1km behind hotel. Med, some hdstg, pt sl, pt shd; htd wc; chem disp; shwrs inc; el pnts (6-16A) inc; Indtte (inc dryer); tradsmn; rest; snacks; bar; playgrnd; htd pool; internet; TV; 5% statics; dogs; Eng spkn; quiet, but some rd noise; CCI. "Special pitches for NH (don't need to unhitch); fair." € 15.00 2009*

⊞ **VIRTON** *D3* (2km N Rural) *49.57915, 5.54892* **Camping Colline de Rabais, 1 Rue Clos des Horlès, 6760 Virton [(063) 571195; fax 583342; info@collinederabais.be; www.collinederabais.be]** Take junc 29 fr A4/E411 onto N87, 2km fr Virton turn into wood at site sp. At end of rd bef lge building turn R, then 3rd turn R at phone box. Lge, pt sl, terr, pt shd; htd wc; chem disp; mv service pnt; baby facs; shwrs inc; el pnts (16A) €3; Indtte; shop; tradsmn; rest; snacks; bar; playgrnd; pool; lake sw, fishing 1km; tennis 1km; cycle hire; cab TV; 20% statics; dogs €2.50; phone; Eng spkn; adv bkg; quiet; ccard acc; CCI. "Pleasant site; gd facs." ♦ € 24.00 2009*

⊞ **WAASMUNSTER** *A2* (1km N Rural) *51.12690, 4.08455* **Camping Gerstekot, Vinkenlaan 30, 9250 Waasmunster [(0323) 7723424; fax 7727382; maria-lyssens@telenet.be]** Exit A14/E17 at junc 13 Waasmunster onto N446 S; take 1st L in 100m into Patrijzenlaan & L again into Vinkenlaan, foll camp sp. Med, mkd pitch, pt shd; htd wc; chem disp; mv service pnt; baby facs; shwrs; el pnts (16A) inc; Indtte (inc dryer); shop; snacks; bar; BBQ; playgrnd; games area; games rm; wifi; TV; 95% statics; phone; poss cr; adv bkg; quiet; ccard acc; CCI. "Busy at w/end; water use metered; key req for shwrs; gd." ♦ € 18.00 2011*

WACHTEBEKE *A2* (4km Rural) *51.15396, 3.88928* **Camping Puyenbroeck, Puyenbrug 1a, 9185 Wachtebeke [(09) 3424231; fax 3424258; poyenbroeck@oost-vlaanderen.be; www.oost-vlaanderen.be]** Exit N49/A11 sp Wachtebeke. Foll sp to Puyenbroeck, site sp. Lge, pt shd; htd wc; chem disp; shwrs inc; el pnts (10A) inc; Indtte; shops 1.5km; rest; snacks; playgrnd; lake & children's pool; fishing; boating; phone; many statics at w/end but sep area for tourers; no dogs; adv bkg; quiet; red CCI. "Site part of recreational park." 1 Apr-30 Sep. € 20.00 2008*

⊞ **WAIMES** *C4* (6km NE Rural) *50.43916, 6.11793* **Camping Anderegg, Bruyères 4, 4950 Waimes [(080) 679393; www.campinganderegg.be]** Fr W on N632 dir Bütgenbach, turn L onto N676 for 3km. Site on L bef lake x-ing - ent easy to miss. Med, hdg/mkd pitch, pt sl, pt shd; htd wc; chem disp; baby facs; shwrs €0.75; el pnts (6A) €1.50; Indry rm; shop; rest; snacks; bar; BBQ; playgrnd; no statics; bus adj; Eng spkn; no adv bkg; quiet; ccard acc; CCI. "Clean, friendly site; modern san facs; excel." ♦ € 13.50 2008*

BELGIUM

WESTENDE *A1* (SW Coastal) *51.15787, 2.76060* **Kompas Camping Westende, Bassevillestraat 141, 8434 Westende [(058) 223025; fax 223028; westende@kompascamping.be; www.kompascamping.be]** Exit A18/E40 junc 4 onto N369/325 dir Middelkerke. Fr Westender Dorp cent (Hovenierstraat church) turn R in approx 750m into Beukenstraat, site in 200m, sp. Lge, hdg/mkd pitch, some hdstg, pt shd; htd wc; chem disp; baby facs; fam bthrm; shwrs inc; el pnts (10A) €2.40; gas; Indtte (inc dryer); shop; rest; snacks; bar; playgrnd; sand beach 500m; tennis; games area; covrd play area; wifi; TV rm; 60% statics; dogs; adv bkg; quiet; ccard acc. ♦ 1 Apr-14 Nov. € 33.50 (CChq acc) 2009*

WESTENDE *A1* (3km SW Coastal) *51.15728, 2.76561* **Camping Westende, Westendelaan 341, 8434 Westende [(058) 233254; fax 230261; info@campingwestende.be; www.campingwestende.be]** Fr Middelkerke foll N318; just after Westende vill church take dir Nieupoort, site on L in 150m. Lge, mkd pitch, unshd; htd wc; chem disp; mv service pnt; shwrs inc; el pnts (10A) inc; gas; Indtte; shops adj; rest; snacks; playgrnd; htd pool; sand beach 1km; wifi; 90% statics; dogs €2; bus adj; tram 1km; phone; poss cr; Eng spkn; quiet; ccard not acc; CCI. "Sm but tidy touring area; friendly owners; beach nr; excel cycling; gd." ♦ 1 Apr-14 Nov. € 34.00 2011*

⊞ **WESTENDE** *A1* (W Coastal) *51.15423, 2.76046* **KACB Camping Duinendorp, Bassevillestraat 81, 8434 Westende [(058) 237343; fax 233505; campingkacbwestende@pi.be; www.kacbcamping.be]** Site clearly sp off N318 in Westende vill. Fr cent turn R dir Lombardsijde (Beukenstraat). Turn almost opp TCB site. Lge, unshd; htd wc; chem disp; baby facs; shwrs inc; el pnts (10A) inc; gas; Indtte (inc dryer); rest; snacks; bar; playgrnd; sand beach 600m; games area; golf adj; TV; 60% statics; poss cr; adv bkg; quiet; ccard acc; red long stay/CCI. ♦ € 28.00 2010*

⊞ **WESTOUTER** *B1* (3km SW Urban) *50.78222, 2.74249* **Douve Camping, Bellestraat 58, 8954 Westouter [(057) 444546; info@douve.be; www.douve.be]** Fr Ypres take rd SW thro Dikkebus & cont to Mont Noir on Belgium/France border. Site on L behind Douve Rest & household shop, at end of main high street. Sm, hdg pitch, sl, pt shd; wc; own san rec in winter; shwrs €1; el pnts inc (long lead poss req); rest; snacks; playgrnd; dogs; bus; Eng spkn; quiet. "Conv for Ypres (14km) & Mont Noir military cemetary; pitch on car park in winter (no water avail at this time of year); access to pitches v steep & narr in parts; rough path & 36 steps to facs & chem disp point; forest walks; gd." € 12.00 2010*

WEZEMBEEK see Bruxelles *B2*

YPRES/IEPER *B1* (1km SE Urban) *50.8467, 2.8994* **Camping Jeugdstadion, Bolwerkstraat 1, 8900 Ypres [(057) 217282; fax 216121; info@jeugdstadion.be; www.jeugdstadion.be]** Fr S ent town cent on N336, after rlwy x-ing turn R at rndabt onto ring rd & L at 2nd rndabt (lge, gushing tap in cent). Site in 300m on L, sp fr ring rd. If app town cent fr N on N8 fr Veurne take ring rd N37; at gushing tap rndabt turn L, site in 300m on L, well sp. Fr N38 in Ypres turn off at gushing tap rndabt sp Industrie/Jeugdstadion, take 2nd L, site at end. NB site open all year for m'vans. Med, hdg/mkd pitch, some hdstg, pt sl, pt shd; htd wc; chem disp; mv service pnt; shwrs inc; el pnts (6A) inc (poss rev pol); shop 500m; playgrnd; sports park & pool adj; wifi; statics; dogs €1; poss v cr; Eng spkn; adv bkg rec high ssn; quiet but some noise until evening fr indus unit & fr sports complex adj; ccard acc. "Automatic registration/check out avail when office clsd; peaceful, well-refurbished site conv WW1 battle fields & museums; 10 min walk to Menin Gate; helpful staff; gd, modern san facs; soft grass pitches - ask for one with 'rubber tracks' to avoid sinking; hdstg m'van pitches in sep area like an Aire; site poss v full local public hols; site not fully enclosed; excel site; rec." 1 Mar-12 Nov. € 14.00 2011*

YPRES/IEPER *B1* (9km SW Rural) *50.7853, 2.8199* **Camping Ypra, Pingelaarstraat 2, 8956 Kemmel-Heuvelland [(057) 444631; fax 444881; camping.ypra@skynet.be; www.camping-ypra.be]** On N38 Poperinge ring rd turn S at rndabt onto N304. Foll sp Kemmel. Site on R in 12km on N edge of Kemmel. Med, mkd pitch, some hdstg, pt sl, pt shd; htd wc; chem disp; shwrs inc; el pnts (6A) inc (poss rev pol); Indtte (inc dryer); sm shop & 1km; tradsmn; rest 1km; bar; playgrnd; 90% statics in sep area; dogs €1.90; Eng spkn; adv bkg; quiet; red CCI. "Clean, well-maintained site; gd, modern san facs, but ltd; helpful, friendly staff; access to some pitches poss diff; interesting rest in vill; conv for WW1 battlefields." 1 Mar-30 Nov. € 22.00 2011*

ZELE *A2* (4.5km W Rural) *51.05273, 3.97996* **Camping Groenpark, Gentsesteenweg 337, 9240 Zele [(09) 3679071; groenpark@tiscali.be; www.campinggroenpark.be]** Fr W (Ghent) exit A14 junc 11 onto N449 S & in 2km turn L onto N445. Site in 6km at ent sp to Zele. Sm, mkd pitch, pt shd, htd wc; chem disp; mv service pnt; baby facs; shwrs inc; el pnts (10A) inc; Indtte (inc dryer); shop, rest, bar 1km; snacks; playgrnd; lake sw & sand beach 2km; TV rm; some statics; tram; Eng spkn; adv bkg; quiet; CCI. "Nr Park & Ride to Ghent; wooded area for tourers; gd." 1 Mar-1 Nov. € 23.00 2010*

ZONHOVEN see Hasselt *B3*

BELGIUM

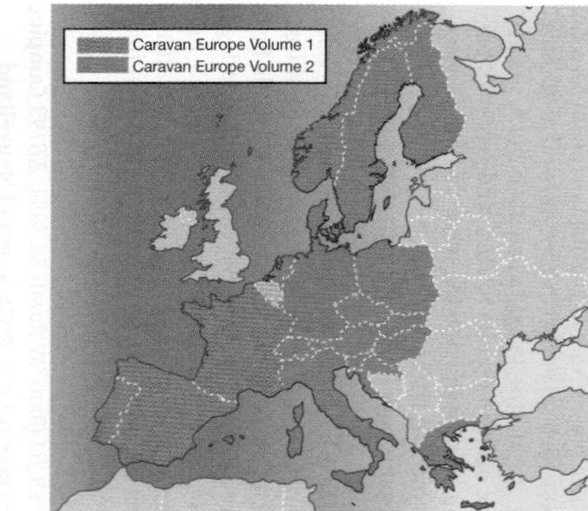

Distances are shown in kilometres and are calculated from town/city centres along the most practical roads, although not necessarily taking the shortest route. 1km = 0.62miles

Eupen to Turnhout = 122km

	Aalst	Aalter	Antwerpen	Arlon	Ath	Bastogne	Brugge	Bruxelles (Brussels)	Charleroi	Clervaux (Luxembourg)	Dinant	Eupen	Gent	Hasselt	Huy	Kortrijk	Leuven	Liège	Luxembourg City	Malmedy	Mechelen	Mons	Namur	Oostende	Oudenaarde	Philippeville	Tournai	Turnhout	Ypres
Aalter	48																												
Antwerpen	53	81																											
Arlon	217	262	233																										
Ath	50	83	112	216																									
Bastogne	178	220	196	39	177																								
Brugge	76	26	107	288	113	247																							
Bruxelles (Brussels)	29	73	55	189	54	151	99																						
Charleroi	82	130	115	166	63	129	154	60																					
Clervaux (Luxembourg)	210	253	230	67	207	32	280	181	159																				
Dinant	121	165	135	120	118	82	190	91	55	113																			
Eupen	163	207	154	136	187	97	234	133	129	82	127																		
Gent	33	27	61	245	70	206	55	56	110	231	147	191																	
Hasselt	114	166	81	172	133	131	188	79	93	139	125	67	145																
Huy	109	157	129	123	117	83	183	84	64	100	62	72	141	74															
Kortrijk	70	46	102	274	58	231	59	92	122	263	159	239	48	189	174														
Leuven	59	102	69	188	82	148	129	28	68	180	92	117	88	51	69	129													
Liège	127	171	124	132	149	93	198	96	92	120	91	42	155	43	36	203	80												
Luxembourg City	244	288	262	28	242	67	315	220	195	60	148	130	272	199	150	299	215	180											
Malmedy	182	226	180	123	185	69	253	152	132	56	101	26	210	110	68	242	136	56	116										
Mechelen	51	95	28	207	84	166	123	27	89	199	109	144	82	80	96	115	24	107	234	163									
Mons	89	97	121	196	25	158	136	69	46	190	85	164	121	164	100	76	87	129	225	168	90								
Namur	90	136	110	127	88	89	164	63	36	120	28	99	120	97	34	144	62	62	155	102	81	72							
Oostende	93	42	122	302	121	264	29	115	166	294	205	249	70	202	198	62	144	214	329	268	137	140	179						
Oudenaarde	47	30	81	283	42	224	71	72	111	255	164	207	29	197	165	35	103	172	310	226	96	67	137	86					
Philippeville	108	155	141	149	90	111	182	86	26	142	30	155	136	156	91	146	94	119	177	130	115	72	62	193	138				
Tournai	67	71	127	244	29	203	88	84	93	235	131	211	71	211	148	29	134	175	270	242	116	48	120	91	37	119			
Turnhout	99	128	45	277	155	236	155	94	161	344	177	122	106	55	171	147	112	105	304	166	54	160	146	170	127	185	174		
Ypres	100	77	132	302	90	263	53	122	151	293	189	269	78	217	205	29	161	232	328	272	146	106	175	56	65	175	58	176	
Zeebrugge	90	40	121	302	128	263	15	114	170	263	205	70	201	156	197	74	143	212	331	263	137	151	177	25	86	195	113	167	68

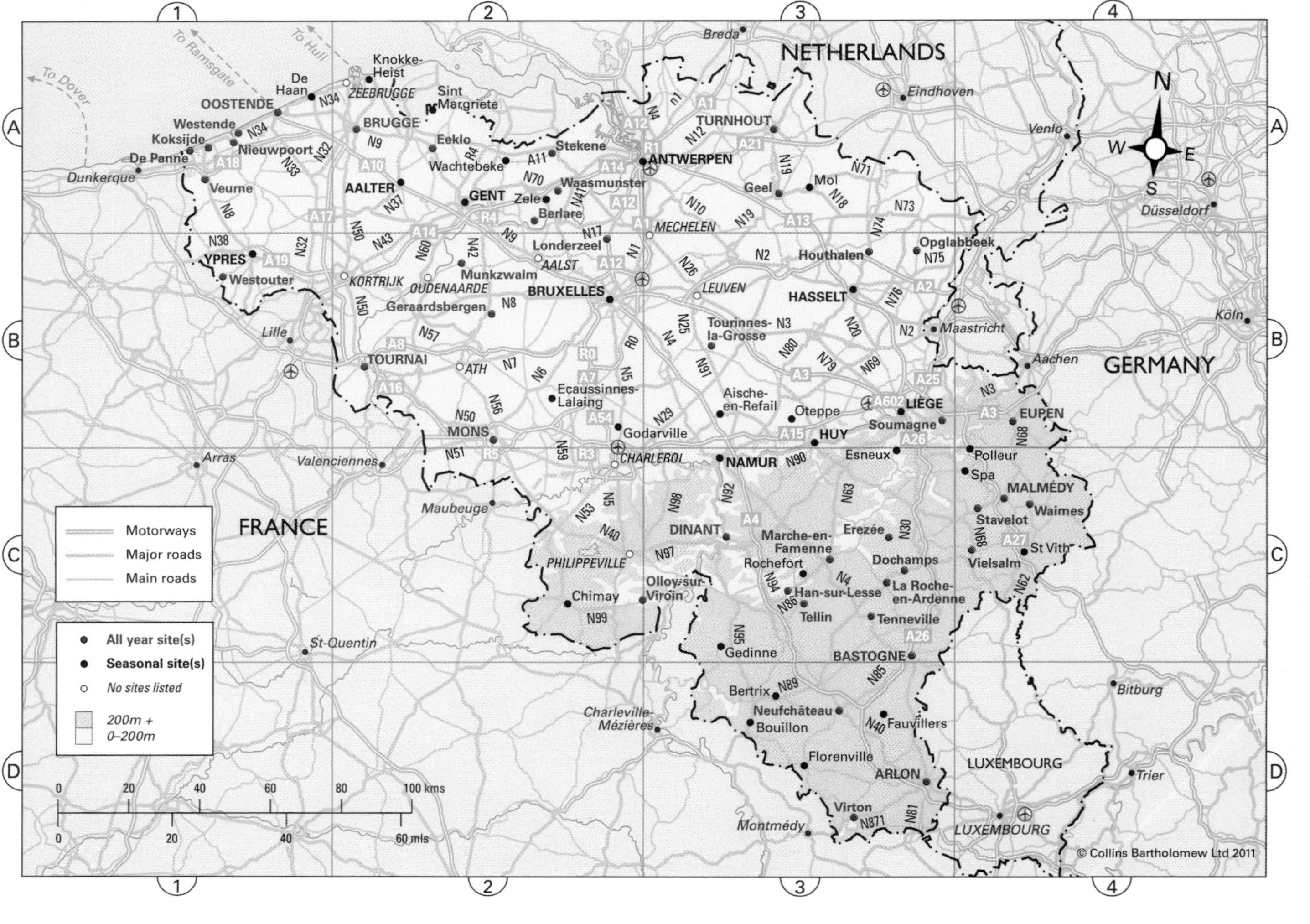
NETHERLANDS
GERMANY
FRANCE
LUXEMBOURG
To Dover
To Ramsgate
To Hull
Dunkerque
De Panne
Koksijde
Westende
OOSTENDE
Nieuwpoort
De Haan
Knokke-Heist
ZEEBRUGGE
BRUGGE
Sint Margriete
Eeklo
Wachtebeke
Stekene
ANTWERPEN
Breda
TURNHOUT
Eindhoven
Venlo
Düsseldorf
Veurne
AALTER
GENT
Zele
Waasmunster
Berlare
Geel
Mol
YPRES
Westouter
KORTRIJK
OUDENAARDE
Munkzwalm
Londerzeel
AALST
MECHELEN
Houthalen
Opglabbeek
Geraardsbergen
BRUXELLES
LEUVEN
HASSELT
Lille
TOURNAI
ATH
Tourinnes-la-Grosse
Maastricht
Köln
Aachen
Ecaussinnes-Lalaing
Aische-en-Refail
Otteppe
LIÈGE
EUPEN
Soumagne
MONS
Godarville
HUY
Arras
Valenciennes
CHARLEROI
NAMUR
Esneux
Polleur
Spa
MALMÉDY
Maubeuge
Waimes
Stavelot
DINANT
Erezée
Marche-en-Famenne
PHILIPPEVILLE
Rochefort
Dochamps
Vielsalm
St Vith
Chimay
Olloy-sur-Viroin
Han-sur-Lesse
La Roche-en-Ardenne
Tellin
Tenneville
St-Quentin
Gedinne
BASTOGNE
Bertrix
Bitburg
Charleville-Mézières
Neufchâteau
Bouillon
Fauvillers
Florenville
ARLON
Trier
Virton
Montmédy
LUXEMBOURG
N
E
S
W
Motorways
Major roads
Main roads
All year site(s)
Seasonal site(s)
No sites listed
200m +
0–200m
0
20
40
60
80
100 kms
0
20
40
60 mls
© Collins Bartholomew Ltd 2011

Croatia

Country Introduction

© iStockPhoto.com/ Damir Spanic

Pula, Croatia

Population (approx): 4.3 million

Capital: Zagreb (population approx 793,000)

Area: 56,540 sqkm, divided into 20 counties

Bordered by: Bosnia and Herzegovina, Hungary, Serbia and Montenegro, Slovenia

Terrain: Flat plains along border with Hungary; low mountains and highlands near Adriatic coast and islands

Climate: Mediterranean climate along the coast with hot, dry summers and mild, wet winters; continental climate inland with hot summers and cold winters

Coastline: 5,835km (inc 4,058km islands)

Highest Point: Dinara 1,830m

Language: Croatian

Local Time: GMT or BST + 1, i.e. 1 hour ahead of the UK all year

Currency: Kuna (HRK) divided into 100 lipa; £1 = HRK 8.69, HRK 10 = £1.15 (October 2011)

Telephoning: From the UK dial 00385 for Croatia and omit the initial zero of the area code of the number you are calling. To call the UK from Croatia dial 0044, omitting the initial zero of the area code

Emergency Numbers: Police 92; Fire brigade 93; Ambulance 94. Or dial 112 and specify the service you need.

Public Holidays in 2012

Jan 1, 6; Apr 8, 9; May 1; Jun 7, 22 (Anti-Fascist Resistance Day), 25 (National Day); Aug 5 (Thanksgiving Day), 15; October 8 (Independence Day); Nov 1; Dec 25, 26.

Public Holidays in 2013

Jan 1, 6; Mar 31; Apr 1; May 1, 30; Jun 22 (Anti-Fascist Resistance Day), 25 (National Day); Aug 5 (Thanksgiving Day), 15; October 8 (Independence Day); Nov 1; Dec 25, 26.

In addition, some Christian Orthodox and Muslim festivals are celebrated locally. School summer holidays from the last week in June to end of August.

Tourist Office

CROATIA NATIONAL TOURIST BOARD
2 THE LANCHESTERS, 162-164 FULHAM PALACE ROAD
LONDON W6 9ER Tel: 020 8563 7979
www.croatia.hr info@croatia-london.co.uk

The following introduction to Croatia should be read in conjunction with the important information contained in the Handbook chapters at the front of this guide.

Camping and Caravanning

There are more than 500 campsites in Croatia including several well-established naturist sites, mainly along the coast. Sites are licensed according to how many people they can accommodate, rather than by the number of vehicles or tents, and are classed according to a grading system of 1 to 4 stars. There are some very large sites catering for up to 10,000 people at any one time but there also many small sites – mainly in Dalmatia – situated in gardens, orchards and farms.

Many sites open from April to October; few open all year. They are generally well-equipped.

Holders of a Camping Card International (CCI) generally benefit from a 5-10% reduction in site fees. If you are travelling in the low season, or are over 60 years of age you may also receive a discount in prices.

A tourist tax is levied of between HRK 4 and HRK 7 per person per day according to region and time of year.

Casual/wild camping is illegal and is particularly frowned on at beaches, harbours or rural car parks. Most campsites have overnight areas for late arrivals and there are a number of rest areas established along main roads for overnight stays or brief stopovers.

Country Information

Electricity and Gas

Current on campsites ranges from 10 to 16 amps. Plugs have 2 round pins. There may not be CEE connections and a long cable might be required.

Campingaz cylinders are not available, so take a good supply of gas with you.

*See **Electricity and Gas** in the section **DURING YOUR STAY.***

Entry Formalities

British and Irish passport holders may visit Croatia for up to three months without a visa.

Unless staying at official tourist accommodation (hotel or campsite) all visitors are obliged to register at the nearest police station or town tourist agency within 48 hours of arrival in the country. Campsites and other tourist accommodation should carry out this function for their guests but make sure you check this with them. If you fail to register you may receive a fine or you may even have to leave Croatia.

British citizens intending to stay for an extended period should register their presence with the Consular Section of the British Embassy in Zagreb, tel: (01) 6009100.

Regulations for Pets

*See **Pet Travel Scheme** under **Documents** in the section **PLANNING AND TRAVELLING.***

Medical Services

For minor ailments, first of all consult staff in a pharmacy (ljekarna).

The European Health Insurance Card (EHIC) is not valid in Croatia but Britain has a reciprocal health care arrangement and British nationals may obtain emergency medical and hospital treatment on presentation of a British passport. You will be expected to pay a proportion of the cost (normally 20%). Doctors and hospitals may expect up-front cash payments for other, non-emergency medical services and full fees are payable for private medical and dental treatment and for prescriptions and other services. Only basic health care facilities are available in outlying areas and islands and this could result in a delay if you require urgent medical care.

Hepatitis A immunisation is may be available for long-stay visitors to rural areas and those who plan to travel outside tourist areas.

If you enjoy hiking and outdoor sports you should seek medical advice before you travel about preventative measures and immunisation against tick-borne encephalitis, a potentially serious and debilitating viral disease of the central nervous system which is endemic from spring to autumn. Lyme disease is an equally serious tick-borne infection for which there is no preventative vaccine. Ticks are found in rural and forested areas, particularly in long grass, bushes, hedgerows and woods, and in scrubland and areas where animals wander. If you think you might be at risk use an insect repellent containing DEET, wear long sleeves and long trousers, inspect the body for ticks after outdoor activity and remove with tweezers, and avoid unpasteurised dairy products in risk areas. See www.tickalert.org, email info@tickalert.org or telephone 01943 468010.

For further information on health risks please visit www.nathnac.org and select Croatia from the country information section of the website.

You are strongly recommended to obtain comprehensive travel and medical insurance before travelling, such as The Caravan Club's Red Pennant Overseas Holiday Insurance – see www.caravanclub.co.uk/redpennant

*See **Medical Matters** in the section **DURING YOUR STAY.***

Opening Hours

Banks – Mon-Fri 7am-7pm; Sat 7am-1pm.

Museums – Tue-Sun 10am-5pm; most museums close Monday and some museums are closed on Sunday afternoons.

Post Offices – Mon-Fri 7am-7pm (2pm in small villages), Sat 7am-1pm.

Shops – Mon-Fri 8am-8pm; Sat & Sun 8am-2pm.

Safety and Security

The level of street crime is low, but you should nevertheless be wary of pickpockets in major cities and coastal areas (pavement cafés are particularly targeted), and take sensible precautions when carrying money, credit cards and passports.

Personal and valuable items should not be left unattended, particularly on the beach. If travelling by train, take special care to guard valuables.

Incidents have been reported of gangs robbing car occupants after either indicating that they are in trouble and require assistance, or pulling alongside a car and indicating that something is wrong with the vehicle. Be extremely cautious should something similar occur.

Unexploded land mines are still a danger in some isolated areas in the mountains and countryside. Highly populated areas and major routes are now clear of mines and are believed to be safe to visit. If you are planning to travel outside the normal tourist resorts you should be aware that there are areas affected by the war, which ended in 1995, where unexploded mines remain. These include Eastern Slavonia, Brodsko-Posavska County, Karlovac County, areas around Zadar County and in more remote areas of the Plitvice Lakes National Park. See the Croatian Mine Action Centre's website at www.hcr.hr/en/protuminUvod.asp for more specific information about mine-affected areas. You should be wary of leaving cultivated land or marked paths without an experienced guide. If in doubt seek local advice.

If you intend to hike in the Croatian mountains always seek local guides' advice, however tame the mountain might seem to you. The weather can change quickly, even in the summer months, and temperatures can plummet overnight. There have been reports of hikers getting lost in the mountains when they have gone out alone and have left marked paths or been caught in stormy weather. If in trouble, call the emergency number 112 and ask for the Croatian Mountain Rescue service – see www.gss.hr for more information and advice.

Croatia shares with the rest of Europe an underlying threat from terrorism. Attacks could be indiscriminate and against civilian targets, including places frequented by tourists.

*See **Safety and Security** in the section **DURING YOUR STAY.***

British Embassy

UL IVANA LUČIĆA 4
HR-10000 ZAGREB
Tel: (01) 6009100
http://ukincroatia.fco.gov.uk

There are also Honorary Consulates in Dubrovnik and Split.

Irish Honorary Consulate

MIRAMARSKA 23 (EUROCENTER)
10000 ZAGREB
Tel: (01) 6310025
irish.consulate.zg@inet.hr

TRUMBICEVA OBALA 3
21000 SPLIT
Tel: (021) 343715
ante.cicin-sain@zg.htnet.hr

Customs Regulations

Customs Posts

Main border crossings are open 24 hours a day.

Duty-Free Import Allowances

Croatia is not a member of the EU and visitors aged 18 or over may import the following duty-free goods into the country:

200 cigarettes or 100 cigarillos or 50 cigars or 250gm tobacco

1 litre spirits

2 litres liqueur or sparkling wine

2 litres wine

1 bottle of perfume (50gm) and 0.25 litres of cologne

Gifts to a value of 300 HRK

Foodstuffs

It is prohibited to import fresh meat into Croatia.

Refund of VAT on Export

VAT at the rate of 23% is levied on all goods and services. Visitors may obtain a refund of VAT paid on goods and services purchased in Croatia if the value of items per one invoice exceeds HRK 740. Ask the vendor for a 'PDV-P' form and have it completed and stamped. When leaving the country you must submit all forms to Customs for verification.

Before you travel check for more detailed information, rules, regulations and updates on customs please visit www.carina.hr

See also ***Customs Regulations*** in the section ***PLANNING AND TRAVELLING.***

Documents

Driving Licence

All types of full, valid British driving licence are recognised but if you have an old-style green licence then it is advisable to change it for a photocard licence in order to avoid any local difficulties which may arise.

Passport

You must be able to show some form of identification if required by the authorities and, therefore, should carry your passport at all times. Keep a copy of the personal details page in a safe place, including details of your next of kin. On entry to Croatia there should be three months' remaining validity on your passport.

Vehicle(s)

Carry your vehicle registration certificate (V5C), insurance details and MOT certificate (if applicable). If you are not the owner of your vehicle then carry a letter of authority from the owner permitting you to drive it.

Green Card

While an International Motor Insurance Certificate (Green Card) is not necessary, you should ensure that your vehicle insurance includes cover for Croatia. Insurance can normally be purchased at the main border crossings, however some of the smaller crossings may not have this facility or have limited hours when the service is available.

If you are driving to or through Bosnia and Herzegovina (for example, along the 20 km strip of coastline at Neum on the Dalmatian coastal highway to Dubrovnik) you should ensure that you have obtained Green Card cover for Bosnia and Herzegovina. For Club members insured under The Caravan Club's Motor Insurance schemes full policy cover is available for this 20km strip but if you have difficulties obtaining such cover before departure contact the Club's Travel Service Information Officer for advice, email travelserviceinfo@caravanclub.co.uk. Alternatively, temporary third-party insurance can be purchased at the country's main border posts, or in Split and other large cities. It is not generally obtainable at the Neum border crossing itself.

As an alternative, you can take the ferry from Ploče to Trpanj on the Pelješac peninsula and avoid the stretch of road in Bosnia and Herzegovina altogether. There are frequent ferries during summer months. It is understood that it may be necessary for motorhomes to reverse onto them.

*See **Insurance** and **Documents** in the section **PLANNING AND TRAVELLING.***

Money

Visitors may exchange money in bureaux de change, banks, post offices, hotels and some travel agencies but it is understood that the most favourable rates are obtained in banks. Exchange slips should be kept in order to convert unspent kuna on leaving the country. Travellers' cheques may be exchanged in banks and bureaux de change. Many prices are quoted in both kuna and euros, and euros are widely accepted.

Most shops and restaurants accept credit cards, but VISA is not as widely accepted as other cards. There are cash machines in all but the smallest resorts.

The police are warning visitors about a recent increase in the number of forged Croatian banknotes in circulation, especially 200 and 500 kuna notes. Take care when purchasing kuna and use only reliable outlets, such as banks and cash points.

Carry your credit card issuers'/banks' 24-hour UK contact numbers in case of loss or theft of your cards.

Motoring

Accidents

Any visible damage to a vehicle entering Croatia must be certified by the authorities at the border and a Certificate of Damage issued, which must be produced when leaving the country. In the event of a minor accident while in Croatia resulting in material damage only, the police must be called and they will assist, if necessary, with the exchange of information between drivers and will issue a Certificate of Damage to the foreign driver. You should not try to leave the country with a damaged vehicle without this Certificate as you may be accused of a 'hit and run' offence.

Confiscation of passport and a court appearence within 24 hours are standard procedures when people are injured in a motoring accident.

The Croatian Insurance Bureau in Zagreb can assist with Customs and other formalities following road accidents, tel (01) 4696600, huo@huo.hr, www.huo.hr

Alcohol

The general legal limit of alcohol is 50 milligrams in 100 millilitres of blood, i.e. less than the level in the UK (80 milligrams). For drivers of vehicles over 3,500 kg and for drivers under 25 years of age the alcohol limit is zero. The general legal limit also applies to cyclists. The police carry out random breath tests and penalties are severe.

It is prohibited to drive after having taken any medicine whose side-effects may affect the ability to drive a motor vehicle.

Croatia has adopted a law expressing zero tolerance on alcohol consumption by those in charge of yachts and other boats, however small.

Breakdown Service

The Hrvatski Auto-Klub (HAK) operates a breakdown service throughout the country, telephone 987 (or 01987 from a mobile phone) for assistance. On motorways use the roadside emergency phones which are placed at 2km intervals. Towing and breakdown services are available 24 hours a day in and around most major cities and along the coast in summer (6am to midnight in Zagreb).

Essential Equipment

Lights

Dipped headlights are compulsory at all times, regardless of weather conditions, from the last Sunday in October to the last Sunday in March, and in reduced visibility at other times of the year. Recent visitors report that the police are diligently fining motorists for not using dipped headlights as they enter Croatia. Bulbs are more likely to fail with constant use and it is compulsory to carry spares, in Croatia, however this rule does not apply if your vehicle is fitted with xenon, neon, LED or similar lights.

Reflective Jacket/Waistcoat

It is obligatory to carry a reflective jacket inside your car (not in the boot) and you must wear it if you need to leave your vehicle to attend to a breakdown, e.g. changing a tyre. It is also common sense for any passenger leaving the vehicle to also wear one.

Warning Triangle(s)

You should carry two triangles if you are towing a caravan or trailer.

Child Restraint Systems

Children under the age of 12 are not allowed to travel in the front seats of vehicles, with the exception of children under 2 years of age who can travel in the front if they are placed in a child restraint system adapted to their size. It must be fitted facing the opposite direction of travel and the airbag must be de-activated.

Children up to 5 years old must be placed in a seat adapted to their size on the back seat. Children between the ages of 5 and 12 must travel on the back seat using a 3 point seat belt with a booster seat if necessary for their height.

Winter Driving

It is compulsory to carry snow chains in your vehicle and they must be used if required by the weather conditions (snow or black ice). The compulsory winter equipment in Croatia consists of a shovel in your vehicle and a set of snow chains on the driving axel.

Snow chains can be hired or purchased from Polar Automotive Ltd, tel 01892 519933, www.snowchains.com, email: polar@snowchains.com (10% discount for Caravan Club members).

*See **Motoring – Equipment** in the section **PLANNING AND TRAVELLING.***

Fuel

Petrol stations are generally open from 6am to 8pm, later in summer. Some of those on major stretches of road stay open 24 hours a day. Payment by credit card is widely accepted. LPG (Autogas) is fairly widely available.

*See also **Fuel** under **Motoring – Advice** in the section **PLANNING AND TRAVELLING.***

Parking

Lines at the roadside indicate parking restrictions. Traffic wardens patrol roads and impose fines for illegal parking. Vehicles, including those registered outside Croatia, may be immobilised by wheel clamps.

Roads

In general road conditions are good in and around the larger towns. The Adriatic Highway or Jadranksa Magistrala (part of European route E65) runs down the whole length of the Adriatic coast and is good for most of its length, despite being mostly single-carriageway. Elsewhere minor road surfaces may be uneven and, because of the heat-resisting material used to surface them, may be very slippery when wet. Minor roads are usually unlit at night.

Motorists should take care when overtaking and be aware that other drivers may overtake unexpectedly in slow-moving traffic. The standard of driving is generally fair.

Road Signs and Markings

Road signs and markings conform to international standards. Motorway signs have a green background; national road signs have a blue background.

Speed Limits

*See **Speed Limits Table** under **Motoring – Advice** in the section **PLANNING AND TRAVELLING.***

In addition to complying with other speed limits, drivers under the age of 25 must not exceed 80 km/h (50 mph) on the open road, 100 km/h (62 mph) on expressways and 120 km/h (74 mph) on motorways.

Traffic Jams

During the summer, tailbacks may occur at the border posts with Slovenia at Buje on the E751 (road 21), at Bregana on the E70 (A3) and at Donji Macelj on the E59 (A1). During July and August there may be heavy congestion, for example at Rupa/Klenovica and at other tourist centres, and on the E65 north-south Adriatic Highway. This is particularly true on Friday evenings, Saturday mornings, Sunday evenings and the Assumption Day holiday. Queues form at ferry crossings to the main islands.

Road and traffic conditions can be viewed on the HAK website (in English), www.hak.hr or telephone HAK on (01) 4640800 (English spoken) or (060) 520520 in the Dubrovnik area for round-the-clock recorded information.

Violation of Traffic Regulations

The police may impose on-the-spot fines for parking and driving offences. If you are unable to pay the police may confiscate your passport. Motoring law enforcement, particularly with regard to speeding, is strictly observed.

Motorways

There is just under 1,000 kilometres of motorways, with the major stretches being shown in the table below. Tolls (cestarina) are levied according to vehicle category. Electronic display panels above motorways indicate speed limits, road conditions and lane closures. Information on motorways can be found on www.hac.hr

Motorway Tolls

Class 1 Vehicle with 2 axles, height up to 1.3m (measured from front axle) excluding vans

Class 2 Vehicle with 2 or more axles, height up to 1.3m (measured from front axle), including car + caravan or trailer, motorhomes and vans.

Class 3 Vehicle with 2 or 3 axles, height over 1.3m (measured from front axle), including van with trailer

Class 4 Vehicle with 4 or more axles, height over 1.3m (measured from front axle)

Touring

There are a number of national parks and nature reserves throughout the country, including the World Heritage site at the Plitvice lakes, the Paklenica mountain massif, and the Kornati archipelago with 140 uninhabited islands, islets and reefs. Dubrovnik, itself a World Heritage site, is one of the world's best-preserved medieval cities, having been extensively restored since recent hostilities.

While Croatia has a long coastline, there are few sandy beaches; instead there are pebbles, shingle and rocks with man-made bathing platforms.

The Croatian National Tourist Board operates 'Croatian Angels', a multi-lingual tourist information and advice service available from the end of March to mid-October, telephone 062 999 999 or 00385 62 999 999 from outside Croatia.

Croatia originated the concept in Europe of commercial naturist resorts and today attracts an estimated 1 million naturist tourists annually. There are approximately 20 official naturist resorts and beaches and numerous other unofficial or naturist-optional 'free' beaches, sometimes controlled and maintained by local tourist authorities. Many beaches outside town centres have both naturist and textile (non-naturist) areas. Naturist beaches and resorts are signposted 'FKK'.

Total Journey	Class 1	Class 2	Class 3
A1 Zabreb to Split (under construction)	171	265	389
A2 Zagreb to Macelj (border with Slovenia)	42	62	96
A3 Zagreb to Bregana	5	7	10
A3 Zagreb (Ivanja Reka) to Lipovac (border with Serbia)	105	160	240
A4 Zagreb (Sveta Helena) to Goričan (border with Hungary)	36	54	81
A5 Beli Manastir (Osijek) to border with Bosnia-Herzegovina)	0	0	0
A6 Zagreb to Rijecka (under construction)	60	108	144
A7 Rijeka to Rupa to Žuta Lokva (under construction)	5	7	10
A10 Mali Prolog to Ploče (under construction)			
A11 Zagreb to Sisak (under construction)			
Učka Tunnel	28	40	82
Krk Bridge	30	40	70
Mirna Bridge (Istria)	14	21	42

Toll charges in Croatian kuna (HRK) 2011, subject to change. Payment in cash (including foreign currency) or by credit or debit card. Tolls are levied on some other roads.

The Adriatic coast offers a wide variety of seafood which is generally excellent. Mussels and langoustines in particular are plentiful and cheap. A popular dish is 'brodet' made with a variety of fish and served with rice. In the interior of the country, meat is served roasted or braised, for example 'pašticada'. Wine is produced in Dalmatia and Istria and local beers are good and inexpensive. Slivovica, plum brandy, is the local spirit.

Smoking is prohibited in restaurants, bars and public places. A service charge is general included in the bill. English is widely spoken.

If you propose to drive to or through Bosnia and Herzegovina (for example along the 20 km strip of coastline at Neum on the Dalmatian coastal highway to Dubrovnik) see information under ***Documents*** earlier in this chapter.

Local Travel

A programme of investment in and modernisation of the railways is underway but, in the meantime, many important routes are still not electrified and allow only single-track travel, making progress slow.

By contrast the bus network offers the cheapest, most extensive and widely-used means of public transport. Buy bus tickets when you board at the front of the vehicle or beforehand from kiosks, and ensure that you validate your ticket once on board. Single and daily tickets are available. Children under six travel free. Trams operate in Zagreb and you can buy tickets from kiosks.

Coastal towns and cities have regular scheduled passenger and car ferry services including links to many inhabited islands. During the summer months hydrofoil services also operate. Most ferries are drive-on/drive-off and are operated by Jadrolinija Line – see www.jadrolinija.hr for sailing schedules and interactive maps.

Car ferries operate from Ancona, Bari, Pescara and Venice in Italy to Dubrovnik, Korčula, Mali Lošinj, Poreč, Pula, Rijecka, Rovinj, Sibenik, Split, Starigrad, Vis and Zadar. Full details from:

VIAMARE TRAVEL LTD
SUITE 3, 447 KENTON ROAD
HARROW
MIDDX HA3 0XY
Tel: 020 8206 3420, www.viamare.com

All place names used in the Site Entry listings which follow can be found in the Croatia & Slovenia Superatlas published by Freytag & Berndt, scale 1cm to 1.5km, see www.freytagberndt.com

Dubrovnik Old City © iStockPhoto.com/Artur Bogacki

BANJOLE see Pula *A3*

BASKA (KRK ISLAND) *A3* (1km NE Urban) *44.96668, 14.74510* **Autocamp Zablaće, Emila Geistlicha 38, 51523 Baška [(051) 856909; fax 856604; campzablace@hotelibaska.hr; www.campingzablace.info]** Fr Rijeka S on Adriatic highway, in approx 23km turn R over bdge & foll so to Krk & Baška. Site sp on R when app Baška. V lge, mkd pitch, hdstg; unshd; wc; chem disp; mv service pnt; sauna; baby facs; shwrs; el pnts (10A) inc; Indtte (inc dryer); shop 200m; rest adj; snacks; bar; BBQ; playgrnd; htd, covrd pool; paddling pool; waterslide; shgl beach; sailing; fishing; tennis; games area; cycle hire; wellness cent 100m; wifi; entmnt; TV rm; 50% statics; dogs HRK25; Eng spkn; quiet; ccard acc; CCI. "San facs overstretched if site full - use facs in main part of site; vg." ♦ 15 Apr-15 Oct. HRK 218 (CChq acc) 2008*

BASKA (KRK ISLAND) *A3* (1km W Coastal) *44.96911, 14.76671* **FKK Camping Bunculuka (Naturist), 51523 Baška [(051) 856806; fax 856595; bunculuka@hotelibaska.hr; www.bunculuka.info]** Fr Rijeka S on Adriatic highway, in approx 23km turn R over bdge, foll sp Krk & Baška. Site sp. V lge, mkd pitch, terr, pt shd; wc; chem disp; mv service pnt; baby facs; shwrs; el pnts (16A) inc (long cable poss req); Indtte; shop; rest; snacks; bar adj; playgrnd; shgl beach; sailing; kayak hire; tennis; internet; some statics; dogs HRK25; phone; poss cr; adv bkg rec high ssn; ccard acc; quiet. "Pleasant coastal mkd walks; superb site." 7 Apr-15 Oct. HRK 200 2008*

BIOGRAD NA MORU *B3 43.88611, 15.53305* **Autocamp Oaza Mira, Ul. Dr. Franje Tudmana 2, 23211 Drage [023 635419; info@oaza-mira.hr or oazamira@globalnet.hr; www.oaza-mira.hr]** A1 Karlovac-Split past Zadar, exit Biograd dir Sibenik on coast rd; sp on coastal side of rd; foll sp site after bay. Med, hdstg, terr, pt shd; wc; chem disp; mv serv pnt; fam bthrm; el pnts inc; Indry rm; shop; bar; BBQ; pool; beach adj; games rm; wifi; dogs €8; Eng spkn; adv bkg; quiet. "Excel new site; generous pitches; 2 beautiful bays adj to site; highly rec." 1 Apr-31 Oct. € 41.00 2011*

BIOGRAD NA MORU *B3* (500m N Coastal) *43.96064, 15.42963* **Camping Moče, Put Primorja 8, 23207 Sveti Filip i Jakov [tel/fax (023) 388436; info@camping-moce.com; www.camping-moce.com]** Sp fr rd 8/E65. Sm, pt shd; wc; chem disp; serviced pitches; shwrs inc; el pnts (16A) HRK20; Indtte; shop 100m; rest, bar 200m; playgrnd; shgl beach adj; cab/sat TV; dogs; phone adj; poss cr; Eng spkn; adv bkg; red long stay; CCI. "CL-type site in garden; excel clean facs; friendly welcome fr owners; beach thro back gate - locked at night." ♦ 1 Apr-15 Oct. HRK 135 2009*

BIOGRAD NA MORU *B3* (3km N Coastal) *43.96083, 15.42472* **Camping Đardin, 23207 Sveti Filip i Jakov [(023) 388960; info@camping-croatia.com; www.camping-croatia.com]** S fr Zadar (approx 23km) on E65/rd 8 turn R immed bef lge blue hotels/site sp twd sea. Site on L just bef lane narrows. Lge, pt sl, shd; wc; chem disp; shwrs inc; el pnts (10A); gas 500m; Indry rm; shop adj; rest, snacks, bar adj; playgrnd; sand beach adj; watersports; boating; 80% statics; bus; poss cr; Eng spkn; adv bkg; quiet; red CCI. "In superb position on edge of resort vill; friendly, helpful staff; gd, clean facs." 15 Apr-15 Oct. HRK 138 2010*

⊞ **BIOGRAD NA MORU** *B3* (3km N Coastal) **Camping Filip, Put Primorja 10a, 23207 Sveti Filip i Jakov [tel/fax (023) 389196; auto.kamp.filip@zd.t-com.hr; www.camping-filip-kroatien.de]** S fr Zadar (approx 23km) turn R immed bef lge blue hotels/site sp twd sea. Site on L just past Autocamp Đardin. Sm, hdg pitch, hdstg, pt sl, shd; wc; chem disp; shwrs inc; el pnts €3; Indtte (inc dryer); shop 500m; rest, snacks, bar adj; BBQ; cooking facs; playgrnd; adj; beach adj; games area; adj; dogs €2.10; phone; bus nr; Eng spkn; quiet; red long stay. "San facs luxurious & clean; friendly owners; private gate to beach; sh walk to town; excel." 1 May-30 Sep. € 19.30 2010*

BIOGRAD NA MORU *B3* (10km NE Coastal) **Autocamp Martin, Sveti Petar na Moru, 23207 Sveti Filip i Jakov [tel/fax (023) 391104]** Fr Zadar on rd 8/E65, lge yellow sp to site. Sm, pt shd; htd wc; chem disp; mv service pnt; shwrs inc; el pnts (16A) inc; supmkt 9km; rest 100m; BBQ; beach adj; dogs HRK10; poss cr; Eng spkn; adv bkg; quiet; CCI. "Family-run site in unique position - some pitches on purpose-built promontory into sea; friendly welcome; excel, unisex facs; highly rec." HRK 130 2010*

BIOGRAD NA MORU *B3* (1km S Coastal) *43.92841, 15.45521* **Camping Soline, Put Solina 17, 23210 Biograd na Moru [(023) 383351; fax 384823; info@campsoline.com; www.campsoline.com]** Site sp fr road 8/E45. Lge, mkd pitch, hdstg, sl, shd; wc; chem disp; mv service pnt; shwrs inc; el pnts (16A) inc; Indtte; shop; rest; snacks; bars; BBQ; playgrnd; aquatic cent in town; shgl beach adj; tennis; sports cent 150m; cycle hire; games area; wifi; entmnt; TV; 50% statics; dogs €4.80; poss cr; Eng spkn; adv bkg; ccard acc; red low ssn/long stay; CCI. "Well laid-out site in pine trees; pitches poss not suitable lge o'fits; friendly, helpful staff; pleasant walk into Biograd; highly rec." 15 Apr-30 Sep. € 30.30 (CChq acc) 2008*

⊞ **BOL (BRAC ISLAND)** *C4* (500m W Urban/Coastal) *43.26373, 16.64799* **Camping Konoba Kito, Bračke Ceste bb, 21420 Bol [(021) 635551; www.bol.hr]** Take ferry fr Makarska to Brač & take rd 113/115 to Bol (37km). On o'skrts do not turn L into town but cont twd Zlatni Rat. Pass Studenac sup'mkt on R, site on L. Sm, pt shd; wc; chem disp; shwrs inc; el pnts (16A) €2.50; gas; Indtte; rest; BBQ; beach 500m; TV; some statics; dogs; poss cr; Eng spkn; adv bkg; quiet. "Excel for beaches & boating; gd local food in rest; vg, friendly, family-run site; clean, well-equipped; well worth effort to get there." € 18.40 2010*

CRES (CRES ISLAND) *A3* (1km N Coastal) *44.96277, 14.39694* **Camping Kovačine (Part Naturist), Melin 1/20, 51557 Cres [(051) 573150; fax 571086; campkovacine@kovacine.com; www.camp-kovacine.com]** Fr N, foll sp bef Cres on R. Fr S app thro vill of Cres. V lge, pt shd; wc; chem disp; baby facs; shwrs inc; el pnts (12A) inc; lndtte; shop; rest, snacks; playgrnd; beach; watersports; tennis; games area; sep area for naturists; wifi; dogs HRK23; Eng spkn; quiet; ccard acc; red long stay/CCI. "Site in olive grove; rocky making driving diff, but amenities gd & well-run; welcoming staff; delightful walk/cycle rte to sm vill of Cres." ♦ 4 Apr-15 Oct. HRK 208 2008*

DRASNICE see Drvenik *C4*

⊞ **DRVENIK** *C4* (10km NW Coastal) *43.16840, 17.20892* **Autocamp Ciste, Tonći Urlić, 21328 Drašnice [tel/fax (021) 679906; camp_ciste@yahoo.com]** Fr N on rd 8/E65 fr Makarska to Dubrovnik, site sp after Živogošće. Sm, terr, pt shd; wc; chem disp; shwrs inc; el pnts (6-10A) HRK20; lndry rm; tradsmn; shop; rest; shgl beach adj; dogs HRK15; poss cr; red long stay. "Delightful site in beautiful setting; friendly, helpful staff; excel, clean, modern san facs; conv ferry to Hvar." ♦ HRK 145 2008*

DRVENIK *C4* (12km NW Coastal) *43.17086, 17.1965* **Camping Dole, 21331 Živogošće [(021) 628749; fax 628750; autocamp-dole@st.hinet.hr; www.hotelizivogosce.com]** Ent at km post 679 on Adriatic Highway, rd 8/E65, sp. V lge, some hdstg, pt sl, terr, pt shd; wc; chem disp; shwrs; el pnts (10A) €4.20; lndry rm; shop; rest; snacks; bar; BBQ; shgl beach adj; tennis; wifi; dogs €2.50; Eng spkn; some rd noise; ccard acc; red CCI. "Beach slopes steeply; used by school groups; vg." ♦ 1 May-30 Sep. € 32.4 2011*

DUBROVNIK *C4* (6km S Rural/Coastal) *42.6240, 18.18856* **Autocamp Kupari, Kupari b.b, 20207 Mlini [(020) 485548; fax 487344; info@campkupari.com; www.campkupari.com]** Fr Dubrovnik along coast rd sp airport & Mlini. Well sp on inland side of rd on ent vill. V lge, hdg/mkd pitch, shd; wc (cont); chem disp; shwrs inc; el pnts (10A) inc; lndtte; shop 200m; rest; snacks; bar; BBQ; shgl beach 400m; internet; entmnt; some statics; dogs €3; Eng spkn; adv bkg; some rd noise; ccard acc; CCI. "San facs need update (2009)." 1 Apr-31 Oct. € 17.90 2009*

DUBROVNIK *C4* (6km S Coastal) *42.62381, 18.19305* **Camping Porto, Srebreno 6, 20207 Mlini [tel/fax (020) 487079; nela.madesko@du.tel.hr]** Take by-pass fr Dubrovnik to vill of Kupari. At sp indicating end of Kupari take 1st R. Site sp off rd 8/E65. Med, pt shd; wc (some cont); chem disp; shwrs; el pnts (6A); shop 500m; rest; snacks; bar; BBQ; shgl beach 200m; dogs; bus & water bus to Dubrovnik; Eng spkn; red CCI. 1 May-31 Oct. € 18.70 2009*

DUBROVNIK *C4* (7km S Coastal) *42.62471, 18.20801* **Autocamp Kate, Tupina 1, 20207 Mlini [(020) 487006; fax 487553; info@campingkate.com; www.campingkate.com]** Fr Dubrovnik on rd 8 foll sp Cavtat or Čilipi or airport into vill of Mlini. Fr S past Cavtat into Mlini. Site well sp fr main rd. Sm, hdstg, pt sl, terr, pt shd; wc; chem disp; shwrs inc; el pnts (10-16A) inc; lndtte; shop adj; rest, bar adj; BBQ; shgl beach 200m; phone; bus to Dubrovnik 150m; dogs €0.50; Eng spkn; adv bkg; some rd noise; red long stay/low ssn; CCI. "Family-run site in lovely setting; helpful, hard-working, welcoming owners; vg clean facs; boats fr vill to Dubrovnik; long, steep climb (steps) down to beach." 1 Apr-1 Nov. € 18.80 2009*

⊞ **DUBROVNIK** *C4* (10km S Coastal) **Autocamp Matkovica, Srebreno 8, 20207 Dubrovnik [(020) 485867; u.o.matkovica@hotmail.com]** Fr Dubrovnik S on coast rd. At Kupari foll sp to site behind Camping Porto. Sm, mkd pitch, shd; wc; chem disp; shwrs inc; el pnts (6A) inc; lndtte; supmkt, rest, snacks, bar 200m; shgl beach adj; wifi; no statics; dogs; Eng spkn; phone; bus 200m; Eng spkn; quiet; red low ssn. "Well-kept site; friendly, helpful owners; san facs old but clean; water bus to Dubrovnik 1km." € 20.00 2009*

DUBROVNIK *C4* (5km NW Urban/Coastal) *42.66191, 18.07050* **Autocamp Solitudo, Vatroslava Lisinskog 17, 20000 Dubrovnik [(020) 448686; fax 448688; solitudo@babinkuk.com; www.camping-adriatic.com]** S down Adriatic Highway to Tuđjman Bdge over Dubrovnik Harbour. Turn L immed sp Dubrovnik & in 700m take sharp U-turn sp Dubrovnik & carry on under bdge. Site on Babin Kuk across harbour fr bdge. Lge, mkd pitch, hdstg, pt sl, pt terr, pt shd; htd wc; chem disp; mv service pnt; baby facs; shwrs inc; el pnts (10A) inc (long lead poss req); lndtte (inc dryer); shop; rest; snacks; bar; BBQ (gas/elec only); pool, paddling pool 200m; shgl beach 500m; tennis; cycle hire; wifi; no statics; dogs HKR26; twin-axles acc (rec check in adv); phone; bus 150m; poss cr; Eng spkn; adv bkg; quiet; ccard acc; red low ssn/CCI. "Friendly, clean, well-run, v busy site; sm pitches poss stony &/or boggy; some lge pitches; levelling blocks poss req; nearest site to city cent; conv Bari ferry." ♦ 1 Apr-31 Oct. HRK 268 (CChq acc) SBS - X01 2011*

DUGA RESA see Karlovac *B2*

FAZANA *A3* (500m S Coastal) *44.91717, 13.81105* **Camping Bi-Village, Dragonja 115, 52212 Fažana [(052) 300300; fax 380711; info@bivillage.com; www.bivillage.com]** N fr Pula on rd 21/A9/E751 at Vodnjan turn W sp Fažana. Foll sp for site. V lge, mkd pitch, pt shd; htd wc; chem disp; mv service pnt; shwrs inc; el pnts (10A) inc; gas; lndtte (inc dryer); supmkt; tradsmn; rest; snacks; bar; BBQ; playgrnd; 3 pools; waterslide; shgl/rocky beach adj; watersports; tennis 1km; games area; cycle & boat hire; golf 2km; wifi; entmnt; 30% statics/apartments; dogs HRK37; phone; bus; poss cr; Eng spkn; adv bkg; quiet; ccard acc; red low ssn/snr citizens; CCI. "Excel, modern, clean san facs; private bthrms avail; site surrounded by pine trees; some beachside pitches; conv Brijuni Island National Park; excel leisure facs for families; vg cycle paths; no emptying point for Wastermaster; vg." ♦ 1 Apr-13 Nov. HRK 263 (5 persons) (CChq acc) 2010*

FUNTANA see Poreč *A2*

HVAR (HVAR ISLAND) *B4* (4km N Coastal) *43.18970, 16.42990* **Autocamp Vira, Mala Vira b.b, 21450 Hvar [(021) 741803; info@campvira.com; www.campvira.com]** N fr Hvar town (cent parking area on L) dir Vira, site sp. Med, mkd pitch, hdstg, pt shd; htd wc; chem disp; mv service pnt; baby facs; shwrs inc; el pnts (10A); gas; lndtte (inc dryer); shop; tradsmn; rest; snacks; bar; BBQ; playgrnd; shgl beach; cycle hire; games area; wifi; entmnt; dogs €5; bus; phone; adv bkg; quiet; red low ssn/long stay. "Excel site; sea views all pitches; vg san facs; ltd water pnts; rest & bar o'look private beach; highly rec." 20 Apr-30 Sep. € 35 (CChq acc) 2011*

ICICI see Opatija *A2*

JELSA (HVAR ISLAND) *C4* (500m E Coastal) *43.16396, 16.70306* **Camping Mina, 21465 Jelsa [(021) 761210; fax 761227; www.tzjelsa.hr]** Fr W take main rd 116. After main town junc ignore sp Hotel Mina & shortly after Autocamp Holiday turn L (rd passes thro part of this site) & cont round bay. Site on R on promontory, sp. Lge, mkd pitch, terr, pt shd; wc; shwrs; el pnts; lndtte; shop; bar; playgrnd; sand beach adj; tennis nr; games area; cycle hire; adv bkg; quiet. "Excel location & lovely vill, but poor facs." 1 May-30 Sep. 2009*

I'll go online and tell the Club what we think of the campsites we've visited – www.caravanclub.co.uk/europereport

JEZERA (MURTER ISLAND) *B3* (800m NW Coastal) *43.79313, 15.62734* **Holiday Village Jezera Lovišća, Zaratic 1, 22242 Jezera [(022) 439600; fax 439215; info@jezera-kornati.hr; www.jezera-kornati.hr]** S on main coast rd turn R 4km SE of Pirovac sp Murter. Foll winding rd into vill & over swing bdge on island. Foll rd round to R. Site on R in 2km. V lge, pt sl, pt shd; wc; chem disp; shwrs inc; el pnts (10A) €3.80; shop, rest, snacks high ssn; bar; playgrnd; shgl beach adj; watersports; tennis; entmnt; internet; TV rm; 50% statics; dogs €6.10; quiet; ccard acc; red long stay/CCI. "Excel site; boat trips organised fr site; excel rest; lots to do in area." ♦ 26 Apr-9 Oct. € 27.80 2009*

JEZERA (MURTER ISLAND) *B3* (5km NW Coastal) *43.81701, 15.57844* **Autokamp Slanica, Jurja Dalmatinca 17, 22243 Murter [(022) 434580; fax 435911; m.j.commerce@murter-slanica.hr; www.murter-slanica.hr]** S on main coast rd turn R 4km SE of Pirovac sp Murter. Foll winding rd into vill & over swing bdge onto island. Foll sp Murter & on ent town turn L sp Slanica. Site clearly sp by beach in 1km. Med, terr, pt shd; wc; chem disp; shwrs inc; el pnts (6A) HRK22; supmkt 1km; rest, bar adj; shgl each adj; 10% statics; dogs HRK15.75; poss cr; Eng spkn; quiet; CCI. "Vg site on headland with spectacular views to Kornati Islands; sm pitches not suitable lge o'fits." HRK 114 2008*

KARLOVAC *B2* (12km SW Rural) *45.41962, 15.48338* **Autocamp Slapić, Mrežničke Brig, 47250 Duga Resa [tel/fax (047) 854754; autocamp@inet.hr; www.campslapic.hr]** Exit A1/E65 junc 3 for Karlovac; strt over traff lts immed after toll booth sp Split & Rijecka.Take D23 to Duga Resa; turn L by church in Duga Resa; cont over bdge & turn R; foll rd keeping rv on your R; cont thro vill of Mrnžnički Brig in 3km; site sp in another 1km. NB Do not app via Belavići as Bailey Bdge totallly unsuitable c'vans & m'vans. Site well sp fr Duga Resa. Sm, mkd pitch, pt shd; wc; chem disp; shwrs inc; el pnts (16A) HRK20; lndtte (inc dryer); shop 500m; rest, snacks, bar adj; BBQ; playgrnd; rv sw & beach adj; fishing; canoeing; tennis; games area; cycle hire; wifi; dogs HRK15; phone; train to Zagreb 500m; Eng spkn; adv bkg; poss noise fr daytrippers; ccard acc. "Friendly, pleasant, family-owned site in gd location on rv; lovely area; gd bar/rest; gd clean facs; lge pitches; long hoses req low ssn; easy drive into Zagreb; excel." ♦ 1 Apr-31 Oct. HRK 150 (CChq acc) 2011*

KASTEL STARI *B4* (Coastal) *43.55305, 16.34666* **Camping Hrabar, Obala Kralja Tomislava 43, 21216 Kaštel-Stari [(091) 8998526; ihrabar77@yahoo.com]** Fr coast rd 8 turn twds coast at Kaštel-Stari, site sp. Site approx 18km fr Split. Med, mkd pitch, pt shd; wc; chem disp; shwrs inc; el pnts; lndtte; rest; snacks; bar; BBQ; shgl beach adj; dogs; bus 500m; poss cr; Eng spkn; adv bkg. "Helpful staff; gd central location for Split & Trogir; Kaštela area worth exploring." 1 May-30 Sep. 2010*

KORCULA (KORCULA ISLAND) *C4* (6km NW Coastal) **Autocamp Vrbovica, 20275 Žrnovo [(020) 721311]** Ferry fr Orebič to Korčula onto rd 118. In approx 4km turn R sp Račišće, site clearly sp, on R in 6km. Sm, mkd pitch, terr, pt shd; wc; chem disp; shwrs inc; el pnts (6A) inc; supmkt 6km; shgl beach adj; dogs; poss cr; quiet. "In garden of villa in beautiful setting; ltd pitches for tourers; excel." 1 May-30 Sep. HRK 115 2008*

KORENICA *B3* (9km SE Rural) **Camping Lička Kapa, Bjelopolje, 53230 Korenica [(053) 753004]** S fr Plitvička Jezera National Park, site by rest/hotel on W side of E71 just bef vill of Bjelopolje. Sm, pt shd; wc (use rest); el pnts; rest; snacks; bar; Eng spkn; rd noise. "Gd NH conv for National Park; friendly owner." HRK 80 2008*

KORENICA *B3* (1.5km NW Urban) *44.76527, 15.68833* **Camping Borje, Vranovaca bb, 53231 Korenica [(053) 751789; fax 751791; autocamp-borje@np-plitvicka-jezera.hr; www.np-plitvicka-jezera.hr]** Exit A1/A6 at Karlovac & take rd 1/E71 S dir Split. Site on R approx 15km after Plitvička Jezera National Park, well sp. Med, mkd pitch, sl, pt shd; wc; chem disp; mv service pnt; baby facs; shwrs inc; el pnts (10A) inc; lndtte (inc dryer); supmkt 2km; rest; snacks; bar; BBQ; playgrnd; lake sw nr; TV in adj rest; wifi; dogs; Eng spkn; adv bkg; ccard acc; quiet; CCI. "Vg, clean, well-kept, spacious, sloping site - levelling poss tricky; gd, modern facs; helpful staff." 1 Apr-15 Oct. € 26.00 (CChq acc) 2011*

CROATIA

KRALJEVICA *A2* (2km SW Coastal) *45.26784, 14.57330* **Camping Oštro, Oštro b.b, 51262 Kravlevica [(051) 281218; fax 281404; novi-turist@ri.t-com.hr; www.novi-turist.hr]** Fr Trieste take Adriatic highway E65 thro Rijeka to Kraljevica. Turn R soon after passing port area, Site situated bef toll bdge to Krk. Med, some hdg pitch, terr, shd; wc; shwrs inc; el pnts inc; shop; rest; snacks; bar; shgl/stone beach adj; 20% statics; poss cr; Eng spkn; adv bkg; noise fr adj oil refinery; ccard acc; red CCI. "Pleasant site but poss unkempt; clean facs but ltd in number & stretched high ssn; NH only." 1 May-30 Sep. 2008*

KRK (KRK ISLAND) *A3* (4km SE Coastal) *45.01638, 14.62833* **Autocamp Pila, Šetalište Ivana Brusića 2, 51521 Punat [tel/fax (051) 854020; pila@hoteli-punat.hr; www.hoteli-punat.hr]** Take coast rd, rte 2 twd Split. At Kraljevica, turn R onto rd 103 over Krk toll bdge. Foll sp for Krk, Punat. Site sp at T-junc after Punat Marina & vill. Lge, pt shd; wc; chem disp; mv service pnt; baby facs; some serviced pitches; shwrs inc; el pnts (10-16A) inc; lndtte (inc dryer); shops adj; rest; snacks; cooking facs; playgrnd; beach adj; fishing; watersports; wifi; entmnt; TV; 80% statics; dogs €3.60; quiet; ccard acc; red CCI. "Well-run site; clean facs; gd for families with sm children; boat hire; boat trips; sm picturesque vill; lots to do." ♦ Easter-15 Oct. € 29.50 (CChq acc) 2010*

KRK (KRK ISLAND) *A3* (5km SE Coastal) *44.98972, 14.62805* **FKK Camp Konobe (Naturist), Obala 94, 51521 Punat [(051) 854049; fax 854036; konobe@hoteli-punat.hr; www.hoteli-punat.hr]** Site is approx 30km fr Krk Bdge, sp fr Krk-Baska rd. Lge, pt shd; wc; mv service pnt; baby facs; shwrs inc; el pnts (16A) inc; lndtte (inc dryer) shop; rest; snacks; BBQ; playgrnd; rocky beach adj; watersports; tennis; wifi; entmnt; 10% statics; dogs €3; sep car park; adv bkg; ccard acc; red CCI. "Vg san facs; beach with crystal clear water." ♦ Easter-30 Sep. € 29.50 (CChq acc) 2010*

KRK (KRK ISLAND) *A3* (16km SE Coastal) *44.96048, 14.68402* **Autocamp Škrila, Stara Baška, 51521 Punat [(051) 844678; fax 844725; skrila@skrila.hr; www.skrila.hr]** Fr Krk E on rd 102, turn S dir Punat & Stara Baška. Site on R at bottom of hill approx 8km after Punat. Lge, hdstg, terr, unshd; wc; chem disp; shwrs inc; el pnts €3.50; shop; tradsmn; rest; shg beach adj; statics; dogs €2.10; poss cr; Eng spkn; quiet. "Approx 50 touring pitches; friendly, helpful staff; gd security; lovely, isolated position." 15 Apr-15 Oct. € 20.00 2008*

KRK (KRK ISLAND) *A3* (2km S Coastal) *45.02444, 14.59222* **FKK Camp Politin (Naturist), 51500 Krk [(051) 221351; fax 221246; politin@valamar.com; www.valamar.com]** Site S of Krk town on Baška rd, sp. Lge, unshd; wc; chem disp; shwrs inc; el pnts (6A) inc; gas; lndtte; shop; rest; playgrnd; shgl beach; watersports; boat-launching; tennis; entmnt; dogs €4.30; poss cr; quiet; ccard acc; red INF/CCI. "Hilly walk to town; gd renovated san facs." ♦ 24 Apr-9 Oct. € 29.00 2009*

⊞ **KRK (KRK ISLAND)** *A3* (800m SW Rural/Coastal) *45.02246, 14.56210* **Autocamp Bor, Crikvenička 10, 51500 Krk [(051) 221581; fax 222429; info@camp-bor.hr; www.camp-bor.hr]** Foll sp to Krk cent. At bottom of hill turn R at rndabt, site well sp up hill. Med, mkd pitch, hdstg, pt sl, terr, pt shd/unshd; wc; mv service pnt; shwrs inc; el pnts (10A) HRK33; lndtte; tradsmn; rest; snacks; bar; shgl beach 800m; cycle hire; many statics; dogs HRK28; poss cr; Eng spkn; adv bkg; quiet. "Well-maintained, family-run site, but some pitches bare earth; close to lovely town & harbour; choice of gd beaches." HRK 172 2011*

KRK (KRK ISLAND) *A3* (300m W Urban/Coastal) *45.01875, 14.56701* **Autocamp Ježevac, Planicka bb, 51500 Krk [(051) 221081; fax 221137; jezevac@valamar.com; www.valamar.com]** Fr main island rd heading S, app Krk, take 1st rd on R (W) sp Centar. At rndabt take 2nd exit sp Autocamp. App to site thro housing estate. V lge, hdstg, pt sl, pt shd; wc; chem disp (wc); mv service pnt; some serviced pitches; shwrs inc; el pnts (10-16A) inc; lndtte (inc dryer); shop; rest; snacks; bar; playgrnd; shgl beach adj; watersports; tennis; games area; wifi; entmnt; dogs €4.40; phone; poss cr; Eng spkn; poss noisy high ssn; ccard acc; red CCI. "Conv for touring Krk Island; pleasant, gd value rest with view of old town; registration fee payable 1st night; busy site; levelling poss diff for m'vans." ♦ 1 Apr-10 Oct. € 30.00 2010*

KRUSCICA *B3* (5km SE Coastal) **Autocamp Punta Šibuljina, 23245 Trbanj-Šibuljina [tel/fax (023) 658004; info@campsibuljina.com; www.campsibuljina.com]** On seaward side of E65 in vill. Med, pt sl, shd; wc; chem disp; mv service pnt; shwrs inc; el pnts (10A) HRK16; lndtte; shop 2km; rest 200m; snacks; bar; BBQ; playgrnd; shg beach adj; games area; entmnt; 60% statics; dogs HRK12; phone; bus adj; poss cr; Eng spkn; adv bkg; CCI. "V friendly welcome; view of Pag & bay; poss untidy site; tired san facs; quiet low ssn; gd." 15 Apr-15 Oct. HRK 106 2010*

KUCISTE see Orebič *C4*

LANTERNA see Poreč *A2*

LOPAR (RAB ISLAND) *A3* (3km E Coastal) *44.82345, 14.73735* **Hotel Village San Marino, 51281 Lopar [(051) 775133; fax 775290; ac-sanmarino@imperial.hr; www.rab-camping.com]** Fr Rab town N to Lopar, sp ferry. At x-rds turn R sp San Marino, site sp. V lge, mkd pitch, some hdstg, terr, shd; wc (some cont); chem disp; mv service pnt; baby facs; fam bthrm; shwrs inc; el pnts (16A) inc; lndtte (inc dryer); shop; rest; snacks; bar; playgrnd; sand beach adj; watersports; tennis; games area; entmnt; TV; 10% statics; dogs HRK29; phone; bus; poss cr; Eng spkn; adv bkg; ccard acc; red CCI. "Superb, family site on delightful island; pitches on sandy soil in pine woods." ♦ 1 Apr-30 Sep. HRK 187 2011*

LOVISTE *C4* (500m N Coastal) *43.02500, 17.03500* **Autokamp Đenka, 20269 Lovište [(020) 718069; fax 321160; autocamp. denka@hi.t-com.hr; www.camping-denka.com]** Fr Orebič W to Lovište. In vill turn R at T-junc, site along sm rd which runs round bay. Sm, hdstg, terr, pt shd; wc; chem disp; shwrs inc; el pnts (16A); shop, rest, snacks, bar 500m; BBQ; shgl beach adj; dogs; adv bkg; quiet. "Beautiful bay for sw & watersports; gd walks & historical sites; warm welcome; well-maintained site." 1 Jun-15 Oct. 2009*

LOVRECICA see Umag *A2*

LOZOVAC see Sibenik *B3*

MALI LOSINJ (LOSINJ ISLAND) *A3* (2km SW Coastal) *44.53599, 14.45064* **Camping Čikat, Drazica 1, 51550 Mali Lošinj [(051) 232125; fax 231708; info@camp-cikat.com; www. camp-cikat.com]** Sp fr town. V lge, hdstg, terr, shd; wc (some cont); chem disp; mv service pnt; baby facs; shwrs inc; el pnts (16A); lndtte; shop; tradsmn; rest; snacks; bar; playgrnd; shgl beach adj; cycle hire; entmnt; many statics; dogs HRK21; poss cr; adv bkg; quiet; ccard acc; CCI. "Touring pitches on terr with sea views; gd san facs; easy walk/cycle to attractive town; boat trips & ferry to Zadar daily fr mid-Jun." ♦ 4 Apr-20 Oct. HRK 171 2009*

MALI LOSINJ (LOSINJ ISLAND) *A3* (500m W Coastal) *44.53397, 14.45461* **Kredo Camping & Hotel, Šet. Dr Von M-Montesole 5, Čikat, 51550 Mali Lošinj [(051) 233595; fax 238274; info@kre-do.hr; www.kre-do.hr]** Hotel & site sp on Čikat road. Med, shd; htd wc; chem disp; mv service pnt; some private bthrms avail; sauna; baby facs; shwrs; el pnts HRK11; lndtte (inc dryer); shop; supmkt 1.5km; rest; snacks; bar; playgrnd; beach adj; watersports; boat hire; cycle hire; tennis 400m; fitness rm; wifi; TV; some statics; dogs HRK30; adv bkg; quiet. 1 Mar-1 Dec. HRK 217 (CChq acc) 2010*

MALI LOSINJ (LOSINJ ISLAND) *A3* (4km NW Coastal) *44.55555, 14.44166* **Camping Village Poljana, Privlaka 19, 51550 Mali Lošinj [(051) 231726; fax 231728; info@poljana.hr info@ baiaholiday.com; www.baiaholiday.com]** On main island rd 1km bef vill of Lošinj, sp. Two ferries a day fr Rijeka take car & c'van on 2hr trip to island. V lge, pt sl, terr, shd; wc (some cont); chem disp; mv service pnt; baby facs; private washrms avail; shwrs; el pnts (6-16A) inc; gas; lndtte (inc dryer); shop; rest; snacks; bar; no BBQ; playgrnd; shgl beach; watersports; sep naturist beach; tennis; games area; boat & cycle hire; wifi; entmnt; 50% statics; dogs €8; phone; poss cr; adv bkg; quiet; ccard acc; CCI. "Site in pine forest; sw with dolphins nrby." ♦ 24 Mar-31 Oct. € 41 2011*

MARTINSCICA (CRES ISLAND) *A3* (500m NW Coastal) *44.82108, 14.34298* **Camping Slatina, 51556 Martinšćica [(051) 574127; fax 574167; info@camp-slatina.com; www. camp-slatina.com]** Fr Cres S on main rd sp Mali Lošinj for 17km. Turn R sp Martinšćica, site in 8km at end of rd. V lge, hdg pitch, hdstg, terr, shd; wc; chem disp; mv service pnt; baby facs; fam bthrm; shwrs inc; el pnts (10A) inc (long lead req); lndtte; shop; rest; snacks; bar; playgrnd; shgl beach adj; boat launching; entmnt; internet; 20% statics; dogs HRK23; phone; poss cr; Eng spkn; adv bkg; quiet; cc acc. "Site on steep slope; newest san facs superb; beautiful island." 4 Apr-10 Oct. HRK 170 2009*

MEDULIN *A3* (1km Coastal) *44.81411, 13.93121* **Camping Village Medulin, Osipovica 30, 52203 Medulin [(052) 572801; fax 576042; marketing@arenaturist.hr; www.arenaturist.hr]** Foll sp to Medulin fr Pula; site 1st R on ent Medulin, L on waterfront & sp. V lge, pt sl, pt shd; wc; chem disp; shwrs; el pnts (6A) HRK22; gas; lndtte; shop; rests; snacks; pool & sports cent nrby; beach adj; fishing; surf & diving school; boat & cycle hire; entmnt; excursions; statics; dogs HRK33; poss cr; quiet except NW corner nr nightclub/casino; ccard acc; red CCI. "Ideal cent for watersports, fishing etc; beautiful situation." ♦ 15 Mar-19 Oct. HRK 216 2008*

MEDULIN *A3* (1km S Coastal) *44.80694, 13.95194* **Camp Kažela (Part Naturist), Kapovica 250, 52203 Medulin [(052) 576050; fax 577460; info@campkazela.com]** Fr Pula foll sp to Medulin. In Medulin site on R in 1.5km, sp. V lge, mkd pitch, pt sl, pt shd; wc (some cont) chem disp; mv service pnt; baby facs; shwrs inc; el pnts (10A) inc; gas; lndtte; shop; rest; snacks; bar; playgrnd; paddling pool; rocky beach; tennis; cycle hire; internet; entmnt; TV; 10% statics; dogs HRK31; phone; adv bkg; v quiet; ccard acc; red snr citizens/ CCI. "Well-maintained site with views; sep naturist site & beach." ♦ 3 Apr-9 Oct. HRK 208 (CChq acc) 2009*

MEDULIN *A3* (3km SW Coastal) *44.79768, 13.91353* **Camping Village Stupice, 52100 Premantura [(052) 575111; fax 575411; acstupice@arenaturist.hr; www.arenaturist.hr]** Foll Pula ring rd & sp Premantura, site sp. V lge, mkd pitch, pt sl, pt shd; wc; chem disp; mv service pnt; shwrs inc; el pnts (10A) HRK22; shop & 2km; rest; snacks; bar; shgl beach adj; boat hire; boat-launching; games area; entmnt; sat TV; 30% statics; dogs HRK31; bus 100m; poss cr; Eng spkn; adv bkg; quiet. ♦ Easter-3 Nov. HRK 205 2008*

MEDVEJA *A2* (2.5km N Coastal) *45.27080, 14.26897* **Autocamp Medveja, Medveja bb, 51416 Lovran [(051) 291191; fax 292471; medveja@liburnia.hr; www.liburnia.hr or www.camping.hr]** Site Pula-Rijeka rd 21/E751, 2km S of Lovran, well sp. Lge, hdg/mkd pitch, pt shd; wc; chem disp; mv service pnt; baby facs; shwrs; el pnts (10-16A) inc; gas; lndtte (inc dryer); shop adj; rest; snacks adj; bar; playgrnd; shgl beach adj; scuba-diving; games area; wifi; entmnt; 20% statics; dogs; bus adj; poss cr; Eng spkn; adv bkg; quiet, a little rd noise; ccard acc; red low ssn/long stay/CCI. "Excel for visiting local area - Lovran lovely town; conv for ferry to Cres; gd, modern san facs; various pitch prices." ♦ 1 Apr-15 Oct. € 33.2 (CChq acc) 2011*

MLINI see Dubrovnik *C4*

MOLUNAT *D4* (Coastal) **Autocamp Adriatic II, 20218 Molunat [(020) 794450]** Fr E65 foll sp Pločice & Đurinići to coast. Site sp. Site is 45km fr Dubrovnik. Sm, terr, pt shd; wc; shwrs; el pnts HRK16; shop 150km; rest nrby; BBQ; sand beach adj; dogs; quiet. "Excel location on beach in unspoilt backwater; poor san facs but gd for sh stay." Easter-31 Oct. HRK 100 2008*

CROATIA

⊞ **MOLUNAT** *D4* (500m N Coastal) *42.45298, 18.4276* **Autokamp Monika, Molunat 28, 20219 Molunat [(020) 794417; fax 794557; info@camp-monika.hr; www.camp-monika.hr]** Site well sp in Molunat off Adriatic Highway E65. Sm, terr, pt shd; wc (some cont); chem disp; mv service pnt; shwrs inc; el pnts (6A) HRK25; Indtte; rest; snacks; bar; BBQ; sand beach adj; internet; dogs HRK8; bus; poss cr; Eng spkn; quiet; red low ssn. "Gd site close to Montenegro border & in quiet cove; sea view fr all pitches; owner's wine & olive oil for sale." HRK 165 2011*

MURTER see Jezera (Murter Island) *B3*

NEREZINE (LOSINJ ISLAND) *A3* (500m N Coastal) *44.66350, 14.39753* **Camping Rapoča, Yu, 51554 Nerezine [(051) 237145; fax 237146; rapoca@lostur.hinet.hr]** Ent on L of main rd on ent Nerezine. Lge, shd; wc; chem disp; baby facs; shwrs; el pnts (10A) HRK24; gas; Indtte; shop; rest 300m; bar; rocky beach adj; watersports; boat-launching; 50% statics; dogs HRK30; poss cr; no adv bkg; quiet; ccard acc; red CCI. "Half-hourly ferry fr Brestova Pier, 35km S of Opatija." ♦ 1 Apr-31 Oct. HRK 210 2008*

NJIVICE (KRK ISLAND) *A2* (400m N Coastal) *45.16971, 14.54701* **Autocamp Njivice, 51512 Njivice [(051) 846168; fax 846185; anton.bolonic@finvestcorp.hr; www.hoteli-njivice.hr]** 8km S of Krk Bdge on rd 102 turn R to Njivice. Site not well sp but foll sp to hotel area N of town cent. V lge, shd; wc (mainly cont); chem disp; mv service pnt; shwrs inc; el pnts (6-10A) €3.70; shop; rest; bar; shgl/rocky beach adj; playgrnd nr; wifi; 60% statics; dogs €3.20; phone; bus; poss cr; Eng spkn; no adv bkg; ccard acc; red CCI. "Less cr than other Krk sites; gd facs." ♦ 1 May-30 Sep. € 20.30 2010*

NOVALJA (PAG ISLAND) *A3* (1.5km SE Coastal) *44.54523, 14.89167* **Autocamp Straško Novalja (Part Naturist), Trg Loža 1, 51291 Novalja [(053) 663381; fax 663430; turno@turno.hr; www.turno.hr]** Take ferry fr Prizna to Stara Novalja, foll sp Novalja, site sp on L on o'skts Novalja. Lge, pt sl, shd; wc (some cont); chem disp; mv service pnt; baby facs; shwrs inc; el pnts (6-10A) inc; Indtte (inc dryer); shop; tradsmn; rest; snacks; bar; BBQ; playgrnd; shgl beach; tennis; watersports; wifi; entmnt; TV; 20% statics; dogs €4; sep naturist area; poss v cr; no adv bkg; quiet; red over 60's; ccard acc. "Facs poss stretched; excel for boating." ♦ 18 Apr-10 Oct. € 33.00 (CChq acc) 2008*

NOVI VINODOLSKI *A3* (7km NE Coastal) *45.15361, 14.72488* **Autocamp Selce, Jasenová 19, 51266 Selce [(051) 764038; fax 764066; kamp-selce@ri.t-com.hr; www.jadran-crikvenica.hr]** Thro Selce town cent, site is 500m SE of town, sp. Lge, hdstg, pt sl, terr, pt shd; wc (some cont) chem disp; mv service pnt; shwrs; el pnts (10A) HRK 25; Indtte; shop; rest; snacks; bar; playgrnd; shgl beach adj; TV; statics; dogs HRK16; phone; poss cr; quiet; ccard acc; red long stay/CCI. "Wooded site; seaside location; excel facs; helpful staff." ♦ 1 Apr-15 Oct. HRK 157 2011*

NOVIGRAD (DALMATIA) *B3* (N Coastal) *44.18472, 15.54944* **Camping Adriasol, 23312 Novigrad [(023) 375111; fax 375619; info@adriasol.com; www.adriasol.com]** Exit A1 at Posedarje & foll sp Novigrad. Site sp at end of vill. Med, pt shd; wc; chem disp; mv service pnt; baby facs; shwrs inc; el pnts (16A) €3; Indtte; shop 500m; rest, snacks, bar adj; cooking facs; playgrnd; beach adj; watersports; cycle hire; games area; internet; some statics; dogs €1; TV; adv bkg; quiet; red CCI. "Well-positioned site - poss windy; gd facs; friendly staff." ♦ 14 May-30 Sep. € 17.00 2009*

NOVIGRAD (ISTRIA) *A2* (1.5km SE Coastal) *45.31541, 13.57563* **Autocamp Sirena, Škversaka 8, 52466 Novigrad [(052) 757159; fax 757076; camping@laguna-novigrad.hr; www.laguna-novigrad.hr]** On rd S fr town dir Poreč, hotel/camping complex sp. V lge, some mkd pitch, pt sl, pt shd; wc; chem disp; baby facs; shwrs inc; el pnts (10-16A) €2.70; Indtte; shop & 1km; rest 1km; snacks, bar in hotel; playgrnd; htd pool; shgl beach adj; boat launch; cycle hire; gym; games area; tennis; 50% statics; dogs €4.60; poss cr; adv bkg; noise fr quarry/stone-crushing plant nrby; ccard acc; red long stay/CCI. "In pine forest - pitches poss diff to access; some unshd pitches in open field; part of hotel complex; excel san facs." ♦ 1 Apr-30 Sep. € 24.40 2008*

NOVIGRAD (ISTRIA) *A2* (4km NW Coastal) *45.34333, 13.54805* **Autocamp Mareda, Škverska bb, 52466 Novigrad [(052) 735291; fax 757035; camping@laguna-novigrad.hr; www.laguna-novigrad.hr]** Fr Novigrad foll coast rd dir Umag, in 4km foll sp to L. Lge, mkd pitch, pt shd; wc (some cont); chem disp; mv service pnt; shwrs inc; el pnts (10-16A) €3; Indtte; shop; rest; bar; BBQ; playgrnd; shgl beach adj; boat lauch; tennis; entmnt; 50% statics; dogs €4.60; poss cr; Eng spkn; quiet; ccard acc; red CCI. "Peaceful site amongst vineyards; modern, clean san facs; cheaper, unmkd pitches avail." ♦ 1 Apr-30 Sep. € 25.40 2009*

⊞ **OMIS** *C4* (8km S Coastal) *43.40611, 16.77777* **Autocamp Sirena, Četvrt Vrilo 10, 21317 Lokva Rogoznica [tel/fax (021) 870266; autocamp-sirena@st.t.hr; www.autocamp-sirena.com]** Thro Omiš S'wards on main coastal rd, site up sm lane on R immed bef sm tunnel. Med, hdstg, sl, terr, pt shd; wc; chem disp; mv service pnt; shwrs inc; el pnts (16A) HRK15; gas; Indtte; shop; tradsmn; rest; snacks; bar; BBQ; shgl beach adj; watersports; internet; dogs HRK15; phone; bus; poss cr; Eng spkn; adv bkg; quiet; CCI. "Enthusiastic, welcoming staff; improving site; easy access lge o'fits; stunning location above beautiful beach; excel stop bet Split & Dubrovnik." HRK 135 2009*

⊞ **OMIS** *C4* (1.5km W Coastal) *43.44040, 16.67960* **Autocamp Galeb, Vukovarska bb, 21310 Omiš [(021) 864430; fax 864458; camping@galeb.hr; www.camp.galeb.hr]** Site sp on rd 2/E65 fr Split to Dubrovnik. Lge, mkd pitch, pt shd; wc; chem disp; mv service pnt; baby facs; serviced pitches; private bthrms avail; shwrs; el pnts (16A) inc; gas; Indtte; tradsmn; supmkt adj; rest; snacks; bar; BBQ (gas, elec); playgrnd; sand beach; watersports; white water rafting; sports area; tennis; wifi; entmnt;. 50% statics; dogs €4.39; bus; poss cr; noisy high ssn; ccard acc; red low ssn/CCI. "Excel, well-maintained site in gd position; extra for waterside pitch; clean san facs; suitable young children; easy walk or water taxi to town." ♦ € 33.87 (CChq acc) SBS - X02 2011*

OMISALJ (KRK ISLAND) *A2* (5km N Coastal) **Camp Municipal Pušća, Pušća bb, 51513 Omišalj [tel/fax (051) 841440; pusca@inet.hr; www.tz-njivice-omisalj.hr]** Cross toll bdge to Krk Island, site sp on R in approx 1km. Med, pt sl, unshd; wc; chem disp (wc); shwrs inc; el pnts (10A) €2.70; shop; rest; BBQ; shgl beach adj; 5% statics; dogs €2; quiet. "Pleasant situation; ltd san facs." 1 May-30 Sep. € 12.00 2008*

OPATIJA *A2* (5km S Coastal) *45.30633, 14.28354* **Autocamp Opatija, Liburnijska 46, 51414 Ičići [(051) 704387; tz-icici@ri.t-com.hr]** Fr Opatija take Pula rd 66. Site sp on R of rd 5km after Opatija. Sp fr Ičići. Med, terr, pt shd; wc; chem disp; mv service pnt; shwrs inc; el pnts (10A); rest, snacks 1km; shgl beach adj; tennis; dogs; Eng spkn; quiet. "Gd site nr coastal promenade; gd facs; diff for lge o'fits without motor mover." 1 May-30 Sep. 2010*

ORASAC *C4* (500m S Coastal) **Autocamping Peča, Na Przini 38, 20234 Orašac [(020) 891161; info@peca.hr; www.peca.hr]** Site on L of Split to Dubrovnik rd, on S edge vill Orašac. Sm, pt shd; wc; chem disp; shwrs inc; el pnts (16A) HRK15; lndry rm; shop 300m; snacks, bar 600m; shgl beach 600m; dogs; phone; poss cr; Eng spkn; adv bkg; quiet; ccard not acc; CCI. "Excel, well-run, friendly site; clean, modern facs; bus to Dubrovnik; gd bar/rest at beach - steep climb down." 1 Jun-30 Sep. HRK 108 2010*

ORASAC *C4* (W Coastal) *42.69919, 18.00578* **Autocamp Pod Maslinom, Na Komardi 23, 20234 Orašac [(020) 891169; orasac@orasac.com; www.orasac.com]** On main coast rd, on seaward side. Sp. Sm, hdstg, pt sl, terr, pt shd; wc; chem disp; shwrs inc; el pnts HRK15; sm shop; rest, bar 200m; BBQ; shgl beach 200m; wifi; dogs; bus; Eng spkn; quiet. "Pleasant site, clean facs; vg value for money." 1 May-20 Oct. HRK 87 2010*

⊞ **OREBIC** *C4* (1km E Coastal) *42.9810, 17.1980* **Nevio Camping, Dubravica bb, 20250 Orebič [(020) 713100; fax 713950; info@nevio-camping.com; www.nevio-camping.com]** Fr N take ferry fr Ploče to Trpanj & take rd 415 then 414 dir Orebič, site sp. Fr S on rd 8/E65 turn W at Zaton Doli onto rd 414 to site. Site ent immed after lge sp - not 100m further on. Sm, terr, pt shd; htd wc; chem disp; mv service pnt; some serviced pitches; baby facs; shwrs inc; el pnts (16A) inc; lndtte (inc dryer); shop 300m; tradsmn; rest; snacks; bar; BBQ; cooking facs; pool; dir access to shgl beach; tennis; cycle hire; wifi; TV rm; 40% statics; dogs €5; Eng spkn; adv bkg; quiet; red low ssn/snr citizens. "Excel new site in gd location; friendly, helpful, welcoming staff; gd views; gd, clean facs; not suitable lge o'fits." ♦ € 32.00 (CChq acc) 2011*

OREBIC *C4* (3km E Coastal) **Camping Glavna Plaža, Kneža Domagoja 49, 20250 Orebič [(020) 713399; fax 713390; info@glavnaplaza.com; www.glavnaplaza.com]** Fr E dir Orebič. At Trstenica beach foll slip rd to L, site sp. Sm, pt shd; wc; chem disp; shwrs inc; el pnts (12A) €4.20; lndtte; shop adj; rest, snacks, bar adj; BBQ; cooking facs; playgrnd; sand beach adj; no statics; no dogs; phone; bus; poss cr; Eng spkn; quiet but noise fr occasional discos nrby. "Vg, attractive, friendly, family-run site in garden of 'Captain's House'; not suitable lge o'fits; some pitches with superb sea views; gd, clean facs; conv for ferry to Korčula." 1 Jun-30 Sep. € 13.00 2008*

OREBIC *C4* (5km W Coastal) *42.97750, 17.12950* **Camping Palme, Kučište 45, 20267 Kučište [tel/fax (020) 719164; info@kamp-palme.com; www.kamp-palme.com]** Fr E thro Orebič on rd 414, site sp. Med, pt sl, terr, pt shd; htd wc; chem disp; mv service pnt; shwrs inc; el pnts (10A) HRK30; gas; lndtte; shop 100m; rest adj high ssn; snacks, bar high ssn; BBQ; shgl beach adj; watersports; boat hire; internet; TV rm; 10% statics; dogs HRK22; bus; poss cr; quiet; red CCI. "Nice, busy family-run site; beautiful wooded location on coast; friendly owners; excel rest; gd walking; ferry to Korčula; not suitable lge o'fits." HRK 163 2011*

PAKOSTANE *B3* (500m S Coastal) *43.90547, 15.51616* **Autocamp Nordsee, Alojzija Stepinca 68, 23211 Pakoštane [tel/fax (023) 381438; info@autocamp-nordsee.com; www.autocamp-nordsee.com]** Site sp in Pakoštane on rd 8/E65. Med, mkd pitch, terr, pt shd; htd wc; chem disp; mv service pnt; baby facs; shwrs inc; el pnts (16A) €3; lndtte (inc dryer); shop 400m; rest; snacks; bar; dir access to beach adj; wifi; 10% statics; dogs €3; adv bkg; quiet. "Pleasant, family site." 1 Mar-31 Oct. € 25.70 (CChq acc) 2010*

PIROVAC *B3* (1km N Coastal) *43.82341, 15.65818* **Autocamp Miran, Zagrebačka bb, 22213 Pirovac [(022) 467064; fax 467022; reservations@rivijera.hr; www.rivijera.hr]** Sp on main coast rd NW Šibenik. Site 300m off Adriatic highway. Med, mkd pitch, some hdstg, pt sl, pt shd; wc; shwrs; el pnts (16A) inc; lndry rm; shops & 2km; rest; playgrnd; pool nr; shgl beach; tennis; cycle hire; entmnt; TV; some statics; dogs €4.50; poss cr; quiet; ccard acc. "Ideal for watersports; sm pitches on water's edge." 23 Apr-30 Sep. € 27.00 2011*

POREC *A2* (10km N Coastal) *45.29625, 13.5944* **Lanternacamp, V Nazora 9, Tar, 52440 Lanterna [(052) 404500 or 465100 (res); fax 404591; lanterna@valamar.com; www.valamar.com]** Site sp 5km S of Novigrad (Istria) & N of Poreč on Umag-Vrsar coast rd. V lge, hdg/mkd pitch, hdstg, pt sl, terr, pt shd; wc; chem disp; mv service pnt; fam bthrm; baby facs; shwrs inc; el pnts (10A); gas; lndtte; supmkts; rest; snacks; bar; BBQ; playgrnd; pool; 2 hydro-massage pools; paddling pool; shgl beach adj; watersports; boat launch; tennis; games area; cycle hire; wifi; entmnt; 10% statics; dogs €5; phone; adv bkg (fee); noise fr ships loading across bay; ccard acc; red CCI (cash payments only). "V busy, well-run site; excel san facs & leisure facs; although many san facs you may still have a long walk; variety of shops; gd sightseeing; extra for seaside/hdg pitch; vg." ♦ 4 Apr-4 Oct. € 42.70 2011*

POREC *A2* (5km S Coastal) *45.19313, 13.59670* **Autocamp Bijela Uvala (Part Naturist), Zelena Luguna, 52440 Poreč [(052) 410551 or 410552; fax 410600; reservations@plavalaguna.hr; www.plavalaguna.hr]** Fr Poreč, take coast rd S to Vrsar, site sp on R. V lge, mkd pitch, some hdstg, pt sl, pt terr, pt shd; wc (some cont); chem disp; mv service pnt; baby facs; fam bthrm; shwrs; el pnts (10A) €3.20; gas; lndtte (inc dryer); shop; rest; snacks; bar; playgrnd; pools; paddling pool; rocky beach; sep naturist beach; watersports; games area; tennis; wifi; entmnt; TV; dogs €6; poss cr; Eng spkn; adv bkg; quiet; ccard acc. "Excel touring base Istrian peninsula; clean, tidy, well-run site; friendly staff." ♦ Easter-30 Sep. € 30.20 2011*

CROATIA

POREC *A2* (5km S Coastal) *45.19193, 13.58916* **Camping Zelena Laguna, 52440 Poreč [(052) 410700; fax 410601; reservations@plavalaguna.hr; www.plavalaguna.hr]** Fr Poreč take rd to Vrsar, site sp on R. V lge, some mkd pitch, hdstg, pt shd; wc; serviced pitches; chem disp; shwrs; el pnts (10A) €3.60; Indtte; shop, supmkt adj; rest; snacks; bar; playgrnd; pool; rocky shgl beach; sep naturist beach; entmnt; dogs €6; poss cr; adv bkg; quiet but noisy disco; ccard acc; red long stay/CCI. "A gd resort site with excel & spotless facs & lge, mainly terr, pitches; gd for touring Istrian peninsula; extra charge if stay fewer than 3 days Jul/Aug; footpath/cycle path to town." ♦ 27 Mar-4 Oct. € 26.60 2011*

POREC *A2* (7km S Coastal) *45.17693, 13.60053* **Autocamp Puntica, 52452 Funtana [(052) 410102; fax 451044; reservations@plavalaguna.hr; www.plavalaguna.hr]** Fr Koper on rte 2 foll sp to Poreč & Vrsar. 7km S of Poreč, turn R (care needed) 200m past Funtana sp. Site on R in 500m. Narr ent. Lge, sl, pt shd; wc (cont); chem disp; mv service pnt; shwrs inc; el pnts (10A) €3.50; Indtte; shop; rest adj; playgrnd; beach adj; watersports; wifi; 50% statics; dogs €4.20; quiet; red CCI. "Sep beach for naturists; located on peninsula nr Funtana complex; extra charge if stay fewer than 3 days." ♦ 24 Apr-3 Oct. € 22.50 2010*

POREC *A2* (7km S Coastal) *45.17453, 13.59213* **Camping Istra Naturist Funtana (Naturist), Ul Grgeti 35, 52450 Funtana [(052) 445123; fax 445306; camping@valamar.com; www.valamar.com or www.camping-adriatic.com]** Fr Poreč S sp Vrsar-Rovinj. After 6km turn R at sp Istra bef Funtana vill. Foll sp to camp in 1km. V lge, hdg/mkd pitch, pt sl, pt shd; wc (some cont); chem disp; mv service pnt; baby facs; fam bthrm; shwrs inc; el pnts (16A) inc; gas; Indtte; shop; rest; snacks; bar; BBQ; playgrnd; shgl beach adj; tennis; games area; boat & cycle hire; wifi; entmnt; TV rm; 10% statics; dogs €5.50; poss cr; Eng spkn; quiet; ccard acc; red low ssn/INF/CCI. "Excel site; beaches v rocky." ♦ 16 Apr-3 Oct. € 29.50 2011*

PREMANTURA see Medulin *A3*

PRIMOSTEN *B4* (2km N Coastal) *43.60646, 15.92085* **Camp Adriatic, Huljerat b.b, 22202 Primošten [(022) 571223; fax 571360; info@camp-adriatic.hr; www.camp-adriatic.hr]** Off Adriatic Highway, rd 8/E65, sp. V lge, all hdstg, pt sl, pt terr, unshd; wc; chem disp; mv service pnt; fam bthrm; baby facs; shwrs inc; el pnts (16A) inc; gas; Indtte (inc dryer); shop & 2km; rest; snacks; bar; rocky beach adj; boat hire; watersports; diving cent; tennis; games area; wifi; entmnt; dogs HRK32; Eng spkn; quiet; red CCI. "Gd sea views; excel san facs; some pitches poss diff to get onto; beautiful views fr beach." ♦ 1 May-15 Oct. HRK 305 (CChq acc) 2010*

PULA *A3* (8km S Coastal) *44.82012, 13.90252* **Autocamp Pomer, Pomer bb, 52100 Pula [(052) 573128; fax 573062; camp-pomer@camp-pomer.com; www.camp-pomer.com]** Fr N on A9 to Pula, take exit to Pula. At bottom of hill turn L after filling stn & foll dir Medulin/Premantura. In Premantura turn L by Consum supmkt & foll sp to Pomer & site. Med, mkd pitch, terr, shd; wc; chem disp; shwrs; el pnts (16A) HRK21 (long lead poss req); Indry rm; shop; tradsmn; rest; snacks; bar; BBQ; playgrnd; rocky beach adj; fishing; watersports; games area; entmnt; some statics; dogs HRK23; phone; Eng spkn; adv bkg; quiet; red CCI. "Clean san facs poss stretched high ssn; friendly owner; quiet, relaxing site." 1 Apr-15 Oct. HRK 147 2009*

When we get home
I'm going to post
all these site report
forms to the Club
for next year's guide.
The deadline's mid September 2013

PULA *A3* (8km S Rural) *44.82472, 13.85885* **Camping Diana, Castagnes b b, 52100 Banjole [(052) 505630; booking@camp-diana.com; www.camp-diana.com]** Fr Pula ring rd foll sp Premantura & Camping Indije. Site 1km bef Cmp Indije. Sm, pt sl, pt shd; wc; chem disp (wc); shwrs inc; el pnts (16A) inc; shop 200m; bar; playgrnd; pool; paddling pool; tennis; games area; wifi; no dogs; adv bkg; quiet. "Pleasant site in garden setting; gd range of facs; immac san facs; welcoming family owners." 1 May-1 Oct. € 27 2010*

PULA *A3* (3km SW Coastal) *44.85957, 13.81470* **Camping Village Stoja, Stoja 37, 52100 Pula [(052) 387144; fax 387748; acstoja@arenaturist.hr; www.arenaturist.hr]** App fr either Piran or Rijeka down to waterfront, turn L & foll rd round bay past naval barracks. Fork R at x-rds & foll site sp. V lge, mkd pitch, pt sl, pt shd; wc (some cont); chem disp; mv service pnt; shwrs inc; el pnts (10A) inc; Indtte; shop; rest; snacks; bar; playgrnd; shgl/rocky beach; watersports; tennis; games area; entmnt; 30% statics; dogs HRK33; phone; bus at gate; tourist info office; adv bkg; ccard acc; red CCI. "Conv visit to Roman amphitheatre & attractions in Pula; bus to city; passport req as well as CCI; variable pitch price structure; helpful staff." ♦ 24 Mar-1 Nov. HRK 220 2008*

PUNAT see Krk (Krk Island) *A3*

RAB (RAB ISLAND) *A3* (2km SE Coastal) *44.75253, 14.77411* **Campsite Imperial Padova III, Banjol 496, 51280 Rab [(051) 724355; fax 724539; padova3@imperial.hr; www.rab-camping.com]** Fr ferry at Mišnjak foll rd 105 N dir Rab town & Banjol, site sp. Lge, mkd pitch, hdstg, terr, pt shd; wc (some cont); chem disp; shwrs inc; el pnts (6-16A) inc; Indtte (inc dryer); shop; tradsmn; rest; snacks; bar; BBQ; playgrnd; 2 pools (1 htd, covrd) at Hotel Padova; sand/shgl beach adj; tennis; internet; phone; bus 2km; poss cr; Eng spkn; adv bkg; ccard acc; red long stay; CCI. "On edge of lovely bay; many sandy beaches on island; coastal path to Rab medieval town." ♦ 1 Apr-14 Oct. € 24.20 (CChq acc) 2008*

RABAC *A3* (500m W Coastal) *45.08086, 14.14583* **Camping Oliva, 52221 Rabac [tel/fax (052) 872258; olivakamp@maslinica-rabac.com; www.maslinica-rabac.com]** On ent Rabac fr Labin, turn R at sp Autocamp; site ent in 500m. V lge, mkd pitch, pt shd; wc (mainly cont); baby facs; shwrs; el pnts (10A) inc (long lead poss req); gas; Indtte (inc dryer); shop 100m; rest; snacks; bar; playgrnd; shgl beach; watersports; boat-launching; sports complex; 30% statics; dogs €2.90; phone; poss cr; adv bkg Aug ess; quiet; ccard acc; red CCI. "Conv historic walled town Labin; walk along beach to shops & rest." ♦ 24 Apr-8 Oct. € 37.10 (CChq acc) 2009*

RAKOVICA *B3* (3km S Rural) *44.97340, 15.64789* **Turist Grabovac Camping, Grabovac 102, 47245 Rakovica [(047) 784192; fax 784189; info@kamp-turist.hr; www.kamp-turist.hr]** On main rd 1/E71 S fr Karlovac, site on R, well sp opp Ina petrol stn. Med, hdg/mkd pitch, hdstg, pt sl, pt shd; wc; shwrs inc; el pnts (6-16A) inc (long lead req); shop, rest adj; cycle hire; 20% statics; dogs; bus to National Park adj; Eng spkn; adv bkg; some rd noise; ccard acc; CCI. "Gd views fr higher pitches; friendly staff; well-maintained site; insufficient facs stretched high ssn; excursions arranged." ♦ 1 Apr-30 Sep. € 21.75 2010*

RAKOVICA *B3* (7km SW Rural) *44.95020, 15.64160* **Camp Korana, Plitvička Jezera, 47246 Drežnik Grad [(053) 751888; fax 751882; info@np-plitvicka-jezera.hr; www.np-plitvicka-jezera.hr]** On A1/E59 2km S of Grabovac, site on L. Site is 5km N of main ent to Plitvička Nat Park, sp. Lge, some hdstg, pt sl, unshd; wc; own san; chem disp; mv service pnt; shwrs inc; el pnts (16A) inc (poss long lead req); Indry rm; shop; rest; snacks; bar; BBQ; wifi; 10% statics; dogs €3; Eng spkn; no adv bkg; ccard acc; CCI. "Lovely site, v busy; poss long way fr facs; gd san facs but inadequate for size of site; efficient, friendly site staff; poss muddy in wet; bus to National Park (6km) high ssn." 1 Apr-15 Oct. € 28.50 (CChq acc) 2010*

RIJEKA *A2* (9km W Coastal) *45.35638, 14.34222* **Camping Preluk, Preluk 1, 51000 Rijeka [(051) 662185; fax 622381; camp.preluk@gmail.com]** On Rijeka to Opatija coast rd. Sm, shd; wc (some cont); own san; chem disp; shwrs; el pnts (10A) inc; shop; snacks; mainly statics; dogs; bus; poss cr; Eng spkn; rd noise. "NH only." 1 May-30 Sep. HRK 140 2009*

ROVINJ *A2* (1km N Coastal) *45.10444, 13.62527* **Camping Valdaliso, Monsena b.b, 52210 Rovinj [(052) 805505; fax 811541; info@rovinjturist.hr; www.campingrovinjvrsar.com]** N fr Rovinj dir Valalta for 2km, turn W to coast, site sp. Lge, hdg/mkd pitch, some hdstg, pt sl, pt shd; htd wc; chem disp; mv service pnt; baby facs; fam bthrm; shwrs; el pnts (16A) inc; gas; Indtte; shop; rest; snacks; bar; BBQ; playgrnd; shgl beach adj; waterslide; tennis; cycle hire; games area; games rm; wifi; entmnt; sat TV; 10% statics; no dogs; phone; bus; water taxi; Eng spkn; adv bkg; quiet; ccard acc; CCI. "Pretty site in olive trees; use of all amenities in hotel adj; excel modern san facs; poss waterlogged after heavy rain; excel." ♦ 1 Apr-8 Oct. € 30.60 2010*

ROVINJ *A2* (5km SE Coastal) *45.05611, 13.68277* **Camping Veštar, 52210 Rovinj [(052) 829150; fax 829151; vestar@maistra.hr; www.campingrovinjvrsar.com]** Clearly sp on ent/exit Rovinj dir Pula. V lge, mkd pitch, pt sl, pt shd; wc; chem disp; mv service pnt; baby facs; shwrs inc; el pnts (16A) inc (poss rev pol); gas; Indtte; supmkt; rest; snacks; bar; playgrnd; pool; paddling pool; shgl beach adj; boat & cycle hire; watersports; tennis; internet; entmnt; TV; 20% statics; dogs €6.20; phone; sep naturist beach adj; cash machine; poss cr; Eng spkn; adv bkg; ccard acc; red long stay/snr citizens/CCI. "Well-run, clean site on beautiful sm bay; coastal cycle track to Rovinj; gd touring base; friendly staff; some lge pitches; ltd el pnts high ssn; extra charge for stay fewer than 3 days." ♦ 25 Apr-3 Oct. € 30.40 2009*

ROVINJ *A2* (4km S Coastal) *45.05944, 13.67333* **Camping Polari, Polari b b, 52210 Rovinj [(052) 801501; fax 811395; polari@maistra.hr; www.campingrovinjvrsar.com]** Clearly sp on ent Rovinj & in town cent. V lge, mkd pitch, hdstg, pt sl, pt shd; wc (some cont); chem disp; mv service pnt; shwrs; el pnts (16A) inc (rev pol); gas; Indtte; supmkt; rest; snacks; bar; BBQ; playgrnd; pool; rocky beach adj; watersports; tennis; games area; games rm; cycle hire; entmnt; internet; TV rm; 40% statics; dogs €5.70; sep naturist site/beach; water taxi/bus; poss cr; Eng spkn; adv bkg req high ssn; quiet but poss noisy nr sports complex; ccard acc; red long stay/CCI. "Excel, busy site; cycle path/footpath to town (can lead to adj naturist area); v helpful staff; vg facs." ♦ 1 Apr-30 Sep. € 29.40 2008*

ROVINJ *A2* (700m NW Coastal) *45.09472, 13.64527* **Autocamp Porton Biondi, Aleja Porton Biondi 1, 52210 Rovinj [(052) 813557; fax 811509; portonbiondi@web.de; www.portonbiondi.hr]** Site sp on ent Rovinj. Lge, pt sl, terr, shd; wc; shwrs inc; el pnts inc; shop adj; rest; snacks; rocky beach nr; watersports; entmnt; dogs HRK24; adv bkg; quiet; ccard acc; red low ssn/long stay/CCI. "Gd site within walking dist Rovinj old town; beautiful views; old facs; sm pitches not suitable lge outfits; excel rest; 2nd & subsequent nights at reduced rate." ♦ 15 Mar-31 Oct. HRK 170 2011*

ROVINJ *A2* (4km NW Coastal) *45.10909, 13.61974* **Camping Amarin, Monsena bb, 52210 Rovinj [(052) 802000; fax 813354; ac-amarin@maistra.hr; www.campingrovinjvrsar.com]** Fr town N in dir Valalta, turn L & foll site sp. V lge, mkd pitch, pt sl, pt shd; wc (some cont), chem disp; mv service pnt; shwrs inc; el pnts (10A) inc; Indtte; shop; rest; snacks; bar; playgrnd; htd pool; paddling pool; waterslide; shgl beach adj; sports facs; tennis; cycle hire; entmnt; internet; TV; 30% statics; dogs €6.20; phone; poss cr; Eng spkn; adv bkg; quiet; ccard acc; red low ssn/CCI. "Excel site; clean, well-maintained san facs & pool; gd entmnt; views of town & islands; lovely situation in pine & olive trees; water taxi to town." ♦ 25 Apr-3 Oct. € 31.30 2011*

SELCE see Novi Vinodolski *A3*

SENJ *A3* (3km N Urban/Coastal) **Autokamp Škver, Škver bb, 53270 Senj [tel/fax (053) 885266; kamp_skver@yahoo.com]** Fr N on rd 8/E65 on ent town turn R opp petrol stn & cont down narr lane to sea. Site sp bef marina. Sm, mkd pitch, hdstg, unshd; wc; chem disp; shwrs inc; el pnts inc; shops 500m; rest; bar; shgl beach adj; phone; poss cr; Eng spkn; adv bkg; rd noise. "Gd views; harbour & rest nrby." 2009*

SENJ *A3* (11km S Coastal) **Eurocamp Rača, Rača bb, 53284 Sveti Juraj [tel/fax (053) 883209; info@sojat.net]** On rte 2 Rjeka-Split, well sp fr Senj. Lge, hdstg, pt sl, terr, pt shd; wc; chem disp (wc); shwrs; el pnts; sm shop; rest adj; snacks; bar; shgle beach adj; boat-launching; watersports; diving school; tennis; games area; entmnt; poss cr; some rd noise; CCI. "In ravine with own beach; beautiful location; ltd facs; conv NH." 2010*

SENJ *A3* (6km NW Coastal) *45.04403, 14.87817* **Autocamp Sibinj, Sibinj 9, 51252 Klenovica [(051) 796916; milieijko. tomijanovic@ri.hinet.hr]** Fr Novi Vinodolski, take rd S. In approx 12km site sp. Med, sl, terr, pt shd; wc (male cont); shwrs inc; el pnts (10A); shops, sm bar & rest; private shgl beach adj; some rd noise. "Well-run site; clean facs but in need of modernising; magnificent views; poss open all yr; some rd noise; NH only." 1 May-31 Oct. € 20 2011*

SIBENIK *B3* (10km NE Rural) *43.80063, 15.94210* **Camp Krka, Skocici 21, 22221 Lozovac [(022) 778495; goran.skocic@ si.t-com.hr; www.camp-krka.hr]** Exit A1 at junc 22 Šibenik, turn E at T-junc, thro tunnel & site in approx 4km. Fr main coast rd at Sibenik turn N onto rte 33 twd Drniš. After 15km turn L dir Skradin, site sp on L. Med, hdstg, pt shd; wc; chem disp; shwrs; el pnts (16A) €3 (poss rev pol; check earth); Indtte; shop 4km; bar; some statics & B&B; Eng spkn; quiet; red low ssn/CCI. "Pleasant, basic site in orchard; friendly owner; gd modern san facs; conv Krka National Park & Krka gorge; gd." 1 Mar-31 Oct. € 15 2011*

SIBENIK *B3* (4km S Coastal) *43.69925, 15.87942* **Camping Solaris, Hotelsko Naselje Solaris, 22000 Šibenik [(022) 364000; fax 364450; info@solaris.hr; www.solaris. hr]** Sp fr E65 Zadar-Split rd, adj hotel complex. V lge, hdg/ mkd pitch, pt shd; htd wc; chem disp; mv service pnt in adj marina; sauna; serviced pitches; shwrs inc; el pnts (6A) inc; Indtte; shop adj; rest; snacks; bar; BBQ; playgrnd; pool; paddling pool; waterslide; watersports; tennis; cycle hire; wifi; entmnt; TV; dogs; bus; poss v cr; some rd noise; ccard acc; red long stay/low ssn/CCI. "Well-situated in olive & pine trees; some pitches adj marina; gd, modern san facs." ♦ 15 Apr-31 Oct. € 29.50 (CChq acc) 2010*

SIBINIK *B3* (10km S Coastal) *43.65238, 15.95066* **Camping Jasenovo, Uvala Jasenovo, 22010 Žaborić-Brodarica [(022) 350550; fax 350953; kamp@jasenovo.hr; www. jasenovo.hr]** Fr Šibinik S on E65, site well sp on R. Sm, hdstg, pt sl, shd; wc; chem disp; shwrs inc; el pnts €3; Indry rm; shop 2km; tradsmn; snacks; bar; shgl beach adj; wifi; dogs €4; bus adj; poss cr; Eng spkn; adv bkg; quiet; CCI. "Vg, family-run site in pine & olive trees; helpful staff; plans to extend." ♦ 1 May-1 Oct. € 22.00 2010*

⊞ **SIMUNI (PAG ISLAND)** *A3* (1km E Coastal) *44.46509, 14.96760* **Camping Village Šimuni, Šimuni bb, 23251 Kolan [(023) 697441; fax 697442; info@camping-simuni. hr; www.camping-simuni.hr]** Site sp on coast rd bet Pag & Novalja. Lge, mkd pitch, hdstg, pt sl, terr, pt shd; wc (some cont); mv service pnt; shwrs inc; private bthrms avail; el pnts (10A) inc; Indtte; shop; tradsmn; rest; snacks; bar; playgrnd; beach adj; tennis; cycle hire; games area; internet; entmnt; TV rm; 30% statics; dogs €5.90; bus adj; Eng spkn; adv bkg; quiet; red snr citizens/low ssn; CCI. "Lovely bay; facs rather care-worn but plenty hot water." € 33.60 (CChq acc) 2008*

⊞ **SPLIT** *B4* (5km SE Coastal) *43.50501, 16.52768* **Camping Stobreč-Split, Sv Lovre 6, 58311 Stobreč [(0521) 325425; fax 325452; info@campingsplit.com; www.campingsplit. com]** Fr N foll E65 & m'way thro Split to sp Stobreč. Site sp R off E65 at traff lts in Stobreč. Lge, mkd pitch, hdstg, pt sl, shd; wc; chem disp; mv service pnt; shwrs; el pnts (16A) inc (long lead poss req); Indtte (inc dryer); shop; rest; snacks; bar; playgrnd; sand beach; games area; wifi; dogs €3.50; bus to Split; poss cr; Eng spkn; some rd noise. "Superb, well-run site in lovely setting with views; helpful, welcoming staff; gd facs; own sandy beach; public footpath thro site; rec arr early to secure pitch." ♦ € 28.70 (CChq acc) 2011*

STARIGRAD (HVAR ISLAND) *B4* (SW Coastal) **Camping Jurjevac, Njiva b b, 21460 Starigrad [(021) 765843; fax 765128; info@hoteli-helios.hr; www.hoteli-helios.hr]** Ferry fr Split to Starigrad, fr dock dir Starigrad, site on L in 1km on SW town o'skts. Med, pt shd; chem disp (wc); shwrs inc; el pnts (10A) €3; shop 100m; BBQ; rocky beach 300m; watersports; cycle hire; 25% statics; dogs €3; phone; bus 500m; poss cr; Eng spkn; adv bkg; quiet; red CCI. "Gd." 1 May-30 Sep. € 15.00 2010*

STARIGRAD PAKLENICA *B3* (3.5km N Coastal) *44.32263, 15.39158* **Camping Pinus, 23244 Starigrad-Paklenica [tel/fax (023) 658652; info@camping-pinus.com; www. camping-pinus.com]** On seaward side of E65, clearly sp. Sm, terr, pt shd; wc; chem disp (wc); shwrs inc; el pnts (10-15A) HRK17; shop, rest, snacks, bar 4km; shgl beach; dogs HRK14; poss cr; quiet. "Beautiful sea views to Pag; simple site; not suitable lge o'fits." 1 May-30 Sep. HRK 130 2008*

STARIGRAD PAKLENICA *B3* (300m S Coastal) *44.28694, 15.44666* **Autocamp Paklenica, Dr Franje Tuđjmana 14, 23244 Starigrad-Paklenica [(023) 209050; fax 209073; camping.paklenica@bluesunhotels.com; www. bluesunhotels.com]** On rd 8/E65 Adriatic H'way at ent to Paklenica National Park in Zidine vill. Hotel Alan is lge, 10-storey block - ent & continue to site. Lge, pt sl, shd; wc; chem disp; shwrs inc; el pnts (16A) inc (long lead poss req); Indtte; shop; rest; bar; playgrnd; pool adj; paddling pool; beach adj; tennis; games area; cycle hire; wifi; entmnt; TV; 5% statics; dogs €4.80; phone; Eng spkn; poss cr nr shore; adv bkg; ccard acc; red long stay/low ssn/CCI. "Gd clean facs; conv National Park; excel walking & rockclimbing; use of facs at adj hotel; site muddy when wet." ♦ 2 Apr-5 Nov. € 30.70 2011*

STARIGRAD PAKLENICA *B3* (1km S Coastal) *44.28713, 15.44761* **Autocamp Nacionalni Park Paklenica, Dr Franje Tudmana 14, 23244 Starigrad-Paklenica [(023) 369202 or 369155; fax 359133; alan@bluesunhotels.com; www. bluesunhotels.com]** On seaward side of rd 8/E65 adj Hotel Alan. Sm, gravel, pt shd; wc (some cont); chem disp; shwrs inc; el pnts (10-15A) HRK16-22; shop adj; rest, snacks adj & 700m; bar; shgl beach; boating; no statics; dogs HRK15; phone; bus; poss cr; ccard acc. "Ent to National Park 2km; hiking; rock-climbing; v pleasant staff; lack of privacy in shwrs." ♦ 1 Apr-15 Nov. HRK 160 2010*

STOBREC see Split *B4*

CROATIA

STON *C4* (3km S Coastal) *42.81775, 17.67591* **Autocamp Prapratno, Dubrovačko Primorje, 20230 Ston [(020) 754000; fax 754344; dubrovacko-primorje.dd@inet.hr]** SE on Adriatic highway thro Neum. Take R turn after 15km for Ston & Pelješac Island, skirt Ston, up winding hill & after 8.5km turn L on sharp bend, site sp. Easy access due improved rd. Site adj ferry to Korčula. Lge, pt shd; wc; chem disp; mv service pnt; shwrs inc; el pnts (6A) €3; shop; rest; snacks; bar; playgrnd; sand beach; tennis; games area; TV; dogs €2.70; poss cr; quiet; ccard acc; red CCI. "Beautiful setting on gd sand beach; ideal for sailing & watersports; gd san facs; welcoming owner." 15 May-30 Sep. € 25.00 2010*

SVETI JURAJ see Senj *A3*

TROGIR *B4* (2km S Coastal) *43.50510, 16.25833* **Camping Rožac, Okrug Gornji, 21220 Trogir [(021) 806105; booking@camp-rozac.hr; www.camp-rozac.hr]** Fr A8 foll sp Trogir. Cross bdge onto Trogir Island, keep L & cross 2nd bdge to Čiovo Island. Turn R & foll sp Okrug Gornji, site in 1.5km on R. NB Narr app rd to site poss diff lge o'fits. Lge, hdg/mkd pitch, shd; wc; chem disp; mv service pnt; baby facs; shwrs inc; el pnts (16A) €3.50; lndtte (inc dryer); shop 200m; tradsmn; rest; snacks; bar; beach adj; watersports; wifi; entmnt; 5% statics; dogs €2; bus to Trogir; adv bkg; quiet, but poss noise fr nrby beach resort; red low ssn/snr citizens. "Pleasant, wooded site on headland; narr approach rds - not rec for lge o'fits; gd, modern facs; excel." ♦ 1 Apr-31 Oct. € 26.8 (CChq acc) 2011*

TROGIR *B4* (2km W Coastal) *43.51910, 16.22442* **Camping Seget, Hrvatskih Žrtava 121, 21218 Seget-Donji [(021) 880394; kamp@kamp-seget.hr; www.kamp-seget.hr]** Exit A1 at junc Prgomet & foll sp Trogir twd coast. Pass under coast rd at Trogir-Seget rd, turn R & site in 300m on L. Fr coast rd going SE take minor rd that runs thro Trogir & Seget Donji. Med, pt sl, pt shd; wc; chem disp; shwrs; el pnts (10A) €3; shop & 300m; rest 300m; shgl beach adj; dogs €1.50; bus 300m; poss cr; Eng spkn; poss noisy high ssn. "Busy site; old, poor san facs; friendly staff; public access to beach via site; water bus to Trogir fr site; pleasant vill with excel seafood rests etc; mkt in Trogir every day except Sun." ♦ 1 May-31 Oct. € 28.10 2010*

TROGIR *B4* (5km W Coastal) *43.51150, 16.19430* **Camping Vranjica-Belvedere, Seget Vranjica bb, 21218 Seget Donji [(021) 894141; fax 894151; vranjica-belvedere@st.htnet.hr; www.vranjica-belvedere.hr]** Site clearly sp on coast rd, W of Trogir, 100m bef start of by-pass. V lge, mkd pitch, terr, pt sl, pt shd; wc (some cont); chem disp; mv service pnt; baby facs; private san facs avail; shwrs inc; el pnts (10-16A) €4.20; lndtte (inc dryer); shop; rest; snacks; bar; BBQ; playgrnd; shgl beach adj; watersports; tennis; games area; wifi; entmnt; TV rm; 30% statics; dogs €2.90; phone; bus, water taxi; poss cr; Eng spkn; adv bkg; quiet; ccard acc; red lw ssn/long stay/CCI. "Beautiful position with views of bay; lovely town; gd facs; helpful staff; vg site." 14 Apr-15 Oct. € 27 (CChq acc) 2011*

TUHELJSKE TOPLICE *B2* (Urban) *46.06583, 15.78513* **Camping Terme Tuhelj, Ljudevita Gaja 4, 49215 Tuhelj [(049) 203000; info@terme-tuhelj.hr; www.terme-tuhelj.hr]** N fr Zagreb on A2 for approx 24km, exit junc 5 Zabok & foll rds 24/301/205 to sp Tuheljske Toplice. Check in at Hotel Toplice. Sm, pt shd; wc; chem disp; mv service pnt; shwrs inc; el pnts (6A) HRK25; lndry rm; rest; snacks; bar; playgrnd; htd pool; waterslide; paddling pool; thermal spa adj; games area; games rm; wifi; TV; no dogs; phone; bus; Eng spkn; adv bkg; quiet. "Gd, new site (2010); conv Zagreb & gd alt to Zagreb site." ♦ 1 Apr-31 Oct. HRK 200 2010*

UMAG *A2* (2.5km N Coastal) *45.45055, 13.52265* **Camping Stella Maris, Savudrijska Cesta b.b, 52470 Umag [(052) 710900; fax 710909; camp.stella.maris@istraturist.hr; www.istracamping.com]** Site sp on o'skts of Umag. Lge, pt shd; wc; chem disp; mv service pnt; shwrs inc; el pnts (10A) inc; gas; lndtte; shop; rest, snacks adj; playgrnd; pool 200m; shgl beach; watersports; cycle hire; entmnt; 25% statics; dogs €3.50; m'van o'night area; Eng spkn; adv bkg; ccard acc; red long stay/CCI. "Gd for touring Istrian peninsula; helpful staff; lge pitches; gd, modern san facs; use of amenities in hotel adj." ♦ 26 Mar-31 Oct. € 30.50 2010*

UMAG *A2* (10km N Coastal) *45.48550, 13.56523* **FKK Camping Kanegra (Naturist), Kanegra b.b, 52470 Umag [(052) 709000; fax 709499; camp.kanegra@istraturist.hr; www.istracamping.com]** Fr Trieste foll sp Slovenia, then Umag. Bef Umag foll sp Savudrija, site well sp. Lge, mkd pitch, pt shd; htd wc; chem disp (wc); mv service pnt; baby facs; shwrs; el pnts (10A) inc; gas; lndtte; shop; tradsmn; rest; snacks; bar; playgrnd; beach adj; tennis; watersports; tennis; cycle hire; games area; internet; entmnt; TV; 40% statics; dogs €3.50; phone; poss cr; Eng spkn; adv bkg; quiet; ccard acc; red CCI. "Clean san facs; excel." ♦ 23 Apr-26 Sep. € 30.50 2010*

UMAG *A2* (6km S Coastal) *45.39271, 13.54193* **Autocamp Finida, Križine br 55A, 52470 Umag [(052) 756296; fax 756295; camp.finida@instraturist.hr; www.istracamping.com]** Site clearly sp. Lge, mkd pitch, pt sl, pt shd; wc; chem disp; mv service pnt; baby facs; shwrs inc; el pnts (10A) inc; lndtte; shop; rest; snacks; bar; playgrnd; shgl beach adj; cycle hire; TV; 50% statics; dogs €3.20; phone; bus; poss cr; Eng spkn; adv bkg; quiet; ccard acc; red long stay/CCI. "Gd base for touring Istria; gd, clean, modern facs; lovely site amongst oak trees; friendly staff." 23 Apr-30 Sep. € 27.90 2009*

UMAG *A2* (8km S Coastal) *45.36540, 13.54473* **Camping Park Umag, Karigador b.b, 52466 Lovrečica [(052) 725040; fax 725053; camp.park.umag@istraturist.hr; www.istracamping.com]** Fr Novigrad, take coast rd N twd Umag. Site in 6km twd sea. V lge, mkd pitch, pt sl, pt shd; wc; chem disp; mv service pnt; baby facs; fam bthrm; shwrs inc; el pnts (6A) inc; gas; lndtte; supmkt; rest; snacks; bar; playgrnd; pools; paddling pool; boat anchorage & own rocky beach adj; tennis; games area; wifi; entmnt; TV; 20% statics; dogs €3.20; m'van o'night area; Eng spkn; adv bkg; ccard acc; red long stay/CCI. "Excel site for beach holiday; many leisure facs inc dog shwrs! immac san facs; narr site rds; sm pitches & v muddy after rain." ♦ 10 Apr-4 Oct. € 38.40 2010*

VODICE *B3* (2.5km E Coastal) *43.75268, 15.78981* **Camping Imperial, Vatroslava Lisinskog 2, 22211 Vodice [tel/fax (022) 454412 or (022) 454488 (LS); reservations@rivijera.hr; www.rivijera.hr]** Fr N on E65 pass INA service stn in Vodice, then at rndabt foll Hotel Imperial & site sps. Fr S site sp at ent to town. Med, mkd pitch, terr, pt shd; wc; chem disp; baby facs; shwrs inc; el pnts (16A) inc; shop; rest; snacks; bar; BBQ; playgrnd; 2 pools (1 htd covrd); waterslide; paddling pool; shgl beach adj; fishing; watersports; tennis; cycle hire; games rm; entmnt; internet; 8% statics; dogs €7; bus; poss cr; Eng spkn; entmnt; ccard acc; red low ssn/long stay; CCI. "Vg site." ♦ 21 Apr-30 Sep. € 36 SBS - X08 2011*

VRSAR *A2* (500m N Urban/Coastal) *45.15555, 13.61055* **Camping Orsera, 52450 Vrsar [(052) 441330; fax 441010; camping@valamar.com; www.valamar.com]** S fr Poreč pass Autocamp Funtana, site on R. V lge, hdg/mkd pitch, pt sl, pt shd; wc; chem disp; mv service pnt; baby rm; fam bthrm; shwrs inc; el pnts (10A) inc; gas; lndtte; shop; rest; snacks; bar; playgrnd; shgl/rocky beach adj; waterslide; boat slipway; watersports; games area; games rm; 15% statics; dogs €5.10; phone; money exchange; poss v cr; Eng spkn; adv bkg rec high ssn; quiet; ccard acc; red CCI. "Gd situation nr Vrsar vill & harbour; clean san facs; muddy in rain; conv for town; vg." ♦ 1 Apr-3 Oct. € 29.30 2010*

VRSAR *A2* (2km N Coastal) *45.16505, 13.60796* **Camping Valkanela, Petalon 1, 52450 Vrsar [(052) 445216; fax 445394; valkanela@maistra.hr; www.campingrovinjvrsar.com]** Site sp N of town fr coast rd. V lge, pt sl, terr, pt shd; wc (some cont); chem disp; mv service pnt; fam bthrm; baby rm; shwrs inc; el pnts (6A) inc; gas 1km; lndtte; supmkt; shops; 2 rests; snacks; bar; playgrnd; rocky beach; watersports; tennis; games area; cycle hire; entmnt; TV; 40% statics; dogs €6; phone; poss cr; Eng spkn; adv bkg; quiet; ccard acc; red CCI. "Excel for watersports; vg san facs; vg site for children." ♦ 25 Apr-3 Oct. € 27.70 2008*

VRSAR *A2* (1km SE Coastal) *45.14144, 13.60196* **Camping Porto Sole, Petalon 1, 52450 Vrsar [(052) 441198; fax 441830; portosole@maistra.hr; www.campingrovinjvrsar.com]** Site sp in dir Koversada. V lge, mkd pitch, hdstg, pt shd; wc (some cont); chem disp; mv service pnt; fam bthrm; baby facs; shwrs inc; el pnts (10A) inc; gas; lndtte (inc dryer); supmkt; rest; snacks; bar; playgrnd; pool; paddling pool; rocky beach adj; watersports; diving school; tennis; games area; cycle hire; wifi; entmnt; TV rm; 20% statics; dogs €6.50; adv bkg req high ssn; quiet; ccard acc; red long stay/CCI. "Lovely area & site; excel sports facs; easy walk to town cent; vg." ♦ 24 Apr-1 Oct. € 31.30 2010*

VRSAR *A2* (1km SE Coastal) *45.14233, 13.60541* **Naturist-Park Koversada (Naturist), Petalon 1, 52450 Vrsar [(052) 441378; fax 441761; koversada-camp@maistra.hr; www.campingrovinjvrsar.com]** Site sp fr Vrsar in dir Koversada. V lge, hdg/mkd pitch, pt sl, terr, pt shd; wc (some cont); chem disp; mv service pnt; baby facs; fam bthrm; shwrs inc; el pnts (10-16A) inc; gas 500m; lndtte; supmkt; shops; rests; snacks; bar; playgrnd; rocky/sandy beach; tennis; games area; diving school; watersports; cycle hire; entmnt; internet; TV rm; 50% statics; dogs €6; phone; poss cr; Eng spkn; adv bkg; quiet; ccard acc; red long stay/CCI. "Vg, modern san facs; excel leisure facs; peaceful situation; excel." ♦ Easter-23 Sep. € 36.00 2011*

ZADAR *B3* (3.5km N Coastal) *44.13485, 15.21599* **Autocamp Borik, Majstora Radovana 7, 23000 Zadar [(023) 332074; fax 332065; camp@hoteliborik.hr; www.hoteliborik.hr]** On ent Zadar foll sps to Borik. Site poorly sp. V lge, shd; wc; own san; chem disp; mv service pnt; shwrs; el pnts (10A) inc; shop; rest; snacks; bar; playgrnd; 2 pools (1 htd, covrd) nrby; shgl beach; watersports; tennis; no dogs; phone; bus 450m; Eng spkn; no adv bkg; ccard acc; 10% red CCI. "Part of resort complex of 6 hotels; facs poor & some cold water only; poor security; gd sw beach; gd rests nrby; site run down; NH only." ♦ 1 May-30 Sep. € 30 2010*

ZAGREB *B2* (12km SW Urban) *45.77389, 15.87778* **Camping Motel Plitvice, Lučko, 10090 Zagreb [(01) 6530444; fax 6530445; motel@motel-plitvice.hr]** Site at motel attached to Plitvice services on A3/E70. Access only fr m'way travelling fr N, otherwise long m'way detour fr S. Lge, pt shd; htd wc; chem disp; shwrs inc; el pnts (16A) inc; lndry rm; shop; rest; snacks; bar; tennis; TV; phone; bus to town fr site; m'way noise; ccard acc; red CCI. "Ask at motel recep (excel Eng) for best way back fr city &/or details minibus to city; Zagreb well worth a visit; site shabby but facs clean & adequate - stretched when site full & in need of update." 1 May-30 Sep. € 26.00 2010*

ZATON *B3* (1.5km N Coastal) *44.22960, 15.17320* **Autocamp Peroš, Put Petra Zoranica 14, 23232 Zaton [(023) 265830; fax 265831; info@autocamp-peros.hr; www.autocamp-peros.hr]** Site sp 16km N of Zadar fr rd 306 dir Nin. Foll sp to Zaton Holiday Vill & fork R to site. Sm, mkd pitch, hdstg, pt shd; wc; chem disp; mv service pnt; shwrs inc; el pnts (16A) inc; lndtte; shop 1.5km; tradsmn; snacks; bar; cooking facs; htd pool; paddling pool; watersports; shgl beach 300m; cycle hire; wifi; TV rm; dogs €5 (no Rottweillers or Dobermans); phone; bus 1.5km; Eng spkn; adv bkg; quiet; ccard acc; red low ssn/long stay. "Excel, peaceful, pleasant, family-run site; vg new facs; helpful staff; cycle rtes to local areas of interest; close to sea & gd access to Zadar; friendly owners." 1 Mar-30 Nov. € 30.00 (CChq acc) 2011*

ZATON *B3* (1.5km N Coastal) *44.23434, 15.16605* **Autocamp Zaton, Široka ulica bb, 23232 Zaton [(023) 280215 or 280280; fax 280310; camping@zaton.hr; www.zaton.hr]** Site 16km NW of Zadar on Nin rd. Part of Zaton holiday vill. Wel sp. V lge, pt shd; htd wc; chem disp; mv service pnt; shwrs inc; el pnts (10A) inc; gas; lndtte; supmkt; rest; snacks; bar; playgrnd; pool; paddling pool; sand beach adj; boat hire; watersports; tennis; games area; entmnt; internet; 15% statics; dogs €8.50; phone; adv bkg; quiet; ccard acc; red low ssn; CCI. "Excel, well-run, busy site; own beach; excel san facs; cent of site is 'village' with gd value shops & rests; gd for all ages; nr ancient sm town of Nin, in walking dist; conv National Parks; excel." ♦ 1 May-30 Sep. € 41.20 2011*

ZIVOGOSCE see Drvenik *C4*

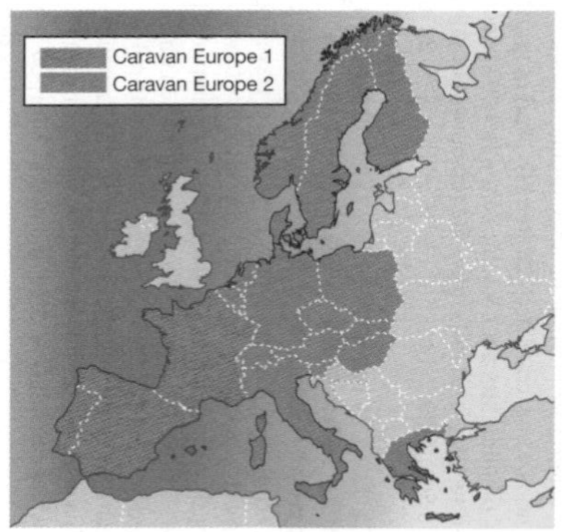

Distances are shown in kilometres and are calculated from town/city centres along the most practical roads, although not necessarily taking the shortest route. 1km = 0.62miles

Porec to Virovitica = 410km

	Dubrovnik	Karlovac	Korenica	Krk	Metkovic	Ogulin	Osijek	Pag	Porec	Pula	Rijeka	Šibenik	Senj	Sisak	Split	Trieste (Italy)	Varaždin	Virovitica	Zadar
Karlovac	526																		
Korenica	439	134																	
Krk	659	184	220																
Metkovic	96	481	343	563															
Ogulin	524	49	85	135	432														
Osijek	902	336	463	513	810	378													
Pag	465	288	154	327	369	239	617												
Porec	678	206	242	132	589	157	535	324											
Pula	711	236	275	168	622	190	568	357	56										
Rijeka	601	126	165	58	512	80	462	231	77	110									
Šibenik	305	282	181	333	230	266	644	139	423	416	296								
Senj	251	322	188	408	159	273	651	186	430	463	353	123							
Sisak	667	94	218	278	575	133	235	382	300	333	223	409	406						
Split	225	309	181	430	133	299	677	236	456	503	393	97	26	425					
Trieste (Italy)	684	209	245	135	592	160	538	247	83	190	80	426	433	303	459				
Varaždin	670	154	272	322	619	187	236	426	344	390	280	436	460	149	463	347			
Virovitica	777	204	338	388	685	253	131	492	410	443	333	519	526	110	552	413	102		
Zadar	377	232	131	282	302	216	594	67	301	334	224	72	195	359	169	304	386	469	
Zagreb	572	56	190	261	537	105	280	344	262	292	182	338	378	67	365	265	82	150	288

Motorways
Major roads
Main roads
AUSTRIA
SLOVAKIA
HUNGARY
SLOVENIA
SERBIA
BOSNIA-HERZEGOVINA
MONTENEGRO
ITALY
ADRIATIC SEA
VIENNA
BRATISLAVA
BUDAPEST
Graz
Maribor
Nagykanizsa
LJUBLJANA
VARAŽDIN
Tuheljske Toplice
Pécs
Novo Mesto
ZAGREB
VIROVITICA
Sombor
Trieste
Umag
Opatija
RIJEKA
KARLOVAC
SISAK
OSIJEK
Novigrad (Istria)
POREČ
Vrsar
Rovinj
Medveja
Kraljevića
Omišalj
Njivice
OGULIN
Fažana
PULA
Medulin
Rabac
Cres
CRES
KRK
Baška
Lopar
Rab
RAB
Novi Vinodolski
SENJ
Rakovica
Bihać
Martinšćica
Nerezine
Mali Lošinj
LOŠINJ
KORENICA
Banja Luka
Novalja
PAG
Simuni
Kruscica
Starigrad Paklenica
Zaton
ZADAR
Novigrad (Dalmatia)
Biograd na Moru
Pakoštane
Jezera
Pirovac
MURTER
Vodice
ŠIBENIK
SARAJEVO
Primošten
Trogir
Kastel-Stari
SPLIT
Omiš
BRAČ
Bol
Starigrad
Hvar
Jelsa
HVAR
Drvenik
Mostar
Loviste
Orebić
METKOVIĆ
Korčula
KORČULA
Ston
Orašac
DUBROVNIK
Molunat
PODGORICA
All year site(s)
Seasonal site(s)
No sites listed
200m +
0–200m
0 50 100 150 kms
0 50 100 mls
© Collins Bartholomew Ltd 2011

Czech Republic

Country Introduction

© iStockphoto.com/Nikada

Prague

Population (approx): 10.5 million

Capital: Prague (approx population 1.25 million)

Area: 78,864 sq km

Bordered by: Austria, Germany, Poland, Slovakia

Terrain: Diverse landscape with rolling hills and plains in the west (Bohemia) surrounded by low mountains; higher hills and heavily forested mountains in the east (Moravia)

Climate: Temperate continental with warm, showery summers and cold, cloudy, snowy winters

Highest Point: Snezka 1,602m

Language: Czech

Local Time: GMT or BST + 1, i.e. 1 hour ahead of the UK all year

Currency: Czech crown (CZK); £1 = CZK 30, CZK 100 = £3.38 (September 2011)

Telephoning: From the UK dial 00420. All numbers have 9 digits which incorporate the area code. All 9 digits must be dialled even when calling locally within the same town. To call the UK from the Czech Republic dial 0044 and omit the initial zero of the area code

Emergency numbers: Police 112; Fire brigade 112; Ambulance 112 (operators speak English)

Public Holidays 2012/2013

Jan 1; Easter Monday; May 1, 8 (National Liberation Day); Jul 5, 6 (Johannes Hus Festival); Sep 28 (St Wenceslas), Oct 28 (Independence Day); Nov 17 (Day of Freedom and Democracy); Dec 24, 25, 26.
School summer holidays are from the beginning of July to the end of August.

Tourist Office

CZECH TOURISM GREAT BRITAIN
13 HARLEY STREET
LONDON W1G 9QG
Tel: 020 7631 0427
www.czechtourism.com
info@czechtourism.com
Postal, email or telephone enquiries only

The following introduction to the Czech Republic should be read in conjunction with the important information contained in the Handbook chapters at the front of this guide.

Camping and Caravanning

Campsites are divided into four categories from 1 to 4 stars. Normally campsites are open from May to mid September, although some campsites stay open all year. They usually close at night between 10pm and 6am. A Camping Card International entitles the holder to a discount at some sites.

Campsites are generally good value and in recent years many have upgraded their facilities. Many also offer cabins, often operating as motels, and sanitary facilities may become strained if a coach party arrives for the night. Privacy in the showers may be a problem due to a shortage of, or lack of, shower curtains and only a communal dressing area. At the beginning and end of the season some facilities may be closed, making a longer walk necessary to use the facilities at an adjacent hotel/motel.

Some sites have communal kitchen facilities which enable visitors to make great savings on their own gas supply.

Motorhomes are recommended to carry a very long hose with a variety of tap connectors. Refill the onboard tank whenever possible as few sites have easily accessible mains water.

Casual/wild camping is not permitted and fines are imposed for violation of this law, especially in national parks. It is prohibited to sleep in a caravan or motorhome outside a campsite.

Country Information

Cycling

There are around 2,500 km of cycle tracks, known as Greenways, in tourist areas. A long-distance cycle track links Vienna and Prague and there are many tracks linking the Czech Republic to Austria and Poland. Helmets are compulsory for cyclists under the age of 18.

Other Activities

There are many other great outdoor activities in the Czech Republic, from walking, hiking, horseriding and geocaching, to golf, water sports and winter sports. Visit www.czechtourism.com for further information.

Electricity and Gas

Current on campsites varies between 6 and 16 amps. Plugs have two round pins. A few campsites have CEE connections but not many. Reversed polarity may be encountered.

Recent visitors report that Campingaz 907 cylinders are available from large DIY warehouses.

*See **Electricity and Gas** in the section **DURING YOUR STAY.***

Entry Formalities

British and Irish passport holders may visit the Czech Republic for up to three months without a visa. If intending to stay longer, visitors must register with the police. There are no identity checks at the borders with neighbouring countries and normally it is not necessary for a driver to stop when crossing the border. However, random identity checks may be made at any time at the border or inside the country itself.

Regulations for Pets

*See **Pet Travel Scheme** under **Documents** in the section **PLANNING AND TRAVELLING.***

Medical Services

For minor ailments first consult staff at a pharmacy (lékárna) who are qualified to give advice and are sometimes able to sell drugs which are normally only available on prescription in the UK. Language may be a problem outside Prague; if you need particular drugs or a repeat prescription, take an empty bottle or remaining pills with you. For more serious matters requiring a visit to a doctor go to a medical centre (poliklinika) or hospital (nemocnice).

British nationals may obtain emergency medical and hospital treatment and prescriptions on presentation of a European Health Insurance Card (EHIC). You may have to make a small contribution towards costs. Make sure that the doctor or dentist you see is contracted to the public health insurance service, the CMU (most are), otherwise you will have to pay in full for private treatment and for any prescription medicines and the Czech insurance service will not reimburse you. See www.cmu.cz, email info@cmu.cz for advice on healthcare in the Czech Republic.

In parts of the country where few foreign visitors venture, medical staff may not be aware of the rights conferred on you by an EHIC. If you have difficulties contact the British Embassy in Prague – see contact details on the next page.

If you enjoy hiking and outdoor sports you should seek medical advice before you travel about preventative measures and immunisation against tick-borne encephalitis, a potentially serious and debilitating viral disease of the central nervous system which is endemic from spring to autumn. Lyme disease is an equally serious tick-borne infection for which there is no preventative vaccine. Ticks are found in rural and forested areas, particularly in long grass, bushes, hedgerows and woods, and in scrubland and areas where animals wander. If you think you might be at risk use an insect repellent containing DEET, wear long sleeves and long trousers, inspect the body for ticks after outdoor activity and remove with tweezers, and avoid unpasteurised dairy products in risk areas. See www.tickalert.org, email info@tickalert.org or telephone 01943 468010.

Outbreaks of hepatitis A occur sporadically, particularly in the Prague and Central Bohemia areas, and immunisation is advised for long-stay visitors to rural areas and those who plan to travel outside tourist areas. Take particular care with food and water hygiene.

You are strongly recommended to obtain comprehensive travel and medical insurance before travelling, such as The Caravan Club's Red Pennant Overseas Holiday Insurance – see www.caravanclub.co.uk/redpennant

*See **Medical Matters** in the section **DURING YOUR STAY.***

Opening Hours

Banks – Mon-Fri 9am-5pm.

Museums – Tue-Sun 10am-7pm; closed Monday

Post Offices – Mon-Fri 8am-5pm, some open on Saturday morning; main post office in Prague (Jindrisska Street 14) is open 24 hours

Shops – Mon-Fri 9pm-6pm, small shops usually close at lunchtime; Sat 9am-1pm; some food shops open on sundays

Safety and Security

There is a high incidence of petty theft, particularly in major tourist areas in Prague, and pickpocketing is common at popular tourist attractions. Particular care should be taken around the main railway station and on trains and trams, particularly routes to and from Prague Castle. Try to avoid the especially busy carriages on the metro and on trams, which are favoured by pickpockets. Theft on trams and the metro may involve gangs of up to ten people surrounding their victims and even threatening violence.

Despite the above comment you may wish to travel into Prague by public transport owing to incidents of theft from cars. Leave valuables in your caravan safe and do not carry large quantities of cash.

Beware of bogus plain-clothes police officers asking to see your foreign currency and passport. If approached, decline to show them your money but offer instead to go with them to the nearest police station or find a uniformed officer. If you suspect that you are dealing with bogus police officers, you can call 158 or 112 to check their identity. No police officer has the right to check your money or its authenticity. Never leave drinks or food unattended or accept drinks from strangers. There has been a small number of incidents where visitors' drinks have been spiked and their valuables stolen.

Be aware of consumption charges in night clubs as they can be high. Be careful with consumption cards which carry high financial penalties if they are lost before bills are paid. Make sure you know where your belongings are at all times, particularly while in restaurants, bars and night clubs.

If your passport, wallet or other items are lost or stolen you should report the incident immediately to the nearest police station and obtain a police report. A police station that is used to dealing with foreign travellers and is open 24 hours, is at Jungmannovo Náměstí 9, Praha 1; nearest metro: Můstek. In any event, any theft of property anywhere in the country must be reported in person to the police within 24 hours in order to obtain a crime number. It is understood that it is possible to obtain this once you are back home by writing (in English) describing the event to: Policejni Prezidium-Podatelna, Strojnícka 27, 170 89 Praha 7, Czech Republic.

Seasonal flooding – usually in spring – occurs occasionally.

The Czech Republic shares with the rest of Europe an underlying threat from terrorism. Attacks could be indiscriminate and against civilian targets, including tourist attractions.

*See **Safety and Security** in the section **DURING YOUR STAY.***

British Embassy

THUNOVSKÁ 14
118 00 PRAGUE 1
Tel: 257402111
http://ukinczechrepublic.fco.gov.uk/en/ info@britain.cz

Irish Embassy

VELVYSLANECTVÍ IRSKA
TRŽIŠTĚ 13, 118 00 PRAHA 1
Tel: 257530061
www.embassyofireland.cz

Customs Regulations

Alcohol and Tobacco

For import allowances for alcohol and tobacco products see ***Customs Regulations*** in the section ***PLANNING AND TRAVELLING.***

Documents

Driving Licence

The Czech Republic authorities require foreign drivers to carry a driving licence bearing a photograph of the holder. You should, therefore, obtain a photocard driving licence, or failing that, an International Driving Permit to accompany your British driving licence.

Passport

You must have a valid passport to enter Czech Republic and it is recommended that your passport is valid after your planned departure date in case of an unforeseen emergency, such as illness, which may prevent you from leaving.

British nationals with passports in poor condition have been refused entry so you should ensure that your passport is in an acceptable state.

The Foreign & Commonwealth Office recommends that you carry a photocopy of your passport data page (including photograph and any visa pages) with you at all times for identification purposes. Failure to do so may result in a fine.

If you hold a British passport where your nationality is shown as anything other than British Citizen contact the Czech Embassy in London to determine whether you require a visa for entry.

Vehicle(s)

Carry your vehicle registration certificate (V5C), insurance details and MOT certificate (if applicable). If you are not the owner of your vehicle you are advised to carry a letter of authority from the owner permitting you to drive it.

*See **Documents** in the section **PLANNING AND TRAVELLING.***

Money

Travellers' cheques are accepted as a means of payment in some hotels, shops, etc. They may be changed at authorised exchange offices, banks, main post offices and other designated agencies. Check the commission and exchange rates as they can vary substantially.

It is better to exchange foreign currency at banks where commission rates are generally lower. In Prague some foreign exchange bureaus are open 24 hours. Scottish and Northern Irish bank notes will not be changed. Never exchange money with vendors on the street as notes are often counterfeit.

Credit cards are often accepted in tourist areas. Cash points are widely available but take care using them from a personal security point of view. Many retail outlets accept payment in euros.

Carry your credit card issuers'/banks' 24-hour UK contact number in case of loss or theft of your cards.

Motoring

Accidents

If an accident causes injury or damage in excess of CZK 50,000 it must be reported to the police immediately. You should wait at the scene of the accident until the police arrive and then obtain a police report.

If your vehicle is only slightly damaged it is still a good idea to report the accident to the police as they will issue a certificate which will facilitate the exportation of the vehicle.

Alcohol

It is prohibited to drink alcohol before or whilst driving. No degree of alcohol is permitted in the blood and driving under the influence of alcohol is considered a criminal offence. This rule also applies to cyclists and horseriders. Frequent random breath-testing takes places and drivers are likely to be breathalysed after an accident, even a minor one.

Breakdown Service

The motoring organisation ÚAMK provides roadside assistance and towing services 24 hours a day, telephone 1230 or 261104123. Emergency operators speak English. Breakdown assistance is provided for all motorists at a basic cost of approximately CZK 330 for 30 minutes + CZK 20 per kilometre travelled, payable in cash (2010). Extra charges apply at night, at weekends and for towing.

The vehicles used for road assistance are yellow Skodas, bearing the ÚAMK and/or ARC Transistance logos or the words 'Silnični Služba', together with the telephone number of the emergency centre. ÚMAK also uses the services of contracted companies who provide assistance and towing. These vehicles are also marked with the ÚAMK logo and the telephone number of the emergency centre.

Essential Equipment

*See also **Motoring – Equipment** in the section **PLANNING AND TRAVELLING.***

Glasses

If you wear prescription glasses when driving you must keep a spare pair in your vehicle.

Lights

Dipped headlights are compulsory at all times, regardless of weather conditions. Bulbs are more likely to fail with constant use and you are required to carry a complete set of spares.

Drivers are required to signal when leaving a roundabout and when overtaking cyclists.

Reflective Jacket/Waistcoat

If your vehicle has broken down, or in the event of an emergency, you must wear a reflective jacket or waistcoat on all roads, carriageways and motorways when getting out of your vehicle. Passengers who leave the vehicle, for example to assist with a repair, should also wear one. Jackets should, therefore, be kept inside your vehicle, and not in the boot.

Child Restraint System

Children under the weight of 36kg and under the height of 1.5m are not allowed to travel in the rear or front of a vehicle unless they are using a suitable restraint system adapted to their size.

Winter Driving

Winter tyres are compulsory from November to March on some road sections (including the D1 motorway between Prague and Brno) where the use of salt is prohibited. However, from November 2011 it is very likely that winter tyres will become compulsory on all roads in the Czech Republic in winter weather conditions. Please check before you travel.

Sign for winter tyres (if shown with a line through indicates the end of restriction)

Vehicles over 3,500 kg must be fitted with winter tyres on the driving wheels or carry snow chains. A full list of roads where this rule applies can be found on www.uamk.cz

Snow chains can be hired or purchased from Polar Automotive Ltd, tel 01892 519933, fax 01892 528142, www.snowchains.com, email: polar@snowchains.com (10% discount for Caravan Club members).

Fuel

Some petrol stations on main roads, international routes and in main towns are open 24 hours a day. Most accept credit cards.

Diesel pumps are marked 'Nafta'. LPG is called 'Autoplyn' or 'Plyn' and is widely available at many filling stations. A list of these is available from the ÚAMK and a map is available from filling stations, or see www.lpg.cz and click on 'Čerpací stanice'.

See also ***Fuel*** *under* ***Motoring – Advice*** *in the section* ***PLANNING AND TRAVELLING.***

Parking

Vehicles may only be parked on the right of the road. In a one-way road, parking is also allowed on the left.

Continuous or broken yellow lines along the carriageway indicate parking prohibitions or restrictions. Visitors are advised to park only in officially controlled and guarded parking areas since cars belonging to tourists may be targetted by thieves. Illegally-parked vehicles may be clamped or towed away.

Prague city centre is divided into three parking zones: the orange and green zones are limited to two and six hours respectively between 8am and 6pm, and the blue zones are for residents only. Parking meters have been introduced in both Prague and Brno.

See also ***Parking Facilities for the Disabled*** *under* ***Motoring – Advice*** *in the section* ***PLANNING AND TRAVELLING.***

Priority

At uncontrolled intersections which are not marked by a priority road sign, priority must be given to vehicles coming from the right. Where there are priority signs, these may easily be missed and care is therefore needed at junctions which, according to recent visitors, may have no road markings.

Trams turning right have priority over traffic moving alongside them on the right. Drivers must slow down and, if necessary, stop to allow buses and trams to merge with normal traffic at the end of a bus lane. On pedestrian crossings pedestrains have right of way, except if the vehicle approaching is a tram.

Roads

Czech drivers are sometimes described as reckless (particularly when overtaking) and inconsiderate. Speeding is common and the law on the wearing of seat belts is sometimes ignored.

In general roads are in a good condition and well-signposted. Roads are being upgraded and many have new numbers. It is essential, therefore, to have an up-to-date road map or atlas.

Care is required where roads follow an old route through a village when there may be sudden bends in an otherwise straight road.

Road Signs and Markings

Road signs and markings conform to international standards. Continuous white lines indicate no overtaking, but are often ignored.

The following road signs may be encountered:

Bez poplatků – *Free of charge (some motorway or express roads)*

Chod'te vlevo – *Pedestrians must walk on the left*

Dálkový provoz – *By-pass*

Nebezpečí smyku – *Danger of skidding*

Nemocnice – *Hospital*

Objizdka – *Diversion*

Pozor děti – *Attention children*

Průjezd zakázán – *Closed to all vehicles*

Rozsvit' světla – *Lights needed*

Úsek častých nehod – *Accident blackspot*

Zákaz zastavení – *Stopping prohibited*

Traffic Lights

A traffic light signal with a green arrow shows that drivers may turn in the direction indicated by the arrow. If a yellow light in the form of a walking figure accompanies the signal, this means that pedestrians may cross the road and drivers must give them right of way. A green light lit at the same time as a red or yellow light means that drivers may turn in the direction indicated by the arrow on condition that they give way to other traffic and to pedestrians.

An illuminated speed signal indicates the speed at which to travel in order to arrive at the next set of traffic lights when they are green.

Speed Limits

*See **Speed Limits Table** under **Motoring – Advice** in the section **PLANNING AND TRAVELLING.***

Motorhomes over 3,500 kg and cars towing a caravan or trailer are restricted to
80 km/h (50 mph) on motorways and main roads and lower limits in urban areas.

Speed limits are strictly enforced and drivers exceeding them may be fined on the spot. Police with radar guns are much in evidence.

The use of radar detectors is prohibited and GPS systems which indicate the position of fixed speed cameras must have that function deactivated.

Traffic Jams

The volume of traffic has increased considerably in recent years, particularly in and around Prague, including its ring road. Traffic jams may also occur on the E50/D1 (Prague-Mirošovice), the E48/R6 (Prague-Kladno), the E50/D5 (Plzeň-Rozvadov) and on the E50/D1 (Prague-Brno).

Traffic may be heavy at border crossings from Germany, Austria and Slovakia, particularly at weekends, resulting in extended waiting times. Petrol is cheaper than in Germany and you may well find queues at petrol stations near the border.

Traffic information can be obtained from the ÚAMK Information Centre, tel 261104333, or from their website www.uamk.cz.

Violation of Traffic Regulations

The police are authorised to impose and collect on-the-spot fines up to CZK 5,000 and to withdraw a driving licence in the case of a serious offence. An official receipt should be obtained. Efforts are under way to improve enforcement of traffic regulations and a points system has been introduced, together with stricter penalties.

Motorways

There are approximately 950 km of motorways and express roads. New sections of motorways are being built and recent visitors report that motorway junctions are being renumbered to correspond with kilometre markers.

There is a good network of service areas with petrol stations, restaurants and shops, together with rest areas with picnic facilities. Emergency telephones connected to the motorway police are placed at 2 km intervals.

Motorway Tolls – Vignette

To use motorways and express roads you must purchase a vignette (windscreen sticker) which must be displayed on the right hand side of your windscreen. This is available from post offices, ÚAMK branch offices, petrol stations and border posts where euros may be used in payment. If you have been to the Czech Republic before, make sure you remove your old sticker.

Charges in 2011 (subject to change) are CZK 1,200 for an annual vignette, CZK 350 for one month and CZK 250 for 10 consecutive days. For more information please visit www.motorway.cz/stickers

Vehicles over 3,500 kg

Vehicles over 3,500 kg are subject to an electronic toll (mýto) and vehicle owners must register with the toll-collection service to obtain an on-board device called a Premid which must be fixed on your windscreen inside the vehicle and for which a deposit is required.

Tolls vary according to the emissions category and weight of the vehicle and distance driven. You must be able to show your vehicle documentation when obtaining the device but if your vehicle registration certificate (V5C) does not give an emissions category, then your vehicle will be classified in category Euro 2 for the purposes of this system. For more information please visit www.premid.cz before you travel.

Touring

Assorted cold meats, pickles, cabbage, beef, pork and dumplings are national favourites. Sweet dishes, such as fruit dumplings, strudel and pancakes are also very popular. Apart from carp, fresh fish is rare but venison and other game feature on some menus. Beer is regarded as the national drink – there are more than 470 varieties and brewery tours are available. Locally produced wine, both red and white, is excellent. It is not necessary to tip in restaurants but if you have received very good service add 10% to the bill or round it up.

Smoking is not permitted in public places (public transport, places of entertainment, etc) and restaurant owners must provide an area for non-smokers.

The historic centre of Prague is a World Heritage Site, as are the centres of Český Krumlov, Kutná Hora, Telč and Třebíč, together with a number of other monuments and attractions.

A Prague Card offers entrance to over 50 tourist attractions and discounts on excursions and activities. It is available from tourist offices, main metro stations, some travel agents and hotels or order online from www.praguecard.biz

German is the most widely spoken foreign language and a basic understanding is particularly helpful in southern Bohemia. However, many young people speak English as it is now the main foreign language taught in schools and is commonly spoken in popular tourist areas.

Local Travel

There is little point in driving into Prague city centre, so park outside and use buses, trams or the metro which is efficient and cheap. There are guarded Park and Ride facilities at a number of metro stations around Prague.

Public transport tickets must be purchased before travelling and are available from newspaper stands ('Trafika'), tobacconists, convenience stores and from vending machines at stations. Tickets must be validated before the start of your journey at the yellow machines at metro stations or on board trams and buses, including before boarding the funicular tram at Petřín. Failure to do so may result in an on-the-spot fine.

Take extra care when in the vicinity of tram tracks and make sure you look both ways. Trams cannot stop quickly nor can they avoid you if you are on the track.

As a pedestrian you may be fined if you attempt to cross the road or cross tram tracks within 50 metres of a designated crossing point or traffic lights. You may also be fined if you cross at a pedestrian crossing if the green pedestrian light is not illuminated.

For reasons of safety and economy use major taxi companies wherever possible. If you telephone to order a taxi these companies are usually able to tell you in advance the type, number and colour of the car allocated to you. If you do pick up a taxi in the street always check the per kilometre price before getting in. The price list must be clearly displayed and the driver must provide a receipt if requested.

All place names used in the Site Entry listings that follow can be found in the Czech Republic Superatlas published by Freytag & Berndt, scale 1 cm to 1.5 km, see www.freytagberndt.com

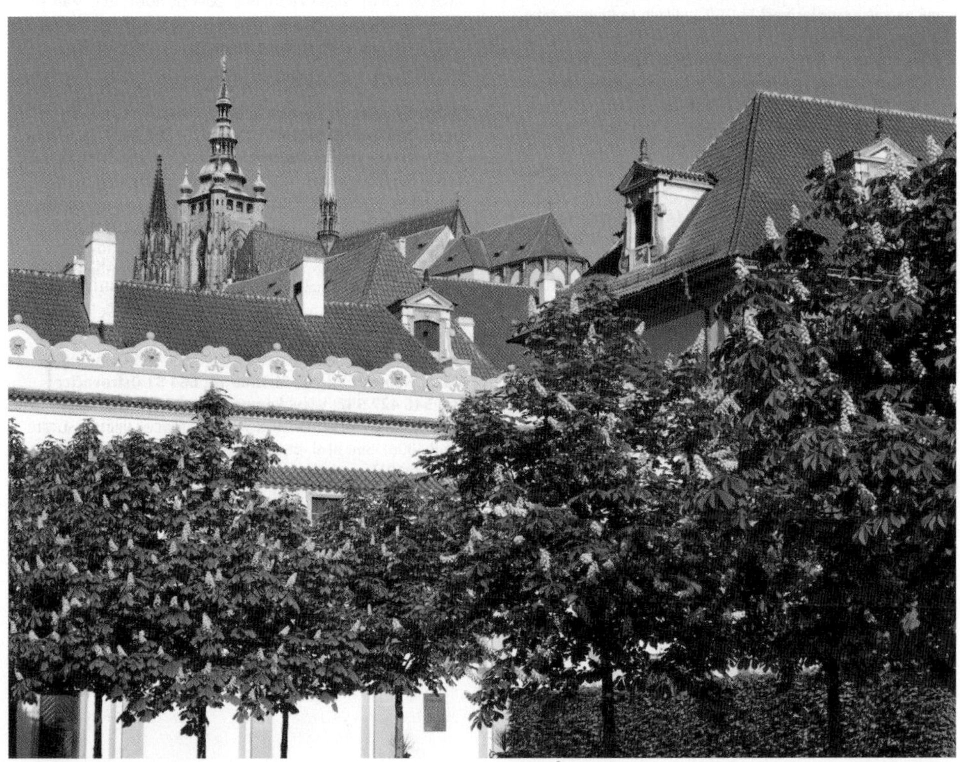

Prague © *iStockphoto.com/travelif*

BENESOV *B2* (1km SW Rural) *49.77159, 14.67036* **Motelcamping Konopiště, 256 01 Benešov u Prahy [tel 301 722 732; fax 301 722 053; reserve@cckonopiste.cz]** Fr Prague on D1 Prague-Brno m'way. At Mirošovice turn R onto E55/rd 3. Cont past Benešov turn R twd Jarcovice sp Motel Konopiště. Turn R, site up wooded lane into ent for motel. Med, terr, pt shd; wc; chem disp; mv service pnt; sauna; shwrs inc; el pnts (12A) inc; lndtte; rest; snacks; bar; BBQ; cooking facs; playgrnd; pool high ssn; tennis; cycle hire; fitness cent; golf 5km; internet; TV rm; dogs CZK50; rlwy stn nr; Eng spkn; adv bkg rec; some rd noise; ccard acc; red CCI (for cash). "Some pitches diff when wet; dated san facs; helpful staff; poss security probs; sh walk to stn - 1 hr by train to Prague." ♦ 1 May-31 Oct. CZK 660 2008*

BEROUN *B2* (300m N Urban) *49.96910, 14.07563* **Autocamping Na Hrázi, Závodí, 266 01 Beroun [tel/fax 311 623 294]** On NE bank of rv, 200m upstream fr bdge dir Krivoklát. Exit D5/E50 junc 14, turn R after uneven level x-ing opp factory, then in 100m L down ul Mostnikovska (turn easy to miss). Med, pt shd; htd wc; shwrs; el pnts (4A) inc (rev pol); lndtte; shop 500m; playgrnd; pool 1.5km; phone; quiet; ccard not acc; CCI. "Basic san facs; walking dist to rlwy stn to Prague; excel base for Prague & Karlstein; waymkd walks fr Beroun." CZK 180 2009*

BEROUN *B2* (2km N Rural) *49.98588, 14.07016* **Autocamping Plešivec, Lidická ul, Závodí, 266 01 Beroun [tel 311 624 577; www.aa.cz/campplesivec]** Fr D5/E50 Plzen to Prague, take exit 14 or 18 to Beroun. On ent town, take rd sp Kladno on E side of rv bet rlwy line & rv; fork L after 800m. Site well sp. NB App is under narr arch under rlwy - caution. Med, pt sl, unshd; wc; shwrs CZK20; el pnts inc; shop 200m; rest; snacks; fishing adj; some statics; dogs CZK20; quiet but some rlwy noise. "Conv Prague & Plzeň; pretty site; primitive facs." 1 May-30 Sep. CZK 235 2008*

BEROUN *B2* (8km NE Rural) *50.0115, 14.1505* **Camping Valek, Chrustenice 155, 267 12 Chrustenice [tel/fax 311 672 147; info@campvalek.cz; www.campvalek.cz]** SW fr Prague on E50; take exit 10 twd Loděnice then N to Chrustenice. Foll sp. Lge, pt shd; wc; chem disp; mv service pnt; shwrs inc; el pnts (10A) CZK110; lndtte; sm shop & 4km; tradsmn; rest; snacks; bar; BBQ; playgrnd; pool; tennis; entmnt at w/end; TV; 10% statics; dogs CZK45; phone; Eng spkn; adv bkg; quiet; red long stay/CCI. "Vg location; money change on site; excel rest; metro to Prague at Zličín (secure car park adj)." 1 May-30 Sep. CZK 460 2010*

⊞ **BESINY** *C1* (500m SW Rural) *49.29533, 13.32086* **Eurocamp Běšiny, Běšiny 150, 339 01 Běšiny [tel/fax 376 375 0011; eurocamp@besiny.cz; www.eurocamp.besiny.cz]** Fr E53/rd 27 take rd 171 twd Sušice. Site just outside vill on L. Med, unshd; htd wc; chem disp; shwrs; el pnts (6A) inc; lndtte; shop 500m; tradsmn; rest; bar; BBQ; cooking facs; pool; paddling pool; tennis; games area; wifi; 50% statics; dogs; poss cr; adv bkg; quiet; ccard acc; CCI. "Pleasant setting." ♦ € 11 2011*

BITOV *C3* (2km S Rural) *48.94086, 15.72066* **Camp Bítov, 671 10 Bítov [tel/fax 515 296 204 or 515 294 611; info@camp-bitov.cz; www.camp-bitov.cz]** Site is 20km SW of Moravské Budějovice. Fr rd 408 turn S dir Bítov & Lake Vranovská. Foll rd S fr Bítov, over bdge & turn R to site. Lge, mkd pitch, unshd; htd wc; chem disp; mv service pnt; shwrs CZK20; el pnts (12-16A) CZK45; lndry rm; shop; rest; bar; cooking facs; playgrnd; lake beach; fishing; cycle hire; 50% statics; dogs CZK60; quiet. "Beautiful situation; pretty site." ♦ 1 May-30 Sep. CZK 265 2008*

BOJKOVICE see Uherský Brod *C4*

BOSKOVICE *C3* (15km SE Rural) *49.42296, 16.73585* **Camping Relaxa, 679 13 Sloup [tel 516 435 291; info@staraskola.cz]** Fr Boskovice take dir Valchov; at Ludikov head S & onto rte 373 to Sloup. Site sp up track on R. Sm, pt sl, unshd; htd wc; chem disp; shwrs inc; el pnts (6A) inc (poss rev pol); lndry rm; shop, rest 1km; bar; pool 250m; dogs; bus 1km; poss cr; quiet; CCI. "Conv Moravski Kras karst caves; immed access walking/cycling trails." 1 May-20 Sep. € 11.00 2010*

BRECLAV *D3* (5km NW Rural) *48.78549, 16.82663* **Autocamp Apollo, Charvátská Nová Ves, 691 44 Břeclav [tel 519 340 414; info@atcapollo.cz; www.atcapollo.cz]** Fr Breclav take Lednice rd. Site is 3km S of Lednice vill. Lge, pt sl, pt shd; wc; chem disp; shwrs inc; el pnts CZK30; shops 3km; rest adj; lake sw 500m; dogs CZK30; bus; poss cr; noisy; CCI. "Fair sh stay; site in beautiful area; excel cycling & walking; Lednice Castle worth a visit; poss school parties." 1 May-30 Sep. CZK 280 2009*

BRNO *C3* (10km W Rural) *49.20640, 16.41565* **Camping Alpa, Osvobození, 664 81 Ostrovačice [tel 602 715 674 or 728 066 609 (mob); sitar@campalpa.cz; www.campalpa.cz]** Leave E65/E50/D1 exit 178 to Ostrovačice, site well sp. Med, hdg pitch, pt shd; wc; chem disp; shwrs inc; el pnts CZK60; shop, rest 200m; cooking facs; playgrnd; htd, covrd pool 500m; 10% statics; dogs free; phone; Eng spkn; adv bkg; quiet, some rd noise; ccard not acc; CCI. "If site unattended, site van yourself - owner calls eves; clean facs." 15 Apr-15 Oct. CZK 390 2010*

BRNO *C3* (15km W Rural) *49.21182, 16.40745* **Camping Oáza, Náměstí Viléma Mrštíka 10, 664 81 Ostrovačice [tel 546 427 552; www.kempoaza.cz]** Leave E65/E50 Prague-Brno at junc 178 for Ostrovačice. At T-junc in vill turn L, site on R 100m. Sm, pt sl, pt shd; wc; chem disp (wc); shwrs inc; el pnts (10A) inc; lndtte; shop & 500m; rest 500m; sm pool; playgrnd; phone 500m; quiet; CCI. "Excel CL-type site, v clean facs; friendly, helpful lady owner; narr, uneven ent poss diff lge outfits; poss unreliable opening dates." 1 May-31 Oct. CZK 300 2009*

BRNO *C3* (12km NW Rural) *49.27618, 16.4535* **Camping Hana, Dlouhá ul 135, 664 71 Veverská Bítýška [tel 549 420 331 or 607 905 801 (mob); camping.hana@quick.cz; www.campinghana.com]** On E50 Prague-Brno m'way, exit junc 178 at Ostrovačice & turn N on 386 for 10km to Veverská Bítýška. Site sp bef & in vill. Med, mkd pitch, pt shd; wc; chem disp; shwrs CZK10; el pnts (10A) CZK60; Indtte (inc dryer); shop; tradsmn; rest in vill 1km; snacks adj; BBQ; cooking facs; wifi; no statics; dogs CZK40; Eng spkn; quiet; twin-axles extra; CCI. "Peaceful, well-run site; family owned; clean, dated san facs; hot water runs out by evening if site full; gd security; interesting caves N of town; bus/tram/boat to Brno; excel rest in vill; flexible open-closing dates if reserved in advance; helpful, friendly owners; pleasant walk along rv to vill; gd NH." 15 Apr-15 Oct. CZK 370 2011*

BUCHLOVICE see Uherské Hradiště *C4*

BUDISOV NAD BUDISOVKOU *B4* (500m SE Urban) *49.79089, 17.63668* **Autokemp Budišov, Nábřeží č. 688, 747 87, Budišov nad Budišovkou [tel 556 305 283; autokemp@budisov.cz; www.autokemp.budisov.cz]** Ent town fr E on rd 443; at T junction turn L sp; foll rd which will take you under rlwy; site on R in 100m. Sm, sl, unshd; wc; shwrs; el pnts (6A) CZK80; shop 500m; rest; snacks; bar; BBQ; playgrnd; pool; wifi; 50% statics; dogs CZK30 (valid vacination card req); quiet; CCI. "Space for 20 vans only, with 4 elec pnts; mini-golf onsite & bike hire avail." 01 May-30 Sep. CZK 240 2011*

CERNA V POSUMAVI see Horni Plana *C2*

CESKA SKALICE see Náchod *B3*

CESKE BUDEJOVICE *C2* (10km N Rural) *49.07305, 14.41155* **Autocamping Křivonoska, Munice 75, 373 41 Hluboká nad Vltavou [tel/fax 387 965 285; info@krivonoska.cz; www.krivonoska.cz]** Fr E49, turn N 5km fr České Budějovice (avoid minor rd thro woods). Site sp fr rte 105 (České Budějovice) 2km N of vill of Hluboká nad Vltavou on L. Lge, pt shd; wc; chem disp; cold shwrs; el pnts (16A) CSK60; Indtte; shop; rest; snacks; playgrnd; lake sw; beach adj; dogs CSK40; quiet; red CCI. "Walk thro pinewoods to facs; castle (copy of Windsor Castle) open in vill." ♦ 1 May-30 Sep. CZK 225 2008*

CESKE BUDEJOVICE *C2* (20km N Rural) *49.13701, 14.47413* **Camping Kostelec, Kostelec 8, 373 41 Hluboká nad Vltavou [tel 731 272 098; info@campingkostelec.nl; www.campingkostelec.nl]** Fr České Budějovice N twd Hluboká nad Vltavou, then foll unnumbered rd thro forest to Poněšice & Kostelec for approx 14km. Med, pt sl, terr, pt shd; wc; chem disp; shwrs inc; el pnts (10A) inc; gas; Indtte (inc dryer); shop & 14km; tradsmn; rest; snacks; BBQ (gas/elec); playgrnd; sm pool; fishing; games rm; wifi; entmnt; dogs free; bus adj; poss cr; Eng spkn; adv bkg; quiet; red low ssn; CCI. "Remote, peaceful site; gd walking; conv Prague, České Budějovice & Český Krumlov." ♦ 30 Apr-15 Sep. CZK 570 2011*

⊞ **CESKE BUDEJOVICE** *C2* (2km S Urban) *48.89633, 14.97818* **Autocamping-Motel Dlouhá Louka, Stromokva 8, 370 01 České Budějovice [tel 387 203 601; fax 387 203 595; motel@dlouhalouka.cz; www.dlouhalouka.cz]** On Ceske Budějovice to Cesky. Krumlov/Linz rd. Site sp on R on o'skts of town. Fr town foll sp for C. Krumlov; after exit ring rd turn R in 300m at motel sp, 60m bef Stromovka site. Can take new ring rd round town. Site next to Interhotel Autocamping Stomovka - foll sp. Med, some hdstg, pt shd; htd wc; serviced pitches; chem disp; shwrs inc; el pnts (10A) inc (rev pol); Indtte (inc dryer); supmkt 1km; rest, snacks, bar high ssn; cooking facs; playgrnd; 10% statics; dogs CZK30; phone adj; poss cr; some Eng spkn; quiet; red low ssn; ccard not acc; CCI. "Clean facs; supmkt nr; easy walk to interesting town or gd bus service; grassy area rough & uneven - poss diff wet weather; conv Český Krumlov & area; gd cycle paths along rv." CZK 530 2010*

CESKY KRUMLOV *C2* (4km SW Rural) *48.81888, 14.26645* **Caravan Camp Petrášku Dvur, Topolová 808, 383 01 Prachatice [tel 602 130 418; fax 388 314 125; milan.sebesta@seznam.cz; www.petraskuv-dvur.cz]** Fr Český Krumlov on rd 39 dir Černá for 3km. Take 2nd R after Motorest Krumlov at site sp, then 300m R again for site. Med, pt sl, pt shd; wc; chem disp; shwrs CZK10; el pnts (16A) CZK70; Indtte; shop 3km; rest; bar; games area; wifi; dogs CZK50; Eng spkn; quiet; red long stay; CCI. "Site yourself if recep clsd; vg san facs, inc disabled; gd & clean; pleasant walk to town, or cycle path." ♦ 1 May-30 Sep. CZK 320 2011*

CESKY KRUMLOV *C2* (9km NW Rural) *48.85962, 14.21549* **Camping Chvalšiny, Chvalšiny 321, 382 08 Chvalšiny [tel 380 739 123; info@campingchvalsiny.nl; www.campingchvalsiny.nl]** Take rd 39 fr Český Krumlov twd Černá; after 4km turn R at Kájov onto rd 166 to Chvalšiny 6km. Turn R thro main sq of town; site 300m on L. Fr Germany on A3 exit junc 114 to Freyung & Philippsreut to Czech border. Foll sp to Volary then rd 39 to Český Krumlov, & rd 166 to Chvalšiny. Med, mkd pitch, terr, pt sl, unshd; wc; chem disp; mv service pnt; shwrs CZK15; pnts (6A) CZK50; gas; Indtte; shop 300m; tradsmn; supmkts 11km; rest; bar; BBQ; playgrnd; lake sw nr; dogs CZK50; phone; bus 500m; Eng spkn; adv bkg; quiet; no ccard acc; CCI. "Dutch-run; v clean, friendly, spacious, well-maintained site; vg facs; C Krumlow beautiful unspoilt, medieval town; secure car park adj castle." 28 Apr-15 Sep. CZK 500 2008*

⊞ **CHEB** *B1* (4km N Rural) *50.11773, 12.32713* **Hotel Jadran Autocamping, Jezerní 84/12, 351 01 Františkovy Lázně [tel/fax 354 542 412 or 603 845 789 (mob); info@atcjadran.cz; www.atcjadran.cz]** Fr rte 6 turn N dir Libá. After 2km, immed N of new by-pass over bdge, fork L to vill; on o'skirts turn L & foll site/hotel sp, then R in 100m onto narr lane. In 700m turn R. Site in 400m, well sp. Lge, pt shd; wc; mv service pnt; shwrs inc; el pnts (16A) inc (rev pol & long cable req); shop 2km; rest; bar; lake sw; cycle hire; many cabins; dogs CZK60; poss noisy w/end; red long stay; CCI. "Delightful site beside sm lake; many places of interest nr; walk thro woods to beautiful spa town; supmkt on rd to Cheb." CZK 480 2008*

CHEB *B1* (5km SE Rural) *50.04931, 12.41326* **Camping am See Václav, Jesenická Přehrada, 350 02 Podhrad [tel/fax 354 435 653; info@kempvaclav.cz; www.kempvaclav.cz]** E fr Cheb on rte 606 sp Praha & Karlovy Vary. After 3km take minor rd to R (150m bef petrol stn) to Podhrad. At Podhrad under rlwy bdge take immed L fork & cont thro houses for 2km (rlwy on R). Site sp fr town on NW shore Lake Jesenice. Fr N on E48/6 exit junc 164 onto rd 606 & foll sp Cheb. Turn L at site sp 150m after petrol stn, foll site sp. Med, pt sl, terr, pt shd; wc; chem disp; shwrs inc; el pnts (16A) inc; Indtte; shop; rest; snacks; bar; playgrnd; beach & lake sw adj; fishing; watersports; games area; TV; wifi; dogs CZK60; poss cr; Eng spkn; adv bkg; quiet but some rlwy noise; red long stay/low ssn; CCI. "Friendly, improving, spacious, family-run site; well managed & scenic; choose own pitch; gd, clean, modern san facs; boats, pedalos for hire; scenic area; conv Mariánské Lázně, Karlovy Vary, hot springs at Soos." 25 Apr-25 Sep. CZK 735 2011*

CHRUSTENICE see Beroun *B2*

CHVALSINY see Český Krumlov *C2*

DOLNI BREZANY see Praha *B2*

DOMAZLICE *C1* (11km SE Rural) *49.40314, 13.05763* **Autocamping Hájovna, Na Kobyle 209, 345 06 Kdyně [tel 379 731 233; fax 379 731 595; automotoklub@kdyne.cz; www.camphajovna.cz]** In Kdyně going twd Klatovy on rd 22, turn L at end of town sq; then 1st R twd cobbled rd (for 300m); site on L in 2km. Med, some hdstg, pt sl, pt shd; wc; shwrs CZK10; el pnts (10A) inc (poss rev pol); Indtte; shop; rest adj; playgrnd; pool; TV; some cabins; dogs CZK35; phone; quiet; CCI. "Hořovský Týn & Domažlice interesting towns; gd walking; friendly owner; ltd level pitches." 1 May-30 Sep. CZK 250 2009*

FRANTISKOVY LAZNE see Cheb *B1*

FRYDEK MISTEK *B4* (1km W Rural) *49.66459, 18.31161* **Autokemp Olešná, Nad Přehradou, 738 02 Frýdek-Místek [tel 558 434 806; fax 558 431 195; olesna@tsfm.cz; www.katalog-kempu.cz/autokemp-olesna/]** Nr Tesco on S side of E462/rte 48 on lakeside. Sm, sl, unshd; wc; chem disp; shwrs; el pnts (10A); shop; rest; bar; cooking facs; fishing; dogs; Eng spkn; quiet. "Unisex san facs; indiv shwr cabins." 1 May-30 Sep. 2009*

FRYDLANT *A2* (6km SE Urban) *50.90116, 15.14147* **Rekreační a sportovní areál, Raspenava, U Stadionu 181, 46361 [tel 482 360 431; mesto.raspenava@raspenava.cz; www.raspenava.cz]** Ent Raspenava fr E on rd 290, do not cross rv; turn R round filling stn (dir Nove Mesto Pod Smrkem) & immed L along R side of rv for approx 500m; site sp on the R. Sm, pt shd; wc; shwrs inc; el pnts; shop 1km; rest; snacks, bar; playgrnd; pool; games area; games rm; 50% statics; bus 500m; train 500m; quiet; CCI. "In Jizerske Hory mountains area & close to Polish border; Frydlant has chateau/castle & interesting centre; sm campsite on a sports centre with pool & hall; only 8 elec pnts." 1 May-30 Sep. CZK 200 2011*

FRYMBURK *D2* (800m S Rural) *48.65556, 14.17008* **Camping Frymburk, Frymburk 20/55, 382 79 Frymburk [tel 380 735 284; fax 380 735 283; info@campingfrymburk.cz; www.campingfrymburk.cz]** Fr Černa on lake, take rd 163 dir Loucovice to site. Fr Český Krumlov take Rožmberk nad Vltavou rd, turn R at Větřni on rd 162 sp Světlik. At Frymburk turn L to Lipno then site 500m on R on lake shore. Med, v sl, terr, pt shd; wc; chem disp; private san facs some pitches; shwrs CZK15; el pnts (6A) inc; Indtte; shop & 600m; tradsmn high ssn; rest 200m; snacks; playgrnd; lake sw; fishing; boating; cycle & boat hire; entmnt & child entmnt high ssn; wifi; TV rm; some cabins; dogs CZK60; poss v cr; adv bkg; quiet. "Beautiful lakeside site; modern, clean san facs; some pitches poss tight for lge o'fits; gd rest nrby; helpful Dutch owners; gd walking; adv bkg rec bef 1st Apr." 25 Apr-1 Oct. CZK 640 2009*

HLUBOKA NAD VLTAVOU see České Budějovice *C2*

HLUBOKE MASUVKY see Znojmo *C3*

HOLICE see Pardubice *B3*

HORNI PLANA *C2* (14km E Rural) *48.74617, 14.11945* **Autocamp Olšina Lipno, Čkyně 212, 382 23 Černá v Pošumaví [tel 608 029 982 (mob); info@campingolsina.cz; www.campingolsina.cz]** Fr Horní Planá E to Černá v Pošumaví on rd 39. Cont on this rd 1.5km N to site on lakeside. Sm, pt shd; wc; chem disp; mv service pnt; shwrs CZK20; el pnts (6A) CZK80; Indtte; tradsmn; rest; snacks; playgrnd; lake sw adj; watersports; windsurfing 1.5km; boat & cycle hire; wifi; 25% statics; dogs CZK60; quiet; CCI. "Vg; lovely countryside; welcoming owner; lovely site." ♦ 2 Apr-31 Oct. CZK 370 2011*

HORNI PLANA *C2* (1.5km SE Rural) *48.75098, 14.04328* **Autocamp Jenišov, 382 26 Horní Planá [tel/fax 337 738 156; info@autocampjenisov.cz; www.autocampjenisov.cz]** Site is on rd 39; well sp. Med, pt sl, pt shd; wc; chem disp; mv service pnt; shwrs CZK20; el pnts (6-10A) CZK80; Indtte; shop; rest; snacks; bar; playgrnd; lake sw & beach adj; watersports; fishing; boat & cycle hire; tennis; wifi; 10% statics; dogs CZK60; bus, train nr; poss cr; quiet; CCI. "Beautiful quiet setting on lake; gd, clean san facs; conv Český Krumlov." ♦ 10 Apr-31 Oct. CZK 350 2008*

HORNI PLANA *C2* (500m S Rural) *48.76086, 14.02584* **Camping Horní Planá, Málek Václav Veršová 19, 382 26 Horní Planá [tel 380 738 339 or 602 660 264 (mob); anderlep@quick.cz; www.caravancamping-hp.cz]** Fr Český Krumlov take rd SW to Černá. In Černá take Volary rd W. In Horní Planá vill turn twd lake. Over rlwy x-ing fork L after 100m & strt on to office immed L again. Med, some hdstg, pt shd; wc; chem disp; shwrs CZK10; el pnts (10A) CZK90; Indtte; shop; bar; BBQ; playgrnd; lake sw & sand beach adj; watersports; tennis; fishing; boat hire; dogs CZK50; poss cr; quiet; CCI. "Modern, v clean facs; lake ferry adj; superb views; cycle rtes." ♦ 1 May-31 Oct. CZK 360 2008*

HRANICE *C4* (1km SE Rural) *49.54194, 17.74111* **Autocamp Hranice, Pod Hůrkou 2103, 753 01 Hranice [tel/fax 581 601 633; autokemphranice@seznam.cz]** Fr Olomouc head E on rd 35/E442/E462 to Hranice. On app to town turn R onto E442 sp Valašské-Meziřičí for 2km thro town, sp to site on R. Site in 500m, turn R then L up steep hill & under rlwy bdge (3.2m high) to site. Sm, pt sl, pt shd; wc; chem disp; shwrs; el pnts (10A); Indtte; shops 500m; rest; snacks; bar; cooking facs; playgrnd; htd pool 1.5km; dogs; poss cr; some rlwy noise; red CCI. "Gd 24hr security; lovely site; conv for Helfstýn Castle & Zbrašov Caves." 1 May-30 Sep. 2011*

The opening dates and prices on this campsite have changed. I'll send a site report form to the Club for the next edition of the guide.

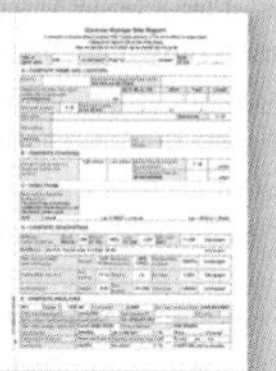

JABLONNE V PODJESTEDI *A2* (1km N Rural) *50.77345, 14.76636* **Autocamping Jablonné, Markvartice 22, 471 25 Jablonné v Podještědí [tel 424 762 343; fax 487 762 364; ts_jablonne_vp@volny.cz; www.automkemp.jabl.euroregin.cz]** On rte 13/E442, within 1km vill of Jablonné v Podještědí. Ent to site opp petrol stn. Med, mkd pitch, pt sl, pt shd; wc; shwrs inc; el pnts (10A) CZK80; Indtte; shop & 1km; snacks; bar; playgrnd; pool; lake/beach nr; fishing 3km; some cabins; dogs CZK80; quiet; ccard not acc; CCI. 15 May-30 Sep. CZK 520 2008*

JEDOVNICE *C3* (1km SE Rural) *49.33350, 16.76299* **Autokemp Olšovec, Havlíčkovo Náměstí 71, 679 06 Jedovnice [tel/fax 516 442 216; kemp@olsovec.cz; www.olsovec.cz]** Fr S on rd 373 or fr N on rd 379, site sp on W side of lake. Med, pt shd; htd wc; chem disp; mv service pnt; shwrs; el pnts (10A) CZK50; Indtte; shop; tradsmn; rest; snacks; bar; BBQ; playgrnd; lake sw adj; fishing; TV rm; 25% statics; dogs CZK50; bus 1km; poss cr; noisy due fairgrnd adj; red CCI. "Conv Moravský Kra karst show caves; gd walking/cycling; lively site." 1 May-30 Sep. CZK 320 2010*

⊞ **JESENIK** *B3* (2km W Rural) *50.22444, 17.17472* **Autocamping Bobrovník, 790 61 Lipová-Lázně [tel 584 411 145; camp@bobrovnik.cz; www.bobrovnik.cz]** Fr S on rd 44, at rndabt on app to town turn L sp Lipová-Lázně. Site on R in 3km. Med, unshd; wc; shwrs CZK5; el pnts (10A) CZK50; Indtte; shop; rest; snacks; bar; cooking facs; playgrnd; cycle hire; 10% statics; dogs CZK45; quiet; CCI. "Gd touring base." CZK 255 2008*

JIHLAVA *C3* (6km N Rural) *49.44655, 15.60185* **Autocamping Pávov, Pávov 90, 586 01 Jihlava [tel 567 210 295; fax 567 210 973; atcpavov@volny.cz]** Fr D1/E50/E65 exit junc 112 sp Jihlava. Foll sp Pávov & site for 2km. Fr N/S on rte 38, nr a'bahn pick up sp for Pávov. Recep in adj pension/rest. Med, mkd pitch, unshd; wc; shwrs CZK14; el pnts (6A); Indtte; shop; rest; snacks; playgrnd; lake sw & beach adj; fishing; tennis; 30% statics; m'way noise. "Grand Hotel in Jihlava gd, friendly rest." 1 May-30 Sep. 2011*

KARLOVY VARY *B1* (7km NE Rural) *50.26450, 12.90013* **Autokamp Sasanka, Sadov 7, 360 01 Sadov [tel/fax 353 590 130 or 603 202 051 (mob); campsadov@seznam.cz]** Fr Karlovy Vary on rd 13/E442 to Bor, exit to Sadov, site sp. Med, pt sl, pt shd; wc; chem disp; mv service pnt; shwrs inc; el pnts (16A) CZK60 (poss rev pol); Indtte; shops 200m; tradsmn; snacks; bar; playgrnd; wifi; dogs CZK50; poss cr; no adv bkg; quiet but some rlwy noise; red long stay/CCI. "Lovely, well-run site; friendly, helpful staff; modern, clean san facs; picturesque vill of Loket a must; gd bus service fr vill to Karlovy Vary; take care height restriction on app to Tesco fr m'way; rec." 1 Apr-31 Oct. CZK 380 2011*

KARLOVY VARY *B1* (3km S Rural) *50.19558, 12.86282* **Camping Březová Háj, Staromlýnská 154, 362 15 Březová [tel/fax 353 222 665; info@brezovy-haj.cz; www.brezovy-haj.cz]** Fr Cheb-Karlovy Vary R6/E48, turn R on edge of town onto rd 20/E49 S twd Plzeň. In 7km keep L where rd goes across dam, site on R Med, wc; shwrs; el pnts (6A) inc; rest, bar at hotel adj; games area; adv bkg; quiet. "Ltd space for c'vans; poss lge, noisy youth groups; some barrack-like buildings; NH/sh stay only." 1 Apr-30 Sep. CZK 300 2010*

KARLSTEJN *B2* (1km W Rural) *49.93515, 14.16490* **Autocamping Karlštejn, Ve Spáleném 326, 267 18 Karlštejn [tel 311 681 263; hc@obeckarlstejn.cz; www.mestys-karlstejn.cz]** 30km SW fr Prague on D5/E50 dir Beroun. Turn L onto rd 116 dir Řevnice to Karlštejn. Rd winding & hilly fr Beroun. Med, shd; wc; chem disp; shwrs CZK10; el pnts CZK50; gas; Indtte; shop; rest 1km; snacks; playgrnd; tennis; games area; cabins; dogs CZK15; adv bkg. "Delightful rvside site; conv lge castle & crystal glass." 9 Apr-3 Oct. CZK 220 2008*

KDYNE see Domažlice *C1*

KLATOVY *C1* (10km SW Rural) *49.28614, 13.14478* **Autocamping Nýrsko, Tylová 778, 340 22 Nýrsko [tel 376 571 220; fax 376 570 437; alena-hostalkova@seznam.cz; www.autokemp-nyrsko.cz]** S fr Klatovy on rd 191; turn L at x-rds on S o'skts of town onto rd 190 twd water tower; after 100m fork L, sp camping. Med, unshd; wc; chem disp; shwrs inc; el pnts; Indtte; rest; shop; sw adj; tennis adj; poss cr; quiet. 1 May-30 Sep. € 10.60 2008*

KONSTANTINOVY LAZNE *B1* (1km N Rural) *49.8869, 12.97168* **Camping La Rocca, 349 52 Konstantinovy Lázně [tel/fax 374 625 287; laroccacamp@seznam.cz; www.larocca.cz]** Fr rd 230 turn onto rd 201 to Konstantinovy Lázně in 18km, site sp. Med, mkd pitch, pt shd; wc; chem disp; mv service pnt; shwrs; el pnts (4-10A) CZK100; shop adj; rest; bar; playgrnd; htd pool 100m; paddling pool; games area; cycle hire; entmnt; 30% statics; dogs CZK50; adv bkg; quiet. "Friendly, spacious site; conv for spa towns, Pilzen & Tepla Monastery." ♦ 1 May-30 Sep. CZK 320 2010*

⊞ **KRALIKY** *B3* (3km NE Rural) *50.11582, 16.76904* **Camping Collins, Horní Lipka 80, 561 69 Králíky [tel 465 632 068 or 728 713 436 (mob); G.Collins@seznam.cz; www.pension-collins.info]** Fr Králíky foll sp for Hanušovice on rd 312; after 2km turn L sp Prostřední Lipka. Cont over rlwy x-ing, turn R sp Horní Lipka. Site in 1km sp on L. Sm, hdstg, pt sl, unshd; wc; chem disp; shwrs; el pnts (10A) CZK70; shop 200m; sw & boating 15km; dogs CZK30; adv bkg; quiet; no ccard acc; red long stay; CCI. "Nr Polish border; excel for walking, cycling, skiing in winter; helpful British/Czech owners." ♦ CZK 200 2009*

KUTNA HORA *B2* (2.5km NE Urban) *49.96416, 15.30250* **Autocamp Transit, Malín 35, 284 05 Kutná Hora [tel 327 523 785; egidylada@seznam.cz; www.transit.zde.cz]** Fr N on rd 38 fr Kolín, turn W onto rd 2, site in 1km on L immed bef rlwy bdge. Sm, pt shd; wc; chem disp (wc); shwrs inc; el pnts (16A) CZK75; shop 200m; rest 1km; cooking facs; wifi; TV; dogs free; phone; bus 800m; Eng spkn; poss noisy; CCI. "Clean, well-kept, CL-type site with garden area." 1 Apr-30 Sep. CZK 290 2010*

KUTNA HORA *B2* (500m NW Urban) *49.95444, 15.26003* **Camping Santa Barbara, Česká 988, 284 01 Kutná Hora [tel 327 512 051 or 602 361 330 (mob); info@santabarbara.cz; www.santabarbara.cz]** Site off minor ring rd to NW of town, turn uphill (NW) into Ceska Ulice just below crest, site 200m on on L. Site sp is set back (not easy to see). Sm, hdg/mkd pitch, pt shd; wc; chem disp; shwrs CZK25; el pnts (6A) CZK80; lndtte; shop 200m; snacks; bar; htd pool nr; dogs CZK50; Eng spkn; adv bkg; ccard acc; CCI. "Nice shady site; welcoming owner; vg, modern san facs; 5 min walk to historic cent of Kutná Hora with many attractions; site locked at night, if locked on arrival call for owner." ♦ 1 Apr-31 Oct. CZK 370 2010*

⊞ **KYSELKA** *B1* (2km N Rural) *50.27038, 12.99445* **Camping Na Špici, Radošov 87, 362 72 Kyselka [tel 353 941 152 or 777 145 710 (mob); fax 353 941 285; naspici@quick.cz; http://naspici.sweb.cz/naspiciAN.htm]** Fr Karlovy Vary N on rd 222 along Rv Ohře. Site nr hotel, S of Radošov. Or take rd 13/E442 fr Karlovy Vary & turn R to Bor. Cont on rd & cross wooden bdge (max height 3m) & turn R. Site in 500m on R. Site behind Na Špici Hotel. Med, terr, pt shd; wc; chem disp; shwrs inc; el pnts (10A); lndtte; shop 500m; rest; snacks; bar; playgrnd; rv sports; wifi; TV; 25% statics; dogs CZK70; phone; bus; site poss clsd mid Jan to mid-Mar & Xmas, rec phone in adv; Eng spkn; adv bkg; quiet; red long stay; CCI. "Vg site in beautiful valley; rest gd value; gd walking & rv sports; conv Karlovy Vary." ♦ CZK 410 2011*

⊞ **LIBEREC** *A2* (2km NW Rural) *50.7387, 15.1079* **Autocamping Liberec-Pavlovice, ul Letná, 460 01 Liberec [tel/fax 485 123 468; info@autocamp-liberec.cz; www.autocamp-liberec.cz]** App fr W on rte 13, take 1st exit sp town cent. Foll to rndabt; sp ahead to Pavlovice (site sp after rndabt). Site on L immed after footbdge. Med, pt shd; wc; shwrs CZK10; el pnts (10A) CZK80; lndtte; shop 200m; rest; snacks 200m; playgrnd; pool high ssn; tennis; karting track adj; dogs CZK50; quiet; red CCI. "Conv Jizerské Hory mountains." CZK 290 2009*

LIPNO NAD VLTAVOU *D2* (1km W Rural) *48.63891, 14.20880* **Autocamp Lipno Modřín, 382 78 Lipno nad Vltavou [tel 380 736 272; camp@lipnoservis.cz]** Site sp on rd 163 on lakeside. Lge, mkd pitch, unshd; wc; chem disp; shwrs CZK20; el pnts (6A); lndtte (inc dryer); shop 500m; rest; snacks; bar; playgrnd; htd pool complex 500m; lake beach & sw; boat & cycle hire 500m; tennis; games area; wifi; some statics; dogs CZK41; adv bkg; quiet. "Pleasant, popular site." ♦ 1 Apr-30 Sep. CZK 450 (CChq acc) 2009*

LITOMERICE *A2* (500m SE Urban) *50.53200, 14.13866* **Autocamping Slavoj, Střelecký Ostrov, 412 01 Litoměřice [tel 416 734 481; kemp.litomerice@post.cz; www.autokempslavojlitomerice.w1.cz]** Fr N on rd 15 N of rv make for bdge over Rv Elbe (Labe) sp Terezín; R down hill immed bef bdge (cobbled rd), L under rlwy bdge, L again, site 300m on R bef tennis courts at sports cent beside rv. Fr S on rod 15 turn L immed after x-ing rv bdge to cobbled rd. Sm, pt shd; wc; chem disp; shwrs inc; el pnts (8-16A) CZK75; supmkt 1.5km; rest; pool; tennis; some cabins; dogs CZK30; poss cr; Eng spkn; quiet but rlwy noise; CCI. "Friendly, family-run site; gd, modern san facs; vg rest; 10 mins walk town cent; Terezín ghetto & preserved concentration camp." 1 May-30 Sep. CZK 300 2010*

LITOMERICE *A2* (3km S Rural) *50.50805, 14.14305* **Autocamping Kréta, Kréta 322, 411 55 Terezín [tel 416 782 473; camp@terezin-camp.cz; http://autocamp.kreta.sweb.cz/]** Fr rd 8 (E55) Prague to Lovosice. In Terezín at L-hand bend turn R at museum & ghetto sp. Take 4th turning on R (with caution), foll camp sp at T-junc, turn L & immed R, site on R. Sm, pt shd; wc; own san; shwrs inc; el pnts CZK80; shop 200m; rest; playgrnd; watersports; some statics; dogs CZK50; quiet; CCI. "Basic site & tired facs; no privacy in unisex san facs; gd rest; ltd space for tourers; historic forts & Jewish museum in town; fair NH/sh stay when not full." 1 Apr-30 Sep. CZK 390 2010*

LITOMYSL *B3* (500m E Urban) *49.86776, 16.32440* **ATC Primátor Camping, Strakovská, 570 01 Litomyšl [tel/fax 461 612 238 or 732 148 723 (mob); primator@camplitomysl.cz; www.camplitomysl.cz]** Fr S on E442/35 turn R at sp on edge of town, site on L in 500m. Sm, some hdstg, sl, pt shd; wc; shwrs CZK10; el pnts (6A) CZK60; lndtte; shop, rest in town; playgrnd; pool & sports facs 300m; TV; 80% statics; dogs CZK45; Eng spkn; quiet but some rd noise; CCI. "Worth visit to Litomyšl - steep walk; easy (paid) parking in town sq; vg san facs; v sloping site; friendly owner." 1 May-30 Sep. CZK 230 2010*

MARIANSKE LAZNE *B1* (1.5km SE Rural) *49.94419, 12.72797* **Camping Stanowitz-Stanoviště, Stanoviště 9, 353 01 Mariánské Lázně [tel 165 624 673; info@stanowitz.com; www.stanowitz.com]** Fr Cheb on rd 215, then rd 230 dir Karlovy Vary/Bečov. Site sp on R after passing under rlwy bdge. Sm, pt sl, pt shd, some hdstg; htd wc; chem disp; mv service pnt; shwrs inc; el pnts (16A) CZK90; lndtte; shop & 3km; tradsmn; rest; snacks; bar; BBQ; TV; dogs CZK30; phone; Eng spkn; ccard not acc; CCI. "Excel CL-type site with gd rest; conv spa towns & Teplá Monastery; mkd walks in woods; helpful staff." ♦ Easter-31 Oct. CZK 370 2009*

MARIANSKE LAZNE *B1* (4km SW Rural) *49.95238, 12.66799* **Autocamping Luxor, Plzeňská ul, 354 71 Velká Hleďsebe [tel 354 623 504; autocamping.luxor@seznam.cz; www.luxor.karlovarsko.com]** Site on E side of rd 21 fr Cheb-Stříbro at S end of vill. Med, hdstg, pt sl, unshd; wc; chem disp; shwrs inc; el pnts (10A) inc; shops 1km; rest; snacks; bar; cooking facs; sm lake 100m; some cabins; dogs free; poss cr; quiet; ccard not acc; CCI. "Site in woodland clearing; gd, modern san facs; gd walking; delightful town; ground poss unrel in wet." 1 May-30 Sep. CZK 360 2009*

MLADA BOLESLAV *B2* (2km NW Urban) *50.44432, 14.91561* **Autocamp Škoda, Pod Oborou, 293 06 Kosmonosy [tel 326 724 134; fax 326 321 344; camp@skskoda.cz; www.akskoda.cz]** Fr Mladá Boleslav head N to Kosmonosy. Turn W off main rd in vill cent & foll site sp. Sm, pt sl, pt shd; wc; shwrs; el pnts inc; lndry rm; rest; cooking facs; games area; tennis; 70% statics; dogs; quiet. "Fair site; conv Škoda museum." 1 May-30 Sep. 2010*

MOHELNICE *B3* (500m W Urban) *49.78308, 16.90808* **Autocamping Morava, ul Petra Bezruče 13, 789 85 Mohelnice [tel 583 430 129; fax 583 433 011; info@atc-morava.cz; www.atc-morava.cz]** Fr E keep on D35/E442 to town boundary, turn R down rd 35. Site sp 300m on R. Lge, pt shd; wc; shwrs inc; el pnts (10A) inc; shop; rest in motel adj; snacks; bar; playgrnd; pool high ssn; tennis; cycle hire; TV rm; 20% statics; poss cr; Eng spkn; no adv bkg; quiet; red CCI. "Pleasant, well-run site; v quiet low ssn; san facs & water in motel; hourly trains to Olomouc." 15 May-15 Oct. CZK 188 2008*

⊞ **NACHOD** *B3* (8km SW Rural) *50.39866, 16.06302* **Autocamping Rozkoš, Masaryka 836, 552 03 Česká Skalice [tel 491 451 112 or 491 451 108; fax 491 452 400; atc@atcrozkos.com; www.atcrozkos.com]** On rd 33/E67 fr Náchod dir Hradec Králové, site sp 2km bef Česká Skalice on lakeside. V lge, wc; sauna; baby facs; shwrs; el pnts (16A) CZK60; lndtte; shop; rest; snacks; playgrnd; paddling pool; lake sw & beach adj; watersports; windsurfing school; cycle hire; entmnt; 10% statics; dogs CZK30; poss cr; no adv bkg; ccard acc. "Lovely countryside." ♦ CZK 290 2010*

NEPOMUK *C2* (1.2km W Rural) *49.48356, 13.53446* **Autokemping Nový Rybník, Plzeňská 456, 335 01 Nepomuk [tel 371 591 336; kemp@novyrybnik.cz; www.novyrybnik.cz]** Fr Plzeň foll E49/rd 20 twd Písek. At o'skirts of Nepomuk turn R onto rd 191 & foll sp. Med, unshd; wc; chem disp; shwrs; el pnts (10A) CZK70; lndtte; shop; tradsmn; rest; snacks; playgrnd; lake sw; tennis; boating; cycle hire; wifi; poss noisy; adv bkg; CCI. "Gd forest walks." 15 May-30 Sep. CZK 220 2010*

NETOLICE *C2* (1km S Rural) *49.03767, 14.18457* **Autocamping Podroužek, Tyršova 226, 384 11 Netolice [tel 338 324 315; post@autocamp-podrouzek.cz; www.autocamp-podrouzek.cz]** Fr Netolice cent take rd 122 dir Český Krumlov, site sp on R in 1km adj lake. Med, pt shd; wc; shwrs CZK5; el pnts CZK85; shop; lndtte; rest; snacks high ssn & in vill; playgrnd; lake sw; tennis; games area; internet; some cabins; dogs CZK25; quiet; CCI. "V quiet site; poss problematic el pnts; modern san facs; conv Kratochvile & museum of animated film - delightful." 1 May-30 Oct. CZK 220 2010*

NOVE STRASECI *B2* (4.5km W Rural) *50.17221, 13.83951* **Camping Bucek, Trtice 170, 271 01 Nové Strašecí [tel 313 564 212; info@campingbucek.cz; www.campingbucek.cz]** Site sp fr E48/rd 6, 2km S of Řevničov on lakeside & approx 40km fr Prague. Med, mkd pitch, pt sl, pt shd; wc; chem disp; mv service pnt; shwrs inc; el pnts (6A) inc; lndtte (inc dryer); shop 2km; tradsmn; rest; snacks; bar; BBQ; playgrnd; htd pool; sw & boating on adj lake; wifi; TV; dogs CZK60; Eng spkn; no adv bkg; quiet. "Helpful owner; modern san facs; gd walks in woods." 25 Apr-15 Sep. CZK 400 2009*

NYRSKO see Klatovy *C1*

OPATOV *C3* (2km S Rural) *49.20888, 15.65611* **Camping Vidlák, Jur en Lilian Vinke, C.p. 322, 675 28 Opatov na Morave [tel 736 678 687; campingvidlak@tiscali.cz; www.campingvidlak.cz]** Fr Prague foll dir Brno (E50, E55, E65), take exit 112 dir Jihlava; in Jihlava foll E59 (rd no. 38) dir Znojmo/Vienna for approx 20km; in Dlouhá Brtnice turn L after first few houses sp Opatov; in Opatov foll sp for camping. Fr S (Vienna) drive via Znojmo on the E59 (rd no. 38) dir Jihlava for approx 50km; turn R dir Třebíč (rd no. 23); in Předín turn L sp Opatov; in Opatov foll sp for camping. Sm, pt sl, pt shd; htd wc; chem disp; mv service point; shwrs inc; el pnts (10A) CZK110; lndtte; BBQ; playgrnd; lake sw; games area; internet; TV rm; dogs CZK30; bus 1.5km; Eng spkn; adv bkg; quiet; red low ssn/CCI. "Well-kept site in picturesque location nr lake; friendly, helpful Dutch owners; spacious pitches; first class san facs; bread order during summer months; special m'van pitches avail; forest walks; cycle rtes for mountain bikes; site is exceptional." ♦ 15 Apr-15 Sep. CZK 415 2011*

ORLIK NAD VLTAVOU *C2* (7km N Rural) *49.52458, 14.15563* **Camping Velký Vír, Kožlí 23, 398 07 Orlík nad Vltavou [tel 382 275 192; fax 382 275 171; obec.kozli@seznam.cz; www.velkyvir.cz]** Fr Milevsko head W on rte 19; turn N to Orlík vill; foll camp sp 7km N to Velký Vír. Med, pt sl, unshd; wc; chem disp; shwrs CZK10; el pnts (6A) CZK60; shop; rest; snacks; playgrnd; rv sw adj; tennis; some cabins; dogs CZK60; poss v cr; adv bkg; quiet; CCI. "V quiet site by rv; few el pnts & may not work." 1 May-30 Sep. CZK 310 2009*

OSECNA *A2* (1km NE Rural) *50.70428, 14.93898* **Camping 2000, Junův Důl 15, 463 52 Janův Důl [tel/fax 485 179 621; camping2000@wanadoo.nl; www.camping2000.com]** Fr Liberec on rd 35/E442 turn W sp Ještěd then Osečná. Med, mkd pitch, unshd; wc; chem disp; mv service pnt; shwrs inc; el pnts (6A) inc; lndtte (inc dryer); tradsmn; rest; snacks; bar; cooking facs; playgrnd; pool; paddling pool; waterslide; tennis; horseriding; cycle hire; wifi; TV rm; 5% statics; dogs €2.50; Eng spkn; adv bkg; quiet. "Pleasant site; conv Ještěd Mountains." ♦ 15 Apr-15 Sep. € 25.80 2011*

OSTROVACICE see Brno *C3*

CZECH REPUBLIC

⊞ **PARDUBICE** *B3* (14km E Rural) *50.08701, 15.9728* **Camping Hluboký, Podlesí 89, 534 01 Holice [tel/fax 466 682 284; camp-hluboky@iol.cz; www.camp-hluboky.cz]** Site on E side of rd 35/E442 (Holice to Hradec Králové); take rd 36, E fr Pardubice & turn onto rd 35 in Holice; site sp in 3km on R. Med, shd; htd wc; shwrs CZK10; el pnts (16A) CZK90; Indtte; shop; rest; snacks; bar; playgrnd; lake sw adj; entmnt; internet; 80% statics; dogs CZK50: poss noisy. "Site adj to lake in pine wood; popular at w/end; gd walks, rec visit old town & sq." CZK 200 2008*

PASOHLAVKY *C3* (2km E Rural) *48.89914, 16.56738* **Autocamp Merkur, 691 22 Pasohlávky [tel 519 427 714; fax 519 427 501; camp@pasohlavky.cz; www.pasohlavky.cz]** S fr Brno on E461/rd 52. After Pohořelice site 5km on R, sp. V lge, hdg/mkd pitch, pt shd; wc; chem disp; mv service pnt; shwrs; el pnts inc; Indtte; shop; rest; snacks; bar; BBQ; cooking facs; playgrnd; lake sw & beach adj; watersports; tennis; games area; cycle hire; entmnt; TV rm; some statics; dogs CZK60; phone; poss cr; Eng spkn; adv bkg; ccard acc; CCI. "Vg, secure, pleasant site." ♦ 1 Apr-31 Oct. CZK 440 2011*

PLANA *B1* (5km SW Rural) *49.82043, 12.75463* **Camping Karolina, Brod nad Tichou, 348 15 Planá [tel 777 296 990; camping@campingkarolina.com; www.campingkarolina.com]** S fr Planá on rd 21 to Brod nad Tichou, site sp 1km SE of Brod. Narr app rd. Med, pt shd; wc; chem disp; shwrs; el pnts (10A) €2.50; Indtte; snacks; bar; BBQ; playgrnd; sm pool; games area; TV; some statics; adv bkg; quiet. "Pretty site; gd walking." 1 May-15 Oct. € 15.00 (CChq acc) 2009*

PLUMLOV see Prostějov *C3*

PLZEN *B1* (4km N Rural) *49.77747, 13.39047* **Autocamping Ostende, 315 00 Plzeň-Malý Bolevec [tel/fax 377 520 194; atc-ostende@cbox.cz; www.cbox.cz/atc-ostende]** Head N fr Plzeň on rd 27 dir Kaznějov; site sp R on o'skts Plzeň. Foll minor rd over rlwy bdge & sharp R bend to site on L. Beware earlier turning off rd 27 which leads under rlwy bdge with height restriction. Med, pt sl, shd; wc; shwrs CZK20; el pnts (10A) CZK140 (poss rev pol); gas; Indtte; shop; rest; snacks; playgrnd; lake sw; beach adj; entmnt; dogs CZK70; bus to town; poss cr; Eng spkn; no adv bkg; red CCI. "Pretty, well-run site; bar/rest area untidy - needs upgrade (2009); facs poss gd walk fr c'van area - no shwr curtains; gates not locked at night (2011); cycle rte & walk around lake, site needs upgrading (2011)." 1 May-30 Sep. CZK 420 2011*

PODEBRADY *B2* (1km E Rural) *50.13549, 15.13794* **Autocamping Golf, U Nové Vodárny 428, 290 01 Poděbrady [tel 325 612 833; ATCAutokemp@gmail.com; www.kemp-golf.cz]** Fr D11/E67 (Prague/Poděbrady) take Poděbrady exit N onto rd 32 for 3km; at junc with rte 11/E67 turn W sp Poděbrady (care needed, priority not obvious); site sp on L on E edge of town; site opp town name sp 400m down lane; app fr E if poss. Med, pt shd; wc (own san rec); chem disp; shwrs inc; el pnts (long cable req); snacks; bar; lake 2km; cabins; quiet; CCI. "Conv for touring area; gd supmkt with parking in town; basic site." 1 May-31 Sep. 2010*

PRAGUE see Praha *B2*

⊞ **PRAHA** *B2* (5km N Urban) *50.11715, 14.42775* **Autocamp Trojská, Trojská 157/375, 171 00 Praha 7 [tel 233 542 945; autocamp-trojska@iol.cz; www.autocamp-trojska.cz]** Fr Plzeň (E50/D5) head into cent to rte D8/E55 sp Treplice. Foll sp N to c sp. Immed after rv x-ing take exit under rte 8 & foll camp sp & site on L. Fr Dresden on E55/D8 foll sp to Centrum. Exit just N of Vltava Rv sp Troja & zoo. R (W) fr exit ramp twd Troja & zoo, turn L at traff lts, site on L in 400m. NB: There are 5 sites adj to each other with similar names. Sm, mkd pitch, shd; wc; chem disp (wc); shwrs inc; el pnts (16A) inc; Indtte; shop; rest; snacks; cooking facs; BBQ; TV; some cabins; dogs CZK50; bus for city at ent; tram stop 500m; poss cr; adv bkg; quiet. "Friendly & welcoming; poss diff lge o'fits due trees on site; peaceful, clean & conv site; gd security." CZK 600 2010*

⊞ **PRAHA** *B2* (10km N Rural) *50.15277, 14.4506* **Camping Triocamp, Ústecká ul, Dolní Chabry, 184 00 Praha 8 [tel/fax 283 850 793; triocamp.praha@telecom.cz; www.triocamp.cz]** Fr N on D8/E55 take junc sp Zdiby, strt on at x-rds to rd 608 dir Praha. Camp sp in 2km on R just after city boundary. Med, pt sl, pt shd; wc; chem disp; mv service pnt; baby facs; shwrs inc; el pnts (6-10A) CZK90; gas; Indtte; shop; rest; snacks; bar; cooking facs; playgrnd; sw 4km; internet; 30% chalets; dogs CZK80; phone; bus/tram to city (tickets fr recep); barrier clsd at 2200; poss cr; Eng spkn; rd noise & daytime aircraft noise; ccard acc; red CCI. "Well-organised, clean, family-run site; excel facs; rec arr early; free cherries in ssn; helpful staff." ♦ CZK 730 2008*

PRAHA *B2* (10km E Urban) *50.11694, 14.42361* **Camping Sokol, Národnich Hrdinů 290, 190 12 Dolní Počernice [tel/fax 281 931 112; info@campingsokol.cz; www.campingsokol.cz]** Site sp 400m off main rd 12 to Koĺin in vill of Dolní Počernice. Med, pt shd; wc; shwrs inc; el pnts (16A) €4; Indtte (inc dryer); shop; rest; snacks; bar; cooking facs; playgrnd; paddling pool; cycle hire; wifi; some chalets; dogs €2; poss cr; Eng spkn; adv bkg; some rd noise; red long stay; ccard acc; CCI. "Friendly owners; gd, clean facs; excel meals; 1 hr to Prague by public transport." ♦ 1 Apr-31 Oct. € 25.00 2010*

PRAHA *B2* (18km E Urban) *50.09833, 14.68472* **Camping Praha Klánovice, V Jehličině 391, 190 14 Klánovice [tel 774 553 542; info@campingpraha.cz; www.campingpraha.cz]** Fr Prague ring rd exit at Běchovice onto rd 12 dir Kolin. At Újezd nad Lesy turn L at x-rds twd Klánovice & in approx 3km turn R into Šlechtitelská, site on R in approx 1km. Med, mkd pitch, pt shd; wc; chem disp; mv service pnt; sauna; shwrs inc; el pnts (16A) €4; gas; Indtte (inc dryer); shop; tradsmn; supmkt 3km; rest; snacks; bar; BBQ; playgrnd; pool; paddling pool; cycle hire; games area; games rm; cycle hire; wifi; TV; 50% statics; dogs €2; phone; bus to Prague; poss cr; Eng spkn; adv bkg; quiet; ccard acc. "New site 2010; gd public transport to city." ♦ 9 Apr-22 Oct. € 25.00 (CChq acc) 2010*

PRAHA *B2* (10km SE Urban) *50.01271, 14.51183* **Camp Prager, V Ladech 3, Šeberov, 149 00 Praha 4 [tel 244 912 854, 244 911 490 or 603 418 391 (mob); fax 244 912 854; petrgali@login.cz; www.pensioncampprague.com]** Fr W on D1/E50 fr Prague exit 2 sp Praha-Šeberov, turn L at rndabt. Fr SE fr Brno take exit 2A. After traff lts take outside lane & go strt over at next rndabt & in 700m turn R into V. Ladech. Site L in 100m. Ring bell if gate shut. Site well sp. Sm, pt shd; wc; chem disp; shwrs inc; el pnts (10A) CZK80; shops 500m; games area; games rm; wifi; dog CZK30; bus 100m; metro 1km; Eng spkn; adv bkg; quiet; CCI. "Gd, secure site in orchard; facs impeccable; helpful & friendly owner; phone ahead to check if open low ssn; flexible opening dates with adv notice; guarded park & ride facs adj Opatov metro stn; bus/metro tickets fr recep." 1 May-30 Sep. CZK 400 2011*

PRAHA *B2* (7km S Rural) *50.03254, 14.40421* **Intercamp Kotva Braník, ul Ledáren 55, 147 00 Praha 4 [tel 244 461 712; fax 244 466 110; kotva@kotvacamp.cz; www.kotvacamp.cz]** Site well sp fr main rd fr Plzeň & fr S ring rd. Med, unshd; wc; shwrs inc; el pnts (10A) inc; Indtte; shop & 500m; snacks; cooking facs; boating; fishing; tennis; games area; wifi; some cabins; poss cr; Eng spkn; adv bkg; some rlwy/rd/airport noise; no ccard acc; red CCI. "Conv Prague - buy tram tickets fr recep; tents & vans pitched v close; 26 steps to wc; site guarded." 1 Apr-31 Oct. 2009*

PRAHA *B2* (12km S Rural) *49.95155, 14.47455* **Camping Oase, Zlatníky 47, 252 41 Dolní Břežany [tel 241 932 044; info@campingoase.cz; www.campingoase.cz]** Fr Prague on D1 (Prague-Brno). Exit 11 (Jesenice). Head twd Jesenice on rd 101. In vill turn R then immed L at rndabt dir Zlatníky. At Zlatníky rndabt turn L dir Libeň, site in 500m. Beware 'sleeping policemen' on final app. Med, pt shd; htd wc; chem disp; mv service pnt; fam bthrm; serviced pitches; sauna; shwrs inc; el pnts (6A) inc (poss rev pol); gas; Indtte (inc dryer); shop; tradsmn; rest; snacks; bar; cooking facs; BBQ; playgrnd; 2 pools (1 htd covrd); paddling pool; fishing lake 1km; horseriding; cycle hire; games area; games rm; wifi; entmnt; sat TV rm; dogs CZK50; no c'vans/m'vans over 12m high ssn; phone; bus, tram to city; metro 10km; Eng spkn; adv bkg; quiet; ccard acc (discount for cash); red low ssn/senior citizens. "Lovely site; v helpful owners; excel, clean san facs; vg pool; swipe card for barrier & all chargeable amenities; well-guarded; bus/train/metro tickets fr recep; rec use metro Park & Ride to city." ♦ 28 Apr-15 Sep. CZK 650 SBS - X07 2011*

PRAHA *B2* (15km S Rural) *49.93277, 14.37294* **Camp Matyáš, U Elektrárny, 252 46 Vrané nad Vltavou [tel 257 761 228; fax 257 761 154; campmatyas@centrum.cz; www.camp-matyas.com]** Exit D1 junc 11 onto rd 101 to Dolní Břežany. Turn S thro Ohrobec & foll sp Vrané nad Vltavou, site sp on rvside. Or S fr Prague on rd 4/102, cross Rv Vltava at Zbraslav to Dolní Břežany, then as above. Med, pt shd; wc; chem disp; mv service pnt; shwrs inc; el pnts (10A) CZK110; Indtte; shop & 800m; tradsmn; rest; snacks; bar; cooking facs; playgrnd; paddling pool; rv sw & fishing adj; wifi; 2% statics; dogs free; bus, train to city; Eng spkn; adv bkg; quiet; red low ssn; CCI. "In lovely location; friendly owners; train & tram service to Prague (1 hr); boat trips on Rv Vltava." 20 Apr-30 Sep. CZK 600 2010*

⊞ **PRAHA** *B2* (2km SW Urban) *50.05583, 14.41361* **Caravan Camping Praha, Císařská Louka 162, Smíchov, 150 00 Praha 5 [tel 257 317 555; fax 257 318 763; info@caravancamping.cz; www.caravancamping.cz]** Foll dir as for Prague Yacht Club Caravan Park. This site just bef on R, look for lge yellow tower. Sm, unshd; wc; chem disp; shwrs inc; el pnts CZK95; Indtte; shop; rest; snacks; poss v cr; Eng spkn; quiet; CCI. "V helpful staff; busy sh stay site on island; conv for Prague cent metro - St Wenceslas Sq 15/20mins." CZK 545 2008*

⊞ **PRAHA** *B2* (2km SW Urban) *50.05194, 14.40222* **Praha Yacht Club Caravan Park, Cisařská Louka 599, Smíchov, 150 00 Praha 5 [tel 257 318 681 or 060 2343701 (mob); fax 257 318 387; convoy@volny.cz; www.volny.cz/convoy]** Fr E50 access only poss fr S by travelling N on W side of rv. After complex junc (care needed), turn sharp R bef Shell petrol stn to Cisařská Island, foll rd to end. Nr Caravan Camping CSK. Diff app fr N due no L turns on Strakonická. Sm, pt shd; wc; chem disp; shwrs CZK20; el pnts (16A) inc; shops 1.5km across rv; rest, snacks, bar high ssn; pool 1km; tennis 100m; dogs CZK53; poss v cr; adv bkg; quiet; ccard acc. "Boats for hire; launch trips on rv; 1 minute to ferry & metro to Prague; water taxi fr Prague, book at site recep; helpful staff; friendly, secure site; v basic san facs; excel location; views of city; milk etc avail fr Agip petrol stn on Strakonická." CZK 564 2010*

⊞ **PRAHA** *B2* (5km SW Rural) *50.01984, 14.35579* **Camping Auto Servis Slivenic, Ke Smíchovu 25, 154 00 Slivenec-Praha 5 [tel/fax 251 817 442; info@camp-autoservis.cz; www.camp-autoservis.cz]** App Prague fr E on E50, turn R into Slivenec, Turn R in vill after pond immed bef shop. Sm, sl, shd; htd wc; chem disp; shwrs; el pnts (10A) inc; Indtte; rest; tram to city; quiet. "Site in garden - recep at back of house; facs old/sparse but clean; sm pitches; conv city cent." CZK 380 2011*

PRAHA *B2* (10km SW Rural) *50.04388, 14.28416* **Camp Drusus, Třebonice 4, 155 00 Praha 5 [tel/fax 235 514 391; drusus@drusus.com; www.drusus.com]** Fr Plzeň take E50/D5 to exit 1/23 Třebonice, then E50 dir Brno. Fr Brno exit E50/D5 at junc 19 sp ŘŘeporyje, site in 2km, sp. Sm, sl, unshd; wc; chem disp; mv service pnt; shwrs CZK20; el pnts (10A) CZK90; gas; Indtte (inc dryer); shop 1.5km; rest; bar; playgrnd; internet; TV; dogs free; 10% statics; bus; Eng spkn; adv bkg; ccard acc; red low ssn/CCI. "Reg bus service to Prague nrby - tickets fr site; owner v helpful." 1 Apr-15 Oct. CZK 540 2011*

⊞ **PRAHA** *B2* (15km SW Urban) *50.03944, 14.31305* **Sunny Camp, Smíchovská ul 1989, Stodůlky, 155 00 Praha 5 [tel/fax 251 625 774; sunny-camp@post.cz; www.sunny-camp.cz]** Fr E50 take Stodůlky & Řeporyje exit (Ikea), in 2.5km turn R at g'ge & foll site sp. Med, pt sl, pt shd; htd wc; chem disp; mv service pnt; shwrs inc; el pnts (16A) CZK70; gas; Indry facs; shop & 500m; tradsmn; rest; snacks; bar; wifi; TV; dogs free; metro 500m; poss v cr; Eng spkn; quiet; ccard acc; red CCI. "Conv metro, bus, tram to city - ticket fr recep; v clean facs but ltd; units v close together, gd security 24 hrs; excel rest; helpful owner & family." ♦ CZK 710 2011*

PRAHA *B2* (3km W Rural) *50.09890, 14.33569* **Camping Džbán, Nad Lávkou 5, Vokovice, 160 05 Praha 6 [tel 235 359 006; fax 235 351 365; info@campdzban.eu; www.campdzban.eu]** Exit 28 off ring rd onto rd 7 Chomutov-Prague; site approx 4km after airport twd Prague; at traff lts on brow of hill just bef Esso stn on L turn L; take 2nd L & strt on for 600m; site adj go-kart racing. Lge, pt sl, unshd; wc; chem disp; shwrs inc; el pnts (10A) CZK90; Indtte; shop & 2km; rest; snacks; bar; pool & lake 500m; tennis; games area; wifi; dogs CZK60; tram 200m; poss cr; some Eng spkn; ccard acc; red CCI. "Tram direct to Prague (Republic Sq) 25 mins, tickets at bureau; gd security; long way bet shwrs & wcs; san facs old but clean; communal male shwrs; narr pitches." 1 May-30 Sep. CZK 550 2010*

PRAHA *B2* (3km W Urban) *50.06730, 14.34681* **University Sporting Klub (USK) Camping, Plzeňska, 150 00 Praha 5 [tel/fax 257 215 084; caravancamp@uskprague.cz; www.caravancampprague.cz]** Fr D5/E50 Plzeň-Praha m'way, foll sp 'Centrum-Motol'. Head for Centrum & turn R at traff lts into Plzeňska, pass golf club, site on R in 600m. Med, pt sl, pt shd; wc; chem disp; mv service pnt; shwrs; el pnts (10A) CZK120; rest; bar; pool high ssn; TV; dogs CZK60; phone; tram 100m; Eng spkn; adv bkg; some tram noise; CCI. "No. 9 tram fr site to Wencelas Sq; fair site." 1 Apr-31 Oct. CZK 730 2008*

⊞ **PRAHA** *B2* (5km NW Urban) *50.11694, 14.42361* **Camping Sokol Trója, Trojská 171a, 171 00 Praha 7 [tel/fax 233 542 908 or 283 850 486; info@camp-sokol-troja.cz; www.camp-sokol-troja.cz]** Fr Pilsen (E50/D5) head into cent to rte D8/E55 sp Treplice. Foll N to Trója sp. Immed after rv x-ing take exit under rte 8 & foll camp sp & site on L 100m past Autocamp Trojská. Fr Dresden on E55/D8 foll sp to Centrum to Trója exit on R, foll camping sp. NB: There are 5 sites adj to each other with similar names. Best app fr Treplice. Med, some hdstg, pt shd; wc; shwrs inc; el pnts (10A) CZK150; Indry service; shop high ssn; rest; snacks; bar; internet; dogs CZK50; poss cr; ccard acc; noise fr bar; red CCI. "Easy tram transport to city; Trója Palace & zoo 1km; v helpful owner; bar & rest gd value." CZK 540 2010*

PROSTEJOV *C3* (8km W Rural) *49.46265, 17.01391* **Autocamping Žralok, Rudé Armády 302, 798 03 Plumlov [tel/fax 582 393 209; atczralok@seznam.cz; www.camp-zralok.cz]** Fr cent of Prostějov foll sp to Boskovice & thro Čechovice & Plumlov, site clearly sp. Down steep narr lane, cross dam & R to site. Med, sl, unshd; wc; shwrs inc; el pnts (10A) CZK90; long cable req; shop; rest; snacks; paddling pool; 20% statics; dogs CZK25; quiet; CCI. "Overlkng lake; facs basic but clean." 1 May-30 Sep. CZK 245 2008*

PROTIVIN *C2* (400m S Rural) *49.19038, 14.21723* **Camping Blanice, Celčického 889, 398 11 Protivín [tel 721 589 125; info@campingblanice.nl; www.campingblanice.nl]** Fr E49 take 1st exit Protivin going N or 2nd exit going S. Site sp bef town cent. Sm, mkd pitch, pt shd; wc; chem disp; mv service pnt; shwrs inc; el pnts (8-16A) €3-4.50; Indtte (inc dryer); shop 500m; rest; snacks; bar; rv sw adj; wifi; 5% chalets; dogs free; train 1km; Eng spkn; adv bkg; quiet but some rlwy noise. "Friendly, peaceful Dutch-run site; easy walk thro fields beside rv into town." 1 Apr-1 Nov. € 19.50 2010*

⊞ **REJSTEJN** *C1* (500m NW Rural) *49.14222, 13.51344* **Camping Klášterský Mlýn, Klášterský Mlýn 9, 341 92 Rejštejn [tel 376 582 833; info@klasterskymlyn.nl; www.klasterskymlyn.nl]** S fr Susice on rd 169 dir Kašperské Hory for 12 km. In Kašperské Hory turn L onto rd 145 to Rejštejn. In Rejštejn take 1st R, cross bdge & foll site sp. Med, mkd pitch, pt shd; htd wc; chem disp; baby facs; fam bthrm; sauna; shwrs; el pnts (6-16A) CZK100; Indtte; shop; rest; snacks; bar; cooking facs; playgrnd; tennis; games area; cycle hire; fitness rm; wifi; some statics; dogs CZK50; quiet. "Friendly, family-run, renovated site; gd, modern facs; gd touring base." CZK 300 (CChq acc) 2009*

ROZNOV POD RADHOSTEM *C4* (1km E Rural) *49.46654, 18.16376* **Camping Rožnov, Radhošťská 940, 756 61 Rožnov pod Radhoštěm [tel 571 648 001; fax 571 620 513; info@camproznov.cz; www.camproznov.cz]** On rd 35/E442; on E o'skts of Rožnov on N of rd 200m past ent to Camping Sport, take L fork opp Benzina petrol stn (site sp obscured by lamp post). Med, pt shd; htd wc; chem disp; shwrs inc; el pnts (16A) inc; Indtte (inc dryer); shop; tradsmn; rest 300m; snacks; playgrnd; htd pool; tennis; 60% statics; phone; some Eng spkn; no adv bkg; quiet; ccard acc; red CCI. "Welcoming; gd cooking & washing facs; pitches v close together, but annexe has more space (extra charge); basic, worn san facs; nr open-air museum (clsd Mon); gd walking cent; cycle to town thro park." 1 Apr-15 Oct. € 16.45 (CChq acc) 2011*

ROZNOV POD RADHOSTEM *C4* (1km E Rural) *49.46555, 18.1613* **Camping Sport, Pod Strání 2268, 756 61 Rožnov pod Radhoštěm [tel 571 648 011; fax 571 648 012; kempsport-tjroznov@wo.cz; www.beskydy-valassko.cz/tj-roznov]** On E442/rd 35 heading E, about 500m thro vill of Rožnov pod Radhoštěm on R. Sp nr Camping Rožnov & adj Hotel Stadion. Lge, pt shd; wc; chem disp; shwrs inc; el pnts (10A) CZK90; Indtte; shop; rest in hotel on site; snacks; playgrnd; 3 pools; tennis; horseriding; fishing; no dogs; quiet; red CCI. "Gd NH." 15 Jun-15 Sep. CZK 315 2008*

SADOV see Karlovy Vary *B1*

SLOUP see Boskovice *C3*

SOBESLAV *C2* (3km S Rural) *49.22988, 14.72062* **Autocamp Karvánky, Jirásková 407/2, 392 01 Soběslav [tel 381 521 003; fax 381 522 011; karvanky@post.cz; www.karvanky.cz]** Site well sp on rte 3/E55. Lge, pt sl, pt shd; wc; shwrs CZK25; el pnts (10A) CZK90; snacks; playgrnd; lake sw; cycle hire; TV; 10% statics; dogs CZK60; phone; rd noise; ccard acc. "Conv NH." 15 May-27 Sep. CZK 170 2009*

⊞ **SPINDLERUV MLYN** *A3* (1.5km N Rural) *50.73566, 15.6072* **Autocamping Správy Krnap, 543 51 Špindlerův Mlýn [tel 499 523 534; fax 499 433 369; tesspindl@quick.cz; www.krnap.cz]** N on rd 295 fr Špindlerův Mlýn, site sp fr town. Med, hdstg, pt shd; htd wc; chem disp; mv service pnt; shwrs CZK20; el pnts (10A) inc; Indtte; shop 1km; rest; snacks; bar; cooking facs; lake sw 4km; skilift 100m; some statics; dogs; phone; bus; poss cr; Eng spkn; adv bkg (bkg fee); quiet; CCI. "Site in Krkonošský National Park; vg waymkd walks; vg downhill & x-country skiing." ♦ € 13.00 2008*

SRNI *C1* (5km SE Rural) *49.05764, 13.51206* **Autokemp Antýgl, Srní 97, 341 92 Kašperské Hory [tel 376 599 331]** S fr Sušice on rte 169 dir Modrava. In Srní bear L in vill uphill to site. Med, pt sl, unshd; wc; own san; shwrs CZK10; el pnts (5-10A) CZK80 (long lead poss req); shop; tradsmn; rest; snacks; bar; cooking facs inc; dogs; phone; bus; quiet. "Lovely site; san facs basic but clean; excel base for walking & cycling; gd fishing." 5 May-5 Oct. CZK 240 2008*

I'll fill in a report online and let the Club know – www.caravanclub.co.uk/europereport

This is a wonderful site.

STAHLAVY *B1* (2.5km SE Rural) *49.66392, 13.53704* **Hotel Hájek & Camping, Štáhlavice 158, 332 03 Štáhlavy [tel 377 969 369; fax 377 969 135; info@hajek.cz; www.hajek.cz]** Fr E49 S of Plzen foll sp Starý Plzenec, then Štáhlavy. In vill turn L & cont to Štáhlavice. Site sp turn R & immed R then 4km thro woods. Site ent on L thro main gate Areál Hájek hotel. Recep in hotel. Sm, pt sl, pt shd; wc; chem disp (wc); shwrs inc; el pnts CZK200; rest; bar; tennis; games area; 30% statics; dogs CZK50; Eng spkn; quiet. "Lovely site in deep woodland; gd walking & cycling." CZK 390 2008*

STERNBERK *B3* (2km N Rural) *49.74800, 17.30641* **Autocamping Šternberk, Dolní Žleb, 785 01 Šternberk [tel 585 011 300; info@campsternberk.cz; www.campsternberk.cz]** Fr Olomouc take rte 46 to Šternberk. At Šternberk go thro town cent & foll sp Dalov, site just bef vill of Dolní Žleb. Or circumnavigate to W on rds 444 & 445, site sp. Med, pt shd; wc; chem disp; shwrs inc; el pnts (10A) CZK60 (poss rev pol); lndtte; shop & 500m; rest 500m; snacks; bar; cooking facs; playgrnd; lake 1km; TV; phone; 30% statics; dogs CZK30; poss cr; adv bkg; quiet; red CCI. "Gd, clean facs even when full; helpful staff." 15 May-15 Sep. CZK 190 2010*

STRMILOV *C2* (1km S Rural) *49.14956, 15.20890* **Autokemp Komorník, 378 53 Strmilov [tel 384 392 468; recepce@autokempkomornik.cz; www.autokempkomornik.cz]** Sp fr rd 23 at Strmilov. Lge, pt sl, pt shd; wc; chem disp (wc); shwrs CZK20; el pnts (10A) CZK60 (long lead rec); shop; rest; snacks; bar; BBQ; playgrnd; lake & sand beach adj; 20% statics; quiet; CCI. "V pleasant setting by lake; clean, modern san facs; gd rest & bar; conv Telč & Slavonice historic towns." ♦ 1 Jun-15 Sep. CZK 300 2009*

⊞ **TABOR** *C2* (5km E Rural) *49.40985, 14.73157* **Autocamping & Hotel Knížecí Rybník, Měšice 399, 39156 Tábor [tel 381 252 546; knizecak@seznam.cz; www.knizecirybnik.cz]** On N side of rd 19 fr Tábor to Jihlava, in woods by lake adj hotel. Lge, hdg/mkd pitch, pt shd; wc; shwrs CZK20; el pnts (6-10A) inc; lndtte; shop & 3km; rest; snacks; bar; lake sw & beach adj; fishing; tennis; some statics; dogs; poss cr; rd noise; ccard acc; CCI. "Pleasant, lakeside site; modern san facs." CZK 280 2010*

⊞ **TANVALD** *A2* (2km W Rural) *50.74205, 15.28269* **Camping Tanvaldská Kotlina (Tanvald Hollow), Pod Špičákem 650, 46841 Tanvald [tel 483 311 928; kotlina@tanvald.cz; www.tanvald.cz]** Fr S on rte 10, in cent Tanvald at rndabt turn foll sp Desnou & Harrachov. In 500m take L fork under rlwy bdge, then immed turn L & foll rd past hospital. Turn R bef tennis courts, site in 600m. Sm, pt shd; wc; chem disp; mv service pnt; shwrs; el pnts CZK30 + metered; lndtte; rest; BBQ; cooking facs; playgrnd; pool in town; games area; entmnt; dogs CZK20; quiet - occasional motor cycle trials nrby. "Excel site." CZK 190 2009*

TELC *C2* (7km NW Rural) *49.20250, 15.38444* **Camping Javořice, Pension Javořice, Lhotka 10, 58856 Telč [tel 567 317 111; fax 567 317 516; info@javorice.cz; www.javorice.cz]** Fr Telč foll rd 23 W to Mrákotin & turn R in vill twd Lhotka. Turn L in cent of Lhotka & foll sp to site. Sm, pt sl, terr, pt shd; htd wc; chem disp; shwrs inc; el pnts CZK50; shop nr; BBQ; cooking facs; no statics; dogs CZK20; bus in vill; Eng spkn; adv bkg; quiet; CCI. "Delightful sm site in old orchard; v peaceful; poss diff for lge o'fits due terrs; B&B in main house; Telč stunning." 15 May-30 Sep. CZK 220 2008*

⊞ **TELC** *C2* (10km NW Rural) *49.22785, 15.38442* **Camp Velkopařezitý, Řásná 10, 58856 Mrákotín [tel 567 379 449; fax 567 243 719; campvelkoparezity@tiscali.cz; www.campvelkoparezity.cz]** Exit Telč on Jihlava rd; turn L in 300m (sp) & foll sp to site beyond Rásná. Well sp fr Telč. Steep site ent. Sm, pt sl, pt shd; wc; chem disp; shwrs; el pnts CZK100; rest; shop; beach 1km; some statics; dogs CZK30; poss cr. "Friendly atmosphere; poor san facs; gd walking & cycling; Telć wonderful World Heritage site." CZK 270 2010*

TEPLICE NAD METUJI *A3* (2km W Rural) *50.60006, 16.15151* **Camping Bučnice, Dolní Adršpach 104, 54957 Teplice nad Metují [tel 447 581 387; kubik.vladimir@seznam.cz; www.autokemp.wz.cz]** N fr Náchod on rte 303 to Police, rd sp Teplice. Site 2km beyond Teplice on rd to Adršpach. Med, unshd; wc; chem disp; shwrs inc; el pnts CZK30; lndtte; shops 1km; rest 300m; cooking facs; lake sw 1km; sailing; fishing; quiet; red CCI. "Ideal for visiting Adršpach Rocks." 1 May-30 Sep. CZK 230 2008*

TEREZIN **see Litoměřice** *A2*

TREBIC *C3* (1.5km W Urban) *49.21671, 15.85904* **Autocamping Třebíč-Poušov, Poušov 849, 67401 Třebíč [tel 568 850 641]** Foll sp for Telč fr town cent. After 3km turn R after 2nd rlwy x-ing, site at bottom of hill. Sm, pt shd; own san rec; shwrs CZK20; el pnts inc; lndry rm; shop 1km; snacks; bar; cooking facs; some statics; dogs; adv bkg; quiet, some rd noise; CCI. "Excel san facs; cycle rte to town along rv." 1 Jun-30 Sep. CZK 300 2009*

TREBON *C2* (5km SE Rural) *48.96432, 14.93705* **Camping Sever, 37804 Chlum u Třeboně [tel/fax 384 797 189; post@campsever.cz; www.campsever.cz]** S fr Třeboň on E49 dir Vienna, turn L in 5km to Chlum u Třeboně. Site sp thro vill on N side of lake. Med, pt sl, pt shd; wc; chem disp; mv service pnt; shwrs CZK10; el pnts (6A) CZK60; Indtte; shop 300m; tradsmn; rest 300m; snacks; bar; playgrnd; lake sw; fishing; canoeing; games area; cycle hire; golf 15km; wifi; 20% statics; dogs CZK20; phone; bus; adv bkg; quiet; ccard acc; red CCI. "Lovely situation; excel value site; basic san facs; gd touring base; excel cycling, walking." 9 Apr-31 Oct. CZK 280 2010*

TREBON *C2* (1km S Rural) *48.99263, 14.76753* **Autocamp Třeboňsky Ráj, Domanin 285, 37901 Třeboň [tel/fax 384 722 586; info@autocamp-trebon.cz; www.autocamp-trebon.cz]** Exit town by rd 155 sp Borovany heading SW. Site on L just past lake. Med, pt sl, pt shd; wc; shwrs CZK10; el pnts (6A) CZK45 (long cable req & poss rev pol); Indtte; shop; rest; snacks; bar; cooking facs; playgrnd; lake sw; cycle hire; entmnt; internet; some cabins; dogs CZK50; quiet; CCI. "Attractive unspoilt town; helpful owner; facs stretched when site full; communal shwrs; insect repellant rec; gd cycle paths; gd rest on site." 25 Apr-30 Sep. CZK 320 2008*

TURNOV *A2* (5km SE Rural) *50.5580, 15.1867* **Autocamping Sedmihorky, Sedmihorky 72, 51101 Turnov [tel 481 389 162; fax 481 389 160; camp@campsedmihorky.cz; www.campsedmihorky.cz]** Fr rte 35/E442 fr Turnov. Turn SW over rlwy x-ing at camping sp S of Sedmihorky. 300m along ave take 1st R. Lge, pt sl, pt shd; wc; chem disp; shwrs CZK10; el pnts (10A) CZK60; Indtte; shop; rest; snacks; bar; playgrnd; lake sw; cycle hire; dogs CZK50; phone; poss cr; Eng spkn; quiet; ccard acc; CCI. "V beautiful site in National Park, sometimes called Bohemian Paradise; v busy site high ssn; dep bef 1000 otherwise charge for extra day." ♦ 1 Apr-31 Oct. CZK 410 2010*

UHERSKE HRADISTE *C4* (10km W Rural) *49.08505, 17.34563* **Camping Smraďavka, Tyršova 801, 687 08 Buchlovice [tel 572 595 367]** Fr Uherské take E50 W for 10km to Buchlovice. Site sp on L. Med, mkd pitch, pt sl, pt shd; wc (own san rec); shwrs inc; el pnts CZK40; shop; rest 300m; cooking facs; lake sw; fishing; watersports; some statics; dogs; Eng spkn; poss noisy w/end; CCI. "Tricky ent; conv for Buchlovice Château & monastery; steep walk to facs; ltd san facs low ssn; fair NH." 1 May-30 Sep. CZK 160 2008*

UHERSKE HRADISTE *C4* (10km NW Rural) *49.1186, 17.38038* **Autocamping Velehrad, Velehrad 31, 68706 Velehrad [tel 572 571 183]** Foll rd 428 to Velehrad, site 1km N of vill. Sm, pt sl, pt shd; wc; shwrs inc; el pnts (10A) CZK30; Indtte; shop 1km; rest; bar; playgrnd; tennis; dogs CZK10; adv bkg; CCI. "Well sp cycle & hiking routes; Velehrad interesting vill; NH only." 1 May-30 Sep. CZK 200 2009*

UHERSKY BROD *C4* (10km E Urban) *49.04034, 17.79993* **Eurocamping Bojkovice, Stefánikova, 68771 Bojkovice [tel/fax 572 641 717; info@eurocamping.cz; www.eurocamping.cz]** Off E50 at Uherský Brod turn onto rd 495. Find rlwy stn at Bojkovice on rd 495 at SW end of town. Cross rlwy at NE (town) end of stn & foll sp round L & R turns to site. Med, pt sl, terr, pt shd; wc; chem disp; shwrs inc; el pnts (6A) inc; Indry rm; shop; tradsmn; rest; snacks; bar; cooking facs; playgrnd; pool high ssn; paddling pool; games area; entmnt; dogs CZK50; adv bkg; poss noisy. "Gd walking area." 1 May-30 Sep. CZK 520 2008*

VELEHRAD see Uherské Hradiště *C4*

VELESIN *C2* (4km W Rural) *48.83558, 14.40857* **Guesthouse Rajka, Mojné 7, 38232 Velesin [tel/fax 380 743 855; info@guesthouserajka.com; www.guesthouserajka.com]** S fr České Budějovice on rd 3/E55, turn onto rd 155 dir Římov, foll sp Mojné & Guesthouse. Sm, pt sl, pt shd; wc; chem disp (wc); shwrs inc; el pnts (4A) CZK90; Indtte; shop, bar 1km; lake sw 4km; 60% statics; dogs; phone; Eng spkn; adv bkg; quiet. "Site on a farm; excel touring base." 1 Jun-30 Sep. CZK 440 2008*

VRANE NAD VLTAVOU see Praha *B2*

⊞ **VRCHLABI** *A3* (300m E Rural) *50.62406, 15.64056* **Euro Air Camp, 54311 Vrchlabí [tel 499 421 292 or 603 235 743 (mob); fax 499 422 179; info@euro-air-camp.cz; www.euro-air-camp.cz]** E of Vrchlabí on rd 14, site close to airfield. Med, mkd pitch, pt sl, pt shd; htd wc; chem disp; mv service pnt; baby facs; shwrs inc; el pnts (16A) inc; Indtte; shop; rest; snacks; bar; cooking facs; playgrnd; pool high ssn; lake fishing; tennis 200m; wifi; dogs; Eng spkn; adv bkg; quiet; ccard acc; red low ssn/CCI. "Nr Giant Mountains & Polish border; facs dated but clean; friendly, helpful owners; gd walking; gliding fr adj grass strip." ♦ € 16.45 2010*

⊞ **VRCHLABI** *A3* (1.5km S Rural) *50.61036, 15.60263* **Holiday Park Liščí Farma, Dolní Branná 350, 54362 Vrchlabí [tel 499 421 473; fax 499 421 656; info@liscifarma.cz; www.liscifarma.cz]** S fr Vrchlabí on rd 295, site sp. Lge, mkd pitch, pt shd; htd wc; chem disp; mv service pnt; sauna; private bthrms avail; shwrs inc; el pnts (6A) inc; Indtte; shop 500m; tradsmn; rest; bar; cooking facs; playgrnd; pool high ssn; canoeing; tennis; games area; cycle hire; horseriding 2km; golf 5km; entmnt; TV; dogs CZK90; adv bkg; quiet; ccard acc. ♦ CZK 640 2009*

ZAMBERK *B3* (1km E Urban) *50.08638, 16.47527* **Autocamping Jan Kulhanek, U koupaliště, 564 01 Žamberk [tel 465 614 755; kemp@orlicko.cz; www.autocamping.cz]** Fr Zamberk centre on rd 11, foll sp. Sm, pt shd; wc; shwrs; el pnt (16A) CZK70; Indtte; shop 1km; rest, snacks & bar 200m at sports centre; cooking facs; playgrnd, pool, games area, games rm at sports centre; TV rm; 50% statics; wifi; dogs CZK50; phone; bus adj; train 1km; Eng spkn; quiet; CCI. "Site is part of sports centre & aqua park with many diff facs inc mini-golf, volleyball & bowling; site leaflet avail at recep showing town plans with supmkts & info office; gd site." 01 Apr-31 Oct. CZK 241 2011*

ZDAR NAD SAZAVOU *C3* (3km N Rural) *49.58908, 15.92825* **Camping Pilák, Cerum, 59102 Žďár nad Sázavou [tel 566 623 267; fax 566 625 086; remarova@cerum.cz; www.cerum.cz]** N fr Žďár on rd 37. In 3km bear L where main rd bears R. Turn L (sp) pass Tálský Mlýn Hotel, cross narr bdge & foll tarmac rd for 1km thro woods to clearing. Med, sl, pt shd; wc; shwrs; el pnts (16A) CZK50; shops 3km; rest 1km in hotel; cooking facs; cycle hire; few cabins; dogs CZK20; phone; CCI. "Lakeside site; UNESCO protected pilgrim church & monastery Zelená Hora nrby; poss security problems, open to general public." 1 May-30 Sep. CZK 150 2008*

ZNOJMO *C3* (7km N Rural) *48.92018, 16.02588* **Camping Country, 67152 Hluboké Mašůvky [tel/fax 515 255 249; camping-country@cbox.cz; www.camp-country.com]** N fr Znojmo on E59/38 4km; turn E on 408 to Přímětice; then N on 361 4km to Hluboké Mašůvky. Sharp turn into site fr S. Med, sl, pt shd; wc; chem disp; shwrs inc; el pnts (16A) CZK80 (long lead poss req); Indtte; shop 500m; rest in ssn; playgrnd; sm pool; tennis; lake sw 1km; cycle hire; horseriding; TV rm; 20% cabins; dogs CZK50; phone 500m; Eng spkn; quiet; no ccard acc; red CCI. "Gd, clean, well-manicured site; v helpful owner & family; not easy to find level pitch; excel meals." ♦ 1 May-30 Oct. CZK 410 2009*

CZECH REPUBLIC

Distances are shown in kilometres and are calculated from town/city centres along the most practical roads, although not necessarily taking the shortest route. 1km = 0.62miles

Caravan Europe 1
Caravan Europe 2

Klatovy to Tábor = 119km

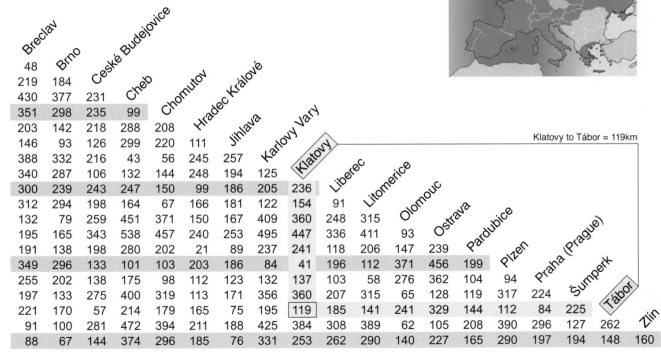

	Breclav	Brno	Ceské Budejovice	Cheb	Chomutov	Hradec Králové	Jihlava	Karlovy Vary	Klatovy	Liberec	Litomerice	Olomouc	Ostrava	Pardubice	Plzen	Praha (Prague)	Šumperk	Tábor	Zlín
Brno	48																		
Ceské Budejovice	219	184																	
Cheb	430	377	231																
Chomutov	351	298	235	99															
Hradec Králové	203	142	218	288	208														
Jihlava	146	93	126	299	220	111													
Karlovy Vary	388	332	216	43	56	245	257												
Klatovy	340	287	106	132	144	248	194	125											
Liberec	300	239	243	247	150	99	186	205	236										
Litomerice	312	294	198	164	67	166	181	122	154	91									
Olomouc	132	79	259	451	371	150	167	409	360	248	315								
Ostrava	195	165	343	538	457	240	253	495	447	336	411	93							
Pardubice	191	138	198	280	202	21	89	237	241	118	206	147	239						
Plzen	349	296	133	101	103	203	186	84	41	196	112	371	456	199					
Praha (Prague)	255	202	138	175	98	112	123	132	137	103	58	276	362	104	94				
Šumperk	197	133	275	400	319	113	171	356	360	207	315	65	128	119	317	224			
Tábor	221	170	57	214	179	165	75	195	119	185	141	241	329	144	112	84	225		
Zlín	91	100	281	472	394	211	188	425	384	308	389	62	105	208	390	296	127	262	
Znojmo	88	67	144	374	296	185	76	331	253	262	290	140	227	165	290	197	194	148	160

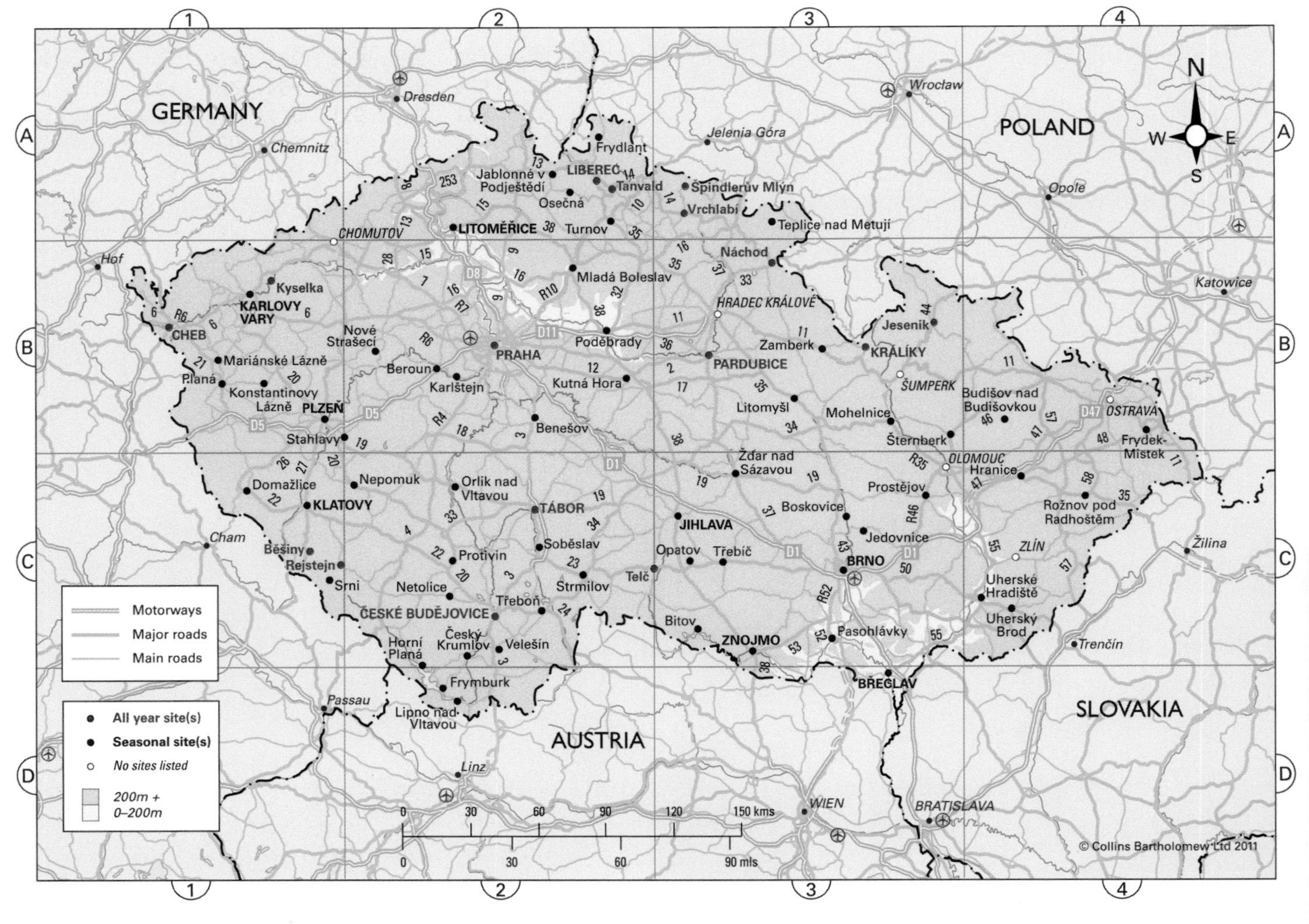

GERMANY
POLAND
SLOVAKIA
AUSTRIA
N
W
E
S
Dresden
Chemnitz
Hof
Cham
Passau
Linz
WIEN
BRATISLAVA
Wrocław
Opole
Katowice
Jelenia Góra
Žilina
Trenčín
CHEB
Planá
Mariánské Lázně
Konstantinovy Lázně
KARLOVY VARY
Kyselka
CHOMUTOV
Nové Strašecí
PLZEŇ
Stahlavy
Domažlice
KLATOVY
Běšiny
Rejstejn
Srni
Nepomuk
Beroun
Karlštejn
PRAHA
LITOMĚŘICE
Jablonné v Podještědí
LIBEREC
Frydlant
Tanvald
Osečná
Turnov
Mladá Boleslav
Poděbrady
Kutná Hora
Benešov
Orlik nad Vltavou
Protivin
Netolice
ČESKÉ BUDĚJOVICE
Horní Planá
Český Krumlov
Frymburk
Lipno nad Vltavou
Velešín
Třeboň
TÁBOR
Soběslav
Strmilov
Telč
Opatov
JIHLAVA
Třebíč
Bitov
ZNOJMO
Špindlerův Mlýn
Vrchlabí
Teplice nad Metují
Náchod
HRADEC KRÁLOVÉ
PARDUBICE
Zamberk
Litomyšl
Žďar nad Sázavou
Boskovice
BRNO
Jedovnice
Pasohlávky
BŘECLAV
Prostějov
Mohelnice
KRÁLÍKY
Jeseník
ŠUMPERK
Šternberk
OLOMOUC
Hranice
Budišov nad Budišovkou
OSTRAVA
Frydek-Mistek
Rožnov pod Radhoštěm
ZLÍN
Uherské Hradiště
Uherský Brod
Motorways
Major roads
Main roads
All year site(s)
Seasonal site(s)
No sites listed
200m +
0–200m
150 kms
90 mls
© Collins Bartholomew Ltd 2011

Denmark

Country Introduction

© iStockphoto.com/Jet Chen Tan

Copenhagen

Population (approx): 5.5 million

Capital: Copenhagen (population approx 1.8 million)

Area: 43,094 sq km (excl Faroe Islands and Greenland)

Bordered by: Germany

Terrain: Mostly fertile lowland, undulating hills, woodland, lakes and moors

Climate: Generally mild, changeable climate without extremes of heat or cold; cold winters but usually not severe; warm, sunny summers; the best time to visit is between May and September

Coastline: 7,314km

Highest Point: Ejer Bavnehøj 173m

Languages: Danish

Local Time: GMT or BST + 1, ie 1 hour ahead of the UK all year

Currency: Krone (DKK) divided into 100 øre; £1 = DKK 8.66, DKK 10 = £1.15 (September 2011)

Telephoning: From the UK dial 0045 for Denmark followed by the 8-digit number; there are no area codes. To call the UK from Denmark dial 0044, omitting the initial zero of the area code

Emergency numbers: Police 112 (114 for non-urgent calls); Fire brigade 112; Ambulance 112 (operators speak English).

Public Holidays 2012

Jan 1; Apr 1, 5, 6, 8, 9; May 4, 17, 27, 28; Jun 5 (Constitution Day); Dec 25, 26.

Public Holidays 2013

Jan 1; Mar 24, 28, 29, 31; Apr 1, 26; May 9, 19, 20; Jun 5 (Constitution Day); Dec 25, 26.

School summer holidays extend from end June to mid August.

Tourist Office

VisitDenmark
55 SLOANE STREET
LONDON SW1X 9SY
FAX: 020 7259 5955
www.visitdenmark.com
london@visitdenmark.com

The following introduction to Denmark should be read in conjunction with the important information contained in the Handbook chapters at the front of this guide.

Camping and Caravanning

Denmark has approximately 500 approved, well-equipped, annually inspected campsites. A green banner flies at each campsite entrance, making it easy to spot. Campsites are graded from 1 to 5 stars, many having excellent facilities including baby-changing areas, private family bathrooms, self-catering cooking facilities and shops. Prices are regulated and there is very little variation.

All except the most basic 1-star sites have water and waste facilities for motorhomes and at least some electric hook-ups. You may find it useful to take your own flat universal sink plug. During the high season it is advisable to book in advance as many Danish holidaymakers take pitches for the whole season for use at weekends and holidays resulting in minimal space for tourers.

A camping pass is required on all classified campsites. You should be in possession of a Camping Card International (CCI) or you may purchase a Camping Card Scandinavia (CCS), which is also valid in Finland, Norway and Sweden, on arrival at your first campsite or from local tourist offices or online at www.danskecampingpladser.dk. The price is DKK 100 (2011) for an individual, couple or family for the year. The CCS entitles the holder to discounts on petrol and diesel, and on some ferry fares and campsites.

Approximately 190 campsites have a 'Quick Stop' amenity which provides safe, secure overnight facilities on or adjoining campsites, including the use of sanitary facilities. Quick Stop rates are about two thirds of the regular camping rate but you must arrive after 8pm and leave by 10am next morning. Reception at most sites closes at 11pm at the latest. A list of Quick Stop sites may be obtained from local tourist offices or downloaded from DK-Camp www.dk-camp.dk. You will also find information about small campsites, city sites and 'elite' sites on their website, or alternatively you can email them on info@dk-camp.dk for further information.

Whenever possible you should obtain permission before parking a caravan or putting up a tent anywhere other than on an organised campsite. This especially applies when camping on or near cultivated ground or in forests, woods and parks. Camping is prohibited on common or state land, in lay-bys and car parks, in the dunes or on beaches, unless within an organised campsite.

Casual/wild camping is not allowed and is particularly frowned on near beaches where on-the-spot fines may be incurred.

Motorhomes

Motorhomes who enjoy small, rural or farm sites may like to obtain a copy of a Camper Guide published by DACF, an organisation for people with motorhomes, which lists approximately 250 sites throughout the country. The guide is available from tourist offices and some motorway service areas – see www.dacf.dk

A Nordic Motorhome Guide listing approximately 800 sites in Denmark, Finland, Norway, Sweden and Estonia is also available from DACF and you can order online from www.shop.womoweb.de (click on Stellplatzlisten Scandinavien).

Country Information

Cycling

Although not as flat as the Netherlands, Denmark is very cyclist-friendly and many major and minor roads, including those in all major towns, have separate cycle lanes or tracks. They have their own traffic lights and signals. Cyclists often have the right of way and, when driving, you should check cycle lanes before turning left or right.

In Århus and Copenhagen the use of city centre bicyles is free, on payment of a returnable deposit, between mid-April and November. Simply look for one of the many bicycle racks around the central area; see www.visitcopenhagen.com for more information.

There are many separate cycle routes, including eleven national routes, which may be long distance, local or circular, mainly on quiet roads and tracks. Local tourist offices can provide information. When planning a route, take the prevailing (often strong) westerly winds into account.

Transportation of Bicycles

Bicycles may be carried on the roof of a car as well as at the rear. When carried at the rear, the lights and number plate must remain visible.

Electricity and Gas

Current on campsites varies between 6 and 16 amps, a 10 amp supply being the most common. Plugs have 2 round pins. Some sites have CEE17 electric hook-ups or are in the process of converting. If a CEE17 connection is not available site staff will usually provide an adaptor. Visitors report that reversed polarity is common.

Campingaz 904 and 907 butane cylinders are readily available from campsites, or some Statoil service stations and at camping or hardware shops. If travelling on to Norway, it is understood that Statoil agencies there will exchange Danish propane cylinders.

*See **Electricity and Gas** in the section **DURING YOUR STAY.***

DENMARK

Entry Formalities

Visas are not required by British or Irish passport holders for a stay of up to three months. Visitors planning to stay longer should contact the Danish Embassy in London before they travel www.denmark.org.uk.

Regulations for Pets

Between April and September all dogs must be kept on a lead. This applies not only on campsites but throughout the country in general.

Medical Services

The standard of healthcare is high. Citizens of the UK are entitled to the same emergency medical services as the Danish, including free hospital treatment, on production of a European Health Insurance Card (EHIC). Tourist offices and health offices (kommunes social og sundhedforvaltning) have lists of doctors and dentists who are registered with the public health service. For a consultation with a doctor you may have to pay the full fee but you will be refunded if you apply to a local health office if they are registered with the Danish Public Health Service. Partial refunds may be made for dental costs and approved medicines. Prescriptions are dispensed at pharmacies (apotek).

You are strongly recommended to obtain comprehensive travel and medical insurance before travelling to Denmark, such as The Caravan Club's Red Pennant Overseas Holiday Insurance – see www.caravanclub.co.uk/redpennant

*See **Medical Matters** in the section **DURING YOUR STAY.***

Opening Hours

Banks: Mon-Fri 10am-4pm (Thu to 6pm). In the Provinces opening hours vary from town to town.

Museums: Tue-Sun 9am/10am-5pm; most museums close Monday.

Post Offices: Mon-Fri 9am/10am-5pm/6pm, Sat 9am/10am-12pm/1pm/2pm or closed all day.

Shops: Mon-Fri 9.30am-5.30pm (Fri to 7pm); Sat 9am-1pm/2pm; supermarkets open Mon-Fri 9am-7pm & Sat 9am-4pm/5pm; open on first Sunday of the month 10am-5pm. Most shops close on public holidays but you may find some bakers, sandwich shops, confectioners, kiosks and florists open.

Safety and Security

Denmark has relatively low levels of of crime and most visits to the country are trouble-free. The majority of public places are well lit and secure, most people are genuinely friendly and the police courteous, helpful and often speak good English.

Visitors should, however, be aware of the risk of pickpocketing or bag-snatching in Copenhagen, particularly around the central station and in the Christiania and Nørrebro areas, as well as in other large cities and tourist attractions, and should take the usual common-sense precautions. Car break-ins have increased in recent years; never leave valuables in your car.

Denmark shares with the rest of Europe a general threat from terrorism. Attacks could be indiscriminate and against civilian targets in public places, including tourist sites.

*See **Safety and Security** in the section **DURING YOUR STAY.***

British Embassy

KASTELSVEJ 36/38/40
DK-2100 Copenhagen Ø
Tel: 35 44 52 00
http://ukindenmark.fco.gov.uk/en

There are also Honorary Consulates in Aabenraa, Århus, Fredericia and Herning

Irish Embassy

ØSTBANEGADE 21
DK-2100 Copenhagen Ø
Tel: 35 47 32 00
www.embassyofireland.dk

Customs Regulations

Alcohol and Tobacco

*For import allowances for alcohol and tobacco products see **Customs Regulations** in the section **PLANNING AND TRAVELLING.***

Documents

Passport

Your passport must be valid for the proposed duration of your stay, however in case of any unforseen delays it is strongly recommeneded to have a period of extra validity on your passport.

Vehicle(s)

Carry your vehicle documentation, including vehicle registration certificate (V5C), certificate of insurance and MOT certificate (if applicable). You may be asked to produce your V5C if driving a motorhome over the Great Belt Bridge between Funen and Zealand in order to verify the weight of your vehicle. See ***Toll Bridges*** later in this chapter.

*See **Documents** in the section **PLANNING AND TRAVELLING.***

Money

Some shops and restaurants, particularly in the larger cities, display prices in both krone and euros and many will accept payment in euros.

Travellers' cheques may be cashed at banks and hotels and can be used at most restaurants and shops.When changing travelling cheques for Kroners a commission per cheque exchanged may be charged.

The major credit cards are widely, but not always, accepted. Credit cards are not normally accepted in supermarkets). Cash machines are widespread. A 5% surcharge is usually applied to credit card transactions. Recent visitors report that some banks and/or cash machines may not accept debit cards issued by non-Danish banks.

It is advisable to carry your passport or photocard driving licence if paying with a credit card as you may well be asked for photographic proof of identity.

Carry your credit card issuers'/banks' 24-hour UK contact numbers in case of loss or theft of your cards.

Motoring

Alcohol

The level of alcohol cannot exceed 50 milligrams in 100 millilitres of blood (80 milligrams in the UK). Drivers caught over this limit will be fined and their driving licence withdrawn. Police carry out random breath tests.

Breakdown Service

Assistance can be obtained 24 hours a day from Dansk Autohjælp (Danish Automobile Assistance). The number to call throughout Denmark is 70 27 91 12.

The hourly charge between Monday and Friday is DKK 638 + VAT and an administration charge; higher charges apply at night and at weekends and public holidays. On-the-spot repairs and towing must be paid for in cash.

On motorways use the emergency telephones, situated every 2 km, to call the breakdown service. The telephone number to dial in case of an accident is 112.

Essential Equipment

*See **Motoring – Equipment** in the section **PLANNING AND TRAVELLING**.*

Lights and Indicators

Dipped headlights are compulsory at all times, regardless of weather conditions. Bulbs are more likely to fail with constant use and you are recommended to carry spares.

On motorways drivers must use their hazard warning lights to warn other motorists of sudden queues ahead or other dangers such as accidents.

By law indicators must be used when overtaking or changing lanes on a motorway. Their use is also compulsory when pulling out from a parked position at the kerb.

Child Restraint System

Children under three years of age must be seated in an approved child restraint system adapted to their size. Children under three years old and under 1.35 metres in height must be seated in an approved child restraint suitable for both their height and weight. If the vehicle is fitted with an active airbag children must not be placed in the front with their back to the road.

Since May 2009 all rear seat passengers must wear a seat belt, therefore it is no longer possible to transport three children if there are only two seat belts available.

Fuel

Some petrol stations in larger towns stay open 24 hours a day and they are increasingly equipped with self-service pumps which accept DKK 50, 100 and occasionally DKK 200 notes. Few display instructions in English and it is advisable to fill up during normal opening hours when staff are on hand. Unleaded petrol pumps are marked 'Blyfri Benzine'. Leaded petrol is no longer available and has been replaced by Lead Replacement Petrol, called Millennium, which contains an additive. The major credit cards are normally accepted.

LPG (Autogas or Bilgas) is available from a handful of BP, OK, Q8, Uno-X, YX, Shell and Statoil service stations – the Danish Tourist Board publishes a list of outlets on its website www.visitdenmark.com

*See also **Fuel** under **Motoring – Advice** in the section **PLANNING AND TRAVELLING**.*

Parking

Parking prohibitions and limitations are indicated by signs. Hours during which parking is not allowed are displayed in black for weekdays, with brackets for Saturdays and in red for Sundays and public holidays. Parking meters and discs are used and discs are available free of charge from post offices, banks, petrol stations and tourist offices. The centre of Copenhagen is divided into red, green and blue zones and variable hourly charges apply round the clock Monday to Friday (Saturday to 5pm; Sunday and public holidays free). 'Pay and display' tickets may be bought from machines with cash or a credit card. Cars must be parked on the right-hand side of the road (except in one-way streets). An illegally parked vehicle may be removed by the police.

*See also **Parking Facilities for the Disabled** under **Motoring – Advice** in the section **PLANNING AND TRAVELLING**.*

Priority

At intersections where there are 'give way' or 'stop' signs and/or a transverse line consisting of triangles (shark's teeth) with one point facing towards the driver, drivers must give way to traffic at an intersection. If approaching an intersection of two roads without any signs you must give way to vehicles coming from the right.

Give way to cyclists and to buses signalling to pull out. Motorists should take special care on the Danish islands where many people travel by foot, bicycle or on horseback.

Roads

Roads are generally in good condition, well-signposted and largely uncongested and driving standards are fairly high.

Caravanners should beware of strong crosswinds on exposed stretches of road. Distances are short; it is less than 500 km (310 miles) from Copenhagen on the eastern edge of Zealand, to Skagen at the tip of Jutland, and the coast is never more than an hour away.

Road Signs and Markings

Signs directing you onto or along international E-roads are green with white lettering. E-roads, having been integrated into the Danish network, usually have no other national number.

Signs above the carriageway on motorways have white lettering on a blue background. Signs guiding you onto other roads are white with red text and a hexagonal sign with red numbering indicates the number of a motorway exit.

Primary (main roads) connecting large towns and ferry connections have signs with black numbers on a yellow background. Secondary (local) roads connecting small towns and primary routes are indicated by signs with black numbers on a white background. Signs of any colour with a dotted frame refer you to a road further ahead. Road signs themselves may be placed low down and, as a result, may be easy to miss.

'Sharks teeth' markings at junctions indicate stop and give way to traffic on the road you are entering.

General roads signs conform to international standards. You may see the following:

Place of interest

Recommended speed limits

Dual Carriage-way ends

The following are some other common signs:

Ensrettet kørsel – *One-way street*

Fare – *Danger*

Farligt sving – *Dangerous bend*

Fodgægerovergang – *Pedestrian crossing*

Gennemkørsel forbudt – *No through road*

Hold til hojre – *Keep to the right*

Hold til venstre – *Keep to the left*

Omkørsel – *Diversion*

Parkering forbudt – *No parking*

Vejen er spærret – *Road closed*

Speed Limits

*See **Speed Limits Table** under **Motoring – Advice** in the section **PLANNING AND TRAVELLING.***

Vehicles over 3,500 kg are restricted to 70 km/h (44 mph) on the open road and on motorways.

When roads are wet or slushy reduce your speed to avoid splashing other road users. It is prohibited to use radar detectors.

Traffic Jams

British drivers will enjoy the relatively low density of traffic. At most, traffic builds up during the evening rush hours around the major cities of Copenhagen, Århus, Aalborg and Odense. During the holiday season traffic jams may be encountered at the Flensburg border crossing into Germany, on the roads to coastal areas, on approach roads to ferry crossings and on routes along the west coast of Jutland.

Violation of Traffic Regulations

The police are authorised to impose and collect on-the-spot fines for traffic offences. Driving offences committed in Denmark are reported to the UK authorities.

Motorways

There are approximately 1,000 km of motorways, mainly two-lane and relatively uncongested. No tolls are levied except on bridges. Lay-bys with picnic areas and occasionally motorhome service points are situated at 25 km intervals. These often also have toilet facilities. Service areas and petrol stations are situated at 50 km intervals and are generally open from 7am to 10pm. These offer a kiosk, toilets and cafeteria together with road and traffic information.

Toll Bridges

The areas of Falster and Zealand are linked by two road bridges, 1.6 km and 1.7 km in length respectively.

The areas of Funen and Zealand are linked by an 18 km suspension road bridge and rail tunnel known as the Great Belt Link (Storebæltsbroen), connecting the towns of Nyborg and Korsør. The toll road is part of the E20 between Odense and Ringsted and tolls for single journeys on the bridge are shown in Table 1 below (2011 prices subject to change).

Table 1 – Great Belt Bridge

Vehicle(s)	Price
Car, motorhome up to 6 metres	DKK 220
Car + trailer/caravan up to 6 metres	DKK 335
Car or motorhome (under 3,500 kg) over 6 metres	DKK 335
Car + trailer/caravan over 6 metres	DKK 335
Motorhome (over 3,500 kg) up to 10 metres	DKK 665
Motorhome (over 3,500 kg) over 10 metres	DKK 1,050

You may be asked to produce your Vehicle Registration Certificate (V5C) to verify the weight of your vehicle. Day return and weekend return tickets are also available. For more information see www.storebaelt.dk/english

DENMARK

The 16 km Øresund Bridge links Copenhagen in Denmark with Malmö in Sweden and means that it is possible to drive all the way from mainland Europe to Sweden by motorway. The crossing is via a 7.8 km bridge to the artificial island of Peberholm, and a 4 km tunnel. Tolls for single journeys (payable in cash, including euros, or by credit card) are levied on the Swedish side, and are shown in Table 2 below (2011 prices subject to change).

Table 2 – Øresund Bridge

Vehicle(s)	Price
Car, motor home up to 6 metres	€ 40
Car + caravan/trailerup to 6 metres or motorhome over 6 metres	€ 80

Speed limits apply, and during periods of high wind the bridge is closed to caravans. Bicycles are not allowed. Information on the Øresund Bridge can be found on www.oeresundsbron.com

On both the Øresund and Storebælts bridges vehicle length is measured electronically and even a slight overhang over six metres, e.g. tow bars, projecting loads and loose items, will result in payment of the higher tariff.

Touring

The peak holiday season and school holidays are slightly earlier than in the UK and by mid-August some attractions close or operate on reduced opening hours.

Danish cooking is excellent and fish and dairy produce are especially good and plentiful.

Denmark is famous for its cold table and its range of open sandwiches called 'smørrebrod'. In country districts good places for meals are the local 'kros' or inns. The national drinks are lager and schnapps.

Service charges are automatically added to restaurant bills although you may round up the bill if service has been good, but it is not expected. Tips for taxi drivers are included in the fare. No further tipping is required. Smoking is not allowed in enclosed public places, including restaurants and bars.

The 3,500 km Marguerite Route, marked by brown signs depicting a flower (see below), takes motorists to the best sights and scenic areas in Denmark.

A route map and guide (in English) are available from bookshops, tourist offices and Statoil service stations all over Denmark. Stretches of the route are not suitable for cars towing caravans as some of the roads are narrow and twisting.

Tourist Route

The capital and major port, Copenhagen, is situated on the island of Zealand. Grundtvig Cathedral, Amalienborg Palace and the Viking Museum are well worth a visit, as are the famous Tivoli Gardens open from mid April to the third week in September and again for a few days in October and from mid November to the end of December (excluding Christmas). The statue of the Little Mermaid, the character created by Hans Christian Andersen, can be found at the end of the promenade called Langelinie. Copenhagen is easy to explore and from there visitors may travel to the north of Zealand along the 'Danish Riviera' to Hamlet's castle at Kronborg, or west to Roskilde with its Viking Ship Museum and 12th century cathedral.

A Copenhagen Card (CPH Card) offers unlimited use of public transport throughout Greater Copenhagen and North Zealand, free entry to over 60 museums and attractions (including the Tivoli Gardens) and discounts at restaurants and other attractions. Cards are valid for 24 or 72 hours and may be purchased from selected tourist offices, travel agents, hotels and railway stations or online from www.visitcopenhagen.com. Two children up to the age of nine are included free of charge on an adult card. It is also available to buy and use the Copenhagen Card via a free iPhone app.

The first national park on the Danish mainland, Thy National Park near Thisted along Jutland's north-west coast, opened in 2008, followed in 2009 by the Mols Bjerge National Park in eastern Jutland and in 2010 by the Wadden Sea National Park in the south-west of the country. Another two areas are being developed as national parks and are due to open in the near future. See www.visitdenmark.com for more information.

The Danish Tourist Board publishes a brochure for disabled people travelling in the West Jutland region which contains information about accommodation (including campsites), restaurants, museums, sightseeing, entertainment, events and useful addresses. See www.disabledtravelguide.com or write to Turistgruppen Vestjylland, Kirkevej 4, 6960 Hvide Sande, tel 0045 75 28 74 00.

English is widely spoken throughout the country.

Local Travel

Public transport is excellent and you can buy a variety of bus, train and metro tickets at station kiosks and at some supermarkets. Children under the age of 12 travel free on buses and metro trains in the Greater Copenhagen area when accompanied by an adult. Tickets must be purchased for dogs and bicycles.

Numerous car ferry connections operate daily between different parts of the country. The ferry is a common mode of transport in Denmark and there may be long queues, especially at weekends in summer. The most important routes connect the bigger islands of Zealand and Funen with Jutland using high-speed vessels on day and night services. Vehicle length and height restrictions apply on routes between Odden (Zealand) and Århus and Æbeltoft (Jutland) and not all sailings transport caravans – check in advance.

The Danish Tourist Board can provide general information on car ferry services or contact Scandlines for information on inter-island services including timetables and prices www.scandlines.dk, email scandlines@scandlines.com or telephone 0045 33 15 15 15.

International ferry services are particularly busy during July and August and it is advisable to book in advance. Popular routes include Frederikshavn to Gothenburg (Sweden), Helsingør to Helsingborg (Sweden), Copenhagen to Oslo (Norway), and Rødby to Puttgarden in Germany (this route involves a road bridge which is occasionally closed to high-sided vehicles because of high winds). The ferry route from Copenhagen to Hamburg is a good alternative to the busy E45 motorway linking Denmark and Germany.

All place names used in the Site Entry listings which follow can be found in Kraks Vejkort Danmark atlas, scale 1 cm to 2 km, see www.krak.dk

SITES IN DENMARK

AALBORG *B1* (1.5km W Urban) *57.05500, 9.88500* **Strandparken Camping, Skydebanevej 20, 9000 Aalborg [tel 98 12 76 29; fax 98 12 76 73; info@strandparken.dk; www.strandparken.dk]** Turn L at start of m'way to Svenstrup & Aalborg W, foll A180 (Hobrovej rd) twd town cent. Turn L bef Limfjorden bdge onto Borgergade for 2km, site on R. Fr N turn R after bdge onto Borgergade. Med, shd; wc; chem disp; mv service pnt; baby rm; shwrs DKK10; el pnts (10A) DKK30 (poss rev pol); kiosk & shops 500m; cooking facs; playgrnd; pool adj; TV; some cabins; dogs DKK10; phone; bus nr; Eng spkn; adv bkg; poss noisy tent campers high ssn; ccard acc; CCI. "Gd cent for town & N Jutland; gd security." ♦ 1 Apr-12 Sep. DKK 175 2010*

AALESTRUP *B2* (S Rural) *56.69166, 9.49991* **Aalestrup Camping, Parkvænget 2, 9620 Aalestrup [tel 98 64 23 86; pouledb@ofir.dk; www.rosenparken.dk]** Fr E45 turn W onto rd 561 to Aalestrup; 500m after junc with rd 13 turn L into Borgergade, cross rlwy line. Site sp. Med, pt shd; wc; shwrs; chem disp; mv service pnt; el pnts DKK25; shop nr; rest; snacks; playgrnd; quiet. "Free entry to beautiful rose garden; gd touring base; friendly staff." 1 Mar-1 Nov. DKK 120 2010*

AARS *B2* (1km N Rural) *56.81530, 9.50695* **Aars Camping, Tolstrup Byvej 17, 9600 Aars [tel 98 62 36 03; fax 98 62 52 99; camping@aars.dk; www.aarscamping.dk]** Fr E45 exit junc 33 W to Aars on rd 535. Turn N onto rd 29 (Aggersundvej), site sp. Med, pt sl, pt shd; htd wc; chem disp; mv service pnt; shwrs DKK5; el pnts (16A) DKK30; gas; Indtte; shop; rest; snacks; bar & 1km; BBQ; cooking facs; playgrnd; tennis; horseriding; internet; TV; some statics; dogs; poss cr; Eng spkn; adv bkg; quiet; ccard acc; CCI. "Vg." ♦ 1 Apr-1 Nov. DKK 150 2011*

AEROSKOBING (AERO ISLAND) *C3* (1km W Urban/Coastal) *54.89452, 10.40118* **Ærøskøbing Campingplads, Sygehusvej 40B, 5970 Ærøskøbing [tel 62 52 18 54; fax 62 52 14 36; info@aeroecamp.dk; www.aeroecamp.dk]** Fr Ærøskøbing ferry take 1st or 2nd R, sp to Sygehus & site. Med, some mkd pitch. Pt sl, pt shd; wc; chem disp; mv service pnt; baby facs; fam bthrm; shwrs DKK3; el pnts (16A) DKK25; gas; shop 1km; rest, snacks, bar 1km; cooking facs; playgrnd; sand/shgl beach; boating; TV; phone; no adv bkg; quiet; CCI. ♦ 1 May-30 Sep. DKK 138 2008*

ALBAEK *C1* (6km N Coastal) *57.64433, 10.46179* **Bunken Camping, Ålbækvej 288, Bunken Klitplantage, 9982 Ålbæk [tel 98 48 71 80; fax 98 48 89 05; dancamp@mail.tele.dk; www.dancamp.dk]** Site in fir plantation E of A10. V lge, hdg pitch, pt shd; wc; chem disp; mv service pnt; baby rm; fam bthrm; shwrs DKK5; el pnts DKK25 (adaptor on loan fr recep) (poss rev pol); gas; Indtte; shop; cooking facs; playgrnd; sand beach 150m; fishing; boating; TV; dogs DKK15; phone; adv bkg; some rd noise. "Beautiful site in trees; spacious pitches." ♦ 3 Apr-18 Oct. DKK 158 2009*

ALSGARDE see Helsingør *D2*

⊞ **ARHUS** *C2* (9km N Rural) *56.22660, 10.16260* **Århus Camping, Randersvej 400, Lisbjerg, 8200 Århus Nord [tel 86 23 11 33; fax 86 23 11 31; info@aarhuscamping.dk; www.aarhuscamping.dk]** Exit E45 junc 46 Århus N, then to Ikea rndabt. Then foll sp Lisbjerg & head for smoking factory chimney. Site 400m N of Lisbjerg. Med, pt sl, pt shd; wc; chem disp; mv service pnt; baby facs; fam bthrm; shwrs DKK5; el pnts (16A) metered; gas; Indtte (inc dryer); shop; snacks; BBQ; cooking facs; playgrnd; htd pool; paddling pool; beach 9km; games area; golf 10km; wifi; TV rm; 10% statics; dogs DKK10; phone; poss cr; adv bkg; rd noise; red CCI. "Conv Århus; gd, tidy site; modern san facs." ♦ DKK 174 2009*

ARHUS *C2* (5km S Coastal) *56.11030, 10.23209* **Blommehaven Camping, Ørneredevej 35, 8270 Højbjerg [tel 86 27 02 07; fax 86 27 45 22; info@blommenhaven.dk; www.blommehaven.dk]** Fr S on E45 at junc 50 take rd 501 twd Århus. In 10km this becomes 01 ring rd. Take 2nd R Dalgas Ave, at T-junc turn L & immed R into Strandvejen. Site 3km on L in Marselisborg Forest. Lge, hdg/mkd pitch, terr, pt shd; wc; chem disp; mv service pnt; fam bthrm; baby facs; shwrs; el pnts DKK35; Indtte; shop; BBQ; cooking facs; playgrnd; sand beach adj; TV rm; 4% statics; dogs DKK10; phone; bus; Quickstop o'night facs; poss cr; Eng spkn; adv bkg; quiet. "Some pitches sm & bare earth; helpful staff; clean facs; easy reach woods, cliffs & beach; conv for open-air museum." ♦ 21 Mar-18 Oct. DKK 180 2011*

ASAA *C1* (SE Urban/Coasal) *57.1460, 10.4023* **Asaa Camping, Vodbindervej 13, 9340 Aså [tel 98 85 13 40; fax 98 85 00 38; info@asaacamping.dk; www.asaacamping.dk]** Fr Aalborg take E45 NE for approx 20km, turn E to Aså at junc 16 onto rd 559, then R onto rd 541, site sp. Lge, pt shd; wc; chem disp; mv service pnt; shwrs; fam bthrm; baby facs; el pnts DKK30; Indtte; shop; snacks; cooking facs; playgrnd; pool; sw 2km; games area; fishing; TV; some cabins; dogs free; phone; Eng spkn; adv bkg; red low ssn; quiet; CCI. "Pleasant location; facs for anglers." ♦ 15 Mar-28 Sep. DKK 180 2011*

ASSENS *B3* (W Urban/Coastal) *55.26569, 9.88390* **Camping City Camping (formerly Willemoes), Næsvej 15, 5610 Assens [tel 64 71 15 43; fax 64 71 15 83; info@camping-willemoes.dk; www.camping-willemoes.dk]** Site on beach at neck of land W of town adj marina. Med, pt shd; wc; chem disp; mv service pnt; fam bthrm; baby facs; shwrs DKK5; el pnts (10A) DKK30; gas; Indtte; shop; playgrnd; sand beach adj; fishing; watersports; TV; 20% statics; phone; adv bkg; red low ssn. "Pleasant site on beach." ♦ Easter-13 Sep. DKK 155 2009*

AUGUSTENBORG see Sønderborg *B3*

⊞ **BILLUND** *B3* (2km NE Rural) *55.73131, 9.13565* **FDM Billund Camping, Ellehammers Allé 2, 7190 Billund [tel 75 33 15 21; fax 75 35 37 36; c-billund@fdm.dk; www.billund.fdmcamping.dk]** In vill of Billund take rd twd Grindsted & Vejle. In 1km turn N foll sp to Legoland, site on R. V lge, pt shd; wc; chem disp; mv service pnt; shwrs inc; el pnts (10A) DKK32; gas; Indtte; shop & 2km; rest; bar; playgrnd; pool 500m; games area; internet; TV; some statics; dogs DKK12; phone; Quickstop o'night facs; poss cr; Eng spkn; adv bkg; some aircraft noise; ccard acc; red long stay/CCI. "Impersonal but excel; open 24 hrs; sh walk to Legoland (free entry for last 90 mins of day)." ♦ DKK 162 2010*

We can fill in site report forms on the Club's website – www.caravanclub.co.uk/europereport

⊞ **BILLUND** *B3* (7km SE Rural) *55.68877, 9.26864* **Randbøldal Camping, Dalen 9, 7183 Randbøl [tel 75 88 35 75; fax 75 88 34 38; info@randboldalcamping.dk; www.randboldalcamping.dk]** Fr Vejle take Billund rd. After approx 18km take L turn to Randbol & Bindebolle. Foll sp, site located approx 5km on L. Med, pt sl, shd; htd wc; chem disp; mv service pnt; baby facs; fam bthrm; shwrs inc; el pnts (10A) DKK30; Indtte; shop; snacks; cooking facs; playgrnd; lake sw, waterslide & fishing nr; TV; 15% statics; dogs DKK10; phone; poss cr; Eng spkn; adv bkg; quiet; ccard acc. "Wooded site nr rv & trout hatchery; facs stretched high ssn; conv Legoland & Lion Park." ♦ DKK 175 2009*

BINDSLEV *C1* (4km N Coastal) *57.58994, 10.18716* **Tannisby Camping, Tannisbugtvej 86, 9881 Tversted/Bindslev [tel 98 93 12 50; info@tannisbycamping.dk; www.tannisbycamping.dk]** Fr S on E39 dir Hirtshals, turn R dirÅlbæk & foll sp to Tversted & site. Med, mkd pitch, some hdstg, pt shd; htd wc; chem disp; mv service pnt; baby facs; fam bthrm; private san facs avail; sauna; shwrs inc; el pnts (13A) DKK30; Indtte (inc dryer); shop; tradsmn; BBQ; cooking facs; playgrnd; sand beach 500m; wifi; TV rm; some statics; dogs DKK5; Quickstop o'night facs; Eng spkn; adv bkg; quiet. "Peaceful, friendly site." 1 Apr-26 Sep. DKK 180 2010*

⊞ **BJERGE** *C3* (3km SW Coastal) *55.56295, 11.16500* **FDM Camping Bjerge Sydstrand, Osvejen 30, Bjerge Sydstrand, 4480 Store Fuglede [tel 59 59 78 03; fax 59 59 37 20; c-bjerge@fdm.dk; www.bjerge.fdmcamping.dk]** E22 to Bjerge. Foll sp Bjerge Systrand on Filipsdalsvej rd, then onto Osvejen rd, site sp. Med, hdg/mkd pitch, pt shd; htd wc; mv service pnt; fam bthrm; shwrs inc; el pnts (6A) DKK30; Indtte; shop, tradsmn high ssn; rest 6km; snacks 300m; playgrnd; sand beach adj; watersports; fishing; internet; TV rm; 50% statics; dogs DKK15; adv bkg; quiet; ccard acc. "Pleasant, peaceful site." DKK 189 2009*

BLAVAND see Vejers Strand *A3*

BLOMMENSLYST see Odense *C3*

BOESLUNDE see Korsor *C3*

BOGENSE *C3* (S Coastal/Urban) *55.56144, 10.08530* **Bogense Strand Camping, Vestre Engvej 11, 5400 Bogense [tel 64 81 35 08; fax 64 81 27 17; info@bogensecamp.dk; www.bogensecamp.dk]** Fr E20 at junc 57 & take 317 NE to Bogense. At 1st traff lts turn L for harbour, site sp at side of harbour. Lge, pt shd; wc; chem disp; mv service pnt; baby facs; fam bthrm; shwrs DKK5; el pnts (12A) DKK35; Indtte; shop & 200m; cooking facs; playgrnd; pool; paddling pool; shgl beach adj; TV; some statics; dogs DKK17; phone; adv bkg; quiet; red low ssn; CCI. "Well-run site; excel facs; interesting sm town 5 mins walk." ♦ 3 Apr-18 Oct. DKK 250 2009*

BOJDEN see Faaborg *C3*

BORK HAVN *A2* (Coastal) *55.84822, 8.28333* **Bork Havn Camping, Kirkehøjvej 9a, 6893 Bork Havn/Hemmet [tel 75 28 00 37; mail@borkhavncamping.dk; www.borkhavncamping.dk]** Fr Tarm take rd 423 thro Hemmet; 500m bef Nørre Bork turn R to Bork Havn, site on L in town just bef harbour. Lge, mkd pitch, pt shd; htd wc; chem disp; mv service pnt; baby facs; shwrs; el pnts (10A) DKK22; Indtte (inc dryer); shop, rest, snacks, bar adj; cooking facs; playgrnd; htd, cov'rd pool in Tarm; shgl beach 200m; watersports nr; fishing; games rm; TV rm; 25% statics; dogs; Eng spkn; adv bkg; quiet; red low ssn; CCI. "Conv Esbjerg ferry to UK; excel." 1 Apr-1 Nov. DKK 144 2010*

BORRE *D3* (3km SE Rural) *54.97971, 12.52198* **Camping Møns Klint, Klintevej 544, 4791 Magleby [tel 55 81 20 25; fax 55 81 27 97; camping@klintholm.dk; www.campingmoensklint.dk]** Site nr end of metalled section of rd 287 fr Stege to E of Magleby, site sp. Lge, pt sl, pt shd; wc; chem disp; mv service pnt; shwrs DKK7; el pnts (10A) DKK40; Indtte; gas; shop; rest; snacks; cooking facs; playgrnd; pool; shgl beach 3km; fishing; boating; tennis; games area; cycle hire; wifi; TV; 20% statics; dogs; phone; poss cr; Eng spkn; adv bkg; quiet; ccard acc; red low ssn; CCI. "150m chalk cliffs adj - geological interest; much flora, fauna, fossils; gd walks; friendly staff; excel facs." 1 Apr-31 Oct. DKK 195 2009*

BOSORE *C3* (1km N Coastal) *55.19295, 10.80633* **Bøsøre Strand Feriepark, Bøsørevej 16, 5874 Hesselager [tel 62 25 11 45; fax 62 25 11 46; info@bosore.dk; www.bosore.dk]** Fr Hesselager N on rd 163, site sp. Lge, mkd pitch, pt shd; htd wc; mv service pnt; chem disp; baby facs; fam bthrm; serviced pitches; sauna; shwrs DKK4; el pnts (10A) DKK35; Indtte (inc dryer); shop; rest; snacks; bar; cooking facs; playgrnd; htd, covrd pool; sand beach adj; games area; cycle hire; golf 18km; wifi; entmnt; TV rm; 15% statics; dogs DKK20; phone; poss cr high ssn; red low ssn/snr citizens; Quickstop o'night facs. "Superb san facs; gd facs young children; on-site bakery; swipe card for facs - settle on departure." ♦ 26 Mar-23 Oct. DKK 236 2011*

DENMARK

BRAEDSTRUP *B2* (5km S) *55.93552, 9.65314* **Gudenåcamping Brædstrup, Bolundvej 4, 8740 Brædstrup [tel 75763070; info@gudenaacamping.dk; www.gudenaacamping.dk]** Fr Silkeborg take rd 52 towards Horsens; site sp R off rd 52 approx 4km fr Braedstrup. Sm, mkd pitch, unshd; htd wc; chem disp; MV service pnt; baby facs; fam bthrm; shwrs metered; el pnts (10A) metered; Indtte; tradsmn; rest; snacks; bar; BBQ; playgrnd; pool; games rm; wifi; TV rm; 25% statics; dogs DKK10; adv bking; quiet; CCI. "Sm, attractive site beside River Gudenå; v well run fam site; fishing fr site; excel san facs." ♦ 08 Apr-25 Sep. DKK 178 2011*

⊞ **BREDERBRO** *B3* (10km W Rural/Coastal) *55.06877, 8.66012* **Ballum Camping, Kystvej 37, 6261 Ballum [tel 74 71 62 63; ballum.camping@bbsyd.dk; www.ballum-camping.dk]** At Bredebro on rd 11 turn W on rd 419 twd coast. Site sp 2km S of Ballum. Med, pt shd; htd wc; chem disp; mv service pnt; shwrs DKK1/min; el pnts (10A) DKK30; Indtte (inc dryer); shop & 2km; tradsmn; rest 1km; playgrnd; sand beach 1km; games area; cycle hire; wifi; 50% statics; dogs DKK10; quiet; CCI. "Close German border; conv Rømø Island with v lge sand beach; gd birdwatching; immac facs." DKK 136 2010*

CHARLOTTENLUND see København *D3*

COPENHAGEN see København *D3*

EBELTOFT *C2* (8km N Rural) *56.25241, 10.60325* **Krakær Camping, Gl Kærvej 18, Krakær, 8400 Ebeltoft [tel 86 36 21 18; fax 86 36 21 87; info@krakaer.dk; www.krakaer.dk]** Fr N on rd 21 twd Ebeltoft, 4km after Feldballe, turn R to site, sp. Lge, pt shd; htd wc; chem disp; mv service pnt; baby facs; fam bthrm; shwrs inc; el pnts (6A) DKK25; Indtte; shop; rest; snacks; bar; cooking facs; playgrnd; htd pool; paddling pool; sand beach 3km; games area; golf 8km; internet; TV rm; 20% statics; dogs DKK10; phone; adv bkg; quiet. "Gd walking area in Mols Bjerge National Park; peaceful." ♦ 1 Apr-20 Oct. DKK 150 2008*

EBELTOFT *C2* (6km NE Coastal) *56.22153, 10.73836* **Dråby Strand Camping, Dråby Strandvej 13, 8400 Ebeltoft [tel 86 34 16 19; fax 86 34 03 48; info@draaby.dk; www.draaby.dk]** Fr N on rd 21 on o'skts of Ebeltoft, turn L just after Shell g'ge at sp Dråby. In 50m take 2nd L sp Dråby. Foll sp Dråby Strand & site. Lge, mkd pitch, unshd; htd wc; chem disp; mv service pnt; baby facs; fam bthrm; shwrs metered; el pnts (10A) DKK26; gas; Indtte; shop & 6km; tradsmn; rest, snacks, bar 6km; cooking facs; playgrnd; htd, covrd pool 6km; shgl beach adj; TV rm; 2% statics; dogs free; phone; Eng spkn; adv bkg; quiet; red long stay; CCI. "Lovely location; excel base for peaceful holiday; conv historic Ebeltoft; v helpful owners." ♦ 15 Mar-14 Sep. DKK 161 2008*

⊞ **EBELTOFT** *C2* (3km S Coastal) *56.1683, 10.7231* **Elsegårde Camping, Kristoffervejen 1, Elsegårde, 8400 Ebeltoft [tel 86 34 12 83; fax 86 34 07 75; eg@egcamp.dk; www.egcamp.dk]** Fork L fr rd 21 on E o'skts of Ebeltoft. Foll sps to Elsegårde, camping sp. Site at end of lane overlkg sea. Med, terr, pt shd; wc; chem disp; mv service pnt; shwrs inc; fam bthrm; baby rm; el pnts (10A) DKK30; gas; Indtte; shop; snacks; cooking facs; playgrnd; pool; beach nr; fishing & horseriding 1km; wifi; TV; statics; dogs free; poss cr; adv bkg; "Quiet; well-maintained; excel views over Kattegat; open in winter by arrangement." ♦ DKK 160 2008*

⊞ **EBELTOFT** *C2* (1km W Coastal) *56.20997, 10.67838* **Ebeltoft Strand Camping, Nordre Strandvej 23, 8400 Ebeltoft [tel 86 34 12 14; fax 86 34 55 33; info@ebeltoftstrandcamping.dk; www.ebeltoftstrandcamping.dk]** Fr N site on R of rd 21 as ent Ebeltoft. Lge, pt shd; wc; chem disp; mv service pnt; fam bthrm; baby facs; shwrs inc; el pnts (10A) DKK30; Indtte; gas; shop; rest 200m; snacks; playgrnd; sand beach adj; wifi; TV; some statics; phone; Eng spkn; quiet; ccard acc; red snr citizens; CCI. "Adv bkg ess 1 Nov-1 Apr as facs open/htd by arrangment only; gd location; 10 mins walk to interesting old town cent; conv Mols Peninsula; excel." ♦ DKK 210 2009*

⊞ **EGTVED** *B3* (1.5km W Rural) *55.60670, 9.27873* **Egtved Camping, Verstvej 9, 6040 Egtved [tel 75 55 18 32; fax 75 55 08 32; post@egtvedcamping.dk; www.egtvedcamping.dk]** Fr junc 63 E20/E45 (Kolding) take rd 176. At Egtved L onto rd 417, site sp on L. Lge, mkd pitch, pt sl, pt shd; wc; chem disp; mv service pnt; baby facs; fam bthrm; shwrs; el pnts (10A) DKK25; gas; Indtte (inc dryer); shop; tradsmn; rest; snacks; cooking facs; playgrnd; htd pool; fishing; games rm; wifi; 60% statics; phone; poss cr; Eng spkn; adv bkg; quiet; ccard acc; CCI. "Clean san facs; conv Legoland, 20km." ♦ DKK 155 2010*

ENGESVANG *B2* (1.5km N Rural) *56.18736, 9.35627* **Bøllingsø Camping, Kragelundvej 5, 7442 Engesvang [tel 86 86 51 44; fax 86 86 41 71; post@bollingso-camping.dk; www.bollingso-camping.dk]** Fr A13 dir Viborg, turn E to N of Engesvang & foll minor rd so Kragelund. Site on L 1km after museum. Med, mkd pitch, pt sl, pt shd; htd wc; chem disp; mv service pnt; fam bthrm; baby facs; shwrs; el pnts (16A) DKK25; Indtte (inc dryer); shop; snacks; rest 3km; cooking facs; playgrnd; pool; paddling pool; games area; lake fishing 250m; TV; 2% statics; dogs DKK10; phone; poss cr; adv bkg; red low ssn; quiet; CCI. "Conv NH for A13; well-kept family site; clean, dated facs; nr Danish lake district." ♦ 1 Apr-1 Oct. DKK 135 2010*

ERSLEV *B2* (5km W Coastal) *56.81754, 8.67203* **Dragstrup Camping, Dragstrupvej 87, 7950 Erslev [tel 97 74 42 49; fax 97 74 45 49; dragstrup.camping@mail.dk; www.dk-camp.dk/dragstrup]** Fr Nykøbing (Mors) head NW along rte 26. Turn L level with Øster Jolby sp Hvidberg, foll sp Dragstrup & site - well sp fr rte 26. Lge, mkd pitch, pt sl, pt shd; wc; chem disp; mv service pnt; baby facs; fam bthrm; shwrs DKK5; el pnts (10A) DKK26; Indtte; shop & 5km; tradsmn; BBQ; cooking facs; playgrnd; sand beach 200m; fishing; 20% statics; dogs DKK10; phone; Quickstop o'night facs; Eng spkn; adv bkg; quiet; CCI. "V attractive site; gd touring base; trout-fishing on site." ♦ 1 Apr-30 Sep. DKK 189 2011*

DENMARK

ERTEBOLLE see Farsø *B2*

⊞ **ESBJERG** *A3* (6km NW Coastal) *55.51180, 8.39350* **Ådalens Camping, Gudenåvej 20, Sædding, 6710 Esbjerg Vest [tel 75 15 88 22; fax 75 15 97 93; info@adal.dk; www.adal.dk]** Exit E20 junc 75 & at rndabt take 2nd exit twd Esjberg N. In 5km turn R at major x-rds with traff lts. Turn L at 1st rndabt into Gudenåvej, site sp. Site on R in 300m. Lge, hdg pitch, pt shd; htd wc; chem disp; mv service pnt; serviced pitches; baby facs; fam bthrm; shwrs; el pnts (10A) DKK30; Indtte (inc dryer); shop; cooking facs; playgrnd; htd pool; paddling pool; waterslide; beach 500m; golf 10km; internet; some statics; dogs DKK10; phone; Eng spkn; CCI. "Gd, clean site & modern facs; excel play areas; friendly, helpful recep; conv ferry to Harwich; worth more than a nights stay, ideal for cycling, lovely quiet site, free dog wash." ♦ DKK 200 2011*

There aren't many sites open at this time of year. We'd better phone ahead to check the one we're heading for is open.

ESBJERG *A3* (8km NW Rural/Coastal) *55.54359, 8.33921* **Sjelborg Camping, Sjelborg Standvej 11, Hjerting, 6710 Esbjerg Vest [tel 75 11 54 32; fax 76 13 11 32; info@sjelborg.dk; www.sjelborg.dk]** Fr Esbjerg take coast rd N twds Hjerting & Sjelborg. At T-junc, Sjelborg Vej, turn L & in 100m turn R onto Sjelborg Kirkevej (camping sp); in 600m turn L into Sjelborg Strandvej (sp); site on R in 600m. Lge, hdg/mkd pitch, pt shd; wc; chem disp; mv service pnt; shwrs inc; fam bthrm; el pnts (10A) DKK35; Indtte (inc dryer); shop; sand/shgl beach nr; lake adj; fishing; golf 5km; bus to town; phone; adv bkg; quiet. "Excel site in a quiet country setting; wild flowers & butterflies; superb facs & activities all ages; spacious on edge of conservation area; mkd walks & bird sanctuary." ♦ 9 Apr-18 Sep. DKK 155 2011*

⊞ **FAABORG** *C3* (2km NE Rural) *55.11704, 10.24487* **Faaborg Camping, Odensevej 140, 5600 Faaborg [tel 62 61 77 94; fax 62 61 77 83; info@faaborgcamping.dk; www.faaborgcamping.dk]** Fr Faaborg cent dir Odense on rd 43, site sp on R. Med, pt sl, terr, unshd; htd wc; chem disp; mv service pnt; baby facs; shwrs; el pnts (10A) DKK27; gas; Indtte; kiosk; shop, rest 1km; cooking facs; playgrnd; cycle & surfboard hire; wifi; TV rm; some statics; dogs free; phone; Eng spkn; adv bkg; quiet; CCI. "Attractive setting; gd base S Funen; friendly owners; clean facs; excel." DKK 160 2008*

FAABORG *C3* (4km NE Rural) *55.10987, 10.29592* **Diernæs Camping, Bjerregardsvej 1, Diernæs, 5600 Faaborg [tel 62 61 13 76; fax 62 61 13 74; diernaes@dk-camp.dk; www.dk-camp.dk/diernaes]** Fr Faaborg foll sp Diernæs, then site. Med, pt sl, pt shd; wc; chem disp; mv service pnt; baby facs; fam bthrm; shwrs DKK2; el pnts (10A) DKK27; Indtte; shop; cooking facs; playgrnd; pool; TV; quiet. "Faaborg pretty town conv for ferries to nrby islands; site in quiet, isolated area." ♦ 1 May-5 Sep. DKK 150 2009*

FAABORG *C3* (6km SE Coastal) *55.06405, 10.31373* **Nab Camping, Kildegårdsvej 8, Åstrup, 5600 Faaborg [tel 62 61 67 79; fax 62 61 67 69; info@nabcamping.dk; www.nabcamping.dk]** Fr Faaborg SE on rd 44 dir Svendborg, turn R after 5km at centre bollards; after 1km turn R onto gravel rd, cont 500m to site. Med, sl, pt shd; wc; chem disp; mv service pnt; baby facs; fam bthrm; shwrs DKK2; el pnts (10A) DKK25; gas; Indtte; shop; rest 1km; snacks; BBQ; playgrnd; sand beach 1km; boating; Wifi; some statics; dogs free; phone; Eng spkn; quiet; ccard acc; red long stay; CCI. "Superb views over archipelago; conv Egeskov Castle & Gardens; excel site; gd cycling & bird watching nrby; m'vans will need levelling blocks; very quiet, views you dream about." 30 Apr-31 Aug. DKK 190 2011*

FAABORG *C3* (10km W Coastal) *55.10568, 10.10776* **Bøjden Strandcamping, Bøjden Landevej 12, 5600 Bøjden [tel 62 60 12 84; fax 62 60 12 94; info@bojden.dk; www.bojden.dk]** Rd 8 W fr Fåborg dir Bøjden/Fynshav, site sp nr ferry. Lge, some hdg/mkd pitch, pt sl, terr, pt shd; htd wc; chem disp; mv service pnt; serviced pitches; baby facs; fam bthrm; shwrs DKK5; el pnts (10A) DKK31; Indtte; shop; rest adj; cooking facs; playgrnd; htd pool & paddling pool; sand beach adj; cycle & boat hire; games rm; golf 12km; entmnt; internet; TV rm; 80% statics; dogs DKK15; sep car park; Eng spkn; adv bkg; ccard acc. "Excel family site with activity cent; blue flag beach; sea views fr pitches; interesting area." ♦ 14 Mar-20 Oct. DKK 234 2008*

⊞ **FAKSE** *D3* (12km E Coastal) *55.23913, 12.23964* **Vemmetofte Strand Camping, Ny Strandskov 1, Vemmetofte, 4640 Fakse [tel 53 71 02 26; fax 53 71 02 59; camping@vemmetofte.dk; www.vemmetofte.dk/camping]** Fr rd E47/E55 turn E on rd 154 to Faske & onto Faske Ladeplads. Head NE for 7km, R for Vemmeltofte-Strand to site in 1.5km. Lge, hdg/mkd pitch, pt shd; wc; chem disp; mv service pnt; baby facs; fam bthrm; sauna; shwrs DKK5; el pnts (10A) DKK30; gas; Indtte (inc dryer); shop; rest, snacks 100m; BBQ; playgrnd; sand beach adj; cycle hire; wifi; 50% statics; dogs DKK20; poss cr; Eng spkn; adv bkg; ccard acc. "Quiet site; Copenhagen 50km; ferry port at Rødby 90km." DKK 159 2010*

⊞ **FAKSE** *D3* (9km S Coastal) *55.17486, 12.1027* **Feddet Camping, Feddet 12, Fed Strand, 4640 Fakse [tel 56 72 52 06; fax 56 72 57 90; info@feddetcamping.dk; www.feddetcamping.dk]** Exit E45 junc 37 onto rd 154 to Fakse. Take rd 209 S, site sp after 9km on L, S of Vindbyholt. Site adj TopCamp Feddet (4 star & more expensive). V lge, mkd pitch, pt shd; htd wc; chem disp; mv service pnt; fam bthrm; el pnts (10A) DKK30; gas; Indtte; shop; rest; snacks; BBQ; cooking facs; playgrnd; indoor play area; sand beach adj; watersports; 60% statics; dogs DKK15; phone; poss cr; Eng spkn; adv bkg; quiet; ccard acc; CCI. "Superb san blocks; 50% pitches with sea views; excel wooded, sheltered area for walking & cycling; gd playgrnd." ♦ DKK 170 2008*

DENMARK

FARSO *B2* (6km W Rural/Coastal) *56.75751, 9.24267* **Farsø Fjord Camping, Gamle Viborgvej 13, Stistrup, 9640 Farsø [tel 98 63 61 76; fax 98 63 61 73; info@farso-fjordcamping.dk; www.farso-fjordcamping.dk]** Fr Viborg take rd 533 N dir Løgstør. 5km N of junc with 187 turn R, site sp on R in 300m. Med, mkd pitch, unshd; htd wc; chem disp; mv service pnt; fam bthrm; baby facs; shwrs DKK5; el pnts (10A) DKK30; gas; Indtte (inc dryer); sm shop; tradsmn; rest; snacks; playgrnd; sm htd pool; shgl beach adj; TV; some statics; dogs free; phone; Eng spkn; adv bkg; quiet; CCI. "Gd, clean san facs; well-kept; friendly staff; site only 500m fr fjord edge." ♦ 27 Mar-24 Sep. DKK 128 2010*

FARSO *B2* (10km NW Coastal) *56.81230, 9.18197* **Ertebølle Strand Camping, Ertebøllevej 42, 9640 Ertebølle [tel 98 63 63 75; fax 98 63 64 34; escamp@escamp.dk; www.escamp.dk]** Fr Viborg foll 26 twds Skive for 1.6km. Turn R along 533 twd Løgstør; 1km N of Strandby turn L for 1km & foll sp to site. Lge, mkd pitch, pt sl, shd; wc; chem disp; mv service pnt; serviced pitch; shwrs DKK5; el pnts (6A) DKK25; Indtte; shop; playgrnd; pool; sand beach 300m; TV; 30% statics; dogs free; phone; Eng spkn; adv bkg; quiet; ccard acc; CCI. "Friendly site in attractive surroundings." 1 Apr-21 Oct. DKK 130 2008*

⊞ **FARUM** *D3* (5km W Rural) *55.81400, 12.26430* **Undinegårdens Camping, Undinevej 3, 3660 Ganløse [tel 48 18 30 32; fax 48 18 47 32; info@undine.dk; www.undine.dk]** Exit rd 16 junc 10 W dir Lynge. Site on rd 233 bet Ganløse & Lynge, just S of Bastrup x-rds. Sp fr rds 233 & 207. Med, hdg/mkd pitch, pt shd; htd wc; chem disp; mv service pnt; baby facs; fam bthrm; shwrs; el pnts (10A) (metered); gas; Indtte; shop; cooking facs; playgrnd; lake fishing adj; TV; 40% statics; dogs; Eng spkn; adv bkg; quiet; CCS. "Vg site; gd walking; conv Hillerod." DKK 185 2011*

FERRING see Lemvig *A2*

FJELLERUP *C2* (2.5km W Coastal) *56.51209, 10.54980* **FDM Camping Hegedal Strand, Ravnsvej 3, 8585 Glesborg [tel 86 31 77 50; fax 86 71 77 40; c-hegedal@fdm.dk; www.hegedal.fdmcamping.dk]** Fr rd 16 turn N onto rd 547 dir Fjellerup. Cont W of Fjellerup to Hegedal, site sp. Med, hdg/mkd pitch, pt shd; htd wc; chem disp; mv service pnt; shwrs; el pnts (6A) DKK32; Indtte; shop; rest 3km; BBQ; cooking facs; playgrnd; sand beach adj; watersports; golf 10km; internet; TV rm; some statics; dogs DKK15; adv bkg; quiet; ccard acc. "Well-maintained family site; gd walking, cycling." ♦ 26 Mar-12 Sep. DKK 184 2010*

⊞ **FJERRITSLEV** *B1* (10km N Coastal) *57.13233, 9.17166* **Klim Strand Camping, Havvejen 167, 9690 Fjerritslev [tel 98 22 53 40; fax 98 22 57 77; ksc@klimstrand.dk; www.klimstrand.dk]** W fr Ålborg on rd 11, at Fjerritslev take rd 569 dir Klim & in 4km turn R to Klim Strand, site sp. V lge, pt shd; wc; mv service pnt; shwrs; child & fam bthrm; el pnts (10A) DKK30; Indtte; shop; rest; snacks; bar; cooking facs; playgrnd; pool; waterslides; sand beach adj; tennis; games area; cycle hire; entmnt; TV; 10% statics; dogs DKK25; phone; adv bkg; ccard acc. "Excel family site." ♦ DKK 355 2008*

⊞ **FJERRITSLEV** *B1* (12km W Rural) *57.10912, 9.09998* **Jammerbugt Camping, Thistedvej 546, 9690 Fjerritslev [tel 98 22 51 36; fax 98 22 55 12; kj@jamcamp.dk; www.jammerbugtcamping.dk]** Fr Ferritslev take rd 569 thro Klim & Vester Torup, site on R 1km beyond Vester Torup. Lge, hdg/mkd pitch, pt shd; htd wc; chem disp; mv service pnt; baby facs; fam bthrm; shwrs; el pnts (16A) DKK32; Indtte; ice; shop; rest; snacks; bar; BBQ; cooking facs; playgrnd; htd pool; paddling pool; sand beach 4km; games area; games rm; internet; entmnt; TV; 80% statics; dogs; phone; bus adj; poss cr; Eng spkn; adv bkg; quiet; CCI. "Vg; friendly owners." ♦ DKK 144 2010*

FOLLENSLEV *C3* (3km NW Coastal) *55.74323, 11.30858* **Vesterlyng Camping, Ravnholtvej 3, Havnsø, 4591 Føllenslev [tel/fax 59 20 00 66; info@vesterlyng-camping.dk; www.vesterlyng-camping.dk]** Fr rd 23 at Jyderup turn R onto rd 225, thro Snertinge. After Særslev turn L to Føllenslev, then turn R twd Havnsø. Foll sp in 1km to Vesterlyng & site. Lge, unshd; htd wc; mv service pnt; shwrs; el pnts (6A) DKK28; Indtte; shop; snacks; cooking facs; playgrnd; htd pool; sand beach 800m; cycle hire; internet; TV rm; 30% statics; dogs free; phone; adv bkg; quiet. "Gd views & beach." ♦ 23 Mar-21 Oct. DKK 176 2008*

⊞ **FREDERICIA** *B3* (6km NE Coastal) *55.6243, 9.8335* **Trelde Næs Camping, Trelde Næsvej 297, Trelde Næs, 7000 Fredericia [tel 75 95 71 83; fax 75 95 75 78; trelde@mycamp.dk; www.mycamp.dk]** Fr E20 exit jund 59 onto rd 28 or fr E45 exit junc 61 onto rd 28. Foll sp Trelde Næs & site. Lge, pt sl, unshd; htd wc; chem disp; mv service pnt; baby facs; fam bthrm; sauna; shwrs DKK4; el pnts (10A) DKK32; Indtte (inc dryer); shop; snacks; BBQ; cooking facs; playgrnd; htd pool; waterslide; sand beach adj; wifi; TV rm; 10% statics; dogs DKK16; phone; poss cr; adv bkg; quiet; ccard acc; red low ssn. "Vg; friendly; fine views over fjord; conv Legoland & island of Fyn; swipecard for all services - pay on departure." ♦ DKK 210 2009*

FREDERIKSHAVN *C1* (2km N Coastal) *57.46415, 10.52778* **TopCamp Nordstrand, Apholmenvej 40, 9900 Frederikshavn [tel 98 42 93 50; fax 98 43 47 85; info@nordstrand-camping.dk; www.nordstrand-camping.dk]** Fr E45/Rd40 foll rd N twd Skagen to outside town boundary (over rlwy bdge), turn R at rndabt into Apholmenvej; site sp. Lge, mkd pitch, unshd; wc; chem disp; shwrs; fam bthrm; baby facs; el pnts (10A) DKK30; gas; Indtte; shop; tradsmn; snacks; playgrnd; covrd pool; beach 1km; entmnt; excursions; TV; some statics; phone; dogs DKK12; poss cr; Eng spkn; adv bkg; ccard acc; red/snr citizens/long stay/CCS. "Vg NH for ferries; recep open 24hrs peak ssn; well-run, clean site; some pitches sm; cycle track to town." ♦ Easter-19 Oct. DKK 194 2008*

GANLOSE see Farum *D3*

DENMARK

GILLELEJE *D2* (12km SW Coastal) *56.09051, 12.14977* **DCU Rågeleje Strand Camping, Hostrupvej 2, 3210 Rågeleje [tel 48 71 56 40; fax 48 71 56 85; raageleje@dcu.dk; www.camping-raageleje.dk]** Fr Gilleleje foll sp to Rågeleje on rd 237. Site on coast rd 2km SW of Rågeleje dir Vejby Lge, hdg pitch, unshd; wc; chem disp; mv service pnt; shwrs; baby facs; fam bthrm; el pnts (10A) DKK30; gas; lndtte (inc dryer); supmkt; rest 1km; cooking facs; playgrnd; sand beach 300m; wifi; TV; dogs DKK20; phone; poss cr; adv bkg; ccard acc; quiet. ♦ 27 Mar-19 Oct. DKK 193 2010*

GIVE see Jelling *B3*

⊞ **GRAM** *B3* (7km W Rural) *55.28884, 8.94758* **Enderupskov Camping, Ribe Landevej 30, Enderupskov, 6510 Gram [tel 74 82 17 11; fax 74 82 07 82; info@enderupskov.dk; www.enderupskov.dk]** Fr Ribe on rd 24 E twds Gram; site on L of main rd (sp) just bef L turn to Fole. Sm, hdg pitch, pt sl, pt shd; wc; chem disp; mv service pnt; shwrs DKK5; el pnts (10A) DKK20; lndtte (inc dryer); shop & 5km; tradsmn; rest; snacks; bar; playgrnd; fishing; some statics; dogs free; phone; Eng spkn; adv bkg; quiet; CCI. "Conv stop after Esbjerg for Ribe & sw coast; woodland walks; friendly owner." ♦ DKK 125 2009*

GRASTEN *B3* (2km SW Coastal) *54.9007, 9.57121* **Lærkelunden Camping, Nederbyvej 17-25, Rinkenæs, 6300 Gråsten [tel 74 65 02 50; fax 74 65 02 25; info@laerkelunden.dk; www.laerkelunden.dk]** Fr Kruså E on rd 8 twds Gråsten & Sønderborg; on E o'skts of Rinkenæs turn R Nederbyvej (car dealer on corner) & foll sp to site in 400m. Lge, few hdstg, pt sl, unshd; wc; chem disp; mv service pnt; fam bthrm; baby facs; 4% serviced pitches; sauna; shwrs inc; el pnts (10A) DKK30; gas; lndtte; shop; cooking facs; BBQ; playgrnd; htd, covrd pool; sm sand beach adj; boat launching; solarium; TV; 10% statics; dogs free; phone; poss v cr; Eng spkn; quiet; ccard acc (5% surcharge); CCI. "Gd sailing/surfing; views over Flensburg fjord; coastal footpath; gd cent for S Jutland & N Germany; excel." ♦ Easter-19 Oct. DKK 210 2008*

I'll go online and tell the Club what we think of the campsites we've visited – www.caravanclub.co.uk/europereport

GRENAA *C2* (2km S Coastal) *56.38957, 10.91213* **Grenaa Strand Camping, Fuglsangsvej 58, 8500 Grenå [tel 86 32 17 18; fax 86 30 95 55; info@grenaastrandcamping.dk; www.grenaastrandcamping.dk]** Fr Grenå harbour foll coast rd due S foll sp. V lge, unshd; wc; chem disp; mv service pnt; fam bthrm; baby facs; shwrs; el pnts (10A) DKK35; gas; lndtte; shop; snacks; playgrnd; pool; solarium; sand beach 250m; entmnt; TV; some statics; dogs DKK30; phone; poss cr; adv bkg; red low ssn; poss noisy high ssn. "Conv for ferries to Sweden; busy site." ♦ 1 Apr-16 Sep. DKK 264 2011*

⊞ **GREVE** *D3* (5km NE Urban/Coastal) *55.59434, 12.34315* **Hundige Strand Familiecamping, Hundige Strandvej 72, 2670 Greve [tel 43 90 31 85; info@hsfc.dk; www.hsfc.dk]** Leave E20/47/55 at junc 27 & foll sp Hundige, cont strt ahead until T-junc with rd 151. Turn L, ent 200m on L. Or leave at junc 22 & foll rd 151 down coast to site on R in 8km. Med, some mkd pitch, terr, pt shd; wc; chem disp; mv service pnt; shwrs; el pnts DKK30; gas; lndtte; shop, hypmkt 1km; tradsmn; rest; snacks; bar adj; BBQ; cooking facs; playgrnd; sand beach 1km; lge sw stadium 5km; TV; 25% statics (sep area); dogs DKK5; phone; site clsd Xmas & New Year; poss cr; Eng spkn; adv bkg; quiet but some rd noise; ccard acc (surcharge); CCS. "Sh walk to rlwy stn & 15 mins to Copenhagen; friendly, helpful staff; office open morning & eves only low ssn; facs clean." DKK 195 2008*

GRINDSTED *B3* (1km SW Rural) *55.75005, 8.91740* **Grindsted Aktiv Camping, Søndre Boulevard 15, 7200 Grindsted [tel 75 32 17 51; fax 75 32 45 75; grindsted@dk-camp.dk; www.dk-camp.dk/grindsted]** Foll sp on Varde-Vejle rd to site on SW o'skts of town nr open-air pool. Med, hdg pitch, pt shd; wc; chem disp; mv service pnt; fam bthrm; baby facs; shwrs DKK5; el pnts (10A) DKK28; lndtte; kiosk; shops 1km; rest 100m; bar; playgrnd; pool 600m; tennis adj; cycle hire; TV; some statics; dogs DKK15; phone; poss cr w/end; adv bkg; quiet. "Sports complex adj with golf & tennis; clean facs; friendly staff; conv Legoland; gd walking & cycle rtes; nh only, site poss untidy; some rd noise." ♦ 1 Apr-1 Oct. DKK 152 2011*

GUDHJEM (BORNHOLM ISLAND) *A1* (2km S Coastal) *55.19566, 14.98602* **Sannes Familiecamping, Melstedvej 39, 3760 Melsted [tel 56 48 52 11; fax 56 48 52 52; sannes@familiecamping.dk; www.familiecamping.dk]** SW fr Gudhjem on rd 158, in 2km site on L. Pass other sites. NB: Bornholm Is can be reached by ferry fr Sassnitz in Germany or Ystad in Sweden. Med, mkd pitch, hdstg, terr, pt shd; wc; chem disp; mv service pnt; sauna; shwrs; el pnts (6A) DKK30; gas; lndtte; shop & supmkt 1km; tradsmn; rest 500m; playgrnd; htd pool; paddling pool; sand beach adj; fishing; fitness rm; cycle hire; wifi; TV rm; 10% statics; dogs; phone; Eng spkn; adv bkg; quiet; ccard acc; CCI. "Friendly & helpful staff; gd cycle paths in area; bus service fr site." ♦ 1 Apr-18 Sep. DKK 270 2011*

HADERSLEV *B3* (1km W Urban) *55.24431, 9.47701* **Haderslev Camping, Erlevvej 34, 6100 Haderslev [tel 74 52 13 47; fax 74 52 13 64; info@haderslev-camping.dk; www.haderslev-camping.dk]** Turn of E45 at junc 68 sp Haderslev Cent; turn R onto rd 170. on ent town. Cross lake & turn R at traff lts. Site on R at rndabt in 500m. Med, mkd pitch, hdstg, pt sl, pt shd; htd wc; chem disp; mv service pnt; fam bthrm; shwrs; el pnts (16A) DKK25; lndtte (inc dryer); shop 1km; rest; snacks; bar; BBQ; cooking facs; playgrnd; pool 1km; lake sw 1km; games rm; internet; TV; some statics; phone; bus 1km; Eng spkn; adv bkg; quiet; ccard acc (surcharge); CCI. "Gd, well-kept site conv E45; all facs to high standard; attractive old town." 15 Mar-31 Oct. DKK 149 2010*

⊞ **HAMPEN** *B2* (1km SE Rural) *56.01433, 9.36365* **Hampen Sø Camping, Hovedgaden 31, 7362 Hampen [tel 75 77 52 55; fax 75 77 52 66; info@hampen-soe-camping.dk; www.hampencamping.dk]** Fr Vejle leave E45 at junc 59 onto rd 13. After approx 35km turn L when app Hampen at site sp, site on R in 1km. Lge, mkd pitch, pt shd; htd wc; chem disp; mv service pnt; baby rm; shwrs DKK5; el pnts (16A) DKK30; gas; Indtte (inc dryer); shop; tradsmn; rest; snacks; bar; playgrnd; pool high ssn; lake sw 1km; fishing 4km; games area; wifi; entmnt; TV rm; phone; dogs DKK10; Eng spkn; adv bkg; quiet; ccard acc; CCI/CCS. "Surrounded by moorland; forests & lakes; conv Legoland (tickets sold) & lake district; welcoming & friendly." ♦ DKK 149 (CChq acc) 2009*

⊞ **HANSTHOLM** *B1* (4km E Coastal) *57.10913, 8.66731* **Hanstholm Camping, Hamborgvej 95, 7730 Hanstholm [tel 97 96 51 98; fax 97 96 54 70; info@hanstholm-camping.de; www.hanstholm-camping.dk]** Ent town fr S on rte 26. At rndabt turn R onto coast rd sp Vigsø. Site on L in about 4km. Lge, hdg/mkd pitch, pt sl, pt shd; htd wc; chem disp; mv service pnt; baby facs; fam bthrm; sauna; shwrs DKK5; el pnts (10A) DKK35; gas; Indtte (inc dryer); shop; snacks; BBQ; playgrnd; htd pool; paddling pool; sand beach 1km; fishing; horseriding; wifi; TV rm; 30% statics; dogs DKK10; phone; Eng spkn; adv bkg; ccard acc; CCI. "Fine view of North Sea coast; nr wildlife area; gd cycling/walking on coast path; excel, busy, well-maintained site." ♦ DKK 226 2010*

⊞ **HAVNEBY (ROMO ISLAND)** *A3* (500m N Coastal) *55.09883, 8.54395* **Kommandørgårdens Camping, Havnebyvej 201, 6792 Rømø [tel 74 75 51 22; fax 74 75 59 22; info@kommandoergaarden.dk; www.kommandoergaarden.dk]** Turn S after exit causeway fr mainland onto rd 175 sp Havneby. Site on L in 8km. V lge, mkd pitch, pt shd; htd wc; chem disp; mv service pnt; baby facs; fam bthrm; shwrs; el pnts (10A) DKK25; gas; Indtte; shop; rest; snacks; playgrnd; htd pool; paddling pool; sand beach 1km; tennis; wellness & beauty cent on site; TV; 30% statics; dogs DKK15; phone; poss cr; adv bkg; quiet. "Family-owned site; ferry to German island of Sylt." ♦ DKK 180 2009*

HEJLSMINDE *B3* (1km NW Coastal) *55.36847, 9.60097* **Hejlsminde Strand Camping, Gendarmvej 3, Hejlsminde, 6094 Hejls [tel 75 57 43 74; fax 75 57 46 26; info@hejlsmindecamping.dk; www.hejlsmindecamping.dk]** 14km NE of Haderslev & 8km E of Christiansfeld. Only site 1km fr harbour at Hejlsminde. Med, mkd pitch, terr, pt shd; wc; chem disp; mv service pnt; shwrs DKK5; fam bthrm; baby facs; el pnts (10A) DKK35; gas; Indtte (inc dryer); shop & 1km; tradsmn; rest 1km; playgrnd; htd, covrd pool; sand/shgl beach 500m; cycle hire; wifi; TV; 40% statics; dogs free; phone; Eng spkn; adv bkg; quiet; ccard acc; CCI. "Well-equipped; friendly owner; excel." ♦ 27 Mar-19 Sep. DKK 209 2010*

HELNAES BY *B3* (2km S Coastal) *55.13253, 10.0357* **Helnæs Camping, Strandbakken 21, Helnæs, 5631 Ebberup [tel 64 77 13 39; fax 64 77 13 54; info@helnaes-camping.dk; www.helnaes-camping.dk]** Fr Assens to Ebberup on rd 323, in town cent foll sp Helnæs island, site sp. Med, hdg/mkd pitch, htd wc; chem disp; mv service pnt; fam bthrm; private san facs some pitches; shwrs inc; el pnts (6A) DKK30; Indtte; shop; tradsmn; rest 900m; snacks; bar; BBQ; cooking facs; playgrnd; sand beach 300m; fishing; watersports; games area; wifi; TV rm; 50% statics; dogs free; adv bkg; quiet. 1 Apr-30 Sep. DKK 166 (CChq acc) 2010*

⊞ **HELSINGOR** *D2* (NE Urban/Coastal) *56.04393, 12.60433* **Helsingør Camping Grønnehave, Strandalleen 2, 3000 Helsingør [tel 49 28 49 50 or 25 31 12 12; fax 49 28 49 40; campingpladsen@helsingor.dk; www.helsingorcamping.dk]** Site in NE o'skts of town, twd Hornbæk. Site nr beach overlkg channel to Sweden on E side of rd. Foll sps on app or in town (beware: sp are sm & low down). Med, pt shd; wc; chem disp; mv service pnt; shwrs DKK5; el pnts (10A) DKK30; Indtte; shop; cooking facs; playgrnd; htd pool nr; beach; 25% statics; phone; poss v cr. "Sh walk fr Hamlet's castle; max stay 14 days 15 Jun-15 Aug; Baltic ships w/end mid-Aug; conv rlwy stn adj site; v busy/cr high ssn." ♦ DKK 165 2011*

HELSINGOR *D2* (12km S Coastal) *55.93949, 12.51643* **Niva Camping, Sølyst Allé 14, 2290 Nivå [tel 49 14 52 26; fax 49 14 52 40; nivaacamping@post8.tele.dk; www.nivaacamping.dk]** Take coast rd bet Copenhagen & Helsingør. Fr N foll sp to Nivå, & site 500m fr main rd, sp. Fr S site 2km after vill. Lge, pt sl, pt shd; wc; chem disp; mv service pnt; baby facs; fam bthrm; shwrs; el pnts (16A); Indtte (inc dryer); shop; tradsmn; rest, snacks 500m; beach 800m; fishing adj; games rm; wifi; TV; some statics; dogs; adv bkg; quiet but nr busy rlwy; red snr citizens; CCI. "Conv Helsingborg ferry, Copenhagen, Kronborg Castle (Hamlet)." 23 Mar-2 Oct. DKK 184 2010*

HELSINGOR *D2* (8km SW Rural) *55.96777, 12.45611* **Højsager Camping, Humlebækvej 31; 3480 Fredensborg [tel 4919 44 48; hojsager@dk-camp.dk; www.hojsager.dk-camp.dk]** Leave E47 at junc 5 sp fredensborg; cont along Humleboekvej Rd; site sp on R. Med, hdg pitch, pt shd; wc; chem disp; shwrs DKK10; el pnts (10A) DKK25; gas; Indtte; shop; BBQ; wifi (ltd); 50% statics; dogs; Eng spkn; adv bkg; quiet. "V conv for Helsingborg-Helsingor ferry & Fredensborg Palace; gd cycle paths adj; basic CL type site; NH/short stay only; helpful, friendly owner." 1 Apr-30 Sep. DKK 155 2011*

HELSINGOR *D2* (10km NW Urban) *56.08104, 12.51348* **Skibstrup Camping, Stormlugen 20, 3140 Ålsgårde [tel 49 70 99 71; fax 49 70 99 61; info@skibstrup-camping.dk; www.skibstrup-camping.dk]** Fr Helsingør take N coast rd to Ålsgårde; then foll site sp. Lge, shd; wc; chem disp; mv service pnt; baby facs; fam bthrm; shwrs; el pnts (10A) DKK35; Indtte (inc dryer); shop 1km; cooking facs; playgrnd; pool; paddling pool; beach 500m; wifi; TV; some statics; dogs free; phone; adv bkg; ccard acc; quiet. "Pleasant site amongst trees; conv for ferry & Copenhagen." ♦ 1 Apr-31 Oct. DKK 155 2010*

DENMARK

HENNE *A3* (S Rural) *55.73258, 8.22189* **Henneby Camping, Hennebysvej 20, 6854 Henne [tel 75 25 51 63; fax 75 25 65 01; info@hennebycamping.dk; www.henneby camping.dk]** Fr Varde on rd 181 & 465 foll sp Henne Strand. Turn R after Kirkeby. Site sp. Lge, hdg pitch, pt shd; htd wc; chem disp; mv service pnt; baby facs; fam bthrm; shwrs DKK2; el pnts (10A) DKK30; gas; Indtte; shop; rest; cooking facs; playgrnd; pool 2.5km; beach 2km; cycle hire; TV rm; some statics; dogs DKK15; poss cr; Eng spkn; quiet; ccard acc; CCI. "Superb facs; gd, clean site." ♦ 3 Apr-25 Oct. DKK 192 2009*

HILLEROD *D2* (500m W Urban) *55.9246, 12.2941* **Hillerød Camping, Blytækkervej 18, 3400 Hillerød [tel 48 26 48 54; info@hillerodcamping.dk; www.hillerodcamping.dk]** Fr Roskilde or Copenhagen on A16 twd Hillerød, take 1st L at traff lts sp Hillerød & Frederiksborg Slot Rv233. Site in town cent, not well sp. Med, pt sl, pt shd; wc; chem disp; mv service pnt; fam bthrm; baby facs; shwrs inc; el pnts (10A) DKK35 (long lead poss req); gas; Indtte; shop, rest nrby; snacks; cooking facs; common/dining rm; playgrnd; cycle hire; TV; phone; bus, train nr; poss cr; Eng spkn; adv bkg; quiet; ccard acc. "Frederiksborg castle in town cent; gd base for N Seeland; 30 min by train to Copenhagen; v helpful, charming owner; pleasant, well-run site; excel, new san facs 2010." 4 Apr-27 Sep. DKK 270.75 2011*

HIRTSHALS *C1* (5.5km SW Coastal) *57.55507, 9.93254* **Tornby Strand Camping, Strandvejen 13, 9850 Tornby [tel 98 97 78 77; fax 98 97 78 81; mail@tornbystrand.dk; www.tornbystrand.dk]** Take rd 55 fr Hjørring twd Hirtshals. In 12km turn L sp Tornby Strand & Camping, site on L in 200m. Lge, pt shd; wc; chem disp; mv service pnt; baby facs; fam bthrm; shwrs; el pnts (10A) DKK30; gas; Indtte; shops adj; snacks; playgrnd; pool 2km; sand beach 1km; TV; dogs DKK5; phone; some statics; Eng spkn; poss cr; adv bkg; quiet; CCI. "Useful for ferries to Kristiansand & Arendal." ♦ 1 Apr-1 Oct. DKK 170 2009*

HIRTSHALS *C1* (W Urban) *57.58650, 9.94583* **Hirtshals Camping, Kystvejen 6, 9850 Hirtshals [tel 98 94 25 35; fax 98 94 33 43; hirtshals@dk-camp.dk; www.dk-camp.dk/ hirtshals]** Located 16km N of Hjørring. Turn L off rd 14 3km SW of Hirtshals & site on L. Fr ferry foll sp town cent, then site sp. Med, terr, unshd; wc; chem disp; mv service pnt; baby facs; fam bthrm; shwrs DKK5; el pnts (10A) DKK30; kiosk; rest 500m; snacks 300m; playgrnd; beach 200m; fishing & sw 200m; cycle hire; TV; dogs DKK10; phone; quiet; red low ssn. "Open site on cliff top; san facs past their best; friendly staff; conv ferries; on coastal cycle path; late arr area." ♦ 23 Apr-12 Sep. DKK 150 2010*

HOBRO *B2* (7km NE Rural) *56.65161, 9.86876* **Camping Bramslev Bakker, Valsgård, 9500 Hobro [tel 40 29 52 53; mail@bramslevbakker.dk; www.bramslevbakker.dk]** Fr E45 turn E at junc 34 onto rd 541 dir Hadsund. Foll sp fr Valsgaard, site above fjord at end of rd. Med, hdg/mkd pitch, pt sl, unshd; htd wc; chem disp; mv service pnt; shwrs inc; el pnts (10-16A) DKK23; Indtte (inc dryer); shop 3km; rest adj; BBQ; cooking facs; playgrnd; lake sw & beach 300m; fishing, watersports adj; 80% statics; dogs; phone; poss cr; Eng spkn; quiet; red long stay; CCI. "In nature reserve." ♦ 15 Apr-2 Oct. DKK 112 2011*

HOBRO *B2* (1km NW Urban/Coastal) *56.63589, 9.78109* **Hobro Camping Gattenborg, Skivevej 35, 9500 Hobro [tel 98 52 32 88; fax 98 52 56 61; hobro@dk-camp.dk; www.hobrocamping.dk]** Exit E45 junc 35 dir Hobro. Site sp in 3km. Med, mkd pitch, terr, pt shd; htd wc; chem disp; mv service pnt; baby facs; fam bthrm; shwrs DKK5; el pnts (10A) DKK28; Indtte; shop; snacks; cooking facs; playgrnd; pool; games area; TV; 5% cabins; Quickstop o'night facs; Eng spkn; quiet; CCI. "Excel, clean site; easy walk to town; views over fjord; friendly site; vg playgrnd; Viking sites in area." ♦ 1 Apr-30 Sep. DKK 280.25 2011*

HOJBJERG see Århus *C2*

HOJER *A3* (4km NW Coastal) *54.98713, 8.66325* **Vadehavs Camping, Emmerlev Klev 1, 6280 Højer [tel 74 78 22 38; fax 74 78 20 58; vadehavscamping@mail.dk; www. vadehavscamping.dk]** Take rd 419 W fr Tønder; on ent Højer turn R sp Emmerlev. In 1.5km turn L at campsite sp to end of rd. Med, hdg/mkd pitch, pt shd; wc; chem disp; mv service pnt; baby facs; shwrs inc; el pnts (10A) DKK25; Indtte (inc dryer); shop high ssn; rest 100m; snacks high ssn; BBQ; playgrnd; pool; beach 200m; fishing; cycle hire; wifi; 30% statics; dogs DKK10; Eng spkn; quiet; CCI. 26 Mar-24 Oct. DKK 146 2010*

⊞ **HOLBAEK** *D3* (2.5km E Coastal) *55.71799, 11.76020* **FDM Holbæk Fjord Camping, Sofiesminde Allé 1, 4300 Holbæk [tel 59 43 50 64; fax 59 43 50 14; c-holbaek@fdm.dk; www.holbaek.fdmcamping.dk]** Fr Rv21 exit junc 20 (fr N) or junc 18 (fr S) & foll sp to harbour. Turn R (E) at harbour - Munkholmvej. Approx 1.5km along Munkholmvej, after traff lts, turn L into Sofiesminde Allé dir marina. Site on R, close to marina. Lge, hdg/mkd pitch, pt shd; htd wc; chem disp; mv service pnt; baby facs; fam bthrm; sauna; shwrs inc; el pnts (10A) inc; gas; Indtte (inc dryer); shop; rest; snacks; cooking facs; BBQ; playgrnd; htd pool; paddling pool; whirlpool; spa; watersports, fishing, golf nr; games area; games rm; wifi; TV rm; 80% statics; dogs DKK15; no c'vans/m'vans over 10m high ssn; phone; adv bkg; quiet; ccard acc; red low ssn. "Well-run site in attractive position; helpful staff; pitches poss tight lge o'fits; clean san facs; gd walks & cycle tracks." ♦ DKK 238 SBS - H17 2011*

HOLSTEBRO *B2* (2km S Rural) *56.34930, 8.64496* **Mejdal Camping, Birkevej 25, 7500 Holstebro [tel 97 42 20 68; fax 97 41 24 92; mejdal@dcu.dk; www.camping-mejdal.dk]** Sp off ring rd A11 & A16, SE of town, sp at km 44. Med, pt sl, pt shd; wc; chem disp; mv service pnt; shwrs inc; fam bthrm; baby facs; el pnts (10A) DKK25; gas; Indtte; shop; rest 2km; playgrnd; fishing; boating; golf 5km; TV; dogs DKK15; phone; adv bkg; ccard acc. "Site adj to lge lake in quiet surroundings, but v cr high ssn; open air museum adj." ♦ 21 Mar-22 Sep. DKK 158 2009*

⊞ **HORSENS** *B2* (4km W Rural/Coastal) *55.85928, 9.91747* **Husodde Camping, Husoddevej 85, 8700 Horsens [tel 75 65 70 60; fax 75 65 50 72; husodde@dk-camp.dk; www.husodde-camping.dk]** Site sp to R of Horsens-Odder rd (451), foll rd to fjord, site sp. Med, mkd pitch, pt sl, pt shd; wc; chem disp; mv service pnt; baby facs; fam bthrm; shwrs DKK5; el pnts (10A) DKK35; Indtte; kiosk & shops 500m; rest, snacks, bar 5km; cooking facs; BBQ; playgrnd; pool 3km; sand beach & fishing adj; TV; 10% statics; dogs DKK10; phone; Eng spkn; quiet; CCI. "Lovely location; lge pitches; well-maintained, well-managed site; friendly welcome; cycle tracks." ♦ DKK 195 2011*

HUMBLE (LANGELAND ISLAND) *C3* (5km W Coastal) *54.81940, 10.63995* **Camping & Feriecenter Ristinge, Ristingevej 104, 5932 Humble [tel 62 57 13 29; fax 62 57 26 29; info@ristinge.dk; www.ristinge.dk]** S on A9 to Rudkøbing. Turn R dir Bagenkop. At Humble foll sp Ristinge on R, site sp. Lge, mkd pitch, pt shd; htd wc; mv service pnt; fam bthrm; shwrs DKK5; el pnts (10A) DKK28; Indtte; shop; rest; snacks; cooking facs; playgrnd; htd pool; paddling pool; waterslide; sand beach 200m; watersports; tennis; games area; boat & cycle hire; TV rm; some statics; adv bkg; quiet. "Pleasant site; gd touring base." ♦ 1 May-31 Aug. DKK 180 2008*

HVIDE SANDE *A2* (4.5km S Coastal) *55.96253, 8.14221* **Camping Holmsland Klit, Tingodden 141, Årgab, 6960 Hvide Sande [tel 97 31 13 09; fax 97 31 35 20; c-holmsland@fdm.dk; www.holmsland.fdmcamping.dk]** Fr Ringkøbing rd 15 then rd 181 twd Søndervig, Hvide Sande & Årgab. Site on R. Med, hdstg, pt sl, unshd; wc; chem disp; mv service pnt; fam bthrm; baby facs; shwrs; el pnts (6-10A) DKK30; gas; Indtte (inc dryer); shop; rest 4.5km; bar; beach adj; playgrnd; fishing; wifi; TV; 20% statics; dogs DKK12; phone; Eng spkn; adv bkg; quiet; ccard acc; red CCI. "Superb beach; next to 40km cycle track; excel for sm children; Legoland 1 hour; friendly." ♦ Easter-26 Sep. DKK 187 (CChq acc) 2010*

HVIDE SANDE *A2* (6km S Coastal) *55.94975, 8.15030* **Nordsø Camping & Badeland, Tingodden 3, Årgab, 6960 Hvide Sande [tel 96 59 17 22; fax 96 59 17 17; info@nordsoe-camping.dk; www.nordsoe-camping.dk]** Fr E20 take exit 73 onto rd 11 to Varde. Then take rd 181 twd Nymindegab & Hvide Sande. Lge, some hdstg, unshd; htd wc; chem disp; mv service pnt; baby facs; fam bthrm; serviced pitches; sauna; private san facs avail; shwrs inc; el pnts (10A) DKK30; Indtte (inc dryer); shop; rest; snacks; bar; playgrnd; 2 pools (1 htd, covrd); paddling pool; waterslides; sand beach 200m; fishing; tennis; wifi; entmnt; TV rm; 10% statics; dogs DKK20; phone; adv bkg; quiet. "Well-maintained facs; extra charge seaview pitches; vg." ♦ 15 Apr-31 Oct. DKK 199 (CChq acc) 2011*

IDESTRUP see Nykøbing (Falster) *D3*

ISHOJ HAVN see København *D3*

JELLING *B3* (10km NW Rural) *55.83138, 9.29944* **Topcamp Riis & Feriecenter, Østerhovedvej 43, 7323 Give [tel 75 73 14 33; fax 75 73 58 66; info@topcampriis.dk; www.topcampriis.dk]** Fr S exit E45 at junc 61, turn L & foll rd 28 for approx 8km. Turn R onto rd 441 for 15km, then turn R into Østerhovedvej for 2km & turn L into site. Or fr N on E45 exit junc 57, turn R & foll rd for 25km; turn L & foll 442 for 500m; turn R into Østerhovedvej & cont for 1.5km; turn R into site. Lge, pt shd; wc; chem disp; mv service pnt; serviced pitch; baby facs; fam bthrm; jacuzzi; sauna; shwrs DKK5; el pnts (13A) inc; gas; Indtte (ind dryer); shop; bar; BBQ; playgrnd; htd pool; waterslide; paddling pool; fishing 3.5km; cycle hire; games rm; child entmnt high ssn; golf 4km; wifi;TV rm; 60% statics; dogs DKK20; no o'fits over 15m high ssn; phone; recep 0800-2200; poss cr; adv bkg; quiet; ccard acc; red low ssn; CCI. "Attractive, well laid-out, well-run site in beautiful countryside; vg san facs; conv Legoland, Safari Park, Center Mobilium museum in Billund, lakes & E coast." ♦ 31 Mar-30 Sep. DKK 320 SBS - H11 2011*

JUELSMINDE *B3* (W Urban) *55.71330, 10.01562* **Juelsminde Strand Camping, Rousthøjs Allé 1, 7130 Juelsminde [tel 75 69 32 10; fax 75 69 32 28; juelsmin@image.dk; www.juelsmindecamping.dk]** Nr beach in SE corner of town; site sep fr public beach. Nr ferry terminal to Kalundborg. Lge, hdg/mkd pitch, pt shd; htd wc; chem disp; mv service pnt; baby facs; fam bthrm; shwrs; el pnts (10A) DKK15; Indtte (inc dryer); shop, rest, snacks & bar; cooking facs; playgrnd; sand beach 200m; fishing; boating; wifi; TV; phone; poss cr; dogs DKK10; Eng spkn; adv bkg; quiet; CCI. "Conv to town & harbour; poss cr." ♦ 1 Apr-27 Sep. DKK 258 (CChq acc) 2011*

JYDERUP *C3* (1km S Rural) *55.65251, 11.39555* **Skarresø Camping, Slagelsevej 40, 4450 Jyderup [tel 59 24 86 80; fax 59 24 86 81; info@skarresoecamping.dk; www.skarresoecamping.dk]** Approx 25km fr Kalundborg dir Copenhagen rte 23 turn L dir Jyderup. Fr town cent foll sp to site on RV225 dir Slagelse, site on R in 1km. Med, pt sl, pt shd; htd wc; chem disp; mv service pnt; baby facs; fam bthrm; shwrs DKK2; el pnts (10A) metered or DKK30; gas; Indtte (inc dryer); shop; tradsmn; rest 1km; BBQ; cooking facs; playgrnd; lake adj; fishing; cycle hire; games area; wifi; TV rm; 25% statics; dogs free; Eng spkn; adv bkg; quiet. "Pleasant site; gd walks round lake fr site; tourist info fr site office." ♦ 26 Mar-26 Sep. DKK 140 2010*

⊞ **KARISE** *D3* (3km S Rural) *55.27086, 12.22281* **Lægårdens Camping, Vemmetoftevej 2A, Store Spjellerup, 4653 Karise [tel 56 71 00 67; fax 56 71 00 68; info@laegaardenscamping.dk; www.laegaardenscamping.dk]** Turn S off rd 209 in Karise, site sp. Med, hdg/mkd pitch, pt shd; htd wc; chem disp; mv service pnt; shwrs DKK5; el pnts DKK30; Indtte; rest, snacks 1km; playgrnd; beach 3km; TV; 60% statics; dogs DKK10; Eng spkn; adv bkg; CCI. DKK 150 2011*

KARREBAEKSMINDE see Næstved *D3*

DENMARK

KERTEMINDE *C3* (1.5km N Coastal) *55.46348, 10.67077* **Kerteminde Camping, Hindsholmvej 80, 5300 Kerteminde [tel 65 32 19 71; fax 65 32 18 71; kerteminde@mycamp.dk; www.kertemindecamping.dk]** On L of coast rd on N o'skts of town on rd 315. Lge, pt shd; htd wc; chem disp; mv service pnt; shwrs DKK6; fam bthrm; baby facs; el pnts (10A) DKK30; Indtte; gas; kiosk; tradsmn; rest 2km; BBQ; cooking facs; playgrnd; beach 100m; watersports; cycle hire; wifi; TV rm; 10% statics; dogs DKK15; phone; poss cr; adv bkg; quiet; ccard acc (surcharge); CCI. "Excel facs; Viking burial ship in cave nrby." ♦ 27 Mar-24 Oct. DKK 173 2010*

KOBENHAVN *D3* (6km N Coastal) *55.74536, 12.58331* **Camping Charlottenlund Fort, Strandvejen 144B, 2290 Charlottenlund [tel 39 62 36 88; fax 39 61 08 16; camping@gentofte.dk; www.campingcopenhagen.dk]** Take København-Helsingør coast rd 02/152, site on seaside 2km N of Tuborg factory. Sm, mkd pitch, few hdstg, shd; wc; chem disp; mv service pnt; shwrs DKK5; el pnts (10A) metered; Indtte (inc dryer); shops 500m; rest, bar adj; cooking facs; sand beach; bus; poss v cr; Eng spkn; adv bkg rec; quiet but noisy during mid-summer festivities; ccard acc; CCI. "Experimentarium Science Park at Tuborg brewery; in grounds of old moated fort; conv Copenhagen & Sweden; gd facs but inadequate high ssn; friendly staff." ♦ 30 Apr-6 Sep. DKK 245 2009*

KOBENHAVN *D3* (15km N Rural) *55.80896, 12.53062* **Nærum Camping, Ravnebakken, 2850 Nærum [tel 42 80 19 57; fax 45 80 11 78; naerum@dcu.dk; www.camping-naerum.dk]** Fr Copenhagen take E47/E55/rd 19 N for 16km, turn W to Nærum at junc 14, over bdge x-ing m'way & sharp L. Lge, pt sl, pt shd; wc; chem disp; mv service pnt; shwrs inc; el pnts inc (lead on loan fr recep) DKK35; gas; Indtte; shop; playgrnd; pool 10km; TV rm; train/bus 500m; poss cr; Eng spkn; adv bkg; some rlwy & m'way noise; ccard acc; CCI. "Popular nr woods; conv Copenhagen & Helsingor; shopping cent nrby over m'way bdge; gd cycle paths; path fr site for suburban rlwy to Copenhagen; if arr bet 1200 & 1400 select pitch & report to office after 1400." ♦ 21 Mar-18 Oct. DKK 162 2010*

KOBENHAVN *D3* (S Urban) *55.65903, 12.55785* **City Camp, Fisketorvet/Vasbygade, 1560 København [tel 45 21 42 53 84; reservation@citycamp.dk]** Fr S on E20, cont over 02 over 'Sjællandsbroen' to R on Scandiagade, cont on Vasbygade, turn R at 1st traff lts. Site is behind Fisketorv shopping cent on 'brown field' site - looks like car park - S of rlwy line by canal. Suggest phone for dirs. M'vans only. Med, hdstg, unshd; wc; shwrs inc; chem disp; mv service pnt; el pnts (16A) DKK35; shops nr; dogs; open 0800 to 2200; poss cr; Eng spkn; poss noisy. "Conv city cent & Tivoli; boat ride to cent; facs sufficient but simple; friendly." 29 May-30 Aug. DKK 225 2009*

KOBENHAVN *D3* (14km S Rural/Coastal) *55.60721, 12.38123* **FDM Camping Tangloppen, Tangloppen 2, 2635 Ishøj Havn [tel 43 54 07 67; fax 43 54 07 64; c-tangloppen@fdm.dk; www.tangloppen.fdmcamping.dk]** S fr København on E20 or 151, site sp at Ishøj on beach rd; on L of 151 on lakeside. Med, unshd; htd wc; chem disp; mv service pnt; baby facs; fam bthrm; shwrs inc; el pnts (4-10A) DKK30; gas 1km; Indtte; shop; supmkt 1km; snacks; cooking facs; playgrnd; sand beach 500m; watersports; cycle hire; internet; TV; some statics; dogs DKK12; phone; bus to rlwy stn 1.2km; poss cr; Eng spkn; quiet; ccard acc; CCI. "Lakeside site in lovely setting; friendly & helpful staff; gd birdwatching; train to Copenhagen nr; no dogs allowed on nrby beach; nr contemporary art gallery; office clsd 1200-1400; facs stretched high ssn; poss unkempt low ssn." ♦ 29 Mar-19 Oct. DKK 189 2008*

⊞ **KOBENHAVN** *D3* (9km W Urban) *55.67055, 12.43353* **DCU Absalon Camping, Korsdalsvej 132, 2610 Rødovre [tel 36 41 06 00; fax 36 41 02 93; absalon@dcu.dk; www.camping-absalon.dk]** Fr E55/E20/E47 exit junc 24 dir København, site on L in 1km, sp. Or fr København foll A156 W for 9km. Sp Rødovre then Brøndbyøster, shortly after this site sp to R at traff lts; ent on L after 100m down side rd, sp. V lge, mkd pitch, pt shd; htd wc; chem disp; mv service pnt; baby facs; fam bthrm; shwrs inc; el pnts (10-16A) DKK30 or metered + conn fee; gas; Indtte (inc dryer); shop & 500m; rest 2km; BBQ; cooking facs; playgrnd; htd pool 300m; golf 10km; wifi; TV rm; 10% statics; dogs DKK20; bus/train nr; poss cr; ccard acc (surcharge). "Well located nr Brøndbyøster rlwy stn & bus Copenhagen (rail tickets fr recep); some pitches unreliable in wet & dusty when dry; vg, modern san facs; office clsd 1200-1400 low ssn; sep area for c'vans & m'vans; helpful staff; cycle rte to city; vg." ♦ DKK 193 (CChq acc) 2010*

⊞ **KOGE** *D3* (10km SE Coastal) *55.44601, 12.19240* **Stevns Camping, Strandvejen 29, 4671 Strøby [tel 56 57 70 03; info@stevnscamping.dk; www.stevnscamping.dk]** Exit E20/E55 junc 33 twd Køge. In Køge take rd 209 & 260 to Strøby. In Strøby turn L onto Strandvejen. Lge, mkd pitch, unshd; htd wc; chem disp; mv service pnt; fam bthrm; baby facs; shwrs inc; el pnts (10A) inc; Indtte (inc dryer); shop; tradsmn; rest, bar 400m; BBQ; cooking facs; playgrnd; htd pool; paddling pool; shgl beach 400m; wifi; some statics; dogs DKK10; phone; Eng spkn; quiet; CCI."Gd site nr coast & Koge; access to Copenhagen by public transport." ♦ DKK 190 (CChq acc) 2011*

KOGE *D3* (1km S Coastal) *55.44561, 12.19280* **Vallø Camping, Strandvejen 102, 4600 Køge [tel 56 65 28 51; fax 56 65 10 25; vallo.camp@mail.dk; www.valloecamping.dk]** Exit Køge head SE on rd 261, sp Store Heddinge for 500m. Site on R on o'skts of town. Lge, pt sl, pt shd; wc; chem disp; mv service pnt; shwrs; fam bthrms; baby facs; el pnts (10A) DKK34; gas; Indtte; shop; cooking facs; playgrnd; sand beach 500m; TV; phone; poss cr; adv bkg; quiet. "Poss some traff noise fr boundary rd; DKK100 deposit for card to use facs - automatically deducted; pitches & san facs run down (Jun 09); excel rlwy links to Copenhagen, Roskilde & Helsingør 15 mins walk fr site." ♦ 1 Apr-30 Sep. DKK 168 2009*

DENMARK

KOLDING *B3* (15km E Coastal) *55.46777, 9.67972* **Gammel Ålbo Camping, Gammel Aalbovej 30, 6092 Sønder Stenderup [tel 75 57 11 16; camping@gl-aalbo.dk; www.gl-aalbo.dk]** Foll rd SE fr Kolding to Agtrup then on to Sønder Bjert & Sønder Stenderup. Foll site sp thro vill twd coast, site at end of rd. Med, hdg pitch, some hdstg, terr, pt shd; htd wc; chem disp; mv service pnt; fam bthrm; shwrs inc; el pnts (16A) DKK32; lndry rm; shop; cooking facs; shgl beach adj; fishing; boat hire; skindiving; dogs free; 10% statics; poss cr; Eng spkn; quiet; CCI. "Well-kept, relaxing site o'looking Lillebælt." 1 Apr-15 Sep. DKK 168 2010*

⊞ **KOLDING** *B3* (3km S Urban) *55.46290, 9.47290* **Kolding City Camp, Vonsildvej 19, 6000 Kolding [tel 75 52 13 88; fax 75 52 45 29; info@koldingcitycamp.dk; www.koldingcitycamp.dk]** Heading N exit E45 sp Christiansfeld at junc 66; then onto rd 170 to Kolding; site 10km N on R. Heading S exit E45 at Kolding Syd, junc 65; R at x-rds to Vonsild; site 800m on L. Lge, pt sl, pt shd; htd wc; chem disp; mv service pnt; baby facs; fam bthrm; private san facs avail; shwrs inc; el pnts (10A) DKK30; gas; lndtte (inc dryer); shop high ssn; supmkt 800m; tradsmn; rest 3km; BBQ; cooking facs; playgrnd; htd, covrd pool 3km; lake beach & fishing 5km; tennis; wifi; TV rm; dogs DKK10; phone; bus to town; poss cr; Eng spkn; adv bkg; some rd noise; ccard acc; 10% red CCI. "Friendly & v quiet; conv NH Legoland; vg san facs." ♦ DKK 185.75 (CChq acc) 2011*

KOLLUND see Kruså *B3*

KORSOR *C3* (3km N Coastal) *55.34951, 11.1064* **Storebælt Camping & Feriecenter, Storebæltsvej 85, 4220 Korsør [tel 58 38 38 05; fax 58 38 38 65; info@storebaeltferiecenter.dk; www.storebaeltferiecenter.dk]** Exit E20 junc 43 & foll sp to site on S side of bdge. Lge, mkd pitch, unshd; htd wc; chem disp; mv service pnt; baby facs; fam bthrm; serviced pitches; shwrs DKK5; el pnts (10A) metered + conn fee; lndtte; shop; snacks; bar; cooking facs; playgrnd; pool; beach adj; games area; games rm; wifi; some statics; dogs free; bus 1km; Eng spkn; adv bkg; quiet; ccard acc (surcharge); CCI. "Some m'way noise; sea views; exposed site poss v windy." ♦ 1 Mar-31 Oct. DKK 170 2009*

KORSOR *C3* (10km SE Rural) *55.28991, 11.2649* **Campinggaarden Boeslunde, Rennebjergvej 110, 4242 Boeslunde [tel 58 14 02 08; fax 58 14 03 40; info@campinggaarden.dk; www.campinggaarden.dk]** Take rd 265 S out of Korsør & in 8km, bef Boeslunde at camping sp, turn R. Site on L in 2km. Lge, pt sl, shd; wc; chem disp; mv service pnt; shwrs inc; fam bthrm; baby facs; el pnts DKK30 (long lead poss req); gas; lndtte; shop; bar; playgrnd; paddling pool; beach 1.5km; sat TV; dogs DKK10; phone; poss cr w/ends; adv bkg; quiet; red CCI. "Gd size, grassy pitches." ♦ 1 Apr-30 Sep. DKK 190 2009*

⊞ **KRUSA** *B3* (1km N Rural) *54.85370, 9.40220* **Kruså Camping, Åbenråvej 7, 6340 Kruså [tel 74 67 12 06; fax 74 67 12 05; info@krusaacamping.dk; www.krusaacamping.dk]** S on E45, exit junc 75 twd Kruså. Turn L onto rd 170, site on L. Lge, pt shd, pt sl; wc; chem disp; mv service pnt; fam bthrm; baby facs; shwrs DKK5; el pnts (10A) DKK30; gas; lndtte (inc dryer); shop; rest; snacks; bar; cooking facs; playgrnd; htd pool; TV; dogs; phone; rd noise; CCI. "Gd NH; bus to Flensburg (Germany) 1km fr site; new san facs 2010." ♦ DKK 176 2010*

KRUSA *B3* (5km E Coastal) *54.84538, 9.46715* **DCU Camping Kollund, Fjordvejen 29A, 6340 Kollund [tel 74 67 85 15; fax 74 67 83 85; c-kollund@fdm.dk]** Take coastal rd E fr Kruså dir Sønderborg; site on L 500m after Kollund. Med, mkd pitch, pt sl, unshd; wc; chem disp; mv service pnt; shwrs DKK5; el pnts (6A) DKK45; lndtte; shop; rest adj; cooking facs; playgrnd; internet; 40% statics; dogs DKK15; phone; Eng spkn; adv bkg; ccard acc. "Friendly owners; gd." ♦ Easter-14 Oct. DKK 175 2009*

⊞ **KRUSA** *B3* (5km E Coastal) *54.84231, 9.45896* **Frigård Camping, Kummelefort 14, 6340 Kollund [tel 74 67 88 30; fax 74 67 88 72; fricamp@fricamp.dk; www.fricamp.dk]** Take coast rd 8 fr Kruså dir Sønderborg. Turn R at 2nd set traff lts dir Kollund, site sp on L after 3km. V lge, pt sl, pt shd; htd wc; chem disp; mv service pnt; baby facs; fam bthrm; sauna; shwrs DKK5; el pnts (16A) DKK35; lndtte (inc dryer); shop; snacks; cooking facs; playgrnd; htd pool; paddling pool; games area; cycle hire; wifi; 50% statics; dogs free; phone; poss cr; no adv bkg; quiet. "Conv Sønderborg & fjord." ♦ DKK 241 2010*

KULHUSE *D2* (1km S Coastal) *55.93168, 11.90907* **DCU Camping Kulhuse, Kulhusevej 199, 3630 Kulhuse [tel 47 53 01 86; fax 47 53 51 28; kulhuse@dcu.dk; www.camping-kulhuse.dk]** Fr Jægerspris on rd 207 N sp Kulhuse. Well sp on L 1km bef vill. Lge, pt sl, terr, pt shd; htd wc; chem disp; mv service pnt; fam bthrm; baby facs; shwrs inc; el pnts (4A) DKK30; lndtte; shop & 1km; rest 1km; snacks; bar 1km; BBQ; cooking facs; playgrnd; sand beach 500m; TV; 20% statics; dogs DKK20; phone; poss cr; Eng spkn; adv bkg; quiet; CCI. "Gd children's playgrnd facs; pleasant site." ♦ 24 Mar-21 Oct. DKK 194 2011*

LAKOLK (ROMO ISLAND) *A3* (Coastal) *55.14478, 8.49460* **Lakolk Strand Camping, Kongsmark, 6792 Lakolk [tel 74 75 52 28; fax 74 75 53 52; lakollk@c.dk; www.lakolkcamping.dk]** Foll rd 175 to Rømø Island, strt at traff lts, foll sp Lakolk. Site 4km on L at end of rd. Lge, mkd pitch, unshd; htd wc; chem disp; mv service pnt; shwrs inc; el pnts (10A) DKK26; gas; lndry rm; shop, rest, snacks, bar adj; cooking facs; BBQ; sand beach; playgrnd; entmnt; TV rm; dogs DKK15; phone; poss cr; Eng spkn; adv bkg; quiet; CCI. "Excel 11km sand beach; gd for watersports." ♦ 14 Mar-19 Oct. DKK 150 2008*

LAVEN see Ry *B2*

DENMARK

LEMVIG *A2* (12km W Coastal) *56.52608, 8.12633* **Bovbjerg Camping, Julsgårdvej 13, 7620 Ferring [tel 97 89 51 20; fax 97 89 53 43; bc@bovbjergcamping.dk; www.bovbjergcamping.dk]** Fr Lemvig foll rd 181 past Nissum Fjord, take rd to L for Ferring. Site to N of vill. Med, hdg/mkd pitch, pt shd; wc; chem disp; mv service pnt; baby facs; fam bthrm; shwrs DKK2; el pnts (10A) DKK29; lndtte; shop; rest 400m; cooking facs; htd pool; paddling pool; sand beach 300m; cycle hire; golf 13km; TV rm; 30% statics; dogs; phone; Eng spkn; adv bkg; quiet; red long stay/snr citizens; CCI."Lge pitches with view." 20 Mar-18 Oct. DKK 178 2009*

LEMVIG *A2* (3km NW Coastal) *56.56733, 8.29399* **Lemvig Strand Camping, Vinkelhagevej 6, 7620 Lemvig [tel 97 82 00 42; fax 97 81 04 56; lemvig@dk-camp.dk; www.lemvigstrandcamping.dk]** Foll camping sps in Lemvig to site. Med, mkd pitch, unshd; wc; chem disp; mv service pnt; baby facs; fam bthrm; sauna; shwrs DKK2; el pnts (10A) DKK30; lndtte; shop; rest adj; cooking facs; playgrnd; htd, covrd pool; beach 300m; games area; games rm; internet; TV rm; 30% statics; dogs; phone; adv bkg; ccard acc. "Vg sailing cent; pretty area." ♦ Easter-13 Sep. DKK 198 2009*

⊞ **LOHALS (LANGELAND ISLAND)** *C3* (1km N Urban) *55.13383, 10.90578* **Lohals Camping, Birkevej 11, 5953 Lohals [tel 58 37 50 80; info@lohalscamping.dk; www.lohalscamping.dk]** On island of Langeland. Cross to Rudkøbing, fr island of Tåsinge, then 28km to N of island (only 1 main rd); site in middle of vill nr ferry to Sjælland Island. Med, shd; wc; chem disp; mv service pnt; baby facs; fam bthrm; shwrs; el pnts (10A) DKK30; gas in vill; lndtte; shop; rest, snacks 200m; playgrnd; htd pool; paddling pool; sand beach 1km; boat & cycle hire; fishing; tennis; games area; TV; some statics; dogs free; phone; adv bkg; quiet. "Conv ferry (Lohals-Korsor) 500m." ♦ DKK 178 2009*

LOKKEN *B1* (6km S Coastal) *57.32070, 9.67760* **Grønhøj Strand Camping, Kettrupvej 125, Ingstrup, 9480 Løkken [tel 98 88 44 33; fax 98 88 36 44; info@gronhoj-strand-camping.dk; www.gronhoj-strand-camping.dk]** S fr Løkken on rd 55, sp on rd Grønhøj Strandvej Lge, unshd; htd wc; chem disp; mv service pnt; serviced pitches; sauna; baby facs; fam bthrm; shwrs DKK5; el pnts (13A) DKK30; lndtte (inc dryer); shop; tradsmn; rest 2km; BBQ; cooking facs; playgrnd; sand beach 700m; tennis adj; games area; wifi; TV rm; 30% statics; dogs; phone; Eng spkn; adv bkg; quiet; ccard acc; red snr citizens. ♦ 15 Apr-18 Sep. DKK 158 (CChq acc) 2011*

LUNDEBORG *C3* (700m N Coastal) *55.14560, 10.78136* **Lundeborg Strand-Camping, Gammel Lundeborgvej 46, 5874 Hasselager [tel 62 25 14 50; fax 62 25 20 22; ferie@lundeborg.dk; www.lundeborg.dk]** Fr rd 163 turn E at Oure, site sp fr Lundeborg. Med, pt sl, unshd; wc; chem disp; mv service pnt; shwrs DKK5; fam bthrm; baby facs; el pnts (6A) DKK35; lndtte; shop; cooking facs; playgrnd; beach adj; boat-launching; TV; some cabins; dogs DKK15; phone; poss cr; adv bkg; quiet. "Attractive sm fishing vill; pay in advance on arrival." Easter-13 Sep. DKK 192 2009*

MALLING *C2* (5km E Coastal) *56.04122, 10.26390* **Ajstrup Strand Camping, Ajstrup Strandvej 81, Ajstrup Strand, 8340 Malling [tel 86 93 35 35; fax 86 93 15 84; info@ajstrupcamping.dk; www.ajstrupcamping.dk]** Fr S turn R in Odder off rd 451 sp Sakslid. Foll rd for 8km thro Norsminde, then turn R & foll site sp. Lge, mkd pitch, pt shd; htd wc; chem disp; mv service pnt; baby facs; fam bthrm; private san facs avail; shwrs; el pnts (6A) DKK30; lndtte (inc dryer); shop; snacks; BBQ; cooking facs; playgrnd; beach adj; cycle & canoe hire; wifi; TV rm; 6% statics; dogs DKK10; Eng spkn; CCI. "Adj to excel cycle track thro forest to Århus." ♦ 15 Apr-23 Oct. DKK 164 (CChq acc) 2009*

MARIAGER *B2* (N Coastal) *56.65424, 9.97500* **Mariager Camping, Ny Havnevej 5A, 9550 Mariager [tel 98 54 13 42; fax 98 54 25 80; info@mariagercamping.dk; www.mariagercamping.dk]** E fr Hobro on rd 555, do not take R sp Mariager, but on to bottom of hill, turn L at camp sp. Med, mkd pitch, unshd; wc; chem disp; mv service pnt; baby facs; fam bthrm; shwrs DKK2; el pnts (16A) DKK25; gas; lndtte; shop; snacks; playgrnd; sand/shgl beach adj; sea & rv fishing; boat launch; 50% statics; dogs free; phone; Eng spkn; adv bkg; quiet; CCI. "Beautiful vill with museum & abbey; fjord views fr site; vg facs." ♦ 5 Apr-23 Sep. DKK 178 2009*

MARIBO *C3* (500m SW Rural) *54.77260, 11.49463* **Maribo Sø Camping, Bangshavevej 25, 4930 Maribo [tel 54 78 00 71; fax 54 78 47 71; camping@maribo-camping.dk; www.maribo-camping.dk]** Exit E47 junc 48 at Maribo. At rndabt take rd to 'Centrum' strt on into Vesterbrogade; turn R into Bangshavevej & foll site sp. Lge, pt shd; wc; chem disp; mv service pnt; baby facs; fam bthrm; shwrs inc; el pnts (6A) DKK32; lndtte; shop; cooking facs; playgrnd; sand beach & lake adj; internet; TV rm; 30% statics; phone; poss cr; Eng spkn; adv bkg; quiet; CCI. "Clean facs; 5 mins walk into Maribo; museum adj; helpful staff; useful as NH after ferry fr Puttgarden, Germany; site clsd 1300-1500, site yourself; late arrivals area avail at night." ♦ 30 Mar-21 Oct. DKK 177 2011*

⊞ **MARSTAL (AERO ISLAND)** *C3* (500m S Urban/Coastal) *54.84666, 10.51823* **Marstal Camping, Eghovedvej 1, 5960 Marstal [tel 63 52 63 69; fax 62 53 36 40; marstal.camping@mail.tele.dk; www.marstalcamping.dk]** Fr Ærøskobing ferry to E end of Ærø Island, thro town of Marstal & turn R at harbour twd sailing club; site adj to club. Med, mkd pitch, pt shd; wc; chem disp; mv service pnt; baby facs; fam bthrm; shwrs DKK5; el pnts (16A) DKK28; lndtte (inc dryer); shop; rest, snacks, bar 500m; BBQ; playgrnd; TV; 10% statics; dogs DKK15, phone; poss cr; adv bkg; poss noisy; ccard acc; red low ssn/CCI. ♦ DKK 163 (CChq acc) 2009*

MIDDELFART *B3* (7km NE Coastal) *55.51948, 9.85025* **Vejlby Fed Camping, Rigelvej 1, 5500 Vejlby Fed [tel 64 40 24 20; fax 64 40 24 38; mail@vejlbyfed.dk; www.vejlbyfed.dk]** Exit E20 junc 57 or 58. Site sp in Vejlby Fed, NE fr Middelfart dir Bogense, on coast. Lge, mkd pitch, pt shd; wc; chem disp; mv service pnt; fam bthrm; baby facs; sauna; shwrs DKK6; el pnts (10A) DKK28; lndtte; shop; tradsmn; snacks; bar; cooking facs; playgrnd; htd pool; paddling pool; sand beach adj; boating; fishing; tennis; wifi; 30% statics; dogs DKK15; phone; Eng spkn; adv bkg; CCI. ♦ 15 Mar-14 Sep. DKK 178 2008*

DENMARK

MIDDELFART *B3* (6km SE Rural/Coastal) *55.43995, 9.82464* **Ronæs Strand Camping, Ronæsvej 10, Ronæs Strand, 5580 Nørre Aaby [tel 64 42 17 63; fax 64 42 17 73; campingferie@hotmail.com; www.camping-ferie.dk]** Leave E20 at Nørre Aaby junc 57, take 313 S twd Assens. In 5km turn R (NW) to Udby. In Udby turn L to Ronaes, turn R in vill. Site on L, sp. Med, mkd pitch, terr, pt sl, pt shd; wc; chem disp; mv service pnt; baby facs; fam bthrm; shwrs DKK6; el pnts (10A) DKK30; gas; Indtte (inc dryer); shop; rest 6km; snacks high ssn; playgrnd; sand beach adj; fishing; boat hire & launching facs; cycle hire; wifi; TV; 10% statics; dogs DKK15; phone; Eng spkn; adv bkg; quiet; ccard acc; CCI. "Gd for families; vg facs." ♦ Easter-19 Sep. DKK 200 2010*

MIDDELFART *B3* (3km SW Rural) *55.51694, 9.68225* **Gals Klint Camping, Galsklintvej 11, 5500 Middelfart [tel 64 41 20 59; fax 64 41 81 59; mail@galsklint.dk; www.galsklint.dk]** Fr W on E20 take rd 161. At traff lts turn L & cross Little Belt Bdge. In 300m turn R into Galsklintvej & foll sp. Lge, hdg/mkd pitch, pt shd; htd wc; chem disp; mv service pnt; baby facs; fam bthrm; shwrs DKK3; el pnts (16A) DKK28; Indtte; shop; rest; snacks; BBQ; cooking facs; playgrnd; shgl beach adj; fishing; boat hire; 10% statics; dogs; Eng spkn; adv bkg; quiet; ccard acc (surcharge); CCI. "Site surrounded by forest; gd cycling/walking; vg." ♦ Easter-2 Oct. DKK 151 2008*

NAERUM see København *D3*

NAESTVED *D3* (6km SW Rural/Coastal) *55.20051, 11.66438* **De Hvide Svaner Camping, Karrebækvej 741, 4736 Karrebæksminde [tel 55 44 24 15; svaner@mail.dk; www.dehvidesvaner.dk]** Fr Næstved take Karrebæksminde rd 265. Site on L 200m after turn for Skælskør. Lge, hdg/mkd pitch, pt sl, pt shd; wc; chem disp; mv service pnt; baby facs; fam bthrm; shwrs inc; el pnts (10A) DKK30; gas; Indtte; sm shop; rest; playgrnd; htd pool; paddling pool; beach nrby; cycle hire; games area; wifi; TV; many statics; dogs DKK10; phone; Quickstop o'night facs; Eng spkn; adv bkg; quiet."Excel, modern san facs; friendly staff; well situated nr lake." ♦ Easter-16 Oct. DKK 192 2009*

NAKSKOV *C3* (13km SW Coastal) *54.79180, 10.98110* **Albuen Strand Camping, Vesternæsvej 70, Ydø, 4900 Nakskov [tel 54 94 87 62; fax 54 94 90 27; mail@albuen.dk; www.albuen.dk]** S fr Nakskov dir Langø. In approx 10km at Ydø, foll sp to site. Lge, unshd; htd wc; chem disp; mv service pnt; baby facs; fam bthrm; shwrs DKK2; el pnts (10A) DKK30; Indtte (inc dryer); shop; tradsmn; cooking facs; playgrnd; htd pool; paddling pool; sand beach adj; cycle hire; games area; wifi; TV rm; 15% statics; dogs DKK20; phone; adv bkg; quiet. ♦ 17 Apr-25 Sep. DKK 200 (CChq acc) 2010*

NAKSKOV *C3* (2.5km W Coastal) *54.83303, 11.09083* **Hestehoved Camping, Hestehovedet 2, 4900 Nakskov [tel 54 95 17 47; fax 54 95 69 20; hestehovedet@tdcadsl.dk; www.hestehovedetcamping.dk]** Cont on main rd fr Tårs after exit ferry fr Spodsbjerg. Site sp R after passing town boundary. Med, mkd pitch, pt shd; wc; chem disp; mv service pnt; baby facs; fam bthrm; shwrs DKK2; el pnts (10A) DKK27; Indtte; shop 3km; rest 200m; sand beach 2km; playgrnd; marina adj; sand beach 250m; cycle hire; TV; 70% statics; phone; adv bkg; quiet. "Conv for ferry Spodsbjerg-Tårs." ♦ 7 Apr-30 Sep. DKK 140 2009*

NEXO (BORNHOLM ISLAND) *A1* (4km S Coastal) *55.02895, 15.11130* **FDM Camping Balka Strand, Klynevej 6, Snogebæk, 3730 Nexø [tel 56 48 80 74; fax 56 48 86 75; c-balka@fdm.dk; www.balka.fdmcamping.dk]** Fr ferry at Rønne on rd 38 to Nexø, foll sp to site N of Snogebæk. Lge, mkd pitch, pt shd; htd wc; chem disp; mv service pnt; baby facs; shwrs inc; el pnts (6A) DKK30; Indtte; shop; supmkt 500m; tradsmn; rest, snacks 500m; BBQ; cooking facs; playgrnd; sand beach 200m; fishing 500m; windsurfing 1km; cycle hire; games area; golf 5km; internet; TV; some cabins; dogs DKK15; adv bkg; quiet; ccard acc. "Superb beach; vg touring base Bornholm Is." ♦ 25 Apr-13 Sep. DKK 189 2009*

⊞ **NIBE** *B2* (500m SW Coastal) *56.97268, 9.62487* **Sølyst Camping, Løgstørvej 2, 9240 Nibe [tel 98 35 10 62; fax 98 35 34 88; soelyst@dk-camp.dk; www.dk-camp.dk/soelyst]** Fr Aalborg go W on rd 187 & 567 to Nibe; site 500m past Nibe; do not turn into vill. Lge, hdg pitch, unshd; htd wc; chem disp; mv service pnt; baby facs; fam bthrm; shwrs; el pnts (12A) DKK29; Indtte; shop; snacks; playgrnd; pool; waterslide; beach adj; fishing; cycle hire; TV; 5% statics; phone; Quickstop o'night facs; Eng spkn; adv bkg; quiet; CCI. "Wonderful sea views most pitches; friendly owners; secure barrier, no cars on site after 2300." ♦ DKK 161 2008*

⊞ **NORDBORG** *B3* (4km N Rural/Coastal) *55.07762, 9.71482* **Augustenhof Strand Camping, Augustenhofvej 30, 6430 Nordborg [tel/fax 74 45 03 04; augustenhof@dk-camp.dk; www.dk-camp.dk/augustenhof]** Take rd N out of Nordberg to Købingsmark. In 1km turn W to Stærbækvej. Cont twd Augustenhofvej. Turn NW & foll rd to camp nr lighthouse. Med, mkd pitch, pt shd; htd wc; chem disp; mv service pnt; baby facs; fam bthrm; shwrs DKK2; el pnts (6-13A) DKK26.50; gas; Indtte; shop; rest, bar 4km; playgrnd; pool 5km; beach; boat-launching; TV; 60% statics; dogs DKK9; phone; Quickstop o'night facs; adv bkg; quiet. "Conv for Nordberg Castle; adv bkg rec low ssn." DKK 167 2009*

⊞ **NORDSKOV** *C3* (1km N Coastal) *55.60648, 10.62190* **Fyns Hoved Camping, Fynshovedvej 748, Nordskov, 5390 Martofte [tel 65 34 10 14; fax 65 34 25 14; fynshoved@dk-camp.dk; www.fynshovedcamping.dk]** Fr E20 foll sp N to Kerteminde then take 315 dir Martofte & Nordskov. Or fr Odense/Nyborg take 165 N to Kerteminde, then as above. Lge, mkd pitch, pt shd; wc; chem disp; 50% serviced pitches; mv service pnt; baby facs; fam bthrm; shwrs; el pnts (10A) DKK30 (long lead poss req); gas; Indtte; shop; tradsmn; rest; snacks; bar; BBQ; cooking facs; playgrnd; shgl beach adj; entmnt; TV rm; some statics; dogs; poss cr; Eng spkn; adv bkg; quiet; ccard acc; CCI. "Excel scenic, rural area; ideal for cycling; vg." ♦ DKK 165 2010*

NORRE AABY see Middelfart *B3*

DENMARK

NORRE NEBEL *A2* (6km NW Rural) *55.82675, 8.21552* **Vesterlund Camping & Café, Vesterlundvej 101, 6830 Nørre Nebel [tel 86 85 56 65; mai-britt.schulze@teliamail.dk; www.vesterlundcamping.dk]** Fr rte 181 thro Nørre Nebel dir Hvide Sande, turn R at site sp in approx 5km, site in 1km on L. Reception in site rest. Med, hdg pitch, pt shd; htd wc; chem disp; mv service pnt; fam bthrm; shwrs; lndry rm; rest; cooking facs; playgrnd; few statics; Eng spkn; quiet; CCI. "Peaceful, relaxing, well-kept site; helpful owner." 27 Mar-24 Oct. DKK 150 2010*

NYBORG *C3* (2km SE Coastal) *55.3042, 10.82461* **Nyborg Strandcamping, Hjejlevej 99, 5800 Nyborg [tel 65 31 02 56; fax 65 31 07 56; mail@strandcamping.dk; www.strandcamping.dk]** Exit E20 at junc 44. Turn N, site sp in 1km. Lge, mkd pitch, pt shd; wc; chem disp; mv service pnt; fam bthrm; baby facs; shwrs DKK8; el pnts metered; gas; lndtte; shop; rest 500m; snacks; playgrnd; sand beach adj; fishing; golf 1km; internet; TV; 50% statics; dogs; phone; Eng spkn; adv bkg; CCI. "Conv m'way, rlwy & ferry; excel views of bdge; gd facs." ♦ 12 Apr-21 Sep. DKK 204 2011*

NYBORG *C3* (9km S Rural) *55.23693, 10.8080* **Tårup Stand Camping, Lersey Allé 25, Tårup Strand, 5871 Frørup [tel 65 37 11 99; fax 65 37 11 79; mail@taarupstrandcamping.dk; www.taarupstrandcamping.dk]** S fr Nyborg take 163 twds Svendborg; after 6.5km turn L sp Tårup. In 2.7km turn L sp Tårup Strand. Site 1.5km on R. Med, mkd pitch, terr, pt shd; wc; chem disp; mv service pnt; fam bthrm; baby facs; shwrs DKK5; el pnts (6-10A) DKK26; lndtte; kiosk; playgrnd; shgl beach; lake; TV; 70% statics; phone; adv bkg; quiet; poss cr high ssn; CCI. "Quiet family site; excel views of bdge." 4 Apr-7 Sep. DKK 162 2008*

NYKOBING (FALSTER) *D3* (8km E Coastal) *54.74057, 12.02801* **Campinggården Ulslev Strand, Strandvejen 3, Ulslev Strand, 4872 Idestrup [tel 54 14 83 50; fax 54 14 83 47; ulslev@dk-camp.dk; www.campinggaarden-ulslev.dk]** Foll E55 around Nykøbing to E, at rndabt turn L twd Horbelev. In 2km turn R & foll sp Ulslev Strand. Fr Gedser ferry turn R (E) at rndabt on app Nykøbing, then as above. Lge, mkd pitch, pt sl, pt shd; wc; chem disp; mv service pnt; fam bthrm; baby facs; sauna; shwrs; el pnts (10A) DKK30; gas; lndtte; shop; rest; playgrnd; sand beach adj; games area; TV; 20% statics; dogs free; phone; Eng spkn; adv bkg; quiet; ccard acc; CCI. "Gd beaches; gd cycling; nr several theme parks; day ferry to Rostok fr Gedser." 20 Mar-3 Oct. DKK 174 2010*

NYKOBING (MORS) *B2* (5km SW Coastal) *56.76435, 8.8148* **Jesperhus Camping, Legindvej 30, 7900 Nykøbing [tel 96 70 14 00; fax 96 70 14 17; jesperhus@jesperhus.dk; www.jesperhus.dk]** Exit rd 26 at sp Nykøbing Syd (S) & foll sp to Salling Sund for 1km; foll sp for Billund. Site on R 200m past Jesperhus Blomsterpark (Flower Park). V lge, hdg pitch, terr, pt shd; wc; chem disp; mv service pnt; fam bthrm; baby facs; sauna; shwrs inc; el pnts (6A) DKK40; lndtte (inc dryer); shop; rest; snacks; bar; cooking facs; playgrnd; htd pools (1 covrd); waterpark; beach 1km; fishing; tennis; games area; entmnt; TV; 50% statics; dogs DKK30; phone; adv bkg; quiet. "Jesperhus Blomsterpark (open May-Oct) excel; site vg for families; many activities." ♦ 26 Mar-25 Oct. DKK 260 2010*

NYMINDEGAB *A2* (600m S Rural) *55.81263, 8.20001* **Nymindegab Familie Camping, Lyngtoften 12, 6830 Nymindegab [tel 75 28 91 83; fax 75 28 94 30; info@nycamp.dk; www.nycamp.dk]** Clear sp on L of rd 181 at ent to vill fr Esbjerg & SE via Nørre Nebel. If app fr N, thro vill & look for Int'l sp on R. Lge, mkd pitch, pt shd; wc; chem disp; mv service pnt; baby facs; fam bthrm; sauna; shwrs DKK2; el pnts (16A) DKK25; gas; lndtte; shop; rest 500m; bar; playgrnd; pool; paddling pool; sand beach 2km; games area; TV; internet; dogs; phone; adv bkg; poss cr; quiet; ccard acc; red low ssn. "Adj army firing ranges troublesome at times; helpful warden." ♦ 1 Apr-27 Sep. DKK 151 2009*

NYSTED *D4* (2km SE Coastal) *54.65426, 11.73167* **Nysted Camping, Skansevej 38, 4880 Nysted [tel 54 87 09 17; fax 54 87 14 29; nystedcamping@post.tele.dk; www.nysted-camping.dk]** Foll sp for site in Nysted. Med, mkd pitch, pt shd; htd wc; chem disp; mv service pnt; baby facs; fam bthrm; shwrs; el pnts (10A) DKK30; gas; lndtte; shop; snacks; cooking facs; playgrnd; sand beach adj; cycle hire; games area; TV; wifi; 10% statics; dogs; phone; site open in winter on request; adv bkg; ccard acc; red CCI. "Noisy at w/end; conv for Rødbyhavn-Puttgarden ferry; castle & vintage car museum in 4km." ♦ Easter-19 Oct. DKK 150 2009*

⊞ **ODENSE** *C3* (4km S Rural) *55.36966, 10.39316* **DCU Camping Odense, Odensevej 102, 5260 Odense [tel 66 11 47 02; fax 65 91 73 43; odense@dcu.dk; www.camping-odense.dk]** Exit E20 junc 50 foll sp 'centrum' (Stenlosevej). After rndabt site on L just after 3rd set traff lts. Ent to R of petrol stn. Lge, pt shd; htd wc; chem disp; mv service pnt; fam bthrm; baby facs; shwrs inc; el pnts (10A) DKK30; gas; lndtte; shop; rest 1.5km; playgrnd; pool; TV rm; dogs DKK15; phone; bus; Eng spkn; adv bkg; quiet; ccard acc (surcharge); CCI. "Hans Christian Andersen's house; many attractions; excel, friendly, family-run site; busy high ssn & facs stretched; lovely, easy cycle rte into town cent." ♦ DKK 193 2010*

⊞ **ODENSE** *C3* (9km W Rural) *55.3894, 10.2475* **Campingpladsen Blommenslyst, Middelfartvej 464, 5491 Blommenslyst [tel/fax 65 96 76 41; info@blommelyst-camping.dk; www.blommenslyst-camping.dk]** Exit E20 onto 161 (junc 53); sp 'Odense/Blommenslyst', site on R after 2km; lge pink Camping sp on side of house. Sm, pt sl, shd; htd wc; chem disp; mv service pnt; shwrs DKK5; el pnts (4A) DKK26; lndtte; shop; café 500m; playgrnd; sm lake; some statics; dogs DKK10; bus; Eng spkn; adv bkg; some rd noise; CCI. "Picturesque setting round sm lake; gd, clean facs; welcoming owners; frequent bus to town outside site; excel." ♦ DKK 119 2010*

⊞ **OKSBOL** *A3* (1km N Rural) *55.64048, 8.28204* **Camp West, Baunhøjvej 34, 6840 Oksbøl [tel 75 27 11 30; fax 75 27 11 31; info@campwest.dk; www.campwest.dk]** N fr Oksbøl dir Øster Vrøgum & Henne, site sp. Med, hdg pitch, pt shd; wc; chem disp; mv service pnt; fam bthrm; baby facs; shwrs inc; el pnts (10A) DKK30; gas; lndtte; shop; playgrnd; sand beach 12km; TV; dogs free; phone; Quickstop o'night facs; adv bkg; ccard acc; quiet; CCI. "Pleasant, rural site; less cr than beach sites." DKK 174 2011*

DENMARK

⊞ **OSLOS** *B1* (1km E Rural/Coastal) *57.0269, 9.0196* **Bygholm Camping & Motel, Bygholmvej 27, Øsløs, 7742 Vesløs [tel 97 99 31 39; fax 97 99 38 02; info@bygholmcamping.dk; www.bygholmcamping.dk]** NE fr Thisted on A11 to Vesløs (22km), turn L twd Øsløs, site sp after 3km. Med, mkd pitch, pt shd; htd wc; chem disp; mv service pnt; baby facs; fam bthrm; htd shwrs; el pnts (10A) DKK29; gas; Indtte; shop; tradsmn; rest; snacks; bar; cooking facs; playgrnd; pool; sand beach adj; TV; 60% statics; dogs DKK5; phone; poss cr; Eng spkn; adv bkg; quiet; ccard acc (5% surcharge). "Well placed for bird reserve; gd cycle track." ♦ DKK 139 2008*

OTTERUP *C3* (6km NE Coastal) *55.56295, 10.45390* **Hasmark Strand Camping, Strandvejen 205, Hasmark Strand, 5450 Otterup [tel 64 82 62 06; fax 64 82 55 80; info@hasmark.dk; www.hasmark.dk]** Exit rd 51 thro Odense onto rd 162 & foll sp Havn Otterup, then dir Hasmark. Site sp. Lge, pt shd; htd wc; chem disp; mv service pnt; fam bthrm; private san facs avail; shwrs; el pnts (10A) DKK35; Indtte; shop; rest; snacks; bar; cooking facs; playgrnd; pool complex; sand beach adj; games area; cycle hire; golf 15km; wifi; TV rm; 25% statics; dogs DKK10; adv bkg; quiet. "Pleasant site on superb beach." ♦ 1 Apr-25 Sep. DKK 175 (CChq acc) 2009*

OTTERUP *C3* (10km NW Coastal) *55.61994, 10.30155* **DCU Flyvesandet Camping, Flyvesandsvej 37, 5450 Otterup [tel 64 87 13 20; flyvesandet@dcu.dk; www.camping-flyvesandet.dk]** Fr Otterup on rd 162 foll sp dir Bogense for approx 8km, turn R to Flyvesandet, foll sps for further 10km. Med, pt shd; htd wc; chem disp; mv service pnt; baby facs; fam bthrm; shwrs; el pnts (13A) metered; Indtte; shop; snacks; cooking facs; playgrnd; shgl beach; TV; no statics; phone; adv bkg. "Gd touring area; vg facs; excel beach & bird sanctuary." ♦ 19 Mar-23 Sep. DKK 140 2008*

RAGELEJE see Gilleleje *D2*

⊞ **RANDERS** *B2* (6km SW Rural) *56.44984, 9.95287* **Randers City Camp, Hedevej 9, Fladbro, 8900 Randers [tel/fax 86 42 93 61; info@randerscitycamp.dk; www.randerscitycamp.dk]** Take exit 40 fr E45 & turn twd Randers. Approx 100m fr m'way turn R at traff lts dir Langå. Site clearly sp in 3km & also sp fr rd 16. Lge, pt shd; wc; chem disp; mv service pnt; baby facs; fam bthrm; shwrs inc; el pnts (10A) DKK30; Indtte (inc dryer); shop 2km; cooking facs; playgrnd; htd pool; fishing; games rm; golf adj; TV; some statics; dogs DKK10; phone; Eng spkn; ccard acc. "On heather hills with view of Nørreå valley; rec arr early for pitch with view; golf course." ♦ DKK 164 2010*

⊞ **RIBE** *B3* (2km SE Rural) *55.3171, 8.7603* **Parking Storkesøen, Haulundvej 164, 6760 Ribe [tel 75 41 04 11; fax 41 08 57; info@storkesoen.dk; www.storkesoen.dk]** Fr S on rte 11, turn R at 1st rndabt onto rte 24 & R at next rndabt. Site 100m on R, sp fishing. Fr S on rte 24, at 1st rndabt after rlwy turn L, site 200m on R. M'vans only - check in at fishing shop on R. Sm, all hdstg, unshd; wc; own san; chem disp; shwrs inc; el pnts (5A/16A) inc; fishing shop; snacks; lake fishing. "Picturesque, quiet site o'looking fishing lakes; walking distance Denmark's oldest city; m'vans & c'vans acc, ideal m/home stopover." DKK 140 2011*

RIBE *B3* (1km W Rural) *55.34115, 8.76506* **Ribe Camping, Farupvej 2, 6760 Ribe [tel 75 41 07 77; fax 75 41 00 01; info@ribecamping.dk; www.ribecamping.dk]** Fr S foll A11 by-pass W of Ribe to traff lts N of town; turn W off A11 at traff lts; site 500m on R. Fr N (Esbjerg ferry) to Ribe, turn R at traff lts sp Farup. Site on R, sp. Lge, pt shd; htd wc; chem disp; mv service pnt; baby rm; fam bthrm; some serviced pitches; shwrs DKK5; el pnts (10A) DKK34; gas; Indtte; shop; snacks; cooking facs; playgrnd; htd pool; games rm; internet; TV; 10% statics; dogs DKK12; phone; Quickstop o'night facs; poss cr; adv bkg; quiet; ccard acc (transaction charge); CCI. "Ribe oldest town in Denmark; much historical interest; helpful staff; well-run, friendly site; excel, modern san facs; conv Esbjerg ferry." ♦ 4 Apr-21 Oct. DKK 210 2011*

RINGE *C3* (W Urban) *55.24024, 10.47439* **Midtfyns Camping, Søvej 30-34, 5750 Ringe [tel 62 62 21 51; fax 62 62 21 54; mfc@midtfyns-frididscenter.dk; www.midtfyns-fritidscenter.dk]** Exit A9 Odense-Svendborg at Ringe N & foll site sp. Register at recep adj sports cent. Med, hdg/mkd pitch, pt sl, pt shd; wc; chem disp; mv service pnt; shwrs; el pnts DKK24; Indtte; shops 500m; rest; snacks; playgrnd; pool; sand beach 20km; tennis; some statics; phone; Quickstop o'night facs; quiet; ccard acc; CCI. "Egeskov Castle (10km) worth a visit." ♦ 1 May-30 Sep. DKK 157 2009*

RINGKOBING *A2* (5km E Rural) *56.08856, 8.31659* **Æblehavens Camping, Herningvej 105, 6950 Ringkøbing [tel/fax 97 32 04 20; ablehave@post12.tele.dk; www.ablehave.dk-camp.dk]** Take rd 15 fr Ringkøbing dir Herning, site on L. Med, hdg/mkd pitch, pt shd; wc; chem disp; mv service pnt; shwrs DKK2; el pnts (10A) DKK29; gas; Indtte; shop; playgrnd; sand beach 3km; playgrnd; TV; phone; dogs DKK10; Quickstop o'night facs; poss cr; adv bkg; quiet. "Beautiful site in mixed forest; friendly welcome; excel facs; gd walks; 3km to fjord; 14km to sea." ♦ 1 Apr-30 Sep. DKK 226 2011*

RINGSTED *D3* (8km NE Rural) *55.49644, 11.85796* **Camping Skovly, Nebs Møllevej 65, Ortved, 4100 Ringsted [tel 57 52 82 61; fax 57 52 86 25; info@skovlycamping.dk; www.skovlycamping.dk]** Take junc 35 off E20 onto rd 14 N. Turn W at sp in Ortved. Med, hdg/mkd pitch, pt sl, shd; wc; chem disp; mv service pnt; fam bthrm; baby facs; shwrs DKK6; el pnts (6A) metered + DKK15; Indtte (inc dryer); shop; tradsmn; cooking facs; playgrnd; htd pool; paddling pool; games rm; wifi; TV; 50% statics; dogs DKK15; phone; Eng spkn; adv bkg; quiet; ltd facs low ssn; ccard acc (surcharge); CCI. "Pleasant, wooded site; friendly, family-run, well-organised site; clean san facs; conv Viking Cent & other attractions." 1 Apr-1 Oct. DKK 182 2010*

⊞ **RODBYHAVN** *C4* (5km NE Urban) *54.69873, 11.39218* **Camping Rødby Lystskov, Strandvej 3, 4970 Rødby [tel 54 60 12 16; info@rodbycamping.dk; www.rodbycamping.dk]** Fr N Zeeland or Rødby ferries, foll sps for site in Rødby, NE of town cent. Med, pt shd; wc; chem disp; mv service pnt; baby facs; shwrs inc; el pnts (16A) DKK25; gas; Indtte (inc dryer); shop; cooking facs; playgrnd; beach 4km; TV; 20% statics; dogs free; poss cr; Eng spkn; adv bkg; CCI. "Clean facs; helpful owner; liable to flooding; sh walk to town cent; conv for ferries." ♦ DKK 150 2010*

RODDING *B3* (8km E Rural) *55.3550, 9.21151* **Jels Sø Camping, Søvej 32, Jels, 6630 Rødding [tel 74 55 22 38; fax 74 55 33 38; jelscamping@mail.dk; www.jelscamping.dk]** Nr x-rds rtes 25 & 403, site sp. Med, mkd pitch, shd; wc; chem disp; mv service pnt; shwrs DKK3; el pnts (9A) DKK25; Indtte; shop; rest 300m; bar; cooking facs; playgrnd; pool 100m; lake sw; fishing; 10% statics; dogs DKK5; phone; Eng spkn; quiet. "Pleasant site & area." 1 Apr-21 Oct. DKK 132 2008*

RODOVRE see København *D3*

⊞ **RONDE** *C2* (4.5km W Rural/Coastal) *56.2936, 10.4026* **Kaløvig Strandgård Camping, Strandvejen, Følle Strand, 8410 Rønde [tel/fax 86 37 13 05; kalovig.camping@get2net.dk; www.kaloevig-camping.dk]** Exit E15 at Ugelbolle & foll camp sps. Med, mkd pitch, terr, pt shd; htd wc; chem disp; mv service pnt; baby facs; fam bthrm; shwrs DKK5; el pnts DKK30; gas; Indtte; shop; rest; snacks; bar; BBQ; cooking facs; playgrnd; pool; beach adj; games rm; TV; o'night area; 50% statics; dogs DKK15; Eng spkn; quiet. "Sea views fr some pitches; gd." DKK 170 2008*

RONNE (BORNHOLM ISLAND) *A1* (1km S Coastal) *55.08978, 14.70565* **Galløkken Camping, Strandvejen 4, 3700 Rønne [tel 56 95 23 20; info@gallokken.dk; www.gallokken.dk]** Fr Rønne cent foll dir airport, site well sp. Med, hdg/mkd pitch, pt shd; htd wc; chem disp; mv service pnt; baby facs; fam bthrm; private san facs avail; shwrs; el pnts (13A) DKK25; Indtte (inc dryer); shop; tradsmn; supmkt 500m; rest 600m; BBQ; cooking facs; playgrnd; sand beach 200m; tennis 1km; cycle hire; games rm; wifi; TV; some statics; dogs; adv bkg; quiet. "Lovely location; gd, modern san facs." ♦ 1 May-31 Aug. DKK 168 (CChq acc) 2010*

ROSKILDE *D3* (4km N Rural) *55.67411, 12.07955* **Roskilde Camping, Baunehøjvej 7-9, 4000 Veddelev [tel 46 75 79 96; fax 46 75 44 26; camping@roskildecamping.dk; www.roskildecamping.dk]** Leave rd 21/23 at junc 11 & turn N on rd 6 sp Hillerød. Turn R onto rd 02 (E ring rd); then rejoin 6; (watch for camping sp). At traff lts with camping sp turn L twds city & foll site sp. Lge, mkd pitch, pt sl, pt shd; wc; own san; chem disp; baby facs; shwrs DKK6; el pnts (10A) DKK30; gas; Indtte; shop; rest; playgrnd; shgl beach; watersports; games rm; TV; poss cr high ssn; Eng spkn; adv bkg; quiet; ccard acc (surcharge); CCI. "Beautiful views over fjord; nr Viking Ship Museum (a must) - easy parking; beautiful cathedral; excel rest & shop open 0800-2000; bus service to stn, frequent trains to Copenhagen; facs in dire need of refurb (2008); ltd flat pitches." 5 Apr-14 Sep. DKK 142 2008*

ROSLEV *B2* (10km NW Rural/Coastal) *56.74333, 8.86884* **Glyngøre Camping, Sundhøj 20A, Glyngøre, 7870 Roslev [tel 97 73 17 88; fax 97 73 17 99; post@glyngore-camping.dk; www.glyngore-camping.dk]** Site sp fr rd 26 dir Glyngøre, immed S of Sallingsund bdge. Lge, hdg/mkd pitch, pt sl, pt shd; htd wc; chem disp; mv service pnt; baby facs; fam bthrm; shwrs metered; el pnts (16A) inc; Indtte (inc dryer); ice; shop; rest; snacks; bar; BBQ; cooking facs; playgrnd; htd, covrd pool; sand beach 1km; games area; games rm; internet; TV; 30% statics; dogs; phone; Eng spkn; adv bkg; quiet; ccard acc; CCI. "Excel, welcoming, spacious site in attractive position; gd touring base." ♦ 1 Apr-12 Oct. DKK 202 2010*

RY *B2* (1km S Rural) *56.07692, 9.76527* **Holmens Camping, Klostervej 148, 8680 Ry [tel 86 89 17 62; fax 86 89 17 12; info@holmens-camping.dk; www.holmens-camping.dk]** Exit Skanderborg on 445 sp Ry & Silkeborg. In Ry immed after level x-ing turn L on rd sp Øm-Kloster & camping sp. Site on R in 2km. Lge, mkd pitch, pt sl, pt shd; wc; chem disp; mv service pnt; baby facs; fam bthrm; shwrs DKK7; el pnts (6A) DKK28; gas; Indtte; shops 2km; rest 2km; snacks; cooking facs; playgrnd; lake sw, fishing, caneoing & watersports (no windsurfing); TV; 25% statics; phone; Eng spkn; adv bkg; quiet; ccard acc; red long stay. "Ry cent of Danish lake district; vg, well organised site." 1 Apr-15 Sep. DKK 175 2009*

RY *B2* (2km NW Rural) *56.10388, 9.74555* **Birkede Camping, Lyngvej 14, 8680 Ry [tel 86 89 13 55; fax 86 89 03 13; info@birkhede.dk; www.birkhede.dk]** Fr S on rd 52 exit onto rd 445 to Ry, then foll sp N on rd dir Laven. Turn R in 1km to site on lakeside. Clearly sp in cent of Ry. Lge, mkd pitch, pt sl, pt shd; wc; chem disp; mv service pnt; baby facs; shwrs DKK6; el pnts (10A) metered + conn fee; gas; Indtte (inc dryer); shop; tradsmn; rest; bar; cooking facs; playgrnd; htd pool; cycle & boat hire; fishing; games rm; golf 10km; wifi; TV rm; 60% statics; dogs; phone; poss cr; Eng spkn; adv bkg; CCI. "Gd site." ♦ 8 Apr-15 Sep. DKK 212 2009*

RY *B2* (6km NW Rural) *56.12421, 9.71055* **Terrassen Camping, Himmelbjergvej 9a, 8600 Laven [tel 86 84 13 01; fax 86 84 16 55; info@terrassen.dk; www.terrassen.dk]** In Silkeborg take Åarhus rd 15 to Linå. In Linå turn R for Laven. In Laven turn R parallel to lake; site up hill on R in 300m. Sharp turn R into ent. Lge, terr, pt shd; wc; chem disp; mv service pnt; baby facs; fam bthrm; sauna; shwrs DKK7; el pnts (10A) DKK32; gas; Indtte (inc dryer); rest adj; snacks 1.5km; shops adj; playgrnd; htd pool; fishing; lake sw; games area; pet zoo; wifi; entmnt; TV rm; 15% statics; dogs DKK15; phone; poss cr; adv bkg; ccard acc; quiet. "Excel views of lake & woods; British owner." ♦ Easter-26 Sep. DKK 230 2010*

RY *B2* (7km NW Rural) *56.13603, 9.68978* **Askehøj Camping, Askehøjvej 18, 8600 Laven [tel 86 84 12 82; fax 86 84 12 80; askehoj@dk-camp.dk; www.askehoj.dk]** Fr Silkeborg take rte 15 twd Århus. In approx 5km site is sp. Lge, mkd pitch, pt sl, terr, pt shd; wc; chem disp; mv service pnt; shwrs inc; el pnts (10A) DKK30; Indtte; shop & 8km; rest 3km; playgrnd; htd pool; paddling pool; waterslide; some statics; dogs DKK5; poss v cr; Eng spkn; adv bkg; quiet; ccard acc; CCI. "Excel site in scenic location; rec." ♦ Easter-27 Sep. DKK 185 2009*

SAEBY *C1* (2km N Coastal) *57.35498, 10.51026* **Hedebo Strandcamping, Frederikshavnsvej 108, 9300 Sæby [tel 98 46 14 49; fax 98 40 13 13; hedebo@dk-camp.dk; www.hedebocamping.dk]** Sp on rd 180. Lge, hdg/mkd pitch, unshd; htd wc; chem disp; mv service pnt; baby facs; fam bthrm; shwrs DKK5; el pnts (10A) inc; Indtte (inc dryer); shop; rest; snacks; bar; BBQ; cooking facs; playgrnd; htd pool; beach adj; wifi; 60% statics; dogs; phone; bus adj; poss cr; Eng spkn; adv bkg; quiet; CCI. 7 Apr-7 Sep. DKK 240 2009*

SAKSKOBING *C3* (Urban) *54.79840, 11.64070* **Sakskøbing Grøn Camping, Saxes Allé 15, 4990 Sakskøbing [tel 54 70 47 57; fax 54 70 70 90; sax.groen.camp@mail.dk; www.saxcamping.dk]** N fr Rødby exit E47 at Sakskøbing junc 46, turn L twd town: at x-rds turn R. In 300m turn R into Saxes Allé, site sp. Med, hdg/mkd pitch, pt shd; wc; mv service pnt; fam bthrm; baby rm; shwrs; el pnts (6A) DKK30; gas; Indtte; shop; rest adj; cooking facs; sand beach 15km; pool 100m; fishing; phone; adv bkg; quiet. "Conv for Rødby-Puttgarden ferry; gd touring base; excel site in pretty area." 15 Mar-28 Sep. DKK 134 2008*

SILKEBORG *B2* (10km SE Rural) *56.12468, 9.64015* **Skyttehuset's Camping, Svejbækvej 3, Virklund, 8600 Silkeborg [tel 86 84 51 11; fax 86 84 50 38; mail@skyttehusetscamping.dk; www.skyttehusetscamping.dk]** Fr S on rd 52 dir Silkeborg turn R onto rd 445 dir Ry. In 5km turn L twd lake, site in 6km, sp. Med, mkd pitch, hdstg, terr, shd; htd wc; chem disp; baby facs; fam bthrm; shwrs DKK6; el pnts (10A) DKK31; Indtte (inc dryer); shop; rest; snacks; bar; playgrnd; lake sw 500m; fishing; canoe & cycle hire; crazy golf; TV; dogs DKK10; phone; Eng spkn; quiet; ccard acc; CCI. "Campsite marina; sh walk to Denmark's cleanest lake; forest location; vg." ♦ 27 Mar-12 Sep. DKK 183 2010*

SILKEBORG *B2* (1.5km S Rural) *56.15716, 9.56395* **Gudenåens Camping Silkeborg, Vejlsøvej 7, 8600 Silkeborg [tel 86 82 22 01; fax 86 80 50 27; mail@gudenaaenscamping.dk; www.gudenaaenscamping.dk]** Fr S on Rv52 at rndabt at beg of Silkeborg bypass take rd sp 'Centrum'. Take 1st R to site, sp. Med, mkd pitch, pt sl, shd; htd wc; chem disp; mv service pnt; baby facs; fam bthrm; el pnts (16A) DKK28; Indtte; shop; rest, snacks 500m; BBQ; cooking facs; playgrnd; internet; TV; many statics; dogs free; Eng spkn; adv bkg; ccard acc; CCI. "Vg site; heavily wooded; easy walk/cycle to Silkeborg; steamer to Himmelbjerget 5 mins fr site." 3 Apr-18 Oct. DKK 283 2009*

⊞ **SILKEBORG** *B2* (10km W Rural) *56.14869, 9.39697* **DCU Hesselhus Camping, Moselundsvej 28, Funder, 8600 Silkeborg [tel 86 86 50 66; fax 86 86 59 49; hesselhus@dcu.dk; www.camping-hesselhus.dk]** Take rd 15 W fr Silkeborg twd Herning; after 6km bear R, sp Funder Kirkeby, foll camping sps for several km to site. Lge, mkd pitch, pt shd; wc; chem disp; mv service pnt; shwrs inc; fam bthrm; baby facs; shwrs; el pnts DKK35; gas; Indtte; supmkt; snacks; playgrnd; htd pool; TV; 40% statics; dogs DKK20; phone; adv bkg; quiet; 10% red CCI. "Great family site; beautiful natural surroundings; 1 hour fr Legoland; busy at w'ends." ♦ DKK 144 2011*

SINDAL *C1* (2.5km N Rural) *57.4899, 10.2013* **Soldalens Camping, Gaden 91, 9870 Sindal [tel 98 93 52 55; fax 98 93 52 56; camping@pmu.dk; www.soldalenscamping.dk]** Site sp on L on W app to town on ring rd. Med, hdg pitch, pt shd; htd wc; chem disp; mv service pnt; baby facs; shwrs inc; el pnts (10A) metered; Indtte; shop 1.5km; rest, snacks; cooking facs; playgrnd; sand beach 20km; TV; some statics; phone; Eng spkn; adv bkg; CCI. "Well-maintained site; vg." 1 Apr-1 Oct. DKK 190 2008*

⊞ **SINDAL** *C1* (1km W Rural) *57.46785, 10.17851* **Sindal Camping, Hjørringvej 125, 9870 Sindal [tel 98 93 65 30; fax 98 93 69 30; info@sindal-camping.dk; www.sindal-camping.dk]** On rte 35 due W of Frederikshavn on S side of rd. Lge, hdg pitch, pt shd; wc; chem disp; mv service pnt; baby facs; fam bthrm; shwrs; el pnts (16A) metered; gas; Indtte; shop; playgrnd; pool; paddling pool; sand beach 11km; gold 3km; TV; dogs DKK5; phone; poss cr; Eng spkn; adv bkg; quiet; CCI. "Train & bus v conv; lovely beaches 30 mins; excel modern san facs." ♦ DKK 155 2009*

⊞ **SKAELSKOR** *C3* (500m W Rural) *55.25648, 11.28461* **Skælskør Nør Camping, Kildehusvej 1, 4230 Skælskør [tel 58 19 43 84; fax 58 19 25 50; kildehuset@cafeer.dk; www.campnor.dk]** Exit E20 junc 42 sp Korsør. Take rd 265 S sp Skælskør, site on L just bef town, nr Kildehuset Rest. Med, mkd pitch, unshd; wc; chem disp; baby facs; fam bthrm; shwrs DKK5; el pnts DKK35; Indtte; shop 1km; rest; bar; cooking facs; playgrnd; shgl beach 2km; TV; phone; Eng spkn; adv bkg; rd noise; ccard acc (surcharge); CCI. "Lovely location by lake in nature reserve; woodland walks; excel facs; helpful owners." ♦ DKK 150 2009*

⊞ **SKAERBAEK** *B3* (500m E Rural) *55.16776, 8.78326* **Skærbæk Familie Camping, Ullerupvej 76, 6780 Skærbæk [tel 74 75 22 22; fax 74 75 25 70; skaerbaekfamiliecamping@c.dk; www.skaerbaekfamiliecamping.dk]** On rd 11 fr Ribe to Tønder, site well sp. Med, hdg/mkd pitch, pt shd; htd wc; chem disp; mv service pnt; fam bthrm; shwrs inc; el pnts DKK25; tradsmn; BBQ; cooking facs; playgrnd; games area; wifi; 50% statics; phone; Eng spkn; quiet; CCI. "Helpful owner; gd tourist info; conv Rømø Island." ♦ DKK 140 2010*

SKAGEN *C1* (1.5km N Coastal) *57.7319, 10.61458* **Grenen Camping, Fryvej 16, 9990 Skagen [tel/fax 98 44 25 46; info@grenencamping.dk; www.grenencamping.dk]** Site on rd 40, sp 500m after white lighthouse. Lge, hdg/mkd pitch, pt shd; htd wc; chem disp; mv service pnt; baby facs; fam bthrm; shwrs DKK5; el pnts (16A) DKK35; Indtte; shop; rest, snacks, bar 1km; cooking facs; playgrnd; sand/shgl beach adj; cycle hire; TV rm; 50% statics; dogs DKK15; phone; poss cr; Eng spkn; quiet; ccard acc; CCI. "Immac site nr pretty town; conv Grenen Point where Baltic & North Seas meet; gd cycling; friendly, helpful staff." ♦ 1 Apr-19 Sep. DKK 240 2010*

SKAGEN *C1* (3km S Rural) *57.71987, 10.53991* **Øster Klit Camping, Flagbakkevej 55, 9990 Skagen [tel/fax 98 44 31 23; skagen-camping@mail.dk]** Fr Albæk on rte 40, site sp to R of rd. Med, mkd pitch, pt shd; wc; chem disp; mv service pnt; baby facs; fam bthrm; shwrs; el pnts; Indtte; shop; rest; snacks; cooking facs; playgrnd; pool; sand beach 2km; TV; 10% statics; phone; Eng spkn; adv bkg; quiet; ccard acc. "Well-run site, suitable for disabled; clean facs; friendly staff; Skagen worth visit." ♦ Easter-12 Sep. DKK 200 2009*

DENMARK

SKAGEN *C1* (10km S Rural) *57.65546, 10.45008* **Råbjerg Mile Camping, Kandestedvej 55, 9990 Hulsig [tel 98 48 75 00; fax 98 48 75 88; info@990.dk; www.990.dk]** Fr rd 40 Frederiskshavn-Skagen, foll sp Hulsig-Råbjerg Mile, site sp. Lge, hdg/mkd pitch, unshd; wc; chem disp; fam bthrm; shwrs DKK2; el pnts (10A) DKK30; lndtte; shop; rest 1km; snacks; bar; cooking facs; playgrnd; htd pool; paddling pool; beach 1.5km; tennis; cycle hire; golf 1.5km; TV; 25% statics; dogs DKK10; phone; poss cr; Eng spkn; adv bkg; ccard acc; CCI. "Gd touring base N tip of Denmark; gd cycling." ♦ Easter-19 Oct. DKK 210 2011*

SKAGEN *C1* (1.5km NW Coastal) *57.73448, 10.60412* **Poul Eeg Camping, Bøjlevejen 21, 9990 Skagen [tel 98 44 14 70; fax 98 45 14 60; info@pouleegcamping.dk; www.pouleeg camping.dk]** Take rd 40 thro Skagen twd Grenen; by hexagonal white tower on N o'skts turn L; site sh distance on L. Lge, pt shd;htd wc; chem disp; mv service pnt; baby facs; fam bthrm; shwrs DKK5; el pnts (10A) DKK35; lndtte (inc dryer); shop; rest 1km; snacks; cooking facs; playgrnd; beach 1km; cycle hire; wifi; TV rm; some statics; dogs DKK15; phone; poss cr; Eng spkn; adv bkg; quiet; ccard acc (surcharge); CCI. "Excel, well-run, peaceful site & facs; friendly, helpful staff; gd sea fishing & cycling; conv touring base." ♦ 20 Apr-4 Sep. DKK 195 2010*

SKANDERBORG *B2* (4km SW Rural) *56.02088, 9.89023* **Skanderborg Sø Camping, Horsensvej 21, 8660 Skanderborg [tel 86 51 13 11; fax 86 51 17 33; info@campingskanderborg.dk; www.campingskanderborg.dk]** N on E45 approx 10km beyond Horsens exit junc 54 to Trebstrup on rd 170 to site on R in 5km. Camping sp on R at top of hill after passing lake. Med, pt sl, pt shd; wc; chem disp; mv service pnt; fam bthrm; baby facs; shwrs DKK8; el pnts (6A) DKK25; gas & 5km; lndtte; shop; rest 1km; snacks; cooking facs; playgrnd; lake sw; boating; fishing; TV; some statics; dogs DKK10; phone; poss cr; adv bkg; Eng spkn; quiet; ccard acc. "In Jutland's lake district; clean, pleasant, well-spaced, friendly site in former orchard; friendly, helpful owner; gd touring base." ♦ 16 Apr-26 Sep. DKK 188 2010*

SKIVE *B2* (3km N Coastal) *56.59783, 9.03783* **FDM Skive Fjord Camping, Marienlyst Strand 15, 7800 Skive [tel 97 51 44 55; fax 97 51 44 75; c-skive@fdm.dk; www.skive.fdmcamping.dk]** Fr Skive foll rd 26 dir Nykøbing. Turn R dir Fur onto rd 551 & foll blue site sp, site on R. Lge, pt sl, terr, unshd; htd wc; chem disp; mv service pnt; baby facs; fam bthrm; shwrs DKK5; el pnts (6A) DKK30; lndtte; supmkt 1km; tradsmn; rest 3km; cooking facs; playgrnd; htd pool; paddling pool; sm waterslide; games area; internet; TV rm; 30% statics; dogs DKK12; phone; Eng spkn; adv bkg; quiet; ccard acc. "Excel san facs; some pitches o'look fjord; cycle track beside fjord to Skive." ♦ 15 Mar-12 Oct. DKK 189 2008*

SKIVE *B2* (6km SW Rural) *56.52181, 8.95806* **Flyndersø Camping, Flyndersøvej 29, 7800 Estvad [tel/fax 97 53 40 24; g-astrup@ofir.dk; www.flyndersoecamping.dk]** Fr Skive take A34 sp Herning. Site sp approx 1km past Estvad on R. Med, pt sl, pt shd; wc; chem disp; mv service pnt; fam bthrm; shwrs DKK5; el pnts (6A) DKK25; lndtte; shop 6km; snacks; playgrnd; TV; 75% statics; dogs DKK10; phone; quiet; Eng spkn; CCI. "Wonderful views; ltd facs for size of site; school parties term time." 1 Apr-23 Oct. DKK 100 2008*

⊞ **SONDER FELDING** *B2* (500m W Rural) *55.93960, 8.78418* **Sønder Felding Camping & Hytteby, Søndergade 7, 7280 Sønder Felding [tel/fax 97 19 81 89; http://sdrfelding.dk-camp.dk]** Fr rd 12 turn W onto rd 439, site sp. Call at Q8 filling stn to check in. Sm, pt shd; htd wc; chem disp; mv service pnt; shwrs DKK5; el pnts (10A) inc (long lead req); lndtte; shop; rest; snacks; cooking facs; playgrnd; quiet; CCI. "If not staffed - pay at petrol stn; rvside walk; gd." DKK 126 2010*

SONDER STENDERUP see Kolding *B3*

SONDERBORG *B3* (4.5km NE Rural) *54.93518, 9.84591* **Madeskov Camping, Madeskov 9, 6400 Sønderborg [tel 74 42 13 93]** Exit E45 at junc 75 onto rd 8 to Sønderborg. Turn L at rndabt with tent sp. Med, unshd; wc; chem disp; mv service pnt; baby facs; shwrs DKK4; el pnts (10A) DKK20; lndtte; shop; rest 5km; playgrnd; sw 300m; cycle hire; TV rm; 20% statics; phone; poss cr; Eng spkn; aircraft noise during day; CCI. "On shores of Augustenborg fiord; under airport flight path." ♦ 15 Mar-18 Oct. DKK 130 2009*

SONDERHO (FANO ISLAND) *A3* (1km N Coastal) *55.35988, 8.46426* **Sønderho Ny Camping, Gammeltoft Vej 3, 6720 Sønderho [tel 75 16 41 44; fax 75 16 44 33; nycamping@mail.dk; www.nycamping.dk]** Nr S tip of Fanø Island, on E of rd. Med, hdg/mkd pitch, pt shd; htd wc; chem disp; mv service pnt; baby facs; fam bthrm; sauna; shwrs DKK2; el pnts (10A) DKK20; gas; lndtte; shop; rest 1km; cooking facs; playgrnd; pool; tennis; cycle hire; TV; 50% statics; dogs DKK10; phone; adv bkg; CCI. ♦ 1 Apr-15 Oct. DKK 136 2008*

SONDERVIG *A2* (750m S Coastal) *56.11179, 8.11680* **Søndervig Camping, Solvej 2, 6950 Søndervig [tel/fax 97 33 90 34; post@soendervigcamping.dk; www.soendervigcamping.dk]** Fr Ringkøbing E on rd 15. At traff lts in Søndervig turn L, site on R in 600m. Lge, hdg/mkd pitch, unshd; htd wc; chem disp; mv service pnt; baby facs; shwrs DKK6; el pnts (10A) DKK30 or metered + conn fee; lndtte (inc dryer); shop; rest, snacks 600m; playgrnd; htd, covrd pool 700m; cycle hire 600m; wifi; TV rm; 10% statics; dogs DKK15; phone; bus 600m; poss cr; Eng spkn; adv bkg; quiet; CCI. "Excel; gd, modern san facs." ♦ Easter 31 Oct. DKK 177 2010*

SORO *C3* (1km W Urban) *55.43806, 11.54705* **Sorø Camping, Udbyhøjvej 10, 4180 Sorø [tel 57 83 02 02; fax 57 82 11 02; info@soroecamping.dk; www.soroecamping.dk]** On rd 150 fr Korsør, 300m bef town name board turn L at camping sp, site in 100m on lakeside. Med, pt sl, pt shd; wc; chem disp; mv service pnt; fam bthrm; baby facs; shwrs DKK2 per min; el pnts (10A) DKK30; lndtte; shop; tradsmn; rest 500m; snacks 1km; cooking facs; playgrnd; lake sw adj; fishing; boating; TV; some statics; dogs free; phone; Eng spkn; adv bkg; quiet; ccard acc; CCS or CCI ess. "Conv Copenhagen, friendly owners; busy site; clean facs - up to C'van Club standands." ♦ 1 Mar-31 Oct. DKK 150 2009*

DENMARK

SPODSBJERG (LANGELAND ISLAND) *C3* (1.5km S Rural/ Coastal) *54.92317, 10.80479* **Billevænge Camping, Spodsbjergvej 182, 5900 Spodsbjerg [tel 62 50 10 06; fax 62 50 10 46; info@billevaenge-camping.dk; www.billevaenge-camping.dk]** Fr Spodsbjerg ferry turn L into town. Site on L in approx 2km. Med, mkd pitch, pt terr, pt shd; wc; chem disp; mv service pnt; baby facs; shwrs DKK5; el pnts (16A) inc; gas; Indtte; shop; cooking facs; playgrnd; sand/shgl beach 500m; games area; internet; dogs DKK10; Eng spkn; adv bkg; quiet; ccard acc; CCI. "Helpful owner; gd, clean beach." 1 Apr-21 Oct. DKK 169 2011*

STEGE *D3* (6km N Coastal) *55.03783, 12.2820* **Ulvshale Camping, Ulvshalevej 236, 4780 Stege [tel 55 81 53 25; fax 55 81 55 23; info@ulvscamp.dk; www.ulvscamp.dk]** Exit E47 junc 41 onto rd 59 over bdge to Møn Island dir Stege. Take rd N at W end of Stege. Site on R. Med, pt sl, pt shd; htd wc; chem disp; mv service pnt; baby facs; shwrs DKK5; el pnts (10A) DKK25; Indtte; gas; shop; shop; tradsmn; playgrnd; sand beach adj; cycle hire; dogs €5; phone; adv bkg; ccard acc; CCI. "Vg clean facs; friendly owner; conv for touring Møn Is; undulating sandy site." ♦ 1 Apr-30 Sep. DKK 144 2008*

STEGE *D3* (8km E Rural) *54.9924, 12.3592* **Keldby Camping Møn, Pollerupvej 3, Keldby Møn, 4780 Stege [tel 40 40 11 56; fax 55 81 30 76; keldby@campingmoen.dk; www.keldbycampingmoen.dk]** Exit E47 junc 41 onto rd 59 E thro Stege twds Møns Klint. Fr Stege take rd 287 E & in 4.7km turn L onto minor rd sp Pollerup; site in L after 80m. Med, hdg/mkd pitch, pt shd; wc; chem disp (wc); mv service pnt; baby facs; shwrs DKK4; el pnts (10A) DKK25; gas; Indtte; shop 4km; tradsmn; playgrnd; pool; beach 8km; TV; some statics; dogs DKK10; phone; Eng spkn; adv bkg; quiet; CCI. "Central for Møn Is & sightseeing etc." 1 Apr-21 Oct. DKK 130 2008*

STENBJERG *A2* (500m W Rural) *56.91835, 8.36483* **Krohavens Familie Camping, Stenbjerg Kirkevej 21, 7752 Stenbjerg [tel 97 93 88 99; fax 97 93 86 55; stenbjerg@kh-camp.dk; www.kh-camp.dk]** On rd 571 fr Snedsted, site sp on ent vill. Med, hdg pitch, unshd; htd wc; chem disp; mv service pnt; fam bthrm; shwrs; el pnts DKK25; Indtte; shop; rest; bar; cooking facs; playgrnd; sand beach 2km; games area; TV; some statics; dogs free; Eng spkn; quiet; CCI. 1 Apr-1 Oct. DKK 160 2011*

STOUBY *B3* (3.5km E Rural) *55.70761, 9.84385* **Løgballe Camping, Løgballevej 12, 7140 Stouby [tel/fax 75 69 12 00; camping@logballe.dk; www.logballe.dk]** N of Vejle turn onto rd 23 dir Juelsminde, thro vill of Stouby, site on R. Med, hdg/mkd pitch, pt sl, pt terr, pt shd; wc; chem disp; mv service pnt; baby facs; fam bthrm; shwrs DKK5; el pnts (6-10A) DKK27; Indtte; shop; tradsmn; snacks; bar; BBQ; cooking facs; playgrnd; pool; paddling pool; beach 6km; cycle hire; games area; TV rm; some statics in sep area; dogs; phone; bus 500m; poss cr; adv bkg; quiet; CCI. "Excel facs for children." ♦ Easter-4 Oct. DKK 140 2009*

STOUBY *B3* (4km S Coastal) *55.67674, 9.81319* **Rosenvold Camping, Rosenvoldvej 19, 7140 Stouby [tel 75 69 14 15; info@rosenvoldcamping.dk; www.rosenvoldcamping.dk]** Exit E45 at junc 59 E twd Daugard & Juelsminde on rd 23. Watch for site sp in approx 20km & turn R to coast, site sp. Med, mkd pitch, unshd; wc; chem disp; mv service pnt; baby facs; fam bhtrm; shwrs DKK6; el pnts (10A) DKK30; Indtte (inc dryer); shop; tradsmn; snacks; BBQ; cooking facs; playgrnd; beach adj; fishing at marina; games area; entmnt; 80% statics; Eng spkn; quiet; ccard acc; CCI. "Vg site." ♦ 1 Apr-30 Sep. 2009*

STROBY see Koge *D3*

STRUER *B2* (1.5km N Rural) *56.5031, 8.58195* **Bremdal Camping, Fjordvejen 12, 7600 Struer [tel 97 85 16 50; fax 97 84 09 50; www.bremdal-camping.dk]** Fr S turn R at S o'skts after c'van showground & foll camping sps thro town. Fr N turn L 5km N of town at camping sp. Site over causeway on E of rd to N of town in plantation nr popular beach. No direct access fr rd 11. Med, pt shd; wc; chem disp; mv service pnt; baby facs; fam bthrm; shwrs; el pnts (16A) DKK20; Indtte; shop; rest 1km; snacks; bar; cooking facs; playgrnd; lake sw; fishing; boating; TV; phone; Eng spkn; adv bkg; quiet. "Swipe card for all services." ♦ 20 Mar-19 Oct. DKK 120 2008*

⊞ **STRUER** *B2* (7.5km NW Rural) *56.54028, 8.53048* **Toftum Bjerge Camping, Gl Landevej 4, 7600 Toftum Bjerge [tel 97 86 13 30; fax 97 86 13 48; toftum-bjerge@dk-camp.dk; www.dk-camp.dk/toftum-bjerge]** N on rd 11 fr Struer. Turn L on 565 at Humlum. Site sp on R in about 1.5km. Med, pt sl, pt shd; wc; chem disp; mv service pnt; baby facs; fam bthrm; shwrs; el pnts (10A) DKK25; Indtte; shop; rest 1km; snacks; cooking facs; playgrnd; shgl beach & sw 500m; cycle hire; TV; phone; adv bkg; quiet. DKK 144 2008*

SVENDBORG *C3* (5km SE Coastal) *55.0537, 10.6304* **Vindebyøre Camping, Vindebyørevej 52, Tåsinge, 5700 Svendborg [tel 62 22 54 25; fax 62 22 54 26; mail@vindebyoere.dk; www.vindebyoere.dk]** Cross bdge fr Svendborg (dir Spodsbjerg) to island of Tåsinge on rd 9; at traff lts over bdge turn L, then immed 1st L to Vindeby, thro vill, L at sp to site. Med, pt sl, pt shd; htd wc; chem disp; mv service pnt; fam bthrm; baby facs; shwrs; el pnts DKK30; Indtte; shop; snacks; cooking facs; BBQ; playgrnd; sand beach; cycle & boat hire; entmnt; internet; TV; some statics; dogs DKK10; phone; o'night area; poss cr; adv bkg; quiet; ccard acc; CCI. "V helpful owners; swipe card for facs; excel touring base & conv ferries to islands; beautiful views; immac, excel site." ♦ Easter-27 Sep. DKK 173 2009*

SVENDBORG *C3* (5km S Rural) *55.03336, 10.61403* **Carlsberg Camping, Sundbrovej 19, Tåsinge, 5700 Svendborg [tel 62 22 53 84; fax 62 22 58 11; mail@carlsberg-camping.dk; www.carlsberg-camping.dk]** Fr Svendborg cross bdge on A9 S to Rudkøbing. After traffic lts in approx 4km sp camping on E side of rd. Enter sm rd & up steep hill for 300m. Steep & narr app. Med, pt shd; wc; chem disp; mv service pnt; fam bthrm; baby facs; shwrs inc; el pnts (6A) DKK30; gas; Indtte (inc dryer); shop; snacks; playgrnd; htd pool inc; beach 4km; games area; games rm; TV; poss cr; quiet; ccard acc; red low ssn. "Gd facs; scenic area." ♦ 1 Apr-25 Sep. DKK 184 2010*

DENMARK

⊞ **TAPPERNOJE** *D3* (E Urban) *55.16568, 11.98195* **Heino's Camping, Hovedvejen 47B, Lille Røttinge, 4733 Tappernøje [tel 55 96 53 22; fax 55 96 01 22; www.heinoscamping.dk]** Fr E47/55 exit 38 twd coast. Site sp. Med, hdg pitch, pt shd; wc; chem disp; shwrs; el pnts DKK20; lndry rm; shop, rest 500m; playgrnd; sand beach 2km; cycle hire; 10% cabins; quiet; CCI. "Gd size pitches." DKK 100 2009*

⊞ **TARM** *A2* (1km S Rural) *55.89309, 8.51278* **Tarm Camping, Vardevej 79, 6880 Tarm [tel 97 37 13 30; fax 97 37 30 15; tarm.camping@pc.dk; www.tarm-camping.dk]** Fr rd 11 S of Tarm take exit twds Tarm; immed turn R, site on L in 500m, sp. Med, mkd pitch, pt shd; wc; chem disp; mv service pnt; fam bthrm; baby facs; shwrs DKK2; el pnts (10A) DKK30; gas; lndtte; snacks; cooking facs; playgrnd; pool; some cabins; dogs; phone; Eng spkn; adv bkg; some rd noise; CCI. "Friendly & helpul staff; vg." ♦ DKK 130 2011*

THISTED *B2* (1km N Coastal) *56.95226, 8.71286* **Thisted Camping, Iversensvej 3, 7700 Thisted [tel 97 92 16 35; fax 97 92 52 34; mail@thisted-camping.dk; www.thisted-camping.dk]** On side of fjord on o'skts of Thisted, sp fr rd 11. Med, pt sl, unshd; wc; chem disp; mv service pnt; baby facs; fam bthrm; shwrs DKK2; el pnts (16A) DKK30; gas; lndtte; shop; rest; cooking facs; playgrnd; pool; TV; Eng spkn; adv bkg; quiet; CCI. "Attractive views fr some pitches." ♦ 1 Apr-31 Oct. DKK 186 2011*

THORSMINDE *A2* (500m N Coastal) *56.37726, 8.12330* **Thorsminde Camping, Klitrosevej 4, 6990 Thorsminde [tel 97 49 70 56; fax 97 49 72 18; mail@thorsmindecamping.dk; www.thorsmindecamping.dk]** On rd 16/28 to Ulfborg, turn W twd coast & Husby Klitplantage. Turn N onto rd 181 to Thorsminde, 1st turn R past shops, site sp. Lge, unshd; wc; chem disp; mv service pnt; fam bthrm; baby facs; sauna; shwrs; el pnts (10A) DKK30; lndtte; shop; rest; cooking facs; playgrnd; covrd pool; beach 300m; TV; few statics; phone; poss cr; adv bkg; quiet. "Pleasant site; helpful staff; excel sea fishing." ♦ 8 Apr-23 Oct. DKK 200 2011*

TOFTUM (ROMO ISLAND) *A3* (Rural/Coastal) *55.16267, 8.54768* **Rømø Familiecamping, Vestervej 13, 6792 Toftum [tel 74 75 51 54; fax 74 75 64 18; romo@romocamping.dk; www.romocamping.dk]** Cross to Rømø Island on rd 175, turn R at 1st traff lts & turn L in 1km to site, sp. Lge, hdg/mkd pitch, some hdstg, pt shd; htd wc; chem disp; mv service pnt; baby facs; fam bthrm; shwrs; el pnts (10A) DKK30; lndtte; shop; BBQ; cooking facs; playgrnd; sand beach, windsurfing 4km; games area; cycle hire; wifi; TV rm; some statics; dogs; adv bkg; quiet. "Pleasant site." 15 Apr-23 Oct. DKK 152 (CChq acc) 2009*

TONDER *B3* (1km E Rural) *54.93409, 8.87957* **Tønder Campingplads, Sønderport 4, 6270 Tønder [tel/fax 74 72 35 00; tonder@danhostel.dk; www.tondercamping.dk]** W fr junc A8 & A11 twd town, in 800m turn R at camping sp. Ent on L in 100m. Med, hdg/mkd pitch, unshd; wc; chem disp; mv service pnt; shwrs; baby facs; el pnts (10A) DKK30; lndtte; shop 1km; bar; playgrnd; sand beach 10km; TV; 50% statics; dogs DKK10; phone; poss cr; Eng spkn; adv bkg; quiet; CCI. "Pleasant old town with gd shopping cent; gd site with modern san facs; helpful recep." ♦ 26 Mar-24 Oct. DKK 150 2011*

ULFBORG *A2* (4km S Rural) *56.23373, 8.3092* **Rejkjær Camping, Ringkøbingvej 24, 6990 Ulfborg [tel 97 49 12 11; fax 97 49 28 09; info@rejkjaer-camping.dk; www.rejkjaer-camping.dk]** Fr S on rd 16/28, site on L 4km N of Tim. Med, hdg/mkd pitch, pt shd; htd wc; chem disp; mv service pnt; fam bthrm; baby facs; shwrs; el pnts (10A) DKK28; lndtte; shop; rest; snacks; BBQ; cooking facs; playgrnd; htd pool; paddling pool; games area; wifi; TV rm; some statics; dogs DKK10; adv bkg; quiet. "Pleasant, welcoming site." 27 Mar-24 Oct. DKK 190 2008*

ULFBORG *A2* (10km W Coastal) *56.25961, 8.14625* **Vedersø Klit Camping, Øhusevej 23, Vedersø Klit, 6990 Ulfborg [tel 97 49 52 02; fax 97 49 52 01; vedersoklit@dk-camp.dk; www.dk-camp.dk/vedersoklit]** W fr Ulfborg on rd 537, turn S onto rd 181 & foll site sp. Lge, mkd pitch, pt shd; wc; chem disp; mv service pnt; fam bthrm; baby facs; shwrs inc; el pnts (10A) DKK25; lndtte (inc dryer); shop; snacks; cooking facs; playgrnd; pool; paddling pool; beach 500m; games area; TV; some statics; dogs DKK10; phone; adv bkg; quiet. ♦ 27 Mar-26 Sep. DKK 190 2010*

ULSTRUP *B2* (2.5km W Rural) *56.38678, 9.76341* **Bamsebo Camping ved Gudenåen, Hagenstrupvej 28, Hvorslev, 8860 Ulstrup [tel 86 46 34 27; fax 86 46 37 18; bamsebo@dk-camp.dk; www.bamsebo.dk]** Fr W twd Ulstrup on rd 525, turn R at traff lts to Ulstrop, take 1st exit at rndabt at top of Ulstrup dir Busbjerg, site sp on R in 2km on rv. Med, hdg pitch, pt sl, pt shd; htd wc; chem disp; mv service pnt; baby facs; fam bthrm; shwrs; el pnts (16A) DKK30; lndry rm; shop & 2.5km; snacks; playgrnd; htd pool; canoes for hire; tennis; games area; TV rm; 60% statics; dogs DKK15; poss cr; Eng spkn; adv bkg; CCI. ♦ 17 Apr-2 Oct. DKK 184 2011*

VAMMEN see Viborg *B2*

⊞ **VEJERS STRAND** *A3* (Coastal) *55.61916, 8.13650* **Vejers Familie Camping, Vejers Havvej 15, 6853 Vejers Strand [tel 75 27 70 36; fax 75 27 72 75; ftj@vejersfamiliecamping.dk; www.vejersfamiliecamping.dk]** Well sp in Vejers Strand on coast. Lge, hdg/mkd pitch, pt shd; wc; chem disp; mv service pnt; fam bthrm; baby facs; shwrs DKK6; el pnts (8A) DKK30; lndtte (inc dryer); shop; rest; snacks; cooking facs; BBQ; playgrnd; pool; paddling pool; sand beach 1km; fishing; wifi; TV rm; some statics; dogs DKK13; phone; Eng spkn; some noise fr adj military firing range; CCI. "Site open all yr but in winter telephone ahead; gd, modern facs." DKK 188 (CChq acc) 2010*

VEJERS STRAND *A3* (8km S Coastal) *55.54403, 8.13386* **Blåvand Camping, Hvidbjerg Strandvej 27, 6857 Blåvand [tel 75 27 90 40; fax 75 27 80 28; info@hvidbjerg.dk; www.hvidbjerg.dk]** Exit rd 11 at Varde on minor rd, sp Blåvand, turn L at sp to Hvidbjerg Strand 2km; site 1km on L. V lge, hdg pitch, pt shd; wc; chem disp; mv service pnt; baby facs; fam bthrm; serviced pitches; shwrs inc; el pnts (6A) inc; gas; lndtte; supmkt; rest; snacks; bar; cooking facs; playgrnd; htd, covrd pool; sand beach; tennis; games area; entmnt; TV; 10% statics; dogs DKK27; phone; adv bkg; quiet; ccard acc. "Superb facs; excel family site." ♦ 7 Apr-22 Oct. DKK 270 2008*

VEJERS STRAND *A3* (1km W Coastal) *55.61998, 8.11931* **Vejers Strand Camping, Vejers Sydstrand 3, 6853 Vejers Strand [tel 75 27 70 50; fax 75 27 77 50; info@vejersstrandcamping.dk; www.vejersstrandcamping.dk]** Site at end of rd 431 fr Varde (23km). Lge, unshd; htd wc; chem disp; mv service pnt; fam bthrm; baby facs; shwrs; el pnts (10A) DKK28; Indtte (inc dryer); shop; rest; snacks; bar; cooking facs; playgrnd; beach 250m; TV; phone; 50% statics; dogs DKK15; adv bkg; quiet but some aircraft noise; ccard acc. "Pt sheltered in dunes; fine beach." ♦ 1 Apr-16 Sep. DKK 180 2009*

When we get home
I'm going to post
all these site report
forms to the Club
for next year's guide.
The deadline's mid September 2013

VEJLE *B3* (2km NE Urban) *55.7151, 9.5611* **Vejle City Camping, Helligkildevej 5, 7100 Vejle [tel 75 82 33 35; fax 75 82 33 54; vejlecitycamping@mail.dk; www.vejlecitycamping.dk]** Exit E45 m'way at Vejle N. Turn L twd town. In 250m turn L at camping sp & 'stadion' sp. Med, pt sl, pt shd; wc; chem disp; mv service pnt; fam bthrm; baby facs; shwrs DKK5; el pnts (6-10A) DKK30; Indtte; shop & 1km; snacks; cooking facs; playgrnd; sand beach 2km; TV; dogs DKK5; phone; poss cr; Eng spkn; adv bkg; quiet; 25% red long stays; ccard acc; red snr citizens. "Site adj woods & deer enclosure; Quickstop o'night facs; walk to town; conv Legoland (26km)." ♦ 17 Apr-14 Sep. DKK 150 2009*

VIBORG *B2* (10km N Rural/Coastal) *56.53452, 9.33117* **Hjarbæk Fjord Camping, Hulager 2, Hjarbæk, 8831 Løgstrup [tel 86 64 23 09; fax 86 64 25 91; info@hjarbaek.dk; www.hjarbaek.dk]** Take A26 (Viborg to Skive) to Løgstrup, turn R (N) to Hjarbæk, keep R thro vill, site sp. Lge, mkd pitch, terr, pt shd; htd wc; chem disp; baby facs; fam bthrm; shwrs inc; el pnts metered; gas; Indtte (inc dryer); shop; rest; bar; cooking facs; BBQ; playgrnd; pool; sand beach adj; lake fishing; wifi; TV; 3% statics; phone; dogs DKK10; quiet; Eng spkn; adv bkg; ccard acc; red snr citizens; CCI. "Friendly & well-run; gd views; close to attractive vill & harbour." ♦ 1 Apr-24 Oct. DKK 179 (CChq acc) 2011*

VIBORG *B2* (14km NE Rural) *56.52268, 9.59470* **Vammen Camping, Langsøvej 15, 8830 Vammen [tel 86 69 01 52; fax 86 69 03 58; info@vammencamping.dk; www.vammencamping.dk]** Fr E45 exit junc 36 onto rd 517 twds Viborg. In 5km turn R at Tjele, sp Vammen, foll sp to site on Tjele Langsø (lake). Med, terr, pt shd; wc; chem disp; mv service pnt; baby facs; 75% serviced pitch; shwrs inc; el pnts (16A) DKK22; Indtte; shop 2km; tradsmn; bar; playgrnd; lake sw/fishing/boating adj; dogs; Eng spkn; adv bkg; quiet; CCI. "Site on edge of lge lake in nature reserve; friendly, helpful owners; some provisions fr site office; lovely views & atmosphere." ♦ 1 May-1 Sep. DKK 150 2008*

VINDERUP *B2* (Rural) *56.45933, 8.87111* **Sevel Camping, Halallé 6, Sevel, 7830 Vinderup [tel 97 44 85 50; fax 97 44 85 51; mail@sevelcamping.dk; www.sevelcamping.dk]** Fr Struer on rd 513. In Vinderup L nr church then R past Vinderup Camping. Site sp on R on edge of vill. Sm, hdg pitch, pt sl, pt shd; htd wc; chem disp; mv service pnt; baby facs; fam bthrm; shwrs DKK5; el pnts (16A) DKK27; Indtte; shop 100m; cooking facs; rest 1km; snacks; playgrnd; 10% statics; dogs DKK6; Eng spkn; adv bkg; quiet; ccard acc; CCI. "Family-run site; pleasant, helpful owners; picturesque, historic area." ♦ 1 Apr-30 Sep. DKK 142 2009*

VINDERUP *B2* (5km NW Coastal) *56.5186, 8.74626* **DCU Camping Ejsing, Ejsingholmvej 13, Ejsing, 7830 Vinderup [tel 97 44 61 13; fax 97 44 63 21; ejsing@dcu.dk; www.camping-ejsing.dk]** On edge of fjord in Ejsing, sp fr rd 189 fr Vinderup. Lge, mkd pitch, pt shd; wc; chem disp; mv service pnt; baby facs; fam bthrm; shwrs; el pnts (10A) DKK27; Indtte; shop; rest 5km; bar; cooking facs; playgrnd; lake sw & watersports 200m; TV; 10% statics; dogs DKK10; phone; adv bkg. ♦ 15 Mar-19 Sep. DKK 176 2008*

VIPPEROD see Holbæk *D3*

⊞ **VORDINGBORG** *D3* (1km SW Urban/Coastal) *55.00688, 11.87509* **Ore Strand Camping, Orevej 145, 4760 Vordingborg [tel 55 77 8822; mail@orestrandcamping.dk; www.orestrandcamping.dk]** Fr E55/47 exit junc 41 onto rd 59 to Vordingborg 7km. Rd continues as 153 sp Sakskøbing alongside rlwy. Turn R at site sp into Ore, site on L. Med, pt shd; wc; chem disp; mv service pnt; baby facs; shwrs; el pnts (6A) DKK30; Indtte; shop; cooking facs; playgrnd; shgl beach adj; phone; adv bkg; poss cr; quiet; Eng spkn; ccard acc. "Gd touring cent; fine views if nr water; interesting old town." DKK 140 2011*

Distances are shown in kilometres and are calculated from town/city centres along the most practical roads, although not necessarily taking the shortest route. 1km = 0.62miles

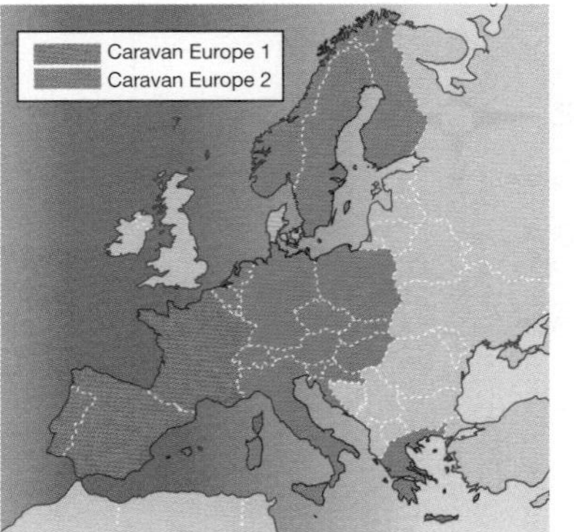

Kolding to Thisted = 195km

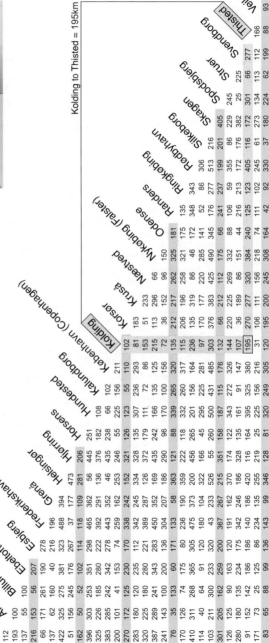

	Aalborg	Århus	Billund	Ebeltoft	Esbjerg	Frederikshavn	Grenå	Helsingør	Hjørring	Horsens	Hundested	Kalundborg	København (Copenhagen)	Kolding	Korsør	Kruså	Næstved	Nykøbing (Falster)	Odense	Randers	Ringkøbing	Rødbyhavn	Silkeborg	Skagen	Spodsbjerg	Struer	Svendborg	Thisted	Vejle
Århus	112																												
Billund	193	100																											
Ebeltoft	137	55	100																										
Esbjerg	216	153	56	207																									
Frederikshavn	66	171	261	190	278																								
Grenå	137	62	160	40	216	196																							
Helsingør	422	325	275	381	323	488	394																						
Hjørring	51	156	245	176	267	37	177	473																					
Horsens	162	50	52	102	114	118	109	281	206																				
Hundested	396	303	253	351	298	465	362	56	445	251																			
Kalundborg	325	226	185	280	222	392	291	136	376	182	108																		
København (Copenhagen)	383	285	242	342	278	443	352	46	435	238	66	102																	
Kolding	200	101	41	153	74	259	162	253	246	55	225	156	211																
Korsør	270	172	125	230	170	338	242	152	321	126	123	55	110	102															
Kruså	283	180	120	235	112	342	245	334	328	135	307	236	293	81	183														
Næstved	320	225	180	280	221	389	287	126	372	179	111	72	86	153	51	233													
Nykøbing (Falster)	387	289	241	343	283	450	352	169	435	242	166	135	125	215	113	296	66												
Odense	241	143	100	200	136	304	207	186	290	96	170	100	156	72	36	152	96	150											
Randers	76	35	133	60	171	133	58	363	121	88	339	265	320	135	212	217	262	325	181										
Ringkøbing	170	126	74	175	80	236	190	359	222	118	332	260	317	115	206	196	258	321	175	135									
Rødbyhavn	410	311	268	365	305	475	373	200	456	265	201	156	164	236	135	319	86	46	172	348	343								
Silkeborg	114	40	64	91	120	180	104	322	166	45	295	225	281	97	170	177	220	285	141	52	86	306							
Skagen	103	211	300	233	320	43	233	526	55	260	500	431	485	303	376	383	425	490	345	176	277	513	216						
Spodsbjerg	301	205	162	259	200	367	267	215	351	158	187	115	176	132	66	212	112	175	66	241	237	199	201	405					
Struer	126	125	90	163	120	191	162	370	174	122	343	272	326	144	220	225	269	332	88	106	59	355	86	229	245				
Svendborg	280	180	135	234	175	342	246	186	328	135	161	91	147	107	36	189	86	151	44	216	213	172	176	382	25	225			
Thisted	91	152	142	186	186	140	186	420	116	164	395	325	380	195	270	277	320	384	240	125	123	405	116	172	301	66	277		
Vejle	171	73	25	125	86	234	135	255	219	25	225	156	216	31	106	111	156	218	74	111	102	245	61	273	134	113	112	166	
Viborg	83	65	88	99	136	143	99	346	128	81	320	249	305	120	195	200	245	308	164	42	92	330	37	180	224	62	199	88	93

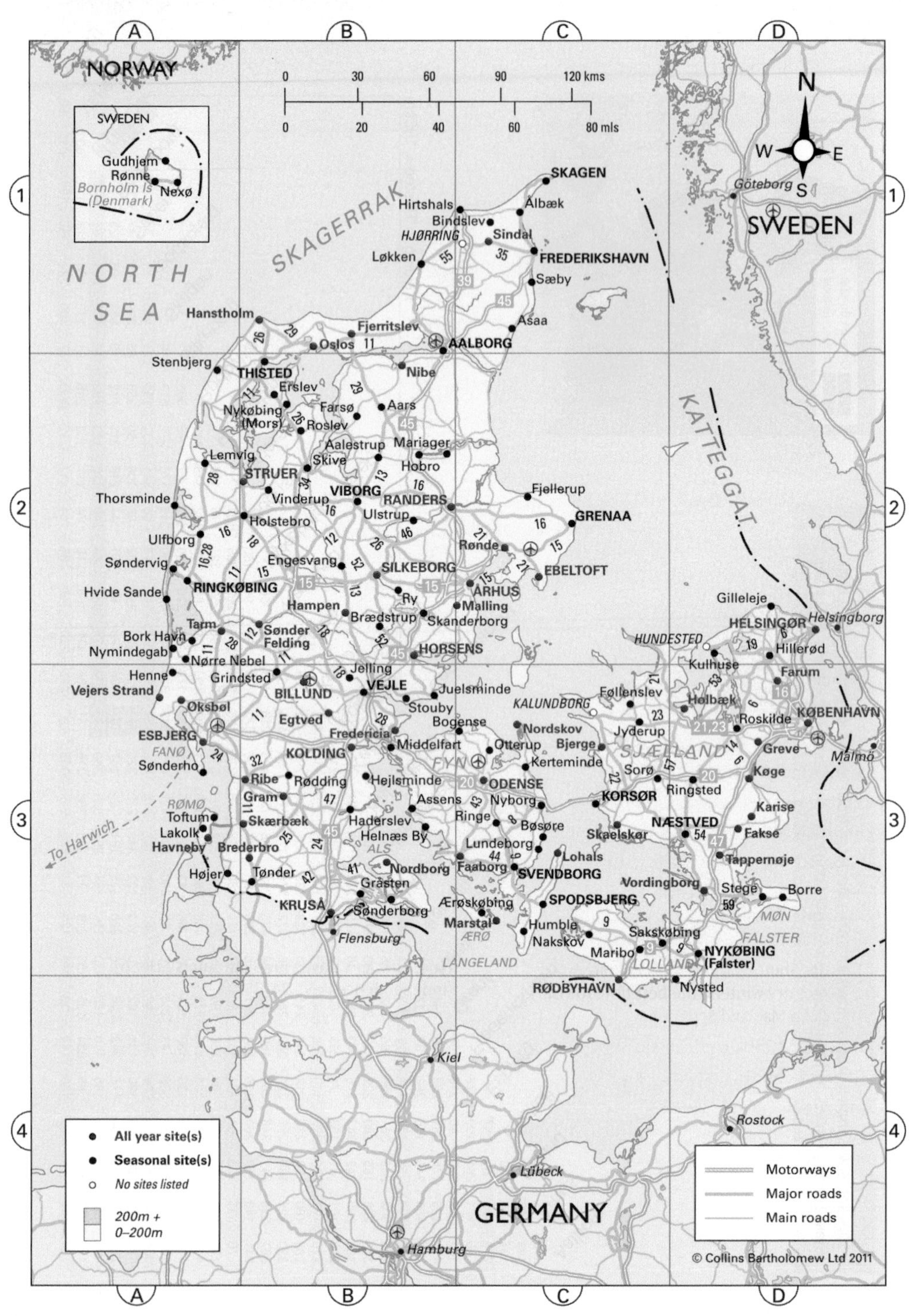
NORWAY
SWEDEN
Gudhjem
Rønne
Nexø
Bornholm Is (Denmark)
NORTH SEA
SKAGERRAK
KATTEGAT
SWEDEN
Göteborg
0 30 60 90 120 kms
0 20 40 60 80 mls
N
W
E
S
SKAGEN
Hirtshals
Ålbæk
Bindslev
HJØRRING
Sindal
FREDERIKSHAVN
Løkken
Sæby
Hanstholm
Asaa
Fjerritslev
Oslos
AALBORG
Stenbjerg
THISTED
Nibe
Erslev
Nykøbing (Mors)
Farsø
Aars
Roslev
Aalestrup
Mariager
Lemvig
Skive
Hobro
STRUER
Thorsminde
Vinderup
VIBORG
RANDERS
Fjellerup
Ulstrup
GRENAA
Holstebro
Ulfborg
Rønde
Søndervig
Engesvang
SILKEBORG
EBELTOFT
RINGKØBING
Hvide Sande
ÅRHUS
Ry
Hampen
Malling
Brædstrup
Skanderborg
Tarm
Sønder Felding
Bork Havn
Nymindegab
HORSENS
Nørre Nebel
Henne
Grindsted
Jelling
Vejers Strand
BILLUND
VEJLE
Juelsminde
Oksbøl
Stouby
Egtved
Bogense
ESBJERG
Fredericia
Middelfart
KOLDING
FANØ
Sønderho
Ribe
Rødding
Hejlsminde
Gram
RØMØ
Toftum
Skærbæk
Haderslev
Lakolk
Havneby
Brederbro
Helnæs By
ALS
Højer
Tønder
Nordborg
Gråsten
KRUSÅ
Sønderborg
Flensburg
To Harwich
Gilleleje
HELSINGØR
Helsingborg
HUNDESTED
Hillerød
Kulhuse
Farum
Føllenslev
KALUNDBORG
Holbæk
KØBENHAVN
Nordskov
Jyderup
Roskilde
Otterup
Bjerge
SJÆLLAND
Greve
Malmö
FYN
Kerteminde
Køge
ODENSE
Sorø
Ringsted
Assens
Nyborg
KORSØR
Karise
Ringe
Bøsøre
NÆSTVED
Skælskør
Fakse
Lundeborg
Lohals
Tappernøje
Faaborg
SVENDBORG
Vordingborg
Stege
Borre
Ærøskøbing
SPODSBJERG
Marstal
Humble
MØN
ÆRØ
Nakskov
Sakskøbing
FALSTER
Maribo
NYKØBING (Falster)
LANGELAND
LOLLAND
RØDBYHAVN
Nysted
Kiel
Rostock
Lübeck
GERMANY
Hamburg
All year site(s)
Seasonal site(s)
No sites listed
200m +
0–200m
Motorways
Major roads
Main roads
© Collins Bartholomew Ltd 2011

Finland

Country Introduction

© iStockPhoto.com/97

Helsinki

Population (approx): 5.4 million

Capital: Helsinki (population approx 583,000)

Area: 338,145 sq km

Bordered by: Norway, Sweden, Russia

Terrain: Flat, rolling, heavily forested plains interspersed with low hills and more than 60,000 lakes; one third lies within the Arctic Circle

Climate: Short, warm summers; long, very cold, dry winters; the best time to visit is between May and September

Coastline: 1,250km (excluding islands)

Highest Point: Haltiatunturi 1,328m

Languages: Finnish, Swedish

Local Time: GMT or BST + 2, ie 2 hours ahead of the UK all year

Currency: Euros divided into 100 cents; £1 = €1.14, €1 = 87 pence (September 2011)

Telephoning: From the UK dial 00358 for Finland and omit the initial zero of the area code of the number you are calling. To call the UK from Finland dial 0044, omitting the initial zero of the area code

Emergency numbers: Police 112; Fire brigade 112; Ambulance 112 (operators speak English).

Public Holidays 2012

Jan 1, 6; Apr 6, 8, 9; May 1, 17. 27; Jun 23 (Midsummer's Day); Nov 3 (All Saints); Dec 6 (Independence Day), 24, 25, 26.

Public Holidays for 2013 not confirmed at date of publication.

School summer holidays from early June to mid-August.

Tourist Office

FINNISH TOURIST BOARD
PO BOX 33213
LONDON W6 8JX
Tel: 020 8600 7260
www.visitfinland.com
finlandinfo.lon@mek.fi

The following introduction to Finland should be read in conjunction with the important information contained in the Handbook chapters at the front of this guide.

Camping and Caravanning

There are around 300 campsites in Finland, usually located by a lake or river or on the coast. Of these 200 belong to the Finnish Travel Association's national network. Campsites are graded from 1 to 5 stars according to facilities available. Most have cabins for hire in addition to tent and caravan pitches, and most have saunas.

At some sites visitors who do not hold a Camping Card International must purchase a Camping Card Scandinavia (CCS) which is also valid in Denmark, Norway and Sweden. The CCS costs €9 (2011) when you buy it direct from a campsite and it is valid for a year. Holders of a CCI/CCS are entitled to a reduction in rates on some campsites. For more information please visit www.camping.fi

During the peak camping season from June to mid-August it is advisable to make advance reservations. Prices at many campsites may double (or treble) over the midsummer holiday long weekend in June and advance booking is essential for this period. Approximately 70 campsites stay open all year.

Casual/wild camping is not permitted.

Country Information

Cycling

Finland is good for cyclists as it is relatively flat. Most towns have a good network of cycle lanes which are indicated by traffic signs. In built up areas pavements are sometimes divided into two sections, one for cyclists and one for pedestrians. It is compulsory to wear a safety helmet.

Electricity and Gas

Current on campsites is usually between 10 and 16 amps. Plugs are round with two pins. Some sites have CEE connections.

Butane gas is not generally available and campsites and service stations do not have facilities for replacing empty foreign gas cylinders. You will need to travel with sufficient supplies to cover your needs while in Finland or purchase propane cylinders locally, plus an adaptor. The Club does not recommend the refilling of cylinders.

*See **Electricity and Gas** in the section **DURING YOUR STAY.***

Entry Formalities

Holders of British and Irish passports are permitted to stay up to three months in any six month period in the Nordic countries, including Finland, before a visa is required. Campsites, hotels, etc, automatically register their foreign guests with the police within 24 hours of arrival.

Regulations for Pets

*See **Pet Travel Scheme** under **Documents** in the section **PLANNING AND TRAVELLING.***

Medical Services

The local health system is good and Finland generally has a high level of health and hygiene. British citizens are entitled to obtain emergency health care at municipal health centres on presentation of a European Health Insurance Card (EHIC). Treatment will either be given free or for a standard fee. Dental care is provided mainly by private practitioners.

There is a fixed non-refundable charge for hospital treatment, whether for inpatient or outpatient visits. Refunds for the cost of private medical treatment may be obtained from local offices of the Sickness Insurance Department, KELA, (www.kela.fi – English option) up to six months from the date of treatment.

Prescribed drugs can be obtained from pharmacies (apteekki), some of which have late opening hours. Some medicines that are available in stores and supermarkets in other countries, such as aspirin and various ointments, are only available in pharmacies in Finland.

If you enjoy hiking and outdoor sports you should seek medical advice before you travel about preventative measures and immunisation against tick-borne encephalitis, a potentially serious and debilitating viral disease of the central nervous system which is endemic from spring to autumn. Lyme disease is an equally serious tick-borne infection for which there is no preventative vaccine. Ticks are found mainly in the Åland Islands, the Turku archipelago and around Kokkola, in rural and forested areas, particularly in long grass, bushes and hedgerows, and in scrubland and areas where animals wander.

If you think you might be at risk use an insect repellent containing DEET, wear long sleeves and long trousers, inspect the body for ticks after outdoor activity and remove with tweezers, and avoid unpasteurised dairy products in risk areas. See www.tickalert.org, email info@tickalert.org or telephone 01943 468010

Mosquitoes are a nuisance, rather than a hazard, but you should arm yourself with repellent if travelling to the north of the country and to the lakes during warm weather. Cities are generally mosquito free.

There are very few public telephone boxes and visitors to remote areas should consider the relative inaccessibility of the emergency services.

You are strongly recommended to obtain comprehensive travel and medical insurance before travelling to Finland, such as The Caravan Club's Red Pennant Overseas Holiday Insurance – see www.caravanclub.co.uk/redpennant

*See **Medical Matters** in the section **DURING YOUR STAY.***

Opening Hours

Banks – Mon-Fri 9.15am-4.15pm.

Museums – Check locally as times vary, possibly closed Mondays.

Post Offices – Mon-Fri 9am-5pm. During winter some post offices may stay open until 6pm.

Shops – Mon-Fri 7am/8am/9am-9pm;
Sat 7am/8am/9am/10am-6pm; Sunday noon to 6pm (some supermarkets until 11pm). On the eve of a public holiday some shops close early.

Safety and Security

The crime rate is relatively low in Finland although the tourist season attracts pickpockets in crowded areas. You should take the usual commonsense precautions to safeguard your person and property.

During the winter months Finland endures severe cold weather. Be prepared for harsh conditions and prepare your vehicle(s). See ***Winter Driving*** later in this chapter.

There is a low threat from international terrorism but you should be aware of the global risks of indiscriminate terrorist attacks which could be against civilian targets in public places, including tourist sites.

*See **Safety and Security** in the section **DURING YOUR STAY.***

British Embassy

ITÄINEN PUISTOTIE 17, 00140 HELSINKI
Tel: (09) 22865100 Fax: (09) 22865262
http://ukinfinland.fco.gov.uk
info.helsinki@fco.gov.uk

There are also Honorary Consulates in Åland Islands, Jyväskylä, Kotka, Kuopio, Oulu, Rovaniemi, Tampere, Turku and Vaasa.

Irish Embassy

EROTTAJANKATU 7A, FIN-00130 HELSINKI
Tel: (09) 6824240
www.embassyofireland.fi

Customs Regulations

Alcohol and Tobacco

*For import allowances for alcohol and tobacco products see **Customs Regulations** in the section **PLANNING AND TRAVELLING.***

Border Posts

The main border posts with Sweden are at Tornio, Ylitornio and Kaaresuvanto. Those with Norway are at Kilpisjärvi, Kivilompolo, Karigasniemi, Utsjoki Ohcejohka and Nuorgam. Border posts are open day and night. The Finnish-Russian border can only be crossed by road at certain official points – contact the Finnish Tourist Board for details.

In order to deter illegal immigrants border guards patrol the area close to the Russian border and it is important, therefore, to carry identification at all times when visiting the region.

Documents

Driving Licence/Vehicle(s)

When driving you should carry your driving licence, vehicle registration certificate (V5C), insurance certificate plus MOT certificate (if applicable).

Passport

You should also carry your passport at all times.

*See **Documents** in the section **PLANNING AND TRAVELLING.***

Money

Currency and travellers' cheques may be exchanged at banks and at bureaux de change. Travellers' cheques are accepted by some large shops in tourist areas.

All the major credit cards are widely accepted and cash machines are widespread.

Carry your credit card issuers'/banks' 24-hour UK contact numbers in case of loss or theft of your cards.

Motoring

Accidents

Accidents must be reported to the police and if a foreign motorist is involved the Finnish Motor Insurers Bureau (Liikennevakuutuskeskus) should also be informed. Their address is Bulevardi 28, FIN-00120 Helsinki, tel (09) 680401, fax (09) 68040391, www.liikennevakuutuskeskus.fi. At the site of an accident other road users must be warned by the use of a warning triangle.

Alcohol

The maximum permitted level of alcohol is 50 milligrams in 100 millilitres of blood, i.e. lower than that permitted in the UK (80 milligrams). It is advisable to adopt the 'no drink and drive' rule at all times as anyone exceeding this limit will be arrested immediately and could face a prison sentence. Breath tests and blood tests may be carried out at random.

Breakdown Service

The Automobile & Touring Club of Finland, Autoliitto, has approximately 300 roadside patrols manned by volunteers and these can be called out at weekends and on public holidays. At other times, or if the Autoliitto patrol cannot be reached, contracted partners will provide assistance. For 24-hour assistance telephone (0)200 8080. Charges are made for assistance and towing, plus a call-out fee.

Emergency telephone boxes are installed around Helsinki, Kouvola, Jamsa, and Rovaniemi, and on the roads Kouvola-Lappeenranta-Imatra-Simpele and Rovaniemi-Jaatila. Drivers are connected to the national breakdown service.

Essential Equipment

Lights

Dipped headlights are compulsory at all times, regardless of weather conditions. Bulbs are more likely to fail with constant use and you are recommended to carry spares.

Reflective Jacket/Waistcoat

Pedestrians must wear reflective devices during the hours of darkness (any type of reflector is acceptable). If you get out of your vehicle you are, therefore, required to wear one and the standard reflective jacket is probably the best option for driver and passengers.

Warning Triangles

All vehicles must carry a warning triangle.

Child Restraint System

Children under the height of 1.35m must be seated in a suitable child restraint.

If there is not a child restraint/seat available a child of 3 years and older must travel in the rear seat using a seat belt or other safety device attached to the seat. Unless in a taxi a child under the age of 3 must not travel in a vehicle without a child restraint.

It is the responsibility of the driver to ensure all children under the age of 15 years old are correctly and safely restrained.

Winter Driving

Winter tyres are compulsory from 1 December to 28 February. Snow chains may be used temporarily when conditions necessitate and they can be hired or purchased from Polar Automotive Ltd, tel 01892 519933, www.snowchains.com, email: polar@snowchains.com (10% discount for Caravan Club members).

The main arctic road leads from Kemi on the Gulf of Bothnia through Rovaniemi to the Norwegian border. During the winter, all high volume, main roads are kept open including routes to Norway and Sweden. In total between 6,000 and 7,000km of roads are mainly kept free of ice and snow by the use of salt. Other roads will consist of compacted snow. Drivers should expect winter conditions as early as October.

*See **Motoring – Equipment** in the section **PLANNING AND TRAVELLING.***

Fuel

Petrol stations are usually open from 7am to 9pm on weekdays and for shorter hours at weekends, although a few stay open 24 hours. Their frequency reduces towards the north, so it is advisable not to let your tank run low. Credit cards are accepted at most manned petrol stations. There are many unmanned stations, which have automatic petrol pumps operated with bank notes or credit cards.
It is understood that automatic payment machines at petrol pumps do not accept cards issued outside Finland.

LPG is not available.

*See also **Fuel** under **Motoring – Advice** in the section **PLANNING AND TRAVELLING.***

Parking

A vehicle that has been illegally or dangerously parked may be removed by the police and the owner fined. Parking fines may be enforced on the spot, the minimum charge being €10. Parking meters operate for between 15 minutes and four hours; the free use of unexpired time is allowed. In some built-up areas you will need a parking disc obtainable from petrol stations or car accessory shops.

8-17	(8-13)	8-14
Restriction applies 8-17 hrs (Mon-Fri)	Restriction applies 8-13 hrs (Sat)	Restriction applies 8-14 hrs (Sun)

In some towns streets are cleaned on a regular basis and road signs indicate which day the cleaning takes place and, therefore, when the street should be kept clear of parked vehicles. Vehicles which cause an obstruction will be removed and drivers fined.

If you have a low emission car you may be entitled to 50% off parking fees in Helsinki. To qualify for this reduction the parking fees must be made by mobile phone and you will need to have obtained a green sticker with the letter 'P' from the Helsinki town authorities, which then needs to be attached to the windscreen. For further information please visit www.easypark.fi or www.nextpark.com

*See also **Parking Facilities for the Disabled** under **Motoring – Advice** in the section **PLANNING AND TRAVELLING.***

Priority

At intersections, vehicles coming from the right have priority, except when otherwise indicated. The approach to a main road from a minor road is indicated by a sign with a red triangle on a yellow background. When this sign is supplemented by a red octagon with STOP in the centre, vehicles must stop before entering the intersection. Trams and emergency vehicles, even coming from the left, always have priority. Vehicles entering a roundabout must give way to traffic already on the roundabout, i.e. on the left.

Roads

In general there is a good main road system, traffic is light and it is possible to cover long distances quickly, but there are still some gravelled roads in the countryside and speed restrictions are imposed on these roads in spring during the thaw so as to avoid the danger of windscreens being broken by loose stones. During the spring thaw and during the wet season in September, gravelled roads may therefore be in a poor condition. Of necessity roadworks take place during the summer months and sections under repair can extend for many miles.

There are large numbers of elk in Finland and they often wander across roads, especially at dawn and dusk. The same applies to reindeer in Lapland.

Warning signs showing approximate lengths of danger zones are posted in these areas. If you collide with an elk, deer or reindeer you must notify the police.

The Finnish Transport Agency operates an information service on weather and road conditions, recommended driving routes and roadworks, tel 0206 90300 or visit www.liikennevirasto.fi

Road Signs and Markings

Road markings are generally white. Road signs conform to international conventions. Signs for motorway and end of motorway are on a green background while those for main roads are on a blue background. The following written signs may also be found:

Aja hitaasti – *Drive slowly*

Aluerajoitus – *Local speed limit*

Kelirikko – *Frost damage*

Kokeile jarruja – *Test your brakes*

Kunnossapitotyö – *Roadworks (repairs)*

Lossi färja – *Ferry*

Päällystetyötä – *Roadworks (metalling or resurfacing of road)*

Tulli – *Customs*

Tie rakenteilla – *Roadworks (road under construction)*

Varo irtokiviä – *Beware of loose stones*

Do not cross a central continuous central white or yellow line.

Speed Limits

*See **Speed Limits Table** under **Motoring – Advice** in the section **PLANNING AND TRAVELLING.***

On all roads outside built-up areas throughout the country, other than motorways, differing speed limits between 70 and 100 km/h (44 and 62 mph) apply – except where vehicles are subject to a lower limit – according to the quality of the road and traffic density. Where there is no sign, the basic speed limit is usually 80 km/h (50 mph) on main roads and 70 km/h (44 mph) on secondary roads, whether solo or towing. The road sign which indicates this basic limit bears the word 'Perusnopeus' in Finnish, and 'Grundhastighet' in Swedish.

Reduced speed limits apply during the winter from October to March and these are generally 20 km/h (13 mph) lower than the standard limits. At other times temporary speed limits may be enforced locally.

The maximum speed limit for motorhomes up to 3,500kg is 100 km/h (62 mph).

Recommended maximum speed limits are indicated on some roads by square or rectangular signs bearing white figures on a blue background. The maximum speed limit in residential areas is 20 km/h (13 mph).

Slow moving vehicles must let others pass wherever possible, if necessary by moving onto the roadside verge. Maintain a sufficient distance behind a slow moving vehicle to allow an overtaking vehicle to pull in front.

Radar detectors are prohibited.

Violation of Traffic Regulations

The police are empowered to impose, but not collect, fines in cases where road users violate traffic regulations. Fines should be paid at banks.

Motorways

There are 700km of motorway (moottoritie) in Finland linking Helsinki, Tampere and Turku. No tolls are levied. There are no emergency phones located on motorways. In the case of breakdown on a motorway drivers of all vehicles must use a warning triangle.

Touring

Both Finnish and Swedish are official languages. As a result, many towns and streets have two names, e.g. Helsinki is also known as Helsingfors, and Turku as

Åbo. Finnish street names usually end 'katu', while Swedish street names usually end 'gatan' or 'vägen'. Swedish place names are more commonly used in the south and west of the country.

Smoking is not permitted in public buildings, restaurants or bars, except in designated smoking zones, nor on public transport.

The Helsinki Card offers free entry to approximately 50 museums and other attractions, and unlimited travel for 24, 48 or 72 hours on public transport, plus discounts for sightseeing, restaurants, shopping, concert tickets, sports, etc. For more information see www.helsinkicard.fi

Finnish cuisine places a strong emphasis on fish, especially salmon, but also rainbow trout, pike and sprats. Meat dishes, with the exception of reindeer and game, are largely continental (mainly French) in flavour. Desserts are often made with Finnish berries.

The sale of wine and spirits is restricted to Alko shops which are open Monday to Friday until 6pm or 8pm, Saturday until 4pm or 6pm, and closed on Sunday and public holidays. Medium strength beer is also sold in supermarkets and other stores.

A service charge is generally included in most restaurant bills and tips are not expected, but if the service has been good it is customary to round up the bill.

Most lakes are situated in the south east of the country and they form a web of waterways linked by rivers and canals, making this a paradise for those who enjoy fishing, canoeing and hiking. In Lapland the vegetation is sparse, consisting mostly of dwarf birch. Reindeer roam freely so motorists must take special care and observe the warning signs. Rovaniemi is the biggest town in Lapland, just south of the Arctic Circle. It has a special post office and 'Santa Claus Land'.

A number of 'Uniquely Finnish' touring routes have been established including the King's Road along the south coast which takes you through many places of interest including Porvoo, a small town with well-preserved, old, wooden houses, Turku, the former capital, and the famous Imatra waterfall near the southern shore of Lake Saimaa. Swedish influence is evident in this area in local customs, place names and language. These 'Uniquely Finnish' touring routes are marked with brown sign posts; contact the Finnish Tourist Board for more information.

Southern and central Finland are usually snow covered from early December to mid or late April, although in recent years the south coast has had little or no snow. Northern Finland has snow falls from October to May and temperatures can be extremely low. Thanks to the Gulf Stream and low humidity, Finland's winter climate does not feel as cold as temperature readings might indicate but if you plan a visit during the winter you should be prepared for harsh weather conditions.

In the summer many Finnish newspapers have summaries of main news items and weather forecasts in English and radio stations have regular news bulletins in English. English is taught in all schools and is widely spoken.

Turku was selected as European Capital of Culture in 2011, together with Tallinn in Estonia.

The Midnight Sun and Northern Lights

Areas within the Arctic Circle have 24 hours of daylight in the height of summer and no sun in winter for up to two months. There are almost 20 hours of daylight in Helsinki in the summer.

The Northern Lights (Aurora Borealis) may be seen in the arctic sky on clear dark nights, the highest incidence occurring in February/March and September/October in the Kilpisjärvi region of Lapland when the lights are seen on three nights out of four.

The Order of Bluenosed Caravanners

Visitors to the Arctic Circle from anywhere in the world may apply for membership of the Order of Bluenosed Caravanners which will be recognised by the issue of a certificate by the International Caravanning Association (ICA). For more information contact Ann Sneddon on telephone 01236 723339, or email: ann.sneddon@o2.co.uk and attach a photograph of yourselves and your outfit under any Arctic Circle signpost, together with the date and country of crossing and the names of those who made the crossing. This service is free to members of the ICA (annual membership £20); the fee for non-members is £5. Coloured plastic decals for your outfit, indicating membership of the Order, are also available at a cost of £2. Cheques should be payable to the ICA. See www.icacaravanning.org

Local Travel

The public transport infrastructure is of a very high standard and very punctual. You can buy a variety of bus, train, tram and metro tickets at public transport stations, HKL service points, newspaper kiosks and shops all over the country. Single tickets, which are valid for 60 minutes, can be purchased from ticket machines or from bus or tram drivers or train conductors. Tourist tickets valid for one, three or five days can also be purchased from kiosks, ticket machines and from drivers and are valid on all forms of public transport including the Suomenlinna ferry. For a public transport route planner (in English) see http://aikataulut.ytv.fi/reittiopas/en/

Within the Helsinki city area you may hire city bicycles in the summer for a token fee (refundable) from one of 26 Citybike stands.

Vehicle ferries operate all year on routes to Estonia, Germany and Russia and it is now possible to enjoy a visa free ferry trip to St Petersburg for up to 72 hours from Helsinki; see www.visitfinland.com for a link to more information or contact the Finnish Tourist Board.

Internal ferry services (in Finnish 'lossi') transport motor vehicles day and night. Those situated on the principal roads, taking the place of a bridge, are state-run and free of charge. There are regular services on Lake Paijanne, Lake Inari and Lake Pielinen, and during the summer vessels operate daily tours as well as longer cruises through Finland's lake region. Popular routes are between Hameenlinna and Tampere, Tampere and Virrat, as well as the Saimaa Lake routes. Full details are available from the Finnish Tourist Board.

All place names used in the Site Entry listings which follow can be found in GT Tiekartasto Road Atlas Suomi, scale 1 cm = 2 km.

ALAND ISLANDS Campsites in towns in the Aland Islands are listed together at the end of the Finnish site entry pages.

ENONTEKIO *B1* (500m W Urban) *68.3856, 23.6094* **Camping Hetan Lomakyla, Ounastie 23, 99400 Enontekiö/ Hetta [(016) 521521; info@hetanlomakyla.fi; www. hetanlomakyla.fi]** Fr W on rd 93 fr Palojoensuu, strt on in Enontekiö. Where rd 93 turns L, site on R in 400m. Sp fr rd 93. Sm, mkd pitch, hdstg, terr, pt shd; htd wc; chem disp; sauna; shwrs inc; el pnts (16A) €4 (poss rev pol); gas 500m; Indtte; sm shop & 1km; rest; snacks; bar; cooking facs; playgrnd; htd, covrd pool 3km; rv sw adj; watersports nr; TV rm; 40% statics; dogs; bus; poss cr; some Eng spkn; adv bkg; quiet; ccard acc; CCI. "Immac facs; friendly, helpful staff; gd walking area." ♦ 1 Mar-30 Oct. € 20.00 2008*

HAMEENLINNA *B4* (5km NE Rural) *61.03263, 24.47209* **Camping Aulangon Lomäkylä, Heikkiläntie 168, 13990 Hämeenlinna [(03) 6759772; myynti@aulangonlomakyla. fi; www.aulangonlomakyla.fi]** E12 exit Hämeenlinna onto rd. Site clearly sp fr Hämeenlinna in Aulanko. Lge, terr, shd; wc; chem disp; mv service pnt; sauna; shwrs inc; el pnts (10A) €5; gas; Indtte; shop; rest; snacks; bar; playgrnd; lake sw & sand beach; cycle hire; tennis; golf course adj; wifi; some cabins; poss cr; quiet; ccard acc; red CCI. "Beautiful location." 1 May-17 Aug. € 20.00 2010*

HANKO/HANGO *B4* (3km N Coastal) *59.85271, 23.01716* **Camping Silversand, Hopeahietikko, 10960 Hanko Pohjoinen [(019) 2485500; fax 713713; info@silversand. fi; www.silversand.fi]** Site sp fr rd 25. Lge, shd; wc; chem disp; mv service pnt; sauna; shwrs inc; el pnts (16A) €5; Indtte; shop & 1km; rest 3km; snacks; cooking facs; playgrnd; fishing; boat & cycle hire; games rm; wifi; TV; 10% statics; poss cr; Eng spkn; no adv bkg; ccard acc; red CCS. "Beautiful location on edge of sea in pine forest." ♦ 25 Apr-30 Sep. € 20.00 2009*

⊞ **HELSINKI/HELSINGFORS** *C4* (15km E Coastal/ Urban) *60.20668, 25.12116* **Rastila Municipal Camping, Karavaanikatu 4, Vuosaari, 00980 Helsinki [(09) 31078517; fax 31036659; rastilacamping@hel.fi; www.hel.fi/rastila]** E fr Helsinki on rte 170, over Vuosaari bdge; or get to ring rd 1, turn E dir Vuosaari, site sp. Also sp fr Silja & other ferry terminals & fr rte 170 to Porvoo. Also sp on rte 167. V lge, hdstg, pt shd; wc; chem disp; mv service pnt; sauna; shwrs inc; el pnts (16A) €4.50; Indtte; shops 100m; supmkt 400m; rest; snacks; cooking facs; playgrnd; sand beach 1.2km; wifi; TV & games rm; 10% statics; metro nr; poss cr; Eng spkn; quiet; ccard acc; red long stay/CCS. "Conv Helsinki & district; pleasant site; gd san facs; helpful staff; poss itinerant workers but site clean & tidy; weekly rates avail." ♦ € 25.00 2010*

⊞ **HOSSA** *C2* (500m NW Rural) *65.44293, 29.55108* **Erä-Hossa Camping, Hossantie 278B, 89220 Ruhtinansalmi [(08) 732310; fax 732316; era-hossa@luukku.com; www. hossa.fi]** At Peranka on rd 5/E63 Kuusamo to Suomussalmi, turn E onto 9190; at T-junc after 29km turn N on rd 843/9193 sp Hossa; site on L 3km. Med, hdstg, pt shd; wc; chem disp; sauna; shwrs inc; el pnts (10A) inc; Indtte; rest; bar; cooking facs; playgrnd; lake sw adj; boating; fishing; cycle hire; quiet; ccard acc; red CCI. "Deep in Karelian Forest; lakeside site in holiday cabin complex with central facs; many hiking & ski trails 4km in National Park." € 21.00 2009*

IISALMI *C3* (5km N Rural) *63.5947, 27.16165* **Camping Koljonvirta, Ylemmäisentie 6, 74120 Iisalmi [(017) 825252; fax 822559; info@campingkoljonvirta.fi; www.camping koljonvirta.fi]** Fr S on rd 5/E63 past Iisalmi, take rd 88 twd Oulu, strt over rndabt, site in 1km on L. Lge, mkd pitch pt sl, pt shd; htd wc; chem disp; mv service pnt; sauna; shwrs inc; el pnts (10A) €5; Indtte; shops adj; rest; snacks; sand beach adj; boating & fishing; poss cr; Eng spkn; quiet; ccard acc; red CCI. "Vg." ♦ 20 May-30 Sep. € 20.00 2011*

IKAALINEN *B4* (1.2km NW Rural) *61.77872, 23.0445* **Camping Toivolansaari, Toivolansaarentie 3, 39500 Ikaalinen [(03) 4586462; fax 4501206; kylpylakaupunki@ikaalinen. fi; www.kylpylakaupunki.fi]** Fr rd 3/E12 exit twd Ikaalinen cent onto rd 2595 Silkintie. Take 4th L in approx 1km sp Keskusta & foll Vanha Tampereentie thro town cent to lake, site sp on tip of promontory on Kyrösjärvi Lake. Med, pt shd; wc; chem disp; mv service pnt; sauna; shwrs inc; el pnts (16A) €4; Indtte; shops 1km; rest; BBQ; playgrnd; pool nr; sand beach & lake sw; boat hire; tennis nr; games rm; entmnt; TV rm; 5% statics; dogs; boat to hotel 800m; poss cr; Eng spkn; adv bkg; quiet; CCI. "Vg, attractive lakeside site; friendly, accommodating staff." ♦ 1 Jun-31 Aug. € 18.00 2009*

IMATRA *C4* (3km SW Rural) *61.20718, 28.72692* **Camping Ukonniemi, Leiritie 1, 55420 Imatra [(05) 5151310; fax (09) 713713; camping@imatrakylpyla.fi]** Turn S on rte 6 on app lge bdge in cent of Imatra & foll sps Kylpylä Spa & site. Lge, shd; htd wc; chem disp; mv service pnt; sauna; shwrs inc; el pnts (16A) inc; Indtte; shop & shop 2km; tradsmn; snacks; cooking facs; playgrnd; lake sw; TV; Eng spkn; no adv bkg; quiet; ccard acc; red CCS. ♦ 23 Jun-17 Aug. € 26.00 2008*

⊞ **INARI** *B1* (500m SE Rural) *68.90233, 27.0370* **Holiday Village/Lomakylä Inari, Inarintie 26, 99780 Inari [(016) 671108; fax 671480; info@lomakyla-inari.fi; www. saariselka.fi/lomakylainari]** Fr S on rte 4/E75, site on R app Inari, clearly sp. Fr N on E75 500m past town cent, site on L, sp. Sm, some hdstg, unshd; wc; chem disp; mv service pnt; sauna; shwrs inc; el pnts (16A) inc (long lead poss req); Indtte; shops, rest 500m; snacks; playgrnd; lake sw adj; sand beach adj; motorboat & canoe hire; 40% statics; dogs free; poss cr; no adv bkg; some rd noise; ccard acc; red CCI. "Gd for walking; midnight sun cruises on Lake Inari; excel Lapp museum; poss boggy in wet; poss low voltage if site full; some lge pitches suitable RVs & lge o'fits; clean site." € 22.00 (4 persons) 2009*

INARI *B1* (2km SE Rural) *68.90216, 27.07141* **Uruniemi Camping, Uruniementie 7, 99870 Inari [(050) 3718826; pentti.kangasniemi@uruniemi.inet.fi; www.uruniemi.com]** N on rte 4/E74, site S of Inari on R, sp. Sm, pt sl, pt shd; wc; sauna; shwrs €0.20; el pnts (10A) €4.50; lndtte; shop & 2km; snacks; cooking facs; playgrnd; lake adj; fishing & boating; cycle hire; TV; 10% statics; quiet; ccard acc. "Vg for viewing midnight sun; boggy in wet; slightly makeshift facs." 1 Jun-20 Sep. € 19.00 2010*

IVALO *B1* (2km S Rural) *68.64369, 27.52714* **Holiday Village Näverniemi, 99800 Ivalo [(016) 677601; fax 677602]** Sp on W side of rte 4/E75. Lge, unshd; wc; chem disp; sauna; shwrs inc; el pnts (10A) €2.50; lndtte; shop; rest; snacks; playgrnd; lake sw adj; entmnt; TV; adv bkg; quiet; ccard acc.; red CCI "Gd cent for birdwatchers; rvside site; reindeer herds nr site; insufficient el hook-ups; helpful, friendly owner; phone ahead early ssn to check open - poss flooding during spring thaw." 1 May-31 Oct. 2009*

JAMSA *B4* (10km N Rural) *61.95586, 25.15016* **Rasua Camping, Koskenpääntie 383, 42300 Jämsänkoski [tel/fax (014) 781124; info@rasuacamping.fi]** Fr Jämsä turn N onto rd 604, site is 3.5km N of Jämsänkoski, sp. Med, pt shd; htd wc; chem disp; mv service pnt; sauna; shwrs inc; el pnts (16A) €3; lndtte; shop 3.5km; rest, snacks; cooking facs; playgrnd; lake sw; boating; fishing; bicycle hire; TV; quiet; red CCS. "In wooded area; beautiful situation." ♦ 1 Jun-1 Sep. € 18.00 2008*

JOENSUU *D3* (1km W Urban) *62.59765, 29.73939* **Linnunlahti Camping, Linnunlahdentie 1, 80110 Joensuu [(013) 126272; fax 525486; info@linnunlahticamping.fi; www.linnunlahticamping.fi]** In town cent, foll sp 'Keskusta' & camp sp. Med, shd; htd wc; chem disp; mv service pnt; baby facs; sauna; shwrs inc; el pnts (16A) €3; lndtte; shop; snacks; playgrnd; fishing; TV; dogs €5; ccard acc; CCI. ♦ 1 Jun-12 Aug. € 12.00 (4 persons) 2008*

JUUKA *C3* (5km SE Rural) *63.22607, 29.34165* **Piitterin Lomakylä Camping, Piitterintie 144, 83900 Juuka [(013) 472000; fax 673220; piitteri@piitteri.fi; www.piitteri.fi]** Turn E off R6 just S of Juuka; site in 5km; sp. Med, hdstg, pt shd; wc; chem disp; sauna; shwrs inc; el pnts (15A) inc; lndtte; snacks; BBQ; cooking facs; playgrnd; sand beach adj; lake sw & boating; tennis; some cabins; Eng spkn; ccard acc; red CCS. ♦ 1 Jun-15 Aug. € 20.00 2010*

JUVA *C4* (2.5km W Rural) *61.89444, 27.82138* **Juva Camping, Hotellitie 68, 51900 Juva [(015) 451930; camping@juvacamping.com; www.juvacamping.com]** Sp fr x-rds of rds 5 and 14. Sm, hdstg, shd; htd wc; chem disp; mv service pnt; baby facs; el pnts €3; lndtte; shop & 700m; rest; snacks; bar 700m; playgrnd; sand beach adj; boat/canoe hire; games area; internet; some statics; dogs free; Eng spkn; adv bkg; quiet; ccard acc; red CCS. "Vg, well-kept site on lakeside; friendly, helpful staff." ♦ 1 May-31 Oct. € 18.00 2009*

⊞ **JYVASKYLA** *C3* (4km N Urban) *62.25536, 25.6983* **Laajis Camping, Laajavuorentie 15, 40740 Jyväskylä [207 436 436; fax (014) 624888; gasthaus@laajis.fi; www.laajavuori.com]** Well sp fr N on E75 & E63 fr S, site sp adj youth hostel. Med, mkd pitch, hdstg, unshd; htd wc; chem disp; mv service pnt; sauna; shwrs inc; el pnts (16A) inc; lndtte; shop 500m; tradsmn; rest; snacks; cooking facs; htd pool 3km; lake 2km; ski lift/jumps adj; wifi; entmnt; cab TV; dogs; Eng spkn; quiet; red long stay; CCS/CCI. "Facs stretched if site full; ski lifts, ski jump adj; c'vans only." ♦ € 29.00 2011*

KALAJOKI *B3* (7km SW Coastal) *64.23237, 23.8016* **Top Camping Hiekkasärkät, Rivelinpolku, 85100 Kalajoki [(08) 4695200; fax 4695220; myynti@camping-hiekkasarkat.fi; www.camping-hiekkasarkat.fi]** Site sp on rte 8. V lge, pt shd; wc; chem disp; mv service pnt; sauna; shwrs inc;el pnts (16A) €5; lndtte; rest; snacks; bar; cooking facs; playgrnd; pool 2km; sand beach; fishing; cycle hire; games area; wifi; entmnt; TV; 50% statics; no adv bkg; ccard acc; red CCI. "Site is part of amusement park." ♦ 17 May-14 Sep. € 26.00 2008*

KAMMENNIEMI *B4* (4km NW Rural) *61.65423, 23.77748* **Camping Taulaniemi, Taulaniementie 357, 34240 Kämmenniemi [(03) 3785753; taulaniemi@yritys.soon.fi; www.taulaniemi.fi]** Fr Tampere take rte 9/E63 dir Jyvaskyla. In 10km take rte 338 thro Kämmenniemi. Foll sp Taulaniemi on unmade rd to lakeside site. Sm, pt sl, terr, unshd; htd wc; chem disp; mv service pnt; sauna; shwrs inc; el pnts (16A) €3; lndtte; shop; rest; snacks; cooking facs; playgrnd; sandy beach/lake on site; boat hire; TV; adv bkg; v quiet; CCI. "Beautiful site." 21 May-13 Sep. € 20.00 2009*

KARIGASNIEMI *B1* (200m N Rural) *69.39975, 25.84278* **Camping Tenorinne, Ylätenontie 55, 99950 Karigasniemi [(016) 676113; camping@tenorinne.com; www.tenorinne.com]** N of town cent on rd 970 Karigasniemi to Utsjoki. Sm, pt shd; htd wc; chem disp; sauna; shwrs inc; el pnts (16A) €4; lndtte; shop, rest 200m; playgrnd; TV; some cabins; no adv bkg; quiet; ccard acc; red CCI. 5 Jun-20 Sep. € 18.00 2010*

KEMIJARVI *C2* (500m SW Urban) *66.71689, 27.41908* **Camping Hietaniemi, Hietaniemenkatu, 98100 Kemijärvi [tel/fax (016) 813640; sales@hietaniemicamping.info; www.hietaniemicamping.info]** In cent of town on lake. Nr x-rds of rte 5 & rte 82, sp. Med; htd wc; chem disp; sauna; shwrs inc; el pnts (16A) inc; lndtte; shop 500m; snacks; bar; playgrnd; pool 1km; fishing; TV; ccard acc; red CCS. "Gd site; helpful staff." ♦ 25 May-31 Aug. € 24.00 2010*

KESALAHTI *D4* (17km N Rural) *62.01883, 29.68420* **Karjalan Lomakeskus Camping, Vääramäentie 147A, 59800 Kesälahti [(013) 378121; fax 378130; info@karjalan-lomakeskus.fi; www.karjalan-lomakeskus.fi]** Fr Kesalähti N on rd 6 to Aittolahti then on rd 4800 for 14km, site sp. Last 400m on narr rd. Med, pt shd; wc; chem disp; mv service pnt; sauna; shwrs inc; el pnts (10A) £3 or metered; lndtte (inc dryer); shop 10km; rest, snacks high ssn; bar; playgrnd; lake sw & sand beach; fishing; tennis; games area; TV; some cabins; dogs; no adv bkg; red CCS. 1 May-30 Sep. € 19.00 2009*

KEURUU *B4* (2.5km S Rural) *62.24435, 24.70893* **Camping Nyyssänniemi, Nyyssänniementie 10, 42700 Keuruu [(040) 7002308; leena.ikalainen@nic.fi; www.nyyssanniemi.fi]** Clearly sp W of rd 58 on S o'skirts of Keuruu. Med, some hdstg, pt shd; wc; chem disp; sauna; shwrs inc; el pnts (16A) €5; Indtte; shops in town; snacks; cooking facs; playgrnd; lake sw; boating; wifi; TV; Eng spkn; adv bkg; quiet; ccard acc; red CCS. 20 May-11 Sep. € 21.00 2011*

⊞ **KILPISJARVI** *A1* (E Rural) *69.01413, 20.88235* **Kilpisjärvi Holiday Village, Käsivarrentie 14188, 99490 Kilpisjärvi [(016) 537801; fax 537803; info@kilpisjarvi.net; www.kilpisjarvi.net]** On main rd 21 almost opp g'ge, in middle of vill, sp. Lge, hdstg, unshd; htd wc; chem disp; baby facs; shwrs €2; el pnts (10A) inc; Indtte; supmkt 100m; rest; snacks; bar; BBQ; cooking facs; bus adj; Eng spkn; quiet. "Gd NH to/fr N Norwegian fjords; access to Saana Fells for gd walking/trekking; winter sports cent." ♦ € 20.00 2011*

KOKKOLA *B3* (2.5km N Coastal) *63.85500, 23.11305* **Kokkola Camping, Vanhansatamanlahti, 67100 Kokkola [tel/fax (06) 8314006; info@kokkola-camping.fi; www.kokkola-camping.fi]** Exit A8 at Kokkola onto rte 749. Site on R, sp fr town. Sm, pt shd; wc; chem disp; mv service pnt; sauna; baby facs; shwrs inc; el pnts €4; shop; snacks; cooking facs; playgrnd; sand beach adj; games area; poss cr; quiet; red CCS. "New owner 2008 - improvements ongoing." 1 Jun-31 Aug. € 20.00 2009*

KOLI *D3* (7km NE Rural) *63.15028, 29.84301* **Loma-Koli Camping, Merilänrannantie 65, 83960 Koli [(013) 673212; fax 223337; info@lomakolicamping.fi; www.lomakolicamping.fi]** Site 16km off rte 6, down rte 504. 64km N of Joensuu. Lge, pt shd; wc; chem disp; sauna; shwrs inc; el pnts (16A) €3; Indtte; shop; snacks; rest 1km; BBQ; playgrnd; lake sw & sand beach; cycle hire; games rm; TV; some cabins; dogs; poss cr; no adv bkg; quiet; ccard acc; red CCI. 1 Jun-12 Aug. € 12.00 2009*

KOUVOLA *C4* (5km E Rural) *60.88788, 26.77481* **Tykkimäki Camping, Rantatie 20, 45200 Kouvola [(05) 3211226; fax 3211203; camping@tykkimaki.fi; www.tykkimaki.fi]** Sp fr rte 6. Lge, mkd pitch, pt shd; wc; chem disp; mv service pnt; sauna; shwrs inc; el pnts (16A) €5; Indtte; shop 2km; rest 500m; snacks; bar; cooking facs; playgrnd; lake sw fishing; tennis; TV; 20% statics; ccard acc; red long stay/CCS. ♦ 23 May-31 Aug. € 20.00 2008*

KRISTIINANKAUPUNKI *B4* (1.5km SW Coastal) *62.26443, 21.36267* **Pukinsaari Camping, Salantie 32, 64100 Kristiinankaupunki [(06) 2211484]** S fr Vaasa turn off E8 at sp Kristiinankaupunki onto rd 662. Foll sp thro town, site on L after old town. Med, pt shd; htd wc; chem disp; baby facs; shwrs inc; el pnts (16A) €4.80; Indtte; shop 1.5km snacks; BBQ; cooking facs; playgrnd adj; beach adj; boat hire; 10% statics; dogs; Eng spkn; quiet; ccard acc; red CCS. "Vg site on edge interesting town; gd views; helpful staff." ♦ 16 May-31 Aug. € 18.00 2008*

KUOPIO *C3* (5km S Rural) *62.86432, 27.64165* **Rauhalahti Holiday Centre, Kiviniementie, 70700 Kuopio [(017) 473000; fax 473099; rauhalahti.camping@kuopio.fi; www.rauhalahti.com]** Well sp fr rte 5 (E63). Site 1.5km fr E63 dir Levänen, on Lake Kallavesi. Lge, hdstg, pt sl, pt shd; htd wc; chem disp; mv service pnt; baby facs; sauna; shwrs inc; el pnts (16A) €5; gas; Indtte; shop; rest; snacks; bar; cooking facs; playgrnd; lake sw; boat trips; watersports; TV rm; ccard acc; red CCI. "Hdstg for cars, grass for van & awning." ♦ 30 May-31 Aug. € 20.00 2009*

⊞ **KUUSAMO** *C2* (5km N Rural) *66.00143, 29.16713* **Camping Rantatropiikki, Kylpyläntie, 93600 Kuusamo/Petäjälampi [(08) 8596000; fax 8521909; myyntipalvelu.tropiikki@holidayclub.fi]** Three sites in same sm area on rd 5/E63, sp. Med, pt shd; htd wc; chem disp; mv service pnt; sauna; shwrs inc; el pnts (10A) inc; Indtte; pool in hotel adj; sand beach; lake sw; tennis; cycle hire; internet; dogs; no adv bkg; quiet; ccard acc; CCI. "Conv falls area; low ssn site recep at hotel 500m past site ent." € 20.00 2009*

⊞ **LAHTI** *C4* (4km N Rural) *61.01599, 25.64855* **Camping Mukkula, Ritaniemenkatu 10, 15240 Lahti [(03) 7535380; fax 7535381; tiedustelut@mukkulacamping.fi; www.mukkulacamping.fi]** Fr S on rte 4/E75 foll camping sps fr town cent. Med, pt shd; htd wc; chem disp; mv service pnt; baby facs; sauna; shwrs inc; el pnts (10A) inc; Indtte; shop 1km; rest, snacks, bar 1km; cooking facs; playgrnd; lake sw; fishing; tennis; cycle hire; internet; TV; no dogs; no adv bkg; quiet; ccard acc; red CCS. "Beautiful lakeside views." ♦ € 22.00 2009*

LAPPEENRANTA *C4* (2.5km SW Rural) *61.05115, 28.15293* **Huhtiniemi Camping, Kuusimäenkatu 18, 53810 Lappeenranta [(05) 4515555; fax 4515558; info@huhtiniemi.com; www.huhtiniemi.com]** Sp on N of rte 6; situated on Lake Saimaa. Lge, pt shd; htd wc; shwrs; chem disp; mv service pnt; sauna; shwrs inc; el pnts (16A) €5; Indtte; rest; snacks; bar; playgrnd; sw 1km; fishing; ski jump; boating; TV; ccard acc; CCI. "Gd; canal trips avail to Vyborg." 18 May-15 Sep. € 19.00 2008*

LEPPAVIRTA *C3* (2km SE Rural) *62.4890, 27.7689* **Camping Mansikkaharju, Kalmalahdentie 6, 79100 Leppävirta [(017) 5541383; fax 5533008; mansikkaharju@mansikkaharju.net; www.mansikkaharju.net]** On rte 5 Varkaus to Kuopio, site on R bef turn to Leppävirta. Well sp. Sm, pt shd; wc; chem disp; sauna; shwrs inc; el pnts (16A) €5; Indtte; shops 1km; snacks; playgrnd; shgl lake beach; games area; TV; adv bkg; quiet; CCI. "Excel for touring Finnish lakes; friendly owners." 1 May-31 Oct. € 20.00 2008*

LIEKSA *D3* (2.5km S Rural) *63.30666, 30.00532* **Timitranniemi Camping, Timitra, 81720 Lieksa [(013) 521780; fax 525486; loma@timitra.com; www.timitra.com]** Rte 73, well sp fr town on Lake Pielinen. Med, pt sl, pt shd; wc; chem disp; sauna; shwrs inc; el pnts (16A) €4; Indtte; shop; rest 2km; snacks; cooking facs; playgrnd; lake sw; fishing; boat & cycle hire; internet; TV; ccard acc; red CCI. "Part of recreational complex; Pielinen outdoor museum worth visit." 15 May-20 Sep. € 20.00 2010*

FINLAND

LUUMAKI/TAAVETTI *C4* (3km E Rural) *60.93403, 27.63388* **Taavetti Holiday Centre & Camping, Rantsilanmäki 49, 54510 Uro [(05) 6152500; fax (09) 713713; myyntipalvelu@lomaliittoo.fi; www.lomaliitto.fi]** Clearly sp to N of rd 6 on o'skts of Luumäki. App thro leisure & games area. Lge, sl, pt shd; wc; chem disp; mv service pnt; sauna; shwrs inc; el pnts (16A) €4; lndtte; sm shop & in town; rest; snacks; bar; playgrnd; lake sw & sand beach; watersports; cycle hire; TV; some cabins; dogs €7; quiet; ccard acc; red CCS. 2 Jun-10 Aug. € 18.00 2008*

MERIKARVIA *B4* (2km W Coastal) *61.84777, 21.47138* **Mericamping, Palosaarentie 67, 29900 Merikarvia [tel/fax (02) 5511283; mericamping.merikarvia@luukka.com; www.mericamping.fi]** Fr E8 foll sp to Merikarvia, site sp 2km W beyond main housing area. Med, mkd pitch, unshd; wc; chem disp; mv service pnt; shwrs inc; el pnts €3.50; rest; snacks; beach adj; wifi; some cottages; Eng spkn; quiet; ccard acc; red CCS. "Vg site on water's edge; friendly, helpful staff." € 12.00 2009*

NAANTALI *B4* (1km SW Coastal) *60.4686, 22.0422* **Naantali Camping, Leirintäalueentie, 21100 Naantali [(02) 4350855; fax 4350052; camping@naantalinmatkailu.fi; www.naantalinmatkailu.fi]** 10km W of Turku. Fr Turku ferry terminal, turn W, dir Pori, but foll Naantali sps as they appear. Avoid Naantali cent, cont twd Naantali ferry. Well sp. Med, steep sl, shd; htd wc; chem disp; sauna; shwrs inc; el pnts (16A) €5; lndtte; shop; rest 500m; snacks; playgrnd; sand beach; TV; poss cr; no adv bkg; quiet; ccard acc; red CCI. "Steep access to pitches; conv ferry; public footpath thro town to town - poor security; 30 min bus journey to Turku fr town; Moominworld theme park." ♦ 1 Jun-31 Aug. € 21.00 2008*

⊞ **NOKIA** *B4* (5km SW Rural) *61.44798, 23.49247* **Camping Viinikanniemi, Viinikanniemenkatu, 37120 Nokia [(03) 3413384; fax 3422385; info@viinikanniemi.com; www.viinikanniemi.com]** SW fr Tampere on rd 12, site well sp. Med, mkd pitch, hdstg, pt sl, pt shd; htd wc; chem disp; mv service pnt; fam bathrm; shwrs inc; el pnts (16A) €5.90-10; gas; lndtte; shop; rest; snacks; bar; BBQ; playgrnd; sand beach & lake sw adj; boat hire; fishing; cycle hire; games area; entmnt; internet; some statics; dogs; Eng spkn; adv bkg; quiet; ccard acc; CCI. "Excel site; conv Tampere." ♦ € 21.00 2011*

NURMES *C3* (4km E Rural) *63.53274, 29.19889* **Hyvärilä Camping, Lomatie 12, 75500 Nurmes [(013) 6872500; fax 6872510; hyvarila@nurmes.fi; www.hyvarila.com]** On rte 73 to Lieksa, turn R 4km fr rte 6/73 junc. Well sp on Lake Pielinen. Check in at hotel. Lge, unshd; wc; chem disp; mv service pnt; sauna; shwrs inc; el pnts (16A) €5; lndtte; shop 2km; rest; snacks; playgrnd; lake sw; tennis; games area; some cabins; dogs; quiet; ccard acc; red long stay/CCI. "Gd base for N Karelia; part of recreational complex." 15 May-15 Sep. € 19.00 2009*

⊞ **OULU/ULEABORG** *B2* (2km NW Coastal) *65.0317, 25.4159* **Camping Nallikari, Leiritie 10, Hietasaari, 90500 Oulu/Uleäborg [(08) 55861350; fax 55861713; nallikari.camping@ouka.fi; www.nallikari.fi]** Off Kemi rd. Sp fr town & rte 4/E75 fr Kemi. (Do not take Oulu by-pass app fr S). Lge, pt shd; htd wc; chem disp; mv service pnt; sauna; shwrs inc; el pnts (16A) €4.50; lndtte; shop; rest 300m; snacks; bar; BBQ; cooking facs; playgrnd; pool & spa adj; sw 500m; cycle hire; games area; child entmnt high ssn; wifi; TV; 20% statics; dogs; poss cr; no adv bkg; quiet; ccard acc; red CCI/CCS. "Gd cycling; excel modern services block." ♦ € 23.00 2009*

PELLO *B2* (1km W Rural) *66.78413, 23.94540* **Camping Pello, Nivanpääntie 58, 95700 Pello [(016) 512494; fax 515601; era.ahjo@oy.inet.fi]** Foll site sp fr town cent. Med, hdstg, pt shd; htd wc; chem disp; mv service pnt; sauna; shwrs; el pnts (16A) inc; lndtte; shop, rest 1km; snacks; playgrnd; rv adj; fishing; boat hire; 30% statics; Eng spkn; quiet; ccard acc. "Rvside pitches avail - insects!" 1 Jun-20 Sep. € 21.00 2009*

PERANKA *C2* (2km E Rural) *65.39583, 29.07094* **Camping Piispansaunat, Selkoskyläntie 19, 89770 Peranka [(040) 5916784]** Take rte 5/63 N or S; at Peranka turn E on rd 9190 for 2km; site on R in trees. Sm, hdstg, pt sl, shd; wc; chem disp; sauna; shwrs inc; el pnts (10A) €4; lndtte; shop 2km; snacks; BBQ; cooking facs; playgrnd; lake sw & sand beach adj; fishing; dogs; Eng spkn; quiet; red CCI. 1 Jun-31 Aug. € 25.00 2011*

PIETARSAARI/JAKOBSTAD *B3* (3km N Rural) *63.7059, 22.7305* **Svanen-Joutsen Camping, Luodontie 50, 68600 Pietarsaari [(06) 7230660; fax 7810008; svanen@cou.fi; www.multi.fi/svanen]** On Kokkola-Nykarleby rd (rte 749) E of town to fly-over. Take this fly-over twd Pietarsaari. In 1km turn R at site sp with lge car dealers on R. After 23km turn R on rd sp Kokkola, in 1km turn R into site. Lge, pt shd; htd wc; chem disp; mv service pnt; baby facs; sauna; shwrs; el pnts (10A) €4.50; lndtte; shop 3km; snacks; bar; playgrnd; sand beach 1km; cycle hire; TV; adv bkg; quiet; ccard acc; CCI. "Pleasant town; san facs old but clean." ♦ 1 Jun-20 Aug. € 14.00 2008*

PORVOO/BORGA *C4* (2km SE Rural) *60.3798, 25.66673* **Camping Kokonniemi, Uddaksentie 17, 06100 Porvoo [(019) 581967; myynti@suncamping.fi; www.fontana.fi]** Fr E on rte 7/E18 m'way ignore 1st exit Porvoo, site sp fr 2nd exit. Med, some hdstg, sl, pt sh; wc; chem disp; mv service pnt; sauna; shwrs inc; el pnts (16A) €5; lndry rm; shop, rest 2km; snacks; playgrnd; poss cr; Eng spkn; no adv bkg; quiet; ccard acc; red CCS. "Access to old town & rv walk; conv Helsinki & ferry." 4 Jun-22 Aug. € 19.00 2010*

⊞ **PUNKAHARJU** *D4* (9km NW Rural) *61.80032, 29.29088* **Punkaharjun Camping, Tuunaansaarentie 4, 58540 Punkaharju [(020) 7529800; fax (015) 441784; punkaharju@fontana.fi]** 27km SE of Savonlinna on rte 14 to Imatra, sp on R. V lge, pt shd; wc; chem disp; mv service pnt; sauna; shwrs inc; el pnts (16A) €5; lndtte; shop; rest; snacks; bar; playgrnd; lake sw; waterslide; fishing; tennis; games area; TV; poss cr; no adv bkg; quiet but noise fr bar; ccard acc; red CCI. "Theme park nrby (closes 15/8); Kerimäki, world's largest wooden church; Retretti Art Cent adj." € 19.00 2009*

PUUMALA *C4* (2km N Rural) *61.53943, 28.15923* **Koskenselkä Holiday Village, Koskenseläntie 98, 52200 Puumala [(015) 4681119; fax 4681809; info@koskenselka.fi; www.koskenselka.fi]** Fr N on rd 434 turn R on unclassified rd 5km bef Puumala vill. Fr S bear L immed after x-ing ferry. Site sp. Med, pt sl, pt shd; wc; chem disp; baby facs; sauna; shwrs inc; el pnts (16A) €3; Indtte; shop & 2km; snacks; playgrnd; shgl beach & lake sw; cycle hire; TV; quiet; ccard acc; CCI. 15 May-15 Aug. € 15.00 2008*

⊞ **PYHAJARVI** *C3* (4km SW Rural) *63.66492, 25.89863* **Emolahti Camping, Pellikantie 430, 86800 Pyhajärvi/ Pyhäsalmi [(08) 783443; fax 781255; emolahti.camping@pyhajarvi.fi; www.pyhajarvi.fi/emolahticamping]** Sp fr E75/ rd 4, S of x-rds with rd 27. On lakeside. Med, pt shd; htd wc; chem disp; mv service pnt; shwrs inc; el pnts (16A) inc; rest; bar; BBQ; cooking facs; playgrnd; lake sw adj; games area; cycle hire; entmnt; TV; dogs; train 4km; some statics; Eng spkn; adv bkg; quiet; ccard acc; CCI. "Gd NH; ground soft in wet weather." ♦ € 21.00 2008*

RAUMA *B4* (2km NW Coastal) *61.13318, 21.4726* **Poroholma Camping, Poroholmantie, 26100 Rauma [(02) 83882500; fax 83882400; poroholma@kalliohovi.fi; www.visitrauma.fi]** Enter town fr coast rd (8) or Huittinen (42). Foll campsite sp around N part of town to site on coast. Site well sp. Lge, pt sl, shd; wc; chem disp; sauna; shwrs inc; el pnts (16A) €3; Indtte; shop; snacks; bar; playgrnd; pool 250m; sand beach; dogs; no adv bkg; quiet; ccard acc; red CCI. "Attractive, peaceful location on sm peninsula in yacht marina & jetty for ferry (foot passengers only) to outlying islands; excel beach; warm welcome fr helpful staff; clean facs." 15 May-31 Aug. € 18.00 2009*

RISTIJARVI *C3* (3km S Rural) *64.48979, 28.18267* **Camping Ristijärven Pirtti, Viitostie 48, 88400 Ristijärvi [(08) 681221; hannukainen_t@hotmail.com]** N fr Kajaani on E63/rd 5, sp on L on lakeside. Sm, pt sl, pt shd; wc; chem disp; baby facs; sauna; shwrs inc; el pnts inc; Indry rm; shop 2km; rest; snacks; BBQ; cooking facs; playgrnd; lake sw; fishing; sat TV; dogs; Eng spkn; adv bkg; quiet; ccard acc; CCI. "Conv NH; modern, clean san facs; friendly, helpful staff." ♦ 1 Jun-30 Oct. € 21.00 2008*

ROVANIEMI *B2* (500m E Urban) *66.49743, 25.74340* **Ounaskoski Camping, Jäämerentie 1, 96200 Rovaniemi [tel/fax (016) 345304]** Exit rte 4 onto rte 78 & cross rv. Over bdge turn S on rvside along Jäämerentie. Site on R in approx 500m immed bef old rd & rail bdge, sp. Med, mkd pitch, pt shd, some hdstg; htd wc; chem disp; mv service pnt; baby facs; sauna; shwrs inc; el pnts (16A) €4.90; Indtte; shop; rest 400m; snacks; cooking facs; playgrnd; pool 1km; rv sw & sand beach; wifi; TV rm; poss v cr; Eng spkn; adv bkg; quiet; ccard acc; red CCI/CCS. "Helpful staff; excel site beside rv in parkland; gd facs; suitable RVs & twin-axles; 9km fr Arctic Circle; 6km to Santa Park, 'official' home of Santa; Artikum Museum worth visit; easy walk to town cent." ♦ 25 May-15 Sep. € 24.00 2010*

FINLAND

ROVANIEMI *B2* (7km E Rural) *66.51706, 25.84678* **Camping Napapiirin Saarituvat, Kuusamontie 96, 96900 Saarenkylä [tel/fax (016) 3560045; reception@saarituvat.fi; www.saarituvat.fi]** Fr town cent take rd 81, site on R at side of rd on lakeside. NB ignore 1st campsite sp after 2km. Sm, terr, pt shd; htd wc; chem disp; sauna; shwrs inc; el pnts (16A) €5.50; Indtte; shop 4km; rest; bar; BBQ; playgrnd; dogs; Eng spkn; adv bkg; quiet; red CCI. "Excel; friendly staff; vg base for Santa Park & Vill." 1 May-30 Sep. € 18.00 2009*

The opening dates and prices on this campsite have changed. I'll send a site report form to the Club for the next edition of the guide.

SALO *B4* (4km SW Rural) *60.36359, 23.06626* **Vuohensaari Camping, 24100 Salo [(02) 7312651; fax 7784810]** N fr Lahti, foll sp on rd 101 at edge of town. Med, pt sl, pt shd; htd wc; chem disp (wc); shwrs inc; el pnts (16A) inc; Indry rm; shop & 4km; snacks; cooking facs; playgrnd; quiet; CCI. "Lge mkt on Thurs in town." ♦ 1 Jun-30 Sep. € 18.50 2009*

SIMO *B2* (500m S Rural) *65.65902, 25.06655* **Lapin Rinki Camping, Lohitie 14, 95200 Simo [(016) 266444; fax 266044]** Fr S just off E75/rd 4 on L, well sp. Sm, pt shd; htd wc; shwrs inc; some el pnts; tradsmn; 50% statics; dogs; poss cr; Eng spkn; quiet; CCI. "Super NH or longer stay for salmon fishing - rv adj, licence avail." ♦ 20 May-25 Sep. € 14.00 2009*

⊞ **SIRKKA LEVI** *B1* (1km W Rural) *67.80407, 24.78827* **Muumari Huoneistot & Caravan, Konttisentie 1, 99130 Sirkka-Levi [(016) 644240; www.peak.fi]** Fr rd 79 at rndabt in Sirkka take exit W sp for tourist info, then foll site sps. Recep in kiosk by lake. Sm, mkd pitch, pt shd; htd wc; chem disp; shwrs inc; el pnts (10A) inc; Indtte (inc dryer); snacks; bar; BBQ; lake sw 150m; 20% statics; dogs; Eng spkn; quiet; rec CCS. "Gd, friendly site." € 25.00 2009*

SODANKYLA *B2* (E Urban) *67.41741, 26.60781* **Nilimella Camping, Kelukoskentie 5, 99600 Sodankylä [(016) 612181; antti.rintala@naturex-ventures.fi]** Fr S on rte 4 (E75), turn R on ent town; site on rte 5 sp Kemijärvi; foll sp. Med, hdg/mkd pitch, unshd; wc; chem disp; mv service pnt; sauna; shwrs inc; el pnts (16A) €3.50; Indtte; shops 1.5km; rest, snacks high ssn; bar; playgrnd; rv sw 500m; TV; dogs €5; adv bkg; quiet; ccard acc. "Conv central Lapland; old wooden church (1689) worth visit; public rd runs thro site; busy; rec NH only." ♦ 1 Jun-30 Aug. € 22.00 2008*

SYSMA *C4* (500m SE Rural) *61.49743, 25.69478* **Camping Sysmä, Huitilantie 3, 19700 Sysmä [(03) 7171386; fax 7172693; timo.puheloinen@luukku.com]** On lakeside on Heinola-Sysma rd 410, sp fr all dirs. Sm, pt sl, shd; wc; chem disp; shwrs inc; el pnts (16A) €4; Indtte; shop & 500m; snacks; playgrnd; lake sw; sailing; boat hire; TV; 20% statics; quiet; red CCI. 1 May-7 Sep. € 15.00 2008*

TAMPERE *B4* (4km S Rural) *61.47183, 23.7390* **Camping Härmälä, Leirintäkatu 8, 33900 Tampere [(03) 2651355; fax (09) 713713; myyntipalvelu@lomaliitto.fi; www.lomaliitto.fi]** Foll camping sp fr Tampere cent to site on Lake Pyhajärvi. Lge, pt shd; wc; chem disp; baby facs; sauna; shwrs inc; el pnts (16A) €5.50; Indtte; shop 4km; snacks; playgrnd; sand beach; cycle & boat hire; TV; poss cr; adv bkg; quiet; ccard acc; red long stay; CCS. 13 May-18 Sep. € 24.00 2011*

TIAINEN *B2* (2km W Rural) *66.8984, 26.19996* **Korvalan Kestikievari Camping, Sodankyläntie 5901, 97540 Tiainen [(016) 737211; fax 737212; korvalan.kestikievari@co.inet.fi; www.korvala.fi]** On W side of rte 4 (E75) 60km N of Rovaniemi, just N of Korvala. Sm, unshd; wc; chem disp; mv service pnt; sauna; shwrs inc; el pnts (16A) €4; shop, snacks, rest high ssn; playgrnd; lake sw; boating; fishing; dogs; CCI. 15 May-30 Sep. € 18.00 2008*

I'll fill in a report online and let the Club know – www.caravanclub.co.uk/europereport

This is a wonderful site.

TORMA *B2* (2km N Rural) *65.89288, 24.63571* **Camping Törmä, Rovaniementie 1298, 95315 Törmä [(016) 276210 or 0414 353882 (mob); maritta.knuuti@luukku.com]** N fr Kemi on E75 turn R onto Rovaniementie at sp Törmä & camping. In 2km turn R, site on L in 1km beside Rv Kemijoki. Sm, unshd; htd wc; chem disp; own san rec; mv service pnt; baby facs; shwrs inc; el pnts (16A) inc; Indry rm; kiosk; BBQ; cooking facs; playgrnd; fishing; 30% statics; dogs; Eng spkn; quiet; CCI. "Peaceful site with rv views; helpful owners." ♦ 1 Jun-10 Sep. € 20.00 2008*

TORNIO *B2* (2.5km S Rural) *65.83211, 24.19953* **Camping Tornio, Matkailijantie, 95420 Tornio [(016) 445945; fax 445030; camping.tornio@co.inet.fi; www.campingtornio.com]** App Tornio on E4 coast rd fr Kemi sp on L of dual c/way; turn L at traff lts then immed R. Site well sp. Lge, pt shd; wc; chem disp; sauna; shwrs inc; el pnts (16A) €3.50; Indtte (inc dryer); shop 3km; snacks; cooking facs; playgrnd; tennis; cycle hire; TV; quiet; ccard acc; red CCI. "Poss boggy in wet." ♦ 15 May-30 Sep. € 20.00 2010*

TURKU/ABO *B4* (9km SW Rural) *60.42531, 22.10258* **Ruissalo Camping (Part Naturist), Saaronniemi, 20100 Turku [(02) 2625100; fax 2625101; ruissalocamping@turku.fi]** Well sp fr m'way & fr Turku docks; recep immed after sharp bend in a layby. Med, pt shd, some hdstg; htd wc; chem disp; mv service pnt; sauna; shwrs inc; el pnts (16A) inc; Indtte; shop; rest 200m; snacks; playgrnd; sand beach adj; watersports; games area; wifi; TV; some statics; sep area for naturists; bus; Eng spkn; quiet; ccard acc; red CCI/CCS. "Conv for ferry; modern, clean san facs; ltd el pnts some parts." ♦ 15 May-31 Aug. € 26.00 2009*

VAASA/VASA *B3* (2km NW Coastal) *63.1008, 21.57618* **Top Camping Vaasa, Niemeläntie 1, 65170 Vaasa [(06) 2111255; fax 2111288; info.topcampingvaasa@aspro-ocio.es; www.topcamping.fi/vaasa]** Fr town cent foll sp to harbour (Satama), site sp. Lge, pt shd; htd wc; chem disp; mv service pnt; baby facs; sauna; shwrs inc; el pnts (10A) €5; Indtte; shop; snacks; bar; playgrnd; cycle hire; TV; 10% statics; dogs; no adv bkg; ccard acc; red long stay/CCI. ♦ 25 May-10 Aug. € 22.00 2009*

VARKAUS *C3* (3km SE Rural) *62.29914, 27.92244* **Taipale Camping, Leiritie 1, 78250 Varkaus [tel/fax (017) 5526644]** Fr rd 5 foll sp Joensuu, site sp on lakeside. Med, pt shd; htd wc; chem disp; mv service pnt; sauna; shwrs inc; el pnts (16A) €3.50; Indtte; shop 1.5km; rest 3km; snacks; playgrnd; lake sw; fishing; games area; cycle hire; TV; adv bkg; quiet; ccard acc. ♦ Jun-Aug. € 16.00 2009*

VIITASAARI *C3* (5km S Rural) *63.03682, 25.81277* **Camping Hännilänsalmi, Naurismaantie 80. 44500 Viitasaari [tel/fax (014) 572550; info@hannilansalmi.fi; www.hannilansalmi.fi]** Site sp fr E75/rd 4 fr both dirs. Site on edge of Lake Keitele approx 200m fr E75. Sm, pt sl, pt shd; htd wc; chem disp; mv service pnt; sauna; shwrs inc; el pnts (16A) €3.50; Indtte; shop; playgrnd; lake sw & beach; boat, canoe hire; some statics; Eng spkn; some rd noise; red CCS. "Picturesque setting." ♦ 1 Jun-3 Sep. € 14.00 2008*

VIRRAT *B4* (3km SE Rural) *62.20883, 23.83501* **Camping Lakarin Leirintä, Lakarintie 405, 34800 Virrat [(03) 4758639; fax 4758667; virtain.matkailu@phpoint.net; www.virtainmatkailu.fi]** Fr Virrat on rte 66 twd Ruovesi. Fr Virrat pass info/park & take 2nd L, then 1st L. Site 1.7km on R (poor surface), sp. Med, pt sl, pt shd; htd wc; chem disp; sauna; shwrs inc; el pnts (16A) €3.40; Indry rm; shop in Virrat; snacks; playgrnd; lake sw adj; boating; fishing; 50% statics; Eng spkn; quiet; red CCS. "Beautiful lakeside pitches." 1 May-30 Sep. € 20.00 2011*

⊞ **VUOSTIMO** *C2* (1km N Rural) *66.95783, 27.50350* **Camping Kuukiurun, Sodankyläntie, 98360 Vuostimo [(016) 882535; fax 882540; kuukiuru@webinfo.fi; www.kuukiuru.fi]** N fr Kemijarvi on rd 5, site on R of rd leaving Vuostimo adj rv. Sm, mkd pitch, pt sl, unshd; wc; chem disp; sauna; shwrs; el pnts inc; snacks; fishing; boat hire; x-country skiing; TV; many cabins; dogs; quiet. "Beautiful, peaceful site; friendly owners." € 20.00 2009*

Aland Islands

ECKERO *A4* (8km SE Coastal) *60.19351, 19.62164* **Notvikens Camping, Södra Överbyvägen 239, 22270 Eckerö/Överby [(018) 38020; fax 38329; info@notviken.aland.fi; www.notviken.aland.fi]** Fr Eckerö ferry take rd 1 E & turn R at site sp in hamlet of Överby. Site in 2km. Med, pt sl, pt shd; wc; chem disp; mv service pnt; shwrs €1; el pnts (10A) inc; Indtte; sm shop; rest; snacks; bar; BBQ; cooking facs; playgrnd; sand beach adj; games area; 5% statics; dogs; phone; bus 2km; Eng spkn; adv bkg; quiet; CCI. "Well-maintained, family-run site in lovely location by long inlet; facs rustic but clean & well-equipped." ♦ 15 May-31 Aug. € 18.00 2009*

FOGLO *A4* (10km E Coastal) *60.05981, 20.51586* **CC Camping, Finholmavägen, 22270 Föglö [(018) 51440; fax 51455; cc.camp@aland.net; http://home.aland.net/cc.camp]** Fr ferry at Degerby on Föglö Island foll main island rd E then N. Site sp fr ferry. Sm, pt sl, unshd; htd wc; chem disp; baby facs; shwrs €1; el pnts €3.50; Indtte; shop 10km; rest; snacks; bar; BBQ; cooking facs; playgrnd; shgl beach adj; no statics; dogs; phone; no twin axles; Eng spkn; adv bkg; quiet; CCI. "Beautiful, quite site on attractive island; gd birdwatching & walks fr site." ♦ 1 Jun-31 Aug. € 10.00 2009*

MARIEHAMN/MAARIANHAMINA *A4* (1km SE Coastal) *60.09079, 19.95038* **Gröna Uddens Camping, Östernäsvägen, 22100 Mariehamn/Maarianhamina [(018) 21121; fax 19041; gronaudden@aland.net; www.gronaudden.com]** Sp fr ferry. Lge, sl, pt shd; wc; chem disp; baby facs; sauna; shwrs; el pnts (10A) inc (long lead req); Indtte; shop; rest 1km; snacks; bar; playgrnd; sand beach; watersports; games area; cycle hire; quiet; ccard acc. "Superb natural scenery, worth long haul; unrel in wet; modern san facs but poss long walk." 1 May-17 Sep. € 23.50 2009*

SUND *A4* (8km SE Coastal) *60.21252, 20.23508* **Puttes Camping, Bryggvägen 40, Bomarsund, 22530 Sund [(018) 44040; fax 44047; puttes.camping@aland.net; www.visitaland.com/puttescamping]** N fr Mariehamn on rd 2 for 40+ km, site at Bomarsund fortress ruins. Med, pt sl, pt shd; wc; chem disp; mv service pnt; shwrs €1; el pnts (10A) inc; Indtte; shop; rest; snacks; bar; BBQ; cooking facs; shgl beach adj; cycle hire; games area; 5% statics; dogs; phone; bus adj; Eng spkn; adv bkg; quiet; CCI. "Basic, but clean & welcoming; vg." ♦ 15 May-11 Sep. € 12.10 2009*

VARDO *A4* (5km N Coastal) *60.27073, 20.38819* **Sandösunds Camping, Sandösundsvägen, 22550 Vårdö [tel/fax (018) 47750; info@sandocamping.aland.fi; www.sandocamping.aland.fi]** Site sp fr ferry at Hummelvik & fr rd 2. Med, pt sl, pt shd; htd wc; chem disp; mv service pnt; baby facs; shwrs inc; el pnts (10A) €3.50 (long lead poss req); Indtte; shop; rest; snacks; bar; BBQ; cooking facs; playgrnd; sand beach adj; cycle & kayak hire; games area; wifi; 5% statics; dogs; phone; Eng spkn; adv bkg; quiet; CCI. "Well-run site in beautiful location; excel facs." ♦ 15 Apr-31 Oct. € 14.00 2009*

Distances are shown in kilometres and are calculated from town/city centres along the most practical roads, although not necessarily taking the shortest route. 1km = 0.62miles

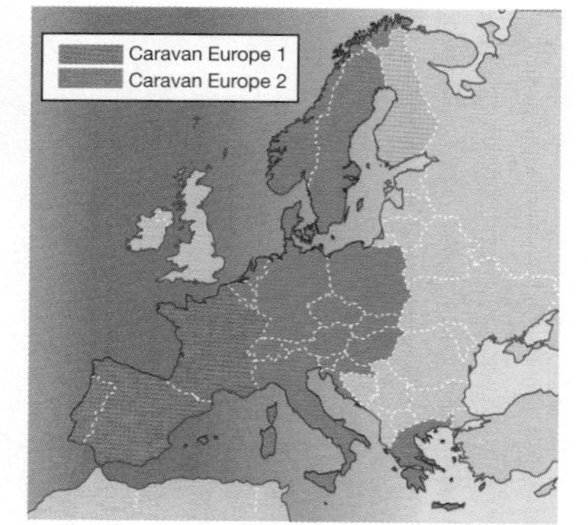

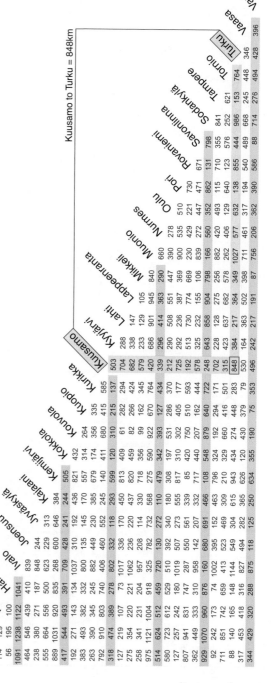

Kuusamo to Turku = 848km

	Forssa	Hanko	Helsinki	Hämeenlinna	Ivalo	Joensuu	Jyväskylä	Kajaani	Kemijärvi	Kokkola	Kouvola	Kuopio	Kurikka	Kuusamo	Kyyjärvi	Lahti	Lappeenranta	Mikkeli	Muonio	Nurmes	Oulu	Pori	Rovaniemi	Savonlinna	Sodankylä	Tampere	Tornio	Turku	Vaasa
Hanko	150																												
Helsinki	114	129																											
Hämeenlinna	56	195	100																										
Ivalo	1091	1238	1122	1041																									
Joensuu	464	546	439	410	839																								
Jyväskylä	238	380	271	187	848	244																							
Kajaani	555	664	556	500	623	229	313																						
Kemijärvi	889	1031	920	835	268	600	646	384																					
Kokkola	417	544	493	391	709	428	241	244	505																				
Kouvola	192	271	143	134	1037	310	192	436	821	432																			
Kuopio	383	493	382	332	800	135	145	170	557	314	264																		
Kurikka	263	390	345	245	882	449	230	385	679	174	356	335																	
Kuusamo	792	910	803	740	406	460	552	245	140	411	680	415	585																
Kyyjärvi	318	474	389	278	802	332	118	293	599	120	310	215	137	503															
Lahti	127	219	107	73	1017	336	170	450	813	409	61	282	294	704	288														
Lappeenranta	275	354	220	221	1062	236	220	437	820	459	82	266	424	682	338	147													
Mikkeli	258	341	231	204	957	208	114	330	718	356	99	162	345	579	233	129	105												
Muonio	975	1121	1004	918	325	782	732	568	275	590	922	670	764	420	686	901	945	840											
Nurmes	514	624	512	459	720	130	272	110	479	342	393	127	434	339	296	414	363	290	660										
Oulu	580	723	612	529	510	392	340	180	308	197	531	286	370	212	290	508	551	447	390	278									
Pori	127	257	242	180	1019	507	273	555	817	310	302	405	177	725	292	236	387	369	900	535	510								
Rovaniemi	807	941	831	747	287	550	561	339	85	420	750	510	593	192	513	730	774	669	230	429	221	730							
Savonlinna	362	449	333	310	958	142	207	332	717	440	207	162	444	578	325	232	155	106	839	272	447	471	671						
Sodankylä	929	1070	960	876	160	680	691	466	108	548	879	640	722	248	643	858	904	798	166	560	352	862	131	798					
Tampere	92	242	173	74	1002	395	152	463	796	324	192	294	171	702	228	128	275	256	882	420	493	115	710	355	841				
Tornio	711	851	742	659	413	523	469	309	210	329	660	416	501	315	423	637	682	578	262	406	129	640	123	576	252	621			
Turku	88	140	165	148	1144	549	304	615	943	434	274	448	283	848	384	217	364	349	1027	577	632	138	855	444	986	153	764		
Vaasa	317	453	418	316	827	494	282	365	626	120	430	379	79	530	164	363	502	398	711	461	317	194	540	489	668	245	448	346	
Varkaus	344	429	320	288	875	118	125	250	634	355	190	75	353	496	242	217	191	87	756	206	362	390	586	88	714	276	494	428	396

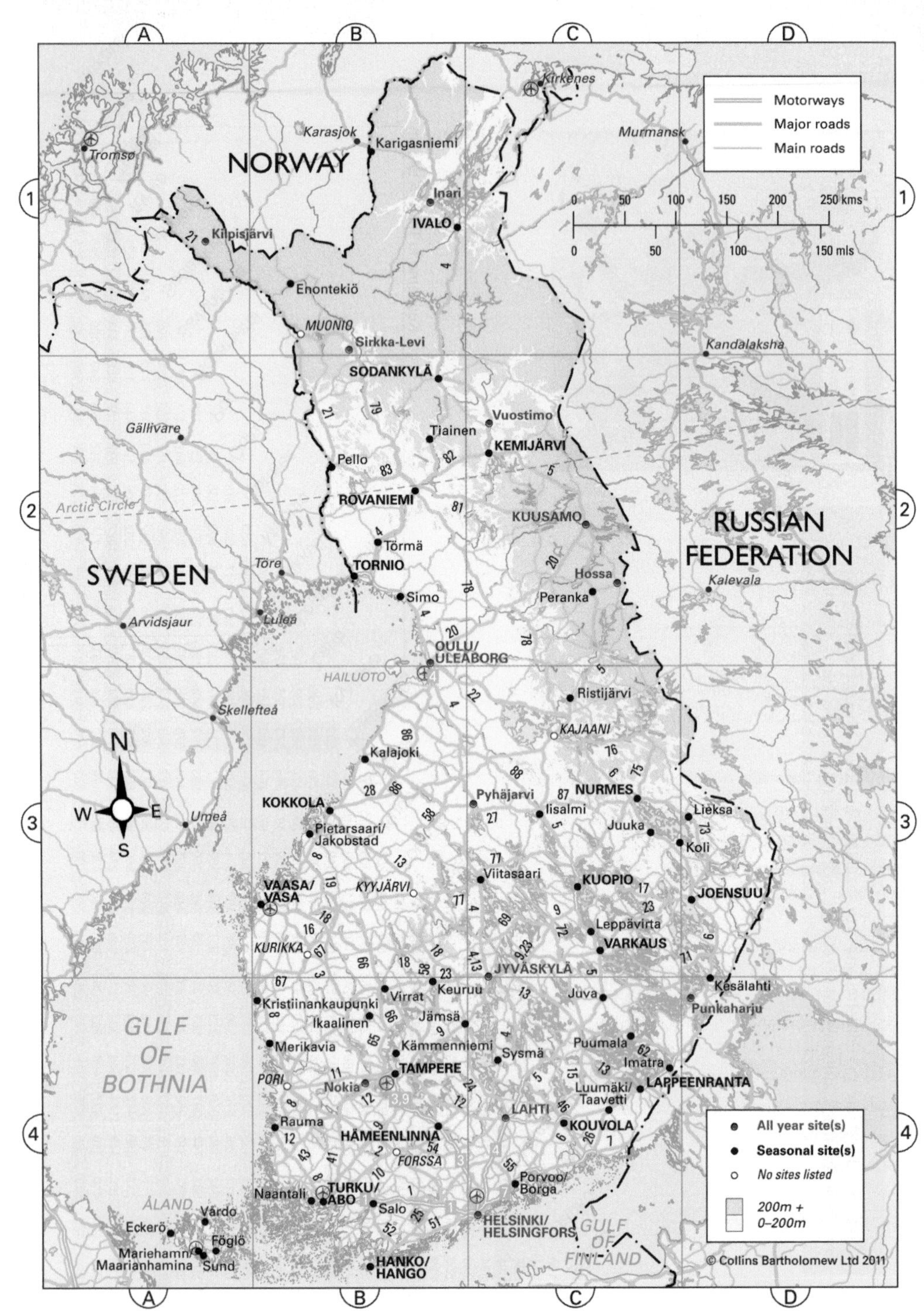
NORWAY
SWEDEN
RUSSIAN FEDERATION
GULF OF BOTHNIA
GULF OF FINLAND
Motorways
Major roads
Main roads
All year site(s)
Seasonal site(s)
No sites listed
200m +
0–200m
© Collins Bartholomew Ltd 2011
Kilpisjärvi
Enontekiö
MUONIO
Sirkka-Levi
SODANKYLÄ
Inari
IVALO
Karigasniemi
Karasjok
Kirkenes
Murmansk
Tromsø
Kandalaksha
Vuostimo
Tiainen
KEMIJÄRVI
Pello
ROVANIEMI
Arctic Circle
Gällivare
KUUSAMO
Törmä
TORNIO
Töre
Hossa
Peranka
Simo
Kalevala
Luleå
Arvidsjaur
OULU/ ULEABORG
HAILUOTO
Ristijärvi
KAJAANI
Skellefteå
Kalajoki
KOKKOLA
Pyhäjarvi
Iisalmi
NURMES
Lieksa
Juuka
Koli
Umeå
Pietarsaari/ Jakobstad
Viitasaari
KUOPIO
JOENSUU
VAASA/ VASA
KYYJÄRVI
Leppävirta
VARKAUS
KURIKKA
JYVÄSKYLÄ
Kesälahti
Punkaharju
Keuruu
Virrat
Juva
Kristiinankaupunki
Ikaalinen
Jämsä
Puumala
Merikarvia
Kämmenniemi
Sysmä
Imatra
TAMPERE
PORI
Nokia
LAPPEENRANTA
Luumäki/ Taavetti
Rauma
LAHTI
KOUVOLA
HÄMEENLINNA
FORSSA
Porvoo/ Borga
Naantali
TURKU/ ABO
Salo
HELSINKI/ HELSINGFORS
ÅLAND
Vårdo
Eckerö
Föglö
Mariehamn/ Maarianhamina
Sund
HANKO/ HANGO

Germany

Country Introduction

© iStockPhoto.com/ © Nikada

Brandenburg Gate,Berlin

Population (approx): 82 million

Capital: Berlin (population approx 3.4 million)

Area: 357,050 sq km

Bordered by: Austria, Belgium, Czech Republic, Denmark, France, Luxembourg, Netherlands, Poland, Switzerland

Terrain: Lowlands in north; uplands/industrialised belt in the centre; highlands, forests and Bavarian alps in the south

Climate: Temperate throughout the year; warm summers and cold winters; rain throughout the year

Coastline: 2,389km

Highest Point: Zugspitze 2,963m

Language: German

Local Time: GMT or BST + 1, i.e. 1 hour ahead of the UK all year

Currency: Euros divided into 100 cents; £1 = €1.14, €1 = 87 pence (October 2010)

Telephoning: From the UK dial 0049 for Germany and omit the initial zero of the area code of the number you are calling. To call the UK from Germany dial 0044, omitting the initial zero of the area code

Emergency numbers: Police 112; Fire brigade 112; Ambulance 112. Operators speak English

Public Holidays 2012

Jan 1, 6; Apr 6, 9; May 5, 17, 28; Jun 7; Aug 15; Oct 3, 31; Nov 1, 21; Dec 25, 26.

Public Holidays 2013

Jan 1, 6; Mar 29; Apr 1; May 1, 9, 20, 30; Aug 15; Oct 3, 31; Nov 1, 20; Dec 25, 26.

Public holidays vary according to region. The dates shown here may not be celebrated throughout the country. School summer holidays vary by region but are roughly July to mid/end Aug or Aug to mid Sept.

Tourist Office

GERMAN NATIONAL TOURIST OFFICE
www.germany.travel
office-britain@germany.travel

The following introduction to Germany should be read in conjunction with the important information contained in the Handbook chapters at the front of this guide.

Camping and Caravanning

There are approximately 3,500 campsites in Germany, which are generally open from April to October. Many (mostly in winter sports areas) stay open in winter and have all the necessary facilities for winter sports enthusiasts. Sites may have a very high proportion of statics, usually in a separate area. In the high summer season visitors should either start looking for a pitch early in the afternoon or book in advance.

Campsites are usually well equipped with modern sanitary facilities, shops and leisure amenities, etc. Some sites impose a charge for handling rubbish, commonly €1 to €2 a day. Separate containers for recycling glass, plastic, etc, are now the norm. A daily tourist tax may also be payable of up to €2 or €3 per person per night.

Naturism is popular, particularly in eastern Germany, and sites which accept naturists will generally display a sign 'FKK'.

Credit and/or debit cards are accepted at many campsites but some campsites will not accept this as a form of payment. You may also find payment by this method refused for overnight or short stays because of high transaction charges. As such it is wise to make sure you have access to cash if needed. Cash machines are widely available.

Many sites close for a two hour period between noon and 3pm (known as Mittagsruhe) and you may find barriers down so that vehicles cannot be moved on or off the site during this period. Some sites provide a waiting area but where a site entrance is off a busy road parking or turning may be difficult.

For a list of small sites (up to 150 pitches) see www.kleincamp.de

Casual/wild camping is discouraged and is not allowed in forests and nature reserves. In the case of private property permission to pitch a tent or park a caravan should be obtained in advance from the owners, or on common land or state property, from the local town hall or police station.

The German motoring organisation, ADAC, publishes an annual guide 'Stellplatz Führer' listing over 3,500 dedicated overnight or short stay parking areas specifically for motorhomes, many with good security and electricity, together with coin or credit card operated water and waste disposal facilities (called Sani-Stations or Holiday-Clean). In addition, many campsites in popular tourist areas have separate overnight areas of hardstanding with appropriate facilities, often just outside the main campsite area. Fees are generally very reasonable.

A Camping Card International (CCI) is recommended.

Country Information

Cycling

There is an extensive network of over 40,000 km of well laid-out cycle paths in all regions. Children under eight years are not allowed to cycle on the road. Up to the age of 10 years they may ride on the pavement but must give way to pedestrians and dismount to cross the road. Bicycles must have front and rear lights and a bell. The wearing of safety helmets is not compulsory, but it is strongly recommended.

Cyclists can be fined €25 for using a mobile phone while cycling.

Electricity and Gas

Current on campsites varies between 2 and 16 amps, 6 to 10 amps being the most common. Plugs have two round pins. Most campsites have CEE connections.

Many sites make a one-off charge – usually €1 or €2 however long your stay – for connection to the electricity supply, which is then metered at a rate per kilowatt hour (kwh) of approximately €0.50-€0.70, with or without an additional daily charge. This connection charge can make one night stays expensive. During the summer you may find only a flat, daily charge for electricity of €2-€5, the supply being metered during the rest of the year.

Campingaz is available and it is understood that the blue cylinders in general used throughout Europe may be exchanged for German cylinders which are green-grey. At some campsites in winters sports areas a direct connection with the gas mains ring is available and the supply is metered.

*See **Electricity and Gas** in the section **DURING YOUR STAY.***

Entry Formalities

British and Irish passport holders may stay in Germany for up to three months without a visa. While there are no Customs controls at Germany's borders into other EU countries, when you enter or leave the Czech Republic and Poland you may still have to show your passport.

Regulations for Pets

Certain breeds of dogs, such as pit bull terriers and American Staffordshire terriers, are prohibited from entering Germany. Other large dogs and breeds such as Dobermann, Mastiff and Rottweiler may need to be kept on a lead and muzzled in public, which also means in your car. You are advised to contact the German embassy in London before making travel arrangements for your dog and check the latest available information from your vet or from the PETS Helpline on 0870 241 1710.

*See **Pet Travel Scheme** under **Documents** in the section **PLANNING AND TRAVELLING.***

Medical Services

Local state health insurance fund offices offer assistance round-the-clock and telephone numbers can be found in the local telephone directory. EU citizens are entitled to free or subsidised emergency care from doctors contracted to the state health care system on presentation of a European Health Insurance Card (EHIC). Private treatment by doctors or dentists is not refundable under the German health service. You will be liable for a percentage of prescribed medication charges at pharmacies and this is also non-refundable. Pharmacies offer an all-night and Sunday service and the address of the nearest out-of-hours branch will be displayed on the door of every pharmacy.

There is a fixed daily charge for a stay in hospital (treatment is free for anyone under 18 years of age) which is not refundable. If you are required to pay an additional patient contribution for treatment then reduced charges apply to holders of an EHIC. For refunds of these additional charges you should apply with original receipts to a local state health insurance fund office.

If you enjoy hiking and outdoor sports you should seek medical advice before you travel about preventative measures and immunisation against tick-borne encephalitis, a potentially serious and debilitating viral disease of the central nervous system which is endemic from spring to autumn. Lyme disease is an equally serious tick-borne infection for which there is no preventative vaccine. Ticks are found in rural and forested areas, particularly in long grass, bushes, hedgerows and woods, and in scrubland and areas where animals wander.

The areas affected are Baden-Württemberg and Bavaria, as well as certain regions within Hessen, Rhineland-Palatinate and Thuringia. If you think you might be at risk use an insect repellent containing DEET, wear long sleeves and long trousers, inspect the body for ticks after outdoor activity and remove with tweezers, and avoid unpasteurised dairy products in risk areas. See www.tickalert.org, email info@tickalert.org or telephone 01943 468010.

You are strongly recommended to obtain comprehensive travel and medical insurance before travelling to Germany, such as The Caravan Club's Red Pennant Overseas Holiday Insurance – see www.caravanclub.co.uk/redpennant

*See **Medical Matters** in the section **DURING YOUR STAY.***

Opening Hours

Banks – Mon-Fri 8.30am-12.30pm & 1.30pm-3.30pm (to 5.30pm on Thurs); hours may vary slightly and are dependent on each bank, closed weekends.

Museums – Daily 10am-5pm/6pm; possibly closed Monday – check locally.

Post Offices – Mon-Fri 8am-6pm; Sat 8am-12pm.

Shops – Mon-Fri 8/9am-6pm/8pm. Sat 8/9am-12/4pm; in some places bakers are open on Sunday mornings.

Safety and Security

Most visits to Germany are trouble free but visitors should take the usual commonsense precautions against mugging, pickpocketing and bag snatching, particularly in areas around railway stations, airports in large cities and at Christmas markets. Do not leave valuables unattended.

Germany shares with the rest of Europe a general threat from terrorism. Attacks could be indiscriminate and against civilian targets in public places, including tourist sites. You should maintain a high level of vigilance at all times.

*See **Safety and Security** in the section **DURING YOUR STAY.***

British Embassy

WILHELMSTRASSE 70, D-10117 BERLIN
Tel: (030) 204570,
http://ukingermany.fco.gov.uk/en/

British Consulates-General

YORCKSTRASSE 19, D-40476
DÜSSELDORF
Tel: (0211) 94480
MÖHLSTRASSE 5, 81675 MÜNCHEN
Tel: (089) 211090

There are also Consulates or Honorary Consulates in Bremen, Frankfurt, Hamburg, Hannover, Kiel, Nürnberg and Stuttgart

Irish Embassy

JÄGERSTRASSE 51, 10117 BERLIN
Tel: (030) 220720
www.embassyofireland.de

There are also Irish Honorary Consulates in Frankfurt, Hamburg, Köln (Cologne) and München (Munich).

Customs Regulations

Alcohol and Tobacco

*For import allowances for alcohol and tobacco products see **Customs Regulations** in the section **PLANNING AND TRAVELLING.***

Documents

Passport

It is a legal requirement to carry your passport at all times. German police have the right to ask to see identification and for British citizens the only acceptable form of ID is a valid passport.

Vehicle(s)

Carry your valid driving licence, insurance and vehicle documents with you in your vehicle at all times. It is particularly important to carry your vehicle registration document V5C – see ***Low Emission Zones*** later in this chapter.

If you are driving a hired or borrowed vehicle, you must be in possession of a letter of authorisation from the owner or a hire agreement.

*See **Documents** in the section **PLANNING AND TRAVELLING.***

Money

Travellers' cheques are best exchanged at a bureau de change (Wechselbüro) as they may not be accepted in payment for goods and services. Banks may decline to change them.

The major debit and credit cards, including American Express, are widely accepted by shops, hotels, restaurants and petrol stations. However, you may find that credit cards are not as widely accepted in smaller establishments as they are in the UK, including many shops and campsites, due to the high charges imposed on retailers, and debit cards are preferred. Cash machines are widespread and have instructions in English.

British visitors have been arrested for possession of counterfeit currency and the authorities advise against changing money anywhere other than at banks or legitimate bureaux de change.

Carry your credit card issuers'/banks' 24-hour UK contact numbers in case of loss or theft of your cards.

Motoring

Roads in Germany are of an excellent standard but speed limits are higher than in the UK and the accident rate is greater. Drivers undertaking long journeys in or through Germany should plan their journeys carefully and take frequent breaks.

Accidents

In the event of a road accident the police must always be called even if there are no injuries.

Alcohol

The maximum permitted level of alcohol is 50 milligrams per 100 millilitres of blood, i.e. lower than that in the UK (80 milligrams). For novice drivers, including foreign residents, who passed their driving test less than two years ago, and for drivers under the age of 21, no alcohol is permitted in the bloodstream. Penalties for driving under the influence of alcohol or drugs are severe.

Breakdown Service

The motoring organisation Allgemeiner Deutscher Automobil-Club (ADAC) operates road patrols on motorways and in the event of a breakdown, assistance can be obtained by calling from emergency phones placed every 2 km. Members of clubs affiliated to the AIT or FIA, such as The Caravan Club, must ask specifically for roadside assistance to be proviced by ADAC as they should be able to receive assistance free of charge. You must pay for replacement parts and towing. ADAC breakdown vehicles are yellow and marked 'ADAC Strassenwacht'.

If ADAC Strassenwacht vehicles are not available, firms under contract to ADAC provide towing and roadside assistance, against payment. Vehicles used by firms under contract to ADAC are marked 'Strassendienst im Auftrag des ADAC'.

On other roads the ADAC breakdown service can be reached 24 hours a day by telephoning 01802-22 22 22 (local call rates) or 22 22 22 from a mobile phone.

Essential Equipment

Lights

Dipped headlights are recommended at all times and must always be used in tunnels, as well as when visibility is poor and during periods of bad weather. Bulbs are more likely to fail with constant use and you are recommended to carry spares.

Child Restraint Systems

Children under three years of age must be placed in an approved child restraint and cannot be transported in a vehicle otherwise. Children of three years and over must travel in the rear of vehicles. Children under 12 years old and 1.5 metres in height must be seated in an approved child restraint. If a child restraint is not available because other children are using a child restraint, then children of three years and over must use a seat belt or other safety device attached to the seat.

Winter Driving

Since December 2010, when a new regulation was introduced, tyres on all vehicles, including those registered outside Germany, must be fitted with winter tyres (or all season tyres) during winter conditions, bearing the mark 'M+S' or the snowflake. Failure to use them can result in a fine and penalty points. There must also be anti-freeze in the windscreen cleaning fluid.

The use of snow chains is permitted and for vehicles fitted with them there is a maximum speed limit of 50 km/h (31 mph). In mountainous areas the requirement for chains is indicated by signs.

Snow chains may be hired or purchased from Polar Automotive Ltd, tel 01892 519933, www.snowchains.com, email: polar@snowchains.com (10% discount for Caravan Club members).

*See **Motoring – Equipment** in the section **PLANNING AND TRAVELLING.***

Fuel

Most petrol stations are open from 8am to 8pm. In large cities many are open 24 hours. In the east there are fewer petrol stations than in the south and west. Some have automatic pumps operated using credit cards.

LPG (autogas or flussiggas) is widely available. You can view a list of approximately 800 outlets throughout the country, including those near motorways, from the website www.autogastanken.de (follow the links under 'Tanken' and 'Tankstellan-Karte).

On some stretches of motorway petrol stations may be few and far between, e.g. the A45, A42 and A3 to the Dutch border, and it is advisable not to let your fuel tank run low.

*See also **Fuel** under **Motoring – Advice** in the section **PLANNING AND TRAVELLING.***

Low Emission Zones

A number of German cities and towns now require motorists to purchase a 'Pollution Badge' (Umwelt Plakette) in the form of a windscreen sticker in order to enter city centre 'Umwelt' or green zones. The areas where restrictions apply are indicated by signs showing coloured vignettes, the colour of the vignette issued (red, yellow or green) depending on your vehicle's engine type and its Euro emission rating.

You must present your vehicle registration document, V5C, at an 'Umwelt Plakette' sales outlet, which can be found at vehicle repair centres, car dealers, MOT (Tüv) stations and vehicle licensing offices and it is understood that badges are also available from ATU motoring supplies shops. The cost varies between €5 and €10 + VAT and postage.

Failure to display a badge could result in a fine of €40. Enforcement is managed by the police, local authorities and traffic wardens. Older vehicles without a catalytic converter or a particulate filter (generally emission-rated Euro 1) will not be issued with a badge and will not be permitted to enter the centres of those cities and towns participating in the scheme.

For more information see www.lowemissionzones.eu or www.umwelt-plakette.de (you may also be able to purchase your badge here before you travel to Germany). Alternatively cntact The Club's Travel Service Information Officer (Club members only), email: travelserviceinfo@caravanclub.co.uk.

Parking

Zigzag lines on the carriageway indicate a stopping (waiting) and parking prohibition, e.g. at bus stops, narrow roads and places with poor visibility, but double or single yellow lines are not used. Instead look out for 'no stopping', 'parking prohibited' or 'no parking' signs.

Except for one-way streets, parking is only permitted on the right-hand side. Do not park in the opposite direction to traffic flow. Parking meters and parking disc schemes are in operation and discs may be bought in local shops or service stations.

*See also **Parking Facilities for the Disabled** under **Motoring – Advice** in the section **PLANNING AND TRAVELLING.***

Priority

At crossroads and junctions, where no priority is indicated, traffic coming from the right has priority. Trams do not have absolute priority over other vehicles but priority must be given to passengers getting on or off stationary trams. Trams in two-way streets must be overtaken on the right. Drivers must give way to a bus whose driver has indicated his intention to pull away from the kerb. Do not overtake a stationary school bus which has stopped to let passengers on or off. This may be indicated by a red flashing light on the bus.

Traffic already on a roundabout has right of way, except when signs show otherwise. Drivers must use their indicators when leaving a roundabout, not when entering.

Always stop to allow pedestrians to cross at marked pedestrian crossings. In residential areas where traffic-calming zones exist, pedestrians are allowed to use the whole street, so drive with great care.

Road Signs and Markings

Most German road signs and markings conform to the international pattern. Other road signs that may be encountered are:

Keep distance shown

Street lights not on all night

Lower speed limit applies in the wet

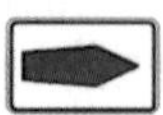

Recommended route on motorways

One way street

Tram or bus stop

Einsatzfahrzeuge Frei – *Emergency vehicles only*

Fahrbahnwechsel – *Change traffic lane*

Freie Fahrt – *Road clear*

Frostchaden – *Frost damage*

Gefährlich – *Danger*

Glatteisgefahr – *Ice on the road*

Notruf – *Emergency roadside telephone*

Radweg Kreuzt – *Cycle-track crossing*

Rollsplitt – *Loose grit*

Stau – *Traffic jam*

Strassenschaden – *Road damage*

Umleitung – *Diversion*

Vorsicht – *Caution*

Road signs on motorways are blue and white, whereas on B roads (Bundesstrasse) they are orange and black. If you are planning a route through Germany using E road numbers, be aware that E roads may be poorly signposted and you may have to navigate using national A or B road numbers.

Speed Limits

*See **Speed Limits Table** under **Motoring – Advice** in the section **PLANNING AND TRAVELLING.***

There is a speed limit of 50 km/h (31 mph) in built-up areas for all types of motor vehicles, unless otherwise indicated by road signs. A built-up area starts from the town name sign at the beginning of a town or village.

The number of sections of autobahn with de-restricted zones, i.e. no upper speed limit, is diminishing and the volume of traffic makes high speed motoring virtually impossible. Regulations on many stretches of two-lane motorway restrict lorries, together with cars towing caravans, from overtaking.

Be aware that speed cameras are frequently in use but they may be deliberately hidden behind crash barriers or in mobile units. A GPS navigation system which indicates the location of fixed speed cameras must have the function deactivated. The use of radar detectors is prohibited.

A car towing a caravan or trailer is prohibited to 80km/h (50 mph) on motorways and other main roads. You may occasionally see car/caravan combinations displaying a sign indicating that their maximum permitted speed is 100 km/h (62 mph). This is only permitted for vehicles who have passed a TUV test in Germany, who will then need to apply for a sticker at a Zulassungsstelle. The application process can be complicated as some Zulassungsstelles will insist they see a registration certificate for your caravan. Obtaining a 100km/h sticker without a registration certificate is best done in Aachen as they are the only Zulassungsstelle familiar with this process. If you are having difficulty at a different Zulassungsstelle ask them to call the Zulassungsstelle in Aachen to confirm that a registration document is not required.

In bad weather when visibility is below 50 metres, the maximum speed limit is 50 km/h (31 mph) on all roads.

Towing

Drivers of cars towing caravans and other slow-moving vehicles must leave enough space in front of them for an overtaking vehicle to get into that space, or they must pull over from time to time to let other vehicles pass.

Motorhomes are prohibited from towing a car. Anyone wishing to do this should put the car on a trailer so that all four wheels are off the ground. Outside built-up areas the speed limit for such vehicle combinations is 80 km/h (50 mph) or 60 km/h (37 mph) for vehicles over 3,500 kg.

Traffic Jams

Roads leading to popular destinations in Denmark, the Alps and Adriatic Coast become very congested during the busy holiday period of July and August and on public holidays. In those periods traffic jams of up to 60 km are not unheard of.

Congestion is likely on the A3 and A5 north-south routes. Traffic jams are also likely to occur on the A7 Kassel-Denmark, the A8 Stuttgart-Munich-Salzburg and on the A2 and A9 to Berlin. Other cities where congestion may occur are Würzburg, Nürnberg (Nuremberg), Munich and Hamburg. Alternative routes, known as U routes, have been devised; those leading to the south or west have even numbers and those leading to the north or east have odd numbers. These U routes often detour over secondary roads to the following motorway junction and the acquisition of a good road map or atlas is recommended.

ADAC employs 'Stauberater' (traffic jam advisors) who are recognisable by their bright yellow motorbikes. They assist motorists stuck in traffic and will advise on alternative routes.

Upgrading of motorways to Berlin from the west and improvements to many roads in the old east German suburbs may result in diversions and delays, and worsened traffic congestion.

Violation of Traffic Regulations

Police are empowered to impose and collect small on-the-spot fines for contravention of traffic regulations. Fines vary according to the gravity of the offence and have in recent years been increased dramatically for motorists caught speeding in a built-up area (over 50 km/h – 31 mph). A deposit may be required against higher fines and failure to pay may cause the vehicle to be confiscated.

It is an offence to use abusive language, make derogatory signs to other drivers or run out of petrol on a motorway.

Pedestrians should be aware that it is illegal to cross a pedestrian crossing when the red pedestrian light is displayed, even if there is no traffic approaching the crossing. Offenders could be fined and will find themselves liable to all costs in the event of an accident.

Motorways

With around 12,600 toll free kilometres, Germany's motorways (autobahns) constitute one of the world's most advanced and efficient systems. Together with an excellent network of federal and state highways, it is possible for motorists to reach any destination in Germany quickly and comfortably. For a complete list of autobahns, including the location of all junctions and roadworks in progress, see www.autobahn-online.de.

Recent visitors report that some motorways are so heavily used by lorries that the inside lane has become heavily rutted. These parallel ruts are potentially dangerous for caravans travelling at high speed and vigilance is necessary. It is understood that the A44 and A7 are particularly prone to this problem. Caution also needs to be exercised when driving on the concrete surfaces of major roads.

On motorways emergency telephones are placed at 2 km intervals; some have one button to request breakdown assistance and another to summon an ambulance. Other telephones connect the caller to a rescue control centre. A vehicle that has broken down on a motorway must be towed away to the nearest exit.

There are more than 700 motorway service areas offering, at the very least, a petrol station and a restaurant or cafeteria. Tourist information boards are posted in all the modern motorway service areas. Recent visitors have reported an increase in service facilities just off Autobahn exit ramps, in particular with 'Autohof' (truck stops). The facilities at Autohofs are reported to be comparable to service areas, but usually with considerably lower prices.

Touring

German beers and wines are famous and there is plenty of regional choice. Visitors cannot fail to be impressed by the generally high quality of German food and its regional range and diversity. In the country there is at least one inn – 'gasthof' or 'gasthaus' – in virtually every village. In September and early October the numerous wine and beer festivals of the Rhineland, Mosel and Bavaria are lively and good fun. A service charge is usually included in restaurant bills but it is usual to leave some small change or round up the bill by 5-10% if satisfied with the service.

Smoking is generally banned on public transport and in restaurants and bars, but regulations vary from state to state.

The German National Tourist Office produces pocket guides to walking and cycle paths throughout the country, as well an extensive range of other brochures and guides. The individual tourist offices for the 16 federal states can also supply a wealth of information about events, attractions and tourist opportunities within their local regions. Obtain contact details from the GNTO.

Christmas markets are an essential part of the run-up to the festive season and they range in size from a few booths in small towns and villages, to hundreds of stalls and booths in large cities. The markets generally run from mid November to 22 or 23 December.

There are 32 UNESCO World Heritage sites in Germany, including the cities of Lübeck, Potsdam and Weimar, the cathedrals of Aachen, Cologne and Speyer, together with numerous other venues of great architectural and archaeological interest.

The Berlin Welcome Card is valid for 2, 3 or 5 days and includes free bus and train travel (including free travel for three accompanying children up to the age of 14), as well as discounted or free entrance to museums, and discounts on tours, boat trips, restaurants and theatres. It can be extended to include Potsdam and the Museuminsel and is available from tourist information centres, hotels and public transport

GERMANY

centres or from www.visitberlin.de. A 3 day museum card – SchauLUST-MuseenBERLIN – is also available, valid in more than 60 national museums in and around the city.

Other cities, groups of cities or regions also offer Welcome Cards, including Bonn, Cologne, Dresden, Düsseldorf, Frankfurt, Hamburg, Heidelberg and Munich. These give discounts on public transport, museums, shopping, dining and attractions. Enquire at a local tourist office or at the German National Tourist Office in London.

Local Travel

Most major German cities boast excellent underground (U-bahn), urban railway (S-bahn), bus and tram systems whose convenience and punctuality are renowned. On public transport services, pay your fare prior to boarding the vehicle using the automated ticketing machines. Your ticket must then be date stamped separately using the machines onboard the vehicle or at the entry gates at major stops. Daily tickets permit the use of trains, buses and trams. Berlin's integrated transport system extends as far as Potsdam.

A number of car ferries operate across the Weser and Elbe rivers which allow easy touring north of Bremen and Hamburg. Routes across the Weser include Blexen to Bremerhavn, Brake to Sandstedt and Berne to Farge. The Weser Tunnel (B437) connects the villages of Rodenkirchen and Dedesdorf, offering an easy connection between the cities of Bremerhaven and Nordenham. Across the Elbe there is a car ferry route between Wischhafen and Glückstadt. An international ferry route operates all year across Lake Constance (Bodensee) between Konstanz and Meersburg. There is also a route between Friedrichshafen and Romanshorn in Switzerland.

All place names used in the Site Entry listings which follow can be found in the AA's Big Road Atlas for Germany, scale 3 miles to 1 inch (1 cm to 1.5 km).

SITES IN GERMANY

⊞ **AACHEN** *1A4* (15km SE Rural) *50.69944, 6.22194* **Camping Vichtbachtal, Vichtbachstrasse 10, 52159 Roetgen-Mulartshütte [tel/fax (02408) 5131; camping@vichtbachtal.de; www.vichtbachtal.de]** On E40/A44 exit junc 3 Aachen/Brand onto B258 dir Kornelimünster. In 5km at R-hand bend turn L sp Mulartshütte. Thro Venwegen. Site ent on L 50m bef T-junc app Mulartshütte, site sp. Med, pt sl, shd; wc; chem disp; mv service pnt; shwrs inc; el pnts (16A) €1.50 or metered; Indtte; shop; rest 150m; playgrnd; 80% statics; site clsd Nov; poss cr; quiet; CCI. "Sm area for tourers."
€ 17.00 2010*

⊞ **AACHEN** *1A4* (2.3km S Urban) *50.76140, 6.10285* **Aachen Platz für Camping, Branderhoferweg 11, 52066 Aachen-Burtscheid [(0241) 6088057; fax 6088058; mail@aachen-camping.de; www.aachen-camping.de]** Exit A44 junc 2 onto L233 Monschauerstrasse dir Aachen. In 3.8km at outer ring rd Adenauer Allee L260 turn R, then in 800m L at 2nd traff lts onto Branderhoferweg twd Beverau. Site on R at bottom of hill. Sm, mkd pitch, hdstg, unshd; htd wc; chem disp; mv service pnt; el pnts (16A) inc; tradsmn; dogs; shwr €1 (5 mins); bus 500m; poss cr; Eng spkn; no adv bkg; quiet, but poss noise fr bar. "Nice, clean, well-run municipal site; gd, modern san facs; max stay 3 nights; excel o'night stop; rec arr bef 1600 high ssn; ideal Xmas mkts." ♦ € 14.00 2011*

⊞ **AALEN** *3D3* (7km SW Rural) *48.78583, 9.98218* **Camping Hirtenheich, Hasenweide 2, 73457 Essingen-Lauterburg [(07365) 296; fax 251; camphirtenteich@aol.com; www.campingplatz-hirtenteich.de]** Exit A7/E43 at Aalen onto B29. Site sp beyond Essingen dir Lauterburg. Med, pt sl, unshd; wc; chem disp; mv service pnt; sauna; shwrs inc; el pnts (16A) metered; Indtte; shop; rest; playgrnd; pool; wintersports; ski-lift 300m; 70% statics; dogs; Eng spkn; quiet; debit cards acc. "Clean facs; pleasant site." ♦ € 17.50 (CChq acc) 2009*

ABTSGMUND *3D3* (9km NW Rural) *48.94650, 9.97628* **Camping Hammerschmiede-See, Hammerschmiede 2, 73453 Abtsgmünd [(07963) 369; fax 840032; hug.hammerschmiede@t-online.de; http://camping.hug-hammerschmiede.de]** Exit B19 (Aalen-Schwabisch Hall) at W end of Abtsgmünd by-pass dir Pommertsweiler. Site sp on lake. Lge, terr, pt sl, pt shd; wc; shwrs €0.50; el pnts (10A) metered + conn fee; gas; shop, rest, snacks 2km; playgrnd; games area; 60% statics; dogs €1.60; no adv bkg; quiet. "Direct rd fr Schwabisch Hall, not suitable for lge outfits; lakeside pitches long walk to san facs." 1 May-30 Sep.
€ 11.80 2009*

⊞ **ACHERN** *3C3* (2km W Rural) *48.64578, 8.03728* **Camping am Achernsee, Oberacherner Strasse 19, 77855 Achern [(07841) 25253; fax 508835; camping@achern.de; www.achern.de]** Exit A5/E35/E52 junc 53 to Achern, site sp in 1km. Med, mkd pitch, shd; wc; shwrs €0.50; chem disp; mv service pnt; el pnts (10A) €2.50; Indtte (inc dryer); shop 2km; rest adj; BBQ; playgrnd; fishing; lake sw; 80% statics; dogs €3.50; quiet, but noise nr m'way. ♦ € 19.00 2009*

ADELBERG see Göppingen *3D3*

AEGIDIENBERG see Bad Honnef *1B4*

AICHELBERG see Göppingen *3D3*

AITRACH see Memmingen *3D4*

AITRANG see Marktoberdorf *4E4*

ALLENSBACH see Radolfzell am Bodensee *3C4*

⊞ **ALPIRSBACH** *3C3* (1.5km N Rural) *48.35576, 8.41224* **Camping Alpirsbach, Grezenbühler Weg 18-20, 72275 Alpirsbach [(07444) 6313; fax 917815; info@camping-alpirsbach.de; www.camping-alpirsbach.de]** On B294 leave Alpirsbach twds Freudenstadt. 1st site sp on L. Med, pt shd, serviced pitch; wc; chem disp; mv service pnt; shwrs inc; el pnts (16A) metered; gas; Indtte; shop; tradsmn; rest; snacks; bar; playgrnd; tennis; golf 5km; 10% statics; dogs €1; o'night area for m'vans €10; poss cr; Eng spkn; quiet; ccard not acc; red long stay/CCI. "Excel site; helpful, informative & friendly owner; v gd welcome with free bottle of local beer per person; immac san facs; gd rest; gd walking; guest card gives free transport on some local transport; some rvside pitches (v shady)."
♦ € 20.20 2011*

ALSFELD *1D4* (10km W Rural) *50.73638, 9.15222* **Camping Heimertshausen, Ehringshäuserstrasse, 36320 Kirtorf-Heimertshausen [(06635) 206; fax 918359; info@camping-heimertshausen.de; www.camping-heimertshausen.de]** Exit A5 junc 3 Alsfeld West onto B49 dir Frankfurt. Turn R in vill of Romrod to Heimertshausen & L to site. Site also sp fr B62. Med, shd; wc; chem disp; shwrs €0.55; el pnts (10-16A) €2 or metered; Indtte; shop; rest; snacks; playgrnd; htd pool adj; dogs €1; 65% statics; clsd 1300-1500 & 2200-0800; o'night area for m'vans; Eng spkn; adv bkg; quiet; red CCI. "Beautiful, wooded area; lovely 'hunting lodge' type cosy rest." 1 Apr-30 Sep.
€ 17.00 2011*

⊞ **ALTEFAHR (RUGEN ISLAND)** *2F1* (300m Nw Coastal) *54.33200, 13.12206* **Sund Camp, Am Kurpark 1, 18573 Altefähr [(038306) 75483; fax 60306; info@sund-camp.de; www.sund-camp.de]** Fr Stralsund, cross bdge on B96 to Rügen Island. Take 2nd turning to Altefähr (fewer cobbles), after 1km turn R & then L along poor rd to site. Well sp. Med, mkd pitch, pt shd; wc; chem disp; mv service pnt; shwrs inc; el pnts (16A) inc (poss rev pol); shops 500m; tradsmn; Indtte; sm shop; rest 400m; shgl beach 500m; cycle hire; TV; 15% statics; dogs €2; poss cr; phone; sep car park; poss cr; quiet; red long stay. "Conv Rugen Is (walks, cycle tracks, beaches, steam rlwy); easy walk to vill & harbour; splendid, but busy island; well worth visit; ferry to Stralsund Altstadt nrby; excel, friendly site; muddy when wet; gd, clean san facs." € 20.50 2010*

ALTENAHR *3B1* (1km W Rural) *50.51328, 6.98637* **Campingplatz Altenahr, Im Pappelauel, 53505 Altenahr-Altenburg [(02643) 8503; fax 900764; info@camping-altenahr.de; www.camping-altenahr.de]** Foll B257 thro narr town cent; site visible on R, on opp bank of Rv Ahr; care needed for lge o'fits over bdge. Lge; wc; shwrs €0.50; el pnts (6A) €3.50; Indtte (inc dryer); shop & 500m; rest; snacks; bar; playgrnd; 30% statics; dogs €1.50; bus; poss cr; some rd & rlwy noise; ccard acc; CCI. "Clean, friendly, well-kept site amongst vineyards; excel facs; conv for x-country rte Koblenz/Aachen; sh walk to pretty vill." ♦ 1 Apr-31 Oct. € 17.00 2010*

ALTENAU see Goslar *1D3*

⊞ **ALTENBERG** *4G1* (1km W Rural) *50.76666, 13.74666* **Camping Kleiner Galgenteich (Naturist), Galgenteich 3, 01773 Altenberg [(035056) 31995; fax 31993; mail@camping-erzgebirge.de; www.camping-erzgebirge.de]** Leave A4 at Dresden-Nord onto B170 sp Zinnwald then Altenberg. On SW side of B170; clearly sp. Lge, pt sl, pt shd; wc; chem disp; mv service pnt; shwrs €0.50; el pnts (10A) metered + conn fee; Indtte; shop; rest; snacks adj; playgrnd; lake sw & sailing adj; skilift 500m; 50% statics; dogs €1; poss cr; quiet. "Sep area for naturists." € 18.50 2009*

ALTENKIRCHEN *2F1* (2km E) *54.63157, 13.37250* **Campingplatz Drewoldke, Zittkower Weg 27, 18556 Altenkirchen [038391 12965; info@camping-auf-ruegen.de; www.camping-auf-ruegen.de]** Take rd from Sassnitz to Altenkirchen (L30), site sp on R before you reach Altenkirchen. Lge, pt shd; htd wc; chem disp; MV service pnt; baby facs; shwrs (metered); el pnts (16A) €2.50; Indtte; shop; tradsmn; rest; snacks; bar; playgrnd; beach adj; dogs €4.50; phone. "Site being updated & has gd modern san facs; site located just outside of Altenkirchen on the Baltic Sea clse to ferry point Sassnitz (plse note there is another place in Germany named Altenkirchen, do not get this confused); gd site." 01 Apr-31 Oct. € 25.40 2011*

ALVERN see Celle *1D3*

AMBACH see Wolfratshausen *4E4*

AMORBACH *3D2* (7km SW Rural) *49.60730, 9.15876* **Azur Campingpark Odenwald, Siegfriedstrasse 2, 63931 Kirchzell [(09373) 566; fax 7375; kirchzell@azur-camping.de; www.azur-camping.de]** Exit A81 at junc 3 Tauberischofsheim onto B27 dir Mosbach. At Walldürn take B47 to Amorbach & turn L dir Kirchzell. Site sp 1km S of Kirchzell dir Amorbach Lge, hdg pitch, pt shd; wc; mv service pnt; sauna; shwrs; el pnts (10A) €2.80; Indtte (inc dryer); shop; rest; snacks; playgrnd; htd, covrd pool; games area; 60% statics; dogs €3; Eng spkn; adv bkg; quiet; CCI. ♦ 1 Apr-31 Oct. € 24.00 2010*

ANNABERG BUCHHOLZ *4G1* (7km SE Rural) *50.55666, 13.04666* **Camping Königswalde, Mildenauerstrasse 50A, 09471 Königswalde [tel/fax (03733) 44860]** Fr B95 Oberwiesenthal-Chemnitz rd, turn E to Königswalde, site sp in vill. Sm, pt shd; wc; shwrs; el pnts (6-10A) metered; gas; shop nr; snacks; bar; playgrnd; dogs €1; no adv bkg; quiet. "Sm CL-type site in lovely vill; walks in hills; no chem disp or waste water points; no drinking water; gd." 1 May-15 Oct & 1 Dec-6 Jan. € 13.00 2008*

⊞ **ANNABERG BUCHHOLZ** *4G1* (15km NW Rural) *50.64291, 12.91496* **Camping Greifensteine, 09427 Ehrenfriedersdorf [(037346) 1454; fax 1218; webmaster@greifenbachstauweiher.de; www.greifenbachstauweiher.de]** On B95 S fr Chemnitz turn W at Thum sp Jahnsbach; after 2km at Jahnsbach turn S & site on R after 3km, sp. V lge, pt sl, pt shd; wc; shwrs €0.50; el pnts (10A) €2; Indtte; shop; rest; snacks; bar; playgrnd; pool; lake; boating; windsurfing; cycle hire; 60% statics; dogs €3; Eng spkn; red long stay; CCI. "Conv for Ore mountains or en rte to Czech Republic; woodland surroundings; friendly staff; excel value." ♦ € 14.00 2009*

ANNWEILER AM TRIFELS see Landau in der Pfalz *3C3*

ASBACHERHUTTE see Idar Oberstein *3B2*

⊞ **ATTENDORN** *3C1* (5km NE Rural) *51.13694, 7.93969* **Campingplatz Hof Biggen, Finnentroperstrasse 131, 57439 Attendorn [(02722) 95530; info@biggen.de; www.biggen.de]** Exit A55 junc 16 Meinerzhagen onto L539 E dir Attendorn. Thro Attendorn, site sp on Ahauser Stausee, 4km fr Biggesee. Lge, some hdstg, terr, unshd; htd wc (some cont); chem disp; mv service pnt; el pnts (16A); Indtte (inc dryer); shop; tradsmn; rest; snacks; bar; BBQ; playgrnd; games area; games rm; wifi; entmnt; TV; 75% statics; dogs; adv bkg; quiet. "Excel, scenic site." ♦ (CChq acc) 2011*

AUGSBURG *4E3* (2km N Rural) *48.43194, 10.92388* **Camping Ludwigshof am See, Augsburgerstrasse 36, 86444 Mühlhausen-Affing [(08207) 96170; fax 961770; info@bauer-caravan.de; www.bauer-caravan.de]** Exit A8/E52 junc 73 at Augsburg Ost/Pöttmes exit; foll sp Pöttmes; site sp on L on lakeside. Lge, unshd; wc; chem disp; mv service pnt; shwrs inc; el pnts (6-16A) €3.50 (long cable req); Indtte; supmkt 500m; bar; rest; playgrnd; lake sw; 70% statics sep area; dogs €2; bus; clsd 1300-1500; poss cr; Eng spkn; quiet; 10% red 3+ days; ccard not acc; CCI. "Pleasant site; lge unmkd field for tourers, close to san facs but long walk to recep; both 6A panel & 16A panels for el pnts -16A only accepts German type of plug; beautiful clean, modern facs; nr m'way; conv NH on way to E Italy or gd for a long stay." 1 Apr-31 Oct. € 15.50 2011*

⊞ **AUGSBURG** *4E3* (7km N Rural) *48.41168, 10.92371* **Camping Bella Augusta, Mühlhauserstrasse 54B, 86169 Augsburg-Ost [(0821) 707575; fax 705883; info@caravaningpark.de; www.caravaningpark.de]** Exit A8/E52 junc 73 dir Neuburg to N, site sp. Lge, pt shd; wc; chem disp; mv service pnt; shwrs inc; el pnts (10A) inc; Indry rm; shop; supmkt 4km; rest; snacks & bar adj; playgrnd adj; lake sw & shgl beach adj; boating; 80% statics; dogs €2.55; noise fr a'bahn; ccard acc. "V busy NH; excel rest; camping equipment shop on site; vg san facs but site looking a little run down; cycle track to town (map fr recep); vg." € 20.00 2008*

AUGSBURG *4E3* (10km NE Rural) *48.4375, 10.92916* **Lech Camping, Seeweg 6, 86444 Affing-Mühlhausen [(08207) 2200; fax 2202; info@lech-camping.de; www.lech-camping.de]** Exit A8/E52 at junc 73 Augsburg-Ost; take rd N sp Pöttmes; site 3km on R. Sm, mkd pitch, pt shd; htd wc; chem disp; mv service pnt; shwrs inc; el pnts (16A) €3.60 or metered + conn fee (poss rev pol); Indtte; shop 300m; supmkt opp; rest; snacks; bar; playgrnd; lake sw adj; boating; wifi; statics sep area; dogs €3; bus to Augsburg; train Munich; Eng spkn; some rd noise; ccard acc. "Lovely, well-ordered site; friendly, helpful owners; excel san facs; gd play area; deposit for san facs key; camping accessory shop on site; cycle rte to Augsburg; excel NH for A8; excel site espec lakeside pitch." ♦ 1 Apr-31 Oct. € 28.50 2011*

BACHARACH see Oberwesel *3B2*

⊞ **BAD BEDERKESA** *1C2* (1km S Rural) *53.62059, 8.84879* **Regenbogen-Camp Bad Bederkesa, Ankeloherstrasse 14, 27624 Bad Bederkesa [(04745) 6487 or (0431) 2372370; fax 8033; urlaub@regenbogen-camp.de; www.regenbogen-camp.de]** Exit A27 junc 5 Debstedt, dir Bederkesa, site sp. V lge, pt shd; wc; chem disp; mv service pnt; shwrs inc; el pnts (16A) metered + conn fee; Indtte (inc dryer); shop 800m; rest; snacks; bar; playgrnd; games area; golf 4km; wifi; TV; 60% statics; dogs €4; clsd 1300-1500; o'night area for m'vans; adv bkg; quiet; ccard acc; red long stay/CCI. ♦ € 25.00 2010*

BAD BELLINGEN see Lörrach *3B4*

⊞ **BAD BENTHEIM** *1B3* (2km E Rural) *52.29945, 7.19361* **Campingplatz am Berg, Suddendorferstrasse 37, 48455 Bad Bentheim [(05922) 990461; rbhaksteen@t-online.de; www.campingplatzamberg.de]** Exit A30 ad junc 3 onto B403, foll sp to Bad Bentheim. After sh incline, passing g'ge on R at traff lts, at next junc turn R round town to hospital (sp Orthopäde). Turn L & cont past hospital to rndabt, strt over then 1.5km on L. Sm, mkd pitch, pt shd; htd wc; chem disp; shwrs inc; el pnts (16A) €2.50; gas; Indtte; shop 2.5km; tradsmn; rest; bar; cooking facs; playgrnd; 50% statics in sep area; dogs; phone; site clsd 24 Dec-26 Jan; poss v cr; Eng spkn; adv bkg; quiet; CCI. "Friendly, helpful owners; easy drive to Europort & ferries; rlwy museum on Dutch side of border." ♦ € 15.00 2009*

BAD BRAMSTEDT *1D2* (1km N Rural) *53.9283, 9.8901* **Kur-Camping Roland, Kielerstrasse 52, 24576 Bad Bramstedt [(04192) 6723; fax 2783]** Exit A7 junc 17 dir Bad Bremstedt; site sp, ent immed at Nissan g'ge at top of hill at start of dual c'way. Fr N exit A7 junc 16 dir Bad Bremstedt; site on L in 4km. Sm, shd; wc; chem disp; shwrs inc; el pnts (6-16A) €2 & metered; Indtte; shop; tradsmn; rest 300m; snacks; dogs €2; Eng spkn; some rd noise; CCI. "Excel CL-type site; friendly owner; el hook-ups not rec if site v full; gd sh stay/NH." ♦ 1 Apr-31 Oct. € 18.00 2008*

BAD BREISIG see Remagen *3B1*

BAD DOBERAN *2F1* (5km N Coastal) *54.15250, 11.89972* **Ferien-Camp Borgerende (Part Naturist), Deichstrasse 16, 18211 Börgerende [(038203) 81126; fax 81284; info@ostseeferiencamp.de; www.ostseeferiencamp.de]** In Bad Doberan, turn L off B105 sp Warnemunde. In 4km in Rethwisch, turn L sp Börgerende. In 3km turn R at site sp. V lge, hdg pitch, unshd; wc; chem disp; mv service pnt; baby facs; fam bthrm; sauna; shwrs inc; el pnts (10-16A) €3; Indtte (inc dryer) shop; tradsmn; rest; snacks; bar; cooking facs; playgrnd; shgl beach adj; sep naturist beach; cycle hire; games area; internet; child entmnt; 10% statics; dogs €4; bus 500m; phone; o'night area for m'vans; Eng spkn; quiet; red low ssn/snr citizens; CCI. "Excel beaches; cycle paths; excel site." ♦ 1 Apr-31 Oct. € 28.00 2010*

⊞ **BAD DURKHEIM** *3C2* (2.5km NE Rural) *49.47361, 8.19166* **Knaus Campingplatz Bad Dürkheim, In den Almen 3, 67098 Bad Dürkheim [(06322) 61356; fax 8161; badduerkheim@knauscamp.de; www.knauscamp.de]** Fr S on A61/E31 exit junc 60 onto A650/B37 twds Bad Dürkheim. At 2nd traff lts turn R, site sp nr local airfield. Fr N on A6 exit junc 19 onto B271 to Bad Dürkheim. At traff lts after Ungstein turn L dir Lugwigshafen, at next traff lts turn L, then 1st R. Site at end of rd. Ent strictly controlled. Site well sp fr all dir on town o'skts. V lge, mkd pitch, pt shd; htd wc; chem disp; mv service pnt; child/baby facs; sauna; shwrs inc; el pnts (16A) €2.50; gas; Indtte (inc dryer); shop; tradsmn; BBQ; rest; playgrnd; sand beach adj; lake sw adj; tennis; games area; solarium; TV rm; cycle hire; golf 8km; 45% statics; phone; bus; m'van o'night facs; poss v cr; quiet but some daytime noise fr adj sports airfield; poss cr; Eng spkn; no ccard acc; red long stay; CCI. "Well-equipped site in vineyards; sm, well-worn pitches; some modern san facs - all clean; no access 1300-1500; gd pool in Bad Dürkheim; wine-fest & wurst-fest Sep excel; conv NH Bavaria & Austria." ♦ € 27.00 2010*

BAD DURKHEIM *3C2* (2km S Rural) *49.43741, 8.17036* **Campingplatz im Burgtal, Waldstrasse 105, 67157 Wachenheim [(06322) 2689; fax 791710; touristinfo@vg-wachenheim.de]** Fr Bad Dürkheim, take B271 S dir Neustadt for approx 2km. After passing Villa Rustica rest area, turn L for Wachenheim, then R. Go strt at traff lts, up hill thro vill (narr). Site on L. Med, hdg/mkd pitch, hdstg, pt shd; wc; chem disp; mv service pnt; serviced pitches; shwrs inc; el pnts (16A) €2; Indtte (inc dryer); shop & 1.5km; rest; bar; playgrnd; tennis; golf 12km; 50% statics; dogs €0.70; poss cr; quiet; CCI. "Forest walks in Pfalz National Park; in heart of wine-tasting country; v busy during wine festival - adv bkg rec; helpful owners; gd facs." ♦ 1 Mar-30 Nov. € 17.50 (3 persons) 2008*

⊞ **BAD DURRHEIM** *3C4* (4km SE Rural) *48.00388, 8.5831* **Naturcamping Sunthausen See, Am Steigle 1, 78073 Bad Dürrheim-Sunthausen [(07706) 712; fax 922906; info@naturcamping-badduerrheim.de; www.naturcamping-badduerrheim.de]** Fr A81/E41 exit junc 36 onto B523 & B33 dir Bad Dürrheim. Foll sp Sunthausen & site. Lge, hdg pitch, terr; wc; chem disp; mv service pnt; shwrs; el pnts (6A) €2.50; Indtte; shop 500m; many statics; dogs €1.50; adv bkg; ccard acc; quiet; CCI. "Friendly warden; best pitches occupied by statics (Aug 08) - tourers on gravel area by site ent where lorries also park; token for hot water/shwrs €5 - pt refund if not used in full." ♦ € 20.00 2008*

GERMANY

BAD EMS *3B2* (3km E Rural) *50.31870, 7.73400* **Campingplatz Bad Ems, Lahnstrasse, 56130 Bad Ems [(02603) 4679; fax 4487; 026034679-0001@t-online.de; www.marktplatz-rhein-lahn.de/campingplatz-bad-ems]** Exit town cent on B260/417 twd Limburg. In approx 3km fr cent, 1st site on R at sharp L bend. Med, pt shd; wc; shwrs €1; el pnts (16A) metered; gas; shop & 2km; snacks; bar; playgrnd; pool; rv fishing & boating; sep car park; 60% statics; dogs €1; adv bkg; Eng spkn; quiet. "Poss flooding after heavy rain/high water." 15 Mar-31 Oct. € 12.50 2008*

BAD EMS *3B2* (4km E Rural) *50.32773, 7.75483* **Camping Lahn-Beach, Hallgarten 16, 56132 Dausenau [(02603) 13964; fax 919935; info@canutours.de; www.campingplatz-dausenau.de]** Foll rv E fr Bad Ems twd Nassau on B260/417. At ent to vill of Dausenau turn R over bdge, site visible on S bank of Lahn Rv. Med, pt shd; wc; chem disp; mv service pnt; shwrs €1; el pnts (6-16A) metered + conn fee; Indtte; shop 400m; rest; snacks; playgrnd; boat-launching; cycle hire; 40% statics; dogs free; sep car park; poss cr; adv bkg; rd noise. "Pleasant situation; interesting rv traffic & sightseeing around Lahn Valley; liable to flood at v high water." 1 Apr-31 Oct. € 15.00 2009*

BAD FEILNBACH see Rosenheim *4F4*

⊞ **BAD FUSSING** *4G3* (2km S Rural) *48.33255, 13.31440* **Kur & Feriencamping Max I, Falkenstrasse 12, 94072 Egglfing-Bad Füssing [(08537) 96170; fax 961710; info@campingmax.de; www.campingmax.de]** Across frontier & bdge fr Obernberg in Austria. Site sp in Egglfing. On B12 Schärding to Simbach turn L immed bef vill of Tutting sp Obernberg. Site on R after 7km, sp. Med, pt shd; htd wc; chem disp; mv service pnt; private san facs avail; shwrs inc; el pnts (16A) metered + conn fee; Indtte (inc dryer); shop; rest 300m; snacks; bar; cooking facs; playgrnd; pool 3km; lake sw; fishing; thermal facs in Bad Füssing; tennis 2km; cycle hire; wellness cent; golf 2km; wifi; entmnt; TV; 20% statics; dogs €2; quiet; red CCI "Gd rest for snacks & meals on site." ♦ € 20.80 (CChq acc) 2011*

⊞ **BAD FUSSING** *4G3* (NW Rural) *48.35801, 13.30661* **Camping Holmernhof, Am Tennispark 10, 94072 Bad Füssing [(08531) 24740; fax 2474360; info@holmernhof.de; www.holmernhof.de]** Exit A8/E56 junc 118 Pocking. Foll sp Bad Füssing, then sp 'Freibad' & 'Tenniszentrum', site sp. Med, mkd pitch, hdstg, pt shd; wc; chem disp; mv service pnt; baby facs; private bthrms avail; sauna; shwrs inc; el pnts (16A) metered; gas; Indtte (inc dryer); shop; rest adj; snacks; bar; playgrnd; htd pool, tennis 200m; games area; golf 2km; wifi; entmnt; TV; no dogs; phone; o'night area for m'vans; Eng spkn; quiet; CCI. "Excel site." ♦ € 22.70 2010*

⊞ **BAD GANDERSHEIM** *1D3* (1.5km E Rural) *51.86694, 10.04972* **DCC-Kur-Campingpark, 37581 Bad Gandersheim [(05382) 1595; fax 1599; info@camping-bad-gandersheim.de; www.camping-bad-gandersheim.de]** Exit A7/E45 at junc 67 onto B64 dir Holzminden & Bad Gandersheim. Site on R shortly after Seboldshausen. Lge, pt shd; wc; chem disp; mv service pnt; shwrs €0.50; el pnts (10A) metered + conn fee; Indtte; shop; rest; snacks; playgrnd; pool 1.5km; cycle hire; 40% statics; dogs €1; sep o'night area; poss cr; quiet. "Excel; always plenty of space." ♦ € 16.90 2011*

⊞ **BAD HARZBURG** *2E3* (3.5km W Rural) *51.89158, 10.51100* **Freizeitoase-Harz Camp, Kreisstrasse 66, 38667 Bad Harzburg-Göttingerode [(05322) 81215; fax 877533; harz-camp@t-online.de; www.harz-camp.de]** Fr A395 to Bad Harzburg, foll sp Oker & Goslar. Site on L at traff lts. Lge, hdstg, pt sl, terr, pt shd; wc; chem disp; mv service pnt; fam bthrm; sauna; shwrs €0.50; el pnts (10A) metered + conn fee; gas; Indtte; shop; tradsmn; rest; bar; cooking facs; playgrnd; pool; solarium; games area; entmnt; sat TV; 40% statics in sep area; dogs €2; phone; bus 100m; Eng spkn; no adv bkg; quiet; CCI. "Friendly owners; excel facs; conv walk to town." ♦ € 18.00 2009*

BAD HERRENALB see Bad Wildbad im Schwarzwald *3C3*

⊞ **BAD HONNEF** *1B4* (9km E Rural) *50.65027, 7.30166* **Camping Jillieshof, Ginsterbergweg 6, 53604 Bad Honnef-Aegidienberg [(02224) 972066; fax 972067; information@camping-jillieshof.de; www.camping-jillieshof.de]** Exit E35/A3 junc 34 & foll sp Bad Honnef. In Himburg bef pedestrian traff lts turn L, then R. Site in 300m. Lge, mkd pitch, sl, pt shd; wc; chem disp; mv service pnt; shwrs inc; el pnts (16A) €2 or metered; shop; playgrnd; pool 9km; fishing; 85% statics; dogs €2; Eng spkn; quiet; red low ssn. "Excel facs; gated." € 17.50 2010*

BAD KISSINGEN *3D2* (500m S Urban) *50.18972, 10.07194* **Campingpark Bad Kissingen, Euerdorferstrasse 1, 97688 Bad Kissingen [(0971) 5211; info@campingpark-badkissingen.de; www.campingpark-badkissingen.de]** Exit A7/E45 junc 96 dir Bad Kissingen onto B286. After Garitz take major turn L turn onto B287 immed bef Südbrücke (bdge) - caution tight R-hand bend - take L-hand lane & turn L in cent of this bend. Site on R. Med, pt shd; wc; chem disp; mv service pnt; some serviced pitches; baby facs; shwrs €0.50; el pnts (16A) €2.80; gas; Indtte (inc dryer); shop; rest; playgrnd; adj rv in park; fishing; golf 1km; wifi; some statics; dogs €2.50; adv bkg; quiet; red long stay/CCI. "Site immac; excel facs; some daytime rd noise; pleasant spa town." ♦ 1 Apr-31 Oct. € 24.50 2010*

BAD KOSEN *2E4* (1.5km S Rural) *51.12285, 11.71743* **Camping an der Rudelsburg, 06628 Bad Kösen [(034463) 28705; fax 28706; campkoesen@aol.com; www.campingbadkoesen.de]** Site sp fr town. Med, pt shd; wc; chem disp; baby facs; shwrs €1; el pnts (16A) metered + conn fee; gas; Indtte; shop 1.5km; tradsmn; rest 1.5km; snacks; bar; playgrnd; 10% statics; dogs €2; o'night area for m'vans; quiet; CCI. ♦ 1 Apr-1 Nov. € 17.00 2009*

BAD KREUZNACH *3C2* (6km S Rural) *49.80542, 7.84236* **Camping Nahe-Alsenz-Eck, Auf dem Grün, 55583 Bad Münster-am-Stein-Ebernburg [(06708) 2453; cnae@gmx.de; www.campingplatz-nahe-alsenz-eck.de]** Exit A61 junc 51 for Bad Kreuznach, take B48 dir Kaiserslauten thro town. Site well sp on rvside. Med, mkd pitch, pt shd; wc; chem disp; shwrs €0.50; el pnts (10A) metered + conn fee; Indtte (inc dryer); shop 200m; tradsmn; rest 300m; snacks; bar; playgrnd; htd pool 300m; 80% statics; dogs €2.10; clsd 1300-1500; poss cr; quiet; CCI. "Pleasant spa town; gd facs; sm pitches; gd atmosphere; many long stay residents; site poss muddy in wet & liable to flood." 1 Apr-15 Oct. € 16.10 2010*

⊞ **BAD KREUZNACH** *3C2* (6km NW Rural) *49.88383, 7.85712* **Campingplatz Lindelgrund, Im Lindelgrund 1, 55452 Guldental [(06707) 633; fax 8468; info@lindelgrund.de; www.lindelgrund.de]** Fr A61 exit junc 47 for Windesheim. In cent immed after level x-ing, turn L & pass thro Guldental. Site sp on R in 500m. Sm, some hdstg, terr, pt shd; wc; chem disp; shwrs €0.50; el pnts (10-16A) €2 or metered; tradsmn; rest; snacks; playgrnd; htd, covrd pool 2km; tennis; golf 12km; 60% statics in sep area; dogs €1.50; poss cr; no adv bkg; quiet; red long stay. "Lovely, peaceful site; friendly owner; improved san facs; wine sold on site; narr gauge rlwy & museum adj; gd NH." € 14.50 2009*

BAD LIEBENZELL see Calw *3C3*

⊞ **BAD MERGENTHEIM** *3D2* (3km SE Rural) *49.46481, 9.77673* **Camping Willinger Tal, Willinger Tal 1, 97980 Bad Mergentheim [(07931) 2177; fax 5636543; info@campingplatz-willinger-tal.de; www.campingplatz-willinger-tal.de]** Fr Bad Mergentheim foll B19 S, sp Ulm. After 1km take rd to L (sps). Ent 2.7m. Med, sl, pt shd; wc; chem disp; shwrs inc; el pnts (10A) metered + conn fee or €1.90; gas; lndtte; shop; snacks; playgrnd; htd, covrd pool; paddling pool; tennis; 20% statics; dogs €2.50; bus nr; sep o'night area; quiet; ccard not acc; CCI. "Nice site; friendly, helpful owner." € 17.00 2011*

⊞ **BAD NEUENAHR AHRWEILER** *3B1* (1km W Urban) *50.53892, 7.09612* **Camping Ahrweiler Am Ahrtor, Kalvarienbergstrasse 1, 53474 Bad Neuenahr-Ahrweiler [(02461) 26539; camping-ahrweiler@online.de; www.camping-ahrweiler.de]** Exit A9 B266 W bet Remagen & Sinzig; then take L84 S to Ahrweiler. Site on S side of city wall sp Nürburgring; after x-ing bdge, sharp R into site on rv bank. Sm, pt shd; wc; shwrs €1; el pnts (16A) €2.50; lndtte (inc dryer); shop, rest, bar 500m; 50% statics on rv bank pitches (rv fast flowing & unfenced); no statics; dogs free; o'night m'van area; Eng spkn; adv bkg; quiet; CCI. "Excel, modern san facs; interesting walled city; conv for m'way." € 16.50 2010*

BAD NEUENAHR AHRWEILER *3B1* (6km W Rural) *50.53400, 7.04800* **Camping Dernau, Ahrweg 2, 53507 Dernau [(02643) 8517; www.camping-dernau.de]** Exit A61 junc 30 for Ahrweiler. Fr Ahrweiler on B267 W to Dernau, cross rv bef Dernau & turn R into Ahrweg, site sp. Sm, some hdstg, shd; htd wc; chem disp; mv service pnt; shwrs €1.50; el pnts €2; shops 500m; playgrnd; dogs €1; bus; train; some rlwy noise. "In beautiful Ahr valley - gd wine area; train to Ahrweiler Markt rec; immac, modern san facs." ♦ 1 Apr-31 Oct. € 15.40 2011*

BAD PETERSTAL *3C3* (2km W Rural) *48.42944, 8.18166* **Kurcamping Traiermühle, Renchtalstrasse 53a, 77740 Bad Peterstal-Griesbach [(07806) 8064; fax 910528; camping@traiermuehle.de; www.traiermuehle.de]** Fr French border at Strasbourg take B28 to Bad Peterstal, site sp after Löcherberg site. Sm, unshd; wc; chem disp; shwrs €0.20; el pnts (10-16A) €2 or metered; lndtte (inc dryer); rest 300m; playgrnd; 70% statics; dogs; train 2km; Eng spkn; quiet, but some daytime rd noise; CCI. "Excel, peaceful site; walking distance to town with rests, shops etc." 1 Apr-31 Oct. € 11.00 2009*

⊞ **BAD PYRMONT** *1D3* (1.5km NE Rural) *51.99651, 9.27608* **Campingpark Schellental (formerly Camping Bad Pyrmont), Am Schellenhof 1-3, 31812 Bad Pyrmont [(05281) 8772; fax 968034; info@camping-badpyrmont.de; www.camping-badpyrmont.de]** Fr B1 Hameln-Paderborn rd, exit into Bad Pyrmont. Foll rd to Löwensen, L to Friedensthal & site. Med, pt sl, pt shd; wc; chem disp; mv service pnt; shwrs inc; el pnts (6A) inc; lndtte; rest; shop; snacks; sw 2km; 50% statics; dogs €2; o'night parking for m'vans €10; quiet; red long stay/CCI. "Gd rest on site." ♦ € 22.00 2008*

We can fill in site report forms on the Club's website – www.caravanclub.co.uk/europereport

⊞ **BAD PYRMONT** *1D3* (10km S Rural) *51.89800, 9.25533* **Camping Eichwald, Obere Dorfstrasse 80, 32676 Lügde-Elbrinxen [(05283) 335; fax 640; info@camping-eichwald.de; www.camping-eichwald.de]** Fr W 7km after Schwalenberg in dir Höxter turn L at sp Bad Pyrmont & Lügde. In 2km site sp bef vill of Elbrinxen. Fr N take Bad Pyrmont rd to Lugde & foll camp sps. Med, mkd pitch, pt sl, pt shd; wc; chem disp; mv service pnt; sauna; shwrs €0.50; el pnts (16A) €1.50; gas; lndtte; shop 500m; rest; playgrnd; htd pool 400m; 60% statics; dogs €1.30; o'night area for m'vans; poss cr; quiet; ccard acc; CCI. "Gd for country lovers; pretty site." ♦ € 14.40 2009*

BAD PYRMONT *1D3* (10km W Rural) *51.98671, 9.10833* **Ferienpark Teutoburgerwald, Badeanstaltsweg 4, 32683 Barntrup [(05263) 2221; info@ferienparkteutoburgerwald.de; www.ferienparkteutoburgerwald.de]** On B1 bet Blomberg & Bad Pyrmont turn W for 1km to Barntrup & foll sp fr vill cent. Med, some hdstg, terr, pt shd; wc; chem disp; mv service pnt; shwrs inc; el pnts (16A) inc; gas; lndtte (inc dryer); shop, rest, snacks 500m; playgrnd; pool, tennis adj; wifi; 10% statics; dogs €2.25; sep m'van area; adv bkg; quiet; red long stay. "Excel site; vg san facs but poss stretched in high ssn; conv Hameln (Hamelin)." 1 Apr-31 Oct. € 26.50 2010*

BAD REICHENHALL *4G4* (2km N Rural) *47.74645, 12.8958* **Campingplatz Staufeneck, Streilachweg, 83451 Piding [(08651) 2134; fax 710450; info@camping-berchtesgadener-land.de; www.camping-berchtesgadener-land.de]** Exit A8/E52/E60 junc 115 onto B20 for approx 3km, site sp. Cannot ent site fr S, so if coming fr S, turn at m'way junc & return on B20, as above. Med, mkd pitch, some hdstg, pt shd; wc; chem disp; mv service pnt; shwrs €0.50; el pnts (16A) €3 or metered + conn fee; lndtte (inc dryer); shop; supmkt 500m; rest 300m; playgrnd; 30% statics; dogs €1.50; bus; Eng spkn; quiet; red CCI. "Excel views; site clsd 2200-0700; office open am & evenings, site yourself if office clsd; Bad Reichenhall v pleasant; conv Salzburg, Berchtesgaden & Tirol - gd bus service; clean, dated facs; excel walking/cycle tracks; v welcoming - nothing too much trouble; pitches on gravel; fast-flowing rv adj; excel site." 1 Apr-30 Oct. € 20.00 2010*

GERMANY

⊞ **BAD RIPPOLDSAU** *3C3* (8.5km S Rural) *48.38396, 8.30168* **Schwarzwaldcamping Alisehof, Rippoldsauerstrasse 8, 77776 Bad Rippoldsau-Schapbach [(07839) 203; fax 1263; info@camping-online.de; www.camping-online.de]** Exit A5/E35 junc 55 Offenburg onto B33 dir Gengenbach & Hausach to Wolfach. At end of Wolfach vill turn N dir Bad Rippoldsau. Site on R over wooden bdge after vill of Schapbach. Or fr Freudenstadt take B28 SW for 12km. Turn L (S) thro Bad Rippolsdau, S to Schapbach. Med, mkd pitch, pt sl, pt shd; htd wc; chem disp; mv service pnt; 30% serviced pitches; baby facs; fam bthrm; shwrs inc; el pnts (16A) metered + conn fee; gas; Indtte; shop; tradsmn; rest; snacks; bar; playgrnd; pool 2km; entmnt; 20% statics; dogs €2.30; phone; site clsd 1230-1430; poss cr; Eng spkn; adv bkg; quiet; red 7+ nts/CCI. "Highly rec; clean, friendly site; many gd walks in area." ♦ € 19.90 2009*

BAD SCHANDAU *2G4* (5km NE Rural) *50.93503, 14.21165* **Panorama-Camping Kleine Bergoase, Oberestrasse 19, 01855 Kirnitzschtal (OT Mittelndorf) [0176 22906538 (mob); fax (035971) 809891; berg-oase@t-online.de; www.panorama-camping.de]** Fr Bad Schandau take rd 154 dir Sebnitz. In 5km at Mittelndorf turn R at end of vill, site sp. Sm, mkd pitch, terr, pt shd; htd wc; chem disp; shwrs €0.50; el pnts (10) metered; shop 5km; tradsmn; rest, snacks, bar 5km; BBQ; pool 5km; spa; wifi; dogs €1.50; bus adj; poss cr; Eng spkn; adv bkg; quiet; CCI. "Vg site, new in 2009; spectacular views; gd hiking; adv bkg rec - not many pitches; close Czech border, Dresden." Mar-Oct. € 20.00 2011*

⊞ **BAD SCHANDAU** *2G4* (3km E Rural) *50.92996, 14.19301* **Campingplatz Ostrauer Mühle, Im Kirnitzschtal, 01814 Bad Schandau [(035022) 42742; fax 50352; info@ostrauer-muehle.de; www.ostrauer-muehle.de]** SE fr Dresden on B172 for 40km (Pirna-Schmilka). In Bad Schandau turn E twds Hinterhermsdorf; site in approx 3km. Med, terr, pt shd; wc; chem disp; mv service pnt; shwrs €0.50; el pnts (10A) €1.75 + conn fee; Indtte; shop; supmkt 4km; rest; sm playgrnd; dogs €2; sep car park; quiet; CCI. "In National Park; superb walking area; rec arr early high ssn; site yourself if office clsd on arr." ♦ € 18.50 2011*

⊞ **BAD SEGEBERG** *1D2* (5km NE Rural) *53.96131, 10.33685* **Klüthseecamp Seeblick, Stripdorfer Weg, Klüthseehof 2, 23795 Klein Rönnau [(04551) 82368; fax 840638; info@kluethseecamp.de; www.kluethseecamp.de]** Exit A21 junc 13 at Bad Sedgeberg Süd onto B432; turn L sp Bad Sedgeberg; cont on B432 dir Scharbeutz & Puttgarden thro Klein Rönnau, then turn R for site. V lge, unshd; wc; chem disp; mv service pnt; some serviced pitches; baby facs; sauna; steam rm; shwrs inc; el pnts (16A) inc; gas; Indtte (inc dryer); shop; tradsmn; rest; snacks; BBQ; playgrnd; htd pool; lake sw 200m; fishing; horseriding; tennis; cycle hire; golf 6km; internet; games/TV rm; 75% statics (sep area); dogs €2; twin-axles acc (rec check in adv); train to Hamburg, Lübeck; site clsd Feb; poss cr; Eng spkn; adv bkg; quiet; ccard acc; red low ssn/CCI. "Spacious, well-kept lakeside site; relaxing atmophere; lge pitches; helpful staff; gd facs & pool; wide range of activities; gd cycling, walking; conv Hamburg, Lübeck; excel." ♦ € 24.00 (CChq acc) SBS - G12 2011*

⊞ **BAD SOBERNHEIM** *3B2* (1km S Urban) *49.77861, 7.65861* **Reisemobilplatz Am Nohfels, Hömigweg 1, 55566 Bad Sobernheim [(06751) 854611; fax 854626; info@amnohfels.de; www.amnohfels.de]** Exit A6/E31 junc 51 onto B41 Bad Kreuznach-Saarbrücken into Sobernheim. Foll sp 'Freilichtmuseum' & sp with m'van symbol. M'vans only. Sm, pt shd; wc; shwrs inc; el pnts (12A) €2; rest 200m; pool 800m; dogs; adv bkg; quiet. € 7.00 2009*

⊞ **BAD SOBERNHEIM** *3B2* (3km NW Rural) *49.79505, 7.57786* **Camping Nahemühle, 55569 Monzingen [(06751) 7475; fax 7938; info@campingplatz-nahemuehle.de; www.campingplatz-nahemuehle.de]** On B41 W fr Bad Kreuznach cross rlwy at traff lts & turn R to stadium, site sp. Sm, unshd; wc; chem disp; mv service pnt; sauna; shwrs inc; el pnts (16A) metered + conn fee; Indtte; shop 1.2km; tradsmn; rest; snacks; bar; playgrnd; fishing; horseriding; 60% statics; dogs; Eng spkn; adv bkg; quiet; red CCI. "Gd cycling area; wine vills." ♦ € 14.90 2009*

⊞ **BAD TOLZ** *4E4* (5km S Rural) *47.70721, 11.55023* **Alpen-Camping Arzbach, Alpenbadstrasse 20, 83646 Arzbach [(08042) 8408; fax 8570; campingplatz-arbach@web.de; www.arzbach.de]** S fr Bad Tölz on B13. Exit Lenggries, turn R to cross rv & R on Wackersburgerstrasse twds Arzbach; in 5km on ent Arzbach turn L. Site ent past sw pool. Med, pt shd; wc; chem disp; shwrs €1; el pnts (16A) inc; gas; Indtte; shop 4km; tradsmn; rest; snacks 300m; playgrnd; covrd pool; tennis 100m; 60% statics; no dogs €1; bus 300m; poss cr; no adv bkg; quiet; CCI. "Gd walking, touring Bavarian lakes, excel facs & rest; care needed with lge c'vans due trees & hedges." ♦ € 20.00 2008*

⊞ **BAD TOLZ** *4E4* (4km W Rural) *47.75047, 11.50144* **Campingplatz Demmelhof, Stallau 148, 83646 Bad Tölz [(08041) 8121; info@campingplatz-demmelhof.de; www.campingplatz-demmelhof.de]** W fr Bad Tölz on B472, site sp on R just after Blomberg ski lift. Med, terr, unshd; htd wc; chem disp; mv service pnt; baby facs; shwrs €0.50; el pnts (10-16A) metered; Indtte (inc dryer); shop 2km; rest, snacks adj; bar; playgrnd; lake sw adj; 70% statics; dogs inc; phone; adv bkg; quiet; CCI. "Pretty area with gd walking in alpine foothills; immac san facs; vg site." ♦ € 18.00 2008*

⊞ **BAD URACH** *3D3* (2.5km NE Rural) *48.50333, 9.42388* **Camping Pfählhof, Pfählhof 2, 72574 Bad Urach [(07125) 8098; fax 8091; camping@pfaehlhof.de; www.pfaehlhof.de]** Fr Stuttgart or Reutlingen to Bad Urach & on twd Blaubeuren. 1km after Bad Urach cent nr town exit sp turn L bef long steep climb sp Oberlenningen & Grebenstetten to site on L in 1.6km. Lge, mkd pitch, pt shd; wc; shwrs; chem disp; baby facs; shwrs €0.50; el pnts (16A) metered + conn fee; Indtte; shop 2km; rest; cooking facs; playgrnd; pool 2km; skilift 8km; 80% statics; dogs €1.65; gates clsd 1300-1500 & 2200-0700; adv bkg in high ssn rec; quiet; CCI. "Site admission gives reduced fees at spa facs; gd rest on site; picturesque sm town; gd walking area; barrier with no access 1300-1500 & 2200-0700; helpful staff." € 16.60 2011*

⊞ **BAD URACH** *3D3* (9km E Rural) *48.48598, 9.50761* **Camping Lauberg, Hinter Lau 3, 72587 Römerstein-Böhringen [(07382) 1509; fax 1074; lauberg@risky.de; www.lauberg.de]** Fr Bad Urach, take rd twd Grabenstetten & foll sp to Böhringen, then sp to site. NB Rd to Grabenstetten avoids long, steep climb on B28. Med, mkd pitch, terr, unshd; htd wc; chem disp; 90% serviced pitch; shwrs inc; el pnts (16A) metered + conn fee; Indtte; shop, rest high ssn; supmkt 1.5km; bar; BBQ; playgrnd; htd pool 9km; wintersports; skilift 5km; 80% statics; dogs €1.50; poss cr; quiet; adv bkg; 10% red 10+ days. "Ideal walking area, castles, caves, Bad Urach baths." ♦ € 15.50 2008*

⊞ **BAD WILDBAD IM SCHWARZWALD** *3C3* (9km E Rural) *48.73745, 8.57623* **Camping Kleinenzhof, Kleinenzhof 1, 75323 Bad Wildbad [(07081) 3435; fax 3770; info@kleinenzhof.de; www.kleinenzhof.de]** Fr Calmbach foll B294 5km S. Site sp on R, in rv valley. Lge, pt sl, pt shd; wc; chem disp; mv service pnt; serviced pitches; sauna; shwrs inc; el pnts (16A) metered + conn fee; gas; Indtte; shop; rest; snacks; playgrnd; 2 pools (1 htd & covrd); cycle hire; skilift 8km; entmnt; 80% statics; dogs €2.10; o'night area for m'vans; clsd 1300-1500; poss cr; adv bkg; quiet; red long stay. "Nature trails from site; mountain views; distillery on site; modern san facs; sm pitches." ♦ € 23.00 2009*

⊞ **BAD WILDBAD IM SCHWARZWALD** *3C3* (4km S Rural) *48.69777, 8.52027* **Camping Kälbermühle, Kälbermühlenweg 57, 75323 Bad Wildbad [(07085) 7322 or 7353; fax 1043; information@kaelbermuehle.de; www.kaelbermuehle.de]** Take Enzklösterle rd S fr Bad Wildbad, site sp on rv bank. Med, pt shd; wc; chem disp (wc); shwrs €0.50; el pnts (16A) metered + conn fee; Indtte (inc dryer); playgrnd; 60% statics; dogs €0.80; bus; adv bkg; quiet. "Friendly owners; beautifully kept, peaceful site; superb rest; mkd forest walks." € 18.00 2010*

⊞ **BAD WILDBAD IM SCHWARZWALD** *3C3* (14km S Rural) *48.66641, 8.46820* **Campingplatz Müllerwiese, Hirschtalstrasse 3, 75337 Enzklösterle [tel/fax (07085) 7485; info@muellerwiese.de; www.muellerwiese.de]** Fr Bad Wildbad take tunnel S; site well sp in vill. Med, hdg/mkd pitch, pt shd; wc; chem disp; mv service pnt; shwrs €0.50; el pnts (10-16A) €2.50 or metered; gas; Indtte; shop, rest in vill; playgrnd; cab/sat TV; 75% statics; dogs €2; bus; site clsd mid-Nov to 19 Dec; Eng spkn; adv bkg; quiet; CCI. "Gd walking, cycling in heart of Black Forest; gd local entmnt high ssn; friendly owners; clean but dated facs; vg." € 16.50 2009*

BAD WILDBAD IM SCHWARZWALD *3C3* (10km NW Urban) *48.79268, 8.42908* **Campingplatz Jungbrunnen, Schwimmbadstrasse 29, 76332 Bad Herrenalb [(07083) 932970; fax 932971; info@camping-jungbrunnen.de; www.camping-jungbrunnen.de]** On S o'skirts Bad Herrenalb on L564 to Gernsbach & Baden-Baden. Foll sp on L down slope. NB: Rd distance fr Bad Wildbad is much more than crow flies due to no direct rds & inclines. If app fr Gernsbach, pass site & proceed into Bad Herrenalb to rndabt, then return. This avoids diff turn. Med, terr, pt shd; wc; chem disp; shwrs €0.50; el pnts (16A) metered; gas; Indtte; shop; snacks; bar; cooking facs; pool; paddling pool; 60% statics; dogs €1.50; bus; Eng spkn; adv bkg; quiet; red CCI. "Friendly owner; easy walk into interesting sm town." 1 Apr-31 Oct. € 15.50 2009*

BAD WILDUNGEN *1C4* (6km NW Rural) *51.16431, 9.08521* **Camping Affolderner See, Mühlengraben 15, 34549 Edertal-Affoldern [(05623) 4290; fax 1489; schuette.v@t-online.de; www.campingplatz-affoldernersee.de]** Fr Bad Wildungen, take B485 N to Edertal, foll sps to Affoldern & site. Med, mkd pitch, shd; wc; chem disp; mv service pnt; shwrs €1; el pnts (16A) €2; Indtte; shop; rest; snacks; playgrnd; lake sw 200m; 40% statics; dogs €2; office clsd 1300-1500; adv bkg; quiet; red long stays. "Situated nr Edersee Dam (Dambusters); gd walking country." 1 Mar-30 Nov. € 15.00 2008*

⊞ **BADEN BADEN** *3C3* (1km NW Urban) *48.7720, 8.2215* **Stellplatz, Aumattstrasse, 76530 Baden-Baden [(07221) 275200; info@baden-baden.com]** Exit A5/E35/E52 at junc 51 for Baden-Baden & foll B500 twd cent. Turn R at traff lts into Aumattstrasse, dir 'stadion' (stadium). Make for coach/bus park, site sp. Free, sm parking place for m'vans only; wc; shop 800m; no other facs. 2010*

BADENWEILER see Neuenburg am Rhein *3B4*

⊞ **BAMBERG** *4E2* (5km S Rural) *49.86138, 10.91583* **Camping Insel, Am Campingplatz 1, 96049 Bamberg-Bug [(0951) 56320; fax 56321; buero@campinginsel.de; www.campinginsel.de]** Exit A70/E48 junc 16 or A73 exit Bamberg-Süd onto B22 dir Würzburg. Site on L of rd along Rv Regnitz. Bug sm vill suburb of Bamburg to S of rv. Fr S on A3 exit junc 79 dir Bamberg. In 12km turn L dir Pettstadt; turn R at rndabt, site in 2km. Lge, shd; htd wc; baby facs; shwrs inc; chem disp; mv service pnt; el pnts (16A) metered (long lead poss req); gas; Indtte; shop; snacks; playgrnd; TV; 40% statics; dogs €1.10; clsd 1300-1500 & 2300-0700; bus to Bamburg; Eng spkn; quiet; ccard not acc; red long stay/CCI. "Lovely historic town; rvside site; excel cycle facs to town; bus to town €1.50; excel, modern san facs." ♦ € 22.00 2011*

BAUTZEN *2G4* (2km NE Rural) *51.20194, 14.46083* **Natur & AbenteuerCamping am Stausee Bautzen, Nimschützerstrasse 41, 02625 Bautzen [(03591) 271267 or (035828) 76430; fax 271268; camping-bautzen@web.de; www.camping-bautzen.de]** Exit A4 junc 90 onto B156. Site sp on lakeside. Med, hdstg, pt shd; htd wc; chem disp; mv service pnt; all serviced pitches; baby facs; shwrs inc; el pnts (16A) €2.50 (poss rev pol); Indtte (inc dryer); shop & 2km; tradsmn; BBQ; cooking facs; playgrnd; lake sw & beach adj; watersports; games rm; entmnt; internet; TV; dogs €2.50; phone; bus adj; Eng spkn; adv bkg; quiet; ccard acc; CCI. "V high quality site; lovely location; Bautzen interesting town; gd cycling & walking; excel." 1 Apr-31 Oct. € 24.50 2010*

BENSERSIEL *1B2* (W Coastal) *53.67531, 7.57001* **Familien & Kurcampingplatz Bensersiel, 26427 Esens-Bensersiel [(04971) 917121; fax 4988; info@bensersiel.de; www.bensersiel.de]** Fr B210 turn N at Ogenbargen; thro Esens to Bensersiel. Site adj to harbour in cent of vill - clearly sp. V lge, unshd; wc; chem disp; mv service pnt; shwrs €0.50; el pnts (16A) €2.50; gas; Indtte; shop; rest; snacks; playgrnd; htd pool; beach adj; spa complex nr; tennis; games area; cycle hire; entmnt; TV; 70% statics; no dogs; poss cr; adv bkg; debit card acc. "Cycling country; gd boat trips; gd san facs; open site adj sea; gd access vill, rests & island ferries; elec metered after 3 days - if staying longer, check meter on arr." ♦ Easter-15 Oct. € 17.00 2008*

⊞ **BERCHTESGADEN** *4G4* (3km NE Rural) *47.64742, 13.03993* **Camping Allweglehen, Allweggasse 4, 83471 Berchtesgaden-Untersalzberg [(08652) 2396; camping@allweglehen.de; www.allweglehen.de]** On R of rd B305 Berchtesgaden dir Salzburg, immed after ent Unterau; sp. App v steep in places with hairpin bend; gd power/weight ratio needed. Lge, pt sl, terr, pt shd, some hdstg; htd wc; serviced pitches; chem disp; mv service pnt; baby facs; shwrs inc; el pnts (16A) metered + conn fee; Indtte (inc dryer); shop; rest; bar; playgrnd; htd pool; cycles; free wifi; entmnt; 20% statics; dogs €2.95 ; bus 500m; ski lift; phone; poss cr; Eng spkn; adv bkg rec high ssn; quiet; ccard acc; 10% red CCI. "Gd touring/walking cent; wonderful views most pitches; beautiful scenery; Hitler's Eagles' Nest worth visit (rd opens mid-May) - bus fr Obersalzburg; site rds poss o'grown & uneven; steep app some pitches - risk of grounding for long o'fits; friendly, family-run site; excel rest." ♦ € 29.25 2011*

There aren't many sites open at this time of year. We'd better phone ahead to check the one we're heading for is open.

⊞ **BERCHTESGADEN** *4G4* (11km NW Rural) *47.67666, 12.93611* **Camping Winkl-Landthal, Klaushäuslweg 7, 83483 Bischofswiesen [(08652) 8164; fax 979831; camping-winkl@t-online.de; www.camping-winkl.de]** Fr Munich-Salzburg m'way take rd 20 sp Bad Reichenhall. Where rd turns L, foll rd 20 twd Berchtesgaden. Site on R in 9km. Med, mkd pitch, pt shd; wc; chem disp; some serviced pitches with sat TV; shwrs inc; el pnts (10A) metered + conn fee (poss rev pol); gas; Indtte; shop & 500m; tradsmn; rest; playgrnd; htd pool 3.5km; golf 15km; wifi; 50% statics; dogs €1.50; site clsd Nov; Eng spkn; adv bkg; some rd & rlwy noise; red long stay/CCI. "Some pleasant, shd pitches adj sm rv; clean san facs." € 21.00 2009*

⊞ **BERGEN** *1D3* (9km E Rural) *52.80443, 10.10376* **Camping am Örtzetal, Dicksbarg 46, 29320 Oldendorf [(05052) 3072; www.campingplatz-oldendorf.de]** Fr S, exit A7/E45 junc 52 dir Celle, in 5km turn L sp Winsen, Belsen & Bergen. Fr N exit A7/E45 at junc 45 onto B3 to Bergen. Foll rd to Bergen. In Bergen foll sp Hermannsburg. In about 7km at T-junc turn R, then 1st L sp Eschede & Oldendorf. In Oldendorf turn L at 2nd x-rds. Site on R in 1km. Lge, pt shd; wc; chem disp; shwrs €0.80; el pnts (6A) metered + conn fee; Indtte (inc dryer); shop 4km; tradsmn; rest 500m; snacks; bar; htd pool 4km; lake 4km; playgrnd; cycle hire; 40% statics; dogs €1.50; phone; quiet; CCI. "Ideal for walking & cycling on Lüneburg Heath; conv Belsen memorial; welcoming, friendly owner; peaceful site; barrier clsd 1300-1500." € 15.50 2009*

BERGWITZ see Lutherstadt Wittenberg *2F3*

⊞ **BERLIN** *2G3* (15km SW Rural) *52.40027, 13.18055* **City Campingplatz Hettler & Lange, Bäkehang 9a, 14532 Kleinmachnow-Dreilinden [(033203) 79684; fax 77913; kleinmachnow@city-camping-berlin.de; www.city-camping-berlin.de]** Fr S exit A115/E51 junc 5 sp Kleinmachnow, turn L at T-junc & cont to rndabt. Turn L & foll site sp in 800m. Lge, pt sl, pt shd; htd wc; chem disp; mv service pnt; baby facs; shwrs inc; el pnts (6A) €2.50; gas; Indtte (inc dryer); sm shop & 5km; tradsmn; rest; snacks; playgrnd; lake sw 2km; boats for hire; dogs €2; phone; bus nr; poss v cr; some Eng spkn; adv bkg; quiet but some barge & rd noise; CCI. "Excel location on canal side; immac, modern san facs; twin-axles by arrangement; gd walking in woods; gd public transport conv Berlin 45 mins - parking at Wannsee S-bahn (family ticket avail for bus & train); vg." € 20.00 2011*

⊞ **BERLIN** *2G3* (15km SW Rural) *52.4650, 13.16638* **DCC Campingplatz Gatow, Kladower Damm 207-213, 14089 Berlin-Gatow [(030) 3654340; fax 36808492; gatow@dccberlin.de; www.dccberlin.de]** Fr A10 to W of Berlin turn E on rd 5 sp Spandau/Centrum. Go twd city cent & after 14km turn R onto Gatowerstrasse (Esso g'ge) sp Kladow/Gatow. Site 6.5km on L almost opp Kaserne (barracks). Med, pt shd; htd wc; chem disp; mv service pnt; shwrs inc; fam bthrm; el pnts (10-16A) metered + conn fee; gas; Indtte (inc dryer); supmkt 2km; tradsmn; snacks; bar; playgrnd; sand beach 1km; 60% statics; dogs €1.80; bus at gate; poss cr; Eng spkn; rd noise; red CCI. "Excel site; gd disabled facs; bus tickets fr recep; frequent bus to Berlin centre at gate; barrier clsd 1300-1500; highly rec; ex san facs." ♦ € 21.50 2011*

⊞ **BERLIN** *2G3* (19km SW Urban) *52.45361, 13.11361* **DCC Campingplatz Berlin-Kladow, Krampnitzerweg 111-117, 14089 Berlin-Kladow [(030) 3652797; fax 3651245; kladow@dccberlin.de; www.dccberlin.de]** Exit E55/A10 junc 26 Berlin-Spandauonto B5 E, Hamburger Chaussee. In 10km turn R onto B2 dir Potsdam. In 5km bear L to Kladow & look for camp sp. Site 1km S of S end Gross-Glienickesee. NB Camping sp for Kladow & Gatow can lead to either site. V lge, mkd pitch, pt shd; wc; chem disp; shwrs €0.50; el pnts (10A) metered + conn fee; Indtte; shop; supmkt 2.5km; rest; lake sw 500m; 70% statics; dogs €1.75; bus 1km; poss cr; adv bkg; quiet; no ent/exit for cars 1300-1500 & 2200-0700; 10% red CCI. "San facs tired; busy, well-organised site; avoid mid-July w/end 'Love Party' on site; Luftwaffe Museum 2km; gd free parking & cycling in Berlin." ♦ € 19.60 2008*

⊞ **BERLIN** *2G3* (10km NW Urban) *52.54861, 13.25694* **City-Camping Hettler & Lange, Gartenfelderstrasse 1, 13599 Berlin-Spandau [(030) 33503633; fax 33503635; spandau@city-camping-berlin.de; www.hettler-lange.de]** Fr N on A111/A115/E26 exit junc 10 sp Tegel Airport & head W on Saatwinkler Damm. Fr S on A100 exit junc 11 onto Saatwinkler Damm. Cont 3.2km to traff lts, turn R, then R again immed bef 2nd bdge. Site on island in rv. Med, pt sl, shd; wc; chem disp; shwrs €1; el pnts (10A) €2; Indtte; shop 2km; tradsmn; rest; bar; dogs €2; Eng spkn; no adv bkg; aircraft noise; ccard acc; CCI. "Conv Berlin; gd location but aircraft noise; gd san facs; NH/sh stay only." € 17.50 2008*

BERNKASTEL KUES *3B2* (2km NE Rural) *49.96556, 7.10475* **Camping Rissbach, Rissbacherstrasse 155, 56841 Traben-Trarbach [(06541) 3111; info@moselcampings.de; www.moselcampings.de]** Fr Bernkastel on B53, after Kröv do not cross Mosel bdge but cont strt on twd Traben, site on R in 1km. NB 20km by road fr Bernkastel to site. Med, mkd pitch, pt sl, shd; htd wc; chem disp; mv service pnt; shwrs €0.25/min; el pnts (16A) €2.50; gas 500m; Indtte; shop & 2km; rest 1km; snacks; BBQ; playgrnd; htd pool adj; boat-launch; wifi; 30% statics; dogs €3.50; phone; quiet. "In lovely position nr rv; extra for pitches nr rv; well-run site; excel san facs; magnificent sw pools in town; poss flooding at high water." ♦ 1 Apr-31 Oct. € 16.00 2010*

BERNKASTEL KUES *3B2* (2km SW Rural) *49.90883, 7.05600* **Kueser Werth Camping, Am Hafen 2, 54470 Bernkastel-Kues [(06531) 8200; fax 8282; camping-cueser-werth@web.de; www.camping-kueser-werth.de]** A'bahn A1/48 (E44) exit Salmtal; join rd sp Bernkastel. Before rv bdge turn L sp Lieser, thro Lieser cont by rv to ent on R for boat harbour, foll camping sp to marina. Diff access via narr single-track rd. Lge, pt shd, wc; chem disp; mv service pnt; shwrs inc; el pnts (16A) metered; Indtte; sm shop; tradsmn; rest; snacks; playgrnd; cycle hire; TV rm; 20% statics; dogs €2; bus 1km; poss cr; Eng spkn; adv bkg; some rd noise & rv barges; 5% red CCI. "Excel cent for touring Mosel Valley; Bernkastel delightful sm town with gd parking, sailing, boat excursions, wine cent; cycle lanes; site low on rv bank - poss flooding in bad weather; efficient staff; gd site with excel facs, inc disabled; not rec for NH/sh stay high ssn as pitches & position poor." ♦ 1 Apr-31 Oct. € 18.00 2009*

BERNKASTEL KUES *3B2* (4km NW Rural) *49.93736, 7.04853* **Camping Schenk, Hauptstrasse 165, 54470 Bernkastel-Wehlen [(06531) 8176; fax 7681; info@camping-schenk.de; www.camping-schenk.com]** On Trier/Koblenz rd B53, exit Kues heading N on L bank of rv & site on R in 4km at Wehlen, sp. Steep exit. Med, mkd pitch, some hdstg, pt sl, some terr, pt shd; htd wc; chem disp; mv service pnt; some serviced pitches; shwrs €0.50; el pnts (16A) metered + conn fee; gas; Indtte; shops 1km; tradsmn; rest adj; snacks; bar; playgrnd; pool; 40% statics; dogs; phone; bus; poss cr; Eng spkn; adv bkg; quiet; CCI. "In apple orchard on Rv Mosel; price according to pitch size; friendly owners; debit cards acc; pool deep - not suitable non-swimmers; poorly ventilated san facs; rv walks & cycle path to town; friendly owner - excel English." ♦ 27 Mar-31 Oct. € 25.40 2011*

BERNRIED see Deggendorf *4G3*

⊞ **BIELEFELD** *1C3* (4km W Rural) *52.00624, 8.45681* **Campingpark Meyer Zu Bentrup, Vogelweide 9, 33649 Bielefeld [(0521) 4592233; fax 459017; bielefeld@meyer-zu-bentrup.de; www.camping-bielefeld.de]** Exit A2 junc 27 & foll sp Osnabrück on B68; site sp on L - approx 14km fr a'bahn. Lge, pt sl, unshd; wc; chem disp; mv service pnt; shwrs €0.30/min; el pnts (10-16A) €1; Indtte (inc dryer); farm shop; tradsmn; bar; cooking facs; playgrnd; games area; games rm; wifi; 95% statics; dogs €2; quiet; red CCI. "Gd; immac, excel san facs." ♦ € 19.50 2010*

BINAU AM NECKAR see Neckarelz *3D3*

⊞ **BINGEN AM RHEIN** *3C2* (5km NW Rural) *50.00428, 7.85528* **Camping Marienort, Zum Friedhof, 55413 Trechtingshausen [tel/fax (06721) 6133; www.campingplatz-marienort.de]** NW fr Bingen on B9, site on R under rlwy with winding & 1-way app rd. NB Bdge 3.2m high. (Do not app via level x-ing). Site sp. Ent narr & poss diff lge m'vans. Med, pt shd; wc; chem disp; mv service pnt; shwrs €1; el pnts (18A) €1.50; Indtte; shop high ssn; rest; playgrnd; 65% statics; train 400m; poss cr; Eng spkn; v noisy trains, boats & aircraft; red long stay/CCI. "On W bank of Rhine; beautiful scenery; friendly; rec phone 1st for availability." € 13.50 2008*

BINZ (RUGEN ISLAND) *2G1* (2km NW Coastal) *54.42315, 13.57808* **Camping Meier, Proraer Chaussee 30, 18609 Prora [(038393) 2085; fax 32624; info@camping-meier-ruegen.de; www.camping-meier-ruegen.de]** On B96 Stralsund to Bergen cont on 196 to Karow. Turn L on 196a to Prora, at traff lts turn R onto L29 to Binz. After 1.5km at camp sp turn R thro wood to site. Med, mkd pitch, pt shd; wc; chem disp; mv service pnt; shwrs €0.50; el pnts (6A) €2.50; gas 1km; Indtte; shops 1km; tradsmn; rest; bar; playgrnd; sand beach 500m; tennis; cycle hire; dogs €3.50; phone; Eng spkn; adv bkg (bkg fee); quiet; red 7+ days; ccard acc (Visa only). "Gd location for touring Rügen area; gd sandy beach thro woods; vg rest; vg san facs." ♦ 1 Apr-31 Oct. € 23.00 2011*

BIRKENFELD *3B2* (1.5km E Rural) *49.65501, 7.18211* **Campingpark Waldwiesen (Naturist), 55765 Birkenfeld [(06782) 5215; fax 5219; info@waldwiesen.de; www.waldwiesen.de]** Exit A62 junc 4 N to Birkenfeld. Site sp off rd B41. Med, hdg pitch, pt sl, pt shd; wc; chem disp; mv service pnt; shwrs inc; el pnts 16A) metered + conn fee; gas; Indtte; shops 500m; tradsmn; rest 600m; snacks 1km; playgrnd; lake sw adj; cycle hire; 10% statics; dogs €2.50; adv bkg; quiet; ccard acc; CCI. "Sep area for naturists; excel facs for children; gd base for Saar-Hunsruck area." Easter-14 Oct. € 21.75 2009*

⊞ **BISCHOFSHEIM** *3D2* (1km SE Rural) *50.39558, 10.02011* **Camping am Schwimmbad, Kissingerstrasse 53, 97653 Bischofsheim [(09772) 1350; fax 931350; info@rhoencamping.de; www.rhoencamping.de]** Fr A7 exit junc 93 at Fulda onto B279 E to Bischofsheim, site sp 1km down minor rd dir Bad Kissingen. Fr A71 exit junc 25 Bad Neustadt onto B279 W. Med, hdg/mkd pitch, hdstg, pt shd; wc; chem disp; mv service pnt; shwrs €0.50; el pnts (16A) metered; gas; Indtte; shop & 500m; tradsmn; rest, bar 500m; BBQ; playgrnd; 2 htd pools (1 covrd); paddling pool; waterslide; tennis; solarium; cycle hire; 30% statics; dogs €1; sep m'van area; adv bkg; quiet; red CCI. "In cent of Rhon Nature Park, ideal for walking; ski adj in winter; office hrs 0800-1230 & 1430-1800; if arr after 1800 phone in adv & ent key will be left for you." ♦ € 19.50 2011*

⊞ **BISPINGEN** *1D2* (4km W Rural) *53.10828, 9.96561* **Campingplatz Brunautal-am-See, Seestrasse 17, 29646 Bispingen [(05194) 840; fax 970812; brunautal@gmx.de; www.campingplatz-brunautal.de]** Exit A7 junc 43 onto L211. Site immed sp twd Behringen, in 800m. Site in Lüneburger Heide nature park. Med, hdg/mkd pitch, pt shd; wc; chem disp; shwrs inc; el pnts (10A) metered; Indtte; shop; rest 200m; BBQ; playgrnd; wifi; TV rm; 20% statics; dogs €1.30; Eng spkn; adv bkg; quiet; CCI. "Friendly owners; excel." € 18.00 2008*

GERMANY

BITBURG *3B2* (9km NE) *50.03750, 6.59111* **Camping Kyllburg, Karl-Kaufmann-Weg 5, D-54655 Kyllburg [65 63 81 33; info@campingkyllburg.de; www.campingkyllburg.de]** Site on E o'skts of Kyllburg on banks of rv Kyll. App fr W turn R immed after x-ing rv. Ent down hill on R immed bef sharp LH bend. Steep & narr descent. Med, unshd; htd wc; chem disp; mv service pnt; baby facs; shwrs inc; el pnts (16A) €0.80; gas; lndtte; shop 500m; tradsmn; rest; snacks; bar; BBQ; playgrnd; pool; rv adj; wifi; 30% statics; dogs €1.80; bus 500m; train 500m; Eng spkn; adv bking; quiet; cc acc; red low ssn; CCI. "Gd for sh stays; 5 swimming pools with waterslide; cycling & walking paths; v gd site." ♦ Mar-Oct. € 18.60 2011*

⊞ **BITBURG** *3B2* (10km W Rural) *49.95895, 6.42454* **Prümtal Camping, In der Klaus 5, 54636 Oberweis [(06527) 92920; fax 929232; info@pruemtal.de; www.pruemtal.de]** On B50 Bitburg-Vianden rd. On ent Oberweis sharp RH bend immed L bef rv bdge - sp recreational facs or sp Köhler Stuben Restaurant-Bierstube. V lge, pt shd; htd wc; chem disp; shwrs inc; el pnts (16A) €2.75 or metered; lndtte; shop; rest; snacks; bar; playgrnd; pool; cycle hire; internet; entmnt; 60% statics; dogs €2.10; Eng spkn; poss v cr high ssn; adv bkg; ccard acc; CCI; "Excel facs; san facs stretched high ssn; vg rest." ♦ € 22.70 2010*

⊞ **BLEKEDE** *2E2* (5km SE Rural) *53.25921, 10.80535* **ADAC Campingplatz Alt Garge, Am Waldbad 23, 21354 Bleckede-Alt Garge [(05854) 311; fax 1640; adac-camping-altgarge@t-online.de; www.camping-altgarge.de]** Fr Lüneburg E on L221 to Blekede, then turn S on L222/K22 to site in 5km. Sm, hdstg, pt shd; htd wc; chem disp; shwrs €0.50; lndtte; shops 10km; cooking facs; playgrnd; dogs; bus adj; Eng spkn; adv bkg; quiet; ccard not acc; CCI. "Pleasant, well-kept, family-run site; gd cent for walks in Elbe Valley; conv Lüneburg; vg." ♦ € 18.50 2008*

⊞ **BLEKEDE** *2E2* (10km SE Rural) *53.23619, 10.84918* **Campingplatz Mutter Grün, Bruchdorferstrasse 30, 21354 Walmsburg [(05853) 310; fax 978653; camping-mutter-gruen@t-online.de; www.camping-mutter-gruen.de]** S fr Blekede dir Neu Darchau on K24 on S bank Rv Elbe, site on R in vill of Walmsburg. Sm, hdg pitch, pt shd; htd wc; chem disp; shwrs €0.50; el pnts (16A) metered; lndtte; shop 10km; cooking facs; dogs; bus adj; Eng spkn; adv bkg; quiet; CCI. "Well-kept, family-run, pleasant site; gd walking in Elbe valley; conv Lüneburg." ♦ € 12.00 2008*

⊞ **BONN** *1B4* (20km S Rural) *50.65388, 7.20111* **Camping Genienau, Im Frankenkeller 49, 53179 Bonn-Mehlem [(0228) 344949; fax 3294989; genienau@freenet.de]** Fr B9 dir Mehlem, site sp on Rv Rhine, S of Mehlem. Med, pt shd; wc; chem disp; shwrs €1; el pnts (6A) €3 or metered; lndtte; rest & shop 600m; rest, snacks 1km; 60% statics; dogs €2; bus; Eng spkn; no adv bkg; some rv & rlwy noise; CCI. "Excel site on rv bank; liable to flood when rv v high; nr ferry to cross Rhine; late arr no problem; san facs up steps but disabled facs at grnd level; lots to see & do." ♦ € 23.00 2011*

BOPPARD *3B2* (5km N Rural) *50.24888, 7.62638* **Camping Sonneneck, 56154 Boppard [(06742) 2121; fax 2076; info@campingpark-sonneneck-boppard.de; www.campingpark-sonneneck.de]** On Koblenz-Mainz rd B9, on W bank of Rhine, in vill of Spay. Lge, mkd pitch, pt shd; wc; chem disp; mv service pnt; serviced pitches; sauna; shwrs inc; el pnts (4A) €2.50; gas; lndtte; shop; rest; snacks; bar; playgrnd; pool high ssn; shgl beach nr; fishing; crazy-golf; 18-hole golf 2km; 10% statics; dogs €2.40; phone; night watchman; poss cr; Eng spkn; rlwy & barge noise; CCI. "V pleasant staff; clean san facs, poss long way fr pitches; ltd waste water points; extra for rvside pitch; site poss liable to flood; gd cycle path along Rhine." ♦ Easter-31 Oct. € 19.60 2009*

BOPPARD *3B2* (8km N Rural) *50.27333, 7.63333* **Camping Die Kleine Rheinperle, Am Rhein 1, 56321 Brey [(02628) 8860; fax 8865; info@camping-freizeitzentrum-brey-de; www.camping-freizeitzentrum-brey.de]** On B9 S of Koblenz, sp in Brey cent 200m fr B9 on bank of Rv Rhein. Sm, pt sl, terr, pt shd; wc (own san rec); chem disp; shwrs inc; el pnts (6A) metered & conn fee; lndry rm; shop & supmkt 1km; tradsmn; snacks; bar; playgrnd; boat-launching; cycle hire; 50% statics; dogs €1; poss cr; some rlwy noise; CCI. 1 May-30 Oct. € 15.60 2008*

BORGERENDE see Bad Doberan *2F1*

BRANDENBURG AN DER HAVEL *2F3* (5km SW Rural) *52.38691, 12.49875* **Camping Buhnenhaus, Buhnenhaus 1, 14776 Brandenburg-an-der Havel [(03381) 6190091; fax 6190092; info@buhnenhaus.de; www.buhnenhaus.de]** Fr S on B102 turn W twds lake & foll sp Wilhelmsdorf & Buhnenhaus marina, site sp adj guesthouse. Med, pt shd; wc; chem disp; shwrs; el pnts inc; rest; bar; playgrnd; lake sw adj; dogs; quiet. "Gd, clean facs; lge pitches; gd rest & beer garden; lovely town." € 13.00 2008*

BRAUBACH see Lahnstein *3B2*

BRAUNFELS see Wetzlar *3C1*

⊞ **BRAUNLAGE** *2E4* (6km NE Rural) *51.75713, 10.68345* **Campingplatz am Schierker Stern, Hagenstrasse, 38879 Schierke [(039455) 58817; fax 58818; info@harz-camping.com; www.harz-camping.com]** Fr W on B27 fr Braunlage for 4km to Elend. Turn L & cross rlwy line. Site on L in 2km at x-rds. Med, hdstg, pt sl, pt shd; htd wc; chem disp; mv service pnt; shwrs inc; el pnts (6A) €2.60; lndtte; sm shop & 8km; tradsmn; rest 200m; snacks 1km; BBQ; cooking facs; TV rm; no statics; dogs €1.30; bus at site ent; train 1km; adv bkg; quiet. "Conv & pleasant site in Harz mountains; excel san facs; friendly, helpful owners live on site; sm pitches; vg." € 19.50 2009*

⊞ **BRAUNLAGE** *2E4* (10km SE Rural) *51.65697, 10.66786* **Campingplatz am Bärenbache, Bärenbachweg 10, 38700 Hohegeiss [(05583) 1306; fax 1300; campingplatz-hohegeiss@t-online.de; www.campingplatz-hohegeiss.de]** Fr Braunlage S on B4 thro Hohegeiss; site sp on L downhill (15%) on edge of town. Med, terr, pt shd; htd wc; chem disp; mv service pnt; baby facs; fam bthrm; shwrs inc; el pnts (6A); lndtte (inc dryer); shops 500m; rest; snacks; bar; cooking facs; BBQ; playgrnd; htd pool; paddling pool; cycle hire; wifi; some statics; dogs €1.50; quiet; Eng spkn; adv bkg; red snr citizens. "Gd walking; friendly." € 15.70 (CChq acc) 2009*

⊞ **BRAUNLAGE** *2E4* (1.5km SW Rural) **Camping Hohe Tannen, Am Campingplatz 1, 38700 Braunlage [(05520) 413; fax 417; campingplatz.hohetannen@t-online.de]** Take B27 fr Braulage dir Bad Lauterberg, site sp. Med, mkd pitch, terr, pt shd; htd wc; shwrs inc; chem disp; mv service pnt; el pnts (16A) metered + conn fee; lndtte; shop; rest; snacks 1km; playgrnd; pool; 50% statics; dogs €1.20; skilift 1km; bus; adv bkg; quiet; red CCI. "Excel facs, ltd low ssn." € 15.30 2009*

BREISACH AM RHEIN *3B4* (5km E Rural) *48.03104, 7.65781* **Kaiserstuhl Camping, Nachwaid 5, 79241 Ihringen [(07668) 950065; fax 950071; info@kaiserstuhlcamping.de; www.kaiserstuhlcamping.de]** Fr S exit A5/E35 junc 64a, foll sp twds Breisach, then camping sp to Ihringen. At Ihringen site sp dir Merdingen. Fr N exit junc 60 & foll sp. Med, unshd; wc; chem disp; mv service pnt; baby facs; shwrs €0.50; el pnts (16A) metered + conn fee; lndtte; shop 800m; rest adj; snacks; bar; playgrnd; htd pool, tennis adj; golf 8km; 10% statics; dogs €2.50; poss cr; quiet; 10% red long stay/CCI. ♦ 14 Mar-30 Oct. € 22.50 2009*

BREISACH AM RHEIN *3B4* (2km S Rural) *48.01972, 7.60861* **Campingplatz Münsterblick Breisach, Hochstetterstrasse 11, 79206 Breisach-Hochstetten [(07667) 93930; fax 939393; adler-hochstetten@t-online.de; www.adler-hochstetten.de]** Fr E5/A5 exit 63 sp Breisach. Site sp off B31 rd app Breisach, adj to Gasthof Adler in Hochstetten. Or cross Rv Rhine fr France at Neuf-Brisach on D415. Site sp at Breisach in approx 1km (L of rd). Sm, pt shd; wc; shwrs inc; chem disp; shwrs €0.50; el pnts (10A) metered + conn fee; lndtte; shop 2km; rest; bar; 10% statics; dogs €1.20; poss cr; adv bkg; quiet; red CCI. "Excel NH; modern, clean san facs; gates clsd 2100." 27 Mar-2 Nov. € 16.30 2009*

⊞ **BREMEN** *1C2* (12km SW Rural) *53.01055, 8.68972* **Camping Wienberg, Zum Steller See 83, 28816 Stuhr-Gross Mackenstedt [(04206) 9191; fax 9293; info@camping-wienburg.de; www.camping-wienberg.de]** Exit A1/E37 junc 58a onto B322 sp Stuhr/Delmenhorst. Foll Camping Steller See sp. Lge, mkd pitch, pt sl, hdstg, pt shd; htd wc; chem disp; mv service pnt; baby facs; shwrs €1; el pnts (16A) metered or €3; lndtte (inc dryer); shop; tradsmn; rest; snacks; bar; playgrnd; pool; cycle hire; entmnt; TV; 50% statics; dogs €2; some Eng spkn; adv bkg; rd noise; ccard acc; CCI. "Helpful staff; basic facs; gd." € 23.70 2011*

⊞ **BREMEN** *1C2* (5km NW Rural) *53.11483, 8.83263* **Camping am Stadtwaldsee, Hochschulring 1, 28359 Bremen [(0421) 8410748; fax 8410749; contact@camping-stadtwaldsee.de; www.camping-stadtwaldsee.de]** Fr A27 exit junc 18 onto B6. At 1st junc turn R sp University, site on R in approx 2km. Foll 'Campingplatz' sp. Lge, mkd pitch, hdstg, unshd; htd wc; chem disp; mv service pnt; baby facs; fam bthrm; shwrs inc; el pnts (16A) metered; gas; lndtte (inc dryer); shop; tradsmn; rest; snacks; bar; cooking facs; BBQ; playgrnd; lake sw adj; wifi; some statics; dogs €4; phone; bus 100m; poss cr; Eng spkn; adv bkg; some rd noise; ltd ccard acc; red long stay; CCI. "Excel, spacious lakeside site; vg san & kitchen facs; cycle path to beautiful city; gd bus service." ♦ € 30.00 2011*

⊞ **BRETTEN** *3C3* (8km E Rural) *49.03478, 8.83352* **Stromberg Camping, Diefenbacherstrasse 70, 75438 Knittlingen-Freudenstein [(07043) 2160; fax 40405; info@strombergcamping.de; www.strombergcamping.de]** Take B35 E fr Bretten, foll sp Knittlingen then Freudenstein, site sp in approx 1lm on L. V lge, mkd pitch, pt shd; wc; chem disp; mv service pnt; shwrs inc; el pnts (16A) €1.50 (rev pol); lndtte (inc dryer); shop; tradsmn; rest high ssn; snacks; bar; cooking facs; playgrnd; pool; paddling pool; pony riding; games area; entmnt; 90% statics; dogs €2.50; poss cr; quiet; red long stay; CCI. "Clsd to vehicles 1300-1500 & 2200-0700; gd touring base for Black Forest; ltd number touring pitches cr nr ent." ♦ € 17.00 2010*

⊞ **BRIESELANG** *2F3* (500m W Rural) *52.57138, 12.96583* **Campingplatz Zeestow im Havelland, 11 Brieselangerstrasse, 14665 Brieselang [(033234) 88634; fax 22863; info@campingplatz-zeestow.de; www.campingplatz-zeestow.de]** Exit A10/E55 junc 27; turn W dir Wustermark; site on L after canal bdge in 500m. Lge, pt sl, unshd; wc; chem disp; shwrs €1; el pnts (16A) metered; gas; lndtte; shop; rest; bar; 75% statics; dogs €2; bus; poss cr; CCI. "Gd NH nr a'bahn; facs dated but clean; 13km fr Berlin & 25km fr Potsdam; fair." ♦ € 14.00 2011*

⊞ **BRODENBACH** *3B2* (1km S Rural) *50.21963, 7.44285* **Campingplatz Vogelsang, Rhein-Mosel Strasse 63, 56332 Brodenbach [(02605) 1437; fax 8254; info@erholungsgebiet-vogelsang.de; www.erholungsgebiet-vogelsang.de]** Fr Cochem, take B49, sp Koblenz; in 26km on ent Brodenbach turn R onto L206 sp Emmelshausen & site on L in 800m. Rec app only fr B49. Site 16km by rd fr Boppard. Med, pt shd; wc; chem disp; mv service pnt; shwrs €0.80; el pnts (6A) metered or €1.30; lndtte; shop; rest; snacks; playgrnd; 60% statics; dogs €1.10; poss cr; adv bkg; quiet. "Conv NH; vg." 2008*

⊞ **BRUGGEN** *1A4* (2km E Rural) *51.23416, 6.19815* **Camping-Forst Laarer See, Brüggenerstrasse 27, 41372 Niederkrüchten [(02163) 8461 or 0172 7630591 (mob); info@campingforst-laarersee.com; www.campingforst-laarersee.com]** Exit A92 junc 3 onto B221 to Brüggen. Foll sp Laarer See & site.Small sp on R. Lge, pt sl, pt shd; htd wc; chem disp; mv service pnt; baby facs; fam bthrm; shwrs €1; el pnts (16A) inc; lndtte; shop 2km; rest; snacks; bar; BBQ; playgrnd; games area; 80% statics; dogs €1; Eng spkn; adv bkg; quiet; CCI. "Unspoilt area nr pretty town; many leisure amenities nr site - gd for children; vg site." ♦ € 19.00 2011*

GERMANY

⊞ **BRUHL** *1B4* (1km W Rural) *50.8294, 6.8780* **Camping Heider Bergsee, Willy Brandt Strasse, 50321 Brühl [(02232) 27040; fax 25261; schirmer@heiderbergsee.de; www.heiderbergsee.de]** Exit A4/E40 junc 11 or A1/E31 junc 108 onto B265 & foll sp Heider Bergsee. Lge, pt shd; wc; chem disp; shwrs €1; el pnts (16A) €2; Indtte; shop; rest; snacks; bar; playgrnd; shgl beach & sw; fishing; 70% statics; dogs €1; poss v cr; quiet; ccard acc; CCI. "Conv for Bonn, Cologne & Phantasialand Pleasure Park; poor pitches for NH only." € 13.50 2008*

BRUNNEN see Füssen *4E4*

BUCHHOLZ see Ratzeburg *2E2*

⊞ **BUHL** *3C3* (5km W Rural) *48.72719, 8.08074* **Ferienpark & Campingplatz Adam, Campingstrasse 1, 77815 Bühl-Oberbruch [(07223) 23194; fax 8982; www.campingplatz-adam.de; www.campingplatz-adam.de]** Exit A5 at Bühl take sp Lichtenau & foll sp thro Oberbruch, then L twd Moos to site in 500m. If app on rd 3 take rd sp W to Rheinmünster N of Bühl. Site sp to S at W end of Oberbruch. Lge, mkd pitch, hdstg, pt shd; serviced pitches; wc; chem disp; mv service pnt; shwrs €0.50; el pnts (10A) €2.20; Indtte; shop; supmkt 1km; rest; snacks; bar; playgrnd; tennis; lake sw; boating; sailing; fishing; entmnt; 60% statics; dogs €2.50; o'night area tarmac car park; extra for lakeside pitches; poss cr; Eng spkn; adv bkg; quiet; ccard acc; red long stay/low ssn; CCI. "Facs clean; conv for Strasbourg, Baden-Baden & Black Forest visits; if recep clsd use area outside gate; vg." ♦ € 25.50 2010*

BULLAY see Zell *3B2*

BURGEN *3B2* (300m N Rural) *50.21457, 7.38976* **Camping Burgen, 56332 Burgen [(02605) 2396; fax 4919; Camping Burgen@gmx.de; www.camping-burgen.de]** On B49 on S bank of Rv Mosel at NE end of Burgen vill, bet rd & rv. Med, mkd pitch, unshd; wc; mv service pnt; shwrs inc; el pnts (10A) metered + conn fee (poss rev pol); Indtte; gas; shop; rest 200m; snacks adj; playgrnd; pool; boat-launching; entmnt; 30% statics; dogs €2; Eng spkn; some rd, rlwy & rv noise; red CCI. "Scenic area; ideal for touring Mosel, Rhine & Koblenz areas; gd facs; gd shop; poss liable to flood; lovely, clean site; new, excel san facs; rec." 3 Apr-25 Oct. € 20.00 2011*

BUSUM *1C1* (1km N Coastal) *54.13855, 8.84333* **Camping Nordsee Büsum, Dithmarscher Strasse 41, 25761 Büsum [(04834) 2515; fax 9281; camping-nordsee.buesum@t-online.de; www.camping-nordsee.de]** Fr A23 exit junc 2 onto B203 sp Büsum. On ent town ignore 'Centrum' sp, foll ring rd N & camping sp. Med, mkd pitch, unshd; wc; chem disp; mv service pnt; shwrs inc; el pnts (6A) €2; Indry rm; shop & 1km; snacks; bar; htd, covrd pool 1km; sand beach adj; 25% statics; dogs €3; poss cr; adv bkg; quiet; CCI. "Gd, flat walking & cycling; gd." ♦ 1 Mar-31 Oct. € 21.50 2008*

⊞ **CALW** *3C3* (8km N Rural) *48.77884, 8.73130* **Campingpark Bad Liebenzell, Pforzheimerstrasse 34, 75378 Bad Liebenzell [(07052) 935680; fax 935681; campingpark@abelundneff.de]** N fr Calw on B463 twd Pforzheim. Site on N edge of Bad Liebenzell on R sp & visible fr rd. Lge, hdg pitch, shd; wc; chem disp; mv service pnt; shwrs inc; el pnts (16A) metered or €2.40; gas; Indtte; shop & 500m; tradsmn; rest; snacks; bar; playgrnd; htd pool adj; waterslide; tennis; 50% statics; dogs €1.50; phone; m'van o'night area; poss cr; adv bkg; poss noisy; ccard acc; red CCI. "Excel pool complex adj; ltd san facs & site slightly scruffy; popular with young families; lovely area; gd walking." ♦ € 18.10 2009*

⊞ **CALW** *3C3* (7km S Rural) *48.67766, 8.68990* **Camping Erbenwald, 75387 Neubulach-Liebelsberg [(07053) 7382; fax 3274; info@camping-erbenwald.de; www.camping-erbenwald.de]** On B463 S fr Calw, take R slip rd sp Neubulach to go over main rd. Foll Neubulach sp until camping sp at R junc. Site well sp. Lge, hdg/mkd pitch, pt shd; wc; chem disp; mv service pnt; baby facs; shwrs €0.50; el pnts (10A) metered; Indtte; shop; tradsmn; rest; snacks; bar; playgrnd; htd pool; paddling pool; games area; internet; 60% statics; dogs €2; phone; Eng spkn; adv bkg; quiet. "Gd size pitches; child-friendly site; no vehicles in or out fr 1300-1500; excel." ♦ € 20.50 2011*

⊞ **CANOW** *2F2* (2km E Rural) *53.19636, 12.93116* **Camping Pälitzsee, Am Canower See 165, 17255 Canow [(039828) 20220; fax 26963; info@mecklenburg-tourist.de; www.mecklenburg-tourist.de]** Fr N on B198 turn S dir Rheinsberg to Canow vill, site sp. Lge, pt shd; wc; chem disp; shwrs €1; el pnts (16A) metered or €3; Indtte; shop high ssn; supmkt 2km; rest 2m; snacks; bar; playgrnd; lake sw & boating; 50% statics; dogs €2; adv bkg; quiet. "Canow charming vill; vg touring base for lakes." ♦ € 19.50 2009*

⊞ **CELLE** *1D3* (10km NE Rural) *52.65305, 10.19361* **Camping Alvern, Beedenbostelerweg 7, 29229 Celle-Alvern [(05145) 6000; schaefer@alvern.com]** NE fr Celle on B191. After 5km at Garssen turn R onto K29 & foll sp thro Alvern. Site sp. Med, pt shd; wc; chem disp; shwrs €0.50; el pnts (10A) inc; Indtte (inc dryer); shop; BBQ; playgrnd; games area; 80% statics; quiet; CCI. "Gd site; gd cycling tracks." € 14.00 2009*

⊞ **CHEMNITZ** *2F4* (10km SW Rural) *50.76583, 13.01444* **Waldcampingplatz Erzgebirgsblick, An der Dittersdorfer Höhe 1, 09439 Amtsberg [(0371) 7750833; fax 7750834; info@waldcamping-erzgebirge.de; www.waldcamping-erzgebirge.de]** Fr A4 take A72 S & exit junc 15. Foll sp 'Centrum' & join 'Südring' ring rd. Turn onto B174 & foll sp Marienberg twd junc with B180. Site sp 500m fr junc. Med, mkd pitch, pt shd; htd wc; chem disp; mv service pnt; baby facs; shwrs €0.50; el pnts (16A) metered; gas; Indtte; shop; tradsmn; supmkt 4km; playgrnd; games area; TV rm; dogs free; bus 800m; site clsd 6-27 Nov; Eng spkn; red long stay; ccard not acc; red long stay/snr citizens/CCI. "Gd san facs; relaxing site; gd walking; vg standard of site." € 17.00 2009*

⊞ **CLAUSTHAL ZELLERFELD** *1D3* (4km SE Rural) *51.78490, 10.35060* **Campingplatz Prahljust, An den Langen Brüchen 4, 38678 Clausthal-Zellerfeld [(05323) 1300; fax 78393; camping@prahljust.de; www.prahljust.de]** Fr Clausthal turn onto B242 dir Braunlage, in 3km turn R, site sp. V lge, terr, pt shd; htd wc; chem disp; mv service pnt; baby facs; sauna; shwrs inc; el pnts (10-16A) metered; gas; lndtte (inc dryer); shop; tradsmn; rest; snacks; bar; cooking facs; playgrnd; htd pool; lake sw adj; cycle hire; skilift 8km; wifi; TV rm; 30% statics; dogs €2; phone; bus 1km; Eng spkn; adv bkg; CCI. "Beautiful wooded location adj lake; gd hiking & cycling; vg." ♦ € 17.40 (CChq acc) 2010*

I'll go online and tell the Club what we think of the campsites we've visited – www.caravanclub.co.uk/europereport

⊞ **COBURG** *4E2* (9km SW Rural) *50.19433, 10.83809* **Campingplatz Sonnland, Bahnhofstrasse 154, 96145 Sesslach [(09569) 220; fax 1593; info@camping-sonnland.de; www.camping-sonnland.de]** Exit A73 junc 10 Ebersdorf onto B303 W. Then at Niederfüllbach turn S onto B4, then turn W dir Sesslach. Site sp N of Sesslach dir Hattersdorf; turn R at sp opp filling stn, site in 150m. Med, mkd pitch, some hdstg, terr, pt shd; htd wc; chem disp; mv service pnt; serviced pitches; shwrs €1.50; el pnts (16A) metered; lndtte (inc dryer); shop 300m; rest 400m; BBQ; playgrnd; lake sw; 70% statics; dogs €1.50; adv bkg; CCI. "Sesslach unspoilt, medieval, walled town; site well laid-out." € 15.00 2010*

COCHEM *3B2* (1.5km N Rural) *50.15731, 7.17360* **Campingplatz am Freizeitzentrum, Moritzburgerstrasse 1, 56812 Cochem [(02671) 4409; fax 910719; info@campingplatz-cochem.de; www.campingplatz-cochem.de]** On rd B49 fr Koblenz, on ent town go under 1st rv bdge then turn R over same bdge. Foll site sp. Lge, mkd pitch, pt sl, pt shd; wc; chem disp; mv service pnt; shwrs €0.90; el pnts (10-16A) €2.50 + conn fee (some rev pol); gas; lndtte (inc dryer); snacks; shops/supmkt, rest nrby; playgrnd; cycle hire; dogs €3; poss cr; some rd/rlwy/rv noise; red low ssn; CCI. "Gd, clean site adj Rv Mosel; pitches tight & poss diff access fr site rds; gd for children; easy walk along rv to town; train to Koblenz, Trier, Mainz." 1 Apr-31 Oct. € 17.00 2010*

COCHEM *3B2* (5km NE Rural) *50.16861, 7.26555* **Camping Pommern, Moselweinstrasse 12, 56829 Pommern [(02672) 2461; fax 912173; campingpommern@netscape.net; www.campingplatz-pommern.de]** On W edge of vill of Pommern bet B49 & Rv Mosel. Med, pt shd; htd wc; chem disp; mv service pnt; baby facs; shwrs; el pnts (16A) metered + conn fee; gas; lndtte; shop; tradsmn; rest; snacks; bar; BBQ; cooking facs; playgrnd; htd pool; watersports; games area; internet; 30% statics; dogs €1.60; bus; train adj; poss cr; adv bkg; rd noise. "Well-kept, friendly site in lovely location; clean, modern san facs." 1 Apr-31 Oct. € 13.90 2010*

COCHEM *3B2* (10km E Rural) *50.17056, 7.29285* **Camping Mosel-Boating-Center, Jachthafen, 56253 Treis-Karden [(02672) 2613; fax 990559; info@mosel-islands.de; www.mosel-islands.de]** Fr Cochem take B49 to Treis-Karden (11km), cross Mosel bdge bear L then 1st sharp L back under Mosel bdge & parallel with rv. After 300m at bdge over stream turn R then thro allotments. Site over bdge by boating cent. Fr A61 Koblenz/Bingen a'bahn descend to rv level by Winningen Valley Bdge, turn L onto B49 (Moselweinstrasse). Do not descend thro Dieblich as caravans are prohibited. After 25km; turn R immed bef Mosel bridge & then as above. Avoid Treis vill (narr with thro traffic priorities). Med, mkd pitch, pt shd; wc; serviced pitches; shwrs €0.80; el pnts (6A) metered & conn fee; gas; lndtte; shops 200m; rest; BBQ; pool 1km; tennis 300m; 50% statics; dogs €3.50; adv bkg; some rv & rlwy noise. "Ideal for touring Mosel valley; rv cruising & historical sites; vg san facs 1st floor; midges!" ♦ 1 Apr-31 Oct. € 18.00 2008*

COCHEM *3B2* (6km SE Rural) *50.10999, 7.23542* **Campingplatz Happy-Holiday, Moselweinstrasse, 56821 Ellenz-Poltersdorf [(02673) 1272; fax 962367; www.camping-happy-holiday.de]** Fr Cochem, take B49 S to Ellenz; site sp on bank of Rv Mosel. Med, pt sl, shd; htd wc; chem disp; shwrs €1; el pnts (6A) metered; gas; lndtte (inc dryer); sm shop; tradsmn; rest; snacks; bar; pool 300m; fishing; watersports; wifi; 70% statics; dogs €1; poss cr; Eng spkn; quiet but rd & rv noise. "Pleasant situation; gd value rest; clean facs; conv touring base." 1 Apr-31 Oct. € 15.00 2011*

COCHEM *3B2* (7km SE Rural) *50.08231, 7.20796* **Camping Holländischer Hof, Am Campingplatz 1, 56820 Senheim [(02673) 4660; fax 4100; holl.hof@t-online.de; www.moselcamping.com]** Fr Cochem take B49 twd Traben-Trarbach; after approx 15km turn L over rv bdge sp Senheim; site on rv island. Med, mkd pitch, pt shd; wc; chem disp; mv service pnt; baby facs; shwrs €0.85; el pnts (6-10A) metered; lndtte; gas; shop & 1km; tradsmn; rest; snacks; bar; playgrnd; rv sw adj; tennis; wifi; 20% statics; no dogs; phone; poss cr; Eng spkn; adv bkg; quiet; debit card acc; red long stay; CCI. "Pleasant, well-run site; beautiful location; helpful staff; sm pitches on loose pebbles; excel cycle paths; poss flooding when wet weather/high water." ♦ 15 Apr-1 Nov. € 16.20 2011*

COCHEM *3B2* (8km SE Rural) *50.13253, 7.23029* **Campingplatz Bruttig, Am Moselufer, 56814 Bruttig-Fankel [(02671) 915429; www.campingplatz-bruttig.de]** Leave Cochem on B49 twd Trier. In 8km turn L over bdge to Bruttig-Fankel. Thro vill, site on R on banks Rv Mosel. Sm, mkd pitch, pt shd; htd wc; chem disp; shwrs €0.50; el pnts (16A) metered; lndtte; snacks; bar; playgrnd; rv sw adj; 50% statics; phone; Eng spkn; quiet. "Pleasant site in pretty vill; gd walking, cycling." Easter-31 Oct. € 14.00 2009*

GERMANY

COCHEM *3B2* (6km S Rural) *50.0804, 7.19298* **Campingplatz Nehren, Moselufer 1, 56820 Nehren [(02673) 4612; fax 962825; info@campingplatz-nehren.de; www.camping platz-nehren.de]** Fr Cochem take B49 twd Bernkastel-Kues site on rv bank at ent to Nehren - 15km by rd. Lge, mkd pitch, pt sl, pt shd; htd wc; chem disp; mv service pnt; shwrs inc; el pnts (6A) €2.20; Indtte (inc dryer); shop; tradsmn; rest 100m; snacks; bar; boat-launching; 40% statics; dogs €1.20; bus adj; poss cr; Eng spkn; adv bkg; quiet; red CCI. "V pleasant setting; san facs up 2 flights stairs; helpful owners; poss flooding at high water; poss midges; excel cycle paths along Mosel." 1 Apr-24 Oct. € 20.00 2011*

COCHEM *3B2* (7km S Rural) *50.09162, 7.16319* **Campingplatz zum Feuerberg, 56814 Ediger-Eller [(02675) 701; fax 911211; prokop@zum-feuerberg.de; www.zum-feuerberg.de]** On A49 fr Cochem to Bernkastel Kues, just bef vill of Ediger on L - 17km by rd. Lge, hdg/mkd pitch, pt shd; wc; chem disp; mv service pnt; shwrs €0.90; el pnts (16A) metered + conn fee; gas; Indtte; shop adj; tradsmn; snacks; bar; playgrnd; pool; boat mooring; cycle hire; internet; 40% statics; dogs €2; phone; bus, train to Cochem; Eng spkn; adv bkg; quiet; CCI. "Well-kept site in lovely area; charming vill; helpful staff; facs at 1st floor level; gd selection of rests & pubs; rv bus high ssn; gd touring base; gd." 1 Apr-31 Oct. € 16.50 2010*

⊞ **COLBITZ** *2E3* (2km N Rural) *52.33158, 11.63123* **Campingplatz Heide-Camp, Angerschestrasse, 39326 Colbitz [(039207) 80291; fax 80593; info@heide-camp-colbitz.de; www.heide-camp-colbitz.de]** Exit A2/E30 junc 70 onto B189 N dir Stendal. In Colbitz foll sp Angern. Site in 2km. Lge, mkd pitch, pt shd; wc; chem disp; mv service pnt; shwrs inc; el pnts (6-16A) metered + conn fee; gas; Indtte; shop, rest adj; snacks; playgrnd; pool adj; games area; 20% statics; dogs €2.80; Eng spkn; adv bkg; quiet; ccard acc, red CCI. "Site on woodland, lge pitches." ♦ € 18.70 2008*

COLDITZ *2F4* (2km E Rural) *51.13083, 12.83305* **Campingplatz am Waldbad, Im Tiergarten 5, 04680 Colditz [tel/fax (034381) 43122; info@campingplatz-colditz.de; www.campingplatz-colditz.de]** Fr Leipzig A14 to Grimma, foll B107 to Colditz. Cross rv, foll B176 sp Dobeln. Turn L immed bef town exit sp. Site 1km on R immed after outdoor sw pool, sm sp. App to site narr. Med, mkd pitch, pt sl, pt shd; wc; chem disp; mv service pnt; sauna; shwrs €1; el pnts (10A) inc; Indtte (inc dryer); shop 1km; tradsmn; sm rest & 500m; leisure cent/pool adj; 30% statics; dogs €1; phone; quiet but some daytime noise fr leisure cent adj; some Eng spkn; red CCI. "V nice peaceful site; gd clean facs; gd value; tight turn into site fr narr rd; helpful, friendly manager; 30 mins walk to Colditz Castle." 1 Apr-30 Sep. € 19.00 2011*

COLOGNE see Köln *1B4*

COSWIG *2G4* (1km W Rural) *51.12055, 13.56388* **Campingplatz am Badesee Coswig-Kötitz, Brockwitzerstrasse 33, 01640 Coswig-Kötitz [(03523) 700220; camping@tw-coswig.de; www.campingplatz-coswig.de]** Exit A4 junc 79 onto S82 dir Meissen for 9km. Pass Autocentre Coswig & under rlwy bdge then in 400m turn L into Brockwitzerstrasse. Foll sp to site. Med, hdg pitch, pt shd; htd wc; chem disp; mv service pnt; serviced pitches; shwrs inc; el pnts (10A) €2.20; Indtte (inc dryer); shop 2km; rest; snacks; bar; BBQ; playgrnd; pool; paddling pool; lake sw adj; games area; 10% statics; dogs €1.70; bus 2km; Eng spkn; quiet; CCI. "Adj Rv Elbe & cycle path to Dresden & Meissen; gd touring area; easy access to lge pitches." ♦ 1 Apr-31 Oct. € 15.60 2010*

CREGLINGEN *3D2* (3.5km S Rural) *49.43945, 10.04210* **Campingpark Romantische Strasse, Münster 67, 97993 Creglingen-Münster [(07933) 20289; fax 990019; camping.hausotter@web.de; www.camping-romantische-strasse.de]** Fr E43 exit A7/junc 105 at Uffenheim. At edge of Uffenheim turn R in dir of Bad Mergentheim; in approx 17km at T-junc turn L for Creglingen, thro vill & then R sp Münster with camping sp - approx 8km further. Site on R after Münster. (Avoid rte bet Rothenburg & Creglingen as includes some v narr vills & coaches). Med, pt shd; 10% serviced pitches; htd wc; chem disp; mv service pnt; baby facs; sauna; shwrs inc; el pnts (6A) €2.20; Indtte (inc dryer); shop; rest; snacks; bar; BBQ; playgrnd; htd, covrd pool; paddling pool; lake fishing; cycle hire; wifi; 20% statics; dogs €1; phone; clsd 1300-1500; poss cr; quiet; debit card acc (surcharge); red CCI. "Site ent needs care; helpful owner; lovely welcome; excel rest & facs; Romantische Strasse with interesting medieval churches locally; gd cent for historic towns; gd value." ♦ 15 Mar-15 Nov. € 19.70 (CChq acc) 2011*

DAHME *2E1* (1.5km N Coastal) *54.24254, 11.08030* **Camping Stieglitz, Im Feriengebiet Zedano, 23747 Dahme [(04364) 1435; fax 470401; info@camping-stieglitz.de; www.camping-stieglitz.de]** Exit A1/E47 junc 12 at Lensahn E twd coast. Fr B501 foll sp Dahme-Nord to sea wall, site sp. Lge, mkd/hdg pitch; pt shd; htd wc; chem disp; mv service pnt; baby facs; shwrs €0.50; el pnts (16A) €2.20 or metered; Indtte (inc dryer); shop; tradsmn; rest; playgrnd; sand beach 200m; fishing; watersports; cycle hire; wifi; entmnt; TV rm; 50% statics; dogs (not Jul-Aug) €4; adv bkg; ccard acc; quiet. ♦ 26 Mar-24 Oct & 5-31 Dec. € 23.00 (CChq acc) 2010*

DAHN *3B3* (500m W Rural) *49.14416, 7.76805* **Campingplatz Büttelwoog, Im Büttelwoog, 66994 Dahn [(06391) 5622; fax 5326; buettelwoog@t-online.de; www.camping-buettelwoog.de]** Fr rte 10 Pirmasens-Karlsruhe turn S at traff lts at Hinterweidenthal onto B427 to Dahn. In Dahn cent turn R, foll Youth Hostel sp; over single track rlwy & up hill; site on R in 500m, clearly sp opp Youth Hostel (Jugendherberge). Med, terr, pt shd; wc; chem disp; mv service pnt; shwrs inc; el pnts (4A) €2 (rev pol); gas; Indtte; shop; tradsmn; sm rest; snacks; bar; playgrnd; covrd pool adj; cycle hire; 10% statics; dogs €3; Quickstop o'night facs; poss cr; Eng spkn; adv bkg; quiet; red CCI. "Welcoming, informal site; clsd to arrivals 1200-1400 & 2200-0800; facs dated & stretched high ssn; picturesque area; gd walks fr site." ♦ 1 Mar-15 Nov. € 18.00 2011*

DANNENBERG *2E2* (800m SE Rural) *53.09726, 11.10993* **Campingplatz Dannenberg, Bäckergrund 35, 29451 Dannenberg [tel/fax (05861) 4183]** Sp off B191 on o'skts of Dannenberg. Med, hdg pitch, shd; wc; chem disp; mv service pnt; shwrs inc; el pnts (16A) metered + conn fee; Indtte; shop; rest, snacks, bar adj; htd pool adj; 60% statics; dogs €1.10; phone; poss cr; Eng spkn; adv bkg; quiet; red CCI. "Gd NH/sh stay." ♦ 15 Mar-31 Oct. € 14.30 2008*

⊞ **DAUN** *3B2* (7km SE Rural) *50.13540, 6.92219* **Feriendorf Pulvermaar, Auf der Maarhöhe, Vulkanstrasse, 54558 Gillenfeld [(06573) 287; info@feriendorf-pulvermaar.de; www.feriendorf-pulvermaar.de]** Fr A1/A48/E44 exit junc 121 onto B421 dir Zell/Mosel. After approx 5km turn R to Pulvemaar, site sp nr lakeside. Med, sl, pt shd; wc; chem disp; shwrs inc; el pnts (16A) metered + conn fee; Indtte; shop; snacks; BBQ; playgrnd; pool; fishing adj; games area; 60% statics; dogs €1; Eng spkn; adv bkg; quiet; CCI. "Conv Mosel valley & Weinstrasse; attractive site." € 17.00 2010*

⊞ **DAUN** *3B2* (9km NW Rural) *50.25483, 6.77946* **Campingpark Zur Dockweiler Mühle, Mühlenweg, 54552 Dockweiler [(06595) 961130; fax 961131; info@campingpark-dockweiler-muehle.de; www.campingpark-dockweiler-muehle.de]** Exit A1/A48 at junc 121 onto B421 dir Daun & Gerolstein. Site sp at ent to Dockweiler vill. Lge, terr, unshd; wc; chem disp; mv service pnt; shwrs €0.50; el pnts (16A) inc; Indtte; gas; shop 500m; rest high ssn; BBQ; playgrnd; covrd pool; 60% statics; dogs €2; sep car park; ccard acc; red long stay/snr citizens; quiet. ♦ € 23.50 2009*

DAUSENAU see Bad Ems *3B2*

DEGGENDORF *4G3* (1.5km W Rural) *48.83083, 12.94611* **Camping Donaustrandhaus, Egingerstrasse 42, 94469 Deggendorf [(0991) 4324; fax 4349; hirt.hj@t-online.de]** Exit A3 junc 110 onto A92. Exit junc 25 Deggendorf. At N end of bdge bear R sp Stadtmitte & foll sp 'Festplatz'. Sm, pt shd; wc; chem disp; shwrs €0.50; el pnts (16A) €1.50; Indtte; rest; snacks; htd pool 1km; sw 5km; fishing; boating; tennis adj; 60% statics; dogs €1.50; bus; poss cr; some noise fr barges & rlwy; CCI. "Gd NH; check earth on el pnts." 1 Mar-31 Oct. € 14.50 2009*

⊞ **DEGGENDORF** *4G3* (8km NW Rural) *48.91533, 12.8860* **Campingland Bernrieder Winkl, Grub 6, 94505 Bernried [tel/fax (09905) 8574; campingland.bernried@vr-web.de; www.camping-bernried.de]** Exit A3/E56 junc 108 or 109 & foll sp Bernried. Site at S ent to vill. Sm, hdg/mkd pitch, hdstg, terr, pt shd; htd wc; chem disp; mv service pnt; fam bthrm; serviced pitches; shwrs; el pnts (10A) metered + conn fee; Indtte (inc dryer); shop 1km; tradsmn; rest; snacks; bar; BBQ; playgrnd; tennis; 50% statics; dogs €2.50; adv bkg; quiet; red long stay. "Excel, well-organised, attractive site in National Park; gd walking, cycling, skiing; conv Passau, Regensburg; helpful owner." ♦ € 19.50 2011*

⊞ **DESSAU** *2F3* (5km E Rural) *51.81206, 12.30973* **Campingplatz Adria, Waldbad Adria 1, 06842 Dessau-Mildensee [(0340) 2304810; fax 2508774; info@cuct.de; www.cuct.de]** Exit A9 junc 10 Dessau-Ost onto B185 dir Oranienbaum, site sp almost immed on R; down track, on lakeside. Sm, pt shd; htd wc; chem disp; shwrs €1; el pnts (16A) €2.50; Indtte; snacks; bar; sand beach & lake sw 150m; 90% statics; no dogs; sep car park; little rd noise. "Excel touring base; vg." ♦ € 16.00 2009*

When we get home
I'm going to post
all these site report
forms to the Club
for next year's guide.
The deadline's mid September 2013

DETTELBACH *3D2* (5km E Rural) *49.80378, 10.21703* **Campingplatz Mainblick, Mainstrasse 2, 97359 Schwarzach-Schwarzenau [(09324) 605; fax 3674; info@camping-mainblick.de; www.camping-mainblick.de]** Exit A7/E45 junc 103 or A3/E43 junc 74 dir Dettelbach. Cross Rv Main bdge, site sp. Med, pt shd; wc; chem disp; mv service pnt; shwrs €0.50; el pnts (10A) €2.10 or metered; gas; Indtte; shop; rest; playgrnd; pool; boating; 30% statics; dogs €1.50; o'night area for m'vans; adv bkg; poss noisy; CCI. "Touring pitches on rvside; vg san facs." 1 Apr-31 Oct. € 15.00 2008*

DETTELBACH *3D2* (6km S Rural) *49.82603, 10.20083* **Camping Katzenkopf, Am See, 97334 Sommerach [(09381) 9215; fax 6028; www.camping-katzenkopf.de]** Fr A7/E45 junc 101 dir Volkach. Cross rv & foll sp S to Sommerach, site sp. Fr S exit A3/E43 junc 74 dir Volkach & foll sp. NB Town unsuitable c'vans; foll site sps bef town ent (beware - sat nav rte poss thro town). Lge, pt shd; wc; chem disp; mv service pnt; baby facs; shwrs inc; el pnts (16A) €2.50 or metered; gas; Indtte; shop; rest; snacks; playgrnd; lake sw & beach; fishing & boating; golf 10km; dogs €2; poss v cr; no adv bkg; quiet; ccard acc; red low ssn/CCI. "Beautiful surroundings; sm pitches; clean, modern facs; m'van o'night area outside site; barrier clsd 1300-1500; easy walk to wine-growing vill; gd rest; gd NH nr A3." ♦ 1 Apr-25 Oct. € 20.20 2009*

DIERHAGEN STRAND see Ribnitz Damgarten *2F1*

DIESSEN *4E4* (1.5km N Rural) *47.96528, 11.10308* **Camping St Alban, Seeweg Süd 85, 86911 St Alban [(08807) 7305; fax 1057; ivian.pavic@t-online.de]** Exit A96 junc 29 & foll rd S to Diessen; site on L 150m after Diessen town sp. Med, unshd; wc; chem disp; baby facs; shwrs inc; el pnts (16A) €4; Indtte; rest; lake sw; shgl beach; boating; windsurfing; games rm; 60% statics in sep area; dogs €1; train nr; Eng spkn; adv bkg; ccard acc. "Helpful staff; excel rest; gd facs; clsd 1200-1400." ♦ 15 Apr-15 Oct. € 24.00 2009*

DINGELSDORF see Konstanz *3D4*

⊞ **DINKELSBUHL** *3D3* (2km N Rural) *49.08194, 10.33416* **DCC Campingpark Romantische Strasse, An der Kobeltsmühle 12, 91550 Dinkelsbühl [(09851) 7817; fax 7848; campdinkelsbuehl@aol.com; www.campingpark-dinkelsbuehl.de]** On Rothenburg-Dinkelsbühl rd 25. Turn sharp L at camp sp immed bef rlwy x-ing (at Jet petrol stn) at N end of town. Site on R in 1km on lakeside. Or exit A7/E43 junc 112; turn R at T-junc. Site well sp. Lge, mkd pitch, terr, pt shd; wc; chem disp; mv service pnt; baby facs; shwrs inc; el pnts (16A) metered; gas; lndtte; sm shop; rest; snacks; bar; playgrnd; lake sw; boating; internet; 40% statics; dogs €1; phone; dog-washing facs; site clsd 1300-1500 & 2200-0800; m'van o'night area with el pnts; adv bkg; quiet; 10% red CCI. "Pitches poss long way fr san facs; gd, modern san facs; NH area with easy access; m'van o'night area; close to beautiful medieval town; quiet, peaceful & well-managed site; excel rest; gd cycle paths in area; gd" ♦ € 20.80 2011*

DOCKWEILER see Daun *3B2*

⊞ **DONAUESCHINGEN** *3C4* (2km SE Rural) *47.93754, 8.53422* **Riedsee-Camping, Am Riedsee 11, 78166 Donaueschingen [(0771) 5511; fax 15138; info@riedsee-camping.de; www.riedsee-camping.de]** Fr Donaueschingen on B31 to Pfohren vill, site sp. Lge, mkd pitch, pt shd; wc; chem disp; mv service pnt; shwrs inc; el pnts (16A) metered (check for rev pol); lndtte; shop (poss ltd opening); rest; snacks; bar; lake sw; boating; tennis; cycle hire; golf 9km; entmnt; 90% statics; dogs €3.50; Eng spkn; ccard acc; CCI. "Vg facs; clean, well-run site; sm pitches; site busy at w/end; office clsd Mon (poss low ssn only); gd value rest; conv Danube cycle way." ♦ € 19.55 2011*

⊞ **DONAUWORTH** *4E3* (5km SE Rural) *48.67660, 10.84100* **Donau-Lech Camping, Campingweg 1, 86698 Eggelstetten [tel/fax (09090) 4046; info@donau-lech-camping.de; www.donau-lech-camping.de]** Fr B2 take Eggelstetten exit & foll sp to vill. Site immed bef vill on R, foll 'International Camping' sp. Med, hdg/mkd pitch, hdstg, pt shd; htd wc; chem disp; mv service pnt; sauna; shwrs inc; el pnts (16A) inc (some rev pol); gas; lndtte; shop adj; tradsmn; rest 200m; snacks; bar; BBQ (gas/elec); playgrnd; lake sw; boat hire; golf, horseriding & fishing nr; archery; wellness studio; wifi; games/TV rm; 80% statics; dogs €2.20; phone; site clsd Nov; Eng spkn; adv bkg; v quiet; no ccard acc; CCI. "Superb, well-maintained, site but poss unkempt & boggy low ssn; ltd area for tourers; friendly, helpful staff & owner; facs clean but update req; owner sites vans; conv base for touring Danube & Romantic Rd; nr Danube cycle way." € 19.80 2010*

DORNSTETTEN HALLWANGEN see Freudenstadt *3C3*

⊞ **DORSEL** *3B2* (1km W Rural) *50.37708, 6.79768* **Camping Stahlhütte an der Ahr, 53533 Dorsel [(02693) 438; fax 511; www.campingplatz-stahlhuette.de]** Take B258 SE fr Blankenheim dir Nürburgring for approx 12km to Dorsel vill. Site on W side of rd. Med, hdg pitch, pt shd; wc; chem disp; serviced pitch; shwrs €0.75; el pnts (16A) metered; lndtte; shop; rest; snacks; bar; playgrnd; cycle hire; golf 10km; 60% statics; dogs €2.50; barrier clsd 1300-1500 & 2130-0730; ccard not acc; red CCI. € 20.00 2009*

⊞ **DORTMUND** *1B4* (10km SE Rural) *51.42078, 7.49514* **Camping Hohensyburg, Syburger Dorfstrasse 69, 44265 Dortmund-Hohensyburg [(0231) 774374; fax 7749554; info@camping-hohensyburg.de; www.camping-hohensyburg.de]** Exit Dortmund a'bahn ring at Dortmund Sud onto B54 sp Hohensyburg. Foll dual c'way S & strt at next traff lts. Turn L twd Hohensyburg, up hill to Y junc. Turn L (camping sp) & cont over hill to Gasthof. Turn R immed bef Gasthof down narr, steep rd (sharp bends) to site in 100m. Lge, pt sl, pt shd; wc; chem disp; mv service pnt; shwrs inc; el pnts (10A) €2.50 or metered; lndtte; shop; rest; playgrnd; boat launch adj; golf 3km; 80% statics; dogs €3; poss cr; adv bkg; quiet, but some aircraft noise; "Lovely, friendly site; narr lane at ent not suitable lge outfits; excel, clean san facs; gd." € 23.00 2011*

DRAGE see Geesthacht *1D2*

⊞ **DRANSFELD** *1D4* (1km S Rural) *51.49177, 9.76180* **Camping am Hohen Hagen, Hoher-Hagenstrasse 12, 37127 Dransfeld [(05502) 2147; fax 47239; camping.lesser@t-online.de; www.campingplatz-dransfeld.de]** Exit A7 junc 73 onto B3 to Dransfeld; foll sp to S of town & site. Lge, mkd pitch, terr, pt shd; htd wc; chem disp; mv service pnt; baby facs; sauna; shwrs inc; el pnts (16A) metered + conn fee; gas; lndtte (inc dryer); shop; rest; snacks; BBQ; cooking facs; playgrnd; htd pool; paddling pool; waterslide; tennis 100m; games area; wifi; entmnt; 95% statics; dogs €1.50; o'night area for m'vans; Eng spkn; quiet; ccard acc. "Beautiful area; gd san facs; diff after heavy rain; helpful staff." ♦ € 17.00 (CChq acc) 2009*

DRESDEN *2G4* (7km N Rural) *51.13833, 13.71861* **Campingplatz Oberer Waldteich - Dresden Nord, Sandweg, 01468 Volkersdorf [(035207) 81469; fax 81499; camping-dresden@t-online.de; www.camping-dresden.de]** Exit A4/E40 junc 81A (Dresden-Flughafen) onto S81 W - Wilschdorfer Landstrasse. In approx 600m turn R at x-rds dir Volkersdorf, then L to site on lakeside, sp. Med, hdg pitch, pt sl, shd; wc; chem disp; shwrs inc; el pnts (16A) €2.70 (poss rev pol); lndtte (inc dryer); shop; tradsmn; snacks; bar; BBQ; playgrnd; lake sw; 60% statics; dogs €1; adv bkg; quiet; CCI. "Gd; poss cr at w/end; touring pitch at lake v attractive; san facs v clean but poss a bit distant." 15 Apr-15 Oct. € 18.50 2011*

⊞ **DRESDEN** *2G4* (17km NE Rural) *51.12027, 13.98000* **Camping Lux-Oase, Arnsdorferstrasse 1, 01900 Kleinröhrsdorf [(035952) 56666; fax 56024; info@luxoase.de; www.luxoase.de]** Leave A4/E40 at junc 85 dir Radeberg. S to Leppersdorf, Kleinröhrsdorf. Sp on L end vill, well sp fr a'bahn. Lge, mkd pitch, pt shd; wc; chem disp; mv service pnt; fam bthrm; some serviced pitches; baby facs; sauna; shwrs; el pnts (10A) inc; gas; lndtte (inc dryer); shop; tradsmn; rest; snacks; bar; BBQ; playgrnd; covrd pool; beach adj; lake sw adj; fishing; horesriding; cycle hire; games area; wifi; entmnt; games/TV rm; 30% statics; dogs €3.50; twin-axles acc (rec check in adv); bus to city; trains 3km; poss v cr w/end; Eng spkn; quiet; site clsd 6-29 Feb; ccard acc; red low ssn/long stay/CCI. "Excel site by lake; vg san facs; new luxury toilet block in operation for 2011; v helpful staff; gd rest; site bus to Dresden Tues - 15 mins walk to regular bus; weekly bus to Prague fr site & other attractions in easy reach; excel." ♦ € 26.60 SBS - G14 2011*

⊞ **DRESDEN** *2G4* (4.5km S Urban) *51.01416, 13.7500* **Campingplatz Mockritz, Boderitzerstrasse 30, 01217 Dresden-Mockritz [(0351) 4715250; fax 4799227; camping-dresden@t-online.de; www.camping-dresden.de]** Exit E65/A17 junc 3 onto B170 N sp Dresden. In approx 1.5km turn E at traff lts sp Zschernitz, site sp. Med, mkd pitch, pt sl, pt shd; htd wc; chem disp; mv service pnt; baby facs; shwrs €0.50; el pnts (10A) €2.70; Indtte; shop; rest; snacks; bar; pool; wifi; bus; quiet; 5% statics; dogs €1.50; site clsd Christmas to end Jan; poss cr w/ends; Eng spkn; CCI. "V conv city cent & buses; office clsd 1300-1600; poss muddy after rain; helpful staff; excel." ♦ € 16.80 2011*

DROLSHAGEN see Olpe *1B4*

DULMEN *1B3* (3km S Rural) *51.78757, 7.27186* **Camping Tannenwiese, 217 Borkenbergstrasse, 48249 Dülmen [(02594) 991759; www.camping-tannenwiese.de]** Fr A43 take junc 7 Haltern/Lavesum dir Dülmen. In Hausdülmen foll sp Flugplatz Borkenberge to site in approx 3km. Med, hdg/mkd pitch, pt shd; wc; chem disp; shwrs €0.50; el pnts (10A) €2.10 or metered; gas; Indtte (inc dryer); shop & 3km; rest 2km; playgrnd; 80% statics; dogs free; CCI. "Tidy & tranquil; lge pitches; gd for families with sm children; away fr main rds; sep area for tourers." 1 Mar-31 Oct. € 13.20 2010*

DUSSELDORF *1B4* (6km N Urban) *51.30180, 6.72560* **Rheincamping Meerbusch (formerly Azur Campingplatz), Zur Rheinfähre 21, 40668 Meerbusch [(02150) 911817; fax 912289; info@rheincamping.com; www.rheincamping.com]** Exit A44 junc 28, turn R twd Strümp. Thro vill, turn L at sp for Kaiserswerth ferry, site on rv. Lge, pt shd; htd wc; chem disp; mv service pnt; baby facs; shwrs inc; el pnts (10A) €3; gas; Indtte; shop; rest adj; snacks; bar; BBQ; playgrnd; boat slipway; wifi; 40% statics; dogs €2.80; ferry/tram; site may flood when rv at v high level; poss cr; Eng spkn; adv bkg; some rv noise; CCI. "Pleasant, open site with gd views of rv; all facs up steps - not suitable disabled; ferry x-ring rv, then tram/train to Dusseldorf." 1 Apr-15 Oct. € 22.50 2010*

DUSSELDORF *1B4* (10km SE Rural) *51.19921, 6.88630* **Campingplatz Unterbacher See/Nord, Kleiner Torfbruch 31, 40627 Düsseldorf [(0211) 8992038; fax 8929132; service@unterbachersee.de; www.unterbachersee.de]** Fr A3 turn W onto A46 dir Düsseldorf/Neuss & exit junc 27 to Erkrath/Unterbach. Foll sp Unterbacher See Nordufer to harbour, site sp. Lge, pt shd; wc; chem disp; mv service pnt; sauna; shwrs; el pnts (6A) €2; gas; Indtte; shop 500m; rest 200m; snacks; gas BBQ only; playgrnd; boating & sw in adj lake; games area; cycle hire; 60% statics; no dogs; poss cr; adv bkg. "Gd NH; pitches close together & poss cr; gd san facs; gd rest & lake nrby." ♦ 3 Apr-24 Oct. € 23.50 2009*

⊞ **DUSSELDORF** *1B4* (1.5km NW Rural) *51.25225, 6.72813* **Campingplatz Lörick, Niederkasseler Deich 305, 40547 Düsseldorf-Lörick [tel/fax (0211) 591401; duesselcamp@web.de; www.duesselcamp.de]** Fr city take rd 52 to Monchengladbach & turn R at sp Düsseldorf-Oberkassel & Düsseldorf-Lörick. Turn L at traff lts, then strt on at next traff lts. In 1.5km turn R at traff lts (camping sp). Foll cobbled rd to site. Fr E, cross Theodor Heuss Brücke (bdge) & immed after bdge fork R then in 1.5km turn R at traff lts, then as above. Med, shd; wc; snacks; shwrs €1; el pnts (4A) €3; Indtte; shop 2km; 2 pools & lake adj; bus to city nr; poss cr; 10% statics; dogs €3; noise fr adj airport; CCI. "Conv NH; ltd facs low ssn." € 16.00 2011*

EBERBACH *3C2* (9km SW Rural) *49.45241, 8.87816* **Odenwald Camping Park, Langenthalerstrasse 80, 69434 Hirschhorn-am-Neckar [(06272) 809; fax 3658; odenwald-camping-park@t-online.de; www.odenwald-camping-park.de]** Fr Eberbach or Neckargemünd leave B37/45 for Hirschorn; foll Int'l Camping sps at Hirschhorn Cent (not Hirschhorn Ost); site on L in 2km NW of town on Heddesbach rd L3105. Med, mkd pitch, pt shd; wc; chem disp; mv service pnt; sauna; shwrs inc; el pnts (6A) €2.50 or metered; gas; Indtte; shop; rest; bar; playgrnd; htd pool; tennis; cycle hire; cab TV; 50% statics; dogs €2.50; quiet; ccard not acc; CCI. "Friendly, helpful staff; sep area for 20 tourers." ♦ 1 Apr-4 Oct. € 18.50 2009*

EBERBACH *3C2* (W Urban) *49.46068, 8.98241* **Campingpark Eberbach, Alte Pleutersbacherstrasse 8, 69412 Eberbach [(06271) 1071; fax 942712; info@campingpark-eberbach.de; www.campingpark-eberbach.de]** Fr Heidelberg-Heilbronn rd B37, ent Eberbach & cross Rv Neckar, turn R at end of bdge. Site 100m on rv bank, sp. Med, pt sl, pt shd; htd wc; chem disp; shwrs €0.50; el pnts (6A) €2.50; Indtte (inc dryer); shops adj; rest; playgrnd; htd pools adj; 10% statics; dogs €2; poss cr w/end; adv bkg; some rd & rlwy noise at night; CCI. "Rv cruises fr opp bank; ferry adj; annual fair last week Aug; excel cycling; NB - cash only." 1 Apr-31 Oct. € 16.70 2011*

ECHTERNACHERBRUCK *3A2* (500m E Rural) *49.81240, 6.43160* **Camping Freibad Echternacherbrück, Mindenerstrasse 18, 54668 Echternacherbrück [(06525) 340; fax 93155; info@echternacherbrueck.de; www.echternacherbrueck.de]** Fr Bitburg on B257/E29 site is at Lux'burg border, sp. Fr Trier take A64 dir Luxembourg; exit junc 15 onto N10 to Echternacherbrück; cross bdg dir Bitburg, then 1st L sp camping & foll sp. Lge, pt shd; htd wc; chem disp; mv service pnt; private bthrms avail; baby facs; shwrs inc; el pnts (10A) €2.40 + conn fee; Indtte (inc dryer); shop 100m; rest 100m; snacks; bar; playgrnd; 2 htd pools 400m (1 covrd); paddling pool; waterslide; rv sw & sandy beach adj; tennis 400m; boat & cycle hire; horseriding 4km; games area; wifi; entmnt; TV rm; 30% statics; dogs €2.40; o'night m'van area; Eng spkn; quiet; CCI. "Poss flooding in v wet weather; excel facs; gd, well-organised site; gd bus service to Luxembourg and Trier." ♦ 1 Apr-15 Oct. € 24.00 (CChq acc) 2011*

EDIGER ELLER see Cochem *3B2*

EGGELSTETTEN see Donauwörth *4E3*

GERMANY

⊞ **EGING AM SEE** *4G3* (1km NE Rural) *48.72135, 13.26540* **Bavaria Kur-Sport-Campingpark, Grafenauerstrasse 31, 94535 Eging [(08544) 8089; fax 7964; info@bavaria-camping.de; www.bavaria-camping.de]** Exit A3 junc 113 at Garham dir Eging, site sp in 4.5km twd Thurmansbang. Med, hdg/mkd pitch, some hdstg, pt sl, terr, pt shd; htd wc; chem disp; mv service pnt; baby facs; shwrs inc; el pnts (16A) €2.50; Indtte (inc dryer); shop; rest; bar; htd pool 300m; lake sw; fishing; tennis nr; games area; cycle hire; golf 10km; wifi; TV rm; 30% statics; dogs €2.60; Eng spkn; quiet; ccard acc; red low ssn/CCI. "Lovely site nr Bavarian National Park; gd walking/cycling fr site; Wild West theme town, Pullman City, 2.5km; vg NH & longer." ♦ € 18.50 (CChq acc) 2011*

⊞ **EHRENBERG** *3D1* (500m N Rural) *50.50653, 10.01065* **Rhön Camping Park, An der Ulster 1, 36115 Ehrenberg-Wüstensachsen [(06683) 1268; fax 1269; info@rhoen-camping-park.de; www.rhoen-camping-park.de]** Exit A7 junc 93 at Fulda onto B27 dir Bad Brückenau. In Döllbach turn L to Gersfeld & Ehrenberg. Site on R immed bef vill, well sp. Med, mkd pitch, pt shd; htd wc; chem disp; mv service pnt; baby facs;100% serviced pitches; sauna; shwrs €0.50; el pnts (16A) metered; Indtte; shop; tradsmn; rest 300m; BBQ; playgrnd; sm water theme park; solarium; gym; skilift 5km; gliding 5km; TV; 25% statics; dogs €2.50; phone; adv bkg; quiet; CCI. "Gd walking; excel." ♦ € 21.00 2009*

EHRENFRIEDERSDORF see Annaberg Buchholz *4G1*

⊞ **EISENACH** *1D4* (10km S Rural) *50.90888, 10.29916* **Campingplatz Eisenach am Altenberger See, 99819 Wilhelmsthal [(03691) 215637; fax 215607; campingpark-eisenach@t-online.de; www.campingpark-eisenach.de]** Leave E40/A4 at junc 39 Eisenach Ost onto B19 sp Meiningen; site 2km S of Wilhelmsthal, sp. Med, pt sl, pt hdstg, pt shd; wc; chem disp; mv service pnt; serviced pitches; sauna; shwrs €0.80; el pnts (16A) inc; Indtte; shop; tradsmn; rest; snacks; bar; sm playgrnd; lake adj; boating; 80% statics; dogs €2; bus to Eisenach nr; clsd 1300-1500; site clsd Nov; poss cr; quiet; ccard acc; CCI. "Helpful staff; scruffy statics area; conv Wartburg & Thuringer Wald; Bach & Luther houses in Eisenach." € 22.00 2011*

ELBINGERODE see Wernigerode *2E3*

ELLWANGEN (JAGST) *3D3* (4km E Rural) *48.9750, 10.25222* **Campingplatz am Sonnenbach, Beersbach 6, 73479 Ellwangen [(07964) 1232; fax 300993; g-b.veile@t-online.de; www.sonnenbach-camping.de]** Leave A7/E43 junc 113 (Ellwangen) dir Nördlingen. Turn E to Röhlingen then L to Pfalheim. In Pfalheim turn L sp Beersbach Stausee; site 1km on L at bottom of hill. Med, terr, unshd; htd wc; chem disp; mv service pnt; baby facs; shwrs inc; el pnts (16A) metered + conn fee; Indtte; shop & 1km; rest 800m; snacks; bar; playgrnd; lake sw adj; 75% statics; dogs €1; poss cr; quiet; red CCI. "Helpful, friendly staff; excel rest." 1 Apr-15 Oct. € 12.80 2008*

ENGEHAUSEN *1D3* (Rural) *52.68916, 9.69774* **Camping Aller-Leine-Tal, Marschweg 1, 29690 Engehausen [(05071) 511549; camping@camping-aller-leine-tal.de; www.camping-aller-leine.tal.de]** Exit A7/E45 at 'Rasthof Allertal', keep R & at x-rds turn L twd Celle. Site in 800m. Med, mkd pitch, pt shd; htd wc; chem disp; mv service pnt; baby facs; shwrs inc; el pnts (10A) €3; Indtte (inc dryer); supmkt 7km; tradsmn; rest 4km; snacks; bar; playgrnd; rv sw & fishing; games area; games rm; wifi; TV rm; 20% statics; dogs €2.50; Quickstop o'night facs; adv bkg; quiet. "Peaceful site conv m'way." 1 Mar-31 Oct. € 16.50 2009*

⊞ **ENGEN** *3C4* (2km NW Urban) *47.86283, 8.7646* **Camping Sonnental, Im Doggenhardt 1, 78234 Engen [(07733) 7529; fax 2666; info@camping-sonnental.de; www.camping-sonnental.de]** Exit A81/E41 junc 39 twd Engen. Do not go into 'Altstadt' (old town) but foll by-pass rd. At T-junc turn L & foll sp to 'Schwimmbad' & site. Med, mkd pitch, some hdstg, sl, pt shd; wc; chem disp; mv service pnt; serviced pitches; shwrs inc; el pnts (10-16A) metered + conn fee or €2.50; gas; Indtte; shop 1.5km; rest; bar; playgrnd; pool 200m; golf 9km; 50% statics; dogs €2; Eng spkn; red long stay/CCI. "Vg; all facs excel." ♦ € 15.00 2008*

ENZKLOSTERLE see Bad Wildbad im Schwarzwald *3C3*

EPPSTEIN NIEDERJOSBACH see Frankfurt am Main *3C2*

ERFTSTADT LIBLAR see Brühl *1B4*

⊞ **ERKNER** *2G3* (3km S Rural) *52.38530, 13.78160* **Camping Jägerbude, Jägerbude 3, 15537 Erkner [(03362) 888084; fax 888094; post@spreecamping.de; www.spreecamping.de]** A10/E55 E of Berlin exit junc 7 Freienbrink to Erkner. Site sp on W side of a'bahn. Lge, hdg/mkd pitch, pt shd; htd wc; chem disp; mv service pnt; sauna; shwrs €0.50; el pnts (16A) €3 or metered; Indtte (inc dryer); shop; tradsmn; rest; BBQ; cooking facs; playgrnd; rv sw; games rm; wifi; few statics; dogs €2; poss cr; CCI. "Conv Berlin; some pitches lake view; gd NH." ♦ € 18.00 (CChq acc) 2010*

ERLANGEN *4E2* (7km NW Rural) *49.63194, 10.9425* **Camping Rangau, Campingstrasse 44, 91056 Erlangen-Dechsendorf [(09135) 8866; fax 724743; infos@camping-rangau.de; www.camping-rangau.de]** Fr A3/E45 exit junc 81 & foll camp sp. At 1st traff lts turn L, strt on at next traff lts, then L at next traff lts, site sp. Med, pt shd; htd wc; shwrs inc; chem disp; el pnts (6A) €2.50 (long lead poss req); Indtte; shop 2km; rest; snacks; playgrnd; pool; lake sw; boat hire; dogs €2.50; gates closed 1300-1500 & 2200 hrs; poss cr; Eng spkn; adv bkg; quiet; ccard acc; red long stay/CCI. "Gd site, espec for families; clean facs; welcoming & well-run; some sm pitches; popular NH - overflow onto adj sports field; vg NH." ♦ 1 Apr-30 Sep. € 16.50 2010*

⊞ **ERNST** *3B2* (800m W Rural) *50.1425, 7.23194* **Wohnmobil Parkplatz, Weingartenstrasse 97, 56814 Ernst [(02671) 980310; fax 980312; info@mosella-schinkenstube.de; www.mosella-schinkenstube.de]** Site on o'skts of vill behind winery, sp fr B49. Sm, mkd pitch, hdstg, pt sl, unshd; el pnts inc; shop, rest, snacks, bar adj; bus; poss cr; no adv bkg; quiet. "Gd NH for m'vans only; drinking water & rubbish points; pay at nrby butchers (Metzgerei-Gaststatte). € 8.00 2011*

⊞ **ESCHWEGE** *1D4* (1km NE Rural) *51.19166, 10.06861* **Knaus Campingpark Eschwege, Am Werratalsee 2, 37269 Eschwege [(05651) 338883; fax 338884; eschwege@knauscamp.de; www.knauscamp.de]** Fr B249 foll sp Werratalsee, site sp. Med, pt shd; wc; chem disp; mv service pnt; serviced pitches; baby facs; fam bthrm; shwrs inc; el pnts (16A) €2.40; gas; Indtte; supmkt 1km; rest 1km; snacks; bar; playgrnd; lake sw; games area; wifi; TV rm; 40% statics; dogs €3; adv bkg; quiet; red snr citizens. € 21.00 2008*

⊞ **ESSEN** *1B4* (8km S Urban) *51.38444, 6.99388* **DCC Campingpark Stadtcamping, Im Löwental 67, 45239 Essen-Werden [(0201) 492978; fax 8496132; Stadtcamping-Essen@t-online.de; www.dcc-stadtcamping-essen-werden.de]** Exit A52 junc 28 onto B224 S dir Solingen. Turn R bef bdge over Rv Ruhr at traff lts & immed sharp R into Löwental, site sp. Med, mkd pitch, hdstg, pt shd; wc; chem disp; mv service pnt; shwrs; el pnts (16A) metered; gas; Indtte; shop; rest; bar; playgrnd; games area; games rm; 95% statics; no dogs; phone; poss cr; Eng spkn; adv bkg; site clsd 1300-1500 & 2130-0700; car park adj; quiet; no ccard acc. "Rv trips; poss itinerant workers; gd." € 16.40 2009*

ETTENHEIM see Lahr (Schwarzwald) *3B3*

⊞ **ETTLINGEN** *3C3* (5km SE Rural) *48.91465, 8.45567* **Campingplatz Albgau, Kochmühle 1, 76337 Waldbronn-Neurod [tel/fax (07243) 61849; kiosk-albgau@t-online.de; www.campingplatz-albgau.de]** Exit A8/E52 at junc 42 & foll sp Bad Herrenalb. When rlwy on R, site sp in 4km on R. Lge, pt shd; wc; own san rec; chem disp; shwrs €0.50; el pnts (16A) €2.30; gas; Indtte (inc dryer); shop; snacks; bar; playgrnd; 80% statics; dogs €3; gates locked 1300-1500 & 2200-0700; quiet but poss noisy at w/end & fr rlwy; ccard not acc. "On edge of Black Forest; footpath walks in vicinity; adj field for NH; modern san facs; helpful owner." ♦ € 18.40 2010*

⊞ **FASSBERG** *1D2* (6km E Rural) *52.87593, 10.22718* **Ferienpark Heidesee (Part Naturist), Lüneburger-Heidesee, 29328 Fassberg-Oberohe [(05827) 970546; fax 970547; heidesee@ferienpark.de; www.campingheidesee.com]** Leave A7/E45 at exit 44 onto B71. Turn S to Müden, then dir Unterlüss. Foll site sp. V lge, terr, pt shd; htd wc; chem disp; mv service pnt; sauna; private bthrms avail; baby facs; shwrs inc; el pnts (10A) €3; Indtte (inc dryer); gas; shop; tradsmn; rest; snacks; playgrnd; pool 250m; lake sw; fishing; tennis; cycle hire; horseriding; games rm; entmnt; 65% statics; dogs €2; ccard acc; CCI. "Naturist camping in sep area." ♦ € 18.50 (CChq acc) 2010*

⊞ **FELDBERG** *2G2* (2km NE Rural) *53.34548, 13.45626* **Camping am Bauernhof, Hof Eichholz 1-8, 17258 Feldberg [(039831) 21084; fax 21534; scholverberg@feldberg.de; www.campingplatz-am-bauernhof.de]** Fr B198 at Möllenbeck turn dir Feldburg, thro Feldburg dir Prenzlau, site sp. Med, mkd pitch, pt sl, unshd; wc; chem disp; shwrs inc; el pnts (16A) metered + conn fee; Indtte; shop; tradsmn; rest 800m; snacks; playgrnd; lake sw; fishing; 30% statics; dogs €3; quiet; CCI. "Well-situated, vg site among lakes; many cycle paths in area." ♦ € 18.00 2011*

FERCH *2F3* (3km N Rural) *52.33122, 12.93105* **Campingplatz Neue Scheune, Fercherstrasse 55, Schwielowsee, 14548 Ferch [(033209) 70957; fax 70958; Camping-Neue-Scheune-Ferch@t-online.de; www.camping-schwielowsee.de]** Exit A10/E55 Berlin ring rd junc 18 twd Ferch. In Ferch foll sp Petzow & Neue Scheune. Site on L after stretch of rough cobbles. Sm, pt shd; htd wc; chem disp; shwrs; el pnts (13A) €2.50; shop 2km; BBQ (gas only); playgrnd; games area; some statics; dogs €1.10; poss cr; Eng spkn; adv bkg; quiet; CCI. "Site on edge woodland on W side Schwielowsee; helpful staff; conv Potsdam." Easter-31 Oct. € 14.90 2009*

⊞ **FICHTELBERG** *4F2* (2.5km N Rural) *50.01673, 11.85525* **Kur-Camping Fichtelsee, Fichtelseestrasse 30, 95686 Fichtelberg [(09272) 801; fax 909045; info@camping-fichtelsee.de; www.camping-fichtelsee.de]** Exit junc 39 fr A9/E51. Foll B303 twd Marktredwitz. After Bischofsgrün take R turn sp Fichtelberg, site on L in 1km. Lge, mkd pitch, hdstg, terr, pt sl, pt shd; wc (some cont); chem disp; mv service pnt; shwrs inc; el pnts (16A) metered + conn fee (poss rev pol); Indtte; shop 2km; tradsmn; rest 200m; playgrnd; pool 800m; entmnt; internet; TV; 20% statics; dogs €2.50; dog-washing facs; phone; site clsd 7 Nov-15 Dec; Eng spkn; ccard acc; CCI. "Gd cent for walking in pine forests round lake & wintersports; peaceful site; barrier clsd 1230-1430; excel san facs." ♦ € 22.00 2009*

⊞ **FINSTERAU** *4G3* (1km N Rural) *48.94091, 13.57180* **Camping Nationalpark-Ost, Buchwaldstrasse 52, 94151 Finsterau [(08557) 768; fax 1062; berghof-frank@berghof-frank.de; www.camping-nationalpark-ost.de]** Fr B12 turn N dir Mauth. Cont to Finsterau & site 1km adj parking for National Park. Sm, pt shd; wc; chem disp; shwrs €1; el pnts (6-16A) metered + conn fee or €2.50; gas; Indtte (inc dryer); shop 1km; wifi; TV rm; dogs €2; quiet; red CCI. "Gd walking & mountain biking; site in beautiful Bavarian forest." ♦ € 17.60 2009*

FLENSBURG *1D1* (5km S Rural) *54.72600, 9.43900* **Camping Sankelmark, Am Krug 7, 24988 Sankelmark-Bilschau [(04630) 457]** Exit A7/E45 junc 3 onto B200 sp Flensburg. In 2km turn R sp Schleswig. At T-junc with B76 turn R dir Bilschau, site sp on R. Sm, pt sl, shd; wc; shwrs €1; el pnts inc; shop 5km; Eng spkn; some rd noise; CCI. "Pretty, secluded CL-type site; warm welcome; ltd facs but clean." 1 May-3 Sep. € 14.00 2008*

⊞ **FLOSSENBURG** *4F2* (1.5km N Rural) *49.74457, 12.34414* **Camping Gaisweiher, Gaisweiher 1, 92696 Flossenbürg [(09603) 644; fax 914666; kontakt@gaisweiher-camping.de; www.campingauer-hellas.de]** Exit A93 to Neustadt. Take minor rd E thro Floss to Flossenbürg, site sp. Lge, pt sl, pt shd; wc; shwrs €0.50; chem disp; mv service pnt; el pnts (16A) metered + conn fee; Indtte; shop; rest; snacks; bar; playgrnd; sw adj; cycle hire; entmnt high ssn; TV rm; 50% statics; dogs €2; quiet; CCI. "Recep 0930-1130, site self other times; barrier clsd 1300-1500; facs old & dark; gd." € 15.50 2009*

⊞ **FRANKFURT AM MAIN** *3C2* (11km W Rural) *50.1475, 8.36166* **Taunuscamp Hubertushof, Bezirkstrasse 2, 65817 Eppstein-Niederjosbach [(06198) 7000; fax 7002; info@taunuscamp.de; www.taunuscamp.de]** Fr A3/E35 exit junc 46 dir Niedernhausen B455 & foll sp for Eppstein (Niederjosbach). Fr B455 take minor rd K792 x-ing rlwy bef vill, foll rd & take 1st R into Bezierkstrasse, site on L in 1km. Med, mkd pitch, terr, pt shd; htd wc; chem disp; mv service pnt; 50% serviced pitch; shwrs inc; el pnts (16A) €2 or metered; gas; Indtte; shop & 500m; rest 1km; snacks; playgrnd; pool nr; 60% statics; dogs free; barrier closes 1300-1500; poss cr; Eng spkn; adv bkg; quiet; ccard acc; red long stay/CCI. "Friendly, pleasant site; steep terr diff for underpowered or long twin-axle o'fits & diff disabled; some sm pitches; excursions arranged." ♦ € 21.00 2009*

⊞ **FRANKFURT AM MAIN** *3C2* (5km NW Urban) *50.16373, 8.65055* **City-Camp Frankfurt, Am der Sandelmühle 35b, 60439 Frankfurt-Heddernheim [(069) 570332; info@city-camp-frankfurt.de; www.city-camp-frankfurt.de]** Exit A661 junc 7 dir Heddernheim, site in park, sp. Med, hdstg, pt shd; wc; chem disp; mv service pnt; shwrs €1.10; el pnts (10A) €3; gas; Indtte; shop 800m; tradsmn; snacks 800m; rest 500m; 30% statics; dogs €2.50; poss cr; Eng spkn; poss noisy; CCI. "Conv for city via adj U-Bahn (20 min to cent); clean but has seen better days; v busy when trade fair on." ♦ € 22.50 2010*

⊞ **FREIBURG IM BREISGAU** *3B4* (12km NE Rural) *48.02310, 8.03473* **Camping Steingrubenhof, Haldenweg 3, 79271 St Peter [(07660) 210; fax 1604; info@camping-steingrubenhof.de; www.camping-steingrubenhof.de]** Exit A5 junc 61 onto B294. Turn R sp St Peter. Steep hill to site on L at top of hill. Or fr B31 dir Donaueschingen, after 4km outside Freiburg turn N sp St Peter; by-pass vill on main rd, turn L under bdge 1st R. Fr other dir by-pass St Peter heading for Glottertal; site on R 200m after rd bdge on by-pass. Med, hdg/mkd pitch, hdstg, pt terr, unshd; wc; chem disp; mv service pnt; serviced pitches; shwrs €0.50; el pnts (16A) metered + conn fee; Indtte (inc dryer); shop & 1km; rest & bar adj; BBQ; playgrnd; wifi; 70% statics; dogs €2; phone; Eng spkn; adv bkg; quiet; ccard acc; 10% red long stay; CCI. "Peaceful site in heart of Black Forest; wonderful location; pleasant staff; immac facs; gate clsd 1200-1400 & 2200-0800; v diff to manoeuvre twin-axle vans onto pitches as narr access paths; pitches are sm & few for tourers; great site." ♦ € 16.00 2011*

⊞ **FREIBURG IM BREISGAU** *3B4* (1km E Rural) *47.99250, 7.87330* **Camping Hirzberg, Kartäuserstrasse 99, 79104 Freiburg-im-Breisgau [(0761) 35054; fax 289212; hirzburg@freiburg-camping.de; www.freiburg-camping.de]** Exit A5 at Freiburg-Mitte & foll B31 past town cent sp Freiburg, Titisee. Foll camping sp twd Freiburg-Ebnet, nr rocky slopes on R. Then approx 2.5km on narr, winding rd. Site on R just after start of blocks of flats on L. Med, pt sl, terr, pt shd; htd wc; chem disp; mv service pnt; shwrs inc; el pnts (10A) €2.50; gas; Indtte; sm shop; tradsmn; rest; snacks; bar; BBQ; playgrnd; pool 500m; cycle hire; internet; 40% statics; dogs €1; bus 300m/tram; clsd 1300-1500; poss v cr; Eng spkn; adv bkg; quiet; CCI. "Pleasant, helpful owner; site clsd 2000 - ltd outside parking; gd cycle path & easy walk to town; busy in high ssn; excel san facs; gd value rest." € 22.50 2011*

FREIBURG IM BREISGAU *3B4* (2.5km E Urban) *47.98095, 7.86666* **Camping Möslepark, Waldseestrasse 77, 79117 Freiburg-im-Breisgau [(0761) 7679333; fax 7679336; information@camping-freiburg.com; www.camping-freiburg.com]** Fr A5 exit junc 62 onto B31 & foll sp Freiburg strt thro city sp Donauschingen. Bef ent to tunnel take L lane & foll site sp (do not go thro tunnel). Site nr Möselpark Sports Stadium. Med, pt sl, shd; wc; chem disp; mv service pnt; sauna; shwrs inc; el pnts (16A) €2.50; Indtte (inc dryer); shop 100m; supmkts 500m; rest adj; playgrnd; htd, covrd pool nr; tennis 1km; cycle hire; wifi; dogs €1.90; tram to city nr; o'night m'van area; Eng spkn; no adv bkg; noise fr stadium adj; ccard acc; red CCI. "Conv Freiburg & Black Forest (footpath adj); wooded site easily reached fr a'bahn; clsd 1200-1430 & 2200-0800 - waiting area in front of site; excel, modern san facs; helpful staff; public transport tickets fr recep; parking nr tram stop." 26 Mar-24 Oct. € 20.10 2010*

⊞ **FREIBURG IM BREISGAU** *3B4* (7km SE Rural) *47.96015, 7.95001* **Camping Kirchzarten, Dietenbacherstrasse 17, 79199 Kirchzarten [(07661) 9040910; fax 61624; info@camping-kirchzarten.de; www.camping-kirchzarten.de]** Sp fr Freiburg-Titisee rd 31; into Kirchzarten; site sp fr town cent. Lge, mkd pitch, pt shd; htd wc; chem disp; mv service pnt; serviced pitches; baby facs; fam bthrm; shwrs inc; el pnts (16A) €1.30 or metered; Indtte; shops 500m; rest adj; snacks; bar; BBQ; playgrnd; 3 htd pools adj; tennis adj; wintersports area; entmnt; 20% statics; dogs €1.50 (not acc Jul/Aug); train 500m; office clsd 1300-1430; Quickstop o'night area; poss cr; Eng spkn; adv bkg (ess Jul/Aug); quiet; ccard acc; red long stay/red low ssn; CCI. "Gd size pitches; choose pitch then register at office; spacious, well-kept site; excel san facs; gd rest; site fees inc free bus & train travel in Black Forest region; helpful staff." ♦ € 26.60 2008*

⊞ **FREIBURG IM BREISGAU** *3B4* (8km NW Rural) *48.06390, 7.82263* **Breisgau Camping am Silbersee, Seestrasse 20, 79108 Freiburg-Hochdorf [tel/fax (07665) 2346]** Fr E35/A5 take Freiburg Nord exit 61, keep to R lane at traff lts & foll camp sp under 2nd bdge. Site on L; awkward app rd. Med, mkd pitch, unshd; wc; chem disp; mv service pnt; shwrs €0.50; el pnts (10A) €1.50; Indtte; shop; tradsmn; rest; snacks; bar; playgrnd; 20% statics; quiet; CCI. € 15.50 2008*

FREIBURG IM BREISGAU *3B4* (10km NW Rural) *48.06350, 7.81421* **Camping Tunisee, Seestrasse, 79108 Freiburg-Hochdorf [(07665) 2249; fax 95134; info@tunisee.de; www.tunisee.de]** Fr E35/A5 exit junc 61, keep to R lane at traff lts & foll camp sp under 2nd bdge. Site on L; awkward app rd. Lge, mkd pitch, pt shd; serviced pitches; wc; chem disp; mv service pnt; shwrs €0.55; el pnts (16A) €2 or metered; lndtte; shop; rest; snacks; bar; playgrnd; lake sw adj; 75% statics; dogs €1; Eng spkn; some rd noise; red long stay; ccard acc; CCI. "Pleasant site; conv Freiburg & Black Forest; gd san facs but quite far fr touring pitches; recep clsd 1300-1500." ♦ 1 Apr-31 Oct. € 17.20 2010*

⊞ **FREUDENSTADT** *3C3* (5km E Rural) *48.48011, 8.5005* **Höhencamping Königskanzel, Freizeitweg 1, 72280 Dornstetten-Hallwangen [(07443) 6730; fax 4574; info@camping-koenigskanzel.de; www.camping-koenigskanzel.de]** Fr Freudenstadt head E on rte 28 foll sp Stuttgart for 7km. Camping sp on R, sharp R turn foll sp, sharp L on narr, winding track to site in 200m. Fr Nagold on R28, 7km fr Freudenstadt fork L; sp as bef. NB: 1st sharp R turn is v sharp - take care. Med, some hdg pitch, pt sl, terr, pt shd; wc; chem disp; mv service pnt; serviced pitch; sauna; shwrs inc; el pnts (10A) metered; gas; lndtte (inc dryer); shop; tradsmn; sm rest; snacks; bar; BBQ; playgrnd; htd pool; cycle hire; golf 7km; skilift 7km; wifi; 60% statics sep area; dogs €2; phone; site clsd 3 Nov-15 Dec; Eng spkn; adv bkg (bkg fee); quiet; ccard not acc; red long stay/CCI. "Pleasant owners; friendly welcome; excel shwr facs, inc for dogs; well run family site; hill top location with gd views of Black Forest; recep clsd 1300-1400; excel value rest." ♦ € 21.30 2011*

FREUDENSTADT *3C3* (3km W Rural) *48.45840, 8.37255* **Camping Langenwald, Strassburgerstrasse 167, 72250 Freudenstadt-Langenwald [(07441) 2862; fax 2893; info@camping-langenwald.de; www.camping-langenwald.de]** Foll sp fr town on B28 dir Strassburg. Med, terr, pt shd; htd wc; chem disp; mv service pnt; fam bthrm; serviced pitch; shwrs inc; el pnts (16A) metered; gas; lndtte; shop; tradsmn; rest; snacks; playgrnd; htd pool; cycle hire; golf 4km; 10% statics; dogs €2; Eng spkn; noisy nr rd; ccard acc (not VISA); red long stay/low ssn/CCI. "Gd, clean san facs; woodland walks fr site; gd rest; friendly owners." ♦ 1 Apr-31 Oct. € 21.00 2009*

FRICKENHAUSEN AM MAIN *3D2* (1km W Rural) *49.66916, 10.07444* **Knaus Campingpark Frickenhausen, Ochsenfurterstrasse 49, 97252 Frickenhausen-am-Main [(09331) 3171; fax 5784; frickenhausen@knauscamp.de; www.knauscamp.de]** Turn off B13 at N end of bridge over Rv Main in Ochsenfurt & foll camping sp. Lge, hdg/mkd pitch, pt shd; wc; serviced pitches; chem disp; mv service pnt; baby facs; shwrs inc; el pnts (16A) €2.40 or metered; gas; lndtte; shop; rest high ssn; bar; playgrnd; htd pool; cycle hire; TV; 40% statics; dogs €3; site clsd 1300-1500; Eng spkn; adv bkg; quiet; red long stay/snr citizens. "Vg, well-managed site on rv island; excel facs; located on Romantischestrasse with many medieval vills." 31 Mar-5 Nov. € 22.50 2008*

FRIEDRICHSHAFEN *3D4* (1km SE Rural) *47.6498, 9.49683* **Campingplatz CAP-Rotach, Grenzösch 3, 88046 Friedrichshafen-Fischbach [(07541) 73421; fax 376174; info@cap-rotach.de; www.cap-rotach.de]** Fr Friedrichshafen take B31 twd Lindau; in 1km turn R into site; sp. Med, pt shd; htd wc; chem disp; mv service pnt; shwrs inc; el pnts (10A) €2; lndtte; supmkt 1km; tradsmn; rest; snacks; bar; lake beach adj; internet; 40% statics; dogs €2.50; m'van o'ight area outside site; clsd 1200-1430; poss cr; Eng spkn; no adv bkg; ccard acc; CCI. "Well-run site adj to Lake Constance; helpful recep; excel facs inc for disabled; gd rest; lake ferries 15 mins walk; Lindau, beautiful town on lake 20km." ♦ Easter-31 Oct. € 21.50 2008*

FRIEDRICHSHAFEN *3D4* (6km W Rural) *47.66896, 9.40253* **Camping Fischbach, Grenzösch 3, 88048 Friedrichschafen-Fischbach [(07541) 42059; fax 44599; info@camping-fischbach.de; www.camping-fischbach.de]** Take B31 fr Friedrichshafen to Meersburg. Site sp on L. Easy access off busy rd. Med, mkd pitch, some hdstg, pt shd; wc; chem disp; mv service pnt; shwrs €0.50; el pnts (10-16A) €2 (poss rev pol); lndtte (inc dryer); shop; rest; snacks; bar; lake sw adj; sand beach adj; 40% statics; no dogs; phone; poss v cr; Eng spkn; no adv bkg; rd noise; CCI. "Tranquil, relaxing site; some lake view pitches - worth the extra; excel, clean, modern san facs; ferries to Konstanz nrby; beautiful medieval towns nr." 1 Apr-10 Oct. € 19.60 2010*

FRIEDRICHSHAFEN *3D4* (6km NW Rural) *47.66583, 9.37694* **Campingplatz Schloss Helmsdorf, Friedrichshafenerstrasse, 88090 Immenstaad-am-Bodensee [(07545) 6252; fax 3956; campingplatz@schloss-helmsdorf.org; www.schloss-helmsdorf.org]** Site sp fr B31 bet Meersburg & Friedrichshafen at Immenstaad. Lge, pt sl, pt shd; htd wc; chem disp; mv service pnt; shwrs €0.50; el pnts (6A) €2; lndtte; shop; rest; snacks; lake beach & sw; boating; windsurfing; 80% statics; no dogs high ssn; poss cr; quiet. "Vg, well-run site; gd position on lakeside; gd, clean san facs; helpful owners; sh walk to lake ferries." ♦ 1 Apr-15 Oct. € 20.00 2009*

FURSTENBERG *2F2* (1km W Rural) *53.18680, 13.13111* **Campingplatz am Röblinsee, Röblinsee Nord 1, 16798 Fürstenberg [(033093) 38278; fax 38613]** Fr S on E251/B96, L turn 500m N of Fürstenburg to N side of lake, site sp. Med, pt shd; wc; chem disp; mv service pnt; shwrs inc; el pnts (16A) €1.50 or metered; lndtte; shop 800m; tradsmn; rest 600m; snacks; lake sw; dogs €1; sep car park high ssn; CCI. "Conv for German Lake District & NH to Poland/Baltic Coast." 1 Apr-31 Oct. € 16.00 2009*

FURTH *3C2* (1km E Rural) *49.65944, 8.78388* **Campingplatz Tiefertswinkel, Im Tiefertswinkel 20, 64658 Fürth [(06253) 5804; fax 3717; info@camping-fuerth.de; www.camping-fuerth.de]** Exit A5 junc 31 at Heppenheim onto B460 or junc 33 at Weinheim onto B38a. Site on L behind sw pool after passing thro Fürth vill. Sm, mkd pitch, pt shd; wc; mv service pnt; shwrs €0.60; chem disp; mv service pnt; serviced pitches; el pnts (16A) metered + conn fee or €2; lndtte; shop, rest, snacks 100m; playgrnd; htd pool 100m; entmnt; 60% statics; no dogs high ssn; poss cr; adv bkg; v quiet; red CCI. "Gd touring base; pleasant views." 1 Mar-30 Nov. € 13.80 2008*

GERMANY

FURTWANGEN *3C4* (6km E Rural) *48.02449, 8.22727* **Camping Michelhof, Linachstrasse 9, 78120 Furtwangen [tel/fax (07723) 7420; post@michelhof-schwarzwald.de; www.michelhof-schwarzwald.de]** On S edge of Furtwangen on rd 500, turn E at camping sp. Site behind Gasthof Michelhof in 6km. Sm, terr, unshd; htd wc; shwrs €1; el pnts metered + conn fee; shop 6km; rest; bar; BBQ; sm playgrnd; 50% statics; dogs €2; quiet; CCI. "Basic but v clean site; helpful owner; beautiful, isolated location; free local public transport." 1 Apr-31 Oct. € 14.00 2011*

⊞ **FUSSEN** *4E4* (2km N Urban) *47.58222, 10.70083* **Camper's Stop, Abt-Hafnerstrasse 9, 87629 Füssen [(08362) 940104; fax 925829; info@wohnmobilplatz.de]** Foll sp (mv symbol) fr town cent. Fr N or W after junc B310 & B16 turn R bef chapel (sp), then 2nd L. Fr B17 thro' town, turn L after chapel. Sm, hdstg, unshd; wc; own san rec; chem disp; mv service pnt; shwrs €1; el pnts (16A) €2; Indtte (inc dryer); supmkt 500m; tradsmn; sw adj; sports cent opp (free use of san facs); wifi; quiet. "Popular site open 24 hrs; warden attends 1700-2100 (site managed fr sports cent); sm pitches; chem disp & water fr machine during day; full facs open 1900-1000 for NH; conv Neuschwanstein Castle; sh walk to Füssen; m'vans only; excel." € 11.00 2010*

The opening dates and prices on this campsite have changed.
I'll send a site report form to the Club for the next edition of the guide.

⊞ **FUSSEN** *4E4* (2km N Urban) *47.58250, 10.70098* **Caravan Zentrum Allgäu/Wohnmobilstellplatz, Abt-Hafnerstrasse 1, 87629 Füssen [(08362) 9261097; fax 921291; info@caravanzentrum-allgaeu.de]** Foll sp (mv symbol) fr town cent. Fr N or W after junc B310 & B16 turn R bef chapel (sp), then 2nd L. Fr B17 thro' town, turn L after chapel. This site is 50m bef Camper's Stop. Med, hdstg, unshd; htd wc; chem disp; mv waste; shwrs €0.50; el pnts (6A) €2; shop 200m; supmkt 500m; sw 500m; phone; poss cr; quiet. "M'vans only; excel, clean san facs; gd rest; cycle paths to town, castle & lake; gd value." € 14.30 (4 persons) 2011*

FUSSEN *4E4* (6km N Rural) *47.61553, 10.7230* **Camping Magdalena am Forggensee, Bachtalstrasse 10, 87669 Osterreinen [(08362) 4931; fax 941333; campingplatz.magdalena@t-online.de; www.sonnenhof-am-forggensee.de]** Fr Füssen take rd 16 sp Kaufbeuren & Forggensee for 5km; R sp Osterreinen for 500m; L at T-junc foll site sp; site on R in 50m; app rd steep with sharp bends. Site well sp. Med, mkd/hdg pitch, terr, pt shd; wc; chem disp; shwrs €0.50; el pnts (10A) metered + conn fee (poss rev pol); gas; Indtte (inc dryer); shop; tradsmn; rest; bar; playgrnd; beach on lake; sailing; watersports; 40% statics; dogs €3; poss cr; Eng spkn; adv bkg rec; v quiet; ccard acc; CCI. "Ltd touring pitches; superb views over lake; peaceful; gd site; sm pitches; conv for Zugspitze, Royal Castles, Oberammergau; lakeside cycle track to Füssen & to Neuschwanstein Castle." 1 Apr-31 Oct. € 20.00 2011*

⊞ **FUSSEN** *4E4* (10km N Rural) *47.64295, 10.73321* **Campingplatz Warsitzka, Tiefental 1, 87699 Rieden [(08367) 406; fax (0721151) 298460; info@camping-warsitzka.de; www.camping-warsitzka.de]** N out of Füssen on B16 sp Forggensee & Kaufbeuren. Med, mkd pitch, pt shd; wc; shwrs inc; gas; chem disp; mv service pnt; shops 2km; el pnts (16A) metered or €1.50; Indtte; shop; rest; playgrnd; lake sw & shgl beach; sailing; internet; entmnt; 30% statics; dogs €2.50; m'van o'night area; site clsd 5 Nov-15 Dec; poss cr; adv bkg (rec high ssn); quiet; debit card acc. "Royal Castles & Bavarian Alps; attractive site in beautiful area; lakeside cycle track Füssen; barrier clsd 1230-1430." € 19.40 2008*

⊞ **FUSSEN** *4E4* (5km NE Rural) *47.59638, 10.73861* **Camping Brunnen, Seestrasse 81, 87645 Brunnen [(08362) 8273; fax 8630; info@camping-brunnen.de; www.camping-brunnen.de]** S on rte 17 twd Füssen turn R in vill of Schwangau N to Brunnen; turn R at ent to vill at Spar shop, site clearly sp. Fr Füssen N on B17; turn L in Schwangau; well sp on lakeside. Lge, mkd pitch, hdstg, pt sl, pt shd; wc; chem disp; mv service pnt; serviced pitches; shwrs inc; el pnts (10-16A) metered + conn fee; gas; Indry rm; sm shop; tradsmn; rest/bar adj; playgrnd; sw & yachting in Lake Forggensee adj; beach adj; cycle hire; golf 3km; dogs €4; bus; site clsd 5 Nov-20 Dec; poss cr; Eng spkn; adv bkg; ccard acc; CCI. "Lovely location; outfits poss tightly packed; steel pegs ess; excel san facs; some pitches cramped; gd for Royal castles; gd cycle rtes; 10% red visits to Neuschwanstein Castle nrby; gates clsd 2200-0700; excel, busy site." ♦ € 28.00 2009*

⊞ **FUSSEN** *4E4* (6km NE Rural) *47.59194, 10.77222* **Camping Bannwaldsee, Münchenerstrasse 151, 87645 Schwangau [(08362) 93000; fax 930020; info@camping-bannwaldsee.de; www.camping-bannwaldsee.de]** On side of B17 rd fr Füssen to Munich & on shore of Bannwaldsee 3km after Schwangau vill. Fr N on B17 5km after Buching vill. Site name only visible at site ent. V lge, mkd pitch, pt sl, pt shd; htd wc; chem disp; mv service pnt; shwrs inc; shop; el pnts (16A) metered + conn fee; Indtte; shop; rest; snacks; bar; playgrnd; lake sw, fishing, boat hire; wintersports area; wifi; entmnt; 30% statics; dogs €3.50; poss cr; poss noisy; red long stay. "Narr site rds & poss diff pitch access; some lge pitches; excel san facs; gd facs young children; gd cycle paths in area." ♦ € 23.10 2009*

⊞ **FUSSEN** *4E4* (5km NW Rural) *47.60198, 10.68333* **Camping Hopfensee, Fischerbichl 17/Uferstrasse, 87629 Hopfen-am-See [(08362) 917710; fax 917720; info@camping-hopfensee.de; www.camping-hopfensee.com]** Fr Füssen N on B16 twd Kaufbeuren in 2km L on rd sp Hopfen-am-See, site at ent to vill on L thro c'van car park. Lge, mkd pitch, hdstg, pt shd; wc; chem disp; mv service pnt; baby facs; all serviced pitches; sauna; shwrs inc; el pnts (16A) metered; gas; Indtte; shop; rest; snacks; bar; playgrnd; htd covrd pool; shgl beach & lake sw adj; boating & fishing; fitness cent; solarium; wintersports area; entmnt; dogs €4.15; internet; clsd 8 Nov-13 Dec; poss cr; Eng spkn; adv bkg rec high ssn; quiet; ccard not acc; red low ssn; CCI. "Gd location; excel facs; helpful staff; gd rest on site; no tents allowed except for awnings; tight squeeze in high ssn; vans need manhandling; gd walking & cycling; lakeside pitches rec." ♦ € 33.80 2009*

FUSSEN *4E4* (5.5km NW Rural) *47.60883, 10.66918* **Haus Guggemos, Uferstrasse 42, 87629 Hopfen-am-See [(08362) 3334; fax 6765; haus.guggemos@t-online.de; www.haus-guggemos.de]** Fr Füssen take B16 N dir Kaufbeuren; in 2km turn L sp Hopfen-am-See. Drive thro vill; site on R opp lake. Sm, some hdstg, pt shd; wc; chem disp; shwrs inc; el pnts (10A) metered; lndtte; shop 500m; rest, snack & bar 200m; playground; lake sw adj; dogs €2; bus adj; Eng spkn; adv bkg; quiet; CCI. "Excel, family-run, farm site in beautiful area; views across lake to Alps." 1 Apr-31 Oct. € 16.00 2011*

GAIENHOFEN HORN see Radolfzell am Bodensee *3C4*

GANDERKESEE *1C2* (5km W Rural) *53.04666, 8.46388* **Feriencenter Falkensteinsee (Part Naturist), Am Falkensteinsee 1, 27777 Ganderkesee-Steinkimmen [(04222) 8214; fax 1043; campingpark@t-online.de; www.falkensteinsee.de]** Exit A28/E22 junc 18 dir Habbrügge. Site on R in 2km. Lge, pt shd; wc; sauna; shwrs inc; el pnts (16A) €2.50 or metered; lndtte; shop; rest 1km; snacks; playgrnd; lake sw adj; sep naturist beach; golf 8km; 70% statics; dogs €1.50; o'night m'van area; quiet; ccard not acc; 5% red CCI. "Conv Oldenburg & Bremen; gd site." ♦ 1 Apr-15 Oct. € 17.00 2010*

GARBSEN see Hannover *1D3*

⊞ **GARMISCH PARTENKIRCHEN** *4E4* (2km SW Rural) *47.50444, 11.10694* **Alpencamp am Wank, Wankbahnstrasse 2, 82467 Garmisch-Partenkirchen [(08821) 9677805; fax 76866; info@alpencamp-gap.de; www.alpencamp-gap.de]** A9/E533 exit onto B2 to Garmisch. Foll m'van symbol/sp to site. M'vans only. Med, hdstg, terr, unshd; htd wc; chem disp; mv service pnt; shwrs €1; el pnts (16A) metered; gas; lndtte; shop 2km; tradsmn; rest; wifi; dogs; bus to town; Eng spkn; quiet. "M'vans only; v clean facs; view fr all pitches of Zugspitze; excel for walking & winter sports; gd for NH or poss longer; diposal point/water coin operated." € 14.00 2011*

⊞ **GARMISCH PARTENKIRCHEN** *4E4* (4km W Rural) *47.4798, 11.05331* **Campingplatz Zugspitze, Griesenerstrasse 4, 82491 Garmisch-Grainau [(08821) 3180; fax 947594; info@zugspitzecamping.de; www.zugspitzcamping.de]** Fr Garmisch-Partenkirchen on rd 23 dir Griesen, site sp. Lge, pt shd; htd wc; chem disp; mv service pnt; shwrs inc; el pnts (6A) metered + conn fee €2; gas; lndtte; shop opp; snacks; rest; htd pool 2km; skilift 2.5km; 30% statics; dogs €2; phone; poss cr; quiet; CCI. "Conv Oberammergau, Zugspitze & castles; cycle track to Garmisch; facs clean but need refurb; pitching haphazard & site becoming run down (2008); sh stays sited adj noisy rd." € 18.00 2008*

GARTOW *2E2* (5km NW Rural) *53.03972, 11.41583* **Camping Laascher See, Ortsteil Laasche 13, 29471 Gartow [(05846) 342; pewsdorf@campingplatz-laascher-see.de; www.campingplatz-laascher-see.de]** Fr S on B493 to Gartow, turn N on L256 (Rondelerstrasse) dir Gartower See & Laasche See, site sp on R. Or E fr Dennenberg on L256 dir Gorleben & Gartow, site sp approx 5km after Gorleben. Med, hdg pitch, pt sl, pt shd; wc; chem disp; mv service pnt; shwrs €0.80; el pnts (6A) inc; lndtte (inc dryer); shop, rest 2.5km; bar; playgrnd; lake sw 300m; 60% statics; dogs €1.50; adv bkg; quiet; CCI. "Pleasant owners; clean, modern san facs; vg." ♦ 1 Apr-31 Oct. € 15.90 2010*

⊞ **GEESTHACHT** *1D2* (5km SW Rural) *53.42465, 10.29470* **Campingplatz Stover Strand International, Stover Strand 10, 21423 Drage [(04177) 430; info@stover-strand.de; www.camping-stover-strand.de]** Fr N on A25 to Geesthacht, then B404 dir Winsen to Stove. Site at end Stover Strand on banks of Rv Elbe. Fr S on A7 to Maschen, then A250 to Winsen then B404, as above. V lge, mkd pitch, pt shd; htd wc; chem disp; mv service pnt; baby facs; shwrs €0.50; el pnts (6-16A) €2 or metered; lndtte (inc dryer); shop; rest; snacks; bar; BBQ; cooking facs; playgrnd; rv sw & beach; fishing; watersports; marina; cycle hire; games area; wifi; entmnt; 80% statics; dogs €2; poss cr; adv bkg; quiet; ccard acc; CCI. "Excel rvside site; poss cr even low ssn; site clsd 1300-1500; Hamburg Card avail." ♦ € 18.00 (CChq acc) 2010*

⊞ **GELSENKIRCHEN** *1B4* (Urban) *51.56081, 7.07114* **Mobilcamp Gelsenkirchen, Adenauerallee 100, 45891 Gelsenkirchen [tel/fax (0176) 78569829; mobilcamp@web.de; www.mobilcamp.de]** Fr W exit A2/E34 junc 6, at rndabt at end of sliprd turn R into Emil Zimmerman Allee, then R again. Site on R. M'vans only. Med, pt shd; wc; chem disp; mv service pnt; shwrs €1; el pnts; gas; shop; rest; bar; dogs; Eng spkn; adv bkg; quiet. "Gd NH." € 7.00 2009*

GEMUNDEN AM MAIN *3D2* (2km W Rural) *50.05260, 9.65656* **Spessart-Camping Schönrain, Schönrainstrasse 4-18, 97737 Gemünden-Hofstetten [(09351) 8645; fax 8721; info@spessart-camping.de; www.spessart-camping.de]** Rd B26 to Gemünden, cross Rv Main & turn R dir Hofstetten, site sp. Lge, hdg/mkd pitch, some hdstg, terr, pt shd; htd wc; chem disp; mv service pnt; sauna; shwrs €0.50; el pnts (10A) metered + conn fee €2.15; lndtte (inc dryer); shop & 2km; tradsmn; rest; snacks; bar; playgrnd; children's pool; games area; cycle hire; fitness rm; solarium; TV; 50% static (sep area); dogs €2.80; phone; variable pitch sizes/prices; poss cr; Eng spkn; quiet; CCI. "Clean, well-kept, wooded site; interesting towns nrby; excel." ♦ 19 Mar-30 Sep. € 22.50 2009*

GEORGENTHAL see Ohrdruf *2E4*

GERA *2F4* (6km N Rural) *50.95361, 12.08722* **Campingplatz am Strandbad, Reichenbacherstrasse 18, 07544 Aga [tel/fax (036695) 20209; strandbad.aga@thueringencamping.de; www.campingplatz-strandbad-aga.de]** Exit E40/A4 junc 58a N onto B2 dir Bad Köstrutz; at 1st junc turn R onto B2 Zeitz. In 2km turn L sp Aga & int'l campsite. Med, pt shd; htd wc; chem disp; mv service pnt; shwrs €0.80; el pnts (16A) €1.50 + conn fee; lndtte; tradsmn; rest high ssn; snacks; BBQ; playgrnd; lake sw & beach; 70% statics; dogs free; poss cr; Eng spkn; red CCI. "Beautiful site with lake; sep sw area for naturists; gd rest." ♦ 1 Apr-31 Oct. € 14.00 2008*

GERMANY

GERMANY

GERBACH see Rockenhausen *3C2*

⊞ **GEROLSTEIN** *3B2* (4km NW Rural) *50.23910, 6.61477* **Campingplatz Oosbachtal, Müllenbornerstrasse 31, 54568 Gerolstein-Müllenborn [(06591) 7409; fax 3635; camping-oosbach@t-online.de; www.camping-oosbachtal.de]** Site well sp fr rte 410 Prüm to Gerolstein. Med, pt sl, hdstg, pt shd; wc; chem disp; mv service pnt; fam bthrm; shwrs inc; el pnts (16A) metered or €1.50; Indtte (inc dryer); shop; rest; bar; BBQ; playgrnd; 2 pools (1 htd, covrd); 60% statics; dogs €2; adv bkg; poss cr; Eng spkn; quiet; CCI. "Scenic area for touring Eifel region; owners friendly & helpful." ♦ € 16.50 2010*

⊞ **GERSFELD (RHON)** *3D2* (1.5km N Rural) *50.46223, 9.91953* **Camping Hochrhön, Schachen 13, 36129 Gersfeld-Schachen [tel/fax (06654) 7836; campinghochrhoen@aol.com; www.rhoenline.de/camping-hochrhoen]** Exit A7 exit Fulda-Süd S onto B27/B279 to Gersfeld, then B284 sp Ehrenberg, Turn L dir Schachen, site poorly sp. Med, hdg/mkd pitch, hdstg, pt shd; wc; chem disp; mv service pnt; shwrs €0.60; el pnts (16A) metered; Indtte; shops 1.5km; rest 500m; playgrnd; ski-lift 3km; some statics (sep area); dogs free; poss cr; red CCI. "Conv for gliding & air sports at Wasswerkuppe; friendly." € 18.00 2011*

GETTORF *1D1* (6km NE Coastal) *54.47485, 10.02910* **Campingplatz Grönwohld, Kronshörn, 24229 Schwedeneck [(04308) 189972; fax 189973; info@groenwohld-camping.de; www.groenwohld-camping.de]** Fr A7 exit junc 6 or 8 to Eckernförde, then onto B503, site sp bet km 8.9 & 9. V lge, hdg/mkd pitch, hdstg, pt shd; wc; chem disp; mv service pnt; sauna; shwrs inc; el pnts (10-16A) metered + conn fee; Indtte; shop; tradsmn; rest; playgrnd; beach adj; fishing; sailing; entmnt; 75% statics; dogs €2.10; adv bkg; quiet; ccard not acc; CCI. "Conv NH; gd, modern facs." ♦ 1 Apr-31 Oct. € 14.10 2011*

GIESELWERDER *1D4* (5.5km S Rural) *51.56600, 9.59500* **Camping Weissehütte, Weissehütte 1, 34399 Oberweser-Weissehütte [(05574) 211939; info@camping-weser.de; www.camping-weser.de]** S fr Bad Karlshafen on B80 along W bank of Rv Weser. Site on L. Sm, hdg pitch, pt shd; wc; chem disp; shwrs; el pnts (10A) €2.30; shop 5km; tradsmn; snacks; mainly statics; dogs €1.50; bus adj; Eng spkn; adv bkg; quiet; CCI. "Gd cycle rtes N & S." € 14.00 2011*

GIROD see Montabaur *3C2*

GLUCKSBURG (OSTSEE) *1D1* (6km NE Coastal) *54.85901, 9.59109* **Ostseecamp, An der Promenade 1, 24960 Glücksburg-Holnis [(04631) 622071; fax 622072; info@ostseecamp-holnis.de; www.ostseecamp-holnis.de]** Fr Flensburg on rd 199 turn off thro Glücksburg & further 6km to Holnis. Med, mkd pitch, some hdstg, pt shd; htd wc; chem disp; mv service pnt; baby facs; shwrs inc; el pnts (16A) €3; Indtte (inc dryer); shop; rest 200m; snacks; BBQ; cooking facs; playgrnd; pool; sand beach adj; fishing; windsurfing 1km; cycle hire; wifi; entmnt; 30% statics; dogs €2.50; adv bkg; quiet; CCI. ♦ 1 Apr-15 Oct. € 20.30 (CChq acc) 2011*

GOHREN (RUGEN ISLAND) *2G1* (7km S Coastal) *54.28133, 13.71308* **Camping Oase, Hauptstrasse 4, 18586 Thiessow [(038308) 8226; fax 8297; info@campingruegen.de; www.campingruegen.de]** Fr Bergen-Göhren B196, turn R at Göhren sp Thiessow, site on R bef vill. Lge, mkd pitch, pt shd, pt sl; wc; chem disp; mv service pnt; serviced pitch; baby facs; shwrs inc; el pnts (16A) €3; Indtte; shop; rest; bar; playgrnd; sand beach adj; windsurfing; entmnt; internet; TV; dogs €3; poss cr; quiet; ccard acc; adv bkg. "Vg." ♦ 1 Apr-31 Oct. € 27.00 2008*

⊞ **GOPPINGEN** *3D3* (7km W Rural) *48.63946, 9.55508* **Campingplatz Aichelberg, Bunzenberg 1, 73101 Aichelberg [(07164) 2700; fax 903029]** Exit E52/A8 junc 58 sp Aichelberg-Goppingen & foll sp to camp site in 1km. Med, pt shd; wc; chem disp; shwrs inc; el pnts (10A) €2; shop; rest 500m; bar; poss cr; adv bkg; 80% statics; dogs €2; poss cr; quiet. "Fills up after 1600 hrs but gd overflow field with el pnts for NH; family-run site; new excel facs; owner helpful." € 20.00 2011*

⊞ **GOPPINGEN** *3D3* (10km NW Rural) *48.75972, 9.59527* **Klosterpark Camping, 73099 Adelberg [(07166) 912100; fax 9121029; klosterpark@adelberg.de; www.adelberg.de]** Fr Göppingen take B297 dir Lorch, turn L to Adelberg. Site on L. Long 9% hill on app. Lge, pt sl, pt shd; wc; chem disp; mv service pnt; shwrs inc; el pnts (16A) metered; Indtte (inc dryer); shop 1.5km; rest/bar adj; snacks; playgrnd; htd pool adj; cycle hire; entmnt; 90% statics; no dogs; recep clsd 1230-1430; poss cr; quiet; ccard acc; red CCI. ♦ € 17.00 2008*

⊞ **GOSLAR** *1D3* (2km S Rural) *51.90113, 10.32743* **Campingplatz Sennhütte, Clausthalerstrasse 28, 38644 Goslar [(05321) 22498; sennhuette@campingplatz-goslar.de; www.sennhuette-goslar.de]** Fr Goslar on B241 twd Clausthal, Zellerfeld site on R in 2km. Ent thro car pk of Hotel Sennhütte. Med, pt shd; wc; chem disp; shwrs €0.50; el pnts (16A) metered + conn fee (poss long lead req); Indtte (inc dryer); shop; rest; 30% statics; dogs; bus at ent to town; no adv bkg; noisy nr rd; ccard acc. "Gd NH/sh stay nr beautiful town." € 15.50 2010*

⊞ **GOSLAR** *1D3* (9km S Rural) *51.82166, 10.43722* **Campingplatz Okertalsperre, Kornhardtweg 2, 38707 Altenau [(05328) 702; fax 911708; info@campingokertal.de; www.campingokertal.de]** Fr Goslar B498 S, site on L of N o'skts of Altenau. Med, hdg/mkd, pt shd; wc; chem disp; mv service pnt; serviced pitches; shwrs inc; el pnts (16A) metered + conn fee; gas; Indtte (inc dryer); shop; tradsmn; snacks; BBQ; playgrnd; lake sw; shgl beach; watersports; wintersports; skilift 2km; games area; games rm; wifi; entmnt; 50% statics (sep area); dogs €2; adv bkg; Eng spkn; quiet; ccard not acc; red CCI. "Beautiful setting 20 mins walk fr cent of Altenau; gd welcome; sm pitches; excel play area; excel cycle paths around lake; ltd facs low ssn; excel." ♦ € 16.50 2010*

⊞ **GOSLAR** *1D3* (7km SW Rural) *51.90110, 10.32724* **Camping am Krähenberg, Harzstrasse 8, 38685 Langelsheim [(05326) 969281; fax 969282; post@campingplatz-Wolfshagen.de; www.campingplatz-wolfshagen.de]** Foll rd 82 W fr Goslar twd Langelsheim. Turn L to Wolfshagen 1km bef Langelsheim. In Wolfshagen foll site sp, site in SE corner of vill uphill. Lge, mkd pitch, terr, pl sl, pt shd; wc; chem disp; mv service pnt; shwrs inc; el pnts (16A) metered + conn fee; gas; Indtte (inc dryer); shop; rest; playgrnd; htd pool adj; tennis; horseriding 1km; internet; 75% statics; dogs €1.20; ccard acc; red CCI. "Gate clsd 1300-1430; shwrs remote (in rest block); lge pitches; charge for sw pool poss automatically added to bill - check bef departure if not req; gd." ♦ € 14.20 2010*

I'll fill in a report online and let the Club know – www.caravanclub.co.uk/europereport

This is a wonderful site.

GOTTSDORF *4G3* (500m NW Rural) *48.53578, 13.72866* **Ferienpark Bayerwald, Mitterweg 11, 94107 Gottsdorf-Untergriesbach [(08593) 880; fax 88111; info@beter-uit.nl; www.ferienparkbayerwald.com]** Fr N bank of Rv Danube in Passau foll N388 to Untergriesbach (22km). At Untergriesbach turn R immed after town. Site bef Gottsdorf. Long pull out of Obernzell to Untergriesbach needs gd power/weight ratio. Lge, mkd pitch, pt sl, pt shd; wc; chem disp; mv service pnt; baby facs; shwrs €0.60; el pnts (10A) €3; Indtte; shop; rest high ssn; snacks; playgrnd; pool & paddling pool 200m; tennis; sports facs; entmnt; 40% statics; dogs €3; red CCI. "Lovely area; gd cycling, walking; friendly staff." ♦ 1 May-30 Sep. € 20.50 2008*

⊞ **GRAFENDORF** *3D2* (5km E Rural) *50.10678, 9.78241* **Camping Rossmühle, 97782 Gräfendorf-Weickersgrüben [(09357) 1210; fax 832; www.campingplatz-rossmuehle.de]** Exit A7 junc 96 onto B27 sp Karlstadt. At Hammelburg foll sps to Gräfendorf & site in 8km on rvside, beyond Weickersgrüben. Lge, mkd pitch, terr, pt shd; wc; chem disp; mv service pnt; shwrs €1; el pnts (6-10A) €2; Indtte; shop, rest high ssn; bar; playgrnd; watersports; fitness rm; cycle & canoe hire; solarium; entmnt; TV; 50% statics; dogs €2; o'night area for m'vans; adv bkg; quiet. "Poss liable to flooding after heavy rain; clean san facs; excel." ♦ € 18.00 2008*

GRAMBIN *2G2* (700m N Coastal/Rural) *53.75944, 14.01000* **Campingpark Oderhaff, Dorstrasse 661, 17375 Grambin [tel/fax (039774) 20420; info@campingpark-oderhaff.de; www.campingpark-oderhaff.de]** Exit A20 junc 28 onto B110 dir Anklam. After approx 23km turn R onto B109 & in 15km turn L in Ducherow onto L31 & foll sp Grambin. Site on L in 17km. Med, pt sl, pt shd; htd wc; chem disp; shwrs €1; el pnts (10-16A) €2.50; Indtte (inc dryer); shop 700m; tradsmn; rest 200m; bar; BBQ; cooking facs; playgrnd; sand beach adj; games area; 60% statics; dogs €2; bus nr; adv bkg; quiet. "Vg site; conv day trips Poland & Peenemunde." ♦ 1 Apr-15 Oct. € 17.40 2010*

⊞ **GREFRATH** *1A4* (1km N Rural) *51.36492, 6.32328* **Campingplatz Waldfrieden, An der Paas 13, 47929 Grefrath [(02158) 3855; fax 3685; ferienpark@waldfrieden@t-online.de; www.ferienpark-waldfrieden.de]** Fr A40-E34 S to Duisburg; turn S at exit 3 sp Grefrath; site sp on L in 3km. Lge, hdg pitch, hdstg, pt shd; wc; chem disp; mv service pnt; shwrs; el pnts (10A) metered + conn fee; gas; Indtte; shop 1.2km; playgrnd; lake sw adj; sw pools 1.5km; 80% statics; dogs €2; poss cr; Eng spkn; quiet; CCI. "Conv NH North Sea ports; WWII cemetaries at Reichswald; site over-used & weary." € 17.75 2008*

GREIFSWALD *2G1* (8km NE Coastal) *54.12666, 13.52196* **Campingplatz Loissin (Part Naturist), 17509 Loissin [(038352) 243; fax 725; info@campingplatz-loissin.de; www.campingplatz-loissin.de]** Fr Greifswald E to Kemnitz, then head N towards Loissin; site on coast N, well sp from the village. Lge, mkd pitch, pt shd; wc; chem disp; mv service pnt; shwrs €0.50; el pnts (16A) inc; Indtte; shop; rest; snacks; bar; playgrnd; sand beach adj; sep naturist beach; windsurfing; games area; cycle hire; internet; entmnt; 40% statics; dogs €2; clsd 1300-1430 & 2200-0800; adv bkg; quiet; red CCI. "Vg site; approx 40km to foot x-ing fr car park to Poland for shopping; excel san facs - no toilet paper, main attraction is immed proximity to sea." ♦ Easter-31 Oct. € 21.00 2011*

⊞ **GREVEN** *1B3* (4km SW Rural) *52.08328, 7.55806* **Campingplatz Westheide, Altenbergerstrasse 23, 48268 Greven [(02571) 560701; kontakt@campingplatz-westheide.de; www.campingplatz-westheide.de]** Exit A1 junc 76 onto B481 around E side of Greven, then turn L onto B219 for 2km. Turn R onto L555 Nordwalderstrasse & in 2km at Westerode turn L into Altenbergerstrasse, site on L in 1km. Med, hdg pitch, pt shd; htd wc; chem disp; fam bthrm; shwrs €0.50; el pnts (16A) metered; Indtte; tradsmn; snacks; bar; playgrnd; lake & sand beach adj; fishing; games rm; 80% statics; dogs €1; quiet; ccard acc; CCI. "Gd for sh stay; walks around lake." € 18.00 2009*

GROSS QUASSOW see Neustrelitz *2F2*

GROSSENBRODE (FEHMARN ISLAND) *2E1* (1.5km SE Coastal) *54.36035, 11.08743* **Camping Strandparadies, Südstrand 3, 23775 Grossenbrode [(04367) 8697; fax 999031; camping@strandparadies-grossenbrode.de; www.camping-strandparadies-grossenbrode.de]** Fr E47/B207 fr Lübeck dir Puttgarden turn R to Grossenbrode & foll 'campingplatz' sp. Turn L after sports hall, foll rd round & turn L into site in front of yellow phone box. Lge, hdg pitch, unshd; wc; chem disp; all serviced pitches; baby facs; shwrs €0.50; el pnts (16A) inc; gas; Indtte; shop, rest, snacks 300m; playgrnd; sand beach 200m; watersports; windsurfing; internet; 75% statics; dogs €2.50; phone; bus; clsd 1300-1500; poss cr; adv bkg; quiet; red long stay. "Superb beach; gd cycle paths; book in after 1800 for special 1 night fee; conv ferries to Denmark & Fehmarn Island; gd for wheelchair users; vg." ♦ 1 Apr-31 Oct. € 21.00 2011*

GERMANY

GERMANY

⊞ **GROSS-SEEHAM** *4F4* (1km S Rural) *47.85166, 11.86222* **Camping Seehamer See, Hauptstrasse 32, 83629 Gross-Seeham [(08020) 396; fax 1400; info@seehamer-see.de; www.seehamer-see.de]** Along W side of A8/E45/E52 a'bahn between juncs 98 Weyarn & 99 Irschenberg exit at km 37 into parking layby; site sp. If fr S take Weyarn exit & in Weyarn turn L opp maypole, site in 4km Lge, pt sl, unshd; wc; chem disp; mv service pnt; shwrs €1; el pnts (16A) €2; Indtte; shop; rest high ssn; snacks; shop 500m; lake sw; shgl beach; mainly statics; poss cr; no adv bkg; rd noise; red CCI. "V friendly owner; sm, sep area for tourers." ♦ € 22.00 2009*

GRUNBERG *3C1* (1km E Urban) *50.59105, 8.97361* **Camping Spitzer Stein, 35305 Grünberg [(06401) 6553; s.moebus@gruenberg.de; www.gruenberg.de]** Exit A5/E40 junc 7 S to Grünberg. At traff lts turn L onto B49; site in 1km on R. Lge, pt sl, pt shd, some hdstg; wc; chem disp; shwrs €0.50; el pnts (5A) metered + conn fee; Indtte; shop, rest & snacks adj; playgrnd; htd pool adj; golf 8km; 95% statics; poss cr; adv bkg; poss noisy; ccard acc; red CCI. "Site surrounded by pleasant wooded hills; sm, unmkd area for tourers; interesting old town; OK, busy NH." 1 Mar-31 Oct. € 12.00 2009*

GUNZBURG *3D3* (5km S Rural) *48.42688, 10.29842* **Legoland Feriendorf, Legoland Allee 2, 89312 Günzburg [(08221) 700789; fax 700199; info@legoland-feriendorf.de; www.legoland-feriendorf.de]** Exit A8/E52 junc 67 S onto B16. Follow sp Lego-Park & Feriendorf to site. Med, unshd; htd wc; chem disp; mv service pnt; fam bthrm; shwrs; el pnts (16A) inc; Indtte (inc dryer); shop 2km; rest; playgrnd; pool 3km; entmnt; no dogs; adv bkg; ccard acc. "New site 2008; opening dates/times dependent on Legoland Deutschland adj - www.legoland.de." ♦ 9 Apr-6 Nov. € 42.00 (inc Legoland tickets) (CChq acc) 2009*

⊞ **GUNZENHAUSEN** *4E3* (3km NW Rural) *49.12555, 10.71666* **Camping Zum Fischer-Michl, Wald-Seezentrum 4, 91710 Gunzenhausen [(09831) 2784; fax 80397; info@campingplatz-fischer-michl.de; www.campingplatz-fischer-michl.de]** Exit junc 52 fr A6 dir Gunzenhausen & then foll sp Nördlingen/Altmühlsee, site sp. Med, mkd pitch, unshd; htd wc; mv waste; baby facs; shwrs €0.50; el pnts (16A) €2; gas; Indtte; rest; snacks; bar; playgrnd; lake sw adj; watersports; fishing; cycle hire; dogs €2; quiet; CCI. "Pleasant lakeside site; gd." € 18.40 2008*

⊞ **GYHUM** *1D2* (2km S Rural) *53.19308, 9.33638* **Waldcamping Hesedorf, Zum Waldbad 3, 27404 Gyhum-Hesedorf [(04286) 2252; fax 924509; info@waldcamping-hesedorf.de; www.waldcamping-hesedorf.de]** Exit A1/E22 junc 49 in dir Zeven. In 1km turn R sp Gyhum & foll site sp to Hesedorf. Med, unshd; htd wc; chem disp; mv service pnt; shwrs; el pnts (16A) inc; Indtte; shop 1km; rest; playgrnd; htd pool 150m inc; wifi; 70% statics (sep area); dogs €0.50; barrier clsd 1300-1500; Eng spkn; quiet; CCI. "Clean, well-kept site; attractive area; gd rest; lge sep area for tourers." € 20.00 2010*

HAAG *4F4* (5km S Rural) *48.10588, 12.20565* **Camping am Soyensee, Seestrasse 28, 83564 Soyen [(08071) 3860; fax 51969; campingplatz@soyensee.de; www.soyensee.de]** E fr Munich on E94/B12 dir Mühldorf. At x-rds with B15 Haag turn R, site on L in 5km. Med, pt sl, pt shd; htd wc; chem disp; shwrs €0.50; el pnts (16A) metered; Indtte; shop; tradsmn; rest; bar; lake sw; sailing; 75% statics; poss cr; adv bkg; quiet. "Wasserburg interesting old town; helpful recep; gd site." ♦ 1 Apr-31 Oct. € 15.00 2008*

HAGNAU see Meersburg *3D4*

⊞ **HALBERSTADT** *2E3* (2km NE Rural) *51.90981, 11.0827* **Camping am See (Part Naturist), Warmholzberg 70, 38820 Halberstadt [(03941) 609308; fax 570791; info@camping-am-see.de; www.camping-am-see.de]** Sp on B81 (Halberstadt-Magdeburg). Med, terr, unshd; wc; chem disp; shwrs inc; el pnts (10A) metered + conn fee €2.50 (poss rev pol); Indtte; shop; snacks; pool adj; lake beach & sw adj (sep naturist beach); 75% statics; dogs €2; sep car park; quiet; red CCI. "Conv Harz mountains & Quedlinburg (770 houses classified as historic monuments by UNESCO); quiet, green site; communal shwrs; clsd 1300-1500." € 18.00 2010*

⊞ **HAMBURG** *1D2* (1.5km NW Urban) *53.5900, 9.93083* **Campingplatz Buchholz, Keilerstrasse 374, 22525 Hamburg-Stellingen [(040) 5404532; fax 5402536; info@camping-buchholz.de; www.camping-buchholz.de]** Exit A7/E45 junc 26 & foll dir 'Innenstadt' - city cent. Site sp in 600m on L Sm, hdg/mkd pitch, all hdstg, pt shd; wc; shwrs €1; chem disp; el pnts (16A) €3; Indtte; shop, rest, snacks 200m; bar; 10% statics; dogs €3.80; bus, train nr; poss v cr; adv bkg; rd noise; no ccard acc. "Fair NH nr a'bahn & Hamburg cent; conv transport to city - tickets fr recep; friendly management; sm pitches; busy site, rec arr early." ♦ € 32.60 2011*

HAMBURG *1D2* (9km NW Urban) *53.64916, 9.92970* **Camping Schnelsen-Nord, Wunderbrunnen 2, 22457 Hamburg [(040) 5594225; fax 5507334; service@campingplatz-hamburg.de; www.campingplatz-hamburg.de]** Heading N on A7 exit junc 23 to Schnelsen Nord; L at traff lts, foll sp Ikea & site behind Ikea. Med, pt shd, mkd pitch; wc; chem disp; mv service pnt; shwrs inc; el pnts (6A) €2.50; Indry rm; shop; tradsmn; rest adj (in Ikea); snacks; bar; playgrnd; TV rm; no statics; no dogs; phone; bus to city; stn adj; deposit for key to san facs & el box; Eng spkn; quiet but some rd noise; ccard acc; CCI. "Useful NH; helpful staff; gates clsd 2200 hrs & 1300-1600 low ssn; elec pylons & cables cross site; 3-day Hamburg card excel value." ♦ 1 Apr-28 Oct. € 25.50 2008*

⊞ **HAMELN** *1D3* (500m S Urban) *52.09638, 9.35805* **Wohnmobilstellplatz Hannes-Weserblick, Ruthenstrasse 14, 31785 Hameln [(05151) 957810; fax 931099; hannes@hwg-hameln.de; www.wohnmobilstellplatz-hameln.de]** Fr B1 to Hameln & foll sp Gewerbegebiet Süd & m'van park. Sm, hdstg; mv service pnt; el pnts (6A) €1; shop 700m; snacks; quiet. "Situated bet buildings of Hameln Youth Training Cent; footpath along Rv Weser to town; m'vans only." € 8.00 2011*

HAMELN *1D3* (500m W Urban) *52.10916, 9.3475* **Campingplatz zum Fährhaus, Uferstrasse 80, 31787 Hameln [(05151) 67489; fax 61167; campingplatz-faehrhaus-hameln@t-online.de; www.campingplatz-faehrhaus-hameln.de]** Fr A2/E30 at Bad Eilsen junc 35 onto B83 to Hameln on NE side of Rv Weser; in town foll sp Detmold/Paderborn; cross bdge to SW side (use Thiewall Brücke); turn R on minor rd twd Rinteln; foll site sp. Med, mkd pitch, unshd; htd wc; chem disp; mv service pnt; shwrs inc; el pnts (10-16A) metered; Indtte; supmkt 500m; rest; bar; htd pool high ssn; 40% statics; dogs €1; phone; clsd 1300-1430; quiet; red CCI. "Picturesque & historic district; open-air performance of Pied Piper in town on Sun to mid-Sep; sm pitches & poss uneven; helpful staff; san facs need update (2009); site poss muddy & untidy; gd cycle paths by rv to town; dog owners - beware owners' own dogs." ♦ € 15.00 2009*

HAMELN *1D3* (4km NW Rural) *52.10725, 9.29588* **Camping am Waldbad, Pferdeweg 2, 31787 Halvestorf [tel/fax (05158) 2774; info@campingamwaldbad.de; www.campingamwaldbad.de]** Fr Hameln on B83 dir Rinteln. In approx 10km turn L, cross rv & foll sp Halvestorf & site. Med, pt sl, unshd; wc; chem disp; shwrs €0.50; el pnts (16A) €2; Indtte (inc dryer); shops 2km; snacks; playgrnd; htd pool; paddling pool; 80% statics; dogs free; adv bkg; quiet. "Pleasant site - better than site in Hameln." ♦ 1 Apr-31 Oct. € 14.00 2009*

HAMM *1B3* (10km S Rural) *51.6939, 7.9710* **Camping Uentrop, Dolbergerstrasse 80, 59510 Lippetal-Lippborg [(02388) 437; fax 1637; info@camping-helbach.de; www.camping-helbach.de]** Exit A2/E34 junc 19, site sp; behind Hotel Helbach 1km fr a'bahn. Lge, pt sl, pt shd; htd wc; chem disp; shwrs inc; el pnts (16A) €2; gas; Indtte; shops adj; tradsmn; rest adj; playgrnd; 90% statics; dogs €2; poss cr; Eng spkn; rd noise; ccard acc. "Friendly; gd security; barrier clsd 1300-1500 & 2200-0500; fair NH." € 18.00 2011*

HAMMELBACH *3C2* (300m S Rural) *49.63277, 8.83000* **Camping Park Hammelbach, Gasse 17, 64689 Grasellenbach/Hammelbach [(06253) 3831; info@camping-hammelbach.de; www.camping-hammelbach.de]** Exit A5/E35 exit junc 31 onto B460 E. Turn S in Weschnitz to Hammelbach & foll site sp. Med, hdg pitch, pt shd; htd wc; chem disp; mv service pnt; baby facs; fam bthrm; sauna adj; shwrs inc; el pnts (16A) metered; gas; Indtte (inc dryer); shop 300m; tradsmn; rest, snacks, bar 300m; BBQ; htd pool 300m; wifi; 70% statics; dogs €1.50; bus 300m; poss cr; Eng spkn; adv bkg; quiet; ccard acc; red low ssn; CCI. "Excel site with views; vg san facs; v pleasant, helpful staff; red for seniors; conv Heidelberg." ♦ 1 Apr-31 Oct. € 16.60 2011*

HANAU *3C2* (5km NE Rural) *50.15226, 8.95763* **Camping Bärensee, Oderstrasse 44, 63486 Bruchköbel bei Hanau [(06181) 12306; fax 1807961; info@baerensee-online.de; www.baerensee.de]** Fr A66 exit junc 37 or 38 sp Erlensee/Langendiebach, site sp. V lge, pt shd; wc; shwrs inc; el pnts (10A) €2.60 or metered; gas; Indry rm; shop; rest; snacks; lake sw; entmnt high ssn; 90% statics; dogs €2.60; clsd 1300-1500 & 2200-0700; poss cr w/end high ssn; adv bkg; quiet; red CCI. "Touring area on shore of sm lake." ♦ 1 Mar-31 Oct. € 12.80 2008*

HANNOVER *1D3* (7km S Rural) *52.30133, 9.74716* **Campingplatz Arnumer See, Osterbruchweg 5, 30966 Hemmingen-Arnum [(05101) 8551490; fax 85514999; info@camping-hannover.de; www.camping-hannover.de]** Leave A7 junc 59 onto B443 dir Pattensen, then B3 dir Hannover. Site sp in Hemmingen dir Wilkenburg. Lge, hdg/mkd pitch, pt shd; htd wc; chem disp; mv service pnt; baby facs; shwrs €0.50; el pnts (16A) €2.50; gas; Indtte (inc dryer); shop 500m; rest; snacks; bar; cooking facs; playgrnd; lake sw; fishing; tennis; cycle hire; wifi; 95% statics; dogs €1.50; bus to Hannover 1.5km; quiet; CCI. "Friendly staff; excel, modern, clean san facs; sm area for tourers - gd size open pitches; gd lake sw & boating; insect repellent essential!" € 23.00 2011*

We can fill in site report forms on the Club's website – www.caravanclub.co.uk/europereport

HANNOVER *1D3* (8km S Rural) *52.30447, 9.86216* **Camping Birkensee, 30880 Laatzen [(0511) 529962; birkensee@camping-laatzen.de; www.camping-laatzen.de]** Fr N leave A7 junc 59 dir Laatzen, turn L & site well sp on L after traff lts. Fr S exit junc 60 twd Laatzen, site sp on L on lakeside. Lge, pt shd; wc; chem disp; mv service pnt; sauna; shwrs inc; el pnts (10A) €2.50 (poss rev pol); Indtte; snacks; bar; playgrnd; covrd pool; lake sw & fishing; games area; 60% statics; dogs €2.50; Eng spkn; rd noise; CCI. "Gd, clean facs; sm touring area." ♦ € 17.50 2010*

HANNOVER *1D3* (13km NW Rural) *52.42083, 9.54638* **Camping Blauer See, Am Blauen See 119, 30823 Garbsen [(05137) 89960; fax 899677; info@camping-blauer-see.de; www.camping-blauer-see.de]** Fr W exit A2 at junc 41 onto Garbsen rest area. Thro service area, at exit turn R, at T-junc turn R (Alt Garbson), at traff lts turn R. All sp with int'l camp sp. Fr E exit junc 40, cross a'bahn & go back to junc 41, then as above. Lge, some hdstg, pt shd; htd wc; chem disp; mv service pnt; some serviced pitches; baby facs; shwrs €0.80; el pnts (16A) €2.70; gas; Indtte (inc dryer); shop; tradsmn; rest; snacks; bar; BBQ: lge playgrnd; lake sw & watersports adj; 90% statics; dogs €2.50; phone; bus to Hannover 1.5km; barrier clsd 2300-0500 & 1300-1500; poss cr; Eng spkn; rd noise; ccard acc; CCI. "Excel san facs; well-organised site; helpful staff; conv bus/train to Hannover; rec pitch by lake." ♦ € 26.00 2010*

HANNOVERSCH MUNDEN *1D4* (7km SE Rural) *51.39500, 9.72527* **Camping Zella im Werratal, Zella 1-2, 34346 Hannoversch-Münden [(05541) 904711; info@zella-im-werratal.de; www.zella-im-werratal.de]** Exit A7/E45 junc 75 onto B80 dir Hann-Münden. In 4km turn L over rv bdge, site in 1km. Med, pt shd; wc; shwrs €0.60; el pnts (16A) inc; gas; Indtte (inc dryer); shop; tradsmn; rest, bar adj; cooking facs; playgrnd; 30% statics; dogs €2; some train noise; red long stay/CCI. "Facs across rd; vg rest; gd NH." € 22.50 2009*

GERMANY

GERMANY

HANNOVERSCH MUNDEN *1D4* (W Rural) *51.41666, 9.64750* **Campingplatz Grüne Insel Tanzwerder, Tanzwerder 1, 34346 Hannoversch-Münden [(05541) 12257; fax 660778; info@busch-freizeit.de; www.busch-freizeit.de]** A7/E45 exit junc 76 onto B496 to Hann-Münden. Cross bdge & site sp on an island on Rv Fulda next to town cent. App over narr swing bdge. Fr junc 75 foll sp to Hann-Münden. At Aral g'ge in town take next L & foll sp to site (sp Weserstein). Med, mkd pitch, pt shd; wc; chem disp; mv service pnt; shwrs €1; el pnts (16A) metered + conn fee; Indtte; shops, rest, snacks, bar 1km; playgrnd; htd pool 1km; wifi; dogs €2; poss cr; Eng spkn; adv bkg; noisy bdge traff; red long stay; CCI. "Pleasant site on island bordered by rv both sides; historic old town." 30 Mar-15 Oct. € 21.00 2010*

HASELUNNE *1B3* (1.5km E Rural) *52.66563, 7.51225* **Comfort-Camping Hase-Ufer, Am Campingplatz 1, 49740 Haselünne [(05961) 1331; fax 7145; info@comfortcamping.de; www.comfortcamping.de]** On B213 fr Enschede to Bremen, foll sp fr Haselünne town cent, well sp. Lge, mkd pitch, pt shd; wc; chem disp; serviced pitches; sauna; shwrs inc; el pnts (16A) inc; gas; Indtte; shop; supmkt 1km; snacks; playgrnd; pool 1km; sand beach; lake sw adj; horseriding; sailing; angling; fitness cent; internet; 50% statics; dogs €2; quiet. "Extra for lger pitches." ♦ 1 Mar-3 Nov. € 25.00 2008*

⊞ **HASLACH IM KINZIGTAL** *3C3* (4km NW Rural) *48.29587, 8.04770* **Camping Kinzigtal, Welschensteinacherstrasse 34, 77790 Steinach [(07832) 8122; fax 6619; webmaster@campingplatz-kinzigtal.de; www.campingplatz-kinzigtal.de]** S on rd 33 fr Offenburg to Haslach. Turn off by-pass thro vill of Steinach; on o'skts of vill turn R under sm rlwy arch. Foll camping sp to site in 1km. Lge, mkd pitch, pt shd; wc; shwrs €0.50; el pnts €2 or metered; Indtte; shop; rest; snacks; playgrnd; htd pool adj; tennis; wifi; entmnt; 30% statics; dogs €1.55; bus 600m; clsd 1300-1500; poss v cr; adv bkg ess; quiet. "Site rds narr; clsd 1300-1500 & 2200-0700." ♦ € 17.50 2007*

HASSENDORF see Rotenburg (Wümme) *1D2*

⊞ **HATTINGEN** *1B4* (2km N Rural) *51.41722, 7.20666* **Camping an der Kost, An der Kost 18, 45527 Hattingen [(02324) 60915; info@hattingencamping.de; www.hattingencamping.de]** Fr A43 exit junc 21 Herbede/Hattingen exit. Site sp just bef bdge over Rv Ruhr. Sm, unshd; wc; chem disp; shwrs inc; el pnts (16A) €3 or metered; shop; rest 2km; 60% statics; dogs €2; phone; site clsd 1300-1500; quiet. "Pleasant situation on rvside." ♦ € 18.00 2008*

HATTINGEN *1B4* (1km NW Urban) *51.40611, 7.17027* **Camping Ruhrbrücke, Ruhrstrasse 6, 45529 Hattingen [(02324) 80038; info@camping-hattingen.de; www.camping-hattingen.de]** Fr A40 bet Essen & Bochum exit junc 29 dir Höntrop & Hattingen. Foll sp Hattingen on L651 & B1, site sp bef rv bdge. Med, pt sl, unshd; htd wc; chem disp; shwrs €1; el pnts (16A) €3; shop 1km; rest, snacks 1km; bar 800m; BBQ; rv sw adj; canoeing, windsurfing adj; dogs €2; phone; bus, train adj; Eng spkn; adv bkg; quiet; CCI. "Beautiful rvside setting; plentiful, clean facs; friendly owner; excel cycle tracks." ♦ 1 Apr-10 Oct. € 18.00 2010*

HAUSBAY see Lingerhahn *3B2*

HAUSEN IM TAL *3C4* (300m E Rural) *48.08365, 9.04290* **Camping Wagenburg, 88631 Hausen [(07579) 559; fax 1525; camping-wagenburg-donautal@alice-dsl.net]** Fr E on B32 stay on Sigmaringen by-pass & take minor rd L227 sp Gutenstein/Beuron to Hausen, site in vill beside Rv Donau. Med, hdstg, pt shd; wc; chem disp; mv service pnt; shwrs €0.50; el pnts (16A) metered + conn fee; Indtte; shop 50m; tradsmn; rest adj; bar; playgrnd; rv sw adj; tennis 300m; TV; no statics; dogs €1.50; poss cr; Eng spkn; adv bkg; red long stay. "Beautiful location in Danube Gorge; friendly, helpful owner; clsd 1230-1430; poss flooding in wet weather/high rv level; gd walking/cycling; vg." ♦ 10 Apr-3 Oct. € 15.00 2007*

⊞ **HECHTHAUSEN** *1D2* (3km W Rural) *53.62525, 9.20298* **Ferienpark & Campingpark Geesthof, Am Ferienpark 1, 21755 Hechthausen-Klint [(04774) 512; fax 9178; info@geesthof.de; www.geesthof.de]** Site sp on B73 rd to Lamstedt. Med, hdg/mkd pitch, pt shd; wc; chem disp; mv service pnt; sauna; baby facs; shwrs inc; el pnts (10A) €2; Indtte (inc dryer); shop; tradsmn; rest; snacks; playgrnd; 2 pools (1 htd, covrd); paddling pool; waterslide; watersports; fishing; boat & cycle hire; wifi; entmnt; 60% statics; dogs €2; Eng spkn; quiet; red 7+ nts. "Superb site with mature trees around pitches; peaceful surroundings adj to rv, lake & woods; friendly staff." ♦ € 19.00 (CChq acc) 2010*

HEIDELBERG *3C2* (5km E Rural) *49.40175, 8.77916* **Campingplatz Haide, Ziegelhäuser Landstrasse 91, 69151 Neckargemünd [(06223) 2111; fax 71959; info@camping-haide.de; www.camping-haide.de]** Take B37 fr Heidelberg, cross Rv Neckar by Ziegelhausen bdge by sliprd on R (avoid vill narr rd); foll site sp. Site on R bet rv & rd 1km W of Neckergemünd on rvside. Lge, unshd; wc; chem disp; mv service pnt; shwrs €1; el pnts (6A) €2.50 (long lead req); Indtte (inc dryer); shop 2km; tradsmn; rest; snacks; BBQ; playgrnd; cycle hire; wifi; 5% statics; dogs €2; bus 1.5km; Eng spkn; some rd, rlwy (daytime) & rv noise; red CCI. "Conv Neckar Valley & Heidelberg; NH/sh stay only." ♦ 1 Apr-31 Oct. € 17.80 2011*

HEIDELBERG *3C2* (10km E Urban) *49.39638, 8.79472* **Campingplatz an der Friedensbrücke, Falltorstrasse 4, 69151 Neckargemünd [tel/fax (06223) 2178; j.vandervelden@web.de]** Exit Heidelberg on S side of rv on B37; on ent Neckargemünd site sp to L (grey sp) mkd Poststrasse; site adj rv bdge. Fr S on B45 turn L sp Heidelberg, then R at camping sp. Fr A6 exit junc 33 onto B45 sp Neckargemünd, then as above. Lge, unshd; htd wc; chem disp; mv service pnt; baby facs; shwrs €0.75; el pnts (6-10A) €5 or metered (poss rev pol); gas; Indtte; shop; rest adj; snacks; bar; playgrnd nr; pool adj; kayaking 500m; tennis; wifi; TV rm; dogs €1.50; phone; transport to Heidelberg by boat, bus & train 10 mins walk fr site; poss cr; Eng spkn; adv bkg; rd & rv noise; ccard not acc. "Gd location by busy rv, but poss liable to flood; immac, well-run, relaxing site; ask for rvside pitch (sm) - extra charge; owner will site o'fits; warm welcome; helpful staff; no plastic groundsheets; 26 steps up to main san facs block; excel facs for less able behind recep with gd access; gd rvside walks & cycling; tourist office 500m." 1 Apr-15 Oct. € 21.50 2011*

⊞ **HEIDENAU** *1D2* (1.5km SW Rural) *53.30851, 9.62038* **Ferienzentrum Heidenau, Minkens Fuhren, 21258 Heidenau [(04182) 4272 or 4861; fax 401130; info@ferienzentrum-heidenau.de; www.ferienzentrum-heidenau.de]** Exit A1 Hamburg-Bremen m'way junc 46 to Heidenau; foll sp. Lge, pt shd; htd wc; chem disp; mv service pnt; sauna; shwrs inc; el pnts (16A) €2 (poss long lead req); Indtte; shop; rest; snacks; bar; BBQ (sep area); playgrnd; htd pool; fishing lakes; gd cycling; tennis; games area; internet; 75% statics; no dogs; phone; Eng spkn; quiet; CCI. "Pleasant, wooded site; tourers on grass areas by lakes; clean, modern facs; ltd shop; gd." € 18.00 2010*

HEIDENBURG see Trittenheim *3B2*

HEINSEN see Holzminden *1D3*

HELLENTHAL see Schleiden *3B1*

⊞ **HELMSTEDT** *2E3* (8km SW Rural) *52.19295, 10.86173* **Camping und Erholungspark Nord-Elm, 38375 Räbke [(05335) 8352; bschafberg@t-online.de]** Exit A2/E30 at junc 59 to Königslutter. In 7km at traff lts, turn E onto B1 sp Helmstedt. At 4km turn S on minor rd to Räbke, foll site sp. Med, pt sl, unshd; wc; chem disp; mv service pnt; shwrs inc; el pnts (16A) €2.50; gas; Indtte; shop 1km; rest adj; pool adj; paddling pool; playgrnd; lake sw; 80% statics; dogs €1.50; poss cr; Eng spkn; adv bkg; quiet; red CCI. "Beautiful pool complex adj; helpful staff; gd walking & cycling; gd family site. ♦ € 15.50 2008*

HEMMINGEN ARNUM see Hannover *1D3*

HEMSBACH see Weinheim *3C2*

HENNSTEDT *1D1* (4km N Rural) *54.31351, 9.18953* **Camping-Ferienpark Eider, Eiderstrasse 20, 25779 Hennstedt-Horst [tel/fax (04836) 611; eidercamping@t-online.de; www.eidercamping.de]** Fr B203 Rendsburg-Heide rd, turn N in Tellingstedt to Hennstedt, then to Horst. Site sp on Rv Eider. Med, hdg/mkd pitch, pt shd; wc; chem disp; shwrs €0.50; el pnts (6A) €1.60; Indtte; shop; rest 4km; snacks; bar; cooking facs; playgrnd; pool; fishing; boat-launching; golf 5km; 40% statics; dogs €2; CCI. 1 Apr-31 Oct. € 14.50 2009*

HERBOLZHEIM *3B3* (500m E Rural) *48.21625, 7.78796* **Terrassen-Campingplatz Herbolzheim, Im Laue 1, 79336 Herbolzheim [(07643) 1460; fax 913382; s.hugoschmidt@t-online.de; www.laue-camp.de]** Fr E35/A5 exit 58 to Herbolzheim. Turn R in vill. Turn L on o'skts of vill. Site in 1km next to sw pool, sp. Med, terr, pt shd; wc; chem disp; mv service pnt; shwrs inc; el pnts (10A) €2; Indtte; shop; rest; playgrnd; pool & tennis nrby; 30% statics; dogs €2 (not acc mid-Jul to mid-Aug); o'nights facs for m'vans; clsd 1300-1500; adv bkg; quiet; ccard acc; red long stay; CCI. "Excel friendly, well-maintained site; conv Vosges, Black Forest & Europapark." 5 Apr-4 Oct. € 21.00 2009*

HERFORD *1C3* (1.5km S Urban) *52.10305, 8.68388* **Camping Herforder Kanu-Klub, Gauss-strasse 6A, 32052 Herford [(05221) 70174; ochwet@t-online.de; www.hkk-herford.de]** Leave A2/E34 at junc 29 onto B239 dir 'Centrum', then R at traff lts & R again at next traff lts. Take 1st L, site sp. Sm, pt shd; wc; chem disp (wc); mv service pnt; shwrs inc; el pnts (10A) metered; Indtte; shop & 1km; rest; bar; rv adj; dogs; quiet; red CCI. "Key issued to shwrs in clubhouse (on 1st floor); fair NH." 1 Apr-30 Sep. 2008*

HERSBRUCK *4E2* (3km E Rural) *49.51884, 11.49200* **Pegnitz Camping, Eschenbacherweg 4, 91224 Hohenstadt [(09154) 1500; fax 91200]** Exit A9 junc 49 onto B14 dir Hersbruck & Sulzbach-Rosenberg. By-pass Hersbruck & after 8km turn L sp Hohenstadt. Bef vill, cross rv bdge & immed turn R at site sp. Med, pt shd; wc; chem disp; mv service pnt; shwrs inc; el pnts (10A) inc; gas; Indtte; tradsmn; shop & rest 1km; cycle hire; 10% statics; trains nrby; Eng spkn; adv bkg; quiet; CCI. "Lovely, peaceful, friendly site; Gd walking & cycling area; helpful owner; v gd san facs; train to Nuremberg; gd." 1 Mar-31 Oct. € 15.00 2011*

HERSBRUCK *4E2* (6km NW Rural) *49.53900, 11.37200* **Berghof Glatzenstein M'van Parking, Jurastrasse 14, 91233 Weissenbach [(09153) 7906; fax 9229926]** Exit A9/E51 junc 49 dir Hersbruck. In 2km turn L on minor rd sp Speikern & Kersbach. Foll sp Weissenbach & Berg Glatzenstein, up winding rd to Berghof. O'night parking area is opp hotel. Sm (5 pitches); no facs, no fee on condition have meal in rest; gd views; m'vans only. May-Sep. € 11.73 2009*

HILSBACH see Sinsheim *3C3*

HIRSCHAU *4F2* (4km E Rural) *49.55608, 12.00634* **Campingplatz am Naturbad, Badstrasse 13, 92253 Schnaittenbach [tel/fax (09622) 1722; info@campingplatz.schnaittenbach.de; www.schnaittenbach.de]** On B14 bet Rosenberg & Wernberg, clearly sp in vill. Med, sl, unshd; wc; chem disp; shwrs inc; el pnts (16A) €1.50 or metered + conn fee; Indtte (inc dryer); shop 1.5km; rest adj; playgrnd; pool; games area; 80% statics; quiet; red CCI. "Gd NH; scenic area." ♦ 1 Apr-30 Sep. € 12.70 2010*

⊞ **HIRSCHAU** *4F2* (2km S Rural) *49.53088, 11.96525* **Camping Monte Kaolino, Wolfgang-Drossbach Strasse 115, 92242 Hirschau [(09622) 81502; fax 81555; info@montekaolino.eu; www.montekaolino.eu]** Exit A93 junc 27 onto B14, site sp. Med, terr, pt sl, pt shd; wc; chem disp; baby facs; shwrs; el pnts (16A) metered + conn fee; Indtte; shop 1.5km; rest; snacks; playgrnd; htd pool; paddling pool; games area; dry-ski & lift; 60% statics dogs €1.50; poss v cr; adv bkg; quiet; red CCI. "Vg for children; poss diff access to pitches for tourers; interesting area." ♦ € 15.00 2009*

HIRSCHHORN see Eberbach *3C2*

GERMANY

⊞ **HOF** *4F2* (8km NW Rural) *50.37494, 11.83804* **Camping Auensee, 95189 Joditz-Köditz [(09295) 381; fax (09281) 706666; rathaus@gemeinde-koeditz.de; www.gemeinde-koeditz.de]** Exit A9 at junc 31 Berg/Bad Steben. Turn R fr m'way & in 200m L to Joditz, foll site sp in vill (1-way ent/exit to site). Med, terr, unshd; wc; mv service pnt; shwrs; el pnts (16A) €1.80 or metered; lndtte; shops adj; rest high ssn; playgrnd; lake sw; fishing; tennis; 75% statics; dogs €1.50; clsd 1230-1500; quiet; red CCI. € 13.00 2010*

HOFHEIM AM RIEGSEE see Murnau am Staffelsee *4E4*

HOHENFELDE *2E1* (2km N Coastal) *54.38630, 10.49165* **Camping Ostseestrand, Strandstrasse, 24257 Hohenfelde [(04385) 620; fax 593846; info@campingostseestrand.de; www.campingostseestrand.de]** Fr Kiel on B502 dir Lütjenburg, foll sp to site in Hohenfelde. Med, mkd pitch, unshd; htd wc; chem disp; mv service pnt; shwrs €0.50; private san facs avail; el pnts (10A); €2.50; lndtte (inc dryer); shop; rest, snacks, bar adj; playgrnd; sand beach adj; watersports; horseriding 2km; golf 5km; internet; TV; 70% statics; dogs €2; o'night facs for m'vans; adv bkg; quiet; ccard acc. "Pleasant area of lakes & forests; ltd pitches for tourers; gd, clean san facs; vg." ♦ 1 Apr-24 Oct. € 19.50 (CChq acc) 2009*

HOHENFELDEN see Kranichfeld *2E4*

HOHENSTADT see Hersbruck *4E2*

⊞ **HOHENSTADT** *3D3* (500m NE Rural) *48.54693, 9.66794* **Camping Waldpark Hohenstadt, Waldpark 1, 73345 Hohenstadt [(07335) 6754; camping@waldpark-hohenstadt.de; www.waldpark-hohenstadt.de]** Exit A8/E52 junc 60 Behelfs & foll sp to Hohenstadt & site in approx 5km. Med, some hdstg, pt sl, pt shd; htd wc; chem disp; mv service pnt; baby facs; shwrs €0.50; el pnts (16A) €2.50; lndtte (inc dryer); tradsmn; rest; snacks; bar; BBQ; playgrnd; htd pool; wifi; 70% statics; dogs free; Eng spkn; quiet; red low ssn; CCI. "Gd, peaceful NH to/fr Austria; handy off A8; helpful & friendly staff; gd facs; long walk to shwrs fr tourer parking; lovely site; area ideal for walking, cycling, climbing, skiing and cross country skiing; excel." € 17.10 2011*

HOHENWARTE *4E1* (13km E Rural) *50.37416, 11.72121* **Campingplatz Mutschwiese, Mutschwiese 1, 07338 Drognitz [(036737) 3300; fax 33020]** Fr Saalfeld S on B90 to Kaulsdorf, then foll sp Hohenwarte, Drognitz & site. Med, terr, unshd; htd wc; chem disp; mv service pnt; sauna; shwrs €1; el pnts (16A) metered + conn fee; gas; lndtte; shop 1km; tradsmn; rest; bar; BBQ; cooking facs; playgrnd; lake sw & boat hire 800m; 50% statics; dogs €2; phone; Eng spkn; quiet but poss noise at w/end; CCI. "Gd walking area; vg." 1 Apr-30 Nov. € 15.00 2008*

HOLLE *1D3* (4km NE Rural) *52.10285, 10.13877* **Seecamp Derneburg, 31188 Holle-Derneburg [(05062) 565; fax 8785; info@campingplatz-derneburg.de; www.seecamp-derneburg.de]** Exit A7/E45 junc 63 at Derneberg onto B6, dir Hildesheim. Site in 300m. Med, unshd; wc; chem disp; shwrs €0.50; el pnts (16A) metered; shop high ssn; rest; playgrnd; lake adj; cycle hire; 50% statics; dogs €2; Eng spkn; ccard acc. "Quiet site; locked at 2200, barrier key ess after this time; helpful; gd rest." 1 Apr-15 Sep. € 18.40 2011*

HOLZMINDEN *1D3* (6km N Rural) *51.88618, 9.44335* **Weserbergland Camping, Weserstrasse 66, 37649 Heinsen [(05535) 8733; fax 911264; info@weserbergland-camping.de; www.weserbergland-camping.de]** Fr Holzminden on B83 twd Hameln, site sp in Heinsen cent twd rv bank. Med, pt sl, pt shd; wc; chem disp; sauna; shwrs €0.50; el pnts (10A) €1.90; gas; lndtte (inc dryer); shop 600m; tradsmn; rest; bar; playgrnd; htd pool; cycle hire; entmnt in high ssn; 50% statics; dogs €2; adv bkg; 10% red long stay/CCI. "Beautiful site on rv bank; gd san facs; gd area for walking/cycling; gd local bus service; new owners 2010 & renovations in hand." 15 Mar-31 Oct. € 15.50 2010*

⊞ **HOLZMINDEN** *1D3* (8km SE Rural) *51.77086, 9.54873* **Campingplatz Silberborn, Glashüttenweg 4, 37603 Holzminden-Silberborn [tel/fax (05536) 664; info@naturcamping-silberborn.de; www.naturcamping-silberborn.de]** S fr Holzminden on B497; turn L to Silberborn. Lge, mkd pitch; pt shd; htd wc; chem disp; baby facs; shwrs €0.50; el pnts (16A) €2 or metered; gas; lndtte (inc dryer); shop 500m; rest; bar; BBQ; playgrnd; pool; 50% statics; dogs €2; phone & bus 500m; adv bkg; quiet; red long stay/CCI. "V clean, well-kept site; popular with bikers; gd value rest; vg." ♦ € 17.10 2010*

HOOKSIEL *1C2* (1.5km N Coastal) *53.64100, 8.03400* **Nordsee Camping Hooksiel (Part Naturist), Bäderstrasse, 26434 Wangerland [(04425) 958080; fax 991475; camp-hooksiel@wangerland.de; www.wangerland.de]** Exit A29 at junc 4 sp Fedderwarden to N. Thro Hooksiel, site sp 1.5km. V lge, some hdstg, unshd; wc; chem disp; mv service pnt; baby facs; shwrs inc; el pnts (6-10A) inc; gas; lndtte (inc dryer); shop; rest; snacks; playgrnd; muddy beach; fishing; sailing; watersports; games area; cycle hire; wifi; entmnt; 50% statics; dogs €3.10; naturist site adj with same facs; poss cr; quiet. "Main san facs excel but up 2 flights steps - otherwise facs in Portakabin." ♦ 25 Mar-17 Oct. € 21.40 2010*

⊞ **HORB AM NECKAR** *3C3* (4km W Rural) *48.44513, 8.67300* **Camping Schüttehof, Schütteberg 7-9, 72160 Horb-am-Neckar [(07451) 3951; fax 623215; camping-schuettehof@t-online.de; www.camping-schuettehof.de]** Fr A81/E41 exit junc 30; take Freudenstadt rd out of Horb site sp. Med, mkd pitch, pt sl, pt shd; wc; chem disp; shwrs €0.50; el pnts (16A) metered + conn fee; gas; lndtte; shop; rest; playgrnd; htd pool; paddling pool; internet; entmnt; 75% statics; dogs €2; poss cr; adv bkg; quiet. "Horb delightful Black Forest town; site close to saw mill & could be noisy; steep path to town; site clsd 1230-1430." € 17.00 2009*

HORSTEL *1B3* (4.5km N Rural) *52.32751, 7.60061* **Campingplatz Herthasee, Herthaseestrasse 70, 48477 Hörstel [(05459) 1008; fax 971875; contact@hertha-see.de; www.hertha-see.de]** Exit A30/E30 junc 10 to Hörstel, then foll sp Hopsten. Site well sp fr a'bahn. V lge, pt sl, shd; wc; chem disp; mv service pnt; baby facs; shwrs €0.50; el pnts (16A) €2.40 or metered + conn fee (poss long lead req); gas; Indtte; shop; rest 2km; snacks; bar; BBQ; playgrnd; lake sw & beach adj; tennis; cycle hire; TV; 70% statics; no dogs; Eng spkn; quiet; CCI. "Excel site." ♦ 15 Mar-12 Oct. € 19.60 2008*

⊞ **HOSSERINGEN** *1D2* (1km S Rural) *52.86940, 10.42274* **Campingplatz am Hardausee, Am Campingplatz 1, 29556 Suderburg-Hösseringen [(05826) 7676; fax 8303; info@camping-hardausee.de; www.camping-hardausee.de]** S fr Uelzen on B4/B191 for 9km to Suderburg & Hösseringen, site sp. Med, pt shd; wc; chem disp; mv service pnt; shwrs inc; el pnts (16A) €2; Indtte; shop (high ssn); rest 1km; snacks; playgrnd; sw 300m; dogs €1.50; quiet. "Ltd touring pitches; excel, clean facs; excel cycling & walking; conv Lüneberg." € 17.00 2009*

HOXTER *1D3* (500m E Rural) *51.76658, 9.38308* **Wesercamping Höxter, Sportzentrum 4, 37671 Höxter [tel/fax (05271) 2589; info@campingplatz-hoexter.de; www.campingplatz-hoexter.de]** Fr B83/64 turn E over rv sp Boffzen, turn R & site sp almost on rv bank. Turn R in 300m at green sp, turn L in car park. Med, pt shd; wc; chem disp; baby facs; shwrs €0.50; el pnts (10-16A) €2; Indtte (inc dryer); shop; rest; playgrnd; internet; child entmnt; 60% statics; dogs €1.50; quiet; red CCI. "Lge open area for tourers; clsd 1300-1500." 15 Mar-15 Oct. € 13.00 2010*

⊞ **HUCKESWAGEN** *1B4* (3km NE Rural) *51.15269, 7.36557* **Campingplatz Beverblick, Grossberghausen 29, Mickenhagen, 42499 Hückeswagen [(02192) 83389; info@beverblick.de; www.beverblick.de]** Fr B237 in Hückeswagen at traff lts take B483 sp Radevormwald. Over rv & in 500m turn R sp Mickenhagen. In 3km strt on (no thro rd), turn R after 1km, site on R. Steep app. Med, hdstg, pt sl, unshd; htd wc; chem disp (wc); shwrs €1.10; el pnts (10A) metered; shop & 5km; tradsmn; rest; bar; 90% statics; dogs; quiet. "Few touring pitches; helpful owners; gd rest & bar; gd touring base; vg." € 15.00 2010*

⊞ **HUNFELD** *1D4* (3.5km SW Rural) *50.65333, 9.72388* **Knaus Campingpark Praforst, Dr Detlev-Rudelsdorff Allee 6, 36088 Hünfeld [(06652) 749090; fax 7490901; huenfeld@knauscamp.de; www.knauscamp.de]** Exit A7 junc 90 dir Hünfeld, foll sp thro golf complex. Med, mkd pitch, pt sl, pt shd; wc; shwrs; chem disp; mv service pnt; el pnts (16A) metered or €2.50; Indtte; shop; tradsmn; playgrnd; pool; fishing; games rm; games area; golf adj; wifi; 40% statics; dogs €2; quiet. "Excel san facs; gd walking/cycling." ♦ € 22.00 2009*

HUSUM *1D1* (6km SW Coastal) *54.45557, 8.97224* **Nordseecamping Zum Seehund, Lundenbergweg 4, 25813 Simonsberg [(04841) 3999; fax 65489; info@nordseecamping.de; www.nordseecamping.de]** L off B5 Heide-Husum at Darigbull sp Simonberg. Site sp. Lge, unshd; wc (htd); chem disp; mv service pnt; baby facs; shwrs inc; el pnts (16A) €2.50; gas; Indtte (inc dryer); shop 6km; tradsmn; rest; snacks; bar; BBQ; playgrnd; mud beach adj; lake sw 300m; wellness cent; golf 10km; 60% statics; dogs €2; poss cr; Eng spkn; quiet; CCI. "Superb family run site with excel facs; modern air-con san facs; gd value for money; really gd for cycling & bikes avail for hire on site." ♦ 1 Mar-15 Nov. € 22.00 2011*

GERMANY

IBBENBUREN *1B3* (3km S Rural) *52.24555, 7.69861* **Camping Dörenther Klippen, Münsterstrasse 419, 49479 Ibbenbüren [(05451) 2553; fax 9615; roesch-ibbenbueren@freenet.de; www.doerenther-klippen.de]** Fr A30/E30 exit junc 11b on B219 dir Greven. Site sp in 1.7km. Sm, hdg/mkd pitch, pt sl, pt shd; wc; chem disp; shwrs inc; el pnts (16A) €2.50 (rev pol); Indtte; rest; bar; pool 5km; many statics; dogs; Eng spkn; quiet but some rd noise; ccard acc; CCI. "Friendly, gd walking; ltd space for tourers; barrier clsd 2200-0700; site poss unkempt/untidy low ssn; NH only." 1 Mar-31 Oct. € 21.50 (4 persons) 2010*

⊞ **IBBENBUREN** *1B3* (5km S Rural) *52.21829, 7.66502* **Camping Eichengrund, Im Brook 2, 49479 Ibbenbüren [(05455) 521; fax 287]** Exit A30/E30 junc 11b onto B219 dir Greven for 5.8km; site sp on R 200m after x-ing canal bdge. Lge, hdg pitch, pt shd; wc; chem disp; mv service pnt; private bathrms avail; shwrs €0.50; el pnts (16A) €1.50; gas; Indtte; shop; rest; playgrnd; 90% statics; quiet; CCI. "Excel site; barrier & office clsd 1300-1500; ltd shwrs & san facs." € 14.00 2009*

⊞ **IDAR OBERSTEIN** *3B2* (10km N Rural) *49.80455, 7.26986* **Camping Harfenmühle, 55758 Asbacherhütte [(06786) 7076; fax 7570; mail@harfenmuehle.de; www.camping-harfenmuehle.de]** Fr rte 41 fr Idar twd Kirn, turn L at traff lts at Fischbach by-pass sp Herrstein/Morbach, site 3km past Herrstein vill. Sharp turn to site. Med, pt shd; wc; chem disp; mv service pnt; sauna; shwrs €0.50; el pnts (16A) metered; Indtte; gas; shop; tradsmn; rest; snacks; bar; playgrnd; lake sw adj; fishing; tennis; games area; games rm; golf 10km; internet; TV rm; 50% statics; dogs €2; phone; o'night area for m'vans; adv bkg; Eng spkn; 10% red CCI. ♦ € 19.00 2009*

IHRINGEN see Breisach am Rhein *3B4*

⊞ **ILLERTISSEN** *3D4* (9km S Rural) *48.14138, 10.10665* **Camping Christophorus Illertal, Werte 6, 88486 Kirchberg-Sinningen [(07354) 663; fax 91314; info@camping-christophorus.de; www.camping-christophorus.de]** Exit A7/E43 junc 125 at Altenstadt. In cent of town turn L, then R immed after level x-ing. Foll site sp. Lge, pt shd; htd wc; chem disp; sauna; shwrs; el pnts (16A) €2.80 or metered; Indtte; shop high ssn; rest; snacks; playgrnd; covrd pool; lake sw adj; fishing; cycle hire; 80% statics; dogs €3.50; Eng spkn; adv bkg; red CCI. "Gd site; sm sep area for tourers; excel san facs." € 18.40 2008*

GERMANY

ILLERTISSEN *3D4* (1km SW Rural) *48.21221, 10.08773* **Camping Illertissen, Dietenheimerstrasse 91, 89257 Illertissen [(07303) 7888; fax 2848; campingplatz-illertissen@t-online.de; www.camping-illertissen.de]** Leave A7 at junc 124, twd Illertissen/Dietenheim; after rlwy x-ing turn R then L foll site sp. Off main rd B19 fr Neu Ulm-Memmingen fr N, turn R in Illertissen, foll sp. Sm, mkd pitch, terr, pt shd; wc; chem disp; mv service pnt; shwrs inc; el pnts (16A) €2 or metered; gas; Indtte; shop & 1.5km; tradsmn; snacks; rest in hotel adj; playgrnd; pool; 65% statics; dogs €2; poss cr; quiet; ccard acc; 10% red CCI. "Trains to Ulm & Kempten; 20 mins walk to town or cycle track; some pitches poss unreliable in wet; site clsd bet 1300-1500 & 2200-0700; obliging owner; conv a'bahn; vg." ♦ 1 Apr-30 Oct. € 19.50 2009*

IMMENSTAAD AM BODENSEE see Friedrichshafen *3D4*

⊞ **IMMENSTADT IM ALLGAU** *3D4* (2.5km NW Rural) *47.57255, 10.19358* **Buchers Alpsee Camping, Seestrasse 25, 87509 Bühl-am-Alpsee [(08323) 7726; fax 2956; camping-allgaeu@t-online.de; www.camping-allgaeu.de]** Fr Immenstadt, W on B308; turn R dir Isny & Missen. In 1.3km turn L sp Bühl & site sp. Lge, unshd; wc; shwrs inc; el pnts (16A) €2.50 (poss rev pol); gas; Indtte; shop; rest; playgrnd; pool 2km; lake sw adj; skilift 3km; dogs €3; poss cr; Eng spkn; adv bkg; quiet. "Lake sm but pleasant; gd mountain walks; friendly welcome; excel site, first class facs." € 27.70 2008*

⊞ **INGOLSTADT** *4E3* (3.5km E Rural) *48.75416, 11.46277* **Azur Campingpark Am Auwaldsee, 85053 Ingolstadt [(0841) 9611616; fax 9611617; ingolstadt@azur-camping.de; www.azur-camping.de]** Exit A9/E45 junc 62 Ingolstadt Süd, foll sp for camp site & Auwaldsee. V lge, pt shd; wc; shwrs inc; chem disp; mv service pnt; el pnts (16A) €2.80; gas; Indtte (inc dryer); shop 1.5km; rest, snacks; adj; bar; playgrnd; pool 1km; rv beach & sw; fishing & boating; wifi; 50% statics; dogs €3.50; bus; clsd 1300-1500; poss cr; adv bkg. "Basic wooded site by lake; useful NH nr m'way." ♦ € 24.00 2010*

⊞ **IRREL** *3A2* (700m S) *49.84175, 6.45750* **Campingplatz Südeifel, Hofstraße 19, 54666 Irrel [06525 510; info@camping-suedeifel.de; www.camping-suedeifel.de]** Take Irrel exit off B257; site sp. Lge, pt shd; wc; shwrs; el pnts (6A) €2; gas; Indtte; rest; bar; BBQ; playgrnd; wifi; dogs €2; quiet; CCI. "Cycling in area & walks fr site; pleasant town; tourist info in town; gd site." 2011*

ISNY IM ALLGAU *3D4* (1.3km S Rural) *47.67828, 10.0306* **Isny Camping (Campingplatz Waldbad), Lohbauerstrasse 59-69, 88316 Isny-im-Allgäu [(07562) 2389; fax 2004; info@isny-camping.de; www.isny-camping.de]** Thro town twds Lindau; L at traff lts; after 500m turn R & foll sp uphill. Site sp fr B12. Sm, hdstg, hdg pitch, wc; chem disp; shwrs €0.50; el pnts (16A) metered + conn fee; (poss rev pol); Indtte; shop 1.3km; tradsmn; rest; snacks; playgrnd; beach; sw; cycle hire; adv bkg; Eng spkn; dogs €1; quiet; red 10+ days; CCI. "Ideal for young children; v peaceful & friendly; local walks; gd base Munich & Bodensee; poss need insect repellent; modern san facs." ♦ 1 Jan-31 Oct. € 22.50 2008*

ISNY IM ALLGAU *3D4* (8km NW Rural) *47.75400, 10.00432* **Campingplatz am Badsee, Allmisried 1, 88316 Isny-Beuren [(07567) 1026; fax 1092; campingbadsee@t-online.de; www.campingbadsee.de]** On Isny-Leutkirch rd turn W on N side of Friesenhofen sp Beuren. In 4km at Beuren turn N onto sm rd sp to site, Badsee & Winnis. Med, pt sl, pt terr, pt shd; wc; chem disp; mv service pnt; baby facs; fam bthrm; shwrs €1; el pnts (16A) metered + €2.50; Indtte; shop high ssn snacks; rest; playgrnd; lake sw & beach; 80% statics; dogs €2.30; clsd 1300-1500; adv bkg. "Isny interesting; excel facs; vg." ♦ 15 Apr-15 Oct. € 18.50 2010*

ISSIGAU *4F2* (S Rural) *50.37413, 11.72103* **Camping Schloss Issigau, Altes Schloss 3, 95188 Issigau [(09293) 7173; fax 7050; info@schloss-issigau.de; www.schloss-issigau.de]** Exit A9/E51 junc 31 dir Berg. In Issigau foll sp over bdge to site. Sm, pt sl, pt shd; wc; chem disp; mv service pnt; shwrs inc; el pnts (16A) metered; gas; Indtte; shop 300m; rest; snacks; bar; playgrnd; TV rm; dogs €1.50; phone; Eng spkn; adv bkg; quiet; ccard not acc; CCI. "Gd walking & cycling; friendly, helpful owners; delightful, well-kept site; vg facs & rest; visit to Mödlareuth worthwhile." 15 Mar-31 Oct & 17 Dec-6 Jan. € 17.50 2011*

⊞ **JENA** *2E4* (2km NE Rural) *50.93583, 11.60833* **Campingplatz Unter dem Jenzig, Am Erlkönig 3, 07749 Jena [(03641) 666688; post@camping-jena.com; www.camping-jena.com]** Exit A4/E40 junc 54 to Jena, then B88 N dir Naumberg. Turn R just outside Jena past Walmart at site sp, R over blue bdge; site nr sports stadium on L, sp. Med, unshd; wc; chem disp; mv service pnt; shwrs inc; el pnts (10A) €2.50 or metered; Indtte; rest 500m; snacks; bar; playgrnd; pool adj; dogs €1; phone; bus 1km; some Eng spkn; adv bkg; quiet. "Gd san facs in Portakabin; poss itinerants; sh walk to interesting town; gd cycle paths." ♦ € 17.50 2011*

JESTETTEN *3C4* (Urban) *47.64802, 8.56648* **Campingplatz & Schwimmbad, Waldshuterstrasse 13, 79798 Jestetten [(07745) 1220; info@jestetten.de; www.jestetten.de]** Site in town on B27 main rd, sp. Sm, pt sl, pt shd; htd wc; chem disp (wc); shwrs inc; el pnts (10A) metered; shop, rest in town; snacks; playgrnd; htd pool; no dogs; bus at gate; train 500m; Eng spkn; adv bkg; quiet. "Gd for walk or train Rhine Falls & Switzerland." ♦ Easter-30 Sep. € 16.60 2009*

JODITZ KODITZ see Hof *4F2*

⊞ **KALKAR** *1A3* (2km N Rural) *51.76100, 6.28483* **Freitzeitpark Wisseler See, Zum Wisseler-See 15, 47546 Kalkar-Wissel [(02824) 96310; fax 963131; info@wisseler-see.de; www.wisseler-see.de]** Fr A3 take junc 4 onto B67 dir Kalkar & Wissel. Fr Kleve take B57 SE for 8km twd Kalkar, E to Wissel & foll camp sp. V lge, hdg/mkd pitch, pt shd; serviced pitches; wc; chem disp; mv service pnt; shwrs inc; el pnts (16A) inc; Indtte; shop; rest; snacks; pool; playgrnd; beach; watersports; tennis; cycle hire; games area; wifi; entmnt; 75% statics; dogs €2.50; Eng spkn; adv bkg;. "Commercialised & regimented but conv NH Rotterdam ferry; gd facs; gd for children & teenagers." ♦ € 24.00 2009*

⊞ **KALKAR** *1A3* (500m E Rural) *51.74000, 6.30111* **Wohnmobilplatz Kalkar, Wayschestrasse, 47546 Kalkar [(02824) 13120 (TO); fax 13234; info@kalkar.de]** Fr Arnhem (N'lands) on E35, exit junc 4 onto B67 to Kalkar. Or fr S exit A57/E31 junc 3 onto B67 to Kalkar. Foll m'van sps to site. Sm, hdstg, pt shd; mv service pnt; el pnts (16A); shop 800m; rest 400m; dogs; quiet. "M'vans only; pleasant, wooded site; interesting church in Kalkar worth visit." € 3.00 2008*

⊞ **KAMENZ** *2G4* (4km NE Rural) *51.30465, 14.15272* **Campingplatz Deutschbaselitz, Grossteichstrasse 30, 01917 Kamenz [(03578) 301489; fax 308098; info@campingplatz-deutschbaselitz.com; www.campingplatz-deutschbaselitz.com]** Fr Kamenz N on rd S95 dir Wittichenau; at Schiedel turn R twd lake, site sp. Med, pt shd; htd wc; chem disp; mv service pnt; baby facs; fam bthrm; shwrs inc; el pnts (16A) €3; Indtte (inc dryer); shop; tradsmn; snacks; BBQ; cooking facs; playgrnd; lake sw & beach adj; watersports; cycle hire; games area; games rm; 10% statics; dogs; adv bkg; quiet; CCI. ♦ € 15.60 (CChq acc) 2009*

⊞ **KAPPELN** *1D1* (7km SW Rural) *54.61945, 9.88402* **Campingpark Schlei-Karschau, Karschau 56, 24407 Rabenkirchen-Faulück [(04642) 920820; fax 920821; info@campingpark-schlei.de; www.campingpark-schlei.de]** Exit A7 junc 5 onto B201 dir Kappeln, site sp dir Faulück & Karschau. Lge, mkd pitch, pt sl, unshd; htd wc; mv service pnt; baby facs; shwrs €0.50; el pnts (6A) inc; Indtte (inc dryer); shop; rest; snacks; playgrnd; sand beach & private beach, rv sw adj; fishing; boat & cycle hire; tennis; games area; golf 5km; 70% statics; dogs €2; adv bkg; quiet. "Gd, peaceful site." ♦ € 20.60 (CChq acc) 2011*

⊞ **KARLSHAGEN** *2G1* (1km E) *54.11769, 13.84477* **Dünencamp, Zeltplatzstraße; 17449 Ostseebad; Karlshagen [038371 20291; camping@karlshagen.de; www.duenencamp.de]** Site sp from karlshagen along Zeltplatzstrasse. Lge, mkd pitch, pt sl, shd; htd wc; chem disp; MV service pnt; baby facs; fam bthrm; shwrs (metered); elec pnt (16A) €2 (or metered); Indtte; playgrnd; beach adj; dogs €4; phone; Eng spkn; quiet. "Site has direct access to long clean sandy beach; long mains lead may be needed for some pitches; conv for visiting Peenemünde; gd site." € 26.10 2011*

KARLSRUHE *3C3* (1.5km E Rural) *49.00788, 8.48303* **Azur Campingpark Turmbergblick, Tiengenerstrasse 40, 76227 Karlsruhe-Durlach [(0721) 497236; fax 497237; karlsruhe@azur-camping.de; www.azur-camping.de]** Exit A5/E35 junc 44 dir Durlach/Grötzingen onto B10 & foll sp to site 3km. Lge, mkd pitch, pt shd; htd wc; chem disp; mv service pnt; baby facs; shwrs inc; el pnts (10A) €3 (long lead poss req); gas; Indtte; shop; tradsmn; supmkt 500m; rest; snacks; bar; playgrnd; 2 pools nr; tennis; entmnt; internet; 20% statics; dogs €3.50; Eng spkn; adv bkg; some rd & rlwy noise; ccard acc; CCI. "NH conv to a'bahn; adequate san facs; clsd 1230-1400." ♦ 1 Apr-31 Oct. € 25.50 2011*

⊞ **KASSEL** *1D4* (3.5km S Urban) *51.29055, 9.48777* **Wohnmobilstellplatz Kassel, Giesenallee, 34121 Kassel [(0561) 707707; strassenverkehrsamt@stadt-kassel.de]** Exit A49 junc 5; strt on at traff lts; 1st R sp camping. Site 80m beyond Fulda Camp. M'vans only. Sm, hdstg, unshd; chem disp; mv service pnt; el pnts (10A) metered; dogs; bus adj. "Max stay 3 nights." € 7.00 2010*

⊞ **KASTELLAUN** *3B2* (1.5km SE Rural) *50.06846, 7.45382* **Burgstadt Camping Park, Südstrasse 34, 56288 Kastellaun [(06762) 40800; fax 4080100; info@burgstadt.de; www.burgstadt.de]** Exit A61 junc 42 dir Emmelshausen onto L206/L213 for 1.2km; turn L onto B327; cont for 13.5km to Kastellaun. Site adj hotel on B237. Med, mkd pitch, hdstg, terr, unshd; htd wc; chem disp; mv waste; baby facs; sauna; solarium; shwrs inc; el pnts (16A) metered; Indtte; shop; tradsmn; rest; snacks; bar; BBQ; playgrnd; htd, covrd pool 300m; tennis, cycle hire, riding & kayaking nrby; wifi; no statics; dogs €2; o'night m'van area; Eng spkn; adv bkg; quiet; ccard acc; CCI. "Lge pitches; clean site; excel san facs; helpful staff; conv touring base; fitness & beauty centre in hotel adj; excel." ♦ € 18.00 2009*

⊞ **KEHL** *3B3* (9km E Rural) *48.54375, 7.93518* **Europa-Camping, Waldstrasse 32, 77731 Willstätt-Sand [tel/fax (07852) 2311; europa.camping@t-online.de; www.europa-camping-sand.de]** Exit A5/E35/E52 at junc 54 almost immed turn R at Int'l Camping sp; foll site sp. Med, some hdstg, pt shd; htd wc; shwrs inc; el pnts (16A) €2.50 (long lead poss req); Indtte (inc dryer); shop & 5km; rest; cooking facs; playgrnd; 30% statics; dogs €2; poss cr; Eng spkn; quiet but some rd noise; ccard acc; red long stay/CCI. "Easy reach Black Forest & Strasbourg; 1km fr a'bahn exit; well-managed, clean, tidy site; gd san facs; some pitches gravel." € 16.00 2011*

KEHL *3B3* (1km S Urban) *48.5615, 7.80861* **DCC Campingpark Kehl-Strassburg, Rheindammstrasse 1, 77694 Kehl-Kronenhof [(07851) 2603; fax 73076; CampingparkKehl@aol.com; www.campingplatz-kehl.de]** Fr A5/E35, take exit 54 onto B28 at Appenweier twd Kehl & foll site sp. Lge, pt shd; htd wc; chem disp; mv service pnt; shwrs €0.50; el pnts (16A) metered + conn fee (long lead poss req); gas; Indtte; shop & 1km; tradsmn; rest; snacks; bar; playgrnd; sw pool adj; 15% statics; dogs €1; bus 1km; poss cr; Eng spkn; adv bkg; quiet but noise fr adj stadium w/end; ccard acc; red CCI. "Peaceful site adj Rv Rhine; excel rest & modern san facs; sm pitches; pleasant rv walk & cycle paths to town; barrier clsd 1300-1500." ♦ 15 Mar-31 Oct. € 16.90 2011*

⊞ **KELBRA** *2E4* (2km W Rural) *51.42551, 11.00307* **Seecamping Kelbra, Langestrasse 150, 06537 Kelbra [(034651) 45290; fax 45292; info@seecampingkelbra.de; www.seecampingkelbra.de]** Exit A38 at Berga (bet junc 12 & 14); on app to town turn L at traff lts onto B85 to Kelbra; go thro chicane in vill, then R onto L234/L1040 dir Sonderhausen; site sp. L234 is Langestrasse. Lge, pt sl, unshd; htd wc; chem disp; mv service pnt; shwrs €0.50; el pnts (16A) €2; Indtte; shop; rest; snacks; bar; BBQ (gas/elec); playgrnd; lake sw adj; sand beach 1km; games area; internet; TV; dogs €2; phone; bus adj; poss cr; Eng spkn; adv bkg; quiet; CCI. "Gd touring base & walking area; boat hire on site; vg." € 15.50 2011*

GERMANY

⊞ **KEMPTEN (ALLGAU)** *3D4* (6km SE Rural) *47.67485, 10.33386* **Camping Öschlesee, 87477 Sulzberg [(08376) 93040; fax 93041; info@camping.oeschlesee.de; www.camping.oeschlesee.de]** Exit A7 at junc 136 Dreieck Allgäu onto rd 980 dir Lindau/Oberstdorf. Turn L to Sulzberg in 1.5km, site sp. Lge, some hdstg, pt sl, pt shd; wc; mv service pnt; shwrs inc; el pnts (16A) €2; gas; lndtte; shop; supmkt 1km; rest adj; snacks; bar; cooking facs; playgrnd; lake sw 300m; TV; 70% statics; dogs €2; bus 200m; poss cr; Eng spkn; quiet; CCI. "Some pitches views of Alps; vg san facs; gd rest 300m; some pitches diff in wet; gd walks." ♦ € 22.00 2010*

KIEL *1D1* (5km N Coastal) *54.41198, 10.18388* **Campingplatz Kiel-Falckenstein, Palisadenweg 171, 24159 Kiel-Friedrichsort [tel/fax (0431) 392078; falckenstein1@aol.com; www.campingkiel.de]** N fr Kiel foll sp to 'Flughafen' & Friedrichsort on B503. Foll 'Olympiazentrum', site sp. Access rd narr with bends, but ent gd. Lge, pt sl, unshd; wc; sauna; shwrs; el pnts (16A) metered + conn fee; gas; lndtte; shop; rest; bar; playgrnd; pool 1km; shgl beach adj; 60% statics; dogs €1.90; poss cr; quiet. "Poor san facs; NH only." ♦ 1 Apr-31 Oct. € 18.50 2011*

⊞ **KINDING** *4E3* (5km E Rural) *49.00328, 11.45200* **Camping Kratzmühle, Mühlweg 2, 85125 Kinding-Pfraundorf [(08461) 64170; fax 641717; info@kratzmuehle.de; www.kratzmuehle.de]** Exit A9/E45 junc 58, dir Beilngries. Site sp. Lge, pt shd; wc; chem disp; mv service pnt; baby facs; some serviced pitches; sauna; shwrs inc; el pnts (16A) €2.50; gas; lndtte; shop; rest; cooking facs; playgrnd; lake sw adj & shgl beach; games area; 40% statics; dogs €2; clsd 1300-1500; poss cr; adv bkg; 10% red 2+ days; quiet; ccard acc; CCI. "Beautiful situation; conv NH for a'bahn; ideal boating & bathing, public access to lake; poss mosquito prob; helpful staff." ♦ € 23.50 2010*

KIPFENBERG *4E3* (500m W Rural) *48.9486, 11.38859* **Azur Campingpark Altmühltal, Campingstrasse 1, 85110 Kipfenberg [(08465) 905167; fax 3745; kipfenberg@azur-camping.de; www.azur-camping.de/kipfenberg]** Exit A9/E45 junc 58 or 59 & foll sp to Kipfenberg, site sp on rvside. Lge, pt shd; htd wc; mv service pnt; shwrs inc; chem disp; mv service pnt; baby facs; el pnts (6A) €2.80; gas; lndtte; tradsmn; shop, rest, snacks 100m; bar; cooking facs; playgrnd; tennis; fishing; excursions; wifi; TV rm; 20% statics; dogs €3.50; sep o'night area; quiet; red CCI. "On edge of attractive old vill; cent for walking, cycling & canoeing; charming site." ♦ 1 Apr-31 Oct. € 23.00 2009*

KIRCHBERG SINNINGEN see Illertissen *3D4*

⊞ **KIRCHHEIM** *1D4* (5km SW Rural) *50.81435, 9.51805* **Camping Seepark, Reimboldshäuserstraße, 36275 Kirchheim [(06628) 1525; fax 8664; info@campseepark.de; www.campseepark.de]** Exit A7 at Kirchheim junc 87, site clearly sp. Lge, mkd pitch, pt sl, terr, mkd pitch, pt shd; htd wc; chem disp; mv service pnt; sauna; shwrs €1; el pnts (16A) €2.50; metered; gas; lndtte; dishwashers; shop; tradsmn; rest; snacks; bar; playgrnd; covrd pool; lake sw & sand beach; tennis; games area; golf 3km; entmnt; 50% statics; dogs €2; bus 500m; phone; o'night area for m'vans; adv bkg; quiet but poss noisy high ssn; ccard acc; red long stay/CCI. "Gd walking; helpful owner; excel site - leisure facs part of lge hotel complex." ♦ € 19.80 (6 people) 2009*

KIRCHZARTEN see Freiburg im Breisgau *3B4*

KIRCHZELL see Amorbach *3D2*

⊞ **KIRKEL** *3B3* (300m W Urban) *49.28175, 7.22860* **Caravanplatz Mühlenweiher, Unnerweg 5c, 66458 Kirkel-Neuhäusel [(06849) 1810555; fax 1810556; info@camping-kirkel.de; www.caravanplatz-kirkel.de]** Fr A6 junc 7 & fr A8 junc 28, take dir into town & foll sp for 'schwimmbad'. Site on L past pool, well sp. Med, mkd pitch, hdstg, pt shd; htd wc; chem disp; mv service pnt; baby facs; shwrs inc; el pnts (10A) €3 or metered + conn fee (poss rev pol); gas; lndtte (inc dryer); shop 1km; rest; bar; pool adj; wifi; TV cab/sat; 60% statics; dogs €1.15; phone; noise fr pool & church bells all night; CCI. "Gd welcome; excel area for cycling; site/office clsd 1230-1500." ♦ € 15.00 2010*

KIRTORF HEIMERTSHAUSEN see Alsfeld *1D4*

KITZINGEN *3D2* (1km SE Urban) *49.73233, 10.16833* **Camping Schiefer Turm, Marktbreiterstrasse 20, 97318 Kitzingen-Hohenfeld [(09321) 33125; fax 384795; info@camping-kitzingen.de; www.camping-kitzingen.de]** Fr A3 take exit junc 74 sp Kitzingen/Schwarzach or exit 72 Würzburg-Ost, or fr A7 exit junc 103 Kitzingen. Site sp in town 'Schwimmbad'. Med, mkd pitch, pt shd; wc; chem disp; mv service pnt; shwrs €0.50; el pnts (16A) €2 or metered; gas; lndtte; shop; supmkt 200m; rest; snacks; pool adj; dogs €1.50; bus; poss cr w/end & high sn; ccard acc. "Bird reserve; pleasant town in evening; gd cycling; busy NH high ssn; san facs up steps." 1 Apr-15 Oct. € 18.00 2009*

KLAIS KRUN see Mittenwald *4E4*

KLEIN RONNAU see Bad Segeberg *1D2*

KLEINROHRSDORF see Dresden *2G4*

KOBLENZ *3B2* (500m N Urban) *50.36611, 7.60361* **Camping Rhein-Mosel, Schartwiesenweg 6, 56070 Koblenz-Lützel [(0261) 82719; fax 802489; info@camping-rhein-mosel.de; www.camping-rhein-mosel.de]** Fr Koblenz heading N on B9 turn off dual c'way at sp for Neuendorf just bef Mosel rv bdge; foll sp to Neuendorf vill. Or heading S on B9 exit dual c'way at camping sp (2nd sp) bef Koblenz; fr Koblenz cent foll sp for 'Altstadt' until Baldwinbrücke (bdge); N over bdge instead of foll sp along S bank of Rv Mosel; R after bdge, then foll sp; site on N side of junc Rhine/Mosel rvs. Lge, some hdstg, pt sl, pt shd; wc; chem disp; mv service pnt; shwrs inc; el pnts (6-16A) €2.05 or metered (long lead poss req); lndtte (inc dryer); shop; supmkt 500m; cooking facs; rest; snacks; bar; dogs; poss v cr; Eng spkn; no adv bkg; heavy rv & rlwy noise; no ccard acc; CCI. "Pleasant, informal site in beautiful location; muddy in wet; staff helpful; no veh acc after 2200; adj ferry to city + easy cycle rte; mkt Sat; flea mkt Sun; 'Rhine in Flames' fireworks 2nd Sat in Aug - watch fr site; site undergoing renovation 2010 & will be used for Horticultural Show Apr-Sep 2011 - adv bkg rec." ♦ 1 Apr-20 Oct. € 17.00 2010*

⊞ **KOBLENZ** *3B2* (8km SW Rural) *50.33194, 7.55277* **Camping Gülser Moselbergen, Am Gülser Moselbogen 20, 56072 Koblenz-Güls [(0261) 44474; fax 44494; info@moselbogen.de; www.moselbogen.de]** Fr A61/E31 exit 38 dir Koblenz/Metternich. After 400m turn R at rndabt dir Winningen. Stay on this rd to T-junc in Winningen, turn L dir Koblenz-Güls, site sp on R in 3km. Med, hdg/mkd pitch, pt shd; htd wc; chem disp; mv service pnt; baby facs; fam bthrm; shwrs €0.50; el pnts (16A) €1.50 + conn fee; gas; lndtte (inc dryer); shop 2km; tradsmn; rest 200m; playgrnd; cab/sat TV; 50% statics; dogs €2; phone; poss cr; Eng spkn; adv bkg; rd & rlwy noise; ccard acc; CCI. "High quality, high-tech san facs; no vehicles 1200-1400; poss subject to flooding; excel." ♦ € 21.00 2010*

KOBLENZ *3B2* (9km SW Urban) *50.30972, 7.50166* **Campinginsel Winningen (previously Campingplatz Ziehfurt), Raiffeisenstraße 16, 56333 Winningen [(02606) 357 or 1800; fax 2566; ferieninsel-winningen@t-online.de; www.mosel-camping.com]** Exit A61/E31 junc 38 to Winningen. In Winningen onto B416. Turn R twd Cochem & cross bdge, turning twd Winningen, site on L by sw pool on island in Mosel Rv. Lge, pt shd; wc; chem disp; mv service pnt; shwrs €0.90; el pnts (16A) €2.50; lndtte; shop; rest; snacks; playgrnd; pool 300m; rv adj; 50% statics; dogs €3; poss v cr; Eng spkn; no adv bkg; some noise fr rd & rlwy. "Cent of wine-growing country; boat trips avail fr Koblenz; cycle rtes; scenic area; poss flooding if v high water; lively site when busy; gd, modern san facs up steep steps but poss stretched on busy w/ends; excel rest; excel site." Easter-1 Oct. € 20.50 2011*

KOLLMAR *1D2* (1km SE Rural/Coastal) *53.72408, 9.50182* **Elbdeich Camping, Kleine Kirchenreihe 22, 25377 Kollmar [(04128) 1379; www.camping-schleswig-holstein.de]** Exit A23 junc 14 Elmshorn-Süd & then take B431 dir Kollmar, site sp on rvside. Med, unshd; htd wc; chem disp; mv service pnt; shwrs inc; el pnts (6A) metered; lndtte; shop, rest, snacks, bar 1km; rv beach adj; 60% statics; dogs €1; phone; bus 1km; site clsd 1200-1500; some Eng spkn; quiet; CCI. "Conv Glückstadt ferry; vg." 1 Apr-31 Oct. € 15.00 2008*

⊞ **KOLN** *1B4* (3km N Urban) *50.96305, 6.98361* **Reisemobilhafen Köln, An der Schanz, 50735 Köln [017 84674591 (mob); info@reisemobilhafen-koeln.de]** Fr A1 Köln ring rd exit junc 100 dir Köln 'Zentrum' until reach rv. Turn L & foll sp to site. M'vans only. Sm, mkd pitch, hdstg; own san; mv service pnt; el pnts (10A) €1 for 12 hrs; shop, rest, snacks, bar 500m; dogs; bus, train nr. "Adj Rv Rhine; must have change for elec, water (metered), parking etc; easy access to city cent; site is unmanned." € 8.00 2011*

⊞ **KOLN** *1B4* (10km NE Rural) *50.99551, 7.06021* **Camping Waldbad, Peter Baum Weg, 51069 Köln-Dünnwald [(0221) 603315; fax 608831; info@waldbad-camping.de; www.waldbad-camping.de]** Exit A3/E35 at junc 24. E for 2km on Willy Brandt ringrd, turn R onto B51 (Mülheimstrasse). In 2.7km turn L into Odenthalerstrasse then foll site sp. Med, pt sl, pt shd; wc; chem disp; mv service pnt; baby facs; shwrs inc; el pnts (10-16A) metered & conn fee; lndtte; shop; rest adj; pool adj; 75% statics; dogs €2; phone; metro to city 10 mins drive; no adv bkg; v quiet. "Close to wildpark, pool & sauna; no ent/exit for cars 1300-1500 & 2200-0700; friendly warden." ♦ € 16.00 2010*

KOLN *1B4* (3km SE Urban) *50.90263, 6.99070* **Campingplatz der Stadt Köln, Weidenweg 35, 51105 Köln-Poll [(0221) 831966; fax 4602221; info@camping-koeln.de; www.camping-koeln.de]** Exit fr A4 (E40) at junc 13 for Köln-Poll-Porz at E end of bdge over Rv Rhine, 3km S of city. At end of slip rd, turn L twd Poll & Köln. Cont about 500m turn L at sp just bef level x-ing, then foll site sp. Narr lane to ent. Lge, pt shd; wc; chem disp; mv service pnt; shwrs €0.50; el pnts (10A) €1.50 (some rev pol & long lead poss req); gas; lndtte; basic shop; tradsmn; snacks; rest 200m; cooking facs; dogs €1.50; phone; trams 1.5km; clsd 1230-1430; poss cr at w/ends; Eng spkn; no adv bkg; some rd & aircraft noise; ccard acc; CCI. "Tram to city over rv bdge; rural site in urban setting on bank of Rv Rhine & subject to flooding; gd undercover cooking facs; gd refurbished san facs on 1st floor; friendly site; v busy at w/end; rvside cycle track to city." ♦ Easter-16 Oct. € 20.00 2011*

⊞ **KOLN** *1B4* (7km SE Rural) *50.8909, 7.02306* **Campingplatz Berger, Uferstrasse 71, 50996 Köln-Rodenkirchen [(0221) 9355240; fax 9355246; camping.berger@t-online.de; www.camping-berger-koeln.de]** Fr A4 turn S onto A555 at Köln-Sud exit 12. Leave A555 at Rodenkirchen exit 3. At 1st junc foll site sp to R. Fr A3 Frankfurt/Köln a'bahn, take A4 twd Aachen (Köln ring rd); exit at Köln Sud; foll sp Bayenthal; at lge rndabt turn R sp Rheinufer & R again at camp sp, under a'bahn. App rd narr & lined with parked cars. Lge, pt shd; htd wc; chem disp; mv service pnt; shwrs inc; el pnts (4-10A) €1.50; gas; lndtte; shop; tradsmn; supmkt 1km; rest; snacks; bar; cooking facs; playgrnd; cycle hire; wifi; 80% statics; dogs €1; phone; bus 500m; poss v cr; Eng spkn; no adv bkg; quiet but some noise fr Rhine barges; ccard acc; red long stay; CCI. "Pleasant, popular, wooded site on banks of Rhine; rvside pitches best; excel rest; helpful staff; gd dog walking; cycle path to city cent; conv cathedral, zoo & museums; do not arr early eve at w/end as narr app rd v busy; pitches poss muddy after rain; san facs up steps - poss clsd 2300-0600." ♦ € 22.20 2011*

KOLPIN see Storkow *2G3*

⊞ **KONIGSSEE** *4G4* (500m N Rural) *47.59445, 12.98583* **Camping Grafenlehen, Königsseer Fussweg 71, 83471 Königssee [(08652) 4140; fax 690768; camping-grafenlehen@t-online.de; www.camping-grafenlehen.de]** On B20 fr Berchtesgaden 5km to Königssee. Where car park with traff lts is ahead, turn R sp Schönau, site on R. Lge, terr, pt shd; htd wc; chem disp; mv service pnt; shwrs inc; el pnts (16A) metered; lndtte; shop; rest; snacks; playgrnd; 10% statics; dogs €2; site clsd Nov to mid-Dec; quiet; red CCI. "Pleasant, quiet site; spectacular views; gd san facs; superb walking; cycle path by rv; gd value rest; 30 mins drive Salzburg Park & Ride; conv Berchtesgaden." € 25.00 2011*

⊞ **KONIGSSEE** *4G4* (1km N Rural) *47.5992, 12.98933* **Camping Mühlleiten, Königsseerstrasse 70, 83471 Königssee [(08652) 4584; fax 69194; info@muehlleiten.eu; www.camping-muehlleiten.eu]** On on R of B20 Berchtesgaden-Königssee. Med, unshd; wc; chem disp; shwrs inc; el pnts (16A) €3 or metered; gas; lndtte; shop & 1km; rest adj; snacks; bar; beach 1km; skilift 500m; golf 6km; entmnt; dogs €2.50; poss cr; quiet; red CCI. "Beautiful area; friendly staff; excel san facs." € 17.50 2009*

GERMANY

KONIGSTEIN *2G4* (1km E Rural) *50.92222, 14.08833* **Camping Königstein, Schandauerstrasse 25e, 01824 Königstein [(035021) 68224; fax 60725; info@camping.koenigstein.de; www.camping-koenigstein.de]** Foll B172 SE fr Dresden/Pirna. Site 500m past Königstein rlwy stn. Turn L over rlwy x-ing & R into site ent on Rv Elbe. Med, pt sl, unshd; wc; chem disp; mv service pnt; shwrs €0.70; el pnts (16A) €2.60; gas; Indtte; shop 1km; rest; playgrnd; 15% statics; dogs €3 (not acc Jul/Aug); sep car park & no dogs Jul/Aug; adv bkg; rlwy noise; red 5+ days. "Gd san facs; lovely location nr national parks & Czech border; on Elbe cycle path; frequent trains to Dresden; boat trips; gates clsd 1300-1500." ♦ 1 Apr-31 Oct. € 23.00 2011*

⊞ **KONIGSTEIN** *2G4* (2.5km E Rural) *50.91500, 14.10730* **Caravan Camping Sächsische Schweiz, Dorfplatz 181d, 01824 Kurort-Gohrisch [caravan-camping@web.de; www.caravan-camping-saechsischeschweiz.de]** Fr Königstein foll B172 E dir Bad Schandau. Fork R dir Gohrisch for 2.5km, turn L into Dorfplatz & foll site sp. Med, hdg/mkd pitch, hdstg, pt sl, pt shd; wc; chem disp; mv service pnt; baby facs; fam bathrm; sauna; shwrs €0.50; el pnts (16A) metered; Indtte (inc dryer); shop; tradsmn; rest; bar; BBQ; cooking facs; playgrnd; htd, covrd pool 4km; padding pool; games area; cycle hire; wifi; sat/cable TV; 5% statics; dogs €2; bus 500m; Eng spkn; adv bkg; quiet; red low ssn/long stay. "Excel site; gd touring base; interesting area; guided walks." ♦ 2010*

KONIGSWALDE see Annaberg Buchholz *4G1*

KONSTANZ *3D4* (7km N Rural) *47.74596, 9.14701* **Camping Klausenhorn, Hornwiesenstrasse, 78465 Dingelsdorf [(07533) 6372; fax 7541; info@camping-klausenhorn.de; www.konstanz.de/tourismus/klausenhorn]** Site sp N of Dingelsdorf on lakeside. Lge, mkd pitch, hdstg, pt shd; htd wc; chem disp; baby facs; shwrs €0.50; el pnts (10A) inc; Indtte; shop & 1.5km; rest 800m; snacks; bar; BBQ; playgrnd; shgl beach & lake adj; boating; games area; wifi; entmnt; 50% statics; no dogs; bus 500m; sep car park; poss cr; Eng spkn; adv bkg; quiet; ccard acc; CCI. "Excel site." ♦ 1 Apr-4 Oct. € 25.50 2009*

KONSTANZ *3D4* (4km NE Urban) *47.67416, 9.20944* **Camping Bruderhofer, Fohrenbühlweg 50, 78464 Konstanz-Staad [(07531) 31388; fax 31392; www.campingplatz-konstanz.de]** Fr Swiss border (Kreutzlingen) take main rd & cross Rhine; NE into Mainaustrasse & foll camp sp to site. Fr bdge to site 2.5km. Fr town cent foll sp for Meersburg ferry, turn R at 2nd traff lts (400m) opp 'Lotto' kiosk; pass houses & woodland for 1.7km & turn R into narr lane. Med, mkd pitch, pt sl, pt shd; wc; chem disp; mv service pnt; shwrs €1; el pnts (16A) €2; Indtte; shop 1km; tradsmn; rest; snacks; bar; playgrnd; lake sw adj; watersports; car park; 30% statics (sep area); dogs free; clsd 1300-1500; poss cr; adv bkg; ccard acc; CCI. "Basic, well-kept site; facs clean; excel walks & cycling; gd for watersports." ♦ 1 Apr-30 Sep. € 19.30 2008*

KONSTANZ *3D4* (10km W Rural) *47.69871, 9.04603* **Camping Sandseele, Bradlengasse 24, 78479 Niederzell [(07534) 7384; fax 98976; beyer@sandseele.de; www.sandseele.de]** Clearly sp off B33 Konstanz-Radolfzell rd. Foll sp on island & sm multiple sp. Lge, pt shd; wc; chem disp; mv service pnt; shwrs inc; el pnts (16A) €3; gas; Indtte; shop; rest; snacks; playgrnd; lake sw & beach; watersports; 30% statics; no dogs; sep car park high ssn; poss v cr; poss noisy. "Insect repellent rec." ♦ 15 Mar-5 Oct. € 20.50 2008*

KONZ see Trier *3B2*

⊞ **KORBACH** *1C4* (13km S Rural) *51.17500, 8.89138* **Camping & Ferienpark Teichmann, Zum Träumen 1a, 34516 Vöhl-Herzhausen [(05635) 245; fax 8145; info@camping-teichmann.de; www.camping-teichmann.de]** Fr Korbach, take B252 S. In 12m cross Rv Eder. Site in 1km on R by lake. Lge, mkd pitch, pt shd, wc; chem disp; mv service pnt; baby facs; sauna; shwrs inc; el pnts (10A) €2.60; Indtte (inc dryer); shop; rest; snacks; bar; playgrnd; lake sw & beach; boat & cycle hire; tennis; cycle & boat hire; games area; horseriding 500m; wellness cent; winter sports; entmnt high ssn; wifi; TV; 50% statics; dogs €3.60; sep car park; o'night area for m'vans; adv bkg; ccard acc; red CCI. "Excel family site in lovely situation; friendly, helpful staff; gd walking in area." ♦ € 30.30 2011*

See advertisement

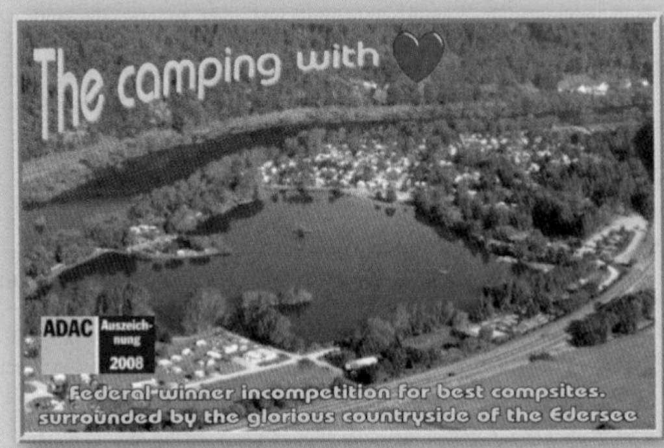

The camping with
ADAC Auszeichnung 2008
Federal winner in competition for best campsites.
surrounded by the glorious countryside of the Edersee

Camping-und Ferienpark
TEICHMANN
34516 Vöhl-Herzhausen . Tel. 05635-245 . Fax 05635-8145
Internet: www.camping-teichmann.de . E-Mail: camping-teichmann@t-online.de

Our family-friendly campsite, in the heart of Germany offers unforgettable holiday enjoyment.

young persons tent area . animation . tennis court . beach volleyball . minigolf boat hire . motorhome friendly . swimming & fishing lake . barbecue hut bicycle hire . restaurant . mini-market . sauna & solarium . holiday homes at the nationalpark info centre . new: w-lan . wellness station . Internetroom

⊞ **KOTZTING** *4F3* (6km NE Rural) *49.20610, 12.92381* **Camping Hohenwarth Fritz-Berger, Ferienzentrum 3, 93480 Hohenwarth [(09946) 367; fax 477; info@campingplatz-hohenwarth.de; www.campingplatz-hohenwarth.de]** Fr Cham, take B85 SW to Miltach, Kötzting & site sp on L on Hohenwarth by-pass. Lge, mkd pitch, some hdstg, unshd; wc; chem disp; mv service pnt; sauna; shwrs inc; el pnts (16A) metered + conn fee; gas; Indtte; shop; tradsmn; rest; snacks; bar; playgrnd; pool; lake sw; skilift 7km; entmnt; internet; 10% statics; dogs €2; phone; site clsd 5 Nov-10 Dec; adv bkg; quiet; ccard acc; CCI. "Gd walking & cycling area; office clsd 1200-1400 & 1800-0800; conv NH for Bavaria & Czech Rep." ♦ € 18.00 2011*

⊞ **KRANICHFELD** *2E4* (4km NW Rural) *50.87216, 11.17843* **Campingplatz Stausee Hohenfelden, 99448 Hohenfelden [(036450) 42081; fax 42082; info@stausse-hohenfelden.de; www.stausee-hohenfelden.de]** Fr A4/E40 take exit 47a S twd Kranichfeld. Site clearly sp by lake along rough rd. Lge, sl, pt terr, pt shd; wc; chem disp; mv service pnt; shwrs €0.80; el pnts (10A) €2.60; Indtte (inc dryer); supmkt 3km; tradsmn; snacks; boating; cycle hire; TV; 60% statics; dogs €2.50; no adv bkg; ccard acc; CCI. "Woodland, lakeside walks; gates clsd 1300-1500 & 2200-0700; poss noisy, scruffy; poss lge youth groups; gd san facs but diff access." ♦ € 17.40 2010*

KRESSBRONN AM BODENSEE *3D4* (7km N Rural) *47.63395, 9.6477* **Gutshof-Camping Badhütten (Part Naturist), Badhütten 1, 88069 Laimnau [(07543) 96330; fax 963315; gutshof.camping@t-online.de; www.gutshof-camping.de]** Fr Kressbronn take B467 to Tettnang & Ravensburg. In 3km immed after x-ing Rv Argen turn R & site sp for approx 3km. V lge, hdg/mkd pitch, pt shd; wc; chem disp; mv service pnt; serviced pitches; baby facs; shwrs inc; el pnts (16A) metered; gas; Indtte; shop; rest; snacks; bar; playgrnd; pool; lake 7km; entmnt; 40% statics; dogs €2; adv bkg; quiet; red long stay; CCI. "Sep area for naturists; gd facs; v rural site; clean, quiet & pleasant; excel." ♦ 30 Mar-5 Nov. € 27.80 2011

KRESSBRONN AM BODENSEE *3D4* (1km W Rural) *47.58718, 9.58281* **Campingplatz Irisweise, Tunau 16, 88079 Kressbronn [(07543) 8010; fax 8032; info@campingplatz-irisweise.de; www.campingplatz-iriswiese.de]** Fr E or W take exit off B31 bypass for Kressbronn, site well sp. Lge, hdg/mkd pitch, pt shd; htd wc; chem disp; mv service pnt; baby facs; shwrs inc; el pnts (10A) metered + conn fee; gas; Indtte; shop; rest; bar; BBQ; playgrnd; beach, lake sw adj (sep naturist beach); sailing; watersports; internet; 10% statics; dogs €2; phone; poss v cr; Eng spkn; no adv bkg; quiet; CCI. "Steamer trips on lake; no car access 2100-0700, park outside site; excel san facs but some distance fr touring pitches; gd." ♦ 8 Apr-15 Oct. € 25.50 2010*

KROV see Wittlich *3B2*

KRUMBACH *4E4* (4km SW Rural) *48.22720, 10.29280* **See Camping Günztal, Oberrieder Weiherstrasse 5, 86488 Breitenthal [(08282) 881870; info@see-camping-guenztal.de; www.see-camping-guenztal.de]** W fr Krumbach on rd 2018, in Breitenthal turn S twd Oberried & Oberrieder Weiher, site sp on lakeside. Med, mkd pitch, some hdstg; pt shd; htd wc; chem disp; mv service pnt; baby facs; shwrs inc; el pnts (10A) inc; Indtte (inc dryer); shop 800m; tradsmn; rest 1.5km; snacks; bar; BBQ; playgrnd; lake sw; watersports; fishing; games area; wifi; TV; 30% statics; dogs €2; adv bkg; quiet. ♦ 1 Apr-30 Oct. € 19.50 (CChq acc) 2010*

There aren't many sites open at this time of year. We'd better phone ahead to check the one we're heading for is open.

KUHLUNGSBORN *2E1* (600m W Coastal) *54.15137, 11.71947* **Campingpark Kühlungsborn, Waldstrasse 1b; 18225 Kühlungsborn [(038293) 7195; fax 7192; info@topcamping.de; www.topcamping.de]** On rd B105 turn N in Neubukow sp Kühlungsborn. In 15km, at W Kühlungsborn stn, rd turns N; foll sp. V lge, pt sl, shd; wc; chem disp; mv service pnt; serviced pitches; baby facs; shwrs inc; el pnts (16A) inc; Indtte; shop adj; rest; snacks; rest; shop; playgrnd; htd pool 300m; beach (sep naturist beach); sailing; windsurfing; games area; cycle hire; entmnt; TV; 20% statics; dogs €5; poss cr; quiet; ccard acc. "Excel site; upgraded & modernised facs, esp new luxurious toilet block (even has a luxury dog wash!); v cln & well managed; town a pleasant, old-fashioned holiday resort." ♦ 30 Mar-26 Oct. € 34.00 2011*

⊞ **KULMBACH** *4E2* (300m NE Urban) *50.11083, 11.46160* **Parkplatz am Schwedensteg, 95326 Kulmbach [(09221) 95880; fax 958844; touristinfo@stadt-kulmbach.de; www.stadt-kulmbach.de]** Exit A70/E48 junc 24 onto B289 dir Kulmbach Stadtmitte. Foll sp 'Festplatz am Schwedensteg' to area behind bus & truck park. Sm, hdstg, unshd; own san; chem disp; mv service pnt; water €1/100 litres; el pnts (16A) metered; shop, rest, snacks, bar 500m; m'vans only. "Historic town cent." ♦ € 3.00 2009*

⊞ **KULMBACH** *4E2* (8km NE Rural) *50.16050, 11.51605* **Campingplatz Stadtsteinach, Badstrasse 5, 95346 Stadtsteinach [(09225) 800394; info@campingplatz-stadtsteinach.de; www.campingplatz-stadtsteinach.de]** Fr Kulmbach take B289 to Untersteinach (8km); turn L to Stadtsteinach; turn R at camping sp & foll rd for 1km. Site also sp fr N side of town on B303. Or fr A9/E51 exit junc 39 onto B303 NW to Stadtsteinach. Med, pt shd; htd wc; chem disp; mv service pnt; shwrs inc; el pnts (16A) €2.10; Indtte; shop 600m; rest; snacks; bar; cooking facs; playgrnd; htd pool adj; paddling pool; rv fishing; tennis; cycle hire; games area; 75% statics; dogs €2; Eng spkn; adv bkg; ccard acc; CCI. "Excel site in beautiful countryside; excel, modern facs." ♦ € 21.00 2009*

GERMANY

LABOE *1D1* (2km NE Coastal) *54.41399, 10.24846* **Camping Fördeblick, Kreisstrasse 30, 24235 Stein [(04343) 7795; fax 7790; info@camping-foerdeblick.de; www.camping-foerdeblick.de]** Exit B76/B202 into Kiel & take sp Gaarden-Ost. Then turn L onto B502 dir Heikendorf. Foll sp Laboe & Stein. Lge, mkd pitch, pt sl, unshd; htd wc; chem disp; mv service pnt; baby facs; shwrs inc; el pnts (10A) €2.60; gas; lndtte; shop; tradsmn; rest; snacks; bar; playgrnd; sand/shgl beach adj; watersports nrby; games area; golf 5km; wifi; entmnt; 75% statics (sep area); no dogs; phone; bus 500m; poss cr; Eng spkn; adv bkg; CCI. "Facs dated but vg; site on cliffs, some pitches excel views; narr access lanes to pitches; pleasant walk into Laboe." ♦ 1 Apr-28 Oct. € 26.00 2011*

LABOE *1D1* (4km E Coastal) *54.42698, 10.29646* **Camping Oase-Bonanza, Schleusenweg 25, 24235 Wendtorf [(04343) 9688; fax 9899; camping@camping-oase-bonanza.de; www.camping-oase-bonanza.de]** N fr Kiel on B502 sp Laboe take turning N sp Stein & Wendtorf. Drive to end past marina ignoring all sps, site on R behind dyke. Med, hdg/mkd pitch, pt shd; htd wc; chem disp; mv service pnt; shwrs €0.60; el pnts (12A) €3; gas; lndtte; shop; supmkt 1km; rest; snacks; bar; playgrnd; sand beach adj (inc naturist); 70% statics; dogs €3; phone; adv bkg; quiet; ccard acc; CCI. "Excel cycle paths; friendly owners; excel san facs; stunning beach." 1 Apr-30 Sep. € 20.50 2011*

I'll go online and tell the Club what we think of the campsites we've visited – www.caravanclub.co.uk/europereport

LAHNSTEIN *3B2* (2.5km E Urban) *50.30565, 7.61313* **Kur-Campingplatz Burg Lahneck, Am Burgweg, 56112 Lahnstein-Oberlahnstein [(02621) 2765; fax 18290]** Take B42 fr Koblenz over Lahn Rv, if fr low bdge turn L immed after church & sp fr there; if fr high level bdge thro sh tunnel turn L at 1st rd on L sp to Burg-Lahneck - site sp on L. Med, pt sl, pt shd; wc; chem disp; mv service pnt; shwrs €0.50; el pnts (16A) metered + conn fee; lndtte; shop; tradsmn; rest; playgrnd; pool adj; 10% statics; dogs €1; poss cr; Eng spkn; quiet but distant rlwy noise at night; ccard not acc. "Gd views over Rhine; scenic area; delightful, helpful owner v particular about pitching; gd size pitches; immac, well-run site." 1 Apr-31 Oct. € 21.50 2010*

LAHNSTEIN *3B2* (8km SE Urban) *50.27393, 7.64098* **Campingplatz Uferwiese, Am Campingplatz 1, 56338 Braubach [tel/fax (02627) 8762; info@campingplatz-braubach.de; www.campingplatz-braubach.de]** Take B42 S twd Rüdesheim. Site behind hotel opp church. Med, shd; wc; chem disp; shwrs €1; el pnts (16A) €2 (poss rev pol); lndtte; shop 300m; rest 200m; snacks; bar; 50% statics; dogs €1; bus; rd & rlwy noise; no ccard acc; CCI. "Scenic on Rv Rhine; poss flooding after heavy rain; gd san facs." 15 Apr-25 Oct. € 18.00 2009*

⊞ **LAHR (SCHWARZWALD)** *3B3* (8km SE Rural) *48.29999, 7.94395* **Ferienparadies Schwarzwälder Hof, Tretenhofstrasse 76, 77960 Seelbach [(07823) 960950; fax 9609522; camping-rezeption@seelbach.org; www.campingplatz-schwarzwaelder-hof.de]** Fr A5 take exit 56 to Lahr. In 5km turn R twd Seelbach & Schuttertal. Thro town & site on S o'skts of Seelbach just after town boundary. Med, mkd pitch, some hdstg, pt sl, terr, pt shd; serviced pitches (extra charge); wc; chem disp; mv service pnt; shwrs inc; el pnts (10A) metered + conn fee; gas; lndtte; shop; tradsmn; rest; snacks 1km; bar; playgrnd; htd pool adj; lake adj; 10% statics; dogs €3.50; o'night area for m'vans; poss v cr; Eng spkn; adv bkg ess high ssn; quiet; ccard acc; red CCI. "Vg touring base; well-laid out pitches & excel facs; many gd mkd walks; gd programme of events in Seelbach." ♦ € 29.70 2011*

LAHR (SCHWARZWALD) *3B3* (5km S Rural) *48.24739, 7.82804* **Terrassen-Campingpark Oase, Mühlenweg 34, 77955 Ettenheim [(07822) 445918; fax 445919; info@campingpark-oase.de; www.campingpark-oase.de]** Exit A5/E35 at junc 57a, foll site sp. Lge, shd; wc; shwrs; chem disp; mv service pnt; baby facs; shwrs €0.50; el pnts (6A) €2; lndtte; shop; rest; snacks; playgrnd; pool adj; tennis adj; cycle hire; 30% statics; dogs €1.50; quiet; CCI. "Modern san facs; variable pitch size/price; short walk/cycle track to attractive town; conv glassworks at Wolfach & House of 1000 clocks nr Triberg." ♦ 15 Mar-8 Oct. € 22.00 2009*

⊞ **LAICHINGEN** *3D3* (2km S Rural) *48.47560, 9.7458* **Camping & Freizeitzentrum Heidehof, Heidehofstrasse 50, 89150 Laichingen-Machtolsheim [(07333) 6408; fax 21463; heidehof.camping@t-online.de; www.camping-heidehof.de]** Exit A8 junc 61 dir Merklingen. At T-junc turn R sp Laichingen. In 3km site sp to L. V lge, hdg/mkd pitch, hdstg, pt sl, pt shd, some hdstg; wc; chem disp; mv service pnt; baby facs; fam bthrm; sauna; shwrs inc; el pnts (10-16A) €2 or metered; gas; lndtte; shop; tradmsn; rest; playgrnd; htd pool; cycle hire; 95% statics; adv bkg; red long stay/CCI. "Blaubeuren Abbey & Blautopf (blue pool of glacial origin) worth visit; sep area for o'nighters immed bef main camp ent - poss unreliable when wet; hdstg pitches sm & sl; vg rest; gd NH." ♦ € 18.00 2008*

LAIMNAU see Kressbronn am Bodensee *3D4*

LANDAU IN DER PFALZ *3C3* (10km W Rural) *49.20138, 7.97222* **Camping der Naturfreunde, Victor von Scheffelstrasse 18, 76855 Annweiler-am-Trifels [(06346) 3870; fax 302945; info@naturfreunde-annweiler.de; www.naturfreunde-annweiler.de]** Fr Landau take B10 dir Pirmasens, take 1st exit to Annweiler then turn L into vill along Landauerstrasse. Turn L immed after VW/Audi g'ge, site sp. Tight access at ent. Sm, hdstg, pt shd; htd wc; chem disp; mv service pnt; shwrs inc; el pnts (10A) €2; lndtte; shops 500m; rest adj; playgrnd; 80% statics; dogs €2; poss cr; quiet; CCI. "Friendly, helpful owner poss on site evenings only; immac, modern san facs; ltd space for tourers but adequate facs; vg views across valley & forest." ♦ 1 Apr-31 Oct. € 16.00 2010*

⊞ **LANDSBERG AM LECH** *4E4* (3km SE Rural) *48.03195, 10.88526* **DCC Campingpark Romantik am Lech, Pössinger Au 1, 86899 Landsberg-am-Lech [(08191) 47505; fax 21406; campingparkgmbh@aol.com; www.campingplatz-landsberg.de]** Not rec to tow thro Landsberg. If app fr S, get onto rd fr Weilheim & foll sp on app to Landsberg. Fr other dir, exit junc 26 fr a'bahn A96 Landsberg Ost, then app town via Muchenstrasse. At rndabt bef town cent, foll sp dir Weilheim, after 400m turn R & foll site sp. Lge, hdg/mkd pitch, pt sl, pt shd; wc; chem disp; mv service pnt; shwrs inc; el pnts (16A) metered (some rev pol); gas; Indtte; shop; rest 2km; snacks; bar; playgrnd; pool 3km; tennis; cycle hire; 50% statics; dogs €1; adv bkg; Eng spkn; quiet; red CCI. "V pleasant site; excel, clean facs; nature reserve on 2 sides; gd walking & cycling; attractive old town; site clsd 1300-1500 & 2200-0700." ♦ € 16.90 2011*

LANDSHUT *4F3* (3km NE Urban) *48.55455, 12.1795* **Camping Landshut, Breslauerstrasse 122, 84028 Landshut [tel/fax (0871) 53366; www.landshut.de]** Fr A92/E53 exit junc 14 onto B299 dir Landshut N. After approx 5km turn L at int'l camping sp & foll site sp. Med, pt shd; wc; chem disp; mv service pnt; shwrs inc; el pnts (16A) €2.50; Indtte; shop 500m; rest 200m; snacks; bar; BBQ; htd pool 3km; 10% statics; dogs €1.50; poss cr; quiet; CCI. "Well-run, friendly site; gd san facs; beautiful medieval town & castle - easy cycle rte." ♦ 1 Apr-30 Sep. € 17.00 2009*

LANGELSHEIM see Goslar *1D3*

LANGSUR METZDORF see Trier *3B2*

⊞ **LANGWEDEL** *1D1* (1km W Rural) *54.21465, 9.91825* **Caravanpark am Brahmsee, Mühlenstrasse 30a, 24631 Langwedel [(04329) 1567; info@caravanpark-sh.de; www.caravanpark-sh.de]** Exit A7 at junc 10 dir Tierpark Warder (animal park) & foll site sp to lakeside. Or exit A215 at Blumenthal onto L298 thro Langwedel dir Tierpark Warder, site sp. Med, hdg/mkd pitch, some hdstg, pt shd; htd wc; chem disp; mv service pnt; shwrs inc; el pnts €2.50; Indtte (inc dryer); shop 1km; tradsmn; rest 1km; cooking facs; BBQ; playgrnd; lake sw 100m; fishing; wifi; 80% statics; dogs; adv bkg; quiet. "Peaceful site in nature park; gd." ♦ € 15.00 (CChq acc) 2010*

⊞ **LECHBRUCK** *4E4* (2.8km NE Rural) *47.71169, 10.81872* **Via Claudia Camping (formerly DCC Campingpark Lechsee), Via Claudia 6, 86983 Lechbruck [(08862) 8426; fax 7570; info@camping-lechbruck.de; www.via-claudia-camping.de]** A95 exit junc 10 Murnau/Kochel & then via Murnau, Saulgrub, Steingaden to Lechbruck. Then foll sps. V lge, mkd pitch, terr, pt shd; wc; chem disp; mv service pnt; baby facs; shwrs inc; el pnts (10-16A) €2.65; gas; Indtte (inc dryer); shop; tradsmn; rest; bar; playgrnd; pool 500m; lake beach & sw; watersports; minigolf; volleyball; archery; wifi; entmnt; 50% statics; dogs €3.50; o'night m'van area; Eng spkn; adv bkg; quiet; ccard acc; red CCI. "Pleasant, peaceful, lakeside site; fac to a high standard; gd welcome; v helpful; cont investment in site fr new owners." ♦ € 24.70 2011*

LEEDEN see Osnabrück *1C3*

⊞ **LEER (OSTFRIESLAND)** *1B2* (3km W Rural) *53.22416, 7.41891* **Camping Ems-Marina Bingum, Marinastrasse 14-16, 26789 Leer-Bingum [(0491) 64447; fax 66405; into-camping-bingum@t-online.de; www.bingumcamper.de]** Leave A32/E12 junc 12; site 500m S of Bingum; well sp. Lge, pt shd; wc; chem disp; mv service pnt; baby facs; shwrs €1; el pnts (16A) €2.50 or metered; gas; Indtte (inc dryer); shop 500m; rest; snacks; playgrnd; cycle hire; 65% statics; dogs €3.50; gate clsd 1230-1500; adv bkg; quiet; red long stay/CCI. ♦ € 20.00 2010*

LEINATEL see Ohrdruf *2E4*

⊞ **LEIPHEIM** *3D3* (2km W Rural) *48.46566, 10.2035* **Camping Schwarzfelder Hof, Schwarzfelderweg 3, Riedheim, 89340 Leipheim [(08221) 72628; fax 71134; info@schwarzfelder-hof.de; www.schwarzfelder-hof.de]** Fr A8 exit junc 66 Leipheim onto B10. In Leipheim foll sp Langenau & Riedheim, site sp. Do not confuse with Laupheim 25km S of Ulm on B30. Sm, hdstg, pt shd; htd wc; chem disp (wc); serviced pitches; shwrs inc; el pnts (16A) €2.10 or metered; Indtte; shop 2km; tradsmn; rest 1.5km; snacks; bar; BBQ; playgrnd; 50% statics; dogs €3.20; train 1km; poss cr; Eng spkn; quiet. "Peaceful, farm-based site on site of old quarry; welcoming, helpful owner; lge pitches; vg san facs but ltd; farm animals & riding for children; conv Ulm; recep open 0800-1000 & 1730-2000; poss noisy youth groups; conv NH for m'way." € 18.70 2010*

⊞ **LEIPZIG** *2F4* (6km NW Urban) *51.37030, 12.31375* **Campingplatz Auensee, Gustav-Esche Strasse 5, 04159 Leipzig [(0341) 4651600; fax 4651617; info@camping-auensee.de; www.camping-auensee.de]** Fr A9/E51 exit junc 16 onto B6 two Leipzig. In Leipzig-Wahren turn R at 'Rathaus' sp Leutzsch (camping symbol), site on R in 1.5km, sp. Lge, mkd pitch, some hdstg, pt shd; htd wc; chem disp; mv service pnt; shwrs inc; el pnts (16A) €3; Indtte (inc dryer); supmkt 1.5km; rest; snacks; bar; BBQ; cooking facs; playgrnd; Lake Auensee 500m; TV; dogs €2; phone; bus; tram 1.5km; poss cr; Eng spkn; adv bkg; ccard acc; CCI. "Roomy, well-run, clean site; plentiful san facs; gd size pitches; vg rest; friendly, helpful staff; 10 mins walk to tram for city cent or bus stop at site ent, tickets avail fr recep; excel." ♦ € 23.50 2011*

⊞ **LEMGO** *1C3* (500m S Urban) *52.02503, 8.90874* **Campingpark Lemgo, Regenstorstrasse 10, 32657 Lemgo [(05261) 14858; fax 188324; info@camping-lemgo.de; www.camping-lemgo.de]** Exit A2 junc 28 onto L712N to Lemgo; at traff lts turn L following L712; at rnd abt take Bismarckstrasse exit; at traff lts turn R into Regenstorstrasse. Site sp. Med, pt shd; wc; shwrs €0.50; el pnts (6A) metered + conn fee; Indtte (inc dryer); shop 500m; rest 300m; snacks 500m; playgrnd; pool 200m; wifi; 25% statics; dogs €2; adv bkg. "Slightly scruffy site but in cent of lovely medieval town; o'night area for m'vans - modern san facs." € 19.50 2010*

GERMANY

⊞ **LENGERICH** *1C3* (2km W Rural) *52.18854, 7.80439* **Campingplatz auf dem Sonnenhügel, Zur Sandgrube 40, 49525 Lengerich [(05481) 6216; fax 845829; info@sonnenhuegel-camping.de; www.sonnenhuegel-camping.de]** Leave A1 Lengerich/Tecklenburg, turn R at bottom of slip rd onto S ring rd; L into Ibbenbüren Str; R & immed R again into Antruper Str; foll rd under S ring; R into Sonnenhügeldamm; foll sp. Med, pt shd; wc; chem disp; shwrs €0.50; el pnts €2 or metered; gas; Indtte; rest 1km; bar; shop; playgrnd; lake sw adj; fishing; 80% statics; dogs €2; clsd 1300-1500; Eng spkn; adv bkg; a'bahn noise; ccard acc; CCI. "Immac facs; vg value." ♦ € 14.00 2011*

LENZEN *2E2* (5km E Rural) *53.11000, 11.54083* **Naturcampingplatz am Rudower See, Leuengarten 9, 19309 Lenzen [(038792) 80075 or (030854) 4020 (winter); fax 80076; info@naturcampingplatz.de; www.naturcampingplatz.de]** Fr B195 turn N along S side of Rudower See, site sp. Site at E end of lake. Med, terr, pt shd; htd wc; chem disp; fam bthrm; shwrs inc; el pnts (16A) €1.75; gas; Indtte; shop 4km; tradsmn; rest & bar 2km; snacks; playgrnd; lake sw adj; boat hire; games area; 20% statics; dogs €2.50; phone; adv bkg; quiet. "Peaceful site in nature park; gd facs; helpful owners; gd walking, cycling, birdwatching; gd NH." ♦ 1 Apr-15 Oct. € 17.00 2010*

LICHTENFELS *4E2* (2.5km N Rural) *50.15598, 11.08654* **Main-Camping, Krösswehrstrasse 52, 96215 Lichtenfels-Oberwallenstadt [(09571) 71729; fax 946851; campingplatz@lichtenfels-city.de; www.lichtenfels-city.de]** Site well sp fr rd B173 at Lichtenfels-Ost dir Oberwallenstadt. Med, mkd pitch, hdstg, pt shd; htd wc; chem disp; shwrs inc; el pnts (16A) €2.10; Indtte; shop 1km; rest 300m; cooking facs; playgrnd; lake sw adj; tennis; 40% statics; dogs €1.50; phone; quiet; ccard acc; CCI. "Lovely site; gd, clean, modern facs; friendly, helpful warden; poss flooding after heavy rain; rec." ♦ 1 Apr-15 Oct. € 10.80 2007*

LIETZOW *2G1* (300m N) *54.48358, 13.50846* **Störtebecker Camp, Gästehaus Lietzow, Waldstraße 59a, 18528 Lietzow [038302 2166; info@lietzow.net; www.lietzow.net]** On rd 96, E22 fr Stralsund to ferry harbour at Sassnitz; when you arr at Lietzow site sp 'Gästehaus Lietzow' on RH side of rd; sh, steep incline fr main rd. Med, hdg pitch, pt shd; wc; chem disp; MV waste; shwrs inc; el pnts inc; gas; Indtte; tradsmn; rest; snacks; bar; playgrnd; beach 250m; dogs €2.50; adv bking; CCI. "Pleasant site, central for the island, sightseeing & useful stopover nr ferry point." 15 Mar-15 Dec. € 28.50 2011*

LIMBURG AN DER LAHN *3C2* (4km SW Rural) *50.38151, 8.00046* **Camping Oranienstein, Strandbadweg, 65582 Diez [(06432) 2122; fax 924193; post@camping-diez.de; www.camping-diez.de]** In Diez on L bank of Lahn. Exit A3 junc 41 Diez or junc 43 Limburg-Süd. Site sp 1km bef Diez, 8km fr a'bahn. Lge, pt shd; wc; chem disp; mv service pnt; shwrs; el pnts (6A) €2.20 or metered; gas; Indtte; shop; rest; playgrnd; children's pool; watersports; cycle hire; 60% statics; dogs; adv bkg; ccard acc; CCI. "Pleasant vill; gd rests; hot water metered." ♦ 1 Apr-30 Oct. € 16.30 2009*

LIMBURG AN DER LAHN *3C2* (200m W Urban) *50.38916, 8.07333* **Lahn Camping, Schleusenweg 16, 65549 Limburg-an-der-Lahn [(06431) 22610; fax 92013; info@lahncamping.de; www.lahncamping.de]** Exit A3/E35 junc 42 Limburg Nord, site sp. By Rv Lahn in town, easy access. Lge, pt shd; wc; chem disp; mv service pnt; baby facs; shwrs €1; el pnts (6A) €2.50 (long lead poss req); gas; Indtte; shop; rest; playgrnd; htd pool 100m; rv sw & fishing; 20% statics; dogs €1.50; bus; poss v cr; Eng spkn; rd & rlwy noise; red CCI. "Busy, well-organised site; sm pitches - some poss diff to manoeuvre; gd views; friendly staff; poss flooding in wet weather; sh walk to interesting town; gates clsd 1300-1500; useful NH." ♦ 29 Mar-24 Oct. € 18.10 2011*

LINDAU (BODENSEE) *3D4* (5km N Rural) *47.58509, 9.70667* **Campingpark Gitzenweiler Hof, Gitzenweiler 88, 88131 Lindau-Gitzenweiler [(08382) 94940; fax 949415; info@gitzenweiler-hof.de; www.gitzenweiler-hof.de]** Exit A96/E43/E54 junc 4 onto B12 sp Lindau. Turn off immed after vill of Oberreitnau twd Rehlings. Site well sp fr all dirs. Lge, mkd pitch, pt sl, pt shd; wc; chem disp; mv service pnt; serviced pitches; baby facs; shwrs inc; el pnts (6A) €2.50; gas; Indtte; shop; rest; snacks; playgrnd; pool; sm boating/fishing lake; lake sw 6km; entmnt high ssn; TV; 50% statics; dogs €2.50; bus 1km; o'night facs for m'vans; Eng spkn; adv bkg; poss noisy high ssn; red long stay; CCI. "Well-run, busy site in scenic area; gd facs; friendly staff; excel site for children; gd cycling; poss prone to flooding after v heavy rain." ♦ 25 Mar-7 Nov. € 24.50 2010*

LINDAU (BODENSEE) *3D4* (4km SE Rural) *47.53758, 9.73143* **Park-Camping Lindau am See, Fraunhoferstrasse 20, 88131 Lindau-Zech [(08382) 72236; fax 976106; info@park-camping.de; www.park-camping.de]** On B31 fr Bregenz to Lindau, 200m after customs turn L to site in 150m; ent could be missed; mini-mkt on corner; ent rd crosses main rlwy line with auto barriers. B31 fr Friedrichshafen, site well sp fr o'skts of Lindau. Lge, mkd pitch, hdstg, pt shd; wc; chem disp; mv service pnt; shwrs inc; el pnts (10A) €1 (long lead poss req); Indtte (inc dryer); sm shop; mini-mkt nr; rest; snacks; playgrnd; shgl beach; lake sw; cycle hire; golf 3km; wifi; entmnt high ssn; 20% statics; dogs €3; m'van o'night area €10; poss cr; Eng spkn; rd & rlwy noise. "Busy site; immac san facs; sh stay pitches poss diff to manoeuvre as v cramped; office/gate clsd 1300-1400; helpful staff; shwr rm for dogs; excel walking in Pfänder area; excel." ♦ 15 Mar-10 Nov. € 26.50 2010*

LINDAUNIS *1D1* (1km S Rural) *54.58626, 9.8173* **Camping Lindaunis, Schleistrasse 1, 24392 Lindaunis [(04641) 7317; fax 7187; info@camping-lindaunis.de; www.camping-lindaunis.de]** Exit A7/E45 junc 5 onto B201 sp Brebel & Süderbrarup. At Brebel turn R & foll dir Lindaunis, site approx 12km on R beside Schlei Fjord. Lge, mkd pitch, pt shd; htd wc; chem disp; baby facs; shwrs €0.50; el pnts (16A) €2.50; Indtte; shop; tradsmn; rest; snacks; bar; playgrnd; sw in fjord; boating; canoing; fishing; boat & cycle hire; entmnt; TV; 80% statics; dogs €1.50; phone; Eng spkn; adv bkg rec; quiet; red CCI. "Vg, family-run site ideally placed for exploring Schlei fjord & conv Danish border; gd san facs; gd cycle rtes." ♦ 1 Apr-15 Oct. € 16.60 2008*

LINDENBERG IM ALLGAU *3D4* (1km S Rural) *47.59789, 9.90047* **Camping Alpenblick, Schreckenmanklitz 18, 88171 Weiler-Simmerberg [(08381) 3447; fax 942195; info@camping-alpenblick.de; www.camping-alpenblick.de]** On S of B308 bet Lindau & Immenstadt. Turn off B308 opp hotels sp 'Schreckenmanklitz. Diff ent - do not attempt to turn fr dir Lindau - cont 200m to turning point (mkd 'wendelplatz') & return. Site in 200m on L, visible fr rd. Med, mkd pitch, terr, pt shd; wc; chem disp; mv service pnt; shwrs €0.20; el pnts (10A) metered + conn fee; Indtte; shops 700m; tradsmn; rest 800m; snacks; playgrnd; lake sw; 60% statics; dogs €3; adv bkg; quiet; red CCI. "Pleasant site with gd views fr some pitches; gd san facs; not suitable for disabled; gd." 1 Mar-30 Oct. € 19.50 2011*

⊞ **LINGERHAHN** *3B2* (4km N Rural) *50.10612, 7.56804* **Country-Camping Schinderhannes, Hausbayerstrasse, 56291 Hausbay [(06746) 80280; fax 802814; info@countrycamping.de; www.countrycamping.de]** Fr A61/E31 exit junc 43, foll sps for 3km to Pfalzfeld & onto Hausbay, site sp. V lge, pt sl, terr, pt shd; htd wc; chem disp; mv service pnt; some serviced pitches; baby facs; shwrs inc; el pnts (8-16A) inc; gas; Indtte; shop; rest; snacks; bar; playgrnd; htd pool 8km; lake sw; fishing; tennis; internet; entmnt; TV rm; internet; 60% statics; dogs €2; sep NH area; adv bkg; quiet; red CCI. "Pleasant, peaceful, clean site; spacious pitches, some far fr san facs; helpful, friendly staff; excel san facs; scenic area close Rv Rhine; vg cycle track; conv m'way, excel NH." ♦ € 23.00 2011*

LIPPETAL LIPPBORG see Hamm *1B3*

LOISSIN see Greifswald *2G1*

LORCH *3C2* (5km SE Rural) *50.01820, 7.85493* **Naturpark Camping Suleika, Im Bodenthal 2, 65391 Lorch-bei-Rüdesheim [(06726) 9464; fax 9440; suleika-camping@t-online.de; www.suleika-camping.de]** Site off B42 on E bank of Rv Rhine, 3km NW of Assmannshausen. 3km SE of Lorch foll sp over rlwy x-ing on narr winding, steep rd thro vineyards to site. App poss diff for lge o'fits. Sm, pt sl, terr, pt shd; wc; mv service pnt; serviced pitches; shwrs inc; el pnts (16A) metered + conn fee; Indtte; shop; rest; snacks; playgrnd; cycle hire; dogs €2; poss cr; quiet; sep car park; red CCI. "Vg site in magnificent setting; excursions by Rhine steamer, local places of interest, wine district; access & exit 1-way system; helpful staff; excel rest." 15 Mar-31 Oct. € 18.00 2010*

⊞ **LORRACH** *3B4* (1.5km N Rural) *47.62461, 7.66275* **Drei-Länder Camp, Grüttweg 8, 79539 Lörrach [(07621) 82588; fax 165034; info@dreilaendercamp.de; www.dreilaendercamp.de]** Exit A98/E54 junc 5. Turn L at 1st traff lts after rv bdge on ent Lörrach & site 100m on L, sp. Med, unshd; wc; chem disp; mv service pnt; baby facs; shwrs €0.60; el pnts (16A) metered + €3 conn fee; Indtte; shop & 300m; rest; snacks; playgrnd; tennis; internet; 30% statics; dogs €3.50; Eng spkn; ccard acc; red CCI. "Gd facs; lge park adj; clsd 1300-1500; gd NH." ♦ € 24.60 2011*

⊞ **LORRACH** *3B4* (12km NW Rural) *47.71211, 7.54686* **Kur & Erlebnis-Camping Lug ins Land, Römerstrasse 3, 79415 Bad Bellingen-Bamlach [(07635) 1820; fax 1010; info@camping-luginsland.de; www.camping-luginsland.de]** Exit junc 67 fr A5/E35 onto U5, site 5km up hill with sharp bend at S end of Bemlach. Sp in town. Lge, terr, pt shd; wc; chem disp; mv service pnt; serviced pitches; shwrs inc; el pnts (16A) metered or €2; gas; Indtte; shop, rest, snacks high ssn; playgrnd; htd pool; tennis; cycle hire; golf 500m; wifi; entmnt; TV; 40% statics; dogs €3.50; poss cr; adv bkg; quiet; red long stay; CCI. "Immac san facs; late arr area with el pnts; excel." ♦ € 24.00 2008*

When we get home
I'm going to post
all these site report
forms to the Club
for next year's guide.
The deadline's mid September 2013

⊞ **LOSHEIM AM SEE** *3B2* (3km NW Rural) *49.31833, 6.73972* **Azur Camping und Reiterhof Girtenmühle, Girtenmühle 1, 66679 Losheim-Britten [(06872) 90240; fax 902411; losheim@azur-camping.de; www.azur-camping.de]** Fr Trier, take B268 S & site on L 3km bef Losheim-am-See, sp. Fr A8/E29 exit junc 6 for Merzig & foll sp Losheim. Sm, pt sl, unshd; wc; chem disp; sauna; shwrs inc; el pnts (10A) €2.30; Indtte; shop 3km; rest; bar; playgrnd; 75% statics; dogs €2.80; adv bkg; quiet; red CCI. € 18.00 2008*

⊞ **LOWENSTEIN** *3D3* (1km NW Rural) *49.11697, 9.38321* **Camping Heilbronn Breitenauer See, 74245 Löwenstein [(07130) 8558; fax 3622; info@breitenauer-see.de; www.breitenauer-see.de]** Exit m'way A81 (E41) at Weinsberg/Ellhofen exit & on B39 twd Löwenstein/Schwäbisch Hall; site in approx 8km. V lge, mkd pitch, pt shd; htd wc; chem disp; mv service pnt; baby facs; fam bthrm; shwrs inc; el pnts (16A) €2 or metered + conn fee; gas; Indtte; shop; rest; snacks; bar; playgrnd; lake sw adj; boating; watersports; golf 15km; dog-washing facs; child entmnt high ssn; 50% statics; dogs €5; poss cr; Eng spkn; adv bkg; quiet; ccard acc; 10% red long stay/low ssn; red CCI. "Lake walks; beautiful location; pleasant site close to A6 & A81; all facs highest quality; some fully serviced pitches; excel." ♦ € 21.00 2009*

⊞ **LUBBEN** *2G3* (8km SE Rural) *51.86965, 13.9799* **Spreewald-Natur-Camping am Schlosspark, Schlossbezirk 20, 03222 Lübbenau [tel/fax (03542) 3533; info@spreewaldcamping.de; www.spreewaldcamping.de]** Leave A13 at junc 9, foll rd 115 into Lübbenau. Site well sp. Med, hdstg, pt shd; wc; chem disp; mv service pnt; shwrs €1; el pnts (16A) metered + conn fee; gas; Indtte; shop; bar; snacks & rest adj; BBQ; canoe hire; cycle hire; dogs €2; phone; poss cr; adv bkg; quiet; CCI. "Cent of Spreewald nature reserve; Lehde Vill open-air heritage museum 2km; boat trips on Rv Spree in punts; excel walking, cycling, canoeing; highly rec; excel site, gd san facs." ♦ € 19.50 2011*

GERMANY

GERMANY

LUBBEN *2G3* (500m S Urban) *51.93641, 13.89490* **Spreewald Camping, Am Burglehn 218, 15907 Lübben [(03546) 7053 or 3335 or 8874; fax 181815; info@spreewald-camping-luebben.de; www.spreewald-camping-luebben.de]** Fr N on A13 exit junc 7 at Freiwalde onto B115 twd Lübben. In town cent turn R to stay on B115 sp Lübbenau. Site on L - well sp. Or fr S exit junc 8 onto B87 to Lübben. Cross rlwy, cont along Luckauerstrasse. Turn R at traff lts into Puschkinstrasse, sp Cottbus. Site on L, well sp. Lge, pt shd; wc; chem disp; mv service pnt; shwrs €0.50; el pnts (10A) metered; gas; Indtte (inc dryer); shop 400m; rest; playgrnd; wifi; 20% statics; dogs free; Eng spkn; adv bkg; quiet; CCI. "Excel location; modern, clean facs; excel cycle rtes; adj rv for boating; conv for Berlin." ♦ 15 Mar-31 Oct. € 19.50 2011*

⊞ **LUBECK** *2E2* (3.5km W Rural) *53.86943, 10.63086* **Campingplatz Lübeck-Schünböcken, Steinrader Damm 12, 23556 Lübeck-Schönböcken [tel/fax (0451) 893090; campingplatz.luebeck@gmx.de; www.camping-luebeck.de]** Fr A1 exit junc 23 for Lübeck-Moisling & foll sp to Schönböcken & then camp sp (not v obvious); turn R at traff lts bef Dornbreite, site in 1km on L. Med, pt sl, unshd; wc; chem disp; mv service pnt; shwrs €0.50; el pnts (6A) €2.50; gas; Indtte; shop; playgrnd; dogs €1; bus to town; Eng spkn; quiet; CCI. "Helpful owners; busy site; gd san facs but poss stretched if site full; conv Travemünde ferries; Lübeck interesting town; cycle path to town; vg." € 16.00 2011*

⊞ **LUNEBURG** *1D2* (4km S Rural) *53.20303, 10.40976* **Camping Rote Schleuse, Rote Schleuse 4, 21335 Lüneburg [(04131) 791500; fax 791695; camproteschleuse@aol.com; www.camproteschleuse.de]** Exit A250 junc 4 onto Neu Häcklingen twd Lüneburg. Site sp to R in 300m. Med, pt shd; wc; chem disp; shwrs €0.50; el pnts (10A) €2.25 or metered; Indtte; shop; tradsmn; rest adj; snacks; bar; playgrnd; pool; cycle hire; internet; 60% statics; dogs €1; bus fr site ent; clsd 1300-1500; poss cr; Eng spkn; adv bkg; quiet. "Pleasant owners; interesting town." € 19.00 2009*

⊞ **LUTHERSTADT WITTENBERG** *2F3* (1.5km S Rural) *51.85465, 12.64563* **Marina-Camp Elbe, Brückenkopf 1, 06888 Lutherstadt-Wittenberg [(03491) 4540; fax 454199; info@marina-camp-elbe.de; www.marina-camp-elbe.de]** Site on S side of Elbe bdge on B2 dir Leipzig; well sp. Med, pt shd; wc; chem disp; mv service pnt; serviced pitches; baby facs; sauna; shwrs inc; el pnts (16A) metered + conn fee; gas; Indtte (inc dryer); shop 1.5km; tradsmn; BBQ; cooking facs; snacks; marina adj; cycle hire; wifi; TV; dogs €1.50; bus at gate; quiet; ccard acc; CCI. "Delightful rvside site; excel, modern san facs." ♦ € 23.00 2011*

MAGDEBURG *2E3* (12km N Rural) *52.21888, 11.65944* **Campingplatz Barleber See, Wiedersdorferstrasse, 39126 Magdeburg [(0391) 503244; fax 2449692; campingplatz@cvbs.de; www.cvbs.de]** Exit A2/E30 junc 71 sp Rothensee-Barleber See; site 1km N of a'bahn. Lge, mkd pitch, pt shd; wc; chem disp; mv service pnt; shwrs inc; el pnts (10A) €2; gas; Indtte; shop; tradsmn; rest; snacks; bar; playgrnd; pool; sand beach adj; lake sw; cycle hire; wifi; 60% statics; dogs €2; poss cr; Eng spkn; no adv bkg; poss noisy w/end; fairly quiet; red long stay/CCI. "Gd beach & watersports; pleasant site; helpful staff; gd sports facs; gd touring base." ♦ 1 May-30 Sep. € 17.00 2011*

MAINZ *3C2* (2.5km SE Urban) *50.00296, 8.28556* **Camping Internationaler Mainz-Wiesbaden Maaraue, Maaraue 48, 55246 Mainz-Kostheim [(06134) 4383; fax 707137; camping@camping-maaraue.de; www.krkg.de/camping]** App fr A671 exit 'Hochheim Süd' foll sp for Kostheim then Int'l camping sp. Med, mkd pitch, pt shd; wc; chem disp; shwrs inc; el pnts (16A) inc; gas; Indtte; shop; rest adj; bar; pool adj; tennis; dogs €3; adv bkg; quiet; ccard not acc; red CCI. "Site on island next to Rv Rhine/Maine junc; o'looks city on opp bank; excel for Rhine cruises; gd NH." 1 Apr-31 Oct. € 23.00 2009*

⊞ **MALCHOW** *2F2* (5km NE Rural) *53.49216, 12.37412* **Naturcamping Malchow am Plauer See, Am Plauser See 1, 17213 Malchow [(039932) 49907; fax 49908; malchow@campingtour-mv.de; www.campingtour-mv.de]** Exit A19/E55 junc 16 onto B192 dir Schwerin. Turn L at camping sp in 500m down narr lane. Lge, mkd pitch, pt shd; wc; chem disp; mv service pnt; baby facs; shwrs metered; el pnts (10A) €2.50; gas; Indtte; shop; tradsmn; rest; bar; BBQ; cooking facs; playgrnd; sand beach & lake sw adj; 30% statics; dogs €2.90; phone; poss cr; Eng spkn; adv bkg; quiet; CCI. "Vg NH bet Rostock ferry & Berlin; excel, modern facs; all hot water metered; Malchow swing bdge worth visit." ♦ € 20.20 2011*

⊞ **MALLISS** *2E2* (2km SE Rural) *53.19596, 11.34046* **Camping am Wiesengrund, Am Kanal 4, 19294 Malliss [tel/fax (038750) 21060; sielaff-camping@t-online.de; www.camping-malliss.m-vp.de]** Sp in Malliss on rd 191 fr Ludwigslust to Uelzen. Sm, pt shd; wc; chem disp; mv service pnt; shwrs €0.75; el pnts (16A) €2; gas; Indtte; shop & 2km; tradsmn; rest 2km; snacks; bar; playgrnd; rv sw adj; watersports; cycle hire; 30% statics; dogs €2.50; phone; m'van o'night facs; quiet; red CCI. "Well-run, pleasant, family site; beautiful surroundings; barrier clsd 1200-1400; visit Ludwigslust Palace & Dömitz Fortress; vg." € 16.50 2009*

⊞ **MALSCH** *3C3* (2km S Rural) *48.86165, 8.33789* **Campingpark Bergwiesen, Waldenfelsstrasse 1, 76316 Malsch [(07246) 1467; fax 5762; email@Campingpark-Bergwiesen.eu; www.Campingpark-Bergwiesen.eu]** Fr Karlsruhe on B3 thro Malsch vill over level x-ing to Waldprechtsweier. Foll site sp, take care tight L turn & steep app thro residential area. Lge, hdg/mkd pitch, hdstg, terr, pt shd; wc; chem disp; serviced pitches; shwrs inc; el pnts (16A) metered + conn fee; gas; Indtte; shop 200m; tradsmn; rest; bar; playgrnd; pool 1km; sw adj; 80% statics; dogs €2; Eng spkn; adv bkg (no fee); quiet; red CCI. "1st class facs; well-run site in beautiful forest setting; v friendly site & owner; not rec for long outfits or lge m'vans; gd walks fr site." € 18.80 2011*

MANDERSCHEID see Wittlich *3B2*

MANNHEIM *3C2* (3km S Urban) *49.44841, 8.44806* **Camping am Strandbad, Strandbadweg 1, 68199 Mannheim-Neckarau [(0621) 8619967; fax 8619968; anfrage@campingplatz-mannheim.de]** Exit A6 Karlsruhe-Frankfurt at AB Kreuz Mannheim (junc 27) L onto A656 Mannheim-Neckarau. Exit junc 2 onto B36 dir Neckarau, site sp. Med, pt shd; wc; mv service pnt; shwrs €1; el pnts (16A) metered; gas; Indtte; shop 2km; rest 300m; snacks; shgl beach & rv sw; wifi; 60% statics; dogs €1.50; poss cr; quiet; CCI. "Some noise fr barges on Rhine & factories opp; poss flooding at high water; interesting area." 1 Apr-31 Oct. € 20.00 2009*

The opening dates and prices on this campsite have changed. I'll send a site report form to the Club for the next edition of the guide.

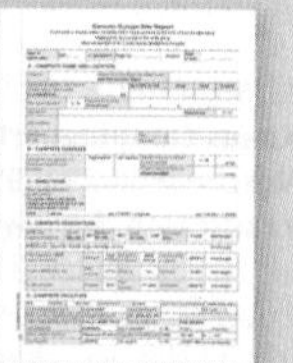

⊞ **MARBURG AN DER LAHN** *1C4* (1.5km S Urban) *50.80000, 8.76861* **Camping Lahnaue, Trojedamm 47, 35037 Marburg-an-der-Lahn [tel/fax (06421) 21331; info@lahnaue.de; www.lahnaue.de]** Site by Rv Lahn, app fr sports cent. Exit a'bahn at Marburg Mitte & sp fr a'bahn. Med, mkd pitch, pt shd; wc; chem disp; shwrs €0.50; el pnts (10A) €2; Indtte (inc dryer); shops 1km; tradsmn; rest 1.5km; snacks; bar; pool adj; rv canoeing; tennis, sw & boating nrby; 10% statics; dogs €2.50; clsd 1300-1500; poss cr; Eng spkn; quiet but m'way & rlwy noise; ccard acc; CCI. "Busy site; some pitches v narr; cycle & footpath to interesting town; excel pool adj; gd." ♦ € 17.00 2011*

MARKDORF *3D4* (2km E Rural) *47.71503, 9.40925* **Camping Wirthshof, Steibensteg 12, 88677 Markdorf [(07544) 96270; fax 962727; info@wirthshof.de; www.wirthshof.de]** Take B33 Markdorf to Ravensburg; site on R sp Camping/Schwimbad/Mini-Golf, in vill of Steibensteg. Lge, pt shd; wc; mv service pnt; sauna; shwrs inc; el pnts (6A) inc; Indtte; shop; rest; playgrnd; pool; cycle hire; golf 10km; entmnt; dogs €4 (reservation req Jul & Aug); clsd 1200-1400; poss cr; debit cards acc. "Excel; activities for children & teenagers; gd sightseeing; special pitches for m'vans in quiet area with el pnts; immac facs; excel rest; helpful owners; Markdorf vill picturesque; gd walking/cycling rtes; Thurs mkt; boat trips on Bodensee; gd tourist info; wonderful." ♦ 1 Mar-30 Oct. € 27.70 2009*

⊞ **MARKTHEIDENFELD** *3D2* (3km S Rural) *49.81885, 9.58851* **Camping Main-Spessart-Park, Spessartstrasse 30, 97855 Triefenstein-Lengfurt [(09395) 1079; fax 8295; info@camping-main-spessart.de; www.camping-main-spessart.de]** Exit A3/E41 junc 65 or 66 sp Lengfurt. In Lengfurt foll sp Marktheidenfeld; site in 1km. Lge, pt sl, terr, pt shd; wc; chem disp; mv service pnt; serviced pitches; shwrs inc; el pnts (6-10A) €3; Indtte; shop; rest; playgrnd; pool adj; watersports; 50% statics; dogs €2.50; Eng spkn; adv bkg; ccard acc; red CCI. "Excel, high quality site; vg rest; vg san facs; easy access A4; sep NH area; helpful owners; access diff parts of site due steep terrs." ♦ € 19.60 2009*

⊞ **MARKTOBERDORF** *4E4* (6km NW Rural) *47.80285, 10.55360* **Campingplatz Elbsee, Am Elbsee 3, 87648 Aitrang [(08343) 248; fax 1406; info@elbsee.de; www.elbsee.de]** W fr Marktoberdorf on B472 onto B12. Turn N foll sp to Elbsee. Fr Kempten E on B12 to Unterthingau N to Aitrang, site 2km S of vill. Lge, mkd pitch, pt sl, pt shd; htd wc; chem disp; mv service pnt; serviced pitches; sauna; shwrs inc; el pnts (16A) metered + conn fee; Indtte (inc dryer); shop; tradsmn; rest adj; BBQ; playgrnd; lake sw & boating adj; solarium; cycle hire; wifi; TV rm; 60% statics; dogs €4.50; phone; o'night facs for m'vans; site clsd 4 Nov-16 Dec; Eng spkn; adv bkg; ccard acc; red CCI. "Excel, friendly, family-owned site; clean, modern facs; dog shwr rm + hairdryer; well marked walk signs from site." ♦ € 24.70 (CChq acc) 2011*

⊞ **MEDELBY** *1D1* (300m W Rural) *54.81490, 9.16361* **Camping Kawan Mitte, Sonnenhügel 1, 24994 Medelby [(04605) 189391; info@camping-mitte.de; www.camping kawanmitte.eu]** Exit A7 junc 2 onto B199 dir Niebüll to Wallsbüll, turn N dir Medelby, site sp. Lge, mkd pitch, pt shd; htd wc; chem disp; mv service pnt; baby facs; fam bthrm; sauna; shwrs inc; el pnts (16A) metered; Indtte (inc dryer); shop; supmkt 600m; rest 600m; snacks; BBQ; cooking facs; playgrnd; 2 htd pool; games area; fitness rm; cycle hire; horseriding 600m; golf 12km; wifi; TV rm; 20% statics; dogs free; adv bkg; quiet; CCI. "Conv m'way & Danish border; vg." ♦ € 28.30 (CChq acc) SBS - G03 2011*

MEERBUSCH **see Düsseldorf** *1B4*

MEERSBURG *3D4* (5km SE Rural) *47.67201, 9.32748* **Camping Alpenblick, Strandbadstrasse 13, 88709 Hagnau [(07532) 495760; fax 495761; info@campingplatz-alpenblick.de; www.campingplatz-alpenblick.de]** On B31 SE fr Meersburg, after traff lts at Hagnau in 650m (0.4 miles) take slip rd R sp Hagnau & almost immed turn R twd lake, site sp. Fr Friedrichshafen 5.28km (3.3 miles) afer Camping Fischbach turn L sp Schloss Kirchberg (lge white house). (If this turn missed, go into lge car park in Meersburg & return as above.) Foll lane alongside B31 to site. Med, mkd pitch, pt sl, terr, pt shd; wc; chem disp; shwrs €0.50; el pnts (10A) €2.50; Indtte; tradsmn; supmkt 3km; rest; bar; lake sw; fishing; cycle hire; 90% statics; dogs €3; poss v cr high ssn; Eng spkn; no adv bkg; no ccard acc; rd noise; CCI. "Lakeside pitches diff access when site busy; warm welcome & staff helpful; san facs due to be renewed 2008; pretty vill with ferries to all ports Lake Constance; vill walking dist; excel cycle tracks; poss youth groups high ssn." 1 Apr-30 Oct. € 24.50 2008*

⊞ **MEININGEN** *3D2* (1km E Rural) *50.56944, 10.43638* **Campingplatz Rohrer Stirn, 98617 Meiningen [(03693) 484421; fax 484422; campingplatz@stadtwerke-meiningen.de]** Exit A71 junc 21, site sp in 2km on R. Sm, mkd pitch, terr, unshd; htd wc; chem disp; mv service pnt; baby facs; shwrs inc; el pnts (16A) metered; Indtte; shop; tradsmn; rest; snacks; bar; BBQ; htd pool adj; TV; dogs €1.50; phone; bus adj; poss cr; adv bkg; quiet. "Excel little site; gd mkt." ♦ € 13.40 2008*

GERMANY

MEISSEN *2G4* (3km SE Rural) *51.13942, 13.49883* **Camping Rehbocktal, Rehbocktal 4, 01665 Scharfenberg-bei-Meissen [(03521) 452680; fax 459206; info@camping-rehbocktal.de; www.camping-rehbocktal.de]** Exit E40/A4 at Dresden Altstadt; foll sp Meissen on B6 to Scharfenberg; site on L opp Rv Elbe. Med, pt sl, pt shd; wc; chem disp; shwrs inc; el pnts (16A) €2; Indtte; shop & 3km; tradsmn; rest adj; snacks; bar; playgrnd; 10% statics; dogs €2; bus; poss cr; no adv bkg; v quiet; ccard acc; CCI. "In wooded valley opp vineyard; friendly staff; conv Colditz; Meissen factory & museum worth visit; cycle path to Meissen nr." 1 Mar-30 Nov. € 20.00 2011*

MEISSENDORF see Winsen (Aller) *1D3*

⊞ **MELLE** *1C3* (3km W Rural) *52.22428, 8.2661* **Campingplatz Grönegau-Park Ludwigsee, Nemdenerstrasse 12, 49326 Melle [(05402) 2132; fax 2112; info@ludwigsee.de; www.ludwigsee.de]** Exit A30/E30 junc 22 twd Bad Essen, site sp on lakeside. Lge, hdg/mkd pitch, pt shd; wc; chem disp; mv service pnt; shwrs €1; el pnts (10A) inc; Indtte; shop 1.5km; rest; snacks; bar; playgrnd; lake sw; games area; cycle hire; internet; entmnt; 80% statics; dogs €2; sep car park; barrier clsd 1300-1500; adv bkg; quiet; ccard acc; red CCI. "Beautiful & pleasant site; helpful owners; sep area for tourers." € 22.00 2009*

MEMMINGEN *3D4* (10km S Rural) *47.94871, 10.08578* **Park-Camping Iller, Illerstrasse 57, 88317 Aitrach [(07565) 5419; fax 5222; info@camping-iller.de; www.camping-iller.de]** Exit A96/E43/E54 junc 11, site in 3km, sp. Or fr Memmingen take rd dir Leutkirch. In Ferthofen vill look for camping sp & turn R after rv bdge. In Aitrach turn R, site 1km on L. Lge, pt shd; htd wc; chem disp; mv service pnt; serviced pitches; baby facs; fam bthrm; shwrs inc; el pnts (10A) €2.50; gas; Indtte (inc dryer); shop; tradsmn; rest 1.5km; snacks; bar; playgrnd; pool; paddling pool; tennis; games rm; internet; 75% statics; dogs €2; o'night area for m'vans; poss cr; adv bkg; quiet; Eng spkn; ccard acc; red snr citizens/CCI. "Gd family site; helpful staff; gd walking, cycling." ♦ 1 May-15 Oct. € 24.50 2011*

⊞ **MENDIG** *3B2* (2km Rural) *50.38646, 7.27237* **Camping Siesta, Laacherseestrasse 6, 56743 Mendig [(02652) 1432; fax 520424; service@campingsiesta.de; www.campingsiesta.de]** Fr A61 exit junc 34 for Mendig dir Maria Laach; foll camp sps; site on R in 300m by ent to car park. Med, some hdg pitch, sl, pt shd; wc; chem disp; shwrs inc; el pnts (16A) €1.80; gas; Indtte; tradsmn; rest; bar; playgrnd; sm pool; sw pool 500m; 60% statics; dogs €1.30; poss v cr; Eng spkn; noise fr nrby a'bahn; CCI. "Useful NH; easy access fr A61; owner helpful in siting NH outfits; longest waterslide in Europe; gd base for region's castles & wines." € 17.90 2011*

MENDIG *3B2* (4km N Rural) *50.42151, 7.26448* **Camping Laacher See, Am Laacher See, 56653 Wassenach [(02636) 2485; fax 929750; info@camping-laacher-see.de; www.camping-laacher-see.de]** Fr A61, exit junc 34 Mendig. Foll tents sp to Maria Laach. Site on Laacher See. Lge, hdg/mkd pitch, hdstg, pt sl, pt terr, pt shd; htd wc; chem disp; mv service pnt; baby facs; shwrs €0.50; el pnts (16A) metered + conn fee; gas; Indtte (inc dryer); shop; tradsmn; rest; snacks; bar; playgrnd; lake sw; sailing; fishing; wifi; 50% statics; dogs €4; bus 500m; Eng spkn; quiet; adv bkg; ccard acc; CCI. "Neat, clean, relaxing site; all pitches lake views; busy at w/end; modern san facs; gd woodland walks, cycling & sw; excel sailing facs; excel." ♦ 1 Apr-30 Sep. € 25.00 2010*

⊞ **MESCHEDE** *1C4* (7km S Rural) *51.29835, 8.26425* **Knaus Campingpark Hennesee, Mielinghausen 7, 59872 Meschede [(0291) 952720; fax 9527229; hennesee@knauscamp.de; www.knauscamp.de]** S fr Meschede on B55 for 7km; at sp for Erholungszentrum & Remblinghausen turn L over Lake Hennesee, site on L in 500m, sp. Lge, mkd pitch, terr, pt shd; wc; chem disp; mv service pnt; sauna; serviced pitches; shwrs inc; el pnts (6A) metered + conn fee; gas; Indtte; supmkt; rest; snacks; bar; playgrnd; lake sw 200m; cycle hire; entmnt high ssn; internet; 70% statics; dogs €2; poss cr; adv bkg; Eng spkn; 60% statics; dogs €3.80; quiet; red CCI. "Conv Sauerland mountains & lakes; 50m elec cable advisable; vg." € 25.40 2009*

MESENICH see Trier *3B2*

⊞ **METTINGEN** *1B3* (1.5km SW Rural) *52.31251, 7.76202* **Camping Zur Schönen Aussicht, Schwarzestrasse 73, 49497 Mettingen [(05452) 606; fax 4751; info@camping-schoene-aussicht.de; www.camping-schoene-aussicht.de]** Exit A30 junc 12 dir Mettingen. Go thro town cent, uphill turn R at traff lts, site sp. Med, hdg/mkd pitch, pt sl, pt shd; wc; chem disp; mv service pnt; shwrs €1.30; el pnts (10A) €3 or metered; Indtte; shop; rest; bar; playgrnd; htd, covrd pool; internet; 50% statics; no dogs; Eng spkn; adv bkg; quiet; CCI. "Nice, friendly site; gd walking, cycling; easy walk to town; gd facs." € 18.50 2010*

MILTENBERG *3D2* (500m N Urban) *49.70366, 9.25417* **Camping Mainwiese, 12 Steingasserstrasse, 63897 Miltenberg [(09371) 3985; fax 68723; info@campingplatz-miltenberg.de; www.campingplatz-miltenberg.de]** On B469 to Miltenberg. Cross rv bdge dir Klingenberg. Ent in 200m on R, sp. Lge, unshd; wc; chem disp; mv service pnt; baby facs; shwrs inc; el pnts (16A) €2; Indtte; shop; rest adj; playgrnd; golf 10km; 25% statics; dogs €2; quiet; red long stay. "Poss long walk to san facs." 1 Apr-30 Sep. € 14.50 2009*

⊞ **MINHEIM** *3B2* (1km E Rural) *49.86527, 6.94222* **Reisemobilpark Minheim, Am Moselufer, 54518 Minheim [(06887) 1553]** Exit A1/E44 junc 127, thro Klausen dir Rv Mosel. Med, chem disp; mv service pnt; el pnts (6A) €1.50; shops, rest nr; m'vans only. "Gd wine vill on Rv Mosel." € 5.00 2008*

⊞ **MITTENWALD** *4E4* (4km N Rural) *47.47290, 11.27729* **Naturcamping Isarhorn, Am Horn 4, 82481 Mittenwald [(08823) 5216; fax 8091; camping@mittenwald.de; www.camping-isarhorn.de]** E fr Garmisch-Partenkirchen on rd 2; at Krün turn S on D2/E533 dir Mittenwald. Site on R in approx 2km at int'l camping sp. Ent on R fr main rd. NB: Rd thro to Innsbruck via Zirlerberg improved & no longer clsd to c'vans descending S; long & steep; low gear; not to be attempted N. Lge, pt shd, unmkd gravel/grass pitches; wc; chem disp; mv service pnt; shwrs €0.50; el pnts (16A) €2.80 or metered; Indtte; shop; snacks; rest; BBQ; htd, covrd pool 4km; canoeing (white water); skilift; tennis; wifi; dogs €2.90; bus adj; site clsd 1300-1500 & 2200-0700; site clsd 1 Nov-mid Dec; Eng spkn; quiet but some rd noise; ccard acc; red low ssn; CCI. "Relaxed, secluded site in pines; mountain views; excel base for walking; cycle track to attractive town; poss some noise fr nrby military base; owner v keen on recycling waste; facs gd but insufficient for size of site; highly rec." € 18.50 2010*

MOHNESEE see Soest *1C4*

MONSCHAU *3A1* (1.5km SW Rural) *50.54305, 6.23694* **Camping Perlenau, 52156 Monschau [(02472) 4136; fax 4493; familie.rasch@monschau-perlenau.de; www.monschau-perlenau.de]** Fr N (Aachen) foll B258 past Monschau dir Schleiden. Site on L just bef junc with B399 to Kalterherberg. Steep & narr app. Fr Belgium, exit A3 junc 38 for Eupen & foll rd thro Eupen to Monschau. Site on rvside. Med, hdg/mkd pitch, hdstg, pt sl, terr, pt shd; htd wc; chem disp; mv service pnt; baby facs; fam bthrm; shwrs; el pnts (10-16A) €2.60 or metered; gas; Indtte; shop; tradsmn; rest; snacks; bar; BBQ; cooking facs; playgrnd; 20% statics; dogs €2.60; phone; bus 500m; poss cr; Eng spkn; adv bkg; quiet; red long stay; CCI. "Gd touring base for Eifel region; attractive site beside stream; historic town in walking dist." ♦ 15 Mar-31 Oct. € 18.60 2009*

⊞ **MONTABAUR** *3C2* (6km SE Rural) *50.43761, 7.90498* **Camping Eisenbachtal, 56412 Girod [(06485) 766; fax 4938]** S on A3/E35 exit junc 41 dir Montabaur; at Girod turn L to site, well sp. Med, hdg/mkd pitch, some hdstg, pt sl, pt shd; htd wc; chem disp; mv service pnt; some serviced pitches; shwrs €0.50; el pnts (4A) inc; (poss rev pol); gas; Indtte; tradsmn; 2 x rest adj; playgrnd; sw 5km; 75% statics; dogs €2; poss cr; Eng spkn; adv bkg; quiet; red long stay; CCI. "Beautiful, well-equipped site in Naturpark Nassau; conv NH fr a'bahn & worth longer stay; friendly, welcoming staff; gd for nature lovers & children; gd walking & cycling; adj rest excel; site clsd 1300-1500 but car park opp; conv Rhine & Mosel valleys." ♦ € 18.00 2011*

⊞ **MORFELDEN** *3C2* (2km E Rural) *49.97986, 8.59461* **Campingplatz Mörfelden, Am Zeltzplatz 5-15, 64546 Mörfelden-Walldorf [(06105) 22289; fax 277459; info@campingplatz-moerfelden.de; www.campingplatz-moerfelden.de]** Exit A5/E451 at Langen/Gross Gerau junc 24 for Mörfelden onto B486. Site sp. Med, pt shd; wc; shwrs €1; el pnts (10A) metered or €2; gas; shop; rest; snacks 1km; playgrnd; dogs €1.50; poss cr; Eng spkn; quiet but some aircraft noise; no adv bkg. "Conv NH/sh stay for Frankfurt; excel, modern san facs; helpful owner." € 20.00 2008*

MORITZBURG *4G1* (3km S Rural) *51.1450, 13.67444* **Campingplatz Bad Sonnenland, Dresdnerstrasse 115, 01468 Moritzburg [(0351) 8305495; fax 8305494; bad-sonnenland@t-online.de; www.moritzburg.de]** Leave A4/E40 exit 80. Turn R sp Moritzburg, foll site sp thro Reichenberg. Site on L 3km bef Moritzburg. Lge, pt shd; wc; chem disp; mv service pnt; shwrs €0.50; el pnts (10A) €2.50; gas; Indtte; shop; supmkt 2km; rest; snacks; bar; playgrnd; lake sw adj; games rm; games area; statics in sep area; dogs €2.50; bus to Dresden; poss v cr; quiet; ccard acc; CCI. "Scenic area; friendly staff; excel, immac facs; site clsd 1300-1500 & 2200-0700; also holiday vill with many huts; conv Dresden, Meissen; narr gauge steam train Dresden-Moritzburg; day trip to Prague; ask for 'Camping Tour' leaflet for discounts on other sites." 1 Apr-30 Oct. € 20.00 2009*

MOSCHWITZ see Plauen *4F1*

MUDEN AN DER ORTZE see Fassberg *1D2*

⊞ **MUHLBERG** *2E4* (3km SW Rural) *50.87516, 10.80843* **Campingplatz Drei Gleichen, Am Gut Ringhofen, 99869 Mühlberg [(036256) 22715; fax 86801; service@campingplatz-muehlberg.de; www.campingplatz-muehlberg.de]** Leave A4/E40 at junc 43 (Wandersleben) S twds Mühlberg; site well sp in 2km on rd to Wechmar. Med, hdg/mkd pitch, pt sl, unshd; wc; chem disp; mv service pnt; shwrs €1; el pnts (16A) €1.80 + conn fee; Indtte; shop 3km; rest adj; bar; playgrnd; sw adj; 50% statics; dogs €2.20; site clsd 1300-1500; adv bkg; quiet; CCI. "Gd facs; helpful staff; conv a'bahn." ♦ € 16.00 2011*

MUHLHAUSEN see Augsburg *4E3*

MUNCHEN *4E4* (5km S Urban) *48.09165, 11.54516* **Camping München-Thalkirchen, Zentralländstrasse 49, 81379 München [(089) 7231707; fax 7243177; campingplatz.muenchen@web.de; www.camping-muenchen.de]** Fr S on A95/E533 at end of a'bahn keep strt on (ignore zoo sp). After tunnel exit R at sp Thalkirchen. Turn L at traff lts & foll sp to camp. If app fr S on A8/E45 turn L at traff lts at end twd Garmish & strt on to tunnel, site sp. Fr NW at end of A8 in 200m turn R & foll sp to zoo (Tierpark). Cont to foll zoo sp until in approx 10km pick up sp to site. (Zoo on E side of Rv Isar, site on W side.) App fr N not rec due v heavy traffic. V lge, mkd pitch, pt shd; htd wc; chem disp; mv service pnt; many serviced pitches; shwrs €1; el pnts (10A) €2 (long lead req); Indtte (inc dryer); shop; rest 500m; snacks; playgrnd; pool & rv 500m; internet; dogs inc; phone; bus 100m; poss cr esp Oktoberfest; Eng spkn; quiet; ccard not acc; CCI. "Busy site; some m'van/o'night pitches v sm; bus/U-bahn tickets avail fr recep; cycle track/walk along rv to town cent, avoiding traffic; helpful staff; san facs stretched when site full; gd site when visiting Munich, clean san facs." ♦ 15 Mar-31 Oct. € 20.90 2011*

GERMANY

GERMANY

MUNCHEN *4E4* (8km NW Rural) *48.17421, 11.44645* **Waldcamping München-Obermenzing, Lochhausenerstrasse 59, 81247 München [(089) 8112235; fax 8144807; campingplatz-obermenzing@t-online.de; www.campingplatz-muenchen.de]** Foll sp around Munich ring rd to ent of A8 Munich/Stuttgart a'bahn; passing m'way ent on L cont on Pippingerstrasse & site on Lochhausenerstrasse; heavy traff to/fr S of site. Lge, hdg/mkd pitch, pt shd; htd wc; chem disp; mv service pnt; serviced pitches; shwrs €1; el pnts (10A) metered; gas; Indtte; shop; tradsmn; snacks; bar; cooking facs; pool 3km; internet; 10% statics; dogs €1; bus to city 1km, train 2km; poss cr; Eng spkn; no adv bkg; m'way noise; CCI. "Pleasant management; Park & Ride to city 3km; variable size pitches, some narr, & poss overgrown; v busy & noisy during beer festival & prices increased." 15 Mar-31 Oct.
€ 21.90 2009*

⊞ **MUNCHEN** *4E4* (10km NW Urban) *48.19888, 11.49694* **Campingplatz Nord-West, Auf den Schrederwiesen 3, 80995 München-Moosach [(089) 1506936; info@campingplatz-nord-west.de; www.campingplatz-nord-west.de]** Fr N exit A99 junc 10 Lugwigsfeld onto B304 S - Dachauerstrasse, sp München. Turn L in approx 800m at traff lts. Turn R at T-junc to site on R. Med, hdstg, shd; htd wc; chem disp; mv service pnt; shwrs €1.50; el pnts (10-16A) €5 or metered; Indtte (inc dryer); shop & 1km; tradsmn; rest 3km; snacks; bar; entmnt; 50% statics; dogs €2; phone; bus to city; poss cr; Eng spkn; adv bkg; quiet; ccard acc; CCI. "Friendly, helpful welcome; enquire about public transport tickets; ltd facs low ssn; Dachau - pretty town 10km; gd." ♦
€ 24.40 2010*

⊞ **MUNCHEN** *4E4* (12km NW Rural) *48.19821, 11.41161* **Campingplatz am Langwieder See, Eschenriederstrasse 119, 81249 München-Langwied [(089) 8641566; fax 8632342; info@camping-langwieder-see.de; www.camping-langwieder-see.de]** Exit A8 junc 80 at Langwieder See & foll sp Dachau; site within 200m. Fr ring rd A99 junc 8 join A8 to N, then as above. Med, hdstg, pt shd; htd wc; chem disp; shwrs €0.50; el pnts (10A) metered + conn fee €1; gas; Indtte; shop; snacks; rest; bar; lake sw adj; 95% statics; dogs €1.70; poss v cr; Eng spkn; no adv bkg; m'way noise; CCI. "Pleasant owners; tourers in a row outside recep area parked v close together; v sm pitches, mostly on gravel; gd san facs; site used by workers; easy access to Munich by train fr Dachau; lge free car park at stn; nh/short stay only."
€ 21.50 2011*

I'll fill in a report online and let the Club know – www.caravanclub.co.uk/europereport

MUNCHSTEINACH see Neustadt an der Aisch *4E2*

MUNICH see München *4E4*

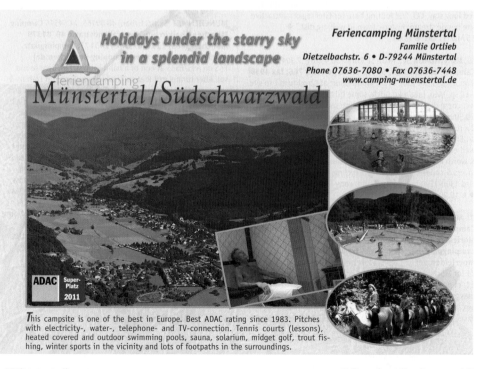

Holidays under the starry sky in a splendid landscape

Feriencamping Münstertal
Familie Ortlieb
Dietzelbachstr. 6 • D-79244 Münstertal
Phone 07636-7080 • Fax 07636-7448
www.camping-muenstertal.de

feriencamping
Münstertal / Südschwarzwald

ADAC Super-Platz 2011

This campsite is one of the best in Europe. Best ADAC rating since 1983. Pitches with electricity-, water-, telephone- and TV-connection. Tennis courts (lessons), heated covered and outdoor swimming pools, sauna, solarium, midget golf, trout fishing, winter sports in the vicinity and lots of footpaths in the surroundings.

⊞ **MUNSTER** *1B3* (3km SE Rural) *51.94638, 7.69027* **Camping Münster, Laerer Wersuefer 7, 48157 Münster [(0251) 311982; fax 3833985; campingplatz-muenster@t-online.de; www.campingplatz-muenster.de]** Fr A43 exit junc 2 or A1/E37 exit junc 78 onto B51 dir Münster then Bielefeld. On leaving built-up area, turn R after TV mast on R. Cross Rv Werse & turn L at 1st traff lts, site sp. (Site is also sp fr Münster S by-pass). Lge, mkd pitch, some hdstg, pt shd; htd wc; chem disp; mv service pnt; serviced pitches; shwrs €0.50; el pnts (16A) inc; lndtte; shop; rest; snacks; playgrnd; htd pool adj; fishing; tennis; cycle hire; wifi; 50% statics; dogs €3; bus 300m; o'night m'van area; barrier clsd 1300-1500; poss v cr w/e; Eng spkn; adv bkg; quiet; red CCI. "Excel; quiet mid wk; Münster v interesting; radio/tv mast useful landmark fr S; gd cycle rtes." ♦ € 26.00 (3 persons) 2011*

⊞ **MUNSTERTAL** *3B4* (1.5km W Rural) *47.85995, 7.76370* **Feriencamping Münstertal, Dietzelbachstrasse 6, 79244 Münstertal [(07636) 7080; fax 7448; info@camping-muenstertal.de; www.camping-muenstertal.de]** Exit A5 junc 64a at Bad Krozingen-Staufen-Münstertal. By-pass Stauffen & foll Münstertal sps. Site on L 1.5km past Camping Belchenblick off rd L123. Lge, mkd pitch, shd; wc; chem disp; mv service pnt; serviced pitches; sauna; steam rm; solarium; private bathrms avail; shwrs inc; el pnts (16A) metered; gas; lndtte; shop; rest; snacks; adventure playgrnd; 2 htd pools (1 covrd); fishing; wintersports nr; skilift 10km; tennis; horseriding; games area; games rm; beauty treatments avail; wifi; entmnt; cab TV; some statics; dogs €3.50; phone; rlwy stn 200m; gates clsd 1300-1430 & 2200-0730; m'van o'night area; adv bkg rec school hols; quiet; red long stay/CCI. "Superb, well-managed site; luxurious, clean facs; many activities for all family; gd walking; vg rest; conv Freiburg & Black Forest." ♦ € 31.55 2011*

See advertisement

MURNAU AM STAFFELSEE *4E4* (5km N Rural) *47.70680, 11.21821* **Camping Brugger am Riegsee, Seestrasse 1, 82418 Hofheim-am-Riegsee [(08847) 728; fax 228; office@camping-brugger.de; www.camping-brugger.de]** Fr A95/E533 exit 9 for Sindelsdorf, dir Habach. Foll sp Hofheim & site. Med, hdg/mkd pitch, hdstg, terr, pt shd; htd wc; chem disp; mv service pnt; serviced pitches; shwrs €0.50; el pnts (16A) €2.50 or metered; gas; lndtte; shop; snacks; playgrnd; pool 5km; shgl beach & lake sw adj; boating; windsurfing; tennis 2km; games area; games rm; internet; entmnt; 60% statics; dogs €2.50; m'van o'night area; clsd 1230-1430; Eng spkn; adv bkg; quiet; red long stay; CCI. "Friendly/helpful owners; beautiful lake & mountain views; gd, modern facs; excel site. panoramic pitches get booked up early for the peak sssn." 1 May-1 Oct. € 25.00 2011*

MURNAU AM STAFFELSEE *4E4* (2km NW Rural) *47.68493, 11.17918* **Camping Halbinsel Burg, Burgweg 41, 82418 Murnau-Seehausen [(08841) 9870; fax 626071; camping-halbinsel-burg@t-online.de]** Exit A95 junc 9 Sindelsdorf/Peissenberg to Murnau. Site sp at traff lts in cent of Murnau, dir Seehausen. Med, pt shd; wc; chem disp; mv service pnt; shwrs inc; el pnts (16A) €1.80; lndtte; shop; rest; playgrnd; lake sw & beach; watersports; entmnt high ssn; 20% statics; no dogs; no adv bkg; red CCI. "Wonderful sw & boating; pleasant site." ♦ 6 Jan-25 Oct. € 26.20 2008*

MURNAU AM STAFFELSEE *4E4* (5km NW Rural) *47.69861, 11.15833* **Campingplatz Aichalehof, Aichalehof 4, 82449 Uffing-am-Staffelsee [(08846) 211; camping@aichalehof.de; www.aichalehof.de]** N fr Murnau dir Seehausen & Uffing - Murnaustrasse. In Murnau turn L into Seestrasse to site in 2km. Site on L after sailing club. Or exit A95 junc 9 onto B472 W to Uffing, then as above. Med, pt sl, pt shd; wc; chem disp; mv service pnt; baby facs; shwrs €0.50; el pnts (10A) €2; lndtte (inc dryer); shop, rest 2km; snacks; bar; BBQ; playgrnd; lake sw adj; watersports; fishing; 70% statics; dogs €2; Eng spkn; adv bkg; quiet; CCI. "Excel, peaceful, scenic site, cycle/walking path around lake, steamer on lake, trains and buses from Uffing." ♦ 1 May-3 Oct. € 21.00 2011*

⊞ **NAUMBURG (HESSEN)** *1C4* (800m NW Rural) *51.25070, 9.16060* **Kneipp Kur Camping, Am Schwimmbad 12, 34311 Naumburg [(05625) 922448; fax 922449; info@camping-naumburg.de; www.camping-naumburg.de]** Exit A44 junc 67 onto B251 thro Istha. At Bründersen foll sp Altenstadt & Naumburg. Foll int'l camping sp, well sp. Lge, mkd pitch, terr, pt shd; htd wc; chem disp; mv service pnt; shwrs; el pnts (16A) €2 or metered (poss rev pol); lndtte; shop; tradsmn; rest, snacks, bar 800m; BBQ; cooking facs; playgrnd; pool adj; tennis; horseriding 5km; golf 15km; spa treatments; 30% statics; dogs €2.50; bus 500m; clsd 1300-1500; Eng spkn; adv bkg; quiet. "Charming site; excel, modern san facs; spacious pitches; friendly, helpful staff; interesting town; gd walks fr site." ♦ € 17.00 2008*

NECKARELZ *3D3* (2km SE Rural) *49.31841, 9.12718* **Camping Cimbria, Wiesenweg 1, 74865 Neckarzimmern [(06261) 2562; fax 35716; info@camping-cimbria.de; www.camping-cimbria.de]** Site bet B27 & Rv Neckar heading S fr Neckarelz; narr app. Med, pt shd; wc; chem disp; mv service pnt; shwrs €0.80; el pnts (10A) €2; lndtte; shop; rest; snacks; bar; playgrnd; htd pool; watersports; tennis; wifi; 30% statics; dogs €3; adv bkg; quiet. "On rvside, but not noisy; poss flooding at high water." 1 Apr-31 Oct. € 18.20 2008*

NECKARGEMUND see Heidelberg *3C2*

NECKARGERACH *3C2* (400m W Rural) *49.39665, 9.07003* **Campingplatz zur Alten Fähre, Bannwiesen, 69437 Neckargerach [tel/fax (06263) 8309; camp_volz@gmx.de; www.camping-zur-alten-faehre.beep.de]** Exit A5/E35 at Heidelberg & take B37 up Neckar valley. Or fr A6/E50 exit Heilbronn junc 37 onto B27 N up valley. Site on banks of rv. Med, mkd pitch, hdstg, pt shd; wc; chem disp; mv service pnt; shwrs inc; el pnts (16A) metered; lndtte; shop 400m; snacks; bar; 50% statics; dogs €1.50; adv bkg; quiet; CCI. "Beautiful location; welcoming warden; well-maintained, peaceful site but san facs poss insufficient high ssn & key req; church clock strikes day & night; ground v soft after heavy rain." 1 Mar-15 Nov. € 17.50 2008*

⊞ **NECKARSULM** *3D3* (2km E Urban) *49.18734, 9.24776* **Camping Reisachmühle, Reisachmühlweg 6, 74172 Neckarsulm [(07132) 2169; fax 308633; info@campingplatz-reisachmuehle.de; www.campingplatz-reisachmuehle.de]** Exit A6/E50 junc 37 onto B27 to Neckarsulm, site well sp nr Aquatoll. Med, mkd pitch, unshd; wc; chem disp; shwrs inc; el pnts (16A) €2 or metered; gas; lndtte; shop; rest 500m; playgrnd; 40% statics; dogs €2; some Eng spkn; CCI. "Conv NH nr a'bahn; rec arr early high ssn." € 16.00 2011*

NEEF *3B2* (200m N Rural) *50.09500, 7.13694* **Wohnmobilplatz Am Frauenberg, Am Moselufer, 56858 Neef** Exit A1/E44 junc 125 onto B49 to Neef. In Neef cross rv bdge, site sp on L beside rv. M'vans only. Med, pt shd; chem disp; mv service pnt; el pnts (10A) inc; shop 400m; rest 100m; tradsmn; some rlwy & rv noise. "Gd; owner calls am & pm for payment." 1 Mar-30 Oct. € 7.00 2009*

NEHREN see Cochem *3B2*

NENNIG *3A2* (1km N Rural) *49.54331, 6.37207* **Camping Mosella am Rothaus (formerly Moselplatz), Rothaus 1, 66706 Perl-Nennig [(06866) 510 or 26660222 (Lux'bourg); fax 1486; info@mosella-camping.de; www.rothaus.lu]** Site on bank of Mosel opp Remich (Luxembourg), access on R just bef bdge. Fr Luxembourg cross rv bdge, turn L after former border post, site is ahead, opp Mosel-Camping Dreiländereck. Med, hdg pitch, pt shd; htd wc; chem disp; mv service pnt; shwrs inc; el pnts (10A) inc; gas 1km; shop 500m; rest; snacks; bar; BBQ; 50% statics; dogs; bus 100m; poss cr; Eng spkn; quiet; CCI. "Lovely site by rv for short or long stay; helpful, friendly owner; adequate facs; rest adj; rvside pitch sm extra charge; gd touring base." ♦ 15 Mar-15 Oct. € 14.50 2011*

NENNIG *3A2* (1km N Rural) *49.54303, 6.37066* **Mosel-Camping Dreiländereck, Am Moselufer, 66706 Perl-Nennig [(06866) 322; fax 1005; info@mosel-camping.de; www.mosel-camping.de]** Site on bank of Mosel opp Remich (Luxembourg), access on R just bef bdge (fr German side). Fr Luxembourg cross rv bdge, turn L after former border post cont to rv & turn L under bdg; site is ahead. Med, unshd; htd wc; chem disp; mv service pnt; shwrs €1.30; el pnts (16A) inc; lndtte; shops 400m; tradsmn; rest; snacks; bar; BBQ; playgrnd; fishing; cycling; golf 15km; 65% statics; dogs €1; phone; poss cr; adv bkg; quiet; no ccard acc; Eng spkn; 10% red long stay; 5% red CCI. "Nice site; dishwashing & chem disp adj; ltd facs; conv vineyards, Roman mosaic floor in Nennig; cycle track along rv; sh walk to Remich." 1 Apr-18 Oct. € 18.00 2010*

NESSELWANG *4E4* (10km SE Urban) *47.56315, 10.57843* **Campingplatz Pfronten, Tirolerstrasse 109, 87459 Pfronten-Steinach [(08363) 377 or 8353]** Fr Nesselwang on B309/E532, go thro Pfronten, site on R by 'Osterreich 1km' sp. Med, pt sl, pt shd; wc; chem disp; mv service pnt; shwrs inc; el pnts (10A) €1.40 (poss rev pol); lndtte; shop & 1km; tradsmn; rest 300m; bar; pool 2km; dogs €0.50; phone; no adv bkg; quiet; CCI. "Gd mountain walks; castles & lakes adj; helpful & friendly staff; no groundsheets allowed, duckboards provided; immac facs." 15 May-27 Sep. € 17.00 2009*

⊞ **NESSELWANG** *4E4* (2km NW Rural) *47.62925, 10.45878* **Camping Wertacher Hof, Hauptstrasse, 87466 Haslach [(08361) 770; fax 9344]** Leave A7/E532 junc 137 W onto B309/310. At 1st rndabt strt on for 200m, L for Haslach, site on R in 500m. Med, pt sl; htd wc; shwrs inc; chem disp; mv service pnt; el pnts (10A) metered; lndtte; shop; rest; playgrnd; pool adj; skilift 2km; Eng spkn; ccard acc; red long stay; CCI. "Gd facs; friendly owner; gravel pitch for NH." ♦ € 17.00 2008*

⊞ **NESSLBACH** *4G3* (500m NW Rural) *48.69400, 13.11638* **Donautal Camping, Schillerstrasse 14, 94577 Nesslbach-Winzer [(08545) 1233 or 0121; fax 911562; info@camping-donautal.de; www.camping-donautal.de]** Exit A3/E56 junc 112 to Nesslbach. Site adj sports stadium, sp. Sm, mkd pitch, unshd; htd wc; chem disp; mv service pnt; shwrs inc; el pnts (6A) inc; lndtte; shop 100m; tradsmn; rest 300m; snacks 100m; games area; 20% statics; dogs free; quiet. "Adj Danube cycleway; lovely, open site; friendly staff; lge pitches - easy access lge o'fits; ltd san facs but clean; site yourself instructions if site not manned; vg." € 18.00 2010*

⊞ **NETZEBAND** *2F2* (500m NE Rural) *52.99722, 12.63416* **Landhotel Märkische Höfe, Dorfstrasse 7, 16818 Netzeband [(033924) 8980; fax 89860; info@maerkischehoefe.de]** Exit A24 junc 21 onto minor rds via Fretzdorf, Rossow & Rägelin to Netzeband. Turn R into main street, site on L in 500m at hotel. Sm, hdstg; no mv service pnt; shwrs €5 (in hotel); el pnts (16A); rest; dogs; quiet. "Site fee waived if meal taken in hotel; space for 3 m'vans only." € 10.00 2008*

⊞ **NEUENBURG AM RHEIN** *3B4* (9km E Rural) *47.81000, 7.67694* **Feriencamping Badenweiler, Weilertalstrasse 73, 79410 Badenweiler [info@camping-badenweiler.de; www.camping-badenweiler.de]** Exit A5 junc 65 at Neuenburg onto B378 dir Müllheim, then L131. Site sp on L bef R turn to Badenweiler. Med, terr, pt shd; htd wc; chem disp; mv service pnt; fam bthrm; shwrs inc; el pnts (16A) metered; lndtte (inc dryer); shop; tradsmn; rest; snacks; bar; playgrnd nr; pool 500m; wifi; no statics; dogs €3; phone; bus 300m; site clsd mid-Dec to mid-Jan; Eng spkn; adv bkg; quiet; red low ssn; CCI. "Excel, well-managed site; strenuous cycle rides; thermal baths nr." ♦ € 29.10 2009*

⊞ **NEUENBURG AM RHEIN** *3B4* (2km SW Rural) *47.79638, 7.55083* **Gugel-Dreiländer Camping & Freizeitpark, Oberer Wald, 79395 Neuenburg-am-Rhein [(07631) 7719; fax (07635) 3393; info@camping-gugel.de; www.camping-gugel.de]** Exit A5/E35 junc 65. Site sp fr Neuenburg cent thro indus est. Lge, mkd pitch, pt sl, pt shd; wc; chem disp; mv service pnt; some serviced pitches; shwrs inc; el pnts (6A) €2.60; gas; lndtte; shop; tradsmn; rest; snacks; playgrnd; cov'rd pool; sm lake nr; tennis; cycle hire; entmnt; TV rm; 60% statics; dogs €3; poss cr; quiet; red long stay. "Excel, wooded site; gd sports facs; vg rest; o'night area poss v cr." ♦ € 22.90 2008*

NEUERBURG *3A2* (3km N Rural) *50.0272, 6.2765* **Camping In der Enz, In der Enz 25, 54673 Neuerburg [(06564) 2660; fax 2979; camping@basse.de; www.camping-neuerburg.de]** Fr Bitburg W on B50, leave at Sinspelt dir Neuerburg. Drive thro vill, site well sp. Med, unshd; htd wc; chem disp; mv service pnt; shwrs €0.50; el pnts; (16A) metered; lndry rm; rest; snacks; bar; BBQ; playgrnd; htd pool; waterslide; tennis; cycle hire; horseriding; wifi; 50% statics (sep area); dogs €2; bus 100m; Eng spkn; adv bkg; quiet; ccard acc; CCI. "Vg site; gd walks & cycle tracks." ♦ Easter-31 Oct. € 15.00 2008*

NEUHAUSEN SCHELLBRONN see Pforzheim *3C3*

NEUKLOSTER *2E2* (500m E Urban) *53.86597, 11.69792* **See-Camping Neukloster, Bützowerstrasse 27a, 23992 Neukloster [(038422) 20844; fax 20461; info@see-camping-neukloster.de; www.see-camping-neukloster.de]** Exit A20 junc 10 or 11 & foll sp Neukloster, then camping sp. Med, pt sl, shd; htd wc; chem disp; shwrs €0.80; el pnts (10-16A) €1.50 (poss rev pol); Indtte; shop 300m; rest 200m; playgrnd; lake adj; 50% statics; dogs €1.50; bus 500m; quiet; CCI. "Conv touring base; easy walk to town; sep site for m'vans sp in town." ♦ 1 Apr-31 Oct. € 13.50 2010*

NEUMAGEN DHRON see Trittenheim *3B2*

⊞ **NEUMARKT IN DER OBERPFALZ** *4E3* (4.5km N Rural) *49.32944, 11.42876* **Campingplatz Berg, Hausheimerstrasse 31, 92348 Berg [tel/fax (09189) 1581; campingplatz-herteis@t-online.de; www.camping-in-berg.de]** Exit A3 junc 91 & foll sp Berg bei Neumarkt. In cent of Berg, turn R, site on R in 800m, sp. On ent turn R to tourers area & walk to recep. Med, pt sl, unshd; wc; chem disp; mv service pnt; baby facs; shwrs €0.60; el pnts (20A) €2.50; Indtte; shop 400m; rest 400m; snacks; golf 8km; 60% statics (sep area); dogs €2; Eng spkn; quiet. "Well-run, friendly, family-owned site; excel san facs; sh walk to Berg cent." € 18.20 2011*

We can fill in site report forms on the Club's website – www.caravanclub.co.uk/europereport

⊞ **NEUMUNSTER** *1D1* (2km SW Rural) *54.04636, 9.92306* **Familien-Camping Forellensee, Humboldredder 5, 24634 Padenstedt [(04321) 82697; fax 84341; info@familien-campingplatz.de; www.familien-campingplatz.de]** Exit A7 junc 14 for Padenstedt, join dual c'way for 1km & turn L sp Centrum. In 1km turn L at traff lts sp Padenstedt for 3km, under m'way. Site on L in vill. Lge, mkd pitch, pt shd; wc; chem disp; mv service pnt; shwrs inc; el pnts (16A) €3 or metered; Indtte; tradsmn; rest 500m; snacks; bar; playgrnd; lake sw; trout-fishing; tennis; games area; 75% statics; phone; poss cr; Eng spkn; some rd noise; CCI. "Gd NH; conv for trains to Hamburg/Lübeck." ♦ € 17.00 2009*

NEUNKIRCHEN *3B2* (3km SE Rural) *49.32777, 7.19416* **Camping Volkssonnengarten, Kirkelerstrasse, 66539 Neunkirchen [(0160) 94753613; fax (06821) 24564]** Leave A8 at junc 24; N twd Neunkirchen; 1st L (camping sp); next L into Kirkelerstrasse sp Kirkel; sharp turn L immed after passing under a'bahn into rd sp as no thro rd. Med, terr, pt shd; wc; chem disp; shwrs inc; el pnts (16A) metered + conn fee or €1.50; Indtte; shops 600m; rest; snacks; bar; playgrnd; pool adj; paddling pool; tennis 200m;90% statics; dogs €2; phone; clsd 1300-1500; poss cr; some Eng spkn; quiet but some rd noise; red CCI. "V friendly, helpful staff; tight pitches; adj pool free to campers; gd NH/sh stay." 1 Mar-31 Oct. € 14.50 2009*

NEUREICHENAU *4G3* (9km NE Urban) *48.74861, 13.81694* **Knaus Campingpark Lackenhäuser, Lackenhäuser 127, 94089 Neureichenau [(08583) 311; fax 91079; lackenhaeuser@knauscamp.de; www.knauscamp.de]** Leave A3/E56 at junc 14 (Aicha-vorm Wald) & go E for 50km via Waldkirchen, Jandelsbrunn, Gsenget & Klafferstrasse to Lackenhäuser. Lge, some hdg/mkd pitch, pt sl, terr, pt shd; wc; chem disp; mv service pnt; some serviced pitches; baby facs; sauna; shwrs inc; el pnts (16A) €2.60 or metered; gas; Indtte; shop; rest; snacks; bar; BBQ; playgrnd; 2 pools (1 htd); paddling pool; tennis 500m; cycle hire; fishing; horesriding adj; games rm; entmnt; solarium; hairdresser; internet; games/TV rm; 40% statics; dogs €2.50; adv bkg; quiet; ccard acc; red low ssn/long stay. "Lge site with little waterfalls & walkways; ski-lift on site - equipment for hire; mv service pnt diff to access; excel shop; 2km to 3 point border with Austria & Czech Republic; excursions booked; recep clsd 1200-1500 & after 1800." ♦ 10 Jan-7 Nov. € 25.90 2010*

NEUSTADT *3C2* (7km S Rural) *49.30083, 8.09027* **Campingplatz Wappenschmiede, Talstrasse 60, 67487 St Martin [(06323) 6435; cpWappenschmiede@hotmail.de; www.campingplatz-wappenschmiede.beep.de]** Exit A65 at junc 13 or 14 to Maikammer, then foll sp St Martin & site (blue/white or yellow/brown sp). At end houses take 1st L into touring area (do not go up hill to statics area). Sm, shd; wc; chem disp; shwrs €1; el pnts €2; Indtte; supmkt 5km; rest; bar; playgrnd; 50% statics; dogs; Eng spkn; adv bkg; quiet; red long stay; CCI. "Poss long walk to facs - not suitable disabled; friendly site; St Martin v picturesque; gd rests; gd walking area." 1 Apr-1 Nov. € 20.00 2011*

NEUSTADT AM MAIN *3D2* (2.5km S Rural) *49.91173, 9.59998* **Main-Spessart-Camping International, 97845 Neustadt-am-Main [(09393) 639; fax 1607; info@camping-neustadt-main.de; www.camping-neustadt-main.de]** Exit A3/E41 junc 65 sp Marktheidenfeld. Do not cross bdge to Marktheidenfeld but turn L up rv sp Lohr. Site on R past Rothenfels on W bank of Rv Main. Med, mkd pitch, pt shd; wc; chem disp; mv service pnt; baby facs; shwrs €0.50; el pnts (16A) metered + conn fee; gas; Indtte (inc dryer); shop; rest 2.5km; snacks; playgrnd; htd pool; paddling pool; boating, waterskiing & fishing; golf 10km; entmnt; 70% statics; dogs €2.50; clsd 1200-1400; Eng spkn; adv bkg; quiet but some rd noise; ccard acc; red CCI. "Beautiful countryside; rvside cycle track 500m; sm pitches; excel." 1 Apr-30 Sep. € 18.50 2010*

⊞ **NEUSTADT AN DER AISCH** *4E2* (6km N Rural) *49.64058, 10.59975* **Campingplatz Münchsteinach, Badstrasse 10, 91481 Münchsteinach [(09166) 750; fax 278; gemeinde@muenchsteinach.de; www.muenchsteinach.de]** Turn NW fr rd 470 Neustadt-Höchstadt at camp sp 8km fr Neustadt & thro Gutenstetten. Int'l camping sp in 5km turn R, foll camp sp. Lge, unshd; wc; mv service pnt; chem disp; shwrs inc; el pnts (16A) metered; Indtte (inc dryer); shop, snacks 500m; pool adj; 60% statics; dogs €2; quiet; red long stay; CCI. "Sm touring area; clean facs; site muddy when wet." ♦ € 11.00 2010*

GERMANY

⊞ **NEUSTADT AN DER WALDNAAB** *4F2* (500m NW Urban) *49.73750, 12.17222* **Waldnaab Camping, Gramaustrasse 64, 92660 Neustadt-an-der-Waldnaab [(09602) 3608; fax 943466; poststelle@neustadt-waldnaab.de; www.neustadt-waldnaab.de]** Exit A93 junc 21a onto B15 for 4km N into Neustadt. Site sp fr N side of vill. Sm, hdg pitch, pt shd; htd wc; chem disp; mv service pnt; shwrs €0.50; el pnts (16A) metered + conn fee; Indtte; supmkt 500m; rest 1km; snacks; bar; playgrnd; pool; games area; dogs €1.50; quiet. "Helpful owners; clean facs; excel value for money." € 13.00 2010*

NEUSTADT IN HOLSTEIN *2E1* (2km E Coastal) *54.09286, 10.82583* **Camping am Strande, Sandbergweg 94, 23730 Neustadt-in-Holstein [(04561) 4188; fax (04361) 7125; info@amstrande.de; www.amstrande.de]** Exit A1/E47 junc 13 or 14 for Neustadt; thro Neustadt twd Pelzerhaken for 2km, site on R past hospital. Lge, hdg/mkd pitch, pt sl, pt shd; wc; chem disp; mv service pnt; shwrs €0.50; el pnts (10A) €2; gas; Indtte; shop 100m; rest 200m; playgrnd; sw & shgl beach adj; watersports; cycle hire; 70% statics; dogs €3; poss cr; Eng spkn; adv bkg; quiet; ccard acc; CCI. "Gd area, gd beaches, & cycling; v pleasant site." ♦ 1 Apr-30 Sep. € 18.00 2009*

⊞ **NEUSTRELITZ** *2F2* (8km S Rural) *53.30895, 13.00305* **Ferienpark Havelberge am Woblitzee, An der Havelbergen 1, 17237 Gross Quassow [(03981) 24790; fax 247999; info@haveltourist.de; www.haveltourist.de]** Fr Neustrelitz foll sp to Userin on L25 & bef Userin turn L sp Gross Quassow. Turn S in vill at camping sp, cross rlwy line & rv, sm ent in 1.5km. Site 1.7km S of Gross Quassow twd lake, sp. Lge, pt sl, pt shd; wc; chem disp; mv service pnt; sauna; shwrs €0.90; el pnts (10A) €2.90; Indtte (inc dryer); shop adj; rest high ssn; snacks; bar; playgrnd; lake sw; watersports; cycle hire; wifi; entmnt & 30% statics; dogs €4.40; quiet. "Lovely wooded area; poss diff lge o'fits; not rec as NH." ♦ € 24.60 2010*

⊞ **NIDEGGEN** *1A4* (2km SW Rural) *50.68530, 6.46966* **Campingplatz Hetzingen, Campingweg 1, 52385 Brück [(02427) 508; fax 1294; info@campingplatz-hetzingen.de; www.campingplatz-hetzingen.de]** Fr Nideggen take rd sp Schmidt/Monschau, ent 2km on L at R-hand bend on ascent fr level x-ing. Lge, pt sl, pt shd; wc; chem disp; sauna; baby facs; shwrs €0.80; el pnts (10-16A) metered; gas; Indtte; shop; rest; snacks; bar; playgrnd; cycle hire; 75% statics; dogs €2.50; train 500m; poss cr; Eng spkn; adv bkg; some rlwy noise; red CCI. "C'van may need manhandling onto pitch; site in wildlife reservation." € 16.00 2009*

NIEDERAU see Meissen *2G4*

NIEDERZELL see Konstanz *3D4*

NIESKY *2H4* (3km W Rural) *51.30156, 14.80302* **Campingplatz Tonschächte (Part Naturist), Raschkestrasse, 02906 Niesky [(03588) 205771; camping_tonschacht@gmx.de]** Leave A4/E40 at junc 93 onto B115 sp Niesky; cont on B115 site sp on L; do not go into Niesky but stay on B115. Lge, shd; wc; shwrs €0.75; el pnts (10A); Indtte; shop; rest 1km; snacks; playgrnd; games area; 50% statics; dogs; poss cr. "Conv Polish border x-ing & a'bahn; sep naturist area." ♦ 15 Apr-15 Oct. € 12.50 2011*

⊞ **NOHFELDEN** *3B2* (5km SW Rural) *49.56072, 7.06105* **Campingplatz Bostalsee, 66625 Nohfelden-Bosen [(06852) 92333; fax 92393; campingplatz@bostalsee.de; www.bostalsee.de]** Fr A62 exit junc 3 sp Nohfelden/Türkismühle & Bostalsee. Turn R & foll camp sp. Site on R in 1.6km after passing thro vill of Bosen. V lge, mkd pitch, pt sl, unshd; htd wc; chem disp; mv service pnt; baby facs; fam bthrm; sauna; shwrs €0.50; el pnts (16A) €2; Indtte (inc dryer); shop 1km; rest; snacks adj; playgrnd; lake sw 800m; watersports; golf 7km; wifi; entmnt; 75% statics; dogs €2; clsd to vehicles 1300-1500 & 2200-0700; adv bkg; quiet. "Vg san facs; pleasant lakeside site but poss unrel in wet; spacious, hdstg pitches; conv NH." ♦ € 20.00 2010*

NORDEN *1B2* (2km W Coastal) *53.60471, 7.13863* **Nordsee-Camp Norddeich, Deichstrasse 21, 26506 Norden-Norddeich [(04931) 8073; fax 8074; www.Nordsee-Camp.de]** Off B70 N of Norden. Well sp. V lge, mkd pitch, pt shd; wc; chem disp; mv service pnt; baby facs; shwrs inc; el pnts (6A) €2.20; Indtte; shop; rest; snacks; playgrnd; beach 200m; fishing; cycle hire; internet; entmnt; 25% statics; dogs; €3.80; ccard acc; red CCI. "Immac san facs; friendly atmosphere; day trips to Frisian Islands; excel rest; v gd site." ♦ 8 Mar-25 Oct. € 20.80 2011*

NORDLINGEN *4E3* (8km SW Rural) *48.82622, 10.40933* **Campingplatz Ringlesmühle, 73469 Riesbürg-Utzmemmingen [(07362) 21377; fax 923516; info@ringsmuehle.de; www.ringlesmuehle.de]** Exit Nördlingen on B466 dir Ulm. In approx 5km turn R in Holheim sp Utzmemmingen. Site sp fr B466 500m beyond Utzmemmingen. Med, pt sl, unshd; wc; chem disp; shwrs; el pnts (6A) €1.50; BBQ; dogs; quiet. "Beautiful setting, cycle rte to Nördlingen; relaxed, friendly site; poss w/end rallies." Easter-31 Oct. € 12.00 2009*

NORDSTRAND *1C1* (2km SE Coastal) *54.46948, 8.90997* **Camping Margarethenruh, Süderhafen 8, 25845 Nordstrand [(04842) 8553 or (04841) 968033; fax (4841) 968033; info@camping-nordstrand.de; www.camping-nordstrand.de]** Fr Husum foll sp to Nordstrand, then S to Süderhafen. On Nordstrand island & reached by causeway. Sm, unshd; htd wc; chem disp; mv service pnt; shwrs inc; el pnts (16A) €2.50 or metered; Indtte; rest 200m; TV; 10% statics; dogs; Eng spkn; quiet; CCI. "Friendly owner; gd, modern san facs; easy cycle path around island; boat trips to nrby islands; vg." 8 Apr-31 Oct. € 17.00 2007*

⊞ **NORTHEIM** *1D4* (3.5km NW Rural) *51.72900, 9.98374* **Camping Sultmerberg, Am Sultmerberg 3, 37154 Northeim [(05551) 51559; fax 5656; campingplatzmajora@web.de; www.campingplatzsultmerberg.de]** Exit 69 fr A7/E45 onto B3, site sp. Med, pt shd; wc; shwrs inc; el pnts (10A) €3 or metered + conn fee; Indtte; shop; rest 100m; snacks; playgrnd; sm pool; 30% statics; dogs €2; poss some rd & rlwy noise; clsd 1-14 Jan; ccard acc; red long stay/CCI. "Delightful, well-kept, woodland site; gd, clean san facs; superb views Harz mountains; plenty space; conv NH." € 21.80 2010*

NUREMBERG see Nürnberg *4E2*

⊞ **NURNBERG** *4E2* (5km SE Urban) *49.42305, 11.12138* **Knaus Campingpark Nürnberg, Hans-Kalb-Strasse 56, 90471 Nürnberg [(0911) 9812717; fax 9812718; nuernberg@knauscamp.de; www.knauscamp.de]** Exit E45/A9 junc 52 or E50/A6 junc 59 dir Nürnberg-Langwasser heading N, or Nürnberg-Fischbach exit travelling S; foll sp to 'Stadion', turn L. Site ent off wide rd opp Nürnberg Conference Centre. Lge, pt mkd pitch, pt shd; htd wc; chem disp; mv service pnt; shwrs inc; el pnts (6-16A) €3 (long cable rec); gas; lndtte (inc dryer); shop; rest 1km; playgrnd; htd, pool adj; tennis; wifi; TV; 25% statics; dogs €2; tram/metro 1.2km; poss cr; Eng spkn; adv bkg; noise fr rd & poss fr stadium; red long stay; ccard acc; CCI. "Friendly, helpful staff; peaceful, surrounded by trees; san facs poss stretched high ssn; v quiet midwk low ssn; gd security; office & access clsd 1300-1500 & 2200-0700; gd cycle rte to town; national rlwy museum in town worth visit; 1.2km to metro to town cent; red squirrels on site." ♦ € 26.80 2011*

⊞ **OBERAMMERGAU** *4E4* (1km S Rural) *47.58988, 11.0696* **Campingpark Oberammergau, Ettalerstrasse 56B, 82487 Oberammergau [(08822) 94105; fax 94197; service@camping-oberammergau.de; www.campingpark-oberammergau.de]** Fr S turn R off B23, site on L in 1km; fr N turn L at 2nd Oberammergau sp. Do not ent vill fr N - keep to bypass. Med, plenty hdstg, hdg/mkd pitch, pt shd; wc; chem disp; mv service pnt; fam bthrm; baby facs; shwrs inc; el pnts (16A) metered + conn fee; gas; lndtte (inc dryer); shop in vill; tradsmn; rest adj; playgrnd; cycle hire; wifi; entmnt; 75% statics; dogs €2; sep car park; bus; poss cr; Eng spkn; adv bkg ess high ssn; red lont stay/low ssn; CCI. "Plenty of space; helpful recep; excel san facs; excel rest adj; easy walk to vill." ♦ € 23.00 2010*

⊞ **OBERSTDORF** *3D4* (1km N Rural) *47.42370, 10.27843* **Rubi-Camp, Rubingerstrasse 34, 87561 Oberstdorf [(08322) 959202; fax 959203; info@rubi-camp.de; www.rubi-camp.de]** Fr Sonthofen on B19, just bef Oberstdorf at rndabt take exit sp Reichenbach, Rubi. Site in 1km over level x-ing, 2nd site on R. Med, hdstg, unshd; htd wc; chem disp; mv service pnt; baby facs; serviced pitches; shwrs inc; el pnts (8A) metered; lndtte; shop 1km; tradsmn; rest; snacks; bar; BBQ; playgrnd; skiift 1km; TV; 10% statics; dogs €2.70; phone; bus; site clsd Nov; Eng spkn; adv bkg; quiet; CCI. "Well-run, well-maintained site; immac facs; block paved paths to pitches; block hdstg with grass growing thro; excel scenery; excel facs." ♦ € 31.20 2011*

⊞ **OBERSTDORF** *3D4* (1.5km N Rural) *47.42300, 10.27720* **Campingplatz Oberstdorf, Rubingerstrasse 16, 87561 Oberstdorf [(08322) 6525; fax 809760; camping-oberstdorf@t-online.de; www.camping-oberstdorf.de]** Fr B19 dir Oberstdorf, foll site sp. Med, hdstg, pt shd; wc; chem disp; mv service pnt; serviced pitches; shwrs inc; el pnts (10A) metered; lndtte (inc dryer); shops 1.5km; tradsmn; rest; snacks; golf 5km; skilift 3km; skibus; wifi; 45% statics (sep area); dogs €0.50; Eng spkn; rd & rlwy noise. "Cable cars to Nebelhorn & Fellhorn in town; Oberstdorf pedestrianised with elec buses fr o'skirts; ask for Allgäu Walser card for free local buses & shop discounts; vg." € 19.40 2010*

OBERWEIS see Bitburg *3B2*

⊞ **OBERWESEL** *3B2* (5km N Rural) *50.14188, 7.72101* **Camping Loreleyblick, An der Loreley 29-33, 56329 St Goar-am-Rhein [(06741) 2066; fax 7233; info@camping-loreleyblick.de; www.camping-loreleyblick.de]** Exit A61/E31 sp Emmelshausen junc 42 & foll sp for St Goar; site adj B9 1km S of St Goar opp Loreley rock on rv bank. Or exit A48 junc 10 dir Koblenz, then B9 St Goar. Lge, pt sl, unshd; htd wc; chem disp; mv service pnt; shwrs inc; el pnts (6A) €2.50; gas; lndtte; shop & 500m; tradsmn; rest, snacks, bar adj (hotel opp); pool 3km; 10% statics; dogs €1.70; phone adj; poss v cr; Eng spkn; no adv bkg; much noise fr rlwy 24 hrs, plus noise fr rd & rv barges; red long stay; CCI. "Lovely setting in scenic area; friendly, helpful owner; excel modern san facs, stretched when site full; pool complex in hills behind; conv boat trips & car ferry across Rhine 500m; if office clsd site self & report later; site clsd if rv in flood Dec-Feb; el voltage drops when site v cr; easy walk to town; castles & museums; wine cents; chair lift at Boppard; gd range of shops in St Goar." ♦ € 18.80 2011*

OBERWESEL *3B2* (6km SE Rural) *50.05111, 7.7750* **Camping Sonnenstrand, Strandbadweg 9, 55422 Bacharach [(06743) 1752; fax 3192; info@camping-sonnenstrand.de; www.camping-sonnenstrand.de]** Fr Koblenz to Bingen, sp at S edge of Bacharach; site bet rd & rv on W bank. NB: Beware of sharp turn into site if travelling fr N. Rec do not app thro Bacharach - narr, cobbled streets & sm archways. Med, pt shd; wc; chem disp; cold shwrs inc; ltd el pnts (6A) €2.50 or metered (poss 2 x 25m cab req); gas; lndtte; shops 300m; rest; bar; beach adj; boating; golf 6km; 30% statics; dogs €1.50; Eng spkn; adv bkg; rv, rd & rlwy noise; red low ssn/long stay/CCI. "Helpful, knowledgeable owner; poss lge groups m'cyclists; scenic area; busy, noisy rvside site; sm pitches; wine cellar visits; shwrs/san facs ltd & poss stretched high ssn; plenty of rv activities; excel rest; sh walk to sm medieval town; sh stay/NH only." 1 Apr-31 Oct. € 16.00 2008*

OBERWESEL *3B2* (600m S Urban) *50.10251, 7.73664* **Camping Schönburgblick, Am Hafendamm 1, 55430 Oberwesel [(06744) 714501; fax 714413; camping-oberwesel@t-online.de; www.camping-oberwesel.de]** Fr A61/E31 exit sp Oberwesel, site sp on L at ent to sports stadium, on rvside. Sm, pt shd; wc; chem disp; mv service pnt; shwrs inc; el pnts (6A) €8.50; supmkt 200m; rest 200m; snacks; bar; tennis adj; o'night area for m'vans; poss cr; adv bkg; some rlwy noise; red long stay; CCI. "Clean, modern san facs in Portacabins - stretched when site full; rv trips, cycling, walking." 15 Mar-31 Oct. € 17.00 2011*

OBERWESEL *3B2* (5km NW Rural) *50.14976, 7.69478* **Camping Friedenau, Gründelbach 103, 56329 St Goar-am-Rhein [tel/fax (06741) 368; info@camping-friedenau.de; www.camping-friedenau.de]** App on B9 fr Boppard or Bingen; turn under rlwy bdge 1km N of St Goar; keep L; site on L in 1km. Sm, pt sl, shd; wc; chem disp; mv service pnt; shwrs inc; el pnts (16A) €2.50; gas; lndtte; shops 1.5km; tradsmn; rest; bar; playgrnd; pool 1.5km; dogs €1; bus; poss cr; Eng spkn; adv bkg; quiet; red CCI. "Quieter than other sites in area - uphill fr busy Rhine & resorts; some pitches uneven & poss diff after heavy rain; vg welcome." ♦ 15 Mar-31 Oct. € 16.10 2009*

OHNINGEN WANGEN see Radolfzell am Bodensee *3C4*

GERMANY

⊞ **OHRDRUF** *2E4* (8km S Rural) *50.73363, 10.75671* **Oberhof Camping Lütschesee, Am Stausee 9, 99330 Frankenhain [(036205) 76518; fax 71768; info@oberhofcamping.de; www.oberhofcamping.de]** Fr A4/E40 exit junc 42 onto B247 S twd Oberhof. After approx 25km at Gasthaus Wegscheide turn L onto forest rd to site. Also accessible fr B88, sp in vill of Frankenhain via tarmac rd - 5km. Lge, shd; htd wc; chem disp; mv service pnt; shwrs inc; el pnts (10A) inc; gas; lndtte (inc dryer); shop; tradsmn; rest 1.5km; rest; snacks; bar; BBQ; playgrnd; lake sw; boat & cycle hire; wifi; TV rm; 60% statics; dogs €2; adv bkg; ccard acc; red long stay/CCI. "Vg, busy site in heart of Thüringer Forest; excel san facs; gd walking & cycling." ♦ € 22.00 (CChq acc) 2010*

⊞ **OHRDRUF** *2E4* (6km W Rural) *50.82452, 10.61060* **Campingplatz Paulfeld, Catterfeld, 99894 Leinatal [(036253) 25171; fax 25165; info@paulfeld-camping.de; www.paulfeld-camping.de]** Fr E exit A4 junc 41a onto B88 sp Friedrichroda & foll sp Catterfeld & site on R. Or fr W exit junc 42 at Gotha. Take B247 S twd Ohrdruf. After 6km bear R sp Georgenthal. In Georgenthal vill, bear R onto B88. After 2km site sp L on app Catterfeld vill. Foll rd 2km thro forest to site, sp. Site approx 12km fr A4. Lge, some hdg, pt shd; chem disp; mv service pnt; wc; sauna; shwrs €0.80; el pnts (16A) inc; gas; lndtte (inc dryer); shop; rest; snacks; bar; BBQ; playgrnd; sm pets corner; lake sw & fishing; solarium; games area; cycle hire; games rm; internet; 40% statics in sep area; dogs €2; twin-axles acc (rec check in adv); poss cr w/end; quiet; ccard not acc; red low ssn/long stay; CCI. "Excel, well-kept site; gd access to pitches; helpful staff; clean san facs; gd for families with young children; woodland walks; conv stop en route eastern Europe." ♦ € 20.50 SBS - G17 2011*

OLCHING *4E4* (3.5km NE Rural) *48.23033, 11.35863* **Camping Ampersee, Josef-Kistlerweg 5, 82140 Olching [(08142) 12786; fax 45114; info@campingampersee.de; www.campingampersee.de]** Exit E52/A8 junc 78 sp Fürstenfeldbruck, turn R & foll site sp. Sm, mkd pitch, pt shd; wc; chem disp; shwrs €0.50; el pnts (4A) €2.50; lndtte; shop; hypmkt nr; rest; snacks; playgrnd; lake sw; 60% statics; dogs €1.80; phone; poss cr; Eng spkn; m'way noise; ccard not acc. "Sm pitches; charge for all hot water." 1 May-3 Oct. € 20.10 2008*

OLDENDORF see Bergen *1D3*

⊞ **OLPE** *1B4* (6km N Rural) *51.0736, 7.8564* **Feriencamp Biggesee - Vier Jahreszeiten, Am Sonderner Kopf 3, 57462 Olpe-Sondern [(02761) 944111; fax 944141; info@camping-sondern.de; www.camping-biggesee.de]** Exit A45/E41 junc 18 & foll sp to Biggesee. Pass both turnings to Sondern. Take next R in 200m. Ent on R in 100m. NB: Other sites on lake. Lge, mkd pitch, terr, pt shd; wc; chem disp; mv service pnt; baby facs; sauna; shwrs inc; el pnts (16A) inc; gas; lndtte; shop & 6km; rest; snacks; bar; cooking facs; playgrnd; shgl beach & lake sw adj; watersports inc diving; tennis; rollerskating rink; cycle hire; solarium; entmnt; internet; 20% statics; dogs €2.50; poss cr; Eng spkn; adv bkg; quiet; CCI; "Gd facs; well-organised site; barrier clsd 1300-1500 & 2200-0700; conv Panorama Theme Park & Cologne; vg cycling area; footpaths." ♦ € 24.00 2010*

⊞ **OSNABRUCK** *1C3* (4.5km NE Rural) *52.29181, 8.10593* **Camping Niedersachsenhof, Nordstrasse 109, 49084 Osnabrück [(0541) 77226; fax 70627; osnacamp@aol.com; www.osnacamp.de]** Exit A30/E30 junc 19 onto A11 sp Diepholz. At traff lts (end of m'way) at junc with B51/65 turn L sp Osnabrück & L again at next traff lts into minor rd (Nordstrasse). Site on R in 600m - do not take 1st ent. Fr Osnabrück, take B51/65 sp Diepholz, & turn R at traff lits in approx 4km by TV tower. Sp throughout Osnabrück. Med, mkd pitch, pt sl, pt shd, pt sl; wc; chem disp; shwrs €0.50; el pnts (16A) €2.80 or metered; lndtte (inc dryer); supmkt 2km; rest adj; snacks 1.5km; BBQ; playgrnd; entmnt; 30% statics; dogs; phone; bus; Eng spkn; adv bkg; quiet but some rd noise; CCI. "V friendly; spacious pitches with views; mv service pnt outside site & diff to use; excel" € 18.50 2010*

There aren't many sites open at this time of year. We'd better phone ahead to check the one we're heading for is open.

⊞ **OSNABRUCK** *1C3* (11km SW Rural) *52.22944, 7.89027* **Regenbogen-Camp Tecklenburg, Grafenstrasse 31, 49545 Leeden [tel/fax (05405) 1007; tecklenburg@regenbogen-camp.de; www.regenbogen-camp.de]** Exit A1/E37 junc 73 or fr A30/E30 junc 13; foll sp to Tecklenburg, then Leeden & foll site sp. V lge, pt sl, pt shd; wc; chem disp; mv service pnt; serviced pitches; baby facs; shwrs; el pnts (16A) €2.90; lndtte; shop, rest, snacks high ssn; playgrnd; htd, covrd pool; paddling pool; games area; cycle hire; entmnt; 45% statics; dogs €3.25; o'night area for m'vans open all yr; site clsd 1 Nov-15 Dec; clsd 1300-1500; poss cr; adv bkg; quiet; ccard acc; red CCI. "Gd views; excel san facs; gd rest." ♦ € 27.75 2009*

⊞ **OSTERODE AM HARZ** *1D3* (3.6km E Rural) *51.7357, 10.3049* **Harzcamp am Sösestausee, Schimpfstrasse, 37520 Osterode-am-Harz [(05522) 3319; fax 72378; harzcamp@t-online.de; www.harzcamp.de]** Take B498 fr Osterode, site on R adj reservoir. Med, mkd pitch, terr, pt shd; wc; chem disp; mv waste; shwrs €0.50; el pnts (16A) metered + conn fee; lndtte; shop 3.5km; tradsmn; playgrnd; lake sw; fishing; 50% statics; dogs €1.50; phone; poss cr; Eng spkn; quiet; CCI. "Fair NH." ♦ € 16.00 2008*

OSTERREINEN see Füssen *4E4*

OSTRINGEN *3C3* (5km SE Rural) *49.20035, 8.76066* **Kraichgau-Camping Wackerhof, Schindelberg 10, 76684 Ostringen-Schindelberg [(07259) 361; fax 2431; info@wackerhof.de; www.wackerhof.de]** Exit A5 junc 41 Kronau; E on B292 to cent Ostringen 9km; turn SE foll camp sp. Site in 5km. Med, mkd pitch, pt sl, terr, pt shd; wc; chem disp; mv service pnt; shwrs inc; el pnts (16A) metered; gas; lndtte; shop; rest, snacks 5km; playgrnd; 60% statics; rd & rlwy noise; some Eng spkn; 10% red CCI. "Friendly; gd, clean facs." 25 Mar-15 Oct. € 10.00 2011*

OTTERNDORF *1C2* (4km NE Coastal) *53.82524, 8.87613* **Campingplatz See Achtern Diek, Deichstrasse 14, 21762 Otterndorf [(04751) 2933; fax 3016; campingplatz.otterndorf@ewetel.net; www.otterndorf.de]** Fr Cuxhaven W to Otterndorf on B73. Take 1st L after rlwy to traff lts, turn L twd Müggendorf, foll site sp, site on Rv Elbe. V lge, hdg/mkd pitch, hdstg; wc; chem disp; mv service pnt; baby facs; serviced pitches; shwrs inc; el pnts (16A) €1.80; gas; lndtte; shop 3.5km; rest, snacks, bar adj; playgrnd; pool; sand beach & sw adj; entmnt; 40% statics; dogs €3.50; phone; adv bkg; quiet; ccard acc; red CCI. "Friendly; efficiently run; easy cycle rtes to town; gd touring cent; site clsd 1300-1500; conv for ferry." ♦ 1 Apr-31 Oct. € 20.00 2009*

⊞ **PAPENBURG** *1B2* (3km SE Rural) *53.06481, 7.42691* **Camping Poggenpoel, Am Poggenpoel, 26871 Papenburg [(04961) 974026; fax 974027; campingpcp@aol.com; www.papenburg-camping.de]** Fr B70, site sp fr town. Med, pt shd; htd wc; chem disp; mv service pnt; baby facs; shwrs €2; el pnts (10A) €2; lndtte; shop; rest; snacks 1km; bar; playgrnd; lake sw adj; games area; golf 1km; entmnt; cab TV; 40% statics; dogs €2; phone; o'night facs for m'vans; quiet; red long stay/CCI. ♦ € 19.00 2009*

PAPPENHEIM *4E3* (W Rural) *48.93471, 10.96993* **Camping Pappenheim, Badweg 1, 91788 Pappenheim [(09143) 1275; fax 837364; info@camping-pappenheim.de; www.camping-pappenheim.de]** B2 heading S, site sp after passing thro Weissenburg, on edge of Pappenheim. Med, pt shd; wc; shwrs; chem disp; mv service pnt; el pnts (16A) €2; lndtte; shop; rest 500m; snacks; lake sw; 25% statics; dogs €1.50; quiet. "Mountain views." 1 Apr-25 Oct. € 16.50 2010*

PASSAU *4G3* (10km W Rural) *48.60605, 13.34583* **Drei-Flüsse Campingplatz, Am Sonnenhang 8, 94113 Irring [(08546) 633; fax 2686; dreifluessecamping@t-online.de; www.dreifluessecamping.privat.t-online.de]** On A3/E56, junc 115 (Passau Nord); foll sps to site. Med, pt sl, terr, pt shd; wc; chem disp; mv service pnt; 60% serviced pitches; shwrs inc; el pnts (16A) €2.50 or metered; gas; lndtte; shop; rest; BBQ; playgrnd; cov'rd pool May-Sep; dogs €1.50; phone; bus 200m; poss cr; adv bkg; ccard acc; red 5+ days; CCI. "Interesting grotto on site; gd rest; rec arr early; facs need updating; poor surface drainage after heavy rain; interesting town at confluence of 3 rvs; on Danube cycle way; conv NH fr A3/E56." ♦ 1 Apr-31 Oct. € 28.00 2011*

⊞ **PEINE** *1D3* (8km NW Rural) *52.35158, 10.12657* **Camping Waldsee, Am Waldsee 1, 31275 Lehrte-Hämelerwald [(05175) 4767; fax 5632]** Exit A2 junc 51 dir Hämelerwald. Thro Hämelerwald, under rlwy bdge. Strt over 1st traff lts, immed L after 2nd pedestrian x-ing in 300m. Site sp. Med, shd; htd wc; chem disp; mv service pnt; shwrs inc; el pnts (10A) inc; lndtte (inc dryer); shop 2km; rest high ssn; snacks; bar; playgrnd; pool 3km; lake sw adj; 5% statics; dogs; Eng spkn; rlwy noise; CCI. "Woodland site; rather run down (2010) but conv NH." ♦ € 15.00 2010*

PETERSDORF (FEHMARN ISLAND) *2E1* (4km NW Coastal) *54.48760, 11.01858* **Strandcamping Wallnau (Part Naturist), 23769 Wallnau [(04372) 456; fax 1829; wallnau@strandcamping.de; www.strandcamping.de]** Site is to W of Fehmarn peninsula 4km W of Petersdorf, sp. V lge, mkd pitch, pt shd; htd wc; mv service pnt; serviced pitches; sauna; baby facs; shwrs; el pnts (16A) €2.50; gas; lndtte (inc dryer); shop; tradsmn; rest; snacks; bar; BBQ; playgrnd; sand beach adj; sep naturist beach; cycle hire; wellness cent; games area; cycle hire; wifi; entmnt; 50% statics; dogs €5.50; poss cr; adv bkg; quiet; red low ssn. "Nature reserve & bird sanctuary nr; excel for families." ♦ 1 Apr-30 Oct. € 29.80 (CChq acc) 2011*

⊞ **PFEDELBACH** *3D3* (2km S Rural) *49.15356, 9.49894* **Camping Seewiese, 11 Seestrasse; 74629 Pfedelbach-Buchorn [fax (07941) 33827; campingseewiese@t-online.de; www.camping-seewiese.de]** Exit A6 junc 40 at Öhringen; foll sp Pfedelbach & Camping. Lge, pt sl, pt shd; wc; chem disp; shwrs; el pnts (16A) €2 or metered; gas; lndtte (inc dryer); ice; rest; sacks; bar; BBQ; playgrnd; htd pool; lake fishing; games rm; TV; 90% statics; phone; dogs €1.50; Eng spkn; adv bkg; quiet; CCI. "Mainly statics, OK NH." ♦ € 19.00 2009*

⊞ **PFORZHEIM** *3C3* (12km SE Rural) *48.81800, 8.73400* **International Camping Schwarzwald, Freibadweg 4, 75242 Neuhausen-Schellbronn [(07234) 6517; fax 5180; fam.frech@t-online.de; www.camping-schwarzwald.de]** Fr W on A8 exit junc 43 for Pforzheim; fr E exit junc 45. In town cent take rd 463 sp Calw, immed after end of town sp take minor rd L thro Huchenfeld up hill to Schellbronn. Site in vill of Schellbronn on N side of rd to Bad Liebenzell - sp at church on R. Lge, pt sl, pt shd; wc; chem disp; mv service pnt; shwrs €0.50; el pnts (17A) €2 or metered; gas; lndtte; shop; rest; snacks; bar; playgrnd; htd pool adj; dance & fitness cent; cycle hire; entmnt high ssn; internet; 80% statics; no dogs; bus; no vehicle access after 2200; poss cr; adv bkg; quiet; red long stay; CCI. "Scenic area; v clean, well-maintained site; vg san facs; excel rest/takeaway; v rural." ♦ € 18.00 2011*

PFRONTEN STEINACH see Nesselwang *4E4*

PIDING see Bad Reichenhall *4G4*

⊞ **PIELENHOFEN** *4F3* (1.5km S Rural) *49.05896, 11.95820* **Campingplatz Naabtal, Distelhausen 2, 93188 Pielenhofen [(09409) 373; fax 723; camping-pielenhofen@t-online.de; www.camping-pielenhofen.de]** Exit A3/E56 junc 97 onto B8 dir Etterzhausen. Thro Etterzhausen turn L to Pielenhofen/Amberg. In Pielenhofen turn R over bdge. Med, mkd pitch, pt shd; htd wc; chem disp; mv service pnt; sauna; shwrs €0.50; el pnts (10A) metered + conn fee €0.60; gas; lndtte; sauna/solarium; shop; rest; bar; playgrnd; tennis; cycle hire; skittle alley; summer curling rink; games area; dogs €2.20; 65% statics; Eng spkn; CCI. "In beautiful valley; helpful warden; v nice site in gd location; liable to flooding; gd rv access for boating; family-run site; lots of facs; spacious pitches; gd rest; conv Regensburg." ♦ € 17.60 2011*

GERMANY

GERMANY

⊞ **PIRMASENS** *3B3* (12km NE Rural) *49.27546, 7.72121* **Camping Clausensee, 67714 Waldfischbach-Burgalben [(06333) 5744; fax 5747; info@campingclausensee.de; www.campingclausensee.de]** Leave a'bahn A6 at junc 15 Kaiserslautern West; S onto B270 for 22km. E 9km on minor rd sp Leimen, site sp. Lge, mkd pitch, pt shd; chem disp; htd wc; mv service pnt; some serviced pitches; shwrs €0.50; el pnts (6-16A) inc; gas; Indtte (inc dryer); shop; tradsmn; rest; snacks; bar; BBQ; playgrnd; lake sw adj; fishing; boating; games/TV rm; quiet; 50% statics; dogs €4.20; no twin-axles; poss cr; Eng spkn; adv bkg; quiet; ccard acc; red low ssn/long stay; CCI. "Peaceful situation in Pfalzerwald Park; helpful staff; clean san facs; busy at w/ends; gd walking & cycling; gd." ♦ € 23.50 2009*

PIRNA *4G1* (2km N Urban) *50.98169, 13.92508* **Waldcampingplatz Pirna-Copitz, Aussere Pillnitzerstrasse 19, 01796 Pirna [(03501) 523773; fax 764149; waldcamping@stadtwerke-pirna.de; www.waldcamping-pirna.de]** Fr B172 fr Dresden to Pirna-Copitz or fr A17/E55. Site well sp. Med, mkd pitch, pt shd; htd wc; chem disp; mv service pnt; baby facs; shwrs inc; el pnts (10A) €3; Indtte; shop 700m; tradsmn; rest 400m; snacks 700m; playgrnd; 20% statics; dogs €2.50; bus 1km; adv bkg; quiet. "Clean, well-run site; modern facs." ♦ 1 Apr-31 Oct. € 21.00 2011*

⊞ **PLAU** *2F2* (3km SE Rural) *53.43832, 12.28699* **Campingpark Zuruf am Plauer See, Seestrasse 38d, 19395 Plau-Plötzenhöhe [(038735) 45878; fax 45879; campingpark-zuruf@t-online.de; www.campingpark-zuruf.de]** N on B103, turn E at x-rds 200m after int'l camping sp. Site on lakeside. Lge, pt shd; wc; chem disp; mv service pnt; shwrs €0.80; el pnts (10A) €2.20; Indtte; shop; rest 1km; snacks; playgrnd; lake sw & beach; watersports; cycle hire; entmnt; dogs €2.50; adv bkg; quiet; CCI. "Pleasant, friendly site; sm pitches, tight access; muddy when wet." € 18.00 2010*

PLAUEN *4F1* (5km N Rural) *50.53860, 12.18495* **Camping Gunzenberg Pöhl, 08543 Möschwitz [(037439) 6393; fax 45013; tourist-info@poehl.de; www.camping-poehl.de]** Exit A72/E441 junc 7 & foll sp for Möschwitz & white sp for Talsperre Pöhl. V lge, pt hdg/mkd pitch, terr, pt shd; wc; chem disp; mv service pnt; shwrs inc; el pnts (10A) €2 or metered + conn fee; Indtte (inc dryer); shop; rest; snacks; bar; playgrnd; shgl beach & lake sw adj; golf 2km; wifi; entmnt; 60% statics; dogs €3; clsd 1230-1400; poss cr; quiet; red CCI. "Excel, v formal, clean site; helpful, friendly staff." ♦ 26 Mar-2 Nov. € 17.00 2010*

PLON *1D1* (3km SE Rural) *54.12855, 10.45510* **Campingpark Augstfelde, Am See, 24306 Augstfelde [(04522) 8128; fax 9528; info@augstfelde.de; www.augstfelde.de]** Fr Plön on B76 twd Bosau, sp. Lge, mkd pitch, terr, pt shd; htd wc; chem disp; mv service pnt; baby facs; sauna; private bthrms avail; shwrs €0.75; el pnts (10-16A) €2.50; gas; Indtte (inc dryer); shop; rest; snacks 3km; bar; playgrnd; lake sw & sand beach adj; fishing; boat, canoe & cycle hire; tennis; fitness cent; games area; golf 100m; wifi; entmnt; 60% statics; dogs €2; o'night area for m'vans; Eng spkn; adv bkg; ccard acc; red long stay; CCI. "Lovely situation; superb sailing, windsurfing; gd for families; excel." ♦ 1 Apr-24 Oct. € 20.30 (CChq acc) 2010*

PLON *1D1* (1.5km SW Rural) *54.14746, 10.39823* **Naturcamping Spitzenort, Ascheberger Strasse 76, 24306 Plön [(04522) 2769; fax 4574; info@spitzenort.de; www.spitzenort.de]** On L of rd B430 fr Plön to Ascheberg at pensinsular. Lge, pt shd; wc; chem disp; mv service pnt; baby facs; some serviced pitches; shwrs inc; el pnts (6A) €2; gas; Indtte; shop; rest; playgrnd; lake sw; shgl beach; watersports; cycle hire; internet; TV; 20% statics; dogs €2; adv bkg; ccard acc. "Vg site in excel location; gd facs for families." ♦ 15 Mar-19 Oct. € 22.60 2008*

PLON *1D1* (6km SW Rural) *54.11928, 10.33670* **Camping Seeblick, Dorfstrasse 59, 24326 Dersau [(04526) 1211; fax 1218; info@camping-dersau.de; www.camping-dersau.de]** Exit A21/B404 junc 8 dir Plöner See, turn R bef lake to Dersau, site on L in 2km, sp. Lge, pt sl, unshd; wc; chem disp; mv service pnt; shwrs inc; el pnts (10-16A) €2 (poss rev pol); Indtte (inc dryer); shop; rest 200m; snacks; playgrnd; lake sw & sand beach adj; boating; wifi; 75% statics; no dogs; adv bkg; quiet; red long stay/low ssn; CCI. "Excel site bet vill & lake; gd walks; gd site shop." 1 Apr-25 Oct. € 16.00 2010*

⊞ **PLOTZKY** *2E3* (1.5km N Rural) *52.06249, 11.79998* **Ferienpark Plötzky, Kleiner Waldsee 1, 39245 Plötzky [(039200) 50155; fax 76082; info@ferienpark-ploetzky.de; www.ferienpark-ploetzky.de]** Exit A14 junc 7 onto B246a dir Schönebeck & Gommern for 13km. Site on L immed after vill of Plötzky, site sp. Lge, pt shd; htd wc; chem disp; mv service pnt; private bthrms avail; baby facs; shwrs €1; el pnts (16A) €2 or metered; Indtte (inc dryer); shop 1.5km; tradsmn; rest 1.5km; snacks; bar; playgrnd; lake sw; boat & cycle hire; games area; horseriding; archery; entmnt; internet; TV rm; 70% statics; dogs €2; adv bkg; quiet; ccard acc. "Gd walking, cycling in wooded area; peaceful, relaxing, well-run site." ♦ € 17.00 2010*

POMMERN see Cochem *3B2*

PORSTENDORF see Jena *2E4*

⊞ **PORTA WESTFALICA** *1C3* (2km SW Rural) *52.22146, 8.83995* **Camping Grosser Weserbogen, Zum Südlichen See 1, 32457 Porta Westfalica [(05731) 6188 or 6189; fax 6601; info@grosserweserbogen.de; www.grosserweserbogen.de]** Fr E30/A2 exit junc 33, foll sp to Vennebeck & Costedt. Site sp. Site 12km by rd fr Bad Oeynhausen. Site sp fr m'way. Lge, mkd pitch, some hdstg, pt shd; wc; chem disp; shwrs; el pnts (10A) €2.90; Indtte; shop & 5km; tradsmn; rest; snacks; bar; playgrnd; lake sw adj (w/ends only); fishing; watersports; dogs €1.50; some Eng spkn; adv bkg; quiet, poss noisy w/end; debit card acc; 10% red CCI. "Site in cent of wildlife reserve; v tranquil; gd base Teutoburger Wald & Weser valley; barrier clsd 1300-1500 & o'night; many statics; lge area for tourers; gd for families; excel san facs & rest; shwrs charged to electronic card; level access; highly rec." ♦ Easter-31 Oct. € 19.00 2010*

POTSDAM *2F3* (8km S Rural) *52.35278, 12.98981* **Naturcampingplatz Himmelreich, Wentorfinsel, 14548 Caputh [(033209) 70475; fax 20100; himmelreich@campingplatz-caputh.de; www.campingplatz-caputh.de]** Exit A10 junc 20 or 23 to Glindow. Take B1 to Geltow, turn L immed after rlwy x-ring & foll sp Caputh. Lge, shd; htd wc; chem disp; mv service pnt; shwrs €1; el pnts (10A) €1.50; Indtte; shop; tradsmn; rest; snacks; bar; sand beach & lake adj; boat hire; 65% statics; dogs €2; phone; metro 500m; poss cr; adv bkg; quiet - rlwy noise some pitches; CCI. "Lovely position on waterfront; modern san facs; poss haphazard pitching; cycle rtes & walks." ♦ 1 Apr-31 Oct. € 17.00 2010*

POTSDAM *2F3* (8km SW Rural) *52.36088, 12.94663* **Camping Riegelspitze, Fercherstrasse, 14542 Werder-Petzow [(03327) 42397; fax 741725; info@campingplatz-riegelspitze.de; www.campingplatz-riegelspitze.de]** Fr A10/E55 Berlin ring a'bahn take exit 22 dir Glindow or Werder exits & foll sp to Werder; then foll B1 for 1.5km twd Potsdam, R after Strengbrücke bdge twd Petzow. Med, terr, pt shd; wc; chem disp; mv service pnt; shwrs (metered); el pnts (16A) €1.80 (poss rev pol & long lead req); Indtte; shop; lge supmkt 1km; rest; snacks; bar; playgrnd; lake sw & sand beach; watersports; cycle hire; 50% statics; dogs €2.50, no dogs high ssn; bus; poss cr; adv bkg; quiet. "Friendly recep; haphazard pitching; transport tickets fr recep; recep clsed 1300-1500; bus outside site; Sanssouci visit a must." ♦ 1 Apr-25 Oct. € 23.00 2011*

POTSDAM *2F3* (10km SW Rural) *52.36055, 13.00722* **Camping Sanssouci, An der Pirschheide 41, 14471 Potsdam [tel/fax (0331) 9510988; info@camping-potsdam.de; www.camping-potsdam.de]** Fr A10 Berlin ring rd take exit 22 at Gross Kreutz onto B1 twd Potsdam cent for approx 17km, past Werder (Havel) & Geltow. Site sp approx 2km after Geltow immed bef rlwy bdge. Lge, shd; wc; chem disp; mv service pnt; 50% serviced pitches; baby facs; shwrs inc; el pnts (10A) inc (poss rev pol); gas; Indtte; shop; tradsmn; rest; bar; BBQ; playgrnd; covrd pool 200m; lake sw & sand beach adj; watersports; fishing; horseriding 8km; cycle hire; games rm; wifi; 25% statics; dogs €4.90; mini-bus to stn; poss cr; Eng spkn; adv bkg; quiet; ccard not acc; CCI. "Helpful, friendly owners; lovely area; sandy pitches; poss diff lge outfits manoeuvring round trees; excel facs inc music in san facs; vg rest; camp bus to/fr stn; gate clsd 1300-1500; gd security; conv Schlosses & Berlin by rail." ♦ 1 Apr-3 Nov. € 38.90 SBS - G16 2011*

⊞ **POTSDAM** *2F3* (11km W Rural) *52.36002, 12.91677* **Camping Glindowsee, Jahnufer 41, 14542 Glindow [(03227) 40855; info@hogab.de; www.hogab.de]** Fr A10/E55 a'bahn exit junc 23 dir Werder. In 4km at beginning of Glindow turn R (S). Thro Glindow, site sp on L. Med, pt shd; htd wc; chem disp; mv service pnt; shwrs inc; el pnts (16A) €3; gas 3km; Indtte; shop 1.5km; rest; bar; BBQ; playgrnd; sand beach & lake sw adj; 80% statics; dogs €1; poss cr; quiet; CCI. "Sm grassy area for tourers; gd, clean, modern facs." € 21.00 2010*

⊞ **POTTENSTEIN** *4E2* (2km NW Rural) *49.77942, 11.38411* **Feriencampingplatz Bärenschlucht, 12 Weidmannsgesees, 91278 Pottenstein [(09243) 206; fax 880; info@baerenschlucht-camping.de; www.baerenschlucht-camping.de]** Exit A9 junc 44 onto B470 dir Forchheim; cont past Pottenstein; site in 2km on R. Med, pt sl, pt shd; htd wc; chem disp; mv service pnt; baby facs; shwrs €0.50; el pnts (8-16A) €1.90; gas; Indtte; cooking facs; shops 2km; rest; bar; 40% statics; dogs €1.90; poss cr; quiet. "A naturalized quarry surrounded by trees & rocky cliffs; Vg." ♦ € 19.00 2011*

I'll go online and tell the Club what we think of the campsites we've visited – www.caravanclub.co.uk/europereport

GERMANY

PREETZ *1D1* (5km SE Rural) *54.21073, 10.31720* **Camp Lanker See, Gläserkoppel 3, 24211 Preetz-Gläserkoppel [(04342) 81513; fax 789939; camp-lanker-see@t-online.de; www.campingplatz-lanker-see.de]** Sp off B76 bet Preetz & Plön. Lge, mkd pitch, terr, pt shd; wc; chem disp; shwrs €0.50; el pnts (6A) metered; Indtte; shop; rest; snacks; bar; playgrnd; lake sw; boating; horseriding; some statics; dogs €1; phone; adv bkg; quiet; ccard acc; red low ssn; CCI. "Barrier clsd 1300-1500 & o'night; gd." 1 Apr-31 Oct. € 22.00 2009*

PRIEN AM CHIEMSEE *4F4* (1.5km S Rural) *47.8387, 12.35078* **Camping Hofbauer, Bernauerstrasse 110, 83209 Prien [(08051) 4136; fax 62657; ferienhaus.campingpl.hofbauer@t-online.de; www.camping-prien-chiemsee.de]** Exit A8/E52/E60 junc 106 dir Prien. Site on L in 3km immed after rndabt. Med, mkd pitch, pt sl, pt shd; wc; chem disp; mv service pnt; shwrs inc; el pnts (16A) metered + conn fee; shop; snacks; playgrnd; pool; lake sw 1km; cycle hire; internet; 50% statics; dogs €2; some rd noise; ccard acc (surcharge); CCI. "Well-kept site; helpful owners; sm pitches - siting poss diff; pts of site flooded after heavy rain, but some raised pitches; solar htd water; gd." ♦ 1 Apr-30 Oct. € 19.00 2009*

PRIEN AM CHIEMSEE *4F4* (2km S Rural) *47.83995, 12.37170* **Panorama-Camping Harras, Harrasserstrasse 135, 83209 Prien-Harras [(08051) 904613; fax 904616; info@camping-harras.de; www.camping-harras.de]** Exit A8/E52/E60 junc 106 dir Prien. After 2.5km turn R at rndabt sp Krankenhaus & site. Lge, pt shd; htd wc; chem disp; mv service pnt; baby facs; fam bthrm; shwrs €0.80; el pnts (6A) €2 (poss no earth); gas; Indtte (inc dryer); shop; tradsmn; rest; snacks; bar; playgrnd; htd, covrd pool 3km; lake sw; canoeing; boat & cycle hire; golf 3km; wifi; 20% statics; dogs €3.20; poss v cr; Eng spkn; quiet but poss noisy disco at w/end; ccard acc; CCI. "Beautiful, scenic area; on Chiemsee lakeside (extra for lakeside pitches); 15% extra if staying fewer than 4 nights; sm pitches; popular, busy site - rec arr early; modern, clean facs; poor drainage after rain; site rather run down end of ssn." ♦ 8 Apr-31 Oct. € 18.30 (CChq acc) 2010*

GERMANY

PRORA see Binz *2G1*

PRUCHTEN *2F1* (800m NW Rural/Coastal) *54.37960, 12.66181* **Naturcamping Pruchten, Zeltplatzstrasse 30, 18356 Pruchten [(038231) 2045; fax 038231 66346; info@naturcamp.de; www.naturcamp.de]** Fr Rostock on B105, at Löbnitz take L23 N sp Barth & Zingst to Pruchten & foll site sp. Lge, mkd pitch, pt shd; htd wc; chem disp; mv service pnt; baby facs; shwrs €1; el pnts (16A) €2; Indtte; shop; tradsmn; rest; snacks; bar; playgrnd; sand beach 500m; games area; horseriding 500m; wifi; 20% statics; dogs €2; m'van o'night area; adv bkg; quiet. "Gd birdwatching, surfing, fishing; vg." 1 Apr-31 Oct. € 16.00 2008*

⊞ **PRUM** *3A2* (1.5km NE Rural) *50.21906, 6.43811* **Waldcamping Prüm, 54591 Prüm [(06551) 2481; fax 6555; info@waldcamping-pruem.de; www.waldcamping-pruem.de]** Site sp fr town cent dir Dausfeld. Med, pt shd; wc; chem disp; mv service pnt; baby facs; shwrs inc; el pnts (10-16A) inc; gas; Indtte (inc dryer); shop; rest 1km; snacks; playgrnd; pool complex adj; tennis adj; cycle hire; skilift 2km; entmnt high ssn; internet; 60% statics; dogs €1.50; o'night facs for m'vans; poss cr; Eng spkn; adv bkg; quiet; ccard acc; red CCI. "Pleasant site in lovely surroundings; friendly staff; clean facs; m'van o'night facs; do not arr bef 1900 on Sundays due local rd closures for family cycling event." ♦ € 22.00 2009*

PUTTGARDEN (FEHMARN ISLAND) *2E1* (8km SE Coastal) *54.45806, 11.27203* **Camping Klausdorfer Strand, 23769 Klausdorf [(04371) 2549; fax 2481; info@camping-klausdorferstrand.de; www.camping-klausdorferstrand.de]** Fr Puttgarden on minor rd (not main E47) sp Burg, turn left after 6km sp Klausdorf. Foll site sp through Klausdorf to coast. Lge, hdg/mkd pitch, unshd; htd wc; chem disp; mv service pnt; some serviced pitches; baby facs; fam bthrm; shwrs inc; el pnts (16A) metered or €2; Indtte; shop; rest; playgrnd; sand beach adj; cycle hire; golf 10km; entmnt; 50% statics; dogs €4; phone; poss cr; Eng spkn; adv bkg; quiet; red CCI. "Conv for ferry to Denmark; excel cycling area; bird sanctuary nr; gd access to pitches; excel." 1 Apr-15 Oct. € 23.00 2011*

PUTTGARDEN (FEHMARN ISLAND) *2E1* (1km NW Coastal) *54.5029, 11.21635* **Camping Puttgarden, Strandweg, 23769 Puttgarden [tel/fax (04371) 3492 or 2185]** N on B207/E47, on app Puttgarden ferry terminal take L turn & foll sp Strand to site on R. Med, hdstg, unshd; wc; mv service pnt; shwrs €0.50; el pnts (16A) metered; Indtte; shop; rest; snacks; playgrnd; fishing; sailing; many statics; dogs €1; poss cr; adv bkg; quiet; ccard acc. "Conv NH for ferry to Denmark." 1 Apr-15 Oct. € 18.00 2009*

⊞ **RADEVORMWALD** *1B4* (4km NE Rural) *51.18400, 7.31300* **Camping-Ferienpark Kräwinkel, Kräwinkel 1, 42477 Radevormwald [(02195) 6887899; fax 689597; info@ferienpark.de; www.ferienpark.de]** Exit A1 Remscheid onto B229 Radevormwald. In Radevormwald 1st mini island turn R, site on L in 4km. Sm, hdg pitch, terr, pt shd; htd wc; chem disp; shwrs inc; el pnts (20A) inc; rest; bar; playgrnd; lake sw nr; 80% statics; dogs €2; Eng spkn; adv bkg; quiet; CCI. "Lge pitches; pleasant area." ♦ € 15.00 2009*

RADOLFZELL AM BODENSEE *3C4* (3km E Rural) *47.73888, 9.00305* **Camping Markelfingen, Unterdorfstrasse 19, 78315 Radolfzell-Markelfingen [(07732) 10611; fax 10727; info@campingplatz-markelfingen.de; www.campingplatz-markelfingen.de]** Fr B33 turn twd Radolfzell. Turn L in 2km at traff lts sp Markelfingen then R at traff lts in Markelfingen. Site sp. Med, hdstg, pt shd; wc; chem disp; shwrs €1; el pnts (10A) metered; Indtte; shop; tradsmn; rest; snacks; bar; BBQ; lake sw & shgl beach; boat launch; 50% statics; dogs €2.30; phone; train adj; poss cr; Eng spkn; quiet; CCI. "Recep clsd 1230-1400; gd train service to Radolfzell & Konstanz; modern san facs." ♦ 15 Mar-15 Oct. € 18.80 2008*

RADOLFZELL AM BODENSEE *3C4* (10km E Rural) *47.71111, 9.07972* **Campingplatz Himmelreich, Strandweg 34, 78472 Allensbach [(07533) 6420; fax 934031; info@campingplatz-himmelreich.de; www.campingplatz-himmelreich.de]** On rte 33 Radolfzell to Konstanz, take R turn sp Allensbach; shortly after rlwy stn turn R sp Strand & Camping; site over bdge, turn L sp Camping. Med, pt shd; wc; chem disp; mv service pnt; shwrs €0.80; el pnts (16A) €2.50 or metered; gas; Indtte; shop; tradsmn; rest; snacks; bar; playgrnd; shgl beach & lake sw; boat-launching; TV; 30% statics; dogs; phone; sep car park high ssn; bus 200m; train to Konstanz; poss v cr; Eng spkn; adv bkg; quiet; no ccard acc; 10% red long stay; CCI. "Vg facs but restricted access to some at night." ♦ 15 Mar-15 Oct. € 19.50 2008*

RADOLFZELL AM BODENSEE *3C4* (6km S Rural) *47.68796, 8.99428* **Campingdorf Horn, Strandweg 3-18, 78343 Gaienhofen-Horn [(07735) 685; fax 8806; campingdorf.horn@t-online.de]** Fr Stein-am-Rhein take L192 along N of Untersee for approx 13km. Site on app to Horn vill, sp. Fr Radolfzell, take rd S on E bank of Zellersee, site on L exit Horn vill. Med, pt shd; wc; chem disp; some serviced pitches; shwrs €1; el pnts (16A) metered + conn fee; Indtte; shop; tradsmn; rest; snacks 200m; bar; playgrnd; lake sw; watersports; entmnt; 20% statics; no dogs; bus; phone; sep car park; adv bkg; quiet; ccard acc; red CCI. "Vg." ♦ 15 Mar-7 Oct. € 26.00 2011*

RADOLFZELL AM BODENSEE *3C4* (10km S Rural) *47.65972, 8.93388* **Campingplatz Wangen, Seeweg 32, 78337 Öhningen-Wangen [(07735) 919675; fax 919676; info@camping-wangen.de; www.camping-wangen.de]** Site in Wangen vill. Med, hdstg, pt shd; wc; chem disp; mv service pnt; shwrs inc; el pnts (16A) metered + conn fee; Indtte; shop 300m; rest; snacks; bar; playgrnd; lake sw & sand beach adj; fishing; 60% statics; dogs €2 (check with site before arr to make sure they will acc); phone; adv bkg; quiet; CCI. "Lovely scenery; site in vill but quiet; helpful recep; gd cycling & sw; lake steamer trips; Stein-am-Rhein 5km." ♦ 6 Apr-7 Oct. € 23.50 2011*

RATZEBURG *2E2* (5km NW Rural) *53.73845, 10.74008* **Naturcamping Buchholz, Am Campingplatz 1, 23911 Buchholz [(04541) 4255; fax 858550; office@naturcampingbuchholz.de; www.naturcampingbuchholz.de]** Fr S on B207 dir Lübeck; turn R sp Buchholz; also R turn when travelling fr N; turns under main rd; foll camp sp. NB: App rd narr, care needed. Med, hdg pitch, few hdstg, terr, pt shd; wc; chem disp; mv service pnt; shwrs inc; el pnts (8A) €1.80; gas; Indtte; rest; adj to lake with slipway for sm boats & sw; cycle path network; 50% statics; o'night facs for m'vans; poss cr; Eng spkn; quiet; ccard not acc; CCI. "Pleasant site; helpful owners; pitches tight - may need to manhandle; fish mkt in Lübeck; Ratzeburg worth a visit." ♦ 1 Apr-30 Sep. € 18.10 2008*

RAVENSBURG *3D4* (8km SW Rural) *47.73935, 9.47187* **Camping am Bauernhof, St Georg Strasse 8, 88094 Oberteuringen-Neuhaus [(07546) 2446; fax 918106; kramer@camping-am-bauernhof.de; www.camping-am-bauernhof.de]** Fr Ravensburg twd Meersburg on B33. In Neuhaus foll sp on R; site bef chapel. Sm, pt shd; wc; chem disp; shwrs inc; el pnts (10A) €2; Indtte; shop 300m; BBQ; playgrnd; lake sw; 20% statics; dogs €2; quiet; CCI. "CL-type but with full facs inc shwrs for wheelchair users; vg, clean, modern san facs; relaxed atmosphere; gd cycling area." ♦ 1 Mar-31 Oct. € 18.00 2010*

⊞ **REGENSBURG** *4F3* (2km W Rural) *49.02779, 12.05899* **Azur Campingpark Regensburg, Weinweg 40, 93049 Regensburg [(0941) 270025; fax 299432; regensburg@azur-camping.de; www.azur-camping.de]** Fr A93/E50 exit junc 40 Regensburg W, dir Weiden; turn W away fr town onto dual c'way; R at traff lts, site sp fr next T-junc. Lge, some hdstg, pt shd; htd wc; chem disp; mv service pnt; shwrs inc; el pnts (4A) €3 (poss long lead req); Indtte; shop high ssn; supmkt 400m; rest high ssn; bar; playgrnd; covrd pool 300m; cycle hire; 40% statics (sep area); dogs €3.50; phone; bus at site ent; o'night area for m'vans; poss cr; quiet; ccard not acc; red CCI. "Helpful owner; vg facs; san facs gd & kept cln; large block san facs unisex; sm pitches poss diff lge o'fits; cycle path into town along Rv Danube; gates clsd 1300-1500 & 2200-0800; gd." ♦ € 28.00 2011*

REINSBERG *2G4* (750m S Rural) *51.00381, 13.36012* **Campingplatz Reinsberg, Badstrasse 17, 19629 Reinsberg [(037324) 82268; fax 82270; campingplatz-reinsberg@web.de; www.campingplatz-reinsberg.de]** Exit A4/E40 junc 75 Nossen. Take 1st R to Siebenlehn & foll sp Reinsberg. In Reinsberg take 1st R sp camping & 'freibad' to site. Med, pt shd; htd wc; chem disp (wc); shwrs inc; el pnts (16A) €2; Indtte; sm shop; tradsmn; rest, bar 500m; snacks; playgrnd; pool & sports facs adj; 40% statics; dogs €2; phone; Eng spkn; adv bkg; quiet. "Friendly, helpful owner; excel san facs; gd walking; conv Meissen, Dresden & Freiberg." ♦ 1 Apr-31 Oct. € 15.00 2010*

⊞ **REINSFELD** *3B2* (1km W Rural) *49.68612, 6.86781* **Azur Campingpark Hunsrück, Parkstrasse 1, 54421 Reinsfeld [(06503) 95123; fax 95124; reinsfeld@azur-camping.de; www.azur-camping.de/reinsfeld]** Fr A1 exit junc 132 Reinsfeld onto B407; site well sp. Lge, pt sl, pt shd; htd wc; chem disp; private bthrms avail; shwrs inc; el pnts (10A) €3; gas; Indtte; shop; rest; snacks; bar; playgrnd; htd pool 200m; paddling pool; sm lake; tennis; games area; entmnt; TV; 40% statics; dogs €3; clsd 1300-1500; poss cr; Eng spkn; adv bkg; no ccard acc; red CCI. "Aircraft exhib worthwhile; some pitches v muddy in wet weather; scenic area; conv Trier & Luxembourg." ♦ € 22.00 2010*

When we get home I'm going to post all these site report forms to the Club for next year's guide. The deadline's mid September 2013

REIT IM WINKL *4F4* (5km E Rural) *47.65845, 12.54114* **Camping Seegatterl, Seegatterl 7, 83242 Reit-im-Winkl [(08640) 98210; fax 5150; info@camping-reit-im-winkl.com; www.camping-reit-im-winkl.com]** On B305, site sp behind lge car park. Camping sp obscured in vill. Med, pt sl, unshd; htd wc; chem disp; mv service pnt; sauna; shwrs inc; el pnts (16A) metered; gas; Indtte (inc dryer); shop; tradsmn; rest; snacks; BBQ; playgrnd; lake sw & beach 2km; cycle hire; skilift fr site; skibus 100m; golf 5km; internet; 50% statics; dogs €2; adv bkg; quiet. "Gd family site; friendly; excel skiing & walking; mainly for winter sport users." 1 Dec-31 Mar & 15 May-15 Oct. € 20.00 2009*

⊞ **REIT IM WINKL** *4F4* (7.5km NW Rural) *47.73556, 12.41565* **Camping Zellersee, Zellerseeweg 3, 83259 Schleching-Mettenham [(08649) 986719; fax 816; info@camping-zellersee.de; www.camping-zellersee.de]** Fr A8 exit junc 109 S sp Reit im Winkel. Just after Marquartstein turn R onto B307 sp Schleching, site sp just N of Schleching. Med, mkd pitch, pt sl, terr, pt shd; htd wc; chem disp; baby facs; shwrs inc; el pnts (16A) metered; gas; Indtte; shop & 1.2km; tradsmn; rest, bar 600m; lake sw; tennis; 50% statics; no dogs; phone; Eng spkn; adv bkg; quiet; ccard acc; red long stay/CCI. "Excel, high quality facs; many footpaths fr site; mountain views; nr Alpenstrasse." ♦ € 19.00 2008*

REMAGEN *3B1* (7km N Rural) *50.64500, 7.20694* **Camping Siebengebirgsblick, Wickchenstrasse, 53424 Remagen-Rolandswerth [(02228) 910682; fax (02633) 472008; info@siebengebirgsblick.de; www.siebengebirgsblick.de]** Site sp close to car ferry to Königswinter, opp Nonnewerth Is. Fr B9, foll sp to site on rvside. Lge, mkd pitch, unshd; wc; chem disp; shwrs €0.50; el pnts (8A) metered or €2.50; sm shop 500m; rest; snacks; bar; playgrnd; TV; 40% statics; dogs €1; Eng spkn; quiet; red long stay; CCI. "Extra for pitches on rvside; facs in Portacabins; minimal rv & rlwy noise; cycle tracks along rv to Bonn & Remagen; gd NH." 15 Apr-20 Oct. € 17.00 2010*

GERMANY

⊞ **REMAGEN** *3B1* (1km SE Rural) *50.57666, 7.25083* **Campingplatz Goldene Meile, Simrockweg 9-13, 53424 Remagen [(02642) 22222; fax 1555; info@camping-goldene-meile.de; www.camping-goldene-meile.de]** Fr A61 exit dir Remagen onto B266; foll sp 'Rheinfähre Linz'; in Kripp turn L, site sp. Or fr B266 1km beyond Bad Bodendorf at rndabt take B9 (dir Bonn & Remagen); in 1km take exit Remagen Süd; foll sp to sports cent/camping. Site adj Luddendorf Bridge. Fr S on A48 exit junc 10 onto B9 twd Bonn. Site sp in 22km after junc with B266. Lge, hdg/mkd pitch, some hdstg, pt shd; wc; chem disp; mv service pnt; some serviced pitches; shwrs €0.75; el pnts (16A) €2.60 (50m cable rec some pitches); gas; Indtte; shop (ltd opening); tradsmn; rest high ssn; snacks; bar; playgrnd; pool adj; cycle hire; wifi; entmnt; 50% statics; dogs €1.70; m'van o'night area adj; poss cr; Eng spkn; adv bkg; quiet but some noise fr rlwy across rv; red CCI. "Tourers on flat field away fr rvbank; sm pitches tightly packed in high ssn; gd rest; helpful staff; el pnts up ladder; access to facs not gd for disabled; cycle path along Rhine; site clsd 1300-1500; v gd site." ♦ € 28.40 2011*

RETGENDORF *2E2* (750m N Rural) *53.72947, 11.50279* **Campingplatz Retgendorf, Seestrasse 7A, 19067 Retgendorf [(03866) 400040; fax 400041; info@camping-retgendorf.de; www.camping-retgendorf.m-vp.de]** Exit A241 at junc 4 onto B104 dir Schwerin, in 2km turn N onto lakeside rd dir Retgendorf & Flessenow. On ent Retgendorf, site on L by bus stop. Med, mkd pitch, pt shd; wc; chem disp; shwrs €1; el pnts (10A) €2; Indtte; shop 1km; snacks; bar; lake sw & sand beach adj; fishing; 70% statics; dogs €1.50; phone; quiet. "Views of lake; conv beautiful towns of Schwerin & Wismar; gd cycling area." ♦ 1 Apr-15 Oct. € 15.00 2009*

RETGENDORF *2E2* (3.5km N Rural) *53.75194, 11.49638* **Seecamping Flessenow, Am Schweriner See 1a, 19067 Flessenow [(03866) 81491; info@seecamping.de; www.seecamping.de]** Exit A14 at junc 4 Schwerin-Nord onto B104 dir Schwerin. In 2km turn R along lakeside sp Retgendorf & Flessenow, site in approx 10km at end of surfaced rd. Med, mkd pitch, pt shd; htd wc; chem disp; mv service pnt; baby facs; shwrs €0.80; el pnts (10A) €2.50; gas; Indtte (inc dryer); shop; tradsmn; snacks; bar; playgrnd; sand beach & lake sw adj; watersports; games area; 35% statics; dogs free; phone; bus adj; quiet; CCI. "Fair site in gd location." ♦ 1 Apr-31 Oct. € 22.50 2009*

⊞ **RHEINMUNSTER** *3C3* (1km NW Rural) *48.77330, 8.04041* **Freizeitcenter Oberrhein, Am Campingpark 1, 77836 Rheinmünster-Stollhofen [(07227) 2500; fax 2400; info@freizeitcenter-oberrhein.de; www.freizeitcenter-oberrhein.de]** Exit A5 junc 51 at Baden Baden/Iffezheim sp to join B500. At traff lts turn L onto B36 dir Hügelsheim & Kehl. In 8km turn R at rndabt immed on ent Stollhofen & cont to end of lane. V lge, hdg/mkd pitch, pt shd; 60% serviced pitches; wc; chem disp; mv service pnt; fam bthrm; shwrs inc; el pnts (16A) €2.50 + conn fee; gas; Indtte; shop; 2 rests; snacks; bar; playgrnd; lake sw; watersports; windsurfing; fishing; tennis; golf 6km; cycle hire; internet; entmnt; 70% statics (sep area); dogs €4.50; phone; clsd 1300-1500; m'van o'night area outside site; poss cr; Eng spkn; adv bkg; ccard acc; quiet. "Conv touring base Baden-Baden, Strasbourg; Black Forest; helpful staff; excel san facs; highly rec." ♦ € 25.00 2008*

⊞ **RIBNITZ DAMGARTEN** *2F1* (8km NE Coastal) *54.28194, 12.31250* **Camping in Neuhaus, Birkenallee 10, 18347 Dierhagen-Neuhaus [(038226) 539930; fax 539931; ostsee@camping-neuhaus.de; www.camping-neuhaus.de]** Exit E55/A19 junc 6 onto B105 N. At Altheide turn N thro Klockenhagen dir Dierhagen, then turn L at camping sp & foll site sp to sea. Med, pt hdg pitch, pt shd; htd wc; chem disp; baby facs; shwrs €0.50; el pnts (16A) €3; Indtte (inc dryer); shop; rest 1.5km; snacks; playgrnd; beach 100m; wifi; 40% statics; dogs €3; adv bkg; quiet; ccard not acc. "Friendly site; vg." ♦ € 26.00 2009*

RIBNITZ DAMGARTEN *2F1* (8km NW Coastal) *54.29188, 12.34375* **Ostseecamp Dierhagen, Ernst Moritz Arndt Strasse, 18347 Dierhagen-Strand [(038226) 80778; fax 80779; info@ostseecamp-dierhagen.de; www.ostseecamp-dierhagen.de]** Take B105 fr Rostock dir Stralsund. Bef Ribnitz, turn L sp Dierhagen & Wustrow & cont for 5km to traff lts & camp sp. Turn L to site on R in 300m. Lge, pt shd; wc; chem disp; mv service pnt; shwrs €0.50; el pnts (6A) €3; gas; Indtte; shop; supmkt 500m; rest 1km; snacks; playgrnd; sand beach 800m; cycle hire; 20% statics; dogs €2.80; phone; adv bkg (fee); quiet. "Site low-lying, poss v wet after heavy rain; charge for chem disp." ♦ 15 Mar-31 Oct. € 21.50 2009*

RIEGEL AM KAISERSTUHL *3B4* (1.5km N Rural) *48.16463, 7.74008* **Camping Müller-See, Zum Müller-See 1, 79359 Riegel-am-Kaiserstuhl [(07642) 3694; fax 923014; info@muellersee.de; www.muellersee.de]** Exit A5/E35 at junc 59 dir Riegel, foll site sp. Med, unshd; htd wc; chem disp; mv service pnt; baby facs; shwrs €0.30; el pnts (16A) €2; Indtte; shop in vill; tradsmn; rest, snacks in vill; bar; playgrnd; lake sw adj; no dogs; phone; quiet; red CCI. "Excel cycle paths in area; excel san facs; gd NH." ♦ 1 Apr-31 Oct. € 16.00 2011*

⊞ **RIESTE** *1C3* (2km W Rural) *52.48555, 7.99003* **Alfsee Camping-park, Am Campingpark 10, 49597 Rieste [(05464) 92120; fax 5837; info@alfsee.de; www.alfsee.de]** Exit A1/E37 junc 67; site in 5km, sp. V lge, mkd pitch, pt shd; htd wc; chem disp; mv service pnt; baby facs; fam bthrm; shwrs inc; el pnts (16A) metered; Indtte (inc dryer); shop; rest; snacks; bar; playgrnd; lake sw & sand beach adj; watersports; tennis; cycle hire; 50% statics; dogs €3; phone; poss cr at w/end with day visitors; Eng spkn; poss noisy; ccard acc; 10% red CCI. "Site part of lge, busy watersports complex; modern san facs; gd for famiies." ♦ € 23.90 2009*

⊞ **RINTELN** *1C3* (10km S Rural) *52.05118, 9.10223* **Camping Extertal, Eimke 4, 32699 Extertal-Eimke [(05262) 3307; info@campingpark-extertal.de; www.campingpark-extertal.de]** Fr Rinteln on B238 S twd Barntrup; about 1.5km S Bösingfeld turn L at sp to site over level x-ing. Sm, mkd pitch, terr, unshd; wc; chem disp; mv service pnt; serviced pitches; shwrs inc; el pnts (16A) €1.50 or metered; Indtte (inc dryer); shop; tradsmn; rest 500m; snacks high ssn; bar; cooking facs; playgrnd; lake sw; games rm; wifi; entmnt; 75% statics in sep area; dogs €1.50; some Eng spkn; quiet; red long stay/CCI. "Excel site; dry & well-drained in v wet weather; all facs clean; forest walks & cycle paths fr site." ♦ € 14.00 2010*

⊞ **RINTELN** *1C3* (2km W Rural) *52.1865, 9.05988* **Camping Doktorsee, Am Doktorsee 8, 31722 Rinteln [(05751) 964860; fax 964888; info@doktorsee.de; www.doktorsee.de]** Exit A2/E30 a'bahn, junc 35; foll sp 'Rinteln' then 'Rinteln Nord'. Turn L at traff lts, foll 'Stadtmitte' sp over rv bdge. immed turn R, bear L at fork, site in 1km on R. V lge, pt shd; wc; chem disp; mv service pnt; shwrs inc; el pnts (16A) €1.90; Indtte; shop; rest; snacks; bar; playgrnd; lake sw adj; tennis; cycle hire; entmnt high ssn; 60% statics; dogs €1.60; phone; poss cr; Eng spkn; adv bkg; quiet; ccard acc; red CCI. "NH on hdstg by ent; picturesque town with gd shops; 1 excel san facs block, other run down; pleasant staff." ♦ € 19.30 2008*

ROCKENHAUSEN *3C2* (7km NE Rural) *49.67000, 7.88666* **Azur Campingpark Pfalz, Kahlenbergweiher 1, 67813 Gerbach [(06361) 8287; fax 22523; gerbach@azur-camping.de; www.azur-camping.de]** Fr Rockenhausen take local rd to Gerbach then foll site sp on rd L385. Med, pt shd; wc; chem disp; mv service pnt; baby facs; shwrs inc; el pnts (16A) metered or €2.80; gas; Indtte; supmkt; rest; snacks; bar; cooking facs; playgrnd; pool; paddling pool; tennis; entmnt; 60% statics; dogs €2.80; adv bkg; quiet; red CCI. "Conv Rhein & Mosel wine regions; gd walking." 1 Apr-31 Oct. € 22.00 2008*

RODENKIRCHEN see Köln *1B4*

⊞ **ROSENBERG** *3D3* (8km S Rural) *48.97407, 10.02644* **Waldcamping Hüttenhof, Hüttenhof 1, 73494 Rosenberg [(07963) 203; fax 8418894; huettenhof@web.de; www.waldcamp.de]** Exit A7 junc 113 Ellwangen onto B290 dir Schwäbisch Hall; 1km beyond Ellwangen turn L, sp Adelmannsfelden, site sp. Med, mkd pitch, pt shd; htd wc; chem disp; mv service pnt; baby facs; shwrs €0.20; el pnts (16A) metered or €1.80; Indtte; tradsmn; supmkt 8km; rest; snacks; bar; BBQ; playgrnd; lake sw; canoeing; horseriding; games area; games rm; entmnt; dogs €1.80; quiet; red long stay. "Beautiful situation." € 13.00 2008*

⊞ **ROSENHEIM** *4F4* (9km N Rural) *47.92518, 12.13571* **Camping Erlensee, Rosenheimerstrasse 63, 83135 Schechen [(08039) 1695; fax 9416]** Exit A8 junc 102, avoid Rosenheim town cent by foll B15 sp Landshut. Site on E side of B15 at S end Schechen. Med, pt shd; wc; chem disp; some serviced pitches; shwrs €0.50; el pnts (16A) €2; Indtte; shop 1km; rest; lake sw; 60% statics; dogs €2; poss cr; Eng spkn; adv bkg; quiet; red CCI. "Pleasant site; helpful owners; excel facs; mosquito prob." ♦ € 19.40 2009*

⊞ **ROSENHEIM** *4F4* (12km SW Rural) *47.78978, 12.00575* **Tenda-Park, Reithof 2, 83075 Bad Feilnbach [(08066) 884400; fax 8844029; info@tenda-camping.de; www.tenda-camping.de]** Take exit 100 fr A8/E45/E52 & foll sp to Brannenburg. Site in 5km on R, 1km N of Bad Feilnbach. V lge, pt shd; wc; baby facs; shwrs inc; el pnts (16A) €2.50 or metered + conn fee (poss rev pol); gas; Indtte (inc dryer); shop; rest; playgrnd; htd pool; paddling pool; cycle hire; ski-lift 12km; entmnt high ssn; wifi; 80% statics; dogs €3; Eng spkn; adv bkg; quiet. "V busy, clean, well-run site; pleasant, wooded pitches; useful NH." ♦ € 22.00 2010*

⊞ **ROSSHAUPTEN** *4E4* (500m N Rural) *47.65800, 10.71900* **Wohnmobilstellplatz Rosshaupten, Augsburgerstrasse 23, 87672 Rosshaupten [(08367) 913877; fax 913876; info@womomi.de]** Fr N twd Forggensee on B16, site on R immed after taking Rosshaupten exit. Sm, mkd pitch, hdstg, pt shd; htd wc; chem disp; mv service pnt; shwrs €1; el pnts (10A) €2; gas; Indtte; shop, rest, bar 500m; sat TV; dogs; bus; Eng spkn; some rd noise; red long stay. "OK for m'vans but will acc cars/c'vans if site not busy; gd, modern san facs; helpful, friendly owners; c'van dealer/repair on site - can be like parking in a c'van sales yard!; gd location for castles, Forggensee & Austrian border." ♦ € 9.00 (4 persons) 2010*

⊞ **ROTENBURG (WUMME)** *1D2* (3km E Rural) *53.06977, 9.49413* **Camping Ferienpark Hanseat, Am Campingplatz 4, 27386 Bothel [(04266) 335; fax 8424; info@campingpark-hanseat.de; www.campingpark-hanseat.de]** Exit A1 junc 50 Sottrum twd Rotenburg, then take B71 E dir Soltau. Site sp in Bothel. Med, unshd; htd wc; chem disp; mv service pnt; shwrs; el pnts; Indtte (inc dryer); shop; rest; snacks; BBQ; playgrnd; htd pool 100m; lake sw & fishing 1km; tennis; games area; TV rm; 60% statics; dogs €2; adv bkg; quiet. ♦ € 21.80 (CChq acc) 2011*

ROTENBURG (WUMME) *1D2* (8km W Rural) *53.12027, 9.27833* **Camping Stürberg, 27367 Hassendorf [(04264) 9124; fax 821440; campingpark-stuerberg@gmx.de; www.stuerberg.de]** Exit A1/E22 Ottersberg-Rotenburg at Sottrum exit, junc 50. Turn E on B75, site on N side of B75 3km after Sottrum. Fr Rotenburg, take B75 turn S sp Hassendorf; site well sp. Med, pt shd; wc; chem disp; mv service pnt; shwrs inc; el pnts (10A) €2 & metered; gas; Indtte (inc dryer); shop 3km; tradsmn; rest 200m; snacks; bar; playgrnd; pool 3km; 30% statics; dogs €2; Eng spkn; some rd noise; red long stay/CCI. "Grassy, open plan pitches; peaceful; pleasant staff; excel, clean facs." ♦ 15 Mar-31 Oct. € 15.00 2009*

ROTENBURG AN DER FULDA *1D4* (1km E Urban) *50.99348, 9.74303* **Camping der Stadt, Campingweg, 36199 Rotenburg-an-der-Fulda [(06623) 5556; petra.reinhardt@rotenburg.de; www.rotenburg.de]** Fr A4/E40 junc 32 N to Bebra on B27 Kasselerstrasse. Thro Bebra twd Rotenburg on B83; site sp on N side of Rv Fulda. Med, hdstg, pt shd; wc; chem disp; mv service pnt; shwrs inc; el pnts (16A) €2; Indtte (inc dryer); shop; rest 600m; snacks; covrd pool 400m; cycle hire; TV; dogs €0.70; quiet; red CCI. "Basic facs; few mins walk to town." 1 Apr-15 Oct. € 12.90 2010*

⊞ **ROTHENBURG OB DER TAUBER** *3D2* (1km S Urban) *49.37083, 10.18361* **Wohnmobil Park (P2), Bensenstrasse, 91541 Rothenburg-ob-der-Tauber [(09861) 404800; fax 404529; info@rothenburg.de]** Exit A7/E43 junc 108. Just S of Rothenburg, foll sp P2 (car park no. 2). M'vans only. Med, mkd pitch, hdstg, pt sl, unshd; wc; chem disp; mv service pnt & water €1; el pnts (metered); shop 500m; rest opp; rd & rlwy noise. "M'vans only; clean, tidy o'night stop; wcs avail in car park; pay at machine; 5 min walk beautiful, interesting medieval town." € 10.00 2011*

GERMANY

ROTHENBURG OB DER TAUBER *3D2* (2km NW Rural) *49.38805, 10.16638* **Camping Tauber-Idyll, Detwang 28, 91541 Rothenburg-ob-der-Tauber [(09861) 3177 or 6463; fax 92848; camping-tauber-idyll@t-online.de; www.rothenburg.de/tauberidyll]** NW on Rothenburg-Bad Mergentheim rd in vill of Detwang. Sp. Site behind inn nr church. Care on tight R turn into ent. Sm, pt shd; htd wc; chem disp; mv service pnt; shwrs inc; el pnts (6-16A) €2 or metered + conn fee; gas; Indtte; shop; rest at inn; cycle hire; dogs €1; bus; poss v cr; Eng spkn; adv bkg. "Church clock chimes each hour; clsd to vehicles 2200-0800; old walled town, gd cent for Romantische Strasse & Hohenlohe Plain; owners helpful; pleasant site; gd san facs; sm c'van pitches at busy times; gd cycle route along valley." Easter-31 Oct. € 24.40 2011*

The opening dates and prices on this campsite have changed. I'll send a site report form to the Club for the next edition of the guide.

ROTHENBURG OB DER TAUBER *3D2* (2km NW Rural) *49.38888, 10.16722* **Campingplatz Tauber-Romantik, Detwang 39, 91541 Rothenburg-ob-der-Tauber [(09861) 6191; fax 86899; info@camping-tauberromantik.de; www.camping-tauberromantik.de]** NW on Rothenburg-Bad Mergentheim rd in vill of Detwang; turn L at camp sp & immed R; site sp fr Rothenburg. Sharp turn into site ent. Med, some hdstg, pt sl, terr, pt shd; htd wc; chem disp; mv service pnt €1; shwrs inc; el pnts (16A) €2.20; gas; Indtte (inc dryer); sm shop; rest nr; snacks; bar; playgrnd; pool 2km; some statics; dogs €1.50; phone; bus adj; poss cr; Eng spkn; adv bkg; ccard acc; quiet, but constant church bells; CCI. "Pleasant, gd value site; excel, clean facs; gd sized pitches; picturesque town; gd cycle rte; pleasant atmosphere; gd facs for children; conv NH for Austria, Italy." ♦ 15 Mar-4 Nov & 30 Nov-7 Jan. € 21.00 2010*

⊞ **ROTTENBUCH** *4E4* (1km S Rural) *47.72763, 10.96691* **Terrasencamping am Richterbichl, Solder 1, 82401 Rottenbuch [(08867) 1500; fax 8300; info@camping-rottenbuch.de; www.camping-rottenbuch.de]** S fr Schongau for 10km on B23 dir Oberammergau, site just S of Rottenbuch. Med, mkd pitch, terr, pt shd; wc; chem disp; mv service pnt; shwrs inc; el pnts (10A) metered + conn fee; gas; Indtte (inc dryer); shop; rest 300m; snacks; bar; playgrnd; lake sw adj; wifi; 40% statics; dogs €2; Eng spkn; adv bkg; quiet; ccard acc; red long stay/CCI. "Walks & cycle paths fr site; local castles, churches & interesting towns; excel facs; friendly, helpful owners." ♦ € 18.00 2010*

RUDESHEIM *3C2* (500m E Urban) *49.97777, 7.94083* **Camping am Rhein, Auf der Lach, 65385 Rüdesheim-am-Rhein [(06722) 2528 or 49299 (LS); fax 406783; mail@campingplatz-ruedesheim.de; www.campingplatz-ruedesheim.de]** Fr Koblenz (N) on B42 pass car ferry to Bingen on app to Rüdesheim; turn L & over rlwy x-ing, foll Rheinstrasse & rlwy E for 1km; cont under rlwy bdge, turn R sp to Car Park 6; turn R at T-junc, pass coach park; turn L at x-rds & foll rd to site on R. When arr via Bingen ferry turn R onto B42 & foll above dir fr level x-ing. Fr S on B42 ent Rüdesheim, turn L immed after o'head rlwy bdge (2.8m); foll camping sp. Lge, pt shd; htd wc; chem disp; mv service pnt; baby facs; shwrs €1; el pnts (10A) inc (poss rev pol & poss long lead req); gas; Indtte (inc dryer); shop; tradsmn; rest 600m; bar; BBQ (gas/charcoal); playgrnd; htd pool, paddling pool, tennis adj; cycle hire; horesriding 4km; no statics; dogs €2.70; no c'vans/m'vans over 11m; bus 500m; recep 0800-2200; poss v cr; Eng spkn; adv bkg; quiet but rlwy & rv traff noise; ccard not acc; CCI. "Pleasant, busy, family-run site; well-kept & well-run; gd facs; poss long walk to water supply; pleasant 1km walk/cycleway by rv to town; warden sites you & connects elec - no mkd pitches; perforated ground sheets only allowed; rallies welcome; Harley Davidson w/end bike festival in June." ♦ 1 May-3 Oct. € 27.00 SBS - G08 2011*

RUDESHEIM *3C2* (3km E Urban) *49.97944, 7.95777* **Camping Geisenheim Rheingau, Am Rheinufer, 65366 Geisenheim [tel/fax (06722) 75600; info@rheingaucamping.de; www.rheingau-camping.de]** Well sp fr B42, on rvside. Lge, mkd pitch, pt shd; htd wc; chem disp; baby facs; fam bthrm; shwrs inc; el pnts (16A) inc; Indtte (inc dryer); shop 2km; rest; snacks; bar; BBQ; playgrnd; htd pool 1km; games area; 50% statics; dogs €1.50; phone adj; bus adj; Eng spkn; adv bkg; quiet; CCI. "Vg site bet Rv Rhine & vineyards. Walks and cycling by river." ♦ 1 March to 31 October. € 23.00 2011*

⊞ **RUHPOLDING** *4F4* (3km S Rural) *47.7424, 12.66356* **Camping Ortnerhof, Ort 5, 83324 Ruhpolding [(08663) 1764; fax 5073; camping-ortnerhof@t-online.de; www.camping-ruhpolding.de]** Exit A8/E52/E60 junc 112, thro Ruhpolding, turn L onto B305 dir Berchtesgaden, site sp. Med, mkd pitch, some hdstg, unshd; htd wc; chem disp; mv service pnt; shwrs inc; el pnts (10A) metered + conn fee; Indtte; shop 1.5km; tradsmn; rest; snacks; playgrnd; pool 3km; skilift 3km; skibus; internet; quiet; 30% statics; no dogs; poss cr; 10% red CCI 2+ nts. "Restful, friendly site in gd location; helpful recep; sep area for m'vans adj hotel; barrier clsd 1200-1400." € 18.50 2010*

SAALBURG *4F2* (1km N Rural) *50.51542, 11.73072* **Campingplatz Kloster, Klosterstrasse 1b, 07929 Saalburg-Kloster [tel/fax (036647) 22441; bb@saalburg-ebersdorf.de; www.saalburg-ebersdorf.de]** Exit A9/E51 junc 28 dir Saalburg. Site sp on lakeside. Lge, pt sl, unshd; wc; chem disp; mv service pnt; baby facs; shwrs €1; el pnts (10-16A) €1.50; gas; Indtte (inc dryer); shop 1km; rest; snacks; bar; playgrnd; lake sw adj; games area; 80% statics; dogs €2; sep car park; quiet. "Gd." ♦ 1 Apr-31 Oct. € 19.00 2010*

⊞ **SAARBURG** *3B2* (1.5km S Rural) *49.60083, 6.52833* **Campingplatz Waldfrieden, Im Fichtenhain 4, 54439 Saarburg [(06581) 2255; fax 5908; info@campingwaldfrieden.de; www.campingwaldfrieden.de]** Fr B51/B407 bypass foll sp 'krankenhaus' (hospital). Site sp off L132. Med, hdg pitch, some hdstg, pt sl, pt shd; wc; chem disp; mv service pnt; some serviced pitches; shwrs inc; el pnts (16A) €2 or metered; gas; lndtte; shop 600m; tradsmn; rest; snacks; bar; BBQ; cooking facs; playgrnd; pool 1km; cycle hire; wifi; TV rm; 60% statics; dogs €2; Eng spkn; adv bkg; quiet; red low ssn/long stay/CCI. "Highly rec; helpful owners; warm welcome; clean facs; pitches poss tight lge o'fits." ♦ € 18.50 2010*

SAARBURG *3B2* (4km W Rural) *49.62010, 6.54274* **Camping Landal Warsberg, In den Urlaub, 54439 Saarburg [(06581) 91460; fax 914646; warsberg@landal.de; www.landal.de]** Fr Trier take B51 SW with Rv Mosel on R for approx 5km dir Saarbrücken. On leaving Ayl vill turn L sp Wiltingen & Biebelhausen & in 20m R to Saarburg. Pass under Rv Saar bdge & cont 3km to site on R, sp. App rd steep with hairpins but well-surfaced & wide. V lge, mkd pitch, pt sl, pt shd; wc; chem disp; mv service pnt; baby facs; shwrs inc; el pnts (6A) inc; gas; lndtte; shop; rest; snacks; bar; BBQ; playgrnd; htd, covrd pool; tennis; cycle hire; games rm; entmnt high ssn; dogs €3; site clsd 1300-1500; poss noisy, quiet at far end; ccard acc. "Excel; gd san facs; chem disp diff to use; excel pool; chairlift to attractive town cent; gd views; many activities all ages." ♦ 3 Apr-9 Nov. € 32.00 2009*

SAARLOUIS *3B2* (1km NW Urban) *49.31833, 6.73972* **Campingpark Saarlouis Dr Ernst Dadder, Marschall-Ney-Weg 2, 66740 Saarlouis [(06831) 3691; fax 122970; campsls@aol.com; www.camping-saarlouis.de]** Exit A620/E29 junc 2. Foll sp to city cent. At 500m approx turn L at traff lts sp 'Schiffanlegestelle'. At 500m approx site on R. Med, pt shd; wc; mv service pnt; shwrs inc; el pnts (16A) €2.30 or metered; gas; lndtte; shop 500m; rest; snacks; htd pool 150m; 30% statics; dogs €0.60; adv bkg; quiet; ccard acc; red long stay/snr citizens/CCI. "Castles, Roman remains, ruins & forest rds at Saarland & Saarbrücken; friendly owner; gd rest." 15 Mar-31 Oct. € 18.00 2011*

ST GOAR AM RHEIN see Oberwesel *3B2*

ST GOARSHAUSEN *3B2* (5km S Rural) *50.14021, 7.73469* **Campingplatz auf der Loreley, Auf de Loreley 5, 56346 Bornich [(06771) 802697; fax 802698; info@loreley-camping.de; www.loreley-camping.de]** Fr St Goarshausen on E bank of Rhine, take minor, steep rd to Bornich for 2.5km. Turn R twds Loreley rock, site on L 1km downhill. Med, mkd pitch, pt sl, pt shd; htd wc; chem disp; shwrs inc; el pnts (16A) metered + conn fee; lndtte (inc dryer); shop 2km; tradsmn; rest; snacks; bar; BBQ; playgrnd; htd, covrd pool; wifi; 20% statics; dogs €1.50; Eng spkn; quiet; CCI. "Lovely, peaceful, spacious site with views of Rv Rhine; gd, clean san facs; gd bar & rest; friendly, helpful owner with fund of local knowledge." 1 Mar-31 Oct. € 19.00 2010*

ST LEON ROT see Wiesloch *3C3*

ST MARTIN see Neustadt *3C2*

ST PETER see Freiburg im Breisgau *3B4*

SALEM *3D4* (1.5km E Rural) *47.76926, 9.30693* **Gern-Campinghof Salem, Weildorferstrasse 46, 88682 Salem-Neufrach [(07553) 829695; fax 829694; info@campinghof-salem.de; www.campinghof-salem.de]** Site well sp on all app to Neufrach on rvside. Med, mkd pitch, pt sl, unshd; htd wc; chem disp; baby facs; shwrs inc; el pnts (16A) €2; gas; lndtte (inc dryer); tradsmn; rest, snacks 2km; bar; BBQ; cooking facs; playgrnd; htd, covrd pool 4km; lake sw nr; tennis; games rm; internet; cab/sat TV; 5% statics; dogs €2 (not Jul/Aug); phone; bus; poss cr; Eng spkn; adv bkg; quiet; ccard acc; CCI. "Excel touring base for Lake Constance away fr busy lakeside sites; barrier clsd 1230-1500 & 2200-0700; avoid pitches facing recep - noise & dust; gd, clean san facs; friendly, helpful, young owners; gd for families; vg." 1 Apr-31 Oct. € 17.50 2010*

⊞ **SALZHEMMENDORF** *1D3* (6km S Rural) *52.00390, 9.64302* **Campingpark Humboldtsee, Humboldtsee 1, 31020 Salzhemmendorf-Wallensen [(05186) 957140; fax 957139; info@campingpark-humboldtsee.se; www.campingpark-humboldtsee.de]** E fr Hameln on B1, at Hemmendorf turn S twd Salzhemmendorf & Wallensen, site sp 2km SE of Wallensen. V lge, hdg/mkd pitch, pt shd; htd wc; chem disp; mv service pnt; baby facs; shwrs €0.50; el pnts (6A) inc; lndtte (inc dryer); shop & 2km; rest; snacks; cooking facs; playgrnd; pool 3km; paddling pool; lake sw & beach; fishing; boat hire; games rm; entmnt; 60% statics; dogs €2; adv bkg; quiet; ccard acc; red snr citizens/CCI. "Gd facs for families; Hameln (Hamlin) 30km." € 22.50 (CChq acc) 2011*

SCHAPRODE (RUGEN ISLAND) *2F1* (N Coastal) *54.51610, 13.16510* **Camping am Schaproder Bodden, Langestrasse 24, 18569 Schaprode [tel/fax (038309) 1234; camping.schaprode@t-online.de; www.camping-schaprode.de]** Fr Stralsund on B96 to Rügen Island, N to Samtens then turn N thro Gingst; at Trent turn W to Schaprode; site sp on ent to vill. Lge, mkd pitch, pt shd; wc; chem disp; mv service pnt; shwrs €0.50; el pnts (6A) €1.50; lndtte; shop; tradsmn; rest; snacks; bar; BBQ; playgrnd; sand/shgl beach adj; watersports; cycle hire; 20% statics; dogs €1.25; Eng spkn; adv bkg; quiet; CCI. "Pleasant beach position; some great pitches; cheerful, family-owned site; trips to island of Hiddensee (nature reserve) - unspoilt island; rec." 1 Apr-31 Oct. € 18.00 2011*

SCHIERKE see Braunlage *2E4*

⊞ **SCHILLINGSFURST** *3D3* (1.5km S Rural) *49.27353, 10.26587* **Campingplatz Frankenhöhe, Fischhaus 2, 91583 Schillingsfürst [(09868) 5111; fax 959699; info@campingplatz-frankenhoehe.de; www.campingplatz-frankenhoehe.de]** Fr A7/E43 exit junc 109; fr A6/E50 exit junc 49. Site situated bet Dombühl & Schillingsfürst. Med, pt sl, pt shd; htd wc; chem disp; mv service pnt; baby facs; shwrs inc; el pnts (16A) €2.50 or metered + conn fee; gas; lndtte; shop; tradsmn; rest; playgrnd; lake sw 200m; wifi; 40% statics; dogs €1.50; phone; poss cr; adv bkg; red long stay/CCI. "Very clean facs; barrier clsd 1300-1500 & 2100-0700; poss unkempt early season (2009); gd cycle paths." ♦ € 16.50 2011*

GERMANY

SCHILTACH *3C3* (W Urban) *48.29061, 8.33746* **Camping Schiltach, Bahnhofstrasse 6, 77761 Schiltach [(07836) 7289; fax 7466; campingplatz-schiltach@t-online.de]** Site on B294 sp on ent to vill; short, steep ent & sharp turns. Sm, mkd pitch, pt shd; htd wc; chem disp; mv service pnt; shwrs inc; baby facs; el pnts (16A) metered + conn fee; Indtte (inc dryer); shop 500m; tradsmn; rest 200m; snacks; bar; BBQ; playgrnd; covrd pool 2km; shgl beach adj; 2% statics; no dogs; phone; recep clsd 1230-1430; train 200m; Eng spkn; adv bkg; quiet; CCI. "Vg, clean, tidy site on rv bank adj indus est; picturesque vill; disused rlwy bdge over part of site, 2.60m headroom; friendly staff." ♦ 1 Apr-10 Oct. € 15.00 2010*

SCHLECHING METTENHAM see Reit im Winkl *4F4*

⊞ **SCHLEIDEN** *3B1* (1km W Rural) *50.52833, 6.46277* **Campingplatz Schleiden, Im Wiesengrund 39, 53937 Schleiden [(02445) 7030; fax 5980; www.schleiden.de]** Fr Schleiden take B258 twd Monschau. Site on L in approx 1km. Sm, mkd pitch, pt shd; wc; chem disp; shwrs; el pnts (10A) metered; gas; Indtte; shop; rest 1km; snacks 1km; playgrnd; sports cent & pool adj; cab TV; 80% statics; dogs €1.50; poss cr; adv bkg; quiet. ♦ 2008*

⊞ **SCHLEIDEN** *3B1* (6km NW Rural) *50.52752, 6.41195* **Camping Schafbachmühle, 53937 Schleiden-Harperscheid [(02485) 268; info@schafbachmuehle.de; www.schafbachmuehle.de]** Fr Schleiden take B258 twd Monschau. In 3.5km turn R sp Schafbachmühle. Site in 2.5km on L. Med, mkd pitch, hdstg, terr, pt shd; htd wc; chem disp; mv service pnt; baby facs; shwrs €1; el pnts (10A) metered + conn fee; Indtte (inc dryer); shop 800m; tradsmn; rest; snacks; bar; BBQ; playgrnd; games area; 60% statics; dogs €2.20; phone; Eng spkn; adv bkg; quiet. "Tranquil site; gd for touring Eifel, Mosel Valley, Rhine Valley." ♦ € 14.80 2010*

⊞ **SCHLESWIG** *1D1* (7.5km E Coastal) *54.52563, 9.71543* **Campingplatz am Missunder Fährhaus, Missunder Fährstrasse 33, 24864 Brodersby [(04622) 626; fax 2543; missunder-faehrhaus@t-online.de; www.missunder-faehrhaus.de]** Exit A7 junc 5; take B201 sp Kappeln; in 10km turn R sp Scholderup & Brodersby; foll sp Missunder ferry. Site 100m bef ferry x-ing. Sm, sl, unshd; wc; chem disp; shwrs €1; el pnts (16A) €2.50; rest, snacks & bar adj; sailing & canoeing; dogs; quiet; gd. "Watersports; deposit for wc key; rest rec." € 12.00 2009*

SCHLESWIG *1D1* (2km S Rural) *54.50111, 9.57027* **Wikinger Camping Haithabu, 24866 Haddeby [(04621) 32450; fax 33122; info@campingplatz-haithabu.de; www.campingplatz-haithabu.de]** Leave A7/45 N & S junc 6. Travel E two Schleswig & turn R onto B76 sp Kiel & Eckernförde. Site on L in 2km sp. Med, pt shd; wc; chem disp; mv service pnt; shwrs €0.50; el pnts (4A) €2; Indtte; shop 3km; tradsmn; rest; snacks; playgrnd; lake sw adj; boating facs; dogs €2; poss cr; Eng spkn; adv bkg; some rd noise; CCI. "Lovely site on rv; foot & cycle paths to Schleswig (4.5km) & ferry; gd area for children; Schloss Gottorf worth visit; vg Viking museum adj." 1 Apr-25 Oct. € 18.00 2009*

SCHLOSS HOLTE STUKENBROCK *1C3* (4km N Rural) *51.87205, 8.67183* **Campingplatz am Furlbach, Am Furlbach 33, 33785 Schloss-Holte [(05257) 3373; fax 940373; info@campingplatzamafurlbach.de; www.campingplatzamfurlbach.de]** Exit A33 junc 23. Foll sp for Stukenbrock & Safari Park. Site on L. Med, pt shd; wc; chem disp; mv service pnt; shwrs €0.50; el pnts (16A) metered; gas; Indtte; shop; tradsmn; rest 1.5km; snacks; bar; playgrnd; pool 6km; games area; fishing 500m; 75% statics; dogs €2; poss cr; Eng spkn; adv bkg; quiet; 10% red long stay; CCI. "Well-run, friendly site; clsd 2200-0700 & 1230-1430." ♦ 1 Apr-1 Nov. € 16.00 2007*

I'll fill in a report online and let the Club know – www.caravanclub.co.uk/europereport

This is a wonderful site.

⊞ **SCHLUCHSEE** *3C4* (1km NW Rural) *47.82236, 8.16273* **Campingplatz Wolfsgrund, Sägackerweg, 79859 Schluchsee [(07656) 573; fax 7759; info@schluchsee.de; www.camping-schluchsee.de]** Site sp fr rd B500 - rec app fr N only. Lge, hdg/mkd pitch, terr, pt sl, pt shd; wc; chem disp; mv service pnt; shwrs inc; el pnts (10A) metered; gas; Indtte (inc dryer); shop 500m; rest; snacks; playgrnd; shgl beach & lake sw 200m; games area; wifi; dogs €1.50; site clsd 1300-1500 & 2200-0800; poss cr; Eng spkn; quiet; ccard acc; red CCI. "Fishing & sailing on lake adj; wintersports area; gd walking & cycling country with excel views." € 27.50 2011*

⊞ **SCHOMBERG** *3C3* (2km N Rural) *48.79820, 8.63623* **Höhen-Camping, Schömbergstrasse 32, 75328 Langenbrand [(07084) 6131; fax 931435; info@hoehencamping.de; www.hoehencamping.de]** Fr N exit A8 junc 43 Pforzheim, take B463 dir Calw. Turn R sp Schömberg & foll sp Langenbrand. Med, hdg/mkd pitch, pt sl, pt shd; htd wc; chem disp; fam bthrm; shwrs €0.50; el pnts (10-16A) €3; Indtte; shop 200m; playgrnd; TV; 70% statics; dogs €2; phone; adv bkg; quiet; CCI. "Clean, well-maintained site in N of Black Forest; vg san facs; no recep - ring bell on house adj site ent; blocks req for sl pitches." € 18.60 2011*

SCHONAU (RHEIN-NECKAR) *3C2* (5km N Rural) *49.46593, 8.80307* **Camping Steinachperle, Altneudorferstrasse 14, 69250 Schönau-Altneudorf [(06228) 467; fax 8568; campingplatz-steinachperle@t-online.de; www.camping-steinachperle.de]** Fr Heidelberg foll B37 alongside Rv Neckar to Neckarsteinach, turn L at traff lts in cent to Schönau, thro Schönau to Altneudorf, site behind Inn Zum Pflug on L thro vill of Altneudorf. Steep ent/exit. Med, hdg pitch, pt sl, pt shd; wc; chem disp; shwrs €0.50; el pnts (16A) metered + conn fee; Indtte (inc dryer); shop; rest; snacks; bar; playgrnd; pool 2km; beach sw 2km; dogs €1.10; phone; Eng spkn; v quiet; CCI. "Well-kept site; gd san facs but climb to san blocks not suitable disabled; gd sized pitches; barrier clsd 1300-1500; ideal for Neckar Valley - rec." 1 Apr-30 Sep. € 16.00 2011*

⊞ **SCHONAU IM SCHWARZWALD** *3B4* (800m N Rural) *47.79127, 7.90076* **Camping Schönenbuchen, Friedrichstrasse 58, 79677 Schönau [(07673) 7610; fax 234327; info@camping-schoenau.de; www.camping-schoenau.de]** Fr Lörrach on B317 dir Todtnau for approx 23km. Site thro Schönau main rd on R on rvside, ent thro car park. Narr access diff for l'ge o'fits. Med, hdg pitch, pt shd; wc; chem disp; mv service pnt; baby facs; sauna; shwrs; el pnts (16A) €2 (poss rev pol); lndtte; shop 400m; rest; bar; playgrnd; htd pool; sw & watersports adj; tennis; horseriding; cycle hire; 70% statics; dogs €1; adv bkg; quiet; red long stay; CCI. "Friendly staff; site poss not well-kept; gd walking & cycling; lovely old town." ♦ € 25.50 2008*

⊞ **SCHONENBERG KUBELBERG** *3B2* (1.5km E Rural) *49.41172, 7.40479* **Campingpark Ohmbachsee, Miesauerstrasse, 66901 Schönenberg-Kübelberg [(0673) 4001; fax 4002; jungfleisch@campingpark-ohmbachsee.de; www.campingpark-ohmbachsee.de]** Exit A6/E50 junc 10 or 11 twd Schönenberg, site sp on Lake Ohmbach. Lge, mkd pitch, terr, pt shd; htd wc; chem disp; mv service pnt; baby facs; sauna; shwrs inc; el pnts (6A) €2.50 or metered; lndtte (inc dryer); shop; rest; snacks; bar; BBQ; cooking facs; playgrnd; htd pool; paddling pool; canoeing; boat & cycle hire; tennis; games area; horseriding 7km; golf driving range; wifi; entmnt; 50% statics; dogs €3; adv bkg; quiet. "Lake views fr some pitches (ltd); excel facs & rest." ♦ € 19.50 (CChq acc) 2009*

SCHORTENS *1C2* (1km W Rural) *53.55055, 7.93722* **Friesland Camping, Am Schwimmbad 2, 26419 Schortens [(04461) 758727; fax 758933; info@friesland-camping.de; www.friesland-camping.de]** Exit A29 junc 5 onto B210 dir Schortens & Jever. Site on L past Schortens vill. Med, mkd pitch, shd; htd wc; chem disp; mv service pnt; baby facs; serviced pitches; shwrs inc; el pnts (16A) €2.40 or metered; lndtte (inc dryer); shop 800m; snacks; cooking facs; playgrnd; pool; sand beach 15km; lake sw adj; golf 8km; wifi; 20% statics; dogs €3; phone; bus 800m; Eng spkn; adv bkg; quiet; red long stay. "V pleasant site; gd facs; aquapark at Schortens & Jever worth visit; vg." ♦ Easter- 24 Oct. € 20.00 2010*

⊞ **SCHOTTEN** *3D1* (3km SW Rural) *50.48333, 9.09628* **Campingplatz am Nidda-Stausee, Ausserhalb 13, 63679 Schotten [(06044) 1418; fax 987995; campingplatz@schotten.de; www.schotten.de]** Fr A4/E451 exit junc 10 & foll sp to Schotten. Site on R of rd B455. Lge, mkd pitch, some hdstg, terr, pt shd; htd wc; chem disp; mv service pnt; shwrs inc; el pnts (16A) metered + conn fee; lndtte; tradsmn; supmkt 2km; rest; snacks; bar; playgrnd; pool, tennis 3km; lake beach & sw adj; watersports; fishing; golf 6km; 80% statics; dogs; phone; poss cr; adv bkg; quiet; red CCI. ♦ € 12.50 2008*

⊞ **SCHWAAN** *2F2* (2km S Rural) *53.92346, 12.10688* **Camping Schwaan, Güstrowerstrasse 54/Sandgarten 17, 18258 Schwaan [(03844) 813716; fax 814051; info@campingplatz-schwaan.de; www.campingplatz-schwaan.de]** Fr A20 exit junc 13 to Schwaan, site sp. Fr A19 exit junc 11 dir Bad Doberan & Schwaan. Site adj Rv Warnow. Lge, mkd pitch, pt shd; htd wc; mv service pnt; sauna; baby facs; shwrs inc; el pnts (16A) €2.20 or metered; lndtte (inc dryer); shop high ssn; supmkt 800m; rest; snacks; bar; cooking facs; playgrnd; canoeing; boat & cycle hire; tennis 700m; games area; wifi; entmnt; TV; 30% statics; dogs €2; site clsd 21 Dec-4 Jan; adv bkg; quiet. "Pleasant rvside site; gd touring base." ♦ € 19.50 (CChq acc) 2011*

SCHWABISCH HALL *3D3* (2km S Urban) *49.09868, 9.74288* **Camping am Steinbacher See, Mühlsteige 26, 74523 Schwäbisch Hall-Steinbach [(0791) 2984; fax 9462758; thomas.seitel@t-online.de; www.camping-schwaebisch-hall.de]** Fr A6/E50 exit junc 43 fr W or junc 42 fr E to Schwäbisch Hall. On ent town foll site sp to Comburg. Turn sharp R after castle at pedestrian x-ing to site. Site well sp. Med, mkd pitch, pt shd; htd wc; chem disp; mv service pnt; shwrs €0.50; el pnts (10A) metered + conn fee; lndtte; shop 3km; rest 200m; snacks; bar; BBQ; playgrnd; cycle hire; 50% statics; dogs €2; clsd 1300-1500; poss cr; Eng spkn; adv bkg; red CCI. "Lovely well kept idiosyncratic site; friendly; walking dist to interesting medieval town; cycle track to town." ♦ 1 Feb-30 Nov. € 16.70 2011*

SCHWANGAU see Füssen *4E4*

SCHWEDENECK see Gettorf *1D1*

⊞ **SCHWERIN** *2E2* (10km N Rural) *53.69725, 11.43715* **Ferienpark Seehof, Am Zeltzplatz 1, 19069 Seehof [(0385) 512540; fax 5814170; info@ferienparkseehof.de; www.ferienparkseehof.de]** Take B106 N fr Schwerin for approx 5km: turn R at city boundary & site within 5km at end of vill, sp. Lge, pt sl, pt shd; wc; chem disp; mv service pnt; serviced pitches; shwrs €1; el pnts (4A) inc (poss rev pol); gas; lndtte; shop; rest; snacks; bar; playgrnd, lake sw & sand beach; windsurfing; sailing school; cycle hire; entmnt; 30% statics; dogs €1; poss cr; adv bkg; quiet; ccard acc. "Lge pitches; vg." € 27.00 2009*

⊞ **SEEBURG** *2E4* (800m NW Rural) *51.49400, 11.69400* **Camping Seeburg am Süsser See, Nordstrand 1, 06317 Seeburg [(034774) 28281; fax 41757; info@campingplatz-seeburg.de; www.campingplatz-seeburg.de]** W fr Halle on B80 twd Eisleben, sp fr Seeburg. Site on N shore of Lake Süsser See. Lge, pt shd; wc; chem disp; shwrs €0.52; el pnts (16A) €1.10; rest 500m; playgrnd; lake sw; fishing; 95% statics; dogs €1.20. "Attractive, busy site by lake; facs old but clean; excel base for medieval towns nr & 'Martin Luther country'; gd.' ♦ € 23.60 2011*

⊞ **SEESHAUPT** *4E4* (3.5km NE Rural) *47.82651, 11.33906* **Camping beim Fischer, Buchscharnstrasse 10, 82541 St Heinrich [(08801) 802; fax 913461; info@camping-beim-fischer.de; www.camping-beim-fischer.de]** Exit A95 junc 7 & foll sp Seeshaupt for 1.6km to T-junc. Turn R, site in 200m on R. Med, mkd pitch, unshd; htd wc; chem disp; baby facs; shwrs inc; el pnts (16A) metered; gas; Indtte; tradsmn; rest, snacks, bar 200m; playgrnd; lake sw adj; games area; TV; 45% statics; dogs free; bus adj; Eng spkn; adv bkg; quiet; CCI. "Well-maintained, friendly, family-run site; immac facs; conv Munich & Bavarian castles." ♦ € 18.00 2008*

⊞ **SEESHAUPT** *4E4* (2km E Rural) *47.81945, 11.3275* **Camping Seeshaupt, St Heinricherstrasse 127, 82402 Seeshaupt [(08801) 1528; fax 911807; info@campingplatz-seeshaupt.de; www.campingplatz-seeshaupt.de]** Fr A95/E533 exit junc 7. In St Heinrich, turn L for 3km on lake, site sp on R on lakeside. Med, hdstg, pt shd; wc; chem disp; mv service pnt; shwrs inc; el pnts (16A) €2; Indtte; shop & 2km; tradsmn; rest high ssn; snacks; bar high ssn; playgrnd; lake sw & shgl beach; tennis adj; cycle hire; 75% statics; dogs €1.50; phone; Eng spkn; quiet; CCI. "Pretty area; excel san facs; vg." ♦ € 22.00 2008*

SENHEIM see Cochem *3B2*

SESSLACH see Coburg *4E2*

⊞ **SIGMARINGEN** *3D4* (500m SW Urban) *48.08366, 9.20794* **Erlebnis-Camp Sigmaringen, Georg-Zimmererstrasse 6, 72488 Sigmaringen [(07571) 50411; fax 50412; info@erlebnis-camp.de; www.erlebnis-camp.de]** App town fr N or SW, ent town over Danube bdge, turn into car pk (camp sp). To far end of car park & cont on rv bank. Ent camp fr far end. Site adj to stadium by rv, sp fr town. Med, pt shd; wc; chem disp; mv service pnt; shwrs €0.50; el pnts (6-16A) €3; Indtte; shop 300m; tradsmn; rest; snacks 300m; playgrnd; htd pool 300m; cycle hire; internet; 10% statics; dogs €1; CCI. "On Danube cycle way; gd outdoor activities." ♦ € 17.50 2010*

⊞ **SIMMERATH** *1A4* (10km NE Rural) *50.62753, 6.3853* **Campingplatz Woffelsbach, Promenadenweg, 52152 Woffelsbach [(02473) 2704; fax 929445; www.campingplatz-woffelsbach.de]** Fr Simmerath B266 W to Kesternich; L166 to Rurberg; L128 to Woffelsbach; clear sps in vill. Sm, hdstg, terr, unshd; wc; chem disp; mv service pnt; serviced pitches; shwrs €1; el pnts (16A) inc; Indtte; shop adj; rest 200m; snacks 100m; lake sw adj; few statics; no dogs; site clsd Jan; quiet; no ccard acc. "Most pitches with lake views; site rather run down (2010)." € 16.00 2010*

⊞ **SIMMERATH** *1A4* (6km SE Rural) *50.56388, 6.33333* **Camping Hammer, An der Streng 7, 52152 Simmerath-Hammer [(02473) 929041; fax 937481; info@camp-hammer.de; www.camp-hammer.de]** Fr Monschau take B399 N for 5km to Imgenbroich, minor rd E to Hammer. Fr Simmerath take B399 SW for 2km L sp Hammer to site on R in vill. Med, pt shd; htd wc; chem disp; mv service pnt; shwrs €1; el pnts (10A) €3; gas; Indtte; shop & 5km; rest 800m; playgrnd; 60% statics; no dogs; quiet; cash only; CCI. "Excel rvside site; pleasant bistro; unique san facs! walking area, non-touristy." € 18.00 (CChq acc) 2011*

SIMONSBERG see Husum *1D1*

SIMONSWALD see Waldkirch *3C4*

SOEST *1C4* (10km S Rural) *51.47722, 8.10055* **Camping Delecke-Südufer, Arnsbergerstrasse 8, 59519 Möhnesee-Delecke [(02924) 5010; fax 1288; info@camping-berndt.de; www.camping-berndt.de]** Exit A44/E331 at junc 56 onto B229 sp Korbecke/Möhnesee. Cont to lake, cross bdge. At next junc turn L & site immed on L, sp. Med, hdg pitch, pt sl, unshd; wc; chem disp; mv service pnt; shwrs €1; el pnts (16A) €2.20 + conn fee; tradsmn; snacks; bar; rest 800m; Indtte; shop; playgrnd; lake sw & beach adj; boating; 50% statics; phone; no dogs; poss cr; quiet; clsd 1300-1500 & 2000-0800; Eng spkn; adv bkg; CCI. "Excel site on boating lake; san facs locked o'night; gd walking & sailing; v busy at w/ends." ♦ 1 Apr-3 Oct. € 22.50 2010*

⊞ **SOLINGEN** *1B4* (5km S Rural) *51.13388, 7.11861* **Waldcamping Glüder, Balkhauserweg 240, 42659 Solingen-Glüder [(0212) 242120; fax 2421234; info@camping-solingen.de; www.camping-solingen.de]** Exit A1 junc 97 Burscheid onto B91 N dir Hilgen. In Hilgen turn L onto L294 to Witzhelden then R on L359 dir Solingen. Site sp in Glüder by Rv Wupper. Med, hdg/mkd pitch, some hdstg, unshd; htd wc; chem disp; shwrs inc; chem disp; el pnts (6-10A) metered; gas; Indtte; tradsmn; shop 3km; rest adj; snacks; bar; playgrnd; TV; 80% statics; dogs €2.10; bus; Eng spkn; quiet; CCI. "Beautiful location in wooded valley; clsd 1300-1500; resident owner; excel san facs; easy walk to Burg-an-der-Wupper Schloss - worth visit. € 14.50 2008*

⊞ **SOLTAU** *1D2* (1.5km N Rural) *53.00075, 9.8366* **Kur & Fereincamping Röders Park, Ebsmoor 8, 29614 Soltau [(05191) 2141; fax 17952; info@roeders-park.de; www.roeders-park.de]** Exit A7/E45 junc 45 onto B3 dir Soltau. Turn L onto B71 in Soltau cent, then R onto B3 sp Hamburg. Site sp on L at town boundary. Med, mkd pitch, pt shd; wc; chem disp; mv service pnt; some serviced pitches; shwrs inc; el pnts (6A) metered + conn fee; gas; Indtte; shop; rest; snacks; playgrnd; cycle hire; 25% statics; dogs €2; office clsd 1300-1500; ccard acc; red CCI. "Delightful, family-run site; helpful staff; excel rest; vg san facs; gd walking nrby." ♦ € 23.50 2009*

⊞ **SOLTAU** *1D2* (6km SW Rural) *52.94801, 9.85403* **Freizeithof Imbrock, Imbrock 4, 29614 Soltau [(05191) 5202; fax 15960; www.camping-imbrock.de]** Exit A7/E45 junc 45 Soltau-Süd. Foll sp Soltau then Brock, site sp fr main rd. V lge, pt shd; wc; mv service pnt; baby facs; shwrs €0.50; el pnts (10A) €2; Indtte; shop; rest; snacks; playgrnd; lake sw; tennis; games area; 60% statics; dogs €1.50; quiet. "San facs poss stretched." € 16.00 2009*

SOMMERACH see Dettelbach *3D2*

SONNENBUHL ERPFINGEN see Engstingen *3D3*

⊞ **SONTHOFEN** *3D4* (1.5km SW Rural) *47.50636, 10.27353* **Camping an der Iller, Sinwagstrasse 2, 87527 Sonthofen [(08321) 2350; fax 68792; info@illercamping.de; www.illercamping.de]** Clearly sp fr Sonthofen Süd junc on B19; on Rv Iller. Med, mkd pitch, hdstg, unshd; wc; shwrs inc; chem disp; mv service pnt; el pnts (16A) metered; gas; Indtte; shop; rest 200m; snacks; bar; playgrnd; htd pool adj; dogs €2; clsd 1300-1500; some Eng spkn; adv bkg; quiet but some rlwy noise; CCI. "Scenic wintersports area; gd walking, cycling; excel, well-maintained facs; helpful owner; some rd noise; site quite bare; site designed on feng shui principles!" ♦ € 18.00 2011*

⊞ **SOTTRUM** *1D2* (3km SW Rural) *53.08335, 9.17697* **Camping-Paradies Grüner Jäger, Everinghauser Dorfstrsse 17, 27367 Sottrum/Everinghausen [(04205) 319113; fax 319115; info@camping-paradies.de; www.camping-paradies.de]** Exit A1 junc 50 at Stuckenborstel onto B75 dir Rotenburg. In approx 500m turn R & foll sp Everinghausen. Site in 4km. Med, mkd pitch, unshd; htd wc; chem disp; mv service pnt; baby facs; shwrs €0.15 per min; el pnts (16A) €2.50; Indtte; shop 6km; rest; bar; playgrnd; pool; paddling pool; 30% statics; dogs free; Eng spkn; some rd noise; CCI. "Excel NH." € 23.50 2011*

⊞ **SPANGENBERG** *1D4* (500m SE Rural) *51.11373, 9.67391* **Campingplatz Municipal am Sportplatz, Jahnstrasse 23, 34286 Spangenberg [(05663) 222; fax 509026; service-center@stadt-spangenberg.de; www.stadt-spangenberg.de]** Fr A7 exit sp Melsungen & take B487 to Spangenberg. Site on SE of town, clearly visible fr rd. Narr app. Med, mkd pitch, terr, unshd; htd wc; chem disp; shwrs inc; el pnts (16A) metered; Indtte; supmkt 1km; cooking facs; playgrnd; pool & sports complex adj; 60% statics; dogs; clsd 1300-1500; some rd noise; CCI. "Historic old town; welcoming staff; gd clean facs; gd walking/cycling; gd NH & longer." ♦ € 16.80 2010*

SPEYER *3C3* (2km N Rural) *49.33600, 8.44300* **Camping Speyer, Am Rübsamenwühl 31, 67346 Speyer [(06232) 42228; fax 815174; info@camping-speyer.de; www.camping-speyer.de]** Fr Mannheim or Karlsruhe take rd 9 to exit Speyer Nord dir Speyer. At 3rd traff lts turn L into Auestrasse, then at 2nd rndabt L into Am Rübsamenwühl. Site in 500m. Sm, some mkd pitch; shwrs €1; el pnts €3; supmkt 500m; rest; snacks; bar; playgrnd; lake sw & sand beach; 90% statics; dogs €2; no adv bkg; quiet; red long stay. "Speyer pleasant town, cathedral & Technik Museum worth visit; v basic site; scruffy & not well-kept (Aug 2008); fair NH/sh stay." 15 Mar-15 Oct. € 20.00 2008*

⊞ **SPEYER** *3C3* (1km SE Urban) *49.31250, 8.44916* **Camping Technik Museum, Am Technik Museum 1, Geibstrasse, 67346 Speyer [(0632) 67100; hotel.speyer@technik-museum.de; www.hotel-am-technik-museum.de]** Exit A61/E34 at junc 64, foll sp to museum. Med, unshd; htd wc; chem disp; mv service pnt; shwrs inc; el pnts inc; shop 1km; rest, snacks, bar adj; dogs free; phone (hotel); bus; poss cr; Eng spkn; adv bkg. "Book in at hotel adj; excel museum & IMAX cinema on site; conv Speyer cent." ♦ € 20.00 2009*

⊞ **SPIEGELAU** *4G3* (2km W Rural) *48.91737, 13.33150* **Camping am Nationalpark, Bergstrasse 44, 94518 Klingenbrunn [(08553) 727; fax 6930; info@camping-nationalpark.de; www.camping-nationalpark.de]** Fr A3 exit 111 at Hengersberg onto B333 dir Schönberg, turn N onto B85 (Regen-Passau) & foll sp Klingenbrunn. At T-junc in vill cent R & bear L in 300m to site on R in 1km. Med, mkd pitch, terr, pt shd; serviced pitches; mv service pnt; wc; shwrs inc; chem disp; mv service pnt; el pnts (16A) metered + conn fee; Indtte; shop 1km; rest; playgrnd; covrd pool; fishing; horseriding 1km; skilift 3km; entmnt; 15% statics; dogs €1; site clsd 9 Nov-14 Dec; adv bkg; quiet; ccard acc; red CCI. "Peaceful, family-run site." € 13.70 2010*

We can fill in site report forms on the Club's website – www.caravanclub.co.uk/europereport

⊞ **STADTKYLL** *3B2* (1km S Rural) *50.33903, 6.53966* **Camping Landal Wirfttal, Wirftstrasse 81, 54589 Stadtkyll [(06597) 92920; fax 929250; wirfttal@landal.de; www.landal.de]** Exit A1 onto B51 dir Prüm to Stadtkyll, site well sp on minor rd to Schüller fr town cent. Fr SE app town on B421 then foll sps. Lge, pt shd; htd wc; chem disp; mv service pnt; baby facs; sauna; baby facs; shwrs inc; el pnts (8A) inc; gas; Indtte (inc dryer); shop; rest; snacks; bar; playgrnd; htd pool adj; paddling pool; waterslides; tennis; games area; horseriding adj; cycle hire; entmnt; TV; 30% statics; dogs €3; phone; adv bkg; quiet; ccard acc. "Excel site; all facs htd & clean." ♦ € 32.00 2009*

STADTSTEINACH see Kulmbach *4E2*

⊞ **STAUFEN IM BREISGAU** *3B4* (500m SE Rural) *47.87194, 7.73583* **Ferien-Campingplatz Belchenblick, Münstertälerstrasse 43, 79219 Staufen-im-Breisgau [(07633) 7045; fax 7908; info@camping-belchenblick.de; www.camping-belchenblick.de]** Exit A5/E35 junc 64a dir Bad Krozingen-Staufen-Münstertal. Avoid Staufen cent, foll Münstertal sp. Camp on L 500m past Staufen. Visibility restricted fr Münstertal dir. Lge, pt shd; wc; chem disp; mv service pnt; baby facs; fam bthrm; sauna; shwrs inc; el pnts (16A) metered; gas; Indtte (inc dryer); shop; rest 500m; snacks; bar; BBQ area; sm htd indoor pool; playgrnd, public pool & tennis nrby over unfenced rv via footbdge; cycle hire; horseriding 500m; wifi; entmnt; games/TVrm; 60% statics; dogs €2.50; no c'vans/m'vans over 8m high ssn; phone; no veh access 1230-1500 & night time - parking area avail; poss cr; Eng spkn; adv bkg rec high ssn; some rd & rlwy noise in day; no ccard acc; red low ssn/CCI. "Well-run, family-owned site; some pitches sm; excel modern san facs; strict pitching rules; beautiful area & Staufen pleasant town; beware train app round blind corner at x-ing; gd walking, cycling, horseriding." ♦ € 27.50 SBS - G02 2011*

GERMANY

STECHOW *2F3* (6km N Rural) *52.65472, 12.42972* **Campingpark Buntspecht Ferchesar, Weg zum Zeltplatz 1, 14715 Stechow-Ferchesar [(03387) 490072; camping-park-buntspecht@web.de; www.campingpark-buntspecht.de]** Fr Rathenow NE on B188 to Stechow, then turn L sp Ferchesar & foll site sp to lakeside. Or fr A10 exit junc 26 sp Nauen & take B5 for approx 25km to junc with B188 to Stechow. At Stechow rurn R sp Ferchesar then as above. Lge, mkd pitch, pt shd; htd wc; chem disp; mv service pnt; baby facs; private san facs avail; shwrs inc; el pnts (16A) €2; Indtte (inc dryer); shop; tradsmn; rest; snacks; BBQ; cooking facs; playgrnd; lake sw; fishing; boat, canoe, cycle hire; games area; wifi; 10% statics; dogs €3.50; Eng spkn; adv bkg; quiet. "Pleasant, peaceful, family site; gd walking/cycling in area." ♦ 1 Apr-31 Oct. € 23.00 2011*

STEINACH see Haslach im Kinzigtal *3C3*

STEINENSTADT *3B4* (W Urban) *47.76895, 7.55115* **Camping Vogesenblick, Eichwaldstrasse 7, 79395 Steinenstadt [(07635) 1846]** Exit A5/E35 junc 65 Neuenburg-am-Rhein. Turn S at traff lts for Steinenstadt, site sp. Sm, pt shd; wc; chem disp; mv service pnt; shwrs €0.50; el pnts (16A) metered; Indtte; shop, rest adj; bar; htd, covrd pool 5km; 20% statics; dogs €1.50; bus nr; poss cr; adv bkg; quiet. "Peaceful, friendly site; gd cycling beside Rv Rhine; easy access Black Forest, Freiburg etc." 15 Mar-31 Oct. € 18.00 2009*

STOCKACH *3C4* (4km S Rural) *47.80860, 8.97000* **Campinggarten Wahlwies, Stahringerstrasse 50, 78333 Stockach-Wahlwies [(07771) 3511; fax 4236; info@camping-wahlwies.de; www.camping-wahlwies.de]** Exit A98 junc 12 Stockach West onto B313 to Wahlwies. In vill turn L immed after level x-ing, site on R bef next level x-ing, sp. Med, pt shd; wc; chem disp; mv service pnt; shwrs inc; el pnts (16A) €2; Indtte; shop 1km; tradsmn; rest 1km; snacks; bar; lake sw 5km; 50% statics; dogs free; phone; poss cr; Eng spkn; adv bkg rec bank hols; quiet; CCI. "Pleasantly situated, friendly, orchard site 6km fr Bodensee; female san facs inadequate; gd touring cent; gd local train service; excel cycle tracks." 20 Mar-7 Nov. € 19.30 2011*

⊞ **STOCKACH** *3C4* (1.5km SW Urban) *47.84194, 8.99500* **Camping Papiermühle, Johann Glatt Strasse 3, 78333 Stockach [(07771) 91651333; campingplatz@caramobil.de; www.caramobil.de/stockach/freizeitpark]** Fr Stockach at junc rndabt of B31 & B313, turn L (E) to Caramobil C'van Sales Depot. Site adj under same management. Med, mkd pitch, some hdstg, pt sl, terr, pt shd; htd wc; chem disp; mv service pnt; shwrs inc; el pnts (6A) €2; Indtte (inc dryer); shop; tradsmn; rest adj; snacks; bar; BBQ; playgrnd; 50% statics; dogs €2.20; phone; bus 200m; poss cr; Eng spkn; adv bkg; quiet; ccard acc; CCI. "Sep m'van area adj; gd walking & cycling; vg site." ♦ € 18.90 2010*

⊞ **STORKOW** *2G3* (6km NE Rural) *52.29194, 13.98638* **Campingplatz Waldsee, 15526 Reichenwalde-Kolpin [(033631) 5037; fax 59891; mail@campingplatz-waldsee.de; www.campingplatz-waldsee.de]** Fr A12/E30, exit junc 3 Storkow. Just bef ent Storkow, turn N twd Fürstenwalde. In 6km turn R leaving Kolpin, site sp. Med, pt sl, pt shd; wc; chem disp; sauna; shwrs €0.50; el pnts (16A) €2; Indtte; shops 2km; rest 6km; rest 6km; snacks; bar; playgrnd; lake sw adj; cycle hire; 60% statics; dogs €1; Eng spkn; adv bkg; quiet; ccard acc; red CCI. "Gd san facs; haphazard pitching; conv NH en rte to/fr Poland; gd cycling area; Bad Saarow lakeside worth visit." € 14.50 2009*

STRAUBING *4F3* (1km N Urban) *48.89346, 12.5766* **Camping Straubing, Wundermühlweg 9, 94315 Straubing [(09421) 89794; fax 182459; campingplatzstraubing@gmx.de; www.campingplatzstraubing.de]** Fr A3/E56 exit junc 105 or 106 to Straubing. Foll sp over Danube bdge, site sp on R in approx 1km. Also foll sp to stadium. Med, pt shd; htd wc; chem disp; mv service pnt; shwrs inc; el pnts (16A) inc; Indtte; supmkt 250m; tradsmn; snacks; bar; playgrnd; pool 5km; golf 2km; dogs (not acc Aug); phone; bus; 10% red CCI. "Gd, clean, well-kept site In grounds of sports stadium; quaint town with attractive shops; gd san facs; conv Danube cycle way." ♦ 1 May-15 Oct. € 21.50 2008*

STUHR see Bremen *1C2*

⊞ **STUTTGART** *3D3* (4km E Urban) *48.79395, 9.21911* **Campingplatz Cannstatter Wasen, Mercedesstrasse 40, 70372 Stuttgart [(0711) 556696; fax 557454; info@campingplatz-stuttgart.de; www.campingplatz-stuttgart.de]** Fr B10 foll sp for stadium & Mercedes museum & then foll camping sp. Access poss diff when major events in park adj. Lge, all hdstg, pt shd; htd wc; chem disp; mv service pnt; serviced pitches; shwrs inc; el pnts (16A) metered + conn fee; Indtte; shop 1.5km; tradsmn; rest; BBQ; playgrnd; pool 2km; dogs €3; bus nr; stn 1.5km; poss v cr; Eng spkn; adv bkg; poss noise fr local stadium; ccard acc; CCI. "Helpful staff; clean san facs but site run down/shabby (2010); town cent best by train - tickets fr recep; cycle ride to town thro park; Mercedes museum 15 mins walk; fr Sep site/office open 0800-1000 & 1700-1900 only." ♦ € 22.00 2011*

⊞ **STUTTGART** *3D3* (8km E Urban) *48.83111, 9.32222* **Parkplatz am Hallenbad, An der Talaue, 71332 Waiblingen [(07151) 5001155; parkierungsgesellschaft@waiblingen.de]** Fr N exit A81/E41 junc 16 at Ludwigsburg Süd, foll sp dir Remseck & Waiblingen. Fr S or E on B29 take B14 to Waiblingen town cent. Foll sp swimming pool, sports park & parking. M'vans only. Sm, mkd pitch, hdstg, pt shd; wc; chem disp; mv service pnt; water €1/80 litres; el pnts €1/8 hrs; pool; dogs; rd noise. "Fair NH." € 6.00 2010*

SULZBERG see Kempten (Allgäu) *3D4*

⊞ **SULZBURG** *3B4* (1.5km SE Rural) *47.83583, 7.72333* **Terrassen-Camping Alte Sägemühle, Badstrasse 57, 79295 Sulzburg [(07634) 551181; fax 551182; info@camping-alte-saegemuehle.de; www.camping-alte-saegemuehle.de]** Exit A5 junc 64b to Heitersheim & Sulzburg. Fr cent of Sulzburg, foll camp sps SE past timber yard on rd to Bad Sulzburg hotel. Sm, mkd pitch, terr, pt shd; htd wc; chem disp; mv service pnt; shwrs inc; el pnts (16A) metered + conn fee; gas 1km; lndtte; shop; tradsmn; rest, snacks, bar 1.5km; BBQ; lake sw adj; 10% statics; dogs €2; Eng spkn; quiet; 10% red CCI. "Excel san facs - poss long walk; v friendly, helpful owners site van with tractor; restful site in beautiful hilly countryside; gd walking, cycling." € 21.00 2011*

⊞ **SULZBURG** *3B4* (1km NW Rural) *47.84778, 7.69848* **Camping Sulzbachtal, Sonnmatt 4, 79295 Sulzburg [(07634) 592568; fax 592569; a-z@camping-sulzbachtal.de; www.camping-sulzbachtal.de]** Fr A5/E35 exit junc 64a Bad Krozingen onto L120/L123 dir Staufen-in-Breisgau. Cont on L125, site sp on L. Med, mkd pitch, hdstg, terr, pt shd; htd wc; chem disp; mv service pnt; 65% serviced pitches; baby facs; shwrs inc; el pnts (16A) metered; lndtte (inc dryer); shop 1km; tradsmn; snacks; rest 1km; playgrnd; pool; tennis; wifi; 10% statics; dogs €2.60; phone; m'van o'night facs; Eng spkn; adv bkg; quiet; ccard acc; red long stay/CCI. "Gd base for S Black Forest & Vosges; well laid-out site; clean facs; conv m'way; 45 mins to Basel; helpful, pleasant owners; ask about bus/train pass." ♦ € 22.40 (CChq acc) 2010*

SUTEL *2E1* (1km E Coastal) *54.33356, 11.06885* **Campingplatz Seepark Sütel, 23779 Sütel [(04365) 7474; fax 1027; info@camping-seekamp.de; www.seepark-suetel.de]** Fr B501 foll sp to Sütel; drive thro vill to beach & site. V lge, mkd pitch, unshd; wc; chem disp; baby facs; shwrs €0.50; el pnts (16A) €2; lndtte (inc dryer); shop, rest 500m; snacks; bar; playgrnd; beach adj; 90% statics; dogs €1.50; quiet; phone; adv bkg; CCI. "San facs poss inadequate if site full; helpful owner." ♦ 1 Apr-3 Oct. € 14.00 2009*

⊞ **TANGERMUNDE** *2F3* (300m E Urban) *52.54250, 11.97000* **Reismobilstellplatz Tangerplatz, 29590 Tangermünde [(039322) 22393; fax 22394; buero@tourismus-tangermuende.de]** S on B188 fr Stendal, in 3km take L30 to Tangermünde. Site sp nr Rv Elbe. Sm, hdstg, pt shd; wc; mv service inc; el pnts (16A); shop 600m; rest 100m; covrd pool 300m; dogs; quiet. "Max stay 3 nights; interesting old town; m'vans only." € 4.00 2008*

⊞ **TEGERNSEE** *4F4* (3km SW Rural) *47.68875, 11.74836* **Camping Wallberg, Rainerweg 10, 83700 Weissach [(08022) 5371; fax 670274; campingplatz-wallberg@web.de; www.campingplatz-wallberg.de]** Fr Kreuth on rd 307 to Rottach-Egern, take Bad Wiessee rd B318 at traff lts, site well sp on L in 500m. Lge, some hdstg, unshd; wc; chem disp; mv service pnt; shwrs inc; el pnts 10A) metered; lndtte; shop; supmkt 2km; tradsmn; rest; snacks; bar; playgrnd; lake sw 500m; 50% statics; dogs €2.50; phone; poss cr; some Eng spkn; quiet; red CCI. "Lovely mountain views; gd walking & cycling; site poss run down/unclean low ssn; NH only." ♦ € 18.00 2008*

TELLINGSTEDT *1D1* (200m SW Urban) *54.21833, 9.27583* **Camping Tellingstedt, Teichstrasse 8, 25782 Tellingstedt [(04838) 657; fax 786969; info@amt-tellingstedt.de]** E fr Heide on B203, site sp. Sm, pt sl, pt shd; wc; chem disp (wc); shwrs inc; el pnts; lndtte; supmkt nr; snacks 500m; rest 300m; playgrnd 200m; htd pool adj; 5% statics; quiet; red long stay/CCI. "Pleasant municipal site." 1 May-15 Sep. 2008*

⊞ **TENGEN** *3C4* (600m NW Rural) *47.82365, 8.65296* **Hegau Familien-Camping, An der Sonnenhalde 1, 78250 Tengen [(07736) 92470; fax 9247124; info@hegau-camping.de; www.hegau-camping.de]** Exit A81 junc 39 thro Engen dir Tengen, site sp. Lge, mkd pitch, hdstg, pt sl, pt shd; htd wc; chem disp; mv service pnt; serviced pitches; baby facs; fam bthrm; sauna; shwrs inc; el pnts (16A) metered or €2; gas; lndtte (inc dryer); shop; supmkt 500m; tradsmn; rest; snacks; bar; playgrnd; htd, covrd pool; paddling pool; lake sw; canoeing; tennis adj; games area; games rm; cycle hire; horseriding 2km; wifi; entmnt; 40% statics; dogs €4 inc dog shwr; bus 500m; clsd 1230-1430; o'night area for m'vans; Eng spkn; adv bkg; quiet; ccard acc; red long stay/low ssn/CCI. "Site of high standard; fairly isolated; gd family facs; excel." ♦ € 35.00 2010*

THIESSOW see Göhren (Rügen Island) *2G1*

⊞ **TIEFENSEE** *2G3* (700m E Rural) *52.68019, 13.85063* **Country-Camping Tiefensee, Schmiedeweg 1, 16259 Tiefensee [(033398) 90514; fax 86736; info@country-camping.de; www.country-camping.de]** Site sp fr B158 on lakeside. Lge, hdg/mkd pitch, pt shd; htd wc; chem disp; mv service pnt; sauna; baby facs; shwrs €0.50; el pnts (16A) metered or €2.50; lndtte (inc dryer); shop; rest; snacks; bar; BBQ; playgrnd; lake sw & beach adj (sep naturist area); fishing; games area; internet; TV; 75% statics; dogs €1.50; sep car park; o'night area for m'vans; clsd 1300-1500; poss cr; Eng spkn; adv bkg; quiet; ccard acc; red long stay. "Family-owned site; sep m'van pitches; gd cycling & walking; train to Berlin fr Arensfeldt; working ship lift at Niederfinow; vg." ♦ € 20.00 (CChq acc) 2010*

TITISEE NEUSTADT *3C4* (1.5km SW Rural) *47.88693, 8.13776* **Terrassencamping Sandbank, Seerundweg 5, 79822 Titisee-Neustadt [(07651) 8243 or 8166; fax 8286 or 88444; info@camping-sandbank.de; www.camping-sandbank.de]** Fr rte 31 Freiberg-Donauschingen turn S into Titisee. Fork R after car park on R, foll sp for Bruderhalde thro town. After youth hostel fork L & foll sp at T junc. Gravel track to site. Lge, mkd pitch, terr, mainly hdstg by lake; wc (htd); chem disp; mv service pnt; baby facs; shwrs €0.50; el pnts (16A) €1.40; lndtte; shop; rest; snacks; bar; playgrnd; lake sw; boating; cycle hire; 50% statics; dogs €1.50; poss cr; Eng spkn; no adv bkg; quiet but some rlwy noise; ccard acc; red long stay/CCI. "Ltd touring pitches; steel pegs ess; clean, well-run, well laid-out site in gd position; terr gives gd lake views; helpful owner; gd welcome; lger pitches avail at extra cost; gd touring base for Black Forest; gd walks round lake; lakeside walk into town thru woods (approx 30 mins); ask for Konus card for free travel on local buses; clsd 1200-1400; excel." ♦ 1 Apr-20 Oct. € 22.00 2011*

GERMANY

GERMANY

⊞ **TITISEE NEUSTADT** *3C4* (2km SW Rural) *47.88611, 8.13993* **Camping Bühlhof, Bühlhofweg 13, 79822 Titisee-Neustadt [(07652) 1606; fax 1827; herta-jaeger@t-online.de; www.camping-buehlhof.de]** Take rd 31 out of Freiburg to Titisee; R fork on ent Titisee; bear R to side of lake, site on R after end of Titisee, up steep but surfaced hill, sharp bends. Lge, mkd pitch, pt sl, terr, pt shd; wc; chem disp; mv service pnt; serviced pitch; baby facs; shwrs €0.50; el pnts (16A) €1.80; gas; Indtte (inc dryer); rest 300m; BBQ; playgrnd; htd pool 1km; tennis; 300m fr Lake Titisee (but no access); watersports; wintersports area - skilift 6km; boats for hire; horseriding; wifi; 30% statics; dogs €2.30; recep 0700-2200; site clsd Nov to mid-Dec; Eng spkn; ccard not acc; CCI. "Beautiful situation on hillside above Lake Titisee; lower terr gravel & 50% statics; top terr for tents & vans without elec; pitches sm; woodland walks; pleasant walk to town." € 17.00 2010*

⊞ **TITISEE NEUSTADT** *3C4* (2.5km SW Rural) *47.88633, 8.13055* **Camping Bankenhof, Bruderhalde 31, 79822 Titisee-Neustadt [(07652) 1351; fax 5907; info@camping-bankenhof.de; www.camping-bankenhof.de]** Fr B31 Frieberg-Donaueschingen, turn S into Tittisee & fork R after car park on R, foll sp Bruderhalde thro town. In 2.5km fork L after youth hostel; foll sp to site in 200m. If app Titisee fr Donausechingen (B31) do not take Titisee P sp exit but exit with int'l camping sp only, then as above. Lge, mkd pitch, hdstg, pt shd; wc; chem disp; mv service pnt; fam bthrm; shwrs inc; el pnts (16A) metered (poss rev pol); gas; Indtte (inc dryer); shop; rest; bar; playgrnd; lake sw adj; cycle hire; wifi; entmnt high ssn; boat-launching 200m; 20% statics; dogs €2 inc shwr; o'night area for m'vans €12; poss cr; Eng spkn; adv bkg; quiet; ccard acc; red CCI. "Gd walk to town & in forest; lovely scenery; helpful staff; vg san facs; excel rest; most pitches gravel; ask at recep for reduced/free tickets on public transport; excel, well-run, clean site." ♦ € 23.00 2010*

TITISEE NEUSTADT *3C4* (3km SW Rural) *47.88996, 8.13273* **Natur-Campingplatz Weiherhof, Bruderhalde 26, 79822 Titisee-Neustadt [(07652) 1468; fax 1478; info@camping-titisee.de; www.camping-titisee.de]** Fr B31 Frieberg-Donaueschingen, turn S into Titisee & fork R after car park on R, foll sp Bruderhalde thro town. Site on L on lakeside. Lge, shd; htd wc; chem disp; shwrs inc; el pnts (10A) €2.50; Indtte; shop; rest; snacks; bar; playgrnd; pool 1km; lake sw adj; cycle hire; golf 2km; 20% statics; dogs €2; phone; poss cr; quiet; CCI. "Site in woodland next to the lake; no mkd pitches but ample room; vg." ♦ 1 May-15 Oct. € 22.50 2011*

⊞ **TODTNAU** *3C4* (6km NW) *47.86400, 7.91670* **Feriencamping Hochschwarzwald, Oberhäuser Strasse 6, 79674 Todtnau-Muggenbrunn [(07671) 1288 or 530; fax 95190; camping.hochscharzwald@web.de; www.camping-hochschwarzwald.de]** Freiburg rd fr Todtnau past vill of Muggenbrunn; site ent at top end of vill. Med, terr, pt sl, pt shd; htd wc; chem disp; shwrs €0.50; el pnts (10-16A) metered; gas; Indtte; shop; rest; snacks; playgrnd; htd, covrd pool 1km; tennis 1km; sm lake; wintersports; 70% statics; dogs €1.50; sep car park winter ssn; poss cr; quiet; red CCI. "Beautiful location; gd walking area; sm pitches unsuitable lge o'fits; san facs stretched; helpful staff." ♦ € 16.00 2011*

TORGAU *2F4* (1km S Rural) *51.54589, 12.98991* **Campingplatz am Grosser Teich, Turnierplatzweg, 04860 Torgau [(03421) 902875; SV_info@torgau.de; www.torgau.de]** S on B182 fr Torgau, turn R at site sp onto Tunierplatzweg, site sp on L in 700m. Sm, pt shd; wc; shwrs; el pnts (10A) inc; shop 500m; pool; lake sw; quiet. "Sm, old san facs block, but clean; pleasant hosts; lake famous for rare birds & visiting beavers; conv Elbe cycle path." Mid-Apr to Mid-Oct. € 19.00 2009*

TRABEN TRARBACH see Bernkastel Kues *3B2*

⊞ **TRAUNSTEIN** *4F4* (8km S Rural) *47.81116, 12.5890* **Camping Wagnerhof, Campingstrasse 11, 83346 Bergen [(08662) 8557; fax 5924; info@camping-bergen.de; www.camping-bergen.de]** Exit A8/E52/E60 junc 110. On ent Bergen take 2nd R turn (sp). Med, mkd pitch, pt shd; wc; chem disp; mv service pnt; shwrs €0.50; el pnts (16A) metered; Indtte; shop & 500m; rest 400m; playgrnd; htd pool adj; shgl beach 10km; tennis; 30% statics; dogs €2; site clsd 1230-1500; some Eng spkn; adv bkg; quiet; debit card acc; red long stay; CCI. "Excel, v clean, pleasant site in beautiful location; helpful owner; when not full owner tries to offer pitches with empty pitches adjoining; conv a'bahn; cable car to Hockfelln." € 20.50 2011*

There aren't many sites open at this time of year. We'd better phone ahead to check the one we're heading for is open.

⊞ **TRAVEMUNDE** *2E2* (2km SW Rural) *53.94196, 10.84417* **Camping Ivendorf, Frankenkrogweg 2, 23570 Ivendorf [(04502) 4865; fax 75516]** Fr A1 exit junc 19 take B226 to Ivendorf, then B75 dir Travemünde, site well sp. Med, mkd pitch, pt shd; wc; chem disp; baby facs; shwrs inc; el pnts €3.50 or metered; Indtte (inc dryer); shop; rest 200m; playgrnd; pool 4km; 10% statics; dogs €2; train 2km; poss cr; CCI. "Sep disabled pitches & vg disabled san facs; conv ferries to/fr Sweden; easy access to Lübeck, a beautiful city." ♦ € 23.00 2010*

TRECHTINGSHAUSEN see Bingen am Rhein *3C2*

TREIS KARDEN see Cochem *3B2*

⊞ **TRENDELBURG** *1D4* (S Rural) *51.57250, 9.42416* **Campingplatz Trendelburg, Zur Alten Mühle, 34388 Trendleburg [(05675) 301; fax 5888; conradi-camping@t-online.de; www.campingplatz-trendelburg.de]** Enter Trendelburg fr Karlshafen on B83 turn R immed bef x-ing Rv Diemel, site on L in 800m. Sm, pt shd; wc; chem disp; baby facs; shwrs €0.50; el pnts (16A) metered + conn fee; gas; Indtte; shop; tradsmn; rest; snacks; bar; playgrnd; canoeing in adj rv; tennis; 40% statics; dogs €2.20; poss cr; adv bkg; quiet; 10% red CCI. "Pleasant, rvside site." ♦ € 12.20 2011*

TRIER *3B2* (2km S Urban) *49.74385, 6.62523* **Camping Treviris, Luxemburgerstrasse 81, 54290 Trier [(0651) 8200911; fax 8200567; info@camping-treviris.de; www.camping-treviris.de]** On E side of Rv Mosel on A1/A603/B49/B51 cross to W side of rv on Konrad Adenauerbrücke. Cont in R lane & foll sp Koln/Aachen - Luxemburgerstrasse. In 500m turn R to site, site on R. Well sp fr W bank of rv. Med, mkd pitch, pt shd; wc; chem disp; mv service pnt; baby facs; shwrs inc; el pnts (6A) €2.90; Indtte (inc dryer); shop 500m; tradsmn; rest; snacks; bar; BBQ; playgrnd; dogs €1.30; bus 200m; poss cr; site clsd 1-10 Jan; quiet; ccard acc; CCI. "Cycle/walk to town cent; m'van park adj open all yr - ltd facs; clean, modern san facs; swipe card for all facs; electric pylon in cent of site; gd touring base; gd sh stay/NH." ♦ 15 Mar-15 Nov. € 29.45 2011*

TRIER *3B2* (6km SW Rural) *49.70460, 6.57398* **Camping Konz, Saarmünding, 54329 Konz [(06501) 2577; fax 947790; camping@campingplatz-konz.de; www.campingplatz-konz.de]** On B51 S of rv at rndabt just bef rv x-ing, go L & foll sp Camping Konz (not Konz-Könen). Do not go into Konz. Med, mkd pitch, pt shd; wc; mv service pnt; shwrs €1; el pnts metered + conn fee; Indry rm; shops 500m; rest; snacks; playgrnd; watersports; dogs €0.70; Eng spkn; some rd noise. "Conv NH/sh stay for Trier - cycle rte or public transport; facs clean; poss flooding." 15 Mar-15 Oct. € 13.20 2010*

TRIER *3B2* (8km SW Rural) *49.70555, 6.55333* **Campingplatz Igel, Moselstrasse, 54298 Igel [(06501) 12944; fax 601931; info@camping-igel.de; www.camping-igel.de]** SW on A49 Luxembourg rd fr Trier; in cent of Ige vill, turn L by Sparkasse Bank, thro narr tunnel (3.6m max height); in 200m turn L along rv bank; site 300m on L; café serves as recep. Med, pt shd; htd wc; chem disp; mv service pnt; shwrs €1; el pnts (6A) €2 (poss rev pol); Indtte; shop in vill; rest; bar; playgrnd; fishing lakes adj; 90% statics (sep area); dogs €1.50; bus/train to Trier & Roman amphitheatre; poss cr; quiet but some noise fr rlwy & rv barges; CCI. "Excel, friendly, well-run site; immac san facs; gd onsite rest; ltd touring pitches; rv bank foot & cycle path to Trier; conv Roman amphitheatre in Trier; close to Luxembourg border for cheap petrol." 1 Apr-31 Oct. € 14.50 2011*

⊞ **TRIER** *3B2* (15km W Rural) *49.75416, 6.50333* **Campingplatz Alter Bahnhof-Metzdorf, Uferstrasse 42, 54308 Langsur-Metzdorf [(06501) 12626; fax 13796; info@camping-metzdorf.de; www.camping-metzdorf.de]** Fr W leave A64/E44 junc 15 & foll sp Wasserbillig; at T-junc in Wasserbillig turn L onto B49 sp Trier. Ignore campsite in 500m. On ent Germany at end of bdge turn sharp L onto B418 sp Ralingen/Metternich. In 3km turn L sp Metzdorf; in 750m turn L, site in 750m. Fr N (Bitburg) join A64 at junc 3 sp Luxembourg, then as above. Fr SE on A1/E422 join A602 (Trier) & approx 1km past end of a'bahn turn R over Kaiser Wilhelm Bdge sp A64 Lux'bourg) & immed L at end of bdge. In 9km in Wasserbillig turn R under rlwy bdge & keep R on B418 sp Ralingen/Mesenich. In 3km turn L sp Melzdorf, in 750m turn L, site in 750m. Med, pt sl, pt shd; htd wc; chem disp; mv service pnt; shwrs €0.50; el pnts (6-16A) €2 or metered (10A); Indtte; tradsmn; rest; bar; playgrnd; wifi; 75% statics; dogs €1; phone; bus 500m; m'van o'night €9; poss cr; Eng spkn; adv bkg; quiet; ccard not acc; red long stay/low ssn; CCI. "Rvside location; gd san facs but poss long walk & steep climb; cycle rte to Trier; vg NH." ♦ € 15.00 2009*

⊞ **TRIPPSTADT** *3B2* (1km E Rural) *49.35145, 7.78117* **Kawan Village Camping Freizeitzentrum Sägmühle, Sägmühle 1, 67705 Trippstadt [(06306) 92190; fax 2000; info@saegmuehle.de; www.saegmuehle.de]** Fr Kaiserslautern take B270 or B48 S for 14km, foll sp Trippstadt. Cont thro vill in dir of Karstal; site sp. Lge, mkt pitch, pt sl, pt terr, pt shd; htd wc; chem disp; mv service pnt; baby facs; fam bthrm; shwrs inc; el pnts (4A) inc; Indtte (inc dryer); shop; rest; snacks; bar; playgrnd; lake fishing; boat & cycle hire; tennis; games area; wifi; entmnt; TV rm; 50% statics; dogs €2.60; site clsd 1 Nov-13 Dec; poss cr; adv bkg; quiet. "Excel walking area; san facs on edge of site nr tents vg & under-used but long way fr pitches; san facs in cent stretched; c'van spares shop/dealer on site." ♦ € 25.70 (CChq acc) 2011*

TRITTENHEIM *3B2* (300m N Urban) *49.82472, 6.90305* **Reisemobil/Wohnmobilstellplatz (Motorhome Camping), Am Moselufer, 54349 Trittenheim [(06507) 5331; info@trittenheim.de; www.trittenheim.de]** Fr Trier foll B53 dir Bernkastel Kues. Site sp in Trittenheim dir Neumagen-Dhron, on rvside. Sm, hdstg, pt sl, unshd; own san req; chem disp; mv service pnt; el pnts (16A) €2.50; shop, rest, snacks nr; dogs; poss cr; quiet. "M'vans only; pleasant site poss clsd if rv floods; warden calls for payment." 1 Apr-31 Oct. € 5.00 2010*

⊞ **TRITTENHEIM** *3B2* (4km N Urban) *49.84933, 6.89283* **Camping Neumagen-Dhron, Moselstrasse 100, 54347 Neumagen-Dhron [(06507) 5249; fax 703290; camping-neumagen@t-online.de; www.campingneumagen.de]** On B53 fr Trittenheim twd Piesport. Immed after x-ing rv turn R, then R again sp Neumagen. Site sp in vill on rvside. Med, mkd pitch, pt shd; wc; chem disp; baby facs; shwrs inc; el pnts (6-10A) metered + conn fee; Indtte (inc dryer); shop; rest; snacks; bar; BBQ; playgrnd; boating; 40% statics; dogs free; phone adj; poss cr; Eng spkn; adv bkg; quiet; CCI. "Gd; site clsd if rv in flood." € 19.30 2010*

TRITTENHEIM *3B2* (300m SE Rural) *49.82131, 6.90201* **Campingplatz im Grünen, Olkstrasse 12, 54349 Trittenheim [(06507) 2148; fax 992089; cp-trittenheim@t-online.de; www.camping-trittenheim.de]** Foll B53 along Rv Mosel fr Trier dir Bernkastel Kues; turn R in Trittenheim at camping symbol sp Leiwen as if to go over rv & site on R immed bef x-ring rv. Sm, mkd pitch, pt shd; wc; chem disp; fam bthrm; shwrs €1; el pnts €2.60 or metered + conn fee; Indtte; shop, rest in vill; 20% statics in ssn; dogs €1.50; recep clsd 1200-1500; Eng spkn; some rv noise; no ccard acc; CCI. "Lovely, quiet site by Rv Mosel o'looking vineyards; boat trips; beautiful area; excel, clean san facs; mv service pnt point in adj vills; friendly owner; gd cycle paths; close to vill; infrequent bus to Trier; interesting area." 1 Apr-31 Oct. € 17.10 2010*

GERMANY

⊞ **TRITTENHEIM** *3B2* (4km S Rural) *49.79956, 6.92715* **Campingplatz Moselhöhe, Bucherweg 1, 54426 Heidenburg [(06509) 99016; fax 99017; dieter@qasem.de; www.campingplatz-moselhoehe.de]** Leave A1/E422 at junc 131, foll sp twd Thalfang. After 4km take 2nd L over bdge sp Heidenburg (2 hairpin bends). Thro Büdlich to Heidenbrug, foll sp in vill. Med, mkd pitch, terr, unshd; htd wc; chem disp; mv service pnt; serviced pitch; shwrs inc; el pnts (16A) metered; lndtte; shops 1km; tradsmn; snacks; rest 200m; bar; games rm; playgrnd; paddling pool; 25% statics; dogs €1.70; site clsd mid-Nov to mid-Dec; Eng spkn; adv bkg; quiet; ccard acc; red long stay; CCI. "Excel, clean, hilltop site surrounded by meadows; well-maintained; generous terraces; excel san facs; water & waste disposal points nr every pitch; wonderful views; friendly owner; conv Rv Mosel attractions 4km." ♦ € 16.70 2011*

TUBINGEN *3C3* (1km S Rural) *48.50926, 9.03616* **Neckarcamping Tübingen, Rappenberghalde 61, 72070 Tübingen [(07071) 43145; fax 793391; mail@neckarcamping.de; www.neckarcamping.de]** B28 to Tübingen, site well sp fr main rds. Site on N bank of Rv Neckar. Med, pt shd; wc; chem disp; mv service pnt; shwrs inc; el pnts (6A) metered + conn fee (rev pol); lndtte; shop; rest; snacks; playgrnd; cycle hire; 70% statics; dogs €1.50; clsd 1230-1430 & 2200-0800; noisy at w/end; red CCI. "Easy walk to attractive old town & lge pool complex; Neckar cycle path rn; cramped pitches; NH only." ♦ 1 Apr-31 Oct. € 18.80 2008*

UBERLINGEN *3D4* (3km SE Rural) *47.75186, 9.19315* **Campingplatz Nell, Zur Barbe 7, 88662 Überlingen-Nussdorf [(07551) 4254; info@campingplatz-nell.de; www.campingplatz-nell.de]** Exit B31 to Nussdorf. In vill cent turn L under rlwy bdge at 2nd campsite sp, site on R on lakeside. Sm, pt shd; wc; chem disp; snacks; shwrs €0.50; el pnts (6A) metered; lndry rm; shop, rest, snacks, bar 200m; BBQ; shgl beach & lake sw adj; no dogs; adv bkg; quiet. "Beautifully-kept site; friendly owner; all amenities nr; gd cycling; excel." Easter-20 Oct. € 20.60 2011*

UBERLINGEN *3D4* (2km NW Rural) *47.77081, 9.13813* **Campingplatz Überlingen, Bahnhofstrasse 57, 88662 Überlingen [tel/fax (07551) 64583; info@campingpark-ueberlingen.de; www.campingpark-ueberlingen.de]** Heading SE on B31, bef Überlingen turn R at sp Campingplatz Goldbach down slip rd; after 1.75km turn R; foll rd parallel with rlwy; after level x-ing site immed on R by lakeside. Lge, pt sl, pt shd; htd wc; chem disp; mv service pnt; shwrs €0.50; el pnts (16A) metered; gas; lndtte; shop; rest; snacks; bar; BBQ; playgrnd; lake sw & boating adj; 30% statics; dogs €2.50; bus; ltd Eng spkn; no adv bkg; rd & rlwy noise; red long stay/snr citizens/low ssn; no ccard acc; CCI. "Extra for lake pitches; high ssn poss diff for lge c'vans to manoeuvre; gd rest; gd facs for disabled; strict rule no vehicles in after 2230; rec arr early to secure pitch." 1 Apr-9 Oct. € 25.00 2011*

UBERLINGEN *3D4* (10km NW Rural) *47.81783, 9.03856* **Camping See-Ende, Radolfzellerstrasse 23, 78346 Bodman-Ludwigshafen [(07773) 937518; fax 937529; info@see-ende.de; www.see-ende.de]** Exit A98/E54 junc 12 onto B34, site sp. Med, pt sl, pt shd; wc; chem disp; mv service pnt; shwrs inc; el pnts (16A) metered + conn fee; gas; lndtte; shop; rest 1.5km snacks; gas; lake sw & shgl beach; 50% statics; no dogs; Eng spkn; quiet; ccard acc; CCI. "Excel position on lake; poor san facs; fair NH." 1 May-30 Sep. € 19.50 2009*

UBERSEE *4F4* (3km N Rural) *47.8412, 12.47166* **Chiemsee-Campingplatz Rödlgries, Rödlgries 1, 83236 Übersee-Feldwies [(08642) 470; fax 1636; info@chiemsee-camping.de; www.chiemsee-camping.de]** Exit A8/E52 junc 108 Übersee, foll sp Chiemseestrand, veer L at wooden sign of sites. V lge, mkd pitch, some hdstg, pt shd; 50% serviced pitch; htd wc; chem disp; mv service pnt; shwrs inc; el pnts (16A) metered + conn fee; gas; lndtte; shop; rest; snacks; bar; playgrnd; sand/shgl beach; lake sw; boating; entmnt & dogs €2.50 (July/Aug by agreement only); phone; train 3km; poss cr w/end; adv bkg; quiet but some rd noise. "Superb facs; vg for children; highly rec; extra for lakeside/serviced pitches; vg touring base; v conv nr A8; cycle track around lake." ♦ 1 Apr-31 Oct. € 24.00 2011*

UCKERITZ *2G1* (1km E Coastal) *54.01666, 14.06833* **Naturcamping Ückeritz (Part Naturist), Strandstrasse, 17459 Ückeritz [(038375) 2520; fax 25218; kv.campingplatz@ueckeritz.de; www.campingplatz-ueckeritz.de]** Sp fr B111. V lge, pt shd; wc; chem disp; mv service pnt; shwrs €1; el pnts (10A) metered + conn fee; lndtte (inc dryer); shop; rest; snacks; bar; playgrnd; sand beach (sep naturist area); games area; cycle hire; 60% statics; dogs €3; phone; bus 500m; poss cr; adv bkg; poss noisy high ssn. ♦ Easter-31 Oct. € 20.70 2010*

UETZE *1D3* (3km W Rural) *52.46565, 10.16000* **Camping Irenensee, Dahrenhorst 2A, 31311 Uetze [(05173) 98120; fax 981213; info@irenensee.de; www.irenensee.de]** Fr A2 exit junc 51 N dir Burgdorf & Uetze, then B188 dir Uetze & site. Lge, hdg/mkd pitch, hdstg, pt shd; htd wc; chem disp; mv service pnt; some serviced pitches; shwrs €0.70; el pnts (10A) €1.70; gas; lndtte; rest; snacks; bar; playgrnd; lake sw; boat hire; games area; cycle hire; entmnt; internet; 20% statics; dogs €3.10; o'night area; Eng spkn; adv bkg; quiet; red long stay/CCI. 1 Apr-31 Oct. € 25.10 2008*

⊞ **UFFENHEIM** *3D2* (1km S Rural) *49.52277, 10.12583* **Camping Paradies Franken, Walkershofen 40, 97215 Simmershofen [(09848) 969633; camping-paradies-franken@web.de; www.camping-paradies-franken.de]** Fr N exit A7 junc 105 Gollhofen or fr on B13 to Uffenheim. In Uffenheim turn W thro Adelhofen to Simmershofen, then turn L twd Walkershofen, site sp. Med, mkd pitch, pt shd; htd wc; mv service pnt; baby facs; shwrs; el pnts inc; lndtte (inc dryer); shop; tradsmn; rest; snacks; bar; BBQ; playgrnd; htd pool nr; games area; cycle hire; wifi; some statics; dogs €1.50; adv bkg. "Interesting area; gd touring base; gd." ♦ € 20.00 (CChq acc) 2010*

UFFENHEIM *3D2* (500m SW Urban) *49.54426, 10.2248* **Naturcamping am Freibad, Sportstrasse, 97215 Uffenheim [(09842) 1568; fax (09381) 716821; maempel-volkach@t-online.de]** Fr A7/E43 exit junc 105 onto B13 dir Uffenheim, site sp. Med, hdg pitch, pt shd; wc; chem disp; shwrs inc; el pnts (16A) €3 or metered + conn fee; Indtte; shops 1km; tradsmn; rest 300m; snacks; bar; pool adj; dogs €1; adv bkg; quiet; CCI. "Charming town; excel site; quite, v friendly CL type site; gd cycling area." 1 May-15 Sep. € 15.60 2011*

URNSHAUSEN *1D4* (2km NE Rural) *50.74308, 10.20200* **Camping Am Schönsee, Schönsee, 36457 Urnshausen (Thüringen) [(036964) 7451]** Exit B285 at Urnshausen; turn L sp Schönesee; site in 2km at end of rd/track. Med, sl, pt shd; wc; chem disp; shwrs €0.50; el pnts inc; shop 2km; rest; snacks; BBQ (charcoal); playgrnd; lake sw adj; 30% statics; dogs; bus 2km; adv bkg; quiet. "Rustic site adj sm lakes; basic, clean san facs; gd walking in woods; gd value; gd." May-Oct. € 12.00 2009*

URZIG see Wittlich *3B2*

⊞ **VIECHTACH** *4F3* (3km NE Rural) *49.08275, 12.85282* **Knaus Campingpark Viechtach, Waldfrieden 22, 94234 Viechtach [(09942) 1095; fax 902222; viechtach@knauscamp.de; www.knauscamp.de]** Site sp fr B85 at Viechtach, thro indus area. Lge, mkd pitch, terr, pt shd; wc; chem disp; mv service pnt; sauna; solarium; shwrs inc; el pnts (10-16A) €2.40; gas; Indtte; shop; rest; snacks; bar; playgrnd; htd covrd pool; paddling pool; games area; cycle hire; skilift 7km; entmnt; TV rm; 40% statics; dogs €3; poss cr; Eng spkn; adv bkg; quiet, some rd noise daytime; ccard acc; red snr citizens/long stay/ CCI. "Many walks, delightful countryside, wintersports; excel." ♦ € 20.00 2008*

⊞ **VLOTHO** *1C3* (3km NE Rural) *52.17388, 8.90666* **Camping Sonnenwiese, Borlefzen 1, 32602 Vlotho [(05733) 8217; fax 80289; info@sonnenwiese.com; www.sonnenwiese.com]** Fr S exit A2 junc 31 to Vlotho; cross rv bdge (Mindenerstrasse) & in 500m turn R into Rintelnerstrasse to site - 2 sites share same access. Lge, some hdstg, unshd; htd wc; chem disp; mv service pnt; baby facs; some serviced pitches inc private san facs; shwrs inc; el pnts (10A) inc; Indtte (inc dryer); shop; rest; snacks; bar; BBQ; playgrnd; paddling pool; lake sw; games rm; wifi; entmnt; cab TV; 75% statics; dogs €2.20; phone; bus/train 4km; Eng spkn; adv bkg; quiet; CCI. "Excel site." ♦ € 20.80 2010*

VOHL HERZHAUSEN see Korbach *1C4*

WAGING AM SEE *4F4* (1.5km E Rural) *47.93596, 12.7602* **Camping Schwanenplatz, Am Schwanenplatz 1, 83329 Gaden [(08681) 281; fax 4276; info@schwanenplatz.de; www.schwanenplatz.de]** Exit 112 fr A8 to Traunstein, then foll sp to Waging-am-See. Site sp on rd to Freilassing. Lge, pt shd; wc; chem disp; mv service pnt; baby facs; shwrs €0.50; el pnts (10A) inc; Indtte; shop; rest; snacks; bar; playgrnd; lake sw; boating; windsurfing school; wifi; entmnt; no dogs; o'night area; poss cr; Eng spkn; adv bkg; quiet; red long stay. "Vg in lovely setting; extra for lakeside pitches (adv bkg req)." 1 Apr-3 Oct. € 20.00 2008*

WAHLHAUSEN see Witzenhausen *1D4*

WALDBREITBACH *3B1* (1.5km NE Rural) *50.55389, 7.42518* **Campingplatz Wiedhof, Wiedhof 1, 56588 Waldbreitbach [(02638) 4258; camping@wiedhof.de; www.wiedhof.de]** Exit A3 junc 36 onto B256 W to Bonefeld, then take L257 Kurtscheiderstrasse to Niederbreitbach, then L255 to Waldbreitbach, site sp on rvside. This route avoids steep hills. Sm, unshd; wc; chem disp; shwrs; el pnts (10A) inc; Indtte (inc dryer); tradsmn; snacks; bar; BBQ; playgrnd; fishing; TV; 80% statics; dogs; adv bkg; quiet; CCI. "Conv A3 m'way; vg, peaceful site; gd walks." Easter-30 Sep. € 14.00 2010*

WALDFISCHBACH BURGALBEN see Pirmasens *3B3*

WALDKIRCH *3C4* (4km NE Rural) *48.10256, 7.99045* **Camping Elztalblick, Biehlstrasse 10, 79183 Waldkirch-Siensbach [(07681) 4212; fax 4213; elztalblick@t-online.de; www.camping-elztalblick.de]** Exit Waldkirch by B294 NE; within 1km of town cent fork R, sp Siensbach & Camping 2km. After 2km Siensbach vill, turn R into narr rd (camping sp), site at top of hill with 1 in 7 app. If app fr m'way do not go into Waldkirch but foll sp to Waldkirch-Siensbach. Med, hdstg, terr, pt shd; wc; chem disp; mv service pnt; shwrs inc; el pnts (10A) €2; Indtte; shop; tradsmn; rest; snacks; bar; playgrnd; golf 2km; TV rm; 70% statics; dogs €1; Eng spkn; quiet; CCI. "Wonderful views; friendly, family-run site." 1 Apr-20 Oct. € 18.00 2009*

I'll go online and tell the Club what we think of the campsites we've visited – www.caravanclub.co.uk/europereport

WALDKIRCH *3C4* (10km NE Rural) *48.10023, 8.05215* **Camping Schwarzwaldhorn, Ettersbachstrasse 7, 79263 Simonswald [(07683) 477 or 1048; fax 909169; evers@schwarzwald-camping.de; www.schwarzwald-camping.de]** Exit Waldkirch by B294 NE twd Elzach. Turn E dir to Bleibach/ Simonswald onto L173. After 3km turn R at camping sp & site on R. Sm, mkd pitch, pt sl, pt shd; htd wc; chem disp; mv service pnt; shwrs €0.50; el pnts (16A) metered or €1.50; Indtte; shop; tradsmn; rest adj; playgrnd; htd pool 200m; 40% statics; dogs €2.50; phone; bus 500m; sep car park; adv bkg; quiet; CCI. "Pleasant owners; vg site amongst fruit trees; excel base for Black Forest, Freiburg; modern san facs." 1 Apr-20 Oct. € 31.00 2011*

⊞ **WALDMUNCHEN** *4F2* (2km N Rural) *49.39598, 12.69913* **Camping am Perlsee, Alte Ziegelhütte 6, 93449 Waldmünchen [(09972) 1469; fax 3782; info@see-camping.de; www.see-camping.de]** N fr Cham on B22 to Schontal, NE to Waldmünchen for 10km. Foll site sp 2km. Med, hdg/mkd pitch, terr, pt shd; htd wc; chem disp; mv service pnt; baby facs; shwrs inc; el pnts (16A) metered; Indtte (inc dryer); shop & 1km; tradsmn; rest; snacks; bar; BBQ; playgrnd; lake sw adj; watersports; games area; 50% statics; dogs €2; quiet; CCI. "Vg san facs; superb site." ♦ € 17.50 2010*

GERMANY

GERMANY

⊞ **WALDSHUT** *3C4* (1km SE Urban) *47.61083, 8.22526* **Rhein Camping, Jahnweg 22, 79761 Waldshut [(07751) 3152; fax 3252; rheincamping@t-online.de; www.rheincamping.de]** Site on rvside on E o'skts of vill. Fr N foll rd 500 in dir Tiengen fr Switzerland, take 1st L after Koblenz border x-ing & foll site sp. Med, mkd pitch, hdstg, pt shd; wc; chem disp; mv service pnt; shwrs €0.50; el pnts (16A) metered + conn fee €1; gas; lndtte (inc dryer); shop; rest; snacks; bar; pool 200m; paddling pool; rv adj; tennis 100m; wifi; TV; 40% statics; dogs €1.50; poss cr; Eng spkn; adv bkg; quiet; debit cards acc; red long stay/CCI. "Nr Rhine falls at Schaffhausen; boat for Rhine trips fr site; immac facs; sm, tight pitches; helpful staff; gd rest; pleasant walk along Rhine; excel." ♦ € 21.20 2010*

⊞ **WALKENRIED** *2E4* (1km NE Rural) *51.58944, 10.62472* **Knaus Campingpark Walkenried, Ellricherstrasse 7, 37445 Walkenried [(05525) 778; fax 2332; walkenried@knauscamp.de; www.knauscamp.de]** A7, exit Seesen, then B243 to Herzberg-Bad Sachsa-Walkenried, sp. Lge, mkd pitch, terr, pt sl, pt shd; wc; chem disp; mv service pnt; sauna; solarium; shwrs inc; el pnts (6-10A) €2.40; gas; lndtte; shop; rest; snacks; bar; playgrnd; htd covrd pool; games area; wintersports; entmnt; TV; 20% statics; dogs €3; site clsd Nov; Eng spkn; adv bkg; quiet; ccard not acc; red long stay/snr citizens. "Vg rest; lovely old vill; excel site." ♦ € 21.80 2011*

WALMSBURG see Blekede *2E2*

⊞ **WALSRODE** *1D2* (4km S Rural) *52.82277, 9.63805* **Camping zum Alten Mühlenteich, Mühlenstrasse 33-35, 29664 Walsrode-Düshorn [(05161) 8989; fax 73190; muehlenteich@online.de]** Exit A7 junc 47 dir Walsrode or junc 49 dir Krelingen to Düshorn. Site sp on edge of vill. Med, pt shd; wc; chem disp; mv service pnt; shwrs inc; el pnts (16A) €1.80; lndtte; shop; rest 1km; snacks; bar; BBQ; playgrnd; 60% statics; dogs €1.50; Eng spkn; quiet; red CCI. "Conv Walsrode Bird Park; pleasant site." € 15.20 2007*

⊞ **WARBURG** *1C4* (1km E Rural) *51.48600, 9.16590* **Camping Eversburg, Zum Anger 1, 34414 Warburg [(05641) 8668; www.camping-eversburg.de]** Exit A44 junc 65 Warburg; turn R onto B7 twd Kassel; site in approx 4km on R (tight turn) just aft bdge. Sm, pt sl, unshd; wc; chem disp; mv service pnt; shwrs €1; el pnts €1.50 or metered (poss long lead req); gas; lndtte; shops 1km; rest; pool 2km; dogs €1; adv bkg; quiet; red long stay. "Pleasant town." ♦ € 19.50 2011*

⊞ **WAREN** *2F2* (3.5km S Rural) *53.50025, 12.66525* **Camping Ecktannen, Fontanestrasse 66, 17192 Waren [(03991) 668513; fax 664675; camping-ecktannen@waren-tourismus.de; www.camping-ecktannen.de]** Exit A19/E55 Berlin-Rostock dir Waren on B192; in Waren foll site sp. Lge, pt sl, pt shd; wc; chem disp; mv service pnt; shwrs inc; el pnts (10A) €2.30 (long lead poss req); gas; lndtte; shop; supmkt 2km; tradsmn; rest; snacks; bar; playgrnd; sand beach & lake sw adj; cycle hire; internet; 10% statics; dogs €2.10; o'night area; poss cr; quiet; ccard acc; CCI. "Open plan site amongst trees; insects poss a problem in spring; gd for cycling; public transport nrby." ♦ € 17.70 2011*

WARNITZ *2G2* (500m SW Rural) *53.17751, 18.87395* **Camping Oberuckersee, Lindenallee 2, 17291 Warnitz [(039863) 459; fax 78349; info@camping-oberuckersee.de; www.camping-oberuckersee.de]** Fr A11/E28 exit 7. Site sp fr Warnitz on lakeside. Lge, pt sl, shd; wc; chem disp; mv service pnt; shwrs €0.80; el pnts (10A) €2; lndry rm; shop 500m; rest 100m; snacks adj; playgrnd; lake sw & beach; fishing; boating; cycle hire; TV; 50% statics; dogs €2; clsd 1300-1500; quiet. "Lovely site in pine trees on edge lge lake; conv NH en route to Poland; deposit for san facs key; gd cycle rte nrby." ♦ 1 Apr-5 Oct. € 16.00 2011*

WASSENACH see Mendig *3B2*

WAXWEILER *3A2* (300m N Rural) *50.09270, 6.35866* **Eifel Ferienpark Prümtal, Schwimmbadstrasse 7, 54649 Waxweiler [(06554) 92000; fax 920029; info@ferienpark-waxweiler.de; www.ferienpark-waxweiler.de]** Exit A60/E42/E29 junc 5 to B410 to Waxweiler. Site sp dir Prüm on rvside. Med, hdg/mkd pitch, pt shd; htd wc; chem disp; mv service pnt; sauna; shwrs inc; el pnts (10A) inc; lndtte (inc dryer); shop; tradsmn; rest 800m; snacks; bar; BBQ; playgrnd; htd pool adj; paddling pool; waterslide; fishing; tennis; cycle hire; games area; wifi; entmnt; 50% statics (sep area); dogs €2.50; Eng spkn; adv bkg; quiet. "V nice site in the valley; v warm welcome fr staff; lovely pool adj." ♦ 1 Apr-31 Oct. € 27.00 (CChq acc) 2011*

⊞ **WAXWEILER** *3A2* (3km N Rural) *50.10833, 6.34945* **Camping Heilhauser-Mühle, 54649 Heilhausen [(06554) 805; fax 900847; walter-tautges@t-online.de; www.campingplatz-heilhauser-muehle.de]** Exit A60/E29/E42 junc 5 thro Waxweiler on B410. Site sp 300m off rd sp Arzfeld & Lichtenborn. Med, mkd pitch, pt shd; wc; chem disp; mv service pnt; shwrs €0.50; el pnts (10A) metered or €1.50; lndtte; shops 3km; snacks; bar; playgrnd; 50% statics; dogs €1; quiet. "Pleasant country; gd walking area." € 12.00 2008*

⊞ **WEBERSTEDT** *1D4* (1km SW Rural) **Campingplatz am Tor zum Hainich, Hainichstrasse, 99947 Weberstedt [(036022) 98690; fax (36022) 98691; nh@camping-hainich.de; www.camping-hainich.de]** Leave B247 Mühlhausen to Bad Langensalza rd at Schönstedt sp Weberstedt; on entering vill look for sp on L; 1km up cobbled rd. Med, hdstg, unshd; wc; chem disp; mv service pnt; baby facs; el pnts (10A) metered; lndtte; sm shop; shop, rest & bar 1km; playgrnd; cycle hire; horseriding nrby; TV rm; dogs €1; quiet; ccard acc; CCI. "Close to Hainich National Park; modern san facs; recep 0700-1300 & 1500-2200." € 14.40 2011*

WEHLEN see Bernkastel Kues *3B2*

WEILBURG *3C1* (3km SW Rural) *50.4757, 8.23966* **Campingplatz Odersbach, Runkelerstrasse 5A, 35781 Weilburg-Odersbach [(06471) 7620; fax 379603; camping-odersbach@t-online.de; www.camping-odersbach.de]** Fr Limburg exit B49 sp Weilburg & Bad Homburg, turn S (R) opp Shell stn at top of hill at Weilburg o'skts. Site on L at foot of hill in Odersbach. Lge, unshd; wc; shwrs €0.90; el pnts (16A) metered + conn fee; lndtte; shops at ent; rest 100m; snacks; bar; playgrnd; pool; paddling pool; boating; cycle hire; golf 8km; 75% statics; dogs €1; poss cr; quiet; ccard acc; CCI. ♦ 1 Apr-31 Oct. € 13.40 2008*

WEIMAR *2E4* (8km S Rural) *50.92456, 11.34785* **Camping Mittleres Ilmtal, Auf den Butterberge 1, 99438 Oettern [(036453) 80264; fax 808519; weil-camping@freenet.de; www.camping-oettern.de]** Exit A4/E40 junc 50 & foll B87 to SW to Oettern, take 1st L after narr bdge, site on L in 600m along narr rd, sp 'Camperbaude'. Med, some hdstg, pt sl, terr, pt shd; wc; chem disp; shwrs €1; el pnts (16A) €2; tradsmn; rest; snacks; bar; 50% statics; dogs €2; phone; quiet. "Conv Weimar & Buchenwald; recep open 0800-1000 & 1700-2000; welcoming; gd NH/sh stay." 15 Apr-31 Oct. € 14.00 2011*

⊞ **WEINHEIM** *3C2* (4km N Rural) *49.59776, 8.64013* **Camping Wiesensee, Ulmenweg 7, 69502 Hemsbach [(06201) 72619; fax 493426; familie.herwig@camping-wiesensee.de; www.camping-wiesensee.de]** Exit A5/E35 junc 32; foll sp Hemsbach. On ent vill strt at 1st rndbt & traff lts, at 2nd rndabt turn L & foll camping sp about 1km. Lge, hdg pitch, pt shd; wc; chem disp; mv service pnt; serviced pitches; shwrs €0.60; el pnts (16A) €1.90 or metered + conn fee; gas; Indtte (inc dryer); shop; rest high ssn; snacks; playgrnd; htd pool 100m; lake sw; boating; tennis 100m; cycle hire; golf 12km; 75% statics; dogs €2; Eng spkn; adv bkg rec high ssn; quiet but some rlwy noise. "Superb facs to C'van Club standard; friendly welcome; helpful staff; supmkt in walking dist; gd NH for A5." € 18.00 2010*

WEISSACH see Tegernsee *4F4*

WEISSENSEE *2E4* (1.5km N Rural) *51.20593, 11.06735* **Camping Weissensee, Grünstedterstrasse 4, 99631 Weissensee [(036374) 36936; fax 36937; info@campingplatz-weissensee.de; www.campingplatz-weissensee.de]** App on B4 fr Erfurt, turn R after Straussfurt onto B86. Site on R exit Weissensee past lake, clearly sp fr town cent. Med, unshd; wc; chem disp; mv service pnt; shwrs inc; el pnts (10A) metered + conn fee; Indtte (inc dryer); shop high ssn; rest adj; snacks; playgrnd; pool & paddling pool; cycle hire; wifi; 50% statics; dogs €1; no adv bkg; quiet. 1 Apr-30 Sep. € 16.50 2009*

WEMDING *4E3* (2km N Rural) *48.8845, 10.73561* **Campingpark Waldsee Wemding, Wolferstädterstrasse 100, 86650 Wemding [(09092) 90101; fax 90100; info@campingpark-waldsee.de; www.campingpark-waldsee.de]** Exit B25 at Nördlingen E'wards sp Deiningen, Fessenheim & Wemding. Site sp fr B25. Lge, mkd pitch, pt sl, terr, unshd; wc; chem disp; mv service pnt; shwrs inc; el pnts (16A) €2.10 or metered; gas; Indtte; shop; rest; snacks high ssn, bar; playgrnd; pool; waterslide; lake sw adj; boat & cycle hire; tennis 1km; entmnt; 60% statics; dogs €2.10; sep car park; adv bkg; quiet; ccard acc; red CCI. "Medieval towns in area & scenic Altmuhltal Valley; gd for Romantische Strasse; barrier clsd 1300-1500; v friendly, helpful staff." ♦ 1 Mar-31 Oct. € 19.50 2008*

WENNINGSTEDT see Westerland *1C1*

WERDER PETZOW see Potsdam *2F3*

⊞ **WERNIGERODE** *2E3* (8km S Rural) *51.77586, 10.7965* **Camping am Brocken, Schützenring 6, 38875 Elbingerode [(039454) 42589; hobittner@ngi.de; www.campingambrocken.de]** S on B244 fr Werningerode. Turn R at int'l camping sp at bottom of hill ent Elbingerode. Foll sp for 1km - take care on app fr N. Lge, mkd pitch, some hdstg, pt sl, unshd; wc; chem disp; mv service pnt; shwrs €0.50; el pnts (16A) metered + conn fee (poss rev pol); gas; Indtte; shop; tradsmn; rest, snacks 100m; playgrnd; pool 200m; dogs €2; poss cr; adv bkg; quiet; 10% red CCI. "Lovely, friendly site; vg facs; easy for c'vans; sep area for m'vans; highly rec; excel." ♦ € 20.00 2011*

When we get home
I'm going to post
all these site report
forms to the Club
for next year's guide.
The deadline's mid September 2013

⊞ **WERTACH** *4E4* (1km E Rural) *47.60861, 10.41750* **Camping Waldesruh, Bahnhofstrasse 19, 87497 Wertach [(08365) 1004; fax 706369; info@camping-wertach.de; www.camping-wertach.de]** Fr A7 exit junc 137 at Oy & take B310 dir Wertach; 2km bef Wertach turn R into Bahnhofstrasse & foll site sp. Med, mkd pitch, pt sl, pt shd; htd wc; chem disp; mv service pnt; baby facs; shwrs inc; el pnts (10A) metered; gas; Indtte (inc dryer); shop, rest, snacks, bar 500m; BBQ; playgrnd; lake sw 2km; games area; games rm; wifi; TV rm; 50% statics; dogs €2; phone; bus; Eng spkn; adv bkg; quiet; red long stay; CCI. "V picturesque area; friendly site; gd walks; winter sports site & conv NH in rte Austria/Italy." ♦ € 14.50 2011*

⊞ **WERTACH** *4E4* (1km E Rural) *47.61030, 10.44618* **International Grüntensee-Camping, Grüntenseestrasse 41, 87497 Wertach [(08365) 375; fax 1221; info@gruentensee.de; www.gruentensee.de]** Exit A7 junc 137 to Nesselwang. Site on rd fr Nesselwang to Wertach, sp. Lge, terr, pt shd; wc; chem disp; mv service pnt; baby facs; shwrs; el pnts (10-16A) metered + conn fee; Indtte; shop 2km; tradsmn; playgrnd; lake sw & beach; watersports; entmnt; golf 4km; ski-lift nr; wifi; 40% statics; dogs €2.50; o'night m'van facs; adv bkg; quiet; red CCI. "Excel location; extra charge for lakeside pitches; gd walking." € 22.00 2009*

WERTHEIM *3D2* (5km E Rural) *49.78097, 9.56553* **Campingpark Wertheim-Bettingen, Geiselbrunnweg 31, 97877 Wertheim-Bettingen [(09342) 7077; fax 913077]** Fr A3/E41 exit junc 66 - 2nd Wertheim exit; then turn off to vill of Bettingen; site sp. Med, pt sl, unmkd pitch, pt shd; wc; chem disp; mv service pnt; shwrs €0.50; el pnts (16A) €2; gas; Indtte (inc dryer); shop; rest; snacks; playgrnd; boating; fishing; cycle hire; 60% statics; dogs €1; poss v cr; adv bkg; red long stay; Eng spkn; many statics; quiet; ccard acc; red 3+ days; CCI. "On bank of Rv Main; conv, popular NH for A3 - rec arr early; NH tourers on sep, lge, level meadow outside main site (but within barrier); gd rest; gd san facs." ♦ 1 Apr-31 Oct. € 14.50 2010*

GERMANY

WERTHEIM *3D2* (2km NW Urban) *49.77805, 9.50916* **Azur Campingpark Wertheim, An den Christwiesen 35, 97877 Wertheim-Bestenheid [(09342) 83111; fax 83171; wertheim@azur-camping.de; www.azur-camping.de/wertheim]** Exit A3/E41 junc 66 onto L2310 thro Wertheim, site on W bank of Rv Main sp dir Bestenheid. V lge, mkd pitch, hdstg, pt shd; htd wc; chem disp; mv service pnt; baby facs; shwrs inc; el pnts (6A) €3; gas; lndtte; shop; supmkt 1km; rest 1km; snacks; bar; cooking facs; playgrnd; htd pool; paddling pool; waterslide; fishing; boat hire; tennis 500m; games area; 30% statics; dogs €3; phone; bus 100m; train 1km; poss cr; adv bkg; Eng spkn; rush hour rd noise; red low ssn/CCI. "Interesting town in walking dist; helpful staff; gd pitches on rv (extra charge); san facs OK (1 block needs upgrade); site clsd 2200; gd rvside cycle paths; gd." ♦ 1 Apr-31 Oct. € 22.50 (CChq acc) 2011*

⊞ **WESTERHEIM** *3D3* (2km SW Rural) *48.51055, 9.60933* **Alb-Camping Westerheim, Albstrasse, 72589 Westerheim [(07333) 6197 or 6140; fax 7797; info@alb-camping.de; www.alb-camping.de]** Exit A8/E52 at junc 61 (Merklingen) to Laichingen; turn R to Westerheim; foll camp sp (thro housing estate) for 2km to top of hill. Or exit A8 junc 60 thro Westerheim. V lge, mkd pitch, hdstg, pt sl, pt shd; wc; shwrs inc; chem disp; el pnts (16A) €2.50; gas; lndtte; shop; rest; snacks; playgrnd; 3 free pools; tennis 500m; games area; skibus; entmnt; 80% statics; poss cr with long stay vans; Eng spkn; adv bkg ess high ssn; quiet; no ccard acc; red long stay/CCI. "Huge, holiday-camp style site; gd walking & touring area; wintersports; ski lift adj; lge pitches; helpful staff; gd facs for children; immac san facs; office clsd 1200-1300 (check-in at bar)." € 20.60 2010*

WESTERLAND (SYLT ISLAND) *1C1* (3km N Coastal) *54.94251, 8.32685* **Camping Wenningstedt, Am Dorfteich, 25996 Wenningstedt [(04651) 944004; fax 44740; camp@wenningstedt.de; www.wenningstedt.de]** Fr Westerland foll sp to Wenningstedt or List. Site app rd on sharp bend bef Wenningstedt. Lge, pt sl, unshd; wc; chem disp; mv service pnt; baby facs; shwrs inc; el pnts (16A) metered; lndtte (inc dryer); shop; rest; playgrnd; htd, covrd pool; fishing 300m; wifi; entmnt; dogs €3.20; adv bkg; quiet. Easter-31 Oct. € 25.00 2010*

⊞ **WESTERSTEDE** *1C2* (1km S Rural) *53.2508, 7.93506* **Camping Westerstede, Süderstrasse 2, 26655 Westerstede [tel/fax (04488) 78234; camping@westerstede.de; www.westerstede.de/camping]** Exit E35/A28 junc 6 to Westerstede; cont thro town dir Bad Zwischenahn on L815 for 1km; then foll L815 to L onto Oldenburgerstrasse (rd conts strt on as L821); in 200m turn L to site. Med, mkd pitch, hdstg, pt shd; htd wc; chem disp; mv service pnt; shwrs inc; el pnts (9A) inc; lndtte; shop 300m; rest; playgrnd; bus; train 400m; poss cr; Eng spkn; quiet; red CCI. "Pleasant, friendly, relaxing, well-managed site; clsd 1300-1500; sm pitches; outer field cheaper but rd noise & remote fr facs; o'night m'van facs; gd touring base; many cycle paths; gd town for shopping." ♦ € 15.50 2009*

⊞ **WETTRINGEN** *1B3* (8km N Rural) *52.27408, 7.3204* **Campingplatz Haddorfer Seen, Haddorf 59, 48493 Wettringen [(05973) 2742; fax 900889; info@campingplatz-haddorf.de; www.campingplatz-haddorf.de]** Exit A30 junc 7 at Rheine Nord dir Neuenkirchen. At end city limits turn R dir Salzbergen then L in 4km & foll site sp. V lge, mkd pitch, pt shd; htd wc; chem disp; mv service pnt; shwrs inc; el pnts (16A) metered + conn fee; lndtte (inc dryer); shop; tradsmn; supmkt 10km; rest; snacks; bar; playgrnd; lake sw; fishing; watersports; boat hire; games area; 90% statics; dogs €3; adv bkg; quiet; red CCI. "Family-friendly site; modern san facs; gd bistro; gd walking/cycling." ♦ € 19.00 2010*

⊞ **WETZLAR** *3C1* (10km SW Rural) *50.51155, 8.38293* **Campingpark Braunfels, Am Weiherstieg 2, 35619 Braunfels [(06442) 4366; fax 6895; www.braunfels.de]** Take B49 fr Wetzlar to Braunfels. Site on R at S end of town. Med, hdg/mkd pitch, pt sl, pt shd; wc; chem disp; shwrs €0.50; el pnts (16A) metered + conn fee; lndtte (inc dryer); shop 300m; rest; snacks; htd pool 200m, tennis 300m; horseriding 1km; 60% statics; dogs €1; adv bkg; quiet. "Braunfels beautiful health resort in easy reach Taunus mountains; fair NH." € 19.40 2010*

⊞ **WIESLOCH** *3C3* (5km SW Rural) *49.28146, 8.58445* **Camping St Leoner See, 68789 St Leon-Rot [(06227) 59009; fax 880988; info@st.leoner-see.de; www.st.leoner-see.de]** Fr A5/E35 exit junc 39 & turn S onto L 546 for 5km. Thro St Leon-Rot two Reilingen, site sp on R. Avoid Walldorf & Wiesloch. V lge, pt shd; wc; chem disp; mv service pnt; baby facs; shwrs inc; el pnts (6-16A) €2; lndtte; shop; rest; snacks; playgrnd; lge watersports complex inc fishing, windsurfing, waterskiing, lake sw; golf 4km; entmnt; internet; 60% statics; no dogs; phone; sep car park; gates clsd 1300-1500 & 2200-0700; poss cr; Eng spkn; adv bkg; quiet except w/end; ccard acc; red CCI. "Touring vans on hdstg in mkd bays at ent - no space for chairs, awning, etc - NH only; otherwise gd family site; excel sports/water facs." ♦ € 21.00 2009*

WIESLOCH *3C3* (6km W Urban) *49.31643, 8.63481* **Campingplatz Walldorf-Astoria, Schwetzingerstrasse 98, 69190 Walldorf [tel/fax (06227) 9195]** Fr A5, exit junc 39 for Walldorf & Wiesloch; take B291/L598 N sp Walldorf Nord; in 2km turn R onto Schwetzingerstrasse; site sp in 250m. Med, pt shd; wc; chem disp; mv service pnt; shwrs inc; el pnts (16A) €2.50; shop; rest; indoor pool 200m; 50% statics in sep area; no dogs; Eng spkn; CCI. "Vg rest on site; sm zoo & sports complex adj; bus to Heidelberg at gate; gates clsd 1200-1500; excel NH/sh stay; rec arr bef 1700 high ssn; conv for Hockenheim Circuit." ♦ 15 Apr-15 Oct. € 18.00 2009*

⊞ **WIETZENDORF** *1D2* (2km NW Rural) *52.93136, 9.96486* **Südsee Camp, Im Lindhorst-Forst 6, 29647 Wietzendorf [(05196) 980116; fax 980284; info1@suedseecamp.de; www.suedsee-camp.de]** Exit A7/E45 junc 45 & take rd B3 dir Celle. Turn R at viaduct in Bokel, site sp. V lge, mkd pitch, shd; chem disp; mv service pnt; htd wc; baby facs; fam bthrm; serviced pitches; sauna; shwrs; el pnts (4A) €1.50; gas; lndtte; shop; rest; snacks; bar; playgrnd; tropical pool + waterchute; solarium; lake sw & sand beach adj; watersports; tennis; squash; games area; cycle hire; entmnt; internet; TV; 30% statics; dogs €3; phone; adv bkg. "Superb holiday complex." ♦ € 26.00 2008*

⊞ **WILDESHAUSEN** *1C2* (4km N Rural) *52.93400, 8.40200* **Camping Aschenbake, Zum Sande 18, 27801 Dötlingen [(04433) 333; fax 1531; aschenbeck@nwn.de; www.aschenbeck-camping.de]** Exit E37/A1 Osnabrück/Bremen junc 60 dir Wildeshausen. Turn R in traff lts in 800m + foll sp to site in 4km. Single track for last km. Med, hdg/mkd pitch, pt shd; wc; chem disp; shwrs €0.60; el pnts (16A) €2; lndtte; shop; rest; snacks; playgrnd; lake sw & beach adj; dogs €2; quiet. "Walks in woods; office clsd 1300-1500." ♦ € 14.00 2009*

⊞ **WILDESHAUSEN** *1C2* (2km W Rural) *52.89916, 8.35444* **Camping Auetal, Aumühlerstrasse 75, 27793 Aumühle [(04431) 1851; fax 2203]** Exit a'bahn A1/E37 junc 61. Take rd B213 E; site on L in 1.5km. Sm, pt shd; wc; shwrs inc; el pnts (16A) €1.50; lndtte (inc dryer); rest; bar; BBQ; playgrnd; lake sw adj; CCI. "Statics site but sm field for tourers; vg rest; NH only." ♦ € 13.00 2009*

WILDESHAUSEN *1C2* (3km W Rural) *52.8995, 8.3281* **Camping Bürgerpark, Aumühle 78A, 27793 Wildeshausen [(04435) 3752]** Exit A1/E37 junc 61 onto B213 dir Cloppenburg. Site in 300m on R. Med, pt sl, pt shd; wc; chem disp; shwrs; el pnts (6A) inc; shops 500m; snacks; 50% statics; adv bkg; quiet but some rd noise. "Fair NH; pleasant, wooded o'night area; conv for a'bahn." 1 Apr-30 Sep. € 14.00 2008*

WILHELMSTHAL see Eisenach *1D4*

WILLSTATT SAND see Kehl *3B3*

⊞ **WILSUM** *1B3* (3.5m S Rural) *52.51689, 6.87390* **Wilsumerberge Resort, Zum Feriengebiet 1, 49849 Wilsum [(05945) 995590; fax 9955899; info@wilsumerberge.nl; www.wilsumerberge.nl]** Site sp on B403. V lge, pt shd; htd wc; chem disp; mv service pnt; baby facs; shwrs inc; el pnts (6A) inc; lndtte (inc dryer); shop; rest; snacks; bar; playgrnd; lake sw; waterslide; fishing; tennis; cycle hire; games area; games rm; wifi; entmnt; 60% statics; dogs €3; adv bkg; ccard acc; red low ssn. "Attractive site in forest; extra for serviced pitches; vg facs, espec for youngsters." ♦ € 22.00 (CChq acc) 2010*

WINGST *1C2* (2km NE Rural) *53.75277, 9.08361* **Knaus Campingpark Wingst, Schwimmbadallee 13, 21789 Wingst [(04778) 7604; fax 7608; wingst@knauscamp.de; www.knauscamp.de]** A27 to Cuxhaven, B73 to Ottendorf-Neuhaus-Cadenberge. Exit Wingst, well sp. Lge, hdg/mkd pitch, terr, pt shd; wc; chem disp; mv service pnt; sauna; solarium; shwrs inc; el pnts (4-10A) €2; gas; lndtte; shop; rest; playgrnd; games rm; TV; indoor pool 300m; sand beach 6km; sports field 200m; entmnt; 30% statics; dogs €2; site clsd Nov; Eng spkn; 20% red 25+ days/snr citizens; ccard not acc; CCI. "Excel; in wooded area with rolling hills, many attractions for children." 1 Jan-31 Oct. € 20.00 2007*

WINNINGEN see Koblenz *3B2*

⊞ **WINSEN (ALLER)** *1D3* (1.5km W Rural) *52.67506, 9.89968* **Campingplatz Winsen, Auf der Hude 1, 29308 Winsen [(05143) 93199; fax 93144; info@camping-winsen.de; www.camping-winsen.de]** Fr A7/E45 exit junc 50 Wietze onto B214Thro Wietze & in 6km turn L to Oldau & Winsen. Foll site sp. Med, mkd pitch, pt shd; htd wc; chem disp; mv service pnt; shwrs inc; el pnts (10-16A) €2.50 or metered; gas; lndtte (inc dryer); shop; tradsmn; supmkt 1km; rest; snacks; bar; playgrnd; htd, covrd pool 200m; rv beach adj; wifi; 50% statics; dogs €2; phone; bus 1km; m'van o'night area; quiet; red CCI. "Attractive site; helpful staff; some rvside pitches - poss liable to flood; easy walk to picturesque town cent; lovely cycle paths." € 19.00 2009*

⊞ **WINSEN (ALLER)** *1D3* (8km NW Rural) *52.71983, 9.82521* **Campingpark Hüttensee, Hüttenseepark 1, 29308 Meissendorf [(05056) 941880; fax 941881; info@campingpark-huettensee.de; www.campingpark-huettensee.de]** Fr N on A27/A7 exit at Westenholz & cont twd Westenholz/Ostenholz to Meissendorf, site sp. Fr S exit at Allertal rest stop twd Celle/Winsen-Aller. Turn L at traff lts & L again to Meissendorf. Lge, mkd pitch, pt shd; htd wc; chem disp; mv service pnt; baby facs; shwrs €0.50; el pnts (16A) inc; lndtte (inc dryer); shop; tradsmn; supmkt 800m; rest; snacks; bar; playgrnd; lake sw & sand beach; fishing; tennis 500m; boat & cycle hire; games area; wifi; entmnt; 60% statics; dogs €2.50; clsd 1300-1500; adv bkg; quiet; ccard acc; red CCI. ♦ € 24.80 (CChq acc) 2011*

⊞ **WISMAR** *2E2* (200m N Urban) *53.89388, 11.45166* **Wohnmobilpark Westhafen, Schiffbauerdamm 12, 23966 Wismar [(03841) 706070; info@wohnmobilpark-wismar.de]** Exit A20/E22 junc 8 to cent of Wismar; foll sp to 'hafen', site sp. Sm, hdstg, unshd; wc; shwrs €1; el pnts (10A) €1 for 8 hrs; shop adj; rest 200m; adv bkg; quayside noise. "Superb NH in stunning town; m'vans only - no c'vans allowed." € 9.00 2011*

⊞ **WISMAR** *2E2* (5km NW Coastal) *53.93441, 11.37160* **Ostsee Camping, Sandstrasse 19c, 23968 Zierow [(038428) 63820; fax 63833; info@ostsee-camping.de; www.ostsee-camping.de]** Fr Wismar-Lübeck rd B105/22 to Gägelow, turn N to Zierow; thro vill to site at end of rd. V lge, unshd; htd wc; chem disp; mv service pnt; sauna; baby facs; shwrs €1; el pnts (16A) €2.80; lndtte (inc dryer); shop; tradsmn; rest; snacks; playgrnd; beach adj; cycle hire; games area; horseriding adj; wifi; TV; 75% statics (sep area); dogs €2.70; CCI. "Busy site in superb location; gd san facs; a first class campsite." ♦ € 32.30 2011*

WITTENBERG see Lutherstadt Wittenberg *2F3*

WITTLICH *3B2* (8km E Urban) *49.97861, 7.00750* **Wohnmobilstellplatz (M'van Park), Moseluferstrasse, 54539 Ürzig [(06532) 954888; info@uerzig-mosel.de]** Foll B50 fr Wittlich, then B53 for 3km along rv bank to Ürzig. M'vans only, sp. Sm, own san; chem disp; mv service pnt; el pnts €1.50 (16A); shop 200m; rest, bar 100m; dogs; adv bkg. 1 Apr-5 Nov. € 6.50 2009*

⊞ **WITTLICH** *3B2* (11km E Rural) *49.98986, 7.07780* **Camping Sportzentrum Kröverberg, 54536 Kröv [(06541) 70040; fax 700444; www.kroeverberg.de]** Exit A1/A48 junc 125; then B49 dir Koblenz; then L62 Ürzig; L in Ürzig sp Kröv-Bergstrecke up hill (10%) for 2km; foll sp on this rd (do not go downhill into Mosel Valley). Med, hdg/mkd pitch, terr, unshd; wc; shwrs inc; chem disp; mv service pnt; el pnts (10A) metered; gas; Indtte; shop 4km; rest; snacks; playgrnd; games area; statics; dogs €1.80; quiet; adv bkg. "Friendly site high above Mosel; lovely scenery; boat trips on Mosel; mkd walks thro vineyards; excel facs." € 14.00 2011*

WITTLICH *3B2* (12km NW Rural) *50.09680, 6.79797* **Natur-Camping Vulkaneifel, Feriendorf Moritz, Herbstwiese 1, 54531 Manderscheid [(06572) 92110; fax 921149; info@vulkan-camping.de; www.vulkan-camping.de]** Exit A1/E44 junc 122 dir Manderscheid, then foll sp Daun. Site sp. Med, mkd pitch, terr, pt shd; wc; chem disp; mv service pnt; shwrs inc; el pnts (2A) €2.50; Indtte; shop 2km; rest 700m; snacks; playgrnd; htd pool; games area; 10% statics; dogs €1.50; o'night m'van area; red CCI. "Gd walking, cycling; facs shared with football club." ♦ 1 Apr-31 Oct. € 20.00 2009*

⊞ **WITZENHAUSEN** *1D4* (1.5km N Rural) *51.3499, 9.86916* **Camping Werratal, Am Sande 11, 37213 Witzenhausen [(05542) 1465; fax 72418; info@campingplatz-werratal.de; www.campingplatz-werratal.de]** Exit A7/E45 junc 75 to Witzenhausen. Cross rv & immed R foll sp rte around town cent. Site nr rv, sp. Med, unshd; wc; chem disp; mv service pnt; shwrs €0.70; el pnts (16A) €2.30; Indtte (inc dryer); shop; rest, snacks adj; playgrnd; htd, covrd pool 200m; cycle hire; wifi; 50% statics; dogs €2.30; red long stay. "Pleasant, family-run site; poss flooding at high water." € 24.80 2011*

⊞ **WITZENHAUSEN** *1D4* (10km SE Urban) *51.28889, 9.97638* **Camping Oase, Kreisstrasse 32, 37318 Wahlhausen [tel/fax (036087) 98671; www.camping-oase.de]** Take B27 dir Wahlhausen, site sp bet Bad Sooden & Allendorf. Med, pt sl, pt shd; wc; chem disp; shwrs inc; el pnts (16A) metered; Indtte (inc dryer); shop adj; rest; playgrnd; Rv Werra nr; dogs €1; adv bkg; quiet. € 14.50 2010*

⊞ **WOLFACH** *3C3* (2km E Rural) *48.29083, 8.27805* **Trendcamping Wolfach (previously named Schwarzwald Camp Wolfach), Schiltacherstrasse 80, 77709 Wolfach-Halbmeil [(07834) 859309; fax 859310; info@trendcamping.de; http://www.trendcamping.de]** Fr Wolfach E 5km on B294 dir Schiltach. Site on L opp rv bdge. Med, hdstg, terr, unshd; wc; chem disp; mv service pnt; serviced pitches; shwrs; el pnts (16A) metered + conn fee; gas; Indtte; shop; rest; snacks; playgrnd; wifi; some sat TV; 30% statics; dogs €2; o'night m'van area; Eng spkn; adv bkg; quiet but some rd noise; red long stay. "Scenic views across valley; excel, modern, clean san facs; barrier clsd 1230-1430; NH area for m'vans; rock pegs req for awning; free bus & train pass for Black Forest; gd cycling & walking." € 25.00 2011*

⊞ **WOLFACH** *3C3* (5km S Rural) *48.26750, 8.23777* **Campingplatz zur Mühle, Talstrasse 79, 77709 Kirnbach [(07834) 775; fax 8670975; camping-kirnbach@t-online.de; www.camping-kirnbach.de]** Turn S off B294 dir Kirnbach, site sp. Steep access. Sm, hdg/mkd pitch, terr; pt sl, pt shd; htd wc; chem disp (wc); shwrs €0.50; el pnts metered + conn fee; Indtte; shop; tradsmn; snacks; bar; BBQ; rv 500m; TV rm; few statics; no dogs high ssn; phone; quiet. "Pleasant site but not suitable lge o'fits; poss boggy in wet weather; friendly owners help with van placing; gd touring base; gd views Black Forest; gd walks & rests nrby." € 18.00 2009*

⊞ **WOLFRATSHAUSEN** *4E4* (11km SW Rural) *47.85403, 11.33866* **Camping Hirth, Am Schwaiblbach 3, 82541 Ambach [(08177) 546; fax 8820; campingplatzhirth@t-online.de; www.campingplatzhirth.de]** Fr S exit A95 junc 7 twd St Heinrich, turn R on lakeside rd twd Starnberg. Site approx 4km further, sp Café/Restaurant Hirth to L & camping sp below. Fr N exit A95 junc 6 thro Münsing then S to Ambach. Lge, unshd; wc; shwrs €1; chem disp; el pnts (16A) metered + conn fee; Indtte; shop; rest; lake sw 100m; TV; 60% statics; dogs €1; site clsd Dec; some rd noise; ccard acc. "Lakeside walks; chem disp not suitable c'vans - m'vans only." ♦ € 19.50 2008*

⊞ **WOLFSBURG** *2E3* (2km NE Urban) *52.4316, 10.8158* **Camping am Allersee, In den Allerwiesen 5, 38446 Wolfsburg [(05361) 63395; fax 651271; allerseecamping@gmx.de; www.camping-allersee.de]** Exit A39 junc 3 onto B188, foll sp VW Autostadt sp. Turn L over canal, then R past stadium. Med, mkd pitch, hdstg, pt shd; htd wc; chem disp; shwrs €0.50; el pnts (10A) €2.50 or metered; Indtte; shops 2km; rest; bar; cooking facs; playgrnd; beach adj; lake sw 100m; sailing & canoeing; entmnt; 80% statics; dogs €1; clsd 1300-1500 & 2200-0700; o'night area for m'vans; poss cr; Eng spkn; adv bkg; quiet, but poss noise fr pop concerts in VW stadium. "Vg, clean site beside lake; conv VW factory visits (not w/end or bank hols) - check time of tour in Eng; gd lake perimeter path adj; friendly, helpful owners; ice rink & indoor water cent other side of lake." ♦ € 22.00 2011*

⊞ **WOLFSTEIN** *3B2* (2km S Rural) *49.5803, 7.6187* **Azur Camping am Königsberg, Am Schwimmbad 1, 67752 Wolfstein [(06304) 4143; fax 7543; nfo@CampingWolfstein.de; http://www.campingwolfstein.de]** Exit A61 at junc 15 Kaiserslauten West onto B270 dir Lauterecken, site on R 200m bef Wolfstein, sp. Sm, mkd pitch, hdstg, pt sl, unshd; wc; chem disp; serviced pitches; shwrs inc; el pnts (16A) €3 + conn fee; Indtte; ice shop 200m; rest; bar; playgrnd; htd pool adj; games area; wifi; 60% statics; dogs €2.30; poss cr; adv bkg; site clsd 1300-1500; Eng spkn; quiet; ccard acc; red snr citizens/CCI. "Gd." € 22.00 2011*

⊞ **WULFEN (FEHMARN ISLAND)** *2E1* (1km E Coastal) *54.40611, 11.1772* **Camping Wulfener Hals (Part Naturist), Wulfener Hals Weg, 23769 Wulfen [(04371) 86280; fax 3723; camping@wulfenerhals.de; www.wulfenerhals.de]** Turn off B207/E47 to Avendorf, site sp. V lge, mkd pitch, shd; htd wc; chem disp; mv service pnt; serviced pitches; sauna; baby rm; fam bthrm; shwrs; el pnts (10A) €2.10; gas; Indtte; shop; rest; snacks; bar; playgrnd; pool; sand beach adj; sailing; watersports; golf adj; wifi; entmnt; 60% statics; dogs €7.50; phone; adv bkg; ccard acc; red CCI. "Excel." ♦ € 39.50 2011*

⊞ **WUNSIEDEL** *4F2* (5km S Rural) *50.01537, 11.99272* **Camping Luisenburg, Luisenburg 7, 95632 Wunsiedel [(09232) 3301; fax 700294; info@camp-luisenburg.de]** Fr A93 exit junc 13 Marktredwitz Nord onto B303. After 7km exit sp Luisenburg. Foll sp 'Felsenlabyrinth' & site in 1km. Sm, pt sl, pt shd; wc; chem disp; shwrs; el pnts (16A) metered; Indtte; shop; rest 200m; pool 5km; sailing & windsurfing adj; wintersports; spa 2km; 50% statics; dogs €1; site clsd Nov; clsd 1300-1500; Eng spkn; adv bkg; quiet; CCI. "Views over hills & forest; lge open-air theatre nr - red Jul & Aug; gd walking country; friendly welcome; gd NH to/fr Czech Rep." € 11.20 2007*

WURZBURG *3D2* (6km NE Urban) *49.83286, 9.99783* **Camping Estenfeld, Maidbronnerstrasse 38, 97230 Estenfeld [(09305) 228; fax 8006; cplestenfeld@freenet.de; www.camping-estenfeld.de]** Exit A7/E45 junc 101. Foll sp to Estenfeld & site sp. Sm, some hdstg, pt shd; wc; chem disp; shwrs €0.75; el pnts (16A) €2.50 or metered & conn fee; Indtte; shop; tradsmn; rest adj; snacks; bar; playgrnd; some statics; dogs €1.50; clsd 1300-1500; poss v cr high ssn; Eng spkn; quiet; red long stay; CCI. "Helpful owner; clean, tidy site; rec NH." 10 Mar-23 Dec. € 15.00 2010*

WURZBURG *3D2* (2km S Urban) *49.77973, 9.92636* **Kanu-Club Würzberg, Mergentheimerstrasse 13b, 97082 Würzburg [(09317) 72536; www.kc-wuerzburg.de]** Fr A3/E43 exit junc 70, Heidingsfeld. Turn L onto B19 & foll sp for Heidingsfeld. Turn R at site sp to cross tram line, sp Zeltplatz. Site L in 30m on W bank of rv, not well sp. Sm, mkd pitch, pt shd; wc; chem disp; shwrs €0.50; el pnts €2; shop 1.5km; rest; bar; 80% statics; bus/tram adj; dogs €1.50; Eng spkn; adv bkg; CCI. "Site is private club with ltd touring pitches; gd access to lovely, historic city; gd cycling by rv; friendly staff; not suitable lge outfits due sm pitches & restricted access; long walk to san facs; adv bkg ess holiday w/ends; attractive quiet site." Mar-Dec. € 13.00 2011*

⊞ **WURZBURG** *3D2* (4km S Rural) *49.74471, 9.98433* **Camping Kalte Quelle, Winterhäuserstrasse 160, 97084 Würzburg-Heidingsfeld [(0931) 65598; fax 612611; info@kalte-quelle.de; www.kalte-quelle.de]** Exit A3/E43 at Heidingsfeld junc 70 onto A19 dir Würzburg. Take 1st exit & foll sp Ochsenfurt + camping sp. Site on L in approx 5km. Med, mkd pitch, pt shd; wc; chem disp; mv service pnt; shwrs €1; el pnts (16A) conn fee + €2; Indtte; shop; rest; bar; playgrnd; cycle hire; 50% statics; dogs free; clsd 1330-1430; poss cr; Eng spkn; adv bkg; some rd, rv & rlwy noise; ccard acc; CCI. "No doors on shwrs & run down facs, but clean; pleasant situation on rv; NH only; conv Würzburg & Nürnberg." € 16.00 2009*

WUSTENWELSBERG *4E2* (500m SE Rural) *50.13750, 10.82777* **Camping Rückert-Klause, Haus Nr 16, 96190 Wüstenwelsberg [tel/fax (09533) 288]** Fr Coburg on B4, turn W at Kaltenbrunn; site sp thro Untermerzbach & Obermerzbach. Or fr B279 fr Bamberg to Bad Königshofen, turn R just S of Pfarrweisch, sp. Sm, pt sl, pt shd, wc; chem disp; shwrs inc; el pnts (16A) metered + conn fee; Indtte; shops 3km; snacks; bar; playgrnd; 50% statics; Eng spkn; adv bkg; quiet; ccard not acc; CCI. "Many castles nrby; beautiful countryside; super situation." 1 Apr-31 Oct. € 14.00 2009*

ZELL *3B2* (1.5km W Rural) *50.03375, 7.17365* **Campingplatz Mosella, 56856 Zell-Kaimt [tel/fax (06542) 41241]** Fr Cochem S on B49, in Alf take B53 dir Bernkastel-Kues. In Zell site sp to Kaimt. Med, mkd pitch, unshd; wc; chem disp; mv service pnt; shwrs; el pnts (16A) inc; gas; Indtte; snacks; playgrnd; watersports; dogs €1; poss cr; quiet. "Scenic area; v quiet at night; site soggy after rain." 1 Apr-31 Oct. € 25.00 2011*

ZELL *3B2* (3km NW Rural) *50.05889, 7.13027* **Bären Camp, Am Moselufer 1-3, 56859 Bullay [(06542) 900097; info@baeren-camp.de; www.baeren-camp.de]** Exit A1 junc 125 at Wittlich onto B49 to Alf. At Alf cross rv to Bullay & foll sp to site. Med, pt shd; wc; chem disp; mv service pnt; baby facs; shwrs €1; el pnts (16A) metered; Indtte (inc dryer); shop; BBQ; playgrnd; dogs €2; Eng spkn; quiet. "Conv Cochem, Bernkastel-Kues; gd cycling along tow-path; extra for rvside pitch." ♦ Easter-1 Nov. € 20.20 2010*

ZELL *3B2* (4km NW Rural) *50.03305, 7.11527* **Camping Moselland, Im Planters, 56862 Pünderich [(06542) 2618; fax 960696; www.campingplatz-moselland.de]** Foll Rv Mosel S fr Zell on B53. In 6km turn R sp Pünderich & site. Turn immed L, then immed R & foll narr rd to site in 1km. Med, mkd pitch, pt shd; wc; chem disp; shwrs €1; el pnts (16A) metered + conn fee; Indtte; tradsmn; rest; snacks; bar; playgrnd; boat-launching; 30% statics; dogs €2; phone; Eng spkn; adv bkg; quiet. "Pleasant rvside site in vineyards & orchards; vg." 1 Apr-31 Oct. € 16.00 2009*

⊞ **ZEVEN** *1D2* (1.5km NE) *53.30401, 9.29793* **Campingplatz Sonnenkamp Zeven, Sonnenkamp 10, 27404 Zeven [(04281) 951345; fax 951347; info@campingplatz-sonnenkamp.de; www.campingplatz-zeven.de]** Fr A1 exit 47 or 49 to Zeven. Fr Zeven dir Heeslingen/Buxtehude rd, site sp fr all dir twd stadium Lge, mkd pitch, some hdstg, unshd; htd wc; chem disp; mv service pnt; baby facs; sauna; shwrs inc; el pnts (16A) metered; gas; Indtte (inc dryer); shop; tradsmn; rest; snacks; bar; playgrnd; pool, paddling pool, waterslide & sports facs adj; tennis; cycle hire; games area; games rm; wifi; entmnt; 75% statics; dogs €0.50; phone; Eng spkn; poss cr; adv bkg; ccard acc; quiet; red snr citizens; CCI. € 22.60 2011*

⊞ **ZIERENBERG** *1D4* (500m E Rural) *51.36809, 9.31494* **Campingplatz Zur Warme, Im Nordbruch 2, 34289 Zierenberg [tel/fax (05606) 3966; campingplatz-zierenberg@t-online.de; www.campingplatz-zierenberg.de]** Exit A44 at junc 67 to Zierenberg. In vill cent foll sp for Freizeit Centrum. Site on R on leaving vill, well sp. Med, mkd pitch, some hdstg, unshd; htd wc; chem disp; shwrs inc; el pnts (16A) €1.70 or metered; Indtte (inc dryer); shop 500m; tradsmn; rest; snacks; bar; playgrnd; covrd pool; fishing; TV; 75% statics; dogs €1.50; poss v cr; Eng spkn; adv bkg; quiet. "Scenic, well-kept site with stream & sm lake adj; clean, modern facs but poss stretched if site full." ♦ € 16.50 2011*

ZIEROW see Wismar *2E2*

GERMANY

GERMANY

⊞ **ZINGST AM DARSS** *2F1* (500m W Coastal) *54.44055, 12.66031* **Camping am Freesenbruch, Am Bahndamm 1, 18374 Zingst-am-Darss [(038232) 15786; fax 15710; info@camping-zingst.de; www.camping-zingst.de]** On rd 105/E22 at Löbnitz take rd thro Barth to Zingst; site on coast rd. Lge, mkd pitch, pt shd; wc; chem disp; mv service pnt; shwrs inc; el pnts (16A) metered + conn fee; lndtte; shop; rest; snacks; bar; playgrnd; beach adj; games area; cycle hire; entmnt; 20% statics; dogs €2; sep car park; o'night facs for m'vans; poss cr; adv bkg; quiet; ccard acc; CCI. "Well-maintained site in National Park; sep fr beach by sea wall & rd; well-maintained; card operated barrier." ♦ € 20.00 2009*

⊞ **ZISLOW** *2F2* (2km N Rural) *53.44555, 12.31083* **Naturcamping Zwei Seen, Waldchaussee 2, 17209 Zislow [(039924) 2550; fax 2062; info@zwei-seen-naturcamping.de; www.zwei-seen-naturcamping.de]** A19/E55 exit 17 dir Adamshoffnung. Turn R at x-rds in 4km. Site sp. Also sp fr W of Stuer on B198.. Lge, pt shd; wc; chem disp; mv service pnt; shwrs €0.50; el pnts (6A) €2; lndtte (inc dryer); shop; tradsmn; rest; snacks; bar; playgrnd; lake sw; watersports; games area; cycle hire; wifi; entmnt; 40% statics; dogs €2.50; phone; poss cr; Eng spkn; adv bkg; quiet; ccard acc; red CCI. "Ideal for country lovers; remote spot; vg lakeside pitches." ♦ € 17.50 2010*

⊞ **ZITTAU** *2H4* (3km S Rural) *50.8943, 14.77005* **See-Camping Zittauer Gebirge, Zur Landesgartenschau 2, 02785 Olbersdorf [(03583) 69629-2; fax 696293; info@seecamping-zittau.com; www.seecamping-zittau.com]** Fr Zittau foll Olbersdorfer See sp, site on lakeside. Lge, sl, unshd; wc; chem disp; shwrs €0.70; el pnts (10A) €2; lndtte (inc dryer); shop; tradsmn; rest, snacks, bar adj; lake sw adj; entmnt; 10% statics; dogs €2; Eng spkn; quiet; ccard acc; CCI. "Excel san facs; excel base for hill walking; close Polish & Czech borders." ♦ € 19.00 2010*

⊞ **ZORGE** *2E4* (1km NE Urban) *51.64176, 10.65083* **Camping im Waldwinkel, Im Kunzental 2, 37449 Zorge [(05586) 1048; fax 8113]** Fr N via Bad Harzburg, Braunlage, Hohegeiss, turn L at ent to Zorge vill, site sp dir 'Schwimmbad'. Fr S on B243, turn N at Bad Sachsa, dir Walkenried & Zorge, turn R in vill. Med, pt sl, unshd; wc; chem disp; mv service pnt; shwrs; baby rm; el pnts (16A) metered + conn fee; gas; lndtte (inc dryer); shop 1km; rest, snacks adj; playgrnd; htd pool 200m; tennis; skilift 4km; skibus; entmnt; TV; dogs €1; o'night area for m'vans; adv bkg; quiet; red CCI. "Beautiful location." ♦ € 16.00 2010*

ZWEIBRUCKEN *3B3* (1km E Urban) *49.25368, 7.37736* **Campingplatz Zweibrücken, Geschwister-Scholl-Allee 11, 66482 Zweibrücken [(06332) 482984; info@campingplatz-zw.de; www.campingplatz-zw.de]** Exit A8 junc 32 for Zweibrücken town cent. Sp infrequent so foll sp to Rosegarten site beyond show-jumping arena. Turn R at camping sp immed over bdge. Med, unshd; wc; chem disp; shwrs inc; el pnts (10A) metered + conn fee; lndtte; shop 300m; rest; snacks; playgrnd; htd pool 150m; rv & beach adj; cycle hire; wifi; 50% statics; dogs €1; noisy at w/end; red CCI. "Poss diff access due parked cars for sw pool; 15 min walk to town cent; gd NH." ♦ 1 Apr-30 Sep. € 21.90 2009*

ZWEIBRUCKEN *3B3* (3km SW Rural) *49.20638, 7.33111* **Camping Hengstbacher-Mühle, Hengstbacher Mühle 1, 66482 Zweibrücken-Mittelbach [(06332) 18128; fax 904001]** Fr A8 exit junc 33 onto B424 sp Zweibrücken-Ixheim & Mittelbach. At T-junc turn R dir Bitsch & in 50m turn R at camping sp. Site on L in 4km after end of Mittelbach vill. Sm, pt shd; wc; chem disp; mv service pnt; shwrs inc; el pnts (15A) €2.50 or metered (poss rev pol); shops 4km; 70% statics in sep area; liable to flooding; Eng spkn; quiet. "Friendly owner; lovely setting; basic site but clean san facs; gd NH." 15 Apr-31 Oct. € 10.50 2009*

ZWEIBRUCKEN *3B3* (11km SW Rural) *49.15888, 7.24388* **Camping am Schwimmbad, Am Campingplatz 1, 66453 Gersheim-Walsheim [(06843) 1030; fax 80138; freizeitbetrieb@gersheim.de; www.gersheim.de]** Fr A8/E50 exit junc 9 onto B423 dor Blieskastel. In Webenheim turn L twd Gersheim, after 11km turn L for Walsheim. Site on L beyond vill. Med, pt sl, pt shd; wc; chem disp; shwrs inc; el pnts €2 or metered; lndtte (inc dryer); shop in vill; tradsmn; rest, bar adj; BBQ; htd pool adj; 85% statics; dogs €0.50; phone; poss cr; adv bkg; quiet; red CCI. "Helpful warden; sep area for tourers; pleasant countryside; walking & cycle paths nr; site barrier clsd 1300-1500 & 2200." ♦ 15 Mar-15 Oct. € 14.00 2010*

⊞ **ZWIESEL** *4G3* (1.5km E Rural) *49.02611, 13.22055* **Azur Ferienzentrum Bayerischer Wald, Waldesruhweg 34, 94227 Zwiesel [(09922) 802595; fax 802594; zwiesel@azur-camping.de; www.azur-camping.de/zwiesel]** App on B11 fr Regen, thro Zwiesel, sp fr S side of town. V lge, mkd pitch, pt sl, unshd; wc; chem disp; mv service pnt; shwrs inc; el pnts (16A) €2.50; gas; lndtte; shop; rest; snacks 2.5km; bar; playgrnd; htd, covrd pool 200m; health spa facs; skilift 3km; ice rink; golf 3km; wifi; 30% statics; dogs €2.80; poss cr; adv bkg; quiet; ccard acc; red long stay/CCI. "Close to National Park in Bavarian Forest; clsd 1300-1500." ♦ € 20.00 lovely setting; basic site but clean san facs; gd NH." 15 Apr-31 Oct. 2008*

Distances are shown in kilometres and are calculated from town/city centres along the most practical roads, although not necessarily taking the shortest route. 1km = 0.62miles

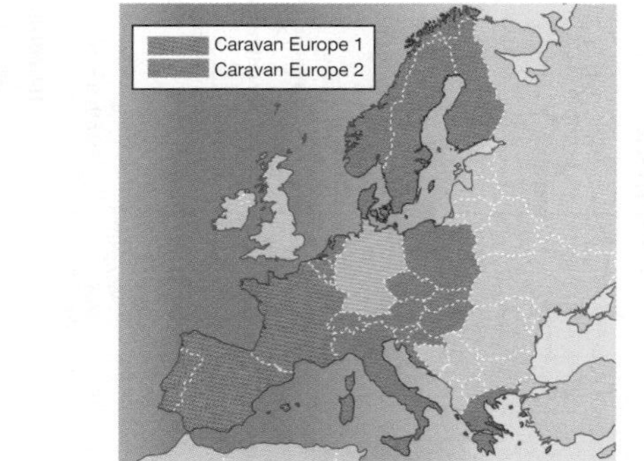

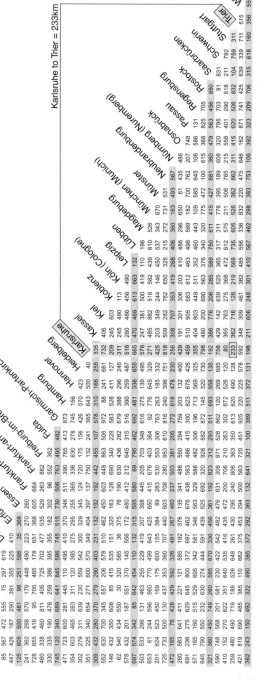

Karlsruhe to Trier = 233km

	Aachen	Augsburg	Bayreuth	Berlin	Bonn	Bremen	Dresden	Düsseldorf	Erfurt	Essen	Frankfurt-am-Main	Frankfurt-an-der-Oder	Freiburg-im-Breisgau	Fulda	Garmisch-Partenkirchen	Hamburg	Hannover	Heidelberg	Karlsruhe	Kassel	Kiel	Koblenz	Köln (Cologne)	Leipzig	Lübben	Magdeburg	München (Munich)	Münster	Neubrandenburg	Nürnberg (Nuremberg)	Osnabrück	Passau	Regensburg	Rostock	Saarbrücken	Schwerin	Stuttgart	Trier	Wilhelmshaven
Augsburg	565																																						
Bayreuth	538	243																																					
Berlin	642	600	356																																				
Bonn	90	482	406	585																																			
Bremen	369	723	580	380	340																																		
Dresden	651	473	237	216	611	479																																	
Düsseldorf	85	567	472	555	75	297	619																																
Erfurt	447	426	187	290	391	355	225	410																															
Essen	125	605	500	481	98	251	586	35	368																														
Frankfurt-am-Main	241	362	268	570	179	448	490	223	270	260																													
Frankfurt-an-der-Oder	728	655	416	95	705	465	178	651	368	605	664																												
Freiburg-im-Breisgau	460	338	460	811	405	725	702	477	535	529	263	882																											
Fulda	330	335	190	476	259	386	395	355	182	302	96	552	362																										
Garmisch-Partenkirchen	745	120	340	689	641	845	586	745	515	730	506	763	495	482																									
Hamburg	471	723	600	281	445	110	495	410	370	346	511	390	765	413	873																								
Hannover	354	603	465	263	311	120	385	275	295	255	365	336	630	278	745	156																							
Heidelberg	302	279	311	639	230	559	542	300	329	345	124	720	175	156	426	570	423																						
Karlsruhe	351	225	340	654	271	600	570	349	404	397	137	750	132	241	365	643	500	40																					
Kassel	309	432	280	370	279	290	403	231	132	192	192	442	455	107	578	310	166	255	335																				
Kiel	552	830	700	345	557	206	578	510	462	450	603	448	863	506	972	88	241	661	732	406																			
Koblenz	146	432	350	608	85	415	535	151	320	163	128	690	340	228	583	526	411	127	209	245	603																		
Köln (Cologne)	62	540	434	550	30	320	585	36	375	76	190	630	436	282	679	386	296	246	311	245	490	113																	
Leipzig	578	432	201	187	551	370	145	556	172	480	412	212	645	315	516	390	259	487	516	280	486	456	490																
Lübben	697	574	342	85	642	454	110	132	315	595	580	69	795	462	692	481	336	655	665	470	469	613	663	132															
Magdeburg	503	533	296	131	463	255	229	419	207	388	445	205	703	348	616	275	139	495	578	247	381	500	419	110	196														
München (Munich)	653	61	244	596	560	770	499	643	425	650	415	676	403	384	92	776	645	329	271	485	882	516	582	439	610	526													
Münster	201	624	523	450	169	175	600	155	384	89	283	530	553	306	763	263	185	332	425	203	349	244	146	450	537	343	670												
Neubrandenburg	725	733	500	130	437	353	360	707	440	603	708	280	953	610	816	240	396	751	818	509	282	762	650	325	215	272	731	531											
Nürnberg (Nuremberg)	472	185	76	428	429	592	326	481	267	460	237	503	381	205	272	618	478	230	256	308	707	353	419	268	406	360	163	493	567										
Osnabrück	260	583	641	411	221	121	585	192	376	135	341	488	550	294	759	203	132	400	429	191	301	306	203	410	486	296	650	61	435	486									
Passau	691	236	275	629	645	800	372	697	462	676	438	563	486	415	300	823	678	426	459	510	905	583	612	463	498	569	182	700	762	207	748								
Regensburg	571	165	160	515	529	695	342	581	346	563	329	588	482	306	196	713	569	325	355	404	803	449	511	352	460	443	109	585	645	108	586	131							
Rostock	645	790	550	232	630	274	444	591	439	525	692	320	926	582	872	145	320	730	798	480	200	690	563	376	340	320	775	472	100	615	368	825	705						
Saarbrücken	321	360	450	749	260	585	670	330	456	361	192	823	312	293	511	693	558	135	192	386	776	206	285	589	750	611	415	427	881	360	479	563	456	850					
Schwerin	590	748	568	201	581	230	422	542	482	476	631	308	871	528	862	120	269	685	756	429	142	639	525	365	317	311	776	395	189	608	320	795	703	91	831				
Stuttgart	410	152	270	622	351	640	535	416	435	472	200	706	210	263	302	672	526	120	80	365	763	275	368	472	612	575	211	506	765	215	558	401	290	818	211	792			
Trier	259	480	490	719	188	526	648	261	430	295	240	806	363	350	613	620	490	128	233	362	716	128	219	569	735	605	526	362	862	311	415	620	506	832	104	759	311		
Wilhelmshaven	421	819	690	485	385	110	662	375	453	294	500	563	720	451	925	220	225	578	592	348	309	461	362	485	556	336	832	220	475	646	162	871	741	425	639	339	711	515	
Würzburg	362	243	150	492	322	490	385	372	292	363	132	641	321	100	389	511	372	131	196	211	606	248	301	410	567	462	298	383	753	106	392	323	209	706	315	618	160	356	559

All year site(s)
Seasonal site(s)
No sites listed
200m +
0–200m
0 20 40 60 80 100 kms
0 10 20 30 40 50 60 mls
© Collins Bartholomew Ltd 2011
NORTH SEA
DENMARK
NETHERLANDS
BELGIUM
Aabenraa
Westerland
Glücksburg (Ostsee)
Medelby
Flensburg
Kappeln
Lindaunis
Schleswig
Nordstrand
Husum
Laboe
Gettorf
KIEL
Hennstedt
Tellingstedt
Preetz
Langwedel
Büsum
Neumünster
Bad Bramstedt
Bad Segeberg
CUXHAVEN
Otterndorf
Wingst
Kollmar
Bensersiel
Norden
Hooksiel
Bad Bederkesa
Hechthausen
Schortens
WILHELMSHAVEN
HAMBURG
Geesthacht
Leer (Ostfriesland)
Westerstede
Groningen
Zeven
Heidenau
Lüneburg
Gyhum
Papenburg
BREMEN
Sottrum
Rotenburg (Wümme)
Bispingen
Ganderkesee
Soltau
Wildeshausen
Wietzendorf
Emmen
Walsrode
Hösseringen
Bergen
Haselünne
Engehausen
Winsen (Aller)
Celle
Wilsum
Rieste
Uetze
HANNOVER
Bad Bentheim
Hörstel
Mettingen
Ibbenbüren
OSNABRÜCK
Porta Westfalica
Peine
Enschede
Melle
Wettringen
Greven
Lengerich
Herford
Rinteln
Hameln
Vlotho
Arnhem
Bielefeld
Lemgo
Salzhemmendorf
MÜNSTER
Schloss Holte-Stukenbrock
Bad Pyrmont
Nijmegen
Bad Gandersheim
Dülmen
Holzminden
Clausthal-Zellerfeld
Kalkar
Höxter
Osterode am Harz
Hamm
Northeim
Gelsenkirchen
Dortmund
Soest
Trendelburg
Gieselwerder
ESSEN
Dransfeld
Eindhoven
Warburg
Hannoversch Münden
Hattingen
Grefrath
Brüggen
Meschede
Zierenberg
Witzenhausen
DÜSSELDORF
KASSEL
Korbach
Solingen
Radevormwald
Naumburg (Hessen)
Eschwege
Hückeswagen
Bad Wildungen
Spangenberg
Olpe
Maastricht
KÖLN
Rotenburg an der Fulda
Eisenach
AACHEN
Brühl
Marburg an der Lahn
Kirchheim
Nideggen
BONN
Bad Honnef
Alsfeld
Urnshausen
Liège
Simmerath
Monschau
Bad Neuenahr-Ahrweiler
Remagen
Hünfeld
Schleiden
Wetzlar
Grünberg
A
B
C
D
1
2
3
4

Map 1

© Collins Bartholomew Ltd 2011

NETHERLANDS
Eindhoven
BELGIUM
LUXEMBOURG
FRANCE
SWITZERLAND
Essen
Dortmund
Grefrath
Hattingen
Brüggen
Düsseldorf
Radevormwald
Solingen
Hückeswagen
Köln
Maastricht
Aachen
Brühl
Bonn
Liège
Nideggen
Bad Honnef
Simmerath
Monschau
Remagen
Schleiden
Altenahr
Bad Neuenahr-Ahrweiler
Waldbreitbach
Stadtkyll
Dorsel
Mendig
Montabaur
Koblenz
Bad Ems
Limburg an der Lahn
Prüm
Gerolstein
Brodenbach
Lahnstein
Daun
Burgen
Boppard
Cochem
St Goarshausen
Waxweiler
Ernst
Lingerhahn
Neuerburg
Neef
Oberwesel
Bitburg
Wittlich
Zell
Kastellaun
Lorch
Mainz
Irrel
Bernkastel-Kues
Rüdesheim
Echternacherbrück
Schweich
Minheim
Trittenheim
Bingen am Rhein
Trier
Idar-Oberstein
Bad Kreuznach
Luxembourg
Reinsfeld
Bad Sobernheim
Saarburg
Birkenfeld
Rockenhausen
Nennig
Nohfelden
Wolfstein
Losheim am See
Schönenberg-Kubelberg
Saarlouis
Neunkirchen
Bad Dürkheim
Trippstadt
Neustadt
Saarbrücken
Kirkel
Zweibrücken
Pirmasens
Dahn
Metz
Nancy
Attendorn
Olpe
Meschede
Marburg an der Lahn
Wetzlar
Weilburg
Grünberg
Trendelburg
Gieselwerder
Warburg
Dransfeld
Hannoversch Münden
Zierenberg
Kassel
Witzenhausen
Korbach
Eschwege
Bad Wildungen
Spangenberg
Rotenburg an der Fulda
Eisen
Kirchheim
Alsfeld
Urnshausen
Hünfeld
Fulda
Schotten
Ehrenberg
Gersfeld (Rhön)
Meinin
Bischofsheim
Bad Kissingen
Hanau
Gräfendorf
Frankfurt am Main
Gemünden am Main
Mörfelden
Neustadt am Main
Marktheidenfeld
Dettelb
Wertheim
Würzburg
Miltenberg
Kitzingen
Fürth
Frickenhausen am Main
Weinheim
Hammelbach
Amorbach
Bad Mergentheim
Uffenheim
Mannheim
Eberbach
Creglingen
Heidelberg
Schönau (Rhein-Neckar)
Neckargerach
Rothenburg ob der Tauber
Speyer
Neckarelz
Wiesloch
Schillingsfürst
Landau in der Pfalz
Östringen
Neckarsulm
Pfedelbach
Schwäbisch Ha
Karlsruhe
Bretten
Löwenstein
Dinkelsbü
Rosenberg
Ettlingen
Ellwangen (Jagst)
Malsch
Pforzheim
Schömberg
Abtsgmünd
Rheinmünster
Baden-Baden
Stuttgart
Bühl
Bad Wildbad im Schwarzwald
Calw
Göppingen
Strasbourg
Achern
Kehl
Tübingen
Hohenstadt
Freudenstadt
Westerheim
Günzbu
Bad Urach
Leipheim
Bad Rippoldsau
Horb am Neckar
Bad Peterstal
Alpirsbach
Laichingen
Lahr (Schwarzwald)
Wolfach
Schiltach
Herbolzheim
Haslach im Kinzigtal
Illertissen
Riegel am Kaiserstuhl
Waldkirch
Breisach am Rhein
Hausen im Tal
Furtwangen
Sigmaringen
Freiburg im Breisgau
Bad Dürrheim
Titisee-Neustadt
Memmingen
Neuenburg am Rhein
Staufen im Breisgau
Donaueschingen
Münstertal
Todtnau
Engen
Stockach
Sulzburg
Tengen
Überlingen
Salem
Steinenstadt
Schluchsee
Meersburg
Ravensburg
Kemp (Allgä
Mulhouse
Schönau im Schwarzwald
Radolfzell am Bodensee
Markdorf
Konstanz
Lörrach
Lindenberg im Allgäu
Isny in Allgä
Waldshut
Jestetten
Friedrichshafen
Basel
Kressbronn am Bodensee
Immenstadt im Allgäu
Lindau (Bodensee)
Sonthofen
Oberstd
Zürich
Bludenz
0 20 40 60 80 100 kms
0 10 20 30 40 50 60 mls
N
W
E
S
All year site(s)
Seasonal site(s)
No sites listed
200m +
0–200m
© Collins Bartholomew Ltd 2011

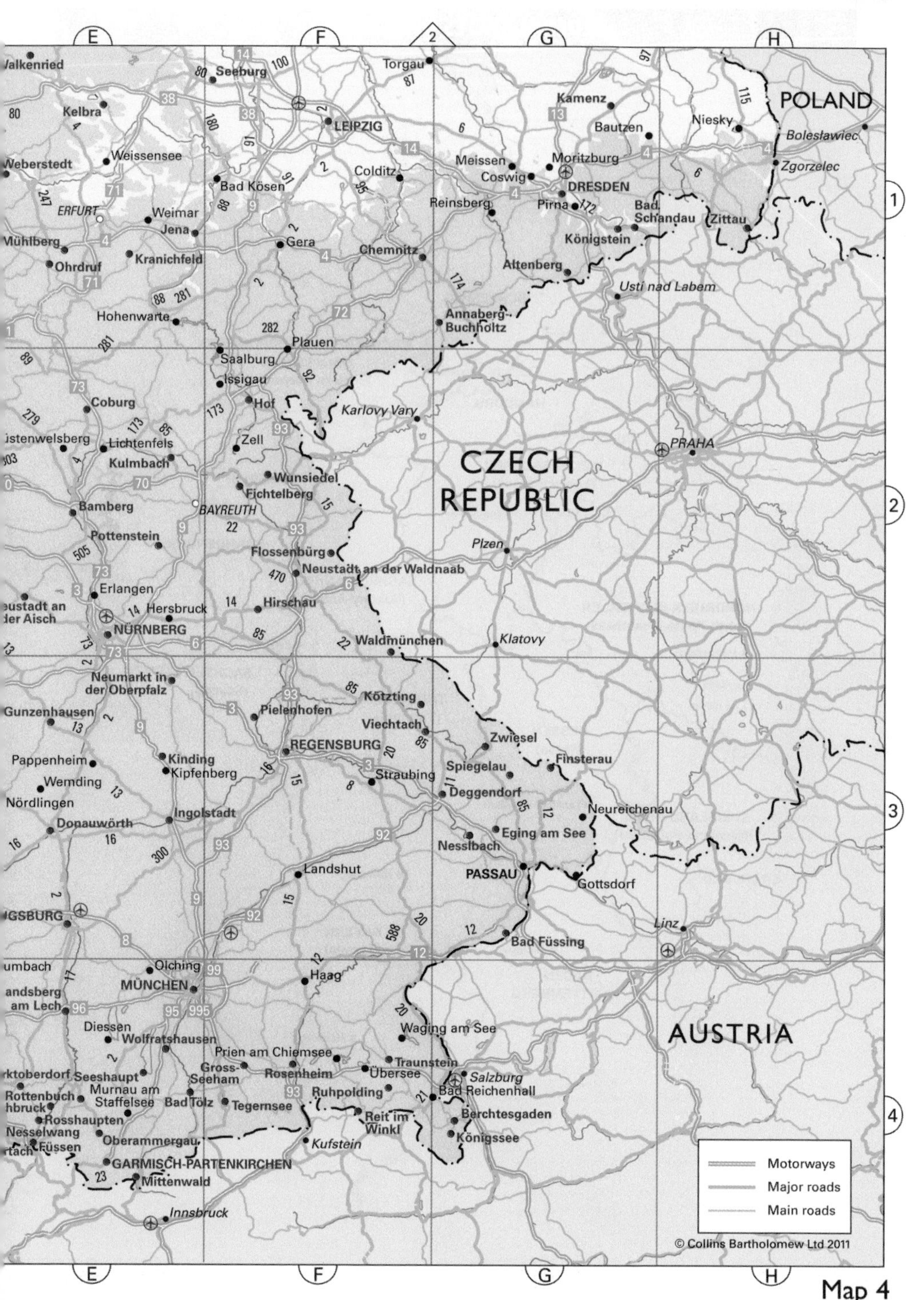
POLAND
CZECH REPUBLIC
AUSTRIA
LEIPZIG
DRESDEN
NÜRNBERG
REGENSBURG
PASSAU
MÜNCHEN
PRAHA
Plzen
Karlovy Vary
Salzburg
Innsbruck
Linz
Motorways
Major roads
Main roads
© Collins Bartholomew Ltd 2011

FEDERAL STATES OF GERMANY

Greece

Country Introduction

© iStockphoto.com/Suze Piat

Delphi, Greece

Population (approx): 10.7 million

Capital: Athens (population approx 3.7 million)

Area: 238,537 sq km (inc islands)

Bordered by: Albania, Bulgaria, Macedonia, Turkey

Coastline: 13,676km

Terrain: Mainly mountain ranges extending into the sea as peninsulas and chains of islands

Climate: Warm mediterranean climate; hot, dry summers; mild, wet winters in the south, colder in the north; rainy season November to March; winter temperatures can be severe in the mountains

Highest Point: Mount Olympus 2,917m

Language: Greek

Local Time: GMT or BST + 2, i.e. 2 hours ahead of the UK all year

Currency: Euros divided into 100 cents; £1 = €1.14, €1 = 87 pence (September 2011)

Telephoning: From the UK dial 0030 and the full area code of the number you are calling. All landline area codes start with a number 2 and mobile numbers with a 6. To call the UK from Greece dial 0044, omitting the initial zero of the area code

Emergency numbers: Police 112; Fire brigade 112; Ambulance 112. Operators speak English. Dial 171 for emergency tourist police.

Public Holidays 2012

Jan 1, 6, 30; Feb 27; Mar 25; Apr 13, 15, 16; May 1; Jun 3, 4; Aug 15; Oct 28; Nov 17; Dec 25, 26.

Public Holidays 2013

Jan 1, 6; Mar 18, 25; May 1, 3, 5, 6; Jun 23, 24; Aug 15; Oct 28; Dec 25, 26.

School summer holidays run from the beginning of July to the first week in September.

Tourist Office

GREEK NATIONAL TOURISM ORGANISATION
4 CONDUIT STREET, LONDON W1S 2DJ
Tel: 020 7495 9300
www.visitgreece.gr
visitgreece@gnto.gr

The following introduction to Greece should be read in conjunction with the important information contained in the Handbook chapters at the front of this guide.

Camping and Caravanning

There are over 340 campsites licensed by the Greek National Tourist Office. These can be recognised by a sign displaying the organisation's blue emblem. Most are open from April until the end of October, but those near popular tourist areas stay open all year. There are other unlicensed sites but visitors to them cannot be assured of safe water treatment, fire prevention measures or swimming pool inspection.

The Camping Card International (CCI) is accepted at all sites and at some a discount will be given to holders of a CCI and members of AIT/FIA clubs on presentation of a membership card.

The Harmonie Campsite chain and the Sunshine Campsite chain operate over 60 campsites collectively and offer up to 20% discount to members. Details are available directly from campsites in the chains, or contact the Harmonie chain on tel (226) 5082888, www.greekcamping.gr and the Sunshine Camping Club on tel (27410) 25766 (summer), or tel (210) 8070834 (winter), email info@sunshine-campings.gr, www.sunshine-campings.gr

Casual/wild camping is not allowed outside official sites.

GREECE

Country Information

Electricity and Gas

Usually current on campsites varies between 4 and 16 amps. Plugs have two round pins. There are few CEE connections.

The full range of Campingaz cylinders are available from hypermarkets and other shops, but you may not be given a refundable deposit receipt. Recent visitors report that it is possible to have a gas cylinder refilled (The Caravan Club does not recommend this practice) but it may be taken away for a few days and may come back re-painted. Similarly, Campingaz cylinders may also be painted when exchanged and suppliers in other countries are understandably reluctant to accept them.

*See **Electricity and Gas** in the section **DURING YOUR STAY.***

Entry Formalities

Visas are not required by British or Irish passport holders for a stay of up to three months. Visitors planning to stay longer should contact the Greek Embassy in London before they travel www.greekembassy.org.uk

Regulations for Pets

*See **Pet Travel Scheme** under **Documents** in the section **PLANNING AND TRAVELLING.***

Medical Services

For minor complaints seek help at a pharmacy (farmakio). Staff are generally well trained and in major cities there is usually one member of staff in a pharmacy who speaks English. You should have no difficulty finding an English speaking doctor in large towns and resorts.

Medications containing codeine are restricted. If you are taking any regular medication containing it, you should carry a letter from your doctor and take no more than one month's supply into the country.

There are numerous public and private hospitals and medical centres of varying standards. Wards may be crowded and the standards of nursing and after care, particularly in the public health sector, are generally below what is normally acceptable in Britain. Doctors and facilities are generally good on the mainland, but may be limited on the islands. The public ambulance service will normally respond to any accident but there are severe shortages of ambulances on some islands.

Emergency treatment at public medical clinics (yiatria) and in state hospitals registered by the Greek Social Security Institute, IKA-ETAM, is free on presentation of a European Health Insurance Card (EHIC) but you may face a long wait. You will be charged for prescriptions so keep the adhesive labels from the medicines packages in order to claim a refund at an IKA-ETAM office. See www.ika.gr for a list of local offices.

You may consult a doctor or dentist privately but you will have to present your EHIC and pay all charges up front. You can then claim back the charges later from the IKA-ETAM.

You are strongly recommended to obtain comprehensive travel and medical insurance before travelling to Greece, such as The Caravan Club's Red Pennant Overseas Holiday Insurance – see www.caravanclub.co.uk/redpennant

If staying near a beach, ensure that you have plenty of insect repellent as sand flies are prevalent. Do not be tempted to befriend stray dogs as they often harbour diseases which may be passed to humans.

In 2011 cases of West Nile Virus were reported and The Health Protection Agency have also reported a small number of cases of maleria. The risk of catching malaria in Greece remains very low and as such it is currently advised that you do not need to take anti-malerials, however if you are visiting Greece make sure you take measures to prevent being bitten, which will also protect you against West Nile Virus.

If you experinece symptoms of maleria, which include fever, headache and muscle pain, seek medical advice immediately. As with any country that you plan to visit always check for updates before you travel.

If you enjoy hiking and outdoor sports you should seek medical advice before you travel about preventative measures and immunisation against tick-borne encephalitis, a potentially life-threatening and debilitating viral disease of the central nervous system which is endemic from spring to autumn. Lyme disease is an equally serious tick-borne infection for which there is no preventative vaccine. Ticks are found in rural and forested areas, particularly in long grass, bushes and hedgerows, and in scrubland and areas where animals wander.

If you think you might be at risk use an insect repellent containing DEET, wear long sleeves and long trousers, inspect the body for ticks after outdoor activity and remove with tweezers, and avoid unpasteurised dairy products in risk areas. See www.tickalert.org, email info@tickalert.org or telephone 01943 468010.

*See **Medical Matters** in the section **DURING YOUR STAY.***

Opening Hours

Banks – Mon-Fri 8am-2pm (1.30pm on Friday); 8am-6pm in tourist areas.

Museums – Check locally for opening hours. Normally closed on Tuesdays and sometimes on Mondays and some bank holidays.

Post Offices – Mon-Fri 8am-2pm; 8am-7pm in tourist areas; many in the Athens area open on Saturday mornings in summer months.

Shops – Mon-Fri 8am/8.30am/9am-2pm/4.30pm & on some days 5pm-8.30pm; Sat 8.30am-3pm; check locally as hours vary according to season.

Safety and Security

Normally visits to Greece are trouble-free, but the tourist season results in an increase in incidents of theft of passports, wallets, handbags, etc, particularly in areas or at events where crowds gather. The use of 'date-rape' drugs has also increased. Personal attacks are rare but visitors are advised to maintain the same level of personal security awareness as in the UK.

Take care when visiting well-known historical sites; they are the favoured haunts of pickpockets, bag-snatchers and muggers. Women should not walk alone at night and lone visitors are strongly advised never to accept lifts from strangers or passing acquaintances at any time.

Multi-lingual tourist police operate in most resorts offering information and help; they can be recognised by a 'Tourist Police' badge, together with a white cap band. There is also a 24-hour emergency helpline for tourists; dial 171 from anywhere in Greece.

Whilst the people of Greece are renowned for their hospitality, and the Greek police are used to dealing with large numbers of foreign tourists (especially on the islands) and do so in a low-key manner, indecent behaviour is not tolerated. The police have made it clear that they will not hesitate to arrest and courts impose heavy fines or prison sentences on people who behave indecently.

Certain areas near the Greek borders are militarily sensitive and you should not take photographs or take notes near military or official installations. Seek permission before photographing individuals.

There is a general threat from domestic terrorism. Attacks could be indiscriminate and against civilian targets in public places. Public protests are a standard feature of Greek politics and it is wise to avoid public gatherings and demonstrations which have the potential to turn violent and are often quelled with tear gas. Domestic anarchist groups remain active but so far their actions have primarily been directed against the Greek state, Greek institutions and commercial and diplomatic interests.

During especially hot and dry periods there is a danger of forest fires. Take care when visiting or driving through woodland areas. Ensure that cigarette ends are properly extinguished, do not light barbecues and do not leave rubbish or empty bottles behind.

Some motorists have encountered stowaway attempts while waiting to board ferries to Italy from Patras. Keep a watch on your vehicle(s).

In order to comply with the law, always ensure that you obtain a receipt for goods purchased. If you buy pirate CDs or DVDs you could be penalised heavily.

*See **Safety and Security** in the section **DURING YOUR STAY.***

British Embassy

1 PLOUTARCHOU STREET
106 75 ATHENS
Tel: (210) 7272600
http://ukingreece.fco.gov.uk

There are also British Consulates/Vice-Consulates/ Honorary Consulates in Corfu, Heraklion (Crete), Rhodes. Patras, Thessaloniki and Zakynthos.

Irish Embassy

7 LEOF.VAS
KONSTANTINOU, 106 74 ATHENA
Tel: (210) 7232771
www.embassyofireland.gr

There are also Honorary Consulates in Corfu, Crete, Rhodes and Thessaloniki.

Customs Regulations

Alcohol and Tobacco

*For import allowances for alcohol and tobacco products see **Customs Regulations** in the section **PLANNING AND TRAVELLING.***

Border Posts

Borders between Greece and Bulgaria and Turkey may be crossed only on official routes where a Customs office is situated. These are usually open day and night. Customs offices at ports are open from 7.30am to 3pm Monday to Friday.

Documents

Passport

Carry your passport at all times as a means of identification.

Vehicle(s)

Carry your vehicle registration certificate (V5C), insurance certificate and MOT certificate (if applicable) at all times.

*See **Documents** and **Insurance** in the section **PLANNING AND TRAVELLING.***

Money

Travellers' cheques are no longer widely accepted.

The major credit cards are accepted in hotels, restaurants and shops and at some petrol stations. They may not be accepted at shops in small towns or villages.

There is an extensive network of cash machines in major cities.

Carry your credit card issuers'/banks' 24-hour UK contact numbers in case of loss or theft.

Motoring

Accidents

While it is not essential to call the police in the case of an accident causing material damage only, motorists are advised to call at the nearest police station to give a description of the incident to the authorities.

Whenever an accident causes physical injury, drivers are required to stop immediately to give assistance to the injured and to call the police. Drivers who fail to meet these requirements are liable to imprisonment for up to three years.

If a visiting motorist has an accident, especially one causing injuries, they should inform the motoring organisation, ELPA, preferably at its head office in Athens, on (210) 606880, email: info@elpa.gr, as they should be able to offer you assistance.

Alcohol

The maximum permitted level of alcohol is 50 milligrams in 100 millilitres of blood, i.e. lower than that permitted in the UK (80 milligrams). A level of 20 milligrams in 100 millilitres of blood applies to drivers who have held a driving licence for less than two years and to motorcyclists. Police carry out random breath tests and refusal to take a test when asked by the police, and/or driving while over the legal limit, can incur high fines, withdrawal of your driving licence and even imprisonment.

Breakdown Service

The Automobile & Touring Club of Greece (ELPA) operates a roadside assistance service (OVELPA) 24 hours a day on all mainland Greek roads as well as on most islands. The number to dial from most towns in Greece is 10400.

Members of AIT/FIA affiliated clubs, such as The Caravan Club, should present their valid membership card in order to qualify for reduced charges for on-the-spot assistance and towing. Payment by credit card is accepted.

Essential Equipment

*See **Motoring – Equipment** in the section **PLANNING AND TRAVELLING.***

Warning Triangles

The placing of a warning triangle is compulsory in the event of an accident or a breakdown. It must be placed 100 metres behind the vehicle.

Child Restraint System

Children under three years of age must be seated in a suitable and approved child restraint. Children between the ages of 3 and 11 years old that are less than 1.35 metres in height must be seated in an appropriate child restraint for their size. From 12 years old children that are over 1.35 metres in height can wear an adult seat belt.

A rear facing child restraint can be placed in the front seat but only on condition that the airbag is deactivated.

Fuel

Petrol stations are usually open from 7am to 7pm; a few are open 24 hours. Some will accept credit cards but those offering cut-price fuel are unlikely to do so. In rural areas petrol stations may close in the evening and at weekends, so keep your tank topped up. There are no automatic petrol pumps operated with either credit cards or bank notes.

LPG (autogas) is available from a limited number of outlets.

*See also **Fuel** under **Motoring – Advice** in the section **PLANNING AND TRAVELLING.***

Parking

No parking is permitted in the Athens 'Green Zone' except where there is parking meters. Special parking sites in other areas have been reserved for short-term parking for tourists and caravans are also admitted.

There may be signs on the side of the road indicating where vehicles should be parked. Parking restrictions are indicated by yellow lines at the side of the road. The police are entitled to remove vehicles. They can also confiscate the number plates of vehicles parked illegally and, while this usually applies only to Greek-registered vehicles, drivers of foreign registered vehicles should nevertheless avoid illegal parking.

Parking is not permitted within three metres of a fire hydrant, five metres of an intersection, stop sign or traffic light, and fifteen metres of a bus stop, tram stop and level crossings.

*See also **Parking Facilities for the Disabled** under **Motoring – Advice** in the section **PLANNING AND TRAVELLING.***

Roads

The surfaces of all major roads and of the majority of other roads are in good condition. Some mountain roads, however, may be in poor condition and drivers must beware of unexpected potholes (especially on corners), precipitous, unguarded drops and single-carriageway bridges. Even on narrow mountain roads you may well encounter buses and coaches.

British motorists visiting Greece should be extra vigilant in view of the high incidence of road accidents. Driving standards are generally poorer than in the UK and you may well have to contend with dangerous overtaking, tailgating, weaving motorcycles and scooters, constant use of the horn, roaming pedestrians and generally erratic driving. Greece has one of the highest rate of road fatalities in Europe and overtaking and speeding are the commonest causes of accidents, particularly on single lane carriageways. Drive carefully and be aware of other drivers at all times.

August is the busiest month of the year for traffic and the A1/E75 between Athens and Thessalonika is recognised as one of the most dangerous routes, together with the road running through the Erimanthos mountains south of Kalavrita. Mountain roads in general can be dangerous owing to narrow carriageways, blind bends and unprotected embankments, so keep your speed down.

You are strongly advised against hiring motorcycles, scooters and mopeds, as drivers of these modes of transport are particularly at risk. The wearing of crash helmets is a legal requirement. Never hand over your passport when hiring a vehicle.

Greece has a high level of pedestrian fatalities. Where there is a shortage of parking spaces drivers park on pavements so that pedestrians are forced to walk in the road. Collisions between pedestrians and motorcycles are common.

Road Signs and Markings

Road signs conform to international conventions. Motorway signs have white lettering on a green background, signs on other roads are on a blue background. All motorways, major and secondary roads are signposted in Greek and English.

Some open roads have a white line on the nearside, and slower-moving vehicles are expected to pull across it to allow vehicles to overtake.

Traffic Jams

There is heavy rush hour traffic in and around the major cities and traffic jams are the norm in central Athens any time of day. During the summer months traffic to the coast may be heavy, particularly at weekends. Traffic jams may be encountered on the A1/E75 Athens to Thessalonika road and on the A8/E65 Athens to Patras road. Traffic may also be heavy near the ferry terminals to Italy and you should allow plenty of time when travelling to catch a ferry. Delays can be expected at border crossings

to Turkey and Bulgaria.

Speed Limits

*See **Speed Limits Table** under **Motoring – Advice** in the section **PLANNING AND TRAVELLING.***

Violation of Traffic Regulations

The Greek police are authorised to impose fines in cases of violation of traffic regulations, but they are not allowed to collect fines on-the-spot. Motorists must pay fines within ten days, otherwise legal proceedings will be started.

Motorways

There are over 2,000 km of motorways in Greece. Service areas provide petrol, a cafeteria and shops. The main motorways are A1 Agean, A2 Egnatia, A6 Attiki, A7 Peloponissos, A8 Pathe, A29 Kastorias. For further information visit *www.greek-motorway.net*

Motorway Tolls

Tolls are charged according to vehicle classification and distance travelled. By European standards the tolls are generally quite low. Cash is the preferred means of payment.

The Egnatia Highway

The 804 km Egnatia Highway (the A2), part of European route E90 linking the port of Igoumenitsa with the Turkish border at Kipoi, has undergone extensive upgrade and improvement in recent years. The route includes many bridges and tunnels with frequent emergency telephones for which the number to call from a landline or mobile phone is 1077. The road provides a continuous high speed link from west to east and will eventually connect with Istanbul. An electronic toll collection system is planned for the future.

Patras – Antirrio Bridge

A 2.8 km long toll suspension bridge between Rio (near Patras) and Antirrio links the Peloponnese with western central Greece and is part of the A8/E55 motorway. It has cut the journey time across the Gulf of Corinth – formerly only possible by ferry – to just five minutes. Tolls are charged.

Preveza – Aktio Tunnel

This undersea toll tunnel links Preveza with Aktio near Agios Nikolaos on the E55 along the west coast of mainland Greece and is part of a relatively fast, scenic route south from Igoumenitsa to central and southern regions.

Touring

Mainland Greece and most of the Greek islands that are popular with British tourists are in seismically active zones, and small earth tremors are common. Serious earthquakes are less frequent but can, and do, occur.

Greek cooking is excellent. Food tends to be simple, rarely involving sauces but making full use of local olive oil and charcoal grills. Along the coast the emphasis is on fish and seafood, and fresh vegetables and salads are a major part of the diet all over the country. Smoking is prohibited in bars and restaurants.

In restaurants, if the bill does not include a service charge, it is usual to leave a 10 to 20% tip. Taxi drivers do not normally expect a tip but it is customary to round up the fare.

The best known local wine is retsina but there is also a wide range of non-resinated wines. Beer is brewed under licence from German and Danish breweries; ouzo is a strong aniseed-flavoured aperitif.

The major Greek ports are Corfu, Igoumenitsa, Patras, Piraeus and Rhodes. Ferry services link these ports with Cyprus, Israel, Italy and Turkey. The routes from Ancona and Venice in Italy to Patras and Igoumenitsa are very popular and advance booking is recommended.

For further information contact:

VIAMARE TRAVEL LTD
SUITE 3, 447 KENTON ROAD, HARROW
MIDDX HA3 0XY
Tel: 020 8206 3420, Fax: 020 8206 1332
www.viamare.com
ferries@viamare.com

Some ferries on routes from Italy to Greece have 'camping on board' facilities whereby passengers are able to sleep in their caravan or motorhome. Mains hook-ups are available, together with showers and toilets.

There are 18 World Heritage Sites in Greece (with more under consideration), including such famous sites as the Acropolis in Athens, the archeological sites at Olympia and Mistras, and the old towns of Corfu and Rhodes. See www.worldheritagesite.org for more information. When visiting churches and monasteries dress conservatively, i.e. long trousers for men and no shorts, skimpy/sleeveless T-shirts or mini-skirts for women.

Local Travel

Greece has a modern, integrated public transport system, including an extensive metro, bus, tram and suburban railway network in and around Athens – see www.ametro.gr for a metro map. A metro system is under construction in Thessaloniki and is due for completion in 2014.

Buy bus/tram tickets from special booths at bus stops, newspaper kiosks or from metro stations.
A ticket is valid for a travel time of 90 minutes.

Taxis are relatively cheap. All licensed taxis are yellow and are equipped with meters (the fare is charged per kilometre) and display a card detailing tariffs and surcharges. In certain tourist areas, you may be asked to pay a predetermined (standard) amount for a ride to a specific destination. Taxis run on a share basis, so they often pick up other passengers on the journey.

There are numerous ferry and hydrofoil services from Piraeus to the Greek islands and between islands. Sailings are most frequent in the summer and it is well to book in advance. Useful websites for information on ferries around the islands are www.ferries.gr/greek-islands-ferry and www.greeceathensaegeaninfo.com (this website also contains a wealth of general information about visiting Greece).

All place names used in the Site Entry listings which follow and the spellings used are as found in Michelin's Europe Tourist & Motoring Atlas.

SITES IN GREECE

⊞ **AGIOI THEODOROI** *B3* (8km E Coastal) *37.95212, 23.17868* **Camping Glaros, Kineta, 19100 Agioi Theodoroi [(22960) 62805; info@camping-glaros.gr; www.camping-glaros.gr]** E fr Korinthos on A8 dir Athens, site sp. Med, pt sl, pt shd; wc; chem disp; shwrs; el pnts; lndtte; shop; rest; snacks; bar; cooking facs; playgrnd; sand beach; internet; some statics; dogs; quiet. "Well-situated for archeological sites; pleasant." (CChq acc) 2011*

AGIOS KONSTANTINOS see Kamena Vourla *B2*

AKRATA *B3* (2km W Coastal) **Akrata Beach Camping, Porrovitsa, 25006 Akrata [(26960) 31988; fax 34733; tzabcamp@otenet.gr; www.akrata-beach-camping.gr]** Bet Patra & Corinth exit E65 dir Akrata, then W on old national rd, thro Akrata. After 2km just over bdge site sp on R. Sm, hdstg, shd; wc; chem disp; mv service pnt; shwrs inc; el pnts (10A) €3.20; gas; lndtte; shop & 2km; tradsmn; snacks; bar; BBQ; cooking facs; shgl beach adj; 50% statics; dogs; phone; bus 2km; poss cr; Eng spkn; adv bkg; quiet; ccard acc; CCI. "V friendly, family-run site; helpful owners." ♦ 1 Apr-31 Oct. € 18.30 2008*

⊞ **ALEXANDROUPOLI** *C1* (1.5km W Coastal) *40.84679, 25.85614* **Camping Alexandroupolis Beach, Makris Ave, 68100 Alexandroupolis [tel/fax (25510) 28735; camping@ditea.gr; www.ditea.gr]** Site on coast - after drainage channel, at 2nd set traff lts close together. Lge, hdg/mkd pitch, pt hdstg, shd; wc (some cont); chem disp; shwrs inc; el pnts (8A) €3.60; gas; shop; snacks; bar; playgrnd; sand beach adj; watersports; tennis; games area; wifi; 20% statics; phone; Eng spkn; quiet but cr & noisy high ssn; red CCI. "Spacious, secure, well-run site; clean, hot shwrs; easy walk to pleasant town cent." € 18.50 2011*

ALISSOS see Patra *A2*

AMALIADA *A3* (6km SW Coastal) *37.75423, 21.30618* **Camping Palouki, Palouki-Amaliados, 27200 Amalias [(26220) 24942 or 24943; fax 24943; info@camping-palouki.gr; www.camping-palouki.gr]** Fr Patras take main coastal rd twds Pirgos; pass Amaliada turn-off & cont for approx 2km to x-rds with lge site sp. Turn R (W) & foll sp to beach & site, site ent on L. Med, hdg pitch, shd; htd wc; chem disp; mv service pnt; shwrs inc; el pnts (16A) €3.80; lndtte; shop; tradsmn; rest; snacks; bar; sand beach adj; TV; phone; Eng spkn; adv bkg; quiet, but some aircraft noise; red CCI. "Immac facs; well shd pitches; friendly family owners; excel rest; Sat mkt in Amaliada." ♦ € 21.00 2008*

AMALIADA *A3* (5km W Coastal) *37.76645, 21.29891* **Camping Kourouta, 27200 Kourouta [(26220) 22901; fax 24921; info@campingkourouta-bungalows.gr]** Fr main Pirgos-Patras rd turn W at Amaliada x-rds approx 20km NW of Pirgos; foll sp to site. Med, mkd pitch, pt shd; wc; chem disp; shwrs; el pnts (16A) €3.50; gas; lndtte; shop; tradsmn; rest; snacks; bar; playgrnd; sand beach adj; watersports; dogs; phone; Eng spkn; quiet; no ccard acc; CCI. "V friendly staff; beautiful beach." 1 Apr-31 Oct. € 20.80 2008*

ANTIRRIO see Nafpaktos *B2*

⊞ **ASPROVALTA** *B2* (6km NE Coastal) *40.75797, 23.75183* **Camping Achilles, 57021 Asprovalta [(23970) 22374 or 22384; fax 22859; achilleas@fastmail.gr]** On L of coast rd bet Asprovalta & Akrogiali. Lge, hdstg, pt sl, pt shd; wc; chem disp; shwrs; el pnts (6A) inc; lndry rm; shop & 2km; rest, snacks, bar adj; playgrnd; shgl beach adj; 25% statics; quiet; CCI. "Diff for lge o'fits due narr rds & o'hanging trees; site in need of maintenance; NH only." € 15.00 2008*

ASSINI see Nafplio *B3*

ATHENS see Athina *B3*

⊞ **ATHINA** *B3* (16km NE Urban) *38.09944, 23.79166* **Camping Nea Kifissia, Potamou 60, Adames, 14564 Athina [tel/fax (210) 8075579 or 6205646; camping@hol.gr; www.camping-neakifissia.gr]** Sp both dirs on E75 Athens-Lamia rd. Heading twd Athens exit at sp, to U-turn onto service rd then take 1st L & foll sp. Sm, hdg pitch, hdstg, terr, shd; wc; chem disp; shwrs inc; el pnts (10A) €4; lndry rm; shop 800m; pool high ssn; TV; 50% statics; dogs; phone; bus to metro stn 200m; poss cr; Eng spkn; aircraft, rlwy & rd noise; red CCI. "Conv base for Athens - metro at Kifissia; pleasant, quiet, well-run site; excel pool; clean san facs but tired; helpful recep staff; san facs down 30+ steps." € 28.00 2010*

⊞ **ATHINA** *B3* (7km NW Urban) *38.00916, 23.67236* **Camping Athens, 198 Leoforos Athinon, 12136 Peristeri [(210) 5814114 or 5814101 winter; fax 5820353; info@campingathens.com.gr; www.campingathens.com.gr]** Fr Corinth on E94 m'way/highway, stay on this rd to Athens o'skts; site is approx 4km past Dafni Monastery, set back on L of multi-lane rd, sh dist beyond end of underpass. Go past site to next traff lts where U-turn permitted. Fr N use old national rd (junc 8 if on toll m'way). Med, pt shd; wc (some cont); chem disp; mv service pnt; shwrs inc; el pnts (16A) €4; lndtte; shop, rest high ssn; snacks; bar; no BBQ; internet; TV; dogs; frequent bus to Athens; poss v cr; rd noise; ccard acc; red low ssn. "V dusty but well-managed site; gd san facs but poss insufficient high ssn; helpful staff; bus tickets to Athens sold; visitors rec not to use sat nav to find site, as it misdirects!" € 25.00 2008*

CHRISSA see Delfi *B2*

CORINTH see Korinthos *B3*

DASSIA see Corfu/Kerkira (Corfu Island) *A2*

DELFI *B2* (7km S Coastal) *38.42502, 22.45824* **Camping Ayannis, 33200 Itea-Kirra [(22650) 32555; fax 33870; m.anagnostakos@hotmail.com]** App Itea fr Delfi; 1km bef Itea take ring rd sp Desfina; site on R after 4km; ent site on rough track for 200m. Med, pt shd; wc (some cont); chem disp; 100% serviced pitches; shwrs inc; el pnts (6A) inc; gas; lndtte; shop; tradsmn; rest; snacks; bar; BBQ; sm shgl beach adj; Eng spkn; quiet; ccard acc; CCI. "Friendly owner; conv for Delphi; poss diff access lge o'fits; fair sh stay." 1 May-30 Oct. € 22.50 2010*

⊞ **DELFI** *B2* (1.5km W Rural) *38.4836, 22.4755* **Camping Apollon, 33054 Delfi [(22650) 82762 or 82750; fax 82888; apollon4@otenet.gr; www.apolloncamping.gr]** Site on N48 fr Delfi twd Itea & 1st of number of campsites on this rd. Site 25km fr Parnassus ski cent. Med, mkd pitch, pt sl, pt terr, pt shd; wc; chem disp; mv service pnt; shwrs inc; el pnts (16A) €3; gas; Indtte; shop; rest; bar; playgrnd; pool; TV; cycle hire; 30% statics; dogs free; phone; Harmonie Group site; poss cr; adv bkg; ccard acc; red CCI. "Magnificent views over mountains & Gulf of Corinth; site cooler than some other sites due to its elevation; vg site; popular with groups of students." ♦ € 22.50 2011*

⊞ **DELFI** *B2* (7km W Rural) *38.47305, 22.45926* **Chrissa Camping, 33055 Chrissa [(22650) 82050; fax 83148; info@chrissacamping.gr; www.chrissacamping.gr]** First site on Itea to Delfi rd, sp. Med, pt sl, terr, shd; wc; chem disp; shwrs inc; el pnts (10A) €4; gas; Indtte; shop; tradsmn; rest, snacks; bar; playgrnd; pools; paddling pool; shgl beach 10km; tennis 300m; games area; wifi; TV rm; adv bkg; quiet; ccard acc; red CCI. "Excel, scenic site." € 26.00 (CChq acc) 2011*

DELFI *B2* (4km NW Rural) *38.47868, 22.47461* **Camping Delphi, Itea Road, 33054 Delfi [(22650) 82209; fax 82363; info@delphicamping.com; www.delphicamping.com]** App fr Itea-Amfissa rd or Levadia; well sp. Med, terr, shd; wc; chem disp; mv service pnt; shwrs inc; el pnts (16A) €3.90; gas; Indtte; shop, rest, snacks high ssn; bar; pool; tennis; wifi; TV; dogs free; phone; bus to Delfi; Sunshine Group site; poss cr; adv bkg; ccard acc; red CCI. "Visit grotto, refuge of Parnassus; Delfi archaeological sites 3km; friendly, helpful staff; magnificent views; gd pool; tired facs; 20% discount for Minoan Line ticketholders; delightful site." 1 Apr-31 Oct. € 21.40 2008*

DREPANO see Nafplio *B3*

⊞ **EGIO** *B2* (10km NW Coastal) *38.32078, 21.97195* **Tsoli's Camping, Lambíri Egion, 25100 Lambiri [(26910) 31469 or 31621; fax 32473]** Fr A8/E65 exit Kamaras, site clearly sp 1km W of Lambiri. Med, hdstg, shd; wc; chem disp; shwrs inc; el pnts (16A) inc; gas; Indtte; shop; rest high ssn; snacks; bar; BBQ; playgrnd; shgl beach adj; watersports; fishing; boat-launching; entmnt; TV; 10% statics; phone; bus; sep car park; Eng spkn; adv bkg; some rd & rlwy noise & noise fr bar; ccard acc; red low ssn; CCI. "Bus & train service to Athens & Patras; gd site with gd facs in delightful position; few shd pitches for tourers & poss diff for high o'fits." € 24.00 2008*

⊞ **FINIKOUNDAS** *A3* (1km W Coastal) *36.80555, 21.79583* **Camping Thines, 24006 Finikoundas [(27230) 71200; fax 71027; thines@otenet.gr; www.finikounda.com]** Fr Methoni dir Finikoundas, turn R 1km bef vill, site on L. Sm, hdg/mkd pitch, hdstg, pt shd; wc; chem disp; shwrs inc; el pnts (6-10A); gas; Indtte; shop & 1km; tradsmn; snacks; bar; BBQ; cooking facs; sand beach adj; boat-launching; wifi; TV; no statics; dogs; poss cr; Eng spkn; quiet; ccard acc; red winter long stay; CCI. "Excel facs; helpful, friendly management; wonderful scenery & beach; lovely vill in walking dist." ♦ € 25.00 (CChq acc) 2011*

FINIKOUNDAS *A3* (2.5km W Coastal) *36.80525, 21.79097* **Camping Ammos, 24006 Finikoundas [(27230) 71262; fax 71124; ammos@finikunda.com]** Fr Pylos S to Methoni; then E on unclassifed rd 14km twd Finikoundas; sp on R bef town. Med, hdstg, pt sl, pt shd; wc; chem disp; shwrs inc; el pnts (16A); gas; Indtte; shop & 1km; tradsmn; rest; snacks; bar; playgrnd; sand beach adj; watersports; TV; Eng spkn; adv bkg; quiet; ccard not acc; CCI. "Vg; rec." 15 Apr-31 Oct. € 24.00 2008*

⊞ **FINIKOUNDAS** *A3* (3km W Coastal) *36.80283, 21.78098* **Camping Finikes, 24006 Finikoundas [(27230) 28524; fax 28525; camping-finikes@otenet.gr; www.finikescamping.gr]** Well sp on rd fr Methoni to Finikoundas. Med, hdg/mkd pitch, pt shd; wc; chem disp; mv service pnt; shwrs inc; el pnts (10A) €3.50; Indtte; shop; tradsmn; rest; snacks; bar; BBQ; cooking facs; playgrnd; beach adj; wifi; TV; dogs; poss cr; Eng spkn; adv bkg; quiet; red long stay; CCI. "Vg site; gd san facs; walk along beach to town." € 19.50 2008*

GERAKINI *B2* (1.5km SE Coastal) *40.26464, 23.46338* **Camping Kouyoni, 63100 Gerakini [tel/fax (23710) 52052; info@kouyoni.gr; www.kouyoni.gr]** Take main rd S fr Thessaloniki to Nea Moudania, then turn E twd Sithonia. Site is 18km on that rd past Gerakini on R, past filling stn. Well sp. Med, hdg/mkd pitch, pt sl, shd; wc; chem disp; shwrs inc; el pnts (16A) €3.30; Indtte; shop & 1km; rest; snacks; bar; BBQ; playgrnd; pool; paddling pool; sand beach adj; games area; boat-launching; TV rm; 30% statics; dogs; phone; adv bkg; quiet; red long stay/CCI. "Gd touring base set in olive grove; friendly owner; gd facs; gd beach; influx of w/enders high ssn." 24 Apr-30 Sep. € 25.90 2009*

GIALOVA see Pylos *A3*

GIANNITSOCHORI see Kyparissia *A3*

⊞ **GITHIO** *B3* (4km S Coastal) *36.72847, 22.54215* **Camping Mani Beach, Mavrovouni, 23200 Githio [(27330) 23450; fax 25451; info@manibeach.grr; www.manibeach.gr]** Fr Githio dir Aeropolis, site sp on L on Mavrovouni beach. Lge, hdg/mkd pitch, hdstg, shd; htd wc; chem disp; shwrs inc; el pnts (16A) €4; gas; Indtte; shop; tradsmn; rest; snacks; bar; BBQ; playgrnd; shgl beach adj; games area; wifi; cab TV; 10% statics; dogs; phone; Eng spkn; adv bkg; ccard acc; red long stay/snr citizens/CCI. "Less cr & noisy than other sites along this rd; set in olive grove; lovely mountain views; conv ferries to Crete; vg." ♦ € 22.00 2011*

⊞ **GITHIO** *B3* (4km SW Coastal) *36.72913, 22.54519* **Gythion Bay Camping, 23200 Githio [(27330) 22522; fax 23523; info@gythiocamping.gr; www.gythiocamping.gr]** Sp fr Githio town, on E of Githio-Areopolis rd. Med, shd; wc (some cont); chem disp; mv service pnt; shwrs inc; el pnts (16A) inc; gas; Indtte; shop; rest; snacks; bar; playgrnd; beach adj; surfing school; boating; games area; wifi; entmnt; TV; no dogs; poss cr; no adv bkg; quiet; Harmonie Group site; ccard acc; 10% red CCI. "Facs clean; mv service pnt up ramp - risk of grounding; site in orange grove; ferries to Crete in ssn." ♦ € 23.90 (CChq acc) 2009*

GREEK ISLANDS Campsites in towns on Greek Islands are listed together at the end of the Greek site entries.

GREECE

IERISSOS *B2* (500m NW Coastal) *40.40369, 23.87608* **Camping Ierissos, 63075 Ierissos [(23770) 21130; fax 21132; desa@ierissos.gr]** Sp at major x-rds in town cent. Med, mkd pitch, unshd; wc; chem disp (wc); shwrs inc; el pnts (10A) €3.15; Indtte; shop, rest, snacks, bar in town/on beach; BBQ; sand beach adj; 80% statics; dogs; poss cr; Eng spkn; poss noisy high ssn. "Fair sh stay; a few dogs roaming site." 1 May-30 Sep. € 15.50 2009*

IGOUMENITSA *A2* (7km SE Coastal) *39.47437, 20.23919* **Camping Kalami Beach, 46100 Plataria [(26650) 71211; fax 71245; info@campingkalamibeach.gr; www.campingkalamibeach.gr]** S fr Igoumenitsa on coast rd, turn sharp R at camping sp down lane to sea & site. Site is 4km N of Platariá. Lge, terr, pt shd; wc; chem disp; mv service pnt; shwrs inc; el pnts (10A) €3; gas; Indtte (inc dryer); shop; tradsmn; rest; snacks; bar; BBQ; shgl beach; watersports; games rm; wifi; TV; some statics; dogs; phone; poss cr; adv bkg; quiet but some rd noise; Sunshine Group site. "Access diff for lge o'fits due tight corners & sm pitches; ltd lge pitches & some diff due trees; pleasant, relaxing site; helpful staff; excel, clean san facs; 20% discount for Minoan Line ticketholders." 20 Mar-31 Oct. € 28.00 2011*

IGOUMENITSA *A2* (10km S Coastal) *39.46346, 20.26037* **Camping Elena's Beach, 46100 Platariá [(26650) 71031; fax 71414; bteo@altecnet.gr; www.epirus.com/campingelena]** Sp on Igoumenitsa-Preveza rd, 2km NW of Platariá. Med, hdstg, pt terr, pt shd; wc; chem disp; shwrs inc; el pnts (5A) inc; gas; Indtte; shop; tradsmn; rest; snacks; bar; BBQ; playgrnd; shgl beach adj; a few statics; dogs; phone; bus; adv bkg; quiet; red long stay; CCI. "Well-maintained, family-run, friendly site; clean, modern san facs; beautiful location with pitches next to sea; excel rest; conv ferries Corfu, Paxos." ♦ 1 Apr-31 Oct. € 22.50 2009*

IGOUMENITSA *A2* (14km S Coastal) *39.44390, 20.25813* **Nautilos Camping, 46100 Plataria [(26650) 71416; fax 71417; wassosf@otenet.gr]** S fr Igoumenitsa on coast rd to Plataria; turn R at end of Plataria Beach; site at top of hill with flags clearly visible, 2km SW of Plataria. Lge, mkd pitch, some hdstg, terr, pt sl, shd; wc; chem disp; shwrs inc; el pnts (16A) inc; gas; Indtte; shop; tradsmn; rest; bar; BBQ; cooking facs; playgrnd; pool; private beach; tennis; wifi; some statics; dogs; phone; Eng spkn; adv bkg; quiet; red CCI. "Helpful staff; lovely quiet site; picturesque setting." 1 Apr-20 Oct. € 27.50 2011*

IOANINA *A2* (1.5km NW Urban) *39.67799, 20.84279* **Camping Limnopoula, Kanari 10, 45001 Ioanina [(26510) 25265; fax 38060]** At Ioanina Nautical Club on Igoumenitsa rd at W o'skts of town on rd that runs along lake fr citadel; site well sp fr all dirs. Med, pt shd; wc; chem disp; shwrs inc; el pnts (10A) inc; gas; Indtte; shop; tradsmn; rest, snacks, bar adj; BBQ; playgrnd; watersports; dogs free; phone; Eng spkn; quiet. "Beautiful situation on lake, mountain views; excel touring base; helpful staff; gd facs; clean; san facs refurbished to excel standard; may close earlier; adv bkg acc 1-2 days ahead only low ssn; popular with groups low ssn; vg." 1 May-15 Oct. € 28.00 2011*

KALAMBAKA *A2* (2km SE Rural) *39.69017, 21.64564* **Camping International Rizos, Trikala Road, Meteora, 42200 Kalambaka [(24320) 22239; fax 22239; info@meteorarizoscamp.gr; www.meteorarizoscamp.gr]** Site visible on S of E92 rd. Med, hdg/mkd pitch, pt shd; htd wc; chem disp; shwrs inc; el pnts (16A); gas; Indtte; shop; rest; snacks; bar; playgrnd; pool; paddling pool; TV; bus to town; adv bkg; CCI. ♦ 1 Apr-31 Oct. 2010*

KALAMBAKA *A2* (2.5km SE Rural) *39.68250, 21.65510* **Camping Philoxenia, 42200 Kalambaka [(24320) 24466; fax 24944; philoxeniacamp@ath.forthnet.gr]** Site on N side of E92 Trikala rd, behind barrier. Med, some hdstg, shd; htd wc; chem disp; mv service pnt; shwrs inc; el pnts (6A) inc; gas; Indtte; shop; tradsmn; rest 1km; snacks; bar; BBQ; cooking facs; playgrnd; pool; paddling pool; waterslide; cycle hire; TV; 30% statics; dogs free; poss cr; Eng spkn adv bkg; quiet; ccard acc; red CCI. "Interesting area particularly during Easter religious festivals." ♦ 1 Mar-30 Nov. € 20.00 (CChq acc) 2011*

KALAMBAKA *A2* (1km NW Rural) *39.70820, 21.60866* **Camping Meteora Garden, 42200 Kastraki [(24320) 22727 or 75566; fax 23119; info@camping-meteora-garden.gr; www.camping-meteora-garden.gr]** App fr Trikala, turn L on ent & by-pass Kalambaka; site approx 1km on R, past town. App fr Ionanina, site on L approx 3km fr Grevena rd junc, shortly after sight of mountains. Med, shd; wc (some cont); chem disp; shwrs inc; el pnts (16A) €3 (poss no earth); Indtte; shop; rest; snacks; bar; playgrnd; pool; TV; dogs; phone; Sunshine Group site; poss cr; Eng spkn; adv bkg; quiet but rd noise; ccard acc; red CCI. "Friendly staff; rec for spectacular monasteries & Katara Pass." ♦ 1 Apr-31 Oct. € 21.00 2008*

⊞ **KALAMBAKA** *A2* (2km NW Rural) *39.7120, 21.61625* **Camping Vrachos, Meteoron Street, 42200 Kastraki [(24320) 22293; fax 23134; campingkastraki@yahoo.com; www.campingkastraki.gr]** Fr cent of Kalambaka take rd at app to vill of Kastraki. Site is 2km N of E92. Med, hdg/mkd pitch, pt sl, terr, shd; wc; chem disp; mv service pnt; shwrs inc; el pnts (16A) inc; gas; Indtte; shop; rest; snacks; bar; BBQ; cooking facs; playgrnd; pool; TV; internet (ltd); dogs free; phone; poss cr; Eng spkn; adv bkg; Harmonie Group site; red CCI. "Friendly management; clean san facs; vg views fr some pitches; ltd facs open in winter; conv for monasteries." ♦ € 18.00 2011*

KALAMITSI *B2* (600m N Coastal) *39.99230, 23.99138* **Camping Porto, 63072 Kalamitsi [tel/fax (23750) 41346; camporto@otenet.gr; www.kalamitsi.com]** Site sp on coast rd on S tip of Sithonia peninsula. Sharp R turn into Kalamitsi fr W. Med, mkd pitch, pt shd; wc; chem disp; shwrs inc; el pnts (6A) €2; Indtte; supmkt; tradsmn; rest, snacks, bar & 500m; sand beach 300m; internet; 20% statics; phone; poss cr; Eng spkn; CCI. "Excel, clean beach; scuba-diving & snorkelling cent." 1 May-31 Oct. € 28.00 2008*

KALIVIA VARIKOU see Plaka Litohorou *B2*

GREECE

KAMENA VOURLA *B2* (5km N Coastal) *38.82310, 22.71543* **Venezuela Camping, Paralia, Agios Serafeim; 35009 Malos [tel/fax (22350) 41691; camping@venezuela.gr; www.venezuela.gr]** Fr Lamia on E75, turn L twd Skarfeia & foll site sp. Fr Athens turn R sp Agios Serafeim, site sp. Med, hdg/mkd pitch, some hdstg, shd; wc; chem disp; shwrs inc; el pnts (10A) €4; shop; tradsmn; rest; snacks; bar; cooking facs; beach adj; wifi; TV; dogs; phone; Eng spkn; adv bkg; quiet; CCI. "Conv NH bet Athens & N; peaceful." 1 May-30 Sep. € 20.00 2011*

KARDAMILI see Stoupa *B3*

⊞ **KASSANDRIA** *B2* (10km SW Coastal) *39.96416, 23.36472* **Camping Kalandra, 63077 Possidi [(23740) 41345; fax 41123]** Fr Thessaloniki foll sp to Nea Moudania, down peninsula to Kalithea, W to Kassandria, S thro Fourka, W to Kalandra, fork R to Possidi & foll sps to end of rd. Lge, pt shd; wc; chem disp; shwrs; el pnts (15A); gas; lndtte; shop; rest; snacks; bar; sand beach adj; no adv bkg; 40% statics; dogs; red CCI. "Quiet but fills up end Jun for Greek hols." 2009*

KASTRAKI see Kalambaka *A2*

KATAFOURKO *A2* (Coastal) *38.99256, 21.15525* **Camping Stratis Beach, 30500 Katafourko [(26420) 51123; fax 51165; harmocamp@europe.com; www.camping.gr/stratis]** Fr N, site on R 25km S of Arta, after vill of Katafourko. Fr S, site on L bef Katafourko, via diff hairpin for lge o'fits. Med, pt shd; wc; chem disp; shwrs inc; el pnts (4A); gas; shop; rest 200m; snacks; bar; sand beach down 110 steps; adv bkg; quiet. 15 Apr-15 Oct. 2008*

KATO ALISSOS see Patra *A2*

KATO GATZEA see Volos *B2*

⊞ **KAVALA** *C1* (4km SW Urban/Coastal) *40.91573, 24.37851* **Camping Multiplex Batis, 65000 Kavala [(2510) 243051; fax 245690; nfo@batis-sa.gr; www.batis-sa.gr]** On W app to town on old coast rd, ent on a curving hill. Med, hdg/mkd pitch, pt sl, shd; htd wc; chem disp; shwrs inc; el pnts (6A) €4; lndry rm; shop; tradsmn; rest; snacks; bar; pool; paddling pool; sand beach adj; entmnt; phone; bus; poss cr; Eng spkn; adv bkg; ccard acc; red CCI. "Beautiful location but v developed; conv ferry to Thassos & archaeological sites; clean facs but site poss unkempt low ssn; vg." ♦ € 26.00 2009*

KERAMOTI *C1* (Coastal) **Camping Keramoti, 64011 Keramoti [(25910) 51279]** E fr Kavála on E90, turn S to Karamoti, site well sp fr town cent. Med, pt shd; wc; chem disp; shwrs inc; el pnts (10A) inc; shop, rest, snacks, bar in town; sand beach adj; 10% statics; Eng spkn; CCI. "Vg site; conv ferry to Thassos; beware soft sand on pitches." 15 Jun-15 Sep. € 13.50 2008*

KORINTHOS *B3* (5km SE Coastal) *37.88886, 23.00575* **Camping Isthmia Beach, Epidauros, 20100 Isthmia [(27410) 37447 or 37720; fax 37710; info@campingisthmia.gr; www.campingisthmia.gr]** Fr Athens/Patras highway 8/E94 cross Corinth canal & turn S onto rd dir Epidaurus; site after 4km on L of rd; sp. Med, mkd pitch, shd; wc; chem disp; mv service pnt; shwrs inc; el pnts (10A) €3.90; gas; lndtte; shop & 3km; rest, bar (high ssn); cooking facs; playgrnd; pool adj; shgl beach adj; TV; no dogs Jul & Aug; poss cr; adv bkg; quiet; Harmonie Group site; ccard acc; red CCI. "Excel beach; conv Corinth Canal; discount for Blue Star/Superfast ferry ticket holders; lovely site." 1 Apr-15 Oct. € 21.00 2008*

KORINTHOS *B3* (5km W Coastal/Urban) *37.93470, 22.86543* **Blue Dolphin Camping, 20006 Lecheon [(27410) 25766 or 25767; fax 85959; info@camping-blue-dolphin.gr; www.camping-blue-dolphin.gr]** Best app fr E to avoid town; Fr A8 exit sp Ancient Corinth, then N (R) to T-junc end of rd, W (R) past pipe factory, sp 400m N (R) at bottom of bdge sl. Fr W take exit sp Ancient Corinth after toll point. Fr Old National rd turn N (L) immed over rlwy bdge bef pipe factory. Fr Corinth foll old National rd twd Patras, past pipe factory. Med, mkd pitch, hdstg, pt shd; wc; chem disp; shwrs inc; el pnts (6A) €3.50; gas; lndtte; shop; tradsmn; rest; snacks; bar; BBQ; playgrnd; shgl beach; games area; wifi; TV; dogs; Sunshine Group site; Eng spkn; quiet; ccard acc; red CCI. "V obliging owners; pleasant site; sm pitches." ♦ 1 Apr-30 Oct. € 22.50 2011*

KORONI *B3* (200m S Coastal) *36.79932, 21.95013* **Camping Koroni, 24004 Koroni [(27250) 22119; fax 22884; info@koronicamping.com; www.koronicamping.com]** Sp on Kalamata to Koroni rd. Med, mkd pitch, pt sl, terr, shd; wc; shwrs inc; el pnts (6A) €4; lndtte; shop; rest; snacks; bar; cooking facs; pool; sand beach adj; wifi; TV; dogs; phone; site clsd Nov; Sunshine Group site; Eng spkn; red CCI. "Pleasant site; friendly owners; basic but adequate facs; gd pool; easy walk to lovely fishing vill; dusty in summer." 1 Mar-20 Oct. € 25.00 2009*

⊞ **KYLLINI** *A3* (10km S Coastal) *37.83828, 21.12972* **Camping Aginara Beach, Lygia, 27050 Loutra Kyllinis [(26230) 96211; fax 96271; info@camping-aginara.gr; www.camping-aginara.gr]** S fr Patras on E55 twds Pyrgos; exit Gastouni & turn W thro Vartholomio twd Loutra Kyllinis; turn L about 3km bef Kyllinis then foll sps. Lge, hdg pitch, hdstg, pt sl, shd; wc; chem disp; mv service pnt; shwrs inc; el pnts (10A); gas; lndtte; shop; tradsmn; rest; snacks; bar; BBQ; playgrnd; sand/shgl beach adj; watersports; wifi; TV; 25% statics; dogs; phone; Eng spkn; adv bkg; quiet; ccard acc; red CCI. "Friendly proprietor; excel, modern facs; site on lovely beach; beautiful views." ♦ € 25.00 (CChq acc) 2011*

KYLLINI *A3* (6km SW Coastal) *37.89944, 21.11666* **Camping Fournia Beach, 27050 Kastro-Kyllini [(26230) 95095; fax 95096]** W fr Patras on E55, for about 61 km, exit Kyllini/Zakinthos, turn R & foll sp for 15km to Kastro-Kyllini. Site sp. Med, mkd pitch, pt shd; wc; chem disp; shwrs; el pnts (16A) inc; lndtte; shop; tradsmn; rest; bar; BBQ; playgrnd; sand beach adj; wifi; TV; some statics; dogs; phone; Eng spkn; adv bkg; ccard acc; CCI. 1 Apr-1 Nov. € 21.30 (CChq acc) 2011*

GREECE

KYPARISSIA *A3* (1km N Coastal) *37.25697, 21.67120* **Camping Kyparissia, 24500 Kyparissia [(27610) 23491; fax 24519; info@campingkyparissia.com; www.campingkyparissia.com]** S fr Pirgos take R fork on ent Kyparissia, foll sp via beach rd; site in view ahead; fr Pilos turn N on o'skts of town. Med, pt sl, shd; wc; chem disp; mv service pnt; shwrs; el pnts (16A) €3.50; Indtte; shop & 1km; rest; snacks; bar; playgrnd; sand beach; watersports; wifi; TV; dogs free; phone; Eng spkn; Sunshine Group site; quiet; red long stay/CCI. "Excel, attractive site; friendly staff; ltd number of shd pitches for high o'fits." 1 Apr-20 Oct. € 19.50 2009*

The opening dates and prices on this campsite have changed. I'll send a site report form to the Club for the next edition of the guide.

KYPARISSIA *A3* (18km N Coastal) *37.39690, 21.67738* **Camping Apollo Village, 27054 Giannitsochori [tel/fax (26250) 61200]** Fr Pirgos S dir Kyparissía, 11km after Zaharo at sp for Giannitsochori, turn R, cross rlwy line & foll site sp. Lge, shd; wc; chem disp; shwrs inc; el pnts (16A) inc; Indtte; shop; rest; snacks; bar; BBQ; sand beach adj; games rm; TV; 10% statics; dogs; phone; quiet; red long stay; CCI. "Excel beach." 1 May-31 Oct. € 24.00 2010*

LAMBIRI see Egio *B2*

LECHEON see Korinthos *B3*

LEONIDI *B3* (20km N Coastal) *37.27566, 22.84054* **Camping Zaritsi, Paralia Tirou, 22300 Tiros [(27570) 41429; fax 41074; camping@zaritsi.gr; www.zaritsi.gr]** Foll main N-S rd down E coast; site immed off this rd on coast 4km N of Tirós, well sp. Steep rd down, but practical for lge o'fits. Site not sp fr S. Med, hdstg, pt shd; wc; chem disp; mv service pnt; shwrs inc; el pnts (16A) inc; gas; Indtte; shop; rest (high ssn); snacks; bar; playgrnd; shgl beach adj; watersports; TV rm; 50% statics; phone; Eng spkn; adv bkg; quiet; no ccard acc; CCI. "Fine site on exceptionally beautiful Arcadia coast rd; friendly owner; stunning mountain scenery; gd rest." 15 Apr-30 Sep. € 27.00 2009*

MARATHONAS *B3* (4km SE Rural/Coastal) *38.13178, 24.00721* **Camping Ramnous, Schinias, 19007 Marathonas [(22940) 55855 or 55244; fax 55242; ramnous@otanet.gr]** Fr Marathon S dir Neo Makri for 3km, turn E & foll sps 5km to site. Med, shd; wc; chem disp; shwrs; el pnts (4A) €3.50; Indtte; shop, rest, snacks high ssn; bar; playgrnd; 2 pools; beach adj; watersports; games area; entmnt; internet; 50% statics; dogs free; phone; bus; red CCI. "Excel pool complex; poss unisex san facs low ssn." 1 Mar-31 Oct. € 24.50 2008*

METHONI *A3* (500m E Coastal) *36.81736, 21.71515* **Camp Methoni, 24006 Methoni [(27230) 31228]** Fr Pylos on rd 9, strt thro Methoni to beach, turn E along beach, site sp. Med, hdstg, pt shd; wc (some cont); shwrs inc; el pnts (10A) inc; Indry rm; tradsmn; rest; snacks; bar; BBQ; playgrnd; sand beach; dogs; phone; Eng spkn; adv bkg; some rd noise; ccard not acc; CCI. "Superb Venetian castle; close to pleasant vill; park away fr taverna & rd to avoid noise; excel sw; v dusty site; clean san facs." 1 Jun-30 Sep. € 17.80 2010*

METHONI PIERIAS *B2* (5km S Coastal) *40.42712, 22.60401* **Hotel & Camping Agiannis, 60066 Methoni-Pierias [(23530) 41216; fax 51840]** Leave E75 Thessaloniki/Athens m'way dir Magrigialos/Methoni, foll sp Camping & Hotel. Med, hdg pitch, pt sl, terr, shd; wc (some cont); chem disp (wc); mv service pnt; shwrs inc; el pnts (6-10A) €3.50 (poss no earth/rev pol); shop; tradsmn; rest high ssn; snacks; playgrnd; pool; sand beach adj; entmnt; TV; 80% statics; dogs free; Eng spkn; red long stay; CCI. "Friendly family-run site; clean facs; gd touring base; excel rest o'looking beach." 1 May-15 Oct. € 18.00 2009*

⊞ **MIKINES** *B3* (500m N Urban) **Camping Mikines/Mykenae, 21200 Mikines [(27510) 76247; fax 76850; dars@arg.forthnet.gr; www.ecogriek.nl]** In town of Mikines (Mycenae) nr bus stop. On R as heading to archeological site, sp. Sm, mkd pitch, hdstg, pt shd; wc; chem disp (wc); shwrs inc; el pnts (10A) €4.50; Indtte; shops 500m; meals served; dogs; Eng spkn; quiet; CCI. "Quaint family-run site; v warm welcome; conv ancient Mycenae; vg." ♦ € 19.00 2008*

⊞ **MIKINES** *B3* (1km W Rural) *37.71915, 22.74081* **Atreus Camping, Argolida, 21200 Mikines [(27510) 76221; fax 76760; atreus@otenet.gr]** Fr E65 twd Mycenae (Mikines), site on L when heading twd archeological site. Sm, pt shd; wc; chem disp; shwrs inc; el pnts (10A) €4; Indtte; shop; tradsmn; rest; bar; pool; paddling pool; wifi; TV; no statics; Sunshine Camping Group site; Eng spkn; CCI. "Sm pitches; poss noise fr barking dogs; san facs antiquated but clean; 2km fr archeological site." € 24.00 (CChq acc) 2010*

NAFPAKTOS *B2* (7km SW Coastal) *38.34297, 21.77006* **Camping Dounis Beach, Neromana, 30200 Antirrio [(26340) 31565; fax 31131]** Foll sp to Antirrio off E55 Mesolongi to Nafpaktos rd. Site situated 1.5km E of Antirrio. Med, pt shd; wc; chem disp; mv service pnt; shwrs inc; el pnts (16A) €4; gas; Indtte; shop; rest, snacks adj; playgrnd; shgl beach; entmnt; no dogs; adv bkg; quiet; red CCI. "San facs in need of upgrade; gd size pitches; ltd facs low ssn; rather run down." 1 May-30 Oct. € 24.50 2010*

NAFPLIO *B3* (N Coastal) *37.52862, 22.86533* **Camping Lido, Sfakes Tolon, 21056 Tolon [(27520) 59396; fax 59596; lidotolo@otenet.gr; www.camping-lido.com]** App Tolon fr Nafplio, site just bef vill on L. Med, pt sl, terr, shd; wc; chem disp; shwrs inc; el pnts (16A); gas; Indtte; shop adj; snacks; sand beach adj; watersports; TV; poss cr; quiet; ccard acc; red CCI. "Excel beach; easy walk to town - many rests & boat trips; sm pitches; some pitches excel views; newer san facs block gd." 1 Apr-30 Oct. € 26.00 2010*

GREECE

NAFPLIO *B3* (10km SE Coastal) *37.53226, 22.89143* **New Triton Camping, Plaka Drepano, 21060 Drepano [(27520) 92128; fax 92121; campnewtriton@yahoo.gr]** E fr Nafplio to Epidhuros; in 5km turn R twds Drepano; in Drepano centre turn R; in one block turn slight L; may not be sp but foll sp for Camping Triton II which is 100m beyond New Triton. Sm, hdg pitch, hdstg, well shd; wc (some cont); chem disp; mv service pnt; serviced pitches; shwrs inc; el pnts (16A) inc; gas 1km; Indtte; shop; rest; snacks; bar; BBQ; cooking facs; beach adj; watersports; games area; wifi; TV; dogs free; poss cr; Eng spkn; CCI. "Immac site & facs; wheelchair-friendly; excel site." ♦ 1 Apr-31 Oct. € 25.00 2011*

⊞ **NAFPLIO** *B3* (12km SE Coastal) *37.53173, 22.89056* **Camping Triton II, Plaka Drepano, 21060 Drepano [(27520) 92228; fax 92510; tritonii@otenet.gr; www.tritonii.gr]** Take rd E fr Nafplio dir Epidavros; after 5km turn R for Drepano vill & foll site sps. Med, hdg/mkd pitch, hdstg, pt shd; wc; chem disp; mv service pnt; baby facs; shwrs; el pnts (6A) inc; Indtte (inc dryer); shop & 1km; tradsmn; rest; snacks; shgl beach adj; tennis; games area; wifi; 30% statics; dogs; phone; Eng spkn; adv bkg (Jul/Aug); ccard acc; red low ssn/long stay; CCI. "Vg low ssn; excel, clean facs; all supplies in walking dist in vill." € 25.00 (CChq acc) 2011*

NAFPLIO *B3* (12km SE Coastal) *37.5287, 22.87553* **Kastraki Camping, Kastraki Assinis, 21100 Assini [(27520) 59386 or 59387; fax 59572; sgkarmaniola@kastrakicamping.gr; www.kastrakicamping.gr]** Fr Nafplio take rd to Tolon. Immed after Assini, take L fork sp Ancient Assini. Site 3km on L. Lge, shd; wc; chem disp; mv service pnt; baby facs; shwrs €0.20; el pnts (16A) €4; Indtte; shop; rest; snacks; bar; playgrnd; sand beach; tennis; games area; TV; dogs; quiet; red facs low ssn; ccard acc. "Vg location with own private beach & excel facs; day trips to several islands fr Tolón harbour; beware if pitch adj beach as public have access; many pitches too sm for lge m'vans." ♦ 1 Apr-20 Oct. € 34.80 2009*

NAFPLIO *B3* (10km S Coastal) *37.53006, 22.86528* **Sunset Camping, 21056 Tolon [(27520) 59566; fax 59195; info@camping-sunset.gr; www.camping-sunset.gr]** Visible on R as app Tolón fr Nafplio, approx 200m bef Tolon. Med, hdstg, terr, pt shd; wc; chem disp; mv service pnt; shwrs inc; el pnts (16A) €4.50; Indtte; shop; tradsmn; rest; snacks; bar; rest; BBQ; cooking facs; playgrnd; sand beach 200m; games rm; wifi; TV rm; some statics; dogs; Eng spkn; adv bkg; quiet; red CCI. "Lovely seaside site; v friendly; pleasant town." 1 Apr-31 Oct. € 26.50 2010*

NEA MOUDANIA *B2* (3.5km S Coastal) *40.21598, 23.31825* **Camping Ouzouni Beach, 63200 Nea Moudania [(23730) 42100; fax 42105; info@ouzounibeach.gr; www.ouzounibeach.gr]** N on Kassandria rd cross Potidea Canal where site sp; take narr rd to site on L; look out for flags - easily missed. Med, hdg pitch, terr, shd; wc (some cont); chem disp; mv service pnt; shwrs inc; el pnts (6A) inc; gas; Indtte; shop, snacks, bar high ssn; playgrnd; beach adj; watersports; internet; TV; phone; Eng spkn; quiet; Sunshine Group site; red CCI. "V clean site; friendly owner; poss vicious stinging insects; excel." ♦ 1 May-30 Sep. € 21.50 2008*

NEOS MARMARAS *B2* (3km N Coastal) *40.12537, 23.76548* **Camping Castello, 63081 Neos Marmaras [(23750) 71094 or 71095; fax 72003; castello@otenet.gr]** Fr Thesssaloniki to Nea Moudania. Take coast rd on W side of peninsular: site 16km S of Nikitas. Med, pt shd; wc; chem disp; shwrs inc; el pnts (6A) €4; gas; Indtte; shop; rest; snacks; bar; playgrnd; sand beach; tennis; watersports; TV; phone; Eng spkn; adv bkg; quiet. "Vg sports facs; friendly staff." 1 Jun-30 Sep. € 23.00 2008*

NEOS MARMARAS *B2* (12km S Coastal) *40.04252, 23.81391* **Camping Stavros, Agia Kyriaki, 63081 Neos Marmaras [tel/fax (23750) 71375; info@campingstavros.gr]** Site on W side of Sithonia Peninsular. Fr Nikitas go S thro Neos Marmaras & Porto Carrasi; sp on R on winding rd. Med, shd; wc (some cont); chem disp; mv service pnt; el pnts (10A) €4; gas; Indtte; shop; rest; bar; playgrnd; beach adj; watersports; games area; TV; phone; Eng spkn; adv bkg; quiet. "Excel facs; friendly, helpful management; gd rest & bar; clean, well-run, peaceful site." 1 May-10 Oct. € 22.00 2009*

NEOS PANTELEIMONAS see Platamonas *B2*

⊞ **OLIMBIA** *A3* (150m S Urban) *37.64518, 21.6228* **Camping Diana, 27065 Olimbia [(26240) 22314 or 22945; fax 22425; harmocamp@europe.com; www.campingdiana.gr]** Fr E55 Pyrgos to Tripoli rd take exit sp 'Ancient Olympia' & foll site sp. Sm, sl, terr, pt shd; wc; chem disp; shwrs inc; el pnts (16A) €5; gas; Indry rm; shop; snacks; bar; pool; TV; dogs; Eng spkn; adv bkg; quiet but some rd noise; Harmonie Group site; red CCI. "Pretty site; san facs clean & tidy; helpful & friendly management; closest campsite to archaeological sites; noisy roosters in morning!" € 23.00 2011*

⊞ **OLIMBIA** *A3* (500m SW Urban) *37.65103, 21.62475* **Camping Olympia, 27065 Olimbia [(26240) 22745; fax 22812; vaggelismamousis@yahoo.com; www.tggr.com/camping-olympia]** Fr E55 Pyrgos to Tiípoli rd take exit sp 'Ancient Olympia' & foll site sp. Med, mkd pitch, hdstg, pt sl, terr, pt shd; wc (some cont); chem disp; mv service pnt; shwrs inc; el pnts (10A) €4; Indry rm; rest high ssn; bar; pool; paddling pool; dogs; TV; Eng spkn; Sunshine Group site; CCI. "V conv for archaeological sites; easy access & level walk into town; san facs antiquated but clean; poss run down low ssn; friendly welcome." ♦ € 19.00 2008*

OLIMBIA *A3* (850m W Rural) *37.64337, 21.61943* **Camping Alphios, 27065 Olimbia [(26240) 22951; fax 22950; alphios@otenet.gr; www.campingalphios.gr]** Fr E55 Pyrgos to Tripoli rd take exit sp 'Ancient Olympia' & foll site sp. Med, hdg/mkd pitch, hdstg, terr, pt sl, pt shd; wc; chem disp; mv service pnt; shwrs inc; el pnts (16A) inc; gas; Indtte; shop; rest; snacks; bar; BBQ; cooking facs; playgrnd; pool; wifi; TV; quiet; ccard acc. "Superb views fr some pitches; excel pool." 1 Apr-15 Oct. € 23.30 2010*

OLYMPIA see Olimbia *A3*

GREECE

PALEA EPIDAVROS *B3* (200m S Coastal) *37.61616, 23.15851* **Camping Nicolas II, Gialassi, 21059 Palea Epidavros [(27530) 41218; fax 41492; info@nicolasgikas.gr; www.nicolasgikas.gr]** Fr Athens/Patras m'way take Epídavros rd. Pass Nea Epidavros & turn E into Ancient/Palea Epidavros. Foll steep rd into town, site sp. Med, shd; wc; chem disp (wc); mv service pnt; shwrs inc; el pnts (16A) inc; Indtte; shop; tradsmn; rest; snacks; bar; pool; shgl beach adj; TV; 10% statics; Eng spkn; quiet; CCI. "Pleasant site in orange grove; shwrs slightly neglected (2007); close to ancient theatre & sanctuary; tourer pitches adj beach - poss tight lge o'fits." ♦ 1 Apr-31 Oct. € 27.00 2008*

PALEA EPIDAVROS *B3* (2km S Coastal) *37.61868, 23.15599* **Camping Bekas, Gialasi, 21059 Palea Epidavros [(27530) 41524; fax 41394; info@bekas.gr; www.bekas.gr]** S fr Korinthos past Nea (New) Epidavros. Do not take 1st sp to Palea (Ancient) Epidavros but exit R 3km later & foll sp to vill. On ent vill turn sharp R at Bekas sp, site in 1.5km. Med, hdstg, terr, shd; wc; chem disp; mv service pnt; baby facs; fam bthrm; shwrs inc; el pnts (16A) €4; gas; Indtte; ice; shop; tradsmn; supmkt 4km; rest; snacks; bar; BBQ; cooking facs; shgl beach adj; tennis; wifi; TV; 10% statics; dogs free; phone; poss cr; Eng spkn; adv bkg; quiet; ccard acc; red low ssn/long stay; CCI. "Sheltered beach in beautiful bay; friendly, family-run site in orange grove; some beachfront pitches; excel." 25 Mar-20 Oct. € 23.50 2009*

PARGA *A2* (2km N Coastal) *39.28550, 20.38997* **Camping Valtos, Valtos Beach, 48060 Parga [(26840) 31287; fax 31131; info@campingvaltos.gr; www.campingvaltos.gr]** Foll sp fr Parga twd Valtos Beach, site sp. Site at far end of beach behind bar/club. Med, mkd pitch, pt sl, shd; wc; chem disp; shwrs inc; el pnts (10A); Indtte; shop; rest; snacks; bar; sand beach adj; no statics; dogs; poss cr; Eng spkn; poss noise fr tents; CCI. "Helpful owners; gd walking area; steep walk to town." 1 May-30 Sep. € 24.50 2008*

⊞ **PARGA** *A2* (1km E Coastal) *39.28474, 20.41088* **Parga Camping, Krioneri, 48060 Parga [(26840) 31161; fax 31661; pargacam@otenet.gr; www.pargacamping.gr]** Fr Igoumenitsa-Preveza rd turn W to Parga, site 1km bef town in olive grove on L, well sp Med, some hdstg, shd; wc; chem disp; mv service pnt; shwrs inc; el pnts (10A) inc; Indry rm; shop, rest, snacks high ssn; bar 400m; BBQ; playgrnd; sand/shgl beach 400m; phone; Eng spkn; adv bkg; quiet; red long stay/low ssn; CCI. "Delightful, peaceful site amongst olive trees in walking dist pretty vill; friendly, helpful owners live on site." € 27.80 2009*

PARGA *A2* (3km E Coastal) *39.2822, 20.43478* **Enjoy Lichnos Camping, 48060 Lichnos-Parga [(26840) 31371 or 31171; fax 32076; holidays@enjoy-lichnos.net; www.enjoy-lichnos.net]** On Igoumenitsa-Preveza rd turn W at sp Parga; sp 3km bef vill, steep app down private rd. Lge, terr, shd; wc; chem disp; shwrs; el pnts (16A) €3.80; Indtte; shop, rest high ssn; snacks; bar; shgl beach; watersports; dogs free; wifi; sep car park; Sunshine Camping Group site; adv bkg; quiet; red CCI. "Vg facs, excel location; some pitches adj excel beach; water taxis to Parga." 1 May-15 Oct. € 22.00 2011*

⊞ **PATRA** *A2* (9km NE Urban/Coastal) *38.30583, 21.77894* **Camping Rion Beach, Odos Poseidonos 11, 26500 Rio [(2610) 991585]** Site is 300m fr bdge, W of Rio. Sm, pt shd; wc; chem disp; shwrs inc; el pnts (16A); gas; Indtte; shop; rest; snacks; bar; BBQ; cooking facs; shgl beach across rd; TV; dogs; site clsd mid-Dec to mid-Jan; poss cr; Eng spkn; rd & rest/disco noise; CCI. "Gd facs; sm pitches; poss mosquitoes; conv NH." € 27.00 2010*

PATRA *A2* (19km SW Coastal) *38.14367, 21.58772* **Camping Golden Sunset Beach, 25002 Alissos [(26930) 71276; fax 71556; goldensunset@patrascamping.gr; www.patrascampings.gr]** 1st site on old national rd W of Patras to Pirgos-Olimbia, sp. Med, pt shd; wc; shwrs inc; el pnts (6A) €4; gas; Indtte; shop; rest; snacks; bar; playgrnd; 3 pools; waterslides; shgl beach; boating; tennis; games area; sat TV; 10% statics; poss cr; Eng spkn; adv bkg; quiet; ccard acc; red long stay; Harmonie Group site. "Helpful management; gd base for tours; site poss clsd Jun-Aug for exclusive use parties of students - phone ahead to check; excel." ♦ 1 May-30 Sep. € 28.00 2009*

PATRA *A2* (21km SW Coastal) *38.14986, 21.57740* **Camping Kato Alissos, 25002 Kato Alissos [(26930) 71249; fax 71150; demiris-cmp@otenet.gr; www.camping-kato-alissos.gr]** W of Patra on old national rd turn R at Kato Alissos & foll site sp for 600m. Med, shd; wc; chem disp; shwrs inc; el pnts (10A) €3.80; Indtte; shop; rest; snacks; bar; cooking facs; playgrnd; shgl beach adj (down 50 steps); watersports; wifi; 10% statics; dogs; phone; bus 1km; Sunshine Camping Group site; poss cr; Eng spkn; adv bkg; quiet; ccard acc; red snr citizens; CCI. "Clean facs; gd NH." 1 Apr-25 Oct. € 21.00 2011*

PETALIDI *B3* (2.5km N Coastal) *36.98167, 21.92886* **Camping Petalidi Beach, 24005 Petalidi [(27220) 31154; fax 31690; info@campingpetalidi.gr; www.campingpetalidi.gr]** Turn L off Kalamata-Pylos rd at Rizomylos. Site sp in 2km. Lge, hdstg, pt shd; wc; chem disp; mv service pnt; shwrs inc; el pnts (16A) inc; gas; Indtte (inc dryer); shop; rest; snacks; bar; BBQ; playgrnd; shgl beach adj; watersports; games area; entmnt; TV; dogs; phone; Eng spkn; adv bkg; Harmonie Group site; red CCI. 1 Apr-30 Sep. € 23.50 2011*

⊞ **PLAKA LITOHOROU** *B2* (6km N Coastal) **Camping Stani, 60200 Kalivia Varikou [(23520) 61277]** Leave E75 (Athens-Thessaloniki) at N Efesos/Varikou, foll sp Varikou & site. Lge, mkd pitch, shd; wc; chem disp; shwrs inc; el pnts; Indtte; shop; rest; snacks; bar; TV rm; dogs; phone; poss cr; CCI. "Ltd facs low ssn; conv Dion; fair site." € 22.00 2008*

PLAKA LITOHOROU *B2* (5km SE Coastal) *40.10185, 22.56198* **Camping Olympos Beach, 60200 Plaka Litohorou [(23520) 22112; fax 22300; info@olympos-beach.fr; www.olympos-beach.gr]** S on Thessaloniki-Athens rd, turn E at sp to sites across rlwy bdge, site on coast rd on L going S, sp as 'Plaka'. Med, hdg pitch, pt sl, shd; wc (some cont); chem disp; shwrs inc; el pnts (8A) inc; gas; Indtte; shop; tradsmn; rest; snacks; bar; playgrnd; shgl beach adj; watersports; TV; entmnt; 50% statics; phone; Sunshine Group site; poss cr; Eng spkn; adv bkg; quiet; CCI. "At foot of Mt Olympus; pleasant beach down steep steps." ♦ 1 May-30 Sep. € 24.00 2008*

GREECE

PLATAMONAS *B2* (5km N Coastal) *40.01055, 22.59192* **Camping Heraklia Beach, 60065 Neos Panteleimonas [(23520) 41403 or 41971; fax 41714; www.tggr.com/heraklia-beach/]** Fr E75 Athens-Thessaloniki rd turn to Panteleimonas, site sp. Med, mkd pitch, shd; wc (some cont); chem disp; shwrs inc; el pnts inc; lndtte; shop; rest; bar; sand beach adj; 60% statics; Sunshine Camping Club site; Eng spkn; adv bkg; quiet. "Warm welcome; pleasant atmosphere; clean san facs; gd beach." 1 May-30 Sep. € 19.00 2008*

PLATAMONAS *B2* (6km N Coastal) *40.01291, 22.59053* **Camping Poseidon Beach, Paralia Pandeleimonas, 60065 Platamonas [(23520) 41654 or 41792; fax 41994; info@poseidonbeach.net; www.poseidonbeach.net]** Exit Katerini to Larissa toll rd 1/E75 & foll site sp over rlwy line (2km) & turn L (sp camping), use underpass, turn R at junc, site in 400m. Lge, hdg pitch, pt shd; wc; chem disp; shwrs inc; el pnts (16A) €3.50; gas; lndtte; shop; rest; bar; sand beach; TV; 80% statics; no dogs; bus 1km; poss cr; Eng spkn; quiet; red long stay/CCI. "Well-managed site; immac facs; sm pitches & narr roads may be diff for lge o'fits; vg beach; pleasant area." 1 Apr-15 Oct. € 23.50 2011*

PLATARIA see Igoumenitsa *A2*

POSSIDI see Kassandria *B2*

PREVEZA *A2* (3km NW Coastal) *38.97395, 20.7161* **Camping Kalamitsi Beach, 48100 Preveza [(26280) 23268; fax 28660; kalamitsi_camping@hotmail.com]** Fr Preveza on E55 twds Igoumenitsa on L of rd; clearly sp. Best app fr N. Med, shd; wc; chem disp; shwrs inc; el pnts (16A); gas; lndtte; shop; rest; bar; playgrnd; pool; beach adj; watersports; wifi; TV; Eng spkn; adv bkg; quiet; red long stay; CCI. "Attractive site; nr archaeological sites; friendly owner; poss diff to manoeuvre onto pitches high ssn." ♦ 15 Jun-1 Oct. € 26.00 2009*

⊞ **PYLOS** *A3* (5km N Coastal) *36.94784, 21.70635* **Camping Navarino Beach, 24001 Gialova [(27230) 22761; fax 23512; info@navarino-beach.gr; www.navarino-beach.gr]** Fr Pylos N twds Kiparissia for 5km around Navarino Bay, site at S end of Gialova vill; sp. Med, some hdstg, pt shd, wc; chem disp; mv service pnt; shwrs inc; el pnts (16A) €4; gas; lndtte; shop 300m; tradsmn; rest; snacks; BBQ; cooking facs; playgrnd; beach; windsurfing, boat-launch; internet; dogs; bus; Eng spkn; adv bkg; quiet; ccard acc; red long stay; CCI. "Management v helpful; gd, clean, modern facs; several rest & shops in easy walking dist; vg." € 22.00 2011*

PYLOS *A3* (7km N Coastal) *36.95291, 21.69565* **Camping Erodios, 24001 Gialova [(27230) 28240; fax 28241; info@erodioss.gr; www.erodioss.gr]** Fr N side of Gialova foll sp 'Golden Beach, site sp. Med, pt shd; wc; chem disp; mv service pnt; baby facs; shwrs; el pnts (10A) €4.50; lndtte; shop; rest; snacks; bar; cooking facs; playgrnd; beach adj; watersports; surfing; cycle hire; wifi; sat TV; 10% statics; bus 500m; Eng spkn; adv bkg; quiet; ccard acc; red long stay/CCI. "Excel facs; welcoming; beautiful situation & sea views fr some pitches; some v lge pitches - can be pre-booked; friendly, helpful staff." ♦ 1 Apr-31 Oct. € 27.50 2011*

RAFINA *B3* (2km N Coastal) *38.03120, 23.99992* **Camping Kokkino Limanaki, 19009 Rafina [(22940) 31604; fax 31603; info@athenscampings.com; www.athenscampings.com]** On Marathon/Athens rd, 25km fr Athens turn L sp Rafina 3km; after 1.6km turn L; after 1.2km thro x-rds & turn L after 200m; site on R in 150m. Med, pt sl, terr, pt shd; wc (some cont); chem disp; shwrs inc; el pnts (10A) inc; gas; lndtte; shop; rest; snacks; bar; BBQ; sand beach; dogs; quiet low ssn; ccard acc. "Site on cliff 100m above sea with excel mountain & ocean views; some pitches sm & poss diff lge o'fits." 1 Apr-15 Oct. € 26.00 2010*

⊞ **RIZA** *A2* (1km NW Coastal) *39.13493, 20.58415* **Camping Acrogiali, Mitos Apostolos, 48100 Riza [(26820) 56382; fax 56283; campacro@hol.gr; www.camping-acrogiali.com]** Fr S foll E44 N fr Preveza, site sp on L in approx 28km. Fr N approx 20km S of Igoumenitsa after x-ring rd bdge, start to climb & at sharp R-hand bend (sign for Riza to L) turn R onto winding, tarmac rd, downhill to coast. In approx 4km, site on L. Sm, mkd pitch, shd; wc; chem disp; mv service pnt; shwrs inc; el pnts (16A) inc; lndtte; shop; rest; bar; BBQ; shgl beach adj; wifi (in rest); TV rm; 50% statics; Eng spkn; adv bkg; quiet; ccard acc. "Gd facs & swimming; excel, new, modern san facs; pitches poss a challenge but location of site on beach worth effort!" € 20.00 (CChq acc) 2011*

SARTI *B2* (12km N Coastal) *40.15233, 23.91293* **Camping Armenistis, Akti Armenistis, 63072 Sarti [tel/fax (23750) 91487; info@armenistis.com.gr; www.armenistis.com.gr]** Fr Nikitas, turn E at junc down E side of Sithonia along coast rd sp Sarti/Sikia; site on E side 28km fr junc; last few km diff driving. Lge, mkd pitch, pt shd; wc; mv service pnt; shwrs inc; el pnts (6A) €3.70; lndtte; shop; rest; snacks; bar; BBQ; playgrnd; beach; games area; entmnt; 30% statics; Sunshine Camping Group site; ccard acc; red CCI. "Gd location with views of Mount Athos; excel for families." 1 May-15 Sep. € 26.40 2009*

SISI (CRETE) *C4* (1.2km W Coastal) *35.30371, 25.50858* **Sisi Camping, 72400 Sisi [tel/fax (28410) 71247; info@sisicamping.gr; www.sisicamping.gr]** E fr Iraklio/Heraklion on E75, after Malia look for Sisi turn approx 5km after Malia. Site sp. Sm, mkd/hdg pitch, pt shd; wc (cont); chem disp; mv service pnt; shwrs inc; el pnts (10A) €3.50; lndtte; shop 800m; tradsmn; rest 250m; snacks; bar; BBQ; pool; paddling pool; sand beach 1km; watersports; wifi; dogs free; phone; Eng spkn; adv bkg; quiet; red low ssn; CCI. "Sisi pretty vill; gd touring base attractions & archaeological sites; warm welcome; vg." 1 May-15 Oct. € 23.30 2010*

⊞ **SOUNIO** *B3* (5km N Coastal) *37.67620, 24.04884* **Camping Bacchus, Ave Lavrio, 19500 Sounio [tel/fax (22920) 39572; campingbacchus@hotmail.com; www.tggr.com/camping-bacchus]** Site sp on N89 coastal rd at km stone 71. Sm, pt shd; wc; chem disp; shwrs inc; el pnts (6A) €4; gas; lndtte; shop, rest (high ssn); snacks; bar; cooking facs; playgrnd; sand beach adj; fishing, windsurfing nr; TV; 50% statics; phone; Sunshine Group site; quiet; ccard acc; red low ssn. "Basic facs; solar water heating, open air wash basins with cold taps only, no privacy cubicles (2009); 4.5km fr Temple of Poseidon; easy access coastal walks & views." € 25.50 2009*

GREECE

⊞ **SPARTI** *B3* (3km W Rural) *37.0716, 22.4049* **Camping Paleologio, 23100 Mistras [(27310) 22724; fax 25256; alixiaba@hotmail.com]** Fr Sparti foll sp to Mistras. Site ent thro filling stn on L. Med, shd; wc; chem disp; shwrs inc; el pnts (16A) €4; gas; Indtte (inc dryer); shop; rest; snacks; bar; playgrnd; pool; TV; phone; quiet; red CCI. "Conv Ancient Mistras & Sparti adj for major shopping; gd pool; facs clean & spacious but ltd low ssn." € 25.00 2008*

SPARTI *B3* (5km W Rural) *37.06941, 22.38163* **Camping Castle View, 23100 Mistras [(27310) 83303; fax 20028; info@castleview.gr]** Fr Kalamata take 1st turning to Mistras, past castle then thro vill dir Sparti. Site in approx 1km on L, well sp. Med, pt shd; wc; chem disp; shwrs inc; el pnts (16A) inc; gas; Indtte; shop; tradsmn; rest; snacks; bar; playgrnd; pool; wifi; TV; some statics; dogs; phone; Eng spkn; quiet; red CCI. "Gd clean facs; gd rest; close to archaeological remains; helpful owner." 1 Apr-20 Oct. € 26.00 2011*

STOUPA *B3* (100m N Coastal) *36.84934, 22.25877* **Camping Kalógria, Barbecer Nicda 29, 24024 Stoupa [(27210) 77319]** S fr Kalamata, turn R at site sp just bef Stoupa, site 200m on L. Med, some hdstg, pt sl, pt shd; wc; chem disp; mv service pnt; shwrs; el pnts (16A) inc; Indtte; shop; tradsmn; rest, snacks, bar 100m high ssn; BBQ; playgrnd; sand beach adj; phone; poss cr; Eng spkn; quiet; CCI. "Nice location; friendly staff; pitches on loose earth amongst trees; pleasant resort town." ♦ 5 May-31 Oct. € 24.30 2011*

STOUPA *B3* (2km N Coastal) *36.86071, 22.25220* **Camping Ta Delfinia, Neo Proastio, 24022 Kardamili [(27210) 77318; perdikeas@in.gr]** Site sp in lay-by; go thro gate & keep going. Sm, some hdstg, pt sl, shd; wc (some cont); chem disp; shwrs; ltd el pnts (16A) inc; Indtte; shop high ssn; rest 1.5km; snacks, bar high ssn; BBQ; playgrnd; sand/shgl beach adj; wifi; TV; poss cr; Eng spkn; red snr citizens; CCI. "Friendly welcome; ltd facs low ssn." 1 Mar-31 Oct. € 26.20 2010*

⊞ **STYLIDA** *B2* (3km E Coastal) *38.89638, 22.65555* **Camping Interstation, Rd Athens-Thessalonika, Km 230, 35300 Stylida [(22380) 23827; fax 23828; interstation@hotmail.com; www.tggr.com/interstation/]** Fr Lamia take rd E to Stylis; cont for further 3km & site situated to side of dual-c'way opp petrol stn. Med, shd; wc; chem disp; shwrs €0.30; el pnts (16A) €3.60; gas; Indtte; shop, rest high ssn; playgrnd; beach adj; tennis; watersports; TV; entmnt; some statics; no dogs; Eng spkn; adv bkg; quiet but some rd noise; red CCI. "Day visitors have access to beach via site; do not confuse with Cmp Paras adj - not rec; Sunshine Camping Group site; poss poor san facs low ssn; NH only." ♦ € 22.60 2009*

THERMISSIA *B3* (1km W Coastal) **Hydra's Wave Camping, 21051 Thermissia Argolidas [(27540) 41095; fax 41055; galanopoulos49@yahoo.gr; www.camping.gr/hydras-wave]** Fr Kranidi turn E on rd to Ermioni & then foll coast rd dir Póros. Site sp on R after 6km. Med, hdg pitch, shd; wc (some cont); chem disp; shwrs inc; el pnts (16A) €4; Indtte; shop; rest; snacks; bar; playgrnd; shgl beach adj; TV; dogs €2.50; bus 500m; Eng spkn; adv bkg; quiet; ccard acc; CCI. "Gd cent for Poros, Hydra, Spetses; helpful owner; dated facs but clean; OK touring base." 1 Mar-30 Nov. € 21.00 2010*

TIROS see Leonidi *B3*

TOLON see Nafplio *B3*

⊞ **VARTHOLOMIO** *A3* (8km SW Coastal) *37.83555, 21.13333* **Camping Ionion Beach, 27050 Glifa [(26230) 96395; fax 96425; ioniongr@otenet.gr; www.ionion-beach.gr]** Fr E55 Patras-Pirgos rd turn W to Gastouni, Ligia & Glifa, then Glifa Beach. Site is 1km SW of Glifa. Med, hdg pitch, hdstg, pt shd; htd wc; chem disp; mv service pnt; serviced pitch; shwrs; el pnts (16A); gas; Indtte (inc dryer); shop in vill; tradsmn; rest; snacks; bar; BBQ; playgrnd; pool; paddling pool; beach adj; watersports; games area; wifi; TV; statics; dogs; Eng spkn; adv bkg; poss noisy; ccard acc; red low ssn; CCI. "Excel, well-run site; superb facs." ♦ € 27.00 2010*

VLYCHO see Lefkada (Lefkas Island) *A2*

I'll fill in a report online and let the Club know – www.caravanclub.co.uk/europereport

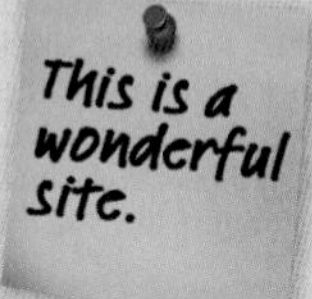
This is a wonderful site.

VOLOS *B2* (17km SE Coastal) *39.31105, 23.10922* **Camping Hellas International, 38500 Kato Gatzea [(24230) 22267; fax 22492; info@campinghellas.gr; www.campinghellas.gr]** Fr Volos take coast rd N34 to Kato Gatzea; sp on R immed bef & adj Sikia (Fig Tree) Camping. Med, shd; wc; chem disp; baby facs; shwrs inc; el pnts (16A) inc; gas; Indtte; shop high ssn; tradsmn; rest, snacks high ssn; BBQ; shgl beach adj; boating; cycle hire; internet; 30% statics; dogs; phone; Harmonie Group site; Eng spkn; adv bkg; ccard acc; red low ssn; CCI. "Excel san facs - poss stretched with site full; friendly, helpful family-run site; great location; vg touring base." ♦ 15 Mar-31 Oct. € 27.50 2010*

VOLOS *B2* (17km SE Coastal) *39.31027, 23.10972* **Camping Sikia Fig Tree, 38500 Kato Gatzea [(24230) 22279 or 22081; fax 22720; info@camping-sikia.gr; www.camping-sikia.gr]** Fr Volos take coast rd S to Kato Gatzea site on R, sp immed next to Camping Hellas. Med, terr, shd; wc; chem disp; mv service pnt; shwrs inc; el pnts (16A) €3; gas; Indtte; shop; rest; snacks; shgl beach; internet; entmnt; 20% statics; dogs; phone; poss cr; Eng spkn; adv bkg; quiet; Sunshine Group site; ccard acc; red long stay/CCI. "Highly rec; some beautiful, but sm, pitches with sea views; excel, friendly family-run site; v clean; v helpful staff; take care o'hanging trees." ♦ 1 Apr-30 Oct. € 19.00 2011*

ZACHARO *A3* (8km S Coastal) **Camping Tholo Beach, Tholo, 27054 Zacharo [(26250) 61345 or 33454 (winter); campingtholo@hotmail.com]** S fr Pyrgos on E55 dir Kyparissia, 8km S of Zacharo turn R to Tholo. Site sp in 500m on L. Med, shd; wc; chem disp; mv service pnt; shwrs inc; el pnts €4; Indry rm; shop; rest; bar; BBQ; playgrnd; sand beach adj; wifi; TV; no statics; dogs; Eng spkn; adv bkg; quiet; CCI, "Excel, quiet, clean site; gd, clean san facs; friendly staff; excel sandy beach where loggerhead turtles lay eggs; dolphins off shore." 1 Apr-30 Oct. € 20.05 2010*

GREECE

Greek Islands

⊞ **AGIA GALINI (CRETE)** *C4* (500m E Rural/Coastal) *35.10004, 24.69514* **Camping No Problem!, 74056 Agia Galini [(28320) 91386; www.agia-galini.com]** Site sp on Tympaki rd. Sm, mkd pitch, pt shd; wc; chem disp; mv service pnt; shwrs; el pnts (6A) €4; Indtte; shop; tradsmn; rest; snacks; bar; BBQ; pool; paddling pool; sand/shgl beach 500m; wifi; some statics; dogs free; bus 500m; poss cr; Eng spkn; adv bkg; quiet. "Vg, family-run site; gd walks." ♦ € 25.50 2010*

CORFU/KERKIRA (CORFU) *A2* (12km N Coastal) *39.68558, 19.83845* **Karda Beach Camping, 49100 Dassia [tel/fax (26610) 93595; campco@otenet.gr]** Fr port, head N & join main rd to Palaeokastritsa after 9.5km (vill of Tzaurou); take R fork then 4.5km to Dassia; site on R of rd 1km fr Club Mediterranée & beyond Chandris Hotel. Lge, shd; wc; chem disp; mv service pnt; shwrs inc; el pnts (16A) €4.20; gas; Indtte; shop; rest; snacks; bar; BBQ; pool; paddling pool; shgl beach adj; watersports; entmnt; internet; sat TV; 40% statics; dogs; phone; Eng spkn; adv bkg; quiet; Sunshine group; ccard acc; red CCI. "Well-run site, gd, clean facs; friendly, helpful staff; vg esp low ssn." ♦ 20 Apr-30 Oct. € 22.80 2008*

ERETRIA (EVIA) *B2* (1km W Coastal) *38.39148, 23.77562* **Milos Camping, 34008 Eretria [(22290) 60420; fax 60360; info@camping-in-evia.gr; www.camping-in-evia.gr]** Fr Chalkida for 20km; ignore any previous sp for Milos Camping. Med, mkd pitch, terr, pt shd; wc; chem disp; mv service pnt; shwrs inc; el pnts (16A) inc; gas; Indtte; shop; rest; snacks; bar; BBQ; playgrnd; shgl beach adj; internet; TV; 50% statics; dogs; phone; Eng spkn; quiet but some rd noise; red CCI. "Friendly site; excel rest; rather scruffy (5/09) but facs OK." ♦ 10 Apr-30 Sep. € 26.10 2009*

HANIA (CRETE) *C4* (5km W Coastal) *35.51183, 23.98482* **Camping Hania, Agii Apostoli, Kato Daratso, 73100 Hania [(28210) 31138; fax 33371; camhania@otenet.gr; www.camping-chania.gr]** W fr cent of Hania on main rd to Kissamos. Med, hdstg, pt sl, shd; wc (some cont); chem disp; mv service pnt; shwrs inc; el pnts (16A) inc; gas; Indtte; shop; rest; snacks; bar; BBQ; cooking facs; playgrnd; pool; paddling pool; sand beach 200m; cycle hire; games rm; TV; some statics; dogs; bus; phone; poss cr; Eng spkn; adv bkg; quiet; ccard acc; red long stay; CCI. "Take care low olive trees; vg." 1 Apr-30 Oct. € 30.00 2011*

IRAKLIO (CRETE) *C4* (16km E Coastal) *35.33290, 25.29182* **Camping Creta, Gouviana Kamara, 71201 Gouves [(28970) 41400]** Take old rd outside Iraklio dir Ag. Nikolaos. After approx 14km turn L to Gouves, site sp. Lge, mkd pitch, pt shd; wc; chem disp; shwrs inc; el pnts (10A) inc; Indtte; shop; rest; snacks; bar; BBQ; playgrnd; beach adj; wifi; dogs; poss cr; Eng spkn; ccard acc; red low ssn/CCI. "Closest site to Knossos; gd." ♦ 1 Apr-31 Oct. € 25.50 2008*

KOS (KOS) *D3* (3km E Coastal) **Kos Camping, 85300 Psalidi [(22420) 29886; fax 29887; grigoris70@hotmail.gr]** On Ag Fokas rd fr Kos town, site on R. Only site on island. Med, mkd pitch, pt shd; wc; shwrs inc; el pnts; gas; shop; rest; snacks; playgrnd; shgl beach across rd; tennis; cycle hire; 30% statics; phone; sep car park; poss cr; adv bkg; quiet. 1 May-5 Oct. 2009*

LEFKADA (LEFKAS) *A2* (2km S Rural/Coastal) *38.80138, 20.71333* **Camping Kariotes Beach, Spasmeni, 31100 Kariotes [(26450) 71103; fax 71103; info@campingkariotes.com; www.campingkariotes.com]** S fr Lefkada on rd dir Nidri. Site on R, sp. Sm, pt sl, pt shd; wc; chem disp; shwrs inc; el pnts (10A); €3.50; Indry rm; shop; rest; bar; cooking facs; pool; sand beach nr; TV; internet; Sunshine Camping Club site; Eng spkn; some rd noise; red CCI. 1 May-30 Sep. € 19.00 2008*

LEFKADA (LEFKAS) *A2* (20km S Coastal) *38.67285, 20.71046* **Camping Dessimi Beach, 31100 Vlycho [(26450) 95374 or 95225; fax 95190; info@dessimi-beach.gr]** Fr Vlycho S side foll sp Dessimi-Geni for 2km. Med, mkd pitch, pt shd; wc; chem disp; mv service pnt; shwrs inc; el pnts (8A) €3.40; Indtte; shop, rest, snacks high ssn; playgrnd; sand beach; diving, fishing & boating; dogs free; phone; sep car park; no adv bkg; quiet; red low ssn. "Gd location." 1 Apr-31 Oct. € 28.30 2008*

LEFKADA (LEFKAS) *A2* (20km S Coastal) *38.67511, 20.71475* **Camping Santa Maura, Dessimi, 31100 Vlycho [(26450) 95007; fax 95493; www.lefkada.biz/campingsantamavra/]** Take coast rd S fr Lefkada to Vlycho, turn L for Dessimi, site in 2.5km (after Camping Dessimi). Access via v steep hill - severe gradients both sides. Med, mkd pitch, terr, pt shd; wc; chem disp; mv service pnt; shwrs inc; el pnts (12A) inc; gas; Indtte; shop; rest; snacks; bar; BBQ; sand/shgl beach adj; TV rm; phone; quiet; CCI. "Excel site & beach; gd,clean san facs; friendly owners." 20 Apr-20 Oct. € 25.00 2009*

PEFKARI (THASSOS) *C2* (250m W Coastal) *40.61630, 24.60021* **Camping Pefkari, 64002 Pefkari [tel/fax (25930) 51190; campingpefkari@hotmail.com]** SW fr Thassos port approx 43km to Limenaria, Pefkari is next sm vill. Site well sp in vill. Med, hdstg, pt shd; own san; chem disp; shwrs inc; el pnts (6A) €2.90; Indry rm; shop; rest; snacks; bar; BBQ; sand beach adj; 5% statics; bus 1km; Eng spkn; quiet; CCI. "Lovely spot; worth putting up with poor, dated san facs; gd local rest; vg." 1 May-15 Oct. € 13.00 2008*

⊞ **RETHYMNO (CRETE)** *C4* (3km E Coastal) *35.36795, 24.51487* **Camping Elizabeth, Ionias 84 Terma, 74100 Missiria [tel/fax (28310) 28694; wallydewever@yahoo.gr; www.camping-elizabeth.com]** W fr Iraklio/Heraklion exit Platanes/Arkadi. Site 1km before Platanes, on R on short unsurfaced rd. Lge, hdg pitch, shd; wc; chem disp; mv service pnt; shwrs; el pnts (12A) inc; Indtte (inc dryer); shop; tradsmn; rest; snacks; bar; BBQ; cooking facs; beach adj; wifi; 3% statics; dogs; phone; bus 500m; poss cr; Eng spkn; adv bkg; quiet; red low ssn; CCI. "Gd walking on mkd rtes; gd cycling; excursion programme; vg." ♦ € 28.20 2010*

RODA (CORFU) *A2* (500m W Coastal) *39.78446, 19.78486* **Camping Roda Beach International, 49081 Roda [(26630) 63120; fax 63081; info@rodacamping.gr; www.rodacamping.gr]** N fr port to join main rd to Palaeokastritsa. Turn R for Sidari & foll sp to Roda. Turn L 30m bef rndabt, 200m on R, sp. Med, pt shd; wc; mv service pnt; shwrs inc; el pnts €3.80; Indtte; shop; rest; snacks; bar; playgrnd; pool; beach 700m; cycle hire; entmnt; internet; TV; no statics; dogs free; Eng spkn; some rd noise; red snr citizens/CCI. 15 Apr-15 Oct. € 22.50 2010*

GREECE - GREEK ISLANDS

ROVIES (EVIA) *B2* (3km N Coastal) *38.83276, 23.19886* **Camping Rovies Beach, 34005 Rovies [(22270) 71120; info@campingevia.com; www.campingevia.com]** Fr N on ferry fr Glifa to Agiokampos foll coast rd S for 23 km. Med, hdg pitch, hdstg, terr, pt shd; wc; chem disp; shwrs inc; el pnts (12A) inc; lndry rm; shop; BBQ; shgl beach adj; 5% statics; CCI. "Delightful location; facs dated & plagued by moths (5/09); many pitches diff for m'vans due low branches; gd." 1 Apr-30 Oct. € 29.00 2009*

SAMI (CEPHALONIA) *A2* (1km N Coastal) *38.25088, 20.63803* **Camping Karavomilos Beach, 28080 Sami [(26740) 22480; fax 22932; info@camping-karavomilos.gr; www.camping-karavomilos.gr]** Site sp. Lge, hdg/mkd pitch, pt shd; wc; chem disp; mv service pnt; shwrs inc; el pnts (16A) inc; lndtte (inc dryer); shop; tradsmn; rest; snacks; bar; playgrnd; pool; paddling pool; shgl beach adj; wifi; TV rm; dogs; phone; poss cr; Eng spkn; adv bkg; some rd noise; ccard acc; red CCI. "Friendly owner; wonderful scenery; easy walk to town; v lge outfits ring ahead for easy access; excel." 1 May-30 Sep. € 28.50 2010*

THASSOS (THASSOS) *C1* (8km S Coastal) *40.72561, 24.7567* **Camping Golden Beach, 64004 Panagia [(25930) 61472; fax 61473; info@camping-goldenbeach.gr; www.camping-goldenbeach.gr]** S fr Thassos to Panagia. Turn L to Hrissi Armoudia & site. Site sp in Panagia. Lge, hdg/mkd pitch, pt shd; wc (some cont); shwrs inc; el pnts €4.30; lndtte; shop; rest adj; snacks; bar; playgrnd; sand beach adj; games area; entmnt; TV; 50% statics; poss cr; Eng spkn; quiet. "Beautiful, long, sandy beach." ♦ 1 May-15 Oct. € 19.90 2011*

THASSOS (THASSOS) *C1* (14km SW Coastal) *40.71472, 24.53534* **Camping Daedalos, 64010 Skala Sotiros [(25930) 58251; fax 71152; tseltha@otenet.gr]** Fr Thassos foll sp to Skala Sotiros, site sp. Med, hdg pitch, pt shd; wc; chem disp (wc); shwrs inc; el pnts €3; lndry rm; shop; tradsmn; rest 2km; snacks; bar; playgrnd; sand beach adj; 20% statics; dogs; bus; Eng spkn; adv bkg; quiet; red long stay; CCI. "Friendly, family-run site; helpful owner & staff; ltd facs low ssn." ♦ 1 May-30 Sep. € 15.00 2008*

TINOS (TINOS) *C3* (500m E Coastal) *37.53994, 25.16377* **Tinos Camping, Louizas Sohou 5, 84200 Tinos [(22830) 22344; fax 24373; tinoscamping@thn.forthnet.gr; www.tinos-info.gr/tinoscamping]** Clearly sp fr port. Sm, hdg/mkd pitch, hdstg; shd; wc; chem disp (wc); shwrs inc; el pnts €4.50; lndry rm; shop; rest; snacks; BBQ; cooking facs; sand/shgl beach 500m; dogs; phone; Eng spkn; adv bkg; ccard acc; red long stay/CCI. "1,600 Venetian dovecots & 600 churches on island; monastery with healing icon." ♦ 1 May-31 Oct. € 21.50 2009*

VASILIKI (LEFKAS) *A2* (500m W Coastal) *38.63108, 20.60663* **Camping Vasiliki Beach, 31082 Vasiliki [(26450) 31308; fax 31458]** On arr in Vasiliki, turn R in 300m, site sp. Med, some hdstg, shd; wc; chem disp; mv service pnt; shwrs; el pnts (10A); gas; lndtte; shop; rest; snacks; bar; BBQ; playgrnd; beach adj; games rm; TV; dogs; phone; poss cr; Eng spkn; red CCI. "Popular with windsurfers; easy walk to town along beach." ♦ 15 Apr-15 Oct. € 36.00 2011*

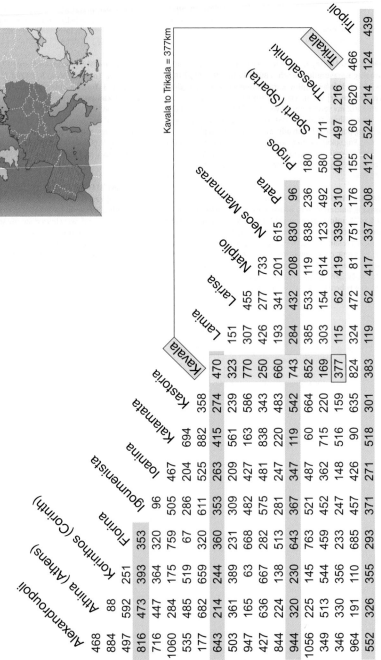

Distances are shown in kilometres and are calculated from town/city centres along the most practical roads, although not necessarily taking the shortest route. 1km = 0.62miles

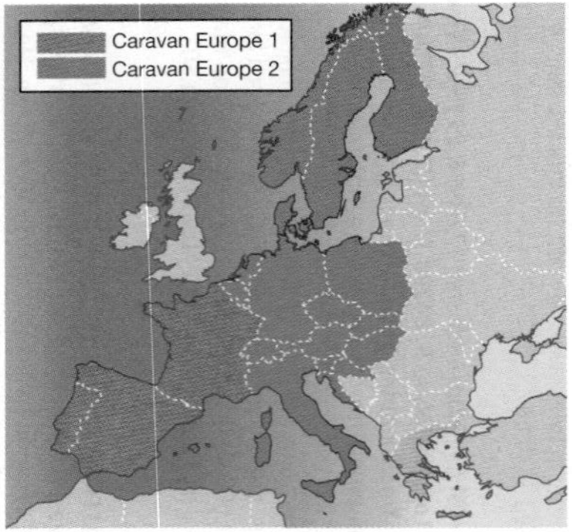

Caravan Europe 1
Caravan Europe 2

Kavala to Trikala = 377km

	Alexandroupoli	Athina (Athens)	Korinthos (Corinth)	Florina	Igoumenista	Ioanina	Kalamata	Kastoria	Kavala	Lamia	Larisa	Nafplio	Neos Marmaras	Patra	Pirgos	Sparti (Sparta)	Thessaloniki	Trikala	Tripoli
Athina (Athens)	468																		
Korinthos (Corinth)	884	88																	
Florina	497	592	251																
Igoumenista	816	473	393	353															
Ioanina	716	447	364	320	96														
Kalamata	1060	284	175	759	505	467													
Kastoria	535	485	519	67	286	204	694												
Kavala	177	682	659	320	611	525	882	358											
Lamia	643	214	244	360	353	263	415	274	470										
Larisa	503	361	389	231	309	209	561	239	323	151									
Nafplio	947	165	63	668	482	427	163	586	770	307	455								
Neos Marmaras	427	636	667	282	575	481	838	343	250	426	277	733							
Patra	844	224	138	513	281	247	220	483	660	193	341	201	615						
Pirgos	944	320	230	643	367	347	119	542	743	284	432	208	830	96					
Sparti (Sparta)	1056	225	145	763	521	487	60	664	852	385	533	119	838	236	180				
Thessaloniki	349	513	544	459	452	362	715	220	169	303	154	614	123	492	580	711			
Trikala	346	330	356	233	247	148	516	159	377	115	62	419	339	310	400	497	216		
Tripoli	964	191	110	685	457	426	90	635	824	324	472	81	751	176	155	60	620	466	
Volos	552	326	355	293	371	271	518	301	383	119	62	417	337	308	412	524	214	124	439

SERBIA
MONTENEGRO
KOSOVO
BULGARIA
MACEDONIA
ALBANIA
TURKEY
AEGEAN SEA
MEDITERRANEAN SEA
SOFIYA
Burgas
Blagoevgrad
Plovdiv
SKOPJE
Edirne
TIRANË
Bitola
FLORINA
KAVALA
Keramoti
Thassos
Pefkári
THASSOS
ALEXANDROUPOLI
THESSALONIKI
Asprovalta
Methoni Pierias
Ierissos
KASTORIA
Nea Moudania
Gerakini
Gjirokastër
Plaka Litohorou
Kassandria
Sarti
NEOS MARMARAS
Kalamitsi
LEMNOS
Platamonas
Roda
Corfu
IOANINA
Kalambaka
LARISA
IGOUMENITSA
TRIKALA
VOLOS
CORFU/KERKIRA
Parga
Riza
Preveza
Katafourko
LESBOS
Stylida
LAMIA
EUBOEA/EVIA
Lefkada
LEVKAS
Vasiliki
Kamena Vourla
Rovies
Izmir
Delfi
Eretria
CHIOS
Sami
Nafpaktos
PATRA
Egio
Akrata
Agioi Theodoroi
Marathonas
Rafina
CEPHALONIA
Kyllini
Vartholomio
Amaliada
KORINTHOS
ATHINA
Mikines
Palea Epidavros
Sounio
ZANTE
PYRGOS
Olimbia
TINOS
Tinos
Zacharo
TRIPOLI
NAFPLIO
Kyparissia
Thermissia
CYCLADES
Leonidi
Bodrum
KALAMATA
SPARTI
Kos
KOS
Pylos
Petalidi
Methoni
Stoupa
Finikoundas
Koroni
Githio
RHODES
Hania
Rethymno
Iraklio
Sisi
Agia Galini
CRETE
N
W
E
S
All year site(s)
Seasonal site(s)
No sites listed
200m +
0–200m
0 50 100 150 200 250 kms
0 50 100 150 mls
Motorways
Major roads
Main roads
© Collins Bartholomew Ltd 2011

Hungary

Country Introduction

© iStockPhoto.com/Ammit

Hungarian Parliament Building, Budapest

Population (approx): 10 million

Capital: Budapest (population approx 2 million)

Area: 93,030 sq km

Bordered by: Austria, Croatia, Romania, Serbia, Slovakia, Slovenia, Ukraine

Terrain: Mostly flat and rolling plains; hills and low mountains to the north

Climate: Temperate, continental climate; cold, cloudy winters; warm, sunny summers; changeable in spring and early summer with heavy rain and storms; the best times to visit are spring and autumn

Highest Point: Kekes 1,014m

Language: Hungarian

Local Time: GMT or BST + 1, i.e. 1 hour ahead of the UK all year

Currency: Forint (HUF); £1 = HUF 340, HUF 1000 = £2.94 pence (October 2011)

Telephoning: From the UK dial 0036 followed by a 1 or 2-digit area code and the number. To call the UK from Hungary dial 0044, omitting the initial zero of the area code

Emergency numbers: Police 112; Fire brigade 112; Ambulance 112. Operators speak English.

Public Holidays 2012

Jan 1; Mar 15 (National Day); Apr 8, 9; May 1, 27, 28; Aug 20 (Constitution Day); Oct 23 (Republic Day); Nov 1; Dec 25, 26.

Public Holidays 2013

Jan 1; Mar 15 (National Day); Mar 31; Apr 1; May 1, 19, 20; Aug 20 (Constitution Day); Oct 23 (Republic Day); Nov 1; Dec 25, 26.

School summer holidays are from mid-June to the end of August

Tourist Office

HUNGARIAN NATIONAL TOURIST OFFICE
46 EATON PLACE
LONDON SW1X 8AL
Tel: 09001 171200 (for brochure requests) or 00800 3600 0000
www.gotohungary.co.uk
info@gotohungary.co.uk

The following introduction to Hungary should be read in conjunction with the important information contained in the Handbook chapters at the front of this guide.

Camping and Caravanning

There are approximately 100 organised campsites in Hungary rated from 1 to 4 stars. These are generally well signposted off main routes, with the site name shown below a blue camping sign. Most campsites open from May to September and the most popular sites are situated by Lake Balaton and the Danube. A Camping Card International is essential.

Facilities vary from site to site, but visitors will find it useful to carry their own flat universal sink plug. There has been much improvement in recent years in the general standard of campsites, but communal changing areas for showers are not uncommon. Many sites have communal kitchen facilities which enable visitors to make great savings on their own gas supply.

Many campsites require payment in cash. Visitors report that prices in local currency have risen sharply in recent years. Therefore, prices in this guide for sites not reported on for some time might not reflect the true picture, although they are still low in real terms.

Casual/wild camping is prohibited.

Country Information

Cycling

There are approximately 2,000km of cycle tracks, 100km of which are in Budapest and 200km around Lake Balaton. Tourinform offices in Hungary will provide a map of cycling routes.

Children under 14 years are not allowed to ride on the road and all cyclists must wear a reflective jacket at night and in poor daytime visibility.

Electricity and Gas

Current on campsites varies between 6 and 16 amps. Plugs have two round pins. There are some sites that do not have CEE connections.

Only non-returnable and/or non-exchangeable Campingaz cylinders are available.

*See **Electricity and Gas** in the section **DURING YOUR STAY.***

Entry Formalities

British and Irish passport holders may stay for a period of three months without a visa. Your passport needs to be valid for the duration of your stay and it is always recommended when visiting a foreign country to have an additional period of validity on your passport in case of any unforeseen delays.

Anyone planning to stay longer than three months should contact the Hungarian Embassy for further information

There are no longer any immigration or Customs checks at borders with other EU countries, i.e. Slovakia, Slovenia and Austria. Border crossings with other countries are generally open 24 hours.

Regulations for Pets

*See **Pet Travel Scheme** under **Documents** in the section **PLANNING AND TRAVELLING.***

Medical Services

British nationals may obtain emergency medical and dental treatment from practitioners contracted to the national health insurance scheme, Országos Egészségbiztosítási (OEP), together with emergency hospital treatment, on presentation of a European Health Insurance Card (EHIC) and a British passport. Fees are payable for treatment and prescribed medicines, and are not refundable in Hungary. You may be able to apply for reimbursement when back in the UK.

Pharmacies (gyógyszertár)) are well stocked. The location of the nearest all-night pharmacy is displayed on the door of every pharmacy.

If you enjoy hiking and outdoor sports you should seek medical advice before you travel about preventative measures and immunisation against tick-borne encephalitis, a potentially serious and debilitating viral disease of the central nervous system which is endemic from spring to autumn. Lyme disease is an equally serious tick-borne infection for which there is no preventative vaccine. Ticks are found in rural and forested areas, particularly in long grass, bushes, hedgerows and woods, and in scrubland and areas where animals wander.

If you think you might be at risk use an insect repellent containing DEET, wear long sleeves and long trousers, inspect the body for ticks after outdoor activity and remove with tweezers, and avoid unpasteurised dairy products in risk areas. See www.tickalert.org, email info@tickalert.org or telephone 01943 468010.

You are strongly recommended to obtain comprehensive travel and medical insurance before travelling to Hungary, such as The Caravan Club's Red Pennant Overseas Holiday Insurance – see www.caravanclub.co.uk/redpennant

*See **Medical Matters** in the section **DURING YOUR STAY.***

Opening Hours

Banks – Mon-Thurs 8am-4pm

Museums – Tue-Sun 10am-6pm; closed Monday.

Post Offices – Mon-Fri 8am-6pm; post office at Budapest post offices at main railway stations open Mon-Sat 7am-9pm.

Shops – Mon-Fri 10am-6pm (supermarkets from 7am to 7pm with some grocery stores open 24 hours); open half day Saturdays.

Safety and Security

Petty theft in Budapest is common in areas frequented by tourists, particularly on busy public transport, at markets and at popular tourist sites. Beware of pickpockets and bag snatchers and leave valuables in your caravan safe.

Do not carry large amounts of cash. Take care when receiving bank notes as change as some that are no longer valid are still in circulation, e.g. HUF 200 notes were withdrawn in 2009. There has been a small number of instances of taxi drivers deliberately passing these notes to tourists. Be aware especially when paying with a HUF 10,000 or 20,000 bank note.

Theft of and from vehicles is common. Do not leave your belongings, car registration documents or mobile phones in your car and ensure that it is properly locked with the alarm on, even if leaving it for just a moment. Beware of contrived 'incidents', particularly on the Vienna-Budapest motorway, designed to stop motorists and expose them to robbery.

Visitors have reported in the past that motorists may be pestered at service areas on the Vienna to Budapest motorway by people insisting on washing windscreens and demanding paper money.

During the summer season in Budapest, uniformed tourist police patrol the most frequently visited areas of the city. Criminals sometimes pose as tourist police and ask for visitors' money, credit cards or travel documents in order to check them. Always ensure that a uniformed police officer is wearing a badge displaying the word 'Rendörség' and a five-digit identification number, together with a separate name badge. Plain clothes police carry a badge and an ID card with picture, hologram and rank. If in doubt, insist on going to the nearest police station.

There are still occasional incidents of exhorbitant overcharging in certain restaurants, bars and clubs in Budapest, accompanied by threats of violence. Individuals who have been unable to settle their bill have frequently been accompanied by the establishment's security guards to a cash machine and made to withdraw funds. Visitors are advised to ask for a menu and only order items which are priced realistically. A five digit price for one dish is too high. Never accept menus which do not display prices and check your bill carefully.

Taxi drivers are sometimes accomplices to these frauds, receiving 'commission' for recommending restaurants and bars which charge extortionate prices to visitors. Never ask a taxi driver to recommend a bar, club or restaurant. If a driver takes you to one or you are approached on the street with an invitation to an unfamiliar bar or restaurant, you should treat such advice with extreme caution.

Do not change money or get involved in any form of gambling in the street; these activities are illegal.

If you need help, go to the nearest police station or to the 24 hour tourist assistance office in Budapest, which is open from 1 June to 1 September at the police headquarters at Teve Utca 6 in District 13, tel (1) 4435259. District police stations in Districts 1, 5, 11 and 14 also have 24 hour tourism desks where complaints can be dealt with and assistance given in English.

There is a low threat from terrorism. Attacks could be indiscriminate and against civilian targets in public places, including tourist sites.

*See **Safety and Security** in the section **DURING YOUR STAY.***

British Embassy

HARMINCAD UTCA 6, BUDAPEST 1051
Tel: (1) 2662888
http://ukinhungary.fco.gov.uk

Irish Embassy

SZABADSÁG TÉR 7,
BANK CENTRE, GRANIT TOWER, V. FLOOR
1054 BUDAPEST
Tel: (1) 3014960
www.embassyofireland.hu

Customs Regulations

Alcohol and Tobacco

*For import allowances for alcohol and tobacco products see **Customs Regulations** in the section **PLANNING AND TRAVELLING.***

Documents

Passport

Carry your passport at all times. A photocopy is not acceptable.

Vehicle(s)

Carry your vehicle registration certificate (V5C), vehicle insurance certificate and MOT certificate (if applicable) with you when driving.

Do not leave these documents in your vehicle when it is unattended.

*See also **Documents** and **Insurance** in the section **PLANNING AND TRAVELLING***

Money

Hungarian currency is available from banks in Austria before crossing the border. For emergency cash reserves, it is advisable to have euros, rather than sterling. Foreign currency is best exchanged at banks as, by law, this is at the rate shown on the banks' currency boards and they are not permitted to charge commission for travellers' cheques or currency. Private bureaux de change, however, do charge commission, but the rate of exchange may be better.

Credit cards are accepted at many outlets in large towns and cities and cash dispensers, 'bankomats', are widespread even in small towns. There is a high incidence of credit card fraud and payment in cash wherever possible is advisable. Carry your credit card issuers'/banks' 24 hour UK contact numbers in case of loss or theft of your cards.

Recent visitors report that some newer types of debit and credit cards issued in the UK do not work in certain cash machines in Hungary. The banks are working on a solution but, in the meantime, if you encounter this problem you should try a cash machine at a different bank. It is possible to obtain cash from post offices with a debit or credit card.

Euros are widely accepted in shops and restaurants frequented by tourists, but check the exchange rate.

When leaving Hungary on the MI motorway (Budapest-Vienna), it is important to change back your forints on the Hungarian side of the border by crossing the carriageway to the left at the designated crossing-point, as visitors report that there are no facilities on the right hand side and none on the other side in Austria.

Motoring

Accidents

Accidents causing damage to vehicles or injury to persons must be reported to the nearest police station and to the Hungarian State Insurance Company (Hungária Biztositó) within 24 hours. The police will issue a statement which you may be asked to show when leaving the country.

If entering Hungary with a conspicuously damaged vehicle, it is recommended that you obtain a report confirming the damage from the police in the country where the damage occurred, otherwise difficulties may arise when leaving Hungary.

Alcohol

It is illegal to drive after consuming any alcoholic drinks whatsoever.

Breakdown Service

The motoring organisation, Magyar Autóklub (MAK), operates a breakdown service 24 hours a day on all roads. Drivers in need of assistance should telephone 188 or (1) 3451755 (operators speak English on this number). The number (1) is the area code for Budapest. On motorways emergency phones are placed at 2km intervals.

MAK road patrol cars are yellow and marked 'Segélyszolgálat'. Their registration numbers begin with the letters MAK.

The roadside breakdown service is chargeable, higher charges applying at night. There is a scale of charges by vehicle weight and distance for towing vehicles to a garage. Payment is required in cash.

Essential Equipment

*See **Motoring – Equipment** in the section **PLANNING AND TRAVELLING.***

First Aid Kit

It is a legal requirement that all vehicles should carry a first aid kit.

Lights

Outside built-up areas dipped headlights are compulsory at all times, regardless of weather conditions. Bulbs are more likely to fail with constant use and you are recommended to carry spares. At night in built-up areas dipped headlights must be used as full beam is prohibited.

Headlight flashing often means that a driver is giving way, but do not carry out a manoeuvre unless you are sure that this is the case.

Reflective Jackets/Waistcoats

If your vehicle is immobilised on the carriageway outside a built-up area, or if visibility is poor, you must wear a reflective jacket or waistcoat when getting out of your vehicle. Passengers who leave the vehicle, for example, to assist with a repair, should also wear one. Keep the jackets inside your vehicle, not in the boot.

In addition, pedestrians and cyclists walking or cycling at night or in poor visibility along unlit roads outside a built-up area must also wear a reflective jacket.

Warning Triangles

In the event of accident, it is compulsory to place a warning triangle 100 metres behind the vehicle on motorways and 50 metres on other roads.

Child Restraint System

Children under the height of 1.5m and over the age of three years must be seated in a suitable child restraint system appropriate for their size in the rear of the vehicle.

Children under the age of three years old can only travel in a vehicle if they are seated in a suitable child restraint system for their size. They can travel at the front of the vehicle but only if the child restraint system is rear facing and if the airbag has been deactivated.

Winter Driving

The use of snow chains can be made compulsory on some roads when there is severe winter weather.

Snow chains can be hired or purchased from Polar Automotive Ltd, tel 01892 519933, www.snowchains.com, email: sales@snowchains.com (10% discount for Caravan Club members).

Fuel

Leaded petrol is no longer available. The sign 'Ólommentes üzemanyag' or 'Bleifrei 95' indicates unleaded petrol. LPG is widely available – see www.mpe.mtesz.hu

Most petrol stations are open from 6am to 8pm. Along motorways and in large towns they are often open 24 hours. Virtually all petrol stations accept credit and debit cards, possible exceptions being in remote, rural areas.

*See also **Fuel** under **Motoring – Advice** in the section **PLANNING AND TRAVELLING.***

Parking

Zigzag lines on the carriageway and road signs indicate a stopping/parking prohibition. Illegally-parked vehicles will be towed away or clamped.
On two-way roads, vehicles must park in the direction of traffic; they may park on either side in one-way streets. In certain circumstances, parking on the pavement is allowed.

Budapest is divided into various time restricted parking zones (maximum three hours) where tickets must be purchased from Monday to Friday from a machine. For longer periods you are advised to use 'Park and Ride' car parks located near major metro stations and bus terminals.

*See also **Parking Facilities for the Disabled** under **Motoring – Advice** in the section **PLANNING AND TRAVELLING.***

Priority

Pedestrians have priority over traffic at pedestrian crossings and at intersections. They do not have priority on the roadway between central tramloading islands and pavements, and drivers must exercise care on these sections. Major roads are indicated by a priority road ahead sign. At the intersection of two roads of equal importance, where there is no sign, vehicles coming from the right have priority. Trams and buses have priority at any intersection on any road and buses have right of way when leaving bus stops after the driver has signalled his intention to pull out.

Roads

Hungary has a good system of well surfaced main roads and driving standards are higher than in many other parts of Europe. There are few dual carriageways and care is required, therefore, when overtaking with a right-hand drive vehicle. Extra care is required on provincial roads which may be badly lit, poorly maintained and narrow. In the countryside at night be on the alert for unlit cycles and horse drawn vehicles.

Road Signs and Markings

Road signs and markings conform to international conventions. Square green road signs indicate the number of kilometers to the next town. At traffic lights a flashing amber light a indicates a dangerous intersection.

Destination signs feature road numbers rather than the names of towns, so it is essential to equip yourself with an up-to-date road map or atlas. Signs for motorways have white lettering on a blue background; on other roads signs are white and green.

Speed Limits

*See **Speed Limits Table** under **Motoring – Advice** in the section **PLANNING AND TRAVELLING.***

A speed limit of 30 km/h (18 mph) is in force in many residential, city centre and tourist resort areas.

Traffic Jams

Roads around Budapest are busy on Friday and Sunday afternoons. In the holiday season roads to Lake Balaton (M7) and around the lake (N7 and N71) may be congested. There are regular traffic hold ups at weekends at the border crossings to Austria, the Czech Republic and Serbia. Motorway traffic information (in English) is available on www.motorway.hu

Violation of Traffic Regulations

The police make spot vehicle document checks and are keen to enforce speed limits. They are permitted to impose, but not collect, on-the-spot fines of up to HUF150,000. Credit cards are not accepted for the payment of fines.

Motorways

All motorways (autópálya) and main connecting roads run to or from Budapest. In recent years the road network has been extended and improved and there are now approximately 900 kilometres of motorway and dual carriageways or semi-motorways, as listed overleaf. However, most roads are still single carriageway, single lane and care is recommended. The M0 motorway is a 75km ringroad around Budapest which links the M1, M7, M6, M5 and Highway 11. The recently built Megyeri Bridge on the Danube is part of the M0 and its opening has considerably reduced traffic congestion to the north of Budapest.

Motorway No.	Route	Distance in km
M0	Budapest ringroad – M1 – M5	28.7
M0	Budapest ringroad – M5 – Road 11	46.7
M1	Budapest to Hegyeshalom	160.2
M2	M0 – Vác, Road 2	30.7
M3	Budapest to Nyíregyháza	223.0
M5	Budapest – Kecskemét – Szeged – Röszke	174.0
M6	Érd – Dunaújváros – Szekszárd – Pécs	205
M7	Budapest to Letenye (Croatian border)	228.7
M8	M6 Danube – Road 51	5.2
M9	Danube Highway – Szekszárd	20.5
M15	M1 – Rajka (Slovakian border)	13.8
M19	M1 – Road 1	9.7
M30	M3 to Miskolc	27.5
M31	M0 Pécel – Gödöllő	12.0
M35	M3 – Debrecen	43.0
M43	Szeged North – Road 5	33.7
M70	Letenye to Tornyiszentmiklós (Slovenian border)	21.4

Motorways M1 and M7 have a common section for 20 km.

Motorway Vignettes

Approximately 30% of motorways are toll-free; for the majority you must purchase an electronic vignette (matrica) or e-vignette (sticker) before entering the motorway.

They are available online and from motorway customer service offices and at petrol stations throughout Hungary. Payment may be made in forints or by credit card.

Leaflets are distributed to motorists at the border and a telephone information centre is available in Hungary – tel 06 40 40 50 60. Vignettes should only be purchased from outlets where the prices are clearly displayed at the set rates.

For full details (in English), including how to buy online and toll-free sections, see www.motorway.hu

When purchasing an e-vignette a confirmation message will be sent or a coupon issued and this must be kept for a year after its expiry date. There is no need to display the vignette in your windscreen as the motorway authorities check all vehicles electronically (without the need for you to stop your vehicle) and verify registration number, category of toll paid and validity of an e-vignette. Charges in forints (2011 charges subject to change) are as shown opposite.

Category of Vehicle	Period of Validity		
	4 days	1 week	1 month
Vehicle up to 3,500kg with or without caravan or trailer	1,650	2,750	4,500
Vehicle between 3,500kg and 7,500kg with or without caravan or trailer	n/a	7,750	13,000

Touring

Hungary boasts eleven World Heritage sites including the national park at Aggtelek which contains Europe's largest cave network, the Christian cemetary at Pécs and the monastery at Pannonhalma. Lake Balaton, the largest lake in Central Europe, attracts lovers of bathing, sailing, fishing and windsurfing. With 200km of sandy shoreline and shallow warm waters, it is very popular with families and easily Hungary's favourite tourist area.

A Budapest Card is available, allowing unlimited travel on public transport for two or three consecutive days, free city walking tours, discounted entry to museums and other attractions, plus discounts on many guided tours, events, shops and restaurants. Cards are available from metro stations, tourist information offices, many travel agencies, hotels, museums and main Budapest transport ticket offices, as well as from the Hungarian National Tourist Office in London. A child under 14 travelling with the cardholder is included free of charge. You may also order online from www.budapestinfo.hu

Download a tourist and cultural guide to Budapest on www.culturalbudapest.com

Hungarian cuisine is renowned for its goulash, but there are countless other specialities characterised by the use of distinctive spices and ingredients such as green peppers, melted pork fat and sour cream. Venison is widely available together with a variety of fish from Lake Balaton. Hungarian wines are excellent, notably Tokay (white) and Bull's Blood (red), and varieties of cherry, plum and apricot brandies are popular. Restaurants are of a good standard with menus often written in German or English, and based on German style dishes of meat, fish or game. A tip of 10-15% of the bill is expected in restaurants. Check your bill first to ensure that a service charge has not already been added.

Take your own supply of plastic carrier bags to supermarkets, as generally they are not supplied.

Hungarian is a notoriously difficult language for native English speakers to decipher and pronounce. English is not widely spoken in rural areas, but it is becoming increasingly widespread elsewhere as it is now taught in schools. German is widely spoken and a dictionary may be helpful in restaurants and shops, etc.

Local Travel

Cars are not permitted within the Castle District and on Margaret Island in Budapest. It is advisable and convenient to use public transport when travelling into the city and there is an excellent network of bus, tram and metro routes (BKV). All public transport in Hungary is free to those aged 65 and over, and this also applies to foreign visitors on presentation of proof of age (passport).

There are a number of ticket options, including family tickets, 1, 3 and 7 day tickets, and they can be bought at metro stations, ticket machines, tobacconists and newsagents. Validate your bus and metro tickets before use at each stage of your journey at the red machines provided and note that you have to validate another ticket every time you change metro lines. Tickets are often checked on vehicles or at metro station exits by controllers wearing arm bands and carrying photo ID. For further information (in English) on public transport in Budapest see www.bkv.hu

As a general rule, it is better to phone for taxis operated by reputable local companies, rather than flag them down in the street, and always ensure that fares are metered. Inspect your change carefully, especially notes. Outside the capital, taxi drivers are less prone to unscrupulous pricing and can usually be flagged down without any problems. Ask what the fare will be to your destination before departure and always check that there is a meter running in the taxi. A tip of approximately 10% of the fare is customary.

Mahart, the Hungarian Shipping Company, operates a regular hydrofoil service from April to October along the Danube between Budapest and Vienna. The journey lasts six hours and covers 288km.
A stop in Bratislava can be arranged. Information on timetables and tickets is available on tel (1) 4844013, www.mahartpassnave.hu

Local companies, Legenda (www.legenda.hu) and Mahart also offer city cruises between April and October, as well as regular trips to tourist attractions outside Budapest, such as Szentendre, Visegrád and Esztergom.

A ferry service takes cars across Lake Balaton from Szántód to Tihany. There are crossings every 10 minutes from June to September and every hour during the low season. Regular bus and train services link the towns and villages along the lakeside.

All place names used in the Site Entry listings which follow can be found in the Hungary Supertouring Autoatlas published by Freytag & Berndt, scale 1cm to 2.5km, see www.freytagberndt.com

AGGTELEK *A3* (500m NW Rural) *48.47094, 20.49446* **Baradla Camping, Baradla Oldal 1, 3759 Aggtelek [tel/fax (48) 503000; szallas@anp.hu]** Fr Slovakia turn off E571/A50 at Plesivec onto rd 587 S via Dlha Ves to border x-ing. Cont S for approx 800m & hotel/campsite complex is on L. Fr Miskolc 45km N on rte 26, turn onto rte 27 sp Perkupa then foll sp Nemzeti National Park & Aggtelek. Site sp in vill. Med, pt sl, pt shd; wc; shwrs; el pnts (16A) inc; rest, snacks, bar at motel; BBQ; cooking facs; playgrnd; some cabins; quiet. "Gd NH to/ fr Slovakia; ent to lge Barlang Caves system adj; facs poss stretched high ssn." 15 Apr-15 Oct. € 13.50 2010*

ALSOORS see Balatonfüred *C2*

BADACSONY *C1* (S Rural) *46.78978, 17.47495* **Camping Eldorado, Vízpart 1, 8262 Badacsonylábdihegy [(87) 432369; fax 432770; balaton@balatoneldoradocamping.hu; www.balatoneldoradocamping.hu]** Nr km 81.5 on rte 71 bet Badacsonytördemic & Badacsony. Ent adj rest & motel. Med, hdg pitch, shd; wc; chem disp; mv service pnt; shwrs inc; el pnts (10A) inc; lndtte; shop; rest; bar; playgrnd; htd pool; paddling pool; lake sw adj; 5% statics; dogs HUF860; bus, train 300m; phone; Eng spkn; daytime train noise; ccard acc; CCI. "V clean facs & site; gd rest; red snr citizens." ♦ 1 May-15 Sep. HUF 6100 2008*

BALATONAKALI *C1* (200m SE Rural) *46.8834, 17.76913* **Balatontourist Camping Strand-Holiday, Strand u 2, 8243 Balatonakali [(87) 544021; fax 544022; strand@balatontourist.hu; www.balatontourist.hu]** Site sp on rte 71 at km 53.6 at E end of Balatonakali. Lge, hdg/mkd pitch, pt shd; wc; chem disp; mv service pnt; baby facs; private bthrms avail; shwrs inc; el pnts (6-10A) inc; lndtte; shop high ssn; rest & 500m; playgrnd; sand beach & lake sw; windsurfing; watersports; fishing; cycle hire; games area; internet; entmnt; TV rm; some statics; dogs HUF900; adv bkg; daytime rlwy noise; ccard acc. "Excel san facs; some lakeside pitches; cycle track around lake adj." ♦ 2 Apr-10 Oct. HUF 8250 (CChq acc) 2010*

BALATONAKALI *C1* (300m SW Rural) *46.87939, 17.74190* **Balatontourist Camping Levendula (Naturist), Hókuli u 25, 8243 Balatonakali [(87) 544011; fax 544012; levendula@balatonturist.hu; www.balatontourist.hu]** NE on rte 71 on N shore of Lake Balaton twds Tihany. Site sp on W app to Balatonakali. Turn R twds lake; go over level x-ing, site ent on R. Med, mkd pitch, pt shd; wc; chem disp; mv service pnt; sauna; shwrs inc; el pnts (4A) inc; gas; lndtte (inc dryer); shop; supmkt 1km; rest; snacks; bar; playgrnd; sand beach & lake sw; fishing; windsurf school; games area; cycle hire; wifi; TV rm; dogs HUF950; adv bkg; Eng spkn; quiet at night, train noise fr early morning; ccard acc; CCI. "Superb site." ♦ 7 May-12 Sep. HUF 6800 (CChq acc) 2010*

BALATONALMADI *C2* (1km SW Rural) *47.0205, 18.00828* **Balatontourist Camping Yacht, Véghely Dezsö út 18, 8220 Balatonalmádi [(88) 584101; fax 584102; yacht@balatontourist.hu; www.balatontourist.hu]** Fr rd 71, km post 25.5, site sp at lakeside. Lge, hdg/mkd pitch, pt shd; wc; chem disp; mv service pnt; shwrs inc; el pnts (4A) inc (rev pol); lndtte; shop; rest; snacks; bar; playgrnd; beach adj; watersports; cycle hire; entmnt; TV; 10% statics; dogs HUF990; Eng spkn; adv bkg; ccard acc; CCI. "Excel san facs; excel rest; friendly staff; several sites in close proximity." ♦ 29 Apr-18 Sep. HUF 8800 2011*

BALATONBERENY *C1* (500m W Rural) *46.71340, 17.31080* **FKK Naturista Camping (Naturist), Kossuth Tèr 1, 8649 Balatonberény [tel/fax (85) 377715; bereny@balatontourist.hu]** Fr Keszthely foll rte 71 & rte 76 round SW end of lake. Lge sp indicates Balatonberény & site. Sps change fr Naturista Camping to FKK at turn off main rd. Med, hdg/mkd pitch, pt shd; wc; chem disp; shwrs inc; el pnts (12-16A) inc; lndtte; shop; tradsmn; rest; snacks; bar; BBQ; direct access lake sw adj; playgrnd; windsurfing; watersports; games area; wifi; entmnt; TV; few statics; dogs €2.60; phone; quiet; poss cr; adv bkg; red INF. "vg site; gd sized pitches." 15 May-15 Sep. € 23.75 2011*

BALATONFURED *C2* (7km NE Rural) *46.9769, 17.95691* **Europa Camping, 8226 Alsóörs [(87) 555021; fax 555022; europa@balatontourist.hu; www.balatontourist.hu]** Fr Veszprém on rte 73 turn L onto rte 71 twd Balatonalmádi. Site well sp fr 31.7km marker on rte 71 on R. Lge, pt shd; wc; chem disp; mv service pnt; shwrs inc; el pnts (6-10A) inc; gas; lndtte; sm supmkt adj; playgrnd; pool; paddling pool; lake sw; sand beach; windsurfing; tennis; cycle hire; internet; TV; dogs HUF650; phone; barrier key; adv bkg; ccard acc. ♦ 10 May-14 Sep. HUF 7480 2008*

⊞ **BALATONFURED** *C2* (9km NE Rural) *46.99722, 17.98944* **Présház Camping, Présház út 1, 8226 Alsóörs [(87) 447736]** Rd 71 fr Balatonfüred, site just past vill of Alsóörs on L. Sm, pt sl, pt shd; wc; chem disp; shwrs inc; el pnts (10A) inc; lake sw 1km; games area; dogs; quiet. "Vg CL-type site in orchard of wine shop; friendly owner; wine-tasting; paid in Euros but Forint preferred; sighting of wild boar nearby!" € 14.00 2011*

BALATONFURED *C2* (1km SW Rural) *46.94660, 17.87590* **Balatontourist Camping Füred, Széchenyi út 24, 8230 Balatonfüred [(87) 580241; fax 580242; fured@balatontourist.hu; www.balatontourist.hu]** Exit M3 or rte 70 on rte 71 sp Balatonfüred. Site sp 1km SW of Balatonfüred on SE side of rd 71 on N side of lake. V lge, pt shd; htd wc; chem disp; mv service pnt; baby facs; sauna; shwrs inc; el pnts (4A) inc; lndtte (inc dryer); shop; rest; snacks; bar; playgrnd; pool; paddling pool; waterslides; beach & lake sw; watersports; tennis; cycle hire; wifi; entmnt; TV rm; 10% statics; no dogs; phone; bus; poss cr; adv bkg; quiet except nr rd; ccard acc; red low ssn. "Many attractions in this holiday area; lovely lakeside town; gd facs, but ltd low ssn; prices vary depending on pitch size; excel." ♦ 22 Apr-2 Oct. HUF 8700 (CChq acc) 2011*

BALATONGYOROK *C1* (2km NE Rural) *46.76888, 17.3646* **Castrum Camping, Szépkilátó, 8313 Balatongyörök [(83) 346666; fax 314422; balatongyorok@castrum.eu; www.castrum-group.hu]** E on rd 71 fr Keszthely for approx 11km. Turn R immed past panorama lookout, site in 500m over rlwy line. Lge, hdg/mkd pitch, pt shd; wc; chem disp; shwrs inc; el pnts (6A) €3; Indtte; shop; rest; snacks; bar; playgrnd; lake sw & beach adj; games area; cycle hire; entmnt; 5% statics; dogs €4; rlwy noise; ccard acc; CCI. "Lake view not poss due tall reeds; facs looking tired." 1 May-30 Sep. € 18.60 (CChq acc) 2008*

BALATONGYOROK *C1* (400m S Rural) *46.75095, 17.35075* **Carina Camping, Balatoni út 13, 8313 Balatongyörök [tel/fax (83) 349084; carinacamping@t-online.hu; www.carinacamping.hu]** On ent country fr Austria (Eisenstadt-Sopron) on rte 84 to Lake Balaton, W on rte 71. Approx 10km bef Keszthely at km 95.5 turn L to Balatongyörök, sp. Turn R into site at end of vill bef rlwy line. Med, pt shd; wc; chem disp; snacks; shwrs inc; el pnts (10A) HUF450; Indtte; shops adj; rest adj; snacks; sw in lake; dogs HUF350; poss cr; adv bkg; rlwy noise; red long stay/CCI. "Beautifully laid-out in lovely area; 100m to beach across rlwy x-ing; avoid pitch adj to dusty rd; gd cycle rtes round lake." 1 Apr-30 Sep. HUF 3250 2008*

BALATONGYOROK *C1* (3km NW Urban) *46.75146, 17.3335* **Balaton Tourist Camping Park, Szentmihàly Domb, 8314 Vonyarcvashegy [tel/fax (83) 348044; park@balatontourist.hu; www.balatontourist.hu]** Fr Keszthely take rte 71 NE & exit at km 96.8, site sp in 1.5km. Med, hdg/mkd pitch, hdstg, pt shd; wc; chem disp; mv service pnt; shwrs inc; el pnts (10A) inc; gas; Indtte; shop; rest; snacks; bar; playgrnd; paddling pool; lake sw/beach adj; tennis; fishing; watersports; wifi; 30% statics; TV; dogs HUF750; poss cr; Eng spkn; quiet; ccard acc; red long stay/CCI. "Sm, med & lge pitches; mkt every day; Hévíz thermal baths nr." ♦ 19 Apr-30 Sep. HUF 5500 2008*

BALATONKENESE *C2* (W Rural) **Romantik Camping, Gesztenye Fasor 1, 8174 Balatonkenese [tel/fax (88) 482360; romantikcamping@invitel.hu]** Off rte 71 on N shore of lake, sp. Med, pt terr, pt shd; wc; shwrs; el pnts HUF400; Indry rm; shop; snacks; cooking facs; 250m to lake; quiet. "Reasonable facs; site has potential." Jun-Sep. 2009*

BALATONSZEMES *C2* (4km SW Rural) *46.79360, 17.72880* **Balatontourist Camping Vadvirág, Arany János ut, 8636 Balatonszemes [(84) 360114; fax 360115; vadvirag@balatontourist.hu; www.balatontourist.hu]** On E71 S coast rd of lake, km stone 134. Site clearly sp over rlwy line. V lge, shd; wc; chem disp; mv service pnt; fam bthrm; shwrs; el pnts (10-16A) inc; gas; Indtte; shop; rest; snacks; bar; playgrnd; lake sw; tennis; games area; cycle hire; entmnt; TV; 50% statics; dogs; poss cr; adv bkg; noise fr rlwy & disco; ccard acc. "Some pitches sm; wine-growing area; buses to Budapest." ♦ 18 Apr-7 Sep. € 29.30 2008*

BALATONSZEPEZD *C1* (2km NE Rural) *46.8610, 17.67335* **Balatontourist Camping Venus, Halász út 1, 8252 Balatonszepezd [(87) 568061; fax 568062; venus@balatontourist.hu; www.balatontourist.hu]** On rte 71; site sp at km post 61, over level x-ing into site. Med, pt shd; wc; chem disp; mv service pnt; shwrs inc; el pnts (4-10A) inc; Indtte; shop; rest; snacks; playgrnd; beach; watersports; fishing; games area; dogs HUF750; Eng spkn; noise fr rlwy; ccard acc. "Excel lakeside position; gd rest; gd value." ♦ 14 May-5 Sep. HUF 5400 2010*

We can fill in site report forms on the Club's website – www.caravanclub.co.uk/europereport

BALATONSZEPEZD *C1* (4km SW Rural) *46.82960, 17.64014* **Balatontourist Camping Napfény, Halász út 5, 8253 Révfülöp [(87) 563031; fax 464309; napfeny@balatontourist.hu; www.balatontourist.hu]** Take m'way E71/M7 & exit junc 90 along N shore of lake, passing Balatonalmádi & Balatonfüred to Révfülöp. Site sp. Lge, mkd pitch, pt shd; wc; chem disp; mv service pnt; baby facs; private san facs avail; shwrs inc; el pnts (6A) inc; Indtte (inc dryer); shop; supmkt 500m; tradsmn; rest; snacks; bar; BBQ; playgrnd; paddling pool; lake sw & beach adj; fishing; watersports; cycle & boat hire; tennis 300m; horseriding 5km; games area; games rm; wifi; entmnt; TV rm; 2% statics; dogs HUF900; twin-axles acc (rec check in adv); phone; adv bkg; quiet; ccard acc; red low ssn. "Warm welcome; excel, well-organised lakeside site; gd pitches; gd for families; fees according to pitch size & location." ♦ 27 Apr-30 Sep. HUF 7150 (CChq acc) SBS - X06 2011*

BIATORBAGY *B2* (200m W Urban) *47.46999, 18.81758* **Camping Margaréta Bia, Bethlen Gábor ut 25, 2051 Biatorbágy [(23) 312465; fax 312143; biacamping@t-online.hu; http://web.t-online.hu/biacamping]** Fr M1/E60 Budapest-Györ exit at Biatorbágy onto rte 1. At rndabt (km 14) sp Biatorbágy, cont for 2km then R on Jókai Mor, then 1st L, site sp. Site on L in 200m, sp fr town. Sm, pt shd; wc; chem disp; mv service pnt; shwrs inc; el pnts (6A) HUF550; Indtte; shop 300m; cooking facs; rest, bar 300m; TV rm; dogs HUF275; bus 400m; phone 1km; Eng spkn; adv bkg; quiet; red CCI. "CL-type, family-run site in orchard; gd sat TV recep; wine-tasting; bus/tram to Budapest; v friendly." ♦ 15 Apr-30 Sep. HUF 4400 2008*

BOLDOGASSZONYFA *D2* (1km S Rural) **Camping Horgásztanya, Petöfi út 53, 7937 Boldogasszonyfa [(73) 702003; horgasztanya@ceginfo.net; www.horgasztanya.hu]** Take rte 67 S fr Kaposvár. Immed after vill of Boldogasszonyfa turn L, site sp on rvside. Sm, hdg pitch, pt sl, shd; wc; chem disp (wc); shwrs inc; el pnts (10A); rest; bar; fishing; quiet; CCI. "Simple, rural site; conv Pécs & border area." ♦ 1 May-30 Sep. 2009*

HUNGARY

BOZSOK see Köszeg *B1*

⊞ **BUDAPEST** *B2* (10km N Urban) *47.57434, 19.05179* **Római Camping, Szentendrei út 189, 1031 Budapest [(1) 3887167; fax 2500426; info@romaicamping.hu; www.romaicamping.hu]** Fr Gyor/Budapest m'way M1/E50 foll rte 11 twd Szentendre/Esztergom for approx 9km. Turn R at site sp. Site adj Római Fürdő rlwy stn. Med, mkd pitch, shd; wc; chem disp; shwrs inc; el pnts (16A) HUF600; Indtte (inc dryer); shop 500m; rest; snacks; BBQ; playgrnd; htd pool; playgrnd; waterslide; TV; dogs HUG590; train 300m; phone; Eng spkn; poss noisy; ccard not acc; CCI. "V conv for city." HUF 5560 2010*

BUDAPEST *B2* (11km N Rural) *47.6013, 19.0191* **Jumbo Camping, Budakalászi út 23, 2096 Üröm [tel/fax (26) 351251; jumbo@campingbudapest.com; www.jumbocamping.hu]** Best app fr N on rd 10 or 11. Fr M1 take Zsámbék exit thro Perbál to join rd 10 & turn W twd Budapest. After Pilisvörösvar turn L in 8km sp Üröm Site well sp. Med, hdg pitch, hdstg, pt sl, terr, pt shd; wc; chem disp; shwrs inc; el pnts (6-10A) inc; Indtte; shop 500m; rest 300m; snacks; bar; playgrnd; htd pool high ssn; TV; 10% statics; dogs; bus to Budapest fr vill; Eng spkn; adv bkg; quiet. "Highly rec; v helpful owners; clean, modern facs; immac, family-run site." 1 Apr-31 Oct. € 21.00 2010*

BUDAPEST *B2* (3.5km SE Urban) *47.47583, 19.08305* **Haller Camping, 27 Haller út, 1096 Budapest [(1) 4763418 or 020 3674274 (mob); info@hallercamping.hu; www.hallercamping.hu]** Fr S on M5 twd Budapest cent. At ring rd foll dir Lagnymanyosi Hid (bdge). Bef bdge by lge shopping cent (Lurdy-Ház) turn R. Site sp. Or fr SE on rd 4 sp airport/Cegléd, turn R 100m bef new church steeple on L, foll sp Haller Piac. Med, hdstg, pt shd; wc; chem disp; mv service pnt; shwrs inc; el pnts (16A) inc; Indtte; lge shoping cent 500m; rest adj; snacks; BBQ; wifi; no statics; dogs free; phone; tram & bus 100m; poss cr; Eng spkn; adv bkg; quiet; red long stay/CCI. "V friendly; vg security; san facs a bit rustic but cln; tram stop opp site; conv for city cent; vg." ♦ 10 May-30 Sep. HUF 6800 2011*

⊞ **BUDAPEST** *B2* (5km NW Urban) *47.51645, 18.9741* **Zugligeti Niche Camping, Zugligeti út 101, 1121 Budapest [tel/fax (1) 2008346; camping.niche@t-online.hu; www.campingniche.hu]** Fr W approx 12km bef Budapest exit M1/E60/E75 N'wards sp Budakesi. Foll sp Budakeszi & Budapest - bumpy, rough rd. Clear sp for Zugligeti. Or fr W on M1 foll sp Budapest cent & Moszkva Tér. Keep to NW side of Moszkva, site clearly sp. Site nr new Tesco. Sm, terr, pt sl, shd; wc; chem disp; mv service pnt; shwrs inc; el pnts (6A) HUF1200; gas adj; Indtte; shop 700m; rest; snacks; bar; playgrnd; pool 3km; wifi; dogs HUF600; bus to city; Eng spkn; adv bkg; red long stay/CCI. "Site converted former tram terminus; gd, modern san facs; ltd facs low ssn; gd security; friendly, helpful owners; buffet breakfast inc in price; pitches for twin-axles (rec check in adv)." ♦ HUF 7390 2011*

BUDAPEST *B2* (12km NW Urban) *47.60451, 19.06931* **Mini Camping, Királyok út 307, 1039 Budapest [(6) 302003752]** N fr Budapest on rte 11 dir Szentendre, 3.5km past Roman ruins turn R just after Shell stn. Cont E for 1km & turn N at 'give way' sp & site sp. Site in 1.3km (sp poss obscured by trees). Sm, mkd pitch, pt shd; wc; chem disp; shwrs inc; el pnts (10A) inc; Indry rm; shop 300m; rest adj; BBQ; playgrnd; pool 1km; dogs HUF400; boat, bus or tram to Budapest; poss cr; quiet; CCI. "Gd security; sh walk to Danube; 40 mins by public transport to city cent; helpful staff; quiet, pleasant oasis in scruffy area." 1 May-30 Sep. € 17.75 2011*

⊞ **BUK** *B1* (2.5km E Rural) *47.38433, 16.79051* **Romantik Camping, Thermál Krt 12, 9740 Bükfürdõ [(94) 558050; fax 558051; info@romantikcamping.com; www.romantikcamping.com]** Fr Sopron on rte 84 twd Lake Balaton for approx 45km, foll sp & exit Bükfürdõ. After service stn turn R then cont for 5km sp Thermalbad & site. Lge, pt shd; htd wc; chem disp; mv service pnt; shwrs inc; el pnts (10-16A) metered; Indtte; shop; rest; bar 100m; playgrnd; pool high ssn; thermal cent 500m; tennis 500m; cycle hire; entmnt; 10% statics; dogs €2; adv bkg; quiet; ccard acc; red long stay/CCI. ♦ € 17.60 2009*

CEGLED *B3* (8km W Rural) *47.2009, 19.73553* **Thermalcamping Cegléd, Fürdo út 27-29, 2700 Cegléd [tel/fax (53) 501177; camping@cegleditermal.hu; http://cegleditermal.hu]** On rd 4/E60 dir Budapest, foll sp thermal pool & aquapark. Med, hdg/mkd pitch, pt shd; htd wc; chem disp; mv service pnt; baby facs; serviced pitches; shwrs inc; el pnts (6-10A) HUF750; Indtte; shop; tradsmn; rest, snacks 100m; cooking facs; playgrnd; htd, covrd pool & spa complex adj; 30% statics; dogs HUF1000; phone; bus; quiet; ccard acc; red CCI. "Highly rec, clean site; superb thermal facs - open late at night." ♦ 15 Apr-15 Oct. HUF 3400 2010*

CELLDOMOLK *B1* (6km W Rural) *47.21466, 17.10043* **Vulkán Resort, Szabadság út 023/2, 9553 Kemeneskápolna [(95) 446070; fax 446056; info@vulkanresort.com; www.vulkanresort.com]** S fr Sárvár on rd 84, turn L dir Gérce & Kemeneskápolna, site sp. Sm, mkd pitch, pt shd; htd wc; chem disp; mv service pnt; sauna; shwrs inc; el pnts (10A) €3.50; Indtte (inc dryer); supmkt 6km; tradsmn; rest 2km; snacks; bar; BBQ; cooking facs; playgrnd; 2 pools (1 htd, covrd); wellness cent; cycle hire; horseriding; wifi; cab TV; some statics; dogs free; adv bkg; quiet; red CCI. "Pleasant, welcoming, peaceful; site in lovely surroundings; gd cycling in area; a feng-shui site!" ♦ 1 Mar-31 Oct. € 19.50 (CChq acc) 2010*

⊞ **CSERKESZOLO** *C3* (W Urban) *46.86386, 20.2019* **Thermal Camping Cserkeszölö, Beton út 5, 5465 Cserkeszölö [(6) 56568450; fax 56568464; hotelcamping@cserkeszolo.hu]** On rte 44 bet Kecksemet & Kunszentmárton. Site sp in Cserkeszölö. Lge, pt shd; htd wc; chem disp; mv service pnt; sauna; shwrs inc; el pnts (10A) inc; Indtte; shop 200m; rest; snacks; BBQ; cooking facs; 2 pools (1 htd, covrd); paddling pool; waterslide; tennis; games area; 10% statics; dogs; phone; bus 200m; poss cr; quiet; CCI. "Use of sw pools & thermal pools inc in site fee; gd." € 20.25 2011*

HUNGARY

DOMOS *B2* (500m E Rural) *47.7661, 18.91495* **Dömös Camping, Dömös Dunapart, 2027 Dömös [(33) 482319; fax 414800; info@domoscamping.hu; www.domoscamping.hu]** On rd 11 fr Budapest, site on R on ent Dömös, adj Rv Danube. Med, hdg pitch, pt shd; wc; chem disp; shwrs inc; el pnts (10A) HUF950; Indtte (inc dryer); rest; snacks; bar; cooking facs; playgrnd; pool; paddling pool; wifi; TV rm; dogs HUF500; phone; bus to Budapest; poss cr; Eng spkn; adv bkg; some rd & rlwy noise; red long stay/CCI. "Delightful site with views Danube bend; spacious pitches - lower ones poss subject to flooding; excel, clean facs & rest." ♦ 1 May-15 Sep. HUF 4200 2011*

⊞ **DUNAFOLDVAR** *C2* (500m NE Rural) *46.81227, 18.92664* **Kék-Duna Camping, Hösök Tere 23, 7020 Dunafoldvár [tel/fax (75) 541107; ddifzrt@freemail.hu]** Fr rndabt S of Dunafoldvár turn twd town cent. At traff lts turn R down to rv, then turn L, under green bdge & foll towpath 300m to site. Sm, shd; wc; shwrs inc; el pnts (16A) inc; Indtte; shop high ssn & 500m; rest; BBQ; 2 pools adj (1 covrd); paddling pool; watersports; fishing; tennis; cycle hire; adv bkg; quiet; 10% red CCI. "Pleasant position o'looking Danube; adequate, clean san facs but dated; gd touring base Transdanubia." HUF 4100 2010*

EGER *B3* (9km N Rural) *47.98935, 20.32951* **Öko-Park Panzió Kemping, Borsod út 9, 3323 Eger-Szarvaskö [tel/fax (36) 352201; info@oko-park.hu; www.oko-park.hu]** Fr Eger N on rd 25. On app vill 500m fr vill name sp, turn R (sp parking) into car park. Cross sm wooden bdge at back of square. Sm, hdg/mkd pitch, pt shd; htd wc; chem disp; baby facs; shwrs inc; el pnts (16A) inc; Indtte; shop adj, rest; snacks; bar; playgrnd; wifi; TV; 5% statics; dogs; phone; bus; Eng spkn; adv bkg; rd & rlwy noise; ccard acc. "Well-laid out; well-managed site; clean facs; lge o'fits stop in car park & walk in; friendly owner; vg." ♦ 15 Mar-15 Nov. HUF 5600 2010*

EGER *B3* (1km SW Urban) *47.89396, 20.36992* **Tulipán Camping, Szépasszonyvölgy 71, 3300 Eger [tel/fax (36) 311542; info@tulipancamping.com; www.tulipancamping.com]** Enter Eger fr S on rte 25 & foll sp to site. Med, mkd pitch, pt shd; wc; chem disp; shwrs inc; el pnts (10A) HUF700; shop 500m; rest; bar; snacks; htd pool; phone; dogs HUF400; poss cr; Eng spkn; adv bkg. "Clean, modern san facs; sm pitches; sh walk to local wine cellars; v interesting town; painting of Council of Trent on library ceiling is a must; waterlogged after heavy rain; pleasant site." 15 Mar-15 Oct. HUF 2980 2010*

ERD *B2* (2km N Urban) *47.39388, 18.93638* **Flamingo Camping, Fürdö út 4, 2030 Érd [(23) 375328; flamingocamp@t-online.hu]** Fr Vienna on M1, then M0, exit at Diósd/Érd & foll sp to site on rd 70. Med, pt shd; htd wc; chem disp; shwrs inc; el pnts (6A) HUF1000; Indtte; shop 200m; rest; snacks; bar; cooking facs; pool high ssn; tennis; TV rm; few statics; dogs HUF1000; bus 50m; rlwy stn 1km; quiet; red long stay/CCI. "Conv Budapest (12km)." 1 Apr-1 Nov. HUF 5000 2010*

ESZTERGOM *B2* (1km W Urban) *47.7910, 18.73165* **Gran Camping, Nagy-Duna Sétány 3, 2501 Esztergom [(33) 402513; fax 411953; fortanex@t-online.hu; www.grancamping-fortanex.hu]** Fr rte 11 site well sp into town. Fr cent turn twds Danube along street to old bdge, foll sp to site on rv bank. Med, mkd pitch, pt shd; wc; chem disp; shwrs inc; el pnts (20A) HUF400; shop high ssn; tradsmn; rest; snacks; bar; BBQ; playgrnd; htd pool; rv cruises; tennis; games area; wifi; 5% statics; dogs HUF500; bus; poss cr; Eng spkn; quiet; red long stay/CCI. "Basilica worth a visit; poss youth groups; gd clean facs." 1 May-30 Sep. HUF 4200 2011*

FERTOD *B1* (5km W Urban) *47.62116, 16.78513* **Termál Camping, Fürdö út 1, 9437 Hegykö [tel/fax (99) 376818; termalkemping@freemail.hu; www.termalkemping.hu]** Fr Sopron on rd 85 turn N at km 60.2 to Hegykö, site in 4.5km on S side of main rd, sp. Sm, pt shd; wc; chem disp; shwrs inc; el pnts (6A) HUF600; Indtte; shop, rest, snacks 500m; htd, covrd pool 500m; no statics; dogs free; poss cr; ccard acc; CCI. "Economical NH; excel spa complex adj; Lake Fertőd & Esterházy Palace worth visit." 15 Apr-15 Oct. HUF 2700 2009*

FONYOD *C1* (3km SW Rural) *46.73312, 17.53198* **Napsugár Camping, Wekerle út 5, 8644 Fonyód-Bétatelep [(85) 361211; fax 361024; napsugar@balatontourist.hu; www.balatontourist.hu]** On NW side of rte 7/E71 on S side of Lake Balaton, sp. V lge, hdg pitch, shd; wc; chem disp; shwrs inc; el pnts (16A) inc; Indtte; shop & 1km; rest, snacks adj; playgrnd; rocky beach adj; 5% statics; dogs; rd & rlwy noise; ccard acc. 1 May-15 Sep. € 17.70 2010*

GYENESDIAS see Keszthely *C1*

⊞ **GYULA** *C4* (2km N Urban) *46.64538, 21.29851* **Thermál Camping & Motel, Szlésö út 16, 5700 Gyula [(66) 463704; fax 463551; gyulacamping@t-online.hu; www.gyulacamping.hu]** Site sp on every app rd to Gyula. Med, some hdstg, shd; wc; chem disp; shwrs inc; el pnts (16A) inc (poss no earth); shop & 500m; Indtte; shop 500m; rest 200m; snacks; cooking facs; thermal baths 1.5km; tennis; dogs HUF500; adv bkg; quiet; CCI. "Site 5km fr Romanian border." HUF 4100 2010*

⊞ **HAJDUSZOBOSZLO** *B4* (1km E Urban) *47.45756, 21.39396* **Thermál Camping, Böszörményi út 35A, 4200 Hajdúszoboszló [tel/fax (52) 558552; thermalcamping@hungarospa-rt.hu; www.hungarospa.hu]** Fr W on rte 4/E573 thro town, site sp on L. Fr Debrecen, turn R 500m past Camping Hadjdútourist on lakeside. Lge, hdg pitch, pt shd; wc; chem disp; mv service pnt; shwrs inc; el pnts (12A) inc; gas 1km; Indtte; shop, rest high ssn; snacks; BBQ; cooking facs; playgrnd; htd, covrd pool & thermal baths adj; paddling pool; waterslide; TV rm; dogs HUF440; phone; poss cr; Eng spkn; no adv bkg; quiet; ccard acc; red CCI. "Pleasant site; sm naturist island in lake." HUF 6435 2010*

HEGYKO see Fertöd *B1*

HEVIZ see Keszthely *C1*

JASZAPATI *B3* (500m S Urban) *47.50537, 20.14012* **Tölgyes Strand Camping, Gyöngyvirág u 11, 5130 Jászapáti [(57) 441187; fax 441008; info@tolgyesstrand.hu; www.tolgyesstrand.hu]** Fr Budapest E on M3, exit at Hatvan & take rd 32 to Jászberény then foll rd 31 to Jászapáti. Site sp fr town cent. Med, mkd pitch, pt shd; wc; chem disp; mv service pnt; shwrs; el pnts (10A); lndtte (inc dryer); rest; snacks; bar; playgrnd; 2 pools (1 htd, covrd); tennis 200m; games area; cycle hire; internet; TV rm; some statics; dogs; site clsd 1 Nov to mid-Dec; adv bkg; quiet. "Gd, modern facs." 1 Apr-30 Nov. (CChq acc) 2009*

KEMENESKÁPOLNA see Celldomolk *B1*

KESZTHELY *C1* (5km N Rural) *46.80803, 17.21248* **Camping Panoráma, Köz 1, 8372 Cserszegtomaj [(83) 314412; fax 330215; matuska78@freemail.hu; www.panoramacamping.com]** Exit Keszthely by direct rd to Sümeg. After turn to Hévíz (Thermal Spa). Clearly sp on R of side rd. Med, terr, pt shd; htd wc; chem disp; shwrs €0.90; el pnts (16A) €2.50; lndtte; shops 200m; rest; lake sw 2km; TV; 30% statics; dogs €1; phone; quiet; red CCI. "Conv Lake Balaton area; v friendly & clean; remedial massage avail." 1 Apr-31 Oct. € 11 2008*

⊞ **KESZTHELY** *C1* (14km N Rural) *46.89442, 17.23166* **Camping St Vendal, Fö út Hrsz 192, 8353 Zalaszántó [tel/fax (83) 370147; camping.stvendal@freemail.hu; www.szallas.net/st.vendel-camping]** Fr N on rd 84 turn dir Bazsi/Hévíz at Sümeg. Site at ent to town. Fr S take Sümeg/Hévíz off rd 71 bef Keszthely & foll sp Sümeg & Zalaszántó. Sm, pt shd; htd wc; chem disp; shwrs inc; el pnts (6A) HUF540; lndtte; rest; snacks; bar; BBQ; cooking facs; internet; TV rm; dogs HUF250; quiet; CCI. "Friendly welcome; gd walking/cycling; conv for thermal lake at Heviz & Lake Balaton but without crowds, noise of lakeside sites; delightful site in orchard - awkward for lge o'fits." HUF 2945 2010*

KESZTHELY *C1* (1km E Rural) *46.76797, 17.25936* **Camping Castrum Keszthely, Móra Ferenc u 48, 8360 Keszthely [(83) 312120; fax 314422; keszthely@castrum.eu; www.castrum-group.hu]** Clearly sp W fr Budapest. Fr all other dir take rd 71 out of town; 300m past church turn twd Lake Balaton. Lge, hdg pitch, pt shd; wc; chem disp; shwrs inc; el pnts (6-15A) HUF900; shop & 200m; lndtte; rest; snacks; playgrnd; pool; paddling pool; lake & watersports 300m; tennis; TV; dogs HUF900; phone; poss cr; adv bkg; some rlwy noise. "Attractively laid-out with excel facs; rlwy runs close to site; friendly staff; Festetics Palace & gardens worth visit." ♦ 1 Apr-31 Oct. HUF 5200 (CChq acc) 2010*

KESZTHELY *C1* (3km E Urban) *46.7648, 17.28945* **Camping Caravan, Madách út 43, 8315 Gyenesdiás [(83) 316020; fax 316382; info@caravancamping.hu; www.caravancamping.hu]** On rte 71 E fr Keszthely, sp bet km 100 & 101. Med, mkd pitch, pt shd; wc; chem disp; mv service pnt; shwrs inc; el pnts (16A) HUF590; lndtte; shop; rest; snacks; playgrnd; pool; lake sw & beach 500m; tennis; 30% statics; dogs free; phone; poss cr; quiet; adv bkg. 1 Apr-1 Oct. HUF 2700 2008*

KESZTHELY *C1* (2km S Rural) *46.7461, 17.2437* **Balatontourist Camping Zala, Entz Géza Sétány, 8360 Keszthely [tel/fax (83) 312782; zala@balatontourist.hu; www.balatontourist.hu]** Fr NE on A71 after traff lts with no entry ahead, turn L & keep R at forks. Foll 1-way system to town cent, then in 200m at junc turn L, site sp on L. Cross rlwy & turn immed R, site in 300m Lge, mkd pitch, pt shd; wc; chem disp; mv service pnt; shwrs inc; el pnts (10A) inc; lndtte; shop; rest; snacks; bar; playgrnd; pool; lake adj; watersports; TV; 25% statics; dogs HUF600; phone; quiet; ccard acc; red CCI. "Town cent 30 min walk; rlwy runs by site; tennis court poorly maintained; gd facs; lake sw not rec; marshy land, mosquitoes at dusk." ♦ 19 Apr-30 Sep. HUF 5800 2008*

⊞ **KESZTHELY** *C1* (7km NW Rural) *46.78393, 17.19575* **Kurcamping Castrum, Tópart, 8380 Héviz [(83) 343198; fax 314422; heviz@castrum.eu; www.castrum-group.hu]** Fr Keszthely foll sp to Héviz & site 700m to E, opp Héviz thermal lake. Lge, mkd pitch, pt shd; htd wc; chem disp; mv service pnt; 20% serviced pitches; shwrs inc; el pnts (6-16A) €3; lndtte; shop; tradsmn; rest; bar; htd pool adj; lake sw adj; sat TV; dogs €4; poss cr; Eng spkn; adv bkg; quiet; CCI. "Lake fed by hot springs so gd for sw; casino adj; easy cycle ride/walk into lovely spa town & cycle path to Keszthely; excel san facs; excursions Budapest fr gate." € 19.60 2008*

⊞ **KOSZEG** *B1* (500m N Urban) *47.39336, 16.54291* **Gyöngyvirág Camping, Bajcsy-Zsilinszky út. 6, 9730 Köszeg [(94) 360454; fax 360574; info@gyongyviragpanzio.hu; www.gyongyviragpanzio.hu]** Foll sp in town cent to site adj hotel. Sm, pt shd; htd wc (cont); shwrs inc; el pnts (10A) HUF400; shop 200m; BBQ; playgrnd; quiet; no ccard acc; red low stay. "Superb, welcoming, orchard site; clean, modern facs; site diff in wet weather; access diff lge o'fits; nature reserve adj town; gd walking; sh walk to one of prettiest towns in Hungary." HUF 3300 2010*

⊞ **LENTI** *C1* (1km SW Urban) *46.61736, 16.5305* **Kurcamping Castrum Lenti, Tancsics M út 18-20, 8960 Lenti [tel/fax (92) 351368; lenti@castrum.eu; www.castrum-group.hu]** Foll sp fr rd 75 on W side of town. Med, hdg/mkd pitch, hdstg, pt shd; htd wc; chem disp; mv service pnt; serviced pitches; shwrs inc; el pnts (6A) €3; lndtte; shop 1km; rest; cooking facs; thermal pools adj; dogs €3; phone; poss cr; quiet; CCI. "Excel facs." ♦ € 20.00 2008*

MATRAFURED *B3* (2km N Rural) *47.84416, 19.95725* **Mátra Camping Sástó, Farkas út 4, 3232 Mátrafüred [tel/fax (37) 374025; info@matrakemping.hu; www.matrakemping.hu]** Take rte 24 N fr Gyöngyös. Site on L 2km after Mátrafüred. Med, some hdstg, pt sl, pt shd; wc; shwrs inc; el pnts (10A) inc; shop, rest, snacks, bar adj; cooking facs; TV; some statics; dogs HUF500; phone adj; poss cr; ccard acc. "Site part of controlled sports complex; vg secure site." 15 Apr-10 Oct. HUF 3500 2010*

HUNGARY

MEZOKOVESD *B3* (3km W Rural) *47.7969, 20.5291* **Autóscamping Zsóry, Zsóry-fürdö, 3400 Mezökövesd [tel/fax (49) 411436; zsoryamping@freemail.hu; www.zsory-camping.lhcom.hu]** Fr W leave M3/E71 at exit Eger/Füzesabony for 3km N twd Eger. Turn E onto rd 3 sp Miskolc, site on L in 8km. Lge, hdg pitch, pt shd; wc; chem disp; mv service pnt; baby facs; shwrs inc; el pnts (16A) HUF550; Indtte; shop 500m; tradsmn; rest; snacks; bar; cooking facs; playgrnd; htd, covrd thermal pool 500m; some statics; dogs HUF330; phone; Eng spkn; quiet; ccard acc; red CCI. "Thermal baths adj; helpful staff; nr National Park." 1 May-30 Sep. HUF 3200 2011*

There aren't many sites open at this time of year. We'd better phone ahead to check the one we're heading for is open.

MISKOLC *A3* (10km W Rural) *48.09623, 20.62128* **Camping Lillafüred, Erzsébet Sétány 39, 3517 Miskolc-Lillafüred [(46) 333146; kovatt@lillacamp.hu; http://kovatt.lillacamp.hu]** Fr Miskolc take rd to Lillafüred. After passing under 2 low bdges (max height 3.4m) site sp on L. Sm, hdg/mkd pitch, pt shd; wc; own san; chem disp (wc); shwrs inc; el pnts (16A) HUF500; shop in vill; rest in hotel nrby; cooking facs; dogs; phone; bus 1km; adv bkg; quiet. "Basic site; gd mkd walks; friendly owner; not suitable lge o'fits; 1km to narr gauge rlwy; NH." ♦ 1 May-30 Sep. HUF 3700 2009*

MOGYOROD *B2* (1km E Rural) **Marcel Camping, Sörfözö u 5, 2146 Mogyoród [(28) 540645; fax 540646; marcelpanzio@vnet.hu; www.marcelpanzio.hu]** Exit M3 fr Budapest dir Mogoród. Turn R at junc, site on R in 400m. Sm, pt sl, unshd; wc; chem disp (wc); shwrs inc; el pnts inc; shops 500m; rest; bar; no statics; bus/metro 1km; adv bkg; rd noise. "2km fr Hungaroring F1 circuit; variable prices up to €49/night for F1 w/end - adv book req." 1 Apr-30 Sep. 2008*

MOSONMAGYAROVAR *B1* (1km E Urban) **Termál Aqua Camping, Kigyó út 1, 9200 Mosonmagyaróvár [tel/fax (96) 579168; aquahotel@t-online.hu; www.tha.hu]** Foll sp fr town cent to Termál Hotel Aqua; site in grounds, just behind lge thermal baths. Sm, hdg/mkd pitch, shd; htd wc; chem disp; mv service pnt; shwrs inc; el pnts €3; Indtte; shop 1km; rest; snacks; bar; BBQ; cooking facs; htd, covrd thermal & sw pool adj; dogs €2; bus, train 1km; phone; Eng spkn; quiet. "Vg site; price inc ent to thermals & sauna." 1 Apr-30 Oct. € 29.00 2009*

⊞ **MOSONMAGYAROVAR** *B1* (2km SE Urban) *47.84224, 17.28591* **Camping Kis-Duna, Gabonarakpart 6, 9200 Mosonmagyaróvár [tel/fax (96) 216433; www.hotels.hu/kis_duna]** Site on L of M1 Mosonmagyaróvár-Gyõr in grounds of motel & rest, 15km fr border. Sm, some hdstg, unshd; wc; chem disp; shwrs inc; el pnts (16A) HUF500; Indtte; shop 1km; rest; thermal pool 2.5km; TV; dogs HUF500. "Gd, clean, facs; rest gd but busy; gd alt to Bratislava site (Slovakia); ideal NH." HUF 3150 2011*

NESZMELY *B2* (3km E Rural) *47.74421, 18.40258* **Éden Camping, Dunapart, 2544 Neszmély [(33) 474183; fax 474327; eden@mail.holop.hu; www.edencamping.com]** Site sp on rte 10 bet Neszmély & Süttõ, on rvside. Lge, hdg pitch, pt shd; htd wc; chem disp; mv service pnt; baby facs; shwrs inc; el pnts (6-10A) HUF600; Indtte (inc dryer); shop; tradsmn; rest; snacks; bar; playgrnd; pool high ssn; rv sw adj; canoeing; watersports; boat & cycle hire; tennis 3km; games area; entmnt; excursions; 10% statics; dogs HUF470; phone; bus 500m; Eng spkn; adv bkg; some rd/rlwy noise; ccard acc; red CCI. "V pleasant, tranquil site in gd location; helpful staff." ♦ 1 Apr-31 Oct. HUF 4310 2010*

ORFU *D2* (1km NW Rural) *46.14638, 18.13750* **Panoráma Camping, Dollar út 1, 7677 Orfü [tel/fax (72) 378434; campingorfu@freemail.hu; www.panoramacamping.hu]** Rte 66 fr Pécs dir Kaposvár. In Magyarszék take rd to Orfü & at lake turn R & foll rd down W side of lake. Site shortly bef end of lake. Lge, mkd pitch, terr, pt shd; wc; chem disp; shwrs inc; el pnts (6A) HUF700; Indtte; shop; snacks; playgrnd; pool, tennis, watersports 1km; lake sw 500m; tennis; cycle hire; games area; TV; some statics; phone; quiet on higher terr; ccard acc; 10% red CCI. "Lovely situation; twin-axles on lower terr only; site badly in need of refurb; gd base for Pécs." 1 May-30 Sep. HUF 3900 2010*

OZD *A3* (12km E Rural) *48.21281, 20.40603* **Camping Amedi, Rákóczi út 181, 3658 Borsodbóta [tel/fax (48) 438468; info@campingamedi.hu; www.campingamedi.hu]** Fr Budapest N on M3/E71, exit at Hatvan N onto rd 21. At Kisterenye turn R onto rd 23 dir Ózd. In Ózd foll sp Borsodbóta for 12km to site. Sm, mkd pitch, pt shd; wc; shwrs inc; el pnts (10A) €3.75; Indtte; supmkt 500m; rest 6km;bar; BBQ; cooking facs; pool; cycle hire; games area; entmnt; some statics; dogs €2; adv bkg; quiet. "Peaceful, Dutch-owned site." 15 Apr-15 Oct. € 17.50 2010*

PANNONHALMA *B2* (500m E Urban) *47.54916, 17.75777* **Panoráma Camping, Fenyvesalja 4/A, 9090 Pannonhalma [(96) 471240; fax 470561; akosprikkel@axelero.hu]** Fr Györ take rte 82 twd Veszprém. After approx 20km turn L on sm loop rd to vill of Pannonhalma. Site at top of v steep slope, low gear needed but site worth diff app. Med, hdg pitch, terr, pt shd; htd wc; chem disp (wc); shwrs inc; el pnts (10A) HUF800; Indry rm; shop 300m; rest in vill; snacks; TV rm; dogs HUF450; adv bkg; quiet; red CCI. "Panoramic views; v helpful owners; clean facs; levelling blocks req; conv for visit to basilica." 1 May-15 Sep. HUF 3500 2009*

⊞ **PECS** *D2* (1.5km E Urban) *46.08601, 18.26319* **Familia Privat Camping, Gyöngyösi Istvan út 6, 7627 Pécs [(72) 327034]** On rte 6 fr Budapest (N side) well sp fr city o'skts. Tight ent for lge o'fits. Sm, pt sl, terr, hdstg, pt shd; htd wc; chem disp; shwrs inc; el pnts (10A) inc (long lead req); Indtte; shop 800m; adv bkg; quiet. "V congested site; arr early to ensure pitch; OK NH." HUF 4200 2010*

REVFULOP see Balatonszepezd *C1*

SAROSPATAK *A4* (2km NE Rural) *48.33274, 21.58245* **Tengerszem Camping, Herceg Ferenc ut 2, 3950 Sárospatak [(47) 312744; fax 323527; info@tengerszem-camping.hu; www.tengerszem-camping.hu]** NW fr Tokaj on R38; then NE on R37 to Sárospatak; foll camp sp. Med, hdg pitch, pt shd; wc; mv service pnt; shwrs; el pnts (10A) inc; shop; rest; snacks; playgrnd; pool; tennis; games area; TV; rlwy noise; CCI. "Refurbished thermal sw baths next door; gd site for mountains." 15 Apr-15 Oct. HUF 4000 2010*

⊞ **SARVAR** *B1* (1km SE Urban) *47.24671, 16.9473* **Sárvár Thermal Camping, Vadkert út 1, 9600 Sárvár [(95) 320292; fax 523612; info@thermalcamping.com; www.thermalcamping.com]** E fr Szombathely via rtes 86 & 88. Site on Sopron-Lake Balaton rte 84. Med, some hdstg, pt shd; htd wc; chem disp; mv service pnt; sauna; baby facs; private san facs avail; shwrs; el pnts (16A) €3; lndtte; shop; tradsmn; rest, snacks adj; BBQ; cooking facs; playgrnd; htd thermal pools adj; paddling pool; waterslide; lake fishing; tennis 500m; wifi; some statics; dogs €2; poss cr; 10% statics; ccard acc; quiet; red long stay; CCI. "Barrier clsd 1330-1500; free ent to spa & fitness cent adj." ♦ € 33.00 (CChq acc) 2010*

SIOFOK *C2* (5km NE Urban) *46.92838, 18.10245* **Balatontourist Camping Aranypart, Szent László út 183-185, 8604 Siófok [(84) 353399; fax 352801; aranypart@balatontourist.hu; www.balatontourist.hu]** Fr Budapest on M7 take exit Siófok onto rd 70. Site sp at Balatonszabadi rlwy stn. V lge, hdg pitch, pt shd; wc; chem disp; mv service pnt; shwrs inc; el pnts (10A) inc; lndtte; shop; rest; snacks; bar; BBQ; cooking facs; playgrnd; lake sw, fishing adj; waterslide; cycle hire; tennis 500m; games area; wifi; entmnt; TV rm; 15% statics; dogs HUF950; phone; poss cr; Eng spkn; adv bkg; quiet; CCI. "Price varies according to pitch size; well-maintained, attractive site." ♦ 22 Apr-11 Sep. HUF 6700 (CChq acc) 2011*

⊞ **SOPRON** *B1* (7km SE Rural) *47.6525, 16.6575* **Kurcamping Castrum Balf-Sopron, Fürdö Sor 59-61, 9494 Balf [(99) 339124; fax (83) 314422; castrum.sopronbalf@rlan.hu; www.sopron-balf-castrum.hu]** On rte 84 S of Sopron turn E sp Balf. In 2km turn N sp Sopron & foll sps. Site at W end Balf vill. Med, hdg/mkd pitch, pt shd; htd wc (cont); chem disp; sauna; shwrs inc; el pnts (6A) HUF800; lndtte (inc dryer); shops 350m; rest 250m; pool & 250m; cycle hire; TV; dogs €2.50; phone; Eng spkn; rd noise; ccard acc; CCI. "Thermal baths avail; Tesco hypmkt on app to Sopron 6km, with ATM; pitches uneven; ltd facs low ssn & poss unkempt; poss cold shwrs but new owners (2010) plan refurb." HUF 4730 2010*

SOSTOFURDO see Nyiregyháza *B4*

SZENTES *C3* (1km W Urban) *46.65052, 20.24812* **Thermál Camping Szentes (Szentesi Üdülökozpont), Csallány Gáborpart 4, 6600 Szentes [tel/fax (63) 400123; udulohazak@udulokozpont-szentes.hu; www.udulokozpont-szentes.hu]** Fr N fr Csongrád on rte 451, site on R at ent to town in park, int'l camping sp. Sm, pt shd; wc; chem disp (wc); shwrs inc; el pnts (16A) HUF1000; shop 1km; rest, snacks, bar in park; 4 htd pools; tennis; horseriding; dogs HUF600; phone; poss cr; Eng spkn; quiet; ccard acc; CCI. "Attractive park; thermal pools open to day visitors; helpful staff." ♦ 1 Apr-30 Sep. HUF 4300 2010*

SZILVASVARAD *A3* (500m S Rural) *48.09615, 20.38783* **Hegyi Camping, Egri út 36, 3348 Szilvásvárad [tel/fax (36) 355207; hegyi.camping@axelero.hu; www.hegyicamping.com]** App fr Eger, site sp just bef vill. Turn R at petrol stn Med, pt sl, pt shd; wc; chem disp; shwrs inc; el pnts (16A) inc; lndtte; shop 1km; rest; bar; cooking facs; internet; TV; 40% statics; phone; poss noisy; ccard acc; red CCI. "Lipizzaner horse stud farm nr; conv touring Bükk National Park; conv narr gauge rlwy into Szalajka Valley; gd rests within 10 mins walk; facs inadequate & tired; poss school parties on site; friendly staff." 1 May-15 Oct. HUF 4000 2010*

SZOLNOK *B3* (2km SE Urban) **Tiszaligeti Motel & Camping, Tiszaligeti Sétány 34, 5000 Tiszaligeti [tel/fax (56) 424403; tiszaligetimotel@gmail.com; www.tiszaligetimotel.hu]** Leave rte 4 onto rd 442 sp Martfü, but foll sp 'Centrum' into Szolnok. Bef bdge look for sps to turn L & foll rd for 800m, site on L. Med, pt shd; wc; chem disp (wc); shwrs inc; el pnts HUF700; shop 2km; rest; BBQ; playgrnd; pool 300m; canoeing, tennis nr; cycle hire; some cabins; dogs HUF1500; phone; bus; poss cr; quiet; CCI. "Pleasant location; vg, modern facs." 1 May-30 Sep. HUF 3200 2009*

TAHITOTFALU *B2* (500m E Rural) *47.75117, 19.08043* **Duna Camping, Kemping út 1, 2022 Tahitótfalu [(26) 385216; fax (33) 412294; juhaszjozsef@mailbox.hu]** In cent Tahitótfalu at km 30.3 on rte 11 to Budapest, site sp. Med, shd; wc; chem disp; shwrs inc; el pnts (10A) inc; lndtte; shops adj; rest; snacks; bar; BBQ; playgrnd; boating; TV; 20% statics; dogs; poss noisy; ccard acc. "Beautiful situation on Danube bend; Szentendre worth visit; basic site; NH only." 15 Apr-15 Oct. € 14.25 2009*

TAKSONY *B2* (6km S Rural) *47.28711, 19.09990* **Camping Rukkel-tó Waterpark, Rukkel-tó 1, 2335 Taksony [(70) 3860852; rukkel@waterpark.hu; www.waterpark.hu]** Exit M0/E71 onto rd 51 dir Taksony & Dunavarsány. Waterpark sp 6km S of Taksony dir Bugyi. Med, mkd pitch, pt shd; wc; shwrs; el pnts; lndtte; rest; snacks; bar; playgrnd; pools; waterslides; boat hire; no dogs; quiet. "Clean site adj waterpark; excel." 1 May-7 Sep. HUF 4800 2009*

TAMASI *C2* (1km S Urban) *46.62577, 18.28734* **Thermál Camping, Hársfa út 1, 7090 Tamási [(74) 471738; camping@tamasistrand.hu; www.tamasistrand.hu]** Site & thermal baths sp on rd 65 adj motel. Med, pt shd; wc; shwrs inc; el pnts (10A) HUF575 (long lead req); lndtte; shop 500m; rest 200m; htd pool; 10% statics; phone; CCI. "Security gate; free access to lge thermal pool complex; vg." 1 May-15 Oct. HUF 5100 2009*

TATABANYA *B2* (12km N Rural) *47.6679, 18.3090* **Fényes Camping, Környei út 24, 2890 Tata [(34) 481208; fax 588144; fenyes@fenyesfurdo.hu; www.fenyesfurdo.hu]** Exit junc 67 fr M1 to Tata town cent; foll sp for 3km E to site. Lge, shd; wc; own san rec; shwrs inc; el pnts; shop; rest; playgrnd; 3 pools; games area; dogs HUF500; Eng spkn; CCI. "Tata interesting town; fair site set in lge park." 1 May-15 Sep. 2009*

TISZAFURED *B3* (1km N Urban) **Dieter's Camping, Fürdö út 5-7, 5350 Tiszafüred [(59) 353132; fax 353300; heinrich@indamail.hu]** S of rte 33, turn L immed after town sp, cross rlwy line. Site sp on R. Sm, hdg pitch, pt shd; htd wc; chem disp; shwrs inc; el pnts inc; Indtte; rest; BBQ; thermal pools adj; dogs; poss cr; CCI. "Excel cycling area; v friendly owner." ♦ HUF 3200 2008*

TISZAFURED *B3* (1km W Urban) *47.62418, 20.7489* **Thermál-Strand Camping, Fürdö út 2, 5350 Tiszafüred [tel/fax (59) 352911; thermalcamping@vipmail.hu]** Fr N on rd 33, immed after town sp cross rlwy & turn R in 100m sp Thermál, site on R in 100m, ent opp Lidl. Med, hdg pitch, pt shd; wc; chem disp; shwrs inc; el pnts (10A) HUF580; Indtte; shop; rest; cooking facs; playgrnd; 2 pools adj (1 htd, covrd) & thermal baths; rv/lake sw; tennis; games area; 10% statics; dogs HUF380; Eng spkn; adv bkg; quiet; ccard acc; red snr citizens/CCI. "Free thermal baths; facs clean but poss inadequate when full; friendly staff." 1 Apr-31 Oct. HUF 2420 2008*

⊞ **TISZAKECSKE** *C3* (500m E Rural) *46.93649, 20.12091* **Camping Tisza-Parti Termálfürdö, Szabolcska út 43a, 6060 Tiszakécske [(76) 441363; fax 540363; thermal@thermaltiszapart.hu; www.thermaltiszapart.hu]** Fr Kecskemét E on rd 44, foll sp Tiszakécske & site on banks of Rv Tisza. Lge, mkd pitch, pt shd; htd wc; private bthrms avail; sauna; shwrs; el pnts inc; Indtte; shop 200m; rest; snacks; bar; playgrnd; htd, coverd pool; waterslide; tennis; games area; some statics; dogs; adv bkg; quiet. HUF 3250 2008*

⊞ **TOROKBALINT** *B2* (1km S Rural) *47.43305, 18.90027* **Fortuna Camping, Dózsa György út 164, 2045 Törökbálint [(23) 335364; fax 339697; fortunacamping@axelero.hu; www.fortunacamping.hu]** Fr M1 or M7 take exit for Törökbálint & foll camp sp to Törökbálint. Leave on rd sp Erd, rd bends L, go under m'way into vill. At T-junc site sp, turn R, rd swings L; site ent halfway up hill on L. Med, some hdg pitch, sl, terr, pt shd, htd wc; chem disp; baby facs; shwrs inc; el pnts (4-16A) €2; Indtte; shop 1.5km; tradsmn; hypmkt 5km; rest high ssn; playgrnd; 2 pools (1 htd, covrd); dogs €2; phone; bus to city 1km; Eng spkn; CCI. "Friendly, helpful, family-run site adj vineyards, but untidy; gd, clean san facs; gd security; variable elec supply & san facs block poss poorly lit; bus/tram tickets to Budapest fr site; excursions arranged; easy access Budapest - tickets fr recep; excel rest; ltd facs low ssn." ♦ € 18.00 2011*

⊞ **TURISTVANDI** *A4* (SW Rural) *48.04710, 22.64300* **Vizimalom Camping, Malom út 3, 4944 Túristvándi [(44) 721082; turvizimalom@freemail.hu; www.turvizimalom.hu]** Fr Fehérgyarmat foll rd 491 NE for 4km to Penyige, turn L to Túristvándi. After approx 12km site on R adj 18thC water mill on Rv Túr. Sm, some hdstg, pt shd; wc; shwrs; el pnts (10A); shop 500m; rest; snacks; bar; BBQ; playgrnd; canoeing; games area; games rm; TV; internet; dogs; quiet. "Excel location; no hdstg." € 14.60 2010*

UROM see Budapest *B2*

VAJTA *C2* (1km N Rural) *46.72859, 18.65587* **Aucost Holiday Parc, Termálsor 1, 7041 Vajta [tel/fax (25) 229700 or 0031 0416 543258 (N'lands); holiday@aucost.nl; www.aucost.nl]** Take rd 63 S fr Cece dir Szekszárd, site on R bef Vajta. Med, mkd pitch, pt sl, pt shd; wc; chem disp; shwrs inc; el pnts €1.95; Indtte;shop 1km; tradsmn; rest 1km; bar; playgrnd; thermal pool; 400m; games rm; internet; TV; 10% statics; dogs €1; Eng spkn; adv bkg; quiet. "Friendly, helpful Dutch owners; gd birdwatching area; vg site." 18 Apr-14 Sep. € 23.80 2009*

VELENCE *B2* (1km W Rural) *47.2375, 18.64225* **Panoráma Camping, Kemping út 2, 2481 Velence [(22) 472043; fax 472964; info@campingpanorama.hu; www.campingpanorama.hu]** Exit M7/E71 junc 42, foll sp to Velence & site. Site on N extremity of lake. V lge, pt shd; wc; chem disp; shwrs inc; el pnts (4A) HUF840; Indry rm; shop; rest; snacks; playgrnd; lake sw; fishing; watersports; 5% statics; dogs HUF700; phone; quiet; red long stay. "Gd area for cycling & walking; 1 san facs block needs refurb; expensive for facs avail." 15 Apr-30 Sep. HUF 4780 2008*

VONYARCVASHEGY see Balatongyörök *C1*

ZALAKAROS *C1* (2km S Rural) *46.53165, 17.12443* **Kurcamping Castrum, Ady Endre út, 8754 Galambok [tel/fax (93) 358610; zalakaros@castrum.eu; www.castrum-group.hu]** Fr rte 7 N dir Zalakaros, site sp. Med, hdg/mkd pitch, pt shd; htd wc; chem disp; sauna; shwrs inc; el pnts (6A) inc; Indtte; shop, rest 1km; snacks; bar; BBQ; htd, covrd pool; thermal complex 2km; wifi; some statics; dogs; bus; quiet; ccard acc; CCI. ♦ 1 Mar-31 Oct. € 25.20 (CChq acc) 2010*

ZALASZANTO see Keszthely *C1*

Distances are shown in kilometres and are calculated from town/city centres along the most practical roads, although not necessarily taking the shortest route. 1km = 0.62miles

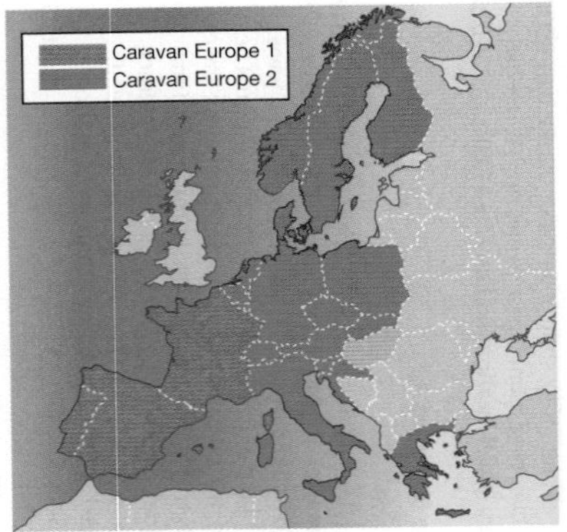

Salgótarján to Tatabánya = 168km

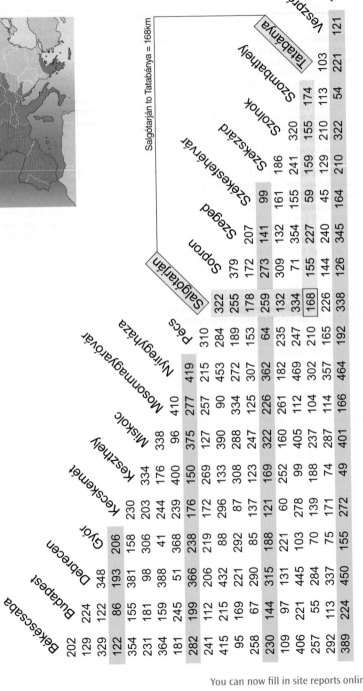

	Békéscsaba	Budapest	Debrecen	Gyór	Kecskemét	Keszthely	Miskolc	Mosonmagyaróvár	Nyíregyháza	Pécs	Salgótarján	Sopron	Szeged	Székesfehérvár	Szekszárd	Szolnok	Szombathely	Tatabánya	Veszprém
Budapest	202																		
Debrecen	129	224																	
Gyór	329	122	348																
Kecskemét	122	86	193	206															
Keszthely	354	155	381	158	230														
Miskolc	231	181	98	306	203	334													
Mosonmagyaróvár	364	159	388	41	244	176	338												
Nyíregyháza	181	245	51	368	239	400	96	410											
Pécs	282	199	366	238	176	150	375	277	419										
Salgótarján	241	112	206	219	172	269	127	257	215	310									
Sopron	415	215	432	88	296	133	390	90	453	284	322								
Szeged	95	169	221	292	87	308	288	334	272	189	255	379							
Székesfehérvár	258	67	290	85	137	123	247	125	307	153	178	172	207						
Szekszárd	230	144	315	188	121	169	322	226	362	64	259	273	141	99					
Szolnok	109	97	131	221	60	252	160	261	182	235	132	309	132	161	186				
Szombathely	406	221	445	103	278	99	405	112	469	247	334	71	354	155	241	320			
Tatabánya	257	55	284	70	139	188	237	104	302	210	168	155	227	59	159	155	174		
Veszprém	292	113	337	75	171	74	287	114	357	165	226	144	240	45	129	210	113	103	
Zalaegerszeg	389	224	450	155	272	49	401	166	464	192	338	126	345	164	210	322	54	221	121

SLOVAKIA
UKRAINE
AUSTRIA
ROMANIA
SERBIA
CROATIA
WIEN
BRATISLAVA
Nové Zámky
Lučenec
Košice
Aggtelek
Sárospatak
Berehove
Ózd
Szilvásvárad
MISKOLC
SALGÓTARJÁN
Túristvándi
Eisenstadt
MOSONMAGYARÓVÁR
SOPRON
Fertod
GYŐR
Esztergom
Dömös
Tahitótfalu
Neszmély
Mátrafüred
Eger
Mezőkövesd
Satu Mare
TATABÁNYA
Pannonhalma
Mogyoród
Tiszafüred
DEBRECEN
Kőszeg
Bük
Biatorbágy
BUDAPEST
Törökbálint
Érd
Jászapáti
Hajdúszoboszló
Sárvár
Celldömölk
Velence
Taksony
SZÉKESFEHÉRVÁR
Cegléd
SZOLNOK
VESZPRÉM
Balatonalmádi
Balatonkenese
Balatonfüred
Oradea
ZALAEGERSZEG
Balatonakali
Balatonszepezd
Siófok
Badacsony
Tiszakecske
Cserkeszőlő
KESZTHELY
Balatonszemes
Dunaföldvár
Fonyód
Balatongyörök
Balatonberény
BÉKÉSCSABA
Lenti
Tamási
Vajta
Szentes
Gyula
Zalakaros
Varaždin
SZEKSZÁRD
Boldogasszonyfa
Orfű
PÉCS
Arad
Subotica
Virovitica
Timişoara
Osijek
M1
M3
M5
M6
M7
M15
M30
M35
M43
M60
M0
N
E
S
W
0 10 20 30 40 50 kms
0 10 20 30 mls
All year site(s)
Seasonal site(s)
No sites listed
200m +
0-200m
Motorways
Major roads
Main roads
© Collins Bartholomew Ltd 2011
A
B
C
D
1
2
3
4

Italy

Country Introduction

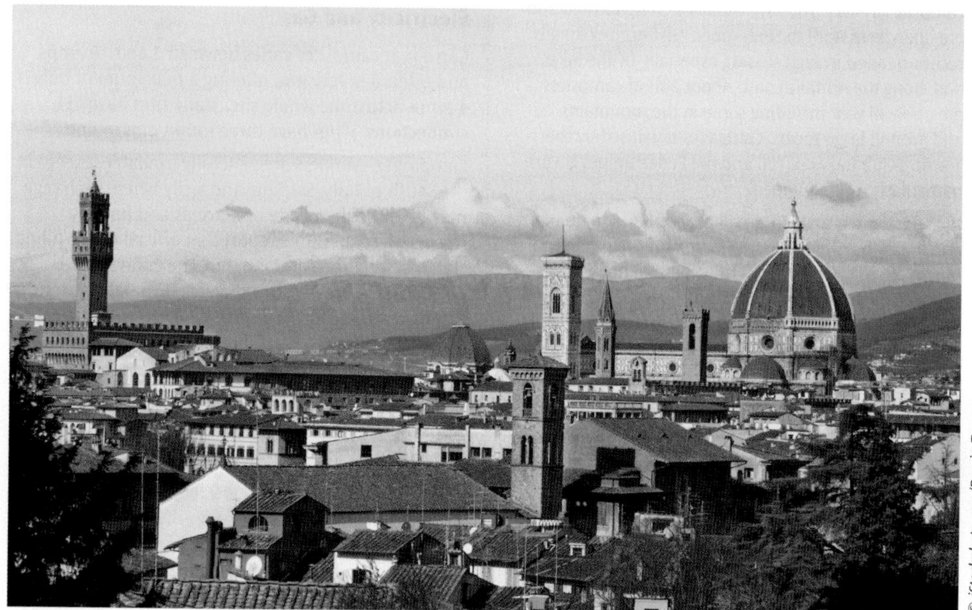

© iStockphoto.com/Burcin Tuncer

Florence Cityscape

Population (approx): 60.6 million

Capital: Rome (population approx 2.7 million)

Area: 301,318 sq km (inc Sardinia & Sicily)

Bordered by: France, Switzerland, Austria, Slovenia

Terrain: Mountainous in the north descending to rolling hills in the centre; some plains and coastal lowlands

Climate: Predominantly Mediterranean climate, alpine in the far north, hot and dry in the south

Coastline: 7,600km

Highest Point: Monte Bianco (Mont Blanc) 4,807m

Language: Italian, German (in the northern Alps)

Local Time: GMT or BST + 1, i.e. 1 hour ahead of the UK all year

Currency: Euros divided into 100 cents; £1 = €1.14, €1 = 87 pence (September 2011)

Telephoning: From the UK dial 0039 for Italy. All area codes start with zero which must be dialled even for local and international calls. To call the UK from Italy dial 0044, omitting the initial zero of the area code.

The country code for San Marino is 00378 followed by a 10-digit number, including the initial zero of the area code.

Emergency numbers: Police 112; Fire brigade 112; Ambulance 112

Public Holidays 2012

Jan 1, 6; Apr 8, 9, 25 (Liberation Day); May 1; Jun 2 (Republic Day); Aug 15; Nov 1; Dec 8 (Immaculate Conception), 25, 26.

Public Holidays 2013

Jan 1, 6; Mar 31; Apr 1, 25 (Liberation Day); May 1; Jun 2 (Republic Day); Aug 15; Nov 1; Dec 8 (Immaculate Conception), 25, 26. Each locality also celebrates its patron saint's day, e.g. Apr 25 (Venice), Jun 24 (Florence), Jun 29 (Rome). School summer holidays run from mid June to mid September

Tourist Office

ITALIAN STATE TOURIST BOARD (ENIT)
1 PRINCES STREET, LONDON, W1B 2AY
Tel: 020 7408 1254
www.enit.it
london@enit.it

The following introduction to Italy should be read in conjunction with the important information contained in the Handbook chapters at the front of this guide.

Camping and Caravanning

There are approximately 2,000 organised and supervised campsites in Italy. They are usually well signposted and are open from April to September. Advance booking is recommended in high season, especially by the lakes and along the Adriatic coast. About 20% of campsites are open all year including some in the mountains and around large towns. Campsites organised by the Touring Club Italiano (TCI) and the Federcampeggio are particularly well equipped.

In general pitch sizes are small at about 80 square metres and it may be difficult to fit a large outfit plus an awning onto a pitch. You will frequently find that hot water is supplied to showers only, for which you will be charged. Published opening and closing dates may be unreliable, especially in Sicily which is a popular winter retreat – phone ahead if travelling during the low season.

It is not compulsory to have a Camping Card International, but it is recommended as a means of identification. If for any reason details are missing from the CCI a site will insist on holding a visitor's passport instead. Outside the high season it is always worth asking for a discount (sconto) when presenting a Camping Card International or in recognition of the lack of full amenities, e.g. pool, restaurant or shop.

Casual camping is not recommended and is not permitted in national parks or in state forests.

Motorhomes

Many local authorities permit motorhomes to park overnight in specially designated places known as 'Camper Stops' or 'Aree di Sosta' and a list of their locations and the services provided are contained in a number of publications and on a number of websites including the French 'Guide Officiel Aires de Service Camping-Car' published by the Fédération Française de Camping et de Caravaning, www.ffcc.fr. You will also find a list of 'Camper Stops' on www.turismoitinerante.com (put 'sosta' in the search box).

Country Information

Cycling – Transportation of Bicycles

An overhanging load must be indicated by an aluminium square panel (panello) measuring 50cm x 50cm with reflectorised red and white diagonal stripes. The load must not exceed 30% of the length of the vehicle, may only overhang at the rear and the regulation applies to a car or caravan carrying bicycles at the rear or windsurf boards on the roof. A fine may be imposed for failure to display the approved sign which is made by Fiamma and in the UK may be purchased from or ordered through motorhome or caravan dealers/accessory shops.

At night outside built-up areas cyclists must wear a reflective jacket and must ride in single file.

Electricity and Gas

Current at campsites varies between 2 and 16 amps and often it is very low, offering a maximum of only 4 amps across the whole site. Many sites have CEE connections. Plugs have three round pins in line.

Campingaz cylinders are generally available, except in the south of Italy, Sardinia and Sicily where exchange may be difficult outside of marinas and holiday resorts. Recent visitors report that official gas re-filling stations are quite common, but The Caravan Club does not recommend this practice for safety reasons – incorrectly filled cylinders can be dangerous.

*See **Electricity and Gas** in the section **DURING YOUR STAY.***

Entry Formalities

British and Irish passport holders may stay in Italy for up to three months without a visa.

Regulations for Pets

All dogs, including those temporarily imported, must be on a leash and wear a muzzle in public places. A domestic animal may be transported in a car provided it does not distract the driver. More than one animal may be transported provided they are kept in the rear of the car, separated from the driver by bars, or kept in special cages.

*See **Pet Travel Scheme** under **Documents** in the section **PLANNING AND TRAVELLING.***

Medical Services

Ask at a pharmacy (farmacia) for the nearest doctor registered with the state health care scheme (SSN) or look in the telephone directory under 'Unita Sanitaria Locale'. The services of a national health service doctor are normally free of charge.

A European Health Insurance Card (EHIC) entitles you to emergency treatment and medication at local rates and to hospital treatment under the state healthcare scheme. Any charges you do incur are non-refundable in Italy but you may be able to make a claim on your return to the UK. Dental treatment is expensive and you will be charged the full fee.

Emergency services (Guardia Medica) are available at weekends and at night and there are first aid posts at major train stations and airports. Staff at pharmacies can advise on minor ailments and at least one pharmacy remains open 24 hours in major towns.

You are strongly recommended to obtain comprehensive travel and medical insurance before travelling to Italy, such as The Caravan Club's Red Pennant Overseas Holiday Insurance – see www.caravanclub.co.uk/redpennant

*See **Medical Matters** in the section **DURING YOUR STAY.***

Opening Hours

Banks – Mon-Fri 8.30am-1pm & 3pm-4pm.

Museums – Tue-Sun 8.30am-6.30pm (check locally as may vary); closed Monday. The Vatican museums and Sistine Chapel are not open to visitors on Sundays. Visitors under 18 or over 60 are admitted free to State museums on production of a passport.

Post Offices – Mon-Fri 8.30am-2pm/5.30pm, Sat 8.30am-12 noon.

Shops – Mon-Sat 8.30am/9am-1pm & 3.30pm/4pm-7.30pm/8pm. In southern Italy and tourist areas shops may open later. There is no lunch time closing in large cities. Shops are closed half a day each week (variable by region).

Safety and Security

Most visits to Italy are trouble free and, in general, levels of crime are low, but visitors should take care on public transport and in crowded areas where pickpockets and bag snatchers may operate. In Rome take particular care around the main railway station, Roma Termini, and on the number 64 bus to and from St Peter's Square. Also take care in and around railway stations in large cities. Be particularly wary of groups of children who may try to distract your attention while attempting to steal from you. Do not carry your passport, credit cards and cash all together in one bag or pocket and only carry what you need for the day. Do not wear expensive jewellery, particularly in the south of Italy.

Take care in bars and try not to leave drinks unattended. Recently there have been cases of drinks being spiked. Check prices before ordering food and insist on seeing a priced menu. Be particularly careful when ordering items, such as lobster, which are charged by weight.

When driving in towns keep your car windows shut and doors locked and never leave valuables on display. Around Rome and Naples moped riders may attempt to snatch bags from stationary cars at traffic lights. Always lock your vehicle and never leave valuables in it, even if you will only be away for a short time or are nearby. Avoid leaving luggage in cars for any length of time or overnight.

Increasingly robberies are taking place from cars at rest stops and service stations on motorways. Treat with caution offers of help, for example with a flat tyre, particularly on the motorway from Naples to Salerno, as sometimes the tyre will have been punctured deliberately.

Do not be tempted to enter or bathe in Italy's many fountains – there are heavy fines if you do. Dress conservatively when visiting places of worship, i.e. cover shoulders and upper arms and do not wear shorts. Avoid queues in the peak season by visiting early in the morning.

The authorities are making strenuous efforts to stamp out the illegal production and sale of counterfeit goods. Illegal traders operate on the streets of all major cities, particularly tourist cities such as Florence and Rome. You are advised not to buy from them at the risk of incurring a fine.

Italy shares with the rest of Europe a general threat from terrorism. Attacks could be indiscriminate and against civilian targets in public places, including tourist sites. There continue to be isolated cases of domestic terrorism by extreme left wing and secessionist groups, aimed primarily at official Italian targets.

*See **Safety and Security** in the section **DURING YOUR STAY.***

British Embassy

VIA XX SETTEMBRE 80A, I-00187 ROMA RM
Tel: 06 42200001
http://ukinitaly.fco.gov.uk/en

British Consulate-General

VIA SAN PAOLO 7, I-20121 MILANO MI
Tel: 02 723001

There is also a British Consulates in Naples.

Irish Embassy

PIAZZA DI CAMPITELLI 3
00186 ROMA
Tel: 06 6979121
www.embassyofireland.it

There is also an Irish Honorary Consulate in Milan.

Customs Regulations

Alcohol and Tobacco

*For import allowances for alcohol and tobacco products see **Customs Regulations** in the section **PLANNING AND TRAVELLING.***

Foodstuffs

If you are travelling from Croatia you must not import eggs, meat or meat products into Italy

Documents

Driving Licence

The standard pink UK paper driving licence is recognised in Italy but holders of the old-style green UK licence are recommended to change it for a photocard licence. Alternatively an International Driving Permit may be purchased from the AA, Green Flag or the RAC.

ITALY

Vehicle(s)

You must be able to present to the police on demand your vehicle and insurance documents, i.e. vehicle registration certificate (V5C), insurance certificate and MOT certificate (if applicable) and, if you are not the owner of your vehicle(s), authorisation for its use from the owner.

*See **Documents** in the section **PLANNING AND TRAVELLING.***

Money

There are few bureaux de change, so change travellers' cheques or cash at a bank. Travellers' cheques are accepted as a means of payment in many hotels, restaurants and shops.

The major credit cards are widely accepted including at petrol stations, but not as widely as in some other European countries. Automatic cash machines (Bancomat) are widespread.

Carry your credit card issuers'/banks' 24-hour UK contact numbers in case of loss or theft of your cards.

Motoring

Alcohol

The maximum permitted level of alcohol is 50 milligrams in 100 millilitres of blood, i.e. less than in the UK (80 milligrams). For drivers with less than three years' driving experience, the limit is zero. It is advisable to adopt the 'no drink and drive' rule at all times as penalties are severe.

Breakdown Service

The motoring organisation, Automobile Club d'Italia (ACI) operates a breakdown service 24 hours a day throughout Italy, including San Marino and Vatican City. Telephone 803116 from a landline or mobile phone. ACI staff speak English. This number also gives access to the ACI emergency information service, operated by multi-lingual staff, for urgent medical or legal advice. You may also use the emergency phones placed every 2km on motorways.

On all roads, including motorways, a charge of €101 is made for assistance and/or recovering a vehicle weighing up to 2,500kg to the nearest ACI garage. Higher charges apply at night, over weekends and public holidays and for towing to anywhere other than the nearest ACI garage. Vehicles over 2,500kg also incur higher charges. Payment is required in cash.

Road police, 'Polizia Stradale', constantly patrol all roads and motorways and can assist when vehicles break down.

Essential Equipment

*See **Motoring – Equipment** in the section **PLANNING AND TRAVELLING.***

Lights

It is compulsory for all vehicles to have dipped headlights at all times when driving outside built-up areas, on motorways and major roads, when driving in tunnels and when visibility is poor, e.g. in rain or snow. Bulbs are more likely to fail with constant use and you are recommended to carry spares.

Reflective Jackets/Waistcoats

If your vehicle is immobilised on the carriageway outside a built-up area at night, or in poor visibility, you must wear a reflective jacket or waistcoat when getting out of your vehicle. This rule also applies to passengers who may leave the vehicle, for example, to assist with a repair. Keep the jackets to hand inside your vehicle, not in the boot.

Warning Triangle

At night a warning triangle must be used to give advance warning of any vehicle parked outside a built-up area near a bend, or on a hill if rear side lights have failed, or in fog. Place the triangle at least 50 metres behind the vehicle (100 metres on motorways). Failure to use a triangle may result in a fine.

Child Restraint System

Children travelling in a UK registered car must be secured according to legislation in force in the UK.

Winter Driving

In the area of Val d'Aosta vehicles must be equipped with winter tyres or snow chains must be carried between 15 October and 15 April. This rule may apply in other areas and over other periods as conditions dictate.

Snow chains can be hired or purchased from Polar Automotive Ltd, tel 01892 519933, www.snowchains.com, email: polar@snowchains.com (10% discount for Caravan Club members).

Fuel

Unleaded petrol is sold from pumps marked 'Super Unleaded' or 'Super Sensa Piombo'. Diesel is called 'gasolio' and LPG is known as 'gas auto' or 'GPL'.

Fuel is sold 24 hours a day on motorways but elsewhere petrol stations may close for an extended lunch break and overnight from approximately 7pm. Opening hours are clearly displayed, as are the addresses of the nearest garages which are open.

Major credit cards are accepted, but possibly not in rural areas, so always carry some cash. Look for the 'Carta Si' sign. Recent visitors report that many petrol stations in rural areas and on major routes between towns are now unmanned and automated. Payment may be made with bank notes but the machines will usually only accept credit cards issued by Italian banks.

*See also **Fuel** under **Motoring – Advice** in the section **PLANNING AND TRAVELLING.***

Overtaking

On roads with three traffic lanes, the middle lane is reserved for overtaking, but overtaking is only allowed if a vehicle travelling in the opposite direction is not already in the middle lane.

When pulling out to overtake on motorways check for cars travelling at well over the maximum speed limit of 130km/h (81 mph).

Parking

In major towns there are parking zones where payment is required and these are indicated by blue road signs. Pay either at a machine with coins or buy a card from local tobacconists or newspaper shops and display it inside your vehicle. Some cities also have green zones where parking is prohibited on working days during the morning and afternoon rush hours.

Parking against the traffic flow and parking on the pavement are not allowed. Illegally parked vehicles may be clamped or towed away.

*See also **Parking Facilities for the Disabled** under **Motoring – Advice** in the section **PLANNING AND TRAVELLING.***

Pollution Charge in Milan

A 'pollution' charge was introduced in 2008 for vehicles entering the centre of Milan, reputedly one of Europe's most polluted cities. It is in force on weekdays between 7.00 or 7.30am and 7.00 or 7.30pm. Under the scheme vehicles, including those registered outside Italy, are classified according to their emissions level and the daily toll ranges from €2 to €10 (2011). Motorists must buy an 'ecopass' at one of 43 entrance points around the city centre, or from tobacconists, newsagents and ATM points. There is no charge for vehicles displaying a disabled passenger blue badge.

Other places in Italy also have low emmission zones in operation. See the website www.lowemissionzones.eu for further information.

Priority

In general, priority must be given to traffic coming from the right except if indicated by roadsigns. At traffic lights a flashing amber light indicates that traffic must slow down and proceed with caution, respecting the priority rules.

Roads

The road network is of a high standard and main and secondary roads are generally good. Many main roads are winding and hilly but provide a more interesting route than the motorways. Stopping places for refreshments may be few and far between in some areas.

Standards of driving may be erratic, especially overtaking, and lane discipline poor; some roads have a particularly bad reputation for accidents. Those where special vigilance is called for include the Via Aurelia between Rome and Pisa, which is mostly two lane and is extremely busy at weekends, the A12 to the north with its series of tunnels and curves, the A1 between Florence and Bologna, the Rome ring road, roads around Naples and Palermo, and mountain roads in the south and in Sicily.

Road Signs and Markings

Road signs conform to international standards. White lettering on a green background indicates motorways (autostrada), whereas state and provincial roads outside built-up areas have white lettering on a blue background. This is a reversal of the colouring used in France and may initially cause confusion when driving from one country to the other.

Other frequently encountered signs include the following:

Snow chains required

Horizontal traffic light

Carabinieri (police)

Ecopass zone (Milan)

Attenzione – *Caution*

Autocarro – *Lorries*

Coda – *Traffic jam*

Curva pericolosa – *Dangerous bend*

Destra – *Right*

Deviazione – *Diversion*

Divieto di accesso – *No entry*

Divieto di sorpasso – *No overtaking*

Divieto di sosta – *No parking*

Ghiaia – *Gravel*

Incidente – *Accident*

Incrocio – *Crossroads*

Lavori in corso – *Roadworks ahead*

Pericoloso – *Danger*

Rallentare – *Slow down*

Restringimento – *Narrow lane*

Senso unico – *One-way street*

Senso vietato – *No entry*

Sinistra – *Left*

Sosta autorizzata – *Parking permitted (at times shown)*

Sosta aietata – *No parking*

Svolta – *Bend*

Uscita – *Exit*

Vietato ingresso veicili – *No entry for vehicles*

A single or double unbroken line in the centre of the carriageway must not be crossed.

Speed Limits

*See **Speed Limits** under **Motoring – Advice** in the section **PLANNING AND TRAVELLING.***

Motorhomes over 3,500kg are restricted to 80 km/h (50 mph) outside built-up areas and 100 km/h (62 mph) on motorways.

Speed on some sections of Italian motorways is electronically controlled. When you leave a motorway at a toll booth electronic tills calculate the distance a vehicle has travelled and the journey time. The police are automatically informed if speeding has taken place, and fines are imposed.

In bad weather the maximum speed is 90 km/h (56 mph) on roads outside built-up areas and 110 km/h (68 mph) on motorways.

The transportation or use of radar detectors is prohibited.

Traffic Jams

During the summer months, particularly at weekends, in general the roads to the Ligurian and Adriatic coasts and to the Italian lakes, are particularly busy, as are the narrow roads around the lakes. Travelling mid week may help a little. Bottlenecks are likely to occur on the A1 north-south motorway at stretches between Milan and Bologna, Rioveggio and Incisa and on the ring road around Rome. Other traffic jams occur on the A14 to the Adriatic coast; on the A4 between Milan and Brescia caused by heavy traffic to Lakes Iseo and Garda; the A11 Florence to Pisa (before the A12 junction); the A12 Rome to Civitavecchia; the A23 Udine to Tarvisio and before the tunnels on the A26 between Alessandria and Voltri.

Italians traditionally go on holiday during the first weekend of August when traffic density is at its worst. Rush hour traffic jams regularly occur on the ring roads for Milan, Rome and Naples.

Violation of Traffic Regulations

The police may impose on the spot fines, which are particularly heavy for speeding and drink and/or drug related driving offences. Payment is required in cash and a receipt must be given. It can take up to a year for notice of a traffic violation and resulting fine to reach the owner of a foreign registered vehicle.

Motorways

There are approximately 6,500km of motorway (autostrade) in Italy. Tolls (pedaggio) are levied on most of them.

On some motorways, tolls are payable at intermediate toll booths for each section of the motorway used. On a few others the toll must be paid on entering the motorway.

Tolls

Category A	Cars with height from front axle less than 1.30m.
Category B	Motor vehicles with 2 axles with height from front axle over 1.30m (motorhomes).
Category C	Motor vehicles with 3 axles, e.g car plus caravan.
Category D	Motor vehicles with 4 axles, e.g. car plus twin-axle caravan.

To calculate the tolls payable on your planned route see www.autostrade.it (English option) which allows you to enter your route and class of vehicle. Alternatively, see the AA's website, www.theaa.com

Tolls can prove expensive especially over long distances. For example, a car plus caravan travelling from Florence to Rome (254km) will pay €22, a motorhome €16.20. For the 768km stretch from Naples to Milan the cost is €68.20 and €50.20 respectively (2011 tolls subject to change).

The same website, www.autostrade.it, also contains details of motorway service areas and traffic information.

Payment

Cash, including major foreign currencies, debit and credit cards are accepted. Credit cards are also accepted for payment in the Fréjus, Mont-Blanc and Grand St Bernard tunnels. However, visitors advise that on some stretches of motorway automated pay desks which accept credit cards will only do so for solo vehicles. If you are towing a caravan it is advisable to have cash available as you may need to pass through the manned white channel for cash payments.

The prepaid Viacard, available in values of €25, €50 and €75, is also accepted on the majority of motorways and is obtainable from motorway toll booths, service areas and PuntoBlu points of sale along the motorways. The card may be used for any vehicle. When leaving a motorway on which the Viacard is accepted (use the blue or white lanes – do not use the yellow 'Telepass' lanes), insert your entry ticket and card into the machine or give them to the attendant who will deduct the amount due. A Viacard is valid until the credit expires and may be used on a subsequent visit to Italy but cannot be refunded. Viacards are not accepted on Sicilian motorways.

Touring

Italy's great cities, with their religious, artistic and historic treasures, are high on the short break list and are worthy destinations in their own right. Rome is one of the world's great artistic and historic cities and merits more than just a fleeting visit. Visitors over 65 often qualify for reduced or free entrance to museums and other attractions, so carry your passport as proof of age.

In Rome an Archaeological Card is available, valid for up to seven days, offering entry (ahead of any queues) to many of the most famous sites, together with discounts on guided tours. The cards are available from participating sites and museums.

Sampling the country's culinary diversity, along with its fine wines, is high on most visitors' agenda. There is much more to Italian cooking than pasta and pizza; try the range of veal dishes, such as saltimbocca or ossobuco, and sample some of the delicious pastries, desserts and ice cream.

Smoking is not permitted in public places including restaurants and bars.

In bars prices shown are for drinks taken standing at the bar. Prices are higher if you are seated at a table. In restaurants a service or cover charge is usually added to the bill but it is customary to add 50 cents or €1 per person if you are happy with the service provided. Not all restaurants accept credit cards; check before ordering.

The east coast of Italy has many holiday resorts with fine, sandy beaches, from Ravenna, to Pescara and beyond. However, most beaches in Italy are commercially managed and unless a campsite or hotel has its own private beach, be prepared to pay to enjoy a day by the sea. By law a part of every beach must have free access, but usually it is the least attractive part.

Many parts of Italy lie on a major seismic fault line and tremors and minor earthquakes are common. Visitors climbing Mount Etna should follow the marked routes and heed the advice of guides. There is also ongoing low-intensity volcanic activity on the island of Stromboli.

Visitors to Venice should note that parts of the city are liable to flood in late autumn and early spring.

There are more than 40 World Heritage Sites in Italy (more than any other country) including the historic centres of Florence, Siena, Naples, Pienza, Urbino and the Vatican City.

The Vatican museums and Sistine Chapel are closed on Sundays, except on the last Sunday of the month. When visiting art galleries in Florence, in particular the Uffizi and Accademia, you are advised to buy timed tickets in advance, either online or in person. Otherwise you will inevitably encounter very long queues.

There are numerous ferry services transporting passengers and vehicles between Italy and neighbouring countries. Major ports of departure for Croatia, Greece and Turkey are Ancona, Bari, Brindisi, Trieste and Venice. Services also operate to Corsica from Citavecchia, Genoa, Livorno, Porto Torres (Sardinia), Santa Teresa di Gallura (Sardinia) and Savona.

For further information contact:

VIAMARE TRAVEL LTD
SUITE 3, 447 KENTON ROAD
HARROW
MIDDX HA3 0XY
Tel: 020 8206 3420, Fax: 020 8206 1332
www.viamare.com
ferries@viamare.com

If you are planning a skiing holiday contact the Italian State Tourist Board for advice on safety and weather conditions before travelling. Off-piste skiing is highly dangerous and all safety instructions should be followed meticulously in view of the dangers of avalanches in some areas.

Italy has introduced a law requiring skiers and snowboarders to carry tracking equipment if going off-piste. The law also obliges children up to 14 years of age to wear a helmet. There are plans for snowboarders to be banned from certain slopes.

Easy Italia

Easy Italia is a multi-lingual service providing tourist information and assistance by telephone (9am-10pm) 039 039 039.

Local Travel

Traffic is restricted or prohibited at certain times in the historical centre of most Italian cities in order to reduce congestion and pollution levels, and you are advised to use out of centre car parks and public transport. The boundaries of historic centres are usually marked with signs displaying the letters ZTL (zona traffico limitato). A crossed hammer on the sign means the restriction does not apply on Sundays and public holidays. Do not pass the ZTL sign as your registration number is likely to be caught on camera and notice of a fine – or fines if you cross more than one ZTL zone – will probably be sent to your home address. Fines are around €100 each time you enter a ZTL.

In addition many northern Italian regions have banned traffic in town and city centres on Sundays. Buses and taxis are permitted to operate.

ITALY

Public transport is usually cheap and efficient. All the major cities have extensive bus networks and Messina, Milan, Padova, Rome and Turin also have trams. At present only Rome and Milan have an extensive underground network and Perugia has recently inaugurated a 'minimetro'. Bus and metro tickets cannot be purchased on board and must be obtained prior to boarding from newsagents, tobacconists, ticket kiosks or bars. Books of tickets and daily, weekly and monthly passes are also available.

Validate your ticket when using public transport at the yellow machines positioned at the entrance to platforms in railway stations, in the entrance hall of metro stations and on board buses and trams. Officials patrol all means of public transport and will issue an on the spot fine if you do not hold a validated ticket. Tickets for buses and the metro tend to be time limited (75 minutes) and it is therefore necessary to complete your journey within the allotted time and purchase a new ticket for any additional travel.

Only use taxis which are officially licensed. They will have a neon taxi sign on the roof and are generally white or yellow. Also ensure that the meter in the taxi has been reset before starting your journey. Fares are quite high and there are additional charges for luggage and pets, at night and on public holidays. A tip is expected (up to 10%) and this is sometimes added to the fares for foreigners.

Car ferry services operate between Venice and the Lido, the Italian mainland and the Aeolian Islands, Sardinia, Sicily, Elba and Capri, Corsica (France) and on Lakes Maggiore, Como and Garda. Parking in Venice is very difficult; instead park at a mainland car park and use a bus or ferry to the city. However, be aware that thieves may operate in car parks in Mestre. Driving and parking in Naples are not recommended in any circumstances.

Cars towing caravans are prohibited at all times from using the S163 south of Naples because it is narrow and has many bends. Motorhomes are prohibited in summer between Positano and Vietri-a-Mare.

All place names used in the Site Entry listings which follow can be found in Michelin's Tourist & Motoring Atlas for Italy, scale 1:200,000 (1cm = 2km).

⊞ **AGEROLA** *3A3* (2km E Urban) **Camping Beata Solitudo, Piazza Generale Avitabile 4, San Lazzaro, 80051 Agerola (NA) [tel/fax 081 8025048; beatasol@tiscalinet.it; www.beatasolitudo.it]** Exit A3/S145 at Castellammare-di-Stabia & foll dirs S on S366 to Agerola. Turn L sp San Lazzaro, site in vill square - narr access rds. Do not app via Amalfi coast rd. Sm, terr, shd; wc (cont); chem disp; mv service pnt; shwrs inc; el pnts (3A) inc; lndry rm; shop, rest, snacks, bar in vill; sm playgrnd; shgl beach 16km; wifi; 70% statics; dogs free; bus adj; poss cr; Eng spkn; adv bkg; quiet; red CCI. "Vg access to Amalfi coast via bus; site at 650m - sea views; v helpful owner; bungalows & hostel accomm avail in restored castle building on site; vg but suitable m'vans only." € 20.00 2009*

⊞ **ALBA** *1B2* (1km SW Urban) *44.68507, 8.01019* **Camping Village Alba, Corso Piave 219, San Cassiano, 12051 Alba (CN) [0173 280972; fax 288621; info@albavillagehotel.it; www.albavillagehotel.it]** Fr A21 exit Asti Est onto S231 to Alba ring rd. Take Corso Piave dir Roddi & Castiglione Falletto, site sp (Campo Sportivo) on L - red block. Or fr A6 exit at SP662 & foll sp Cherasco & Marene, then at rndabt foll sp Pollenza, then Roddi. Fr Roddi site sp dir Alba. Med, hdg/mkd pitch, pt shd; htd wc; chem disp; mv service pnt; shwrs inc; el pnts (16A) €3; lndtte; shop 150m; rest; bar; BBQ; htd pool adj; paddling pool; sports cent adj; cycle hire; games area; internet; some statics/apartmnts; dogs; bus; Eng spkn; adv bkg; quiet; ccard acc; red CCI. "Excel, friendly, clean site; open country to rear; vg facs; conv Barolo vineyards; attractive town & area." ♦ € 27.00 2011*

ALBENGA *1B2* (5km N Rural) *44.09636, 8.20709* **Parco Vacanze Ali Baba, Via Nostra Signora delle Grazie 80, Peagna, 17023 Ceriale (SV) [tel/fax 0182 990182; info@campingalibaba.it; www.campingalibaba.it]** On N side of main coast rd SS1 at Ceriale on rd bet Albenga & Loano. Med, pt sl, shd; wc; shwrs; el pnts inc; lndtte; shop; rest; bar; playgrnd; pool & paddling pool; beach 2km; 90% statics; poss cr; quiet; ccard acc. "Excel san facs; gd." 1 May-30 Sep. € 32.00 2008*

ALBENGA *1B2* (2km E Rural/Coastal) *44.08277, 8.21611* **Camping Baciccia, Via Torino 19, 17023 Ceriale (SV) [0182 990743; fax 993839; info@campingbaciccia.it; www.campingbaciccia.it]** Exit A10 for Albenga, turn L onto SS1 Via Aurelia dir Savona for 3km. Turn L inland at traff lts bef Famiglia Supmkt in Ceriale, site in 200m on L, sp. Med, mkd pitch, pt sl, pt shd; htd wc (some cont); chem disp; mv service pnt; serviced pitches; baby facs; shwrs inc; el pnts (6A) inc; gas; lndtte; shop; supmkt nr; rest; snacks; bar; BBQ; playgrnd; pool high ssn; paddling pool; public shgl beach 600m, private beach nrby; tennis 500m; cycle hire; horseriding 2km; golf 10km; wifi; entmnt; TV rm; 5% statics; dogs €4; bus to private beach; sep car park; poss cr; Eng spkn; adv bkg; quiet; ccard acc; red long stay/low ssn/CCI. "Family-run site; ltd touring pitches; narr site rds & ent & sm pitches; friendly owners; gd san facs & pool; busy w/ends; lovely pool & café; conv many historical attractions." 1 Apr-3 Nov & 1 Dec-10 Jan. € 49.00 (3 persons) 2011*

ALBENGA *1B2* (5km NW Rural) *44.08472, 8.21027* **Camping Bella Vista, Via Campore 23, 17030 Campochiesa-d'Albenga (SV) [0182 540213; fax 554925; info@campingbellavista.it; www.campingbellavista.it]** Exit A10 at Borghetto S Spirito & foll sp Ceriale. In Ceriale turn R at 3rd traff lts, R at next traff lts & foll site sp. Med, hdg/mkd pitch, terr,pt shd; htd wc (some cont); chem disp; mv service pnt; baby facs; shwrs inc; el pnts (3-6A) €2.50 (poss rev pol); lndtte; shop; tradsmn; rest; snacks; bar; BBQ; htd pool; paddling pool; beach 1.5km; games rm; internet; entmnt; 30% statics; dogs €6.50; phone; bus 900m; poss cr; Eng spkn; adv bkg; quiet. "Pleasant, friendly, clean, Dutch family-run site; helpful staff; narr site rds; mostly sm pitches; owner will site c'van with tractor on request; poss diff lge o'fits." ♦ 15 Mar-15 Nov & 15 Dec-15 Jan. € 33.50 2011*

⊞ **ALBEROBELLO** *3A4* (1.5km N Rural) *40.80194, 17.25055* **Camping Dei Trulli, Via Castellana Grotte, Km 1.5, 70011 Alberobello (BA) [0804 323699; fax 322145; info@campingdeitrulli.it; www.campingdeitrulli.com]** Fr Alberobello, site sp on R. Lift barrier to ent if clsd. Med, mkd pitch, hdstg, pt shd; wc; mv service pnt opp; shwrs €0.50; el pnts (6A) €2.50; shop &1.5km; rest; snacks; bar; 2 pools high ssn; cycle hire; wifi; entmnt; phone; Eng spkn; ccard acc; red long stay/CCI. "Gd touring base; helpful, friendly owner; some pitches sm due trees; ltd facs low ssn; hot water to shwrs only." € 27.00 2010*

ALBEROBELLO *3A4* (1km S Rural) *40.77507, 17.24040* **Camping Bosco Selva, 27 Via Bosco Selva, 70011 Alberobello (BA) [080 4323726; campingboscoselva@libero.it; www.campingboscoselva.it]** Sp fr S172/S239 Alberobello ring rd. Med, some hdstg, pt sl, pt shd; htd wc (some cont); chem disp; mv service pnt; shwrs inc; el pnts (2A) inc; lndtte; shop 1km; rest; bar; games rm; some statics; Eng spkn; quiet; CCI. "In heart of 'Trulli' region of sm beehive-shaped houses; wooded site; friendly owner; vg facs." 1 Apr-10 Oct. € 23.00 2010*

ALBINIA see Orbetello *1D4*

AMEGLIA see Sarzana *1C2*

⊞ **ANITA** *2E2* (10km E Rural) **Camping Prato Pozzo, Rifugio di Valle, Via Rotta Martinella 34/A, 44010 Anita (FE) [tel/fax 0532 801058; info@pratopozzo.com; www.pratopozzo.com]** Fr Comacchio take rd round W side of lagoon twd Anita. Turn L twd ferry over Rv Reno, site on R bef ferry - not obvious. Sm, pt shd; wc; chem disp; mv service pnt; shwrs inc; el pnts inc; rest; playgrnd; sand beach 15km; horseriding; 5% statics; Eng spkn; adv bkg; quiet, "Delightful CL-type 'Agrituristico' site; poss horses & ponies on site; excel private nature reserve adj; excel cent for Po Delta National Park; unfenced ponds not suitable sm children; vg san facs; poss mosquito prob." ♦ € 14.00 2007*

ITALY

⊞ **ANTERSELVA DI SOPRA/ANTHOLZ OBERTAL** *2E1* (500m NE Rural) *46.86450, 12.10966* **Camping Anterselva/Antholz, Obertal 34, 39030 Anterselva-di-Sopra/Antholz-Obertal (BZ) [0474 492204; fax 492444; info@camping-antholz. com; www.camping-antholz.com]** E fr Brunico on S49. Turn N at Rasun & Antholz valley; cont 12km, well sp, app not steep. Site is 2km N of Antholz. Med, pt sl, unshd; htd wc; chem disp; mv service pnt; baby facs; shwrs inc; el pnts (4A) inc; gas; Indtte; shop; rest snacks; bar; playgrnd; tennis 500m; cycle hire; wifi; TV; dogs €3; bus nr; adv bkg; quiet. ♦ € 25.00 2009*

I'll go online and tell the Club what we think of the campsites we've visited – www.caravanclub.co.uk/ europereport

AOSTA *1B1* (1km N Rural) *45.74666, 7.31897* **Camping Ville d'Aoste, Viale Gran San Bernardo 67, Loc Les Fourches, 11100 Aosta (AO) [0165 267213]** 1st site on L off old rd fr Aosta to Grand St Bernard tunnel rte S27. Nr Hotel Rayon du Soleil. Sm, pt shd; wc (some cont); chem disp; mv service pnt; shwrs inc; el pnts (4-10A) inc; gas; Indtte; shop; snacks; bar; playgrnd; TV; phone; train at Saraillon; some rd noise; ccard acc; CCI. "Interesting town with many Roman historic remains; uncr, even in high ssn; unreliable opening dates." 9 Jul-31 Oct. € 17.00 2008*

AOSTA *1B1* (4km E Rural) *45.74088, 7.39355* **Camping Aosta, Villaggio Clou 29, 11020 Quart (AO) [tel/fax 0165 765602; info@campingaosta.com]** Site 1km fr Villefranche at Quart on SS26. Med, pt sl, terr, shd; wc (some cont); chem disp; shwrs inc; mv service pnt; el pnts (6A) inc; Indtte; sm shop; supmkt 2km; rest; bar; playgrnd; pool 5km; cycle hire; mainly statics; phone; rlwy noise. "Ltd touring pitches; poorly-maintained site; NH only." 15 May-15 Sep. € 21.00 2010*

⊞ **AOSTA** *1B1* (3km SE Rural) *45.73338, 7.36006* **Camping Les Iles, Loc Les Iles 17, 11020 Pollein (AO) [tel/fax 0165 53154; camping_les_iles@hotmail.it]** Fr N exit A5 Aosta Est sp St Christophe/Pollein, go under a'strada, cross Rv Dora, site sp. Med, pt shd; wc; chem disp; mv service pnt; shwrs; el pnts metered; snacks; bar; playgrnd; tennis; some statics; dogs €3; bus nr; some rd noise; ccard acc; CCI. "Beautiful location; conv Mont Blanc & St Bernard tunnels." ♦ € 29.00 2009*

AOSTA *1B1* (4km W Rural) *45.72190, 7.26985* **Camping International Touring, Fraz. Arensod 10, 11010 Sarre (AO) [tel/fax 0165 257061; campingtouring@libero.it; www. campingtouring.com]** Exit A5/E25 Aosta West, site sp fr rd S26. Lge, pt shd; wc (some cont); own san rec; chem disp; mv service pnt; shwrs inc; el pnts (3-6A) €2.80; gas; Indtte; sm supmkt 100m; rest; snacks; bar; playgrnd; pool high ssn; tennis; 10% statics; dogs €1; poss cr; quiet; 10% red CCI. "Lovely scenery; conv for Val d'Aosta with historical castles; somewhat run down site; NH only." 15 May-15 Sep. € 24.50 2009*

AOSTA *1B1* (5km W Rural) *45.71706, 7.26161* **Camping Monte Bianco, St Maurice 15, 11010 Sarre (AO) [0165 257523; info@ campingmontebianco.it; www.campingmontebianco.it]** Fr A5/E25 exit Aosta W twd Aosta, site on R, well sp. Fr Mont Blanc tunnel on S26 site on R at Sarre 500m past St Maurice sp. W fr Aosta, site on L 100m past boundary sp St Maurice/ Sarre, yellow sp. Turn into site poss tight for lge o'fits. Sm, terr, pt shd; wc (some cont); chem disp; mv service pnt; shwrs €0.50; el pnts (6-10A) €2.80; gas; Indry rm; shop adj; supmkt 500m; rest 200m; bar 100m; playgrnd; pool 4km; phone; Eng spkn; adv bkg; quiet; red long stay low ssn; CCI. "Sm, family-run site set in orchard on rv; friendly, helpful; excel tourist info; beautiful alpine scenery & walks; do not rely on sat nav to site nor Via Michelin rte." 1 Apr-30 Sep. € 32.00 2011*

AQUILA, L' *2E4* (11km NE Rural) *42.4202, 13.52596* **Camping Funivia del Gran Sasso, Fonte Cerreto, 67010 Assergi (AQ) [tel/fax 0862 606163; campingfuniviagransasso@virgilio. it]** Fr A24 take Assergi exit. Turn R sp Funivia del Gran Sasso. At T-junc in 800m turn R, site well sp on R in 1.8km. Sm, pt shd; wc (cont); chem disp; shwrs €0.70; el pnts (4A) €1.50; Indry rm; shop 8km; rest, bar 200m; BBQ; 5% statics; dogs €1; sep car park high ssn; poss cr; quiet; ccard acc. "Spectacular mountain scenery; excel walking; clean tho' ltd basic facs." 15 May-15 Sep. € 24.50 2008*

AQUILEIA *2E1* (300m NE Rural) *45.77786, 13.36943* **Camping Aquileia, Via Gemina 10, 33051 Aquileia (UD) [0431 91042; fax 919583; info@campingaquileia.it; www. campingaquileia.it]** Fr A4/E70 take Grado/Palmanova exit & foll sp Grado on SS352. Turn L at traff lts at ent to Aquileia. Site in 400m on R. Fr SS14 turn onto SS352, site sp. Med, shd; wc (some cont); chem disp; mv service pnt; shwrs inc; el pnts (6A) inc; Indry rm; supmkt adj; rest; snacks; playgrnd; pool; paddling pool; some statics; dogs €3; bus 300m; quiet; red long stay; ccard acc; CCI. "Excel site; lge pitches; 10 mins walk thro Roman ruins to magnificent, unique basilica & mosaics; poss noisy concerts July festival week; gd, friendly site." 21 Apr-15 Sep. € 27.50 2011*

AQUILEIA *2E1* (3km S Coastal) *45.72640, 13.39860* **Camping Village Belvedere Pineta, 33051 Belvedere-di-Grado (UD) [0431 91007; fax 918641; info@belvederepineta.it; www. belvederepineta.it]** Fr Venezia/Trieste a'strada, exit for Palmanova & foll Grado sp on S352 to Aquileia. Drive thro Belvedere, & site is nr lagoon. Slow app to site due to uneven surface. V lge, mkd pitch, shd; wc; chem disp; mv service pnt; baby facs; shwrs inc; el pnts (3-6A) inc; gas; Indtte (inc dryer); supmkt; rest; snacks; bar; BBQ; playgrnd; pool; paddling pool; waterslide; sand beach adj; watersports; tennis; games area; games rm; cycle hire; excursions; entmnt; golf 5km; 50% statics; dogs €7.50; rlwy stn 10km at Cervignano; adv bkg; quiet; red long stay/snr citizens; CCI. "Wooded site - poss mosquitoes; steamer trips fr Grado; gd touring base, inc Venice; discount for Seniors; excel site with v cln san facs." ♦ 1 May-30 Sep. € 38.50 (CChq acc) 2011*

ARCO *1D1* (1km N Rural) *45.92694, 10.8925* **Camping Arco, Loc Prabi, Via Legionari Cecoslovacchia 12, 38062 Arco (TN) [0464 517491; fax 515525; arco@arcoturistica.com; www.arcoturistica.com]** Fr N foll sp Arco Centre at rndabt at start of ring rd & turn R immed after x-ing rv bdge. Fr S foll ring rd sp Trento. Turn L at Camping/Prabi (climbing area) sp. Lge, shd; wc (some cont); chem disp; mv service pnt; shwrs inc; el pnts (4A) inc; gas; Indtte; shop; rest 300m; snacks adj; bar; playgrnd; pool adj; tennis; games area; cycle hire; wifi; 10% statics; dogs €4; quiet; ccard acc. "V busy site; v clean." ♦ 21 Mar-8 Nov. € 28.10 2009*

ARCO *1D1* (700m W Rural) *45.8740, 10.8675* **Camping Arco Lido, Loc Linfano, 38062 Arco (TN) [0464 505077; fax 548668; lido@arcoturistica.com; www.arcoturistica.com]** Site sp on lake shore between Riva-del-Garda & Torbole. Lge, mkd pitch, pt shd; wc (some cont); chem disp; mv service pnt; baby facs; shwrs inc; el pnts (2A) inc; gas 400m; Indtte; shop & 600m; rest, snacks, bar 200m; playgrnd; lake sw & shgl beach adj; internet; no statics; dogs €4; phone; bus 300m; poss cr; Eng spkn; adv bkg; quiet; ccard acc. "Direct access to super beach; beachside walk to attractive, lively town; site v busy at w/end; well-stocked shop." ♦ 3 Apr-10 Oct. € 26.50 2008*

ARENZANO see Genova *1C2*

⊞ **AREZZO** *1D3* (10km SW Rural) *43.45181, 11.79041* **Camping Villaggio Le Ginestre, Loc Ruscello 100, 52100 Arezzo [0575 363566; fax 366949; info@campingleginestre.it; www.campingleginestre.it]** Ont A1 sp Arezzo. Foll sp to Battifolle & Ruscello, proceed for 2km to rdbt, turn L to Ruscello and foll signs to site which will be on the L Med, some hdstg, terr, pt sl, pt shd; htd wc; chem disp; mv service pnt; shwrs inc; el pnts (5-10A) inc; Indtte; shop 500m; rest; snacks; bar; playgrnd; pool; tennis; games area; games rm; 5% statics; dogs; bus; site clsd Jan; poss cr; adv bkg; ccard acc; CCI. "Pleasant, grassy site with views; friendly owner; gd rest; trains fr Arezzo to Florence, Rome etc; gd touring base." ♦ € 43.00 2011*

ARONA *1B1* (7km N Rural) *45.81583, 8.54992* **Camping Solcio, Via al Campeggio, 28040 Solcio-de-Lesa (NO) [0322 7497; fax 7566; info@campingsolcio.com; www.campingsolcio.com]** Foll S33 N fr Arona, thro Meina campsite on R of rd app Solcio; well sp, adj boatyard. Med, mkd pitch, pt shd; htd wc (some cont); chem disp; mv service pnt; baby facs; shwrs inc; el pnts (6A) inc; gas; Indtte (inc dryer); shop & 1km; rest; snacks; bar; BBQ; lake sw & shgl beach adj; fishing; watersports; wifi; entmnt; 40% statics; dogs €7.80; phone; rlwy noise; poss cr; Eng spkn; adv bkg; red low ssn/long stay; CCI. "Gd site adj lake; some sm pitches; premium for lakeside pitches; gd rest; gd cent for area; conv Stresa; friendly." 19 Mar-16 Oct. € 41.50 (3 persons) 2011*

⊞ **ARONA** *1B1* (2km S Rural) *45.73741, 8.57651* **Camping Lago Azzurro, Via Enrico Fermi 2, 28040 Dormelletto (NO) [tel/fax 0322 497197; info@campinglagoazzurro.it; www.campinglagoazzurro.it]** Exit A8/A26/E62 dir Castelletto Ticino onto SS33. Site 1km N of Dormelletto, on W shore of lake. Rec app fr Dormelletto, not Arona. Med, hdg/mkd pitch, shd; wc (some cont); mv service pnt; shwrs €0.70; el pnts (3A) €3.50; Indtte; shop; rest 1km; snacks; bar; pool high ssn; tennis; private shgl beach; boating; tennis adj; games area; entmnt; sat TV; 50% statics; dogs €4; phone; poss cr; adv bkg; quiet but motor boats noisy w/end, noisy entmnt high ssn. "Facs stretched high ssn due tented teenage vill on site; sm pitches." ♦ € 29.50 2010*

ARONA *1B1* (2km S Urban) *45.73648, 8.57564* **Camping Röse, Via Fermi 3, 28040 Dormelletto (NO) [0322 497979; fax 498970; info@campingrose.it; www.campingrose.it]** Site 2km N of Dormelletto, on W shore of lake. Rec app fr Dormelletto, not Arona. Med, some mkd pitch, shd; wc (some cont); chem disp; shwrs; el pnts (3A) €3; gas; Indtte; shop; rest adj; snacks; bar; playgrnd; beach adj; fishing; watersports; 80% statics; dogs €5; adv bkg; ccard acc; quiet. "Friendly site; inadequate shwrs; lake ferry boats at Arona." ♦ 1 Apr-12 Oct. € 26.00 2010*

⊞ **ARONA** *1B1* (5km S Rural) *45.72825, 8.57966* **Camping Lido Holiday Inn, Via Marco Polo 1, 28040 Dormelletto (NO) [tel/fax 0322 497047; info@campingholidayinn.com; www.campingholidayinn.com]** Exit A8/A26/E62 at Castelletto Ticino dir Arona, foll sp Dormelletto. Lido sp on R. Lge, hdg/mkd pitch, pt sl, pt shd; wc; chem disp; mv service pnt; baby facs; shwrs inc; el pnts (3A) €4.50; gas; Indtte; shop; tradsmn; rest; snacks; bar; BBQ; playgrnd; pool; lake sw & shgl beach; tennis; golf 8km; 30% statics; dogs €5; phone; train 400m; Eng spkn; adv bkg; quiet; red CCI. "Ent thro fountain (it stops on ent!)" ♦ € 37.00 2009*

ARSIE *1D1* (1km S Rural) *45.96333, 11.76027* **Camping Al Lago, Via Campagna 14, 32030 Rocca di Arsie (BL) [0439 58540; fax 58471; info@campingallago.bl.it; www.campingallago.bl.it]** Fr Trento on S47, turn E dir Feltre/Belluno rd SS50B, take 1st exit after long tunnel. Fr Belluno on S50 & S50B take Arsié exit & foll site sp. Med, pt shd; wc; chem disp (wc); shwrs inc; el pnts (3A) inc; gas 2.5km; shop 3km; rest high ssn; bar; playgrnd; lake sw adj; 15% statics; dogs; phone; poss cr; adv bkg; quiet; ccard acc; CCI. "Excel, well-run, clean, tidy site in unspoilt area of historical & cultural interest; simple facs, basic but clean; boat hire locally; ent clsd 1400-1530 & 0000-0800; passport req to register." 1 Apr-4 Oct. € 23.00 2009*

ARSIE *1D1* (3km S Rural) *45.96777, 11.76583* **Gajole - Quiet & Lake Camping, Loc Soravigo, 32030 Arsie (BL) [tel/fax 0439 58505; info@campinggajole.it; www.campinggajole.it]** Fr S47 take S50bis dir Feltre, Belluno. Turn 1st R after long tunnel, site well sp. Med, hdstg, pt sl, terr, pt shd; wc (some cont); chem disp; mv service pnt; shwrs inc; el pnts (4A) inc; Indtte; shop; snacks; bar; lake sw 200m; 50% statics; dogs; Eng spkn; quiet. "Excel, peaceful site." ♦ 1 Apr-30 Sep. € 22.00 2009*

ASSERGI see Aquila, L' *2E4*

ITALY

⊞ **ASSISI** *2E3* (1km E Rural) *43.06605, 12.63056* **Camping Fontemaggio, Via Eremo delle Carceri 8, 06081 Assisi (PG) [075 813636 or 812317; fax 813749; info@fontemaggio.it; www.fontemaggio.it]** Fr Perugia on S75, turn L onto rd SS147 twd Assisi; keeping Assisi walls on L past coach car park & foll sp to Porta Nuova. In square at front of gate turn R & foll sp to Eremo delle Carceri, Foligno & Cmp Fontemaggio. Foll sp 1km to square in front of next gate, turn R (sharp hairpin), site sp 800m on R at gate with narr arch, site 800m on R. Diff long, winding uphill app; recep in hotel. Lge, terr, hdstg, pt shd; htd wc (some cont); chem disp; mv service pnt; some serviced pitches; shwrs inc; el pnts (6A) inc (long lead rec); gas; lndry rm; shop (high ssn) & 1km; rest; snacks (high ssn); bar; htd pool 3km; TV cab/sat; some statics; dogs; phone; poss cr; Eng spkn; adv bkg; quiet; ccard acc; CCI. "Lovely, spacious site in olive grove; views; footpath to attractive town; steep site rds diff when wet; order bread at hotel recep; firefly displays on site." ♦ € 20.50 2009*

ASSISI *2E3* (3km W Rural) *43.07611, 12.57361* **Camping Internazionale Assisi, Via San Giovanni Campiglione 110, 06081 Assisi (PG) [075 813710; fax 812335; info@campingassisi.it; www.campingassisi.com]** Fr Perugia SS75 to Ospedalicchio, then SS147 twd Assisi. Site well sp on R bef Assisi. Fr Assisi take SS147 to Perugia. Site on L in 3km adj Hotel Green. Lge, mkd pitch, shd; wc (mainly cont); chem disp; mv service pnt; shwrs inc; el pnts (3A) inc (rev pol), 6A avail; gas; lndtte (inc dryer); shop & supmkt 3km; rest; pizzeria; bar; playgrnd; pool high ssn; tennis; 40% statics; dogs €2; phone; bus; car wash; poss cr; Eng spkn; adv bkg rec high ssn; quiet; ccard acc; red low ssn; CCI. "Helpful staff; minibus to Assisi; lovely, tidy, clean site; busy even in low ssn; immac san facs; gd rest; sm pitches; caves at Genga worth visit; excel; 10% red on next site if part of same chain." ♦ 1 Apr-31 Oct. € 34.00 2011*

ASTI *1B2* (2km NW Rural) *44.94087, 8.18726* **Camping Umberto Cagni, Loc Valmanera 152, 14100 Asti [0141 271238; info@campingcagniasti.it; www.campingcagniasti.it]** Fr town cent head N uphill & foll site sp. Do not foll lorry rte to Alessandria when coming fr Turin. Diff app on long narr rd. Med, pt sl, shd; wc (mainly cont); shwrs; el pnts €3; shop; rest; snacks; bar; games area; entmnt; 50% statics; dogs €2; poss cr & noisy; 10% red CCI. "Fair NH/sh stay; friendly staff; not suitable lge o'fits; poss itinerants; gates clsd 1300-1500." 1 Apr-30 Sep. € 21.00 2007*

AURONZO DI CADORE *2E1* (3km NW Rural) **Camping Europa, Via Pause 21, 32041 Auronzo di Cadore (BL) [tel/fax 0435 400688; info@campingeuropa.org; www.campingeuropa.org]** Site sp on rd SR48. Sm, mkd pitch, pt shd; htd wc; chem disp; mv service pnt; shwrs inc; el pnts (6A) inc; lndtte; shops nr; tradsmn; rest; snacks; bar; playgrnd; cycle hire; TV; 10% statics; dogs €2; bus adj; Eng spkn; adv bkg; quiet; ccard acc; CCI. "Excel touring base; rvside walk to town; excel walking; vg site." ♦ 1 Jun-30 Sep. € 23.00 2008*

⊞ **AVIGLIANA** *1B2* (1km S Rural) *45.05917, 7.38646* **Camping Avigliana Lacs, Via Giaveno 23, 10051 Avigliana (TO) [0331 5050822; fax 011 8190117; info@aviglianalacs.it]** W of Turin exit A32 at Avigliana Est onto SP589 S. Foll sp 'Laghi' & Sacra Di San Michele to Lago Grande, site sp. Sm, mkd pitch, terr, pt shd; htd wc (some cont); chem disp; mv service pnt; shwrs inc; el pnts (15A) inc; lndtte (inc dryer); tradsmn; snacks; bar; BBQ; playgrnd; lake sw; no statics; dogs; poss cr; Eng spkn; some rd noise; red snr citizens; CCI. "Lake views; helpful owner; renovations in hand 2009." ♦ € 17.50 2009*

BAIA DOMIZIA see Marina di Minturno *2F4*

BALISIO DI BALLABIO see Lecco *1C1*

BARBERINO VAL D'ELSA see Poggibonsi *1D3*

BARDOLINO *1D2* (800m N Rural) *45.5570, 10.7181* **Camping Continental, Loc Reboin, 37011 Bardolino (VR) [045 7210192; fax 7211756; continental@campingarda.it; www.campingarda.it/continental]** Exit A22/E45 Lago di Garda Sud onto SR249. Site bet km 52/III & 52IV. Lge, shd; wc (some cont); mv service pnt; shwrs inc; el pnts (3A) inc; lndtte (inc dryer); shop; rest; snacks; bar; playgrnd; lake sw & beach adj; car wash; 50% statics; dogs not acc end Jun-end Aug; poss cr; adv bkg; quiet. ♦ 16 Apr-9 Oct. € 33.60 2011*

BARDOLINO *1D2* (1.2km N Rural) *45.56388, 10.71416* **Camping La Rocca, Loc San Pietro, Via Gardensana 37, 37011 Bardolino (VR) [045 7211111; fax 7211300; info@campinglarocca.com; www.campinglarocca.com]** Exit A22/E45 Affi/Lago di Garda Sud & foll SR249 sp Bardolino. Camp 1st site on both sides of rd exit town at km 53/IV. V lge, shd; wc (some cont); chem disp; mv service pnt; shwrs inc; el pnts (6A) inc; lndtte; shop; tradsmn; rest; snacks; bar; BBQ; playgrnd; pool; paddling pool; shgl beach adj; lake sw; fishing; cycle hire; TV rm; 15% statics; dogs €5; phone; poss cr; Eng spkn; no adv bkg; some rd noise (rd thro site); ccard acc; red CCI. "Pleasant, popular site; gd views; avoid field nr lake; lakeside walk to Garda or Bardolino 20mins; mkt Thurs Bardolino, Fri Garda;red snr citizens." ♦ Easter-6 Oct. € 36.50 2011*

BARDOLINO *1D2* (1.5km N Rural) *45.55944, 10.71666* **Camping Serenella, Loc Mezzariva 19, 37011 Bardolino (VR) [045 7211333; fax 7211552; serenella@camping-serenella.it; www.camping-serenella.it]** Site on R SR249. Lge, pt sl, pt shd; wc; chem disp; mv service pnt; shwrs inc; el pnts (6A) inc; lndtte (inc dryer); shop; rest; snacks; bar; playgrnd; pool; paddling pool; lake sw; boat launching; waterski; games rm; cycle hire; entmnt; 50% statics; no dogs; poss v cr; Eng spkn; no ccard acc. "Bus to Verona; lakeside walk to Garda or Bardolino; excel, clean facs; sm pitches poss diff lge o'fits - check bef pitching; vg supmkt, rest." ♦ 1 Apr-18 Oct. € 36.50 2009*

BARDOLINO *1D2* (500m S Rural) *45.54275, 10.72513* **Camping Europa, Loc Mandracci, Via Santa Cristina 12, 37011 Bardolino (VR) [045 7211089; fax 7210073; europa@campingarda.it; www.campingarda.it]** N fr Peschiera on SR249, site on W side of rd opp 2nd Bardolino 50 km/h sp at S of vill, adj lge petrol stn & Hotel du Lac. Med, mkd pitch, pt shd; wc; chem disp; shwrs inc; el pnts (6A) inc; lndtte (inc dryer); shop; rest 500m; snacks; bar; lake sw & watersports adj; TV; 40% statics; no dogs Jul & Aug; adv bkg; rd noise. "Lovely lakeside setting; helpful staff." ♦ 1 Apr-9 Oct. € 32.50 2010*

BARDOLINO *1D2* (2km S Rural) *45.52525, 10.72977* **Camping Cisano/San Vito, Via Peschiera 48, 37010 Cisano (VR) [045 6229098; fax 6229059; cisano@camping-cisano.it; www.camping-cisano.it]** Sites on S boundary of Cisano, on SE shore of Lake Garda. V lge, mkd pitch, terr, sl, shd; wc; chem disp; mv service pnt; shwrs inc; el pnts (4A) inc; gas; lndtte (inc dryer); supmkt; rest; snacks; bar; pool; paddling pool; waterslide; private beach & lake sw adj; waterskiing; windsurfing; canoeing; tennis; games area; cycle hire; entmnt; TV rm; statics; no dogs; Eng spkn; quiet; red low ssn. "Two lovely, clean, lakeside sites run as one - San Vito smaller/quieter; helpful staff; san facs in need of refurb; some pitches diff access & chocks req; passport req at site check-in; Verona Opera excursions arranged high ssn; gd." ♦ 26 Mar-8 Oct. € 43.00 (CChq acc) 2011*

⊞ **BARDONECCHIA** *1A2* (5km SW Rural) *45.04954, 6.66510* **Camping Bokki, Loc Pian del Colle, 10052 Bardonecchia (TO) [tel/fax 0122 99893; info@bokki.it; www.bokki.it]** Fr A32 ent Bardonecchia & foll sp Melezet. After Melezet foll rd uphill for 1.5km. Bokki is 2nd site on R. Med, mkd pitch, pt sl, pt shd; htd wc; chem disp; mv service pnt; baby facs; fam bthrm; shwrs inc; el pnts (2-10A) inc; lndtte; shop 3km; rest; snacks; bar; playgrnd; lake sw adj; TV rm; 95% statics; dogs €1; phone; Eng spkn; adv bkg; quiet; CCI. "Helpful owners; beautiful location; conv Fréjus tunnel." € 27.00 2007*

BAROLO *1B2* (1km W Rural) *44.61246, 7.92106* **Camping Sole Langhe, Piazza della Vite e Del Vino, Frazione Vergne, 12060 Barolo (CN) [0173 560977; info@solelanghe.com; www.campingsolelanghe.it]** Fr S exit A6 E sp Carru. At Carru turn N onto SP12 & foll sp Barolo. Site sp on ent Barolo. Sm, hdg pitch, pt shd; wc; chem disp; mv service pnt; shwrs inc; el pnts (6A) inc; lndtte; shop; rest; snacks, bar 1km; BBQ; playgrnd; games area; no statics; dogs; Eng spkn; quiet. "Lovely orchard site in cent Barolo wine region; v helpful owner." 1 Mar-30 Nov. € 26.00 2010*

⊞ **BARREA** *2F4* (500m S Rural) *41.74978, 13.99128* **Camping La Genziana, Loc Tre Croci 1, 67030 Barrea (AQ) [tel/fax 0864 88101; pasettanet@tiscalinet.it; www.campinglagenzianapasetta.it]** Fr S83 to S end Lago di Barrea, thro Barrea S, site immed on L on uphill L-hand bend. Med, mkd pitch, terr, pt shd; wc; chem disp; mv service pnt; shwrs; el pnts (3A) €2.60; lndtte; sm shop; rest 300m; bar; BBQ: playgrnd; sand beach & lake sw 3km; dogs €3; bus; Eng spkn; adv bkg; quiet. "Knowledgeable owner; delightful site but unreliable hot water & poor facs; excel area cycling; trekking, skiing; ltd shops Barrea 10 mins walk; conv Abruzzi National Park." € 26.40 2009*

BASCHI *2E3* (3.5km NE Rural) *42.72235, 12.26067* **Camping Gole del Forello, Lago di Corbara, Salviano, 05023 Baschi [0335 6671902 (mob); info@goledelforello.it; www.goledelforello.it]** Fr Orvieto take SS205 dir Baschi then S448 alongside Lago di Corbaro. Site sp on lakeside. Med, mkd pitch, some hdstg, terr, pt shd; htd wc; chem disp; mv service pnt; shwrs; el pnts (6A) inc; lndry rm; shop; tradsmn; rest; snacks; bar; BBQ; pool; paddling pool; fishing; watersports; tennis; games area; wifi; some statics; dogs; adv bkg; quiet; ccard acc; red long stay/low ssn. "Gd position with lake views; pleasant, peaceful site." ♦ Easter & 1 May-30 Sep. € 23.20 2010*

⊞ **BASTIA MONDOVI** *1B2* (1km N Rural) *44.44871, 7.89417* **Camping La Cascina, Loc Pieve 4, 12060 Bastia-Mondovi (CN) [tel/fax 0174 60181; info@campinglacascina.it; www.campinglacascina.it]** Fr Cuneo on S564 turn R at rndabt adj to Rv Tanaro sp to Bastìa Mondovi, site on R in 500m. Lge, pt shd; wc; chem disp; mv service pnt; shwrs inc; el pnts (6A) €2.50; lndtte; shop; rest 1km; bar; playgrnd; pool; games area; 90% statics; phone; site clsd Sep; poss cr; Eng spkn; ccard acc; CCI. "Touring vans on edge of sports field; conv wine vills; hot water poss erratic; v busy w/end high ssn." ♦ € 19.50 2010*

BAVENO see Stresa *1B1*

BELLAGIO *1C1* (1.5km S Rural) **Clarke Camping, Via Valassina 170/C, 22021 Bellagio [031 951325; info@villa-magnolia.co.uk; www.bellagio-camping.com]** Fr Como, on arr in Bellagio foll sp Lecco to R, foll site sps uphill. Narr rds & site ent. Med, terr, pt shd; wc (some cont); chem disp; mv service pnt; shwrs inc; el pnts €2; shop 500m; rest, snacks, bar 1.5km; lake sw 1.5km; no statics; no dogs; ferries, water taxis 1.5km; quiet. "British owner; views over lake; uphill walk fr town to campsite; town is on lakeside; site & app not suitable lge o'fits; no twin-axles; beautiful, peaceful site. basic san facs but clean, friendly owners." 15 May-15 Sep. € 28.00 2011*

BELLARIA *2E2* (3km N Coastal) *44.16606, 12.43563* **Camping Delle Rose, Via Adriatica 29, 47043 Gatteo-a-Mare (FC) [0547 86213; fax 87583; info@villaggiorose.com; www.villaggiorose.com]** Exit A14/E55 dir Rimini Nord onto S16. Exit S16 at Gatteo a Mare, turn R at junc, over rndabt. Site on L in 100m at km 186. Lge, mkd pitch, shd; wc (some cont); chem disp; mv service pnt; shwrs inc; el pnts (6A) €3; gas; lndtte; shop; rest; snacks; bar; playgrnd; pool; paddling pool; sand beach 300m; games area; entmnt; TV; 30% statics; dogs €8.10 (sm only); free shuttle bus to beach; poss cr; Eng spkn; adv bkg; quiet, some rlwy & rd noise; ccard acc; red CCI. "Easy reach San Marino & Urbino." ♦ 24 Apr-20 Sep. € 36.00 2009*

ITALY

⊞ **BELLARIA** *2E2* (2km NE Coastal) *44.16076, 12.44836* **Happy Camping Village, Via Panzini 228, San Mauro a Mare, 47814 Bellaria (RN) [0541 346102; fax 346408; info@happycamping.it; www.happycamping.it]** Fr A14 exit Rimini Nord onto S16 N. Turn off dir San Mauro Mare & Bellaria Cagnona, foll sp Aquabell Waterpark. Over rlwy x-ing, turn R, site on L. Lge, mkd pitch, hdstg, pt sl, pt shd; wc (some cont); chem disp; mv service pnt; baby facs; fam bthrm; shwrs inc; el pnts (8-10A) €3.50; gas; Indtte (inc dryer); shop; rest; snacks; bar; playgrnd; pool; paddling pool; sand beach adj; tennis; games area; games rm; wifi; TV; 40% statics; dogs €6; phone; poss cr & noisy; ltd Eng spkn; adv bkg; red low ssn; CCI. "Conv Rimini, San Marino; variable size pitches; clean, private beach; pool clsd 1300-1530 & after 1900; lge shopping cent & cinema complex 2km; Bellaria pleasant resort with port & marina." € 39.00 2010*

BELLARIA *2E2* (1.5km NW Coastal/Urban) *44.16235, 12.44231* **Camping Green, Via Vespucci 8, 47030 San Mauro-Mare (FO) [tel/fax 0541 341225; info@campinggreen.it; www.campinggreen.it]** Exit A14/E55 at Rimini Nord onto S16. Foll sp N to San Mauro-Mare, site sp. Med, shd; wc; chem disp; mv service pnt; shwrs inc; el pnts (6A) €2.50; gas; Indtte; shop 200m; rest 100m; playgrnd; sand beach adj; watersports; cycle hire; wifi; some statics; dogs €4; poss cr; quiet but some rlwy noise. "Excel, family-run, friendly site." ♦ 9 Apr-24 Sep. € 27.50 2011*

BELLARIA *2E2* (3km NW Coastal) *44.16483, 12.44065* **Camping Rubicone, Via Matrice Destra 1, 47039 Savignano-Mare (FO) [0541 346377; fax 346999; info@campingrubicone.com; www.campingrubicone.com]** Exit A14 at Rimini Nord onto SS16. N to Bellaria & San Mauro a Mare. Turn L immed after level x-ing, site sp. V lge, mkd pitch, pt shd; wc; chem disp; mv service pnt; serviced pitches; private bthrms some pitches; shwrs inc; el pnts (6A) €2.40; Indtte; shop; rest; bar; playgrnd; pool; paddling pool; sand beach adj; watersports; windsurfing; tennis; entmnt; no dogs; poss cr; Eng spkn; some rlwy noise. "Plenty of activities, excel for family beach holidays." ♦ 10 May-27 Sep. € 36.50 2008*

BELVEDERE DI GRADO see Aquileia *2E1*

⊞ **BERCETO** *1C2* (1km E Rural) *44.51225, 9.9985* **Camping I Pianelli, Pianelli, Via Nazionale 109, 43042 Berceto (PR) [0525 629014; fax 629421; camping-ipianelli@libero.it; www.campingipianelli.com]** Exit A15/E31 Berceto; foll Berceto sp for 6km, site sp thro & beyond vill 1km. Lge, some hdstg, terr, unshd; wc; chem disp; shwrs; el pnts (10A) inc; Indtte; shop; rest; playgrnd; tennis; gym; walking; horseriding; 75% statics; Eng spkn; adv bkg; quiet; ccard acc. "Splendid mountain top with views of Appennines; ltd facs low ssn; well-run, friendly site; gd security; v ltd touring pitches." ♦ € 24.00 2008*

BIBIONE *2E1* (2km W Coastal) *45.6350, 13.0375* **Villagio Turistico Internazionale, Via delle Colonie 2, 30020 Bibione (VE) [0431 442611; fax 43620; info@vti.it; www.vti.it]** Fr A4 exit at Latisana & foll sp Bibione. In Bibione turn R & foll Via Baseleghe for 2km, then foll Via Toro & at end of td turn R to site. Lge, pt shd; wc (some cont); mv service pnt; chem disp; baby facs; shwrs inc; el pnts (10A) inc; gas; Indtte; shop; rest; snacks; bar; pool; paddling pool; playgrnd; watersports; cycle hire; games area; tennis; wifi; entmnt; TV; 45% statics; dogs €7; phone; bungalows & aptmnts; adv bkg; quiet; red low ssn. "Excel for families; well-equipped site; gd security." ♦ 24 Apr-28 Sep. € 44.40 2008*

BIBIONE *2E1* (6km W Coastal) *45.63055, 12.99444* **Camping Village Capalonga, Viale della Laguna 16, 30020 Bibione-Pineda (VE) [0431 438351 or 0431 447190 LS; fax 438370 or 0431 438986 LS; capalonga@bibionemare.com; www.capalonga.com]** Well sp approx 6km fr Bibione dir Bibione Pineda. V lge, shd; wc (some cont); chem disp; mv service pnt; baby facs (on request); shwrs inc; el pnts (10A) inc; gas; Indtte; shop; rest; snacks; bar; BBQ; playgrnd; pool; private Blue Flag sand beach adj; watersports; fishing; tennis; archery; cycle hire nrby; horseriding 6km; golf 10km; games rm; excursions; various activities; wifi; entmnt; TV; 25% statics; no dogs; no c'vans/m'vans over 10m high ssn; phone; adv bkg; quiet; ccard acc; red low ssn. "Well-organised site; gd for families; extra for pitches on beach; spacious, clean san facs; rest o'looking lagoon; voracious mosquitoes!" ♦ 24 Apr-23 Sep. € 51.80 SBS - Y15 2011*

BIBIONE *2E1* (6km W Coastal) *45.63472, 13.01583* **Camping Village Il Tridente, Via Baseleghe 12, 30020 Bibione-Pineda (VE) [0431 439600; fax 439193; tridente@bibionemare.com; www.bibionemare.com]** Sp on rd fr Bibione to Bibione Pineda. Lge, shd; wc (some cont); mv service pnt; chem disp; baby facs; shwrs inc; el pnts (5A) inc; gas; Indtte; shop; rest; snacks; bar; playgrnd; pool; paddling pool; watersports; tennis; cycle hire; games area; entmnt; TV; 50% statics; phone; no dogs; quiet; adv bkg. "Gd family site." ♦ 8 May-14 Sep. € 39.00 2008*

⊞ **BOBBIO** *1C2* (1.5km S Rural) *44.75340, 9.38456* **Camping Ponte Gobbo Terme, Via San Martino 4, 29022 Bobbio (PC) [0523 936927; fax 960610; camping.pontegobbe@iol.it; www.campingpontegobbo.it]** Heading twd Genova on S45 turn L on long bdge & immed R. Site sp. Lge, pt sl, shd; htd wc (some cont); chem disp; shwrs €0.50; el pnts (4A) €2; gas; shop & 1km; rest 300m; bar; playgrnd; games area; entmnt; TV; 40% statics; phone; sep car park; Eng spkn; no adv bkg; quiet; ccard acc; red low ssn/CCI. "Trout-fishing in rv; gd scenery; lovely town; hot water to shwrs only; site scruffy low ssn." ♦ € 22.50 2007*

BOGLIASCO see Genova *1C2*

⊞ **BOLOGNA** *1D2* (2km NE Rural) *44.52333, 11.37388* **Centro Turistico Campeggio Città di Bologna, Via Romita 12/4a, 40127 Bologna [051 325016; fax 325318; info@hotelcamping.com; www.hotelcamping.com]** Fr N on A1 take A14 sp Ancona. Foll m'way (ignore sp leading to Tangenziale) dir Fiera & take exit (unnumbered) for Fiera. Site sp on R after toll booth. Site also accessible fr junc 7 off A14, Via Stalingrado - narr & winding app. Fr S on A13 leave at sp Fiera & Tangenziale. Med, mkd pitch, pt shd; htd wc; chem disp; mv service pnt; shwrs inc; el pnts (6A) inc; Indtte (inc dryer); shop; tradsmn; supmkt nrby; rest; snacks; bar; BBQ (charcoal/gas); playgrnd; pool; games rm; wifi; TV rm; dogs €2; no c'vans/m'vans over 15m on hdstg & over 9m on grass; bus to city; site clsd 20 Dec-9 Jan; Eng spkn; adv bkg; some rd & aircraft noise; ccard acc; red low ssn/long stay/CCI. "Conv Bologna Trade Fair & Exhibition cent; friendly, helpful staff; excel, clean san facs; excel pool; tourist pitches at rear nr san facs block; gd bus service fr ent into city; access to pitches poss diff lge o'fits; sat nav dir may take you down narr rds; poss voracious mosquitoes!" ♦ € 32.00 SBS - Y14 2011*

BOLSENA *1D3* (400m S Urban) *42.63866, 11.98466* **Camping Internazionale Il Lago, Viale Cadorna 6, 01023 Bolsena (VT) [tel/fax 0761 799191; info@campingillago.it; www.campingillago.it]** Fr S71 at traff lts in town cent turn L, foll street past 2 petrol stns (1 on each side) & turn R twds lake. Site strt ahead at T-junc in 400m. Site sp in town on lakeside. Sm, hdg/mkd pitch, pt shd; wc; chem disp; mv service pnt; shwrs inc; el pnts (5A) inc; shop; rest; bar; lake sw & private sand beach adj; dogs; poss cr; adv bkg; quiet; CCI. "Gd site not suitable lge outfits; friendly, helpful staff." ♦ 1 Apr-30 Sep. € 21.50 2008*

BOLSENA *1D3* (1km S Rural) *42.63120, 11.99453* **Blu International Camping, Loc Pietre Lanciate, 01023 Bolsena (VT) [tel/fax 0761 798855; info@blucamping.it; www.blucamping.it]** Fr SS2 Via Cassia, turn twd lake at km 111.6, site sp. Med, mkd pitch, pt shd; wc; chem disp; mv service pnt; shwrs inc; el pnts (5-8A) inc; Indtte; shop; supmkt 1km; rest; snacks; bar; pool; lake sw & sand beach adj; tennis 1km; horseriding 2km; TV rm; 25% statics; dogs €3; sep car park high ssn; Eng spkn; adv bkg; quiet; ccard acc; red low ssn. ♦ Easter-30 Sep. € 24.00 (3 persons) 2008*

BOLSENA *1D3* (2km S Rural) *42.62722, 11.99444* **Camping Village Lido di Bolsena, Via Cassia, Km 111, 01023 Bolsena (VT) [0761 799258; fax 796105; info@bolsenacamping.it; www.bolsenacamping.it]** Fr S on a'strada A1 foll sp Viterbo & Lago di Bolsena, then take SR2 N to site; sp. Fr N exit A1 at Orvieto onto SS71 to Bolsena. At traff lts in cent of town turn L, site on R in approx 2km. V lge, pt shd; wc; chem disp; mv service pnt; private bthrms avail; shwrs €0.50; el pnts (3A) inc (poss rev pol); gas; Indtte (inc dryer); shop; rest; snacks; bar; playgrnd; pool; private sand beach adj; lake sw; watersports; tennis; cycle hire; games area; entmnt; some statics; no dogs; phone; sep car park; Eng spkn; adv bkg; quiet; ccard not acc. "Beautiful lakeside location; gd size pitches; all facs excel; cycle path around lake to town." 24 Apr-30 Sep. € 34.50 2010*

BOLSENA *1D3* (1km SW Rural) **Camping Le Calle, Via Cassia, Km 111.2, 01023 Bolsena (VT) [0761 797041]** On S2 bet Lido Camping Vill & Camping Blu, ent by Fornacella rest. Sm, mkd pitch, pt shd; wc; chem disp; mv service pnt; shwrs inc; el pnts (6A) inc; Indry rm; rest adj; lake sw & beach adj; dogs €2; adv bkg; quiet; CCI. "Family-run CL-type 'Agrituristico' site; friendly, helpful owners offer own produce inc wine & olive oil; vg san facs; foot/cycle path to Bolsena." ♦ 1 Mar-31 Oct. € 17.00 2008*

BOLSENA *1D3* (700m W Rural) *42.64595, 11.97492* **Camping Pineta, Viale Armando Diaz 48, 01023 Bolsena (VT) [0761 796905; fax 796021; info@campingpinetabolsena.it; www.campingpinetabolsena.it]** Sp fr town cent, at lakeside. Med, mkd pitch, pt shd; htd wc (some cont); shwrs €0.50; el pnts (5A) inc; gas; shop & 1km; tradsmn; rest; snacks; bar; lake sw adj; wifi; 50% statics; dogs €0.50; phone; adv bkg; quiet; CCI. "Friendly owners; pleasant lakeside walk to attractive town; clean, smart facs; recep clsd 1300-1600; gd." 1 Apr-30 Sep. € 18.00 2008*

BOLSENA *1D3* (6km W Rural) *42.65340, 11.93120* **Camping Valdisole, Via Cassia, Km 117, 01023 Bolsena (VT) [tel/fax 0761 797064 or 03349 952575 LS; valdisolecamping@virgillio.it; www.campingvaldisole.com]** Fr N on A1 exit Orvieta & foll S71 to junc with S74; turn R twd San Lorenzo Nuovo. Then take S2 (Via Cassia) to site on R, 10km after San Lorenzo Nuovo. Fr S exit at Orte onto S204 sp Viterbo, then S2 Via Cassia N dir Montefiascone & Bolsena. Thro town & site in approx 500m after g'ge. Lge, mkd pitch, shd; wc (cont); chem disp; shwrs inc; el pnts (8A) inc (check pol); gas; Indtte; shop; tradsmn; rest; snacks; pizzeria adj; bar; BBQ; playgrnd; lake sw & (black) sand beach; fishing; watersports; horseriding 5km; golf 500m; guided walks 5km; wifi; games/TV rm; dogs; Eng spkn; adv bkg rec Jul/Aug; poss noisy high ssn; ccard acc; red low ssn/CCI. "Beautiful location; charming owners; lge grassed pitches, shd or sunny (poss dusty high ssn); vg san facs; easy transport Rome, Siena & Orvieto; rallies welcome; mkt Tues." ♦ 1 May-30 Sep. € 33.00 2009*

BOLZANO/BOZEN *1D1* (8km S Rural) *46.4300, 11.34305* **Camping-Park Steiner, Kennedystrasse 32, 39055 Laives/Leifers (BZ) [0471 950105; fax 951572; info@campingsteiner.com; www.campingsteiner.com]** Fr N take Bolzano/Bozen-Sud exit fr A22/E45 & pick up rd S12 twd Trento to site; site on R on ent Laives at N edge of vill. Fr S leave A22 at junc for Egna onto rd S12 dir Bolzano. Poorly sp. Lge, hdg/mkd pitch, pt sl, shd; htd wc; (some cont) chem disp; mv service pnt; baby facs; shwrs inc; el pnts (6A) inc; gas; Indtte; shop; rest; snacks; pizzeria; bar; playgrnd; 2 pools (1 covrd); cycle hire; wifi; TV; some statics; dogs €5; phone; Eng spkn; adv bkg rec; some rd & rlwy noise; CCI. "Pleasant, well-run, excel site on edge of Dolomites; attractive pitches; helpful staff; gd, clean, modern san facs; gates clsd 1300-1500 & 2200-0700; beautiful area; vg walking." ♦ 10 Apr-6 Nov. € 32.00 2011*

ITALY

⊞ **BOLZANO/BOZEN** *1D1* (2km NW Rural) *46.50333, 11.3000* **Camping Moosbauer, Via San Maurizio 83, 39100 Bolzano [0471 918492; fax 204894; info@moosbauer.com; www.moosbauer.com]** Exit A22/E45 at Bolzano Sud exit & take S38 N dir Merano (keep L after toll booths). After tunnel take 1st exit sp Eppan & hospital, & turn L at top of feeder rd sp Bolzano. After approx 2km at island past 08 G'ge turn L & foll site sp. Site on R in 1km by bus stop on S38, sp. Med, hdg/mkd pitch, hdstg, pt sl, pt shd; htd wc; chem disp; mv service pnt; serviced pitches; baby facs; shwrs inc; el pnts (5A) inc; lndtte; shop; tradsmn; rest; snacks; bar; playgrnd; htd pool; games rm; cab/sat TV; entmnt; dogs €4; bus; poss cr; Eng spkn; adv bkg; quiet but some rd noise; CCI. "Popular, well-maintained, attractive site; gd welcome fr friendly owners; pitches narr; excel, modern san facs; gate shut 1300-1500; bus service adj for archaeological museum (unique ice man); gd cent for walks in Dolomites." ♦ € 33.90 2010*

⊞ **BOLZANO/BOZEN** *1D1* (14km NW Rural) *46.56235, 11.17629* **Naturcaravan Park Tisens, Via Lido/Schwimmbadstrasse 39, 39010 Tesimo/Tisens (BZ) [0328 0173571; fax 0473 927130; info@naturcaravanpark-tisans.com; www.naturcaravanpark-tisens.com]** Fr Brenner Pass on A22 exit sp Merano/Meran & Lana. At Lana take S238 & foll sp thro Tesimo/Tisens. Site sp to E of vill. App fr S not rec. Med, mkd pitch, pt shd; htd wc; chem disp; mv service pnt; serviced pitches; baby facs; shwrs inc; private san facs avail; el pnts (6A) inc; lndtte; shop; tradsmn; rest; snacks; bar; BBQ; htd pool; paddling pool; tennis; games area; entmnt; sat TV; adv bkg; quiet; ccard acc. € 27.00 2008*

When we get home
I'm going to post
all these site report
forms to the Club
for next year's guide.
The deadline's mid September 2013

⊞ **BOMBA** *2F4* (2km W Rural) *42.0175, 14.36138* **Campeggio Isola Verde, Via del Lago 2, 66042 Bomba (CH) [0872 860475; fax 860450; isolaverde@tin.it; www.isolaverdeonline.it]** Exit A14 at Val di Sangro exit & take SS652 for Bomba. Site clearly sp. Med, some hdstg, terr, pt shd; wc; chem disp; shwrs inc; el pnts (10A) inc; shop; rest; snacks; bar; playgrnd; pool; lake sw & beach; tennis; cycle hire; entmnt; 50% statics; dogs; bus/train 500m; Eng spkn; adv bkg; quiet; ccard acc. "Excel position above lake in beautiful countryside; gd base winter sports; excel rest." € 38.00 2011*

BORGO SAN LORENZO *1D3* (7km SE Rural) *43.93087, 11.46426* **Camping Vicchio Ponte, Via Costoli 16, 50039 Vicchio [055 8448306; fax 579405; info@campingvecchioponte.it; www.campingvecchioponte.it]** On SP551 adj to sw pool in Vicchio. Med, pt shd; wc (cont); chem disp; mv service pnt; shwrs inc; el pnts (4A) inc; lndry rm; shop, rest, bar in vill; htd pool adj; dogs; train to Florence 1km; poss cr; Eng spkn; quiet; CCI. "Simple, municipal site." 1 Jun-15 Sep. € 24.00 2009*

BORGO SAN LORENZO *1D3* (5km W Rural) *43.96144, 11.30918* **Camping Mugello Verde, Via Massorondinaio 39, 50037 San Piero-a-Sieve (FI) [055 848511; fax 8486910; mugelloverde@florencecamping.com; www.florencecamping.com]** Exit A1 at Barberino exit & foll Barberino sp twd San Piero-a-Sieve & Borgo San Lorenzo. Turn S on S65 twd Florence. Site sp immed after Cafaggiolo. Lge, sl, terr, pt shd; htd wc (some cont); chem disp; mv service pnt; shwrs inc; el pnts (6A) inc; gas; lndtte (inc dryer); shop; rest; snacks; bar; playgrnd; pool (bathing caps req); tennis; cycle hire; wifi; entmnt; 25% statics; bus/train; no adv bkg; quiet; ccard acc; red low ssn; CCI. "Hillside site; bus to Florence high ssn (fr vill low ssn) or 20 mins drive; hard ground diff for awnings; poss long walk to recep & shop; helpful, friendly staff; refurbed, gd, clean san facs; avoid early Jun - Italian Grand Prix!." ♦ 19 Mar-6 Nov. € 29.50 2008*

⊞ **BORMIO** *1D1* (5km S Rural) *46.41608, 10.35264* **Camping Cima Piazzi, Loc Tola, Via Nazionale 29, 23030 Valdisotto (SO) [0342 950298; info@cimapiazzi.it; www.cimapiazzi.it]** S on S38 dir Tirano & Sondrio, site sp fr Bormio. Med, mkd pitch, terr, unshd; htd wc (some cont); chem disp; shwrs €1; el pnts €2.30; lndtte (inc dryer); shop 1km; rest; bar; playgrnd; htd, covrd pool; games rm; TV; 90% statics; bus adj; quiet; cccard; CCI. "Few touring pitches & access poss diff; excel rest; conv Stelvio, Gavia passes & Livigno (duty-free zone)." € 23.00 2008*

BOTTAI see Firenze *1D3*

BRACCIANO *2E4* (3km N Rural) *42.1300, 12.17333* **Kawan Village Roma Flash Sporting, Via Settevene Palo 42, 00062 Bracciano [tel/fax 0699 805458 or 3389 951738 LS; info@romaflash.it; www.romaflash.it]** Fr A1 exit at Magliano Sabina dir Civita Castellana. Then foll sp Nepi, Sutri, Trevignano & Bracciano. Sp on lakeside rd N of Bracciano. Lge, mkd pitch, pt shd; wc (some cont); chem disp; mv service pnt; baby facs; sauna; shwrs inc; el pnts (6A) inc; lndtte (inc dryer); shop high ssn; rest; snacks; bar; BBQ (charcoal, gas); playgrnd; pool; lake sw & free beach; watersports; fishing; horseriding 4km; tennis; cycle hire; games rm; wifi; entmnt; TV; 5% statics; dogs €5.50; no c'vans/m'vans over 12m; shuttle bus to Bracciano; bus/train to Rome; sep car park; Eng spkn; quiet; ccard acc; red low ssn. "Attractive, well-kept lakeside site; clean, modern san facs; conv Rome." ♦ 1 Apr-30 Sep. € 42.00 (CChq acc) SBS - Y16 2011*

BRACCIANO *2E4* (8km N Rural) *42.14673, 12.26905* **Camping Internazionale Lago di Bracciano, Via Del Pianoro 4, 00069 Trevignano-Romano (RM) [0699 85032; fax 826781; robertocarrano@tin.it; www.camping-interlagodibracciano.com]** Fr SS2 exit at Lake Bracciano & cont twd Trevignano then Anguillara. Site on lakeside at end of lane. Lge, pt shd; wc (some cont); chem disp; mv service pnt; shwrs; el pnts (3-6A) inc; lndtte (inc dryer); shop; rest; snacks; cooking facs; playgrnd; paddling pool; cycle hire; games area; internet; TV rm; 20% statics; dogs €3.70; adv bkg; quiet; ccard acc. "Set in Due Laghi Nature Park; peaceful." 1 Apr-30 Sep. € 28.00 2009*

BRACCIANO *2E4* (1.5km SE Rural) *42.10505, 12.18595* **Camping Porticciolo, Via Porticciolo, 00062 Bracciano [06 99803060; fax 99803030; info@porticciolo.it; www.porticciolo.it]** Avoid town cent. Fr Rome circular rd take S2 dir Viterbo, then Anguillara & dir Bracciano. Keep to lakeside; at traff lts turn twds town & after rlwy bdge turn immed R & foll site sp. Avoid town cent. Med, hdg/mkd pitch, shd; wc; chem disp; shwrs €0.50; el pnts (3-6A) €3.40-5; Indtte; shop; tradsmn; rest; snacks; bar; playgrnd; shgl beach & lake adj; sand beach 15km; sailing; watersports; wifi; 10% statics; dogs €4.50; sep car park Jul/Aug; site bus to stn; excursions; Eng spkn; adv bkg; quiet; red low ssn/long stay; ccard acc; CCI. "Lovely position on lakeside; gd base for touring; frequent trains to Rome fr Bracciano; new, modern san facs; lge pitches; haphazard site layout; vg." ♦ 1 Apr-30 Sep. € 26.00 2010*

BRESSANONE/BRIXEN *1D1* (1km SE Rural) *46.73472, 11.64555* **Camping Löwenhof, Brennerstrasse 60, 39040 Varna/Vahrn (BZ) [0472 836216; fax 801337; info@loewenhof.it; www.loewenhof.it]** On main Brenner rd SS12 at 481km mark, on R at minor rd junc adj hotel; easily seen fr main rd. Sm, mkd pitch, wc; shwrs inc; el pnts (4A) €2; Indtte; shop & 2km; rest; snacks; bar; htd pool; paddling pool; hotel sauna, solarium, whirlpool & steambaths avail for use; tennis; games rm; cycle hire; dogs €5 (not acc Jul/Aug); poss cr; Eng spkn; adv bkg; quiet but rd noise behind hotel; red low ssn/long stay/CCI. "Vg." 1 Apr-30 Oct. € 33.00 2009*

BRIATICO *3B4* (W Coastal) *38.72378, 16.02538* **Villaggio Camping L'Africano, 89817 Briatico (VV) [tel/fax 0963 391150; info@villaggiocampinglafricano.it; www.villaggiocampinglafricano.it]** Exit A3/E45 or S18 at Pizzo onto S522 W dir Tropea, site sp. Lge, pt shd; wc; mv service pnt; shwrs inc; el pnts €3; Indtte; shop high ssn; rest high ssn; rest; snacks; bar; pool; paddling pool; sand beach 200m; games area; entmnt; TV rm; some statics; dogs €2; adv bkg; quiet. 1 Apr-31 Oct. € 31.50 2009*

BRUNICO/BRUNECK *1D1* (10km E Rural) *46.77600, 12.03688* **Camping Residence Corones, Niederrasen 124, 39030 Rasun-di-Sotto/Niederrasen (BZ) [0474 496490; fax 498250; info@corones.com; www.corones.com]** On SS49 dir Rasun, turn N to site to Antholz, bear L in front of Gasthof, over bdge turn L, site in 400m. Med, pt shd; wc; chem disp; mv service pnt; serviced pitches; sauna; shwrs inc; private bthrms avail; el pnts (3A) metered; gas; Indtte; shop; rest; snacks; bar; playgrnd; htd pool; paddling pool; tennis; games area; cycle hire; solarium; some statics; dogs €4.20; phone; Eng spkn; adv bkg; quiet; ccard acc (poss not in rest); red low ssn. "Gd cent for walking & skiing - outings arranged; superb facs, inc in winter; conv day visit to Dolomites; helpful owner & staff; excel." ♦ 1 Dec-19 Apr & 20 May-25 Oct. € 28.80 2010*

BRUNICO/BRUNECK *1D1* (9km S Urban) *46.69472, 11.93805* **Camping Al Plan, Via Catarina Lanz 63, 39030 San Vigilio-di-Marebbe/Sankt Vigil-in-Enneberg (BZ) [0474 501694; fax 506550; camping.alplan@rolmail.net; www.campingalplan.com]** Fr A22 take S49 twd Brunico. At San Lorenzo take S244 S & foll sp San Vigilio & site on W edge of town. Med, mkd pitch, hdstg, terr, pt shd; htd wc; chem disp; mv service pnt; baby facs; shwrs inc; el pnts (3A) inc; gas; Indtte; shop; tradsmn; rest; snacks 500m; bar 500m; pool; ski bus; skilift 1km; cab/sat TV; 50% statics; phone; dogs €3; poss cr; adv bkg; poss noisy; ccard acc; CCI. "Excel rest; gd walks & access to pistes." ♦ 6 Dec-15 Apr & 1 Jun-31 Oct. € 26.00 2008*

ITALY

⊞ **BRUNICO/BRUNECK** *1D1* (3km SW Rural) *46.78137, 11.89904* **Camping Wildberg, Dorfstrasse 9, 39030 St Lorenzen/San Lorenzo-di-Sebato (BZ) [0474 474080; fax 474626; info@campingwildberg.com; www.campingwildberg.com]** Sp on Brenner/Brunico rd S49, SW of San Lorenzo, sp. Med, pt sl, pt shd; htd wc; chem disp; mv service pnt; shwrs €0.50; el pnts (6A) €2.50; Indtte; shop 400m; rest 300m; bar; BBQ; htd pool; paddling pool; playgrnd; games area; cycle hire; dogs €3; bus 400m; phone; site clsd Nov; poss cr; adv bkg; quiet; red long stay; ccard acc. "Vg; excel, modern facs & pool; gd walks & cycle tracks; friendly staff." € 26.00 2007*

BRUNICO/BRUNECK *1D1* (8km W Rural) *46.80805, 11.81305* **Camping Gisser, Via Val Pusteria 26, San Sigismondo, 39030 Chienes/Kiens (BZ) [0474 569605; fax 569657; camping@hotelgisser.it; www.hotelgisser.it]** On SS49 at 20.8km post in San Sigismondo. Lge, pt sl, pt shd; wc; shwrs inc; el pnts (5A) €2; Indtte; shop 100m; rest; snacks; bar; htd pool; canoeing; dogs €2.50; no adv bkg; quiet. "NH en rte Venice; ltd facs low ssn & basic." 1 May-15 Oct. € 22.00 2009*

CALCERANICA AL LAGO see Levico Terme *1D1*

⊞ **CANAZEI** *1D1* (200km E Rural) *46.47326, 11.77586* **Camping Marmolada, Via Pareda 60, 38032 Canazei (TN) [0462 601660; fax 601722; campingmarmolada@virgilio.it; www.campingmarmolada.com]** On R bank of Rv Avisio on rd S641. Sp fr cent of Canazei. Lge, hdstg, pt shd; wc; chem disp; shwrs; el pnts (4A) €3; Indtte (inc dryer); snacks; bar; BBQ; htd pool adj; 45% statics; dogs €3; winter ski cent; poss cr; Eng spkn; no adv bkg ess high ssn; poss noisy high ssn; ccard acc. "Opp cable car & stn; gd for walking/skiing; excel views all round; vg san facs; 10 min walk to town." € 30.50 2010*

CANAZEI *1D1* (2km W Rural) *46.47479, 11.74067* **Camping Miravalle, Strèda de Greva 39, 38031 Campitello-di-Fassa (TN) [0462 750502; fax 751563; info@campingmiravalle.it; www.campingmiravalle.it]** In vill cent on rte 48 site sp down side rd. Lge, sl, unshd; wc (some cont); chem disp; mv service pnt; baby facs; shwrs inc; el pnts (3A) inc (poss rev pol), extra €2 for 6A; Indtte; shop 100m; rest, snacks; 100m; bar; dogs €4; poss cr; Eng spkn; adv bkg; quiet; ccard acc; CCI. "Excel facs; conv cable car." ♦ 1 Jun-30 Sep & 1 Dec-30 Apr. € 28.50 2009*

ITALY

CANNOBIO *1C1* (200m N Rural) *46.06515, 8.6905* **Camping Riviera, Via Casali Darbedo 2, 28822 Cannobio (VB) [tel/fax 0323 71360; riviera@riviera-valleromantica.com; www.riviera-valleromantica.com]** N of Cannobio twd Switzerland on main rd. Over rv at o'skts of town, site ent on R in 30m; sp. Lge, hdg/mkd pitch, shd; wc; chem disp; mv service pnt; private san facs some pitches; shwrs inc; el pnts (4A) €4; gas; lndtte; shop; rest; snacks; bar; playgrnd; private shgl beach & lake sw adj; boat hire; windsurfing; some statics; dogs €4.50; poss cr; adv bkg. "Popular, peaceful, well-maintained site bet rv & lake; extra for lakeside pitch; gd sailing; v helpful staff." ♦ 1 Apr-18 Oct. € 30.00 2009*

CANNOBIO *1C1* (500m N Urban) *46.06678, 8.69507* **Camping Del Sole, Via Sotto i Chiosi 81/A, 28822 Cannobio (VB) [0323 70732; fax 72387; info@campingsole.it; www.campingsole.it]** Fr S fr A26 foll Verbania sp then sp Cannobio or Locarno. Ent vill, over cobbles, 2nd R in 750m. Bef rv bdge immed sharp R under main rd, site on L after quick R turn. Fr N ent Cannobio, 1st L after x-ing rv, then as above. Lge, hdg pitch, pt shd; wc; chem disp; shwrs inc; el pnts (4A) €3; gas; lndtte; supmkt 150m; rest; bar; playgrnd; pool; shgl beach & lake sw 250m; 60% statics; dogs €4; poss cr; Eng spkn; adv bkg; poss noisy; ccard acc; red long stay/low ssn; CCI. "Attractive vill & lake frontage; friendly, family-run site; poss tight access some pitches; clean facs; lovely pool area." 1 Apr-10 Oct. € 24.00 2009*

CANNOBIO *1C1* (1km N Rural) *46.07791, 8.69345* **Villaggio Camping Bosco, Punta Bragone, 28822 Cannobio (VB) [0323 71597; fax 739647; bosco@boschettoholiday.it; www.boschettoholiday.it/bosco]** On W side of lakeshore rd bet Cannobio & Swiss frontier. Sh steep app to site & hairpin bend fr narr rd, unsuitable for car/c'van o'fits & diff for m'vans. Med, terr, pt shd; wc; chem disp; shwrs €0.50; el pnts (3A) €3.50; gas; lndtte; shop; BBQ; bar; playgrnd; private shgl beach; lake sw; dogs €3.50; Eng spkn; adv bkg - ess in high ssn; quiet; CCI. "All pitches with magnificent lake view; beautiful town; hot water to shwrs only." ♦ 1 Apr-30 Sep. € 28.50 2011*

CANNOBIO *1C1* (1.5km SW Rural) *46.05756, 8.67831* **Camping Valle Romantica, Via Valle Cannobina, 28822 Cannobio (VB) [tel/fax 0323 71249; valleromantica@riviera-valleromantica.com; www.riviera-valleromantica.com]** Turn W on S o'skirts of Cannobio, sp Valle Cannobina. In 1.5km at fork keep L. Site immed on R. On ent site cont to bottom of hill to park & walk back to recep. Lge, hdg/mkd pitch, pt sl, terr, pt shd; wc; chem disp; mv service pnt; shwrs inc; el pnts (4-6A) €4.00; lndtte; shop; rest; snacks; bar; playgrnd; pool; golf 12km; 25% statics; dogs €4; adv bkg; quiet. "Vg; some sm pitches; particularly helpful staff; narr site rds poss diff m'vans; masses of flowers; beautiful situation; footpath to town, poss cr high ssn." ♦ 24 Mar-30 Sep. € 32.00 2011*

CA'NOGHERA see Mestre *2E2*

CAORLE *2E2* (3km SW Coastal) *45.57388, 12.81166* **Centro Vacanze Pra' delle Torri, Via Altanea 201, 30021 Caorle (VE) [0421 299063; fax 299035; torri@vacanze-natura.it; www.pradelletorri.it]** Fr A4 exit dir Santo Stino di Livenze, then foll sp Caorle & Porto Santa Margherita. by-pass town & cont on coast rd. Site clearly sp on L. V lge, shd, mkd pitch, serviced pitch; wc (some cont); mv service pnt; chem disp; baby facs; shwrs inc; el pnts (5A) inc; lndtte; shop; snacks; rest; shop; htd pool complex; sand beach; boat hire; windsurfing; tennis; cycle hire; games area; car wash; internet; entmnt; 30% statics; phone; no dogs; poss cr; adv bkg (min 3 nts); quiet; red senior citizens; ccard acc. "Extensive, excel sport & entmnt facs for children; lge water park inc; entmnt inc; excel family holiday cent." ♦ 4 Apr-27 Sep. € 41.80 2009*

CAORLE *2E2* (5km SW Coastal) *45.56694, 12.79416* **Camping Villaggio San Francesco, Via Selva Rosata 1, Duna Verde, 30020 Porto-Santa-Margherita (VE) [0421 299333; fax 299284; info@villaggiostrancesco.com; www.villaggiosfrancesco.com]** Fr A4/E70 exit Santo Stino di Livenza, then dir Caorle. By-pass town & cont on coast rd, site sp on L. V lge, shd; wc (some cont); chem disp; mv service pnt; baby facs; shwrs inc; el pnts (6A) inc; gas; lndtte (inc dryer); shop; 3 rests; snacks; bar; 5 pools; waterslide; private beach adj; boat hire; windsurfing; waterskiing; tennis; games area; games rm; cycle hire; solarium; internet; entmnt; TV; 60% statics; dogs €3; phone; min 2 nights' stay; poss cr; quiet; ccard not acc; red snr citizens/CCI. "Excel family facs." ♦ 24 Apr-25 Sep. € 44.60 (CChq acc) 2009*

CAPALBIO *1D3* (8km S Coastal) *42.38086, 11.44660* **Campeggio di Capalbio, Strada del Chiarone, Loc Graticciala, 58010 Capalbio (GR) [0564 890101; fax 890437; mauro.ricci@ilcampeggiodicapalbio.it; www.ilcampeggiodicapalbio.it]** Exit SS1 heading S twd Rome at sp Chiarone Scalo twd sea. Cross rlwy, site sp. Lge, mkd pitch, pt sl, shd; wc (some cont); mv service pnt; shwrs; el pnts (3-5A); gas; lndtte (inc dryer); shop; tradsmn; rest; snacks; bar; BBQ; playgrnd; sand beach adj; cycle hire; games area; entmnt; 70% statics; no dogs; sep car park; poss cr; adv bkg; quiet; ccard acc."narrow lanes, diff for lge o'fits without mover." 10 Apr-4 Oct. € 47.00 2011*

CAPANNOLE see Montevarchi *1D3*

CAPOLIVERI (ELBA ISLAND) *1C3* (3km NW Coastal) *42.75810, 10.36070* **Camping La Calanchiole, Loc Calanchiole, 57031 Capoliveri (LI) [0565 933488; fax 940001; info@lecalanchiole.it; www.lecalanchiole.it]** Fr Portoferraio, take rd twd Porto Azzuro & Marina de Campo. Then foll sp Capoliveri, site sp. Lge, mkd pitch, pt shd; wc (some cont); chem disp; mv service pnt; shwrs; el pnts (3A) inc; lndtte (inc dryer); rest; snacks; bar; BBQ; paddling pool; private sand beach; watersports; boat & cycle hire; tennis; wifi; entmnt; some statics; adv bkg; quiet; ccard acc. ♦ 1 Apr-31 Oct. € 53.50 (CChq acc) 2011*

CAPRAROLA *2E4* (4km W Rural) **Camping Natura, Loc Sciente Le Coste, 01032 Caprarola (VT) [tel/fax 0761 612347; info@camping-natura.com; www.camping-natura.com]** Fr Viterbo take Via Cimina sp Ronciglione. After approx 19km bef Ronciglione turn R sp Nature Reserve Lago di Vico, in 200m turn R, site sp on R in 3km. Med, mkd pitch, pt shd; wc; chem disp; mv service pnt; shwrs; el pnts (4A) €3; shop; rest; snacks; bar; lake sw adj; dogs €3; quiet; red low ssn; ccard acc. "Friendly site; guided walks in nature reserve; run down low ssn & ltd facs." Easter-30 Sep. € 18.00 2007*

The opening dates and prices on this campsite have changed. I'll send a site report form to the Club for the next edition of the guide.

CAPRESE MICHELANGELO *1D3* (9km N Rural) *43.69710, 11.92488* **Camping La Verna, Loc Vezzano 31, 52010 Chiusi-della-Verna (AR) [0575 532121; fax 532041; info@campinglaverna.it; www.campinglaverna.it]** Fr Arezzo foll sp Rassina then Chuisi della Verna. Fr Florence E on S67/S70 via Pontassieve, Consuma & Poppi to S208 to La Verna. Or exit E45 at Pieve St Stefano W to La Verna. Med, mkd pitch, sl, terr, pt shd; wc (some cont); chem disp; mv service pnt; shwrs inc; el pnts (3A) inc; Indtte; shop 900m; rest; snacks; bar; BBQ; playgrnd; htd pool high ssn; TV rm; 5% statics; dogs; adv bkg; quiet. "Delightful, interesting, historical area; excel touring base; nr Casentinesi Forest National Park; many mkd walks; lovely site in little visited area." Easter-7 Oct. € 22.50 2007*

CAPRESE MICHELANGELO *1D3* (500m S Rural) *43.63661, 11.98752* **Camping Michelangelo, Loc Zenzano, 52033 Caprese-Michelangelo (AR) [0575 793886; fax 791183; campmichelangelo@libero.it]** Exit E45 at Pieve Santo Stefano; in Pieve foll sp to Caprese; site on S edge of vill on rd to S Cristoforo. Sm, mkd pitch, hdstg, terr, pt shd; wc (some cont); chem disp; shwrs (solar heating); el pnts (5A) inc; Indtte; shop 300m; rest 200m; snacks; bar; playgrnd; tennis; games area; 50% statics; quiet; CCI. "Helpful management; gd walks & excel views; gd sized pitches, well-spaced in woodland; excel." 1 Apr-31 Oct. € 21.00 2007*

CARLAZZO see Porlezza *1C1*

CAROVIGNO *3A4* (5km N Coastal) *40.76643, 17.67850* **Camping Villaggio Lamaforca, SS379, Km 25, Contrada da Mindelli, 72012 Carovigno (BR) [0831 968496; fax 968070; informazioni@lamaforca.it; www.lamaforca.it]** Exit SS379 sp Torre Pozella, site sp. Lge, pt shd; wc; mv service pnt; baby facs; shwrs inc; el pnts inc; Indtte; shop; rest; snacks; bar; playgrnd; pool; paddling pool; waterslide; sand beach adj; cycle hire; games rm; TV rm; 70% statics; dogs €2.50; phone; adv bkg; quiet; ccard acc; red low ssn/snr citizens. "Conv Brindisi, Ostuni." ♦ 1 Apr-18 Sep. € 39.00 (CChq acc) 2009*

CAROVIGNO *3A4* (8km NE Coastal) *40.73972, 17.7375* **Camping Pineta al Mare, Viale dei Tamerici 33, 72012 Specchiolla-di-Carovigno (BR) [0831 994057; fax 987803; info@campingpinetamare.com; www.campingpinetamare.com]** About 18km fr Brindisi on main coast rd S379, turn NE twd coast nr bdge over rd, sp Specchiolla 1km. Well sp. Lge, pt sl, pt shd; wc (cont); chem disp; mv service pnt; shwrs; el pnts (3A) €2.50; Indtte; shop; rest; snacks; bar; playgrnd; 2 pools; waterslide; private sand beach opp; windsurfing; tennis; games area; entmnt; 70% statics; dogs €8; poss cr; no adv bkg; quiet; ccard acc; red CCI. "NH for Brindisi ferries; helpful owners; excel pools; vg rest; low ssn go to rear gate & ring bell for entry - site may appear clsd; poss poor san facs & run down low ssn." ♦ 1 Apr-20 Sep. € 36.00 2007*

CASAL BORSETTI see Marina di Ravenna *2E2*

CASALBORDINO *2F4* (7km NE Coastal) *42.20018, 14.60897* **Camping Village Santo Stefano, S16, Km 498, 66020 Marina-di-Casalbordino (CH) [0873 918118; fax 918193; info@campingsantostefano.com; www.campingsantostefano.com]** Exit A14 Vasto N onto S16 dir Pescara, site at km 498 on R. Med, mkd pitch, shd; wc; chem disp; shwrs inc; el pnts (6A) inc; shop; rest; snacks; bar; playgrnd; pool; paddling pool; beach adj; entmnt; 10% statics; no dogs; Eng spkn; adv bkg; quiet but some rlwy noise; CCI. "Pleasant, well-maintained, family-run site; sm pitches; beautiful private beach & pool area; gd rest." 24 Apr-12 Sep. € 41.00 2010*

CA'SAVIO see Punta Sabbioni *2E2*

⊞ **CASCIANO** *1D3* (800m S Rural) *43.15555, 11.33166* **Camping Le Soline, Via delle Soline 51, 53016 Casciano (SI) [0577 817410; fax 817415; camping@lesoline.it; www.lesoline.it]** SS223 S fr Siena, L to Fontazzi, R to Casciano. Long, steep climb & narr rd thro vill. Site well sp. Med, mkd pitch, hdstg, terr, pt shd; htd wc; chem disp; mv service pnt; baby facs; shwrs €0.75; el pnts (4-16A) €1.50; gas; Indtte; shop & 1km; rest; snacks; bar; playgrnd; htd pool; games area; horseriding; TV; some statics; dogs €1; adv bkg; quiet; red long stay; red CCI. "Conv Siena 20km; panoramic views of hills; friendly, clean site; gd san facs." ♦ € 23.00 2007*

⊞ **CASSA, LA** *1B2* (600m N Rural) *45.18689, 7.51599* **Camping Club Le Betulle (Naturist), Via Lanzo 33, 10040 La Cassa (TO) [011 9842962; fax 9842819; info@lebetulle.org; www.lebetulle.org]** Exit Turin by-pass at Collegno & foll sp Pianezza. In 200m bear R at traff lts sp San Gillio & La Cassa. In La Cassa foll sp Fiano, site on L. Site is 25km fr Turin cent. Lge, hdstg, pt sl, pt shd; htd wc (some cont); chem disp (wc); baby facs; fam bthrm; shwrs inc; el pnts (16A) inc; Indtte; shop 600m; tradsmn; rest; snacks; bar; playgrnd; pool; TV rm; 90% statics; dogs €2; poss cr; Eng spkn; adv bkg; INF card. "Friendly staff." € 38.00 2011*

CASSONE see Malcesine *1D1*

ITALY

⊞ **CASTEL DEL PIANO** *1D3* (500m S Urban) *42.88454, 11.53646* **Camping Residence Amiata, Via Roma 15, Montoto, 58033 Castel-del-Piano (GR) [0564 956260; fax 955107; info@amiata.org; www.amiata.org]** Fr Siena on S223 to Paganico. Turn L (via overpass) twd Castel del Piano. On reaching town, turn R, sp Ospedale (Hospital). Strt over rndabt site on R up hill (1km). Lge, hdg/mkd pitch, hdstg, shd; htd wc; chem disp; mv service pnt; baby facs; shwrs; el pnts (3-6A) inc; gas; Indtte (inc dryer); shop & 1km; tradsmn; rest; snacks; bar; BBQ; playgrnd; pool 3km; games area; solarium; TV rm; some statics; dogs €2.70; poss cr; Eng spkn; adv bkg; quiet; ccard acc; red long stay; red CCI. "Friendly owners; dated san facs; lovely views; excel touring base medieval towns & vills." ♦ € 22.20 (CChq acc) 2010*

CASTELDIMEZZO see Pesaro *2E3*

CASTELLETTO SOPRA TICINO see Sesto Calende *1B1*

CASTELLINA IN CHIANTI see Poggibonsi *1D3*

⊞ **CASTELNUOVO DI GARFAGNANA** *1C2* (NE Rural) *44.12006, 10.42321* **Camping Parco La Piella, 55032 Castelnuovo-di-Garfagnana (LU) [tel/fax 0583 62916]** Fr Pieve Fosciana foll site sp for 2.5km. Winding app not rec c'vans. Med, terr, pt shd; wc; shwrs; mv service pnt; el pnts inc; sm shop; snacks; bar; quiet. "Peaceful green site conv for Garfagnana; best suited tents & sm camper vans; if gate locked on arr, tel & owner will unlock." ♦ € 21.00 2008*

CASTIGLIONE DEL LAGO *2E3* (500m N Rural) *43.13460, 12.04383* **Camping Listro, Via Lungolago, Lido Arezzo, 06061 Castiglione-del-Lago (PG) [tel/fax 075 951193; listro@listro.it; www.listro.it]** Fr N A1 Val di Chiana exit 75 bis Perugia, site clearly sp on N edge of town on lakeside. Med, mkd pitch, pt shd; wc; chem disp; mv service pnt; shwrs inc; el pnts (3A) inc (poss rev pol); gas; Indtte; shop & 500m; rest 200m; snacks; bar; playgrnd; pool nr; private sand beach & lake sw adj; tennis nr; cycle hire; poss cr; Eng spkn; adv bkg; rd noise; ccard acc; red long stay/low ssn; CCI. "On W shore of Lake Trasimeno; facs stretched when site full; v helpful staff; bus to Perugia; rlwy stn 1km for train to Rome; 'tree fluff' a problem in spring." ♦ 1 Apr-30 Sep. € 18.70 2011*

CASTIGLIONE DEL LAGO *2E3* (6km N Rural) *43.18028, 12.0163* **Camping Badiaccia, Via Pratovecchio 1, 06061 Castiglione-del-Lago (PG) [0759 659097; fax 650919; info@badiaccia.com; www.badiaccia.com]** Leave A1 m'way at Val-di-Chiana exit & foll sp for Castiglione-del-Lago. Site on L immed past Shell g'ge. Lge, mkd pitch, sl, pt shd; wc (cont); chem disp; mv service pnt; baby facs; shwrs inc; el pnts (4A) inc; gas; Indtte (inc dryer); shop; tradsmn; rest; snacks; bar; BBQ; playgrnd; 2 pools; lake sw; boat & cycle hire; windsurfing; tennis; games area; wifi; 10% statics; dogs €2.50; adv bkg ess; quiet; red 7+ days. "Refurbished san facs; gd site." ♦ 1 Apr-30 Sep. € 25.00 2010*

CASTIGLIONE DEL LAGO *2E3* (8km N Rural) *43.19156, 12.07486* **Villaggio Turistico Punta Navaccia, Via Navaccia 4, 06069 Tuoro-sul-Trasimeno (PG) [075 826357; fax 8258147; info@puntanavaccia.it; www.puntanavaccia.it]** Exit A1 dir Lago di Trasimeno & foll sp Punta Navaccia; site sp fr rd. Lge, shd; wc (some cont); chem disp; mv service pnt; shwrs inc; el pnts (2-6A) inc; gas; Indtte; shop; rest; snacks; bar; playgrnd; htd pool; paddling pool; lake sw & beach; watersports; games area; tennis; entmnt; 50% statics; dogs free; phone; poss cr; adv bkg; quiet; ccard acc; red long stay/CCI. "Vg for watersports; direct access to lake & lakeside pitches - poss mosquitoes; Isla Maggiore ferry nr." ♦ 15 Mar-31 Oct. € 28.50 2008*

CASTIGLIONE DELLA PESCAIA *1D3* (2km N Coastal) *42.77361, 10.84398* **Camping Maremma Sans Souci, Strada delle Collacchie, Casa Mora, 58043 Castiglione-della-Pescaia (GR) [0564 933765; fax 935759; info@maremmasanssouci.it; www.maremmasanssouci.it]** Exit SS1 Via Aurelia at Follonica onto SS322, site at km post 12, sp. Lge, mkd pitch, shd; wc; chem disp; mv service pnt; shwrs; el pnts (3A) inc; Indtte; shop; rest; snacks; bar; no BBQ; sand beach adj; TV; dogs €2 (not acc Jun-Aug); phone; sep car park; Eng spkn; adv bkg ess Jul-Aug; ccard acc; red low ssn. "Most pitches diff lge outfits; lovely location; direct access to beach; poss mosquito problem." ♦ 1 Apr-31 Oct. € 43.00 (CChq acc) 2011*

CASTIGLIONE DELLA PESCAIA *1D3* (6km W Coastal) *42.77760, 10.79384* **Camping Village Baia Azzurra, Via delle Rocchette, 58043 Castiglione-della-Pescaia (GR) [0564 941092; fax 941242; info@baiaazzurra.it; www.baiaazzurra.it]** Fr Castiglione della Pescaia on S322, turn L sp Rocchette, site on R in 3km. Med, mkd pitch, shd; wc (some cont); chem disp; shwrs inc; el pnts (3A) inc; gas; Indtte; shop; tradsmn; rest nr; snacks; bar; no BBQ; playgrnd; pool high ssn; paddling pool; private sand beach adj; tennis; cycle hire; wifi; entmnt; TV; 10% statics; dogs €6; phone; sep car park; bus; poss cr; Eng spkn; adv bkg; quiet; ccard acc; red low ssn. "Beautiful location; 24 hr security." ♦ 15 Apr-17 Oct. € 54.00 (CChq acc) 2011*

CAVALLINO *2E2* (2.5km S Coastal) *45.46726, 12.53006* **Camping Union Lido, Via Fausta 258, 30013 Cavallino (VE) [041 968080 or 2575111; fax 5370355; info@unionlido.com; www.unionlido.com]** Exit a'strada A4 (Mestre-Trieste) at exit for airport or Quarto d'Altino & foll sp for Jesolo & then Punta Sabbiono; site on L 2.5km after Cavallino. V lge, mkd pitch, shd; htd wc; chem disp; mv service pnt; 60% serviced pitches; baby facs; sauna; shwrs inc; el pnts (6A) inc; gas; Indtte (inc dryer); 30 shops & supmkt; 7 rests; snacks; bars; playgrnd; pools & children's lagoon with slides; dir access private beach; tennis; gym; golf; fishing; boating; horseriding; watersports; cycle hire; skating rink; hairdressers; babysitting; wifi; entmnt; sat TV some pitches; late arrival (after 2100) o'night parking area with el pnts; church; banking facs; 1st aid cent; Italian lessons; wellness cent; 50% statics; no dogs; Eng spkn; adv bkg; ccard acc. "Variable pitch size & price; min stay 7 days in high ssn; some pitches soft sand (a spade useful!); many long-stay campers; no admissions 1230-1500 (poss busy w/end); excursions; varied entmnt programme high ssn inc firework displays; well-organised, well-run; clean facs; no need to leave site; worth every penny! excel." ♦ 30 Apr-26 Sep. € 48.00 2010*

CAVALLINO *2E2* (2.5km S Coastal) *45.45710, 12.50702* **Camping Village Vela Blu, Via Radaelli 10, 30013 Cavallino (VE) [041 968068; fax 5371003; info@velablu.it; www.velablu.it]** Site sp on leaving Ca'ballarin. Lge, mkd pitch, pt shd; wc; chem disp; mv service pnt; 50% serviced pitches; baby facs; shwrs inc; el pnts (6A) inc; Indtte Inc dryer); shop; rest; snacks; bar; BBQ; playgrnd; private beach adj; cycle hire; wifi; entmnt; sat TV; 50% statics; dogs €4.50; phone; poss cr; Eng spkn; adv bkg; ccard acc; red long stay/snr citizens; CCI. "Well-kept site; excel san facs; excel rest; gd facs for children; gd beach; bus/ferry tickets to Venice fr recep; friendly site." ♦ 30 Apr-30 Sep. € 33.00 (CChq acc) 2009*

CAVALLINO *2E2* (5km SW Coastal) *45.45638, 12.4960* **Camping Enzo Stella Maris, Via delle Batterie 100, 30010 Cavallino-Treporti (VE) [041 966030; fax 5300943; info@enzostellamaris.com; www.enzostellamaris.com]** Exit A4 at sp for airport. Foll sp Jesolo, Cavallino, Punta Sabbioni rd SW. Site sp after Ca'Ballarin, NB Cmp Stella Maris & Cmp Enzo now combined as 1 site. Lge, mkd pitch, pt shd; wc; chem disp; mv service pnt; baby facs; serviced pitches; shwrs inc; el pnts (6A) inc; gas; Indtte; shop; rest; snacks; bar; no BBQ; playgrnd; pool; sand beach adj; fitness rm; games area; wifi; entmnt; TV rm; 25% statics; no dogs; phone; clsd 1230-1600 & 2300-0700; poss cr; Eng spkn; no adv bkg; quiet; ccard acc; red snr citizens/long stay; CCI. "Well-run, friendly, family-owned site; excel facs; beware mosquitoes." ♦ 17 Apr-2 Oct. € 48.60 2011*

CAVALLINO *2E2* (5km SW Coastal) *45.45666, 12.50066* **Camping-Village Cavallino, Via delle Batterie, 164 - 30013 Cavallino-Treporti (VE) [041 966133; fax 5300827; info@campingcavallino.com info@baiaholiday.com; www.baiaholiday.com]** Foll rd Jesolo/Cavallino, lge sp at L turn into camp. V lge, hdstg, pt shd; wc; chem disp; mv service pnt; serviced pitches; shwrs inc; el pnts (6A) inc; Indtte; supmkt; shop; rest; snacks; bar; playgrnd; 2 pools; sand beach adj; waterskiing; golf 2km; internet; entmnt; 25% statics; dogs €8; poss cr; adv bkg - ess in high ssn; quiet; red snr citizens. "Lovely, wooded, well-organised, clean site; gd facs; poss mosquito prob." ♦ 24 Mar-31 Oct. € 46.20 2011*

CAVALLINO *2E2* (6km SW Coastal) *45.44872, 12.47116* **Camping Dei Fiori, Via Vettor Pisani 52, 30010 Cavallino-Treporti (VE) [041 966448; fax 966724; fiori@vacanze-natura.it; www.deifiori.it]** Fr Lido di Jesolo foll sp to Cavallino; site on L approx 6km past Cavallino & bef Ca'Vio. Lge, mkd pitch, shd; wc; chem disp; mv service pnt; serviced pitch; shwrs inc; el pnts (5A) inc (poss rev pol); gas; Indtte; shop; supmkt; rest; snacks; bar; playgrnd; pool; sand beach adj; hydro massage; games area; entmnt; internet; no dogs; Eng spkn; adv bkg ess Jul/Aug; quiet; ccard acc; red snr citizens/long stay. "V clean & quiet even in Aug; excel facs & amenities; conv water bus stop at Port Sabbioni; 3/5 day min stay med/high ssn; highly rec; excel." ♦ 19 Apr-30 Sep. € 43.50 2009*

CA'VIO see Cavallino *2E2*

CAVRIGLIA see Montevarchi *1D3*

CECINA *1D3* (5km E Rural) *43.30043, 10.58153* **Camping Valle Gaia, La Casetta, Via Cecinese 87, 56040 Casale-Marittimo (PI) [0586 681236; fax 683551; info@vallegaia.it; www.vallegaia.it]** Fr Cecina E on S68 foll sp Guardistallo & Casale Marittimo, site poorly sp - look for Robin Hood rest. Med, hdg pitch, pt shd; wc; chem disp; baby facs; shwrs inc; el pnts (6A) inc; gas; Indtte; shop; rest; snacks; bar; BBQ; playgrnd; 2 pools; tennis; games area; cycle hire; entmnt; TV rm; 10% statics; dogs €3; phone; poss cr; Eng spkn; adv bkg; quiet; red CCI. "Best site in area; scenic location; gd sized pitches; excel, modern facs; helpful staff; excursions arranged; conv Siena, San Gimignano, Pisa." ♦ 4 Apr-10 Oct. € 29.60 2009*

CECINA *1D3* (5km S Rural) *43.25388, 10.55291* **Camping Le Capanne, SS Aurelia, Km 273, 57020 Marina-di-Bibbona (LI) [0586 600064; fax 600198; info@campinglecapanne.it; www.campinglecapanne.it]** Fr E side of rd SS1 fr La California to Marina di Bibbona, sp at km 273. Lge, shd; wc (some cont); chem disp; mv service pnt; shwrs inc; el pnts (3A) inc; gas; Indtte; shop; rest; snacks; bar; playgrnd; pool; paddling pool; beach 1.5km; tennis; games area; cycle hire; entmnt; 10% statics; dogs €8.20; adv bkg; quiet; cc acc; red low ssn. 24 Apr-30 Sep. € 38.00 2009*

CECINA *1D3* (8km S Coastal) *43.24638, 10.52555* **Camping Casa di Caccia, Via del Mare 40, 57020 Marina-di-Bibbona (LI) [tel/fax 0586 600000; info@campingcasadicaccia.com; www.campingcasadicaccia.com]** On S1/E1 rd turn W at sp Marina-di-Bibbona, foll camping sp CCC. Med, pt shd; wc; shwrs €0.30; el pnts (6A) inc; Indtte; shop; rest; snacks; bar; playgrnd; sand beach; entmnt; 10% statics; no dogs; poss cr; adv bkg; quiet; ccard acc. "Pitches sm, access poss diff; 10 days min stay fr end Jun to beg Sep; tours to Pisa, Florence, Elba, Rome." ♦ 15 Mar-31 Oct. € 39.00 2008*

⊞ **CECINA** *1D3* (2km W Urban/Coastal) *43.30464, 10.48809* **Camping Bocca di Cecina, Via Guado alle Vacche 2, 57023 Marina-di-Cecina (LI) [0586 620509; fax 621326; bocca.cecina@tin.it; www.ccft.it]** Fr Livorno ignore 1st sp to Cecina Mare Centu. At cent of Marina di Cecina turn R, site bef rv bdge. Lge, shd; wc; shwrs; el pnts (2A); gas; Indtte; shop; rest high ssn; snacks; bar; beach; windsurfing; tennis; games area; many statics; no dogs; sep car park; poss cr; ccard acc. "Lovely situation." € 29.00 2009*

CECINA *1D3* (3km NW Coastal) *43.31850, 10.47440* **Camping Mareblu, Via dei Campilunghi, Mazzanta, 57010 San Pietro-in-Palazzi (LI) [0586 629191; fax 629192; info@campingmareblu.com; www.campingmareblu.com]** Fr S on SS1 exit sp Cecina Nord & foll dir Mazzanta, site sp. Fr N exit sp Vada then Mazzanta. Lge, hdg/mkd pitch, pt shd; wc (some cont); chem disp; mv service pnt; shwrs inc; el pnts (3A) inc; gas; Indtte (inc dryer); shop; tradsmn; rest; snacks; bar; BBQ (gas only); playgrnd; pool; paddling pool; sand beach adj; wifi; 10% statics; dogs free (not accepted Jul & Aug); phone; sep car park; ATM; poss cr; Eng spkn; adv bkg; red low ssn; ccard acc; red CCI. "Lge pitches; gd facs & pool area; car must be parked in sep car park; well-organised, friendly site." ♦ 26 Mar-15 Oct. € 37.00 (CChq acc) 2011*

ITALY

CECINA *1D3* (6km NW Coastal) *43.33206, 10.46021* **Camping Molino a Fuoco, Via Cavalleggeri 32, 57018 Vada (LI) [0586 770150; fax 770031; info@campingmolinoafuoco.com; www.campingmolinoafuoco.com]** Sp fr SS1 Aurelia at cent of vill of Vada, adj Camping Rada Etrusca. Lge, shd; wc (some cont); chem disp; mv service pnt; baby facs; shwrs inc; el pnts (4A) inc; lndtte (inc dryer); shop; rest; snacks; bar; BBQ; playgrnd; shgl beach adj; games area; cycle hire; wifi; 30% statics; dogs €2 (not acc Jul/Aug); sep car park; phone; poss cr; ccard acc; red low ssn. "Pleasant site; helpful staff; gd san facs." ♦ 2 Apr-16 Oct. € 34.00 2010*

I'll fill in a report online and let the Club know – www.caravanclub.co.uk/europereport

This is a wonderful site.

CECINA *1D3* (6km NW Coastal) *43.34305, 10.45833* **Camping Tripesce, Via dei Cavalleggeri 88, 57018 Vada (LI) [0586 788167; fax 0568 789159; info@campingtripesce.com; www.campingtripesce.com]** Sp in Vada cent. On Vada to Cecina rd S of Vada, 1st on R fr Vada. Lge, pt shd; wc (some cont); chem disp; serviced pitches; shwrs inc; el pnts (4A) inc; lndtte; shop; rest; snacks; bar; playgrnd; sand beach adj; sailing; windsurfing; wifi; no dogs (Jul & Aug); quiet; red low ssn/CCI. "Lovely beach; site clsd 1400-1600; cycle path to Vada." ♦ 15 Mar-18 Oct. € 36.00 2008*

CERIALE see Albenga *1B2*

CERVIA *2E2* (5km N Coastal) *44.30472, 12.3425* **Camping Nuovo International, Via Meldola 1/A, 48020 Lido-di-Savio (RA) [0544 949014; fax 949085; info@camping-international.it]** 2km fr Ravenna-Rimini rd S16, sp in Savio at x-rds. Lge, shd; wc; baby facs; shwrs inc; el pnts (3A) €1; gas; lndtte; shop; rest; snacks; bar; playgrnd; pool; beach 200m; entmnt; no dogs; 90% statics; Eng spkn; no adv bkg; ccard acc. "Well-run, clean site; friendly staff." ♦ 1 May-16 Sep. € 23.00 2008*

CERVIA *2E2* (1.5km S Coastal) *44.24760, 12.35901* **Camping Adriatico, Via Pinarella 90, 48015 Cervia (RA) [0544 71537; fax 72346; info@campingadriatico.net; www.campingadriatico.net]** On SS16 S fr Cervia twd Pinarella, turn L at km post 175, over rlwy line & take 1st R, site sp. Lge, shd; wc (some cont); chem disp; mv service pnt; baby facs; shwrs inc; el pnts (6A) inc; lndtte; shop; tradsmn; rest; snacks; bar; playgrnd; htd pool; paddling pool; sand beach 600m; fishing; tennis 900m; golf 5km; entmnt; TV rm; 40% statics; dogs €6; Eng spkn; adv bkg; ccard acc; red CCI. "V pleasant site; friendly staff; gd san facs." ♦ 21 Apr-15 Sep. € 34.10 (CChq acc) 2010*

CERVO see Diano Marina *1B3*

⊞ **CESENATICO** *2E2* (1.5km N Coastal) *44.21545, 12.37983* **Camping Cesenatico, Via Mazzini 182, 47042 Cesenatico (FC) [0547 81344; fax 672452; info@campingcesenatico.it; www.campingcesenatico.com]** Travelling S on S16 look for Esso g'ge on R on app Cesenatico. Take 2nd L after Erg g'ge, over rlwy x-ing, site on L, sp. V lge, mkd pitch, hdstg, pt shd; htd wc (some cont); chem disp; mv service pnt; shwrs inc; el pnts (4A) €3.60; gas; lndtte; shop; snacks; rest; bar; playgrnd; htd pool; private sand beach adj; tennis; games area; entmnt; hairdresser; medical cent; wifi; entmnt; TV; 80% statics; dogs €8.70; phone; poss cr; Eng spkn; adv bkg; ccard acc; red long stay/low ssn/CCI. "Many long stay winter visitors; gd touring base; unspoilt seaside resort with canal (designed by Da Vinci), port & marina; excel." ♦ € 47.80 (CChq acc) 2009*

CESENATICO *2E2* (2km N Coastal) *44.21584, 12.37798* **Camping Zadina, Via Mazzini 184, 42047 Cesenatico (FC) [0547 82310; fax 672802; info@campingzadina.it; www.campingzadina.it]** Leave A14 at Cesena Sud; foll sp Cesenático; after 10.5km turn R at T-junc onto SS16; after 2km fork L over level x-ing; site on L. V lge, mkd pitch, pt terr, shd; wc; chem disp; shwrs inc; el pnts (6A) inc; gas; lndtte; shop; rest; snacks; bar; private sand beach; fishing; 80% statics; dogs €7; sep car park; poss cr; adv bkg; noisy in high ssn; ccard not acc; red low ssn. "Sea water canal runs thro site; pitches poss tight lge o'fits; gd." ♦ 19 Apr-20 Sep. € 34.00 2009*

CHATILLON see St Vincent *1B1*

⊞ **CHIAVENNA** *1C1* (3km E Rural) *46.33153, 9.43279* **Camping Acquafraggia, Via San Abbondio 1, 23020 Piuro (SO) [tel/fax 0343 36755; info@campingacquafraggia.com; www.campingacquafraggia.com]** On S37 dir St Moritz, site well sp. Sm, mkd pitch, terr, pt shd; htd wc; chem disp; mv service pnt; shwrs inc; el pnts €2.50; lndtte; shop, rest, snacks, bar 300m; BBQ; playgrnd; games rm; internet; 5% statics; bus 200m; phone; quiet. "Beautiful setting by waterfall; superb san facs; excel." € 20.00 2008*

CHIENES/KIENS see Brunico/Bruneck *1D1*

CHIOGGIA *2E2* (2km E Coastal) *45.20533, 12.29856* **Camping Adriatico, Lungomare Adriatico 82, 30019 Sottomarina (VE) [041 492907; fax 5548567; info@campingadriatico.com; www.campingadriatico.com]** Fr rd S309 foll sp for Sottomarina Lido, foll dual c'way on sea front, site on L. Med, mkd pitch, shd; wc (cont); chem disp; mv service pnt; some serviced pitches; shwrs inc; el pnts (6A) inc (some rev pol); gas; lndtte; shop; rest; snacks; bar; playgrnd; pool; sand beach adj; sailing; watersports; TV; 30% statics; phone; dogs (not acc Jun-Aug); poss v cr; quiet; some traff noise; adv bkg; Eng spkn; red long stay; ccard acc; red low ssn; CCI. "Water bus to Venice; Chioggia worth visit; money exchange." ♦ 4 Apr-20 Sep. € 32.50 2009*

CHIOGGIA *2E2* (2km E Urban/Coastal) *45.19027, 12.30361* **Camping Miramare, Via A. Barbarigo 103, 30019 Sottomarina (VE) [tel/fax 041 490610; campmir@tin.it; www.miramarecamping.com]** Fr SS309 foll sp Sottomarina. In town foll brown sp to site. Lge, mkd pitch, pt shd; wc; chem disp; mv service pnt; shwrs inc; el pnts (6A) inc; gas; lndtte; shop; rest; snacks; bar; playgrnd; pool; private sand beach; games area; wifi; entmnt; 75% statics; no dogs; poss cr; adv bkg; ccard acc; CCI. "Busy site - field across rd quieter; friendly staff; gd entmnt facs for children; cycle tracks to picturesque Chioggia." ♦ 22 Apr-21 Sep. € 31.00 2008*

CHIOGGIA *2E2* (3km SE Coastal) *45.18138, 12.3075* **Kawan Village Camping Oasi, Via A. Barbarigo 147, 30019 Sottomarina (VE) [041 5541145; fax 490801; info@campingoasi.com; www.campingoasi.com]** Exit SS309/E55 sp Sottomarina, Chioggia & foll Viale Mediterraneo twd coast. Site sp on R - last one along Via Barbarigo. Med, hdg/mkd pitch, pt shd; wc (some cont); chem disp; mv service pnt; baby facs; shwrs inc; el pnts (6A) inc; lndtte (inc dryer); shop; rest; snacks; bar; BBQ; playgrnd; pool; paddling pool; private sand beach adj; watersports; games area; tennis; cycle hire; wifi; entmnt; TV; 50% statics; dogs €3; phone; poss cr; adv bkg; quiet; ccard acc; red low ssn. "Pleasant, welcoming site; vg facs; excel beach; water bus to Venice." ♦ 25 Mar-30 Sep. € 34.00 (CChq acc) 2011*

We can fill in site report forms on the Club's website – www.caravanclub.co.uk/europereport

CHIOGGIA *2E2* (4km S Coastal) *45.22768, 12.29747* **Camping Tropical, Via San Felice, Zona Diga 10/C, 30019 Sottomarina (VE) [041 403055; fax 550593; info@campingtropical.com; www.campingtropical.com]** Fr Chioggia by-pass foll sp Sottomarina, last site of many, well sp. Med, mkd pitch, pt shd; wc; chem disp; shwrs inc; el pnts (4A) inc; lndtte; sm shop & 3km; rest; snacks; bar; playgrnd; sand beach adj; watersports; many statics; no dogs high ssn; poss cr; adv bkg. "Vg family site; private beach." ♦ Easter-21 Sep. € 29.20 2008*

CHIOGGIA *2E2* (10km S Coastal) *45.1625, 12.32277* **Villagio Turistico Isamar, Via Isamar 9, 30010 Sant' Anna (VE) [041 5535811; fax 490440; info@villaggioisamar.com; www.villaggioisamar.com]** Take SS309 S fr Venice. Immed after x-ing Rv Brenta 2km S of Chioggia, turn L & foll Isola Verde & Ca' Lino sp. In Ca' Lino turn L & foll site sp. V lge, shd; wc (some cont); chem disp; mv service pnt; serviced pitches; shwrs inc; el pnts (4A) inc; gas; lndtte; pizzeria; shop; supmkt; rest; snacks; bar; 6 pools; private beach adj; watersports; tennis; games area; horseriding; cycle hire; internet; entmnt; 55% statics; no dogs; adv bkg (fee); ccard acc; red CCI. "Many sports & activities; excel for families." ♦ 4 May-16 Sep. € 52.40 6 persons 2008*

⊞ **CHIUSA/KLAUSEN** *1D1* (1km N Rural) *46.64138, 11.57361* **Camping Gamp, Via Griesbruck 10, 39043 Chiusa/Klausen (BZ) [0472 847425; fax 845067; info@camping-gamp.com; www.camping-gamp.com]** Exit A22 Chiusa/Klausen & bear L at end of slip rd (sp Val Gardena). Site on L at rd fork 800m, sp. Sm, mkd pitch, pt shd; htd wc; chem disp; shwrs inc; mv service pnt; baby facs; el pnts (6A) €2.60; lndtte; shop & 500m; tradsmn; rest; snacks; bar; playgrnd; pool; table tennis; htd ski & boot rm; internet; sat TV: dogs €3.50; phone; sep m'van o'night facs; Eng spkn; some rd & rlwy noise; CCI. "Excel cent for mountain walks; Chiusa attractive town; immac facs, sep m'van overnight area." ♦ € 30.50 2011*

CHIUSI DELLA VERNA see Caprese Michelangelo *1D3*

CIRO MARINA *3B4* (2km N Coastal) *39.38526, 17.14255* **Camping Villaggio Punta Alice, 88811 Ciro-Marina (KR) [0962 31160; fax 373823; info@puntalice.it; www.puntalice.it]** Fr N on S106 twd Crotone, exit Cirò Marina. Cross rlwy line, foll site sp thro town (rds narr) to site. Lge, mkd pitch, pt shd; wc; chem disp; mv service pnt; shwrs inc; el pnts (6A) inc; lndtte; shop; rest; snacks; bar; playgrnd; pool; private sand/shgl beach; games area; cycle hire; entmnt; cinema; TV rm; 50% statics; dogs €5.50; phone; sep car park high ssn; poss cr; Eng spkn; poss noisy; CCI. "Vg, clean site; friendly staff; excel rest." ♦ 1 Apr-30 Sep. € 44.00 2010*

CISANO see Bardolino *1D2*

CITTA DI CASTELLO *2E3* (3km W Rural) *43.45142, 12.22205* **Camping La Montesca, Loc Montesca, 06012 Città di Castello (PG) [0758 558566; fax 520786; info@lamontesca.it; www.lamontesca.it]** W fr SS3bis on winding rd; foll sp to town cent then sm brown site sp. Med, hdg/mkd pitch, terr, pt shd; wc; shwrs; el pnts (6A) inc; lndtte; shop & 3km; rest, bar high ssn; pool; entmnt; dogs; quiet; red CCI. "Superb views; ltd, sm touring pitches, but made welcome; poor san facs (2009); beautiful town." ♦ 15 Apr-20 Sep. € 27.00 2009*

COGNE *1B1* (3km SW Rural) *45.58764, 7.34157* **Camping Lo Stambecco, Frazione Valnontey, 11012 Cogne (AO) [0165 74152; infotiscali@campeggiolostambecco.it; www.campeggiolostambecco.it]** On Aosta-Mont Blanc rd (S26) heading W, after Sarre turn L to Cogne. In Cogne turn R sp Valnontey (Gran Paradiso). Site on L at ent to Valnontey vill. Use easier 2nd ent opp car park. Long 10% app fr S26. Med, pt sl, pt shd; wc (some cont); chem disp; mv service pnt; shwrs inc; el pnts (3A) €2; gas; lndtte; shop 3km; bar; 20% statics; Eng spkn; poss cr; quiet; ccard not acc; CCI. "In magnificent Gran Paradiso National Park; botanic garden highly rec; gd facs; excel walks." 20 May-20 Sep. € 22.00 2011*

COLTANO see Pisa *1C3*

ITALY

COMACCHIO *2E2* (7km N Coastal) *44.73444, 12.23138* **Camping Tahiti, Viale Libia 133, 44020 Lido-delle-Nazioni (FE) [0533 379500; fax 379700; info@campingtahiti.com; www.campingtahiti.com]** Fr a'strade Ferrara-Comacchio take exit dir Porto Garibaldi. Take S309 N to km 32.5, site sp. Lge, mkd pitch, shd; wc (some cont); chem disp; mv service pnt; serviced pitches; baby facs; fam bthrm; sauna; shwrs inc; el pnts (10A) inc; gas; Indtte; supmkt; rest; snacks; bar; playgrnd; pool complex; private beach adj; tennis; cycle hire; wellness cent; wifi; entmnt; 30% statics; no dogs; phone; adv bkg (fee); ccard acc. "Excel family site; many sports & activities." ♦ 18 Apr-21 Sep. € 48.60 2008*

COMACCHIO *2E2* (1km SE Coastal) *44.70130, 12.23810* **Kawan Village Florenz, Via Alpi Centrali 199, 44020 Lido-degli-Scacchi (FE) [0533 380193; fax 313166; info@campingflorenz.com; www.campingflorenz.com]** Fr a'strade Ferrara-Comacchio take exit dir Porto Garibaldi, site sp on coast rd. V lge, hdg pitch, pt shd; wc (some cont); chem disp; mv service pnt; baby facs; shwrs inc; el pnts (3A) inc; gas; Indtte; shop; rest; snacks; playgrnd; pool; paddling pool; sand beach adj; beauty cent; cycle hire; games area; golf 5km; wifi; entmnt; TV rm; 60% statics; dogs €5.90; poss cr; quiet; ccard acc; red snr citizens; CCI. ♦ 1 Apr-1 Nov. € 37.60 (CChq acc) 2011*

COMACCHIO *2E2* (2km SE Coastal) *44.68944, 12.23833* **Camping Spiaggia e Mare, S.P. Ferrara-Mare 4, 44029 Porto Garibaldi (FE) [0533 327431; fax 325620; info@campingspiaggiamare.it; www.campingspiaggiamare.it]** Fr a'strada Ferrara-Comacchio take exit dir Porto Garibaldi, then S on S309 dir Ravenna. In 1km take sliprd on R to Porto Garibaldi. Strt over traff lts, site on L just bef RH bend. Fr S take slip rd on R at km 27 sp, then as above. Lge, mkd pitch, pt shd; wc (mainly cont); chem disp; mv service pnt; shwrs inc; el pnts inc (6A) inc; gas; Indtte; supmkt; rest; snacks; bar; playgrnd; 2 pools; paddling pool; sand beach adj; watersports; games area; cycle hire; wifi; entmnt; 50% statics; dogs €6.30; poss cr; poss noisy; red snr citizens. "Excel beach; excel sw pool; active fishing port." ♦ 10 Apr-20 Sep. € 38.70 2009*

COMO *1C1* (5km S Urban) *45.78385, 9.06034* **International Camping-Sud, Breccia, Via Cecilio, 22100 Como [tel/fax 031 521435; campingint@hotmail.com; www.camping-internazionale.it]** Fr E to Como, on SS35 Milano rd foll sp a'strada Milano; site on Como side of rndabt at junc S35 & S432; ent/exit diff unless turn R. Or take 2nd exit off m'way after border (Como S), site sp. Med, pt sl, pt shd; wc; shwrs inc; el pnts (4-6A) €2.50 (rev pol); gas; Indtte; shop; supmkt nr; rest; snacks; bar; playgrnd; pool; cycle hire; golf 5km; dogs €2; poss cr; no adv bkg; rd noise; red low ssn; ccard acc. "Conv NH for m'way." 1 Apr-31 Oct. € 21.00 2010*

⊞ **CORIGLIANO CALABRO** *3A4* (8km N Coastal) *39.68141, 16.52160* **Camping Il Salice, Contrada da Ricota Grande, 87060 Corigliano-Calabro (CS) [0983 851169; fax 851147; info@salicevacanze.it; www.salicevacanze.it]** Exit A3 dir Sibari onto SS106 bis coast rd dir Crotone. At 19km marker after water tower on L, turn L sp Il Salice - 1.5km to new access rd to site on L. Site sp easily missed. Lge, mkd pitch, hdstg, pt sl, pt shd; htd wc (cont); chem disp; mv service pnt; serviced pitches; baby facs; fam bthrm; shwrs inc; el pnts (3-6A) inc; gas; Indtte; shop & 2km; rest; snacks; bar; BBQ; playgrnd; pool; sand beach adj; watersports; tennis; games area; games rm; cycle hire; TV; 70% statics; dogs €4; phone; poss cr; Eng spkn; red low ssn; CCI. "Narr rds thro vill to site - care needed when busy; v popular, well-run winter destination; haphazard siting in pine trees; clean, private beach; modern san facs; ltd facs low ssn; big price red low ssn; scenic area." ♦ € 48.00 2008*

CORTENO GOLGI see Edolo *1D1*

CORTINA D'AMPEZZO *2E1* (5km N Rural) *46.57222, 12.11583* **Motor Caravan Park, Loc Fiames, 32043 Cortina d'Ampezzo (BL) [tel/fax 04 364571; serviampezzo@tin.it]** Exit A22/E45 at Bressanone/Brixen onto SS49 to Dobbiaco/Toblach. Then take SS51 dir Cortina & foll Fiames sp. Situated on old airfield. Water; mv service pnt inc; bus; stay ltd to 48 hrs. 1 Jul-10 Sep. € 15.00 2008*

CORTINA D'AMPEZZO *2E1* (9km NE Rural) *46.58775, 12.25814* **Camping Alla Baita, Via Col Sant'Angelo 4, 32040 Misurina (BL) [tel/fax 0435 39039; labaita@misurina.com; www.misurina.com]** Sp just outside Misurina vill. Med, mkd pitch, hdstg, pt sl, unshd; wc (some cont); mv service pnt; shwrs inc; el pnts (2A) inc; shops 1km; rest; bar adj; dogs €3; poss cr; ccard acc; red low ssn; CCI. "Chairlift in vill to Col de Varda; bus to Tre Cime/Dreisinnen fr site; magnificent scenery; altitude 1756m; refurbed facs but hot water only for shwrs; m'van park adj." 15 Jun-15 Sep. € 24.00 2007*

CORTINA D'AMPEZZO *2E1* (1.5km SE Rural) *46.52241, 12.13413* **Camping Rocchetta, Via Campo 1, 32043 Cortina-d'Ampezzo (BL) [tel/fax 0436 5063; camping@sunrise.it; www.campingrocchetta.it]** Fr Cortina on SS51 dir Belluno & Venice, site sp. Fr Belluno on S51 on app Cortina turn L, brown sp at junc, site sp. Lge, shd; htd wc (some cont); chem disp; mv service pnt; shwrs inc; el pnts (3A) inc; Indtte (inc dryer); shop; rest adj; bar; pool 2km; 10% statics; dogs €1; poss cr; Eng spkn; adv bkg; quiet; ccard acc; red low ssn; CCI. "Gd, clean facs; 30 min walk to Cortina; mountain views." 1 Jun-20 Sep & 3 Dec-3 Apr. € 26.00 2010*

CORTINA D'AMPEZZO *2E1* (3.5km S Rural) *46.51858, 12.1370* **Camping Dolomiti, Via Campo di Sotto, 32043 Cortina-d'Ampezzo (BL) [0436 2485; fax 5403; campeggiodolomiti@tin.it; www.campeggiodolomiti.it]** 2km S of Cortina turn R off S51. Site beyond Camping Cortina & Rocchetta. Lge, mkd pitch, pt shd; htd wc; shwrs inc; chem disp; mv service pnt; el pnts (4A) inc (check earth); gas; Indtte; shop; rest 1km; bar; playgrnd; htd pool; games area; games rm; 10% statics; dogs; phone; bus; poss cr; Eng spkn; no adv bkg; quiet; red low ssn; ccard acc. "Superb scenery in mountains, gd walks; cycle rte into Cortina; excel disabled facs; helpful owner." ♦ 1 Jun-20 Sep. € 24.00 2010*

⊞ **CORTINA D'AMPEZZO** *2E1* (1.5km SW Rural) *45.51993, 12.13611* **Camping Cortina, Loc Campo di Sopra 2, 32043 Cortina-d'Ampezzo (BL) [0436 867575; fax 867917; campcortina@tin.it]** Site sp fr Cortina town cent. Fr S on SS51 turn L foll camp sp on app to Cortina. Site at bottom of valley. Lge, shd; wc; shwrs inc; el pnts (3A) inc; gas; lndtte; shop; rest; snacks; bar; playgrnd; pool; 80% statics; dogs; poss cr; Eng spkn; ccard acc; CCI. "Excel position & area; gd facs; card operated barrier; helpful staff; site poss unkempt in low ssn; bus into Cortina." ♦ € 25.00 2007*

CORVARA IN BADIA *1D1* (2km W Rural) *46.55111, 11.8575* **Camping Colfosco, Via Sorega 15, 39030 Corvara-in-Badìa (BZ) [0471 836515; fax 830801; info@campingcolfosco.org; www.campingcolfosco.org]** Fr Brenner Pass take A22/E45 S & turn E onto S49 to Brunico; 4km bef Brunico turn S onto S244 to Corvara in Badia. Turn W in Corvara for Gardena Pass onto S243. After 900m bear L bef bdge. Site in 300m. Med, hdstg, pt sl, unshd; wc; chem disp; shwrs inc; el pnts (10A) inc; lndtte; shop; rest 500m; bar; playgrnd; golf 4km; skilift 300m; ski bus; dogs €2.50; sep car park; site clsd 1200-1500; poss cr; no adv bkg; quiet; ccard acc. "Fine scenery & walks; well-managed site; sh walk to vill; gd base for skiing (ski in & out of site) & mountain biking; lift/bus passes avail; vg san facs; somewhat bleak hdstg area." 1 Jan-6 Apr & 18 May-5 Oct. € 26.50 2008*

COSTACCIARO *2E3* (3km W Rural) *43.35096, 12.6846* **Camping Rio Verde, Loc Fornace, Via Flaminia, Km 206.5, 06021 Costacciaro (PG) [075 9170138; fax 9170181; info@campingrioverde.it; www.campingrioverde.it]** Fr Costacciaro N on SS3 for 1km, turn L & foll brown site sp. Fairly steep ent. Sm, mkd pitch, pt sl, shd; wc (some cont); chem disp; mv service pnt; shwrs inc; el pnts (6A) inc; lndtte; shop & 4km; rest; bar; playgrnd; pool; 10% statics; dogs free; Eng spkn; adv bkg; quiet; red long stay/CCI. "Gd walking in Monte Cucco National Park; hang-gliding nrby." ♦ 18 Apr-30 Sep. € 26.50 2008*

COURMAYEUR *1A1* (6km NE Rural) **Camping Tronchey, Val Ferret, 11013 Courmayeur (AO) [tel/fax 0165 869707; info@tronchey.com; www.tronchey.com]** Take S26 N fr Courmayeur dir Mont Blanc Tunnel. Turn R sp Val Ferret at La Palud, site in 5km on L. Rd steep initially. Med, terr, pt shd; wc (cont); own san; chem disp; mv service pnt; shwrs €1; el pnts (6A) €1.60; lndtte; shop; tradsmn; rest, bar adj; bar; playgrnd; dogs; bus to Courmayeur & top of valley; poss cr; Eng spkn; adv bkg; quiet; ccard acc; CCI. "Superb mountain views; gd walking & golf adj; m'vans not permitted to park in upper valley beyond site in high ssn." 15 Jun-15 Sep. € 15.00 2008*

⊞ **COURMAYEUR** *1A1* (6km SE Rural) *45.76333, 7.01055* **Camping Arc en Ciel, Loc Feysoulles, 11017 Morgex (AO) [0165 809257; fax 807749; info@campingarcenciel.it; www.campingarcenciel.it]** Fr A5/E25 take Morgex exit, turn L to vill & foll sp dir Dailley. Site in 1km on L, sp. Fr tunnel take SS25 to Morgex, then as above. Med, terr, pt shd; wc; chem disp; shwrs inc; el pnts (4-6A) €1.50; lndtte; shop; rest; snacks; bar; rafting; mountain climbing; ski-lift 8km; ski bus; 30% statics; dogs €1; sep car park; site clsd 6 Nov-8 Dec; poss cr; adv bkg; quiet; ccard acc; red CCI. "Gd, clean san facs; views Mont Blanc fr some pitches; vg; Views of the mountains marvellous." € 21.50 2011*

CREMONA *1C2* (1km SW Rural) *45.11978, 10.0088* **Camping Parco al Po, Via Lungo Po Europa 12, 26100 Cremona [0372 21268; fax 27137; campingcr@libero.it; www.campingcremonapo.it]** Exit A21 at Castelvetro or Cremona onto S10 ring rd. Site well sp fr ring rd, adj to sports complex nr rvside. If lost foll sp Paziena, then site, Med, mkd pitch, shd; wc (some cont); mw service pnt; chem disp; shwrs €0.50; el pnts (4A) inc; lndtte; shop 2km; bar; snacks; rest; rv sw 1km; cycle hire; 20% statics; dogs €2; phone; poss cr; adv bkg; ccard acc; some rd noise. "In spacious park; some pitches gloomy due excessive shading; facs old; gates locked 1400-1530; gd rest; interesting town; mosquitoes." ♦ 1 Apr-30 Sep. € 22.00 2011*

⊞ **CUNEO** *1B2* (9km S Rural) *44.32777, 7.60515* **Camping Il Melo, Loc Miclet, Via Don Peirone 57, 12016 Peveragno (CN) [0171 383599; fax 336977; info@campingilmelo.it; www.campingilmelo.it]** Fr E on P564 turn L at Beinette dir Peveragno. In town turn R at traff lts & in 300m turn L, site sp. Sm, pt sl, pt shd; htd wc (some cont); chem disp; mv service pnt; shwrs €1; el pnts (6A) €1.60; lndtte; shop, rest, snacks, bar nr; pool; sports cent adj inc gym & tennis; rv fishing; horseriding 2km; cycle hire; 90% statics; dogs; site clsd mid-Feb to mid-Mar; adv bkg; quiet. "Gd views; conv for ski areas; peaceful location; friendly owner; ltd pitches for tourers; clean, well-maintained facs." ♦ € 15.40 2008*

CUNEO *1B2* (3km SW Rural) *44.36443, 7.51483* **Camping Communale Bisalta, Via San Maurizio 33, 12010 San Rocco-Castagnaretta (CN) [tel/fax 0171 491334; campingbisalta@libero.it]** App Cuneo on S20 fr S fr Col de Tende (France) dir. On o'skts of town turn L at traff lts by cemetary, foll site sp. Lge, shd; wc; chem disp; mv service pnt; shwrs inc; el pnts (3A) inc; lndtte; shop; rest 1km; snacks; bar; BBQ; cooking facs; pool; tennis; cycle hire; 85% statics; dogs; 10% red long stay/CCI. "Pleasant site; friendly atmosphere; fair facs poss stretched high ssn; gd touring base." ♦ € 21.50 2009*

CUPRA MARITTIMA *2F3* (1km W Urban/Coastal) *43.02054, 13.84925* **Villaggio Verde Cupra, Via Lazio 26, 63012 Cupra-Marittima (AP) [0735 777411; fax 777666; info@verdecupra.it; www.verdecupra.it]** Fr N leave A14 dir Pedaso, then S on SS16 in dir Pescara. In 10km site sp in town on R. Med, mkd pitch, pt shd; wc; shwrs inc; el pnts (4A) inc; gas 2km; lndtte; shop; rest; snacks; bar; playgrnd; pool; beach 1km; tennis; cycle hire; entmnt; TV rm; phone; poss cr; some Eng spkn; adv bkg; poss noisy; CCI. "Helpful owner & staff; quite a climb up a hill to the site." ♦ 1 Apr-31 Oct. € 33.00 2011*

CUPRA MARITTIMA *2F3* (2km W Rural/Coastal) *43.04211, 13.85103* **Camping Il Frutteto, Via Baccabianca 99, 63012 Cupra-Marittima (AP) [0735 777459; fax 778165; www.campingilfrutteto.it]** Fr N leave A14 dir Pedaso, then S on SS16 dir Pescara for 9km. Site sp on R shortly after Camping Led Zeppelin. Med, mkd pitch, sl, pt shd; wc; chem disp (wc); shwrs inc; el pnts (6A) inc; gas 1km; lndry rm; shop; rest; bar; playgrnd; pool; paddling pool; beach 1km; 10% statics; dogs; train 2km; rd & rlwy noise; ccard acc; CCI. "Friendly, helpful owner." 20 Apr-20 Sep. € 29.00 2008*

DARE see Tione di Trento *1D1*

DEIVA MARINA *1C2* (1km NE Rural) *44.22520, 9.53250* **Villaggio Turistico Arenella, Loc Arenella, 19013 Deiva-Marina (SP) [0187 825259; info@campingarenella.it; www.campingarenella.it]** Exit A12/E80 Deiva Marina. In approx 6.8km site sp on R, easy access. Med, hdstg, terr, pt shd; wc (some cont); chem disp; mv service pnt; shwrs inc; el pnts (3A) €2; Indtte; shop; rest; snacks; bar; BBQ; beach 2.2km; wifi; 40% statics; dogs; phone; bus to stn (trains to Cinque Terre) high ssn; Eng spkn; adv bkg; quiet; red low ssn/CCI. "Pleasant site with stream running thro it; helpful staff; vg." ♦
1 May-31 Oct & 5-31 Dec. € 33.00 2010*

⊞ **DEIVA MARINA** *1C2* (3km E Rural) *44.22630, 9.55013* **Camping La Sfinge, Loc Gea 5, 19013 Deiva-Marina (SP) [tel/fax 0187 825464; info@campinglasfinge.com; www.campinglasfinge.com]** Fr a'strada A12 exit Deiva Marina, site on R in approx 4.5km Med, hdg/mkd pitch, hdstg, terr, pt shd; wc (cont); mv service pnt; chem disp; serviced pitches; shwrs inc; el pnts (3A) inc; gas; Indtte; shop; tradsmn; rest; snacks; bar; playgrnd; shgl beach 3km (free bus high ssn); entmnt; fishing; watersports; trekking; internet; 50% statics; dogs €2; phone; bus to beach/stn high ssn; sep car park; poss cr; Eng spkn; adv bkg ess high ssn; quiet; 10% red 5+ days; red low ssn; ccard acc; 10% red CCI. "Excel san facs; v popular inc low ssn - rec arr early; gd, clean site; ltd touring pitches & some sm/diff for lge o'fits; conv Genova, Pisa, Portofino, Cinque Terre, marble quarry at Carrara; gd walking." ♦
€ 31.50 2010*

There aren't many sites open at this time of year. We'd better phone ahead to check the one we're heading for is open.

⊞ **DEIVA MARINA** *1C2* (3km E Coastal) *44.22476, 9.55146* **Villaggio Camping Valdeiva, Loc Ronco, 19013 Deiva-Marina (SP) [0187 824174; fax 825352; camping@valdeiva.it; www.valdeiva.it]** Fr A12 exit Deiva Marina, site sp on L in approx 4km by town sp. Med, mkd pitch, hdstg, pt sl, pt shd; wc (some cont); chem disp; shwrs inc; el pnts (3A) inc; Indtte; shop; tradsmn; rest; snacks; bar; BBQ; playgrnd; pool; shgl beach 3km; wifi; entmnt; sat TV; 90% statics; dogs; phone; bus to stn; sep car park high ssn; poss cr; Eng spkn; adv bkg essential high ssn; ccard acc; red low ssn; CCI. "Spacious site in pine woods; free minibus to stn - conv Cinque Terre or Portofino; helpful, friendly staff; gd rest; excel walking." € 35.00 (3 persons) 2009*

DEIVA MARINA *1C2* (1km SE Coastal) *44.21473, 9.51874* **Camping Fornaci al Mare, Loc Fornaci, 19014 Framura (SP) [tel/fax 0187 816295]** Foll 1-way to L in town, sp La Spezia-A'strada, over narr bdge. Site immed S of rv bdge. Med, pt sl, pt shd; wc (some cont); chem disp; mv service pnt; shwrs €0.50; el pnts (2A) inc; shop, rest, snacks, bar nr; beach adj; 80% statics; no dogs; train nr; phone; poss cr; rlwy noise; CCI. "Not suitable lge o'fits; v friendly; san facs dated; sh walk to stn for Cinque Terra towns, some railway noise." ♦
1 Apr-31 Oct. € 25.00 2011*

⊞ **DEMONTE** *1B2* (1.5km N Rural) *44.32260, 7.29222* **Campeggio Il Sole, Frazione Perosa 3/B, 12014 Demonte (CN) [0334 1132724; fax 071 955630; erikamelchio@virgilio.it]** Fr lge town square on S21 go E for 100m, fork L & in 100m turn L. Pass 2 churches on L, turn L, then R over rv into Via Colle dell'Urtica to N. Foll this rd uphill for 1.2km, turn L at T-junc & in 300m L at T-junc again. Site on R. Town cent side streets v narr with arches & app rd narr & steep in places. Sm, mkd pitch, unshd; wc; chem disp; mv service pnt; shwrs €1; el pnts €2; Indry rm; rest; bar; BBQ; playgrnd; dogs; quiet. "Lovely, peaceful site in mountains; vg value rest." ♦
€ 17.00 2009*

DEMONTE *1B2* (1.5km W Rural) *44.31357, 7.27275* **Camping Piscina Demonte, Loc Bagnolin, 12014 Demonte (CN) [0171 214889; fax 011 2274301; info@campingdemonte.com; www.campingdemonte.com]** App only fr Borgo on S21, 500m after Demonte turn L, foll sp. Med, pt shd; wc; chem disp; shwrs €0.60; el pnts (6A) €1.50; gas; Indtte; shop, rest 1.5km; bar; pool; 90% statics; dogs €1.60; poss cr; adv bkg; quiet; ccard acc; CCI. "Gd NH bef Col d'Larche; helpful, friendly owner; gd mountain scenery." 15 Jun-15 Sep.
€ 16.50 2008*

DESENZANO DEL GARDA *1D2* (4km N Rural) *45.4957, 10.5108* **Camping Villa Garuti, Via del Porto 5, 25080 Padenghe-sul-Garda (BS) [030 9907134; fax 9907817; info@villagaruti.it; www.villagaruti.it]** Fr Desenzano foll sp for Salò on S572 - site on R. Sharp R turn at site ent. Med, pt shd; wc; chem disp; mv service pnt; shwrs inc; el pnts (6-9A) inc; gas; rest; bar; pool; lake sw & private beach adj; fishing; 30% statics; dogs €3-6; bus adj; poss cr; Eng spkn; quiet. "Sm marina adj; sm pitches, some lakeside; friendly, helpful staff; gd value low ssn; clean, adequate facs; lovely old villa in grounds." ♦
19 Mar-10 Oct. € 32.00 2008*

DESENZANO DEL GARDA *1D2* (5km SE Rural) *45.46565, 10.59443* **Camping San Francesco, Strada V San Francesco, 25015 Desenzano-del-Garda (BS) [030 9110245; fax 9119464; moreinfo@campingsanfrancesco.com; www.campingsanfrancesco.com]** E fr Milan on A4 a'strada take exit Sirmione & foll sp twd Sirmione town; join S11 twd Desenzano & after Garden Center Flowers site 1st campsite on R after rndabt; site sp twd lake bet Sirmione & Desanzano. Or fr Desenzano, site just after Rivoltella. Lge, mkd pitch, pt sl, shd; wc; chem disp; baby facs; shwrs inc; el pnts (6A) inc; gas; Indtte (inc dryer); shop; rest; snacks; bar; BBQ (charcoal/gas); playgrnd; pool; lake sw & shgl beach; boat hire; windsurfing; sailing; canoe hire; fishing; tennis; games area; cycle hire; golf 10km; wifi; entmnt; TV rm; 50% statics; dogs free; no c'vans/m'vans over 6m high ssn; phone; recep clsd 1300-1500 & no vehicle movement; poss cr; Eng spkn; adv bkg; noisy entmnt high ssn; ccard acc; red low ssn; CCI. "Lovely lakeside pitches for tourers (extra); muddy if wet; poss diff lge o'fits due trees; helpful staff, well managed site, gd position on edge of lake; handy for local bus." ♦ 1 Apr-30 Sep. € 46.00 (CChq acc) 2011*

DESENZANO DEL GARDA *1D2* (8km NW Rural) *45.51276, 10.52327* **Camping La Ca', Via San Cassiano 12, 25080 Padenghe-sul-Garda (BS) [0309 907006; fax 907693; info@campinglaca.it; www.laca.it]** N fr Desenzano on S572 twd Salo & site on R, clearly sp. Med, mkd pitch, terr, shd; wc; shwrs; el pnts (5A) €1.90; gas; Indtte; shop; rest; bar; pool; paddling pool; lake sw; 30% statics; dogs €4; poss cr; adv bkg. "Steep gradient fr lower terr pitches - tractor avail for tow if req; excel san facs." ♦ 1 Mar-31 Oct. € 27.30 2007*

⊞ **DIANO MARINA** *1B3* (1.5km NE Coastal) *43.92146, 8.09859* **Camping Rosa, Via al Santuario 4, 18016 San Bartolomeo-al-Mare (IM) [0183 400473; fax 400475; info@campingrosa.it; www.campingrosa.it]** Exit a'strada A10 at San Bartolomeo/Diano Marina onto Via Aurelia S1 dir Cervo. At traff lts turn R dir Diano Marina, then R in 400m, site sp in cul-de-sac in 200m - poss narr due parked cars. Med, hdg/mkd pitch, hdstg, pt sl, pt shd; htd wc (some cont); chem disp; serviced pitches; shwrs inc; el pnts (6A) inc; Indtte; shop; rest high ssn; snacks; bar; playgrnd; 2 pools; shgl beach 200m; entmnt; TV rm; many statics; no dogs; phone; Eng spkn; quiet but church bells; red low ssn; ccard acc; CCI. "V ltd touring pitches; pleasant resort; best beach at Alássio; gd NH." ♦ € 44.00 (4 persons) 2008*

DIANO MARINA *1B3* (4km NE Coastal) *43.92177, 8.10831* **Camping del Mare, Via alla Foce 29, 18010 Cervo (IM) [0183 400130; fax 402771; info@campingdelmare-cervo.com; www.campingdelmare-cervo.com]** Exit A10/E80 at San Bartolomeo/Cervo onto Via Aurelia. Turn L at traff lts twd Cervo. Sp adj rv bdge. R turn acute - long o'fits app fr NE. Med, hdg/mkd pitch, hdstg, shd; wc; chem disp; baby facs; shwrs; el pnts (6A) €2; gas; Indtte; shop; snacks; shgl beach adj; internet; TV; 40% statics; dogs; phone; Eng spkn; adv bkg rec Jun-Aug; quiet; ccard acc. "Immac site; spacious pitches; friendly staff; picturesque beach & perched vill (Cervo); easy walk San Bartolomeo; gd mkts; highly rec site." ♦ 26 Mar-17 Oct. € 40.00 2009*

DIANO MARINA *1B3* (4km NE Urban/Coastal) *43.92345, 8.10924* **Camping Lino, Via Nazario Sauro 4, 18010 Cervo (IM) [0183 400087; fax 400089; info@campinglino.it; www.campinglino.it]** Exit A10 dir San Bartolomeo al Mare. Inside Cervo boundary where main coast rd N bends L to pass under rlwy. Turn R clearly sp. Site ent visible fr rd. Med, mkd pitch, shd; wc (some cont); chem disp; fam bthrm; serviced pitches; shwrs; el pnts (6A) metered; gas; Indtte; shop; rest 100m; snacks; playgrnd; cycle hire; internet; 10% statics; dogs; adv bkg; red low ssn; quiet. "Lge pitches completely shd; vans manhandled onto pitch fr ent; sw & boating for children in lagoon; clean, tidy site, but regimented; minimum stay 3 nights; various pitch sizes & prices; park outside bef checking in as diff to turn once inside site." ♦ 1 Apr-20 Oct. € 43.00 (4 persons) 2009*

DIANO MARINA *1B3* (4km NE Urban/Coastal) *43.92384, 8.11100* **Camping Miramare, Via Nazario Sauro 12, 18010 Cervo (IM) [tel/fax 0183 400285; info@campingmiramare.im.it; www.campingmiramare.im.it]** In Cervo where coastal main rd bends L under rlwy bdge, turn R 50m beyond Camping Lino. Sm, mkd pitch, shd; wc; chem disp; shwrs inc; el pnts (4A) €2; Indtte; shop; rest 100m; snacks; bar; shgle beach adj; 10% statics; dogs; phone; poss cr; quiet but some rlwy noise. "Pleasant, family-run site." 1 Apr-3 Oct. € 43.00 (3 persons) 2010*

⊞ **DIANO MARINA** *1B3* (500m S Coastal) *43.90556, 8.07647* **Camping Marino, Via Angiolo Silvio Novaro 3, 18013 Diano-Marina (IM) [0183 498288; fax 494680; info@campingmarino.it; www.campingmarino.it]** At S end of town on coast rd, cross over rlwy bdge & immed turn R. Foll rd to L, site on L in 100m. Lge, hdg/mkd pitch, pt terr, pt shd; htd wc; chem disp; shwrs inc; el pnts (6A) inc; gas; Indtte; shop; rest; snacks; bar; playgrnd; pool (high ssn); sand beach 300m; tennis; games area; entmnt; 30% statics; dogs; phone; train 200m; poss cr; Eng spkn; adv bkg; rlwy noise; ccard acc; red low ssn. "Vg site & san facs; gd mkt Tues." ♦ € 40.00 2008*

⊞ **DIANO MARINA** *1B3* (500m W Urban/Coastal) *43.90667, 8.07097* **Camping Oasi Park, Via Sori 5, 18013 Diano-Marina (IM) [tel/fax 0183 497062; oasi-park@libero.it; www.oasipark.it]** On W o'skts Diano Marina, cross rlwy bdge & immed turn R. Foll rd to L past Camping Marino. In 200m turn L, site 200m ahead. M'vans only. Lge, hdstg, terr, pt shd; wc (cont); own san; chem disp; mv service pnt; shwrs €1; el pnts (8A) €2; gas; Indtte; shop 200m; tradsmn; playgrnd; sand beach 500m; 20% statics; dogs; phone; bus, train 500m; poss v cr; Eng spkn; quiet; ccard acc; CCI. "Conv pleasant town & gd beaches; helpful owner; awnings not allowed." € 15.00 2009*

DIMARO *1D1* (1km W Rural) *46.32611, 10.86222* **Dolomiti Camping Village, Via Gole 105, 38025 Dimaro (TN) [0463 974332; fax 973200; info@campingdolomiti.com; www.campingdolomiti.com]** Site sp on S42 nr rv bdge. Med, terr, pt shd; wc; chem disp; sauna; baby facs; shwrs inc; el pnts (5A) €1.30 or metered; gas; Indtte (inc dryer); shop; rest; snacks; bar; playgrnd; 2 htd pools (1 covrd); tennis; canoeing; cycle hire; ski lift 1.5km; free skibus; mountain biking; extreme sports; wifi; entmnt; TV; 25% statics; dogs €4 (not acc Jul/Aug); sep car park high ssn; gate clsd 1300-1500; quiet; ccard acc; red long stay/CCI. "Helpful staff; gd facs; some pitches poss diff lge o'fits & m'vans; excel walking." ♦ 20 May-25 Sep & 3 Dec-15 Apr. € 33.40 2010*

⊞ **DIMARO** *1D1* (11km W Rural) *46.30980, 10.74010* **Camping Cevedale, Via di Sotto Pilla 4, 38026 Fucine-di-Ossana (TN) [tel/fax 0463 751630; info@campingcevedale.it; www.campingcevedale.it]** Exit A22 at San Michele sull' Adige onto SS43/SS42 twd Dimaro & Fucine. Foll sp Ossana & site over bdge. Lge, mkd pitch, terr, pt shd; htd wc (some cont); chem disp; mv service pnt; shwrs; el pnts (3A) inc; Indtte (inc dryer); shop 500m; snacks; bar; playgrnd; games area; ski shuttle bus; internet; TV rm; 30% statics; no dogs; adv bkg; quiet; ccard acc. "Excel, clean san facs; beautiful area." ♦ € 32.00 2011*

⊞ **DOBBIACO/TOBLACH** *2E1* (3km E Urban) **Aree di Sosta Trattoria da Claudia, Via Stazione 7, 39038 San Candido/Innichen (BZ) [0474 913324; fax 912570; trattoriadamirko@alice.it]** Fr W just bef Austrian border on SS49. On W edge San Candido turn R over rlwy line into Via Pizach, then L into Via Matthias Schranzhofer; at T-junc into Via Stazione, site sp. M'vans only. Sm, hdstg, pt shd; wc; mv service pnt; shwrs €1; el pnts inc; shop, rest in vill; dogs; Eng spkn; rd & rlwy noise. € 15.00 2007*

⊞ **DOBBIACO/TOBLACH** *2E1* (2km S Rural) *46.70642, 12.21834* **Camping Toblachersee, Toblacher-See 3, 39034 Dobbiaco/Toblach (BZ) [0474 972294 or 973138; fax 976647; info@toblachersee.com; www.toblachersee.com]** Site sp fr rd SS51 dir Cortina d'Ampezzo - last 200m v narr. Lge, mkd pitch, pt sl, terr, pt shd; htd wc; chem disp; mv service pnt; fam bthrm; shwrs inc; el pnts (16A) metered; gas; lndtte; shop & 3km; rest; snacks; bar; playgrnd; htd, covrd pool 2km; lake adj & shgl beach adj; tennis 1.5km; ski slopes nr; dogs €4; Eng spkn; adv bkg; quiet. "Beautiful area; gd walking & skiing; luxurious san facs; some sm pitches; walk/cycle rte into town." ♦ € 29.30 2007*

⊞ **DOBBIACO/TOBLACH** *2E1* (2km W Rural) *46.73431, 12.19362* **Camping International Olympia, Via Pusteria 1, 39034 Dobbiaco/Toblach (BZ) [0474 972147; fax 972713; info@camping-olympia.com; www.camping-olympia.it]** Trun off S49 at E end of Villabassa/Niederdorf by-pass, sp 'camping'. Site 1km E of Villabassa. Lge, mkd pitch, pt shd; wc; chem disp; mv service pnt; some serviced pitches; sauna; shwrs inc; el pnts (6A) inc; gas; lndtte; shop; rest; snacks; bar; playgrnd; pool; paddling pool; cycle hire; solarium; ski school; entmnt; TV; 30% statics; dogs €4.50; Eng spkn; adv bkg; quiet; ccard acc; CCI. "Vg, luxurious facs; magnificent views; cycle tracks; gd walks; sm zoo; excel." ♦ € 31.00 2010*

⊞ **EDOLO** *1D1* (1.5km W Rural) *46.17648, 10.31333* **Camping Adamello, Via Campeggio 10, Loc Nembra, 25048 Edolo (BS) [tel/fax 0364 71694; info@campingadamello.com; www.campingadamello.com]** On rd 39 fr Edolo to Aprica; after 1.5km turn sharp L down narr lane by rest; camping sp on rd; diff app. Med, pt sl, terr, pt shd; wc; chem disp; shwrs inc; el pnts (6A) €1.50; lndtte; shop; rest, snacks 1km; bar; 50% statics; dogs €3; poss cr; quiet; no ccard acc. "Useful NH; beautiful mountain site; steep rds all round; very diff approach from West, quiet for couples nothing for children." ♦ € 27.00 2011*

⊞ **ENTRACQUE** *1B2* (1km NW Rural) *44.24965, 7.38939* **Camping Valle Gesso, Strada Provinciale per Valdieri 3, 12010 Entracque (CN) [tel/fax 0171 978247; info@campingvallegesso.com; www.campingvallegesso.com]** Fr Cuneo on S20 to Borgo S Dalmazzo, R to Valdieri, then twd Entracque, site sp. Med, mkd pitch, shd; htd wc (some cont); chem disp; mv service pnt; shwrs €1; el pnts (3-6A) €2.80-3.80; lndtte; shop; snacks; bar; playgrnd; pool high ssn; paddling pool; entmnt; TV; 30% statics; dogs €3.80; phone; sep car park; poss cr; Eng spkn; quiet; ccard acc. "Mountain walking area in Argentera National Park." € 21.50 2008*

ERACLEA MARE see Lido di Jesolo *2E2*

⊞ **FALZE DI PIAVE** *2E1* (700m S Rural) **Parking Le Grave, Via Passo Barca, 31010 Falze-di-Piave (TV) [0339 2348523; fax 0438 86896; belleluigi@libero.it; www.legrave.it]** Fr A27 exit Conegliano & turn R onto SP15 then SS13 to Susegana. At Ponte-della-Priula turn onto SP34 to Falze-di-Piave. Fr town cent turn L just past war memorial into Via Passo Barca, site on R. Sm, unshd; no wc or shwrs; chem disp; mv service pnt; el pnts(4A) inc; BBQ; playgrnd; quiet. "CL-type site in delightful area; friendly, helpful owner; gd walking/cycling. Wine tasting last w/end May." € 10.00 2011*

FANO *2E3* (6km SE Coastal) *43.81138, 13.07694* **Camping Mare Blu, Torrette, SS Adriatica Sud, 61032 Torrette-di-Fano (PU) [0721 884201; fax 884389; mareblu@camping.it; www.camping.it/mareblu]** A14/E55 exit Fano onto SS16, site bet km 256 & 257. Lge, mkd pitch, pt shd; wc; chem disp; mv service pnt; some serviced pitches; shwrs inc; el pnts (4-6A) inc; lndtte; shop; rest; snacks; bar; playgrnd; sand beach adj; 80% statics; no dogs high ssn; phone; poss cr; adv bkg; quiet; red CCI. ♦ 5 Apr-22 Sep. € 32.00 2008*

FANO *2E3* (8km S Rural) *43.74600, 13.08140* **Camping Mar y Sierra, Via delle Grazia 22, 61039 Stacciola-di-San Costanza (PU) [tel/fax 0721 930044; info@marysierra.it; www.marysierra.com]** Exit A14 at Marotta onto SS424 dir Pergola. In 4.5km at Ponte Rio pass Opel/Alfa Romeo g'ge & turn R onto SP154 dir Stacciola. Site on R in 2km. Med, mkd pitch, terr, pt shd; wc; chem disp; mv service pnt; shwrs inc; el pnts (16A) inc; lndtte; shop 8km; tradsmn; rest; snacks; bar; playgrnd; pool; paddling pool; private sand beach 8km; tennis; cycle hire; fitness rm; TV rm; 10% statics; bus at site ent; poss cr; Eng spkn; quiet. "Vg, peaceful site with lovely views; helpful staff; facs stretched high ssn; hot water in 1 block only." ♦ 1 Apr-15 Oct. € 28.00 2008*

FARRA D'ALPAGO *2E1* (S Rural) *46.11879, 12.35367* **Camping Sarathei, Lago di Santa Croce, Via al Lago 13, 32016 Farra-d'Alpago (BL) [tel/fax 0437 46996; info@sarathei.it; www.sarathei.it]** Stay on S51 (not a'strada) sp Farra d'Alpago & sp thro vill to site. Lge, mkd pitch, hdstg, pt shd; wc (some cont); chem disp; mv service pnt; shwrs inc; el pnts (3A) inc; lndtte; rest; bar; playgrnd; shgl beach; watersports; cycle hire; 20% statics; dogs free; Eng spkn; no adv bkg; quiet; ccard acc; CCI. "Vg site & san facs; busy at w/end; frequent trains to Venice fr Conegliano; gd windsurfing; 2 hrs m'way to Adriatic coast." ♦ 1 Apr-30 Sep. € 18.50 2007*

FERIOLO see Verbania *1B1*

⊞ **FERRARA** *1D2* (2km NE Rural) *44.85303, 11.63328* **Campeggio Comunale Estense, Via Gramicia 76, 44100 Ferrara [tel/fax 0532 752396; campeggio.estense@freeinternet.it]** Exit A13 Ferrara N. After Motel Nord Ovest on L turn L at next traff lts into Via Porta Catena. Rd is 500m fr city wall around town; foll brown/yellow sps - well sp fr all dirs. Med, pt shd; htd wc (some cont); chem disp; mv service pnt; shwrs inc; el pnts (6A) €3; lndtte; shops, rest 200m; pool in park nrby; cycle hire; golf adj; some stored c'vans; dogs €1.50; site clsd early-Jan to end-Feb; Eng spkn; quiet; ccard acc €50+; 10% red CCI. "Peaceful, well-kept, clean site; helpful staff; lge pitches; ltd privacy in shwrs; interesting town; gd cycle tracks round town; rlwy stn in town for trains to Venice." ♦ € 18.50 2010*

FIANO ROMANO *2E4* (2km W Rural) *42.15167, 12.57670* **Camping I Pini, Via delle Sassete 1/A, 00065 Fiano-Romano [0765 453349; fax 1890941; ipini@camping.it; www.camping.it/roma/ipini or www.ecvacanze.it]** Fr A1/E35 exit sp Roma Nord/Fiano Romano (use R-hand lane for cash toll), foll sp Fiano at rndabt. Take 1st exit at next rndabt sp I Pini & stay on this rd for approx 2km. Take 2nd exit at next rndabt, L at T-junc under bdge, site sp on R. Med, hdg/mkd pitch, pt sl, terr, pt shd; htd wc; chem disp; mv service pnt; shwrs inc; el pnts (6A) inc (poss rev pol); Indtte (inc dryer); shop; rest; snacks; bar; BBQ; playgrnd; pool; paddling pool; tennis; cycle hire; horseriding nrby; fishing; wifi; entmnt; games rm; TV; 60% statics (tour ops); dogs €2; no c'vans/m'vans over 10m high ssn; phone; bus; poss cr; Eng spkn; adv bkg rec high ssn; quiet, but noisy nr bar; ccard acc; red low ssn/CCI. "Well-run, clean, family owned site; excel san facs; helpful, friendly staff; excel rest; access poss diff lge o'fits; kerbs to all pitches; excursions by coach inc daily to Rome or gd train service." ♦ 28 Apr-26 Sep. € 39.00 SBS - Y13 2011*

I'll go online and tell the Club what we think of the campsites we've visited – www.caravanclub.co.uk/europereport

⊞ **FIE/VOLS** *1D1* (3km N Rural) *46.53334, 11.53335* **Camping Alpe di Siusi/Seiser Alm, Loc San Constantino 16, 39050 Fiè-allo-Sciliar/Völs-am-Schlern (BZ) [0471 706459; fax 707382; info@camping-seiseralm.com; www.camping-seiseralm.com]** Leave Bolzano on SS12 (not A22) sp Brixen & Brenner. After approx 7km take L fork in tunnel mouth sp Tiers, Fiè. Foll rd thro Fiè, site in 3km dir Castelrotto, sp on L. Lge, mkd pitch, hdstg, terr, unshd; htd wc; chem disp; mv service pnt; baby facs; sauna; shwrs inc; el pnts (16A) metered; Indtte (inc dryer); shop; rest; snacks; bar; playgrnd; golf 1km; sat TV; 20% statics; dogs €4.50; bus; phone; site clsd 5 Nov to 20 Dec; poss cr; Eng spkn; adv bkg; quiet; CCI. "Well-organised site with gd views; impressive, luxury undergrnd san facs block; private san facs avail; vg walking/skiing; an amazing experience!" € 29.50 2009*

⊞ **FIESOLE** *1D3* (1km NE Rural) *43.80666, 11.30638* **Camping Panoramico, Via Peramonda 1, 50014 Fiesole (FI) [055 599069; fax 59186; panoramico@florencecamping.com; www.florencecamping.com]** Foll sp for Fiesole & Camping Panoramico fr Florence; site on R. Rd to Fiesole v hilly & narr thro busy tourist area. Lge, terr, pt shd; wc; chem disp; shwrs inc; el pnts (3A) inc; gas; Indtte; shop; bar; rest in high ssn; playgrnd; pool; internet; 20% statics; dogs free; poss cr; Eng spkn; quiet; ccard acc. "Access v diff - more suitable tenters; site soggy in wet; ltd water points; Florence 20 mins bus but 1.5km steep walk to stop; excel views." ♦ € 38.80 2009*

FIGLINE VALDARNO *1D3* (2.5km W Rural) *43.61111, 11.44940* **Camping Norcenni Girasole Club, Via Norcenni 7, 50063 Figline-Valdarno (FI) [055 915141; fax 9151402; girasole@ecvacanze.it; www.ecvacanze.it]** Fr a'strada A1, dir Rome, take exit 24 (sp Incisa SS69) to Figline-Valdarno; turn R in vill & foll sp to Greve; site sp Girasole; steep app rd to site with some twists for 3km. V lge, some hdg pitch, terr, pt shd; wc (some cont); chem disp; mv service pnt; baby facs; private bthrm extra; sauna; shwrs inc; el pnts (6A) inc; gas; Indtte (inc dryer); shop; tradsmn; rest; snacks; bar; BBQ; playgrnd; 2 pools (1 covrd); paddling pool; jacuzzi; tennis; games area; horseriding; cycle hire; fitness cent; games rm; wifi; entmnt; TV; dogs free; twin-axles acc (rec check in adv); station 1.5km; bus to Florence; excursions; initial cash payment to smart card req for all expenses on site (cash not acc); busy at w/end in ssn & poss v cr; Eng spkn; adv bkg; ccard acc; red low ssn/long stay; CCI. "Excel, well-run site; some pitches sm; steep site rds poss diff lge outfits; steel pegs rec; upper level pool area excel for children; site clsd 1330-1530; poss long walk to san facs block; site hilly, poss unsuitable elderly & disabled; wine tasting trips; gd touring base." ♦ 1 Apr-13 Oct. € 45.50 SBS - Y07 2011*

FINALE LIGURE *1B2* (1.5km N Rural) *44.18395, 8.35349* **Eurocamping Calvisio, Via Calvisio 37, 17024 Finale-Ligure (SV) [019 600491; fax 601240; info@eurocampingcalvisio.it; www.eurocampingcalvisio.it]** On SS1 Savona-Imperia, turn R at ent to Finale-Ligure; sp to site in Calvisio vill. Med, hdg/mkd pitch, shd; wc (some cont); chem disp; shwrs €0.50; el pnts (6A) inc; Indtte (inc dryer); shop; rest; snacks; bar; playgrnd; pool high ssn; paddling pool; sand beach 2km; solarium; wifi; entmnt; 80% statics; dogs; sep car park high ssn; poss cr; adv bkg; quiet; ccard acc; red low ssn. "Security guard at night; clean, well-maintained san facs." ♦ Easter- 5 Nov. € 54.50 2010*

⊞ **FINALE LIGURE** *1B2* (5km NE Rural) *44.1960, 8.3740* **Camping San Martino, Le Manie, 17029 Varigotti (SV) [tel/fax 019 698250; campingsanmartino@campingsanmartino.it; www.campingsanmartino.it]** Exit A10 for Spotorno, turn R & foll sp Tosse, Magnone, Le Manie. Half hour of mountain rds to site. Care needed with app. Med, pt sl, shd; htd wc (some cont); chem disp; mv service pnt; shwrs; el pnts (3A); Indtte; shop & 4km; rest; bar; playgrnd; sand beach 4km; tennis; games area; cycle hire; 50% statics; dogs €2; phone; poss cr; adv bkg ess Jul/Aug; quiet; ccard acc; red long stay. "Winter storage arranged; quiet among pines clear of busy coastal strip, 1000m up; excel san facs." € 23.00 2007*

⊞ **FIRENZE** *1D3* (3km NE Urban) *43.79066, 11.29005* **Camp & Ostello Municipal Villa di Camerata, Viala Augusto Righi 2/4, 50100 Firenze [055 601451; fax 610300; firenze@ostellionline.org]** Exit a'strada at Firenze Sud. Foll any sp for Fiesole several km fr a'strada. Rd crosses Rv Arno at Ponte G da Verrazzano, then cross rlwy & cont along Via Lungo L'Affrico. Watch for camp sp/Youth Hostel sp (Ostello) on L at rndabt into Viale Augusto Righi. Turn L, site is 50m on R in Youth Hostel grounds. V poor sp around Florence & poss diff to find. Med, pt sl, pt shd, mkd pitch, hdstg; wc; chem disp; mv service pnt; shwrs inc; el pnts (5A) inc; Indtte; shop 700m; rest 700m; snacks; bar; bus; poss cr; Eng spkn; adv bkg; noisy; red CCI. "Bus to Florence every 20 mins (tickets fr hostel office); access to Youth Hostel facs low ssn; hot water to shwrs only - other san facs basic but clean; gd local rest; poss unkempt low ssn." € 30.00 2009*

⊞ **FIRENZE** *1D3* (3km SE Urban) *43.76183, 11.26801* **Camping Michelangelo, Viale Michelangelo 80, 50125 Firenze [055 6811977; fax 689348; michelangelo@evacanze.it; www.ecvacanze.it]** Exit a'strada A1/E35 at Firenze Certosa or Firenze Sud; foll sp for Piazzale Michelangelo; site on L (N) in approx 6km, 200m past Piazzale (lge view point); steep site ent. Lge, some hdstg, pt sl, pt shd; wc (mainly cont); chem disp; mv service pnt; shwrs inc; el pnts (2-5A) inc; gas; Indtte; supmkt high ssn; rest 1km; snacks; bar; playgrnd; cycle hire; golf 10km; wifi; 30% statics; dogs €2; phone; bus; poss v cr; Eng spkn; quiet; ccard acc (€103 min); CCI. "Views over city fr some pitches; noise fr jukebox & bar at top end of site high ssn; cr, busy, backpacker site but well-run; gd rests walking dist; bus (tickets fr recep); v conv to visit city on foot; arr early for gd pitch; diff sl pitches in wet weather; check for suitable place bef booking in; care using light switches; old san facs in poor condition; few pitches suitable c'vans & most diff for m'vans." € 37.70 2011*

FIRENZE *1D3* (12km SE Rural) *43.70138, 11.40527* **Camping Village Il Poggetto, Via Il Poggetto 143, 50010 Troghi (FI) [tel/fax 055 8307323; info@campingilpoggetto.com; www.campingilpoggetto.com]** Fr S on E35/A1 a'strada take Incisa exit & turn L dir Incisa. After 400m turn R dir Firenze, site in 5km on L. Fr N on A1 exit Firenze-Sud dir Bagno a Ripoli/S. Donato; go thro S. Donato to Troghi, site on R, well sp. Narr, hilly app rd & sharp turn - app fr S easier. Lge, hdg/mkd pitch, pt sl, pt terr, pt shd; wc (some cont); chem disp; mv service pnt; baby facs; private san facs avail; shwrs inc; el pnts (7A) inc (poss rev pol); gas; Indtte; shop; tradsmn; rest; snacks; bar; playgrnd; 2 pools; cycle hire; table tennis; internet; 5% statics; dogs €2.20; phone; bus adj; money change; poss cr; Eng spkn; adv bkg ess high ssn; quiet but some m'way noise; red long stay; ccard acc over €200; 10% red CCI (low ssn). "Superb, picturesque,family-run site in attractive location inc vineyard; clean, modern facs; lovely pool; bus to Florence 45mins - tickets fr recep; trains fr Incisa Valdarno (free parking at stn); excursions; gd rest on site; low ssn offers for long stay (7+ days)." ♦ 1 Apr-15 Oct. € 34.00 2009*

⊞ **FIRENZE** *1D3* (3km SW Rural) *43.72146, 11.21861* **Camping Internazionale Firenze, Via San Cristofano 2, 50029 Bottai (FI) [055 2374704; fax 2373412; internazionale@florencecamping.com; www.florencecamping.com]** Exit A1/E35 for Firenze/Certosa & foll sp twds Florence. Site well sp in 1.4km. Fairly steep climb on narr, v congested app rd. Med, pt sl, terr, pt shd; wc; shwrs; chem disp; mv service pnt; el pnts (6A) inc (rev pol); gas; Indtte; shop; rest; snacks; bar; playgrnd; pool; internet; entmnt; 50% statics; dogs; bus; poss cr; Eng spkn; rd noise; ccard acc. "Conv Florence, Siena; gates clsd 0000-0700 ; vg, clean facs; friendly recep; touring pitches on hilltop only - levelling poss diff; site diff in wet weather; poss cr." ♦ € 34.00 2011*

FLORENCE see Firenze *1D3*

FOCE DI VARANO see Rodi Garganico *2G4*

FOLLONICA *1D3* (6km E Rural) *42.91291, 10.85253* **Camping Vallicella, Loc Vallicella, 58020 Scarlino (GR) [0566 37229; fax 37232; info@vallicellavillage.com; www.vallicellavillage.com]** Fr E80, S1 Via Aurelia exit for Scarlino-Scalo, foll sp Scarlino & site. Lge, hdg/mkd pitch, terr, pt shd; wc (some cont); chem disp; mv service pnt; baby facs; private san facs avail; shwrs inc; el pnts (4-6A) inc; Indtte (inc dryer); shop; rest; snacks; bar; no BBQ; playgrnd; pool; paddling pool; sand beach 6km; tennis; cycle & boat hire; tennis; archery; horseriding 3km; golf 10km; wifi; TV rm; 40% statics; dogs €4.50; sep car park; adv bkg; quiet; ccard acc. ♦ 23 Apr-1 Oct. € 35.00 (CChq acc) 2011*

⊞ **FOLLONICA** *1D3* (3km NW Coastal) *42.94339, 10.71522* **Camping Parco Vacanze Il Veliero, Isole Eolie, 58022 Follonica (GR) [0566 260099; fax 260100; ilveliero@sivacanze.it; www.sivacanze.it]** Exit SS1 Follonica Nord S onto SP152 Pratoranieri, site sp. Lge, pt shd; wc; chem disp; mv service pnt; private san facs on pitches; sauna; shwrs; el pnts inc; Indtte; shop; rest; snacks; bar; playgrnd; pool; paddling pool; sand beach 1km; tennis; cycle hire; golf 12km; some statics; adv bkg; quiet. € 50.00 2009*

FOLLONICA *1D3* (5km NW Coastal) *42.95029, 10.68681* **Camping Village Pappasole, Loc Torre Mozza, Via di Carbonifera 14, 57020 Vignale-Riotorto (LI) [0565 20414 or 20420; fax 20346; info@pappasole.it; www.pappasole.it]** Fr SS1 take Follonica Nord exit onto SS322 & foll sp twd Piombino. After approx 1km turn L twd Torre Mozza onto overpass over m'way. Site in 1km. V lge, hdg/mkd pitch, hdstg, pt shd; wc; chem disp; mv service pnt; baby facs; private san facs + kitchen avail; shwrs inc; el pnts (3-10A) inc; gas; Indtte (inc dryer); shop; rest; snacks; bar; BBQ; playgrnd; pool; sand beach adj; watersports; tennis; cycle hire; games area; wifi; entmnt; 70% statics; dogs €9; phone; poss cr; Eng spkn; adv bkg; rd & rlwy noise & poss noisy at w/end; ccard acc; red long stay/low ssn; CCI. "Excel site; helpful staff; vg beach; lots of tourist info." ♦ 3 Apr-16 Oct. € 56.50 2010*

FOLLONICA *1D3* (9km NW Rural) *42.96705, 10.65611* **Campeggio Riotorto, Loc Campo al Fico 15, 57020 Vignale-Riotorto (LI) [0565 21008; fax 21118; info@campingriotorto.com; www.campingriotorto.com]** Fr SS1 Via Aurelia exit Vignale-Riotorto. At x-rds turn R & go over by-pass, site sp. Lge, shd; wc; mv service pnt; shwrs inc; el pnts inc; shop; snacks; bar; playgrnd; pool; paddling pool; sand beach 2km; tennis; cycle hire; statics; dogs €5; sep car park; adv bkg; quiet. "Sm pitches; gd touring base." ♦ 22 Apr-19 Sep. € 35.00 2008*

FONDOTOCE see Verbania *1B1*

⊞ **FORNI DI SOPRA** *2E1* (2km E Rural) *46.42564, 12.56928* **Camping Tornerai, Stinsans. Via Nazionale, 33024 Forni-di-Sopra (UD) [0433 88035]** Site sp on SS52 Tolmezzo-Pieve di Cadore rd, 2km E of Forni-di-Sopra (approx 35km by rd fr Pieve-di-Cadore). Sm, pt sl, pt shd; wc (cont); chem disp (wc); el pnts (2A) €1 (extra for 6A) (long lead poss req); 50% statics; dogs €2; poss cr; Eng spkn; quiet; ccard acc. "Conv CL-type site for Forni-di-Sopra chairlift & Passo-della-Mauria; gd san facs." € 20.00 2009*

FORTE DEI MARMI *1C3* (1km NE Rural) *43.97979, 10.17397* **Camping Internazionale Versilia, Via Vittoria Apuana 33, Loc Querceta, 55042 Forte-dei-Marmi (LU) [0584 880764; fax 752118; campingversilia@camping.it; www.camping.it/toscana/versilia]** Site sp fr Versilia exit fr a'strada. Med, shd; wc; own san rec; chem disp; shwrs €0.60; el pnts (5A) inc; Indtte; shop; rest; snacks; bar; sand beach 2km; cycle hire; solarium; games rm; TV rm; noise fr m'way & rlwy; Eng spkn; noisy; ccard acc. "Easy cycle to v smart town; spacious pitches; many midges; NH only." 19 Apr-30 Sep. € 29.00 2008*

FUCINE DI OSSANA see Dimaro *1D1*

FUSINA see Venezia *2E2*

⊞ **GAGLIANO DEL CAPO** *3A4* (E Rural/Coastal) *39.82444, 18.36861* **Centro Vacenze Santa Maria di Leuca, SS 275, Km 35.700, 73034 Gagliano del Capo (LE) [0833 548157; fax 548485; centrovacanze@campingsmleuca.com; www.campingsmleuca.com]** S on S613 to Lecce then S101 to Gallipolli & S274 dir Santa Maria di Leuca. Foll S275 sp Gagliano del Capo & site in 3km. V lge, shd; wc; chem disp; mv service pnt; private san facs avail; shwrs; el pnts €2; Indtte; shop & 2km; rest & 200m; snacks; bar; playgrnd; pool; paddling pool; tennis; sand beach 3km; entmnt; TV; some statics; dogs €2; shuttle bus to beach; adv bkg; quiet. "Pleasant site amongst pine, eucalyptus & olive trees." ♦ € 43.00 2008*

⊞ **GALLIPOLI** *3A4* (3km N Coastal) *40.07444, 18.00888* **Centro Vacanze La Masseria, Via Garibaldi 89, 73014 Gallipoli (LE) [0833 202295; fax 281014; info@lamasseria.net; www.lamasseria.net]** N fr Gallipoli on coast rd, site on R adj beach. Lge, mkd pitch, shd; wc; chem disp; mv service pnt; private bthrms avail; shwrs inc; el pnts (3-6A) inc; Indtte; shop; rest; snacks; bar; BBQ; playgrnd; pool 3km; private rock/shgl beach adj; tennis; games area; entmnt; 5% statics; dogs; bus; poss cr; quiet; ccard acc; CCI. "Vg site; modern san facs." € 35.00 (3 persons) 2008*

GALLIPOLI *3A4* (4km SE Coastal) *39.99870, 18.02590* **Camping Baia di Gallipoli, Litoranea per Santa Maria di Leuca, 73014 Gallipoli (LE) [0833 273210; fax 275405; info@baiadigallipoli.com; www.baiadigallipoli.com]** Fr Brindisi/Lecce take S101 to Gallipoli. Exit at sp Matino-Lido Pizzo & foll sp to site, on coast rd bet Gallipoli & Sta Maria di Leuca. V lge, pt shd; htd wc; chem disp; mv service pnt; shwrs inc; el pnts inc; Indtte (inc dryer); shop; rest; snacks; bar; BBQ; playgrnd; pool; paddling pool; sand beach 800m (free shuttle bus); tennis; games area; wifi; entmnt; excursions; TV rm; statics; dogs (sm only) €2.50; sep car park; quiet; ccard acc. ♦ 1 Apr-30 Sep. € 40.00 (CChq acc) 2009*

GEMONA DEL FRIULI *2E1* (1km W Rural) *46.29086, 13.12975* **Camping Ai Pioppi, Via Bersaglio 118, 33013 Gemona-del-Friuli (UD) [tel/fax 0432 980358; bar-camping-taxi@aipioppi.it; www.aipioppi.it]** Exit A23/E55 at Gemona-Ossopo exit, R onto SS13. Site well sp fr N & S on SS13. Med, some hdstg, sl, pt shd; wc; chem disp; shwrs inc; el pnts (5-16A) inc; gas; Indtte; shop & 1km; rest 200m; snacks; bar; dogs; adv bkg; quiet. "Friendly site; some awkward pitches; gd facs; ltd el pnts; NH only." 15 Mar-15 Nov. € 20.00 2008*

GEMONA DEL FRIULI *2E1* (12km NW Rural) *46.32506, 13.06289* **Camping Lago dei Tre Comuni, Via Tolmezzo 52, Alesso, 33010 Trasaghis (UD) [0432 979199; info@campinglagodeitrecomuni.com]** Leave A23 exit sp Gemona-de-Friuli. On ent Gemona foll sp for Alesso & Lago di Cavazzo. Site sp on ent Alesso. Med, mkd pitch, pt sl, pt shd; wc; chem disp; shwrs inc; el pnts inc; Indtte; shops 2km; rest adj; snacks; bar; BBQ; playgrnd; lake adj; canoeing; windsurfing; dogs free; quiet; ccard acc. "Excel, grassy pitches; gd, clean, modern facs; walking trails; gd cycling; attractive vills; friendly, helpful owner." ♦ 1 May-30 Oct. € 22.00 2008*

GEMONA DEL FRIULI *2E1* (12km NW Rural) *46.32570, 13.06317* **Camping Val del Lago, Loc Alesso, Via Tolmezzo 54, 33010 Trasaghis (UD) [0432 979164; fax 979455]** Exit A23 sp Gemona-del-Friuli onto S13 N. Foll sp for Alesso, Trasaghis & Lago di Cavazzo. Site adj Camping Lago dei Tre Comuni. Sm, mkd pitch, shd; wc; chem disp; shwrs inc; el pnts inc (poss rev pol); shop 2km; rest; snacks; bar; lake sw adj; statics; dogs €3; Eng spkn; quiet. "Superbly situated; friendly owner; gd facs." 1 Apr-30 Sep. € 24.00 2009*

GENOA see Genova *1C2*

GENOVA *1C2* (10km E Rural/Coastal) *44.38085, 9.07215* **Camping Genova Est, Via Marconi, Loc Cassa, 16031 Bogliasco (GE) [tel/fax 010 3472053; info@camping-genova-est.it; www.camping-genova-est.it]** Sp fr SS1 (Via Aurelia) in both dir. Exit A12/E80 Genova/Nervi exit & foll La Spezia sp to Bogliasco, look for sp on wall on L. V steep narr access, unsuitable without high power/weight ratio. Med, terr, pt shd; wc; mv service pnt; shwrs; el pnts (5A) €2.70; gas; Indtte; shop; rest, snacks, bar high ssn; BBQ; playgrnd; shgl beach 1.5km; dogs €2; bus; sep car park; Eng spkn; quiet; ccard acc. "Narr pitches; manhandling vans poss req; upper facs better than lower; steep footpath to Bogliasco; adv bkg rec during boat show in Oct." 15 Mar-20 Oct. € 25.00 2010*

⊞ **GENOVA** *1C2* (9km W Urban/Coastal) *44.43055, 8.81364* **Camping Villa Doria, Via al Campeggio Villa Doria 15, 16156 Pegli [tel/fax 010 6969600; villadoria@camping.it]** Take SS1 coast rd W fr Genova to cent Pegli, past airport thro dock waterfront & look out for brown site sp on R by bus stop at traff lts. Foll narr & steep app to site - care needed. Site sp on wall on R round blind L-hand bend. Or exit A26 sp Pegli, turn W & foll site sp. Sm, mkd pitch, pt sl, unshd; htd wc (some cont); chem disp; mv service pnt; shwrs inc; el pnts (3-10A) inc; gas; Indtte (inc dryer); shop; rest 1km; snacks; bar; playgrnd; beach 1km; solarium; TV; dogs; phone; bus; sep car park; site clsd Jan; poss cr; Eng spkn; ccard acc; CCI. "Friendly, helpful owner; conv trains to Genoa & La Spezia; not rec for lge o'fits due narr access rd & o'hanging branches; footpath to vill; gd site but needs some TLC." ♦ € 30.00 2010*

ITALY

ITALY

⊞ **GENOVA** *1C2* (15km W Coastal) *44.41437, 8.70475* **Caravan Park La Vesima, Via Aurelia, Km 547, 16100 Arenzano (GE) [010 6199672; fax 6199686; info@caravanparklavesima.it; www.caravanparklavesima.it]** E of Arenzano on coast rd, clearly sp. Or leave A10 at Arenzano & go E on coast rd. Med, mkd pitch, hdstg, unshd; htd wc (cont); chem disp; baby facs; fam bthrm; shwrs €0.50; el pnts (3A) inc (poss rev pol); gas; Indtte; shop high ssn & 3km; rest, snacks, bar high ssn; private shgl beach adj; 90% statics; no dogs; poss cr; Eng spkn; adv bkg; rd, rlwy noise; CCI. "Useful low ssn NH/sh stay; gd security; gd, clean san facs; v cr, noisy high ssn & some pitches tight." € 32.60 2010*

GIGNOD see Aosta *1B1*

GIOVINAZZO *2H4* (1km S Coastal) *41.18246, 16.6826* **Camping Campofreddo, Loc Ponte, 70054 Giovinazzo (BA) [080 3942112; fax 3943290; torraco@libero.it; www.campofreddo.it]** Exit A14/E55 at Bitonto dir Giovinazzo. Site sp on coast rd. Lge, pt shd; wc; chem disp; mv service pnt; shwrs €0.30; el pnts (3A) inc; Indtte rm; shop; rest, snacks adj; rocky beach; fishing; tennis; 90% statics; dogs; adv bkg; quiet; ccard acc. "Poss unreliable el pnts; Many beautiful churches in area." ♦ 20 May-20 Sep. € 23.00 2008*

GIOVINAZZO *2H4* (1km NW Coastal) *41.19167, 16.65769* **Camping La Baia, Loc Trincea, 70054 Giovinazzo (BA) [tel/fax 0803 945165; camping.labaia@libero.it; www.campinglabaia.it]** Well sp fr S16bis onto S16, then no sp. Turn L at traff lts sp 'Lungomare', then L at end. Cont for 1km, site on L. Med, mkd pitch, some hdstg; pt shd; wc (mainly cont); shwrs €0.50; el pnts (6A) €3; Indtte; shop 1km; tradsmn; snacks; bar; shgl beach adj; 40% statics; dogs €3; poss noisy (rd & disco adj); ccard acc; red CCI. "Attractive town & close to cathedral town of Trani & 13thC Castel de Monte; no sea views; gd NH." ♦ 1 May-30 Sep. € 26.00 2010*

GIULIANOVA LIDO *2F3* (2.9km N Coastal) *42.77790, 13.95613* **Camping Don Antonio (formerly Baviera Holiday Ovest), Lungamare Zara Nord 127, 64022 Giulianova-Lido (TE) [085 8008928; fax 8004420; baviera@camping.it; www.campingbaviera.it]** Exit A14/E55 dir Giulianova, site sp at Lido, 2km N of Giulianova, sp adj Camping Holiday. Med, mkd pitch, pt shd; wc; serviced pitches; shwrs inc; el pnts (6A) inc; Indtte; shop, rest, snacks in Cmp Holiday adj; pool; sand beach adj; playgrnd; games area; tennis adj; watersports; entmnt; excursions; sep car park high ssn; statics; dogs free (not acc Jul/Aug); adv bkg; quiet but some rlwy noise; red low ssn/snr citizens; ccard acc; red CCI. "Excel family site; lots to do in area." ♦ 16 May-13 Sep. € 42.00 2011*

GIULIANOVA LIDO *2F3* (2.9km N Coastal) *42.77790, 13.95588* **Camping Village Holiday, Lungamare Zara, 64022 Giulianova-Lido (TE) [085 8000053; fax 8004420; holiday@camping.it; www.villaggioholiday.it]** Exit A14/E55 dir Giulianova, site sp at Lido, adj Baviera Camping. Lge, pt shd; wc (some cont); chem disp; mv service pnt; serviced pitches; shwrs inc; el pnts (6A) €1.86; Indtte; supmkt; rest; snacks; bar; playgrnd; pool; sand beach adj; watersports; tennis; games area; entmnt;TV; sep car park; 20% statics; dogs free (not acc Jul/Aug); poss cr; adv bkg; quiet but some rlwy noise & tannoy; ccard acc; red low ssn; red CCI. "Excel family site; sm pitches; site clsd 1400-1600." ♦ 24 Apr-20 Sep. € 42.00 2009*

GIULIANOVA LIDO *2F3* (500m S Coastal) *42.73510, 13.98095* **Camping Stork, Viale Del Mare 11, 64020 Cologna-Spiaggia (TE) [0858 937076; fax 937542; info@campingstork.com; www.campingstork.com]** Fr a'strada foll sp on SS80 to Giulianova; at junc with SS16 turn R for 300m, turn L at traff lts, site sp. V lge, mkd pitch, shd; wc; chem disp; mv service pnt; baby facs; shwrs inc; el pnts (6A) inc; Indtte; supmkt; rest; snacks; bar; playgrnd; pool; paddling pool; sand beach adj; watersports; tennis; games area; cycle hire; wifi; entmnt; TV; cash machine; 40% statics; dogs €2.50; phone; sep car park high ssn; adv bkg; ccard acc; red long stay. ♦ 19 Apr-13 Sep. € 38.50 (CChq acc) 2011*

GIUNCUGNANO *1C2* (2km W Rural) *44.20680, 10.23520* **Camping Argegna, Via Argegna, 55030 Giuncugnano (LU) [0583 611182; fax 611536; info@toscanacampclub.com; www.toscanacampclub.com]** Exit A1 at Aulla. After bdge turn R; at rndabt foll sp Fivizzano. Approx 5km bef Fivizzano turn R onto rd SR445; foll sp Lucca to Carpinelli Pass, site sp in 4km on L - foll rd (approx 4m wide) to site. NB Fr Giuncugnano rte to site narr & winding for 20km; poor surface in parts. Sm, mkd pitch; shd; wc; mv service pnt; shwrs; el pnts €2.20; Indtte; shop; rest, snacks, bar 100m; BBQ; cooking facs; games area; WiFi; TV rm; some statics; dogs; adv bkg; quiet. "Peaceful site in lovely, little-known, interesting area." 1 May-15 Oct. € 26.00 (CChq acc) 2011*

GLURNS/GLORENZA see Mals/Malles Venosta *1D1*

GRADO *2E1* (8km NE Rural) *45.70750, 13.48728* **Camping All'Argine (Part Naturist), Via Averto 6, 34070 Fossalon-di-Grado (GO) [tel/fax 0431 88156; agriargine@libero.it]** Fr Monfalcone dir Grado on SP19, turn L at sp Fossalon (adj water tower), then R into Via Averto. Sm, pt shd; wc; chem disp; shwrs; el pnts inc; Indry rm; shop 5km; sand beach 2km; adv bkg; quiet; CCI. "Quiet farm site adj nature reserve." ♦ 25 Apr-30 Sep. € 20.00 2008*

GRADO *2E1* (2km E Coastal) *45.67848, 13.42021* **Camping Al Bosco, Loc La Rotta, 34073 Grado (GO) [043 180485; fax 181008; info@campingalbosco.it; www.campingalbosco.it]** Site in dunes E of Grado. App via narr rd, ent 3.6km, sp. Lge, pt shd; wc; shwrs €0.30; el pnts (3A) inc; Indtte (inc dryer); shop; rest; snacks; bar; playgrnd; sand beach 500m; cycle hire; no dogs; poss cr; adv bkg ess Jul/Aug; ccard acc. "Poss long walk to facs; reasonable site." 1 May-15 Sep. € 28.00 2009*

GRAVEDONA *1C1* (3km NE Rural) *46.15070, 9.33129* **Camping Europa, Via Case Sparse 16, 22013 Domaso (CO) [0344 96044; fax 96024; info@hotelcampingeuropa.com; www.hotelcampingeuropa.com]** Site on L bef x-ing rv bdge on ent Domaso fr N. Med, mkd pitch, pt shd; wc; shwrs €0.75; el pnts (3-6A) inc; Indtte; rest 100m; bar; shgl beach; pool; lake sw; watersports; some statics; dogs €2.50; poss noise fr adj hotel at w/end; red CCI. 1 Apr-18 Oct. € 23.50 2008*

GRAVEDONA *1C1* (3km NE Rural) *46.15438, 9.33701* **Camping Le Vele, 244 Via Case Sparse, 22013 Domaso [0344 965049; fax 536107; levele@domaso.it; www.levele.domaso.it]** Site sp fr SS340. Med, mkd pitch, pt shd; htd wc; chem disp; mv service pnt; sauna; shwrs inc; el pnts (3A) inc; Indtte (inc dryer); shop nr; rest; snacks; bar; BBQ; playgrnd; htd pool; lake sw & beach adj; watersports; fitness cent; internet; 15% statics; dogs free; bus 200m; adv bkg; quiet; ccard acc. "Clean, well-run site; excel san facs; vg situation - direct access to lake; sm pitches." 26 Mar-24 Oct. € 38.00 2010*

When we get home I'm going to post all these site report forms to the Club for next year's guide. The deadline's mid September 2013

GRAVEDONA *1C1* (2km SW Rural) *46.1255, 9.2842* **Camping La Breva, Via Cimitero 19, Loc Cossognini, 22014 Dongo (CO) [tel/fax 034 480017; info@campinglabreva.com; www.campinglabreva.com]** On E o'skts Dongo on SS340, site sp. Rec app fr Colico - avoid Julier Pass fr N if towing. Med, mkd pitch, some hdstg, pt sl, pt shd; htd wc (some cont); chem disp; mv service pnt; shwrs €0.80; el pnts (6A) €1.50; gas; shop 500m; tradsmn; snacks; bar; BBQ; playgrnd; pool 2km; shgl beach adj; lake sw; 5% statics; no dogs; phone; sep car park; poss cr; Eng spkn; adv bkg; red long stay. "Clean, well-run, family-owned site; v helpful staff; pitches tight for lge o'fits; good location next to lake; san facs basic diff to fill van with water or empty; elec usage very poor." ♦ 1 Mar-31 Oct. € 26.00 2011*

GRAVEDONA *1C1* (2km SW Rural) *46.13268, 9.28954* **Camping Magic Lake, Via Vigna del Lago 60, 22014 Dongo (CO) [tel/fax 034 480282; camping@magiclake.it; www.magiclake.it]** Site sp on S340d adj Lake Como. Sm, pt sl, pt shd; htd wc; chem disp; mv service pnt; baby facs; shwrs inc; el pnts (6A) inc; Indtte; shop adj; tradsmn; snacks; bar; BBQ; playgrnd; lake sw adj; TV; 40% statics; dogs €3; bus 100m; poss cr; Eng spkn; adv bkg; quiet; red long stay; CCI. "Excel, friendly, family-run site; walk, cycle to adj vills along lake; excel facs; v.clean mod facs, cycle/kayak hire on site, cycle repairs on site." ♦ 8 Apr-11 Oct. € 29.00 2011*

GROSSETO *1D3* (10km SW Coastal) *42.71390, 11.00870* **Camping Cieloverde, Via della Trappola 180, 58046 Marina-di-Grosseto (GR) [0564 321611; fax 30178; info@cieloverde.it; www.cieloverde.it]** Fr Grosseto take SS322 twd Marina-di-Grosseto, then twd Principina-a-Mare. Site on R. V lge, pt shd; wc; private san facs avail; baby facs; shwrs inc; el pnts (3-6A) inc; Indtte (inc dryer); supmkt; tradsmn; rest; snacks; bar; BBQ; playgrnd; sand beach 800m (free shuttle); watersports; tennis 500m; games area; cycle hire; wifi; entmnt; cinema; TV rm; some statics; adv bkg; ccard acc. "Conv Maremma Nature Reserve; some pitches for RVs." ♦ 9 May-20 Sep. € 49.00 (CChq acc) 2009*

GROSSETO *1D3* (12km SW Coastal) *42.74598, 10.94936* **Camping Le Marze, Strada Statale 322 della Collacchie, Le Marze, 58046 Marina-di-Grosseto (GR) [0564 35501; fax 744503; lemarze@boschettoholiday.it; www.boschettoholiday.it/lemarze]** Fr E80/SS1 S fr Livorno foll dual c'way round Grosseto by-pass. Leave at 4th exit Grossetto Sud; cont dir Grosseto for 5km on SP154; look for sp Marina on L & foll rd for 9km; at traff lts turn R onto SP158 sp Castiglione-della-Pescia, site on R in approx 5km. Lge, shd; wc (cont); chem disp; mv service pnt; baby facs; shwrs inc; el pnts (3A) inc; gas; Indtte (inc dryer); sm shop; rest; pizzeria; bar; BBQ areas (gas/elec); playgrnd; pool; private beach 1km; cycle hire; fishing 500m; games rm; cinema; wifi; entmnt; TV; dogs €4.50; no c'vans/m'vans over 7m; sep car park; 15% statics; adv bkg; quiet; red facs low ssn; ccard acc; red long stay/low ssn; CCI. "Site in pine forest; excel staff; vg san facs; some pitches uneven & poss tight lge o'tfits, espec when site busy; free standing pool not suitable disabled or unsupervised childen; poss mosquitoes; excursions Elba, Florence, Rome, Siena." ♦ 1 Apr-7 Oct. € 49.15 SBS - Y09 2011*

GROTTAMMARE see Martinsicuro *2F3*

GUBBIO *2E3* (3.5km SW Rural) *43.32105, 12.56778* **Camping Citta di Gubbio, Frazione. Cipolleto 49, 06024 Gubbio (PG) [075 9272037; fax 9276620; info@gubbiocamping.com; www.gubbiocamping.com]** Fr E3 take 1st Gubbio exit onto Gubbio by-pass & take Perugia rd. Fork R in 500m beside garden cent into narr lane, site 1.5km on R. Fr Perugia on S298 site sp on L 4km bef Gubbio at bottom of hill at Ponte d'Assi, well sp. Med, pt shd; wc; chem disp; shwrs; el pnts (3A) €3; Indtte; shop, rest, snacks, bar 3.5km; playgrnd; pool; paddling pool; tennis; games area; cycle hire; dogs €2.50; phone; Eng spkn; adv bkg; quiet; red long stay; ccard acc; red CCI. "Excel, friendly, spacious site; clean facs; Gubbio sm medieval city well worth a visit." ♦ 1 Apr-15 Sep. € 29.50 2011*

IDRO *1D1* (2km NE Rural) *45.7540, 10.4981* **Azur Ferienpark Idro Rio Vantone, Via Vantone 45, 25074 Idro (BS) [0365 83125; fax 823663; idro@azur-camping.de; www.azur-camping.de]** Fr Brescia, take S237 N. At S tip of Lago d'Idro, turn E to Idro. thro Crone, on E shore of lake, thro sh tunnel, site 1km on L, last of 3 sites. Lge, shd; wc; chem disp; mv service pnt; baby facs; serviced pitches; shwrs; el pnts (6-16A) €2.50; Indtte; gas; shop; rest; snacks; bar; playgrnd; paddling pool; tennis; lake adj; boat hire; windsurfing; games area; cycle hire; internet; entmnt; TV rm; dogs €2.80; phone; poss cr; adv bkg; quiet; ccard acc; 5% red CCI. "Idyllic on lakeside with beautiful scenery; superb san facs; excel." ♦ 15 Mar-15 Nov. € 27.20 2007*

IMER *1D1* (1km E Rural) *46.14805, 11.79666* **Camping Calavise, Villaggio Sass Maor 36, Loc Pezze, 38050 Imer (TN) [tel/fax 0439 67468; info@campingcalavise.it; www.campingcalavise.it]** Fr Trento on S47 then N on S50 - take care as narr in places. Turn R at traff lts in Imer in front hotel Al Bivio to site in 1km. Med, mkd pitch, terr, pt shd; wc (mainly cont); chem disp; shwrs inc; el pnts (2A) inc; Indtte; shop 500m; rest, snacks 1km; bar; playgrnd; pool; wifi; TV rm; 80% statics; dogs €3; bus 1km; poss cr; Eng spkn; adv bkg; quiet; CCI. "V helpful owner; beautiful area; excel walking in National Park; easy 10km cycle track along rv; vg." ♦ 1 Jun-30 Sep & 8 Dec-30 Apr. € 22.50 2010*

ITALY

⊞ **IMPERIA** *1B3* (1km SW Coastal) *43.86952, 7.99810* **Camping de Wijnstok, Via Poggi 2, 18100 Porto-Maurizio (IM) [tel/fax 0183 64986; info@campingdewijnstok.com; www.campingdewijnstok.com]** Exit A10/E80 Imperia W twds sea, take coast rd SS1 Via Aurelia dir San Remo. At km 651/1 turn dir Poggi, site sp. Med, shd; wc (some cont); chem disp; shwrs €0.70; el pnts (3A) €2; gas; Indtte; shop 200m; snacks; bar; shgl beach 500m; wifi; TV; 80% statics; phone; sep car park; site clsd mid-Dec to mid-Jan; quiet but some rd noise; ccard acc. "Shabby facs ltd low ssn; sm pitches diff for lge o'fits; sh walk to town; NH only." ♦ € 25.00 2010*

⊞ **IMPERIA** *1B3* (2km SW Coastal) *43.87152, 8.00362* **Camping Eucalyptus, Via D'Annunzio 32, 18100 Imperia [tel/fax 0183 61534; info@campingeucalyptus.com; www.campingeucalyptus.com]** Exit A10 Imperia W. Turn L after tolls. Site well sp. Diff access lge o'fits - rec site ent via 2nd gate 100m beyond 1st. Med, hdstg, pt terr, shd; wc; chem disp; mv service pnt; shwrs inc; el pnts (6A) €1.50; Indtte; gas; bar; rest 100m; shop 200m; sand beach 500m; wifi; some statics; dogs; Eng spkn; red low ssn; CCI. "Quiet on terr pitches away fr rd; each pitch set in own garden & site in grounds of villa; interesting owner; mosquitoes." € 26.00 2010*

⊞ **IMPERIA** *1B3* (2km SW Coastal) *43.87244, 7.99997* **Camping Parco La Pineta, Via Tommaso Littardi 68, 18100 Imperia [0183 61498]** Exit A10 Imperia W. Turn L after tolls. Site well sp. Med, hdstg, terr, pt shd; wc; chem disp; shwrs €1; el pnts (3A) €2; Indry rm; shop & 200m; rest by beach; sand beach adj; 95% statics; poss cr; Eng spkn; ccard not acc; quiet. "Site in grounds of 17thC house; a few sm touring pitches - no room for awnings; clean san facs; pleasant owners; smart town 30 mins walk; gd." ♦ € 26.00 2009*

ISEO *1C1* (500m NE Rural) *45.66416, 10.05722* **Camping Iseo, Via Antonioli 57, 25049 Iseo (BS) [tel/fax 030 980213; info@campingiseo.it; www.campingiseo.com]** Fr A4 exit sp Rovato & immed foll brown sp Lago d'Iseo. Site well sp in vill. Med, some hdg pitch, pt shd; wc (some cont); chem disp; mv service pnt; baby facs; fam bthrm; some serviced pitches; shwrs inc; el pnts (6-10A) inc; gas; Indtte; shop; rest 300m; snacks; bar; playgrnd; beach adj; windsurfing; games area; cycle hire; golf 3km (red for campers); wifi; entmnt; some statics; dogs €3.50; phone; poss v cr; Eng spkn; adv bkg; quiet; red CCI. "V scenic; friendly, welcoming owner; well-organised, smart site; sm pitches; extra for lakeside pitches; well-maintained, clean facs but ltd; cruises on lake; many rests nr; excel; site next to a railway line, poss some noise; sm pitches." ♦ 1 Apr-1 Nov. € 39.00 2011*

ISEO *1C1* (500m NE Rural) *45.66388, 10.05638* **Camping Punta d'Oro, Via Antonioli 51-53, 25049 Iseo (BS) [tel/fax 030 980084; info@camping-puntadoro.com; www.puntadoro.com]** Fr Brescia-Boario Terme into Iseo, look for `Camping d'Iseo' sp on corner; after 200m cross rlwy, 1st R to site in 400m on lakeside. Med, pt sl, pt shd; wc; chem disp; mv service pnt; shwrs inc; el pnts (4A) inc; Indtte; shop 500m; rest 500m; snacks; bar; playgrnd; shgl beach; lake sw; boating; golf 6km; wifi; dogs €3.50; poss v cr high ssn; Eng spkn; some rlwy noise; red snr citizens; CCI. "Strictly-run but friendly site; gd security; beautiful area; friendly family run site cheerful and eager to help." ♦ Easter-19 Oct. € 32.00 2011*

ISEO *1C1* (1km NE Rural) *45.66527, 10.06277* **Camping Quai, Via Antonioli 73, 25049 Iseo (BS) [030 9821610; fax 981161; info@campingquai.it; www.campingquai.it]** Fr Brescia-Boario Terme rd by-passing Iseo, take NE exit; look for 'Camping d'Iseo' sp on corner. After 200m cross rlwy, site sp - sps obscured - go slow. Site adj Punta d'Oro on lakeside. Med, mkd pitch, shd; wc (some cont); chem disp; mv service pnt; shwrs inc; el pnts (4A) inc (poss rev pol); Indtte; shop, rest 1km; tradsmn; snacks; bar; BBQ; playgrnd; shgl beach & lake sw adj; watersports; games area; boat-launching; 25% statics; dogs; phone; bus, train 1km; sep car park; poss cr; Eng spkn; adv bkg; some rd noise; ccard acc; red long stay/snr citizens. "Well-kept; lake views fr some pitches; helpful manager; some noise fr nrby rlwy." ♦ 1 Apr-30 Sep. € 28.00 2011*

ISEO *1C1* (1.5km W Rural) *45.65689, 10.03739* **Camping Del Sole, Via per Rovato 26, 25049 Iseo (BS) [030 980288; fax 9821721; info@campingdelsole.it; www.campingdelsole.it]** Exit Brescia-Milan a'strada at Rivato-Lago d'Iseo exit & foll sp to Iseo. At complex rd junc with rndabts on Iseo o'skirts, site ent on L (lge sp). Site bet lakeside & rd, bef API petrol stn on R. Lge, mkd pitch, shd; wc; chem disp; mv service pnt; htd private bthrms avail; shwrs; el pnts (6A) inc; Indtte (inc dryer); supmkt; rest; snacks; bar; playgrnd; htd pool; paddling pool; shgl beach & lake sw: tennis; waterskiing; cycle hire; games area; wifi; entmnt; TV rm; 75% statics; dogs €3; sep car park; poss cr; Eng spkn; adv bkg; quiet; ccard acc. "Glorious views; excel facs; well-run, pleasant, popular lakeside site; pitches poss closely packed; ltd waste/water disposal; narr site rds." ♦ 15 Apr-25 Sep. € 40.90 (CChq acc) 2011*

ISEO *1C1* (1.5km W Rural) *45.65690, 10.03429* **Camping Sassabanek, Via Colombera 2, 25049 Iseo (BS) [030 980300; fax 9821360; sassabanek@sassabanek.it; www.sassabanek.it]** On periphery of Iseo by lakeside. Lge, pt shd; wc (some cont); chem disp; mv service pnt; sauna; shwrs inc; el pnts (3A) inc; gas; Indtte; shop; tradsmn; rest; snacks; bar; BBQ; playgrnd; pool; paddling pool; boating; windsurfing; tennis; cycle hire;TV; 50% statics; no dogs; phone; sep car park; adv bkg; quiet; ccard acc. "Clean facs; sh walk to pretty lakeside & vill; helpful staff; gd NH/sh stay." ♦ 1 Apr-30 Sep. € 35.30 2010*

ISPRA see Sesto Calende *1B1*

⊞ **LACES/LATSCH** *1D1* (700m E Rural) *46.62222, 10.86388* **Camping Latsch, Reichstrasse/Via Nazionale 4, 39021 Làces/Latsch (BZ) [0473 623217; fax 622333; info@camping-latsch.com; www.camping-latsch.com]** On L of SS38 Merano-Silandro (main rd by-passes vill of Latsch); do not go into vill; ent thro car park of Hotel Vermoi adj petrol stn. Fr N do not confuse with vill of Lasa/Laas. Med, hdg/mkd pitch, terr, pt shd; htd wc; chem disp; sauna; 15% serviced pitch; shwrs inc; el pnts (16A) €2.50; Indtte; shop; rest; snacks; bar; playgrnd; 2 pools (1 covrd, htd); paddling pool; waterslide; canoeing; tennis; solarium; ski school; ski lift 6km; free ski bus; underground car park; 20% statics; dogs €5.20; site clsd mid-Nov to mid-Dec; recep clsd 1300-1500; Eng spkn; quiet; ccard acc; red long stay; CCI. "Immac shwr block; gym equipment; if erecting awning take care strong wind fr mountains in N; excel walking." € 29.00 2008*

LAGO DI CORBARA see Baschi *2E3*

LAIVES/LEIFERS see Bolzano/Bozen *1D1*

⊞ **LAMA MOCOGNO** *1D2* (7km S Rural) *44.24568, 10.71155* **Camping Parco dei Castagni, Via del Parco 5, 41025 Montecreto (MO) [0536 62902; camping@parcodeicastagni.it; www.parcodeicastagni.it]** On S o'skirts Lama-Mocogno turn S at sp Camping Valverde. Cont past site on rd S40 & foll sp Sestola. Site on R, sp 'Montcreto Camping'. Med, mkd pitch, terr, pt shd; htd wc; chem disp; mv service pnt; some serviced pitches; shwrs inc; el pnts (3A) inc; Indtte; shop; rest, bar 500m; playgrnd adj; pool; 90% statics; dogs €3; poss cr; adv bkg. "Pleasant site amongst chestnut trees; friendly, helpful owner applies rules strictly; chairlift 1.6km; gd, modern san facs." ♦ € 30.00 2007*

⊞ **LAVENA** *1C1* (9km SW Rural) *45.95960, 8.86340* **International Camping di Rimoldi Claudio, Via Marconi 18, 21037 Lavena-Ponte-Tresa (VA) [0332 550117; fax 551600; info@internationalcamping.it; www.internationalcamping.com]** On rte S233 going SW into Italy fr Switzerland, turn SE after border twd Lavena-Ponte-Tresa. Going twd Switzerland fr Italy on same rte turn R twd vill. Site sp in vill. Med, pt sl, hdg pitch; pt shd; wc (some cont); shwrs; el pnts (2-6A) €1 inc; Indtte; supmkt opp; rest; snacks; bar; playgrnd; sand beach on lake; mainly statics; poss cr; adv bkg; quiet; CCI. "On smallest, most W bay of Lake Lugano; excel facs; friendly, helpful staff, wall arnd site so no direct views of Lake." € 24.00 2011*

LAZISE *1D2* (1.5km N Urban) *45.50807, 10.73166* **Camp Municipale, Via Roma 1,37017 Lazise (VR) [045 7580020; fax 7580549; camping.municipale@comune.lazise.vr.it; www.comune.lazise.vr.it]** N on S249 fr Peschiera, thro Pacengo & Lazise, at rndabt cont on S249 then turn L into Via Roma. Site sp at end of rd. Care req in 100m, sharp R turn; site ent pt hidden. Med, hdg/mkd pitch, pt shd; wc; chem disp; mv service pnt; shwrs inc; el pnts (10A) inc; Indtte; shop 250m; rest, snacks, bar adj; lake sw & beach adj; 5% statics; dogs €3; Eng spkn; quiet; ccard acc. "Gd touring cent; some pitches v muddy; gd, clean facs; friendly staff; avoid arr bef 1500 Wed (mkt on app rd); easy walk along lake to interesting sm town." ♦ 22 Mar-2 Nov. € 32.00 2010*

LAZISE *1D2* (500m S Rural) *45.49861, 10.7375* **Camping Du Parc, Loc Sentieri, 37017 Lazise (VR) [045 7580127; fax 6470150; duparc@camping.it; www.campingduparc.com]** Site on W side of lakeside rd SR249. Lge, pt sl, hdg pitch, pt shd; wc; chem disp; mv service pnt; shwrs; el pnts (5A) inc (rev pol); Indtte; shop; rest; snacks; bar; playgrnd; pool; waterslides; sand beach & lake sw; watersports; boat & cycle hire; gym; entmnt; 15% statics; dogs €5.70; poss cr at w/end; Eng spkn; adv bkg; red low ssn; ccard acc; red low ssn. "Sh walk to old town & ferry terminal; lovely lakeside position; excel, well-maintained site; vg san facs; gd size pitches, some on lake - long walk to water point; vg pizzeria & pool; quiet low ssn; ideal for families; gd security; Magic of Europe discount; vg." ♦ 12 Mar-31 Oct. € 40.00 2010*

LAZISE *1D2* (1km S Urban) *45.49722, 10.73694* **Camping Spiaggia d'Oro, Loc Bottona, Via Sentieri 1, 37017 Lazise (VR) [045 7580007; fax 7580611; info@campingspiaggiadoro.com; www.campingspiaggiadoro.com]** Fr A4/E70 exit dir Peschiera & take SR249 N; site sp. Fr Innsbruck on A22 exit Lago di Garda S. At rndabt take SR450 for Peschiera, then in 8km exit to Lazise. V lge, mkd pitch, pt sl, pt shd; wc; chem disp; mv service pnt; shwrs inc; el pnts (3-5A) inc (rev pol on 3A); gas; Indtte; shop & supmkt; snacks; bar; playgrnd; 3 pools; sandy private beach & sw adj; boat hire; dogs €7; quiet; Eng spkn; ccard not acc; CCI. "Helpful staff; lovely location nr historic walled town; gd facs." ♦ 27 Mar-15 Oct. € 49.40 2009*

LAZISE *1D2* (1.5km S Rural) *45.49277, 10.73305* **Camping La Quercia, Loc Bottona, 37017 Lazise (VR) [045 6470577; fax 6470243; laquercia@laquercia.it; www.laquercia.it]** Exit A22/E45 at Affi/Lago di Garda Sud or exit A4/E70 at Peschiera-del-Garda. Site on SR249, on SE shore of lake. V lge, hdg/mkd pitch, pt sl, shd; htd wc; chem disp; mv service pnt; baby facs; fam bathrm; shwrs inc; el pnts (6A) inc; gas; Indtte (inc dryer); shops; rest; snacks; bar; playgrnd; pool; paddling pool; waterslide; jacuzzi; private sand beach; watersports; tennis; games area; gym; wifi; entmnt; 15% statics; dogs €6.90; phone; vehicle safety checks for cars/m'vans; poss cr; adv bkg. "Superb site for family holidays; many excel sports & leisure facs; some pitches on lakeside; easy walk to town along beach; highly rec." ♦ 25 Mar-3 Oct. € 59.00 2011*

⊞ **LAZISE** *1D2* (2km S Urban) *45.47912, 10.72635* **Camping Amici di Lazise, Loc Fossalta Nuova, Strada del Roccolo 8, 37017 Lazise (VR) [045 6490146; fax 6499448; daniela@campingamicidilazise.it]** S fr Lazise, immed bef high rest with Greek columns (bef Gardaland) take side rd on R, site on R. Med, pt shd; wc (some cont); chem disp; mv service pnt; some serviced pitches; shwrs inc; el pnts (6A) inc; Indtte; shop; rest; bar; playgrnd; pool; paddling pool; shgl beach 300m; entmnt; 40% statics; dogs €4.50; poss cr; Eng spkn; adv bkg; quiet; red low ssn. "Gd." ♦ € 32.00 2011*

LAZISE *1D2* (2.5km S Rural) *45.48027, 10.7225* **Camping Fossalta, Via Fossalta 4, 37017 Lazise (VR) [045 7590231; fax 7590999; info@fossalta.com; www.fossalta.com]** Site on SR249 on SE shore of lake. Lge, pt sl, terr, shd; wc; chem disp; mv service pnt; shwrs inc; el pnts (4A) inc; gas; Indtte; shop; rest 500m; snacks; playgrnd; htd pool; lake sw; private beach adj; tennis; games area; cycle hire; dogs €5; bus to Verona; Eng spkn; noise fr nrby Caneva World attraction; ccard not acc; red long stay/low ssn; CCI. "Gd site in gd position; gd rest; clean & relaxed; well-kept, modern san facs; helpful staff." ♦ Easter-25 Sep. € 30.50 2008*

⊞ **LECCE** *3A4* (6km W Rural) *40.36417, 18.09889* **Camping Lecce Namaste, 73100 Lecce [0832 329647; info@camping-lecce.it; www.camping-lecce.it]** Fr Lecce ring rd exit junc 15 W dir Novoli, in 5km immed after (abandoned) sm petrol stn turn R at sp Namaste. App rd to site potholed/gravelled. Site may appear clsd - sound horn for attention. Sm, some hdstg, pt shd; wc; shwrs inc; el pnts (10A) inc; shop 2km; beach 16km; bus to Lecce; quiet. "Gd, clean site but dated facs; conv for Baroque city of Lecce & coast around heel of Italy." € 19.00 2011*

ITALY

ITALY

⊞ **LECCO** *1C1* (8km NE Rural) *45.92075, 9.43831* **Camping Grigna, Via Prato Caminaccio 1, 23811 Balisio-di-Ballabio (LC) [0341 232045; fax 232631; campinggrigna@libero.it; www.campinggrigna.it]** Fr Lecco take SP62 dir Ballabio & Barzio, site on L at top of pass. Med, terr, unshd; htd wc (cont); chem disp; mv service pnt; shwrs inc; el pnts (4A) inc; Indtte; shop; rest; snacks; bar; BBQ; playgrnd; 50% statics; dogs; poss cr; quiet; CCI. "Fair." ♦ € 26.00 2008*

LECCO *1C1* (3km S Urban) *45.8227, 9.41715* **Camping Rivabella, Via alla Spiaggia 35, 23900 Chiuso [tel/fax 0341 421143; rivabellalecco@libero.it; www.rivabellalecco.3000.it]** Well sp fr SS639. Exit 3km S of Lecco nr rlwy bdge & foll lane for 300m to site on L. Med, mkd pitch, pt shd; wc; mv service pnt; shwrs €0.50; el pnts (3A) inc; Indtte; gas; shop; rest 500m; snacks; bar; playgrnd; lake sw; beach adj; golf 10km; 60% statics; dogs €3; poss cr; adv bkg; quiet. "Charming lakeside site; friendly, helpful staff; poss v cr at w/end as facs used by public for sw etc; facs need refurb; exit fr site poss v diff due to crowds; gd cycle path to Lecco; friendly staff." ♦ 15 Apr-30 Sep. € 22.10 2008*

LECCO *1C1* (4km W Rural) *45.81730, 9.34307* **Camping Due Laghi, Via Isella 34, 23862 Civate (LC) [tel/fax 0341 550101]** S side of Lecco-Como rd on lake. Use slip rd marked Isella/Civate. Turn L at T-junc, then L over bdge; foll v narr app rd to site, sp. Med, pt sl, shd; wc (cont); shwrs inc; el pnts (4A) inc; gas; Indtte; shop; rest; snacks; bar; pool; paddling pool; games area; mainly statics; dogs €3; quiet; Eng spkn. "Unkempt site; gd, modern san facs." 1 Apr-30 Sep. € 25.00 2008*

LECCO *1C1* (9km NW Rural) *45.92138, 9.28777* **Camping La Fornace, Onno, Via Garibaldi 52, 23865 Oliveto-Lario (LC) [tel/fax 031 969553; laformace@libero.it; www.lafornace.it]** Fr Lecco SP583 twd Bellagio. Site on R at '37km' sp. Fr Bellagio on SP583 site on L 100m after Onno boundary sp. V sharp L turn at yellow sp. App diff for lge o'fits, narr app rd. Sm, mkd pitch, hdstg, pt sl, pt shd; wc (male cont); chem disp; mv service pnt; shwrs inc; el pnts (5A) inc; shop; rest; snacks; bar; beach & lake sw adj; games rm; dogs; poss cr; adv bkg; quiet; red low ssn; CCI. "Peaceful, lakeside site but poss loud music fr bar until sm hours; delightful setting; simple, clean facs." 1 Apr-30 Sep. € 22.00 2011*

LENNO see Menaggio *1C1*

LEVANTO *1C2* (1km NE Coastal) *44.17364, 9.62550* **Camping Cinque Terre, Sella Mereti, 19015 Levanto (SP) [tel/fax 0187 801252; info@campingcinqueterre.it; www.campingcinqueterre.it]** Clearly sp fr cent of Lèvanto. Fr E turn L off SS1 to Lèvanto, sp Carradano, site on R bef town. Sm, hdg/mkd pitch, terr, shd; htd wc (mainly cont); chem disp; mv service pnt; shwrs €1; el pnts (3A) inc; gas; Indtte; shop 500m; tradsmn; rest 500m; snacks; bar; sm playgrnd; shgl/sand beach 1km; games rm; wifi; TV; no dogs high ssn; sep car park; bus to beach high ssn; poss cr; adv bkg; quiet; ccard not acc; red low ssn; CCI. "Excel, friendly, family-run site; modern san facs; steepish ent, but site level." ♦ Easter-30 Sep. € 34.50 2010*

LEVANTO *1C2* (1km E Coastal) *44.17505, 9.62289* **Camping Pian di Picche, Pian di Picche, 19015 Levanto (SP) [tel/fax 0187 800597; piandipicche@libero.it]** Clearly sp fr cent of Lèvanto. Fr E turn L off SS1 to Lèvanto, sp Carradano, site on R bef town; adj Camping Cinque Terre. Med, hdg pitch, terr, pt shd; wc (some cont); chem disp; shwrs €0.50; el pnts (3A) inc; gas; Indtte; sm shop; tradsmn; rest 200m; bar; BBQ; shgl beach 800m; TV; dogs; sep car park high ssn; Eng spkn; quiet; ccard acc. "Basic facs; access to site/pitches diff - narr rds; early arr rec in Aug; conv Cinque Terre vills; friendly, helpful staff." ♦ 1 Apr-30 Sep. € 34.00 2010*

⊞ **LEVANTO** *1C2* (300m S Coastal/Urban) *44.16656, 9.61366* **Camping Acqua Dolce, Via Guido Semenza 5, 19015 Levanto (SP) [0187 808465; fax 807365; mail@campingacquadolce.com; www.campingacquadolce.com]** Site sp fr town cent, app rd to Levanto steep & winding. Site ent steep. Med, mkd pitch, hdstg, terr, shd; wc (some cont); chem disp; mv service pnt; serviced pitches; shwrs inc; el pnts (6A) €2.50; Indtte; shops adj; rest; snacks; bar; playgrnd; pool 250m; sand beach 300m; dogs; phone; sep car park; site clsd mid-Jan to end Feb; poss cr; Eng spkn; adv bkg; quiet; ccard acc; red low ssn. "Site ent poss diff; sm pitches; vg, modern san facs but unisex; o'fits parked v close high ssn; not rec c'vans over 6m; gd touring base Cinque Terre vills; gd walks fr site; lovely, clean beach; easy walk to boat terminal & rlwy stn." ♦ € 46.50 2011*

LEVICO TERME *1D1* (1km S Rural) *46.00638, 11.28944* **Camping Jolly, Via Pleina 5, 38056 Levico-Terme (TN) [0461 706934; fax 700227; mail@campingjolly.com; www.campingjolly.com]** Foll sp to Levico fr A22 or SS12 onto SS27; site sp. Lge, mkd pitch, shd; wc; chem disp; mv service pnt; serviced pitches; baby facs; shwrs inc; el pnts (6A) inc; gas; Indtte (inc dryer); shop & 500m; rest 200m; snacks; bar; BBQ; playgrnd; pool high ssn; paddling pool; shgl beach 200m; golf 7km; internet; entmnt; 30% statics; dogs €5; poss cr; adv bkg; quiet; red snr citizens. "Health spa nr; vg." ♦ 1 Apr-10 Oct. € 38.00 2011*

LEVICO TERME *1D1* (1km SW Urban) *46.00791, 11.28416* **Camping Levico, Via Pleina 1, 38056 Levico-Terme (TN) [0461 706491; fax 707735; mail@campinglevico.com; www.campinglevico.com]** Foll sp for Levico fr SS47 (under viaduct). In Levico turn L at junc & in 400m turn L foll sp to site on R. Lge, pt shd; wc (some cont); chem disp; mv service pnt; baby facs; shwrs; el pnts (6A) inc; gas; Indtte; shop; rest; snacks; playgrnd; private shgl beach & lake sw; boat hire; windsurfing; tennis; cycle hire; 20% statics; dogs €5; poss cr; no adv bkg; quiet. "Gd sw in warm lake; gd san facs; use of pool at Camping Jolly." ♦ 5 Apr-5 Oct. € 31.00 2008*

LEVICO TERME *1D1* (1km SW Rural) *46.00392, 11.25838* **Camping Spiaggia, Viale Venezia 12, 38050 Calceranica al Lago (TN) [tel/fax 0461 723037; info@campingspiaggia.net; www.campingspiaggia.net]** Foll sp to Levico fr Trento; after exit rd turn L & in 400m turn L foll sp to site. Site after Camping Jolly on S side of lake. Med, hdg/mkd pitch, pt shd; wc; chem disp; mv service pnt; private san facs avail; shwrs inc; el pnts inc; playgrnd; private shgl beach & lake sw (across rd); some statics; dogs €3; poss cr; Eng spkn; quiet. "Gd site." 10 Apr-15 Oct. € 22.50 2009*

LEVICO TERME *1D1* (2km W Rural) *46.00444, 11.28527* **Camping Due Laghi, Loc Costa 3, 38056 Levico-Terme (TN) [0461 706290; fax 707381; info@campingclub.it; www.campingclub.it]** E fr Trento on S47 to Levico Terme; L at junc & in 100m turn L up Trento slip rd & foll sp to site immed on R on lake. Lge, pt shd; wc (some cont); chem disp; mv service pnt; baby facs; sauna; shwrs inc; el pnts (3-6A) inc; gas; lndtte (inc dryer); shop; rest; snacks; bar; BBQ; htd pool; paddling pool; shgl beach 500m; tennis; games area; cycle hire; wifi; entmnt; TV rm; 5% statics; dogs €4; phone; poss cr; Eng spkn; adv bkg; some rd noise; ccard acc; red long stay/snr citizens. "Friendly, helpful owner; clean facs; individ washrms avail; scenic area & pretty town." ♦ 14 Apr-11 Sep. € 34.00 (CChq acc) 2011*

LEVICO TERME *1D1* (5km W Rural) *46.00194, 11.25527* **Camping Al Pescatore, Via dei Pescatori 1, 38050 Calceranica-al-Lago (TN) [0461 723062; fax 724212; trentino@campingpescatore.it; www.campingpescatore.it]** Exit Trento-Padova rd (SS47) either end of lake for Calceranica. Turn W in vill over rlwy x-ing & R on to lakeside. Site sp in 300m. Lge, pt shd; wc; chem disp; mv service pnt; shwrs inc; el pnts (3A) inc; lndtte (inc dryer); shop; rest, snacks 200m; bar; pool; paddling pool; shgl beach & lake sw adj; wifi; entmnt; 10% statics; dogs €3; poss cr; quiet. "Vg, modern san facs; lovely lakeside location; cycle routes fr site." ♦ 7 May-11 Sep. € 32.50 2011*

LEVICO TERME *1D1* (5km W Rural) *46.00458, 11.26034* **Camping Mario Village, Via Lungolago 4, 38052 Caldonazzo (TN) [0461 723341; fax 723106; direzione@campingmario.com; www.campingmario.com]** Exit A22 onto SS47 E. Past Pergine foll sp Calceranica & Caldonazzo. Site on lakeside. Med, mkd pitch, pt sl, pt shd; wc; chem disp; mv service pnt; baby facs; shwrs inc; el pnts (6A) inc; gas; lndtte; shop; rest, snacks adj; bar; playgrnd; pool; solarium; lake sw; games area; wifi; entmnt; some statics; dogs €3; phone; poss cr; Eng spkn; adv bkg; quiet; red low ssn. "Lovely location; mountain views; cycle paths; vg, modern san facs." ♦ 1 May- 13 Sep. € 25.00 2009*

LIDO DELLE NAZIONI see Comacchio *2E2*

LIDO DI JESOLO *2E2* (300m W Coastal) *45.48425, 12.58762* **Jesolo International Club Camping, Via Alberto da Guissano 1, 30017 Lido-di-Jesolo (VE) [0421 971826; fax 972561; info@jesolointernational.it; www.jesolointernational.it]** Site at W end of Lido-di-Jesolo, twd Cavallino. V lge, mkd pitch, shd; wc; serviced pitches; chem disp; mv service pnt; shwrs inc; el pnts (10A) inc; gas; lndtte; shop; rest; snacks; bar; playgrnd; pool; paddling pool; sand beach adj; watersports; tennis; boat hire; games area; golf 3km; wifi; entmnt; sat TV; 10% statics; no dogs; site boat to Venice; sep car par; poss cr; quiet; ccard acc; red long stay/low ssn. "Superb site; many activities." ♦ 1 May-30 Sep. € 50.00 2010*

LIDO DI JESOLO *2E2* (6km NW Coastal) *45.55356, 12.76705* **Portofelice Camping Village, Viale dei Fiori, 30020 Eraclea-Mare (VE) [0421 66441; fax 66021; info@portofelice.it; www.portofelice.it]** Exit A4 sp Caorle. In Caorle foll coast rd S to Eraclea-Mare, site sp. V lge, hdg/mkd pitch, shd; wc; chem disp; baby facs; some serviced pitches; shwrs inc; el pnts (6A) inc; gas; lndtte; shop; tradsmn; rest; snacks; bar; playgrnd; pools; paddling pool; sand beach 400m; tennis; games area; golf 6km; entmnt; 50% statics; no dogs; phone; bus; sep car park; poss cr; Eng spkn; adv bkg; ccard acc; red long stay/snr citizens. "Excel pool complex." ♦ 9 May-16 Sep. € 41.30 2009*

LIDO DI METAPONTO *3A4* (Coastal) *40.35878, 16.83380* **Camping Internazionale, Viale Magna Grecia, 75010 Lido-di-Metaponto (MT) [0835 741916; fax 741987; info@villageinternazionale.com; www.villageinternazionale.com]** Well sp in vill. Med, mkd pitch, all hdstg, pt shd; wc (mainly cont); mv service pnt; chem disp; shwrs €0.50; el pnts (3A) €3; lndtte; shop 200m; rest; snacks; bar; playgrnd; sand beach adj; entmnt; 50% statics; dogs €4; sep car park high ssn; poss cr; noise fr local bars until late; ccard acc; CCI. "Well-organised, clean site; sm, narr pitches, gd san facs; barrier clsd 1400-1600." ♦ 1 Mar-30 Sep. € 28.00 2008*

⊞ **LIDO DI OSTIA** *2E4* (6km S Coastal) *41.70583, 12.34000* **Camping Internazionale di Castelfusano, Via Litoranea 132, 000122 Lido-di-Ostia [06 5623304; fax 56470260; info@romacampingcastelfusano.it; www.romacampingcastelfusano.it]** Fr Rome leave ring rd at junc 27, take Via C Colombo dir W. At sea front (approx 18km) turn L & fork L into Via Litoranea, site on R on dual c'way. Lge, mkd pitch, pt sl, pt shd; wc; chem disp; mv service pnt; shwrs inc; el pnts (3A) €2.50 (poss no earth); gas; lndtte; shop; rest; snacks; bar; playgrnd; sand beach adj; entmnt; internet; 20% statics; dogs; adv bkg; noisy; ccard acc; CCI. "Gd base for Rome; conv buses, metro & rlwy; conv archaeological site at Ostia; best pitches in shady part at S end; low trees at N end; poss scruffy low ssn & resident workers/contractors; facs poss stretched if busy; rest & playgrnd not rec; NH only." ♦ € 30.00 2008*

LIDO DI SAVIO see Cervia *2E2*

LIGNANO SABBIADORO *2E1* (2km NE Urban) *45.68196, 13.12580* **Camping Sabbiadoro, Via Sabbiadoro 8, 33054 Lignano-Sabbiadoro (UD) [0431 71455; fax 721355; campsab@lignano.it; www.campingsabbiadoro.it]** Fr Latisano strt rd 20km to Lignano. Bear L & foll sp to Sabbiadoro. After 3km thro pine trees on edge of town turn R. Rndabt with BP g'ge after 400m. Site opp. V lge, pt shd; shwrs; wc; el pnts (4A) inc; lndtte; shop; rest; snacks; bar; playgrnd; htd pool; paddling pool; tennis; cycle hire; games area; internet; some statics; dogs €2; adv bkg; ccard acc; quiet. "Vg; fine beach for children 20 mins walk." ♦ 4 Apr-18 Oct. € 35.50 2009*

LIMONE SUL GARDA *1D1* (1km S Rural) *45.80555, 10.7875* **Camping Garda, Via 4 Novembre, 25010 Limone-sul-Garda (TN) [0365 954550; fax 954357; horstmann.hotel@tin.it]** Site sp fr SS45b. Sm, mkd pitch, hdstg, pt sl, terr, pt shd; wc (cont); chem disp; shwrs €0.25; el pnts (3A) €1; Indtte; shop 250m; rest, snacks high ssn; pool; paddling pool; shgl beach & lake sw; cycle hire; 10% statics; dogs €4; poss cr; Eng spkn; adv bkg; quiet; CCI. "Splendid views; v friendly owner; clean, well-kept site adj to lake; excel pool." ♦ 1 Apr-28 Oct. € 28.40 2008*

LIMONE SUL GARDA *1D1* (1.5km S Rural) *45.80111, 10.78583* **Camping Nanzel, Via IV Novembre 3, 25010 Limone-sul-Garda (BS) [0365 954155; fax 954468; campingnanzel@libero.it; www.limonesulgarda.it]** On rd SS45 bis ent at San Giorgio Hotel at km post 101.2. Diff app & not rec for lge o'fits. Sh 1 in 8 descent & low bdge (2.3m) past hotel. Med, terr, pt shd; wc; shwrs €0.50; el pnts (3A) €1; Indtte; shop; rest 500m; snacks; bar; beach adj; boat launching facs; windsurfing; sep car park; poss cr; ccard acc. "Helpful owner; site in olive grove; beautiful views across lake." ♦ 1 Apr-15 Oct. € 26.80 2008*

⊞ **LIVORNO** *1C3* (10km S Coastal) *43.48119, 10.33327* **Camping Village Miramare, Via del Littorale 220, 57100 Antignano (LV) [0586 580402; fax 587462; contact@campingmiramare.com; www.campingmiramare.com]** Fr Livorno foll SS1 in dir Grosseto/Rome. Site on R just after 2nd rd tunnel. Med, hdg pitch, hdstg, pt shd; wc (cont); chem disp; mv service pnt; shwrs inc; el pnts (10A) inc; Indtte; shop & 5km; rest; snacks; bar; BBQ; playgrnd; pool; paddling pool; shgl beach adj; wellness cent; entmnt; internet; TV; 10% statics; bus; phone; no dogs; quiet but some rlwy noise; adv bkg; Eng spkn; red long stay; ccard acc. "Extra for beachside pitches; ltd space/access for twin-axle vans; conv visits Pisa, Siena, Florence & wine areas; lovely setting." ♦ € 52.00 2009*

⊞ **LUCCA** *1D3* (800m NW Urban) *43.85000, 10.48583* **Camper Il Serchio, Via del Tiro a Segno 704, Santa Anna, 55100 Lucca (LU) [tel/fax 0583 317385; info@camperilserchio.it; www.camperilserchio.it]** Sp fr main rds to Lucca & fr town. Gd access rds. Med, hdg/mkd pitch, hdstg, pt shd; wc; chem disp; mv service pnt; shwrs inc; el pnts (5A) inc; Indtte (inc dryer); rest nr; BBQ; playgrnd; pool €5; tennis, games area opp; cycle hire; wifi; no statics; dogs; bus; poss cr; adv bkg; quiet but disco noise nrby. "New site 2007; attractive pitches; mainly for m'vans - not suitable lge car/c'van o'fits or lge tents." ♦ € 25.00 2011*

LUINO *1C1* (6km N Rural) *46.03888, 8.73277* **Azur Parkcamping Maccagno, Via Corsini, 21010 Maccagno (VA) [0332 560203; fax 561263; maccagno@azur-camping.de; www.azur-camping.de]** Fr S up E side of Lake Maggiore on S394, thro Luino, Maccagno in 6km (twisting, narr rd). Site on L down narr lane, then diff R, site on L. Site sp easy to miss, access narr & tight. Med, pt sl, mkd pitch, pt shd; wc; chem disp; mv service pnt; baby facs; shwrs; el pnts (6A) €2.80; gas; Indtte; shop; bar; playgrnd; shgl beach on lake; boating; fishing; tennis; 20% statics; dogs €2.80; poss cr; adv bkg; red CCI. "Conv Luino; lovely lakeside setting; popular with local families; rec sm m'vans & o'fits only - sm pitches." ♦ 15 Mar-15 Nov. € 28.60 2008*

LUINO *1C1* (6km N Rural) *46.04189, 8.73279* **Camping Lido Boschetto Holiday, Via Pietraperzia 13, 21010 Maccagno (VA) [tel/fax 0332 560250; lido@boschettoholiday.it; www.boschettoholiday.it/lido]** On E shore of Lake Maggiore on SS394 bet Bellinzona & Laveno. Fr Luino pass under 2 rlwy bdges & foll sp L twd lake, site clearly sp. Med, pt shd; wc; shwrs inc; chem disp; shwrs inc; el pnts (3-4A) €3.50; (poss rev pol); Indtte; shop; snacks adj; playgrnd; lake sw & beach adj; watersports; some statics; dogs €3; adv bkg; quiet; ccard acc; CCI. "Hydrofoil/ferries fr vill to all parts of lake; trains to Locarno." 1 Apr-30 Sep. € 29.00 2011*

MACCAGNO see Luino *1C1*

MAGIONE *2E3* (10km S Rural) *43.08140, 12.14340* **Camping Polvese, Via Montivalle, 06060 Sant' Arcangelo-sul-Trasimeno (PG) [075 848078; fax 848050; polvese@polvese.com; www.polvese.com]** Fr A1 exit dir Lake Trasimeno to Castiglione-del-Lago, then S599 to San Arcangelo. Med, mkd pitch, pt shd; wc (cont); chem disp; mv service pnt; shwrs inc; el pnts (10A) inc; gas; Indtte; shop; tradsmn; snacks; bar; playgrnd; 2 pools; paddling pool; sand beach adj; watersports; lake fishing; cycle hire; games area; wifi; entmnt; 40% statics; dogs €2; phone; poss cr; adv bkg; quiet; red long stay; CCI. "Gd touring base for Umbria; lakeside pitches avail." ♦ 1 Apr-30 Sep. € 22.00 (CChq acc) 2011*

MAGIONE *2E3* (5km SW Rural) *43.12422, 12.16700* **Camping Riva Verde, Loc Trasiemeno, Via Ghandi 5/7, 06063 San Feliciano (PG) [tel/fax 075 8479351; info@rivaverdecamping.com; www.rivaverdecamping.com]** Exit SS75 at Magione, foll SS599 twd Chiusi. In 4km R on SP316 to San Feliciano & foll to site at N end of vill on lakeside. Med, shd; wc; shwrs; el pnts inc; shops 1km; bar; rest; BBQ; pool adj high ssn; lake sw; waterskiing; games area; entmnt;lge new pool (2011), many statics; no dogs; sep car park; poss cr; adv bkg; quiet. "Excel for touring Umbria; indiv washrooms; lovely lake views; hot water to shwrs only; diff for lge o'fits." ♦ 1 Apr-30 Sep. € 22.00 2011*

MAGIONE *2E3* (6km SW Rural) *43.08835, 12.15630* **Camping Villaggio Italgest, Via Martiri di Cefalonia, 06060 Sant' Arcangelo-sul-Trasimeno (PG) [075 848238 or 848292; fax 848085; camping@italgest.com; www.italgest.com]** Fr Magione, take SS599 on S edge of Lake Trasimeno; site sp to R on app to Sant' Arcangelo. Lge, mkd pitch, pt shd; wc (some cont); chem disp; mv service pnt; baby facs; shwrs inc; el pnts (6A) inc; gas; Indtte (inc dryer); shop; tradsmn; rest; snacks; bar; cooking facs; playgrnd; pool; paddling pool; waterslides; lake sw & private sand beach adj; fishing; watersports; tennis; boat, cycle hire; games area; games rm; wifi; entmnt; sat TV rm; 60% statics; dogs €2.50; sep car park; poss cr esp w/end; Eng spkn; adv bkg (dep); ccard acc; CCI. "High standard, well-maintained site; mosquitoes poss a prob; friendly owner; helpful staff; clean facs; noisy nr disco & recep; quiet low ssn; highly rec." ♦ 20 Apr-30 Sep. € 28.50 (CChq acc) 2009*

MALCESINE *1D1* (Urban) *45.76583, 10.81096* **Camping Villaggio Turistico Priori, Via Navene 31, 37018 Malcesine (VR) [045 7400503; fax 6583098; antpriori@katamail.com; www.appartement-prioriantonio.it]** Well sp in town cent. Take care if app fr N. Sm, mkd pitch, hdstg, pt sl, terr, pt shd; wc; chem disp; shwrs inc; el pnts (3A) inc; Indtte; shop adj; rest, snacks, bar adj; lake sw & shgl beach 200m; no dogs; phone; poss cr; some rd noise; adv bkg; Eng spkn; CCI. "Vg; conv all amenities & Monte Baldo funicular." 15 Apr-16 Oct. € 24.00 2011*

The opening dates and prices on this campsite have changed. I'll send a site report form to the Club for the next edition of the guide.

MALCESINE *1D1* (2km N Rural) *45.78741, 10.82209* **Camping Campagnola, Via Gardesana 8, 27018 Malcesine (VR) [tel/fax 045 7400777; info@campingcampagnola.it; www.campingcampagnola.it]** Fr Malcesine on rd SS249, sp. Med, mkd pitch, terr, pt shd; wc; chem disp (wc); shwrs inc; el pnts (8A) inc; gas; Indtte; sm shop; tradsmn; rest; snacks; bar; BBQ; lake sw & beach adj; watersports; 50% statics; dogs; bus adj; poss cr; Eng spkn; adv bkg; quiet. "Clean, well-run, family-run site." Easter-5 Oct. € 22.00 2008*

MALCESINE *1D1* (2km N Rural) *45.7850, 10.82027* **Camping Tonini, Via Gardesana 378, Loc Campagnola, 37018 Malcesine (VR) [tel/fax 0457 401341; info@campingtonini.com; www.campingtonini.com]** Site sp on SS249 on lakeside, sp at gate. Med, mkd pitch, terr, pt sl, pt shd; wc; chem disp; mv service pnt; shwrs inc; el pnts (6A) €2; Indtte; sm shop; rest, snacks, bar 2km; shgl beach thro tunnel; dogs €2; poss cr; Eng spkn; some rd noise; CCI. "In beautiful position, walking dist town; gd sized pitches; clean, modern san facs; gd views; friendly owner; gd cent mountain walking/biking & windsurfing; excel." ♦ 1 Apr-5 Oct. € 25.00 2009*

MALCESINE *1D1* (3km N Rural) *45.78846, 10.82307* **Camping Claudia, Loc Campagnola, 37018 Malcesine (VR) [tel/fax 045 7400786; info@campingclaudia.it.; www.campingclaudia.it]** On SS249 Torbole-Garda rd by Hotel Anna, sp. Med, mkd pitch, pt sl, terr, pt shd; wc; chem disp; mv service pnt; fam bthrm; shwrs; el pnts inc; shop; tradsmn; rest adj; bar; beach & lake sw 100m; watersports; dogs €2.50; bus adj; poss v cr; adv bkg; quiet but some rd noise. "Gd, well-situated site; sm pitches; modern san facs; cash only." 19 Apr-12 Oct. € 26.00 2008*

MALCESINE *1D1* (3km N Rural) *45.78971, 10.82609* **Camping Martora, Campagnola, Martora 2, 37018 Malcesine (VR) [045 4856733; fax 4851278; martora@martora.it; www.martora.it]** On E side of lake on rd SS249 at km 86/11. Ent up concrete rd bet iron gates at 'Prinz Blau' sp. Med, mkd pitch, pt sl, pt shd; wc; chem disp; shwrs; el pnts (4A) inc; gas 200m; rest 100m; lake sw, windsurfing adj; wifi; 10% statics; poss cr; adv bkg; quiet. "Lakeside cycle path to town." 1 Apr-3 Oct. € 27.00 2011*

⊞ **MALCESINE** *1D1* (5km S Rural) *45.7300, 10.78333* **Camping Bellavista, Via Gardesana 4, Loc Vendemme, 37010 Cassone (VR) [tel/fax 045 7420244; info@campingbellavistamalcesine.com; www.campingbellavistamalcesine.com]** 1km S of Cassone on R of rd SS249. Steep access rd. Lge, terr, pt shd; wc; mv service pnt; shwrs; el pnts (5A) inc (poss rev pol); gas; Indtte; shop; rest adj; bar; playgrnd; shgl beach & lake sw; no dogs; poss cr; adv bkg; quiet. "Ltd facs low ssn; footpath along lake shore; lovely views over lake; on arr park 20m past STOP sp at reception; v clean san facs." € 31.00 2009*

⊞ **MALS/MALLES VENOSTA** *1D1* (1km S Rural) *46.68416, 10.55055* **Mals Camping, Bahnhofstrasse/Via Stazione 51, 39024 Mals (BZ) [0473 835179; fax 845172; info@campingmals.it; www.campingmals.it]** Exit A12 to Landeck. In Landeck take 1st exit at rndabt over rv bdge, then turn L & foll sp Reschen Pass. On app Mals do not take any of L turns into town (v narr rds); stay on main rd until traff lts then turn R twd stn. Site in 500m on L. Sm, hdg/mkd pitch, terr, pt shd; htd wc; chem disp; mv waste; shwrs inc; el pnts (16A) inc; gas; Indtte; shop 500m; tradsmn; snacks; bar; playgrnd; htd, covrd pool, tennis nr; cycle hire adj; wifi; dogs €3; bus/train 250m; skibus 100m; Eng spkn; adv bkg; quiet; ccard acc; CCI. "Gd walking, cycling area, free ent to local pools; vg, high-quality, modern site." ♦ € 32.00 2009*

MALS/MALLES VENOSTA *1D1* (3km S Rural) *46.67305, 10.5700* **Campingpark Gloria Vallis, Wiesenweg 5, 39020 Glurns/Glorenza (BZ) [0473 835160; fax 835767; info@gloriavallis.it; www.gloriavallis.it]** Sp on rd S41 E of Glorenza. Med, mkd pitch, terr, unshd; htd wc; chem disp; mv service pnt; baby facs; shwrs inc; el pnts (10A) inc; gas; Indtte; shop; tradsmn; snacks; bar; playgrnd; pool 1km; tennis; games area; entmnt; 5% statics; dogs €4; phone; o'night parking place for m'vans; Eng spkn; adv bkg; quiet; ccard acc; CCI. "Excel mountain views; dog shwr rm; higher prices in winter." ♦ 1 Apr-31 Oct. € 34.80 2009*

MALS/MALLES VENOSTA *1D1* (3km S Rural) **Stadt-Camping im Park (Municipal), 39026 Glurns/Glorenza (BZ) [0473 835160; fax 845767]** Fr W (Ofenpass) on rd 28/S41 at Glorenza take v sharp L turn immed after bdge & bef town walls. Site 500m along v narr rd, not suitable lge/wide o'fits. Sp 'MV Parking' fr town but all units acc. NB Height restriction fr S (S40) 2.8m; fr N (Mals) 3.4m. Sm, pt sl, pt shd; wc; chem disp; mv service pnt; shwrs €0.50; el pnts (10A) €2.50; shop, rest, snacks, bar 400m; no statics; dogs; CCI. "Spacious, tranquil CL-type site; beautiful views; easy walking, cycling; attractive medieval town with all facs; v clean san facs; owner calls in evening." 1 Apr-30 Oct. € 12.00 2010*

MANERBA DEL GARDA *1D2* (1.5km N Rural) *45.56194, 10.56361* **Camping Belvedere, Via Cavalle 5, 25080 Manerba-del-Garda (BS) [0365 551175; fax 552350; info@camping-belvedere.it; www.camping-belvedere.it]** Fr Salo-Desenzano rd SS572 turn E at sp to Manerba. Site sp fr Manerba, 1.5km N. Med, terr, shd; wc (some cont); chem disp; shwrs €0.30; el pnts; (6A) inc; gas; Indry rm; shop; rest; bar; pool; private shgl beach & lake sw; tennis; sat TV; 30% statics; dogs €4; poss cr; quiet; ccard acc. "Excel, well-organised site; views lake/mountains; Manerba pleasant vill; close to Iron Age hill fort." ♦ 15 Mar-15 Oct. € 28.50 2008*

ITALY

ITALY

MANERBA DEL GARDA *1D2* (1.5km N Rural) *45.56194, 10.56472* **Camping La Rocca, Via Cavalle 22, 25080 Manerba-del-Garda (BS) [0365 551738; fax 552045; info@laroccacamp.it; www.laroccacamp.it]** Fr Desenzano-Salo rd SS572 turn E at sp Manerba. Site sp fr Manerba. Be careful to head for 'Camping La Rocca' & not 'La Rocca'. Sh, steep app rd, site on R. Lge, pt shd; wc (some cont); chem disp; mv service pnt; shwrs inc; el pnts (4A) inc; shop; rest 200m; snacks; bar; playgrnd; pool & paddling pool; shgl beach & lake sw adj; tennis; games area; cycle hire; wifi; 20% statics; €4.50; adv bkg; quiet; "Excel site & facs; some pitches with lake views, some with low olive trees - care req; amusing, helpful owner; highly rec." 1 Apr-30 Sep. € 35.00 2010*

MANERBA DEL GARDA *1D2* (1.5km N Rural) *45.56333, 10.56611* **Camping San Biagio, Via Cavalle 19, 25080 Manerba-del-Garda (BS) [0365 551549; fax 551046; info@campingsanbiagio.net; www.campingsanbiagio.net]** Fr S572 rd turn E at sp Manerba, site sp 1.5km N fr Manerba. Lge, mkd pitch, hdstg, terr, shd; htd wc; baby facs; shwrs inc; el pnts (16A) metered; Indtte (inc dryer); shop; rest; snacks; bar; BBQ; playgrnd; shgl beach & lake sw; wifi; dogs €5; poss cr; Eng spkn; adv bkg; quiet; ccard acc. "Terr pitches with views over Lake Garda; v clean, modern san facs; easily got twin axle into lge pitch (reserved); excel." ♦ 1 Apr-30 Sep. € 45.00 2011*

MANERBA DEL GARDA *1D2* (2km N Rural) *45.56138, 10.55944* **Camping Rio Ferienglück, Via del Rio 37, 25080 Manerba-del-Garda (BS) [0365 551450 or 551075; fax 551044; rioferiengluck@gardalake.it; www.gardalake.it/rioferiengluck]** Fr S572 rd turn E at traff lts sp Manerba Centro. At tourist office turn L down hill & at petrol stn turn R into Viale Degli Alpini. At next rndabt turn L & foll site sp. Site 1.5km N of Manerba opp Hotel Zodiaco. Lge, mkd pitch, pt shd; wc (some cont); chem disp; mv service pnt; shwrs inc; el pnts (6A); gas; Indtte (inc dryer); shop; tradsmn; rest nr; snacks; bar; BBQ; playgrnd; htd pool; paddling pool; shgl beach & lake sw adj; watersports; wifi; some statics; dogs; Eng spkn; no adv bkg; quiet; CCI. "Excel, family-run lakeside site with lge, level, grass pitches; welcoming vill nr; central for Garda sightseeing; conv for train to Venice & Milan; beautiful area." ♦ 1 Apr-30 Sep. € 29.50 2010*

MANERBA DEL GARDA *1D2* (1km SE Rural) *45.53040, 10.55487* **Camping Sivino's, Via Gramsci 78, 25080 Manerba-del-Garda (BS) [0365 552767; fax 550678; info@sivinos.it; www.campingsivinos.it]** Exit A4/E70 to Desenzano & foll sp dir Salo. In Moniga-del-Garda turn R at traff lts to vill sq & foll sp to Sivino's. Med, mkd pitch, terr, pt shd; wc; chem disp; shwrs inc; el pnts (6A) inc; gas 3km; Indtte; shops 1km; tradsmn; rest, snacks, bar at adj holiday vill; lake sw & shgl beach adj; 5% statics; dogs €8; phone; bus 500m; poss cr; Eng spkn; adv bkg; quiet. "Beautiful site; excel facs; dir access to lake; extra for superior lakeside pitches; noise poss high ssn due parties/discos nrby; this part of lake poss v windy - extra storm straps essential." ♦ 1 Apr-30 Sep. € 43.00 2009*

MANERBA DEL GARDA *1D2* (1km S Rural) *45.53916, 10.55555* **Camping Zocco, Via del Zocco 43, 25080 Manerba-del-Garda (BS) [0365 551605; fax 552053; info@campingzocco.it; www.campingzocco.it]** Fr Desenzano rd N twd Riva. In 5km take minor rd to Manerba. Shortly after Irish pub turn R dir Moniga-del-Garda, thro vill & foll site sp. Lge, mkd pitch, terr, shd; wc (some cont); some serviced pitches; baby facs; fam bthrm; shwrs inc; el pnts (4A) inc; gas; Indtte; shop; rest; bar; playgrnd; pool; paddling pool; beach & lake sw adj; tennis; games area; wifi; entmnt; 60% statics; dogs €4; ccard acc; red long stay/low ssn/CCI. "Beautiful situation; excel pool complex." ♦ 4 Apr-20 Sep. € 30.60 2009*

MANERBA DEL GARDA *1D2* (3km S Rural) *45.52555, 10.54333* **Camping Fontanelle, Via del Magone 13, 25080 Moniga-del-Garda (BS) [0365 502079; fax 503324; info@campingfontanelle.it; www.campingfontanelle.it]** Exit A4 m'way dir Desenzano del Garda & foll sp Salo. In 10km arr at Moniga del Garda take 2nd exit off 1st rndabt twd Salo, then 1st R into Via Roma sp Moniga Centro. Immed after 'Api' g'ge on L turn R into into Via Caccinelli; at end of this narr rd turn R into Via del Magone; site on L by lake. Access poss diff lge o'fits due narr vill rds. Lge, mkd pitch, sl, terr, pt shd; wc; chem disp; mv service pnt; baby facs; shwrs inc; el pnts (6A) inc; gas; Indtte (inc dryer); shop; supmkt; rest; snacks; bar; BBQ (gas/charcoal only); playgrnd; pool; paddling pool; lake sw & shgl beach; watersports; boat trips; fishing; tennis; golf 5km; horseriding 8km; cycle hire 2km; wifi; entmnt; games/TV rm; 20% statics; dogs €7; no c'vans/m'vans over 6.50m high ssn; phone; poss cr nr lake; Eng spkn; adv bkg; ccard acc; red low ssn/snr citizens; extra for lakeside pitches; CCI. "Vg site; excursions to Venice, Florence, Verona; friendly staff; excel san facs; levellers needed all pitches; pitches poss tight lge o'fits due trees; mkt Mon; lovely site, cheerful & helpful staff & nothing was too much trouble." ♦ 28 Apr-23 Sep. € 43.00 SBS - Y01 2011*

MANERBA DEL GARDA *1D2* (3.5km S Rural) *45.52006, 10.52945* **Camping Piantelle, Via San Michele 2, 25080 Moniga-del-Garda (BS) [0365 502013; fax 502637; info@piantelle.com; www.piantelle.com]** Fr Desenzano take SP572 sp Salo. In Moniga turn R twd lake & foll site sp. Lge, hdg/mkd pitch, some terr, pt shd; wc; chem disp; some serviced pitches; el pnts (6A) inc; Indtte; shop; rest; snacks; bar; playgrnd; pool; paddling pool; lake sw & beach adj; watersports; games area; gym; wifi; entmnt; TV; 25% statics; dogs €7.50; extra for lakeside pitches; Eng spkn; adv bkg; quiet; red low ssn/snr citizens. "Friendly, helpful staff; gd touring base; excel, well-kept, well-managed site & facs; sep area for v lge o'fits; site produces own olive oil." ♦ 1 Apr-26 Sep. € 35.00 2009*

⊞ **MANERBA DEL GARDA** *1D2* (2km SW Rural) *45.53186, 10.52741* **Camping Trevisago, Via Prato Negro 10, 25080 Moniga-del-Garda (BS) [tel/fax 0365 502252; info@trevisago.com; www.trevisago.com]** Fr Desenzano take SP572 sp Salo. In Moniga foll brown sp. Med, hdg/mkd pitch, pt shd; wc (some cont); chem disp; shwrs €1; el pnts (10A) €2.50; Indtte; shop 1km; rest; snacks; bar; playgrnd; pool; paddling pool; lake beach 1km; watersports; TV; 80% statics; dogs €2.50 (not acc mid-July to end Aug); phone; bus 400m; poss cr high ssn w/end; Eng spkn; adv bkg; quiet; CCI. "Owner v helpful; well-maintained facs; mountain views; gd." € 30.50 2010*

MARCIALLA CERTALDO see Poggibonsi *1D3*

MARINA DI BIBBONA see Cecina *1D3*

MARINA DI CAMEROTA *3A4* (4km N Coastal) *40.02650, 15.32583* **Camping Nessuno, Via Mingardo 3, 84059 Marina-di-Camerota (SA) [tel/fax 0974 931457; info@villaggionessuno.com; www.villaggionessuno.com]** On coast rd N twd Palinuro, site on L 1.5km after series of sh tunnels. NB Height restriction 3.3m & width 2.3m at Lentiscosa. Lge, mkd pitch, pt shd, terr, shd; wc; chem disp; mv service pnt; shwrs inc; el pnts (3A) inc; gas; Indtte; shop & 1km; rest; bar; playgrnd; sand beach adj; games area; cash machine; entmnt; 10% statics; dogs; phone; sep car park; poss cr; Eng spkn; no adv bkg; some rd noise; ccard acc. "On sand in pine forest; dir access to beach; most pitches reasonable size; friendly, helpful staff." ♦ 29 May-5 Sep. € 46.00 2010*

MARINA DI CAMPO (ELBA ISLAND) *1C3* (E Coastal) *42.75194, 10.24472* **Camping Ville degli Ulivi, Via della Foce 89, 57034 Marina-di-Campo nell'Elba (LI) [0565 976098; fax 976048; info@villedegliulivi.it; www.villedegliulivi.it]** Fr Portoferraio take rd sp 'tutti le direzione', then foll sp Procchio, Marina-di-Campo & La Foce, site sp. Lge, pt shd; wc (some cont); chem disp; mv service pnt; baby facs; shwrs inc; el pnts (4A) €2.50; gas; Indtte; shop; rest; snacks; bar; no BBQ; playgrnd; pool; paddling pool; waterslides; sand beach adj; watersports; tennis 300m; horseriding 2km; cycle hire; golf 15km; archery; 30% statics; dogs €6; dog shwrs; internet; adv bkg; quiet; ccard acc. "Lovely, well-preserved island; gd, modern site." ♦ 1 Apr-15 Oct. € 45.00 2007*

MARINA DI CAULONIA *3B4* (1km NE Coastal) *38.35480, 16.48375* **Camping Calypso, Contrada Precariti, 89040 Marina-di-Caulonia (RC) [tel/fax 0964 82028; info@villaggiocalypso.com; www.villaggiocalypso.com]** On o'skts of Marina-di-Caulonia on S106. Med, mkd pitch, shd; wc (mainly cont); mv service pnt; chem disp; baby facs; shwrs €0.50; el pnts (2A) €3.50; Indtte; shop; rest; snacks; bar; playgrnd; sand beach adj; games area; tennis 500m; games area; entmnt; TV rm; 5% statics; dogs €2.50; phone; sep car park high ssn; Eng spkn; ccard acc; CCI. "Superb sandy beach; gd (if dated) facs; close to early Byzantine church at Stilo & medieval hill vill of Gerace." 1 Apr-30 Sep. € 28.50 2009*

MARINA DI EBOLI see Paestum *3A3*

MARINA DI GROSSETO see Grosseto *1D3*

MARINA DI MASSA *1C3* (1km N Coastal) *44.0250, 10.07388* **Camping Giardino, Via delle Pinete 382, Loc Partaccia, 54037 Marina-di-Massa (MS) [0585 869291; fax 240781; info@campinggiardino.com; www.campinggiardino.com]** On coast rd bet Marina-di-Massa & Marina-di-Carrara, sp. Lge, shd; wc (some cont); chem disp; mv service pnt; shwrs; el pnts (3A) (check pol); gas; Indtte; shop; rest 200m; snacks; bar; playgrnd; pool adj; paddling pool; sand beach 100m; 50% statics; dogs (not Jun-Aug); phone; sep car park; poss cr; adv bkg; rd noise; ccard acc; red low ssn. "Spacious pitches low ssn; conv NH for A12." ♦ 1 Apr-26 Sep. € 38.00 2010*

MARINA DI MASSA *1C3* (3km N Coastal) *44.02509, 10.08627* **Camping Oasi, Via Silcia, Loc Partaccia, 54037 Marina-di-Massa (MS) [0585 780305; fax 788190; info@campingoasi.it; www.campingoasi.it]** Exit A12 at Massa & foll sp Marina-di-Massa thro traff lts. At next traff lts turn R, then turn R at 3rd traff lts, Via Silcia is 3rd R; site sp. Narr, twisty rd to site. Med, pt shd; wc (some cont); chem disp (wc); shwrs inc; el pnts (5A) inc; gas; Indtte; shop 400m; rest; snacks; bar; playgrnd; pool; sand beach 800m; 75% statics; dogs €6 (sm dogs only); phone; sep car park; poss cr; Eng spkn; adv bkg; quiet; ccard acc; red long stay/CCI. "Friendly, helpful staff but tatty site; diff to manoeuvre c'vans around site; tight pitches; gd rest; conv Pisa, Florence; mountain views; NH only." ♦ Easter-15 Sep. € 34.00 2008*

⊞ **MARINA DI MASSA** *1C3* (1km NW Coastal) *44.02764, 10.06803* **Campeggio Italia, Via delle Pinete 412, Loc Partaccia, 54037 Marina-di-Massa (MS) [0585 780055; fax 631733; info@campeggioitalia.com; www.campeggioitalia.com]** Exit A12 at Massa, foll sp Marina-di-Massa. Head twd Marina di Carrera, site sp. V lge, shd; htd wc; chem disp (wc); mv service pnt; shwrs inc; el pnts (3A) inc (long lead poss req); Indtte (inc dryer); shop; tradsmn; rest; bar; private sand beach 800m; wifi; TV rm; 90% statics; no dogs; bus adj; poss cr; Eng spkn; no adv bkg; rd noise; ccard acc. "Basic site; friendly staff; vg touring base." ♦ € 34.00 (CChq acc) 2008*

MARINA DI MINTURNO *2F4* (6km SE Coastal) *41.20731, 13.79138* **Camping Villlagio Baia Domizia, Via Pietre Bianche, 81030 Baia-Domizia (CE) [0823 930164; fax 930375; info@baiadomizia.it; www.baiadomizia.it]** Exit A1 at Cassino onto S630, twd Minturno on S7 & S7quater, turn off at km 2, then foll sp Baia Domizia, site in 1.5km N of Baia-Domizia. V lge, hdg pitch, shd; wc (some cont); chem disp; mv service pnt; baby facs; shwrs inc; el pnts (3-10A) inc (poss rev pol); gas; Indtte; shop; rest; snacks; bar; 2 pools; sand beach adj; boat hire; windsurfing; tennis; games area; cycle hire; entmnt; TV; no dogs; poss cr; quiet; ccard acc; red low ssn. "Excel facs; 30/7-16/8 min 7 night stay; site clsd 1400-1600 but adequate parking area; top class site with all facs; gd security." ♦ 30 Apr-20 Sep. € 45.40 2009*

MARINA DI MINTURNO *2F4* (3km S Coastal) *41.22891, 13.75482* **Camping Golden Garden, Via Dunale 74, 04020 Marina-di-Minturno (LT) [tel/fax 0771 614985; servizio.clienti@goldengarden.it; www.goldengarden.it]** S on S7 Via Appia; bef x-ing Rv Garigliano turn R foll N bank of rv almost to mouth. Turn R, site on L in 300m. Or fr Gaeta (16km S) foll old S7 Via Appia, thro Scauri, turn R at traff lts after km 153 sp, Bar Marina on corner, foll sp. Med, mkd pitch, pt shd; wc; chem disp; shwrs inc; el pnts (4A) inc; gas 5km; Indtte; shop 5km; bar; sand beach adj; waterskiing; games area; solarium; entmnt; 50% statics; dogs €5; phone; sep car park; poss cr; Eng spkn; adv bkg; ccard acc; red low ssn. "Gd sand beach; slightly run down area." ♦ 30 Apr-5 Sep. € 35.00 2010*

ITALY

MARINA DI MONTENERO *2F4* (1km NW Coastal) *42.06500, 14.77700* **Centro Vacanze Molise, SS Adriatica, Km 525, 86036 Marina-di-Montenero (CB) [tel/fax 0873 803570; info@campingmolise.it; www.campingmolise.it]** Exit A14 at Vasto Sud to SS16 dir S. On R Centro Commerciale Costa Verde, site opp on L. Med, mkd pitch, pt shd; wc (some cont); chem disp; mv service pnt; shwrs inc; el pnts (3A) inc; gas; Indtte; shop opp; tradsmn; rest; snacks; bar; private sand beach adj; tennis; games area; dogs €1; phone; bus; poss cr; Eng spkn; adv bkg; poss noisy high ssn; CCI. "Excel site; helpful staff; vg beach; Aqualand Water Park nr; Tremiti Isands rec; gd touring base; conv for m'way A14." ♦ 14 May-15 Sep. € 31.00 2011*

I'll fill in a report online and let the Club know – www.caravanclub.co.uk/europereport

This is a wonderful site.

MARINA DI PISA *1C3* (1km S Coastal) *43.65294, 10.28365* **Camping Internazionale, Via Litoranea 7, 56103 Marina-di-Pisa (PI) [050 35211; fax 36553; campinternazionale@alice.it; www.campeggiointernazionale.com]** On L of coast rd fr Marina de Pisa to Livorno. Lge, hdg/mkd pitch; shd; wc; chem disp; mv waste; shwrs €0.50; el pnts (3A) inc; Indtte; shop; snacks; bar; private beach adj; statics; dogs €2; adv bkg; quiet; ccard acc. "Fair site." 1 May-30 Sep. € 24.00 2008*

MARINA DI PISA *1C3* (6km S Coastal) *43.64720, 10.29603* **Camping Village St Michael, Via della Bigattiera 24, 56018 Tirrenia (PI) [050 33103; fax 33041; info@campingstmichael.com; www.campingstmichael.com]** Fr A12/E80 exit Pisa Sud & foll sp Tirrenia. In vill turn N twd Marina di Pisa, sp along coast rd to R. Lge, hdg pitch, pt shd; wc (some cont); chem disp; shwrs €0.50; el pnts (3A) inc; gas; Indtte; shop; rest; snacks; bar; playgrnd; private sand beach 600m; games area; golf 1.5km; entmnt; TV; 25% statics; no dogs; bus to Pisa & Livorno 600m; phone; poss cr; quiet; ccard acc. "Nr Livorno for ferries to Sardinia & Corsica; helpful staff." ♦ 1 Jun-15 Sep. € 29.00 2009*

MARINA DI RAVENNA *2E2* (6km N Coastal) *44.55895, 12.27995* **Camping Adria, Via Spallazzi 30, 48010 Casal-Borsetti (RA) [0544 445217; fax 442014; adria@camping.it; www.villaggiocampingadria.it]** Fr Ravenna take SS309 N for 17km, then at km 13 R (E) to sea & Casal-Borsetti & foll camp sp. Lge, pt shd; wc (some cont); chem disp; baby facs; shwrs inc; el pnts (4A) inc; gas; Indtte (inc dryer); shop; tradsmn; rest; snacks; bar; BBQ; playgrnd; pool; paddling pool; private beach 200m; wifi (recep area); entmnt; TV rm; 75% statics; dogs €4; phone; bus; poss cr; Eng spkn; adv bkg; ccard acc; red low ssn; CCI. "Conv Venice/gd NH bet Ancona & Venice; 1st class beach; new pool complex; many interesting buildings." ♦ 16 Apr-15 Sep. € 30.60 (CChq acc) 2011*

MARINA DI VASTO see Vasto *2F4*

MARONE *1C1* (1km S Rural) *45.73166, 10.09361* **Campeggio Riva di San Pietro, Via Cristini 9, 25054 Marone (BS) [tel/fax 030 9827129; info@rivasanpietro.it; www.rivasanpietro.it]** Site well sp on lakeside on L of SS510 on app Marone dir Pisogne. Turn sharp L, site adj Camping Breda. Med, mkd pitch, pt shd; wc (some cont); chem disp; mv service pnt; baby facs; shwrs inc; el pnts (4A) inc; gas; Indtte; shop; tradsmn; rest, snacks, bar 150m; playgrnd; 2 pools; lake sw; boat hire; windsurfing; canoeing; solarium; cycle hire; 30% statics; dogs €3; sep car park; poss v cr; Eng spkn; adv bkg (ess high ssn); rd/rlwy noise; red long stay; ccard acc; CCI. "Welcoming, helpful owners; poss v cr & cramped, even low ssn; gd dog exercise area." ♦ 1 May-30 Sep. € 31.00 2009*

MARTINSICURO *2F3* (Coastal/Urban) *42.88027, 13.92055* **Camping Riva Nuova, Via dei Pioppi 6, 64014 Martinsicuro (TE) [0861 797515; fax 797516; info@rivanuova.it; www.rivanuova.it]** Fr N exit A14/E55 sp San Benedetto-del-Tronto onto S16 dir Pescara to Martinsicuro, site sp. Lge, shd; wc (some cont); chem disp; mv service pnt; baby facs; shwrs inc; el pnts inc; Indtte; shop; rest; snacks; bar; playgrnd; pool; paddling pool; sand beach adj; watersports; games area; gym; cycle hire; entmnt; TV rm; excursions; adv bkg; ccard acc. ♦ 26 Apr-20 Sep. € 39.30 2008*

MARTINSICURO *2F3* (10km N Coastal) *42.97238, 13.87748* **International Camping Don Diego, Lungomare De Gasperi 124, 63013 Grottammare (AP) [0735 581285; fax 583166; info@dondiegocamping.it; www.campingdondiego.it]** Exit A14/E55 dir Grottammare, site bet San Bernadetto & Grottammare off SS16 coast rd, well sp. Lge, shd; wc (some cont); shwrs inc; el pnts (6A) €3.50; gas; Indtte; shop; rest; snacks; bar; no BBQ; playgrnd; beach adj; games area; internet; entmnt; 50% statics; no dogs; adv bkg; quiet; ccard acc; red low ssn; CCI. "Gd facs; vg." ♦ 29 May-12 Sep. € 44.50 2010*

MASSA LUBRENSE see Sorrento *3A3*

⊞ **MATERA** *3A4* (2km S Rural) *40.65305, 16.60694* **Azienda Agrituristica Masseria del Pantaleone, Contrada Chiancalata 27, 75100 Matera (MT) [0835 335239; info@agriturismopantaleonematera.it; www.agriturismopantaleonematera.it]** Fr S on SS7 take Matera Sud exit, site 2km on L, not well sp. Opp Ospedale Madonna delle Grazie. Sm, all hdstg, terr, pt shd; wc; chem disp; mv service pnt; shwrs €1; el pnts (16A) inc; rest; bar; BBQ; dogs; Eng spkn; quiet; CCI. "Conv Matera - World Heritage site; helpful owners provide transport to/fr Matera cent." € 12.00 2010*

MATTINATA *2G4* (2km Coastal) *41.70510, 16.06681* **Camping Mattinata, Contrada Funni, 71030 Mattinata (FG) [tel/fax 0884 550313; mattinata@camping.it]** Exit a'strada A14 at Foggia, sp Manfredonia. Fr Manfredonia on SS89 foll sp to Mattinata. Turn twds sea at km 145.8 & foll sp 'Lido'. Tight turn R into site fr W. Lge, pt shd; wc; shwrs €0.50; el pnts (4A) €2.07; gas; Indtte; shop; snacks; bar; playgrnd; sand/shgl beach adj; watersports; tennis; entmnt; 30% statics; no dogs; sep car park; poss cr; adv bkg; quiet. 25 May-25 Sep. € 39.00 (3 persons) 2009*

⊞ **MATTINATA** *2G4* (2km NE Coastal) **Villagio Camping Il Principe, Via del Mare, Loc Puntone del Principe, 71030 Mattinata (FG) [0884 550903; fax 552042; campingilprincipe@alice.it; www.villaggioilprincipe.it]** Sp on coast rd fr Manfredonia dir Vieste, opp marina. Lge, mkd pitch, hdstg, shd; wc (some cont); chem disp; baby facs; shwrs inc; el pnts (4A) inc; gas; lndtte; shop 2km; tradsmn; rest; snacks; bar; BBQ; playgrnd; pool; sand beach 300m; tennis; games area; boat hire; TV & games rm; 70% statics; dogs; phone; bus; poss cr; Eng spkn; adv bkg; some rd noise; red long stay; CCI. "Gd, clean site & facs; ltd touring pitches; sea views; friendly owners; pleasant town; conv Gargano National Park & Forest of Umbra; poss clsd winter - phone ahead." ♦ € 33.50 2007*

⊞ **MATTINATA** *2G4* (2km E Coastal) *41.69779, 16.06393* **Camping Punta Grugno, 71030 Mattinata (FG)** Exit A14 at Foggia onto SS89 dir Manfredonia. On o'skts Manfredonia foll sp to Mattinata, then foll sp Litorale & Vieste. Turn R at sp for multiple sites & foll sp to end of rd. Med, hdstg, pt shd; wc; chem disp; mv service pnt; shwrs €0.75; el pnts (6A) €2.50; shop; snacks, bar adj; shgl beach adj; dogs; poss cr; quiet. "Clean, pleasant site under olive trees; basic facs; narr access not suitable lge o'fits; most suitable m'vans; useful out of ssn when adj sites clsd." € 17.50 2007*

MENAGGIO *1C1* (500m N Rural) *46.02516, 9.23996* **Camping Europa, Loc Leray, Via dei Cipressi 12, 22017 Menaggio (CO) [0344 31187]** On ent Menaggio fr S (Como) on S240 turn R & foll 'Campeggio' sp along lakeside prom. On ent fr N turn L at 'Campeggio' sp, pass site ent & turn in boatyard. Sm, mkd pitch, terr, pt shd; wc; shwrs; el pnts; shop; rest 300m; snacks; bar; lake sw; boat hire; cycle hire; 80% statics; dogs; poss v cr; Eng spkn; adv bkg; rd noise; CCI. "V sm pitches cramped high ssn; narr site rds diff for lge o'fits; old-fashioned facs but clean; poor security; helpful owner; m'vans rec to arr full of water & empty of waste; hardly any road noise, Menaggio delightful place." 1 Apr-30 Sep. € 21.00 2011*

MENAGGIO *1C1* (6km S Urban) *45.96937, 9.19298* **Camping La'vedo, Via degli Artigiani 1, 22016 Lenno (CO) [0344 56288]** Fr Como foll S340 along W shore of lake, site SE of Lenno 200m fr lake, adj to supmkt. Sm, pt sl, pt shd; wc (cont); chem disp; mv service pnt; shwrs €0.50; el pnts (3A) inc; lndtte; shop adj; rest opp; bar; BBQ; games area; entmnt; 25% statics; dogs; rd noise; CCI. "Picturesque, friendly site in sm town; basic facs; 15 mins to boat stn for other towns on lake; great care needed on S340 - v narr & busy rd." ♦ 1 Apr-30 Sep. € 20.00 2008*

MERANO/MERAN *1D1* (500m S Urban) *46.66361, 11.15638* **Camping Merano, Via Piave/Piavestrasse 44, 39012 Merano/Meran (BZ) [0473 231249; fax 235524; info@meran.eu]** Exit S38 at Merano Sud & foll rd into town. Brown site sps to Camping & Tennis (no name at main juncs in town cent). Site ent mkd 'Camping Tennis'. Site also sp fr N. Med, hdstg, pt shd; wc; chem disp; mv service pnt; shwrs inc; el pnts (6A) €2.40; shop opp; supmkt 500m; rest, snacks, bar adj; htd pool; tennis adj; no statics; dogs €3.30; phone; poss cr; some rd noise; red long stay days; CCI. "Sh walk to town cent; fine site surrounded by spectacular mountain scenery; helpful staff; pitches soft after rain." Easter-3 Nov. € 25.10 2008*

MERANO/MERAN *1D1* (9km S Rural) *46.59861, 11.14527* **Camping Völlan, Zehentweg 6, 39011 Völlan/Foiana [0473 568056; fax 557249; info@camping-voellan.com; www.camping-voellan.com]** Leave S38 dual c'way (Merano-Bolzano) S of Merano sp Lana. Drive thro Lana, turn uphill sp Gampenpass. Turn R sp Foliana/Völlan & foll sp to site. Sm, mkd pitch, terr, pt shd; wc; chem disp; mv service pnt; some serviced pitches; shwrs €0.50; el pnts (4A) €2.50; lndtte (inc dryer); shop; rest 800m; playgrnd; pool; golf 6km; 10% statics; dogs €3; phone; Eng spkn; quiet; CCI. "Long drag up to site fr Lana, but worth it; beautiful situation o'looking Adige Valley; excel facs & pool; barriers clsd 1300-1500 & 2200-0700; v helpful owners." 19 Mar-7 Nov. € 24.00 2010*

⊞ **MESTRE** *2E2* (3km E Urban) *45.48098, 12.27516* **Venezia Camping Village, Via Orlanda 8/C, 30170 Mestre (VE) [tel/fax 041 5312828; info@veneziavillage.it; www.veneziavillage.it]** On A4 fr Milan/Padova take exit SS11 dir Venice. Exit SS11 for SS14 dir Trieste & airport. 200m after Agip g'ge on R watch for sp and take first exit R from rdbt between two major dealerships. Keep in R lane all way to site. Med, mkd pitch, pt shd; wc; chem disp; mv service pnt; shwrs inc; el pnts (6A) inc (poss rev pol); gas; lndtte (inc dryer); shop high ssn; rest; snacks; bar; playgrnd; pool 3km; sand beach 6km; rv sw 2km; wifi; TV; 20% statics; dogs; phone; buses to Venice; poss cr & noisy high ssn; Eng spkn; adv bkg; red long stay/CCI. "V conv Venice - tickets/maps fr recep; clean, well-run site; popular with m'vanners; friendly, helpful owners; pitches poss cramped when site full; mosquitoes. new recep/bar/rest/shop/wellness area; new toilet block 2011; excel." € 33.00 2011*

MESTRE *2E2* (4km E Urban) *45.48425, 12.28227* **Camping Rialto, 16 Via Orlanda, Loc Campalto, 30175 Mestre (VE) [041 900785; info@campingrialto.com; www.campingrialto.com]** Fr A4 take Marco Polo Airport exit, then fork R onto SS14 dir Venice. Site on L 1km past Campalto opp lge car sales area, well sp. Do not enter Mestre. Med, pt shd; wc (mainly cont); chem disp; mv service pnt; shwrs inc; el pnts (15A) €1.50; lndtte; shop; no statics; dogs €3; phone; bus to Venice; poss cr; Eng spkn; adv bkg; some rd noise; red CCI. "Site in need of refurb but v conv Venice; bus tickets fr recep; friendly, helpful staff." 1 Feb-30 Oct. € 31.00 2010*

MESTRE *2E2* (3km S Urban) *45.47138, 12.21166* **Camping Jolly delle Querce, Via G De Marchi 7, 30175 Marghera (VE) [tel/fax 041 920312; info@jollycamping.com; www.jollycamping.com]** App fr Milan, exit A4/E70 immed after toll, sp Mestre/Ferrovia/Marghera, then onto SS309 at rndabt sp Chioggia, then 1st R, site sp on R. Lge, shd; wc; chem disp; shwrs; el pnts (4A) inc (rev pol); gas; lndtte; shop; snacks; bar; pool; paddling pool; 80% statics; dogs free; poss cr; v noisy fr adj airport & m'way; 10% red CCI. "Bus to Venice 15 min walk." 1 Feb-30 Nov. € 30.60 2008*

⊞ **MILANO** *1C2* (8km W Urban) *45.47390, 9.08233* **Camping Citta di Milano, Via Gaetano Airaghi 61, 20153 Milano [0248 207017; fax 202999; info@campingmilano.it; www.campingmilano.it]** Fr E35/E62/A50 Tangentiale Ovest ring rd take Settimo-Milanese exit & foll sp San Siro along Via Novara (SS11). Turn R in 2km at Shell petrol stn, then R at traff lts in 500m & L to site in 600m. Site ent at Gardaland Waterpark, poorly sp. Lge, mkd pitch, pt shd; wc; chem disp; mv service pnt; shwrs inc; el pnts (3A) inc; lndtte; shop 500m; rest; snacks; bar; waterspark adj; dogs €3.50; phone; bus 500m; poss cr; Eng spkn; no adv bkg; rd, aircraft noise, disco at w/end & waterpark adj; ccard acc; red low ssn/CCI. "Gd san facs; noise fr adj concerts high ssn; conv bus/metro Milan; properly penned animals for children to enjoy." ♦ € 32.00 2011*

MISURINA see Cortina d'Ampezzo *2E1*

⊞ **MODENA** *1D2* (3km N Urban) *44.65429, 10.86884* **Camping International, Via Cave di Ramo 111, 41100 Modena (MO) [059 332252 or 06771259 (mob); fax 823235; info@internationalcamping.org; www.internationalcamping.org]** Exit A1/E35/E45 to Modena Nord; after toll station turn 1st L & immed L again at rndabt, then R; site nr motel rest adj to toll booth. Alt rte fr city cent: take S9 Via Emilia fr cent sp dir Milan; camp sp clear on R of main rd; turn R; foll sp. Med, mkd pitch, pt shd; wc (cont); chem disp; mv service pnt; shwrs inc; el pnts (6-10A) €3 (poss rev pol); gas; lndtte; ice shop; rest; snacks; bar; playgrnd; pool; dogs €2; phone; poss cr; Eng spkn; rd noise; ccard not acc; CCI. "Easy to find; poss itinerants; parts of site waterlogged after heavy rain; facs clean but inadequate for size of site high ssn; conv for m'way; call mobile no. if arr low ssn; mosquitoes NH only." ♦ € 27.00 2009*

⊞ **MODENA** *1D2* (2km SE Urban) *44.61361, 10.94444* **Camper Club Mutina, Strada Collegarola 76A, 41100 Modena (MO) [059 4557043; fax 39 1782732524; camperclub.mutina@tiscali.it; www.camperclubmutina.it]** Exit A1 Modena Sud onto SP623 dir 'Centro'. In approx 4km site sp on L (also sp Camper Market). Site adj rugby club. M'vans only. Sm, hdstg, unshd; htd wc (cont); chem disp; mv service pnt; shwrs inc; el pnts (6A) inc; gas; lndry rm; BBQ; wifi; bus 1km; vehicle-washing facs; red CCI. "Vg facs; easy access to Modena; phone first if car+c'van - poss acc, good security, mini-bus to city, cycle path to city 60m, very friendly site." € 15.00 2011*

MOLINA DI LEDRO see Pieve di Ledro *1D1*

⊞ **MOLVENO** *1D1* (1km SW Rural) *46.13916, 10.95916* **Camping Spiaggia Lago di Molveno, Via Lungolago 25, 38018 Molveno (TN) [0461 586978; fax 586330; info@campingmolveno.it; www.campingmolveno.it]** Fr Molveno head S on W side of lake, 1km on L. Lge, shd, mkd pitch; wc; shwrs inc; chem disp; mv service pnt; el pnts (5A) inc; gas 1km; lndtte; shop; rest; snacks; bar; lake sw; windsurfing; tennis; games area; cycle hire; ski school; hiking; TV; 60% statics; dogs €4; phone; poss cr w/end; Eng spkn; quiet; ccard acc; red low ssn. "Beautiful vill & mountains; well-maintained, high quality, friendly, busy site; clean san facs; vg." € 35.00 2009*

MONFALCONE *2E1* (8km SE Coastal) *45.77241, 13.6245* **Camping Mare Pineta, Via Sistiana 60/D, 34019 Sistiana (TS) [040 299264; fax 299265; info@marepineta.com; www.baiaholiday.com]** Well sp on SS14 on NW o'skirts of Sistiana. V lge, pt sl, terr, shd; wc (mainly cont); mv service pnt; some serviced pitches; shwrs inc; el pnts (3A) inc; lndtte; shop; rest; snacks; bar; playgrnd; pool; beach 600m; tennis; cycle hire; solarium; 30% statics; dogs €8; quiet; ccard acc; red long stay/CCI. "Free bus to beach; overlkg Adriatic & Bay of Trieste; site tight for lge m'vans." ♦ 1 Apr-15 Oct. € 40.00 2011*

MONFALCONE *2E1* (9km SE Rural/Coastal) *45.76742, 13.64214* **Camping Alle Rose, Via Sistiana 24/D, 34013 Sistiana (TS) [040 299457]** Exit A4 at Sistiana exit & foll sp Sistiana. On app to vill turn R at T-junc, pass supmkt set back on R & look for blue site sp on L bef shops. Narr ent poss diff lge o'fits. Sm, shd; wc (some cont); shwrs; el pnts (6A) inc; gas adj; rest 200m; shgl beach 1km; dogs; bus to Trieste 300m; Eng spkn; quiet. "Shops & rests in walking dist; sand beach at Monfalcone; friendly, helpful owner; lovely spot - like a gd CL." 10 May-30 Sep. € 21.00 2010*

MONIGA DEL GARDA see Manerba del Garda *1D2*

MONOPOLI *2H4* (2.5km SE Coastal) *40.92646, 17.33185* **Camping Santo Stefano, 70043 Monopoli (BA) [080 777065]** Site clearly sp on coast rd. Lge, pt sl, pt shd; wc; chem disp; shwrs €0.33; el pnts (3A) €2.50; shop & 6km; rest 100m; beach adj; 65% statics; dogs €4; poss cr in ssn; quiet; CCI. Apr-Sep. € 27.00 2008*

MONTALTO DI CASTRO *1D4* (5.5km SW Coastal) *42.30494, 11.62260* **California International Camping Village, Loc Le Castellette, 01014 Marina-di-Montalto (VT) [0766 802848; fax 801210; info@californiacampingvillage.com; www.californiacampingvillage.com]** Fr SS1 Via Aurelia at km 105.5 turn twds Marina-di-Montalto, site sp. V lge, mkd pitch, shd; wc; mv service pnt; shwrs inc; el pnts (4A) inc; lndry rm; shop; rest; snacks; bar; playgrnd; pool; paddling pool; waterslides; sand beach adj; watersports; fishing; games area; fitness rm; entmnt; TV rm; 25% statics; no dogs; adv bkg. "Sm pitches; peaceful site." ♦ 1 May-20 Sep. € 37.00 2008*

MONTECATINI TERME *1D3* (3km N Rural) *43.90505, 10.79190* **Camping Belsito, Via delle Vigne 1/A, Loc Vico, 51016 Montecatini-Terme (PT) [tel/fax 0572 67373; info@campingbelsito.it; www.campingbelsito.it]** Fr Montecatini-Terme foll sp to Montecatini-Alto for 3km; site sp fr rd junc nr vill. NB Steep app with hairpins but OK with care & balanced o'fit. Med, mkd pitch, some hdstg, pt sl, pt shd; wc (some cont); chem disp; mv service pnt; 50% serviced pitch; private bthrms some pitches - extra charge; shwrs inc; el pnts (6A) €1.50 (check pol); lndtte (inc dryer); sm shop; rest; bar; BBQ; playgrnd; htd pool; games rm; internet; TV; 10% statics; dogs; phone; bus; Eng spkn; adv bkg ess; quiet; ccard acc; red low ssn/long stay/CCI. "Superb, well-kept site; excel facs; beautiful situation in high ground o'looking Tuscan hills/valleys; helpful staff; conv for Florence, Pisa & Lucca; gate clsd 1300-1500; excel pool & rest; traditional Easter lunch at camp rest was outstanding." ♦ 1 Apr-30 Sep. € 33.00 2011*

MONTECRETO see Lama Mocogno *1D2*

MONTEGROTTO TERME see Padova *1D2*

MONTESE *1D2* (3km S Rural) *44.25569, 10.93254* **Camping Ecochiocciola, Via Testa 80, 41055 Maserno-di-Montese (MO) [059 980065; fax 980025; info@ecochiocciola.com; www.ecochiocciola.com]** Exit A1 Modena Sud onto S623 dir Vignola, then rd P4. At Verica turn L to Montese & foll sp 'Chiocciola' to Maserno & site. Med, mkd pitch, pt sl, pt shd; wc (mainly cont); mv service pnt; shwrs inc; el pnts (6A) inc; shop 200m; rest; bar; BBQ; pool high ssn; tennis; games rm; TV; 30% statics; dogs €5; bus 100m; sep car park; site clsd 5 Nov-5 Dec; Eng spkn; quiet; CCI. "Beautiful setting; friendly owner knowledgeable about local ecology; excel cent for walking; ltd touring pitches suitable sm m'vans only; gd rest." ♦ 4 Apr-2 Nov & Xmas/New Year. € 35.00 2010*

MONTEVARCHI *1D3* (10km S Rural) *43.44500, 11.61855* **Camping La Chiocciola, Via G Cesare, 52020 Capannole (AR) [tel/fax 055 995776; info@campinglachiocciola.com; www.campinglachiocciola.com]** Exit A1 at Valdarno & foll sp Levane. In Levane strt on at traff lts sp Bucine, site on R in 7km. NB Do not ent Bucine - narr rds. Med, hdg/mkd pitch, terr, pt shd; wc; chem disp; mv service pnt; all serviced pitch; shwrs inc; el pnts (6A) inc; gas; lndtte; hypmkt 13km; tradsmn; rest adj; playgrnd; htd pool adj; statics inc tour ops; dogs €2; poss v cr; Eng spkn; adv bkg (rec book in Jan for Jul/Aug); ccard acc; noise of barking dogs; CCI. "Excel for Tuscany, Florence & Siena easy drive; vg, clean san facs; lge pitches; site v cr early ssn - rec book mkd pitch; vg pool." ♦ 1 Mar-25 Oct. € 40.00 2011*

MONTEVARCHI *1D3* (12km W Rural) **Camping Piano Orlando, Loc Cafaggiolo, 52022 Cavriglia (FI) [tel/fax 055 967422; info@campingchianti.com; www.campingchianti.com]** Fr Montevarchi take P408 to Cavriglia & foll sp for Castelnuovo-dei-Sabbiono. Site is 5km W of Castelnuovo, sp. Steep, narr rd. Easier rte on R222, turn E at Greve-in-Chianti & foll sp. Med, mkd pitch, pt sl, shd; wc; chem disp; mv service pnt; shwrs inc; el pnts (3A) inc; gas; lndtte; shop; rest; snacks; bar; pool; 10% statics; dogs; phone; poss cr; Eng spkn; ccard acc. "Site high on Monti di Chianti, surrounded by forests; 500m fr ent of Parco di Cavriglia; gd walking." 1 Mar-31 Oct. € 30.00 2009*

⊞ **MONTOPOLI IN VAL D'ARNO** *1D3* (1km N Rural) *43.67611, 10.75333* **Kawan Toscana Village, Via Fornoli 9, 56020 Montópoli (PI) [0571 449032; fax 449449; info@toscanavillage.com; www.toscanavillage.com]** Bet Pisa & Florence; exit Fi-Pi-Li dual c'way at Montópoli, foll site sps. Turn L bef Montópoli vill - site well sp. Med, mkd pitch, terr, pt shd; htd wc (some cont); chem disp; mv service pnt; some serviced pitches; baby facs; shwrs inc; el pnts (10A) €2.50; gas; lndtte (inc dryer); shop; tradsmn; supmkt 4km; rest; snacks; bar; BBQ; playgrnd; pool high ssn; cycle hire; golf 7km; wifi; TV rm; 15% statics; dogs; phone; train 3km; poss cr; Eng spkn; adv bkg req; some rd noise; ccard acc; red long stay; CCI. "Helpful staff; gravel site rds, steep in places; some v sm pitches; spotless facs; gd food in rest; gd pool; well organised; excel for Florence, Pisa & Tuscany." ♦ € 31.00 (CChq acc) 2011*

MONZA *1C2* (4km N Urban) *45.62305, 9.28027* **Camping Autodromo, Via Santa Maria alle Selve, 20046 Biassono (MI) [tel/fax 039 387771; campmonza@libero.it; www.monzanet.it/eng/campeggi.aspx]** Fr E exit A4 at Agrate-Brianza; fr W A4 exit Sesto San Giovanni onto S36. Foll sp to Autodromo/Biassono, then to site in Parco Reale complex. NB: Do not go to Monza Centro or exit main rd to Autodromo as no access to site; site clearly sp by g'ge. Lge, shd; wc (cont); own san rec; mv service pnt; shwrs €0.50; el pnts (5A) €2; lndtte (inc dryer); shop; rest adj; snacks; bar; playgrnd; pool adj; games area; 10% statics; dogs; phone; bus to Milan nr; poss cr; Eng spkn; no adv bkg; quiet except during racing. "Day ticket for all transport; bus 200m fr gate to Sesto FC (rlwy stn, bus terminal & metro line 1) - fr there take metro to Duomo; poor facs; NH/sh stay only for racing." ♦ 21 Apr-30 Sep. € 24.00 2009*

MORGEX see Courmayeur *1A1*

MUGGIA see Trieste *2F1*

NARNI *2E3* (6km S Rural) *42.48459, 12.51516* **Camping Monti del Sole, Strada Borgaria 22, 05035 Narni (TR) [tel/fax 0744 796336; montisole@libero.it; www.campingmontidelsole.it]** Fr Narni on S3 dir Rome, then foll sp Borgheria, R in 1km. Diff rd to site. Med, shd; wc (some cont); chem disp; mv service pnt; shwrs inc; el pnts (5A) inc; lndtte; rest high ssn; snacks; bar; pool high ssn; paddling pool; tennis; games area; 20% statics; no dogs; phone; adv bkg; quiet. "Beautiful wooded site in heart of Umbria; off-the-beaten-track; lge pitches; dated san facs, but clean; friendly, welcoming owner; conv Rome, Perugia, Spoleto." ♦ 1 Apr-30 Sep. € 27.50 2010*

NATURNO/NATURNS *1D1* (500m S Rural) *46.6475, 11.00722* **Camping Adler, Via Lido 14, 39025 Naturno (BZ) [0473 667242; fax 668346; info@campingadler.com; www.campingadler.com]** Fr E on S38 turn L at rndabt into Naturno, L at traff lts & foll sp to site. Fr W after passing thro tunnel bypass, turn R at rndabt then as above. Med, pt shd; htd wc; chem disp; mv service pnt; shwrs inc; el pnts (4-6A) €2.50-3; lndtte; shop, rest 200m; snacks; htd pool 300m; wifi; TV; 20% statics; dogs €2.50; bus; poss cr; Eng spkn; adv bkg; ccard acc; CCI. "Well-kept site; conv town cent; gd hill walks; friendly staff." ♦ 1 Mar-15 Nov. € 25.00 2008*

NATURNO/NATURNS *1D1* (1km S Rural) *46.64305, 11.00805* **Waldcamping, Via Dornsberg 8, Cirlano, 39025 Naturno/Naturns (BZ) [0473 667298; fax 668072; info@waldcamping.com; www.waldcamping.com]** At E end of tunnel on S38 by-passing Naturno turn at rndabt into town, foll camping sp L at traff lts. Cont past Camping Adler round RH end to T-junc. Turn L over rv & rlwy & foll sp to site. Med, pt shd; wc; chem disp; htd shwrs inc; el pnts (6A) €3; shop; lndtte; rest, snacks adj; playgrnd; pool; tennis adj; cab/sat TV; dogs €2.50; phone; adv bkg ess high ssn; quiet; red long stay. "Superb views; mountain walks & climbs; excel facs." ♦ 15 Mar-5 Nov. € 25.00 2008*

ITALY

⊞ **NUMANA** *2F3* (2km N Urban/Coastal) *43.51931, 13.61907* **Camping Reno, Via Moriconi 7, 60020 Sirolo (AN) [tel/fax 071 7360315; reno.sirolo@camping.it; www.camping.it/marche/reno]** Exit m'way A14 at Ancona Sud onto Pescara rd. In 7km sp Sirolo & Numano. In Sirolo turn L & sp on R. Site sps brown & yellow or white - site poss diff to find. Sm, terr, pt shd; wc; chem disp; shwrs inc; el pnts (3A) €2.50; lndry rm; shops 300m; rest 300m; snacks; bar; beach 2km; games area; 10% statics; dogs; site clsd Nov; poss cr; Eng spkn; adv bkg; quiet; red low ssn; CCI. "Friendly owner; Sirolo a gem; lovely, scenic area; poss diff lge o'fits due low trees & no turning space; v sm pitches; clean facs; site o'looked by adj tall buildings." ♦ € 35.00 2007*

OLIVETO LARIO see Lecco *1C1*

OLMO, L' see Perugia *2E3*

⊞ **OPI** *2F4* (3km E Rural) *41.77914, 13.86282* **Camping Il Vecchio Mulino, Via Marsicana, Km 52, 67030 Opi (AQ) [tel/fax 0863 912232; ilvecchiomulino@tiscalinet.it; www.campingvecchiomulino.it]** Turn off A1 twd Frosinone, 35km NE on S214 to Sora, 40km E on S509 to Opi, 5km E on S83 twd Villetta Barrea. Site on R. Med, pt shd; htd wc (some cont); chem disp; mv service pnt; shwrs inc; el pnts (8A) inc; lndtte; shop 3km; rest; snacks; bar; BBQ; playgrnd; games area; some statics; dogs; phone; Eng spkn; adv bkg rec Jul/Aug; quiet; ccard acc; CCI. "Wonderful walking country; excel rest; lovely site but facs stretched if site full." ♦ € 28.50 2010*

We can fill in site report forms on the Club's website – www.caravanclub.co.uk/europereport

ORA/AUER *1D1* (NE Urban) *46.34779, 11.29980* **Camping Markushof, Via Truidn 1, 39040 Ora/Auer (BZ) [0471 810025; fax 810603; info@campingmarkushof.it; www.hotelmarkushof.it]** Exit A22 at Bolzano Sud onto SS12, then S to Ora. Site on main street, sp. Sm, mkd pitch, some hdstg, unshd; wc; chem disp; mv service pnt; some serviced pitches; el pnts (16A) inc; lndtte (inc dryer); shop adj; rest; snacks; bar adj; playgrnd; htd pool; paddling pool; some statics; dogs €4; quiet; CCI. "Part of hotel complex; excel facs." ♦ 1 Apr-20 Oct. € 27.00 2010*

ORA/AUER *1D1* (500m E Rural) *46.34225, 11.30276* **Camping Cascata/Wasserfall, Via Cascata 36, 39040 Ora/Auer (BZ) [0471 810519; fax 810150; c.rosamaria@virgilio.it]** A22/E45 take exit Egna/Ors & fr Ora/Auer take S48 dir Cavalese, turn L after bdge & foll lge sp. V sharp R turn at site ent - poss diff lge o'fits. Med, mkd pitch, pt sl, shd; wc; shwrs inc; el pnts (6A) inc; gas; lndtte; shop 500m; rest 500m; snacks in high ssn; playgrnd; pool & paddling pool; no dogs; phone; poss cr; quiet; ccard not acc; red low ssn. "Gd facs; clean, tidy site; easy walk to Ora; conv for m'way." 1 Apr-2 Nov. € 24.00 2008*

ORBETELLO *1D4* (7km N Coastal) *42.49611, 11.19416* **Argentario Camping Village, Torre Saline, 58010 Albinia (GR) [0564 870302; fax 871380; info@argentariocampingvillage.com; www.argentariocampingvillage.com]** Turn W off Via Aurelia at 150km mark, sp Porto S. Stefano, site on R, clearly sp in 500m. Ignore sps Zona Camping. Lge,mkd pitch; shd; wc; mv service pnt; shwrs inc; el pnts (6A) inc; lndtte; rest; snacks; bar; shop; playgrnd; pool & paddling pool; sand/shgl beach; boat hire; games area; 90% statics; no dogs; phone; sep car park; poss cr; adv bkg; quiet. ♦ 1 Apr-30 Sep. € 42.00 2010*

ORBETELLO *1D4* (8km N Coastal) **Camping Ideal, Via Aurelia, Km 156, 58010 Osa-Fonteblanda (GR) [tel/fax 0564 885379; campingideal@libero.it]** S on Via Aurelia fr Grosseto, past Fonteblanda over rlwy bdge at km 157, camp on R of main rd after Hotel & Agip petrol stn. Most N of string of pine-shaded beach-side sites. Lge, shd; wc; mv service pnt; shwrs €0.25; el pnts (4A) inc; gas; lndtte; rest 500m; snacks; bar; sand beach; 95% statics; no dogs; sep car park; poss cr; quiet; ccard acc. "Helpful, friendly staff." Easter-20 Sep. € 22.00 2009*

ORBETELLO *1D4* (8km N Coastal) *42.53258, 11.18593* **Camping Il Gabbiano, SS Aurelia, Km 154.2, 58010 Albinia (GR) [tel/fax 0564 870202; info@ilgabbianocampingvillage.com; www.ilgabbianocampingvillage.com]** On W side of Via Aurelia at km stone 154. Lge, mkd pitch, shd; wc; shwrs inc; el pnts (3A) inc; gas; lndtte; shop; rest; snacks; bar; BBQ; playgrnd; private sand beach adj; entmnt; 90% statics; no dogs Jul/Aug; sep car park high ssn; poss cr; adv bkg; poss noisy; red low ssn. "Vg; v clean facs." ♦ 1 Apr-13 Sep. € 37.50 2010*

⊞ **ORBETELLO** *1D4* (8km N Coastal) **Camping Regio, SS Aurelia, Km 154.350, 58010 Albinia (GR) [0564 870163; fax 871572; info@campingcamporegio.it; www.campingcamporegio.it]** Fr N on Via Aurelia, after km 157 & Camping Ideal, take camping side rd on R. Site 3rd on this rd. Lge, mkd pitch, hdstg, pt shd; wc (some cont); chem disp; baby facs; shwrs €0.40; lndtte (inc dryer); shop & 4.5km; rest & 1.5km; bar; BBQ; playgrnd; sand beach adj; 95% statics; dogs; phone; bus; poss cr; Eng spkn; adv bkg; ccard acc; some rlwy noise. ♦ € 32.00 2008*

ORIAGO see Venezia *2E2*

ORTA SAN GIULIO *1B1* (500m N Rural) *45.80125, 8.42093* **Camping Orta, Via Domodossola 28, Loc Bagnera, 28016 Orta San Giulio (NO) [tel/fax 0322 90267; info@campingorta.it; www.campingorta.it]** Fr Omegna take rd on SS229 for 10km to km 44.5 sp Novara. Site both sides of rd 500m bef rndabt at Orta x-rds. Recep on L if heading S; poor access immed off rd. Med, pt sl, pt terr, pt shd; htd wc (some cont); chem disp; shwrs €0.20; el pnts (3-6A) €2.50; gas; lndtte (inc dryer); shop; rest 500m; bar; playgrnd; lake sw adj; waterskiing; wifi; dogs €4; Eng spkn; adv bkg; rd noise; ccard not acc; red low ssn. "Popular site in beautiful location; sm pitches; narr site rds & tight corners; arr early for lakeside pitch (extra charge); slipway to lake; friendly, helpful owner; Orta a gem." ♦ 1 Mar-31 Dec. € 28.75 2010*

ORTA SAN GIULIO *1B1* (3km N Rural) *45.81212, 8.41076* **Camping Verde Lago, Corso Roma 76, 28028 Pettenasco (NO) [0323 89257; fax 888654; campingverdelago@campingverdelago.it; www.campingverdelago.it]** Site bet SS229 & lake at km 46, 500m S of Pettenasco on Orta Lake. Gd access. Sm, pt sl, pt shd; wc (some cont); chem disp; shwrs inc; el pnts (6A) €2.50; Indry rm; shop, rest; snacks; bar; BBQ; playgrnd; lake sw & sand beach adj; games rm; TV; 60% statics; no dogs; poss cr at w/end; Eng spkn; quiet; ccard acc. "Vg family-run site; friendly, helpful; clean facs; dir access private beach & boat mooring; recep 0930-1200 & 1630-1900." 1 Apr-31 Oct. € 16.00 2008*

⊞ **ORTA SAN GIULIO** *1B1* (4km N Rural) *45.83117, 8.39664* **Camping La Punta di Crabbia, Via Crabbia 2, 28028 Pettenasco (NO) [tel/fax 0323 89117; infotiscali@campingpuntacrabbia.it; www.campingpuntacrabbia.it]** Site situated on L (E) of rd 229 fr Omegna to Orta, 1.5km N of Pettenasco. Steep access rd to site. Med, sl, shd; wc (cont); chem disp; mv service pnt; shwrs; el pnts (6A) €2.50; Indtte; ice shop & 3km; rest 700m; snacks; bar; lake adj; windsurfing; solarium; 90% statics; dogs €4; quiet; Eng spkn; ccard not acc; red low ssn. "Gd view of lake fr some pitches but with rd noise; v helpful recep." € 24.00 2009*

ORTA SAN GIULIO *1B1* (E Rural) *45.79785, 8.42087* **Camping Cusio Lyons Edda, Via Giovanni Bosco 5, 28016 Orta San Giulio (NO) [tel/fax 0322 90290; cusio@tin.it; www.campingcusio.it]** S fr Omegna, turn L at traff lts (sp Miasino) & site on L in 100m. Access via steep, rough track. Med, pt sl, pt shd; wc; shwrs; el pnts €2.70; gas; Indtte; shop 150m; snacks; bar; sm pool; beach 2km; tennis; games rm; internet; some statics; dogs €3.70; quiet. "Views over Lake Orta; gd, clean facs; conv for walk into town." 1 Apr-30 Nov. € 27.60 2009*

ORTONA *2F4* (7km SE Coastal) *42.30772, 14.44221* **Camping Costa d'Argento, Via Murata 135, 66035 Marina-di-San Vito (CH) [0872 816731; fax 596262; info@costadargento.net; www.costadargento.net]** S fr Ortona on S16, in Marina-di-San Vito foll sp at km 478.8 to site. Med, pt shd; wc (cont); chem disp; shwrs inc; el pnts (3-6A) €2; Indtte; shop 500m; rest, snacks, bar; playgrnd; 2 pools; sand beach 500m; 30% statics; dogs €1.50; phone; Eng spkn; quiet. "Pleasant site, esp nr ent & pools; hot water in shwrs only." ♦ 7 Jun-29 Sep. € 29.00 2008*

ORTONA *2F4* (5km NW Coastal) *42.37623, 14.37394* **Camping Torre Mucchia, Loc Lido Riccio, 66026 Ortona (CH) [0859 196298; taoceti@supereva.it]** Exit SS16 at Ortona. In 500m turn sharp L & site sp. Med, shd; wc; shwrs; el pnts inc; gas; Indtte; shops 300m; snacks; bar; sand beach 200m; dogs; sep car park; adv bkg; quiet; CCI. "Sm, friendly, family-run site but poss scruffy." Easter-15 Sep. 2009*

⊞ **ORVIETO** *2E3* (500m S Urban) *42.72379, 12.13162* **Aree di Sosta Parcheggio Funicolare, Via della Direttissima, 05018 Orvieto (TR) [0763 300161; renzo.battistelli@hotmail.com; www.orvietoonline.com]** At Orvieto foll sp rlwy stn & funicular parking. Site on L just beyond funicular parking & behind rlwy stn. Foll sp 'Parcheggio Camper'. Sm, mkd pitch, hdstg, unshd; htd wc; chem disp; shwrs inc; el pnts (10A) inc; Indtte (inc dryer); shops 500m; rest, snacks, bar 200m; dogs; phone; bus, train 200m; rlwy noise; CCI. "M'vans only but c'vans poss acc low ssn; conv A1." ♦ € 18.00 2010*

OSTRA *2E3* (200m SW Rural) *43.61032, 13.15351* **Camping 'L Prè, Viale Matteotti 45, 60010 Ostra (AN) [tel/fax 071 68045; info@lpre.it; www.lpre.it]** Exit A14 at Senigallia onto S360. After approx 10km turn R to Ostra. Sp in vill. Sm, terr, pt shd; wc (some cont); chem disp; shwrs inc; el pnts (3A) €2.50; shop 300m; rest 100m; sand beach 10km; games rm; dogs; red long stay. "Gd san facs; v friendly owners; lovely simple site with easy access Ancona, Esini Valley." 1 Apr-30 Sep. € 24.50 2010*

OSTUNI *3A4* (9km NE Coastal) *40.76602, 17.65044* **Camping Cala dei Ginepri, Contrada da Montanaro, SS 379, Km 23.500, 72017 Ostuni (BR) [tel/fax 0831 330402; info@caladeiginepri.com; www.caladeiginepri.com]** Fr SS379 exit Cala dei Ginepri & foll sp to site. Lge, hdg/mkd pitch, shd; htd wc; mv service pnt; htd private san facs on pitches; shwrs inc; el pnts inc; Indtte; shop; rest; snacks; bar; pool; sand beach 700m; watersports; cycle hire; entmnt; TV rm; some statics; adv bkg; quiet. "Gd touring base." 1 May-12 Sep. € 38.00 (CChq acc) 2009*

OTRANTO *3A4* (1.5km NW Urban/Coastal) *40.16665, 18.47620* **Camping Mulino d'Acqua, Via Santo Stefano, 73028 Otranto (LE) [0836 802191; fax 802196; mulino.camping@anet.it; www.mulinodacqua.it]** Clearly sp on S611 coast rd. Lge, pt sl, pt shd; wc (cont); chem disp; mv service pnt; baby facs; shwrs €0.50; el pnts (6A) €3; gas; Indtte; shop; rest; snacks; bar; pool; sand beach adj; playgrnd; tennis; games area; cycle hire; entmnt; TV; statics; dogs €6; sep car park; adv bkg; quiet; ccard acc; red low ssn. 21 May-12 Sep. € 56.00 2010*

PACENGO see Peschiera del Garda *1D2*

PADENGHE SUL GARDA see Desenzano del Garda *1D2*

PAESTUM *3A3* (N Coastal) *40.42780, 14.98244* **Camping Villaggio Ulisse, Via Ponte di Ferro, 84063 Paestum (SA) [tel/fax 0828 851095; info@campingulisse.com; www.campingulisse.com]** Foll site sp in cent Paestum, well sp. Lge, mkd pitch, shd; wc (some cont); chem disp; shwrs inc; el pnts (3A) inc; Indtte; shop; rest; snacks; bar; playgrnd; sand beach adj; games area; 80% statics; dogs; poss cr; quiet; CCI. "Direct access to beach; gd, clean, friendly site." ♦ 1 Apr-30 Sep. € 35.00 2009*

ITALY

PAESTUM *3A3* (9km N Coastal) *40.49248, 14.94196* **Camping Villaggio Paestum, Loc Foce Sele, 84025 Marina-di-Eboli (SA) [tel/fax 0828 691003; info@campingpaestum.it; www.campingpaestum.it]** Fr Salerno/Battipaglia foll sp S to Paestum, turn R at site sp, site 150m on L after T-junc with coast rd. Lge, shd; htd wc (some cont); chem disp; mv service pnt; shwrs inc; el pnts (6A) inc; lndtte; shop; rest; snacks; bar; playgrnd; pool; paddling pool; sand beach 300m; tennis; games area; wifi; 50% statics; no lge dogs; phone; poss cr; adv bkg; poss noisy at w/end; ccard acc; CCI. "Gd rest & pool; sm pitches; Greek temples at Paestum superb." ♦ 15 Apr-15 Sep. € 36.00 2010*

⊞ **PAESTUM** *3A3* (5km NW Coastal) *40.41330, 14.99140* **Camping Villaggio Dei Pini, Via Torre, 84063 Paestum (SA) [0828 811030; fax 811025; info@campingvillaggiodeipini.com; www.campingvillaggiodeipini.com]** Site 50km S of Salerno in vill of Torre-de-Paestum. Foll a'strada to Battipaglia onto main rd to Paestum, site sp bef Paestum on rd S18, foll to beach. Med, hdg/mkd pitch, shd; wc (mainly cont); chem disp; mv service pnt; shwrs inc; el pnts (6A) inc; lndtte; shop; tradsmn; rest; snacks; bar; BBQ; playgrnd; private sand beach adj; games area; internet; entmnt; 30% statics; no dogs Jul/Aug; phone; adv bkg; quiet low ssn; red low ssn; ccard acc; CCI. "Historical ruins nr; narr access rd fr vill due parked cars; lge o'fits may grnd at ent; some sm pitches - c'vans manhandled onto pitches." ♦ € 51.00 (4 persons) 2009*

⊞ **PALMI** *3B4* (4km N Coastal) *38.39194, 15.86555* **Camping San Fantino, Via San Fantino 135, Loc Taureana, 89015 Lido-di-Palmi (RC) [0966 479729; fax 479430; info@campingsanfantino.it; www.campingsanfantino.it]** Leave A3/E45 at Palmi exit & take S18 N dir Gioia. After 4km turn L sp Taureana, site well sp. Lge, hdstg, terr, shd; wc; chem disp; shwrs; el pnts (4A) €2 (rev pol); gas; lndtte; shop; tradsmn; rest; bar; playgrnd; sand beach 400m; 20% statics; Eng spkn; 10% statics; adv bkg; quiet; CCI. "Site on cliff top with path to beach; gd views fr some pitches; conv NH bef Sicily ferry; gd rest; rough site rds - care needed." ♦ € 20.00 2008*

⊞ **PALMI** *3B4* (8km N Coastal) *38.40676, 15.86912* **Villaggio Camping La Quiete, Contrada Scinà, 89015 Palmi (RC) [0966 479400; fax 479649; info@villaggiolaquiete.it; www.villaggiolaquiete.it]** N fr Lido-di-Palmi on Contrada Pietrenere coast rd dir Gioia Tauro, site sp. Lge, all hdstg, pt shd; wc; chem disp; shwrs inc; el pnts (10A) €3; gas; lndry service; rest; snacks; bar; sand beach 200m; 5% statics; dogs; phone; site clsd Oct; Eng spkn; adv bkg; ccard acc; red low ssn/long stay; CCI. "Sm pitches; fair sh stay/NH." ♦ € 26.50 2008*

PASSIGNANO SUL TRASIMENO *2E3* (800m E Rural) *43.18397, 12.15089* **Camping La Spiaggia, Via Europe 22, 06065 Passignano-sul-Trasimeno (PG) [tel/fax 075 827246; info@campinglaspiaggia.it; www.campinglaspiaggia.it]** Exit A1 at Bettolle-Valdichiana & foll sp Perugia for 30km. Exit at Passignano Est & foll sp to site. Sm, mkd pitch, shd; htd wc (some cont); chem disp; mv service pnt; baby facs; fam bthrm; shwrs inc; el pnts (6A) inc; lndtte; shop 800m; rest; snacks; bar; BBQ; playgrnd; pool; lake & sand beach adj; games area; boat & cycle hire; wifi; sat TV; no statics; dogs €2; phone; bus/train 800m; poss cr; Eng spkn; adv bkg; quiet; ccard acc; red long stay/low ssn. "Lovely lakeside site; friendly owner; lge pitches; excel san facs but hot water variable; gd rest; interesting lakeside town; excel touring base for hill towns." ♦ 27 Mar-3 Oct. € 28.00 2011*

PASSIGNANO SUL TRASIMENO *2E3* (1km E Rural) *43.18338, 12.15085* **Camping Kursaal, Viale Europa 24, 06065 Passignano-sul-Trasimeno (PG) [075 828085; fax 827182; info@campingkursaal.it; www.campingkursaal.it]** Fr Perugia on S75 to Lake Trasimeno. Exit at Passignano-Est twd lake; site on L past level x-ing adj hotel, well sp. Med, hdg/mkd pitch, pt sl, pt shd; wc; chem disp; mv service pnt; baby facs; shwrs inc; el pnts (6A) €2 (poss rev pol); lndtte (inc dryer); shop; rest; snacks; bar; playgrnd; pool; private shgl lake beach; cycle hire; wifi; TV; dogs €1.50; phone; poss v cr; Eng spkn; adv bkg ess; some rlwy noise; red low ssn; ccard acc; red CCI. "Pleasant site; vg rest; some pitches have lake view; ltd space & pitches tight." ♦ 1 Apr-31 Oct. € 28.00 2010*

PASSIGNANO SUL TRASIMENO *2E3* (2km E Rural) *43.18176, 12.16517* **Camping Europa, Loc San Donato 8, 06065 Passignano-sul-Trasimeno (PG) [tel/fax 075 827405; info@camping-europa.it; www.camping-europa.it]** Fr A1 E on SS75 bis twd Perugia; exit SS75 at Passignano Est & cont E on smaller parallel rd for 2km. Site on R via subway under rlwy. Med, pt shd; wc (some cont) chem disp; mv service pnt; shwrs inc; el pnts (6A) inc; gas; lndtte; shop; rest; snacks; bar; playgrnd; pool; private sand beach by lake; boat hire; watersports; games area; cycle hire; wifi; 20% statics; bus; Eng spkn; quiet, some rlwy noise; ccard acc. "Well-run, clean, friendly, gd value site; san facs in need of renovation; ltd (plunge-type pool); conv Assisi, Perugia, lake trips to islands." ♦ 28 Mar-10 Oct. € 23.00 2009*

PAVIA *1C2* (2.5km NW Rural) *45.19453, 9.12005* **Camping Ticino, Via Mascherpa 10, San Lanfranco, 27100 Pavia [tel/fax 0382 527094; info@campingticino.it; www.campingticino.it]** On S35 fr S (Tangenziale Uvest) ring rd turn off at sp Pavia (Riviera). Foll brown camping sp R at end of slip rd, site in 500m. Med, shd; wc; chem disp; shwrs inc; el pnts (4A) inc; shop 200m; rest 200m; snacks; playgrnd; pool; 20% statics; dogs; poss cr; quiet; ccard acc; red CCI. "Excel site; superb, modern san facs; helpful staff." ♦ 1 Apr-30 Sep. € 28.10 2011*

PEGLI see Genova *1C2*

⊞ **PEIO** *1D1* (1.5km S Rural) *46.35833, 10.68138* **Camping Panoramico Val di Sole, Via Dossi di Cavia, 38020 Peio (TN) [0463 753177; fax 753176; info@valdisolecamping.it; www.valdisolecamping.it]** Travelling W fr Dimaro on SS42 twd Tonale Pass, turn R into Val-de-Peio thro Cogolo twd Peio-Fonti. Site in 1.8km on R. Med, mkd pitch, terr, pt shd; htd wc (some cont); chem disp; mv service pnt; baby facs; shwrs inc; el pnts (3A) inc; lndtte (inc dryer); shop; rest 2km; snacks high ssn; bar; playgrnd; 60% statics; dogs €2; phone; bus 300m; site clsd end May & Nov; poss cr Aug; quiet; ccard acc; red CCI. "Excel for mountain walking in Stelvio National Park." ♦ € 23.50 2009*

PERGINE VALSUGANA see Trento *1D1*

PERTICARA *2E3* (2km N Rural) *43.89608, 12.24302* **Camping Perticara, Via Serra Masini 10/d, 61017 Perticara (PS) [0541 927602; fax 927707; info@campingperticara.com; www.campingperticara.com]** Fr A14 at Rimini take S258 to Novafeltria. Foll sp Perticara & site. Steep, hairpins on part of route. Med, hdg/mkd pitch, hdstg, terr, unshd; htd wc; chem disp; mv service pnt; baby facs; serviced pitches; shwrs inc; el pnts (10A) inc; gas; Indtte; shop & 2km; tradsmn; rest; snacks; bar; playgrnd; pool; paddling pool; wifi; entmnt; TV rm; 5% statics; dogs; phone; bus; poss cr; Eng spkn; adv bkg; quiet; ccard acc; red low ssn; CCI. "Clean, well-maintained, scenic site; hospitable Dutch owners; many activities arranged; immac san facs; poss diff egress to SW (hairpins with passing places) - staff help with 4x4 if necessary; not rec disabled due terrain." 1 May-20 Sep. € 34.00 2010*

There aren't many sites open at this time of year. We'd better phone ahead to check the one we're heading for is open.

PERUGIA *2E3* (6km NW Rural) *43.10985, 12.32726* **Camping Il Rocolo, Strada Fontana la Trinita 1/N, 06074 L'Olmo (PG) [075 5178550; ivano@ilrocolo.it; www.ilrocolo.it]** Exit E45 at sp Ferro-di-Cavallo. At rndabt turn L. Foll rd parallel to a'strada for 1km & turn R at site sp. Med, terr, pt shd; wc; chem disp; mv service pnt; shwrs; el pnts (10A) inc; gas; Indtte; shop; rest 1km; snacks; bar; playgrnd; Eng spkn; adv bkg; quiet; ccard acc; red CCI. "In olive grove; peaceful low ssn; helpful staff." ♦ Apr-Sep. € 22.50 2008*

PERUGIA *2E3* (8km NW Rural) *43.12030, 12.31328* **Camping Paradis d'Eté, Colle della Trinita, Strada Fontana 29/H, 06074 Perugia [075 5173121; fax 0755 176056; jnlagu@tin.it; www.wel.it/cparadis]** Exit Perugia-Firenze a'strada A1 at Ferro-di-Cavallo exit to N. At traff lts turn L (W) & foll rd parallel to a'strada for approx 1km. Turn R at camp sp, & site 3km up steep hill on R. Sm, pt sl, terr, shd; wc; mv service pnt; shwrs inc; el pnts (6A) €1.50; Indtte; shop; supmkt 3km; snacks; bar; playgrnd; pool; games rm; dogs; bus to Perugia; quiet; ccard acc; CCI. "Peaceful site; steep incline in & out of site; dated facs, but clean." 1 Mar-31 Aug. € 29.00 2009*

PESARO *2E3* (10km N Coastal) *43.95993, 12.80136* **Camping Paradiso, Via Rive del Faro 2, 61010 Casteldimezzo (PS) [tel/fax 0721 208579; info@campingparadiso.it; www.campingparadiso.it]** Turn of SS16 at Colombare, turn in vill (by bank). Steep & narr - best turn by church N of vill. Site sp. Med, terr, shd; wc (some cont); chem disp; shwrs inc; el pnts (6A) inc; Indtte; shop; tradsmn; rest adj; snacks; bar; playgrnd; sand & shgl beach adj; internet; 10% statics; dogs €2.50; phone; poss cr; adv bkg; some rlwy noise; red low ssn; ccard acc. "Gd views; beach down v steep cliff rd." ♦ 1 Mar-31 Dec. € 35.50 2010*

PESCARA *2F4* (11km SE Coastal) *42.40397, 14.32075* **Camping Paola, Via Francesco Paola Tosti 101, 66023 Francavilla-al-Mare (CH) [tel/fax 085 817525; info@campingpaola.com; www.campingpaola.com]** Exit A14 a'strada at Pescara S onto rd S16, site bet sea & rlwy, sp. For c'vans under 3m high: fr S on S16 at junc with S263 turn R under rlwy bdge twd sea; turn R at rndabt, site on R in 100m. For c'vans over 3m high: fr S on S16 cont past junc with S263 for 4km. Nr stadium turn R into Via Paola under rlwy bdge (4m), immed R into Via Foume, site on R in 4km. Take care sharp bends & narr ent/access rds. Med, shd; wc; shwrs; el pnts (5A) inc; gas; Indry rm; shop in ssn & supmkt 1km; snacks; rest & bar in ssn; playgrnd; sand beach adj; games area; dogs (sm only) €2.50; some rd & rlwy noise; red low ssn. "Poor, outdated facs; sm, narr pitches with many trees; Pescara lovely, lively town." 1 May-30 Sep. € 33.00 2008*

⊞ **PESCASSEROLI** *2F4* (500m S Rural) *41.79888, 13.79222* **Camping Sant' Andrea, Loc Sant' Andrea, Via San Donato, 67032 Pescasseroli (AQ) [tel/fax 0863 912725; info@campingsantandrea.com; www.campingsantandrea.com]** Site sp on R bet Pescasseroli & Opi. If gate clsd ent thro side gate & turn key to open main gate. Sm, mkd pitch, pt shd; htd wc (some cont); chem disp; mv service pnt; shwrs inc; el pnts (10A) inc; shop, rest, snacks, bar in town; playgrnd; statics in sep area; dogs; phone; CCI. "Beautiful, open pitches in lovely area; clean facs but ltd high ssn." € 15.00 2008*

PESCHICI *2G4* (10km E Coastal) *41.94361, 16.04855* **Villaggio Camping Internazionale Manacore, 71010 Manacore (FG) [0884 911020; fax 911049; manacore@grupposaccia.it; www.grupposaccia.it]** Coast rd thro town of Peschici to Vieste, site sp. If app fr W, do NOT enter town. Turn R twd Vieste; at rndabt in 2km turn L, sp Manacore. V lge, pt sl, pt shd; wc; chem disp; mv service pnt; shwrs inc; private bthrms avail; el pnts (3A) inc; gas; Indtte; shop; rest; snacks; bar; playgrnd; sand beach; boat hire; windsurfing; tennis; cycle hire; games area; entmnt; 25% statics; dogs; sep car park high ssn; poss cr; no adv bkg; quiet; ccard acc; CCI. "Magnificent scenery; excel for boats & sw; excel facs." ♦ 1 May-11 Oct. € 49.00 2010*

PESCHICI *2G4* (5km SE Rural) *41.93815, 16.04963* **Camping La Gemma, Loc Baia di Manaccora, 71010 Peschici (FG) [0884 911010; fax 962777; info@la-gemma.it; www.la-gemma.it]** Exit A14 at Poggio Imperiale onto SS89 E to Peschici. Turn off & foll sp to Manaccora & site. Med, shd; htd wc; mv service pnt; shwrs; el pnts; Indtte; shop; rest; snacks; bar; playgrnd; pool; paddling pool; sand beach 300m; watersports; fishing; tennis; entmnt; internet; TV rm; some statics; adv bkg; quiet. 1 Apr-1 Oct. € 26.50 2009*

PESCHICI *2G4* (1.5km S Coastal) *41.94237, 16.03054* **Centro Turistico San Nicola, Punta San Nicola, 71010 Peschici (FG) [0884 964024; fax 964025; sannicola@sannicola.it; www.sannicola.it]** Site clearly sp on S89 bet Peschici & Vieste. V lge, mkd pitch, sl, terr, pt shd; wc (some cont); chem disp; mv service pnt; shwrs inc; el pnts (5A) inc; gas; Indtte; shop; rest; snacks; sand beach; windsurfing; tennis; gym; entmnt & some statics; no dogs high ssn; adv bkg; noisy; ccard acc; red long stay/CCI. "Excel for families; lovely site in beautiful location; surface water on pitches after heavy rain." ♦ 1 Apr-15 Oct. € 37.00 2009*

PESCHIERA DEL GARDA *1D2* (1km N Urban) *45.44780, 10.70195* **Camping del Garda, Via Marzan 6, 37019 Castelnuovo-del-Garda (VR) [045 7550540; fax 6400711; info@camping-delgarda.com; www.campingdelgarda.it]** Exit A4/E70 dir Peschiera onto SR249 dir Lazise. Turn L in 500m dir Lido Campanello, site in 1km on L on lakeside. V lge, shd; wc (mainly cont); chem disp; mv service pnt; shwrs inc; el pnts (4A) inc; gas; lndtte; shop; rest; snacks; bar; playgrnd; 3 pools; shgl beach; lake sw; tennis; games area; entmnt; 60% statics; no dogs; phone; adv bkg; quiet. "Busy, well-organised site; helpful staff, discount snr citizens." ♦ 1 Apr-30 Sep. € 51.00 2011*

PESCHIERA DEL GARDA *1D2* (1km N Rural) *45.46722, 10.71638* **Eurocamping Pacengo, Via del Porto 13, 37010 Pacengo (VR) [tel/fax 045 7590012; eurocamping.pacengo@camping.it; www.camping.it/garda/eurocamping]** On SS249 fr Peschiera foll sp to Gardaland, Pacengo in 1km. Turn L at traff lts in cent of vill, site on L. Lge, mkd pitch, sl, pt shd; wc (some cont); chem disp (wc); mv service pnt; shwrs €0.30; el pnts (6A) inc; lndtte; shop & 500m; rest; snacks; bar; playgrnd; pool adj; lake sw, boat-launching adj; entmnt; 25% statics; dogs €2.10; phone; poss cr; Eng spkn; adv bkg; quiet; CCI. "Well-equipped site on shore Lake Garda; helpful staff; some sm pitches; especially gd end of ssn; excel rest; conv Verona." ♦ 1 Apr-24 Sep. € 24.30 2008*

PESCHIERA DEL GARDA *1D2* (2.5km N Rural) *45.45480, 10.70200* **Camping Gasparina, Loc Cavalcaselle, 37010 Castelnuovo-del-Garda (VR) [045 7550775; fax 7552815; info@gasparina.com; www.gasparina.com]** On SS249 dir Lazise, turn L at site sp. Lge, mkd pitch, sl, pt shd; wc; chem disp; mv service pnt; shwrs inc; el pnts (3A) inc; gas; lndtte; shop; tradsmn; rest; snacks; bar; playgrnd; pool; lake adj; games area; entmnt; some statics; dogs; poss cr; adv bkg; poss noisy; ccard acc. "Popular, busy site; variable pitch sizes; lake views some pitches." 1 Apr-30 Sep. € 27.00 2009*

PESCHIERA DEL GARDA *1D2* (4km N Rural) *45.46472, 10.71416* **Camping Le Palme, Via del Tronchetto 2, 37010 Pacengo (VR) [045 7590019; fax 7590554; info@lepalmecamping.it; www.lepalmecamping.it]** A4/E70 exit at Peschiera onto SS249, sp Lazise. Site sp bef Pacengo in approx 5km. Lge, mkd pitch, terr, pt shd; wc; chem disp; serviced pitches; baby facs; shwrs inc; el pnts (6A) inc; lndtte (inc dryer); shop; rest 300m; snacks; bar; playgrnd; htd pool; paddling pool; waterslide; lake sw & shgl beach adj; wifi; 40% statics; dogs €4.60; Eng spkn; adv bkg; ccard acc; red low ssn. "Well-maintained site; excel, clean facs; extra for lakeside pitches; helpful staff; sh walk to vill; 4 theme parks nr; excel." ♦ 1 Apr-25 Oct. € 31.10 2011*

PESCHIERA DEL GARDA *1D2* (700m W Rural) *45.44555, 10.69472* **Camping Butterfly, Lungo Lago Garibaldi 11, 37019 Peschiera (VR) [045 6401466; fax 7552184; info@campingbutterfly.it; www.campingbutterfly.it]** Fr A4/E70 exit twd Peschiera for 2km. At x-rds with bdge on L, strt over & foll rv to last site after RH bend at bottom. Lge, shd; wc (some cont); shwrs; el pnts inc; gas; lndtte; shop; rest; snacks; bar; playgrnd; pool; paddling pool; lake sw; entmnt; 75% statics; dogs €5; poss cr; adv bkg; quiet except w/end; ccard acc. "Busy holiday site; conv town & lake steamers; sm pitches; clean san facs." ♦ 13 Mar-31 Nov. € 43.50 (4 persons) 2009*

PESCHIERA DEL GARDA *1D2* (1km W Urban) *45.44222, 10.67805* **Camping Bella Italia, Via Bella Italia 2, 37019 Peschiera (VR) [045 6400688; fax 6401410; info@camping-bellaitalia.it; www.camping-bellaitalia.it]** Fr Brescia or Verona on SS11, take W exit for town cent; site sp on L on lakeside. V lge, slight sl, shd; wc; chem disp; mv service pnt; baby facs; shwrs inc; el pnts (6A); gas; lndtte (inc dryer); shop; 2 rests; snacks; bar; BBQ; playgrnd; pool; paddling pool; waterslides; lake sw adj; windsurfing; tennis; games area; cycle hire; archery; wifi; entmnt; many static tents; no dogs; bus to Verona; poss cr; Eng spkn; adv bkg rec; poss noisy high ssn; red low ssn; CCI. "Busy, popular site, nr theme park, Aqua World, Verona; suits all ages; v clean; rests gd & gd price; easy walking & cycling distances." ♦ 26 Mar-23 Oct. € 51.80 (CChq acc) 2011*

PESCHIERA DEL GARDA *1D2* (1.5km W Urban) *45.44825, 10.66978* **Camping San Benedetto, Strada Bergamini 14, 37019 San Benedetto (VR) [045 7550544; fax 7551512; info@campingsanbenedetto.it; www.campingsanbenedetto.it]** Exit A4/E70 dir Peschiera-del-Garda, turn N at traff lts in cent of vill, site on lake at km 274/V111 on rd S11. Lge, pt sl, shd; wc; mv service pnt; shwrs inc; el pnts (3A) inc; lndtte; shop; rest; snacks; bar; playgrnd; pool; paddling pool; lakeside shgl beach nr; boat hire; windsurfing; canoeing; cycle hire; games area; entmnt; 30% statics; dogs; poss cr; adv bkg; quiet; red snr citizens. "Pleasant, well-run; sm harbour; site clsd 1300-1500." 28 Mar-4 Oct. € 32.00 2008*

PETTENASCO see Orta San Giulio *1B1*

PEVERAGNO see Cuneo *1B2*

PIENZA *1D3* (6km E Rural) **Camping Il Casale, 53026 Pienza (SI) [tel/fax 0578 755109; podereilcasale@libero.it]** Fr Pienza dir Montepulciano on S146, turn R in 4km onto sm, gritted track sp Monticchiello (sm, brown sp easily missed). Site in 3km on L sp Podereilcasale. Fr Montepulciano dir Pienza rd to L sp Il Borghetto (Fago). Sm, pt shd; wc; shwrs inc; el pnts (16A) inc; shop; tradsmn; rest; bar; playgrnd; lake adj; dogs; phone; poss cr; Eng spkn; adv bkg; quiet; ccard acc. "4 pitches only for c'vans/mvans; simple farm site; friendly family; price inc breakfast; panoramic views; rec phone to check availability." ♦ 1 Apr-3 Nov. € 17.00 2008*

PIETRAMURATA *1D1* (Rural) *46.02388, 10.94333* **Camping Daino, Viale Daino 17, 38070 Pietramurata (TN) [tel/fax 464 507451; campingdaino@gardaqui.net; www.gardaqui.net/campingdaino]** On Trento-Riva rd S45 bis, site adj hotel. Sp fr both N & S dir. Med, mkd pitch, pt sl, pt shd; wc; chem disp; shwrs inc; el pnts (6A) €2; lndtte; supmkt 3km; rest; pool; lake sw & shgl beach 10km; 10% statics; dogs €3; phone; poss cr; adv bkg; quiet; CCI. 10 Mar-31 Oct. € 23.00 2008*

PIEVE DI LEDRO *1D1* (Rural) *45.88527, 10.73138* **Camping Azzurro, Via Alzer, 38060 Pieve-di-Ledro (TN) [0464 508435 or 591276; fax 508150; info@campingazzurro.net; www.campingazzurro.net]** Fr Riva-del-Garda foll sp Val di Ledro on S240. Ent vill on by-pass, at x-rds turn L, site on L in 200m on lakeside. Med, mkd pitch, some hdstg, shd; wc; chem disp; mv service pnt; shwrs inc; el pnts (2-6A) inc; Indtte; supmkt adj; rest 100m; snacks; playgrnd; pool; lake sw; fishing; watersports; internet nr; 50% statics; dogs €5; bus nr; adv bkg; quiet; red low ssn. "Attractive vill; cycle track around lake; friendly staff; well-run site." ♦ 1 May-30 Sep. € 30.00 (CChq acc) 2011*

PIEVE DI LEDRO *1D1* (3km E Rural) *45.87805, 10.76777* **Camping Al Sole, Loc Besta, Via Maffei 127, 38060 Molina-di-Ledro (TN) [tel/fax 0464 508496; info@campingalsole.it; www.campingalsole.it]** Exit A22 at Rovereto S onto SS240 twd Riva-del-Garda then Vall di Ledro & Molina, site sp on Lake Ledro. Lge, mkd pitch, pt shd; wc; shwrs inc; el pnts (3A) inc; Indtte (inc dryer); shop; rest; snacks; bar; playgrnd; pool; lake sw & beach adj; watersports; tennis adj; wifi; entmnt; TV rm; 10% statics; dogs; adv bkg; quiet. "Peaceful site; busy but clean & well-ordered; some lake view pitches; gd outdoor activities." ♦ 1 Apr-30 Sep. € 31.00 2010*

PIEVE DI LEDRO *1D1* (500m S Rural) *45.88361, 10.73157* **Camping Al Lago, Via Alzer 7-9, 38060 Pieve-di-Ledro (TN) [tel/fax 0464 591250; info@camping-al-lago.it; www.camping-al-lago.it]** Exit A22 W onto SS240 to Riva-del-Garda, then cont on SS240 to Pieve-di-Lago. Turn L into Via Alzer & foll sp to site (after Cmp Azzurro). Med, mkd pitch, some hdstg, pt shd; wc (some cont); chem disp; mv service pnt; shwrs; el pnts (3A) inc; Indtte (inc dryer); shop 500m; rest 250m; snacks; bar; BBQ; playgrnd; lake sw adj; fishing; tennis; games area; cycle & canoe hire; wifi; entmnt; TV; 10% statics; dogs; Eng spkn; adv bkg; quiet; ccard acc; CCI. "Vg site; gd walking area." ♦ 2 Apr-10 Oct. € 30.00 2010*

⊞ **PIEVE TESINO** *1D1* (6km N Rural) *46.11361, 11.61944* **Villaggio Camping Valmalene, Loc Valmalene, 38050 Pieve-Tesino (TN) [0461 594214; fax 592654; info@valmalene.com; www.valmalene.com]** Fr Trento E for 50km on S47. Turn N at Strigno to Pieve-Tesino, site sp. Med, mkd pitch, pt shd; htd wc; mv service pnt; sauna; private bthrms avail; baby facs; shwrs; el pnts inc; Indtte; shop; supmkt 6km; tradsmn; rest; snacks; bar; playgrnd; htd pool; padding pool; tennis; cycle hire; games area; fitness rm; internet; some statics; dogs €4; site clsd Nov; adv bkg rec; quiet; ccard acc. "Gd base for summer & winter hols." ♦ € 27.00 2009*

PINETO *2F3* (2km NE Coastal) *42.62617, 14.05436* **Camping Heliopolis, Contrada Villa Fumosa, 64025 Pineto (TE) [0859 492720; fax 492171; info@heliopolis.it; www.heliopolis.it]** Exit A14 at Atri Pineto, then dir Pineto cent. Turn L at traff lts, then dir Conad (supmkt). Turn R at intersection, then R & R again. Cross level x-ing & foll sp to site. Med, pt shd; wc; chem disp; mv service pnt; shwrs; el pnts (4-6A) inc; Indtte; shop; rest; snacks; bar; playgrnd; pool; paddling pool; sand beach adj; watersports; fishing; tennis; internet; entmnt; TV; some statics; dogs; sep car park; adv bkg; ccard acc. ♦ 1 Apr-30 Sep. € 49.00 (4 persons) 2008*

PINETO *2F3* (9km S Coastal) *42.5675, 14.0925* **Camping Europe Garden, Via Belvedere 11, 64028 Silvi-Marina (TE) [085 930137; fax 932846; info@europegarden.it; www.europegarden.it]** Exit A14/E55 for Atri/Pineto or Pescara N onto coast rd SS16, bet Silvi-Marina & Pineto, turn W away fr coast at Europe Garden at km 5 & site sp. Lge, terr, shd; wc (some cont); mv service pnt; baby facs; shwrs inc; el pnts (5A) €2.50; gas; Indtte; shop; hypmkt 2km; rest; snacks; bar; playgrnd; pool; paddling pool; sand beach adj; tennis; archery; cycle hire; entmnt; 90% statics; no dogs; sep car park high ssn; Eng spkn; adv bkg; ccard acc; red CCI. "Well laid-out; steep slopes on site not rec for disabled; tractor help for c'vans avail; sm pitches diff for l'ge o'fits; site muddy in wet weather; panoramic views; pleasant staff; conv Appenines, Atri walled town & Abruzzo National Park." 1 May-1 Sep. € 36.50 2009*

PINZOLO *1D1* (5km N Rural) *46.18535, 10.78027* **Camping Fae', 38080 Sant' Antonio-di-Mavignola (TN) [tel/fax 0465 507178; campingfae@campiglio.it; www.campiglio.it/campingfae]** Site well sp on SS239 bet Pinzolo & Madonna-di-Campiglio. Med, mkd pitch, terr, pt shd; htd wc (some cont); chem disp; mv service pnt; shwrs inc; el pnts (6A) inc; Indtte; shop 1km; tradsmn; bar; BBQ; playgrnd; games rm; TV; 40% statics; dogs; bus adj; poss cr; adv bkg; quiet; ccard acc; red low ssn. "Well-run, family owned site; clean san facs; gd walking." ♦ 1 Jun-30 Sep & 1 Dec-30 Apr. € 31.50 2009*

⊞ **PISA** *1C3* (500m N Urban) **Camper Parking, Via Pietrasantina, 56100 Pisa** On Via Aurelia SS1 fork R app Pisa, then turn E approx 1km N of Arno Rv, sp camping. After 1km turn L into Via Pietrasantina. Site on R behind lge Tamoil petrol stn, sp coach parking. Max height under rlwy bdge 3.30m. C'vans acc. Lge, hdstg, unshd; own san ess; mv service pnt; no el pnts; shop; rest, snacks, bar 100m; dogs; bus adj; quiet. "Excel NH; parking within walking dist of leaning tower; water & waste inc; plenty of space." ♦ € 12.00 2010*

PISA *1C3* (1km N Urban) *43.72416, 10.3830* **Camp Torre Pendente, Viale delle Cascine 86, 56100 Pisa [050 561704; fax 561734; info@campingtorrependente.com; www.campingtorrependente.com]** Exit A12/E80 Pisa Nord onto Via Aurelia (SS1). After 8km & after x-ing rlwy bdge, turn L after passing Pisa sp at traff lts. Site on L, sp. Lge, mkd pitch, pt shd; wc; mv service pnt; chem disp; baby facs; fam bthrm; shwrs inc; el pnts (5A) inc (poss rev pol); gas; Indtte (inc dryer); shop; supmkt 400m; rest; pizzeria; snacks; bar; BBQ; playgrnd; pool; sand beach 10km; cycle hire; wifi; TV rm; dogs €1.60; phone; poss cr; Eng spkn; no adv bkg; ccard acc over €100; red long stay; CCI. "Gd base Pisa; leaning tower 15 mins walk; immac, modern, well-maintained san facs; private san facs avail; pitches typically 50sqm; poss tight lge outfits due narr site rds & corners; many pitches shd by netting; site rds muddy after rain; friendly staff; excel, well-run site." ♦ 1 Apr-15 Oct. € 33.50 2011*

ITALY

PISA *1C3* (7km S Rural) *43.63083, 10.36277* **Agricampeggio Lago Le Tamerici, Via della Sofina 6, 56121 Coltano (PI) [050 989007; info@lagoletamerici.it; www.lagoletamerici.it]** S fr Pisa on SS1 Via Aurelia, turn L sp Coltano, then Lago Le Tamerici. Or fr S on SS206 foll sp Coltano etc. Sm, hdg/mkd pitch, pt shd; wc; chem disp; mv service pnt; el pnts (10A) inc; Indtte (inc dryer); shop; tradsmn; rest; snacks; bar; BBQ; playgrnd; pool; lake fishing; canoe & cycle hire; games area; adv bkg; quiet. ♦ 12 Mar-16 Oct. € 28.00 (CChq acc) 2010*

PISOGNE *1C1* (200m N Rural) *45.80611, 10.1050* **Camping Eden, Loc Goia, Via Piangrande 3/A, 25055 Pisogne (BS) [tel/fax 0364 880500; info@campeggioeden.com; www.campeggioeden.com]** Exit P510 at Pisogne Sud, over rlwy line, site sp. Med, mkd pitch, shd; wc; shwrs inc; el pnts (2A) €1.30; Indtte; shop 200m; rest, snacks 100m; playgrnd; sand beach; watersports; tennis; some statics (sep area); dogs €1.50; adv bkg; quiet. "Lovely, wooded site; excel facs." ♦ 1 May-15 Sep. € 24.50 2010*

PISTOIA *1D3* (10km S Rural) *43.84174, 10.91049* **Camping Barco Reale, Via Nardini 11, 51030 San Baronto-Lamporecchio (PT) [0573 88332; fax 856003; info@barcoreale.com; www.barcoreale.com]** Leave A11 at Pistoia junc onto P9 & foll sp to Vinci, Empoli & Lamporecchio to San Baronto. In vill turn into street by Monti Hotel & Rest, site sp. Last 3km steep climb. Lge, mkd pitch, pt sl, terr, shd; wc; chem disp; mv service pnt; 30% serviced pitch; baby facs; shwrs inc; el pnts (3-6A) inc (poss rev pol); gas; Indtte; shop; tradsmn; rest; snacks; bar; playgrnd; pool; games area; cycle hire; internet; entmnt; dogs; phone; Eng spkn; adv bkg ess; quiet; red long stay/low ssn; ccard acc; red long stay; CCI. "Excel site in Tuscan hills; helpful staff; gd touring base; excel mother & baby facs; vg rest; poss diff access some pitches but towing help provided on request; unsuitable lge o'fits; well-organised walking & bus trips." ♦ 1 Apr-30 Sep. € 34.60 2007*

PIZZO *3B4* (6km N Coastal) *38.72213, 16.15104* **Camping Villaggio Pinetamare, 88812 Pizzo (VV) [0963 264067; fax 534871; info@villaggiopinetamare.it]** Exit A3/E45 dir Pizzo. Fr Pizzo go N on S18 twd Santa Eufemia-Lamezia, km 392; site sp. Lge, mkd pitch, hdstg, shd; wc (some cont); chem disp; shwrs inc; el pnts (6A) €3.50; gas; Indry rm; shop; rest; snacks; bar; playgrnd; 3 pools; private sand/shgl beach adj; windsurfing; tennis; entmnt & no dogs; Eng spkn; adv bkg; ccard acc; CCI. "Vg family site under pine trees." 15 Jun-15 Sep. € 37.00 2009*

POGGIBONSI *1D3* (8km N Rural) *43.54625, 11.17848* **Camping Semifonte, Via Foscolo 4, 50021 Barberino-Val-d'Elsa (FI) [tel/fax 055 8075454; semifonte@semifonte.it; www.semifonte.it]** Heading S on a'strada Florence-Siena exit at Tavarnelle junc, thro Tavarnelle to Barberina-Val-d'Elsa; take 1st L turn on ent vill; site in 500m. Med, terr, mkd pitch, hdstg, pt shd; wc (some cont); chem disp; mv service pnt; shwrs inc; el pnts (4A) inc (poss rev pol & reduced mains voltage); gas; Indtte; shop; snacks 500m; pool; paddling pool; lake sw 8km; dogs; phone; Eng spkn; adv bkg; quiet; 5% red long stay/low ssn/snr citizens; ccard acc; CCI. "Pitches sm - steep pull out of site; some manual parking of vans poss necessary on narr terrs; rec report to office & walk round site to select pitch; helpful staff; lovely peaceful situation; conv Florence, Siena, San Gimignano & Chianti vineyards." 15 Mar-5 Oct. € 29.00 2008*

POGGIBONSI *1D3* (12km N Rural) *43.58198, 11.13801* **Camping Panorama Del Chianti, Via Marcialla 349, 50020 Marcialla-Certaldo (FI) [tel/fax 0571 669334; info@campingchianti.it; www.campingchianti.it]** Fr Florence-Siena a'strada exit sp Tavarnelle. On reaching Tavernelle turn R sp Tutti Direzione/Certaldo & foll by-pass to far end of town. Turn R sp to Marcialla, in Marcialla turn R to Fiano, site in 1km. NB Some steep hairpins app site fr E. Med, mkd pitch, hdstg, terr, pt shd; wc (some cont); chem disp; mv service pnt; shwrs inc; el pnts (3A) inc; shop, rest, snacks, bar 800m; tradsmn; sm pool; cycle hire; dogs €2; phone; adv bkg; Eng spkn; quiet; red long stay; ccard not acc; CCI. "Gd tourist info (in Eng); sports facs in area; cultural sites; helpful staff; friendly owner; san facs clean - hot water to shwrs only; 4 excel rests nr; panaromic views; midway bet Siena & Florence; popular site - arr early to get pitch." 15 Mar-15 Oct. € 29.50 2010*

POGGIBONSI *1D3* (10km E Rural) *43.39916, 11.24888* **Camping Luxor Quies, Loc Trasqua, 53011 Castellina-in-Chianti (SI) [tel/fax 0577 743047; info@luxorcamping.com; www.luxorcamping.com]** Fr Siena take SS2 rd (not a'strada) dir Florence; camp turn 12km on R (sp). Fr Florence-Siena a'strada A1, take Firenze Certosa exit, foll non-a'strada dual c'way (sp Corsie 4) to Siena exit at Monteriggioni & turn R sp Siena. After 2km turn L sp Trasqua onto dirt rd. Site 2km up narr dirt track with severe hairpin bends but not really diff for balanced o'fit. Med, hdg/mkd pitch, pt sl, shd; wc (some cont); shwrs €0.50; el pnts (4A) €1; gas; Indtte; shop; rest; snacks; bar; playgrnd; pool; dogs; poss cr; adv bkg ess high ssn; quiet; ccard acc; CCI. "Conv Siena, San Gimignano; excel wine cellar in vill; lovely wooded, hilltop site; sm, dusty, bare pitches; beautiful pool open to public & poss cr; site diff lge o'fits due trees & gullies." 17 May-14 Sep. € 24.00 2008*

⊞ **POMPEI** *3A3* (1km S Urban) *40.74638, 14.48388* **Camping Spartacus, Loc Pompei Scavi, Via Plinio 117, 80045 Pompei (NA) [tel/fax 081 8624078; spartacuscamping@tin.it; www.campingspartacus.it]** Fr N on A3 exit Pompei Ovest. At T-junc turn L & site on R just after passing under rlwy bdge. Fr S exit Pompei Est & foll sp Pompei Scavi (ruins). Sm, mkd pitch, shd; wc; chem disp; mv service pnt; shwrs inc; el pnts (5A) €2.50 (poss rev pol); gas; Indtte; shop; supmkt 400m; rest, snacks, bar in high ssn; internet; TV rm; poss v cr; Eng spkn; adv bkg; some rd/rlwy noise; ccard acc; red low ssn/CCI. "Nice, family-run, welcoming site, 50m fr historical ruins; conv train to Naples, boats to Capri; stray dogs poss roam site & ruins; v popular with students high ssn; best of 3 town sites; gd site for exploring area." ♦ € 22.50 2011*

PORLEZZA *1C1* (4km E Rural) *46.04074, 9.16827* **Camping Ranocchio, Via Lago 7, Loc Piano Porlezza, 20010 Carlazzo (CO) [tel/fax 0344 70385; info@ranocchio.eu; www.ranocchio.eu]** On main rd bet Menaggio & Porlezza. Ent in vill of Piano on S side. Sp. Steep app in Lugano with hairpin bends; 15% gradient. V narr rd fr Lugano - clsd to c'vans at peak times. Lge, terr, shd, pt sl; wc; chem disp; mv service pnt; baby facs; shwrs €0.50; el pnts inc; gas; Indtte (inc dryer); shop adj; rest; snacks; bar; playgrnd; pool; paddling pool; lake sw & fishing; horseriding 2km; wifi; TV rm; dogs €2; Eng spkn; quiet; CCI. "Friendly recep; gd for exploring Como & Lugano; steamer trips on both lakes; lovely site." ♦ 1 Apr-30 Sep. € 25.00 (CChq acc) 2010*

PORTESE see San Felice Del Benaco *1D2*

PORTO CESAREO *3A4* (6.5km NE Coastal) *40.29077, 17.82711* **Camping Porto Cesareo, Via Torre Lapillo-Torre Columena, Km 0.7, 73010 Porto-Cesareo (LE) [tel/fax 0833 565312; info@portocesareocamping.it; www.portocesareocamping.it]** S fr Manduria or N fr Nardo on SP359, foll sp Porto Cesareo & site. Med, hdg/mkd pitch, shd; wc; chem disp; mv service pnts; shwrs inc; el pnts (4A) inc; Indtte; shop & 1km; tradsmn; rest; snacks; bar; BBQ; playgrnd; pool; sand beach 400m; cycle hire; games area; wifi; entmnt; TV rm; 15% statics; dogs free; Eng spkn; adv bkg; quiet; ccard acc. "Scenic, well-maintained site; vg, modern san facs; lovely pool; bus transfer to beach - gd snorkelling area; friendly, helpful staff." ♦ 1 Jun-12 Sep. € 32.00 (CChq acc) 2010*

PORTO RECANATI *2F3* (4km N Coastal) *43.47123, 13.64150* **Camping Bellamare, Lungomare Scarfiotti 13, 62017 Porto-Recanati (MC) [071 976628; fax 977586; info@bellamare.it; www.bellamare.it]** Exit A14/E55 Loreto/Porto-Recanati; foll sp Numana & Sirolo; camp on R in 4km on coast rd Lge, unshd; wc; chem disp; shwrs; el pnts (6A) €3; gas; Indtte; shop; rest; snacks; bar; playgrnd; pool; paddling pool; sand & shgl beach (shelves steeply); cycle hire; games area; games rm; entmnt; internet; some statics; no dogs; phone; Eng spkn; ccard acc; red low ssn; CCI. "V well-run site; NH tarrif of €19 (inc elec) for a pitch at the edge of the site but ok; beach access." ♦ 23 Apr-30 Sep. € 42.50 2011*

PORTO SAN GIORGIO *2F3* (1km S Coastal) *43.16015, 13.80819* **Camping Gemma, Via Campofiloni, Santa Maria-a-Mare, 63023 Fermo (AP) [tel/fax 0734 53411; info@campinggemma.it; www.campinggemma.it]** Exit A14 at Porto-San Giorgio, turn S onto SS16. Take 1st exit at rndabt then immed L by church. Foll sp to site adj to Camping Spinnaker. Med, mkd pitch, pt shd; wc (cont); shwrs inc; el pnts (3A); Indtte; shop; rest, snacks, bar high ssn; playgrnd; pool; shgl beach adj; 70% statics; no dogs; phone; poss cr; Eng spkn; adv bkg; quiet but some noisy fr adj site & some rlwy noise; red long stay/low ssn; CCI. "Red facs low ssn but only €75 per week for 4 persons." ♦ 1 May-14 Sep. € 34.00 2008*

PORTO SAN GIORGIO *2F3* (1km S Coastal) *43.15905, 13.80823* **Camping Spinnaker, Via Campofiloni, Santa Maria-a-Mare 27, 63023 Fermo (AP) [0734 53412; fax 53737; info@vacanzespinnaker.it; www.vacanzespinnaker.it]** Exit A14 at junc for Porto-San Giorgio onto S16 S, foll site sp. V lge, mkd pitch, pt shd; wc; chem disp; mv service pnt; baby facs; shwrs inc; el pnts €3; Indtte; shop; rest; snacks; bar; playgrnd; pool; waterslide; sand beach adj; watersports; tennis; games area; cycle hire; entmnt; cash machine; some statics; dogs €3 (sm only); poss cr; adv bkg. 16 May-13 Sep. € 44.00 2009*

PORTO SANTA MARGHERITA see Caorle *2E2*

⊞ **POZZA DI FASSA** *1D1* (2km N Rural) *46.44477, 11.69650* **Camping Soal, Strada Dolomites 190, 30836 Pera-di-Fassa (TN) [tel/fax 0462 764519; info@campingsoal.com; www.campingsoal.com]** On R of SS48. Foll sp fr Pozza. Lge, pt shd; wc; chem disp; shwrs; el pnts (3A) inc; gas; shop; rest; snacks; bar; games area; entmnt; skibus; excursions; dogs €3; adv bkg (except Aug); some rd noise; ccard acc. "Gd walking/skiing cent; pleasant site & scenery." ♦ € 28.50 2008*

⊞ **POZZA DI FASSA** *1D1* (1km SE Rural) *46.42015, 11.70730* **Caravan Garden Vidor, Loc Vidor 5, 38036 Pozza-di-Fassa (TN) [0462 763247; fax 764780; info@campingvidor.it; www.campingvidor.it]** Exit A22 at Ora/Auer onto SS48 to Pozza-di-Fassa cent, turn R (E) over bdge dir Val di Nicolo, site in 2km on L on rvside. Other rds in area clsd to c'vans. Med, mkd pitch, hdstg, terr, pt shd; htd wc (some cont); chem disp; mv service pnt; baby facs; fam bthrm; sauna; shwrs inc; el pnts (2-16A) metered; gas (fixed supply to some pitches); Indtte (inc dryer); shop; tradsmn; rest adj & 2km; snacks; bar; BBQ; playgrnd; htd pool; paddling pool; sh tennis; cable car 1km; wifi; TV rm; 30% statics; dogs €4.50; phone; site clsd Nov; poss cr; Eng spkn; adv bkg; quiet; ccard acc; CCI. "Beautiful location; friendly, family-run site; excel views & facs; above hubbub of main valley; gd walking." ♦ € 31.00 2010*

⊞ **POZZA DI FASSA** *1D1* (500m SW Rural) *46.42638, 11.68527* **Camping Rosengarten, Via Avisio 15, 38036 Pozza-di-Fassa (TN) [0462 763305; fax 763501; info@catinacciorosengarten.com; www.catinacciorosengarten.com]** Fr S SS48 site sp just after San Giovanni. Lge, hdstg, pt shd; wc; chem disp; mv service pnt; shwrs inc; el pnts (2A) inc (extra for higher amperage); Indtte; shop 500m; rest, snacks adj; bar; pool 300m; skilift 1km; ski bus; 30% statics; dogs €4; site clsd Oct; poss cr; Eng spkn; adv bkg ess; quiet; 10% red 14+ days; ccard acc; CCI. "Superb scenery; helpful staff; luxury san facs; free taxi (2010) to Vigo di Fassa cable car; excel site." € 29.80 2010*

POZZUOLI *3A3* (1km N Urban) *40.82933, 14.13788* **Camping Vulcano Solfatara, Via Solfatara 161, 80078 Pozzuoli (NA) [081 5262341; fax 5263482; info@solfatara.it; www.solfatara.it]** Fr Rome on A1 join Tangenziale & leave at junc 11 sp Agnano. Foll Via Domitiana to site on R, set back fr rd on brow of hill. Ent thro narr arch. Med, pt shd; wc (some cont); chem disp (wc); mv service pnt; shwrs inc; el pnts (4A) inc (rev pol & long lead poss req); Indtte; shop; rest; snacks; bar; pool high ssn; TV; dogs free; phone; bus/metro; Eng spkn; quiet but poss noisy school parties visiting volcano; ccard acc; CCI. "Dormant volcanic crater adj site, volcanic activity in evidence - free access to campers; bus to port for trips to Ischia; conv Naples (by metro); friendly, well-run site; gd, clean facs; vg pool." 1 Apr-5 Nov. € 32.80 2008*

⊞ **POZZUOLI** *3A3* (3km N Coastal) *40.84120, 14.08696* **Camping Averno, Via Montenuovo Licola Patria 85, 80072 Pozzuoli (NA) [081 8042666; fax 8042570; www.averno.it]** N on Domiziana rd at km 55. Exit ring rd sp Cuma. Sm, pt shd; wc; sauna; shwrs; el pnts inc; shop 100m; rest; bar; snacks; pool & htd thermal pools; paddling pool; solarium; tennis; games area; wifi; 30% statics; bus to Naples; sep car park; poss cr; adv bkg; noisy; ccard acc. € 27.00 2007*

ITALY

PRAIA A MARE *3A4* (500m S Coastal) *39.88198, 15.78529* **International Camping Village, Lungomare F. Sirimarco, 87028 Praia-a-Mare (CS) [tel/fax 0985 72211; reception@campinginternational.it; www.campinginternational.it]** On beach rd just bef rocky island. Lge, hdg/mkd pitch, hdstg, shd; wc (some cont); chem disp; mv service pnt; shwrs inc; el pnts (5A) inc; lndtte; shop, rest, bar high ssn; BBQ; playgrnd; paddling pool; private shgl beach adj; tennis; games area; entmnt; some statics; dogs; phone; rlwy noise; ccard acc; red low ssn. "Welcoming, clean site; hot water to shwrs only." ♦ 23 Apr-30 Sep. € 38.50 2009*

PRAIA A MARE *3A4* (2km S Coastal) *39.87654, 15.78867* **Camping Villaggio Turistico La Mantinera, Contrada de Mantinera, 87028 Praia-a-Mare (CS) [0985 779023; fax 779009; lamantinera@tiscali.it; www.lamantinera.it]** On old coast rd, exit SS18 at sp to Praia. Fr N thro town on L; fr S immed at bottom of hill on R. Lge, hdg/mkd pitch, shd, all serviced pitches; wc; shwrs inc; el pnts (7A) inc; rest (Jul/Aug); bar; snacks; shop; lndry rm; playgrnd; shgl beach 750m; pool; boat hire; windsurfing; tennis; cycle hire; 30% statics; no dogs high ssn; poss cr; adv bkg; noisy disco & traff; ccard acc; 10% red CCI. "Indiv tree-lined bays with own water & el pnts; free transport to beach; tours to Naples, Pompei & organised activities." ♦ 30 Apr-30 Sep. € 42.00 (3 persons) 2009*

⊞ **PRATO ALLO STELVIO** *1D1* (1.5m E Rural) *46.61777, 10.59555* **Camping Sägemühle, Dornweg 12, 39026 Prato-allo-Stélvio (BZ) [0473 616078; fax 617120; info@campingsaegumuehle.com; www.camping.saegemuehle.suedtirol.com]** Fr rd S40 turn E at Spondigna onto rd S38 dir Stélvio, site sp in vill. Med, hdg/mkd pitch, hdstg, pt sl, pt shd; htd wc; chem disp; mv service pnt; baby facs; fam bthrm; sauna; shwrs inc; el pnts (16A) inc; lndtte (inc dryer); shop 200m; rest; bar; playgrnd; 2 pools (1 htd, covrd); paddling pool; games area; skilift 10km; skibus; wifi; TV; phone; dogs €4; site clsd 8 Nov to 18 Dec; adv bkg; quiet; 10% red low stay; ccard acc; CCI. "Excel, well-run site; gd, clean facs; helpful staff; gd walking area in National Park." € 38.00 2010*

PRATO ALLO STELVIO *1D1* (500m NW Rural) *46.62472, 10.59388* **Camping Kiefernhain, Via Pineta 37, 39026 Prato-allo-Stélvio (BZ) [0473 616422; fax 617277; kiefernhain@rolmail.net; www.camping-kiefernhain.it]** Fr rd S40 turn SW at Spondigna onto rd S38 dir Stélvio, site sp in vill. Lge, mkd pitch, pt shd; wc; chem disp; mv service pnt; baby facs; private bthrms avail; shwrs inc; el pnts (6A) €2.50; lndtte; shop; tradsmn; rest 300m; snacks; bar; BBQ; playgrnd; htd pool; waterslide; sports cent adj; dogs €4; phone; dog shwr; Eng spkn; adv bkg rec high ssn; quiet; red long stay. "V modern, clean san facs; superb views." ♦ 1 Apr-4 Oct. € 29.00 2008*

PRECI *2E3* (2km NW Rural) *42.88808, 13.01483* **Camping Il Collaccio, 06047 Castelvecchio-di-Preci (PG) [0743 939005; fax 939094; info@ilcollaccio.com; www.ilcollaccio.com]** S fr Assisi on S75 & S3, turn off E sp Norcia, Cascia. Then foll sp for Visso on S209. In approx 30km turn R for Preci, then L, site sp. Rte is hilly. Med, mkd pitch, terr, pt shd; htd wc (some cont); chem disp; mv service pnt; baby facs; shwrs inc; el pnts (6A) inc (long lead poss req); lndtte; shop & 2km; tradsmn; rest; snacks; bar; playgrnd; 2 pools; tennis; games area; horseriding; paragliding; cycle hire; TV rm; 20% statics; dogs; phone; Eng spkn; adv bkg; quiet; ccard acc; red CCI. "Beautiful views; well-maintained, clean site; pleasant rest; maganificent pool area; sm pitches; gd walking in Monti Sibillini National Park; conv Assisi & historic hill towns." ♦ 1 Apr-30 Sep. € 33.00 2010*

I'll go online and tell the Club what we think of the campsites we've visited – www.caravanclub.co.uk/europereport

PREDAZZO *1D1* (1.5km E Rural) *46.31027, 11.63138* **Camping Valle Verde, Loc Ischia 2, Sotto Sassa, 38037 Predazzo (TN) [0462 502394; fax 501147; info@campingvalleverde.it; www.campingvalleverde.it]** Exit A22 dir Ora onto rd S48 dir Cavalese/Predazzo. Fr Predazzo take SS50 W, turn R in 1.5km, site on L in 500m. Med, mkd pitch, pt shd; htd wc (some cont); chem disp; mv service pnt; shwrs inc; el pnts (4A) €1.50 (6A avail); lndtte; rest; snacks; bar; playgrnd; pool 500m; 10% statics; poss cr; adv bkg; quiet; red low stay/snr citizens; ccard acc; CCI. "Gd." ♦ 1 May-30 Sep. € 25.00 2008*

PUNTA MARINA TERME see Ravenna *2E2*

PUNTA SABBIONI *2E2* (2km N Coastal) *45.43773, 12.43881* **Camping Marina di Venezia, Via Montello 6, 30010 Punta-Sabbioni (VE) [041 5300955; fax 966036; camping@marinadivenezia.it; www.marinadivenezia.it]** Exit A4 dir Marco Polo Airport, foll dir Jesolo. At Jesolo where rd splits, bear R dir Cavallino/Punta-Sabbioni. Site well sp. V lge, hdg/mkd pitch, pt shd; wc; chem disp; shwrs inc; el pnts (6A) inc; gas; lndtte; shops & supmkt; rest; snacks; bar; playgrnd; 2 pools; sand beach adj; boat hire; windsurfing; tennis; cycle hire; solarium; games area; 5% statics; dogs €3.50; phone; bus fr site to waterbus to Venice; adv bkg rec; quiet; ccard acc; red low ssn/snr citizen. "Lge pitches; high quality site, wonderfully equipped and well run; min stay 2 nts (7 nts Jul/Aug); excel, clean facs; some pitches avail v lge o'fits; superb pool complex; pleasant, helpful staff; within easy reach of Venice; highly rec." ♦ 16 Apr-30 Sep. € 44.10 2011*

PUNTA SABBIONI *2E2* (2km NE Coastal) *45.44560, 12.46100* **Campéole Camping Ca'Savio, Via di Ca'Savio 77, 30010 Ca'Savio (VE) [041 966017; fax 5300707; info@casavio.it; www.casavio.it or www.campeole.com]** Fr Lido di Jesolo head twd Punta-Sabbioni; at x-rds/rndabt in cent of Ca'Savio turn L twd beach (La Spiaggia) for 800m; turn L into site just bef beach. Or at L turn at rndabt - rd poss clsd at night - cont to Punta-Sabbioni, turn L at sp to beach; L at T-junc, then R at x-rds. V lge, hdg/mkd pitch, shd; wc (some cont); chem disp; mv service pnt; baby facs; shwrs; el pnts (5A) inc (check pol); gas; Indtte (inc dryer); supmkt; rest; pizzeria; snacks; bar; playgrnd; pool; paddling pool; direct access to adj sandy beach; water sports; canoeing/kayaking; games area; archery; cycle hire; wifi; entmnt; games rm; TV; 50% statics; no dogs; no c'vans/m'vans over 7m high ssn; phone; bus to Venice ferry; ccard acc; red low ssn; CCI. "Well laid-out, well-run, busy site - noisy high ssn; helpful staff; conv Venice by ferry fr Punta Sabbioni; excel, clean san facs; facs ltd low ssn; long, narr pitches; access poss diff lge o'fits; gd supmkt; min 3 nights stay high ssn; barriers clsd 1300-1500." ♦ 21 Apr-30 Sep. € 37.50 (CChq acc) SBS - Y02 2011*

PUNTA SABBIONI *2E2* (700m S Coastal) *45.44035, 12.4211* **Camping Miramare, Lungomare Dante Alighieri 29, 30010 Punta-Sabbioni (VE) [041 966150; fax 5301150; info@camping-miramare.it; www.camping-miramare.it]** Take rd Jesolo to Punta-Sabbioni, pass all camps & go to end of peninsula. Turn L at boat piers & foll rd alongside beach; site 500m on L. Med, hdg/mkd pitch, pt shd; htd wc; chem disp; mv service pnt; shwrs inc; el pnts (6A) inc (rev pol); gas; Indtte; shop; rest & pizzeria adj; playgrnd; internet; statics; dogs €4 (only sm dogs allowed); phone; bus to beach 2km & ferry; min 3 nights stay high ssn; Eng spkn; quiet; ccard acc (min €100); red low ssn/snr citizens. "Excel, well-organised, family-owned site closest to boat terminal for Venice - 10 mins walk (tickets fr recep) - can leave bikes at terminal; gd security; helpful, friendly staff; new part of site v pleasant wooded area; clean facs; poss mosquito problem; superior to many other sites in area; min stay 2 nights Jul/Aug; don't miss camping supmkt on way in - an Aladdin's cave; avoid dep on Sat due traffic; Magic of Italy site." ♦ 1 Apr-1 Nov. € 34.00 2011*

PUNTA SABBIONI *2E2* (700m S Coastal) *45.44141, 12.42127* **Parking Dante Alighieri, Lungomare Dante Alighieri 26, 30010 Punta-Sabbioni (VE)** Take rd Jesolo to Punta-Sabbioni, pass all camps & go to end of peninsula. Turn L at boat piers & foll rd alongside beach; site on L just bef Camping Miramare. Sm, pt shd; wc; chem disp; mv service pnt; shwrs inc; el pnts (8A) inc; shop, rest, snacks, bar 500m; bus 500m; dogs; poss cr; Eng spkn; quiet. "M'vans only; friendly, helpful owner; 10 min walk for boats to Venice; vg." € 23.00 2011*

QUART see Aosta *1B1*

RAPALLO *1C2* (2km N Urban) *44.35805, 9.2100* **Camping Miraflores, Via Savagna 10, 16035 Rapallo (GE) [0185 263000; fax 260938; info@campingmiraflores.it; www.campingmiraflores.it]** Exit A12/E80 at Rapallo. In 100m fr toll gate sharp L across main rd, sharp L again, site sp 200m on R. Site almost immed beside toll gate but not easily seen. Sp fr town. Med, hdg/mkd pitch, hdstg, terr, pt shd; wc (some cont); chem disp; mv service pnt; shwrs €0.60; el pnts (3A) €1.80; gas; Indry rm; shop 300m; rest 200m; snacks; bar; playgrnd; sm pool; 10% statics; dogs free; bus 200m to stn & town cent; sep car park; poss cr; rd noise; ccard acc; red low ssn/CCI. "Excel htd pool adj; gd, modern san facs; grass pitches for tents, earth only for m'vans & c'vans; v noisy & dusty as under m'way; v friendly staff; ferries to Portofino fr town; conv NH; rec phone ahead if lge o'fit." ♦ 1 Mar-31 Dec. € 26.50 2011*

RAPALLO *1C2* (2.5km W Urban) *44.35691, 9.1992* **Camping Rapallo, Via San Lazzaro 4, 16035 Rapallo (GE) [tel/fax 0185 262018; campingrapallo@libero.it; www.campingrapallo.it]** Exit A12/E80 dir Rapallo, turn immed R on leaving tolls. Site sp in 500m on L at bend (care), over bdge then R. Narr app rd. Site sp. Med, hdg/mkd pitch, pt shd; wc (some cont); chem disp; mv service pnt; shwrs inc; el pnts (3A) €2.20; gas; Indtte; supmkt 500m; rest 200m; bar; htd pool; shgl beach 2.5km; cycle hire; 10% statics; dogs; bus (tickets fr recep); poss cr; Eng spkn; adv bkg; some daytime rd noise; ccard acc; CCI. "Clean, family-run site; conv Portofino (boat trip) & train to Cinque Terre; beautiful coastlline; shwrs clsd during day but hot shwrs at pool; v busy public hols - adv bkg rec; awkward exit, not suitable for lge o'fits; NH only." 1 Feb-30 Nov. € 25.00 2009*

RASUN DI SOTTO/NIEDERRASEN see Brunico/Bruneck *1D1*

RAVENNA *2E2* (7km E Coastal) *44.43335, 12.29680* **Camping Park Adriano, Via dei Campeggi 7, 48020 Punta-Marina-Terme (RN) [0544 437230; fax 438510; info@campingadriano.com; www.campingadriano.com]** Fr S309 Ravenna-Venezia rd foll sp to Lido Adriano. Site at N end of Lido. Lge, shd; wc; chem disp; mv service pnt; shwrs inc; el pnts (5A) inc (poss rev pol/no earth); Indtte (inc dryer); shop; tradsmn; rest; snacks; bar; BBQ; playgrnd; pool; paddling pool; beach 300m; cycle hire; golf 10km; wifi; entmnt; TV rm; 70% statics; dogs €3; bus to Ravenna; ATM; Eng spkn; adv bkg; poss noisy disco; ccard acc; red snr citizens/CCI. "Site in pine forest; excel san facs; sh walk to beach." ♦ 22 Apr-19 Sep. € 40.00 (CChq acc) 2009*

RAVENNA *2E2* (9km E Coastal) *44.43147, 12.30034* **Camping Villaggio dei Pini, Via della Fontana, 48020 Punta-Marina-Terme (RA) [0544 437115; fax 531863; villaggiodeipini@gestionecampeggi.it; www.gestionecampeggi.it]** Foll sp to Punta Marina fr S67; in cent of Punta-Marina take sm rd S; site at end of rd on L. Lge, pt shd; wc (some cont); chem disp; mv service pnt; shwrs inc; el pnts (5A) inc; gas; Indtte; shop; rest; snacks; bar; playgrnd; beach adj; cycle hire; entmnt; 90% statics; no dogs; phone; clsd 1400-1600 & 0000-0700; poss v cr; quiet; ccard acc. "Conv for mosaics; pitches v sm." ♦ 23 Apr-13 Sep. € 31.30 2010*

ITALY

RICCIONE *2E3* (1km SE Coastal) *43.9850, 12.67916* **Camping Riccione, Via Marsala 10, 47838 Riccione (RN) [0541 690160; fax 690044; info@campingriccione.it; www.campingriccione.it]** Exit A14/E55 onto SS16 thro Riccione ignoring numerous other camp sp & look for site sp. Turn L and site in 150m on R. Lge, shd; wc; mv service pnt; some serviced pitches; shwrs inc; el pnts (5A) inc; gas; Indtte; shop; rest; snacks; bar; playgrnd; pool & paddling pool; sand beach 500m; tennis; games area; cycle hire; solarium; wifi; sat TV; 10% statics; dogs (not acc mid-Jul to mid-Aug); poss cr; adv bkg; traff noise (rd, rlwy & air); ccard acc; red CCI. "Pitch acc poss diff due to trees." ♦ 18 Apr-21 Sep. € 47.10 2011*

RICCIONE *2E3* (2km S Coastal) *43.98610, 12.68806* **Camping Alberello, Viale Torino 80, 47838 Riccione (RN) [tel/fax 0541 615248; direzione@alberello.it; www.alberello.it]** Exit A14/E55 dir Riccione on SS16. Site is sp off this rd dir Misano Adriatico, twds sea. Lge, hdg/mkd pitch, shd; wc; shwrs inc; el pnts (4A) €2.50; gas; Indtte; shop; rest; snacks; bar; playgrnd; sand beach adj; games area; golf 1km; entmnt; TV rm; no dogs; car wash; no adv bkg; quiet but rlwy/rd noise. "Gd for families." ♦ 9 Apr-28 Sep. € 32.70 2009*

RIVA DEL GARDA *1D1* (2.5km E Rural) *45.88111, 10.86194* **Camping Monte Brione, Via Brione 32, 38066 Riva-del-Garda (TN) [0464 520885; fax 520890; info@campingbrione.com; www.campingbrione.com]** Exit A22 Garda Nord onto SS240 to Torbole & Riva; on app to Riva thro open-sided tunnel; immed R after enclosed tunnel opp Marina; site ent 700m on R. Med, mkd pitch, terr, pt shd; wc (some cont); chem disp; mv service pnt; shwrs inc; el pnts (6A) inc; gas; Indtte; shop; rest 200m; snacks; bar; BBQ; playgrnd; htd pool; shgl beach & lake sw 500m; watersports; cycle hire; solarium; wifi; dogs €4; barriers clsd 1300-1500 & 2300-0700; Eng spkn; adv bkg; quiet; ccard acc; CCI. "Olive groves adj; pleasant site with lge pitches; gd, modern san facs." ♦ 1 Apr-30 Sep. € 28.50 2009*

RIVA DEL GARDA *1D1* (SE Urban) *45.88044, 10.85579* **Camping Bavaria, Viale Rovereto 100, 38066 Riva-del-Garda (TN) [0464 552524; fax 559126; camping@bavarianet.it; www.bavarianet.it]** Exit A22 Garda Nord dir Tarbole & Riva. On app Riva thro enclosed tunnel, past marina. Site on L immed bef Bavaria Rest. Med, pt shd; wc; shwrs; el pnts inc; shop adj; snacks; rest 100m; shgl beach; windsurfing school; dogs €2; poss cr; ccard acc; red CCI. "Views of Lake Garda, pleasant scenery; lakeside walk adj; pitches poss tight lge outfits; clean san facs; busy site conv for town." ♦ 1 Apr-31 Oct. € 25.00 2007*

RIVA DI SOLTO *1C1* (1km S Rural) *45.77045, 10.03536* **Camping Trenta Passi, Via XXV Aprile 1, 24060 Riva-di-Solto (BG) [035 980320; fax 985119; info@trentapassi.it; www.trentapassi.it]** Site sp fr SS469 along lakeside. Sm, mkd pitch, unshd; wc; shwrs inc; el pnts inc; Indtte; rest; bar; BBQ (gas only); playgrnd; private sand beach adj; entmnt; 90% statics (sep area); dogs; quiet. "Delightful little site; gd facs & rest; friendly staff; conv vill - mkt Wed." 1 Apr-31 Oct. € 19.00 2007*

⊞ **RIZZOLO** *1C2* (3km S Rural) **Camping Cascinotta, 29019 Rizzolo (Postal address: San Giorgio-Piacentino (PC)) [0523 530113; fax 0523 530451; rose@cittadellerose.it; www.cittadellerose.it]** Site is 10km S of San Giorgio-Piacentino on rd fr Rizzolo to Ponte-dell'Ollio. Med, mkd pitch, pt terr, pt shd; wc; chem disp; mv service pnt; shwrs inc; el pnts €2; Indtte; bar; BBQ; playgrnd; 5% statics; dogs; adv bkg; CCI. "Site attached to religious sanctuary & pilgrimage cent; set in parkland; vg touring base." € 24.00 2009*

ROCCA PIETORE *1D1* (8km E Rural) *46.43538, 12.09781* **Camping Cadore, Via Peronaz 3, 32020 Selva-di-Cadore (BL) [tel/fax 0437 720267; cadore@sunrise.it; www.camping.dolomiti.com/cadore]** Fr Cortina-d'Ampezzo S on SR48 then SP638; site bet Selva-di-Cadore & Forno-di-Zoldo, 3km N of summit of Passo Staulanza. Lge, hdstg, terr, pt shd; htd wc; chem disp; shwrs; el pnts inc; shop; rest 200m; bar; playgrnd; 90% statics; dogs €4; poss cr; adv bkg; quiet. "Excel walking Pelmo mountains; gd views fr site." ♦ 1 Dec-25 Apr & 5 Jun-26 Sep. € 29.00 2007*

ROCCA PIETORE *1D1* (6km W Rural) *46.42525, 11.90394* **Camping Malga Ciapela Marmolada, Malga Ciapela, 32020 Rocca-Pietore (BL) [tel/fax 0437 722064; camping.mc.marmolada@dolomiti.com; www.camping.dolomiti.com/malgaciapela/]** Fr Canazei take S641 sp Passo-di-Fedaia, site sp on R at Malga-Ciapela. NB Site not accessible fr E or W for towed c'vans - banned fr steep stretches of S641. Med, mkd pitch, hdstg, pt sl, pt shd; htd wc; chem disp; shwrs inc; el pnts inc; Indtte; shop; rest; bar; BBQ; cooking facs; playgrnd; 30% statics; phone; skibus; quiet. "Vg, peaceful site; gd walking base." 1 Dec-30 Apr & 1 Jun-30 Sep. € 21.20 2008*

⊞ **ROCCARASO** *2F4* (2km NE Rural) *41.84194, 14.10277* **Camping Del Sole, Piana del Leone, Via Pietransieri, 67037 Roccaraso (AQ) [0864 62532; fax 619328; delsole@camping.it; www.camping.it/english/abruzzo/delsole/]** Turn E fr S17 at sp Petransieri & site on R in 2km. Med, pt sl, pt shd; wc; chem disp; shwrs inc; el pnts inc (poss no earth - long lead rec); gas; Indtte; shop 2km; rest; bar; playgrnd; sw 2km; ski school; 5% statics; dogs (sm only); bus; quiet; ccard acc; CCI. "Excel & conv National Park; ltd facs low ssn." ♦ € 19.00 2007*

RODI GARGANICO *2G4* (7.5km E Rural) **Camping Village Valle d'Oro, Via degli Ulivi, Loc Aia del Cervone, 71010 San Menaio (FG) [tel/fax 0884 991580; info@campingvalledoro.it; www.campingvalledoro.it]** Exit A14 at Poggio Emperiate onto S89 E dir Peschici & Vieste thro Rodi Garganico. At San Menaio turn R twd Vico del Gargano for 4km, site on R, well sp. Sm, terr, pt shd; htd wc; chem disp; shwrs inc; el pnts (3A) €2.50; Indry rm; shop; rest; snacks; bar; playgrnd; sm pool; sand beach 4km; games area; dogs; poss cr; Eng spkn; adv bkg; quiet; red low ssn; CCI. "Pleasant site in olive trees away fr busy coastal sites; friendly, welcoming, helpful owners; vg rest; shuttle bus to beach high ssn; Vico-del-Gargano interesting town." ♦ 1 Jun-15 Sep. € 23.50 2009*

RODI GARGANICO *2G4* (4km W Coastal) *41.91209, 15.72950* **Camping 5 Stelle, C da Pagliai dei Combattenti, Km 34.500, 71010 Foce-di-Varano (FG) [tel/fax 0884 917583; info@camping5stelle.it; www.camping5stelle.it]** Exit A14 at Poggio-Imperiale E twd Vieste. Turn N at Sannicandro & foll sp Torre-Mileto, Porto-Capoiale & Isola-Varano. Site sp. Lge, pt shd; wc; chem disp; mv service pnt; private bthrms some pitches; baby facs; shwrs; el pnts (5A) €2.50; Indtte; shop; rest; snacks; bar; BBQ; playgrnd; pool; paddling pool; sand beach adj; lake fishing; tennis; cycle hire; games area; entmnt; TV rm; 20% statics; dogs €3; poss cr; quiet; ccard acc; red low ssn. ♦ 1 Apr-30 Sep. € 49.00 (CChq acc) 2011*

⊞ **ROMA** *2E4* (8km N Urban) *41.95618, 12.48240* **Camping Village Flaminio, Via Flaminia Nuova 821, 00191 Roma [06 3332604 or 3331429; fax 3330653; info@villageflaminio.com; www.villageflaminio.com]** Exit GRA ring rd at exit 6 & proceed S along Via Flaminia twd Roma Centrale. In 3km where lanes divide keep to L-hand lane (R-hand land goes into underpass). Cross underpass, then immed back to R-hand lane & slow down. Site on R 150m, sp as Flaminio Bungalow Village. No vehicular access to site fr S or exit to N. Lge, pt sl, pt shd; htd wc; chem disp; mv service pnt; shwrs inc; el pnts (3-12A) inc; gas; Indtte (inc dryer); shop; supmkt 200m; rest; snacks; bar; playgrnd; pool (sw caps req); cycle hire; wifi; TV rm; some statics; phone; bus (cross v busy rd); train nr; site clsd mid-Jan to end Feb; poss cr; no adv bkg; red long stay/low ssn; ccard acc (min €155). "Well-run site; excel, clean san facs; poss long walk fr far end of site to ent (site transport avail); poss dusty pitches; take care sap fr lime trees; cycle/walking track to city cent nrby; train 10 mins walk (buy tickets on site); local excursions pick-up fr site (tickets fr recep)." ♦ € 42.60 (CChq acc) 2009*

ROMA *2E4* (9km N) *42.00353, 12.45283* **Happy Village & Camping, Via Prato della Corte 1915, 00100 Roma [06 33626401; fax 33613800; info@happycamping.net; www.happycamping.net]** Take exit 5 fr Rome ring rd sp Viterbo. Site sp on ring rd, fr N & S on dual c'way Rome/Viterbo at 1st exit N of ring rd. Lge, pt terr, pt shd; wc; chem disp; mv service pnt; shwrs inc; el pnts (6A) inc; gas; Indtte; shop; rest; snacks; bar; BBQ; playgrnd; pool high ssn; some statics; dogs free; train into Rome; poss cr; adv bkg; poss noisy; ccard acc; red CCI. "Friendly, busy site in hills; sm pitches; vg rest; mini bus shuttle to train stn; gd site." ♦ 1 Mar-6 Jan. € 36.00 2011*

ROMA *2E4* (12km N Urban) *42.0102, 12.50368* **Camping Tiber, Via Tiberina, Km 1.4, 00188 Roma [06 33610733; fax 33612314; info@campingtiber.com; www.campingtiber.com]** Fr Florence, exit at Rome Nord-Fiano on A1 & immed after tolls turn S on Via Tibernia, site sp. Fr any dir on Rome ring rd take exit 6 N'bound on S3 Via Flaminia. Site 1km S of Prima Porta. Lge, pt shd; wc; mv service pnt; shwrs inc; el pnts (4-6A) inc (long lead req & poss rev pol); gas; Indtte (inc dryer); shop; rest; snacks; bar; pool high ssn; games area; wifi; some statics; dogs; free bus to metro stn; Eng spkn; quiet; ccard acc; red long stay/CCI. "Ideal for city by metro (20 mins) & bus; helpful staff; recep 0700-2300; modern san facs; some lge pitches; poss ant/mosquito prob; Magic of Europe discount; perfectly comfortable." ♦ 25 Mar-20 Oct. € 36.50 2011*

ROMA *2E4* (10km SW Rural) *41.77730, 12.39605* **Camping Fabulous, Via Cristoforo Colombo, Km 18, 00125 Acilia (RM) [06 5259354; fax 83517789; fabulous@ecvacanze.it; www.ecvacanze.it]** Exit junc 27 fr Rome ring rd into Via C Colombo. At 18km marker turn R at traff lts, site 200m on R. V lge, mkd pitch, pt sl, shd; htd wc; baby facs; shwrs inc; el pnts (6-10A) inc; Indtte; shop; rest; snacks; bar; BBQ; playgrnd; pool; paddling pool; waterslide; sand beach 12km; tennis; games area; entmnt; quiet at night; 80% statics; dogs €1.50; phone; bus on main rd; Eng spkn; adv bkg; ccard acc; CCI. "Set in pinewoods; gd sh stay." ♦ 12 Mar-31 Oct. € 34.90 2009*

⊞ **ROMA** *2E4* (4km W Urban) *41.88741, 12.40468* **Roma Camping, Via Aurelia 831, Km 8.2, 00165 Roma [06 6623018; fax 66418147; campingroma@ecvacenze.it]** Site is on Via Aurelia approx 8km fr Rome cent on spur rd on S side of main dual c'way opposite lge Panorama Hypmkt. Fr GRA ring rd exit junc 1 Aurelio & head E sp Roma Cent & Citta del Vaticano. In approx 3km take spur rd on R 50m bef covered pedestrian footbdge x-ing dual c'way & 250m bef flyover, sp camping; site gates on R (S) in 100m. W fr Rome take spur rd 8km fr cent sp camping just after Holiday Inn & just bef Panorama Hypmkt. At top turn L (S) over flyover & immed R sp camping; site gates on L in 200m. V lge, hdstg, terr, pt shd; wc (some cont); baby facs; shwrs inc; el pnts (4-6A) inc; Indtte; supmkt opp; rest; snacks; bar; playgrnd; pool high ssn; games area; wifi; 75% statics; dogs €1.50; bus to city; poss cr; Eng spkn; rd noise; ccard acc; red low ssn/CCI. "Gd, clean site; excel san facs & pool; friendly staff; popular site - rec arr early; rec not leave site on foot after dark." ♦ € 36.80 2009*

ROME see Roma *2E4*

ROSETO DEGLI ABRUZZI *2F3* (1.5km N Urban/Coastal) *42.69879, 13.99960* **Camping Surabaja, Via Makarska, Lungomare Nord, 64026 Roseto-degli-Abruzzi (TE) [tel/fax 085 8933181; info@campingsurabaja.it; www.campingsurabaja.it]** Exit A14 to Roseto-degli-Abruzzi, foll sp Lungomare Nord. Site on R almost at end of prom. Avoid low bdges, use level x-ing in town cent to reach prom. Med, mkd pitch, pt shd; wc (mainly cont); chem disp; mv service pnt; shwrs €0.35; el pnts (3A) €2; gas; Indtte; shop; rest; snacks; bar; playgrnd; sand beach adj; entmnt; no dogs Aug; phone; bus to town high ssn; sep car park; poss cr; Eng spkn; quiet. "Friendly, family-run site; excel private beach." ♦ 1 May-15 Sep. € 34.00 2007*

ROSETO DEGLI ABRUZZI *2F3* (3km S Coastal) *42.65748, 14.03568* **Eurcamping Roseto, Lungomare Trieste Sud 90, 64026 Roseto-degli-Abruzzi (TE) [085 8993179; fax 8930552; eurcamping@camping.it; www.eurcamping.it]** Fr A14 exit dir Roseto-degli-Abruzzi to SS16. At rndabt turn R, next L & under rlwy bdge to promenade. Turn R at sea front, site at end of promenade. Med, shd, hdg/mkd pitch; wc; chem disp; mv service pnt; shwrs inc; el pnts (3A) inc; Indtte (inc dryer); shop; rest; snacks; bar; playgrnd; pool; paddling pool; private sand & shgl beach adj; tennis; cycle hire; games area; wifi; entmnt; 20% statics; dogs €5; poss cr; Eng spkn; adv bkg; quiet but some rlwy noise; red low ssn; CCI. "Phone to check if open low ssn; gates close 2300; pitches poss flood after heavy rainfall; Roseto excel resort." ♦ 1 May-31 Oct. € 40.50 (CChq acc) 2010*

ITALY

⊞ **ST VINCENT** *1B1* (10km N Rural) *45.78729, 7.60361* **Camping Dalai Lama Village, Loc Promiod, 11024 Châtillon (AO) [0166 548688; fax 549921; info@dalailamavillage.com; www.dalailamavillage.com]** Exit A5/E25 at Châtillon & take R46 N to Antey-St André. In cent of town fork R over sm bdge & climb for approx 5km to site, sp. Care needed lge m'vans. Lge, mkd pitch, pt shd; htd wc; chem disp; mv service pnt; sauna; shwrs inc; el pnts inc; Indtte; rest; snacks; bar; playgrnd; htd, covrd pool; games area; games rm; gym; entmnt; 50% statics; dogs €4; adv bkg; quiet. "Stunning views; superb, peaceful site & san facs; vg bar/rest terr; highly rec; diff narrow rd for lge o'fits, 1km single track without passing places, excep views, 80% statics, shwrs not incl or pool/sauna €29 for session." ♦ € 39.00 2011*

⊞ **SALBERTRAND** *1A2* (1km SW Rural) *45.06200, 6.86821* **Camping Gran Bosco, SS24, Km 75, Monginevro, 10050 Salbertrand (TO) [0122 854653; fax 854693; info@campinggranbosco.it; www.campinggranbosco.it]** Leave A32/E70 (Torino-Fréjus Tunnel) at Oulx Ouest junc & foll SS24/SS335 sp Salbertrand. Site sp 1.5km twd Salbertrand at km 75. Fr S (Briançon in France) on N94/SS24 to Oulx cent, foll SS24 thro town & foll sp Salbertrand, then as above. Lge, pt shd; htd wc (mainly cont); chem disp; mv service pnt; shwrs; el pnts (3-6A) inc; gas; Indtte; shop; rest 1km; snacks; bar; playgrnd; tennis; games area; entmnt; 80% statics (sep area); some rd & rlwy noise; ccard acc. "Beautiful setting; excel NH bef/after Fréjus Tunnel or pass to/fr Briançon; gates open 0830-2300; excel, modern, clean san facs; sm pitches; ground soft in wet - no hdstg." € 26.00 2009*

SALSOMAGGIORE TERME *1C2* (3km E Rural) *44.80635, 10.00931* **Camping Arizona, Via Tabiano 42, 43039 Tabiano-Salsomaggiore Terme (PR) [0524 565648; fax 567589; info@camping-arizona.it; www.camping-arizona.it]** Exit A1 for Fidenza & foll sps for Salsomaggiore fr Co-op supmkt, to Tabiano; sp on S side of rd. Not rec to attempt to find site fr S9 fr Piacenza. Lge, pt sl, shd; wc (some cont); chem disp (wc); mv service pnt; shwrs inc; el pnts (3A) inc (rev pol); Indtte (inc dryer); shop; rest; snacks; bar; playgrnd; 4 pools high ssn; 2 waterslides; jacuzzi; fishing; tennis; games rm; games area; cycle hire; golf 7km; wifi; entmnt; 30% statics; dogs €3; phone; sep car park; bus to Salsomaggiore; phone; quiet; red low ssn; ccard not acc. "Vg site; friendly, helpful staff; interesting, smart spa town; excel touring base; gd for families." ♦ 1 Apr-15 Oct. € 32.00 2011*

SALTO DI FONDI see Terracina *2E4*

SAN BARONTO LAMPORECCHIO see Pistoia *1D3*

SAN BENEDETTO IN ALPE *1D3* (500m N Rural) *43.98238, 11.68657* **Camping Acquacheta, Via Acquacheta 7, 47010 San Benedetto-in-Alpe (FO) [0543 965245; fax 951289; info@campingacquacheta.it; www.campingacquacheta.it]** Take SS67 fr Florence or Forli. Foll camping sp in cent of San Benedetto-in-Alpe by bdge. Site half way up hill with ent on sharp bend. App steep with hairpin bends. Sm, mkd pitch, terr, pt shd; wc; shwrs inc; el pnts (3A); Indry rm; shop 500m; rest; snacks; BBQ; shops; playgrnd; 74% statics; quiet; CCI. "Ltd touring pitches; scenic area." ♦ 15 Apr-15 Oct. € 17.50 2008*

SAN CANDIDO/INNICHEN see Dobbiaco/Toblach *2E1*

SAN FELICE DEL BENACO *1D2* (1km N Rural) *45.59972, 10.54972* **Camping Eden, Via Preone 45, 25010 Portese (BS) [0365 62093; fax 559311; mail@camping-eden.it; www.camping-eden.it]** Best app fr Salo (N), foll lakeside twd Porto Portese. Site ent up steep slope on R. Lge, hdg/mkd pitch, hdstg, terr, shd; wc; chem disp; mv service pnt; baby facs; shwrs inc; el pnts (3A) inc; Indtte; shop; rest; snacks; bar; playgrnd; pool; lake sw & shgl beach adj; golf 3km; 85% statics; dogs €10; phone; Eng spkn; adv bkg; quiet; red low ssn/snr citizen; CCI. "Beach down steep rd opp site; 10 mins walk to boat terminal for lake; steep steps to san facs; manhandling req to get c'vans onto pitches; site not rec lge o'fits." ♦ 11 Apr-27 Sep. € 42.00 2009*

When we get home
I'm going to post
all these site report
forms to the Club
for next year's guide.
The deadline's mid September 2013

SAN FELICE DEL BENACO *1D2* (1km E Rural) *45.58500, 10.56583* **Camping Fornella, Via Fornella 1, 25010 San Felice-del-Benaco (BS) [0365 62294; fax 559418; fornella@fornella.it; www.fornella.it]** N fr Desenzano on S572 twd Salo. Turn R to San Felice-del-Benaco, over x-rds & take 2nd R turn at sp to site. R into app rd, L into site. Rd narr but accessible. Avoid vill cent, site sp (with several others) fr vill by-pass just bef g'ge. Lge, pt sl, terr, pt shd; htd wc (some cont); chem disp; mv service pnt; baby facs; shwrs inc; el pnts (6A) inc; gas; Indtte (inc dryer); shop; rest; snacks; bar; BBQ (charcoal); playgrnds; pool; paddling pool; sw & shgl beach on lake; fishing; boat hire & windsurfing; cycle hire; tennis; games area; entmnt; games rm; wifi; entmnt; TV (in bar); 20% statics; dogs €7; no c'vans/m'vans over 7m high ssn; sep car park; recep 0800-1200 & 1400-2000; poss v cr; Eng spkn; adv bkg; quiet; ccard acc; extra for lge pitches & lakeside pitches; red low ssn & snr citizens low ssn; CCI. "Family-run site in vg location; park outside until checked in; excel pool; excursions to Venice, Florence & Verona opera." ♦ 1 May-23 Sep. € 44.10 SBS - Y11 2011*

SAN FELICE DEL BENACO *1D2* (1km SE Rural) *45.57861, 10.55388* **Camping Ideal Molino, Via Gardiola 1, 25010 San Felice-del-Benaco (BS) [0365 62023; fax 559395; info@campingmolino.it; www.campingmolino.it]** Site approx 6km S of Salo on W shore of lake. Foll sp Porto & San Felice. Site 1km past San Felice; narr app. Med, mkd pitch, pt shd; wc; chem disp; baby facs; shwrs inc; el pnts (4A) inc; gas; Indtte; shop; rest; bar; playgrnd; shgl beach; boat hire; fishing; 30% statics; no dogs; phone; adv bkg rec; quiet; red low ssn/snr citizens. "Steamer trips on lake; some v sm pitches; excel lakeside rest." ♦ 24 Mar-30 Sep. € 38.60 2009*

SAN FELICE DEL BENACO *1D2* (1km NW Rural) *45.59517, 10.53313* **Camping Villaggio Weekend, Via Vallone della Selva 2, 25010 San Felice-del-Benaco (BS) [0365 43712; fax 42196; info@weekend.it; www.weekend.it]** Well sp fr Desenzano. Ignore 1st sp San Felice-del-Benaco, turn R at rndabt to vill then 2nd L. Do not app fr Riva-del-Garda end of lake - narr tunnels. Nearest town Salo. Lge, mkd pitch, terr, shd; wc; chem disp; some serviced pitches; baby facs; shwrs inc; el pnts (6A) inc; Indtte (inc dryer); supmkt; rest; snacks; bar; BBQ; playgrnd; pool; paddling pool; waterslide; lake sw & scuba diving; cycle hire; games area; wifi; entmnt; 20% statics; dogs €7.50; poss cr; Eng spkn; adv bkg ess; quiet; ccard acc; red low ssn; CCI. "Excel, family site in olive grove; excel entmnt; bathing caps req in pool; views of lake & mountains fr some pitches; low branches some pitches diff for m'vans; some sm pitches - lge avail; tight corners poss diff lge o'fits; office clsd 1300-1500." ♦ 16 Apr-25 Sep. € 52.00 2010*

SAN GIMIGNANO *1D3* (2km S Rural) *43.45331, 11.05375* **Camping Il Boschetto di Piemma, Santa Lucia, 53037 San Gimignano (SI) [0577 940352; fax 907453; info@boschettodipiemma.it; www.boschettodipiemma.it]** App fr Poggibonsi, 1km bef San Gimignano turn L dir Volterra & almost immed turn L on rd for Santa Lucia; site 2km on L by tennis club. Med, pt sl, pt shd, hdstg; wc (few cont); own san rec; shwrs inc; el pnts (6A) inc; gas; shop; rest; snacks; bar; pool adj high ssn; tennis; games area; cycle hire; internet; sat TV; statics; dogs; bus; sep car park high ssn; poss cr; Eng spkn; quiet but some music fr café; red long stay; CCI. "No views fr site but scenic country outside; arr early, site fills up; recep clsd 1300-1500 & 2330-0800; 20 min walk San Gimignano; poss v cr with many tenters, ltd space for c'vans high ssn; vg, modern san facs." ♦ 25 Mar-2 Nov. € 31.80 2008*

SAN GIMIGNANO *1D3* (3km S Rural) *43.49805, 11.10702* **Area di Sosta, Loc Racciano-Santa Chiara, 53037 San Gimignano (SI) [0577 940695; fax 943090; info@jolly-pentacar.com; www.jolly-pentacar.com]** App San Gimignano fr Poggibonsi. At edge of town by car parks turn L sp Santa Chiara car park/coach park. Site on L in 1km, clearly sp. Sm, hdstg, unshd; htd wc; chem disp; mv service pnt; shwrs inc; el pnts (16A) inc; Indtte; shop, rest 1.5km; bar; snacks; games area; dogs; poss v cr; Eng spkn. "Transfer to town inc in price; ideal way to see San Gimignano; ltd facs low ssn." ♦ € 22.00 2008*

⊞ **SAN GIOVANNI ROTONDO** *2G4* (700m SE Rural) **Aree di Sosta Giovanni di Cerbo, Contrada Coppa Mazzanelle, 71013 San Giovanni-Rotondo (FG) [0882 453900]** Fr A14 exit onto SS272 dir San Marco-in-Lamis. Foll sp to San Giovanni-Rotondo. On town o'skts at rndabt turn R dir Foggia. Site on R bef next rndabt - 1km down narr lane. Fr S fr Foggia foll sp Manfredonia then San Giovanni. On o'skts of town turn L at rndabt, site in 50m. Sm, all hdstg, pt sl, unshd; wc; chem disp; mv service pnt; shwrs inc; el pnts (10A) metered (poss rev pol/no earth); shop 500m; rest; bar; htd pool 8km; sand beach 20km; dogs; poss cr; Eng spkn; adv bkg; noisy dogs in area; CCI. "V popular with m'vanners; off beaten track in scenic area; ltd san facs; minibus to town cent; conv Gargano National Park & Forest of Umbra." ♦ € 15.00 2010*

SAN LORENZO DI SEBATO see Brunico/Bruneck *1D1*

⊞ **SAN MARINO** *2E3* (4km N Rural) *43.95990, 12.46090* **Centro Vacanze San Marino, Strada San Michele 50, 47893 Cailungo, Repubblica di San Marino [0549 903964; fax 907120; info@centrovacanzesanmarino.com; www.centrovacanzesanmarino.com]** Exit A14 at Rimini Sud, foll rd S72 to San Marino. Pass under 2 curved footbdges, then 800m after 2nd & 13km after leaving a'strada, fork R. Cont uphill for 1.5km then turn R at Brico building, site sp. Steep long-haul climb. Lge, hdg pitch, hdstg, terr, pt shd; htd wc; chem disp; mv service pnt; serviced pitch; shwrs inc; el pnts (6A) inc (poss rev pol); Indtte; sm shop, rest high ssn; snacks; bar; BBQ; cooking facs; playgrnd; htd pool; paddling pool; tennis; games area; cycle hire; solarium; mini-zoo; wifi; sat TV; some statics; dogs €5; bus; poss v cr; Eng spkn; adv bkg; quiet; red 7+ days; ccard acc; CCI. "V busy at w/end - rec arr early; superb hill fort town; excel rest & pool; sm pitches; conv Rimini 24km; excel, clean site; bus calls at site ent for San Marino." ♦ € 38.50 (CChq acc) 2011*

SAN MENAIO see Rodi Garganico *2G4*

SAN MICHELE ALL'ADIGE *1D1* (3km S Rural) **Camping Moser, Via Nazionale 64, 38015 Nave San Felice (TN) [0461 870248]** 12km N of Trento on SS12. Sm, mkd pitch, shd; wc; chem disp; shwrs; el pnts inc; shop in vill; rest; bar; dogs; bus 500m; poss cr; Eng spkn; adv bkg; rd & rlwy noise. "Gd, friendly NH." 1 May-31 Oct. € 18.00 2009*

SAN PIERO A SIEVE see Borgo San Lorenzo *1D3*

⊞ **SAN REMO** *1B3* (2.5km W Coastal) *43.80244, 7.74506* **Camping Villaggio Dei Fiori, Via Tiro a Volo 3, 18038 San Remo (IM) [0184 660635; fax 662377; info@villaggiodeifiori.it; www.villaggiodeifiori.it]** Fr A10/E80 take Arma-di-Taggia exit & foll sp San Remo Centro. At SS1 coast rd turn R sp Ventimiglia. At 2.5km look for red/yellow Billa supmkt sp on R; 50m past sp take L fork, site on L in 50m. Fr W on A10 take 1st exit dir San Remo - winding rd. Turn R & site on L after Stands supmkt. Fr Ventimiglia on SS1, 150m past San Remo boundary sp turn sharp R (poss diff lge outfits) to site. Lge, some hdg/mkd pitch, all hdstg, pt terr, pt shd; htd wc (some cont); chem disp; mv service pnt; baby facs; fam bthrm; shwrs inc; el pnts (3A) €3; Indtte (inc dryer); supmkt 200m; rest; snacks; bar; BBQ; playgrnd; htd pool; shgl beach adj; tennis; games area; cycle hire; wifi; entmnt; 60% statics; no dogs; train to Monaco & bus San Remo nr; poss cr; Eng spkn; adv bkg rec high ssn; rd & fairground noise; red long stay/low ssn; ccard acc.; CCI "Gd location; well-kept, tidy, paved site; vg, clean facs; beach not suitable for sw; some pitches superb sea views (extra charge), some sm; lge outfits not acc high ssn as sm pitches; vg rest; conv Monaco; gates locked at night." ♦ € 55.00 (4 persons) 2010*

SAN ROCCO CASTAGNARETTA see Cuneo *1B2*

⊞ **SAN VALENTINO ALLA MUTA** *1D1* (500m W Rural) *46.7700, 10.5325* **Camping Thöni, Landstrasse 83, 39020 San Valentino-alla-Muta/St Valentin-an-der-Haide (BZ) [0473 634020; thoeni.h@rolmail.net; www.camping-thoeni.it]** N twd Austrian border site on L on edge of vill on S edge of Lago di Resia. Sm, pt sl, unshd; htd wc; chem disp; shwrs inc; el pnts (6A) €1.50; shop, rest, snacks, bar 300m; pool 7km; dogs; site clsd Nov; quiet. "Conv sh stay/NH en route Austria; cycle route around lake." € 20.50 2010*

SAN VINCENZO *1D3* (8km S Coastal) *43.02815, 10.5345* **Camping Park Albatros, Pineta di Torre Nuova, 57027 San Vincenzo (LI) [0565 701018; fax 703589; albatros@camping.it; www.camping.it/toscana/albatros]** Fr N exit SS1 San Vincenzo Nord, fr S exit Sud. As app town foll sp Piombino on SP23 Via Della Principessa, just after 7km post turn L on reaching pine wood, site sp. V lge, pt shd; wc; chem disp; mv service pnt; baby facs; shwrs; el pnts (5A) inc; lndtte; gas; shop; rest; snacks; bar; playgrnd; pool complex; sand beach 900m; games area; cycle hire; wifi; entmnt; 40% statics; dogs €3; phone; poss cr; Eng spkn; loud music in pool area all day; ccard acc; red low ssn. "Gd, improving, busy site; lge pitches; gd, modern san facs; excel pool complex." ♦ 24 Apr-25 Sep. € 47.70 2010*

SANT' ANTONIO DI MAVIGNOLA see Pinzolo *1D1*

SANT' ARCANGELO SUL TRASIMENO see Magione *2E3*

SANTA MARIA DI MERINO see Vieste *2G4*

SAPPADA *2E1* (2km E Rural) *46.57160, 12.71815* **Camping Gorte, Borgata Cretta 32, 32047 Sappada (BL) [0435 469815; info@campinggorte.com; www.campinggorte.com]** Fr W on R355 thro Sappada, site on R just bef rv bdge. NB fr E v sharp L turn. Med, pt sl, pt shd; wc (cont); own san; shwrs inc; shop; supmkt 2km; snacks; bar; BBQ; 30% statics; dogs; bus adj; poss cr; quiet. "Spectacular rv gorge 2km W of town; OK NH." 1 Jun-30 Sep & 15 Dec-15 Mar. € 24.00 2008*

SARDINIA Campsites in towns in Sardinia are listed together at the end of the Italian site entry pages.

SARNONICO *1D1* (Rural) *46.4226, 11.13221* **Campingpark Baita Dolomiti, Via Cesare Battisti 18, 38011 Sarnonico (TN) [tel/fax 0463 830109; info@baita-dolomiti.it; www.baita-dolomiti.com]** Exit A22 Bolzano Sud; take Mendola Pass to Sarnonico on S42; site on L sp just beyond vill church, 3km S of Fondo. Towed c'vans: Exit A22 at Mezzocorona & take SS43 to Dermulo; turn R for Sanzeno & Sarnonico. Med, pt sl, pt shd; wc; chem disp; mv service pnt; sauna; shwrs inc; el pnts (4A) inc; lndtte; rest; bar; shop 100m; rest; playgrnd; pool; games area; golf 1km; wifi; entmnt; 10% statics; dogs €3; site clsd 1300-1500; Eng spkn; quiet; ccard acc; red long stay/CCI. "Lovely, unspoilt rural area; nr to Dolomites; splendid walking area; modern facs." ♦ 1 Jun-30 Sep. € 31.00 2008*

SARRE see Aosta *1B1*

Dedicated Services Only For You

Italia. La Spezia. Ameglia. T : + 39 0187 65920 | F : + 39 0187 65183
E : info@campingriver.com | booking@campingriver.it
Numero Verde Toll-free **800 953 253 *Fast Line***

SARTEANO *1D3* (W Rural) *42.9875, 11.86444* **Camping Parco Delle Piscine, Via del Bagno Santo, 53047 Sarteano (SI) [0578 26971; fax 265889; info@parcodellepiscine.it; www.parcodellepiscine.it]** Exit A1/E35 onto S478 at Chiusi & foll sp to Sarteano. Site at W end of vill, sp. Lge, pt shd; wc (some cont); chem disp; mv service pnt; serviced pitches; shwrs inc; el pnts (5A) inc; Indtte; shops 100m; rest; snacks; bar; playgrnd; 3 pools; tennis; solarium; wifi; entmnt; 60% statics; no dogs; poss cr; Eng spkn; quiet; ccard acc. "Clean, well-run; security guard 24 hrs; no vehicles during quiet periods 1400-1600 & 2300-0700; poss long walk to wc/shwrs; Florence 90 mins on m'way, Siena 1 hr; site at 600m, so cool at night; excel." ♦ 1 Apr-30 Sep. € 50.50 2008*

⊞ **SARZANA** *1C2* (6km SE Rural) *44.10354, 10.00733* **Camping Cascina dei Peri, Via Montefrancio 71, 19030 Castelnuovo-Magra (SP) [tel/fax 0187 674085; info@lacascinadeiperi.com; www.lacascinadeiperi.it]** Exit A12 onto S1 dir Sarzana, Massa, Pisa. In 2km, 800m after km post 392, turn L in Colombiera dir Castelnuovo-Magra. In 1km after exiting 40 km/h limit turn L into Via Montefrancio sp Cascina dei Peri. Site on L in 2km, sp but diff to find & rd narr. Sm, hdg pitch, hdstg, pt shd; wc; chem disp; mv service pnt; shwrs; el pnts (16A) inc; gas 3km; shop 2km; supmkt 3km; rest & 2km; snacks, bar 2km; sand beach 8km; adv bkg; quiet; ccard acc. "CL-type site; meals can be taken with family; own wine & olive oil sold; gd views; conv Cinque Terre & Pisa; m'vans only - not suitable lge vans." € 15.00 2008*

SARZANA *1C2* (8km S Rural/Coastal) *44.07638, 9.97027* **Camping River, Loc Armezzone, 19031 Ameglia (SP) [0187 65920; fax 65183; river@campingriver.com; www.campingriver.com]** Exit A12 at Sarzana & foll sp Ameglia & Bocca di Magra on SP432. In 7km turn L into Via Crociata to site (blue sp). Narr app rd with few passing places. Lge, mkd pitch; pt shd; wc (mainly cont); chem disp; mv service pnt; sauna; shwrs inc; el pnts (3-6A) inc; Indtte (inc dryer); supmkt 700m; rest; snacks; pizzeria; bar; playgrnd; 2 pools; paddling pool; beach 2km; rv fishing; tennis 200m; games area; boat & cycle hire; horseriding 200m; golf driving range; wifi; entmnt; TV rm; 50% statics; dogs €3; bus to beach; poss cr; adv bkg; red low ssn. "Gd touring base Cinque Terre; pleasant, helpful staff; vg, well-situated site; gd shop & rest; nice location by rv." ♦ 1 Apr-30 Sep. € 50.00 (3 persons) 2011*

See advertisement

SASSELLO *1B2* (5km NE Rural) *44.49672, 8.52794* **Club Naturista Costalunga (Naturist), 17046 Sassello (SV) [tel/fax 019 720004; info@costalunga.org; www.costalunga.org]** Fr A10 exit at Albissola & turn L after toll booth sp Sassello. In Sassello bear R sp Palo & Urbe, in 5km turn L at site sp, site on L in 500m. Sm, hdstg, pt sl, terr, pt shd; wc; chem disp; shwrs inc; el pnts (6A) €3; Indtte; shop 5km; pre-ordered snacks; playgrnd; pool; TV rm; 30% statics; dogs €2; bus 500m; adv bkg; quiet; ccard not acc; red long stay; INF card. "Friendly, helpful owners; views fr some pitches; gd." 1 Apr-30 Sep. € 25.00 2011*

⊞ **SASSO MARCONI** *1D2* (2.5km SE Rural) *44.37289, 11.24961* **Camping Piccolo Paradiso, Via Sirano 2, 40043 Marzabotto (BO) [051 842680; fax 6756581; piccoloparadiso@aruba.it; www.campingpiccoloparadiso.eu]** Exit A1 (Bologna-Florence) Sasso Marconi & foll sp Sasso at 1st rndabtr. L at next rndabt, site sp. App & ent steep with hairpin junc. Lge, mkd pitch, shd; htd wc (some cont); chem disp; serviced pitches; baby facs; shwrs inc; el pnts (3A) inc (extra for 6A); gas; Indtte; shop; tradsmn; rest; snacks; bar; BBQ; playgrnd; pool, tennis, fishing 200m; games area; cycle hire; 50% statics; dogs €3; phone; sep car park; Eng spkn; loud music on Sat fr adj sports complex & some rd noise. "Conv Florence & Bologna; scenic area of historic interest; conv NH nr a'strada; friendly staff." ♦ € 26.50 2008*

⊞ **SASSO MARCONI** *1D2* (11km SW Rural) **Centro Naturista Ca'Le Scope (Naturist), Loc San Martino/La Quercia, 40043 Marzabotto (BO) [tel/fax 051 932328; calescope@virgilio.it; www.calescope.com]** Fr A1 exit at Rioveggio, turn R after toll booth. In 200m turn R onto S325 sp Bologna. In 3.5km turn sharp L sp Quercia, over rv & foll rd for 4km (narr & uneven in parts - care req). Turn L at x-rds sp to site, site in 1.5km on L. Med, hdg/mkd pitch, hdstg, pt sl, pt shd; wc (some cont); chem disp (wc); baby facs; shwrs inc; el pnts (6A) €3.15; gas; Indtte; basic shop; tradsmn; rest; snacks; bar; playgrnd; pool; internet; TV rm; 50% statics; dogs; train 6km; poss cr; Eng spkn; adv bkg; quiet; ccard acc; INF card. "Spectacular views over Monte Sole National Park; friendly Dutch owners; site rds steep in parts - care req." € 31.20 2011*

SAVONA *1B2* (10km NE Rural) *44.38105, 8.50151* **Camping Dolce Vita, Via Riobasco 62, 17040 Stella-San Giovanni (SV) [tel/fax 019 703269 or 03939 836543 (mob); campingdolcevita@libero.it; www.campingdolcevita.it]** Foll sp Albisola off Genoa-Savona a'strada, Turn L in town onto rd SS334 dir Sassello. Site in 5km on L on rd twd mountains. Site sp faces S only; if app fr N look for flags. Sm, pt shd; wc; mv service pnt; chem disp; shwrs €1; el pnts (4-8A) €3; gas; Indtte; shop 2.5km; rest; snacks; bar; playgrnd; pool; beach 5.5km; TV; 75% statics; dogs €3; Eng spkn; no adv bkg; quiet; CCI. "Sm touring pitches unsuitable lge o'fits; v busy at w/end; gd welcome; poss untidy low ssn; gd NH." ♦ 1 Jan-20 Oct. € 31.00 2009*

SAVONA *1B2* (1km SW Coastal) **Camping Charly, Via Nizza 93/R, Zinola, 17100 Savona (SV) [0198 62265; fax 0192 63427; info@campingcharly.it; www.campingcharly.it]** Take SS1 fr Savona twd Sportorno. Site in vicinity of Zinola bet AGIP & BP g'ges on dual c'way. Med, shd; wc; shwrs €0.50; el pnts (5A) inc; shop; snacks; bar; pool; paddling pool; sm sand beach across rd; 50% statics; no dogs; poss cr; Eng spkn; adv bkg; some rd & rlwy noise at night; red low ssn; CCI. "Hot water to shwrs only." 15 Apr-14 Sep. € 30.00 2009*

SAVONA *1B2* (2km SW Coastal) *44.29079, 8.45331* **Camping Vittoria, Via Nizza 111/113, Zinola, 17040 Savona (SV) [0198 81439; www.campingvittoria.com]** Exit Savona heading SW, site on L on seashore immed bef Shell petrol stn behind bar Vittoria. Med, unshd; wc (some cont); shwrs; el pnts inc; shops adj; rest adj; bar; private sand beach adj; 90% statics; poss v cr; Eng spkn; adv bkg; quiet; CCI. "Excel location with views; busy site; helpful, friendly owner; pitches adj beach; clean, simple facs; ltd sm touring pitches." 1 Apr-30 Sep. € 31.00 2010*

SAVONA *1B2* (9km SW Coastal) *44.22731, 8.40795* **Camping Rustia, Via La Torre 4, 17028 Spotorno (SV) [019 745042; fax 743035; info@campingrustia.it; www.campingrustia.it]** Exit A10/E80 for Spotorno, site sp on app rd to m'way. V steep app rd. C'vans returning to m'way use ent at Albissola Marina. Lge, shd; wc; shwrs €1; el pnts (3A) €3; shop; bar; rest, snacks 300m; sand beach 600m; 30% statics; dogs; poss cr; no adv bkg; rd & rlwy noise; Eng spkn; ccard acc. "Site diff for lge outfits due narr paths & many trees - manhandling necessary onto pitches; gd san facs; gates locked at night. ♦ 1 Apr-30 Sep. € 30.00 2008*

SCARLINO see Follonica *1D3*

SELVA DI CADORE see Rocca Pietore *1D1*

SENIGALLIA *2E3* (1km S Coastal) *43.70416, 13.23805* **Villaggio Turistico Camping Summerland, Via Podesti 236, 60019 Senigallia (AN) [tel/fax 071 7926816; info@campingsummerland.it; www.campingsummerland.it]** Exit A14/E55 onto SS16 to Senigallia S. Site on R after lge car park at side of rd. Lge, shd; wc (cont); mv service pnt; baby facs; shwrs; el pnts (5A) €2.50; gas; lndtte; shop; rest; snacks; bar; playgrnd; 2 pools & paddling pool; beach 200m; tennis; games area; entmnt; TV rm; some statics; no dogs Jul/Aug; sep car park; poss cr; adv bkg. ♦ 1 Jun-15 Sep. € 31.50 2007*

SESTO CALENDE *1B1* (1km N Rural) *45.72988, 8.61989* **Camping La Sfinge, Via Angera 1, 21018 Sesto-Calende (VA) [0331 924531; fax 922050; info@campeggiolasfinge.it; www.campeggiolasfinge.it]** Take rd fr Sesto-Calende to Angera. Site 1km on L bef junc for Sant' Anna. Med, mkd pitch, shd; wc (mainly cont); shwrs; el pnts; gas; lndtte; shop 1km; snacks; bar; playgrnd; pool; boating; games area; 90% statics; dogs €4; poss cr; quiet; ccard acc. "Friendly owners; gd lakeside location; poss mosquitoes." ♦ 15 Jan-30 Oct. € 26.00 2008*

SESTO CALENDE *1B1* (4km N Rural) *45.74892, 8.59698* **Camping Okay Lido, Via per Angera 115, Loc Lisanza, 21018 Sesto Calende (VA) [tel/fax 0331 974235; campingokay@camping-okay.com; www.camping-okay.com]** Exit A8 at Sesto Calende onto SP69 N dir Angera, site sp. Med, mkd pitch, terr, pt shd; wc; chem disp; mv service pnt; private san facs avail; baby facs; shwrs €0.60; el pnts (6A) €3; lndtte; supmkt 3km; rest; snacks; bar; playgrnd; htd pool; paddling pool; lake sw; watersports; games area; games rm; wifi; entmnt; TV rm; some statics; dogs €5; Eng spkn; adv bkg; quiet. "Friendly, welcoming site; NH pitches by lakeside; diff exit up steep gravel rd." ♦ 8 Mar-3 Oct. € 30.00 2010*

SESTO CALENDE *1B1* (7.5km N Rural) *45.82712, 8.62722* **International Camping Ispra, Via Carducci 11, 21027 Ispra (VA) [0332 780458; fax 784882; info@internationalcampingispra.it; www.internationalcampingispra.it]** Site 1km NE of Ispra on E side of lake. Med, pt terr, shd; wc (cont); own san; shwrs €0.20; el pnts (6A) €3; lndtte; shop; tradsmn; rest; snacks; bar; BBQ; playgrnd; pool (sw caps req); beach & lake sw; boating; fishing; games area; TV rm; 90% statics; dogs €6; poss cr; Eng spkn; adv bkg; quiet; red low ssn; CCI. "Gd views of lake - muddy beach." 20 Mar-1 Nov. € 29.00 2009*

SESTO CALENDE *1B1* (3km NW Rural) *45.72441, 8.60946* **Camping Italia Lido, Via Cicognola 88, 28053 Castelletto-Sopra-Ticino (NO) [tel/fax 0331 923032; info@campingitalialido.it; www.campingitalialido.it]** Fr Sesto Calende take S33 dir Arona/Stresa. Site in 3km, approx 1.5km after x-ing Rv Ticino. Site sp on R. Lge, pt shd; wc; shwrs; el pnts (3A) €2.50; gas; lndtte; shop; supmkt 1km; rest; snacks; bar; lake sw & sand beach adj; boat hire; games area; cycle hire; 70% statics; dogs €4; phone; Eng spkn; aircarft noise; red long stay/low ssn. "Gd views of lake & Alps; narr, twisting ent to site; clean, tidy site." 1 Mar-31 Oct. € 25.60 2008*

⊞ **SESTO/SEXTEN** *2E1* (3km SE Rural) *46.66806, 12.39935* **Caravan Park Sexten, Via San Guiseppe 54, 39030 Sesto/Sexten (BZ) [0474 710444; fax 710053; info@caravanparksexten.it; www.caravanparksexten.it]** Fr S49 take S52 SE fr San Candido thro Sexten & Moos. After sh, steep climb site on W of S52 midway bet Moos & Kreuzberg pass. Lge, mkd pitch, pt sl, pt shd; wc; chem disp; mv service pnt; serviced pitches; sauna; private bthrms avail; shwrs inc; el pnts (16A) metered; gas; lndtte; shop; rest; bar; playgrnd; pool; paddling pool; solarium; tennis; wintersports; internet; entmnt; beauty & wellness treatments; TV; dogs €6; poss cr; Eng spkn; adv bkg ess high ssn; quiet; CCI. "Excel, clean facs; Waldbad worth visit; rock climbing wall; lovely scenery; mountain walks." ♦ € 39.00 2010*

⊞ **SETTIMO VITTONE** *1B1* (2.5km N Rural) *45.56474, 7.81668* **Camping Mombarone, Torre Daniele, 10010 Settimo-Vittone (TO) [0125 757907; fax 757396; info@campingmombarone.it; www.campingmombarone.it]** On E side of Ivrea-Aosta rd (SS26), 100m S of Pont-St Martin. Exit A5 at Quincinetto, turn R onto SP69 across bdge, R at end onto SP26 & site on L in 150m. (App fr S, sp at ent but if overshoot go on 100m to rndabt to turn). Tight ent off busy rd. Med, pt sl, pt shd; wc; chem disp; shwrs inc; el pnts (4A) €2.50; lndtte; shop 400m; tradsmn; rest adj; snacks; bar; sm pool; games area; wifi; 80% statics; poss v cr & noisy high ssn; ccard not acc; red CCI. "Gd base Aosta valley; superb views; Quincinetto medieval vill walking dist; lovely, grassy, well-kept site; ltd space for tourers; v pleasant owner who speaks gd Eng, friendly welcome; san facs immac; gd NH." € 18.00 2011*

SETTIMO VITTONE *1B1* (11km N Rural) **Camping Nosy, Trovinasse, 10010 Settimo-Vittone (TO) [0125 659970; www.settimovittone.info/camping]** Fr A5 exit at Quincinetto, over bdge & turn R for 2km. In Settimo-Vittone turn L at traff lts & foll narr, twisting mountain rd for 10km. M'vans only. Sm, pt sl, pt shd; wc (some cont); shwrs; el pnts €1.50; shop, rest 11km; bar; BBQ; 20% statics; adv bkg; quiet. "Vg, peaceful site; superb walking & views." 1 May-30 Oct. € 20.00 2008*

SIBARI *3A4* (4km E Coastal) *39.77944, 16.47889* **Camping Villaggio Pineta di Sibari, 87070 Sibari (CS) [0981 74135; fax 74302; info@pinetadisibari.it; www.pinetadisibari.it]** Exit A3 at Frascineto onto SS106, then exit at Villapiana-Scalo. Site sp on beach. Lge, pt shd; wc; mv service pnt; shwrs inc; el pnts (6A) inc; lndtte; shop; rest; snacks; bar; playgrnd; sand beach adj; tennis; cycle hire; internet; entmnt; TV rm; 20% statics; dogs €5; poss cr; poss noisy; ccard acc. "Vg beach; site in pine forest; noisy bar/music; gd touring base." ♦ 1 Apr-20 Sep. € 42.00 2009*

SICILY Campsites in towns in Sicily are listed together at the end of the Italian site entry pages.

SIENA *1D3* (2.5km N Urban) *43.33750, 11.33055* **Camping Siena Colleverde, Via Scacciapensieri 47, 53100 Siena [0577 334080; fax 334005; info@campingcolleverde.com; www.campingcolleverde.com]** Site sp ('Camping' or symbol) on all app to Siena, foll sp for 'Ospedale' (hospital). Use exit Siena Nord & foll site sp, but take care as some sp misleadingly positioned. Lge, hdg/mkd pitch, hdstg, pt sl, terr, pt shd; htd wc; chem disp; mv service pnt; shwrs inc; el pnts (10A) inc; gas; Indtte; shop; rest; snacks; bar; playgrnd; pool high ssn; wifi; TV rm; dogs; phone; bus; poss cr; Eng spkn; adv bkg; some rd noise; CCI. "Attractive location; gd views old town wall fr upper pitches (no shade); excel touring base; upgraded site - gd, well kept, modern san facs; easy access by bus to town fr site ent." ♦ 1 Mar-03 Jan. € 35.00 2011*

SIENA *1D3* (10km W Rural) *43.2815, 11.21905* **Camping La Montagnola, Strada della Montagnola 39, 53100 Sovicille (SI) [tel/fax 0577 314473; montagnolacamping@libero.it; www.camping.it/toscana/lamontagnola]** Fr N on S2 or S on S223 site well sp fr junc with S73. Avoid Siena town cent. Med, mkd pitch, hdstg, terr, pt shd; wc; chem disp; mv service pnt; shwrs inc; el pnts (6A) inc; gas; Indtte; shop & 5km; rest 800m; snacks; bar; playgrnd; games area; 7% statics; dogs free; phone; bus to Siena; sep car park; poss cr; adv bkg rec; Eng spkn; quiet; ccard acc (over €50); red CCI. "Super site; sm pitches; sharp stone chippings on hdstg pitches; v clean facs; vg refuge fr summer heat in wooded hills; facs poss stretched high ssn & rubbish bins o'flowing; gd walks fr site (booklet fr recep); Magic of Italy disc, conv bus service to Siena from site." Easter-30 Sep. € 25.00 2011*

⊞ **SIENA** *1D3* (2km NW Urban) **Siena Parcheggi, Viale Achille Sclavo, 53100 Siena** Fr Florence on SR2 twd Siena cent, fork L into Viale Achille Sclavo at rndabt just bef rlwy/bus stn. Site on L in 50m, well sp. Part of car park - manned during day. Med, hdstg, pt shd; wc (daytime only); own san; chem disp; mv service pnt; shop, rest, snacks, bar nrby; dogs; quiet. "Excel, basic NH for Siena; easy walk to town cent." € 20.00 2008*

SILVI MARINA see Pineto *2F3*

SIRMIONE *1D2* (3km S Rural) *45.46845, 10.61028* **Camping Sirmione, Via Sirmioncino 9, 25010 Colombare-di-Sirmione (BS) [tel/fax 030 919045; info@camping-sirmione.it; www.camping-sirmione.it]** Exit S11 at traff lts sp Sirmione, in 500m R at site sp. Lge, mkd pitch, pt sl, some hdstg, pt shd; wc (cont); mv service pnt; shwrs; el pnts (6A) inc; Indtte; shop; tradsmn; rest; snacks; bar; pool; paddling pool; lake sw; private beach; watersports; games area; 30% statics; dogs; poss cr; adv bkg; quiet; ccard acc. "Excel lakeside site; facs poss stretched when site busy; vg rest/bar." ♦ 25 Mar-5 Oct. € 40.00 2010*

SISTIANA see Monfalcone *2E1*

SOLCIO DE LESA see Arona *1B1*

SORICO *1C1* (500m E Rural) *46.17152, 9.39302* **Camping La Riva, Via Poncione 3, 22010 Sorico (CO) [tel/fax 0344 94571; info@campinglariva.com; www.campinglariva.com]** Fr Lecco take SS36 twd Colico & Sondrio. At end of tunnels fork L sp Como & Menaggio. At end of dual c'way turn L onto S340 to Sorico sp Como & Menaggio. Cross bdge & site 500m down lane on L bef cent Sorico, sp Cmp Poncione & La Riva. Easiest app on SS36 on E side of lake (pt dual c'way). Rd on W side narr & congested. Med, mkd pitch, pt shd; wc (some cont); chem disp; mv service pnt; shwrs €0.80; el pnts (6A) inc; gas 50m; Indtte; sm shop; tradsmn; rest nr; snacks; bar; BBQ; playgrnd; pool; sw & rv/lakeside beach adj; canoeing; waterskiing; fishing; cycle & boat hire; games/TV rm; dogs €4 (must be kept on lead); no c'vans/m'vans over 7.50m high ssn; phone; Eng spkn; quiet; red low ssn; CCI. "Excel, family-run site; gd views of lake & mountains; clean, well-kept & tidy; immac san facs; v warm welcome; less commercialised than some other sites in area; cycle track to vill; poss mosquito problem in Jun." ♦ 1 Apr-4 Nov. € 37.00 SBS - Y12 2011*

SORICO *1C1* (S Rural) *46.17200, 9.38590* **Camping Boothill, Via Don A Pasini 2, 22010 Sorico (CO) [tel/fax 0344 84079; boothill@boothillcamping.com]** Fr Como on S340 on W side of lake ent Sorico & turn R immed after petrol stn, site sp. Best app fr E side of lake (dual c'way). Sm, mkd pitch, unshd; wc; chem disp; shwrs inc; el pnts inc; Indtte; shop, rest 1km; snacks; bar; pool; lake sw & beach 500m; rv sw adj; games area; dogs; Eng spkn; quiet; CCI. "Excel san facs; friendly, obliging family owners; vg site." May-Oct. € 22.50 2008*

⊞ **SORRENTO** *3A3* (3km N Coastal) *40.63541, 14.41758* **Camping I Pini, Corso Italia 242, 80063 Piano-di-Sorrento (NA) [081 8786891; fax 8788770; info@campingipini.com; www.campingipini.com]** S fr Naples on A3; Exit A3 sp Castellammare di Stabia & take SS145 sp to Sorrento; pass thro vill of Meta; site on R immed over bdge; lge sp on main rd. Med, hdg/mkd pitch, pt sl, pt shd; wc; chem disp; mv service pnt; shwrs inc; el pnts (4A) inc; shops 500m; rest; snacks; bar; pool (in winter htd & open fr 8.30-15.00); beach 1km; 50% statics; dogs; bus 50m; Eng spkn; adv bkg; quiet; ccard acc; red long stay/low ssn; CCI. "Spacious site in mountains bet 2 vills; pool restricted to campers; sh walk to public transport to sites of interest; best site in Sorrento to avoid narr gridlocked rds." ♦ € 33.50 2011*

SORRENTO *3A3* (5km NE Coastal) *40.65953, 14.41835* **Camping Sant Antonio, Via Marina d'Equa 20/21, Seiano, 80069 Vico-Equense (NA) [tel/fax 081 8028570; info@campingsantantonio.it; www.campingsantantonio.it]** Fr A3 exit at Castellamare-di-Stabia. Foll sp for Sorrento; app Vico-Equense take L fork thro tunnel, at end of viaduct R to Seiano-Spaggia. Last site of 3 on L down narr twisting rd after 1km (poss v congested). Access to pitches poss diff due to trees. Med, pt sl, shd; wc; chem disp; shwrs €0.50; el pnts (5A) inc; gas; Indry rm; shop; tradsmn; rest; snacks; bar; shgl beach 100m; boat hire; excursions; solarium; some statics; no dogs Aug; phone; bus adj, train 800m; poss cr; Eng spkn; adv bkg; quiet; ccard acc; 10% red CCI. "Ideal base Amalfi coast, Capri, Naples; lovely harbour adj; v helpful, friendly staff; bus & train tickets avail fr site; gd rest." ♦ 15 Mar-31 Oct. € 24.00 2008*

ITALY

SORRENTO *3A3* (5km NE Coastal) *40.66022, 14.42048* **Camping Seiano Spiaggia, Marina Aequa, Seiano, 80069 Vico-Equense [tel/fax 081 8028560; info@campingseiano.it; www.campingseiano.it]** Fr A3 exit at Castellammare-di-Stabia & foll sp Sorrento. On app Vico-Equense take L fork thro tunnel & turn R at end of viaduct to Seiano-Spiagga. Site on L in 800m. Med, mkd pitch, terr, shd; htd wc; chem disp; shwrs €0.50; el pnts (6A) inc; gas; shop; tradsmn; rest, snacks adj; bar; BBQ; pool 200m; sand/shgl beach adj; no statics; dogs; bus, train to Sorrento nrby; Eng spkn; adv bkg; quiet but some rd noise at front of site; red long stay/CCI. "Clean, well-maintained site; helpful, welcoming staff; conv sightseeing base." ♦ 1 Apr-30 Sep. € 27.50 2009*

SORRENTO *3A3* (5km NE Coastal) *40.65990, 14.42153* **Villaggio Turistico Azzurro, Via Marina Aequa 9, 80066 Seiano-di-Vico-Equense (NA) [081 8029984; fax 8029176; info@villaggioazzurro.net; www.villaggioazzurro.net]** Fr A3 exit sp Castellammare-di-Stabia, foll sp Sorrento. App Vico-Equense take L fork thro tunnel. At end of viaduct turn R to Seiano-Spaggia, Site on L in 800m down steep, narr, twisting rd - poss congested espec at w/ends & used by buses. Sm, mkd pitch, shd; wc (some cont); chem disp; mv service pnt; shwrs €0.50; el pnts (6A) inc; Indtte (inc dryer); shop; tradsmn; rest; snacks; bar; BBQ; playgrnd; shgl beach 400m; cycle hire; some statics; dogs; bus to stn high ssn; ferry; Eng spkn; adv bkg; rd noise; ccard acc; red long stay/CCI. "Conv Naples, Pompei etc; v helpful owner; site in orange grove & pitching poss diff lge o'fits due trees; vg." 1 Mar-1 Dec. € 30.00 2009*

SORRENTO *3A3* (10km S Coastal) *40.58389, 14.35220* **Camping Nettuno, Via A Vespucci, Marina-del-Cantone, 80068 Massa-Lubrense (NA) [081 8081051; fax 8081706; info@villaggionettuno.it; www.villaggionettuno.it]** Fr Castellammare to Sorrento rd, turn L in Meta dir Positano. Site well sp in dir St Agate, then Marina-del-Cantone. Tortuous rd to site & steep, diff ent to site. Sm, shd; wc (some cont); chem disp; mv service pnt; shwrs inc; el pnts (3A) €2.50; gas; Indtte; shop; rest; snacks; bar; BBQ; shgl/rock beach adj; diving cent; boat hire; tennis; internet; entmnt; TV rm; some statics; phone; Eng spkn; quiet; ccard acc. "Lovely situation; sea views fr some pitches (extra cost); v muddy when wet; san facs need refurb (2009); ltd/primitive water & drainage facs; coastal walks; gd public transport; 10% red on next site if part of same chain." ♦ 1 Mar-2 Nov. € 32.00 (CChq acc) 2009*

SORRENTO *3A3* (1.5km SW Coastal) *40.62555, 14.36583* **Camping Nube d'Argento, Via Capo 21, 80067 Sorrento (NA) [081 8781344; fax 8073450; info@nubedargento.com; www.nubedargento.com]** Exit a'strada for Castellamare. Foll sp to Sorrento. At 1-way system foll sp out of Sorrento dir Massa Lubrense on SS148. On exit Sorrento site ent on R. App diff; rec head approx 500m beyond ent to wide rd, make 'U' turn & rtn to site. Driving thro town cent diff. Med, pt sl, terr, pt shd; wc (some cont); chem disp (wc); mv service pnt; shwrs inc; el pnts (4-6A) inc; gas; Indtte; shop; rest; snacks; bar; playgrnd; pool; boat hire; entmnt; TV; 15% statics; dogs; phone; bus/train; Eng spkn; no adv bkg; rd noise; ccard acc; red low ssn/CCI. "Some excel pitches with sea views, others v sm; steep, narr rds thro site, obstacles, o'hanging trees & tight bends - suitable sm o'fits only; pitches muddy after rain; san facs old & basic; hot water to shwrs only; site nr sewage plant; friendly & helpful staff; excel rest; sh walk to town; red facs low ssn." 20 Dec-10 Jan & 15 Mar-10 Nov. € 41.00 2010*

SORRENTO *3A3* (2km W Coastal) *40.62722, 14.35666* **Camping Villaggio Santa Fortunata, Via Capo 39, 80067 Capo-de-Sorrento (NA) [081 8073579; fax 8073590; info@santafortunata.com; www.santafortunata.com]** Only app fr a'strada, exit Castellamare. Foll sp into Sorrento then sp Massa-Lubrense. Site poorly sp fr Sorrento on R, gd wide ent. V lge, mkd pitch, terr, shd; wc (some cont); chem disp; mv service pnt; shwrs inc; el pnts (6A) inc; gas; Indtte; shop; rest; snacks; bar; playgrnd; pool high ssn; internet; entmnt; TV; 50% statics; dogs free; phone; bus adj; sep car park; poss cr; Eng spkn; red long stay/CCI. "Gd facs; pitches sm for lge o'fits (7m+) & poss dusty; bus fr gate, ticket fr recep; boat trips to Capri fr site beach; noisy nr rest, disco & 18-30 tours; many scruffy statics; facs dated; steep access & tight hairpins to some pitches." ♦ 1 Apr-18 Oct. € 38.50 2009*

SOTTOMARINA see Chioggia *2E2*

SOVICILLE see Siena *1D3*

SPERLONGA *2E4* (1km SE Coastal) *41.25514, 13.44625* **Camping Villaggio Nord-Sud, Via Flacca, Km 15.5, 04029 Sperlonga (LT) [0771 548255; fax 557240; info@campingnordsud.it; www.campingnordsud.it]** Site on seaward side of S213 at km post 15.9. Lge sp visible fr both dirs. Lge, mkd pitch, hdstg, shd; wc (mainly cont); chem disp; shwrs inc; el pnts (4A) inc; Indtte; shop, rest high ssn; snacks; bar; private sand beach; windsurfing; tennis; fitness rm; games area; entmnt; some statics; no dogs; adv bkg; quiet; red low ssn. "Mostly statics but great location; pleasant site; picturesque beach." ♦ 1 Apr-31 Oct. € 48.00 2010*

⊞ **SPEZIA, LA** *1C2* (4km SE Urban) *44.10333, 9.86000* **La Spezia Camper Club, Loc Pagliari, Via Pitelli, 19138 La Spezia [0187 519154; areacampersp@libero.it]** Sp to Camper Area at intersection with Via S Bartolomeo in front of shipyard S Marco & INMA). Adj to ferry slipway (ferries to Sardinia, Corsica, Tunisia). Well sp fr SP331. Sm, hdstg, unshd; wc; water; own san; chem disp; mv service pnt; 24-hr security; no shwrs or el pnts; bus to town. "Unattractive area & site but conv NH bef ferry or for Cinque Terre; m'vans only; gd security; helpful staff; no rest or shops locally; managed by local ambulance service - voluntary contributions welcome." 2009*

SPOTORNO see Savona *1B2*

STACCIOLA DI SAN COSTANZA see Fano *2E3*

STELLA SAN GIOVANNI see Savona *1B2*

STIA *1D3* (5km N Rural) *43.83028, 11.70061* **Camping Falterona, Loc Montalto, 52017 Stia (AR) [tel/fax 0575 582360; info@campingfalterona.it; www.campingfalterona.it]** E fr Florence on R69 to Pontassieve, then R70 to Poppi. Turn N onto R310 to Stia then foll dir Forli to Papiano & site. Med, some hdstg, terr, pt shd; wc (some cont); chem disp; mv service pnt; shwrs; el pnts (3A) €1.50; shop; tradsmn; snacks; bar; BBQ; playgrnd; sm pool; games area; Eng spkn; quiet. "Beautiful area; vg walking." 29 May-5 Sep. € 21.50 2010*

STRESA *1B1* (4km NW Urban) *45.91246, 8.50410* **Camping Parisi, Via Piave 50, 28831 Baveno (VB) [0323 924160; campingparisi@tiscalinet.it; www.campingparisi.it]** Exit A26 at Baveno, after x-ing bdge on o'skirts Baveno, turn L off main rd bet Hotel Simplon & Agip g'ge & foll sp. Fr Stresa drive thro Baveno. At end of prom, take R fork at Dino Hotel up a minor 1-way street (poss congested by parked cars); foll Parisi sp. Med, pt sl, pt shd; wc; chem disp; mv service pnt; shwrs inc; el pnts (6A) €3.50; Indtte; shop, supmkt 500m; rest, snacks 500m; bar adj, playgrnd; lake sw; sm shgl beach adj; boat-launching; fishing; wifi; 10% statics; dogs €4; bus; phone; poss cr; Eng spkn; adv bkg; quiet but w/end evening noise fr adj lido; red CCI. "Well-managed site on Lake Maggiore; fine views; extra for lakeside pitches; frequent lake steamers nr site; gd rests adj; long hose rec for m'van fill up; sm pitches; busy at w/end; supervise children carefully when sw in lake; many repeat visitors; clean facs; welcoming recep; conv base for visiting Borromeo Islands." ♦ 1 Apr-2 Oct. € 29.00 2011*

STRESA *1B1* (4km NW Rural) *45.91185, 8.48913* **Camping Tranquilla, Via Cave 2, Oltrefuime, 28831 Baveno (VB) [tel/fax 0323 923452; info@tranquilla.com; www.tranquilla.com]** Fr N go into Baveno & turn R 200m past Hotel Splendide; fr S turn L immed after x-ing bdge. Foll brown sp to site up steep hill 1km. Med, hdg/mkd pitch, some hdstg, pt sl, terr, pt shd; wc (some cont); chem disp; mv service pnt; serviced pitch; shwrs inc; el pnts (6A) €2.60; Indtte (inc dryer); shops 1km; rest 400m; bar; shgl lake beach 800m; pool; watersports; cycle hire; entmnt at w/end; 25% statics; dogs €2.50; train to Milan 2km; car wash; Eng spkn; adv bkg; quiet; red long stay/snr citizens/CCI. "Clean, well-managed, family-owned site; v helpful staff; excel rest; sm pitches; conv Lake Maggiore; day trip by train to Milan; site was clean and comfortable the owner is pleasant and helpful." 15 Mar-15 Oct. € 26.00 2011*

STRESA *1B1* (6km NW Urban) *45.90323, 8.50807* **Camping Calaverde, Sempione 24, 28831 Baveno (VB) [0323 924178; info@calaverde.it]** Fr Stresa N on S33, site ent on R 100m after 87km post. Tight, concealed ent. Sm, pt shd; wc, chem disp; shwrs inc; el pnts inc; Indry rm; shop opp; bar; lake & private shgl beach adj; quiet but some rd/rlwy noise; Eng spkn; dogs; phone; quiet. "Helpful, friendly owner; clean site; boat-launching; gd size pitches; lake steamer 2km." € 26.00 2009*

TALAMONE *1D3* (1.5km SE Coastal/Rural) *42.56507, 11.13942* **Talamone International Camping, 58010 Talamone (GR) [0564 887026; fax 887170; info@talamonecampingvillage.com; www.talamonecampingvillage.com]** Fr SS1 25km S of Grosseto take exit R twd Talamone. Site on R after 4km, 1km bef vill. Lge, mkd pitch, pt terr, pt shd; wc; shwrs inc; el pnts (4A) inc; gas; Indtte; shop; rest; snacks; bar; playgrnd; pool; paddling pool; beach 1km; tennis; watersports; boat & fishing trips; internet; entmnt; TV; 1% statics; dogs (not acc Jul/Aug; phone; bus to beach high ssn; adv bkg; quiet; red 30+ days. "Friendly, helpful recep & staff." ♦ Easter-15 Sep. € 34.50 2007*

TARQUINIA *1D4* (5km SW Coastal) *42.23058, 11.69968* **Camping Village Tuscia Tirrenica, Viale delle Nereidi, 01010 Tarquinia-Lido (VT) [0766 864294; fax 846200; info@campingtuscia.it; www.campingtuscia.it]** Site on seashore; exit S1 at km 92 twds coast, in 5km thro Tarquina-Lido vill; turn R to site at end of metalled rd; sp fr o'skts of Tarquinia Lido. Lge, pt shd; wc (mainly cont); chem disp; shwrs; el pnts (3A) inc; Indtte; shop; rest; snacks; bar; playgrnd; pool; beach adj; tennis; windsurfing; games area; entmnt; sep car park; no dogs; poss cr; poss noisy at w/end; ccard acc; red low ssn CCI. "Site yourself in wooded area; lovely site but gloomy due trees; hot water to shwrs only." ♦ 1 Apr-30 Sep. € 24.00 2008*

TERLAGO see Trento *1D1*

⊞ **TERMOLI** *2F4* (6km SE Coastal) *41.93861, 15.08194* **Camping La Pineta, Contrada Ramitelli 5/A, 86042 Campomarino-Lido (CB) [0875 539402; fax 538143; info@lapinetacamping.it; www.lapinetacamping.it]** Leave a'strada A14 at Termoli onto SS16 dir Foggia. After approx 2km turn sp Lido-di-Campomarino; cross over rlwy bdge twds sea, foll site sp. Lge, pt shd; wc (some cont); shwrs; el pnts (3A) €3; gas; Indtte; shop; tradsmn; rest; snacks; bar; sand beach adj; tennis; games area; entmnt; 80% statics; no dogs Jul/Aug; poss cr; some rd & rlwy noise; red low ssn; CCI. "Friendly, family-run site; site grubby & gloomy low ssn; tight turns & narr pitches poss diff lge o'fits; pitches boggy after rain; gd san facs; hot water only in shwrs; beach access; v friendly staff; NH only." € 29.00 2011*

TERNI *2E3* (7km E Rural) *42.54801, 12.71878* **Camping Marmore, Loc Campacci, 05100 Cascata-delle-Marmore (TN) [0744 67198; www.campinglemarmore.com]** E fr Terni on S79 dir Marmore & Rieti. Foll site sp. Med, hdstg, pt sl, shd; htd wc (some cont); chem disp; shwrs inc; el pnts inc; shop & 1km; rest; bar; rv sw adj; watersports on lake nrby; games rm; 90% statics; dogs €4; phone; poss cr; Eng spkn; quiet. "Spectacular waterfalls adj & mountain scenery; gd." ♦ 1 Apr-30 Sep. € 21.00 2009*

TERRACINA *2E4* (6km S Coastal) *41.29539, 13.31965* **Camping Settebello, Via Flacca, Km 3.600, 04020 Salto-di-Fondi (LT) [0771 599132; fax 57635; settebello@settebellocamping.com; www.settebellocamping.com]** Site sp fr S213 bet Terracina & Sperlonga. Lge, some hdstg, pt shd; wc; chem disp; mv service pnt; shwrs inc; el pnts inc; gas; Indtte (inc dryer); shop; rest; snacks; bar; BBQ; playgrnd; pool; paddling pool; beach adj; watersports; tennis; games area; internet; entmnt; TV; cinema; 50% statics; sep car park high ssn; poss cr; quiet, but poss noisy w/end; some rd noise; red low ssn. "Gd touring base; pleasant site." ♦ 1 Apr-30 Sep. € 55.00 (CChq acc) 2008*

TERRACINA *2E4* (4km W Coastal) *41.28285, 13.19610* **Camping Internazionale Badino (Naturist), Via Badino, Km 4.8, Porto Badino, 04019 Terracina (LT) [tel/fax 0773 764430]** Fr Latina on S148 (SS Mediana) foll sp Port Badino & site. Med, mkd pitch, pt shd; wc; shwrs €1; chem disp; el pnts (1.50A) inc; gas; Indtte; shop, rest 100m; bar; sand beach adj; games area; solarium; no dogs Jul/Aug; quiet. ♦ 1 Apr-15 Oct. € 35.00 2009*

ITALY

TIONE DI TRENTO *1D1* (5km N Rural) *46.07077, 10.71970* **Camping Val Rendena, Via Civico 117, 38080 Dare (TN) [tel/fax 0465 801669; info@campingvalrendena.com; www.campingvalrendena.com]** Fr Trento take S237 sp Sarche & Ponte Arche. At Tione-di-Trento turn R for Pinzolo, site sp on R. Fr N on S42 turn S onto S239 rd dir Madonna-di-Campiglio & Tione-di-Trento. V steep app; rec only with gd power/weight ratio. Med, mkd pitch, pt shd; htd wc (some cont); chem disp; mv service pnt; baby facs; shwrs inc; el pnts (16A) inc; Indtte; shop; rest; snacks; playgrnd; htd pool; paddling pool; rv fishing; tennis; cycle hire; games area; some statics; dogs €3; phone; poss cr; adv bkg; quiet. "Clean, tidy site in wooded valley; quiet & peaceful; charming owners; excel." ♦ 13 May-24 Sep & 1 Dec-30 Apr. € 24.90 2008*

TORBOLE *1D1* (Urban) *45.87138, 10.87416* **Camping Al Cor, Via Matteotti 26, 38069 Tórbole (TN) [tel/fax 0464 505222; www.camping-al-cor.com]** Fr Riva take S240 to Torbole, x-ing rv. Site on R in 100m bef rndabt, opp g'ge (turning easily missed). Med, hdstg, pt shd; wc; chem disp; mv service pnt; shwrs inc; el pnts (3A) inc; Indry rm; shop; rest; snacks; bar; BBQ; lake sw & shgl beach adj; windsurf & cycle hire; wifi; 10% statics; dogs €1.50; phone; poss cr; Eng spkn; adv bkg; quiet; ccard acc; red low ssn; CCI. "Excel; take care netting over pitches." ♦ 1 Apr-5 Oct. € 26.00 2008*

TORBOLE *1D1* (Urban) *45.8725, 10.87361* **Camping Al Porto, Via Al Cor, 38069 Tórbole (TN) [tel/fax 0464 505891; info@campingalporto.it; www.campingalporto.it]** On ent Tórbole fr S take rd twd Riva-del-Garda for approx 600m. Petrol stn & car park on R, turn L into narr lane after shops; site sp. Med, mkd pitch, pt shd; wc (some cont); chem disp; mv service pnt; shwrs inc; el pnts (5A) inc; Indtte; shops 300m; tradsmn; rest 100m; snacks; bar; BBQ; playgrnd; lake sw & shgl beach 100m; watersports; dogs €2.50; poss cr; quiet; red long stay/low ssn; CCI. "Excel san facs." ♦ 14 Mar-2 Nov. € 26.60 2008*

TORBOLE *1D1* (Urban) *45.87277, 10.87166* **Camping Europa, Via Al Cor 21, 38069 Torbole (TN) [0464 505888; fax 549879]** On ent Torbole fr S take rd twd Riva-del-Garda for approx 600m. Petrol stn & car park on R, turn L into narr lane after shops; site sp. Med, hdg/mkd pitch, hdstg, shd; wc; chem disp; shwrs inc; el pnts (3A) inc (poss no earth); Indtte; shops 400m; rest 300m; lake sw; windsurfing; beach adj; dogs €2.60; min stay 4 nights high ssn; poss cr; quiet; ccard not acc. "Views of Lake Garda; clean, spacious facs; narr site rds, lge outfits may need to unhitch to get round some corners; excel." ♦ 1 Apr-1 Nov. € 25.90 2008*

TORRE CANNE *3A4* (500m SE Coastal) *40.82897, 17.47563* **Lido Fiume Piccolo - Camper Service, Via Appia Antica 47, Torre-Canne (BR) [0338 8447311]** Leave E55/S379 at sp Torre-Canne, thro vill dir Brindisi. Site on L on beach nr Hotel Serena. Sm, mkd pitch, hdstg, pt shd; wc (cont); mv service pnt; shwrs; el pnts (6A); shop 1km; rest; snacks; bar; BBQ; sand beach adj; dogs; phone; CCI. "M'vans only; charge for fresh water & water disposal." 1 Apr-30 Sep. 2007*

TORRE DEL LAGO PUCCINI see Viareggio *1C3*

TORRETTE DI FANO see Fano *2E3*

TORRI DEL BENACO *1D1* (2km N Rural) *45.65750, 10.72472* **Camping Ai Salici, Via Pai di Sotto, Frazione Pai, 37010 Torri-del-Benaco (VR) [tel/fax 045 7260196; aisalici@tiscali.it; www.campingaisalici.eu]** N fr Garda along edge of lake on SR249, site sp. Narr site ent. Sm, mkd pitch, terr, pt sl, pt shd; wc (some cont); chem disp; shwrs inc; el pnts (4A) inc; Indtte; shop, rest, snacks, bar 200m; lake sw & beach adj; watersports nr; 25% statics; dogs €1.50; bus 500m; poss cr; Eng spkn; adv bkg; some; rd noise; CCI. "Friendly, helpful owners; v clean san facs; generous pitches; lovely, quiet site in olive grove beside lake." ♦ 5 May-16 Sep. € 22.00 2008*

TOSCALANO MADERNO *1D1* (N Urban) *45.63777, 10.61277* **Camping Toscolano, Via Religione 88, 25088 Toscolano-Maderno (BS) [0365 641584; fax 642519; toscolano@hg-hotels.com; www.hghotels.com]** Site at lakeside bet Gargnano & Maderno. Narr archway on app. Lge, pt shd; wc (some cont); shwrs inc; el pnts (3A) inc; gas; Indtte; shop; rest; snacks; bar; playgrnd; pool; paddling pool; shgl beach & lake sw; tennis; games area; golf 5km; entmnt; 50% statics; dogs €3.50; poss v cr; adv bkg rec. ♦ 1 Apr-30 Sep. € 34.50 2010*

TRASAGHIS see Gemona del Friuli *2E1*

TRENTO *1D1* (12km NW Rural) *46.11111, 11.04805* **Camping Laghi di Lamar, Via alla Selva Faeda 15, 38070 Terlago (TN) [0461 860423; campeggio@laghidilamar.com; www.laghidilamar.com]** Head W fr Trento for 10km on SS45b dir Riva-del-Garda/Brescia. Turn R twd Monte-Terlago; site sp on R. Last section via SS45 v steep. Med, terr, pt shd; wc (some cont); chem disp; mv service pnt; shwrs inc; el pnts (6A) inc; gas; Indtte (inc dryer); shop; rest 100m; rest; snacks; bar; BBQ; playgrnd; pool; lake sw 700m; games area; games rm; cycle hire; wifi; TV; 30% statics; dogs €2.50; phone; Eng spkn; quiet; ccard acc; red snr citizens/CCI. "Excel site." ♦ 1 Apr-15 Oct. € 27.50 2010*

TREPORTI see Cavallino *2E2*

⊞ **TRIESTE** *2F1* (4km N Rural) **Camping Obelisco, Strada Nuova Opicina 37, 34016 Opicina (TS) [040 212744; fax 212744; info@campeggiobelisco.it; www.campeggiobelisco.it]** Sp fr S58. Med, hdstg, pt sl, terr, shd; wc (cont); own san; mv service pnt; shwrs inc; el pnts €2.50; rest; snacks; bar 1km; playgrnd; 95% statics; dogs €2.50; Eng spkn; quiet; CCI. "V steep, narr, twisting ent/exit to site - suitable sm c'vans only & diff in wet; excel views Trieste harbour; interesting tram ride into city fr obelisk; demanding up hill walk to top of site, both Turkish & European wcs." € 18.00 2011*

TROGHI see Firenze *1D3*

TROPEA *3B4* (7km NE Coastal) *38.70610, 15.97024* **Villaggio Camping Sambalon, Via del Mare, 89868 Marina-di-Zambrone (VV) [0963 392828; fax 45385; info@sambalon.com; www.sambalon.com]** Fr N exit A3 at Pizzo Calabro onto S522 dir Tropea for 20km. Foll sp Marina di Zambrone & site. Med, mkd pitch, some hdstg, pt shd; wc; mv service pnt; shwrs; el pnts; Indtte; shop & 1km; rest; snacks; bar; playgrnd; sand beach adj; wifi; entmnt; TV; some statics; dogs; adv bkg; quiet. 1 Jun-30 Sep. (CChq acc) 2011*

The opening dates and prices on this campsite have changed. I'll send a site report form to the Club for the next edition of the guide.

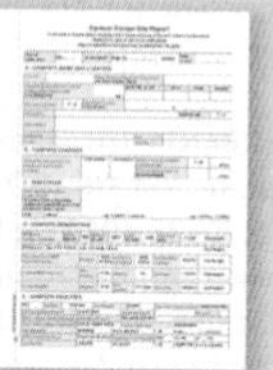

UGENTO *3A4* (6km S Coastal) *39.87331, 18.14261* **Camping Riva di Ugento, Loc Fontanelle, 73059 Ugento (LE) [0833 933600; fax 933601; info@rivadiugento.it; www.rivadiugento.it]** Fr Bari take Brindisi rd to Lecce, then SS101 to Gallipoli, then SR274 twd Sta Maria di Leuca & exit at Ugento. Turn R at traff lts on SS91, site well sp. V lge, mkd pitch, shd; htd wc (some cont); mv service pnt; shwrs inc; el pnts (3A) inc; gas; Indtte (inc dryer); shop; rest; snacks; bar; BBQ; playgrnd; pool; paddling pool; sand beach adj; watersports; tennis; cycle hire; games area; horseriding 1km; boat & cycle hire; wifi; TV rm; cinema; excursions; 10% statics; no dogs; no adv bkg; ccard acc. "Excel beach; some pitches at water's edge; tranquil site." ♦ 15 May-30 Sep. € 45.00 (CChq acc) 2011*

URBINO *2E3* (2.5km E Rural) *43.73055, 12.65710* **Camping Pineta, Via Ca' Mignore, 5, 61029 San Donato (PS) [0722 4710; fax 4734; campeggiopinetaurbino@email.it; www.camping-pineta-urbino.it]** Site sp fr rndabout just below city walls on S423 fr Pesaro. Med, terr, pt shd; wc (mainly cont); chem disp (wc); shwrs inc; el pnts (4-6A) inc (long lead poss req); Indtte; shop in ssn; tradsmn; supmkt 1km; rest, bar 2km; pool; sand beach 20km; dogs €3; bus to town (ltd); Eng spkn; adv bkg red Jul/Aug; quiet; ccard acc; red long stay/low ssn. "Lovely setting on hill o'looking Urbino; v interesting area; sm, steep, tight pitches unsuitable lge o'fits; tired, old facs poss stretched; gd pool." Easter-30 Sep. € 50.00 2010*

⊞ **URBISAGLIA** *2E3* (6km NE Rural) **Centro Agrituristico La Fontana, Via Selva 8, Abbadia-di-Fiastra, 62010 La Fontana (MC) [tel/fax 0733 514002]** Fr SP77 turn S to Abbadia-di-Fiastra onto SP78. On reaching Abbadia turn L & immed R, then uphill for 2km & foll sp to site on R just after sharp RH bend. Sm, terr, pt shd; wc; chem disp; mv service pnt; shwrs inc; el pnts (6A) inc; rest; snacks; bar; BBQ; playgrnd; sand beach 35km; TV cab/sat; quiet. "Fair sh stay/NH; CL-type site on farm; not suitable lge o'fits; attactive countryside; v helpful owners." ♦ € 21.00 2010*

VADA see Cecina *1D3*

VALLECROSIA *1B3* (Coastal) *43.78411, 7.63368* **Camping Vallecrosia, Lungomare Marconi 149, 18019 Vallecrosia (IM) [tel/fax 0184 295591; info@campingvallecrosia.com; www.campingvallecrosia.com]** Fr SS1 Via Aurelia cont W dir Bordighera & Vallecrosia, foll sp. Site on seafront. Fr A10 exit at Ventimiglia & take SS1 dir San Remo, foll site sp. Do not take m'way exits at San Remo or Bordighera as rds unsuitable c'vans & m'vans. Sm, mkd pitch, hdstg, pt shd; htd wc; chem disp; mv service pnt; shwrs inc; el pnts (6A) €3; Indtte; shop; rest, snacks, bar 200m; playgrnd; shgl beach 100m; wifi; 25% statics; dogs €3; phone; quiet; CCI. "Lovely, well-spaced site; excel beach opp with beach bar; popular with windsurfers; helpful staff; v clean san facs; longer vans may req manhandling onto mkd pitches; ideal NH bet Italy & France." ♦ 1 Apr-30 Sep. € 30.00 2010*

VALMADONNA see Alessandria *1B2*

VALSAVARENCHE *1B1* (5km S Rural) *45.54889, 7.21250* **Camping Gran Paradiso, Loc Plan de la Pesse 1, 11010 Valsavarenche (AO) [tel/fax 0165 905801; campinggranparadiso@libero.it; www.campinggranparadiso.it]** Exit A5 Aosta Ovest onto S26 W dir Monte Bianco. In 3km at Villeneuve turn S & foll sp Valsavarenche for approx 18km. Approx 5km after passing cent of Degioz site sp just bef rd crosses rv. Sm, mkd pitch, terr, shd; wc; chem disp; mv service pnt; fam bthrm; shwrs inc; el pnts (3A) €2; Indtte (inc dryer); tradsmn; snacks; bar; BBQ; cooking facs; games area; games rm; dogs; phone; Eng spkn; adv bkg; quiet. "Well-situated, scenic site for hiking, canyoning, rafting; guided walks; excel." ♦ 1 Jun-30 Sep. € 18.00 2010*

VARIGOTTI see Finale Ligure *1B2*

VASTO *2F4* (5km N Coastal) *42.15508, 14.71601* **Camping Grotta del Saraceno, Punta Pena, Via Osca 6, 66054 Vasto (CH) [0873 310213; fax 310295; info@grottaadelsaraceno.it; www.grottadelsaraceno.it]** Site sp on rd S16. Lge, pt shd; wc; shwrs; el pnts inc; gas; Indtte; shop; rest; snacks; bar; beach adj; watersports; tennis; games area; entmnt; some statics; dogs €6; quiet; ccard acc. ♦ 15 Jun-15 Sep. € 31.50 2008*

VASTO *2F4* (2km SE Coastal) *42.08489, 14.73830* **Camping Pioppeto, SS16, Km 521, 66055 Marina-di-Vasto (CH) [0873 801466; fax 0873-364074; infocampeggio@ilpioppeto.it; www.ilpioppeto.it]** Site on L of main rd SS16 SE dir Termoli. Med, shd; wc; shwrs; el pnts (4A) €2.80; shop; rest; snacks; bar; sand beach 100m; playgrnd; dogs €5; some rd noise; ccard acc. "Well-equipped site; helpful staff." ♦ 15 May-15 Sep. € 33.10 2008*

ITALY

⊞ **VENEZIA** *2E2* (5km S Coastal) *45.41916, 12.25666* **Camping Fusina, Via Moranzani 79, 30030 Fusina (VE) [041 5470055; fax 5470050; info@camping-fusina.it; www.campingfusina.com]** Exit A4 at sp Ravenna/Chiogga onto SS309 S, & foll sp to site. Take care when turning into rd leading to Fusina as L-hand turning lane used by locals for o'taking. Lge, pt shd; htd wc; chem disp; mv service pnt; shwrs inc; el pnts (6A) inc (poss rev pol); gas; Indtte; shop; rest; snacks; bar; playgrnd; boat hire; games area; wifi; entmnt; TV rm; 50% statics; dogs free; poss cr; no adv bkg; some ship & aircraft noise + noise fr bar & adj indus complex; ccard acc; red CCI. "Pleasant, busy site; some pitches overlkng lagoon; many backpackers, educational groups & 18-30s; gd san facs; gd public transport/boat dir to Venice; helpful staff; poss mosquitoes; some pitches diff due trees & soft when wet; Magic of Europe discount (ask on arr); ltd facs low ssn & poss itinerants." € 33.00 2011*

VENEZIA *2E2* (12km W Rural) *45.45222, 12.18305* **Camping Della Serenissima, Via Padana 334/A, 30030 Oriago (VE) [041 5386498; fax 920286; campingserenissima@shineline.it; www.campingserenissima.com]** Exit A4 at Oriago/Mira exit. At 1st rndabt foll sp Ravenna/Venezia; at next rndabt take 1st exit sp Padova/Riviera del Brenta (SR11) twd Oriago. Rv on L, site on R in approx 2km. Med, hdg pitch, pt shd; wc (some cont); shwrs inc; el pnts (16A) inc; gas; Indtte; shop; supmkt 5km; rest; snacks; bar; playgrnd; pool 3km; sand beach 10km; cycle & boat hire; 25% statics; dogs free; poss cr; Eng spkn; no adv bkg; quiet; ccard acc; red snr citizens; CCI. "Bus to Venice - buy tickets on site; friendly owners; efficient recep; some sm pitches; excel, clean san facs; poss mosquitoes; conv Padova." ♦ Easter-8 Nov. € 30.00 2009*

VENEZIA (VENICE) See also sites listed under Cavallino, Lido di Jesolo, Mestre and Punta Sabbioni.

⊞ **VERBANIA** *1B1* (8km N Rural) *45.99669, 8.65290* **Aire de Oggebbio Gonte, Via Martiri, 28824 Oggebbio (VB) [0348 9286475 or 7336392; eurnaser@libero.it]** S fr Locarno/Cannobio on SS34 in Oggebbio turn R up steep, narr rd. Site well sp. M'vans only. Sm, mkd pitch, hdstg, terr, unshd; wc; chem disp (wc); mv service pnt; shwrs inc; el pts (10A) inc; shop, rest, bar 500m; playgrnd 500m; dogs; quiet. "Modern, clean facs; tight pitches; water to each pitch; fees collected; lake views." € 10.00 2008*

VERBANIA *1B1* (6km NE Rural) *45.97659, 8.63385* **Camping La Sierra, Belvedere 337, 28823 Ghiffa (VB) [0333 7815534; info@campinglasierra.it; www.campinglasierra.it]** Fr Verbania N on SS34 dir Cannobio, site on L just after exit fr Ghiffa. Sm, mkd pitch, hdstg, terr, pt shd; wc; chem disp; shwrs inc; el pnts (6A) inc; Indtte; shop 1km; tradsmn; rest; snacks; bar; BBQ; playgrnd; shgl beach adj; fishing; watersports; 8% statics; dogs €3; bus; phone; poss cr; Eng spkn; adv bkg; rd noise; CCI. "Vg site; views of lake." 1 Mar-1 Nov. € 20.00 2009*

VERBANIA *1B1* (5km E Rural) *45.93916, 8.50055* **Village-Camping Isolino, Via per Feriolo 25, 28924 Fondotoce (VB) [0323 496080; fax 496414; info@isolino.com; www.campingisolino.com]** Exit A26/E62 at Baveno onto SS33 dir Verbania. Site sp 1.5km W of Fondotoce. V lge, mkd pitch, shd; wc (some cont); chem disp; mv service pnt; baby facs; shwrs inc; el pnts (6A) inc; Indtte; supmkt; rest; snacks; bar; playgrnd; pool & paddling pool; sand beach & lake adj; boat hire; windsurfing; tennis; cycle hire; golf 2km; wifi; entmnt; 25% statics; dogs €7.60; poss cr; adv bkg; red long stay/low ssn; ccard acc; CCI. "Busy, popular site; gd for children." ♦ Easter-22 Sep. € 41.75 3 persons 2008*

VERBANIA *1B1* (4km W Rural) *45.95365, 8.47698* **Camping La Quiete, Via Turati 72, Lago di Mergozzo, 28924 Fondotoce (VB) [0323 496013; fax 496139; info@campinglaquiete.it; www.campinglaquiete.it]** Exit A26 at Gravellona Toce onto SS34 to Fondotoce, then SP54 to Lago di Mergozzo. Site on E edge Lago di Mergozzo, sp. Lge, mkd pitch, pt shd; wc; chem disp; mv service pnt; shwrs; el pnts (6A) €3; Indtte; shop; rest; bar; lake sw adj; canoing; fishing; windsurfing; games area; games rm; golf 2km; some statics; dogs €5.50; some Eng spkn; adv bkg rec; quiet; ccard not acc. "Lovely site with view of alps & lake; extra for lakeside pitches; friendly, welcoming owner; excel." 1 Apr-30 Sep. € 27.00 2010*

I'll fill in a report online and let the Club know – www.caravanclub.co.uk/europereport

This is a wonderful site.

VERBANIA *1B1* (6km W Rural) *45.93731, 8.48615* **Camping Conca d'Oro, Via 42 Martiri 26, 28835 Feriolo (VB) [0323 28116; fax 28538; info@concadoro.it; www.concadoro.it]** Foll S33 NW fr Stresa, thro Bavena to Feriolo. At traff lts in Feriolo fork R, sp Verbania & in 800m immed over rv bdge, turn R into site. Clearly sp. Lge, mkd pitch, pt sl, shd; wc; chem disp; mv service pnt; shwrs inc; el pnts (6A) inc; Indtte; supmkt; rest; snacks; bar; playgrnd; private sand beach adj; windsurfing; games area; cycle hire; internet; entmnt; 10% statics; dogs €5.00 (not acc Jul/Aug); Eng spkn; adv bkg; quiet; ccard acc; CCI. "Helpful staff; gd, clean, modern san facs; discount for local services; extra for lakeside pitches; vg site." ♦ 01 Apr-30 Sep. € 35.00 2011*

VERBANIA *1B1* (6km W Urban) *45.93283, 8.48266* **Camping Orchidea, Via 42 Martiri, 28835 Feriolo (VB) [0323 28257; fax 28573; info@campingorchidea.it; www.camping orchidea.it]** Exit A26/E62 sp Baveno onto SS33 dir Verbania. Past traff lts in Feriolo to site on R in 500m. Lge, pt shd; wc; mv service pnt; baby facs; shwrs; el pnts (6A) €2.60; gas; Indtte; shop; rest; snacks; bar; playgrnd; sand beach & lake sw adj; cycle hire; wifi; 25% statics; dogs €5; poss cr; adv bkg ess high ssn; quiet but rd noise; ccard acc. "Beautiful situation at lake end, splendid views; lake shore walk to vill; 3 gd rests in 10 mins walk; boats fr Stresa to Locarno; sm pitches." 1 Mar-1 Oct. € 32.00 2009*

VERBANIA *1B1* (7km W Rural) *45.94970, 8.48114* **Camping Continental Lido, Via 42 Martiri 156, 28924 Fondotoce (VB) [0323 496300; fax 496218; info@campingcontinental.com; www.campingcontinental.com]** Fr Verbania to Fondotoce; turn R to Gravellona; in 150m turn R; track thro fields to Lake Mergozzo 250m; sp. V lge, pt shd; wc; chem disp; mv service pnt; baby facs; shwrs inc; el pnts (5A) inc (poss rev pol); gas; Indtte (inc dryer); shop; tradsmn; rest; snacks; bar; playgrnd; pool complex; padding pool; waterslide; beach & lake sw adj; canoeing; fishing; tennis; cycle hire; games area; golf 500m; wifi; entmnt; TV; 25% statics; dogs €5.85; phone; poss cr; Eng spkn; adv bkg rec; quiet; no ccard acc; CCI. "No cash acc on site - all transactions by key system; pitches muddy if wet; gd touring cent Lake Maggiore; beautiful area." ♦ 15 Apr-26 Sep. € 38.00 (3 persons) 2008*

VERONA *1D2* (1.5km N Rural) *45.44985, 11.00415* **Camping San Pietro, Via Castel San Pietro 2, 37100 Verona [tel/fax 045 592037; info@campingcastelsanpietro.com; www.campingcastelsanpietro.com]** Exit A4/E70 to San Martino-Buon-Albergo & foll S11 dir Verona cent, site sp adj Castel San Pietro. Sm, mkd pitch, hdstg, shd; wc (cont); chem disp (wc); shwrs inc; no el pnts; Indtte; shop; rest 500m; snacks; bar; BBQ; wifi; no dogs; some statics; bus 1km; no vehicles/o'fits over 7m; adv bkg ess; some rd noise. "Basic site in park, more suited to tents or sm m'vans only - no el pnts; beautiful views over city; easy walk to town cent, but many steps." ♦ 2 May-30 Sep. € 27.00 2008*

⊞ **VERONA** *1D2* (1km NE Urban) *45.45150, 10.95456* **Camper Park Verona, Via Eraclea, 37100 Verona [0348 7328589; camperparkverona@libero.it]** Fr W on SR11 Corso Milano, site sp to L behind Esselunga supmkt; sp. Sm, unshd; el pnts; water fill. "New m'van parking area; v conv town cent." 2007*

⊞ **VERONA** *1D2* (10km W Rural) *45.44553, 10.83443* **Camping El Bacàn, Via Verona 11, 37010 Palazzolo di Sona (VR) [045 6080708; info@el-bacan.it; www.el-bacan.it]** Exit A4 onto A22 N & foll sp for Brescia (W) on SR11. Site in 7km on R, sp 150m bef site ent. Sm, hdg/mkd pitch, unshd; wc (cont); chem disp; el pnts (16A) inc; Indtte; shop (farm produce); tradsmn; rest, snacks, bar 2km; BBQ; playgrnd; internet; TV; no statics; dogs; bus 1km; Eng spkn; adv bkg; quiet, some rd noise; cc acc; CCI. "Charming site on working farm; conv Verona, Lake Garda; helpful, friendly staff." ♦ € 20.00 2011*

VIAREGGIO *1C3* (3km N Urban/Coastal) *43.90340, 10.22605* **Centro Sportivo Camping Versilia Mare, Via Trieste 175, 55043 Lido-di-Camaiore (LU) [0584 619862; fax 618691; info@campingversiliamare.com; www.versiliamare.com]** Fr A12 exit Viareggio Nord & foll sp Lido di Camaiore. To seafront along Viale Pistelli, turn R at site sp, then L to site on R. Med, mkd pitch, shd; wc (some cont); mv service pnt; shwrs inc; el pnts inc; Indtte; hypmkt 300m; tradsmn; bar; BBQ; playgrnd; 2 pools; sand beach 400m; tennis; games rm; 80% statics; dogs €3; poss cr; Eng spkn; quiet. "Friendly, helpful staff; cycle track along coast to nrby resorts; bus to Pisa, Florence, Lucca; mountain caves inland worth visit." 20 Mar-5 Oct. € 36.00 2008*

VIAREGGIO *1C3* (2km S Coastal) *43.85133, 10.25963* **Camping Viareggio, Via Comparini 1, 55049 Viareggio (LU) [0584 391012; fax 395462; info@campingviareggio.it; www.campingviareggio.it]** Fr sea front at Viareggio, take rd on canal sp Livorno; after x-ing canal bdge turn L (but not immed on canal) & 2nd R to site in 2km. Lge, shd; wc (some cont); chem disp; mv service pnt; baby facs; shwrs €0.50; el pnts (4A) (poss rev pol); gas; Indtte; shop; rest; bar; playgrnd; pool; beach 800m; games area; TV; internet; phone; dogs €4 (not permitted Aug); adv bkg; quiet; red low ssn/CCI. "Gd site & facs; hot water to shwrs only; cycle rte/footpath to town." ♦ 1 Apr-4 Oct. € 30.00 2009*

VIAREGGIO *1C3* (4km S Rural) *43.82693, 10.27182* **Camping Dei Tigli, Viale del Tigli 54, 55048 Torre-del-Lago Puccini (LU) [0584 359182; fax 341278; info@campingdeitigli.com; www.campingdeitigli.com]** Leave A11/12 at Viareggio, foll rd parallel to a'strada sp Torre-del-Lago-Puccini & after 6km turn R twd Torre. When thro town turn L at traff lts, over rlwy, L at rndabt & foll brown camp sp. V lge, hdg pitch, pt shd; wc; chem disp (wc); shwrs €0.50; el pnts (5A) inc; gas; Indtte; shop; rest; snacks; bar; BBQ; sand beach 1.2km; entmnt; 50% statics; dogs €6 (only small); phone; poss cr w/end; Eng spkn; adv bkg; quiet but poss disco noise high ssn; ccard acc; red long stay/CCI. "Pleasant, friendly site; facs old but clean; sep area for tourers; cycle path to town cent." 1 Apr-30 Sep. € 35.00 (3 persons) (CChq acc) 2011*

VIAREGGIO *1C3* (5km S Coastal) *43.82920, 10.2727* **Camping Italia, Viale dei Tigli, 55048 Torre-del-Lago Puccini (LU) [0584 359828; fax 341504; info@campingitalia.net; www.campingitalia.net]** Fr A12 N exit sp Viareggio, fr S exit Pisa N onto SS1 & turn twd Torre del Lago at S junc, site well sp thro vill. Do not turn L at vill cent but cont for 2km N, then L at rlwy bdge. At rndabt turn L, site on R in 250m. Avoid Viareggio town cent. Med, shd; wc (some cont); chem disp; mv service pnt; shwrs €0.50; el pnts (6A) €1.30; gas; Indtte (inc dryer); shop; rest; snacks; bar; lge playgrnd; pool; sand beach 1.5km; tennis; cycle hire; wifi; entmnt; TV rm; some statics (sep area); no dogs Jun-Aug; sep car park; Eng spkn; adv bkg; noisy w/ends high ssn; ccard acc; red low ssn. "Vg for Lucca - Puccini's birthplace; bus tickets fr site for Pisa & Lucca; some pitches diff for lge o'fits due trees & low branches; gd clean facs; poss problem with mosquitoes." ♦ 8 Apr-25 Sep. € 30.50 2009*

VIAREGGIO *1C3* (6km S Rural) *43.83105, 10.2707* **Camping Europa, Viale dei Tigli, 55048 Torre-del-Lago Puccini (LU) [0584 350707; fax 342592; info@europacamp.it; www.europacamp.it]** Exit A12/E80 at Pisa Nord exit, foll sp dir Viareggio to Torre-del-Lago & turn L. Site well sp fr vill cent. Lge, shd; wc (some cont); shwrs €0.40; el pnts (3A) inc (poss rev pol); gas; Indtte; shop & 2km; rest; snacks; bar; playgrnd; pool; paddling pool; sand beach 1km; tennis; games area; cycle hire; entmnt; 50% statics; dogs €2 (not acc Jul/Aug); poss cr; Eng spkn; adv bkg; quiet; ccard acc; red long stay/CCI. "Excel, clean, tidy site in regional coastal park; facs poss stretched when site full; helpful, friendly staff; poss mosquitoes; 1km to bus to Pisa, Lucca, Florence." ♦ Easter-1 Oct. € 33.00 2011*

VICCHIO see Borgo San Lorenzo *1D3*

ITALY

ITALY

VICENZA *1D2* (5km E Urban) *45.5175, 11.60222* **Camping Vicenza, Strada Pelosa 239, 36100 Vicenza [0444 582311; fax 582434; info@campingvicenza.it; www.ascom.vi.it/camping/]** Exit A4 Vicenza Est dir Torri di Quartesole; turn R immed after toll; site on L 300m fr Vicenza exit, hidden behind Viest Quality Inn. Fr city foll sp Padua & a'strada; sp. Med, pt sl, pt shd; wc (some cont); chem disp; mv service pnt; baby facs; shwrs inc; el pnts (3A) inc (rev pol); Indtte; shops 1km; rest, snacks 500m; bar; BBQ; playgrnd; tennis; cycle hire; internet; entmnt; bus; Eng spkn; adv bkg; rd noise; 10% red long stay; ccard acc; red CCI. "Cycle path to interesting town; poss ant problem; functional site." ♦ 1 Apr-30 Sep. € 32.20 2010*

VICO EQUENSE see Sorrento *3A3*

VIESTE *2G4* (2km N Coastal) *41.89901, 16.14964* **Camping Punta Lunga, Loc Defensola, 71019 Vieste (FG) [0884 706031; fax 706910; puntalunga@puntalonga.com; www.puntalunga.com]** N fr Vieste 1.5km fr end of long beach, turn R at traff lts down narr lane. Site sp. Lge, mkd pitch, pt terr, pt shd; htd wc (some cont); chem disp; mv service pnt; baby facs; shwrs inc; el pnts (3-5A) inc; gas; Indtte; shop; rest; snacks; playgrnd; beach adj; windsurfing; canoeing; cycle hire; wifi; entmnt; TV; 15% statics (sep area); no dogs; phone; bus; sep car park; poss cr; Eng spkn; adv bkg; quiet; ccard acc; red low ssn/CCI. "Friendly, helpful staff; well-run site on lovely cove; tight pitches - beware pitch marker posts; v clean facs; rec use bottled water; beautiful coastal area; gd rest; lovely cove; excel beaches." 1 May-30 Sep. € 36.00 2011*

VIESTE *2G4* (2km S Coastal) *41.85914, 16.17405* **Camping Adriatico, Lungomare. Enrico Mattei 110, 71019 Vieste (FG) [info@campingadriatico.it; www.campingadriatico.it]** S fr Vieste on coast rd SP53, site on both sides of rd. Med, mkd pitch, pt shd; wc (cont); chem disp; mv service pnt; shwrs inc; el pnts (6A) inc; Indtte; shop; tradsmn; rest; snacks; bar; BBQ; playgrnd; sand beach adj; windsurfing; games area; wifi; some statics; phone; bus; poss cr; Eng spkn; adv bkg; red low ssn. "Vg family-run site." ♦ 1 Apr-31 Oct. € 32.00 2010*

VIESTE *2G4* (6km NW Coastal) *41.91473, 16.11635* **Camping Umbramare, 71019 Santa Maria-di-Merino (FG) [tel/fax 0884 706174; umbramare@tiscali.it; www.umbramarevieste.it]** On Vieste-Peschici coast rd, sp. Med, mkd pitch, pt shd; wc (mainly cont); mv service pnt; shwrs inc; el pnts (4A) inc; rest; Indtte; shop; tradsmn; rest; snacks; bar; playgrnd; pool 300m; sand beach adj; windsurfing; games area; entmnt; no dogs; phone; sep car park; adv bkg; poss noisy; CCI. "Excel walks in Umbra Forest National Park - wild boar etc; excel windsurfing." ♦ 1 Apr-31 Oct. € 31.50 2007*

VIESTE *2G4* (8km NW Coastal) *41.92487, 16.10801* **Villagio Capo Vieste, Spiaggia Santa Maria-di-Merino, 71019 Vieste (FG) [0884 706326; fax 705993; info@capovieste.com; www.capovieste.com]** On P52 coast rd, Peschichi-Vieste. Site sp on R after Covo-di-Saraceni. Lge, pt shd; wc (some cont); chem disp; shwrs inc; el pnts (3A) inc; gas; Indtte; shop; rest; snacks; bar; playgrnd; beach adj; tennis; windsurfing; boat hire; cycle hire; entmnt; TV; some statics; sep car park; poss cr; adv bkg; quiet; 25% red CCI. "Boat trips to grottoes; ancient (pre-Greek) necropolis adj; friendly owners; excel rest." ♦ 1 Apr-24 Oct. € 37.00 2007*

VIGNALE RIOTORTO see Follonica *1D3*

VILLANOVA D'ALBENGA see Albenga *1B2*

⊞ **VIPITENO/STERZING** *1D1* (S Urban) *46.88737, 11.43098* **Autoporto, 00098 Vipiteno [0472 760620; info@hotel-brenner.com]** S fr Brenner Pass approx 17km, take exit immed bef toll booths Vipiteno & foll sp 'Autoporto'. Site well sp fr toll booth - 500m. Can also be accessed fr SS12. Push button on site barrier if office clsd. Med, hdstg, pt shd; wc; mv service pnt; shwrs; el pnts inc; shop, rest adj. "Excel NH for c'vans or m'vans; conv Austrian border." € 15.00 2009*

We can fill in site report forms on the Club's website – www.caravanclub.co.uk/europereport

VIVERONE *1B2* (3km S Rural) *45.40544, 8.05313* **Camping Internazionale del Sole, Loc Comuna 45, 13886 Viverone (BI) [tel/fax 0161 98169; www.campeggiodelsole.com]** Exit A5/A4 m'way network at junc for Cavaglia/Santhia. Foll S143 to Cavaglia approx 4km. At Cavaglia join S228 for Viverone/Ivrea. Immed after Viverone town sp turn L at rndabt. After 2km site sp strt on past hotel on R, recep on L. Lge, terr, pt sl, pt shd; wc (some cont); chem disp; shwrs €1; el pnts (3A) €1.50; Indtte; shop; rest; snacks; bar; playgrnd; lake sw; boating & fishing in lake; games rm; 90% statics; poss cr; adv bkg; poss noisy; red CCI. "Conv Aosta Valley, National Park & mountain resorts below Matterhorn; lovely situation by lake but facs minimal for such a lge site, espec low ssn; NH only." 1 Apr-30 Sep. € 21.50 2010*

VIVERONE *1B2* (1km SW Rural) *45.41644, 8.04874* **Camping Rocca, Via Lungo Lago 35, 13040 Viverone (BI) [tel/fax 0161 98416; laroccaviverone@hotmail.com; www.la-rocca.org]** On lakeside sp fr S228. Not well sp. Sm, pt shd; wc (mainly cont); chem disp; mv service pnt; shwrs €0.50; el pnts (2A) €1.80; shop 1km; rest; snacks; bar; playgrnd; lake sw & beach adj; 50% statics; phone; CCI. "Somewhat tatty (06/09); NH only." ♦ 1 Apr-30 Sep. € 22.00 2011*

VOLLAN/FOIANA see Merano/Meran *1D1*

VOLTERRA *1D3* (1km NW Rural) *43.41271, 10.8509* **Camping Le Balze, Via di Mandringa 15, 56048 Volterra (PI) [tel/fax 0588 87880; campinglebalze@hotmail.it; www.campinglebalze.com]** Take Pisa rd (S68) fr town; site clearly sp ('Camping' or symbol) after 1km. Watch out for R turn at sharp L corner. Med, pt sl, terr, pt shd; wc (some cont); chem disp; shwrs inc; el pnts (6A) inc; gas; Indtte; shop; tradsmn; supmkt 300m; rest 150m; bar; pool; paddling pool; dogs free; bus adj; poss cr; Eng spkn; no adv bkg; quiet; ccard acc; CCI. "Beautifully situated with views of Volterra & hills; gd, modern san facs; select own pitch; easy walk to town; Etruscan walls just outside site." ♦ 1 Apr-15 Oct. € 38.00 2011*

ZAMBRONE see Tropea *1B4*

SARDINIA

AGLIENTU *1C4* (6km N Coastal) *41.12701, 9.07071* **Camping Village Saragosa, Pineta di Vignola-Mare, 07020 Aglientu (SS) [079 602077; fax 602037; info@campingsaragosa.it; www.campingsaragosa.it]** Take coastal rd SW fr Santa Teresa Gallura (ferries fr Corsica) to Vignola Mare - approx 20km, site sp. Lge, shd; wc; mv service pnt; shwrs; el pnts (3A) inc; Indtte; shop; tradsmn; rest; snacks; bar; playgrnd; sand beach adj; games area; entmnt; 50% statics; dogs €4; phone; poss cr; Eng spkn; adv bkg; ccard acc; red low ssn. "Direct access to superb beach; some pitches adj beach." ♦ 1 May-30 Sep. € 37.00 2010*

ALGHERO *3A1* (1.5km N Coastal) *40.57916, 8.31222* **Camping La Mariposa, Via Lido 22, 07041 Alghero (SS) [079 9950480; fax 984489; info@lamariposa.it; www.lamariposa.it]** N fr Alghero on coast rd dir Fertilia. Site on L just beyond pool. Lge, pt sl, hdstg, terr, pt shd; wc; chem disp; mv service pnt; shwrs €0.50; el pnts (6-10A) €3; gas; Indtte; shop; rest; snacks; bar; BBQ; private sand beach adj; watersports; cycle hire; games rm; wifi; entmnt; TV; dogs; 20% statics; dogs; bus nr; sep car park; Eng spkn; ccard acc; red CCI. "Lovely wooded site; gd clean facs; gd security; friendly staff; boat fr Alghero to caves at Cape Caccia or by rd + 625 steps." 1 Apr-15 Oct. € 46.00 2011*

See advertisement

ALGHERO *3A1* (6km NW Coastal) **Camping Calik, 07040 Fertilia (SS) [tel/fax 079 930111; info@campeggiocalik.it; www.campeggiocalik.it]** Fr Alghero W on coast rd, site bet rndabt & rv bdge 500m bef Fertilia on R. Med, shd; wc; chem disp; shwrs inc; el pnts (3A); Indtte; shop; rest; snacks; bar; playgrnd; sand beach 200m; entmnt; 50% statics; dogs €3; bus at gate; poss cr; adv bkg; ccard acc. "Well-situated by rv with easy access to beach; cycle track to Fertilia." 15 Mar-30 Sep. € 35.50 2009*

ALGHERO *3A1* (12km NW Coastal) *40.64110, 8.18960* **Camping Torre del Porticciolo, Loc Porticciolo, 07041 Alghero (SS) [079 919007; fax 919212; info@torredelporticciolo.it; www.torredelporticciolo.it]** N fr Alghero sp SS127 to Capo Caccia; in 18km site sp R at T-junc then L in 300m. V lge, shd; wc (some cont); private san facs avail; shwrs inc; el pnts (4A) inc; gas; Indtte; shop; rest; snacks; bar; BBQ; playgrnd; sand beach; pool; paddling pool; watersports; tennis; games area; games rm; wifi; entmnt; TV; some statics; dogs €6; quiet; adv bkg; ccard acc; CCI. "Excel; close to Grotto di Nettuno; beautiful area." 1 May-10 Oct. € 73.00 (CChq acc) 2011*

ARBOREA *3A1* (2km NW Coastal) *39.81667, 8.55337* **Camping Village S'Ena Arrubia, Strada Ovest 29, 09092 Arborea (OR) [tel/fax 0783 809011; info@senarrubia.it; www.senarrubia.it]** Fr N on SS131 dir Oristano at km 94.5 foll sp Oristano-Sorgono. In 2km foll sp Oristano-Fenosu, then Santa Giusta (Oristano-Sud) to site. Lge, mkd pitch, pt sl, shd; wc; mv service pnt; shwrs inc; el pnts €3; Intte; shop; rest; snacks; bar; BBQ; playgrnd; pool; sand beach nr; lake sw & fishing; watersports; tennis; cycle & boat hire; games area; entmnt; some statics; adv bkg; red snr citizens. "Wooded site; excel touring base; gd modern san facs; cycle rtes." 10 May-30 Sep. € 41.00 (CChq acc) 2011*

ARZACHENA *1C4* (7km NW Coastal) *41.13156, 9.44064* **Camping Centro Vacanze Isuledda, 07020 Cannigione (OT) [0789 86003; fax 86089; info@isuledda.it; www.isuledda.it]** Fr S125 foll sp Cannigione, site 3km N of Cannigione, sp on R. V lge, mkd pitch, pt shd; wc (some cont); chem disp; mv service pnt; shwrs; el pnts (4A); Indtte (inc dryer); shop; tradsmn; rest; bar; BBQ; sand beach adj; watersports; boat & cycle hire; fitness/beauty rm; wifi; entmnt; TV; some statics; no dogs; adv bkg; quiet; ccard acc. 1 Apr-30 Oct. € 54.00 (CChq acc) 2011*

07041 ALGHERO (SS)
Tel. +39 079950480
E-mail: info@lamariposa.it
Http: www.lamariposa.it
la Mariposa
★★★ camping con bungalows
il gioco, ritrovarsi

Camping La Mariposa is very well equipped with bar, grocer's, market and private beach. It is well-known because of its care and hospitality. The camping site provides equipped pitches for tents, caravans and motocaravans, but also double rooms, 4 bedded bungalows, 2/4 bedded caravans and 4 bedded mini-villas. Camping La Mariposa is looking forward to welcoming you for a pleasant holiday from 1st April till 15th October with booking facilities avaiable all the year long.

New 2012: Mobilhome 4/5 pers. with cookingcorner and bathroom

BOSA *3A1* (2km S Coastal) *40.27424, 8.48811* **Camping Turas, Bosa Marina, 08013 Bosa (OR) [tel/fax 0785 359270; mussitta81@yahoo.it]** Fr SS129bis foll sp Bosa Marina. At seafront foll site sp for 500m; site on L. Med, mkd pitch, pt shd; wc; mv service pnt; shwrs; el pnts (4A) inc; shop 1km; tradsmn; rest, snacks; bar; sand/shgl beach 200m; some statics; no dogs; adv bkg; quiet; ccard acc. "Pleasant site with gd san facs; Bosa elegant city." 1 Jun-30 Sep. € 30.00 2008*

⊞ **CAGLIARI** *3B1* (1km SE Urban) *39.21129, 9.12883* **Camper Cagliari Park, 13 Via Stanislao Caboni, 09125 Cagliari [070 303147 or 0328 3348847 (mob); info@campercagliaripark.it; www.campercagliaripark.it]** Well sp on main rds into Cagliari. Sm, unshd; wc; chem disp; mv service pnt; el pnts (10A) €4; Indtte nr; bus 200m; Eng spkn; CCI. "Gd secure site; v helpful owner; walking dist historical cent, rests etc; c'vans enquire 1st." € 15.00 2007*

CANNIGIONE see Arzachena *1C4*

CASTIADAS *3B2* (4km E Coastal) *39.24450, 9.56980* **Villaggio Camping Capo Ferrato, Via delle Ginestre, Loc Costa Rei-Monte Nai, 09040 Castiadas (CA) [070 991012; fax 885653; info@campingcapoferrato.it; www.campingcapoferrato.it]** Fr Cagliari take coastal rd E twd Villasimius, then N to Monte Nai, site sp. Or fr Cagliari take S125 to San Priamo, then S to Monte Nai & site. Med, pt shd; wc; chem disp; mv service pnt; shwrs inc; el pnts (2-6A) €2.30-3.40; Indtte; shop; supmkt 500m; rest; snacks; bar; BBQ; playgrnd; sand beach adj; windsurfing 100m; tennis; cycle hire; horseriding 3km; games area; wifi; entmnt; TV; 10% statics; Eng spkn; adv bkg; quiet; ccard acc. "Welcoming, family-run site; might be diff for lge o'fits; Discover Sardinia theme weeks end Jun & beg Sep; conv Capo Carborana Nature Park." 1 Apr-2 Nov. € 44.20 (CChq acc) 2011*

CUGLIERI *3A1* (15km S Rural) *40.07083, 8.49055* **Camping Bella Sardinia - Village Europa, Loc Torre del Pozzo, 09073 Cuglieri (OR) [0785 38058; info@bellasardinia.it; www.bellasardinia.it]** S fr Olbia on SS131 dir Alghero, foll sp to Caglieri on SS15, then S on SS292, site sp in 15km. Lge, mkd pitch, pt shd; wc (some cont); chem disp; mv service pnt; shwrs; el pnts (3A); Indtte; shop; rest; snacks; bar; BBQ; playgrnd; pool; paddling pool; tennis; games area; games rm; wifi; entmnt; TV; some statics; adv bkg; quiet; ccard acc. "Pleasant, forested site." 9 Apr-15 Oct. € 44.00 (CChq acc) 2010*

DORGALI *3A2* (7km W Coastal) *40.28486, 9.63370* **Camping Villaggio Calagonone, Via Collodi 1, 08022 Cala-Gonone (NU) [0784 93165; fax 93255; info@campingcalagonone.it; www.campingcalagonone.it]** Fr S125 turn E twd Cala Gonone, thro tunnel. Site sp on L of main rd Med, terr, shd; wc; chem disp; mv service pnt; el pnts (6A) €5; shop; rest; snacks; bar; BBQ; playgrnd; pool; sand/shgl beach 400m; tennis; games area; 30% statics; dogs €5; phone; poss cr; adv bkg; ccard acc. "Beautiful situation in pine forest on edge of pretty town; nrby coves & grottoes accessible by boat or on foot." ♦ 1 Apr-3 Nov. € 39.00 2009*

⊞ **NARBOLIA** *3A1* (6km W Coastal) *40.06956, 8.48375* **Camping Nurapolis, Loc Is Arenas, 09070 Narbolia (OR) [0783 52283; fax 52255; camping@nurapolis.it; www.nurapolis.it]** Fr Oristano take sp to Cuglier on rd SS292i. Site sp fr rd approx 5km fr S. Caterina-di-Pittinura. Lge, pt shd; wc; shwrs; el pnts (3A) €3; gas; shop; rest; snacks; bar; sand beach adj; tennis; entmnt; watersports; dogs; poss cr; adv bkg; ccard acc; red CCI. "Site in pine forest; many sports, guided walks Easter to Oct; v pleasant owners." ♦ € 26.50 2007*

NORBELLO *3A1* (7km NW Rural) *40.17472, 8.77305* **Camping Villaggio Nuragheruiu, Loc Sant' Ignacio, 09070 Norbello [0785 825101; info@nuragheruiu.it; www.nuragheruiu.it]** Fr SS131 take Norbello/Sant' Ignacio exit; site in 4km. Lge, mkd pitch, some hdstg, pt sl, pt shd; wc; chem disp; mv service pnt; shwrs inc; el pnts (5A) inc; Indtte; shop; tradsmn; rest; snacks; bar; BBQ; playgrnd; pool; paddling pool; games area; cycle hire; wifi; entmnt; TV; some statics; dogs €3.50; Eng spkn; adv bkg; quiet; ccard acc; red CCI. "Gd touring base; gd." ♦ 1 May-30 Sep. € 39.00 2010*

OLBIA *3A2* (8km N Coastal) *41.08805, 9.58138* **Villaggio Camping Cugnana, Loc Cugnana, 07026 Olbia (SS) [0789 33184; fax 33398; info@campingcugnana.it; www.campingcugnana.it]** Fr Olbia N on SS125 for 8km. Turn R twd Porto-Rotondo, site on R in 4km. Med, pt sl, pt shd; wc (some cont); mv service pnt; shwrs; el pnts (16A) €3; gas; Indtte; shop; tradsmn; rest; snacks; bar; pool; shgl beach 1km; tennis; games area; 50% statics; dogs (sm only) free; shuttle bus to beach; Eng spkn; quiet; red long stay/low ssn; ccard acc. "Gd touring base Costa Smeralda." ♦ 15 Mar-15 Oct. € 38.50 2008*

ORISTANO *3A1* (5km W Coastal) *39.90388, 8.53111* **Camping Spinnaker, Via del Pontile, Marina-di-Torre Grande, 09170 Oristano [0783 22074; fax 22071; info@campingspinnaker.com; www.spinnakervacanze.com]** Fr Cagliari on S131 exit at Sta Giusta & foll sp Oristano & Torre-Grande. Med, mkd pitch, pt shd; htd wc; mv service pnt; baby facs; shwrs €0.50; el pnts €3; Indtte; shop; tradsmn; rest; snacks; bar; BBQ; playgrnd; pool; paddling pool; beach 200m; watersports; fishing; tennis 500m; cycle & boat hire; entmnt; TV rm; some statics; dogs €3; adv bkg; quiet. "Easy access to Sinis Peninsula for birdwatching & Tharros archaeological site." ♦ 1 Apr-30 Sep. € 46.00 (CChq acc) 2009*

PALAU *1C4* (500m N Coastal) *41.18586, 9.37700* **Villagio Camping Acapulco, Loc Punta Palau 07020 Palau [0789 709497; fax 706380; info@campingacapulco.com; www.campingacapulco.com]** Take rd S133 SE fr Sta Teresa-Gallura (ferry fr Corsica) sp Palau/Olbia, site sp in Palau. Med, mkd pitch, terr, some hdstg, pt shd; wc (some cont); chem disp; shwrs inc; el pnts (4A) €3; Indtte (inc dryer); shop 500m; rest; snacks; pizzeria; bar; BBQ; playgrnd; sand beach adj; boat-launching; watersports; wifi; entmnt; TV; 30% statics/cabins; phone; sep car park; Eng spkn; no adv bkg; ccard acc; quiet. "Superb situation; vg Mexican rest; helpful staff; vg site." 1 Mar-31 Oct. € 36.00 2009*

PALAU *1C4* (400m E Coastal) *41.17916, 9.39333* **Villaggio Camping Baia Saraceno (Part Naturist), Punta Nera, 07020 Palau (SS) [0789 709403; fax 709425; info@baiasaraceno.com; www.baiasaraceno.com]** Take rd S133 SE fr Sta Teresa-Gallura (ferry fr Corsica) sp Palau/Olbia, site sp dir Capo d'Orso. Lge, mkd pitch, pt shd; wc (some cont); chem disp; mv service pnt; shwrs inc; el pnts (3A) €3; gas; Indtte (inc dryer); supmkt high ssn; rest; snacks; pizzeria; bar; BBQ; playgrnd; beach adj; watersports; boat-launching; wifi; entmnt; 25% statics/cabins; no dogs; sep area & beach for naturists; no adv bkg; ccard acc. "Superb situation on water's edge; helpful, friendly staff; vg rest; site busy in ssn; ferry to La Maddalena islands; conv day trips to Corsica." ♦ 1 Mar-31 Oct. € 40.00 2009*

PALAU *1C4* (5km SE Coastal) *41.16116, 9.40300* **Camping Capo d'Orso, Loc Le Saline, 07020 Palau (SS) [0789 702007; fax 702006; info@capodorso.it; www.capodorso.it]** Site sp on coast rd dir Arzachena. Lge, mkd pitch, pt sl, terr, shd; wc (some cont); chem disp; mv service pnt; shwrs; el pnts (3A) €3; gas; Indtte; shop; rest; snacks; pizzeria; bar; playgrnd; pool; private sand beach adj; boat hire; sailing & diving school; watersports; tennis; cycle hire; games area; games rm; entmnt; TV; 50% statics; dogs; phone; bus (high ssn); extra for pitches adj beach high ssn; sep car park high ssn; poss cr; Eng spkn; adv bkg; quiet; CCI. "Excel family site in beautiful position; vg facs." 15 May-30 Sep. € 41.00 2009*

⊞ **PORTO SAN PAOLO** *3A2* (2km S Coastal) *40.85870, 9.64296* **Camping Tavolara, Loc Porto Taverna, 07020 Loiri-Porta San Paolo (SS) [0789 40166; fax 40000; info@camping-tavolara.it; www.camping-tavolara.it]** On SS125, sp. Med, hdg/mkd pitch, shd; wc (mainly cont); mv service pnt; shwrs inc; el pnts (3-6A) €3.50; Indtte; shop & 2km; rest; snacks; bar; playgrnd; sand beach 500m; tennis; cycle hire; entmnt; 50% statics; dogs €3; phone; site clsd Dec & early Jan; Eng spkn; adv bkg; ccard acc; red CCI. "Friendly staff; conv ferries & boat trips." € 43.00 2011*

PORTO TORRES *3A1* (7km E Coastal) *40.81607, 8.48541* **Camping Golfo dell'Asinara-Cristina, Loc Platamona, 07037 Sorso (SS) [079 310230; fax 310589; info@campingasinara.it; www.campingasinara.it]** Foll coast rd SP81 E fr Porto-Torres to site. Sp. Lge, pt shd; wc; mv service pnt; shwrs; el pnts (4A) €4; gas; Indtte; shop; rest; snacks; bar; playgrnd; pool; sand beach adj; tennis; games area; cycle hire; 40% statics; no dogs; sep car park; poss cr; quiet; ccard acc; red long stay/CCI. "Gd position." ♦ 1 May-30 Sep. € 34.00 2010*

⊞ **PULA** *3B1* (4km S Coastal) *38.96779, 8.97799* **Camping Flumendosa, Santa Margherita, Km 33.800, 09010 Pula (CA) [070 9208364; fax 9249282; info@campingflumendosa.it; www.campingflumendosa.it]** Fr Cagliari take SS195 past Pula, sp. Turn L, foll track for 500m to site ent. Med, hdstg, pt shd; wc; chem disp; mv service pnt; shwrs €0.50; el pnts (3A) €3; gas; Indtte; shop; rest 1km; snacks; bar; playgrnd; sand beach; boat & cycle hire; windsurfing; waterskiing; canoeing; golf 4km; 20% statics; dogs €2.50; sep car park; poss cr; Eng spkn; adv bkg; quiet; ccard acc; red low ssn. "Beautiful coastline; excel for children; sand flies abound." ♦ € 27.00 2011*

QUARTU SANT' ELENA *3B1* (7km SE Coastal) *39.20584, 9.31996* **Camping Pini e Mare, Viale Leonardo Da Vinci, Capitana, 09045 Quartu-Sant'Elena (CA) [tel/fax 070 803103; info@piniemare.com; www.piniemare.com]** Fr Cagliari take Villasimius rd. Site just past Capitana on L, sp. Med, mkd pitch, pt sl, terr, shd; wc (mainly cont); shwrs €0.50; el pnts (6A) inc (long lead, rev pol); Indtte; shop; snacks; bar; sand beach adj; 30% statics; dogs €3; phone; bus to Cagliari adj; poss cr; Eng spkn; some rd noise; red CCI. "Bus tickets fr recep; rec 'trenino verdi' (little green train); beach via tunnel under rd." 15 Mar-31 Oct. € 36.00 2007*

SANT' ANTIOCO *3B1* (12km SW Coastal) *39.00691, 8.38752* **Tonnara Camping, Cala Sapone, 09017 Sant' Antioco (CA) [0781 809058; fax 809036; mail@camping-tonnara.it; www.campingtonnara.co.uk]** Fr Cagliari take S130 & then S126. Site on W coast of Isola-di-S. Antiocio. Lge, hdg/mkd pitch, shd; wc; mv service pnt; shwrs; el pnts (6A) inc; gas; Indtte; shop; rest; bar; pool; sand/shgl beach; tennis; games area; scuba-diving school; sep car park; dogs €6; phone; bus 100m; poss cr; adv bkg; quiet; ccard acc; red low ssn. "Delightful, peaceful site in gd location; some narr lanes." 1 Apr-30 Sep. € 49.00 2011*

SINISCOLA *3A2* (7km E Coastal) *40.57853, 9.77306* **Camping Selema, Thiria Soliana, 08029 Santa Lucia-di-Siniscola (NU) [tel/fax 0784 819068; info@selemacamping.com; www.selemacamping.com]** Sp fr coast rd S125. Lge, mkd pitch, pt sl, terr, pt shd; wc; chem disp; mv service pnt; shwrs inc; el pnts (6A) €4.50; Indtte; shop; rest; snacks; bar; playgrnd; pool; paddling pool; sand beach adj; tennis; games area; horseriding; cycle hire; wifi; 30% statics; poss cr; adv bkg; red low ssn; CCI. "Excel clean facs; site in pine forest; might be diff for lge o'fits if cr." 1 Apr-31 Oct. € 45.50 (CChq acc) 2011*

SORSO see Porto Torres *3A1*

TEULADA *3B1* (7km SW Coastal) *38.92669, 8.71153* **Camping Proturismo Portu Tramatzu, 09019 Teulada (CA) [0709 283027; fax 283028; coop.proturismo@libero.it]** Sp fr Teulada on SP71 & fr coast rd. Med, terr, pt shd; wc; mv service pnt; shwrs; el pnts (5A) inc; gas; Indtte; shop; rest, snacks, bar high ssn; BBQ; playgrnd; sand beach adj; games area; entmnt; some statics; dogs €3; sep car park high ssn; Eng spkn; adv bkg; red CCI. "Vg." ♦ Easter-31 Oct. € 33.00 2010*

⊞ **TONARA** *3A1* (200m N Rural) *40.02851, 9.17578* **Camping Sa Colonia, Via Muggianeddu 4, 08039 Tonara (NU) [03921 282340; info@campingsacolonia.it; www.campingsacolonia.it]** Fr S fr Cagliari on SS128/SS295, site sp. Sp route unsuitable lge car + c'van o'fits or v lge m'vans. Avoid town cent streets - v narr & steep. Med, mkd pitch, terr, shd; wc; chem disp (wc); shwrs; el pnts (5A) inc; shop in town; rest; bar; playgrnd; no statics; Eng spkn; quiet. CCI. "Mountain scenery; rds gd but steep, twisty & slow." € 15.00 2010*

TORTOLI *3A2* (5km E Coastal) *39.90810, 9.67830* **Camping Orri, Loc Orri, 08048 Tortoli (NU) [0782 624695; fax 624685; camping.orri@tiscali.it; www.campingorri.it]** E fr Tortoli to Arbatax, site sp along coast rd. Med, shd; wc (some cont); chem disp; mv service pnt; shwrs inc; el pnts (4A) €2.50; Indtte; shop; tradsmn; rest; snacks; bar; BBQ; playgrnd; pool; paddling pool; sand beach adj; lake fishing; cycle hire; games area; horseriding 1km; entmnt; TV rm; statics; dogs; adv bkg; quiet; red CCI. "Eng spkn." ♦ 1 May-20 Sep. € 42.00 (CChq acc) 2011*

There aren't many sites open at this time of year. We'd better phone ahead to check the one we're heading for is open.

VALLEDORIA *1B4* (1km W Coastal) *40.93333, 8.81694* **Camping La Foce, Via Ampurias 1, 07039 Valledoria (SS) [079 582109; fax 582191; info@foce.it; www.foce.it]** Fr Porto Torres N via Castelsardo to Valledoria, site sp twd sea. Lge, shd; wc (some cont); chem disp; mv service pnt; shwrs inc; el pnts (4A) €1.50; gas; Indtte (inc dryer); shop; rest; snacks; bar; no BBQ; playgrnd; pool; paddling pool; sand beach adj; fishing; canoeing; watersports; tennis; cycle hire; games aea; wifi; 10% statics; dogs €3; sep car park; poss cr; adv bkg; ccard acc. 25 Apr-30 Sep. € 35.00 (CChq acc) 2011*

SICILY

⊞ **ACIREALE** *3C4* (1km N Coastal/Urban) *37.60638, 15.17027* **Camping Panorama, Via Santa Caterina 55, 95024 Acireale (CT) [095 7634124; fax 605987; info@panoramavillage.it; www.panoramavillage.it]** A18 a'strada fr Messina to Catania take Acireale exit. Panorama situated nr Aloha Hotel. Lge, shd; wc (some cont); chem disp; mv service pnt; shwrs inc; el pnts (4A) €3; gas; Indtte; shop; rest; snacks; pizzeria; bar; playgrnd; pool; beach nr; boat hire/trips; tennis; games area; entmnt; TV; mainly statics; phone; adv bkg; quiet; ccard acc. "Excursions to Etna volcano, Siracusa & Taormina; facs need maintenance, clean but basic." ♦ € 33.00 2008*

⊞ **ACIREALE** *3C4* (1.5km NE Coastal) *37.62015, 15.17320* **La Timpa International Camping, Via Santa Maria La Scala 25, 95024 Acireale (CT) [095 7648155; fax 7640049; info@campinglatimpa.com; www.campinglatimpa.com]** Exit A18/E45 onto rd S114 dir Acireale. Foll sp for Santa Maria La Scala; site on L after 1.5km; steep & diff access rds Med, pt shd; wc; shwrs; el pnts (6A) €3.50; Indtte; shop high ssn; rest; snacks; bar; playgrnd; beach adj; 60% statics; dogs €4 (not acc Jul/Aug); sep car park; poss noisy; ccard acc; red CCI. "Site in orchard, surfaced in black volcanic ash; ltd open-air shwrs only; nearest chem disp in g'ge uphill; trips to Etna; lift down to rocky beach; sh, steep walk to vill & harbour." ♦ € 31.50 2009*

⊞ **AGRIGENTO** *3C3* (4km SE Coastal) *37.24395, 13.61423* **Camping Internazionale Nettuno, Via Lacco Ameno 3, San Leone, 92100 Agrigento [tel/fax 0922 416268; info@campingnettuno.com; www.campingnettuno.com]** Fr Agrigento to San Leone on SS115, foll rd SE out of San Leone alongside beach until sharp L away fr beach. Turn immed R into lane, site on R. Med, hdg pitch, hdstg, terr, pt shd; wc (some cont); chem disp; mv service pnt; shwrs inc; el pnts (6A) €2.50 (rev pol); gas; Indtte; shop; tradsmn; rest; snacks; bar; BBQ; sand beach adj; wifi; entmnt; TV rm; 15% statics; dogs free; phone; poss cr; adv bkg; ccard acc; red long stay/CCI. "Bus to temples at Agrigento; peaceful, unspoilt beach; steep slope to pitches - towed c'vans rec to keep to upper levels if poss; gd rest; take care low branches." ♦ € 24.00 2009*

⊞ **AGRIGENTO** *3C3* (8km S Coastal/Urban) *37.26936, 13.58299* **Camping Valle dei Templi, Viale Emporium, 92110 San Leone [tel/fax 0922 411115; info@campingvelledeitempli.com; www.campingvalledeitempli.com]** Sp S of Agrigento, foll sp San Leone, site on L bef beach. Lge, some hdstg, pt sl, terr, pt shd; wc; chem disp; mv service pnt; shwrs inc; el pnts (6A) €3; Indtte; shop adj; rest; snacks; bar; beach 800m; tennis; cycle hire; 20% statics; dogs; phone adj; bus; site clsd 8 Dec-15 Jan; poss cr; Eng spkn; adv bkg; ccard acc; red long stay/CCI. "Gd modern facs; no potable water on site; bus to temples fr site ent." ♦ € 26.50 2009*

⊞ **AVOLA** *3C4* (4km N Coastal) *36.93631, 15.17462* **Camping Sabbiadoro, 96012 Avola (SR) [tel/fax 0931 560000; info@campeggiosabbiadoro.com; www.campeggiosabbiadoro.com]** Fr N exit A18/E45 at Cassibile onto S115 dir Avola, site sp in 4km. Last 500m on narr, winding rd. Med, mkd pitch, terr, pt sl, shd; wc; chem disp; mv service pnt; shwrs €0.50; el pnts (2A) €4; Indtte; shop & 2km; snacks; bar; dir access to sand beach; horseriding; wifi; 20% statics; dogs; phone; sep car park Jul-Aug; adv bkg; quiet; ccard acc. "V attractive site with clean, ltd facs; rec visit Noto." € 32.00 (CChq acc) 2011*

AVOLA *3C4* (5km NE Coastal) *36.93853, 15.17756* **Camping Paradiso del Mare, Contrada Gallinara Fondolupo, 96012 Avola (SR) [tel/fax 0931 561147; info@paradisodelmare.com; www.paradisodelmare.com]** Best app fr N on S115 fr Siracusa, site on L, well sp. Tight turn if app fr Avola. Sm, mkd pitch, pt shd; wc; chem disp; shwrs inc; el pnts (5A) €3; Indtte; shop; tradsmn; rest 3km; snacks; bar; beach adj; dogs; bus 200m; Eng spkn; quiet; CCI. "Pleasant site." ♦ 1 May-30 Sep. € 23.00 2007*

⊞ **BRUCOLI** *3C4* (E Coastal) *37.28191, 15.18941* **Camping Baia del Silenzio, Campolato Basso, 96010 Brucoli (SR) [0931 981881; fax 982288; www.baiadelsilenzio.net; www.baiadelsilenzio.net]** Sp fr Brucoli stn level x-ing, E of rd SS114. Lge, mkd pitch, pt sl, shd; wc (some cont); chem disp; mv service pnt; shwrs inc; el pnts (2A) €8; Indtte; shop; tradsmn; rest; snacks; bar; sm sandy/rocky beach adj; tennis; 20% statics; dogs €5 (not acc Jul/Aug); phone; sep car park high ssn; adv bkg; poss noisy; ccard acc; red low ssn; CCI. "Clean, well-maintained site with gd facs; conv Siracusa, Catania & Mt Etna." ♦ € 43.00 2009*

CALATABIANO see Taormina *3C4*

You can now fill in site reports online

CAPO D'ORLANDO *3B3* (1km W Coastal) *38.12866, 14.70936* **Camping Santa Rosa, Via Trazzera Marina 761, 98071 Capo-d'Orlando (ME) [0941 901723; info@campingsantarosa.com; www.agatirno.it/santarosa/]** Fr S113 fr Palermo in Capo d'Orlando cross over rlwy line at level x-ing or carry on to end of town & acc 'lungomare' at E end. Site well sp. Med, hdg pitch, pt shd; wc; chem disp; mv service pnt; shwrs inc; el pnts (6A) €3; Indry rm; shop; rest; bar; playgrnd; pool; sand/shgl beach adj; TV rm; 20% statics; phone; poss cr; rec CCI. "Pleasant, friendly, simple site." 15 Jun-15 Sep. € 27.50 2010*

CASTELLAMMARE DEL GOLFO *3C3* (1km E Coastal) *38.02393, 12.89348* **Nausicaa Camping, C/da Spiaggia-Plaia, Loc Forgia, 91014 Castellammare-del-Golfo (TP) [0924 33030; fax 35173; info@nausicaa-camping.it; www.nausicaa-camping.it]** Site 1km E fr Castellammare on R of rte 187. Well sp. Awkward ent for lge outfits as steep ramp. Sm, mkd pitch, hdstg, pt shd; wc; chem disp; shwrs inc; el pnts €3; gas; Indry rm; shop; rest 100m; snacks; playgrnd; sand beach adj; tennis; some statics; quiet; ccard acc; CCI. "Nr Roman temple at Segesta; gd 1st stop fr Palermo if touring historical sites." 1 Mar-31 Oct. € 42.00 2009*

CASTELLAMMARE DEL GOLFO *3C3* (4.5km NW Coastal) *38.05596, 12.83868* **Camping Baia di Guidaloca, Corso Garibaldi, 91014 Scopello (TP) [0924 541262; fax 531277; giovannitod@libero.it]** Fr SS187 foll sp bet km 34 & 33 dir Scopello, site sp on L. Med, pt shd; wc; chem disp; shwrs inc; el pnts (3A) €2.50; shop 2km; rest 2km; snacks; bar; sand beach adj; 10% statics; phone; bus; sep car park high ssn; poss cr; adv bkg; quiet; CCI. "Conv Zingaro nature reserve - v beautiful; vg." 1 Apr-30 Sep. € 27.00 2008*

⊞ **CASTELVETRANO** *3C3* (12km SE Rural) *37.59764, 12.84269* **Camping Maggiolino, Contrada Garroffo, 91022 Marinella di Selinunte (TP) [tel/fax 0924 46044; info@campingmaggiolino.it; www.campingmaggiolino.it]** Exit SS115 (Castelvetrano-Sciacca) at sp to Selinunte, site on L bef Selinunte. Sm, pt shd, hdstg; wc; shwrs; el pnts (3A) €2; shop 1km; Indtte; snacks; bar; playgrnd; sand beach 1.5km; tennis; cycle hire; dogs; Eng spkn; quiet; ccard acc; red CCI. "Ideal for Greek city of Selinunte, temples, etc; not suitable lge outfits." ♦ € 21.00 2009*

⊞ **CASTELVETRANO** *3C3* (13km SE Coastal) *37.59571, 12.84139* **Camping Athena, Loc Marinella, Contrada Garraffo, 91022 Castelvetrano (TP) [tel/fax 0924 46132; info@campingathenaselinunte.it; www.campingathenaselinunte.it]** Exit SS115 (Castelvetrano-Sciacca) at sp to Selinunte, site on L bef Selinunte. Sm, some hdstg, pt shd; wc; mv service pnt; shwrs inc; el pnts (10A) inc; Indtte; shop 1km; rest; snacks; bar; BBQ; sand beach 800m; dogs; phone; ccard acc; red CCI. "Can take lger outfits than Maggiolino site; conv temples at Selinunte." 2008*

⊞ **CATANIA** *3C4* (6km NE Coastal) *37.53194, 15.12055* **Camping Jonio, Loc Ognina, Via Villini a Mare 2, 95126 Catania [095 491139; fax 492277; info@campingjonio.com; www.campingjonio.com]** Fr A18 foll sp Catania Est, then foll lge brown sp for site. Med, hdstg, terr; pt shd; wc; baby facs; shwrs; el pnts €3.20; gas; Indtte; shop, supmkt nrby; rest; snacks; bar; playgrnd; rocky beach; waterskiing; games area; wifi; 85% statics; no dogs high ssn; bus to Catania; sep car park; no adv bkg; ccard acc; red low ssn/CCI. "Mt Etna 45 mins drive N; owner v helpful; some pitches sm." ♦ € 31.50 2008*

CEFALU *3B3* (3km W Coastal) *38.02703, 13.98283* **Camping Costa Ponente, C de Ogliastrillo, 90015 Cefalù (PA) [0921 420085; fax 424492]** Fr Palermo E twd Cefalù, on rd SS113 at km stone 190.3, site sp. Lge, hdstg, terr, shd; wc (some cont); chem disp; shwrs; el pnts (3A) €5; gas; Indry rm; shop & 4km; tradsmn; rest high ssn; snacks; bar; pool; paddling pool; sand beach (down steep steps); tennis; 10% statics; dogs €3.50 (not acc Aug); bus nr; sep car park (high ssn); poss cr; no adv bkg; poss noisy; ccard acc; 5% red CCI. ♦ 1 Apr-31 Oct. € 30.00 2009*

⊞ **DONNALUCATA** *3C3* (2km E Rural/Coastal) **Camping Club Piccadilly, Via Mare Adriatico, Contrada da Spinasanta, 97010 Donnalucata (RG) [0932 938704; fax 931113; info@club-piccadilly.it; www.club-piccadilly.it]** Site sp fr coast rd bet Donnalucata & Cava d'Aliga, Med, mkd pitch, hdstg, pt shd; wc; chem disp; mv service pnt; shwrs €0.80; el pnts (5A) €3; gas 2km; Indtte; shop 2km; tradsmn; rest, snacks, 2km bar; playgrnd; htd, covrd pool 15km; sand beach adj; internet; TV rm; dogs €2; poss cr; Eng spkn; adv bkg; red long stay; CCI. "Gd touring base; excursions to Malta high ssn; v friendly owner sells own wine." ♦ € 26.00 2008*

⊞ **FINALE** *3B3* (500m W Coastal) *38.02305, 14.15388* **Camping Rais Gerbi, SS119, Km 172.9, 90010 Finale (PA) [0921 426570; fax 426577; camping@raisgerbi.it; www.raisgerbi.it]** Direct access fr SS113 immed after bdge W of Finale. Lge, hdg/mkd pitch, mainly hdstg, terr, pt shd; wc; chem disp; mv service pnt; shwrs inc; el pnts (6A) €4; Indtte; shop; tradsmn; rest; snacks; bar; BBQ; playgrnd; pool; private shgl beach 600m; tennis; games area; cycle hire; horseriding 200m; entmnt; internet; TV rm; 13% statics; dogs free; phone; bus; poss cr; Eng spkn; adv bkg (min 10 day stay); quiet but some rlwy noise; ccard acc; red long stay/CCI. "Gd touring base Cefalu & N coast; friendly, helpful staff; excel, clean site & facs." ♦ € 37.00 2008*

GIARDINI NAXOS see Taormina *3C4*

ISOLA DELLE FEMMINE see Palermo *3B3*

LETOJANNI see Taormina *3C4*

ITALY - SICILY

⊞ **MARINA DI RAGUSA** *3C3* (1km E Coastal) **Camping Baia del Sole, Lungomare Andrea Doria, 97010 Marina-di-Ragusa (RG) [0932 239844; fax 230344]** Foll sp in Marina di Ragusa for Hotel Baia del Sole. Site in hotel grounds on dual c'way on seafront. Med, shd; wc; shwrs inc; el pnts (3A) inc; Indtte; shop high ssn; supmkt 1.5km; rest; snacks; bar; playgrnd; pool; beach adj; tennis; cycle hire; sep car park; adv bkg; quiet but noise fr disco; ccard acc. "3m height barrier at ent - 2nd gate further on - go to recep 1st." € 28.50 2007*

MASCALI see Taormina *3C4*

MAZARA DEL VALLO *3C3* (1km E Coastal) *37.63630, 12.61722* **Sporting Club Camping, Contrada da Bocca Arena, 91026 Mazara-del-Vallo (TP) [tel/fax 0923 947230; info@sportingcampingvillage.com; www.sportingclubvillage.com]** Site 1km fr S115, clearly sp (brown) fr all dirs. Lge, pt shd; wc (some cont); chem disp; mv service pnt; shwrs inc; el pnts (6A) €5; Indtte; shop; rest; snacks; bar; BBQ; playgrnd; pool; beach 500m; tennis; games area; games rm; entmnt; 5% statics; dogs; bus 500m; dogs €4; poss cr; Eng spkn; red long stay/low ssn; ccard acc; CCI. "Interesting area." ♦ 1 Apr-1 Oct. € 32.00 2009*

⊞ **MENFI** *3C3* (6km S Coastal) *37.56500, 12.96416* **Camping La Palma, Contrada Fiore, Via delle Palme 29, 92013 Menfi (AG) [tel/fax 0925 78392; campinglapalma@libero.it; www.camping-lapalma.com]** Foll sp fr SS115 past Menfi to coast. Med, pt shd; wc; chem disp; shwrs; el pnts €3; gas; Indtte; rest; snacks; bar; shop; playgrnd; sand beach adj; quiet; CCI. "Lovely, unspoilt beach with dunes; v helpful owner & staff." € 23.50 2007*

MESSINA *3B4* (12km W Coastal) *38.25920, 15.46779* **Camping Il Peloritano, Contrada Tarantonia, Km 28, 98161 Rodia-Messina (ME) [tel/fax 090 348496; il_peloritano@yahoo.it; www.peloritanocamping.it]** Fr Messina on A20 take exit Villafranca. Turn R onto rd S113 dir Rodia, site 2km on R. Fr Palermo exit sp Rometta, under m'way & turn R, site on R in approx 5km. Med, mkd pitch, pt sl, pt shd; htd wc; chem disp; mv service pnt; shwrs €0.50; el pnts (6A) €4; gas; Indtte; shop; tradsmn; rest; snacks; bar; playgrnd; htd, covrd pool; sand beach; wifi; entmnt; excursions; dogs; phone; bus; poss cr; Eng spkn; adv bkg; quiet; red long stay/CCI. "Local bus to Messina; site in olive grove; low trees & tight ent poss diff lge o'fits; old but clean san facs; conv Messina ferry; vg." ♦ 1 Mar-31 Oct. € 27.00 2009*

MILAZZO *3B4* (4km N Coastal) *38.26222, 15.24387* **Villaggio Turistico Cirucco, Strada Panoramica 66, Capo di Milazzo, 98057 Milazzo (ME) [090 9284746; fax 9287384; info@cirucco.it; www.cirucco.it]** Foll Capo di Milazzo sp fr Milazzo, site sp adj Camping Riva Smeralda. Diff, narr app. Med, hdstg, pt sl, terr, pt shd; wc; chem disp; mv service pnt; shwrs inc; el pnts (6A); shop; rest; snacks; bar; playgrnd; private shgl beach 100m; internet; entmnt; 30% statics; sep car park high ssn; poss cr; Eng spkn; red long stay. "Insufficient san facs; private beach down steps; barrier clsd 1400-1600; gd base Stromboli." 1 Apr-31 Oct. € 35.00 2009*

⊞ **MILO** *3C4* (1km S Rural) *37.71434, 15.11703* **Camping Mareneve, Via del Bosco 30/B, 95010 Milo (CT) [095 7082163; fax 7083417; campmareneve@tiscalinet.it]** Foll sp S fr Milo or N fr Zafferana Etnea, sp on rd SP59. Med, pt sl, terr, pt shd; wc; shwrs inc; el pnts (3A) inc; rest; snacks; bar; pool; 20% statics; dogs; poss cr; adv bkg; cccard acc; CCI. "On E flank of Mount Etna; basic site & not well-maintained; fair sh stay only." € 22.00 2008*

⊞ **MONTALLEGRO** *3C3* (5km S Rural/Coastal) **Camping Torre Salsa Agriturismo, 92010 Montallegro (AG) [tel/fax 0922 847074; info@torresalsa.it; www.torresalsa.it]** Fr SS115 take exit Montallegro West & foll sp to site. On leaving site turn 1st L, then R to get back to SS115. Sm, mkd pitch, hdstg, pt sl, pt shd; wc (some cont); chem disp; mv service pnt; shwrs €1; el pnts (10A) €2.50; Indtte; shop 5km; tradsmn; sand beach adj; some statics; dogs €1; phone; Eng spkn; adv bkg; quiet; CCI. "Beautiful, well-kept site on hilltop farm o'looking beach in nature reserve; san facs ltd but excel; helpful, friendly owners; 3 night min stay preferred; conv Agrigento." ♦ € 22.00 2008*

⊞ **NICOLOSI** *3C3* (1km N Rural) *37.62303, 15.00854* **Camping Etna, Via Goethe s/n, Monti Rossi, 95030 Nicolosi (CT) [tel/fax 095 914309; campingetna@tiscali.it]** Fr Nicolosi on SP92 foll sp Etna Sud, turn L just bef Titanic rest. Site on L in pinewood, sp. Med, mkd pitch, terr, shd; wc; chem disp; mv service pnt; el pnts (6A) inc; Indtte; shop 1km; tradsmn; rest 500m; snacks; bar; BBQ; playgrnd; pool; paddling pool; entmnt; TV rm; 50% statics; dogs; poss cr; Eng spkn; poss noisy; CCI. "Gd, modern san facs; friendly staff; v conv Etna." ♦ € 22.80 2010*

NOTO *3C4* (1.8km SE Rural) **Noto Parking Camper & Caravan, Contrada Faldino, 96017 Noto [0328 8065260]** E fr Ragusa on SS115, turn R on ent o'skts of Noto onto SP35 at sp, site 100m on L. Sm, hdstg, pt shd; chem disp; mv service pnt; shwrs (cold); BBQ; sand beach 5km; dogs; train 1.8km; quiet; CCI. "Conv Neto; train to Siracusa; v helpful, friendly owners provide transport to Neto & stn; gd." Apr-Sep. € 10.00 2008*

⊞ **OLIVERI** *3B4* (1.5km N Coastal) *38.12913, 15.05813* **Camping Villaggio Marinello, Via del Sole 17, Marinello, 98060 Oliveri (ME) [0941 313000; fax 313702; marinello@camping.it; www.camping.it/sicilia/marinello]** Exit A20 Falcone dir Oliveri, site well sp. Lge, hdg/mkd pitch, hdstg, pt shd; wc; chem disp; mv service pnt; shwrs inc; el pnts (6A) inc; Indtte; shop; rest high ssn; snacks bar; playgrnd; sand/shgl beach adj; watersports; tennis; excursions; 20% statics; dogs free (not acc Jul/Aug); phone; train; poss cr; Eng spkn; quiet but some rlwy noise; red CCI. "Basic, clean, well-managed site not suitable lge o'fits; excel but shelving beach; helpful staff." ♦ € 32.50 2008*

camping luminoso

OPEN WHOLE YEAR

Modern camping by the sea - Private beach - Wi-Fi
Private baths with hot water
Shady pitches and bounded
Children's playground
Comfortable Mobile homes
Cars available

www.campingluminoso.com

Viale dei Canalotti - Punta Braccetto
S. Croce Camerina (Rg) Sicilia
Tel. 0039 0932 918401
Fax 0039 0932 918455
Mobile 0039 338 2202010
e-mail: info@campingluminoso.com
GPS 14° 27' 57" E - 36° 49' 02" N

PALERMO *3B3* (12km NW Coastal) *38.19686, 13.24455* **Camping La Playa, Viale Marino 55, 90040 Isola delle Femmine (PA) [tel/fax 091 8677001; campinglaplaya@virgilio.it; www.campinglaplaya.net]** On Palermo-Trapani rd take A29 exit Isola-delle-Femmine & foll sp. Med, hdstg, pt shd; wc; chem disp; mv service pnt; shwrs €0.50; el pnts (6A) inc; gas; lndtte (inc dryer); shop; rest; snacks; bar; BBQ; playgrnd; sand beach adj; dogs; Eng spkn; adv bkg; quiet; ccard acc; red CCI. "V helpful staff; bus into Palermo hourly; barrier clsd 1400-1600; v clean, well-managed, busy site." 15 Mar-15 Oct. € 27.00 2008*

⊞ **PALERMO** *3B3* (13km NW Urban/Coastal) *38.19805, 13.28083* **Camping Degli Ulivi, Via Pegaso 25, 90148 Sferracavallo (PA) [tel/fax 091 533021; mporion@libero.it; www.campingdegliulivi.com]** Fr W on A29 exit sp Tommaso & foll dual c'way twd Mondello. Do U-turn at 1st opportunity to Sferracavallo - poorly sp. Sm, pt sl, pt shd; wc; shwrs €0.50; el pnts (10A) €3; lndtte; shops 400m; rest 600m; snacks 400m; rocky beach 300m; sand beach 700m; bus to Palermo; sep car park; Eng spkn; quiet; CCI. "Helpful staff; pleasant ambience; well-maintained site nr nature park - excel views, popular site." ♦ € 25.00 2008*

⊞ **PETROSINO** *3C3* (2km W Coastal) *37.70118, 12.47748* **Camping Biscione, Via Biscione, 91020 Petrosino (TP) [tel/fax 0923 731444; leonardo.urso@tiscali.it]** Take Petrosino exit fr SS115, take beach rd out of town & foll brown camping sps. Lge, pt shd; wc; chem disp; mv waste; shwrs inc; el pnts (4A) inc; lndtte; shop 3km; tradsmn; rest; bar; playgrnd; sand beach 400m; tennis; games area; entmnt; few statics; Eng spkn; quiet; red long stay/CCI. "Gd site; helpful owner." ♦ € 25.00 2008*

⊞ **PIAZZA ARMERINA** *3C3* (4km SE Rural) *37.20239, 14.23155* **Camping Agriturismo Agricasale, C da Ciavarini, 94015 Piazza-Armerina (EN) [tel/fax 0935 686034; www.agricasale.it]** In Piazza-Armerina town foll sp twd Mirabella but at rndabt with stone cross bear R (red fox sign) & foll red fox to site. Sm, pt sl, pt shd; wc; chem disp; mv service pnt; shwrs inc; el pnts (6A) inc; lndtte; shop 4km; rest; bar; BBQ; playgrnd; pool; TV rm; dogs; poss cr; Eng spkn; adv bkg; quiet; CCI. "Excel site close Palazzo Romana mosaics; pony-trekking, archery & other activities high ssn; all inclusive rate of €50 avail per day inc excel banquet!" ♦ € 15.00 2010*

⊞ **PUNTA BRACCETTO** *3C3* (Coastal/Urban) *36.81722, 14.46583* **Camping Luminoso, Viale dei Canalotti, 97017 Punta Braccetto - Santa Croce Camerina (RG) [0932 918401; fax 918455; info@campingluminoso.com; www.campingluminoso.com]** W fr Marina di Ragusa on SP80/SC25 coast rd. Site sp. Med, mkd pitch, hdstg, shd; wc; chem disp; mv service pnt; private bathrms avail; some serviced pitches; shwrs; el pnts (6A) €5; lndtte; shop & 400m; tradsmn; rest; snacks; bar; direct access to private sand beach adj; cycle hire; wifi; child entmnt; TV; some statics; dogs free; adv bkg rec high ssn; ccard acc; red low ssn/CCI. "Well-run site in gd location; easy access to pitches - suitable lge o'fits/m'vans; excel." ♦ € 44.00 2011*

See advertisement

⊞ **PUNTA BRACCETTO** *3C3* (Coastal/Urban) *36.81713, 14.46736* **Camping Scarabeo, Via dei Canaletti 120, Punta-Braccetto, 97017 Santa Croce Camerina (RG) [0932 918096; fax 918391; info@scarabeocamping.it; www.scarabeocamping.it]** W fr Marina di Ragusa on SP80/SC25 coast rd. Site sp. Sm, mkd pitch, hdstg, pt sl, pt shd; wc; chem disp; mv service pnt; private bthrm €4; shwrs €0.60; el pnts (3-6A) €3.50-4.50; lndtte (inc dryer); shop & 4km; tradsmn; rest, snacks 600m, bar nr; BBQ; direct access to sand beach adj; wifi; child entmnt; 5% statics; dogs €2.50; phone; poss cr; Eng spkn; adv bkg; quiet; red long stay; CCI. "Beautiful situation; well-maintained, friendly, family-run site; gd, clean, modern facs; vg security; friendly, helpful staff; excel." ♦ € 37.50 (CChq acc) 2011*

See advertisement on next page

SAN VITO LO CAPO *3B3* (Urban/Coastal) *38.17471, 12.73218* **Camping La Fata, Via Mattarella 68, 91010 San Vito-lo-Capo (TP) [tel/fax 0923 972133; lafata@trapaniweb.it; www.trapaniweb.it/lafata]** Fr E exit A29 at Castellammare-del-Golfo onto S187. After 24km turn R sp San Vito-lo-Capo, site sp. Fr Trapani foll S187 sp Valderice for 16km, turn L at sp San Vito. Med, mkd pitch, hdstg, pt sl, pt shd; wc; chem disp; shwrs €0.50; el pnts (6A) €3; gas 500m; lndtte; shop & 500m; rest 500m; snacks, bar high ssn; sand beach 500m; entmnt; 35% statics; dogs; phone adj; poss cr; Eng spkn; adv bkg; quiet; ccard acc; CCI. "Pleasant, friendly site; site ent poss diff; conv town, beach & Zingaro nature park; some manhandling of vans poss req." ♦ 1 Jun-30 Sep. € 24.50 2008*

Scarabeo
Camping ★★★
I-97017 Santa Croce Camerina
(RAGUSA) Punta Braccetto
Tel. 0039.0932.918391-918096
Tel. 0039.0932.918459
Fax 0039.0932.918391
info@scarabeocamping.it
www.scarabeocamping.it
CAMPING FAMILY RUN CAMPSITE
OPEN ALL YEAR. Situated directly on the beautiful bay of Punta Braccetto with its fine golden sand, this family-run campsite distinguishes itself for its tranquillity and cleanliness, its well-tended gardens and its ablutions, all with private bathrooms. Excellent starting point for excursions (guided tours also organised by the owners) towards places of archeological, historical and cultural interest. Free tastings of wines and other local products.
WINTER OFFERS: from 01/01/2012 to 31/03/2012 and from 01/10/2012 to 31/12/2012, from € 7 .- exl. electricity per night for a minimum stay of 30 nights. The offer includes: 2 people, a camper or camping, caravans and cars, electricity, hot water and private bathroom. OFFER BUNGALOW FOR TWO PEOPLE: from 01/01/2012 to 31/03/2012 and from 01/10/2012 to 31/12/2012, from €13.00 per night for a minimum stay of 60 nights.
GPS: N 36° 49' 01.7" E 14° 28' 02.5"

⊞ **SAN VITO LO CAPO** *3B3* (1km E Coastal) *38.17395, 12.74795* **Camping La Pineta, Via del Secco 88, 91010 San Vito-lo-Capo (TP) [0923 972818; fax 974070; info@campinglapineta.it; www.campinglapineta.it]** Foll sp fr town. Lge, mkd pitch, hdstg, pt sl, shd; htd wc; chem disp; mv service pnt; shwrs €0.50; el pnts (6A) €5; Indtte; shop; rest; bar; BBQ; playgrnd; pool; paddling pool; sand beach 1km; cycle hire; games area; wifi; entmnt; 30% statics; phone; site clsd Nov; Eng spkn; ccard acc; red low ssn/CCI. "Gd, clean site; easy walk to vill." ♦ € 38.00 (CChq acc) 2009*

SAN VITO LO CAPO *3B3* (3km S Coastal) *38.15067, 12.73184* **El Bahira Camping Village, Contrada Salinella, 91010 San Vito-lo-Capo (TP) [0923 972577; fax 972552; info@elbahira.it; www.elbahira.it]** W fr Palermo on A29 dir Trapani. Exit at Castellammare del Golfo onto SS187, then turn N onto SP16 sp San Vito-lo-Capo. At Isolidda foll site sp. Lge, mkd pitch, shd; wc (some cont); chem disp; el pnts (6A) inc; Indtte; shops; rest; snacks; bar; pizzeria; BBQ; playgrnd; pool (sw caps req); paddling pool; sand/shgl beach adj; watersports; tennis; games area; games rm; entmnt; excursions; TV; some statics; phone; bus nr; sep car park; Eng spkn; ccard acc; quiet; CCI. "Excel, secure site in vg location; gd facs for families." ♦ 1 Apr-4 Oct. € 35.40 2009*

⊞ **SECCAGRANDE** *3C3* (Coastal) *37.43833, 13.2450* **Kamemi Camping Village, Contrada Camemi Superiore, 92016 Seccagrande-di-Ribera (AG) [tel/fax 0925 69212; info@kamemicamping.it; www.kamemicamping.it]** Foll sp fr S115 to Seccagrande & site. Med, hdstg, pt shd; wc; shwrs inc; el pnts (6A) €5; Indtte; rest; snacks; bar; playgrnd; 2 pools; sand beach 1km; tennis; games area; entmnt; 30% statics; dogs free; sep car park high ssn; Eng spkn; adv bkg. ♦ € 34.00 2008*

SFERRACAVALLO **see Palermo** *3B3*

⊞ **SIRACUSA** *3C4* (Urban) *37.07716, 15.28756* **Area Van Platen, Via Augusto Von Platen, 96100 Siracusa (SR)** In town cent, v close to archeological museum. Foll sp. Med, mkd pitch, unshd; wc; chem disp; mv service pnt; shwrs inc; el pnts inc; shop, rest, snacks, bar nr; BBQ; bus adj; poss cr; Eng spkn; adv bkg; quiet. "Excel location; 24 hr access & guard; friendly, helpful staff; walking dist archeological sites; m'vans & c'vans acc." € 15.00 2008*

⊞ **SIRACUSA** *3C4* (4km SW Rural) *37.03841, 15.25063* **Camping Agritourist Rinaura, Strada Laganelli, Loc Rinaura, SS115, 96100 Siracusa [tel/fax 0931 721224; marinas@sistenia.it]** S fr Siracusa on S115 twd Avola. Turn R 300m past Hotel Albatros then immed R after rlwy x-ing. Narr lane to site in 300m. Lge, pt shd; wc; chem disp (wc); shwrs €0.60; el pnts (16A) €3; shop high ssn; rest 2km; bar; playgrnd; sand beach 2km; cycle hire; phone; bus 1km; poss cr; Eng spkn; adv bkg; noise fr nrby hol camp; red long stay/CCI. "CL-type site in lge orchard; basic but adequate san facs; rather neglected low ssn; helpful owners." ♦ € 21.00 2008*

TAORMINA *3C4* (7km N Coastal) *37.89718, 15.3268* **Camping Paradise, Loc Meliano, 98037 Letojanni (ME) [tel/fax 0942 36306; campingparadise@campingparadise.it; www.campingparadise.it]** Exit A18 dir Taormina & foll SS114 dir Messina to site at km post 41. Med, hdstg, pt shd; wc (some cont); chem disp; mv service pnt; shwrs inc; el pnts (3A) €4; gas; Indtte; shop 2km; rest; bar; no BBQ; playgrnd; sand beach adj; tennis; 20% statics; no dogs; phone; poss cr; CCI. "Rec arr early; gd." ♦ 1 Apr-30 Aug. € 35.00 2008*

I'll go online and tell the Club what we think of the campsites we've visited – www.caravanclub.co.uk/europereport

TAORMINA *3C4* (12km S Coastal) *37.74928, 15.20616* **Camping Mokambo, Via Spiaggia 211, Fondachello, 95016 Máscali (CT) [095 938731; fax 934369; info@campingmokambo.it; www.campingmokambo.it]** Exit A18/E45 at Fiumefreddo & take S114 sp Catania. In Máscali turn L twd Fondachello. At Fondachello turn R & foll site sp, site 1km on R. Med, pt shd; wc; chem disp; shwrs €0.50; el pnts (3A) €2.80; rest; snacks; BBQ; playgrnd; beach adj; games area; wifi; 10% statics; no dogs Jul/Aug; Eng spkn; quiet; ccard acc; red CCI. "V pleasant site, gd views Etna; conv beach & Taormina." ♦ 1 Apr-30 Sep. € 25.20 2009*

⊞ **TAORMINA** *3C4* (7km SW Coastal) *37.8047, 15.2444* **Camping Internazionale Almoetia, Via San Marco 19, 95011 Calatabiano (CT) [tel/fax 095 641936; info@camping almoetia.it; www.campingalmoetia.it]** Exit a'strada dir Giardini Naxos. Turn S onto S114 dir Catania, foll sp L onto Via San Marco, site clearly sp. Med, pt shd; wc (some cont); chem disp; shwrs inc; el pnts (6A) €2.50; gas; Indtte; shop & 1.5km; rest; snacks; bar; BBQ; shgl beach 500m; cycle hire; tennis; canoeing; TV rm; dogs; phone; poss cr; adv bkg; quiet but noise fr bar in eve; red low ssn/long stay; CCI. "Conv Etna, Taormina; surrounded by orchards; used by tour groups in motor hotels; poss unkempt low ssn." ♦ € 27.00 2009*

TRAPANI *3C3* (12km NE Coastal) *38.07029, 12.63115* **Camping Lido Valderice, Via del Dentice 15, 91010 Valderice (TP) [tel/fax 0923 573477; info@campinglidovalderice.it; www.campinglidovalderice.com]** On coast 7km N of Valderice off rd S187. Fr Trapani foll sp Capo San Vito, site well sp. Med, mkd pitch, shd; wc (mainly cont); mv service pnt; shwrs inc; el pnts (2A) €2; Indtte; shop 200m; snacks, bar 200m; sand beach adj; some statics; poss noisy; ccard acc; red long stay; CCI. "Conv Erice medieval hill-top vill, Scopello & National Park; no facs low ssn." 1 Jun-30 Sep. € 23.00 2007*

VALDERICE see Trapani *3C3*

ITALY

REGIONS AND PROVINCES OF ITALY

ABRUZZO
Chieti
L'Aquila
Pescara
Teramo

BASILICATA
Matera
Potenza

CALABRIA
Catanzaro
Cosenza
Crotone
Reggio di Calabria
Vibo Valentia

CAMPANIA
Avellino
Benevento
Caserta
Napoli
Salerno

EMILIA-ROMAGNA
Bologna
Ferrara
Forlì
Modena
Parma
Piacenza
Ravenna
Reggio Emilia
Rimini

FRIULI-VENEZIA GIULIA
Gorizia
Pordenone
Trieste
Udine

LAZIO
Frosinone
Latina
Rieti
Roma
Viterbo

LIGURIA
Genova
Imperia
La Spezia
Savona

LOMBARDIA
Bergamo
Brescia
Como
Cremona
Lecco
Lodi
Mantova
Milano
Pavia
Sondrio
Varese

MARCHE
Ancona
Ascoli Piceno
Macerata
Pesaro e Urbino

MOLISE
Campobasso
Isernia

PIEMONTE
Alessandria
Asti
Biella
Cuneo
Novara
Torino
Verbano-Cusio-Ossola
Vercelli

PUGLIA
Bari
Brindisi
Foggia
Lecce
Taranto

SARDEGNA
Cagliari
Nuoro
Oristano
Sassari

SICILIA
Agrigento
Caltanissetta
Catania
Enna
Messina
Palermo
Ragusa
Siracusa
Trapani

TOSCANA
Arezzo
Firenze
Grosseto
Livorno
Lucca
Massa Carrara
Pisa
Pistoia
Prato
Siena

TRENTINO-ALTO ADIGE
Bolzano
Trento

UMBRIA
Perugia
Terni

VALLE D'AOSTA
Aosta/Aoste

VENETO
Belluno
Padova
Rovigo
Treviso
Venezia
Verona
Vicenza

Distances are shown in kilometres and are calculated from town/city centres along the most practical roads, although not necessarily taking the shortest route. 1km = 0.62miles

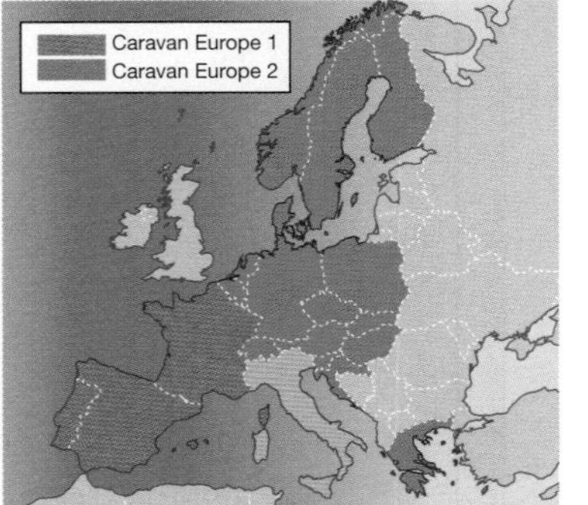

Milano (Milan) to Venezia (Venice) = 274km

	Ancona	Aosta	Bari	Bologna	Bolzano	Brindisi	Como	Cortina d'Ampezzo	Desanzano del Garda	Firenze (Florence)	Foggia	Genova (Genoa)	Grosseto	Imperia	L'Aquila	La Spezia	Livorno	Messina	Milano (Milan)	Napoli (Naples)	Orbetello	Palermo	Parma	Perugia	Pescara	Piacenza	Pisa	Ravenna	Reggio di Calabria	Roma (Rome)	Salerno	Siena	Siracusa (Syracuse)	Taranto	Torino (Turin)	Trento	Trieste	Venezia (Venice)	Verona
Aosta	619																																						
Bari	467	1075																																					
Bologna	220	404	677																																				
Bolzano	498	447	944	278																																			
Brindisi	573	1188	113	786	1062																																		
Como	475	207	929	258	290	1037																																	
Cortina d'Ampezzo	529	543	981	317	102	1090	381																																
Desanzano del Garda	385	296	839	170	188	937	134	243																															
Firenze (Florence)	262	472	724	104	369	836	355	419	261																														
Foggia	343	947	138	552	825	249	803	864	718	635																													
Genova (Genoa)	508	245	948	299	422	1062	186	497	255	225	842																												
Grosseto	324	556	634	242	512	745	497	561	463	142	552	303																											
Imperia	622	322	1066	403	529	1170	292	602	363	343	946	122	358																										
L'Aquila	203	794	392	411	697	512	675	730	586	372	272	562	305	722																									
La Spezia	428	348	872	212	370	984	274	432	247	146	773	101	232	220	498																								
Livorno	415	419	768	203	446	882	353	506	321	119	678	174	135	295	437	95																							
Messina	910	1445	455	1088	1342	457	525	1367	1469	975	556	1210	893	1317	731	1124	1022																						
Milano (Milan)	426	178	881	212	290	990	50	376	127	301	760	149	438	244	625	223	296	1272																					
Napoli (Naples)	411	962	263	596	858	374	845	1064	746	487	177	718	410	832	247	841	534	731	788																				
Orbetello	308	585	595	275	540	708	525	602	444	170	508	336	41	455	260	260	176	852	471	364																			
Palermo	1147	1682	692	1325	1579	694	1565	427	1604	1212	793	1447	1130	1554	968	1361	1265	237	1584	708	1089																		
Parma	314	315	767	98	243	879	170	315	78	185	644	205	329	310	513	122	194	1398	120	675	358	1127																	
Perugia	141	626	636	264	521	745	511	575	417	155	550	379	180	501	179	301	272	1127	457	434	169	1127	340																
Pescara	153	766	299	363	643	415	623	676	531	406	191	655	396	762	100	574	526	980	574	388	352	980	458	262															
Piacenza	365	252	815	150	261	933	115	356	115	242	703	145	379	247	565	162	236	1452	66	725	411	1452	63	399	508														
Pisa	358	401	787	182	446	902	329	487	302	100	700	162	150	270	419	77	19	1279	279	554	179	1279	172	253	499	214													
Ravenna	149	477	605	78	355	716	334	306	245	137	488	374	279	478	353	292	255	1317	285	636	306	1317	173	196	295	229	235												
Reggio di Calabria	910	1441	452	1093	1346	459	1333	1367	1232	975	557	1205	890	1315	728	1128	1018	237	1268	499	576	237	1166	890	741	1219	1035	1086											
Roma (Rome)	286	748	450	379	645	563	632	697	535	276	362	503	192	618	113	427	322	947	571	226	145	942	463	188	206	515	342	382	707										
Salerno	450	1000	240	634	898	355	885	924	787	532	152	763	448	869	286	881	578	684	830	220	405	684	715	442	295	772	599	636	446	260									
Siena	247	535	677	172	435	785	422	486	328	68	590	291	75	411	281	173	121	1165	366	534	105	1165	252	110	379	304	108	205	929	231	480								
Siracusa (Syracuse)	1064	1599	609	1242	1496	611	1482	1521	1386	1129	710	1364	1047	1471	885	1278	1136	154	135	638	1004	259	1315	1044	897	1369	1196	1234	155	859	601	1082							
Taranto	549	1156	98	760	1031	70	1009	1062	922	805	217	1028	722	1149	479	948	850	627	965	305	660	627	852	713	386	906	865	688	392	517	256	755	544						
Torino (Turin)	547	110	1006	333	412	1116	165	503	257	393	883	172	477	208	715	275	345	1607	142	885	502	1607	245	548	699	178	326	405	1375	674	927	463	1524	1089					
Trento	442	394	893	297	60	998	233	135	100	312	773	365	452	475	642	342	413	1525	242	799	485	1525	192	472	582	210	392	296	1286	593	845	381	1442	974	353				
Trieste	506	582	958	295	347	1072	421	236	286	396	839	537	538	643	706	502	492	1607	415	884	567	1607	361	550	652	395	468	288	1374	670	923	465	1524	1045	540	292			
Venezia (Venice)	364	441	816	154	214	931	279	165	147	255	694	399	399	505	566	364	348	1464	274	741	427	1464	218	413	508	255	332	143	1229	533	781	322	1381	899	403	158	159		
Verona	354	331	811	140	155	917	172	236	30	234	689	289	374	388	555	220	295	1439	167	716	403	1439	105	389	503	142	279	215	1206	505	761	295	1356	889	289	103	253	115	
Vicenza	360	376	814	150	183	925	216	167	81	252	693	334	394	439	562	374	347	1464	209	746	424	1464	155	410	505	191	327	166	1223	528	785	322	1381	901	342	144	213	73	52

SWITZERLAND
FRANCE
CORSICA (France)
BERN
Lausanne
Genève
Martigny
Chamonix-Mont-Blanc
Courmayeur
AOSTA
Cogne
Valsavarenche
St Vincent
Orta San Giulio
Settimo Vittone
Viverone
Verbania
Stresa
Arona
Sesto Calende
Cannobio
Porlezza
Luino
Lavena
COMO
MILANO
Grenoble
La Cassa
Bardonecchia
Salbertrand
Avigliana
TORINO
Briançon
Gap
Pavia
Cremona
PIACENZA
Asti
Alba
Barolo
Cuneo
Bastia Mondovi
Demonte
Entracque
Sassello
GENOVA
Savona
Finale Ligure
Albenga
IMPERIA
Diano Marina
San Remo
Vallecrosia
Nice
MONACO
Salsomaggiore Terme
Bobbio
Rizzolo
PARMA
Berceto
Rapallo
Deiva Marina
Levanto
LA SPEZIA
Sarzana
Giuncugnano
Castelnuovo di Garfagnana
Marina di Massa
Forte dei Marmi
Viareggio
Lucca
Montecatini Terme
Pistoia
PISA
Marina di Pisa
LIVORNO
FIRENZE
Fiesole
Montopoli in Val d'Arno
San Gimignano
Volterra
Poggibonsi
SIENA
Cecina
Casciano
San Vincenzo
Follonica
Marina di Campo
Capoliveri
ELBA
Castiglione della Pescaia
GROSSETO
Talamone
Capalbio
ORBETELLO
Montalto di Castro
Tarquinia
Ferrara
Modena
BOLOGNA
Lama Mocogno
Montese
Sasso Marconi
San Benedetto in Alpe
Borgo San Lorenzo
Stia
Caprese Michelangelo
Figline Valdarno
Montevarchi
Arezzo
Pienza
Sarteano
Castèl del Piano
Bolsena
Palau
Arzachena
Aglientu
Valledoria
see inset on Map 2
N
W
E
S
All year site(s)
Seasonal site(s)
No sites listed
200m +
0–200m
Motorways
Major roads
Main roads
0 50 100 150 kms
0 50 100 mls
© Collins Bartholomew Ltd 2011

AUSTRIA
SLOVENIA
CROATIA
BOSNIA-HERZEGOVINA
SAN MARINO
ADRIATIC SEA
Anterselva di Sopra/Antholz Obertal
Dobbiaco/Toblach
Sesto/Sexten
CORTINA D'AMPEZZO
Sappada
Auronzo di Cadore
Forni di Sopra
Gemona del Friuli
Farra d'Alpago
Monfalcone
Aquileia
Lignano Sabbiadoro
Bibione
Grado
TRIESTE
Caorle
Lido di Jesolo
Cavallino
Punta Sabbioni
Chioggia
Pula
Comacchio
Marina di Ravenna
RAVENNA
Cervia
Cesenatico
Bellaria
San Marino
Riccione
Pesaro
Fano
Urbino
Senigallia
ANCONA
Ostra
Numana
Porto Recanati
Citta di Castello
Gubbio
Costacciaro
Magione
PERUGIA
Assisi
Urbisaglia
Porto San Giorgio
Cupra Marittima
Martinsicuro
Preci
Giulianova Lido
Roseto degli Abruzzi
Pineto
Orvieto
Baschi
Narni
Terni
PESCARA
Ortona
L'AQUILA
Caprarola
Fiano Romano
Bracciano
ROMA
Lido di Ostia
Casalbordino
Vasto
Marina di Montenero
Bomba
Termoli
Rodi Garganico
Peschici
Vieste
Pescassèroli
Roccaraso
Opi
Barrea
San Giovanni Rotondo
Mattinata
FOGGIA
Terracina
Sperlonga
Marina di Minturno
Giovinazzo
BARI
Monopoli
Split
SARAJEVO
0 50 kms
0 25 mls
St Moritz
Vipiteno/Sterzing
Brunico/Bruneck
San Valentino alla Muta
Mals/Malles Venosta
Merano/Meran
Bressanone/Brixen
Chiusa/Klausen
Prato allo Stelvio
Laces/Latsch
Naturno/Naturns
Corvara in Badia
Fie/Vols
Bormio
BOLZANO/BOZEN
Canazei
Pozza di Fassa
Peio
Ora/Auer
Rocca Pietore
Chiavenna
Sarnonico
Dimaro
Predazzo
Sorico
San Michele All'Adige
Gravedona
Menaggio
Edolo
Molveno
Pieve Tesino
Pinzolo
Imer
Bellagio
TRENTO
Tione de Trento
Levico Terme
Pietramurata
Lecco
Pieve di Ledro
Arco
Arsie
Riva del Garda
Pisogne
Torbole
Limone sul Garda
Malcesine
Riva di Solto
Marone
Idro
Toscolano-Maderno
Iseo
Torri del Benaco
Monza
San Felice del Benaco
Manerba del Garda
Bardolino
VICENZA
Sirmione
Lazise
DESENZANO DEL GARDA
VERONA
Peschiera del Garda

Map 3

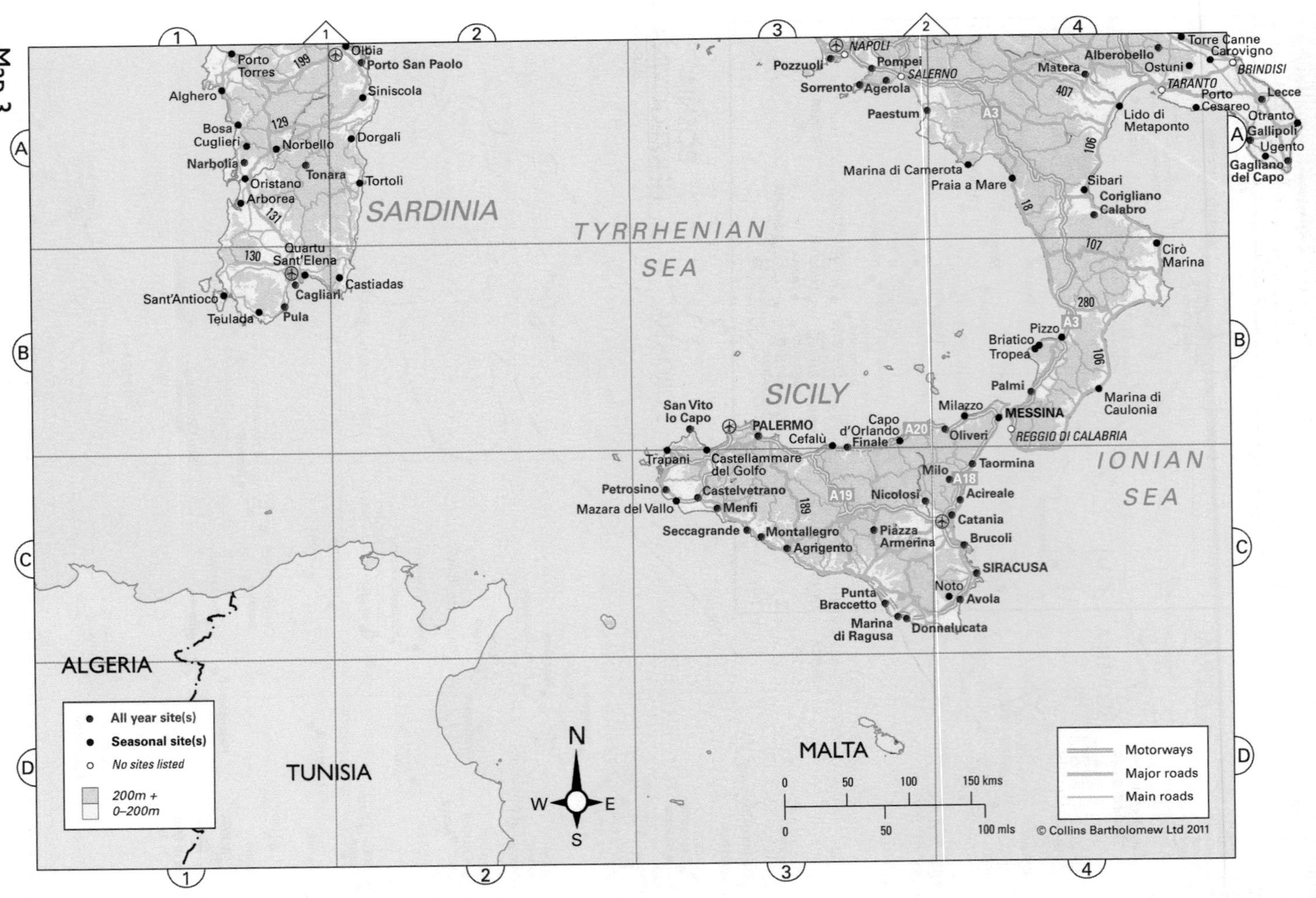

Porto Torres
Olbia
Porto San Paolo
Alghero
Siniscola
Bosa
Cuglieri
Norbello
Dorgali
Narbolia
Tonara
Oristano
Tortolì
Arborea
SARDINIA
TYRRHENIAN SEA
Quartu Sant'Elena
Castiadas
Cagliari
Sant'Antioco
Teulada
Pula
NAPOLI
Pozzuoli
Pompei
SALERNO
Sorrento
Agerola
Paestum
Marina di Camerota
Praia a Mare
Matera
Alberobello
Torre Canne
Carovigno
BRINDISI
Ostuni
TARANTO
Porto Cesareo
Lecce
Otranto
Gallipoli
Ugento
Gagliano del Capo
Lido di Metaponto
Sibari
Corigliano Calabro
Cirò Marina
Pizzo
Briatico
Tropea
Palmi
Marina di Caulonia
Milazzo
MESSINA
REGGIO DI CALABRIA
SICILY
San Vito lo Capo
PALERMO
Capo d'Orlando
Cefalù
Finale
Oliveri
Trapani
Castellammare del Golfo
Taormina
IONIAN SEA
Milo
Petrosino
Castelvetrano
Nicolosi
Acireale
Mazara del Vallo
Menfi
Catania
Seccagrande
Montallegro
Piazza Armerina
Brucoli
Agrigento
SIRACUSA
Noto
Punta Braccetto
Avola
Marina di Ragusa
Donnalucata
ALGERIA
TUNISIA
MALTA
All year site(s)
Seasonal site(s)
No sites listed
200m +
0–200m
Motorways
Major roads
Main roads
0 50 100 150 kms
0 50 100 mls
© Collins Bartholomew Ltd 2011

Luxembourg

Country Introduction

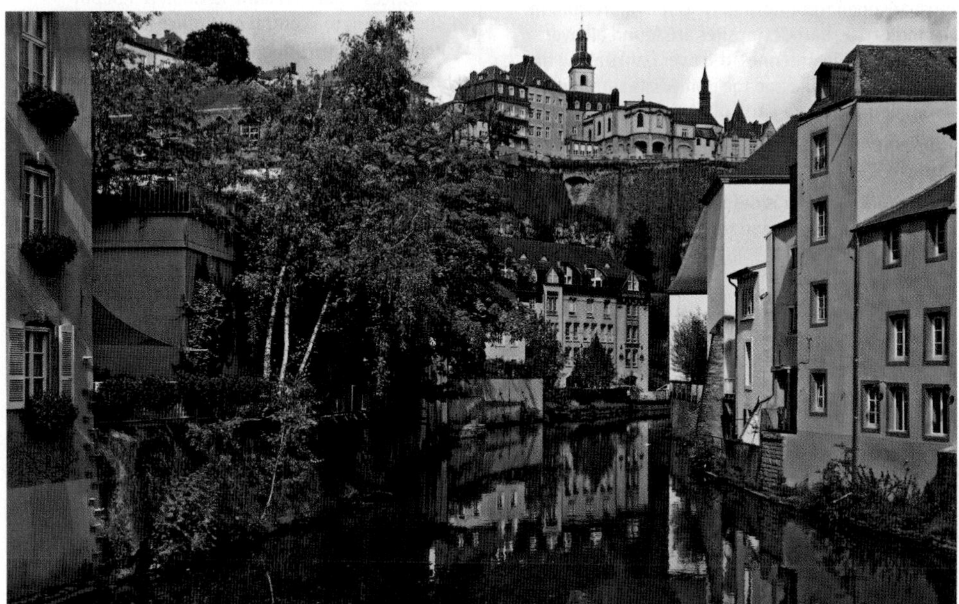

© iStockPhotos.com/rusm

Luxembourg old town

Population (approx): 500,000

Capital: Luxembourg City (population approx 90,000)

Area: 2,586 sq km

Bordered by: Belgium, France, Germany

Terrain: Rolling hills to north with broad, shallow valleys; steep slope to Moselle valley in south-east

Climate: Temperate climate without extremes of heat or cold; mild winters; warm, wet summers; July and August are the hottest months; May and June have the most hours of sunshine.

Highest Point: Burgplatz 559m

Languages: French, German, Lëtzebuergesch (Luxembourgish)

Local Time: GMT or BST + 1, i.e. 1 hour ahead of the UK all year

Currency: Euros divided into 100 cents; £1 = €1.14, €1 = 87 pence (September 2011)

Telephoning: From the UK dial 00352 for Luxembourg followed by the 6, 7 or 8-digit number; there are no area codes. To call the UK from Luxembourg dial 0044, omitting the initial zero of the area code

Emergency numbers: Police 112; Fire brigade 112; Ambulance 112. Operators speak English

Public Holidays 2012

Jan 1; Apr 6, 9; May 1, 17, 28; Jun 23 (National Day); Aug 15; Nov 1; Dec, 25, 26.

Public Holidays 2013

Jan 1; Mar 29; Apr 1; May 1, 9, 20; Jun 23 (National Day); Aug 15; Nov 1; Dec, 25, 26.

Please note 20 Feb 2012 & 11 Feb 2013 (Carnival), 3 Sep 2012 & 2 Sep 2013 (Luxembourg City Fete) and 2 Nov 2012 & 2013 (All Souls Day) are not officially bank holidays but many businesses, banks and shops may be closed. School summer holidays run from mid-July to mid-September

Tourist Office

LUXEMBOURG TOURIST OFFICE
SUITE 4.1, SICILIAN HOUSE, 7 SICILIAN AVENUE
LONDON WC1A 2QR
Tel: 020 7434 2800
www.luxembourg.co.uk tourism@luxembourg.co.uk

The following introduction to Luxembourg should be read in conjunction with the important information contained in the Handbook chapters at the front of this guide.

Camping and Caravanning

There are approximately 120 campsites in Luxembourg; most are open from April to October. Apart from in the industrial south, campsites are found all over the country. The Ardennes, the river banks along the Moselle and the Sûre and the immediate surroundings of Luxembourg City are particularly popular.

The Camping Card International (CCI) is accepted at all sites but is not compulsory.

Casual/wild camping is only permitted with a tent, not a caravan, but permission must first be sought from the landowner.

Motorhomes

Many campsites have motorhome amenities and some offer Quick Stop overnight facilities at reduced rates.

Country Information

Electricity and Gas

Most campsites have a supply of between 6 and 16 amps and many have CEE connections. Plugs have two round pins. The full range of Campingaz cylinders is widely available.

*See **Electricity and Gas** in the section **DURING YOUR STAY.***

Entry Formalities

British and Irish passport holders may stay for up to three months without a visa.

Regulations for Pets

*See **Pet Travel Scheme** under **Documents** in the section **PLANNING AND TRAVELLING.***

Medical Services

Emergency medical treatment is available on presentation of a European Health Insurance Card (EHIC) but you will be charged both for treatment and prescriptions. Refunds can be obtained from a local sickness insurance fund office, Caisse de Maladie des Ouvriers (CMO). Emergency hospital treatment is normally free apart from a non-refundable standard daily fee.

You are strongly recommended to obtain comprehensive travel and medical insurance before travelling to Luxembourg, such as The Caravan Club's Red Pennant Overseas Insurance – see www.caravanclub.co.uk/redpennant

*See **Medical Matters** in the section **DURING YOUR STAY.***

Opening Hours

Banks – Mon-Fri 8.30am-12 noon & 1.30pm-4.30pm (some do not close for lunch); Sat 9am -12 noon (some banks only).

Museums – Tue-Sun 10am-5pm (check locally); most museums close Monday.

Post Offices – Mon-Fri 8am-12 noon & 1.30pm-4.30pm/5pm; the central post office in Luxembourg City is open 7am-7pm Mon to Fri & 7am-5pm Sat.

Shops – Mon-Sat 9am/10am-6pm/6.30pm. Some shops close for lunch and some do not open Mon mornings. Large malls may be open to 8pm or 9pm.

Safety and Security

There are few reports of crime but visitors should take the usual commonsense precautions against pickpockets. Do not leave valuables in your car.

Luxembourg shares with the rest of Europe an underlying threat from terrorism. Attacks could be indiscriminate and against civilian targets in public places, including tourist sites.

*See **Safety and Security** in the section **DURING YOUR STAY.***

British Embassy

5 BOULEVARD JOSEPH II, L-1840 LUXEMBOURG
Tel: 22 98 64
http://www.ukinluxembourg.fco.gov.uk

Irish Embassy

Résidence Christina (2nd floor)
28 ROUTE D'ARLON, L-1140 LUXEMBOURG
Tel: 450 6101~
www.embassyofireland.lu

Customs Regulations

Alcohol and Tobacco

*For import allowances for alcohol and tobacco products see **Customs Regulations** in the section **PLANNING AND TRAVELLING.***

Documents

Passport

When driving it is easy to cross into neighbouring countries without realising it. Although you are unlikely to be asked for it, you must have your valid passport with you.

Vehicle(s)

Drivers of foreign-registered vehicles must be able to produce on demand a current driving licence, vehicle registration document (V5C) insurance certificate, insurance certificate and MOT certificate (if applicable).

Money

Money may be exchanged at banks and bureaux de change including at the central railway station. Travellers' cheques can be cashed at banks and are widely accepted.

The major credit cards are widely accepted and cash machines are widespread. Carry your credit card issuers'/banks' 24-hour UK contact numbers in case of loss or theft of your cards.

Motoring

Alcohol

The maximum permitted level of alcohol is 50 milligrams in 100 millilitres of blood, i.e. lower than that permitted in the UK (80 milligrams). For drivers who have held a driving licence for less than two years the permitted level is 20 milligrams i.e. virtually nil. Breath tests are compulsory following serious road accidents and road offences.

Breakdown Service

A 24-hour breakdown service 'Service Routier' is operated by the Automobile Club De Grand-Duche de Luxembourg (ACL) on all roads, telephone 26000. Operators speak English. Payment by credit card is accepted.

Essential Equipment

*See **Motoring – Equipment** in the section **PLANNING AND TRAVELLING.***

Lights

The use of dipped headlights in the daytime is recommended for all vehicles.

Reflective Jacket/Waistcoat

It is compulsory to wear a reflective jacket when getting out of your vehicle on a motorway or main road. Pedestrians walking at night or in bad visibility outside built-up areas must also wear one.

Child Restraint System

Children under the age of 3 years old must be seated in an approved child restraint system.

Children from the ages of 3 to 18 and/or under the height of 1.5m must be seated in an appropriate restraint system. If they are over 36kg in weight they can use a seat belt but only if they are in the rear of the vehicle.

Rearward facing child restraint systems are not allowed on seats with frontal airbags unless the airbag has been deactivated.

Fuel

Petrol stations are generally open from 8am to 8pm with 24 hour service on motorways. Most accept credit cards and many have automatic pumps operated with a credit card.

LPG is available at a handful of petrol stations – see www.luxembourg.co.uk and look for a list under FAQ about petrol.

*See also **Fuel** under **Motoring – Advice** in the section **PLANNING AND TRAVELLING.***

Overtaking

When overtaking at night outside built-up areas it is compulsory to flash headlights.

Parking

Parking is prohibited where there are yellow lines or zigzag white lines. Blue zone parking areas exist in Luxembourg City, Esch-sur-Elzette, Dudelange and Wiltz. Parking discs are obtainable from the ACL, police stations, tourist offices and shops. Parking meters operate in Luxembourg City. The police will clamp or remove illegally parked vehicles.

There are free car parks two to three kilometres outside Luxembourg City and Esch-sur-Elzette from which regular buses leave for the city.

If there is no public lighting when parking on a public road sidelights are required to be switched on.

*See also **Parking Facilities for the Disabled** under **Motoring – Advice** in the section **PLANNING AND TRAVELLING.***

Priority

Where two roads of the same category intersect, traffic from the right has priority. In towns give priority to traffic coming from the right, unless there is a 'priority road' sign (yellow diamond with white border) indicating that the driver using that road has right of way.

Road Signs and Markings

Road signs and markings conform to international standards and are shown in French and German. Traffic lights pass from red immediately to green (no red and amber phase). A flashing amber light allows traffic to turn in the direction indicated, traffic permitting. In Luxembourg City some bus lanes and cycle lanes are marked in red.

Speed Limits

*See **Speed Limits Table** under **Motoring – Advice** in the section **PLANNING AND TRAVELLING.***

The top speed of 130 km/h (81 mph) for solo cars is reduced to 110 km/h (68 mph) in wet weather.

The speed limit for drivers who have held a licence for less than a year is 90 km/h (56 mph) on motorways and 75 km/h (47 mph) outside built-up areas. In some residential areas and commercial areas called 'Zones de Rencontre' the maximum permitted speed is 20 km/h (13 mph).

Traffic Jams

Many holidaymakers travel through Luxembourg in order to take advantage of its cheaper fuel. In the summer, queues at petrol stations are often the reason for traffic congestion, in particular along the 'petrol route' past Martelange (N4 in Belgium), at Dudelange on the A3/E25 at the Belgium-Luxembourg border, and at the motorway junction near Steinfort on the A6 where waiting cars may encroach onto the hard shoulder.

Other bottlenecks occur, particularly during weekends in July and August, at the junctions on the A1/E44 near Gasperich to the south of Luxembourg City, and the exit from the A3/E25 at Dudelange. To avoid traffic jams between Luxembourg City and Thionville (France), leave the western ring road around Luxembourg and take the A4 to Esch-sur-Alzette and then the D16. When past Aumetz join the N52 which then connects to the A30 to Metz.

In order to avoid traffic jams when travelling through Luxembourg see the website www.cita.lu which offers webcam views of all motorways and information on traffic flow.

Violation of Traffic Regulations

Police officers may impose on the spot fines for infringement of regulations. These must be settled in cash and a receipt given. Non-residents of Luxembourg are liable, in the same way as residents, to receive penalty points for serious infringements of traffic law.

Motorways

There are approximately 115km of motorways, all of which are toll-free for private vehicles. Motorway service areas are situated at Capellen on the A6 near Mamer, at Pontpierre on the A4, and at Berchem near Bettenbourg on the A3.

Emergency telephones are situated every 1.5km along main roads and motorways and link motorists to the 'Protection Civile'.

Touring

Luxembourg is the only Grand Duchy in the world and measures a maximum of 81km (51 miles) from north to south and 51km (32 miles) from east to west. The fortifications and old town of Luxembourg City have been designated as a UNESCO World Heritage site.

The cuisine is a combination of French, Flemish and German dishes. Specialities include smoked pork with beans, Ardennes ham, meatballs and sauerkraut, trout and pike. Local beers and wines are recommended. There are reputed to be more Michelin starred restaurants per square kilometre than in any other country. Smoking is not allowed in bars and restaurants. A service charge is usually added to restaurant bills and it is normal practice to leave a little extra if the service is good.

The Luxembourg Card is valid for one, two or three days, and entitles the holder to free public transport throughout the Grand Duchy, free admission to numerous museums and tourist attractions, and discounts on sightseeing trips. It is available from tourist offices, campsites, hotels, information and public transport offices as well as from participating attractions. You can also buy it online at www.ont.lu

There are many marked walking trails throughout the country – see www.hiking-in-luxembourg.co.uk for full details. A Christmas market is held in the pedestrianised Place d'Armes in Luxembourg City. Others are held in towns and villages throughout the country.

French is the official language, but Lëtzebuergesch is the language most commonly used. English is widely spoken in Luxembourg City, but less so elsewhere.

Local Travel

A transport network ticket (billet réseau) is available at railway stations throughout the country and at the airport. It allows unlimited travel on city buses, trains and country coaches for one day (until 8am the next morning) throughout Luxembourg. Public transport maps can be downloaded from the Luxembourg Tourist Office website, www.luxembourg.co.uk

Despite its cliffs and ramparts, Luxembourg is a compact city and walking around it is easy and pleasant. It is served by an efficient network of buses. You can buy bus tickets valid either for two hours (billet de courte durée) or one day (billet de longue durée). A discount is offered on a block of 10 tickets. Tickets must be validated at the machines on buses and train platforms. Dogs are allowed free of charge on city buses. People over 65 years of age may qualify for travel concessions; show your passport as proof of age.

An interactive parking map (including GPS co-ordinates) is available for Luxembourg City on www.lcto.lu – look under 'travel'. Park and Ride schemes operate from the outskirts of the city.

All place names used in the Site Entry listings which follow can be found in Michelin's Benelux & North of France Touring & Motoring Atlas, scale 1:150,000 (1 cm = 1.5 km).

ALZINGEN see Luxembourg City *C3*

BERDORF see Echternach *C3*

BORN SUR SURE *C3* (200m NE Rural) *49.76081, 6.51672* **Camping Officiel Born-Sûre, 9 Rue du Camping, 6660 Born-sur-Sûre [tel/fax 730144; syndicat@gmx.lu; www.camping-born.lu]** E along E44 sp Trier; leave immed bef ent Germany. On N10 go N sp Echternach; ignore sat nav & drive to end of vill, site sp. Med, mkd pitch, pt shd; wc; chem disp; shwrs inc; el pnts (10A) inc; Indtte; supmkt 8km; tradsmn; rest; snacks; bar; BBQ; htd pool 8km; fishing; boating; 70% statics; dogs €2.50; phone; Eng spkn; adv bkg; some rd noise; ccard acc; CCI. "Gd, clean site; all tourers on rvside; if barrier clsd find contact in bar; excel." ♦ 1 Apr-1 Oct. € 16.00 2010*

CLERVAUX *B2* (11km SW Rural) *49.97045, 5.93450* **Camping Kaul, Rue Joseph Simon, 9550 Wiltz [tel 950359; fax 957770; icamping@campingkaul.lu; www.campingkaul.lu]** Turn N off rd 15 (Bastogne-Ettelbruck) to Wiltz, foll sp N to Ville Basse & Camping. Lge, mkd pitch, unshd; htd wc; chem disp; mv service pnt; baby facs; fam bthrm; shwrs €0.50; el pnts (6-10A) €2.50-2.75; gas; Indtte; shop high ssn & 500m; snacks; playgrnd; pool adj; waterslides; tennis; dogs €1.50; poss cr; quiet; adv bkg. "Gd site; pitches tight for awnings if site full; excel san facs & take-away; local children use playgrnd." ♦ 1 Apr-31 Oct. € 17.00 2009*

CLERVAUX *B2* (200m W Rural) *50.05471, 6.02391* **Camping Officiel de Clervaux, 33 Klatzewe, 9714 Clervaux [tel 920042; fax 929728; campingclervaux@internet.lu; www.camping-clervaux.lu]** Site sp fr town cent & fr all dirs at foot of Abbey Hill; some sharp bends. Med, hdg/mkd pitch, pt shd; htd wc; chem disp; mv service pnt; baby facs; shwrs €1; el pnts (10A) €2.50; gas; Indtte (inc dryer); shop & 1km; tradsmn; snacks; BBQ; playgrnd; htd pool; tennis 200m; games area; internet; TV; 50% statics; dogs €2; phone; poss cr; Eng spkn; some rlwy noise; CCI. "Friendly, helpful staff; pleasant town; gd walking; trains to Liège & L'bourg City; rv on site unfenced; 5 mins walk town; vg." ♦ 1 Apr-15 Oct. € 17.10 2010*

⊞ **DIEKIRCH** *C2* (10km E Rural) *49.86852, 6.26430* **Camping de la Rivière, 21 Rue de la Sûre, 9390 Reisdorf [tel/fax 836398; campingreisdorf@pt.lu; www.campingreisdorf.com]** Fr Diekirch take N19 (sp Echternach) for 10km to where rd crosses Rv Sûre. Site on L after bdge. Med, mkd pitch, pt shd; htd wc; chem disp; shwrs €1.10; el pnts (6-10A) €2.75; gas; Indtte (inc dryer); shop adj; rest; snacks; bar; playgrnd; internet; 20% statics; dogs €1.50; bus; poss cr; Eng spkn; quiet; red CCI. "Lovely site in beautiful countryside; excel for walking/cycling; helpful, friendly owners; gd touring base." ♦ € 15.00 2011*

Birkelt
Larochette
tel + 352 87 90 40

Kohnenhof
Obereisenbach
tel +352 92 94 64

Nommerlayen
Nommern
tel +352 87 80 78

Trois Frontières
Lieler
tel +352 99 86 08

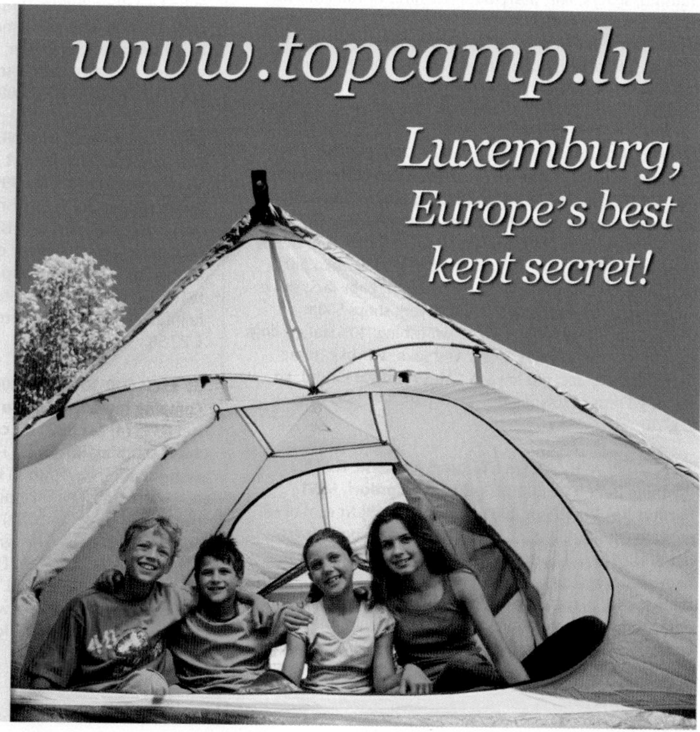

www.topcamp.lu
Luxemburg,
Europe's best
kept secret!

DIEKIRCH *C2* (500m SE Urban) *49.86635, 6.16513* **Camping de la Sûre, 34 Route de Gilsdorf, 9234 Diekirch [tel 809425; fax 802786; tourisme@diekirch.lu; www.diekirch.lu]** Fr town cent take N14 twds Larochette, then 1st L after x-ing rv bdge. Well sp. Lge, mkd pitch, pt shd; htd wc; chem disp; baby facs; shwrs €1; el pnts (10A) €2.50; Indtte; shop 500m; bar; playgrnd; pool 200m; 50% statics; dogs €2; m'van o'night area outside gates; Eng spkn; adv bkg; quiet; red CCI; ccard acc. "Nice welcome; excel, clean facs; pleasant rvside site 5 mins walk fr town cent; vg touring base, Battle of Bulge Museum nearby." ♦ 1 Apr-30 Sep. € 17.75 2011*

⊞ **DIEKIRCH** *C2* (500m S Rural) *49.86768, 6.16984* **Camping op der Sauer, Route de Gilsdorf, 9201 Diekirch [tel 808590; fax 809470; info@campsauer.lu; www.campsauer.lu]** On rd 14 to Larochette, on S o'skts of Diekirch. 1st L after x-ing rv bdge, site well sp on L past Camping de la Sûre and behind sports facs. Lge, mkd pitch, pt shd; htd wc; chem disp; shwrs inc; el pnts (6A) €3; gas; Indtte; shop & 400m; tradsmn; rest; snacks; bar; playgrnd; pool 400m; dogs €2.50; bus 800m; Eng spkn; adv bkg; CCI. "On banks Rv Sûre; sh walk/cycle to town; spacious site; friendly owners; ltd facs low ssn; gd, basic site." € 16.00 2010*

ECHTERNACH *C3* (2km SE Rural) *49.79681, 6.43122* **Camping Alferweiher, Alferweiher 1, 6412 Echternach [tel/fax 720271; info@camping-alferweiher.lu; www.camping-alferweiher.lu]** Fr S on N10 on ent Echternach turn R at sp (pictogram fishing/camping) then L at sp to Alferweiher. Lge, mkd pitch, pt shd; htd wc; chem disp; mv service pnt; baby facs; shwrs inc; el pnts (10A) €2.75; gas; Indtte; shop; tradsmn; snacks; bar; playgrnd; cycle hire; TV rm; entmnt; dogs €2; poss cr; Eng spkn; adv bkg; quiet; CCI. "Gd walking; office open 0900-1300 & 1400-1800; if shut site yourself - el boxes not locked; hot water in individ cubicles in san facs block only - other basins cold water." ♦ 23 Apr-15 Sep. € 20.00 2010*

ECHTERNACH *C3* (1km NW Rural) *49.81716, 6.41058* **Camping Officiel, 5 Rue de Diekirch, 6430 Echternach [tel 720272; fax 26720747; info@camping-echternach.lu; www.camping-echternach.lu]** Fr Luxembourg City cont thro Echternach on N10 sp Diekirch & Ettelbruck. Site clearly sp on L overlkg rd & rv; diff exit fr site. Lge, hdg/mkd pitch, terr, pt shd; wc; chem disp; mv service pnt; baby facs; shwrs inc; el pnts (16A) €2.50; Indtte (inc dryer); shops 500m; tradsmn; playgrnd; pool; rv/lake sw; fishing; 10% statics; dogs €2; bus to Luxemb'g City 500m; Eng spkn; adv bkg; some rd noise; ccard acc; red low ssn. "Music festival Jun/Jul; gd walks; gd rests in town; rvside cycle path." ♦ 15 Mar-30 Oct. € 17.10 2011*

⊞ **ECHTERNACH** *C3* (6km NW Rural) *49.81958, 6.34737* **Camping Belle-Vue 2000, 29 Rue de Consdorf, 6551 Berdorf [tel 790635 or 808149; fax 799349]** Nr cent of vill on rd to Consdorf. 2nd of 3 adj sites with facs on L on way out of vill. Lge, hdg pitch, terr, pt shd; htd wc; chem disp; baby facs; shwrs inc; el pnts (6A); gas; Indtte; shop; tradsmn; snacks; BBQ; playgrnd; pool 500m; games rm; 50% statics; dogs; phone; adv bkg; quiet; CCI. "Gd walking; attractive vill with gd rests; open in Jan only if no snow; pitches poss soft after rain." € 15.00 2008*

ECHTERNACH *C3* (6km NW Rural) *49.81904, 6.34694* **Camping Bon Repos, 39 Rue de Consdorf, 6551 Berdorf [tel 790631; fax 799571; irma@bonrepos.lu; www.bonrepos.lu]** In cent Echternach at x-rds take Vianden rd, then in 2km turn L to Berdorf thro vill twds Consdorf. Site nr cent vill on L adj Camping Belle-Vue. Fr Luxembourg thro Consdorf to Berdorf, site on R on ent to vill, clearly sp. Med, hdg/mkd pitch, terr, pt sl, pt shd; htd wc; chem disp; baby facs; shwrs inc; el pnts (16A) €2.80 (poss rev pol); gas; Indtte; tradsmn; shop adj; rest & bar 100m; playgrnd; pool 5km; games rm; wifi; TV; no dogs; bus 100m; Eng spkn; adv bkg; quiet; red long stay; CCI. "Clean, tidy site - best in area; clean facs; helpful, friendly owners; some pitches sm; forest walks fr site; conv for trips to Germany." 1 Apr74 Nov. € 18.00 2010*

When we get home I'm going to post all these site report forms to the Club for next year's guide. The deadline's mid September 2013

⊞ **ESCH SUR ALZETTE** *B3* (500m E Rural) *49.4846, 5.9861* **Camping Gaalgebierg, 4001 Esch-sur-Alzette [tel 541069; fax 549630; gaalcamp@pt.lu; www.gaalgebierg.lu]** Sp in cent of town, turn L dir Kayl. Under rlwy bdge sharp R, up steep hill. Lge, hdstg, terr, shd; htd wc; baby facs; shwrs inc; el pnts (16A) €1.50 but elec for heating metered & restricted in bad weather; Indtte; shop; snacks; bar; playgrnd; pool 2km; TV conn all pitches; mainly statics; bus 1km; train to Luxembourg city; Eng spkn; quiet; ccard acc; CCI. "V clean san facs; gd walks; park & sm zoo adj site; well-kept site; poss boggy when wet." ♦ € 15.00 2010*

ESCH SUR SURE *B2* (6km NE Rural) *49.91420, 6.00098* **Camping Toodlermillen, 1 Op der Millen, 9181 Tadler-Moulin [tel 839189; fax 899236; keisera@gms.lu; www.toodlermillen.lu]** Fr Ettelbrück on N15 twd Esch-sur-Sûre, turn E onto N27 dir Goebelsmühle. Site is 4km on R. Med, mkd pitch, unshd; htd wc; chem disp; baby facs; shwrs €1; el pnts (6A) €3; Indtte; shop, rest, bar adj; playgrnd; BBQ; rv fishing; canoeing; 20% statics; dogs €3; Eng spkn. "V helpful owner; beautiful area; excel san facs." 15 Apr-15 Oct. € 22.50 2010*

⊞ **ESCH SUR SURE** *B2* (500m E Rural) *49.90693, 5.94220* **Camping Im Aal, 7 Rue du Moulin, 9650 Esch-sur-Sûre [tel 839514; fax 899117; camping-im-aal@hotmail.com; www.camping-im-aal.lu]** Fr N turn R off N15 onto N27 sp Esch-sur-Sûre. Pass thro sh tunnel, site on L in 500m on banks of Rv Sûre. Lge, hdg/mkd pitch, pt sl, pt shd; htd wc; chem disp; shwrs inc; el pnts (6A) €2; Indtte (inc dryer); shop & 500m; tradsmn; bar; playgrnd adj; fishing; 30% statics; dogs €2; site clsd 1 Jan-14 Feb; Eng spkn; quiet; red CCI. "Well-kept, clean site; gd welcome; gd, modern facs; some rvside pitches; walks along towpath & in woods; gd for wheelchair users; gd fishing, walking; gd NH & longer." ♦ € 16.00 2010*

LUXEMBOURG

ETTELBRUCK *B2* (3km E Rural) *49.85043, 6.13461* **Camping Gritt, 2 Rue Gritt, 9161 Ingeldorf [tel 802018; fax 802019; apeeters@pt.lu; www.campinggritt.lu]** On N15 fr Bastogne turn R at rndabt in Ettelbrück sp Diekirch, go under A7 sp Diekirch. In 3km at end of elevated section foll slip rd sp Diekirch, Ettelbrück, Ingeldorf. At rndabt take 2nd exit sp Ingledorf, site on R over narr rv bdge. Fr Diekirch on N7 fork L twd Ingeldorf. Site on L over rv bdge. Lge, mkd pitch, pt shd; htd wc; chem disp; baby facs; shwrs inc; el pnts (6A) inc; gas; Indtte; supmkt 1.5km; tradsmn; rest; snacks; bar; BBQ (charcoal/gas only); rv sw 1.5km; fishing, canoe hire, tennis nrby; ltd wifi; entmnt; games/TV rm; 30% statics; dogs €2; twin-axles acc (rec check in adv); bus/train to Luxembourg City; recep 0900-1800 high ssn; poss cr; adv bkg; quiet; red for groups; red low ssn/CCI. "Peaceful site; helpful, welcoming Dutch owners; lge pitches with open aspect; gd, modern san facs; pitching still OK after heavy rain; on banks of Rv Sûre (swift-flowing & unfenced); gd walking & sightseeing." ♦ 1 Apr-30 Oct. € 25.30 SBS - H07 2011*

ETTELBRUCK *B2* (2km NW Rural) *49.84600, 6.08193* **Camping Kalkesdelt, 88 Chemin du Camping, 9022 Ettelbrück [tel 812185; fax 813186; kalkesdelt@ettelbruck-info.lu; www.ettelbruck-info.lu]** Exit Ettelbrück on Bastogne rd N15. Site visible as approach town; approx 200m fr town cent fork L into lane, turn R at sp at foot of hill, narr rd. Site sp fr town. Lge, mkd pitch, terr, pt shd; htd wc; chem disp; mv service pnt; baby facs; shwrs inc; el pnts (16A) €2.90; Indtte; shop; rest; snacks; bar; playgrnd; pool 3km; TV; 15% statics; dogs €2.50; phone; poss cr; Eng spkn; adv bkg; quiet; CCI. "Gd, well-maintained, friendly, family-run site in woods; excel san facs; lge pitches; gd walks; train to Luxumbourg city fr town; excel site." ♦ 1 Apr-30 Oct. € 22.50 2011*

⊞ **ETTELBRUCK** *B2* (10km NW Rural) *49.87748, 5.99288* **Camping Fuussekaul, 4 Fuussekaul, 9156 Heiderscheid [tel 268888; fax 26888828; info@fuussekaul.lu]** Take N15 fr Bastogne twd Ettelbrück, site 1.5km past Heiderscheid on R. Lge, pt sl, pt shd; htd wc; chem disp; mv service pnt; sauna; shwrs €1; el pnts (10A) inc; gas; Indtte; shop high ssn; rest; snacks; bar; playgrnd; 2 pools; waterslide; lake sw 8km; tennis; games area; archery; internet; entmnt; 30% statics; dogs €2; bus; poss cr; adv bkg; quiet; red long stay. "Vg site." € 35.00 2009*

GRAVENMACHER *C3* (500m NE Urban) *49.68302, 6.44891* **Camping La Route du Vin, 32 Route de Thionville, 6791 Grevenmacher [tel 750234 or 758275; fax 758666; sitg@pt.lu; www.grevenmacher.lu]** Fr E44/A1 exit junc 14 onto N1 to Grevenmacher. After 1km turn R at T-junc opp Esso g'ge. Site sp in town, ent off rndabt. Med, sl, pt shd; wc; chem disp; shwrs inc; el pnts (6A) €1.50; shop, rest, snacks 500m; bar; pool nr; tennis; child entmnt; 60% statics; dogs €1; Eng spkn; some rd noise; CCI. "Easy walk to town cent; wine festival in Sep; pleasant site but rather scruffy (8/09); NH only." 1 Apr-30 Sep. € 11.60 2009*

HEIDERSCHEID see Ettelbrück *B2*

INGELDORF see Ettelbrück *B2*

⊞ **KAUTENBACH** *B2* (N Rural) *49.95387, 6.02730* **Camping Kautenbach, An der Weierbaach, 9663 Kautenbach [tel 950303; fax 950093; info@campingkautenbach.lu; www.campingkautenbach.lu]** Travelling E fr Bastogne on N84, approx 5km after Luxembourg border take N26 to Wiltz & foll sp to Kautenbach/Kiischpelt. In 10km turn L over bdge into vill, site sp 800m. Lge, mkd pitch, pt shd; htd wc; chem disp; shwrs inc; baby facs; el pnts (6A) inc; gas; Indtte; shop; tradsmn; rest; snacks; bar; BBQ; playgrnd; entmnt; cycle hire; wifi; TV rm; 20% statics; phone; dogs; site clsd 21 Dec-14 Jan; Eng spkn; adv bkg; quiet but some rlwy noise; ccard acc. "Gd for walking & mountain biking; long site along beautiful, secluded rv valley." ♦ € 22.25 2009*

KOCKELSCHEUER see Luxembourg City *C3*

LAROCHETTE *C3* (1.5km W Rural) *49.78525, 6.21010* **Camping Birkelt, 1 Rue Birkelt, 7633 Larochette [tel 879040; fax 879041; info@camping-birkelt.lu; www.camping-birkelt.lu]** Fr Diekirch take N14 to Larochette; turn R in town on CR118 (N8), foll sp for Mersch. At top of hill foll site sp. Fr Luxembourg take N7 foll sp for Mersch & Ettelbruck (ignore Larochette sp bef Mersch). Turn R bef rv bdge at Mersch onto CR118 & foll rd to o'skts of town. Site on R beyond municipal sports cent - fairly steep, winding app rd. Lge, hdg/mkd pitch, pt sl, pt shd; htd wc; chem disp; mv service pnt; serviced pitch; baby facs; sauna; shwrs inc; el pnts (10A) inc; gas; Indtte (inc dryer); shop; rest; snacks; bar; BBQ (gas/charcoal only); playgrnd; 2 pools (1 htd, covrd); paddling pool; tennis; fitness rm; horseriding; fishing, canoeing, golf 5km; cycle hire; games rm; games area; wifi; entmnt; TV rm; 50% statics; dogs €2.50; no c'vans/m'vans over 9m; poss cr; Eng spkn; ccard acc; red low ssn; CCI. "Excel, well-kept, busy site in pleasant wooded hilltop location; friendly, helpful staff; ideal for families; gd san facs; access poss diff lge o'fits; late arrivals report to rest/bar." ♦ 24 Mar-4 Nov. € 37.70 (CChq acc) SBS - H08 2011*

See advertisement on page 479

LAROCHETTE *C3* (4km W Rural) *49.78521, 6.16596* **Europacamping Nommerlayen, Rue Nommerlayen, 7465 Nommern [tel 878078; fax 879678; nommerlayen@vo.lu; www.nommerlayen-ec.lu]** N7 Luxembourg to Diekirch. At Mersch N8 E dir Larochette & Nommern. Site is 1km S of Nommern. Lge, hdg/mkd pitch, terr, pt shd; htd wc; mv service pnt; chem disp; baby facs; sauna; shwrs inc; private bthrms avail; el pnts (2A) inc (16A €3.75); gas; Indtte (inc dryer); shop; tradsmn; rest; snacks; bar; playgrnd; htd pool; paddling pool; tennis, games area; games rm; cycle hire; wifi; entmnt; TV; 10% statics; dogs €2.85; phone; Eng spkn; adv bkg; quiet; red low ssn/snr citizens. "Superb site & facs." ♦ 1 Feb-1 Dec. € 40.00 2011*

See advertisement on page 479

LUXEMBOURG

LAROCHETTE *C3* (2.5km NW Rural) *49.79991, 6.19816* **Camping auf Kengert, Kengert, 7633 Larochette [tel 837186; fax 878323; info@kengert.lu; www.kengert.lu]** N8 dir Mersch, CR19 dir Schrondweiler. Site sp fr cent Larochette. Lge, mkd pitch, sl, shd; htd wc; chem disp; mv service pnt; baby facs; sauna; shwrs inc; el pnts (4-16A) €2; gas; Indtte; shop; rest; snacks; bar; 2 playgrnds (1 indoor); solar htd pool; solarium; wifi; some statics; dogs €1.25; poss cr; Eng spkn; adv bkg; quiet; CCI. "Vg facs; Luxembourg Card (red on attractions & public transport) avail at recep; peaceful site; gd rest; gd local walks/cycle rtes." ♦ 1 Mar-8 Nov. € 28.00 2008*

⊞ **LIELER** *B2* (300m W Rural) *50.12365, 6.10509* **Camping Trois Frontières, Hauptstroos 12, 9972 Lieler [tel 998608; fax 979184; camp.3front@cmdnet.lu; www.troisfrontieres.lu]** Fr N7/E421 turn E sp Lieler, site sp. Med, mkd pitch, pt shd; htd wc; chem disp; mv service pnt: baby facs; shwrs; el pnts (6A) €2.75; Indtte (inc dryer); tradsmn; rest; snacks; bar; playgrnd; 2 htd pools (1 covrd); paddling pool; cycle hire; games rm; games area; wifi; entmnt; TV; some statics; dogs €2.20; adv bkg; quiet. "V pleasant site; gd touring base." € 25.00 2011*

See advertisement on page 479

LUXEMBOURG CITY *C3* (4km S Rural) *49.57220, 6.10857* **Camping Kockelscheuer, 22 Route de Bettembourg, 1899 Kockelscheuer [tel 471815; fax 401243; caravani@pt.lu; www.camp-kockelscheuer.lu]** Fr N on A6 then A4 exit junc 1 sp Leudelange/Kockelscheuer, at top of slip rd turn L N4. After about 1.5km turn R N186 sp Bettemburg/Kockelscheuer & foll camp sp. Foll sp 'Park & Ride', site is 1st R. Fr S exit A3 junc 2 sp Bettembourg & Kockelscheuer. In 700m turn R dir Kockelscheuer & in 3km turn L & foll site sp. Lge, some hdg/mkd pitch, pt terr, pt shd; htd wc; chem disp; mv service pnt; shwrs inc; el pnts (10-16A) metered or €2.50 (check pol); gas; Indtte (inc dryer); shop; tradsmn; rest adj; snacks; bar; playgrnd; pool 4km; sports complex adj; internet; sat TV; bus to city 400m (tickets fr site recep); office & gates clsd 1200-1400 & 2230-0700; Eng spkn; adv bkg; some rd & aircraft noise during day; ccard not acc; low ssn weekly rate for snr citizens; 10% red CCI. "Rec arr early afternoon as popular, well-run, clean, pretty site; helpful, pleasant staff; gd san facs; pitch access on lower level needs care; gd size pitches on terr; poss boggy after rain; el pnts metered after 2 days; gd dog walks nrby; useful NH for Zeebrugge." ♦ Easter-31 Oct. € 13.00 2011*

LUXEMBOURG CITY *C3* (5km S Rural) *49.56907, 6.16010* **Camping Bon Accueil, 2 Rue du Camping, 5815 Alzingen [tel/fax 26362199; sydicat.dinitiative@internet.lu]** Fr Luxembourg city take A3/E25 S, exit junc 1 sp Hespérange. Cont thro town to Alzingen, site sp on R after Mairie, well sp. Med, some hdstg, pt shd; wc; chem disp; shwrs inc; el pnts (16A) inc (poss rev pol); gas; Indtte; shop, rest adj; pool 3km; playgrnd; dogs €3; bus to city nr; poss cr; quiet. "Pleasant, open, clean, tidy site; gd size pitches; friendly staff; vg, clean, modern san facs; hot water metered; lovely gardens adj; clsd 1200-1400 - ltd waiting space; excel base for city." 1 Apr-15 Oct. € 19.00 2011*

LUXEMBOURG CITY *C3* (7km W Rural) *49.63012, 6.04761* **Camping Mamer, 4 Rue de Mersch, 8251 Mamer [tel/fax 312349; campingmamer@hotmail.com; www.campingmamer.tk]** App Luxembourg on A6/E25. Exit m'way at Mamer junc on N6. Pass thro Mamer vill, turn L in 1km at 2nd rndabt, site sp. Bef m'way viaduct turn R into site. Med, pt sl, pt shd; htd wc; chem disp; shwrs inc; el pnts (6A) inc (poss rev pol); gas; shops 1.5km; hypmkt nr; rest; snacks; bar; playgrnd; dogs; poss v cr; Eng spkn; adv bkg; CCI. "V pleasant site; helpful owners; easy access to city; bus into city fr hypmkt; o'night/late arrivals area in gravel car park under m'way (noisy); poss long walk to facs; many o'nighters." 1 Apr-30 Sep. € 18.00 2010*

MAMER see Luxembourg City *C3*

MERSCH *B3* (800m SW Rural) *49.74403, 6.09075* **Camping Um Krounebierg, Rue de Camping, 7501 Mersch [tel 329756; fax 327987; contact@campingkrounebierg.lu; www.campingkrounebierg.lu]** In Mersch town cent fr main N7 foll site ss. Fr A7, exit Kopstal dir Mersch, then foll site sps. Lge, hdg/mkd pitch, some hdstg, pt sl, terr, pt shd; htd wc; chem disp; mv service pnt; baby facs; shwrs inc; el pnts (6A) inc; gas; Indtte; shop; rest; snacks; bar; BBQ; playgrnd; htd, covrd pool adj; paddling pool; tennis; skate park; TV; 5% statics; dogs €2.60; phone; quiet; red low ssn. "Gd touring & walking cent; conv for trains to Luxembourg City; warden v helpful - only on site 2 hrs morning & 2 hrs evening low ssn; site guarded; excel clean facs." ♦ 1 Apr-31 Oct. € 31.90 (3 persons) 2008*

NOMMERN see Larochette *C3*

OBEREISENBACH *C2* (1.5m N Rural) *50.01640, 6.13680* **Camping Kohnenhof, Maison 1, 9838 Obereisenbach [tel 929464; fax 929690; kohnenho@pt.lu; www.campingkohnenhof.lu]** Fr N on N7/E421 turn E onto N10 at Marbourg, foll rd S to Kohnenhof, site sp on rvside. Med, mkd pitch, pt sl, terr, pt shd; htd wc; chem disp; mv service pnt; baby facs; shwrs inc; el pnts (6A) inc; gas; Indtte; shop; tradsmn; hypmkt 10km; rest; snacks; bar; BBQ; playgrnd; htd pool 12km; rv sw adj; boating; tennis 4km; games area; cycle hire; golf 18km; wifi; TV rm; 5% statics; dogs €3; phone; poss cr; Eng spkn; adv bkg rec; red low ssn; CCI. "Clean site in lovely setting; gd walking & interesting town; self-operated ferry on site to cross rv to forest; vg touring base; excel." 20 Mar-9 Nov. € 28.00 (CChq acc) 2011*

See advertisement on page 479

REMICH See also sites listed under Nennig in Germany, map ref 3A2

LUXEMBOURG

REMICH *C3* (5km S Rural) *49.5106, 6.36302* **Camping Le Port, 5447 Schwebsange [tel 23664460; fax 26 66 53 05; commune@wellenstein.lu]** Fr Remich take N10 S on W bank of Moselle. Site 1km E of Schwebsange. Or fr S leave A13 at junc 13 onto N10. Site sp. Lge, mkd pitch, pt shd; wc; chem disp; mv service pnt; serviced pitch; shwrs inc; el pnts (10A) inc; gas; Indtte; shop 4km; tradsmn; bar; playgrnd; pool 4km; marina & rv activities; 80% statics; dogs; Eng spkn; poss cr; adv bkg rec high ssn; rd, rv & port noise; Switch cards acc (no cc); CCI. "Busy transit site for Austria/Italy; clean facs; helpful staff; office open 1830-2030; sep area for m'vans on far side of port; red facs low ssn; gd cycle rtes fr site." ♦ 1 Apr-31 Oct. € 14.00 2011*

SCHWEBSANGE see Remich *C3*

⊞ **SEPTFONTAINES** *B3* (4km NE Rural) *49.69274, 5.98514* **Camping Simmerschmelz, Rue de Simmerschmelz 1, 8363 Septfontaines [tel 307072; fax 308210; info@campingsimmer.lu; www.campingsimmer.lu]** Head NE fr Arlon sp Mersch. In 4km at Gaichel (Bel/Lux frontier) foll valley of Rv Eisch thro Hobscheid, Septfontaines & in 2km at rd junc turn R. Site on L in 100m. Or fr E25 m'way exit at Windhof. Head N to Koerich & onto Septfontaines, as above. Med, pt sl, pt shd; htd wc; chem disp; shwrs inc; el pnts (6A) €2.50; gas; Indtte; shop high ssn; snacks; pool high ssn; TV; 40% statics; dogs €3; phone; Eng spkn; adv bkg; quiet. "Pleasant site in valley - wet in winter; 1 hdstg pitch; helpful owner." € 21.00 2009*

TROISVIERGES *B2* (500m S Urban) *50.11908, 6.00251* **Camping Walensbongert, Rue de Binsfeld, 9912 Troisvierges [tel 997141; fax 26957799; wbongert@pt.lu; www.walensbongert.lu]** Fr Belgium on E42/A27 exit at junc 15 St Vith on N62 sp Troisvierges. Site sp. Med, hdg/mkd pitch, pt shd; htd wc; chem disp; mv service pnt; baby facs; shwrs inc; el pnts (16A) €2.50; Indtte (inc dryer); shop 500m; tradsmn; rest 500m; snacks; bar; pools adj; paddling pool; tennis; games rm; 10% statics; dogs €2; phone; train 1km; Eng spkn; adv bkg; quiet; ccard acc; red low ssn; CCI. "Pretty town; gd hiking; charming, helpful owners." ♦ 1 Apr-30 Sep. € 17.00 2010*

VIANDEN *C2* (SE Urban) *49.93213, 6.21554* **Camping op dem Deich, Rue Neugarten, 9420 Vianden [tel 834375; fax 834642; info@campingopdemdeich.lu; www.campingopdemdeich.lu]** Fr Diekirch take N19 E for 3km. Turn L on N17 to Vianden. Site sp 500m fr town cent twd Bitburg. Lge, mkd pitch, hdstg, unshd; htd wc; chem disp; baby facs; shwrs; el pnts (16A) €2.20; Indtte (inc dryer); shops 500m; BBQ; playgrnd; pool 2km; fishing; games rm; wifi; some statics; dogs €1.50; phone; poss cr; quiet. "Some rvside pitches; excel scenery; sh walk along rv to lovely old town & castle." 1 Apr-11 Oct. € 17.00 2010*

VIANDEN *C2* (2km S Rural) *49.92673, 6.21990* **Camping du Moulin, Rue de Bettel, 9415 Vianden [tel/fax 834501; info@campingdumoulin.lu; www.campingdumoulin.lu]** Fr Diekirch take N17 dir Vianden. In 8km at Fouhren take rd N17B sp Bettel then sp Vianden. Site on R behind yellow Vianden sp. Lge, mkd pitch, pt shd; htd wc; chem disp; mv service pnt; baby facs; shwrs; el pnts (10-16A) €2.20; Indtte; shop; tradsmn; rest, bar; playgrnd; pool 2km; rv adj; wifi; cab TV; no statics; dogs €1.50; phone; Eng spkn; quiet; CCI. "Lovely location; spacious pitches, some on rv bank; gd, modern san facs; superb children's san facs." 24 Apr-5 Sep. € 17.00 2011*

The opening dates and prices on this campsite have changed.
I'll send a site report form to the Club for the next edition of the guide.

WASSERBILLIG *C3* (Urban) *49.71536, 6.50592* **Camping Schützwiese, 41 Rue des Romains, 6649 Wasserbillig [tel 740543; fax 26 714203; info@camping-schuetzwiese.eu]** Fr A1/E44 exit 14, B49 sp Trier, site sp 150m fr frontier bdge. Med, pt sl, pt shd; wc; chem disp; mv service pnt; shwrs inc; el pnts (6A) €2; shops adj; rest 4km; tennis 500m; 40% statics; dogs €1.50; poss cr; adv bkg ess; quiet. 1 Apr-31 Oct. € 11.50 2009*

WASSERBILLIG *C3* (2km SW Rural) *49.70241, 6.47717* **Camping Mertert, Rue du Parc, 6684 Mertert [tel 748174; fax 749808; emejos@web.de]** On E of rte 1 (Wasserbillig-Luxembourg), clearly sp in both dir. Immed R after rlwy x-ing. Site on rv. Med, some mkd pitch, shd; htd wc; chem disp; baby facs; shwrs; el pnts (10A) inc; Indtte; shops 250m; playgrnd; pool 4km; sm boating pond; 70% statics; buses & trains nr; adv bkg; quiet; ccard not acc. "Grassed tourer area open fr Apr, but owner allows pitching on tarmac rd adj office; excel, clean facs; scruffy statics area; recep clsd 1300-1500; vg." ♦ 15 Apr-15 Oct. € 12.50 2008*

WEISWAMPACH *B2* (500m W Rural) *50.13806, 6.06335* **Camping du Lac, Klackepëtzn, 9990 Weiswampach [tel 9972811; fax 9972812; camping.weiswampach@pt.lu; http://camping.weiswampach.lu]** Foll N7/E421 fr Luxembourg. Site sp on L 500m fr vill of Weiswampach. Lge, hdg/mkd pitch, terr, pt shd; htd wc; chem disp; mv service pnt; baby facs; fam bthrm; shwrs €0.50; el pnts (10A) €1.90; gas; Indtte (inc dryer); shop; supmkt 1km; rest; snacks; bar; BBQ; cooking facs; playgrnd; lake sw adj; fishing; watersports; entmnt; TV; 50% statics; dogs €1.80; phone; poss cr; Eng spkn; adv bkg; quiet; red long stay/CCI. "Wonderful site on edge of 2 lakes; gd facs; warm welcome." ♦ 1 Apr-31 Oct. € 16.40 2010*

WILTZ see Clervaux *B2*

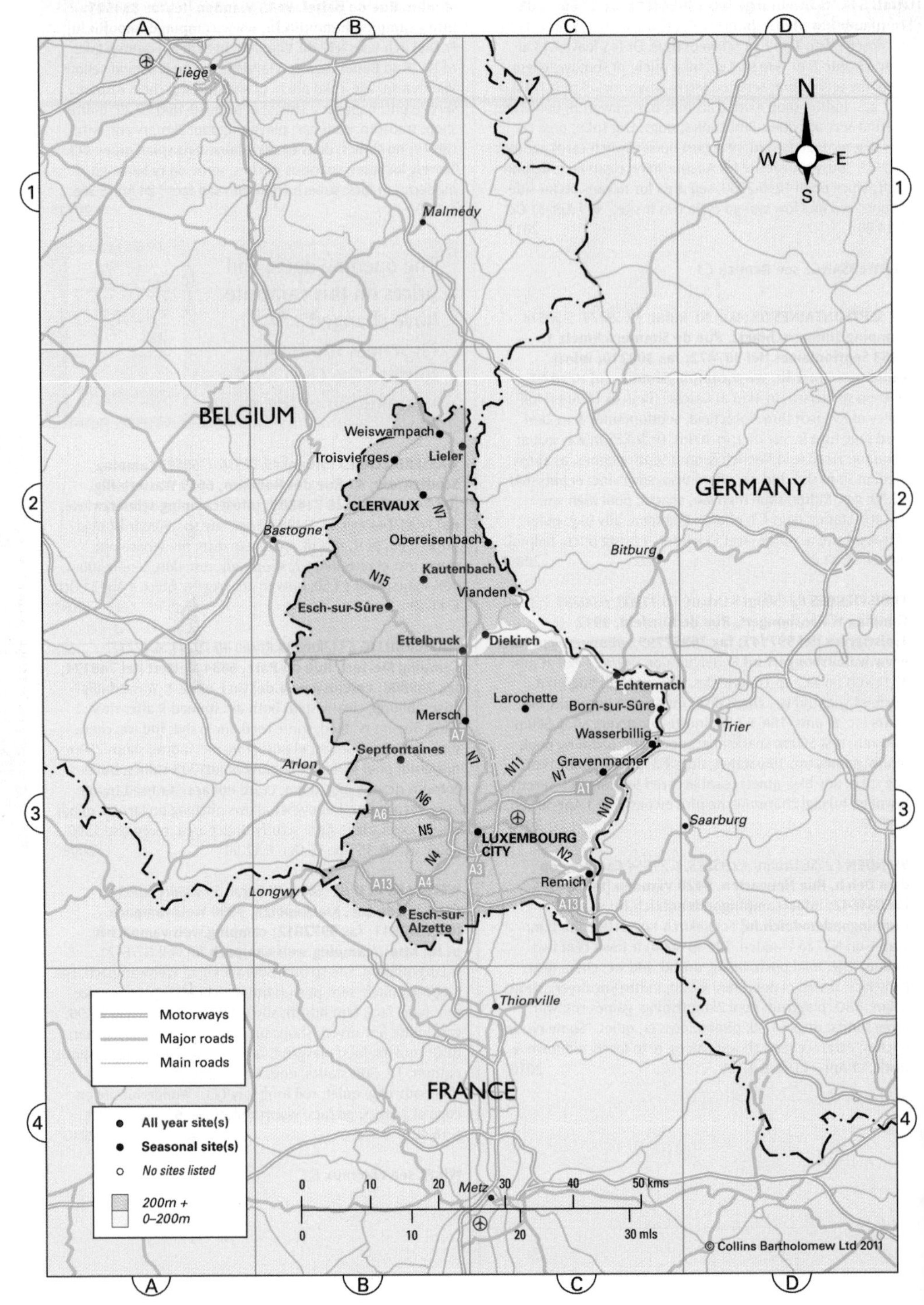
A
B
C
D
1
2
3
4
N
W
E
S
Liège
Malmédy
BELGIUM
GERMANY
FRANCE
Weiswampach
Lieler
Troisvierges
CLERVAUX
N7
Bastogne
Obereisenbach
Bitburg
N15
Kautenbach
Vianden
Esch-sur-Sûre
Ettelbruck
Diekirch
Echternach
Larochette
Born-sur-Sûre
Trier
Mersch
Wasserbillig
A7
Septfontaines
N7
N11
Arlon
Gravenmacher
N1
A1
N6
A6
N10
Saarburg
N5
LUXEMBOURG CITY
N4
N2
A3
Longwy
A13
A4
Remich
A13
Esch-sur-Alzette
Thionville
Motorways
Major roads
Main roads
All year site(s)
Seasonal site(s)
No sites listed
200m +
0–200m
0
10
20
30
40
50 kms
Metz
0
10
20
30 mls
© Collins Bartholomew Ltd 2011

Netherlands

Country Introduction

©Netherlands Board of Tourism

Amsterdam © iStockPhotos.com/ Nikada

Population (approx): 16.6 million

Capital: Amsterdam (population approx 783,000)

Area: 41,532 sqkm

Bordered by: Belgium, Germany

Terrain: Mostly coastal lowland and reclaimed land (polders) dissected by rivers and canals; hills in the south-east

Climate: Temperate maritime climate; warm, changeable summers; cold/mild winters; spring is the driest season

Coastline: 451km

Highest Point: Vaalserberg 321m

Language: Dutch

Local Time: GMT or BST + 1, i.e. 1 hour ahead of the UK all year

Currency: Euro divided into 100 cents; £1 = €1.14, €1 = 87 pence (September 2011)

Telephoning: From the UK dial 0031 and omit the initial zero of the area code of the number you are calling. To call the UK from the Netherlands dial 0044, omitting the initial zero of the area code

Emergency numbers: Police 112; Fire brigade 112; Ambulance 112. Operators speak English

Public Holidays 2012

Jan 1; Apr 6, 8, 9, 30 (Queen's Day);
May 5 (Liberation Day), 17, 27, 28; Dec 25, 26.

Public Holidays 2013

Jan 1; Mar 29, 31; Apr 1, 30 (Queen's Day);
May 5 (Liberation Day), 9, 19, 20; Dec 25, 26

School summer holidays vary by region, but are roughly early/mid July to end August/early September

Tourist Office

THE NETHERLANDS BOARD OF TOURISM
PO BOX 30783, LONDON WC2B 6DH
Tel: 0906 8717777 (brochure requests) or 020 7539 7950
www.holland.com/uk
info-uk@holland.com

The following introduction to the Netherlands should be read in conjunction with the important information contained in the Handbook chapters at the front of this guide.

Camping and Caravanning

There are approximately 2,500 officially classified campsites which offer a wide variety of facilities. Most are well equipped with modern sanitary facilities and they generally have a bar, shop and leisure facilities.

A number of sites require cars to be parked on a separate area away from pitches and this can present a problem for motorhomes. Some sites allow motorhomes to park on pitches without restrictions, but others will only accept them on pitches if they are not moved during the duration of your stay. Check before booking in.

A tourist tax is levied at campsites of between €0.50 and €1.00 per person per night. It is not generally included in the prices quoted in the Site Entry listings which follow this chapter.

Visitors in search of quiet simplicity may stay at country farm sites. VeKaBo is an organisation offering hundreds of CL type farm sites; contact them at Amerweg 54, 9444 TG Grolloo, info@vekabo.nl, www.vekabo.nl, tel (0591) 377627. Another organisation offering good value farm sites is SVR, c/o Camping De Victorie, Broeksweg 75-77, 4231 VD Meerkerk, tel (0)183 352741, info@svr.nl, www.svr.nl. British caravanners may join both organisations for a small annual subscription.

The Nederlandse Caravan Club runs 26 campsites, most of which are well equipped with basic facilities. Admission to NCC sites is open to members only, but members of FICC-affiliated clubs, such as The Caravan Club, are welcome providing they make advance reservations through the NCC head office at Nieuwe Concordialaan 12, 6712 GM Ede (PO Box 8177, 6710 AD Ede), tel (0)318 619124, email info@ncc.nl, www.ncc.nl. You should carry a Camping Card International as well as a valid membership card issued by your own club.

A Camping Card International is essential for those wishing to stay on a country or farm site and, while it is not compulsory, it is recommended on other sites to avoid handing in a passport.

The periods over, and immediately after, the Ascension Day holiday and the Whitsun weekend are very busy for Dutch sites and you can expect to find many of them full. Advance booking is highly recommended.

Casual/wild camping is prohibited as is overnight camping by the roadside or in car parks. There are overnight parking places specifically for motorhomes all over the country – see the website of the Camper Club Nederland, www.campervriendelijk.nl and look under 'camperplaatsen NL' or write to CCN at Postbus 70, 7240 AB Lochem, tel (0)643 582790. Alternatively see www.campercontact.nl

Many campsites also have motorhome amenities and some offer Quick Stop overnight facilities at reduced rates.

Country Information

Cycling

There are twice as many bicycles as cars in the Netherlands and as a result cyclists are catered for better than in any other country. Owing to the flat nature of much of the countryside, it is a pastime all members of the family can enjoy. There are 15,000 kilometres of well-maintained cycle tracks in both town and country, all marked with red and white road signs and mushroom-shaped posts indicating the quickest and/or most scenic routes. Local tourist information centres (VVV) sell maps of a wide range of cycling tours and a cycling fact sheet and maps are available from the Netherlands Board of Tourism in London. Motorists should expect to encounter heavy cycle traffic, particularly during rush hours.

Obligatory separate bicycle lanes for cyclists are indicated by circular blue signs displaying a white bicycle. Small oblong signs with the word 'fietspad' or 'rijwielpad' indicate optional bicycle lanes. White bicycles and dotted white lines painted on the road surface indicate cycle lanes which may be used by motor vehicles providing they do not obstruct cyclists. Cycle lanes marked by continuous white lines are prohibited to motor vehicles.

Cyclists must obey traffic light signals at crossroads and junctions; elsewhere, where no traffic lights are in operation, they must give way to traffic from the right.

Cycle tracks are also used by invalid vehicles and mopeds which can travel at high speeds. Pedestrians should be especially cautious when crossing roads, especially on zebra crossings. Look out for both cyclists and riders of mopeds, who often ignore traffic rules as well as red lights. In Amsterdam in particular, many cyclists do not use lights at night.

Transportation of Bicycles

Bicycles may be carried on the roof of a car providing the total height does not exceed 4 metres. They may also be carried at the rear providing the width does not extend more than 20cm beyond the width of the vehicle.

Electricity and Gas

Most campsites have a supply ranging from 4 to 10 amps and almost all have CEE connections. Plugs have two round pins.

The full range of Campingaz cylinders is available.

*See **Electricity and Gas** in the section **DURING YOUR STAY.***

Entry Formalities

British and Irish passport holders may stay in the Netherlands for up to three months without a visa.

Regulations for Pets

*See **Pet Travel Scheme** under **Documents** in the section **PLANNING AND TRAVELLING**.*

Medical Services

Pharmacies (apotheek) dispense prescriptions whereas drugstores (drogisterij) sell only over-the-counter remedies, amongst other items. Pharmacies may require a photocopy of the details on your European Health Insurance Card (EHIC). You will need to show your EHIC to obtain treatment by a doctor contracted to the state health care system (AGIS Zorgverzekeringen) and you will probably have to pay a fee. You will be charged for emergency dental treatment. Charges for prescriptions vary. Refunds are obtained from AGIS.

Inpatient hospital treatment is free provided it is authorised by AGIS. Local state health insurance fund offices can give advice on obtaining emergency medical services and provide names and addresses of doctors, health centres and hospitals. Tourist offices also keep lists of local doctors.

You are strongly recommended to obtain comprehensive travel and medical insurance before travelling to the Netherlands, such as The Caravan Club's Red Pennant Overseas Holiday Insurance – see www.caravanclub.co.uk/redpennant

*See **Medical Matters** in the section **DURING YOUR STAY.***

Opening Hours

Banks – Mon-Fri 9am-4pm/5pm (some open Saturdays).

Museums – Tue-Fri 10am-5pm; Sat & Sun 11am/1pm-5pm.

Post Offices – Mon-Fri 9am-5pm; some post offices Sat 9am-12 noon/1.30pm.

Shops – Mon-Fri 8am/8.30am-6pm/8pm; Sat 8am/8.30am-4pm/5pm; late night shopping in many towns on Thursday or Friday to 9pm. Shops close one day or half day in the week in addition to Sunday.

Safety and Security

In relative terms there is little crime but visitors should take the usual precautions in central Amsterdam (particularly in and around Central Station), in Rotterdam and The Hague. As in many large cities, pickpocketing and bag snatching are commonplace. Pickpockets often operate in gangs (usually, but not exclusively, on trams especially on numbers 2 and 5 in Amsterdam); while one distracts you, often by asking for directions, another picks your pocket or steals your bag.

Opportunist thieves are prevalent and sometimes enter restaurants with the excuse of selling you something or looking for someone. It has been known for bags to be stolen from between people's feet while they are distracted. Ensure you keep your valuables safely with you at all times and do not leave them unattended or hanging on the back of a chair. Bicycle theft is a common occurrence in the major cities.

Fake, plain clothes policemen are in action pretending to be investigating counterfeit money and false credit cards. You may be identifiable as a tourist and asked to hand over your money and credit cards for verification; sometimes you may also be asked for your PINs and/or searched for drugs. The fake policemen may show shiny police badges. Dutch police do not have badges and plain clothes police will rarely carry out this kind of inspection. Always ask for identity, check it thoroughly and do not allow yourself to be intimidated. Call 0900 8844 to contact the nearest police station if you are suspicious.

Several deaths occur each year due to drowning in canals. Take particular care when driving, cycling or walking alongside canals.

Avoid confrontation with anyone offering to sell you drugs and stay away from quiet or dark alleys, particularly late at night.

There have been incidences of drinks being spiked in city centre locations. Always be aware of your drink and do not leave it unattended. Young women and lone travellers need to be especially vigilant.

The Netherlands shares with the rest of Europe a general threat from terrorism. Attacks could be indiscriminate and against civilian targets in public places, including tourist sites.

*See **Safety and Security** in the section **DURING YOUR STAY.***

British Embassy

LANGE VOORHOUT 10, 2514 ED THE HAAG
Tel: (070) 4270427
http://ukinnl.fco.gov.uk/en/

British Consulate-General

KONINGSLAAN 44,1075 AE AMSTERDAM
Tel: (020) 6764343

Irish Embassy

SCHEVENINGSEWEG 112, 2584 AE THE HAGUE
Tel: (070) 3630993
www.embassyofireland.nl

There is also an Irish Honorary Consulate-General in Rhoon (Rotterdam).

Customs Regulations

Alcohol and Tobacco

*For import allowances for alcohol and tobacco products see **Customs Regulations** in the section **PLANNING AND TRAVELLING.***

Documents

Passport

Everyone from the age of 14 is required to show a valid identity document to police officers on request and you should, therefore, carry your passport at all times.

Vehicle(s)

When driving carry your driving licence, vehicle registration certificate (V5C), insurance certificate and MOT certificate, if applicable. If driving a vehicle that does not belong to you, carry a letter of authority from the owner.

*See **Documents** in the section **PLANNING AND TRAVELLING.***

Money

Money may be exchanged at main border crossing posts, major post offices, banks, VVV tourist information offices and some ANWB offices. Other bureaux de change may not give such favourable rates. Recent visitors report difficulties in finding banks that will cash travellers' cheques, even euro ones. As a last resort bureaux de change at stations in major towns will usually cash them.

The major credit and debit cards are widely accepted (VISA more widely than others) but supermarkets will not generally accept credit cards. As a precaution carry enough cash to cover your purchases as you may find that debit cards issued by banks outside the Netherlands are not accepted. Cash machines are widespread.

Carry your credit card issuers'/banks' 24-hour UK contact numbers in case of loss or theft of your cards.

Motoring

The Dutch drive assertively and are not renowned for their road courtesy. Pedestrians should be very careful when crossing roads, including on zebra crossings.

Accidents

All accidents which cause injuries or major damage must be reported to the police. Drivers involved in an accident must exchange their identity details and their insurance company information.

Alcohol

The maximum permitted level of alcohol is 50 milligrams in 100 millilitres of blood, i.e. lower than that permitted in the UK (80 milligrams). Penalties for driving under the influence of alcohol can be severe. A lower level of 20 milligrams applies to drivers who have held a driving licence for less than five years. It is wisest to adopt a 'no drinking and driving' rule.

Breakdown Service

There are emergency telephones every 2km on all motorways and they are directly linked to the nearest breakdown centre.

ANWB, the motoring and leisure organisation, has a road patrol service which operates 24 hours a day on all roads. Drivers requiring assistance may call the 'Wegenwacht' road patrol centre by telephoning 088 2692888. Alternatively call the ANWB Emergency Centre on (070) 3147714. Operators speak English.

Charges apply for breakdown assistance and towing is charged according to distance and time of day. Members of clubs affiliated to the AIT/FIA, such as The Caravan Club, incur lower charges. Payment by credit card is accepted. In some areas the ANWB Wegenwacht has contracts with local garages to provide assistance to its members and affiliates.

Essential Equipment

Lights

The use of dipped headlights during the day is recommended.

Child Restraint System

Children under the age of 18 years, measuring less than 1.35m, must be seated in an approved child restraint adapted to their size (ECE 44/03 or 44/04 safety approved). Children under 3 years of age are not permitted to travel in the vehicle if it is not fitted with rear seat belts. Children under 3 years old are able to travel in the front if they are seated in a rear facing child seat with the airbag deactivated.

*See **Motoring – Equipment** in the section **PLANNING AND TRAVELLING.***

Fuel

Unleaded petrol is available from green pumps marked 'Loodvrije Benzine'. LPG (autogas) is widely available along main roads and motorways.

Petrol stations along motorways and main roads and in main towns are open 24 hours, except in parts of the north of the country where they close at 11pm. Credit cards are accepted but some all night petrol stations only have automatic pumps which may operate with bank notes only.

*See **Fuel** under **Motoring – Advice** in the section **PLANNING AND TRAVELLING.***

Parking

Parking meters or discs are in use in many towns allowing parking for between 30 minutes and two or three hours; discs can be obtained from local shops. A sign 'parkeerschijf' indicates times when a disc is compulsory. Paid parking is expensive and there are insufficient parking spaces to meet demand. Clamping and towing away of vehicles are commonplace and fines are high. Check signs for the precise times you are allowed to park, particularly on main roads in Amsterdam.

*See also **Parking Facilities for the Disabled** under **Motoring – Advice** in the section **PLANNING AND TRAVELLING.***

Priority

Yellow diamond shaped signs with a white border indicate priority roads. In the absence of such signs drivers must give way to all traffic approaching from the right. At the intersection of two roads of the same class where there are no signs, traffic from the right has priority.

At junctions marked with a 'priority road ahead' sign, a stop sign or a line of white painted triangles ('shark's teeth') across the road, drivers must give way to all vehicles on the priority road, including bicycles and mopeds. Be particularly careful when using roundabouts – on some you have the right of way when on them, but on others you must give way to vehicles entering the roundabout, i.e. on your right.

Trams have priority at the intersection of roads of equal importance, but they must give way to traffic on priority roads. If a tram or bus stops in the middle of the road to allow passengers on and off, you must stop. Buses have right of way over all other vehicles when leaving bus stops in built-up areas.

Roads

Roads are generally good and well maintained, but are overcrowded and are frequently subject to strong winds. Most cities have a policy of reducing the amount of nonessential traffic within their boundaries. Narrowing roads, obstacles, traffic lights and speed cameras are often in place to achieve this.

Road Signs and Markings

National motorways are distinguished by red signs, and prefixed with the letter A, whereas European motorways have green signs and are prefixed E. Dual carriageways and other main roads have yellow signs with the letter N and secondary roads are prefixed B.

In general road signs and markings conform to international standards. The following are some road signs which may also be seen:

Cycle path

Cycle route

District Numbers

Hard shoulder open as rush-hour lane

Afrit – *Exit*

Doorgaand verkeer gestremd – *No throughway*

Drempels – *Humps*

Langzaam rijden – *Slow down*

Omleiding – *Detour*

Oprit – *Entrance*

Ousteek u lichten – *Switch on lights*

Parkeerplaats – *Parking*

Pas op! – *Attention*

Stop-verbod – *No parking*

Wegomlegging – *Detour*

Werk in uitvoering – *Road works*

Woonerven – *Slow down (in built-up area)*

A continuous central white line should not be crossed even to make a left turn.

Speed Limits

*See **Speed Limits Table** under **Motoring – Advice** in the section **PLANNING AND TRAVELLING**.*

Be vigilant and observe the overhead illuminated lane indicators when they are in use, as speed limits on motorways are variable. Speed cameras, speed traps and unmarked police vehicles are widely used. The use of radar detectors is prohibited. For the location of speed cameras throughout the country see www.fixedspeedcamera.com

Motorhomes over 3,50kg are restricted to 50 km/h (31 mph) in built-up areas and to 80 km/h (50 mph) on all other roads.

Since March 2011 a new speed limit of 130 km/h is being tested for solo cars on certain sections of motorways. This is indicated by signposts.

The beginning of a built up area is indicated by a rectangular blue sign with the name of the locality in white. The end of a built up area is indicated by the same sign with a white diagonal lines across it.

Traffic Jams

The greatest traffic congestion occurs on weekdays at rush hours around the major cities of Amsterdam, Den Bosch, Eindhoven, Rotterdam, Utrecht, The Hague and Eindhoven.

Summer holidays in the Netherlands are staggered and, as a result, traffic congestion is not too severe. However during the Christmas, Easter and Whitsun holiday periods, traffic jams are common and bottlenecks regularly occur on the A2 (Maastricht to Amsterdam), the A12 (Utrecht to the German border) and on the A50 (Arnhem to Apeldoorn). Roads to the Zeeland coast, e.g. the A58, N57 and N59, may become congested during periods of fine weather.

Many Germans head for the Netherlands on their own public holidays and the roads are particularly busy during these periods.

Violation of Traffic Regulations

Police are empowered to impose on-the-spot fines (or confiscate vehicles) for violation of traffic regulations and fines for speeding can be severe. If you are fined always ask for a receipt.

Motorways

There are over 2,340 kilometres of toll-free motorway. There are rest areas along the motorways, most of which have a petrol station and a small shop. Tolls are charged on some bridges and tunnels, notably the following:

Westerschelde Toll Tunnel

A road tunnel links Terneuzen (north of Gent) and Ellewoutsdijk (south of Goes) across the Westerschelde. It provides a short, fast route between Channel ports and the road network in the west of the country. The tunnel is 6.6km long (just over 4 miles) and the toll (2011) for a car + caravan (maximum height 2.5m measured from front axle) is €7.15 and for a motorhome €4.80 (height under 2.5m) or €17.50 (height over 2.5m). Credit cards are accepted. See www.westerscheldetunnel.nl

Touring

The southern Netherlands is the most densely populated part of the country but, despite the modern sprawl, ancient towns such as Dordrecht, Gouda, Delft and Leiden have retained their individuality and charm. Rotterdam is a modern, commercial centre and a tour of its harbour – the busiest in Europe – makes a fascinating excursion. The scenery in the north of the country is the most typically Dutch – vast, flat landscapes, largely reclaimed from the sea, dotted with windmills. Some of the most charming towns and villages are Marken, Volendam and Alkmaar (famous for its cheese market). Aalsmeer, situated south of Amsterdam, stages the world's largest daily flower auction.

It is worth spending time to visit the hilly provinces in the east such as Gelderland, known for its castles, country houses and its major city, Arnhem, which has many links with the Second World War. Overijssel is a region of great variety and the old Hanseatic towns of Zwolle and Kampen have splendid quays and historic buildings. Friesland is the Netherland's lake district.

An Amsterdam Card entitles you to free admission to many of the city's famous museums, including the Rijksmuseum and Van Gogh Museum, and to discounts in many restaurants, shops, attractions and at Park & Ride car parks. It also entitles you to discounts on tours as well as free travel on public transport and a free canal cruise. The Card is valid for one, two or three days and is available from tourist information offices, some Shell petrol stations, Canal Bus kiosks, Park & Ride car parks and some hotels. Alternatively purchase online from www.iamsterdamcard.com

There are few dishes that can be described as essentially Dutch but almost every large town has a wide selection of restaurants specialising in international cuisine. As a result of the Dutch colonisation of the former East Indies, Indonesian food is particularly popular. Dutch gin 'genever' and 'advocaat' are the best known drinks and local beer is excellent. Service charges are included in restaurant bills and tips are not necessary. Smoking is not permitted in bars or restaurants.

Spring is one of the most popular times to visit the Netherlands, in particular the famous Keukenhof Gardens near Lisse, open from 22 March to 20 May in 2012, see www.keukenhof.nl. Visitors enjoy a display of over seven million flowering bulbs, trees and shrubs. Special events take place here at other times of the year, including a National Bulb Market in October.

Local Travel

There is an excellent network of buses and trams, together with metro systems in Amsterdam (called the GVB), Rotterdam and The Hague. An electronic card 'OV Chipkaart' is gradually replacing the previous system of 'Strippenkaart' which were strips of 15 or 45 tickets valid throughout the country.

OV-Chip cards can be bought at vending machines at stations or ticket offices and on board buses and trams and are available for periods from one hour to seven days allowing unlimited travel on trams, buses and the metro. Children under the age of 12 and people over the age of 65 qualify for reduced fares (show your passport as proof of age). For more information see www.gvb.nl

Tickets must be validated before travel either at the yellow machines on trams and at metro stations or by your bus driver or conductor.

In Amsterdam canal transport includes a regular canal shuttle between Centraal Station and the Rijksmuseum. A 'circle tram' travels from Centraal Station through the centre of Amsterdam past a number of local visitor attractions, such as Anne Frank's house, the Rijksmuseum, Van Gogh museum and Rembrandthuis.

There are Park & Ride facilities at most railway stations. Secure parking is also offered at 'transferiums', a scheme offering reasonably priced guarded parking in secure areas on the outskirts of major towns with easy access by road and close to public transport hubs. Transferiums have heated waiting rooms and rest rooms as well as information for travellers, and some even have a shop.

Frequent car ferry services operate on routes to the Frisian (or Wadden) Islands off the north west coast, for example, from Den Helder to Texel Island, Harlingen to Terschelling Island and Holwerd to Ameland Island. Other islands in the group do not allow cars but there are passenger ferry services. In the summer island-hopping round tickets are available to foot passengers and cyclists.

If you use P & O Ferries' Hull to Rotterdam service then recent visitors recommend making a particular note of the berth ('haven') number on arrival at Rotterdam in preparation for your return sailing. There are thousands of berths and it is understood that signposting may be difficult as you approach the port.

All place names used in the Site Entry listings which follow can be found in Michelin's Benelux & North of France Touring & Motoring Atlas, scale 1:150,000 (1 cm = 1.5 km).

AARDENBURG see Sluis *A4*

AERDT see Zevenaar *C3*

⊞ **AFFERDEN** *C3* (1km N Rural) *51.63845, 6.00325* **Camping Klein Canada, Dorpsstraat 1, 5851 AG Afferden [(0485) 531223; fax 532218; info@kleincanada.nl; www.kleincanada.nl]** Fr Nijmegen on A77/E31 exit junc 2 to Afferden. Site is 1km N of Afferden on N271. Lge, mkd pitch, some hdstg, pt shd; htd wc; chem disp; mv service pnt; fam bthrm; baby facs; serviced pitches; sauna; shwrs inc; el pnts (6-10A) inc; gas; Indtte (inc dryer); shop; rest; snacks; bar; playgrnd; 2 pools (1 htd, covrd); paddling pool; waterslide; cycle hire; animal park; wifi; entmnt; TV rm; 80% statics; dogs; phone; Holland Tulip Parcs site; poss cr; Eng spkn; adv bkg; quiet; ccard acc; CCI. "Excel san facs & rest; gd touring base E Holland & W Germany; in Maasduinen National Park; child friendly; highly rec." ♦ € 29.00 2008*

ALKMAAR *B2* (2km N Rural) *52.64200, 4.72390* **Camping Alkmaar, Bergerweg 201, 1817 ML Alkmaar [(072) 5116924; info@campingalkmaar.nl; www.campingalkmaar.nl]** Fr W ring rd (Martin Luther Kingweg) foll Bergen sp, bear R at T-junc & site 150m on L. Site well sp. Med, mkd pitch, hdstg, pt shd; htd wc; chem disp; mv service pnt; fam bthrm; shwrs €0.50; el pnts (4-10A) inc; Indtte; shop 1km; BBQ; playgrnd; pool adj; sand beach 6km; golf 2km; cab TV; some cabins; dogs €3; bus at gate; poss cr; Eng spkn; adv bkg; quiet; ccard acc; red CCI. "Clean, friendly site; sm pitches; buses to town; 10 mins walk to cent; cheese mkt on Friday in ssn." ♦ 1 Apr-1 Oct. € 25.00 2009*

ALKMAAR *B2* (3km N Rural) *52.69425, 4.77080* **Camping DroomPark Molengroet, Molengroet 1, 1723 PX Noord-Scharwoude [(0226) 393444; fax 391426; info@molengroet.nl; www.molengroet.nl]** Fr Amsterdam, Haarlem take A9 to end at rndabt, then onto Ring Alkmaar & foll sp Schagen. Take N245 sp Schagen (dual carr'way). Exit at km post 25.2 W sp Geestmeerambacht. Site sp on R. Lge, hdg/mkd pitch, unshd; htd wc; chem disp; mv service pnt; baby facs; fam bthrm; some serviced pitches; private san facs some pitches; shwrs inc; el pnts (4-10A) inc; gas; Indtte (inc dryer); shop; rest; snacks; bar; BBQ; htd pool; sand beach 10km; lake sw 300m; entmnt; cycle hire; sat TV; 50% statics; dogs €3; sep car park; free bus to cheese mkt (Fri) & beach (Sat); Holland Tulip Parcs site; adv bkg; quiet; ccard acc. "Located in recreation park with lge lake; site bus to cheese mkt & beach; modern, clean san facs." Easter-31 Oct. € 26.00 (CChq acc) 2009*

ALKMAAR *B2* (4km SW Rural) *52.60841, 4.68899* **Camping Klein Varnebroek, De Omloop 22, 1852 AB Heiloo [(072) 5331627; fax 5331620; info@kleinvarnebroek.nl; www.kleinvarnebroek.nl]** Exit A9 Haarlem-Alkmaar at Heiloo. At 1st traff lts in Heiloo foll sp twds Egmond; then foll sp to site & sw baths (Zwembad), site opp pool. Lge, pt shd; htd wc; chem disp; fam bthrm; private bthrms avail; shwrs inc; el pnts (4-6A) €3.50; gas; Indtte; shop, rest, snacks, bar high ssn; playgrnd; pool opp; games area; cycle hire; TV; 50% statics; no dogs; phone; sep car park; quiet; ccard acc; red low ssn. "Excel facs; gd family site." 26 Mar-19 Sep. € 23.50 (4 persons) 2010*

ALKMAAR *B2* (5km SW Rural) *52.60649, 4.69016* **Camping Heiloo, De Omloop 24, 1852 RJ Heiloo [(072) 5355555; fax 5355551; info@campingheiloo.nl; www.campingheiloo.nl]** Exit A9 at Heiloo. At 1st traff lts in Heiloo turn L sp Egmond, foll sp to site. Med, pt shd; htd wc; chem disp; mv service pnt; baby facs; shwrs inc; el pnts (4A) inc; Indtte; shop 100m; rest; snacks; bar; playgrnd; htd, covrd pool adj; sand beach 5km; internet; TV; 50% statics; no dogs; train nr; sep car park (extra for car on pitch); Eng spkn; adv bkg; quiet, but occasional aircraft noise; ccard acc (surcharge). "San facs unisex low ssn; Heiloo quiet & untouristy; easy cycling to coast, bulbfields, Alkmaar; gd." ♦ 4 Apr-20 Sep. € 26.75 2009*

⊞ **ALKMAAR** *B2* (6km SW Rural) *52.63100, 4.69500* **Camping Hoeve Engeland, Egmondermeer 9, 1934 PN Egmond aan den Hoef [(072) 5116370; rus.jan@tiscali.nl]** Take A9 to Alkmaar & take N9 ring rd W. Take 1st L turn after rlwy viaduct at traff lts opp ING bank. Foll sm rd past garden cent, site in approx 250m - sp on gate. Sm, pt shd; htd wc; shwrs inc; el pnts (16A) inc (poss rev pol); beach 8km; bus 1km; poss cr; Eng spkn; adv bkg; quiet. "Friendly, CL-type farm site; clean (ltd) facs; mosquitoes; gd cycling to historic Alkmaar & coastal dunes." € 12.00 2010*

ALMERE *C3* (2km S Rural) *52.35688, 5.22505* **Camping Waterhout, Archerpad 6, 1324 ZZ Almere [(036) 5470632; fax 5344096; info@waterhout.nl; www.waterhout.nl]** Exit A6 junc 4, site sp fr slip rd on S edge Weerwater. Med, mkd pitch, shd; wc; chem disp; baby facs; fam bthrm; shwrs €0.50; el pnts (10A) inc; Indtte (inc dryer); shop; tradsmn; rest; snacks; bar; playgrnd; sand beach & lake sw adj; entmnt; TV rm; 30% statics; dogs €2.50; phone; bus 200m; poss cr; Eng spkn; adv bkg; quiet; red CCI. "Well laid-out site; conv Amsterdam by bus or train - 30 mins; Almere ultra-modern city." 1 Apr-31 Oct. € 18.50 2009*

⊞ **ALPHEN AAN DEN RIJN** *B3* (5km NE Rural) *52.15039, 4.70524* **NCC Camping Oudshoorn, Westkanaalweg 18a, 2403 NA Alphen aan den Rijn [(0172) 424666; alphen@ncc.nl; www.ncc.nl]** Fr N on A4/E19 exit onto N207 dir Alphen ann den Rijn. Keep on N207 at Ring Noord, cross Aar Kanal & at rndabt turn L sp Zegersloot Noord, then turn L/double-back immed & cross back over Aar Canal on bdge section for local traff. Turn L at end of U-bend, foll canal for 800m, site on L. Med, hdg/mkd pitch, pt shd; htd wc; chem disp; mv service pnt; shwrs inc; el pnts (4A) €2.20; Indtte; shop; playgrnd; pool 5km; dogs; bus 2km; poss cr; adv bkg; some rd & aircraft noise. "Free use bikes for children; boules every evening; site ideally situated for historic towns; members only - C'van Club members welcome but must pre-book." ♦ € 10.00 2008*

AMERSFOORT *C3* (9km S Rural) *52.07975, 5.38151* **Vakantiepark De Heigraaf, De Haygraeff 9, 3931 ML Woudenberg [(033) 2865066; info@heigraaf.nl; www.heigraaf.nl]** Exit A12 at Maarn junc 21 or junc 22 & foll sp to site on N224, 2km W of Woudenberg. V lge, mkd pitch, pt shd; htd wc; chem disp; mv service pnt; baby facs; shwrs €0.50; el pnts (4-6A) inc; Indtte (inc dryer); shop; rest; snacks; bar; playgrnd; lake sw 150m; wifi; entmnt; 50% statics; no dogs; phone; bus 500m; Eng spkn; adv bkg; quiet. "Vg, well-managed site; modern san facs." ♦ 1 Apr-31 Oct. € 18.00 2008*

⊞ **AMERSFOORT** *C3* (5km NW Rural) *52.15996, 5.33690* **King's Home Park, Birkstraat 136, 3768 HM Soest [(033) 4619118; fax 4610808; camping@kingshome.nl; www.kingshome.nl]** Leave A28 Utrecht to Amersfoort rd at junc 5 (Maarn). Foll sps with elephant picture for 4km to zoo, turn L at traff lts. Turn L, site on L in 200m. Med, pt shd, all serviced pitches; htd wc; chem disp; fam bthrm; baby facs; shwrs €0.60; el pnts (10A) inc; gas; lndtte; shops 5km; snacks, bar high ssn; playgrnd; pool 800m; tennis; TV; cycle hire; entmnt; 95% statics; dogs €2.50; bus; sep car park; Eng spkn; adv bkg; quiet but noise fr kennels adj; red long stay/snr citizen; CCI. "Touring pitches not rec m'vans or lge o'fits; excel, refurbished facs." ♦ € 24.00 2008*

AMSTELVEEN see Amsterdam *B3*

⊞ **AMSTERDAM** *B3* (5km N Rural) *52.43649, 4.91445* **Camping Het Rietveen, Noordeinde 130, 1121 AL Landsmeer [(020) 4821468; fax 4820214; info@camping hetrietveen.nl; www.campinghetrietveen.nl]** Fr A10 ring rd exit junc 117. At junc off slip rd turn L dir Landsmeer, site sp. Sm, mkd pitch, mkd pitch; wc; chem disp; mv service pnt; shwrs inc; el pnts (10A) inc; shop, rest, bar 500m; lake sw & fishing; tennis; cycle hire; dogs free; phone adj; bus to Amsterdam 200m; poss cr; Eng spkn; adv bkg; quiet; CCI. "Vg, pretty lakeside site, like lge CL, in well-kept vill; no recep - site yourself & owner will call; sep field avail for rallies; excel touring base; city 30 mins by bus." € 25.00 2010*

⊞ **AMSTERDAM** *B3* (3km E Urban) *52.36555, 4.95829* **Camping Zeeburg, Zuider Ijdijk 20, 1095 KN Amsterdam [(020) 6944430; fax 6946238; info@campingzeeburg.nl; www.campingzeeburg.nl]** Fr A10 ring rd exit at S114 & foll site sps. Lge, unshd; wc; chem disp; mv service pnt; shwrs €0.80; el pnts (6-10A) inc; gas; lndtte; shop; snacks; cycle hire; internet; some statics; dogs €3; bus/tram to city nr; poss cr; adv bkg. "Used mainly by tents in summer, but rest of year suitable for c'vans; conv city cent." € 28.00 2011*

AMSTERDAM *B3* (10km S Urban) *52.31258, 4.99035* **Gaasper Camping, Loosdrechtdreef 7, 1108 AZ Amsterdam-Zuidoost [(020) 6967326; fax 6969369; www.gaaspercamping.nl]** Fr A2 take A9 E sp Amersfoort. After about 5km take 3rd exit sp Gaasperplas/Weesp S113. Cross S113 into site, sp. Lge, hdg/mkd pitch, some hdstg, pt shd; htd wc; chem disp; mv service pnt; serviced pitches; shwrs metered; el pnts (10A) €3.50 (care needed); gas; lndtte; shop; rest; snacks; bar; playgrnd; 20% statics; dogs €2.50; metro 5 mins walk (tickets fr site recep); poss cr; Eng spkn; quiet but some rd & air traffic noise; CCI. "Immac site set in beautiful parkland; well-run with strict rules; night guard at barrier (high ssn); vans must be manhandled onto pitch (help avail); high ssn arr early to ensure pitch - no adv bkg for fewer than 7 nights; poss cold shwrs & ltd shop low ssn." 15 Mar-1 Nov. € 22.00 2010*

AMSTERDAM *B3* (12km SW Rural) *52.29366, 4.82316* **Camping Het Amsterdamse Bos, Kleine Noorddijk 1, 1187 NZ Amstelveen [(020) 6416868; fax 6402378; info@campingamsterdam.com; www.campingamsterdamsebos.com]** Foll A10 & A4 twd Schiphol Airport. Fr junc on A4 & A9 m'way, take A9 E twd Amstelveen; at next exit (junc 6) exit sp Aalsmeer. Foll Aalsmeer sp for 1km bearing R at traff lts then at next traff lts turn L over canal bdge onto N231. In 1.5km turn L at 2nd traff lts into site. Fr S exit A4 junc 3 onto N201 dir Hilversum (ignore other camp sps). Turn L onto N231 dir Amstelveen, at rd junc Bovenkirk take N231 dir Schiphol, site on R in 200m, sp. V lge, pt shd; htd wc; chem disp; mv service pnt; shwrs €0.80; el pnts (10A) €4.50; gas; lndtte; shop; supmkt nr; rest; snacks; bar; waterpark nr; 20% statics; dogs €2.50; bus to city; poss cr; Eng spkn; no adv bkg; some aircraft noise; ccard acc; CCI. "Conv Amsterdam by bus - tickets sold on site; poss migrant workers resident on site; san facs stretched high season; gd walking & cycling paths; spectacular daily flower auctions at Aalsmeer; conv bulbfields." ♦ 15 Mar-1 Dec. € 25.50 2011*

AMSTERDAM *B3* (10km W Rural) *52.39548, 4.75308* **Camping Parc Spaarnwoude (formerly Houtrak), Zuiderweg 2, 1105 NA Halfweg [(020) 4972796; fax (087) 7844089; info@campinghoutrak.nl; www.parcspaarnwoude.nl]** Fr A9 dir Haarlem exit onto A200 sp Halfweg. In 1.5km sp for Spaarnwoude, go L under A200, over rlwy x-ing & take 4th on L. Site on R in 100m. Fr Amsterdam foll N202, Spaarnwoude & site sp. Sm, mkd pitch, pt shd; htd wc; chem disp; mv service pnt; baby facs; shwrs €0.50; el pnts (6A) €2.20; lndtte; playgrnd; pool 11km; internet; TV; dogs €5; poss cr; noise fr aircraft. "Under flightpath into Schiphol airport; min stay 3 nights Aug." 1 Apr-31 Oct. € 17.40 2009*

APELDOORN *C3* (7km N Rural) *52.29066, 5.94520* **Camping De Helfterkamp, Gortelseweg 24, 8171 RA Vaassen [(0578) 571839; fax 570378; info@helfterkamp.nl; www.helfterkamp.nl]** Leave A50 junc 26; foll sp to Vaassen; site sp on ent to town - 2.5km W of Vaassen. Med, mkd pitch, pt shd; htd wc; chem disp; baby facs; fam bthrm; shwrs €0.50; el pnts (6A) metered (poss rev pol); gas; lndtte; shop; playgrnd; lake sw 1.5km; cycle hire; 40% statics; dogs €1.75; phone; Eng spkn; adv bkg ess high ssn; quiet; ccard acc; 10% red long stay; CCI. "Excel, immac, well-maintained, busy site in beautiful woodland area; key for shwrs & hot water; v friendly owners; conv for Apeldoorn/Arnhem areas & De Hooge Veluwe National Park; gd walking/cycling." 16 Feb-31 Oct. € 19.20 2008*

APELDOORN *C3* (13km N Rural) *52.31366, 5.92705* **Recreatiecentrum De Wildhoeve, Hanendorperweg 102, 8166 JJ Emst [(0578) 661324; fax 662965; info@wildhoeve.nl; www.wildhoeve.nl]** Exit 26 fr A50, site sp 3.5km W of Emst. Lge, mkd pitch, pt shd; htd wc; chem disp; mv service pnt; serviced pitches; fam bthrm; baby facs; shwrs; el pnts (6A); gas; lndtte (inc dryer); shop; tradsmn; rest; snacks; bar; playgrnd; 2 pools (1 htd, covrd); paddling pool; waterslide; games area; tennis; cycle hire; wifi; TV; 20% statics; no dogs; sep car park; Holland Tulip Parcs site; adv bkg. ♦ 1 Apr-30 Sep. € 31.75 (CChq acc) 2011*

⊞ **APELDOORN** *C3* (8km S Rural) *52.15096, 6.02197* **Camping De Vinkenkamp, Vinkenkamp 10, 7364 CD Lieren [(055) 5051253; info@vinkenkamp.nl; www.vinkenkamp.nl]** Exit A1 junc 20 Apeldoorn Sud & foll sp Loenen-Eerbeek. Site sp. Med, mkd pitch, pt shd; htd wc; chem disp; mv service pnt; baby facs; shwrs inc; el pnts (6-16A) inc; gas; Indtte; shop; snacks; bar; playgrnd; entmnt; TV; some statics; dogs €1.70; Eng spkn; quiet; ccard acc. "Beautiful part of Holland; excel site." € 22.50 2010*

⊞ **APELDOORN** *C3* (10km S Rural) *52.11771, 5.90641* **Camping De Pampel, Woeste Hoefweg 35, 7351 TN Hoenderloo [(055) 3781760; fax 3781992; info@pampel.nl; www.pampel.nl]** Exit A50 Apeldoorn-Arnhem m'way W at junc 19 Hoenderloo. Fr Hoenderloo dir Loenen, site sp. Lge, hdg/mkd pitch, pt shd; htd wc; chem disp; mv service pnt; serviced pitches; baby facs; fam bthrm; private bthrms avail; shwrs inc; el pnts (16A) €3; Indtte; shop & 1km; tradsmn; rest in ssn; snacks; bar; playgrnd; 2 pools; cycle hire; go-kart hire; no dogs €3 (not acc high ssn); poss cr; adv bkg ess high ssn & Bank Hols; quiet but rd noise some pitches; red low ssn. "V pleasant setting 2km fr National Park; excel facs; free 1-day bus ticket; private bthrms avail; some site rds diff for lge o'fits; vg for children; many mkd walks/cycle paths; friendly staff." € 25.00 2008*

APELDOORN *C3* (13km SW Rural) *52.15040, 5.74080* **Camping De Harskamperdennen, Houtvester van 't Hoffweg 25, 3775 KB Kootwijk [(0318) 456272; fax 457695; info@harskamperdennen.nl; www.harskamperdennen.nl]** Exit A1/E30 at junc 17 dir Harskamp, site sp on L in 6km. Lge, shd; htd wc; chem disp; mv service pnt; baby facs; shwrs €0.50; el pnts (4-6A) inc; gas; Indtte; tradsmn; playgrnd; games area; cycle hire; TV; no dogs; phone; sep car park; quiet; ccard acc. "All pitches in sm glades in forest; military base nr & explosions heard from time to time, otherwise peaceful; neat, tidy site; friendly staff." ♦ 1 Apr-25 Oct. € 25.90 2009*

⊞ **ARCEN** *D4* (3km N Rural) *51.49616, 6.18395* **Recreakiepark Klein Vink, Klein Vink 4, 5944 EX Arcen [(077) 4732525 or 4731564; info@kleinvink.nl; www.roompotparken.nl/parken/kleinvink]** N fr Venlo on N271; by-pass Arcen on dual c'way. Site on R in 6km. Med, mkd pitch, pt shd; htd wc; chem disp; mv service pnt; baby facs; fam bthrm; shwrs inc; el pnts (6A) inc; Indtte; shop; rest; snacks; bar; BBQ; playgrnd; htd pool; paddling pool; lake sw adj; games area; entmnt; cab/sat TV; 80% statics; dogs; phone; Eng spkn; adv bkg; quiet; red low ssn. "Well-run site in lge holiday park with full amenities; v busy in summer." ♦ € 42.00 2007*

ARCEN *D4* (3km NE Rural) *51.49130, 6.20638* **Camping De Maasvallei, Dorperheiderweg 34, 5944 NK Arcen [(077) 4731564; fax 4731573; info@demaasvallei.nl]** N fr Venlo on N271. Take dual c'way by-passing vill of Arcen. At traff lts sp Lingsfort turn R sp Geldern & foll site sp. Lge, mkd/hdg pitch, pt shd; htd wc; chem disp; mv service pnt; baby facs; fam bthrm; shwrs inc; el pnts (6A) inc; Indtte; shop; rest; snacks; bar; playgrnd; htd pool & use of Klein Vink pool; lake sw; tennis; games area; cycle hire; TV rm; 80% statics; dogs; phone; poss cr; adv bkg; quiet; CCI. "Well-run site; same owners as Klein Vink; if recep clsd contact Klein Vink." 1 Jan-31 Oct. 2008*

ARNHEM *C3* (5km W Rural) *51.99365, 5.82203* **Camping Aan Veluwe (formerly De Bilderberg), Sportlaan 1, 6861 AG Oosterbeek [(0224) 563109; fax 563093; info@aannoordzee.nl; www.aanveluwe.nl]** Fr S fr Nijmegen, cross new bdge at Arnhem. Foll Oosterbeek sp for 5km, cont past memorial in Oosterbeek, in 1km turn R at rndabt, 500m L to site. Or fr A50 exit junc 19 onto N225 twd Osterbeek/Arnhem. In 3km at rndabt turn L, site on L in 500m. Med, pt sl, pt shd; htd wc; chem disp; shwrs inc; el pnts (16A) inc; gas; shop; bar; playgrnd; pool 3km; adv bkg; few statics; dogs €1.80; sep car park; quiet; red for long stays. "Conv Airborne Museum & Cemetery & Dutch Open Air Museum; sports club bar open to site guests; shwr facs for each pitch; lovely walks." 1 Apr-31 Oct. € 26.50 2010*

ARNHEM *C3* (2km NW Rural) *52.02405, 5.85875* **Recreatiepark Arnhem, Kemperbergerweg 771, 6816 RW Arnhem [(026) 4431600; fax 4457705; info@recreatieparkarnhem.nl; www.vakantiebundel.nl]** Fr Utrecht on m'way A12/E35, exit 25 sp Oosterbeek, after 1.5km turn L sp Hooge Veluwe. After 1.5km turn R & & in 1.8km turn R foll site sp. Immed after bdge turn R to site ent (bad rd). Lge, mkd pitch, shd; htd wc; chem disp; mv service pnt; baby facs; serviced pitches inc sat TV; shwrs inc; el pnts (4-10A) €2.50 (poss rev pol); gas; Indtte; shop; rest; snacks; bar; playgrnd; pool & paddling pool; tennis; games area; entmnt; TV; poss cr; 25% statics; quiet but some m'way noise; CCI. "Many tourist attractions in area; site in fir trees; beware 'sleeping policemen'; secluded pitches; excel facs for children." ♦ Easter-25 Oct. € 32.00 2008*

ARNHEM *C3* (3km NW Rural) *52.0072, 5.8714* **Camping Warnsborn, Bakenbergseweg 257, 6816 PB Arnhem [(026) 4423469; fax 4421095; info@campingwarnsborn.nl; www.campingwarnsborn.nl]** Fr Utrecht on E35/A12, exit junc 25 Ede (if coming fr opp dir, beware unnumbered m'way junc 200m prior to junc 25). Take N224 dual c'way twd Arnhem & foll sp Burgers Zoo, site sp. Beware oncoming traff & sleeping policeman nr site ent. Med, pt shd; htd wc; chem disp, mv service pnt; baby facs; fam bthrm; shwrs €1; el pnts (4A) inc; gas; Indtte; sm shop & 3km; tradsmn; rest 1km; BBQ; playgrnd; internet; 5% statics; dogs €3; phone; bus 100m; poss cr; Eng spkn; adv bkg; quiet; ccard acc; red long stay/CCI. "Excel, spacious, clean, well-maintained, wooded site; san facs clean; friendly, helpful family owners & staff; airborne museum & cemetery; cycle rtes direct fr site; conv Hooge Veluwe National Park & Kröller-Müller museum (Van Gogh paintings)." ♦ 1 Apr-31 Oct. € 19.40 2011*

ARNHEM *C3* (5km NW Rural) *52.03192, 5.86652* **Droompark Hooge Veluwe, Koningsweg 14, Schaarsbergen, 6816 TC Arnhem [(026) 4432272; fax 4436809; info@dehoogeveluwe.nl; www.hoogeveluwe.nl]** Fr Utrecht A12/E35, Oosterbeck exit 25 & foll sp for Hooge Veluwe to site in 4km on R. Lge, pt shd; htd wc; chem disp; mv service pnt; baby facs; fam bthrm; serviced pitches; shwrs inc; el pnts (6-16A) inc; gas; Indtte; shop; rest; snacks; bar; playgrnd; 2 pools (1 htd, covrd); paddling pool; games area; entmnt; dogs €3.50; 50% static in sep area; sep car park; some rd noise; poss cr; adv bkg; Eng spkn; ccard acc. "Vg, espec for children." ♦ 1 Apr-31 Oct. € 28.00 2010*

NETHERLANDS

⊞ **ASSEN** *D2* (4km SW Rural) *52.98020, 6.50530* **Camping Buitencentrum Witterzomer, Witterzomer 7, 9405 VE Assen [(0592) 393535; fax 393530; www.witterzomer.nl]** Exit A28/E232 junc 33 onto N371 dir Bovensmilde. Site sp. V lge, shd; htd wc; chem disp; baby facs; fam bthrm; private san facs avail some pitches; shwrs inc; el pnts (4-6A €3; gas; lndtte; shop; rest; snacks; bar; playgrnd; pool; waterslide; tennis; games area; entmnt; TV; 50% statics; dogs €4; adv bkg; quiet. "Gd touring cent; conv Assen TT circuit." € 26.00 2007*

BAARLAND see Kruiningen *A4*

BARENDRECHT see Rotterdam *B3*

BEERZE see Ommen *D2*

BEILEN *D2* (7km S Rural) *52.80166, 6.52501* **Camping De Otterberg, Drijberseweg 36A, 9418 TL Wijster [(0593) 562362; fax 562941; info@otterburg.nl; www.otterberg.nl]** Take A28 Hoogeveen-Assen exit Dwingeloo/Wijster. In Wijster turn R & foll sps approx 1.5km dir Dribjer. Lge, mkd pitch, pt shd; htd wc; fam bthrm; baby facs; chem disp; shwrs €0.20; el pnts (6A) inc; gas; lndtte (inc dryer); shop; snacks; rest; playgrnd; pool; tennis; cycle hire; TV; 60% statics; dogs €3; phone; poss cr; Eng spkn; adv bkg. "Helpful, friendly site adj National Park; gd, modern san facs." ♦ 1 Apr-1 Oct. € 25.00 2010*

BEILEN *D2* (2.5km NW Rural) *52.85285, 6.59010* **Camping De Valkenhof, Beilerstraat 13a, 9431 GA Westerbork [(0593) 331546; fax 333278; info@camping-de-valkenhof.nl; www.camping-de-valkenhof.nl]** Exit A28 junc 30 Beilen, dir Westerbork, site sp to W of Westerbork. Lge, some hdstg, pt shd; htd wc; chem disp; mv service pnt; baby facs; fam bthrm; shwrs inc; el pnts (6A) inc; gas; lndtte (inc dryer); supmkt high ssn; snacks; BBQ; playgrnd; htd pool; paddling pool; waterslide; games area; cycle hire; wifi; cab TV; 20% statics; dogs €4.35; sep car park; Holland Tulip Parcs site; Eng spkn; adv bkg; quiet. "Gd walking area." 1 Apr-1 Oct. € 25.00 (CChq acc) 2011*

BELT SCHUTSLOOT see Meppel *C2*

BERG EN TERBLIJT see Valkenburg aan de Geul *C4*

BERGEIJK see Eersel *C4*

BERGEN OP ZOOM *B4* (3km NW Rural) *51.51122, 4.31652* **Camping De Heide, Bemmelenberg 12, 4614 PG Bergen op Zoom [(0164) 235659 or 253522; fax 254377; info@campingdeheide.nl; www.campingdeheide.nl]** Exit A58 at Bergen op Zoom Noord, foll sp to town until De Heide sps are picked up. Lge, hdg pitch, pt shd; wc; chem disp; mv service pnt; baby facs; fam bthrm; serviced pitch; shwrs €0.50; el pnts (4A) €2.50; gas; lndtte; shop; rest; snacks; playgrnd; pool; sand beach 3km; TV; 75% statics; dogs €3; phone; adv bkg; quiet; red snr citizens; CCI. "Gd NH." ♦ 1 Apr-26 Sep. € 30.00 2009*

BERLICUM see 'S-Hertogenbosch *C3*

BIDDINGHUIZEN see Harderwijk *C3*

BILTHOVEN see Utrecht *B3*

BLADEL *C4* (1km S Rural) *51.35388, 5.22254* **Mini-Camping De Hooiberg, Bredasebaan 20, 5531 NB Bladel [(0497) 369619 or 06 54341822 (mob); info@minicampingdehooiberg.nl; www.minicampingdehooiberg.nl]** Exit A67 junc 32 onto N284 to Bladel, turn L at traff lts to Bladel-Zuid, site on L in 2km. Sm, pt shd; htd wc; chem disp; shwrs inc; el pnts (6A) inc; lndtte (inc dryer); no statics; dogs free; bus adj; sep car park; Eng spkn; adv bkg; quiet. "Gd site." ♦ 15 Mar-31 Oct. € 14.00 2009*

BLADEL *C4* (2km S Rural) *51.34325, 5.22740* **Camping De Achterste Hoef, Troprijt 10, 5531 NA Bladel [(0497) 381579; fax 387776; info@achterstehoef.nl; www.achterstehoef.nl]** Fr A67 exit junc 32 onto N284 to Bladel, then Bladel-Zuid, site sp. V lge, pt shd; htd wc; chem disp; mv service pnt; baby facs; fam bthrm; private san facs avail; shwrs; el pnts (6A) inc; lndtte (inc dryer); supmkt; rest; snacks; bar; playgrnd; 2 pools (1 htd, covrd); paddling pool; waterslide; tennis; games area; games rm; cycle hire; wifi; entmnt; 45% statics; dogs; Holland Tulip Parcs site; adv bkg; ccard acc. ♦ 8 Apr-31 Oct. € 37.50 (CChq acc) 2011*

BLARICUM *C3* (500m N Rural) *52.28172, 5.24302* **Camping De Woensberg, Woensbergweg 5, 1272 JP Huizen [(0577) 411556 or 0900 4004004; fax 711767; info@paasheuvelgroep.nl; www.woensberg.nl]** Fr S on A27 exit junc 35 Blaricum/Huizen, go over m'way to traff lts & cont strt. Site sp on L. Med, mkd pitch, pt shd; htd wc; chem disp; mv service pnt; baby facs; shwrs inc; el pnts (4A) €2.85 (poss rev pol); lndtte; shop; rest; snacks; bar; playgrnd; sports facs 3km; TV; 40% statics; dogs €3.30; sep car park; poss cr; Eng spkn; quiet; CCI. ♦ 1 Apr-30 Oct. € 14.90 2008*

BOURTANGE *D2* (W Rural) *53.01014, 7.18494* **NCC Camping 't Plathuis, Bourtangerkanaal Noord 1, 9545 VJ Bourtange [(0599) 354383; fax 354388; info@plathuis.nl; www.plathuis.nl]** Exit A47 junc 47 onto N368 sp Blijham to Vlagtwedde. Turn L onto N365 to Bourtange, site sp on R. Med, pt shd, htd wc; chem disp; mv service pnt; baby facs; fam bthrm; shwrs €0.50; el pnts (6A) inc (extra for 10A); gas; lndtte; shop; tradsmn; snacks; bar; playgrnd; lake sw; fishing; games area; cycle canoe hire; wifi; 50% statics; dogs; phone; bus; adv bkg; quiet; red CC1. "Site adj historic fortress town 2km fr German border; sm marina at ent; part of site belongs to NCC (C'van Club members welcome at reduced rates but must phone ahead); gd, clean facs; friendly, helpful owners; vg." ♦ 1 Apr-31 Oct. € 17.50 2010*

BREDA *B3* (8km E Rural) *51.58270, 4.90721* **Camping D'n Mastendol, Oosterhoutseweg 7-13, 5121 RE Rijen [(0161) 222664; fax 222669; info@mastendol.nl; www.mastendol.nl]** Take main rd fr Breda twd Tilburg (not m'way). After 9km turn L, on rd sp Oosterhout 9km; camp 500m on L. Lge, pt shd; htd wc; chem disp; mv service pnt; baby facs; shwrs €0.75; el pnts (10A) inc; lndtte; shops 2km; snacks; bar; playgrnd; pool; TV; 90% statics; dogs €3; phone; rd noise; ccard acc. "Conv touring base; pitches in pine woods; friendly staff." ♦ 21 Mar-31 Oct. € 23.00 2010*

BREDA *B3* (10km SE Rural) *51.49334, 4.89964* **Camping RCN De Flaasbloem, Flaasdijk 1, 4861 RC Chaam [(0161) 491654; fax 492054; flaasbloem@rcn.nl; www.rcn.nl/centra/deflaasbloem]** A58 Breda-Tilberg, exit junc 14 for Chaam. Fr vill on Alphen rd, site sp. V lge, mkd pitch, pt sl, pt shd; htd wc; chem disp; mv service pnt; baby facs; fam bthrm; shwrs inc; el pnts (10A) inc; gas; Indtte (inc dryer); shop; supmkt; rest; snacks; playgrnd; 2 pools (1 htd, covrd) lake sw & beach; wifi; TV; 75% statics; dogs €4.75; adv bkg; quiet, but poss noisy w/end; Eng spkn; CCI. "Cycling cent in flat woodland; many sports facs; many facs for children; well-run site." ♦ 1 Apr-31 Oct. € 28.00 2010*

BREDA *B3* (2.5km SW Rural) *51.56488, 4.69628* **Camping Liesbos, Liesdreef 40, 4838 GV Breda [(076) 5143514; fax 5146555; info@camping-liesbos.nl; www.camping-liesbos.nl]** Fr A16 take exit 16 dir Etten-Leur. Fr A58/E312 take exit 18; site sp. Lge, pt shd; wc; chem disp; mv service pnt; shwrs €0.75; el pnts (6A) inc; gas; Indtte; shop; rest; snacks; bar; playgrnd; pool; paddling pool; tennis; cycle hire; TV; 95% statics; dogs €2.50; phone; poss v cr; quiet; ccard acc. "Narr site rds; sm pitches; v clean san facs; NH only." 1 Apr-1 Oct. € 20.00 2009*

⊞ **BRESKENS** *A4* (1km W Coastal) *51.40090, 3.53505* **Camping DroomPark Schoneveld, Schoneveld 1, 4511 HR Breskens [(0117) 383220; fax 383650; info@droompark schoneveld.nl; www.droomparkschoneveld.nl]** Fr S on N58, take 2nd exit to Breskens & foll site sp. Fr N on A28, thro Westerschelde Tunnel & take N61 twd Breskens. Take 2nd exit at rndabt & foll site sp. Lge, pt shd; htd wc; chem disp; mv service pnt; baby facs; fam bthrm; shwrs €0.65; el pnts (6A) inc; gas; Indtte (inc dryer); supmkt 800m; rest & 100m; snacks, bar; BBQ; playgrnd; htd, covrd pool; paddling pool; sand beach adj; watersports; fishing; tennis; games area; cycle hire; wifi; TV; 60% statics; dogs €3; sep car park; Holland Tulip Parcs site; Eng spkn; adv bkg; quiet; ccard acc. "Excel beach; lge pitches; lovely area; poss v muddy after heavy rain." ♦ € 33.00 (CChq acc) 2008*

⊞ **BRESKENS** *A4* (3km W Coastal) *51.40360, 3.51310* **Molecaten Park Napoleon Hoeve, Zandertje 30, 4511 RH Breskens [(0117) 383838 or 381428; fax 383550; camping@napoleonhoeve.nl; www.napoleonhoeve.nl]** Fr S on N58 twd Breskens, turn L onto N675 dir Groede. Approx 500m bef Groede turn N onto Noordweg twd coast, then L into Zandertje. Site sp on coast rd. Lge, mkd pitch, unshd; htd wc; chem disp; mv service pnt; baby facs; private san facs avail; shwrs €0.50; fam bthrm; el pnts (10A) inc; gas; Indtte; supmkt; rest; snacks; bar; playgrnd; 2 pools (1 htd, covrd); sand beach adj; sep naturist beach; tennis; cycle hire; entmnt; TV; 60% statics; dogs €3.90; phone; adv bkg; ccard acc. "Friendly, family site; excel facs; gd bar, rest & children's play area." ♦ € 37.00 2010*

BRESKENS *A4* (3km NW Coastal) *51.39513, 3.48833* **Camping Groede, Zeeweg 1, 4503 PA Groede [(0117) 371384; info@campinggroede.nl; www.campinggroede.nl]** S fr Breskens on N58 then W on N675 to Groede; site sp 3km W Groede by sea; sp. V lge, some hdg/mkd pitch, pt shd; htd wc; mv service pnt; chem disp; baby facs; fam bthrm; 50% serviced pitches; shwrs inc; el pnts (4-10A) inc; gas; Indtte; supmkt; rest; playgrnd; pool; sand beach; games area; internet; TV; 40% statics; dogs €2.50; poss cr; Eng spkn; quiet; 10% red low ssn; CCI. "Friendly, family-run; v clean san facs; conv Bruges, Waterland." ♦ 17 Mar-31 Oct. € 34.00 2008*

I'll fill in a report online and let the Club know – www.caravanclub.co.uk/europereport

This is a wonderful site.

BRIELLE *B3* (1km NE Urban) *51.90969, 4.18533* **Camping De Krabbeplaat, Oude Veerdam 4, 3231 NC Brielle [(0181) 412363; fax 412093; info@krabbeplaat.nl; www.krabbeplaat.com]** Exit A15 fr Rotterdam junc 12 onto N57. Foll sp Brielse Maas-Noord, then site sp. Site sp fr N57. Lge, hdg/mkd pitch, pt shd; wc; chem disp; mv service pnt; baby facs; shwrs inc; el pnts (4-10A) inc; gas; Indtte (inc dryer); shop; rest; snacks; bar; playgrnd; rv adj; tennis; games area; cycle & boat hire; wifi; cab TV; 70% statics; no dogs; phone; ferry to Brielle; poss cr; Eng spkn; adv bkg; ccard acc; CCI. "Gd for families; easy access to rv." ♦ 1 Apr-24 Oct. € 23.90 2010*

BRIELLE *B3* (5km NE Coastal) *51.91379, 4.18218* **NCC Camping De Lepelaar, Brielse Veerweg, 3231 NA Brielle [(0181) 417338; www.ncc.nl]** Fr Rotterdam foll A15/N15 W dir Europoort. Exit junc 12 at Brielle, over Hartelkanaal & at end sliprd exit Brielse Maas Noord. Turn L on Staaldiepseweg, in 2.3km L into Brielse Veerweg, sp Voetveer Brielle. Site 2nd on R. Sm, mkd pitch, pt shd; htd wc; chem disp; shwrs inc; el pnts (4A) €2.75; Indtte; shop, rest, snacks, bar 9km; BBQ; playgrnd; lake sw & beach 500m; dogs; phone; poss cr; adv bkg req; quiet; CCI. "Excel site; C'van Club members welcome, but must pre-book; ferry to Brielle (high ssn) 200m." ♦ 1 Apr-31 Oct. € 10.00 2009*

BRIELLE *B3* (700m E Urban) *51.90666, 4.17527* **Camping de Meeuw, Batterijweg 1, 3231 AA Brielle [(0181) 412777; fax 418127; info@demeeuw.nl; www.demeeuw.nl]** On A15/N57 foll sp to Brielle. Turn R after passing thro town gates & foll sp to site. Lge, pt shd; wc; chem disp; mv service pnt; fam bthrm; baby facs; shwrs inc; el pnts (6A) €2 (poss rev pol); gas; Indtte; shop; rest; snacks; bar; playgrnd; pool 2km; sand beach; cycle hire; entmnt; 70% statics; dogs €3.75; phone; Eng spkn; red CCI. "Historic fortified town; attractive area for tourers; conv Europoort ferry terminal; gd NH/sh stay." 1 Apr-31 Oct. € 22.50 2009*

BROEKHUIZENVORST see Horst *C4*

⊞ **BUREN (AMELAND ISLAND)** *C1* (1km N Coastal) *53.45355, 5.80460* **Camping Klein Vaarwater, Klein Vaarwaterweg 114, 9164 ME Buren [(0519) 542156; fax 542655; info@kleinvaarwater.nl; www.kleinvaarwater.nl]** Take ferry fr Holwerd to Nes on Ameland Island. Turn R at rndabt twd Buren & strt on to supmkt. At 3-lane intersection turn L twd beach rd & site. Med, mkd pitch, pt shd; htd wc; chem disp; mv service pnt; baby facs; fam bthrm; shwrs; el pnts (16A); gas; lndtte (inc dryer); supmkt; ATM; rest; snacks; bar; BBQ; playgrnd; htd, covrd pool; paddling pool; waterslide; sand beach 800m; tennis; 10-pin bowling; games area; fitness rm; wifi; entmnt; TV; 75% statics; no dogs; Holland Tulip Parcs site; poss cr; adv bkg; red low ssn. "Nature park adj; site in dunes & forest." ♦ (CChq acc) 2011*

BURGUM *C2* (7km SE Rural) *53.19102, 6.02375* **Recreatiecentrum Bergumermeer, Solcamastraat 30, 9692 ND Sumar [(0511) 461385; fax 463955; info@bergumermeer.nl; www.bergumermeer.nl]** Fr N356 or N355 S thro Burgum & at traff lts turn L sp Sumar, foll site sp 3.5km E of Sumar. Lge, pt shd; htd wc; chem disp; mv service pnt; fam bthrm; baby facs; shwrs inc; el pnts (10A) inc; gas; lndtte; shop; rest; snacks; bar; playgrnd; covrd pool; lake adj; sailing; watersports; tennis; cycle hire; entmnt; TV: 60% statics; dogs €4.60; phone; sep car park; Eng spkn; adv bkg; quiet. "Vg site; lge lake adj; ccard acc." ♦ Easter-25 Oct. € 27.50 2007*

⊞ **CALLANTSOOG** *B2* (1.5km NE Coastal) *52.84627, 4.71549* **Camping Tempelhof, Westerweg 2, 1759 JD Callantsoog [(0224) 581522; fax 582133; info@tempelhof.nl; www.tempelhof.nl]** Fr A9 Alkmaar-Den Helder exit Callantsoog, site sp to NE of vill. Lge, mkd pitch, pt shd; htd wc; mv service pnt; chem disp; mv service pnt; serviced pitches; baby facs; fam bthrm; sauna; private bthrms avail; shwrs inc; el pnts (10A) inc; gas; lndtte; rest, snacks, bar high ssn; playgrnd; htd, covrd pool; paddling pool; sand beach 1km; tennis; games area; gym; cycle hire; wifi; entmnt; sat TV; 50% statics; dogs €3.50; phone; adv bkg. "Superb, well-run site & facs." ♦ € 35.00 2008*

CALLANTSOOG *B2* (1.5km NE Coastal) *52.84143, 4.71909* **NCC Camping De Ooster Nollen, Westerweg 8, 1759 JD Callantsoog [(0224) 581281 or 561351; fax 582098; info@denollen.nl; www.denollen.nl]** N fr Alkmaar on A9; turn L sp Callantsoog. Site sp 1km E of Callantsoog. Lge, mkd pitch, pt shd; htd wc; chem disp; mv service pnt; baby facs; shwrs inc; el pnts (10A) inc; gas; lndtte (inc dryer); shop; rest; snacks; bar; playgrnd; pool 400m; sand beach 1.5km; cycle hire; games area; wifi; entmnt; TV; 40% statics; dogs €3; phone; Eng spkn; adv bkg; quiet; ccard acc; 10% red long stay; CCI. "Nature area nr; cheese mkt." 1 Apr-31 Oct. € 25.50 2009*

CHAAM see Breda *B3*

DE KOOG see Den Burg (Texel Island) *B2*

DE VEENHOOP see Drachten *C2*

DEIL *C3* (1km SE Rural) *51.87040, 5.26047* **Camping De Kijfakkers, Hooiweg 6A, 4158 LE Deil [(0345) 651203; fax 651000; famdeheus@kijfakker.nl; www.kijfakker.nl]** Fr A2 exit junc 15 onto N327 E sp Geldermalsen. Turn R at 1st rndabt, L at T-junc into Hooiweg, site on L in 500m, sp. Sm, hdg/mkd pitch, unshd; htd wc; chem disp; shwrs inc; el pnts (6A) inc; lndtte (inc dryer); shop, rest, snacks, bar 3km; BBQ; pool 2km; TV; dogs €1; bus 3km; poss cr; Eng spkn; adv bkg rec; quiet. "CL-type site on farm (cattle, horses); gd cycling, walking espec along Rv Linge; gd touring base." 15 Mar-31 Oct. € 13.50 2010*

DELFT *B3* (1km E Urban) *52.01769, 4.37945* **Camping Delftse Hout, Korftlaan 5, 2616 LJ Delft [(015) 2130040; fax 2131293; info@delftsehout.nl; www.delftsehout.nl]** Fr Hook of Holland take N220 twd Rotterdam; after Maasdijk turn R onto A20 m'way. Take A13 twd Den Haag at v lge Kleinpolderplein interchange. Take exit 9 sp Delft (Ikea on R). Turn L under m'way (3.2m height limit) & immed R at 1st traff lts; then site sp. Lge, hdg/mkd pitch, some hdstg, pt shd; htd wc; chem disp; mv service pnt; baby facs; fam bthrm; shwrs inc; el pnts (10A) inc; gas; lndtte (inc dryer); shop; rest; snacks; bar; BBQ; playgrnd; htd pool; paddling pool; watersports, fishing nrby; cycle hire; golf 5km; wifi; entmnt; games/TV rm; 50% statics; dogs €3.25; no c'vans/m'vans over 7.50m; phone; bus to Delft; Holland Tulip Parcs site; Eng spkn; some rd noise; ccard acc; red low ssn/long stay/snr citizens/CCI. "Located by pleasant park; gd quality, secure, busy site with excel facs; helpful, friendly staff; little shade; sm pitches poss diff lge outfits; excursions by bike & on foot; easy access Delft cent; sm m'van o'night area outside site; mkt Thur; excel." ♦ 23 Mar-31 Oct. € 32.50 (CChq acc) SBS - H06 2011*

See advertisement

⊞ **DELFT** *B3* (2km E Rural) *52.01901, 4.38953* **Camping De Uylenburg, Noordeindseweg 70, 2645 BC Delftgauw [(015) 2143732; fax 2158086; herberg@uylenburg.nl; www.uylenburg.nl]** Exit A13 Rotterdam-Den Haag at junc 9 Delft-Pijnacker, dir Pijnacker. In Delftgauw at traff lts turn L, site on R in 1km on single track local rd, ent thro rest car park. Tight turns into site; take care o'hanging branches. Sm, hdg pitch, pt shd; wc; chem disp; mv service pnt; shwrs €0.50; el pnts (4A) €2.50; shops 2.5km; rest; bar; beach 10km; dogs; sep car park; clsd Xmas & New Year; poss cr; Eng spkn; quiet; CCI. "Vg for children; facs just adequate - poss run down low ssn; gd walking & cycling; adj nature reserve - gd birdwatching; 40 mins walk to Delft - pleasant town; vet in Pijnacker." € 17.50 2010*

DEN BURG (TEXEL ISLAND) *B2* (2km NE Rural) *53.05362, 4.81647* **Camping De Hal, Hallerweg 33, 1791 LR Den Burg [(0222) 312703; camping@dehal.nl; www.dehal.nl]** Exit ferry dir Den Burg, turn R at junc 6, at end of Leemkuil turn L & at T-junc turn R onto Schilderweg. Take 1st L into Hallerweg & when rd bears L turn R to site, sp. Sm, hdg/mkd pitch, pt shd; htd wc; chem disp; shwrs €0.50; el pnts (6A) inc; lndtte; shop, rest, snacks, bar 2km; sand beach 7km; dogs €1.50; bus 2km; poss cr; Eng spkn; adv bkg rec; quiet. "CL-type site on sheep farm; friendly owners; gd walking, cycling, beaches." 15 Mar-31 Oct. € 14.50 2008*

DEN BURG (TEXEL ISLAND) *B2* (6km NW Rural) *53.10346, 4.77107* **Camping Om de Noord, Boodtlaan 50, 1796 BG De Koog [(0222) 327842; fax 327167; info@texelcampings.nl; www.texelcampings.nl]** Fr ferry take rd to De Koog; site sp on R of rd on N of town dir De Cocksdorp. Med, mkd pitch, pt shd; htd wc; mv service pnt; chem disp; fam bthrm; baby facs; private san facs avail; shwrs inc; el pnts (16A) inc; Indtte (inc dryer); playgrnd; pool 1.5km; sand beach 2km; games area; wifi; 10% statics; dogs €4; phone; poss cr; quiet; ccard acc; CCI. "Excel site adj nature reserve; walks in heathland; conv touring Texel; friendly owners." ♦ 1 Apr-31 Oct. € 38.60 2010*

We can fill in site report forms on the Club's website – www.caravanclub.co.uk/europereport

⊞ **DEN HAAG** *B3* (5km SW Coastal) *52.05925, 4.21175* **Vakantiecentrum Kijkduinpark, Machiel Vrijenhoeklaan 450, 2555 NW Den Haag [(070) 3252510; fax 3232457; info@kijkduinpark.nl; www.roompotparcs.com]** Foll E8, Hoek van Holland-Den Haag, S to Loosduinen, turn SW at camping sp (rd runs parallel to sea) to site ent at end of rd. Lge, pt shd; htd wc; chem disp; mv service pnt; baby facs; fam bthrm; shwrs inc; el pnts (10-16A) inc; gas; Indtte; shop; rest; snacks; bar; playgrnd; htd, covrd pool; paddling pool; sand beach 500m; tennis; games area; cycle hire; car washing facs; internet; entmnt; TV; 50% statics; dogs; poss v cr; adv bkg; quiet; red low ssn. "Conv Hague & Scheveningen; lge pitches; many excel facs." ♦ € 45.00 2007*

DEN HELDER *B2* (2km SW Coastal) *52.93672, 4.73377* **Camping de Donkere Duinen, Jan Verfailleweg 616, 1783 BW Den Helder [(0223) 614731; fax 615077; info@donkereduinen.nl; www.donkereduinen.nl]** Fr S turn L off N9 sp Julianadorp (Schoolweg), strt over at x-rds in Julianadorp (Van Foreestweg). Turn R at t-junc onto N502, site on L in approx 4km. Lge, pt shd; wc; chem disp; mv service pnt; baby facs; shwr €0.20; el pnts (4-16A) inc; gas; Indtte; shops 3km; playgrnd; sand beach 800m; tennis; cycle hire; 10% statics; dogs €2.75; poss cr; Eng spkn; adv bkg (fee); quiet; CCI. "V helpful owner; excel walking/cycling; ferry to Texel Is; lge naval museum & submarine." 17 Apr-31 Aug. € 26.00 2008*

DENEKAMP *D3* (3.5km NE Rural) *52.39190, 7.04890* **Camping De Papillon, Kanaalweg 30, 7591 NH Denekamp [(0541) 351670; fax 355217; info@depapillon.nl; www.depapillon.nl]** Fr A1 take exit 32 onto N342 Oldenzaal-Denekamp, dir Nordhorn, site sp just bef German border. Lge, pt shd; htd wc; chem disp; mv service pnt; baby facs; fam bthrm; shwrs €0.20; el pnts (4A) inc; gas; Indtte; shop; rest; snacks; bar; playgrnd; 2 pools (1 htd & covrd); lake sw; tennis; cycle hire; TV; 12% statics; dogs €4.50; phone; quiet; red long stay/low ssn. "Super, clean site; friendly, helpful owners; man-made lake." ♦ 1 Apr-1 Oct. € 24.75 2007*

DEVENTER *C3* (1.5km W Urban) *52.24992, 6.14634* **Camp Municipal De Worp, De Worp 12, 7419 AD Deventer [(0570) 613601; deventer@stadscamping.eu; www.stadscamping.eu]** Fr N on N337 on o'skts of Deventer foll 'Centrum' sp to W of town cent. Go over rv bdge on N344 dir Apeldoorn, site immed on R. sp. Or fr A1 exit junc 22 dir Twello, turn R onto N344, site on L just bef rv bdge on ent Deventer. Med, pt shd; htd wc; chem disp (wc); baby facs; fam bthrm; shwrs €1; el pnts (4-6A) €2.50; Indtte; playgrnd; 10% statics; dogs €2.50; phone; Eng spkn; quiet; CCI. "Foot passenger ferry over rv to Deventer cent adj site; lovely, interesting old town; Terwolde windmill worth visit; refurbished san facs but inadequate if site full." 1 Apr-30 Sep. € 16.50 2011*

DIEVER *D2* (1km N Rural) *52.86684, 6.32004* **Camping Diever, Haarweg 2, 7981 LW Diever [tel/fax (0521) 591644; camping.diever@hetnet.nl; www.campingdiever.nl]** Fr A32 exit 4 dir Havelte & Diever. In Diever take dir Zorgvlied/Wateren, site sp. Lge, mkd pitch; pt sl, shd; htd wc; chem disp; fam bthrm; baby facs; shwrs €0.50; el pnts (10A) €2.75; gas; Indtte; shop; snacks; playgrnd; pool 5km; cycle hire; internet; TV; some statics; dogs €2.25; phone; sep car park; Eng spkn; adv bkg; quiet. "Pleasant, densely wooded site." 1 Apr-1 Oct. € 16.60 2009*

DIEVER *D2* (1km S Rural) *52.82405, 6.31650* **Camping Wittelterbrug, Wittelterweg 31, 7986 PL Wittelte [(0521) 598288; fax 598250; info@wittelterbrug.nl; www.wittelterbrug.nl]** N of Meppel on N371 for approx 12km. Site on R over narr canal bdge. Med, hdg pitch, pt shd; wc; chem disp; mv service pnt; serviced pitch; baby facs; shwrs €0.60; el pnts (10A) inc; gas; Indtte; shop & 5km; rest; snacks; bar; playgrnd; covrd pool; paddling pool; cycle hire; entmnt; TV; 65% statics; dogs €3.60; phone; Eng spkn; adv bkg; quiet. "Lovely family-run site; facs excel." 1 Apr-31 Oct. € 19.50 2009*

DIFFELEN see Hardenberg *D2*

DOETINCHEM *D3* (3km SE Rural) *51.94628, 6.33550* **Camping De Wrange, Rekhemseweg 144, 7004 HD Doetinchem [(0314) 324852; info@dewrange.nl; www.dewrange.nl]** Leave A18 at exit 4 dir Doetinchem Oost, then L dir Doetinchem. In 500m turn R at water tower, foll site sp. Lge, mkd pitch, unshd; htd wc; chem disp; mv service pnt; baby facs; fam bthrm; shwrs €0.70; el pnts (4-6A) €3; gas; Indtte; shop; rest; snacks; bar; BBQ; playgrnd; htd pool; paddling pool; cycle hire; entmnt; TV; 75% statics; dogs €3; phone; sep car park; poss cr; Eng spkn; adv bkg; quiet; CCI. ♦ 1 Apr-31 Oct. € 16.50 2009*

DOKKUM *C2* (E Urban) *53.32611, 6.00468* **Camping Harddraverspark, Harddraversdijk 1a, 9101 XA Dokkum [(0519) 294445; fax 571402; info@campingdokkum.nl; www.campingdokkum.nl]** Best app fr E fr ring rd N361 onto Harddraversdijk alongside rv, site sp. Do not app thro town - narr rds. Med, hdg/mkd pitch, some hdstg, pt shd; wc; chem disp; shwrs €0.50; el pnts (6A) €2.50; gas; Indtte; shop, rest, snacks, bar 400m; tradsmn; playgrnd; tennis; dogs €2; Eng spkn; quiet. "Excel location in cent of lovely town; conv for ferry to Ameland Island (12km)." 1 Apr-31 Oct. € 13.00 2010*

NETHERLANDS

DOMBURG *A3* (1.5km SE Rural) *51.55578, 3.51516* **Camping Westhove, Zuiverseweg 2, 4363 RJ Aagtekerke [(0118) 581809; fax 582502; westhove@ardoer.com; www.ardoer.com]** Fr Middelburg thro Oostkapelle, site sp on L twds Domburg. Lge, mkd pitch, pt shd; htd wc; chem disp; mv service pnt; baby facs; shwrs inc; el pnts (4A) inc; Indtte; shop; rest; snacks; bar; playgrnd; htd, covrd pool; sand beach 2km; cycle hire; entmnt; TV; 25% statics; dogs (not acc Jul/Aug); phone; sep car park; Eng spkn; quiet; ccard acc; CCI. "Gd pool; easy walk/cycle to Domburg & beach." ♦ 27 Mar-25 Oct. € 35.00 (3 persons) 2009*

⊞ **DOMBURG** *A3* (1km W Coastal) *3.4870* **Camping Hof Domburg, Schelpweg 7, 4357 RD Domburg [(0118) 588200; fax 583668; info@roompot.nl; www.roompot.nl]** On main rd fr Domburg twds Westkapelle, site sp on L. Lge, pt shd; htd wc; chem disp; mv service pnt; baby facs; shwrs inc; el pnts (6A) inc; gas; Indtte; shop; rest; snacks; bar; playgrnd; 2 pools (1 covrd); sand beach 300m; tennis; entmnt; watersports; cycle hire; 5% statics; no dogs; phone; car park; poss cr Jul-Aug; adv bkg; ccard acc. ♦ € 45.00 (4 persons) 2007*

DORDRECHT *B3* (3km SE Rural) *51.80738, 4.71862* **Camping 't Vissertje, Loswalweg 3, 3315 LB Dordrecht [(078) 6162751; info@campinghetvissertje.nl; www.hetvissertje.nl]** Fr Rotterdam across Brienenoord Bdge foll sp Gorinchem & Nijmegen A15. Exit junc 23 Papendrecht & turn R onto N3 until exit Werkendam. Turn R & foll sp 'Het Vissertje'. Sm, pt shd; wc; chem disp; shwrs €0.50; el pnts (6A) inc; wifi; 20% statics; dogs €1; Eng spkn; quiet; red long stay. "Lovely site; friendly, helpful manager; modern, clean san facs; gd cycle rtes nr; vg." 1 Apr-31 Oct. € 20.00 2011*

⊞ **DORDRECHT** *B3* (8km W Rural) *51.79279, 4.53679* **Camping De Fruitgaarde, Polderdijk 47, 3299 LL Maasdam [(078) 6765176; www.campercontact.nl]** Exit A16 junc 20 onto N217 W dir Puttershoek & Maasdam thro Kiltunnel (toll). Fork L onto N491 then foll rd round W side of polder dir Binnenmaas & Westmaas. Site sp on L, 1km W of Maasdam. Sm, hdstg, pt shd; htd wc; chem disp; mv service pnt; baby facs; shwrs inc; el pnts (16A) €2; Indtte; shop 6km; tradsmn; rest; snacks 1km; bar; playgrnd; pool 4km; sw adj; no statics; dogs; bus 1km; Eng spkn; quiet. "Site in orchard; helpful owner; water bus, Kinderdijk windmills, historic towns nrby." ♦ € 10.00 2009*

DRACHTEN *C2* (4km S Rural) *53.07095, 6.13672* **Camping Het Koningsdiep, De Mersken 2, 9247 WK Ureterp [(0512) 381844; info@campinghetkoningsdiep.nl; www.campinghetkoningsdiep.nl]** Exit A7/E22 at junc 30 onto N381 dir Oosterwolde. In 1km after Azeven indus est turn R into Selmien West, then in 1km turn L into Selmien/De Mersken, site sp. Sm, pt shd; htd wc; chem disp; fam bthrm; shwrs inc; el pnts (10A) inc; Indry rm; shop 2.5km; rest, snacks, bar 2.5km; BBQ; horseriding; dogs; Eng spkn; adv bkg; quiet; CCI. "Vg, friendly site on working stud farm; gd walking; gd touring base." ♦ 1 Apr-28 Oct. € 20.00 2009*

DRACHTEN *C2* (10km W Rural) *53.12556, 5.98391* **Camping de Stjelp, It West 48, 9216 XE Oudega [(0512) 372270; fax 371053; stjelp@camping-de-stjelp.nl; www.camping-de-stjelp.nl]** W fr Drachten on N31. Turn L at Nijega then bear R to Oudega. Site at W end of vill at bungalow no. 1920. Sm, mkd pitch, unshd; wc; chem disp; shwrs inc; el pnts (4A) metered; Indry rm; shop, snacks, bar 1km; BBQ; lake sw & beach 3km; cycle hire; dogs €1; quiet; CCI. "Attractive farm site, friendly owners; conv Friesland canals & lakes; cycle rtes; vg touring base." ♦ 14 Apr-15 Oct. € 13.60 2011*

DRACHTEN *C2* (13km W Rural) *53.09696, 5.94695* **Camping De Veenhoop Watersport & Recreatie, Eijzengapaed 8, 9215 VV De Veenhoop [(0512) 462289; fax 461057; info@de-veenhoop.nl; www.de-veenhoop.nl]** Exit A7 junc 28 dir Nij Beets, foll De Veenhoop sp to site. Or exit A32 junc 13 & turn W for approx 6km via Aldeboarn. Turn L at Pieter's Rest to De Veenhoop, site on L bef sm bdge. Med, pt shd; htd wc; chem disp; shwrs €0.50; el pnts (6-10A) €3; Indtte; shops 5km; rest 200m; BBQ; sm playgrnd; lake sw; boat hire; 50% statics; dogs; bus adj; Eng spkn; adv bkg; quiet. "Excel, peaceful, friendly site; clean & well-maintained; excel sailing, cycling, walking; well situated for lakes & N N'lands; gd NH." 1 Apr-31 Oct. € 14.50 2010*

⊞ **DRIMMELEN** *B3* (1km E Rural) *51.70690, 4.82290* **Camping Biesbosch Marina, Marinaweg 50, 4924 AD Drimmelen [(0162) 685795; fax 681675; info@campingbiesbosch marina.nl; www.campingbiesboschmarina.nl]** Exit A59 junc 32 at Made & foll sp Drimmelen & site. Med, mkd pitch, unshd; htd wc; chem disp; mv service pnt; baby facs; fam bthrm; serviced pitches; shwrs inc; el pnts (16A) inc; gas; Indtte (inc dryer); shop; tradsmn; rest; snacks; bar; BBQ; playgrnd; lake sw & sand beach; sailing lessons; boat, canoe, cycle hire; games area; wifi; some statics; dogs €3 (max 1); Holland Tulip Parcs site; adv bkg; quiet; ccard acc; red long stay. "Superb site; access to all facs by electronic key; lge, well-drained pitches; excel touring base & conv NH Hook of Holland." € 30.55 (CChq acc) 2009*

DRONTEN *C2* (1km W Rural) *52.52099, 5.69189* **Camping en Horecacentrum 't Wisentbos, De West 1, 8251 ST Dronten [(0321) 316606; info@wisentbos.nl; www.wisentbos.nl]** E fr Lelystad on N309, site well sp. Sm, some hdstg, pt shd; htd wc; chem disp; mv service pnt; baby facs; shwrs €0.50; el pnts (10A) inc; Indtte; rest; snacks; bar; playgrnd; beach & fishing lake adj; 80% statics; dogs €1.55; bus adj; Eng spkn; adv bkg; quiet; ccard acc (not Visa). "Wooded area; friendly, helpful staff; sep area for m'vans; excel." 1 Apr-31 Oct. € 15.00 2009*

⊞ **DWINGELOO** *D2* (2km SE Rural) *52.82216, 6.39258* **Camping De Olde Bârgen, Oude Hoogeveensedijk 1, 7991 PD Dwingeloo [(0521) 597261; fax 597069; info@oldebargen.nl; www.oldebargen.nl]** Exit A28 Zwolle/Assen rd at Spier, turn W sp Dwingeloo, site clearly sp, in wooded area. Sm, mkd pitch, pt shd; wc; chem disp; fam bthrm; shwrs inc; el pnts (4-6A) inc; Indtte; shop 800m; playgrnd; pool 1.5km; few statics; dogs €2; adv bkg; Eng spkn; quiet; CCI. "Excel, well-run site on N side Dwingelderveld National Park; gd for walkers & cyclists; v friendly, helpful owners." ♦ € 17.75 2010*

ECHT *C4* (1km N Rural) *51.09213, 5.91116* **Camping Marisheem, Brugweg 89, 6102 RD Echt [(0475) 481458; fax 488018; info@marisheem.nl; www.marisheem.nl]** Exit A2 Maastricht-Eindhoven junc 45 dir Echt. In Echt foll sp Koningsbosch, site down side rd on L. Lge, mkd pitch, pt shd; htd wc; chem disp; mv service pnt; shwrs; el pnts (6-10A) inc; gas; Indtte; shop; rest; snacks; bar; htd pool; playgrnd; 60% statics; no dogs; quiet; Eng spkn; red low ssn; CCI. "Vg, well-organised site; vg pool; helpful staff; gd train service to Maastricht." 1 Apr-30 Sep. € 31.10 (4 persons) 2011*

⊞ **ECHT** *C4* (2km NE Rural) *51.12075, 5.96888* **Camping Biej De Vogel, Heinsbergerweg 15, 6065 NK Montfort [(0475) 541522; info@campingbiejdevogel.nl; www.campingbiejdevogel.nl]** Exit A2/E25 junc 44 dir Roermond, turn R to Montfort & go thro town to fork & statue. Turn L up narr rd, then strt over x-rds, farm approx 1km on L. Sm, mkd pitch, pt shd; wc; chem disp; shwrs €1; el pnts (10-16A) €1.75; Indtte; shop 2km; pool 2km; dogs; phone; Eng spkn; adv bkg; quiet; red long stay. "Excel CL-type site - 15 pitches." € 12.00 2009*

EDAM *B2* (9km S Rural) *52.42787, 5.07387* **Camping-Jachthaven Uitdam, Zeedijk 2, 1154 PP Uitdam [(020) 4031433; fax 4033692; info@campinguitdam.nl; www.campinguitdam.nl]** Fr Amsterdam foll N247 (Amsterdam-Hoorn), at 10km turn R sp Marken/Monickendam across canal. After 5km turn R at camping sp to site on L after 2km. Lge, pt shd; htd wc; chem disp; mv service pnt; baby facs; shwrs €0.90; el pnts (4-6A) inc; gas; Indtte; shop; rest; snacks; bar; playgrnd; pool 5km; paddling pool; sand beach adj; fishing; boating; cycle hire; entmnt; TV; 50% statics; dogs €5; phone; poss cr; Eng spkn; adv bkg; 20% red low ssn; ccard acc; CCI. "Exposed location low ssn; no water supply nr touring pitches; bus 2km to Amsterdam cent; water taxi to Volendam; excel cycle tracks." 1 Mar-31 Oct. € 23.70 2009*

EDAM *B2* (2km NW Coastal) *52.52457, 5.06478* **Camping Strandbad Edam, Zeevangszeedijk 7A, 1135 PZ Edam [(0299) 371994; fax 371510; info@campingstrandbad.nl; www.campingstrandbad.nl]** Foll N247 Amsterdam-Hoorn; after sp for Edam foll site sp. At traff lts in Edam keep on N247 past bus stn on R, then R at next rndabt. Last 100m to site is single track opp marina. Access thro public car park. Lge, pt shd; htd wc; chem disp; mv service pnt; baby facs; fam bthrm; shwrs €1; el pnts (10A) €2.90; gas; Indtte; shop; rest; snacks; bar; playgrnd; pool 3km; paddling pool; sand beach adj; watersports; cycle hire; wifi; TV; 40% statics; no dogs; phone; no dogs; poss cr; Eng spkn; adv bkg; quiet; ccard acc; red long stay. "Walking dist Edam; landing stage for boats; excel san facs; sm, poss cramped pitches high ssn." 1 Apr-30 Sep. € 20.25 2010*

⊞ **EDE** *C3* (5km N Rural) *52.06544, 5.66504* **NCC Camping de Braamhorst, Zonneoordlaan 45a, 6718 TL Ede [(0318) 617814; www.ncc.nl]** Fr Arnhem on A12 exit Ede Oost & foll N224. In 5km turn R dir Lunteren, in 1km turn R onto Zonneoordlaan, sp crematorium. In 1.5km site sp on L. Med, mkd pitch, pt sl, terr, pt shd; htd wc; chem disp; shwrs inc; el pnts (4A) €2.75; Indtte; dogs; poss cr; adv bkg; quiet; CCI. "Pleasant, well-run, spacious, clean site; lge pitches; phone/write ahead to site or tourist info in Ede to book in - C'van Club memb card ess; gd cycling." ♦ € 10.00 2008*

EDE *C3* (4.5km E Rural) *52.03836, 5.73525* **Camping Zuid Ginkel, Verlengde Arnhemseweg 97, 6718 SM Ede [(0318) 611740; fax 618790; info@zuidginkel.nl; www.zuidginkel.nl]** On rd N224 Ede-Arnhem. Site on L behind lge rest. Med, pt shd; htd wc; chem disp; baby facs; shwrs €0.50; el pnts (6A) €3; gas; Indtte; shops 3km; rest; snacks; BBQ; playgrnd; pool 4.5km; TV rm; 80% statics; dogs €3; sep car park; poss cr; Eng spkn; adv bkg; quiet but rd noise; CCI. "Wooded site close to museums in Arnhem & Oosterbeek; WW2 parachute drop area across rd; many walking/cycling tracks; nature cent nr; v diff twin-axles (sharp turns)." ♦ 1 Apr-26 Oct. € 16.50 2008*

EERSEL *C4* (6km SW Rural) *51.33635, 5.35552* **Camping De Paal, De Paaldreef 14, 5571 TN Bergeijk [(0497) 571977; fax 577164; info@depaal.nl; www.depaal.nl]** Fr A67/E34 Antwerp/Eindoven exit junc 32 sp Eersel & bear R onto N284 & stay in R-hand lane. At rndabt take 1st exit onto Eijkereind. In 500m after rndbt turn L at traffic lts & foll rd around R & L bend. Take R turn sp Bergeijk after lge church (sm sp on sharp L bend). After approx 5km turn L into site road. V lge, pt shd, htd wc (some cont); chem disp; mv service pnt; baby facs; sauna; fam bthrm; shwrs inc; el pnts (6A) inc; gas; Indtte (inc dryer); shop; rest & snacks (high ssn); bar; BBQ (charcoal); playgrnds; 2 htd pools (1 covrd); paddling pool; sand beach, lake sw 7km; watersports 10km; fishing; excursions; sm children's zoo; tennis; cycle hire; horseriding 500m; wifi; entmnt; games rm/TV rm (sat TV); recep 0900-1800; 10% statics; dogs €5; no c'vans/m'vans over 8m high ssn; no twin-axles; phone; sep cark park; poss cr/noisy; ccard not acc; red low ssn. "Excel, family-run site set in woodland; espec gd for young children; lge pitches in groups with sep sm play areas; central play areas; conv Efteling theme park, Hilvarenbeek safari park, Oisterwijk bird park; mkt Mon & Tue pm." ♦ 1 Apr-28 Oct. € 49.00 SBS - H04 2011*

EERSEL *C4* (9km SW Rural) *51.29155, 5.29475* **Camping De Zwarte Bergen, Zwarte Bergendreef 1, 5575 XP Luyksgestel [(0497) 541373; fax 542673; info@zwartebergen.nl; www.zwartebergen.nl]** Fr Eindhoven foll sps to Bergeyk & Luyksgestel; site sp on main rd 2km S of Luyksgestel. V lge, mkd pitch, pt sl, shd; htd wc; chem disp; mv service pnt; some serviced pitches; baby facs; shwrs inc; el pnts (6-16A) inc; gas; Indtte; shop; rest; snacks; bar; playgrnd; pool; paddling pool; 60% statics; phone; sep car park; poss cr & noisy; Eng spkn; adv bkg; CCI. "Vg; well organised; ample facs but ltd low ssn; welcoming staff." ♦ 1 Apr-30 Sep. € 28.50 2009*

⊞ **EINDHOVEN** *C4* (10km SE Rural) *51.37393, 5.55206* **Camping Heezerenbosch, Heezerenbosch 6, 5591 TA Heeze [(040) 2263811; fax 2262422; info@heezerenbosch.nl; www.heezerenbosch.nl]** Exit m'way A56 at junc 34 & foll sp Heeze. Foll rd to town, site sp fr town limits, 2km W of cent. V lge, pt shd; htd wc (cont); chem disp; mv service pnt; baby facs; shwrs inc; el pnts (4A) inc; gas; Indtte; shop; rest; snacks; bar; playgrnd; pool; waterslide; lake sw adj; tennis; games area; cycle hire; TV; 95% statics; dogs €1.50; phone; adv bkg; quiet; red low ssn. "Low ssn site charges per day, ie 1 night's stay costs 2 days' fees; tourers in open field with elec & water - san facs some distance; helpful, friendly staff; busy, poss noisy site; ground poss boggy low ssn." € 30.00 2009*

NETHERLANDS

EINDHOVEN *C4* (10km S Rural) *51.32887, 5.46160* **Recreatiepark Brugse Heide, Maastrichterweg 183, 5556 VB Valkenswaard [(040) 2018304; fax 2049312; info@brugseheide.nl; www.brugseheide.nl]** S fr Eindhoven, exit Waalre; take N69 Valkenswaard; drive thro to rndabt, turn L. At next rndabt strt ahead, at next rndabt turn R, foll sp Achel. Site on L in 1km. Lge, mkd pitch, shd; htd wc; all serviced pitches; chem disp; mv service pnt; baby facs; shwrs inc; el pnts (6A) inc; gas; Indtte (inc dryer); shop 2km; tradsmn; snacks; bar; BBQ; playgrnd; htd pool; paddling pool; cycle hire; wifi; entmnt; TV; 40% statics; dogs; phone; Eng spkn; adv bkg (no dep); quiet (can be v noisy w/end); ccard acc; red low ssn. "Excel, friendly site; gd NH en rte Germany." ♦ Easter-31 Oct. € 23.20 (4 persons) 2010*

ELBURG *C2* (600m E Rural) *52.44294, 5.84318* **Natuurkamping Landgoed Old Putten, Zuiderzeestraatweg Oost 65, 8081 LB Elburg [(0525) 681938; fax 681325; info@oldputten.nl; www.oldputten.nl]** Fr A28 exit junc 16 dir 't Harde & Elburg. Foll sp on Zuiderzeestraatweg. Sm, mkd pitch, pt shd; wc; chem disp; baby facs; shwrs inc; el pnts (4A) €2; Indtte; shops 500m; pool; tennis; 20% statics; sep car park; phone. 1 Apr-1 Oct. € 16.50 2009*

ELLEWOUTSDIJK *A4* (1km W Coastal) *51.38801, 3.82226* **NCC Camping Zuudschorre, P J Israelweg 3, 4437 NE Ellewoutsdijk [(0113) 548598; www.ncc.nl]** Exit A58 junc 35 at 's-Gravenpolder & foll sp S to Ovezande. Turn L dir Oudelande & foll sp Ellewoutsdijk. At statue turn L thro vill onto dyke, turn L & site sp 200m on L. Sm, hdg pitch, pt shd; htd wc; chem disp; shwrs inc; el pnts (4A) €2.75; Indtte; shop & 1km playgrnd; rv sw adj; dogs; bus; quiet. "Lovely setting on Schelde estuary nr charming vill; gd touring base Goes & Middelburg; well-maintained, friendly site; members only - C'van Club members welcome but must pre-book." ♦ 1 Apr-31 Oct. € 10.00 2009*

EMMEN *D2* (5km N Rural) *52.82861, 6.85714* **Vakantiecentrum De Fruithof, Melkweg 2, 7871 PE Klijndijk [(0591) 512427; fax (0591 513572; info@fruithof.nl; www.fruithof.nl]** On N34 N fr Emmen dir Borger, turn R sp Klijndijk, foll site sp. Lge, hdg/mkd pitch, pt shd; htd wc; chem disp; mv service pnt; serviced pitches; baby facs; fam bthrm; shwrs inc; el pnts (6A) inc; gas; Indtte; shop & 5km; rest; snacks; bar; BBQ; playgrnd; htd pool; paddling pool; lake sw & beach adj; tennis; games area; cycle hire; entmnt; TV; 50% statics; dogs; Eng spkn; adv bkg; red low ssn/long stay; CCI. "Excel." Easter-29 Sep. € 27.80 2009*

EMMEN *D2* (7km W Rural) *52.79352, 6.80338* **Minicamping De Brinkhoeve, Brinkweg 1-3, 7846 AW Noord-Sleen [(0591) 361891; camping@debrinkhoeve.nl; www.debrinkhoeve.nl]** Fr Emmen on N381 dir Westerbork & Beilen; exit at junc with N376 to Noord-Sleen & take 3rd exit at rndabt & 3rd exit at next rndabt. At junc nr Café Wielens keep L, site in 150m on R. Sm, hdstg, unshd; wc; chem disp; shwrs inc; el pnts (6A) €2.25; Indtte; shop 7km; rest nr; snacks, bar 1km; cooking facs; wifi; TV rm; bus; Eng spkn; adv bkg; quiet; CCI. "Excel site & facs; pretty vill; friendly, welcoming owners; gd cycle paths." ♦ 17 Mar-30 Sep. € 15.90 2007*

EMST see Apeldoorn *C3*

ENKHUIZEN *C2* (800m N Coastal) *52.70888, 5.28830* **Camping De Vest, Noorderweg 31, 1601 PC Enkhuizen [(0228) 321221; fax 312211; info@campingdevest.nl; www.campingdevest.nl]** When N302 turns R at traff lts, keep strt on to T-junc. Foll site sp to R, site on R in 50m. Sm, pt shd; wc; chem disp; shwrs; el pnts (4A) inc; sand beach 800m; 25% statics; dogs; poss cr; Eng spkn; adv bkg; ccard not acc. "Gates clsd 2300-0800; easy walk to town cent; lively jazz festival last w/end in May; facs old but well-kept - poss stretched when site full." Easter-30 Sep. € 18.50 2011*

ENKHUIZEN *C2* (500m E Coastal) *52.7098, 5.2956* **Camping Enkhuizer Zand, Kooizandweg 4, 1601 LK Enkhuizen [(0228) 317289; fax 312211; info@campingenkhuizerzand.nl; www.campingenkhuizerzand.nl]** Sp in town. Lge, pt shd; htd wc; chem disp; mv service pnt; baby facs; shwrs inc; el pnts (4A) inc; Indtte; shop; snacks; playgrnd; htd, covrd pool adj; sand beach & lake sw; boating; tennis adj; TV; 70% statics; dogs €3.50; phone; sep car park; poss cr; poss noisy; CCI. "Modern san facs; Zuider Zee museum 1km; deer park." ♦ 1 Apr-30 Sep. € 23.50 2009*

ENKHUIZEN *C2* (10km W Rural) *52.72838, 5.09591* **Camping Veerhof, Vereweg 4, 1678 HW Oostwoud [(0229) 201575 or 581823; info@campingveerhof.nl; www.campingveerhof.nl]** Exit A7 junc Medemblik, take 2nd R, site sp. Or fr Enkhuizen on rd 302, turn R dir Oostwoud, site sp in vill. Sm, mkd pitch, unshd; wc; chem disp; serviced pitches; shwrs €0.50; el pnts (6A) €2.50; Indry rm; snacks; cycle, boat hire; 5% statics; dogs €1; sep car park; quiet; Eng spkn; CCI. "Conv Edam & open-air museum; lovely site; fair san facs stretched high ssn." 1 Apr-30 Sep. € 12.50 2008*

⊞ **ENSCHEDE** *D3* (2.5km E Urban) *52.21034, 6.95127* **Euregio Camping de Twentse Es, Keppelerdijk 200, 7534 PA Enschede [(053) 4611372; fax 4618558; info@twentse-es.nl; www.twentse-es.nl]** Fr Germany, cross border at Gronau on B54/N35; twd Enschede. In 2.5km turn R into Oostweg, then in 2km turn R into Gronausestraat, then in 800m turn R into Esmarkelaan. Foll rd thro residential area, turn L at end, site on R. Not rec to foll sat nav due rd building (7/09). Lge, pt shd; htd wc; chem disp; shwrs inc; el pnts (10A) inc; gas; Indtte; shop; rest; snacks; bar; playgrnd; pool; paddling pool; games area; cycle hire; wifi; entmnt; TV rm; 70% statics; dogs free; adv bkg; quiet; ccard acc; red CCI. ♦ € 24.00 2009*

ERICHEM see Tiel *C3*

GENDT *C3* (S Rural) *51.87599, 5.98900* **Waalstrand Camping, Waaldijk 23, 6691 MB Gendt [(0481) 421604; fax 422053; info@waalstrand.nl; www.waalstrand.nl]** Exit A15 to Bemmel, then Gendt. In Gendt foll sp to site on Rv Waal. Med, mkd pitch, terr, unshd; wc; chem disp; baby facs; fam bthrm; el pnts (6A) inc; gas; Indtte; snacks, bar adj; playgrnd; pool; rv beach adj; tennis; cycle hire; wifi; cab TV inc; 50% statics; dogs €3; poss cr; Eng spkn; adv bkg; quiet but some noise fr rv traff. "Excel, well-kept site; clean, modern san facs; interesting rv traff." 1 Apr-1 Oct. € 24.50 2009*

GIETHOORN see Meppel *C2*

GOES *A3* (6km NW Rural) *51.54200, 3.78000* **Minicamping Janse, Muidenweg 10, 4471 NM Wolphaartsdijk [(0113) 581584 or 06 12612728 (mob); fax 581111; info@heerlijkheidwolphaartsdijk.nl; www.heerlijkheidwolphaartsdijk.nl]** Off N256 Zierikzee to Goes rd foll sp Jachthaven Wolphaartsdijk. Shortly after vill turn L twd windmill. Turn R at mini rndabt (ignore camping sp by L turn) sp Arnemuiden, strt on at next rndabt, then L at next rndabt; site on L in 1km on lakeside - ent thro farm gate. Sm, hdg pitch, pt shd; wc; chem disp; shwrs inc; el pnts (6-16A) inc; lndtte; playgrnd; lake sw & beach adj; windsurfing; sailing; dogs €0.50; bus 1km; Eng spkn; quiet; CCI. "CL-type, farm site; modern san facs; friendly owners; bird reserve opp; excel cycling; rec." 15 Mar-31 Oct. € 18.00 2010*

GOES *A3* (7km NW Rural) *51.54685, 3.81339* **Camping De Veerhoeve, Veerweg 48, 4471 NC Wolphaartsdijk [(0113) 581155; fax 581944; info@deveerhoeve.nl; www.deveerhoeve.nl]** Off N256 Zierikzee to Goes rd foll sp Wolphaartsdijk. Site is last of 3 on this rd. Lge, mkd pitch, some hdstg, pt shd; htd wc; chem disp; mv service pnt; serviced pitches; baby facs; fam bthrm; shwrs €0.50; el pnts (10A) inc; gas; lndtte (inc dryer); shop; snacks; playgrnd; pool 8km; watersports cent adj; windsurfing; sport fishing; diving; sailing; tennis; games area; cycle hire; wifi; 50% statics; dogs €4; phone; Holland Tulip Parcs site; poss cr; Eng spkn; adv bkg ess; quiet; ccard acc; CCI. "By nature reserve & lovely lake Veerse Meer." ♦ 1 Apr-30 Oct. € 26.00 (4 persons) (CChq acc) 2009*

GOES *A3* (7km NW Rural) *51.54436, 3.81242* **Camping Veerse Meer, Veerweg 71, 4471 NB Wolphaartsdijk [(0113) 581423; fax 582129; info@campingveersemeer.nl; www.campingveersemeer.nl]** Exit A58 N onto N256 dir Zierikzee, take 2nd sp to Wolphaartsdijk. Go thro town, past windmill, site on R, reception on L. Lge, hdg pitch, hdstg, unshd; htd wc; chem disp; baby facs; shwrs €0.50; el pnts (6A) inc; lndtte (inc dryer); shop, rest 500m; tradsmn; snacks; playgrnd; cycle hire; internet; TV; 95% statics; dogs €2.50; sep car park; poss cr; Eng spkn; quiet; CCI. "Vg site; helpful owners." 1 Apr-31 Oct. € 21.50 2008*

GOOR *D3* (6km N Rural) *52.29639, 6.61444* **Camping 't Schuttenbelt, Vloodweg 7, 7468 RS Enter [0547 381472; schuttenbelt@3onnet.nl]** Leave A1 at exit 28 towards Enter; site sp bef Enter. Sm, mkd pitch, pt shd; wc; chem disp; baby facs; shwrs inc; el pnts (10A) inc; lndtte; snacks; bar; BBQ; playgrnd; pool; entmnt; dogs (extra charge); quiet. "Gd facs with excel pitches; beautiful cycling & walking; gd site." ♦ 15 Apr-15 Sep. € 19.00 2011*

⊞ **GOOR** *D3* (6km SW Rural) *52.1923, 6.5722* **Camping De Mölnhöfte, Nijhofweg 5, 7478 PX Diepenheim [(0547) 351514; fax 351641; mohnhofte@planet.nl; www.molnhofte.nl]** Turn S N346 Hengelo-Zutphen to Diepenheim & foll sps to camp 1km S of Diepenheim, 1.5km fr L turn where VVV sp strt. Med, pt shd; htd wc; chem disp; mv service pnt; baby facs; shwrs inc; el pnts (4A) €2.75; gas; lndtte; shop; snacks; bar; playgrnd; pool high ssn; games area; cycle hire; entmnt; TV; 80% statics; dogs €2.75; adv bkg; Eng spkn; quiet; red CCI. "Clean facs; helpful staff; poss muddy after rain; gd." ♦ € 13.25 2008*

GORINCHEM *B3* (4km NE Rural) *51.84524, 5.03995* **Camping Het Lingebos, Haarweg 6, 4214 KL Vuren [(0183) 630631; fax 637185; info@lingebos.nl; www.lingebos.nl]** Exit A15 exit junc 28 Gorinchem E sp Lingebos. Site at end of lge recreation area. Lge, pt shd; wc; chem disp; mv service pnt; baby facs; shwrs inc; el pnts (4A) €2.50; lndtte; sm shop & 4km; tradsmn; rest; snacks; playgrnd; pool 5km; lake sw; fishing; canoeing; cycle hire; games area; few statics; dogs €3.50; phone; sep car park; poss cr; Eng spkn; adv bkg; quiet but some m'way noise; red long stay; CCI. "Pt grass, pt wooded; paved rdways; muddy when wet; gd rest; excel." ♦ 1 Apr-30 Sep. € 19.00 2009*

GORINCHEM *B3* (10km E Rural) *51.81845, 5.12563* **Camping De Zwaan, Waaldijk 56, 4171 CG Herwijnen [(0418) 582354]** Exit A15 at junc 29 dir Herwijnen. In Herwijnen turn R at T-junc sp Brakel. Turn L in 500m (Molenstraat). At T-junc turn R (Waaldijk), site on L in 150m on Rv Waal. Sm, pt shd; wc; chem disp; shwrs €0.50; el pnts (4A) inc; shop 1km; playgrnd; rv adj; 75% statics; poss cr; adv bkg rec; Eng spkn; quiet but some boat noise; CCI. "Helpful owners; ltd but clean facs." 15 Apr-15 Oct. € 13.00 2008*

⊞ **GOUDA** *B3* (500m E Urban) *52.01226, 4.71544* **Klein Amerika Parking, 2806 Gouda** 500m fr Gouda town cent, sp off Blekerssingel/Fluwelensingel. There are 3 designated parking spaces for m'vans in car park at Klein Amerika supervised by Gouda City Council. Max stay 3 days. Chem disp, water, rubbish bins, all free. Public wc (small fee). Normal car parking fees applicable. € 7.00 2009*

⊞ **GOUDA** *B3* (8.5km E Rural) *52.01719, 4.82943* **Camping De Mulderije, Hekendorpsebuurt 33, 3467 PA Hekendorp [(0348) 563233 or 06 20680521 (mob); demulderije@wxs.nl; www.demulderije.com]** Exit A12 junc 14 Woerden onto N204 S. In 5km turn R to Oudewater N228. Cont dir Hekendorp & in approx 2km site sp on R. Narr rd to site. Sm, hdstg, pt shd; wc; chem disp; shwrs inc; el pnts (6A) inc; lndry rm; shop, rest, snacks, bar 2km; dogs free; quiet. "Vg, clean, friendly site in nature reserve; cycle or boat to Gouda." ♦ € 16.00 2010*

GRIJPSKERKE *A3* (2km E Rural) *51.53200, 3.56700* **Mini-Camping Het Munniken Hof, Jacob Catsweg 4, 4364 TE Grijpskerke [(0118) 591659; fax 594826]** Fr S via Westerschelde Tunnel to Middelburg, N on N57 & foll sp L dir Domburg & Grijpskerke. At vill sp take 1st R (opp windmill). In 300m 1st R, site on R 200m. Sm, pt shd; htd wc; chem disp; shwrs inc; el pnts (6A) inc; lndtte; shop, rest, snacks, bar 1km; playgrnd; sand beach 7km; dogs €0.50; sep car park; poss cr; Eng spkn; adv bkg; quiet. "Pleasant farm site; excel for cyling; vg touring base; v helpful owners." Easter-31 Oct. € 17.50 2009*

GROEDE see Breskens *A4*

⊞ **GROENLO** *D3* (1.5km SE Rural) *52.03680, 6.63185* **Camping Marveld, Elshofweg 6, 7141 DH Groenlo [(0544) 466000; fax 465295; info@marveld.nl; www.marveld.nl]** Fr Groenlo take N319 dir Winterswijk, site well sp. V lge, mkd pitch, pt shd; htd wc; chem disp; mv service pnt; baby facs; fam bthrm; private san facs some pitches; sauna; shwrs €0.20; el pnts (6A) inc; gas; Indtte (inc dryer); shop; tradsmn; rest; snacks; bar; BBQ; playgrnd; htd, covrd pools; paddling pool; lake fishing; cycle hire; games area; wifi; entmnt; TV rm; 60% statics; dogs €2.50; phone; sep car park; Holland Tulip Parcs site; poss cr; adv bkg; Eng spkn; ccard acc (surcharge); CCI. "Huge leisure complex; something for everyone; immac." € 22.60 (CChq acc) 2009*

GRONINGEN *D2* (2km SW Urban) *53.20128, 6.53577* **Camping Stadspark, Campinglaan 6, 9727 KH Groningen [(050) 5251624; fax 5250099; info@parkcampings.nl; www.campingstadspark.nl]** Sp fr Groningen ring rd. Med, shd; wc; chem disp; mv service pnt; fam bthrm; shwrs €0.45; el pnts (6A) €2.50 (poss rev pol); gas; Indtte (inc dryer); shop in ssn; tradsmn; snacks; bar; playgrnd; pool 3km; cycle hire; internet; TV; 20% statics; dogs €2; phone; sep car park; poss cr; Eng spkn; adv bkg; quiet; ccard not acc. "Municipal site adj parkland with gd sports facs; park & ride into town; plenty of space, tents & vans mixed; extensive cycle paths; car park adj to each set of pitches; gd san facs." 15 Mar-15 Oct. € 18.00 2010*

GULPEN *C4* (2km S Rural) *50.80720, 5.89430* **Panorama Terrassencamping De Gulperberg, Berghem 1, 6271 NP Gulpen [(043) 4502330; fax 4504609; info@gulperberg.nl; www.gulperberg.nl]** Fr Maastricht on N278 twd Aachen. At 1st traff lts in Gulpen turn sharp R & foll site sp for 2km (past sports complex). Narr final app. Lge, mkd pitch, some hdstg, terr, pt shd; htd wc; chem disp; baby facs; fam bthrm; shwrs inc; el pnts (6A) inc; gas; Indtte (inc dryer); shop; tradsmn; rest; snacks; bar; BBQ; playgrnd; pool; paddling pool; cycle hire; games area; wifi; cab/sat TV; 10% statics; dogs €3; phone; Holland Tulip Parcs site; poss cr; Eng spkn; adv bkg; quiet; red snr citizens; CCI. "Nr 3 nations boundary visitor cent & Maastricht with gd walking/views; mkd cycle rtes & footpaths; modern, clean facs - poss long walk; some tourers sited on top terr - long way fr shop & recep; beautiful views; v popular site, poss cr even in low ssn; excel." 1 Apr-30 Oct. € 25.60 (CChq acc) 2010*

GULPEN *C4* (1.5km SW Rural) *50.80688, 5.87175* **Camping Osebos, Reijmerstokkerdorpsstraat, 6271 PP Gulpen [(043) 4501611; info@osebos.nl; www.osebos.nl]** W fr Gulpen on N278 dir Maastricht in 1km turn L, site sp. Lge, mkd pitch, terr, unshd; htd wc; chem disp; mv service pnt; baby facs; fam bthrm; shwrs inc; el pnts (6A) inc; gas; Indtte (inc dryer); shop; rest; snacks; bar & 1.5km; playgrnd; pool; games rm; entmnt; 20% statics; dogs €3; bus; poss cr; Eng spkn; adv bkg; quiet; red long stay. "Excel, popular site; rec book ahead." ♦ 1 Apr-27 Nov. € 24.10 2010*

⊞ **HAARLEM** *B3* (2km E Rural) *52.37700, 4.67500* **Camping De Liede, Lieoever 68, 2033 AD Haarlem [(023) 5358666; fax 5405613; kampeerbedrijfdeliede@hetnet.nl; www.campingdeliede.nl]** Fr Amsterdam on A9 foll sp Haarlem onto A200. On A200 at 1st traff lts turn L, then L again, site sp. Med; wc; chem disp; shwrs; el pnts (4A) €3; gas; Indtte; shop; rest; beach 11km; 20% statics; phone; bus 700m; poss cr; Eng spkn; adv bkg; CCI. "Site in 2 parts both sides of rd." € 17.00 2011*

HAARLEM *B3* (5km SW Rural) *52.32006, 4.56698* **Camping Vogelenzang, Tweede Doodweg 17, 2114 AP Vogelenzang [(023) 5847014; fax 5849249; camping@vogelenzang.nl; www.vogelenzang.nl]** Foll site sp on rd N206. V lge, hdg/mkd pitch, pt shd; htd wc; chem disp; mv service pnt; baby facs; shwrs €0.50; el pnts (4A) inc; Indtte (inc dryer); shop; tradsmn; rest; snacks; bar; playgrnd; pools; paddling pool; sand beach 4km; games rm; golf 7km; TV; 50% statics; no dogs; adv bkg; quiet; ccard acc; CCI. "Gd screening & hedging make site appear much smaller than it is; overflow field has el pnts & wc; gd san facs; vg." ♦ 1 Apr-15 Sep. € 25.25 2010*

HAGUE, THE see Den Haag *B3*

HALFWEG see Amsterdam *B3*

HARDENBERG *D2* (1km E Rural) *52.52246, 6.54563* **NCC Camping De Rolle, Grote Esweg 96, 7795 DD Diffelen [(0523) 251556; hardenberg@ncc.nl; www.ncc.nl]** Fr N34 turn S onto N36 dir Almelo. After 5km turn L sp Marienberg, then L in 300m; after x-ring rv take 1st L, site 1km on L, sp. Sm, mkd pitch, pt shd; htd wc; chem disp; shwrs inc; el pnts (4A) €2.75; shop 3km; rest 1km; snacks, bar 3km; playgrnd; htd, covrd pool 8km; dogs; poss cr; adv bkg; quiet. "C'van Club members welcome but must pre-book (phone ahead bet 1700 & 1800); excel walking, cycling country; historic towns in area; v friendly; vg. 1 Apr-31 Oct. € 10.00 2009*

HARDERWIJK *C3* (4km N Rural) *52.38500, 5.62860* **Camping Flevostrand, Strandweg 1, 8256 RZ Biddinghuizen [(0320) 288480; fax 288617; info@flevostrand.nl; www.molecaten.nl/flevostrand]** Foll A28 dir Amersfoort-Zwolle past Utrecht. At junc 13 turn off onto N302 Harderwijk; cont on N302 over lake bdge; turn R onto N306 sp Veluwemeer & 'Walibi World'; foll rd along lakeside for 1.5km to site on R. V lge, mkd pitch, pt shd; htd wc; chem disp; mv service pnt; fam bthrm; baby facs; sauna; shwrs inc; el pnts (6A) inc; gas; Indtte (inc dryer); shop; rest; snacks; bar; BBQ; playgrnds; 2 htd pools (1 covrd); paddling pool; marina; sand beach & lake sw; free sailing & surfing lessons; waterskiing; cycle & boat hire; horseriding; tennis; two theme parks nrby; organised child activities; entmnt; games rm; wifi; TV; 60% statics; dogs €3.90; no c'vans/m'vans over 8.50m high ssn; various pitch prices; phone; sep car park; poss cr; adv bkg; quiet; ccard acc; red low ssn; CCI. "Full marina facs on Veluwemeer for all types of boating; vg." 1 Apr-1 Nov. € 31.25 SBS - H16 2011*

HARDERWIJK *C3* (7km NE Rural) *52.39470, 5.73230* **Camping De Hooghe Bijsschel, Randmeerweg 8, 8071 SH Nunspeet [(0341) 252406; fax 262565; info@hooghebijsschel.nl; www.hooghebijsschel.nl or www.molecaten.nl/nl/de-hooghe-bijsschel]** Fr A28/E232 exit junc 14 & turn L at rndabt. Go strt over next 3 rndbts foll sp Nunspeet then turn L at 4th rndabt sp Hulshorst, then R at next rndabt sp Veluwemeer. Site on R after 3km (after sharp L-hand bend). Lge, mkd pitch, pt sl, pt shd; htd wc (some cont); chem disp; mv service pnt; serviced pitches; baby facs; fam bthrm; shwrs; el pnts (6A) inc; gas; Indtte (inc dryer); sm shop; supmkt nr; rest; snacks; bar; BBQ; playgrnd; htd pool; lake sw & sand beach adj; watersports; fishing; tennis; cycle hire; horseriding 2km; wifi; entmnt; games/TV rm; 60% statics; dogs €3.90 (1 only per pitch); no c'vans/m'vans over 7.50m; phone; sep car park; recep 0900-2100 high ssn 0900-1700 low ssn; adv bkg; quiet; ccard acc; red low ssn. "Excel, spacious pitches; shop at w/end only low ssn; rec use new san facs block nr rest/pool - not old block; gd walking/cycling & watersports." ♦ 1 Apr-30 Sep. € 34.50 SBS - H05 2011*

HARDERWIJK *C3* (8km W Rural) *52.27155, 5.43550* **Camping Flevo-Natuur (Naturist), Wielseweg 3, 3896 LB Zeevolde [(036) 5228880; fax 5228664; info@flevonatuur.nl; www.flevonatuur.nl]** Fr A28 Harderwijk exit junc 13 onto N302, L onto N305, foll sp Zeevolde & site. V lge, mkd pitch, pt shd; htd wc; chem disp; mv service pnt; sauna; shwrs €0.50; el pnts (4A) inc (poss rev pol); gas; Indtte; shop; tradsmn; rest; snacks; bar; htd, covrd pool; lake sw; games area; TV; 50% statics; dogs; phone; sep car park; Eng spkn; adv bkg; red long stay. "Excel pool complex." € 23.40 2009*

HARICH see Lemmer *C2*

⊞ **HARLINGEN** *C2* (9km NE Urban) *53.18979, 5.55392* **Recreatiepark Bloemketerp, Burg J Dijkstraweg 3, 8801 PG Franeker [(0517) 395099; fax 395150; info@bloemketerp.nl; www.bloemketerp.nl]** In Franeker town cent, adj sw pool. Med, hdg/mkd pitch, pt shd; htd wc; chem disp; mv service pnt; baby facs; shwrs €0.50; el pnts (6-10A) inc; Indtte (inc dryer); shop; rest; snacks; bar; playgrnd; pool; cycle hire; sat TV; phone; quiet; Eng spkn; ccard acc; CCI. "Pleasant site; gd train link to Harlingen." ♦ € 22.50 2010*

HARLINGEN *C2* (1km SW Coastal) *53.16253, 5.41653* **Camping De Zeehoeve, Westerzeedijk 45, 8862 PK Harlingen [(0517) 413465; fax 416971; info@zeehoeve.nl; www.zeehoeve.nl]** Leave N31 N'bound at sp Kimswerd. At rndabt turn L under N31 & foll site sp. Site on R in 1.6km. Lge, pt shd; htd wc; chem disp; mv service pnt; baby facs; fam bthrm; shwrs €0.50; el pnts (6A) inc; gas; Indtte (inc dryer); shop 1km; rest; snacks; bar; playgrnd; beach adj; fishing; watersports; cycle hire; games area; wifi; entmnt; TV; 30% statics; dogs €3.50; phone; Eng spkn; ccard acc (surcharge). "Roomy, well-maintained, open site; clean facs; easy walk to town & harbour; interesting area; vg." ♦ 1 Apr-15 Oct. € 21.50 2011*

See advertisement below

HATTEM see Zwolle *C2*

HEERDE *C3* (2km SW Rural) *52.37764, 6.00601* **Camping De Klippen, De Klippenweg 4, 8181 PC Heerde [(0578) 696690; fax 560258]** Exit A50 junc 28 or 29 & head twd Heerde. Site sp on ent vill on L. Foll sp to De Klippen & also Mussenkamp site. Med, mkd pitch, pt shd; wc; chem disp; shwrs €0.45; el pnts (4A); Indtte; shops 3km; playgrnd; 60% statics; phone; v quiet; CCI. "Excel site; immac facs; ltd space for tourers - phone ahead." ♦ 1 Apr-31 Oct. € 11.50 2009*

HEERENVEEN *C2* (6km S Rural) *52.90814, 5.91828* **Camping De Frije Fries, Schoterweg 2, 8462 TD Rotstergaast [(0513) 636178 or 06 53367727 (mob); fax 647084; info@gebrdevries.nl]** Exit A32 at junc 11 onto N924 W. In 2.5km turn L sp Rotstergaast, site on R in 4km. Sm, pt shd; wc; chem disp (wc); shwrs €0.50; Indtte; shop; BBQ; Eng spkn; quiet. "Vg, friendly site; gd cycling." 15 Mar-1 Nov. € 9.50 2009*

HEERLEN *C4* (6km SW Rural) *50.85213, 5.93594* **Camping Colmont, Colmonterweg 2, 6367 HE Voerendaal [(045) 5620057; fax 5620058; markpot@colmont.nl; www.colmont.nl]** Fr A76 take exit 6 Voerendaal; foll sp Ubachsberg; site sp. Med, pt sl, pt shd; htd wc; chem disp; mv service pnt; baby facs; shwrs inc; el pnts (4-6A) €2; gas; Indtte; shop; rest; snacks; bar; BBQ; playgrnd; htd pool; games area; cycle hire; TV; 30% statics; dogs €2; phone; poss cr; adv bkg (fee); quiet; CCI. "Gd size pitches; friendly owner." ♦ 2 Apr-25 Sep. € 19.00 2010*

CAMPING *DE ZEEHOEVE* **Beside the Waddenzee**

Part of the famous Eleven-City skating route, "De Zeehoeve" is by the city of Harlingen, the only seaport in the beautiful, historical province of Friesland. You can make a day trip to Vlieland or Terschelling, two of the lovely Wadden Islands and our province has many places of interest, most close to the city itself - the Ald Faers Erf-route, Kazemattenmuseum, Technical Activity Centre Aeolus, the Planetarium in Franeker. You can rent bikes, canoe or use pedaloes, cycle, ramble or go sea fishing on the Waddensea - these are just some of the things to see and do in Friesland. The campsite is 1 km. south of Harlingen, with heated modern toilet facilities - launderette - animation in high season - an inland harbour with a trailer slip, and there is accommodation to hire.

Fam. Kleefstra, Westerzeedijk 45, 8862 PK Harlingen
Tel. +31 517-413465, fax +31 517-416971
E-mail: info@zeehoeve.nl www.zeehoeve.nl

online direct booking
and WIFI on the campsite!

NETHERLANDS

Lots of country pleasure in leisure

heumens bos

Camping luxuriously in the " NIJMEGEN Area "

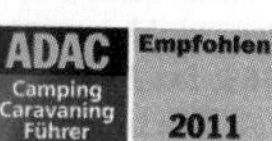

Vosseneindseweg 46
6582 BR Heumen
Tel. +31 24 358 14 81
info@heumensbos.nl
www.heumensbos.nl

HEEZE see Eindhoven *C4*

HEILOO see Alkmaar *B2*

HELLEVOETSLUIS *B3* (2km W Coastal) *51.82918, 4.11606* **Camping 't Weergors, Zuiddijk 2, 3221 LJ Hellevoetsluis [(0181) 312430; fax 311010; weergors@pn.nl; www.weergors.nl]** Via m'way A20/A4 or A16/A15 dir Rotterdam-Europoort-Hellevoetsluis; take N15 to N57, exit Hellevoetsluis, site sp. Lge, hdg/mkd pitch, some hdstg, unshd; htd wc; chem disp; mv service pnt; baby facs; shwrs €0.15/minute; el pnts (16A) €2.80; gas; lndtte (inc dryer); shop; rest; bar; BBQ; playgrnd; paddling pool; lake fishing; tennis; games area; cycle hire; wifi; TV rm; 60% statics; dogs €1.60; sep car park; Holland Tulip Parcs site; poss cr; Eng spkn; quiet; ccard acc. "Delta works 6km worth visit; bird sanctuary adj; nothing too much trouble; flat site; gd san facs; v friendly staff; excel rest; gd walking/cycling; excel site." ♦ 1 Apr-31 Oct. € 19.00 (CChq acc) 2011*

HENGELO *D3* (6km W Rural) *52.25451, 6.72704* **Park Camping Mooi Delden, De Mors 6, 7491 DZ Delden [(074) 3761922; fax 3767539; info@parkcamping.nl; www.parkcamping.nl]** Exit A35 junc 28 onto N346 dir Delden. Fr Delden-Oost, site sp. Site ent is R-hand of 2 via barrier (use intercom on arr.) If you have a high vehicle take the turning after Delden-Oost to avoid low rail bdge (2.3m); turn L immed aft lge rv bdge & foll site sp. Med, mkd pitch, pt shd; htd wc; chem disp; baby facs; fam bthrm; shwrs; el pnts (6-10A) €3.40 (poss rev pol); lndtte; shop & 1km; snacks; bar; playgrnd; pool; tennis; 50% statics; dogs €3.15; poss cr; Eng spkn; adv bkg; quiet. "Ideal for touring beautiful part of Holland; sports complex adj; pleasant, well-kept site; clean facs." ♦ 1 Apr-1 Oct. € 18.65 2011*

HERKENBOSCH see Roermond *C4*

⊞ **HEUMEN** *C3* (1km S Rural) *51.76890, 5.82140* **Camping Heumens Bos, Vosseneindseweg 46, 6582 BR Heumen [(024) 3581481; fax 3583862; info@heumensbos.nl; www.heumensbos.nl]** Take A73/E31 Nijmegen-Venlo m'way, leave at exit 3 sp Heumen/Overasselt. Do not re-cross m'way. After 500m turn R at camp sp. Site on R in approx 1.5km, 1km S of Heumen. V lge, hdg/mkd pitch, shd; htd wc (some cont); chem disp; mv service pnt; baby facs; fam bthrm; shwrs €0.50; el pnts (6A) inc; gas; lndtte (inc dryer); sm supmkt; rest; snacks; bar; BBQ; playgrnd; ' 2 pools (1 htd); paddling pool; jacuzzi; lake sw, sandy beach 2km; fishing 2km; watersports 6km; tennis; games area; cycle hire; horseriding 100m; activities/entmnt in ssn; wifi; games/TV rm; 60% statics in sep area; dogs €4; no c'vans/m'vans over 14m; phone; sep car park; extra €3 for m'vans; adv bkg; noise fr bar high ssn; ccard acc; red low ssn. "Excel, busy, family-run site; modern san facs; lots to do on site & in area - info fr recep; ideal for Arnhem; WW2 museums nr; mkt Sat & Mon in Nijmegen." ♦ € 35.00 SBS - H01 2011*

See advertisement above

HILVARENBEEK *B3* (4km N Rural) *51.52839, 5.12398* **Safaripark Beekse Bergen, Beekse Bergen 1, 5081 NJ Hilvarenbeek [(013) 5491100; fax 5366716; info@beeksebergen.nl; www.safaripark.nl]** Exit A58 m'way junc 10 onto N269, site sp. Lge, pt shd; htd wc; chem disp; mv service pnt; baby facs; fam bthrm; shwrs inc; el pnts (6-10A) inc; gas; lndtte (inc dryer); shop; rest; snacks; bar; BBQ; playgrnds; covrd pool; paddling pool; tennis; games area; cycle hire; internet; entmnt; TV; 30% statics; dogs; phone; adv bkg; ccard acc. "Free ent to adj Safari & Adventure Parks; excel facs; excel value - all sports inc in price." ♦ 1 Apr-15 Oct. € 30.60 2010*

HILVERSUM *C3* (4km SW Rural) *52.19341, 5.15519* **Camping Zonnehoek, Noodweg 15, 1213 PZ Hilversum [(035) 5771926; info@campingzonnehoek.com; www.campingzonnehoek.com]** Exit A27 junc 32 dir Hilversum & Martensdijk. Site sp on L after Hollandse Rading. Ent easily missed. Med, shd; wc; chem disp; baby facs; shwrs €0.50; el pnts (4A) €2.50; Indtte; rest; snacks; bar; playgrnd; pool 2km; entmnt; TV; 60% statics; phone; sep car park; carwash; poss cr; quiet; red CCI. "Woodland site with foot & cycle paths across heathland to Hilversum." 15 Mar-31 Oct. € 13.00 2008*

HILVERSUM *C3* (10km W Rural) *52.20242, 5.03039* **Rekreaticentrum Mijnden, Bloklaan 22A, 1231 AZ Loosdrecht [(0294) 233165; fax 233402; info@mijnden.nl; www.mijnden.nl]** Fr A2/E35 Utrecht-Amsterdam rd exit junc 4 dir Hilversum, in 2km over rlwy bdge & canal then 1st R sp Loenen. After vill, site sp 1st L. V lge, mkd pitch, some hdstg, unshd; htd wc; chem disp; mv service pnt; baby facs; shwrs €0.50; el pnts (4-10A) inc; Indtte; shop; supmkt 3km; rest; snacks; bar; BBQ; playgrnd; lake adj; sailing; TV; phone; dogs; poss cr; Eng spkn; adv bkg; sep area for tourers; ccard acc; CCI. "Marina/sailing site; bus/train to Amsterdam/Utrecht; card-operated security barrier; modern san facs." ♦ 25 Mar-2 Oct. € 23.50 2008*

⊞ **HOEK** *A4* (3km W Rural) *51.31464, 3.72618* **Braakman Holiday Island, Middenweg 101, 4542 PN Hoek [(0115) 481730; fax 482077; info@braakman.nl; www.braakman.nl]** Sp fr N61. V lge, mkd pitch, pt shd; htd wc; chem disp; mv service pnt; shwrs €0.50; fam bthrm; baby facs; serviced pitches; el pnts (4A) inc; gas; Indtte; shop; rest; snacks; bar; playgrnd; sub-tropical pool; lake beach; sailing; tennis; squash; entmnt; cab TV; 50% statics; dogs €5; phone; poss cr; Eng spkn; adv bkg; ccard acc;. "Excel for families; extensive recreation facs; conv Bruges/Antwerp; extra for lake view pitches." € 30.15 2009*

HOEK VAN HOLLAND *B3* (1.5km N Urban) *51.98953, 4.12767* **Camping Hoek van Holland, Wierstraat 100, 3151 VP Hoek van Holland [(0174) 382550; fax 310210; info@campinghoekvanholland.nl; www.campinghoekvanholland.nl]** Fr ferry foll N211/220 Rotterdam. After 2.4km turn L, 50m bef petrol stn on R, sp 'Camping Strand', site 400m on R. Lge, mkd pitch, hdstg, pt shd; htd wc; chem disp; baby facs; shwrs inc; el pnts (6A) inc; gas; Indtte; shop; rest; snacks; bar; playgrnd; pool; sand beach nr; tennis; cycle hire; entmnt; TV; 60% statics; no dogs; phone; bus; sep car park; poss v cr; Eng spkn; quiet; CCI. "Open 0800-2300; modern san facs but poss inadequate when site full & long walk fr m'van area; conv ferry." ♦ 14 Mar-11 Oct. € 28.00 (4 persons) 2009*

HOEK VAN HOLLAND *B3* (2km N Coastal) *51.99685, 4.13347* **Camping Jagtveld, Nieuwlandsedijk 41, KV 2691 'S-Gravenzande [(0174) 413479; fax 422127; info@jagtveld.nl; www.jagtveld.nl]** Fr ferry foll N211/220 sp Rotterdam. After 3.2km, turn L at junc with traff lts gantry into cul-de-sac. Site 200m on L. Med, unshd; wc; chem disp; shwrs inc; shop; el pnts (5A)poss rev pol €2; gas; Indtte; shop; snacks; playgrnd; sand beach 400m; entmnt; some statics; no dogs; phone; sep car park; poss cr; Eng spkn; quiet. "Ideal for ferry port; conv Den Haag & Delft; gd, clean, level, family-run site; diff when wet; helpful owners; excel 8km long beach." 1 Apr-1 Oct. € 23.00 2011*

HOENDERLOO see Apeldoorn *C3*

HOEVEN *B3* (1.5km SW Rural) *51.57020, 4.56020* **Molecaten Bosbad Hoeven, Oude Antwerpsepostbaan 81B, 4741 SG Hoeven [(0165) 520570; fax 504254; info@bosbadhoeven.nl; www.bosbadhoeven.nl]** Exit A58/E312 junc 20 Sint Willebrord dir Hoeven, site sp. V lge, pt sl, terr, pt shd; htd wc; chem disp; baby facs; shwrs €0.50; el pnts (6-10A) inc; Indtte; shop; rest; snacks; bar; 2 pools (1 covrd); paddling pool; waterslide; tennis; games area; cycle hire; entmnt; TV; 75% statics; no dogs; phone; adv bkg. "Popular family site high ssn; excel pool complex." ♦ 1 Apr-31 Oct. € 26.00 2007*

HOORN *B2* (10km SE Rural/Coastal) *52.62474, 5.15505* **Camping Het Hof, Zuideruitweg 64, 1608 EX Wijdenes [(0229) 501435; fax 503244; info@campinghethof.nl; www.campinghethof.nl]** Exit A7 junc 8 onto N506 Hoorn ring rd. Foll sp to Enkhuisen, after approx 10km at Tako's Wok rest, turn to Wijdenes vill, site sp. Med, mkd pitch, pt shd; htd wc; chem disp; baby facs; shwrs inc; el pnts (6A) €3; gas; Indtte; shop; tradsmn; rest; snacks; playgrnd; pool; shgl beach adj; sailing; watersports; cycle hire; TV; 60% statics; dogs €3; phone; sep car park; poss cr; Eng spkn; adv bkg; quiet; red CCI. 1 Apr-30 Sep. € 21.00 2008*

⊞ **HOORN** *B2* (2km SW Rural) *52.63085, 5.00920* **Camping 't Venhop, De Hulk 6, 1647 DP Berkhout [(0229) 551371; fax 553286; info@venhop.nl; www.venhop.nl]** Fr A7, exit junc 7 dir Avenhorn. Turn L under A7, site sp on R. Sm, pt shd; htd wc; chem disp; shwrs €0.55; el pnts (10A) inc; Indtte; shop; snacks; bar; playgrnd; boat hire; wifi; 60% statics; dogs €1.50;; phone; sep car park; Eng spkn; CCI. "Friendly owner; pleasant, well-run site nr canal; full facs low ssn." € 22.00 2008*

HORST *C4* (10km W Rural) *51.50657, 6.15603* **Recreatiepark Kasteel Ooijen, Blitterswijckseweg 2, 5871 CE Broekhuizenvorst [(077) 4631307; fax 4632765; info@kasteelooijen.nl; www.kasteelooijen.nl]** N fr Venlo on A72/73 turn R at junc 11 Horst twd Lottum. At T-junc turn L twd Broekhuizen & Broekhuizenvorst, site sp on R. Lge, hdg/mkd pitch, pt shd; htd wc; chem disp; mv service pnt; 90% serviced pitches; baby facs; fam bthrm; el pnts (4-10A) inc; gas; Indtte; shop; rest; snacks; bar; playgrnd; pool; tennis; games area; cab/sat TV; entmnt; 30% statics; dogs €1; phone; Eng spkn; adv bkg; quiet; ccard acc; CCI. "Gd facs; helpful staff; special area for families with children; gardens at Arcen worth visit." ♦ 27 Mar-31 Oct. € 24.55 2009*

IJHORST see Meppel *C2*

NETHERLANDS

IJMUIDEN *B2* (8km E Rural) *52.43199, 4.70819* **Parc Buitenhuizen, Buitenhuizerweg 2, 1981 LK Velsen Zuid [(023) 5383726; fax 5490078; info@parcbuitenhuizen.nl; www.parcbuitenhuizen.nl]** Fr S take A9 to sp Ijmuiden, then foll sp to Spaarnwoude recreation area at T-junc. Site on R in 5km. Fr Amsterdam, take N202 on N Sea Canal, twd W. In 10km site on L. Fr Ijmuiden port take N202 sp Amsterdam, site on R in approx 4km. V lge, hdg/mkd pitch, pt shd; wc; chem disp; shwrs €0.50; el pnts (6A) inc; gas; Indtte; shop; tradsmn; rest; snacks; bar; pool 2km; lake sw adj; playgrnd; cycle hire; wifi; 40% statics; dogs €3.50; bus to Amsterdam; adv bkg; quiet but aircraft noise; CCI. "Golf course & outdoor sports; conv NH for port; new owners 2008 - improvements in hand." ♦ 1 Apr-31 Oct. € 21.50 2008*

JULIANADORP *B2* (2km S Coastal) *52.90667, 4.72499* **Camping 't Noorder Sandt, Noordersandt 2, 1787 CX Julianadorp [(0223) 641266; fax 645600; info@noordersandt.com; www.noordersandt.com]** On ent Den Helder on N9 turn L sp Julianadorp. Foll sp to site. V lge, mkd pitch, pt shd; htd wc; chem disp; mv service pnt; baby facs; shwrs €0.50; el pnts (10A) inc; Indtte; shop; snacks; playgrnd; covrd pool; waterslide; sand beach 600m; tennis; games area; cab TV; 30% statics; dogs €3.50; phone; adv bkg; quiet; ccard acc; red long stay. "Excel, friendly site; gd for children; excel pool; breakfast avail & bread baked daily; gd foot & cycle paths; conv Alkmaar." 28 Mar-25 Oct. € 33.75 2009*

KAATSHEUVEL *B3* (E Rural) *51.66086, 5.05484* **Mini-Camping De Hoefstal, Horst 7A, 5171 RA Kaatsheuvel [(0416) 273344; fax 284614; info@dehoefstal.com; www.dehoefstal.com]** Turn S off A59 at junc 37 Waalwijk & foll sp Kaatsheuvel & Loonen/Drunense Duinen, site sp. Strt ahead at windmil, site on L in 250m. Sm, pt shd; wc; chem disp; shwrs €0.50; el pnts (4A) inc; Indtte (inc dryer); rest; playgrnd; Eng spkn; poss cr; adv bkg rec; some rd noise. "V clean facs; friendly, helpful owner; cycle path to Efteling theme park." 1 Apr-31 Oct. € 11.00 2009*

KAATSHEUVEL *B3* (1km E Rural) *51.66300, 5.07100* **Boerderij Camping, Van Loon's Hoekske, Van Haestrechtstraat 17a, 5171 RB Kaatsheuvel [(0416) 335758 or 06 20935679 (mob); vanloonshoekske@kpnplanet.nl; www.vanloonshoekske.nl]** Exit A59 junc 37 Waalwijk & foll sp Kaatsheuvel & Park de Loose Drunense Duinen. At windmill turn L, site 1km on L, sp. Sm, mkd pitch, unshd; wc; chem disp; shwrs inc; el pnts (10A) inc; BBQ; tradsmn; rest, snacks, bar 1km; playgrnd; Eng spkn; quiet. "Vg CL-type site on working farm." € 15.00 2009*

⊞ **KAMPERLAND** *A3* (3km W Coastal) *51.5682, 3.6632* **Camping RCN De Schotsman, Schotsmanweg 1, 4493 CX Kamperland [(0113) 371751; fax 372490; schotsman@rcn-centra.nl]** Sited on Noord Beveland on edge of Veersemeer. Fr Goes foll Rotterdam sps to Nood Beveland & N255 to Kamperland, site sp. V lge, hdstg, pt shd; htd wc; chem disp; mv service pnt; fam bthrm; baby rm; shwrs inc; el pnts (10-16A) inc; gas; Indtte; shop; rest; snacks; bar; playgrnd; pool 5km; sand beach 2km; lake sw; watersports; games area; tennis; cycle hire; internet; entmnt; TV; 50% statics; dogs; phone; sep car park; adv bkg; quiet; ♦ € 36.00 2007*

KAMPERLAND *A3* (500m NW Rural) *51.57902, 3.69795* **Camping De Molenhoek, Molenweg 69a, 4493 NC Kamperland [(0113) 371202; molenhoek@zeelandnet.nl; www.demolenhoek.com]** Site sp fr N255. V lge, mkd pitch, pt shd; htd wc; chem disp; mv service pnt; baby facs; shwrs €0.50; el pnts (6A) inc; gas; Indtte (inc dryer); shop; tradsmn; supmkt 800m; rest; snacks; bar; playgrnd; htd tropical pool complex; paddling pool; sand beach 2.5km; games area; games rm; cycle hire; wifi; entmnt; TV; 75% statics; dogs €5; Eng spkn; adv bkg; quiet. "Excel, spacious, family site; gd, clean san facs; gd touring base." ♦ 1 Apr-30 Oct. € 34.00 2010*

⊞ **KATWIJK AAN ZEE** *B3* (500m N Coastal) *52.21137, 4.41019* **Camping De Noordduinen, Campingweg 1, 2221 EW Katwijk [(071) 4025295; fax 4033977; info@noordduinen.nl; www.noordduinen.nl]** Fr A44 Wassenaar-Amsterdam, exit 8 Katwijk, onto N206. Leave at Katwijk Noord (fr S) or Katwijk ann Zee (fr N), R at rndabt & go over 6 sets of traff lts, immed R then L. Lge, hdg/mkd pitch, terr, unshd; htd wc; chem disp; mv service pnt; serviced pitches; baby facs; shwrs inc; el pnts (10A) €4.50 (poss rev pol); Indtte (inc dryer); shop; tradsmn; rest; snacks; bar; BBQ (gas/elec); playgrnd; 2 pools (1 htd/covrd); paddling pool; sand beach adj; tennis; wifi; cab TV; 60% statics; no dogs; sep car park; Holland Tulip Parcs site; poss cr; Eng spkn; adv bkg (dep); ccard acc; red low ssn/snr citizens. "Friendly, helpful management; clean facs; gd security; 'comfort' pitches avail at extra cost." ♦ € 31.50 (CChq acc) 2011*

See advertisement on next page

KATWIJK AAN ZEE *B3* (2km SE Rural) *52.19990, 4.45625* **Camping Koningshof, Elsgeesterweg 8, 2331 NW Rijnsburg [(071) 4026051; fax 4021336; info@koningshofholland.nl; www.koningshofholland.nl]** Fr A44 (Den Haag/Wassenaar-Amsterdam) exit junc 7 (Rijnsburg-Oegstgeest). In Rijnsburg cont twd Noordwijk. Foll blue & white sps thro Rijnsburg, across a bdge & then R twd Voorhout. Site in 2km. Lge, hdg/mkd pitch, hdstg, pt shd; htd wc (some cont); chem disp; mv service pnt; baby facs; shwrs inc; el pnts (10A) inc; gas; Indtte (inc dryer); shop; rest; snacks; bar; BBQ; playgrnd; 2 pools (1 htd, covrd); paddling pool; sand beach 5km; fishing; cycle hire; tennis; games rm; wifi; entmnt; TV cab/sat; 20% statics; dogs €3; c'vans/m'vans over 8m high ssn by request; phone; sep car park for some pitches; recep 0900-1230 & 1330-2000 high ssn; Holland Tulip Parcs site; Eng spkn; adv bkg; quiet; ccard acc; red long stay low ssn/snr citizens; CCI. "Vg, well-run, busy, friendly site; gd for families; excel rest; excel facs & pool; useful tour base for bulb fields; mkt Tues." ♦ 16 Mar-16 Nov. € 30.50 (CChq acc) SBS - H03 2011*

See advertisement on next page

Your home away from home

Recreatiecentrum De Zuidduinen
Zuidduinseweg 1, 2225 JS Katwijk
info@zuidduinen.nl
www.zuidduinen.nl
tel: +31 71-4014750
fax: +31 71-4077097

Recreatiecentrum De Noordduinen
Campingweg 1, 2221 EW Katwijk
info@noordduinen.nl
www.noordduinen.nl
tel: +31 71-4025295
fax: +31 71-4033977

Recreatiecentrum Koningshof
Elsgeesterweg 8, 2231 NW Rijnsburg
info@koningshofholland.nl
www.koningshofholland.nl
tel.: +31 71-4026051
fax: +31 71-4021336

Recreatiecentrum Delftse Hout
Korftlaan 5, 2616 LJ Delft
info@delftsehout.nl
www.delftsehout.nl
tel.: 015-2130040
fax: 015-2131293

KATWIJK AAN ZEE *B3* (1km S Coastal) *52.19319, 4.38986* **Camping De Zuidduinen, Zuidduinseveg 1, 2225 JS Katwijk [(071) 4014750; fax 4077097; info@zuidduinen.nl; www.zuidduinen.nl]** Fr A44 turn off at junc 8 onto N206 to Katwijk & foll 'Zuid-Boulevard' sps. Site sp. Lge, mkd pitch, unshd; htd wc; chem disp; mv service pnt; baby facs; shwrs inc; el pnts (4A) €3.50; gas; lndtte (inc dryer); shop; tradsmn; snacks; bar; no BBQ; playgrnd; sub-tropical pool 2km in Katwijk; sports & organised activities; tennis nr; cycle hire; wifi; cab TV; tour boats; tourist mkt; 50% statics; no dogs; phone; sep secure car park; adv bkg; quiet; ccard acc; red low ssn/snr citizens. "In dunes conservation area; well-run, peaceful site; excel facs." ♦ 1 Apr-30 Sep. € 32.50 (4 persons) 2011*

See advertisement

KLIJNDIJK see Emmen *D2*

KOOTWIJK see Apeldoorn *C3*

⊞ **KOUDUM** *C2* (1.5km S Rural) *52.90290, 5.46625* **Kawan Village De Kuilart, De Kuilart 1, 8723 CG Koudum [(0514) 522221; fax 523010; info@kuilart.nl; www.kuilart.nl]** Fr A50 exit sp Lemmer/Balk. Foll N359 over Galamadammen bdge, site sp. Lge, mkd pitch, pt shd; htd wc; mv service pnt; fam bthrm; baby facs; private bthrms some pitches; 90% serviced pitches; sauna; shwrs €0.35; el pnts (6-16A) €1.50-3.60; gas; lndtte (with dryer); supmkt; rest; snacks; bar; playgrnd; 2 pools (1 htd, covrd); waterslide; sailing; watersports; marina; games area; wifi; entmnt; TV & cinema rm; 50% statics; ltd dogs €3.35 (adv bkg rec); phone; sep car park; poss cr; Eng spkn; adv bkg; Holland Tulip Parcs site; CCI. ♦ € 26.00 (CChq acc) 2011*

KOUDUM *C2* (4.5km S Rural) *52.87526, 5.43887* **Camping Martinus, De Soal 6, 8584 VS Hemelum [tel/fax (0514) 581970 or 06 54632485 (mob); pieterzeldenrust@wanadoo.nl]** W fr Lemmer or E fr Koudum on N359. Turn L sp Hemelum, thro vill into De Soal street. Site on R in 1.5km. Sm, pt shd; htd wc; chem disp; shwrs inc; shop 1.5km; rest; no statics; dogs €1.25; Eng spkn; quiet. "Friendly, helpful owners; excel cycling; gd." 1 Mar-31 Oct. € 10.00 2009*

NETHERLANDS

KRAGGENBURG *C2* (1.5km N Rural) *52.67566, 5.89224* **Camping De Voorst, Leemringweg 33, 8317 RD Kraggenburg [(0527) 252524; devoorst@vdbrecreatie.nl; www.vdbrecreatie.nl]** Exit A6 junc 13 onto N352 sp Nagele & Ens. In Ens turn L at 1st traff lts (still N352) & foll sp Kraggenburg. Site sp at 1st rndabt. Lge, mkd pitch, some hdstg, pt shd; wc; chem disp; mv service pnt; shwrs €0.50; el pnts (4A) inc; lndtte (inc dryer); tradsmn; rest adj; snacks; bar; BBQ; playgrnd; htd pool; paddling pool; waterslide; tennis; games area; cycle hire; wifi; TV; 30% statics; dogs €2; bus; Eng spkn; quiet; CCI. "Excel." 1 Apr-30 Sep. € 19.00 2010*

⊞ **KRUININGEN** *A4* (2km SE Rural) *51.4349, 4.0455* **Camping Den Inkel, Polderweg 12, 4416 RE Kruiningen [(0113) 320030; fax 320031; info@deninkel.nl; www.deninkel.nl]** Exit A58 sp Kruiningen Ferry. In 1.4km at traff lts turn S sp Ferry; L at next traff lts, site sp. Lge, hdg/mkd pitch, pt shd; htd wc; chem disp; mv service pnt; baby facs; shwrs €0.50; el pnts (4-6A) inc; gas; lndtte; shop; rest; snacks; bar; playgrnd; pool 100m; sand/shgl beach 5km; tennis; games area; cycle hire; internet; TV; 60% statics; phone; sep car park; Eng spkn; adv bkg; quiet; ccard acc; CCI. "Friendly site; gd cycling." ♦ € 19.50 2007*

KRUININGEN *A4* (10km SW Coastal) *51.39681, 3.89825* **Comfort Camping Scheldeoord, Landingsweg 1, 4435 NR Baarland [(0113) 639900; fax 639500; Scheldeoord@Ardoer.com; www.scheldeoord.nl]** Take exit 35 off A58 sp 'S-Gravenpolder, foll sp Baarland & site 2km SE of Baarland. Lge, mkd pitch, unshd; htd wc; chem disp; mv service pnt; baby facs; fam bthrm; shwrs inc; baby rm; el pnts (6-16A) inc; gas; lndtte; supmkt; rest; snacks; bar; playgrnd; 2 pools (1 htd, covrd); sand beach adj; tennis; cycle hire; entmnt; internet; TV; phone; sep car park; 60% statics; dogs; sep car park; adv bkg; ccard acc. "Excel facs." 14 Mar-30 Oct. € 39.00 (3 persons) 2008*

LANDSMEER see Amsterdam *B3*

⊞ **LAUWERSOOG** *D1* (2km SE Coastal) *53.40250, 6.21740* **Camping Lauwersoog, Strandweg 5, 9976 VS Lauwersoog [(0519) 349133; fax 349195; info@lauwersoog.nl; www.lauwersoog.nl]** Fr N355 Leeuwarden-Groningen rd, take N361 Dokkum exit. Foll rd to Lauwersoog, site sp. V lge, unshd; htd wc; chem disp; mv service pnt; serviced pitches; baby facs; shwrs; el pnts (10A) inc; gas; lndtte (inc dryer); shop; rest; snacks; bar; playgrnd; pool; tennis; cycle hire; wifi; entmnt; TV; 50% statics; dogs €4.75; phone; sep car park; Holland Tulip Parcs site; poss v cr; Eng spkn; adv bkg; quiet; ccard acc; CCI. "Excel, well-maintained site; vg rest; gd facs." ♦ € 29.50 (CChq acc) 2011*

LEEUWARDEN *C2* (5km E Rural) *53.21644, 5.88714* **Camping De Kleine Wielen, De Groene Ster 14, 8926 XE Leeuwarden [(0511) 431660; fax 432584; info@dekleinewielen.nl; www.dekleinewielen.nl]** E fr Leeuwarden on N355 twds Groningen; in 5km look on S side for site sp. Lge, pt shd; htd wc; chem disp; mv service pnt; baby facs; shwrs €0.40; el pnts (4A) €3.25; gas; lndtte; shop; snacks; playgrnd; sand beach; lake sw; watersports; fishing; entmnt; TV; 60% statics; dogs €2.40; phone; adv bkg; some rd noise; ccard acc; CCI. "Beautiful location; helpful staff; sep area for tourers; vg." ♦ 1 Apr-1 Oct. € 14.65 2009*

LEEUWARDEN *C2* (5km SW Rural) *53.1490, 5.7616* **Camping Weidumerhout, Dekemawei 9, 9024 BE Weidum [(058) 2519888; fax 2519826; welkom@weidumerhout.nl; www.weidumerhout.nl]** Fr A32 exit junc 16 sp Weidum, foll sp for site. Site on R immed over canal bdge 1km E of Weidum. Sm, mkd pitch, pt shd; htd wc; chem disp; fam bthrm; shwrs inc; el pnts (6A) €3.45; lndtte; shop 1km; rest; bar; playgrnd; pool 5km; fishing; boating; cycle hire; sat TV; dogs; phone; sep car park; Eng spkn; adv bkg; quiet; ccard acc; CCI. "Excel rest in hotel adj; ideal touring base Friesland; facs stretched when site full; v ltd facs low ssn; Weidum pleasant, pretty town." ♦ 1 Feb-1 Dec. € 14.00 2007*

LEIDEN *B3* (5km N Rural) *52.20984, 4.51370* **Camping De Wasbeek, Wasbeeklaan 5b, 2361 HG Warmond [(071) 3011380; dewasbeek@hetnet.nl]** Exit A44 junc 4 dir Warmond; in 200m turn L into Wasbeeklaan, then R in 50m. Site sp. Sm, pt shd; wc; chem disp; shwrs €0.70; lndtte; shop, rest, snacks, bar 1km; BBQ; pool 2km; sand beach 8km; 40% statics; dogs free; bus 500m; sep car park; Eng spkn; adv bkg; quiet but some aircraft noise. "Attractive, lawned site close to bulb fields; m'vans by arrangement; twin-axles not acc; friendly, helpful staff; gd cycling (track to Leiden); fishing; boating; birdwatching." 1 Apr-15 Oct. € 13.00 2010*

LELYSTAD *C2* (5km SW Rural) *52.48570, 5.41720* **Camping 't Oppertje, Uilenweg 11, 8245 AB Lelystad [(0320) 253693; info@oppertje.nl; www.oppertje.nl]** Exit A6 junc 10 & take Larserdreef dir Lelystad. In 3km turn L into Buizerdweg & foll sp to site. Med, mkd pitch, pt shd; htd wc; chem disp; mv service pnt; baby facs; fam bthrm; shwrs €0.50; el pnts (10A) €3; lndtte; shop 5km; tradsmn; snacks; bar; BBQ; playgrnd; lake sw & beach adj; fishing; 20% statics; no dogs; sep car park; Eng spkn; quiet; red low ssn/CCI. "Pleasant site in nature reserve; friendly, helpful staff; modern san facs; cycle track adj; excel." ♦ 1 Apr-1 Oct. € 17.00 2010*

LEMMER *C2* (9km SW Rural) *52.87929, 5.62082* **Camping De Tjasker, Iwert 17, 8563 AM Wijckel [(0514) 605869; info@campingdetjasker.nl; www.campingdetjasker.nl]** Fr Lemmer take N359 sp Balk, in approx 7km turn R at caravan sp. Sm, unshd; wc; chem disp; shwrs inc; el pnts (4-6A) €2.20; lndtte; shops 4km; playgrnd; dogs; sep car park; adv bkg; quiet. "Sm farm site with gd facs; gd for exploring Friesland with easy cycling & walking." 15 Mar-1 Oct. € 10.80 2009*

LEMMER *C2* (6km NW Rural) *52.89993, 5.64208* **Camping De Jerden, Lytse Jerden 1, 8556 XC Sloten [(0514) 531389; fax 531837; info@campingdejerden.nl; www.campingdejerden.nl]** Exit A6 at Lemmer onto N359 sp Balk. In 9km foll sp Wijckel & Slotten. In 3km turn R into Heerenhoogweg, L into Lytse Jerden, site along canal on L. Sm, hdg/mkd pitch, unshd; htd wc; chem disp; shwrs €0.50; el pnts (16A) €3; lndtte (inc dryer); shop 500m; rest, bar in vill; playgrnd; lake sw 500m; sand beach; boat & cycle hire; games area; dogs €2; phone; adv bkg; Eng spkn; CCI. "Lovely site in excel position; gd touring base; clean facs; lge pitches." 1 Apr-1 Nov. € 17.00 2009*

LEMMER *C2* (11km NW Rural) *52.92019, 5.57494* **Camping Zwinzicht, Trophornsterweg 2, 8571 MX Harich [tel/fax (0514) 604512 or 06 12145209 (mob); info@zwinzicht.nl; www.zwinzicht.nl]** Fr N359 turn N dir Balk & Woudsend onto N928. Site sp 2km N of Harich. Sm, hdg/mkd pitch, pt shd; htd wc; chem disp; el pnts (6A) inc; Indtte; shop 2km; rest 1km; BBQ; playgrnd; games rm; no statics; dogs €1.75; sep car park; Eng spkn; quiet; red low ssn. "Vg." 1 Apr-2 Oct. € 14.00 2009*

LIEREN see Apeldoorn *C3*

LISSE *B3* (5km S Rural) *52.22175, 4.55418* **Camping De Hof van Eeden, Hellegatspolder 2, 2160 AZ Lisse [(0252) 212573; fax 235200; info@dehofvaneeden.nl; www.dehofvaneeden.nl]** Exit A44 junc 3 & turn N onto N208 dir Lisse. Turn R at rest on R bef 1st set traff lts into narr rd, foll rd to end (under A44) to site. Sm, unshd; wc; chem disp (wc); shwrs €0.50; el pnts (16A) inc; rest; playgrnd; 90% statics; Eng spkn; rlwy noise. "Gd CL-type site, space for 5 tourers - rec phone or email bef arr; interesting location by waterway & lifting rlwy bdge; conv Keukenhof." 15 Apr-15 Oct. € 17.50 2009*

LOCHEM *D3* (2km SW Rural) *52.14251, 6.38210* **Camping Landgoed Ruighenrode, Ploegdijk 2, 7241 SC Lochem [(0573) 253618; fax 253535; info@landgoedruighenrode.nl; www.landgoedruighenrode.nl]** Site sp fr N346 dir Zutphen. V lge, shd; htd wc; chem disp; mv service pnt; baby facs; fam bthrm; shwrs inc; el pnts (4-6A) inc; gas; Indtte (inc dryer); shop; tradsmn; rest; snacks; bar; playgrnd; pool complex 1km; lake sw; tennis; cycle hire; games rm; entmnt; TV; 60% statics; dogs €2; phone; adv bkg; quiet; CCI. "Pleasant wooded site." 1 Apr-30 Oct. € 25.00 2011*

LOENEN *C3* (1km SE Rural) **Camping De Marshoeve, Reuweg 51, 7371 BX Loenen [(055) 5051610; fax 5052710; info@marshoeve.nl; www.marshoeve.nl]** Fr N on N786 or N789 to Loenen, site well sp. Med, hdg pitch, pt shd; htd wc; chem disp; baby facs; shwrs inc; el pnts (6A) inc; Indtte; shop 1km; rest; bar; playgrnd; htd pool; 50% statics (sep area); dogs €3.50; poss cr; Eng spkn; quiet; CCI. "Lge pitches; excel site." 1 Apr-1 Oct. € 18.00 2007*

LOOSDRECHT see Hilversum *C3*

LUTTENBERG see Nijverdal *D3*

LUYKSGESTEL see Eersel *C4*

MAARN *C3* (1km N Rural) *52.07740, 5.37895* **Recreatiepark Laag Kanje, Laan van Laag Kanje, 3951 KD Maarn [(0343) 441348; fax 443295; allurepark@laagkanje.nl; www.laagkanje.nl]** Exit A12 junc 21 onto N227. In 2km turn R onto N224, in 1km turn R sp Laag Kanje. Lge, hdg pitch, pt shd; htd wc; chem disp; mv service pnt; baby facs; fam bthrm; shwrs €0.50; el pnts (4-6A) €2.65; Indtte; shop & 1km; rest; snacks; bar; playgrnd; lake sw & beach; games area; cab TV; 80% statics; no dogs; phone; adv bkg; quiet. "Lovely site in forest; excel sw in lake; excel cycle rtes; conv Utrecht/Arnhem." ♦ 1 Apr-25 Sep. € 19.50 2008*

⊞ **MAASBREE** *C4* (2km NE Rural) *51.3740, 6.0612* **Recreatiepark Bree Bronne, Lange Heide 9, 5993 RE Maasbree [(077) 4652360; fax 4652095; info@breebronne.nl; www.breebronne.nl]** Take exit 38 fr A67 onto N277 then N275 Maasbree. Turn L at rndabt at BP g'ge, go thro Maasbree; 200m & at x-rds nr elect sub-stn turn R & foll narr rd. Site on L after 3 speed bumps, sp. Lge, mkd pitch, shd; htd wc; chem disp; mv service pnt; fam bthrm; baby facs; serviced pitches; shwrs inc; el pnts (10A) inc; gas; Indtte; shop; rest; snacks; bar; playgrnd; 3 pools (1 covrd); sand beach on lake; boating; tennis; cycle hire; entmnt; TV; 50% statics; dogs €5.20; phone; adv bkg (fee); quiet; ccard acc; red low ssn; CCI. "Excel family site; excel, extensive facs; pitches poss muddy in wet; narr site paths poss make pitching diff; office opens 0900-1700; red low ssn over 55s." ♦ € 43.75 2007*

MAASDAM see Dordrecht *B3*

MAURIK *C3* (2km NE Rural) *51.97605, 5.43020* **Recreatiepark Eiland van Maurik, Rijnbandijk 20, 4021 GH Maurik [(0344) 691502; fax 692248; receptie@eilandvanmaurik.nl; www.eilandvanmaurik.nl]** Exit A15 junc 33 at Tiel onto B835 N & foll sp to Maurik & site on rvside. Or exit A2 junc 13 at Culembourg onto N320 to Maurik. Lge, pt shd; htd wc; chem disp; mv service pnt; baby facs; fam bthrm; shwrs €0.50; el pnts (10A) inc; gas; Indtte; shop; rest; snacks; bar; playgrnd; tennis; fishing; watersports; games area; covrd play area; horseriding; entmnt; wifi; TV; 50% statics; dogs €4; Holland Tulip Parcs site; Eng spkn; adv bkg; quiet. ♦ 20 Mar-1 Oct. € 31.00 (CChq acc) 2010*

MEDEMBLIK *B2* (1.5km SW Rural) *52.75900, 5.10873* **Camping & Lodge Arado, Brakeweg 61, 1671 LP Medemblik [(0227) 541671; info@arado.nl; www.arado.nl]** Exit A7/E22 junc 11 onto N239 dir Medemblik. Go strt over rndabt & turn R onto N240 dir Enkhuizen. Site on R in 2km. Sm, unshd; wc; chem disp; shwrs inc; el pnts (16A) inc; Indtte; shop 2km; cooking facs; internet; TV; no statics; dogs free; Eng spkn; adv bkg; CCI. "Vg CL-type site; friendly owners; easy access to pleasant town & yachting harbour; excel san facs; comfortable lounge." ♦ 1 Apr-30 Sep. € 16.00 2011*

MEERKERK *B3* (4km NW Rural) *51.93635, 4.96601* **Camping de Victorie, Broeksweg 75-77, 4231 VD Meerkerk [(0183) 351516 or 352741; fax 351234; info@campingdevictorie.nl; www.campingdevictorie.nl]** Leave m'way A27 10km N of Gorinchem at junc 25 Noordeloos/Meerkerk; take N214 twd Noordeloos. Turn R after Noordeloos sp SVR Camping & after 1.5km turn R. After 4km turn L at T-junc, site on L. NB: Not rec to tow thro Meerkerk due narr streets. Med, mkd pitch, pt shd; wc; chem disp; shwrs €0.50; el pnts (4A) inc; gas; Indtte; shop 4km; tradsmn; playgrnd; cycle hire; beach 35km; rv sw 3km; 50% statics; dogs €0.50; Eng spkn; sep car park; quiet; adv bkg; ccard acc; CCI. "Well-run farm site; HQ of SVR organisation (mem'ship avail); helpful staff; sep areas 60+ & families with children; poss boggy after rain; poss long walk to san facs; gd for touring old world Holland; fruit festival in Tiel mid Sep." 1 Apr-30 Sep. € 10.00 2010*

Send in your site reports by mid September 2013

MEPPEL *C2* (8km W Rural) *52.69395, 6.08130* **Camping de Kettingbrug, Veneweg 270, 7946 LW Wanneperveen [(0522) 281207; fax 282657; info@dekettingbrug.nl; www.dekettingbrug.nl]** N on A28/A32 & exit junc 3 Meppel N onto N375 dir Giethoorn for approx 8km. Turn R onto N334 after x-ing lifting bdge & look for site sp in approx 4km. Sm, hdg/mkd pitch, pt shd; htd wc; chem disp; shwrs inc; el pnts (10A) €3; gas; lndtte; shop 300m; tradsmn; playgrnd; lake sw & grass beach adj; watersports; statics in sep area across rd; dogs €1.50; bus; phone; poss cr; Eng spkn; adv bkg; quiet. "Excel, family-run site; ltd touring pitches, some on lakeside; gd views; conv Giethoorn by cycle rte." 1 Apr-15 Oct. € 19.00 2010*

MEPPEL *C2* (9km W Rural) *52.72164, 6.07484* **Passantenhaven Zuiderkluft, Jonenweg, 8355 LG Giethoorn [(0521) 362312]** Turn off N334 sp Dwarsgracht, over lifting bdge, 1st L over bdge, 1st L again, site on R. Sm, unshd; wc; chem disp; mv service pnt; shwrs €0.50; el pnts (10A) metered; lndtte; drinking water €0.50; Eng spkn; m'vans only; quiet. "Site run by VVV (tourist board) for m'vans only; ltd el pnts; walking dist fr delightful vill on water." € 10.00 2009*

MEPPEL *C2* (10km W Rural) *52.67261, 6.05973* **NCC Camping 't Hoogland, Vaste Belterweg 4, 8066 PT Belt-Schutsloot [(038) 3866313; www.ncc.nl]** Exit A32 junc 3 at Meppel Noord onto N375 sp Genemuiden. At T-junc after bdge turn R onto N334 sp Giethoorn, in 2km turn L sp Belt-Schutsloot. In vill turn R into Kerklaan then in 200m L into Belterweg, site on R. Do not app fr W - sharp turn onto narr bdge. Med, mkd pitch, unshd; wc; chem disp; shwrs inc; el pnts (4A) €2.75; lndtte; shop, rest, snacks, bar adj; playgrnd; htd, covrd pool; lake sw adj; boating; watersports; dogs; phone; adv bkg; quiet. "Lovely area; historic towns & vills; friendly staff; C'van Club members welcome but must pre-book." ♦ 1 Apr-31 Oct. € 12.50 2009*

MEPPEL *C2* (7km NW Rural) *52.72100, 6.06300* **Mini-Camping Van de Werfe Hoeve, Jonenweg 11, 8355 CN Giethoorn [tel/fax (0521) 360492]** In Giethoorn turn L at Smost bdge sp Dwarsgracht & Jonen, immed L to foll rd on L side of canal - narr rd. Site on L in 500m. Sm, unshd; wc; chem disp; shwrs; el pnts (4A) inc; gas 1km; shops 1km; no statics; dogs €0.50; poss cr; Eng spkn; adv bkg; quiet; ccard not acc. "Facs clean; boat hire nrby; gd cycle tracks & footpaths; cycle hire avail locally." € 15.00 2009*

MIDDELBURG *A4* (5km N Rural) *51.55005, 3.64022* **Mini Camping Hoekvliet, Meiwerfweg 3, 4352 SC Gapinge [(0118) 501615; copgapinge@zeelandnet.nl; www.hoekvliet.nl]** Fr Middleburg turn R off N57 at traff lts sp Veere & Gapinge, site sp after Gapinge vill. Sm, mkd pitch, some hdstg, pt shd; wc; chem disp; mv service pnt; shwrs inc; el pnts (6A) inc; lndtte (inc dryer); BBQ; rest, snacks, bar 2km; playgrnd; sand beach 5km; TV cab; cycle hire; 20% statics; dogs €1; sep car park; Eng spkn; quiet; CCI. "Superb little (25 outfits) farm site; excel, modern san facs; helpful owner." ♦ 1 Apr-31 Oct. € 21.00 2011*

MIDDELBURG *A4* (4km NE Rural) *51.53863, 3.65394* **Minicamping Trouw Vóór Goud, Veerseweg 66, 4351 SJ Veere [(0118) 501373; info@trouwvoorgoud.nl; www.trouwvoorgoud.nl]** Take Veere rd N out of Middleburg. Site on L in 4km, bef lge g'ge, sp 'Minicamping'. 1.5km SW of Veere. Sm, pt shd; wc; chem disp; shwrs inc; el pnts (6A) €1.75; lndtte; playgrnd; sand beach 6km; some statics; dogs €0.80; Eng spkn; quiet. "Excel facs; friendly, tidy, spacious, CL-type site; walking distance Veere." 15 Mar-31 Oct. € 14.00 2010*

MONTFORT see Echt *C4*

NIEUWESCHANS *D2* (1km NE Rural) *53.18343, 7.21640* **Camping Holland Poort, Mettingstraat 18, 9693 BX Nieuweschans [(0597) 522178]** Exit A7/E22 junc 49 & foll sp thro vill. Sm, hdg/mkd pitch, pt shd; wc (cont); shwrs €2; el pnts (6A) inc; Eng spkn; quiet. "Useful NH; ltd facs; pitch up & owner will call in evening." 1 Apr-31 Oct. € 12.50 2007*

⊞ **NIEUWVLIET** *A4* (3km N Coastal) *51.3872, 3.4398* **Vakantiepark De Pannenschuur, Zeedijk 19, 4504 PP Nieuwvliet [(0117) 372300; fax 371415; info@pannenschuur.nl; www.roompotparken.nl/parken/pannenschuur]** Fr Westerschelde Tunnel take N58. Foll sp Groede & Cadzand, thro Groede & in 3km turn R sp Nieuwvliet Strand, foll sp Pannenschuur. V lge, pt shd; htd wc; chem disp; mv service pnt; baby facs; fam bthrm; sauna; shwrs; el pnts (6A) inc; gas; lndtte (inc dryer); shop; rest; snacks; bar; playgrnd; covrd pool; sand beach 500m; tennis; cycle hire; wifi; TV; 70% statics; phone; sep car park; adv bkg; quiet; ccard acc. "V gd touring base for N & S Zeeland, Sluis, Bruges, Ghent." ♦ € 44.45 2010*

NIEUWVLIET *A4* (1km NW Rural) *51.37425, 3.44862* **Camping De Waag, Sint Jansdijk 8, 4504 PB Nieuwvliet [(0117) 371666; dewaag@zeelandnet.nl; www.campingdewaag.nl]** S fr Westerschelde Tunnel onto N61 & N58 dir Breskens. S of Breskens turn W sp Groede & Cadzand. In 6.5km beyond Groede at 2nd sp Nieuwvliet turn R; foll camp sp to site on R in 1.3km. Med, pt shd; wc; chem disp; baby facs; shwrs €0.50; el pnts (6A) €2.50; lndtte (inc dryer); shop; playgrnd; pool 1.5km; sand beach 1.5km; games area; wifi; entmnt; TV; 40% statics; dogs €1.20; phone; quiet; adv bkg. "Helpful owners; gd for sm children; conv Bruges, Zeeland & Zeebrugge." 23 Apr-1 Oct. € 14.70 2010*

NIJVERDAL *D3* (1.5km SW Rural) *52.34980, 6.45458* **Camping De Noetselerberg, Holterweg 116, 7441 DK Nijverdal [(0548) 612665; fax 611908; info@camping-noetselerberg.nl; www.camping-noetselerberg.nl]** Exit A1 at junc 28. Foll N347 dir Rijssen & Nijverdal. Turn L at rndabt down Noetselerbergweg, site sp. Lge, hdg/mkd pitch, pt shd; htd wc; chem disp; mv service pnt; fam bthrm; baby facs; shwrs; el pnts (4-6A) inc; gas; lndtte; shop; tradsmn; rest; snacks; bar; playgrnd; 2 pool (1 htd, covrd); cycle hire; entmnt; TV; 30% statics; phone; sep car park; quiet; adv bkg; Eng spkn. "Beautiful area; gd cycle tracks; friendly, helpful staff; excel." ♦ 3 Apr-25 Oct. € 34.00 2009*

NIJVERDAL *D3* (10km NW Rural) *52.39470, 6.36130* **Rekreatiepark De Luttenberg, Heuvelweg 9, 8105 SZ Luttenberg [(0572) 301405; fax 301757; receptie@luttenberg.nl; www.campingluttenberg.nl]** Exit junc 23 fr A1 dir Deventer. Head twds Raalte/Ommen on N348 & exit dir Luttenberg. Site 800m W of Luttenberg, sp. Lge, hdg pitch, some hdstg, pt shd; htd wc; mv service pnt; chem disp; baby facs; fam bthrm; private san facs avail; shwrs inc; el pnts inc (10A) inc; gas; Indtte (with dryer); shop; rest; snacks; bar; playgrnd; htd pool; paddling pool; waterslide; tennis; cycle hire; games area; wifi; entmnt; TV rm; 30% statics; dogs; phone; sep car park; poss cr; Eng spkn; adv bkg ess; Holland Tulip Parcs site; quiet; CCI. "Excel; conv Sallandse Heuvelrug National Park; water supply each pitch - key req fr office." ♦ 26 Mar-1 Oct. € 25.00 (CChq acc) 2008*

NOORD SLEEN see Emmen *D2*

NOORDEN see Alphen aan de Rijn *B3*

NOORDWIJK AAN ZEE *B3* (4km N Rural) *52.27102, 4.47686* **Camping De Carlton, Kraaierslaan 13, 2204 AN Noordwijk aan Zee [(0252) 372783; fax 370299; info@campingcarlton.nl; www.campingcarlton.nl]** Fr N206 take Noordwijkerhout turn off, foll sp to town & drive thru to rndabt. Take R exit sp Congrescentrum Leeuwenhorst, then take 1st L & foll site sp. Med, mkd pitch, pt shd; htd wc; chem disp; mv service pnt; shwrs €0.50; el pnts (4A) inc; Indtte (inc dryer); shops 1km; rest, snacks, bar; playgrnd; pool; cycle hire; TV; 40% statics; phone; sep car park; poss cr; Eng spkn; quiet; ccard acc; CCI. "Conv Keukenhof; gd clean site; friendly owners." ♦ 1 Apr-1 Nov. € 26.60 2009*

NOORDWIJK AAN ZEE *B3* (5km N Rural) *52.26896, 4.47359* **Camping Club Soleil, Kraaierslaan 7, 2204 AN Noordwijk aan Zee [(0252) 374225; fax 376450; info@parcdusoleil.nl; www.parcdusoleil.nl]** Fr Amsterdam/Den Haag m'way A4/A44 take exit 3, cont to 3rd rndabt (Congrescentrum), turn R, site sp. On N206 N of Noordwijk turn L onto N443; at next rndabt turn R into Gooweg. Turn L at rndabt onto Schulpweg, site in 400m, sp. Lge, hdg/mkd pitch, unshd; htd wc; chem disp; baby facs; fam bthrm; shwrs inc; el pnts (10A) inc; gas; Indtte (inc dryer); shop; rest; snacks; bar; playgrnd; htd, covrd pool & waterslide; sand beach 2km; tennis; cycle hire; games rm; wifi; TV; 10% statics; dogs; phone; sep car park; poss cr; Eng spkn; quiet. "Vg, clean, family site; conv tulip fields; gd cycling rtes." ♦ 1 Apr-30 Oct. € 47.00 (4 persons) 2008*

⊞ **NOORDWIJK AAN ZEE** *B3* (2km NE Rural) *52.24874, 4.46358* **Camping op Hoop van Zegen, Westeinde 76, 2211 XR Noordwijkerhout [(0252) 375491; info@campingophoopvanzegen.nl; www.campingophoopvanzegen.nl]** Exit A44 junc 6 dir Noordwijk aan Zee. Cross N206 & turn R in 1km into Gooweg dir Leeuwenhorst. In 1km turn L into Hoogweg & foll sp to site. Med, hdg/mkd pitch, unshd; htd wc; chem disp; mv service pnt; baby facs; fam bthrm; shwrs; el pnts (6A) €2.25; Indtte (inc dryer); shop 2km; playgrnd; sand beach 2.5km; cycle hire; games area; dogs €2.50; phone; poss cr; adv bkg rec when Keukenhof open; Eng spkn; quiet; ccard acc; CCI. "Gd site; modern san facs; sm pitches; conv bulb fields, beaches." € 15.50 2009*

NOORDWIJKERHOUT see Noordwijk aan Zee *B3*

NUNSPEET see Harderwijk *C3*

⊞ **OIRSCHOT** *C3* (1km N Rural) *51.51684, 5.30854* **Camping De Bocht, Oude Grintweg 69, 5688 MB Oirschot [(0499) 550855; info@campingdebocht.nl; www.campingdebocht.nl]** Fr A58/E312 take exit 8 to Oirschot. Site in 4km on Boxtel rd. Site sp. Med, hdg pitch, shd; htd wc; chem disp; baby facs; shwrs €0.50; el pnts (10A) €3; gas; Indtte (inc dryer); rest; snacks; bar; playgrnd; pool high ssn; paddling pool; cycle hire; wifi; entmnt; TV; 60% statics; dogs €2.50; phone; poss cr; adv bkg; quiet; Eng spkn. "Gd touring base; gd for families; pleasant town." € 21.70 2011*

OIRSCHOT *C3* (1km S Urban) *51.49606, 5.32156* **Camping Latour, Bloemendaal 7, 5688 GP Oirschot [(0499) 575625; fax 573742; info@campinglatour.nl; www.campinglatour.nl]** Fr Eindhoven-Tilburg A58, exit 8, sp Oirschot. Turn R at junc & foll c'van sp keeping R approx 1.5km after A58. Med, mkd pitch, pt shd; htd wc; chem disp; mv service pnt; baby facs; fam bthrm; shwrs inc; el pnts (6A) inc; gas; Indtte; shop 1km; tradsmn; rest; snacks; bar; cooking facs; playgrnd; htd pool; tennis; cycle hire; entmnt; TV; 40% statics; sep car park; Eng spkn; adv bkg; quiet; CCI. "Vg site; lge sports complex with sw/tennis etc; immac san facs; helpful staff." ♦ 1 Apr-30 Sep. € 21.00 2007*

OISTERWIJK see Tilburg *B3*

OMMEN *D2* (7km E Rural) *52.51033, 6.51564* **Camping de Roos, Beerzerweg 10, 7736 PJ Beerze [(0523) 251234; fax 251903; info@camping-de-roos.nl; www.camping-de-roos.nl]** Fr N34 at Ommen turn S onto N347. Cross rv & immed turn E. Site on L in Beerze. Lge, pt shd; htd wc; chem disp; baby facs; shwrs inc; el pnts (6A) €2.70; gas; Indtte; shop; snacks; playgrnd; lake & rv sw adj; boating; fishing; cycle hire; 10% statics; no dogs; phone; sep car park; quiet; ccard acc; red low ssn. "Excel family site; lots of play space." 2 Apr-3 Oct. € 17.00 2010*

OMMEN *D2* (3km W Rural) *52.51911, 6.36461* **Resort de Arendshorst, Arendshorsterweg 3A, 7731 RC Ommen [(0529) 453248; fax (0059) 453045; info@resort-de-arendshorst.nl; www.resort-de-arendshorst.nl]** W fr Ommen on N34/N340 turn L at site sp, then 500m along lane past farm, site on rvside. Lge, mkd pitch, pt shd; htd wc; chem disp; serviced pitches; baby facs; shwrs €0.20; el pnts (10A) inc; gas; Indtte; shop; rest; snacks; bar; no BBQ; playgrnd; pool 3km; paddling pool; sw in canal; games area; cycle hire; TV rm; 50% statics; dogs; phone; Eng spkn; adv bkg (fee); quiet; red 7+ days/snr citizens; CCI. "Beautiful area; many cycle rtes; gd children's facs." 1 Apr-31 Oct. € 28.50 2009*

OOSTERBEEK see Arnhem *C3*

⊞ **OOSTEREND (TERSCHELLING ISLAND)** *C1* (E Rural) *53.40562, 5.37947* **Camping 't Wan Tij, Oosterend 41, 8897 HX Oosterend [(0562) 448522; fax 4433495; info@wantij-terschelling.nl; www.wantij-terschelling.nl]** Fr Harlingen to Terschelling by ferry. Take rd to Oosterend, site ent on L 250m after vill sp, past bus stop & phone box. Sm, mkd pitch, pt shd; htd wc; chem disp; shwrs €0.50; el pnts (6A) €3 (poss rev pol); Indtte; shop 3km; rest, snacks, bar 100m; cooking facs; playgrnd; sand beach 2km; internet; TV; dogs €1.75; bus adj; Eng spkn; adv bkg; quiet; CCI. "Gd area for birdwatching; many cycle/foot paths across dunes; horsedrawn vehicles for conducted tours; Elvis memorabilia 2km at Heartbreak Hotel - rest on stilts; excel site." ♦ € 15.00 2010*

There aren't many sites open at this time of year. We'd better phone ahead to check the one we're heading for is open.

⊞ **OOSTERHOUT** *B3* (2km SW Rural) *51.63039, 4.83167* **Vakantiepark De Katjeskelder, Katjeskelder 1, 4904 SG Oosterhout [(0162) 453539; fax 454090; kkinfo@katjeskelder.nl]** On A27 m'way N fr Breda exit junc 17 Oosterhout Zuit & foll site sp. Lge, mkd pitch, pt sl, pt shd; htd wc; chem disp; mv service pnt; baby facs; fam bthrm; shwrs inc; el pnts (6A) inc; gas; Indtte; shop; rest; snacks; bar; playgrnd; covrd pools; waterslides; tennis; cycle hire; internet; TV; 70% statics; dogs; phone; sep car park; poss cr; Eng spkn; adv bkg; quiet; ccard acc; red low ssn; CCI. "Gd rds to Rotterdam, Amsterdam, en rte to Rhineland; well-run site; no m'vans due soft ground." ♦ (4 persons) 2008*

OOSTERHOUT *B3* (2km NW Rural) *51.65358, 4.82736* **Mini-Camping Vrachelen, Vrachelsestraat 48, 4911 BJ Den Hout [(0162) 454032; fax 430680; jan@pheninckx.nl; www.pheninckx.nl]** Leave A59 at junc 32 S twd Oosterhout West. At 1st rndabt foll sp Oosterhout, at next rndabt turn R sp Den Hout & site. Site on R in 400m. Sm, mkd pitch, unshd; htd wc; chem disp; shwrs inc; el pnts (6A) inc; shop; tradsmn; playgrnd; TV; many statics; poss cr; Eng spkn; quiet; red low ssn; CCI. "Perfect level lawn in mkt garden; farm produce for sale; v helpful, friendly owners; pitches have hdstg for awnings; highly recommended." 15 Mar-1 Nov. € 15.00 2011*

OOSTKAPELLE *A3* (300m S Rural) *51.56382, 3.55676* **Camping in De Bongerd, Brouwerijstraat 13, 4356 AM Oostkapelle [tel/fax (0118) 581510; info@campingdebongerd.nl; www.campingdebongerd.nl]** Fr Middelburg foll sps to Domburg. Oostkapelle vill 4km bef Domburg, on ent foll 1-way system then sp to site 600m fr cent. Lge, pt shd; htd wc; chem disp; mv service pnt; serviced pitches; baby rm; fam bthrm; shwrs inc; el pnts (6A) inc; gas; Indtte; supmkt 300m; rest 300m; snacks; bar; playgrnd; covrd pool & paddling pool; sand beach 3km; internet; entmnt; TV; 15% statics; dogs €2.95 (low ssn only); phone; Holland Tulip Parcs site; poss cr; adv bkg; quiet. "Sm seaside resort on island; friendly staff." ♦ 14 Mar-2 Nov. € 38.50 2008*

OOSTKAPELLE *A3* (200m W Rural) *51.56253, 3.54627* **Zeeland Camping Ons Buiten, Aagtekerkseweg 2A, 4356 RJ Oostkapelle [(0118) 581813; fax 583771; onsbuiten@ardoer.com; www.ardoer.com/nl/camping/ons-buiten]** Fr Middelburg foll sps to Domburg; Oostkapelle vill 4km bef Domburg, on ent foll 1-way system, foll sps to site, 400m fr cent. Lge, mkd pitch, pt shd (in orchard); htd wc; chem disp; mv service pnt; private bthrms some pitches; baby facs; fam bthrm; shwrs inc; el pnts (6A) inc; gas; Indtte (inc dryer); shop; rest; snacks; playgrnd; covrd pools; sand beach 3.5km; tennis; cycle hire; wifi; entmnt; TV; 10% statics; phone; sep car park; no dogs; adv bkg; quiet. "Friendly staff; ideal for sm children." ♦ 1 Apr-1 Nov. € 40.50 2010*

OOSTWOUD see Enkhuizen *C2*

OPENDE *D2* (2km SE Rural) *53.16465, 6.22275* **NCC Camping de Watermolen, Openderweg 26, 9865 XE Opende [tel/fax (0594) 659144; info@campingdewatermolen.nl; www.campingdewatermolen.nl]** Exit A7 junc 32 dir Kornhorn. In Noordwijk turn L at church & in 3 km turn R into Openderweg. Site in 700m on L. Med, mkd pitch, hdstg, pt shd; htd wc; chem disp; shwrs €0.50; el pnts (4-10A) €2.50; Indtte; rest; bar; playgrnd; lake sw; internet; some statics; dogs €2.50; phone; adv bkg; quiet. "Friendly owners; part of site for NCC members - C'van Club members welcome but must book ahead." 1 Apr-31 Oct. € 16.75 2008*

OPENDE *D2* (3km S Rural) *53.15262, 6.19175* **Camping 't Strandheem, Parkweg 2, 9865 VP Opende [(0594) 659555; fax 658592; info@strandheem.nl; www.strandheem.nl]** E22/A7 Amsterdam to Groningen m'way take Frieschepalen exit 31. Foll N358 to Suirhesterveen; site sp. Lge, mkd pitch, some hdstg, pt shd; htd wc; mv service pnt; chem disp; serviced pitches; some pitches individ san facs; baby facs; fam bthrm; shwrs inc; el pnts (10A) €2.50; gas; Indtte (inc dryer); shop; tradsmn; rest; snacks; bar; playgrnd; htd, covrd pool; sand beach 5km; wifi; entmnt; 30% statics; dogs €4.25; poss cr; Eng spkn; adv bkg; quiet; Holland Tulip Parcs site; CCI. "Lge pitches; friendly owners; gd well-run site." ♦ 1 Apr-30 Sep. € 25.50 (CChq acc) 2011*

OTTERLO *C3* (2km S Rural) *52.08657, 5.76934* **Camping De Wije Werelt, Arnhemseweg 100-102, 6731 BV Otterlo [(0318) 591201; fax 592101; info@wijewerelt.nl; www.wijewerelt.nl]** Exit A50 junc 22 dir Hoenderlo & N304 to Otterlo. Site on R after Camping de Zanding. Lge, mkd pitch, unshd; htd wc; chem disp; mv service pnt; baby facs; fam bthrm; shwrs inc; el pnts (6-10A) inc; Indtte; shop; tradsmn; rest; snacks; bar; playgrnd; pool; paddling pool; games area; 40% statics; dogs €4; phone; Eng spkn; adv bkg; quiet; ccard acc. "Excel, well-run site; immac san facs; vg for families; conv Arnhem." 27 Mar-31 Oct. € 33.00 2009*

OTTERLO *C3* (1km SW Rural) *52.09310, 5.77762* **Camping De Zanding, Vijverlaan 1, 6731 CK Otterlo [(0318) 596111; fax 596110; info@zanding.nl; www.zanding.nl]** Leave A1 at exit 17 onto N310 thro Otterlo, or junc 19 onto N304. Foll camp sp to site. Fr A50 exit junc 22 dir Hoenderloo & N304 to Otterlo. V lge, mkd pitch, some hdstg, pt shd; htd wc; chem disp; mv service pnt; serviced pitches; baby facs; shwrs inc; el pnts (4-10A) inc; gas; Indtte (inc dryer); rest; shop; playgrnd; lake sw & sand beach; tennis; wifi; entmnt; TV; 45% statics; dogs €3.50; Holland Tulip Parcs site; poss cr; Eng spkn; adv bkg ess hol periods; red low ssn; ccard acc; CCI. "Peaceful, wooded site; modern, well-organised & well laid-out; friendly, helpful staff; gd for families; excel facs; conv National Park, Kröller Müller museum; excel." ♦ 26 Mar-31 Oct. € 35.00 (CChq acc) 2011*

OUDDORP *A3* (3.5km W Rural) *51.8161, 3.8995* **Camping De Klepperstee, Vrijheidsweg 1, 3253 LS Ouddorp [(0187) 681511; fax 683060; info@klepperstee.com; www.klepperstee.com]** Fr Europoort (Rotterdam) take A15 (8km) then turn S onto rte 57. Travel approx 25km to Ouddorp turn R onto Oosterweg then L into Vrijheidsweg. V lge, hdg pitch, hdstg, pt shd; htd wc; chem disp; mv service pnt; baby facs; shwrs; el pnts (6-10A) €2.50; gas; shop & 3.5km; Indtte; rest; snacks; bar; playgrnd; paddling pool; sand beach adj; tennis; games area; cycle hire; TV; 60% statics; no dogs; phone; sep car park; poss cr; Eng spkn; quiet; CCI. "Excel." 1 Apr-31 Oct. € 31.00 (4 persons) 2007*

OUDEGA see Drachten *C2*

OUDEMIRDUM *C2* (1.5km N Rural) *52.86005, 5.54450* **Camping De Wigwam, Sminkewei 7, 8567 HB Oudemirdum [(0514) 571223; fax 571725; camping@dewigwam.nl; www.dewigwam.nl]** Exit A6 junc 17 onto N359 to Balk. Approx 3km beyond Balk turn L at sp Oudemirdum & foll site sp in woodland N of vill. Lge, mkd pitch, pt shd; wc; chem disp; baby facs; shwrs €0.75; el pnts (16A) inc; gas; Indtte; snacks; playgrnd; lake sw & sand beach 3km; cycle hire; golf adj; wifi; TV; 60% statics (sep area); dogs €2.70; Eng spkn; quiet; ccard acc; red snr citizens/low ssn. "Close to Ijsselmeer; lge pitches; gd cycling area; easy walk to pleasant vill; charge for all hot water." 1 Apr-1 Nov. € 17.30 2010*

OUDEMIRDUM *C2* (500m NW Rural) *52.85436, 5.53147* **Boskampeerterrein De Waps, Fonteinwei 14, 8567 JT Oudemirdum [tel/fax (0514) 571437; waps@planet.nl; www.dewaps.nl]** Fr Lemmer take N359 twd Balk. In 12km turn L sp Oudemirdum, site sp fr church in vill. Med, hdg/mkd pitch, pt shd; htd wc; chem disp; shwrs inc; baby facs; fam bthrm; el pnts (10A) inc; Indtte; shop 500m; tradsmn; rest; snacks; bar; playgrnd; sand beach 3km; games area; cycle hire; entmnt; 25% statics; dogs €2; phone; Eng spkn; quiet; ccard acc. "In pine forest; excel walks; clean facs; friendly staff." 1 Apr-31 Oct. € 24.30 2009*

PETTEN *B2* (200m W Coastal) *52.77057, 4.65908* **Camping Corfwater, Strandweg 3, 1755 LA Petten [(0226) 381981; fax 383371; camping@corfwater.nl; www.corfwater.nl]** On A9 N of Alkmaar, foll sp for Petten. Thro vill, site behind sea wall. Lge, mkd pitch, unshd; htd wc; chem disp; mv service pnt; baby facs; fam bthrm; shwrs inc; el pnts (6A) inc; gas; Indtte; shop; no BBQ; playgrnd; pool 3km; sand beach adj; 20% statics; no dogs; phone; sep car park; Eng spkn; quiet; ccard acc; CCI. "Vg site; busy in high ssn." ♦ 1 Apr-31 Oct. € 26.00 2011*

PLASMOLEN *C3* (S Rural) *51.73566, 5.91756* **Jachthaven en Camping Eldorado, Witteweg 9-18, 6586 AE Plasmolen [(024) 6961914; fax 6963017; info@eldorado-mook.nl; www.eldorado-mook.nl]** S on N271 fr Nijmegen to Venlo; site bet Mook & Milsbeek, turn R at Plasmolen, site sp. In 50m on R. Lge, mkd pitch, pt shd; wc; chem disp; shwrs €1; el pnts (6A) €3; gas; Indtte; shop; rest; snacks; bar; playgrnd; pool; fishing; watersports; cycle hire; 70% statics; dogs €2; poss cr; Eng spkn; adv bkg; poss noisy; CCI. "Site is part of marina/watersports complex avail to campers; v busy." ♦ 1 Apr-30 Sep. € 17.00 2008*

RAALTE *D3* (2km E Rural) *52.37419, 6.31261* **Minicamping 't Linderhof, Raamsweg 23, 8106 RH Mariënheem [06 10808636 (mob); info@campinglinderhof.nl; www.campinglinderhof.nl]** E on N35 fr Raalte, in Mariënheem turn R by church, site sp on R in 300m. Sm, pt shd; wc; chem disp; shwrs; el pnts (4A) inc; Indtte; playgrnd; games rm; quiet. "Pleasant, peaceful site; modern san facs." 15 Mar-31 Oct. € 14.00 2007*

RAVENSTEIN *C3* (E Urban) *51.79600, 5.65500* **NCC Camping De Pollepel, Bleek 5, 5371 AP Ravenstein [(0486) 413849; info@ncc.nl; www.ncc.nl]** Fr N exit A50 junc 17 dir Ravenstein, strt on at rndabt into Ravenstein. Fr S exit A50 junc 17 turn R at rndabt into Ravenstein. Foll sp for NCC camping; pass sm marina on RH side; turn L into Walstraat; then L immed after car park, site ent 50m thro gates. Sm, mkd pitch, pt shd; htd wc; chem disp; shwrs inc; el pnts (4A) £2.75; Indtte; shop, rest, snacks, bar 500m; playgrnd; htd, covrd pool 4km; rv sw adj; TV rm; train 3km; poss cr; adv bkg; some rd noise. "Beautiful site; located in cent picturesque fortress town on Rv Maas; gd cycling, walking; interesting area; C'van Club members welcome but must phone ahead." 1 Apr-31 Oct. € 12.00 2011*

REEUWIJK see Gouda *B3*

RENESSE *A3* (1km N Coastal) *51.73917, 3.77611* **Camping Duinhoeve, Scholderlaan 8, 4328 EP Renesse [(0111) 461309; fax 462760; info@campingduinhoeve.nl; www.campingduinhoeve.nl]** On rd 102 fr Renesse to Haamstede, turn R on ent to Haamstede bef T-junc. Last site on long picturesque lane. Lge, hdg/mkd pitch, pt shd; htd wc; chem disp; mv service pnt; baby facs; shwrs inc; el pnts (4-6A) inc; gas; Indtte; shop; rest; snacks; bar; playgrnd; sand beach nr; games area; cycle hire; TV; 20% statics; dogs €3.50; poss cr; adv bkg; quiet; ccard acc. "Charming area; Delta works worth visit; wide dunes on sea shore." ♦ 1 Feb-31 Oct. € 28.20 2009*

NETHERLANDS

⊞ **RENESSE** *A3* (1km SW Coastal) *51.71840, 3.76769* **Camping de Wijde Blick, Lagezoom 23, 4325 CK Renesse [(0111) 468888; fax 468889; wijdeblick@ardoer.com; www.ardoer.com/wijdeblick]** Sp fr rd 106 fr Haamstede. Lge, mkd pitch, pt shd; htd wc; chem disp; mv service pnt; serviced pitches; baby facs; fam bthrm; shwrs inc; el pnts (6-16A) inc; gas; lndtte; shop; rest; snacks; bar; playgrnd; pool; games area; entmnt; TV; 50% statics; no dogs; phone; bus to beach high ssn; sep car park; adv bkg; quiet. "Excel family site." ♦ € 34.50 2008*

RETRANCHEMENT see Sluis *A4*

RIJEN see Breda *B3*

RIJNSBURG see Katwijk aan Zee *B3*

ROCKANJE *A3* (NW Coastal) *51.88000, 4.05422* **Molecaten Park Waterbos, Duinrand 11, 3235 CC Rockanje [(0181) 401900; fax 404233; info@waterboscamping.nl; www.waterboscamping.nl]** Site clearly sp fr Rockanje vill. Lge, hdg pitch, pt shd; htd wc; chem disp; mv service pnt; baby facs; private san facs avail; shwrs €0.50; el pnts (6A) inc; lndtte; shop; rest; snacks; bar; playgrnd; sand beach/dunes 1km; entmnt; cab/sat TV; 80% statics; phone; no dogs; phone; poss cr; adv bkg; quiet; CCI. "Lovely base for Voorne area." ♦ 1 Apr-1 Oct. € 19.00 2009*

ROERMOND *C4* (5km SE Rural) *51.16424, 6.06523* **Mini Camping 't Haldert, Stationsweg 76, 6075 CD Herkenbosch [(0475) 531387; fax 531101; info@haldert.nl; www.haldert.nl]** Fr N end of town foll sp Roermond-Ost, then Herkenbosch. Under rlwy bdge, L at rndabt, 4km to petrol stn then immed L. Site in 500m, 2km N of Herkenbosch. Sm, pt shd; chem disp; wc; chem disp; shwrs €1; el pnts (6A) €1.50; lndtte; shop, rest in vill; playgrnd; pool 3km; adv bkg; quiet. "Excel, friendly, family-run, clean, CL-type site adj De Meinweg National Park; peaceful; gd clean facs." 1 Apr-31 Oct. € 11.00 2008*

ROERMOND *C4* (15km W Rural) *51.20947, 5.83008* **Camping Geelenhoof, Grathemerweg 16, 6037 NR Kelpen-Oler [(0495) 651858; geelenhoof@hetnet.nl; www.geelenhoof.nl]** 1km S of Kelpen-Oler; bet Roermond & Weert; exit N280 foll sp; well mkd. Med, hdg/mkd pitch, pt shd; htd wc; chem disp; mv service pnt; baby facs; shwrs inc; el pnts (6A) €3; rest; snacks; bar; playgrnd; games area; games rm; dogs (on request) €2.50; Eng spkn; adv bkg; quiet; CCI. "Cars not to be parked with c'van; vg site." 1 Mar-31 Oct. € 16.00 2011*

ROOSENDAAL *B3* (8km E Rural) *51.56334, 4.55341* **Camping Landgoed De Wildert, Pagnevaartdreef 3, 4744 RE Bosschenfhoofd [(0165) 312582; fax 310941; www.landgoeddewildert.nl]** Fr A58 exit junc 20 dir Hoeven or junc 21 Bosschenhoofd, foll sp to site to E of vill. Med, mkd pitch, shd; htd wc; chem disp; mv service pnt; baby facs; fam bthrm; shwrs inc; el pnts (6A) inc; lndtte; rest; bar; BBQ; playgrnd; games area; tennis; 50% statics; no dogs; Eng spkn; adv bkg; quiet; CCI. "Peaceful, wooded site; gd birdwatching." ♦ 1 Apr-30 Sep. € 21.00 2008*

ROOSENDAAL *B3* (5km SE Rural) *51.49430, 4.48536* **Camping Zonneland, Turfvaartsestraat 6, 4709 PB Nispen [(0165) 365429; info@zonneland.nl; www.zonneland.nl]** Take A58 exit 24 onto N262 dir Nispen. Foll site sps. Lge, some hdstg, shd; wc; chem disp; mv service pnt; shwrs €0.50; el pnts (4-10A) €2; lndtte; shop; supmkt 4km; snacks; bar; pool; playgrnd; entmnt; 80% statics; no dogs; phone; Eng spkn; adv bkg; quiet; ccard acc. 1 Mar-15 Oct. € 15.00 2008*

⊞ **ROTTERDAM** *B3* (2.5km N Urban) *51.93100, 4.44200* **Stadscamping Rotterdam, Kanaalweg 84, 3041 JE Rotterdam [(010) 4153440; fax 4373215; info@stadscamping-rotterdam.nl; www.stadscamping-rotterdam.nl]** Adj to junc of A13 & A20, take slip rd sp Rotterdam Centrum & Camping Kanaalweg sp to site. Dist fr m'way 2.5km with 3 L turns. Lge, pt shd; wc; chem disp; baby facs; shwrs inc; el pnts (6A) €3.75; gas; lndtte; shop; snacks; bar; internet; pool 500m; dogs €2; bus; poss cr; adv bkg; quiet but rds, rlwy adj; ccard acc. "Gd bus service to city cent; few water taps." ♦ € 18.70 2007*

ROTTERDAM *B3* (12km SE Rural) *51.83454, 4.54673* **Camping De Oude Maas, Achterzeedijk 1A, 2991 SB Barendrecht [(078) 6772445; fax 6773013; www.campingdeoudemaas.nl]** Leave A29 (Rotterdam-Bergen op Zoom) junc 20 Barendrecht, foll sp for Heerjansdam, site sp, Fr A16 (Breda-Dordrecht) foll Europort sp, then Zierikzee, Barendrecht, site sp. Lge, pt shd; htd wc; chem disp; mv service pnt; baby facs; fam bthrm; shwrs inc; el pnts (10A) inc; lndtte; shop; snacks; playgrnd; TV; 80% statics in sep area; dogs; phone; quiet; ccard acc. "Excel site on Rv Maas inc sm marina & joins rec park; excel facs; some pitches rough & long way fr facs; ferry fr site in ssn; check recep opening time if planning dep bef midday (espec Sun) for return of deposit & barrier key." ♦ 1 Mar-1 Nov. € 18.80 2007*

RUINEN *D2* (2km N Rural) *52.77570, 6.37170* **Camping Ruinen, Oude Benderseweg 11, 7963 PX Ruinen [(0522) 471770; fax 472614; info@camping-ruinen.nl; www.camping-ruinen.nl]** Exit A28 junc 28 sp Ruinen & foll sp to site; narr lanes. Lge, mkd pitch, some hdstg, pt shd; htd wc; chem disp; mv service pnt; baby facs; fam bthrm; shwrs inc; el pnts (6A) inc; gas; lndtte (inc dryer); supmkt high ssn; rest; snacks; playgrnd; htd pool; paddling pool; waterslide; tennis; cycle hire; wifi; entmnt; cab TV; 30% statics; dogs €3.35; sep car park; Holland Tulip Parcs site; Eng spkn; adv bkg; quiet. "V pleasant site." ♦ 1 Apr-1 Oct. € 25.00 (CChq acc) 2011*

RUURLO *D3* (2km N Rural) *52.1024, 6.44219* **Camping Tamaring, Wildpad 3, 7261 MR Ruurlo [(0573) 451486; fax 453891; info@camping-tamaring.nl; www.camping-tamaring.nl]** E fr Zutphen on N346 to Lochem. Turn R onto N312 dir Barchem, site sp bef Ruurlo. Med, hdg/mkd pitch, hdstg, pt shd; htd wc; chem disp; baby facs; shwrs inc; el pnts (4A) €2; gas; lndtte; shop; tradsmn; rest, snacks, bar 2km; playgrnd; paddling pool; cycle hire; 25% statics; dogs €2.10; adv bkg; quiet. ♦ 15 Mar-31 Oct. € 14.00 2008*

RUURLO *D3* (3km SE Rural) *52.06778, 6.50236* **Camping de Meibeek, Bekkenwal 2,7261 RG Ruurlo [(0573) 491236; info@campingdemeibeek.nl; www.campingdemeibeek.nl]** Site on N319, sp. Med, hdg/mkd pitch, pt shd; htd wc; chem disp; mv service pnt; baby facs; shwrs €0.50; el pnts (6A) metered; Indtte (inc dryer); tradsmn; rest; snacks; bar; playgrnd; pool; fishing nr; tennis 3km; golf 10km; games area; wifi; entmnt; 50% statics; dogs; Eng spkn; adv bkg; quiet. "Friendly, enthusiastic young owners; excel." 1 Apr-31 Oct. 2009*

⊞ **SEVENUM** *C4* (5km SW Rural) *51.38310, 5.97590* **Camping De Schatberg, Midden Peelweg 1, 5975 MZ Sevenum [(077) 4677777; fax 4677799; receptie@schatberg.nl; www.schatberg.nl]** Fr A2/A67 exit junc 38 for Helden; foll sp Sevenum & site by sm lake. V lge, shd; htd wc; chem disp; mv service pnt; fam bthrm; baby facs; private san facs some pitches; sauna; shwrs inc; el pnts (6-10A) inc; gas; Indtte (inc dryer); shop; rest; snacks; bar; playgrnd; 2 pools (1 htd, covrd); paddling pool; waterslide; jacuzzi; lake sw & sand beach; watersports; fishing; tennis; games area; cycle hire; entmnt; TV; 60% statics; dogs (in sep area); phone; Holland Tulip Parcs site; Eng spkn; adv bkg; quiet; CCI. "Excel leisure facs, espec for children; vg site but impersonal; tourers pitched amongst statics; Venlo Sat mkt worth visit." ♦ € 41.30 (4 persons) (CChq acc) 2011*

'S-HEERENBERG *D3* (3km NE Rural) *51.8871, 6.29980* **Mini Camping De Hartjens, Hartjensstraat 7, 7045 AH Azewijn [(0314) 652653; fax 652850; info@dehartjens.nl; www.dehartjens.nl]** Fr Arnhem take A12/E25 junc 30 onto N335 dir Beek, Zeddam & Terborg. Turn R to Azewijn on Ompertsestraat & in 1.5km turn R to site. Fr E exit A3 junc 3 onto N316 to 's-Heerenberg & Zeddam. Turn R onto N335 then as above. Sm, hdg pitch, unshd; htd wc; chem disp; baby facs; fam bthrm; shwrs inc; el pnts (6A) €1.75; playgrnd; TV rm; Eng spkn; quiet. "Excel, family-run site on working farm/vineyard; v clean san facs." 15 Mar-1 Nov. € 12.00 2008*

'S-HEERENBERG *D3* (3km W Rural) *51.87795, 6.21125* **Camping Brockhausen, Eltenseweg 20, 7039 CV Stokkum [(0314) 661212; fax 668563; info@brockhausen.nl; www.brockhausen.nl]** Fr A12 exit junc sp 's-Heerenberg, cont past 's-Heerenberg sp & pick up sp to Stokkum & site on L. Med, mkd pitch, pt shd; htd wc; chem disp; mv service pnt; baby facs; shwrs metered; el pnts (4-6A) inc; Indtte (inc dryer); shop 3km; playgrnd; cab TV; 40% statics; dogs €3.45; Eng spkn; adv bkg; quiet. "V clean, eco-friendly site; facs charged on electronic key; friendly, helpful staff; lovely area walking, cycling; excel." ♦ 1 Apr-31 Oct. € 21.80 2011*

⊞ **'S-HEERENBERG** *D3* (3km W Rural) *51.87855, 6.21453* **Camping De Slangenbult, St Isidorusstraat 12, 7039 CW Stokkum [(0314) 662798; info@deslangenbult.nl; www.deslangenbult.nl]** Fr Germany on A12/E35 exit junc 3 sp 's-Heerenberg. Thro town & foll sp to Stokkum & Beek, site sp. Lge, pt sl, unshd; wc; chem disp; baby facs; shwrs inc; el pnts (6A) €2; gas; Indtte; BBQ; playgrnd; games area; cycle hire; cab TV; 60% statics; dogs €2.50; phone; Eng spkn; adv bkg; quiet; CCI. "Gd, modern san facs; spacious site; gd walking/cycling; lovely nature area; interesting town." € 14.50 2007*

'S-HERTOGENBOSCH *C3* (6km E Rural) *51.6938, 5.4148* **Camping de Hooghe Heide, Werstkant 17, 5258 TC Berlicum [(073) 5031522; fax 5037351; info@hoogheheide.nl; www.hoogheheide.nl]** Fr A59/A2 circular rd around 's-Hertogenbosch exit junc 21 dir Berlicum. Foll sp Berlicum & site. Site is NE of Berlicum. Med, mkd pitch, pt shd; wc; chem disp; baby facs; shwrs inc; el pnts (10A) €3; Indtte; shop; snacks; playgrnd; pool; paddling pool; games area; TV; 70% statics; dogs €4.25; phone; poss cr/noisy high ssn; Eng spkn; adv bkg ess; quiet; CCI. "Nice, peaceful wooded site; narr site rds for lge outfits; tourers on open field; excel." ♦ 1 Apr-16 Oct. € 26.50 2010*

SINT OEDENRODE *C3* (1km N Rural) *51.57741, 5.44648* **Camping De Kienehoef, Zwembadweg 37, 5491 TE Sint Oedenrode [(0413) 472877; fax 477033; info@kienehoef.nl; www.kienehoef.nl]** Exit A50 junc 9; go towards Sint Oedenrode; foll sp to Centrum at rndabt; foll sp. Lge, hdg/mkd pitch, some hdstg, pt shd; htd wc; chem disp; mv service pnt; fam bthrm; baby facs; shwrs inc; el pnts (6A) inc; gas; Indtte (inc dryer); shop; rest; snacks; bar; BBQ; playgrnd; htd, covrd pool; paddling pool; lake sw; fishing; tennis; cycle hire; wifi; entmnt; TV rm; 50% statics; no dogs; phone; sep car park; Holland Tulip Parcs site; Eng spkn; adv bkg; ccard acc; CCI."Lovely CL type site; v gd facs; 1.50 miles fr lovely sm town with plenty of shops & rests." 1 Apr-25 Sep. € 30.00 (CChq acc) 2011*

⊞ **SINT OEDENRODE** *C3* (1km N Rural) *51.57800, 5.4400* **NCC Camping 't Roois Klumpke, Vliegden 1, 5491 VS Sint Oedenrode [(0413) 474702; www.ncc.nl]** Exit A2 junc 26 to Sint Oedenrode; site sp on Schijndel rd - 100m bef Camping Kienehoef turn R onto Vliegden, site 400m on L. Med, mkd pitch, pt shd; htd wc; chem disp; shwrs inc; el pnts (4A) €2.75; Indtte; BBQ; Eng spkn; poss cr; Eng spkn; adv bkg; quiet; CCI. "Members only - C'van Club members welcome but must pre-book; shop, rest, snacks avail at Camping de Kienehoef." ♦ € 11.00 2009*

SINT OEDENRODE *C3* (1km W Rural) *51.5690, 5.44388* **Camping De Donkershoeve, Ollandsweg 119, 5491 XA Sint Oedenrode [(0413) 473034; fax 490165; info@donkershoeve.nl; www.donkershoeve.nl]** Exit A58 junc 27 to Sint Oedenrode then dir Olland. Site sp. Sm, mkd pitch, unshd; htd wc; chem disp; baby facs; fam bthrm; shwrs inc; el pnts (16A) inc; Indtte; bar; playgrnd; htd, covrd pool 1km; fishing; games area; TV; 20% statics; dogs; phone; bus 1km; poss cr; Eng spkn; adv bkg; quiet. "Pleasant, CL-type site; site caters specially for disabled; owners former care workers; tents & statics also have disabled facs." ♦ 1 Apr-1 Oct. € 15.25 2008*

SLUIS *A4* (400m NE Rural) *51.31395, 3.38863* **Camping De Meidoorn, Hoogstraat 68, 4524 LA Sluis [tel/fax (0117) 461662; meidoorn@zeelandnet.nl]** Fr Zeebrugge, ignore 1st turn L to Sluis, cont to rndabt sp Sluis 1km. At windmill keep R (do not go to town cent). After LH bend turn R, foll sps. Lge, pt shd; htd wc; chem disp; mv service pnt; baby facs; shwrs €0.50; el pnts (6A) €3; gas; shop; rest; snacks; bar; playgrnd; tennis; TV; 80% statics; dogs €1.75; phone; Eng spkn; red CCI. "Quiet, friendly, well-kept site; helpful owners; sh walk to lovely town - many shops & rests; conv for Bruges; gd cycle rtes to coast;first class location; highly rec." ♦ 1 Apr-28 Oct. € 20.00 2011*

SLUIS *A4* (5km SE Rural) *51.28682, 3.43580* **Camping de Oliepot, Draaibrugseweg 8, 4527 PA Aardenburg [(0117) 491518; fax 493286; s.van.male@agroweb.nl; www.oliepot.nl]** Fr Knokke take N376 onto Sluis by-pass N58; turn R onto N251 Aardenburg. At next rndat in 1km turn L sp Draaibrug & immed R onto service rd. Site on L in 1km. Sm, mkd pitch, pt shd; wc; chem disp; shwrs €0.50; el pnts (4-16A) €1.65-6.30; lndtte; shop 1km; playgrnd; pool 3km; sand beach 6km; no statics; dogs €1.30; Eng spkn; adv bkg rec high ssn; quiet; ccard not acc; CCI. "V well-run site, clean & tidy; friendly, helpful owners; conv Bruges & Ghent. 1 Apr-30 Sep. € 11.00 2009*

SNEEK *C2* (1km NE Urban) *53.03557, 5.67630* **Jachthaven Camping De Domp, De Domp 4, 8605 CP Sneek [(0515) 412559; fax 439846; www.dedomp.nl]** Fr cent of Sneek on Leeuwarden rd, turn R sp De Domp. Med, pt shd; htd wc; chem disp; mv service pnt; serviced pitches; baby facs; shwrs €0.50; el pnts (6A) inc; gas; lndtte; rest; snacks; bar; supmkt nr; playgrnd; boating; sep car park; dogs; adv bkg; Eng spkn. "Many canals in Sneek; marina on site; easy walk to pleasant town; gd cycling cent." ♦ 1 Apr-1 Nov. € 18.20 2009*

STADSKANAAL *D2* (1km W Urban) *52.99079, 6.94159* **Camping 't Nije Hof, Spoorstraat 29b, 9503 AM Stadskanaal [599 658 892; info@nijehof.nl; www.nijehof.nl]** Fr Groningen take exit 44 off A7 Winschoten onto N33 dir Pekela; take N366 dir Stadskanaal & foll this rd until junction & take exit Stadskanaal (N) onto Van Boekerenweg; drive strt on for several km and pass hospial; turn L after hospital at traff lts island onto Handlestraat, which becomes Postraat; rd alongside canal, turn R over bridge sp Drouwener; take first R into Spoorstraat; pass over railway lines and immed sharp L into site. Sm, pt shd; htd wc; chem disp; baby facs; shwrs inc; elec pnts inc; lndtte; playgrnd; 15% statics; dogs €1.50; adv bkings; quiet; CCI. "Pleasant quiet site; friendly owners; pay on arr; handy for exploring Dolmen on Dutch/German border." Apr-Sep. € 17.50 2011*

STEENBERGEN *B3* (4km NW Rural) *51.60887, 4.27303* **Camping De Uitwijk, Dorpsweg 136, 4655 AH De Heen [(0167) 560000; info@de-uitwijk.nl; www.de-uitwijk.nl]** Fr N259 at Steenbergen turn W onto N257 dir Zierikzee. In 2km turn N thro De Heen & turn R at T-junc. Site recep on R, site on L. Do not take c'van to recep, but ent site, park on R & walk back. Med, mkd pitch, pt shd; htd wc; chem disp; mv service pnt; baby facs; shwrs inc; el pnts (4-10A) inc; lndtte (inc dryer); shop 4km; rest; snacks; bar; playgrnd; games rm; wifi; entmnt; sat TV; 60% statics; dogs €3.20; bus 750m; poss cr; Eng spkn; adv bkg; CCI. "Pleasant, quiet site adj marina; friendly staff; excel." 4 Apr-31 Oct. € 19.50 2009*

⊞ **STEENWIJK** *C2* (3km N Rural) *52.81494, 6.12007* **Camping De Kom, Bultweg 25, 8346 KB Steenwijk [(0521) 513736; fax 518736; info@vakantieparkdekom.nl; www.campingdekom.nl]** Take exit 6 fr A32 dir Vledder, site sp. Lge, mkd pitch, some hdstg, shd; htd wc; chem disp; baby facs; fam bthrm; shwrs €0.60; el pnts (4A) €3.30; gas; lndtte; shop; rest; snacks; bar; playgrnd; pool; paddling pool; games area; games rm; entmnt; internet; TV; cycle hire; 65% statics; sep car park; adv bkg; quiet. € 18.50 2008*

STEENWIJK *C2* (6km NE Rural) *52.84123, 6.17674* **Camping de Moesberg, Hoofdweg 14, 8383 EG Nijensleek [(0521) 381563; fax 383285; info@moesberg.nl; www.moesberg.nl]** Exit A32 junc 6 at Steenwijk N onto N855 sp Frederiksoord & Vledder; thro Nijensleek, site on L. Med, mkd pitch, unshd; htd wc; chem disp; mv service pnt; baby facs; shwrs inc; el pnts (10A) inc; lndry rm; shop 2km; rest adj; bar; playgrnd; pool 3km; wifi; sat TV; 10% statics; dogs; poss cr; Eng spkn; adv bkg; quiet. "Paved patio area at each pitch; helpful, friendly owners; gd rest adj." 1 Apr-1 Nov. 2009*

SUMAR see Burgum *C2*

THORN *C4* (600m SW Rural) *51.1596, 5.8340* **Camping Viverjerbroek, Kessenicherweg 20, 6017 AA Thorn [(0475) 561914; fax 565565; info@campingthorn.com]** Take junc 41 of A2, foll sp to Thorn. Turn R in vill down Wilhelminalaan, R into Holstraat, foll rd to site. Sm, hdg/mkd pitch, pt shd; wc; chem disp; shwrs €1; el pnts (4A) inc (rev pol); shop 500m; rest; bar; BBQ; lake sw & sand beach 1km; watersports; boating; 80% statics; dogs; phone; adv bkg; quiet; CCI. "Nr attractive vill; conv motorway; site run down (May 2010); NH only." 1 Apr-30 Oct. € 17.50 2010*

TIEL *C3* (4km W Rural) *51.89964, 5.35948* **Camping de Vergarde, Erichemseweg 84, 4117 GL Erichem [(0344) 572017; fax 572229; info@devergarde.nl; www.devergarde.nl]** Exit A15 at Tiel-West junc 32; foll sp Erichem & site. Lge, mkd pitch, pt shd; htd wc; chem disp; mv service pnt; serviced pitches; baby facs; fam bthrm; shwrs; el pnts (10A) inc; gas; lndtte; shop; rest; snacks; bar; playgrnd; htd pool; fishing; tennis; cycle hire; horseriding; children's farm; entmnt; internet; TV; 60% statics; dogs €3.75; poss cr; Eng spkn; quiet; red low ssn; ccard acc; CCI. "Gd facs." ♦ 1 Apr-18 Oct. € 27.50 2010*

TILBURG *B3* (10km E Rural) *51.57370, 5.23200* **Camping De Reebok, Duinenweg 4, 5062 TP Oisterwijk [(013) 5282309; fax 5217592; reebok@cambiance.nl; www.dereebok.nl]** Fr Tilburg NE on A65/N65, exit to Oisterwijk, over level x-ing, foll camp sps 'Recreatieve Voorzieningen' & De Reebok. Site is 3.5km SW of Oisterwijk. Lge, mkd pitch, shd; htd wc; chem disp; shwrs; el pnts (6A) inc; lndtte; shop; snacks; bar; playgrnd; lake sw 2km; cycle hire; internet; TV; 70% statics; adv bkg; quiet; red low ssn. 1 Apr-31 Oct. € 24.00 2007*

TUITJENHORN *B2* (2km E Rural) *52.73495, 4.77612* **Campingpark de Bongerd, Bongerdlaan 3, 1747 CA Tuitjenhorn [(0226) 391481; fax 394658; info@bongerd.nl; www.bongerd.nl]** N fr Alkmaar on N245, exit at Dirkshorn & foll sp to site. V lge, mkd pitch, pt shd; htd wc; chem disp; baby facs; shwrs inc; el pnts (10A) inc; gas; lndtte (inc dryer); shop; rest; snacks; bar; BBQ; playgrnd; 2 htd pools (1 covrd); paddling pool; waterslide; lake fishing; tennis; games area; cycle hire; wifi; entmnt; 60% statics; dogs €1.90; Eng spkn; adv bkg; ccard acc; quiet. "Excel, attractive family site; vg facs." ♦ 8 Apr-30 Sep. € 43.30 (CChq acc) 2008*

⊞ **UDEN** *C3* (6km NE Rural) *51.6955, 5.6565* **Camping De Heische Tip, Straatsven 4, 5411 RS Zeeland [(048) 6451458; fax 6452634; heischetip@heischetip.nl; www.heischetip.nl]** Fr A50 exit junc 16 sp Oss Ost/Schaijk & Zeeland. Foll sp Zeeland look for int'l camping sp to site, 2km W of Zeeland. Lge, hdg/mkd pitch, pt shd; htd wc; chem disp; baby facs; fam bthrm; shwrs €0.50; el pnts (6-10A); Indtte; shop; rest; snacks; bar; playgrnd; sand beach by lake adj; tennis; internet; cab/sat TV; 90% statics; phone; poss cr; adv bkg; quiet; CCI. € 25.00 2007*

I'll go online and tell the Club what we think of the campsites we've visited – www.caravanclub.co.uk/europereport

UDEN *C3* (11km E Rural) *51.66309, 5.77641* **Mini Camping Boszicht, Tipweg 10, 5455 RC Wilbertoord [(0485) 451565; fax (0845) 471522; boszicht-wilbertoord@planet.nl; www.boszichtcamping.nl]** Fr 's-Hertogenbosch on N279 dir Helmond. At Veghel turn L onto N265. Bef Uden turn R onto N264 to Wilbertoord in 11km. Sm, hdg/mkd pitch, unshd; wc; shwrs; el pnts (6A) metered; shops, rest in vill; playgrnd; games area; quiet. "Family-run farm site in woodland; conv Arnhem, Nijmegen." 20 Mar-19 Oct. € 13.00 2009*

UITDAM see Edam *B2*

UTRECHT *B3* (8km NE Rural) *52.13123, 5.22024* **Camping Bospark Bilthoven, Burg van der Borchlaan 7, 3722 GZ Bilthoven [(030) 2286777; fax 2293888; info@bosparkbilthoven.nl; www.bosparkbilthoven.nl]** Exit A28/E30 Utrecht-Amersfoort at exit sp De Bilt & strt to Bilthoven. Approx 3km after leaving m'way (400m S of level x-ing) turn R sp De Bospark Bilthoven. At edge of town foll sps twd lge brown tower & golf course. Site on L. V lge, pt shd; htd wc; chem disp; mv service pnt; baby facs; fam bthrm; serviced pitches; shwrs inc; el pnts (4-6A) inc (poss rev pol); gas; Indtte; shop 1km; tradsmn; snacks; bar; playgrnd; htd pool; TV; 60% statics; dogs €3.50; phone; poss cr; Eng spkn; adv bkg; quiet but some noise fr air base. "Helpful management; 20 mins walk to stn for trains to Utrecht cent." ♦ 1 Apr-31 Oct. € 25.75 2009*

UTRECHT *B3* (10km E Rural) *52.09272, 5.28287* **Camping de Krakeling, Woudensbergseweg 17, 3707 HW Zeist [(030) 6915374; fax 6920707; info@dekrakeling.nl; www.dekrakeling.nl]** Fr A12 exit junc 20 Driebergen/Zeist. In Zeist foll dir Woudenberg, site sp. V lge, hdg/mkd pitch, pt shd; htd wc; chem disp; mv service pnt; baby facs; shwrs €0.50; el pnts (6-10A); Indtte; shop; rest, snacks, bar w/end only low ssn; playgrnd; pool 3km; lake sw 5km; tennis; internet; cab TV; 90% statics; dogs; phone; adj nature reserve; bus; adv bkg. "Gd touring base Amsterdam/Utrecht; friendly; excel, clean facs; recep open 0900-1700, clsd for lunch." ♦ 1 Apr-4 Oct. € 24.70 2011*

VAALS *C4* (500m W Rural) *50.78159, 6.00694* **Camping Hoeve de Gastmolen, Lemierserberg 23, 6291 NM Vaals [(043) 3065755; fax 3066015; info@gastmolen.nl; www.gastmolen.nl]** Fr A76 exit at Knooppunt Bocholtz onto N281 SW to join N278, turn L twd Aachen. Site on L just bef 1st rndabt as ent Vaals. Med, hdg/mkd pitch, pt sl, pt shd; wc; chem disp; shwrs €0.50; el pnts (4A) €2.70; Indtte; shops 500m; tradsmn; rest 500m; snacks; playgrnd; 10% statics; dogs €2.70; bus 500m; sep car park; poss cr; Eng spkn; adv bkg rec; quiet; CCI. "Sm rural site; conv Aachen; vg san facs; diff in wet - tractor avail; mosquitoes; 'Drielandenpunt' 4km, in walking dist (where Netherlands, Germany & Belgium meet); excel." 1 Apr-31 Oct. € 16.00 2011*

VAASSEN see Apeldoorn *C3*

⊞ **VALKENBURG AAN DE GEUL** *C4* (1.5km N Rural) *50.88013, 5.83466* **Familiecamping De Bron, Stoepertweg 5, 6301 WP Valkenburg [(045) 4059292; fax 4054281; info@camping-debron.nl; www.camping-debron.nl]** Fr A79 exit junc 4 dir Hulsberg. Take 3rd exit fr rndabt onto N298, across next rndabt, then L onto N584, site sp. Fr A76 exit junc 3 dir Schimmert, foll sp Valkenburg & site. Lge, mkd pitch, pt shd; htd wc; chem disp; mv service pnt; baby facs; shwrs inc; el pnts (4-6A) €3-4.50; Indtte; shop; rest; snacks; bar; playgrnd; pool; games area; cycle hire; entmnt; internet; TV; 30% statics; dogs €3.50; phone; adv bkg; CCI. "Vg, well laid-out site; gd facs; muddy in wet weather." ♦ € 20.00 2007*

VALKENBURG AAN DE GEUL *C4* (2.7km E Rural) *50.86845, 5.86912* **Camping Waalheimer Farm, Walem 55, 6342 PA Walem [tel/fax (043) 4591571; waalheimerfarm@live.nl; www.waalheimerfarm.tk]** Fr A79 fr Maastricht exit junc 5 sp Klimmen. Turn R at 1st junc onto Overheek, then strt for 700m to rndabt, L onto Klimmenderstraat then immed R into Achtbunderstraat. Strt for 600m then R at Houtstraat leading to Waalheimerweg. In Walem sp turn R, farm on L under arch. Ent poss tight lge o'fits - watch for sm concrete post in hedge opp. Sm, hdg/mkd pitch, pt sl, pt shd; wc; chem disp; shwrs €0.50; el pnts (6A) €2; Indry rm; shop in vill 2.7km; dogs €2; bus/train; sep car park; v cr public hols; Eng spkn; quiet. "Wonderful views; vg CL-type site on working farm; sm pitches; bus fr Valkenburg to Maastricht." 15 Mar-1 Nov. € 13.00 2008*

VALKENBURG AAN DE GEUL *C4* (5km E Rural) *50.85042, 5.88120* **Camping Schoonbron, Valkenburgerweg 128, 6305 EA Schin op Geul [(043) 4591209; fax 4591486; info@schoonbron.nl; www.schoonbron.nl]** E fr Valkenburg on N595 to Schin op Geul. Site opp Camping Vinkenhof, just after Esso g'ge on L. Clearly sp, but ent pt hidden by RH bend in rd. V lge, mkd pitch, pt sl, pt shd; htd wc; chem disp; mv service pnt; baby facs; fam bthrm; shwrs inc; el pnts (4A) inc; Indtte (inc dryer); shop; rest; snacks; bar; playgrnd; covrd, htd pool; games area; wifi; entmnt; TV; 60% statics; dogs €3.25; Eng spkn; quiet; ccard not acc; CCI. "Clean, modern facs; friendly staff; vg." ♦ 15 Mar-31 Oct. € 23.90 2009*

VALKENBURG AAN DE GEUL *C4* (3km SE Rural) *50.84990, 5.87320* **Camping Vinkenhof, Engwegen 2A, 6305 PM Schin op Geul [(043) 4591389; fax 4591780; info@campingvinkenhof.nl; www.campingvinkenhof.nl]** Exit E2 Eindhoven-Maastricht at Meersen/Valkenburg about 6km bef Maastricht; foll rd E to Valkenburg. In town take rd E to Schin op Geul & foll camping sps. Med, mkd pitch, unshd; htd wc; serviced pitches; chem disp; baby facs; serviced pitches; shwrs €0.75; el pnts (6A) inc; gas; Indtte; shop 1km; rest adj; snacks; playgrnd; pool; cycle hire; TV rm; 5% statics; dogs €3; phone; site clsd 20 Dec-14 Jan; Eng spkn; quiet; CCI. "Gd walking country; well-kept, friendly site." 1 Mar-4 Jan. € 26.50 2010*

VALKENBURG AAN DE GEUL *C4* (500m S Urban) *50.85972, 5.83138* **Stadscamping Den Driesch, Heunsbergerweg 1, 6301 BN Valkenburg [(043) 6012025; fax 6016139; info@campingdendriesch.nl; www.campingdendriesch.nl]** Fr A2 dir Maastricht exit sp Valkenburg-Cauberg. Foll sp Valkenburg N590 & take turning sp Sibbe-Margraten. At rndabt foll sp Valkenburg, pass coal mine & turn R in 250m into sm, sl, unmkd ent. Steep turn off main rd into ent. NB L turn into site diff - proceed to rndabt at top of hill & return downhill to site. Med, mkd pitch, hdstg, pt sl, terr, pt shd; htd wc; chem disp; mv service pnt; shwrs €0.70; el pnts (10A) inc; Indtte; shop & 500m; rest 500m; snacks; no BBQs; htd, covrd pool 1km; cycle hire; 10% statics; dogs €3; phone; Eng spkn; adv bkg; quiet; ccard acc; CCI. "Castle & caves adj; other attractions nr; gd Xmas mkts in caves; easy access Maastricht by bus/train; vg." Easter-21 Dec. € 28.00 2009*

VALKENBURG AAN DE GEUL *C4* (1km S Rural) *50.85672, 5.81891* **Camping De Cauberg, Rijksweg 171, 6325 AD Valkenburg [(043) 6012344; info@campingdecauberg.nl; www.campingdecauberg.nl]** Exit A79 sp Valkenburg, foll Sibbe & Margraten sp to town cent. Take R fork in town sp De Cauberg, site on R at top of hill just past end Valkenburg sp. Med, mkd pitch, pt sl, shd; htd wc; chem disp; baby facs; shwrs inc; el pnts (10A) inc; Indtte; shop, rest; snacks; playgrnd; htd pool 1km; internet; 10% statics; dogs €3.10; bus; phone; site clsd 1-15 Nov; Eng spkn; adv bkg; quiet; red long stay; CCI. "Excel pool 1km; excel, modern, clean san facs; friendly, helpful owner; conv Maastricht; many rests, cafes in Valkenburg." 1 Mar-31 Oct & 19 Nov-31 Dec. € 27.50 2010*

VALKENBURG AAN DE GEUL *C4* (2km W Rural) *50.86057, 5.77237* **Camping Oriëntal, Rijksweg 6, 6325 PE Berg en Terblijt [(043) 6040075; info@campingoriental.nl; www.campingoriental.nl]** Fr A2/E25 exit onto N278 E & in 1km turn L onto N590 sp Berg en Terblijt & Valkenburg. Cont on N590, site on R in 4km at start of vill Lge, mkd pitch, pt shd; htd wc; chem disp; mv service pnt; baby facs; serviced pitches (inc cab TV); shwrs; el pnts (6A) inc (poss rev pol); gas; Indtte; shop; rest 500m; snacks; bar; playgrnd; htd, covrd pool; paddling pool; games area; wifi; 10% statics; dogs €3; phone; bus to Maastricht adj; Eng spkn; adv bkg; quiet; red low ssn; red low ssn; CCI. "Immac, well-run site; some areas flood in heavy rain; gd entmnt prog for young children; conv Maastricht." ♦ Easter-30 Oct. € 22.50 2008*

VALKENSWAARD see Eindhoven *C4*

VEERE see Middelburg *A4*

VELSEN ZUID see Ijmuiden *B2*

⊞ **VENLO** *D4* (2km SE Rural) *51.34823, 6.18548* **Camping/Restaurant De Kraal, Kaldenkerkerweg 186, 5915 PP Venlo [(077) 3514116; fax 3546164; kraal@dekraal.nl; www.dekraal.nl]** Fr rndabt by Venlo rlwy stn, take Kaldenkerkerweg SE for 2km; rest adj petrol stn. Sm, hdstg, pt shd; own san; chem disp; mv service pnt; el pnts inc; rest; snacks; bar; adv bkg. "CL-type site behind excel rest; nature park; watersports; walking; cycling; excel NH; m'vans only." € 6.00 2009*

⊞ **VENLO** *D4* (3km NW Rural) *51.42029, 6.10675* **Camping Californië, Horsterweg 23, 5971 ND Grubbenvorst [(077) 3662049; fax 3662997; info@campingcalifornie.nl; www.camping-californie.tk]** Exit A73 at Grubbenvorst junc 12 dir Sevenum, site sp. Med, pt shd; htd wc; chem disp; mv service pnt; shwrs inc; el pnts (4-10A) metered; Indtte; playgrnd; Eng spkn; quiet. "Pleasant, peaceful, CL-type site on asparagus farm; poss resident workers; warm welcome; unisex shwrs." € 15.50 2009*

VLISSINGEN *A4* (500m N Urban) *51.4684, 3.5546* **Camping De Lange Pacht, Boksweg 1, 4384 NP Vlissingen [tel/fax (0118) 460447; delangepacht@zeelandnet.nl]** Fr E on A58 to Vlissingen, then onto N288 & foll sp Kouderkerke. At rndabt at end built-up area turn L into Lammerenburgweg/Jacoba van Beierenweg then L tinto Vlamingstraat & foll to Boksweg & site. Sm, mkd pitch, pt shd; htd wc; chem disp; shwrs inc; el pnts (4-6A) inc; Indtte (inc dryer); shops 500m; BBQ; sand beach & pool 3km; playgrnd; sand beach 2km; wifi; 40% statics; dogs; phone; sep car park; adv bkg; quiet; CCI. "Clean, friendly site." 1 Apr-31 Oct. € 20.50 2010*

VOORTHUIZEN *C3* (2km NE Rural) *52.1869, 5.6245* **Camping Ackersate, Harremaatweg 26, 3781 NJ Voorthuizen [(0342) 471274; fax 475769; info@ackersate.nl; www.ardoer.com/ackersate]** Exit 16 fr A1 dir Voorthuizen. Take N344 twd Garderen, site sp on leaving town. Lge, pt shd; htd wc; chem disp; mv service pnt; fam bthrm; baby rm; shwrs inc; el pnts (6A) inc; gas; Indtte; shop; rest; snacks; bar; playgrnd; 2 covrd pools; entmnt; cycle hire; TV; 60% statics; dogs €4.50; phone; bus 1km; sep car park; quiet. "Excel site; recep not open Sun am." Easter-26 Oct. € 33.50 2007*

VUREN see Gorinchem *B3*

WASSENAAR *B3* (3km E Rural) *52.15269, 4.43361* **Camping Maaldrift, Maaldriftseweg 9, 2241 BN Wassenaar [(070) 5113688; fax 5170980; campingmaaldrift@hotmail.com]** Fr Hoek take N211/E30 to A4, then A12 & N44. Turn 1st L after Wassenaar & immed R onto rd parallel with main rd. Site sp on L in approx 2km. Sm, mkd pitch, pt shd; wc; chem disp; baby facs; shwrs €0.75; el pnts (6A) €2.25; Indtte (inc dryer); shop; snacks; bar; BBQ; playgrnd; pool 5km; sand beach 8km; 60% statics; dogs €1.25; phone; Eng spkn; quiet. "Excel, quiet base away fr cr commercial sites; narr site rds; lge pitches; clean, modern san facs." 1 Apr-30 Sep. € 16.20 2010*

WASSENAAR *B3* (1.5km W Rural) *52.11147, 4.34363* **Camping Duinhorst, Buurtweg 135, 2244 BH Wassenaar [(070) 3242270; fax 3246053; info@duinhorst.nl; www.duinhorst.nl]** Fr Leiden-Den Haag m'way A44 take Wassenaar exit, site sp. Lge, pt shd; htd wc; chem disp; mv service pnt; baby facs; shwrs €0.50; el pnts (6A) €2.40; gas; Indtte; shop; rest; snacks; bar; playgrnd; pool; sand beach 3km; tennis; cycle hire; games area; 50% statics; phone; no dogs; quiet; Eng spkn; ccard acc; CCI. "Nr Duinrell Theme Park & nature reserve; helpful staff; clean, well-organised site; gd rest; security barrier with card ent; gd for visiting The Hague & coast." ♦ Easter-30 Sep. € 17.80 2008*

⊞ **WASSENAAR** *B3* (300m NW Rural) *52.14638, 4.38750* **Camping Duinrell, Duinrell 1, 2242 JP Wassenaar [tel/fax (070) 5155147 or (070) 5155255; touroperator@duinrell.nl; www.duinrell.nl]** Fr Rotterdam in dir Den Haag on A13/E19, then on A4/E19 foll sp for Amsterdam. On A4 keep R onto A12 in dir Voorburg/Den Haag. At end m'way turn R onto N44 sp Wassenaar. In 8km turn L at traff lts immed bef Mercedes g'ge, foll site sp. On arr at site foll sp to campsite not coach park. Not rec to arrive mid-afternoon/early evening due to heavy traff leaving amusement park. V lge, hdg/mkd pitch, pt shd; htd wc; chem disp; mv service pnt; baby facs; serviced pitches; sauna; private san facs avail; shwrs inc; el pnts (6A) inc; gas; Indtte (inc dryer); shop; rest; snacks; bar; BBQ; playgrnd; 2 pools (1 covrd); paddling pool; waterslide; sand beach 3km; fishing, horseriding nrby; tennis; cycle hire; free ent adj amusement park; golf 1km; games rm; internet; wifi; entmnt; TV; 30% statics; dogs €6; no c'vans/m'vans over 7.75m high ssn; phone; sep car park for some pitches; poss cr; Eng spkn; adv bkg; quiet; red low ssn/snr citizens; ccard acc. "Popular, busy site; some pitches poss diff access, check bef siting; superb, modern facilities; tropical indoor pool; vg security; excel." ♦ € 35.50 SBS - H13 2011*

See advertisement

WEERSELO *D3* (1km W Rural) *52.36530, 6.84285* **Camping De Molenhof, Kleijsenweg 7, 7667 RS Reutum [(0541) 661165; fax 662032; info@demolenhof.nl; www.demolenhof.nl]** Exit A1 junc 33 dir Oldenzaal then Tubbergen. At Weerselo, foll site sp. Lge, pt shd; htd wc; chem disp; mv service pnt; baby facs; fam bthrm; shwrs inc; el pnts (10A) inc; gas; Indtte (inc dryer); shop; rest; snacks; bar; BBQ; playgrnd; 2 pools (1 htd, covrd); waterslide; fishing; tennis; covrd play area; cycle hire; golf 10km; wifi; entmnt; TV rm & cab TV to pitches; 25% statics; dogs €3; Holland Tulip Parcs site; Eng spkn; adv bkg; quiet; ccard acc. ♦ 16 Apr-2 Oct. € 37.00 (CChq acc) 2010*

WEERSELO *D3* (1.5km NW Rural) *52.35930, 6.83740* **Camping De Veldmeijer, Oude Almelosedijk 4, 7595 LJ Weerselo [(0541) 662195; info@develdmeijer.nl; www.develdmeijer.nl]** Exit A1/E30 dir Oldenzaal then N343 dir Tubbergen. After Weerselo foll 'Mini-Camping' sp. Sm, pt shd; htd wc; chem disp; shwrs inc; el pnts (6A) inc; Indtte (inc dryer); shop, snacks 1km; playgrnd; pool nrby; wifi; 25% statics; Eng spkn; adv bkg; quiet. "Welcoming owners; excel facs; lge pitches; gd cycling; vg." ♦ 1 Apr-31 Oct. € 16.00 2009*

WEERT *C4* (6km SE Rural) *51.22480, 5.79916* **Camping Landgoed Lemmenhof, Kampstraat 10, 6011 RV Ell [(0495) 551277; fax 551797; info@lemmenhof.nl; www.lemmenhof.nl]** Exit A2 junc 40 dir Kelpen. In 2km at traff lts turn R; in 50m turn R dir Ell. In 2km immed bef vill sp & De Prairie Cafe turn R into Kempstraat, site in 200m. Sm, hdg/mkd pitch, unshd; htd wc; chem disp; shwrs inc; el pnts (6A) inc; Indtte; shop 500m; rest, bar 200m; playgrnd; dogs €0.70; Eng spkn; adv bkg; quiet; CCI. "Vg; B&B & apartments avail." ♦ 15 Mar-31 Oct. € 15.00 2008*

WEIDUM see Leeuwarden *C2*

WESTERBORK see Beilen *D2*

⊞ **WEZUPERBRUG** *D2* (500m E Rural) *52.84030, 6.72370* **Rekreatiepark 't Kuierpadtien, Oranjekanaal Noordzijde 10, 7853 TA Wezuperbrug [(0591) 381415; fax 382235; info@kuierpad.nl; www.kuierpad.nl]** Fr A28 m'way exit 31 dir Emmen onto N381. Take exit Zweeloo & turn L immed. Go under viaduct twd Wezuperbrug via Wezup. In Wezuperbrug go over bdge, turn R, site sp. V lge, pt shd; htd wc; chem disp; mv service pnt; baby facs; fam bthrm; shwrs inc; el pnts (6A) inc; gas; Indtte (inc dryer); shop; rest; snacks; bar; playgrnd; htd, covrd pool; paddling pool; waterslide; lake sw & boating; tennis; games rm; cycle hire; wifi; entmnt; TV; 30% statics; dogs €5; phone; sep car park; Holland Tulip Parcs site; quiet. "Excel site; great for kids; vg pool & extensive sports facs." ♦ € 36.20 (CChq acc) 2011*

WIER *C2* (1km S Rural) *53.25033, 5.62216* **Tuincamping De Brinkhoeve, Gernierswei 19, 9043 VN Wier [(0518) 462287; info@debrinkhoeve.com; www.debrinkhoeve.com]** Exit A31 junc 21 dir Menaldum, then dir St Jacobiparochie. Site on this rd 6km fr Menaldum on Gernierswei, not in Wier. Sp locally as 'Theeschenkerij Wier'. Sm, pt shd; htd wc; chem disp; baby facs; shwrs inc; el pnts (6A) €2; Indtte; tradsmn; rest; snacks; BBQ; playgrnd; no statics; dogs €1.50; bus 50m; poss cr; Eng spkn; adv bkg rec. "Friendly, nothing too much trouble; like a high quality CL; beautiful gardens; cycle rtes adj." 1 Apr-15 Oct. € 10.50 2010*

WIERINGERWERF *B2* (200m N Rural) *52.85757, 5.02361* **Camping Land Uit Zee, Oom Keesweg 12A, 1771 ME Wieringerwerf [tel/fax (0227) 601893; campinglanduitzee@hetnet.nl; www.campinglanduitzee.nl]** Fr A7/E22 exit junc 13 Wieringerwerf & foll site sp N thro town 200m, site on R. Sm, hdg pitch, pt shd; wc; chem disp; mv service pnt; shwrs €0.80; el pnts (6A) €2.25; gas; shop; playgrnd; cycle hire; TV; 10% statics; dogs €1.55; Eng spkn; adv bkg; quiet; CCI. "Friendly, welcoming owners; gd base for cycling; nrby town Medemblick worth visit; run down statics, unclean facs & itinerants (Apr 2010)." 1 Apr-12 Sep. € 11.50 2010*

WIJCKEL see Lemmer *C2*

WIJDENES see Hoorn *B2*

WIJSTER see Beilen *D2*

WILBERTOORD see Uden *C3*

★★★★ classification **LIMITLESS PLEASURE AT CAMPING DUINRELL!**

- "Super" pitches from about 80 m² - 100 m² with modern facilities and sanitary buildings
- A free amusement park (April - October).
- Tropical Tiki Pool, fun water paradise with spectacular water attractions.
- Entertainment programm in summer.
- Woods and dunes, sea and beach, Den Haag and Scheveningen nearby.
- Luxury bungalows (4/5/6/7 pers.) for hire.

If you spend a night at Duinrell, you will be able to visit the amusement park free of charge.
Duinrell 1, 2242 JP Wassenaar, Holland
Reservations: Tel. 0031 70 5155 255
BOOK ONLINE: www.duinrell.nl

DUINRELL, PUTS SPRING IN YOUR STEP!

⊞ **WINSCHOTEN** *D2* (1km NW Urban) *53.15315, 7.02728* **Stadscamping De Burcht, Bovenburen 46A, 9675 HG Winschoten [(0597) 413290; fax 414467; info@campingdeburcht.nl; www.campingdeburcht.nl]** Exit E22/A7 junc 47 Winschoten exit & foll sp to site on edge of town. Sm, hdg pitch, pt shd; wc; chem disp; shwrs inc; el pnts (4A) €2.60; Indtte; shop 500m; playgrnd; pool 1km; 15% statics; dogs €1.50; quiet; CCI. "Gd site for cyclists; pay site fees on arr; vg NH/sh stay." € 16.00 2009*

WINTERSWIJK *D3* (3km NE Rural) *51.98273, 6.75714* **Camping Kortschot, Vredenseweg 142, 7113 AE Winterswijk-Henxel [(0543) 562347; info@kortschot.nl; www.kortschot.nl]** App Winterswijk fr SE on N319, turn R into Bataafsweg sp Vreden/Meddo. In 1.8km turn R into Vredenseweg, site on R in 1.5km. Sm, unshd; htd wc; chem disp; shwrs inc; el pnts (6A) inc; Indtte; shop, rest, snacks, bar 3km; BBQ; playgrnd; pool 3km; no statics; dogs €0.45; Eng spkn; adv bkg; quiet. "Vg site (18 pitches); friendly, helpful owner; excel facs; gd cycling/walking." ♦ Easter-1 Oct. € 14.10 2008*

WOERDEN *B3* (1km N Rural) *52.09280, 4.88530* **Camping Batenstein, Van Helvoortlaan 37, 3443 AP Woerden [(0348) 421320; fax 409691; campingbatenstein@planet.nl; www.camping-batenstein.nl]** Fr A12 exit junc 14 sp Woerden. Twd cent of town, L at rndabt, R at next rndabt, thro rlwy tunnel. L at traff lts, L again at next traff lts, R at camping sp. Ent narr & small sp. Med, pt shd; wc; chem disp; mv service pnt; baby facs; sauna; shwrs €0.50; el pnts (6-10A) inc; gas; Indtte (inc dryer); shops 1km; snacks; playgrnd; htd, covrd pool; paddling pool; waterslide; games area; wifi; 75% statics; dogs €1.50; phone; bus 750m; sep car park; poss cr; adv bkg; quiet but some noise fr pool during day; ccard acc; red long stay; CCI. "Gd touring base; el conn by site staff only (locked boxes); san facs cramped but gd quality & clean; conv for ferries." 1 Apr-30 Oct. € 18.00 2010*

WOLPHAARTSDIJK see Goes *A3*

WONS *C2* (1.5km S Rural) *53.06569, 5.42389* **Mini-Camping DeWeeren, Weersterweg 35, 8747 NR Wons [(0515) 231374 or 06 18498048 (mob); deweeren@hetnet.nl]** Exit A7 junc 16 dir Makkum. Site on L in 2km. Sm, pt shd; htd wc; chem disp; shwrs inc; el pnts (10A) inc; Indtte; shop, rest, snacks, bar 2km; BBQ; playgrnd; cycle hire; dogs €0.50; sep car park; quiet. "Gd." 1 Apr-31 Oct. € 13.50 2009*

WORKUM *C2* (3km NE Rural) *52.99216, 5.49391* **Minicamping De Klompen, Nummer 19, 8775 XD Nijhuizum [(0515) 541597; info@minicampingdeklompen.nl; www.minicampingdeklompen.nl]** On N359 thro Workumturn R sp Nijhuizum. In vill turn L & foll site sp to end of rd, 2km. Sm, unshd; htd wc; chem disp; shwrs €0.50; el pnts (10A) €2; Indtte; shop, rest, snacks, bar 3km; BBQ; lake & watersports nr; dogs €1; sep car park; Eng spkn; quiet. "Gd very hospitable owners, san facs very clean; communal room if rainy day; peaceful, rural dairy farm." € 14.00 2011*

WOUDENBERG see Amersfoort *C3*

ZANDVOORT *B3* (2km N Coastal) *52.40415, 4.55180* **Kennemer Duincamping De Lakens, Zeeweg 60, 2051 EC Bloemendaal aan Zee [(023) 5411570; fax 5411579; delakens@kennemerduincampings.nl; www.kennemerduincampings.nl]** Site sp N of Zaandvoort on coast rd, site in sand dunes. V lge, unshd; htd wc; chem disp; mv service pnt; baby facs; shwrs inc; el pnts (4-10A) inc; gas; Indtte; shop; rest; snacks; playgrnd; pool 4km; sand beach 200m; windsuring 2km; games area; horseriding 300m; internet; TV rm; 50% statics; no dogs; poss cr; adv bkg rec high ssn; ccard acc; quiet. "V busy May/June public holidays; gd facs; excel walking, cycling fr site." ♦ 1 Apr-1 Nov. € 43.50 2009*

ZEELAND see Uden *C3*

⊞ **ZEEWOLDE** *C3* (4km SE Rural/Coastal) *52.30300, 5.53400* **NCC Camping de Distel, Dasselaarweg 53, 3896 LT Zeewolde [(036) 5221575; zeewolde@ncc.nl; www.ncc.nl]** Exit A28 junc 9 at Nijkerk onto N301 sp Zeewolde. After 4km turn R onto N705 dir Zeewolde. After 5.6km turn R sp NCC Camping. In 300m turn R & foll site sp. Site on L at white stones. Lge, mkd pitch, pt shd; htd wc; chem disp; mv service pnt; baby facs; shwrs inc; el pnts (4A) €3; Indtte; shop; playgrnd; sand beach 500m; watersports; dogs; bus 4km; poss cr; adv bkg; quiet, "Warm, friendly atmosphere; members only - open to C'van Club members, but must pre-book; conv Amsterdam 1hr by rd." ♦ € 12.00 2009*

⊞ **ZEEWOLDE** *C3* (2km SW Rural) *52.27155, 5.43550* **Camping Flevo Natuur (Naturist), Wielseweg 3, 3896 LA Zeewolde [(036) 5228880; fax 5228664; info@flevonatuur.nl; www.flevonatuur.nl]** Exit E232/A28 junc 9 Nijkerk onto N301 N. After x-ing bdge, take 1st R turn & at bottom turn R again, then 1st L. Site sp. Lge, pt shd; wc; chem disp; sauna; shwrs; el pnts (4-10A) inc; lndtte; supmkt high ssn; rest; snacks; bar; playgrnd; 2 pools (1 htd, covrd); games area; tennis; cab/sat TV; some statics; dogs €3.70; Eng spkn; adv bkg; quiet. € 25.50 2008*

ZEIST see Utrecht *B3*

ZEVENAAR *C3* (4.5km S Rural) *51.89666, 6.07041* **Camping De Rijnstrangen, Beuningsestraat 4, 6913 KH Aerdt [(0316) 371941; rijnstrangen@kpn-officedsl.nl; www.derijnstrangen.nl]** Exit A12 junc 29 onto N 336 Elten & Lobith. At sp Aerdt turn R onto dyke (narr) & cont approx 1.5km to church. Turn L in 100m, site on R (500m W of Aerdt). Sm, pt shd; htd wc; chem disp; mv service pnt; shwrs inc; el pnts (6A) inc; lndtte; shop 2km; TV rm; poss cr; adv bkg; quiet. "Friendly, welcoming owners; gd cycling area; excel." 15 Mar-31 Oct. € 14.00 2009*

ZEVENHUIZEN see Gouda *B3*

ZIERIKZEE *A3* (1km NE Rural) *51.65683, 3.91242* **T Uulof Mini-Camping, Zandweg 37, 4301 SL Zierikzee [(0111) 414614; info@tuulof.nl; http://campingtuulof.nl/]** SE fr Serooskerke on N59. In 9km just bef traff lts turn L. Site 300m on R; sp fr N59. Sm, pt shd; wc; chem disp; serviced pitches; shwrs €0.50; el pnts (6A) inc; shop 1km; gas 1km; lndtte; pool 2km; sand beach 13km; 25% statics; dogs €1; Eng spkn; some rd noise; CCI. "Lovely site on farm - produce avail; excel san facs but pt unisex; helpful, friendly owner; interesting town, steamer trips; easy cycling to town." 1 Apr-1 Oct. € 13.50 2010*

ZIERIKZEE *A3* (1km S Coastal) *51.64660, 3.91133* **Camping Kloet, Eerst Weegje 3, 4301 SL Zierikzee [(0111) 414214; fax (0114) 421200; info@campingkloet.nl; www.campingkloet.nl]** Fr S on N256 cross Zeelandbrug & turn L onto N59 twd Zierikzee. After rndabt turn L sp 'Parking'. Site on L after 2nd rndabt. Sm, htd pitch, pt shd; wc; chem disp; mv service pnt; shwrs inc; el pnts (4A) inc; lndtte; shop, rest, bar 1km; playgrnd; games rm; TV; no dogs; bus 1km; Eng spkn; adv bkg; quiet; CCI. "Attractive, historic town in walking distance; excel area for cycling; gd birdwatching." 1 Apr-1 Nov. € 28.00 2011*

ZOETERMEER *B3* (2km W Rural) *52.06716, 4.44862* **Camping De Drie Morgen, Voorweg 155, 2716 NJ Zoetermeer [(079) 3515107; fax 3512084; mail@dedriemorgen.nl; www.dedriemorgen.nl]** Fr Den Haag take A12/E30 sp Zoetermeer. Exit junc 6 sp Zoetermeer cent. In 1.5km turn L onto Amertaweg. In 2km foll sp to Mini-Camping. At rndabt turn R onto Voorweg, site on R. Sm, unshd; wc; chem disp; mv service pnt; shwrs inc; el pnts (6A) €1.75; tradsmn; farm shop; playgrnd; dogs; sep car park; Eng spkn; adv bkg; quiet. "A working farm; gd touring base; pleasant staff; peaceful." 1 Apr-31 Oct. € 12.75 2009*

ZUIDWOLDE *D2* (2km S Rural) *52.65822, 6.42726* **NCC Camping De Krententerp, Ekelenbergweg 2, 7921 RH Zuidwolde DR [(0528) 372847; www.ncc.nl]** Fr S fr Zwolle exit A28 junc 22 dir Dedemsvaart. Turn L at Balkbrug onto N48, then L at junc Alteveer-Linde to site. Sm, mkd pitch, shd; htd wc; chem disp; shwrs inc; el pnts (4A) €2.75 (long lead poss req); lndtte; shop, rest, snacks, bar 2km, playgrnd; htd, covrd pool 2km; dogs; bus 200m; poss cr; adv bkg; quiet. "Peaceful site; friendly, helpful staff; C'van Club members welcome; phone ahead bet 1700 & 1800; excel cycling, walking; Zuidwolde beautiful town." 1 Apr-31 Oct. € 11.00 2009*

ZUNDERT *B4* (5km NW Rural) *51.49492, 4.60208* **Camping Internationaal Priem, Rucphenseweg 51, 4882 KB Zundert [(076) 5972632; fax 5971923; info@internationaalpriem.nl; www.internationaalpriem.nl]** S fr Breda on N263 to Zundert. Take N638 dir Rucphen, camp on S of rd, opp abbey. Sm, hdg pitch, pt shd; wc; chem disp; shwrs €0.50; el pnts (4A) inc; gas; lndtte; rest in ssn; playgrnd; entmnt; TV rm; 75% statics (sep area); dogs €3.50; phone; Eng spkn; adv bkg; quiet; ccard acc; red long stay; CCI. "Well-established, mature site; friendly." 1 Apr-31 Oct. € 17.50 2009*

ZWEELOO *D2* (3km N Rural) *52.80882, 6.75855* **Mini-Camping 't Looveld, Broekstukkenweg 4, 7851 TE Zweeloo [(0591) 371469; fax 377436; looveld@hotmail.com; www.looveld.net]** Exit A28 junc 31 onto N381 E dir Westerbork & Emmen. Turn N twd Schoonoord & in 800m turn R into Broekstukkenweg, site on R in 1.5km down minor rd. Sm, unshd; wc; chem disp; baby facs; shwrs inc; el pnts (4A) €2.30; lndtte; sm shop; no statics; dogs €1; quiet. "Friendly, CL-type farm site; vg." 1 Apr-1 Oct. € 12.00 2007*

ZWOLLE *C2* (1.5km NE Urban) *52.53690, 6.12954* **Camping De Agnietenberg, Haersterveerweg 27, 8034 PJ Zwolle [(038) 4531530; camping@agnietenberg.nl; www.campingagnietenberg.nl]** N fr Zwolle on A28 exit junc 20 Zwolle Oost & turn R at end of slip rd then immed L. In 400m turn L at traff lts into Haersterveerweg & foll site sp. Lge, mkd pitch, pt shd; htd wc; chem disp; mv service pnt; baby facs; shwrs €0.50; lndtte; shop; rest; snacks; bar; BBQ; playgrnd; pool; lake beach & sw adj; fishing; tennis; wifi; entmnt; TV; 60% statics; dogs €3.50; Eng spkn; quiet; ccard acc (Mastercard only). "Excel, family site in pleasant area; gd walking, cycling, water recreation." 1 Apr-31 Oct. € 19.00 2009*

ZWOLLE *C2* (5km SW Rural) *52.45566, 6.04016* **Molecaten Park De Leemkule, Leemkuilen 6, 8051 PW Hattem [(038) 4441945; fax 4446280; info@leemkule.ne; www.leemkule.nl]** Exit A50 junc 29 dir Wezep; foll sp Hattem/Wapenveld, site on L after 3km. Lge, shd; htd wc; chem disp; baby facs; shwrs inc; el pnts (10A) inc; gas; lndtte; shop; rest; snacks; bar; playgrnd; 2 pools (1 htd, covrd); paddling pool; tennis; cycle hire; games area; entmnt; 20% statics; no dogs; phone; sep car park; adv bkg; quiet; ccard acc. 1 Apr-1 Nov. € 25.00 2009*

Distances are shown in kilometres and are calculated from town/city centres along the most practical roads, although not necessarily taking the shortest route. 1km = 0.62miles

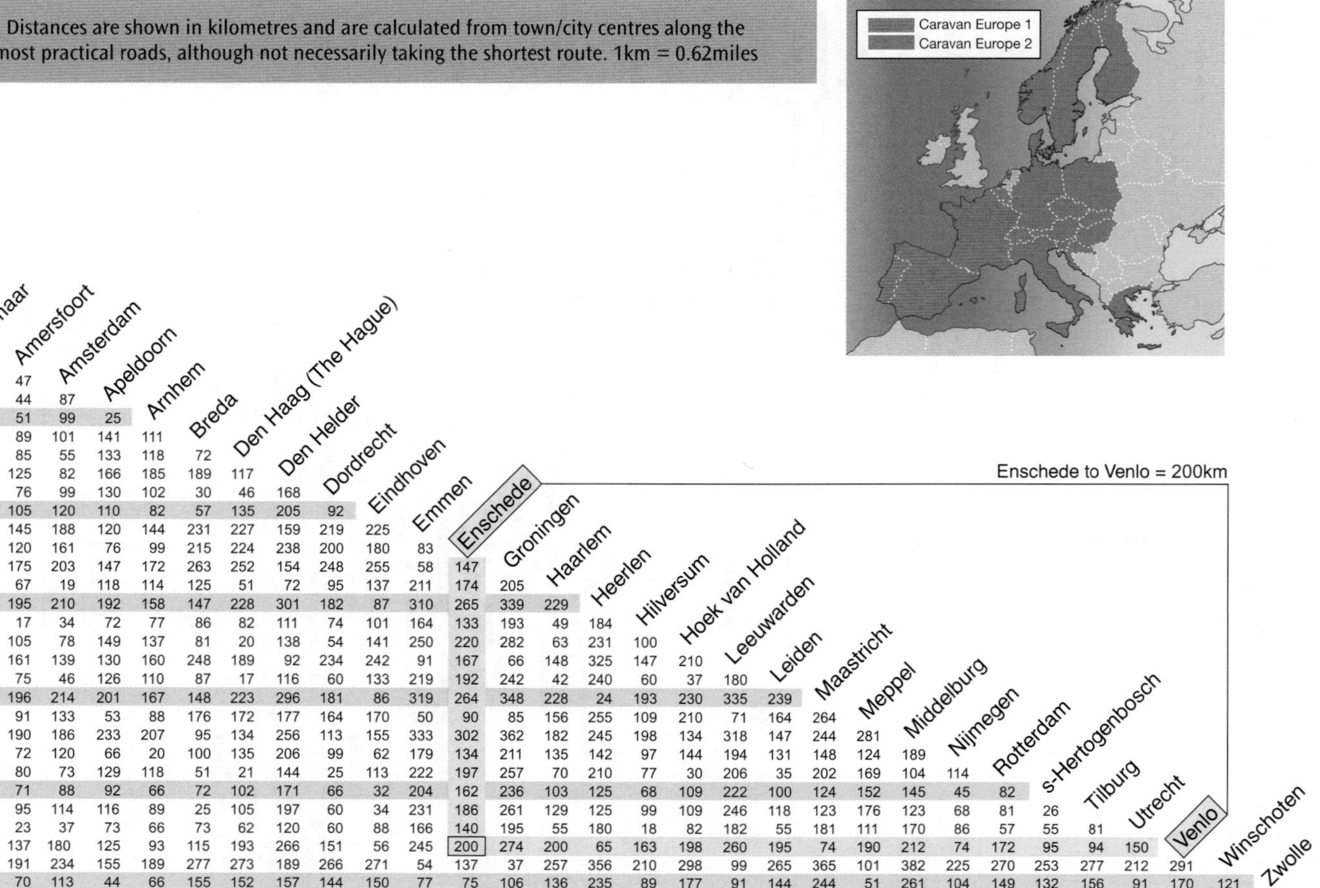

Enschede to Venlo = 200km

	Alkmaar	Amersfoort	Amsterdam	Apeldoorn	Arnhem	Breda	Den Haag (The Hague)	Den Helder	Dordrecht	Eindhoven	Emmen	Enschede	Groningen	Haarlem	Heerlen	Hilversum	Hoek van Holland	Leeuwarden	Leiden	Maastricht	Meppel	Middelburg	Nijmegen	Rotterdam	s-Hertogenbosch	Tilburg	Utrecht	Venlo	Winschoten
Amersfoort	83																												
Amsterdam	40	47																											
Apeldoorn	120	44	87																										
Arnhem	141	51	99	25																									
Breda	145	89	101	141	111																								
Den Haag (The Hague)	85	85	55	133	118	72																							
Den Helder	42	125	82	166	185	189	117																						
Dordrecht	125	76	99	130	102	30	46	168																					
Eindhoven	162	105	120	110	82	57	135	205	92																				
Emmen	179	145	188	120	144	231	227	159	219	225																			
Enschede	194	120	161	76	99	215	224	238	200	180	83																		
Groningen	105	175	203	147	172	263	252	154	248	255	58	147																	
Haarlem	30	67	19	118	114	125	51	72	95	137	211	174	205																
Heerlen	256	195	210	192	158	147	228	301	182	87	310	265	339	229															
Hilversum	69	17	34	72	77	86	82	111	74	101	164	133	193	49	184														
Hoek van Holland	103	105	78	149	137	81	20	138	54	141	250	220	282	63	231	100													
Leeuwarden	111	161	139	130	160	248	189	92	234	242	91	167	66	148	325	147	210												
Leiden	75	75	46	126	110	87	17	116	60	133	219	192	242	42	240	60	37	180											
Maastricht	255	196	214	201	167	148	223	296	181	86	319	264	348	228	24	193	230	335	239										
Meppel	156	91	133	53	88	176	172	177	164	170	50	90	85	156	255	109	210	71	164	264									
Middelburg	201	190	186	233	207	95	134	256	113	155	333	302	362	182	245	198	134	318	147	244	281								
Nijmegen	164	72	120	66	20	100	135	206	99	62	179	134	211	135	142	97	144	194	131	148	124	189							
Rotterdam	102	80	73	129	118	51	21	144	25	113	222	197	257	70	210	77	30	206	35	202	169	104	114						
s-Hertogenbosch	125	71	88	92	66	72	102	171	66	32	204	162	236	103	125	68	109	222	100	124	152	145	45	82					
Tilburg	156	95	114	116	89	25	105	197	60	34	231	186	261	129	125	99	109	246	118	123	176	123	68	81	26				
Utrecht	80	23	37	73	66	73	62	120	60	88	166	140	195	55	180	18	82	182	55	181	111	170	86	57	55	81			
Venlo	225	137	180	125	93	115	193	266	151	56	245	200	274	200	65	163	198	260	195	74	190	212	74	172	95	94	150		
Winschoten	231	191	234	155	189	277	273	189	266	271	54	137	37	257	356	210	298	99	265	365	101	382	225	270	253	277	212	291	
Zwolle	134	70	113	44	66	155	152	157	144	150	77	75	106	136	235	89	177	91	144	244	51	261	104	149	132	156	91	170	121

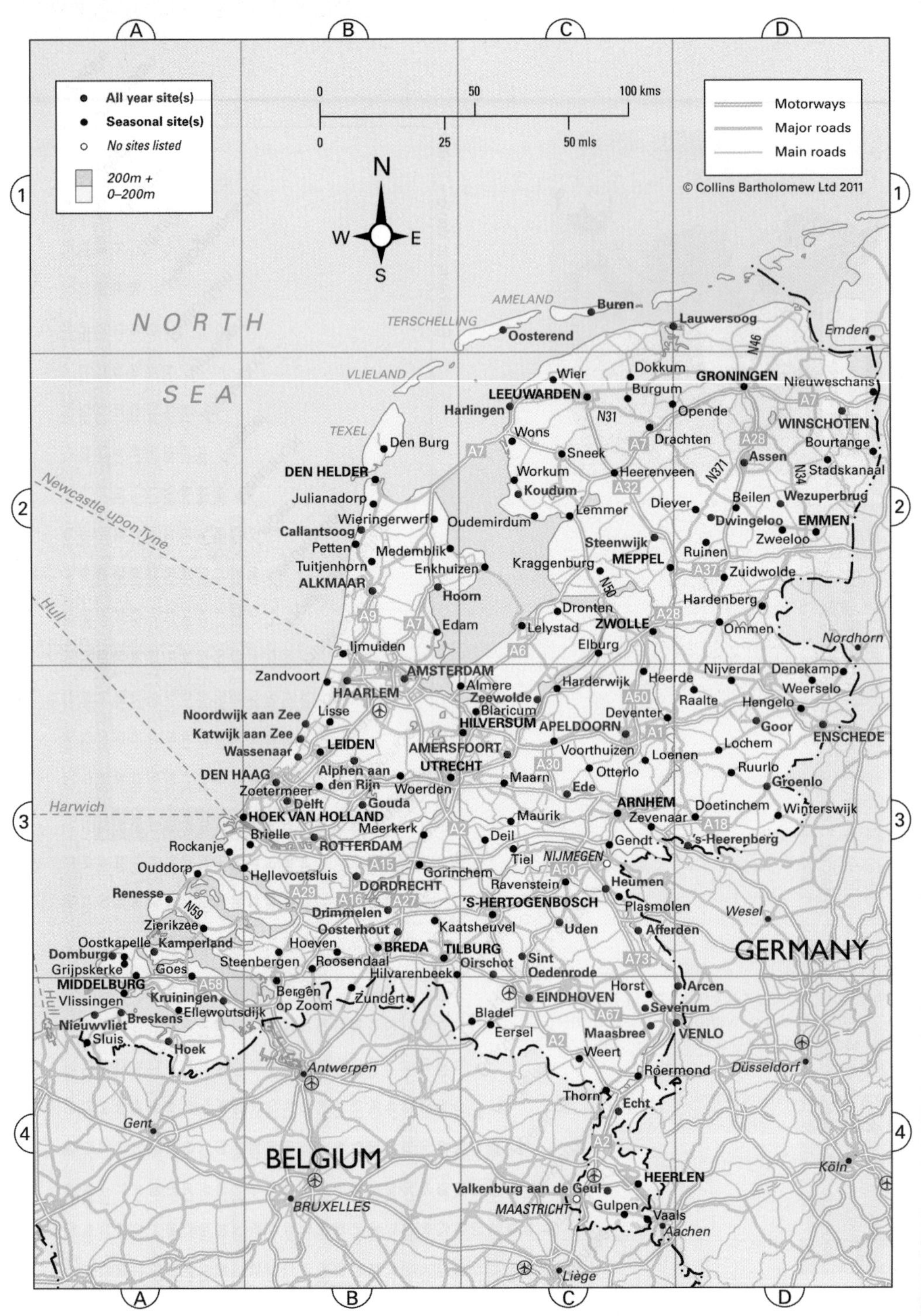

A
B
C
D
1
2
3
4
All year site(s)
Seasonal site(s)
No sites listed
200m +
0–200m
0
50
100 kms
0
25
50 mls
N
W
E
S
Motorways
Major roads
Main roads
© Collins Bartholomew Ltd 2011
NORTH
SEA
AMELAND
Buren
TERSCHELLING
Oosterend
Lauwersoog
Emden
VLIELAND
Wier
Dokkum
GRONINGEN
Nieuweschans
LEEUWARDEN
Burgum
Harlingen
Opende
WINSCHOTEN
TEXEL
Wons
Drachten
Bourtange
Den Burg
Sneek
Assen
Stadskanaal
DEN HELDER
Workum
Heerenveen
Koudum
Julianadorp
Diever
Beilen
Wezuperbrug
Wieringerwerf
Oudemirdum
Lemmer
Dwingeloo
EMMEN
Callantsoog
Steenwijk
Zweeloo
Petten
Medemblik
Ruinen
Tuitjenhorn
Enkhuizen
Kraggenburg
MEPPEL
Zuidwolde
ALKMAAR
Hoorn
Hardenberg
Dronten
Edam
Lelystad
ZWOLLE
Ommen
Nordhorn
Ijmuiden
Elburg
Newcastle upon Tyne
Hull
Zandvoort
AMSTERDAM
Almere
Heerde
Nijverdal
Denekamp
HAARLEM
Zeewolde
Harderwijk
Raalte
Weerselo
Noordwijk aan Zee
Lisse
Blaricum
Deventer
Hengelo
Katwijk aan Zee
HILVERSUM
APELDOORN
Goor
ENSCHEDE
Wassenaar
LEIDEN
AMERSFOORT
Voorthuizen
Loenen
Lochem
DEN HAAG
Alphen aan den Rijn
UTRECHT
Otterlo
Ruurlo
Zoetermeer
Woerden
Maarn
Ede
Groenlo
Delft
Gouda
ARNHEM
Doetinchem
Winterswijk
Harwich
HOEK VAN HOLLAND
Maurik
Zevenaar
Brielle
Meerkerk
Deil
Gendt
's-Heerenberg
Rockanje
ROTTERDAM
Tiel
NIJMEGEN
Ouddorp
Hellevoetsluis
Gorinchem
Ravenstein
Heumen
Renesse
DORDRECHT
Drimmelen
'S-HERTOGENBOSCH
Plasmolen
Wesel
Zierikzee
Oosterhout
Kaatsheuvel
Uden
Afferden
Oostkapelle
Kamperland
Hoeven
BREDA
TILBURG
Sint Oedenrode
GERMANY
Domburg
Grijpskerke
Steenbergen
Roosendaal
Oirschot
Goes
Hilvarenbeek
MIDDELBURG
Vlissingen
Kruiningen
Bergen op Zoom
Zundert
EINDHOVEN
Horst
Arcen
Nieuwvliet
Breskens
Ellewoutsdijk
Bladel
Sevenum
Sluis
Hoek
Eersel
Maasbree
VENLO
Antwerpen
Weert
Roermond
Düsseldorf
Thorn
Echt
Gent
BELGIUM
HEERLEN
Köln
Valkenburg aan de Geul
MAASTRICHT
Gulpen
Vaals
BRUXELLES
Aachen
Liège
A7
A28
N34
N371
N31
A32
N46
A37
N50
A9
A6
A50
A1
A30
A2
A18
A15
A29
A16
A27
N59
A58
A73
A67

Norway

Country Introduction

© iStockPhoto.com/ Mikhail Laptev

Norwegian fjord

Population (approx): 4.8 million

Capital: Oslo (population approx 575,000)

Area: 385,155 sqkm

Bordered by: Finland, Russia, Sweden

Terrain: Mostly high plateaux and mountain ranges broken by fertile valleys; deeply indented coastline; arctic tundra in the north

Climate: Moderate climate along coastal areas thanks to the Gulf Stream; more extreme inland with snowy/rainy winters; arctic conditions in the northern highlands; summers can be unpredictable and May and June can be cool

Coastline: 25,148km (including islands and fjords)

Highest Point: Galdhopiggeh 2,469m

Language: Norwegian; Sami in some areas

Local Time: GMT or BST + 1, i.e. 1 hour ahead of the UK all year

Currency: Krone (NOK) divided into 100 øre; £1 = NOK 8.80, NOK 10 = £1.14 pence (October 2011)

Telephoning: From the UK dial 0047 for Norway, plus the 8-digit number; there are no area codes. To call the UK from Norway dial 0044, omitting the initial zero of the area code

Emergency numbers: Police 112 (or 02800 for non-emergency calls); Fire brigade 110; Ambulance 113. From a mobile phone dial 112 for any service.

Public Holidays 2012

Jan 1; Apr 5, 6, 9; May 1, 17 (Constitution Day), 28; Dec 25, 26.

Public holidays for 2013 not yet confirmed at date of publication. School summer holidays run from mid-June to mid-August.

Tourist Office

NORWEGIAN TOURIST BOARD
CHARLES HOUSE
5 LOWER REGENT STREET
LONDON SW1Y 4LR
Tel: 09063 022003 (brochure requests)
or 020 7839 2650
www.visitnorway.com
infouk@innovationnorway.no

The following introduction to Norway should be read in conjunction with the important information contained in the Handbook chapters at the front of this guide.

Camping and Caravanning

There are more than 1,000 campsites in Norway which are classified 1 to 5 stars and which are generally open between June and mid August.
A camping guide listing 300 sites is available from the Norwegian Automobile Association, Norges Automobilforbund (NAF), see www.nafcamp.no. The Norwegian Tourist Board also distributes a camping guide free of charge – see www.camping.no. Most 3 star sites and all 4 and 5 star sites have sanitary facilities for the disabled and all classified sites have cooking facilities.

Many sites do not open until mid-June and do not fully function until the beginning of July, particularly if the winter has been prolonged. Sites with published opening dates earlier than June may not open on time if the weather has been particularly bad and if, for example, there has been heavy rain and flooding near rivers or lakes where campsites are situated. Campsites which are open all year will usually have very limited facilities for most of the year outside the short holiday season.

Facilities vary; in main tourist centres there are large, well-equipped sites with good sanitary installations, grocery shops, leisure facilities and attendants permanently on duty. Sites are generally maintained to a high standard of cleanliness. In more remote areas, sites are small and sanitary installations and other facilities are very simple.

Many small campsites have no chemical disposal point. Roadside notice boards at the entrance to each local area (kommune) indicate campsites, chemical disposal points (normally sited at petrol stations) and other local amenities. These disposal facilities are usually coin-operated and have instructions in English. It is understood that in some areas in the north, there may be no adequate arrangements for the disposal of waste water, either on site or in the immediate area, and you are advised to make enquiries when arriving at a campsite.

The Camping Card Scandinavia (CCS), which is also valid in Denmark, Finland and Sweden, may be required by some campsites, but where this is the case a Camping Card International (CCI) should be accepted instead as the equivalent of the CCS. The CCS costs NOK 120 (2011 price) and offers holders instant swipe registration at campsites, plus a number of discounts on attractions and services throughout the country; see www.camping.no for details. A CCS may be obtained on arrival at your first campsite or from tourist offices. It is also available in advance from www.camping.no

There are many sites on the E6 to the North Cape, seldom more than 30km apart. These sites may be subject to road noise. Caravans are allowed to stay at the North Cape but no facilities are available – see Nordkapp later in this chapter and in the Site Entry listing.

In the short summer season campsites can be crowded and facilities stretched and you are recommended to arrive before 3pm in order to have a better choice of pitches and have the opportunity to erect an awning. In any event, campsites may close to new arrivals by 4pm, so plan accordingly.

Casual/wild camping is not actively encouraged (and is not permitted for longer than 48 hours in one spot) but the Norwegian 'Right of Access' allows visitors to explore the countryside freely, except for cultivated land, farmland, gardens, nurseries, etc. Off-road driving is not allowed. Visitors must respect nature and take their rubbish away with them when they leave. Open fires (which include Primus stoves) are prohibited in forests or on open land between 15 April and 15 September.

There are many good lay-bys and picnic places along the roads which are meant for short stops and rests. These should not be used for overnight stays.

Motorhomes

Many towns provide parking places for motorhomes close to city centres, known as Bobil Parks, which are open in June, July and August. In general these parking areas provide limited facilities and car and caravan outfits are not permitted. Details, where known, are listed in the Site Entry pages.

Apart from at campsites, motorhome service points are reported to be few and far between and are generally to be found at petrol stations, where water refill may also be available.

Country Information

Cycling

Cyclists are fairly well catered for and some areas, such as Vestfold, Rogaland and the Lillehammer area, have a well-developed network of cycle paths. Some old roads have been converted into cycle paths in the mountains and along western fjords. Paths run through magnificent scenery in the Lofoten and Vesterålen Islands in particular, and from Haugastøl in the Hardangervidda National Park to Flåm. A number of tunnels are prohibited to cyclists, but local detours are generally signposted.

Information is available from the Norwegian Tourist Board or from Sykkelturisme i Norge, Fylkeshuset, N-3706 Skien, fax: 35 52 99 55 email: info@bike-norway.com, www.bike-norway.com

Electricity and Gas

Campsites usually have a minimum 10 amp supply. Plugs are the continental type and have two round pins plus two earth strips. Adaptors may sometimes be borrowed from a site, or purchased from some petrol stations, such as Esso. Some sites do not yet have CEE connections. It is recommended that you take an extension cable of at least 50 metres as this may be necessary on some campsites.

There have been persistent reports about problems with both polarity and the earthing of the electrical supply on some sites. Due to its geology and mountainous nature, Norway's electricity supply network is quite different from that found elsewhere in Europe. There is no national grid as such and electricity systems vary from place to place throughout the country. Any polarity testing system is likely to give false readings. It is understood that progress is being made to improve and standardise the electrical supply throughout the country but, in the meantime, you should exercise caution and, if in any doubt, ask site staff to demonstrate the integrity of the earthing system to your satisfaction.

The Caravan Club recommends that you assure yourself that a proper protective earthing system exists. Failing this, the supply should not be used.

Propane gas cylinders are generally widely available from Esso and Statoil petrol stations. You will need to buy an appropriate adaptor, available from camping shops or Statoil garages. AGA AS dealers will allow you to sell back propane cylinders within six months of purchase prior to leaving Norway at approximately 80% of the purchase price. It is understood that Statoil garages no longer buy them back. Some Statoil garages and AGA AS dealers will exchange Swedish Primus propane cylinders for their Norwegian version but will not accept other foreign propane cylinders. There is no refund for the adaptor.

Gas supplies can be conserved by taking advantage of the kitchens and/or cooking facilities available at classified campsites, and using electrical hook-ups at every opportunity.

*See **Electricity and Gas** in the section **DURING YOUR STAY.***

Entry Formalities

Holders of British and Irish passports may visit Norway for up to three months without a visa.

Regulations for Pets

For details of the regulations regarding the import of pets into Norway, see www.mattilsynet.no (English option) or contact the Norwegian Embassy in London.

*See also **Pet Travel Scheme** under **Documents** in the section **PLANNING AND TRAVELLING.***

Medical Services

British visitors are entitled to the same basic emergency medical and dental treatment as Norwegian citizens, on production of a UK passport or European Health Insurance Card (EHIC), but you will have to pay the standard fees. Ensure you consult a doctor who has a reimbursement arrangement with the NAV (Norwegian Employment and Welfare Organisation). Hotels and tourist offices have lists of local doctors and dentists.

You will have to pay in full for most prescribed medicines which are available from pharmacies (apotek). Emergency in-patient hospital treatment at public hospitals, including necessary medication, is free of charge but you will have to pay for out-patient treatment. NAV Health Service Agencies will reimburse any payments that are refundable.

Visitors to remote areas should consider the relative inaccessibility of the emergency services.

Arm yourself with insect repellant devices as mosquitoes and midges may be a nuisance at certain times of the year, especially near lakes.

You are strongly recommended to obtain comprehensive travel and medical insurance before travelling to Norway, such as The Caravan Club's Red Pennant Overseas Holiday Insurance – see www.caravanclub.co.uk/redpennant

*See **Medical Matters** in the section **DURING YOUR STAY.***

Opening Hours

Banks – Mon-Fri 8.15am-3pm (3.30pm in winter and some open until 5pm on Thursday).

Museums – 9am/10am-4pm/5pm; no regular closing day.

Post Offices – Mon-Fri 8am/8.30am-4pm/5pm; Sat 8am-1pm.

Shops – Mon-Fri 9am-4pm/5pm (Thursday 9am-6pm/8pm); Sat 9am/10am-1pm/3pm. Supermarkets and shopping centres have longer hours and some are open on Sunday.

Safety and Security

Norway is considered to have lower crime rates than some other European countries, even in the large cities, however you should always take the usual precautions against pickpockets and petty theft, especially in areas where crowds gather. Do not leave valuables in your car.

Following some recent incidents of robbery, the police are warning motorists with caravans, motorhomes and trailers not to stop in lay-bys overnight. The Norwegian Automobile Association, Norges Automobilforbund (NAF), has also sent out warnings to campsites urging campers to be careful.

If you plan to go off the beaten track or out to sea you should take local advice about weather conditions, have suitable specialist equipment and respect warning signs. Because of Norway's northerly latitude the weather can change rapidly, producing sudden arctic conditions on exposed mountains – even in summer. The winter is long (it can last well into April) and temperatures can drop to minus 25°C and below, plus any wind chill factor.

Norway shares with the rest of Europe an underlying threat from terrorism. Attacks could be indiscriminate and against civilian targets in public places, including tourist sites.

*See **Safety and Security** in the section **DURING YOUR STAY.***

British Embassy

THOMAS HEFTYES GATE 8, OSLO
Tel: 23 13 27 00
http://ukinnorway.fco.gov.uk/en/

There are also British Consulates or Honorary Consulates in Ålesund, Bergen, Bodø, Kristiansand, Stavanger, Tromsø and Trondheim.

Irish Embassy

HAAKON VIIS GATE 1, N-0244 OSLO
Tel: 22 01 72 00
www.embassyofireland.no

Customs Regulations

Border Posts

Borders with Sweden and Finland may be crossed on all main roads and Customs posts are usually open day and night.

Storskog on the E105, east of Kirkenes, is the only border crossing for tourist traffic from Norway into Russia (visa required).

Duty-Free Import Allowances

Norway is not a member of the EU and therefore it is possible to import goods duty-free into the country from the EU. Duty-free allowances are not particularly generous and are strictly enforced. Visitors may import the following:

200 cigarettes or 250gm tobacco

1 litre spirits and 1½ litres wine

or 3 litres wine and 2 litres beer

or 5 litres beer

Goods to the value of NOK 6,000 (including alcohol and tobacco products)

Visitors must be aged 20 years and over to import spirits and 18 years and over for wine, beer and cigarettes.

Foodstuffs and Medicines

Up to 10kg (combined weight) of meat, meat products and cheese can be imported into Norway from EU countries for personal consumption. The import of potatoes is not permitted but you can take in up to 10kg of fruit, berries and other vegetables. Visitors may only take in medicines for their own personal use with a covering letter from a doctor stating their requirements.

Money

Travellers may import or export currency up to the equivalent of NOK 25,000 in Norwegian and/or foreign notes and coins. Any amount above this must be declared to Customs. There is no limit on travellers' cheques.

Refund of VAT on Export

Some shops have a blue and red sign in their window indicating that visitors may, on presentation of a passport, purchase goods free of VAT. For visitors from the UK the purchase price of individual items (exclusive of VAT) must be at least NOK 250. Shop assistants will issue a voucher and on departure from Norway visitors must present goods and vouchers at a tax-free counter situated on ferries, at airports and at main border crossings where a refund of 11-18% will be made.

*See also **Customs Regulations** in the section **PLANNING AND TRAVELLING.***

Documents

Vehicle(s)

Carry your vehicle registration document (V5C), insurance certificate and MOT certificate (if applicable). If driving a borrowed vehicle carry a letter of authority from the owner.

*See also **Documents** in the section **PLANNING AND TRAVELLING.***

Money

Norway is expensive; bring or have electronic access to plenty of money, especially if you are intending to eat and drink in restaurants and bars.

Bank opening hours are shorter than in the UK, especially in summer, but cash machines are widespread. Bureaux de change are found in banks, post offices, airports, stations, hotels and some tourist offices.

Recent visitors report that post offices give the best exchange rates. Travellers' cheques are accepted in banks, hotels and shops.

The major credit cards are widely accepted and may be used at cash machines (minibanks) throughout the country. In remote areas banks and cash machines may be few and far between.

It is advisable to carry your passport or photocard driving licence if paying with a credit card as you may well be asked for photographic proof of identity.

Carry your credit card issuers'/banks' 24-hour UK contact numbers in case of loss or theft of your cards.

Motoring

Alcohol

Norwegian law is very strict: do not drink and drive. Fines and imprisonment await those who exceed the legal limit of 20 milligrams of alcohol in 100 millilitres of blood, which is considerably lower than that permitted in the UK (80 milligrams), and equates to virtually zero for at least 12 hours before driving. Random roadside breath tests are frequent.

If you are involved in a road accident, whether there is material damage only or both material damage and injured persons, you should not drink any alcohol for six hours following the accident as the police may wish to carry out blood alcohol tests.

If purchasing medicines in Norway you should be aware that some containing alcohol should be avoided if you intend to drive. These are marked with a red triangle.

Breakdown Service

Norges Automobilforbund (NAF) operates a 24-hour breakdown service nationwide. Call 08505 from a landline or 0926 08505 from a mobile phone. Emergency yellow telephones have been installed on difficult stretches of road.

NAF Veipatrulje (road patrols) operate from mid-June to mid-August on difficult mountain passes and in remote areas but in Oslo, Stavanger and Bergen, they operate all year round.

Members of The Caravan Club are recommended to show their Club membership card in order to benefit from special NAF rates for breakdown assistance. Some breakdown vehicles have credit card payment terminals; otherwise payment for services is required in cash.

Essential Equipment

Lights

The use of dipped headlights is compulsory at all times, regardless of weather conditions. Bulbs are more likely to fail with constant use and you are required to carry spares.

Reflective Jacket/Waistcoat

Owners of vehicles registered in Norway are required to carry a reflective jacket to be worn if their vehicle is immobilised on the carriageway following a breakdown or accident. This legislation does not yet apply to foreign registered vehicles but you are strongly advised to carry at least one such jacket. Passengers who leave the vehicle, for example to assist with a repair, should also wear one.

Child Restraint System

Children of four years and under must be seated in a special child restraint system. Children over the age of four must use a child restraint system or seatbelt.

Winter Driving

Vehicles with a total weight of 3,500kg or more must carry chains during the winter season, regardless of road conditions. Checks are often carried out. Snow chains can be hired or purchased from Polar Automotive Ltd, tel 01892 519933, www.snowchains.com, email: polar@snowchains.com (10% discount for Caravan Club members).

Generally spiked tyres can be used from 1st November to the first Sunday after Easter. In an effort to discourage the use of spiked tyres in Bergen, Oslo and Trondheim a tax is levied on vehicles equipped with them. For vehicles up to 3,500kg the tax is NOK 30 for one day and NOK 400 for a month. For vehicles over 3,500kg the fee is doubled. Daily permits are available from vending machines along major roads into the city marked 'Frisk luft i byen'.

*See **Motoring – Equipment** in the section **PLANNING AND TRAVELLING.***

Fuel

Prices vary not only according to region (they are slightly higher in the north and in mountainous areas) but also according to the manner in which fuel is sold; the lowest currently being self-service prices in Oslo. Prices can also vary on different days and fuel tends to be cheaper on Sunday and Monday. There are many automatic petrol pumps where payment is made by credit card or bank notes.

Petrol stations are generally open from 7am to 10pm on weekdays, but you are well advised not to leave filling up until the last minute as opening hours vary greatly and there may be many miles between petrol pumps, particularly in the north.
In cities some petrol stations remain open 24 hours.

Unleaded petrol is dispensed from pumps marked 'Blyfri'. Not all petrol stations stock diesel. If you fill up with it, ensure that you use the correct pump and do not inadvertently fill with 'Afgift Diesel' (red diesel for agricultural vehicles). LPG is available at a limited number of outlets – see www.visitnorway.com for a list.

*See also **Fuel** under **Motoring – Advice** in the section **PLANNING AND TRAVELLING.***

Mountain Passes

If planning a motoring holiday to Norway in the autumn, winter or spring you should check that the mountain passes you intend to use are open. Some high mountain roads close during the winter, the duration of the closure depending on weather conditions, but many others remain open all year. Other passes may close at short notice or at night or during periods of bad weather.

The Norwegian Tourist Board can provide a list, for guidance purposes, of roads which usually close in winter, or contact the Road User Information Centre (Vegtrafikksentralen) which will provide information about roads, road conditions, mountain passes, tunnels, border crossings, etc. The Centre is open round the clock all year, telephone 02030 within Norway or (0047) 91 50 20 30 from abroad. Alternatively a list of roads that are closed in winter or which have limited accessibility can be found at www.vegvesen.no/en/Traffic and click on Truckers' Guide, or email firmapost@vegvesen.no

Yellow emergency telephones are installed on mountain passes.

Parking

A white line on the edge of the carriageway indicates a parking restriction. Do not park on main roads if visibility is restricted or where there is a sign 'All Stans Førbudt' (no stopping allowed). If you do so you may have your vehicle towed away. Parking regulations in towns are very strict and offences are invariably subject to fines. Parking meters and pay and display car parks are in use in the main towns. Free use of unexpired time on meters is allowed.

*See also **Parking Facilities for the Disabled** under **Motoring – Advice** in the section **PLANNING AND TRAVELLING.***

Priority

Priority roads (main roads) are indicated by a road sign bearing a yellow diamond on a white background. A black diagonal bar through the sign indicates the end of the priority rule. If you are not travelling on a priority road then vehicles coming from the right have priority. Traffic already on a roundabout has priority and trams always have priority.

Narrow roads have passing places (møteplass) to allow vehicles to pass. The driver on the side of the road where there is a passing place must stop for an oncoming vehicle. However heavy goods vehicles tend to take right of way on narrow roads, especially if travelling uphill, and it may be necessary to reverse to a passing place to allow one to pass.

Roads

The standard of roads is generally acceptable but stretches of major roads may be bumpy and rutted as a result of use by heavy freight traffic. Caravanners in particular should take care to avoid wheels being caught in such ruts.

Some roads are narrow, especially in the mountains, and may not have a central yellow line. New roads are wider and generally do have a central yellow line. State roads are shown in red on maps and are asphalted but may not have kerbs and may, therefore, easily become cracked and rutted. Many roads have barriers mounted close to the side of the road. Beware sharp bends and proceed with caution, especially where the roadside is a vertical rock wall.

Secondary roads have a gravel surface that can be tricky when wet and may be in poor condition for some weeks during and after the spring thaw.

Do not assume that roads with an E prefix are necessarily up to European road standards. Visitors report that sections of the E39, for example, are still single-track with passing places. The E6 road is asphalted all the way to the Swedish border in the south and to Kirkenes in the north but it is, for the most part, two-lane with a few three-lane overtaking sections. You may encounter reverse camber on both left and right-hand bends, which may throw you off line and cause difficulties when faced with oncoming traffic on narrow roads.

Some roads in the fjord region have many hairpin bends and can be challenging. Roads may narrow to a single carriageway and single-track bridges often appear without any advance warning.

Gradients on main highways are generally moderate, not over 10%, but the inside of hairpin bends may be much steeper than this. There is a gradient of 20% on the E68 from Gudvangen (on the southern tip of the Sognefjord) to Stalheim, but a tunnel under the steepest section of the Stalheim road eliminates this difficult section. The old road remains open to traffic.

Maps showing roads closed to caravans and those only recommended for use by experienced caravanners, together with rest stops, may be obtained from the Norwegian Tourist Board, Norwegian local road authority offices and from the NAF.

It is easy to misjudge distances in Norway; the country stretches over 2,500km from north to south and distances between towns can be hundreds of kilometres. When driving, focus on road numbers rather than place names.

Because of the nature of the country's roads – and the beauty of the scenery – average daily mileage may be less than anticipated. Visitors report that often the average speed attainable is only about 40 mph (approx 70 km/h). Major repairs to roads and tunnels, of necessity, take place during the summer months and traffic controls may cause delays which will slow progress even further. Ferries make up an integral part of a number of routes, particularly when travelling north along the coast, which also causes slow progress.

Care should be taken to avoid collisions with elk, deer and reindeer, particularly at dawn and dusk. Accidents involving any kind of animal must be reported to the police.

A number of roads are closed in winter, including the E69 to the North Cape, due to snow conditions; some do not open until late May or early June. See information under ***Mountain Passes*** earlier in this chapter.

Road Signs and Markings

European highways are prefixed with the letter E and are indicated by signs bearing white letters and figures on a green background, national highways (Riksvei or Stamvei) are indicated by black figures prefixed Rv on a yellow background and local, county roads (Fylkesvei) by black figures on a white background. County road numbers do not generally appear on maps.

Lines in the middle of the carriageway are yellow. Bus, cycle and taxi lanes are marked in white.

Some new signs have been introduced, for example a square blue sign showing a car and '2+' in white means that cars carrying more than two people can use bus lanes. Square signs indicate the presence of speed cameras, small rectangular signs indicate the exit numbers on highways and main roads, and a number of triangular signs with a yellow background indicate a temporary danger. Signs advising maximum speeds on bends, obstructions, etc, should be respected.

In addition to international road signs, the following signs may also be seen:

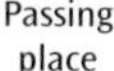

Passing place

Place of intrest

All stans førbudt – *No stopping allowed*

Arbeide pa vegen – *Roadworks ahead*

Enveiskjøring – *One-way traffic*

Ikke møte – *No passing, single line traffic*

Kjør sakte – *Drive slowly*

Løs grus – *Loose chippings*

Møteplass – *Passing place*

Omkjøring – *Diversion*

Rasteplass – *Lay-by*

Speed Limits

*See **Speed Limits Table** under **Motoring – Advice** in the section **PLANNING AND TRAVELLING.***

Drivers should pay close attention to speed limits, which are in general significantly lower than in the UK. Fines for exceeding speed limits are high and often have to be paid on the spot. The use of radar detectors is prohibited.

In residential areas the speed limit may be as low as 30 km/h (18 mph). Frequent speed controls are in operation. Ramps and speed control bumps are not always signposted.

Vehicles over 3,500kg are restricted to 80 km/h (50 mph) on motorways and highways, regardless of signs showing higher general limits.

Towing

Drivers of cars and caravans with a combined length of more than 12.4 metres must check from the list of national highways and/or municipal roads whether it is permitted to drive on their intended route. This information may be obtained from the Road User Information Centre (Vegtrafikksentralen), telephone 02030 within Norway or (0047) 91 50 20 30 from abroad, www.vegvesen.no/en/Traffic and click on Truckers' Guide, or from the Norwegian Tourist Board or NAF. For a motorhome the maximum length is 12 metres (12.4 metres for those registered before September 1997).

Some secondary roads have a maximum width of less than 2.55 metres. If your caravan is wider than 2.3 metres and more than 50cm wider than your car, white reflectors must be mounted on the front of your car mirrors. More information is available from the Road User Information Centre.

It is understood that the Rv55 from Sogndal to Lom and the Rv63 north from Geiranger are not suitable for caravans exceeding 5 metres in length, or those without an adequate power/weight ratio.

Traffic Jams

Roads in general are rarely busy but the roads in and around the cities of Oslo, Bergen, Kristiansand and Trondheim suffer traffic jams during rush hours and at the beginning and end of the holiday season.

The E6 Oslo-Svinesund road at the border with Sweden and the E18 Oslo-Kristiansand road are generally busy during the June to August holiday period. During the summer you should also expect delays at ferry terminals.

Tunnels

The road network includes approximately 950 tunnels, most of which can be found in the counties of Hordaland and Sogn og Fjordane in western Norway. Most tunnels are illuminated and about half are ventilated. There are emergency telephones at the entrance to tunnels and inside them. Tunnels also have refuges which can be used by motorists in the event of an emergency.

Laersdal Tunnel

The Lærsdal road tunnel links the Rv50 from just east of Aurlandsvangen to the E16 east of Lærdalsoyri, by-passing the ferry link from Gudvangen to Lærsdal. The toll-free 24.5km long tunnel is illuminated and ventilated throughout and has a number of caverns at regular intervals which act as turning points and, it is reported, help dispel any feelings of claustrophobia. An alternative route is to take the Rødnes tunnel and then the Rv53, but this involves a steep climb beyond Øvre Ardal.

Lofoten and Vesterålen Islands

The Lofoten Islands can be reached by ferries from Bodø & Skutvik and the Vesteralen Islands can be reached by road (E10) west of Narvik. The individual islands of the Lofoten and Vesterålen groups are connected to each other by bridge or tunnel and the two groups of islands are linked by the E10 Lofast route from Gullesfjordbotn in Vesterålen to Fiskebøl in Lofoten. This route was formerly only possible by ferry.

Oslo Tunnel

A 3km long toll-free tunnel runs from east to west Oslo.

Violation of Traffic Regulations

The police are empowered to impose and collect on-the-spot fines for infringement of traffic regulations.

Motorways

There are 300km of 4 lane motorways signposted by the prefix A, which are situated around the towns of Bergen and Oslo. In addition there are category B motorways with 2 lanes.

There are normally no emergency telephones on motorways.

Motorway Tolls

There are many toll roads throughout the country and most have an electronic toll system. Vehicles are categorised as follows:

Class 1 – Motorcycles

Class 2 – Car, with or without trailer, with a total weight less than 3,500kg and maximum length of 6m.

Class 3 – Vehicle with or without trailer and a total weight more than 3,500kg or between 6m and 12.4m in length.

Payment

If you have not registered your credit card under the ***Visitors' Payment*** scheme (see below) you would normally pass through tolls in the lanes marked 'Mynt/Coin' or 'Manuell'. You either pay manually or at a coin machine – keep a supply of small change handy as it is understood that the machines do not issue change. Most toll roads have a facility for credit card payment. Drivers of vehicles over 3,500kg must, if there is one, drive through the 'Manuell' lane.

In general do not be tempted to pass through unmanned tolls without paying, as checks are made. However, many toll road operators have installed fully automatic toll stations – AutoPASS – where a sign indicates that you should not stop. Drivers without an AutoPASS can stop and pay at a nearby Esso stations (following the 'KR-Service' signs) within three days of being eligible to pay a toll, or they will receive an invoice by post at their home address. This also applies to drivers of foreign-registered vehicles.

Visitors' Payment

Alternatively, and more conveniently, there is now a 'Visitors' Payment' system for which you register and pay NOK 300 (vehicles below 3,500kg) or NOK 1,000 (over 3,500kg) by credit card. You specify how long your account is to be operative (maximum three months) and it is then automatically debited when you pass a pay point. Three months after your 'Visitors' Payment' has expired your account will be credited with any balance remaining. See www.autopass.no (English option) for more information and to open an account.

This system means you can drive through all toll roads in the AutoPASS lane and pay automatically at toll stations and pay points where there is no option for manual payment. You do not need an AutoPASS tag which is designed for residents and long-stay visitors and for which you have to enter into a contract.

City Tolls

Toll ring roads are in place around major cities charging drivers to take their vehicles into city centres (charge applied one-way only). For example, the toll for the use of the Oslo ring road for a car and caravan is NOK 26 (2011).

Other Tolls

Because of the mountainous terrain and the numerous fjords and streams, there are many bridges and tunnels where tolls are normally payable. Tunnels may be narrow and unlit and care is needed when suddenly entering an unlit tunnel from bright daylight. Alternative routes to avoid tolls can be full of obstacles which are not marked on a map, e.g. narrow stretches with sharp turns and/or poor road surface, and are best avoided.

Svinesund Bridge

There is a 700 metre long bridge linking Norway and Sweden on the E6 at Svinesund (Sweden) – the busiest border crossing between the two countries. Tolls are NOK20 (or SEK equivalent) for vehicles up to 3,500kg and NOK100 (or SEK equivalent) for vehicles over 3,500kgs (2011).

Touring

International ferry services operate between Norway and Denmark, Germany, Iceland and Sweden. Routes from Harwich to Denmark and Newcastle to the Netherlands are in operation as gateways to Europe and, in addition, a daily overnight ferry service connects Copenhagen and Oslo.

There are hundreds of tourist offices throughout Norway offering an excellent multi-lingual service. A green 'i' sign indicates a tourist information office which is open all year with extended opening hours in summer, whereas a red sign means that the office is only open during the summer season.

Norwegians take their school and industrial holidays from the middle of June to the middle of August; travelling outside this season will ensure that facilities are less crowded and more economically priced. Winter brings the inevitable snowfall with some of the most reliable snow conditions in Europe. The winter sports season is from November to April.

Alta, on the coast north of the Arctic Circle, boasts the most extensive prehistoric rock carvings in Europe and has been declared a UNESCO World Heritage Site. Other World Heritage Sites include Geirangerfjord, Nærøyfjord, Bryggen in Bergen and the wooden buildings in Røros.

City cards are available for Oslo and Bergen, giving unlimited free travel on public transport, free public parking and free or discounted admission to museums and tourist attractions. They can be bought from tourist information centres, hotels and campsites in or near the city, from some kiosks or online at www.visitoslo.com or www.visitbergen.com

Cod, salmon, prawns and trout provide the basis for the traditional 'cold table' and reindeer and other game are popular menu choices. Wine and spirits are only available from special, state-owned shops (vinmonopolet) usually found in larger towns, and are expensive, as are cigarettes. Beer is available from supermarkets. Smoking in bars, restaurants and public places is prohibited. Tipping is not expected in restaurants.

English is widely spoken, often fluently, by virtually everyone under the age of 60.

The Midnight Sun and Northern Lights

The best time to experience the midnight sun is early or high summer. The sun does not sink below the horizon at the North Cape (Nordkapp) from the second week in May to the last week in July. The whole disc of the midnight sun is visible as follows:

Bodø – June 4 to July 8

Hammerfest – May 16 to July 26

Harstad – May 24 to July 18

North Cape – May 13 to July 29

Svolvær – May 28 to July 14

Tromsø – May 20 to July 22

Vardø – May 17 to July 25

These dates may change by 24 hours from year to year. Midsummer Night's Eve is celebrated all over the country with thousands of bonfires along the fjords.

You can hope to see the Northern Lights (Aurora Borealis) between November and February depending on certain meteorological conditions. You need to go north of the Arctic Circle, which crosses Norway, just south of Bodø on the Nordland coast. Occasionally the Northern Lights may be seen in southern Norway subject to certain weather conditions.

North Cape (Nordkapp)

A tunnel links the island of Magerøya, on which the North Cape is situated, to the mainland and the toll (2011) each way is NOK145 for a motorhome or car up to 6 metres (with or without caravan) including the driver. For a vehicle over 6 metres plus driver the charge is NOK460. Additional passengers are charged NOK47 each. Toll booths in both directions are on the North Cape side. North Cape is open from the beginning of May until the end of September. It is possible to visit in winter; contact the Nordkapp Tourist Office, www.nordkapp.no or telephone (0047) 78 47 70 30.

In addition to these tolls a further charge of NOK 235 per person (2011) is payable to enter the North Cape Hall area. This is a tourist centre where there are exhibitions, displays, restaurants, shops and a

NORWAY

post office, as well as an area of hardstanding for parking. This charge covers a stay of up to 48 hours. More information is given in the campsite entry for Nordkapp or on the website www.nordnorge.com. NB There are no cash machines at North Cape but credit cards are accepted in shops and restaurants, as are euros and sterling.

The true northernmost point of Norway is in fact at Knivskjellodden on a peninsular to the west of North Cape which is marked by a modest monument and a wooden box where you can record your name in a log book. It is possible to walk the 18km round trip from a car park on the E69 to Knivskjellodden but the walk should not be undertaken lightly. Later you can claim a certificate to mark your achievement from the tourist office in Honningsvåg by quoting the reference number of your signed entry in the log book.

The Order of Bluenosed Caravanners

Visitors to the Arctic Circle from anywhere in the world may apply for membership of the Order of Bluenosed Caravanners, which will be recognised by the issue of a certificate by the International Caravanning Association (ICA). For more information contact Ann Sneddon on telephone 01236 723339, or email: ann.sneddon@o2.co.uk and attach a photograph of yourselves and your outfit under any Arctic Circle signpost, together with the date and country of crossing and the names of those who made the crossing. This service is free to members of the ICA (annual membership £20); the fee for non-members is £5. Coloured plastic decals for your outfit, indicating membership of the Order, are also available at a cost of £2. Cheques should be payable to the ICA. See www.icacaravanning.org

Local Travel

The public transport network is excellent and efficient with bus routes extending to remote villages. For economical travel buy a 24 hour bus pass (campsites often sell them), valid when stamped for the first time. Many train routes run through very scenic countryside and special offers and discounts mean that train travel is reasonably priced. Only Oslo has a metro system. Trams operate in Bergen and Trondheim.

Using domestic public ferry services is often the quickest way of travelling around Norway and from place to place along the coast and within fjords. Most operate from very early in the morning until late at night. Booking is not normally necessary except in the height of the holiday season when there may be long queues to the more popular destinations. However, internal ferries can be expensive in high season and you may wish to plan your route carefully in order to avoid them. The Norwegian Tourist Board in London and local tourist offices will provide details of international and domestic ferry services.

The ultimate ferry journey is the Norwegian steamer trip (hurtigrute) up the coast from Bergen to Kirkenes. A daily service operates in both directions and the steamer stops at about 30 ports on the way. The round trip lasts eleven days.

The scenic round trip from Bergen or Oslo, 'Norway in a Nutshell', takes you through some of the most beautiful scenery in the country. It combines rail, boat and coach travel on the scenic Bergen railway, the breathtaking Flåm Railway, and takes in the Aurlandsfjord, the narrow Naerøyfjord and the steep Stalheimskleiva. Further details are available from the Norwegian Tourist Board.

The Norwegian Public Roads Administration is upgrading 18 stretches of road (1,850 kilometres) to form National Tourist Routes running through and showcasing a variety of magnificent natural landscapes away from main highways. Six routes are currently classified as National Tourist Routes and upgrading of the remainder is scheduled for completion by 2015. See www.turistveg.no (English option) for more information.

You can safely hail a taxi off the street or take one from a taxi stand. Most drivers speak English and all taxis are equipped for taking payment by credit card.

All place names used in the Site Entry listings which follow can be found in Freytag & Berndt's Scandinavia Superatlas, scales 1:250,00 and 1:400,000.

AKKERHAUGEN *1C3* (1km SE Rural) *59.38797, 9.26518* **Norsjø Ferieland, 3812 Akkerhaugen (Telemark) [tel 35 95 84 30; fax 35 95 85 60; post@norsjo-ferieland.no; www.norsjo-ferieland.no]** Fr Kristiansand on E18 to Skien, turn L twd Gvarv on Rv36, then Akkerhaugen. Site sp. Fr Oslo take E18 to Drammen, then E134 to Notodden, then Rv360 twd Gvarv & Akkerhaugen. Lge, mkd pitch, pt shd; htd wc; mv service pnt; shwrs; el pnts NOK40; Indtte; shop; rest; snacks; bar; cooking facs; playgrnd; lake sw & beach; watersports; boat hire; 50% statics; dogs; adv bkg; quiet. "Beautiful situation on Lake Nørsjo; gd walking, cycling." ♦ 1 Apr-30 Sep. NOK 280 2008*

AKSDAL see Haugesund *1A3*

ALESUND *1B1* (1km N Coastal) *62.47571, 6.15688* **Ålesund Bobilsenter, Storgata 39, 6015 Ålesund (Møre og Romsdal)** Foll coast to N of town cent & m'van sps; well sp. Sm, hdstg, unshd; wc; mv service pnt; shwrs NOK10; no el pnts; some traff noise; motor c'vans only. "Charge NOK10 per hr; up to NOK140 for 24 hrs; cash req for coin machine - no on-site warden; site on water's edge adj sea wall; conv town cent." May-Sep. NOK 160 2010*

ALESUND *1B1* (1.5km E Urban/Coastal) *62.46986, 6.19839* **Volsdalen Camping, Sjømannsveien, 6008 Ålesund (Møre og Romsdal) [tel 70 12 58 90; fax 70 12 14 94; v.camp@online.no; www.volsdalencamping.no]** Foll Rv136 two Centrum, ignore 1st camping sp (Prinsen), take 2nd site sp Volsdalsberga to exit R, up slip rd. At top turn L over E136 then immed R, site on L. Sm, mkd pitch, hdstg, terr, unshd; htd wc; chem disp; mv service pnt; shwrs NOK10; el pnts (10A) NOK30 (no earth); gas; Indtte; shop & 500m; tradsmn; rest, snacks high ssn; cooking facs; playgrnd; shgl beach & sw; TV rm; 40% statics; dogs; bus 600m; poss cr; Eng spkn; adv bkg; quiet; ccard acc; red long stay. "Conv walking dist Ålesund; stunning location; some pitches o'looking fjord; sm pitches not suitable lge o'fits high ssn." ♦ 1 May-1 Sep. NOK 220 2009*

⊞ **ALESUND** *1B1* (6km SE Coastal) *62.46336, 6.25466* **Prinsen Strandcamping, Grønvika 17, 6015 Ålesund (Møre og Romsdal) [tel 70 15 21 90; fax 70 15 49 96; post@prinsencamping.no; www.prinsencamping.no]** Fr Ålesund foll E136. Ignore sp Prinsen a few km out & foll sp Volsdalen up slip rd on R, at T-junc turn L & cross bdge, then immed R into Borgundvegen. Site on L. Med, pt shd; htd wc; chem disp; mv service pnt; sauna inc; shwrs NOK5; el pnts (16A) NOK30; gas; Indtte; shop & 1km; snacks; dining rm; playgrnd; sand beach; cab TV; bus 500m; Eng spkn; no adv bkg; quiet; ccard acc; CCI. "Vg; poss muddy in heavy rain; poss smell fr creek running thro site." ♦ NOK 200 2008*

ALTA *2G1* (10km NE Coastal) *70.00000, 23.48283* **Solvang Camping & Ungdomssenter, 9505 Alta (Finnmark) [tel 78 43 04 77; fax 78 44 30 20; post@solvangcamping.no; www.solvangcamping.no]** E along E6 fr Alta dir Rafsbotn, sp. Sm, unshd; wc; chem disp; shwrs; el pnts; Indtte; snacks; cooking facs; beach adj; TV rm; some cabins; phone; Eng spkn; adv bkg; quiet; CCI. "Gd NH in lovely area." 1 Jun-30 Aug. 2009*

⊞ **ALTA** *2G1* (7km E Rural) *69.96255, 23.39719* **Kronstad Camping, Altaveien 375, 9507 Alta (Finnmark) [tel 78 43 03 60; fax 78 43 11 55]** Located by E6, 1km E of Alta bdge, sp. Sm, hdstg, pt shd; htd wc; chem disp; mv service pnt; sauna; shwrs NOK10; el pnts (10-16A) inc (poss earth fault); gas; Indtte; rest; snacks; shop; sand beach 2km; fishing; TV; phone; poss cr; some airport noise during day; adv bkg; ccard acc. ♦ NOK 180 2008*

⊞ **ALTA** *2G1* (4.5km S Rural) *69.92728, 23.26901* **Wisløffs Camping (FI65), Steinfossveien, 9518 Øvre Alta (Finnmark) [tel 78 43 43 03; fax 78 44 31 37; lilly@wisloeff.no; www.wisloeff.no]** Fr E6 take E93 S sp Kautokeino for 4km, site clearly sp on L. Med, pt shd; htd wc; chem disp; mv service pnt; shwrs inc; el pnts (16A) NOK40; Indtte; shop; BBQ; cooking facs; playgrnd; wifi; TV rm; 25% statics; dogs; Eng spkn; adv bkg; ccard acc; red long stay; CCI. ♦ NOK 190 2008*

⊞ **ALTA** *2G1* (5km S Rural) *69.92904, 23.26136* **Alta River Camping, Steinfossveien, 9500 Øvre Alta (Finnmark) [tel 78 43 43 53; fax 78 43 69 02; post@alta-river-camping.no; www.alta-river-camping.no]** Fr E6 (by-passing Alta), take E93 S sp Kautokeino. Site clearly sp on L (opp information board). Med, pt shd; htd wc; chem disp; mv service pnt; sauna; shwrs NOK10; el pnts (10-16A) NOK30; Indtte; shop; cooking facs; playgrnd; ltd wifi; TV; adv bkg; quiet; ccard acc; CCI. "Excel facs; o'looks salmon rv." ♦ NOK 170 2008*

⊞ **ALTA** *2G1* (5km S Rural) *69.92735, 23.27075* **Alta Strand Camping & Apartments, Stenfossveien 29, 9518 Øvre Alta (Finnmark) [tel 78 43 40 22; fax 78 43 42 40; mail@altacamping.no; www.altacamping.no]** Fr E6 (W of Alta) take Rv93 S sp Kautokeino. Three sites adj in 3km on L, clearly sp, Strand is last one. Sm, pt shd; htd wc; chem disp; mv service pnt; sauna; shwrs inc; el pnts (10A) NOK40 (poss no earth); Indtte; shop 5km; tradsmn; snacks; bar; BBQ; cooking facs; playgrnd; wifi; some statics; phone; car wash; Eng spkn; adv bkg; ccard acc; CCI. "Gd for visiting rock carvings; midnight sun visible fr nrby Alta museum; vg." NOK 190 (CChq acc) 2010*

⊞ **ALVDAL** *1C2* (4km W Rural) *62.13115, 10.56896* **Gjelten Bru Camping, 2560 Alvdal (Hedmark) [tel 62 48 74 44; fax 62 48 70 20; www.nafcamp.com/gjelten-camping]** Fr Rv3 join rd 29 at Alvdal. Cross rv opp general store to site on rv bank. Sm, mkd pitch, pt shd; wc; chem disp; mv service pnt; baby facs; shwrs NOK5; el pnts (10A) NOK40; Indtte (inc dryer); playgrnd; games area; fishing; dogs; Eng spkn; quiet. "V pleasant site; friendly owner." NOK 160 2010*

AMOT *1B3* (300m N Rural) *59.5725, 7.99158* **Camping Groven, Ytre Vinje, 3890 Åmot (Telemark) [tel 35 07 14 21; fax 35 07 10 87; grovenc@online.no; www.grovencamping.no]** Fr Åmot take Rv37 N, site 200m on R. Med, terr, pt shd; htd wc; chem disp; mv service pnt; baby facs; sauna; shwrs NOK5; el pnts (10A) NOK30; Indtte; shop; playgrnd; pool 100m; winter skiing; TV rm; phone. "Attractive scenery; walking tours arranged; clean, rustic site." 20 May-1 Oct. NOK 150 2009*

ANDALSNES *1B1* (1.5km S Rural) *62.55223, 7.70394* **Åndalsnes Camping & Motell, 6300 Åndalsnes (Møre og Romsdal) [tel 71 22 16 29; fax 71 22 61 63; andalsnes camping@tele2.no; www.andalsnes-camping.com]** Foll E136 to o'skirts of Åndalsnes. Foll sp Ålesund x-ing rv bdge twd W & L immed. Lge, pt shd; wc; chem disp; mv service pnt; shwrs NOK15; el pnts (10-16A) NOK40 (check earth); Indtte; shop; rest; snacks; fishing; boating; wifi; TV; ccard acc; red CCI. "Excel facs; on rv with marvellous mountain scenery; nr Troll Rd & Wall." ♦ 1 May-30 Sep. NOK 195 2010*

ANDALSNES *1B1* (10km S Rural) *62.4940, 7.75846* **Trollveggen Camping, Horgheimseidet, 6300 Åndalsnes (Møre og Romsdal) [tel 71 22 37 00; fax 71 22 16 31; post@ trollveggen.com; www.trollveggen.com]** Sp on W side of E136, dir Dombås. Med, mkd pitch, terr, pt shd; htd wc; chem disp; mv service pnt; baby facs; fam bthrm; shwrs NOK10; el pnts (10A) NOK40; Indtte (inc dryer); kiosk; rest 5km; BBQ; cooking facs; playgrnd; fishing; golf 10km; cycle hire; wifi; statics; dogs; Eng spkn; adv bkg; quiet. "Friendly, family-run site; excel touring base; outstanding scenery; at foot of Trollveggen wall - shd fr late afternoon." ♦ 10 May-19 Sep. NOK 150 2011*

ANDSELV *2F1* (6km SE Rural) *69.03517, 18.64448* **Målselvfossen Turistsenter, 9325 Bardufoss (Troms) [tel 77 83 47 00; fax 77 83 46 99; booking@malselvfossen. com; www.malselvfossen.com]** Fr S leave E6 at Elverom on Rv87, site sp N of Rv87. Fr N take Rv853 fr Bardufoss, then Rv87. Sm, mkd pitch, hdstg, pt shd; wc; chem disp; shwrs NOK10; el pnts (10A) inc; Indtte; shop & 10km; rest; bar; 5% statics; Eng spkn; quiet; CCI. "Conv NH on E6; close to impressive waterfall & rv famous for salmon-fishing." 1 Jun-15 Sep. NOK 160 2008*

ANDSELV *2F1* (18km NW Rural) *69.12022, 18.2170* **Krogstadtunet Camping, Finnset, 9310 Sørreisa (Troms) [tel 77 86 10 71; jostein.paulsen@c2i.net]** Fr Andselv L onto Rv86 dir Finnsnes, site on L 3.5km S fr Sørreisa Sm, pt sl, unshd; htd wc; chem disp; mv service pnt; shwrs inc; el pnts (10A) NOK20; Indry rm; rest; cooking facs; playgrnd; Eng spkn; adv bkg; quiet; CCI. "CL-type site with vg, clean facs; friendly owners; garden for families; welcome change fr lge sites; sm folk museum on site." 15 May-15 Sep. NOK 110 2008*

ARENDAL *1B4* (5km SW Rural) *58.42726, 8.72881* **Nidelv Brygge & Camping, Vesterveien 251, 4817 His (Aust-Agder) [tel/fax 37 01 14 25; nidelv.c@online.no]** Rv420 fr Arendal, site by bdge over Rv Nidelv. Med, unshd; wc; chem disp; shwrs NOK10; el pnts NOK35; gas; Indtte; shop; rest; boating & sw; some cabins; bus; Eng spkn; quiet. "Poss unmanned low ssn." 15 May-15 Sep. NOK 170 2010*

⊞ **AURDAL** *1C2* (2km E Rural) *60.91553, 9.39000* **Aurdal Fjordcamping, 2910 Aurdal (Oppland) [tel 61 36 52 12; fax 61 36 52 13; post@aurdalcamp.no; www.aurdalcamp. no]** Fr S on E16 just bef Aurdal vill turn L opp sm supmkt, site 2.5km down hill on L bef bdge. Med, mkd pitch, pt sl, unshd; htd wc; chem disp; mv service pnt; baby facs; shwrs NOK5; el pnts (6A) NOK30; Indtte; shop & 2.5km; rest; snacks; bar; lake sw & shgl beach adj; 60% statics; dogs; phone; poss cr; Eng spkn; adv bkg; quiet; ccard acc; CCS. "Some excel lakeside pitches, but poss diff when wet; some hdstg with partial views of fjord; vg site." NOK 170 2008*

AURLAND see Flåm *1B2*

BALESTRAND *1B2* (1km S Coastal) *61.20220, 6.53140* **Sjøtun Camping, 6899 Balestrand (Sogn og Fjordane) [tel/fax 57 69 12 23; camping@sjotun.com; www.sjotun.com]** Fr Dragsvik ferry or fr W on by-pass; foll int'l site sp. Sm, pt sl, unshd; htd wc; chem disp (wc); mv service pnt; shwrs inc; el pnts (16A) NOK25; Indtte; shop, rest, snacks 1km; BBQ; cooking facs; shgl beach 1km; few statics; dogs; phone; Eng spkn; adv bkg; quiet; red long stay; CCI. "Neat, well-kept site with gd view of Sognefjord; poss diff if wet due grass pitches." 1 Jun-15 Sep. NOK 110 2010*

BALLANGEN *2F2* (1.5km E Coastal) *68.3383, 16.85776* **Ballangen Camping, 8540 Ballangen (Nordland) [tel 76 92 76 90; fax 76 92 76 92; ballcamp@c2i.net; www.ballangen-camping.no]** Sp on N side of E6 fr Narvik, beside fjord. Lge, mkd pitch, pt shd; htd wc; chem disp; mv service pnt; sauna; shwrs inc; el pnts (10A) NOK40; Indtte (inc dryer); shop; rest; snacks; playgrnd; htd pool; paddling pool; waterslide; shgl fjord beach; tennis; games area; wifi; TV; some statics; dogs; Eng spkn; ccard acc; CCI. "Pleasant site adj fjord; friendly owners; gd facs - ltd san facs high ssn; gd rest; foot/cycle path to town." ♦ 14 Mar-1 Oct. NOK 200 2010*

BARDU see Setermoen *2F2*

⊞ **BEITOSTOLEN** *1C2* (1km S Rural) *61.24128, 8.92068* **Beitostølen Hytter & Camping (OP151), Finntøppvegen 2, 2953 Beitostølen (Oppland) [tel 61 34 11 00 or 95 70 35 05; fax 61 34 15 44; info@beitocamp.no; www.beitocamp.no]** Fr S on Rv51, site on L. Lge, hdstg, pt sl, unshd; htd wc; chem disp; mv service pnt; sauna; baby facs; fam bthrm; shwrs NOK10; el pnts (13A) NOK30; Indtte (inc dryer); shop adj; rest BBQ; cooking facs; playgrnd; htd, covrd pool 1km; canoe & cycle hire; wifi; 90% statics (sep area); dogs; Eng spkn; quiet; ccard acc; CCI. "Wintersports, horseriding nrby; gd walking; excel site." ♦ NOK 200 (CChq acc) 2010*

⊞ **BERGEN** *1A3* (10km E Rural) *60.37381, 5.45768* **Lone Camping, Hardangerveien 697, 5233 Haukeland (Hordaland) [tel 55 39 29 60; fax 55 39 29 79; booking@ lonecamping.no; www.lonecamping.no]** Fr N on E39 until junc with E16. foll sp Voss to rndabt junc with Rv580 sp Nesttun. Foll Rv580 S for approx 5km, site sp on L. Fr S on E39 until Nesttun, foll Rv580 N sp Indre Arna for approx 6km, site sp on R. Recep is sm bureau adj g'ge or, if unmanned, in g'ge. Do NOT go into Bergen city cent. Site is 20km by road fr Bergen. Lge, pt sl, pt shd, some hdstg; wc; chem disp; mv service pnt; shwrs NOK10 (no earth); el pnts (16A) NOK40; gas; Indtte; shop; supmkt adj; snacks; playgrnd; lake sw, fishing & boating; wifi; TV rm; some statics; phone; bus to Bergen; site clsd 5 Nov-19 Dec & New Year; poss v cr; Eng spkn; quiet; red 3+ days; ccard acc; CCI. "Well-organised; helpful staff; peaceful lakeside setting; superb views; lakeside pitches diff when wet; bus at camp ent for Bergen (35 mins)." NOK 205 2010*

BERGEN *1A3* (15km SE Rural) *60.35220, 5.43520* **Bratland Camping, Bratlandsveien 6, 5268 Haukeland (Hordaland) [tel 55 10 13 38; fax 55 10 53 60; post@bratlandcamping.no; www.bratlandcamping.no]** Fr N on E39 until junc with E16, foll sp Voss to rndabt junc with Rv580 sp Nesttun. Foll Rv580 S for approx 4km; site sp on L. Fr Voss on E16, emerge fr tunnel to rndabt, turn L onto Rv580. Then as above. Site 16km by road fr Bergen. Sm, some hdstg, unshd; wc; chem disp; mv service pnt; shwrs NOK10; el pnts (10A) NOK40; lndtte (inc dryer); shop; cooking facs; wifi; TV rm; 10% statics; bus to Bergen at site ent; poss cr; Eng spkn; rd noise; ccard acc; CCI. "Clean, family-run site; gd, modern san facs; v helpful owners; conv Bergen, nrby stave church & Grieg's home." ♦ 20 May-10 Sep. NOK 190 2011*

⊞ **BERGEN** *1A3* (1km S Urban) *60.38232, 5.31794* **Bergen Bobilsenter, Damsgårdsveien 99, 5058 Bergen (Hordaland) [tel 55 34 05 00]** Site on quayside on S side of rv, almost beneath bdge where Rv555 crosses rv. Sm, mkd pitch, hdstg, pt sl, unshd; wc; chem disp; mv service pnt; shwrs NOK20; el pnts (10A) inc; lndry rm; poss cr; Eng spkn; rd/rv noise; m'vans only. "20 min walk to town cent; for sm/med m'vans only; adequate, basic site." NOK 200 2010*

⊞ **BERGEN** *1A3* (10km S Urban) *60.31988, 5.36552* **Midttun Motel & Camping, Middtunvegen 3, 5230 Nesttun (Hordaland) [tel 55 10 39 00; fax 55 10 46 40; midtmot@online.no; www.mmcamp.no]** S fr Bergen turn L at junc R1 & Rv580 (Nesttun) onto Rv580 sp Voss, in 500m turn L at sp. Site 200m on R. Sm, all hdstg, pt sl, unshd; htd wc; chem disp; mv service pnt; fam bthrm; baby facs; sauna; shwrs inc; el pnts (earth fault) inc; lndtte; shop 800m; rest; snacks; bus adj; Eng spkn; adv bkg; rd noise; ccard acc; CCI. "Grieg's home & Fantoft Stave church nr; easy reach of Bergen; basically a car park with el pnts." ♦ NOK 200 2009*

BERLEVAG *2H1* (Coastal) *70.85716, 29.09933* **Berlevåg Camping & Apartments, Havnagata 8, 9980 Berlevåg (Finnmark) [tel 78 98 16 10; post@berlevag-pensjonat.no; www.berlevag-pensjonat.no]** Leave E6 at Tanabru, foll Rv890 to Berlevåg. Site sp at beg of vill. Sm, unshd; htd wc; chem disp; mv service pnt; shwrs NOK10; el pnts (16A) NOK40; lndtte (inc dryer); shop 500m; BBQ; cooking facs; playgrnd; beach; library & lounge; wifi; TV rm; phone; Eng spkn; adv bkg; ccard acc; CCI. "Busy fishing port on edge of Barents Sea; museum, glassworks, WW2 resistance history; v helpful staff as site is also tourist office; site will open outside Jun-Sep on request if contacted ahead; rec arr early; excel site." ♦ 1 Jun-30 Sep. NOK 160 (CChq acc) 2009*

BIRISTRAND see Lillehammer *1C2*

BIRTAVARRE *2G1* (S Rural) *69.49051, 20.82976* **Camping Birtavarre (TR34), 9147 Birtavarre (Troms) [tel/fax 77 71 77 07; mail@birtavarrecamping.com; www.birtavarrecamping.com]** On E6 Olderdalen to Nordkjsobotn, sp. Or foll sp fr vill. Med, unshd; wc; chem disp; mv service pnt; baby facs; shwrs NOK10; el pnts NOK45; lndtte; shop 1km; snacks; cooking facs; fjord sw; Eng spkn; some rd noise; ccard acc; CCI. 1 May-15 Oct. NOK 140 2009*

BJERKA see Korgen *2F2*

⊞ **BO** *1C3* (5km N Rural) *59.44425, 9.06318* **Bø Camping (TE5), Lifjellvegen 51, 3800 Bø (Telemark) [tel 35 95 20 12; fax 35 95 34 64; bocamping@bo.online.no; www.bocamping.com]** Fr Bø cent on Rv36 dir Folkestad; take rd on L to Lifjell, site sp; 500m fr Bø Sommarland amusement park. Med, hdstg, pt shd; htd wc; chem disp; shwrs; el pnts NOK30; gas; lndtte; snacks; shop; playgrnd; pool; paddling pool; fishing; solarium; TV; 20% statics; phone; poss cr; Eng spkn; adv bkg; ccard acc; CCI. NOK 180 2009*

BODO *2F2* (11km NE Coastal) *67.34136, 14.51261* **Geitvågen Bad & Camping, Geitvagen, 8001 Bodø (Nordland) [tel 75 51 01 42; fax 75 52 49 58; post@visitbodo.com]** On ent Bodø on Rv80, turn R onto Rv834 sp Kjerringøy. After 10km turn L at sp, pass car park on R. Med, pt sl, pt shd; wc; chem disp; mv service pnt; shwrs NOK10; el pnts inc; snacks; playgrnd; beach adj. "Arr early for pitch with sea view for midnight sun." 31 May-17 Aug. NOK 150 2008*

⊞ **BODO** *2F2* (2km SE Rural) *67.2695, 14.42483* **Camping Bodøsjoen, Kvernhusveien 1, 8013 Bodø (Nordland) [tel 75 56 36 80; fax 75 56 46 89; bodocamp@yahoo.no; www.bodocamp.no]** Fr E on Rv80 at Bodø sp, turn L at traff lts by Esso g'ge sp airport & camping. L at next rndabt, foll camping sp. Lge, pt sl, unshd; wc; chem disp; shwrs inc; el pnts (10A) NOK20 (no earth); lndtte; shop 1km; rest 2km; beach; bus 1km; boat hire; fishing excursions; bus 250m; Eng spkn; aircraft noise; CCI. "Conv Lofoten ferry; superb views; midnight sun (Jun-Jul); Mt Rønvik 3.2km fr camp." ♦ NOK 180 2010*

BODO *2F2* (12km SE Rural) *67.23409, 14.59756* **Elvegård Camping, Straumøya, 8056 Saltstraumen (Nordland) [tel 94 80 09 00; elvegaard.camping@gmail.com; www.elvegaard-camping.no]** Fr N 14km fr Løding on Rv17 S, turn R after x-ing bdge over fjord - site is approx 33km by rd fr Bodø. Sm, pt sl, unshd; htd wc; chem disp; mv service pnt; shwrs inc; el pnts NOK25; lndtte; shop 600m; rest, snacks 2km; BBQ; cooking facs; playgrnd; fishing; 10% statics; dogs; ccard acc. "Picturesque, pleasant site; 1km fr Mælstrom." ♦ 1 Jun-1 Sep. NOK 175 (3 persons) 2008*

⊞ **BODO** *2F2* (12km SE Coastal) *67.23640, 14.63290* **Saltstraumen Camping, Knapplund, 8056 Saltstraumen (Nordland) [tel 75 58 75 60; fax 75 58 75 40; salcampi@online.no; www.saltstraumen-camping.no]** Fr Bodø take Rv80 for 19km; turn S onto rte 17 at Løding; site sp in Saltstraumen. Site is 33km by road fr Bodø. Med, hdstg, unshd; htd wc; chem disp; mv service pnt; shwrs inc; el pnts (16A) NOK30; gas; lndtte (inc dryer); shop adj; rest adj; cooking facs; playgrnd; fishing; cycling; boating; TV; phone; poss cr; Eng spkn; quiet; ccard acc; CCI. "5 min walk to Mælstrom, the 'angler's paradise'; v busy high ssn - rec arr early." ♦ NOK 200 2010*

BOSBERG see Trondheim *2E3*

BOVERDALEN see Lom *1C2*

BREKKE *1A2* (7km W Coastal) *61.03154, 5.35152* **Botnen Camping, 5961 Brekke (Sogn og Fjordane) [tel 57 78 54 71; www.botnencamping.com]** Fr Brekke off E39, travel W sp Rutledalen & ferry (2 unlit tunnels). Site on R, well sp. Sm, hdstg, pt sl, pt shd; htd wc; chem disp (wc); mv service pnt; baby facs; shwrs NOK5; el pnts (16A) NOK20 (poss rev pol/ no earth); Indtte; kiosk; BBQ; cooking facs; playgrnd; games area; sw; boat hire; fishing; 25% statics; dogs; bus; poss cr; Eng spkn; adv bkg; quiet; ccard acc. "Scenic site on S side of Sognefjord, conv for Oppedal-Lavik ferry; fisherman's paradise; gd." 1 May-30 Sep. NOK 120 2007*

BREKSTAD *2E3* (5km NE Rural/Coastal) *63.69912, 9.74268* **Austrått Camping, 7140 Opphaug (Sør-Trøndelag) [tel 72 52 14 70; fax 72 52 43 72; camping@austraat.no; www.austraat.no]** Take Rv710 SW down Ørland Peninsula to Opphaug; foll sp. Sm, pt sl, unshd; wc; mv service pnt; chem disp; shwrs NOK10; el pnts (6A) NOK30; Indtte; shop 8km; playgrnd; beach adj; poss cr; Eng spkn; quiet. "Frequent car ferry fr Valset to Brekstad - an attractive rte N to Namsos; vg." ♦ 1 May-1 Sep. NOK 150 2007*

⊞ **BREMSNES** *1B1* (1.5km S Coastal) *63.08043, 7.59535* **Skjerneset Brygge Camping, Ekkilsøy, 6530 Averøy (Møre og Romsdal) [tel 71 51 18 94; fax 71 51 18 15; info@skjerneset.com; www.skjerneset.com]** Foll sp to Ekkilsøya Island on Rv64 (off Averøy Island). Site on R over bdge. Sm, some hdstg, pt shd; htd wc; chem disp; mv service pnt; shwrs; el pnts (10-16A) NOK30; Indtte; sm shop; cooking facs; boat hire; fishing; sat TV; apartments to rent; quiet. "Charming, clean site adj working harbour; beautiful outlook; basic san facs; waterside pitches - unfenced deep water in places; museum adj." NOK 150 2009*

BRIKSDALSBRE **see Olden** *1B2*

BRONNOYSUND *2E3* (3km NE Rural) *65.49994, 12.25644* **Mosheim Camping, Torghatten, 8900 Brønnøysund (Nordland) [tel 75 02 20 12; fax 41 46 51 45; post@torghatten.no]** Fr N on Rv17 site sp. Fr town head NE & turn onto Rv17 sp Horn. Sm, hdstg, unshd; htd wc; baby facs; fam bthrm; shwrs NOK10; el pnts (10A) (no earth); Indtte; shop 2km; rest, snacks 3km; bar; playgrnd; TV rm; 20% statics; dogs; Eng spkn; quiet. "V scenic area; coastal steamer calls for day trips." ♦ 2008*

⊞ **BRONNOYSUND** *2E3* (12km SW Coastal) *65.39340, 12.09920* **Torghatten Camping, 8900 Torghatten (Nordland) [tel 75 02 54 95; fax 75 02 58 89; pkha@online.no; www.rv17.no/torghatten-camping/]** Fr Rv17 onto Rv76 to Brønnøysund, foll sp Torghatten. Site at base of Torghatten mountain. Sm, pt sl, unshd; wc; chem disp; mv service pnt; shwrs inc; el pnts (16A) NOK30; Indtte; shop; tradsmn; snacks; bar; playgrnd; sea water pool & beach adj; bus; phone; Eng spkn; quiet. "Take care speed humps in/out Brønnøysund; vg." ♦ NOK 140 2009*

BRUSAND *1A4* (1km NW Coastal) *58.53955, 5.72526* **Camping Brusand, Kvalbein, 4363 Brusand (Rogaland) [tel 51 43 91 23; fax 51 43 91 41; post@brusand-camping.no; www.brusand-camping.no]** On Rv44 N fr Egersund, site sp dir Stavanger. Med, pt sl, pt shd; wc; chem disp; mv service pnt; shwrs NOK10; el pnts (16A) NOK30; gas; Indtte; shop 2km; tradsmn; playgrnd; sand beach adj; horseriding; TV rm; 70% statics; dogs; Eng spkn; adv bkg; quiet; CCI. "Conv NH ferry ports Stavanger & Egersund." ♦ 1 May-30 Sep. NOK 170 2007*

BUD *1B1* (500m E Coastal) *62.9040, 6.92866* **PlusCamp Bud (MR11), 6430 Bud (Møre og Romsdal) [tel 71 26 10 23; bud@pluscamp.no; www.budcamping.no]** Site on Rv664, sp fr Bud. Med, pt sl, unshd; htd wc; chem disp; mv service pnt; baby facs; shwrs NOK10; el pnts (16A) NOK40; Indtte (inc dryer); shop; snacks; cooking facs; playgrnd; sand beach & sw adj; boat hire; fishing; TV rm; 50% statics; dogs; Eng spkn; quiet; ccard acc; CCI. "Waterfront site with beautiful views; 20 min walk to vill shops/rest; gdl facs." ♦ 1 Apr-1 Oct. NOK 195 (5 persons) 2010*

BURFJORD *2G1* (13km N Rural) *70.02728, 22.08860* **Alteidet Camping, Alteidet, 9161 Burfjord (Troms) [tel 78 48 75 59; fax 77 76 93 51; alteidetcamp@hotmail.com]** On W of E6, midway bet Burfjord & Langfjordbotn. Med, pt sl, unshd; wc; chem disp; baby facs; sauna; shwrs NOK10; el pnts (10A) NOK40; Indtte; kiosk; shops 5km; bar; cooking facs; playgrnd; TV; dogs; phone; poss cr; adv bkg; quiet; Eng spkn. "Attractive by rv & fjord; excel base to visit glacier." 15 Jun-15 Aug. NOK 140 2009*

⊞ **BYGLANDSFJORD** *1B4* (2.5km N Rural) *58.68895, 7.80322* **Neset Camping, 4741 Byglandsfjord (Aust-Agder) [tel 37 93 40 50; fax 37 93 43 93; post@neset.no; www.neset.no]** N on Rv9 fr Evje, thro Byglandsfjord, site on L. Lge, pt sl, unshd; htd wc; chem disp; mv service pnt; fam bthrm; sauna; shwrs NOK5; el pnts (10A) NOK30; gas; Indtte (inc dryer); shop; snacks; rest; BBQ; cooking facs; playgrnd; lake sw & beach adj; fishing; windsurfing; boat & cycle hire; wifi; TV rm; 40% statics; dogs; Eng spkn; adv bkg; quiet; ccard acc. "Smart site on lakeside; elk safaris." ♦ NOK 205 (CChq acc) 2009*

BYRKJELO *1B2* (3km S Rural) *61.73026, 6.50843* **Byrkjelo Camping & Hytter, 6826 Byrkjelo (Sogn og Fjordane) [tel 57 86 74 30; fax 57 86 71 54; byrkjelocamping@sensewave.com; www.byrkjelo-camping.tefre.com]** Fr S site ent on L as ent town, clearly sp. Sm, some hdstg, pt shd, wc; chem disp; baby facs; fam bthrm; shwrs NOK5; el pnts (10A) NOK30; Indtte; shop, snacks adj; rest 500m; cooking facs; playgrnd; htd pool; paddling pool; fishing; cycling; solarium; wifi; 25% statics; phone; Eng spkn; adv bkg; quiet but some rd noise; ccard acc; CCI. "Horseriding, mountain & glacier walking; excel site." ♦ Easter & 1 May-1 Oct. NOK 175 2010*

DALEN (TELEMARK) *1B3* (250m S Rural) *59.44223, 8.00758* **Buøy Camping (TE20), Buøyvegen, 3880 Dalen (Telemark) [tel 35 07 75 87; fax 35 07 77 01; info@dalencamping.com; www.dalencamping.com]** Fr E134 at Høydalsmo take Rv45 twd Dalen (approx 20km, 12% gradient). Of fr E134 at Åmot take Rv38 to Dalen (no gradient). Site in cent of Dalen on Rv45, well sp. Med, pt shd; htd wc; chem disp; mv service pnt; baby facs; shwrs inc; el pnts (16A) NOK35; gas; lndtte; shop; rest; cooking facs; playgrnd; leisure cent 500m; cycle hire; wifi; TV; 60% chalets; dogs; phone; Eng spkn; quiet; ccard acc; CCI. "Site on island; gd family base; gd walking." 1 May-28 Aug. NOK 240 2010*

DALSGRENDA see Mo i Rana *2F2*

DOMBAS *1C2* (6km S Rural) *62.02991, 9.17586* **Bjørkhol Camping, 2660 Dombås (Oppland) [tel 61 24 13 31; post@bjorkhol.no; www.bjorkhol.no]** Site on E6. Sm, pt sl, pt shd; htd wc; chem disp; mv service pnt; shwrs NOK5; el pnts (10A) NOK40 (long lead poss req); lndtte; shop; rest, snacks, bar 6km; cooking facs; playgrnd; 10% statics; dogs; phone; Eng spkn; adv bkg; quiet; CCI. "A well-kept, friendly, family-owned, basic site; excel mountain walking in area." 1 May-1 Sep. NOK 130 2010*

⊞ **DOVRE** *1C2* (2km N Rural) *61.9986, 9.2228* **Toftemo Camping, 2662 Dovre (Oppland) [tel 61 24 00 45; fax 61 24 04 83; post@toftemo.no; www.toftemo.no]** On W of E6. Clearly sp, 10km S of Dombås. Lge, pt sl, pt shd; htd wc; chem disp; shwrs NOK10; el pnts (10-16A) inc; lndtte; shop; rest; snacks 10km; bar; htd pool; fishing; cycle hire; TV; dogs; phone; no adv bkg; quiet; ccard acc. ♦ NOK 190 2007*

DRAMMEN *1C3* (4km W Rural) *59.75111, 10.13361* **NAF Camping Drammen, Buskerudveien 97, 3027 Drammen (Buskerud) [tel 32 82 17 98; fax 32 82 57 68; d-camp@online.no; www.drammencampingplass.no]** Fr Drammen take Rv283 dir Hokksund & Kongsberg. After 5km foll sp to rvside & site. Med, pt shd; htd wc; chem disp; mv service pnt; baby facs; shwrs NOK10; el pnts (5A) NOK45; gas; lndtte; shop 4km; rest 1km; snacks; playgrnd; fr sw adj; dogs; phone; bus to Oslo sh walk; poss cr; Eng spkn; quiet; ccard acc; CCS. "Helpful, friendly staff; poss diff when wet; facs stretched high ssn." 1 May-15 Sep. NOK 165 2007*

⊞ **DREVSJO** *1D2* (4km E Rural) *61.89818, 12.00659* **Drevsjø Camping, 2443 Drevsjø (Hedmark) [tel 62 45 92 03; fax 62 45 91 42; tobronke@bbnett.no; www.drevsjocamping.no]** At S end of Femund Lake. Sm, pt sl, pt shd; wc; chem disp; mv service pnt; shwrs; el pnts (10A) inc (earth prob); lndry rm; snacks; BBQ; cooking facs; lake sw & beach adj; phone; bus; Eng spkn; CCI. "Wild area - reindeer roam past site; gd." NOK 170 2007*

EDLAND *1B3* (5km E Rural) *59.72378, 7.69712* **Velemoen Camping, 3895 Edland (Telemark) [tel 35 07 01 09; fax 35 07 02 15; velemoen@frisurf.no; www.velemoen.no]** Fr E site on L off E134 bef Edland; Fr W site is on R, 8km after Haukeligrend on Lake Tveitevatnet Sm, pt sl, shd; wc; baby facs; no chem disp/mv service pnt; shwrs; el pnts; lndtte; shops 1km; cooking facs; playgrnd; lake sw adj; sat TV; some cabins; dogs; Eng spkn; quiet; no ccard acc. "V helpful owner; immac san facs; beautiful lakeside/mountain location; on S side of Hardangervidda National Park; on main E-W rte Oslo-Bergen." ♦ 15 May-1 Oct. NOK 150 2011*

⊞ **EGERSUND** *1A4* (3.5km N Rural) *58.4788, 5.9909* **Steinsnes Camping, Jærveien 190, Tengs, 4370 Egersund (Rogaland) [tel 51 49 41 36; fax 51 49 40 73; post@steinsnescamping.co; www.steinsnescamping.no]** Site located S of Rv44 & on bank of rv; bet filling stn & rv bdge at Tengs Bru. Med, mkd pitch, unshd; wc; chem disp; mv service pnt; shwrs NOK5; el pnts (4A) NOK35; lndtte; shops adj; snacks adj; bar 2km; BBQ; playgrnd; sand beach 8km; horseriding school adj; phone; poss cr; Eng spkn; adv bkg; quiet but some rd noise; ccard acc; CCI. "Spectacular rapids 1km (salmon leaping in July); on North Sea cycle rte; conv ferry to Denmark or Bergen; vg." ♦ NOK 150 2008*

EIDFJORD *1B3* (Urban) *60.46860, 7.07315* **Kjærtveit Camping, 5786 Eidfjord (Hordaland) [tel 53 66 53 71; eidfjord@c21.net]** Sp fr cent of Eidfjord, foll sp for Sima power plant on L less than 500m fr x-rds. Sm, unshd; htd wc; chem disp; mv service pnt; shwrs NOK10; fam bthrm; el pnts NOK30; lndtte; tradsmn; playgrnd; beach adj; boat hire; quiet; CCI. "Excel location beside fjord; antiquated san facs, poss unclean; charge for hot water for washing-up." 1 Apr-15 Oct. NOK 140 2008*

EIDFJORD *1B3* (7km E Rural) *60.42563, 7.12318* **Sæbø Camping (HO11), 5784 Øvre-Eidfjord (Hordaland) [tel 53 66 59 27 or 55 10 20 48; scampi@online.no; www.saebocamping.com]** Site N of Rv7 bet Eidfjord & Geilo, 2nd on L after tunnel & bdge; clearly sp. Med, pt shd; htd wc; chem disp; mv service pnt; fam bthrm; shwrs NOK10; el pnts (10A) NOK30 (earth fault); lndtte (inc dryer); shop; tradsmn; rest, snacks 500m; cooking facs; playgrnd; boating; quiet; CCI. "Vg; beautiful lakeside setting; adj to excel nature cent with museum/shop/theatre; clean san facs; helpful staff." ♦ 1 May-25 Sep. NOK 160 2009*

⊞ **ELVERUM** *1D2* (2km S Rural) *60.86701, 11.55623* **Elverum Camping, Halvdan Gransvei 6, 2407 Elverum (Hedmark) [tel 62 41 67 16; fax 62 41 68 17; booking@elverumcamping.no; www.elverumcamping.no]** Site sp fr Rv20 dir Kongsvinger. Lge, pt shd; htd wc; chem disp; mv service pnt; shwrs inc; el pnts (10A) NOK40; lndtte; shop, rest, snacks, bar 2km; BBQ; playgrnd; 20% statics; phone; dogs; adv bkg; Eng spkn; quiet. "Vg; museum of forestry adj; rlwy museum at Hamar (30km)." NOK 200 2009*

EVJE *1B4* (500m S Urban) *58.5850, 7.79472* **Odden Camping (AA13), Verksmoen, 4735 Evje (Aust-Agder) [tel 37 93 06 03; fax 37 93 11 01; odden@oddencamping.no; www.oddencamping.no]** Close to junc of Rv9 & Rv42 bet rd & rv. Lge, pt sl, pt shd; wc; chem disp; baby facs; fam bthrm; shwrs NOK10; el pnts (10A) NOK30; Indtte; shop; supmkt nr; playgrnd; cycle hire; 50% seasonal statics; quiet; ccard acc; red CCI. "Evje interesting gem-mining area; vg." ♦ 1 May-1 Nov. NOK 170 2007*

EVJE *1B4* (5km S Rural) *58.5534, 7.7826* **Hornnes Camping (AA15), Riksvei 9, 4737 Hornes (Aust-Agder) [tel 37 93 03 05; fax 37 93 16 04; post@hcamp.no; www.hcamp.no]** Site sp fr Rv9 on E side of rd, sp. Med, pt sl, pt shd; wc; chem disp; mv service pnt; shwrs NOK10; el pnts (10A) NOK20; Indtte; cooking facs; playgrnd; lake sw adj; fishing; 50% statics; dogs; phone; Eng spkn; quiet; CCI. "Cent for gem mining; site yourself, owner call eves; gd." ♦ 15 May-15 Sep. NOK 110 2007*

FAGERNES *1C2* (6km N Rural) *61.04015, 9.17148* **Fossen Camping, Holdalsfoss, 2900 Fagernes [tel 61 36 35 34; office@fossencamping.no; www.fossencamping.no]** Site sp off Rv51. Med, pt shd; wc; chem disp; baby facs; shwrs NOK10; el pnts NOK30; Indtte; cooking facs; playgrnd; shgl beach; 30% statics; dogs; Eng spkn; some rd noise. "Modest but comprehensive facs." 1 May-1 Oct. NOK 150 2008*

⊞ **FAGERNES** *1C2* (200m S Rural) *60.9805, 9.2328* **Camping Fagernes, Tyinvegen 23, 2900 Fagernes (Oppland) [tel 61 36 05 10; fax 61 36 07 51; post@fagernes-camping.no; www.fagernes-camping.no]** Site on N side of Fagernes on E16. Lge, some hdg pitch, pt sl, pt shd; htd wc; chem disp; mv service pnt; baby facs; shwrs NOK10; el pnts (10-16A) NOK30; Indtte; shop; rest; snacks; bar; cooking facs; playgrnd; lake sw; activity cent; cycling; skiing; fishing; car wash; TV; 90% statics; dogs; phone; poss cr; Eng spkn; quiet low ssn; ccard acc; CCI. "Helpful owner; modern san facs; ltd water pnts; Valdres folk museum park adj highly rec; fjord views." ♦ NOK 195 2008*

FARSUND *1A4* (4km S Rural) *58.0663, 6.7957* **Lomsesanden Familiecamping, Loshavneveien 228, 4550 Farsund (Vest-Agder) [tel 38 39 09 13; e-vetlan@online.no; www.lomsesanden.no]** Exit E39 at Lyngdal onto Rv43 to Farsund & foll camp sps. (NB Rv465 fr Kvinesdal not suitable for c'vans.) Med, pt shd; wc; chem disp; baby facs; shwrs NOK10; el pnts (10A) NOK45; Indtte; shop; playgrnd; dir access sand beach adj; fishing; TV; 95% statics/cabins; dogs; Eng spkn; adv bkg rec; quiet; ccard acc. "Gd site in beautiful location." 1 May-15 Sep. NOK 185 2009*

⊞ **FAUSKE** *2F2* (12km N Coastal) *67.34618, 15.59533* **Strømhaug Camping, Strømhaugveien 2, 8226 Straumen (Nordland) [tel 75 69 71 06; fax 75 69 76 06; mail@stromhaug.no; www.stromhaug.no]** N fr Fauske on E6, turn off sp Straumen, site sp. Sm, pt sl, pt shd; htd wc; chem disp; mv service pnt; shwrs NOK10; el pnts (6-10A) inc; Indtte; shop, rest, snacks, bar adj; cooking facs; playgrnd; fishing; boating; TV; Eng spkn; red 7+ days. "Site on rv bank; salmon-fishing in Aug." ♦ NOK 220 2010*

⊞ **FAUSKE** *2F2* (4km S Urban) *67.23988, 15.41961* **Fauske Camping & Motel, Leivset, 8201 Fauske (Nordland) [tel 75 64 84 01; fax 75 64 84 13; fausm@online.no]** Fr S site on R of E6, approx 6km fr exit of Kvenflåg rd tunnel, & 2km bef Finneid town board. Fr N site on L approx 1km after rv bdge. Sm, pt sl, pt shd; wc; mv service pnt; baby facs; shwrs NOK10; el pnts (10A) NOK40; Indtte; shop 2km; snacks; cooking facs; playgrnd; sw 2km; fishing; cycling; wifi; dogs; poss cr; some Eng spkn; adv bkg; some rd noise; ccard acc. "Vg; phone ahead low ssn to check open." NOK 165 2009*

When we get home
I'm going to post
all these site report
forms to the Club
for next year's guide.
The deadline's mid September 2013

FAUSKE *2F2* (3km SW Rural/Coastal) *67.24541, 15.3360* **Lundhøgda Camping, Lundeveien, 8200 Fauske (Nordland) [tel 75 64 39 66; fax 75 64 92 49; post@lundhogdacamping.no; www.lundhogdacamping.no]** Site on Rv80 fr Fauske dir Bodø, sp. Sm, sl, pt shd; htd wc; chem disp; mv service pnt; shwrs NOK10; el pnts (16A) NOK40; Indtte; shops 3km; tradsmn; rest 2km; snacks; cooking facs; playgrnd; beach 300m; cycle hire; TV rm; 40% statics; poss cr; Eng spkn; quiet; ccard acc; CCI. "On high open ground on headland but lower slopes boggy; gd views; helpful, friendly staff." 15 Jun-15 Aug. NOK 150 2009*

⊞ **FJAERLAND** *1B2* (4km N Rural) *61.42758, 6.76211* **Bøyum Camping, 5855 Fjærland (Sogn og Fjordane) [tel 57 69 32 52; fax 57 69 29 57; kfodne@frisurf.no; www.fjaerland.org/boyumcamping]** On Rv5 Sogndal to Skei. Shortly after end of toll tunnel on L, well sp. Sm, pt hdstg, unshd; htd wc; chem disp; mv service pnt; shwrs NOK5-10; el pnts NOK30; Indtte; ltd shop; tradsmn; snacks; cooking facs; playgrnd; wifi; TV rm; 30% statics; phone; poss cr; Eng spkn; adv bkg; quiet; ccard acc; CCI. "Adj glacier museum, conv for glacier & fjord trips; beautiful location nr fjord (no views); visit Mundal for 2nd hand books; helpful owner; superb, clean site." ♦ NOK 150 2009*

FLAKK see Trondheim *1C1*

FLAM *1B2* (8km N Rural) *60.90006, 7.20618* **Lunde Camping, 5745 Aurland (Sogn og Fjordane) [tel 57 63 34 12; fax 57 63 31 65; lunde.camping@alb.no; www.lunde-camping.no]** Fr N exit E16 at rndabt immed after S end of 25km tunnel turn for Aurland. R S exit E16 8km fr Flam at rndabt sp Aurland. Site on S side of rd, sp. Steep ent. Med, pt shd; htd wc; chem disp; mv service pnt; shwrs NOK10; el pnts (16A) NOK30 (rev pol); Indtte; shops 1.4km; cooking facs; dogs; phone; Eng spkn; some rd noise; ccard acc; CCS/CCI. "Much quieter than site in Flåm; clean facs; superb setting with views; gd walking." Easter & 1 May-1 Oct. NOK 250 2011*

FLAM *1B2* (400m S Urban) *60.86240, 7.10921* **Flåm Camping, 5743 Flåm (Sogn og Fjordane) [tel 57 63 21 21; camping@flaam-camping.no; www.flaam-camping.no]** Fr Lærdal Tunnel cont on E16 thro 2 more tunnels. At end of 2nd tunnel (Fretheim Tunnel) turn L immed to Sentrum. Turn L at x-rds, site on L. Med, hdstg, pt sl, terr, pt shd; htd wc; chem disp; mv service pnt; serviced pitches; baby facs; shwrs NOK10; el pnts (10A) inc; Indtte (inc dryer); shop; supmkt nrby; rest, snacks & bar 500m; BBQ; cooking facs; playgrnd; cycle hire; watersports; boating; fishing; dogs free; no c'vans/m'vans over 8.50m; phone; poss cr; Eng spkn; quiet but noise fr rd & cruise ships during day; ccard acc; red long stay; CCI. "Well-kept, friendly, busy, family-run site; excel san facs; conv mountain walks, Flambana rlwy, Aurlandsvangen 7km - gd shops; gd cycling base; excel." ♦ 1 May-15 Sep. NOK 260 SBS - H14 2011*

⊞ **FLEKKEFJORD** *1A4* (5km SE Rural) *58.28868, 6.7173* **Egenes Camping (VA7), 4400 Flekkefjord (Vest-Agder) [tel 38 32 01 48; fax 38 32 01 11; post@egenescamping.no; www.egenes.no]** Located N of E39 dir Seland. Med, mkd pitch, pt shd; htd wc; chem disp; mv service pnt; baby facs; shwrs NOK10; el pnts (5A) NOK40; Indtte; shop; snacks; playgrnd; TV; 75% statics; phone; ccard acc; red CCI. "Ltd facs low ssn; sm area for tourers poss cr; lovely situation." ♦ NOK 250 2010*

⊞ **FLORO** *1A2* (2km E Coastal) *61.59420, 5.07244* **Pluscamp Krokane (SF15), Strandgt 30, 6900 Florø (Sogn og Fjordane) [tel 57 75 22 50; fax 57 75 22 60; post@krocamp.no; www.krocamp.no]** On Rv5 Forde to Florø, on ent town turn L at rndabt sp Krokane, then immed R & foll rd to coast. Turn L, pass marina to site, sp. Steep ent/exit. Sm, hdstg, pt sl, pt shd; htd wc; chem disp; mv service pnt; baby facs; fam bthrm; shwrs NOK10; el pnts (10A) NOK30; Indtte; shop 2km; tradsmn; rest, snacks, bar 2km; playgrnd; htd, covrd pool 1km; sand beach adj; boat hire; fishing; internet; 80% statics; phone; bus; Eng spkn; quiet; CCI. "V sm area for tourers; Florø interesting fishing town with boat trips etc." ♦ NOK 130 2010*

FORDE *1A2* (1.5km NE Rural) *61.44940, 5.89008* **Førde Gjestehus & Camping (SF94), Kronborgvegen, Havstad, 6803 Førde (Sogn og Fjordane) [tel 46 80 60 00; post@fordecamping.no; www.fordecamping.no]** Site is on NE o'skirts Forde. At rndabt on E39at Havstad foll sp 'Hospital', site on R in 1km; well sp. Med, mkd pitch, some hdstg, pt shd; htd wc; chem disp; mv service pnt; shwrs inc; baby facs; fam bthrm; el pnts (16A) inc; Indtte; shop; rest; cooking facs; playgrnd; rv sw adj; TV rm; some statics; phone; Eng spkn; adv bkg; quiet; ccard acc; CCI. "Pleasant, peaceful site." ♦ 15 Apr-1 Oct. NOK 230 2010*

FREDRIKSTAD *1C4* (2km SE Coastal) *59.20116, 10.96263* **Fredrikstad Motel & Camping (OF20), Torsnesveien 16, 1630 Fredrikstad (Østfold) [tel 69 32 03 15; fax 69 32 36 66; eivind.enger@hotelcity.no; www.fredrikstadmotel.no]** Fr S on Rv110 at rndabt bef lge span bdge (tourist office at bdge) foll sp Gamlebyen/Torsnes, site on L. Or foll brown sps for old city. Med, hdstg, pt sl, pt shd; htd wc; chem disp; baby facs; fam bthrm; shwrs inc; el pnts (10A) NOK50; Indtte; shop; cooking facs; playgrnd; pool 100m; beaches adj; cycle hire; TV; dogs; adv bkg; quiet but poss noise fr late arrivals fr ferry; CCI. "Guided tours to craft indus; sh walk to lovely walled city; v cr water festival (2nd w/end July)." ♦ 1 Jun-31 Aug. NOK 200 2011*

⊞ **GAUPNE** *1B2* (500m S Rural) *61.40056, 7.30076* **Sandvik Camping (SF20), 6868 Gaupne (Sogn og Fjordane) [tel 57 68 11 53; fax 57 68 16 71; sandvik@pluscamp.no; www.pluscamp.no/sandvik]** Site sp N of Rv55 (Sogndal/Lom) after leaving Gaupne. Med, pt shd; htd wc; chem disp; baby facs; shwrs NOK10; el pnts (16A) (poss earth fault); Indtte (inc dryer); shop; snacks; rest 500m; bar; playgrnd; games area; TV; quiet; ccard acc. "Vg; ltd facs early ssn & poss stretched if site full; lovely, peaceful site; gd touring base." ♦ NOK 150 2009*

⊞ **GEILO** *1B3* (400m S Rural) *60.52915, 8.20705* **Geilo Camping, Skurdalsveien 23, 3580 Geilo (Buskerud) [tel 32 09 07 33; fax 32 09 11 56; post@geilocamping.no; www.geilocamping.no]** Fr W on Rv7 at rndabt in town cent turn R (S) onto Rv40 sp Kongsberg, site on R in 300m by rv. Sm, mkd pitch, hdstg, some terr, pt shd; wc; chem disp; shwrs NOK10; el pnts (10A) NOK30; Indtte (inc dryer); shop; tradsmn; snacks; rv beach adj; fishing; 70% statics; bus 300m; Eng spkn; quiet; ccard acc. "Mountain views; walking & fishing cent; poss muddy after heavy rain; san facs tired." NOK 220 2009*

GEIRANGER *1B1* (2km N Rural) *62.11538, 7.18528* **Geirangerfjorden Feriesenter, Grande, 6216 Geiranger (Møre og Romsdal) [tel 95 10 75 27; geirangerfjorden@adsl.no; www.geirangerfjorden.net]** N fr Geiranger, site on L bef hairpin bends. Sm, unshd; htd wc; chem disp; shwrs NOK10; el pnts (10A) NOK30; gas, Indtte; shop 2km; rest, snacks, bar 500m; BBQ; cooking facs; playgrnd; boat hire; sw & fishing; poss cr; Eng spkn; adv bkg; quiet; ccard acc; red long stay; CCI. "Site on edge of fjord; spectacular views; helpful, friendly owner." 20 Apr-15 Sep. NOK 155 2007*

GEIRANGER *1B1* (1.5km SE Urban) *62.09486, 7.2184* **Vinje Camping, 6216 Geiranger (Møre og Romsdal) [tel 70 26 30 17; fax 70 26 30 15; post@vinje-camping.no; www.vinje-camping.no]** Sp on Rv63, but rd not rec for c'vans. Rec c'vans travel via ferry fr Hellesylt, then S'wards to site (10% max gradient). Med, mkd pitch, pt shd; wc; chem disp; mv service pnt; shwrs NOK5; el pnts (16A) NOK35; Indtte; shop; rest 500m; snacks 1.5km; cooking facs; playgrnd; lake sw; watersports; Eng spkn; quiet; ccard acc. "Beautiful situation nr waterfall; gd facs." 1 Jun-15 Sep. NOK 150 2008*

NORWAY

GEIRANGER *1B1* (500m S Rural) *62.09998, 7.20421* **Camping Geiranger, 6216 Geiranger (Møre og Romsdal) [tel/fax 70 26 31 20; postmaster@geirangercamping.no; www.geirangercamping.no]** Site on fjord edge in vill. On Rv63 Eidsdal-Geiranger take lower rd thro vill to site on R & on both sides of rv. Rv63 not suitable for c'vans - steep hill & hairpins, use ferry fr Hellesylt. Lge, pt sl, unshd; wc; chem disp; mv service pnt; shwrs NOK10; ltd el pnts (16A) NOK35; lndtte (inc dryer); tradsmn high ssn; BBQ; cooking facs; playgrnd; wifi; dogs; poss cr; Eng spkn; adv bkg; quiet but noise of waterfall; ccard acc; CCI. "Busy site in superb location; gd touring base; gd boat trips on fjord; facs (inc el pnts) ltd if site full." ♦ 20 May-10 Sep. NOK 175 2010*

GJERDE *1B2* (Rural) *61.63061, 7.26628* **Jostedal Camping (SF97), Jostedal, 6871 Gjerde (Sogn og Fjordane) [tel 57 68 39 14; fax 57 68 41 36; post@jostedalcamping.no; www.jostedalcamping.no]** N fr Gaupne on Rv604 to Gjerde, site sp on R bef Statoil g'ge; on rvside. Sm, pt shd; htd wc; chem disp; mv waste; fam bthrm; shwrs NOK10; el pnts (16A) NOK30; lndtte; rest, bar 200m; rv sw adj; no dogs; poss cr; Eng spkn; quiet. "Excel, modern san facs; 6km to Nigardsbreen glacier cent - easy access to glacier gd." 20 May-1 Oct. NOK 130 2008*

⊞ **GJOVIK** *1C2* (13km N Rural) *60.88881, 10.67425* **Camping Sveastranda, 2836 Redalen (Oppland) [tel 61 18 15 29; fax 61 18 17 23; resepsjon@sveastranda.no; www.sveastranda.no]** N fr Gjovik on Rv4, site sp on L, 3km S of Mjøsbrua bdge. Lge, mkd pitch, pt shd; htd wc; chem disp; mv service pnt; shwrs NOK10; el pnts (16A) NOK20; lndtte; shop high ssn; rest, snacks 4km; playgrnd; lake sw; boating; TV; 50% statics; poss cr; quiet; ccard acc. "On shore of Lake Mjøsa; modern san facs." NOK 195 2008*

⊞ **GOL** *1C2* (2.5km S Rural) *60.70023, 9.00416* **Gol Campingsenter (BU17), Heradveien 7, 3550 Gol (Buskerud) [tel 32 07 41 44; fax 32 07 53 96; gol@pluscamp.no; www.golcamp.no]** Ent on R of Rv7 fr Gol twd Nesbyen. Lge, pt sl, unshd; htd wc; chem disp; mv service pnt; baby facs; fam bthrm; sauna; shwrs inc; el pnts (16A) inc: lndtte (inc dryer); gas; shop; supmkt 2km; rest; snacks; bar; cooking facs; playgrnd; htd pool; padding pool; rv sw 2km; games area; wifi; TV rm; poss noisy; ccard acc; CCI. "Excel; lge extn with full facs across main rd - modern & clean." ♦ NOK 245 (4 persons) (CChq acc) 2010*

⊞ **GOL** *1C2* (2km W Rural) *60.69161, 8.91909* **Personbråten Camping, 3550 Gol (Buskerud) [tel 32 07 59 70; leif.personbraten@c2i.net]** Fr Gol to Geilo on Rv7, on L on rvside Med, pt shd; wc; chem disp (wc); shwrs inc; el pnts (10A; lndtte; BBQ; cooking facs; playgrnd; fishing; cycling; rv sw 1km; adv bkg; Eng spkn; CCI. "On rvside; v pleasant; poss noise fr rd & rv; honesty box if office unmanned; excel NH." 2009*

GRANLI see Kongsvinger *1D3*

GRANVIN *1B2* (2km N Rural) *60.59220, 6.80680* **Camping Espelandsdalen, 5736 Granvin (Hordaland) [tel 56 52 51 67; fax 56 52 59 62; post@espelandsdalencamping.no; www.esplelandsdalencamping.no]** Fr Granvin on Rv13, take Rv572 sp Espelandsdalen, narr rd. Sm, pt sl, unshd; htd wc; chem disp; shwrs NOK5; el pnts (10A) NOK35; shops 13km; cooking facs; playgrnd; lake sw; some cabins; dogs; adv bkg; quiet. "Ideal for Ulvik & Voss area." 1 May-1 Sep. NOK 130 2009*

GRANVIN *1B2* (14km SW Rural) *60.47239, 6.61173* **Kvanndal Camping, 5739 Kvanndal (Hordaland) [tel 56 52 58 80; fax 56 52 58 55; kvanndal.camping@sensewave.com]** On Rv7 in cent of vill opp ferry port to Kinsarvik & Utne. Sm, pt sl, unshd; wc; baby facs; shwrs NOK10; el pnts NOK30; lndtte; shop; tradsmn; rest; playgrnd; TV rm; 30% statics; phone; Eng spkn; quiet; ccard acc; red long stay/CCI. "Conv ferry fr Bergen & trips to S Hardanger fjord." ♦ 1 Mar-1 Nov. NOK 110 (4 persons) 2007*

⊞ **GRIMSBU** *1C2* (N Rural) *62.15546, 10.17198* **Grimsbu Turistsenter, 2582 Grimsbu (Oppland) [tel 62 49 35 29; fax 62 49 35 62; mail@grimsbu.no; www.grimsbu.no]** On Rv29 11km E of Folldal, well sp. Med, pt sl, pt shd; htd wc; chem disp; mv service pnt; sauna; private san facs avail; shwrs NOK10; el pnts (16A) NOK30; lndtte (inc dryer); shop; rest; snacks; BBQ; cooking facs; playgrnd; lake sw 1.5km; rv fishing; cycle & boat hire; fitness rm; wifi; TV rm; Eng spkn; adv bkg; quiet; ccard acc. "Family-run site; beautiful situation." ♦ NOK 140 (3 persons) (CChq acc) 2009*

⊞ **GRIMSTAD** *1B4* (5km NE Coastal) *58.36888, 8.63722* **Moysand Familiecamping, Moy, 4885 Grimstad (Aust-Agder) [tel 91 19 75 94; mail@moysand-familiecamping.no; www.moysand-familiecamping.no]** Exit A18 junc 78 onto Rv420 E twd Fevik. Foll site sp on rd to Riksveien, site 2km after Riksveien. Lge, mkd pitch, pt shd; htd wc; baby facs; private san facs avail; shwrs; el pnts metered; lndtte (inc dryer); shop; tradsmn; supmkt 5km; rest; BBQ; cooking facs; playgrnd; fishing; boat hire; TV; some statics; dogs; adv bkg; quiet. ♦ NOK 190 2010*

⊞ **GRONG** *2E3* (2km SW Rural) *64.4604, 12.3137* **Langnes Camping, 7870 Grong (Nord-Trøndelag) [tel 47 68 83 33; langnescamping@hero.no; www.nafcamp.com/langnes-camping]** N on E6 turn off S of bdge over rv on by-pass, site sp. Med, mkd pitch, some hdstg, unshd; htd wc; chem disp; mv service pnt; shwrs NOK10; el pnts (10A) NOK35; lndtte (inc dryer); tradsmn; snacks; rest 3km; BBQ; cooking facs; playgrnd; rv sw & beach nr; rv fishing; drying rm for skiers; games area; games rm; wifi; TV; some statics; Quick Stop pitches; Eng spkn; adv bkg; quiet. "Helpful staff; pleasant, family-run site; free phone to owner if site clsd; gd facs." ♦ NOK 140 (CChq acc) 2011*

GUDVANGEN *1B2* (500m SW Rural) *60.87206, 6.82873* **Vang Camping, 5717 Gudvangen (Sogn og Fjordane) [tel/fax 57 63 39 26]** At S end of of Nærøy Fjord on E16 at edge of vill. Sm, some hdstg, unshd; wc; chem disp/mv service pnt at Shell g'ge 1km; shwrs NOK5; el pnts (16A) NOK30 (poss no earth); lndtte; shop 1km; rest 1km at ferry; Eng spkn; quiet but some rd noise; no ccard acc; CCI. "Immac site in beautiful valley with waterfalls; spectacular scenery; cruises on adj fjord." 15 May-10 Sep. NOK 110 2007*

HALDEN *1D4* (1.5km E Rural) *59.11668, 11.39853* **Camping Fredriksten, 1750 Halden (Østfold) [tel 69 18 40 32; fax 69 18 75 73]** Located at old fortress of Fredriksten on hill visible fr town; site sp. Med, pt sl, pt shd; wc; chem disp; mv service pnt; baby facs; shwrs NOK10; el pnts (10A) NOK40; Indtte; sm shop & 250m; snacks; playgrnd; cycle hire; TV; Eng spkn; quiet; ccard acc. "Attractive situation on wooded hill; rv trips to Strømstad; rest at fortress." ♦ 1 May-15 Sep. NOK 150 2007*

HALSA *2E2* (S Coastal) *66.73930, 13.51661* **Furøy Camping, Furøy 6, 8178 Halsa (Nordland) [tel 75 75 05 25; fax 75 75 03 36; post@furoycamp.no; www.furoycamp.no]** Foll Rv17 S fr Ornes, at Forøy ferry x-ing strt on, foll rd sp to site. Sm, pt sl; htd wc; chem disp; shwrs NOK10; el pnts (16A) NOK25; Indtte; kiosk; shop 1km; rest; bar; BBQ; cooking facs; shgl beach adj; fishing; boat hire; some statics; dogs; phone; Eng spkn; adv bkg; quiet. "Lovely position; arr early for prime pitch, site fills up quickly after 1730 high ssn; archaeological site adj; 15km Svartisen glacier; san facs stretched when site full." ♦ 1 May-30 Sep. NOK 175 2009*

HAMALVOLL see Os I Osterdalen *1D1*

HAMMERFEST *2G1* (1km SE Rural) *70.65261, 23.66096* **Hammerfest Turistsenter, Storsvingen, 9600 Hammerfest (Finnmark) [tel 78 41 11 26; fax 78 41 19 26; post@hammerfest-turist.no; www.hammerfest-turist.no]** On Rv94, adj Shell stn. Med, terr, hdstg, unshd; htd wc; chem disp; mv service pnt; shwrs inc; el pnts (10-16A) NOK40; Indtte; shop; snacks; cooking facs; playgrnd; phone; rd noise; ccard acc. "Glorious views inc midnight sun; poss poor site maintenance low ssn & unhtd san facs." ♦ 1 May-1 Oct. NOK 200 2009*

HAMRESANDEN see Kristiansand *1B4*

HARRAN *2E3* (Rural) *64.55916, 12.48376* **Harran Camping, 7873 Harran (Nord-Trøndelag) [tel 74 33 29 90; harrancamping@gmail.com]** Site E of E6 N of Grong in cent Harran behind Statoil filling stn. Med, pt shd; wc; chem disp; mv service pnt; baby facs; fam bthrm; shwrs NOK10; el pnts (10A) NOK50; gas; Indtte (inc dryer); shop & rest 500m; BBQ; playgrnd; fishing; TV; phone; Eng spkn; quiet but some rd noise. "Pleasant site; lovely location." ♦ 1 May-15 Sep. NOK 150 2009*

HAUGE *1A4* (4km NE Rural) *58.36166, 6.30944* **Bakkaåno Camping, Bakka, 4380 Hauge i Dalane (Rogaland) [tel 51 47 78 52 or 91 10 64 91 (mob); eurdal@c2i.net; www.bakkaanocamping.no]** Heading E fr Hauge on Rv44, over rv & immed turn L & foll site sp. Site on L, recep on R over golf course at white house. Rd narr. Med, pt shd; wc; chem disp; mv service pnt; shwrs NOK1; el pnts (5A) NOK30; shop; cooking facs; sw & fishing adj; 80% statics; Eng spkn; quiet. "Sep area for tourers; friendly, welcoming owners." ♦ Easter-30 Sep. NOK 160 2008*

⊞ **HAUGESUND** *1A3* (2km N Coastal) *59.43073, 5.24655* **Haraldshaugen Camping, Gard, 5507 Haugesund (Rogaland) [tel 52 72 80 77; fax 52 86 69 32]** Site off Rv47 dir Leirvik, sp. Med, pt sl, pt shd; htd wc; mv service pnt; chem disp; shwrs NOK10; el pnts (10A) NOK40; Indtte; shop, snacks 500m; rest 1.7km; playgrnd; sw 3km; boating; fishing; 60% statics; no dogs; no adv bkg; quiet; ccard acc. "In easy reach of sea, nature park; gd views." ♦ NOK 200 2008*

HAUGESUND *1A3* (12km E Rural) *59.43453, 5.48243* **Grindafjord Feriesenter, Litlaskog, 5570 Aksdal (Rogaland) [tel 52 77 57 40; fax 52 77 52 12; post@grindafjord.no; www.grindafjord.no]** Fr Haugesund on E134 to Rv515 at Aksdal, site sp. Med, pt shd; htd wc; mv service pnt; shwrs NOK10; el pnts (6A) NOK25; Indtte; shop; rest high ssn; bar; playgrnd; pool high ssn; waterslide; beach & sw; fishiing; boat hire; tennis; games area; internet; TV rm; dogs free; quiet; ccard acc; red long stay. "Modern san facs; gd family site." ♦ 1 Apr-30 Sep. NOK 150 2008*

HAUKELAND see Bergen *1A3*

⊞ **HEIDAL** *1C2* (10km W Rural) *61.73005, 9.12070* **Jotunheim Feriesenter, N2676 Heidal [tel 61 23 49 50; post@jotunheimenferiesenter.no; www.jotunheimenferiesenter.no]** Fr Rv51 turn E at Randsverk onto rd 267. Site on R in approx 2km. Med, pt sl, pt shd; htd wc; chem disp; baby facs; shwrs NOK10; el pnts (12A) NOK45; Indtte (inc dryer); shop 8km; snacks; BBQ; cooking facs; playgrnd; games area; internet; TV; dogs; Eng spkn; adv bkg; quiet; ccard acc; CCI. "Beautiful surroundings & walks; friendly owners; vg site." ♦ NOK 190 2010*

HELLESYLT *1B1* (E Coastal) *62.08333, 6.87016* **Hellesylt Camping, 6218 Hellesylt (Møre og Romsdal) [tel 90 20 68 85; fax 70 26 52 10; postmottak@hellesyltturistsenter.no; www.hellesyltturistsenter.no]** Site on edge of fjord, sp fr cent of vill dir Geiranger. Sm, unshd; htd wc; chem disp; mv service pnt; shwrs NOK10; el pnts (10A) NOK30; Indtte (inc dryer); sm shop; supmkt 100m, rest adj; shgl beach; wifi; 40% statics; dogs; Eng spkn; adv bkg; quiet; no ccard acc; CCI. "Conv ferry to Geiranger; adj fjord surrounded by mountains - views; gd rest in local hotel; beautiful church nr." ♦ 15 Apr-30 Sep. NOK 140 2009*

HJERKINN *1C1* (1.5km E Rural) *62.22148, 9.57801* **Camping Hjerkinn Fjellstue, 2661 Hjerkinn (Oppland) [tel 61 21 51 00; fax 61 21 51 01; fiellstue@hjerkinn.no; www.hjerkinn.no]** At Hjerkinn on E6 turn E onto Rv29 to Folldal for 1km. Site at hotel on L. Med, terr, unshd; wc; chem disp; sauna; shwrs NOK10; el pnts (10A) inc; Indtte (inc dryer); shop 1.5km; jacuzzi; rest; snacks; bar; horseriding school adj; wifi; 30% statics; dogs; no adv bkg; quiet; ccard acc. "O'looks magnificent mountains; walks of historical interest on Old King's Rd; excel." ♦ 1 Jun-1 Oct. NOK 200 2009*

HONEFOSS *1C3* (8km NW Rural) *60.19441, 10.15145* **Elvenga Camping, Elvengveien 3, 3518 Hønefoss (Boskerud) [tel 32 14 43 70; fax 32 13 14 27; elvanga-camp@hotmail.com]** Fr Hønefoss head twds Gol on Rv7; site on R in approx 10km. Sm, pt shd; wc; chem disp; baby facs; shwrs NOK10; el pnts NOK30; Indtte (inc dryer); shop; snacks; bar; playgrnd; TV; Eng spkn; some traff noise; CCI. ♦ 1 May-15 Sep. NOK 150 2009*

NORWAY

NORWAY

HONNINGSVAG *2H1* (7km N Coastal) *71.02625, 25.89091* **Nordkapp Camping, 9751 Honningsvåg (Finnmark) [tel 78 47 33 77; fax 78 47 11 77; post@nordkappcamping.no; www.nordkappcamping.no]** En rte Nordkapp on E69, site clearly sp. Sm, unshd; htd wc; chem disp; shwrs NOK5; el pnts (16A) NOK35; Indtte; shop & 10km; snacks; dogs NOK10; quiet; ccard acc; red CCI. "Gd." ♦ 1 May-30 Sep. NOK 180 2009*

HORTEN *1C3* (2km S Rural/Coastal) *59.39430, 10.47483* **Rørestrand Camping, Parkveien 34, 3186 Horten (Vestfold) [tel 33 07 33 40; fax 33 07 47 90]** Fr Horten foll Rv19 for 500m S to rndabt, then foll sp. Sm, sl, unshd; htd wc; chem disp; baby facs; shwrs NOK10; el pnts (10A) NOK40; Indtte (inc dryer); shop; snacks; playgrnd; games area; 90% statics; dogs; phone; poss cr; Eng spkn; quiet; ccard acc; CCI. "Conv NH en rte Oslo; facs stretched high ssn." ♦ 1 May-15 Sep. NOK 205 2010*

HOVAG see Kristiansand *1B4*

HOVIN *1C3* (N Rural) *59.80455, 9.08536* **Blefjell Camping (TE10), 3652 Hovin (Telemark) [tel 35 09 91 50; blecamp@online.no; www.blefjellcamping.no]** On NE side of Lake Tinnsjøen on Rv364 approx midway bet Kongsberg & Rjukan. Sm; wc; chem disp; mv service pnt; shwrs; el pnts NOK35; snacks; lake sw; fishing; boating; quiet. "Gd, peaceful site on lakeside; friendly welcome; Rjukan museum (heroes of Telemark) attractive drive away." 1 Jun-1 Sep. NOK 140 2008*

IFJORD *2H1* (Rural) *70.46294, 27.10636* **Nilsen Gjestgiveri & Camping, Lebesby, 9740 Ifjord (Finnmark) [tel 78 49 98 17 or 90 88 28 14 (mob); fax 78 49 98 57; halvdanhansen@hotmail.com]** Behind petrol stn at junc of Rv98 and Rv888; recep in café/petrol stn/shop. Sm, hdstg, pt shd; htd wc; sauna; shwrs NOK10; el pnts (10A) inc; snacks; wifi; 10% statics. "Remote area; basic site & facs; conv NH." 1 Jun-31 Aug. NOK 150 2009*

INNHAVET *2F2* (9km S Rural) *67.90305, 15.88076* **Tømmerneset Camping, Tømmernes, 8260 Innhavet (Nordland) [tel 75 77 29 55; fax 75 77 29 65; to.ca@online.no]** Sp on L fr E6 nr Rv835 to Steigen. Med, pt sl, pt shd; wc; chem disp; mv service pnt; sauna; shwrs NOK10; el pnts (5A) inc; Indtte (inc dryer); snacks; cooking facs; playgrnd; solarium; TV; Eng spkn; adv bkg; quiet; CCI. "Vg; rock carvings adj to site; museum of Vikings & Iron Age; canoes avail on adj lake." 1 Jun-31 Aug. NOK 170 2009*

JEVNAKER *1C3* (6km N Rural) *60.28466, 10.41349* **Sløvika Camping (OP125), 3520 Jevnaker (Oppland) [tel 61 31 55 80 or 91 35 42 73; fax 61 31 41 03]** Site on Rv240 on E side of Randsfjord bet Sløvika & Vang. Med, sl, unshd; wc; chem disp; shwrs NOK10; el pnts NOK35 (long lead poss req); Indtte; cooking facs; playgrnd; fishing; slipway for boats; 80% statics; Eng spkn; ccard acc; CCI. "Helpful owner & staff; touring pitches on lge, sl field." 1 May-15 Sep. NOK 185 2007*

JORPELAND *1A3* (3km SE Rural) *58.99925, 6.0922* **Preikestolen Camping (RO17), Jøssang, 4126 Jørpeland (Rogaland) [tel 51 74 97 25 5174 8077; fax 51 74 80 77; info@preikestolencamping.com; www.preikestolencamping.com]** Fr S exit Rv13 to Preikestolen to R, site sp. Rd narr in places, care needed. Med, mkd pitch, hdstg, unshd; wc; chem disp; mv service pnt; shwrs inc; el pnts (16A) NOK40; Indtte; shop & 10km; tradsmn; rest; snacks; bar; playgrnd; rv sw adj; games area; dogs; phone; bus to Preikestolen parking; poss cr; adv bkg; Eng spkn; quiet; red long stay; ccard acc; CCI. "Marvellous views; poss walk to Pulpit Rock but not easy: conv Stavanger by ferry; excel facs, esp shwrs; midge repellent essential." ♦ 1 May-30 Sep. NOK 250 2011*

⊞ **KARASJOK** *2H1* (1km SW Rural) *69.46963, 25.48938* **Camping Karasjok, Kautokeinoveien, 9730 Karasjok (Finnmark) [tel 78 46 61 35; fax 78 46 66 97; karasjokcamping@runbox.no]** Sp in town; fr x-rds in town & N of rv bdge take Rv92 W dir Kautokeino, site 900m on L. Sm, pt shd; htd wc; chem disp; mv service pnt 1km; shwrs NOK5; el pnts (10A) NOK40; Indtte (inc dryer); shops 1km; playgrnd; wifi; Eng spkn; adv bkg; v quiet; ccard acc; CCI. "Youth hostel & cabins on site; gd, clean site & facs; lge pitches suitable RVs & lge o'fits; sh walk to Sami park & museum." ♦ NOK 130 2010*

⊞ **KAUTOKEINO** *2G1* (1km S Rural) *68.99760, 23.03662* **Arctic Motell & Kautokeino Camping, Suomaluodda 16, 9520 Kautokeino (Finnmark) [tel 78 48 54 00; fax 78 48 75 05; samicamp@me.com; www.kauto.no]** Well sp fr Rv93. Sm, pt sl, unshd; htd wc; shwrs NOK10; el pnts NOK30; Indtte; shop; rest; 20% statics; poss cr; Eng spkn; quiet. "No chem disp; Juhls silver gallery worth visit; gd, friendly site; san facs being improved (2009)." NOK 180 2009*

KAUTOKEINO *2G1* (8km S Rural) *68.94737, 23.08892* **Kautokeino Fritidssenter & Camping, Suohpatjávri, 9520 Kautokeino (Finnmark) [tel/fax 78 48 57 33; ellivarsbeck@c2i.net]** Sp on Rv93. Sm, hdstg, unshd; htd wc; chem disp; mv service pnt; shwrs NOK10; el pnts (10A) NOK50; Indtte; shop; cooking facs; rv sw adj; Eng spkn. 30 May-30 Aug. NOK 145 2008*

⊞ **KILBOGHAMN** *2E2* (3km S Coastal) *66.50667, 13.21608* **Hilstad Camping, 8752 Kilboghamn (Nordland) [tel 75 09 71 86; fax 75 09 71 01; post@polarcamp.com; www.polarcamp.com]** N on Rv17 sp to L just bef Kilboghamn ferry. Sm, hdstg, terr, unshd; wc; chem disp; shwrs inc; el pnts (10A); Indtte; shop; tradsmn; rest; snacks; bar; playgrnd; shgl beach adj; fishing; 40% statics; phone; poss cr; Eng spkn; quiet. "Superb location on Arctic Circle; ltd san facs in high ssn; fishing/boat trips arranged." NOK 180 2009*

KINSARVIK *1B3* (10km N Rural) *60.44128, 6.77941* **Ringøy Camping (HO39), 5780 Kinsarvik (Hordaland) [tel 53 66 39 17; fax 53 66 32 05; torleivr@kinsarvik.net; www.ringoy-camping.no]** Site on Rv13 halfway bet Kinsarvik & Brimnes. Do not use 1st access if app fr Brimnes (v tight turn). Sm, sl, pt terr, unshd; wc; chem disp; mv service pnt; shwrs NOK10; el pnts (10A) NOK30 (long lead req); BBQ; cooking facs; fishing; boating; dogs; no adv bkg; quiet. "Delightful meadowland site alongside Hardanger Fjord; no recep - site yourself, owner calls bet 1900 & 2100." 1 Jun-15 Sep. NOK 120 2009*

⊞ **KINSARVIK** *1B3* (500m SW Rural/Coastal) *60.37426, 6.71866* **Kinsarvik Camping, 5780 Kinsarvik (Hordaland) [tel 53 66 32 90; evald@kinsarvikcamping.no; www.kinsarvikcamping.no]** Fr SW edge of vill on rv. At Esso g'ge foll sp uphill fr cent of Kinsarvik. Sm, pt shd; wc; chem disp, mv service pnt at Esso g'ge; baby facs; fam bthrm; shwrs NOK10; el pnts (10A) NOK30 (poss no earth); Indtte; sm shop 400m; snacks; cooking facs; playgrnd; fishing; TV; 80% statics; bus 400m; quiet; CCI. "Wonderful views over Hardanger Fjord." NOK 180 2008*

KINSARVIK *1B3* (6km SW Coastal) *60.33586, 6.65823* **Camping Lofthus, 5781 Lofthus (Hordaland) [tel 53 66 13 64; fax 53 66 15 00; post@lofthuscamping.com; www.lofthuscamping.com]** Drive SW on Rv13, turn L onto narr country rd, site on R, sp fr Rv13. Narr app with passing places. Med, pt sl, pt shd; wc; sauna; shwrs NOK10; el pnts (10A) NOK35; Indtte; shop; rest 800m; playgrnd; pool adj in sports cent; TV; 25% statics; poss cr; no adv bkg; quiet; ccard acc; red CCI. "Excel, o'looking fjord & glaciers; gd walking; gd san facs; pick your own cherries; conv for ferries; v muddy & diff after rain." ♦ 1 May-30 Sep. NOK 190 2008*

KIRKENES *2H1* (7km S Rural) *69.69911, 29.95000* **Kirkenes Camping, Maggadalen, Ekveien 19, 9912 Hesseng (Finnmark) [tel 78 99 80 28; fax 78 99 23 03; eiri-ols@online.no]** Sp W of Hesseng on E6. Sm, hdstg, pt sl, pt shd; htd wc; chem disp; mv service pnt; shwrs NOK10; el pnts (10A) inc; Indtte (inc dryer); playgrnd; fishing; hiking; TV; some cabins; dogs; Eng spkn; CCI. "Conv for Kirkenes & Russian border; helpful staff; gd site." 1 Jun-1 Sep. NOK 190 2010*

⊞ **KOLVEREID** *2E3* (2km S Coastal) *64.82530, 11.58628* **Kvisterø Kystcamping, 7970 Kolvereid (Nord-Trøndelag) [tel 74 39 67 37; info@kvisteroe.com; www.kvisteroe.com]** Fr Rv17 just N of Foldereid take Rv770 S to Kolvereid. After Kolvereid foll sp ferries (Geisnes/Lund), site sp 1km fr ferries & Hoflesja. Sm, some mkd pitch, some hdstg, unshd; htd wc; chem disp; shwrs inc; el pnts (16A) NOK40; Indtte; shop 1km; snacks; cooking facs; playgrnd; shgl beach adj; fishing; boat hire; games rm; wifi; 40% statics; dogs; phone; Eng spkn; adv bkg; quiet; ccard acc; CCI. "Vg site; beautiful views." ♦ NOK 150 2009*

⊞ **KONGSBERG** *1C3* (6km N Rural) *59.71683, 9.61133* **Pikerfoss Camping, Svendsplassveien 2, 3614 Kongsberg (Buskerud) [tel 32 72 49 78 or 91 19 07 41; mail@pikerfoss.no; www.pikerfoss.no]** Fr E134 in Kongsberg turn N bef x-ring rv & go N bet rv (on L) & rlwy line (on R) on Bærvergrendveien. Site on R just after x-ing rlwy line. Sm, mkd pitch, pt shd; htd wc; chem disp; shwrs inc; el pnts (10A) NOK30; Indtte; shop, rest, snacks, bar 6km; playgrnd; 10% statics; Eng spkn; quiet. "Modern, clean facs; lge pitches; excel." NOK 140 2008*

KONGSVINGER *1D3* (8km SE Rural) *60.11786, 12.05208* **Sigernessjøen Familiecamping, Strenelsrud Gård, Arko-Vegen, 2210 Granli (Hedmark) [tel 62 82 72 05; fax 62 82 72 04; post@golfcamping.no; www.golfcamping.no]** On N side of Rv2 Kongsvinger to Swedish border, well sp. Med, pt sl, pt shd; htd wc; chem disp; baby facs; shwrs inc; el pnts (10A) NOK40; Indtte (inc dryer); playgrnd; lake sw adj; golf adj; wifi; 30% statics; Eng spkn; quiet. "Gd." 1 May-30 Sep. NOK 250 2010*

⊞ **KONGSVINGER** *1D3* (11km S Rural) *60.10063, 12.05961* **Sjøstrand Camping, Børslungvegen, 2210 Granli (Hedmark) [tel 62 82 71 59]** On Rv2, fr Kongsvinger, well sp adj Lake Sigernessjøen. Sm, pt sl, pt shd; wc; chem disp; baby facs; shwrs; el pnts (10A); Indtte; shop; playgrnd; lake sw adj; TV; Eng spkn; quiet. 2008*

KOPPANG *1D2* (1.5km W Rural) *61.57163, 11.01745* **Camping Koppang, 2480 Koppang (Hedmark) [tel 62 46 02 34; fax 62 46 12 34; info@koppangcamping.no; www.koppangcamping.no]** Fr Rv3, 25km S of Atna, turn onto Rv30; site on L soon after Shell stn & immed bef rv bdge. Med, pt sl, pt shd; wc; chem disp; baby facs; shwrs NOK10; el pnts (16A) NOK25; gas; Indtte (inc dryer); shop; snacks; rest 100m; cooking facs; playgrnd; fishing; wifi; TV; some cabins; dogs; Eng spkn; adv bkg; quiet; no ccard acc. ♦ 1 May-30 Sep. NOK 175 2010*

KORGEN *2F2* (16km N Rural) *66.15166, 13.83923* **Bjerka Camping, Nergårdsgaten 27, 8643 Bjerka (Nordland) [tel 75 19 05 47; fax 75 19 31 90; post@bjerkacamping.no; www.bjerkacamping.no]** On E6 32km S of Mo-i-Rana on E6. Ignore dirs over bdge - site on R just bef rv bdge. Med, pt shd; wc; chem disp; mv service pnt at filling stn, 2km; baby facs; shwrs NOK10; el pnts (16A) NOK25; Indtte; shop 500m; rest 500m; snacks; playgrnd; lake sw; fishing; boating; cycle hire; disco; TV; 50% statics; dogs; phone; poss cr; adv bkg; quiet; ccard acc. "Pleasant owner; site office open 1700-2100, if arr early, site yourself; ground poss boggy." 1 Jun-1 Sep. NOK 150 2008*

KORGEN *2F2* (1km NE Rural) *66.07453, 13.83851* **Korgen Camping (NO78), Korgsjøen 5, 8646 Korgen (Nordland) [tel 75 19 11 36; fax 75 19 12 26; post@korgen-camping.no; www.korgen-camping.no]** Exit E6 at Korgen church, sp. Med, pt sl, pt shd; wc; chem disp; shwrs NOK5; el pnts (10A) NOK30; Indtte; shop 1km; rest, snacks 1.5km; playgrnd; cycle hire; TV; 20% statics; dogs; phone; no adv bkg; quiet. "Mountain views." ♦ 1 Jun-10 Sep. NOK 160 2008*

NORWAY

⊞ **KRISTIANSAND** *1B4* (12km NE Coastal) *58.19011, 8.08283* **Hamresanden Camping, Hamresandveien 3, 4656 Hamresanden (Vest-Agder) [tel 38 04 72 22; fax 38 04 71 44; info@hamresanden.com; www.hamresanden.com]** Fr E18 foll sp Kjevik airport then Hamresanden & site. Lge, pt shd; htd wc; chem disp; fam bthrm; shwrs NOK15; el pnts (10A) inc; Indtte; rest; snacks; bar; cooking facs; playgrnd; htd pool; waterslides; sand beach & sw adj; watersports; tennis; boat & cycle hire; games area; TV; 10% statics; dogs; bus; poss cr; Eng spkn; noise fr airport; ccard acc. ♦ NOK 275 2010*

KRISTIANSAND *1B4* (2km E Coastal) *58.14701, 8.0303* **Camping Roligheden, Framnesveien, 4632 Kristiansand (Vest-Agder) [tel 38 09 67 22; fax 38 09 11 17; roligheden@roligheden.no; www.roligheden.no]** Sp fr E18 on N side of town. Lge, pt sl, pt shd; wc; chem disp; mv service pnt; shwrs NOK40; el pnts (25A) NOK40; Indtte; supmkt 400m; rest adj; playgrnd; sand beach adj; 5% statics; bus; poss cr; Eng spkn; quiet; ccard acc; red CCI. "Conv for ferry & exploring Kristiansand & district; 40 min walk to town; poss itinerants; site becoming run down; NH/sh stay only." 31 May-1 Sep. NOK 260 2011*

⊞ **KRISTIANSAND** *1B4* (12km E Rural) *58.12187, 8.06568* **Kristiansand Feriesenter, Dvergsnesveien 571, 4639 Kristiansand (Vest-Agder) [tel 38 04 19 80; fax 38 04 19 81; post@kristiansandferiesenter.no; www.dvergsnestangen.no]** Turn S off E18 6km E of Kristiansand after Varoddbrua onto Rv401, cont for 5.5km foll sps to site. Rd narr last 3km. Lge, mkd pitch, sl, shd; htd wc; chem disp; mv service pnt; baby facs; shwrs NOK10; el pnts (16A) inc; Indtte; shop; snacks; cooking facs; playgrnd; sw in fjord but rocky; fishing; boat hire; TV; phone; poss cr; quiet; ccard acc; CCI. "Gd NH; conv for ferry; beautiful location; helpful, friendly staff." ♦ NOK 370 2010*

⊞ **KRISTIANSAND** *1B4* (16km E Coastal) *58.12551, 8.2310* **Skottevik Feriesenter (AA1), Hæstadsvingen, 4770 Høvåg (Aust-Agder) [tel 37 26 90 30; fax 37 26 90 33; post@skottevik.no; www.skottevik.no]** Fr Kristiansand, take E18 E, turn onto Rv401 twd Høvåg; site sp. Lge, pt shd; wc; chem disp; mv service pnt; private bathrms avail; shwrs NOK10; el pnts (10A) NOK45; gas; Indtte; shop; snacks & bar high ssn; rest 3km; playgrnd; htd pool; paddling pool; beach; 9-hole golf course; wifi; entmnt; poss cr; Eng spkn; adv bkg; quiet; ccard acc; CCI. "Beautiful area." ♦ NOK 205 2011*

⊞ **KRISTIANSUND** *1B1* (4km N Rural) *63.12543, 7.74106* **Atlanten Motel & Camping, Dalaveien 22, 6501 Kristiansund (Møre og Romsdal) [tel 71 67 11 04; fax 71 67 24 05; resepsjonen@atlanten.no; www.atlanten.no]** Fr Atlantic Rd (Atlanterhavsveien) & Bremsnes-Kristiansund ferry, foll sp on leaving ferry 5km to site. Med, terr, hdstg, pt shd; htd wc; chem disp; mv service pnt; baby facs; shwrs inc; el pnts (6A) NOK40; Indtte; shops; BBQ; cooking facs; playgrnd; pool 300m; shgl beach 2km; dogs; phone; Eng spkn; adv bkg; quiet; ccard acc; CCI. "Conv Kristiansund & fjords; boat trips to Grip Is with Stave Church; site clsd 20-31 Dec." ♦ NOK 150 2010*

KROKELVDALEN see Tromsø *2F1*

KROKSTRANDA *2F2* (N Rural) *66.46868, 15.08318* **Krokstrand Camping, Saltfjellveien 1573, 8630 Krokstranda (Nordland) [tel/fax 75 16 60 74; toverakvaag@msn.com]** Nr Krokstrand bdge on E6, 18km S of Artic Circle & approx 50km N of Mo i Rana. Med, pt sl, pt shd; htd wc; chem disp; mv service pnt; baby facs; shwrs NOK5-10; el pnts (10A) NOK30; Indtte (inc dryer); shop; rest; snacks bar; cooking facs; playgrnd; fishing; 20% statics; phone; train; Eng spkn; adv bkg; ccard acc; quiet; CCI. "Conv Polar Circle Cent; gd." 1 Jun-20 Sep. NOK 180 2010*

KVAM *1C2* (6km NW Rural) *61.69133, 9.5955* **Kirketeigen Camping (OP18), Bygdahusvegen 11, 2642 Kvam (Oppland) [tel 61 21 60 90; fax 61 21 60 91; post@kirketeigen.no; www.kirketeigen.no]** On E6, sp fr both dirs. Sm, pt shd; wc; el pnts inc; Indtte; kiosk; games area; covr'd pool, tennis nrby; 80% cabins; some rlwy noise. "Conv Peer Gynt rd, war museum." 15 May-1 Sep. NOK 210 2009*

KVANNDAL see Granvin *1B2*

KVISVIKA *1B1* (8km NE Coastal) **Magnillen Camping, 6674 Kvisvika (Møre og Romsdal) [tel 71 53 25 59; jarl-mo@online.no; www.magnillen.no]** Fr W turn L off E39 approx 5km after Vettafjellet (N); thro Kvisvika & after another 9km turn L into site; sp. Sm, unshd; wc; chem disp; mv service pnt; serviced pitches; shwrs NOK10; el pnts (10A) NOK30; gas; Indtte; shop 8km; snacks; BBQ; playgrnd; lake sw & sand beach adj; boat hire; 50% statics; Eng spkn; adv bkg; quiet; ccard acc; red long stay; CCI. "Site adj sm harbour; gd views." ♦ NOK 130 2009*

KYRPING *1A3* (1.5km N Rural) *59.74395, 6.11202* **PlusCamp Kyrping, Kyrping, 5590 Etne (Hordaland) [tel 53 77 08 80; fax 53 77 08 81; post@kyrping-camping.no; www.kyrping-camping.no]** Site sp off E134 on Åkrafjord; tight ent. Med, mkd pitch, some hdstg, sl, terr, pt shd; wc; chem disp; mv service pnt; shwrs NOK10; el pnts (10A) NOK30; Indtte; shop; snacks; cooking facs; TV; sand beach; boating; 50% statics; poss cr; Eng spkn; quiet; ccard acc; CCI. "Popular with fishermen; beautiful waterside location." 1 Apr-1 Oct. NOK 120 2007*

LAERDALSOYRI *1B2* (400m NW Rural/Coastal) *61.10056, 7.47031* **Lærdal Ferie & Fritidspark, Grandavegen 5, 6886 Lærdal (Sogn og Fjordane) [tel 57 66 66 95; fax 57 66 87 81; info@laerdalferiepark.com; www.laerdalferiepark.com]** Site on N side of Lærdal off Rv5/E16 adj Sognefjord. Med, unshd; htd wc; chem disp; mv service pnt; baby facs; fam bthrm; shwrs NOK5; el pnts NOK40 (poss no earth); Indtte (inc dryer); shop; supmkt 400m; rest high ssn; snacks; bar; BBQ; cooking facs; playgrnd; shgl beach adj; boat & cycle hire; tennis; games area; games rm; golf 12km; wifi; TV rm; dogs; phone; Eng spkn; quiet; red long stay; ccard acc; red long stay/CCI. "Modern, clean, gd value site; excel san & cooking facs; lovely location adj fjord ferry terminal & nr attractive vill; gd touring base; friendly, helpful owners - will open on request outside dates shown." ♦ 1 Apr-31 Oct. NOK 180 (CChq acc) 2011*

LAKSELV *2G1* (15km N Rural) *70.17835, 24.90909* **Stabbursdalen Feriesenter, 9710 Stabbursnes (Finnmark) [tel 78 46 47 60; post@stabbursdalen.no; www.stabbursdalen.no]** N fr Lakselv on E6, site on L. Med, mkd pitch, unshd; htd wc; chem disp; shwrs inc; el pnts inc; Indtte; sm shop; tradsmn; rest; snacks; bar; BBQ; cooking facs; playgrnd; fishing; wifi; TV rm; 35% statics; dogs; bus; poss cr; Eng spkn; adv bkg; ccard acc; red long stay; CCI. "Friendly owner; vg NH to/fr Nordkapp. 1 Mar-30 Nov. NOK 180 2008*

LAKSELV *2G1* (1km NE Rural) *70.05100, 25.00860* **Solstad Camping, 9700 Lakselv (Finnmark) [tel 78 46 14 04; fax 78 46 12 14]** Fr N thro town & cont on E6, at rndabt take Rv98. Site on R in 500m. Sm, shd; wc; chem disp at Esso g'ge in town; sauna; shwrs inc; el pnts inc; Indry rm; shops 1km; cooking facs; dogs; phone; Eng spkn; quiet; ccard acc. "Poss poor/red facs low ssn; mosquitoes; last site bef Tana Bru; NH only." 30 May-30 Sep. NOK 180 2009*

LANGFJORDBOTN *2G1* (1km S Rural) *70.02781, 22.2817* **Altafjord Camping, 9545 Langfjordbotn (Finnmark) [tel/fax 78 43 28 24; post@altafjord-camping.no; www.altafjord-camping.no]** On E6, 600m S of exit to Bognelv, site adj to fjord across E6, sp. Distance by rd fr Alta 80km. Med, hdstg, terr, unshd; htd wc; serviced pitches; chem disp; sauna; shwrs NOK5; el pnts (16A); gas; Indtte; shops adj; tradsmn; cooking facs; sand & shgl beach; fjord sw & fishing; cycle hire; TV rm; 50% cabins; dogs; phone; poss cr; Eng spkn; no adv bkg; quiet; ccard acc. "Friendly owner; excel views; boat hire; mountaineering." 1 Jun-1 Sep. 2009*

LARVIK *1C4* (10km S Rural/Coastal) *58.97381, 9.96795* **Kjærstranda Familiecamping, Nalumruta, 3294 Stavern (Vestfold) [tel 33 19 57 50 or 91 77 12 01 (mob); fax 33 19 57 50; kjaerstr@online.no; www.kjarstranda.no]** Fr Larvik W on Rv303 & turn L (S) on Rv301 to Stavern; thro Stavern for approx 6km; then L to Skarabakken; 2nd site on L. Lge, unshd; wc; chem disp; mv service pnt; baby facs; shwrs NOK15; el pnts (8A) NOK45; Indtte (inc dryer); shop 6km; snacks; playgrnd; beach adj; TV; 75% statics; dogs; Eng spkn; CCI. "Fair sh stay/NH." 1 May-1 Sep. NOK 215 2009*

LARVIK *1C4* (10km S Coastal) **Trane Camping, Hummerbakken, 3294 Stavern (Vestfold)** Exit E18 onto Rv303 (Larvik); foll Rv302 (sp Helgeroa); in 13km, turn L onto Rv301 (sp Stavern); in 2km, R nr church (Hummerbakken); site on R in 2km. Sm, unshd; wc; chem disp; shwrs; el pnts (10A); Indtte; playgrnd; 30% statics; phone; Eng spkn; CCI. "Site yourself if recep clsd." ♦ Jun-Sep. 2009*

⊞ **LILLEHAMMER** *1C2* (2km S Urban) *61.10275, 10.46278* **Camping Lillehammer, Dampsagveien 47, 2609 Lillehammer (Oppland) [tel 61 25 33 33; fax 61 25 33 65; resepsjon@lillehammer-camping.no; www.lillehammer-camping.no]** Exit E6 at Lillehammer Sentrum. Turn 1st R at 1st rndabt, foll rd around Strandtorget shopping cent, cont approx 1.5km along lakeside rd. Med, mkd pitch, some hdstg, unshd; wc; chem disp; mv service pnt; baby facs; shwrs NOK10; el pnts (10A) inc (check earth); gas; Indtte Inc dryer); shop 2km; playgrnd; pool 2km; internet; TV rm; statics; dogs; phone; poss cr; Eng spkn; adv bkg; quiet; ccard acc; red CCI. "Excel san facs, site adj Lake Mjøsa; gd views, conv town & skiing areas; site adj to c'van cent, spare parts etc; excel." ♦ NOK 240 2009*

LILLESAND *1B4* (1km E Rural) *58.2560, 8.3896* **Tingsaker Familiecamping, Øvre Tingsaker, 4790 Lillesand (Aust-Agder) [tel 37 27 04 21; fax 37 27 01 47; post@tingsakercamping.no; www.tingsakercamping.no]** E18 take 1st R at Texaco petrol stn past turn for Lillesand. Med, pt sl, unshd; htd wc; chem disp; shwrs NOK10; el pnts (10A) NOK35; Indtte; shop; snacks; playgrnd; sand beach; boating; cycle hire; TV; poss cr; adv bkg; quiet; ccard acc. "Gd situation, friendly owner; rather cramped." ♦ 1 May-31 Aug. NOK 255 2010*

⊞ **LOEN** *1B2* (5km SE Rural) *61.8519, 6.91196* **Pluscamp Sande Camping, 6789 Loen (Sogn og Fjordane) [tel 57 87 45 90; fax 57 87 45 91; post@sande-camping.no; www.sande-camping.no]** Turn inland at Alexander Hotel off rd 60 for Lodalen. Site on R at lakeside after 4.5km. Narr rd with passing places. Med, terr, unshd; wc; chem disp; mv service pnt; sauna; shwrs NOK10; el pnts (16A) NOK30; Indtte; shop; rest; snacks; playgrnd; lake sw; fishing; boating; cycle hire; wifi; 50% statics; quiet; ccard acc. "Beautiful scenery; gd facs; v helpful owner; steep access tracks; easy cycling along lake; many excel walks inc guided glacier walks." ♦ NOK 150 2007*

LOEN *1B2* (1km SW Rural) *61.86558, 6.83303* **Lo-Vik Camping, 6878 Loen (Sogn og Fjordane) [tel 57 87 76 19; fax 57 87 78 11; lo-vik@c2i.net; www.lo-vik.no]** On lake side of Rv60. Med, unshd; htd wc; chem disp; shwrs NOK5; el pnts (10-16A) NOK35; Indtte; shop & 300m; tradsmn; rest adj; snacks; playgrnd; pool in hotel opp; sw adj; TV rm; 50% statics; dogs; poss cr; Eng spkn; adv bkg; some rd noise; red long stay; CCI. "Beautiful views; field adj to fjord exclusively for tourers." ♦ 20 May-15 Sep. NOK 160 2009*

LOFOTEN AND VESTERALEN ISLANDS *2F2* **There are a number of sites on the Lofoten Islands reached by ferries fr Bodø & Skutvik. The Vesteralen Islands can be reached by road (E10) west of Narvik. Campsites in towns in the Lofoten and Vesteralen Islands are listed together at the end of the Norwegian site entry pages.**

LOM *1C2* (300m E Rural) *61.83846, 8.5709* **Camping Nordalturistsenter, 2686 Lom (Oppland) [tel 61 21 93 00; fax 61 21 93 01; booking@nordalturistsenter.no; www.nordalturistsenter.no]** In cent Lom at x-rds R of Rv15. Ent by rndabt bet Esso stn & recep. Site at foot of Sognefjell Pass. Med, pt shd; htd wc; chem disp; mv service pnt; baby facs; fam bthrm; sauna; shwrs NOK10; el pnts (10A) (no earth); Indtte; shop adj; rest; snacks adj; bar; cooking facs; playgrnd; TV rm; some cabins; dogs; Eng spkn; adv bkg; ccard acc; CCI. "Split level site; bottom level quiet; top level adj to recep - often noisy due to rd noise & w/end coach parties; gd, modern san facs; mosquitoes troublesome in hot weather; busy tourist area." 1 May-30 Oct. 2009*

LOM *1C2* (19km SW Rural) *61.72099, 8.34857* **Bøverdalen Vandrerhjem & Galdesand Camping, 2687 Bøverdalen (Oppland) [tel/fax 61 21 20 64]** On Rv55 S of junc with Rv15. Site sp in vill just bef Co-op shop. Sm, pt shd, unshd; wc; shwrs; chem disp; el pnts; Indtte; rest; Eng spkn; quiet. "Immac site." 21 May-?. NOK 120 2009*

NORWAY

NORWAY

LOM *1C2* (7.5km NW Rural) *61.8700, 8.45295* **Gjeilo Camping, 2690 Skjåk (Oppland) [tel 61 21 30 32; s.gjeilo@online.no]** Site on R of Rv15 fr Lom, sp. Med, pt sl, pt shd; htd wc; chem disp; shwrs NOK5; el pnts (10A) NOK25; Indtte (inc dryer); shop 3.5km; snacks; cooking facs; playgrnd; lake sw & sand beach adj; kayak hire; 20% cabins; phone; Eng spkn; adv bkg; quiet; CCI. "Undulating site on lake; gd." 1 Jun-1 Sep. NOK 120 2010*

LOM *1C2* (12km NW Rural) **Storøya Camping, Rv15, 2690 Skjåk (Oppland) [tel 61 21 43 51; post@storoyacamping.com; www.storoyacamping.com]** Site clearly sp N of Rv15. Sm, pt shd; htd wc; shwrs; el pnts (10A); some statics; quiet. "Friendly, little site with basic facs." 15 May-15 Sep. 2008*

LUSTER see Skjolden *1B2*

LYSEBOTN *1A4* (1km E Rural) *59.05489, 6.64919* **Lysebotn Tourist Camp, 4127 Lysebotn (Vest-Agder) [tel 90 03 70 36; mail@lysebotn-touristcamp.com; www.lysebotn-touristcamp.com]** Site sp 100m E of ferry terminal. Do not attempt with c'van - m'vans only (many hairpin bends inc 1 in tunnel). Sm, unshd; htd wc; shwrs NOK10; el pnts (6A) NOK38; Indtte; tradsmn; rest; snacks; bar; playgrnd; shgle beach adj; Eng spkn; quiet; CCI. "Beautiful location at head of Lyse Fjord; ferry to Stavanger; san facs stretched high ssn; fair NH." 18 May-1 Oct. NOK 207 2008*

MAJAVATN *2E3* (500m S Rural) *65.16238, 13.3659* **Majavatn Camping, 8683 Majavatn (Nordland) [tel 47 28 94 69; marianne@majavatncamping.no; www.majavatncamping.no]** S on E6 fr Trofors for approx 45km, site on R on lakeside. Sm, pt sl, pt shd; htd wc; fam bthrm; shwrs NOK15; el pnts (10A) NOK20; Indry rm; BBQ; cooking facs; lake sw; fishing; boating; Eng spkn; rd & rlwy noise. "Rlwy stn nr; few touring pitches - rec arr early." ♦ 1 Jun-31 Aug. NOK 100 2009*

MALMEFJORDEN see Molde *1B1*

MALVIK *1D1* (2.5km E Rural) *63.43243, 10.70778* **Storsand Gård Camping (ST68), 7563 Malvik (Sør-Trøndelag) [tel 73 97 63 60; fax 73 97 73 46; post@storsandcamping.no; www.storsandcamping.no]** On N side of E6 N, site sp. Rec use E6 toll rd fr S, 2nd exit after tunnel. Many lge speed humps on local rd Rv950, care needed. Lge, unshd; wc; chem disp; shwrs NOK10; el pnts (10A) NOK35; Indtte; shop; cooking facs; rest in hotel adj; playgrnd; shgl beach; fishing; games area; TV; some statics; phone; poss cr; rlwy noise. ♦ 1 May-1 Sep. NOK 260 2011*

⊞ **MALVIK** *1D1* (1.5km W Coastal) *63.44064, 10.63978* **Vikhammer Camping, Vikhammerløkka 4, 7560 Vikhammer [tel 73 97 61 64; vikcampi@online.no; www.vikhammer.no]** E fr Trondheim on E6. Immed bef toll plaza take ramp sp Vikhammer/Ransheim & turn R, then foll sp Vikhammer. After approx 6km at traff lts cont strt on Rv950 to rndabt & take 3rd exit sp motel & site. Fr N exit E6 after airport sp Hell, then Malvik/Hommelvik. Then take Rv950 to site. NB Many lge speed humps on Rv950, care req. Sm, terr, unshd; htd wc; chem disp; mv service pnt; shwrs inc; el pnts (16A) NOK30; shop 1km; tradsmn; rest; bar; BBQ; wifi; some statics; dogs; phone; bus adj; Eng spkn; adv bkg; rd & rlwy noise; ccard acc; CCI. ♦ NOK 210 2009*

MANDAL *1B4* (2.5km N Rural) *58.04213, 7.49436* **Sandnes Camping, Holumsveien 133, 4516 Mandal (Vest-Agder) [tel 38 26 51 51; sandnescamping@online.no; www.sandnescamping.com]** On E39 Kristiansand to Stavanger. Turn N onto Rv455, site on R 1.4km. Sm, some hdstg, pt shd; htd wc; chem disp; mv service pnt; baby facs; shwrs NOK5; el pnts (16A) NOK40 (poss rev pol); Indtte; shop, rest, snacks, bar in Mandal; cooking facs; BBQ; sand beach 2.5km; rv sw & beach nr; fishing; boating; 5% statics; dogs; phone; Eng spkn; adv bkg; quiet; CCI. "Excel, well-kept site; friendly, helpful owners; superb scenery; nature trails thro adj pine forest; Mandal pretty town with longest sandy beach in Norway, conv Kristiansand ferry & Lindesnes, Norway's most S point." ♦ 15 May-1 Sep. NOK 160 2010*

MANDALEN/VOLL *1B1* (W Rural/Coastal) *62.53655, 7.43870* **Måna Camping, Voll, 6386 Måndalen (Møre og Romsdal) [tel 71 22 34 35; ifarkvam@online.no; www.manacamping.no]** W fr Åndalnes on E136, site sp by side of fjord. Med, unshd; wc; chem disp; shwrs NOK10; el pnts (10A) NOK30; Indtte; shop 300m; cooking facs; shgl beach adj; 40% statics; dogs free; poss cr; Eng spkn; some rd noise; CCI. "Superb location." 1 Apr-1 Oct. NOK 160 2008*

MAURANGER see Odda *1A3*

⊞ **MAURVANGEN** *1C2* (Rural) *61.48838, 8.84176* **Maurvangen Hyttegrend Camping, Besseggen Fjellpark, 2880 Maurvangen (Oppland) [tel 61 23 89 22; fax 61 23 89 58; post@maurvangen.no; www.maurvangen.no]** At rv bdge turn off Rv51. Foll sp. Med, pt hdstg, pt sl, pt shd; wc; mv service pnt; chem disp; baby facs; fam bthrm; shwrs NOK15; el pnts (10A) inc; Indtte; shop; rest; snacks; BBQ; cooking facs; playgrnd; lake sw 5km; fishing; cycling; TV; phone; Eng spkn; adv bkg; quiet; CCI. "White water rafting; gd views; rd 51 poss clsd Nov to mid-May; gd hill-walking cent." ♦ NOK 170 2008*

MELHUS *1C1* (7km NW Coastal) *63.32713, 10.21947* **Øysand Camping (ST38), Øysandan, 7224 Melhus (Sør-Trøndelag) [tel 72 87 24 15 or 92 08 71 74 (mob); fax 72 85 22 81; post@oysandcamping.no; www.oysandcamping.no]** Fr Melhus, N on E6; then L (W) onto E39; site sp. Med, mkd pitch, unshd; wc; chem disp (wc); shwrs NOK15; el pnts (10A) NOK50; Indtte; shop; tradsmn; rest; snacks; bar; BBQ; cooking facs; playgrnd; lake sw, fishing, boating & beach adj; games area; statics; dogs; phone; poss cr; Eng spkn; noise fr daytrippers; ccard acc; red long stay; CCI. "Fair site with gd views." ♦ 1 May-1 Sep. NOK 170 2008*

MEVIK see Ornes *2E2*

MO I RANA *2F2* (16km SW Rural) *66.23307, 13.89178* **Yttervik Camping, Sørlandsveien 874, 8617 Dalsgrenda (Nordland) [tel 75 16 45 65 or 90 98 73 55 (mob); fax 75 16 92 57; ranjas@online.no; www.yttervikcamping.no]** Sp S of Mo i Rana, on W side of E6, cross sm bdge over rlwy - diff for long o'fits. Sm, mkd pitch, hdstg, unshd; htd wc; chem disp; shwrs NOK5; el pnts (16A) NOK40 (no earth); Indtte; sm shop; rest; playgrnd; fishing; 50% statics; dogs; poss cr; Eng spkn; adv bkg; quiet; ccard acc; CCI. "Pleasant location on edge fjord; friendly owners; clean, well-run site." 1 Jun-15 Sep. NOK 180 2010*

⊞ **MOELV** *1C2* (1km SW Rural) *60.91591, 10.70022* **Steinvik Camping (HE16), Kastbakkveien, 2390 Moelv (Hedmark) [tel 62 36 72 28; fax 62 36 81 67; www.steinvik-camping.net]** Exit E6 Oslo-Lillehammer rd 1km S of Moelv at sp. Site in 400m on dirt track on edge of Lake Mjøsa. Med, pt shd; htd wc; chem disp; mv service pnt; baby facs; shwrs NOK15; el pnts (10-16A) NOK20; Indtte; shop; snacks; cooking facs; playgrnd; sand beach; watersports; fishing; solarium; 90% statics; dogs; quiet; ccard acc; CCI. "Gd family site; no obvious place to dispose of grey water." ♦ NOK 200 2008*

⊞ **MOLDE** *1B1* (3.5km E Rural) *62.74258, 7.2333* **Camping Kviltorp, Fannestrandveien 136, 6400 Molde (Møre og Romsdal) [tel 71 21 17 42; fax 71 21 10 19; kviltorp.camping@molde.online.no; www.kviltorpcamping.no]** On app fr S, Rv64 (toll) turn L onto E39/Rv62, site on L, sp. Nr airport. Med, pt sl, pt shd; htd wc; baby facs; shwrs NOK10; el pnts (10A) NOK30; gas; Indtte; shop & adj; rest; snacks; playgrnd; pool 3km; fjord sw adj; fishing; boating; solarium; TV; phone; Eng spkn; aircraft & rd noise; ccard acc; CCI. "Conv Molde; adj Romsdal Fjord (some pitches avail on fjord-side); wonderful mountain views; excel, clean facs; poor security - site open to rd on 1 side; helpful owners." ♦ NOK 140 2007*

MOLDE *1B1* (8.5km S Coastal) *62.81468, 7.22528* **Bjølstad Camping, 6445 Malmefjorden [tel 71 26 56 56 or 47 23 79 62 (mob); post@bjolstad.no; www.bjolstad.no]** E fr Molde on E39 turn L by airport & foll Rv 64 N. Turn L sp Lindset, site on L in 1km. Sm, pt sl, pt shd; wc; chem disp; mv service pnt; shwrs NOK10; el pnts (10A) NOK30; shop 1km; BBQ; cooking facs; playgrnd; shgl beach adj; boat hire; dogs; Eng spkn; quiet. "Vg site on fjord edge; views." 1 Jun-30 Sep. NOK 170 2009*

MORGEDAL *1B3* (Rural) *59.47478, 8.42138* **Morgedal Camping, 3848 Morgedal (Telemark) [tel 35 05 41 52; morgedalcamping@kviteseid.online.no; www.morgedalcamping.no]** W of Seljord, adj E134, sp. Med, pt shd; wc; chem disp; shwrs NOK10; el pnts (16A) NOK30; Indtte (inc dryer); shop 500m; BBQ; cooking facs; lake sw & fishing; boating; 5% statics; dogs; Eng spkn; quiet; CCI. "Vg site; conv Heddal stave church; on site lgest wooden bowl in world!" 14 May-15 Sep. NOK 150 2009*

⊞ **MOSJOEN** *2E3* (1km S Rural) *65.83453, 13.21971* **Mosjøen Camping & Hotel, Kippermoen, 8651 Mosjøen (Nordland) [tel 75 17 79 00; post@mosjoenhotell.no; www.mosjoencamping.no]** E6 by-passes town, well sp on W side of E6 by rndabt. Fr S only mkd by flag 500m bef rndabt at start Mosjøen bypass. Med, terr, pt shd; htd wc; chem disp (wc); mv service pnt; shwrs inc; baby facs; el pnts (10A) NOK30; Indtte; shop 1km; rest; snacks; bar; playgrnd; pool; bowling alley; entmnt; TV; dogs; phone; poss cr; Eng spkn; adv bkg; rd noise; ccard acc; CCI. "Clean, v basic san facs." ♦ NOK 200 2010*

⊞ **NAMSOS** *2E3* (4km E Rural) *64.47393, 11.57796* **Namsos Camping, 7800 Namsos (Nord-Trøndelag) [tel 74 27 53 44; fax 74 27 53 93; namsos@pluscamp.no; www.pluscamp.no]** Fr Namsen bdge turn E on Rv17. Site on R in 1.5km beside airfield & lake. Sm, hdstg, pt shd; htd wc; chem disp; mv service pnt; fam bthrm; shwrs NOK5; el pnts (16A) NOK35; Indtte; shop; snacks; playgrnd; boating; TV; 60% statics; phone; no dogs; Eng spkn; quiet; ccard acc; CCI. "Well-equipped site." ♦ NOK 215 2009*

NAMSSKOGAN *2E3* (15km N Rural) *65.03986, 13.2861* **Camping Mellingsmo, 7890 Namsskogan (Nord-Trøndelag) [tel 74 33 46 65; fax 74 33 36 65]** E of E6, N of Bjørnstad. Sm, pt shd; wc; shwrs; el pnts (10A) NOK20; Indtte; shop; rest 3km; cooking facs; playgrnd; fishing; 50% cabins; quiet. 1 May-30 Sep. NOK 130 2008*

⊞ **NARVIK** *2F2* (1.5km N Rural) *68.4506, 17.45851* **Camping Narvik, Rombaksveien 75, 8517 Narvik (Nordland) [tel 76 94 58 10; fax 76 94 14 20; narvikcamping@narvikcamping.com; www.narvikcamping.com]** Sp on E6, site by rd. Med, terr, unshd; wc; chem disp; baby facs; fam bthrm; sauna; shwrs NOK10; el pnts (6-10A) inc (no earth); Indtte; shop; rest; BBQ; TV; phone; poss cr; Eng spkn; adv bkg; rd/rlwy noise; ccard acc; red CCI. "Facs 'tired' & stretched high ssn (may need to share electrics) & poss unkempt; no privacy in shwrs; walk/cycle to town, 20 mins; 3-level site, chem disp 3rd level only; fair NH/sh stay only." ♦ NOK 200 2009*

NES I ADAL *1C3* (8.5km S Rural) *60.49379, 10.07103* **Sperillen Camping, Skagnes, 3524 Nes I Ådal (Buskerud) [tel/fax 32 14 32 00; sperillc@start.no; www.sperillencamp.no]** Site sp on E15, 45km N of Hønefoss. Med, mkd pitch, unshd; htd wc; chem disp; fam bthrm; shwrs inc; el pnts (10A) NOK40; Indtte; shop; cooking facs; playgrnd; lake sw & beach; 90% statics; poss cr; Eng spkn; quiet; CCS. "Lovely lakesite position; friendly owner; gd facs for children; RVs acc; if coming out of ssn, give 7 days' notice & owner will open site." ♦ 1 May-1 Oct. NOK 200 2009*

⊞ **NESBYEN** *1C3* (3.5km N Rural) *60.59881, 9.07928* **Sutøya Feriepark, Hallingdal, 3540 Nesbyen (Buskerud) [tel 32 07 13 97; fax 32 07 01 11; sutferie@online.no; www.sutoyaferiepark.no]** On E side of Rv7, sp. Lge, mkd pitch, terr, pt shd; wc; chem disp; shwrs NOK10; el pnts (10A) NOK35; Indtte (inc dryer); sm shop; rest; snacks; playgrnd; rv adj; trout-fishing; skibus; wifi; 40% statics; Eng spkn; quiet; ccard acc; red CCI. NOK 170 (4 persons) 2009*

⊞ **NESNA** *2E2* (500m N Coastal) *66.20273, 13.02278* **Nesna Feriecamp & Motell, Sjåberget 3, 8700 Nesna (Nordland) [tel 75 05 65 40; fax 75 05 66 97; nesnafer@online.no; www.arctic-circle-coast.no]** Foll rds E12 & Rv17 fr Mo i Rana to Nesna & foll site sp on ent vill. Med, pt sl, unshd; htd wc; chem disp; mv service pnt; shwrs; el pnts (10A); Indtte (inc dryer0; shop high ssn; rest, snacks 200m; cooking facs; playgrnd; pool 300m; beach; waterslide; cycle hire; games area; wifi; TV rm; quiet; ccard acc; CCI. "Lovely scenery; boat trips to islands & viewing puffins; trip to Træna a must." ♦ 2010*

NESTTUN see Bergen *1A3*

NORDFJORDEID *1A2* (8km E Rural) *61.90881, 6.11468* **Nesjartun Camping, Nes, 6770 Nordfjordeid (Sogn og Fjordane) [tel 57 86 27 32; nesjartun@c2i.net]** Fr Nordfjordeid E on E39. At Hjelle turn R onto Rv15 along S bank of lake. Site on R in 2km. Sm, terr, pt shd; wc; chem disp; mv service pnt; shwrs NOK5; el pnts (16A) NOK30; Indtte; shop; bar; playgrnd; boating; fishing; 30% statics; no dogs; Eng spkn; adv bkg; ccard acc; quiet but rd noise on lower levels; CCI. "Site up steep slope; stop at bottom to register." 1 May-1 Oct. NOK 190 2008*

NORDKAPP *2H1* **See also Skarsvåg.**

The opening dates and prices on this campsite have changed.
I'll send a site report form to the Club for the next edition of the guide.

⊞ **NORDKAPP** *2H1* (Rural/Coastal) *71.1725, 25.7822* **Nordkapphallen Carpark, 9764 Nordkapp (Finnmark) [tel 78 47 68 60; fax 78 47 68 61; nordkapphallen@rica.no; www.rica.no]** N on E69. Hdstg, pt sl, unshd; wc (0100-1100); own san; rest; bar; shop; 1 Nov-1 Apr private vehicles not permitted - buses in convoy (daily) only. "Max stay 48 hrs; no other o'night or site charges; price inc visit to Nordkapp Cent; no facs; v exposed gravel surface; excel for viewing midnight sun." NOK 235 (per person) 2010*

NORDKJOSBOTN *2G1* (200m S Rural) *69.21623, 19.5553* **Bjørnebo Camping, Sentrumsveien 10, 9040 Nordkjosbotn (Troms) [tel 77 72 81 61]** Fr junc of E6 & E8 (Tromsø) 200m S turn L twd Nordkjosbotn, site 200m on L. Sm, pt shd; htd wc; chem disp; baby facs; shwrs NOK10; el pnts (16A) NOK30; Indtte; shop adj; snacks; bar; playgrnd; TV; dogs; phone; Eng spkn; quiet. "Conv for day trip to Tromsø; friendly owners." ♦ 5 Jun-15 Aug. NOK 150 2008*

NOTODDEN *1C3* (2.5km W Rural) *59.57105, 9.19851* **Notodden Camping, Reshjemveien 46, 3670 Notodden (Telemark) [tel 35 01 33 10; fax 35 01 85 87; notcamp@notoddencamping.com; www.notoddencamping.com]** On E134 by airfield. Med, unshd; wc; baby facs; shwrs NOK10; el pnts (10A) NOK30; Indtte; shops adj; snacks; playgrnd; TV; statics; poss cr; Eng spkn; quiet but some airfield noise; red CCI. "Heddal Stave church 10 mins drive; NH only." ♦ 1 Jul-1 Sep. NOK 230 2009*

⊞ **ODDA** *1A3* (2km S Rural) *60.0533, 6.5426* **Odda Camping, Jordalsveien 29, 5750 Odda (Hordaland) [tel 41 32 16 10; fax 53 64 12 92; post@oddacamping.no; www.oddacamping.no]** Sp on Rv13; adj sports complex, nr lakeside. Med, pt shd; htd wc; mv service pnt; private san facs avail; shwrs NOK10; el pnts (16A) NOK40; Indtte (with dryer); shop 1km; rest 1km; BBQ; lake fishing; watersports; cycle hire; games area; dogs; Eng spkn; quiet. "Beautiful area; nr Hardanger Fjord; watersports with canoes for hire; owner owns a guesthouse where you can use free wifi & organise trips." ♦ NOK 150 (CChq acc) 2011*

ODDA *1A3* (10km W Rural) *60.11335, 6.26456* **Sundal Camping, Sunndal, 5476 Mauranger (Hordaland) [tel 53 48 41 86; fax 53 48 18 20; sundal.camping@c2i.net; www.sundalcamping.no]** W fr Odda thro Folgefonn Tunnel. Site sp. Or fr ferry at Løfallstrand, take Rv551 approx 22km NE along side of fjord dir Gjerde. Med, pt sl, terr, pt shd; wc; chem disp; mv service pnt; shwrs; el pnts (10A) NOK30; Indtte; shop; rest; snacks; bar; playgrnd; shgl beach adj; fishing; boat hire; games area; 50% statics; poss cr Jul/Aug; Eng spkn; adv bkg; CCI. "Beautiful location; fisherman's paradise; walk fr site to Bondhus Glacier & Fureberg Waterfall." ♦ 1 Apr-31 Oct. NOK 110 2009*

OLDEN *1B2* (11km S Rural) *61.75823, 6.81173* **Camping Oldevatn, Sunde, 6788 Olden (Sogn og Fjordane) [tel/fax 57 87 59 15; post@oldevatn.com; www.oldevatn.com]** Turn S off Rv60 in Olden, sp Briksdal, site on R immed after rd crosses lake. Sm, terr, unshd; htd wc; chem disp; mv service pnt; baby facs; fam bthrm; shwrs NOK10; el pnts (16A) NOK30; Indtte; tradsmn; rest 11km; snacks; bar 11km; cooking facs; playgrnd; lake sw & boating; cycle hire; TV rm; few statics; dogs free; phone; bus 50m; Eng spkn; adv bkg; quiet; red CCI. "Lovely lakeside setting; 11km fr base of glacier; well-kept, clean site & facs." ♦ 1 May-30 Sep. NOK 200 2010*

OLDEN *1B2* (12km S Rural) *61.7410, 6.7906* **Gryta Camping, Oldedalen, 6788 Olden (Sogn og Fjordane) [tel/fax 57 87 59 36; gryta@gryta.no; www.gryta.no]** Fr Olden take rd sp Briksdal Glacier, site on L bef sm bdge & Gytri Camping. Sm, terr, pt shd; htd wc; chem disp; shwrs NOK10; el pnts (10A) NOK30; Indtte; BBQ; rest, snacks 12km; shop & 2km; tradsmn; playgrnd; lake sw adj; TV; phone; poss cr; Eng spkn; adv bkg; quiet; ccard acc; red CCI. "Beside Lake Oldevatnet & close Briksdal glacier; excel site with magnificent views; immac san facs; friendly, helpful owner." ♦ 15 May-15 Oct. NOK 140 2008*

OLDEN *1B2* (13km S Rural) *61.73896, 6.78943* **Olden Camping, 6788 Olden (Sogn og Fjordane) [tel 57 87 59 34; fax 57 87 65 50; post@oldencamping.com; www.oldencamping.com]** Turn S off Rv60 in Olden sp Oldedalen & Briksdalsbreen. Site on L after Gryta Camping & sm bdge. Sm, terr, pt shd; htd wc; mv service pnt; baby facs; shwrs NOK10; el pnts (15A) NOK25; Indtte; shop 4km; tradsmn; rest 10km; snacks, bar 13km; BBQ; cooking facs; playgrnd; lake sw; boat hire; dogs free; phone; bus; Eng spkn; adv bkg; quiet; red long stay; ccard acc; red CCI. "Magnificent scenery inc glacier; free use of rowing boats; friendly, helpful owner; pitch yourself; excel facs; excel." ♦ 1 May-15 Sep. NOK 140 2007*

OLDEN *1B2* (20km S Rural) *61.66513, 6.81600* **Camping Melkevoll Bretun, Oldedalen, 6792 Briksdalsbre (Sogn og Fjordane) [tel 57 87 38 64; fax 57 87 38 90; post@melkevoll.no; www.melkevoll.no]** Take rte to Briksdal glacier to end of rd. Med, hdg pitch, terr, unshd; htd wc; chem disp; mv service pnt; baby facs; sauna; shwrs NOK10; el pnts (25A) NOK40; Indtte; shop; snacks; cooking facs; playgrnd; internet; phone; Eng spkn; quiet; ccard acc. "Walks to glacier; excel views glaciers some pitches; excel." 15 Apr-15 Oct. NOK 140 2010*

⊞ **OLDERFJORD** *2G1* (1km N Rural) *70.48121, 25.06321* **Olderfjord Hotel Russenes Camping, 9713 Russenes (Finnmark) [tel 78 46 37 11; fax 78 46 37 91; olderfj@online.no; www.olderfjord.no]** N fr Olderfjord on E69. Site on L. Med, pt sl, pt shd; wc; shwrs NOK10; el pnts NOK20; gas; lndtte; shop; rest; snacks; cooking facs; playgrnd; beach adj; fishing; boating; TV; bus 500m; Eng spkn; ccard acc; CCI. "Gd facs but untidy area & poss stretched; space ltd - rec arr early; conv N Cape tunnel." NOK 150 2009*

⊞ **OPPDAL** *1C1* (2km NE Rural) **Solly Camping, Gorsetråket, 7340 Oppdal (Sør-Trøndelag) [tel 72 42 44 16; anug@online.no]** Site sp on E6. Sm, pt shd; wc; chem disp 10km; mv service pnt; shwrs inc; el pnts (10A) inc; lndtte; shop 2km; rest, snacks, bar 2km; BBQ; sm playgrnd; htd pool 2km; games area 1km; internet; TV; dogs; bus nr; train 2km; poss cr; Eng spkn; adv bkg; quiet; CCI. "Nr Dovrefjell National Park; rv rafting nrby; gd walking & cycle paths; ski area in winter; v pleasant site." NOK 120 2009*

⊞ **OPPDAL** *1C1* (3km NE Rural) *62.61537, 9.74172* **Camping Imi Stølen, 7340 Oppdal (Sør-Trøndelag) [tel 72 42 13 70; fax 72 42 08 70; post@imi-stolen.no; www.imi-stolen.no]** N of Oppdal on E6, site sp on L. Sm, mkd pitch, terr, unshd; wc; baby facs; fam bthrm; shwrs NOK10; el pnts NOK40; lndry rm; shop; snacks; playgrnd; TV; Eng spkn; quiet. ♦ NOK 160 2009*

⊞ **OPPDAL** *1C1* (6.5km S Rural) *62.54779, 9.62911* **Granmo Camping, 7340 Oppdal (Sør-Trøndelag) [tel/fax 72 42 41 47; grancamp@online.no]** On E6 Oppdal to Dombas rd, well sp by Rv Driva. Med, unshd; htd wc; shwrs; el pnts (10A); lndtte; shop 6km; cooking facs; playgrnd; 15% statics; adv bkg; Eng spkn; quiet; CCI. "Simple site; pleasant location; friendly staff; gd hillwalking." 2009*

⊞ **OPPDAL** *1C1* (7.5km S Rural) *62.53411, 9.62536* **Smegarden Camping, Driva, 7340 Oppdal (Sør-Trøndelag) [tel 72 42 41 59; fax 72 42 42 42; smegarden@oppdal.com; www.smegarden.no]** Sp fr E6 dir Dombås on E of rd. Med, pt sl, pt shd; htd wc; chem disp; mv service pnt; baby facs; shwrs NOK10; el pnts (10A) NOK30; lndtte; kiosk; shop 200m; BBQ; playgrnd; fishing; sat TV; 80% statics; dogs; phone; Eng spkn; CCI. "Views of mountains; conv Dovrefjell National Park." ♦ NOK 150 2008*

⊞ **OPPDAL** *1C1* (10km S Rural) *62.49886, 9.58853* **Magalaupe Camping, 7340 Oppdal (Sør-Trøndelag) [tel/fax 72 42 46 84; camp@magalaupe.no; www.magalaupe.no]** On W side of E6 Dombås to Trondheim rd, sp on side of Rv Driva. Med, pt sl, unshd; htd wc; chem disp; mv service pnt; sauna; shwrs NOK10; el pnts (10-16A) NOK20; lndtte; shop; supmkt 11km; snacks; bar; cooking facs; playgrnd; fishing; cycle hire; TV rm; some statics; dogs; Eng spkn; quiet. "Sh walk to waterfalls; musk oxen safaries run by owner; excel." NOK 110 2007*

ORJE *1D3* (4km N Rural) *59.51222, 11.66138* **Sukken Camping (OF5), 1870 Ørje (Østfold) [tel 69 81 10 77; fax 69 81 18 24; sukkan@c2i.net; www.sukken-camping.no]** Fr Oslo on E18, turn L at Statoil g'ge sp Rømskog. In 4km turn R to site. Recep 400m bef site. Sm, pt sl, unshd; wc; chem disp; mv service pnt; shwrs NOK10; el pnts (10A) NOK30; lndtte; shop, rest, snack, bar 6km; cooking facs; playgrnd; 50% statics; Eng spkn; adv bkg; quiet; CCI. "Conv NH for Swedish border; gd woodland walks; ground poss boggy; ltd san facs but clean." 1 May-30 Aug. NOK 179 2007*

ORNES *2E2* (10km N Coastal) *66.94519, 13.73200* **Mevik Camping, 8145 Mevik (Nordland) [tel 75 75 61 34; fax 75 75 91 07; www.mevikcamping.com]** N fr Ørnes on Rv17, site sp in Mevik. Sm, sl, unshd; htd wc; shwrs NOK10; el pnts; shgl beach adj; Eng spkn; quiet. "V basic CL-type site in lovely location on banks of fjord; view of midnight sun; NH only." Jun-Aug. NOK 130 2008*

⊞ **OS I OSTERDALEN** *1D1* (2km NE Rural) *62.50430, 11.25938* **Røste Hyttetun & Camping, 2550 Os I Østerdalen (Sør-Trøndelag) [tel 62 49 70 55; fax 62 49 70 86; post@rostecamping.no; www.rostecamping.no]** Sp on Rv30. Sm; wc; chem disp; shwrs NOK10; el pnts NOK40; lndtte (inc dryer); cooking facs; playgrnd; fishing 150m; TV rm; some cabins; quiet. NOK 150 2010*

OS I OSTERDALEN *1D1* (8km S Rural) *62.44696, 11.11960* **Camping Hummelfjell, 2550 Håmålvoll (Hedmark) [tel 62 49 72 58]** Sp on Rv30. Sm, pt shd; wc; chem disp; baby facs; shwrs NOK10; el pnts NOK35; lndtte; cooking facs; playgrnd; TV rm; quiet. 15 May-15 Sep. NOK 150 2009*

OSEN *2E3* (W Coastal) *64.29650, 10.49858* **Osen Fjordcamping, 7740 Steinsdalen [tel 72 57 79 00 or 41 14 68 02 (mob); booking@osen-fjordcamping.no; www.osen-fjordcamping.no]** Fr Rv17 about halfway bet Namsos & Steinkjer take rd 715 W for approx 40km to sea, site sp. Med, unshd; wc; chem disp; sauna; shwrs NOK10; el pnts NOK30; shop, rest in town; tradsmn; playgrnd; beach adj; wifi; 50% statics; dogs; bus adj; Eng spkn; quiet. "Vg." ♦ 1 May-31 Aug. NOK 165 2009*

⊞ **OSLO** *1C3* (9km N Urban) *59.9623, 10.6429* **NAF Camping Bogstad, Ankerveien 117, Røa, 0757 Oslo [tel 22 51 08 00; fax 22 51 08 50; mail@bogstadcamping.no; www.bogstadcamping.no]** Fr N on E16 cont to E18 & turn E twd Oslo. After approx 7km exit & proceed N twds Røa and Bogstad. Site sp adj Oslo golf club. V lge, some mkd pitch, pt sl, pt shd; htd wc; chem disp; mv service pnt; shwrs NOK10 (swipe card fr recep); el pnts (10A) NOK50 (long lead poss req); lndtte (inc dryer); shop adj; snacks; lake nr; 25% statics; dogs; poss v cr; Eng spkn; adv bkg; bus to Oslo 100m; ccard acc; CCI. "Beautiful area with walking trails; avoid area of site with statics & many itinerant workers (behind recep), but other areas OK esp at far end with lake views; inadequate water points/waste points; modern, clean san facs; helpful staff; recep open 24 hrs; conv Oslo cent." ♦ NOK 260 (4 persons) 2010*

OSLO *1C3* (3km SE Urban) *59.8984, 10.7734* **Ekeberg Camping, Ekebergveien 65, 1181 Oslo [tel 22 19 85 68; fax 22 67 04 36; mail@ekebergcamping.no; www.ekebergcamping.no]** Fr Göteborg to Oslo on E6 leave 2km bef Oslo; sp Ekeberg, foll sp to site. Fr S on E6 just after passing thro Oslo ent toll take slip rd sp Ekeberg; camp sp about 6km, up 10% hill. V lge, sl, unshd; wc; chem disp; mv service pnt; shwrs NOK10; baby facs; ltd el pnts (6-10A) inc (long lead poss req & poss rev pol); gas; Indtte (inc dryer); shop; supmkt 1km; tradsmn; rest 200m; snacks; bar; playgrnd; dogs; internet; bus/tram to city - tickets fr site recep; poss cr; Eng spkn; no adv bkg; ccard acc; CCI. "Insufficient el pnts & leads running across roads; area without hook-ups flatter & quieter; use san facs block taps for fresh water; easy access to Oslo cent & places of interest; avoid site during annual children's football tournament end Jul/beg August - queues for pitches & facs v stretched; poss itinerant workers on site; recep open 0730-2300; helpful staff." ♦ 1 Jun-1 Sep. NOK 310 (4 persons) 2010*

OSLO *1C3* (8km S Rural/Coastal) *59.8350, 10.7817* **Oslo Fjordcamping, Ljanbruksveien 1, 1250 Oslo [tel 22 75 20 55; fjordcamping@yahoo.no; www.oslofjordcamping.no]** S on E18 to exit for Rv155 & sp Fjordcamping, site in 100m. Sm, pt sl, pt shd; wc; chem disp; mv service pnt; shwrs inc; el pnts inc (check earth & long lead poss req); Indtte; shop; snacks; BBQ; playgrnd; sand/shgl beach 300m; 20% statics; dogs; phone; bus adj; poss cr; Eng spkn; little rd noise; ccard acc; CCI. "V easy access by bus to Oslo; gd site but poss run down low ssn & poss itinerants; run down, basic san facs; site muddy in wet; NH only." 1 May-30 Sep. NOK 290 (4 persons) 2009*

OSLO *1C3* (3km W Urban) *59.91866, 10.67500* **Sjølyst Marina Campervan Parking, Drammensveien 160, Sjølyst Båtopplag, 0273 Oslo [tel/fax 22 50 91 93; post@bobilparkering.no; www.bobilparkering.no]** Fr E exit E18 at junc after Bygdøy (museums) junc. At rndabt take last exit, go under E18 & into site. Fr W leave E18 at Sjølyst junc, at bottom of slip rd turn R into site. Sm, hdstg, unshd; own san rec; chem disp; mv service pnt; shwrs NOK10; el pnts inc; snacks; BBQ; dogs; bus adj; clsd 2300-0700; Eng spkn; quiet. "Gd, basic site, pt of marina; m'vans only - pay at machine; san facs clsd o'night; 30 min walk city cent." ♦ 1 Jun-15 Sep. NOK 150 2011*

OTTA *1C2* (1.5km W Rural) *61.77223, 9.50653* **Otta Camping & Motell, Ottadalen 580, 2670 Otta (Oppland) [tel 61 23 03 09; fax 61 23 38 19; post@ottacamping.no; www.ottacamping.no]** Exit E6 twd Vagamo, 2km; turn L over 2 bdges, then R down track by rv. Med, pt shd; htd wc; chem disp; baby facs; shwrs NOK5; el pnts (10A) NOK30; Indtte; shop; rest 1km; playgrnd; cycle hire; sw; TV; dogs; phone; Eng spkn; adv bkg; rd & rv noise; red low ssn; ccard acc. "Conv for local sightseeing; lovely site; gd facs; gd views of rv." ♦ 1 May-15 Oct. NOK 140 2009*

OVERHALLA see Skogmo *2E3*

OVRE EIDFJORD see Eidfjord *1B3*

⊞ **OYER** *1C2* (6km N Rural) *61.27993, 10.35985* **Rustberg Camping, 2636 Øyer (Oppland) [tel 61 27 81 84; fax 61 27 87 05; rustberg@pluscamp.no; www.pluscamp.no/rustberg]** On E side of E6, sp. Med, terr, pt shd; wc; chem disp; mv service pnt; sauna; shwrs NOK10; el pnts (10A) NOK20; Indtte; shop; rest 6km; playgrnd; htd pool; paddling pool; waterslide; lake sw; fishing; boat hire; TV rm; some cabins; poss cr; adv bkg; quiet; ccard acc. "Gd facs for children; modern san facs." ♦ NOK 180 2007*

⊞ **PORSGRUNN** *1C4* (4km S Rural) *59.11183, 9.71208* **Camping Olavsberget, Nystrandveien 64, 3944 Porsgrunn (Vestfold) [tel/fax 35 51 12 05]** Leave E18 at Eidanger onto Rv354 N; foll camp sp for 1km; site on L. Fr Porsgrunn foll Rv36 S; just bef E18 junc turn L; foll sp as above. Med, pt sl, unshd; wc; shwrs; el pnts (16A) NOK30 (no earth); Indtte (inc dryer); sm shop; supmkt 1km; snacks; sand beach adj with diving boards; 60% statics; poss cr; rd noise; no ccard acc; clsd 2300-0700; Eng spkn; CCI. "Well-run site; public access to beach thro site; gd walks in wood; visits to Maritime Brevik & mineral mine, Porsgrunn porcelain factory & shop, Telemark Canal inc boat tour." ♦ 2009*

RAKKESTAD *1D3* (3km S Rural) *59.40282, 11.38202* **Bjørnstad Camping, 1890 Rakkestad (Østfold) [tel/fax 69 22 10 19; han-s@online.no]** N fr Halden for 35km on Rv22. Site on R. Med, pt sl, unshd; htd wc; mv service pnt; chem disp; shwrs NOK10; el pnts (10-16A) inc; Indtte; shop; phone; v quiet; Eng spkn; CCI. "Grassy clearing amid pines; if wet avoid lower pitches." ♦ 15 Mar-15 Sep. NOK 130 2007*

RAMFJORDBOTN see Sakariasjord *2F1*

REDALEN see Gjøvik *1C2*

⊞ **RISNES** *1A2* (10km E Coastal) *60.84492, 5.20355* **Nautesund Camping, Risnes, 5192 Hosteland (Hordaland) [tel 56 36 70 44; fax 56 36 62 30; nautesund@online.no; www.nautesund.no]** N fr Bergen on E39 to Knarrviki then Rv57 to Leirvåg. Take ferry to Sløvag then Rv570 to Risnes, site sp in 2km, between Sløvag & Duesund. Sm, pt hdstg, pt sl; htd wc; chem disp; shwrs NOK10; el pnts NOK30; Indtte; snacks; playgrnd; beach & sw adj; fishing; boat hire; some statics; phone; poss cr; Eng spkn; quiet; CCI. "About 2hrs fr Bergen; lovely coastal inlet." NOK 150 2008*

⊞ **RISOR** *1C4* (5km SW Coastal) *58.69083, 9.16333* **Sørlandet Feriecenter, Sandnes, 4950 Risør [tel 37 15 40 80; sorferie@online.no; www.sorlandet-feriesenter.no]** Fr N take E18 to Sørlandsporten then Rv416 to Risør, then Rv411 to Laget. Foll sp Sørlandet. Fr S exit E18 at Tvedestrand & cont to Laget, then foll site sp. Site is 20km by rd fr Risør. Med, mkd pitch, pt shd; htd wc; chem disp; baby facs; private san facs avail; shwrs; el pnts inc; Indtte (inc dryer); shop; supmkt 1km; rest; bar; cooking facs; playgrnd; sand beach; watersports; boat & cycle hire; tennis 1km; fitness rm; games rm; wifi; cab TV; some statics; dogs; adv bkg; Eng spkn; quiet. ♦ NOK 230 2010*

⊞ **RODBERG** *1C3* (4km S Rural) *60.23533, 9.0040* **Fjordgløtt Camping, Vrenne, 3630 Rødberg (Buskerud) [tel 32 74 13 35; fax 32 74 16 90; info@fjordglott.net; www.fjordglott.net]** Fr Rødberg on Rv40 dir Kongsberg, take R turn sp Vrenne, cross bdge & foll sp past power stn. Med, mkd pitch, terr, pt shd; htd wc; chem disp; 75% serviced pitches; baby facs; sauna; shwrs NOK10; el pnts (10A) NOK30; Indtte; shop; tradsmn; snacks; playgrnd; lake sw; fishing; 40% statics; phone; Eng spkn; quiet; ccard acc; CCI. "Lovely views of fjord; excel facs." ♦ NOK 170 2008*

RODBERG *1C3* (2km W Rural) **Persgård Camping, Nore og Uvdal, 3630 Rødberg (Buskerud) [tel 32 24 32 54]** Site fr Rv40. Sm, unshd; wc; chem disp; shwrs NOK10; el pnts NOK30; sand beach & lake sw adj; 20% statics; quiet. "Beautiful setting; basic, clean facs; gd." ♦ Jul-Sep. NOK 100 2009*

ROGNAN *2F2* (500m N Coastal) *67.10284, 15.40892* **Rognan Fjordcamp, Sandbakkveien 16, 8250 Rognan (Nordland) [tel 75 69 00 88; fax 75 69 14 77; admin@fjordcamp.com; www.fjordcamp.com]** Fr E6 N foll sp Rognan N, site in 500 on R. Fr E6 S foll sp Rognan S, site on L 500m beyond vill. Med, pt shd; htd wc; chem disp (wc); mv service pnt; baby facs; fam bthrm; shwrs NOK10; el pnts (10-16A) NOK40; Indtte; shop & 500m; rest, snacks, bar 500m; cooking facs; playgrnd; shgl beach adj; fishing; boat trips; cab TV; 20% statics; dogs; phone; adv bkg; quiet; CCI. "Friendly, well-run site; beautiful situation on edge of fjord; helpful owners." ♦ 1 May-30 Nov. NOK 150 2007*

ROGNAN *2F2* (5km S Rural) *67.06150, 15.37120* **Medby Camping, 8250 Rognan (Nordland) [tel 75 69 03 15; fax 75 69 07 09]** S on E6, foll sp Medby. Sm, unshd; htd wc; chem disp; mv service pnt; shwrs inc; el pnts NOK20; Indry rm; shop, rest, bar, shop 5km; cooking facs; Eng spkn; quiet. "Lovely, peaceful, CL-type site; gd." 1 Jun-1 Sep. NOK 120 2009*

⊞ **ROLDAL** *1B3* (Rural) *59.83227, 6.81843* **Skysstasjonen Hytter & Camping, Kyrkjevegen 24, 5760 Røldal (Hordaland) [tel 53 64 73 85; fax 53 64 73 44; roldal@roldalstunet.no; www.skysstasjonen.no]** Fr E on E134 turn L down into vill bef petrol stn. Site ent opp supmkt. Med, some hdstg, pt sl, pt terr, pt shd; htd wc; chem disp; sauna; shwrs NOK10; el pnts (10A) NOK35; Indtte (inc dryer); shop adj; rest; snacks; cooking facs; internet; TV; 50% statics; dogs; phone; quiet; CCI. "Vg site in beautiful, sheltered rvside location; wintersports." ♦ NOK 160 2009*

⊞ **ROLDAL** *1B3* (1km SE Rural) *59.83103, 6.82888* **Røldal Hyttegrend & Camping, Kyrkjevegen 49, 5760 Røldal (Hordaland) [tel 53 64 71 33; fax 53 64 39 41; adm@roldal-camping.no; www.roldal-camping.no]** Fr E on E134 turn L on ent vill, site sp. Sm, pt shd; htd wc; chem disp; mv service pnt; baby facs; shwrs NOK10; baby facs; fam bthrm; el pnts (10A) NOK30; gas; Indtte; shop; snacks; cooking facs; playgrnd; rv sw adj; wifi; TV rm; 20% statics; dogs; phone; Eng spkn; adv bkg; ccard acc; red CCI. "Gd walking, angling." ♦ NOK 130 2008*

⊞ **ROLDAL** *1B3* (500m S Rural) *59.83255, 6.82138* **Saltvold Camping, Kirkeveien 34, 5760 Røldal (Hordaland) [tel 53 64 72 45; gulleik@online.no]** Fr W on E134 turn R at 2nd camping sp (immed after 1st camping sp). Site at bottom of hill just bef stave church. Med, pt sl, unshd; wc; chem disp; shwrs NOK5; el pnts (10A) NOK40; Indtte; shop, rest, snacks 100m; 20% statics; Eng spkn; quiet; red CCI. "Mountain views." NOK 135 (4 persons) 2009*

ROLDAL *1B3* (1km SW Rural) *59.83012, 6.81061* **Seim Camping, 5760 Røldal (Hordaland) [tel/fax 53 64 73 71; seim@seimcamp.no; www.seimcamp.no]** App fr SW on E134, site sp at ent town. Turn R off main rd & R again. Med, pt sl, pt shd; htd wc; chem disp; baby facs; fam bthrm; shwrs NOK5; el pnts (20A) NOK40; Indtte; shop, rest, snacks, bar 200m; playgrnd; fishing; boating; dogs; Eng spkn; CCS/CCI. "Gd walks; beautiful views; prehistoric burial mounds & museum on site." ♦ 15 May-1 Oct. NOK 130 2010*

ROROS *1D1* (200m S Urban) *62.57078, 11.38295* **Idrettsparken Hotel & Camping, Øra 25, 7374 Røros (Sør-Trøndelag) [tel 72 41 10 89; fax 72 41 23 77; ihotell@online.no; www.idrettsparken.no]** Heading twd Trondheim on Rv30 to Røros cent, turn L at rndabt into Peter Møllersvei, over rlwy line, left again & foll sp to site. Sm, unshd; htd wc; shwrs NOK10; el pnts (10A) NOK35; shops & pool nr; quiet. "Tours of museums & mines; nature reserve & nature park nr; no chem disp - use dump point at fire stn on Rv30; fair NH." ♦ 1 May-30 Sep. NOK 165 2010*

RORVIK *2E3* (2km N Coastal) *64.8729, 11.2609* **Nesset Camping, Engan, 7900 Rørvik (Nord-Trøndelag) [tel 74 39 06 60]** Fr cent of Rørvik on Rv770, foll sp to site. Med, hdg pitch, hdstg, pt sl, terr, pt shd; htd wc; chem disp; shwrs NOK10; el pnts; sw adj; Eng spkn; quiet. "CL-type site in v scenic location; many pitches with fjord view; facs stretched high ssn." May-Sep. NOK 125 2008*

RUNDE (RUNDE ISLAND) *1A1* (500m NW Coastal) *62.39717, 5.65624* **Runde Camping & Hostel, 6096 Runde (Møre og Romsdal) [tel 90 74 43 43; runde@hihostels.no; www.runde.no]** Fr S via E39 Volda & Ørsta, thro Eiksundsambandet Tunnel, then 25km by rd to Runde. On reaching Runde Island turn R along coast, site sp. Fr N take ferry fr Sulesund (nr Ålesund) to Hareid, then 45km by rd, site sp. Sm, hdstg, unshd; htd wc; chem disp; shwrs; el pnts (16A); Indtte; shop; snacks 300m; BBQ; cooking facs; wifi; beach adj; dogs; phone; o'night area for m'vans; Eng spkn; adv bkg; quiet; ccard acc; CCI. "Lge bird colonies on island; boat trips organised; helpful owner." 1 May-30 Sep. 2010*

⊞ **RUNDE (RUNDE ISLAND)** *1A1* (3km NW Rural/Coastal) *62.40416, 5.62525* **Camping Goksøyr, 6096 Runde (Møre og Romsdal) [tel 70 08 59 05 or 924 12 298 (mob); fax 70 08 59 60; camping@goksoyr.no; www.goksoeyr-camping.com]** Take causeway/bdge to Runde Island. Turn R off bdge & foll rd round island, thro tunnel. Rd ends 1km after site. Sm, hdstg, unshd; wc; chem disp; mv service pnt; shwrs NOK10; el pnts (16A) NOK30; Indtte; shop; snacks; fishing; cycle hire; phone; Eng spkn; adv bkg; quiet; CCI. "Excel birdwatching (inc puffins); site on water's edge; boat trips avail; basic facs poss inadequate when site full; owner helps with pitching; vg." NOK 150 2010*

NORWAY

NORWAY

RYSSTAD *1B4* (1km S Rural) *59.0908, 7.5402* **Sølvgarden Feriesenter, 4748 Rysstad (Aust-Agder) [tel 37 93 61 30; fax 37 93 61 09; post@rysstadferie.no; www.rysstadferie.no]** Site sp on E side of Rv9, S of junc of Rv9 & Rv45. Sm, some hdg/mkd pitch, pt sl, pt shd; htd wc; chem disp; shwrs NOK10; el pnts (10A) NOK35; Indtte (inc dryer); shop; tradsmn; rest; snacks; bar; cooking facs; BBQ; playgrnd; rv sw adj; fishing; canoeing; cycle hire; wifi; TV rm; some cabins; dogs; phone; Eng spkn; ccard acc; CCS/CCI. "Pleasant site; beautiful setting; modern san facs." ♦ 1 May-1 Oct. NOK 320 2010*

SAKARIASJORD (RAMFJORDBOTN) *2F1* (1km NE Rural) *69.51665, 19.24845* **Camping Ramfjord, Sørbotn, 9027 Ramfjordbotn (Troms) [tel 77 69 21 30; fax 77 69 22 60; post@ramfjordcamp.no; www.ramfjordcamp.no]** Approx 27km S of Tromsø on E8, clearly sp. Sm, unshd; wc; chem disp; mv service pnt; baby facs; shwrs NOK5; el pnts (10A) NOK50; gas; Indtte; shop; snacks; cooking facs; playgrnd; shgl beach adj; TV; 75% statics; dogs; phone; poss cr; Eng spkn; adv bkg ess; quiet; ccard acc; red CCI. "Facs ltd when cr; superb views of fjord; conv Tromsø." ♦ 1 Jun-15 Aug. NOK 170 2009*

SALTSTRAUMEN see Bodø *2F2*

⊞ **SANDANE** *1A2* (1.5km W Coastal) *61.76743, 6.19605* **Gloppen Camping, 6823 Sandane (Sogn og Fjordane) [tel 57 86 62 14; fax 57 86 81 05; post@gloppen-camping.no; www.gloppen-camping.no]** Fr town cent on rd E39 take Rv615 sp Rygg & Hyen. Site on R at fjordside. Med, mkd pitch, hdstg, unshd; htd wc; chem disp; mv service pnt; shwrs NOK10; el pnts (16A) NOK30; Indtte; shop; rest, snacks, bar 2km; BBQ; cooking facs; playgrnd; pool high ssn; beach adj; fishing; boat trips; tennis; golf 3km; TV rm; 70% statics; phone; quiet; ccard acc; CCI. "Day trips to Briksdal Glacier; gd." ♦ NOK 200 2011*

SELJORD *1B3* (1km E Urban) *59.4867, 8.65136* **Camping Seljord & Badeplass, 3840 Seljord (Telemark) [tel/fax 35 05 04 71; post@seljordcamping.no; www.seljordcamping.no]** Site on Rv36, sp. Lge, mkd pitch, pt sl, pt shd; htd wc; chem disp; baby facs; fam bthrm; shwrs NOK10; el pnts (10A) NOK30; Indtte; kiosk & shops 500m; rest 1km; snacks; playgrnd; lake sw adj; fishing; boating; Eng spkn; quiet; ccard acc; CCI. "Pleasantly situated on lakeside; lake claimed to have a monster!" ♦ 1 May-30 Sep. NOK 160 2008*

SETERMOEN *2F2* (20km S Rural) **Solbakken Camping, Sollidveien, Salangsdalen, 9360 Bardu (Troms) [tel 77 18 41 34]** On W side of E6, foll sp up hill. Sm, pt sl, terr, unshd; htd wc; shwrs NOK10; cooking facs; games area; 70% statics; some Eng spkn; quiet. "Poss bleak, windswept but gd views; warden calls evenings; gd NH." May-Sep. 2009*

⊞ **SJOHOLT** *1B1* (9km N Rural) *62.52022, 6.91722* **Camping Ørskog Fjellstova, 6249 Ørskog (Møre og Ronsdal) [tel 70 27 03 03; fax 70 27 00 60; post@fjellstova.no; www.fjellstova.no]** Site sp on E39, 50km E of Ålesund & 25km W of Molde. Med, hdstg, unshd; htd wc; chem disp; shwrs inc; el pnts (10A) NOK30; tradsmn; rest; snacks; BBQ; 5% cabins; bus; Eng spkn; quiet; ccard acc. "Dutch owners; gd site mainly for winter use; gd for fishing, cross country, skiing." NOK 150 2011*

SKARNES *1D3* (10km N Urban) *60.34744, 11.60470* **Songnabben Camping, Størjen, 2100 Skarnes (Hedmark) [tel 62 97 37 28; fax 62 97 64 91; songnabben@online.no]** N fr Oslo on E6, turn E onto Rv2 to Skarnes & foll sp to site on Rv24. Sm, pt sl, unshd; wc; chem disp; baby facs; shwrs NOK10; el pnts NOK20; Indtte; kiosk; cooking facs; playgrnd; TV rm; quiet; ccard acc. "Useful NH on rte N." 1 May-15 Sep. NOK 190 2007*

⊞ **SKARNES** *1D3* (5km S Rural) *60.19910, 11.58054* **Sanngrund Camping, Oslovegen 910, 2100 Skarnes (Hedmark) [tel 62 96 46 60; fax 62 96 46 69; booking@sanngrund.no; www.sanngrund.no]** Fr Skarnes foll Rv2 S; site sp on L. Sm, mkd pitch, pt shd; htd wc; chem disp; mv service pnt; baby facs; shwrs inc; el pnts inc; Indtte; shop 10km; rest; snacks; BBQ; cooking facs; playgrnd; rv sw & fishing adj; TV; 50% statics; poss cr; Eng spkn; rd noise; CCS. "Conv NH to/fr Oslo (approx 70km); pleasant rest; fair site." ♦ NOK 235 2010*

SKARSVAG *2G1* (3km S Rural) *71.09286, 25.78521* **Midnattsol Camping, 9763 Skarsvåg (Finnmark) [tel/fax 78 47 52 13]** Sp on E69 at junc for Skarsvåg. Sm, hdstg, unshd; htd wc; chem disp; mv service pnt; shwrs; el pnts (10A); Indtte; rest; bar; some cabins; Eng spkn; quiet. "V friendly." 1 Jun-15 Sep. 2009*

SKARSVAG *2G1* (1km SW Coastal) *71.1073, 25.81238* **Kirkeporten Camping, 9763 Skarsvåg (Finnmark) [tel 78 47 52 33; fax 78 47 52 47; kipo@kirkeporten.no; www.kirkeporten.no]** Foll E69 fr Honningsvåg for 20km to Skarsvåg junc; site sp at junc & on L after 2km immed bef vill. Sm, hdstg, pt sl, unshd; htd wc; chem disp; mv service pnt; sauna; shwrs inc; el pnts (16A) NOK25; Indtte (inc dryer); rest; snacks; bar; TV; poss cr; Eng spkn; adv bkg; quiet; ccard acc; CCI. "Site on edge sm fishing vill 10km fr N Cape, ringed by mountains; exposed location; claims to be world's most N site; helpful, knowledgeable owner; vg rest; clean facs but stretched if site full; poss reindeer on site; highly rec; arr early." ♦ 1 May-1 Oct. NOK 215 2010*

SKIBOTN *2G1* (2km E Rural) *69.39397, 20.26797* **NAF Camping Skibotn, 9143 Skibotn (Troms) [tel 77 71 52 77]** On E6 site 2km bef town. Heading N on E6 site opp supmkt on beach. Sm, pt sl, unshd; wc; chem disp; shwrs NOK10 (10 mins); el pnts (16A) NOK25; gas; Indtte; shops adj; rest; snacks; cooking facs; playgrnd; fishing; Eng spkn; quiet. "NH only, dir access to beach on fjord." 1 Jun-31 Aug. NOK 160 2009*

SKIBOTN *2G1* (1km S Rural) *69.38166, 20.29528* **Olderelv Camping (TR30), 9048 Skibotn (Troms) [tel 77 71 54 44 or 91 13 17 00 (mob); fax 77 71 51 62; firmapost@olderelv.no; www.olderelv.no]** W of E6 1km N of junc at E8. Lge, mkd pitch, pt sl, pt shd; wc; chem disp; sauna; baby facs; shwrs NOK10; el pnts (10A) inc; Indtte (inc dryer); shop; snacks; cooking facs; playgrnd; solarium; wifi; 80% statics; dogs free; phone; quiet; ccard acc. "Well-maintained & clean; dryest area of Troms; gd walking." ♦ 15 May-15 Sep. NOK 220 2009*

SKJAK see Lom *1C2*

SKJOLDEN *1B2* (3km NE Rural) *61.48453, 7.6505* **Vassbakken Camping, 6876 Skjolden (Sogn og Fjordane) [tel 57 68 61 88 or 57 68 67 00; fax 57 68 61 85; vassbakken@skjolden.com; www.skjolden.com/vassbakken]** Site on Rv55. Sm, pt shd; wc; chem disp; mv service pnt; baby facs; sauna; shwrs NOK10; el pnts (10A) NOK30; Indtte; sm shop & 3km; rest; snacks; playgrnd; lake sw & fishing adj; wifi; TV; phone; Eng spkn; no adv bkg; ccard acc. "Mountain setting; waterfall adj; gd walking & fishing." 1 May-30 Sep. NOK 170 2009*

SKJOLDEN *1B2* (1km SE Rural) *61.48977, 7.60709* **Nymoen Leirplass, 6876 Skjolden (Sogn og Fjordane) [tel 57 68 66 03; fax 57 68 67 33; nymoen@skjolden.com; www.skjolden.com/nymoen]** Fr Lom on rd 55 site on R behind petrol stn. Fr Sogndal on exit Skjolden after 2nd bdge site on L. Sm, unshd; wc; chem disp; mv service pnt; shwrs NOK10; el pnts (16A) NOK25; gas; Indtte (inc dryer); shops adj & 500m; cooking facs; lake sw 500m; fishing; poss cr; adv bkg; quiet; ccard acc. "Beautiful situation on lakeside; fine views; walk to vill & Lustrafjorden." 1 May-1 Oct. NOK 159 2010*

SKODJE *1B1* (5km S Coastal) *62.48333, 6.68638* **Vika Feriesenter A/S, Valle, 6260 Skodje (Møre og Romsdal) [tel/fax 70 27 62 06]** On rd E39 30 km E of Ålesund. Site sp fr both dirs. On service rd, site is 2nd on L. Sm, hdstg, unshd; wc; chem disp; mv service pnt; shwrs; el pnts; Indtte; sand/shgl beach adj; fishing; boat hire; 80% statics; phone; Eng spkn; quiet; CCI. "Conv Ålesund, Åndalsnes & ferries." 1 Jun-31 Aug. 2008*

⊞ **SKOGANVARRE** *2G1* (Rural) *69.83826, 25.07673* **Skoganvarre Turist & Camping, 9722 Skoganvarre (Finnmark) [tel 78 46 48 46; fax 78 46 48 97; skoganvarre@c2i.net; www.skoganvarre.no]** Site sp fr E6 on lakeside 27km S of Lakselv. Med, pt shd; htd wc; chem disp; sauna; shwrs NOK10; el pnts (10A) NOK40; Indtte; rest; snacks; lake sw; fishing; cooking facs; TV; quiet. "Useful NH on E6; gd site." NOK 140 2008*

SKOGMO *2E3* (1km W Rural) *64.50393, 11.99123* **Bjøra Camping, 7863 Overhalla (Nord-Trøndelag) [tel 74 28 13 08; fax 74 28 23 16; j-blen@online.no; www.bjora.no]** Fr E6 at Grong turn W onto Rv17 thro Skogmo twd Namsos. Sm, pt sl, pt shd; htd wc; chem disp (wc); mv service pnt (at g'ge across rd); shwrs NOK10; el pnts (10A) NOK20; Indtte; rest, snacks, bar 3km; playgrnd; fishing adj; 10% statics; dogs; Eng spkn; quiet; ccard acc; CCI. "Gd; salmon-fishing adj." 15 May-15 Oct. NOK 130 2008*

⊞ **SKUDENESHAVN** *1A3* (500m N Coastal) *59.15595, 5.24356* **Skudenes Camping, Postveien 129, 4280 Skudeneshavn (Rogaland) [tel 52 82 81 96 or 92 09 85 65; fax 52 82 96 85; skuc@online.no; www.skudenescamping.no]** Sp fr Rv47 Sm, all hdstg, pt sl, unshd; wc; chem disp; mv service pnt; baby facs; shwrs inc; el pnts (10A) NOK30; Indtte (inc dryer); shop, rest, snacks nr; BBQ; cooking facs; playgrnd; fishing; wifi; TV rm; some statics; dogs; phone; bus; Eng spkn; adv bkg; quiet but some rd noise; CCI. "Well-maintained site, well-spaced pitches; attractive fishing vill; conv Stavanger ferry; excel NH." NOK 170 2008*

SKUTVIKA *2F2* (4km E Coastal) *68.00636, 15.41630* **Ness Camping, 8290 Skutvika (Nordland) [tel 75 77 13 88; fax 75 77 19 44; post@ness-camping.no; www.ness-camping.no]** Exit E6 at Ulsvåg onto Rv81. Site 36km, sp, 500m fr Skutvika ferry. Sm, pt sl, unshd; htd wc; shwrs NOK10; el pnts (16A) NOK35; Indtte; sm shop; BBQ; cooking facs; pool; sand beach adj; dogs; Eng spkn; adv bkg; quiet; ccard acc. "Delightful owner; boats & fishing avail in lovely estuary on fjord; conv ferry to/fr Lofoten Islands." 15 May-15 Sep. NOK 150 2008*

SNASA *2E3* (16km SW Rural) *64.17300, 12.09605* **Strindmo Gård Camping, Strindmo, 7760 Snåsa (Nord-Trøndelag) [tel/fax 74 16 39 12]** Fr Snåsa take Rv763 twds Steinkjer; site is sp on L in approx 15km. Sm, hdstg, pt sl, pt shd; htd wc; chem disp; shwrs NOK10; el pnts NOK35; Indtte; cooking facs; playgrnd; rv sw adj; boat & cycle hire; Eng spkn; adv bkg; some rlwy noise; CCI. "V friendly, welcoming, family-owned site; immac san facs; site has own hydro-electric generating plant open for inspection; midges!" 1 Apr-1 Oct. NOK 160 2009*

SOGNDALSFJORA *1B2* (13km NE Rural) *61.30738, 7.21500* **Lyngmo Camping (SF16), Lyngmovegen 12, 6869 Hafslo (Sogn of Fjordane) [tel 57 68 43 66; fax 57 68 39 29; lyngmo@lyngmoinfo.com; www.lyngmoinfo.com]** Fr Rv55 Sogndal-Gaupne turn L at sp Galden. Immed turn R at camping sp & foll gravel rd down to site on lakeside. Sm, pt sl, unshd; wc; chem disp; mv service pnt; baby facs; shwrs; el pnts; Indry rm; cooking facs; lake sw & fishing; some statics; phone; Eng spkn; quiet; ccard acc; CCI. "Beautiful location; steep hill to san facs block." 19 Jun-24 Aug. 2008*

SOGNDALSFJORA *1B2* (3.5km SE Coastal) *61.2118, 7.12106* **Camping Kjørnes, 6856 Sogndal (Sogn og Fjordane) [tel 57 67 45 80; fax 57 67 33 26; camping@kjornes.no; www.kjornes.no]** Fr W foll sp in Sogndal for Kaupanger/Lærdal (Rv5) over bdge. Fr E (Rv55) turn L at T-junc with rd 5 over bdge. Site on R; sharp R turn into narr lane (passing places); site ent on R in approx 500m. Med, pt sl, terr, pt shd; wc; chem disp; shwrs NOK10; el pnts (10-16A) NOK30 (no earth); Indtte; shops; rest, snacks 3.5km; cooking facs; playgrnd; beach adj; boat launching; fishing; wifi; some statics; phone; poss cr; Eng spkn; adv bkg; rd noise; ccard acc; CCI/CCS. "Useful for ferries; stunning location on edge of fjord; superb san facs; excel site." ♦ 1 May-1 Oct. NOK 220 2009*

SOGNDALSFJORA *1B2* (1km S Rural) *61.22505, 7.10271* **Stedje Camping, Kyrkjevegen 2, 6851 Sogndal (Sogn og Fjordane) [tel 57 67 10 12; fax 57 67 11 90; post@scamping.no; www.scamping.no]** W fr Hella to Sogndal, turn L off Rv55 adj Shell petrol stn, site clearly sp, narr ent. Med, sl, pt shd; htd wc; chem disp; mv service pnt; baby facs; shwrs NOK10; el pnts (16A) NOK40 (check earth); Indtte; shop; snacks; playgrnd; lake sw & beach 500m; watersports; solarium; cycle hire; TV; Eng spkn; quiet; CCI. "1st gd site after Vangsnes-Hella ferry - in orchard; poss poor facs early ssn; poss v diff in wet for lge m' vans; conv visit to 12th C Urnes stave church." ♦ 1 Jun-31 Aug. NOK 140 2008*

NORWAY

SOLA *1A4* (6km W Coastal) *58.86713, 5.56485* **Ølberg Camping & Friområde, Ølberg Havneveg 93, Ræg, 4054 Tjelta [tel 51 65 43 75; post@jarenfri.no; www.jarenfri.no]** Fr Stavanger or Sandnes take rds Rv209 & Rv210 to Sola airport & then foll sps for campsite along Fv380. Med, pt sl, unshd; wc; chem disp; mv service pnt; shwrs NOK10; el pnts (10A) NOK45; Indtte (inc dryer); tradsmn; snacks; BBQ; cooking facs; playgrnd; sand beach adj; games area; cycle hire; 30% statics; dogs free; phone; bus 500m; Eng spkn; adv bkg; quiet; CCI. "Adj pretty beach & sm harbour; gd walking & cycling; v relaxed, seaside site; vg, clean & well-run." ♦ 10 May-31 Aug. NOK 180 2010*

SORREISA see Andselv *2F1*

SPANGEREID *1A4* (8km S Coastal) *57.99593, 7.09003* **Lindesnes Camping, Lillehavn, 4521 Spangereid (Vest-Agder) [tel 38 25 88 74; fax 38 25 88 92; gabrielsen@lindesnescamping.no; www.lindesnescamping.no]** Fr E39 at Vigeland turn S onto Rv460 sp Lindesnes lighthouse (Fyr). Approx 8km after vill of Spangereid turn L sp Lillehavn, site sp. Sm, pt sl, pt shd; htd wc; chem disp; mv service pnt; shwrs NOK10; el pnts (16A) NOK40; Indtte; tradsmn; BBQ; cooking facs; dogs; phone; poss cr; Eng spkn; adv bkg; quiet; ccard acc; CCI. "Excel, clean, well-run site; pitches not marked" 1 Apr-30 Sep. NOK 185 2011*

STABBURSNES see Lakselv *2G1*

STAVANGER *1A3* (2km SW Rural) *58.9525, 5.71388* **Mosvangen Camping, Henrik Ibsens Gate, 4021 Stavanger (Rogaland) [tel 51 53 29 71; fax 51 87 20 55; info@mosvangencamping.no; www.mosvangencamping.no]** Fr Stavanger foll sp E39/Rv510; site well sp. Fr Sandnes on E39 exit Ullandhaug; foll camp sp. Med, some hdstg, sl, pt shd; wc; chem disp; mv service pnt; shwrs NOK10; el pnts (10A) NOK40 (no earth & poss intermittent supply); Indtte (inc dryer); kiosk; shop 500m; rest 1km; cooking facs; playgrnd; lake sw adj; sand beach 10km; dogs; phone; bus; poss v cr; Eng spkn; quiet but some rd noise; ccard acc; CCI. "Excel for wooden city of Stavanger; easy, pleasant walk to town cent; soft ground in wet weather; facs well used but clean, may be stretched when site full; helpful manager; excel rustic type of site." ♦ 1 Apr-1 Oct. NOK 200 2011*

STAVERN see Larvik *1C4*

⊞ **STEINKJER** *2E3* (14km N Rural) *64.10977, 11.57816* **Føllingstua Camping, Haugåshalla 6, 7732 Steinkjer (Nord-Trøndelag) [tel 74 14 71 90; fax 74 14 71 88; post@follingstua.no; www.follingstua.com]** N on E6, site on R, well sp. Sm, mkd pitch, hdstg, pt shd; htd wc; chem disp; mv service pnt; shwrs NOK20; el pnts (16A) NOK50; Indtte; shop 11km; rest; snacks; bar; BBQ; playgrnd; lake & beach adj; fishing; boating; TV rm; 60% statics; dogs; bus 200m; poss cr; adv bkg; quiet. "Excel san facs down 10 steps; some lakeside pitches." ♦ NOK 190 2010*

⊞ **STEINKJER** *2E3* (2km E Rural) *64.02246, 11.50745* **Camping Guldbergaunet, Elvenget 34, 7700 Steinkjer (Nord-Trøndelag) [tel 74 16 20 45; fax 74 16 47 35; g-book@online.no; www.rv17.no/guldbergaunet]** E fr town cent on E6. Foll Rv762 at 2km L past school. Site at end. Med, mkd pitch, pt sl, pt shd; htd wc; chem disp; mv service pnt; baby facs; shwrs NOK10; el pnts (10-16A) NOK40; gas; Indtte; shop; rest; snacks; playgrnd; pool 2km; rv sw 2km; fishing; sports cent adj; phone; Eng spkn; some rlwy noise; ccard acc; red long stay/CCI. "On peninsula bet two rvs; friendly; san facs poss stretched; lge pitches, suitable RVs & lge o'fits; gd NH." NOK 170 2008*

STOREN *1C1* (500m E Rural) *63.04465, 10.29078* **Vårvolden Camping (ST17), Volløyan 3A, 7290 Støren (Sør-Trøndelag) [tel/fax 72 43 20 24; varvolden.camping@gauldalen.no]** Leave E6 for Støren & foll site sp. Sm, unshd; htd wc; chem disp; mv service pnt; baby facs; fam bthrm; shwrs; el pnts (16A); Indtte (inc dryer); shop 500m; rest, snacks 1km; cooking facs; playgrnd; 20% statics; dogs; Eng spkn; CCI. "Vg." ♦ 15 May-1 Sep. 2009*

STOREN *1C1* (800m E Rural) *63.04083, 10.29333* **Camping Støren, Frøsetøren 1, 7290 Støren (Sør-Trøndelag) [tel/fax 72 43 14 70; post@storencamping.no; www.gaula.no]** Located at Støren off E6 on sm app rd dir Røros, nr Rv Gaula. Low bdge at ent to site 3.3m. Med, mkd pitch, pt shd; htd wc; chem disp; baby facs; shwrs NOK10; el pnts (10-16A) NOK30; Indtte (inc dryer); shop; snacks; playgrnd; TV; mainly statics; phone. "Gd salmon rv, permit needed." ♦ 1 Jun-31 Aug. NOK 125 2010*

STORFORSHEI *2F2* (6km N Rural) *66.37946, 14.60366* **Camping Skogly Overnatting, Saltfjellveien, Skogly, 8630 Storforshei (Nordland) [tel 75 16 01 57; fax 75 16 60 74; post@skoglyovernatting.com]** N fr Mo i Rana for 30km, site on L of E6. Sm, hdstg, unshd; htd wc; chem disp (wc); baby facs; shwrs inc; el pnts NOK40; cooking facs; Eng spkn; quiet. "Excel facs, inc for disabled; helpful owner." 1 May-20 Sep. NOK 140 2008*

STORFORSHEI *2F2* (12km W Rural) *66.40241, 14.42377* **Storli Camping (NO40), Saltfjellveien 632, 8630 Storforshei (Nordland) [tel 75 16 02 32]** Sp on E6 20km N of Mo i Rana. Sm, pt shd; htd wc; chem disp (wc); mv service pnt; shwrs; el pnts (few only); Indry rm; tradsmn; rest, snacks, bar 12km; phone; no dogs; quiet; Eng spkn; adv bkg. 1 Jun-31 Aug. NOK 80 2008*

⊞ **STORJORD** *2F2* (Rural) *66.81317, 15.40055* **Saltdal Turistsenter, 8255 Storjord (Nordland) [tel 75 68 24 50; fax 75 68 24 51; firmapost@saltdal-turistsenter.no; www.saltdal-turistsenter.no]** Site is 35km S of Rognan by-pass on E6, 700m N of junc of Rv77, adj filling stn. Med, mkd pitch, some hdstg, terr, pt shd; htd wc; chem disp; mv service pnt; shwrs NOK10; el pnts (10A) NOK25; Indtte; shop; rest; snacks; BBQ; cooking facs; playgrnd; 99% statics; phone; Eng spkn; adv bkg; quiet; CCI. "Motorway-style service stn & lorry park; tightly packed cabins & statics; 10 pitches only for tourers; excel rv walks fr site; beautiful area; NH only." ♦ NOK 155 2007*

STORSLETT *2G1* (11km N Coastal) *69.83880, 21.21058* **Fosselv Camping, Straumfjord, 9151 Storslett (Troms) [tel 77 76 49 29; fax 77 76 76 09; fosselv.camping@c2i.net; www.fosselv-camping.no]** Sp fr E6. Sm, pt sl, pt shd; wc; chem disp; mv service pnt; shwrs; el pnts (10A) NOK50; Indtte; cooking facs; playgrnd; shgl beach adj; Eng spkn; rd noise; CCS. "Lovely fjord setting; poss reindeer on site in evening." 10 May-25 Oct. NOK 150 2009*

STRAUMEN see Fauske *2F2*

I'll fill in a report online and let the Club know – www.caravanclub.co.uk/europereport

This is a wonderful site.

STRYN *1B2* (10km E Rural) *61.60008, 6.88866* **Mindresunde Camping (SF43), 6880 Stryn (Sogn og Fjordane) [tel 57 87 75 32; fax 57 87 75 40; post@mindresunde.no; www.mindresunde.no]** 2nd site on Rv15 on N side of rd. Sm, mkd pitch, pt sl, unshd; htd wc; chem disp; mv service pnt; baby facs; fam bthrm; shwrs NOK10; el pnts inc (earth prob); Indtte; shop; snacks; playgrnd; shgl beach; TV; car wash; Eng spkn; adv bkg; little rd noise; CCI. "Well-kept, pleasant site; many pitches on lake; friendly staff; site yourself; vg views; excel facs; conv Geiranger, Briksdal glacier & Strynefjellet summer ski cent; gd walking." ♦ 1 Apr-1 Nov. NOK 190 2007*

STRYN *1B1* (11km E Rural) *61.9314, 6.92121* **Strynsvatn Camping, Meland, 6783 Stryn (Sogn og Fjordane) [tel 57 87 75 43; fax 57 87 75 65; camping@strynsvatn.no; www.strynsvatn.no]** On Rv15 Lom to Stryn, on L. Sm, terr, unshd; wc; chem disp; mv service pnt; sauna; shwrs NOK10; el pnts (10A) inc (poss earth fault); Indtte (inc dryer); shop; snacks; playgrnd; lake adj; TV; 20% statics; Eng spkn; adv bkg; quiet; ccard acc; CCI. "Superb site; excel facs & v clean, gd views/walking; v friendly owners." ♦ 1 Apr-30 Sep. NOK 210 2010*

STRYN *1B2* (20km E Rural) **Grande Camping, 6799 Oppstryn (Sogn og Fjordane) [tel 97 16 97 09; post@grandecamping.no; www.grandecamping.no]** E fr Stryn on Rv15 to head of Strynsvatn lake, thro Hjelle, site sp on lakeside. Med, pt shd; wc; chem disp; mv service pnt; shwrs NOK10; el pnts (5A) NOK35; (poss earth fault); Indry rm; kiosk; shop 5km; cooking facs; playgrnd; private beach & lake sw; boat hire; fishing; quiet. "Beautiful area; if recep clsd site yourself & pay later." ♦ 1 Jun-30 Aug. NOK 125 2007*

TANA *2H1* (4km SE Rural) *70.1663, 28.2279* **Tana Familiecamping, Skiippagurra, 9845 Tana (Finnmark) [tel 78 92 86 30; fax 78 92 86 31; tana@famcamp.net]** On ent Tana fr W, cross bdge on E6, heading E sp Kirkenes; site on L in approx 4km. Sm, pt sl, unshd; htd wc; chem disp; mv service pnt; sauna; shwrs inc; el pnts (16A); Indtte (inc dryer); rest; BBQ; playgrnd; Eng spkn; ccard acc; quiet. 1 May-1 Oct. 2010*

TINN AUSTBYGD *1B3* (1km S Rural) *59.99308, 8.81902* **Sandviken Camping (TE13), 3650 Tinn Austbygd (Telemark) [tel 35 09 81 73; fax 35 09 41 05; kontakt@sandviken-camping.no; www.sandviken-camping.no]** Site is off Rv364 on L after passing thro Tinn Austbygd. Med, pt shd; htd wc; chem disp; mv service pnt; fam bthrm; sauna; shwrs NOK10; el pnts (10A) NOK35 (check earth); gas; Indtte; shop high ssn; BBQ; cooking facs; playgrnd; lake sw; games rm; games area; boat hire; TV rm; some statics; dogs; phone; poss cr; Eng spkn; CCI. "Superb, peaceful location at head of Lake Tinnsjø; sh walk thro woods to shops & bank; conv for museum at Rjukan heavy water plant." ♦ NOK 205 2009*

TISLEIDALEN *1C2* (2km SW Rural) *60.85360, 9.18161* **Vasetdansen Camping (OP15), 2923 Tisleidalen (Oppland) [tel 61 35 99 50; fax 61 35 99 55; camp@vasetdansen.no; www.vasetdansen.no]** On W side of Rv51 bet Leira & Gol. Lge, pt sl, terr, unshd; htd wc; chem disp; mv service pnt; sauna; shwrs NOK10; el pnts (10A) NOK30; Indtte; shop high ssn; tradsmn; rest; snacks; bar; cooking facs; playgrnd; cycle hire; skilift 2km; internet; TV rm; 80% statics; Eng spkn; quiet; ccard acc; CCI. "Gd." ♦ NOK 175 2008*

TJOTTA *2E3* (8km N Coastal) *65.82290, 12.41825* **Offersøy Camping, 8860 Tjøtta (Nordland) [tel 75 04 64 11; fax 75 04 63 72; post@kystferie.no; www.kystferie.no]** At end of Rv17 take L & cont 8km. Site well sp. Sm, hdstg, pt sl, pt shd; htd wc; shwrs inc; el pnts NOK40; Indtte; BBQ; cooking facs; playgrnd; beach adj; boat hire & launching; wifi; 80% statics; dogs; poss cr; Eng spkn; quiet. "Conv for ferry; gd." ♦ 15 Jun-15 Aug. NOK 170 2009*

TRETTEN *1C2* (6km N Rural) *61.3671, 10.2852* **Camping Mageli (OP46), 2635 Tretten (Oppland) [tel 61 27 63 22; fax 61 27 63 50; info@magelicamping.no; www.magelicamping.no]** On W side of E6. Lge, pt sl, pt shd; htd wc; chem disp; mv service pnt; shwrs NOK8; el pnts (10A) inc; shop; gas; Indtte; snacks; playgrnd; sand beach; boating; fishing; phone; poss cr; Eng spkn; quiet but rd noise; ccard acc. ♦ NOK 200 2008*

TRETTEN *1C2* (7km N Rural) *61.38504, 10.26019* **Krekke Camping (OP33), Sør Fåvang, 2634 Fåvang (Oppland) [tel 61 28 45 71; fax 61 28 46 71]** On W side of E6 about 1km N of Mageli Camping, on lakeside. Med, pt sl, unshd; wc; chem disp; mv service pnt; baby facs; shwrs; el pnts inc; Indtte; playgrnd; beach adj; 20% statics; quiet. "Site yourself, warden calls; beautiful views." 1 May-1 Oct. 2009*

TREUNGEN *1B4* (15km N Rural) *59.15560, 8.50611* **Søftestad Camping, Nissedal, 3855 Treungen (Aust-Agder) [tel 41 92 76 20]** N fr Kristiansand on Rv41 to Treungen, then alongside E edge of Nisser Water to Nissedal, site sp. Sm, shd; wc; chem disp; baby facs; shwrs inc; el pnts (10A) inc; Indtte; BBQ; playgrnd; phone; bus adj; Eng spkn; adv bkg; quiet; ccard acc; red long stay; CCI. "Close to Telemarken heavy water plant; beautiful alt rte N fr Kristiansand - rd suitable for towed c'vans." ♦ 1 May-1 Sep. NOK 140 2008*

NORWAY

TROFORS *2E3* (3km S Rural) *65.50846, 13.3951* **Storforsen Camping, Båtfjellmoen, 8680 Trofors (Nordland) [tel 41 28 43 59; storforsen_camping@hotmail.com]** Site is 40km S of Mosjøen on E6, sp. Sm, terr, unshd; wc; chem disp; shwrs NOK10; el pnts (16A); lndtte; rest 3km; playgrnd; some statics; rd noise; CCI. "Waterfall behind recep, forest walks, mountain views; ltd facs but immac." 1 Jun-1 Sep. 2008*

TROGSTAD *1D3* (6km N Rural) *59.68888, 11.29275* **Olberg Camping, Olberg, 1860 Trøgstad (Østfold) [tel 69 82 86 10; fax 69 82 85 55; froesol@online.no]** Fr Mysen on E18 go N on Rv22 for approx 20km dir Lillestrøm. Site is 2km 2 of Båstad Sm, hdg pitch, pt shd; htd wc; chem disp; shwrs; baby facs; el pnts (10-16A) NOK35; lndtte (ind dryer); kiosk; snacks; BBQ; playgrnd; pool; beach 3km; fishing; tennis 200m; ice-skating; TV; phone; Eng spkn; adv bkg; quiet; ccard acc; red long stay/CCI. "Site on lge, working farm with elk safaris; local bread & crafts; farm museum; conv Oslo (40km)." ♦ 1 May-1 Oct. NOK 155 2009*

⊞ **TROMSO** *2F1* (25km NE Coastal) *69.77765, 19.38273* **Skittenelv Camping, Ullstindveien 736, 9022 Krokelvdalen (Troms) [tel 77 69 00 27; fax 77 69 00 50; post@skittenelv camping.no; www.skittenelvcamping.no]** Fr S end of Tromsø Bdge on E8, foll sps to Kroken & Oldervik. Site on N side of rd Fv53. Med, some hdstg, unshd; htd wc; chem disp; sauna; shwrs NOK10; el pnts (10A) NOK50; lndtte (inc dryer); shop; tradsmn; snacks; BBQ; playgrnd; htd pool; paddling pool; waterslide; fishing; games rm; wifi; TV; some statics; dogs free; quiet; ccard acc; red CCI. "Beautiful situation on edge of fjord; arctic sea birds." ♦ NOK 170 (CChq acc) 2011*

⊞ **TROMSO** *2F1* (2km E Rural) *69.64735, 19.01505* **Tromsø Camping, 9020 Tromsdalen (Troms) [tel 77 63 80 37; fax 77 63 85 24; post@tromsocamping.no; www.tromsocamping.no]** At rndabt on edge of Tromsø take 2nd exit under E8 bdge. Shortly turn R & foll sp. Do not cross narr bdge but turn R then fork L to site. Sm, unshd; wc; chem disp; shwrs inc; mv service pnt; el pnts (10-16A) NOK50; lndtte (inc dryer); shops 1.5km; snacks; playgrnd; wifi; dogs; poss cr; Eng spkn; some noise fr stadium; CCS. "V busy site; facs poss stretched when cr, esp el pnts - improvements in hand; surrounded by fast rv after rain; poss mkt traders on site; rec visit to Arctic church at midnight." NOK 230 2010*

⊞ **TRONDHEIM** *1C1* (2km NE Urban) *63.44384, 10.44966* **Lade Municipal Campervan Park, Haakon VII Gate, Lade, 7041 Trondheim (Sør-Trøndelag)** Fr S on E6 foll so E6 bypass (not E6 city). In 5km take Rv836 for 3km. Park is on L immed bef 3rd rndabt where Haakon VII Gate meets Lade Alle. Sm, hdstg, sl, unshd; own san essential - no facs except water tap; bus nr; poss cr. "Unsupervised tarmaced area within 30 mins walk of city cent; rec arr early high ssn; m'vans only." 2008*

TRONDHEIM *1C1* (10km W Rural) *63.44611, 10.20925* **Flakk Camping (ST19), 7070 Flakk (Sør-Trøndelag) [tel 72 84 39 00; contact@flakk-camping.no; www.flakk-camping.no]** Fr N on E6 to Trondheim cent, then foll sp Fosen onto Rv715 W; site sp & adj Flakk ferry terminal; fr S to Trondheim take Rv707 to site & ferry. Med, pt sl, unshd; wc; chem disp; mv service pnt; baby facs; shwrs inc; el pnts (10A) NOK40 (check earth); lndtte; shop 5km; supmkt 8km; dogs; bus to city; poss cr; Eng spkn; adv bkg; some ferry noise at night; no ccard acc; CCI. "V well-kept site; clean facs; pleasant view over fjord; parts poss muddy after rain; site by ferry terminal; helpful owner." ♦ 1 May-1 Sep. NOK 190 2009*

⊞ **TRYSIL** *1D2* (3km N Rural) *61.30400, 12.27459* **Camping Klara, Storvegen, 2420 Trysil (Hedmark) [tel 62 45 13 63; fax 62 45 47 98; klaracamping@trysil.com; www.klaracamping.no]** By Rv26 by Rv Trysilelva, 6km N of Nybergsund, opp hotel. Med, pt sl, pt shd; wc; chem disp; shwrs NOK10; el pnts NOK30; lndtte (inc dryer); shop; snacks; bar; cooking facs; playgrnd; fishing; boating; quiet; CCI. NOK 170 2010*

ULSVAG *2F2* (S Rural) *68.11583, 15.86611* **Ulsvåg Camping, 8276 Ulsvåg (Nordland) [tel 75 77 15 73; fax 75 77 12 81; post@gjestgiveriet.net; www.ulvsvag-gjestgiveri.no]** At junc of rd E6 & Rv81 to Skutvik at Hotel Gjestgiveri on N side of junc. Med, hdstg, pt shd; wc; chem disp; mv service pnt; serviced pitches; shwrs NOK5; el pnts (10A) inc; lndtte; shop adj; rest; snacks; bar; shgl beach & lake sw adj; wifi; dogs; poss cr; Eng spkn; adv bkg; quiet; ccard acc; CCI. "Conv ferries Lofoten Is; beautiful setting & views; gd walking area; useful NH." ♦ NOK 200 2010*

ULVIK *1B2* (500m S Rural) *60.56485, 6.90741* **Ulvik Fjordcamping, Sponheim, 5730 Ulvik (Hordaland) [tel 91 17 96 70; post@ulvikcamping.no]** Fr ferry at Bruravik take rd to Ulvik. Site on R in 9km. Fr Granvin, site visible on descending to Ulvik. Sm, pt sl, pt shd; wc; chem disp; shwrs NOK10; el pnts (10A) inc; gas; lndtte; shops 500m; hotel rest adj; snacks; playgrnd; shgl beach; some cabins; Eng spkn; adv bkg; quiet; CCI. "On fjord edge; spectacular scenery; picturesque vill; Osa waterfall 10km, Solsævatnet Lake 10km; immac facs; gd walking; recep in hotel opp." 1 May-31 Aug. NOK 185 2009*

UTNE *1A3* (5km W Rural) **Lothe Camping (HO50), Lothe, 5778 Utne (Hordaland) [tel 53 66 66 50; fax 53 66 30 58; mail@lothecamping.no; www.lothecamping.no]** Take Rv550 fr Utne ferry quay dir Jondal. Site on R in 5km. Rd steep, single track - not suitable c'vans. Sm, hdstg, pt sl, unshd; wc; chem disp; baby facs; shwrs; el pnts (5A); lndtte; kiosk; snacks; cooking facs; playgrnd; beach adj; sw; fishing; internet; TV rm; some statics; quiet. "Gd location on Hardanger Fjord." ♦ 15 May-15 Sep. 2008*

UTVIKA *1C3* (Rural) *60.02972, 10.26316* **Utvika Camping (BU14), Utstranda 263, 3531 Utvika (Buskerud) [tel/fax 32 16 06 70; post@utvika.no; www.utvika.no]** Site on loop rd fr E16 N of Nes twd Hønefoss. Site sp but sp opp site ent v sm. Med, pt sl, pt shd; wc; chem disp; baby facs; shwrs NOK10; el pnts (10A) NOK30; Indtte; playgrnd; lake sw adj; cab TV; 50% statics; Eng spkn; quiet. "Conv Oslo (40km) & better than Oslo city sites; busy, friendly site." ♦ 1 May-1 Oct. NOK 225 2009*

VADSO *2H1* (15km W Rural) *70.11935, 29.33155* **Vestre Jakobselv Camping, Lilledalsveien 6, 9801 Vestre Jakobselv (Finnmark) [tel 78 95 60 64; s.jankila@imf.no; www.vj-camping.no]** E fr Tana for approx 50km on E6/E75 dir Vadsø, site sp, 1km N of Vestre Jakobselv. Sm, hdstg, pt shd; wc; chem disp; mv service pnt; shwrs inc; el pnts (10A) NOK40; Indtte; shop 1km; rest; snacks; cooking facs; 10% statics; dogs; bus 1km; Eng spkn; quiet; ccard acc; red CCI/CCS. "Conv Vadsø & Vardø - interesting towns." ♦ 15 May-15 Aug. NOK 150 2009*

VAGAMO *1C2* (1km S Rural) *61.86465, 9.11438* **Smedsmo Camping, Vågåvegen 80, 2680 Vågåmo (Oppland) [tel 61 23 74 50; fax 61 23 74 14; smedsmo@online.no]** Behind petrol stn on Rv15 twd Lom. Med, pt shd; wc; chem disp; mv service pnt; baby facs; fam bthrm; shwrs NOK10; el pnts (10A) NOK40; Indtte; shop; snacks at g'ge; playgrnd; TV; some statics; dogs; Eng spkn; ccard acc; CCI. "Gd touring base; pay at petrol stn." ♦ 1 May-30 Sep. NOK 190 2009*

⊞ **VAGSEIDET** *1A2* (4km N Rural) *60.67886, 5.22408* **Camping Bruvoll, Lindås, 5956 Vågseidet (Hordaland) [tel 56 36 35 25; jkonglev@online.no; www.bruvoll-camping.no]** N fr Knarrviki on Rv57. After approx 16km site ent on L immed bef tunnel. Sm, hdstg, pt shd; wc; chem disp; shwrs; el pnts; Indtte; shop 500m; BBQ; playgrnd; fishing; boat & canoe hire; TV rm; some statics; quiet; CCI. "Fedje Island worth visit; gd touring base; poss migrant workers in huts; facs clean; NH only." NOK 150 2008*

VALLE *1B3* (9km N Rural) **Sanden Såre Bobilpark, 4747 Valle (Aust-Agder) [tel 37 93 68 49; td.lunden@online.no; www.setesdal.com]** On Rv9, sp. Sm, mkd pitch, hdstg, pt sl, shd; htd wc; chem disp; mv service pnt; serviced pitches; shwrs inc; el pnts inc; Indry rm; rv adj; TV; quiet. "M'vans & c'vans, but poss diff lge o'fits; honesty box for payment; lovely setting." NOK 150 2009*

VALLE *1B3* (2km S Rural) *59.20288, 7.52115* **Steinsland Familiecamping, 4747 Valle (Aust-Agder) [tel 37 93 71 26; www.setesdal.com]** Site to W of Rv Otra, sp. Sm, hdg pitch, terr, pt shd; htd wc; shwrs NOK10; v ltd el pnts inc; playgrnd; fishing; 50% statics; quiet. "Fair, basic site; clean san facs; gd walking & climbing; gd NH." NOK 200 2008*

⊞ **VANG** *1B2* (1km W Rural) *61.13032, 8.54352* **Bøflaten Camping, 2975 Vang I Valdres (Sogn og Fjordane) [tel 61 36 74 20; fax 22 29 46 87; info@boflaten.com; www.boflaten.com]** Sp on E16 55km NW of Fagernes. Med, mk pitch, pt shd; htd wc; chem disp; mv service pnt; shwrs NOK10; el pnts (10A) NOK45; Indtte; shop 1km; rest, bar adj; BBQ; cooking facs; lake sw & shgl beach adj; 10% statics; phone; Eng spkn; quiet; ccard acc; CCI. "Beautiful area; useful NH & gd winter sports site." ♦ NOK 150 2007*

⊞ **VANGSNES** *1B2* (N Rural) *61.17483, 6.63729* **Solvang Camping & Motel, 6894 Vangsnes (Sogn og Fjordane) [tel 57 69 66 20; fax 57 69 67 55; post@solvangcamping.com; www.solvangcamping.com]** Site at end of peninsula, on S side of Sognefjord on Rv13, immed overlkg ferry terminal. Sm, sl, pt shd; wc; fam bthrm; baby facs; shwrs inc; el pnts NOK30; Indtte; shops adj & 300m; rest; snacks; bar; playgrnd; pool; lake sw; fishing; boating; TV; some noise fr ferries. "Wonderful views; useful sh stay/NH for x-ing Sognefjord; delightful." NOK 185 2010*

VANGSNES *1B2* (3.5km S Rural) *61.14516, 6.62025* **Tveit Camping (SF32), 6894 Vangsnes (Sogn og Fjordane) [tel 57 69 66 00; fax 57 69 66 70; tveitca@online.no; www.tveitcamping.no]** On Rv13; sp. Sm, terr, pt shd; htd wc; chem disp; mv service pnt; baby facs; shwrs NOK10; el pnts (10A) NOK25; Indtte (inc dryer); kiosk; shop, rest, snacks 3.5km; playgrnd; boating; boat & cycle hire; internet; TV; 30% cabins; dogs; phone; quiet; red long stay/CCI. "Views of Sognefjord." ♦ 1 May-1 Oct. NOK 160 2010*

⊞ **VASSENDEN** *1A2* (2km SW Rural) *61.48785, 6.08366* **PlusCamp Jølstraholmen, 6847 Vassenden (Sogn og Fjordane) [tel 57 72 89 07; fax 57 72 75 05; jostraholmen@pluscamp.no; www.jolstraholmen.no]** On R of E39, site is 2km SW of Vassenden at Statoil petrol stn. Med, hdg pitch, terr, pt sl, pt shd; htd wc; mv service pnt; chem disp; baby facs; shwrs NOK6; el pnts (10-16A) NOK40; Indtte (inc dryer); shop; tradsmn; rest; snacks; BBQ; playgrnd; paddling pool; rv & lake sw & fishing; skilift 500m; cab TV; 70% statics; dogs; Eng spkn; no adv bkg; quiet; ccard acc; red CCI. "Rv flows thro site; gd facs; friendly site; ltd facs for tourers; NH." ♦ NOK 180 2010*

VESTRE JAKOBSELV see Vadsø *2H1*

VIKEDAL *1A3* (2km S Coastal) *59.48010, 5.89990* **Camping Søndenaastranden, Søndenå, 5583 Vikedal (Rogaland) [tel 52 76 03 29; fax 53 76 62 63; gunnar@halvorsen-regnskap.no]** Sp on Rv46. Lge, mkd pitch, unshd; wc; chem disp; shwrs NOK10; el pnts (6A); Indtte (inc dryer); shop adj; snacks; bar; cooking facs; playgrnd; shgl beach adj; fishing; boat launching facs; 60% statics; Eng spkn; no ccard acc; CCI. 1 Apr-1 Oct. 2010*

VIKERSUND *1C3* (1km E Rural) *59.97766, 10.02036* **Natvedt Gård & Camping, Øst-Modumveien, 3370 Vikersund (Buskerud) [tel 32 78 73 55; natvedt@frisurf.no]** On Rv35 Hokksund-Hønefoss; in Vikersund R onto Rv284 sp Sylling to site 3km after lake bdge. Clearly sp on L. Med, pt sl, pt shd; chem disp; mv service pnt; shwrs; el pnts (4A) NOK35; Indtte (inc dryer); sm shop & 3km; rest 4km; playgrnd; lake sw; phone; poss cr; quiet. "Hilly - not suitable for disabled." 1 May-15 Sep. NOK 170 2010*

VIKHAMMER see Malvik *1D1*

VIKOYRI *1B2* (W Rural) *61.08416, 6.56786* **Vik Camping, 6891 Vikøyri (Sogn og Fjordane) [tel 57 69 51 25; grolilje@hotmail.com]** Sp in cent of Vikøyri dir Ligtvor; 67km N of Voss on Rv13. Sm, unshd; htd wc; chem disp; shwrs; el pnts (10A) (no earth); lndtte; shop 200m; dogs; quiet; Eng spkn; CCI. "Conv for ferry fr Vangsnes, easier access than other sites; gd NH." ♦ 10 May-30 Sep. 2009*

VIKSDALEN *1A2* (6km E Rural) *61.35805, 6.19371* **Viksdalen Camping, 6978 Viksdalen (Sogn og Fjordane) [tel 57 71 69 25; www.viksdalen.no/camping]** Fr Viksdalen church site on R of Rv13 twds Førde. Sm, unshd; wc; chem disp (wc); shwrs NOK10; el pnts (16A) NOK15; lndtte; BBQ; cooking facs; dogs; adv bkg; quiet except for waterfall. "Superb view Vallestadfossen waterfall; CL-type site in beautiful valley; clean facs; warden visits evenings to collect money; gd." 15 May-15 Oct. NOK 75 2007*

VIKSDALEN *1A2* (11km S Rural) *61.32628, 6.26926* **Hov Camping, 6978 Viksdalen (Sogn og Fjordane) [tel 57 71 79 37; fax 57 71 79 55; ottarhov@c2i.net; www.viksdalen.no/hov-hyttegrend]** Fr Dragsvik N on Rv13, site is approx 9km S of junc with Rv610, sp. Sm, hdstg, unshd; htd wc; baby facs; shwrs NOK10; el pnts (8-10A) NOK20; lndtte (inc dryer); shop; tradsmn; playgrnd; fishing; cycle hire; Eng spkn; quiet; ccard acc; CCI. "Attractive site with boating on lake; wcs by parking area; all other facs 150m; remote area." ♦ 1 Apr-30 Sep. NOK 140 2010*

VISTDAL *1B1* (200m W Rural) *62.71764, 7.92556* **Visa Camping, 6364 Vistdal (Møre og Romsdal) [tel 71 23 51 94]** Site well sp at W end of vill. Med, pt sl, unshd; htd wc; chem disp; shwrs; el pnts NOK30; lndtte; shop 200m; cooking facs; sw 200m; fishing; dogs; Eng spkn; quiet. "Beautiful surroundings; immac san facs; warden visits 2000-2300 to collect money." ♦ 15 May-15 Sep. NOK 120 2007*

⊞ **VOLDA** *1A1* (7km NE Coastal) *62.18979, 6.12020* **Ørsta Camping, Osholane 2, 6150 Ørsta (Hordaland) [tel 70 06 64 77; fax 70 06 85 30; post@orstacamping.no; www.orstacamping.no]** Site is on E side of E39 if ent Ørsta fr Volda & S. Sm, mkd pitch, pt sl, unshd; htd wc; chem disp; shwrs NOK10; el pnts (10A); gas 500m; lndtte; shop, snacks in town; playgrnd; 20% statics; phone; Eng spkn; quiet; 10% red 3 days; ccard acc; CCI. "Facs v ltd; gd position." NOK 150 2007*

⊞ **VOSS** *1A2* (12km NE Rural) *60.72611, 6.48913* **Tvinde Camping, Skulestadmo, 5700 Voss (Hordaland) [tel 56 51 69 19; fax 56 51 30 15; tvinde@tvinde.no; www.tvinde.no]** Fr Voss foll rd Rv13/E16 N sp Gudvangen. Site on L in approx 12km. Sm, pt sl, pt shd; wc; chem disp; baby facs; shwrs NOK10; el pnts (10A) NOK40 (poss earth fault); lndtte; sm shop in ssn; rest 8km; snacks; BBQ; cooking facs; playgrnd; rv nrby; watersports 5km; horseriding, golf 3km; wifi; TV; some statics; dogs; poss cr; recep 0800-2200; ccard acc; CCI. "Excel, clean facs; poor touring pitches; nr waterfall (noisy)." ♦ NOK 140 2008*

VOSS *1A2* (300m S Rural) *60.62476, 6.42235* **Voss Camping, Prestegardsmoen 40, 5700 Voss (Hordaland) [tel 56 51 15 97 or 90 18 11 20; fax 56 51 06 39; post@vosscamping.no; www.vosscamping.no]** Exit town on E16 & camping sp; by lake nr cent of Voss; app fr W on E16, site visible by lake on R; 2nd turn on R in town to site in 300m. Sm, mkd pitch, hdstg, terr, pt shd; htd wc; chem disp; shwrs NOK10; el pnts (10A) NOK45; lndtte; shop 500m; snacks; playgrnd; htd pool; watersports; beach/lake adj; boat & cycle hire; few statics; phone; poss v cr; Eng spkn; no adv bkg; ccard acc; CCI. "Excel cent for fjords; cable car stn in walking dist; tourist bureau; most pitches hdstg gravel but narr/sm." 1 May-30 Sep. NOK 190 2008*

LOFOTEN ISLANDS

FREDVANG see Ramberg *2E2*

KABELVAG see Svolvær *2F2*

KLEPPSTAD see Svolvær *2F2*

⊞ **LAUKVIK** *2F2* (Coastal) **Skippergaarden Camping, 8315 Laukvik [tel/fax 76 07 51 97; skgaarden@gmail.com; http://home.c2i.net/skippergaarden]** Approx 26km N of Svolvær in Laukvik; sp fr E10. Sm, some hdstg, pt shd; wc; chem disp; mv service pnt; shwrs NOK10; el pnts (16A) NOK25; lndtte; shop, rest 200m; playgrnd; few cabins; poss cr; Eng spkn; quiet. "Sh walk to view point for midnight sun; pleasant site with 'local' atmosphere." 2009*

LAUKVIK *2F2* (5km S Rural) *68.33603, 14.49808* **Sandsletta Camping, Sandsletta, 8315 Laukvik [tel/fax 76 07 52 57; sandsletta@camping-lofoten.com; www.camping-lofoten.com]** W of E10 Svolvær-Fiskebøl rd on W side of island; sp at exit. Med, pt sl, unshd; wc; chem disp; mv service pnt; baby facs; shwrs NOK5; el pnts (16A) NOK25; lndtte; shop; snacks; cooking facs; playgrnd; lake sw adj; quiet; CCI. "Gd." 1 Jun-30 Aug. NOK 150 2008*

RAMBERG *2E2* (4km NE Coastal) **Skagen Camping, Flakstad, 8380 Ramberg [tel 95 03 52 83; sm-skage@online.no; www.lofoten-info.no/skagen]** On Flakstadøya Island; on R of E10, 18km fr Nappstraumen tunnel. Site immed after Flakstad church. Sm, pt sl, unshd; wc; shwrs; el pnts (6A); lndtte; beach; Eng spkn; CCI. "Superb views over sea on N shore." 20 Jun-1 Aug. 2007*

RAMBERG *2E2* (2km W Rural) *68.0975, 13.1619* **Strand & Skærgårdscamping, 8387 Fredvang [tel 76 09 42 33; fax 76 09 41 12; mail@fredvangcamping.no; www.fredvangcamp.no]** Foll Fredvang sp fr E10; site sp in vill cent. Sm, unshd; htd wc; chem disp; mv service pnt; shwrs NOK10; el pnts (16A) NOK25; lndtte; kiosk; cooking facs; sand beach adj; boat hire & launching; sat TV; Eng spkn; quiet; CCI. "View of midnight sun; surrounded by sand beach, sea & mountains; peaceful; gd san facs; friendly." 20 May-31 Aug. NOK 150 2009*

SORVAGEN *2E2* (2km N Coastal) *67.90017, 13.04656* **Moskenes Camping, 8392 Sørvågen [tel 99 48 94 05]** Fr ferry turn L, then immed R opp terminal exit, site up sh unmade rd, sp. Med, hdstg, terr, unshd; htd wc; chem disp; mv service pnt; el pnts (10A) NOK10; Indtte; shop 2km; snacks 1km; no statics; Eng spkn; quiet. "Excel NH." May-Sep. NOK 180 2009*

STAMSUND *2F2* (6km N Rural/Coastal) *68.19921, 13.98290* **Brustranda Sjøcamping, Rolfsfjord, 8356 Leknes [tel 76 08 71 00; fax 76 08 71 44; post@brustranda.no; www.brustranda.no]** Take E10 W fr Svolvaer ferry for approx 19km. After 3rd bdge turn L onto Rv815. Site on L in 22km at petrol stn. Sm, pt shd; wc; chem disp; shwrs NOK10; el pnts (10A) NOK40 (poss rev pol); Indtte; shop 16km; snacks; shgl beach adj; sand beach 2km; fishing; boat hire; 30% statics; dogs; Eng spkn; quiet. "Idyllic setting; mountain views; v helpful staff; san facs stretched when site full; highly rec." 1 Jun-31 Aug. NOK 160 2009*

⊞ **SVOLVAER** *2F2* (10km N Coastal) **Sildpollnes Sjøcamp, 8315 Sildpollnes [tel 76 07 58 12; fax 76 07 02 88; www.sildpollnes-sjocamp.no]** N fr Svolvær on E10 for approx 10km, site sp. Med, some hdstg, terr, unshd; wc; chem disp; shwrs inc; el pnts (10A) NOK25 (poss no earth); BBQ; playgrnd; fishing; boat hire; 10% statics; dogs; Eng spkn; quiet; ccard acc; CCI. "Gd, peaceful site adj Sildpollnes church; fjord/mountain views." ♦ NOK 125 2008*

SVOLVAER *2F2* (6km SW Coastal) *68.20573, 14.42576* **Sandvika Fjord & Sjøhuscamping (N09), Ørsvågveien 45, 8310 Kabelvåg [tel 76 07 81 45; fax 76 07 87 09; post@sandvika-camping.no; www.sandvika-camping.no]** Sp on S of E10; app lane thro 1 other site. Lge, mkd pitch, terr, unshd; wc; chem disp; mv service pnt; fam bthrm; sauna; shwrs NOK10; el pnts (16A) NOK35 (poss rev pol); Indtte (inc dryer); shop, rest high ssn; snacks; playgrnd; pool; boating; fishing; cycle hire; wifi; TV; phone; bus nr; currency exchange; poss cr; Eng spkn; quiet; ccard acc. "Ideal for trip thro Lofoten Islands; conv Svolvær main fishing port; vg." ♦ 15 Apr-1 Oct. NOK 185 2010*

SVOLVAER *2F2* (15km W Coastal) *68.22356, 14.21471* **Lofoten Bobilcamp, Lyngvær, 8333 Kleppstad [tel 76 07 87 80 or 76 07 87 81; fax 76 07 82 10; post@lofoten-bobilcamping.no; www.lofoten-bobilcamping.no]** On E10 at SW side of island; approx 3km S of Kleppstad. Fr E fr Kabelvåg 13km on E10. Site on L approx 1km after rd turns N. Med, terr, unshd; htd wc; chem disp; mv service pnt; shwrs NOK10; el pnts (10-16A) NOK35; Indtte; shop, rest 10km; BBQ; cooking facs; playgrnd; sand beach adj; boat hire; salmon/trout pond; sat TV; dogs; poss cr; Eng spkn; quiet; red long stay. "Vg; on edge of fjord; facs poss stretched if site full." 1 May-30 Sep. NOK 110 2009*

VESTERALEN ISLANDS

ANDENES *2F1* (3km S Coastal) *69.30390, 16.06621* **Andenes Camping, Bleiksveien 34, 8480 Andenes [tel 76 14 14 12; fax 76 14 19 33; erna.strong@norlandia.no]** Site on L of Rv82, sp. Sm, some hdstg, unshd; htd wc; chem disp; mv service pnt; shwrs NOK10; el pnts (16A) inc (check earth); shop 250m; cooking facs; sand beach adj; Eng spkn; some rd noise; CCI. "Nice, sandy beaches; conv whale safari, summer ferry to Gryllefjord & Bleiksøya bird cliff; gd for midnight sun." 1 Jun-30 Sep. NOK 190 2007*

⊞ **GULLESFJORDBOTN** *2F2* (N Coastal) *68.53213, 15.72611* **Gullesfjordbotn Camping, Våtvoll, 8409 Gullesfjordbotn [tel 77 09 11 10; fax 77 09 11 11; post@gullesfjordcamping.no; www.gullesfjordcamping.no]** Fr S on E10 then rd 82. At rndabt just bef Gullesfjordbotn take 2nd exit to site, well sp. Sm, hdstg, unshd; htd wc; chem disp; mv service pnt; sauna; shwrs NOK10; el pnts (16A) NOK50; Indtte (inc dryer); shop; snacks high ssn; cooking facs; sw & shgl beach adj; fishing; boat hire; phone; poss cr; Eng spkn; ccard acc; CCI. "On edge of fjord; liable to flood after heavy rain; mountain views; gd san facs; friendly owners." NOK 150 2009*

⊞ **HARSTAD** *2F2* (5km S Coastal) *68.77231, 16.57878* **Harstad Camping, Nessevegen 55, 9411 Harstad [tel 77 07 36 62; fax 77 07 35 02; postsmaster@harstad-camping.no; www.harstad-camping.no]** Sp fr E10/Rv83. Med, pt sl, unshd; wc; chem disp; shwrs NOK10; el pnts (16A) inc; shop; snacks 1km; rest 5km; playgrnd; fishing; boating; quiet; ccard acc; CCI. "San facs poss stretched high ssn; lovely situation." ♦ NOK 260 (6 persons) 2009*

⊞ **RISOYHAMN** *2F1* (10km S Coastal) **Andøy Friluftssenter & Camping, Buksnesfjord, 8484 Risøyhamn [tel/fax 76 14 88 04; post@andoy-friluftssenter.no; www.andoy-friluftssenter.no]** Exit E10 onto Rv82 sp Sortland; in 31km at bdge to Sortland do not cross bdge but cont N on Rv82 sp Andenes. Site on R in 38km at Buknesfjord. Sm, hdstg, pt sl, unshd; htd wc; chem disp; shwrs inc; el pnts (10A) NOK50; Indtte; rest; snacks; playgrnd; lake sw; fishing; 50% statics; Eng spkn; adv bkg; quiet; ccard acc; CCI. "Lake fishing with facs for disabled; guided mountain walks; easy access for whale-watching; v clean facs; gourmet meals." ♦ NOK 150 2009*

⊞ **SORTLAND** *2F2* (1.5km W Rural) *68.70286, 15.3919* **Camping Sortland & Motel, Vesterveien 51, 8400 Sortland [tel 76 11 03 00; fax 76 12 25 78; hj.bergseng@sortland-camping.no; www.sortland-camping.no]** Exit E10 onto Rv82 sp Sortland; in 31km turn L over bdge to Sortland, L again at end bdge. Site sp in approx 1km immed past church. Foll rd uphill for 1km, site on R. Med, pt shd; wc; chem disp; baby facs; fam bthrm; shwrs NOK10; el pnts (16A) NOK30; gas; Indtte; shop; snacks; cooking facs; playgrnd; skiing; cycling; walking; fishing; boating; solarium; gym; TV; phone; poss cr; Eng spkn; quiet; ccard acc; CCI. "Basic, clean site; helpful staff." NOK 220 2009*

STO *2F1* (N Coastal) *69.01891, 15.12215* **Stø Bobilcamp, 8438 Stø [tel 76 13 25 30; fax 76 13 25 31; loleinan@frisurf.no; www.stobobilcamp.com]** Site sp fr cent of Stø. Sm, hdstg, unshd; htd wc; chem disp; mv service pnt; shwrs NOK10; el pnts (16A) NOK30; shop; rest; cooking facs; fishing; cycle hire; some cabins; poss cr; quiet; Eng spkn. "View of midnight sun; 10min walk to whale boat safari; coastal walks, Queen Sonja's walk fr site, v scenic but poss strenuous; facs stretched high ssn; site open to public for parking." ♦ 15 May-1 Sep. NOK 130 2009*

STOKMARKNES *2F2* (1km NE Rural) *68.5717, 14.9273* **Hurtigrutens Hus & Turistsenteret, 8450 Stokmarknes [tel 76 15 29 99; fax 76 15 29 95; www.hurtigrutenhus.com]** Beside E10. Sm, mkd pitch, hdstg, unshd; htd wc; chem disp; baby facs; shwrs; el pnts (16A) inc; gas; lndtte; shop & 1km; rest; snacks high ssn; bar; BBQ; fjord sw adj; tennis; cycle hire; entmnt; TV; dogs; phone; Eng spkn; adv bkg; quiet but poss rd/aircraft noise; ccard acc. "Gd facs." ♦ 1 Jun-31 Aug. NOK 175 2008*

Distances are shown in kilometres and are calculated from town/city centres along the most practical roads, although not necessarily taking the shortest route. 1km = 0.62miles

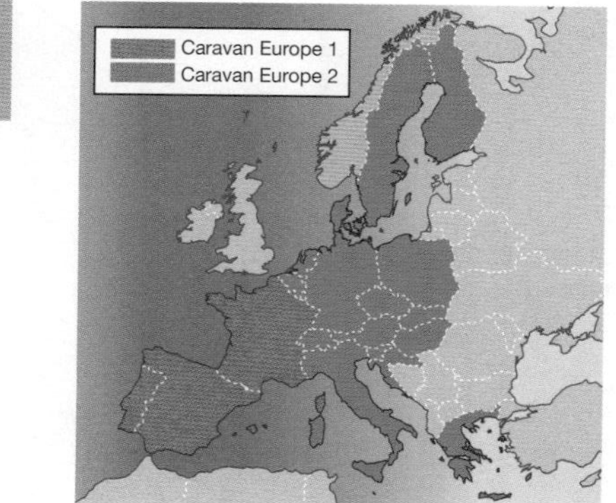

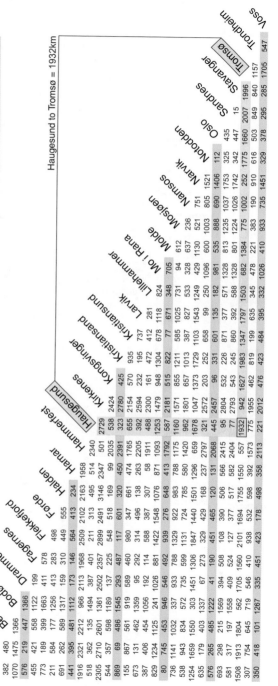

Haugesund to Tromsø = 1932km

	Ålesund	Arendal	Bergen	Bodø	Drammen	Fagernes	Flekkefjord	Førde	Halden	Hamar	Hammerfest	Haugesund	Kirkenes	Kongsvinger	Kristiansand	Kristiansund	Larvik	Lillehammer	Mo i Rana	Molde	Mosjøen	Namsos	Narvik	Notodden	Oslo	Sandnes	Stavanger	Tromsø	Trondheim
Arendal	788																												
Bergen	382	480																											
Bodø	1070	1475	1366																										
Drammen	576	219	447	1366																									
Fagernes	455	421	558	1122	199																								
Flekkefjord	773	189	399	1663	411	578																							
Førde	211	584	177	1256	413	283	498																						
Halden	691	262	589	1317	159	310	449	555																					
Hamar	441	395	481	1112	173	146	564	413	234																				
Hammerfest	1916	2321	2212	966	2113	1968	2509	2102	2163	1958																			
Haugesund	518	362	135	1494	387	401	211	313	495	514	2340																		
Kirkenes	2305	2710	2601	1361	2502	2357	2899	2491	3146	2347	501	2729																	
Kongsvinger	544	357	598	1189	137	225	548	518	169	99	2035	538	2424																
Kristiansand	869	69	486	1545	293	487	117	601	320	450	2391	323	2780	425															
Kristiansund	155	867	561	919	589	460	980	347	661	474	1765	655	2154	570	935														
Larvik	673	131	462	1359	95	292	314	496	138	263	2205	392	2594	232	195	737													
Lillehammer	387	406	454	1056	192	114	588	387	307	58	1911	488	2300	161	472	412	281												
Mo i Rana	829	1234	1125	241	1026	881	1422	1548	1076	871	1093	1253	1479	948	1304	678	1118	824											
Molde	80	745	453	946	546	492	939	276	648	413	1792	587	2181	515	822	77	671	348	705										
Mosjøen	736	1141	1032	337	933	788	1329	922	983	788	1175	1160	1571	855	1211	585	1025	731	94	612									
Namsos	538	943	834	572	735	599	1131	724	785	580	1420	962	1801	657	1013	387	827	533	328	637	236								
Narvik	1254	1659	1550	303	1451	1306	1847	1440	1501	1296	659	1678	1047	1373	1729	1103	1543	1249	429	1130	521	751							
Notodden	635	179	403	1337	67	273	329	429	168	237	2797	321	2572	203	252	658	99	250	1096	600	1003	805	1521						
Oslo	576	265	485	1222	41	190	451	465	120	131	2068	445	2457	96	331	601	135	182	981	535	888	690	1406	112					
Sandnes	693	298	215	1569	394	508	108	390	506	566	2415	95	2804	532	226	871	377	571	1328	813	1235	1037	1753	325	435				
Stavanger	581	317	197	1558	409	524	127	377	517	582	2404	77	2793	543	245	860	392	588	1328	801	1224	1026	1742	342	447	15			
Tromsø	1508	1913	1804	562	1705	1560	2101	1694	1755	1550	557	1932	942	1627	1983	1347	1797	1503	682	1384	775	1002	252	1775	1660	2007	1996		
Trondheim	307	754	645	719	546	410	938	532	598	392	1573	775	1955	462	819	199	635	345	478	221	383	190	910	616	503	849	840	1157	
Voss	350	418	101	1267	335	451	423	178	498	358	2113	221	2012	476	423	484	395	332	1026	410	933	735	1451	329	378	295	285	1705	547

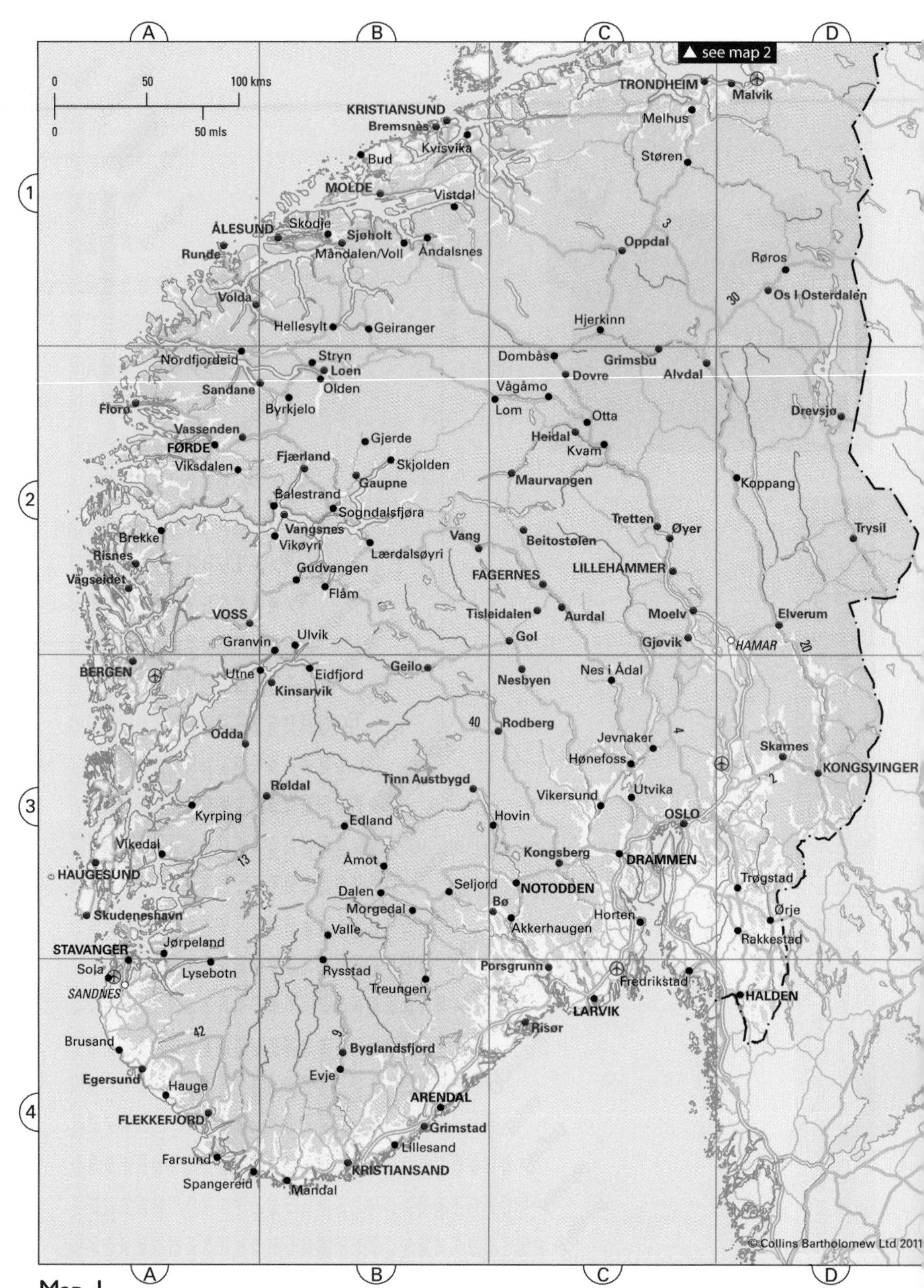
A
B
C
D
1
2
3
4
0
50
100 kms
50 mls
see map 2
TRONDHEIM
Malvik
KRISTIANSUND
Bremsnes
Kvisvika
Melhus
Bud
Støren
MOLDE
Vistdal
ÅLESUND
Skodje
Sjøholt
Måndalen/Voll
Åndalsnes
Runde
Oppdal
Røros
Os I Østerdalen
Volda
Hellesylt
Geiranger
Hjerkinn
Nordfjordeid
Stryn
Loen
Olden
Sandane
Dombås
Dovre
Grimsbu
Alvdal
Florø
Byrkjelo
Vågåmo
Lom
Otta
Drevsjø
Vassenden
FØRDE
Viksdalen
Fjærland
Gjerde
Skjolden
Gaupne
Heidal
Kvam
Maurvangen
Koppang
Balestrand
Sogndalsfjøra
Vangsnes
Vikøyri
Lærdalsøyri
Brekke
Risnes
Vågseidet
Gudvangen
Flåm
Vang
Beitostølen
Tretten
Øyer
Trysil
FAGERNES
LILLEHAMMER
VOSS
Tisleidalen
Aurdal
Moelv
Elverum
Granvin
Ulvik
Gol
Gjøvik
HAMAR
BERGEN
Utne
Eidfjord
Geilo
Kinsarvik
Nesbyen
Nes i Ådal
Odda
Rodberg
Jevnaker
Hønefoss
Skarnes
KONGSVINGER
Røldal
Tinn Austbygd
Vikersund
Utvika
Kyrping
Edland
Hovin
OSLO
Vikedal
Åmot
Kongsberg
DRAMMEN
HAUGESUND
Dalen
Seljord
NOTODDEN
Trøgstad
Morgedal
Bø
Akkerhaugen
Horten
Ørje
Skudeneshavn
Valle
Rakkestad
STAVANGER
Jørpeland
Sola
Lysebotn
Rysstad
Porsgrunn
Fredrikstad
SANDNES
Treungen
HALDEN
LARVIK
Risør
Brusand
Byglandsfjord
Evje
Egersund
Hauge
ARENDAL
FLEKKEFJORD
Grimstad
Lillesand
Farsund
KRISTIANSAND
Spangereid
Mandal
© Collins Bartholomew Ltd 2011

Map 1

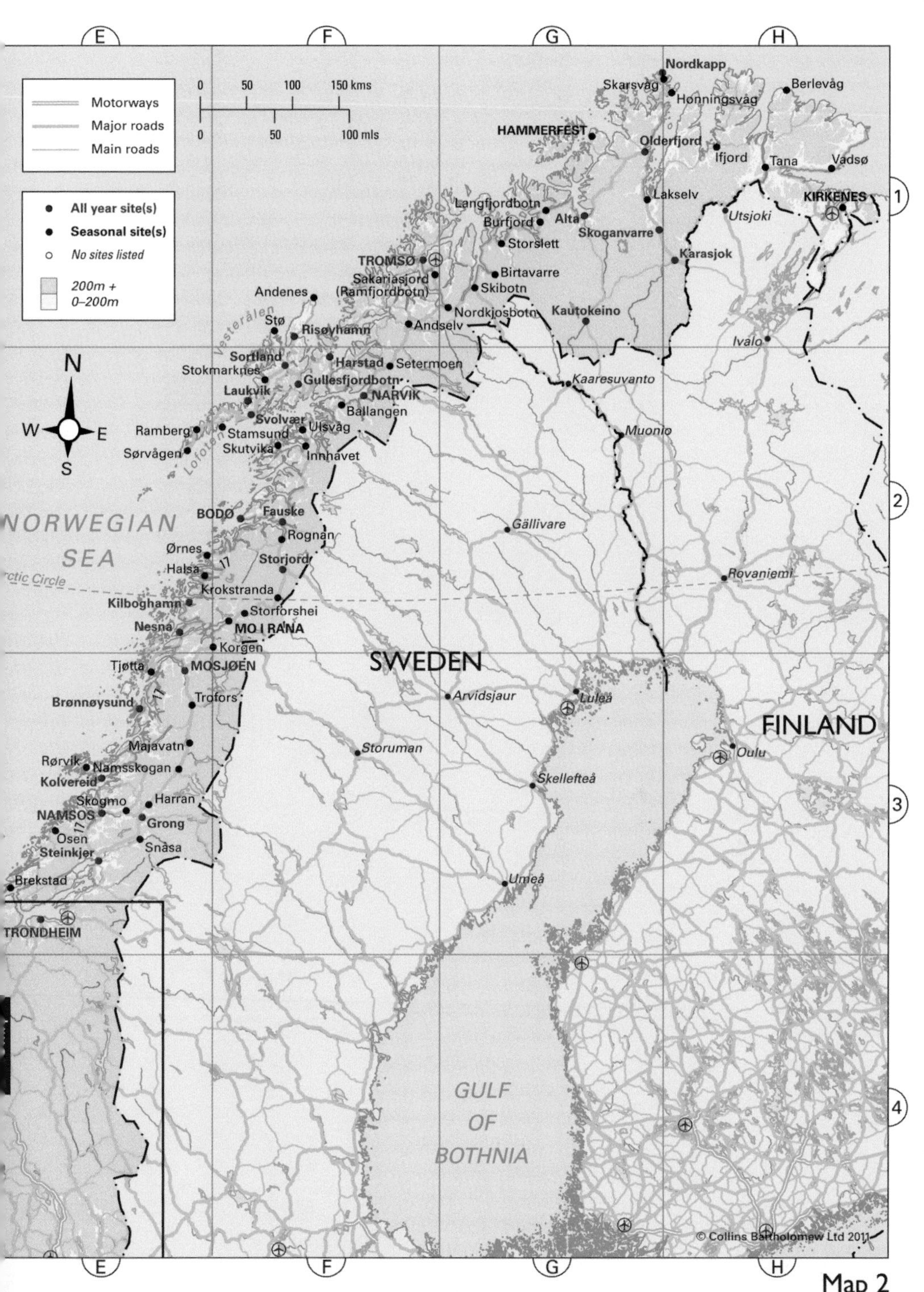

Motorways
Major roads
Main roads
0 50 100 150 kms
0 50 100 mls
All year site(s)
Seasonal site(s)
No sites listed
200m +
0–200m
N
W
E
S
NORWEGIAN SEA
SWEDEN
FINLAND
GULF OF BOTHNIA
Arctic Circle
Vesterålen
Lofoten
Nordkapp
Skarsvåg
Honningsvåg
Berlevåg
HAMMERFEST
Olderfjord
Ifjord
Tana
Vadsø
KIRKENES
Utsjoki
Lakselv
Langfjordbotn
Burfjord
Alta
Skoganvarre
Storslett
Karasjok
TROMSØ
Sakariasjord (Ramfjordbotn)
Birtavarre
Skibotn
Andenes
Nordkjosbotn
Kautokeino
Stø
Risøyhamn
Andselv
Ivalo
Sortland
Harstad
Setermoen
Stokmarknes
Gullesfjordbotn
Kaaresuvanto
Laukvik
NARVIK
Ballangen
Svolvær
Ulsvåg
Ramberg
Stamsund
Muonio
Sørvågen
Skutvika
Innhavet
BODØ
Fauske
Gällivare
Rognan
Ørnes
Storjord
Halsa
Rovaniemi
Krokstranda
Kilboghamn
Storforshei
Nesna
MO I RANA
Korgen
Tjøtta
MOSJØEN
Trofors
Arvidsjaur
Luleå
Brønnøysund
Majavatn
Storuman
Oulu
Rørvik
Namsskogan
Kolvereid
Skellefteå
Skogmo
Harran
NAMSOS
Grong
Osen
Snåsa
Steinkjer
Brekstad
Umeå
TRONDHEIM
E
F
G
H
1
2
3
4
17
© Collins Bartholomew Ltd 2011

Poland

Country Introduction

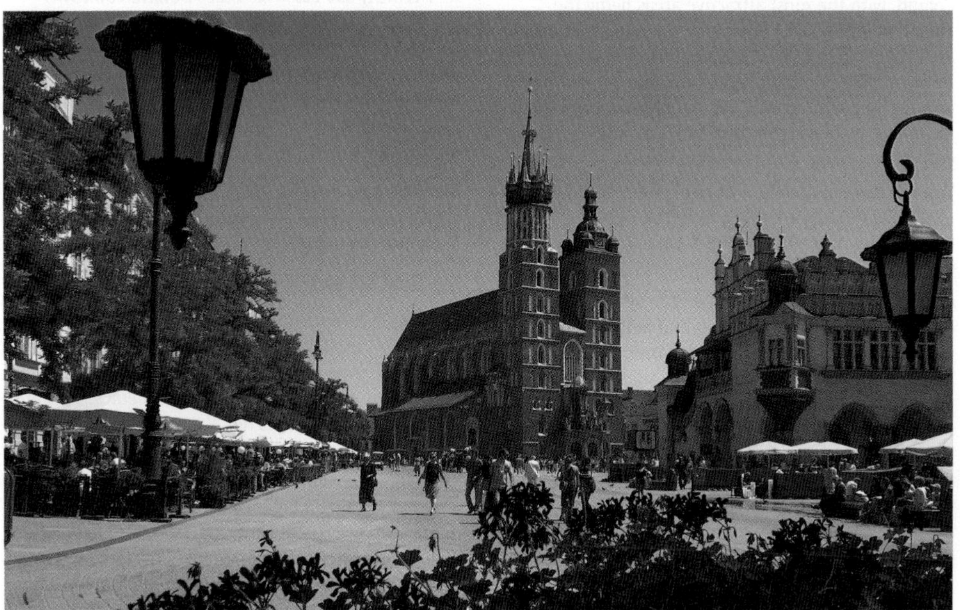

© iStockPhoto.com/puchan

Krakow, Poland

Population (approx): 38.1 million

Capital: Warsaw (population approx 1.6 million)

Area: 312,685 sq km

Bordered by: Belarus, Czech Republic, Germany, Lithuania, Russia, Slovakia, Ukraine

Terrain: Mostly flat plain with many lakes; mountains along southern border

Climate: Changeable continental climate with cold, often severe winters and hot summers; rainfall spread throughout the year; late spring and early autumn are the best times to visit

Coastline: 491km

Highest Point: Rysy 2,499m

Language: Polish

Local Time: GMT or BST + 1, i.e. 1 hour ahead of the UK all year

Currency: Zloty (PLN) divided into 100 groszy; £1 = PLN 5.02; PLN10 = £1.99 (October 2011)

Telephoning: From the UK dial 0048 and omit the initial zero of the area code of the number you are calling. To call the UK from Poland dial 0044, omitting the initial zero of the area code

Emergency numbers: Police 112; Fire brigade 112; Ambulance 112.

Public Holidays 2012

Jan 1; Apr 8, 9; May 1, 3 (Constitution Day); Jun 7; Aug 15; Nov 1, 11 (Independence Day); Dec 25, 26.

Public Holidays 2013

Jan 1; Mar 31; Apr 1; May 1, 3 (Constitution Day); May 30; Aug 15; Nov 1, 11 (Independence Day); Dec 25, 26.

School summer holidays run from the last week of June to the end of August.

Tourist Office

POLISH NATIONAL TOURIST OFFICE
WESTGATE HOUSE, WEST GATE,
LONDON W5 1YY
Tel: 0300 3031812 (brochure requests)
www.poland.travel/en-gb/ london@poland.travel.pl

The following introduction to Poland should be read in conjunction with the important information contained in the Handbook chapters at the front of this guide.

Camping and Caravanning

There are around 250 organised campsites throughout Poland, with the most attractive areas being the Mazurian lake district and along the coast. Campsites are usually open from the beginning of May or June to the middle or end of September, but the season only really starts towards the end of June. Until then facilities may be very limited and grass may not be cut, etc.

You can download details of approximately 160 sites (including GPS co-ordinates) from the website of the Polish Federation of Camping & Caravanning, www.pfcc.eu

Campsites are classified into two categories. Category one sites provide larger pitches and better amenities, but it may still be advisable to use your own facilities. There are also some basic sites which are not supervised and are equipped only with drinking water, toilets and washing facilities. Recent visitors report that sites may be in need of modernisation but, on the whole, sanitary facilities are clean although they may provide little privacy. Some new sites are being built to higher standards. A site may close earlier than its published date if the weather is bad.

Visitors report that many sites are not signposted from main roads and may be difficult to find. It is advisable to obtain a large scale atlas or good maps of the areas to be visited and not rely on one map covering the whole of Poland.

A Camping Card International (CCI) is recommended as it gives proof that the holder is covered by insurance and may lead to a 10% reduction in the overnight rate.

Casual/wild camping is not recommended and is prohibited in national parks (except on organised sites) and in sand dunes along the coast.

Country Information

Cycling

There are several long-distance cycle routes using a combination of roads with light motor traffic, forest trails or tracks along waterways. There are some cycle lanes on main roads where cyclists may not ride two or more abreast.

Electricity and Gas

The current on most campsites is 10 amps. Plugs have two round pins. There are some CEE connections.

It is understood that both propane and butane supplies are widely available, but cylinders are not exchangeable and it may be necessary to refill. The Caravan Club does not recommend this practice and you should aim to take enough gas to last during your stay. Some campsites have kitchens which you may use to conserve your gas supplies.

*See **Electricity and Gas** in the section **DURING YOUR STAY.***

Entry Formalities

British and Irish passport holders may visit Poland for up to three months without a visa. At campsites reception staff should undertake any required registration formalities with local authorities.

Regulations for Pets

*See **Pet Travel Scheme** under **Documents** in the section **PLANNING AND TRAVELLING.***

Medical Services

For simple complaints and basic advice consult staff in a pharmacy (apteka). Some English may be spoken. In general, medical facilities are comparatively inexpensive and of a good standard. Medical staff are well qualified. English is not always widely spoken and you may face language difficulties.

You will need a European Health Insurance Card (EHIC) to obtain emergency treatment from doctors, dentists and hospitals contracted to the state health care system, the NFZ. Reimbursements for any charges that you incur can be claimed from the NFZ office in Warsaw. You will have to pay a proportion of the cost of prescriptions, which is not refundable in Poland.

Private health clinics offering a good standard of medical care can also be found in large cities.

If you enjoy hiking and outdoor sports you should seek medical advice before you travel about preventative measures and immunisation against tick-borne encephalitis, a potentially serious and debilitating viral disease of the central nervous system which is endemic from spring to autumn. Lyme disease is an equally serious tick-borne infection for which there is no preventative vaccine. Ticks are found in rural and forested areas, particularly in long grass, bushes, hedgerows and woods, and in scrubland and areas where animals wander.

If you think you might be at risk use an insect repellent containing DEET, wear long sleeves and long trousers, inspect the body for ticks after outdoor activity and remove with tweezers, and avoid unpasteurised dairy products in risk areas. See www.tickalert.org, email info@tickalert.org or telephone 01943 468010.

You are strongly recommended to obtain comprehensive travel and medical insurance before travelling to Poland, such as The Caravan Club's

Red Pennant Overseas Holiday Insurance – see www.caravanclub.co.uk/redpennant

*See **Medical Matters** in the section **DURING YOUR STAY.***

Opening Hours

Banks – Mon-Fri 9am-4pm; Sat 9am-1pm.

Museums – Tue-Sun 10am-5pm; closed Monday.

Post Offices – Mon-Fri 8am-6pm; Sat 8am-2pm (on rota basis).

Shops – Mon-Fri 11am-8pm; Sat 9am-2pm/4pm; food shops open and close earlier; supermarkets open until 9pm/10pm.

Safety and Security

Most visits to Poland are trouble free and violent crime is rare, but there is a risk of robbery in tourist areas, particularly near hotels, at main railway stations and on public transport. Passengers are most at risk when boarding and leaving trains or trams. Care is needed at all times; keep jewellery, watches, cameras and wallets/purses out of sight. Take particular care of your passport and credit cards. Extra caution should be exercised when carrying out transactions at money exchange facilities or cash dispensers. Avoid walking alone at night, particularly in dark or poorly-lit streets or in public parks.

Some tourists have been the target of a scam in which men claiming to be plain clothes police officers come to their aid, usually when another person has stopped them to ask for help or directions. The fake police officers ask visitors to show their identity documents and bank cards, and then ask for their PIN(s). Although the police are allowed to stop people and request to see identification, under no circumstances should you disclose your bank account details or PIN(s).

Theft of and from vehicles is common so do not leave vehicle documentation or valuables in your car. Foreign registered cars may be targeted, especially in large, busy supermarket car parks. Elsewhere, park in guarded parking areas if possible.

Cases have been reported of vehicles with foreign number plates being stopped by gangs posing as police officers, either claiming a routine traffic control or at the scene of fake accidents, particularly in rural and tourist areas, such as the lake district. If in doubt, when flagged down keep all doors and windows locked, remain in your vehicle and ask to see identification. The motoring organisation, PZM, advises that any car or document inspection performed outside built-up areas can only be carried out by uniformed police officers and at night these officials must use a police patrol car. Although police officers do not have to be in uniform within built-up areas, they must always present their police identity card. More details are available to motorists at Polish road borders.

An emergency helpline for tourists has been set up to assist visitors who have been victims of crime or who require assistance with any other problems encountered during their stay. Telephone 0800 200300 (freephone) or +48 608 599999 (mobile number). The helpline operates from 1 June to 30 September between 10am and 10pm. Please note: this is not a tourist information service.

Do not leave drinks or food unattended or accept drinks from strangers. There has been a small number of reports of drinks being spiked and of visitors having their valuables stolen whilst drugged.

The threat from terrorism is low but you should be aware of the global risk of indiscriminate terrorist attacks which could be in public places, including tourist sites.

*See **Safety and Security** in the section **DURING YOUR STAY.***

British Embassy

UL KAWALERII 12
00-468 WARSZAWA
Tel: (022) 3110000
http://ukinpoland.fco.gov.uk/en/

There are also Honorary Consulates in Gdansk, Katowice, Kraków, Łódz, Lublin, Poznan, Szczecin and Wrocław.

Irish Embassy

UL MYSIA 5, 00-496 WARSZAWA
Tel: (022) 8496633
www.embassyofireland.pl

There is also an Honorary Consulate in Poznan.

Customs Regulations

Alcohol and Tobacco

*For import allowances for alcohol and tobacco products see **Customs Regulations** in the section **PLANNING AND TRAVELLING.***

Border Posts

Customs posts are open 24 hours a day throughout the year. Cars crossing the eastern borders, especially to Lithuania and Belarus, are usually intensively scrutinised by the Polish authorities in an effort to combat widespread smuggling of stolen cars. Travellers should ensure all documents are in order.

Borders may be busy at weekends with cross-border shoppers, and it is understood that in particular the crossing from Germany via Frankfurt-on-Oder can be heavily congested on Saturday mornings.

Documents

Driving Licence

The standard pink UK paper driving licence is recognised, but if you hold the old style green UK licence or a Northern Irish licence issued prior to 1991 you are advised to update it to a photocard licence in order to avoid any local difficulties.

Passport

Carry your passport at all times.

Vehicle(s)

You must carry your original vehicle registration certificate (V5C), insurance documentation and MOT certificate (if applicable) at all times. You may be asked for these if you are stopped by the police and, in particular, when crossing borders. If you do not own the vehicle(s) you will need a letter of authority from the owner, together with the vehicle's original documentation.

*See **Documents** in the section **PLANNING AND TRAVELLING**.*

Money

Cash can easily be obtained from ATMs in banks and shopping centres. ATMs offer an English option.

Travellers' cheques may be cashed at banks, some hotels, travel agents and border crossings, but they are not accepted at exchange bureaux ('kantors'). They are accepted as payment for goods and services in larger cities.

The major credit cards are widely accepted in hotels, restaurants and shops but you may find that supermarkets do not accept them. Take particular care to safeguard your credit/debit cards. You are advised not to lose sight of them during transactions.

Visitors advise that sterling and euros are readily accepted at exchange bureaux but Scottish and Northern Irish bank notes are not generally recognised and you may have difficulties trying to cash them.

Carry your credit card issuers'/banks' 24-hour UK contact numbers in case of loss or theft of your cards.

Motoring

Poland is a major east to west route for heavy vehicles and driving can be hazardous. There are few dual carriageways and even main roads between large towns can be narrow and poorly surfaced. Slow moving agricultural and horse-drawn vehicles are common in rural areas. Street lighting is weak even in major cities.

Local driving standards are poor and speed limits, traffic lights and road signs are often ignored. Drivers rarely indicate before manoeuvring and you may encounter aggressive tailgating, overtaking on blind bends and overtaking on the inside. Take particular care on national holiday weekends when there is a surge in road accidents.

It is not advisable to drive a right hand drive vehicle alone for long distances or to drive long distances at night. At dusk watch out for cyclists riding without lights along the edge of the road or on its shoulder.

Hitchhikers use an up and down motion of the hand to ask for a lift. This may be confused with flagging down.

When visibility is poor, for example, due to fog or rain, you should use your horn when overtaking other vehicles outside built-up areas.

Accidents

A driver involved in an accident must call the police, obtain an official record of damages and forward it to the insurance company of the Polish driver involved (if applicable), for example, the Polish National Insurance Division (PZU) or the Polish Insurance Association (WARTA). Members of AIT/FIA affiliated clubs, such as The Caravan Club, can obtain help from the touring office ('Autotour') of the Polish motoring organisation, Polski Zwiazek Motorowy (PZM), tel (022) 8496904 or (022) 8499361.

If people are injured, you must call an ambulance or doctor. By law, it is an offence for a driver not to obtain first aid for accident victims or to leave the scene of an accident. In such circumstances the authorities may withdraw a tourist's passport and driving licence, vehicle registration certificate or even the vehicle itself and the penalties can be a prison sentence and a fine.

Alcohol

There is zero tolerance for drink-driving; the permitted level of alcohol is 20 milligrams in 100 millilitres of blood, which in practice equates to zero. At the request of the police or if an accident has occurred a driver must undergo a blood test which, if positive, may lead to a prison sentence, withdrawal of driving licence and a fine. Penalty points will be notified to the authorities in the motorist's home country.

Breakdown Service

The PZM runs a breakdown service covering the entire country 24 hours a day. Members of AIT and FIA affiliated clubs, such as The Caravan Club, should call the PZM Emergency Centre on (022) 5328433. Staff speak English. Roadside assistance must be paid for in cash.

Essential Equipment

Strictly speaking, it is not compulsory for visiting motorists to carry a fire extinguisher or first aid kit but you are recommended to do so in order to avoid any possible local difficulties which may arise.

Lights

Dipped headlights must be used at all times. Bulbs are more likely to fail with constant use and you are recommended to carry spares. In bad visibility due to fog, rain, etc, use your horn to indicate that you are going to overtake.

Warning Triangles

Drivers of vehicles must use a warning triangle when a vehicle is stationary on a road in poor visibility (less than 100 metres) and if the vehicle is likely to obstruct traffic. On a normal road the triangle must be placed between 30 and 50 metres behind the vehicle and must be clearly visible to oncoming traffic; on a motorway, it must be placed 100 metres behind the vehicle. Hazard warning lights may be used in addition to, but not instead of, a triangle.

Child Restraint System

Children under the age of 12 years old and under the height of 1.5m must use a suitable restraint system that has been adapted to their size. It is prohibited to place a child in a rear facing seat in the front of the vehicle if the car is equipped with airbags.

*See **Motoring – Equipment** in the section **PLANNING AND TRAVELLING.***

Fuel

The usual opening hours for petrol stations are from 8am to 7pm; many on main roads and international routes and in large towns are open 24 hours. Credit cards are widely accepted. LPG (Autogas) is widely available from service stations.

*See also **Fuel** under **Motoring – Advice** in the section **PLANNING AND TRAVELLING.***

Parking

There are parking meters in many towns and signs display parking restrictions or prohibitions. There are many supervised car parks charging an hourly rate. Illegally parked cars causing an obstruction may be towed away and impounded, in which case a driver will be fined. Wheel clamps are in use.

Sidelights must be used when parking in unlit streets during the hours of darkness.

*See also **Parking Facilities for the Disabled** under **Motoring – Advice** in the section **PLANNING AND TRAVELLING.***

Priority

Priority should be given to traffic coming from the right at intersections of roads of equal importance, however vehicles on rails always have priority. At roundabouts traffic already on a roundabout has priority.

Give way to buses pulling out from bus stops. Trams have priority over other vehicles at all times. Where there is no central reservation or island you should stop to allow passengers alighting from trams to cross to the pavement.

Roads

All roads are hard surfaced and the majority of them are asphalted. However, actual road surfaces may be poor; even some major roads are constructed of cement or cobbles and heavily rutted. Average journey speed is about 50 km/h (31 mph).

Some roads, notably those running into Warsaw, have a two metre wide strip on the nearside to pull onto in order to allow other vehicles to overtake. Oncoming lorries expect other motorists to pull over when they are overtaking.

Overtake trams on the right unless in a one-way street.

Road Signs and Markings

Road signs and markings conform to international standards. Motorway and national road numbers are indicated in red and white, and local roads by yellow signs with black numbering. Signs on motorways are blue with white lettering and on main roads they are green and white.

The following road signs may be seen:

Rondzie – *Roundabout*

Wstep szbroniony – *No entry*

Wyjscie – *Exit*

You may also encounter the following:

Paid parking between 7am and 6pm

Residential area-predestrians have priority

Toll road

Rutted road

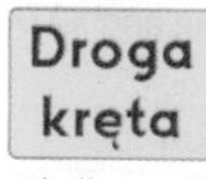

Winding road

Emergency vehicles

Crossroads and road junctions may not be marked with white 'stop' lines, and other road markings in general may be well worn and all but invisible, so always take extra care.

Speed Limits

*See **Speed Limits** under **Motoring – Advice** in the section **PLANNING AND TRAVELLING.***

In built up areas the speed limit is 50 km/h (31 mph) between 5am and 11pm, and 60 km/h (37 mph) between 11pm and 5am. For vehicles over 3,500kg all speed limits are the same as for a car and caravan outfit. In residential zones indicated by entry/exit signs, the maximum speed is 20 km/h (13 mph).

The use of radar detectors is prohibited.

Traffic Lights

Look out for a small, non-illuminated green arrow under traffic lights, which permits a right turn against a red traffic light if the junction is clear.

Violation of Traffic Regulations

Motorists must not cross a road's solid central white line or even allow wheels to run on it. Radar speed traps are frequently in place on blind corners where speed restrictions apply. Police are very keen to enforce traffic regulations with verbal warnings and/or on the spot fines. Fines are heavy and drivers of foreign registered vehicles will be required to pay in cash. Always obtain an official receipt.

Motorways and Tolls

There are approximately 873km of motorways in Poland. Tolls are levied on sections and vary in price, for example, the A1 Rusocin to Nowe Marzy is €41.80 (2011 prices) for a car towing a caravan. There are some stretches of motorway that are toll free.

As of 1 July 2011 a new electronic toll system was introduced in Poland for vehicles over the weight of 3,500kg. These vehicles (which include motorhomes and car and caravan combinations if the total weight is over 3,500kg) will need to be equipped with an electronic device, known as the viaBOX. Tolls vary and are dependent on the type of road, distance travelled and the emissions category of the vehicle. For more information please visit www.viatoll.pl/en/heavy-vehicles/viatoll-system.

Below is an example of toll prices for a vehicle weighing between 3,500kg and 12,000kg on category A and S roads:

EURO 2 = 0.40 PLN per km
EURO 3 = 0.35
EURO 4 = 0.28
EURO 5 = 0.20

From January 2012 an electronic system of payment for vehicles under 3,500kg will be available on motorways, managed by GDDKiA.

There are emergency telephones every 2km along motorways. Recent visitors report that newer stretches of motorway have rest areas with chemical disposal and waste water disposal facilities.

Touring

Polish cuisine is tasty and substantial and restaurants offer good value. Visitors should not miss the opportunity to try pierogi (savoury ravioli), kalduny (stuffed dumplings) and gołabki (stuffed cabbage rolls). Poland's climate does not permit the production of wine, the national drinks being varieties of vodka and plum brandy. It is usual to leave a tip of between 10 to 15%.

There are over 9,000 lakes in Poland, mostly in the north. The regions of Western Pomerania, Kaszubia and Mazuria are a paradise for sailing enthusiasts, anglers and nature lovers. In order to protect areas of great natural beauty, national parks and nature reserves have been created, two of the most interesting of which are the Tatra National Park covering the whole of the Polish Tatra mountains, and the Slowinksi National Park with its 'shifting' sand dunes.

There are 13 UNESCO World Heritage sites including the restored historic centres of Warsaw and Kraków, the medieval, walled town of Toruń as well as Auschwitz Concentration Camp. Other towns worth a visit are Chopin's birthplace at Zelazowa Wola, Wieliczka with its salt mines where statues and a chapel are carved out of salt, and Wrocław.

White and brown signs placed strategically in cities and near sites of interest pinpoint architectural and natural landmarks, places of religious worship, etc. Each sign includes not only information on the name of and distance to a particular attraction, but also a pictogram of the attraction, e.g. Jasna Góra monastery. Themed routes, such as the trail of the wooden churches in the Małopolska Region (south of Kraków), are marked in a similar way.

A Warsaw Tourist Card and a Kraków Tourist Card are available, both valid for up to three days and offering free travel on public transport and free entry to many museums, together with discounts at selected restaurants and shops and on sightseeing and local excursions. Buy the cards from tourist information centres, travel agents or hotels.

The Polish people are generally friendly, helpful and polite. English is becoming increasingly widely spoken in major cities.

Local Travel

For security reasons recent visitors recommend using guarded car parks such as those in Warsaw on the embankment below the Old Town, in the Palace of Culture and near the Tomb of the Unknown Soldier.

Problems have been reported involving overcharging by non-regulated taxi drivers. Use only taxis from official ranks whose vehicles have the name and telephone number of the taxi company on the door and on the roof (beside the occupied/unoccupied light). They also display a rate card in the window of the vehicle. Taxis with a crest but no company name are not officially registered.

There are frequent ferries from Gydnia, Swinoujscie and Gdansk to Denmark, Germany and Sweden. There are no car ferry services on internal waters but passenger services operate along the Baltic Coast, on the Mazurian lakes and on some rivers, for example, between Warsaw and Gdansk.

There is a metro system in Warsaw linking the centre to the north and south of the city. It is possible to buy a daily or weekly tourist pass which is valid for all means of public transport – bus, tram and metro. Buy tickets at newspaper stands and kiosks displaying a sign 'bilety'. Tickets must be punched before travelling at the yellow machines at the entrance to metro stations or on board buses and trams. You will incur an on the spot fine if you are caught travelling without a valid ticket.

Jay walking is an offence and, if caught by the police, you will be fined.

All place names used in the Site Entry listings which follow can be found in the Poland Road Atlas published by Copernicus, scale 1cm to 2.5km, see www.ppwk.pl

AUSCHWITZ see Oświęcim *D3*

BAKOW see Kluczbork *C2*

BARANOWO see Poznań *B2*

BIALOWIEZA *B4* (1km W Rural) *52.69395, 23.83088* **Camping U Michała (No. 124), ul Krzyże 11, 17-230 Białowieża [(085) 6812703]** Exit Bielsk Podlaski onto rd 689; cont past Hajnówka for 17m; site on R at end of vill. Sm, mkd pitch, pt shd; wc; chem disp; shwrs inc; el pnts (16A); lndtte; playgrnd; cycle hire; poss cr; quiet. "Gd san facs." ♦ 15 Apr-30 Sep. PLN 50 2011*

⊞ **BIALYSTOK** *B4* (6.5km N Rural) *53.19364, 23.19364* **Camping Hotel Jard, ul Białostocka 94, 16-010 Wasilków [(085) 7185240; fax 7185511; www.jard.pl]** On L of rte 19 when on app Wasilków fr Białystok. Sm, pt sl, pt shd; own san rec; shwrs inc; el pnts (10A) PLN8; shop 2km; rest; bar; ccard acc. "Fair NH; simple site - only one for some dist." PLN 34 2009*

BIELSKO BIALA *D3* (1.5km S Rural) *49.78031, 19.05318* **Camping Ondraszek (No. 57), ul Pocztowa 43, 43-309 Bielsko-Biała [(033) 8146425; fax 8143601; kemping57ondraszek@op.pl; www.tkkfblonia.ovh.org]** Fr E462 ent BielskO-Biała & foll sp Szczyrk. Site sp on R after Park Hotel. Cont uphill to T-junc, L to gates. Site on edge of town in park. Sm, hdg pitch, pt sl, pt shd; wc; chem disp; mv service pnt; shwrs inc; el pnts; shops 1.5km; rest adj; bar; BBQ; playgrnd; pool & sports facs adj; quiet. "Pretty, well-kept site in woods; daytime noise fr neighbouring sports facs; conv Oswięcim (Auschwitz)." ♦ 15 Apr-30 Sep. € 13.10 2010*

⊞ **BIELSKO BIALA** *D3* (10km S Rural) **Camping Skalite (No. 262), ul Kempingowa 4, 43-370 Szczyrk [(033) 8178760]** Fr Bielsko Biała S on B69 dir Zywiec, turn onto B942 to Szczyrk; on ent town cross sm bdge to site ent. Med, hdg pitch, pt shd; wc; chem disp; shwrs inc; el pnts; shops 500mm; rest, snacks, bar 1.5km; Eng spkn; quiet; red long stay/CCI. "Basic san facs; charge depends on pitch size; conv mountains on Czech border; easy x-ing 50km at Cieszyn/Cesky Tesin." PLN 35 2007*

BIELSKO BIALA *D3* (5km SW Rural) *49.78148, 19.02281* **Camping Pod Dębowcem (No. 99), ul Karbowa 15, 43-316 Bielsko-Biała [(033) 8216181 or (0604) 144186 (mob); 99@camping.org.pl; www.camping.bielsko.com.pl]** Rd 1/E75 out of Bielsko-Biała to Cieszyn or fr B942 foll sp 'Szyndzielnia' (cable car) to site. Med, mkd pitch, some hdstg, terr, pt sl, pt shd; wc; chem disp; shwrs inc; el pnts (6A) PLN10; lndtte; snacks; bar; BBQ; playgrnd; TV; dogs; no adv bkg; quiet; CCI. "Conv Czech border." ♦ 1 May-31 Oct. PLN 48 2010*

BOGACZEWO see Gizycko *A3*

CHMIELNO see Kartuzy *A2*

⊞ **CZESTOCHOWA** *C3* (1km W Urban) *50.81122, 19.09131* **Camping Oleńka (No. 76), ul Oleńki 10, 42-200 Częstochowa [tel/fax (034) 3606066; camping@mosir.pl; www.mosir.pl]** Fr A1/E75 foll sp Jasna Góra monastery, pick up sm white camping sp to site. Lge, pt shd; wc; chem disp; shwrs inc; el pnts (20A); lndtte; shops nrby; rest; bar; playgrnd; pool 2km; internet; TV; 20% statics; dogs; phone; Eng spkn; no adv bkg; quiet; ccard acc; red CCI. "Guided tours; monastery worth visit; gd NH/sh stay nr Jasna Góra & Black Madonna painting; poor security; san facs unclean & poorly maintained (6/09)." ♦ € 19.95 2009*

DZIWNOW *A1* (500m N Coastal) *54.02194, 14.74654* **Camping Korab (No. 93), ul Słowackiego 8, 72-420 Dziwnów [(091) 3813569 or (0607) 683604 (mob); wojciechstudzinski@vp.pl; www.nawczasy.pl/korab]** 200m fr Dziwnów on rd 102. E of bdge over rv, clearly visible fr rd & sp at ent town. Med, shd; wc; shwrs inc; el pnts (10A) PLN8; lndtte; shop; snacks; bar; cooking facs; playgrnd; fishing in lagoon; watersports; TV; some statics; dogs; poss cr; some Eng spkn; quiet. "Helpful, friendly warden; secure site; NH only." 1 May-30 Sep. PLN 43 2008*

DZIWNOW *A1* (2km E Coastal) *54.03404, 14.79978* **Camping Wiking (No. 194), ul Wolności 3, 72-420 Dziwnówek [tel/fax (091) 3813493; camping@campingwiking.pl; www.campingwiking.pl]** Foll rd 102 thro Dziwnówek twd Dziwnów. Site on R in 400m (past ent to diff site). Med, pt sl, shd; wc; chem disp; baby facs; shwrs PLN15; el pnts PLN13.50 (poss rev pol); lndtte; shop; rest; snacks; bar; BBQ; playgrnd; sw & sand beach adj; some statics; dogs PLN7; bus; poss cr; CCI. "Fair sh stay/NH; gd security." ♦ 1 May-10 Sep. PLN 60 2009*

ELBLAG *A3* (N Urban) *54.15349, 19.39403* **Camping Elbląg (No. 61), ul Panieńska 14, 82-300 Elbląg [tel/fax (055) 6418666; camping@camping61.com.pl; www.camping61.com.pl]** Fr rd 7/E77 fr Gdańsk, take slip rd into Elbląg. At traff lts bdge over canal turn L, site on R, well sp fr ring rd. Sm, pt shd; wc; chem disp; shwrs; el pnts (16A) PLN8; lndtte; rest 500m; snacks 400m; playgrnd; wifi; dogs; red low ssn/long stary/CCI. "Helpful staff; old san facs clean but poss stretched high ssn; conv for 'shiplift' canal." 29 Apr-30 Sep. PLN 51 2011*

ELK *A3* (500m SW Urban) *53.81545, 22.35215* **Camping Plaża Miejska (No. 62), ul Parkowa 2, 19-300 Ełk [(087) 6109700; fax 6102723; mosir@elk.com.pl; www.mosir.elk.com.pl]** Fr town cent on rd 16 take rd 65/669 dir Białystok. After 200m cross rv & immed turn R, site 100m on L. Sm, mkd pitch, hdstg, pt shd; htd wc; shwrs inc; el pnts (10A) inc; shop 500m; snacks; bar; cooking facs; lake sw & sand beach 200m; quiet; CCI. "Gd security; well-maintained, clean site adj town cent & attractive lake; gd touring base lake district." ♦ 1 Jun-1 Sep. PLN 65 2011*

FROMBORK *A3* (1km E Rural/Coastal) *54.35877, 19.69572* **Camping Frombork (No. 12), ul Braniewska, 14-530 Frombork [(0506) 803151; kontakt@campingfrombork.pl; www.campingfrombork.pl]** Fr Frombork on rd 504 dir Braniewo, site on L. Med, pt shd; wc; chem disp & mv service pnt at car wash; shwrs inc; el pnts inc; lndtte; shop 1km; bar; BBQ; playgrnd; sand beach 2km; games area; dogs; quiet. "Pleasant, basic site; san facs tatty but clean (2009); pleasant countryside." 1 May-30 Sep. PLN 40 2009*

GAJ see Krakow *D3*

GDANSK *A2* (5km E Coastal) *54.37021, 18.72938* **Camping Stogi (No. 218), ul Wydmy 9, 80-656 Gdańsk [(058) 3073915; fax 3042259; jan@kemping-gdansk.pl; www.kemping-gdansk.pl]** E fr Gdańsk on rd 7 (E77) for approx 2km, then L foll sp for Stogi. Then foll tram rte no. 8 to Stogi Plaza/Beach. Site is 100m fr tram terminus, well sp. Med, hdstg; wc; chem disp; shwrs inc; el pnts (10-16A) PLN10; lndtte; shop; snacks; bar; BBQ; playgrnd; sand beach adj; games area; 75% statics; tram 100m; poss cr & poss noise fr school parties; CCI. "Basic site, with school groups; san facs old but clean; ltd facs low ssn; close to huge, clean beach; gd security." 25 Apr-5 Oct. PLN 54.8 2011*

GIZYCKO *A3* (6km SE Rural) *53.96750, 21.77666* **Camping Echo (No. 55), Mazurska 48, 11-511 Rydzewo-Miłki [(087) 4211186; olanowakowska84@gmail.com; www.mazury.info.pl/echo]** Fr Giżycko rd 63 dir Orzysz; in Ruda foll sp to R Rydzewo & site on lakeside. Sm, pt shd; wc; shwrs inc; el pnts (16A) PLN9; lndtte; shop; rest 1km; snacks high ssn; BBQ; sand beach; lake sw; dogs PLN5; Eng spkn; quiet. "Vg; gd, modern san facs; ideal for touring Masurian Lake District." 1 May-30 Sep. PLN 50 2010*

GIZYCKO *A3* (10km S Rural) **Camping Marina Evelyn, 11-532 Bogaczewo [(087) 4280647; info@camping-marina-evelyn.de; www.camping-marina-evelyn.de]** S fr Giżycko on rd 59 sp Mrągowo, turn L onto rd 643 sp Mikołajki. Site in 7km, sp on L. Med, unshd; wc; chem disp; shwrs inc; el pnts PLN6; lndtte; shop in vill; snacks; bar; lake sw & beach; fishing; boat-launching; watersports; games area; bus; dogs PLN3; quiet. "Well-kept site on lakeside." 1 May-30 Sep. PLN 50 2008*

GIZYCKO *A3* (500m W Urban) *54.03413, 21.76002* **Camping Zamek (No. 1), ul Moniuszki 1, 11-500 Giżycko [(087) 4283410; info@cmazur.pl; www.cmazur.pl]** Fr Olsztyn on rte 59 ent town. After junc with rte 592 fr Kętrzyn bear R to town cent & swing bdge. Site on R bef swing bdge over canal adj Hotel Zamek. NB Swing bridge 2.5T weight & 2m height limit, do not app site thro town. Sm, hdg pitch, pt sl, pt shd; wc; chem disp; shwrs PLN10; el pnts (16A) PLN8; lndtte; shop 500m; rest; snacks; bar; cooking facs; lake 500m; wifi; dogs PLN10; rlwy noise & poss noisy until 2300 as disco adj; CCI. "Adj boat marina & nr beautiful lakes/forests." ♦ 1 May-30 Sep. PLN 41 2011*

⊞ **JELENIA GORA** *C2* (700m SE Urban) *50.89638, 15.74266* **Auto-Camping Park (No. 130), ul Sudecka 42, 58-500 Jelenia Góra [tel/fax (075) 7524525; campingpark@interia.pl; www.camping.karkonosz.pl]** In town foll sp to Karpacz on rd 367. Site 100m fr hotel. Well sp. Med, some hdstg, pt terr, pt shd; wc in recep building; shwrs inc; el pnts (6-10A) PLN10 (poss rev pol); lndtte; shops 100m; rest 200m; snacks; pool, tennis & sports facs 500m; wifi; TV; 20% statics; dogs PLN5; adv bkg; quiet but some rd noise; ccard acc; red CCI. "Conv Karkanosze mountains & Czech border; well-run, neat site nr hotel with gd, modern facs; 20 min walk to pleasant town; staff friendly & helpful; conv NH." ♦ PLN 40 2010*

JELENIA GORA *C2* (8km SW Urban) *50.86566, 15.6644* **Camping Słoneczna Polana, ul Rataja 9, 58-560 Cieplici [tel/fax (075) 7552566; info@campingpolen.com; www.campingpolen.com]** Fr SW on rd 3/E65 twd Jelenia Góra; after Wojcieszyce, then o'head power lines, turn R to Cieplice & watch for church spire strt ahead. Take care at level x-ing, turn R at T-junc to site on L after 1km where rd crosses stream. Fr N app Jelenia Góra on rd 297 & rd 30, turn R on rd 3/E65 sp Szklarska Poręba. After about 3km app x-rds at Wojcieszyce. Turn L to Cieplice, then as above. Med, mkd pitch, pt shd; wc; chem disp; mv service pnt; shwrs inc; el pnts (6-10A) (adaptors free) PLN16; lndtte (inc dryer); shop 300m; tradsmn; rest; snacks; playgrnd; pool; paddling pool; thermal baths nr; games rm; wifi; sat TV; some statics; dogs PLN16; poss cr; Eng spkn; adv bkg; quiet; ccard not acc; red low ssn/snr citizens; CCI. "Excel Dutch-run site; barrier clsd 2200-0700; Cieplici attractive spa." 1 May-30 Sep. PLN 65 2010*

KARPACZ *D2* (3km N Rural) *50.81110, 15.76836* **Camping Wiśniowa Polana (No. 142), Miłków 40A, 58-535 Młków [(0692) 430135 (mob); camping-milkow@karkonosz.pl; www.camping-milkow.karkonosz.pl]** Fr Jelenia Góra to Karpacz on rte 367, turn L at junc with rte 366 at Kowary, site on E of Miłków by rv. Med, some hdstg, pt shd; wc; chem disp (wc); mv service pnt; shwrs inc; el pnts (10A) PLN10; lndtte; shop 500m; snacks; bar; BBQ; playgrnd; pool; paddling pool; fishing; games area; internet; no statics; dogs PLN5; quiet; red snr citizens/CCI. "Well-kept, guarded site & facs; v friendly staff; 7km fr chairlift onto mountain ridge; gd walking - map fr recep." ♦ 1 May-30 Sep. PLN 38 2009*

⊞ **KARTUZY** *A2* (12km W Rural) *54.31983, 18.11736* **Camping Tamowa (No. 181), Zawory 47A, 83-333 Chmielno [tel/fax (058) 6842535; camping@tamowa.pl; www.tamowa.pl]** Fr Gdańsk take rd 7 & rd 211 to Kartuzy, cont for approx 4km on 211. Turn L for Chmielno; site sp fr vill on lakesite along narr, bumpy app rd. Med, terr, unshd; wc; chem disp; sauna; shwrs PLN2; el pnts (10-16A) inc; shop 1km; snacks; bar; BBQ; playgrnd; lake sw adj; boat & cycle hire; Eng spkn; quiet; CCI. "Attractive, well-kept site in beautiful location; friendly owner; not suitable lge o'fits." PLN 54 2009*

POLAND

KATOWICE *D3* (3.5km SE Rural) *50.24355, 19.04795* **Camping Dolina Trzech Statow (No. 215), ul Murckowska 1, 40-266 Katowice [tel/fax (032) 2565939]** Exit A4 at junc Murckowska & foll sp on rd 86 Sosnowiec. In 500m turn R & foll site sp. Med, pt sl, shd; htd wc; shwrs inc; el pnts (16A) PLN2.50/kwh; shop 1km; rest adj; snacks; bar; cooking facs; playgrnd; lake; tennis; dogs PLN5; Eng spkn; adv bkg; quiet; ccard acc; red CCI. "V clean facs but basic & little privacy; vg." ♦ 1 May-30 Sep. PLN 42 2010*

⊞ **KLODZKO** *D2* (10km W Urban) *50.41502, 16.51335* **Camping Polanica-Zdroj (No. 169), ul Sportowa 7, 57-320 Polanica-Zdrój [(074) 8681210; fax 8681211; osir.polanica@neostrada.pl; www.osir.polanica.net/pl]** Foll sp fr rd 8/E67. Site is 1km N of Polanica-Zdrój. Med, pt shd; htd wc; chem disp; shwrs inc; el pnts (6A) PLN9.50; Indtte; shop & 500m; snacks; rest; playgrnd; pool; sandy/shgl beach; tennis; TV; many chalets adj; dogs PLN5; poss cr; Eng spkn; quiet; ccard acc; CCI. "Well-run site; clean san facs; helpful warden; easy walk to pleasant spa town - many rests/cafés; mkd cycle rtes pass site ent." PLN 43 2011*

KLUCZBORK *C2* (6km SE Rural) *50.96486, 18.27743* **Camping Bąków (No. 23), ul Kluczborska, 46-233 Bąków [(077) 4180586; osir@kluczbork.pl; www.osir.kluczbork.pl]** On rd 11 Kluczbork to Olesno. Sp on L of rd. Med, mkd pitch, shd; wc; shwrs inc; el pnts (10A) PLN5; Indtte; rest; snacks; bar; playgrnd; pool; TV; 50% statics; quiet; CCI. "No privacy in shwrs; site poss open outside dates shown; campfires in evening; excel value." 1 May-30 Sep. PLN 23 2009*

KOLOBRZEG *A2* (1km NE Coastal) *54.18131, 15.59338* **Camping Baltic (No. 78), ul 4 Dywizji, 78-100 Kołobrzeg [tel/fax (094) 3524569 or (0606) 411954 (mob); baltic78@post.pl; www.camping.kolobrzeg.pl]** Nr Solny Hotel on NE edge of town over rlwy x-ing; sp fr rndabt in vill. Med, pt shd; wc; chem disp; mv service pnt; shwrs; shops 500m; el pnts (10-16A) PLN10; shop, rest adj; snacks; bar; playgrnd; sand beach 800m; TV; dogs PLN3; phone; poss cr; Eng spkn; adv bkg; rd & rlwy noise; ccard acc; red long stay/CCI. "Helpful staff; easy walk/cycle to town." ♦ 15 Apr-15 Oct. PLN 54 2007*

KRAKOW *D3* (3km N Urban) *50.09454, 19.94127* **Camping Clepardia (No. 103), ul Pachońskiego 28A, 31-223 Kraków [(012) 4159672; fax 6378063; clepardia@gmail.com; www.clepardia.pl]** Fr Kraków cent take rd 7/E77 N twds Warsaw for 3km. Turn L onto rd 79 'Opolska' & foll sp 'Domki Kempingowe - Bungalows'. Fr A4/E40 exit onto E462 then S on rd 79 'Pasternik' thro to 'J Conrada & foll sp. Site is nr lge Elea supmkt & Clepardia Basen (sw pools). Med, mkd pitch, pt shd; wc; chem disp; shwrs inc; el pnts (6A) PLN12; Indtte; supmkt, rest 300m; pool adj; wifi; dogs free; phone; bus nr; poss cr; Eng spkn; no adv bkg; aircraft noise; red low ssn/CCI. "Busy site with tightly packed pitches - rec arr bef 1700 high ssn to secure pitch; excel, clean, modern san facs; ltd el pnts if site full; muddy in wet weather; friendly, helpful staff; gd security." 2 Apr-24 Oct. PLN 69 2010*

KRAKOW *D3* (6km S Urban) *50.01546, 19.92525* **Camping Krakowianka (No. 171), ul Żywiecka Boczna 2, 30-427 Kraków [tel/fax (012) 2681417; hotel@krakowianka.com.pl; www.krakowianka.com.pl]** Exit A4 at Wezel Opatkowice & head N on E77 twd city cent for approx 3km. After passing Carrefour supmkt on R, turn L at next traff lts & foll site sp. Lge, pt shd; wc; chem disp; shwrs; el pnts (16A) PLN8; Indtte; supmkt 400m; rest 1.5km; snacks; playgrnd; pool adj; games area; TV; some cabins; dogs; phone; tram; car wash. "Ltd, basic facs; conv tram to town." 1 May-30 Sep. PLN 50 2009*

KRAKOW *D3* (10km S Rural) *49.9625, 19.89277* **Korona Camping (No. 241), ul Myślenicka 32, 32-031 Gaj [tel/fax (012) 2701318; biuro@camping-korona.com.pl; www.camping-korona.com.pl]** Site on E77, well sp fr all dirs. NB dangerous main rd - rec app fr S cont twd Kraków for approx 2km, then turn at x-rds, back to site. When leaving site & travelling N, drive about 5km S, take R turn after speed limit warnings, cross rd by bdge, then back N. Med, mkd pitch, terr, pt shd; wc; chem disp; mv service pnt; shwrs inc; el pnts (10-16A) PLN12; Indtte; shop; snacks; bar; BBQ; playgrnd; games area; dogs PLN4; bus to city at gate; poss cr; Eng spkn; adv bkg; rd noise; red long stay/CCI. "Friendly, family-run site; clean facs need modernising (2010); lower part of site unreliable in wet." ♦ 1 May-15 Sep. PLN 65 2011*

⊞ **KRAKOW** *D3* (4km W Rural) *50.04638, 19.88111* **Camping Smok (No. 46), ul Kamedulska 18, 30-252 Kraków [tel/fax (012) 4297266; info@smok.krakow.pl; www.smok.krakow.pl]** Fr Kraków W ring rd site sp as No 46. Fr S 1st exit immed after x-ing rv onto rd 780 twd Kraków. Med, pt sl, shd; wc; chem disp; mv service pnt; shwrs inc; el pnts (5-10A) PLN12; Indtte; sm shop; supmkt 4km; rest 1km; playgrnd; lake sw & windsurfing 6km; dogs PLN5; poss v cr; some Eng spkn; adv bkg (rec for upper pitches); quiet but some rd noise; red long stay/CCI. "On rd to Auschwitz; salt mine at Wieliczka; friendly, well-kept site; spotless san facs; lower field (m'vans) poss muddy after rain - tractor tow avail; poss rallies on site; gd tour base; frequent bus to Krakow connects with trams to cent; cycle rte to cent; gd security; tours with pick-up fr site; poss barking dogs; excel." PLN 77 2011*

KRETOWINY see Morąg *A3*

LAGOW *B1* (5km S Rural) *52.29666, 15.24666* **Camping De Kroon, Poźrzadło 16, 66-233 Toporów [(06) 53850782]** Fr German border at Słubice for 55km dir Poznań on rte 2/E30, turn R opp Nevada cent sp Skąpe. Site on R in 300m. Sm, unshd; wc; chem disp (wc); shwrs inc; el pnts inc; shop 500m; snacks; bar; playgrnd; sm pool; dogs; Eng spkn; quiet. "Helpful Dutch owner; friendly site; gd, clean facs; watersports on lake in Łagów." 1 Apr-30 Sep. € 15.00 2007*

LEBA *A2* (Urban) *54.75705, 17.55178* **Camping Marco Polo (No. 81), ul Wspólna 6, 84-360 Łeba [(059) 8662333; marcopolo@leba.info; www.marcopolo.leba.info]** App fr S, foll camping sp L fr main rd. Pass rlwy stn, immed L alongside rlwy, site on R. Med, hdg/mkd pitch, unshd; wc; chem disp; shwrs; el pnts (16A) PLN10; Indry rm; shop; snacks; bar; BBQ; sand beach 700m; games area; some statics; poss cr; Eng spkn; CCI. "Conv Slowinksi National Park sand dunes." 1 Jun-30 Sep. PLN 44 2010*

POLAND

LEBA *A2* (500m N Coastal) *54.76150, 17.53833* **Camping Morski (No. 21), ul Turystyczna 3, 84-360 Łeba [(059) 8661380; fax 8661518; camp21@op.pl; www.camping21.interleba.pl]** N fr Lębork on E214. In Łeba foll sp Camping Raphael & pass rlwy stn on L, over rv bdge twd sea. Site sp. Lge, hdg/mkd pitch, pt shd; htd wc; chem disp; mv service pnt; baby facs; shwrs inc; el pnts (10A) PLN12; Indtte (inc dryer); shop adj; rest; bar; BBQ; cooking facs; playgrnd; sand beach 150m; tennis; wifi; TV; dogs PLN8; phone; poss cr, adv bkg; CCI. "Nice, well-run site in gd position; modern san facs; pleasant resort; excel." ♦ 1 May-30 Sep. PLN 62 (CChq acc) 2011*

LEBA *A2* (500m W Rural) *54.7572, 17.5467* **Camping Rafael (No. 145), ul Turystyczna 4, 84-360 Łeba [(059) 8661972; campingrafael@campingrafael.pl; www.campingrafael.pl]** Fr town cent, site well sp. Med, pt shd; wc; chem disp; shwrs; el pnts (16A) PLN12; Indtte; shop high ssn; snacks, bar high ssn; playgrnd; sand beach 500m; wifi; TV; 5% statics; site open all year for statics, poss also for tourers; dogs PLN5; CCI. "Nice site, but san facs poss poor (2011); easy walk to town; conv beaches." 1 Jun-31 Aug. PLN 55 2011*

LEGNICA *C2* (10km SE Rural) *51.14216, 16.24006* **Camping Legnickie Pole (No. 234), Ul Henryka Brodatego 7, 59-241 Legnickie Pole [(076) 8582397; fax 8627577; osir.legnica@wp.pl; www.osir.legnica.pl]** Fr A4/E40 fr Görlitz take exit dir Legnickie Pole/Jawor, foll sp to vill & site. Sharp L turn after leaving main rd. Site sp on S o'skirts of Legnica on E65 & fr m'way. Sm, pt shd; wc; shwrs inc; el pnts (10A) inc; shop 500m; snacks; bar; playgrnd; pool high ssn; TV; dogs PLN8; poss cr; no adv bkg; CCI. "Helpful, friendly welcome; clean, basic facs (hot water to shwrs only); poss diff after heavy rain; gd NH on way S." ♦ 1 May-30 Sep. PLN 53 2010*

LODZ *C3* (4km NE Rural) *51.81591, 19.50273* **Camping Na Rogach (No. 167), ul Łupkowa 10/16, 91-527 Łódź [(042) 6306111; hotel.spt@hotel.spt.com.pl; www.hotelspt.com.pl]** Turn L off rte N14 (to Warsaw) 100m bef Peugeot dealer. Site not well sp. Call at adj hotel reception bef ent site. Sm, hdg/mkd pitch, hdstg, unshd; wc; shwrs inc; el pnts (16A) inc; shop opp; playgrnd; rest adj; few statics; dogs PLN6; quiet. "Gd NH; facs run down but clean (2009); o'night coach parties." 15 May-30 Sep. PLN 50 2011*

LUBLIN *C4* (7km S Rural) *51.19186, 22.52725* **Camping Graf Marina (No. 65), ul Krężnicka 6, 20-518 Lublin [tel/fax (081) 7441070; info@graf-marina.pl; www.graf-marina.pl]** Take rd 19 S & cross rlwy line; lge parking area after 1.8km then L after 300m (no sp but leads to Zemborzyce); in 5km cross rlwy then L at T-junc; site on R in 5km on lakeside. Med, hdg/mkd pitch, unshd; wc; own san; shwrs inc; el pnts (10A); shop 3km; rest; sand beach & lake sw adj; statics; Eng spkn; quiet but rd & rlwy noise; CCI. "Marina adj; sailing; fishing; site poss run down early ssn." 1 May-30 Sep. € 17 2011*

MALBORK *A2* (1.5km N Urban) *54.04741, 19.03938* **Camping Nogat (No. 197), ul Parkowa 3, 82-200 Malbork [tel/fax (055) 2722413; hotel@osirmalbork.pl; www.osir-malbork.e-tur.com.pl]** Fr Gdańsk on 1/E75 thro Tczew & join rd 22. At Malbork 1st L after main bdge over Rv Nogat. Site adj stadium & Hotel Parkowa. Well sp. Sm, pt shd; wc; chem disp; shwrs inc; el pnts (10A) PLN12; Indtte; supmkt 1.5km; snacks; bar; cooking facs; playgrnd; fishing; canoeing; tennis; games rm; TV; dogs PLN8; phone; quiet; CCI. "Recep at Hotel Parkowa; gd san facs; excel." ♦ 15 Apr-15 Oct. PLN 56 2011*

MIEDZYZDROJE *A1* (1.5km W Coastal) *53.92241, 14.43505* **Camping Gromada (No. 24), ul Polna 134, 72-510 Międzyzdroje [(091) 3280275; fax 3280610; dwgrazyna@poczta.onet.pl; www.nadmorze.pl/polenamiotowe24]** Fr Świnoujście take rd 3/E65 twd Szczecin. After 12km turn L twd Międzyzdroje. Foll sm camping sp fr town cent. Lge, pt shd; wc; chem disp; shwrs ltd; el pnts (10A) PLN9; Indtte; shop; snacks; bar; BBQ; playgrnd; beach 1km; TV; poss cr; quiet; CCI. "Gd NH." 1 May-30 Sep. PLN 49 2009*

MIELNO *A2* (500m E Coastal) *54.26272, 16.07245* **Camping Rodzinny (No. 105), ul Chrobrego 51, 76-032 Mielno [(094) 3189385; fax 3475008; recepcja@campingrodzinny.pl; www.campingrodzinny.pl]** Fr Koszalin W on rd 11, turn N onto rd 165 to Mielno (5km). Bear R in town & foll site sp. Site on L thro narr gate bet gardens - easy to miss. Sm, pt shd; htd wc; chem disp; el pnts (6A) PLN10; Indtte; shop; BBQ; cooking facs; playgrnd; sand beach 500m; games rm; internet; some statics; dogs; poss cr; some Eng spkn; adv bkg; quiet; CCI. "Easy walk to town; secure, well-kept, family-owned site; gd san facs." ♦ 15 Apr-15 Nov. PLN 51 2011*

MIKOLAJKI *A3* (1.5km W Rural) *53.7954, 21.56471* **Camping Wagabunda (No. 2), ul Leśna 2, 11-730 Mikołajki [(087) 4216018; wagabunda-mikolajki@wagabunda-mikolajki.pl; www.wagabunda-mikolajki.pl]** Exit town by rd 16 dir Mrągowo & site sp to L. Med, pt sl, unshd; wc; shwrs inc; el pnts (16A) PLN12; Indtte; shop & 1.5km; rest; snacks; shgl beach 2km; lake sw 400m; games area; TV; 50% statics; dogs PLN6.50; phone; poss cr; adv bkg; quiet; no ccard acc; twin-axles extra charge; red low ssn/CCI. "Pleasant site nr nice town; san facs adequate but need update (2011); conv Masurian Lakes & historical sites." ♦ 3 May-1 Sep. PLN 57 2011*

⊞ **MRAGOWO** *A3* (8km N Rural) *53.94278, 21.32001* **Camping Seeblick, Ruska Wieś 1, 11-700 Mrągowo [tel/fax (089) 7413155; marian.seeblick@gmail.com; www.campingpension.de]** Fr Mrągowo N on rd 591 dir Ketrzyn, site sp. Med, terr, pt shd; htd wc; chem disp; shwrs inc; el pnts inc; Indry rm; shop 500m; rest; bar; lake sw; boating; tennis; games area; entmnt; quiet. "Gd; ltd san facs." PLN 50 2009*

POLAND

⊞ **NIEDZICA** *D3* (2km SE Urban) *49.40477, 20.33411* **Camping Polana Sosny (No. 38), Osiedle Na Polanie Sosny, 34-441 Niedzica [tel/fax (018) 2629403; polana.sosny@niedzica.pl; www.niedzica.pl]** Rte 969 fr Nowy Targ. At Dębno turn R & foll sp to border (lake on L). At 11km pass castle & 1st dam on L twds 2nd Dunajec dam. Site sp. Sm, mkd pitch, unshd; htd wc; chem disp; shwrs; fam bthrm; el pnts inc; lndtte shop 1.5km; rest adj; snacks; bar; cooking facs; rv adj; watersports; games area; phone; quiet but noise fr dam; adv bkg; quiet; red long stay; CCI. "Beautiful, well-maintained site in superb location; friendly, helpful staff; clean, modern san facs; excel walks in mountains; 2km to Slovakian border; vg touring base." ♦ € 10.00 2010*

NOWY SACZ *D3* (E Urban) *49.61975, 20.71548* **Camping Dom Turysty Nowy Sącz (No. 87), ul Nadbrzeżna 40, 33-300 Nowy Sącz [tel/fax (018) 4415012; apazdyk@gmail.com]** Fr W on rd 28 cross Rv Dunajec & in 2km at rndabt turn L into rd 75. Site on L. Sm, mkd pitch, some hdstg, pt shd; wc; chem disp; shwrs; el pnts (16A); lndtte; shops 1km; snacks; bar; BBQ; quiet; CCI. "Close to Slovakian border & lakes." ♦ 1 May-30 Sep. PLN 23 2010*

OLSZTYN *A3* (5km NW Rural) *53.78686, 20.40170* **Agro Camping, ul Młodzieżowa 1, 11-041 Olsztyn [(089) 5238666]** Fr Olsztyn W on rd 16 for approx 5km, turn N thro Łupstych & foll site sp. Sm, pt sl, pt shd; wc; shwr; some Eng spkn; quiet. "Lovely position on Lake Ukiel; CL-type site with facs." 1 May-30 Sep. 2009*

⊞ **OSWIECIM** *D3* (2km W Rural) *50.02262, 19.19891* **Centre for Dialogue & Prayer in Auschwitz, ul Maksymiliana Kolbego 1, 32-600 Oświęcim [(033) 8431000; fax 8431001; biuro@centrum-dialogu.oswiecim.pl; www.centrum-dialogu.oswiecim.pl]** 700m fr Auschwitz museum car park on parallel rd to S, on forecourt of hotel-like building. Sm, hdstg, unshd; wc; shwrs inc; el pnts inc; shops 2km; rest; BBQ; phone; Eng spkn; rd noise; CCI. "Conv Auschwitz museum & Auschwitz-Birkenau (3km); clean, modern, site; gd, clean san facs; v gd disabled shwr rm, on same lines as Caravan Club ones; friendly staff; v nice site." ♦ PLN 60 2011*

⊞ **OSWIECIM** *D3* (2km W Urban) *50.02895, 19.20054* **Parking Przy Museum Auschwitz, 32-600 Oświęcim** Foll sp to Auschwitz museum fr rd 933. Parking area is on opp side of rd (away fr main car park) by tourist office. M'vans only. Sm; el pnts (6A) PLN7; shop; rest; snacks; bar; BBQ; internet; water PLN6; dogs; quiet. "1 night stay only permitted; ltd el pnts; allow 4 hrs for museum tour." PLN 20 2010*

PIECKI *A3* (2km N Rural) *53.77938, 21.33583* **Camping Piecki (No. 269), ul Zwycięstwa 60, 11-710 Piecki [tel/fax (089) 7421025; owpttk@post.pl; www.owpttk.pl]** Site sp bet Mrągowo & Piecki on rd 59. No sps except sm sp at ent. In Masurian Lake District 3km to W of Piecki. NB Ent tight lge o'fits. Med, pt sl, pt shd; wc; chem disp (wc); shwrs inc; el pnts (10A) PLN12; lndtte; shop, rest & snacks 5km; bar; BBQ; playgrnd; lake sw; watersports; games area; TV; 10% statics; dogs PLN10; bus adj; Eng spkn; adv bkg; poss noisy high ssn due school parties; CCI. "San facs poor; NH only." 1 May-30 Sep. PLN 50 2011*

POLANICA ZDROJ see Kłodzko *D2*

⊞ **POZNAN** *B2* (4km E Urban) *52.40343, 16.98399* **Camping Malta (No. 155), ul Krańcowa 98, 61-036 Poznań-Malta [(061) 8766203; fax 8766283; camping@malta.poznan.pl; www.poznan.pl]** Fr A2/E30 Poznań bypass leave at rte 2/11 dir Poznań. Turn R at traff lts onto rte 5/E261 sp Malta, Zoo & camping, site sp. Sm, hdg pitch, pt shd; htd wc; chem disp; shwrs inc; el pnts (16A) inc; lndtte; shop; snacks; bar; shop 1km; lake adj; many cabins; tram to city; Eng spkn; quiet but loud disco across lake at w/end; ccard acc; red CCI. "Clean tidy site on lake with sports but poss unkempt pitches low ssn; 6 tram stops to Poznań Sq; vg 24-hr security; helpful staff." ♦ PLN 80 2011*

We can fill in site report forms on the Club's website – www.caravanclub.co.uk/europereport

⊞ **PRZEMYSL** *D4* (1km SW Rural) **Camping Zamek (No. 233), ul Sanocka 8a, 37-700 Przemyśl [(016) 6750265; fax 6783413; przemysl@neostrada.pl]** Site sp on rd B28. Med, shd; wc; own san rec; shwrs; el pnts (10A); shops adj; snacks; fishing; games area; 50% chalets; phone; quiet. "Interesting town & churches; helpful staff; basic facs; gd pizza rest nrby." PLN 44 2009*

PRZEWORSK *D4* (1km W Urban) *50.06138, 22.48361* **Camping Pastewnik (No. 221), ul Łańcucka 2, 37-200 Przeworsk [(016) 6492300; fax 6492301; zajazdpastewnik@hot.pl; www.pastewnik.prv.pl]** On N side of N4/E40, sp. Sm, pt shd; wc; shwrs inc; el pnts (10A) PLN10; lndtte; shop adj; rest; snacks; bar; playgrnd; Eng spkn; rd noise; ccard acc; CCI. "Conv NH/sh stay with motel & rest; Łańcut Castle & Carriage Museum 25km." 1 May-30 Sep. PLN 38 2007*

ROWY *A2* (500m W Coastal) *54.65940, 17.04926* **Camping Prymorze (No. 156), ul Bałtycka 6, 76-212 Rowy [tel/fax (059) 8141940; biuro@przymorze.com.pl; www.przymorze.com.pl]** Fr Ustka on coast rd, site on rd into Rowy. Med, pt shd; wc; shwrs inc; el pnts (16A) inc; lndtte; shop; snacks; bar; cooking facs; playgrnd; pool 300m; TV; dogs €2; phone; quiet. "Sm fishing port; gd facs; helpful staff." ♦ 1 May-31 Aug. € 17.60 2009*

⊞ **RUCIANE NIDA** *A3* (5km NW Rural) *53.68668, 21.54713* **Camping Nad Zatoka (No. 9), Wygryny 52, 12-220 Ruciane Nida [(087) 4231597; fax 4236342; zbigre@orange.pl; www.ter-lid.com.pl]** Fr rte 58 N onto rd 610 NE twds Piecki for 4km. Turn R for Wygryny 2km, foll sp in vill. Sm, pt sl, unshd; wc; chem disp; mv service pnt; shwrs inc; el pnts (16A) PLN10; lndtte; shop 300m; tradsmn; rest, bar nrby; BBQ; playgrnd; sand beach; lake sw; canoe & cycle hire; dogs PLN6; poss cr; quiet. "Private site in field on lakeside; beautiful scenery; vg san facs; excel." PLN 50 2007*

RYDZEWO MILKI see Giżycko *A3*

POLAND

SANDOMIERZ *C3* (400m E Urban) *50.68010, 21.75502* **Camping Browarny (No. 201), ul Żwirki I Wigury 1, 27-600 Sandomierz [(015) 8332703; fax 8323050; wmajsak@poczta.fm; www.majsak.pl]** Fr S on rd 79, cross rv bdge, site on L. Sm, pt shd; wc; chem disp; mv service pnt; shwrs inc; el pnts (16A) PLN10; Indtte; shop in town; rest nr; bar; BBQ; cooking facs; playgrnd; games rm; dogs; phone; bus adj; poss cr; Eng spkn; adv bkg; some rd noise; CCI. "Attractive sm town in walking dist; vg site." ♦ Easter-30 Oct. PLN 42 2008*

SIERAKOW *B2* (2km SE Rural) *52.63324, 16.09870* **Camping Sieraków Owir (No. 109), ul Poznańska 28, 64-410 Sieraków [(061) 2952868; recepcja@owir.sierakow.pl; www.owir.sierakow.pl]** Fr rd 182 in town cent, SE on ul Ponzańska on L, opp hotel. Not well sp. Med, pt sl, shd; wc; chem disp (wc); shwrs inc; el pnts (5A) PLN5; Indry rm; shop 200m; rest 300m; snacks; bar & 300m; htd covrd pool; lake sw & beach 300m; boating; TV rm; 5% statics; phone; poss cr & noisy w/end; CCI. "Poss pop concerts on beach in summer; gd san facs; site poss diff lge o'fits due tall trees." ♦ 20 Jun-30 Sep. 2009*

SLAWA *C2* (1km W Rural) *51.88145, 16.05817* **Camping Słoneczny (No. 261), ul Odrodzonego Wojska Polskiego 19, 67-410 Sława [tel/fax (068) 3566452; osir.slawa@wp.pl; www.osir.slawa.pl]** Site sp on lakeside. Sm, mkd pitch, pt shd; wc; chem disp; el pnts; Indtte; snacks; lake sw; waterslide; fishing; games area; cycle hire; some cabins; adv bkg; quiet; CCI. "Beautiful location; friendly, helpful owners; san facs unclean (6/09)." 1 May-30 Sep. PLN 50 2009*

SOPOT *A2* (1.8km N Urban) *54.46136, 18.5556* **Camping Kamienny Potok (No. 19), ul Zamkowa Góra 25, 81-713 Sopot [tel/fax (058) 5500445; kempingnr19@wp.pl; www.kemping19.cba.pl]** Fr Gdańsk rte 27 twds Sopot. Site on R just behind Shell petrol stn. Fr N on rte 6/E28 turn S at Gdynia, onto new section of E28, for 7.5km. Turn L onto rte 220 by 'Euromarket' for 5km. Turn R onto rte 27 (S) twd Gdańsk & site nr Shell g'ge on opp c'way. Lge, mkd pitch, pt shd; wc; chem disp; shwrs inc; el pnts (2-20A) PLN10; Indtte; shop 500m; snacks; bar; playgrnd; internet; TV; phone; poss cr; rd & rlwy noise; ccard acc; red CCI. "Pleasant site; friendly & helpful staff; frequent trains for Gdansk 250m; modern, clean san facs; gd security; gd walking/cycling track into town; busy site." 1 May-30 Sep. PLN 54 2011*

STEGNA *A2* (1.5km N Coastal) *54.34186, 19.1176* **Camping Stegna No. 159, ul Morska 26, 82-103 Stegna [(055) 2478303; fax 2478034; camp@camp.pl; www.camp.pl]** Fr Stegna vill on rte 501 turn N at church onto Morska. Site on R, sp. Sm, shd; wc; chem disp; shwrs inc; el pnts (10A) PLN8; Indtte; shop 300m; tradsmn; rest, snacks, bar 100m; playgrnd; sand beach 400m; 10% statics; dogs PLN4; Eng spkn; adv bkg; quiet. "Friendly, family-run site; gd security; gd base Gdansk 30km; rec." 1 May-30 Sep. PLN 56 2009*

STETTIN see Szczecin *B1*

STRZESZYNEK see Poznań *B2*

SULECIN *B1* (3km S Rural) *52.40911, 15.11761* **Camping Marina (No. 50), Ostrów 76, 69-200 Sulęcin [tel/fax (0951) 552294; infos@camping-marina.eu; www.camping-marina.eu]** Cross border fr Frankfurt-an-Oder & take rd 2 to Torzym (35km). In Torzym turn L onto rd 138 dir Sulęcin; thro Tursk & site in 3km. Med, mkd pitch, pt shd; wc; mv service pnt; shwrs; el pnts €2; Indtte; tradsmn; supmkt 4km; snacks; bar; playgrnd; lake sw; fishing; cycle hire; wifi; TV rm; some cabins; dogs €1; adv bkg; quiet; red CCI. "Gd, modern san facs; gd walking/cycling; pleasant, relaxing site; conv Berlin." ♦ 1 Apr-31 Oct. € 15.00 2010*

SUWALKI *A3* (11km NW Rural) *54.0767, 23.0742* **Kajaki Camping Pokoje, 16-412 Stary Folwark 44, Wigry [(087) 5637789; wigry@wigry.info; www.wigry.info]** Fr Suwalki take 653 dir Sejny. In about 11km turn R in Stary Folwark at PTTK sp. Site on R in approx 100m. Sm, unshd; wc; chem disp; shwrs inc; el pnts (10A) inc; Indtte; BBQ; lake sw & kayaking nrby; wifi; Eng spkn; quiet. "Nr lake in National Park; kayaking fr site; vg site." 01 May-30 Sep. PLN 40 2011*

SWIECIE *B2* (1km E Urban) *53.40321, 18.45574* **Camping Zamek (No. 54), ul Zamkowa 10, 86-100 Świecie [(052) 3311726]** S fr Gdańsk on E75 take rd 1 to Chełmno & Świecie. Cross Rv Wisła & L at x-rds in Świecie cent; site sp at traff lts. Sm, shd; wc; own san rec; shwrs; el pnts (10A); Indtte; shop, bar in town 2km; playgrnd; games area; dogs; quiet. "In castle grounds (tower visible fr rd); if gate clsd, ring bell on L." 1 May-15 Sep. PLN 25 2009*

⊞ **SWINOUJSCIE** *A1* (1km N Coastal) *53.91709, 14.25693* **Camping Relax (No. 44), ul Słowackiego 1, 72-600 Świnoujście [(097) 3213912; relax@fornet.com.pl; www.camping-relax.com.pl]** Fr E rd 3/E65 cross rv on free ferry. Fr town cent N for 500m. No vehicle border x-ing fr W. V lge, shd; wc; shwrs inc; el pnts (16A) PLN10; Indtte; shops 500m; snacks; cooking facs; playgrnd; beach 200m; games rm; wifi; phone; quiet; adv bkg; ccard acc. "Nice town; gd beach; gd walking; site popular with families; red snr citizens." PLN 65 2007*

⊞ **SZCZECIN/STETTIN** *B1* (7km E Rural) *53.39505, 14.63640* **Marina Camping (No. 25), ul Przestrzenna 23, 70-800 Szczecin-Dąbie [tel/fax (091) 4601165; camping.marina@pro.onet.pl; www.campingmarina.pl]** Fr E28/A6 take A10 sp Szczecin. Immed after rlwy bdge turn R sp Dąbie. At traff lts in cent Dąbie turn L, site on R in approx 2km on lake. Med, pt shd; htd wc; mv service pnt; baby facs; shwrs; el pnts (6A) inc; Indtte (inc dryer); tradsmn; shop 2km; supmkt 3km; rest; snacks; bar; lake sw; boat hire; tennis; games area; wifi; bus to Stettin; poss cr; noise fr late arrivals & early departures; red CCI. "Pleasant, lakeside site; clean, modern san facs but inadequate if site full; bus tickets fr recep; helpful staff." PLN 65 (CChq acc) 2011*

POLAND

TARNOW *D3* (1km N Rural) *50.02320, 20.98813* **Camping Pod Jabłoniami (No. 202), ul Piłsudskiego 28a, 33-100 Tarnów [(014) 6215124; recepcja@camping.tarnow.pl; www.camping.tarnow.pl]** E fr Kraków on E40, foll sp to Tarnów 'Centrum'. Turn L by Tesco & foll sp to site. Sm, pt sl, pt shd; wc; chem disp; shwrs inc; el pnts (16A) PLN10; Indtte; supmkt 2km; rest, bar 1km; BBQ; playgrnd; pool adj; wifi; TV; poss cr; Eng spkn; some rd noise; red CCI. "Walk to attractive town; gd site." ♦ 1 Apr-30 Oct. PLN 51 2011*

TORUN *B2* (1km S Urban) *53.00138, 18.60472* **Camping Tramp (No. 33), ul Kujawska 14, 87-100 Torún [tel/fax (056) 6547187; tramp@mosir.torun.pl; www.mosir.torun.pl]** Cross bdge S of town & take 1st L at traff lts, site sp in 500m on rvside. Med, shd; wc; chem disp; shwrs; el pnts (10A) inc; Indtte; shop 500m; rest 1.5km; snacks; bar; games area; some statics; dogs PLN4.50; continual traffic noise & poss noise fr bar; red CCI. "Noisy, busy site but reasonable; walking dist fr interesting old town across bdge; gd security; NH/sh stay only." ♦ 1 May-30 Sep. PLN 62 2010*

USTKA *A2* (NE Urban) *54.57655, 16.88088* **Camping Morski (No. 101), ul Armii Krajowej 4, Przewloka, 76-270 Ustka [tel/fax (059) 8144789 or 8144426; cam_mor@pro.onet.pl; www.camping-morski.afr.pl]** Fr Koszalin & Sławno to Łupsk on rd 6/E28 turn L to Ustka. Foll main rd which bears R & foll camping sp to R. After 200m turn R at rndabt & camp on L after 300m. Sm, pt shd; wc; own san; shwrs; el pnts (6A) inc; Indtte; shop 500m; rest adj; snacks; bar; BBQ; playgrnd; beach 1.3km; tennis; dogs; quiet; red long stay/CCI. "Seaside resort with gd shopping & fishing port; vg for children; gd cycling." ♦ 1 May-30 Sep. PLN 60 2011*

POLAND

WALCZ *B2* (12km N Rural) **Camping Zdbice, 78-611 Wałcz [tel/fax (067) 2581677]** Fr N on rd 22 at Szwecja turn R at sp Zdbice, site sp. Site on L bef vill of Zdbice. Med, pt sl, unshd; wc; chem disp (wc); shwrs; el pnts; bar; lake sw adj; statics; quiet. "Pleasant site on lakeside; facs basic but adequate; at site ent, stop to register & ask owner to open gate at 2nd ent - main ent has diff turn & overhanging branches; if arriving late - phone number displayed on barrier." 1 May-30 Sep. PLN 48.50 2010*

WARSZAWA *B3* (9km SE Urban) *52.17798, 21.14727* **Camping Wok (No. 90), ul Odrębna 16, 04-867 Warszawa [(022) 6127951; fax 6166127; wok@campingwok.warszawa.pl; www.campingwok.warszawa.pl]** Fr city cent or fr W on E30, take bdge on E30 over Rv Wisła to E side of rv. Then take rte 801 for approx 8km (dual c'way). At rndabt double back for 600m & take 3rd R into Odrębna. Site 200m on R. Sm, shd; htd wc; chem disp; mv service pnt; baby facs; shwrs inc; el pnts (10-16A) PLN15; gas; Indtte; shop 700m; rest 1km; snacks; bar; BBQ; cooking facs; playgrnd; games area; internet; TV; bus/tram adj; Eng spkn; adv bkg; quiet; ccard acc; red CCI. "Lovely little site; v secure; spotless, modern san facs; helpful staff." 1 Apr-31 Oct. PLN 85 2011*

WARSZAWA *B3* (4km W Urban) *52.2144, 20.96575* **Majawa Camping (No. 123), ul Bitwy Warszawskiej 19/20, 02-366 Warszawa-Szczęśliwice [tel/fax (022) 8233748; biuro@majawa.pl; www.majawa.pl]** Fr W on E30/rd 2 at junc with E67/rd 8 rd goes S thro tunnel under rlwy then strt on under new over-pass. Site on R in 100m. On E67/rd 8 fr Wrocław app concrete monument 3m high in middle of tramway; turn L at traff lts. Hotel Vera on R, site on L. Fr cent of Warsaw, take rd no. 7/8 700m twds Katowice. Not v well sp fr cent of town. Ent & exit diff due v busy rd. Sm, pt shd; wc; chem disp; shwrs inc; el pnts (6A) PLN15; Indry rm; shop 300m; rest 100m; BBQ; playgrnd; pool 100m; tennis; TV; some statics; phone; bus 500m; poss cr; Eng spkn; quiet; ccard acc; red CCI. "Easy access to Warsaw & Royal Castle; gd meals at adj bowling alley or Vera hotel; poss lge rallies on site; friendly; excel security." 1 May-30 Sep. PLN 51 2007*

There aren't many sites open at this time of year. We'd better phone ahead to check the one we're heading for is open.

WEGORZEWO *A3* (2km SW Rural) *54.18647, 21.77018* **Camping Rusałka (No. 175), ul Lesna 2, 11-600 Węgorzewo [(087) 4272191; fax 4272049; camp.175@wp.pl; www.cmazur.pl]** Fr rte 63 fr Giżycko to Węgorzewo turn W approx 3km SW of Węgorzewo. Foll sp to site. Lge, pt shd; wc; chem disp (wc); shwrs inc; el pnts PLN8; Indtte; shops 2km; rest; snacks; bar; playgrnd; lake sw adj; fishing; sailing; many statics; dogs; quiet. "Lovely part of Lake District; delightful situation; all facs at top of steep hill." 1 May-30 Sep. PLN 36 2008*

WIELICZKA *D3* (1.2km E Urban) *49.98273, 20.07611* **Motel Camping Wierzynka, ul Wierzynka 9, 32-020 Wieliczka [tel/fax (012) 2783614; motel@nawierzynka.pl]** Site sp fr E40/rte 4 about 2km fr salt mine. Sm, some hdstg, pt sl, pt shd; wc; shwrs; el pnts (10A) PLN15 (rev pol); shop 1.5km; rest; snacks; bar; cycle hire; wifi; bus to Krakow; train 1km; poss cr; Eng spkn; quiet; ccard acc (fee); CCI. "10 pitches in pleasant setting; helpful staff; facs basic but clean; shwrs erratic; conv public transport; cheap alt to Kraków; 1.5km fr salt mines." 1 May-30 Sep. PLN 48 2010*

WROCLAW *C2* (5km NE Urban) *51.11722, 17.09138* **Stadion Olimpijski Camp (No. 117), ul Padarewskiego 35, 51-620 Wrocław [tel/fax (071) 3484651]** Fr A4 into Wrocław foll N8 sp Warszawa thro city. On N8 dir Warszawa, pass McDonalds, at fork in rd take Sienkiewicza to end, then Rozyckiego to stadium, site on R. If poss foll sp 'stadion' to camp; head for lighting towers of sports stadium if seen thro trees. Lge, pt shd; wc; shwrs inc; el pnts (10A) PLN7.50; Indry rm; shops, rest adj; snacks; bar; BBQ; playgrnd; pool 700m; 10% statics; dogs; tram nr; phone; poss cr; no adv bkg; poss noise fr stadium; red CCI. "San facs basic but clean; site in need of modernisation (2010); gd security; v conv for city but NH only." 1 May-15 Oct. PLN 62.50 2011*

ZAKOPANE *D3* (4km N Rural) *49.32208, 19.96555* **Camping Ustup (No. 207), ul Ustup K/5, 34-500 Zakopane-Ustup [(018) 2063667; camping@ustup.com]** Turn R off Kraków-Zakopane rd 47 at petrol stn/McDonalds just after 1st town sp. Turn R again immed (also sp Cmg Harenda), site on L in 200m. Sm, pt sl, unshd; wc; chem disp; baby facs; shwrs inc; el pnts (10A) inc; shop adj; rest opp; playgrnd; bus to town cent; poss cr; adv bkg; quiet; CCI. "Ideal cent for Tatra region; mountain views; excel, family-run site; v welcoming & helpful; vg, clean san facs; grassy pitches; coach tours arranged fr adj g'ge info desk." 1 May-30 Sep. PLN 65 2011*

⊞ **ZAKOPANE** *D3* (1km S Urban) *49.2830, 19.9690* **Camping Pod Krokwia (No. 97), ul Żeromskiego 26, 34-500 Zakopane [tel/fax (018) 2012256; camp@podkrokwia.pl; www.podkrokwia.pl]** Sp fr town cent. Fr N 2nd exit at 1st rndbt; strt over at 2nd rndbt; turn R at 3rd rndabt, then R in 250m. Site on L. Lge, hdstg, pt sl, shd; wc; chem disp; shwrs inc; el pnts (10A) inc; Indtte; shop 500m; rest; snacks; bar nr; BBQ; cooking facs; playgrnd; pool, tennis adj; bus to Kraków; ski slopes & cable cars; rafting on rapids; wifi; TV; dogs PLN5; phone; poss cr; Eng spkn; quiet; CCI. "Lge tent area; few mkd pitches; poss scruffy low ssn; conv Tatra Mountains - site of 2006 Winter Olympics; mountain walks; town v touristy." PLN 65.4 2011*

⊞ **ZAMOSC** *C4* (2km W Rural) *50.71919, 23.23908* **Camping Duet (No. 253), ul Królowej Jadwigi 14, 22-400 Zamość [tel/fax (084) 6392499; duet@virgo.com.pl; www.duet.virgo.com.pl]** Fr Zamość cent W on rd 74, site on R bef Castorama. Sm, pt shd; wc; chem disp (wc); shwrs inc; el pnts PLN12; shop opp; rest; snacks; bar; pool 150m; some statics; dogs; poss cr; quiet; CCI. "Walk to attractive town; fair sh stay/NH." PLN 31 2011*

⊞ **ZGORZELEC** *C1* (1km N Urban) *51.15957, 15.00069* **Camping Zgorzelec, ul Lubańska 1a, 59-900 Zgorzelec [(075) 7752436; ardi@op.pl]** Ent Zgorzelec fr Germany & foll rd sp Zagan. Turn L at traff lts at BP g'ge. Only sp is at camp gate. Sm, pt sl, unshd; wc; el pnts inc; CCI. "Conv NH." PLN 60 2009*

ZIELONA GORA *C2* (1km NW Urban) **Leśny Camping (No. 52), ul Sulechowska 39, 65-022 Zielona Góra [tel/fax (068) 3253636; hotel.lesny@op.pl; www.lubtour.pti.pl/lesny.php]** Fr N on E65 fr Swebodzin, L to cent of town & immed L again. Hotel Lesny is sp. Go to recep for key. Sm, pt shd; wc; chem disp; shwrs; el pnts (10A); Indtte; shop 1km; rest; cooking facs; playgrnd; games area; adv bkg; ccard acc; CCI. ♦ 1 May-30 Oct. 2010*

ZLOCIENIEC *B2* (10km SW Rural) *53.45880, 15.92430* **Inter Nos Island Camping (No. 110), ul Błędno 1, 78-520 Złocieniec [(094) 3631190 or (0602) 554348 (mob); m.moser@inter-nos.pl; www.inter-nos.pl]** Fr Stettin E on rd 10 to Stargard Szczeciński then rd 20 to Drawsko Pomorski. In Drawsko take rd sp Lubieszewo & foll site sps W to lakeside. Access to site on island by ferry. Med, pt shd; wc; chem disp; sauna; shwrs; el pnts €1.50; Indry rm; shop; rest; snacks; bar; BBQ; playgrnd; lake sw & beach; watersports; tennis; cycle hire; horseriding; TV rm; dogs; adv bkg; quiet. "Scenic area." ♦ 1 May-30 Sep. € 17.00 (CChq acc) 2009*

ZNIN *B2* (2km S Rural) *52.84472, 17.72444* **Camping Żnin (No. 31), ul Szkolna 16, 88-400 Żnin [(052) 3020113; pttk.znin@paluki.pl; www.paluki.pl/pttk]** Fr town sq take rd E sp Inowrocław; in 300m turn R. Site R in 400m adj lge lake. Sm, shd; wc; chem disp; shwrs; el pnts; Indtte; shop 500m; snacks; BBQ; cooking facs; lake sw; CCI. "Busy site."1 May-31 Oct. 2007*

ZYWIEC *D3* (2km N Rural) *49.67347, 19.22310* **Camping Dębina (No. 102), ul Kopernika 4, 34-330 Żywiec-Sporysz [tel/fax (033) 8614888; manager@centrumdebina.pl]** Fr Bielsko-Biała B94, sp Żywiec. In Żywiec foll sp for Korbielów on B945. Site on R nr lake. Lge, pt shd; wc; shwrs inc; el pnts (16A) metered; Indtte; shop 2km; snacks in ssn; bar; playgrnd; tennis; TV; dogs PLN5; phone; Eng spkn; quiet; CCI. "Gd; conv Kraków & Auschwitz; conv border x-ings to Slovakia & Czech Rep; on Rv Stryszawka; site waterlogged after heavy rain." 1 Apr-31 Oct. PLN 42 2007*

POLAND

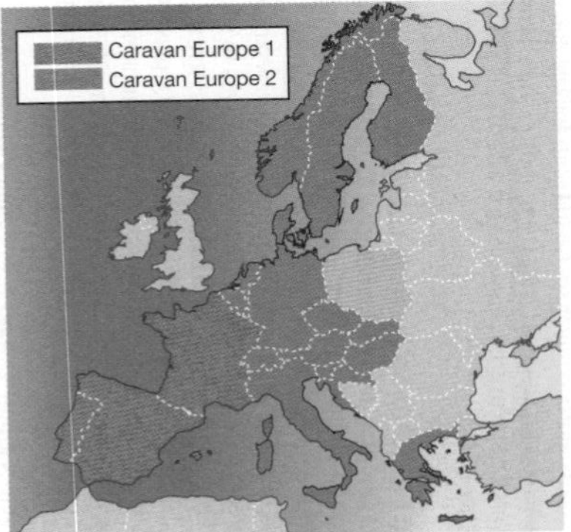

Distances are shown in kilometres and are calculated from town/city centres along the most practical roads, although not necessarily taking the shortest route. 1km = 0.62miles

Koszalin to Warszawa (Warsaw) = 436km

	Biala Podlaska	Bialystok	Bielsko-Biala	Bydgoszcz	Czestochowa	Elblag	Gdansk	Gorzów Wielkopolski	Jelenia Góra	Katowice	Kielce	Koszalin	Kraków	Legnica	Lódz	Lublin	Olsztyn	Plock	Poznan	Przemysl	Radom	Rzeszów	Suwalki	Swinoujscie	Szczecin	Torun	Warszawa (Warsaw)	Wroclaw	Zamosc
Biala Podlaska																													
Bialystok	149																												
Bielsko-Biala	472	543																											
Bydgoszcz	412	392	447																										
Czestochowa	365	410	133	314																									
Elblag	404	320	584	171	451																								
Gdansk	461	379	617	167	473	59																							
Gorzów Wielkopolski	596	603	496	214	415	333	315																						
Jelenia Góra	605	641	348	344	285	515	513	251																					
Katowice	416	485	58	391	75	524	545	456	327																				
Kielce	262	365	207	348	124	461	482	480	415	156																			
Koszalin	596	570	618	198	508	247	188	215	461	560	543																		
Kraków	376	477	86	434	114	567	565	529	403	75	114	621																	
Legnica	567	603	301	288	247	460	455	219	56	291	371	405	341																
Lódz	286	322	252	203	121	325	342	341	313	196	143	395	222	273															
Lublin	127	260	362	421	288	441	500	596	537	323	167	595	269	499	242														
Olsztyn	305	223	537	217	401	99	156	431	536	479	392	344	501	482	279	372													
Plock	267	270	363	150	230	234	276	346	385	305	231	340	327	340	104	271	177												
Poznan	470	488	387	131	289	300	296	131	226	333	354	241	405	170	210	465	323	215											
Przemysl	312	445	319	588	342	622	685	721	618	322	241	778	243	580	384	185	555	444	595										
Radom	184	285	285	322	181	383	444	487	430	232	78	512	192	392	137	107	316	179	358	268									
Rzeszów	297	430	238	513	272	585	642	639	542	243	165	710	165	503	306	170	514	378	517	78	199								
Suwalki	269	117	631	417	497	277	336	613	722	571	449	524	565	675	414	379	200	336	525	562	370	549							
Swinoujscie	730	701	676	312	586	400	341	179	429	636	651	151	701	397	508	728	491	462	297	892	634	816	667						
Szczecin	677	656	603	267	520	374	351	105	356	561	585	160	634	324	446	683	484	415	234	832	585	750	651	110					
Torun	366	347	422	46	290	167	181	260	366	364	307	236	384	312	159	375	172	104	150	542	278	472	370	356	313				
Warszawa (Warsaw)	157	188	355	252	222	280	338	439	452	297	183	436	294	415	136	161	212	112	310	346	103	299	274	601	524	211			
Wroclaw	496	532	230	265	176	436	432	268	109	199	300	420	267	69	204	428	442	276	178	511	321	435	614	442	371	279	344		
Zamosc	180	334	392	514	335	532	589	683	624	367	211	686	320	582	329	90	459	360	554	148	196	155	447	815	770	463	249	508	
Zielona Góra	570	601	387	259	328	430	411	109	142	358	420	322	427	111	301	542	453	351	130	663	433	586	653	290	212	281	413	159	629

BALTIC SEA
BORNHOLM IS (Denmark)
RUSSIA
LITHUANIA
BELARUS
UKRAINE
SLOVAKIA
CZECH REPUBLIC
GERMANY
Kaliningrad
Marijampole
VILNIUS
Hrodna
Slonim
Brest
Kovel'
Rostock
Greifswald
Sassnitz
Pasewalk
BERLIN
Frankfurt an der Oder
Cottbus
Dresden
Görlitz
Liberec
PRAHA
Hradec Králové
Ostrava
Žilina
ŚWINOUJŚCIE
Dziwnów
Międzyzdroje
SZCZECIN
Mielno
Kołobrzeg
KOSZALIN
Ustka
Rowy
Łeba
Sopot
Kartuzy
GDAŃSK
Stegna
Malbork
ELBLĄG
Frombork
OLSZTYN
Mrągowo
Mikołajki
Piecki
Ruciane-Nida
Węgorzewo
Giżycko
Ełk
SUWAŁKI
BIAŁYSTOK
Białowieża
Złocieniec
Wałcz
Świecie
BYDGOSZCZ
TORUŃ
Żnin
GORZÓW WIELKOPOLSKI
Sulecin
Łagów
Sierakow
POZNAŃ
PŁOCK
WARSZAWA
BIAŁA PODLASKA
ZIELONA GÓRA
Sława
ŁÓDŹ
RADOM
LUBLIN
LEGNICA
Zgorzelec
JELENIA GÓRA
Karpacz
WROCŁAW
Kluczbork
CZĘSTOCHOWA
KIELCE
Sandomierz
ZAMOŚĆ
Kłodzko
KATOWICE
Oświęcim
KRAKÓW
Wieliczka
Tarnów
RZESZÓW
Przeworsk
PRZEMYŚL
BIELSKO-BIAŁA
Żywiec
Nowy Sącz
Niedzica
Zakopane
N
S
E
W
All year site(s)
Seasonal site(s)
No sites listed
200m +
0–200m
Motorways
Major roads
Main roads
0 50 kms
0 30 mls
© Collins Bartholomew Ltd 2011

Slovakia

Country Introduction

© iStockPhoto.com/Kajdi Szabolcs

Strbske Pleso

Population (approx): 5.4 million

Capital: Bratislava (population approx 452,000)

Area: 49,035 sq km

Bordered by: Austria, Czech Republic, Hungary, Poland, Ukraine

Terrain: Rugged mountains in the centre and north; lowlands in the south

Climate: Continental climate; warm, showery summers; cold, cloudy, snowy winters; best months to visit are May, June and September

Highest Point: Gerlachovský štít 2,655m

Languages: Slovak, Hungarian, German

Local Time: GMT or BST + 1, i.e. 1 hour ahead of the UK all year

Currency: Euros divided into 100 cents; £1 = €1.14, €1 = 87 pence (September 2011)

Telephoning: From the UK dial 00421 for Slovakia and omit the initial zero of the area code of the number you are calling. To call the UK from Slovakia dial 0044, omitting the initial zero of the area code

Emergency numbers: Police 112; Fire brigade 112; Ambulance 112

Public Holidays 2012

Jan 1, 6; Apr 6, 9; May 1, 8 (VE Day); Jul 5 (St Cyril & St Methodius); Aug 29 (Anniversary of Slovak Uprising); Sep 1 (National Day), 15 (St Mary); Nov 1, 17 (Freedom & Democracy Day); Dec 24, 25, 26.

Public Holidays 2013

Jan 1, 6; Mar 29; Apr 1; May 1, 8 (VE Day); Jul 5 (St Cyril & St Methodius); Aug 29 (Anniversary of Slovak Uprising); Sep 1 (National Day), 15 (St Mary); Nov 1, 17 (Freedom & Democracy Day); Dec 24, 25, 26.

School summer holidays are from the beginning of July to the end of August

Tourist Office

SLOVAK TOURIST BOARD
PO BOX 35, 97405 BANSKA BYSTRICA, SLOVAKIA
www.slovakia.travel/ sacr@sacr.sk

The following introduction to Slovakia should be read in conjunction with the important information contained in the Handbook chapters at the front of this guide.

Camping and Caravanning

There are approximately 175 campsites (Kemping or Autocamp) situated near tourist resorts and classified into four categories. Sites are normally open from 15 June until 15 September, although some may open in May and a handful are open all year. The season is slow to get going and sites which claim to open in May may not do so or there may be only minimal facilities.

Campsites' standards are variable and facilities may be basic. Many consist mainly of cabins and chalets in various states of repair, while others form part of the facilities offered by hotels, guest houses or leisure/thermal spa complexes.

Casual/wild camping is not permitted; it is prohibited to sleep in a caravan or motorhome outside a campsite.

Recent visitors report that prices at campsites and the cost of living in general are still relatively low. Some of the prices shown in the campsite entries that follow have been directly converted from prices previously shown in koruna (crowns) and rounded up. You may find actual prices somewhat higher now that the official currency is the euro. Prices charged include a tourist tax.

Discounts may apply on presentation of a CCI, in low season when there are limited facilities, and for being over 60, but you will probably have to ask for them.

Country Information

Cycling

There are a number of long distance cycle tracks throughout the country (see www.slovakia.travel for more information) including alongside the River Danube between Bratislava and the Gabčikovo Dam.

Cyclists must ride in single file on the right hand side of the road or may use the verge outside built up areas. Children under 10 years of age may not ride on the road unless accompanied by a person over 15 years of age.

Electricity and Gas

Usually the current on campsites varies between 10 and 16 amps. Plugs have two round pins. Some campsites, but not all, have CEE connections.

It is not possible to purchase Campingaz International or any other of the gas cylinders normally available in the UK. Sufficient supplies for your stay should be taken with you. Many sites have communal kitchen facilities which enable visitors to make great savings on their own gas supply.

*See **Electricity and Gas** in the section **DURING YOUR STAY.***

Entry Formalities

Holders of valid British and Irish passports may visit Slovakia for up to three months without a visa. There are no registration formalities for short stay visitors.

Regulations for Pets

*See **Pet Travel Scheme** under **Documents** in the section **PLANNING AND TRAVELLING.***

Medical Services

Medical facilities are variable. Whereas the standard of care from doctors is good and medical equipment is constantly improving, many hospitals suffer from a lack of maintenance. The biggest problem you will probably encounter is language, as many nurses and ancillary workers will probably not speak English.

There is a reciprocal health care agreement with the UK for urgent medical treatment and you should present a European Health Insurance Card (EHIC). Emergency treatment is from doctors and dentists contracted to the Slovak health insurance system, but you will be asked for payment and follow on costs could be considerable. Hospital patients are required to make a financial contribution towards costs.

Charges incurred are not refundable in Slovakia.

A 24 hour first aid service exists in all provincial and district towns, as well as in some small communities. For minor ailments, the first call should be to a pharmacy (lekáren) where staff are qualified to give advice and may be able to prescribe drugs normally available only on prescription in the UK.

If you enjoy hiking and outdoor sports you should seek medical advice before you travel about preventative measures and immunisation against tick-borne encephalitis, a potentially serious and debilitating viral disease of the central nervous system which is endemic from spring to autumn. Lyme disease is an equally serious tick-borne infection for which there is no preventative vaccine. Ticks are found in rural and forested areas, particularly in long grass, bushes, hedgerows and woods, and in scrubland and areas where animals wander.

If you think you might be at risk use an insect repellent containing DEET, wear long sleeves and long trousers, inspect the body for ticks after outdoor activity and remove with tweezers, and avoid unpasteurised dairy products in risk areas. See www.tickalert.org, email info@tickalert.org or telephone 01943 468010.

Hepatitis A immunisation is advised for long stay travellers to rural areas, and those who plan to travel outside tourist areas.

You are strongly recommended to obtain comprehensive travel and medical insurance before travelling to Slovakia, such as The Caravan Club's Red Pennant Overseas Holiday Insurance – see www.caravanclub.co.uk/redpennant

*See **Medical Matters** in the section **DURING YOUR STAY.***

Opening Hours

Banks – Mon-Fri 8.30am-4.30pm.

Museums – Tue-Sun 10am-5pm; closed Monday.

Post Offices – Mon-Fri 8am-6pm; Sat 8am-1pm.

Shops – Mon-Fri 8am-6pm; Sat 8am-12 noon. Hypermarkets usually open Sunday.

Safety and Security

Most visits to Slovakia are trouble free. However, there is a risk of being a victim of petty theft, particularly in Bratislava, and pickpocketing is common at the main tourist attractions and in some bars where foreigners are easily identified and targeted. You should take sensible precautions against bag snatching and mugging. Avoid poorly lit areas at night.

When placing your jacket on the back of a chair in a restaurant your wallet should be kept securely elsewhere. When putting bags down, place one foot through the arm straps or handle to prevent theft. There have been occurrences in Bratislava of visitors being offered 'spiked' drinks and subsequently being robbed. Be wary of drinks offered by people you do not know.

Visitors entering Slovakia via the border crossings on the D2 and D4 motorways should be extremely vigilant. While you leave your vehicle to buy petrol or a motorway vignette, a tyre may be deliberately damaged. Once you are back on the road and have driven a few kilometres other motorists will flag you down and, under the pretext of offering assistance, attempt to steal items from your vehicle. In these circumstances you should stay in your vehicle with the doors locked and call the police (dial 112) or the emergency service of the Slovensky Autoturist Klub (SATC) on 18124 or (02) 68249211.

Robberies from parked cars are on the increase. Cameras, mobile phones and small electrical goods (laptops, mobiles, games, etc) are as attractive as cash and credit cards; don't leave them or other valuables unattended and remove them from your car when parking.

If you intend to ski or hike in the Slovak mountains you are recommended to ensure that you have sufficient insurance to cover potentially high rescue costs should the Slovak Mountain Rescue (HZS) be called out. Take heed of any instructions issued by HZS; if you ignore their advice you may be liable to a heavy fine.

Taking photos of anything that could be perceived as a military establishment or of security interest may result in problems with the authorities.

Slovakia shares with the rest of Europe an underlying threat from terrorism. Attacks, although unlikely, could be indiscriminate and against civilian targets, including places frequented by tourists.

*See **Safety and Security** in the section **DURING YOUR STAY.***

British Embassy

PANSKA 16, 81101 BRATISLAVA
Tel: (02) 59982000
http://ukinslovakia.fco.gov.uk/en/

Irish Embassy

CARLTON SAVOY BUILDING
MOSTOVA 2, 81102 BRATISLAVA
Tel: (02) 59309611
www.embassyofireland.sk

Customs Regulations

Alcohol and Tobacco

For import allowances for alcohol and tobacco products see ***Customs Regulations*** in the section ***PLANNING AND TRAVELLING.***

Documents

Passport

Carry your passport at all times as it is an offence to be without it and you may be fined and held in custody for up to 24 hours. Keep a photocopy of the details page separately. Ensure your passport is in a presentable state as the authorities can refuse you entry if it is worn or damaged or looks as if it may have been tampered with.

Vehicle(s)

You should carry your vehicle registration certificate (V5C), at all times together with your driving licence, insurance certificate and your vehicle's MOT certificate (if applicable). Fines may be imposed by police patrols if you cannot produce these documents on request.

*See **Documents** and **Insurance** in the section **PLANNING AND TRAVELLING.***

Money

Travellers' cheques are the safest way to carry money but make sure that you buy them from an organisation with agents in Slovakia. Change cash and travellers' cheques at banks or bureaux de change. Exchange kiosks, although legal, offer poor exchange rates and there is a risk of being robbed by thieves loitering nearby.

Scottish and Northern Irish bank notes will not be exchanged in Slovakia.

Cash machines which accept UK debit or credit cards are common but do not rely on finding one in remote areas. Shops, particularly in the main tourist areas, increasingly accept credit cards but are sometimes reluctant to accept cards issued by foreign banks. If you intend to pay for something by card do check first that the shop will accept it and that it can be read. You are also recommended to check your statements carefully for transactions you did not make.

Carry your credit card issuers'/banks' 24-hour UK contact numbers in case of loss or theft of your cards.

Motoring

The standard of driving is not high and conduct can be aggressive with drivers often going too fast, especially in bad weather, pushing into dangerously small gaps, tailgating and overtaking dangerously. Drive defensively and allow yourself more 'thinking time'. Beware particularly of oncoming cars overtaking on your side of the road (especially on bends and hills). Older, low-powered cars and trucks travel very slowly.

Accidents

If your vehicle is damaged when you enter Slovakia the border authorities must issue a certificate confirming the visible damage. While in the country if an accident causes bodily injury or material damage exceeding a value of approximately €4,000 it must be reported to the police immediately. If a vehicle is only slightly damaged both drivers should complete a European Accident Report. In the case of foreign motorists driving vehicles registered abroad, it is advisable to report the accident to the police who will issue a certificate which will facilitate the exportation of the vehicle.

Alcohol

Don't drink and drive. Slovakia has a policy of zero tolerance for drinking or consuming drugs before driving. There is no permitted level of alcohol in the bloodstream. Police carry out random breath tests and you will be heavily penalised if there is any trace of alcohol in your system.

Breakdown Service

The motoring organisation, Slovensky Autoturist Klub (SATC), operates an emergency centre which can be contacted 24 hours a day by dialling (0)18124 or (02) 68249211. Operators speak English.

Essential Equipment

*See **Motoring – Equipment** in the section **PLANNING AND TRAVELLING.***

Lights

All vehicles must use dipped headlights at all times.

Reflective Jacket/Waistcoat

If your vehicle is immobilised on the carriageway outside a built up area, or if visibility is poor, you must wear a reflective jacket or waistcoat when getting out of your vehicle. Passengers who leave the vehicle, for example, to assist with a repair, should also wear one.

Sat Nav/GPS Device

A GPS device must not be placed in the middle of the windscreen. The driver's view must not be impeded.

Warning Triangles

Carry a warning triangle which, in an emergency or in case of breakdown, must be placed at least 100 metres behind your vehicle on motorways and highways, and 50 metres behind on other roads. The triangle may be placed closer to the vehicle in built-up areas. Drivers may use hazard-warning lights until the triangle is in position.

In case of breakdown, vehicles left on the edge of the carriageway will be towed away after three hours by the organisation in charge of the motorway or road at the owner's expense.

Child Restraint System

Children under the age of 12 years and anyone under 1.5m in height must not travel in the front seat of a vehicle. Specially adapted child restraint seats must be used for any children weighing less than 36kg.

Winter Driving

In winter equip your vehicle(s) for severe driving conditions and fit winter tyres, which are compulsory when roads are covered in snow or ice. Carry snow chains and use them when there is enough snow to protect the road surface.

Snow chains can be hired or purchased from Polar Automotive Ltd, tel 01892 519933, www.snowchains.com, email polar@snowchains.com (10% discount for Caravan Club members).

Fuel

*See also **Fuel** under **Motoring – Advice** in the section **PLANNING AND TRAVELLING.***

Diesel is sold in service stations with the sign 'TT Diesel' or 'Nafta'. LPG is widely available and is sold under the name ECO Auto-gas or ECO Car-Gas – see www.lpg.szm.sk/slovensko_5.pdf for a list of outlets. If driving a vehicle converted to use LPG you must be in possession of a safety certificate covering the combustion equipment in your vehicle.

Some service stations on international roads and in main towns are open 24 hours but in other areas they may close by 6pm. Credit cards are generally accepted. Service stations may be hard to find in rural areas.

Parking

Visitors are warned to park only in officially controlled parking areas since cars belonging to tourists may be targeted for robbery. There are many restrictions on parking in Bratislava and fines are imposed. Wheel clamps are used in main towns and vehicles may be towed away.

Continuous white/yellow lines along the carriageway indicate that parking is prohibited and broken white/yellow lines indicate parking restrictions.

See also ***Parking Facilities for the Disabled*** *under* ***Motoring – Advice*** *in the section* ***PLANNING AND TRAVELLING.***

Priority

At uncontrolled crossroads or intersections not marked by a priority sign, priority must be given to vehicles coming from the right. Drivers must not enter an intersection unless the exit beyond the crossing is clear.

Drivers must slow down and, if necessary, stop to allow buses and trams to move off from stops and to allow buses to merge with general traffic at the end of a bus lane. A tram turning right and crossing the line of travel of a vehicle moving on its right has priority once the driver has signalled his intention to turn. Trams must be overtaken on the right but do not overtake near a tram refuge.

Roads

Roads are relatively quiet and are generally well maintained. They often follow routes through towns and villages, resulting in sharp bends and reduced speed limits.

Many main roads, although reasonably good, have only a single carriageway in each direction making overtaking difficult. Road markings may be difficult to see in bad weather.

In winter, north south routes through Slovakia can be challenging as they pass through mountain ranges. The passes of Donovaly (Ružomberok to Banská Bystrica), Veľký Šturec (Martin to Banská Bystrica), and Čertovica (Liptovský Mikuláš to Brezno) are the most frequented. Slow moving vehicles travelling uphill should pull over at suitable stopping places to allow vehicles behind to pass.

See ***Winter Driving*** earlier in this chapter.

Road Signs and Markings

Road signs and markings conform to international standards. The following signs may also be seen.

Dialkova premavka – *By-pass*

Hnemocnica – *Hospital*

Jednosmerny premavka – *One-way traffic*

Obchadzka – *Diversion*

Průjezd zakázaný – *Closed to all vehicles*

Zákaz parkovania – *No parking*

Zákaz vjazdu – *No entry*

Signs indicating motorways are red and white and signs on motorways or semi-motorways have a green or blue background; on other roads signs have a blue background.

Speed Limits

See ***Speed Limits Table*** *under* ***Motoring – Advice*** *in the section* ***PLANNING AND TRAVELLING.***

Motorhomes over 3,500kg are restricted to 80/90 km/h (56 mph) on motorways and to 80 km/h (50 mph) on other main roads and dual carriageways. Do not exceed 30 km/h (18 mph) when approaching and going over level crossings.

Speed limits are strictly enforced. The carrying and/or use of radar detectors is prohibited.

Traffic Lights

A green arrow together with a red or amber light indicates that drivers may turn in the direction indicated by the arrow provided they give way to other traffic and to pedestrians. A green arrow accompanied by an amber light in the form of a walking figure means that pedestrians have right on way.

Violation of Traffic Regulations

Police are empowered to collect on the spot fines for contravention of driving regulations. An official receipt should be obtained.

Motorways

There are 350km of motorways. Bratislava has direct motorway connections with Prague and Vienna and a new motorway is planned to connect it with Budapest.

Emergency phones are placed along motorways and callers are connected directly to the police.

Vehicles using motorways and selected highways must display a vignette (windscreen sticker), which may be purchased at border crossings, petrol stations and post offices. Charges in euros in 2011 for vehicles up to 3,500kg with or without a caravan or trailer are as follows (subject to change): €7 for a period of 7 days and €14 for one month. Fines are payable for non-display and old stickers must be removed. The road from the Austrian border crossing at Berg to Bratislava is free of charge.

Drivers of vehicles over 3,500kg must pay motorway tolls by means of an electronic toll collection unit fitted to their vehicle. Tolls vary according to distance driven, vehicle weight and emissions classification. For information see www.emyto.sk or telephone 00421 235 111111.

Touring

Slovakian culture reflects a strong Hungarian influence in terms of food. Assorted cold meats are an important part of the diet, while venison and game, such as duck and pigeon, are plentiful. Apart from carp and occasionally trout or crayfish, fresh fish is rare. Southern Slovakia is an important wine producing area and slivovice, a strong plum brandy, is a national favourite.

Smoking is not allowed on the premises where food is served and a partial smoking ban is in force in some bars and cafés which have a dedicated area for smokers. A tip of between 5 to 10% is usual in restaurants. It is normal to give taxi drivers a small tip by rounding up fares to the nearest 50 cents.

Mains water is heavily chlorinated and may cause stomach upsets. Bottled water is available.

The highest peaks of the Tatras mountains are covered with snow for approximately four months of the year and offer ample scope for winter sports. There are plenty of cableways and ski-lifts.

There are a number of UNESCO World Heritage sites in Slovakia including the town of Bardejov, the mining centre of Banská Štiavnica, the 'gingerbread houses' of Vlkolínec village, Spiš Castle, wooden churches in the Carpathian mountains and the caves of Aggtelek Karst and Slovak Karst.

Slovakia has over a thousand curative mineral and thermal springs, together with extensive deposits of high quality healing peat and mud reputed to cure a variety of diseases and ailments. Visitors from all over the world attend these spas every year.

The Bratislava City Card valid for one, two or three days, offers discounts and benefits at approximately 60 attractions and at restaurants and cafés. In addition, it offers free access to public transport and a free one hour walking tour of the Old Town. The card can be obtained at tourist information centres, at the central railway station and at hotels.

In general Slovakia does not cater for the physically handicapped. For example, it is normal for cars to park on the pavement and dropped kerbs are perceived as helping drivers to achieve this without damaging tyres or suspension! Public transport invariably requires large steps to be climbed and bus and tram drivers tend to accelerate from stops at great speed, catching passengers by surprise. Access to most buildings is by steps, rather than ramps. However effort is now being taken to make buildings more accessible.

German is the most common second language. English is still not widely understood or spoken.

Local Transport

From April to September hydrofoil services operate from Bratislava to Vienna and Budapest.

In Bratislava bus, trolley bus and tram tickets are valid for periods of up to 60 minutes, extending to up to 90 minutes at night and weekends. Buy them from kiosks and yellow ticket machines. Alternatively you can buy tickets valid for one or several city zones for a fixed period, e.g. 24, 48 or 72 hours or for seven days. Ensure that you validate your ticket on boarding the bus or tram.

Passengers aged 70 and over travel free; carry your passport as proof of age. You must buy a ticket for dogs travelling on public transport and they must be muzzled. You must also purchase a ticket for large items of luggage. For more information see www.imhd.zoznam.sk/ba/ (English option).

All place names used in the Site Entry listings which follow can be found in the Slovakia & Europe Superatlas published by Freytag & Berndt, scale 1cm to 1.5km and 1cm to 3.5km, see www.freytagberndt.com

BANSKA BYSTRICA *B2* (7km W Rural) *48.7540, 19.0552* **Autocamping Tajov, 97634 Tajov [(048) 4197320; kukis@slovanet.sk; www.velkydvor.sk/en]** Fr Tajov dir Kordíky. Site well sp 2km NW of Tajov. Sm, pt sl, unshd; htd wc; chem disp; shwrs inc; el pnts (6-10A) inc; shop; snacks; bar; rest 300m; playgrnd; wifi; TV; statics; bus; quiet; red CCI. "Lovely setting in wooded valley; friendly welcome." € 16.00 2011*

BOJNICE *B2* (3km W Rural) *48.78026, 18.56190* **Autocamping Bojnice, Mestszy Urad, 97201 Bojnice [tel/fax (046) 5413845; info@campingbojnice.sk; www.campingbojnice.sk]** Fr S on rd 50 or fr N on rd 64 foll sp for Prievidza then Bojnice & Autocamping. Site on rd to Nitrianske, past 2nd hairpin bend. Foll sp 'Zoo' & 'Sportzentrum'. Sm, pt sl, shd; wc; shwrs inc; el pnts (10A) €3.50; shop; lndtte; snacks; TV. 1 Jun-31 Aug. € 10.00 2008*

BRATISLAVA *C1* (8km NE Urban) *48.18801, 17.18488* **Autocamping Zlaté Piesky, Senecká Cesta 12, 82104 Bratislava [(02) 44257373 or 44450592; fax 44257373; kempi@netax.sk; www.intercamp.sk]** Exit D1/E75 junc sp Zlaté Piesky. Site on S side of rd 61 (E75) at NE edge of Bratislava. Look for pedestrian bdge over rd to tram terminus, ent thro adj traff lts. If x-ing Bratislava foll sp for Žilina. In summer a 2nd, quieter, drier site is opened. For 1st site turn L when ent leisure complex; for 2nd site carry strt on then turn R. Med, shd; wc; shwrs inc; el pnts (10A) €3 (long lead poss req); shop; supmkt (Tesco) 300m; rest; snacks; bar; playgrnd; sw & pedalos on lake; fishing; tennis; golf 10km; entmnt; dogs €2; phone; tram to city; poss cr; Eng spkn; v noisy fr adj m'way & bar; red CCI. "Basic site on lge leisure complex; no privacy in shwrs; ltd hot water; muddy in wet; security guard at night & secure rm for bikes etc but regular, major security problems as site grounds open to public; helpful, friendly staff; interesting city." 1 May-15 Oct. € 13.20 2010*

BREZNO *B3* (6km SE Rural) *48.79501, 19.72867* **Camping Sedliacky Dvor, Hliník 7, 97701 Brezno [(048) 6117218; info@sedliackydvor.com; www.sedliackydvor.com]** Fr cent of Brezno at traff lts nr Hotel Dumbier take rd 530/72 SE sp Tisovec. In approx 5km cross rlwy line & ent vill of Rohozná. At end of vill turn L after Camping sp. Site in 500m. Sm, pt shd; wc; shwrs; el pnts (10A) €3.25; lndtte; cooking facs; pool; games area; wifi; dogs €1; Eng spkn; adv bkg; quiet. "Excel site in lovely orchard setting; welcoming Dutch owners; camp fires in evening; excel facs." 15 Apr-31 Oct. € 12.60 2010*

CEROVO *C2* (8km NE Rural) *48.25228, 19.21783* **Camping Lazy, Cerovo 163, 96252 Cerovo [(090) 8590837; info@campinglazy.eu; www.campinglazy.eu]** S fr Zvolen on rd 66 dir Krupina. S of Krupina turn L onto rd 526 to Bzovik. After church in Bzovik turn R sp Kozí Vrbovok, Trpin & Litava. Cont thro Litava (agricultural co-operative, Družstvo, on R) & cont for approx 5km to T-junc with bus shelter & turn R. Do not foll sp Cerovo on R but cont to forest & look out for sm lane & site sp to R. Sm, pt sl, pt shd; wc; chem disp; shwrs; el pnts (4-6A) €2.50; lndtte; some statics (equipped tents); dogs free; quiet. "Site on working farm; ideal for nature lovers, hikers, dog owners; gd, modern san facs; pleasant, helpful owners." € 12.00 2010*

CERVENY KLASTOR *A3* (500m W Rural) *49.39112, 20.40113* **Camping Dunajec, 05906 Červený Kláštor [(052) 4822656; fax 4822525; info@penzionpltnik.sk; www.penzionpltnik.sk]** E fr Spišská Stará Ves on rd 543, site on Rv Dunajec adj Pltnik Hotel. Sm, pt shd; wc; shwrs; el pnts €2.50; rest, bar adj; quiet. "Beautiful setting." € 10.00 2008*

DEDINKY *B3* (200m S Urban) *48.86255, 20.38501* **Autocamping Dedinky, 04973 Dedinky [(058) 7981212; fax 7881682]** Rd 67 S fr Proprad for approx 40km, foll sp Dedinky onto rd 535. Stop at hotel in vill - also recep for site. Sm, v sl, unshd; wc, shwrs in hotel; shop 500m; rest, bar in hotel; lake sw. "Beautiful location by reservoir; steep access & v sl ground; excel walking; conv spectacular ice caves at Dobšinská; suitable tents & sm m'vans only." 1 May-30 Sep. € 11.00 2008*

DEMANOVSKA DOLINA see Liptovský Mikuláš *B3*

DOBSINA *B3* (1km W Rural) *48.81836, 20.37272* **Camping Chatová Osada Alweg, Zimná 191, 04925 Dobšiná [tel/fax (058) 7941564; alweg@stonline.sk]** App thro back streets of Dobšiná, steep, rough access rd, sp. Sm, pt shd; wc; shwrs; el pnts; rest in hotel; cooking facs; quiet. "Sm, basic site; o'looking wooded hills." € 8.00 2008*

DOLNY KUBIN *B2* (2km W Rural) *49.20661, 19.26476* **Tília Kemp Gäcel, 02601 Dolný Kubin [(043) 5865110; fax 5864950; info@tiliakemp.sk; www.tiliakemp.sk]** W of Dolný Kubin on S bank of Rv Orava. Diff to find. Access fr Dolný Kubin is by narr rd fr church on S side of rv with a no ent sp. Also access fr rd 70 at Veličná. Turn S fr cent of Veličná, over rv bdge into Oravská Poruba & turn L after 1.5km. Site on L in 2km. Sm, hdg pitch, unshd; wc; shwrs; el pnts (16A) €2.50; lndtte; shops 3km; rest adj; fishing; some statics; dogs €1.50; Eng spkn; quiet; ccard acc; red CCI. "Scenic mountain area; old-fashioned, clean facs; poss unreliable opening dates." 1 May-30 Sep. € 18.00 2008*

HRABUSICE *B3* (2.5km SW Rural) *48.96444, 20.38500* **Autocamping Podlesok, Hlavná 171, 05315 Hrabušice [(053) 4299164; fax 4299163; atcpodlesok@gmail.com]** Bet Poprad & Levoca on rd 18 (E 50) turn S at Spišsky Štvrtok & foll sps to Hrabušice. Site sp. Lge, pt sl, pt shd; own san rec; el pnts (6A) €2.50; lndtte; shop; snacks; pool 16km; skilift 1km; 10% statics; dogs €2; Eng spkn; poss noisy at w/end fr school parties. "Magnificent setting; warm welcome; v primitive facs but hot water avail; conv National Park." € 8.50 2008*

JELENEC *C2* (2km N Rural) *48.39750, 18.20611* **Autocamping Jelenec, 95173 Jelenec [(037) 6313232; fax 6313317; obec.jelenec@jelenec.sk; www.jelenec.sk]** Fr rd 65/E571 turn N sp Jelenec, site sp. Sm, unshd; wc; shwrs; el pnts (15A) inc; shop 3km; snacks; lake sw & fishing nr; tennis; sat TV; some statics; quiet. "Simple site on wooded hillside; primitive facs but clean; gd waymkd walks in Tribeč hills to Gýmeš Castle." 15 May-30 Sep. € 8.00 2008*

KOSICE *B4* (4km SW Rural) *48.68746, 21.25583* **Autocamping Salaš Barca, Alejová ul, 04001 Košice [(055) 6233397; fax 6258309; www.autocamping.szm.sk]** Access only avail E'bound on E571/E50/E58. Fr W foll sp Miskolc E571/E50/E58. Site on R 2km after clover leaf junc. Fr N or E foll sp E50/E571 Rožňava W-bound past camp to clover leaf junc & return E-bound on E571/E50/E58. Fr S (Hung border) on ent Košice turn L under ring rd sp Spišská Nová Ves & Rožňava (E571). After approx 2.5km take airport/Rožňava exit over clover leaf & back down E-bound ringrd (E571). Site on R. Sm, unshd; wc; shwrs inc; el pnts (10A) inc; shop 1km; rest; snacks, bar 1km; cooking facs; sand/shgl beach & rv sw 1km; pool 1km; 50% workers' chalets; tram 500m; Eng spkn; rd noise; CCI. "Old but clean facs, ltd low ssn; recep sells tram tickets; 24hr security; gd touring base, but run down (2009); Košice delightful city." 15 May-15 Oct. € 19.30 2009*

I'll go online and tell the Club what we think of the campsites we've visited – www.caravanclub.co.uk/europereport

LEVICE *C2* (5km SE Rural) *48.19055, 18.66178* **Autocamping Margita-Ilona, Nábrezná 1, 93401 Kalinčiakovo [(036) 6312954; fax 6221954; margita-ilona@margita-ilona.sk; www.margita-ilona.sk]** SE fr Levice on rd 564, site sp. Med, pt shd; wc; shwrs inc; el pnts (10-16A) inc; shop; rest 200m; snacks; bar; playgrnd; pool; paddling pool; 30% statics; dogs €1.70; noise fr nightly disco; CCI. "Holiday complex - not rec high ssn; no water fill." 15 May-30 Sep. € 15.00 2008*

⊞ **LEVOCA** *B3* (3km N Rural) *49.04982, 20.58727* **Autocamping Levočská Dolina, 05401 Levoča [(053) 4512705 or 4512701; fax 4513689; rzlevoca@pobox.sk]** Site on E side of minor rd 533 running N fr E50 at Dolina to Levočská Dolina. Steep ent; ltd access lge o'fits. Med, sl, pt shd; wc; chem disp; shwrs inc; el pnts (16A) €3; lndtte; shop 3km; rest; snacks; bar; playgrnd; skilift 2.5km; TV; dogs €1.50; Eng spkn; quiet; CCI. "Diff in wet weather due v sl grnd; friendly staff; interesting old town; Spišský Hrad castle worth visit; walks in forests around site." € 15.00 2009*

LIPTOVSKY MIKULAS *B3* (6km NE Rural) *49.11108, 19.54608* **Autocamp Liptovský Trnovec, 03222 Liptovský Trnovec [(044) 5598459; fax 5598458; atctrnovec@atctrnovec.sk; www.atctrnovec.sk]** E fr Ružomberok on R18/E50 exit on R584 to Liptovský Mikuláš. Site on N side of Lake Liptovský Mara. Med, unshd; wc; chem disp; shwrs inc; el pnts (6A) €2.50; lndtte; shop; rest, bar in ssn; playgrnd; lake sw; boating; cycle hire; internet; 10% cabins; dogs €2; Eng spkn; quiet; red CCI. "Excel; lovely site in beautiful location." ♦ 1 May-31 Oct. € 13.50 2010*

⊞ **LIPTOVSKY MIKULAS** *B3* (6km S Rural) *49.03341, 19.57526* **Hotel Bystrina & Autocamp, 03251 Demänovská Dolina [(044) 5548163; fax 5477079; hotelbystrina@hotelbystrina.sk; www.hotelbystrina.sk]** On D1 m'way take junc at Liptovský Mikuláš S dir Jasná. Site & hotel clearly sp fr rd in 6km. Med, pt sl, terr, pt shd; wc; chem disp; shwrs inc; el pnts (10A) €3.70; lndtte; shop 7km; rest; snacks; bar; playgrnd; dogs €2; bus; no adv bkg; quiet; ccard acc; CCI. "Woodland setting above hotel; gd walking area; ice cave worth visit; poss security prob." € 14.50 2008*

⊞ **LIPTOVSKY MIKULAS** *B3* (10km NW Rural) *49.13608, 19.5125* **Penzión Villa Betula Caravan Club, 03223 Liptovský Sielnica [(044) 5598464; villabetula@villabetula.sk; www.villabetula.sk]** Fr rd 18/E50 exit onto R584 to Liptovský Mikuláš, site on N of lake 6km past Autocamp. Sm, mkd pitch, hdstg, unshd; wc; chem disp; sauna; baby facs; shwrs inc; el pnts (10A) inc; rest; bar; playgrnd; lake sw adj; cycle hire; jacuzzi; wifi; no statics; dogs €3; phone; Eng spkn; quiet; ccard acc; CCI. "Family-friendly, gem of a site in wonderful area of lakes, mountains & forest; welcoming, helpful owners; v clean & well-kept; vg rest." € 22.00 2011*

LIPTOVSKY SIELNICA see Liptovský Mikuláš *B3*

LIPTOVSKY TRNOVEC see Liptovský Mikuláš *B3*

⊞ **MARTIN** *B2* (5km NW Rural) *49.1082, 18.89888* **Autocamping Turiec, Kolónia Hviezda 92, 03608 Martin [(043) 4284215; fax 4131982; recepcia@autocampingturiec.sk; www.autocampingturiec.sk]** Site in town of Vrútky 3km NW of Martin. Foll Autocamping Turiec sps fr rd 18/E50 Žilina-Poprad. Site approx 1km S of this rd on o'skts Vrútky. Med, pt sl, pt shd; wc; chem disp; shwrs inc; el pnts (10A); shops nr; rest; pool 2km; 30% statics; dogs €0.70; Eng spkn; quiet; CCI. "Warm welcome; excel security; pleasant wooded setting." € 15.00 2008*

NAMESTOVO *A2* (9km SE Rural) *49.38442, 19.52976* **Camping Stará Hora, Oravská Priehrada, 02901 Námestovo [(043) 5522223; fax 5591146; camp.s.hora@mail.t-com.sk; www.oravskapriehrada.sk]** N fr Dolný Kubin on E77/rd 59, turn L in Tvrdošín onto rd 520 sp Námestovo. Site on R in 4km on Lake Orava. Med, hdg pitch, pt sl, pt shd; wc; shwrs inc; el pnts (10A) €3; shop; rest; snacks; bar; lake sw & beach adj; 50% statics; dogs €1.20; bus; Eng spkn; quiet; CCI. "Pleasant site in forested area; conv for rd 521 to Polish border - useful alt to busy E77 rte." 1 May-30 Sep. € 9.00 2008*

NITRIANSKE RUDNO *B2* (N Rural) *48.80457, 18.47601* **Autocamping Nitrianske Rudno, 97226 Nitrianske Rudno [(046) 5455403; info@camping-nrudno.sk; www.camping-nrudno.sk]** E fr Bánovce & Dolné Vestenice on rd 50, turn N onto rd 574. Site on shore of Lake Nitrianske Rudno, sp in vill. Med, pt shd; wc; shwrs; el pnts €2.50; lndtte; snacks; bar; cooking facs; playgrnd; lake sw; watersports; games area; internet; entmnt; some statics; dogs €1; adv bkg; quiet; red CCI. "Welcoming, helpful owner; pleasant location." 1 Jun-30 Sep. € 8.70 2008*

SLOVAKIA

⊞ **ORAVICE** *B3* (Rural) *49.29880, 19.74633* **Autocamp Oravice, 02712 Oravice [(043) 5394114; fax 5393249; bajocamp@szm.sk]** Fr Trstená W on rd 520 thro Liesek to Vitanová, turn S to Oravice, site sp. Sm, pt shd; wc; shwrs; el pnts (6A); shop 300m; snacks; bar; thermal spa & pool adj; quiet. "Superb setting in W foothills of Tatras; welcoming owner; facs old-fashioned but clean; worth a detour." 2008*

POVAZSKA BYSTRICA *B2* (3km NE Rural) *49.14409, 18.49107* **Camping Manin, Manínska Tiesňava, 01701 Považská Bystrica [(042) 4381111; fax 4381112; pobyton@stonline.sk; www.maninska.sk]** Site sp on ent Považská Bystrica fr S; thro town & turn R at sp Považská Tepla. Foll sp for 3km. Sm, pt shd; wc; shwrs inc; el pnts €2.50; shops 2km; rest; cooking facs; games rm; games area; statics; Eng spkn; quiet. "Čičmany vill worth visit; helpful recep; basic facs; gd NH." May-Sep. € 10.00 2008*

RAJECKE TEPLICE see Žilina *B2*

ROZNAVA *B3* (5km E Rural) **Autocamping Krásnohorské, Hradná 475, 04941 Krásnohorské Podhradie [(058) 7325457; fax 7921332]** E fr Rožňava on rd 50/E571 foll sp Krásnohorské Podhradie. Site under shadow of castle. Sm, pt shd; wc; shwrs; mainly huts. "Lovely setting in pine woods; primitive facs but plenty of hot water; conv for cave visits." € 8.30 2008*

SENEC *C1* (1.5km SE Urban) *48.21386, 17.41088* **Autocamping Slnečné Jazerá (Die Sonnenseen), Mierové Námestie 19, 90301 Senec [(02) 45924081; fax 45923080; info@slnecnejazerasenec.sk; www.slnecnejazerasenec.sk]** Fr D1/E75 take junc exit for Senec onto rd 503, site sp. Lge, pt shd; wc; shwrs inc; el pnts (16A) inc; lndtte; shop; supmkts in town; rest; snacks; playgrnd; aqua park nr; sand beach; lake sw; boating; tennis; cycling; TV; entmnt; no dogs; phone; bus/train to Bratislava nr; poss cr; noise fr disco, rd & rlwy. "Gd alternative to Bratislava site." 15 Jun-15 Sep. € 19.30 2011*

SNINA *B4* (3km E Rural) **Autocamping Stanový Tábor, 06901 Snina [(090) 5537091; fax 5723862; autocampingsnina@centrum.sk; www.autocampingsnina.sk]** On S side of Rv Kolonička bet Snina & Stakčin. Sp fr rd 74. Sm, pt shd; wc; shwrs €0.30; el pnts €2.50; snacks; bar; dogs €1; quiet. "In birch woods; helpful, welcoming owners; basic, adequate facs; conv touring base." 15 May-15 Oct. € 7.50 2008*

TAJOV see Banská Bystrica *B2*

⊞ **TATRANSKA LOMNICA** *B3* (2km SE Rural) *49.15830, 20.30979* **Intercamp Tatranec, 05960 Tatranská Lomnica [(052) 4467092; hoteltatranec@hoteltatranec.com]** NE fr Poprad on rd 67, after 8km turn L over level x-ing, thro Veľká Lomnica twds Tatranská Lomnica on rd 540. Site on L. Lge, pt sl, unshd; wc; chem disp; shwrs inc; el pnts (6A) inc; lndtte; shop & 4km; rest; bar; playgrnd; wifi; entmnt; Eng spkn; adv bkg; quiet; red CCI. "Superb views of High Tatras; conv cable car, train etc; excel base for walking & holiday resort; hotel adj; poor facs & ltd privacy." € 18.50 2011*

TERCHOVA *B2* (3km W Rural) *49.24779, 18.98866* **Autocamp Belá, Nižné Kamence, 01305 Belá [(041) 5695135; camp@bela.sk; www.camping.bela.sk]** Fr Zilina foll rd 583 twd Terchová. Site on L 3km after vill of Belá. Med, pt shd; wc; chem disp; mv service pnt; shwrs €0.30; el pnts (10A) €3; lndry rm; shop; tradsmn; rest; snacks; BBQ; cooking facs; playgrnd; tennis; 10% statics; dogs €1; rd noise. "Delightful rvside site; gd welcome; clean, modern san facs; conv walking in Malá Fatra mountains." 1 May-15 Oct. € 11.50 2011*

When we get home
I'm going to post
all these site report
forms to the Club
for next year's guide.
The deadline's mid September 2013

TRENCIN *B2* (300m N Urban) *48.90011, 18.04076* **Autocamping Na Ostrove, Ostrov, 91101 Trenčín [(032) 7434013; autocamping.tn@mail.pvt.sk; http://web.viapvt.sk/autocamping.tn]** Fr SW on rd 61/E75 cross rv at Hotel Tatra, 1st L dir Sihot, go under rlwy bdge. 1st L, then immed 1st L again, then R at stadium, cross canal to island, site on L. Sm, unshd; wc; chem disp; shwrs inc; 25% serviced pitches; el pnts (10A) €4; lndtte; shop in town; snacks; bar; cooking facs; pool 500m; 70% cabins; dogs €1.50; poss cr; some Eng spkn; some noise fr rlwy & sports stadium; CCI. "Popular NH en rte Poland, rec arr early high ssn; on rvside in run down part of town adj sports stadium; adj delightful town with fairy-tale castle; poss waterlogged in wet; facs old but clean - some lack privacy." 1 May-15 Sep. € 17.00 2011*

TURANY see Martin *B2*

VARIN see Žilina *B2*

ZILINA *B2* (12km E Rural) *49.20995, 18.87858* **Autocamping Varín, 01303 Varín [(041) 5621478; fax 5623171; selinan@selinan.sk; www.selinan.sk]** Leave Žilina by rte 11/E75 dir Čadca. Immed after x-ing rv bdge take R lane & turn R along N bank of rv dir Tepličká & Bela. Site approx 12km fr rte 11 & 3km beyond Gbel'any on R, visible fr rd. Foll sp Terchova. V lge, pt shd; wc; shwrs inc; el pnts €3.20; shop; rest in ssn; playgrnd; cycling; dogs €1.50; quiet; CCI. "Pleasant site; v basic facs but clean; gd rest; helpful, friendly manager; be aware of ticks in grass; vg walking in National Park; 18km fr cable car." 1 May-15 Oct. € 10.00 2007*

ZILINA *B2* (10km S Rural) *49.14283, 18.71943* **Autocamping Slnečné Skaly, Poluvsie, 01313 Rajecké Teplice [(041) 54949901; fax 5494057; info@camping-raj.sk; www.camping-raj.sk]** On Žilina to Prievidza rd 64 bet Porúbka & Rajecké Teplice. Med, unshd; wc; shwrs inc; el pnts €2; supmkt 3km; snacks; playgrnd; pool, tennis 3km; fishing; games area; horseriding; 10% statics; dogs €1; bus nr; Eng spkn; quiet; red CCI. "Delightful setting by rv but poss liable to flooding; gd walking; conv Čičmany painted houses." 1 May-30 Sep. € 10.00 2007*

ZVOLEN *B2* (1.5km S Rural) *48.56346, 19.13756* **Autocamping Neresnica, Moyzesova 28, 96001 Zvolen [(045) 5332651; www.campneresnica.sk]** Site on E side of rd 66/E77 on S edge of town adj filling stn, sp. Med, pt shd; wc; own san; shwrs inc; el pnts (10A) €2.70; lndry rm; shop 200m; rest nr & 700m; playgrnd; pool adj; bus/train in Zvolen; no adv bkg; rd noise; CCI. "Sited bet busy rd & rlwy, but green & restful; helpful, welcoming staff;." 15 May-15 Oct. € 9.30 2008*

ZVOLEN *B2* (6km NW Rural) *48.60611, 19.10175* **Autocamp Kovácová, Kúpelhá ul, 96237 Kovácová [(045) 5445220; fax 5445363; recent@recent.sk]** Fr E77/66 dir Banská Bystrica turn at sp Kovácová. In vill foll site sp. Med, pt sl, pt shd; wc; chem disp (wc); shwrs inc; el pnts €2.50; lndry rm; shop 500m; snacks; bar; BBQ; cooking facs; htd pool adj; TV rm; 40% statics; Eng spkn; quiet; CCI. "Clean site but run down (6/09); friendly owner." 26 May-2 Sep. € 11.40 2009*

SLOVAKIA

Distances are shown in kilometres and are calculated from town/city centres along the most practical roads, although not necessarily taking the shortest route. 1km = 0.62miles

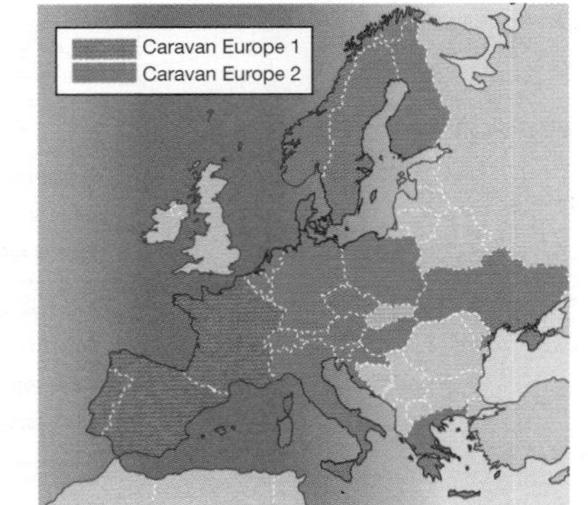

	Banská Bystrica	Bratislava	Budapest (Hungary)	Komárno	Košice	Liptovský Mikuláš	Lučenec	Malacky	Martin	Nitra	Prešov	Poprad	Považská Bystrica	Rimavská Sobota	Svidník	Trenčín	Trnava	Wien (Austria)	Zvolen
Bratislava	214																		
Budapest (Hungary)	183	201																	
Komárno	167	106	94																
Košice	218	404	282	330															
Liptovský Mikuláš	75	291	260	246	166														
Lučenec	77	243	160	168	161	151													
Malacky	223	42	242	144	417	290	258												
Martin	64	233	246	197	225	63	140	232											
Nitra	114	98	165	72	310	194	152	111	142										
Prešov	201	413	316	361	35	140	194	429	199	321									
Poprad	120	335	286	288	110	57	123	343	116	233	84								
Považská Bystrica	120	174	306	210	283	118	197	171	61	144	260	176							
Rimavská Sobota	103	274	187	194	132	132	25	287	164	177	165	97	223						
Svidník	259	471	371	415	90	195	251	484	256	373	55	135	313	221					
Trenčín	145	125	281	161	332	166	183	129	103	99	302	222	47	212	360				
Trnava	169	60	209	117	361	238	204	63	182	54	372	287	120	231	422	74			
Wien (Austria)	281	68	244	175	473	358	314	109	298	125	483	400	240	340	537	194	126		
Zvolen	22	201	162	147	213	99	56	210	85	101	225	142	145	82	280	132	154	267	
Žilina	89	205	273	215	254	87	167	202	26	142	226	145	32	190	282	76	153	271	112

Martin to Wien (Austria) = 298km

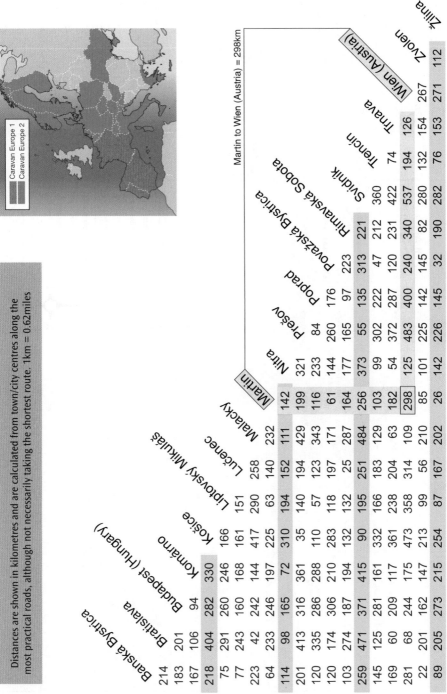

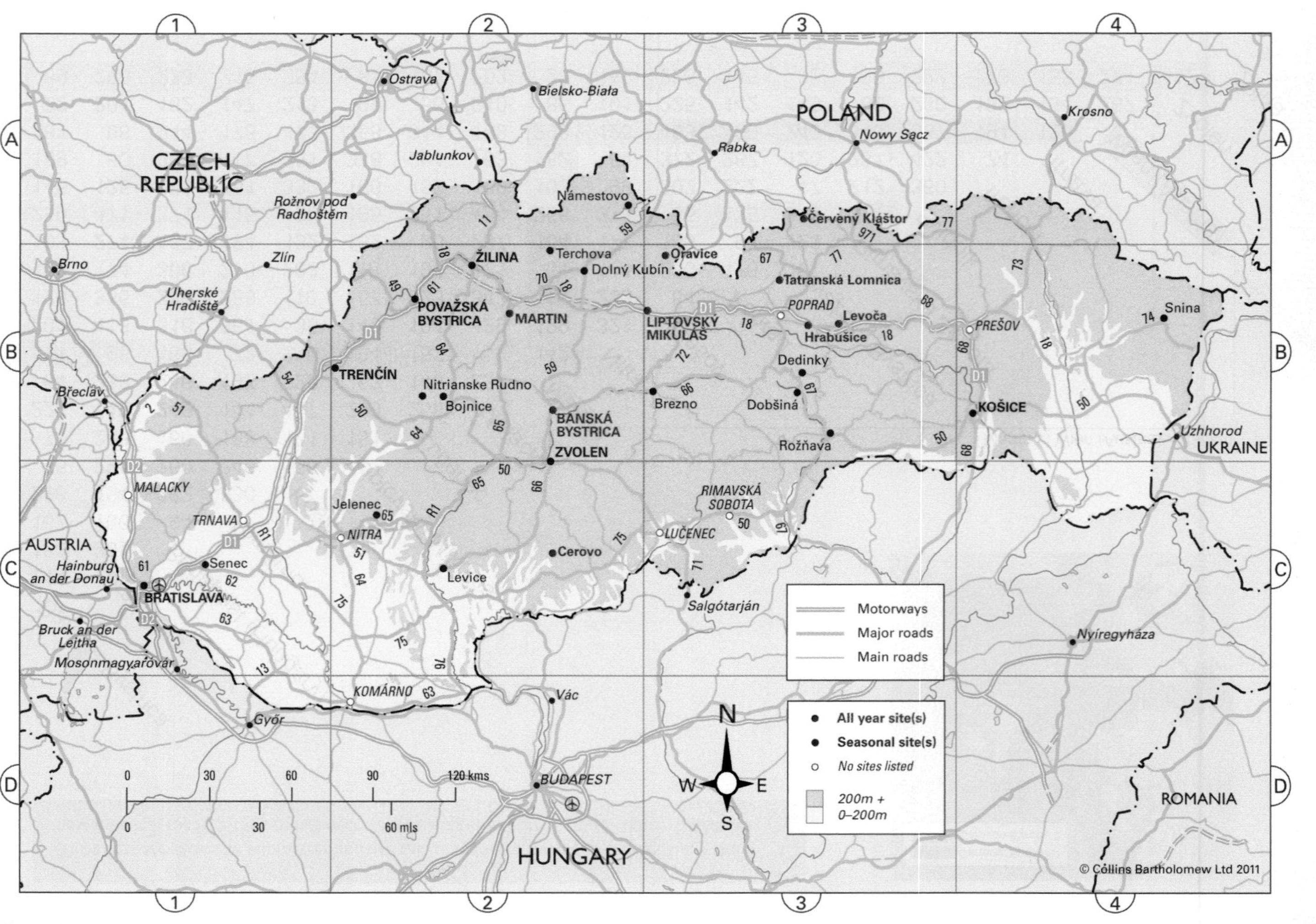

POLAND
CZECH REPUBLIC
AUSTRIA
HUNGARY
UKRAINE
ROMANIA
Ostrava
Bielsko-Biała
Krosno
Nowy Sącz
Rabka
Jablunkov
Rožnov pod Radhoštěm
Zlín
Brno
Uherské Hradiště
Břeclav
Námestovo
Červený Kláštor
Terchova
Oravice
Žilina
Dolný Kubín
Tatranská Lomnica
Považská Bystrica
Martin
Liptovský Mikuláš
Poprad
Levoča
Hrabušice
Prešov
Snina
Trenčín
Dedinky
Nitrianske Rudno
Bojnice
Brezno
Dobšiná
Košice
Banská Bystrica
Rožňava
Uzhhorod
Zvolen
Malacky
Rimavská Sobota
Jelenec
Trnava
Nitra
Lučenec
Cerovo
Hainburg an der Donau
Senec
Levice
Bratislava
Salgótarján
Bruck an der Leitha
Mosonmagyaróvár
Nyíregyháza
Komárno
Vác
Győr
Budapest
Motorways
Major roads
Main roads
All year site(s)
Seasonal site(s)
No sites listed
200m +
0–200m
N
W
E
S
0
30
60
90
120 kms
60 mls
© Collins Bartholomew Ltd 2011

Slovenia

Country Introduction

© iStockphoto.com/gaspr13

Lake Bled, Slovenia

Population (approx): 2 million

Capital: Ljubljana (population approx 276,000)

Area: 20,273 sqkm

Bordered by: Austria, Croatia, Hungary, Italy

Coastline: 46.6km

Terrain: Coastal strip on the Adriatic; alpine mountains in west and north; many rivers and forests

Climate: Mediterranean climate on the coast; hot summers and cold winters in the plateaux and valleys in the east; spring and early autumn are the best times to visit

Highest Point: Triglav 2,864m

Languages: Slovenian; Serbo-Croat

Local Time: GMT or BST + 1, i.e. 1 hour ahead of the UK all year

Currency: Euros divided into 100 cents; £1 = €1.14, €1 = 87 pence (September 2011)

Telephoning: From the UK dial 00386 for Slovenia and omit the initial zero of the area code of the number you are calling. To call the UK from Slovenia dial 0044, omitting the initial zero of the area code

Emergency numbers: Police 112; Fire brigade 112; Ambulance 112. Operators speak English

Public Holidays 2012

Jan 1, 2; Feb 8 (Culture Day); Apr 8, 9, 27; May 1, 2; Jun 25 (National Day); Aug 15; Oct 31 (Reformation Day); Nov 1; Dec 25, 26.

Public Holidays 2013

Jan 1, 2; Feb 8 (Culture Day); Mar 31; Apr 1, 27; May 1, 2; Jun 25 (National Day); Aug 15; Oct 31 (Reformation Day); Nov 1; Dec 25, 26.

School summer holidays are from the last week in June to the end of August

Tourist Office

SLOVENIAN TOURIST BOARD
INFORMATION OFFICE
10 LITTLE COLLEGE STREET, LONDON SW1P 3SH
Tel: 0870 2255305
www.slovenia.info london@slovenia.info
(Telephone and email enquiries only)

The following introduction to Slovenia should be read in conjunction with the important information contained in the Handbook chapters at the front of this guide.

Camping and Caravanning

There are approximately 50 organised campsites in Slovenia rated one to five stars. They are usually open from May to October but a few are open all year. Standards of sites and their sanitary facilities are generally good. Campsites on the coast consist mostly of statics and can be overcrowded during the peak summer season. Casual/wild camping is not permitted.

A Camping Card International (CCI) is not compulsory but is recommended and may result in a price reduction of between 5% and 10%. A tourist tax of up to €1 per person per day is charged.

Country Information

Cycling

There are some cycle lanes which are also used by mopeds. Cyclists under the age of 15 must wear a safety helmet.

Transportation of Bicycles

An overhanging load which exceeds one metre at the rear of a vehicle must be indicated by a red flag or red panel measuring 30cm square. At night the overhanging load must be indicated by a red light and a reflector. Loads may only project rearwards; they must not overhang the sides of vehicles.

Electricity and Gas

Usually the current on campsites varies between 6 and 16 amps. Plugs have two round pins. Hook-up points on most campsites conform to CEE standards.

Campingaz cylinders cannot be purchased or exchanged. Recent visitors report that it is possible to have gas cylinders refilled at premises on Verovškova Ulica 70, Ljubljana. The company's name is Butan-Plin. However, The Caravan Club does not recommend this practice and you should aim to take enough gas to last during your stay.

*See **Electricity and Gas** in the section **DURING YOUR STAY***

Entry Formalities

All foreign nationals must register with the police within three days of arrival in Slovenia. Campsites carry out registration formalities, but if you are staying with friends or family you or your host will need to visit the nearest police station to register your presence in the country.

British and Irish passport holders may stay in Slovenia for up to three months without a visa. For longer stays contact the Slovenian Embassy for further information.

*See **Pet Travel Scheme** under **Documents** in the section **PLANNING AND TRAVELLING** for regulations for pets.*

Medical Services

British visitors may obtain emergency medical, hospital and dental treatment from practitioners registered with the public health service, Health Institute of Slovenia (HIIS) on presentation of a European Health Insurance Card (EHIC). You will have to make a contribution towards costs which will not be refunded in Slovenia. Full fees are payable for private medical and dental treatment.

Health resorts and spas are popular and the medical profession uses them extensively for treatment of a wide variety of complaints.

If you enjoy hiking and outdoor sports you should seek medical advice before you travel about preventative measures and immunisation against tick-borne encephalitis, a potentially serious and debilitating viral disease of the central nervous system which is endemic from spring to autumn. Lyme disease is an equally serious tick-borne infection for which there is no preventative vaccine. Ticks are found in rural and forested areas, particularly in long grass, bushes, hedgerows and woods, and in scrubland and areas where animals wander. If you think you might be at risk use an insect repellent containing DEET, wear long sleeves and long trousers, inspect the body for ticks after outdoor activity and remove with tweezers, and avoid unpasteurised dairy products in risk areas. See www.tickalert.org, email info@tickalert.org or telephone 01943 468010.

You are strongly recommended to obtain comprehensive travel and medical insurance before travelling to Slovenia, such as The Caravan Club's Red Pennant Overseas Holiday Insurance – see www.caravanclub.co.uk/redpennant

*See **Medical Matters** in the section **DURING YOUR STAY.***

Opening Hours

Banks – Mon-Fri 9am-12 noon & 2pm-5pm; banks closed on Sat and Sun

Museums – Mon-Fri 10am-6pm (winter) 9pm (summer); Sat, Sun & public holidays 10am-6pm; closed Monday in winter.

Post Offices – Mon-Fri 8am-6pm; Sat 8am-12 noon.

Shops – Mon-Fri 8am-7pm/9pm; Sat 8am-1pm;

Safety and Security

Slovenia is generally regarded as relatively safe for visitors but the usual sensible precautions should be taken against pickpockets in large towns and cities. Do not leave valuables in your car.

Western Slovenia is on an earthquake fault line and is subject to occasional tremors.

If you are planning a skiing or mountaineering holiday, contact the Slovenian Tourist Board for advice on weather and safety conditions before travelling. You should follow all safety instructions meticulously, given the danger of avalanches in some areas. Off-piste skiing is highly dangerous.

There is a low threat from terrorism but attacks could be indiscriminate and against civilian targets, including places frequented by tourists.

*See **Safety and Security** in the section **DURING YOUR STAY.***

British Embassy

4TH FLOOR, TRG REPUBLIKE 3, 1000 LJUBLJANA
Tel: (01) 2003910 http://ukinslovenia.fco.gov.uk/en

Irish Embassy

POLJANSKI NASIP 6
1000 Ljubljana
Tel: (01) 3008970 www.embassyofireland.si

Customs Regulations

Alcohol and Tobacco

For import allowances for alcohol and tobacco products see ***Customs Regulations*** *in the section **PLANNING AND TRAVELLING.***

Documents

Driving Licence

All European countries recognise the EU format paper UK driving licence introduced in 1990. However, it is a legal requirement to show your driving license with a form of photographic identification, such as your passport, if your driving licence does not include a photograph.

Passport

Carry a copy of your passport at all times as a form of identification.

Vehicle(s)

You should carry your vehicle documentation, i.e. vehicle registration certificate (V5C), insurance certificate, MOT certificate (if applicable) and driver's licence.

If you are driving a hired or borrowed vehicle, you must be in possession of a letter of authorisation from the owner or a hire agreement.

*See **Documents** in the section **PLANNING AND TRAVELLING.***

Money

Travellers' cheques are accepted in some shops and hotels. They may be exchanged in most banks, bureaux de change, travel agencies and post offices. Exchange rates vary and you are advised to compare these prior to exchange.

Cash machines are widespread and the major credit cards are widely accepted. Carry your credit card issuers'/banks' 24-hour UK contact numbers in case of loss or theft of your cards.

Motoring

Accidents

Any visible damage to a vehicle entering Slovenia must be certified by authorities at the border. All drivers involved in an accident while in the country should inform the police and obtain a written report (Potrdilo). Drivers of vehicles which have been damaged will need to present this police report to Customs on departure.

Alcohol

The maximum permitted level of alcohol is 50 milligrams in 100 millilitres of blood, i.e. lower than what is permitted in the UK (80 milligrams). If a driver is under the age of 21 or has held a driving licence for less than three years the permitted level of alcohol is zero. The police carry out tests at random.

Breakdown Service

The motoring organisation, Avto-Moto Zveza Slovenije (AMZS), operates a 24 hour breakdown service which can be contacted by telephoning 1987. On motorways, using a mobile phone, call the AMZS Alarm Centre in Ljubljana on (01) 5305353 or use the emergency telephones and ask for AMZS assistance.

Charges apply for basic on-the-spot repairs and towing, plus supplements at night, weekends and on public holidays. Credit cards are accepted in payment.

Essential Equipment

*See **Motoring – Equipment** in the section **PLANNING AND TRAVELLING***

Lights

Dipped headlights are compulsory at all times, regardless of weather conditions. Bulbs are more likely to fail with constant use and you are required to carry spares. Hazard warning lights must be used when reversing.

Reflective Jacket/Waistcoat

In the event of vehicle breakdown on a motorway, anyone – driver and passengers – who leaves the vehicle must wear a reflective jacket.

SLOVENIA

Child Restraint System

Children under 12 years of age and under the height of 1.5 metres must use a suitable child restraint system for their size and age.

Warning Triangles

Vehicles towing a trailer must carry two warning triangles (single vehicles require only one). In the event of a breakdown to vehicle and trailer combinations, two triangles must be placed one beside the other at least 50 metres behind the vehicles.

At night, drivers must always use hazard warning lights or a torch in addition to the warning triangles.

Winter Driving

From 15 November to 15 March, and beyond those dates during winter weather conditions (snowfalls, black ice, etc), private cars and vehicles up to 3,500kg must have winter tyres on all four wheels or, alternatively, carry snow chains. Minimum tread depth of tyres is 3mm.

Snow chains can be hired or purchased from Polar Automotive Ltd, tel 01892 519933, fax 01892 528142, www.snowchains.com, email: polar@snowchains.com (10% discount for Caravan Club members).

Fuel

*See also **Fuel** under **Motoring – Advice** in the section **PLANNING AND TRAVELLING.***

Petrol stations are generally open from 6am to 10pm Monday to Saturday. Many near border crossings, on motorways and near large towns are open 24 hours. Credit cards are accepted. It is understood that few petrol stations sell LPG.

Parking

Parking meters are used in towns. In city centres white lines indicate that parking is permitted for a maximum of two hours between 7am and 7pm, but a parking ticket must be purchased from a machine. Blue lines indicate places where parking is allowed free of charge for up to 30 minutes. Vehicles parked illegally may be towed away or clamped.

*See also **Parking Facilities for the Disabled** under **Motoring – Advice** in the section **PLANNING AND TRAVELLING.***

Priority

At intersections drivers must give way to traffic from the right, unless a priority road is indicated. The same rule applies to roundabouts, i.e. traffic entering a roundabout has priority.

Roads

Slovenia has a well-developed road system, and international and main roads are in good condition. Secondary roads may still be poorly maintained and generally unlit. Minor roads are often gravelled and are known locally as 'white roads'. Road numbers are rarely mentioned on road signs and it is advisable to navigate using place names in the direction you are travelling.

Roadside verges are uncommon, or may be lined with bollards which make pulling over difficult. Where there is a hard shoulder it is usual for slow vehicles to pull over to allow faster traffic to overtake.

The capital, Ljubljana, can be reached from Munich, Milan, Vienna and Budapest in less than five hours. There are numerous border crossings for quick and trouble free entry into Slovenia.

Care should be taken, especially on narrow secondary roads, where tailgating and overtaking on blind bends are not unknown. Drive defensively and take extra care when driving at night. Be prepared for severe weather in winter.

Information on roads may be obtained by telephoning the AMZS Information Centre on (01) 5305300.

Road Signs and Markings

Road signs conform to international standards. Motorway signs have a green background and national road signs a blue background. On your travels you may see the following signs:

Mountian pass

School area

Toll: Vignette/ card or cash

Speed Limits

*See **Speed Limits Table** under **Motoring – Advice** in the section **PLANNING AND TRAVELLING.***

Motorhomes over 3,500kg are restricted to 80 km/h (50 mph) on open roads, including motorways. Other speed limits are the same as for solo cars.

There is an increasing number of areas where speed is restricted to 30 km/h (18 mph) and these are indicated by the sign 'Zone 30'. In bad weather when visibility is reduced to 50 metres the maximum speed limit is 50 km/h (31 mph).

Traffic Jams

Traffic congestion is much lighter than in other European countries but, as Slovenia is a major international through-route, bottlenecks do occur on the roads to and from Ljubljana, such as the E61/ A2 from Jesinice and the E57 from Maribor. Traffic queues can be expected during summer holiday weekends, particularly Saturday mornings, from the beginning of May to the end of August on the roads around Lake Bled and to the Adriatic and you may experience bottlenecks on the E70/A1 motorway near the Razdrto toll station and near Kozina and Koper. Tailbacks also occur at border posts near the Karawanken Tunnel, Ljubelj and Šentilj/Spielfeld particularly at weekends. Temporary traffic jams can be expected as a result of an extensive road improvement and reconstruction programme.

The motoring organisation, AMZS, provides traffic information in English – telephone (01) 5305300 or see their website www.amzs.si

Violation of Traffic Regulations

The police have powers to stop drivers and levy heavy on-the-spot fines, including penalties for speeding, driving under the influence of alcohol and for using mobile phones without properly installed wireless headsets (bluetooth). Jaywalking is an offence and you could be fined if caught. Fines must be paid in local currency and you should obtain an official receipt.

Motorways

There are about 620km of motorways (autoceste) and expressways (hitre ceste) with more under construction. For more information about motorways see the website www.dars.si

There are service areas and petrol stations along the motorways and emergency telephones are situated every 2km.

Motorway Tolls

Drivers of vehicles weighing up to 3,500kg must purchase a vignette (windscreen sticker) for use on motorways and expressways. Caravans/trailers do not need an additional vignette and the weight of the caravan/trailer is not taken into account. The vignette is available from petrol stations in Slovenia, neighbouring countries and at border posts. The cost of a 7 day vignette is €15, 1 month vignette €30 and an annual vignette €95 (2011 charges subject to change). Tolls on individual stretches of motorway will continue to be charged for vehicles over 3,500kg and are payable with cash or credit card.

Karawanken Tunnel

The 8km Karawanken motorway tunnel links the E61/A11 in Austria and E61/A2 in Slovenia. The toll is €6.50 for car and caravan or motorhome up to 3,500kg and €10.50 for a motorhome over 3,500kg (2011 charges subject to change).

Touring

The cuisine reflects an Austro-German influence with sauerkraut, grilled sausage and apple strudel appearing often on menus. On the Adriatic coast there are specialities based on fish, lobster and crayfish. White wines are especially good, as are local beers or 'pivo'. A 10% tip is usual in restaurants and for taxi drivers.

The capital, Ljubljana, is a gem of a city with many Baroque and Art Nouveau influences. The works of the world renowned architect Jože Plecnik are among the finest urban monuments in the city. A Ljubljana Card is available for one, two or three days and offers free travel on city buses, tourist boat trips, the city funicular, guided tours and the tourist train to Ljubljana Castle, plus free admission to museums together with discounts at a wide range of shops, restaurants and bars. You can buy the card at the main bus and railway stations, hotels and tourist information centres or from www.visitljubljana.si

The largest cave in Europe is situated at Postojna, south west of Ljubljana and is a 'must' for tourists. Also worth visiting are the mountains, rivers and woods of Triglav National Park, which covers the major part of the Julian Alps, together with the oldest town in Slovenia, Ptuj, and the city of Maribor. In Lipica guided tours are available around the stud, home to the world famous Lipizzaner horses.

There is a hydrofoil service between Portorož and Venice from April to November.

Slovenian is the official language although Serbo-Croat is widely spoken. Most Slovenians speak at least one other major European language and many, especially the young, speak English.

Local Transport

There is an extensive bus network in Ljubljana. Buy a yellow 'top-up' Urbana card for a one-off payment of €2 from news-stands, tobacconists, tourist information offices or the central bus station and add credit (between €1 and €50) at the same locations or at the green Urbanomati machines around the city. When boarding a bus simply touch the card to one of the card readers at the front of the bus and €0.80 will be deducted allowing 90 minutes of unlimited travel regardless of how many changes you make. Taxis are generally safe, clean and reliable. Fares are metered. For longer distances ordering a taxi by phone will attract lower rates.

All place names used in the Site Entry listings which follow can be found in the Croatia & Slovenia Superatlas published by Freytag & Berndt, scale 1cm to 1.5km, see www.freytagberndt.com

ANKARAN see Koper *D1*

BLED *B2* (4km E Rural) *46.35527, 14.14833* **Camping Šobec, Šobčeva Cesta 25, 4248 Lesce [(04) 5353700; fax 5353701; sobec@siol.net; www.sobec.si]** Exit rte 1 at Lesce, site sp. Lge, pt shd, pt sl; wc; chem disp; mv service pnt; shwrs; el pnts (16A) €3.20 (poss long lead req); Indtte; shop; rest; snacks; bar; playgrnd; rv pool; many sports & activities; cycle hire; internet; TV; dogs €3.20; bus 2km; Eng spkn; ccard acc; red 7+ days/CCI. "Excel, tranquil rvside site in wooded area surrounded by rv; friendly staff; lge pitches; clean san facs; gd rest; gd walking/ cycling." ♦ 21 Apr-30 Sep. € 25.60 2011*

BLED *B2* (5km SE Urban) *46.34772, 14.17284* **Camping Radovljica, Kopališka 9, 4240 Radovljica [(04) 5315770; fax 5301229; pkrad@plavalnicklub-radovljica.si]** Exit A1/E61 junc Bled/Bohinj, site in cent of Radovljica bet bus & train stn sp Camping & Swimming. Med, pt sl, pt shd; wc; chem disp; shwrs inc; el pnts (16A) inc; shop 500m; rest 300m; snacks adj; bar; playgrnd; pool adj; paddling pool; cycle hire; fitness rm; wifi; 10% statics; dogs; poss cr; quiet; red long stay. "Vg; security gate." 1 Jun-15 Sep. € 26.00 2010*

BLED *B2* (2km SW Rural) *46.36155, 14.08066* **Camping Bled, Kidričeva 10c, 4260 Bled [(04) 5752000; fax 5752002; info@camping.bled.com; www.camping-bled.com]** Fr Ljubljana take E16/A2 & exit dir Bled/Lesce. At rndabt take 2nd exit for Bled & cont along rd 209. In Bled take rd around lake on L (lake on R), site sp - winding rd. Lge, some mkd pitch, pt sl, pt shd; wc; chem disp; mv service pnt; baby facs; shwrs inc; el pnts (16A) inc (long lead req some pitches - fr recep); gas; Indtte (inc dryer); shop, rest adj; snacks; bar; BBQ; playgrnd; shgl beach; lake sw adj; spa centre nrby; fishing; white water rafting; paragliding; horseriding; cycle hire; games area; wifi; entmnt; games/TV rm; dogs €3; twin-axles acc (rec check in adv); m'van & car wash; dog shwrs; bus to Ljubljana adj; Eng spkn; fairly quiet but some rlwy noise; ccard acc; red long stay/low ssn/snr citizens/CCI. "Beautifully situated nr lake; busy, popular, well-run site; well-drained in bad weather altho lower pitches poss muddy; modern, clean san facs; helpful, efficient staff; conv Vintgar Gorge, Bled Castle, Lake Bohinj, Dragna Valley; excel walking/cycling around lake." ♦ 1 Apr-15 Oct. € 30.50 SBS - X03 2011*

BOHINJSKA BISTRICA *B1* (500m W Rural) *46.27438, 13.94798* **Camping Danica, Triglavska 60, 4264 Bohinjska Bistrica [(04) 5721055 or 5723370; fax 5723330; info@camp-danica.si; www.bohinj.si/camping-danica]** Site on o'skts of vill clearly sp. Med, pt shd; wc; chem disp; mv service pnt; shwrs; el pnts (6A) inc (long lead poss req); gas; Indtte; shops 500m; rest; snacks; bar; tennis; entmnt; lake sw 6km; canoe & kayak hire; fly-fishing; wifi; 10% statics; dogs €2; Eng spkn; quiet; ccard acc; red long stay/CCI. "Excel, spacious, open, attractive site in beautiful valley; gd walking & climbing; helpful family owners; gd, clean san facs but poss stretched high ssn; conv bus to Ljubljana & Lake Bohinji." 16 Apr-31 Oct. € 26.50 2011*

BOHINJSKA BISTRICA *B1* (11km W Rural) *46.27902, 13.83606* **Autocamp Zlatarog, Ukanc 2, 4265 Bohinjsko Jezero [(04) 5723482; fax 5723064; info@aaturizem.com; www.aaturizem.com]** On rte 1 exit at Lesce or Jesenice for Bled & Bohinji. Clearly sp fr Bohinji, further 5km on L side of lake. Lge, some mkd pitch, sl, shd; wc; chem disp; shwrs; el pnts (6A) €5 (long lead req); gas; Indtte; shop adj; rest adj (high ssn); snacks; playgrnd; beach adj; lake sw; 50% statics; dogs €3; bus; sep car park high ssn; Eng spkn; adv bkg; ccard acc; red low ssn/long stay/CCI. "Excel walking, watersports; sm, uneven pitches & rather cramped site, but beautiful lakeside location; facs stretched high ssn; poss long walk to facs; site ground rough to walk on (2011); poor security low ssn; gd touring base; cable car nr to Mount Vogel." 15 May-30 Sep. € 25.80 2011*

BOHINJSKO JEZERO see Bohinjska Bistrica *B1*

BOVEC *B1* (400m E Rural) *46.33659, 13.55803* **Autocamp Polovnik, Ledina 8, 5230 Bovec [(05) 3896007; fax 3896006; kamp.polovnik@siol.net; www.kamp-polovnik.com]** Sp on rd 206 down fr Predil Pass (1,156m - 14% gradient) fr Italy - do not turn into vill. Site 200m after turn to Bovec. Sm, pt shd; wc; chem disp; shwrs €0.50; el pnts (16A) €2.50 (poss rev pol); Indtte (inc dryer); shop adj; rest; snacks; bar; BBQ; tennis; fishing; wifi; poss cr; no adv bkg; quiet; ccard acc; CCI. "Helpful staff; clean facs; 1 Apr-15 Oct. € 19.00 2010*

⊞ **BREZICE** *C3* (5km S Rural) *45.89138, 15.62611* **Camping Terme Čatež, Topliška Cesta 35, 8251 Čatež ob Savi [(07) 4936700; fax 4935005; info@terme-catez.si; www.terme-catez.si]** Exit E70 at Brežice, foll brown sp to Terme Čatež, then site sp. Lge, mkd pitch, pt shd; htd wc; chem disp; mv service pnt; sauna; baby facs; shwrs inc; el pnts (10A) inc; gas; Indtte (inc dryer); supmkt; rest; snacks; bar; BBQ area; playgrnd; thermal water complex, inc 10 outdoor & 3 indoor pools, waterfalls & whirlpools, etc; paddling pool; fishing; golf 7km; boating; canoeing; tennis; fitness studio; games area; cycle hire; games rm; wifi; entmnt; TV; 50% statics (sep area); dogs €4; poss cr; Eng spkn; adv bkg; ccard acc; red low ssn; CCI. "Site in lge thermal spa & health resort; many sports, leisure & health facilities; select own pitch - best at edge of site; modern, v clean san facs; gd family site; conv Zagreb." ♦ € 44.30 SBS - X05 2011*

CATEZ OB SAVI see Brežice *C3*

KAMNIK *B2* (500m NE Urban) *46.22724, 14.61902* **Kamp Resnik, Maistrova Ul, Nevlje, 1240 Kamnik [(01) 8317314; fax 8318192; info@kamnik-tourism.si]** Fr Ljubljana foll rd sp Celje then turn N for Kamnik. Fr Kemnik by-pass (E side of rv) bear R thro 2 sets traff lts, site 200m on L just after sports cent - site ent not obvious, turn bef zebra x-ing opp pub. Fr E on rd 414, site sp. Med, pt shd; wc (some cont); own san; chem disp; mv service pnt; shwrs; el pnts (10A) inc; gas; Indtte; shops 500m; rest, snacks 100m; bar; playgrnd; pool adj; thermal spa, golf course nr; 5% statics; dogs; bus; Eng spkn; adv bkg; some daytime rd noise; ccard acc; red CCI. "Conv Ljubljana & Kamnik Alps; basic facs (2010); friendly staff; pleasant, well-kept NH." 1 May-30 Sep. € 20.00 2011*

⊞ **KOBARID** *B1* (500m E Rural) *46.25070, 13.58664* **Kamp Koren, Drežniške Ravne 33, 5222 Kobarid [(05) 3891311; fax 3891310; info@kamp-koren.si; www.kamp-koren.si]** Turn E fr main rd in town, site well sp dir Drežnica. Med, pt shd; htd wc (some cont); chem disp; mv service pnt; shwrs inc; el pnts (16A) €4; shop; Indtte; snacks; rest 500m; playgrnd; cycle hire; canoeing; internet; TV rm; dogs €2; Eng spkn; quiet; ccard acc; red low ssn/long stay/CCI. "Vg, clean facs but stretched; friendly, helpful staff; pitches cramped; pleasant location in beautiful rv valley; excel walk to waterfall (3hrs); WW1 museum in town." ♦ € 23.00 2011*

The opening dates and prices on this campsite have changed. I'll send a site report form to the Club for the next edition of the guide.

KOPER *D1* (5km N Coastal) *45.57818, 13.73573* **Camping Adria, Jadranska Zesta 25, 6280 Ankaran [(05) 6637350; camp@adria-ankaran.si; www.adria-ankaran.si]** Fr A1/E70/E61 onto rd 10 then rd 406 to Ankaran. Or cross Italian border at Lazzaretto & foll sp to site in 3km. Site sp in vill. Lge, mkd pitch, shd; wc; chem disp; mv service pnt; sauna; private san facs avail; shwrs inc; el pnts (10A) €3; Indtte (inc dryer); shop; supmkt adj; rest; snacks; bar; BBQ; playgrnd; 2 pools (1 Olympic-size); waterslide; beach adj; tennis; cycle hire; wifi; entmnt; 60% statics; dogs €4; bus 500m; ccard acc. "Old town of Koper worth a visit; Vinakoper winery rec N of site on dual c'way; poss noisy groups high ssn; insect repellent req; clean san facs but red low ssn; gd rest; vg." ♦ 15 Apr-15 Oct. € 25.00 (CChq acc) 2008*

⊞ **KRANJSKA GORA** *B1* (12km E Rural) *46.46446, 13.95773* **Camping Kamne, Dovje 9, 4281 Mojstrana [tel/fax (04) 5891105; info@campingkamne.com; www.campingkamne.com]** Sp fr rd 201 bet Jesenice & Kranjska Gora, 2km E of Mojstrana. Do not go thro vill of Dovje. Sm, terr, pt shd; some hdstg; htd wc; chem disp; mv service pnt; shwrs €0.50; el pnts (6-10A) €2.50-3.50; Indtte (inc dryer); shop 1km; rest 1.5km; snacks; bar; playgrnd; sm pool; fishing; hiking; tennis; cycle hire; TV rm; 10% statics; dogs €2; bus to Kranjska Gora fr site; Eng spkn; quiet but some rd noise; red long stay/CCI. "Conv Triglav National Park & border; views Mount Triglav; warm welcome; ltd san facs stretched high ssn; gd cycling along old rlwy track." ♦ € 17.60 2011*

⊞ **LENDAVA** *B4* (1km S Rural) *46.55195, 16.45875* **Therman Auto Camp Lipa, Tomšičeva 2a, 9220 Lendava [(02) 5774468; fax 5774412; terme.lendava@terme-lendava.si; www.terme-lendava.si]** Site well sp, adj hotel complex. Med, pt shd; htd wc; chem disp; mv service pnt; private bthrms avail; sauna; shwrs inc; el pnts (16A) €4; Indtte; shop 200m; rest; snacks; bar; no BBQ; playgrnd; 2 pools (1 htd, covrd); paddling pool; waterslide; tennis; games area; cycle hire; fitness rm; internet; TV rm; some statics; dogs €3; adv bkg; ccard acc. "Conv Hungarian & Croatian borders; use of spa inc." € 26.00 2008*

LESCE see Bled *B2*

⊞ **LJUBLJANA** *C2* (5km N Urban) *46.09752, 14.51870* **Ljubljana Resort, Dunajska Cesta 270, 1000 Ljubljana [(01) 5683913; fax 5683912; ljubljana.resort@gpl.si; www.ljubljanaresort.si]** Fr Maribor take A1 twd Ljubljana, at junc Zadobrova take Ljubljana ring rd twd Kranj & exit junc 3 sp Lj - Ježica, Bežigrad. At x-rds turn R twd Črnuče along Dunajska Cesta, turn R 100m bef rlwy x-ing. Fr N (Jesenica/Karawanken tunnel) exit A2/E66 at junc 13 sp Ljubljana Črnuče & foll rd for 3.5km; at rndabt junc with Dunajska Cesta rd turn R (1st exit); site on L in 200m. Lge, hdg/mkd pitch, pt shd; htd wc; chem disp; mv service pnt; shwrs inc; el pnts (10A) inc; Indry/dishwash area; Indtte (inc dryer); shop; supmkt 900m; rest; snacks; bar; BBQ (gas/elec, sep area); playgrnd; htd pool complex adj; whirlpools; paddling pool; naturist sunbathing adj pool; rv fishing; tennis; cycle hire; horseriding 500m; archery; fitness club; wifi; entmnt; games rm; some statics; dogs €4.50; phone; bus to city at site ent (tickets at recep); some rlwy noise; ccard acc; red low ssn/CCI. "Busy site by rv; gd rest; red facs low ssn; pitches nr hotel poss noisy due late-night functions; some pitches muddy when wet; conv for city." ♦ € 27.00 (CChq acc) 2011*

LUCE OB SAVINJI *B2* (1km N Rural) *46.36092, 14.73637* **Autocamp Šmica, Luče 4, 3334 Luče [(03) 5844330; fax 5844333; camp.smica@siol.net; www.camp-smica.com]** Fr rd 428, site sp on rvside. Sm, pt shd; wc; shwrs inc; el pnts (16A) €2.50; gas; Indtte; BBQ; playgrnd; tennis; wifi; 5% statics; dogs; phone; bus 400m; poss cr; Eng spkn; adv bkg; quiet; red long stay; CCI. "Ideal base for mountaineering, hiking, watersports etc; vg." ♦ 1 May-30 Sep. € 13.00 2009*

⊞ **MARIBOR** *B3* (6km SW) *46.5355, 15.60508* **Camping Centre Kekec, Pohorska ulica 35c, 2000 Maribor [040 665 732; info@cck.si; www.cck.si]** Fr S on A1 exit Maribor Jug; foll rd until you see Bauhaus shopping centre on the R, turn L at this x-rd; turn R after approx 400m; turn L after approx 100m; site on L after approx 3km at the Mlada Lipa guesthouse. Sm, mkd pitch, hdstg, pt sl, terr, unshd; htd wc; chem disp; MV service pnt; baby facs; shwrs; el pnts (16A) €3; Indtte; rest & bar 250m; BBQ; wifi; dogs €1.50; Eng spkn; adv bking; ccard acc; CCI. "Site undergoing major refurb; rec for larger o'fits as lge pitches avail but care with narr ent rd." € 18.00 2011*

MOJSTRANA see Kranjska Gora *B1*

⊞ **MORAVSKE TOPLICE** *A4* (S Rural) *46.67888, 16.22165* **Camping Terme 3000, Kranjčeva Ulica 12, 9226 Moravske Toplice [(02) 5121200; fax 5121148; info@terme3000.si; www.terme3000.si]** N fr Murska Sabota for 3km then turn E for 4km, foll sp Moravske Toplice & Terme 3000. Site adj hotels & thermal complex. Lge, some hdstg, pt shd; htd wc; chem disp; mv service pnt; shwrs inc; el pnts (10A) €3.50; Indtte (inc dryer); shop 200m; rest, snacks, bar 100m; BBQ; playgrnd; htd, covrd pool 100m; tennis; cycle hire; watersports; games area; golf; wifi; entmnt; 75% statics; dogs €3; phone; poss cr; Eng spkn; adv bkg; quiet; ccard acc; red long stay; CCI. "Spas, thermal & therapeutic facs; use of pool inc in site fees; excursions arranged; gd cycling rtes; excel." ♦ € 34.00 2008*

MOZIRJE *B3* (6km W Rural) *46.30930, 14.91593* **Camping Savinja, Spodjne Pobrežje 11, 3332 Rečica ob Savinji [tel/ fax (035) 835472; www.sloveniaholidays.com]** SW fr Velenje for 14km to Mozirje. Then foll sp to Pobrežje for 4km, over bdge. Site is sp in vill down lane opp house no 11. Med, pt shd; wc; chem disp; shwrs; el pnts (16A) €3; Indtte; shop; fishing; dogs €1; quiet; CCI; "Scenic Savinja & Logarska Dolina valleys; ideal walking & cycling; clean facs; lovely, peaceful, simple site." 1 May-30 Sep. € 12.00 2010*

MURSKA SOBOTA *A4* (12km S Rural) *46.57332, 16.17174* **Camping Terme Banovici (Part Naturist), 9241 Veržej [(02) 5131400; fax 5871703; terme.banovci@radenska. si; www.radenska-zdravilisce.si]** Fr Murska Sobota head SE twd Lendava. Turn R 2km after Rakičan, Banovci in 7km. Do not confuse with Bakovci nrby. Site is 1.5km S of Veržej. Lge, mkd pitch, pt shd; htd wc; chem disp; mv service pnt; shwrs inc; el pnts (10A) €3.75; tradsmn; rest; bar; playgrnd; htd pool; paddling pool; tennis; bicycle hire; internet; 60% statics; dogs €3; no adv bkg; quiet; ccard acc; red CCI. "Sep naturist area with pool & facs; security gate." ♦ 1 Apr-31 Oct. € 26.00 2008*

⊞ **NAZARJE** *B2* (6km W Rural) *46.31166, 14.90916* **Camping Menina, Varpolje 105, 3332 Rečica ob Savinji [(03) 5835027; fax 35835027; info@campingmenina.com; www.campingmenina.com]** Fr rte E57 bet Ljubljana & Celje, turn N twd Nazarje, then dir Ljubno for 3km. Site sp. Med, mkd pitch, some hdstg, shd; wc; chem disp; mv service pnt; shwrs inc; el pnts (6-16A) €3; Indtte (inc dryer); rest; snacks; bar; playgrnd; lake sw adj; cycle hire; wifi; 10% statics; dogs €3; Eng spkn; adv bkg; quiet; red CCI. "Helpful owners; delightful site in woodland; v ltd facs in winter." € 20.00 2010*

NOVA GORICA *C1* (8km SE Rural) *45.94182, 13.71761* **Camping Lijak - Mladovan Farm, Ozeljan 6, 5261 Šempas [(05) 3088557; fax 53079619; camp.lijak@volja.net; www. camplijak.com]** Fr Nova Gorica take rd 444 twd Ljubljana/ Ajdovščina. Site on L bef turn-off to Ozeljan. Sm, pt shd; htd wc; chem disp; shwrs inc; el pnts (10A) €3 (poss long lead req); shop 1km; snacks; BBQ; wifi; some statics; dogs €1; phone; bus; Eng spkn; slight rd noise; red low ssn. "Farm site in wine-growing area; weekly wine tasting; hang-gliding area, enthusiasts use site; friendly owner; gd san facs." 15 Mar-30 Oct. € 26.00 2011*

PODCETRTEK see Rogaška Slatina *B3*

⊞ **PORTOROZ** *D1* (4km NE Coastal) *45.52536, 13.60754* **Autocamp Strunjan, Strunjan 23, 6320 Portorož [(05) 6782076; amd-piran@siol.net; www.amdpiran-drustvo.si]** Fr Koper on rd 111 at 6.5km marker turn R at traff lts sp Strunjan. In 50m turn L, site in L in 200m, well sp. Med, pt shd; wc; chem disp; shwrs inc; el pnts (6A) inc; Indry rm; shop 300m; bar; shgl beach 500m; 95% statics; dogs; phone; bus adj; Eng spkn; rd noise; rec CCI. "Open all yr for m'vans, but ltd pitches; excel san facs; friendly staff." ♦ € 19.00 2010*

PORTOROZ *D1* (2.5km S Coastal) *45.50138, 13.59388* **Camping Lucija, Obala 77, 6320 Portorož [(05) 6906000; fax 6906900; camp@metropolgroup.si; www. metropolgroup.si]** Fr Koper (N) on rd 111, turn R at traff lts in Lucija. Take next left, then 2nd L into site. Nr Metropol Hotel, site sp. Lge, pt shd; wc; mv service pnt; serviced pitches; shwrs inc; el pnts (6-10A) €4.50; Indtte; shop; rest; bar; beach adj; cycle hire; 60% statics; dogs €5; poss cr; Eng spkn; quiet; ccard acc; red CCI. "Conv Piran old town by bike or bus; sea views; sep area for tourers, extra for beach pitch; sm pitches; vg facs." ♦ 1 Apr-3 Oct. € 33.00 2010*

I'll fill in a report online and let the Club know – www.caravanclub.co.uk/ europereport

This is a wonderful site.

POSTOJNA *C2* (5km NW Rural) *45.80551, 14.20470* **Camping Pivka Jama, Veliki Otok 50, 6230 Postojna [(05) 7203993; fax 7265348; avtokamp.pivka.jama@siol.net; www.venus-trade.si]** From N or S Exit A1/E61 strt over traff lts, R at rdbt then bear L at next, foll sp to caves grotto (Postojnska Jama). Pass caves on R & then foll signs for Predjama Castle. 3km after caves site sp. Narr, winding approach rd. Lge, hdstg, pt sl, terr, hdstg, shd; htd wc; chem disp; mv service pnt; shwrs inc; el pnts (6A) €3.70 (rev pol); Indtte; shop; rest; snacks; bar; cooking facs; playgrnd; pool; paddling pool; tennis; 50% statics; dogs; poss v cr; Eng spkn; adv bkg; quiet but noisy nr sw pool; ccard acc; red low ssn/CCI. "Gd forest site; gd rest with live Tirolean music; gd san facs; used as transit to Croatia, open 24 hrs; caves 4km (take warm clothing!), caves are a must visit." 1 Apr-31 Oct. € 22.80 2011*

PREBOLD *B3* (N Rural) *46.23832, 15.09266* **Camping Park, Latkova Vas 227, 3312 Prebold [(03) 7001986; info@ campingpark.si; www.campingpark.si]** Fr A1/E57 or rd 5 exit at Prebold. Foll site sp for 400m, cross Rv Savinja & site on L. Sm, shd; htd wc; chem disp; shwrs inc; el pnts (6A) inc; Indtte; shops 2km; rest; bar; BBQ; games area; some Eng spkn; adv bkg; quiet; 10% red CCI. "V pleasant, well-kept site but ltd facs; pleasant walks by rv; helpful owners own adj hotel; gd walking & cycling." 1 Apr-31 Oct. € 20.00 2011*

⊞ **PREBOLD** *B3* (200m N Rural) *46.24027, 15.08790* **Camping Dolina, Dolenja Vas 147, 3312 Prebold [(03) 5724378; fax 5742591; camp@dolina.si; www.dolina.si]** On A1/E57 turn R 16km fr Celje sp Prebold & foll sp, site on N edge of vill. Sm, unshd; wc; chem disp; shwrs (inc); el pnts (6-10A) €3.30; gas; Indtte; shop 400m; rest in hotel 800m; htd pool; cycle hire; dogs €2; poss cr; quiet; red long stay; CCI. "Gd clean facs but no changing area in shwrs; helpful, friendly owner; conv Savinja valley; gd walking." € 18.50 2010*

⊞ **PTUJ** *B4* (1km NW Rural) *46.42236, 15.85478* **Autokamp Terme Ptuj, Pot V Toplice 9, 2250 Ptuj [(02) 7494100; fax 7837771; info@terme-ptuj.si; www.terme-ptuj.si]** S fr Maribor on A4 or rd 1/E59; turn L onto rd 2 sp Ptuj (exit junc 2 fr A4); on app Ptuj foll sp Golf/Terme Camping to L off rd 2; site after leisure complex on Rv Drava. Diff to find when app fr SW on rd 432. Med, pt shd; htd wc; chem disp; mv service pnt; sauna; steam rm; shwrs inc; el pnts (10A) €4; gas; Indtte (inc dryer); shop 2km; rest, snacks, bar; BBQ; playgrnd; htd, covrd pools/spa; waterslide; games area; tennis; fitness rm; cycle hire; golf 1km; internet; statics; dogs €4; phone; weekly bus to Vienna; poss cr; Eng spkn; red low ssn/long stay/snr citizens/CCI. "Helpful staff; basic san facs (2010), poss stretched high ssn; pitches muddy in wet; superb water park free to campers; lovely area; castle & monastery in Ptuj old town worth a visit." ♦ € 34.00 (CChq acc) 2011*

RECICA OB SAVINJI see Mozirje *B3*

ROGASKA SLATINA *B3* (8km S Rural) *46.16499, 15.60495* **Camping Natura Terme Olimia, Zdraviliška Cesta 24, 3254 Podčetrtek [(03) 8297000; fax 5829024; info@terme-olimia.com; www.terme-olimia.com]** Fr Celje take rte E dir Rogaška Slatina. Turn S sp Podčetrtek just bef Rogaška. Site on L (waterchutes) alongside Rv Solta on Croatian border in approx 10km. Sm, unshd; htd wc; chem disp; mv service pnt; sauna; shwrs inc; el pnts (10-16A) €3.20; Indtte; shop high ssn; rest 800m; snacks; bar; playgrnd; 2 htd pools (1 covrd); paddling pool; waterslide; fitness rm; tennis; cycle hire; horseriding 2km; golf 4km; wifi; TV rm; phone; adv bkg; ccard acc; red CCI. "Aqualuna Thermal Pk adj; vg walking country with wooded hillsides." ♦ 15 Apr-15 Oct. € 32.00 (CChq acc) 2011*

SKOFJA LOKA *B2* (10km E Rural) *46.17455, 14.41720* **Camping Smlednik (Part Naturist), Dragočajna 14a, 1216 Smlednik [(01) 3627002; camp@dm-campsmlednik.si; www.dm-campsmlednik.si]** Fr Ljubljana N on E61 take turning W onto rd 413 sp Zapoge & Zbilje. After Valburg & bef x-ing rv turn R to Dragočajna & site. Lge, terr, pt shd; wc; chem disp; shwrs inc; el pnts (6-10A) €3-4; shop; snacks; bar; BBQ; canoeing; tennis; many statics; dogs €1; Eng spkn; quiet; CCI. "Pleasant rvside location; steep site; sep sm naturist site; shwrs poss only warm as solar powered; ltd facs low ssn." 1 May-15 Oct. € 16.00 2010*

SOCA see Bovec *B1*

VELENJE *B3* (3km NW Rural) *46.36832, 15.08864* **Autocamp Jezero, Cesta Simona Blatnika 26, 3320 Velenje [(03) 5866466; mastodontbar@gmail.com]** Exit A1/E57 at Velenje & cont to 2nd traff lts, then turn R. Turn L at 3rd traff lts & foll site sp. Site on lakeside. Med, mkd pitch, pt shd; wc; chem disp; mv service pnt; shwrs; el pnts (10A) inc; Indtte; supmkt 2km; rest 300m; snacks; playgrnd; lake sw; watersports; tennis; games area; fitness rm; internet; some statics; dogs €1.50; quiet. "Lovely location but nr coal-powered power stn; poss unkempt low ssn; Velenje coal mining museum worth visit 1km." ♦ 1 May-30 Sep. € 19.00 (CChq acc) 2010*

Caravan Europe 1
Caravan Europe 2

Distances are shown in kilometres and are calculated from town/city centres along the most practical roads, although not necessarily taking the shortest route. 1km = 0.62miles

Kocevje to Rogaška Slatina = 176km

	Bled	Bohinj Bistrica	Brezice	Celje	Dravograd	Ilirska Bistrica	Jesenice	Kobarid	Kocevje	Kranj	Ljubljana	Maribor	Murska Sobota	Nova Gorica	Novo Mesto	Postojna	Ptuj	Rogaška Slatina	Tolmin
Bohinj Bistrica	20																		
Brezice	165	180																	
Celje	129	143	76																
Dravograd	176	191	135	61															
Ilirska Bistrica	137	154	181	159	203														
Jesenice	11	37	168	134	181	139													
Kobarid	106	126	219	197	244	140	95												
Kocevje	124	139	91	144	191	102	127	156											
Kranj	31	46	135	99	149	110	34	109	95										
Ljubljana	57	74	104	76	123	79	62	119	61	30									
Maribor	180	198	126	51	59	210	185	248	195	151	127								
Murska Sobota	237	252	186	108	119	265	240	305	252	210	184	56							
Nova Gorica	165	91	209	188	232	91	171	53	129	138	109	236	295						
Novo Mesto	131	148	42	95	154	144	134	185	48	104	74	147	201	175					
Postojna	107	124	149	127	174	33	110	104	74	80	51	181	238	61	114				
Ptuj	184	199	130	55	109	212	189	252	200	154	132	27	66	242	149	182			
Rogaška Slatina	163	180	58	35	97	191	168	232	176	136	110	48	106	219	98	163	53		
Tolmin	101	58	204	181	232	128	106	14	142	96	104	232	293	41	169	89	239	218	
Velenje	138	157	98	24	39	166	143	206	151	111	83	73	128	195	120	140	77	59	191

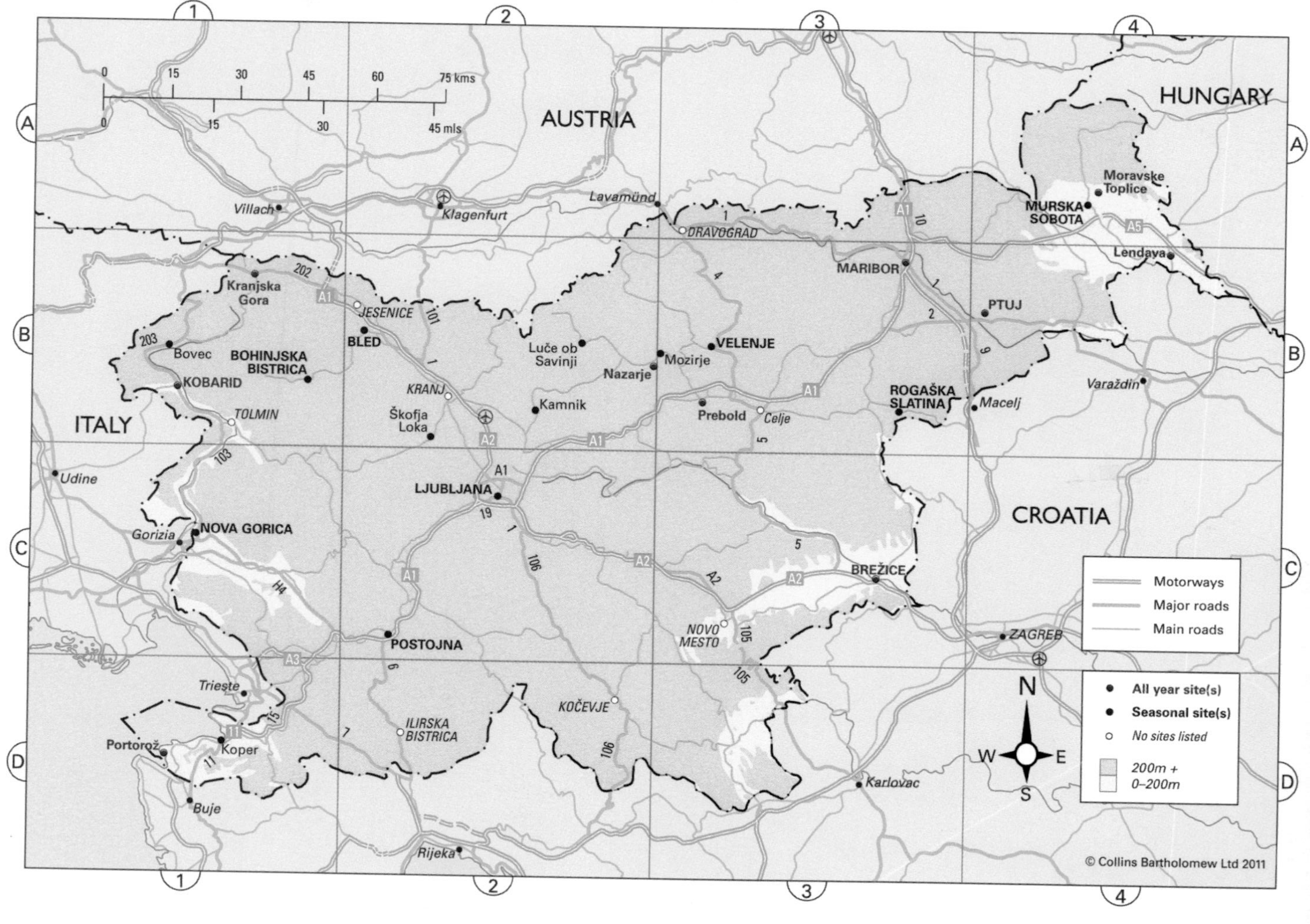
AUSTRIA
HUNGARY
ITALY
CROATIA
0 15 30 45 60 75 kms
0 15 30 45 mls
Villach
Klagenfurt
Lavamünd
DRAVOGRAD
Moravske Toplice
MURSKA SOBOTA
Lendava
MARIBOR
PTUJ
Varaždin
Kranjska Gora
JESENICE
BLED
Bovec
BOHINJSKA BISTRICA
KOBARID
TOLMIN
KRANJ
Škofja Loka
Kamnik
Luče ob Savinji
Nazarje
Mozirje
VELENJE
Prebold
Celje
ROGAŠKA SLATINA
Macelj
Udine
LJUBLJANA
Gorizia
NOVA GORICA
BREŽICE
ZAGREB
NOVO MESTO
POSTOJNA
Trieste
Koper
Portorož
Buje
ILIRSKA BISTRICA
KOČEVJE
Karlovac
Rijeka
Motorways
Major roads
Main roads
All year site(s)
Seasonal site(s)
No sites listed
200m +
0–200m
N
S
E
W
© Collins Bartholomew Ltd 2011

Sweden

Country Introduction

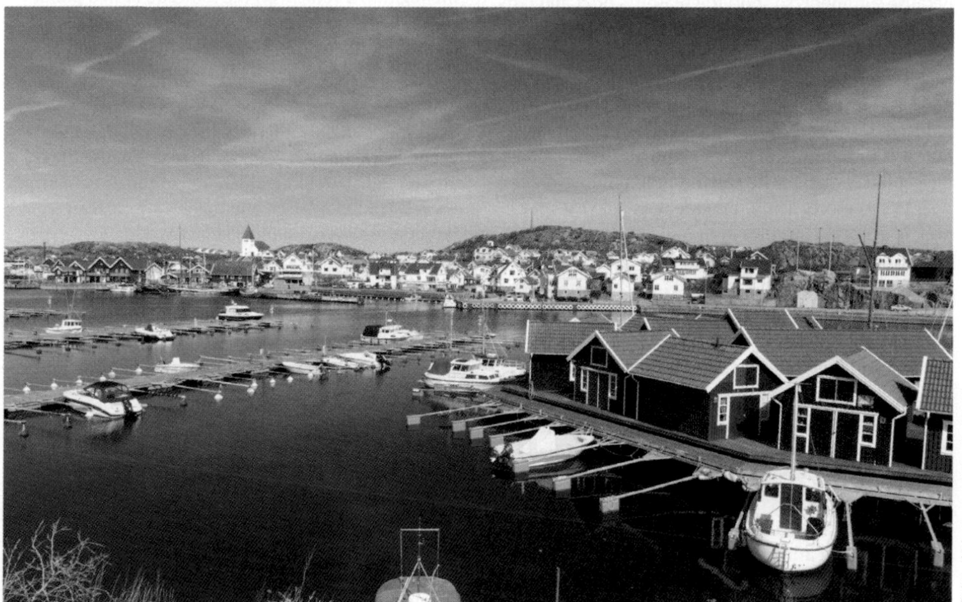

© iStockPhotos.com/ Martin Wahlborg

Marina of Skarhamn

Population (approx): 9.4 million

Capital: Stockholm (population 2 million)

Area: 450,000 sqkm

Bordered by: Finland, Norway

Terrain: Mostly flat or gently rolling lowlands; mountains in the west

Climate: Cold, cloudy winters, sub-arctic in the north; cool/warm summers. The best time to visit is between May and September; August can be hot and wet. Be prepared for occasional sub-zero temperatures and snowfalls, even in summer months

Coastline: 3,218km

Highest Point: Kebnekaise 2,114m

Language: Swedish

Local Time: GMT or BST + 1, i.e. 1 hour ahead of the UK all year

Currency: Krona (SEK) divided into 100 öre; £1 = SEK 10.43, SEK 100 = £9.59 (October 2011)

Telephoning: From the UK dial 0046 for Sweden and omit the initial zero of the area code of the number you are calling. To call the UK from Sweden dial 0044, omitting the initial zero of the area code. Mobile phone coverage may be poor in sparsely inhabited inland areas

Emergency Numbers: Police 112 (or 11414 for non-emergency calls); Fire Brigade 112; Ambulance 112. Operators speak English

Public Holidays 2012

Jan 1, 6; Apr 6, 8, 9; May 1, 17, 27; Jun 6 (National Day), 23 (Midsummer); Nov 3; Dec 25, 26.

Public Holidays 2013

Jan 1, 6; Mar 29, 31; Apr 1; May 1, 9, 19; Jun 6 (National Day), 22 (Midsummer); Nov 2; Dec 25, 26.

School summer holidays are from early June to the second or third week of August

Tourist Office

VISIT SWEDEN
STORTORGET 2-4, SE-83130 ÖSTERSUND, SWEDEN
Tel: 020 7108 6168 (UK)
www.visitsweden.com uk@visitsweden.com

The following introduction to Sweden should be read in conjunction with the important information contained in the Handbook chapters at the front of this guide.

Camping and Caravanning

Camping and caravanning are very popular but because summer is so short the season is brief and lasts only from May to late August/early September, although winter caravanning is enjoying increasing popularity. High season on most sites ends around the middle of August when prices and site office opening hours are reduced or sites are closed altogether. There are more than 1,000 campsites of which about 350 remain open during the winter, particularly in mountainous regions near to ski resorts. Those that are open all year may offer fewer or no facilities from mid-September to April and advance booking may be required.

In late June and July advance booking is recommended, especially at campsites along the west coast (north and south of Göteborg), on the islands of Öland and Gotland and near other popular tourist areas.

Approximately 500 campsites are members of the SCR (Svenska Campingvärdars Riksfärbund – Swedish Campsite Owners' Association), which are classified from 1 to 5 stars. Visitors wishing to use these sites must be in possession of a Camping Card Scandinavia (CCS), which is also valid in Denmark, Finland and Norway, plus an annual validity sticker. The Camping Card International (CCI) is not currently accepted at most SCR campsites but it is accepted at over approximately 500 independent sites and you will find a list of these on www.campinggladje.se/resa/

The CCS is obtainable online from www.camping.se (allow four weeks for delivery) or a temporary one may be obtained from your first campsite. The cost is SEK140 for one year (2011). The Card is valid for a whole family, i.e. one or two adults and accompanying children. It enables instant swipe registration at campsites, provides accident insurance while on site and use of 'Quick Stop' overnight facilities. In addition, holders of a CCS are entitled to discounts on a number of ferry lines including Scandlines, Silja Line, Stena Line and TT-Line, and reduced rates at a range of attractions, retail and food outlets. These discounts do not apply to temporary cards issued at your first campsite, so it is better to purchase your CCS before travelling to Sweden.

Most Swedes use electric hook-ups so caravanners using their battery will obtain a pitch which is on a less congested part of the site. Also aim to arrive by mid afternoon to get a better pitch, since many Swedes arrive late. It is reported that handbasins on sites often do not have plugs so it is advisable to carry a flat universal plug when touring.

Many sites have a 'Quick Stop' amenity which provides safe, secure overnight facilities on, or adjacent to, a site. This normally includes the use of sanitary facilities. 'Quick Stop' rates are about two thirds of the regular camping rate if you arrive after 9pm and leave before 9am.

Casual/wild camping is normally permitted, however for security reasons it is not recommended to spend the night in a vehicle on the roadside or in a public car park. Instead use the 'Quick Stop' amenity at campsites. In any event local parking rules and signposting should always be observed.

Alternatively there are around 150 organised 'ställplatser' mainly intended for motorhomes but generally car and caravan outfits may also use them for an overnight stay at the discretion of the site's manager. For a list of 'ställplatser' and maps showing their location see www.campinggladje.se/resa/

Most designated rest areas along highways are owned and managed by the Vågverket (Swedish Roads Administration) which, although not officially ranked as 'ställplatser', offer adequate parking space and various facilities for motorhomes staying overnight. A map showing these rest areas is available at local tourist offices.

Country Information

Cycling

The network of cycle lanes in Sweden is growing rapidly and many cycle routes are named and signposted. In some cases cycle lanes are combined with foot paths. See www.svenska-cykelsallskapet.se.

The 'Sverigeleden' cycle trail covers the whole country and connects all major ports and cities. The 190km cycle route along the Göta Canal from Sjötorp on Lake Vänern to Mem on the Baltic coast is relatively flat and hence a very popular route.

The wearing of a safety helmet is compulsory for children up to the age of 15 and is recommended for everyone.

Electricity and Gas

On campsites the current is usually 10 amps or more and round two-pin plugs are used. CEE connections are becoming standard.

Propane (gasol) is the gas most widely obtainable at more than 2,000 Primus dealers; you will need to buy an appropriate adaptor. It is understood that it is possible to sell back your propane cylinder at the end of your holiday and outlets will also exchange the corresponding Norwegian Progas cylinders. Recent visitors report that major distributors will refill cylinders but they must be of a recognised make/type and in perfect condition. The Caravan Club does not recommend the refilling of cylinders.

Butane gas is available from a number of outlets including some petrol stations. It is understood that Campingaz 904 and 907 cylinders are available but recent visitors report that they may be difficult to find, and virtually impossible in the north of the country. For more information on butane suppliers contact the Swedish Campsite Owners' Association (SCR) by email: info@scr.se

Ensure that you are well-equipped with gas if venturing north of central Sweden as it may be difficult to find an exchange point. Many sites have communal kitchen facilities which enable visitors to make great savings on their own gas supply.

*See **Electricity and Gas** in the section **DURING YOUR STAY.***

Entry Formalities

Holders of valid British and Irish passports may visit Sweden for up to three months without a visa.

Regulations for Pets

In order to protect the countryside and wildlife, dogs are not allowed to run off the lead from 1 March to 20 August and at other times in certain areas.

Dogs travelling directly from the UK and Ireland must be microchipped and have an EU pet passport. For more information please visit the website link: www.jordbruksverket.se/swedishboardofagriculture/engelskasidor/animals/import/dogsandcats

*See **Pet Travel Scheme** under **Documents** in the section **PLANNING AND TRAVELLING.***

Medical Services

Health care facilities are generally very good and most medical staff speak English. The general practitioner system does not apply; instead visit the nearest hospital clinic (Akutmottagning or Värdcentral) and present your passport and European Health Insurance Card (EHIC). You will be charged a fee for the clinic visit (free for anyone under 20) plus a daily standard charge if it is necessary to stay in hospital. These charges are non-refundable in Sweden.

Prescriptions are dispensed at pharmacies (apotek) which are open during normal shopping hours. Emergency prescriptions can be obtained at hospitals. Dental surgeons or clinics (tandläkare or folktandvård) offer emergency out-of-hours services in major cities but you may have to pay the full cost of treatment.

If you enjoy hiking and outdoor sports you should seek medical advice before you travel about preventative measures and immunisation against tick-borne encephalitis, a potentially serious and debilitating viral disease of the central nervous system which is endemic from spring to autumn.

Lyme disease is an equally serious tick-borne infection for which there is no preventative vaccine. Ticks are found in coastal areas, especially the Stockholm Archipelego, in rural and forested areas, particularly in long grass, bushes, hedgerows and woods, and in scrubland and areas where animals wander.

If you think you might be at risk use an insect repellent containing DEET, wear long sleeves and long trousers, inspect the body for ticks after outdoor activity and remove with tweezers, and avoid unpasteurised dairy products in risk areas. See www.tickalert.org, email info@tickalert.org or telephone 01943 468010.

The use of mosquito repellent is also recommended, particularly from mid June to September when mosquitos are most common. Mosquitos are generally more often encountered in the north of Sweden rather than the south.

Visitors to remote areas should consider the relative inaccessibility of the emergency services. In northern Sweden mobile phone coverage does not generally extend beyond main roads and the coast.

You are strongly recommended to obtain comprehensive travel and medical insurance before travelling to Sweden, such as The Caravan Club's Red Pennant Overseas Holiday Insurance – see www.caravanclub.co.uk/redpennant

*See **Medical Matters** in the section **DURING YOUR STAY.***

Opening Hours

Banks – Mon-Fri 9.30am-2pm/3pm and until 5.30pm one day a week in Stockholme and larger towns. Many banks do not handle cash after 3pm and some banks will not handle cash at all.

Museums – Tue-Sun 10am-4pm; usually closed Monday.

Post Offices – Post offices no longer exist. Mail is dealt with at local shops, kiosks and petrol stations; opening hours vary.

Shops – Mon-Fri 9am-6pm; Sat 9am-1pm/2pm/3pm; supermarkets may open until 8pm and on Sunday. Banks and shops generally close early the day before a public holiday.

Safety and Security

Petty crime levels are much lower than in most other European countries but you should take the usual commonsense precautions. Pickpocketing is common in the summer months in major cities where tourists may be targetted for their passports and cash.

In recent years there have been incidents of 'highway robbery' from motorhomes parked on the roadside, especially on the west coast between Malmö and Gothenburg.

Sweden shares with the rest of Europe an underlying threat from terrorism. Attacks could be indiscriminate and against civilian targets in public places, including tourist sites.

*See **Safety and Security** in the section **DURING YOUR STAY.***

British Embassy

SKARPÖGATAN 6-8,115 93 STOCKHOLM
Tel: (08) 6713000
http://ukinsweden.fco.gov.uk/en/

Irish Embassy

Hovslagargatan 5, 100 55 STOCKHOLM
Tel: (08) 54504040
www.embassyofireland.se

Customs Regulations

Alcohol and Tobacco

For import allowances for alcohol and tobacco products *see **Customs Regulations** in the section **PLANNING AND TRAVELLING.***

Visitors arriving from an EU country via a non-EU country (e.g. Norway) may bring quantities of tobacco and alcohol obtained in EU countries, plus the amounts allowed duty-free from non-EU countries. However, you must be able to produce proof of purchase for goods from EU countries and goods must be for your personal use.

Border Posts

There are approximately 40 Customs posts along the Swedish/Norwegian border. They are situated on all main roads and are normally open Monday to Friday from 8.30am to 4pm/5pm.

Travellers with dutiable goods must cross the land borders during hours when the Customs posts are open. However, travellers without dutiable goods may cross the border outside Customs post opening hours.

The main border posts with Finland are at Haparanda, Övertornea, Pajala and Karesuando.

Documents

Driving Licence

A UK driving licence is only valid when it bears a photograph of the holder, i.e. a photocard licence, or when it is carried together with photographic proof of identity, such as a passport.

*See **Documents** in the section **PLANNING AND TRAVELLING.***

Money

Foreign currency may be exchanged in banks and bureaux de change. Travellers' cheques are not widely accepted as a means of payment in shops and restaurants, but they may be exchanged at some banks and bureaux de change, subject to a high service charge.

The major credit cards are widely used both for major and minor transactions and cash machines (Bankomat or Minuten) are widespread. It is advisable to carry your passport or photocard driving licence if paying with a credit card as you may be asked for photographic proof of identity.

Carry your credit card issuers'/banks' 24-hour UK contact numbers in case of loss or theft of your cards.

Motoring

Accidents

In the case of an accident it is not necessary to call the police unless there are injuries to drivers or passengers and/or vehicles are badly damaged, but drivers are required to give their details to the other persons involved before leaving the accident scene. A driver leaving the scene of an accident without following this procedure may be fined.

If you are involved in an accident with a possible third party claim, you are strongly recommended to report the accident to the national Swedish insurance bureau which will act as claims agent. Contact Trafikförsäkringsforeningen in Stockholm, tel 08 522 78200, info@ tff.se, www.tff.se

Accidents involving wild animals (e.g. elk, reindeer, bear, wolf, etc) must be reported to the police immediately by calling 112 or 11414 and the spot where the accident took place must be marked by putting up reflective tape or anything clearly noticeable so that the police can find it easily. Collisions must be reported even if the animal involved is not injured. After reporting the accident and marking out the place, a driver may leave. Accidents involving smaller animals (badgers, foxes, etc) need not be reported.

Alcohol

Penalties for driving a motor vehicle under the influence of alcohol are extremely severe. The police carry out random breath tests. If the level of alcohol exceeds 20 milligrams in 100 millilitres of blood a fine will be imposed and driving licence withdrawn. This level is considerably lower than that permitted in the UK (80 milligrams) and equates to virtually zero. A level exceeding 100 milligrams is considered to be severe drink driving for which a jail sentence of up to two years will be imposed and licence withdrawn.

Breakdown Service

The motoring organisation, Motormännens Riksförbund (known as the 'M'), does not operate a breakdown service. It does, however, have an agreement with

'AssistanceKåren' (a nationwide road service company) which operates a 24-hour, all-year service and can be contacted free on (020) 912912 or 08 6275757 from a foreign-registered mobile phone. Phone boxes are becoming quite scarce and it is advisable to carry a mobile phone. There are normally no emergency telephones along motorways or dual carriageways. Charges for assistance and towing vary according to day and time and payment by credit card is accepted.

Essential Equipment

*See **Motoring – Equipment** in the section **PLANNING AND TRAVELLING.***

Lights

Dipped headlights are compulsory at all times, regardless of weather conditions. Bulbs are more likely to fail with constant use and you are recommended to carry spares. Fog lights may be used when visibility is poor but they must not be used together with dipped headlights.

Child Restraint System

Children under the height of 135cm must be seated in a child restraint or child seat. A child aged 15 or over, or 135cm in height or taller, can use normal seat belts in the car.

Children under the height of 140cm are only allowed in the front seat if the passenger seat airbag has been deactivated.

Winter Driving

The winter months are periods of severe cold and you should be prepared for harsh conditions. The fitting of winter tyres is compulsory for vehicles up to 3,500kg from 01st December to 31st March in the event of severe winter road conditions, i.e. the road is covered with ice or snow, or if the road is wet and the temperature is around freezing point. Trailers towed by these vehicles must also be equipped with winter tyres. Winter tyre regulations do not apply to vehicles over 3,500kg but if summer tyres are used the tread must be at least 5mm deep. These regulations apply to foreign registered vehicles.

Snow chains may be used if weather and road conditions require. Snow chains can be hired or purchased from Polar Automotive Ltd, tel 01892 519933, www.snowchains.com, email: polar@snowchains.com (10% discount for Caravan Club members).

Fuel

Petrol stations are usually open from 7am to 9pm. Near motorways and main roads and in most cities they may remain open until 10pm or even for 24 hours. Outside large towns garages seldom stay open all night but most have self-service pumps (possibly not for diesel) which accept credit cards. In the far north filling stations may be few and far between so keep your tank topped up. Credit cards are accepted.

LPG (known as gasol) is sold at a very limited number of petrol stations mainly located in central and southern Sweden.

*See also **Fuel** under **Motoring – Advice** in the section **PLANNING AND TRAVELLING.***

Overtaking

Take care when overtaking long vehicles. A typical long-distance Swedish truck is a six-wheeled unit towing a huge articulated trailer, i.e. a very long load.

Many roads in Sweden have wide shoulders or a climbing lane to the right of the regular lane and these permit drivers of slow moving vehicles or wide vehicles to pull over to allow other traffic to pass. These climbing lanes and shoulders should not be used as another traffic lane.

Parking

Parking meters and other parking restrictions are in use in several large towns. Vehicles must be parked facing the direction of the flow of traffic. Wheel clamps are not in use but illegally parked vehicles may be towed away and, in addition to a parking fine, a release fee will be charged.

In an area signposted 'P' parking is permitted for a maximum of 24 hours, unless otherwise stated.

*See also **Parking Facilities for the Disabled** under **Motoring – Advice** in the section **PLANNING AND TRAVELLING.***

Priority

Vehicles driving on roads designated and signposted (with a yellow diamond on an black background) as primary roads always have priority. On all other roads, as a general rule, vehicles coming from the right have priority, unless signs indicate otherwise. This rule is sometimes ignored however, especially by vehicles on roads regarded as major roads but not signposted as such, and care is required.

At most roundabouts signs indicate that traffic already on the roundabout has priority, i.e. from the left.

Give trams priority at all times. Where there is no refuge at a tram stop, you must stop to allow passengers to board and alight from the tram.

Roads

The condition of national and country roads is good although some minor roads may be covered with oil-gravel only. Road surfaces may be damaged following the spring thaw, and some may be closed or have weight restrictions imposed during that period. Gradients are generally slight and there are no roads that need to be avoided for vehicles towing a caravan.

Road repairs tend to be intensive during the short summer season. This may cause problems to outfits towed over the temporary surface. It is recommended that water hose joints, etc, be checked soon after arrival on site. Information on major roadworks and road conditions on E roads and major national roads can be obtained from www.trafikverket.se.

Accidents involving collisions with wild animals, particularly deer, elk and wild boar, are very common (approximately 40,000 a year). Some major roads are fenced to prevent animals crossing, but most roads are unfenced. There is little reaction time as animals may appear without warning on stretches of road or close to populated areas. Continual vigilance is essential, especially at dawn and dusk. A yellow warning triangle with a red border depicts the animal most commonly encountered on a particular stretch of road and these signs should be taken seriously. Accidents involving the larger wild animals must be reported to the police immediately – see ***Accidents*** above. Campsites and tourist information centres have leaflets on the required reporting procedures.

There is a good road link with Norway in the far north of Sweden. The Kiruna-Narvik road is open all year from Kiruna to the border. It is a wide road with no steep gradients.

There is generally little or no heavy goods traffic on roads during the Christmas, Easter and midsummer holidays or on the days preceding these holidays so good progress can be made.

Road Signs and Markings

Road signs and markings conform to international standards. Road markings are white. The middle of the road is indicated by broken lines with long intervals. Warning lines (usually on narrow roads) are broken lines with short intervals which indicate that visibility is limited in one or both directions; they may be crossed when overtaking. Unbroken lines should not be crossed at any time.

National roads (riksvägar) have two-digit numbers and country roads (länsvägar) have three-digit numbers. Roads which have been incorporated into the European road network – E roads – generally have no other national number.

Direction and information signs for motorways and roads which form part of the European road network are green. Signs for national roads and the more important country roads are blue. Signs for local roads are white with black numerals.

In some towns traffic restrictions, including weight restrictions, may apply at certain times and these are signposted. The following are some other signs that you may see:

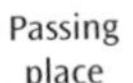
Passing place

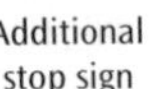
Additional stop sign

Accident

Enkelriktat – *One way*

Farlig kurva – *Dangerous bend*

Grusad väg – *Loose chippings*

Höger – *Right*

Ingen infart – *No entrance*

Parkering förbjuden – *No parking*

Vänster – *Left*

Speed Limits

*See **Speed Limits Table** under **Motoring – Advice** in the section **PLANNING AND TRAVELLING.***

Speed limits are no longer based on the category of road but on the quality and safety level of the roads themselves. As a result limits may vary from one town to another and along stretches of the same road. It is advisable, therefore, to pay close attention to road signs as speed limits are strictly enforced. If in doubt, or if no speed limit is indicated, you are advised to keep to 70 km/h (44 mph) until you see a speed limit sign.

Outside built-up areas, including expressways, speeds up to 100 km/h (62 mph) may be permitted according to road signs, providing a lower maximum speed is not applicable for certain vehicle categories. On motorways the maximum permitted speed is 110 or 120 km/h (68 or 74 mph). During the winter a speed limit of 90 km/h (56 mph) is in force on some motorways and dual carriageways. This limit is signposted.

In most residential areas and during certain periods in areas near schools, speed is limited to 30 km/h (18 mph) according to road signs. Periods indicated in black mean Monday to Friday, those in black in brackets mean Saturday and the eves of public holidays, and those indicated in red mean Sunday and public holidays.

Speed limits for motorhomes under 3,500kg and privately registered motorhomes over 3,500kg are the same as for solo cars.

Speed cameras are in use on many roads. The use of radar detectors is not permitted.

Traffic Lights

A green arrow indicates that traffic may proceed with caution in the direction of the arrow but pedestrians must be given priority. A flashing amber light indicates that a crossing/turning must be made with caution.

Violation of Traffic Regulations

Police are authorised to impose, but not collect, fines for violation of minor traffic offences which must be paid at a bank, normally within two to three weeks. Fines range from SEK400 to 1,200, but if two or more offences are committed and total fines exceed SEK2,500, the offender will be taken to court. Offences, which may qualify for a fine include driving without lights in daylight, speeding, lack of a warning triangle or nationality plate (GB or IRL) or a dirty or missing number plate.

If a fine is not paid and the driver is a resident of another EU country, notice of the fine will be forwarded to the authorities in the driver's country of residence.

Jaywalking is not permitted; pedestrians must use official crossings.

Motorways

There are approximately 1,900 kms of motorway and 560 kms of semi-motorway or dual carriageway, all confined to the south of the country and relatively free of heavy traffic by UK standards. No tolls are levied. There are no service areas or petrol stations on motorways; these are situated near the exits and are indicated on motorway exit signs.

Toll Bridges

The Øresund Bridge links Malmö in Sweden with Copenhagen in Denmark and means that it is possible to drive all the way from mainland Europe by motorway. The crossing is via a 7.8 km bridge to the artificial island of Peberholm and a 4 km tunnel. Tolls (payable in cash, including EUR, SEK or DKK or by credit card) are levied on the Swedish side and are as follows for single journeys (2011 prices subject to change):

Vehicle(s)	Price
Car, motorhome up to 6 metres	€ 40
Car + caravan/trailer or motor caravan over 6 metres	€ 80

Vehicle length is measured electronically and even a slight overhang over six metres will result in payment of the higher tariff.

Speed limits apply in the tunnel and on the bridge, and during periods of high wind the bridge is closed to caravans. Bicycles are not allowed. Information on the Øresund Bridge can be found on www.oeresundsbron.com

Svinesund Bridge

There is a 700 metre long bridge linking Sweden and Norway on the E6, at Svinesund. Tolls are SEK24 (NOK20) for light vehicles and SEK120 (NOK100) for vehicles over 3,500kgs (2011).

Touring

Ferry services connect Sweden with Denmark, Estonia, Finland, Germany, Latvia, Lithuania, Norway and Poland; some services only operate in the summer. Full details are available from Visit Sweden, www.visitsweden.com. Scheduled car ferry services also operate between the mainland and the island of Gotland during the summer season.

In the south and centre the touring season lasts from May to September. In the north it is a little shorter, the countryside being particularly beautiful at each end of the season. Campsites are most crowded over the midsummer holiday period and during the Swedish industrial holidays in the last two weeks of July and first week of August. Tourist attractions may close before the end of August or operate on reduced opening hours.

Sweden has 14 UNESCO World Heritage sites and 29 national parks which, together with nature reserves, cover eight percent of the country. Information on national parks and nature reserves is available in English on www.naturvardsverket.se

Inland, particularly near lakes, visitors should be armed with spray-on, rub-on and electric plug-in insect repellant devices as mosquitoes and midges are a problem.

Discount cards are available in Stockholm and Gothenburg offering free public transport and free admission to many museums and other attractions, plus free boat and canal sightseeing trips. Buy the cards at tourist information offices, hotels, kiosks, some campsites and online – see www.stockholmtown.com or www.goteborg.com

Local tourist offices are excellent sources of information and advice; look for the blue and yellow 'i' signs. Information points at lay-bys at the entrance to many towns are good sources of street maps.

Swedish cuisine places special emphasis on natural ingredients, particularly fresh, pickled and smoked seafood and game. Specialities include crayfish, herring, salmon, eel, reindeer and elk and, of course, the traditional smörgåsbord, which is rather less common these days. A good-value 'dagens rätt' (dish of the day) is available in most restaurants at lunchtime. A service charge is usually included in restaurant bills but an additional small tip is normal if you have received good service.

The most popular alcoholic drink is lager, available in five strengths. Wines, spirits and strong beer are sold only through the state-owned 'Systembolaget' shops, open from Monday to Friday and on Saturday morning, with branches all over the country. Light beer can be bought from grocery shops and supermarkets. The minimum age for buying alcoholic drinks is 20 years at Systembolaget and 18 years in pubs, bars and licensed restaurants.

It is not permitted to smoke in restaurants, pubs or bars or in any place where food and drinks are served.

English is widely spoken.

The Midnight Sun and Northern Lights

The Midnight Sun is visible north of the Arctic Circle from about the end of May until the middle of July, for example:

Abisko: 17 June – 19 July

Björkliden: 17 June – 19 July

Gällivare: 4 June – 12 July

Jokkmokk: 8 June – 3 July

Kiruna: 31 May – 11 July

The Northern Lights (Aurora Borealis) are often visible during the winter from early evening until midnight. They are seen more frequently the further north you travel. The best viewing areas in Sweden are north of the Arctic Circle between September and March.

The Order of Bluenosed Caravanners

Visitors to the Arctic Circle from anywhere in the world may apply for membership of the Order of Bluenosed Caravanners which will be recognised by the issue of a certificate by the International Caravanning Association (ICA). For more information contact Ann Sneddon on telephone 01236 723339, or email: ann.sneddon@o2.co.uk and attach a photograph of yourselves and your outfit under any Arctic Circle signpost, together with the date and country of crossing and the names of those who made the crossing. This service is free to members of the ICA (annual membership £20); the fee for non-members is £5. Coloured plastic decals for your outfit, indicating membership of the Order, are also available at a cost of £2. Cheques should be payable to the ICA. See www.icacaravanning.org

Local Travel

Stockholm has an extensive network of underground trains (T-bana), commuter trains, buses and trams. Underground station entrances are marked with a blue 'T' on a white background. You can buy single tickets for one of three zones at the time of your journey, or save money by buying tickets in advance. A discount applies if you are aged 65 or over. Single tickets and prepaid tickets are valid for one hour after beginning your journey. Travel cards offer reduced price public transport throughout the Greater Stockholm area for periods of 1, 3, 7 or 30 days, regardless of zone – see www.sl.se (click on 'Visitor') for details of routes, fares and tickets.

For information on public transport systems in Göteborg and Malmö, see www.vasttrafik.se and www.skanetrafiken.se

Stockholm is built on an archipelago of islands and island hopping ferries operate all year. You can buy single tickets or an island hopping pass for use on the Waxholmsbolaget and Cinderella fleet of ferries.

Confirm your taxi fare before setting off in the vehicle. Some companies have fixed fares which vary according to the day of the week and time of day. A full price list must be on display. Payment by credit card is generally accepted. It is usual to round up the fare shown on the meter by way of a tip.

Sweden is a country of lakes, rivers and archipelagos and, as a result, there are over 12,000 bridges. Road ferries, which form part of the national road network, make up the majority of other crossings; no bookings are necessary or possible. Most ferries are free of charge and services are frequent and crossings very short.

A congestion charge was introduced in Stockholm in 2007 but drivers of foreign-registered vehicles are exempt from the charge. In some other towns traffic restrictions may apply during certain periods and these are signposted.

When giving directions Swedes will often refer to istances in 'miles'. A Swedish 'mile' is, in fact, approximately ten kilometres. All road signs are in kilometres and so, for example, a distance of 30km to a town, Swedes will tell you is three miles!

All place names used in the Site Entry listings which follow can be found in the Sverige Vägatlas published by Motormännens, scale 1:250,000 (1 cm = 2.5 km).

⊞ **AHUS** *2F4* (1km NE Urban/Coastal) *55.94118, 14.31286* **Regenbogen Camp (L27), Kolonivägen 59, 29633 Åhus [(044) 249530; fax 243523; ahus@regenbogen-camp.se; www.regenbogen-camp.se]** Take rd 118 fr Kristianstad SE twd Åhus. Site well sp fr ent to town. Lge, mkd pitch, hdstg, pt shd; htd wc; chem disp; mv service pnt; baby facs; sauna; shwrs inc; el pnts (10A) SEK29; Indtte (inc dryer); shop; rest, bar 500m; BBQ; playgrnd; htd pool 300m; sand beach 150m; some statics; dogs; site clsd 3 Nov-16 Dec; poss cr; Eng spkn; quiet; ccard acc; CCS. "Gd base for walking, cycling, watersports; excel fishing; famous area for artists." ♦ SEK 260 2011*

ALINGSAS *2E2* (4km SW Rural) **Lövekulle Camping, 44144 Alingsås [(0322) 12372; lovekulle@telia.com; www.lovekulle.com]** Foll sp fr E20. Sm, mkd pitch, some hdstg, unshd; htd wc; chem disp; mv service pnt; shwrs; el pnts (10A); Indtte; shop; snacks; playgrnd; sw; fishing; games area; 10% statics; Eng spkn; quiet; CCI. "Pleasant situation by lake; clean san facs." ♦ 1 May-30 Sep. 2010*

ALMHULT *2F3* (2km N Rural) *56.56818, 14.13217* **Sjöstugans Camping (G5), Campingvägen, Bökhult, 34394 Älmhult [(0476) 71600; fax 15750; info@sjostugan.com; www.sjostugan.com]** Fr Växjö SW on rd 23, at rndabt turn W to Älmhult. Fr town cent turn N on Ljungbyvägen, site in 1.5km on lakeside, well sp. Sm, pt sl, pt shd; htd wc; chem disp; mv service pnt; baby facs; shwrs; el pnts (10A) SEK40; Indtte (inc dryer); shop & 1.5km; rest; snacks; bar; cooking facs; playgrnd; lake & sand beach adj; canoe hire; wifi; some cabins; dogs; Eng spkn; quiet; ccard acc; CCS. "Some lakeside pitches; well-kept site; 1st Ikea store opened here in 1958; gd." 1 May-30 Sep. SEK 165 2009*

⊞ **ALVDALEN** *1B4* (W Urban) *61.22789, 14.03007* **Älvdalens Camping (W2), Ribbholmsvägen 26, 79631 Älvdalen [tel/fax (0251) 12344; kontakt@alvdalenscamping.se; www.alvdalenscamping.se]** Fr S & Mora take rd 70 N; in Älvdalen, 200m after church turn L (W) to site; part of sports & leisure cent; well sp. Lge, hdstg, pt shd; htd wc; chem disp; mv service pnt; baby facs; fam bthrm; shwrs inc; el pnts (10A) SEK40; Indtte (inc dryer); shop, rest, snacks 500m; BBQ; cooking facs; playgrnd; htd, covrd pool, waterslide, ice rink nr; cycle hire; wifi; TV; dogs; Eng spkn; quiet; ccard acc; CCS. "Sh walk to town cent; gd facs." ♦ SEK 175 2011*

⊞ **AMAL** *2E2* (1km SE Urban) *59.0465, 12.7236* **Örnäs Camping (P2), Gamla Örnäsgatan, 66222 Åmål [(0532) 17097; fax 71624; ornascamping@amal.se; www.amal.se]** Leave rd 45 to Åmål, site sp. Sm, some hdstg, pt sl, terr, pt shd; htd wc; chem disp; mv service pnt; sauna; shwrs SEK5; el pnts (10A) inc; Indtte (inc dryer); shop, rest 1km; snacks; bar; playgrnd; sand beach/lake adj; fishing; tennis; boat & cycle hire; wifi; some statics; dogs; Eng spkn; red 7 days; ccard acc; CCS. "Gd views Lake Vänern." ♦ SEK 250 2011*

ANASET *1C3* (1km S Rural) *64.26834, 21.04120* **Lufta Camping (AC15), Galgbacken 1, 91594 Ånäset [(0934) 20488; fax 20215; info@luftacamping.se; www.luftacamping.se]** Exit E4 at Int'l Camp sp at Ånäset. Site immed S of Ånäset & 300m W of E4. Med, pt sl, pt shd; htd wc; chem disp; mv service pnt; sauna; shwrs; el pnts (10A) SEK50; Indtte; shop 500m; rest; snacks; bar; playgrnd; htd pool adj; waterslide; games area; cycle hire; fishing; wifi; TV; some statics; Eng spkn; ccard acc; CCS. "Beautiful setting." ♦ 1 May-30 Sep. SEK 130 2009*

ANGELHOLM *2E4* (2.5km SE Rural) *56.22646, 12.89181* **Solhälls Familjecamping (L34), Höjalandsväg 76, 26293 Ängelholm [(0431) 80400; fax 80845; solhallscamping@telia.com]** Leave E6 (Göteborg-Malmö) at junc 34 Höja twd Ängelholm. Site on L. Med, mkd pitch, pt sl, pt shd; wc; chem disp; shwrs inc; el pnts SEK30; gas 2km; Indtte; farm shop; tradsmn; BBQ; cooking facs; playgrnd; sand beach 2km; games area; dogs; Eng spkn; adv bkg rec; quiet; CCS. "Family-run site, v helpful owners, clean facs, poss stretched if full; conv local amenities all within cycle dist." 15 May-30 Sep. SEK 130 2008*

ANGELHOLM *2E4* (2km W Coastal) *56.2540, 12.8336* **Råbocka Camping (L12), Råbockavägen 101, 26263 Ängelholm [(0431) 10543 or 430600; fax 16144; rabockacamping@telia.com; www.rabockacamping.se]** Fr E6 foll sps to Ängelholm, site 2km fr town cent. Lge, mkd pitch, pt shd; wc; chem disp; mv service pnt; baby facs; shwrs SEK10; el pnts (10A) SEK50; Indtte; shop; snacks; bar; playgrnd; sand beach; TV; 10% statics; poss cr; Eng spkn; adv bkg; ccard acc; CCS. "Excel, busy site; gd beach & nature park nrby." ♦ 16 Apr-11 Sep. SEK 275 2009*

⊞ **ARBOGA** *2G1* (13km S Rural) *59.28134, 15.90509* **Herrfallets Camping (U14), 73293 Arboga [(0589) 40110; fax 40133; reception@herrfallet.se; www.herrfallet.se]** Foll sp fr E20/E18, turn off at Sätra junc twd Arboga, cross rv. Foll sp to Herrfallet/Västermo. Med, mkd pitch, pt shd; htd wc; chem disp; 50% serviced pitches; mv service pnt; baby facs; sauna; shwrs SEK10; el pnts (10A) SEK40; Indtte (inc dryer); shop; tradsmn; rest; bar; BBQ; playgrnd; lake sw & beach; boating; cycle hire; wifi; entmnt; dogs; phone; quiet; ccard acc; CCS/CCI. "Lovely spot on edge Lake Hjälmaren." ♦ SEK 190 2010*

ARBOGA *2G1* (1km SW Rural) *59.38863, 15.82713* **Krakaborgs Camping, Örebrovägen 2A 24B, 73221 Arboga [(0589) 12670; fax 17425; www.arboga.se]** Fr E18 exit sp Arboga. On ent town at rndabt foll site sp, site on L. Sm, pt shd; htd wc; chem disp; baby facs; shwrs; el pnts (10A) SEK35; Indtte; shop; snacks; cooking facs; playgrnd; TV; dogs; phone; adv bkg; quiet. 1 Jun-31 Oct. SEK 150 2009*

ARJANG *2E1* (25km SE Rural) *59.30295, 12.44474* **Camping Grinsby, Grindsbyn 100, Sillerud, 67295 Årjäng [(0573) 42022; fax 40175; campgrinsby@telia.com]** On E18 SE fr Årjäng & Sillerud, turn L at site sp. Site in 2km on Stora Bör lake. Med, some hdstg, terr, pt shd; htd wc; chem disp; mv service pnt; baby facs; shwrs SEK10; el pnts (10A) SEK40; Indtte (inc dryer); shop; tradsmn; BBQ; cooking facs; playgrnd; sand beach & lake sw adj; boat & cycle hire; games rm; some statics; dogs; phone; Eng spkn; adv bkg; quiet; ccard acc; CCI. "A 'wilderness' site in beautiful setting; many walking paths; friendly, helpful staff; vg san facs." ♦ 15 May-31 Aug. SEK 150 2010*

⊞ **ARJANG** *2E1* (3km S Rural) *59.36756, 12.14036* **Årjäng Camping (S13), Strand Sommarvik, 67291 Årjäng [(0573) 12060; fax 12048; booking@sommarvik.se; www.sommarvik.se]** Foll sp fr E18/rd 172. Site sp in Årjäng. At T-junc foll sp Stubgy & site sp on R 400m up hill, steep in parts but strt. Lge, pt sl, pt shd; htd wc; mv service pnt; baby facs; sauna; shwrs SEK10; el pnts (10A) inc; gas; Indtte (inc dryer); shop; rest; snacks; bar; cooking facs; playgrnd; htd pool high ssn; paddling pool; lake sw & beach; fishing; boating; boat & cycle hire; games area; tennis 1.5km; wifi; entmnt; TV rm; 50% statics; dogs; phone; Quickstop o'night facs; quiet; CCS. "Gd family site." ♦ SEK 200 2011*

⊞ **ARJEPLOG** *1C2* (1.5km W Rural) *66.05007, 17.86298* **Kraja Camping (BD1), Krajaudden, 93090 Arjeplog [(0961) 31500; fax 31599; arjeplog@kraja.se; www.kraja.se]** NW fr Arvidsjaur thro Arjeplog vill to site on R. Med, pt shd; htd wc; chem disp; baby facs; sauna; shwrs; el pnts (10A) SEK40; Indtte (inc dryer); shop; rest; bar; cooking facs; playgrnd; htd pool; paddling pool; sand beach; lake sw 4km; fishing; boating; TV; many statics; dogs; phone; poss cr; quiet; CCS. "Gd cent for local Lapp area." ♦ SEK 195 2010*

SWEDEN

⊞ **ARVIDSJAUR** *1C2* (1.5km SE Rural) *65.58185, 19.19026* **Camp Gielas (BD2), Järnvägsgatan 111, 93334 Arvidsjaur [(0960) 55600; fax 10615; gielas@arvidsjaur.se; www.arvidsjaur.se]** Well sp on rd 95. Med, mkd pitch, pt shd; htd wc; chem disp; mv service pnt; sauna; shwrs inc; el pnts (10A) SEK30; Indtte; shop 1km; rest 1.5km; snacks; cooking facs; playgrnd; lake sw & beach adj; waterslide; tennis; sports hall; games area; solarium; wifi; 30% statics; c'van wash point; poss cr & noisy; Eng spkn; no adv bkg; ccard acc; CCS. "Fine for families; ltd facs low ssn; poss problem with mosquitoes high ssn." ♦ SEK 165 2008*

ASA *2E3* (S Coastal) *57.34906, 12.12200* **Åsa Camping (N3), Stora Badviksvägen 10, 43031 Åsa [(0340) 219590; info@asacamping.com; www.asacamping.com]** On E6/E20 S fr Göteborg take exit rd sp Åsa. On app Åsa site sp on R. Med, unshd wc; chem disp; mv service pnt; baby facs; shwrs SEK5; el pnts (10A) SEK40; Indtte (inc dryer); shop & adj; rest; bar; playgrnd; sand beach nr; games area; games rm; golf; fishing; wifi; TV; 80% statics; dogs; phone; adv bkg; quiet; ccard acc; CCS. "Well-organised, family site but dominated by statics; avoid pitches nr access rd & facs block." ♦ 22 Apr-11 Sep. SEK 200 2009*

⊞ **ASARNA** *1B3* (9km S Rural) *62.56340, 14.38786* **Kvarnsjö Camp, Kvarnsjö 696, 84031 Åsarna [tel/fax (0682) 22016; info@kvarnsjocamp.com; www.kvarnsjocamp.com]** Fr N on E45 3km after Åsarna turn R onto rd 316 dir Klövsjo. In 8km turn L sp Cmp Kvarnsjö. In 8km cross rlwy, thro vill, site on L in 1km. Fr S 9km after Rätan turn L dir Klövsjo. In 1.5km bear R at Y-junc site in 4km. Sm, hdstg, terr, unshd; wc; chem disp; mv service pnt; sauna; shwrs inc; el pnts (10A) SEK40; Indtte; shop 16km; no statics; dogs; Eng spkn; adv bkg; quiet. CCI. "CL-type family-run site o'looking woods & mountains; excel walking, fishing; boating, fresh bread/breakfast in high sssn." SEK 130 2011*

ASELE *1C3* (1km E Rural) *64.17063, 17.36215* **Sagorna Åsele Camping, Värdshusvägen 21, 91060 Åsele [(0941) 10904; fax 14079; info@aselecamping.se; www.aselecamping.se]** Site is on L of rd 90 dir Vilhelmina adj Rv Ångermanälven. Med, pt shd; htd wc; chem disp; baby facs; sauna; shwrs inc; el pnts (10A) SEK30; Indtte; kiosk; shop; rest; snacks; playgrnd; pool; paddling pool; boating; cycle hire; TV; 30% statics; phone; ccard acc. "Beautiful site." ♦ 1 May-30 Sep. 2008*

ASKIM see Göteborg *2E3*

BARSEBACK *2E4* (1km W Coastal) *55.77030, 12.92621* **Barsebäckstrand Camping (M19), Kustvägen 125, 24657 Barsebäck [(046) 776079; info@barsebackstrand.se; www.barsebackstrand.se]** Fr S exit E6 junc 23 sp 'Center Syd' & foll sp Barsebäck thro vill. Turn L at T-junc, site in 2km, sp. Fr N exit junc 24 & foll coast rd 'Kustvägen' to site in 5km. Med, mkd pitch, terr, unshd; htd wc; chem disp; mv service pnt; shwrs inc; el pnts (10A) SEK40; Indry rm; shop 4km; tradsmn; rest; snacks; cooking facs; playgrnd; beach & sw adj; 40% statics; dogs free; poss cr; Eng spkn; adv bkg; quiet; CCS. "Vg site; gd beach; excel site rest." ♦ 30 Apr-31 Aug. SEK 210 2011*

⊞ **BENGTSFORS** *2E2* (12km SE Rural) *58.95271, 12.25201* **Laxsjöns Camping & Friluftsgård (P3), 66010 Dals Långed [(0531) 30010; fax 30555; office@laxsjons.se; www.laxsjon.se]** Fr Bengtsfors S on rd 172; 4km after x-ing Dalsland Canal at Billingsfors turn L twd Dals Långed; after 1km site on Lake Laxsjön on L; sp. Ent 4.5m. Lge, mkd pitch, pt sl, pt shd; htd wc; chem disp; sauna; shwrs SEK5; el pnts (10A) SEK40; Indtte (inc dryer); shop; rest in ssn; playgrnd; htd pool; lake sw adj; canoe hire; waterskiing; sailing; fishing; bus 200m/1km; Quickstop o'night facs; Eng spkn; adv bkg; quiet; ccard acc; red 7+ days; CCS. "Vg for quiet holiday & watersports; friendly staff; rec." ♦ SEK 190 2010*

BERGKVARA *2G4* (1km E Coastal) *56.39043, 16.09061* **Dalskärs Camping (H15), Dalskärvägen, 38502 Bergkvara [(0486) 20150; info@dalskarscamping.se; www.dalskarscamping.se]** Exit E22 in Bergkvara twd Dalskärsbadet, site sp. Med, mkd pitch, pt shd; wc; chem disp; mv service pnt; baby facs; sauna; shwrs SEK5; el pnts SEK40; Indtte; shop; rest; bar; htd pool; paddling pool; sand beach adj; boat & cycle hire; games area; wifi; some statics; dogs free; phone; Eng spkn; quiet; ccard acc. "Gd family site." ♦ 24 Apr-11 Sep. SEK 140 2010*

BERGKVARA *2G4* (3km S Rural/Coastal) *56.36108, 16.07481* **Skeppeviks Camping, 38598 Bergkvara [(0486) 20637; info@skeppevik.com; www.skeppevik.com]** N on E22 fr Karlskrona for approx 40km. Site sp fr main rd to R, then 1km. Med, mkd pitch, unshd; htd wc; chem disp; shwrs inc; el pnts (10A) SEK35; shop 3km; rest; snacks; playgrnd; beach adj; minigolf; 30% statics; dogs; phone; Eng spkn; adv bkg; quiet; CCS. "Delightful site; spacious pitches." ♦ 16 Apr-12 Sep. SEK 135 2008*

⊞ **BOCKSJO** *2F2* (5km NW Rural) *58.68058, 14.59911* **Stenkällegårdens Camping Tiveden, 54695 Stenkällegården [(0505) 60015; fax 60085; stenkallegarden@swipnet.se; www.stenkallegarden.nu]** N on rd 49 fr Karlsborg, turn L at Bocksjö, site sp on L in 2km. Pt of rte single track with passing places. Med, mkd pitch, pt sl, terr, pt shd; htd wc; chem disp; mv service pnt; baby facs; sauna; shwrs SEK10, el pnts (10A) SEK40; Indtte (inc dryer); shop; tradsmn; rest; cooking facs; BBQ; playgrnd; lake sw; fishing; boat hire; TV rm; 30% statics; dogs; site clsd last 2 weeks Apr & 1st 2 weeks Oct; Eng spkn; quiet; ccard acc; CCS. "Gd cycling; mkd walking trails; spacious, sheltered site; clean san facs; skiing on site in winter; Tividen National Park 5km." ♦ SEK 170 2009*

BOLLNAS *1C4* (3km E Rural) *61.3475, 16.43245* **Vevlingestrands Camping (X24), Vevlinge 3680, 82150 Bollnäs [(0278) 12684; info@vevlingestrand.com; www.vevlingestrand.com]** Fr Söderhamn take rd 50 twds Bollnäs; turn L at town edge & foll sp for Vevlinge & Segersta. In 600m foll sp Vevlingestrand to site; well sp. Med, mkd pitch, sl, unshd; wc; chem disp; baby facs; shwrs; el pnts (10A) SEK40; Indtte; shop; rest; snacks; cooking facs; playgrnd; lake sw & private beach adj; fishing; games area; Eng spkn; quiet; CCS. "Lovely lakeside setting; pleasant site." 1 May-30 Sep. SEK 150 2009*

⊞ **BORAS** *2E3* (2.5km N Urban) *57.73885, 12.93608* **Caming Borås Salteman (P11), Campinggatan 25, 50602 Borås [(033) 353280; fax 140582; info@borascamping.com; www.borascamping.com]** Exit N40 fr Göteborg for Borås Centrum; foll sps to Djur Park R42 to Trollhätten thro town; well sp. Lge, mkd pitch, pt shd; wc; chem disp; mv service pnt; shwrs inc; el pnts (10A) SEK30; Indry rm; shop 3km; rest; snacks; playgrnd; pool 500m; boating; bus 350m; Quickstop o'night facs; poss cr; Eng spkn; adv bkg; some rd noise; CCS. "Gd pitches adj rv with paths; gd zoo 500m; gd, clean facs." ♦ SEK 220 2008*

BORENSBERG *2G2* (1.5km S Rural) *58.55663, 15.27911* **Strandbadets Camping, 59030 Borensberg [(0141) 40385; info@strandbadetscamping.se; www.strandbadetscamping.se]** Site sp off rd 36. Med, pt shd; wc; mv service pnt; baby facs; shwrs; el pnts (10A) SEK40; Indtte; shop, rest in vill; snacks; cooking facs; playgrnd; lake sw & beach; fishing; few statics; quiet; CCS. "Gd base for Östergötland & Lake Vättern area; cycle rte along Göta Canal." 22 Apr-11 Sep. SEK 175 2008*

BROMMA see Stockholm *2H2*

BYSKE *1D2* (1.5km E Coastal) *64.94771, 21.23483* **Byske Havsbad Camping (AC19), Bäckgatan 40, 93047 Byske [(0912) 61290; fax 61526; byskehavsbad@skelleftea.se; www.byskehavsbad.com]** N on E4 coast rd, turn R (twd sea) at Byske & foll camp sp, site approx 3km fr E4. V lge, shd; htd wc; chem disp; mv service pnt; baby facs; shwrs inc; el pnts (10A) SEK50; Indtte (inc dryer); shop; rest; snacks; bar; playgrnd; htd pool; waterslides; sand beach; watersports; tennis; games area; cycle hire; wifi; entmnt; TV; some cabins; Quickstop o'night facs; adv bkg; quiet; ccard acc; red low ssn; CCS. ♦ 30 May-18 Sep. SEK 230 2008*

DALS LANGED see Bengtsfors *2E2*

DEGERFORS *2F2* (1.5km N Rural) *59.25145, 14.4595* **Degernäs Camping (T7), 69335 Degerfors [(0586) 44999; reception@degernascamping.se; www.degernascamping.se]** Fr rd 204, take rd 243 twds lake, site sp. Med, pt sl, pt shd; htd wc; chem disp; mv service pnt; baby facs; sauna; shwrs inc; el pnts (10A) SEK50; Indtte (inc dryer); shop; rest; snacks 2km; playgrnd; lake beach; fishing; boating; cycle hire; TV; 50% statics; poss cr; no adv bkg; quiet; ccard acc; CCS. ♦ 1 May-18 Sep. SEK 160 2011*

⊞ **DOROTEA** *1C3* (500m SW Rural) *64.26003, 16.39606* **Doro Camping, Storgatan 1A, 91070 Dorotea [(0942) 10238; fax 10779; reception@dorocamp.com; www.dorocamp.com]** Site on E side of E45. Med, pt sl, pt shd; wc; chem disp; sauna; baby facs; shwrs inc; el pnts (10A) SEK50; Indtte (inc dryer); shop; snacks; cooking facs; lake sw; playgrnd; fishing; golf; hiking; internet; some statics; site clsd Nov; poss cr; Eng spkn; quiet. ♦ SEK 135 2010*

⊞ **ED** *2E2* (2km E Rural) *58.89931, 11.93486* **Gröne Backe Camping (P8), Södra Moränvägen 64, 66832 Ed [(0534) 10144; fax 10145; gronebackecamping@telia.com]** App Ed on rd 164/166, site sp on Lake Lilla Le. Med, pt sl, shd; wc; chem disp; sauna; baby facs; shwrs SEK5; el pnts (10A) SEK40; Indtte (inc dryer); shops, rest, snacks 300m; playgrnd; lake sw; cycle hire; wifi; quiet; ccard acc; CCS. "Excel for boating." SEK 180 2009*

EKSHARAD *2F1* (1km E Rural) *60.1760, 13.5090* **Byns Camping (S3), Slätta, 68050 Ekshärad [(0563) 40885; fax 30196; info@bynscamping.eu; www.bynscamping.eu]** Turn E off rd 62 at x-rds by church, site sp on rv bank. Sm, pt shd; htd wc; chem disp; baby facs; shwrs SEK5; el pnts (10A) SEK35; Indtte (inc dryer); shop; snacks; cooking facs; playgrnd; cycle hire; phone; v quiet; ccard acc; CCS. "Pleasant site." ♦ 27 May-31 Aug. SEK 140 2010*

⊞ **EKSJO** *2F3* (1km E Rural) *57.66766, 14.98923* **Eksjö Camping (F13), Prästängsvägen 5, 57536 Eksjö [(0381) 39500; fax 14096; info@eksjocamping.se; www.eksjocamping.se]** Site sp fr town cent on rd 33 twd Västervik, on lakeside. Med, shd; wc; chem disp; mv service pnt; baby facs; shwrs; el pnts (10A) SEK45; Indtte (inc dryer); shop; rest; snacks; bar; playgrnd; covrd pool 100m; lake sw adj; fishing; boating; cycle hire; wifi; 10% statics; dogs; phone; poss cr; no adv bkg; quiet; ccard acc; CCS. "Gd cent glass region; attractive countryside & old town." ♦ SEK 140 2009*

ELDSBERGA see Halmstad *2E3*

SWEDEN

⊞ **ENKOPING** *2H1* (4km S Rural) *59.59334, 17.07146* **Bredsand Camping, Falkstigen 1, 74591 Bredsand [(0171) 80011; fax 80095; info@bredsand.com; http://bredsand.com]** Fr E18 or rd 55 foll sp to site, well sp on Lake Mälaren. Med, mkd pitch, pt sl, pt shd; htd wc; chem disp; mv service pnt; baby facs; shwrs inc; el pnts (10A) SEK50; Indtte (inc dryer); supmkt 4km; rest; snacks; lake sw & beach adj; 50% statics; dogs; quiet; CCS. "Vg site." SEK 210 2011*

ESKILSTUNA *2G2* (10km N Rural) *59.45138, 16.43700* **Mälarbadens Camping (D15), Mälarbadsvägen, 64436 Torshälla [(016) 343187; fax 343559; campingmalarbaden@gmail.com]** Fr Eskilstuna on E20 turn N to Torshälla & foll site sp N twds lake. Sm, hdg pitch, pt sl, pt shd; wc; chem disp; baby facs; el pnts (13A) SEK35; Indtte (inc dryer); shop 2km; tradsmn; rest; snacks; cooking facs; playgrnd; lake sw & beach 1km; sports stadium nr; 60% statics; dogs; phone; Eng spkn; adv bkg; quiet; CCI. "Vg, clean, peaceful site; gd security; gd for children." 1 May-15 Sep. SEK 195 2011*

FALKENBERG *2E3* (10km SE Coastal) *56.8234, 12.60955* **Ugglarps Camping (N30), Strandkantsvägen 2, 31169 Ugglarp [(0346) 43889; info@ugglarp.nu; www.ugglarp.nu]** Exit E6 junc 48, foll sp Slöinge, then site sp. Lge, mkd pitch, terr, pt shd; htd wc; chem disp; mv service pnt; baby facs; some serviced pitches; shwrs inc; el pnts (16A) inc; Indtte (inc dryer); shop; tradsmn; rest; snacks; bar; BBQ; cooking facs; playgrnd; beach adj; games rm; wifi; 15% statics; dogs; phone; Eng spkn; adv bkg; quiet; red low ssn; CCS. "Gd san facs." ♦ 21 Apr-11 Sep. SEK 340 2011*

FALKENBERG *2E3* (3km S Coastal) *56.88315, 12.51495* **Skrea Camping (N12), Strandvägen, 31142 Falkenberg [(0346) 17107; fax 15840; info@skreacamping.se; www.skreacamping.se]** Turn off E20/E6 at junc 50 to Falkenberg S, foll sp Skrea Strand to site. Lge, mkd pitch, pt shd; htd wc; chem disp; mv service pnt; baby facs; shwrs SEK2; el pnts (10-16A) SEK45; gas; Indtte (inc dryer); shop & 500m; rest 200m; BBQ; playgrnd; paddling pool; sand beach 250m; windsurfing; golf 5km; wifi; entmnt; sat TV; 20% statics; dogs; phone; Quickstop o'night facs; barrier clsd 2300-0600; poss cr; adv bkg; ccard acc; CCS. "Vg site; gd san facs." ♦ 20 Apr-4 Sep. SEK 295 2009*

FALKENBERG *2E3* (10km NW Coastal) *56.95551, 12.36641* **Rosendals Camping Morup (N26), Rosendalsvägen 22, 31198 Glommen [(0346) 97300; fax 97302; info@rosendalscamping.se; www.rosendalscamping.se]** Fr N on E6 exit junc 52 sp Morup/Glommen. Foll rd to x-rds by school (ent to Glommen vill). Turn R sp Morup & site on R in 3km at minor rds. Fr Falkenberg take rd sp Glommen at traff lts nr docks; foll 11km along coast rd to x-rds at ent to Glommen vill. Go across x-rds sp Morup & foll rd as above. Med, pt shd; wc; chem disp; baby facs; sauna; shwrs; el pnts (6A) SEK30; Indtte (inc dryer); shop; playgrnd; beach 1km; cycle hire; 60% statics; phone; dogs; Quickstop o'night facs; quiet; ccard acc; CCS. "Site yourself & owner calls." ♦ 1 Apr-11 Sep. SEK 190 2009*

⊞ **FALKOPING** *2F2* (1km W Rural) *58.17595, 13.52726* **Mössebergs Camping & Stugby (R7), Lidgatan 4, 52132 Falköping [(0515) 17349; mossebergscamping@telia.com]** Exit rd 184 at Falköping; foll Int'l Camping sps or sps to Mösseberg; site also sp fr rds 46 & 47 & in town. Site on plateau overlkg town. Med, mkd pitch, pt shd; wc; mv service pnt; baby facs; sauna; shwrs SEK5; el pnts SEK40; Indtte (inc dryer); cooking facs; shops 1km; playgrnd; pool 400m; lake sw 400m; wifi; some cabins; dogs; phone; quiet; ccard acc; CCS. ♦ SEK 150 2009*

⊞ **FALUN** *2G1* (2km NE Rural) *60.61941, 15.6525* **Lugnets Camping (W20), Lugnetvägen 5, 79183 Falun [(023) 83563; info@lugnetscamping.se; www.lugnetscamping.se]** Site sp on ent to town. Med, mkd pitch, terr, unshd; wc; chem disp; baby facs; sauna; shwrs inc; el pnts (10A) SEK40; Indtte (inc dryer); shop; rest; snacks high ssn; bar; playgrnd; htd pool adj; tennis 300m; cycle hire; golf 3km; wifi; Eng spkn; quiet; red 3+ days; CCS. "Adj major sports complex inc lge ski jump; excel." ♦ SEK 150 2008*

⊞ **FALUN** *2G1* (4km S Rural) *60.58111, 15.67675* **Främby Udde Camping (W55), Främby Udde 20, 79153 Falun [(023) 19784; info@frambyudde.com; www.frambyudde.com]** Exit rd 50 at Tallens shopping cent & foll sp to Främby. Fr cent of Falun take Myntgatan twd Källviken. Turn L at Falu riding club & foll track to site. Sm, mkd pitch, hdstg, pt shd; htd wc; chem disp; mv service pnt; shwrs inc; el pnts (10A) SEK40; Indtte (inc dryer); rest; BBQ; cooking facs; playgrnd; beach adj; sw & boating; games area; wifi; entmnt; 30% statics; dogs; Eng spkn; adv bkg; quiet; ccard acc; CCS. "Friendly, family-run site in picturesque area; vg." ♦ SEK 155 2008*

⊞ **FILIPSTAD** *2F1* (1km N Rural) *59.72035, 14.15899* **Munkeberg Camping (S5), Skillervägen, 68233 Filipstad [tel/fax (0590) 50100; alterschwede@telia.com; www.munkeberg.com]** Fr Karlstad take rd 63 to Filipstad. In town foll sp for rd 246 twd Hagfors, site sp in town. Med, pt sl, pt shd; htd wc; chem disp; shwrs inc; el pnts (10A) SEK30; Indtte (inc dryer); shop 1km; snacks; playgrnd; lake sw; boating; fishing; wifi; some statics; dogs; adv bkg; quiet; CCS/CCI. "Beautiful lakeside site; gd for touring old mining district." ♦ SEK 160 2009*

FINNERODJA *2F2* (5km W Rural) *58.92808, 14.33558* **Skagern Camping (T26), 69593 Finnerödja [tel/fax (0506) 33040; camp.skagern@telia.com]** S fr Örebro & Laxå on E20, vill is sp. Med, mkd pitch, sl, pt shd; htd wc; chem disp; mv service pnt; sauna; baby facs; shwrs; el pnts (10A) inc; Indtte (inc dryer); shop; tradsmn; BBQ; playgrnd; sand beach/lake; boat hire; fishing; games area; games rm; wifi; TV; 75% statics; dogs; Quickstop o'night facs; Eng spkn; quiet; ccard acc; CCS/CCI. "Vg site; levelling blocks req." 1 May-30 Sep. SEK 230 2011*

SWEDEN

FJALLBACKA *2E2* (3.5km N Coastal) *58.63125, 11.27283* **Långsjö Camping (O12), Långesjö Vikarna 22, 45071 Fjällbacka [(0525) 12116; info@langsjocamping.se; www.langsjocamping.se]** Exit E6 at junc 103 & foll rd 163 to Fjällbacka. Site sp in vill, narr ent. Sm, pt shd; wc; chem disp; mv service pnt; baby facs; shwrs SEK5; el pnts (10A) SEK45; Indtte (inc dryer); shop; snacks; BBQ; cooking facs; playgrnd; beach adj; fishing; cycle hire; games area; games rm; wifi; entmnt; some statics; dogs; poss cr; Eng spkn; quiet; ccard acc; CCI. "Gd site; beautiful vill." ♦ 1 May 13 Sep. SEK 250 2009*

FJARAS see Kungsbacka *2E3*

FROSON see Östersund *1B3*

⊞ **GADDEDE** *1B2* (1km NE Rural) *64.50400, 14.14900* **Gäddede Camping, Sagavägen 9, 83090 Gäddede [(0672) 10035; fax 10511; info@gaddedecamping.se; www.gaddedecamping.se]** On ent Gäddede cent on rd 342, turn R & site in 500m on R, sp. Med, mkd pitch, pt shd; htd wc; chem disp; sauna; shwrs SEK5; el pnts (10A) SEK50; Indtte; shop 500m; rest 100m; playgrnd; htd pool; paddling pool; canoe hire; fishing; games area; games rm; TV; 40% statics; dogs; poss cr; Eng spkn; adv bkg; quiet; ccard acc; CCI. "Gd touring base 'Wilderness Way'." ♦ SEK 130 2009*

GALLIVARE *1C2* (1km S Urban) *67.1290, 20.6776* **Gällivare Campingplats (BD5), Kvarnbacksvägen 2, 98231 Gällivare [(0970) 10010; fax 10030; info@gellivarecamping.com; www.gellivarecamping.com]** 300m S off rd 45, sp on Rv Vassara. Med, pt shd; htd wc; chem disp; baby facs; sauna; shwrs inc; el pnts (10A) SEK50; Indtte (inc dryer); shop; rest, snacks 1km; rest; playgrnd; cycle hire; wifi; TV; 10% statics; phone; ccard acc; CCS. "Helpful, friendly owners; pleasant pitches on rvside; gd facs." ♦ 16 May-19 Sep. SEK 160 2008*

GAMLEBY *2G2* (1km SE Coastal) *57.88475, 16.41373* **Hammarsbadets Camping (H2), Hammarsvägen 10, 59432 Gamleby [(0493) 10221; fax 12686; info@campa.se; www.campa.se]** On E22 Kalmar-Norrköping, foll sp to site 2km off main rd. Med, mkd pitch, terr, pt shd; wc; chem disp; mv service pnt; baby facs; sauna; shwrs SEK5; el pnts (10A) SEK45; Indtte (inc dryer); shop; tradsmn; rest; snacks; bar; playgrnd; pool; sand beach adj; lake sw; boat & cycle hire; tennis; wifi; some statics; dogs; phone; Quickstop o'night facs; quiet; ccard acc; CCS/CCI. "Clean, well-kept, relaxing site." 30 Apr-13 Sep. SEK 190 2009*

GAVLE *2H1* (10km NE Coastal) *60.72946, 17.29145* **Engesbergs Camping & Stugby, Solviksvägen 7, 80595 Gävle [(026) 99025; fax 99347; info@engesbergscamping.se; www.engesbergscamping.se]** Site sp along coast rd to Bönan. Lge, pt sl, pt shd; wc; chem disp; mv service pnt; shwrs inc; el pnts (10A) SEK40 or metered; shop; snacks; playgrnd; statics; dogs; poss cr; quiet; ccard acc; CCS. "Lovely site, mostly in trees." ♦ 1 May-1 Oct. SEK 150 2009*

⊞ **GESUNDA** *1B4* (2km N Rural) *60.90100, 14.58500* **Solleröns Camping (W60), Levsnäs, 79290 Sollerön [(0250) 22230; fax 22268; info@sollerocamping.se; www.sollerocamping.se]** Fr Gesunda take bdge to Sollerön Island in Lake Siljan. Site immed on R on reaching island; clearly visible fr bdge. Lge, pt sl, pt shd; wc; chem disp; mv service pnt; baby facs; sauna; shwrs inc ; el pnts (10A) SEK30; Indtte (inc dryer); shop; rest; snacks; bar; playgrnd; lake sw adj; canoe & boat hire; tennis; wifi; poss cr; adv bkg; quiet; ccard acc; CCS/CCI. "Beautiful outlook to S across lake; gd base for Dalarna folklore area; gd site & facs; Every 7th day is free." ♦ SEK 190 2011*

We can fill in site report forms on the Club's website – www.caravanclub.co.uk/europereport

GLAVA *2E1* (10km S Rural) *59.4768, 12.68526* **Sölje Camping (S61), Tångeberg, 67020 Glava [(0570) 464141; fax 464142; solje.camping@telia.com]** Fr Arvika take rd 175 S. Just bef Stömne (approx 30km) turn R sp Sulvik. Foll sp at Sölje x-rds. Sm, pt sl, unshd; wc; chem disp; mv service pnt; baby facs; sauna; shwrs SEK5; el pnts SEK40; Indtte (inc dryer); kiosk; cooking facs; playgrnd; lake sw adj, fishing; boat & cycle hire; games area; wifi; entmnt; some statics; dogs; CCS. "Idyllic lakeside location; peaceful - a real find." ♦ 1 Jun-31 Aug. SEK 140 2011*

GLOMMEN see Falkenberg *2E3*

⊞ **GOTEBORG** *2E3* (4km E Rural) *57.7053, 12.0286* **Lisebergsbyn Camping Kärralund (O39), Olbersgatan 1, 41655 Göteborg [(031) 840200; fax 840500; lisebergsbyn@liseberg.se; www.liseberg.se]** Exit E6/E20 junc 71 onto rd 40 E & foll sp Lisebergsbyn, site well sp. Lge, pt sl, terr, pt shd; wc; chem disp; mv service pnt; fam bthrm; baby facs; shwrs inc; el pnts (10A) inc; gas; Indtte (inc dryer); shop (open only once a week low ssn); supmkt nrby; playgrnd; wifi; TV; phone; tram 400m; poss cr/noisy high ssn; Eng spkn; adv bkg rec; ccard acc; red low ssn & Sun-Fri; CCS. "Boat trips arranged; vg, well-run site; low ssn arr early to obtain barrier key; poss itinerants on site; cycle path to Liseberg amusement park & town cent." SEK 450 2011*

GOTEBORG *2E3* (7km S Rural) *57.6461, 11.9935* **Krono Camping Göteberg/Åby (O20), Idrottsvägen 13, 43162 Mölndal [(031) 878884; fax 7760240; kronocamping@telia.com; www.kronocamping.nu]** Take E6 S to Mölndal & exit junc 66 dir Åby, foll sp to site. Lge; wc; chem disp; mv service pnt; some serviced pitches; baby facs; sauna; shwrs inc; el pnts (10A) SEK50 (inc cab TV); Indtte (inc dryer); shop; playgrnd; pool, games area & tennis nr; games rm; wifi; cab TV; 70% statics; dogs; phone; bus/tram; rd noise; ccard acc; CCS. "Low ssn arrive early to obtain barrier key for access to site; many residential/workers' statics: take care security; 20 mins fr ferries." ♦ 1 May-31 Aug. SEK 225 2009*

GOTEBORG *2E3* (10km S Coastal) *57.62871, 11.92080* **Lisebergs Camping Askim Strand (O38), Marholmsvägen 122, 43645 Askim [(031) 840200; fax 681335; askim.strand@liseberg.se; www.liseberg.se]** Fr E6 exit S of Göteborg sp Hamnar/Mölndal, join dual c'way rd 158 & foll int'l camp sps & Askim. Turn off at yellow junc & cont to foll int'l camp sps. Avoid Mölndal cent. Fr ferry head towards Särö & rd 158, foll sp Askim & site. Turn off by Näset junc (yellow bdge) & foll site symbol approx 2 km after exit. Lge, mkd pitch, unshd; htd wc; chem disp; mv service pnt; baby facs; fam bthrm; sauna; shwrs inc; el pnts (10A) inc; gas; Indtte (inc dryer); shop; playgrnd; beach 200m; watersports; fishing; cycle hire; wifi; TV; some statics; dogs; phone; bus; poss cr & noisy high ssn; ccard acc; CCS. "Clean, well-run site; clean, modern facs; private san facs avail; conv for Göteborg & ferries; gd position nr beach; tightly packed pitches high ssn." ♦ 20 Apr-4 Sep. SEK 365 2008*

GOTEBORG *2E3* (15km NW Coastal) *57.7434, 11.7566* **Göteborgs Camping Lilleby (O40), Lillebyvägen 100, 42353 Torslanda [(031) 562240; fax 562246; lillebycamping@gmail.com; www.goteborgscamping.se]** Fr S on E6 pass thro Tingstads Tunnel in Göteborg & immed turn W onto R155 & foll sp Torslanda. Site sp fr N on E6; immed S of Kungälv, exit W at sps for Säve; foll sp to Torslanda; site sp. Med, mkd pitch, pt shd; wc; chem disp; mv service pnt; shwrs inc; el pnts SEK50; gas; Indtte (inc dryer); shop; cooking facs; playgrnd; sw at rocky beach 250m with waterchute; bus adj; poss cr; Eng spkn; poss noisy in ssn; ccard acc; CCS. "V attractive area; meadowland; clean & pleasant with gd bus nr ent; avoid arr or dep rush hr - traffic fr Volvo factory; facs stretched in ssn; friendly, helpful staff." 1 Jun-28 Aug. SEK 200 2010*

GOTHENBURG see Göteborg *2E3*

GRANNA *2F2* (9km N Rural) *58.0962, 14.53271* **Getingaryds Familjecamping (F2), Getingaryd, 56391 Gränna [(0390) 21015; getingaryd.camping@tele2.se]** Leave E4 for lakeside rd at Ödeshög (S) or Gränna (N); site well sp. Med, pt sl, unshd; wc; chem disp; baby facs; shwrs SEK2; el pnts (10A) SEK30; gas; Indtte (inc dryer); sm shop & 9km; tradsmn; bar; playgrnd; fishing; boating; lake adj; pony rides; cycle hire; TV; some statics; dogs; Quickstop o'night facs; some Eng spkn; adv bkg; CCS. "Pleasant, well-run but basic farm site on lake shore; gd san facs but lack of privacy; friendly staff." ♦ 1 May-30 Sep. SEK 140 2008*

GRANNA *2F2* (9km S Rural) *57.92446, 14.32341* **Vätterledens Camping (F4), Vättersmålen 7, 56393 Gränna [(036) 52167; vatterledenscamping@glocalnet.net; www.vatterledenscamping.se]** Site sp off E4 bet Jönköping & Gränna, behind a motel. Sm, pt sl, unshd; htd wc; chem disp; mv service pnt; baby facs; shwrs inc; el pnts (10A) SEK40; Indtte (inc dryer); rest, snacks, bar 200m; wifi; TV rm; some cabins; Eng spkn; quiet; CCS. "Ltd facs but clean; helpful owner; pitches waterlogged after rain, but tractor avail; gd NH." 1 May-14 Aug. SEK 150 2011*

GRANNA *2F2* (500m NW Rural) *58.02783, 14.45821* **Grännastrandens Familjecamping (F3), Hamnen, 56300 Gränna [(0390) 10706; fax 41260; info@grannacamping.se; www.grannacamping.se]** In cent of Gränna down rd twd Lake Vättern, sp Visingsö Island. Lge, unshd; wc; chem disp; mv service pnt; baby facs; shwrs; el pnts (10A) metered + conn fee; Indtte (inc dryer); shop; rest adj; playgrnd; lake sw & beach; wifi; sat TV; some cottages; dogs; poss v cr; CCS. "Ballooning cent of Sweden; Visingsö Island, Brahehus ruined castle, glass-blowing 3km; vg site; gd location; gd san facs; excel camp kitchen." ♦ 30 Apr-3 Oct. SEK 240 2011*

⊞ **GREBBESTAD** *2E2* (1km S Coastal) *58.6832, 11.2625* **Grebbestads Familjecamping (O10), Rörvik, 45795 Grebbestad [(0525) 61211; fax 14319; info@grebbestadfjorden.com; www.grebbestadfjorden.com]** Exit E6 at Tanumshede sp Grebbestad; foll rd thro vill, past harbour; site on R approx 500m after harbour. Lge, mkd pitch, pt sl, unshd; wc; chem disp; mv service pnt; baby facs; sauna; shwrs inc; el pnts (10A) SEK50; Indtte (inc dryer); sm shop & 500m; snacks; cooking facs; htd pool 1km; sand beach 150m; games area; wifi; mainly statics; phone; dogs; poss cr; Eng spkn; adv bkg; quiet; ccard acc; CCS. "Well-maintained site 500m fr busy fishing/yachting harbour; meadowland; excel mv services; helpful staff." ♦ SEK 285 2011*

GRYT *2G2* (2km E Coastal) *58.17378, 16.85228* **KustCamp Ekön (E27), Ekövägen, 61042 Gryt [(0123) 40283; fax 12686; ekon@campa.se; www.campa.se]** Exit E2 sp Valdemarsvik, then rd 212 twd Gryt. Approx 2 km after Gryt turn R into Ekövägen. Foll site sp. Med, unshd; htd wc; chem disp; mv service pnt; baby facs; shwrs inc; el pnts (10A) SEK45; Indtte (inc dryer); shop; rest; snacks; BBQ; cooking facs; playgrnd; beach adj; canoe & boat hire; games area; internet; 30% statics; dogs; poss cr; Eng spkn; quiet; ccard acc; CCI. "Gd walking & cycling; gd." ♦ 1 Apr-13 Sep. SEK 160 2009*

HALMSTAD *2E3* (6km SE Coastal) *56.63587, 12.89996* **Hagöns Camping (N17), Östra Stranden, 30260 Halmstad [(035) 125363; fax 124365; info@hagonscamping.se; www.hagonscamping.se]** Fr S exit A6 junc 43 sp Halmstad-S onto rd 117 Laholmsvägen twd Halmstad. In 300m turn L twds coast & foll sp. Lge, pt shd; wc; mv service pnt; baby facs; shwrs SEK5; el pnts (6-10A) SEK40; Indtte; shop; rest; snacks; bar; playgrnd; pool 12km; sand beach; naturist bathing area; fishing; some statics; dogs; phone; bus; poss cr; Quickstop o'night facs; m'way noise; ccard acc; CCS. "Nr extremely attractive town on W coast; excel beaches, pools; gd golf course; many interesting excursions." ♦ 20 Apr-31 Aug. SEK 240 2008*

⊞ **HALMSTAD** *2E3* (10km S Coastal) *56.59033, 12.94430* **Gullbrannagården Camping (N27), 31031 Eldsberga [tel/fax (035) 42180; mail@gullbrannagarden.se; www.gullbrannagarden.se]** Fr S site sp on E6. Lge, pt sl, pt shd; wc; chem disp; mv service pnt; baby facs; shwrs inc; el pnts SEK45; Indtte; shop; snacks; cooking facs; playgrnd; sand beach 500m; games rm; wifi; entmnt; 60% statics; dogs; poss cr; Eng spkn; adv bkg; quiet. "Christian-run site; church & bible classes; alcohol discouraged; OK for those of like mind." ♦ SEK 290 2009*

SWEDEN

HALMSTAD *2E3* (9km W Coastal) *56.66025, 12.74035* **First Camp Tylösand (N25), Kungsvägen 3, 30270 Tylösand [(035) 30510; fax 32778; tylosand@firstcamp.se; www.firstcamp.se]** Fr E6/E20 foll sps Halmstad Centrum, then Tylösand. Don't turn into Tylösand but foll sps for site. Lge, pt shd; wc; chem disp; sauna; shwrs; el pnts (10A) inc; lndtte (inc dryer); shop; tradsmn; rest 1km; snacks high ssn; cooking facs; playgrnd; sand beach 300m; fishing; cycle hire; games rm; golf 1km; wifi; entmnt; sat TV; some cabins; poss cr; quiet. "Excel site, fine beach; excel, modern facs; some pitches badly worn." ♦ 25 Apr-31 Aug. SEK 320 2008*

⊞ **HAMMARSTRAND** *1C3* (1km E Rural) *63.12030, 16.34330* **Hammarstrands Camping (Z6), Koppelhällsvägen 18, 84070 Hammarstrand [(0696) 10302; info@goragunda.com; www.goragunda.com]** Exit rd 87 N twd Hammarstrand onto rd 323. Cross rv bdge & take 1st R & 1st R again; site along gravel track in 1km. Sm, pt shd; wc; chem disp; shwrs; el pnts (10A) SEK30; lndtte (inc dryer); shop 1km; tradsmn; rest; snacks; bar; cooking facs; playgrnd; htd pool; sand beach 200m; games area; wifi; TV; some statics; dogs free; bus 1km; Eng spkn; adv bkg; quiet; ccard acc; red long stay; CCI. "Pleasant Dutch owners; gd site with basic, clean facs; views across rv; ideal NH." ♦ SEK 150 2011*

⊞ **HAPARANDA** *1D2* (15km N Rural) *65.9620, 24.0378* **Kukkolaforsen Camping (BD27), Kukkolaforsen 184, 95391 Haparanda [(0922) 31000; fax 31030; info@kukkolaforsen.se; www.kukkolaforsen.se]** On rd 99 on banks of Rv Tornionjoki. Med, pt shd; htd wc; chem disp; baby facs; sauna; shwrs inc; el pnts (10A) SEK40; lndtte; shop; rest; snacks; bar; playgrnd; fishing; cycle hire; TV; cabins; phone; adv bkg; ccard acc; CCS. "Friendly staff; rv rapids." SEK 210 2010*

HARNOSAND *1C3* (2.5km NE Coastal) *62.64451, 17.97123* **Sälstens Camping (Y21), Sälsten 22, 87133 Härnösand [tel/fax (0611) 18150; salsten.camping@telia.com]** On Gulf of Bothnia, E of town & on S side of inlet; exit off E4; foll sp for Härnösand town cent, then intn'l camping sp; then site. Sm, mkd pitch, terr, pt shd; htd wc; chem disp; shwrs inc; el pnts (10A) SEK30; lndtte (inc dryer); shop; playgrnd; beach; wifi; TV; Eng spkn; quiet; CCS. "Folk museum in town; excel site." ♦ 15 May-31 Aug. SEK 170 2009*

⊞ **HARNOSAND** *1C3* (8km SW Rural) *62.58648, 17.79083* **Antjärns Camping & Stugby (Y28), Antjärn 113, 87191 Härnösand [(0611) 74150; contact@antjarnscamping.com; www.antjarnscamping.com]** Fr E4 approx 30km N of Sundsvall, turn R at Antjärns & site sp, site on R in 300m. Sm, pt sl, unshd; htd wc; chem disp; sauna; shwrs inc; el pnts (10A) SEK25; lake sw; fishing; wifi; sat TV; dogs; adv bkg; some rd noise; ccard acc; CCI. "Beautiful lakeside setting; lovely town; pleasant owners; immac, modern facs." SEK 160 2009*

HEBERG see Falkenberg *2E3*

⊞ **HEDE** *1B3* (10km E Rural) *62.40899, 13.67394* **Sonfjällscampen, Hedeviken 753, 84093 Hede [tel/fax (0684) 12130; info@sonfjallscampen.se; www.sonfjallscampen.se]** Sp in vill of Hedivikens S of rd 84 on lakeside. Sm, pt shd; htd wc; chem disp; shwrs; el pnts (10A) SEK30; lndtte; shops adj; sand beach; fishing; boat hire; 60% statics; adv bkg; quiet; red facs low ssn; ccard acc; CCS. "Pleasant stay; helpful owner; gd facs; conv Sånfjallet National Park." SEK 130 2009*

HEDESUNDA *2G1* (5km SE Rural) *60.35000, 17.02100* **Sandsnäs Camping, Övägen 68, 81040 Hedesunda [tel/fax (0291) 44123; info@hedesundacamping.se; www.hedesundacamping.se]** Exit rd 67 L at sp Hedesunda. Foll camp sp thro Hedesunda; past church, cont about 4km to Hedesunda Island. Sm, pt shd; htd wc; chem disp; shwrs inc; el pnts (6A) SEK30; gas; lndtte (inc dryer); shop 3km; rest; snacks; cooking facs; playgrnd; sand beach & lake sw adj; boat hire; fishing; TV; poss cr at w/end; Eng spkn; quiet; red 16+ days; CCS. "Peaceful, lakeside site; organised activities in ssn; helpful staff." ♦ 15 Apr-15 Nov. SEK 175 2010*

HEDEVIKEN see Hede *2B3*

⊞ **HELSINGBORG** *2E4* (5km S Coastal) *56.0034, 12.7300* **Campingplatsen Råå Vallar (M3), Kustgatan, 25270 Råå [(042) 182600; fax 107681; raavallar@nordiccamping.se; www.nordiccamping.se]** Exit E6 into Helsingborg onto rd 111 to Råå, foll sp to camp. Lge, pt shd; htd wc; baby facs; sauna; shwrs inc; el pnts (10A) SEK50; gas; lndtte (inc dryer); shop; rest; snacks; bar; playgrnd; pool; paddling pool; sand beach; fishing; sports cent 2km; golf 5km; wifi; some statics; phone; Quickstop o'night facs; poss cr; ccard acc; CCS/CCI. "Excel, secure site with gd facs; friendly staff; excursions to Copenhagen via Helsingør or Landskrona; town bus excursions to King's Summer Palace daily; boat trips to glass works at Hyllinge." ♦ SEK 270 2010*

HELSINGBORG *2E4* (7km S Rural) *56.0020, 12.77265* **Camping Stenbrogårdens (M4), Rausvägen, 25592 Helsingborg [(042) 290600; raavallar@nordiccamping.se]** Exit E6 at Helsingborg S exit & foll sp to site. Sp also on Rausvägen rd fr Helsingborg to Ekeby & Bårslöv. Lge, pt shd; htd wc; chem disp; mv service pnt; shwrs inc; el pnts (10A) SEK50; gas; shop; snacks; playgrnd; pool 3km; sand beach 2km; dogs; phone; Quickstop o'night facs; adv bkg; some rd noise; ccard acc; 10% red long stay; CCS. "Conv for ferry to Denmark; poss itinerants (Jul 08)." ♦ 1 Jul-7 Aug. SEK 170 2008*

HILLERSTORP *2F3* (4km NE Rural) *57.34200, 13.96200* **Ågård Lantgårds Camping, Ågård, 33033 Hillerstorp [(0370) 82170; fax 82450; info@kulantrading.se; www.kulantrading.se]** Fr E4 exit Värnamo (N) junc 85; rd 151 to Hillerstorp; rd 152 n; turn R at sp Ågård & site. Med, unshd; wc; chem disp; shwrs; el pnts (10A); lndtte; shop; rest; snacks; bar; playgrnd; pool; fishing; 5% statics; Eng spkn; adv bkg; some rd noise; ccard acc; 25% red long stay. "Storemosse National Park 4km; High Chaparral Wild West Park 4km; gd for children - farm animals; excel." 1 Apr-30 Sep. 2008*

SWEDEN

⊞ **HINDAS** *2E3* (1km E Urban) *57.70615, 12.4620* **Hindås Camping (O65), Boråsvägen 3, 43063 Hindås [(0301) 10088; fax 10064; hicamp@telia.com; www.hindascamping.se]** Fr Göteborg on rd 40 for approx 35km. Exit at sp Hindås & foll sp for approx 10km. Site adj petrol stn, recep at g'ge. Sm, hdstg, pt shd; htd wc; chem disp; baby facs; shwrs inc; el pnts (10A) inc; Indtte (inc dryer); shop adj & 500m; lake sw & beach adj; sat TV; some statics; dogs; bus 100m; poss cr; adv bkg; rd noise; red long stay; CCS. "Pleasant area." SEK 220 2008*

HJO *2F2* (600m N Rural) *58.30986, 14.30311* **Hjo Camping (R11), Karlsborgsvägen, 54432 Hjo [(0503) 31052; fax 13264; campinghjo@hotmail.com; www.hjocamping.se]** Sp fr town cent on lakeside. Med, mkd pitch; wc, chem disp; mv service pnt; baby facs; shwrs inc; el pnts (10A) SEK40; Indtte (inc dryer); shop; bar; cooking facs; playgrnd; htd pool; lake adj; fishing; games area; wifi; some statics; Eng spkn; ccard acc; CCS. "Delightful wooden town; gd." 1 Apr-1 Oct. SEK 180 2010*

HOGANAS *2E4* (8km N Rural) *56.27061, 12.52981* **FirstCamp Mölle (M1), Kullabergsvägen, 26042 Mölle [(042) 347384; fax 347729; molle@firstcamp.se; www.firstcamp.se]** Site is S of Mölle at junc of rds 11 & 111, at foot of Kullaberg. Lge, pt sl, unshd; htd wc; chem disp; mv service pnt; sauna; shwrs inc; el pnts (10A) inc; Indtte (inc dryer); shop; rest; snacks; bar; cooking facs; playgrnd; beach 1.5km; fishing; games area; walking; golf; wifi; entmnt; 10% statics; dogs; Quickstop o'night facs; Eng spkn; quiet; ccard acc. "Steep slope to san facs; Krapperups Castle & park sh walk fr site; excel outdoor activities." ♦ 1 Feb-14 Nov. SEK 275 2010*

HOGANAS *2E4* (2km S Coastal) *56.18194, 12.55805* **Camping Lerbergets (M2), Lerbergsvägen 108, 26352 Lerberget [(042) 331400; camping@lerberget.se; www.lerbergetscamping.se]** Exit E20 at junc 33 W to Höganäs, then turn S along coast rd. Site in 2km bef Viken. Med, shd; wc; chem disp; mv service pnt; baby facs; shwrs inc; el pnts SEK45; gas; Indtte (inc dryer); shop, rest 1km; playgrnd; sand beach adj; cycle hire; internet; 80% statics; bus adj; Eng spkn; quiet; ccard acc; CCI. "Lovely coast; access to site by phoning for number of box for plastic gate-opener (doubles for shwr); gd." ♦ 1 Apr-25 Sep. SEK 200 2009*

HOVA *2F2* (6 NE) *58.90998, 14.28995* **Otterbergets Bad & Camping, 548 91 Hova [050633 127; info@otterbergetscamping.com; www.otterbergetscamping.com]** Fr Laxa take E20 rd; site sp approx 4km fr Hova; drive 2 km thro woods to site. Med, mkd pitch, pt shd; wc; chem disp; baby facs; shwrs (metered); el pnts (10A) SEK 40; Indtte; snacks; BBQ; playgrnd; sauna; beach adj; 10% statics; poss cr; Eng spkn; adv bking; quiet; red low ssn. "Attractive site with private access to lake; events held such as fishing competition & trade fairs (when site may be busy); v helpful Dutch owners." ♦ 01 May-30 Sep. SEK 190 2011*

⊞ **HOVMANTORP** *2G3* (SE Urban) *56.7839, 15.13081* **Gökaskratts Campingplats (G11), Bruksallén, 36051 Hovmantorp [(0478) 40807; fax 40822; jonnan.s@live.se]** On Lake Rottnen S of town. Med, mkd pitch, pt shd; htd wc; chem disp; baby facs; shwrs; el pnts (10A) inc; Indtte (inc dryer); shop; rest; playgrnd; lake sw adj; fishing; boating; cycle hire; wifi; TV; 10% statics; phone; Quickstop o'night facs; poss cr; quiet; ccard acc; CCS. "Conv rlwy stn for Gothenborg/Kalmar." ♦ SEK 200 2011*

HULT *2G3* (1km N Rural) *57.65583, 15.12435* **Movänta Camping (F14), Badvägen 4, 57592 Hult [(0381) 30028; fax 30166; info@movantacamping.se; www.movantacamping.se]** Fr Eksjö rd 33 E to Hult, turn L into vill, foll sp to lakeside. Med, mkd pitch, some hdstg, pt shd; htd wc; chem disp; mv service pnt; baby facs; shwrs; el pnts (10A) SEK40; Indtte (inc dryer); shop; snacks; bar; playgrnd; lake sw adj; fishing; sailing; wifi; TV; some statics; dogs; phone; Quickstop o'night facs; Eng spkn; quiet; ccard acc; CCS. "Conv Eksjö & Skurugata canyon." ♦ 29 Apr-25 Sep. SEK 185 2011*

⊞ **JARNA** *2H2* (2km E Coastal) *59.09801, 17.64825* **Farstanäs Camping, Farsta 1, 15391 Järna [(08551) 50215; fax 50650; info@farstanashf.se; www.vatterledenscamping.se]** Exit E4 junc 141 for Järna, E fr m'way site sp past filling stn about 6km fr exit. Lge, pt sl, pt shd; wc; mv service pnt; baby facs; shwrs; el pnts (10A) SEK40; Indtte; shop; rest; snacks; bar; playgrnd; pool; sand beach & sw; fishing; boat hire; 25% statics; dogs; phone; poss cr; quiet; CCS. "Conv Södertälje & Stockholm on m'way; superb wooded location." ♦ SEK 250 2011*

JOHANNISHOLM *1B4* (Rural) *60.82630, 14.12660* **Johannisholm Camping, 79292 Johannisholm [tel/fax (0250) 60000; johannisholm@hotmail.com; www.johannisholm.com]** On rd 45 at junc with rd 26 to Vansbro. Site is 35km SW of Mora adj Lake Örklingen. Med, unshd; wc; chem disp; shwrs SEK5; el pnts (10A) SEK30; Indtte; tradsmn; rest, snacks, bar adj; cooking facs; playgrnd; lake sw & sand beach adj; watersports; fishing; boat & cycle hire; some statics; phone; Eng spkn; adv bkg; quiet. "Gd facs; outdoor activity cent; gd NH." 1 Apr-31 Aug. SEK 150 2008*

JOKKMOKK *1C2* (3km SE Rural) *66.59453, 19.89145* **Jokkmokk Camping Center (BD4), Notudden, 96222 Jokkmokk [(0971) 12370; fax 12476; campingcenter@jokkmokk.com; www.jokkmokkcampingcenter.com]** Sp fr rd 45. In Jokkmokk take rd 97 E, site in 3km on N side of rd situated bet rv & rd. Lge, mkd pitch, pt shd; htd wc; chem disp; mv service pnt; sauna; shwrs inc; el pnts (10A) SEK40 (poss rev pol); Indtte (inc dryer); sm shop & 3km; rest; snacks; bar; playgrnd; 3 htd pools high ssn; waterslide; lake sw adj; fishing; cycle hire; internet; some statics; dogs; Eng spkn; adv bkg; ccard acc; quiet; CCS. "Friendly, clean, well-maintained site 5km inside Arctic Circle; gd area for Sami culture; excel playgrnd; lakeside setting, gd pool." ♦ 20 May-31 Aug. SEK 195 2011*

SWEDEN

⊞ **JOKKMOKK** *1C2* (3km W Rural) *66.60500, 19.76200* **Skabram Stugby & Camping, 96224 Skabram [(0971) 10752; info@skabram.com; www.skabram.com]** Site sp fr E45 along rd 97, Storgatan. Sm, pt hdstg, pt shd; htd wc; sauna; shwrs inc; el pnts (10A) SEK25; Indry rm; BBQ; cooking facs; lake sw adj; boating; fishing; Eng spkn; adv bkg; quiet. "Gd; canoe & dog sleigh trips; relaxing site." SEK 125 2008*

⊞ **JONKOPING** *2F3* (2.5km E Urban) *57.7876, 14.2195* **Swecamp Villa Björkhagen (F6), Friggagatan 31, 55454 Jönköping [(036) 122863; fax 126687; info@villabjorkhagen.se; www.villabjorkhagen.se]** Fr N exit E4 junc 99 or fr S exit E4 junc 98a & foll sp Rosenlund/Elmia & site sp nr exhibition cent. Site on Lake Vättern. Lge, mkd pitch, pt sl, pt shd; htd wc; chem disp; mv service pnt; baby facs; sauna; shwrs inc; el pnts (10A) SEK35; Indtte (inc dryer) shop; rest; bar; playgrnd; htd, covrd pool complex, waterslide 300m; lake sw 500m; fishing; cycle hire; wifi; entmnt; sat TV; 50% statics; dogs; phone; Quickstop o'night facs; poss v cr; quiet; ccard acc; CCS. "Gd rest; prone to flooding after heavy rain; some facs run down & site untidy (6/10); site charges increase considerably during exhibitions & site v full." ♦ SEK 265 (CChq acc) 2010*

JONKOPING *2F3* (12km S Rural) *57.66245, 14.18407* **Lovsjöbadens Camping (F7), Hyltena, 55592 Jönköping [(036) 182010; info@lovsjocamping.se; www.lovsjocamping.se]** Exit E4 at Hyltena, site sp on lakeside. Sm, mkd pitch, terr, pt sl; wc; chem disp; baby facs; shwrs inc; el pnts (10-16A) SEK30; Indtte (inc dryer); tradsmn; snacks; BBQ; cooking facs; lake sw; boat & cycle hire; games rm; wifi; TV; some statics; dogs; Eng spkn; adv bkg; quiet; ccard acc; CCS. "V friendly owners; vg site." ♦ 14 May-12 Sep. SEK 190 2011*

KALMAR *2G3* (2km S Coastal) *56.64975, 16.32705* **Stensö Camping (H12), Stensövägen, 39247 Kalmar [(0480) 88803; fax 420476; info@stensocamping.se; www.stensocamping.se]** Fr E22 foll sp Sjukhus (hosp) then camping sp - this avoids town cent. Fr town cent, site sp. Lge, some mkd pitch, pt sl, shd; wc; chem disp; mv service pnt; baby facs; shwrs inc; el pnts (10A) SEK40 (check pol); Indtte (inc dryer); shop; tradsmn; rest; snacks; bar; cooking facs; playgrnd; pool 1km; sand beach adj; fishing; boating; cycling; wifi; some cabins; phone; Quickstop o'night facs; Eng spkn; ccard acc; CCS. "San facs old & run down, but clean; conv Öland Island (over bdge); glass factories in vicinity; walking dist to town; helpful, friendly staff." ♦ 20 Apr-2 Oct. SEK 170 2008*

KAPPELLSKAR *2H1* (500m W Rural) *59.72046, 19.05045* **Camping Kapellskär (B9), Riddersholm 985, 76015 Gräddö [(0176) 44233]** Fr Norrtälje take E18 E sp Kapellskär. At ferry sp turn R, site in 1km, sp. Last 700m on unmade rd. Med, mkd pitch, some hdstg, terr, pt shd; htd wc; chem disp; mv service pnt; baby facs; shwrs inc; el pnts (10A) SEK40; Indtte (inc dryer); shop; rest 1.5km; snacks; bar; playgrnd; cycle hire; games area; 60% statics; dogs; Eng spkn; adv bkg; quiet; ccard acc; CCS. "Conv for ferry terminal; fair site." 1 May-30 Sep. SEK 160 2008*

KARLSBORG *2F2* (1km N Rural) *58.5453, 14.50075* **Karlsborgs Camping (R12), Norra Vägen 3, 54633 Karlsborg [(0505) 44916; fax 44912; info@karlsborgscamping.se; www.karlsborgscamping.se]** Heading N on rd 49 300m N of Göta canal on L of rd on Lake Bottensjö. Med, shd; wc; chem disp; mv service pnt; baby facs; shwrs SEK5; el pnts (10A) SEK40; gas; Indtte (inc dryer); shops adj; rest; snacks; bar; cooking facs; playgrnd; sand beach on lake; fishing; boating; wifi; TV; dogs; phone; poss noisy at w/end; ccard acc; CCS. "Gd touring base in beautiful location; gd fishing." ♦ 24 Apr-30 Sep. SEK 180 2010*

KARLSHAMN *2F4* (3km SE Coastal) *56.15953, 14.89085* **Kolleviks Camping (K7), Kolleviksvägen, 37430 Karlshamn [(0454) 19280; fax 16280; kollevik@karlshamn.se; www.karlshamn.se]** Fr E22 dir Karlshamn & Hamnar (harbour), then site well sp. Med, mkd pitch, pt sl, pt shd; htd wc; chem disp; mv service pnt; baby facs; shwrs SEK5; el pnts (10A) SEK45; Indtte (inc dryer); shop; rest; snacks; playgrnd; pool 1km; sand beach adj; canoeing; 25% statics; Quickstop o'night facs; Eng spkn; adv bkg; quiet; ccard acc; red long stay/low ssn; CCS. "Helpful owner; attractive location inc harbour; gd base for area; ltd facs low ssn; well-kept site." ♦ 26 Apr-14 Sep. SEK 155 2008*

KARLSKRONA *2G4* (4km N Coastal) *56.20158, 15.60546* **Skönstaviks Camping (K12), Ronnebyvägen, 37191 Karlskrona [(0455) 23700; fax 23792; info@skonstavikcamping.se; www.skonstavikcamping.se]** Rd 15/E22 fr Malmö, camp sp on app to Karskrona. Lge, pt sl, pt shd; htd wc; chem disp; mv service pnt; baby facs; shwrs; el pnts (10A) SEK45; Indtte; rest; snacks; bar; shop; playgrnd; sm sand beach; cycle hire; fishing; boating; wifi; entmnt; TV; 10% cabins; dogs; Quickstop o'night facs; quiet; ccard acc; CCS. ♦ 1 Apr-31 Aug. SEK 225 2011*

KARLSKRONA *2G4* (2km NE Coastal) *56.1729, 15.5675* **Dragsö Camping (K10), Dragsövägen, 37124 Karlskrona [(0455) 15354; fax 15277; info@dragso.se; www.dragsocamping.se]** Foll app to town cent, taking m'way. At end of m'way foll sp to Dragsö. Site sp - on its own island. Lge, mkd pitch, pt shd; htd wc; mv service pnt; baby facs; sauna; shwrs; el pnts (10A) inc; Indtte (inc dryer); kiosk; supmkt, rest 3km; snacks; bar; playgrnd; beach adj; fishing; boating; cycle hire; wifi; entmnt; TV rm; some statics; dogs; Quickstop o'night facs; poss v cr; CCS. "Sea bathing; rocky cliffs; scenic beauty; gd." ♦ 15 Apr-9 Oct. SEK 260 2009*

⊞ **KARLSTAD** *2F1* (6km W Rural) *59.37428, 13.38958* **First Camp Karlstad-Skutberget (S10), Skutbergsvägen, 65346 Karlstad [(054) 535120; fax 535121; karlstad@firstcamp.se; www.firstcamp.se]** Sp 1km S of E18, on Lake Vänern, also sp on rd 61 fr N. Lge, unshd; htd wc; mv service pnt; baby facs; sauna; shwrs; el pnts (10A); Indtte (inc dryer); shop; rest adj; snacks; bar; BBQ; cooking facs; playgrnd; sand & shgl beach 500m; fishing; sailing; cycle hire; fitness rm; sport facs adj; wifi; TV; dogs; Quickstop o'night facs; quiet; CCS. ♦ 2011*

SWEDEN

⊞ **KARLSTAD** *2F1* (9km W Rural) *59.36233, 13.35891* **Swecamp Bomstad-Badens (S9), Bomstadsvägen 640, 65346 Karlstad [(054) 535068; fax 535375; info@bomstad-baden.se; www.bomstadbaden.se]** 2km S of E18 on Lake Vänern. Foll sp thro woods. Lge, pt sl, shd; wc; chem disp; mv service pnt; baby facs; shwrs SEK10; el pnts (10A) SEK50; Indtte (inc dryer); shop; supmkt 4km; snacks; bar; BBQ; playgrnd; pool; sand beach; lake sw; fishing; canoeing; cycle hire; wifi; entmnt; statics; phone; adv bkg; CCS. "Excel base; beautiful site in trees; gd walks on mkd trails." ♦ SEK 220 2010*

⊞ **KATRINEHOLM** *2G2* (2km S Rural) *58.9696, 16.21035* **Djulöbadets Camping (D6), Djulögatan 51, 64192 Katrineholm [tel/fax (0150) 57242; djulocamping@hotmail.com; www.djulocamping.se]** At Norrköping on E4 cont twd Stockholm for about 3km, turn L onto rd 55 N twd Katrineholm. Camping site sp in 2km. Lge, hdstg, pt sl; wc; mv service pnt; baby facs; shwrs SEK1; el pnts (10A) SEK35; gas; Indtte (inc dryer); shop 2km; rest 2km; snacks; playgrnd; lake sw; boating; fishing; games area; cycle hire; wifi; poss cr; adv bkg; quiet; ccard acc; CCS. "On lakeside in lge park; well-run, friendly site." ♦ SEK 140 2009*

⊞ **KIL** *2F1* (6km N Rural) *59.54603, 13.34145* **Frykenbadens Camping (S17), Stubberud, 66591 Kil [(0554) 40940; fax 40945; info@frykenbaden.se; www.frykenbaden.se]** Fr Karlstad take rd 61 to Kil, site clearly sp on lakeside. Lge, pt sl, pt shd; wc; chem disp; mv service pnt; baby facs; sauna SEK5; shwrs; el pnts (10A) SEK40; Indtte (inc dryer); shop; snacks; bar; playgrnd; lake sw; fishing; boat-launching; cycle hire; wifi; TV; phone; Quickstop o'night facs; quiet; adv bkg; CCS. ♦ SEK 180 2008*

KINNA *2E3* (3km SE Rural) *57.47400, 12.70415* **DreamCamp Hanatorp (P14), Öresjövägen 26, 51131 Örby [(0320) 48312; fax 49314; info@dreamcamp.se; www.dreamcamp.se]** 3.2km E of junc rds 41 & 156, site sp 650m along rd to Öxabäck. Lge, mkd pitch, hdstg, pt shd; wc; chem disp; mv service pnt; baby facs; shwrs SEK5; el pnts (10A) SEK40; gas; Indtte (inc dryer); shop; rest; snacks; bar; playgrnd; htd, covrd pool 8km; lake sw adj; boat & cycle hire; golf 8km; wifi; TV; 20% statics; dogs; phone; Quickstop o'night facs; adv bkg; quiet; red long stay; ccard acc; CCS/CCI. "Variable pitch price; excel." ♦ 21 Apr-18 Sep. SEK 220 2010*

⊞ **KIRUNA** *1C1* (500m N Urban) *67.8604, 20.2405* **Ripan Hotel & Camping, Campingvägen 5, 98135 Kiruna [(0980) 63000; fax 63040; info@ripan.se; www.ripan.se]** Site sp fr town cent. Med, unshd, mkd pitch, hdstg; htd wc; chem disp; sauna; shwrs SEK20; el pnts (10A) inc; Indtte; shop 500m; rest; bar; playgrnd; htd pool; cab TV; poss cr; quiet; Eng spkn; ccard acc. "No privacy in shwrs; easy walk to town; public footpath thro site (top end) - poss v noisy & disruptive; trips to Kirunavaara Deep Mine fr tourist info office." ♦ SEK 170 2009*

KIVIK *2F4* (1km N Rural/Coastal) *55.69135, 14.21373* **Kiviks Familjecamping (L35), Väg 9, 27732 Kivik [(0414) 70930; fax 70934; info@kivikscamping.se; www.kivikscamping.se]** On rd 9 o'looking sea, sp. Med, mkd pitch, unshd; wc; chem disp; mv service pnt; baby facs; shwrs SEK5; el pnts SEK35; Indtte (inc dryer); shop; rest; BBQ; playgrnd; shgl/sand beach 1km; entmnt; TV rm; phone; 20% statics; dogs; Eng spkn; ccard acc; CCS. "Steam rlwy w/end in summer at Brösarp; cider/apple area; easy walk to town." ♦ 16 Apr-9 Oct. SEK 200 2008*

KLIPPAN *2F4* (1.5km E Urban) *56.13461, 13.16213* **Elfdalens Camping (L25), Vedbyvägen 69, 26437 Klippan [tel/fax (0345) 14678; elfdalens.camping@telia.com]** E fr Helsingborg on rd 21. Take E exit to Klippan & foll local sps. Med, pt shd; wc; chem disp; sauna; shwrs inc; el pnts (6A) SEK30; Indtte (inc dryer); shop 300m; snacks; cooking facs; playgrnd; wifi; 5% statics; phone; bus 3km; Eng spkn; quiet; CCS. "Vg, friendly site; gd touring base; gd walking." ♦ 1 Apr-15 Sep. SEK 130 2009*

KLIPPAN *2F4* (5km W Urban) *56.13186, 13.04481* **Kvidingebadets Camping (L16), Södra Järnvägsgatan 8, 26060 Kvidinge [(0435) 20125]** Fr Helsingborg on E4 sp Jönköping, after 25km at Åstorp turn onto rd 21. In 5km turn L onto minor rd sp Kvidinge. Site in cent of vill at municipal sw pool. Recep at pool closes 1600 hrs. Sm, mkd pitch, unshd; wc; chem disp; shwrs inc; el pnts (10A) SEK25; shop 500m; pool; Eng spkn; some rd noise; CCS. "Gd NH." 2 Jun-21 Aug. SEK 125 2008*

KOLMARDEN *2G2* (2km SE Coastal) *58.6597, 16.4006* **First Camp Kolmården (E3), 61834 Kolmården [(011) 398250; fax 397081; kolmarden@firstcamp.se; www.firstcamp.se]** Fr E4 NE fr Norrköping take 1st Kolmården exit sp Kolmården Djur & Naturpark. Site on sea 2km bef Naturpark. Lge, pt terr, pt shd; htd wc; chem disp; mv service pnt; baby facs; sauna; shwrs SEK5; el pnts (10A); Indtte (inc dryer); shop; kiosk; rest; snacks; bar; cooking facs; playgrnd; beach adj; waterslide; boat & cycle hire; entmnt; TV rm; 10% statics; dogs; phone; ccard acc; CCS. ♦ 30 Apr-11 Sep. 2011*

⊞ **KOSTA** *2G3* (W Rural) *56.84218, 15.39101* **Kosta Bad & Camping (G10), Rydvägen, 36502 Kosta [(0478) 50517; fax 50065; info@glasriketkosta.se; www.glasriketkosta.com]** On rd Rv28 in Kosta turn E at rd 28 by sp. Med, mkd pitch, pt shd; wc; chem disp; mv service pnt; fam bthrm; shwrs inc; el pnts (10A) SEK35; Indtte (inc dryer); shop 250m; snacks; bar; cooking facs; BBQ; playgrnd; htd pool; fishing; TV; some statics; dogs; phone; Eng spkn; CCS. "Situated in cent of 'Kingdom of Glass; Kosta Glassworks nrby worth visit; salmon & trout fishing in area; low ssn site youself, warden calls." ♦ SEK 145 2008*

⊞ **KRISTIANSTAD** *2F4* (4km SW Urban) *56.01988, 14.12586* **Charlottsborgs Camping (L20), Slättingsvägen 38, 29160 Kristianstad [(044) 210767; fax 200278; info@charlottsborgsvandrarhem.com; www.charlottsborgsvandrarhem.com]** On E22, site sp app junc with rd 21, site within 500m. Med, mkd pitch, pt shd; wc; chem disp; mv service pnt; shwrs inc; el pnts (10A) SEK40; Indtte (inc dryer); shop 200m; rest 500m; snacks; playgrnd; pool 3km; wifi; TV cab/sat; dogs; phone; bus to city; Eng spkn; adv bkg; some rd noise; CCS. "Youth Hostel on site." SEK 150 2008*

SWEDEN

KRISTINEHAMN *2F2* (2km E Rural) *59.31408, 14.14696* **Kvarndammens Camping, Bartilsbrovägen, 68100 Kristinehamn [(0550) 88195; fax 12393]** Ent to site 800m fr E18. Exit E18 for Mariested. Site not sp thro town except fr S on R64. Med, pt shd, pt sl; wc; chem disp; mv service pnt; sauna; shwrs inc; el pnts (10A) SEK35; shop; lndtte; snacks; cooking facs; playgrnd; lake sw adj; fishing; phone; poss cr; Eng spkn; CCS. "V pleasant lakeside site amid pine trees." 1 Mar-30 Nov. SEK 130 2008*

KUNGALV *2E2* (1km SE Rural) *57.86211, 11.99613* **Kungälvs Vandrarhem & Camping (037), Färjevägen 2, 44231 Kungälv [(0303) 18900; fax (303) 19295; info@kungalvsvandrarhem.se; www.kungalvsvandrarhem.se]** Exit E6 junc 85 or 86 & foll sp Kungälv cent, then sp 'Bohus Fästning'. Site sp. Sm, mkd pitch, some hdstg, shd; htd wc; chem disp; mv service pnt; baby facs; shwrs inc; el pnts (12A) SEK40; lndtte (inc dryer); shop; rest; snacks; bar; gas BBQ; playgrnd; wifi; some statics; dogs; bus adj; Eng spkn; quiet; ccard acc; red long stay; CC1. "Site adj Bonus Fästning (fort) & Kungälv Church (17th C) on rv bank; find pitch & check in at recep 0800-1000 & 1700-1900; door code fr recep for san facs; gd NH." ♦ 1 May-15 Sep. SEK 160 2008*

KUNGSBACKA *2E3* (5km SE Rural) *57.42492, 12.15860* **Silverlyckans Camping, Varbergsvägen 875, 43433 Fjärås [(0300) 541349; www.silverlyckan.eu]** Exit E6/E20 junc 58 dir Åsa. Site in 400m on L. Med, pt sl, unshd; htd wc; chem disp; mv service pnt (refill only); shwrs SEK5; el pnts (10A) SEK30; lndtte; shop, rest, snacks 3km; cooking facs; playgrnd; htd pool 3km; sand beach 4km; 10% statics; dogs; bus adj; Eng spkn; adv bkg; quiet. "Vg site; rec visit Tjolöholms Slott (castle)." 1 May-15 Sep. SEK 160 2009*

KUNGSHAMN *2E2* (10km NE Rural/Coastal) *58.37825, 11.33095* **Örns Camping (067), Håle 2, 45691 Kungshamn [(0523) 34335; fax 34409; kjell.andersson@ornscamping.com; www.ornscamping.com]** Exit E6 junc 101 onto rd 162/171 twd Kungshamn; 7km after Nordens Ark turn L sp Kungshamn S. In 3km turn L twd Bohus Malmön, site on R in approx 2km (thru vill). Lge, mkd pitch, pt shd; wc; chem disp; mv service pnt; baby facs; shwrs SEK5; el pnts SEK50; lndtte (inc dryer); shop; playgrnd; beach adj; wifi; sat TV; statics; dogs; Eng spkn; quiet; ccard acc. "Beautiful area; gd coastal walks, fishing, boating." ♦ 1 May-30 Sep. SEK 220 2011*

KVIDINGE see Klippan *2F4*

LACKEBY *2G3* (6km SE Coastal) *56.75718, 16.37700* **Kalmar Camping (H73), Rafshagen 430, 38031 Läckeby [(0480) 60464; fax 60424; info@kalmarcamping.se; www.kalmarcamping.se]** On E22 10km N of Kalmar, turn R approx 500m N of junc with rd 125 to Läckeby & foll sp for Rafshagen & site. Med, mkd pitch, pt sl, pt shd; htd wc; chem disp; mv service pnt; baby facs; shwrs inc; el pnts (10A) SEK40; lndtte (inc dryer); rest; snacks; bar; BBQ; cooking facs; playgrnd; shgl beach adj; fishing; boat hire: games area; TV; some statics; dogs; Eng spkn; quiet; ccard acc. "Gd site; pleasant area; gd cycling area; lakeside site amongst trees, helpful owners, Eng spkn; trips across Oland bridge to island, san facs excel." ♦ 1 Mar-31 Oct. SEK 210 2011*

LANDSKRONA *2E4* (2km N Rural) *55.90098, 12.8042* **Borstahusens Camping (M5), Campingvägen, 26161 Landskrona [(0418) 10837; fax 22042; bengt@borstahusenscamping.se; www.borstahusenscamping.se]** Exit E6/E20 at 'Landskrona N' & foll sp for Borstahusen 4.5km fr E6/D20. Lge; htd wc; chem disp; shwrs inc; baby facs; el pnts (10A) SEK40; lndtte (inc dryer); shop; snacks 200m; playgrnd; htd pool 2km; tennis; cycle hire; game reserve; golf; wifi; TV rm; 75% statics; phone; poss v cr; ccard acc; CCS/CCI. "Gd, pleasant site on edge of Kattegat; sm pitches." ♦ 21 Apr-11 Sep. SEK 180 2008*

⊞ **LEKSAND** *2G1* (2km N Rural) *60.7502, 14.97288* **Leksand Camping (W11), Siljansvägen 61, 79327 Leksand [(0247) 13800; fax 14790; info@leksandstrand.se; www.leksand.se]** On Lake Siljan. Foll sp fr town cent. Lge, some mkd pitch, pt shd; wc; mv service pnt; shwrs inc; sauna; el pnts (10A) SEK45; lndtte (inc dryer); kiosk; shop; rest high ssn; bar; cooking facs; playgrnd; htd pool; waterslide; lake sw; fishing; tennis; cycle hire; wifi; sat TV; some statics; dogs; Quickstop o'night facs; ccard acc; CCS. "Friendly, helpful owners; non-elec pitches in gd location." ♦ SEK 200 2008*

LEKSAND *2G1* (4km SW Rural) *60.73061, 14.95221* **Västanviksbadets Camping (W12), Siljansnäsvägen 130, 79392 Leksand [(0247) 34201; fax 13133; info@vastanviksbadetscamping.se; www.vastanviksbadetscamping.se]** L off Borlänge to Leksand rd at Leksand S, dir Siljansnäs. Site ent clearly visible on R in 3km at W end Lake Siljan at Västanvik. Med, pt sl, unshd; wc; chem disp; mv service pnt; baby facs; shwrs inc; el pnts (10A) SEK45; lndtte (inc dryer); shop & 3km; bar; cooking facs; playgrnd; pool; lake sw; boating; fishing; cycle hire; wifi; some statics; dogs free; Quickstop o'night facs; poss cr; Eng spkn; adv bkg; quiet; CCS. "Attractive site on lakeside; friendly welcome; ltd facs low ssn." 1 Apr-6 Oct. SEK 160 2008*

LIDHULT *2F3* (15km NE Rural) *56.89671, 13.64343* **Lökna Camping & Stugby, Lökna Norregård 8, 34010 Lidhult [(035) 92026; fax 92120; lokna-camping@telia.com; www.loknacamping.com]** Fr rd 25 Ljungby to Halmstad turn N to Odensjö. In Odensjö turn R by church dir Lökna, site in 5km on well-maintained dirt rd, sp. Sm, mkd pitch, hdstg, pt shd; htd wc; chem disp; mv service pnt; sauna; shwrs inc; el pnts (16A) SEK30; lndtte (inc dryer); sm shop; BBQ; cooking facs; playgrnd; lake sw adj; fishing; watersports; some statics; dogs; Eng spkn; adv bkg rec high ssn; quiet; ccard not acc. "Wonderful lake views; excel, relaxing site; no shops nr." 21 Apr-13 Sep. SEK 200 2010*

⊞ **LIDKOPING** *2F2* (1km N Rural) *58.51375, 13.14008* **Krono Camping (R3), Läckögaten, 53154 Lidköping [(0510) 26804; fax 21135; info@kronocamping.com; www.kronocamping.com]** On Lake Vänern nr Folkparken, on rd to Läckö; at Lidköping ring rd foll int'l camping sp. Lge, pt shd; serviced pitch; wc; chem disp; mv service pnt; baby facs; some serviced pitches; shwrs inc; el pnts (10A) inc; gas; lndtte (inc dryer); shop; rest 300m; playgrnd; htd pool 300m; lake sw 300m; watersports; wifi; cab TV (via el hook-up); quiet; ccard acc; CCS. "V clean, friendly, well-run site; open pinewoods on lakeside; interesting area." ♦ SEK 360 2009*

SWEDEN

⊞ **LIDKOPING** *2F2* (4km E Rural) *58.49316, 13.24656* **Filsbäcks Camping (R1), Badvägen, 53170 Lidköping [(0510) 546027; fax 546376; filsback@telia.com; www.filsbackscamping.se]** Fr Lidköping on rd 44, site on L, sp. Med, mkd pitch, pt shd; htd wc; chem disp; mv service pnt; baby facs; shwrs SEK15; el pnts (10A) SEK30; Indtte (inc dryer); shop; rest; snacks; BBQ; cooking facs; playgrnd; lake sw & beach adj; games area; cycle hire; internet; TV; some statics; dogs; bus 100m; Eng spkn; adv bkg; ccard acc; red low ssn. "Excel, clean, well-kept site; friendly, helpful staff; lge pitches; v scenic area; cycle & hiking trails." ♦ SEK 160 2008*

LIMHAMN see Malmo *2E4*

⊞ **LINKOPING** *2G2* (4km NW Rural) *58.42140, 15.56230* **Glyttinge Camping (E28), Berggårdsvägen 6, 58437 Linköping [(013) 174928; fax 175923; glyttinge@nordiccamping.se; www.nordiccamping.se]** Exit fr E4 sp Linköping N; foll sp to Centrum & camping sp. Lge, hdg pitch, pt shd; htd wc; chem disp; mv service pnt; baby facs; fam bthrm; shwrs inc; el pnts (10A) SEK50; gas; Indtte (inc dryer); shop; rest; playgrnd; pool adj; cycle hire; fishing; boating; internet; TV; no statics; Quickstop o'night facs; quiet; ccard acc; red low ssn; CCS. "Lovely site but inadequate san facs for size; gd touring base; easy cycle ride to town cent; recep only mornings only low ssn - no access if arr later than 1pm." ♦ SEK 180 2010*

LIT *1B3* (1km E Rural) *63.31928, 14.8651* **Lits Camping/ Little Lake Hill Canoe Centre, 83030 Lit [(0642) 10247; fax 10103; ove.djurberg@swipnet.se; www.litscamping.com]** On rd 45, sp. Med, pt sl, pt shd; wc; chem disp; mv service pnt; baby facs; sauna; shwrs inc; el pnts (10A) SEK35; Indtte; shop, rest 1km; cooking facs; playgrnd; canoeing; fishing; tennis; cycle hire; wifi; some cabins; phone; adv bkg; quiet; ccard acc; CCS. "Pleasant site, gd alt to cr sites in Östersund high ssn." ♦ 29 May-30 Sep. SEK 155 2009*

LJUNGBY *2F3* (1km N Urban) *56.84228, 13.95251* **Ljungby Camping Park, Campingvägen 1, 34134 Ljungby [tel/fax (0372) 10350; reservation@ljungby-semesterby.se; www.ljungby-semesterby.se]** Exit E4 at Ljungby N, site sp. Med, shd; htd wc; chem disp; shwrs inc; el pnts (10A) SEK35; Indtte (inc dryer); shop; rest (Jun-Aug); playgrnd; htd pool adj; paddling pool; cycling; poss cr in ssn; ccard acc; CCS. "Adv bkg ess high ssn; NH only rec low ssn." 1 May-31 Aug. SEK 215 2009*

LJUNGBY *2F3* (14km NW Rural) *56.90406, 13.77996* **SweCamp Sjön Bolmen Camping (G27), Bolmstad Mjälen, 34196 Ljungby [(0372) 92051; fax 92351; swecamp@bolmencamping.se]** Exit E4 at sp Ljungby N, turn L at top of slip rd & 1st L over E4 sp Ljungby. Foll sp to Bolmsö & site sp to Sjön Bolmen. Med, mkd pitch, pt shd; htd wc; chem disp; mv service pnt; baby facs; shwrs inc; el pnts (10A) SEK40; Indtte; shop; tradsmn; rest; playgrnd; lake sw fr pontoon; boating; games area; cycle hire; TV; 5% statics; dogs; phone; poss cr; Eng spkn; quiet; ccard acc; CCS. ♦ 1 Jun-31 Aug. SEK 210 2011*

⊞ **LJUSDAL** *1B3* (3km W Rural) *61.83894, 16.04059* **Ljusdals Camping (X21), Ramsjövägen 56, 82730 Ljusdal [(0651) 12958; info@ljusdalscamping.se; www.ljusdalscamping.se]** Leave Ljusdal on Rv83 dir Ånge, site on R in 3km. Med, pt shd; htd wc; chem disp; mv service pnt; sauna; shwrs inc; el pnts (10A) SEK40; Indtte (inc dryer); tradsmn; rest; snacks; bar; cooking facs; playgrnd; lake sw & beach adj; games area; cycle hire; wifi; entmnt; some cabins; dogs; Eng spkn; adv bkg; ccard acc; CCS. ♦ SEK 150 2009*

LODERUP *2F4* (5km S Coastal) *55.38181, 14.12795* **Löderups Strandbad Camping (M12), Östanvägen, 27645 Löderup [(0411) 526311; fax 526613; www.loderupsstrandbadscamping.se]** Rd 9 fr Ystad, after Nybrostrand turn R sp Kaseberga, site sp. Lge, mkd pitch, pt shd; wc; chem disp; baby facs; shwrs SEK10; el pnts SEK40; Indtte (inc dryer); shop 400m; rest 1km; snacks nr; playgrnd; sand beach adj; TV; 50% statics; dogs; phone; quiet; poss cr; Eng spkn; ccard acc; CCS. "Site in dunes adj nature reserve; facs poss stretched high ssn; uneven ground; gd birdwatching, rambling; nr historical sites." ♦ 21 Apr-27 Sep. SEK 180 2009*

⊞ **LOFSDALEN** *1B3* (SE Rural) *62.11215, 13.27448* **Lofsdalenfjällen Camping (Z61), Lofsdalsvägen 37, 84085 Lofsdalen [(0680) 41233; fax 41525; turistbyra@lofsdalen.com; www.lofsdalen.com]** Site in cent of vill adj Lofssjön lake. Sm, mkd pitch, some hdstg, unshd; htd wc; chem disp; mv service pnt; baby facs; sauna; shwrs SEK5; el pnts (16A) SEK30; Indtte (inc dryer); shop, rest, bar 300m; BBQ; cooking facs; playgrnd; lake sw & beach; boat & cycle hire; fishing; tennis nr; internet; TV; 10% statics; dogs; Eng spkn; adv bkg; quiet; ccard acc; CCS. "Recep in tourist office; clean facs; gd walking area; gd." ♦ SEK 170 2008*

LOMMA see Malmö *2E4*

⊞ **LULEA** *1D2* (8km W Coastal) *65.59565, 22.07221* **First Camp Luleå (BD18), Arcusvägen 110, 97594 Luleå [(0920) 60300; lulea@firstcamp.se; www.firstcamp.se/lulea]** Exit E4 on R 500m N of Luleälv Rv bdge. Foll sp 'Arcus' (recreation complex). V lge, mkd pitch, pt shd; htd wc; chem disp; mv service pnt; baby facs; sauna; shwrs inc; el pnts (10A) inc; Indtte (inc dryer); shop; tradsmn; rest; snacks; bar; cooking facs; playgrnd; htd pool complex 700m; sand beach adj; tennis 300m; cycle hire; wifi; TV; dogs; phone; car wash; Eng spkn; adv bkg; quiet; ccard acc; CCS. "Excel family site; many sports facs; san facs poss stretched high ssn; suitable RVs & twin-axles; adj rlwy museum." ♦ SEK 270 2009*

MALMO *2E4* (11km N Coastal) *55.68873, 13.05756* **Habo-Ljung Camping (M23), Södra Västkustvägen, 23434 Lomma [(040) 411210; fax 414310; info@haboljungcamping.se; www.haboljungcamping.se]** Turn off E6 dir Lomma, head N for Bjärred, site on L. Lge, pt shd; htd wc (cont); chem disp; mv service pnt; baby facs; shwrs inc; el pnts (10A) SEK40; Indtte (inc dryer); shop; snacks; BBQ; cooking facs; playgrnd; sand beach adj; entmnt; 5% statics; phone; poss cr; Eng spkn; poss noisy; ccard acc; CCS. "Conv NH; vg." ♦ 15 Apr-15 Sep. SEK 200 2010*

SWEDEN

⊞ **MALMO** *2E4* (7km SW Urban) *55.5722, 12.90686* **Malmö Camping & Feriesenter (M8), Strandgatan 101, Sibbarp, 21611 Limhamn [(040) 155165; fax 159777; malmo camping@malmo.se; www.malmo.se/malmocamping]** Fr Öresund Bdge take 1st exit & foll sp Limhamn & Sibbarp, then int'l campsite sp. Fr N on E6 round Malmö until last exit bef bdge (sp), then as above. Fr Dragør-Limnhamn ferry turn R on exit dock. Site in 1km on R, nr sea, in park-like setting. V lge, pt sl, pt shd; htd wc; chem disp; mv service pnt; baby facs; shwrs inc; el pnts (10A) inc (poss rev pol); gas; Indtte (inc dryer); shops; rest; snacks; cooking facs; playgrnd; pool 400m; sand beach 250m; windsurfing; cycle hire; wifi; TV rm; phone; bus to Malmo; poss cr; no adv bkg; quiet; ccard acc; CCS. "Easy cycle to town cent; facs poss stretched high ssn; v busy city site; well-laid out but poss long walk to san facs; conv Öresund Bdge." ♦ SEK 290 2010*

⊞ **MALUNG** *2F1* (1km W Rural) *60.68296, 13.70243* **Malungs Camping (W22), Bullsjövägen, 78200 Malung [(0280) 18650; fax 18615; campingen@malung.se; www.malungscamping.se]** Fr Stöllet take rd 45 to Malung, site sp. Lge, pt shd; htd wc; chem disp; baby facs; shwrs inc; el pnts (10A) SEK40; Indtte (inc dryer); shop; snacks; playgrnd; pool; fishing; boating; cycle hire; internet; TV; car wash; Quickstop o'night facs; quiet; ccard acc; CCS. ♦ SEK 160 2009*

MARIEFRED *2H2* (2km E Rural) *59.26301, 17.25503* **Mariefreds Camping (D1), Strandbadet, 64700 Mariefred [(0159) 13250; fax 10230; mariefredscamping@yahoo.se; www.strangnas.se]** On Lake Mälaren, 2km E of Mariefred, sp. If app fr Stockholm on E4, take E20 at Södertälje int'chge; in 28km R at Mariefred junc & foll sp to site. Lge, mkd pitch, pt shd; wc; chem disp; mv service pnt; shwrs inc; baby facs; el pnts (10A) SEK40; Indtte; shop; snacks; playgrnd; shgl beach; lake sw adj; fishing; boating; cycle hire; poss cr; Eng spkn; quiet; ccard acc; red long stay; CCS. "Narr gauge steam rlwy; conv Gripsholm Castle; attractive lakeside setting; sm pitches; path to Mariefred; 4km to rlwy stn to Stockholm - lge car park." 29 Apr-11 Sep. SEK 160 2008*

MARIESTAD *2F2* (2km NW Rural) *58.7154, 13.79516* **Ekuddens Camping (R2), 54245 Mariestad [(0501) 10637; fax 18601; andreas.appelgren@mariestad.se; www.ekuddenscamping.se]** Fr E20 take turn off twd Mariestad. At 1st rndabt foll ring rd clockwise until site sp on Lake Vänern. Lge, shd; wc; mv service pnt; sauna; shwrs inc; el pnts (10A) SEK40; gas; Indtte (inc dryer); shop; rest; bar; playgrnd; htd pool; beach; golf 2km; cycle hire; dogs; phone; Quickstop o'night facs; ccard acc; CCS. "Gd views fr lakeside pitches; friendly, helpful staff; gd san facs." ♦ 1 May-15 Sep. SEK 180 2010*

MARKARYD *2F3* (500m N Urban) *56.46475, 13.60066* **Camping Park Sjötorpet (G4), Strandvägen 4, 28531 Markaryd [(0433) 10316; fax 12391; reservation@sjotorpet-roc.se; www.sjotorpet-roc.se]** E4 fr Helsingborg (ferry) site is bet E4 N turn to Markaryd & rd 117, sp. Narr app. Sm, pt sl, pt shd; htd wc; shwrs inc; chem disp; mv service pnt; baby facs; el pnts (10A) SEK40; Indtte (inc dryer); shop; rest; snacks; bar; cooking facs; playgrnd; lake sw; fishing; boating; cycle hire; wifi; some statics; dogs; phone; poss cr; Eng spkn; quiet; ccard acc; CCS. "Excel san & cooking facs; well-run site; helpful staff." ♦ 1 Apr-31 Oct. SEK 210 2011*

MARSTRAND *2E2* (1.5km NE Coastal) *57.89380, 11.60510* **Marstrands Camping (036), Långedalsvägen 16, 44030 Marstrand [(0303) 60584; fax 60440; info@marstrand camping.se; www.marstrandscamping.se]** Exit A6 dir Kungsälv/Marstrand & foll rd 168 to Marstrand. Site sp on Koön Island. App rd to site v narr. Med, pt sl, pt shd; htd wc; chem disp; mv service pnt; baby facs; shwrs; el pnts (10A) SEK45; Indtte; shop; cooking facs; playgrnd; shgl beach; wifi; TV; 50% statics; dogs; poss v cr; adv bkg; quiet; ccard acc; CCS. "Ferry to Marstrand Island." ♦ 16 Apr-25 Sep. SEK 225 2011*

There aren't many sites open at this time of year. We'd better phone ahead to check the one we're heading for is open.

MELLBYSTRAND *2E3* (1km N Coastal/Urban) *56.51961, 12.94628* **Marias Camping (N18), Norra Strandvägen 1, 31260 Mellbystrand [(0430) 28585; fax 27321; info@mariascamping.se; www.mariascamping.se]** 20km N of Båstad, exit junc 41 fr E6 W onto rd 24, site sp off coast rd N. Lge, hdg/mkd pitch, pt shd; htd wc; chem disp (wc); mv service pnt; baby facs; shwrs; el pnts inc; Indtte (inc dryer); shop; rest; snacks; bar; cooking facs; playgrnd; sand beach adj; games rm; internet; TV; dogs; bus 500m; Eng spkn; adv bkg; quiet; CCS. "Vg site beside dunes; beautiful beach." ♦ 21 Apr-26 Aug. SEK 300 2011*

⊞ **MELLERUD** *2E2* (4km SE Coastal) *58.68933, 12.51711* **Mellerud SweCamp Vita Sandar (P13), 46421 Mellerud [(0530) 12260; fax 12934; mail@vitasandarscamping.se; www.vitasandarscamping.se]** Fr S on rd 45 take Dalslandsgatan Rd on R & foll sp. Fr N turn L twd Sunnanåhamn, Vita Sandar. Med, pt shd; htd wc; chem disp; mv service pnt; sauna; shwrs SEK5; baby facs; el pnts (10A) SEK50; Indtte (inc dryer); shop; rest; snacks; bar; cooking facs; playgrnd; htd pool; waterslides; sand beach & lake sw; boat & cycle hire; fishing; tennis; games area; wifi; TV rm; 20% statics; dogs; Quickstop o'night facs; poss cr; quiet; ccard acc; red low ssn; CCS/CCI. "Pleasant family site in pine trees; excel sw." ♦ SEK 230 (CChq acc) 2009*

MELLERUD *2E2* (2km W Rural) *58.71288, 12.43231* **Kerstins Camping (P21), Hålsungebyn 1, 46494 Mellerud [tel/fax (0530) 12715; epost@kerstinscamping.se; www.kerstinscamping.se]** Fr Mellerud on rd 166 dir Bäckefors & Ed, site sp. Sm, pt shd; htd wc (cont); chem disp; mv service pnt; baby facs; shwrs inc; el pnts (10A) SEK45; Indtte (inc dryer); shop; BBQ; cooking facs; playgrnd; games rm; TV rm; some statics; dogs; phone; Eng spkn; adv bkg; quiet; CCS. "Pleasant area; excel." ♦ 3 May-26 Aug. SEK 175 2011*

MOLLE see Höganäs *2E4*

MOLNDAL see Göteborg *2E3*

SWEDEN

⊞ **MORA** *1B4* (500m N Urban) *61.00853, 14.53178* **Mora Parkens Camping, Parkvägen 1, 79231 Mora [(0250) 27600; fax 12785; info@moraparken.se; www.moraparken.se]** Fr SW site sp on rd 45. Or foll sp in town cent; site in 400m. Recep in adj hotel. Lge, mkd pitch, pt sl, pt shd; htd wc; chem disp; mv service pnt; baby facs; shwrs inc; el pnts (10A) inc; Indtte (inc dryer); shops 500m; rest 300m; covrd, htd pool; paddling pol; waterslide; fishing; sports facs; games rm; TV; wifi; some cabins; Quickstop o'night facs; Eng spkn; no adv bkg; quiet; ccard acc; CCS. "Excel site; ltd facs low ssn & poss unclean; suitable RVs & twin-axles; conv for bear sanctuary at Orsa." ♦ SEK 165 2009*

MOTALA *2F2* (2.5km N Rural) *58.54930, 15.00860* **Z-Parkens Camping, Månvägen Varamon, 59152 Motala [(0141) 211142; fax 217251; campingen@bkzeros.se; www.bkzeros.se]** Site is 2.5km NW of Motala on rd 50; turn W twd lake (sp Varamon), site well sp. Med, mkd pitch, pt shd; wc; chem disp; mv service pnt; shwrs inc; fam bthrm; baby facs; el pnts (16A) SEK30; Indtte; shop; BBQ; playgrnd; lake sw & sand beach adj; TV; dogs; phone; Eng spkn; quiet; CCS. "Adj to Lake Vättern; communal shwrs; ageing facs; gd." ♦ 1 May-21 Sep. SEK 150 2008*

NJURUNDABOMMEN *1C3* (5km E Coastal) *62.26828, 17.45181* **Bergafjärdens Camping & Havsbad (Y29), Bergafjärden, 86286 Njurundabommen [(060) 34598; fax 34841; info@bergafjarden.nu; www.bergafjarden.nu]** Clearly sp on E4 at Njurundabommen. Lge, shd; wc; chem disp; mv service pnt; baby facs; shwrs SEK5; el pnts (6A) SEK40; Indtte (inc dryer); shop; snacks; bar; playgrnd; sand beach; lake sw; cycle hire; wifi; TV; some cabins; dogs; phone; quiet; ccard acc; CCS. ♦ 9 May-18 Sep. SEK 180 2011*

NORA *2G1* (1km N Rural) *59.52576, 15.04386* **Trängbo Camping (T1), 713280 Nora [(0587) 12361; fax 311389; info@trangbocamping.se; www.trangbocamping.se]** Site sp fr sq in cent of town, on rd 244 fr Hällefors to Örebro. Med, pt sl, pt shd; htd wc; chem disp; mv service pnt; baby facs; shwrs; el pnts (10A) SEK35; Indtte (inc dryer); shop & 1km; playgrnd; lake sw; boating; fishing; nature trails; cycle hire; games area; wifi; some cabins; ccard acc; quiet; CCS. ♦ 1 May-30 Sep. SEK 190 2011*

NORA *2G1* (3km N Rural) *59.5342, 15.0405* **Gustavsberg Camping (Naturist), NF Bergslagens Solsport, 71322 Nora [(073) 6425282; info@gustavsbergscamping.com; www.gustavsbergscamping.com]** Fr Örebro take rd N to Nora, site sp fr Nora cent past Trängbo Camping, just outside vill limits on R. Sm, mkd pitch, pt shd; htd wc; chem disp; fam bthrm; sauna; shwrs inc; el pnts (10A) SEK35; Indtte; shop, rest, snacks, bar 3km; BBQ; cooking facs; playgrnd; lake sw adj; fishing; games area; TV rm; 20% statics; dogs; phone; Eng spkn; adv bkg; quiet; ccard acc; red for INF cardholders. "Gd family site; all facs unisex; many preserved buildings & antique shops in Nora." ♦ 1 Jun-31 Aug. SEK 145 2009*

⊞ **NORDMALING** *1C3* (200m W Rural/Coastal) *63.57546, 19.45881* **SweCamp Rödviken (AC43), Rödviksvägen 93, 91431 Nordmaling [tel/fax (0930) 31250; info@rundviksrederi.se]** Site off E4, well sp. Med, unshd; wc; chem disp; mv service pnt; shwrs inc; el pnts (16A) SEK45; Indtte (inc dryer); shop; rest; snacks adj; bar; cooking facs; playgrnd; htd pool; paddling pool; sand beach; rv fishing; sports & ice rink adj; cycle hire; some cabins; dogs; Quickstop o'night facs; quiet; ccard acc; CCS. ♦ SEK 170 2009*

NORRFJARDEN *1D2* (N Rural) *65.42076, 21.5437* **Camping Ladrike (BD11), Hyndgrundsvägen 2, 94591 Norrfjärden [tel/fax (0911) 200250; cai@jussila.nu]** Site on E side of E4, sp. Med, mkd pitch, unshd; htd wc; chem disp; shwrs inc; el pnts SEK30; Indtte (inc dryer) rest; BBQ; playgrnd; pool; games area; wifi; some statics; some rd noise; CCS. ♦ 1 Jun-21 Aug. SEK 165 2008*

NORRFJARDEN *1D2* (8km SE Rural/Coastal) *65.35521, 21.58571* **Borgaruddens Camping (BD31), Borgaruddsvägen, 94521 Norrfjärden [(0911) 203518; borgarudden.nif@telia.com]** Site on E side of E4. Med, mkd pitch, htd wc; chem disp; mv service pnt; baby facs; shwrs inc; el pnts (10A) SEK40; Indtte (inc dryer); snacks; cooking facs; playgrnd; pool; shgl beach adj; wifi; 10% statics; phone; Eng spkn; quiet; ccard acc; CCS. "Conv unique parish vills Luleå, Piteå & Skellefteå." ♦ 1 Jun-31 Aug. SEK 170 2011*

NORRKOPING *2G2* (2km W Urban) *58.59138, 16.14080* **Himmelstalunds Camping (E4), Utställningsvägen, 60234 Norrköping [(011) 171190; fax 170987; info@norrkopingscamping.com; www.norrkopingscamping.com]** Exit Norrköping S fr E4, foll sp sports cent & site. Lge, pt sl, pt shd; htd wc; chem disp; mv service pnt; baby facs; serviced pitches; shwrs inc; el pnts (10A) SEK40; Indtte (dryer); shop; snacks; cooking facs; playgrnd; htd pool & sports facs 200m; cycle hire; wifi; TV; 10% cabins; phone; quiet; ccard acc; CCS. ♦ 15 Apr-15 Oct. SEK 160 2009*

NOSSEBRO *2E2* (500m N Urban) *58.19195, 12.72161* **Nossebrobadets Camping (R22), Marknadsgatan 4, 46530 Nossebro [(0512) 57043; fax 57042; info@nossebrobadet.se; www.nossebrobadet.se]** N fr Alingsås on E20; exit N to Nossebro, site in 16km. Clearly sp. Sm, pt sl, unshd; wc; mv service pnt; sauna; shwrs; el pnts inc; Indtte (inc dryer); shop 500m; playgrnd; 2 pools (1 covrd); fishing; boat hire; sports ground adj; cycle hire; some cabins; dogs; quiet. "Vg NH; stream thro site." ♦ 1 May-31 Aug. SEK 140 2011*

NYKOPING *2G2* (8km SE Coastal) *58.71970, 17.09182* **Strandstuvikens Bad & Camping (D10), 61192 Nyköping [tel/fax (0155) 97810; lilian@bissarna.se; www.strandstuvikencamping.com]** On E4 dir Nyköping foll sp town cent then 'Hamnen' (harbour) & turn R onto rd 53 sp Arno. In approx 3km turn L onto minor rd & foll site sp. Med, mkd pitch, pt shd; htd wc; chem disp; mv service pnt; baby facs; fam bthrm; el pnt (10A) SEK50; Indtte; shop; snacks; cooking facs; playgrnd; sand beach adj; TV; some statics; Eng spkn; quiet; CCI. "Gd site; gd walking, cycling." ♦ 1 May-15 Sep. SEK 150 2009*

⊞ **NYNASHAMN** *2H2* (1km NW Coastal) *58.90717, 17.93805* **Nicksta Camping (B8), Nickstabadsvägen 17, 14943 Nynäshamn [(08) 52012780; fax 52015317; info@nickstacamping.se; www.nickstacamping.se]** Fr Stockholm on Rv 73 to Nynäshamn. Foll site sp, turning R at ICA supmkt, then immed L (sp poss cov'rd by hedge.) Med, pt sl, pt shd; htd wc; chem disp; mv service pnt; baby facs; shwrs inc; el pnts (10A) SEK50; Indtte (inc dryer); shop 700m; snacks; cooking facs; playgrnd; beach adj; waterslide; games area; cycle hire; wifi; some cabins; dogs; train 600m; site clsd mid-Dec to mid-Jan; Quickstop o'night facs; Eng spkn; CCS. "Gd site; ferries to Gotland & Poland." ♦ SEK 165 2009*

OLAND ISLAND Campsites in towns on Öland Island are listed together at the end of the Swedish site entry pages.

OREBRO *2G2* (1km S Rural) *59.2554, 15.18955* **Gustavsviks Camping (T2), Sommarrovägen, 70229 Örebro [(019) 196950; fax 196961; camping@gustavsvik.com; www.gustavsvik.com]** Foll sp fr E18/E20 & rd 51 to site. V lge, mkd pitch, pt sl, pt shd; htd wc; chem disp; some serviced pitches; mv service pnt; baby facs; fam bthrm; shwrs inc; el pnts (10A) SEK80 inc sat TV (poss rev pol); gas; Indtte (inc dryer); shop; kiosk; rest; snacks; bar; BBQ; cooking facs; playgrnd; 2 pools (1 htd, covrd); waterslide; paddling pool; lake sw & beach adj; golf nr; gym; solarium; wifi; entmnt; cab TV; 10% statics; dogs; phone; bus; Eng spkn; quiet; ccard acc; CCS. "Excel family site; superb facs; gentle stroll to town; v highly rec." ♦ 15 Apr-6 Nov. SEK 295 2010*

⊞ **ORSA** *1B4* (1km W Rural) *61.12090, 14.59890* **Orsa SweCamp (W3), Timmervägen 1, 79421 Orsa [(0250) 46200; fax 46260; info@orsagronklitt.se; www.orsacamping.se]** Sp fr town cent & fr rd 45. V lge, pt shd; htd wc; shwrs inc; baby facs; sauna; el pnts (10A) SEK50; mv service pnt; Indtte (inc dryer); shops 500m; rest; bar; cooking facs; playgrnd; 4 htd pools high ssn; waterslide; sand beach & lake sw; fishing; canoe & cycle hire; tennis; wifi; entmnt; sat TV; 5% statics; phone; quiet; CCS. "Excel countryside; bear reserve 15km; gd general facs but ltd low ssn." ♦ SEK 215 (CChq acc) 2010*

⊞ **OSKARSHAMN** *2G3* (3km N Coastal) *57.27800, 16.47500* **Havslätts Café & Camping, Eversvägen 30, 57221 Oskarshamn [(0491) 15325; fax 12449; info@havslatt.se; www.havslatt.se]** N of Oskarshamn turn off E22 at Glabo & foll coast rd thro Saltvik to site. Med, pt shd; htd wc; chem disp; mv service pnt; baby facs; shwrs; el pnts (10A) inc; Indtte; shops 500m; rest; snacks adj; playgrnd; sand beach 100m; cycle hire; 50% statics; dogs; poss cr; quiet; ccard acc. "Ferries to Öland Island fr Oskarshamn Harbour approx 2km." ♦ SEK 190 2008*

OSKARSHAMN *2G3* (3km SE Coastal) *57.2517, 16.49206* **Gunnarsö Camping (H7), Östersjövägen 103, 57263 Oskarshamn [tel/fax (0491) 13298; gunnarso@oskarshamn.se; www.oskarshamn.se]** Fr E22 dir Oskarshamn, site sp on Kalmar Sound. Med, pt shd; htd wc; chem disp; mv service pnt; baby facs; sauna; shwrs SEK5; el pnts (10A) SEK35; Indtte (inc dryer); shop; snacks; playgrnd; 2 pools; watersports; wifi; TV; 40% statics; dogs; phone; adv bkg; quiet; ccard acc; CCS. "Beautiful location; many pitches with gd views; gd walking/cycling." ♦ 1 May-18 Sep. SEK 175 2009*

OSTERFARNEBO *2G1* (1.5km S Rural) *60.29937, 16.80614* **Färnebofjärdens Camping, Berreksvägen 19, 46291 Österfärnebo [0736 505334 (mob); farnebocamping@hotmail.com; www.farnebocamping.se]** Fr rd 67 turn W at Gysinge onto rd 272 dir Österfärnebo. In 5km turn L sp By at football grnd, site in 2km, sp. Med, mkd pitch, unshd; wc; shwrs; el pnts (10A) SEK40; Indtte; lake sw; fishing; boat hire; 20% statics; quiet. "Pleasant site; conv National Park." 1 Jun-30 Sep. SEK 130 2010*

⊞ **OSTERSUND** *2B3* (3km S Rural) *63.15955, 14.6731* **Östersunds Camping (Z11), Krondikesvägen 95, 83146 Östersund [(063) 144615; fax 144323; ostersundscamping@ostersund.se; www.ostersund.se]** At Odensala on lakeside, well sp fr E14. Lge, mkd pitch; pt sl; htd wc; chem disp; mv service pnt; baby facs; sauna; shwrs SEK5; el pnts (10A) SEK50 (poss rev pol); Indtte (inc dryer); shop; rest; bar; cooking facs; playgrnd; pool; paddling pool; tennis; wifi; cab TV; 80% statics; dogs; phone; poss cr; quiet; ccard acc; CCS."gd NH, v helpful staff." ♦ SEK 210 2011*

OSTERSUND *2B3* (4.5km W Rural) *63.17196, 14.54013* **Frösö Camping (Z12), Valla, 83296 Frösön [(063) 43254; fax 43841; froson@nordiccamping.se; www.nordiccamping.se]** Fr E14 (E75) foll sp Frösön across rv bdge. Turn R over bdge & foll sp for airport then site sp for 4.5km. Lge, sl, pt shd, pt sl; wc; baby facs; shwrs; chem disp; el pnts (10A) inc; Indtte (inc dryer); shops 1km; snacks; playgrnd; fishing; boating; golf; wifi; poss cr; quiet; red low ssn; CCS. "Grass pitches poss diff after heavy rain; gd views fr lower pitches." ♦ 23 May-18 Sep. SEK 160 2008*

⊞ **PAJALA** *1D1* (1.5km SE Rural) *67.20381, 23.4084* **Pajala Camping (BD8), Tannavägen 65, 98431 Pajala [tel/fax (0978) 74180; pajalacamping@gmail.com]** Site sp fr rd 99. Med, mkd pitch, hdstg, pt shd; htd wc; chem disp; mv service pnt; baby facs; sauna; shwrs inc; el pnts (10A) SEK30; Indtte (inc dryer); shop; snacks; cooking facs; playgrnd; tennis; cycle hire; wifi; TV rm; dogs; bus 1.5km; Eng spkn; adv bkg; quiet; ccard acc; red long stay; CCS. "Clean, well-presented site; delightful owner; salmon-fishing in rv in ssn (mid-Jun approx)." ♦ SEK 190 2011*

RAMVIK *1C3* (1km S Rural) *62.79911, 17.86931* **Snibbens Camping (Y19), Snibben 139, 87016 Ramvik [tel/fax (0612) 40505; info@snibbenscamping.com; www.snibbenscamping.com]** Fr S on E4, 23km N of Härnösand; after high bdge sighted take slip rd dir Kramfors; site sp in 2.5km on L just bef Ramvik. Med, mkd pitch, pt sl, pt shd; htd wc; chem disp; mv service pnt; baby facs; shwrs inc; el pnts (16A) SEK20; Indtte (inc dryer); shop 1km; rest; snacks; bar; cooking facs; playgrnd; lake sw & beach adj; fishing; boat hire; wifi; TV rm; some cabins; bus; poss cr; Eng spkn; quiet; ccard acc; CCS. "Helpful owners; delightful site with lakeside setting; v peaceful even when busy; spotless facs & lovely camp kitchen with seating areas inside & out; conv Höga Kusten suspension bdge." ♦ 6 May-11 Sep. SEK 160 2011*

SWEDEN

⊞ **RATTVIK** *1B4* (1km N Rural) *60.89103, 15.13115* **Enåbadets Camping (W7), Enåbadsvägen 8, 79532 Rättvik [(0248) 56111; fax 12660; info@enan.se; www.enan.se]** Site sp on N o'skts of town fr Tourist Info board, on rd 70. Lge, shd; wc; chem disp; mv service pnt; serviced pitches; baby facs; sauna; shwrs inc; el pnts (10A) SEK50; Indtte (inc dryer); shop; rest; snacks; bar; cooking facs; playgrnd; pool; lake adj; wifi; entmnt; TV; 10% statics; phone; poss cr; quiet; ccard acc; CCS. "Gd base for touring potteries & local vills; wooded." ♦ SEK 190 2010*

RATTVIK *1B4* (500m W Rural) *60.88891, 15.10881* **Siljansbadets Camping (W8), Långbryggevägen 4, 79532 Rättvik [(0248) 51618; fax 51689; camp@siljansbadet.com; www.siljansbadet.com]** Fr S on rd 70 thro Rättvik. Immed outside town turn L at rndabt, site sp on Lake Siljan. Height restriction 3.5m. V lge, mkd pitch, pt shd; wc; chem disp; baby facs; shwrs inc; el pnts (10A) SEK50; Indtte (inc dryer); shop & 500m; rest & 500m; bar; cooking facs; playgrnd; lake sw & sand beach; boat hire; wifi; TV rm; 15% statics; dogs; bus/train; poss cr; Eng spkn; quiet; ccard acc. "Lovely scenic location; conv town cent." ♦ 21 Apr-10 Oct. SEK 185 2009*

RORBACK *1D2* (Coastal) *65.80030, 22.59516* **Rörbäcks Camping & Havsbad (BD79), Rörbäck 79, 95592 Råneå [tel/fax (0924) 35047; info@rorbackscamping.se]** Off E4 approx 10km SW of junc with E10, at Jämtöfjärden foll sp S to coast, site well sp. Sm, mkd pitch, hdstg, pt shd; htd wc; chem disp; serviced pitches; sauna; shwrs inc; baby facs; el pnts (10A) inc; Indtte; rest; snacks; BBQ; cooking facs; playgrnd; sand beach adj; fishing; canoe hire; TV; phone; poss cr; Eng spkn; adv bkg; ccard acc; CCS. "Cosy, clean site on water's edge in a wood; vg facs." ♦ 1 Jun-31 Aug. SEK 200 2009*

ROSTANGA *2F4* (500m SW Rural) *55.99656, 13.28050* **Röstånga Camping (M20), Blinkarpsvägen 3, 26024 Röstånga [(0435) 91064; fax 91652; info@rostanga camping.se; www.rostangacamping.se]** Site sp in Röstånga along rd 108. Med, pt shd; htd wc; chem disp; mv service pnt; fam bthrm; baby facs; private san facs avail; shwrs inc; el pnts (10A) SEK40; Indtte (inc dryer); shop high ssn; rest 300m; snacks; bar; BBQ; cooking facs; htd pool; paddling pool; waterslide; lake fishing; canoeing; tennis; games area; games rm; wifi; entmnt; TV rm; 15% cabins; dogs; Eng spkn; adv bkg; quiet; ccard acc; CCS. "Pleasant family site; some pitches by stream; superb pool; conv Söderåsens National Park." ♦ 21 Apr-2 Oct. SEK 220 2010*

ROXENBADEN *2G2* (S Rural) *58.54135, 15.62292* **Sandviks Camping, Stjärnorp, 59078 Roxenbaden [tel/fax (013) 61470; sandvik@caravanclub.se]** Fr E4 Jönköping to Linköping turn onto rd 36 & foll sp Göta Canal, Berg. Site sp in Berg & is 3km E of Stjärnorp. Med, mkd pitch, terr, pt shd; wc; chem disp; shwrs inc; el pnts (10A) SEK50; Indtte (inc dryer); shop; playgrnd; lake sw & sand/shgl beach adj; 30% statics; dogs; phone; bus at gate; Eng spkn; quiet; ccard acc; CCS/CCI. "Well-kept, relaxing site; interesting area; gd walks." ♦ 15 Apr-15 Sep. SEK 180 2010*

RYD see Urshult *2F3*

⊞ **SAFFLE** *2F2* (6km S Rural) *59.08326, 12.88616* **Duse Udde Camping (S11), 66180 Säffle [(0533) 42000; fax 42002; duseudde@krokstad.se; www.duseudde.se]** Site sp fr rd 45. Med, pt sl, shd; wc; mv service pnt; baby facs; sauna; shwrs SEK10; el pnts (10A) SEK50; Indtte (inc dryer); shop; rest high ssn; snacks; bar; playgrnd; watersports; pool 6km; beach; lake sw; cycle hire; wifi; entmnt; bus; 20% statics; phone; dogs; Quickstop o'night facs; quiet; ccard acc; red long stay; CCS. "Place to relax; useful base for Värmland area with nature walks." ♦ SEK 180 2010*

I'll go online and tell the Club what we think of the campsites we've visited – www.caravanclub.co.uk/europereport

SALA *2G1* (6km N Rural) *59.95473, 16.5168* **Silvköparens Camping (U2), Gamla Riksväg 70, 73397 Sala [tel/fax (0224) 59003; silvkoparen@caravanclub.se; www.sala.se]** Site on rd 70 bet Sala & Avesta, sp. Med, pt shd; htd wc; chem disp; shwrs inc; el pnts (10A); Indtte (inc dryer); shop adj & 6km; snacks; playgrnd; lake sw adj; boating; canoeing; cycling; TV; some statics; dogs; phone; poss cr; Eng spkn; quiet; ccard acc; CCS. "Sala silver mine & museum; Sätra Brunn spa; lovely situation." ♦ 30 Apr-18 Sep. SEK 205 2011*

SANDARNE see Söderhamn *1C4*

⊞ **SARNA** *1B3* (1km S Rural) *61.69281, 13.14696* **Särna Camping (W32), Särnavägen 6, 79090 Särna [(0253) 10851; fax 32055; camping@sarnacamping.se; www.sarnacamping.se]** Turn R off rd 70 opp fire stn. Med, terr, pt shd; wc; chem disp; mv service pnt; sauna; shwrs SEK5; el pnts (10A) SEK35; Indtte (inc dryer); shop, rest, snacks 200m; playgrnd; shgl beach; cycle hire; poss cr; adv bkg; quiet. "Beautiful setting o'looking lake; pleasant town." ♦ SEK 160 2010*

⊞ **SIMRISHAMN** *2F4* (2km N Coastal) *55.57021, 14.33611* **Tobisviks Camping (L14), Tobisvägen, 27294 Simrishamn [(0414) 412778; fax 412771; hakan@fritidosterlen.se; www.fritidosterlen.se]** By sea at N app to town. Lge, pt shd; wc; chem disp; mv service pnt; shwrs SEK1/min; el pnts (10A) SEK50; Indtte (inc dryer); shop 400m; rest 2km; htd pool; watersports; TV; phone; ccard acc; CCS. SEK 210 2010*

⊞ **SJOBO** *2F4* (1km SE Rural) *55.62613, 13.71981* **Orebackens Camping (M16), Ostergatan, 27534 Sjöbo [(01416) 10984; info@orebacken.se; www.orebacken.se]** Fr rndabt at junc rds 11 & 13 S of Sjöbo, go to town cent. In cent town turn R, site on L in 1km, sp. Med, mkd pitch, hdstg, pt sl, pt shd; htd wc; chem disp; shwrs inc; el pnts (16A) SEK35; Indtte (inc dryer); shop & 1km; rest; snacks; cooking facs; playgrnd; pool; TV; 80% statics; dogs; phone; bus 1km; poss cr; Eng spkn; quiet; CCS. "Basic site but clean; gd touring base; forest walks fr site." ♦ SEK 165 2008*

SWEDEN

SKANOR *2E4* (2km SE Coastal) *55.39750, 12.86555* **Ljungens Camping (M9), Strandbadsvägen, 23942 Falsterbo [(040) 471132; fax 470955; camping@telia.com; www.mamut.net/ljungenscamping]** Fr E6/E22 exit to W sp Höllviken onto rd 100. Foll sp Skanör/Falsterbo. Site sp on L at rndabt at ent to town, dir Falsterbo. Lge, mkd pitch, some hdstg, pt shd; htd wc; chem disp; mv service pnt; baby facs; shwrs SEK5; el pnts (10A) SEK40; Indtte (inc dryer); shop; snacks high ssn; BBQ; cooking facs; playgrnd; sand beach 200m; wifi; TV; 50% statics; dogs; bus; Eng spkn; no adv bkg; aircraft noise (under flight path Copenhagen airport) ccard acc; CCS. "Conv Viking Village museum; nature reserve adj; gd birdwatching, cycling; vg." ♦ 1 Mayr-1 Oct. SEK 220 2011*

SKARHOLMEN see Stockholm *2H2*

⊞ **SKELLEFTEA** *1C3* (1.5km N Rural) *64.76156, 20.97513* **Skellefteå Camping (AC18), Mossgaten, 93170 Skellefteå [(0910) 735500; fax 701890; skellefteacamping@skelleftea.se; www.skelleftea.se/skelleftea camping/]** Turn W off E4; well sp behind g'ge. Also sp as Camping Stugby. Lge, mkd pitch, pt sl, unshd; htd wc; chem disp; mv service pnt; sauna; shwrs inc; el pnts (10A) SEK60; Indtte (inc dryer); shop; rest, snacks 100m; bar 1km; BBQ; cooking facs; playgrnd; htd pool; waterslide; sand beach 5km; fishing; tennis 150m; cycle hire; games area; wifi; TV rm; 10% statics; dogs; phone; poss cr; Eng spkn; quiet; ccard acc; CCS. "Friendly, clean site in pine trees on sheltered inlet; lge pitches suitable RVs & twin-axles; Nordanå Cultural Cent & Bonnstan Church Vill in walking dist; if site clsd book in at Statoil stn 500m S on E4 at rndabt; excel san facs; lge camp kitchen; helpful staff; lge supmkt nearby." ♦ SEK 230 2011*

SKELLEFTEA *1C3* (7km NE Coastal) *64.77681, 21.11993* **Bovikens Havsbad Camping (AC60), 93140 Skellefteå [tel/fax (0910) 54000; www.bovikenscamping.se]** Site sp off E4, site in 5km. Med, mkd pitch, pt shd; wc; chem disp; baby facs; shwrs inc; el pnts SEK50; Indtte (inc dryer); snacks; playgrnd; sand beach adj; tennis nr; TV rm; some statics; dogs; poss cr; Eng spkn; adv bkg; quiet; ccard acc; CCS. "Gd family site by secluded beach; friendly owner; excel birdwatching; avoid shwr cubicles with electric heaters nr floor level!" ♦ 20 Jun-8 Aug. SEK 180 2009*

SKUTSKAR *2H1* (3km SE Coastal) *60.6380, 17.4690* **Rullsands Camping (C8), 81493 Skutskär [tel/fax (026) 86046; info@rullsand.se; www.rullsand.se]** Fr Gavle on rd 76 S, site sp 2km S of Skutskär. Lge, some mkd pitch, pt shd; htd wc; chem disp; mv service pnt; baby facs; shwrs inc; el pnts (10A) SEK35; Indtte (inc dryer); shop high ssn; snacks; cooking facs; playgrnd; sand beach adj; wifi; 20% statics; dogs; phone; Eng spkn; no adv bkg; quiet; CCI. "Well-kept site; forest walks." ♦ 29 Apr-2 Oct. SEK 165 2008*

SLAGNAS *1C2* (SE Urban) *65.58458, 18.17284* **Slagnäsforsens Camping, Campingvägen 5, 93091 Slagnäs [tel/fax (0960) 650093; info@slagnascamping.com; www.slagnascamping.com]** On rd 45 bet Sorsele & Arvidsjaur, nr bdge over Skellefteälvan. Sm, pt sl, unshd; wc; chem disp; sauna; shwrs inc; el pnts (10A) inc; Indtte; shop; rest 700m; cooking facs; playgrnd; dogs; no adv bkg; quiet; CCS. "Gd." 1 May-30 Sep. SEK 150 2009*

SODERALA see Söderhamn *1C4*

SODERFORS *2H1* (S Urban) *60.38265, 17.23393* **Camping Söderfors (C14), Ängsbacksvägen 1, 81576 Söderfors [(0293) 30850; fax 66540; soderfors.camping@gmail.com; www.soderfors.nu]** Site sp in cent of vill, adj sw pool & on edge of lake, approx 13km W of E4 where it is sp along rd 292. Sm, mkd pitch, pt shd; wc; chem disp; shwrs inc (in pool complex); el pnts SEK40; Indtte (inc dryer); BBQ; cooking facs; pool; paddling pool; Eng spkn; CCS. "Picturesque setting; book in at sw pool office." 1 May-14 Sep. SEK 130 2008*

SODERHAMN *1C4* (10km SE Coastal) *61.24843, 17.19506* **Stenö Havsbad Camping (X9), Stenövägen, 82022 Sandarne [(0270) 60000; fax 60005; steno@nordiccamping.se; www.nordiccamping.se]** Exit E4 at sp Bollnäs-Sandarne (S of Söderhamn turn), foll sp Sandarne at Östansjö, turn L at camping sp. Lge, shd; wc; chem disp; baby facs; mv service pnt; shwrs inc; el pnts (10A) SEK50; Indtte (inc dryer); shop; rest; snacks; bar; cooking facs; playgrnd; pool 12km; sand beach; games area; wifi; TV rm; some cabins; phone; bus; poss cr; adv bkg; quiet; ccard acc; CCS. "Adj nature reserve." ♦ 1 May-31 Oct. SEK 150 2009*

⊞ **SODERHAMN** *1C4* (10km W Rural) *61.29318, 16.8266* **Moheds Camping (X6), Mohedsvägen 59, 82692 Söderala [(0270) 425233; fax 425326; info@mohedscamping.se; www.mohedscamping.se]** Take Söderhamn exit fr E4 onto rd 50 twds Bollnäs; site sp after approx 10km. Med, hdstg, pt sl, pt shd; wc; chem disp; mv service pnt; sauna; shwrs SEK5; baby facs; el pnts (10A) SEK35; Indtte (inc dryer); shop; tradsmn; snacks; bar; playgrnd; pool; lake beach, fishing, boating & sw adj; tennis; cycling; wifi; TV; many statics; phone; poss cr; Eng spkn; adv bkg; quiet; ccard acc; CCS. "Skydiving in nrby airfield; attractive coastline; sh walk to bus to town; busy site." ♦ SEK 165 2011*

SODERKOPING *2G2* (1km N Rural) *58.49163, 16.30618* **Skeppsdockans Camping (E34), Dockan 1, 61421 Söderköping [(0121) 21630; korskullenscamp@hotmail.com; www.soderkopingscamping.se]** On E22 immed N of canal bdge. Sm, mkd pitch, unshd; htd wc; shwrs inc; el pnts SEK40; Indtte (inc dryer); rest & shops 1km; cooking facs; canal sw; cycle hire; TV; Eng spkn; quiet; ccard acc; CCS. "On side of Gota Canal with constant boating traffic, but peaceful." ♦ 30 Apr-2 Oct. SEK 160 2009*

SODERKOPING *2G2* (SE Urban) *58.4770, 16.33471* **Korskullen Camping (E17), Skönbergagaten 50, 61421 Söderköping [(0121) 21621; korskullencamp@hotmail.com]** On E22 in town cent. Sm, hdg pitch, pt shd; wc; chem disp; shwrs; el pnts SEK40; Indtte (inc dryer); shop adj; rest; bar; playgrnd; TV; some cabins; dogs; Eng spkn; quiet but some rd noise; ccard acc; CCS. "Well-maintained san facs." 6 May-18 Sep. SEK 180 2011*

SOLLENTUNA see Stockholm *2H2*

SOLLERON see Gesunda *1B4*

SWEDEN

SOLVESBORG *2F4* (4km S Coastal) *56.0280, 14.56366* **Tredenborgs Campingplats (K3), Tredenborgsvägen, 29436 Sölvesborg [(0456) 12116; fax 12022; tredenborgs camping@hotmail.com; www.tredenborgscamping.com]** Exit E22 at Sölvesborg dir Hamn, foll site sp. Lge; wc; chem disp; mv service pnt; shwrs SEK5; el pnts (10A) SEK40; gas; Indtte (inc dryer); shop; rest; snacks; playgrnd; sand beach; cycle hire; games area; games rm; wifi; some statics; dogs; poss cr & noisy high ssn; CCS. "Attractive site set in sand dunes & trees; gd san facs." ♦ 16 Apr-18 Sep. SEK 200 2008*

⊞ **SORSELE** *1C2* (400m W Rural) *65.53428, 17.52663* **Sorsele Camping (AC21), Fritidsvägen, Näset, 92070 Sorsele [(0952) 10124; fax 10625; info@lapplandskatan.nu; www.lapplandskatan.nu]** N on rd 45/363 fr Storuman to Arvidsjaur. In Sorsele vill turn W for 500m; site sp. Med, unshd; htd wc; chem disp; baby facs; shwrs; el pnts (16A) SEK35; Indtte (inc dryer); shop 200m; playgrnd; pool; beach; canoeing; fishing; hiking; cycle hire; wifi; TV; some statics; dogs; phone; poss cr; quiet; ccard acc; CCS. "Nature reserve; interesting ancient Lapp vill; friendly, welcoming; attractive site." ♦ SEK 145 2008*

STENKALLEGARDEN see Bocksjö *2F2*

STOCKEN *2E2* (700m S) *58.14786, 11.42143* **Stocken Camping, 101, 474 92 Ellös [0304 511 00; info@stocken.nu; www.stocken.nu]** Foll rd 160 (sp Orust); at Varekil turn L onto rd 178 (sp Ellös); in approx 15km turn L (sp Stocken) & foll sp to site (on L just before vill). Lge, mkd pitch, pt sl, unshd; wc; chem disp; MV service pnt; baby facs; shwrs metered; el pnts (10-16A) metered; Indtte; shop; rest; snacks; bar; BBQ; playgrnd; beach 500m; games area; games rm; TV; 20% statics; dogs; bus adj; adv bking; quiet; ccard acc; red long stay. "Beautiful coastline; gd walks; vg site." 09 Apr-02 Oct. SEK 285 2011*

⊞ **STOCKHOLM** *2H2* (15km N Rural) *59.43821, 17.99223* **Rösjöbadens Camping (B1), Lomvägen 100, 19256 Sollentuna [(08) 962184; fax 929195; info@rosjobaden.se; www.rosjobaden.se]** Take E18 m'way N fr Stockholm, sp Norrtälje. Pass Morby Centrum on L after 7km. Take Sollentuna exit, turn L & foll Sollentuna rd 265/262 for approx 5km. At 2nd set of traff lts with pylons adj, turn R on sm rd, clear sp to site. Lge, pt sl, pt shd; wc; chem disp; mv service pnt; baby facs; shwrs SEK10; el pnts (10A) SEK45; Indtte (inc dryer); shops; snacks; playgrnd; fishing; boating; lake sw fr pontoons; sat TV; some statics; dogs; bus; Quickstop o'night facs; Eng spkn; quiet; CCS. "Conv Morby Centrum, lge shopping cent, petrol, metro to city; pleasant walks in woods & lakeside." ♦ SEK 215 2011*

STOCKHOLM *2H2* (10km SW Rural) *59.29558, 17.92300* **Bredäng Camping (A4), Stora Sällskapetväg, 12731 Skärholmen [(08) 977071; fax 7087262; bredangcamping@telia.com; www.bredangcamping.se]** Exit E4/E20 to Bredäng junc 152 & foll sp to site. Lge, mkd/hdstg pitch nr ent otherwise grass/unmkd, pt shd; htd wc; chem disp; serviced pitches; mv service pnt; baby facs; sauna; shwrs inc; el pnts (10A) SEK40; Indtte; shop; rest; snacks; bar; cooking facs; playgrnd; lake & beach adj; cycle hire; battery-charging; metro 700m; Quickstop o'night facs; poss cr; quiet; ccard acc; red snr citizens/low ssn; "Facs ltd low ssn & poss stretched in ssn; helpful staff; overspill 3km at Sätra Camping; conv for Stockholm; shopping cent & metro with free car park about 700m; access to Stockholm also poss by lake steamer fr pier (high ssn) - 10 min walk; well-run site." ♦ 1 Apr-10 Oct. SEK 275 2011*

STOCKHOLM *2H2* (2.5km W Urban) *59.32021, 18.03198* **Långholmens Motorcaravan Park (A11), Skutskepparvägen, 11733 Stockholm [(08) 6691890; info@autocamper-stockholm.se; www.autocamper-stockholm.se]** Fr N foll sp Södermalm fr E4. Immed after x-ing Västerbron (bdge) foll 'Autocamper' sp. Site under S end of bdge. Fr S foll sp Södermalm, then sp Långholmen & site Med, mkd pitch, hdstg, unshd; wc; chem disp; mv service pnt; shwrs inc; el pnts (10A) SEK30; Indtte (inc dryer); rest, bar, shop 300m; cycle hire; TV; adv bkg; Eng spkn; recep open 0700-2200; m'vans only; security fence; constant rd noise; ccard acc; CCS. "Site under flyover but conv city cent." 27 May-4 Sep. SEK 190 2009*

⊞ **STOCKHOLM** *2H2* (10km W Rural) *59.33731, 17.90105* **Ängby Campingplats (A3), Blackebergsvägen 25, 16850 Bromma [(08) 370420; fax 378226; reservation@angbycamping.se; www.angbycamping.se]** On E4 fr Stockholm take rd 275 W twd Vällingby. At rndabt turn L for rd 261 dir Ekerö, then R sp Sodra Ängby, site sp. Med, mkd pitch, pt sl, pt shd; wc; chem disp; mv service pnt; sauna; shwrs SEK5; baby facs; el pnts SEK35; Indtte (inc dryer); shop; rest; snacks; bar; sand beach & lake sw adj; waterslide; tennis; wifi; cab TV; some statics; dogs; phone; train; poss v cr; Eng spkn; ltd facs low ssn; ccard acc; CCS/CCI. "Sh walk to metro stn - 20 mins to city; gd situation; walk/cycle to Drottningsholm Palace; some sm pitches; poss diff pitching for lge o'fits; lack of privacy in shwrs; san facs stretched high ssn & need update; workers living on site; site poss muddy after rain; helpful staff." ♦ SEK 250 2010*

STODE *1C3* (200m W Rural) *62.41585, 16.57015* **Stöde Camping (Y39), Kälsta 107, 86013 Stöde [(0691) 10180; stodecampingstode@hotmail.com; www.stodecamping.com]** Fr S on rd 305 site on L after x-ing rv bdge. Fr Sundsvall on E14 turn S onto rd 305, site on R after underpass. Sm, mkd pitch, pt sl, pt shd; htd wc; chem disp; mv service pnt; baby facs; fam bthrm; el pnts (16A) SEK30; Indtte (inc dryer); shop 500m; snacks; playgrnd; htd pool & sports facs adj; paddling pool; lake sw adj; fishing; boat hire; tennis; TV rm; some statics; dogs; phone; Eng spkn; adv bkg; quiet; red long stay; CCI. "Well-kept, friendly site." 15 May-30 Oct. SEK 140 2011*

SWEDEN

STORUMAN *1C2* (200m NW Rural) *65.10022, 17.11427* **Storumans Camping (AC5), Lokgränd 3, 92331 Storuman [(0951) 14300; storumanscamping@storuman.se; www.storuman.se]** On Lake Storuman, site sp fr rd 45/E12. Med, pt shd; wc; chem disp; mv service pnt; sauna; baby facs; shwrs inc; el pnts (10A) SEK30; Indtte (inc dryer); shop; rest, snacks 200m; playgrnd; lake sw & beach adj; watersports; boat hire; tennis; cycle hire; TV; quiet; ccard acc; CCS. "Ltd facs low ssn." ♦ 1 Apr-30 Sep. SEK 165 2011*

⊞ **STROMSTAD** *2E2* (3km S Coastal) *58.91350, 11.20531* **Camping Lagunen (O3), Skärsbygdsvägen 40, 45297 Strömstad [(0526) 755000; fax 12367; info@lagunen.se; www.lagunen.se]** On Uddevalla rd 176 out of Strömstad. Site on L. Lge, pt sl, pt shd; wc; mv service pnt; baby facs; shwrs; el pnts inc; Indtte (inc dryer); shop; rest; snacks; bar; cooking facs; playgrnd; beach adj; boat & cycle hire; wifi; TV rm; some cabins; dogs; poss cr; adv bkg; quiet; ccard acc; red low ssn. SEK 360 (CChq acc) 2009*

⊞ **STROMSTAD** *2E2* (5km S Coastal) *58.9039, 11.20011* **Daftö Feriecenter (O4), Dafter 2511, 45297 Strömstad [(0526) 26040; fax 26250; info@dafto.com; www.dafto.com]** Fr Uddevalla E6 exit at sp Strömstad, turn L at sp approx 6km on R. Fr Oslo exit E6 sp Strömstad; foll ring rd 176 round E side town; foll sp Daftö; site on R. V lge, pt sl, pt shd; wc; mv service pnt; some serviced pitches; baby facs; sauna; shwrs inc; el pnts (10A) SEK50; Indtte (inc dryer); shop; rest, snacks high ssn; bar; cooking facs; playgrnd; htd pool; sand beach; lake sw; boating; canoeing; fishing; games area; wifi; entmnt; 15% statics; Quickstop o'night facs; site clsd Xmas to 8 Jan; poss cr; adv bkg ess in ssn; quiet; ccard acc; CCS. "Holiday complex with many children's activities; busy at w/end; quiet during wk; views fr some pitches." ♦ SEK 425 (5 persons) 2010*

STROMSTAD *2E2* (12km S Coastal) *58.8832, 11.14253* **Bofors Camping (O62), Korsnäs Tjärnö 2821, 45296 Strömstad [(0526) 25036; birgittathyft@hotmail.com; www.boforscamping.com]** Fr S exit E6 L at sp Strömstad; after 5km turn L at sp Tjarnö 7km (pass Camp Daftö on R); after 5km turn R at sp Befors Camping 2; site on L. Fr N exit E6 R of Strömstad; foll as above. Lge, mkd pitch, pt sl, pt shd; wc; chem disp; shwrs SEK5; el pnts (10A) SEK35; Indtte (inc dryer); shop; sand beach adj; fishing; boat-launching facs; wifi; 60% statics; dogs; Eng spkn; adv bkg; quiet; ccard acc. "Attractive rocky coast with sandy bays; v busy - rec adv bkg." 1 May-15 Sep. SEK 245 2011*

STROMSTAD *2E2* (4km NW Coastal) *58.95741, 11.14763* **Seläters Camping (O48), Norrkärr, 45290 Strömstad [(0526) 12290; fax 12238; info@selater.se; www.selater.se]** Exit E6 at sp Strömstad; foll sps to Seläter; site on R. V lge, mkd pitch, pt shd; wc; mv service pnt; baby facs; shwrs inc; el pnts (10A) SEK50; Indtte (inc dryer); shop; rest; playgrnd; beach 800m; watersports; tennis 500m; golf 1km; wifi; 10% statics; bus; phone; dogs; Quickstop o'night facs; CCS. "Pleasant countryside; well-run site." ♦ 1 Apr-30 Sep. SEK 250 2010*

⊞ **STROMSUND** *1B3* (1km SW Rural) *63.84651, 15.53378* **Strömsunds Camping (Z3), Näsviken, 83324 Strömsund [(0670) 16410; fax 13705; turism@stromsund.se; www.stromsund.se/stromsundscamping]** W of rd 45, over bdge S of main town on lakeside. Lge, pt sl, pt shd; htd wc; chem disp; mv service pnt; baby facs; shwrs SEK5; el pnts (10A) SEK30; Indtte (inc dryer); shop adj; rest; snacks; cooking facs; playgrnd; pool; paddling pool; fishing; cycle & boat hire; wifi; 10% statics; dogs; phone; quiet; cccard acc; CCS. "In 2 parts: W side has main facs but E quieter; go to g'ge adj when site office clsd." ♦ SEK 150 2009*

SUNDSVALL *1C3* (4km SE Urban/Coastal) *62.3585, 17.37016* **Fläsians Camping & Stugor (Y26), Norrstigen 15, 85468 Sundsvall [(060) 554475; fax 569601; bernt.ostling@gmail.com]** Clear sps on E4 in both dirs; site on E coast side of rd. Med, mkd pitch, terr, pt shd; htd wc; chem disp; mv service pnt; baby facs; shwrs inc; el pnts (10A) SEK35; Indtte (inc dryer); shop on site & 2km; rest; cooking facs; playgrnd; sand beach adj; fishing; poss cr; quiet; adv bkg; Eng spkn; ccard acc; CCS. "Sea view all pitches; gd access even in wet; suitable RVs & twin-axles; if recep clsd, site yourself & pay later; helpful staff; some traff noise; sw pools in Sundsvall." ♦ 15 May-31 Aug. SEK 150 2008*

⊞ **SVEG** *1B3* (700m S Rural) *62.03241, 14.36496* **Svegs Camping (Z32), Kyrkogränd 1, 84232 Sveg [(0680) 13025; fax 10337; info@svegscamping.se]** Just S of traff lts at junc rds 45 & 84. Opp Statoil at rear of rest, well sp. Med, mkd pitch, pt shd; htd wc; chem disp; shwrs inc; el pnts (16A) SEK25; Indtte (inc dryer); rest, bar nrby; snacks; playgrnd; pool 500m; cycle hire; games area; TV; some statics; dogs; phone; some rd noise; ccard acc; CCS. "Gd for sh stay/NH." SEK 185 2011*

⊞ **SYSSLEBACK** *1B4* (2km S Rural) *60.71113, 12.88493* **Sysslebäcks Fiskecamping (S36), Badhusvägen 2, 68060 Sysslebäck [(0564) 10514; fax 10196; info@syssleback.se; www.syssleback.se]** Site bet rd 62 & Rv Klarälven in Sysslebäck. Med, pt sl, pt shd; wc; chem disp; mv service pnt; baby facs; sauna; shwrs SEK5; el pnts (10A) SEK55; Indtte (inc dryer); shop; rest 2km; snacks 300m; playgrnd; fishing; canoe hire; tennis; games rm; skilift 7km; wifi; TV; 50% statics; dogs; phone; Quickstop o'night facs; ccard acc; CCS. "Quiet site on rv bank." ♦ SEK 155 2008*

⊞ **TARNABY** *1B2* (3km E Rural) *65.71971, 15.3335* **Tärnaby Camping, Ljungvägen 3, 92064 Tärnaby [(0954) 10009; fax 10558; info@tarnabycamping.se; www.tarnabycamping.se]** Take E12 fr Mo-i-Rana (Norway), cross border at Umbukta Fjellstue. Site sp N off E12 adj rv. Ignore site in town. Med, hdstg, pt shd; htd wc; chem disp; shwrs SEK5; el pnts (10A) SEK30; Indtte; shop; rest 3km; BBQ; rv fishing adj; TV; poss cr; quiet; ccard acc; red CCI. "Interesting wildlife area; excel walks & views; clean san facs; chapel on site." ♦ SEK 140 2008*

SWEDEN

⊞ **TIMMERNABBEN** *2G3* (1.5km S Rural/Coastal) *56.94405, 16.46708* **Camping Timmernabben, Varvsvägen 29, 38052 Timmernabben [(0499) 23809; fax 23871; timmernabben-camp@telia.com]** Turn off E22, site sp. Med, mkd pitch, pt sl, shd; htd wc; chem disp; baby facs; shwrs; el pnts (10A) inc; lndtte (inc dryer); tradsmn; BBQ; playgrnd; shgl beach adj; tennis; games area; internet; Eng spkn; quiet. CCS/CCI. "Tranquil site; delightful views; gd walking & windsurfing; paths on site not wheelchair-friendly." 2009*

TIVED *2F2* (2km N Rural) *58.79855, 14.5371* **Camping Tiveden (T24), Baggekärr 2, 69597 Tived [(0584) 474083; fax 474044; info@campingtiveden.com; www.camping tiveden.com]** Fr Karlsborg N on rd 202 to Undernäs. Turn R dir Tived, site on L in 2km. Med, mkd pitch, pt shd; wc; chem disp; mv waste; baby facs; shwrs SEK5; el pnts (10A) SEK40; lndtte (inc dryer); shop 2km; snacks; playgrnd; sand beach 15km; lake sw adj; boat & cycle hire; fishing; dogs; some statics; poss cr; Eng spkn; quiet; CCI. "Friendly owners; gd walks; conv Tiveden National Park & Göta Canal; excel." ♦ 1 Apr-30 Sep. SEK 145 2011*

TOMELILLA *2F4* (N Urban) *55.54578, 13.95856* **Väla Camping, Folkets Park, Parkgatan 4, 27380 Tomelilla [(0417) 18110; fax 14400; www.tomelilla.se/en/turism/]** Fr Ystad take rd 19 NE to Tomelilla; foll sp in town cent; recep at sw pool kiosk. Sm, mkd pitch, pt sl, pt shd; wc; chem disp; sauna; shwrs; el pnts (10A) SEK30; lndtte; shop & snacks 500m; BBQ; cooking facs; playgrnd; htd pool adj; some statics; dogs; Eng spkn; quiet; CCS. "Well-situated for historic sites, coastal towns; some traff noise at rush hrs." 1 Jun-1 Sep. SEK 125 2009*

TOREKOV *2E3* (1km N Coastal) *56.43540, 12.63700* **FirstCamp Båstad (L9), Flymossavägen 5, 26093 Torekov [tel/fax (0431) 364525; torekov@firstcamp.se; www.firstcamp.se]** Exit E6 onto rd 115 & head for Torekov, site on R bef Torekov. Lge, pt sl, pt shd; htd wc; chem disp; mv service pnt; baby facs; fam bthrm; sauna; shwrs inc; el pnts (10A); lndtte (inc dryer); shop; rest; snacks; bar; cooking facs; playgrnd; pool; beach adj; fishing; watersports; cycle hire; games rm; golf; wifi; cab TV; 10% statics; bus 800m; poss v cr high ssn; CCS. "Gd sea fishing; pitches cramped high ssn; Båstad picturesque town." ♦ 15 Apr-25 Sep. 2010*

⊞ **TORSBY** *2F1* (20km N Rural) *60.30529, 13.04200* **Abbas Stugby & Camping, Nötön 1, 68594 Torsby [(0560) 30360; fax 30361; info@abbasstugby.se; www.abbasstugby.se]** N fr Torsby on E45 for approx 20km, turn L after Vägsjöfors at site sp. Sm, pt sl, pt shd; htd wc; chem disp; baby facs; shwrs inc; el pnts (10A) SEK40; lndtte (inc dryer); tradsmn; rest; snacks; bar; BBQ; cooking facs; playgrnd; lake sw adj; games area; cycle & boat hire; wifi; entmnt; some cabins; dogs; Eng spkn; adv bkg; quiet; ccard acc; CCS. "Vg site." SEK 160 2009*

TORSBY *2F1* (5km S Rural) *60.09168, 13.03045* **Torsby Camping Svenneby (S21), Bredviken, 68533 Torsby [(0560) 71095; info@torsbycamping.se; www.torsbycamping. se]** On shore of Lake Fryken, sp fr rd 45. Med; wc; chem disp; mv service pnt; baby facs; sauna; shwrs SEK5; el pnts (10A) inc; lndtte (inc dryer); shop; rest; snacks; bar; playgrnd; lake sw; watersports; wifi; entmnt; TV; 10% statics; dogs; quiet; red long stay; ccard acc; CCI/CCS. 1 May-15 Sep. SEK 230 2008*

TORSHALLA see Eskilstuna *2G2*

TORSLANDA see Göteborg *2E3*

⊞ **TRANAS** *2F2* (3km E Rural) *58.03548, 15.0309* **Hättebadens Camping (F1), Hätte, 57382 Tranås [(0140) 17482; fax 68404; hattebaden@tranas.se; www.hattecamping.se]** On W edge Lake Sommen on rd 131, sp. Med, mkd pitch, pt shd; wc; mv service pnt; baby facs; shwrs; el pnts (10A) SEK40; lndtte (inc dryer); sm shop, rest, snacks adj; bar; playgrnd; lake sw; fishing; boating; cycle hire; wifi; 20% statics; dogs; phone; Quickstop o'night facs; Eng spkn; ccard acc; CCS/CCI. "Generous pitches; spacious site; gd, clean facs." ♦ SEK 180 2009*

⊞ **TRELLEBORG** *2E4* (2.5km E Coastal) *55.3638, 13.20933* **Camping Dalabadet, Dalköpingestrandväg 2, 23132 Trelleborg [(0410) 14905; fax 45068]** Bet sea shore & rd 9 (Trelleborg-Ystad), E of town. Foll sp fr town. Med, shd; htd wc; chem disp; mv service pnt; baby facs; sauna; shwrs inc; el pnts (10A) SEK30; lndtte; shop, rest nr; cooking facs; playgrnd; beach; tennis; cab TV; 20% statics; dogs; phone; ccard acc; CCS. "Conv for ferries; gd." ♦ SEK 200 2009*

TROLLHATTAN *2E2* (1km N Urban) *58.29206, 12.29848* **Trollhättans Camping Hjulkvarnelund (P7), Kungsportsvägen 7, 46139 Trollhättan [(0520) 30613; fax 32961; folketspark. trollhattan@telia.com; www.trollhattansfp.se/camping/]** Foll rd 45, site sp adj rv/canal. Med, pt sl, pt shd; wc; chem disp; mv service pnt; baby facs; shwrs inc; el pnts (10A) SEK40; lndtte (inc dryer); shops 1km; playgrnd; htd pool 300m; tennis; cycles; dogs; poss cr; Eng spkn; no adv bkg; some train & rd noise; CCS. "Access to Trollhätte Canal; beautiful, spacious wooded site; easy walk to town & impressive gorge/ waterfall; modern, clean san facs poss stretched high ssn." ♦ 2 May-4 Sep. SEK 150 2011*

⊞ **TROLLHATTAN** *2E2* (5km S Rural) *58.23946, 12.23605* **Stenrösets Camping (P25), Assarebo Stenröset 2, 46198 Trollhättan [(0520) 70710; fax 70811; stenroset.camping@ telia.com; www.stenrosetscamping.se]** Site visible & sp fr rd 45. Sm, sl, pt shd; htd wc (cont); mv service pnt; baby facs; shwrs inc; el pnts (10A) SEK30; lndtte (inc dryer); shop; BBQ; cooking facs; playgrnd; wifi; 5% statics; dogs; phone; quiet; Eng spkn; adv bkg; some rd noise; red long stay; ccard acc; CCS. "Helpful owners; conv Göteborg (60km); scenic surroundings & interesting area." ♦ SEK 170 2009*

TROSA *2H2* (3km S Coastal) *58.87288, 17.57431* **Trosa Havsbad Camping (D12), Rävuddsvägen 40, 61922 Trosa [(0156) 12494; info@trosahavsbad.se; www.trosahavsbad. se]** Exit E4 at junc 138 onto rd 218 twd Trosa, site sp dir harbour. Lge, pt sl, pt shd; htd wc; baby facs; chem disp; mv service pnt; shwrs; el pnts (10A) SEK40; lndtte (inc dryer); shops 3km; snacks; playgrnd; sand beach; lge sailing marina; fishing; tennis; cycling; wifi; 30% statics; dogs; phone; poss cr; quiet; CCS. ♦ 17 Apr-26 Sep. SEK 200 2010*

SWEDEN

TVAAKER *2E3* (4km NW Rural) *57.06445, 12.3593* **Himle Stugor & Camping (N38), Kärragård Spannarp 182, 43010 Tvååker [(0340) 43010; info@himlecamping.se; www.himlecamping.se]** 12km S fr Varberg fr E6 take exit at Rastplats (layby) Himle (not junc 53), turn L, site on L, sp. Med, unshd; htd wc; chem disp; mv service pnt; baby facs; shwrs inc; el pnts SEK30; Indtte (inc dryer); shop 500m; rest; snacks; bar; cooking facs; beach 7km; golf 1km; 40% statics; phone; Eng spkn; adv bkg; quiet; CCS. "Friendly owner; clean but ltd facs; conv Varberg." ♦ 18 Apr-22 Sep. SEK 170 2008*

TYLOSAND see Halmstad *2E3*

⊞ **UDDEVALLA** *2E2* (8km W Rural) *58.3306, 11.8222* **Unda Camping (030), Unda 149, 45194 Uddevalla [(0522) 86347; fax 86392; undacamping@telia.com; www.undacamping.se]** Exit E6 junc 96 Uddevalla N onto rte 44 twd Uddevalla Centrum. Site sp in 1km on R. Lge, pt sl, pt shd; htd wc; chem disp; mv service pnt; baby facs; sauna; shwrs SEK5; el pnts (10A) SEK45; Indtte (inc dryer); shop; rest; bar; cooking facs; playgrnd; pool; beach sw; fishing; boat & cycle hire; wifi; TV; many statics; phone; o'flow area when full; Quickstop o'night facs; adv bkg; ccard acc; CCS. "Lovely situation in nature reserve; recep hrs erratic low ssn." ♦ SEK 245 2010*

⊞ **UDDEVALLA** *2E2* (15km W Coastal) *58.31470, 11.72310* **Hafsten SweCamp Resort (028), Hafsten 120, 45196 Uddevalla [(0522) 644117; fax 644480; info@hafsten.se; www.hafsten.se]** Fr S take rd 160 thro Island of Orust, 1km N of bdge turn E at site sp for 4km. Fr N, turn W off E6 at junc 96 onto rd 161 sp Lysekil/Fiskebäcksil, after 8km at Rotviksbro rndabt turn onto rd 160 twd Orust. Turn L (E) in 2km, sp as above. App rd narr with passing places. Lge, pt shd, pt sl, terr; htd wc; chem disp; mv service pnt; baby facs; sauna; shwrs SEK5; el pnts (10A) inc; gas; Indtte (inc dryer); shop; snacks; bar; cooking facs; playgrnd; sand beach adj; fishing; tennis; boat & cycle hire; pedalos; horseriding; wifi; TV rm; 50% statics; dogs; phone; bus 4km; Quickstop o'night facs; poss cr & noisy high ssn; ccard acc; CCS. "Excel location; helpful staff; gd facs block; steel or rock pegs req for awnings; o'flow field used in high ssn - no facs." ♦ SEK 315 (CChq acc) 2009*

ULRICEHAMN *2F3* (2km S Rural) *57.77055, 13.40173* **Camping Skotteksgården (P34), Gamla Marbäcksvägen, 52390 Ulricehamn [(0321) 13184; fax 35185; skotteksgarden@telia.com; www.skottek.cc]** On rd 40 take dir Centrum. Foll sp Skotteksgården to Tranemo. Sm, mkd pitch, hdstg, unshd; htd wc; mv service pnt; serviced pitches; baby facs; fam bthrm; sauna; shwrs inc; el pnts SEK45; Indtte (inc dryer); shop & 1.5km; rest; snacks; cooking facs; playgrnd; lake sw adj; fishing; cycle & boat hire; 10% statics; dogs; phone; quiet; ccard acc; CCS. "Friendly, helpful owner; cycle path adj." ♦ 15 Apr-15 Oct. SEK 195 2009*

⊞ **ULRICEHAMN** *2F3* (12km S Rural) *57.67870, 13.37535* **Vegby Camping (P35), Storgatan 2, 52011 Vegby [(0321) 72912; fax 72562; vegbycamping@hotmail.com; www.vegbycamping.com]** Fr Rv 40 at Ulricehamn turn S on rd 157. Turn R at Gällstad & foll sp for Vegby & site. Med, terr, unshd; wc; chem disp; mv service pnt; baby facs; sauna; shwrs inc; el pnts (10A) SEK35; Indtte (inc dryer); shop; snacks; cooking facs; playgrnd; pool nr; lake sw; fishing; wifi; TV; Eng spkn; quiet; ccard acc; red low ssn; CCI. "Vg site; lake views fr all pitches; cycle rtes nr." SEK 190 2009*

⊞ **UMEA** *1C3* (5km NE Coastal) *63.84210, 20.33815* **FirstCamp Umeå (AC12), Nydalasjön 2, 90654 Umeå [(090) 702600; fax 702610; umea@firstcamp.se; www.firstcamp.se]** Sp fr E4 to N of town on lakeside. Lge, mkd pitch, pt shd; wc; chem disp; mv service pnt; 30% serviced pitches; shwrs inc; el pnts (10A) inc; Indtte (inc dryer); shop; snacks; playgrnd; htd pool complex; waterslide; lake sw 500m; tennis; games area; games rm; wifi; some statics; bus; ccard acc; CCS. "Attractive site; lge pitches suitable RVs & twin-axles; excel service block; conv E4." ♦ SEK 260 2009*

UNDERSAKER *1B3* (21km SW Rural) *63.1660, 13.0590* **Camping Vålågården, Östra Vålådalen 120, 83012 Vålådalen [tel/fax (0647) 35173; britta@valagarden.se; www.valagarden.se]** E14 to Undersåker, turn S at hotel sp Vålådalen. Site on L. Sm, pt shd; htd wc; chem disp; baby facs; sauna; shwrs; el pnts (10A); Indtte; shop; snacks; cooking facs; playgrnd; TV; 20% statics; dogs; Eng spkn; quiet; ccard acc; CCI. "Hiking in surrounding nature reserve; magnificent mountain scenery; friendly owners." 15 Feb-30 Apr & 1 Jun-30 Sep. 2008*

⊞ **UPPSALA** *2H1* (1.5km N Urban) *59.87133, 17.61923* **Fyrishov Camping (C12), Idrottsgatan 2, 75333 Uppsala [(018) 7274960; fax 244333; info@fyrishov.se; www.fyrishov.se]** Exit E4 Uppsala N; in 300m at rndabt foll sp Strangnas, Sala. In 2.25km exit via slip rd sp Bjorklinge, Fyrishov. At rndabt foll sp Fyrishov, in 1.6km at traff lts turn R & immed R. Site in Fyrishov Park adj sw & sports complex. Med, unshd; wc; chem disp; mv service pnt; shwrs SEK5; el pnts (10A) SEK45; Indtte (inc dryer); shop adj; rest adj; snacks; playgrnd; pool adj (sports complex behind pool); bus; poss cr; no adv bkg; ccard acc; CCS. "Within easy access of city cent; fair NH." ♦ SEK 180 2010*

URSHULT *2F3* (1km N Rural) *56.54476, 14.80703* **Urshults Camping (G7), Sirkövägen 19, 36013 Urshult [(0477) 20243; fax 48046; info@urshult-camping.com; www.urshult-camping.com]** Rd 30 S fr Växjö, turn W onto rd 120 at Tingsryd. In 10km at Urshult turn R, site sp on lakeside. Med, pt shd; htd wc; chem disp; mv service pnt; baby facs; shwrs; el pnts (10A) SEK45; Indtte (inc dryer); shop; tradsmn; snacks; cooking facs; playgrnd; lake sw adj; 10% statics; dogs; Eng spkn; quiet; CCS. "Well-run site; nr Kurrebo gardens & museum; vg." ♦ 25 Apr-25 Oct. SEK 165 2009*

SWEDEN

URSHULT *2F3* (10km NW Rural) *56.58466, 14.69491* **Getnö Gård Naturcamping (G24), Lake Åsnen Resort, 36010 Ryd [(0477) 24011; fax 24049; info@getnogard.se; www.getnogard.se]** W fr Urshult on rte 120 to junc with rte 126; turn NW onto rte 126, site in 7km via Ålshult to Getnö Gård. Site on shore Lake Åsnen. Med, mkd pitch, pt sl, pt shd; htd wc; chem disp; mv service pnt; baby facs; shwrs inc; el pnts (10A) SEK45; Indtte (inc dryer); shop; rest; snacks; bar; cooking facs; playgrnd; lake & private shgl beach adj; fishing; canoe hire; some cabins; dogs; phone; poss cr; Eng spkn; adv bkg; red long stay; quiet; CCS. "Beautiful location in private nature reserve; well-kept facs." ♦ 1 May-10 Oct. SEK 195 2009*

URSHULT *2F3* (14km NW Rural) *56.62111, 14.71305* **Mjölknabbens Camping, Mjölknabben, Sirkön, 36013 Urshult [(0477) 24018; ije404d@tninet.se; www.mjolknabben.com]** Fr Urshult foll sp Sirkön & Lake Åsnen. Site on lakeside. Sm, pt sl, pt shd; wc; chem disp; shwrs; el pnts; Indtte; shop 14km; tradsmn; BBQ; cooking facs; sand beach adj; fishing; canoe & fishing boat hire; dogs; bus adj; Eng spkn; quiet. "Excel fishing, birdwatching." 1 Apr-25 Oct. 2008*

VADSTENA *2F2* (2km N Rural) *58.46448, 14.9334* **Vadstena Camping (E9), Vätterviksbadets, 59294 Vadstena [(0143) 12730; info@vadstenacamping.se; www.vadstenacamping.se]** On rd 50, 3km N of Vadstena by Lake Vattern. Lge, mkd pitch, pt shd; wc; chem disp; mv service pnt; sauna; shwrs inc; el pnts (10A) SEK50; Indtte (inc dryer); shop; snacks; cooking facs; playgrnd; htd pool 3km; waterslide; sand beach & lake adj; fishing; tennis; wifi; 20% statics; dogs; poss cr; Eng spkn; adv bkg; ccard acc; red low ssn; CCS. "Many local attractions; vg family site; cycle path to town; gd birdwatching nrby." ♦ 29 Apr-11 Sep. SEK 200 2009*

VAGGERYD *2F3* (500m N Rural) *57.50973, 14.1327* **Hjortsjöns Camping (F8), Badplatsvägen, 56731 Vaggeryd [(0393) 12262; hjortsjonscamping@vaggeryd.se; www.hjortsjonscamping.com]** Site is at E side of lake; take turning at N app to Vaggeryd. Med, mkd pitch, pt sl, pt shd; wc; chem disp; baby facs; shwrs; el pnts (10A) SEK40; Indtte (inc dryer); shop; snacks; cooking facs; playgrnd; lake sw, fishing & boating adj; dogs; phone; quiet; CCS. "Lakeside site with woodland walks; gd touring base." ♦ 16 May-18 Sep. SEK 150 2009*

VALADALEN see Undersaker *1B3*

VANERSBORG *2E2* (3km N Coastal) *58.4122, 12.3208* **Ursands Camping (P6), Ursandsvägen, 46221 Vänersborg [(0521) 18666; ursandscamping@telia.com; www.ursandscamping.se]** On rd 45 heading N over rv bdge to site on R in 2km; sp fr bdge. Med, shd; wc; baby facs; mv service pnt; shwrs SEK7; el pnts (10A) SEK40; Indtte (inc dryer); shop high ssn; rest; bar; cooking facs; playgrnd; sand beach & lake sw; fishing; boating; cycle hire; wifi; TV; Quickstop o'night facs; poss cr; adv bkg; quiet; ccard acc; CCS. "Pleasant, family site." ♦ 23 Apr-12 Sep. SEK 205 2010*

VARBERG *2E3* (8km N Coastal) *57.1826, 12.22076* **Kärradals Camping (N7), Torpavägen 21, 43295 Varberg [(0340) 622377; fax 623576; brink@karradalscamping.se; www.karradalscamping.se]** Fr S exit E6 junc 55 Varberg N & foll sp Tångeberg & Kärradal. Fr N exit junc 56 & foll sp Värö & Åskloster, then Kärradal & site. Lge, mkd pitch, pt shd; wc; chem disp; mv service pnt; baby facs; shwrs SEK1; el pnts SEK40; Indtte (inc dryer); shop; rest; snacks; bar; cooking facs; playgrnd; sand beach 500m; games area; cycle hire; wifi; TV rm; 80% statics; dogs; phone; poss cr; Eng spkn; rlwy noise; ccard acc; CCI. "Rec arrive early afternoon high ssn; o'flow field has minimal san facs, but clean." ♦ 23 Apr-5 Sep. SEK 260 2010*

VARBERG *2E3* (4km NW Coastal) *57.1165, 12.21426* **Getteröns Camping (N6), Valvikavägen 1-3, 43293 Varberg [(0340) 16885; fax 10422; info@getteronscamping.se; www.getteronscamping.se]** Exit E6/E20 junc 54 Varberg Centrum, then W dir Getterön, site sp. V lge, mkd pitch, unshd; htd wc; mv service pnt; baby facs; sauna; shwrs; el pnts (6A) SEK45; Indtte (inc dryer); snacks; shop adj; playgrnd; sand beach 200m; fishing; cycle hire; wifi; entmnt; 50% statics; dogs; phone; poss cr; ccard acc; CCS. "Conv ferry to Denmark; Varberg pleasant town; lge nature reserve nr; gd beach walk; clean san facs; well laid-out site." ♦ 25 Apr-14 Sep. SEK 290 2008*

VARNAMO *2F3* (500m N Rural) *57.19055, 14.04615* **Värnamo Camping (F10), Prostsjön, 33183 Värnamo [(0370) 16660; fax 47150; info@varnamocamping.se]** Exit E4 Värnamo N, foll site sp. Site is 2km W of E4. Med, pt shd; wc; mv service pnt; baby facs; shwrs SEK5; el pnts (10A) SEK40; Indtte (inc dryer); shop high ssn; tradsmn; rest, snacks 500m; cooking facs; playgrnd; lake sw; fishing; boating; cycling; games rm; wifi; TV; 20% statics; dogs; phone; quiet; red CCS. "NH only; not particularly welcoming." ♦ 1 May-15 Sep. SEK 230 2010*

⊞ **VASTERVIK** *2G3* (3km SE Coastal) *57.73823, 16.66846* **Camping Lysingsbadets (H3), Lysingsvägen, 59353 Västervik [(0490) 254850; lysingsbadet@vastervik.se; www.lysingsbadet.se]** On coast 3km SE of town. Fr E22 foll sp around S ring rd; on app to Västervik. Site well sp fr E22. V lge, pt shd; htd wc; chem disp; mv service pnt; serviced pitches; sauna; shwrs inc; el pnts (10A) inc; Indtte (inc dryer); shop; 2 rests high ssn; snacks; bar; cooking facs; playgrnd; htd pool; waterslide; sand beach adj; boat & cycle hire; tennis; golf; wifi; entmnt; some statics; dogs; o'night area for m'vans; ccard acc. "Lovely, family site in landscaped, coastal woodland; easy access to islands by wooden footbdge fr site." ♦ SEK 330 2009*

VATTERSMALEN see Gränna *2F2*

VAXHOLM *2H1* (2km W Coastal) *59.40508, 18.3047* **Waxholm Strand & Camping (B6), Eriksövägen, 18521 Vaxholm [(08) 54130101; info@waxholmstrand.com; www.vaxholmstrand.com]** On rd 274 turn R immed after x-ing bdge to Vaxholm Island, foll sp 'Eriksö Camping'. Med, mkd pitch, pt sl, unshd; wc; chem disp; mv service pnt; shwrs inc; el pnts SEK40; Indtte (inc dryer); shop 1km; rest; snacks; playgrnd; sand beach adj; wifi; some statics; dogs; phone; adv bkg; quiet; ccard acc; CCS. "Conv Stockholm; boat trips to city & archipelago." ♦ 30 Apr-25 Sep. SEK 210 2011*

⊞ **VAXJO** *2F3* (5km N Rural) *56.92216, 14.81905* **Växjö SweCamp Evedal (G16), 35263 Växjö [(0470) 63034; fax 63122; evedals.camping@telia.com; www.evedalscamping.com]** Sp fr Växjö on E23. Med, pt shd; htd wc; chem disp; baby facs; sauna; shwrs inc; el pnts (10A) SEK50; Indtte (inc dryer); shop; rest adj; playgrnd; sand beach; watersports; cycle hire; wifi; TV; some statics; dogs; quiet; red 7+ days; ccard acc; CCS. "Ideal for children; in lakeside park in cent of glass industry; Kroneberg castle adj; Småland Museum in Växjö." SEK 225 2011*

VEGBY see Ulricehamn *2F3*

VENJAN *1B4* (1km E Rural) *60.9537, 13.93021* **Venjans Camping, Moravägen, 79293 Venjan [(0250) 62310; fax 62350; info@venjanscamping.se; www.venjanscamping.se]** Fr E45 turn W 3km N of junc of E45/64. Site in 18km, sp. Sm, mkd pitch, pt shd; htd wc; chem disp; mv service pnt; shwrs SEK5; el pnts (10A) SEK35; Indtte; shop 1km; playgrnd; lake sw & sand beach adj; fishing; boat hire; dogs; phone; Eng spkn; adv bkg; quiet; CCS. ♦ 15 May-1 Sep. SEK 130 2010*

VILHELMINA *1C2* (1.5km SE Rural) *64.62131, 16.67846* **Saiva Camping (AC4), Baksjön 1, 91231 Vilhelmina [(0940) 10760; info@saiva.se; www.saiva.se]** Sp on E site of rd 45. Med, pt shd; htd wc; chem disp; baby facs; shwrs SEK1; el pnts (10A) SEK30; Indtte (inc dryer); shop; snacks; playgrnd; lake beach; tennis; cycle hire; wifi; TV; some statics; dogs; phone; poss cr; quiet; ccard acc; CCS. "Gd; excel san facs in log style cabins; v helpful staff; lovely lakeside setting." ♦ 20 May-1 Oct. SEK 160 2011*

⊞ **VILHELMINA** *1C2* (5km NW Rural) *64.64998, 16.59240* **Kolgärdens Camping, Lövliden 16, 91292 Vilhelmina [(0940) 10304; kolgarden@vilhelmina.ac; www.kolgarden.se]** Site sp fr E45 N of Vilhelmina. Sm, pt shd; htd wc; chem disp; mv service pnt; sauna; shwrs inc; el pnts (10A) SEK35; Indtte; shop 5km; cooking facs; fishing; internet; TV rm; 50% statics; dogs; Eng spkn; quiet. "Wonderful lakeside location; clean san facs; helpful, pleasant owner; highly rec." ♦ SEK 145 2011*

VINSLOV *2F4* (500m N Rural) *56.10988, 13.91245* **Vinslövs Camping (L2), Troed Nelsongatan 18, 28834 Vinslöv [(070) 2077679; info@vinslovscamping.se]** Site sp of rte 21, Sm, mkd pitch, pt shd; wc; chem disp; shwrs inc; el pnts (6A) SEK40; Indtte (inc dryer) shop 500m; cooking facs; rest, snacks, bar 500m; playgrnd; htd pool adj; 20% statics; dogs; bus 500m; quiet; CCS. ♦ 1 Apr-30 Sep. SEK 120 2010*

⊞ **VITTSJO** *2F4* (1km N Rural) *56.35106, 13.66541* **Vittsjö Camping, Campingvägen 1, 28022 Vittsjö [(0451) 22489; v.turistforening@telia.com; www.vittsjocamping.se]** Well sp on N edge of vill on rd 117 by Lake Vittsjö, approx 20km N of Hässleholm. Sm, mkd pitch, hdstg, pt shd; htd wc; chem disp; mv service pnt; baby facs; shwrs inc; el pnts (16A); Indtte; shop & 2km; rest 2km; snacks; cooking facs; playgrnd; lake sw adj; cycle hire; wifi; 40% statics; dogs; Eng spkn; quiet; CCS. "Family-run site; security barrier; gd." SEK 160 2010*

YSTAD *2F4* (3km E Coastal) *55.43286, 13.8650* **Camping Sandskogens (M15), Österleden, 27160 Ystad [(0411) 19270; fax 19169; info@sandskogenscamping.se; www.sandskogenscamping.se]** On N side of rd 9. Lge, mkd pitch, shd; wc; chem disp; mv service pnt; baby facs; shwrs SEK5; el pnts (10A) SEK40; Indtte (inc dryer); shop; rest 400m; playgrnd; paddling pool; sand beach 100m; wifi; TV; some cabins; dogs; phone; no adv bkg; rlwy noise; ccard acc; CCS. "On Baltic coast; cycle path to beautiful town; mkd walks nrby; excel, well-managed site; full high ssn expects queues for checking in." ♦ 24 Apr-20 Sep. SEK 250 2011*

OLAND ISLAND

BORGHOLM *2G3* (200m N Coastal) *56.88281, 16.65713* **Camping Kapelludden (H27), Sandgatan 27, 38731 Borgholm [(0485) 560770; fax 560778; info@kapelludden.se; www.kapelludden.se]** Sp fr rd 136, site on edge of town. Lge, mkd pitch, unshd; wc; chem disp; mv service pnt; sauna; shwrs inc; el pnts (10A) SEK40; Indtte (inc dryer); shop & 200m; rest; snacks; bar; playgrnd; htd pool; games area; wifi; entmnt; poss cr; Eng spkn; ccard acc; CCS. "Gd touring base for island of Öland." ♦ 15 Apr-2 Oct. SEK 160 2008*

BORGHOLM *2G3* (3.5km NE Rural/Coastal) *56.88395, 16.72385* **Klinta Camping (H31), Klinta Bodarsväg 20, 38752 Köpingsvik [(0485) 72156; fax 72153; info@klinta.se; www.klintacamping.se]** Fr Borgholm N on rd 136, site on W side of rd N of Köpingsvik. Lge, hdg/mkd pitch, terr, unshd; htd wc; chem disp; baby facs; serviced pitches; shwrs SEK5; el pnts (10A) SEK40; Indtte; shop, rest high ssn; snacks; playgrnds; sand beach adj; tennis; golf 15km; wifi; entmnt; TV; many statics; dogs; poss cr; adv bkg; Eng spkn; ccard acc; CCS. "Most pitches sm for lge outfits; excel beach." ♦ 15 Apr-2 Oct. SEK 230 2008*

BORGHOLM *2G3* (12km S Coastal) *56.7933, 16.5664* **Ekerums Camping & Stugor SweCamp (H26), 38792 Borgholm [(0485) 564700; fax 564701; info@ekerum.nu; www.ekerum.nu]** Cross land bdge fr Kalmar, turn N, site sp on rd 136 bet Färjestaden & Borgholm. V lge, shd; htd wc; chem disp; mv service pnt; baby facs; shwrs inc; el pnts (10A) inc; Indtte (inc dryer); shop; rest; snacks; bar; cooking facs; playgrnd; 2 htd pools; waterslide; sand/shgl beach adj; fishing; boating; golf 1km; cycle hire; tennis 1km; wifi; TV rm; 20% statics; dogs; phone; Quickstop o'night facs; quiet; CCS. "Excel family site; private san facs avail; Borgholm castle worth visit." ♦ 11 Apr-2 Oct. SEK 300 (CChq acc) 2009*

BYXELKROK *2G3* (1km N Coastal) *57.33013, 17.01211* **Neptuni Camping (H41), Småskogsvägen 2, 38075 Byxelkrok [(0485) 28495 or 070 5428495 (mob); neptuni.camping@telia.com; www.neptunicamping.se]** Fr S on rd 136 thro Böda, at Byxelkrok turn R past harbour for 200m. Site on R. Med, pt shd; wc; chem disp; mv service pnt; shwrs SEK5; el pnts (16A) SEK40; Indtte (inc dryer); shop; playgrnd; beach adj; games area; dogs; phone; Eng spkn; quiet; ccard acc; CCS. "Conv touring base N Öland, sh walk to harbour, rest & supmkt." ♦ 30 Apr-31 Aug. SEK 170 2009*

⊞ **DEGERHAMN** *2G4* (12km S Rural) *56.23778, 16.4530* **Ottenby Vandrarhem & Camping (H57), Ottenby 106, 38065 Degerhamn [(0485) 662062; fax 662161; info@ottenbyvandrarhem.se; www.ottenbyvandrarhem.se]** Rd 36 S to Ottenby, bear R for 4km, site on R at youth hostel. Sm, unshd; htd wc; chem disp; mv service pnt; baby facs; shwrs inc; el pnts (10A) SEK40; Indtte (inc dryer); shop 5km; tradsmn; cooking facs; htd pool; paddling pool; cycle hire; 10% statics; dogs free; phone; quiet; ccard acc. "On edge Ottenby nature reserve; excel walks & birdwatching - ssn geared to bird migration; poss noise fr late arrivals & early risers as no barrier; World Heritage Site on S part of island." ♦ SEK 160 2010*

FARJESTADEN *2G3* (1km N Coastal) *56.68681, 16.48253* **Krono Camping Saxnäs/Öland (H25), Södra Saxnäs, 38695 Färjestaden [(0485) 35700; info@kcsaxnas.se; www.kcsaxnas.se]** Cross Öland Bdge fr Kalmar on rd 137, take exit for Öland Zoo/Saxnäs. Site sp. Lge, mkd pitch, pt shd; wc; chem disp; mv service pnt; baby facs; 25% serviced pitches; shwrs inc; el pnts (10A) inc (poss rev pol); Indtte; shop; rest; bar; playgrnd; shgl beach adj; games area; sat TV inc; some cabins; dogs; phone; adv bkg; poss noisy high ssn; ccard acc; red low ssn; CCS. "Öland is beautiful island with 400 19thC windmills." ♦ 12 Apr-2 Oct. SEK 350 2011*

LOTTORP *2G3* (3km N Coastal) *57.17876, 17.03746* **Sonjas Camping (H39), John Emils Gata 43, 38074 Löttorp [(0485) 23212; fax 23255; info@sonjascamping.se; www.sonjascamping.oland.com]** Fr Kalmar over bdge to Öland Island, take rd 136 N thro Borgholm. Cont to Löttorp, site sp. Lge, mkd pitch, pt shd; htd wc; chem disp; mv service pnt; fam bthrm; baby facs; sauna; shwrs SEK5; el pnts (10A) SEK45; Indtte (inc dryer); shop; rest; snacks; bar; cooking facs; playgrnd; htd pool; paddling pool; sand beach adj; fishing; tennis; cycle hire; wifi; entmnt; 10% cabins; adv bkg; quiet. CCS. "Vg beach; excel family site; vg touring base." ♦ 21 Apr-4 Oct. SEK 250 (6 persons) 2010*

MELLBODA *2G3* (500m E Coastal) *57.23891, 17.0698* **Böda Hamns Camping (H43), Bödahamnsvägen 42, 38074 Mellböda [(0485) 22043; fax 22457; info@bodahamnscamping.se; www.bodahamnscamping.se]** N fr Borgholm for 52km on rte 136 twd Mellböda & Böda, turn R twd Böda Hamn, site nr harbour. Lge, mkd pitch, pt shd; chem disp; mv service pnt; shwrs; el pnts (10A) SEK40; Indtte (inc dryer); shop; rest; snacks; bar; BBQ; cooking facs; playgrnd; sand beach adj; games area; wifi; some statics; dogs free; phone; Eng spkn; quiet; ccard acc. "Sep area of beach for dogs; vg site." ♦ 29 Apr-3 Oct. SEK 160 2010*

When we get home I'm going to post all these site report forms to the Club for next year's guide.
The deadline's mid September 2013

MORBYLANGA *2G3* (1km N Coastal) *56.52163, 16.37725* **Mörbylånga Camping, Kalvhagen 1, 38062 Mörbylånga [tel/fax (0485) 40591; info@morbylangacamping.se; www.morbylangacamping.se]** Site sp off rd 136 in Mörbylånga. Med, unshd; wc; chem disp; mv service pnt; baby facs; shwrs inc; el pnts SEK40; Indtte; shop; rest; snacks; bar; cooking facs; sand beach adj; fishing; games area; cycle hire; sat TV; some statics; dogs; phone; Eng spkn; red low ssn; ccard acc; CCS. "Pleasant, relaxing, family-run site with open view; unusual & interesting island." ♦ 15 May-1 Oct. SEK 190 2009*

SWEDEN

Distances are shown in kilometres and are calculated from town/city centres along the most practical roads, although not necessarily taking the shortest route. 1km = 0.62miles

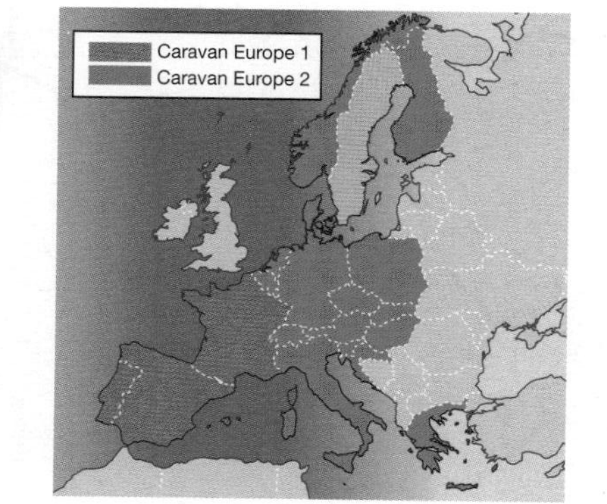

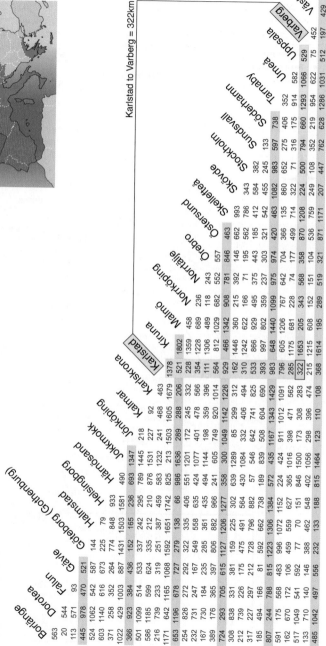

Karlstad to Varberg = 322km

	Borlänge	Dorotea	Falun	Gävle	Göteborg (Gothenburg)	Halmstad	Helsingborg	Härnösand	Jokkmokk	Jönköping	Kalmar	Karlskrona	Karlstad	Kiruna	Malmö	Norrköping	Norrtälje	Örebro	Östersund	Skellefteå	Skövde	Stockholm	Sundsvall	Söderhamn	Tarnaby	Umeå	Uppsala	Varberg	Västerås
Dorotea	563																												
Falun	20	544																											
Gävle	113	571	93																										
Göteborg (Gothenburg)	445	978	470	521																									
Halmstad	524	1062	542	587	144																								
Helsingborg	603	1140	616	673	225	79																							
Härnösand	371	258	352	264	774	848	933																						
Jokkmokk	1022	429	1003	887	1431	1503	1581	490																					
Jönköping	366	923	384	436	152	165	236	693	1347																				
Kalmar	501	1099	514	533	337	242	295	789	1445	218																			
Karlskrona	586	1185	599	624	335	212	210	876	1531	227	92																		
Karlstad	216	739	233	319	251	387	459	583	1232	241	468	463																	
Kiruna	1171	642	1165	1068	1592	1651	1742	825	213	1503	1605	1679	1378																
Malmö	653	1196	678	727	279	138	66	986	1636	289	288	206	521	1802															
Norrköping	254	826	272	292	322	335	406	551	1201	172	245	332	228	1359	458														
Norrtälje	232	731	247	167	549	558	635	424	1077	401	478	566	354	1228	689	236													
Örebro	167	730	184	235	285	361	435	494	1144	198	359	396	111	1306	489	118	243												
Östersund	389	176	365	397	806	882	966	241	605	749	920	1014	564	812	1029	682	552	557											
Skellefteå	724	293	705	615	1127	1206	1277	358	300	1049	1142	1226	929	466	1342	908	781	846	463										
Skövde	308	838	331	381	159	225	302	639	1289	85	299	312	162	1446	360	215	392	146	662	993									
Stockholm	212	739	226	175	475	491	564	430	1084	332	406	494	310	1242	622	166	71	195	562	786	343								
Sundsvall	317	227	297	212	728	796	882	57	546	642	741	825	533	866	929	495	375	443	185	412	584	382							
Söderhamn	185	494	166	81	592	662	738	189	839	508	604	690	393	997	802	359	237	303	321	542	455	245	133						
Tarnaby	807	244	788	815	1223	1306	1384	572	435	1167	1343	1429	983	648	1440	1099	975	974	420	463	1082	983	597	738					
Umeå	591	175	568	483	996	1072	1152	224	424	911	1012	1091	796	605	1206	767	642	704	366	135	860	652	275	406	352				
Uppsala	162	670	172	106	459	559	627	365	1016	398	471	562	285	1175	681	228	74	177	499	714	322	71	316	175	914	582			
Varberg	517	1049	541	592	77	70	151	846	1500	173	308	283	322	1653	205	343	568	358	870	1208	224	500	794	660	1293	1066	529		
Västerås	133	710	140	146	388	462	548	402	1056	298	396	474	215	1215	608	152	151	104	536	759	249	108	352	219	954	622	75	452	
Växjö	485	1042	497	556	232	133	188	815	1464	123	110	108	368	1614	195	289	519	321	871	1171	207	447	762	628	1286	1031	512	197	429

Motorways
Major roads
Main roads
0 50 100 150 kms
0 50 100 mls
All year site(s)
Seasonal site(s)
No sites listed
200m +
0–200m
N
W
E
S
NORWEGIAN SEA
NORWAY
FINLAND
GULF OF BOTHNIA
Arctic Circle
Tromsø
Skibotn
Trædal
Narvik
Muonio
KIRUNA
Pajala
Gällivare
Storjord
JOKKMOKK
Rovaniemi
Mo i Rana
Arjeplog
Haparanda
Rörbäck
TÄRNABY
Arvidsjaur
Luleå
Sorsele
Slagnäs
Norrfjärden
Storuman
Byske
Vilhelmina
SKELLEFTEÅ
Gäddede
DOROTEA
Ånäset
Åsele
UMEÅ
Strömsund
Nordmaling
Trondheim
Undersåker
Lit
ÖSTERSUND
Hammarstrand
Ramvik
HÄRNÖSAND
Åsama
Stöde
Tynset
Hede
SUNDSVALL
Njurundabommen
Lofsdalen
Sveg
Drevsjø
Särna
Ljusdal
Bollnäs
Älvdalen
Orsa
SÖDERHAMN
Venjan
Mora
Gesunda
Sysslebäck
Johannisholm
Rättvik
GÄVLE
see map 2
© Collins Bartholomew Ltd 20

Map 1

see map 1
E
F
G
H
1
2
3
4
Sysslebäck
Malung
Leksand
GÄVLE
Skutskär
FALUN
BORLÄNGE
Hedesunda
Söderfors
Kongsvinger
Ekshärad
Torsby
Österfärnebo
OSLO
Sala
UPPSALA
Filipstad
NORRTÄLJE
Kapellskär
VÄSTERÅS
Enköping
Glava
Kil
Nora
Årjäng
KARLSTAD
Arboga
Vaxholm
Kristinehamn
ÖREBRO
Eskilstuna
STOCKHOLM
Degerfors
Mariefred
Säffle
VÄNERN
Bengtsfors
Åmål
Järna
Strömstad
Ed
Finnerödja
Katrineholm
Hova
Nynäshamn
Trosa
Tived
Mariestad
Nyköping
Grebbestad
Mellerud
Bocksjö
Kolmården
Fjällbacka
Lidköping
Borensberg
Karlsborg
Motala
NORRKÖPING
Uddevalla
Vänersborg
Roxenbaden
Vadstena
Söderköping
SKÖVDE
Linköping
BALTIC
SEA
Trollhättan
Hjo
VÄTTERN
Nossebro
Gryt
Falköping
Gränna
Alingsås
Tranås
Marstrand
Kungälv
Gamleby
GÖTEBORG
Borås
Ulricehamn
JÖNKÖPING
Hindås
Västervik
Hult
GOTLAND
Eksjö
Kungsbacka
Kinna
Vaggeryd
Åsa
Byxelkrok
Hillerstorp
Oskarshamn
Mellböda
VARBERG
Värnamo
Löttorp
Tvååker
Timmernabben
Falkenberg
Lidhult
Ljungby
VÄXJÖ
Kosta
Borgholm
Läckeby
HALMSTAD
Hovmantorp
ÖLAND
KALMAR
Färjestaden
Mellbystrand
Älmhult
Markaryd
Urshult
Torekov
Mörbylånga
Höganäs
Vittsjö
Bergkvara
Degerhamn
Ängelholm
Karlshamn
Klippan
KARLSKRONA
HELSINGBORG
Vinslöv
Sölvesborg
Röstånga
Kristianstad
Landskrona
Åhus
Barsebäck
KØBENHAVN
Kivik
Sjöbo
Simrishamn
DENMARK
MALMÖ
Tomelilla
Skanör
Ystad
Löderup
Trelleborg
BORNHOLM IS
(Denmark)
0
50
100 kms
0
50 mls
© Collins Bartholomew Ltd 2011

Switzerland

Country Introduction

© iStockPhoto.com/ Stefano Sala

Matterhorn

Population: 7.5 million

Capital: Bern (population 121,000)

Area: 41,293 sq km

Bordered by: Austria, France, Germany, Italy, Liechtenstein

Terrain: Mostly mountainous; Alps in the south, Jura in the north-west; central plateau of rolling hills, plains and large lakes

Climate: Temperate climate varying with altitude; cold, cloudy, rainy or snowy winters; cool to warm summers with occasional showers

Highest Point: Dufourspitze 4,634m

Languages: French, German, Italian, Romansch

Local Time: GMT or BST + 1, i.e. 1 hour ahead of the UK all year

Currency: Swiss Franc (CHF) divided into 100 centimes (also called 'rappen' or 'centesimi' in German/Italian areas of the country; £1 = CHF 1.43, CHF 10 = £7.01 (October 2011)

Telephoning: From the UK dial 0041 for Switzerland. All area codes start with a zero which must be dialled when making calls within Switzerland, but not when calling Switzerland from abroad. To call the UK from Switzerland dial 0044, omitting the initial zero of the area code.

The international code for Liechtenstein is 00423

Emergency numbers: Police 117; Fire brigade 118; Ambulance 144 or 112 for any service

Public Holidays 2012

Jan 1, 22; Apr 6, 9, 16; May 13, 17, 28; Aug 1 (National Day); Sep 10, 16, 17; Dec 25, 26.

Public Holidays 2013

Jan 1, 2; Mar 29; Apr 1, 15; May 9, 12, 20; Aug 1 (National Day); Sep 9, 15, 16; Dec 25, 26.

These public holidays are not necessarily celebrated throughout Switzerland and individual cantons may have additional holidays. School summer holidays vary by canton but are approximately from early July to mid/end August.

Tourist Office

SWITZERLAND TOURISM
30 BEDFORD STREET, LONDON WC2E 9ED
Tel: 00800 100 20030
www.myswitzerland.com info.uk@myswitzerland.com

The following introduction to Switzerland should be read in conjunction with the important information contained in the Handbook chapters at the front of this guide.

Camping and Caravanning

There are approximately 340 campsites available to touring caravanners, with around 70 sites remaining open in winter. Some sites may be nearly full with statics, with only a small area for tourers.

There are 29 Touring Club Suisse (TCS) sites and affiliated sites classified into five categories according to amenities available. All TCS campsites have a service station with facilities for emptying sanitary tanks. For further information and current rates see www.reisen-tcs.ch

The Swiss Camp Sites Association (VSC/ACS) produces a camping and road map covering approximately 180 sites, including charges and classification. See www.swisscamps.ch

To download a guide to more than 40 campsites, including those open in winter, in the Bernese Oberland region of Switzerland see www.camping-bo.ch or write to Camping Berner Oberland, Lehnweg 6, CH-3800 Interlaken, fax 0041 033 8231920.

The Swiss are environmentally conscious with only limited scope for removing waste. Recycling is vigorously promoted and it is normal to have to put rubbish in special plastic bags obtainable from campsites. A 'rubbish charge' or 'entsorgungstaxe' of approximately CHF 3 per person per day is commonly charged.

A visitors' tax, varying according to the area, is levied in addition to the site charges. A Camping Card International is not mandatory but recommended. At TCS sites a 10% reduction is granted during low season on presentation of a CCI.

Recent visitors report that pitches are rarely totally level and anyone with a motorhome should take a good supply of blocks or other levelling devices.

The rules on casual/wild camping differ from canton to canton. It may be tolerated in some areas with the permission of the landowner or local police, or in motorway service areas, but local laws – particularly on hygiene – must not be contravened. For reasons of security The Caravan Club recommends that overnight stops should always be at recognised campsites.

Country Information

Cycling

Switzerland has 9,000 km of cycle trails, including nine national cycle routes, which have been planned to suit all categories of cyclist from families to sports cyclists. Routes are marked by red and white signs. The problem of strenuous uphill gradients can be overcome by using trails routed near railway lines. Most trains will transport bicycles and often bicycles are available for hire at stations. Switzerland Tourism can provide more information.

Transportation of Bicycles

Bicycles may be carried on the roof of a car providing they are attached to an adequate roof rack and providing the total height does not exceed 4 metres. Bicycles carried on special carriers at the rear of a vehicle can exceed the width of the vehicle by 20 cm on each side, but the total width must not exceed 2 metres. The rear lights and number plate must remain visible and the driver's view must not be obstructed.

Electricity and Gas

Usually current on campsites varies between 4 and 16 amps. Plugs have two or, more usually, three round pins. Some campsites have CEE connections. Some may lend or hire out adaptors – but do not rely on it – and it may be advisable to purchase an appropriate adaptor cable with a Swiss 3-pin plug. Adaptors are readily available in local supermarkets.

The full range of Campingaz cylinders is available from large supermarkets.

*See **Electricity and Gas** in the section **DURING YOUR STAY.***

Entry Formalities

Holders of valid British or Irish passports may enter Switzerland without a visa for a period of up to six months.

Regulations for Pets

*See **Pet Travel Scheme** under **Documents** in the section **PLANNING AND TRAVELLING.***

Medical Services

There are reciprocal emergency health care arrangements with Switzerland for EU citizens. A European Health Insurance Card (EHIC) will enable you to get reduced cost for emergency treatment in a public hospital but you will be required to pay the full cost of treatment and apply afterwards for a refund from the Department for Work & Pensions on your return to the UK. Ensure that any doctor you visit is registered with the national Swiss Health Insurance Scheme. Dental treatment is not covered.

You will have to pay 50% of the costs of any medically-required ambulance transport within Switzerland and/or Liechtenstein, including air ambulance. There is a fixed charge for in-patient treatment in a public hospital.

If you enjoy hiking and outdoor sports you should seek medical advice before you travel about preventative measures and immunisation against tick-borne encephalitis, a potentially serious and debilitating viral disease of the central nervous system which is endemic from spring to autumn. Lyme disease is an equally serious tick-borne infection for which there is no preventative vaccine. Ticks are found in rural and forested areas, particularly in long grass, bushes, hedgerows and woods, and in scrubland and areas where animals wander.

If you think you might be at risk use an insect repellent containing DEET, wear long sleeves and long trousers, inspect the body for ticks after outdoor activity and remove with tweezers, and avoid unpasteurised dairy products in risk areas. See www.tickalert.org, email info@tickalert.org or telephone 01943 468010.

You are strongly recommended to obtain comprehensive travel and medical insurance before travelling to Switzerland, such as The Caravan Club's Red Pennant Overseas Holiday Insurance – see www.caravanclub.co.uk/redpennant. If you are proposing to participate in sports activities, such as skiing and mountaineering, your personal holiday insurance should be extended to cover these activities and should also include cover for mountain rescue and helicopter rescue costs.

*See **Medical Matters** in the section **DURING YOUR STAY.***

Opening Hours

Banks – Mon-Fri 8.30am-4.30pm (some close for lunch; late opening once a week to 5.30pm/6pm in some towns).

Museums – Tue-Sun 10am-5pm; closed Monday; check locally.

Post Offices – Mon-Fri 7.30am-12pm & 13.45pm-6pm (no lunch break in main towns); Sat 7.30am-11am.

Shops – Mon-Fri 8am/8.30am-6.30pm/7pm (closed lunch time) & Sat 8am-4pm/7pm (sometimes lunch time closing); shops close early on the eve of a public holiday. Food shops may be closed on religious and public holidays.

Safety and Security

Most visits to Switzerland and Liechtenstein are trouble-free and the crime rate is low. However, petty theft is on the increase and you should be alert to pickpockets, confidence tricksters and thieves in city centres, railway stations and other public places.

You should be aware of the risks involved in the more hazardous sports activities and take note of weather forecasts and conditions, which can change rapidly in the mountains. You should be well-equipped; do not undertake the activity alone, study the itinerary and inform someone of your plans. Off-piste skiers should follow the advice given by local authorities and guides; to ignore such advice could put yourselves and other mountain users in danger.

Switzerland and Liechtenstein share with the rest of Europe an underlying threat from terrorism. Attacks could be indiscriminate and against civilian targets in public places, including tourist sites.

*See **Safety and Security** in the section **DURING YOUR STAY.***

British Embassy

THUNSTRASSE 50, CH-3005 BERN
Tel: 031 3597700
http://ukinswitzerland.fco.gov.uk/en

British Consulate-General

AVENUE LOUIS CASAÏ 58
CH-1216 COINTRIN, GENEVE
Tel: 022 9182400

There are also Honorary Consulates/Vice-Consulates/ Consular Agencies in Allschwill (Basel), Lugano, Mollens-Valais, St Légier (Montreux) and Zürich.

Irish Embassy

KIRCHENFELDSTRASSE 68, CH-3005 BERN
Tel: 031 3521442
www.embassyofireland.ch

There is also an Honorary Consulate in Zürich.

Customs Regulations

Alcohol and Tobacco

Switzerland is not a member of the EU and visitors aged 17 years and over may import the following items duty-free:

200 cigarettes or 100 cigarillos or 50 cigars or 250 gm tobacco

1 litre spirits or 2 litres spirits fortified wine

4 litres wine

16 litres beer

Other goods (including perfume) up to a value of €300

Caravans and Motorhomes

Caravans registered outside Switzerland may be imported without formality up to a height of 4 metres, width of 2.55 metres and length of 12 metres (including towbar). The total length of car + caravan/trailer must not exceed 18.75 metres.

Foodstuffs

From EU countries you may import per person 500 gm of fresh, chilled or frozen meat and 3.50 kg of all other meat and meat products.

Refund of VAT on Export

A foreign visitor who buys goods in Switzerland in a 'Tax-Back SA' or 'Global Refund Schweiz AG' shop may obtain a VAT refund (7.6%) on condition that the value of the goods is at least CHF 300 including VAT. Visitors should complete a form in the shop and produce it, together with the goods purchased, at Customs on leaving Switzerland. For more information see www.globalrefund.com or www.myswitzerland.com

*See also **Customs Regulations** in the section **PLANNING AND TRAVELLING.***

Documents

Vehicle(s)

Carry your original vehicle registration certificate (V5C), MOT certificate (if applicable) and insurance documentation at all times. Recent visitors report that drivers may be asked to produce proof of vehicle ownership at the border and failure to do so may mean that entry into Switzerland is refused. If you are driving a vehicle which does not belong to you, you should be in possession of a letter of authorisation from the owner.

*See also **Documents** in the section **PLANNING AND TRAVELLING.***

Money

Travellers' cheques are not widely accepted as a means of payment but can be cashed at banks and bureaux de change, banks offering the best exchange rates.

Prices in shops are often displayed in both Swiss francs and euros.

The major credit cards are widely accepted, although you may find small supermarkets and restaurants do not accept them. In addition, recent visitors report that retail outlets may accept only one kind of credit card (MasterCard or VISA), not both, and it may be advisable to carry one of each. You may occasionally find that a surcharge is imposed for the use of credit cards.

Carry your credit card issuers'/banks' 24-hour UK contact numbers in case of loss or theft of your cards.

Motoring

Accidents

In the case of accidents involving property damage only, when drivers decide not to call the police, a European Accident Statement must be completed.

In the case of personal injury or of damage to the road, road signs, lights, barriers etc, the police must be called.

Alcohol

The maximum permitted level of alcohol is 50 milligrams in 100 millilitres of blood, i.e. lower than that permitted in the UK (80 milligrams). A blood test may be required after an accident, and if found positive, the penalty is either a fine or a prison sentence, plus withdrawal of permission to drive in Switzerland for at least two months. Police carry out random breath tests.

Breakdown Service

The motoring and leisure organisation Touring Club Suisse (TCS) operates a 24-hour breakdown service, 'Patrouille TCS'. To call for help throughout Switzerland and Liechtenstein, dial 140. On motorways use emergency phones and ask for TCS.

Members of clubs affiliated to the AIT, such as The Caravan Club, who can show a current membership card will be charged reduced rates for breakdown assistance and towing, according to the time of day and/or the distance towed. Payment by credit card is accepted.

Essential Equipment

Lights

Dipped headlights are recommended at all times, even during the day. They are compulsory in all tunnels, whether or not they are lit, and in poor visibility. Bulbs are more likely to fail with constant use and you are recommended to carry spares.

Nationality Plate (GB or IRL Stickers)

Strictly-speaking, it is necessary to display a conventional nationality plate or sticker when driving outside EU member states, even when vehicle number plates incorporate the GB or IRL Euro-symbol. However, the Swiss authorities have adopted a commonsense approach and confirm that it is not necessary to display a separate GB or IRL sticker if your number plates display the GB or IRL Euro-symbol. If your number plates do not incorporate this symbol then you will need a separate sticker.

Warning Triangles

All vehicles must be equipped with a warning triangle which has to be within easy reach and not in the boot.

Child Restraint System

Vehicles registered outside of Switzerland that are temporarily imported into the country, have to comply with the country of registration with regards to safety belt equipment and child restraint regulations. All children up to 12 years of age must be placed in an approved UN ECE 44.03 regulation child restraint, unless they measure more than 150cm and are over seven years old.

Winter Driving

Alpine winters often make driving more difficult. You should equip your vehicle(s) with winter tyres and snow chains and check road conditions prior to departure.

A sign depicting a wheel and chains indicates where snow chains are required for the mountain road ahead.

Snow chains are compulsory in areas where indicated by the appropriate road sign. They must be fitted on at least two drive wheels. Snow chains can be hired or purchased from Polar Automotive Ltd, tel 01892 519933, fax 01892 528142, www.snowchains.com email: polar@snowchains.com (10% discount for Caravan Club members).

*See **Motoring – Equipment** in the section **PLANNING AND TRAVELLING.***

Fuel

Prices of petrol vary according to the brand and region, being slightly cheaper in self-service stations. Credit cards are generally accepted.

On motorways, where prices are slightly higher, some service stations are open 24 hours and others are open from 6am to 10pm or 11pm only, but petrol is available outside these hours from automatic pumps where payment can be made by means of bank notes or credit cards.

There are 36 outlets (2011) selling LPG (GPL) – see www.jaquet-ge.ch for a list of outlets and a map showing their location.

*See also **Fuel** under **Motoring – Advice** in the section **PLANNING AND TRAVELLING.***

Mountain Roads and Tunnels

One of the most attractive features of Switzerland for motorists is the network of finely engineered mountain passes, ranging from easy main road routes to high passes that may be open only from June to October. In the Alps most roads over passes have been modernised; only the Umbrail Pass, which is not recommended for caravans, is not completely tarred. Passes have a good roadside telephone service for calling aid quickly in the event of trouble.

A blue rectangular sign depicting a yellow horn indicates a mountain postal road and the same sign with a red diagonal stripe indicates the end of the postal road. On such roads, vehicles belonging to the postal services have priority.

During certain hours, one-way traffic only is permitted on certain mountain roads. The hours during which traffic may proceed in either or both directions are posted at each end of the road. The TCS road map of Switzerland, scale 1:300,000, indicates this type of road.

Speed must always be moderate on mountain passes, very steep roads and roads with numerous bends. Drivers must not travel at a speed which would prevent them from stopping within the distance they can see ahead. When it is difficult to pass oncoming vehicles, the heavier vehicle has priority.

Slow-moving vehicles are required by law to use the lay-bys provided on alpine roads to allow the free flow of faster traffic. This is the case where a car towing a caravan causes a queue of vehicles capable of a higher speed.

*See also **Advice for Drivers** under **Mountain Passes and Tunnels** in the section **PLANNING AND TRAVELLING.***

Parking

Parking in cities is difficult and it is worth using the numerous Park & Ride schemes which operate around major towns and cities. Illegal parking of any kind is much less tolerated in Switzerland than in any of its neighbours and fines are common for even minor violations.

Pay and display car parks and parking meters are used throughout the country and permitted parking time varies from 15 minutes to 2 hours. Feeding meters is not allowed. Wheel clamps are not used, but vehicles causing an obstruction may be removed to a car pound.

You may park in a 'blue zone' for limited periods free of charge providing you display a parking disc in your vehicle. These are available from petrol stations, kiosks, restaurants and police stations. Parking in a marked red zone is free for up to 15 hours with a red parking disc obtainable from police stations, tourist offices, etc.

Parking on pavements is not allowed. Do not park where there is a sign 'Stationierungsverbot' or 'Interdiction de Stationner'. Continuous or broken yellow lines and crosses at the side of the road and any other yellow markings also indicate that parking is prohibited.

*See also **Parking Facilities for the Disabled** under **Motoring – Advice** in the section **PLANNING AND TRAVELLING.***

Priority

In general, traffic (including bicycles) coming from the right has priority at intersections but drivers approaching a roundabout must give way to all traffic already on the roundabout, i.e. from the left, unless otherwise indicated by signs. However, vehicles on main roads – indicated by a yellow diamond with a white border or a white triangle with a red border and an arrow pointing upwards – have priority over traffic entering from secondary roads.

Sometimes pedestrians have right of way and will expect vehicles to stop for them, so please be aware of this.

Roads

Switzerland has some 72,000 kilometres of well-surfaced roads, from motorways to local municipal roads, all well-signposted. Four-wheel drive vehicles must not be driven off road without the permission of the local authority.

During daylight hours outside built-up areas you must sound your horn before sharp bends where visibility is limited. After dark this warning must be given by flashing your headlights.

Dial the following numbers for information:

162: Weather information

163: Road conditions, mountain passes, access to tunnels and traffic news

187: In winter, avalanche bulletins; in summer, wind forecasts for Swiss lakes

It is also possible to obtain updated information on road conditions via teletext in larger motorway service areas.

Motorway Tax

To be able to use national roads (motorways and semi-motorways) in Switzerland, motor vehicles and trailers up to a total weight of 3,500kg must have a vehicle sticker (vignette). The ticket is valid for 14 months from 01st December every year and costs CHF40 (2011). An additional fee of CHF 40 is charged for caravans and trailers. The sticker allows multiple re-entry into Switzerland during the period of validity.

If you enter a motorway or semi-motorway without a sticker you will be fined CHF100 and also the cost of the sticker. The stickers can be bought from custom offices, petrol stations or TCS offices in Switzerland or alternatively they can be purchased from the UK before you travel by calling the Swiss Travel Centre on 00800 100 20030.

Heavy Vehicle Tax

Vehicles (including motorhomes) over 3,500kg must pay a heavy vehicle tax on entry into Switzerland which is applicable for all roads. This charge applies for every day you are in Switzerland and your vehicle is on the road. For a 10-day pass (valid for a year) you self-select the days that your vehicle is on the road and, therefore, you are not penalised if your motorhome is parked at a campsite and not driven on a public road. This heavy vehicle tax applies to any Swiss road and replaces the need for a motorway vignette.

This particular tax is only payable at the border on entry into Switzerland and if there is any doubt about the exact weight of your vehicle it will be weighed. An inspection may be carried out at any time and is likely at the exit border. Failure to pay the tax can result in an immediate fine.

Road Signs and Markings

Road signs and markings conform to international standards.

White lettering on a green background indicates motorways, whereas state and provincial main roads outside built-up areas have white lettering on a blue background. This is the reverse of the colouring used in France and Germany and may initially cause confusion when driving from one country to the other. Road signs on secondary roads are white with black lettering.

The following are some road signs which you may encounter:

Postal vehicles have priority

Parking disc compulsory

Slow lane

One-way street with a two-way cycle lane

Speed Limits

*See **Speed Limits Table** under **Motoring – Advice** in the section **PLANNING AND TRAVELLING.***

The fundamental rule in Switzerland, which applies to all motor vehicles and also to bicycles, is that you must always have the speed of your vehicle under control and must adapt your speed to the conditions of the road, traffic and visibility. On minor secondary roads without speed limit signs speed should be reduced to 50 km/h (31 mph) where the road enters a built-up area. The speed limit in residential areas is 30 km/h (18 mph). Speeding fines are severe.

When travelling solo the speed limit on dual carriageways is 100 km/h (62 mph) and on motorways, 120 km/h (74 mph) unless otherwise indicated by signs. On motorways with at least three lanes in the same direction, the left outside lane may only be used by vehicles which can exceed 80 km/h (50 mph).

Motorhomes with a laden weight of under 3,500 kg are not subject to any special regulations. Those over 3,500 kg may not exceed 80 km/h (50 mph) on motorways.

In road tunnels with two lanes in each direction, speed is limited to 100 km/h (62 mph); in the St Gotthard tunnel and San Bernardino tunnels the limit is 80 km/h (50 mph).

It is prohibited to transport or use radar detection devices. If your GPS navigation system has a function to identify the location of fixed speed cameras, this must be deactivated.

Traffic Jams

Traffic congestion occurs near tunnels in particular, during the busy summer months, at the St Gotthard tunnel on Friday afternoons and Saturday mornings. When congestion is severe and in order to prevent motorists coming to a standstill in the tunnel, traffic police stop vehicles before the tunnel entrance and direct them through in groups.

Other bottlenecks occur on the roads around Luzern (A2) and Bern (A1, A6 and A12), the border crossing at Chiasso (A2), the A9 around Lausanne and between Vevey and Chexbres, and the A13 BellinzonaSargans, mainly before the San Bernardino tunnel.

In order to avoid traffic jams motorists may use secondary roads but this means a much slower journey through the mountains. A number of roads are closed to touring caravans.

*See **Mountain Passes and Tunnels** in the section **PLANNING AND TRAVELLING.***

Traffic Lights

Outside peak rushhours traffic lights flashing amber mean proceed with caution.

Violation of Traffic Regulations

The police may impose and collect on-the-spot fines for minor infringements. In the case of more serious violations, they may require a deposit equal to the estimated amount of the fine. Fines for serious offences are set according to the income of the offender. Drivers of foreign-registered vehicles may be asked for a cash deposit against the value of the fine.

Motorways

There are 1,700 km of motorways and dual carriageways. To use these roads motor vehicles and trailers up to a total weight of 3,500kg must display a vignette (see Motorway Tax on opposite page).

Motorists using roads to avoid motorways and dual carriageways may find it necessary to detour through small villages, often with poor signposting. In addition, due to a diversion, you may be re-routed onto roads where the motorway vignette is required.

Drivers of vehicles over 3,500kg see ***Heavy Vehicle Tax*** on the opposite page.

If you have visited Switzerland before, make sure you remove your old sticker from your windscreen.

There are emergency telephones along motorways.

Touring

If visiting during early and late summer it is worth looking for sites in broad valleys which enjoy more sunshine than those in the shade of mountains.

The peak season for winter sports is from December to the end of April in all major resorts. February and March are the months with the most hours of winter sunshine and good snow for skiing. Summer skiing is also possible in a few resorts. Information on snow conditions, including avalanche bulletins, is available in English from www.slf.ch

If you enjoy walking in the mountains recent visitors advise that September is the best month to visit. Summers can be very hot and wet, with cloud cover below 2,000 metres, whereas September tends to be drier and cooler with the added advantage of reduced pressure on transport and site facilities.

Besides being famous for watches, chocolate and cheese, the Swiss have a fine reputation as restauranteurs, but eating out can be expensive. Local beers are light but pleasant and some very drinkable wines are produced.

There are a number of UNESCO World Heritage Sites in Switzerland including the three castles of Bellinzona, Bern Old Town, the Monastery of St John at Müstair, the Jungfrau, the Aletsch Glacier and the Bietschhoorn region.

Liechtenstein is a principality of 160 sq km sharing borders with Switzerland and Austria. The capital, Vaduz, has a population of approximately 7,000 and German is the official language. The official currency is the Swiss franc. There are no passport or Customs controls on the border between Switzerland and Liechtenstein.

Local Travel

It is common for Swiss drivers to switch off their engines at traffic lights and railway crossings as well as in traffic jams to reduce pollution.

Some towns are inaccessible by road, e.g. Zermatt and Wengen, and can only be reached by train or tram. You will have to park at the bottom of the mountain and take public transport.

The Swiss integrated transport system is well-known for its efficiency, convenience and punctuality. Co-ordinated timetables ensure rapid, trouble-free interchange from one means of transport to another. Yellow post buses take travellers off the beaten track to the remotest regions and are a familiar sight along scenic routes throughout the country. Their safety standards and record of reliability are unrivalled. As far as railways are concerned, in addition to efficient inter-city travel, there is an extensive network of mountain railways, including aerial cableways, funiculars and ski-lifts.

Anyone contemplating a holiday in Switzerland is advised to contact Switzerland Tourism for information on half-fare travel cards and other tourist concessionary tickets such as the Swiss Pass. Half-fare tickets are available for attractions such as cable cars, railways and lake steamers. In addition, Switzerland Tourism offers a public transport map and a number of other useful publications. See www.swisstravelsystem.com

All visitors to campsites and hotels in Interlaken are issued with a pass allowing free bus and train travel in the area.

A ferry operates on Lake Constance (Bodensee) between Romanshorn and Friedrichshafen (Germany) saving a 70km drive. The crossing takes 40 minutes. Telephone 071 4667888 for more information; www.bodensee-schiffe.ch. A frequent ferry service also operates between Konstanz and Meersburg on the main route between Zürich, Ulm, Augsburg and Munich (Germany); more information is available on a German telephone number, 0049 7531 8030; www.stadtwerke.konstanz.de. The crossing takes 20 minutes. Principal internal ferry services are on Lake Lucerne between Beckenried and Gersau, www.autofaehre.ch, and on Lake Zürich between Horgen and Meilen, www.faehre.ch. All these services transport cars and caravans.

All place names used in the Site Entry listings which follow can be found in Schweiz Strassen-und Stådteplan-Atlas published by Kümmerly & Frey, scale 1:300,000 (1 cm = 3 km).

AARBURG *A2* (500m S Rural) *47.31601, 7.89488* **Camping Wiggerspitz, Hofmattstrasse 40, 4663 Aarburg [062 7915810; fax 7915811; info@camping-aarburg.ch; www.camping-aarburg.ch]** Exit A1/A2/E35 junc 46 sp Rothrist/Olten, foll sp to site. Med, mkd pitch, pt shd; htd wc; chem disp; mv service pnt; shwrs CHF1; el pnts (6A) CHF3 (rev pol), long lead req; gas; Indtte; shop; tradsmn; rest 500m; snacks; bar; BBQ; htd pool adj; 25% statics; dogs CHF1; phone; rlwy noise; red CCI. "Conv Luzern, Zürich, Bern; picturesque, walled town; excel, clean site; friendly warden." 1 May-15 Sep. CHF 28.00 2010*

ADLISWIL *A3* (3km S Urban) **Camping Sihlwald, 8135 Langnau-am-Albis [044 7200434; camping.sihlwald@gmx.ch]** Turn off Zürich-Luzern rd dir Adliswil, site sp on L by Forsthaus rest. Med, pt shd; htd wc; chem disp; shwrs; el pnts inc; gas; Indtte; shop; rest; snacks; bar; playgrnd; pool 4km; dogs CHF4; poss cr; Eng spkn; adv bkg; quiet, but some rd noise; red CCI. "Pretty setting by rv; conv Luzern, Zürich & Bern; pitches furthest fr rv unreliable in wet; excel, clean facs; helpful staff." 15 Apr-15 Oct. CHF 27.50 2009*

AESCHI see Spiez *C2*

AGNO see Lugano *D3*

⊞ **AIGLE** *C2* (4km NE Rural) *46.34030, 7.01550* **Camping du Soleil, Route du Suchet, 1854 Leysin [024 4943939; fax 4942121; info@camping-leysin.ch; www.camping-leysin.ch]** Take rd 20 Aigle to Le Sépey, exit at Le Sépey for Leysin, 6 hairpin bends to site. On ent vill pass g'ge on L, in 50m turn L into app rd to lge sports cent. In 100m turn R into narr access rd & bear L; site opp Hotel du Soleil. NB: Fr Aigle distance by rd 16km, last 5km up winding, steep but gd rd. Med, pt sl, pt shd; htd wc; chem disp; baby facs; shwrs inc; el pnts (16A) metered (adaptor avail); gas; Indtte (inc dryer); shops, rest nr; bar; BBQ; playgrnd; covrd pool adj; tennis adj; cycle hire; games area; games rm; horseriding, winter & summer skiing; sports cent & skating rink (all year) 100m; TV; many statics; dogs CHF3; quiet; ccard acc; red CCI. "Mainly winter ski resort but magnificent views; 15 min walk (uphill) to shops etc; conv cablecar; navette 100m; ski & boot rm; friendly, helpful staff; mkt Thu; used by school groups." ♦ CHF 37.00 2011*

AIGLE *C2* (1km NW Rural) *46.32385, 6.96206* **Camping Les Glariers, Ave des Glariers 2, 1860 Aigle [tel/fax 024 4662660]** Turn W off N9 (Aigle-Lausanne) at N edge of Aigle, site sp. Foll rd for 400m, site past pool on L. Med, pt shd; wc; chem disp; mv service pnt; shwrs inc; el pnts (4A) CHF3.50 (adaptor avail); gas; Indtte; sm shop; snacks; bar; playgrnd; pool; tennis; fishing; cycle hire; some statics; dogs CHF4; poss cr; Eng spkn; adv bkg; quiet but a little rlwy noise; ccard acc; red CCI. "V helpful owner; v gd, well-maintained site; pleasant town & gd touring base; outlook on to vineyards." 30 Mar-7 Oct. CHF 35.40 2011*

⊞ **ALTDORF** *B3* (1km N Rural) *46.89256, 8.62800* **Remo-Camp Moosbad, Flüelerstrsse 122, 6460 Altdorf [041 8708541]** Exit A2 at Altdorf junc 36. Foll sp Altdorf to rndabt (enormous yellow watering can) & turn R. Site 200m on L adj cable car & sports cent. Sm, pt shd; wc; chem disp; mv service pnt; shwrs CHF1; el pnts (10A) CHF3 (adaptor loan); Indtte (inc dryer); shop & 200m; rest; bar; BBQ; public pool, waterslide & rest adj; 80% statics; dogs €1; phone; poss cr; Eng spkn; some rd & rlwy noise; ccard not acc; CCI. "Ideal windsurfing; useful NH en rte Italy; friendly welcome; excel san facs; gd rest; superb views; gd base for train trip over St Gotthard pass." CHF 25.00 2010*

ALTDORF *B3* (5km N Rural) *46.91497, 8.62257* **Camping Windsurfing Urnersee, Unterer Winkel 11, 6454 Flüelen-See [041 8709222; fax 8709216; info@windsurfing-urnersee.ch; www.windsurfing-urnersee.ch]** On N4 & Axenstrasse, site sp on ent Flüelen. Steep app, not rec for lge or heavy o'fits. Med, terr, pt shd; wc; chem disp; shwrs CHF1; el pnts CHF3.50; shop; rest; bar; htd, covrd pool 2km; shgl beach; lake sw; fishing; watersports; cycle hire; tennis; no dogs; poss cr; adv bkg; quiet but some rlwy noise; Eng spkn. "Excel watersports." 1 Apr-30 Oct. CHF 36.00 2011*

ALTENRHEIN *A4* (Rural) *47.49173, 9.56538* **Camping Idyll, Mennstrasse 2, 9423 Altenheim [tel/fax 071 8554213; camping.idyll@freenet.ch]** Bet Bregenz & Rorschach on S side of Bodensee on rd 13. Foll sp fr rndabt 2km W of Buriet. Site nr airfield. Med, mkd pitch, pt shd; htd wc; chem disp; shwrs inc; el pnts (10A) CHF2.50; Indtte; shop; rest; snacks; bar; playgrnd; pool; lake sw 1km; games area; 60% statics; phone; Eng spkn; adv bkg; some light aircraft noise; CCI. "Immac, efficient site; clean facs; gd for late arrivals; gd." 1 Apr-30 Sep. CHF 28.00 2008*

ANDEER see Thusis *C4*

ANDELFINGEN *A3* (500m NE Rural) *47.59698, 8.68376* **TCS Camping Rässenwies, Alte Steinerstrasse 1, 8451 Kleinandelfingen [079 2383535; raessenwies@tcs-ccz.ch; www.tcs-ccz.ch]** On N4 Schaffhausen-Winterthur rd, site well sp in Kleinandelfingen, on Rv Thur. Sm, unshd; wc; shwrs; el pnts CHF3.50; gas; Indtte; shop pool 1km; fishing; dogs CHF2.50; quiet. "Beautiful area." 20 Mar-4 Oct. CHF 29.20 2008*

⊞ **APPENZELL** *A4* (3km SW Rural) *47.32236, 9.38703* **Camping Eischen, Kaustrasse 123, 9050 Appenzell-Kau [071 7875030; fax 7875660; info@eischen.ch; www.eischen.ch]** Fr St Gallen foll blue sps thro Herisau for Appenzell. 1km bef Appenzell turn R sp Gonten, then Kau. Steep 10% climb up narr rd fr Appenzell. Med, sl, unshd; wc; chem disp; mv service pnt; shwrs CHF1; el pnts (10A) CHF3; Indtte; rest; playgrnd; pool 3km; golf 3km; wifi; 60% statics (sep area); dogs CHF2; phone; poss cr; quiet; CCI. "A bit of a climb, but worth it; beautiful location & views in unspoilt area; mountain walks; excel rest on site." ♦ CHF 29.50 2008*

⊞ **APPENZELL** *A4* (5km W Rural) *47.31880, 9.33314* **Camping Anker Jakobsbad, 9108 Gonten [071 7941131; fax 7941833; info@camping-jakobsbad.ch; www.camping-jakobsbad.ch]** W fr Appenzell past Gonten, site on L immed bef Jakobsbad rlwy stn; sp. Med, pt sl, unshd; htd wc; chem disp (wc); shwrs CHF1; el pnts (6A) CHF2; gas; lndtte; shop; tradsmn; rest; playgrnd; fishing; adv bkg; 95% statics; dogs CHF2; train 1km; phone; adv bkg; quiet. "Cable car to Kronberg 400m; many walks; skiing in winter; conv base for touring Appenzell Canton; friendly owners." CHF 18.00 2008*

ARBON *A4* (1km W Rural) *47.52449, 9.42049* **Camping Buchorn, Philosophenweg 17, 9320 Arbon [071 4466545; fax 4464834; info@camping-arbon.ch; www.camping-arbon.ch]** Fr N on Kreuzlingen-Romanshorn rd 13, 8km after Romanshorn, site sp at ent to Arbon, on lakeside. Med, mkd pitch, pt shd; wc; chem disp; mv service pnt; baby facs; shwrs; el pnts CHF3; gas; lndtte (inc dryer); sm shop; rest; snacks; BBQ; playgrnd; paddling pool; lake sw; fishing; watersports; boat hire; tennis; games rm; wifi; TV; no dogs; poss cr; adv bkg; quiet but some rlwy noise; ccard acc. "Pleasant location; clean site; helpful owner; steamer trips fr Arbon." ♦ Easter-1 Oct. CHF 38.00 2010*

AVENCHES *B2* (6km N Rural) *46.91320, 7.03345* **TCS Camping Le Chablais, 1585 Salavaux [026 6771476; fax 6773744; camping.salavaux@tcs.ch; www.campingtcs.ch]** Fr N1 take exit Faoug & foll lakeside rd W to Avenches; site sp. V lge, unshd; wc; chem disp; mv service pnt; baby facs; shwrs inc; el pnts (4A) CHF4; gas; lndtte (inc dryer); supmkt; rest; snacks; bar; playgrnd; pool 2km; lake sw 100m; boating; tennis; horseriding; entmnt; 75% statics; dogs CHF4; Eng spkn; poss v cr; adv bkg; ccard acc. "Pitches tight; lovely situation." ♦ Easter-5 Oct. CHF 39.50 2008*

BASEL *A2* (5km S Urban) *47.49963, 7.60283* **Camping Waldhort, Heideweg 16, 4153 Basel-Reinach [061 7116429; fax 7114833; info@camping-waldhort.ch; www.camping-waldhort.ch]** Fr Basel foll m'way sp to Delémont & exit m'way at Reinach-Nord exit; at top of slip rd, turn R & L at 1st traff lts (about 300m). Site on L in approx 1km at curve in rd with tramway on R, sp. Basel best app off German m'way rather than French. Lge, mkd pitch, pt shd; wc; chem disp; mv service pnt; baby facs; shwrs inc; el pnts (6A) inc; gas; lndtte; shop; tradsmn; rest 500m; snacks; playgrnd; pool; paddling pool; 50% statics; dogs CHF3; tram 500m (tickets fr recep); poss cr; Eng spkn; adv bkg; m'way noise; ccard acc; 10% red CCI. "Rec arr early in high ssn; helpful staff; gd sized pitches; m'van pitches sm; excel san facs; gates clsd 2200-0700; site muddy when wet; excel art museums in Basel." ♦ 1 Mar-25 Oct. CHF 36.00 2008*

⊞ **BASEL** *A2* (10km S Rural) *47.45806, 7.63545* **TCS Camping Uf der Hollen, Auf der Hollen, 4146 Hochwald [061 7511398; fax 7120240; info@tcscampingbasel.ch; www.tcscampingbasel.ch]** Exit A18 at Reinach-Sud dir Dornach, S thro Dornach dir Hochwald, uphill thro forest to site. Med, mkd pitch, pt shd; htd wc; chem disp; shwrs CHF0.50; el pnts CHF3; lndtte; playgrnd; htd, covrd pool 10km; games area; 90% statics; adv bkg; quiet; red CCI. "Gd views; peaceful, pleasant site." ♦ CHF 27.00 2010*

BEATENBERG see Interlaken *C2*

BELLINZONA *C3* (1km N Urban) *46.21186, 9.03831* **TCS Camping Bosco di Molinazzo, Via San Gottardo 131, 6500 Bellinzona [091 8291118; fax 8292355; camping.bellinzona@tcs.ch; www.campingtcs.ch]** Fr A13 exit Bellinzona Nord, foll rd over rv & rlwy bdgs. In approx 200m on R, immed after rd to Gorduno, site sp in 200m down ramp to R just bef Shell g'ge. Med, sl, pt shd; wc; chem disp; mv service pnt; baby facs; shwrs; el pnts (6A) CHF4; gas; lndtte (inc dryer); shop; rest; snacks; bar; BBQ; playgrnd; pool; tennis; rv adj; boating; fishing; cycle hire; golf; wifi; entmnt; TV; 20% statics; dogs CHF4; poss v cr; adv bkg; rd & rlwy noise; ccard acc; red CCI. "Pleasant & attractive city; gd NH en route Italy; san facs stretched high ssn & site overcr; early arrivals site yourselves & report later - instructions on barrier." ♦ 1 Apr-10 Oct. CHF 36.20 (CChq acc) 2008*

The opening dates and prices on this campsite have changed. I'll send a site report form to the Club for the next edition of the guide.

BELLINZONA *C3* (7km N Rural) *46.2656, 9.01881* **Camping Al Censo, 6702 Claro [091 8631753; fax 8634022; info@alcenso.ch; www.alcenso.ch]** Exit A2/E35 at Biasca & at rndabt turn L to E side of m'way. Foll sp twd Bellinzona. Site 9km on L, just bef Claro. Med, pt sl, terr, pt shd; wc; chem disp; mv service pnt; sauna; shwrs inc; el pnts (6A) CHF3.50; gas; lndtte; shop & 7km; tradsmn; rest 600m; snacks; playgrnd; pool; jacuzzi; wifi; dogs CHF2.50; site clsd 1200-1400; Eng spkn; adv bkg; quiet but some rlwy noise. "Modern, well-used san facs, poss stretched if site busy; well-maintained, pretty, family-run site; sm pitches; used by school parties; gd NH." 1 Apr-15 Oct. CHF 42.00 2008*

BERN *B2* (3km SE Rural) *46.93285, 7.45569* **Camping Eichholz, Strandweg 49, 3084 Wabern [031 9612602; fax 9613526; info@campingeichholz.ch; www.campingeichholz.ch]** Exit A1/A12 & take 2nd turn-off sp Bern/Bümplitz dir Belp & airport. Turn L under A12 & foll sp Wabern & site. Lge, hdstg, shd; wc; chem disp; mv service pnt; shwrs CHF1.50; el pnts CHF3.50; gas; lndtte; shop; supmkt nr; rest; snacks; bar; BBQ; playgrnd; pool 2km; fishing; tennis; cycle hire; wifi; tram; poss cr; Eng spkn; adv bkg; poss v noisy; ccard acc. "Walk to Bern by rv (steep climb); clean, modern san facs; helpful staff." 20 Apr-30 Sep. CHF 28.50 2009*

BERN *B2* (10km SW Rural) *46.89301, 7.33408* **Freizeitzentrum Thörishaus, Strandheimstrasse 20, 3174 Thörishaus [031 8890271; fax 031 8890296; sense.giardino@hispeed.ch]** Exit m'way Bern-Fribourg at Flamatt. Strt at 1st rndabt, R at 2nd sp Thörishaus. Site on R in 150m. Med, pt shd; wc; shwrs inc; el pnts (10A) CHF3.50; gas; lndtte; shop; rest; snacks; bar; playgrnd; pool 4km; tennis; fishing; 80% statics; sep car park; Eng spkn; adv bkg; ccard acc; 10% red CCI. "Conv Bern; gd cycle paths; vg site." ♦ 1 Apr-31 Oct. CHF 26.00 2009*

⊞ **BERN** *B2* (6km NW Rural) *46.96375, 7.38420* **TCS Camping Bern-Eymatt, Wohlenstrasse 62C, 3032 Hinterkappelen [031 9011007; fax 9012591; camping.bern@tcs.ch; www.campingtcs.ch/bern]** Fr E on A1 exit junc 33 sp Bern-Bethlehem; foll sp for Wohlen & site. In 200m turn R at bottom of hill into site on shores Wohlensee. Fr W take Brunnen-Bern exit, then sp to Wohlen. Access for lge o'fits poss diff. Lge, some hdstg, pt shd; htd wc; chem disp; mv service pnt; baby facs; shwrs inc; el pnts (6A) inc; gas; Indtte; shop; rest; snacks; bar; BBQ (charcoal/gas); playgrnd; htd pool; paddling pool; fishing; cycle hire; games area; wifi; entmnt; TV/games rm; many statics; dogs CHF5; no c'vans/m'vans over 8m high ssn; bus to Bern nry; sep car park; poss cr; ccard acc; red low ssn; CCI. "Recep 0830-1100 & 1700-2000 high ssn, but site yourself; various pitch sizes; clean facs; disabled facs not easily accessible fr all pitches; gd value rest; helpful staff; daily mkt in Bern; 2 supmkts nearby; excel." ♦ CHF 46.10 (CChq acc) SBS - S03 2011*

BERNHARDZELL see St Gallen *A4*

BIEL/BIENNE *B2* (7km SW Rural) *47.10916, 7.01666* **Camping Sutz am Bielersee, Kirchrain 40, 2572 Sutz [032 3971345; fax 3972061; mail@camping-sutz.ch; www.camping-sutz.ch]** Exit A1/E25 Biel cent on rd twd Neuchâtel. Turn L at Biel o'skts, foll sp to Ipsach-Täuffelen along E side of lake. Site sp after Ipsach on R at edge of lake. Lge, unshd; wc; chem disp; baby facs; shwrs inc; el pnts (10A) inc; gas; Indtte; shop; rest 2km; lake sw; fishing; tennis; 90% statics; Eng spkn; adv bkg; quiet; ccard acc. "Gd, modern san facs; extra lge pitches avail; friendly staff; cycle path adj." ♦ 1 Apr-31 Oct. CHF 39.00 2009*

BIEL/BIENNE *B2* (10km SW Rural) *47.08556, 7.11726* **Camping Prêles AG, Route de la Neuveville 61, 2515 Prêles [032 3151716; fax 3155160; info@camping-jura.ch; www.camping-jura.ch]** App Biel fr N on rd 6 approx 2km bef town; immed after emerging fr 2nd long tunnel turn R then L sp Orvin. Cont thro Orvin to Lamboing, in Lamboing turn L dir La Neuveville to Prêles. Drive strt thro vill & look out for tent sp beyond vill when descending hill. App fr S on rd 5 poss via Neuveville or Twann but steep climb, tight bends & narr vill street. Lge, pt sl, shd; wc; chem disp; mv service pnt; baby facs; shwrs CHF0.50; el pnts (10A) CHF3.50; gas; Indtte; sm shop; rest; snacks; BBQ; playgrnd; htd pool; watersports 5km; tennis; cycle hire; horseriding, games rm; entmnt; dogs CHF2; some statics; sep car park high ssn; adv bkg; v quiet; ccard acc; red long stay; CCI. "Nice scenery & gd views; peaceful site surrounded by woods & meadows; recep clsd 1130-1400 & after 1800." ♦ 1 Apr-15 Oct. CHF 31.50 2009*

BLUMENSTEIN see Thun *B2*

BONIGEN see Interlaken *C2*

BOURG ST PIERRE *D2* (500m N Rural) *45.95265, 7.20740* **Camping du Grand St Bernard, 1946 Bourg-St Pierre [tel/fax 027 7871411; grand-st-bernard@swisscamps.ch; www.campinggrand-st-bernard.ch]** Fr Martigny S to Grand St Bernard Tunnel. Site well sp in cent of vill. Med, unshd; wc; chem disp; shwrs; el pnts (4A) CHF3.50; gas; Indtte; shop 200m; tradsmn; rest, snacks, bar adj; htd pool adj; dogs; Eng spkn; quiet; ccard acc; CCI. "Conv St Bernard Tunnel; gd views." 15 May-15 Oct. CHF 28.00 2009*

BOUVERET, LE see Villeneuve *C1*

BRENZIKOFEN see Thun *B2*

BRIENZ *B2* (1km SE Rural) *46.75069, 8.04838* **Camping Seegartli, 3855 Brienz [033 9511351]** Fr Interlaken take N8 sp Luzern/Brienz. Take Brienz exit, ignore sp to site to R & take L in 1km bef Esso stn, sp Axalp. Site in 500m on R immed after passing under rlwy. Site on E shore of lake, next to sawmill. Sm, pt sl, pt shd; wc; chem disp; mv service pnt; shwrs CHF1; el pnts (10A) CHF3; Indtte; shop; lake sw; watersports; fishing; tennis; Eng spkn; quiet CCI. "Beautiful lakeside situation; well-kept site; friendly owner; lakeside pitches boggy in wet weather; long hose req for m'van fill-up; arr bef noon in ssn. No dogs." 1 Apr-31 Oct. CHF 33.00 2011*

BRIENZ *B2* (1.5km SE Urban) *46.74811, 8.04769* **Camping Aaregg, Seestrasse 22, 3855 Brienz [033 9511843; fax 9514324; mail@aaregg.ch; www.aaregg.ch]** Fr Interlaken take N8 sp Luzern/Brienz. Take Brienz exit, ignore sp to site to R & take L in 1km bef Esso stn, sp Axalp. Site in 500m on R after passing under rlwy. Site on E shore of lake, next to sawmill. Med, mkd pitch, hdstg, pt shd; htd wc; chem disp; mv service pnt; some serviced pitches; shwrs inc; el pnts (10A) CHF5; Indtte; shop; rest; snacks; bar; pool 500m; lake sw adj; internet; dogs CHF4; phone; rlwy stn nr; poss cr; Eng spkn; adv bkg rec (lge dep req); quiet; ccard acc; red long stay/low ssn; CCI. "Excel, busy site on lakeside; lakeside pitches sm & poss cr; ideal touring base; min stay 9 nights on best pitches high ssn; excel, modern san facs; many attractions nrby." 1 Apr-31 Oct. CHF 42.00 2009*

BRIG *C2* (3km E Rural) *46.31500, 8.01369* **Camping Tropic, Simplonstrasse 11, 3901 Ried bei Brig [027 9232537]** On Brig-Domodossola rd on Swiss side of Simplon Pass. Fr Brig, exit Simplon rd at sp Ried-Brig Termen. Site on L in 500m. Fr Simplon foll sp to Ried-Brig, site in vill. Med, sl, pt shd; wc; shwrs CHF1; el pnts CHF3; gas; Indtte; shop; playgrnd; pool 2km; TV; Eng spkn; rd noise. "Useful CL-type NH to/fr Italy; welcoming & helpful owners; superb scenery." 1 Jun-15 Sep. CHF 24.00 2008*

BRIG *C2* (700m S Rural) *46.30838, 7.99338* **Camping Geschina, Geschinastrasse 41, 3900 Brig [tel/fax 027 9230688; www.geschina.ch]** Foll sps twd Simplon Pass, site on R at 700m, behind pool at rv bdge. Best app fr Glis. Med, pt sl, pt shd; wc; chem disp; shwrs inc; el pnts (10A) CHF2.50; gas; Indtte; shop; snacks; bar; playgrnd; pool adj; fishing; dogs CHF2; poss cr; Eng spkn; adv bkg; quiet; red long stay/CCI. "Friendly, well-kept, family-run site; vg san facs; superb mountain & glacier views; ideal for Rhône Valley & Simplon Pass; sh walk to town." 1 Apr-15 Oct. CHF 29.00 2011*

⊞ **BRUNNEN** *B3* (2km S Rural) *46.99030, 8.63394* **Camping Ferienhof Rüti, Rüti 4, 6443 Morschach [041 8205309; fax 8205313; info@ferienhof-rueti.com; www.ferienhof-rueti.ch]** N4/E41 S thro Brunnen tunnel, take next L sp Morschach, thro vill & site on R bef cable car. Sm, mkd pitch, pt sl, pt shd; htd wc; chem disp; shwrs inc; shop; tradsmn; BBQ (gas/charcoal); playgrnd; lake sw nrby; games area; games rm; wifi; TV; dogs; bus adj; Eng spkn; quiet; ccard acc; CCI. "Panoramic views; excel site on hobby farm with donkeys, mini-pigs, hens etc." CHF 25.00 2008*

BRUNNEN *B3* (1km NW Rural) *46.99775, 8.59346* **Camping Hopfreben, 6440 Brunnen [041 8201873; www.camping-brunnen.ch]** A4/E41 exit Brunnen-Nord, dir Weggis, site sp on lakeside. Med, pt shd; wc; chem disp; mv service pnt; shwrs CHF1; el pnts (6A) CHF3 (adaptor avail/long cable req); Indtte; shop; rest 1km; snacks; bar; playgrnd; pool 200m; lake sw 500m; boat launch; cycle hire; 20% statics; dogs CHF3; poss cr w/end; adv bkg; quiet but some daytime noise fr gravel barges/lorries adj; CCI. "Delightful location." 15 Apr-24 Sep. CHF 39.00 2011*

BUCHS *B4* (S Rural) *47.16557, 9.46524* **Camping Werdenberg, 9470 Buchs [081 7561507; fax 7565090; verkehrsvereinbuchs@bluemail.ch; www.werdenberg.ch]** Fr bdge over Rv Rhine at Buchs on rd 16 dir Werdenberg & Grabs. Turn L at parking/camping sp, thro car park to site. Sm, unshd; wc; chem disp; shwrs CHF1; el pnts (16A) CHF4; gas; Indtte (inc dryer); shops nr; htd pool 2km; lake sw adj; dogs CHF2; adv bkg; quiet but church bells adj every 15 mins. "Vg, attractive setting by lake with views of old town & castle; friendly owners; gd base for Liechtenstein, Appenzell & Vorarlberg; walking; plenty of activities mini-golf etc; extra charge for vans over 5m; gd for families." ♦ 1 Apr-31 Oct. CHF 34.00 2011*

BULLE *C2* (6km N Rural) *46.67545, 7.08478* **Camping du Lac, 1643 Gumefens [026 9152162; fax 9152168; info@campingdulac-gruyere.ch; www.campingdulac-gruyere.ch]** Fr S on N12 exit junc 4 for Bulle. At T-junc turn N for Riaz. Foll rd thro Riaz & Vuippens. Site on R 500m after Gumefens turning. Fr N exit junc 5 Rossens & foll dir Bulle. In 7km turn L twd lake & site. Med, mkd pitch, unshd; wc; chem disp; mv service pnt; shwrs CHF0.50; el pnts (6A) CHF2.50; gas; Indtte; shop; rest; snacks; bar; playgrnd; private beach; watersports; cycle hire; 60% statics; no dogs; site open w/ends May & Sep; Eng spkn; adv bkg; quiet; ccard not acc; red long stay/CCI. "Lovely lakeside site, mountain views; helpful owner; sm pitches not suitable lge o'fits; exit to main rd sh & steep." 1 Jul-31 Aug. CHF 26.50 2010*

⊞ **BULLE** *C2* (8km N Rural) *46.67373, 7.02492* **Camping La Forêt, Route de Montiollin, 1642 Sorens [026 9151882; fax 9150363; info@camping-la-foret.ch; www.camping-la-foret.ch]** Fr S exit N12 Bulle dir Fribourg. In 6km turn L uphill to Sorens & site in 2km on L twd Malessert, sp. Lge, pt sl, pt shd; wc; chem disp; mv service pnt; shwrs CHF1; el pnts CHF3 (adaptor avail); Indtte; shop; rest; snacks; bar; playgrnd; pool; tennis; cycle hire; 80% statics; dogs CHF2; Eng spkn; adv bkg; quiet; red long stay. ♦ CHF 23.50 2009*

BUOCHS *B3* (500m N Rural) *46.97950, 8.41860* **TCS Camping Sportzentrum, Seefeldstrasse, 6374 Buochs-Ennetbürgen [041 6203474; fax 6206484; camping.buochs@tcs.ch; www.campingtcs.ch]** Fr W on N2 m'way, exit junc 33 Stans-Süd & bear L. Foll sp Buochs. At 1st x-rds in Buochs, turn L to Ennetbürgen, in approx 1km R twd lake, sp. Fr E exit junc 34 for Buochs, turn L onto Beckenriederstrasse; at x-rds in cent of town turn R dir Ennetbürgen & foll sp as above. Med, mkd pitch, pt shd; wc; chem disp; mv service pnt; shwrs inc; el pnts (4A) CHF3.50 (adaptor avail); gas; Indtte (inc dryer); supmkt adj; tradsmn; rest; snacks; bar; playgrnd; pool adj; lake sw adj; fishing; tennis; cycle hire; games rm; wifi; TV rm; 60% statics in sep area; dogs CHF5; Eng spkn; quiet but some light aircraft noise; ccard acc; red low ssn/CCI. "Gd NH twd Italy; helpful staff; well-maintained facs; fine views; boat trip tickets sold on site; ferry close by; if recep clsd find own pitch & sign in later." 1 Apr-3 Oct. CHF 36.70 (CChq acc) 2010*

BURGDORF *B2* (E Rural) *47.05241, 7.63350* **TCS Camping Waldegg, Waldeggweg, 3400 Burgdorf [078 8718780; www.campingtcs.ch]** Exit Bern-Basel N1 m'way at sp Kirchberg. Site in Burgdorf clearly sp. App over narr (2.7m) humpback bdge. Med, pt shd; wc; chem disp; mv service pnt; shwrs inc; el pnts (10A) CHF4; Indry rm; shops 300m; rest 100m; playgrnd; pool 200m; fishing; tennis; golf; wifi; dogs; adv bkg; quiet. "Conv Bern; old town of Burgdorf v interesting; friendly staff; clean san facs; gd NH." 1 Apr-31 Oct. CHF 23.50 2010*

CHABLE, LE *D2* (5km S Rural) *46.05488, 7.24563* **Camping La Sasse, Chemin de la Sasse 11, 1947 Champsec [078 8277342; patricia.gabbud@netplus.ch]** Fr Martigny E on rd 21 & cont dir Verbier. Ent Le Châble & turn R at traff lts. Site on R in 5km. Sm, unshd; wc; chem disp; shwrs CHF1; el pnts CHF4; Indtte; shop, rest 1km; bar; 50% statics; adv bkg; quiet. "Rustic site; ltd facs; superb location." 15 May-31 Oct. CHF 20.00 2009*

⊞ **CHATEAU D'OEX** *C2* (500m SW Rural) *46.46740, 7.12578* **Camping au Berceau, 1660 Château-d'Oex [026 9246234; fax 9242526; piscine@chateau-doex.ch]** On R of rd 11 to Les Mosses, clearly sp. Med, pt shd; wc; mv service pnt; shwrs CHF0.50; el pnts (10A) CHF4 (adaptors avail); gas; Indtte; sm shop & 500m; rest; snacks; bar; playgrnd; pool; tennis; fishing; horseriding; 90% statics; dogs CHF2; poss cr; Eng spkn; ccard acc; red CCI. "Beautiful situation; v cr statics; few touring pitches." ♦ CHF 29.00 2008*

CHAUX DE FONDS, LA *B1* (1km SE Rural) *47.09398, 6.83605* **Camping Bois du Couvent, Bois du Couvent 108, 2300 La Chaux-de-Fonds [079 2405039; fax 032 9144877; campingboisducouvent.ch; www.campingboisducouvent.ch]** On W side of rd fr Neuchâtel/Chaux at 2nd rndbt fr tunnel, turn L. Foll sps. Med, pt sl, pt shd; wc; chem disp; mv service pnt; shwrs; el pnts (10A) CHF3; gas; Indtte; shop adj; rest; snacks; bar; playgrnd; htd pool 200m; table tennis; TV rm; 60% statics; dogs CHF3; phone; ccard acc; CCI. "Conv clock museum, undergrnd mills & Swiss Jura; recep clsd 1300-1600; excel facs; vg." ♦ 1 May-30 Sep. CHF 23.00 2008*

SWITZERLAND

CHAUX DE FONDS, LA *B1* (10km SW Rural) *47.06568, 6.69856* **Camping Lac des Brenets, 2416 Les Brenets [032 9321618; fax 9321639; campinglesbrenets@kfnmail.ch; www.camping-brenets.ch]** Take rd 20 fr La Chaux-de-Fonds to Le Locle, foll sp Les Brenets. Foll twisting rd downhill to lake, turn & ascend to ent site on R. NB Diff L turn on descent. Med, hdstg/grass, terr, unshd; htd wc; chem disp; mv service pnt; shwrs inc; baby facs; el pnts (12A) CHF4; gas; lndtte; shop, rest, snacks, bar high ssn; sm pool; lake sw adj; tennis; 80% statics; dogs CHF3; adv bkg; quiet; red long stay; ccard acc; CCI. "Gd site o'looking Lac des Brenets & Rv Doubs; beautiful views; watch/clock museum 3km; friendly owner." ♦ 1 Apr-31 Oct. CHF 31.00 2008*

CHESSEL see Villeneuve *C1*

⊞ **CHUR** *B4* (1.5km NW Rural) *46.85605, 9.50435* **Camping Au Chur, Felsenaustrasse 61, Obere Au, 7000 Chur [081 2842283; fax 2845683; info@camping-chur.ch; www.camping-chur.ch]** Site sp fr Chur Süd a'bahn exit, foll sp with tent pictogram (easily missed). Lge, pt shd; htd wc; chem disp; mv service pnt; baby facs; shwrs inc; el pnts (10A) CHF3.50; gas; lndtte; shop; rest 400m; snacks; bar; playgrnd; htd pool 200m; tennis; games area; wifi; TV; 65% statics; dogs CHF3; bus nr; poss cr; Eng spkn; ccard acc; red CCI. "Well-ordered, clean site; sm area for tourers; sm pitches; gd, modern facs; v soft when wet; helpful, friendly owners; interesting, old town." ♦ CHF 33.00 2010*

CLARO see Bellinzona *C3*

COLOMBIER see Neuchâtel *B1*

CORCELETTES LA POISSINE see Yverdon *B1*

CRANS MONTANA see Sierre *C2*

CUGNASCO see Locarno *C3*

CULLY see Lausanne *C1*

CUREGLIA see Lugano *D3*

DAVOS *B4* (5km S Rural) *46.74148, 9.77690* **Camping RinerLodge, Landwasserstrasse 64, 7277 Glaris [081 4011321; fax 4011382; rinerlodge@davosklosters.ch]** S fr Davos to Glaris, site opp Rinerhorn cable car. Med, hdstg, unshd; htd wc; chem disp; mv service pnt; shwrs inc; el pnts (16A) inc; tradsmn; rest, snacks, bar; dogs; bus/train; Eng spkn; adv bkg; quiet but slight rlwy noise; ccard acc. "Excel bus & train service - summer card gives free transport inc cable car; stream runs thro site; gd views & walks; ideal ski base." 1 Dec-30 Apr & 1 Jun-31 Oct. CHF 50.00 2008*

DELEMONT *A2* (SW Urban) *47.35753, 7.33620* **TCS Camping La Grande Ecluse, Vies St Catherine 1, 2800 Delémont [tel/fax 032 4227598; camping.delemont@tcs.ch; www.campingtcs.ch]** Turn S off Delémont/Porrentruy rd on exit Delémont & foll sp immed after pool. Med, pt sl, pt shd; wc; chem disp; mv service pnt; shwrs inc; el pnts (4A) CHF4.50; gas; lndtte; shop; rest; snacks; bar; playgrnd; pool 500m; tennis; fishing; 50% statics; dogs CHF4; Eng spkn; adv bkg; quiet; ccard acc; red CCI. "Pleasant owners; sm area for tourers." Easter-5 Oct. CHF 29.20 2008*

DISENTIS MUSTER *C3* (2.5km S Rural) *46.69620, 8.85270* **TCS Camping Fontanivas, Via Fontanivas 9, 7180 Disentis-Mustèr [081 9474422; fax 9474431; camping.disentis@tcs.ch; www.campingtcs.ch]** Fr Disentis S twd Lukmanier Pass for 2.5km. Site on L. Lge, pt shd; htd wc; chem disp; mv service pnt; baby facs; shwrs inc; el pnts (6-10A) CHF4; gas; lndtte (inc dryer); shop; rest; snacks; bar; BBQ; cooking facs; playgrnd; pool 2.5km; lake sw; tennis; cycle hire; wifi; TV rm; 25% statics; dogs CHF6; Eng spkn; adv bkg; quiet; ccard acc; CCI. "Excel san facs; historic old town; gd walks." ♦ 23 Apr-26 Sep. CHF 36.00 2009*

DUDINGEN see Fribourg *B2*

EGLISAU *A3* (4km W Rural) *47.57900, 8.5817* **TCS Camping Steubisallmend, 8416 Flaach [052 3181413; fax 3182683; camping.flaach@tcs.ch; www.campingtcs.ch]** Fr S (Zürich) on A51 to Bülach at end of m'way, then N4 N to Eglisau. Cross rv & cont twd Schaffhausen. Turn R dir Rüdlingen & Flaach. Site 2km W of Flaach; turn N at Rest Ziegelhütte. Steep access rd needs care. Lge, shd; wc; chem disp; mv service pnt; shwrs inc; el pnts (4A) CHF4; gas; lndtte; shops; rest 500m; snacks; bar; playgrnd; pool; fishing; cycle hire; 75% statics; dogs CHF6; poss cr; Eng spkn; adv bkg; ccard acc; red CCI. "Well situated on Rv Rhine; lower area subject to flood in wet." ♦ Easter- 4 Oct. CHF 38.80 2009*

EGNACH see Romanshorn *A4*

⊞ **ENGELBERG** *B3* (1km S Rural) *46.81003, 8.42273* **Camping Eienwäldli, Wasserfallstrasse 108, 6390 Engelberg [041 6371949; fax 6374423; info@eienwaeldli.ch; www.eienwaeldli.ch]** Fr N2 m'way take Stans Süd exit & foll sp to Engelberg for 22km. Foll sp 'Wasserfall', site sp. Final access to vill steep with hairpins. Lge, hdstg, pt shd; wc; chem disp; mv service pnt; sauna; solarium; shwrs CHF1; el pnts (10A) metered + conn fee; gas; lndtte; shop; rest; playgrnd; htd pool; fishing; tennis; cycle hire; cab TV; 75% statics in sep area; dogs CHF2; courtesy bus Jul-Oct; poss cr; adv bkg; quiet; "Mountain views; immac, all weather site; Swiss adaptor provided free; vg san facs; " CHF 35.80 2008*

ERLACH *B2* (500m N Rural) *47.04649, 7.09812* **Camping Erlach, Stadtgraben 23, 3235 Erlach [032 3381646; fax 3381656; camping@erlach.ch; www.erlach.ch]** Fr any dir foll sp for sm town of Ins; fr there foll sp Erlach. In Erlach turn L dir Le Landeron, then R twd Hotel du Port; turn L at hotel, site 200m on L by pier. Med, mkd pitch, shd; wc; chem disp; mv service pnt; baby facs; shwrs CHF1; el pnts inc; gas; Indtte (inc dryer); shop; rest, 200m; snacks; bar; playgrnd; pool 3km; lake sw & beach; tennis; games area; cycle hire; entmnt; TV; 60% statics; dogs CHF3; poss cr; Eng spkn; adv bkg rec; quiet; ccard acc; red CCI. "Scenic area; gd for walking & sightseeing; pleasure steamers on lake; gd, modern san facs; charming site." Easter-15 Oct. CHF 42.00 2011*

ESCHENZ *A3* (1km S Rural) *47.64467, 8.85985* **Camping Hüttenberg, 8264 Eschenz [052 7412337; fax 7415671; info@huettenberg.ch; www.huettenberg.ch]** Fr Schaffhausen dir Kreuzlingen on rd 13, in Eschenz turn R over level x-ing up hill, site sp. Lge, some hdstg, terr, unshd; htd wc; chem disp; mv service pnt; shwrs inc; el pnts (6-10A) CHF3; Indtte; shop; rest; snacks; bar; playgrnd; pool; paddling pool; internet; 80% statics; dogs CHF3; phone; bus 1km; train 2km; o'night area for m'vans; poss cr; Eng spkn; adv bkg; quiet; ccard acc; red low ssn; CCI. "Beautiful site with stunning views over Untersee; Stein am Rhein & Rhine Falls a must; gd, modern san facs; ltd space for tourers." ♦ 9 Apr-18 Oct. CHF 33.00 2009*

ESTAVAYER LE LAC *B1* (1.5km NW Rural) *46.86042, 6.86332* **Camping La Ferme de la Corbière, 1470 Estavayer-le-Lac [026 6633619; fax 6631638; info@corbiere.ch; www.corbiere.ch]** Fr Yverdon foll sp Estavayer-le-Lac. On app Estavayer foll sp Lac de Neuchâtel to pick up site sp. Med, pt shd; wc; shwrs; el pnts (10A) inc (adaptor avail & long lead poss req); shop 3km; BBQ; playgrnd; lake sw adj (steep climb); shgle beach; wifi; dogs; adv bkg; quiet; CCI. "Delightful, quiet alt to busy lakeside sites; helpful owner; CL-type with basic facs; hostel in farm buidings adj; used by lge youth/school tent groups." CHF 31.00 2009*

EVOLENE *C2* (W Rural) *46.11080, 7.49656* **Camping Evolène, 1983 Evolène [027 2831144; fax 2833255; info@camping-evolene.ch; www.camping-evolene.ch]** Fr Sion take rd to Val d'Hérens. As app Evolène take L fork to avoid vill cent. Proceed to Co-op on L, turn sharp R & 1st L to site. Site sp. Sm, unshd; htd wc; chem disp; mv service pnt; shwrs CHF1; el pnts (10A) CHF4.00; gas; Indtte; shop & 400m; rest adj; bar; playgrnd; cycle, x-country ski & snowboard hire; 5% statics; dogs CHF3; Eng spkn; quiet; ccard acc; CCI. "Mountain scenery; well-kept site; vg san facs; attentive owners; sh walk to vill cent, poss cr;." 15 May-15 Oct. CHF 28.40 2011*

⊞ **FAIDO** *C3* (1km SE Rural) *46.47165, 8.81705* **Camping Gottardo, 6764 Chiggiogna [tel/fax 091 8661562]** Exit A2/E35 at Faido, site on R in 500m, sp immed bef Faido. Med, terr, pt shd; htd wc; chem disp; shwrs CHF0.50; el pnts (6A) CHF4; gas; Indtte; sm shop & 2km; rest; snacks; bar; playgrnd; sm pool; few statics; dogs CHF2; phone; bus 400m; train 1.5km; poss v cr; Eng spkn; quiet but some rlwy noise; red long stay. "On main rd fr Italian lakes to St Gotthard Pass; interesting vill; poss diff for lge outfits, especially upper terrs (rec pitch bef white building); excel facs; gd rest - home cooking inc bread, pastries; friendly, helpful staff." CHF 44.52 2011*

⊞ **FIESCH** *C2* (500m NE Rural) *46.41016, 8.13871* **Camping Eggishorn, Fieschertalstrasse, 3984 Fiesch [027 9710316; fax 9710317; info@camping-eggishorn.ch; www.camping-eggishorn.ch]** Fr N19 turn into Fiesch, site sp in town. Med, mkd pitch, pt shd; htd wc; chem disp; mv service pnt; baby facs; shwrs inc; el pnts (16A) CHF4; gas; Indtte (inc dryer); shop 500m; tradsmn; rest; snacks; bar; BBQ; playgrnd; htd, covrd pool; fishing; games area; games rm; wifi; TV; 25% statics; dogs CHF3; bus, train 600m; poss cr; Eng spkn; quiet; ccard acc; CCI. "Beautiful situation - views all dirs; cable cars nr for Aletsch glacier; excel walking; well-kept site; highly rec." ♦ CHF 43.00 2011*

FILISUR *C4* (1.5km SW Rural) *46.67176, 9.67408* **Camping Islas, 7477 Filisur [081 4041647; fax 4042259; info@campingislas.ch; www.campingislas.ch]** Fr Tiefencastel take dir Albula. At Filisur foll camping sp. Long, single track rd to site. Med, some hdstg, unshd; htd wc; chem disp; shwrs inc; el pnts (10A) CHF2; gas; Indtte (inc dryer); shop; tradsmn; supmkt 10km; rest; bar; BBQ; playgrnd; pool; fishing; wifi; TV; 70% statics; dogs free; phone; train 1.5km; Eng spkn; quiet. "Gd touring base; informal management; euros acc." ♦ 1 Apr-31 Oct. CHF 37.00 2010*

FLAACH see Eglisau *A3*

FLEURIER *B1* (N Rural) *46.90643, 6.57508* **Camping Val de Travers, Belle Roche 15, 2114 Fleurier [tel/fax 032 8614262; camping.fleurier@tcs.ch; www.camping-val-de-travers.ch]** On Pontarlier (France) to Neuchâtel rd, site sp in Fleurier to L at start of vill. Med, pt shd; wc; chem disp; mv service pnt; shwrs; el pnts (4A) CHF3; gas; Indtte; shop; rest; bar; playgrnd; htd pool 2km; rv fishing; tennis; games area; cycle hire; 15% statics; dogs CHF3; Eng spkn; adv bkg; quiet; ccard acc. "Helpful owners; wild chamois on rocks behind site visible early morning; vg." 17 Apr-26 Sep. CHF 28.00 2009*

⊞ **FLIMS WALDHAUS** *B3* (500m SW Rural) *46.82441, 9.28183* **Camping Flims, Via Prau la Selva 4, 7018 Flims-Waldhaus [081 9111575; fax 9111630; info@camping-flims.ch; www.camping-flims.ch]** Fr N13 take exit Reichenau on rd 19 W twd Flims, site sp in 10km. Med, hdstg, pt sl, pt shd; wc; chem disp; fam bthrm; shwrs inc; el pnts (16A) CHF3.50; Indtte; shop; playgrnd; pool 3km; fishing; tennis; internet; 90% statics; bus 100m; Eng spkn; adv bkg; quiet; ccard acc. "Sm area for tourers; rec arr early; gd walking all levels; vg san facs; helpful owner." CHF 34.00 2008*

FOREL see Vevey *C1*

FOULY, LA *D2* (500m N Rural) *45.93693, 7.09548* **Camping des Glaciers, 1944 La Fouly-Val Ferret [027 7831735; fax 7833605; info@camping-glaciers.ch; www.camping-glaciers.ch]** Exit Martigny-Grand St Bernard rd at Orsières. Cont thro Val Ferret to vill of La Fouly. At end of vill turn R, site in 500m. V steep rd for 13km fr Orsières. Lge, terr, pt sl, pt shd; wc; chem disp; mv service pnt; baby facs; shwrs inc; el pnts CHF3.50; gas; Indtte; shop 500m; rest 500m; playgrnd; tennis 300m; games area; fishing; horseriding; wifi; TV; dogs CHF2; Eng spkn; adv bkg; quiet; ccard acc; CCI. "Lovely site; excel facs; excel walking, climbing cent; lovely views." 15 May-30 Sep. CHF 30.00 2009*

SWITZERLAND

FRIBOURG *B2* (13km N Rural) *46.87827, 7.19121* **Camping Schiffenensee, Schiffenen 15, 3186 Düdingen [026 4933486; fax 4933474; info@camping-schiffenen.ch; www.camping-schiffenen.ch]** Exit A12 Bern-Fribourg at Düdingen & foll rd for Murten (sp). Ent poss tight lge o'fits. Lge, mkd pitch, pt shd; wc; chem disp; shwrs CHF1; el pnts (10A) CHF3; Indtte; shop; rest; snacks; bar; pool; paddling pool; lake adj; tennis; 80% statics; dogs CHF3; bus; poss cr; Eng spkn; adv bkg; quiet; ccard not acc; CCI. 1 Apr-31 Oct. CHF 27.00 2009*

FRUTIGEN see Kandersteg *C2*

GAMPEL see Leuk *C2*

GAMPELEN see Neuchâtel *B1*

GENEVE *C1* (7km NE Urban) *46.24465, 6.19433* **TCS Camping Pointe à la Bise, Chemin de la Bise, 1222 Vésenaz [022 7521296; fax 7523767; camping.geneve@tcs.ch; www.campingtcs.ch]** Fr Geneva take S lakeside rd N5 sp Evian to Vésanez 4km. Turn L on Rte d'Hermance (D25) at traff lts & foll sp to site in 1km. Med, pt shd; wc; chem disp; mv service pnt; baby facs; shwrs inc; el pnts (4-10A) CHF4.50 (adaptor on loan); gas; Indtte; shop; tradsmn; rest; snacks; bar; playgrnd; paddling pool; lake sw; fishing; cycle hire; wifi; TV; 60% statics; dogs CHF5; bus to Geneva; poss cr; Eng spkn; ccard acc; red CCI. "Pleasant site; excel lake & mountain excursions; helpful staff; muddy when wet." 1 Apr-3 Oct. CHF 45.50 2010*

GENEVE *C1* (6km W Rural) *46.20111, 6.06621* **Geneva City Camping (previously Camping du Bois de Bay), 19 Route du Bois de Bay, 1242 Geneve [022 3410505; fax 3410606; info@geneva-camping.ch; www.geneva-camping.ch]** Fr A1 exit sp Bernex, then foll sp to Vernier, site sp. Lge, hdg pitch, pt shd; htd wc; chem disp; mv service pnt; baby facs; shwrs inc; el pnts (6A) CHF4.50; gas; Indtte (inc dryer); shop; tradsmn; snacks; bar; BBQ; playgrnd; tennis 2km; wifi; 40% statics; dogs CHF3.50; bus 2km; Eng spkn; some aircraft noise; ccard acc; red CCI. "V friendly; modern san facs; park & ride bus to city; don't be put off by indus site outside site." ♦ 1 Mar-31 Dec. CHF 42.50 2011*

GISWIL GROSSTEIL see Sarnen *B3*

⊞ **GOLDAU** *B3* (2km SE Rural) **Bernerhöhe Camping, 6410 Goldau [041 8551887; fax 8551358]** Exit N4 dir Goldau, then turn R dir Lauerz. Site sp on L nr top of hill. Med, terr, unshd; wc; chem disp; shwrs CHF0.50; el pnts (10A) CHF1.50; gas; Indtte; shop; tradsmn; playgrnd; paddling pool; lake sw 2km; TV; 90% statics; no dogs; quiet; CCI. "Great views fr upper sections." CHF 15.00 2008*

GONTEN see Appenzell *A4*

GORDEVIO see Locarno *C3*

GRAFSCHAFT see Ulrichen *C3*

GRINDELWALD *C2* (800m SE Rural) *46.62061, 8.04400* **Camping Gletscherdorf, Lochenbodenweg, 3818 Grindelwald [033 8531429; fax 8533129; info@gletscherdorf.ch; www.gletscherdorf.ch]** Exit N6 at Interlaken & then dir Grindelwald. Turn R just after church at end of main rd thro town at sp Gletscher/Schlucht & down steep descent for 500m, camp on R, sharp R turn to ent. Med, mkd pitch, hdstg, pt sl, unshd; wc; chem disp; mv service pnt; shwrs inc; el pnts (10A) CHF4; gas; Indtte; shop; tradsmn; rest 500m; covrd pool 1km; 60% statics; no dogs; poss cr; Eng spkn; adv bkg; quiet; ccard acc; CCI; "Sh walk to glacier; ideal base for walking; views of Eiger; site yourself & pay later - recep clsd 1000-1730; excel san facs, but ltd; friendly." 1 May-20 Oct. CHF 34.00 2011*

⊞ **GRINDELWALD** *C2* (1.5km W Rural) *46.62211, 8.01550* **Camping Eigernordwand, 3818 Grindelwald [033 8534227 or 8553322 winter; camp@eigernordwand.ch; www.eigernordwand.ch]** At 1st rndabt at ent to town turn R, site sp, no. 27. Med, pt sl, pt shd; htd wc; chem disp; mv service pnt; serviced pitch; shwrs inc; el pnts (10A) CHF5 (poss rev pol); gas; Indtte; shop; rest; snacks; bar; playgrnd; pool 1km; games area; TV; 60% statics; no dogs; bus 1km; site clsd mid-Apr to mid-May; higher winter prices; poss cr; quiet; ccard acc; red long stay. "Superb position at base of Eiger north wall; relaxed atmosphere; friendly, helpful staff; uphill walk to town; ski in/ski out; excel." ♦ CHF 34.00 2010*

GRINDELWALD *C2* (9km W Rural) *46.63769, 7.93211* **Dany's Camping, Baumgarten 7, 3801 Lütschental bei Grindelwald [033 8531824; fax 8536646]** Fr Interlaken, head twd Grindelwald for 12km. After L turn over rlwy go further 2km. Sp on L nr top of steep wooded ravine indicating ent on L up old rd with rest at junc. Site in 500m on R. Sm, pt sl, pt shd; wc; chem disp; mv service pnt; shwrs CHF1; el pnts (10A) CHF3.50; gas; Indtte; shop; rest 400m; playgrnd; fishing nr; dogs CHF1.50; adv bkg; quiet; CCI. "Superb views; conv for mountains & cable rlwy; helpful owners." 1 May-15 Oct. CHF 29.00 2008*

GRUYERES *C2* (2km N Rural) *46.59515, 7.08069* **Camping Les Sapins, 1664 Epagny-Gruyères [026 9129575; fax 9121053; info@gruyeres-camping.ch; www.gruyeres-camping.ch]** Foll rd S fr Bulle sp Châteaux d'Oex. Site on L of rd sp Gruyères-Moléson. Med, pt shd; htd wc; chem disp; mv service pnt; shwrs CHF1; el pnts (6A) CHF3; gas; Indtte; rest 1km; snacks; bar; playgrnd; pool 2km; tennis; 50% statics; phone; adv bkg; quiet. "Neat, tidy site; Gruyères lovely medieval town; visits to cheese factory; lovely countryside; easy reach E end Lake Geneva." ♦ 1 Apr-30 Sep. CHF 25.00 2008*

GRUYERES *C2* (4km S Rural) *46.56080, 7.08740* **Camping Haute Gruyère, Chemin du Camping 18, 1667 Enney [tel/fax 026 9212260; camping.enney@bluewin.ch; www.camping-gruyere.ch]** Well sp fr N (Gruyères) but not by name - foll TCS sp, not well sp fr S. Site E of rd fr Bulle to Château d'Oex, 1km S of Enney vill. Beware trains on x-ing at turn in. Med, unshd; htd wc; chem disp; mv service pnt; fam bthrm; shwrs inc; el pnts (6-10A) CHF4.50 (adaptor on loan); gas; Indtte (inc dryer); shops 1km; rest, snacks; bar; playgrnd; lake sw 10km; fishing; cycle hire; entmnt; TV; 50% statics; dogs CHF4; poss cr; adv bkg; quiet; 10% red long stay; ccard acc. "Friendly owners; vg, modern san facs; sm area for tourers; bread baked to order on site." 1 Apr-31 Oct. CHF 37.20 (CChq acc) 2011*

GSTAAD *C2* (11km S Rural) *46.38197, 7.26316* **Berg-Camping Heiti, 3785 Gsteig-bei-Gstaad [033 7551197]** Fr Gstaad take rd S thro Gsteig vill, site on L. App fr Aigle to S long climb over Col du Pillon. Sm, unshd; wc; shwrs CHF1.50; el pnts CHF3; Indry rm; shops 500m; rest & bar in vill; playgrnd; games area; many statics; dogs CHF2; bus adj; poss cr; Eng spkn; quiet. "Friendly, helpful warden; clean san facs; spectacular setting; gd walking area; cable car to Les Diablerets glacier for summer ski; vill walking dist." 20 May-31 Oct & 18 Dec-19 Apr. CHF 31.00 2008*

⊞ **GSTAAD** *C2* (700m W Rural) *46.48119, 7.27269* **Camping Bellerive, Bellerivestrasse 38, 3780 Gstaad [033 7446330; fax 7446345; bellerive.camping@bluewin.ch; www.bellerivecamping.ch]** App fr Saanen turn R bef Gstaad, sp. Sm, mkd pitch, some hdstg, pt shd; htd wc; chem disp; mv service pnt; shwrs CHF1; el pnts (12A) CHF2.70; gas; Indtte (inc dryer); tradsmn; playgrnd; pool 700m; tennis; fishing; skiing; internet; TV; 60% statics; dogs CHF2.70; Eng spkn; adv bkg; rlwy noise. "Gd touring, walking, wintersports; rvside site; sm pitches; buy Gstaad Card for rd, rail & mountain transport." CHF 28.70 2011*

GSTEIG BEI GSTAAD see Gstaad *C2*

⊞ **GUDO** *C3* (1.5km W Rural) *46.17080, 8.93170* **Camping Isola, Via Campeggi, 6515 Gudo [091 8593244; fax 8593344; roberto@ticino.com; www.camping-isola.ch]** Exit A2 at Bellinzona Sud dir Locarno. In 2.5km turn R twd Gudo, then L & foll site sps; site on banks Rv Tessine. Lge, hdg/mkd pitch, pt shd; htd wc; chem disp; mv service pnt; baby facs; shwrs inc; el pnts (10A) CHF4; Indtte; shop; tradsmn; rest; snacks; bar; playgrnd; htd pool; paddling pool; 25% statics; dogs CHF4; site clsd mid-Dec to mid-Jan; quiet. "Delightful, well-kept site; NH pitches poor with inadequate elec supply; easy access fr main rd." CHF 42.00 2009*

GUMEFENS see Bulle *C2*

GWATT see Thun *B2*

HASLIBERG GOLDERN *B3* (500m S Rural) *46.73727, 8.19588* **Camping Hofstaff-Derfli, Hoffstatt, 6085 Hasliberg-Goldern [033 9713707; fax 9713755; welcome@derfli.ch; www.derfli.ch]** Fr Brünig pass foll sp for Hasliberg. After cable car at Twing foll rd to Gasthof & turn R down narr rd opp. Site well sp. Sm, mkd pitch, pt shd; htd wc; chem disp; mv service pnt; baby facs; shwrs inc; el pnts (10A) metered; gas; Indtte (inc dryer); shop & 2km; tradsmn; rest, snacks, bar 500m; playgrnd; hot tub; cycle hire; games area; games rm; wifi; TV; 20% statics; dogs CHF2; phone; bus 500m; Eng spkn; adv bkg; quiet. "Excel, beautiful site; vg summer walking/winter sports; gd size pitches." ♦ 15 Dec-30 Apr & 15 May-31 Oct. CHF 34.00 2010*

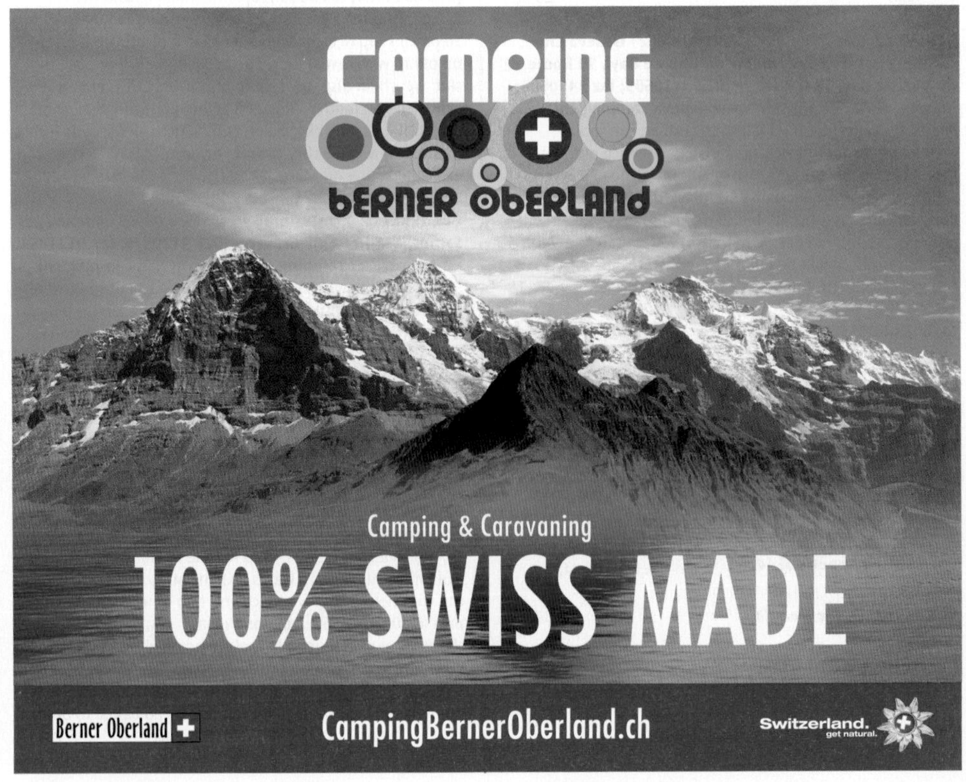

CAMPING
bERNER ObERLAND
Camping & Caravaning
100% SWISS MADE
Berner Oberland
CampingBernerOberland.ch
Switzerland.
get natural.

SWITZERLAND

⊞ **HAUDERES, LES** *D2* (1.5km N Rural) *46.09303, 7.50560* **Camping Molignon, 1984 Les Haudères [027 2831240; fax 2831331; info@molignon.ch; www.molignon.ch]** Fr Sion take rd to Val d'Hérens, turn R 2.5km after Evolène. Site sp but ent poorly mkd on unmade rd. Rd fr Sion steep, twisting & narr in places. Med, mkd pitch, terr, pt shd; wc; mv service pnt; chem disp; baby facs; shwrs inc; el pnts (10A) CHF3.80; gas; lndtte; shop; tradsmn; rest; snacks; bar; playgrnd; htd pool; skilift 3km; TV; 15% statics; dogs CHF3.20; phone; Eng spkn; adv bkg; quiet; ccard acc; red CCI. "V friendly owner; ideal for mountain climbing & walking; beautiful location." CHF 29.20 2008*

HINTERKAPPELEN see Bern *B2*

HORW see Luzern *B3*

⊞ **INNERTKIRCHEN** *C3* (300m N Rural) *46.70211, 8.22619* **Camping Grimselblick, Stapfenweg, 3862 Innertkirchen [033 9713752; info@camping-grimselblick.ch; www.camping-grimselblock.ch]** Foll sp to site on ent vill, well sp. Sm, pt sl, pt shd; htd wc; chem disp; shwrs CHF1; el pnts (10A) CHF2.50; lndtte; shop, rest in vill; games rm; 50% statics; dogs CHF1; Eng spkn; quiet. "Gd site on rv; not suitable lge o'fits due narr ent; refurb of san facs planned 2008." CHF 26.40 2008*

INNERTKIRCHEN *C3* (1km E Rural) *46.70700, 8.24219* **Camping Bauernhof-Wyler, Sustenstrasse 32, 3862 Innertkirchen [033 9718451; camping-wyler@bluewin.ch; www.camping-wyler.com]** App fr Innertkirchen dir Sustenpass, take care hairpin bends. Turn R on ent vill & foll sp. Sm, pt sl, unshd; wc; chem disp; shwrs CHF1; el pnts (10A) CHF2.50 (long lead poss req); lndtte (inc dryer); BBQ; playgrnd; tennis; fishing; games rm; horseriding; 20% statics; dogs CHF2; phone nr; adv bkg; Eng spkn; quiet. "Picturesque location; pleasant owner; CL-type site." ♦ 1 Apr-31 Oct. CHF 27.40 2009*

⊞ **INNERTKIRCHEN** *C3* (500m S Rural) *46.70669, 8.22619* **Camping Grund, Grundstrasse 44, 3862 Innertkirchen [tel/fax 033 9714409; info@camping-grund.ch; www.camping-grund.ch]** App fr Susten or Grimsel Pass, turn L at camping sp immed on ent vill. Foll further sp for 1km. Sm, pt shd; htd wc; chem disp; mv service pnt; shwrs CHF1; el pnts (6A) CHF3; gas; lndtte (inc dryer); shops 200m; BBQ; playgrnd; htd covrd pool 6km; tennis; fishing; horseriding; games rm; dogs CHF2; adv bkg; quiet; 10% red long stay. "V helpful & friendly; gd cent for mountains." CHF 28.60 2011*

INNERTKIRCHEN *C3* (NW Rural) *46.70938, 8.21519* **Camping Aareschlucht, Hauptstrasse 34, 3862 Innertkirchen [033 9715332; fax 9715344; campaareschlucht@bluewin.ch; www.camping-aareschlucht.ch]** On Meiringen rd out of town on R. Sm, pt shd; htd wc; chem disp; shwrs CHF1; el pnts (6-10A) CHF3; gas; lndtte (inc dryer); shop & rests nr; tradsmn; BBQ; playgrnd; pool 5km; games rm; 30% statics; dogs CHF2; adv bkg; Eng spkn; sep car park; quiet, but some rd noise; ccard acc. Red CCI. "Excel site; clean facs; gd walking; gd touring base Interlaken, Jungfrau region; conv Grimsel & Susten passes; rv walk to town." 1 May-31 Oct. CHF 24.00 2011*

INTERLAKEN Sites in the Interlaken area are identified by numbers signposted from the N8. Follow the appropriate number to your site as follows: Manor Farm 1, Alpenblick 2, Hobby 3, Lazy Rancho 4, Jungfrau 5, Interlaken-Ost 6, Jungfraublick 7, Oberoi 8, Seeblick 10, Du Lac 15, Bauernhof Wang 19.

⊞ **INTERLAKEN** *C2* (5km NE Rural) *46.70761, 7.91330* **Camp au Lac, 3852 Ringgenberg [033 8222616; fax 8234360]** Fr Ringgenberg to Brienz, site sp on R when exit Ringgenberg. Cont under rlwy viaduct to site. Med, pt sl, pt shd; wc; chem disp (wc); mv service pnt; shwrs CHF1; el pnts (6A) CHF3 (long cable poss req); lndry rm; shop & 1km; rest (clsd Mon, Tue low ssn); bar; pool 2km; 25% statics; dogs CHF2; bus; poss cr; Eng spkn; adv bkg; quiet; ccard acc; red low ssn; CCI. "Excel site; private access to lake; magnificent setting." ♦ CHF 36.00 2009*

⊞ **INTERLAKEN** *C2* (5km NE Urban) *46.70755, 7.90908* **Camping International Talacker, 3852 Ringgenberg [033 8221128; fax 8229838; camping@talacker.ch]** Fr Ringgenberg to Brienz on L shortly after Camping au Lac, sp fr main rd. Med, pt sl, pt shd; wc; chem disp; mv service pnt; shwrs CHF1; el pnts (10A) CHF4; gas; lndtte (inc dryer); shop tradsmn; snacks; bar; playgrnd; lake sw 3km; fishing; watersports; 10% statics; dogs CHF1; bus to Interlaken; adv bkg; quiet; Eng spkn; red low ssn. "Friendly, helpful family owners; peaceful, spacious, well-maintained site." CHF 35.00 2008*

⊞ **INTERLAKEN (NO. 1)** *C2* (3.5km W Rural) *46.68004, 7.81669* **Camping Manor Farm, Seestrasse 201, 3800 Interlaken-Thunersee [033 8222264; fax 8232991; manorfarm@quicknet.ch; www.manorfarm.ch]** Fr W on A8 exit junc 24 Interlaken West & foll sp Thun & Gunten. At rndabt take 2nd exit twd Thun, sp Gunten; pass Camping Alpenblick on R, then site on L after bdge. V lge, mkd pitch, pt shd; chem disp; mv service pnt; wc; baby facs; serviced pitches; shwrs inc; el pnts (6A) inc (adaptor avail); gas; lndtte (inc dryer); shop; 2 rests adj; snacks; bar; BBQ (charcoal/gas); playgrnd; paddling pool; private beach/lake sw adj; boat & cycle hire; steamer boat trips; excursions; cable car & chairlift nrby; watersports; fishing; golf 300m; horseriding 3km; wifi; entmnt; games/TV rm; 25% statics; dogs CHF5; c'vans/m'vans over 8m by request; money exchange; variable pitch price; poss cr; Eng spkn; adv bkg (bkg fee); quiet, rd noise some pitches; ccard acc; red low ssn; CCI. "Site on banks of Lake Thun; excel views; gd sized pitches; helpful staff; immac san facs; excel facs for children; local bus pass provided free; gd walking; if staying on Super pitch, water hose with pressurised valve fitting req." ♦ CHF 59.60 SBS - S07 2011*

See advertisement on next page

⊞ **INTERLAKEN (NO. 2)** *C2* (3km W Rural) *46.67969, 7.81764* **Camping Alpenblick, Seestrasse 130, 3800 Unterseen-Interlaken [033 8227757 or 8231470; fax 8231479; info@camping-alpenblick.ch; www.camping-alpenblick.ch]** Fr W on A8 exit junc 24 Interlaken West & foll sp Thun & Gunten. At rndabt take 2nd exit twd Thun, sp Gunten. Site adj Motel Neuhaus & Rest Strandbad on Gunten-Thun rd. Lge, mkd pitch, pt shd; htd wc; chem disp; mv service pnt; baby facs; shwrs inc; el pnts (10A) CHF4.50; gas; Indtte (inc dryer); shop; rest; snacks; BBQ; pool 3km; playgrnd; lake sw adj; watersports; fishing; golf adj; wifi; 30% statics; dogs CHF3; phone; bus fr site ent; stn 3km; Eng spkn; ccard acc (surcharge); red low ssn/long stay/CCI. "In beautiful situation; mountain views; excel, modern facs; bread baked on site; lake steamers fr hotel opp; gd walks nr; free bus pass to town; cycle rte to Interlaken." CHF 49.40 2011*

See advertisement

INTERLAKEN (NO. 3) *C2* (2km W Rural) *46.68400, 7.82961* **Camping Hobby, Lehnweg 16, 3800 Unterseen-Interlaken [033 8229652; fax 8229657; info@campinghobby.ch; www.campinginterlaken.ch or www.campinghobby.ch]** On N8 fr Thun at E end of lake exit junc to Unterseen on rd 70. In 200m past petrol stn, turn L into narr lane; site sp. Site next to Camping Lazy Rancho. Or fr Interlaken turn R by side of Landhotel Golf opp g'ge, foll No.3 sp. Med, pt shd, some hdg pitch; htd wc; chem disp; mv service pnt; baby facs; shwrs CHF0.50; el pnts (10A) CHF4.50 (adaptor avail); gas; Indtte (inc dryer); shop; tradsmn; rest, snacks 400m; BBQ; playgrnd; paddling pool; shgl beach & lake sw 1.5km; golf 1km; wifi; 25% statics; dogs free; Eng spkn; adv bkg; quiet but some noise fr shooting range at w/end; ccard not acc; red low ssn; CCI. "Gd for touring Interlaken, Jungfrau region & Bernese Oberland; wonderful views of Eiger & other mountains; v clean facs; friendly staff." ♦ 1 Apr-30 Sep. CHF 50.00 2011*

See advertisement

INTERLAKEN (NO. 4) *C2* (2.5km W Rural) *46.68555, 7.83083* **Camping Lazy Rancho, Lehnweg 6, 3800 Unterseen-Interlaken [033 8228716; fax 8231920; info@lazyrancho.ch; www.lazyrancho.ch]** Fr W on app to Interlaken, exit A8/A6 junc 24 sp Interlaken West. Turn L at slip rd rndabt then at rndabt take a sharp R turn (foll camping sp Nos. 3-5); at Migrol petrol stn foll sp for Lazy Rancho 4 (narr rd on L just bef Landhotel Golf); it is 2nd site. Cent of Interlaken best avoided with c'vans or lge m'vans. Rec arr bef 1900 hrs. Med, hdg/mkd pitch, some hdstg, pt shd; htd wc; some serviced pitches; chem disp; mv service pnt; baby facs; shwrs inc; el pnts (10A) inc (adaptors provided); gas; Indtte (inc dryer); shop; tradsmn; cooking facs; BBQ (charcoal/gas/elec); playgrnd; sm pool; watersports, fishing nrby; cycle hire; tennis 2.5km; horseriding 500m; games rm; wifi; sat TV; 30% statics; dogs CHF3; no c'vans/m'vans over 7.50m high ssn; phone; Eng spkn; quiet but some noise fr shooting range at w/end; ccard acc; red low ssn; CCI. " Superb views Eiger, Monch & Jungfrau; ideal for touring Interlaken, Bernese Oberland; friendly, caring, helpful owners; sm pitches; recep 0900-1200 & 1330-2100 high ssn; 5 mins to bus stop nr Cmp Jungfrau; ask about Swiss red fare rlwy services - excel value; immac, well-maintained site & facs." ♦ 6 Apr-20 Oct. CHF 58.10 SBS - S01 2011*

See advertisement

INTERLAKEN (NO. 5) *C2* (2km W Rural) *46.68688, 7.83411* **Jungfrau Camp, Steindlerstrasse 60, 3800 Unterseen-Interlaken [tel/fax 033 8225730; info@jungfraucamp.ch; www.campinginterlaken.ch or www.jungfraucamp.ch]** Leave N8 at exit Unterseen. In approx 600m turn R at rndabt & foll sp to site. Med, pt shd; htd wc; chem disp (ltd); mv service pnt; baby facs; fam bthrm; shwrs CHF1; el pnts (10A) CHF4; gas; Indtte (inc dryer); shop; rest; snacks; bar; playgrnd; pool; lake sw 1.5km; tennis; 40% statics; dogs CHF4; bus adj; poss cr; Eng spkn; adv bkg; quiet some noise fr shooting range at w/end; red low ssn. "Visits to all Bernese Oberland vills; views of Jungfrau, Mönch & Eiger; town in walking dist; excel, relaxing, well-run site; high standard san facs." 1 Jun-15 Sep. CHF 46.20 2011*

See advertisement

SWITZERLAND

INTERLAKEN (NO. 6) *C2* (E Rural) *46.69256, 7.8689* **TCS Camping Interlaken-Ost, Brienzstrasse 24, 3800 Interlaken [033 8224434; fax 8224456; camping.interlaken@tcs.ch; www.campinginterlaken.ch]** Exit N8 at Ringgenberg & foll sp for Brienz/Luzern. After viaduct turn L & site sp in 100m. Awkward bends on app. Med, mkd pitch, pt shd; wc; chem disp; mv service pnt; shwrs; el pnts (8A) CHF4; gas; Indtte (inc dryer); shop in ssn; rest; bar; playgrnd; pool 300m; sand beach 2km; wellness facs; wifi; 20% statics; dogs CHF5; train opp; poss cr high ssn; Eng spkn; some rd noise; ccard acc; red CCI. "Gd cent for Bernese Oberland; excel walking; helpful staff; easy access to town; lively entmnt on lake cruises; concerts." 1 Apr-10 Oct. CHF 44.00 2011*

See advertisement

INTERLAKEN (NO. 7) *C2* (2km S Rural) *46.67309, 7.86719* **Camping Jungfraublick, Gsteigstrasse 80, 3800 Matten-Interlaken [033 8224414; fax 8221619; info@jungfraublick.ch; www.jungfraublick.ch]** Fr E exit N8 after tunnel at Lauterbrunnen-Grindelwald junc 25, head N twd Matten-Interlaken & site 250m on L. Med, mkd pitch, pt shd; htd wc; chem disp; mv service pnt; shwrs CHF0.50; el pnts (6A) inc (poss rev pol); gas; Indtte (inc dryer); shop; BBQ (gas/charcoal); playgrnd; sm htd pool in ssn; lake sw 3km; fishing; rafting; paragliding; canyoning; cycle hire; golf, horseriding 4km; wifi; TV/games rm; 40% statics; dogs CHF3; no c'van/m'van over 7.50m (inc towbar) high ssn; phone; free local bus; poss cr; Eng spkn; adv bkg; some rd/rlwy noise; ccard acc; red long stay/low ssn; CCI. "Wonderful views Jungfrau; helpful staff; clean facs; adventure sports adj; excursions, walks & cycle rtes around Interlaken; vg." ♦ 1 May-20 Sep. CHF 49.60 SBS - S04 2011*

See advertisement

INTERLAKEN (NO. 8) *C2* (4km S Rural) *46.66161, 7.86500* **Camping Oberei, Obereigasse 9, 3812 Wilderswil-Interlaken [tel/fax 033 8221335; oberei8@swisscamps.ch; www.campinginterlaken.ch or www.campingwilderswil.ch]** Fr Interlaken by-pass take rd sp Grindelwald & Lauterbrunnen to Wilderswil. Site sp 800m past stn on R in vill. Narr ent. Med, mkd pitch, pt sl, pt shd; htd wc; chem disp; baby facs; shwrs CHF1; el pnts (6A) CHF3; gas; Indtte (inc dryer); shop; rest, snacks in vill; pool 3km; TV rm; dogs CHF1; bus adj, bus/train nr; poss cr; Eng spkn; adv bkg; quiet; ccard not acc; CCI. "Well-managed, relaxing, family-run site in superb scenic location; helpful owners; ground sheets supplied if wet/muddy; blocks provided; gd, clean facs; gd touring cent; easy walk to rlwy stn; guest card gives free local train & bus travel; excel popular as ever; rec high ssn." 1 May-15 Oct. CHF 33.00 2011*

See advertisement

INTERLAKEN (NO. 10) *C2* (2.8km E Rural) *46.69125, 7.89353* **TCS Camping Seeblick, Campingstrasse 14, 3806 Bönigen [033 8221143; fax 8221162; camping.boenigen@tcs.ch; www.campingtcs.ch]** Fr A8 exit junc 26 Interlaken-Ost dir Bönigen; on ent vill turn L, site sp on Lake Brienz. Med, some hdstg, shd; htd wc; chem disp; mv service pnt; baby facs; shwrs inc; el pnts (6A) CHF4; gas; Indtte (inc dryer); shop; rest 600m; snacks; bar; playgrnd; htd pool, paddling pool 200m; lake sw; fishing; boating; golf 4km; wifi; entmnt; TV rm; 10% statics; dogs CHF5; phone; Eng spkn; quiet; ccard acc; red low ssn/CCI. "Ideal for fishing or boating; v helpful owner; clean facs; lakeside walk to Interlaken; excel." ♦ 1 Apr-3 Oct. CHF 37.80 (CChq acc) 2011*

See advertisement

INTERLAKEN (NO. 15) *C2* (10km E Rural) *46.71141, 7.96886* **Camping du Lac, Schorren, 3807 Iseltwald [079 3533021; info@campingdulac.ch; www.campingdulac.ch]** Leave N8 at Iseltwald. Site sp fr N8, on Lake Brienz adj hotel. Sm, mkd pitch, terr, unshd; wc; chem disp; shwrs inc; el pnts CHF4.50; Indtte (inc dryer); shop; lakeside rest adj; paddling pool; lake beach & sw 200m; fishing; watersports; mountain biking; internet; TV rm; 80% statics; dogs CHF4; bus 300m; Eng spkn; adv bkg; quiet; red low ssn. "Peaceful site in superb location; friendly owner; vg, modern facs; access poss diff lge o'fits; touring pitches in cent of statics; vg." 1 May-30 Sep. CHF 46.00 2011*

See advertisement

INTERLAKEN (NO. 19) *C2* (10km NW Rural) *46.69025, 7.78469* **Camping auf dem Bauernhof Wang, 3803 Beatenberg [033 8412105; fax 8412185; camping-wang@gmx.ch; www.naturpur.ch/camping-wang]** Exit m'way at junc Unterseen & foll sp to Beatenberg; 300m after church turn L & site sp. GPS route not rec - use these directions. Sm, terr, pt shd; wc; chem disp; shwrs inc; el pnts CHF3; Indtte; tradsmn; playgrnd; htd, covrd pool, tennis 1km; wifi; some statics; dogs CHF2; bus 300m; adv bkg; quiet; red low ssn. "Vg, peaceful, beautiful site in superb location; gd san facs; owner helpful; excel hiking country; conv Interlaken." 20 Apr-15 Oct. CHF 31.00 2011*

See advertisement

ISELTWALD see Interlaken *C2*

⊞ **KANDERSTEG** *C2* (9km N Rural) *46.58188, 7.64150* **Camping Grassi, 3714 Frutigen [033 6711149; fax 6711380; camping grassi@bluewin.ch; www.camping-grassi.ch]** Exit rd to Kandersteg at Frutigen-Dorf & in 400m L to site in 500m. Med, pt shd; htd wc; chem disp; mv service pnt; baby facs; shwrs inc; el pnts (6A) CHF3; gas; Indtte; shops; rest 500m; playgrnd; htd covrd pool 1km; fishing; tennis; cycle hire; wifi; TV; 50% statics; dogs CHF1.50; phone; Eng spkn; adv bkg; red long stay. CHF 28.80 2009*

⊞ **KANDERSTEG** *C2* (E Rural) *46.49800, 7.68519* **Camping Rendez-Vous, 3718 Kandersteg [033 6751534; fax 6751737; rendez-vous.camping@bluewin.ch; www.camping-kandersteg.ch]** In middle of Kandersteg turn E dir Sesselbahn Öschinensee; site sp. Med, some hdstg, pt sl, terr, pt shd; htd wc; chem disp; mv service pnt; shwrs CHF1; el pnts (10A) metered (adaptors avail); gas; Indtte (inc dryer); shop; tradsmn; rest; snacks; bar; BBQ; htd pool 800m; cycle hire; games rm; wifi; dogs CHF3; Eng spkn; adv bkg; quiet; ccard acc; CCI. "Excel, well-supervised site; chair-lift adj; excel walking." CHF 36.00 2009*

KRATTIGEN see Spiez *C2*

I'll fill in a report online and let the Club know – www.caravanclub.co.uk/europereport

This is a wonderful site.

KREUZLINGEN *A3* (E Rural) *47.64676, 9.19810* **Camping Fischerhaus, Promenadenstrasse 52, 8280 Kreuzlingen [071 6884903; info@camping-fischerhaus.ch; www.camping-fischerhaus.ch]** Fr Konstanz take rd 13 dir Romanshorn. Turn L at sp 'Hafen/Indus Est' off main lakeside rd, Kreuzlingen-Arbon. Camping sps fr 5km SE at Customs in Konstanz. Med, pt shd; wc (some cont); chem disp; mv service pnt; shwrs inc; el pnts (10A) inc; gas; Indtte; shop; rest; pool adj; fishing; tennis; 75% statics; phone; no dogs; poss cr; Eng spkn; adv bkg; quiet, but some noise w/end. "Facs for statics excel, but for tourers v basic; gates clsd 1200-1400 & 2200-0700; gd cycle paths." ♦ 1 Apr-17 Oct. CHF 43.00 2008*

KREUZLINGEN *A3* (8km SE Rural) *47.62182, 9.26602* **Camping Ruderbaum, Ruderbaum 3, 8595 Altnau-am-Bodensee [071 6952965; camping@ruderbaum.ch; www.ruderbaum.ch]** Fr Kreuzlingen foll main lakeside rd 13 twd Romanshorn. After passing sp for Altnau, at rndabt turn L, cross rlwy, site on L. Lge, pt sl, pt shd; htd wc; chem disp; mv service pnt; shwrs; el pnts CHF3.50; Indtte; shop; tradsmn; rest, snacks, bar adj; shgl beach & lake adj sw; 80% statics; dogs €2.50; train adj; Eng spkn; quiet; some rlwy noise; CCI. "Sep area for tourers sloping down to lake - poss diff when wet; gd site in beautiful setting; helpful staff; lakeside walks & cycling; landing stage for Lake Constance ships; helpful staff; gd." ♦ 1 Apr-31 Oct. CHF 28.50 2010*

LANDERON, LE *B2* (300m S Rural) *43.05251, 7.06995* **Camping des Pêches, Route du Port, 2525 Le Landeron [032 7512900; fax 7516354; info@camping-lelanderon.ch; www.camping-lelanderon.ch]** A5 fr Neuchâtel, exit Le Landeron or La Neuveville; foll site sp. Med, mkd pitch, pt shd; wc; chem disp; mv service pnt; 20% serviced pitches; baby facs; shwrs CHF1; el pnts (15A) CHF3.50; gas; Indtte; shop; tradsmn; rest; bar; playgrnd; htd pool 100m; fishing; tennis; cycle hire; TV rm; 60% statics; sep car park; poss cr; Eng spkn; adv bkg; noisy; ccard acc; red CCI. "Sep touring section on busy site; walks by lake & rv; interesting old town." ♦ 1 Apr-15 Oct. CHF 32.00 2009*

LANDQUART *B4* (3km E Rural) *46.97040, 9.59620* **TCS Camping Neue Ganda, Ganda 21, 7302 Landquart [081 3223955; fax 3226864; camping.landquart@tcs.ch; www.campingtcs.ch]** Exit A13/E43 dir Landquart, site sp on rd to Davos. Lge, pt sl, pt shd; htd wc; chem disp; mv service pnt; fam bthrm; baby facs; shwrs inc; el pnts (6-10A) CHF4; gas; Indtte (inc dryer); shop; snacks; bar; BBQ; cooking facs; playgrnd; rv fishing; canoeing; tennis 300m; games rm; cycle hire; wifi; entmnt; 60% statics; dogs CHF4; rd noise; ccard acc; red CCI. "Immac san facs; excel site; v helpful owner & staff; poss uneven pitches, mainly grass; gd facs for disabled; if recep clsd find pitch & sign in later; many mkd walks fr site." ♦ 10 Dec-28 Feb & 19 Mar-17 Oct. CHF 31.60 (CChq acc) 2008*

LANGNAU AM ALBIS see Adliswil *A3*

LANGWIESEN see Schaffhausen *A3*

LAUFELFINGEN see Sissach *A2*

LAUSANNE *C1* (9km E Rural) *46.48973, 6.73786* **Camping de Moratel, Route de Moratel 2, 1096 Cully [021 7991914; camping.moratel@bluewin.ch]** Fr Lausanne-Vevey lakeside rd (not m/way), turn R to Cully; sp thro town; site on R on lake shore. Ent not sp. Sm, hdg/mkd pitch, hdstg, pt shd; wc; chem disp; mv service pnt; shwrs inc; el pnts (3-5A) metered (adaptor provided); gas; Indtte; shop; tradsmn; snacks; bar; pool 3km; lake sw; fishing; boating; 80% statics; bus, train, ferry; poss cr; adv bkg; some rlwy noise. "Vg value; attractive, clean site with beautiful views; rec adv bkg for lakeside pitch; friendly staff; siting poss diff for lge o'fits; gd location for best part Lake Geneva; excel san facs." 20 Mar-20 Oct. CHF 22.50 2011*

⊞ **LAUSANNE** *C1* (2km W Rural) *46.51769, 6.59766* **Camping de Vidy, Chemin du Camping 3, 1007 Lausanne [021 6225000; fax 6225001; info@clv.ch; www.clv.ch]** Leave A1 at Lausanne Süd/Ouchy exit; take 4th exit at rndabt (Rte de Chavannes); in 100m filter L at traff lts & foll site sp to L. Site adj to HQ of Int'l Olympic Organisation, well sp all over Lausanne. Lge, mkd pitch, pt shd; htd wc (some cont); chem disp; mv service pnt; baby facs; shwrs inc; el pnts (10A) inc; gas; Indtte (inc dryer); shop; rest; snacks; bar; BBQ; playgrnd; lake beach adj; watersports; tennis 1km; cycle hire; sports & recreation area adj; games rm; wifi; TV; many statics in sep area; recep 0800-2100 high ssn; dogs CHF2; no c'vans/m'vans over 8m high ssn; bus to Lausanne 400m; chem disp up steps; Eng spkn; adv bkg; quiet; ccard acc; CCI. "Excel lakeside site in attractive park; friendly staff; sm pitches; gd san facs; gd train service to Geneva; conv m'way; free bus passes for unltd bus & Metro tavel in Lausanne." ♦ CHF 45.40 SBS - S11 2011*

SWITZERLAND

⊞ **LAUTERBRUNNEN** *C2* (S Rural) *46.59100, 7.91311* **Camping Schützenbach, Witimatte 204B, 3822 Lauterbrunnen [033 8551268; fax 8551275; info@schutzenbach.ch; www.schutzenbach.ch]** S fr Interlaken, site sp after Lauterbrunnen. Med, pt sl, terr, pt shd; htd wc; chem disp; mv service pnt; shwrs CHF0.50; el pnts (15A) CHF4 (poss rev pol); gas; Indtte (inc dryer); shop & 300m; snacks; bar; playgrnd; pool 400m; fishing; tennis; 60% statics; dogs CHF3; bus at site ent; rlwy stn nr; site clsd 6 Nov-9 Dec; Eng spkn; adv bkg; quiet but some noise fr nrby helipad & hostel adj; ccard acc. "Clean, modern san facs; site used by coach camping parties & lge groups; friendly owners." CHF 26.00 2010*

⊞ **LAUTERBRUNNEN** *C2* (500m S Rural) *46.58788, 7.91030* **Camping Jungfrau, Weid 406, 3822 Lauterbrunnen [033 8562010; fax 8562020; info@camping-jungfrau.ch; www.camping-jungfrau.ch]** S o'skts of Lauterbrunnen sp at R fork, site in 500m. Lge, some hdstg, terr, pt shd; htd wc; chem disp; mv service pnt; baby facs; some serviced pitches; shwrs inc; el pnts (15A) CHF4 (metered in winter; poss rev pol); gas; Indtte (inc dryer); supmkt; tradsmn; rest; snacks; bar; playgrnd; pool 600m; tennis; cycle hire; wifi; TV; 30% statics; dogs CHF3; phone; sep car park when site full; ski-bus; ATM; poss cr; Eng spkn; adv bkg rec; quiet; ccard acc; red/long stay/CCI. "Friendly, helpful welcome; fine scenery; rlwy tickets sold; close to town & rlwy stn to high alpine resorts; ski & boot rm; rest clsd Sun, Mon in winter; navette inc; some noise fr helicopter pad & shooting club; top of site quietest; superb site & facs." ♦ CHF 43.10 2011*

See advertisement

⊞ **LAUTERBRUNNEN** *C2* (3km S Rural) *46.56838, 7.90869* **Camping Breithorn, Sandbach, 3824 Stechelberg [033 8551225; fax 8553561; breithorn@stechelberg.ch; www.campingbreithorn.ch]** Up valley thro Lauterbrunnen, 300m past Trümmelbach Falls to ent on R. Med, unshd; wc; chem disp; mv service pnt; shwrs CHF1; el pnts (10A) metered; gas; Indtte (inc dryer); shop; rest 200m; BBQ; sm playgrnd; pool 3km; tennis; fishing; 60% statics; dogs CHF1; phone; Eng spkn; adv bkg; quiet; red CCI. "Quiet site in lovely area; arr early high ssn; fine scenery & gd touring base; friendly helpful owners; frequent trains, funiculars & cable cars fr Lauterbrunnen stn (4km); Schilthorn cable car 1.5km; excel cent for mountain walking & cycling; excel, clean facs." CHF 26.00 2011*

LAUTERBRUNNEN *C2* (6km S Rural) *46.54619, 7.90100* **Camping Rütti, 3824 Stechelberg [033 8552885; fax 8552611; campingruetti@stechelberg.ch; www.campingruetti.ch]** Fr Interlaken thro Lauterbrunnen, past Trümmelbach Falls, site on R at end of valley. Med, pt sl, pt shd; wc; chem disp; shwrs; el pnts (10A) CHF3; gas; Indtte (inc dryer); shop, rest, bar 200m; tradsmn; playgrnd; fishing; tennis; cycle hire; games rm; 10% statics; phone; dogs CHF2.50; bus 200m; poss cr; Eng spkn; adv bkg rec; quiet; CCI. "Frequent buses to Lauterbrunnen stn; gd walking/cycling; superb site." 1 May-30 Sep. CHF 30.40 2009*

⊞ **LENK** *C2* (3km S Rural) *46.42819, 7.47788* **Camping Hasenweide, Hasenweide 1, Oberried, 3775 Lenk im Simmental [033 7332647; fax 7332973; info@camping-hasenweide.ch; www.camping-hasenweide.ch]** Take rd S fr Zweisimmen to Lenk, thro Lenk vill twd Oberreid for 4.5km, ignore 1st site on R, site at end of rd on L. Sm, pt sl, pt shd; htd wc; chem disp; shwrs inc; el pnts (6A) CHF3 (poss long lead req); Indtte (inc dryer); sm shop & 5km; tradsmn; rest adj; BBQ; games rm; internet; 75% statics; dogs CHF2; phone; bus to town; site clsd mid-Oct to mid-Nov; Eng spkn; quiet. "Mostly statics but some rm for tourers, otherwise field outside; poss long walk to san facs; ideal cent walking & skiing; beautiful location at foot of waterfall; vg." CHF 30.00 2009*

⊞ **LENZERHEIDE** *C4* (5km S Rural) *46.69873, 9.55813* **Camping St Cassian, 7083 Lenz bei Lenzerheide [081 3842472; fax 3842489; camping.st.cassian@bluewin.ch]** Fr Chur exit m'way Chur Süd & foll sp Lenzerheide. 2km past Lenzerheide site clearly sp on L. Fr S 1km past Lenz on R. NB Long, hard climb & hairpin bet Lenzerheide & Chur. Med, hdstg, pt sl, terr, shd; wc; all serviced pitches; mv service pnt; chem disp; shwrs CHF1; el pnts (10A) CHF3; gas; Indtte; shop 3km; rest adj; playgrnd; lake sw 2km; wifi; 90% statics; dogs CHF2; phone; poss cr; some Eng spkn; adv bkg; quiet; CCI. "Site in conifer woodland; non-glaciated area gd for walking, touring, mountain biking; mountain views; rec arr early to secure pitch." ♦ CHF 30.50 2009*

Mountain Holiday Park
Camping Jungfrau
Lauterbrunnen
www.camping-jungfrau.ch
– Very modern facilities
– Family-friendly, childrens' playground
– Hiking & skiing areas of the Jungfrau region
– Restaurant, grocery shop, ...
– Specially adapted for motor homes
– Bungalows, caravans, B&B
– Winter season sites
– Free ski bus
LAUTERBRUNNEN
in the Valley of 72 Waterfalls
WiFi Zone
Hotspot
swisscom
Eiger
Mönch
Jungfrau
CAMPING JUNGFRAU AG, CH-3822 LAUTERBRUNNEN, Berner Oberland
Phone ++ 41(0)33 856 20 10, info@camping-jungfrau.ch, www.camping-jungfrau.ch
Open the whole year round!

LENZERHEIDE *C4* (500m SW Rural) *46.72331, 9.55468* **TCS Camping Gravas, Voa Nova 6, 7078 Lenzerheide/Lai [081 3842335; fax 3842306; camping.lenzerheide@tcs.ch; www.campingtcs.ch]** Exit A13 at Chur-Süd onto rd 3 dir Lenzerheide (20km). Site sp fr cent of Lenzerheide. Long, hard climb to site with hairpin. Lge, shd; htd wc; chem disp; shwrs; el pnts (6-10A) CHF4.50; gas; Indtte (inc dryer); shops adj; pool 1km; lake sw 1.2km; 60% statics; dogs CHF5; poss cr; Eng spkn; adv bkg; rd noise; ccard acc; CCI. "Many sports & activities in Lenzerheide; excel walking; sm pitches." 2 Dec-11 Apr & 28 May-2 Nov. CHF 34.60 2010*

LEUK *C2* (6km N Rural) *46.38119, 7.62361* **Camping Sportarena, 3954 Leukerbad [027 4701037; fax 4703707; info@sportarenatop.ch; www.sportarenatop.ch]** Exit A9 at Susten & foll sp N to Leukerbad, site sp. Med, some hdstg, pt sl, pt terr, pt shd; htd wc; chem disp; mv service pnt; shwrs inc; el pnts (10A) CHF5; Indtte; shop 500m; tradsmn; rest; snacks; bar; BBQ; htd, covrd pool 200m; thermal pools nr; sports cent adj; games area; TV rm; 20% statics; dogs CHF2; poss cr; Eng spkn; adv bkg; quiet. "Beautiful situation; pleasant, helpful staff; attractive little town; cable cars; walks; vg." ♦ 1 May-31 Oct. CHF 30.00 2009*

LEUK *C2* (8km E Rural) *46.30719, 7.76388* **Camping Rhône, 3945 Gampel [027 9322041; info@campingrhone.ch; www.campingrhone.ch]** Fr rd A9/E62 exit dir Gampel, site well sp on R bank of Rv Rhône. Lge, pt shd; wc; chem disp; mv service pnt; baby facs; shwrs inc; el pnts CHF3.20; gas; Indtte; shop high ssn; rest high ssn; bar; playgrnd; htd pool & paddling pool; tennis; golf; fishing; 30% statics; dogs CHF3; poss cr; adv bkg; quiet. "Superb location & touring base; gd walking, cycling; driest part of Switzerland." ♦ 1 Apr-31 Oct. CHF 22.50 2009*

LEUK *C2* (1.6km SE Urban) *46.29911, 7.63738* **Camping Bella-Tola, Waldstrasse 57, 3952 Susten [027 4731491; fax 4733641; info@bella-tola.ch; www.bella-tola.ch]** E fr Sierre turn R at ent to Susten, after bdge over Illgraben & foll sp for 1.5km. NB Acute turn off main rd; v steep hill & bad rd surface. Lge, mkd pitch, sl, pt shd; wc; chem disp; mv service pnt; baby facs; shwrs inc; el pnts (10A) CHF3.60; gas; Indtte; shop; tradsmn; rest; snacks; bar; BBQ; playgrnd; htd pool; lake sw & shgl beach; games rm; wifi; TV; 25% statics; dogs CHF2.70; phone; bus 1.6km; poss cr; adv bkg; noisy at w/end; ccard acc; red low ssn. 11 May-30 Sep. CHF 49.35 2011*

LEUK *C2* (3km SE Rural) *46.29780, 7.65936* **Camping Gemmi 'Agarn', Briannenstrasse 4, 3952 Susten [tel/fax 027 4731154 or 4734295; info@campgemmi.ch; www.campgemmi.ch]** Foll A9/E27 SE; then nr Martigny take A9/E62 to Sierre; then take E62 thro Susten. After 2km, by Hotel Relais Bayard, take R lane (Agarn, Feithieren), ignoring sp Camping Torrent, & foll Alte Kantonstrasse sp Agarn. Turn R at site sp into Briannenstrasse; site in 200m. Med, mkd pitch, pt sl, pt shd; wc; chem disp; mv service pnt; serviced pitches; individual san facs some pitches; shwrs inc; el pnts (16A) inc; gas; Indtte (inc dryer); shop; tradsmn; rest; snacks; BBQ (gas/elec); playgrnd; pool 600m; golf, tennis, horseriding nrby; wifi; sat TV; 5% statics; dogs CHF3; no c'vans/m'vans over 9m high ssn; Eng spkn; adv bkg; quiet; various pitch prices; ccard acc; red low ssn; CCI. "Outstanding site; friendly, helpful, hardworking owners; private bthrms avail; gd stop on way Simplon Pass; barrier clsd 2200-0800; excel walking; conv A9." 14 Apr-14 Oct. CHF 40.00 SBS - S12 2011*

LEYSIN see Aigle *C2*

⊞ **LIGNIERES** *B2* (500m E Rural) *47.08545, 7.07093* **Camping Fraso Ranch, Chemin du Grand-Marais, 2523 Lignières [032 7514616; fax 7514614; camping.fraso-ranch@bluewin.ch; www.camping-lignieres.ch]** Fr A5 exit dir Le Landeron. In Le Landeron turn L sp Lignières. In 5km (do not go into vill) keep strt to site on R in further 2km. Bef Lignières keep R & foll camp sp. Lge, pt shd; wc; chem disp; mv service pnt; baby facs; sauna; shwrs CHF0.50; el pnts (10A) CHF3.50; gas; Indtte; shop; cooking facs; playgrnd; htd pool; paddling pool; jacuzzi; tennis; games area; 90% statics (sep area); dogs CHF1.50; sep car park; site clsd 1 Nov-20 Dec; gates clsd 1230-1400; Eng spkn; ccard acc; red CCI. "V well-organised, tidy site." ♦ CHF 31.00 2009*

LOCARNO see also sites under Tenero *C3*

LOCARNO *C3* (9km E Rural) *46.16978, 8.91396* **Park-Camping Riarena, Via Campeggio, 6516 Cugnasco [091 8591688; fax 8592885; camping.riarena@bluewin.ch; www.camping-riarena.ch]** Exit A2/E35 Bellinzona-Süd & foll sp dir airport. Bear R at rndabt & foll site sp to Gudo, site on R in 2km. Lge, shd; wc; chem disp; mv service pnt; shwrs inc; el pnts (10A) CHF5 (adaptor avail); gas; Indtte; shop; rest; snacks; bar; playgrnd; pool & 2 paddling pools; games area; cycle hire; wifi; entmnt; dogs CHF4; Eng spkn; adv bkg; quiet; ccard acc (CHF100+); red long stay. "Friendly, family-run site; excursions arranged; gd cycle rtes; gate shut 1300-1500; clean san facs; dusty site; beware acorn drop September." ♦ 13 Mar-23 Oct. CHF 47.00 2011*

LOCARNO *C3* (5km SE Rural) *46.14256, 8.83899* **Camping Vira-Bellavista, 6574 Vira-Gambarogno [tel/fax 091 7951477; info@campingbellavista.ch; www.campingbellavista.ch]** Leave N13 Bellizona-Locarno rd sp Gamborogno, cont thro Magadino. Site just outside Vira on lakeside. Steep, awkward access to site. Sm, pt shd; wc; mv service pnt; shwrs; el pnts CHF4; Indry rm; shops 300m; lake sw; watersports; boat-launch 1km; fishing; tennis; golf; entmnt; dogs CHF3; bus; poss v cr; Eng spkn; rd noise. "Beautiful area; ideal family site; gd facs but ltd & stretched high ssn." 25 Apr-19 Oct. CHF 33.00 2008*

LOCARNO *C3* (2km S Urban) *46.15587, 8.80258* **Camping Delta, Via Respini 7, 6600 Locarno [091 7516081; fax 7512243; info@campingdelta.com; www.campingdelta.com]** Fr cent of Locarno make for prom & foll sp to Lido. Site in 400m past Lido on L. Fr Simplon Pass SS337 fr Domodossola to Locarno clsd to trailer c'vans; narr rd with many bends. Site well sp fr m'way. Lge, hdg/mkd pitch, pt shd; wc; chem disp; mv service pnt; shwrs; el pnts (10A) CHF5; gas; Indtte (inc dryer); shop; rest; snacks; bar; playgrnd; pool & lake sw 300m; cycle & kayak hire; fitness rm; wifi; no dogs; poss cr; Eng spkn; adv bkg to end Mar; quiet; no radios or musical instruments allowed; red low ssn/snr citizens. "No access for vehicles 2200-0700; superb location walking dist Locarno; excel facs but long walk fr S end of site; premium for lakeside pitches." 1 Mar-31 Oct. CHF 87.00 2011*

SWITZERLAND

LOCARNO *C3* (5km W Rural) *46.17801, 8.73035* **Camping Zandone, Via Arbigo, 6616 Losone [091 7916563; fax 7910047; campeggio.zandone@tiscalinet.ch]** Fr N2 exit Bellinzona Süd to Locarno-Ascona-Losone. In Losone take rd to Intragna, site on R. Lge, pt shd; wc; chem disp; mv service pnt; shwrs; el pnts (10A) CHF5; lndtte; shop; rest 200m; snacks; bar; playgrnd; 20% statics; dogs CHF6; poss cr; CCI. "Gd area for walking/cycling; ltd el pnts." ♦ 1 Apr-31 Oct. CHF 45.30 2008*

LOCARNO *C3* (10km NW Rural) *46.22436, 8.74395* **TCS Camping Bella Riva, 6672 Gordévio [091 7531444; fax 7531764; camping.gordevio@tcs.ch; www.campingtcs.ch]** Fr W end of A13 tunnel under Locarno foll sp Centovalle & Valle Maggia. In 3km turn R to Valle Maggia. Stay on rd which by-passes Gordévio (approx 5km), site on L. Lge, pt shd; wc; chem disp; mv service pnt; baby facs; shwrs; el pnts inc (10A) CHF4.50; gas; lndtte; shop; rest; snacks; playgrnd; pool; rv sw & beach; fishing; tennis; cycle hire; wifi; TV; 30% statics; dogs CHF5; sep car park; poss cr; Eng spkn; adv bkg; quiet; ccard acc; red CCI. "Attractive region; well-run site; lge tent area adj." 1 Apr-15 Oct. CHF 44.00 2009*

LUCERNE see Luzern *B3*

⊞ **LUGANO** *D3* (10km N Rural) *46.09036, 8.91626* **Camping Palazzina, La Cuntrada, 6805 Mezzovico [091 9461467; fax 9463061]** Exit A2/E35 at Rivera. R at T-junc dir Lugano; site on L in approx 3.5km. Med, pt shd; wc; chem disp; shwrs; el pnts (10A) CHF4; gas; shop; rest; snacks; bar; playgrnd; pool 1km; TV; 80% statics; dogs CHF2; adv bkg; rd & rlwy noise; ccard acc. "Helpful owner." CHF 34.00 2011*

LUGANO *D3* (10km N Rural) *46.06921, 8.93675* **Camping Taverne Nord, 6807 Taverne [tel/fax 091 9451198; taverne67@bluewin.ch; http://campeggiotaverne.ch/]** Exit A2/E35 at Rivera or Lugano Nord onto N2. Foll sp for Bellinzona to Taverne. Site ent clearly sp nr long bdge. Med, pt shd; wc; chem disp; mv service pnt; shwrs CHF1; el pnts (6A) CHF4 (poss rev pol); shop; bar; rest 200m; playgrnd; pool high ssn; tennis; 20% statics; dogs CHF2.50; poss cr; adv bkg; rlwy & factory noise; red long stay. "Basic NH site in pleasant situation by shallow stream; Lugano beautiful." 1 Apr-15 Oct. CHF 24.50 2011*

LUGANO *D3* (3km NE Rural) *46.03287, 8.94209* **TCS Camping Moretto, Moretto 3, 6944 Cureglia [091 9667662; fax 9667600; camping.cureglia@tcs.ch; www.tiscover.ch/camping-moretto]** Exit m'way N2 at Lugano Nord, at end of link rd foll sp for Vézia & Rivera. Or fr Lugano cent take rd to Bellinzona & Vezia. Turn off to Vezia immed bef m'way ent. Site sp 600m on L. Fr Bellinzona foll old rd to Lugano, turn L 100m after sp for Vezia, site 600m on L. Lge, pt sl, pt shd; wc; chem disp; mv service pnt; shwrs inc; el pnts (4A) CHF3 - adaptor avail (long lead poss req); gas; lndtte; shop & supmkt 800m; rest; snacks; bar; playgrnd; sm pool; pool 2km; tennis, horseriding nr; entmnt; 40% statics; dogs CHF4; bus to Lugano adj; Eng spkn; adv bkg; quiet; 10% red 3+ days; ccard acc; CCI. "Gd base Lugano & Como area; vg, clean san facs, but in need of refurb; diff access to mv service pnt; friendly, welcoming staff; gd rest on site; alternative to cr lakeside sites." 20 Mar-12 Oct. CHF 35.70 2008*

LUGANO *D3* (6km S Urban) *45.92861, 8.97670* **Camping Monte Generoso, 6818 Melano [091 6498333; fax 6495944; camping@montegeneroso.ch; www.montegeneroso.ch]** S fr Lugano on N2/E35 m'way; exit immed after tunnel sp Bissone & Chiasso. Cross lake & foll sp Chiasso (blue sps) thro Caroggio. Site on R after rlwy stn. Or fr Como & S on m'way, take exit sp Bissone & Melide bef x-ing lake; foll sp Melano. Med, mkd pitch, pt sl, pt shd; wc; chem disp; shwrs CHF0.50; el pnts (6A) CHF4; gas; lndtte; shop & 1km; snacks; bar; playgrnd; pool 2km; shgl lake beach adj; boating; tennis; games area; TV; 20% statics; dogs CHF5; Eng spkn; adv bkg; 50% statics; quiet but rd & rlwy noise; ccard acc; red low ssn. "Wonderful lakeside location; vg san facs; 500m to rlwy stn for Lugano; gd." 26 Mar-24 Oct. CHF 46.00 2009*

LUGANO *D3* (15km S Rural) *45.92273, 8.97981* **Camping Paradiso-Lago, Via Pedreta, 6818 Melano [091 6482863; fax 6482602; campingparadiso@bluewin.ch; www.camping-paradiso.ch]** Fr N2/E35 exit after tunnel sp Bissone, foll sp to Bissone. Turn R to site 1km bef Melano, app rd under m'way & rlwy bdges. Lge, mkd pitch, pt sl, pt shd; wc; chem disp; shwrs inc; el pnts (6A) CHF5 inc; gas; lndtte; shop; tradsmn; rest; snacks; bar; BBQ; playgrnd; pool 2km; lake sw adj; watersports; beach; tennis; 40% statics; no dogs; phone; poss cr; adv bkg; rlwy & rd noise, poss noise bar & fr dog-training site adj; ccard acc; CCI. "Pleasant surroundings; premium for lakeside pitches; sep car park high ssn; excel site; avoid pitches nr office; euros acc; mtn railway stn 3 miles." 30 Mar-15 Nov. CHF 43.20 2011*

LUGANO *D3* (5km W Rural) *45.9927, 8.9006* **Camping Golfo del Sole, 6982 Agno [091 6054802; fax 6054306; info@golfodelsole.ch; www.golfodelsole.ch]** Exit A2 Lugano Nord & foll sp Ponte Tresa & airport. In Agno at junc, turn R dir Ponte Tresa & Varese. Site sp in 500m, turn L immed bef nightclub. Sm, pt shd; wc; chem disp; shwrs CHF1; el pnts (4A) CHF4 (adaptor avail); gas; lndry rm; shop 500m; playgrnd; lake sw & beach; fishing; tennis; 25% statics; phone; bus/train to Lugano; extra charge for lakeside pitch; poss cr; Eng spkn; adv bkg; quiet. "Beautiful setting; friendly owner." 15 Mar-17 Oct. CHF 38.00 2009*

⊞ **LUGANO** *D3* (5km W Rural) *45.99534, 8.90845* **TCS Camping La Piodella, Via alla Force 14, 6933 Muzzano-Lugano [091 9947788 or 091 9858070 LS; fax 9946708; camping.muzzano@tcs.ch; www.campingtcs.ch/muzzano]** Leave A2 at Lugano Nord & foll sp Ponte Tresa & airport. In Agno turn L at traff island; foll camping sp. In 800m, just after La Piodella town sp, look for sm sp at road junc with tent symbol & TCS sticker. NB This may appear to direct you to your R but you must make a 180° turn & take slip rd along R-hand side of rd you have just come along - app rd to site. Lge, some mkd pitch, pt shd; wc; chem disp; mv service pnt; baby facs; serviced pitch; shwrs inc; el pnts (10A) inc (long lead poss req - avail fr recep); gas; lndtte (inc dryer); shop & 800m; rest; snacks; bar; BBQ; playgrnd; htd pool & paddling pool; sand beach by lake; watersports; boating & horseriding 6km; fishing; tennis; games area; wifi; entmnt; games/TV rm; some statics; dogs CHF5.50; no cats; no c'vans/m'vans over 7.50m high ssn; sep car park; poss cr; Eng spkn; adv bkg; day/eve aircraft noise; ccard acc; red low ssn/CCI. "Idyllic location; pitches nr lake higher price; gd welcome; helpful staff; modern san facs; access to pitches poss diff lge o'fits; local train to Lugano 1km, or easy drive; ideal for Ticino Lakes; barrier clsd 1200-1400." ♦ CHF 75.20 SBS - S10 2011*

LUGANO *D3* (6km W Rural) *45.99565, 8.90593* **Camping Eurocampo, Via Molinazzo 9, 6982 Agno [091 6052114; fax 6053187; eurocampo@ticino.com; www.eurocampo.ch]** Exit A2/E34 Lugano N & foll sp airport and Agno. In Agno turn L, then over rlwy x-ing & rnadbt. Turn R down narr lane to site. Lge, pt shd; wc; chem disp; mv service pnt; shwrs CHF1; el pnts CHF3.50 (poss rev pol); gas; Indtte; shop; tradsmn; rest; bar; htd pool 200m; paddling pool; lake sw adj; TV rm; 30% statics; dogs free; phone; train 500m; poss cr; Eng spkn; adv bkg; some aircraft noise morning & evening. "Gd site but facs need upgrade (2008)." 1 Apr-31 Oct. CHF 32.50 2008*

LUGANO *D3* (6km W Rural) *45.99523, 8.90417* **Camping La Palma, Via Molinazzo 21, 6982 Agno [091 6052521]** N2 exit for Lugano & foll sp airport/camping. Site on L ent Agno. Make U-turn at rndabt & turn R. Narr lane ent. Lge, pt shd; wc (cont); own san rec; chem disp; mv service pnt; shwrs CHF0.50; el pnts (6A) CHF4; gas; Indtte; shop & 1km; rest high ssn & 2km; snacks; bar; BBQ; shgl beach adj; lake sw; TV; 30% statics; dogs CHF4; train; some daytime aircraft noise; CCI. "Beautiful lakeside location; gd, modern san facs; conv Lugano." Easter-20 Oct. CHF 39.00 2008*

LUNGERN see Meiringen *C3*

LUTSCHENTAL see Grindelwald *C2*

⊞ **LUZERN** *B3* (2.5km E Rural) *47.0500, 8.33833* **Camping International Lido, Lidostrasse 19, 6006 Luzern [041 3702146; fax 3702145; luzern@camping-international.ch; www.camping-international.ch]** Fr bdge on lake edge in city cent foll sp Küssnacht & Verkehrshaus. Turn R off Küssnacht rd at traff lts by transport museum (sp Lido), site 50m on L beyond lido parking. Fr A2/E35 exit Luzern Centrum. Lge, mkd pitch, hdstg (mv pitch poss diff), pt shd; htd wc; chem disp; mv service pnt; shwrs inc; el pnts (10A) CHF5 (poss rev pol; adaptors avail); gas; Indtte (inc dryer); shop & 400m; rest 1km; snacks; bar; BBQ; playgrnd; pool adj (May-Sep); lake sw & sand beach adj; boat trips; boat-launch; wifi; 10% statics; dogs CHF4; phone; bus; lake ferry 200m; recep open 0830-1200 & 1400-1800 high ssn; money exchange; poss v cr high ssn; Eng spkn; adv bkg rec; ccard acc; red snr citizens/low ssn/CCI. "Various sizes/prices pitches; ltd touring pitches cr in peak ssn, early arr rec; recep in bar low ssn; clean, well-maintained facs stretched high ssn; helpful staff; pleasant lakeside walk to Luzern; conv location; excel rest in Wurzenbach." ♦ CHF 46.80 2011*

LUZERN *B3* (8km E Rural) *47.06164, 8.40239* **Camping Vierwaldstättersee, Luzernerstrasse 271, 6402 Merlischachen [041 8500804; fax 8505041; welcome@seecamping.ch; www.seecamping.ch]** Exit A2/E35 junc 26 to Luzern; exit Luzern dir Merlischachen & Küssnacht. Site on R 500m bef Merlischachen on lakeside, well sp. Med, unshd; htd wc; chem disp; mv service pnt; shwrs inc; el pnts (6A) CHF4; gas; shops 500m; rest, snacks, bar & lake sw adj; pool 6km; 10% statics; no dogs; bus adj; phone 500m; Eng spkn; adv bkg; some rd noise; ccard not acc; red long stay/CCI. "Beautiful lakeside location; wonderful views; excel facs; excel." 1 Apr-30 Sep. CHF 38.00 2011*

LUZERN *B3* (4km S Rural) *47.01201, 8.31113* **TCS Camping Steinibachried, Seefeldstrasse, 6048 Horw [041 3403558; fax 3403556; camping.horw@tcs.ch; www.campingtcs.ch]** Fr A2/E336 exit Horw & foll sp. After x-ing rlwy turn R twd lake in 200m, site sp. Lge, mkd pitch, unshd; wc; chem disp; shwrs CHF1; el pnts (4A) CHF4 (adaptor on loan); gas; Indtte (inc dryer); shop; rest; snacks; bar; playgrnd; lake sw 200m; games rm; 30% statics; dogs CHF5; bus; sep car park; poss cr; Eng spkn; adv bkg; quiet but daytime factory noise; ccard acc; red long stay/CCI. "Excel facs; beautiful location but car park adj high-rise flats; vg." ♦ 1 Apr-2 Oct. CHF 41.00 2011*

MADULAIN *C4* (200m NE Rural) *46.58764, 9.94004* **Camping Madulain, Via Vallatscha, 7523 Madulain [tel/fax 081 8540161; www.campingmadulain.ch]** Sp fr N27 at foot of Albula Pass. Sm, pt sl, terr, pt shd; htd wc; chem disp; shwrs inc; el pnts (10A) CHF2; Indry rm; shop, rest, snacks, bar 1.5km; 70% statics; bus/train adj; quiet. "Simple CL-type site; excel san facs." 15 Dec-15 Apr & 1 Jun-26 Oct. CHF 31.00 2008*

MARTIGNY *D2* (500m SE Urban) *46.09788, 7.07953* **TCS Camping Les Neuvilles, Route du Levant 68, 1920 Martigny [027 7224544; fax 7223544; camping.martigny@tcs.ch; www.campingtcs.ch]** Exit A9/E62 dir Grand St Bernard to Martigny. Camping poorly sp fr town; foll Expo sp, ent past cemetary. Lge, mkd pitch, some hdstg, unshd; htd wc; chem disp; mv service pnt; baby facs; shwrs inc; el pnts (6-10A) CHF4.50; gas; Indtte (inc dryer); shop & 500m; tradsmn; rest; snacks; bar; playgrnd; plunge pool; fishing; tennis; cycle hire; wifi; TV rm; 65% statics; dogs CHF5; poss cr; Eng spkn; adv bkg; quiet, but some rd noise; ccard acc; red CCI. "Excel san facs; conv Valais & Mont Blanc area; Martigny pleasant town; gd cycling." ♦ 1 Apr-31 Oct. CHF 38.60 (CChq acc) 2011*

⊞ **MARTIGNY** *D2* (10km S Rural) *46.03280, 7.10817* **Camping Les Rocailles, 1938 Champex-Lac [027 7831979; fax 7834200; pnttex@netplus.ch; www.champex-camping.ch]** Take B21 fr Martigny dir St Bernard pass, turn R at Orsières. Rd fr Orsières to Champex-Lac v steep with many bends. Med, terr, unshd; htd wc; chem disp; mv service pnt; shwrs inc; el pnts (10A) CHF4; gas; Indtte; shops 200m; rest 400m; bar; playgrnd; pool 1km; lake sw 700m; fishing; boating; tennis; 25% statics; poss cr; quiet; CCI. "Beautiful situation; excel for walking or climbing; nr rd to St Bernard Tunnel; ski-lift adj." CHF 33.70 2008*

MATTEN see Interlaken *C2*

MAUR see Zürich *A3*

MEIERSKAPPEL *B3* (1km S Rural) *47.12175, 8.44670* **Campingplatz Gerbe, Landiswilerstrasse, 6344 Meierskappel [041 7904534; info@swiss-bauernhof.ch; www.swiss-bauernhof.ch]** Exit A4/E41 at Küssnacht & foll sp N to Meierskappel. Bef ent Meierskappel turn L into farm ent for site (sp.) Med, pt sl, pt shd; htd wc; chem disp; mv service pnt; baby facs; shwrs inc; el pnts (10A) CHF3.50 (poss rev pol); Indtte (inc dryer); shop; tradsmn; rest; snacks; bar; BBQ; playgrnd; htd, covrd pool; wifi; 5% statics; dogs CHF2.50; poss cr; quiet; CCI. "Vg, basic farm site with gd facs (unisex); lge field - choose own pitch; conv Luzerne & Zurich." ♦ 1 Mar-31 Oct. CHF 23.50 2010*

⊞ **MEIRINGEN** *C3* (2km E Rural) *46.73257, 8.17092* **Alpencamping, Brünigstrasse 47, 3860 Meiringen [033 9713676; info@alpencamping.ch; www.alpencamping.ch]** Leave A8, then take rd11/6 twd Brünig Pass, at mini-rndabt approx 2km fr Meiringen foll site sp on L. Med, unshd; htd wc; chem disp; mv service pnt; baby facs; shwrs inc; el pnts (10A) CHF3.50; gas; lndtte (inc dryer); shop; tradsmn; rest, snacks nrby; BBQ; cooking facs; playgrnd; pool nr; internet; entmnt; 30% statics; dogs CHF2.50; bus 200m; train 1.3km; site clsd Nov; Eng spkn; adv bkg; CCI. "Meeting point of alpine passes; friendly, family-run site; excel, modern san facs; vg walking/cycling." ♦ CHF 34.00 2010*

⊞ **MEIRINGEN** *C3* (2km S Rural) *46.72538, 8.17088* **Camping Balmweid, Balmweidstrasse 22, 3860 Meiringen [033 9715115; info@camping-meiringen.ch; www.camping-meiringen.ch]** Turn R off A6 Breinz-Innertkirchen rd immed after rndabt at BP petrol stn. Site on L after 200m. Lge, mkd pitch, hdstg, terr, pt shd; htd wc; chem disp; mv service pnt; 20% serviced pitches; baby facs; fam bthrm; shwrs inc; el pnts (10A) CHF4.50; gas; lndtte (inc dryer); shops & 2km; tradsmn; rest; snacks; bar; BBQ; playgrnd; pool; skilift 1km; games rm; wifi; TV; 65% statics; dogs CHF2; adv bkg; quiet; ccard acc; red CCI. "Ideal base for Sherlock Holmes fans (Reichenbach Falls) & 3 passes tour; gd cycle track into town; site poss run down (Sep 2010)." ♦ CHF 35.00 2010*

⊞ **MEIRINGEN** *C3* (10km NW Rural) *46.78499, 8.15157* **Camping Obsee, Campingstrasse 1, 6078 Lungern [041 6781463; fax 6782163; camping@obsee.ch; www.obsee.ch]** S fr Luzern on N8 to Suchseln. Exit m'way for rte 4 to Brienz; thro Lungern; R at end of vill & site on R on lakeside. Best app fr Luzern - turn fr Interlaken diff for lge o'fits. Lge, pt sl, pt shd; htd wc; chem disp; mv service pnt; shwrs CHF2; el pnts CHF3; gas; lndtte (inc dryer); shops 1km; rest; snacks; playgrnd; paddling pool; lake sw; fishing; tennis; games rm; entmnt; TV; 95% statics; dogs CHF3; poss cr; quiet; Eng spkn. "Well-kept site in beautiful situation - ski cent; cable rlwy adj; 10 mins walk to vill; sm area for tourers; gd for families; vg rest; easy access by rd or train to attractions." ♦ CHF 35.00 2010*

MELANO see Lugano *D3*

MENDRISIO *D3* (13km NW Rural) *45.88921, 8.94841* **TCS Camping Parco al Sole, Via Ala Caraa 2, 6866 Meride [091 6464330; fax 6460992; camping.meride@tcs.ch; www.campingtcs.ch]** Fr A2/E35 exit Mendrisio, then foll sp Rancate & Serpiano. Steep climb. Site on L to S of vill. Med, some hdstg, pt sl, pt shd; wc; chem disp; mv service pnt; baby facs; shwrs inc; el pnts (4A) CHF4.50; gas; lndtte (inc dryer); shop 2km; rest; snacks; bar; playgrnd; htd pool; paddling pool; fishing lake; wifi; entmnt; TV rm; 20% statics; dogs CHF5; sep car park; poss v cr; Eng spkn; adv bkg; v quiet; ccard acc. "Attractive, peaceful setting away fr traffic; Unesco World Heritage vill; pitches uneven in parts & v sm, some surrounded by other pitches - make sure you can get off with o'fit; site clsd to arrivals 1100-1700; conv Milan by train." ♦ 23 Apr-26 Sep. CHF 36.90 (CChq acc) 2010*

MERIDE see Mendrisio *D3*

MERLISCHACHEN see Luzern *B3*

MEZZOVICO see Lugano *D3*

MOHLIN see Rheinfelden *A2*

MONTANA see Sierre *C2*

MORGES *C1* (1km W Rural) *46.50360, 6.48760* **TCS Camping Le Petit Bois, Promenade du Petit-Bois 15, 1110 Morges [021 8011270 or 091 9858070 LS; fax 8033869 or 091 9946708 LS; camping.morges@tcs.ch; www.campingtcs.ch/morges]** Exit A1/E25 at Morges Ouest, then foll sp to lake. Site well sp on Lake Léman N shore adj pool. Lge, hdg/mkd pitch, pt shd; wc; chem disp; mv service pnt; baby facs; shwrs; el pnts (10A) inc (adaptor/long lead avail); gas; lndtte (inc dryer); shop; rest; bar; BBQ; playgrnd; htd pool 200m (high ssn) inc; lake sw adj; watersports; boating; tennis 500m; wifi; entmnt; games/TV rm; 50% statics; dogs CHF3-5; no c'vans/m'vans over 7/8m high sn; m'van o'night/late arrivals area; poss cr; adv bkg; Eng spkn; quiet, but rd/rlwy noise some pitches; ccard acc; red low ssn/CCI. "Pleasant site but sm pitches; pleasant, helpful staff; clean san facs; vg pool complex nr (high ssn); conv Lausanne, Geneva & some Alpine passes; tulip festival Apr; easy walk to town & stn; cycle path around lake; vg." ♦ 4 Apr-14 Oct. CHF 56.00 SBS - S14 2011*

MOSEN *B3* (200m W Rural) *47.24497, 8.22451* **Camping Seeblick, Seestrasse, 6295 Mosen [tel/fax 041 9171666; infos@camping-seeblick.ch; www.camping-seeblick.ch]** Fr Lenzburg or Luzern on rd 26 turn E in Mosen at rlwy stn, immed L into site ent. Med, hdg/mkd pitch, some hdstg, pt sl, pt shd; wc; chem disp; mv service pnt; shwrs CHF0.50; el pnts (10A) CHF3; gas; lndtte (inc dryer); shop; rest adj; snacks; BBQ; playgrnd; lake sw adj; fishing; paddling pool; boating; games rm; 60% statics; dogs CHF3; poss cr; quiet; red CCI. "Pleasant site conv Luzern & Zürich; excel shop & san facs; helpful owner." ♦ 1 Mar-31 Oct. CHF 27.00 2011*

MURG *B3* (300m N Rural) *47.11543, 9.21445* **Camping Murg am Walensee, 8877 Murg [081 7381530; info@camping-murg.ch; www.murg-camping.ch]** Exit A3 junc 47 dir Murg, site sp on lake. Med, pt shd; wc; chem disp; shwrs CHF1; el pnts (10A) CHF3.70; shop & 200m; rest 300m; lake sw & beach adj; 30% statics; dogs CHF4.50; phone; poss cr; adv bkg ess high ssn; quiet. "Spectacular outlook at water's edge; sm pitches." 1 Apr-15 Oct. CHF 49.00 2011*

MUZZANO see Lugano *D3*

NEUCHATEL *B1* (7km NE Rural) *47.00198, 7.04145* **TCS Camping Fanel, Seestrasse 50, 3236 Gampelen [032 3132333; fax 3131407; camping.gampelen@tcs.ch; www.campingtcs.ch]** Foll TCS camping sp fr turning off N5 in Gampelen - approx 4km fr vill, on lakeside. V lge, mkd pitch, pt shd; wc; chem disp; mv service pnt; 20% serviced pitch; shwrs; el pnts (4-6A) CHF 3.50-4.50 (adaptor on loan); gas; lndtte (inc dryer); shop; tradsmn; rest; bar; BBQ; playgrnd; htd pool; lake sw & beach; watersports; fishing; tennis; golf; archery; wifi; entmnt; 80% statics; dogs CHF5; Eng spkn; adv bkg; 10% red 3+ days; ccard acc; CCI. "In nature reserve; office/barrier clsd 1200-1400; office & shop hrs vary with ssn; gd, modern facs; helpful staff Euros also accepted." ♦ 1 Apr-2 Oct. CHF 48.00 2011*

NEUCHATEL *B1* (9km W Rural) *46.96727, 6.87029* **Camping Paradis-Plage, La Saunerie, 2013 Colombier [032 8412446; fax 8414305; info@paradisplage.ch; www.paradisplage.ch]** Take Lausanne rd out of Neuchâtel; after tunnel exit at int'chge sp Auvenier, Colombier. Foll Colombier sp thro traff lts. Ent L over tram rails past Inn Des Alleens. Lge, shd; wc; chem disp; mv service pnt; shwrs inc; el pnts (10A) CHF4; gas; Indtte; shop; rest; snacks; playgrnd; paddling pool; lake sw; fishing; watersports; tennis; 60% statics; dogs CHF2; adv bkg; some m'way noise; red long stay. "Gd walks/cycling; v pleasant site." ♦ 1 Mar-31 Oct. CHF 41.00 2009*

NOVILLE see Villeneuve *C1*

We can fill in site report forms on the Club's website – www.caravanclub.co.uk/europereport

ORBE *B1* (500m N Rural) *46.73595, 6.53315* **TCS Camping Le Signal, Route du Signal, 1350 Orbe [024 4413857; fax 4414510; camping.orbe@tcs.ch; www.campingtcs.ch]** A1 exit to N of Orbe & foll sp to cent. Site in 2km adj sw pool. Site sp. Fr A9 exit dir Cossonay, Lausanne & foll sp. Lge, sl, shd; wc; chem disp; mv service pnt; baby facs; private san facs avail; shwrs inc; el pnts (4A) CHF4.50; gas; Indtte (inc dryer); supmkt; snacks; bar; playgrnd; pool & waterslide adj; paddling pool; fishing; tennis; horseriding; cycle hire; wifi; 50% statics; dogs CHF4; phone; poss cr (but o'flow field); Eng spkn; quiet; red 2+ nights; ccard acc. ♦ 1 Apr-3 Oct. CHF 29.20 (CChq acc) 2008*

OTTENBACH see Zürich *A3*

PONTRESINA MORTERATSCH see St Moritz *C4*

PRELES see Biel/Bienne *B2*

⊞ **PRESE, LE** *C4* (Rural) *46.29490, 10.08010* **Camping Cavresc, 7746 Le Prese [081 8440259; camping.cavresc@bluewin.ch; www.campingsertori.ch]** S fr Pontresina on N29 site sp on L 5km S of Poschiavo adj Lake Poschiavo. Med, unshd; htd wc; chem disp; mv service pnt; shwrs CHF0.50; el pnts (10A) CHF4; gas; Indtte; shop adj; rest; snacks; bar; BBQ; playgrnd; sm pool; htd, covrd pool 5km; lake 300m; games area; TV; dogs CHF2; bus/train adj; poss cr; adv bkg; quiet; ccard acc; red long stay; CCI. "Ltd el pnts but more planned for 2009 + internet; stunning scenery; walking/cycling rtes; excel." ♦ CHF 36.00 2008*

RANDA see Zermatt *D2*

RARON see Visp *C2*

RECKINGEN see Ulrichen *C3*

REINACH see Basel *A2*

RHEINFELDEN *A2* (3km NE Rural) *47.57535, 7.83855* **Camping Bachtalen, 4313 Möhlin [061 8515095; info@camping-moehlin.ch; www.camping-moehlin.ch]** Rte 3 to Zürich fr Basel exit Rheinfelden & foll sp Möhlin. Site well sp on L at far end of vill adj sw pool. Med, pt sl, terr, unshd; wc; chem disp; shwrs; el pnts (10A) CHF3 (adaptor loan); Indtte; shops 1km; tradsmn; snacks, bar adj; playgrnd; pool adj; paddling pool; fishing; tennis; 70% statics; dogs CHF4; poss cr; Eng spkn; adv bkg; quiet; ccard acc; red CCI. "Pretty site nr Rhine; superb facs; conv German m'way; sewage treatment plant adj; ltd space for NH." 1 Apr-31 Oct. CHF 29.00 2008*

RINGGENBERG see Interlaken *C2*

ROLLE *C1* (1km N Rural) *46.46192, 6.34613* **Camping Aux Vernes, Chemin de la Plage, 1180 Rolle [tel/fax 021 8251239; reception@campingrolle.ch; www.campingrolle.ch]** Fr A1/E25/E62 exit Rolle, site sp dir Lausanne. Lge, shd; wc; chem disp; mv service pnt; baby facs; shwrs; el pnts (4A) CHF3.50 (loan of adaptor); gas; Indtte (inc dryer); shop; tradsmn; snacks; bar; BBQ; playgrnd; shgl beach & lake sw; boating; watersports; fishing; 20% statics; dogs CHF3; phone; poss cr; Eng spkn; adv bkg; quiet; ccard acc; red long stay/ CCI. "Gd base Geneva, Gruyères, Chillon Castle; attractive site." 1 Apr-1 Oct. CHF 38.50 2011*

ROMANSHORN *A4* (6km SE Rural) *47.53620, 9.39885* **Camping Wiedehorn, 9322 Egnach [071 4771006; fax 4773006; info@wiedehorn.ch; www.wiedehorn.ch]** Site is 2km E of Egnach, dir Arbon. Med, pt sl, pt shd; wc; chem disp; shwrs inc; el pnts (4A) CHF2.50; gas; Indtte; shop; rest; snacks; bar; playgrnd; fishing; TV; 60% statics; dogs CHF2.50; phone; sep car park high ssn; adv bkg; quiet. "Direct access Lake Constance; statics sep." 1 Apr-30 Sep. CHF 30.50 2009*

ROMANSHORN *A4* (3km NW Rural) *47.58736, 9.33468* **Camping Strandbad Amriswil, 8592 Uttwil [tel/fax 071 4634773; camping@amriswil.ch]** Fr Romanshorn, take rte 13 twd Konstanz. After passing thro Uttwil, turn R nr c'van dealers, under rlwy bdge turn L, 1st site. Med, sl, pt shd; wc; chem disp; shwrs CHF0.50; el pnts CHF3 (rev pol); Indtte; shop; snacks; bar; playgrnd; lake sw adj; fishing; tennis; 80% statics; dogs CHF2; poss cr; quiet but some train noise during day. "Busy site; private access to lake; helpful owner; sm area for tourers; poss unreliable in wet; gd walks." 24 Apr-21 Sep. CHF 29.00 2008*

⊞ **SAANEN** *C2* (500m SE Urban) *46.48738, 7.26406* **Camping Beim Kappeli, Campingstrasse, 3792 Saanen [033 7446191; fax 7446184; info@camping-saanen.ch; www.camping-saanen.ch]** On edge of vill bet rv & light rlwy. Site sp fr town cent. Med, pt shd; htd wc; shwrs CHF0.50; el pnts (6-13A) CHF4; Indtte; shop 1km; playgrnd; pool adj; tennis; fishing; 50% statics; dogs CHF3; site clsd Nov; poss cr; Eng spkn; quiet; ccard acc. "Beautiful walks; neat site; excel, clean facs. Buy Gstaad card v.gd value." CHF 35.00 2011*

SWITZERLAND

SAAS FEE *D2* (2km NE) *46.11588, 7.93819* **Camping am Kapellenweg, 3910 Saas-Grund [027 9574997 or 9573316; camping@kapellenweg.ch; www.kapellenweg.ch]** Fr Visp, take Saas Fee rd to Saas Grund, cont twd Saas Almagell, site on R after 1km. Sm, pt sl, pt shd; wc; chem disp; shwrs inc; el pnts CHF3; gas; Indtte; shop & 1km; tradsmn; snacks; golf; fishing; dogs CHF2.50; Eng spkn; red low ssn. "Ideal for walking; family-run site; clean san facs." ♦ 15 May-15 Oct. CHF 21.00 2008*

SAAS FEE *D2* (2km NE Rural) *46.11368, 7.94136* **Camping Mischabel, Unter den Bodmen, 3910 Saas-Grund [027 9572961; fax 9571981; mischabel@hotmail.com]** Fr Visp take Saas Fee rd to Saas Grund & cont twd Saas Almagell for 1.2km. Med, pt shd; wc; chem disp; shwrs inc; el pnts (10A) CHF3; Indtte; shop & 1km; tradsmn; rest; snacks; bar; pool 1km; boating; fishing; TV; no statics; dogs CHF2.50; poss cr; Eng spkn; adv bkg; quiet; CCI. "Lovely scenery; gd walking; helpful, friendly staff." 1 Jun-30 Sep. CHF 21.00 2009*

⊞ **SAAS FEE** *D2* (2.5km NE Rural) *46.11150, 7.94238* **Camping Schönblick, 3910 Saas-Grund [tel/fax 027 9572267; schoenblick@campingschweiz.ch]** Fr Visp take Saas Fee rd to Saas Grund & cont twd Saas Almagell for 1.5km. Site on R over rv. Sm, hdstg, unshd; htd wc; shwrs CHF1; el pnts (10A) CHF3; gas; Indtte; shop 1km; rest; snacks; bar; playgrnd; pool 1km; fishing; tennis; winter & summer skiing; horseriding; TV; 25% statics; adv bkg; open Oct-May with adv bkg only; quiet; ccard acc. "Site ideal for walking & mountain scenery; navette 50m; facs ltd low ssn." CHF 20.00 2009*

SAAS GRUND see Saas Fee *D2*

ST GALLEN *A4* (5km N Rural) *47.46191, 9.36371* **Camping St Gallen-Wittenbach, Leebrücke, 9304 Bernhardzell [071 2984969; fax 2985069; campingplatz.stgallen@ccc-stgallen.ch; www.ccc-stgallen.ch]** Exit A1/E60 St Fiden. L in Wittenbach cent at site sp. Cross Rv Sitter on sharp R bend, turn sharp R at sp. Med, some hdstg, pt shd; wc; chem disp; baby facs; shwrs inc; el pnts (6A) CHF4 (adaptor loan); gas; Indtte (inc dryer); basic shop & 2km; tradsmn; snacks; bar; BBQ; playgrnd; htd, covrd pool nr; canoeing; cycle hire; golf 10km; TV; 30% statics; dogs CHF3; bus; poss cr; Eng spkn; adv bkg; quiet; ccard acc; red CCI. "Gd base for S shore of Bodensee; pleasant rvside setting; friendly staff." 10 Apr-2 Oct. CHF 27.40 2010*

ST MARGRETHEN *A4* (3km N Rural) *47.45114, 9.65650* **Strandbad Camping Bruggerhorn, 9430 St Margrethen [071 7442201; fax 7442757]** Exit N1/E60 dir St Margrethen, site well sp. Med, pt shd; wc; chem disp; shwrs inc; el pnts (10A) CHF2.50 (adaptor avail); gas; Indtte; shop; rest 500m; snacks; playgrnd; 2 pools; lake sw; sports cent adj; tennis; no dogs; poss cr; Eng spkn; adv bkg; quiet; red CCI. "Picturesque, clean site; vg shwrs; helpful staff." 1 Apr-31 Oct. CHF 34.00 2009*

ST MORITZ *C4* (4km NE Rural) *46.50988, 9.87936* **TCS Camping Punt Muragl, Via da Puntraschigna 56, 7503 Samedan [tel/fax 081 8428197; camping.samedan@tcs.ch; www.campingtcs.ch]** Site on S side of rd fr Celerina to Pontresina, adj to rndabt at junc rds 27 & 29. Med, shd; htd wc; mv service pnt; chem disp; shwrs inc; el pnts (6-10A) CHF4 (metered in winter); gas; Indtte; shop; rest 300m; snacks; bar; playgrnd; pool & lake 3km; fishing; tennis; skiing; entmnt; 30% statics; dogs CHF5; adv bkg; quiet; ccard acc. "Excel for mountains & Engadine; close rlwy stns & funicular; walking rtes thro forest; clean, spacious facs; enquire about public transport travel card." 26 Nov-18 Apr & 21 May-10 Oct. CHF 39.30 2011*

There aren't many sites open at this time of year. We'd better phone ahead to check the one we're heading for is open.

ST MORITZ *C4* (1km S Rural) *46.47843, 9.82511* **TCS Camping Olympiaschanze, 7500 St Moritz [081 8334090; fax 8344096; camping.stmoritz@tcs.ch; www.campingtcs.ch]** Turn S off rd N27 immed after park & ride car park. Site 1km fr vill of Champfer. Med, mkd pitch, pt sl, shd; wc; chem disp; mv service pnt; shwrs; el pnts (6A) CHF4 (adaptor on loan); gas; Indtte; shops; rest 700m; snacks; bar; playgrnd; pool 1km; lake sw 500m; tennis; cycle hire; entmnt; dogs CHF4; Eng spkn; v quiet; ccard acc; red low ssn/CCI. "Gd walking area, nr St Moritz & Maloja & Julier passes; site v high & cold (poss snow in Aug); san facs stretched when site full; sh walk town cent." 15 May-28 Sep. CHF 36.40 2008*

ST MORITZ *C4* (4.5km S Rural) *46.46132, 9.93568* **Camping Plauns, Via da Bernina, 7504 Pontresina-Morteratsch [081 8426285; fax 8345136; plauns@bluewin.ch; www.campingplauns.ch]** On Bernina Pass rd 4km SE of Pontresina, turn R at camp sp. If app fr St Moritz or Samedan, keep to Pontresina by-pass, do not turn L where sp Pontresina. Lge, pt sl, pt shd; htd wc; chem disp; mv service pnt; shwrs CHF0.50; el pnts (6-13A) CHF3.50 (adaptor avail & long lead poss req); gas; Indtte; shop; rest 1km; snacks; playgrnd; pool 4km; skilift 3km; ski bus; golf 4km; internet; 20% statics; dogs CHF4; phone; poss cr; some Eng spkn; adv bkg 2 weeks or more only (non-return fee); quiet; ccard acc; CCI. "Idyllic site in forest clearing; magnificent scenery; v clean, modern san facs; conv Morteratsch Glacier, Bernina Pass, St Moritz; walking dist rlwy & rest; cable rlwys, funiculars, chair lifts; high walks; glacier excursions." ♦ 25 May-15 Oct & 15 Dec-15 Apr. CHF 36.80 2010*

SALAVAUX see Avenches *B2*

SALGESCH see Sierre *C2*

SAMEDAN see St Moritz *C4*

SARNEN *B3* (10km SW Rural) *46.8530, 8.1874* **Camping International Sarnersee, Campingstrasse, 6074 Giswil-Grossteil [041 6752355; fax 6752351; giswil@camping-international.ch; www.camping-international.ch]** App W end of Sarnersee ignore Giswil-N Sörenberg exit. Go thro Giswil tunnel & take Giswil-S Grossteil turning. At stop sp, turn R, then immed L. In approx 2km at rndabt turn R (tent sp). In 1km as rd swings L go strt & foll thro unfenced fields to site. Fr Luzern foll sp Giswil-S Grossteil then as above. Med, pt sl, pt shd; wc; mv service pnt; chem disp; shwrs CHF0.50; el pnts (10A) CHF3 or metered; gas; Indtte; sm shop; rest; snacks; bar; playgrnd; sand/shgl beach adj; watersports; boating; 50% statics; dogs CHF4; poss cr; Eng spkn; adv bkg ess Jul/Aug; quiet; red CCI. "Gd san facs; attractive lakeside location." ♦ 1 Apr-14 Oct. CHF 36.00 2008*

⊞ **SAVOGNIN** *C4* (400m NW Rural) *46.59777, 9.59083* **Camping Julia, Veia Sandeilas 10, 7460 Savognin [081 6841444; camping.julia@savogninbergbahnen.ch; www.savogninbergbahnen.ch]** S on rd 3, clearly sp adj Cube Hotel. Sm, hdstg, unshd; htd wc; chem disp; shwrs inc; el pnts (16A) CHF2.50; Indtte (inc dryer); shop 400m; rest, snacks, bar adj; rv sw & shgl beach adj; 80% statics; dogs CHF1; bus 500m; Eng spkn; adv bkg; quiet; ccard acc; CCI. "Not particularly attractive site but superb facs; adj chairlift & postbus use free; best for smaller o'fits; gd NH Julier Pass." ♦ CHF 31.00 2010*

SCHAFFHAUSEN *A3* (2.5km SE Rural) *47.68763, 8.65461* **TCS Camping Rheinwiesen, Hauptstrasse, 8246 Langwiesen [052 6593300; fax 6593355; camping.schaffhausen@tcs.ch; www.campingtcs.ch/schaffhausen]** Fr N, S & W on A4/E41 exit Schaffhausen & foll sp 'Kreuzlingen' on rd 13. Fr E on rd 13 pass under rlwy bdge to Langwiesen about 3km bef Schaffhausen; site sp at Feuerthalen (tent sign only - no site name) down narr rd on L on Rv Rhine. Med, mkd pitch, pt shd; wc; chem disp; mv service pnt; baby facs; htd shwrs inc; el pnts (4A) inc (adaptor avail); gas; Indtte (inc dryer); shop; rest; snacks; bar; BBQ (gas & charcoal); playgrnd; children's pool; covrd pool 4km; rv beach & sw; fishing; horseriding 3km; wifi; games/TV rm; 30% statics; no dogs; no c'vans/m'vans over 7m high ssn; phone; Eng spkn; adv bkg; quiet but some rd/rlwy noise; ccard acc; red low ssn; CCI. "Excel site in beautiful location; conv Rhine Falls & Lake Constance; pitches on rvside (rv v fast-moving & unfenced); clean, adequate san facs; grass pitches poss muddy after rain; poss tight access to pitches; gd facilities sm children; gd cycling." 24 Apr-7 Oct. CHF 41.10 (CChq acc) SBS - S06 2011*

SCHAFFHAUSEN *A3* (14km SE Rural) *47.66216, 8.84034* **Camping Wagenhausen, Hauptstrasse 82, 8260 Wagenhausen [052 7414271; fax 7414157; campingwagenhausen@bluewin.ch; www.campingwagenhausen.ch]** Turn R off Stein-am-Rhein/Schaffhausen rd, site sp. Med, pt shd; wc; chem disp; serviced pitches; shwrs CHF1; el pnts (10A) CHF3; gas; Indtte; shop; rest; bar; playgrnd; pool; paddling pool; fishing; games area; TV rm; 80% statics; dogs CHF4; poss cr; Eng spkn; quiet; ccard acc. "Vg; direct access to Rv Rhine; rvside footpath." ♦ 1 Apr-31 Oct. CHF 33.00 2009*

SCHWYZ *B3* (5km NW Rural) *47.04761, 8.59173* **Camping Buchenhof, Seebad, 6422 Steinen [041 8321429; www.camping-buchenhof.ch]** Fr N4 exit dir Goldau, then R dir Lauerz. Before lake take R fork sp Steinen, over m'way bdge; site sp Seebad. Med, mkd pitch, some hdstg, pt sl, unshd; wc; chem disp; shwrs CHF1; el pnts (4A) CHF2; gas; Indtte; shop; rest; snacks; BBQ; playgrnd; lake sw & beach; fishing; boat hire; tennis; 50% statics; dogs CHF2; Eng spkn; quiet but rlwy noise; CCI. "Mountain scenery; gd facs." ♦ 1 Apr-31 Oct. CHF 44.00 2010*

SCUOL/SCHULS *B4* (1km S Rural) *46.8018, 10.28731* **TCS Camping Gurlaina, 7550 Scuol/Schuls [081 8641501; fax 8640760; camping.scuol@tcs.ch; www.campingtcs.ch]** App fr Zernez foll Landeck sp to avoid Scuol cent. At E end of by-pass turn R sp Scuol. In 250m foll Scuol sp & camp site clearly sp. Med, pt sl; wc; chem disp; mv service pnt; shwrs; el pnts (4-10A) CHF5; shop; snacks; bar; playgrnd; pool 500m; fishing; tennis; skiing; 30% statics; dogs CHF4; poss cr; Eng spkn; quiet; 10% red after 3 days; ccard acc. "Gd cent for Lower Engadine, Swiss National Park; close to Austrian & Italian borders; walking dist historic area & rests; thermal baths in Scuol; excel san facs." 13 Dec-16 Apr & 16 May-22 Oct. CHF 37.00 2008*

SEMPACH *B3* (1.5km S Rural) *47.12447, 8.18924* **TCS Camping Seeland, Seelandstrasse, 6204 Sempach Stadt [041 4601466 or 091 9858070; fax 4604766 or 091 9946708 LS; camping.sempach@tcs.ch; www.campingtcs.ch/sempach]** Fr Luzern on A2 take exit sp Emmen N, Basel, Bern. Join E35 & cont on this road to exit at Sempach sp. Site well sp. Lge, mkd pitch, unshd; htd wc; chem disp; mv service pnt; baby facs; private san facs avail; shwrs inc; el pnts (13A) inc (adaptor avail); gas; Indtte (inc dryer); shop; rest; bar; BBQ (gas/charcoal only); playgrnd; paddling pool; shgl beach & lake sw adj; watersports; fishing; golf 5km; cycle hire; tennis; wifi; entmnt; games/TV rm; 60% statics; dogs CHF5; no c'vans/m'vans over 9m high ssn; sep car parks high ssn; poss cr; Eng spkn; adv bkg; quiet; ccard acc; red low ssn/CCI. "Excel location on Sempacher See, 10 mins drive fr m'way & attractive town; sm pitches; helpful staff; rest & beach open to public; water & bins far fr many pitches; poss tight parking; ltd facs low ssn; lakeside walk to Sempach." ♦ 4 Apr-7 Oct. CHF 60.10 SBS - S08 2011*

SIERRE *C2* (2km E Rural) *46.29362, 7.55777* **Camping Bois de Finges, Route du Bois de Finges, 3960 Sierre [027 4550284; fax 4553351]** Exit A9 Sierre-Est dir Sierre, site in 500m E of Rhône bdge. Med, mkd pitch, terr, shd; wc; chem disp; mv service pnt; shwrs; el pnts (4A) CHF3.50; gas; Indtte; shop; snacks; bar; playgrnd; htd pool; tennis nr; lake fishing 1.5km; TV; 10% statics; dogs CHF5; phone; Eng spkn; adv bkg; quiet; red low ssn/long stay; ccard acc. "Lovely wooded site; slopes/terr poss diff; warm welcome." 1 May-30 Sep. CHF 35.30 2011*

SIERRE *C2* (3km E Rural) *46.30215, 7.56420* **Camping Swiss Plage, Campingweg 3, 3970 Salgesch [027 4556608 or 4816023; fax 4813215; info@swissplage.ch; www.swissplage.ch]** Fr A9/E62 exit at Sierre, turn L & go over bdge, Foll sp Salgesch & Site. Fr town site well sp. Lge, shd; wc; chem disp; mv service pnt; shwrs CHF1; el pnts (10A) CHF3.60; gas; lndtte; shop; rest; snacks; bar; playgrnd; pool 2km; lake sw; tennis; dogs CHF3.50; Eng spkn; adv bkg ess for long stay; quiet; ccard acc. "Pleasant site in lovely location." Easter-1 Nov. CHF 33.40 2011*

When we get home I'm going to post all these site report forms to the Club for next year's guide. The deadline's mid September 2013

SIERRE *C2* (6km NW Rural) *46.30426, 7.48308* **Camping La Moubra, Impasse de la Plage 2, 3962 Crans-Montana [027 4812851; fax 4810551; moubra@campings.ch; www.campingmoubra.ch]** Fr Sierre take rd to Chermignon & Montana. In Montana turn L sp La Moubra; site in 3km by lake. Med, pt shd; wc; mv service pnt; shwrs; el pnts (10A) CHF4; gas; lndtte; rest 300m; snacks; bar; pool 500m; lake sw; tennis; boating; fishing; watersports; golf; 20% statics; dogs CHF3; Eng spkn; adv bkg; quiet; ccard acc. "Ski & boot rm; navette adj; frozen lake - start of x-country skiing; well-maintained site in gd position; lovely situation, quiet, gd walking & cycling on site" 16 May-15 Oct & 15 Dec-18 Apr. CHF 60.00 2011*

SILVAPLANA *C4* (300m SW Rural) *46.45671, 9.79316* **Camping Silvaplana, 7513 Silvaplana [081 8288492; reception@campingsilvaplana.ch; www.campingsilvaplana.ch]** Exit by-pass rd at S junc for Silvaplana (opp camp site). In 100m after g'ge turn R & site sp via underpass, on lakeside. When app fr Julier Pass foll sp for Maloja Pass as above. Lge, pt sl, pt shd; wc; chem disp; mv service pnt; shwrs CHF1.10; el pnts (16A) CHF3.50; gas; lndtte; shop & 300m; playgrnd; pool 3km; lake sw; watersports; fishing; tennis; wifi; many statics in sep area; dogs CHF3; poss cr; Eng spkn; no adv bkg; quiet; ccard acc. "V beautiful location; gd walking; hiking; climbing; vg watersports & windsurfing; excel facs for m'vans." 13 May-18 Oct. CHF 38.00 2011*

⊞ **SION** *C2* (3km SW Rural) *46.20578, 7.27855* **Camping du Botza, Route du Camping 1, 1963 Vétroz [027 3461940 or 079 2203575 (mob); fax 3462535; info@botza.ch; www.botza.ch]** Exit A9/E62 junc 25 S'wards over a'bahn. Site adj Vétroz indus est, foll sp 'CP Nr.33'. Lge, mkd pitch, pt shd; wc; chem disp; mv service pnt; baby facs; serviced pitches; shwrs CHF1; el pnts (10A) CHF3.70; gas; lndtte; shop; tradsmn; rest; snacks; bar; playgrnd; free htd pool high ssn; paddling pool; fishing; tennis; squash; golf 8km; wifi; entmnt; 30% statics; dogs CHF3.50; adv bkg ess; quiet; ccard acc; red low ssn. "Superb site conv m'way & ski resorts; excel facs; gd security; organised excursions; vg rest; fine mountain views." ♦ CHF 41.40 2009*

⊞ **SION** *C2* (4km SW Rural) *46.21165, 7.31380* **TCS Camping Les Iles, Route d'Aproz, 1951 Sion [027 3464347; fax 3466847; camping.sion@tcs.ch; www.campingtcs.ch]** Take A9 W out of Sion on N side of Rhône. In 4km turn L sp Aproz & Fey, foll sp. V lge, pt shd; wc; chem disp; mv service pnt; shwrs; el pnts (4A) CHF3; gas; lndtte (inc dryer); supmkt; rest; snacks; bar; playgrnd; pool & paddling pool; lake sw; boating; tennis; horseriding; cycle hire; wifi; entmnt; TV; 30% statics; dogs CHF3; poss cr; site clsd 3 Nov-18 Dec; Eng spkn; adv bkg; quiet, but some daytime aircraft noise; ccard acc; red CCI. "Ideal for touring; beautiful area but military firing range nr - poss v noisy." ♦ CHF 41.30 2008*

SISSACH *A2* (9km SE Rural) *47.40416, 7.84804* **Camping Neuhaus, 4448 Läufelfingen [062 2991189]** Exit Basel-Luzern m'way at Sissach, S twd Olten. Site 200m after vill Buckten & 1km bef Läufelfingen. Sm, pt sl, unshd; wc; shwrs CHF1; el pnts (5A) CHF2; gas; shop; 90% statics; poss cr; quiet; "Working farm; ltd space for tourers; ltd facs; NH only." ♦ 15 Apr-31 Oct. CHF 17.00 2008*

SOLOTHURN *B2* (1.5km SW Rural) *47.19883, 7.52288* **TCS Camping Lido Solothurn, Glutzenhofstrasse 5, 4500 Solothurn [032 6218935 or 091 9858070 LS; fax 6218939 or 091 9858070 LS; camping.solothurn@tcs.ch; www.campingtcs.ch/solothurn]** Exit A5 dir Solothurn W, cross rv bdge. At traff lts turn L & foll sp to site (new rd 2009). Lge, mkd pitch, pt shd; htd wc; chem disp; mv service pnt; baby facs; 10% serviced pitches; shwrs inc; el pnts (13A) inc; gas; lndtte (inc dryer); shop; tradsmn; rest; snacks; bar; BBQ; cooking facs; playgrnd; htd pool adj; paddling pool; fishing; tennis 200m; cycle & boat hire; golf 100m; games area; wifi; entmnt; games/TV rm; 20% statics; dogs CHF5; no c'vans/m'vans over 12m high ssn; bus 200m; Eng spkn; adv bkg; quiet; ccard acc; red low ssn; CCI. "Gd touring base by Rv Aare; lge pitches; excel facs; helpful staff; 20 mins walk to picturesque town." ♦ 3 Mar-2 Dec. CHF 48.90 (CChq acc) SBS - S13 2011*

SORENS see Bulle *C2*

⊞ **SPIEZ** *C2* (4km SE Rural) *46.65880, 7.71688* **Camping Stuhlegg, Stueleggstrasse 7, 3704 Krattigen [033 6542723; fax 6546703; campstuhlegg@bluewin.ch; www.camping-stuhlegg.ch]** 13km fr Interlaken on hillside on S side of Lake Thun. Advise app fr Spiez. Fr Spiez rlwy stn heading SE turn R over rlwy bdge; foll sp Leissigen & Krattigen for 5km. In Krattigen shortly after modern church turn R (low gear), site 500m on R, sp. Lge, pt sl, terr, pt shd; htd wc; chem disp; mv service pnt; baby facs; shwrs CHF1; el pnts (10A) CHF4 (some rev pol); gas; lndtte (inc dryer); sm shop; rest 300m; snacks; bar; playgrnd; htd pool; entmnt; 60% statics; dogs CHF3; ski bus; phone; site clsd last week Oct to end Nov; adv bkg; quiet; ccard acc; red low ssn/long stay/CCI. "Excel well-kept site; immac facs; helpful staff; recep clsd 1300-1500; mountain views; gd dog-walking in area." CHF 33.00 2011*

See advertisement on next page

camping stuhlegg

A very special 4 star camping site in the Berner Oberland with a natural swimming pool.

****
Stueleggstr. 7,CH-3704 Krattigen
Phone +41 (0)33 654 27 23, Fax +41 (0)33 654 67 03
campstuhlegg@bluewin.ch, www.camping-stuhlegg.ch
Rolf Schweizer & Rita Gasser

Our site is well known for its magnificent view of the Lake of Thun and the mountains as well as the much appreciated tranquillity and cleanliness.
Ideal for people who like hiking, biking and relaxing.

SPIEZ *C2* (14km S Rural) *46.65311, 7.70030* **Camping Panorama-Rossern, Scheidgasse, 3703 Aeschi [033 6544377; postmaster@camping-aeschi.ch; www.camping-aeschi.ch]** Leave N6 Thun to Interlaken rd at Spiez junc on main rd, foll sp Spiezwieler. In Spiezwieler turn L at g'ge sp Aeschi. Strt on at x-rds in Aeschi town cent. Site on R immed after fire stn. Med, pt sl, pt terr, pt shd; wc; chem disp; shwrs CHF1; el pnts CHF3 (adaptor avail); Indtte; sm shop & shops 2km; tradsmn; playgrnd; 40% statics; dogs CHF1; bus; quiet; poss cr. "Views of Blümlisalp, Niesen; some cars parked away fr vans due terraces." 15 May-15 Oct. CHF 30.20 2011*

⊞ **SPLUGEN** *C3* (500m W Rural) *46.55003, 9.31662* **Camping auf dem Sand, Untere Allmend, 7435 Splügen [081 6641476; fax 6641460; camping@splugen.ch; www.campingsplugen.ch]** Exit A13/E61 (Chur-San Bernardino) & take slip rd sp Splügen. Foll rd thro vill, site at end. Med, unshd; wc; chem disp; mv service pnt; shwrs inc; el pnts (10A) CHF3; gas; Indtte; shop 800m; playgrnd; tennis; fishing; wifi; 70% statics; dogs CHF3; adv bkg; quiet; red CCI. "Conv for San Bernardino Tunnel." CHF 45.00 2011*

STECHELBERG see Lauterbrunnen *C2*

SUMVITG *C3* (500m S Rural) *46.72439, 8.92968* **Camping Garvera, Campadi alla Staziun, 7175 Sumvitg [081 9431922; info@garvera.ch; www.garvera.ch]** Fr Chur on rd 19, site well sp in Sumvitg. Sm, terr, pt shd; htd wc; chem disp; shwrs inc; el pnts (10A) CHF4; Indtte; shop 500m; rest; bar; no statics; dogs CHF4; bus/train adj; Eng spkn; quiet - some daytime rlwy noise; red low ssn. "Excel, clean site; friendly owners; beautiful area; gd walking." ♦ 1 May-18 Oct. CHF 32.00 2010*

⊞ **SUR EN** *B4* (E Rural) *46.81859, 10.36594* **Camping Sur En, 7554 Sur En [081 8663544; fax 8663237; www.sur-en.ch]** Visible in valley fr rd 27. Steep access. Sm, unshd; htd wc; chem disp; mv service pnt; shwrs inc; el pnts (6-10A) CHF3; (long lead poss req; warden has adaptors); Indtte (inc dryer); shop; rest (ccard not acc); snacks; bar; BBQ; playgrnd; sm pool; skilift 7km; free ski bus; 30% statics in sep area; dogs CHF3; Eng spkn; no adv bkg; quiet; ccard acc (surcharge); CCI. "Superb facs in out-of-the-way spot; great atmosphere for nature lovers/walkers/cyclists; gd for dog walking but tick treatment essential." CHF 34.00 2010*

⊞ **SURCUOLM** *B3* (500m N Rural) *46.76053, 9.14324* **Panorama Camping Surcuolm, 7138 Surcuolm [081 9333223; fax 9333224; info@camping-surcuolm; www.camping-surcuolm.ch]** Fr N19 to Ilanz & in Ilanz foll sp Valata & Obersaxen. In Valata turn L to Surcuolm, site on L. This is only rec rte - steep climbs. Med, pt sl, unshd; htd wc; chem disp; mv service pnt; shwrs CHF0.50; el pnts (16A) metered; Indtte (inc dryer); shop; tradsmn; rest, snacks nr; bar; playgrnd; ski lift nr; wifi; 10% statics; dogs CHF3; bus 500m; adv bkg; quiet. "Mountain views; popular winter site; quiet in summer; excel facs." CHF 41.00 2009*

SURSEE *B2* (1.5km NW Rural) *47.17505, 8.08685* **Camping Sursee Waldheim, Baslerstrasse, 6210 Sursee [041 9211161; fax 9211160; info@camping-sursee.ch; www.camping-sursee.ch]** Exit A2 at junc 20 & take L lane onto rd 24 dir Basel/Luzern. Turn R at traff lts, foll rd 2 turn R at 2nd rndabt dir Basel to site. Med, shd; wc; chem disp; shwrs CHF0.50; el pnts (10A) CHF3; gas; Indtte; shop; tradsmn; rest in town; snacks; bar; playgrnd; lake sw 1.5km; 60% statics; dogs CHF1; poss cr; Eng spkn; quiet but poss noisy at w/end; CCI. "Pretty site; excel san facs; gd train service to Luzern; sh walk to town cent; popular NH; gd touring base." 1 Apr-30 Sep. CHF 29.00 2008*

SUSCH *B4* (W Rural) *46.74954, 10.07826* **Camping Muglinas, 7542 Susch [079 7875689; tourimus@susch.ch]** Fr Flüela Pass or Zernez cross sm bdge in Susch town cent & turn L on N side of stream. Turn R after 50m. Inspection advised to plan ent (site at 1400m altitude). Med, pt sl, terr, unshd; wc; shwrs opp CHF2; el pnts (10A) CHF3; Indry rm; shops adj; playgrnd; paddling pool; covrd pool 6km; games area; adv bkg; rlwy noise. "Gd area for walking; climbing & canoeing; beautiful setting; CL-type site; modern san facs in basement of council building 3 mins walk." 15 May-20 Oct. CHF 25.00 2008*

SUSTEN see Leuk *C2*

SUTZ see Biel/Bienne *B2*

TAGERWILEN *A3* (500m W Rural) *47.65928, 9.12341* **Restaurant Werkhof Oase, Hauptstrasse 12, 8274 Tägerwilen [071 6691717; oasecamping@hotmail.com]** Fr Kreuzlingen take rd 13 twds Schaffhausen. Site on L on o'skirts of Tägerwilen. Sm, hstg, unshd; wc; chem disp; mv service pnt; shwrs inc; el pnts (10A) CHF4; Indtte (inc dryer); shop 3km; rest; snacks; bar; lake sw & beach 2km; wifi; no statics; dogs; Eng spkn; quiet; red low ssn. "Sm m'van site, but c'vans acc if room; v friendly owners; conv Lake Constance." Jan-Oct. CHF 20.00 2010*

TASCH see Zermatt *D2*

TAVERNE see Lugano *D3*

TENERO *C3* (1km E Urban) *46.16921, 8.8538* **Camping Lago Maggiore, Via Lido 4, 6598 Tenero [091 7451848; fax 7454318; info@clm.ch; www.clm.ch]** Fr A2 take Bellinzona S exit & foll sp Locarno. In about 12km take Tenero exit, at end slip rd foll sp to site. C'vans not permitted on rd S337 fr Domodossola to Locarno. If app fr Simplon Pass cont S of Domodossola & take S34 up W shore of lake. Lge, pt shd; wc; chem disp; mv service pnt; shwrs inc; el pnts (adaptor avail) inc; gas; Indtte (inc dryer); shop; tradsmn; rest; bar; BBQ; playgrnd; lake sw, pools for adults & children; watersports; fishing; tennis; TV; no dogs; adv bkg; Eng spkn; quiet; ccard acc. "Beautiful region; extra for pitches nr lake; vg." 15 Mar-31 Oct. CHF 58.00 (5 persons) 2010*

TENERO *C3* (1.5km E Rural) *46.16890, 8.85561* **Camping Campofelice, Via alle Brere, 6598 Tenero [091 7451417; fax 7451888; camping@campofelice.ch; www.campofelice.ch]** Fr A2 take Bellinzona S exit & foll sp Locarno on A13. In about 12km take Tenero exit, at end slip rd foll sp to site. V lge, mkd pitch, pt shd, 30% serviced pitch; wc; chem disp; mv service pnt; shwrs & hot water inc; el pnts (10A) inc; gas; Indtte; shop; rest adj; snacks; bar; pool 8km; lake with sand beach & boat moorings; playgrnd; tennis; wifi; entmnt; 10% statics; no dogs; Eng spkn; no adv bkg; red 3+days; ccard acc; red long stay; CCI. "Expensive but superb, attractive & well-equipped, v clean facs; min stay 3+ nights high ssn." ♦ 14 Mar-27 Oct. CHF 55.00 (3 persons) 2008*

TENERO *C3* (1km SE Rural) *46.17575, 8.84515* **Camping Tamaro, Via Mappo, 6598 Tenero [091 7452161; fax 7456636; info@campingtamaro.ch; www.campingtamaro.ch]** Fr N2 take Bellinzona Süd exit dir Locarno. In about 12km take Tenero exit, at end slip rd foll sp to site. Lge, unshd; htd wc; chem disp; mv service pnt; baby facs; shwrs inc; el pnts (10A) CHF4; gas; Indtte; shops; adv bkg; rest; bar; lake sw; beach; watersports; fishing; tennis; 30% statics; no dogs; phone; bus; boat to Locarno; adv bkg; quiet; Eng spkn; red low ssn/long stay; debit card acc. "Excel site; helpful staff; extra for lakeside pitches; tight corners & high kerbs on site rd - manhandling poss req; ferry to Locarno fr site." ♦ 6 Mar-1 Nov. CHF 56.00 2009*

⊞ **TENERO** *C3* (500m SW Urban) *46.17292, 8.84808* **Camping Miralago, Via Roncaccio 20, 6598 Tenero [091 7451255; fax 7452878; info@camping-miralago.ch; www.camping-miralago.ch]** Turn L off A13 Bellinzona/Locarno rd at Tenero & foll camping sps. Med, mkd pitch, unshd; htd wc; chem disp; mv service pnt; baby facs; shwrs CHF1; el pnts (10A) inc; Indtte (inc dryer); shop; tradsmn; rest; snacks; bar; BBQ; playgrnd; htd pool; paddling pool; sand beach & lake sw adj; games area; wifi; dogs CHF3; bus adj; poss cr; Eng spkn; adv bkg; quiet; ccard acc; red low ssn/CCI. "Beautiful area; ltd facs low ssn; lake steamer pier." ♦ CHF 51.00 2009*

TENERO *C3* (1km W Rural) *46.1770, 8.84185* **Camping Lido Mappo, Via Mappo, 6598 Tenero [091 7451437; fax 7454808; camping@lidomappo.ch; www.lidomappo.ch]** Fr A2 take Bellinzona Sud exit & foll sp Locarno. In about 12km take Tenero exit, at end slip rd foll sp to site on lakeside. Lge, shd; htd wc; chem disp; mv service pnt; baby facs; shwrs; el pnts (10A) inc; gas; Indtte (inc dryer); supmkt; tradsmn; rest; snacks; bar; BBQ; playgrnd; lake sw; sand/shgl beach; fishing; boating; watersports; cycle hire; wifi; entmnt; TV; no dogs; phone; adv bkg; poss cr; Eng spkn; quiet, but some noise fr local airfield; ccard acc. "Extra for lakeside pitch; cycle rte to Locarno; v helpful staff." ♦ 14 Mar-31 Oct. CHF 53.00 2010*

THORISHAUS see Bern *B2*

THUN *B2* (3km N Rural) *46.81368, 7.60829* **Camping Wydeli, Wydeli 60, 3671 Brenzikofen [031 7711141; fax 7711181; info@camping-brenzikofen.ch; www.camping-brenzikofen.ch]** Fr A6 take Kiesen exit; foll sp Konolfingen-Langnau to Oppligen; site sp. Med, pt shd; wc; chem disp; shwrs; el pnts CHF 2.50; gas; Indtte; shop; rest; snacks; bar; playgrnd; pool; paddling pool; fishing; tennis; horseriding; 60% statics; dogs; Eng spkn; adv bkg. 1 May-30 Sep. CHF 28.20 2009*

THUN *B2* (3km S Rural) *46.72753, 7.62778* **TCS Camping Thunersee, Gwattstrasse 103a, 3645 Gwatt [033 3364067; fax 3364017; camping.gwatt@tcs.ch; www.thunersee.ch]** Fr A6 take Thun-Süd exit & foll sp to Gwatt; on reaching Thun-Speiz main rd turn L, site on R in 500m. Well sp on rte 6 in Gwatt on lake side of rd. Med, unshd, wc; chem disp; mv service pnt; shwrs inc; el pnts (4A) CHF3.50 (adaptor on loan); gas; Indtte; shop; rest; snacks; bar; pool 1km; shgl beach; lake sw adj; watersports; fishing; mooring for boats; tennis; 40% statics; dogs CHF5; bus to Thun; sep car park; poss cr; Eng spkn; adv bkg; quiet; ccard acc; red long stay; red CCI. "Walks by lake; mkd cycle ways; superb views; pretty site; office/barrier clsd 1130-1400; helpful management; gd san facs." ♦ 3 Apr-11 Oct. CHF 41.00 2010*

THUN *B2* (5km W Rural) *46.74514, 7.52014* **Camping Restaurant Bad, 3638 Blumenstein [033 3562954; k.wenger@bad-blumenstein.ch; www.bad-blumenstein.ch]** Fr A6 exit Thun Nord dir Wattenwil & Blumenstein; site sp in vill. Sm, pt sl, unshd; wc; shwrs CHF0.50/2mins; el pnts CHF3; rest & bar (Wed-Sun); pool 3km; fishing; wifi; bus, train nr; Eng spkn; adv bkg; quiet; red long stay/low ssn; CCI. "Basic, CL-type site - v pleasant, but v ltd; gd." 1 May-30 Sep. CHF 25.00 2009*

THUSIS *C4* (500m NE Rural) *46.69945, 9.44547* **Camping Viamala, Pantunweg 1, 7430 Thusis [tel/fax 081 6512472; info@camping-thusis.ch; www.camping-thusis.ch]** Turn off A13 Chur-San Bernardino rd dir Thusis, site well sp. Med, deeply shd; wc; chem disp; shwrs inc; el pnts CHF3; gas; lndtte; shop; rest 500m; snacks; bar; playgrnd; pool adj; tennis; games area; fishing; 20% statics; dogs; phone; Eng spkn; adv bkg; CCI. "Gd cent for mountains; beautiful situation." 1 May-30 Sep. CHF 26.60 2010*

⊞ **THUSIS** *C4* (10km S Rural) *46.60580, 9.42630* **Camping Sut Baselgia, 7440 Andeer [081 6611453; fax 6307077; camping.andeer@bluewin.ch; www.campingandeer.ch]** On N edge of vill of Andeer. Exit N13 at Zillis for Andeer; site sp. Med, pt shd; wc; chem disp; shwrs inc; el pnts (10A) CHF3; gas; lndtte (inc dryer); shop; tradsmn; snacks; bar; 2 pools adj (1 htd, covrd); paddling pool; tennis; cycle hire; games rm; wifi; 90% statics; dogs CHF2; site clsd Nov; quiet; ccard acc. "Beautiful location; helpful owner; gd NH." CHF 33.00 2011*

TRIESEN see Vaduz (Liechtenstein) *B4*

TRUN *B3* (500m S Rural) *46.73721, 8.98435* **Camping Trun, 7166 Trun [081 9431666; fax 9433149; info@camping-trun.ch; www.campingtrun.ch]** Fr Chur (W) turn L 150m bef stn, sp. Lge, some mkd pitch, pt shd; wc; chem disp; shwrs; el pnts (6A) CHF3; gas; lndtte; shop; rest; snacks; bar; playgrnd; fishing; tennis; games area; fitness run; 70% statics; site clsd Oct; poss v cr; Eng spkn; quiet. 1 Apr-30 Nov. CHF 23.60 2008*

ULRICHEN *C3* (1km SE Rural) *46.50369, 8.30969* **Camping Nufenen, 3988 Ulrichen [027 9731437; info@camping-nufenen.ch; www.camping-nufenen.ch]** On NE end of Ulrichen turn R on Nufenen pass rd. After rlwy & rv x-ing (1km), site on R. Med, pt shd; wc; chem disp; shwrs CHF0.50; el pnts (8A) CHF3.50; lndtte; shop, snacks 500m; tradsmn; rest 1km; pool 6km; tennis 2km; 50% statics; dogs CHF2; phone; poss cr; adv bkg; quiet; red long stay/CCI. "Pleasantly situated, mountainous site with gd local facs; gd walking; san facs basic but clean; recep clsd 1230-1400." ♦ 1 Jun-30 Sep. CHF 26.00 2009*

ULRICHEN *C3* (5km SW Rural) *46.46480, 8.24469* **Camping Augenstern, 3988 Reckingen [027 9731395; info@campingaugenstern.ch; www.campingaugenstern.ch]** On Brig-Gletsch rd turn R in Reckingen over rlwy & rv; site sp. Med, unshd; wc; chem disp; mv service pnt; shwrs CHF1; el pnts (10A) CHF4.50; lndtte; shop; rest; snacks; bar; htd pool adj; golf; fishing; 20% statics; dogs CHF2; quiet; red CCI. "Nr Rv Rhône & mountains." 14 May-16 Oct & 10 Dec-13 Mar. CHF 27.50 2009*

ULRICHEN *C3* (7km SW Rural) **Camping Ritzingen, 3989 Grafschaft [027 9731631; fax 9731461]** NE on Brig-Gletsch rd, turn R in vill of Ritzingen to site by Rv Rhône, well sp. Med, pt sl, terr, pt shd; wc; shwrs CHF1; el pnts CHF3; shop; snacks; playgrnd; pool 2km; games area; fishing; TV; quiet; ccard not acc. "Peaceful; beautiful scenery." 1 May-15 Oct. CHF 18.50 2008*

UNTERSEEN see Interlaken *C2*

UTTWIL see Romanshorn *A4*

⊞ **VADUZ (LIECHTENSTEIN)** *B4* (10km S Rural) *47.0866, 9.52666* **Camping Mittagspitze, Saga 29, 9495 Triesen [3923677; info@campingtriesen.li; www.campingtriesen.li]** On rd 28 bet Vaduz & Balzers, sp. Poss diff for lge o'fits. Med, some hdstg, terr, pt shd; wc; chem disp; shwrs inc; el pnts (6A) CHF5; gas; lndtte; shop & 3km; rest; beergarden; BBQ; playgrnd; pool high ssn; fishing; fitness trail; many statics; dogs CHF4; poss cr; Eng spkn; quiet; ccard acc. "Pretty site in lovely location; excel touring base; site yourself, recep open 0800-0830 & 1900-1930 only; steep, diff access to pitches & slippery when wet; gd rest." CHF 33.00 2009*

VALLORBE *B1* (W Urban) *46.71055, 6.37472* **Camping Pré Sous Ville, 10 Rue des Fontaines, 1337 Vallorbe [021 8432309; yvan.favre@vallorbe.com]** Foll camping sp in town. Med, mkd pitch, pt shd; wc; chem disp; mv service pnt; shwrs inc; el pnts (10A) CHF5; gas; lndtte; rest, snacks adj; bar; playgrnd; htd pool adj; fishing; tennis; games area; 20% statics; dogs; Eng spkn; quiet; red CCI. "Gd, clean facs; gd size pitches; site yourself if warden absent; conv for Vallée de Joux, Lake Geneva & Jura; views down valley." ♦ 15 Apr-15 Oct. CHF 25.00 2009*

⊞ **VERS L'EGLISE** *C2* (1km W Rural) *46.35530, 7.12705* **TCS Camping La Murée, 1865 Les Diablerets [079 4019915; dagonch@bluewin.ch; www.camping-caravaningvd.com]** Fr N9 exit Aigle. In 8km at Le Sepey turn R dir Vers-l'Eglise & Les Diablerets; site on R at ent to vill. Med, pt sl, terr; htd wc; shwrs; chem disp; el pnts (6A) CHF3; gas; lndtte; playgrnd; pool 3km; fishing; tennis; wifi; 40% statics; quiet. CHF 21.00 2009*

VESENAZ see Genève *C1*

VETROZ see Sion *C2*

⊞ **VEVEY** *C1* (12km NW Rural) *46.52864, 6.76556* **Camping Les Cases, Chemin des Cases 2, 1606 Forel [021 7811464; fax 7813126; www.campingforel.ch]** Exit A9/E62 Chexbres & foll Lac de Bret & turn L sp Savigny, then immed L. Site 100m on R, 1km S of Forel. Sm, pt sl, unshd; wc; chem disp; mv service pnt; shwrs CHF1; el pnts (13A) CHF4; gas; lndtte; supmkt; rest; snacks; bar; playgrnd; pool; paddling pool; waterslide; fishing; games area; wifi; TV; 75% statics; dogs CHF2; adv bkg; red long stay. "Sep touring area; gd." ♦ CHF 29.00 2010*

VICOSOPRANO *C4* (1km NE Rural) *46.35700, 9.63100* **Camping Mulina-Vicosoprano, 7603 Vicosoprano [081 8221035; fax 8221030; camping.mulina@bluewin.ch; www.camping-vicosoprano.ch]** Sp fr vill on old rd. Med, sl (need blocks), pt shd; wc; chem disp; shwrs CHF0.50; el pnts (10A) CHF2; lndtte; shops 500m; fishing; phone; adv bkg; quiet. "Owned & run by vill of Vicosoprano; scenic, in alpine meadow; office poss not manned until 2000 hrs & el pnts locked." ♦ 1 May-31 Oct. CHF 30.50 2008*

SWITZERLAND

VILLENEUVE *C1* (6km S Rural) *46.38666, 6.86055* **Camping Rive-Bleue, Bouveret-Plage, 1897 Le Bouveret [024 4812161; fax 4812108; info@camping-rive-bleue.ch; www.camping-rive-bleue.ch]** Fr Montreux foll sp to Evian to S side of Lake Geneva. Turn R after sp 'Bienvenue Bouveret'. Foll camp sp. Site on R approx 1km fr main Evian rd. Lge, mkd pitch, pt shd; wc; chem disp; mv service pnt; shwrs inc; el pnts (6A) CHF4.20 (adaptor avail - check earth); gas; Indtte; rest & snacks adj; shop; playgrnd; pool adj; waterslide; lake sw; watersports; tennis; 50% statics; dogs CHF2.60; sep car park; adv bkg; quiet; CCI. "Well-maintained, well-ordered site in lovely setting on lake; friendly staff; water/waste pnts scarce; v gd facs but red low ssn; 15 mins walk to vill with supmkt; conv ferries around Lake Geneva; cars must be parked in sep public car park; gd cyling area." 1 Apr-17 Oct. CHF 35.80 2010*

⊞ **VILLENEUVE** *C1* (4km SW Rural) *46.39333, 6.89527* **Camping Les Grangettes, Rue des Grangettes, 1845 Noville [021 9601503; fax 9602030; noville@treyvaud.com; www.treyvaud.com]** Fr N9 Montreux-Aigle rd, take Villeneuve exit, at end slip rd turn N twds Villeneuve. At 1st traff lts turn L to Noville, turn R by post office, site sp. V narr app rd. Med, mkd pitch, unshd; htd wc; chem disp; mv service pnt; shwrs; el pnts (10A) CHF4; Indtte; shop & 3km; rest; snacks; bar; pool 3km; lake sw; fishing; boating; 80% statics; dogs CHF3; phone; sep car park; Eng spkn; quiet. "Beautifully situated on SE corner Lake Geneva o'looking Montreux; sep tourer area." ♦ CHF 32.00 2009*

⊞ **VILLENEUVE** *C1* (6km SW Rural) *46.35638, 6.89916* **Camping au Grand-Bois, Chemin au Grand Bois 6, 1846 Chessel [024 4814225; fax 4815113; au.grand-bois@bluewin.ch; www.augrandbois.ch]** Fr N9 Montreux-Aigle, take Villeneuve exit, at end of slip rd turn N twds Villeneuve. At 1st traff lts turn L twds Noville, site on R in 4km. Lge, pt shd; wc; chem disp; mv service pnt; shwrs CHF1; el pnts (10A) CHF3 (adaptor avail); Indtte; shop 3km; tradsmn; playgrnd; htd pool; sand beach 6km; 80% statics; adv bkg; red long stay/CCI. "Gd cent for Geneva & part of Alps; clean, peaceful site; poss itinerants." ♦ CHF 24.00 2009*

VIRA GAMBAROGNO see Locarno *C3*

VISP *C2* (500m N Rural) *46.29730, 7.87269* **Camping Schwimmbad Mühleye, 3930 Visp [027 9462084; fax 9467859; info@camping-visp.ch; www.camping-visp.ch]** Exit main rd E2 at W end of town bet Esso petrol stn & rv bdge at Camping sp. Site nr pool. Lge, pt shd; wc; chem disp; shwrs; el pnts (13A) CHF3.50; gas; Indtte; shops 500m; tradsmn; snacks; bar; playgrnd; lge pool adj; tennis; fishing; 20% statics; dogs CHF2; Eng spkn; some noise fr rlwy & sometimes rifle range; red long stay/low ssn/CCI. "Gd for Zermatt & Matterhorn; recep at sw pool ent; gd value espec low ssn; suitable lge o'fits." 10 Mar-31 Oct. CHF 31.80 2010*

VISP *C2* (6km W Rural) *46.30280, 7.80188* **Camping Santa Monica, Kantonstrasse, Turtig, 3942 Raron [027 9342424; fax 9342450; santamonica@rhone.ch; www.santa-monica.ch]** Turn R off Sion-Brig rd after Turtig, just after sm rndabt. Lge, pt shd; wc; chem disp; mv service pnt; private san facs avail; shwrs CHF1; el pnts (16A) CHF4; gas; Indtte; shop 250m; snacks; htd pool; tennis; fishing; 50% statics; dogs CHF3.80 (1 only); Eng spkn; adv bkg; quiet, but some rd noise; red low ssn. "Recep clsd lunchtime, but no barrier so site yourself." 10 Apr-18 Oct. CHF 30.00 2009*

⊞ **VISP** *C2* (6km W Rural) *46.30288, 7.79530* **Camping Simplonblick, 3942 Raron [027 9343205; fax 9675012; simplonblick@bluewin.ch; www.camping-simplonblick.ch]** Site on S of rd 9. Fr Visp site past junc to Raron thro g'ge forecourt. Lge, pt shd; wc; chem disp; shwrs inc; el pnts CHF4 (adaptor loan); gas; Indtte; tradsmn; rest; bar; playgrnd; pool; paddling pool; dogs CHF4; Eng spkn; adv bkg; quiet; ccard acc. "Vg rest; friendly, welcoming staff; recep clsd 1200-1500 fr end Aug." CHF 35.00 2011*

VITZNAU *B3* (SE Rural) *47.00683, 8.48621* **Camping Vitznau, Altdorfstrasse, 6354 Vitznau [041 3971280; fax 3972457; info@camping-vitznau.ch; www.camping-vitznau.ch]** On E edge of Vitznau, sp. Fr Küssnacht twd Brunnen turn L at RC church with tall clock tower. Lge, terr, hdstg, pt shd; wc; chem disp; mv service pnt; shwrs inc; el pnts (10A) CHF4 (adaptors on loan); gas; Indtte; shop & 500m; bar; pool; lake sw & beach 500m; tennis; 40% statics; dogs CHF5; Quickstop o'night facs CHF20; poss cr; Eng spkn; adv bkg rec; quiet; card acc; red low ssn; ccard acc; red long stay; CCI. "Excel, v clean, family-run site; friendly owner will help with pitching; max c'van length 7m high ssn; sm pitches; some site rds tight & steep; recep closes 1830 hrs; fine views lakes & mountains; many activities inc walking; gd dog-walking; conv ferry terminal, cable cars & mountain rlwy (tickets avail on site); gd saving by using 'tell-pass'; lake steamer to Luzern 500m." ♦ 27 Mar-17 Oct. CHF 50.00 2010*

WABERN see Bern *B2*

WAGENHAUSEN see Schaffhausen *A3*

WALENSTADT *B3* (1km W Rural) *47.11688, 9.30086* **See Camping, Ziegelhütte, 8880 Walenstadt [081 7351896 or 7351212; fax 7351841; kontakt@see-camping.ch; www.see-camping.ch]** Fr Zürich on A3 turn R at Walenstadt sp, turn L & go thro town. Foll camping sp 2km, turn R into site. Med, pt shd; htd wc; chem disp; mv service pnt; shwrs inc; el pnts (16A) CHF3; Indtte; shop; snacks; playgrnd; lake sw adj; TV; quiet but some train noise; 75% statics; phone; no dogs; sep car park; no adv bkg; Eng spkn; red long stay; CCI. "Beautiful area; wonderful lake views." 1 May-30 Sep. CHF 38.00 2010*

⊞ **WILDBERG IM TOSSTAL** *A3* (1km NE Rural) *47.43500, 8.82862* **Camping in der Weid, Wildbergerstrasse, 8489 Wildberg-im-Tösstal [052 3853388; seiler.camping@bluewin.ch; www.campingwildberg.ch]** Leave N1/E17 at Winterthur-Ohringen to cent Winterthur. Turn R onto N15 sp Turbenthal. Wildberg sp on ent Turbenthal, turn R, site on L in 1km. Steep access rd. Med, hdstg, pt sl, terr, pt shd; htd wc; chem disp; mv service pnt; shwrs CHF0.50; el pnts (6A) CHF1.50; lndtte; shop; tradsmn; rest; snacks; bar; BBQ; playgrnd; pool 2km; paddling pool; games area; TV; 90% statics; dogs CHF2; Eng spkn; adv bkg; aircraft noise. "Gd NH for Zürich; ltd space for tourers; friendly, helpful staff; gd for children." ♦ CHF 26.00 2010*

WILDERSWIL see Interlaken *C2*

⊞ **WINTERTHUR** *A3* (3km N Rural) *47.51965, 8.71655* **Camping am Schützenweiher, Eichliwaldstrasse 4, 8400 Winterthur [tel/fax 052 2125260; campingplatz@win.ch; www.campingwinterthur.ch]** Fr A1/E60 exit Winterthur-Ohringen dir Winterthur, turn R & foll site sp, site adj police stn in about 200m. Sm, shd; htd wc; chem disp; shwrs CHF1; el pnts CHF3; gas; lndtte; shops adj; rest; playgrnd; pool 3km; 8% statics; dogs CHF4; phone; poss cr; Eng spkn; some m'way noise; red CCI. "Helpful owner; office open 1900-2000 to register & pay; find own pitch outside these hrs; sm pitches; NH only." CHF 28.00 2010*

YVERDON *B1* (2km N Rural) *46.80284, 6.63399* **Camping Le Pécos, Rue du Pécos, 1422 Grandson [024 4454969; fax 4462904; vd24@campings-ccyverdpn.ch; www.campings-ccyverdon.ch]** Foll rd 5 dir Neuchâtel. Site is 800m SW fr Grandson town cent, lakeside site, sp VD24. Med, mkd pitch, hdstg, pt shd; htd wc; chem disp; mv service pnt; baby facs; fam bthrm; shwrs CHF1; el pnts (10A) CHF6 (adaptor avail); gas; lndry rm; shop; rest; snacks; bar; playgrnd; lake sw adj; wifi; 70% statics; dogs CHF3; phone; extra for lakeside pitches; poss cr; Eng spkn; adv bkg; quiet but some rlwy noise; CCI. "Clean san facs; friendly owners; sm pitches." ♦ 1 Apr-30 Sep. CHF 30.00 2010*

YVERDON *B1* (6km N Rural) *46.82013, 6.67091* **Camping Les Pins, 1422 Corcelettes-La Poissine [tel/fax 024 4454740; bauen@camping-les-pins.ch]** Fr Yverdon take rd 5 twd Neuchâtel as far as Corcelettes, site on R on lakeside. (Height restriction of 3.1m at rlwy bdge on app.) Lge, pt shd; wc; chem disp; shwrs CHF1; el pnts CHF4; gas; lndtte; shop; rest; bar; BBQ; playgrnd; shgl beach on lake 1km; fishing; tennis; entmnt; 98% statics; dogs €6; poss cr; Eng spkn; adv bkg; quiet; ccard acc; CCI. "Fair NH; busy rlwy adj." ♦ 1 Apr-30 Sep. CHF 25.00 2008*

YVERDON *B1* (6km NE) *46.8030, 6.71765* **Camping Pointe d'Yvonand, 1462 Yvonand [024 4301655; fax 4302463; vd8@campings-ccyverdon.ch; www.campings-ccyverdon.ch]** Exit Yverdon by rd 79 for Yvonand. Turn sharp L at o'skts of town. Site sp in 2km to S of Yvonand. V lge, shd; htd wc (some cont); chem disp; mv service pnt; baby facs; fam bthrm; shwrs CHF0.50; el pnts (6-9A) CHF6; lndtte; shop; rest; snacks; bar; playgrnd; sand beach; boating; fishing; 30% statics; no dogs; sep car park; Eng spkn; adv bkg; quiet; red long stay. "Site in pine woods; conv for touring Jura; c'vans over 7m not permitted." ♦ 1 Apr-30 Sep. CHF 31.00 2008*

YVONAND see Yverdon *B1*

ZERMATT *D2* (7km N Rural) *46.06450, 7.77500* **Camping Alphubel, 3929 Täsch [027 9673635; welcome@campingtaesch.ch; www.campingtaesch.ch]** Turn down R-hand slip rd over level x-ing & bdge after rlwy stn in Täsch, & foll sp to site. S bend bdge poss diff for lge o'fits at app. Med, unshd; htd wc; chem disp; mv service pnt; shwrs inc; el pnts (10A) CHF5 (long lead poss req); lndtte; shops 200m; rest adj; htd pool 1km; tennis; fishing; dogs CHF2; recep clsd 1200-1400; poss cr; Eng spkn; no adv bkg; quiet but rlwy noise; ccard not acc. "Conv for frequent train to Zermatt fr vill; superb scenery & walking; helpful owner; vg, modern san facs; excel." 15 May-15 Oct. CHF 28.00 2010*

ZERMATT *D2* (7km N Rural) *46.08600, 7.78219* **Camping Attermenzen, 3928 Randa [027 9672555 or 9671379; fax 9676074; sommercamping@oberwallis.ch or wintercamping@oberwallis.ch; www.camping-randa.ch]** Fr A9/E62 turn S in Visp dir Zermatt. Site on L after approx 30km 2km S of Randa vill bef Tasch. Med, pt sl, unshd; wc; shwrs inc; el pnts (5A) CHF4 (adaptors avail); gas; lndtte; shop; tradsmn; rest; snacks; bar; playgrnd; dogs CHF2; shuttle bus to Zermatt; site clsd Jan; poss cr; Eng spkn; quiet; CCI. "Winter c'vanning; main clientele climbers; excel san facs; humourous owner." 15 Jun-15 Sep & 1 Nov-30 Apr. CHF 24.00 2009*

ZERNEZ *C4* (500m W Rural) *46.69716, 10.08718* **Camping Cul, 7530 Zernez [tel/fax 081 8561462; info@camping-cul.ch; www.camping-cul.ch]** Fr N foll sp for St Moritz to edge of town, sp thro woodyard to site. Fr S sp on L on reaching town. Med, mkd pitch, pt shd; wc; chem disp; mv service pnt; shwrs inc; el pnts (8A) CHF2.50; lndtte; shop & 500m; tradsmn; rest high ssn; playgrnd; pool in town; 5% statics; dogs CHF2; poss cr; adv bkg; quiet; 10% red CCI. "Roomy, clean, pretty, well-organised site surrounded by mountains; friendly staff; excel san facs; barrier clsd 1200-1300; conv Swiss National Park & train to St Moritz; conv Livigno (Italy) for tax-free shopping; easy walk into town along Rv Inn & many walking trails." 15 May-31 Oct. CHF 32.00 2009*

ZUG *B3* (1km E Rural) *47.17806, 8.49438* **TCS Camping Zugersee, Chamer Fussweg 36, 6300 Zug [041 7418422; fax 7418430; camping.zug@tcs.ch; www.campingtcs.ch]** Fr A4/E41 take A4a Zug-West, site sp on R in 3km on lakeside. Fr Zug take Luzern rd for 2km. Site on L under rlwy. Med, mkd pitch, pt shd; htd wc; chem disp; mv service pnt; shwrs inc; el pnts (4A) CHF4; gas; lndtte (inc dryer); shop; rest; snacks; bar; playgrnd; pool 3km; lake sw; fishing; tennis; games area; cycle hire; 40% statics; dogs CHF5; phone; poss cr; Eng spkn; rlwy noise; ccard acc; red CCI. "Easy walk to town." 30 Mar-7 Oct. CHF 35.50 2011*

ZURICH *A3* (8km SE Rural) *47.35574, 8.65881* **TCS Camping Maurholz, Fällandenstrasse, 8124 Maur [044 9800266; fax 9800481; maurholz@tcs-ccz.ch; www.tcs-ccz.ch]** On W shore of Greifensee, 2km SE of Fallanden on rd to Maur, clearly sp. Diff app & steep gradient at exit. Med, pt sl, pt shd; htd wc; chem disp; mv service pnt; shwrs; el pnts (10A) CHF3.50; gas; lndtte; shops & 2km; bar; snacks; lake sw; sand beach; dogs CHF2.50; poss cr; no adv bkg. "Lake Greiffensee gd for boating, fishing & sw; site busy & noisy airfield at w/end." Easter-11 Oct. CHF 27.30 2008*

ZURICH *A3* (10km SE Rural) *47.34613, 8.66915* **Camping Rausenbach, Rausenbachweg, 8124 Maur [044 9800959; fax 9800955]** On W shore of Greifensee 500m N of Maur, site sp. Med, unshd; wc; chem disp; mv service pnt; shwrs CHF0.50; el pnts (10A) metered; gas; lndtte; shop in Maur; rest; snacks; playgrnd; lake sw adj; golf 10km; 80% statics; dogs CHF1.50; sep car park; poss cr; noisy (flight path Zürich airport); red CCI. "Fair sh stay; ltd space for tourers." ♦
1 Apr-31 Oct. CHF 27.00 2008*

ZURICH *A3* (3km S Rural) *47.33633, 8.54167* **Camping Seebucht, Seestrasse 559, 8038 Zürich-Wollishofen [044 4821612; fax 4821660; 2008@camping-zurich.ch; www.camping-zurich.ch]** Fr city foll rd 3 (twd Chur) on S side of lake; foll camping sp. Lge, hdstg, pt shd; wc; chem disp; mv service pnt; shwrs CHF2; el pnts (6A) CHF5; gas; lndtte; shop; tradsmn; rest; snacks; bar; BBQ; playgrnd; pool 3km; lake sw; watersports; fishing; tennis; 80% statics; dogs CHF5; bus; poss cr & noisy; Eng spkn; rd & rlwy noise. "Parking in Zürich v diff, use bus; sm area for tourers; conv NH, v sm pitches." ♦
1 May-30 Sep. CHF 39.00 2011*

ZURICH *A3* (14km SW Rural) *47.27970, 8.39570* **Camping Reussbrücke, Muristrasse 32, 8913 Ottenbach [044 7612022; fax 7612042; reussbruecke8913@bluewin.ch; www.camping-ottenbach.ch]** Exit Basel-Zürich m'way at Lenzburg. Foll sps to Zug/Luzern to Muri. Turn L foll sps twd Affoltern thro Birri. Site on L past rv bdge at Ottenbach. Fr Zürich, take rd to Luzern via Birmensdorf. At Affoltern R sp Muri to site on R in 4.5km at Ottenbach, bef rv bdge. Lge, pt shd; wc; shwrs; chem disp; mv service pnt; el pnts (10A) CHF4; gas; lndtte (inc dryer); shop; tradsmn; rest; snacks; playgrnd; pool; fishing; cycle hire; 75% statics; dogs CHF3.50; poss cr; Eng spkn; adv bkg; quiet; ccard acc; CCI. "Excel san facs; friendly welcome; in beautiful area; sep car pk partly outside gates." 26 Mar-15 Oct. CHF 33.50 2011*

⊞ **ZWEISIMMEN** *C2* (1km N Rural) *46.56338, 7.37691* **Camping Fankhauser, Ey Gässli 2, 3770 Zweisimmen [033 7221356; fax 7221351; info@camping-fankhauser.ch; www.camping-fankhauser.ch]** N6 exit Spiez, then foll sp Zweisimmen. On o'skts of town turn L at camping sp immed bef Agip petrol stn, site on L immed after rlwy x-ing. Med, pt sl; htd wc; chem disp; mv service pnt; shwrs CHF0.50; el pnts (10A) CHF3.50 or metered; lndtte; shop 1km; rest, snacks, bar 1km; BBQ; playgrnd; pool 800m; fishing; golf; 90% statics; dogs free; phone; Eng spkn; adv bkg; some rlwy noise & glider tow planes at w/end; CCI. "Gd NH." CHF 27.50 2011*

The opening dates and prices on this campsite have changed.
I'll send a site report form to the Club for the next edition of the guide.

⊞ **ZWEISIMMEN** *C2* (1km N Rural) *46.56219, 7.37780* **Camping Vermeille, Ey Gässli 2, 3770 Zweisimmen [033 7221940; fax 7723625; info@camping-vermeille.ch; www.camping-vermeille.ch]** Fr N6 exist Spiez & foll sp Zweisimmen. Pass Camping Fankhauser. Site sp almost opp Aldi supmkt. Med, pt shd; htd wc; chem disp; mv service pnt; baby facs; shwrs; el pnts (10A) CHF3.50; gas; lndtte (inc dryer); shop; rest 300m; snacks; BBQ; cooking facs; playgrnd; htd pool; fishing; tennis; cycle hire; games rm; golf; wifi; TV; 70% statics; dogs CHF2; Eng spkn; adv bkg; quiet; ccard acc; red CCI. "Well-run site; friendly, helpful staff; clsd 1200-1400; cable car to top of mountains; many walks & excursions; easy walk to vill/rlwy stn; cycle track to vill & up valley." ♦
CHF 32.40 2009*

Distances are shown in kilometres and are calculated from town/city centres along the most practical roads, although not necessarily taking the shortest route. 1km = 0.62miles

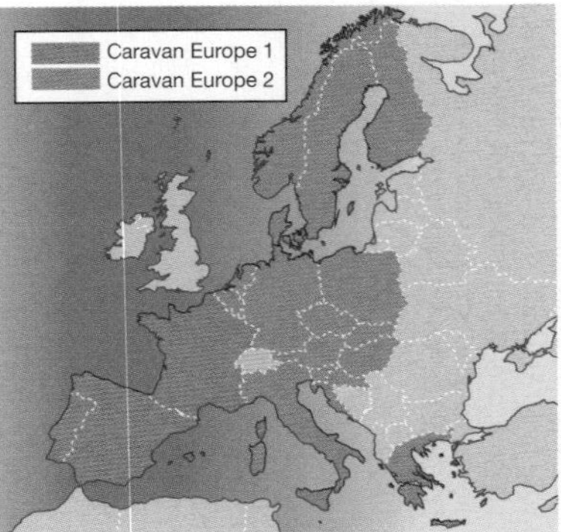

Lausanne to Zermatt = 170km

	Altdorf	Basel	Bellinzona	Bern	Brig	Chur	Delémont	Disentis	Fribourg	Genève (Geneva)	Gstaad	Innertkirchen	Interlaken	La Chaux-de-Fonds	Lausanne	Lugano	Luzern	Martigny	Neuchâtel	Olten	St. Gallen	St. Moritz	Schaffhausen	Scuol/Schuls	Sion	Vaduz (Liechtenstein)	Winterthur	Zermatt	Zug
Basel	144																												
Bellinzona	110	244																											
Bern	155	98	255																										
Brig	118	192	161	166																									
Chur	181	230	115	243	175																								
Delémont	151	44	292	93	182	239																							
Disentis	62	204	80	177	108	66	268																						
Fribourg	188	132	286	35	178	275	124	211																					
Genève (Geneva)	319	268	420	172	216	410	261	324	141																				
Gstaad	159	204	223	81	91	272	172	183	66	145																			
Innertkirchen	68	187	126	91	77	153	178	88	126	263	97																		
Interlaken	99	155	195	59	75	210	144	120	93	230	63	34																	
La Chaux-de-Fonds	189	103	291	68	164	274	61	245	66	145	149	160	126																
Lausanne	257	205	358	107	152	348	201	262	73	62	83	201	166	96															
Lugano	132	264	29	281	189	142	275	108	312	449	284	154	220	315	382														
Luzern	42	102	142	116	151	141	109	103	149	280	134	46	74	145	219	166													
Martigny	281	231	240	136	82	371	225	188	101	136	74	156	192	159	73	267	250												
Neuchâtel	196	142	295	47	142	285	81	223	44	122	149	138	104	23	74	320	155	146											
Olten	96	53	197	69	159	181	64	160	99	235	156	103	122	102	172	220	57	201	111										
St. Gallen	179	191	218	205	289	105	201	156	236	371	318	210	256	237	310	244	139	336	245	145									
St. Moritz	201	313	152	327	242	86	323	145	360	459	406	199	298	362	432	177	218	332	369	268	188								
Schaffhausen	147	159	246	173	262	182	169	209	206	340	291	215	229	208	279	275	110	305	216	115	82	269							
Scuol/Schuls	253	305	186	319	279	105	315	169	348	485	375	256	284	352	425	214	215	337	362	260	181	62	252						
Sion	170	253	215	162	53	401	250	161	129	161	120	115	88	190	99	241	273	27	166	225	356	296	326	317					
Vaduz (Liechtenstein)	110	206	147	203	206	32	213	98	237	371	304	186	241	271	310	184	115	262	249	160	58	117	136	99	221				
Winterthur	119	133	219	145	232	158	141	180	177	311	216	125	188	179	249	243	81	279	188	89	59	245	29	233	299	84			
Zermatt	245	212	185	202	28	199	206	136	204	239	194	114	161	188	170	224	174	99	164	186	325	278	296	313	72	243	267		
Zug	67	125	166	137	181	115	135	130	169	305	164	75	103	172	241	193	28	265	182	79	112	197	82	189	293	86	51	219	
Zürich	65	112	196	123	211	117	122	127	158	292	191	105	128	156	228	223	59	258	165	66	83	201	51	194	280	93	22	245	30

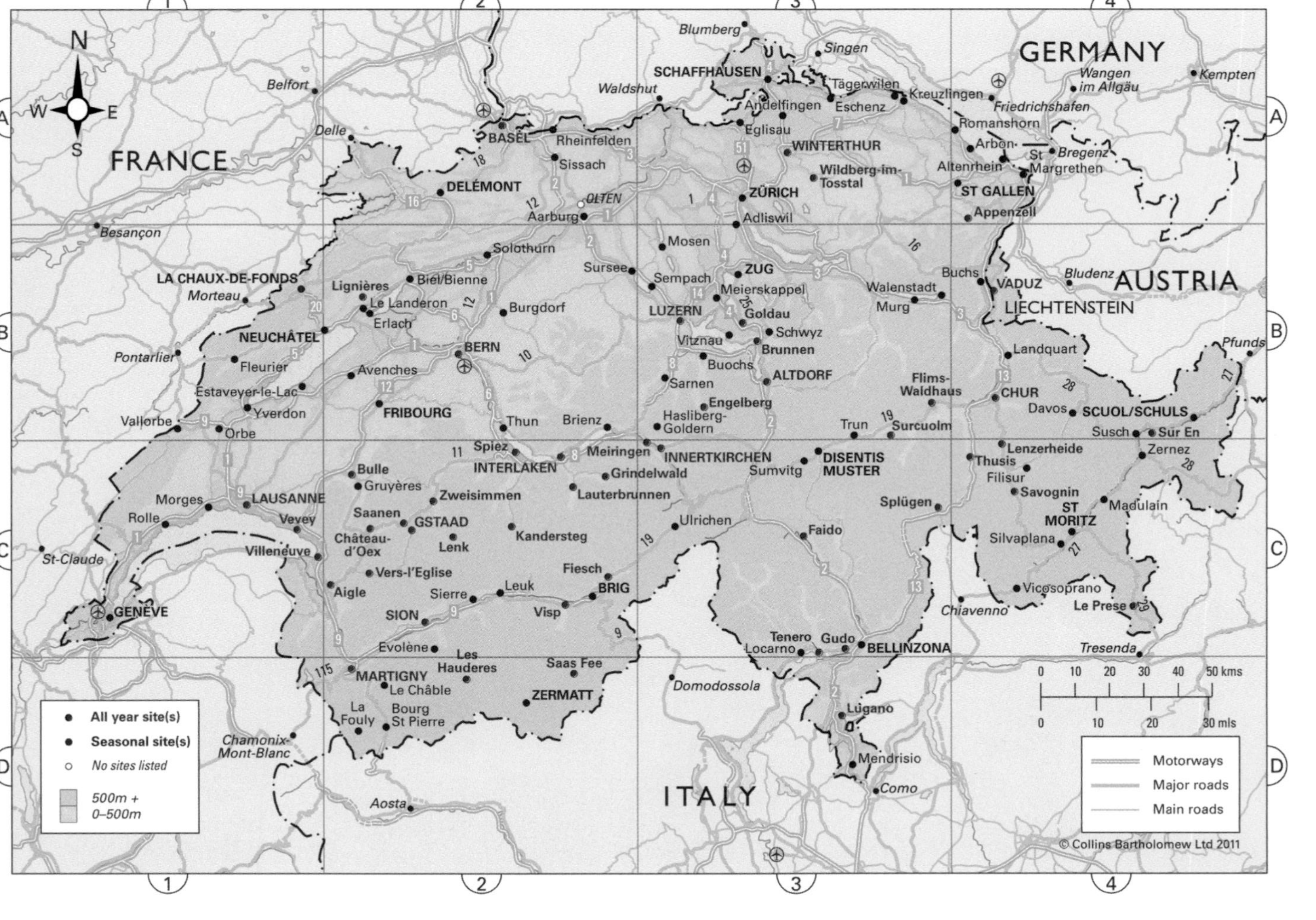
GERMANY
AUSTRIA
LIECHTENSTEIN
FRANCE
ITALY
N
E
S
W
A
B
C
D
1
2
3
4
Belfort
Delle
Besançon
BASEL
Rheinfelden
Sissach
DELÉMONT
OLTEN
Aarburg
Waldshut
Blumberg
Singen
SCHAFFHAUSEN
Tägerwilen
Kreuzlingen
Eschenz
Andelfingen
Eglisau
WINTERTHUR
Wildberg-im-Tosstal
ZÜRICH
Adliswil
Romanshorn
Arbon
Altenrhein
St Margrethen
Bregenz
Friedrichshafen
Wangen im Allgäu
Kempten
ST GALLEN
Appenzell
Solothurn
LA CHAUX-DE-FONDS
Morteau
Lignières
Biel/Bienne
Le Landeron
Erlach
Burgdorf
NEUCHÂTEL
Pontarlier
Fleurier
Avenches
BERN
Estavayer-le-Lac
Yverdon
FRIBOURG
Vallorbe
Orbe
Mosen
Sursee
Sempach
ZUG
Meierskappel
LUZERN
Goldau
Schwyz
Vitznau
Brunnen
Buochs
ALTDORF
Sarnen
Engelberg
Hasliberg-Goldern
Walenstadt
Murg
Buchs
VADUZ
Bludenz
Landquart
Pfunds
Flims-Waldhaus
CHUR
Davos
SCUOL/SCHULS
Susch
Sur En
Zernez
Thun
Brienz
Spiez
INTERLAKEN
Meiringen
INNERTKIRCHEN
Grindelwald
Lauterbrunnen
Trun
Surcuolm
DISENTIS MUSTER
Sumvitg
Lenzerheide
Thusis
Filisur
Savognin
ST MORITZ
Madulain
Silvaplana
Vicosoprano
Le Prese
Chiavenno
Tresenda
Splügen
Bulle
Gruyères
Zweisimmen
Morges
LAUSANNE
Vevey
Rolle
Saanen
GSTAAD
Château-d'Oex
Lenk
Kandersteg
Ulrichen
Faido
St-Claude
Villeneuve
Vers-l'Eglise
Fiesch
Aigle
Sierre
Leuk
BRIG
GENÈVE
SION
Visp
Evolène
Les Hauderes
Saas Fee
MARTIGNY
Le Châble
ZERMATT
La Fouly
Bourg St Pierre
Chamonix-Mont-Blanc
Aosta
Domodossola
Tenero
Locarno
Gudo
BELLINZONA
Lugano
Mendrisio
Como
All year site(s)
Seasonal site(s)
No sites listed
500m +
0–500m
0 10 20 30 40 50 kms
0 10 20 30 mls
Motorways
Major roads
Main roads
© Collins Bartholomew Ltd 2011

Mountain Passes and Tunnels

Passes/Tunnel Report Form

Name of Pass/Tunnel ....

To/From ....

Date Travelled..

Comments (eg gradients, traffic, road surface, width of road, hairpins, scenery)

....

....

....

..Year of Guide used:..

ARE YOU A Caravanner	Motorhome Owner	Trailer-tenter?

==

Passes/Tunnel Report Form

Name of Pass/Tunnel ....

To/From ....

Date Travelled..

Comments (eg gradients, traffic, road surface, width of road, hairpins, scenery)

....

....

Year of Guide used:..

ARE YOU A: Caravanner	Motohome Owner	Trailer-tenter?

CUT ALONG DOTTED LINE

Mountain Passes and Tunnels

Passes/Tunnel Report Form

Name of Pass/Tunnel ....

To/From ....

Date Travelled...

Comments (eg gradients, traffic, road surface, width of road, hairpins, scenery)

....

....

....

..Year of Guide used:..

ARE YOU A Caravanner	Motorhome Owner	Trailer-tenter?

==

Passes/Tunnel Report Form

Name of Pass/Tunnel ....

To/From ....

Date Travelled...

Comments (eg gradients, traffic, road surface, width of road, hairpins, scenery)

....

....

Year of Guide used:...

ARE YOU A: Caravanner	Motorhome Owner	Trailer-tenter?

Caravan Europe Site Report Form **

If campsite is already listed, complete only those sections of the form where changes apply

Please print, type or tick in the white areas

Sites not reported on for 5 years may be deleted from the guide

Year of guide used	20..........	Is site listed?	Listed on page no.	Unlisted	Date of visit	......../........./.........

A – CAMPSITE NAME AND LOCATION

Country		Name of town/village site listed under *(see Sites Location Maps)*			
Distance & direction from centre of town site is listed under *(in a straight line)*	....................km	eg N, NE, S, SW	Urban	Rural	Coastal
Site open all year?	Y / N	Period site is open *(if not all year)*	................./................. to ..../.................		
Site name				Naturist site	Y / N
Site address					
Telephone			Fax		
E-mail			Website		

B – CAMPSITE CHARGES

Charge for car, caravan + 2 adults in local currency	PRICE		EL PNTS inc in this price?	Y / N	Amps ....

C – DIRECTIONS

Brief, specific directions to site (in km) *To convert miles to kilometres multiply by 8 and divide by 5 or use Conversion Table in guide*	
GPS	Latitude...*(eg 12.34567)* Longitude...*(eg 1.23456 or -1.23456)*

D – CAMPSITE DESCRIPTION

SITE size ie number of pitches	Small Max 50	SM	Medium 51-150	MED	Large 151-500	LGE	Very large 500+	V LGE	Unchanged

PITCH size	*eg small, medium, large, very large, various*	Unchanged

Pitch features if **NOT** open-plan/grassy	Hedged	HDG PITCH	Marked or numbered	MKD PITCH	Hardstanding or gravel	HDSTG	Unchanged

If site is **NOT** level, is it	Part sloping	PT SL	Sloping	SL	Terraced	TERR	Unchanged

Is site shaded?	Shaded	SHD	Part shaded	PT SHD	Unshaded	UNSHD	Unchanged

E – CAMPSITE FACILITIES

WC	Heated	HTD WC	Continental	CONT	Own San recommended	OWN SAN REC
Chemical disposal point		CHEM DISP	Dedicated point		WC only	
Motor caravan waste discharge and water refill point			MV SERVICE PNT			
Child / baby facilities (bathroom)		CHILD / BABY FACS	Family bathroom		FAM BTHRM	
Hot shower(s)		SHWR(S)	Inc in site fee?	Y / N	Price....................*(if not inc)*	
ELECTRIC HOOK UP *if not included in price above*		EL PNTS	Price.......................................		Amps..	
Supplies of bottled gas		GAS	On site	Y / N	Or in .... Kms	
Launderette / Washing Machine		LNDTTE	Inc dryer Y / N		LNDRY RM *(if no washing machine)*	

** *You can also complete forms online: www.caravanclub.co.uk/europereport*

CUT ALONG DOTTED LINE

F – FOOD & DRINK

Shop(s) / supermarket	SHOP(S) / SUPMKT	On site		or	.... kms
Bread / milk delivered	TRADSMN				
Restaurant / cafeteria	REST	On site		or	.... kms
Snack bar / take-away	SNACKS	On site		or	.... kms
Bar	BAR	On site		or	.... kms
Barbecue allowed	BBQ	Charcoal	Gas	Elec	Sep area
Cooking facilities	COOKING FACS				

G – LEISURE FACILITIES

Playground	PLAYGRND					
Swimming pool	POOL	On site		or ....km	Heated	Covered
Beach	BEACH	Adj		or ....km	Sand	Shingle
Alternative swimming *(lake)*	SW	Adj		or ....km	Sand	Shingle
Games /sports area / Games room	GAMES AREA	GAMES ROOM				
Entertainment in high season	ENTMNT					
Internet use by visitors	INTERNET	Wifi Internet		WIFI		
Television room	TV RM	Satellite / Cable to pitches		TV CAB / SAT		

H – OTHER INFORMATION

% Static caravans / mobile homes / chalets / cottages / fixed tents on site				................% STATICS
Dogs allowed	DOGS	Y / N	Price per night .... *(if allowed)*	
Phone	PHONE	On site	Adj	
Bus / tram / train	BUS / TRAM / TRAIN	Adj	or .... km	
Twin axles caravans allowed?	TWIN AXLES Y / N	Possibly crowded in high season		POSS CR
English spoken	ENG SPKN			
Advance bookings accepted	ADV BKG	Y / N		
Noise levels on site in season	NOISY / QUIET	If noisy, why?		
Credit card accepted	CCARD ACC	Reduction low season		RED LOW SSN
Camping Card International accepted in lieu of passport	CCI	INF card required *(If naturist site)*		Y / N
Facilities for disabled	Full wheelchair facilities	♦	Limited disabled facilities	♦ ltd

I – ADDITIONAL REMARKS AND/OR ITEMS OF INTEREST

Tourist attractions, unusual features or other facilities, eg waterslide, tennis, cycle hire, watersports, horseriding, separate car park, walking distance to shops etc	YOUR OPINION OF THE SITE:
	EXCEL
	VERY GOOD
	GOOD
	FAIR / POOR
	NIGHT HALT ONLY

Your comments & opinions may be used in future editions of the guide, if you do not wish them to be used please tick ....

J – MEMBER DETAILS

ARE YOU A:	Caravanner		Motor caravanner		Trailer-tenter?
NAME:	CARAVAN CLUB MEMBERSHIP NO:				
	POST CODE:				
DO YOU NEED MORE BLANK SITE REPORT FORMS?	YES		NO		
Address *(Non-members only please complete this section)*					

Please use a separate form for each campsite and do not send receipts. Owing to the large number of site reports received, it is not possible to enter into correspondence. Please return completed form to:

The Editor, Caravan Europe, The Caravan Club
FREEPOST, PO Box 386, (RRZG-SXKK-UCUJ)
East Grinstead RH19 1FH

(This address to be used when mailing within the UK only)

Caravan Europe Site Report Form **

If campsite is already listed, complete only those sections of the form where changes apply

Please print, type or tick in the white areas

Sites not reported on for 5 years may be deleted from the guide

Year of guide used	20..........	Is site listed?	Listed on page no.	Unlisted	Date of visit	......../........./.........

A – CAMPSITE NAME AND LOCATION

Country		Name of town/village site listed under *(see Sites Location Maps)*				
Distance & direction from centre of town site is listed under *(in a straight line)*	....................km	eg N, NE, S, SW	Urban	Rural	Coastal	
Site open all year?	Y / N	Period site is open *(if not all year)*	................./................. to ..../..................			
Site name			Naturist site	Y / N		
Site address						
Telephone		Fax				
E-mail		Website				

B – CAMPSITE CHARGES

Charge for car, caravan + 2 adults in local currency	PRICE		EL PNTS inc in this price?	Y / N	Amps ....

C – DIRECTIONS

Brief, specific directions to site (in km) *To convert miles to kilometres multiply by 8 and divide by 5 or use Conversion Table in guide*	
GPS	Latitude..*(eg 12.34567)* Longitude...*(eg 1.23456 or -1.23456)*

D – CAMPSITE DESCRIPTION

SITE size ie number of pitches	Small Max 50	SM	Medium 51-150	MED	Large 151-500	LGE	Very large 500+	V LGE	Unchanged

PITCH size	*eg small, medium, large, very large, various*	Unchanged

Pitch features if **NOT** open-plan/grassy	Hedged	HDG PITCH	Marked or numbered	MKD PITCH	Hardstanding or gravel	HDSTG	Unchanged
If site is **NOT** level, is it	Part sloping	PT SL	Sloping	SL	Terraced	TERR	Unchanged
Is site shaded?	Shaded	SHD	Part shaded	PT SHD	Unshaded	UNSHD	Unchanged

E – CAMPSITE FACILITIES

WC	Heated	HTD WC	Continental	CONT	Own San recommended — OWN SAN REC
Chemical disposal point	CHEM DISP	Dedicated point		WC only	
Motor caravan waste discharge and water refill point		MV SERVICE PNT			
Child / baby facilities (bathroom)	CHILD / BABY FACS	Family bathroom		FAM BTHRM	
Hot shower(s)	SHWR(S)	Inc in site fee?	Y / N	Price....................*(if not inc)*	
ELECTRIC HOOK UP *if not included in price above*	EL PNTS	Price..		Amps..	
Supplies of bottled gas	GAS	On site	Y / N	Or in .... Kms	
Launderette / Washing Machine	LNDTTE	Inc dryer Y / N		LNDRY RM *(if no washing machine)*	

** *You can also complete forms online: www.caravanclub.co.uk/europereport*

CUT ALONG DOTTED LINE

F – FOOD & DRINK

Shop(s) / supermarket	SHOP(S) / SUPMKT	On site		or	.... kms	
Bread / milk delivered	TRADSMN					
Restaurant / cafeteria	REST	On site		or	.... kms	
Snack bar / take-away	SNACKS	On site		or	.... kms	
Bar	BAR	On site		or	.... kms	
Barbecue allowed	BBQ	Charcoal	Gas	Elec	Sep area	
Cooking facilities	COOKING FACS					

G – LEISURE FACILITIES

Playground	PLAYGRND					
Swimming pool	POOL	On site		or ....km	Heated	Covered
Beach	BEACH	Adj		or ....km	Sand	Shingle
Alternative swimming *(lake)*	SW	Adj		or ....km	Sand	Shingle
Games /sports area / Games room	GAMES AREA	GAMES ROOM				
Entertainment in high season	ENTMNT					
Internet use by visitors	INTERNET	Wifi Internet	WIFI			
Television room	TV RM	Satellite / Cable to pitches	TV CAB / SAT			

H – OTHER INFORMATION

% Static caravans / mobile homes / chalets / cottages / fixed tents on site				................% STATICS
Dogs allowed	DOGS	Y / N	Price per night .... *(if allowed)*	
Phone	PHONE	On site	Adj	
Bus / tram / train	BUS / TRAM / TRAIN	Adj	or .... km	
Twin axles caravans allowed?	TWIN AXLES Y / N	Possibly crowded in high season		POSS CR
English spoken	ENG SPKN			
Advance bookings accepted	ADV BKG	Y / N		
Noise levels on site in season	NOISY / QUIET	If noisy, why?		
Credit card accepted	CCARD ACC	Reduction low season		RED LOW SSN
Camping Card International accepted in lieu of passport	CCI	INF card required *(If naturist site)*		Y / N
Facilities for disabled	Full wheelchair facilities ♦	Limited disabled facilities		♦ ltd

I – ADDITIONAL REMARKS AND/OR ITEMS OF INTEREST

Tourist attractions, unusual features or other facilities, eg waterslide, tennis, cycle hire, watersports, horseriding, separate car park, walking distance to shops etc	YOUR OPINION OF THE SITE:
	EXCEL
	VERY GOOD
	GOOD
	FAIR / POOR
	NIGHT HALT ONLY

Your comments & opinions may be used in future editions of the guide, if you do not wish them to be used please tick ....

J – MEMBER DETAILS

ARE YOU A:	Caravanner		Motor caravanner		Trailer-tenter?	
NAME:	CARAVAN CLUB MEMBERSHIP NO:					
	POST CODE:					
DO YOU NEED MORE BLANK SITE REPORT FORMS?		YES		NO		
Address *(Non-members only please complete this section)*						

Please use a separate form for each campsite and do not send receipts. Owing to the large number of site reports received, it is not possible to enter into correspondence. Please return completed form to:

The Editor, Caravan Europe, The Caravan Club
FREEPOST, PO Box 386, (RRZG-SXKK-UCUJ)
East Grinstead RH19 1FH

(This address to be used when mailing within the UK only)

Caravan Europe Site Report Form **

If campsite is already listed, complete only those sections of the form where changes apply

Please print, type or tick in the white areas

Sites not reported on for 5 years may be deleted from the guide

Year of guide used	20..........	Is site listed?	Listed on page no.	Unlisted	Date of visit	......../........./.........

A – CAMPSITE NAME AND LOCATION

Country		Name of town/village site listed under *(see Sites Location Maps)*				
Distance & direction from centre of town site is listed under *(in a straight line)*	...................km	eg N, NE, S, SW	Urban	Rural	Coastal	
Site open all year?	Y / N	Period site is open *(if not all year)*	................./................. to ..../.................			
Site name				Naturist site	Y / N	
Site address						
Telephone		Fax				
E-mail		Website				

B – CAMPSITE CHARGES

Charge for car, caravan + 2 adults in local currency	PRICE		EL PNTS inc in this price?	Y / N	Amps ....

C – DIRECTIONS

Brief, specific directions to site (in km) *To convert miles to kilometres multiply by 8 and divide by 5 or use Conversion Table in guide*	
GPS	Latitude...*(eg 12.34567)* Longitude...*(eg 1.23456 or -1.23456)*

D – CAMPSITE DESCRIPTION

SITE size ie number of pitches	Small Max 50	SM	Medium 51-150	MED	Large 151-500	LGE	Very large 500+	V LGE	Unchanged
PITCH size	*eg small, medium, large, very large, various*								Unchanged
Pitch features if **NOT** open-plan/grassy	Hedged	HDG PITCH	Marked or numbered	MKD PITCH	Hardstanding or gravel	HDSTG			Unchanged
If site is **NOT** level, is it	Part sloping	PT SL	Sloping	SL	Terraced	TERR			Unchanged
Is site shaded?	Shaded	SHD	Part shaded	PT SHD	Unshaded	UNSHD			Unchanged

E – CAMPSITE FACILITIES

WC	Heated	HTD WC	Continental	CONT	Own San recommended	OWN SAN REC
Chemical disposal point	CHEM DISP	Dedicated point		WC only		
Motor caravan waste discharge and water refill point	MV SERVICE PNT					
Child / baby facilities (bathroom)	CHILD / BABY FACS	Family bathroom	FAM BTHRM			
Hot shower(s)	SHWR(S)	Inc in site fee?	Y / N	Price....................*(if not inc)*		
ELECTRIC HOOK UP *if not included in price above*	EL PNTS	Price..	Amps..			
Supplies of bottled gas	GAS	On site	Y / N	Or in .... Kms		
Launderette / Washing Machine	LNDTTE	Inc dryer Y / N	LNDRY RM *(if no washing machine)*			

** *You can also complete forms online: www.caravanclub.co.uk/europereport*

CUT ALONG DOTTED LINE

F – FOOD & DRINK

Shop(s) / supermarket	SHOP(S) / SUPMKT	On site		or	.... kms
Bread / milk delivered	TRADSMN				
Restaurant / cafeteria	REST	On site		or	.... kms
Snack bar / take-away	SNACKS	On site		or	.... kms
Bar	BAR	On site		or	.... kms
Barbecue allowed	BBQ	Charcoal	Gas	Elec	Sep area
Cooking facilities	COOKING FACS				

G – LEISURE FACILITIES

Playground	PLAYGRND					
Swimming pool	POOL	On site		or ....km	Heated	Covered
Beach	BEACH	Adj		or ....km	Sand	Shingle
Alternative swimming *(lake)*	SW	Adj		or ....km	Sand	Shingle
Games /sports area / Games room	GAMES AREA	GAMES ROOM				
Entertainment in high season	ENTMNT					
Internet use by visitors	INTERNET	Wifi Internet		WIFI		
Television room	TV RM	Satellite / Cable to pitches		TV CAB / SAT		

H – OTHER INFORMATION

% Static caravans / mobile homes / chalets / cottages / fixed tents on site				................% STATICS
Dogs allowed	DOGS	Y / N	Price per night .... *(if allowed)*	
Phone	PHONE	On site	Adj	
Bus / tram / train	BUS / TRAM / TRAIN	Adj	or .... km	
Twin axles caravans allowed?	TWIN AXLES Y / N	Possibly crowded in high season		POSS CR
English spoken	ENG SPKN			
Advance bookings accepted	ADV BKG	Y / N		
Noise levels on site in season	NOISY / QUIET	If noisy, why?		
Credit card accepted	CCARD ACC	Reduction low season		RED LOW SSN
Camping Card International accepted in lieu of passport	CCI	INF card required *(If naturist site)*		Y / N
Facilities for disabled	Full wheelchair facilities	♦	Limited disabled facilities	♦ ltd

I – ADDITIONAL REMARKS AND/OR ITEMS OF INTEREST

Tourist attractions, unusual features or other facilities, eg waterslide, tennis, cycle hire, watersports, horseriding, separate car park, walking distance to shops etc	YOUR OPINION OF THE SITE:	
	EXCEL	
	VERY GOOD	
	GOOD	
	FAIR	POOR
	NIGHT HALT ONLY	

Your comments & opinions may be used in future editions of the guide, if you do not wish them to be used please tick ....

J – MEMBER DETAILS

ARE YOU A:	Caravanner		Motor caravanner		Trailer-tenter?	
NAME:	CARAVAN CLUB MEMBERSHIP NO:					
	POST CODE:					
DO YOU NEED MORE BLANK SITE REPORT FORMS?		YES		NO		
Address *(Non-members only please complete this section)*						

Please use a separate form for each campsite and do not send receipts. Owing to the large number of site reports received, it is not possible to enter into correspondence. Please return completed form to:

The Editor, Caravan Europe, The Caravan Club
FREEPOST, PO Box 386, (RRZG-SXKK-UCUJ)
East Grinstead RH19 1FH

(This address to be used when mailing within the UK only)

Caravan Europe **
Abbreviated Site Report Form

Use this abbreviated Site Report Form if you have visited a number of sites and there are no changes (or only insignificant changes) to their entries in the guide. If reporting on a new site, or reporting several changes, please use the full version of the report form. **If advising prices,** these should be for a car, caravan and 2 adults for one night's stay. **Please indicate high or low season prices and whether electricity is included.**

Remember, if you don't tell us about sites you have visited, they may eventually be deleted from the guide.

Year of guide used	20.........	Page No.	....	Name of town/village site listed under	
Site Name				Date of visit	.... /....... /........
GPS	Latitude...*(eg 12.34567)* Longitude...*(eg 1.23456 or -1.23456)*				
Site is in: Andorra / Austria / Belgium / Croatia / Czech Republic / Denmark / Finland / France / Germany / Greece / Hungary / Italy / Luxembourg / Netherlands / Norway / Poland / Portugal / Slovakia / Slovenia / Spain / Sweden / Switzerland					
Charge for car, caravan & 2 adults in local currency	High Season	Low Season	Elec inc in price?	Y / N	.............amps
			Price of elec (if not inc)		.............amps

Year of guide used	20.........	Page No.	....	Name of town/village site listed under	
Site Name				Date of visit	.... /....... /........
GPS	Latitude...*(eg 12.34567)* Longitude...*(eg 1.23456 or -1.23456)*				
Site is in: Andorra / Austria / Belgium / Croatia / Czech Republic / Denmark / Finland / France / Germany / Greece / Hungary / Italy / Luxembourg / Netherlands / Norway / Poland / Portugal / Slovakia / Slovenia / Spain / Sweden / Switzerland					
Charge for car, caravan & 2 adults in local currency	High Season	Low Season	Elec inc in price?	Y / N	.............amps
			Price of elec (if not inc)		.............amps

Year of guide used	20.........	Page No.	....	Name of town/village site listed under	
Site Name				Date of visit	.... /....... /........
GPS	Latitude...*(eg 12.34567)* Longitude...*(eg 1.23456 or -1.23456)*				
Site is in: Andorra / Austria / Belgium / Croatia / Czech Republic / Denmark / Finland / France / Germany / Greece / Hungary / Italy / Luxembourg / Netherlands / Norway / Poland / Portugal / Slovakia / Slovenia / Spain / Sweden / Switzerland					
Charge for car, caravan & 2 adults in local currency	High Season	Low Season	Elec inc in price?	Y / N	.............amps
			Price of elec (if not inc)		.............amps

Your comments & opinions may be used in future editions of the guide, if you do not wish them to be used please tick ....

Please fill in NAME / MEMBERSHIP NUMBER etc OVER PAGE

Please return completed form to:
The Editor, Caravan Europe, The Caravan Club
FREEPOST, PO Box 386 (RRZG-SXKK-UCUJ)
East Grinstead RH19 1FH
(This address to be used when mailing within UK only)

*** You can also complete forms online: www.caravanclub.co.uk/europereport*

CUT ALONG DOTTED LINE

Year of guide used	20..........	Page No.	....	Name of town/village site listed under		
Site Name					Date of visit	.... /....... /........
GPS	Latitude..(eg 12.34567) Longitude..(eg 1.23456 or -1.23456)					
Site is in: Andorra / Austria / Belgium / Croatia / Czech Republic / Denmark / Finland / France / Germany / Greece / Hungary / Italy / Luxembourg / Netherlands / Norway / Poland / Portugal / Slovakia / Slovenia / Spain / Sweden / Switzerland						
Charge for car, caravan & 2 adults in local currency	High Season	Low Season	Elec inc in price?	Y / N	.............amps	
			Price of elec (if not inc)		.............amps	

Year of guide used	20..........	Page No.	....	Name of town/village site listed under		
Site Name					Date of visit	.... /....... /........
GPS	Latitude..(eg 12.34567) Longitude..(eg 1.23456 or -1.23456)					
Site is in: Andorra / Austria / Belgium / Croatia / Czech Republic / Denmark / Finland / France / Germany / Greece / Hungary / Italy / Luxembourg / Netherlands / Norway / Poland / Portugal / Slovakia / Slovenia / Spain / Sweden / Switzerland						
Charge for car, caravan & 2 adults in local currency	High Season	Low Season	Elec inc in price?	Y / N	.............amps	
			Price of elec (if not inc)		.............amps	

Year of guide used	20..........	Page No.	....	Name of town/village site listed under		
Site Name					Date of visit	.... /....... /........
GPS	Latitude..(eg 12.34567) Longitude..(eg 1.23456 or -1.23456)					
Site is in: Andorra / Austria / Belgium / Croatia / Czech Republic / Denmark / Finland / France / Germany / Greece / Hungary / Italy / Luxembourg / Netherlands / Norway / Poland / Portugal / Slovakia / Slovenia / Spain / Sweden / Switzerland						
Charge for car, caravan & 2 adults in local currency	High Season	Low Season	Elec inc in price?	Y / N	.............amps	
			Price of elec (if not inc)		.............amps	

Name ....

Membership No. ....

Post Code ....

Are you a Caravanner / Motor Caravanner / Trailer-Tenter?

Do you need more blank Site Report forms? YES / NO

Address (if not a Caravan Club member)

Caravan Europe **
Abbreviated Site Report Form

Use this abbreviated Site Report Form if you have visited a number of sites and there are no changes (or only insignificant changes) to their entries in the guide. If reporting on a new site, or reporting several changes, please use the full version of the report form. **If advising prices,** these should be for a car, caravan and 2 adults for one night's stay. **Please indicate high or low season prices and whether electricity is included.**

Remember, if you don't tell us about sites you have visited, they may eventually be deleted from the guide.

Year of guide used	20..........	Page No.	....	Name of town/village site listed under		
Site Name					Date of visit	.... /....... /........
GPS	Latitude..(eg 12.34567) Longitude..(eg 1.23456 or -1.23456)					
Site is in: Andorra / Austria / Belgium / Croatia / Czech Republic / Denmark / Finland / France / Germany / Greece / Hungary / Italy / Luxembourg / Netherlands / Norway / Poland / Portugal / Slovakia / Slovenia / Spain / Sweden / Switzerland						
Charge for car, caravan & 2 adults in local currency	High Season	Low Season	Elec inc in price?	Y / N	.............amps	
			Price of elec (if not inc)		.............amps	

Year of guide used	20..........	Page No.	....	Name of town/village site listed under		
Site Name					Date of visit	.... /....... /........
GPS	Latitude..(eg 12.34567) Longitude..(eg 1.23456 or -1.23456)					
Site is in: Andorra / Austria / Belgium / Croatia / Czech Republic / Denmark / Finland / France / Germany / Greece / Hungary / Italy / Luxembourg / Netherlands / Norway / Poland / Portugal / Slovakia / Slovenia / Spain / Sweden / Switzerland						
Charge for car, caravan & 2 adults in local currency	High Season	Low Season	Elec inc in price?	Y / N	.............amps	
			Price of elec (if not inc)		.............amps	

Year of guide used	20..........	Page No.	....	Name of town/village site listed under		
Site Name					Date of visit	.... /....... /........
GPS	Latitude..(eg 12.34567) Longitude..(eg 1.23456 or -1.23456)					
Site is in: Andorra / Austria / Belgium / Croatia / Czech Republic / Denmark / Finland / France / Germany / Greece / Hungary / Italy / Luxembourg / Netherlands / Norway / Poland / Portugal / Slovakia / Slovenia / Spain / Sweden / Switzerland						
Charge for car, caravan & 2 adults in local currency	High Season	Low Season	Elec inc in price?	Y / N	.............amps	
			Price of elec (if not inc)		.............amps	

Your comments & opinions may be used in future editions of the guide, if you do not wish them to be used please tick ....

Please fill in NAME / MEMBERSHIP NUMBER etc OVER PAGE

Please return completed form to:
The Editor, Caravan Europe, The Caravan Club
FREEPOST, PO Box 386 (RRZG-SXKK-UCUJ)
East Grinstead RH19 1FH
(This address to be used when mailing within UK only)

*** You can also complete forms online: www.caravanclub.co.uk/europereport*

CUT ALONG DOTTED LINE

Year of guide used	20..........	Page No.	....	Name of town/village site listed under	
Site Name				Date of visit	.... /....... /........
GPS	Latitude...(eg 12.34567) Longitude...(eg 1.23456 or -1.23456)				

Site is in: Andorra / Austria / Belgium / Croatia / Czech Republic / Denmark / Finland / France / Germany / Greece / Hungary / Italy / Luxembourg / Netherlands / Norway / Poland / Portugal / Slovakia / Slovenia / Spain / Sweden / Switzerland

Charge for car, caravan & 2 adults in local currency	High Season	Low Season	Elec inc in price?	Y / N	............amps
			Price of elec (if not inc)		............amps

Year of guide used	20..........	Page No.	....	Name of town/village site listed under	
Site Name				Date of visit	.... /....... /........
GPS	Latitude...(eg 12.34567) Longitude...(eg 1.23456 or -1.23456)				

Site is in: Andorra / Austria / Belgium / Croatia / Czech Republic / Denmark / Finland / France / Germany / Greece / Hungary / Italy / Luxembourg / Netherlands / Norway / Poland / Portugal / Slovakia / Slovenia / Spain / Sweden / Switzerland

Charge for car, caravan & 2 adults in local currency	High Season	Low Season	Elec inc in price?	Y / N	............amps
			Price of elec (if not inc)		............amps

Year of guide used	20..........	Page No.	....	Name of town/village site listed under	
Site Name				Date of visit	.... /....... /........
GPS	Latitude...(eg 12.34567) Longitude...(eg 1.23456 or -1.23456)				

Site is in: Andorra / Austria / Belgium / Croatia / Czech Republic / Denmark / Finland / France / Germany / Greece / Hungary / Italy / Luxembourg / Netherlands / Norway / Poland / Portugal / Slovakia / Slovenia / Spain / Sweden / Switzerland

Charge for car, caravan & 2 adults in local currency	High Season	Low Season	Elec inc in price?	Y / N	............amps
			Price of elec (if not inc)		............amps

Name ....

Membership No. ....

Post Code ....

Are you a Caravanner / Motor Caravanner / Trailer-Tenter?

Do you need more blank Site Report forms? YES / NO

Address (if not a Caravan Club member)

Index

A

Abbreviated Site Report Forms .... Back of guide
Abbreviations 11
Accidents & Emergencies 106
Aland Islands – Sites 257
Alcohol – Legal Limits .... Country Intros
Ambulance – Emergencies .... Country Intros
Animals – Entry Regulations .... 40 & Country Intros
AUSTRIA 113

B

Bank Opening Hours .... Country Intros
BELGIUM 149
Bicycle & Motorbike Transportation 70
Boats 35
Booking a Campsite 24
Booking Your Ferry 42
Breakdown Services .... Country Intros
British Consular Services Abroad 112
British & Irish Embassy & Contact Details .... Country Intros

C

Overseas Camping Card International (CCI) 38
Camping Cheques 25
Camping Regulations .... Country Intros
Caravan Club Site Booking Service 24
Campsite Entry – Explanation 10
Campsite Prices .... 28 & Individual Site Entries
Caravan Club Sites Near Ports 44
Caravans Stored Abroad 47
Car, Motorhome & Caravan Insurance 46
Car Telephones .... 70 & Country Intros
Casual/Wild Camping .... Country Intros
Channel Tunnel 44
Checklist 22
Children 40
Contact Details – Sites .... 29 & Individual Site Entries
Continental Campsites 24
Conversion Tables 94
Credit & Debit Cards 52
CRIS document 41
CROATIA 171
Currency Exchange Rates .... Country Intros
Customs Allowances & Regulations 34
Cycling .... Country Intros
CZECH REPUBLIC 193

D

DENMARK 215
Distance Charts .... 64 & Country Intros
Documents 38
Driving Licence 38
Driving Offences .... 56 & Country Intros
Driving on the Continent 56

E

Electrical Connections – CEE17 96
Electricity Supply .... 96 & Country Intros
Emergency Medical Treatment – EHIC 104
Emergency Services .... 106 & Country Intros
Entry Formalities .... Country Intros
Essential Equipment Table 74
Euro, The 53

E cont'd

European Accident Statement 47
European Distance Chart 64
European Health Insurance Card (EHIC) 104
Explanation of a Campsite Entry 10

F

Ferries to the Continent, Ireland & Scandinavia 43
Finding a Campsite 26
Fines .... Country Intros
FINLAND 245
Fire – Prevention & Emergencies .... 109 & Country Intros
Fire Extinguisher 70
First Aid .... 70 & 105
Food & Plants. 35
Foreign Currency Bank Accounts 51
Fuel .... 57 & Country Intros
Fuel Price Guide Table 62

G

Gas Cylinders on Ferries 44
Gas – General Advice 98
GERMANY 261
Glasses (Sight) 70
GPS 72
GREECE 353
Greek Island – Sites 368
Green Card 46

H

Handbook Introduction 6
Holidays – International 50
Holidays – Public .... Country Intros
Hooking up to the Mains 97
How to Use this Guide 6
HUNGARY 373

I

Insect Bites 106
Insurance: 46
– Caravans Stored Abroad 47
– Car, Motorhome & Caravan 46
– Holiday 48
– Home 49
– Marine (Car Ferries/Boats) 49
– Medical 105
– Personal Belongings 49
– Pets 48
– Vehicles Left Behind Abroad 49
International Direct Dial Phone Calls 100
International Driving Permit 38
Irish Embassy & Consular Addresses .... Country Intros
ITALY 391

L

Legal Costs Abroad 47
Liechtenstein .... See Switzerland
Lights .... 70 & Country Intros
Local Currency .... 51 & Country Intros
Local Time .... Country Intros
Local Travel .... Country Intros
Lofoten & Vesteralen Islands – Site Entries 560
Low Emission Zones 58
LPG Supplies .... 58 & Country Intros
Lunch Breaks (on campsites) 27
LUXEMBOURG 475

Index

M

Medical Advice ... 104
Mobile Phones ... 102 & Country Intros
Money ... 51 & Country Intros
MOT Certificate ... 39
Motorhomes – Overnight Stops ... 27
Motorhomes Towing Cars ... 58
Motoring – Advice ... 55
Motoring – Equipment ... 70
Motorway Tolls ... 58 & Country Intros
Mountain Passes & Tunnels ... 75
Mountain Passes & Tunnels Maps ... 90-93
Mountain Passes & Tunnels Report Form ... Back of guide
Municipal Campsites ... 27

N

Nationality Plate (GB/IRL) ... 71
Naturist Campsites ... 27
NETHERLANDS ... 485
NORWAY ... 525

O

Öland Islands – Sites ... 639
Opening Dates ... 28 & Individual Site Entries
Overnight Stops ... 27 & 108
Overseas Site Booking Service ... 24

P

Parking ... 59 & Country Intros
Parking Facilities
for the Disabled ... 59 & Country Intros
Passport ... 39
Pets' Insurance ... 48
Pets on Campsites ... 28
Pets on Ferries & Eurotunnel ... 44
Pet Travel Scheme (PETS) ... 40
Plants & Food ... 35
POLAND ... 567
Police – Emergencies ... Country Intros
Post Office Opening Hours ... Country Intros
Practical Advice ... 16
Priority & Roundabouts ... 59 & Country Intros
Prohibited & Restricted Goods ... 37
Public Holidays ... 50 & Country Intros
Public Transport ... 59 & Country Intros

R

Rabies ... 106
Radar/Speed Camera Detectors ... 71
Radio & Television ... 101
Red Pennant Overseas Holiday Insurance ... 48
Registering at Campsites ... 29
Reversed Polarity ... 98
Road Accidents ... 106
Road Signs & Markings ... 59 & Country Intros
Roundabouts ... 59 & Country Intros
Route Planning & GPS ... 72

S

Safety & Security ... 108
Sanitary Facilities ... 26
Sardinia – Site Entries ... 461
Satellite Navigation ... 7 & 72
Seat Belts ... 72 & Country Intros
Security – Holiday Money ... 53
– Personal ... 111 & Country Intros
Shaver Sockets ... 98

S cont'd

Shop Opening Hours ... Country Intros
Sicily – Site Entries ... 464
Site Booking Service ... 24
Site Facilities Abbreviations ... 11
Site Prices ... 28 & Individual Site Entries
Site Opening Dates ... 28 & Individual Site Entries
Site Report Forms ... 8 & Back of Guide
Sites Location Maps ... End of Site Entries
SLOVAKIA ... 585
SLOVENIA ... 597
Snow Chains ... 61
Spares ... 72
Spare Wheel ... 72
Specimen Site Booking Letters (4 Languages) ... 30-33
Speed Limits ... 60 & 63
Storage Abroad ... 25 & 47
Sun Protection ... 107
SWEDEN ... 609
Swimming Pools – Safety ... 109
SWITZERLAND ... 645
Symbols Used (in Campsite Entries) ... 13

T

Technical Leaflets ... 23
Telephone Cards ... 100
Telephoning ... 102 & Country Intros
Television ... 101
Terrorism ... 112 & Country Intros
Tourist Offices ... Country Intros
Towing Bracket ... 72
Traffic Jams & Traffic Information ... Country Intros
Travellers' Cheques ... 51 & Country Intros
Travel Money Cards ... 52
Travelling with Children ... 40
Tunnels – Rail ... 86
Tunnels – Road ... 87
Tyres ... 73

U

Use of Caravan by Persons
Other Than the Owner ... 36

V

Vaccinations ... 105
Vehicle Excise Licence ... 40
Vehicle Registration Certificate ... 41
Vehicles Left Behind Abroad ... 49
Visas ... 41

W

Warning Triangles ... 73
Waste Disposal ... 26
Water & Food ... 21
Win a Sat Nav ... 8
Winter Driving ... 73
Winter Tyres ... 73